A COLLECTION

OF THE

WORKS

OF

WILLIAM PENN.

In Two VOLUMES.

To Which is PREFIXED

A Journal of His LIFE.

WITH MANY

Original LETTERS *and* PAPERS

Not Before PUBLISHED.

And to Which is Appended
An Index of the Works
Compiled in 1730
by
Henry Portsmouth

VOL. II

AMS PRESS

NEW YORK

A COLLECTION

OF THE

WORKS

OF

WILLIAM PENN.

In Two VOLUMES.

To Which is PREFIXED

A Journal of His LIFE.

WITH MANY

Original LETTERS *and* PAPERS

Not Before PUBLISHED.

VOLUME the SECOND.

Ecclesiastes xii. 11. *The Words of the Wise are as Goads, and as Nails fastened by the Masters of Assemblies, which are given from One Shepherd.*

LONDON:
Printed and Sold by the ASSIGNS of J. SOWLE, at the Bible in George-Yard, Lombard-Street. 1726.

Library of Congress Cataloging in Publication Data

Penn, William, 1644-1718.
   A collection of the works of William Penn, to which is prefixed a journal of life.

   1. Penn, William, 1644-1718. I. Title.
F152.2.P393   1974   974.8'02'0924   79-173942
ISBN 0-404-04982-6

Reprinted with permission from a volume
in the Library, Bryn Mawr College, 1974

Reprinted from the edition of 1726, London
First AMS edition published, 1974
Manufactured in the United States of America

International Standard Book Number:
Complete Set: 0-404-04982-6
Volume II: 0-404-04984-2

AMS PRESS, INC.
New York, N.Y. 10003

THE Contents of the Second Volume.

This VOLUME Contains,

I. Controversial TRACTS, Viz.

Anno 1668. THE Guide Mistaken, and Temporizing Rebuked: Or, A Brief Reply to Jonathan Clapham's Book, entituled, A Guide to the True Religion, *in which his* Religion *is confuted*, Hypocrisy *detected*, Aspersions *reprehended, and* Contradictions *compared*, Page 1.

1671. II. A Serious Apology *for the Principles and Practices of the* People call'd Quakers, *against the Malicious Aspersions, Erroneous Doctrines, and Horrid Blasphemies of* Thomas Jenner, *and* Timothy Taylor, *in their Book, entituled,* Quakerism Anatomiz'd, and Confuted, 32.

1672. III. The Spirit of Truth Vindicated, *against that of* Error *and* Envy, *unseasonably manifested in a Malicious Libel, entituled*, The Spirit of the Quakers Tried, &c. 93.

IV. The New Witnesses prov'd Old Hereticks: Or, Information to the Ignorant; *in which the Doctrines of* John Reeve *and* Lodowick Muggleton, *are proved to be mostly Ancient Whimsies, Blasphemies and Heresies, from the Evidence of* Scripture, Reason, *and several* Historians. *Also an Account of some Discourse between* W. Penn, *and* Lod. Muggleton, 152.

V. Plain Dealing with a Traducing Anabaptist: Or, Three Letters *writ upon Occasion of some Slanderous Reflections, given and promoted against* William Penn, *by one* John Morse, 179.

The Proposed Comprehension, *Soberly, and not Unseasonably considered,* 186.

1673. VI. The Spirit of Alexander the Copper-Smith Justly Rebuked; Or, An Answer *to a late Pamphlet, entituled,* The Spirit of the Hat, *or the* Government of the Quakers, 189.

VII. Judas and the Jews combin'd against Christ and His Followers,

An. 1673. *being a Rejoynder to the late Nameless Reply, call'd,* Tyranny and Hypocrisie detected, *made against a Book, entituled,* The Spirit of Alexander the Copper-Smith, Rebuked. Page 196.

VIII. Quakerism a New Nick-name for Old Christianity, *being an Answer to a Book, entituled,* Quakerism No Christianity, *Subscribed by* J. Faldo. *In which the Rise, Doctrine and Practice of the Abused Quakers, are Truly, Briefly, and Fully Declared and Vindicated, from the False Charges, Wicked Insinuations, and utmost Opposition made by that Adversary,* 227.

IX. The Invalidity of John Faldo's Vindication of his Book, call'd, Quakerism No Christianity: *Being a Rejoynder, in Defence of the Answer, entituled,* Quakerism a New Nick-Name for Old Christianity; *wherein many Weighty Gospel-Truths are handled, and the Disingenuous Carriage of that Adversary is observed, for the Information of Moderate Enquirers,* 314.

X. Wisdom Justified of Her Children, *from the Ignorance and Calumny of* Henry Hallywell, *in his Book called,* An Account of Familism, *as it is Revived and Propagated by the* Quakers, 462.

XI. Reason against Railing, and Truth against Fiction: *Being an Answer to Two Pamphlets, entituled,* A Dialogue between a Christian and a Quaker; *and the* Continuation of the Dialogue, &c. *By one* Thomas Hicks, *an* Anabaptist *Teacher,* 498.

1674. XII. The Counterfeit Christian Detected, and the Real Quaker Justified; *against the Vile Forgeries, Gross Perversions, Black Slanders, Plain Contradictions, and Scurrilous Language of* T. Hicks, *in his Third Dialogue,* call'd

The CONTENTS of the Second Volume.

An. 1674. call'd, The Quaker Condemn'd. By Way of Appeal to all Sober People, especially those called Anabaptists, in, and about the City of London, Page 560.

XIII. A Just Rebuke to One and Twenty Learned and Reverend Divines, so called, being an Answer to an Abusive Epistle against the People called Quakers, 604.

XIV. Urim and Thummim: Or, the Doctrines of Light and Perfection Maintained, against the Opposite Plea of Samuel Grevil, a Pretended Minister of the Gospel, in his Un-Gospel-like Discourse, against a Book entituled, A Testimony of the Light Within; anciently Writ by Alexander Parker, 619.

XV. Naked Truth needs No Shift: Or, an Answer to a Libellous Sheet, entituled, The Quaker's Last Shift found out, 637.

XVI. A Return to John Faldo's Reply, called, A Curb for William Penn's Confidence, 639.

1676. XVII. The Skirmisher Defeated, and Truth Defended; being an Answer to a Pamphlet, entituled, A Skirmish upon Quakerism, 650.

1678. XVIII. A Brief Answer to a False An. 1678. and Foolish Libel, call'd, The Quaker's Opinions; for their Sakes that Writ it, and Read it, Page 668.

XIX. A Brief Examination, and State of Liberty Spiritual, both with Respect to Persons in their Private Capacity, and in their Church-Society & Communion, 691.

1684. XX. A Defence of the Duke of Buckingham's Book of Religion and Worship, from the Exceptions of a Nameless Author, 708.

XXI. Animadversions on the Apology of the Clamorous Squire, against the Duke of Buckingham's Seconds, as Men of No Conscience, 722.

1692. XXII. The New Athenians, No Noble Bereans: Being an Answer to several Athenian Mercuries, in Behalf of the People called Quakers, 792.

1695. XXIII. A Reply by a Nameless Author, to W. Penn's Key; in which the Principles of the People called Quakers, are farther Explained and Confirm'd, 807

1698. XXIV. A Defence of a Paper, entituled, Gospel-Truths, against the Exceptions of the Bishop of Cork's Testimony,

II. Doctrinal BOOKS, Viz.

1692. I. Just Measures: Being an Epistle of Peace and Love, to such Professors of Truth as are under Dissatisfaction about the Order practised in the Church of Christ, 774.

II. A Key, Opening the Way to every Capacity, how to distinguish the Religion Professed by the People called Quakers, from the Perversions and Misrepresentations of their Adversaries. With a Brief Exhortation to all Sorts of People to Examine their Ways, and turn speedily to the Lord, 778.

1695. III. A Visitation to the Jews: To the Seed of Abraham, and House of Israel, after the Flesh, 848.

IV. Primitive Christianity Reviv'd, 1695. in the Faith and Practice of the People called Quakers. Written in Testimony to the present Dispensation of God through them, to the World; that Prejudices may be removed, the Simple informed; the Well-Inclined encouraged, and the Truth, and it's Innocent Friends, rightly represented, 853.

1698. V A Testimony to the Truth of God, as held by the People called Quakers; being a Short Vindication of them, from the Abuses and Misrepresentations often put upon them, by Envious Apostates, and Mercenary Adversaries, 876.

III. Political TREATISES, Viz.

1679. I. England's Great Interest, in the Choice of a New Parliament: Dedicated to all Her Freeholders and Electors, 678.

II. One Project for the Good of England, that is, Our Civil Union is our Civil Safety: Humbly Dedicated to the Great Council, The Parliament of England, 682.

1686. III. A Perswasive to Moderation to Church-Dissenters, in Prudence and Conscience: Humbly submitted to the King, and His Great Council, 727.

1687. IV. Good Advice to the Church of England, Roman Catholick, and Protestant Dissenter; in which it is endeavoured to make appear, that it is their Duty, Principle, and Interest, to abolish the Penal Laws and Tests, 749.

1683. A General Description of the Province of Pennsylvania; its Soil, Air, Water, Seasons, and Produce, both Natural and Artificial, and the Good Increase thereof; with an Account of the Natives, or Aborigines. v. 699.

THE WORKS OF WILLIAM PENN.

The Second VOLUME.

THE
Guide Mistaken, & Temporizing rebuked.

OR,

A Brief REPLY to *Jonathan Clapham's* Book, intitled, *A Guide to the True Religion.*

IN WHICH

His { RELIGION / HYPOCRISY / ASPERSIONS / CONTRADICTIONS } is { Confuted. / Detected. } are { Reprehended. / Compared. }

By *W. Penn*, A Friend to the *True Religion*.

If the Blind lead the Blind, both shall fall into the Ditch, Matt. xv: 14.

To the READER.

AS nothing more imports the Sons of Men, than a judicious Search after the certain Knowledge of that Eternal Truth, in which alone Ability is placed to free from those Sins and Entanglements the lustful Eye and wanton Mind have naturally subjected them unto, and into which they are so deeply intricated; so can there nothing prove more dangerous, than an implicit Reception of such Principles as daily steal out of the Press; Some are so very imbecil, as that they crave a Support from

1668.

the Ingenuity of their Friends to vindicate their Cause; whilst others better skill'd, cunningly can insinuate their Sentiments (however defective, being truly examined) under the Plausibility of Language, and Resemblance of Reason: but tho' I am willing to acknowledge no Age more shatter'd and in Pieces about Religious Concernments than this we live in (some splitting on the Rocks of Atheism, whilst others creep into the shallow Creeks of bare Profession) yet with great Confidence I can impeach Man as the Ground of his own distracted and miserable Estate; for such hath been and is the curious and inquisitive Mind of Man, that as he would be wise above what is written, so is he most impatient in his Search; and over-looking that Sufficiency given him of God, to act in his Divine and Human Capacity, is either busily forming, out of his brain sick Fancies, rather what he would have God, Man and Religion to be, than what they really are; or else, being born under some generally received Apprehensions and Articles of Faith, Worship and Discipline, is so entirely hurried away with the Variety of earthly Pleasures, or diverted by Fears, that he can find no Leisure to enquire how far they bear any Proportion with sound Reason and true Religion: Both these so much experimented Evils, are the undeniable Occasion of that inhuman Entertainment such have met withal, whom God at any Time hath sent to testify against the invented Ways, Words, Works and Worships of this degenerated World; looking on it as an intollerable Affront, that not only they should be exploded for Hereticks, but that the Faith of their Zealous Ancestors should come in Question, it may be by Reformers of no better Rank than poor Mechanicks; forgetting it was the Channel, through which God in all Ages hath been pleased to convey the Streams of Divine Knowledge; and 'twas indeed most congruous with God's Omnipotence, to let the lofty Worldlings know, how able he was by mean and contemptible Instruments to effect the Confusion of them and their Inventions.

This never was more expresly verified, than in the Progress made by that despised Generation of Pilgrims, call'd Quakers, who notwithstanding all that Opposition of Powers Ecclesiastical and Civil, and their many Stratagems imbattelled to scatter and destroy them, are yet a People; and with no other Weapons, than an holy, inoffensive and suffering Conversation, have valiantly warr'd through the many Armies of their Enemies, and in the Wisdom of him that called them forth, been able to undermine and circumvent their most Machiavilian Conspiracies; which leads me to give thee an Account of my thus appearing in thy View: I can assure thee, 'tis no Forwardness to gain the Reputation of a Disputant, since that vain Glory my Principle prohibits, and should most willingly have left this for another, did not Necessity lay it strictly on me.

Amongst the many peevish Adversaries I have met with, who have ventured to oppose and slander that innocent People, I scarce know one who has more made it his Concern than my Antagonist; for besides what either this treats of under my Examination, or another anciently printed, under the Protection of a large Dedicatory Epistle to O. Cromwel, the Acquaintance I have had with him by Paper and personal Conference, as well as the punctual Information I have receiv'd concerning his Practice through all our Revolutions, (which I may term a Touch-stone for Integrity) will by no Means dispense with my passing by this Guide unanimadverted; for truly, Reader, I cannot but in Sincerity assure thee, that a Religious Pity will not have me silent, since when I narrowly observe the Passages of his Life, and then remark the very Drift of his Discourse, (abundantly confused, as will appear in this short Reply) I really find it is to palliate his own Nakedness, and, if possible, not only to confirm all Temporizers like himself, but also by his little Insinuations of pretended Christian Tenderness, to beguile the chaste Minds of others into the Defilement of a Cringing and Conforming Spirit: All which strongly excites me to present thee with a Confutation of his Religion, a Reprehension of his Aspersions, a Detection of his Hypocrisy, and Comparison of his Contradictions; that being once unmask'd, he may appear in all his Imperfections, and his Disguise never prove injurious unto any.

CHAP.

The Guide Mistaken, &c.

CHAP. I.
A Confutation of His Religion.

§. 1. Although I easily shall confess Religion to be Man's chiefest Concernment, and that his Eternal Bliss does indispensibly depend upon the sound Belief and constant Practice of the *True One*, yet when I retrospect upon that Time I once imploy'd in a Conversation with Books, and call to mind the excellent Defence of *Origen*, and Apology of *Tertullian* on the Behalf of those Primitive Christians, and also the Learning, Gravity, and Reason of *Du Plessy*, *Grotius*, *Amiraldus*, &c. who in their Time were truly Honourable, and Modern Writers on the same subject, I cannot but acknowledge my self surpriz'd, to find a Discourse so raw and undigested as *Jonathan Clapham*'s, vent'ring abroad with no less Title, than *A Guide to the True Religion*, thereby implying, either the Insufficiency of what already has been writ, or Self-Conceitedness, that the Abilities of none can better claim so great an Office; whilst in very Truth, he has but shewn himself a Novice in the Task he hath undertook, which will but draw the Eyes of all those *Infidels* and *Hereticks* (against whom he doth so zealously contend) from perusing that which carries with it more of Reason for their Confutation and Convincement, to encounter him, a Match of much less Consequence: So that his Ignorance becomes their Refuge, and his proofless Accusations, gross Contradictions, and often Tautologies, strong Grounds for a Confirmation in their respective Perswasions: And if that which he terms *Christian Religion*, had no better Champion than he seems to be, nor more Zeal to suffer whatever comes, than Reason to defend it, he may as well turn *Jew*, *Turk*, or *Heathen*, as manifestly he hath *Presbyterian*, *Independent*, *Episcopal*; but left I may be censured for condemning that in him, which I allow in my self, *viz.* bare Assertions without a Proof, I shall descend to the examining of those Particulars, which may most deserve our Consideration.

§. 2. In his Epistle to the Reader, which must not slip my Observation, *He much bewails the present State of the Churches of Christ in these Kingdoms, who for many Years* (he says) *have been distracted*: But I'le refer it to thy Judgment, *Reader*, whether this *New Guide* be little better, who dares to call Distracted People, *Christian Churches*, or *Christ's Churches distracted*: *Paul* bore another Record, when he describes the Church of Christ *without Spot, Wrinkle, or Blemish*: But whilst he would seem to allow many Dissenting Parties the Title of *Christian Churches*, it must be remembred he else would have excluded himself from being other than an Infidel, who as Occasion serv'd, has been of four; yet how palpable a Contradiction this will be, not only to the Scripture, but the Design of his whole Discourse, may appear upon the Perusal of it's latter Part, where he not only advises all to acquiesce in the present Constitution of the Church of *England*, but seems to lay it as a Charge upon the rest, pleading strongly (as he thinks) for their Compliance, not considering if they equally deserve the Name of *Christian*, they consequently are independent; and since he doth allow the one to be no more Christian than the others, why any should impose upon, or enjoyn Obedience from it's Sister-Churches, I cannot find any Thing in sound Reason, or Scripture, to warrant it: To mend, or rather marr the Matter, he in so many Words, calls those very Churches he own'd for Christian in one Page, *A Reproach to the Christian Religion, and infamous through the World*, in the very next; but how infamous his Expression is, I beseech thee, *Reader*, to observe, that dares expose such foolish and irreverent Terms to publick View, calling what's Christian, *infamous*, or rather what's infamous, *Christian*; methinks he should better have consulted his own Reputation, since having been a Minister to most of them, his Share has not been small in their Reproach and Infamy.

He marches on without Fear, Wit or Wisdom, telling us, the Intendment of his Book, *Is to help against those Evils, and to direct those who are apt to miscarry, through Occasion of Diversity of Opinions, and Ways, found amongst us*. But how improper this Magisterial Guide is to direct Three Nations which of these many Ways they ought to walk in, will appear, if we consider the Wavering of his own Mind, who as it consisted with his Interest, has been always ready to welcome every New

1668.
Chap. I.

Power with a Leading Compliance; and if none would more concern themselves for his present Opinion, than he has for his past, his Inconstancy would not deceive them in his espousing the next Constitution that may come.

Epist. p. 6, 7.

And that I may not be mistaken in my Conjectures of the Occasion of this Treatise, read but a little farther, and thou wilt find a Confirmation in his own Words, who does not only account those the *Best Christians*, himself, *which (through all those Great Revolutions which have been amongst us) have exercised their Zeal for the maintaining the Fundamental Doctrines of the Gospel, and Practice and Power of Godliness, even to a Degree of Compliance*; but has Confidence to give it as his Judgment, *That such shall appear the most Approved and Judicious Christians unto all.* I shall say little more in this Place, than refer him to such Episcopalians as stood Faithful to their Churches Constitution, during his Compliance with *Presbyter, Independent*, &c. and to the Resentments of those Parties, now he is become *Prelatical.* And thus much for his Preface.

Book, p. 1.

§. 3. His Porch I cannot find to hold the least Proportion, or Harmony, with almost any Part of his confused Building; for he tells us, *The Business of Religion is the Grand Concernment that all of us are sent into the World to mind, and therefore God hath in the framing of Man's Nature, laid so deep an Impression thereof in us, that there is no Nation so barbarous and inhuman, but doth place this amongst the greatest Matters they judge themselves to be interested in.* 'Tis not my Disposition to cavil at Terms, and therefore shall avoid the Occasion he presents me, and rather take his Matter as exprest.

If God Eternal in the Creation of Man, and Infusion of his Soul, gave him that Capacity (for what else can that Impression signifie) whereby he might know and comprehend so much of that Divinity by which he was made, as to Live in a Due and Holy Conformity to His Divine Pleasure manifested therein; what mean his many Exclamations against the *Quaker's Light*, as Natural and Insufficient, since his very Words denominate this of God? Nor can he (I should think) so much forget his *Catechism*, as not to remember and acknowledge the least Ray of that immense Fulness of Glorious Light Supernatural and Perfect; besides, it were to represent the All-wise most indiscreet, in communicating unto Man a Proportion of his Spirit to no Purpose; if then, it will become us better to esteem, both of what he hath imprest, and of the End for which he did bestow that Heavenly Favour, what remains, but that those Inconveniences which have, do, and will attend the World, rise from the over-looking it's Dictates, and giddy following the blind Imaginations and groundless Conjectures of we know not who, transferr'd to us from preceding Generations: Nor will it serve the Turn of any to reply, That whatever Sufficiency this might once have had, it becomes now invalid by Transgression: For though it will be easily granted that Man's Rebellion against the Divine Capacity or Light, has plung'd him into all the dark and confused Practices, with which the World is so universally infected, and becomes thereby so entirely Leavened into the Nature of the Wicked One, (not minding the solid and weighty Things of God, which most concern his Eternal Peace, but rather sporting away this precious Time in the Variety of Delights, exposed to the Enjoyment of his Sense) yet to affirm that it's Vertue is lost, or thereby can be rendred more insufficient to guide Man in all his Performances, than when first bestow'd upon him, is to say, that because a lewd Son will not take his Father's good Advice, therefore it was not the Son's Rebellion, but the Insufficiency of the Father's Counsel; or, because a Servant has not improv'd the Talent given him by his Lord, but conceal'd it in a Napkin, 'therefore 'twas no Talent, or through the Carelesness and idle Practice of the Servant, his Lord's Talent lost the Possibility of Improvement; I shall confess his Negligence might more indispose his Mind to an industrious imploying of his Stock; but that it should thereby lose it's Vertue, Nature, and Capacity of Increase, can by no Means be admitted, because incongruous both to Scripture and Good Reason——*He that tells Man his Thoughts, and the Purpose of his Heart, this is the Lord of Hosts.* But I shall see how this and what follows will consist.

Pag. 2.

§. 4. Although the Beginning of his second Page is manifestly opposite to his own Assertions, and consequently but a farther Proof of my former Section; yet since I am confident he never meant it so, it may be requisite to present thee, *Reader*, with a Confutation in his own Words: *But as it is a Thing all do profess themselves interested in, so there's nothing in all the World Men are at greater Difference about; some taking up one Religion, some another, as pleases themselves best, one serving Baal, another Dagon, some the Sun, others the Moon, or Stars, &c.* If he

See p. 8. 14, 15.

would

would place the Variety of Religions on the Insufficiency of that Instinct, or Impression mentioned in his first Page, and so imply a Necessity of something farther to act Man in that which may be pleasing unto God, then will it manifestly follow that the Capacity given of God, could not discern, nor rightly distinguish betwixt that Eternal, Living, and Omnipotent God, from whence it came, and *Baal, Dagon, Sun, Moon,* or *Stars*, which very gross Absurdity I hope none will have the Confidence to assert: But farther, to repute the Authority of this Impression, pray let these Words of his have but the *Reader's* Consideration *(viz.)* —— *Some of one Religion, some of another, as pleases themselves best.* Can a more Universal Answer be returned, or *Catholick Reason* rendred, to evince the *Verity of the Quaker's Principle to the intelligible World?* For what has been the Original of those great Debates, Contentions, and Religious Duels through the World, but *S E L F*? Which being still impatient to be Taught, and nothing less ambitious to be Wise, hath ever been the Ground of those Distractions, and Womb that hath brought forth those monstrous and mishapen Births, so common among the Sons of Men: And, as the fallible Spirit of a Man, or selfish Part, could not produce a Nature different from it's own, (which ever has been subject to Fluctuation and Incertainty) so have their cross and various Apprehensions in the zealous Prosecution of them, been like the impetuous Billows of a raging Sea, that have dasht each against the other, to their irrecoverable Found'ring in the Ocean of Eternal Misery; whereas if Mankind in that Stilness, and reverent Patience becoming a Creature, had but waited on the Great Creator of all Things, according to that Impression and Measure of his Spirit bestow'd upon him, to incline and guide him in the well-pleasing Path of Righteousness, he doubtless had receiv'd such infallible Instructions, as should have freed him from those otherwise inextricable Disquisitions, and knotty Intanglements, his dark Inventions, and self-exalted Opinions, have perplext the World withal.

§. 5. In the same Page, he goes on thus; *How greatly doth it behove every one, to make a wise Choice of that God he intends to serve, and of that Religion he means to profess in the World, and to live and die in it.* In Page 5. he thus tautologizes (a Fault I find him very often guilty of, with many other more gross Improprieties, whilst he condemns the *Quakers* for illiterate) *to chuse deliberately, what God we will serve, or what Religion we will profess, and then to labour, to be established therein, so as by no Storms or Temptations we be removed.*—— Will any God serve? a very large and libertine Admonition: but he suddenly reprehends himself (the following Lines of the second Page, flatly withstanding that Latitude of serving any God) for says he, *first chuse the true God; and the rather because Man's Eternal Happiness, or Misery depends thereon*:—— Alas for him, that has elected any God, or has by this giddy Guide's Incouragement, chosen what Religion he would profess, with a fix't Resolution, that no Storms should remove him: What Contradiction is here? Can he be esteemed a wise *Counsellor*, that advises to an Undertaking, which by his own Acknowledgment shall never have a prosperous Success? Surely his Fee was very ill deserv'd; and much better were it to have no Religion, but live insensible of all, than to become a very Zealot for a false one: nor is this the only Contradiction of the like Nature, as the Chapter of his Contradictions will more largely manifest.

§. 6. I am now come to take a View of his Proposition, or Basis, on which his Discourse is grounded, viz. *That it's a great Point of Wisdom, to make a right Choice of that Religion he means to take up, and profess in the World, that he intends to live and dye in, and to venture his eternal Salvation upon.*

Since *Paul* who very well knew the Mind of God, has left it as the Spirit's Record in the Scriptures, *That the deep Things of God, knoweth no Man, but the Spirit of God*; and looking on the true Religion, to be what he intends by these following Expressions, [*The Mysteries of God's Kingdom; Heavenly Things, hidden Wisdom, Redemption from all Iniquity, all Things to become new, to be dead with Christ to the World, and risen with him, to seek the Things that are above;* in short, *By the Revelation of the eternal Spirit, to fathom the deep, and behold the mysterious Things of God,* so as thereby, to be translated from *Darkness,* into his most glorious Kingdom, of *Righteousness, Peace and Joy in the holy Spirit*] I can by no Means, subscribe my Assent, to this Guide's Proposition, that Man with his tallest Wisdom, distinct from that Light, or pure Capacity, the *Quakers* affirm God has enlightned and invested all Men with, is able to wade securely into the Depths of Divine Mysteries, nor allow him that *Arbitrium* of working out in his own Strength, Time and Mediums, the Knowledge of true Religion; much less can I concur

1668
Chap. I.

Tautol. p. 2. 4, 5, 6. 12, 13, 14, 15, 16, 18, 22.

Mat. 13. 11. 1 Cor. 2. 7. ch. 4. 1 Joh. 3. 12. Heb. 9. 23. 1 Cor. 2. 7. Tit. 2. 13. 2 Cor. 5. 17. Col. 3. 1. Rom 14. 17.

concur with his esteeming any wise, *in rightly chusing what Religion they would imbrace*, since it doth not limit him to what is true, in which the Choice can only be called right: but rather seems to give him the Liberty of chusing where he will, in which no Election ought to be judged true or wise. And lest I may be here censur'd by the Author of this Discourse, under my Examination, let him peruse not only his Argument, but his 14th Page, where he affirms a Necessity for a Man to be of some Religion; in which by the following Matter, is manifest, as well as from the Words themselves, the exceeding Space given in the Search and espousing of a Religion; yet however necessary, he has made it there, and what Liberty soever he has granted, it's his Advice in the 26th Page, *to do it wisely, lest you be deluded, there being such Diversities of Religion, and so many false Ways in the World, you had need have your Eyes about you, erring herein will not stand with the Safety of your Souls; Eternal Happiness or Misery depends upon it:* Which argues strongly, (or else I know not what Argument means) against the Choice being right in any Religion, and that it only can be so in embracing the true one, let him but peruse the 17th Page, and tell me, if he doth not find this, amongst the many other Contradictions, that the *Opinion or Dream, that every Man may be saved in his own Religion, if he be true to it, is more becoming* Turks *than* Christian. I must confess I have not met of late in any Author, with such palpable Confusion, and can assure thee, *Reader*, I do avoid, for brevity's Sake, the Recital of much more I might instance in. What Superstructure it's possible for the best Artists to erect, on a Foundation, so imperfect and unsound, he need be no exact Architect to determine: but notwithstanding his Mistake in his Way to the true Religion, he may prove Guide sufficient to his following *Errors* and *Defects*.

§. 7. I shall a little insist upon his second Chapter, the Head is this: *Shewing wherein the wise chusing one's Religion lies, and acts concurring thereunto.* He needs must play the crack-Philosopher, and imperfectly has manag'd his little Distinctions, in the pedantick Phrase of the canting Priests and Academists: He tells us, first, what Election is in general, and then divides the right chusing of Religion into three Acts, the intellect precedingly discerning the Nature of the Thing, that by the Will is chosen: And what in the 7th Page he hath defin'd, in the 8th he instances these following Words, to confirm the Definition, viz. *Man being a Religious Creature, by the common Instinct of his natural Conscience, is moved strongly to worship a Deity, as we see in all the Nations of the Earth, much more when he is stirred up by a divine Instinct.*

Answ. It hath been the Unhappiness of many Ages, as it is of this, to darken and confound Matters of Religion (mostly) with Terms, not more affected and difficult, than very often impertinent, of which this Guide is not a little guilty, as must be obvious to such as will examine his most frivolous and contradictory Distinction betwixt Natural and Divine. Not that I shall now allow them to be Terms proper in the Place, but very improper where he puts them: Let me perswade thee, *Reader*, to observe impartially the Confusion; I have to do with one, who characters himself a *Christian*, and not a profest Disciple of the *Heathen Aristotle*; and I should therefore think it may become me best, (as it had him) to use such a sound Form of Words, as are warranted by, and laid down in the Scriptures of Truth; and that he, with all others, may know how far the *Quakers*, are on all Occasions, ready to bring their Principles to be tried, by that which the Spirit there declares, I shall expose both his and theirs, to the Judgment of them, and leave thee, *Reader*, to determine which holds the greatest Harmony therewith; although the Contradiction of his own Words, might have been Confutation evident enough.

Religion is by *James*, a Prophet of the most high God, thus defined: *Pure Religion and undefiled before God and the Father, is this, to visit the Fatherless and Widows in their Affliction, and to keep himself unspotted from the World.* Also, *to believe, as* Paul *has it, in thy Heart, and confess with thy Tongue, in and to the Lord Jesus.* Or, as he hath it in another Place, to wit, *A Subjection and Obedience to that Spirit, Light or Grace manifested from God, to all Men, teaching them that denying Ungodliness and worldly Lusts, they shall live soberly, righteously and godly in this present World.* Taking these Passages, for the clear and compleat Signification of that Term *Religion* (as I shall, till some more ample be produced) and not the whimsical Conjectures of Men, from their wresting of the Scriptures, patcht up into a formal Creed, by their eclipst Understandings, as this Guide must not deny, if he will own Scripture; then will it consequently follow, that no Man can

can be truly ſtiled *Religious*, from a natural Inſtinct or Cauſe: for ſince the one and true *Religion*, or *Primitive*, is *divine*, *Religious* or the *Relative*, muſt neceſſarily participate of the ſame *Divine* Nature; and if by natural Conſcience, he means *Reaſon* abſtractively, the Relative cannot amount to more than rational; for as what is ſimply *Animal*, cannot generate what's *rational*, ſo is it altogether impoſſible for what is but ſimply rational, to produce what is ſpiritual: Nor can I underſtand how he will ſecure himſelf from groſs Impertinency, in nominating Man a *Religious* Creature, from a natural Inſtinct; or to aſſert any Thing, but what is divine, can act Man to worſhip a Divinity; how far he may, to ſave himſelf, extend the Signification of natural, I know not, but if he means it, in the Senſe *Paul* often us'd it, methinks the very Letter of the Scripture, ſhould have barred his unſuitable Expreſſion; for ſaith that Apoſtle, *The natural Man receiveth not the Things of the Spirit of God, neither can he, becauſe they are ſpiritually diſcerned.* But if he will take *Natura φύσις pro Generatione viventium, ſive Animalium, id eſt, Nativitate*; or, if he will rather accept it in the Senſe of him they call *Divine Seneca*, that it imports a Deity, or divine Reaſon, ſown in all Parts of the World, he would do well, to let us know; for the Incongruity of his Aſſertion with good Senſe lies very palpable: He farther confirms his Opinion of the Univerſality of that (by him called *Natural*) *Inſtinct*, with his Parentheſis, *as we ſee in all Nations of the Earth, much more when he is farther ſtirred up by a divine Inſtinct.* I muſt confeſs to the Univerſality of it; but how diſguiſed it is through the various Times of Man's Inventions, and fore-Fathers idle Traditions, a Perſon never ſo little ſpiritualized may ſee, and eaſily deſcry the notorious Foppery of moſt Profeſſions; the Cauſe of which univerſal Darkneſs, has been the Nations ſacrificing their Judgments to the implicit Faith of their deceitful Prieſts; who have been and are a Monopoly to the Souls and Bodies of the whole Creation. And what he ignorantly calls *the farther ſtirring of a divine Inſtinct*, is not a difference from the former, in Reſpect of its Nature or Quality, but Meaſure or Degree. †

† *In this only can the Underſtanding ſoundly judge, and the Will rightly elect.*

I have the longer inſiſted on this Particular, becauſe moſt material, as well to detect his Weakneſs and grand Inability to the Work he forwardly has undertaken, as from his own Expreſſions to elucidate and maintain the *Quakers* Principles to be Orthodox: Although it was againſt them he mainly did deſign his Book; but with what Succeſs the End will manifeſt. I ſhall juſt hint upon his three Branches, into which he has ſplit the firſt Act of his Election. (1) He adviſes *to take a particular View of the Principal Doctrines and Myſteries of Faith, and Duty of Godlineſs taught in the Scriptures*; but doth not tell us by what infallible Expoſitor we ought to peruſe them, that might unfold thoſe Myſteries he ſpeaks of (which imply a dubious, intricate and obſcure Senſe) does he mean the Inſtinct before-mentioned? I fear he is ſcarce ſo Orthodox, or will he have us give our own Conſtructions as Things preſent themſelves to our natural Underſtanding: or muſt we walk by the Crutches of ſome Commentators? For if he will at laſt ſend all to the Scriptures, or can propoſe no better Expedient to reconcile theſe Breaches, and heal thoſe Religious Jars, than that which through Men's Blindneſs (and for want of the infallible Spirit which guides all in the Truth that receive it, and are ſubjected thereunto) has been the very Riſe and Ground of them, the World will be little beholding to this Guide.

p. 10.

His ſecond Branch adviſes to *diſcern the Verity and Certainty of thoſe Doctrines that he may venture his Soul upon them*, as if 'twere poſſible a Man could take *a particular View of the principal Doctrines and Duty of Godlineſs*, and not *diſcern* both *Certainty and Verity*.

p. 11.

His third is like his ſecond, *that a Man muſt know the Excellency thereof*, as if he could *view thoſe Myſteries, behold both, and yet not ſee their Excellency.* Thus Prieſt-like has he ſpoil'd Paper, in ſaying the ſame Thing in differing Expreſſions (as in the Caſe of the Hour-glaſs) that he may hold out.

§. 8. Act the ſecond, he goes on thus; *After the underſtanding doth thus preſent the true Religion before us in the Certainty, Glory and Excellency of it, then the next Act is for the Will to elect, it's that I am reſolved to profeſs whatever Diſgraces, Reproaches, Loſſes, Perſecutions I may meet with:* But beſides his putting Man upon Religion, inſtigating him to run and ſtrive of himſelf (A State the Scriptures declare ſhall never enter, becauſe unlawful) and Points him not to ſuch a Guide as can infallibly direct unto the true Religion, he has been ſo very bad an Example for Conſtancy, that he and his fellow-Temporizers have ſtumbled more into

p. 11.

8   *The Guide Mistaken,*   Vol. II.

1668.

Chap. I.

into a sneaking Conformity, and downright Atheism, than all their Prayers, Preaching, and Printing, will ever regain without a Miracle.

His third Act is little more than a Repetition of the former (a Crime he is very guilty of, as my Marginal in some Place doth observe.)

p. 14.

§. 9. His third Chapter chiefly consists of Considerations, *to evidence it a principal Point of Wisdom for a Man to make a right Choice of that Religion he would profess*: His first is drawn from the Necessity of a Man's being of some Religion: indeed I cannot understand wherefore he should be so often earnest in pressing Men to be of some Religion, who plainly tells them in several other Places there's no Salvation out of the true one; unless he thinks the imploying their Talent to the Service and Adoration of a false God, be more excusable than to worship none: But to inforce this Consideration, he does the *Quakers* the Advantage of farther instancing a Proof for them, and against himself: says he, *in the very framing of the Nature of Man there are such Principles of Religion ingraven on him that cannot be razed out, that have taught the very Heathens to worship a Deity*—Come judge, impartial Reader, betwixt this Guide and the so much condemned *Quakers*, who has here repeated what he had before acknowledged, with this material Addition, *that cannot be razed out*, I would gladly be informed, whether, if he allows the Eternal God to have created and formed Man in Body, Soul and Spirit, that it be not reasonable to conclude no other could invest Man with Religious Principles, and a Propensity to worship a Deity? and can it be admitted by any sober Person, the Principle God hath bestowed on Man should be natural, and yet religious; imperfect, and yet the Gift of God? Surely there can be none so dim-sighted as not to discern these very gross Contradictions: for if God has imprest on Man such a Religious Principle, to teach him to adore a Deity (which must be himself, or else it would not answer the End for which it was given) what is it less than to declare that God hath distributed unto every Man such a Proportion of his pure Spirit, and Measure of his Grace, as might enable him in Thought, Word and Deed to perform that Good, that acceptable and perfect Will of God? And that the Ground of those Divisions in Religion, Fallibility in Judgment, Cruelty in Disposition, and all other Abominations that like a Deluge overflow the World, is not from the Insufficiency of that Divine Principle, but from neglecting and disregarding the Righteous Dictates and Instructions of it: And let him not deny it to be the same it was, who bears this Testimony *that it cannot be razed out*, so deeply (is it his Opinion, as well as Truth) has the infinitly Divine Sculptor ingraven the Characters of his Eternal Law on the Hearts of all Nations, that no Time or Alteration amongst Men can possibly obliterate or deface it.

p. 15.

p. 16.

His second Consideration is *from the many Religions which are in the World, as Heathenism, Mahometanism, Judaism and Christianity*: But in his last he sums up the many Sects and Perswasions that commonly are known therein: he has divided them into such as differ doctrinally or circumstantially; and those which err fundamentally: The first are *Lutherans, Calvinists, Arminians, Anabaptists, Episcopalians, Presbyterians, Independents*, &c. to whom he boldly allots Salvation. But how far his, *&c.* may concern us, he in a few Lines after particularly lets us understand, wherein he has not more exprest his Cunning than his Cowardice; for as he is willing to allow all those Perswasions to be Christian, who are most likely to have the Civil Power in their Hands, (that come any of those seven, with his large, *&c.* he hopes to secure himself Priest of *Wramplingam*, without being condemned for temporizing) so doth he manifest himself exceeding bold, in fighting such for Infidels and Hereticks, as either cannot or will not practise external Violence on those Powers that protect such Caterpillars;) and that he may the better insinuate, he ventures at this Juncture of his Plenty to own his *quondam* Brethren in their Adversity, calling them all Children of the same Father, drest up in different Habits; but that his *Wardrobe* was better furnished than the rest is evident, from his Variety and Change, yet more penurious, for that he never wore a Coat, he has not turn'd.

p. 18.

p. 18.

His last Consideration I rather call the Sequel of the former, *Because*, saith he, *if one should happen of the true Religion, he would never be true unto it, unless he took it upon such a Right Choice as before was spoken of.*

—— What Choice of Religion he has made, or what Arguments he has used to confirm it, I shall refer unto thee, Reader: But I would fain entreat this *Guide* once to be serious with himself, and ask his Heart if ever it had any? And

whether

whether it has not through all Revolutions discover'd it self very deceitful and unsound? Alas, why will he thus nakedly expose his Ignorance and Hypocrisie to publick Censure, unless he would confess? Stiling a Conformity to the Constitution of the Church of *England*, a Right Choice of Religion, methinks it had been rather his Discretion to be silent, contenting himself with his *Stipendium* or Hire, and hiding his Inabilities in the Rusticity of his own Parish; for he must be a very Child that does not see his Weakness and Temerity, that comes abroad reeling and interfering through every Chapter of his Treatise; nor is his Impudence less condemnable, who takes upon him to encourage others to Fidelity, that has himself ever relinquish'd that Perswasion which has sunk under the growing Power of a new Opinion; and this is so notorious, that though I have reserved the Relation of his Carriage for another Place, yet I could not let these Expressions slip my Animadversions.

§. 10. The Business of his fourth Chapter is to invalidate the Religions profest by *Heathens*, *Turks* and *Jews*; and upon better Grounds to extol the *Christian*. It's far from me to justifie the Opinions or Practices of those acknowledged *Infidels*, but I must also say, If the Christian Religion had no better Defendants, and it's Adversaries no stronger Opponents than this Guide, with his proofless Affirmations, it would have as little Reason to owe him it's Acknowledgments, as the others their Ill-Will and Prejudice: —— And one Thing let me tell him, the false *Christian* (for such is he who takes upon him that Profession, and lives not the Holy Life of Him whose Name he bears) is more intolerable than *Heathens*, *Turks*, or *Jews*, and whilst the idle gormandizing *Priests* of *England* run away with above *Fifteen Hundred Thousand Pounds a Year*, under Pretence of being God's Ministers, (who never sent them, but are Preachers of their own chaffie Inventions, not having known his Power, nor seen his Shape) the equal Conversation of those *Infidels* should make both *Priests* and *People* blush; and in the Day that God Almighty shall judge the Works of Men by Jesus Christ, it shall be found more tolerable for them to enter into rest, than the outside washt *Christian*: But, lest I may be censured by thee, Reader, for too severe, let me beseech thee to enquire throughout the Story of the World, where any Kind of Religion has been, or is establisht by Authority, and thou wilt doubtless find upon a diligent Search, that the *People's Judgments* have ever been and are fast chain'd in the *Priests Inquisition*, and that no Sort of People have been so universally through Ages the very Bane of Soul and Body to the Universe, as that abominable Tribe, for whom the Theatre of God's most dreadful Vengeance is reserv'd to act their Eternal Tragedy upon.

§. 11. The Scope of his fifth Chapter is to direct People how to chuse the safest Way amongst the Variety of Sects that are to be found in *Christendom* (so call'd): But before I shall examine the Force and Verity of his Fundamentals, I must take this Passage along with me, which is a Contradiction both to Scripture and other Parts of his own Discourse: —— *Know* (saith he) *that notwithstanding these Diversities of Sects and Variety of Opinions which are found amongst Christians, from which they are not privileged, as neither are those other three Religions*, Heathenism, Judaism, Mahometanism, *nor shall be fully whilst we be imperfect, and know but in Part, and are in part carnal, as well as spiritual, whilst the envious one shall sow Tares in the Field of the Church, and it shall please God to suffer these Things to be, that they which are approved may be made manifest*.

—— I shall not object against the long-suffering of God toward the Sons of Men, who waits that they might return and not be consumed; and till they are reform'd from their gross Darkness, they will not only live (but as Enemies too) amongst the true Circumcision, and those who worship God in Spirit; but how an Impossibility of Perfection in such as do believe, can be argued from the acknowledg'd Imperfection of those who never knew the Blood of Sprinkling, and are not come to Jesus the Saviour from all Iniquity, will scarce hold any Agreement with the very Resemblace of Reason. I well know, that if the World consisted of a Thousand Men, and but one Hundred of them were separated from it's Unrighteousness, or had imbrac'd that pure Religion which keeps unspotted, the whole World cannot be esteem'd *perfect*, since the greater Number remains *Infidel*; however, that which is *Spiritual*, is as certainly *perfect*, as that which is *carnal* is *imperfect*: But to insinuate the Necessity of Imperfection in the *particular*, from the Allowance of it in the *General*; or to deny Perfection attainable by some, because of the confest improbability of being attain'd by all, is false and sophistical:

Gal. 4. 29.

Contrariorum eadem est ratio.

For though all the Individuals of Mankind may not probably be perfect, yet since the Powers, Faculties and Nature of Mankind is as well in the *individual* as the *Species* (there being a Possibility of his Perfection) the Capacity is in all.

And for those two Expressions of Scripture quoted by him, they both are wrested beyond their genuin Sense: I can allow the best of Men to know but in Part, and not submit to his imperfect Apprehensions; for not to mention many Scriptures, nor tediously to argue, there is a Perfection which consists in an entire Separation from the Pollutions of the World, as absolutely necessary and congeneous to the second *Adam*'s State, or Qualification of a true Christian; and a Perfection relating to that more ample and eternal Enjoyment of all Divine Knowledge and Celestial Ravishment, when these earthly Tabernacles shall be dissolv'd: I shall in short say, that as this Place was urg'd to overthrow the Doctrine of Perfection, and consequently insinuate that popularly pleasing Opinion of Sin for Term of Life, so could he never have found a more express Parable to vindicate it by. If Christ's Interpretation ought to be of most Authority, which is this; *The Field is the World, the Good Seed are the Children of the Kingdom, but the Tares are the Children of the wicked One*, he will be greatly disappointed of his End, which also the very Parable refutes from the Nature of the Tares and Wheat: for as I have already said, if he will not argue an Imperfection to *Believers*, from that which is already granted to *Unbelievers*, there needs no more Dispute about the Matter; but if by a confest non-perfection in that greater Number of Tares, or unrighteous Men, he therefore will conclude there is no perfect *Wheat* or godly Men, this were to contradict the express End and very Purpose of the Parable: But since the Nature of the *Wheat* admits no mixture with the Tares parabolically, it follows really that the Children of the Kingdom should have no Relation or Fellowship with, but be separated from, the Nature of the wicked One, and Conversation of his Children, which is more particularly confirm'd in those Places where 'tis said, *He which sinneth is of the Devil, but he that is born of God sinneth not, because the Seed of God abideth in him*: As is the Begetter, so is the begotten. It may be farther observ'd, that into the Kingdom, of which they are called Children or Inhabitants, other Places will not allow an Entrance for any Thing that is unclean or makes a Lye: nor is it congruous with Scripture and common Sense, the same Temple should hold *God* and *Mammon*, *Christ* and *Belial*, or that any can witness a being *dead*, and *crucified* with *Christ*, whilst living in that which has no Share in him. And though he would imply a *Salvo* or Defence for the Admission of all Sorts to *Sacraments* (so call'd) under the Notion of the Field's being the Church, yet, if he well observes, it is call'd the World, out of which the Church of Christ, both as to Doctrine and Conversation, was always gathered; (otherwise those *Heathens*, *Turks*, *Jews*, &c. whom he would exclude, must be Members of his Church;) and whilst he would intrude Tares or the whole Rabble of unrighteous Persons, as Members of Christ's Church, he has forgot the Testimony born by the Apostles concerning that Spotless, Blameless, and Perfect Body, of which Christ Jesus was the Head. And if he would from Christ's Words, of *letting them alone* cover his Practice of admitting all, as being ignorant, who is a Believer, (since none knows, *but in plucking up the Tares he may pluck up the Wheat also*) for this Guide's a Latitudinarian) what need his whole Discourse for a particular Constitution? He might, I am sure, have let that alone as knowing it would be of little Force; yet may he better understand the Passage, if he please, of Persecution; for they were known to be Tares, else how could the Servant say, *Sir, didst not thou sow good Seed in thy Field? from whence then hath it Tares?* If he had not rightly discerned their Nature, and that the Wheat was to hold no Communication in any religious Sort with them? nor were they to express Severity or Force, but (leaving them in supernatural Cases to the Determination and Punishment of the great Judge) live a self-denying Example to the World: — In this Sense *Imperfection* is granted, I mean to the carnal and unregenerate; but to the *Redeemed* of God, and Children of the Kingdom, *Perfection*. I am now come to the Examination of the Essentials of his so much recommended Choice.

§. 12. His First Article is, concerning the Nature of God, and what of Him is to be believed by those that would be Happy: His Words are these, *That there is One God, of an Infinite, Perfect, and Spiritual Nature, subsisting in Three Most Glorious Persons, the Father, Son, and Holy Ghost; who is the Maker, Preserver, and Governour of All Things, and intends His own Glory in All His Works: That the greatest Concernment of Reasonable Creatures, is to know and acknowledge this God,*

God, *fear, love, adore, and glorifie him; and their chiefest Felicity stands in his Love and Favour, in fullest Conformity to his Image, and in no Earthly Good separate from him.*

—— Taking the former Part of his Definition for granted, to wit, *The Perfection, Infinity, and Spirituality of his Nature,* how very unsuitable herewith is the Religion and Practice of this Guide, first, in denying that Revelation by which only a Knowledge of this Glorious and Invisible Deity can be obtained, which was the Testimony Christ bore concerning him, *That no Man knew the Father but the Son, and He to whom the Son revealed Him;* so that if such Revelation as gives to behold the Father, see his Shape, and contemplate the Excellency of his Nature, be wholly rejected by this Guide, methinks it is either Arrogancy to intrude Things he doth not know, or Folly, to tell a Tale received from other People, for infallible Truth, without a Demonstration in himself.

Next, if there be no other Way to have Communion with this *Invisible God,* that thereby the Conformity he talks of may be known, (for being a Spirit, it's preposterous to imagine a Knowledge of *Him* obtainable by other *Mediums,* (than what are adequate to his Divine Nature) but by this Revelation of *Himself* thro' *His Son Christ (in us, except we are Reprobates;)* it will necessarily follow that he must either deny Christ's Doctrine, or else confess himself ignorant of what he writes. And *since the God he would advise all to know, fear and love, is that perfect Spirit,* I fain would know what Worship can be termed suitable thereunto, but the Internal and Spiritual One? Which is altogether void of those *Ceremonies, Formalities, Will-Performances, and Perishing Observations, once used as condescending Signs to the Weakness of some Seasons, which at this Day fill up the Sacrifices, and in which stands the Religion of those called* Christians *through the World;* whose Ignorance of God's once dispensing with Beggarly Elements, for their Sakes whose Understandings were vailed and too weak-sighted to behold at first the Glorious Light, has put many upon the Imitation of past Generations, though void of their Spirit, and not answering the End for which they were then practised, vainly conceiting them *an Offering acceptable to the Eternal Spirit, when it were as well-pleasing to present a Dog's-Neck, as anciently was said.*

What shall I hence conclude, but as the Almighty God is a Spirit, so cannot he otherwise be known or served; and since He has required Homage from his Creatures, and yet is so purely Just as to expect but what he has impow'red them to do, how absolutely necessary is it that all Worship Godward should stand in the Ability given of him thereunto, and how Reasonable to believe that the Occasion of all the Apostacy, Darkness, Inventions, and whole Variety of Forms and Constitutions of Religion, have been from the Neglect of that Pure Spiritual Capacity once given of God to act and order them in all Things that did concern their Duty both to God and Man.

As for his strange Distinction of the *Deity,* which he inforces on the Faith of all that value their Eternal Welfare, I cannot find one Scripture that will bear him out; and if they had been of so much Credit with this *Guide,* as to have been by them led into their undeniable Form of Sound Words, he would not have intruded Tradition for Scripture to the Creed of any, but rather have inserted the Text or Phrase it self, whose Authority might have commanded an Assent: And it had become him to give the World a Reason for his requiring a Submission to, and Credence of his Doctrine, rather than barely to draw up so many Articles, and thus imperiously to call on all for a Subscription as they would be saved; especially since he cannot but know how strongly these very Points have been debated in Ancient Councils, and not less controverted by modern Persons of Reputation and Learning: Some owning One Eternal God, void of all Personal Relations, as *Arrius,* with many Prelates, and some Emperors, in former Centuries: *F. Socinus, L. Socinus, Crellius, Slictingius,* &c. of later Days. Others contend for the Existence of this Divinity in the Relative Persons of Father and Son, as *Macedonius* of old, and many in these Times, to say nothing of Particulars; both which may properly be call'd *Anti-Trinitarians,* or Opposers of this *Guide's* Trinity. But because the Scriptures do not warrant that Division into, and Appellation of *Three Persons,* and that he slightly passes over this Weighty Matter, recommending it for an *Article of Faith,* but never arming him with Reasons that receives it for his Defence against the Strength and great Subtilty of his Adversaries, I here shall offer him by Way of *Query,* what every Sober Person would desire Satisfaction in before he entertains his Principle.

1668.

Chap. I.

Mat. 11. 27.

Isa. 1. 13, 14, 15.
Ch. 66. 3.

1668.
Chap. 1.

Query 1. *Whether that Eternal and Almighty Being, called* GOD, *implies more than One Pure and Simple Act?*

2. *Whether He can be said to subsist in Three Persons?*

3. *Whether any Thing can rightly be called* GOD, *that is not Infinite, and without Beginning?*

4. *Whether if God did beget a Son, that Son had not a Beginning? And if the Holy Ghost proceeded from both, whether he was Contemporary with the Son, and both Co-eternal with God? Since the Begetter precedes the Begotten, and that the Begotten cannot exist before it is?*

5. *Whether these Three Persons are indistinguishable, or distinct from the Godhead, and each other, by incommunicable Properties?*

6. *Whether if* GOD, *implies the Fulness, Perfection and Glory of All; and that no Addition can be to his Greatness and Delight, but what was in his Most Pure and Perfect Self from all Eternity, as that One Pure Act; the Successive Acts of those Personal Relations can soberly be predicated of him, unless they all are Co-eternal; which seems* in terminis, *to confute a Conception, Progression and Perfection of the distinct Relations?*

If he will tell me it is a Mysterious Point, and therefore he did forbear a farther Discussion of it. I answer, it did the more require his Explanation; for that I conceive a Religion, or Hope, will do a Man but little Good, for which he has not a Reason in himself; and to believe Things by Rote, is quite as ineffectual as not to believe at all: If he shall say, That Reason is not to be consulted or rendred in this Case, I answer, That either it's what deserves Silence, and so condemns himself amongst those Fools that will be medling; or if it's to be pried into, then to be understood before believed; or else his Three Philosophical Acts of Election are defeated.

Pag. 37.

§. 13. His Second Fundamental Principle to be received, runs thus: *That God made Man at first in a very Holy and Happy State, from which he soon fell, through Satan's Temptations, and all Mankind became plunged into Sin and Misery; that we are all Heinous Offenders against the God of Heaven, under his Dreadful Wrath, and the Curse of the Law, bar'd out of Heaven and Happiness, and liable to Eternal Torments, if not speedily reconciled to God, and pardoned, and by Renewing Grace, Sanctified and Converted; which neither we, nor any meer Creature, is able to do for us.*

He has here drawn up an Article out of *Scripture-Record*, but never tells us what he has experienced in the Matter, confidently bidding all embrace and believe it, without any farther Examination of its Verity, or Conviction from the Spirit of God, whose Office it is, *To Convince the World of Sin.* And I shall boldly affirm, *That this forward putting People upon the Entertainment of Notions* (though of Truth it self) *whilst the Spirit of the Living God is not at work, or moves not on the Waters, is but the forming up that very Righteousness which is the Second Office of the Eternal Spirit to Convince of,* and condemn the World for. A Confutation to his own Principles and Practices is apparent in the latter Part of this Second Fundamental; *For if they who are sanctified and converted are no Heinous Offenders,* then will it reasonably follow, *That such as are Heinous Offenders, are not sanctified and converted:* But this Guide, with all his Tribe, that are Daily crying, They do the Things they ought not, and have no Health in them, are *Heinous Offenders*; therefore they never knew the *Saving Health of all Nations*, nor yet have felt the Blood that purges, that Spirit which sanctifies, that Word which converts to God. Again, the Holy God is perfect, and has no Fellowship with one unfruitful Work of Darkness; but this Guide allows that Man must be reconciled, or else he lies under the Curse of the Law, therefore there is a Possibility, nay, a Necessity of Man's being Perfect, which to deny, is to contradict his allowed Reconciliation, unless he can tell where to fetch a Proof, That the most Pure God will have Fellowship with, or be reconciled to, whatever is not of his most Perfect Nature; nor is it Sense to say, the Creature can be reconciled, whilst in the Commission of that the Curse for ever lies upon. His Terms *Sanctifie and Convert*, imply as much, especially if he be of *Paul's* Mind, *That prayed the Primitive Saints might be Sanctified throughout*: And if he has an Art to make *Convert* imply more or less than a being changed, turned from, or made new, he would do well to let us know it; for how a Man, in good Sense, can be changed, and the same, *Sanctified and*

John 16. 8, 9, 10.

1 Thes. 5. 23.
Pag. 38.

and Polluted; turned from his Way, and yet in it reconciled, and under the Curse at the same Time, is a Kind of *Antithesis* I never understood. But I haste to his Third.

§. 14. His next Great Principle he recommends, is this, *That the Lord Jesus Christ, the Only Begotten Son of God, Co-essential and Co-eternal with his Father, upon the Appointment and Designation of his Father, voluntarily undertook the Office of a Saviour and Redeemer to Mankind, and being made Man, took upon him our Sins, and the Curse of the Law, and giving himself up a Sacrifice an Offering to God for us, purchased by his Death all Things conducing to Grace and Glory; and having by his own Power risen from the Dead, and ascended into Heaven, he is become an All-Sufficient Saviour, and will effectually confer Pardon, Grace and Salvation, on all those who shall truly believe in him, and that there is no other Name under Heaven to be saved by, but the Name of Jesus Christ.*

O the confused Babble of the World, the by-rote Canting of this *Guide*! How does he wander in the by-paths of vain Tradition and Invention! Romancing over the weighty Mysteries of Eternal Life: And from the dark Results of several Factious and corrupted Councils, has piec'd up a Fundamental to recommend, as indispensibly to be embraced by all: He tells us, *Christ is the Begotten Son of God*: And in his next Words, calls him, *Co-eternal*. I am as far from questioning Christ's Eternity, as ready both to scruple and reject his Phrase, it carrying manifest Opposition to it self. A little farther, he says, *Upon the Father's Designation of the Son, he voluntarily undertook the Office of a Saviour, to effect what after follows on the Behalf of distressed Mankind.* If the Father did appoint the Son, then 'twas not voluntary, or an Act springing from his own *Arbitrium*, (for that's the strict and true Signification of it) but the Father's; so that by Consequence, Christ was not the Cause, but the Effect of God's Love to Man, which contradicts the Ground of that Satisfaction many have conceived themselves secured by, and interested in.

But because this Doctrine has been much controverted, and that the World of those called *Christians* are bearing hard hereupon, according to their Variety of Apprehensions, as the only Support, I shall a little query in the Matter, leaving it to this Guide to direct unto the End of what I ask; for barely to lay down a Doctrine, without the least Proof, is so irrational, as I know none but would be rather forward to reject it, (though in Measure True) because void of a Reason to maintain it. He says, *That Christ took upon him our Sins, and has given himself a Sacrifice*; or in other Terms, has satisfied the Justice of the Father displeased with Man.

Query 1. *Whether he satisfied as God or Man?*
If as God,
(Because no meer Creature can) Then,

Q. 2. *Whether this does not split the Unity of the Godhead?* Which (says this Guide) is the same in Father and Son; *and make a Duality in Natures as well as in Persons; since the one is the Appointer, the other the Appointed; the one Designer, the other Designed; the one Satisfier, the other Satisfied.*

Q. 3. *Whether since the Godhead is but one Pure Act, it's not to say the Father sent the Son, the Son the Father; the Godhead, the Godhead?*

Q. 4. *Whether the Conception of the Appointment, preceded not the Conception of Obedience in the Appointed?*

Q. 5. *Whether Relatives are predicable of a Deity, having their Primitives, which supposes Priority, in Time as well as Nature? Or how commanding, and obeying, Acts can be soberly affirmed of the Divine Being?*

Q. 6. *Whether it is Harmonious with Reason, or according to Scripture, warrantable, to say, That Christ, as God, satisfied his Father? Since 'tis to make God resolved to have Satisfaction somewhere, and none being of Ability, that the same Godhead should pay it; that his Mercy should pay it his Justice, that one Attribute (so called) should deny an Acquittance, till to'ther had solv'd the Debt; God the Father standing off in high Displeasure, and on his Terms, and the same Godhead in the Son designed to satisfie?* Gal. 3. 20.

Q. 7. *Whether if there be not distinct Properties and Attributes in the Father and Son, but are one Pure Being and Godhead, concurring in the Conception, Progression, and Perfection of all Acts, it is less Reasonable and Necessary that the Justice of the Son should have an infinite Satisfaction paid it, than the same Attribute in the Father?*

If

If as Man,

Q. 8. *Whether if the Justice of God be Infinite, his Satisfaction ought not to bear a Proportion therewith?*

Q. 9. *Whether Christ Jesus, as Man, could offer up an infinite Sacrifice, to satisfie the infinite Displeasure of his Father? paying all due Respect to his very great Afflictions, which were sustained by him in his fulfilling his Father's Will, and really were, towards the Salvation of Mankind, as a pleasant Offering.*

If as God and Man,

Q. 10. *Whether if Two Mediums be singly inconsistent with the Nature of the End for which they were propounded, the Conjunction of them does not rather augment, than lessen the Difficulty of atchieving it?*

Q. 11. *Whether 'tis not to paint the Merciful God most Revengeful, that not being able to have his Satisfaction where 'twas owing, would take it where it was not due?*

Q. 12. *Whether it were not more suitable to Truth, and Scripture Record, to avoid all dark Conceits, Schoolmen's Quiddities, and vain Janglings, and to believe, That God was, and is in Christ (who is in us except we be Reprobates) reconciling the World, or Men, unto himself, by removing that unrighteous and self-exalted Nature, which ruled as God in their Hearts; and by His Glorious Light, giving them to know the Glory of God in the Face of Jesus Christ?*

Thou must not, *Reader*, from my querying thus conclude, We do deny (as he hath falsly charged us) those glorious three, which bear Record in Heaven, the *Father*, *Word* and *Spirit*, neither the *Infinity*, *Eternity* and *Divinity* of *Jesus Christ*; for that we know he is the mighty God; nor what the Father sent his Son to do on the Behalf of lost Man, declaring to the whole World, we know no other Name, by which Atonement, Salvation and plenteous Redemption comes; but by his Name, are according to our Measures, made sensible of its mighty Power: But rather to let thee see, how unsatisfactorily he has imposed Religion on the World, and how exceeding open, he has laid his *Principles*, to the *Objection* of every reasonable *Inquirer*; for whilst he undertakes to dress up a Religion, that shall excel all others, and boldly recommends it to such, who are resolved to be of some Religion, (as if there did accompany it such undeniable Evidence, that though it might effect little upon the loose and disolute *Atheist*, to fix his moving Mind, yet questions not the good Success, it might have upon the *Religiously* inclined) he in Reality has not brought a Proof or solid Argument, as Encouragement for any to embrace them.

§. 15. His last *Cardinal Doctrine* I am come to, after which it had been more proper, some may think, to have inserted the preceding Caution; but since this may not give so much Occasion to such as watch for Opportunities, to raise their misty Suspicions, and that it might be too remote from those Passages, for the better Explanation of which it purposely was mentioned, I have the rather placed it here; and now for the Examination of this his last Fundamental,

That our Redeemer, the Lord Jesus Christ, having all Power in Heaven and Earth given to him, hath made a new Law, and caused it to be proclaimed to the World, wherein he promises Pardon and Salvation to all that shall sincerely accept him for their Saviour.

He boldly calls him his Redeemer, not observing how unsutable his Life and Doctrine is with the Redeemed of the World; for whosoever is redeemed by Christ, is perfectly so, inasmuch as all his Works are perfect; but as this Guide's Conversation manifests the contrary, by his very great Miscarriages, so does his Book; for *Paul* testifies to all, *That Jesus Christ was sent to redeem*, not only *from Iniquity* (which might admit of a Distinction, by froward and unclean Spirits) but all *Iniquity*; therefore this Person has spoke too largely, in calling the pure Jesus his Redeemer, for such imperfect Works would very much disgrace their Author; nor is there any Thing, so much stumbles *Infidels*, and brings a Reproach upon the Christian Religion, or Dishonour to the Holy God, as Priests and People, writing, talking, and fighting hard for Christ as Redeemer, whilst every Eye finds them, as polluted and deeply engaged in dishonest and immoral Practices, as those against whom they contend.

And truly repenting of their Sins, shall rest on his Death, and merits, alone for Life, and love him above all Things, and sincerely obey his Gospel, Laws and Commandments, and shall persevere in this Duty to the End.

I hope by this Time, Reader, thou art sufficiently convinced, this Guide is leading thee to a State of Perfection, notwithstanding he would make thee believe it's unattainable in this Life; for he concludes, we ought to love God above all; and is it possible for any Mind, but that which walks with God, is born again, and entirely translated from the Kingdom of Darkness, into the Kingdom of God's marvellous Light, to be so entirely divorced from all, and espoused to God, as *to love him above all?* and *sincerely* (which implies no less than the strongest Activity of an upright Soul) *obey his Gospel, Laws and Commandments, and persevere,* which excludes all Commission or Omission to the contrary.

In short, if Christ's Law be imperfect, then must it's Author be so too, but he is purely perfect, so must his Work or Law: And if the Law be perfect, then is the Observer also perfect, but the Law and Gospel is proved undeniably perfect, therefore must the Observer also. And lest this Guide should offer to retort, that none can observe it, let him answer for me, who says we ought not only to *observe and obey it, but with Sincerity, and Perseverance in fulfilling the Commands of it to the End,* Finis coronat Opus, *The End's Perfection.*

He follows on to this Effect, *And after he shall have sent his Holy Spirit, to work Faith and Conversion in his Elect, he will certainly come again, and by his mighty Power raise the Dead, and convene both quick and dead before his Judgment, and then such as obey his Gospel, he will adjudge to eternal Glory, but Unbelievers to eternal Torments.*

He has here jumbled many Things of moment up together, scraps pickt out of more ample Discourses. Succinctness is commendable, but not in his abrupt Way; cramming and stifling Matters for want of Room to open and explain themselves to the Convincement of the Understanding: And whilst he loudly does exclaim against the *Quakers,* for slighting the Scriptures; who is there found more guilty than himself? that though his Book treats of nothing less than such a Religion, as he assures all must embrace that would be saved, 'tis rare he cites one Passage of them, for a Confirmation of his very Fundamentals; He tells us of the Necessity of believing God *will send his Holy Spirit,* as being otherwise void of *Faith and Conversion,* and yet denies the very Office of the Spirit, which is to reveal the Mysteries of God, and to convert from fallen *Adam's* State, to that glorious *second Adam's,* which never fell, and if he did believe in that eternal Power, which *raises from the Dead,* in Trespasses, it would be to him according to his Faith; *For God is faithful, that hath promised:* But being wholly ignorant of Christ Jesus, the Power, no Wonder if he never knew the Resurrection, and the Life: And how absurd it is for one to draw a Representation of a Thing he never saw, or venture to challenge an Assent to what he ignorantly has fancied to himself, without one Argument to induce, or so much as an Observation, to explain the Obscurity of his Doctrine, I leave the sober Reader to determine.

1 Cor. 1. 24.
John 11. 25.

Thus having endeavoured an Enervation of his four Fundamentals, I shall hasten to the Examining the Force of his Accusations against my Friends, but in my Way thither, I shall a little turn my Eye upon some Passages of lesser Moment.

§. 16. His sixth Chapter mainly intends the recommending to our Consideration, some religious Matters of a secondary Nature; as a preparative to Conformity; for though he seems to express a Tenderness, towards doubting Consciences, yet if we follow him through his 8th and 9th Chapters, it will evidently appear, to be no other than a more facile and probable Way to insinuate the same Conformity-Spirit to the Minds of others which he stands branded with himself; and by his Plea, for a Conformity (as Christian) he palliates his own wicked temporizing, and would so far prevail on others, that none may be left to accuse him of Inconstancy: And if he were the Man he pretends himself to be, what needs he busie himself in scribling, *who has Tenderness enough, he says, to overlook Non-Conformity, and that allows the Non-Conforming-Churches to be Christian*; doth he afford the Church of *England* more? Time was, he would not have acknowledged her so much.

§. 17. His 7th Chapter, is an Application of his preceding Discourse, bringing all Ways amongst the *Christians,* (so called) of these Nations under two, either such an Establishment, *as hath the Sanction of the Law, to warrant and protect it; or those Perswasions, as are espoused by private Men.* Reader, thou may'st be sure he is not of the the last; the first wears the Cap of Maintenance: but he distinguishes amongst those many Ways he fathers on private Spirits; some he indites of holding Principles, that overturn the very Foundation of Christian Religion,

1668.

Chap. I.
Page 56. 57.
Pa. 18. 58, 59, 60, 61, 62.

ligion, whilst he more candidly dismisses others, with the Approbation of *sound Fundamentals*, although he lays it as an Home charge, *that they should not neglect the using such Means, as might better inform their Schismatical Judgments, concerning the Church of* England's *Constitution*.

Those great Impostors or dangerous *Hereticks*, whom this Guide esteems it a foolish Charity to flatter with the Hopes of Salvation, are *Papists, Socinians* and *Quakers*, by which he has at once damn'd Millions of poor Immortal Souls, however strict, serious and sincere, in what they knew, through many Generations; whilst if defective, they owe it to the Idle, Lying, Covetous, Ignorant, and murdering *Spirit*, and Practice of the *Priests*; whose Interest it has ever been to enslave and obscure the People's Understandings, by their many cursed Inventions, and terrifying Punishments; framing and trimming a Religion, with such Variety of external Ceremonies, as probably best might take and influence the carnal Multitude, enacting most severe Laws against such, as should at any Time decry their Fopperies, and testifie against their abominable Inventions; Letting their Canons play, or rather plague, to the Destruction of *Lives, Families*, and *Estates*: —— It's not my Business to apologize for *Papists*, I am not of their Kin; but look upon *Rome Pagan*, to have been much inferiour to the Impieties of *Rome* (called) *Christian*; and the latter greatly transcending the former, in all Sorts of Abomination, capable to be invented by the wicked one. —— As for the *Socinian*, I know him to have Wit and Learning enough, to encounter a more redoubtable Adversary than mine; and however he has expos'd himself to the just Censures of some, his Exemplary Life and Grave Deportment I must acknowledge to be very singular; and if his Cause receive no greater Foil than this Person's bare Reproaches, at least Assertions without Proof, the discreet World will sooner acquiesce in the stronger Arguments of *Socinus*, and his quaint Adherents, than this unreasonable and slandering Guide: Nor does a wrong Opinion gain more Credit or Life, than when oppos'd by Persons indiscreet and incompetent.

CHAP. II. *His Aspersions Reprehended.*

Chap. II.

Pag. 62.

§. 1. IT is an Art this Guide is Curious at, to purchase the Esteem of such whom his Miscarriages may justly have incens'd, at the inhumane Rate of forward and invective Slanders, on such who have for Conscience-sake stept aside from the Establish'd Ministry of the Nations; but more especially the *Quakers*, against whom he ever has been bold to write and speak (being withdrawn from every Form and Constitution, to wait for Life from God, and not from Beggarly Elements) and therefore made a Prey to all Parties, against whom he knew every Hand has been lifted up, (distressed by, and forsaken of all Civil Power) and consequently secure in his Undertaking: He was not slothful under former Powers, nor has he been less diligent since, employing all his wicked Wits to render us a People unfit to hold Society with Men, being not only destructive to Religion, but Government: Nor will the Character he has given of us, in *Pag.* 62, speak much less, where inveighing against *Sects*, he begins with us in this Manner: *I shall only instance in one more of such as err in Fundamental Points, who in respect of their Want of Learning, and outward Accomplishments, are contemptible, yet in respect of their Number, and singular Obstinacy in their Way, whereby they amuse the Vulgar, are not to be past by*, viz. *the* Quakers: *Although* Quakerism *cannot properly be called a* Sect *of* Christians, *but rather a Total Apostacy from Christianity; for excepting they have the Name of Christ in their Mouths, they scarce retain any Article of the Christian Faith*.

Reader, thou need'st not be a Man so very judicious, (although our Cause, being by most perused with a prejudiced Eye, desires thee to be impartial) rightly to taste what the Ingredients and Infusions are that do compose this Spirit, who at the very Entrance manifests himself thus intoxicated, that he has already over-shot both Verity and Good Manners; thereby preparing the Minds of such as read him, to entertain his Falsities the most he can for the Disadvantage of our Persons and Principles: This Front of his Impeachment, calls for my Answer in these Respects; (1.) We stand charg'd as to our *Want of Learning, and External Accomplishments.* It is our Joy, and Matter of Rejoycing, and many Times with unutterable Thanksgivings in Sincerity I can say, that the Everlasting God should now, as frequently at other Times, display the Riches of his Love and Grace to the mean and despised amongst Men; herein is it transcending in our Eye, that he should

abscond

abscond these Things, and leave them still as Mysteries to the Wise World, whilst in extream Love he has so plentifully vouchsafed the Revelation of them unto Babes; and therein made Good that Ancient Observation of *Paul*, in our Times, *Not many Wise, not many Noble*; not that we thereby do exclude any, only we can affirm, that the Entrance of God's Everlasting Gospel of Salvation, or whatever he has had to do amongst the Sons of Men, has been with very seemingly despicable Attendances. This ought not to be dubious unto any intelligent Person that has a moderate Acquaintance with History. If I should go no farther than the Scriptures of Truth, let it be there examined, and 'twill appear if such whom God called at any Time (from the Beginning to the End) were not Handicraft, Labouring, and Husbandmen, Persons inexpert in the Scholastick Adages, Disputations and Opinions of the Heathenish Philosophical World. But left that may not be of sufficient Authority, let them but read the Account that's largely given in this Matter by Heraldus, *who declares the Primitive Christians general Disgust to all human Literature, and Philosophy in particular, the only Accomplishments of that Age; which occasion'd the Gentiles continual upbraiding of the Christians for Idiots and illiterate Persons.* And Origen *in so many Words gives this Account of the very Propagators of the Gospel, that they were* Ἐριέργοι καὶ σκυτοτόμοι, καὶ κναφεῖς, καὶ ἀπαιδεύτοι, καὶ ἀγροικότατοι, *Weavers or Combers of Wooll, Coblers, Fullers, and illiterate and exceeding Rustick*.

But left it may be objected, that though God at first was pleas'd to use such illiterate Preachers, thereby to manifest the Greatness of his Power, yet afterwards the Means of Literature were not to be neglected, as necessary Ingredients to an able and orthodox Minister. Let such but read the Ordinance of the fourth Council of *Carthage*, where it is ordained, *Let every Clergyman get his Livelihood by some Artifice or Husbandry, without Prejudice to his Calling; and, let every Clergyman, tho' learned in the Word of God, have some Artifice or Handicraft; and, let all Clergymen that are able to labour, learn some petty Handicrafts.*

And *Gaudentius* expresly says, *that we do not read that ever the Ancients did teach Philosophy since, they did rather abhor it; I fain, says he, would see any Man that could shew that the Christians, either before, or in the Time of* Justinian, *did openly teach Philosophy.* And as the *Waldenses* of Old answered the Academian Papists (as Warnerius and others, who said concerning their Preachers, Doctores ipsorum sunt Textores & Sutores, *their Teachers are Weavers and Coblers.*) So we return to this Contemner of the Quakers, for their Unacquaintance in Learning; *We are not asham'd of our Ministers, because they labour with their Hands, procuring thereby a Livelihood to themselves, according as they are able, because both the Doctrine and Example of the Apostles doth lead us to such Apprehensions.*

And if this Guide were either learned himself, or but impartial, he may remember, that there was not one at the *Nicene* Council (whose Creed is so famous in *Europe*) who understood the *Hebrew* Tongue: not to make any Comparison between *John's Greek*, and the *Quakers English*; or to instance the great Difference betwixt *Isaiah* and *Jeremiah* in the Old Testament; *And therefore be it known to all those who shall in* Libanus's *Scoffing Stile, say, Let us not hear what these Men speak concerning Heaven, God, and Goodness, who come forth black and sooty from the Smith's Forge and Anvil.* That 'tis not in the Power of Man's Reason, Wit, Study, or Wisdom, to unseal the Book, see, hear, and understand the deep Things of God, nor to give the Light of the Knowledge of the Glory of God in the Face of Jesus Christ: But as the Apostles said, so say we, Everlasting Praises to our God, by the Revelation of his Eternal Spirit he has given us in Measure that *Divine Science*, truly so called: And this Light we are not asham'd to own for our Teacher in the Sight of Nations, but by it's Supream Authority to declare, There is not another Leader by whom Salvation is attainable, and in Obedience to whom the Nations of them that are saved must walk.

Although I needs must say, this Objection of our Ignorance had much better become a Person whose Abilities surpass this *Cantabrigian Sizer's* Education, whose inexpertness in Story, Tongues and Opinions, might have barr'd him from these uncivil as well as untrue Reflections; and so much of Literature is to be found amongst the *Quakers* (though it's not their Strength) as does, and very likely will remain unanswer'd by Scholars of an higher Form than this Conceited Guide.

§. 2.) 2. His Charge of Obstinacy we deny; nor am I much solicitous to enlarge in our Vindication, since 'tis the Sense I know he has of all who withstand a Conformity to that Establishment his Interest leads him to embrace, and bow

1668.
Chap. II.

not with him to the Rising-Sun: In this Sense we own his *Epithet*, and adjunct of *Singular* also, being indeed most *so* in Sufferings; having by all Powers (since we were a People separated by the Lord from their Inventions) been *killed all the Day long* in Reputation, Liberty, Estate, and sometimes Life; but in all other Respects (our Consciences excepted) we are always ready to express Complacency and Willingness to assist our very Enemies.

Rom. 8. 9.
Gal. 5. 16.
John 15. 12.

§. 3.) 3. He does accuse us with a *total Apostacy from Christianity*; but if the Definition *Paul* gives of a Christian ought to decide the Case, then he is one in whom Christ reigns, and by the Fruits of his Spirit manifests to the World he is redeemed from it, and from fulfilling those Lusts which once had absolute Dominion over him: But whether this Guide, or the so much calumniated *Quakers*, are fullest of Self-denyal, most separated from the World, or in greatest Subjection to that pure Spirit of Grace which teaches to deny all Unrighteousness, and to live soberly in this present World, impartial Reader, speak? For if the preceding Qualities denote Men truly Christian, and that a pious, diligent, and inoffensive Conversation, is the most express Character of Christ's Followers; I make my Appeal to thee and the whole World, if there lives among the Sons of Men a People less deserving to be call'd Apostates, and consequently any that so visibly carry with them the Badge of true and Primitive Christianity as they. And whereas he says, we *scarce retain any Article of the Christian Faith*; We do in so many Words reject his Aspersion, being made Partakers of that Divine Faith in Jesus, *which sanctifies, and is held in a pure Conscience*.

Titus 2. 11, 12.

Acts 15. 9.
1 Tim. 3. 9.

§. 4.] 4. His next Accusation is, *That they extol the Light in all Men, as the only sufficient Rule to walk by, to the apparent slighting of Scriptures, and Preaching*.

Reader, If yet thou art a Stranger to this Light he thus explodes and vilifies, let me beseech thee once to observe it in thy self, and tell me then if it has not that Divine Quality to discern betwixt the Precious and the Vile, and manifest every Thought, Word, and Act; whether it is well-pleasing, or the contrary, to the Great God? If it be criminal to own those Scriptures he falsly says we slight, the Case is chang'd, otherwise, we all confess that *God is Light*, and *that he hath enlighten'd every Man*; by heeding and obeying the Dictates of which, we may be preserv'd in that Capacity, as the same Scripture says, shall bring us into the pure Fellowship, and that the *Blood of Jesus shall cleanse us from all Sin*. Nor do they own a Principle in the Clouds, but above all People have demonstrated the Power and Authority of their Principle by that Redemption it has wrought for them, and Alteration it has made from that Condition which nakedly expos'd their immortal Souls to the Snares and Entanglements of this World's perishing Glories, to experience the *Blood which cleanseth from all Iniquity, the unspeakable Peace of perfect Reconciliation with God*.

Jo. 1. 9.
1 Jo. 1. 5. 7.

And for his confident affirming we slight both Scriptures and Preaching, I have this to say, That as there is not any who discover more Respect for them, by a Conformity of Life to what they require, so do they both read, and as often quote them in Preaching, or Declaration, as any who profess them for their Rule. And, Reader, that thou may'st be the better informed concerning the Esteem we have them in, take but the Pains to visit our Assemblies, and that shall be a sufficient Vindication of our Innocency, which also may answer him as to the Advantage, that's confest, the Jew had before the Heathen.

Helps the other wanted.

5. His fifth Reflection is, *Our openly denying the Doctrine of the Trinity*: But methinks it would become him who is reproving others for not paying that Respect they ought unto the Scriptures, to be a little more exemplary in using their unquestionable Phrase, and sound Expression, for I am altogether ignorant of any Scripture that mentions that Word *Trinity*; and 'tis his own Opinion, that Fundamentals should not be drawn from dubious and obscure Places, but rather that the Scriptures were evident and perspicuous, as to what was necessary to be believed; yet, if by Trinity he understands those three Witnesses in Heaven, Father, Word, and Spirit, he should have better acquainted himself with what we disown, than ignorantly thus to blaze Abroad our open Denyal of what we most absolutely credit and believe.

6. His next Slander runs thus: *The Person of Jesus Christ, as to his human Nature, with all his Offices assigned to him by his Father, they utterly reject, (though this is an* Arcanum *that is kept hid from their Novices.)*

Fain

Fain would he here infinuate to People, by his moſt invective Impoſtures, hard Thoughts concerning an inoffenſive People, whilſt in Reality they own no other Name by which Salvation is obtainable than the Chriſt of God; and all the Offices that ever were aſſigned him by his Father, are by them acknowledged; and ſo remote are they from hiding their Sentiments, or being jealous of expoſing them to all, that whoſoever will but give himſelf the Time of frequenting their Meetings, or peruſing their Books, will ſoon perceive how very far this Character is wide of Truth.

7. His next Report is, *We call not upon God, in the Name and Mediation of Jeſus Chriſt.* But, Reader, that thou may'ſt not thus be dogmatized upon, but better ſatisfied in thy ſober Inquiries, aſſure thy ſelf, the *Quakers* never knew any other Name than that of Jeſus Chriſt, through which to find Acceptance with the Lord; nor is it by any other, than Jeſus, the Mediator of the New Covenant, by whom they expect Redemption, and may receive the Promiſe of an Eternal Inheritance.

§. 5. He farther ſays, *They truſt not in his Death for Pardon and Salvation, but in a pretended ſinleſs Perfection.*

They are ſo far from diſowning the Death and Sufferings of Chriſt, that there is not a People on the Earth that ſo aſſuredly witneſs and demonſtrate a Fellowſhip therewith, confeſſing before Men and Angels, that Chriſt died for the Sins of the World, and gave his Life a Ranſom. Perfection from Sin they hold attainable, becauſe *he that's born of God ſins not*, and that nothing which is unclean can enter the Kingdom of God; no Crown without Victory; the little Leaven leavens the whole Lump; the ſtrong Man muſt be caſt out; *Paul* prays they might be *ſanctified wholly: Be ye perfect as God is perfect; be perfect, be of good Comfort; unto a perfect Man; as many as be perfect; that the Man of God may be perfect: The God of Peace make you perfect in every good Work; The God of all Grace make you perfect; let us cleanſe our ſelves from all Filthineſs of Fleſh and Spirit; perfecting Holineſs in the Fear of God; leaving thoſe Things behind, let us go on unto Perfection; and this will we do if God permit*. If Perfection were unattainable, it would be ſtrange that the Scriptures ſhould ſpeak of ſuch a State, and very prepoſterous, that *Paul*, *Peter*, &c. ſhould ſo ſollicite and pray for the ancient Saints, that they might come thither, even to the *Spirits of juſt Men* * *made perfect*; nay, he poſitively avouches to have arrived there, at the Heavenly *Jeruſalem*, at the *Church of the Firſt born*, &c. And notwithſtanding that this excellent State ſhould never be enjoined, ſeems to me no leſs than a giving the Apoſtles Doctrine the Lie, and tacitly impeaching them of groſs Diſſimulation and Contradiction. But, Reader, 'tis not only my Opinion that Perfection is attainable; for if thou pleaſeſt to remember the many Paſſages of his Diſcourſe already paſs'd my Obſervation, as well as to remark the following Chapter of his Contradictions, thou certainly wilt find Perfection an Article of this Guide's Creed, without the leaſt Violation to his Matter.

§. 6. *They deny any Neceſſity of Special Grace of the Spirit to Converſion and Sanctification, ſaying, The Light within is ſufficient hereunto, and ſcoff at them that pray for more.* — His Malice and his Lies run parallel; Are there amongſt the Sons of Men any that ſo contend for that Grace which brings Salvation, and ſo ſtrongly plead, as well with Sufferings as otherwiſe, the abſolute Neceſſity of Faith therein, Subjection thereto, and Sanctification thereby, to this blind-profeſſing World? And for his Diſtinction between the Light and Grace: Reader, if thou doſt well obſerve the Apoſtle *Paul*'s Deſcription of their Properties and Effects, I queſtion not but thou wilt ſoon condemn this Guide for ignorant, and very inobſervant of the Scriptures: For he to the *Epheſians* writes, *That whatſoever makes manifeſt is Light*, and bids them thereby *to walk Circumſpectly*. So that the Apoſtle ſets it as the Diſtinguiſher between Good and Evil, as a Guide or Leader: And thus was Jeſus Chriſt, the Fulneſs of Light, nominated by the Prophet, — *A Light unto the Gentiles, a Leader unto the People, and for Salvation unto the Ends of the Earth*; who by the Evangeliſt, is ſaid, *to have enlightened every Man*; and by the Prophet 'tis determin'd, as well as by the ſame *John* in his *Revelation, That the Nations of them which are ſaved muſt walk in that Light*; and how it can be different from that Grace, whoſe Properties are the ſame, *in teaching to deny Ungodlineſs and worldly Luſts, and to live ſoberly, righteouſly, and godly in this preſent World*, cannot be rationally ſuppos'd; for, ſays the Apoſtle *John*, *If ye walk in the Light, as God is in the Light, ye ſhall be cleanſed from all Sin*; which *Paul* expreſſes

Marginal references:
Heb. 9. 15.
1 John 5. 18.
Rev. 21. 24.
Mat. 13. 33.
1 Theſ. 5. 23.
Mat. 5. 48.
2 Cor. 13. 11.
Epheſ. 4. 13.
Phil. 3. 15.
2 Tim. 3. 17.
Heb. 13. 12.
1 Pet. 5. 10.
2 Cor. 7. 1.
Heb. 6. 1. 3.
* Heb. 12. 22, 23, 24.
Epheſ. 5. 13, 14, 15.
Iſa. 49. 6.
John 1. 9.
Rev. 21. 24.
Tit. 2. 11, 12.
1 John 1. 5. 7.
Gal. 5. 16.

presses thus, *If ye walk in the Spirit, ye shall not fulfil the Lusts of the Flesh*; and, says Christ, *I am the Light of the World, he that follows me shall not walk in Darkness, but shall have the Light of Life*: It must be therefore evident to every common Understanding, that this (so much blasphem'd) Light, Spirit, and Grace, spoken of, (leading to the same Condition, and bringing to the same End) are one in Essence and Virtue, though diversly denominated, according to the Variety of it's Operations; and who is't can be thought a Christian that denies the Sufficiency of this Glorious Light, which graciously is given of God *as a Leader to the Nations, and for Salvation to the Ends of the Earth*? And surely had this Guide but ever been acquainted with it's pure Instructions and walked therein, the Benefit that would have certainly accrued, had better taught him the Excellency of it's Nature, and the reverent Observance he ought to pay it, and not to make a Scoff at it, as he most wickedly says the *Quakers* do at Grace, (who generally are known to be no Mockers, but have been made a Laughing-stock by all Perswasions; *being reviled, they bless; persecuted, they suffer; defamed, they intreat; accounted the off-scouring of all Things unto this Day, and made a Spectacle unto the World, Angels, and Men.*)

§. 7.] 10. He follows on much at the same Rate, *Sabbaths and Sacraments, and all instituted Worship they cast off; the great Doctrines of the Resurrection, Last Judgment, Heaven, and Hell, they turn into Allegories, &c.*

How long wilt thou imagine, write, and utter lying Vanities to bespatter, defame, and expose to vulgar Rage the innocent People, and Royal Inheritance of the most high God? Can'st thou expect thy Days should terminate in Peace, and that the Judge of all will not account with thee for all thy Slanders? Yea, *Clapham*, be it known unto thee, the dreadful God shall recompence it on thy Head; nor shall thy peevish Malice (surpassing all I know) escape a Pledge of God's Displeasure on thee, e'er thou takest thy Farewel of this Earth; he will rebuke thy unclean Spirit, too full of nasty Venom and Lies, ever to have Admittance where nothing enters that defiles or makes a Lye: It's not a Rage I am in, as thou may'st think, and willingly would'st have others to believe, God bears me Record, but the infallible Sense I have upon my Spirit of thy deep ensnaring Hypocrisy to betray (if possible) others more moderate and faithful into the same wicked yielding Spirit with thy self; and also (I fear) thy immortal Enmity to us, the innocent People of the Lord, provokes to an Holy Indignation; and Judgment is for that unrighteous Nature to Eternity.

But that I may not leave the Reader unsatisfied as to this last most impudently wicked Aspersion, know in the Name of all true *Quakers*, the Sabbath that is reserv'd for the People of God, is so far from being by them rejected or deny'd, that they admonish all to the exact and punctual Observation of it, not to think their own Thoughts, speak their own Words, nor do their own Works; — for the Word *Sacraments*, 'tis no where scriptural; and, 'till he explains his Meaning, I am not bound to find him one; but for such Worship as is of Scripture-institution, and perform'd by the Spirit of God, they own and practise, disowning (as there is good Reason) all other Institutions.

The *Doctrine of the Resurrection* of the Just and Unjust, *Last Judgment, Heaven and Hell*, as future Rewards; they believe and confess: — And, as my faithful Testimony both to their Life and Doctrine, I am necessitated to declare, (and be it known to all that ever knew me) that when the unspeakable Riches of God's eternal Love visited me, by the Call of his Glorious Light, from the dark Practices, wandring Notions, and vain Conversations of this polluted World, and that my Heart was influenced thereby, and consequently dispos'd for the more intimate and sincere Reception of it; those very Habits, which once I judg'd impossible, whilst here, to have relinquished, (as well as I was unwilling) and did allow my self a Liberty therein, because not openly gross or scandalous, I thought my self excusable) became not only burdensome, and by that Light manifested to be of another Nature than that which I was called to the Participation of; but in my faithful Adherence to it's Holy Counsel and Instructions, I was immediately endued with that Power and Authority as gave Dominion over them, and being in Measure redeemed from that to which the Curse is pronounc'd, I sensibly enjoy'd the Blessings that attend a Reconciliation; And never since I have been conversant with their Principles, (thus odiously described by him) have I found one Article that did not receive a full and satisfactory Assent from that very Grace, Spirit, or Light of God, which first called me from the gross Impieties, vain Entertainments, tempting Glories and Will-worships of this Generation: And as I have the Seal of God's eternal Spirit of Love upon my Soul, as an infallible Assurance; so, since my first frequenting of them and their Assemblies, I have observ'd that holy, innocent, and righteous Conversation, which harmonizes with the Severity, Circumspection, and Self-denying Life of the Gospel; and testify, (as revealed from God) that since those Centuries, in which the Apostacy eclipsed the Beauty of the Primitive Light, there has not been so glorious a Discovery of Spiritual, Pure and Evangelical Worship, Life and Doctrine, as God hath in his Loving-kindness raised the so much despised *Quakers*, to own, practise and declare amongst the Nations; as the good old Way of Holiness, that leads from Intemperance, Vanity, Pride, Oppression, and the Love of this World's perishing Glories, to that everlasting Joy and Rest which is reserved for the People of the Most High God. In short, they are found in Principles, zealous for God, devout in Worship, earnest in Prayer, constant in Profession, harmless and exemplary in their Lives, patient in Sufferings, orderly in their Affairs, few in Words, punctual in Dealings, merciful to Enemies, Self-denying as to this World's Delights and Enjoyments; and to sum up all, Standards for the God of Heaven, against the Pride, Cruelty, Lust, Avarice, *&c.* of this Godless Generation; —whom the unborn shall call Blessed, when their Testimonies be finished, and they gathered into the unspeakable Solace and Possession of God's eternal Presence; — yet are they concluded by this uncharitable Guide, *not Company for Christians*: But I am perswaded, that the more Discreet will not relax their good Opinion for his slanderous Reflexions, but rather thence renew Occasions of farther expressing their Candour and Humanity: And I hope their discreet and inoffensive Deportment will perswade all People, they are not so deserving their ill Thoughts, as envious and self-interested Priests have endeavoured to insinuate.

CHAP. III. *His Hypocrisy Detected.*

THO' manifold are the Stratagems of Satan, that old Serpent, by which he does surprize the immortal Souls of Men with most deplorable woes, and everlasting Misery, yet is there none that proves so generally effectual as *Hypocrisy*; It's his *Mysterium Maximum*, a Study and Employment fit for none below the Form of his Arch-Angels; such make his archest Emissaries, and most subtil Meanders Sublime Devils, masqu'd with the Vizard of Sincerity, palliating themselves from what they really are, by seeming what as really they are not; outside wash'd Platters; Wolves in Sheeps Cloathing; Inside rotten, but outside whited Sepulchres: In short, the muddy Sensualist refined to a Counterfeit-Fidelity, and Imitation of the Form of Godliness, the more unquestionably to deceive, and securely to insinuate candid Apprehensions of his Purpose; who is the most impudent Despiser of God, Destroyer of Souls, Contemner of Laws, Perverter of Truth, and Treacherous to the End; against whom the sharpest Woes are denounced, and Punishments reserved to Eternity: —— How far this Guide has rendred himself obnoxious to the Character of an Hypocrite, it is our Business mainly in this Chapter to discourse: But lest his dissimulated Condescension, and pretended Christian Instructions, (as inducements to Conformity) should so far prevail upon the Unacquaintance of any with his Spirit, and notorious Practice through all Revolutions as to believe they may deserve my Observation and Reply, (since 'tis irrational to argue the Unsoundness of a Principle from the confess'd Imperfections of it's Defendants) I shall a little hint at the chiefest of his Reasons; as well to manifest 'twas not so much a general as an individual Concern that interested him in this Undertaking, as to prevent (if possible) his ingratiating his Motives to Conformity, with the Minds of such as are inclinable to Temporizing: He states his Question thus.

Whether it be a Duty for Christians to hold Communion with the Church of England, according to her present Administrations?

Had this Guide the least honesty, or been conscientious in his former Perswasions; it should not be a Question with him now (although I fear he is scarce so honest as to make it one, my Paradox is Orthodox) but having ever forfeited the Reputation of a sincere Person, and not being esteem'd other than a gross Temporizer, I easily shall grant it very requisit for him (whose Belly is his God, and that minds earthly Things) to commune with the Church of *England* in her present Administrations; but as for *Christians* I shall not ask his Leave to dissent, unless he

can

1668.

Chap. III.
p. 69.

can produce better Arguments to warrant his confident Assertions: his first runs thus: *It will not be denied by all Dissenters (that have Understanding and Sobriety in them) but that here is a clear Profession of all those fundamental Points of Faith, which are accounted amongst Christians necessary unto Salvation; yea, such a pure Confession of other Points of a secondary Nature, that there's scarce any other Church in the World that God hath blest with a greater Purity.*

What strange Confusion, and unusual Impertinency is this! Would not half-witted People blush to venture abroad in print with such Expressions? Surely this Guide was grosly fond of writing Books, that rather than be quiet, he should with such Greediness expose his Ignorance to vulgar Censure; for if the *Dissenters* he writes against, confess the Church they separate from to be greatly pure in Fundamentals and Things of a secondary Nature, how is it possible, according to good Sense, they can be termed *Dissenters* in Religious Matters? I shall appeal to the intelligent Reader, if this blind Guide is not fallen into the Ditch, that ascribes to such the Title of *Dissenters*, whom he at the same Time characters for absolute Sons of the Church; for, do the highest Conformists to the Church of *England* acknowledge more, than that she's *pure in Fundamentals and Things of a secondary nature*, and yet that such who confess her to be this, should by this silly Guide be stil'd *Dissenters!* away with this apparent Nonsense, since none can properly be so esteem'd that differs not in one or both; and how inconsistent, as well as saucy, his Expression is, that will not allow Dissenters to be *sober* and *intelligent* (when none are such in his Account, that allow not the Church of *England* what they can never do, and properly be counted for Dissenters) sufficiently appears, in his admitting these very Dissenters to be *Christian Churches, and Children of the same Father*, though now he seems to represent them void of both *Understanding* and *Sobriety*. Where his Wits were when these rash and unadvised Words were writ, I leave for the Reader to determine.

p. 72, 73.

§. 3. He speaks largely of the publick Worship, loudly extolling the Constitution of the Church of *England*, professing a Separation therefrom to be unwarrantable; and that Corruption in Manners, both of Ministers and People, should be no Reason for deserting their Assemblies, &c.

Contrary to the whole current of Scripture-record, and the best Accounts that have been transmitted through Ages of the Primitive Christians, who ever have withdrawn themselves from such as *held the Truth in Unrighteousness*; and let the World judge if *Paul* was not thus perswaded, when he strictly enjoyn'd Separation from (not only *Schismaticks, Hereticks,* and *Apostates,* but) *such as held the Form of Godliness*, which consisted in Profession and external Performances, *without* the Everlasting *Power*, which alone could bring into true Obedience, and give the Possession of that Eternal Life, which rightly denominates People Christians, or a Christian Church: But as two strong Pillars, to maintain and underprop his Assertion, he tells us, *otherwise God would have no Publick Worship*; As if an Assembly in an House, Field or Barn, was not as capable to worship God in Spirit, as those who frequent the Parish Steeple-houses; if not, 'tis fit this Guide should pay his Acknowledgements to the Roman Society (he calls *Antichrist*) for his publick Worship; but be it known to him and all the World, that as God's Spirit is not tied to Places, so all Worship standing therein is truly Catholick and Publick Worship, in Field or House, whether Three or Three Thousand; convenient Places being circumstantial, not essential, to God's Worship.

2 Tim. 3. 5.

p. 82.

p. 75.

§. 4. His second Pillar is the Example of *Zacharias, who* (says he) *deserted not his Station in the Jewish-Worship, notwithstanding those many Corruptions that were innovated*, by which he would excuse his continuance in his Priestly Office in *Wramplingam* Parish: But if this Guide will be inform'd, he soon may see his Error in this Particular, (as upon Occasion formerly was exprest to him) the *Jews* were selected from all other Nations, and privileged as God's Peculiar People, by an external Law and Ordinances (all which were typical) over whom he ordained Magistrates, and a Priesthood, which had no Relation to any other Constitution that was contemporary, or should succeed, but were to continue till the Times of Reformation, and then to be abrogated; yet inasmuch as Antitypes are represented by their Types, it must be granted, that many legal Institutions did signifie and shadow forth what afterwards should follow; since therefore it must needs be granted, that the Jewish State relates no farther to us than typically, it will not be unnecessary to examine how far this Guide can secure himself, and justifie his many Turnings, from the confest Constancy of faithful *Zacharias*.

Consider

Confider (1.) that the *Jews* were a People separated from among the Nations, as his visible Church, to whom he gave that intituling Sign of Circumcision.

2. That their Temple, Worship and Laws, moral, judicial and ceremonial, were indisputably of Divine Institution.

3. That as those who were their Priests, were by the high Priest anointed thereunto; so being once dedicated, were to officiate with Integrity and Constancy at the Altar.

4. That no Addition was to be admitted to what God had so punctually ordered, in any Circumstance. Now unless this Guide can prove the Church of *England* the Antitype;

1. In being the Circumcision in Spirit, by which she is rightly intituled to the Priviledges of the Spiritual *Jewish* Church.

2. Can as infallibly and unquestionably prove the Divine Institution of her Faith, Worship and Discipline.

3. That her Ministry is spiritually Anointed of God, by that one High-Priest after the Order of *Melchizedeck*, and by him commissionated to preach the everlasting Gospel.

4. And that in Faith, Worship and Discipline she remains as clear and single from all Inventions, Traditions and Ceremonies (those only allowed as have their footing in the Divine Appointment and Order of God) unless I say this be made good, 'twill declare great Weakness in any to allow this Guide to argue from *Zacharias*'s Case to his own; —— I grant that whosoever is anointed by Jesus Christ to preach his everlasting Salvation, ought to do it incessantly, not mattering the Opposition or Revolution of Powers; and that No defect in the Generality can or ought to unminister him, but rather that he faithfully should decry those Impieties, and keep his Station on God's Behalf, which righteous *Zacharias* did, whose bold withstanding their Inventions, and honest Desire of preserving that Law pure, of which he was instituted Priest, procured no less than his Martyrdom, from the Cruelty of those vain Superstitionists. But what's this to *Clapham*'s Case? *Zacharias* was anointed by the High-Priest; whence was *Clapham*'s Ordination? *Zacharias* was murder'd for opposing their Unrighteousness and wicked Traditions: Where did *Clapham* do so? but has he not preach'd for and against what he at Times has own'd, to keep his Parish. *Zacharias* would not dispense with their Additions to God's Institutions; has *Clapham* done so too? how comes he then to call the Church of *England*, *Pure in secondary Matters*, to wit, her Forms of Prayer, Anthems, Responses, Litanies, Baby-Baptism, Crosses, Altars, Steeple-houses, East and West, Bowings, Organs, Choristers, Surplices, Caps, Rochets, Hoods, with much more such like trash than my Memory will serve at present to insert, which fills up the English Worship, and are known by Persons moderately read in Story, to have been brought forth by the Womb of dark Popery, that sink of Antichristianism: —— But as there ought to be one Temple, Worship and Priesthood to make *Clapham*'s Case resemble *Zacharias*'s, so that his may approach this Guide's, let us suppose amongst the *Jews* three several Temples, Worships and Priesthoods, call'd *Presbyterian, Independent, Episcopal*: If *Zacharias* had first been of the Presbyterian-Priesthood, and as that should decline in esteem, imbraced the Independents, till by Revolution of Government both were violently supprest, as to the Exercise of their Consciences towards God, by the Episcopal; and then that *Zacharias* should divorce his Independent Spouse, crying *All Hail* unto the new Establishment, as *Clapham* undeniably did, he might have quoted *Zacharias* with more Honour, to his own shameful Retreat: but his constant Keeping of his Station in Faithfulness to God, sharply rebukes this Guide's manifest Infidelity both to God and Men.

§. 5. His next great Argument to enforce Compliance, is that Soveraignty bestow'd on Rulers, who (says he) *in particular Circumstances undetermined by God, have Power to order and settle Things according to the general Rules laid down in the Word*; Instancing in several Jewish Kings: Although I need not farther trouble thee nor my self, than barely to recommend the foregoing Page to thy perusal; yet left the Matter may not be so evident, I shall a little observe his very great self-contradiction; his Words are these; *There is not the like Reason to determine all Circumstances in the Christian Churches, as was in the Jewish Church, the one being in it's Minority, the other grown up to a State of greater Liberty. A Boy when he goes to School, in every Particular he is stinted to his Work; but when he goes to*

1668.
Chap. III.

the University, he only hath general Rules for his Study, and is left to his own Disposition for Order and Manner of his Studies. Is it not obvious that he does confute himself, and so has sav'd me the Pains of making any other Answer than what ariseth from his own Assertion and Similitude to prove it: He says the Christian-Church is grown to *greater Liberty*; How so, if still subject to be imposed upon by Civil Power? Is not the Slavery greater, since that the Jews were *stinted* by God himself, but we by Men, and that according to their fallible Apprehensions? yet with such Severity is Obedience enjoyn'd, as Nonconformity costs nothing less than the Price of Liberty and Estate. But since by Boys at School he means the *Jewish* Church, and by those fitted for the University he intends a *State of Liberty* in secondary Matters, what follows but that our Schoolmasters the Magistrates are dismist, and we, being under an Evangelical Constitution, are in those Matters left to that *greater Liberty* relating to the Gospel-State; which flatly contradicts that Power he in other Places does ascribe unto them: Nay, if I should make the most of his Similitude for my Advantage, how apparent would it be that the very Rulers in the Jewish-State were Boys, and stinted in all Religious Circumstances, and consequently not to be our *Schoolmasters* under a Dispensation of greater Freedom, for then the change would be to our apparent Loss and Injury; so that *others* being free as well as *Rulers*, for them to command is gross Usurpation; and for any to yield Obedience is nothing less than High-Treason against the King of Conscience, and a betraying of themselves into the *School-boys* State again——— Sometimes he says the Scriptures are clear in this Particular: in other Places, promiscuous; but his best Argument is the Magistrate, for never wanting a ready Compliance to their Commands (come what will) he has better learnt Interest than to set his Opinion in Competition; — However, I shall propose these Queries, which he may answer if he please, or any else.

Qu. 1. Whether if seven Powers make seven distinct Interpretations of Religious Principles, and erect seven distinct Modes of Worship, according to what they apprehend from the Scriptures; they all may be submitted to notwithstanding their Contrariety?

Q. 2. Whether these seven different Principles and Modes of Worship, enacted to be conformed to, in these seven Dominions, can be rightly said to proceed from the Spirit of God, the Unity; and not their erroneous Apprehensions?

Q. 3. Whether any Prescriptions concerning Faith and Worship, should be allow'd or obey'd, if not from that unerring Spirit in which God's true and only Worship stands?

Q. 4. Whether any Magistrates now in being, do or can pretend to that Infallibility?

Q. 5. Where is that Gospel-Scripture, which impowers Magistrates to concern themselves in Religious Matters?

Q. 6. Whether it be congeneous, or suitable to the second Covenant and Times of Reformation, when the Law is written in the Heart, and the Spirit put in the inward Parts; where there is but one King, and one Lawgiver; where the Offices and Assistance of Sun, Moon and Stars are no more required, but the Lamb *Christ Jesus* is their Light, their Knowledge, their Guide, their All in All; for Rulers to interpose their Civil Authority to pull down or set up Religion?

Q. 7. Whether the first Institution of Magistracy propos'd a Jurisdiction over Consciences, or only the Preservation and Prosperity of the People in Civil and External Matters?

§. 6. Many are his Cautions, and as many his Contradictions, too many for my Observation: In short, the End of all his Tenderness to Dissenters, and kind Titles of *Christian Churches, Children of the same Father, &c.* I find, is a perswading of all into an Acknowledgment of the Church of *England*. But *Reader*, if thou wilt know the Reason why this person *Now* appears so earnest in his Discourse for all to march in his *conforming Steps*, and thus confidently imposes himself a Guide on all to the true Religion, as if we had been at a Loss till now both for the *true Religion* and *a Guide*, I ask thy Patience and thy Credit in the Perusal of this *notorious* (tho' contracted) *Story of his Life*, which a Necessity is upon me to insert, that such who otherwise may let his Hypocritical Insinuations gain their esteem, may (if they please) be furnisht with an Antidote against the Infection of their Nature.

It is not long since (being in those Parts) I had some Hours converse with this Person, and amongst the many Things we touch'd upon, I charg'd him with his Retreat from a certain People to whom he formerly had a Religious Relation: Upon which he sent me this, with other Particulars, by Epistle, in a Way of Apology; *That he never had profest himself of any Party, nor would come under any distinguishing Denomination of* Presbyterian, Independent, Episcopal, *owning no other than that of a* Christian, *avowing, that whatever Apprehensions People had concerning the Church of* England, *and notwithstanding several went as far as* New-England *to enjoy purer Ordinances, yet for our Parts* (including himself as a constant Son of the Church) *we can witness the Lord's Presence is amongst us.*

To all which I then answer'd something, though not so amply; that since he seems to list himself so early amongst the Members of the Church of *England*, Where has he been during the Time of her Captivity and Exile? Did he for Conscience-sake (opposing *Covenant, Engagement*, &c.) quit the Land, contenting himself rather in the Quality of a poor begging Priest beyond the Seas, than to embrace the Perswasions of those Powers, which had reduc'd the Residue of his Brethren to extream Poverty? Or turn'd he Trencher-Chaplain, Tutor, *&c.* Did he traverse the Country, Sprinkling, Marrying, Churching, Burying, the common Trade of those ejected Priests? And can he say, that whilst the King and Bishops were incapacitated by Exile, to act as Officers in the Church and State, he own'd the One for Supream in Matters Civil and Ecclesiastical; and the others, for so many Apostolical Heads in Christ's Church? Did he protest against the Cruelty of those Powers, in the clear Subversion of both? What Prison was he in? What Bonds did he endure, what Loss sustain, Testimony bear, and Loyalty express, on the Behalf of his Episcopal Faith, and it's Defender? — Alas! But was he not in all those strange Occurrences of Times, and Variety of Changes, to be found Priest of *Wramplingam* in *Norfolk*? At the Beginning of the Wars, a most precise Stickler for a Reformation, extolling the great Necessity, as well as Righteousness of the *Solemn League and Covenant*, encouraging others thereunto, both by his Example and Doctrine: Bold for the *Directory*, and busie at *Chusing Elders*, and so went under the Notion of a *Presbyterian*: But 'twas not long before the *Independents*, through their greater Courage and Policy, had undermin'd and vanquisht t'others Interest, and when possest of the Authority, he saw 'twas Folly to expect a Salary as Guide, in that Way the Governing-Party of the Nations had rejected, and therefore was obliged to list himself a Volunteer in *J. Munny's Independent Congregation*; 'twas then the Beheaded King was by this Guide both preach'd and printed, as a *Toe of that Image the little Stone, cut out of the Mountain without Hands, was to smite*; and therefore says, *The Fall of the Ten Kingdoms was begun, the Lord is risen out of his Habitation, gainsay not; for who seeth not the Alteration is of the Lord?* And in his Answer to an Objection, that this Prophecy was accomplish'd when this Nation fell from Popery, says he, *Doctrinally it was, but not Politically; the Government hath continued the same, yea, and hard enough to the Saints* (alias NONCONFORMISTS) *none can deny it.* Now the Change this Prophecy speaks of, respects the Government. In another Place says he, *There can be no clearer Evidence that God is about this Work of breaking down this Great* IMAGE, *and smiting the very Feet and Toes thereof, than this present Victory over the* Scottish *Forces at* Dunbar, *(which we are now to render Thanksgiving to God for) the Cause of this War being, Whether this* IMAGE *shall be upheld, or the Feet and Toes be broken.* In short, *O ye Honoured Worthies, whom the Lord hath raised up to effect these great Changes, carry on the Lord's Work; That your People may not have Cause to say, We have changed our* TYRANTS, *not our* TYRANNY; *although Providence seems to put an Impossibility of setling Government in the former Way:* But Time hath proved him both a Temporizer, and a False Prophet. 'Twas also then he sought, if possible, to ingratiate himself with the Powers and People of the Land, by his most invective and false Discourse against the *Harmless Quakers*, with a large Dedicatory Epistle to O. *Cromwel*, allow'd by him of *England, Scotland, Ireland*, &c. *Protector*, to whom, amongst other extraordinary Complements, I cannot let pass these Expressions, where he invites him, *As God's Delegate, in Honour to Jesus Christ, and out of Love to the Churches of Christ, for whose Welfare you have this Great Power committed to you, to stop these Seducers*, &c. Concluding thus, *The Lord of Heaven and Earth Bless your Highness with the Continuance of His Gracious Presence with you, that as you have done Valiantly in the High Places of the Field,* (that is, fought against King and Bishops) *so you Govern as Righteously*

1668.

Chap. III.

Stone smites the Image on the Feet, p. 16, 17.

Pag. 23.

Pag. 15, 16.

Pref. p. 3.
Pref. p. 4.
Pag. 24.

1668.

Chap. III.

Righteously and Happily in the Gates of the City. O gross Dissimulation! Now 'tis he turns *Engagement-Man*, and is employ'd by the several Churches in *Norfolk*, to *R. Cromwel*, on the Death of *Oliver*, as their Representative about that Petition, or Address made by the Priests in General, which terms the Father *Moses*, and the Son the *Joshua*, that should conduct them to the *Holy-Land*: But he being by the Projections, and angry Resentments of the *Long Parliament*, divested of his Usurped Authority, this Guide finds out a very Honourable Epithet for it; which had not long tasted of Power, before another Revolution took it's Place: But I must needs confess, that when 'twas noised a King was coming in, and the Church of *England* to be restored to all her ancient Emoluments (so called) this Guide grew seemingly dejected, and very forward in expressing his Dislike against their Spiritual Lordships, and not less contumeliously (as he now would think) both of Her Worship and Discipline, hoping the *Presbyterians Testimony of Allegiance*, in their Zealously assisting to facilitate the King's Return, would so far interest him in their Concerns, as not wholly to be excluded from the Exercise of their Religion in the Land: But when 'twas manifest that nothing under an open Conformity would purchase the Enjoyment of their Parishes, (whatever becomes of them) this Guide slinks from his *Independent Church*, and *Presbyterian Hopes*, reads the *Common-Prayer-Book*, subscribes the *Articles*, changes *Oliver*, *Richard*, or *Parliament*, for *Charles*, (once a Toe of the Beast, that the Little Stone was to smite) of *England*, *Scotland*, *Ireland*, &c. And in the Place of *Christ's Churches*, the *Church of England*, with the whole Tribe however dignified or distinguished; the Beheaded King (once the first Broken Toe of the Image,) now he commemorates with an Anniversary-Sermon; and, as the Top of all, boldly renounces his so *Solemnly-taken League and Covenant*; —— What Temporizing's this! O what unheard of Hypocrisie is here! But *Reader*, What's thy Opinion of the Matter? Can *Oliver* be *Moses*? *Richard*, *Joshua*? And *Charles*, *Defender of the Faith*, altogether? Whose Interests were so opposite, as the last to be Exiled, and kept so by both: With whom was God's Presence in all these Times? The Church of *England*? If so, then not with those that turn'd her out, where *Clapham* had his Parish: How plainly have his Actions unmaskt the gross Dissimulation of his Heart, and these corrupt Fruits explain'd the Poisonous Nature of the Tree that brought them forth? But lest I may be thought to wrong him, as if it were impossible for one who pretends himself a Christian Minister, to be Guilty of such abominable Time-serving, *Reader*, peruse these Passages, where he confidently affirms such to have been, *The Best,*

Epist. p. 6, 7.
Book, p. 98.

Wisest, and Most Judicious Christians, who under all those great Changes and Revolutions, amongst us of latter Times, have endeavoured the maintaining the Fundamental Doctrines of the Gospel, even to a Degree of Compliance in Things of a lower Nature; in which he positively concludes all Persons, (from *Canterbury*, to the meanest Curate in the Nation, as also Seculars in their respective Places) have been to blame, both as to their Understanding and Wisdom, in not yielding with *Clapham* in those smaller Matters, *(viz.* an Expulsion of the Church of *England*, a disowning of Monarchical Authority, or Right in the *Stuart's* Family; Preaching and Printing it a *Toe of the Beast*, extolling the Covenant, taking the Engagement, being a *Presbyterian*, an *Independent*, a *Millenary*, &c. Praying, and Swearing for Parliament, Protectors, Parliament again, at last, King and Bishops) since those who have left King, Bishops, Common-Prayer, &c. and espoused the Interest of those other Powers, who Establish'd other Methods both in Church and State, *Were the Best and Most Judicious Christians*; but to excuse this Brazen Impudence and Hypocrisie, he concludes, *Let not any Principles you have inconsiderately taken up, so far engage you, as to make you loath to return to Ways of Truth and Soberness: But it would be considered, it's no Disgrace for the Wisest, Holiest, and most Learned'st Men to retreat, in some Controversial Principles and Practices.* *Reader*, Will this Fig-Leaf Garment cover the Shame of this Guide's Nakedness, from thy Discerning and Censure? I hope not; But does not his Covering stand in Need of one, who says, *The Holiest, Wisest, and most Learned'st Men may still be such, and yet walk not in the Ways of Truth and Sobriety:* What Weakness, what Ignorance, what strange Confusion's here! From which, I also must infer, that since he is but here of late return'd *To the Ways of Truth and Sobriety*, he all his Life-Time before walk'd in the Way of Error and Madness; Judge then how fit he was to Preach others into the Knowledge of the Truth, and a Sober Life: *Have not the People given him Money for that which was not Bread?* And farther, I would observe,

P. 106.

P. 108.

observe, 'twas in that Time of Error and Madness, he writ those wicked Slanders against us who are called *Quakers*.

§. 7. I would observe before I finish, that the Intendment of his Book is not to press Conformity to any one in Opposition to all other Constitutions, otherwise than in a Temporary Sense; for since it is his Principle, *That such are the most Wise and Judicious Christians, that have in all Revolutions complied in lesser Matters*, it follows, that the Church of *England* is no farther concerned in this Discourse, than whilst She keeps the Power and Magistracy on her Side; for which of the Seven Sons, *viz. Lutherans, Calvinists, Anabaptists, Arminians, Episcopalians, Presbyterians, Independents*, (being of the same Father) with that known, or unknown, *&c.* shall gain the Prerogative, he by his own Principles stands ready to embrace him; so that no longer than any of them have external Force to warrant their Commands and Impositions, no longer should they be acknowledged; but any other of them (though remote in smaller Matters, holding the same Fundamentals) is quite as estimable in this Guide's Account, and those Injudicious that concur not with his Sentiments; by which he does at once commend, rather than excuse his past Compliance with those several Persuasions, and palpably discovers his Readiness to do the like, as otherwise conceiving it Unwise, (*they being the Most Wise, and Best Christians, that yield in lesser Matters*) — But that which renders such Alterations suspicious to Sober Men, is the never finding them convenient till Change of Government makes them so; for amongst the many Transactions of this Person's Life, I should not forget, that when the *Fifth-Monarchy Principle* was in Esteem; which would by no Means dispense with an *Earthly Monarch*, (as belonging to the *Great Image*) *J. Clapham* prints a Discourse in the Vindication of it, but the potent Argument of *Cromwel*'s assuming it, under the specious Title of *Protector*, clearly confuted this *Great Millenary*, as he at large acknowledges in his Epistle Dedicatory to him before his Book, anciently writ against the *Quakers*; — so that the only *Constancy* I can remark of *J. Clapham*, has been the keeping of his Parish, through his very *Great Inconstancy*, in his Persuasions.

I hope, by this Time, *Reader*, thou hast well considered, and narrowly inspected the Qualities of this Guide, which surely manifest themselves as detestable as any I have ever met withal; his Ignorance, Impudence, and Hypocrisie, but above all, his Hackney, Mercenary Spirit; which doubtless needs must leave such strong Impressions as shall for ever make thee disesteem his Undertaking, and that the *Quaker*'s Innocency, whom he has so unworthily slandered, without a Proof to warrant his Aspersions, shall not appear the less deserving Favour and Encouragement from thee; however he has not been remiss in putting all his Stratagems on Foot to render them obnoxious to the Fury and Displeasure of such who have Power to execute the Resentments of their Minds, but rather let them have thy Countenance, as a People whose upright and industrious Conversation, renders them not less Serviceable than Exemplary.

Thus have I finish'd my third Chapter, and hasten to my fourth, which is a short Comparison of some of his Contradictions; that whilst he runs insulting upon us for Ignorant, Erroneous, and Contemptible, it may appear that his Discourse requires an *Errata*.

CHAP. IV. *His Contradictions Compared.*

§. 1. GOD *hath in the framing of Man's Nature, laid so deep an Impression of Religion, that there is no Nation but doth judge themselves Interested therein.* P. 1.

In the framing of the Nature of Man, there are such Principles of Religion Engraven in him, as cannot be razed out. P. 8. 15, 16.

BUT *as 'tis a Thing all profess themselves interested in, so there's nothing Men are at greater Difference about; some Worship the Sun, others the Moon or the Stars, and almost any Creature from whence they received any Benefit.* Pag. 2.

We read in the Story of the Israelites, *the Vanity of Man's Nature in Matters of Religion.* P. 3. 4, 5.

Is God's Impression divided, or the Capacity he gave Man so blinded, as that it cannot discern betwixt *Himself, Sun, Moon*, or *Stars*? And is it possible, *That Man's Nature should be Religious, and it's Principles not to be razed out, and yet vain*

1668.

Chap. IV.

vain in those Matters? And what Spiritual Benefit did any ever receive from Sun, Moon, or Stars, that induced them to worship and adore them?

How greatly then doth it behove every Man to make a Wise Choice of that God he intends to serve, and that Religion he means to live and die in? P. 2.	*Man's Eternal Happiness or Misery, depends on the Right Knowing God, or his Mistake about it. P. 2.*
There is a Necessity Men should be of some Religion, P. 14.	*On the Right Chusing one's Religion, or our Mistake about it, Eternal Happiness or Misery, Life or Death depends, P. 16.*
To chuse deliberately what God we will serve, and then resolve to cleave unto him. P. 15.	*The Dream that every Man may be saved in his own Religion, if he be True to it, is more becoming Turks than Christians. P. 17.*

Observ. O strange Contradiction! Has Man a Liberty given, nay, Advice grounded on Necessity to be of some Religion, *And not only to chuse what God he will, but also to Live and Die in his Service;* and yet Damn'd if he hits not on the True One: What's this more, than to say, *It's Necessary Man should do somewhat, though he be Damn'd for it?* And if it's a *Dream* to expect Salvation in being *True to some Religion, is it not a Lethargy of Impertinency, That it's necessary to be of some Religion, and to Live and Die in it?*

There are many False Religions in the World. P. 15.	*It's a Mistake to think that there is such a Multitude of Religions in the World. P. 27.*
There being such Diversities of Religions, you had Need to have your Eyes about you. P. 26.	*There are, to speak properly, but Four Religions. p. 28.*

Observ. These Cross Sayings must needs be manifest to the weakest Capacity; for if he speaks *Properly* on one Side, he speaks very *improperly* on the other.

§. 2. It's not sufficient, that it be delivered unto you, by Tradition from Ancestors, by Education from Godly Parents, commended by the Practice of wise and pious Persons,— but make a wise Choice for your selves. p. 25.	*Man must discern the Verity and certainty of these Doctrines, that he may venture his Soul upon them; for which End, it's exceeding necessary to be conversant in those Treatises which prove the Verity of the Christian Religion. p. 10.*
Those that take up Religion, because it's profest in the Country, and commended by Example, how slight are they therein? p. 19.	*I add one Rule of Caution more, against a common, but dangerous Mistake: Take heed of setting up your own Apprehensions of the Sense of Scripture: Though fundamentals are plainly laid down, yet Points controverted are hidden from ordinary Understandings, that know not the Languages and proper Idioms of Scripture, and other Advantages of Learning. p. 109.*

Observ. In one Side, this Guide is for every Individuals' chusing from a Reason in himself; in the other, that he should accept Things from the Apprehensions and greater Skill of others.

But it's unreasonable to be contending about Things, not so clearly revealed in Scripture; p 44.	*Search the Scriptures and look well to them, they are your Chart and Compass, to steer your Course by; try all Things by them. p. 47.*
But darkly laid down p. 47.	
Take Heed of that great Mistake, that nothing is to be admitted, in and about the Administrations of the Church of Christ, but what is held forth in Scripture. p. 99. 100.	

Observ. O strange Confusion! A Rule and no Rule; revealed, and not revealed: Is it not unreasonable to suppose that Christ, instead of rendering his Church more glorious and infallible than ever, should leave her destitute of Information in those Things

Things, which concern her Peace, since contrary Apprehensions about them, have been the Ground of all Division and Persecution through Ages, and will be yet with most, notwithstanding this Guide's Directions? — Can the Scriptures be clear in deep, and not in shallow Matters?

God hath committed the Care of Religion, and the Settlement of it, to those in Authority, in their Dominions, in such a Way as they judge most agreeable to the Rule of the Word. p. 68.

They are to see all be administred according to the same; and in the particular Circumstances undetermined by God, they have a Power to order and settle Things according to the general Rules laid down in the Word. p. 104.

It's not sufficient that it's commanded by the Laws of the Land, but make a wise Choice for your selves. p. 25.

Let every one be fully perswaded in his own Mind. p. 53.

And Men that act according to Reason, will look into the Oracles of God himself, wherein God hath reveal'd his Will, concerning Faith and Worship. p. 9.

If God has invested Magistrates, with the Power of Interpretation, and Settlement of Religious Matters accordingly; is it not absurd to bid Men chuse for themselves, since they are to be concluded by another's Choice? And how the Oracles of God, should be perspicuous to all Understandings, and yet need an Interpreter, (I mean the Magistrate) I would fain understand.

§. 3. *The Christian Religion was confirm'd by many Signs; by the Means of Propagation of it, by weak and unlearned Men, by whose Preaching it overspread the World.* p. 31.

The Fundamentals of Christianity are so plainly laid down in Scripture, that the weakest Christians may understand them. p. 110.

The Quakers, in Respect of their want of Learning and outward Accomplishments, are contemptible. p. 62.

Controverted Points are hidden from ordinary Understandings that know not the Languages, and proper Idioms of Scripture, and Customs of the Church, and other Advantages of Learning, that it's ordinarily impossible they should find out the Mind of God therein. p. 111.

What Contradiction is here! that what he designs to have been Proof or Argument, to have recommended the more unquestionably the Belief of the Christian Religion in old Times, to the primitive Christians, he here should make the Reason why he rejects and reviles the *Quakers* and their Testimony;—— and that he should tell us, the Spirit they received perfectly inform'd them, and yet that Learning is to be the only Means of knowing God's Mind in these Days, whilst he confesses at the same Time, the weakest Christian may understand the Fundamentals of Religion.

God is to be worshipped in Spirit and in Truth— p. 70.

The Essence of Prayer lies in lifting up true Desires to God in the Name of Christ. p. 71.

To pray, is Part of God's Worship, but whether it be in a Book or out of it, is no Part at all. p. 100.

For who is there that knows not that Forms of Prayer, have been of exceeding long Continuance in the Christian Church. p. 91.

Set-Forms, are not only used and prescribed in the old Testament, but also in the new. p. 94.

How! Worship in Spirit, and yet by Words of Man's Prescription! Can any Man bring the Spirit to so many Words, to begin with I, and end with R? Or who knows the Spirit's Mind, so punctually as to prescribe for Generations to come the Words it will use, for all Persons and Conditions, that may be in the World? Who can pretend to know all States, that he may write Prayers for each? Why not Forms of Sighs and Groans?— Was it not a spiritual Worship, *Christ Jesus* set up, above sixteen Hundred Years ago, in Opposition to the *Jewish* one, and all other particular Worships, in the World? which are known to have been Forms, and such as this Guide pleads for, at least the *Jewish*, and produce me a Form put forth and establish't by any of the Apostles, who were faithful in God's House;— But did not Forms creep up, when the primitive Power and Spirit was lost, imitating Prayer, but not Praying? And did not *Tertullian* in his Apology, (who is generally rank't in the Beginning of the third Century) write, that the Christians prayed not by Book, but as they were moved by the Spirit of God, or to that Purpose; and I challenge this Guide, or any living, to make appear that a Form of

Prayer

1668.

Chap. IV.
Ston. smi.
the Image on
the Feet. p. 29.

Prayer was establish'd, till some Time after his Death; And this Guide himself acknowledges in his *Stone smiting the Image on the Feet*, that the Apostacy was begun, *the Empire yielded up to the Papacy, the primitive Purity of Christian Worship fail'd, and became corrupted*: And let him tell me if the Worship of the Church of *England*, had not it's Beginning there, at least those Things he calls *Additaments and Modes*; so that they are not concluded as necessary by any Light or Prudence, but innovated by a vain, formal and superstitious Nature: Besides, examine the Contradiction of his own Assertions, *God must be worshipped in Spirit, and yet in Form: Forms are not only of Legal, but of Gospel-Institution, and yet whether Prayer be within or without Book, it matters not.*

It's a vain Delusion to think that the Spirit should discover all deep Mysteries. p. 111.

The Spirit of God teaches not by such immediate Enthusiasms [or Revelations]

Wherein you are otherwise minded, he will reveal the Truth, [the Mystery] *unto you.* p. 46.

God will reveal his Secrets to such as fear him, and lead you by his Spirit. p. 46. 47.

Observ.

If it be a vain Delusion, to say the Spirit only can discover all deep Mysteries, pray what is it to say, it shall reveal the Truth, which comprehends all? And that it will reveal God's Secrets, (what are they but Mysteries?) And if God's Spirit does not teach immediately, why does *Clapham* say, that it will reveal God's Secrets, and lead us? Which implies the Familiarity and Constancy of his Presence, What Contradiction's this!

§. 4. For who is there of the highest Form of Christians, that are ascertained that in every particular Doctrine and Practice, these be in the Right, seeing the best of Men are imperfect, and may and do err. p. 53.

Who is in all Things free from Error? What Church or Person upon Earth? p. 65.

For what Churches are so pure, but they have some Defects, Errors, or Corruptions? p. 81.

The Quakers trust in a pretended Sinless Perfection. p. 63.

Let the Doctrines and Mysteries of Faith you receive, influence your Hearts and Lives, sanctifie and change them. Rest not in the Form of Godliness, without the Power of it. p. 27.

God only is to be sanctified of all them that come near to him. p. 70.

In the Church of England, *is a professed Renunciation of the Devil, the World, and the Flesh, with all their Sinful Works and Lusts.* p. 70.

Let this Truth influence your Hearts and Lives, so as you sincerely obey the Gospel, and live in the daily Expectation of the Coming of the Lord, and give Diligence to be found of him, without Spot and Blameless. p. 40.

Observ.

Here's the Perfection of his Contradictions; — 1. Is it Sense to affirm that Societies are sanctified and changed, and yet imperfect, corrupt and erroneous? 2. If God is to be sanctified of all that come near unto him, then such as can't sanctifie him, cannot approach him; but *Clapham*, and such as cry, they have no Health in them, and consequently unsanctified, cannot sanctifie the Lord, therefore can't they approach him. 3. He asks the Question, *What Church is without Corruptions?* and as patly answers it, *The Church of* England (for she) *renounces the Devil, the World and the Flesh, with all their deceitful Works and Lusts*. So that Perfection is an Article of *Clapham's* Faith, as being of that Church. 4. And why should he be angry that the *Quakers trust in a sinless Perfection*, and that which will exceedingly re-joyce, at the Appearance of their Lord? Since he has found so suitable a Defence, that in so many Words, admonishes all to *give Diligence to be found of him in Peace, without Spot, and Blameless.*

And Reader, though he never did intend by his Discourse, a Vindication of the *Quakers Principles*, yet mayst thou easily perceive how he is left of God, in this conceited Undertaking, to manifold gross Contradictions; and whilst he would be thought competent, to enervate such Opinions as don't quadrate, or agree, with his, his Book is made his Confutation: — Nor have I hinted at the Moiety, because I would avoid *Prolixity*, professing in Sincerity, I scarce have ever read such a Compendium of Absurdities, although, when first I saw his Treatise, I was in

Expectation

Expectation of some Essay, or new *Atlantis* in Religion, as might (if not) deserve an Approbation of it's Doctrine, at least have manifested the Ingenuity of its Author; but to find the Gleanings of some mouldy Authors, and dark Suggestions of unwarrantable Tradition, venture to put a Cheat upon the World, under the specious Title of a *Guide*, (who had not gone a Page, before he lost his Way) at once exprest more Ignorance and Impudence, than any Piece I have met with, since I have held the least Intelligence with Books; and I hope what hath been already writ, will by thee be esteemed a sufficient Answer to this Guide, and so unvizard his Designs, as neither thou, or any else, from thence shall take the least Encouragement to embrace his *Religion*, or give Entertainment to his false Aspersions, but rather am willing to believe, that Persons ingenious and deliberate, will never look upon a Time serving Priest, thus circumstantiated with great Variety of Misdemeanours, or any Thing, his Parts or Malice can suggest, so favourably, as to accept his Sentiments to the apparent Prejudice of such, whose Carriage and Correspondence amongst Men, are in the general, confest to be discreet and Friendly; for if the Persons invested with Authority shall once admit of implicit Apprehensions, for their Rule, and that from one, whose very Actions carry such undeniable malignity with them, those different Perswasions against whom he may have treasured up Revenge, must certainly expect the Effects of their Severity and Displeasure, let them in other Matters, where publick Preservation is concerned, appear never so ready and contributory

But such Procedures relish rather of *Romish Bigotry*, and *Inhuman Inquisition*, than Christian Tenderness and Human Prudence: For as a gentle Treatment of *Dissenters* has ever been the most effectual Way for Uniting Differences in Religion, (at least preserving of the Peace) so should all Magistrates remember (if they please) that their Authority cannot reasonably extend beyond the End for which it was appointed, which being not to inthrone themselves Sovereign Moderators in Causes purely Conscientious, and relating to a World in which they cannot pretend the least Jurisdiction, but only to maintain the impartial Execution of Justice, in regulating Civil Matters with most Advantage to the Tranquillity, Enrichment, and Reputation of their Territories, they should not bend their Forces, nor imploy their Strength, to gratifie the *Self-seeking Spirit of the Priests*, or any private Interest whatsoever; — An Exercise below the Dignity of their Office, and much too narrow for that Universal Influence it should have upon the Publick.

§. 5. But to conclude, *Judicious Reader*, hold not so slight an Esteem of the *Quakers Principles*, because decri'd by such as either don't know them, or well know an Entertainment of them would put a Period to their *Gain*: But soberly examine if there be any other Way to perfect Victory over those Corruptions and Fleshly Lusts, to which we naturally are addicted, and most infallibly occasion that Disorder and Confusion we see all Nations subject to, than what they Preach up, Write for, and Walk by, even that *Grace of God which brings Salvation, (from all Iniquity)* which, says this Guide, *is the Sum of all,* viz. *The Grace of God which bringeth Salvation, hath appeared unto all Men, teaching us, that denying Ungodliness and Worldly Lusts, we should Live Soberly, Righteously, and Godly in this present World:* Which being really attended on, it's Instructions cordially embrac'd, and Holy Motions intirely resign'd unto, with that Noble, but necessary Resolution, *Of despising all Shame, and patiently enduring the Cross,* shall make thee a Righteous Magistrate, a Reformed Priest, or an Holy Citizen of the *New Jerusalem*: It leads into Circumspection, and Pure Conformity to the Divine Pleasure: Doubts and Fears, Sighs and Tears, shall fly away, and in that Faithful Stayedness of Heart on God, We can, according to our respective Measures say, *He makes the Rivers of his Peace to overflow, and never-failingly bedews with the Refreshment of his Glorious Presence*: Which Reader, that thou mayst, and all Men, really experience, is the very earnest Desire of him, that God in Everlasting Love, has made a *Friend to the True Religion*, but an Enemy to every False Way.

WILLIAM PENN.

A Serious

A Serious APOLOGY

FOR THE
PRINCIPLES and PRACTICES
Of the PEOPLE call'd
QUAKERS.

Against the Malicious Aspersions, Erroneous Doctrines, and Horrid Blasphemies, of *Thomas Jenner*, and *Timothy Taylor*, in their Book, entituled, *Quakerism Anatomiz'd, and Confuted*.

* *Note*, the First Part was written by *G. Whitehead.*

* The SECOND PART.

By *WILLIAM PENN*.

But these speak Evil of those Things which they know not; raging Waves of the Sea foaming out their own Shame, Jude v. 10 13. *But Wisdom is justified of her Children,* Mat. xi. 19.

The PREFACE.

To the KING's Lieutenant-General, and General-Governour, and Council of *Ireland*: With all other it's Subordinate Magistrates. The Just and Necessary Defence of the People call'd *QUAKERS*.

THO' *it be the usual Design of Dedicatory Epistles, to flatter those Persons whose Names front the ensuing Tracts, with the Protection of them* (and some we confess want it) *yet such is the Dignity of the* TRUTH *we vindicate, that as we cannot attribute it's Original to any Mortal Men, so are it's own Innocence and Certainty the most Convincing Apology against all it's Adversaries: We therefore wave all Gaudy Titles, and chuse to evidence our Respect in a Way less suited to the Education of* Pharisaical Parasites.

Some, mov'd by their own Interests, have been pleas'd to enterprize a Confutation of the Quaker's Doctrines *(at least they think so) in which they let us understand, how much more they design'd to dis-interest us in* Christianity and Civil Government, *than to inforce us of either: But that the* Hope of the Hypocrite may perish, *and their Vain Expectations appear frustrated to all Impartial Readers; we have taken their Discourse into our Serious Examination, otherwise unworthy of our least Notice.*

And though they intend nothing less than a disingaging us in any Claim to Legal Protection, yet, as we only can ascribe the Honour of our Creation to God, so do we attribute our Happiness of Birth unto His Providence, which has not fallen within the Lawless Borders of meer Prerogative, but the more Pleasant Province of Legal Freedoms.

And

And being thus intituled to equal Priviledges with them, we cannot esteem their Partial Characters, Grounds sufficient to cut off that Entail of Liberty, however busily endeavour'd by their meer Rapsody of Folly, Error, and Abuse; Men, whose whole Lives are but the express Instances of Contention: And whilst they seem to represent us undeserving of your Protection, none more Incendiaries than themselves. It is their old Thread-bare Project, to abuse the Civil Magistrate, with the Execution of their Revengeful Designs, under the Pretence of answering some Publick End.

And truly, it ever was the Infelicity of States, to steer by the Sinister Compass of an Avaritious and Enrag'd Clergy.

We judge our selves as rightfully possest of our Demeans as any, and must believe our Lives and Labours as Beneficial to the Publick.

It's not a Meer Credential, or Point of Faith, *that criminates; but an immoral Practice in the Opinion of the Law: And of what Morals those Men are, that dare to instigate Authority to our Subversion, for not believing what they would have us, (whilst they themselves stand Heterodox to the Publick) we may interpret by 'the* Jesuits Bloody Ones.

It's wretched, and almost unpardonable in Men, to pretend themselves Ministers of the Meek and Self-Denying Jesus, *when they are not yet learnt in the School of doing as they would be done by. Their Enmity is the express Image of their Souls, and their envying us your Toleration (whilst they court it for themselves) shews how much it is their Principle to give none; and were you but as subject to their Power, as we are to yours, 'tis shrewdly to be suspected, that our Entertainment would be alike* Cruel.

We hope the Tragical Stories of the Scottish Covenant, *and sad Effects of their strait-laced Engagement, will for ever antidote Sober Men against the Contagion of their Narrow Principles; which rightly understood, are the truest Measures, and plainest* English *of their Christianity, and Obedience to the Civil Magistrate.*

Could we but daub with the untemper'd Mortar of Sin-pleasing Principles, deny our own Judgments, bow to their Dictatorian Censures, flatter their Persons, feed their Pride, augment their Trap-door-Stipends, and excite to Divisions, by aggravating the Miscarriages of Superiors, *we might have more Respect in their Thoughts; who in their implacable Enmity misrepresent us both to you and the Nation, which is the only Cause of our presenting this Defence to you: But 'tis our Desire to give other Testimonies of our Religion, than Animosity; and better Proofs of our Christian Moderation, than the sharp Gusts of a* Scottish-Presbyterian-Directorian-Persecution.

Not that we would be thought to justifie our selves, in condemning them; we make a Difference betwixt seeking Revenge, and giving Men their True Characters.

We are so remote from Vailing our inmost Parts, that we chearfully offer our selves to your narrowest Scrutiny, and most prying Search: Nay, we beseech you do that Justice to your selves and our Adversaries, *as well as to our Cause, to make the strictest Inquisition after us and our Principles.* 'Twas that which rendred the Bereans Noble; *and to* Try all Things, *the Apostle held to be a certain Means of knowing what is Good: For, as it is a Mark of Great Folly, to censure what is neither understood nor known; so may the foulest Error be disguis'd with the fair Pretences of Truth, and Prejudice or Interest, traduce the most in-offensive People upon Earth; which has necessitated us to offer this* Apology, *or, those so often refell'd and refuted Doctrines and Accusations, would not have deserv'd our slightest Notice: But as we can never think our Time better employ'd, than in defending* TRUTH, *against the mean (yet malicious) Essays of her* Adversaries; *so we may reasonably expect (as the just Success of our Endeavours) the Happiness of being better understood, by this renew'd Occasion of once more Remonstrating our real Innocence to the World.*

To conclude, We hope to evidence by the ensuing Discourse, that not We, but our Adversaries, *are the malignant Enemies of* God, Scripture, Religion, *and* Civil Government, *and that by Undeniable Instances.*

At least, it will always appear partial and unmanly, that in a Country, only maintain'd by an English Civil Interest, *those who are themselves* Dissenters, *and esteem* Persecution against them Unchristian, *should express so much Romish Zeal in exasperating the* Civil Magistrate *to our utter Ruin, who are both* English and Dissenters *too.*

We shall omit to mention how far we are conducive to the Publick Good of this Plantation, as well as how far we were Instrumental in procuring it; but this we shall take the Liberty to assert, That since we are as large Contributors to the Government

ment as our Antagonists, we are intituled to as large a Protection from it: *And for our Faith in God, and Worship of Him, we neither are asham'd to confess, nor unable to render a Reason of either; but as we have done both in this* Apology, *so upon all Occasions we chearfully shall express our great Readiness to confess and vindicate the same, against the utmost Strength of all our Enemies.*

We are Your real Friends in all Truth and Righteousness,

G. W. W. P.

The INTRODUCTION.

CHAP. I.

IN my Answer to the latter Part of this Rapsody of *Slander* and *Imposture*, I must take Leave to premise two Things:

First, That as these very Points in Controversy, have been throughly considered, upon several Occasions, (as is evident in the Books of many of our Friends; both of them living, and those that are at Rest with God) so can we find nothing New, either of *Objection* or *Slander*, that might deserve our farther Thoughts; but a meer *Gleaning of that Harvest of Lyes and Error*, in which so many of his *Brethren* (and *Satan's Labourers*) have been, for these twenty Years past, most diligently employ'd: Yet for the Sake of such, as may be imposed upon, and deceived into an Apprehension of the Truth of these detestable *Imputations*, (through their Ignorance, *as well of us and our Principles, as of the Priests and their sinister Practices*) we shall condescend to take them into our serious Examination.

Secondly, Nor would I have the Man conceit it was his Strength of Argument that necessitated Two to answer it; since the Meanest had been more than enough, for an *Adversary so feeble and incompetent:* but being both alive, and particularly concern'd (because abus'd in the Discourse) we can do no less for the Truth, our Brethren, and our selves.

And now I must declare, I am asham'd and troubl'd that any Man should live so long, and to so little Purpose. He recommends his Discourse with Sixty Six Years of Age, as if we ought to infer *Verity* from his *Antiquity*; not considering, *Bis pueri senes*, and that his Age gives but a more just Reflection upon his Folly, whose best *Apology* will be his Doting.

Certainly he must have been very envious in his Youth, in whom the *Flames of Wrath are so unquenchable in old Age*. And instead of *Simeon's* Farewel, *Now let thy Servant depart in Peace* (in Opposition to the Tenor of the Gospel of the Son of God) he is taking his Leave of the World, *with a Proclamation of War and Persecution to his Co-dissenters* (worse than *Amilcar* of old, that made his Son to swear an Implacability to the *Romans*, that he might continue his Hatred with his Posterity) which, however like it was to a Gallant and injur'd *Carthaginian*, was but an ill Copy for a *Christian Minister* to write after (indeed to out-do.) But if that vulgar Fancy were true, of Men's degenerating into the *Irish* Nature by living in the *Irish* Air, we might know whence to derive his Massacring Stile and Doctrine: But as the Innocence and Patience of our Friends there, prove that an Imagination, so his ancient Fierceness against all that suited not the Model of his crazy Brain, shews it to be his very Nature; *And what is bred in the Bone* (we have so far Reason to allow the Proverb) *will never be out of the Flesh*. I shall only say, that the *narrow-spirited envenom'd Presbyter* (who like to that *Ægyptian* King of old, lops all to his Stature that are longer, and stretches all to his Length that are shorter) is the *Metropolitan Canker* to the Serenity and Security of all human Society. But because his Religious Matters first present themselves, I shall suspend my Character of the Man and his Brethren, 'till I have given them their due Consideration.

And that I may begin, I must profess, I have not been more at a Loss for a Beginning in any *Adversary*, that has fallen to my Share. I chose to take my Rise of Answer from his Endeavours to prove, we are against Preaching: But such is the Unhappiness of this miserable *Pedagogue*, that in seeking to imitate a Writer, he plays the Scribler, leaving us strangely in the Dark for a Beginning.

1671.

Chap. I.
Pag. 87, 88.

He calls it Sect. 1. the next is also Sect. 1st, the next to that Sect. 3d, then Sect. 1st again, and Sect. 1st follows that, and then Chap. 3d: But because the *Compositor* has shewn himself more a Master of his Trade in the Punctuality of his Pages, than the *Person* himself a *Doctor* at Writing, by the Mistake of his Sections: I shall refer the Reader to the several Pages for Proof of my true Citation.

As to the Method of my Answer, I have not design'd the common Rode of Printing his Words at large on all Occasions; but having perused an entire *Section* or *Chapter*, I have digested or contracted the Scope and Tendency of the whole into some one or two Positions, which with all convenient Brevity, are fairly examin'd, and, I hope, as rationally confuted.

CHAP. II.

HIS whole Discourse may be considered under these two Heads, *Of Matter of Fact, and Matter of Doctrine*. My Business will be to detect his Falsity in the First, and Error in the Last.

Chap. II.

He confidently chargeth us with a Denial of the Usefulness of Preaching (it is the Title of his Section) and hopes to prove the Charge from this Expression, in a Book, written by G. *Fox*, call'd *Truth's Defence*, viz. *If any Soul be once made one with God by the Spirit, who dare deny but all Scripture is fulfilled in them; therefore they need none to teach them*, For thus (says he) they alledge, *Jer.* 31. 34. *They shall teach no more every Man his Neighbour, &c.* And *Jer.* 2. 27. *You need not any Man teach you*; Also 2 *Pet.* 1. 19. *Ye have a more sure Word of Prophecy, &c.* This then is Matter of Fact, that we deny the Usefulness of Preaching; the Evidence is this Citation out of G. *Fox*'s Book, and the Scriptures quoted.

But certainly he deserves to be begged for a Fool, that could embrace any thing so false and senseless for Truth and Sincerity: The Man has vainly set up the Puppet of his own Fancy, and then pelts as at a real Substance; He rather seems to express what he would have, than what really is; as if he took more Delight that we should be *Heterodox*, than that we were *Orthodox*: And indeed, we have Reason to believe, That his Displeasure against our being in the Right, runs parallel with the Satisfaction he takes to represent us in the Wrong.

What Man of Sense can interpret from *George Fox*'s Expression, the Uselesness of Preaching? If he had said of *Men's Preaching, whom God never sent, but that run of their own Heads, made by the Will and Appointment of Man, that Preach for Hire, and Divine for Money, and prepare War against such as put not into their Mouths; but, like ravenous Curs, seek Gain from their Quarters, stealing their Neighbours Words to supply their own Defects, and the Hour-glass*; I do confess the Inference had been natural. But to affirm G. F. denies Preaching (singly as such) because he says, they need no Teaching that are made one with God's Spirit, were to suppose, he deny'd even the Spirit's Teaching; which were to clear the *Quakers* of what the Priests think to be our most damnable Doctrine, *viz. To Preach by the Spirit*: If then it cannot be supposed, unless they would take that for granted, which they most vehemently deny; namely, *That we disown the Spirit's Teaching*: It follows, that it was not all Teaching; but that which turns to no Profit, *The Traditions and Commandments of Men, the Science, falsly so called*: And that this must needs be the Intent of that Passage, our constant Assemblies (even when our Adversaries dare not to shew their Heads) are pregnant Instances; which tho' urg'd by *Jenner*, to bring a Contradiction upon the *Quakers*, it inverts more strongly upon himself; since that he might conclude, we oppose not all Preaching, against which his Arguments are mostly levelled. He must either begin again, and undertake the Vindication of his *Hackney Homilies, and Hireling Sermons*; or else, relinquish all Pretence to Objection against our Doctrine in this Point.

It is a Piece of *Sophistry*, as black as *Hell*, to say, *That because the* Quakers *deny all human Teaching, or the utmost Knowledge of degenerated, avaricious, proud, persecuting Priests, to be instrumental for the convincing or converting any; that therefore they deny all Preaching, even that which flows from the Divine Power and Spirit of God.*

Besides, had G. F. intended any such Meaning, as is suggested by the Man in Hand, I cannot see the least Unreasonableness in it by his own avow'd Principles: For it is generally agreed upon, That such as have perfect Understanding, need not the Help of any to inform them; and certainly he that is made one with God, can never be ignorant of what is fit for him to know of him, to whom he is perfectly united: This Doctrine the Man himself teaches, saying, That such as are come to Christ, need no Man to teach them; which is an Expression no less comprehensive than that used by G. F. read p. 101.

The *Scriptures* urged to prove the Necessity and Usefulness of Evangelical Teaching, he has not the least Share in; and we profess our selves to be the Men that have fulfilled them: For as that *Mission* of, *Go into all the World, and preach the Gospel*, (with the rest of the same Tendency) was given to a chosen Sort of Men, divinely qualified and inspired for the Work (which none of our *Anti-revelation Adversaries* will dare to derive their Orders from) so do we positively declare to all the World, that we have received a Measure of that same *Anointing*, and by it being qualified in our selves, through much *Travel, Temptation, Sorrow and Experience*, we are become able *Ministers* of the Everlasting Gospel; *and not in Corners, or under the Protection of Earthly Powers, nor yet in set Places for large Stipends, but freely, with our Lives in our Hands, in Perils, in Streights, in Wants, and through great Tribulation, have proclaimed the acceptable Day of the Lord,* namely, that *as many as believe in the Universal Grace, with which God hath indued them, and* (repenting of their former Iniquities) *do obey the same, should have Remission of Sins, and Eternal Salvation:* And this both hath been our Practice, and will be to the Ends of the Earth.

So that his great Pains, and many Scriptures alledged, to maintain the Usefulness of Preaching, are no otherwise of Service, than to detect his own Folly: and therefore wholly useless to the Matter in Hand.

To conclude this Point, I shall advise the Man in his Reply (if he may think it worth his While, and I know no Reason why he should not, since the older he grows the more he dotes) to distinguish between the *Quakers* denying the Spirit's Teaching (which is Free and Universal, without Money and without Price) and the costly Teachings of a Pack of insolent Hirelings: Had he been but informed of this before, he might have saved himself and the Printer, the Pains of so much useless Matter, and me the Trouble of Animadverting: For it was never yet in Controversy with us, whether we own'd, that in an Age as dark, ignorant, and degenerated, (as this manifestly is) it may be necessary for any illuminated and convicted, to Preach the Way of Redemption and Salvation to others, (for in this Sense the Holy Ghost teacheth) since we both assent to and practice it: But the Question ever was on this Hand, *Whether ever men, only qualified with natural Gifts and acquir'd Parts, (not cleans'd, sanctified, and set apart by the Eternal Spirit, for the Work of the Ministry, but Proud, Covetous, and Persecuting) were the undoubted Messengers of the Lord Jesus Christ?* This we utterly renounce, as a damnable Position, and which rests on our *Adversaries* Side to prove. Something he ventureth at in the Sequel of his Book, but with his usual Reason and Success, as shall anon be manifested.

In the mean Time I shall attend his pretended Answer to what he calls our Objection, viz. *That we have Teachers among us, but they are such as are inspired; the contrary, though they may use the Words of Scripture, yet are false Prophets; because they say, The Lord hath said, and yet the Lord never spoke to them,* and we abide by it.

His Answer admits of two Parts; both which I shall faithfully contract into the narrowest Compass I can, without Injury to him or it.

First, *They, who formerly spoke by immediate Revelation, as* Moses *and the Prophets,* Christ *and the Apostles, did confirm what they said by Miracles; the Consequences are plainly this, that there is a mediate Revelation.*

Secondly, *That the only Sign and Evidence of real Inspiration is the working of Miracles.*

To which I Reply, That greater Impertinency no Man can be guilty of, than to affirm or teach, *that there is a Revelation not immediate*; it is a direct Contradiction

diction in Terms; for that which is revealed must be *immediately*, or else it cannot rationally be a *Revelation*, but *Tradition* rather.

Nay, The Scriptures cannot be properly stiled the Revelation of the Will of God, 'till they are first opened by him, who was found worthy to unseal the Book, *That Spirit of Truth, that opens, and none shuts; and shuts, and none opens.*

The Scripture gives this Testimony to what I affirm, That 'tis *the Inspiration of the Almighty which gives Understanding: And none can come to the Father but by me: None knows the Father but the Son, and he to whom the Son reveals him: None knows the Things of God, save the Spirit of God: I will be with you to the End: If any be otherwise minded, God will reveal it to him;* with many the like Expressions, which afford us thus much, *viz.* That since no Man knows the Mind and Will of God, neither can rightly discern of Spiritual Matters, but as they are revealed and manifested by the Spirit of God; the very Scriptures themselves are not a Revelation to him, but the Sense and Purpose of them (so immediately revealed by the Eternal Spirit) *is the only true Revelation, and the Scriptures but a Godly Tradition.*

Moses did not conclude his Predecessors ignorant of the Will of God, who were without a written Law. Nor did *Job* say, That the naked Books of *Moses* were able to give Understanding; *but the Inspiration of the Almighty,* Neither did *Christ* bid them read *the Scriptures, that the Father might be revealed to them.* Nor the *Apostles* require the *Churches to have recourse to their Writings* (then scatter'd amongst them) *as what would only reveal to them the Mind of God.* But as they affirm'd and preacht the Impossibility of knowing the Things of God any other Way, than that of Revelation from God; so did they attribute all such Science, not to their Writings, but to his Spirit; directing all to the Grace, Spirit, and Anointing, as their most infallible Teacher.

Nay, The Lord (in his Wisdom) apprehending, that the People would not believe *Moses*, unless they had some sensible and convincing Evidence, was therefore pleas'd to say to *Moses, Lo I come in a thick Cloud, that the People may hear when I speak with thee, and believe thee for ever,* Exod. 19. 9. This was far from God's speaking so, as that the People should not hear as well as *Moses*, or the Prophets. And truly, the plain *English* why we believe not the Black-Coats of our Age, is because we don't hear God speak to, or by them.

And indeed, it is the very Tenure of the new Covenant, that all should be taught of God, which does not exclude Direction (the Tendency of Preaching under that Covenant, being to direct to that which alone can teach) as I may meet with a Man upon the Road, who not being able to inform me of the Way I would go, directs me to such a *Post*, where the *Town's Names and Cross Ways are inscribed*, for the Information of *Passengers*: He cannot be said to teach me the right Way, but he may be truly allow'd to direct me to what was able to inform me. The *Samaritans* believ'd the Report of the Woman, and embrac'd her Direction; but the Revelation was not from her, but from Christ. For no sooner were they come to him, to whom the Woman had directed them for Satisfaction, but they had this Testimony to bear against all implicit Faith (and that not because of what she said, but what they themselves had seen and known of Christ) that they did believe, *He was the Messiah,* and only begotten Son of God.

Nor would we be thought to lessen the Virtue, Use, and Reputation of the Holy Scriptures, whilst we endeavour the Vindication of the Holy Spirit in his Office of Revelation to Believers.

They are useful in two eminent Respects.

First, Historically, as giving us a true Narrative of the Transactions of those Ages of the World, in reference to the Church or State of both *Jews* and *Christians*, their Trials, Troubles, Temptations, Lapses, Recoveries, and perfect Victories.

Secondly, Doctrinally, as presenting us with a true Account of the Principles and Doctrines of the People of God, their Holy Faith and Patience; I cannot phrase it better, than a Divine Glass, in which we see (I say W E S E E) *who first have that Heavenly Organ and Eye opened by Inspiration and Revelation)* the States and Conditions of the Primitive Saints; which is Matter of unspeakable Comfort and Confirmation, as well as of Good Example to us; yet still, the efficient Cause of all, is the convincing Revelation and Operation of the Eternal Spirit of God; and the Scriptures are only useful, as unfolded by the Inspiration of the same.

This

This is no new Doctrine, but the old and best Ground that the first *Protestants*, as *Luther, Zuinglius, &c.* abroad; and *Whitaker, Reynolds, Jewel, &c.* at home, proceeded on against the *Papists*, in vindication of their Revolt, and separate Faith and Worship from those *Romanists*: Only the Interest of the Mercenary Priests of these Times being varied, they have also chang'd their Way of prosecuting it; and stick not to deny us those Pleas, they once with Confidence employ'd against their *Romish Adversaries*, which this old angry Man might have been pleas'd to observe. But,

Secondly, *That the only Sign and Evidence of Inspiration is Miracles*, I utterly renounce and deny, as what is most false and unworthy of the *Reason, Perspicuity, and Self-evidencing Verity of the Christian Religion*.

I need not go far to detect the Falsity of the Assertion; since many, nay most of the Prophets, are not recorded to have wrought any. And if the Scriptures are acknowledged to have been given forth by the Holy Ghost, how many mention'd in them, whose Words and Works compile them, never wrought so much as one Miracle, and that both under the Old and New Testament?

Besides this wretched Doctrine denies that to be *Revelation*, which is not at the same instant accompanied with *Miracles*; then if it be Revelation to *Thomas Jenner*, and any of his (not Miraculous, but Monstrous) *Crew*, only because attended with Miracles; I hope he will give us leave to infer, that no Man since the World was, had ever any Revelation that had not *Miracles*, which naturally excludes the greatest Part of the *Scripture*, as of Divine *Canon*, and makes the Will of God a sealed Book, to those, to whom the Scriptures testifie it was revealed. But this kind of arguing well becomes an *Anti-revelation-man*, and is an eminent Demonstration how little of the Will of God is known to him.

Nevertheless, I would that all should understand what we mean by Revelation, and that is this, *That from our Conviction of the least Evil, to our Redemption from it; and all the Knowledge we have of God, his Way, and good Pleasure towards us, throughout the whole Exercise of our Religious Life; we ascribe our Knowledge and Instruction to no other Thing than the Discoveries or Revelation of the Spirit of God in our Hearts*: But this not in a Moment, but gradually, through our *Obedience to what we know of him.* For they that do my Will (saith God) *shall know of my Doctrine*, John 7. 17.

And we know not to what else we should impute the eagerness of some Men against this necessary Doctrine of *Daily Revelation* of the Mind and Will of God, than to their greedy Desire of grasping *Divine Knowledge, whilst in a State of Disobedience to what they already know*; and the Impossibility of their obtaining that Heavenly Science in that State of Impurity, makes them so impatient, and angry, and positive in their Denials of it to any other: Although, if they did but consider, *That it is the Inspiration of the Almighty which gives them to understand what is Good, and what is Evil; that they might do the one, and reject the other*: Not a Man in the World needed to be long ignorant of our Meaning of Revelation. And whilst Men and Women continue in such Watchfulness and Obedience, they are daily furnished with such Discoveries from God, as suit their State and Condition.

I know the *monstrous Conceits*, that some have of our Meaning by *Revelation*, fancying we understand *Whimsical Raptures, Strange and Prodigious Trances*; but such imagine Evil of Things they know not: We *disclaim any Share or Interest in those vain Whimsies and idle Intoxications*; professing our Revelation *to be solid and necessary Discovery from the Lord, of those Things that do import and concern our daily Conditions, in reference to the Honour which is due to him, and Care owing to our own Souls*.

But how weak an Argument the Doctrine of *Miracles* is, to prove the Verity of the Christian Faith, or Doctrine of Revelation, at this Time of Day, is best seen by considering 'twas Weakness that occasioned them: For had not the Lord Jesus observ'd the Darkness and Carnality of those Times, to be so great, as without reaching through the black Clouds of their Traditions and Superstitions, by the Hand of his Miracles (or visible Signs to their Understandings, or rather Senses) there was no likelihood of fastning a Conviction on them, there never had been need of an external Miracle in any such Sense. I would that the Man should know, we have receiv'd and maintain'd our Faith in Christ by more noble and sublime Arguments,

guments, than that of Miracles; namely, the *Truth, Reason, Equity, Holiness,* and *Recompence of the Christian Religion*; which *Miracles* can never render more, or less, *Intrinsically* so.

Not that we put a low Esteem upon Miracles, but comparatively only: And to say they are ceast, is in no other Sense true, than that wherein Vision or Revelation is; I mean, they are ceast to them that have not Faith. *For many have, and do know, the Power of taking up their Sick-Beds, and walking; their Faith in God's Power has made them whole.*

His first Part of his Answer being consider'd, I shall apply my self to examine the Weight of the Second.

Secondly, The Substance of the other Part of his Answer, is briefly this, *That the Priests and Levites, who were the People's Instructors under the Law, spoke not by Vision or Revelation, but only what God had spoken by the Prophets, for many Generations were without Prophets, but not Teachers; and that which is now to be taught, ought not to be from any new Revelation; but from what has been already preacht and laid down in the Scriptures, by Christ and his Apostles; the contrary being subject to much Fallacy and Delusion.* To back all which he quoted several Scriptures, but how pertinently to the Matter in Hand, will be the subject of our Inquiry.

Should I grant him his first Assertion, and the Reason he gives for it; of how little Moment would it be to the Business in debate? What if the People then were to have the Law from the Priest's Mouth; is it a good Consequence that therefore under a Gospel Dispensation, and the glorious Covenant of Life, it should be the same? What greater Advantage would redound to Mankind by the second, than the first Covenant, if there were not an universal Priesthood? *You are a Royal Priesthood,* said Peter: *Kings and Priests,* said John; and had that Covenant been perfect in this Particular, there had not been Need of another.

But never let any think that the idle, covetous, self-interested Priests will admit of any Principle or Practice, that may in the least lessen their Tyranny and Simonious Oppression. No, *Let God be dishonoured, let the Covenant of Grace fall to the Ground, and the whole World labour under the Yoak and Bondage of Mercenary Hirelings, rather than they should give their Consent to such a total disbanding and subversion of them, and their Ungodly Gains.*

But besides, That this Consequence is most unnatural, and destructive of the whole Design of the Gospel; he endeavours in his Assertion to obtrude an arrant Lye upon us: For there was Vision and immediate Helps besides the *Mosaical Law:* Nay, the Law being Matter of Duty, did not sufficiently impower such, as were to keep it, to do so; it told them much of what they ought to do, and what not; yet *not the thousandth Part of those Temptations and secret Workings of the Evil One, to defile and alienate their Minds from God; which for all the Law, they must have perished under, had they not had the Discovery of them, and the Remedies against them, from daily Heavenly Vision.* And this cannot but be imply'd from our Adversaries own Words; for they were to teach (or expound) What? their own Inventions, or Experiences? If the former, we may the more easily know of what Tribe he is; if the latter, it's utterly impossible they could do that, *and not have been acquainted with Divine Vision and Revelation:* For what can any experience of God, or Spiritual Things, without a Discovery of them; and that's only by the Spirit's illuminating the Understanding.

But, says he, *God spake by the Prophets, and the Prophets were but at certain Times.*

What then? Therefore did he not speak ordinarily by Visions and Revelations? But that he tells us he is an *Old Man,* and that many Infirmities attend Age, I could scarcely pass this decrepit Inference, without some farther Notice than I am now willing to take: But if this be right Argumentation, then I will say, that because God spoke by the Prophets, *he did not speak by the Apostles.*

Is there any Thing more evident, than that God gave his *good Spirit to the Children of Israel?* And what for? If not to afford them Vision; for every Vision, or Act of the Spirit in the Understanding of the Creature, is *Revelation?* And if God gave them his Good Spirit, neither to appear nor act in them, he gave it to no Purpose; but 'tis most certain his End was, that it should do both.

Secondly, Moses desired that all the Lord's People might be Prophets; and unless the Man will suppose, that *Moses* desired a Thing in-obtainable, or unlawful

(which

1671.
Chap. II.

(which were to impeach him of not a little Ignorance and Presumption) or take for granted, that Men may be Prophets, and not have Revelation (contrary to his own Apprehension and Force of the Word) he must acknowledge, that if every Man had not *Revelation* in that Day, it was not God's Fault, but by Disobedience his own; and if then so, much more now.

Thirdly, *If Vision and Revelation* were not more ordinary and familiar, than is allow'd of by our Adversaries, how comes it, that amongst many others (for I am willing to be brief) the Prophet *Micah* spake after this Manner.

Mic. 3. 6, 7.

Therefore Night shall be unto you, that ye shall not have Vision; and it shall be dark unto you, that ye shall not Divine; and the Sun shall go down over the Prophets, and the Day shall be Dark over them; then shall the Seers be asham'd, and the Diviners confounded; yea, they shall all cover their Lips, for there is no Answer of God.

Certainly the Prophet spake Truth, and as certain then it is that *T. J.* has writ a Lye; for what can be more plain, than that there were Diviners and Prophets among the People? And is it not as evident, that the Reason why the Sun of Vision was set over their Heads, and their Diviners were confounded, was their Rebellion and Disobedience to God, namely, *Their Teaching for Hire, Divining for Money, and Judging for Reward.* (read the following Verses.) And what other Reason can we give, why *Jenner* and his Brethren are Enemies to all Revelation, than that of their Disobedience to God, and horrid Cozenage of the People.

First, *In saying they are Ministers of Christ, and have not One of his Marks.*

Secondly, *In denying the Ministration of the Gospel, by the Revelation of the Spirit.*

Lastly, *In Teaching these Delusions for Hire and Reward.*

I hope by this Time, all *Impartial Readers* will do God, the Scriptures, themselves, and our Friends, the Justice of abhorring the Falseness, Ignorance, and Malicious Imputations of our Adversary; who whilst he pretends to be a Minister of Christ, and their Friend, *Endeavours to overturn the Foundation of his Kingdom, and the most unerring Ground of their Eternal Consolation.*

With what Success can any think he could enterprize the proving of the Non-necessity of *Revelation under the Gospel,* who has so lamely manag'd the same Assertion under the *Law* (where there was more Room, at least for a Pretence) I cannot tell, nor I believe any else: For take away *Revelation,* and take away the *Gospel:* Wherein is a better Covenant, or more Heavenly Dispensation? Or are the Last Days surpassing the First; *If the Times of Restitution leave us still under the Tuition of Mortal Men? If the Law be not writ in the Heart, the Spirit put in the Inward Parts, and every one taught of God?* Nay, *If we are not Temples of the Holy Ghost, and that God tabernacles and dwells not in us;* we do but mock the World with the splendid Names of *Gospel-Days, Covenant of Grace, Glad-Tidings, Times of Refreshment, and perfect Redemption,* &c. But let every such *Jannes* and *Jambres,* and their Gospel be accurst.

Jer. 31. 34.
Heb. 1. 9, 10, 11.
1 Cor. 6. 19.
Revel. 21. 3.

However, the *Man* adventures at a Vindication of his wretched Assertion from the Scriptures, as,

Heb. 12. 25.

First, *See that ye refuse not him that speaketh:* This (says he) *is spoken in the Present Tense, though Christ was in Heaven, and spoke not; but what he at any Time hath spoken, when it is made use of, or apply'd, it must be accounted his present Speaking:* Therefore (says he) *Saints are said to be built upon the Prophets and the Apostles, Jesus Christ himself being the Chief Corner-Stone; and not upon an immediate Voice that comes from God; but upon the Word of God spoken by the Prophets, and is a more sure Word than an immediate Word, for there may be much Falsity and Delusion in that; but we know that God spake with Moses,* &c.

Ephes. 2. 20.

I must frankly profess, that were it not for the Truth's Sake, and their deluded Souls (who through Simplicity have been beguil'd) I should rest for ever silent, from concerning my self in these sordid, weak, and beggarly Cavils, since I shall always despair of working any Change upon a Man, so Grey-headed in his Confidence and Folly.

Deut. 18. 18.

Can a more pregnant Passage be urg'd, to prove the perpetual Speaking of Christ to his Church, than the Place mention'd? Was he not promis'd thus, *I will raise them up a Prophet from their Brethren, like unto thee, and will put my Words in his Mouth; and he shall speak unto them all that I command him: And it shall come to pass, that whosoever will not hearken to my Words, which he shall speak in my Name,*

I will

I will require it of him? And did he not say, *He would be with his to the End of the World? And he would not leave them comfortless, he would come to them; and that He, who was with them, should be in them?*

But I perceive the Scriptures are of as little Reputation with him, as he would falsly render them to be with us.

His *Exposition* I will attend, viz. *That it was not by Revelation, but written Tradition, that Christ spake, which is the Substance of what he would infer.*

The Apostle *Paul* (as is suppos'd) writing to the *Hebrews*, amongst many other weighty Matters, from the eighteenth Verse of the second Chapter, to the five and twentieth of the same, takes Occasion for their Information and Comfort, to tell them, *That they were not come to the Mount that might not be touched, nor to Blackness and Tempest*, which made Moses *exceedingly Fear and Quake,* &c. but to *Mount Zion, to* Jerusalem, *the City of the Living God, to the General Assembly, to the Church of the First-Born, to God the Judge of all, to the Spirits of Just Men made Perfect, and to Jesus the Mediator of the New Covenant: See that ye refuse not him that speaketh; for if they escaped not, who refused him that spoke on Earth, much more shall not we escape, if we turn away from him that speaketh from Heaven:* This Place is the very Tenor of the Gospel. And truly I am beholden to the Man, that since he can find no Scripture for his own Turn, he has provided one Passage so pertinent to mine.

The Law came by Moses, *but Grace and Truth by Jesus Christ:* The first Covenant was for a Time, and imperfect; the second for ever, and most perfect: The Condition of the first was, *To have the Law at the Priest's Mouth*; that of the second is, *To be all taught of God, to learn the Law of the Spirit of Life at the Mouth of our most perfect High-Priest, Christ Jesus the Righteous.* Moses did speak, did give a Law from God, was in the World; but his Day is ended, his Dispensation and Covenant past away (by the bringing in of a better Hope) *but Christ doth speak, he doth give a New Law, he was in the World* (though not of it) *is in the World, and will be to the End thereof; his Day is to Day, and for ever, and his Dispensation always in the Present Tense; for of his Government there shall be no End.*

But how any Man in his Wits, can rationally infer, that because Christ speaketh, *therefore he does not speak, only he did speak*, I leave to the Judgment of any that can distinguish betwixt the Present and Preterperfect Tense, the Time present and past: For because the Apostle saith, *Christ speaketh,* therefore says *T. J.* he did speak, but he does not now speak: What if one should say, *T. Jenner* is an Hireling, would it be a good Consequence to say, therefore he was one, but is not now one; or contrarily, He did write against the *Quakers,* to get a Livelihood by his Books, therefore he does and will write against them for that End, but he did not write against them: Or, that though he says he is sixty six Years old, yet we are to understand he was sixty six Years, but he is not so much now. I can never understand, that the Reason why the Apostle makes Christ a daily present Speaker to his People, should be the Reason why *Jenner* denies he is so, unless from the apparent Contrariety of their Apprehensions.

Indeed, I should stand amaz'd at the Stupidity of the Man, did I not know how Just, as well as frequent, the Lord is, in leaving Men under strange Infatuations; that a Scripture so pertinent for immediate Teaching, should be urg'd against it.

Is it the Gospel State (as the Apostle avows it) *to come to God, the Judge of all, to the Spirits of Just Men made perfect, and to Jesus the Mediator of the New Covenant*, and yet want Revelation and Perfection?

Nor is it less worthy our Observation, that any Man should be so dark, as to imagine, that *Christ's Teaching-Office* was at an end with his outward Life, when he so expresly (and his Apostles after him) makes that to be his chiefest Work, when visibly withdrawn from them.

First, *That he would be with them to the End of the World,* Mat. 28.

Secondly, *That some should not taste of Death, till they saw him come in his Kingdom (and that was within them)* Mat. 16. 28.

Thirdly, *That he that is with them, should be* In *them,* John 14. 17.

Fourthly, *That when the Comforter (or Advocate) came, he would lead them into all Truth; which was himself, in his Spiritual Administration; for the Lord is that Spirit,* John 16. 13. *and the Greek Word in the* 17th *of* John, *is the same Word in* 1 John 2. 1. *If any Man sin we have an* [Advocate] *with the Father, Jesus Christ the Righteous,* &c.

Fifthly, *Except Christ be in you, ye are Reprobates,* 2 Cor. 13. 5.

Sixthly,

Sixthly, said Paul, *When it pleased God to* REVEAL *his Son* IN *me*. Gal. 1. 15. 16.

Seventhly, *Christ in you, the Hope of Glory,* Col. 1. 27.

Eighthly, *If any Man love me, he will keep my Words, and my Father will love him, and we will come unto him, and make our* ABODE *with him,* John 14. which, with many more Places, testifie to Christ's dwelling in, and cohabiting with Believers.

Nor can it reasonably be thought, it should be otherwise, for if under the Gospel, the utmost of our Privilege, must be a Law written, not so much as upon Stone, instead of a Law of Life; we are so far from being advantaged by the Change, that we are upon more uncertain Terms than before. But since it was the Design of God, by giving his Son, *an immediate Light, to enliven and enlighten the dark and dead World, and bring it into a nearer Union, and more intimate Knowledge of him, and Fellowship with him, even to the giving it a Part or Portion of his own Divine Nature, and a being perfectly turned into the Purity and Holiness of it*; For any to deny Revelation, is of all Things, most absurdly ignorant and sacrilegiously abominable.

And thus much the Passage, cited by our Adversary, evidently makes appear; for if the Apostle did not intend that Christ should be understood to be a perpetual immediate Speaker to his Church; why did he not as well phrase Christ's Speaking in the Preterimperfect Tense (it being past) as well as that of *Moses*? But if we ought to understand, that *Moses* did not speak then in *Paul*'s Time, because his Expression of him relates to a Time long since elapst; then by good Reason, may we conclude, that Christ is an immediate perpetual Speaker to his Church; because the Apostle did not use the same Phrase concerning Christ, as he did of *Moses*, though both (as to any external Appearance) are equally gone (Of *Moses*) he says, *For if they escaped not, that refused him that spake on Earth*; (Of Christ) *much more shall not we escape, if we turn away from him that speaketh from Heaven*.

In short, If he design'd we should understand Christ's Speaking, to have been past, why did he not as well say, *speak*, of *Christ*, as he did of *Moses*? But because he said, *spake*, of *Moses*, and *speaketh*, of *Christ*, we must infer, that he intended Christ *was a perpetual immediate Teacher, and Speaker to his People*. Otherwise, if (by *speaketh*) we must understand a Time past, we reasonably ought to conclude, that by *Spake*, is meant the Time present; but if the latter *be ridiculous and false, the former cannot be less impertinent and foolish*.

But perhaps the Word here stumbles him, the Man being so dark, as to conceit *some auricular Sound*, through the visible *Firmament*, but I would have him know, *That Heaven is where Christ inhabits, and he fills Heaven and Earth too*; and though Believers Bodies are on Earth, *their Spirits are in Heavenly Places,* where the Voice of the True Spiritual Shepherd is Spiritually heard and known.

His other Scriptures are as little to his Purpose, viz. *Keep this Commandment until the Appearance of our Lord Jesus Christ. The Things which thou heardest from me, the same commit thou to Faithful Men, who shall be able to teach others. Contend for the Faith which was once delivered to the Saints. Hold the Traditions which ye have been taught, that ye may be able, by Sound Doctrine, both to exhort and convince Gainsayers.*

We greatly want the Consequence. *By no means*, says Thomas Jenner, *Behold here is one at hand; to wit, There is no Certainty in Revelation; an immediate Word is Fallacious, Deceitful, and Delusive; but we know that God spoke to* Moses, *and the Prophets*, &c.

I am weary with wondring; the Frequency of his Folly hath taken away almost the *Sense* of it; and indeed, 'tis unreasonable that a Man should be displeas'd with any for what is so natural to them. *But I answer.*

Did ever any *Quaker* in the World deny the Scriptures quoted? Do they not own, *That the Commandments should be kept for ever? That* Timothy *did well to commit the wholesome Doctrine he had heard of* Paul *to others, and that the Faith should be contended for; and the Tradition, or those Holy Truths, declar'd by the Apostle, should abide with them to whom he spake, and with us too, for evermore.* But what has this to do with the Necessity of Revelation? Does not the same Apostle expresly say, *The Spirit of God only can give to discern the Things of God, and that if any Man is otherwise minded, God will* REVEAL *it to him*.

But what's the Matter with the Man, that an immediate Word is of less Force with him than what's Traditional? Has he endeavour'd to detect us of a Confederacy with the *Papists*, and yet he himself maintain their most Fundamental Error:

Namely,

Namely, *The Infallibility of Tradition:* Have they a stronger Plea? Nay, is it not their most *Dianian* Doctrine, *Calculated to the utter Overthrow both of the Holy Spirit and Scriptures.*

What can be more subject to Variation and Sophistication than Books? And what more certain, than *what we see with our Eyes, hear with our Ears, and handle with our Hands of any Thing.* He that denies the Verity of an immediate Word, and adheres to the Uncertainty of a Report, must disown his own Sense, *and at the same Time embrace that of another Man's.* Certainly he would have made a rare *Papist*; for by his Principles there can be no greater Ground for Faith, *than a mighty Confidence in the Report of another Man.* How Rational the Senseless Opinion of *Transubstantiation* would have appeared to such a Person, is not hard to determine, that esteems a Matter True, *not because he sees or hears it to be,* but because another told him he did, or his Great Grand-father at least.

But if an immediate Word must be so dangerous and deceitful, I wonder upon what Terms he believes the Scriptures to be True: He says, He *is sure that God spake to* Moses *and the Prophets,* I desire to know which Way he came to this mighty Assurance. Is it because it was reveal'd to him? By no Means: He is afraid of nothing more than Inspiration; it must be then because he had been told so; *And is not this a most Scriptural and Protestant Way of Believing* (or much the contrary.)

Has the Man forgot, that in his own Expression he has impeach'd the whole Reformation, whilst he vainly seems to praise the Authors of it; for if the Reason of Believing is not *Inspiration,* it must be *Tradition*; and if *Tradition* be the Ground of Faith, it's high Time he had a *Roman Pension* for his Pains: The very *Papists,* (I mean the more moderate) abhor the Largeness of this Concession, and yet we find it in express Terms in a *Presbyterian* Parson (Whitaker) an ancient *Protestant* Writer, who was of another Opinion, in his Book against *Bellarmine,* betaking himself to the Sanctuary of Divine Revelation, from the Pursuit of that Jesuitical Plea of the Infallibility of Tradition, viz. *That therefore the Scriptures appeared to be True, and their own Constructions of greater Authority than the Ancient Doctors, because the Spirit did witness with their Spirits, that both the Scriptures were from* God, *and the Scope of them truly understood by them:* And thus said *Amesius* on the same Subject. It is a great Shame, as well as manifest Folly, that rather than not abuse the *Quakers,* Men will renounce and oppose the avow'd Principles of their most admir'd Ancestors; but such is the Unhappiness of the Man in Hand, with many more (of his Fraternity) That will violently withstand all Inspiration, though it run them upon the Sands of fallible Tradition.

But there is one material Instance yet omitted, which the Man doubtless confides not a little in, viz.

Well spake (said Paul) *the Holy Ghost by* Isaiah: Paul *did not say, well spake the Holy Ghost by me,* but by Isaiah, *which* Paul *made use of against the* Jews, *to whom he spake, though it were not God's Word immediately, yet mediately; the same is True of the Faithful Ministers of Christ, who therefore are no False Prophets.*

How fatal a Blow our Adversary has given his *Anti-Revelation* Cause, in his Allusion to *Paul,* I proceed to shew.

If *Paul*'s Quotation of those Words were not by Inspiration, then is it no Part or Portion of Scripture, or immediate Revelation, which were both irreverent and absurd to say, upon our Adversaries own Principles. But why none of *Paul*'s, because *Isaiah*'s? As if the same Truth may not be reveal'd to a Thousand several Persons I say, that same Holy Spirit, that spake by *Isaiah,* brought these Words to *Paul*'s Remembrance; and had *Isaiah* never spoken them, if not the very Words, yet the Purpose of them, would have been us'd by that Apostle, as being suitable to the Matter in Hand; and the mentioning of *Isaiah*'s Name, was no otherwise useful, than because he spoke to the *Jews*; that whilst they condemned *Paul* for an *Heretick,* they receiv'd *Isaiah* for a *Prophet.*

But the Parson little thought, that though it should be granted that *Paul* made use of another's Revelation (as the Priests say they do, both of Prophets and Apostles) yet that *Paul* had also Revelations of his own, which they deny, and therefore a most unhappy Instance for the poor Priests.

For if it be a good Argument, that the now Ministers should make use of *Paul*'s Revelation, because he made use of *Isaiah*'s, I am sure it is no bad one, *That because* Paul *also own'd, and had Revelations (as well as that 'tis said he borrow'd* Isaiah*'s) the present Ministers ought to own and have Revelation too.* But if they are

1671.

Chap. II.

are so far from being like *Paul* in the latter, as that they exclaim against Revelation, as a Delusive Thing, *they ought not to borrow and merchandize with the Revelation of other Men.*

The Three Scriptures he pretends to answer, or rather expound in Opposition to what he calls our Sense of them, I might very well omit to consider at this Time, having so largely spoken to the Point, they chiefly are imploy'd by us to vindicate; but that our Adversaries may see how little their Endeavours contribute to their Cause, I shall touch upon them.

Jer. 31. 34.
Heb. 8. 11.
p. 97.

First, *They shall no more teach every Man his Neighbour, and every one his Brother, saying, Know the Lord; for they shall all know me, from the least to the greatest.* Which (saith he) *cannot exclude the Ministry of Man; for the Apostle and Evangelists labour'd in the Word and Doctrine.*

But the poor Man is miserably put to it, to prove his Inference, and indeed, has not so much as rationally attempted it.

We confess it does not exclude God's Teaching by Man; for the Word of Reconciliation was, and is, committed to some of the Sons of Men: *But as* Paul's *Call was not by the Will of Man, so neither his Ministry:* And to assert an humane Ministry from this Passage, or to affirm it not to be destructive of the Ministry of Man, *is to give an high Instance of gross Ignorance.*

And though in the Beginning of the Gospel Administration, Teaching, in the Sense exprest, was allow'd, nay, commendable and necessary; yet, the End of it, is to be brought into such an improv'd State, as shall never need it more, which could never be the Tendency, nor End, of the old Covenant.

In fine, They are taught of God, who are taught by the Spirit of God in another: However the Place totally excludes those, *who borrow their Neighbour's Words, and speak what they have not known and receiv'd of the Lord.*

1 Jo. 2. 27.
p. 99.

Secondly, The Second Scripture is that of John, *But the Anointing, which ye have receiv'd of him, abideth in you; and you need not that any Man teach you, but as the same Anointing teacheth you all Things, and is no Lye.*

To which he offers several Answers, or Expositions, but horribly contradictory to each other.

His first is, *That the Apostle meant, they had no need, who through Grace were anointed with the indwelling saving Operations, and efficacious Influence of the Spirit* (which is the only Teacher) *to hearken to the Doctrine of* Cerinthus, Ebion, *or the* Gnosticks; *who though they pretend to be Ministers of Christ, are indeed Antichrists.*

Where by the way, I must take Liberty to observe, how plainly he vindicates both Revelation, and the Spirit's being the only Teacher or Rule; *If the only Teacher, then no other Teacher; and what then becomes of his Ministry of Man?*

Next, it's strange so old a Man should be so ignorant and impudent at once, as to infer so wrong and so unnatural a Consequence from the Words of the Apostle: How could the Holy Ghost intend, that the Anointing was able to teach them, what were the Words of those Men, *and yet not what was the Way of Truth:* 'Tis not to be supposed, that it was given only to preserve from Error, *and not to lead into all Truth.* But the Parson would not that the Ministry of Man should be totally excluded, and therefore bequeaths to it, the more noble Employment, *viz.* To inform of the Mysteries of the Gospel, but the *Anointing was only to teach to avoid Error*; as if what did the one, was not to do the other: Horrible Folly!

But if the Man will have the Apostle to mean, that because they had received the Anointing, they needed not that *Cerinthus* should teach them his Heresie: I hope he will give us leave to infer, that before they had received the Anointing, they had great Need to embrace his erroneous Teachings; but because such a Construction is most abusively false, it is apparent, that by Man's Teaching was meant the legal Administration, or the utmost Ability, except that which was deriv'd from, or grounded upon, Inspiration.

And that I speak the Truth, let us consider his second Answer, viz. *That this was not spoken to all Men, but of those that are come to Christ, and need no Man to teach them.*

O Stupendious Contradiction! Why? The Man is here become our Proselyte, *he speaks the Language of perfect Revelation*: Certainly, if they were thus qualified that they needed no Man's Teaching, some were come to a State that was above *the so much beloved Ministry of Man*: And how this agrees with the first Answer, viz. *That the Teaching was only to avoid Error, but not of Force enough to inform them of all Truth* (as his Exposition did import) let the sober Man judge.

His third Answer is his third Contradiction, viz. *That the Anointing meant, was the Spirit in the Scripture* (to make the best of his other improper Phrases) *to which no Teaching of Man should be added, but as we are taught there.*

It is as hard for me to understand what he means by the Spirit in the Scriptures, as it is for him to make it out; I hope he does not mean, that when the Bible is in his Pocket, the holy Ghost is there; though that which is their Life and Spirit in the Scriptures, *is the ungodly Gain, they make by them, and that they always love to carry there.*

But 'tis apparent, that though they would seem to joyn the Spirit with the Scriptures, in Reality he means, the Scriptures without the Spirit; for how can the holy Spirit be added to? But the Scriptures may.

What Harmony this third Interpretation has with his two former, that appropriated all to the Anointing, and in Expressions so plain and positive, as no *Quaker* needs to except against them, cannot but be obvious to every unbyast Person.

But that he may not take for granted, that it was the Scripture the Apostle was inspir'd to give forth, but that very *Anointing* which inspir'd the Apostle. Let it be first considered that the Word is plain, *Anointing*, without any other adjunct. And secondly, that little was written, or at least compos'd, but scattered abroad among the several Churches, at that early Time of the Day; or to use his own Words, p. 102. *The New Testament was not then extant.*

Lastly (says he) 'twere well if it were the last of his Absurdities) *These Words are an Hyperbole; there is an Excess in them, as in chap. 2. 20. that they know all Things, which is God's only property. The meaning is, They knew many Things, even so that they needed not that any Man teach them; that is, They knew so much, as that if they persevered, they might be kept without so much Teaching.*

It were (almost) endless to pursue the wretched Folly of this poor Scribler: Was there no other Man among the angry Hirelings, of that Country, to enterprize this Work? Methinks they should (as Men) have scorn'd to suffer so raw and contradictory a Discourse to see the World: What greater Abuse can be put upon the Scriptures than this, to mangle them under the vain Pretence of being skill'd in the Idioms of the Original? 'Tis an Excess (says he (of Folly say I) but what is an Excess? To say that such as have the Holy Spirit need not to be taught by Man, then there is an Excess in pag. 99, and 100. of his own Discourse, where he gives that for his Sense of the Place in controversie; Yes (says he) it is, for the Apostle said, *They knew all Things*, and they did not: But I had rather *Jenner* were a Lyar, than the Apostle: Can such as are taught by the Holy Spirit be ignorant of any Thing that relates to their own Souls? And is the Man so stupid, as to think the Apostle otherwise intended, in his saying, They knew all Things (viz. *That concern them to know*)

Well, but for his meaning now, I would fain be inform'd, *If from knowing all Things*, in the Sense express'd, and needing not to be taught of Men, this meaning of our *Antagonist* may be logically and truly deduc'd? Namely, *That they needed not that any Man should teach them*; that is, *they might be kept without much Teaching*, and this all in a Breath? The first Part of his Meaning is true (if he mean so) however, he was soon weary of it, that in the following line implies the Necessity (after all) of a little of *Man's Ministry* to mix with it; *but that little (with him) is all*. In fine, the Man shews an Ignorance in these Affairs, almost invincible.

His third Passage, by him pretended to be expounded, is this, *We have a more sure Word of Prophesie, whereunto you do well to take heed, as unto a Light that shineth in a dark Place until the Day dawn, and the Day-star shineth in your Hearts.*

He fastens an Interpretation of this Place upon us, but does not tell us whence he takes it. He says it supposeth three Things.

First, *That by the Word of Prophesie is to be understood, the whole Scriptures.*

To which he answers, First, *That the Apostle could not mean the whole Scriptures, since the New Testament was not then extant.* Second, *That it was a Comparison*

parison betwixt the Certainty of the Old Testament, and the Voice upon the Mount; which (says he) Peter *prefer'd not as most true, but as the most sure Ground for Faith of the two.* Third, *That the Voice was not so sure, whilst verbal; but most sure when writ, and made scriptural.*

To all which I say, That as he has obtruded upon us an Interpretation of the Word *Prophesie*, that is neither ours, nor could be the Apostle's (and therefore forc'd.) So to his first Conceit I reply, *That the Spirit of Jesus is the Word of Prophesie*, which is not distinct in Nature from the *Day-star*, but in Degree only; the utmost Attainment being still through the same Power and Spirit, however, diversly denominated, according to it's several Operations; for as the Prophet's State was before that of the Gospel (yet the same Spirit in both) so the Spirit of Prophesie is *the same with the Glorious Day-star*, though in it's Appearance, Service and Tendency, it may be of an inferior Administration.

Besides, It could not be all the Scriptures, because, *The New Testament was not then extant*: How could the Scripture inspir'd by *John* (to use his own Phrase) be the then Saints Rule of Faith and Ground of Knowledge; since he confesses, It was not then in *esse*, in being? But if that was not extant, and yet they were not without a Teacher and a Rule, we hope it will be granted to us, that *the Holy Anointing was both*.

Secondly, I do deny, that the Comparison was betwixt the Old Testament and the Voice in the Mount; for of the two, *without all doubt, the Voice was the most sure*; since two Witnesses are better than one. Of the Old Testament, they could only say they had read it, and they believ'd it to be of God, because they were told so (unless *Tho. Jenner* will allow the Scriptures to be acknowledg'd such, only upon an Inspiration) But of the certainty of that Transaction in the Mount, they had their Eyes and Ears to confirm it, and the Allowance of the Son of God, as afterwards their Discourse about it evidenceth, with their own inward Sense of it, than which nothing could be attended with greater Circumstances of Verity.

But it is worth our Notice, that notwithstanding he has accused us upon the Spot, of disrespect to the Scriptures, he by his own Interpretation and Confession, expresseth our greater Value of them, than the Voice upon the Mount, for if I understand him, he says, the *Quakers make the Scriptures to be the Word of Prophesie*, and by-and-by tells us, *he grants that the Apostle meant the old Testament was so, and that the Comparison lies betwixt it and the Voice.* From whence I conclude, He believes (if he believes what he writes) that because the Scripture is a surer Word of Prophesy than the Voice; and that the *Quakers*, he says, affirm the Scripture is that Word of Prophesy, *the* Quakers *then place more value upon a written and recorded Word, than in an immediate Word or Voice*: Behold the Contradiction of the Man!

But above all, his gross Impertinency in saying, *The Old Testament is not to be preferred as the most true, and yet is the most sure Ground of Faith of the two;* is very remarkable and reprovable.

Thirdly and lastly, If the Certainty of what was heard lay in the writing of it, then it was not certain before; but if they could not write before they heard it, and that it was first certainly heard, before written, what Man in his Wits will dare to affirm that it was therefore only certain, *because Scriptural or Written*.

In short, if it was not as certain before as after, it is uncertain yet, since whatever certainly is heard, was received first by the Hearing of it. But again, What can be more irrational, than that the *Old Testament* should be a Rule to the then *Churches* and *Apostles*, that were Ministers and Congregations of the New One? This very Assertion, besides that, it carries much of Folly in it, *shews how fatal the Spirits of the Priests are to the whole End and Benefit of the Gospel.*

2*d*. The Second Interpretation of the Remainder of that Scripture he makes to be this, viz. *That by the very Dawning and Day-star arising in their Hearts, is to be understood the Spirit of Grace in Regeneration:* But this (says he) *cannot be;* for Peter *wrote to such as had obtained like precious Faith with himself*, Chap. 1. 1.

Of all which I take no farther Notice than this, That though they had received like precious Faith in Kind, yet not in Measure and Degree, for *then they might have as well writ that Epistle to* Peter, *as he did to them.* But if *Peter* had a right Sense of their Conditions, and that the Holy Ghost does nothing needless or in vain; we ought to conclude, that they had not yet arriv'd to that perfect State, albeit,

albeit, they were pressing after it, as that they stood not in Need of a farther Exhortation: And that *Peter* had a more deep Experience, than those to whom he wrote. So much for this, unless he had given us our own Words.

3*d*. His third Branch of Interpretation concerns the Particle [*Until*] *which, be says, we understand to be the limited Instant of Regeneration, though before it we may attend the Scriptures, yet after it we may not.*

To which, by Way of Answer, he makes a wretched Stir about the Particle *Until*. So, like a mean Pedant, and one that would be thought an Originalian, (the Refuge of empty Heads, and defeated Causes) that it would be too tedious to attend his indirect and crooked Motions. But in short, this he means by the whole, that sometimes, [*Until*] in Scripture is taken for no Limitation, and sometimes for a Limitation, Instances he gives us several, but of one Side only, *&c.* *thou shalt by no Means come out thence* [Till] *thou hast paid the utmost Farthing*, Matth. 5. 26. Now, says he, that is meant never: But where's the Consequence? Why this? *that the Scriptures are to be attended upon after the arising of this Day-star.*

To which I answer, That nothing can be more Contradictory to the *Sense* of Scripture, and his own Opinion upon the Place, and by his Folly in this one Particular, the Reader may take a most clear Measure of the whole.

First then, I say, that [*Until*] is not thus to be read, no more than, *do this 'till I come*, in the Case of the Supper, where our Adversaries allow, that when He, the Substance, is come, the Shadow shall disappear; and though we differ about the Substance coming, yet all agree to the Force of the Particle Until; for the Place says, *that they were to take Heed to that sure Word of Prophesy* [*Until*] *the Day-star did arise*; intimating, that when it was risen, it being a greater and more glorious Discovery, it should swallow up the lesser Measure of Light; otherwise, they would rest in a Degree and Condition far short of that Illumination and Enjoyment that belong'd to the Time of the Day-star's arising in the Heart, *and instead of pressing forward and forgetting the Things that are behind*, they would be conforming themselves to them: Not that the Word of Prophesy is to be despised, but that the other is to be preferred: And had we asserted the Scriptures to be the Word of Prophesy, though we acknowledge the Day-star to be of a more infallible and transcending Value, yet we should also have confest, that the Scriptures are, *and yet will be highly valuable and useful to the End of the World.*

But since he restrains not the Force of the Particle [*Until*] to the Instant of Regeneration, but the Vision of the Glory after this Life, (as he conceives) why should he not allow of [*Until*] as I have expressed; since all conclude, that in future Glory there can be no Need of Service, for the Scripture? *Will he both have* [Until] *extend the Authority and Usefulness of the Scriptures beyond and after the arising of the Day-star*, (which, says he, is Eternal Glory) *and yet confess, that in that Cœlestial State there is no Need of them?*

And though his Endeavours are to render our Interpretation (as he calls it) false and irrational, yet can his Sense of the Particle [*Until*] be only Sense and Rational in the Allowance of it.

For which is more sober? To say that the Scriptures are useful, even after Regeneration, or when separated from this visible World, and entred into Eternal Glory? The first is allowed by all, the last is denied by all, so that either he should have made his Particle [*Until*] to signify a Limitation; and so his Notion of the Day-star had been more reconcileable with it, (though false in it self) or else he should not have quarrel'd with that which he calls our Interpretation; that being the most reconcileable. For if he had asserted either (as he does neither) he might have been said to write Sense, though not Truth; but now he miserably misseth both.

So that our Belief of that *Metropolitan and Superintendent Doctrine of Revelation* is so far from receiving any Disadvantage by the Endeavours of the Man in hand, that his most frivolous Objections, but *pertinent Scriptures* by him urg'd, (against himself) have done It the Justice, and Us the Service of a Vindication.

To conclude, There can be no Understanding in this World without Revelation; which is never the less true, because totally unobserv'd, or generally deny'd.

For Instance; What Man alive is capable of the Affairs pertinent and proper to himself as a meer Man in external Matters, without the Discovery and Assistance of that intelligent Principle the Apostle phrases *the Spirit of a Man? Is it not through*

through the *Dictates* or *Revelation* it gives him, that *he is intellectually abilitated to manage the whole Transactions of Human Life?* Thus saith *Paul*, what *Man knoweth the Things of a Man save the Spirit of Man which is in him?* 1 Cor. 2. 11.

And by what Way imaginable can this Knowledge be convey'd, unless by the Manifestation or Discovery of this Spirit of Man, *which I call common, natural, and civil Revelation.*

But as there is this natural and intelligent Spirit, by which Man is daily informed of the Concerns of mortal Life; so is there a divine Principle communicated to him, which we call the Light, that does illuminate and discover to his Understanding the Condition of his Soul, and *give him a true Knowledge of what is good, what he himself is, and what is required at his Hands, either in obeying or suffering.* And to this the Apostle plainly consents in the following Words of the Passage before urged. For when he had ascribed the Knowledge of human Affairs only to the Spirit of Man, he adds, *even so the Things of God knoweth no Man save the Spirit of God.*

I therefore infer, that the most religious, pertinent and authoritative Writings in the World are but so many *senseless Letters and lifeless Words, where that infallible Expositor* (I mean the Holy Spirit) *in his Discovery and Revelation to the Minds of Men, is absent and wanting.*

Since therefore it's Information and Testimonials are the indispensable Requisites to authorize and unfold them to us, 'tis evident that not only no Discourse can otherwise be beneficial to us, *but that it therefore is the most noble and unerring Rule of Faith and Obedience, the Life and Key of all.* Whatever Writings were by Inspiration, are of less Value, than the Spirit that gave them forth; *for the Effect can never be so worthy as the Cause*; and what is liable to Sophistication, *Mistranslation, and false Copies, with almost an Infinity of other Accidents, as the best of Books are,* cannot with any Reverence or good Sense be equalled to the *Unerring, impassible and Eternal Spirit*; which because none can understand the Things of God without, and that 'tis necessary all that would be sav'd should endeavour it, 'tis *greatly necessary that they have Recourse to that Spirit of Truth for sound Conviction and perfect Conversion from the World to God!*

We end the Chapter with this brief Summary of the whole.

First, *That by Revelation we understand the Discovery and Illumination of the Light and Spirit of God relating to those Things that properly and immediately concern the daily Information and Satisfaction of our Souls in the Way of our Duty to him and our Neighbour.*

2d. *That we renounce all fantastical and whimsical Intoxications, or any Pretence to the Revelation of new Matter in Opposition to the ancient Gospel declared by Christ Jesus and his Apostles: And therefore not the Revelation of new Things, but the renewed Revelation of the Eternal Way of Truth.*

3d. *That this Revelation is the Life, Virtue, Condition, and very Soul of the Gospel and second Covenant.*

4th. *That none oppose this, but such as the God of this World has blinded, and that through their Ignorance of the Spirituality of the Evangelical Dispensation, are (whilst they pretend to be under it) Sticklers for a more embondaged State than that of the ancient Jews.*

I must confess I have exceeded my own Design, being thereto led by the plain Discoveries of the Spirit of Truth, how much this Doctrine concerns the Offices of the Lord Jesus, *as he is King, Priest and Prophet,* and that daily Benefit of his Church, without which she must inevitably faint and perish under the dry and mercenary Ministration of very Hirelings.

CHAP. III.

THE first Thing I shall insist upon in this Chapter, (tho' I find little Encouragement to insist upon any Thing) shall be his Answer to what he calls our Second Objection, &c. p. 107, 108.

That the present Ministers take a Text from the Letter of the Scripture, and teach the People from that, which the Prophets never did; The Substance of what he says is this: *That though the Prophets took no Text, (because they were to lay the first Foundation for After-ages) yet Christ himself did, citing that Passage of his going
into*

into the *Synagogues, and reading and expounding on the Sabbath-day recorded by Luke*, &c. *And that they therefore take a Text that the Weight of their Building may have the Prophets and Apostles for it's Foundation.*

To which I need not give any other Reply than what arises from his own Answer.

First, It's a plain Untruth that the Reason of the *Prophets* not taking a Text was their being the first Foundation, *Since the greatest Part of the Old Testament was then in Being, and from whence the present Priests do frequently fetch their Themes.* Nay, the Prophets Works may rather be said to be Prophetical Discourses of the New One.

Secondly, Nor is it less Irreverent that he should make *Christ* the Chief Corner-stone, to be built upon the Foundation of the *Prophets*; For if their Writings are *a Foundation* to After-ages, to build their Preaching upon, then was not *Christ* their Foundation, whom they called the *Foundation* of many Generations, but the *Prophets* his, *because* he quoted their Words: But besides, that this is Irrational, What Foundation had *Enoch, Noah, Abraham, Isaac, Jacob, Moses,* &c?

Thirdly, Neither is *Christ's* Practice, in this Particular, to be imitated, any more than all the rest of his Condescensions to the *Jewish Church*: It was not therefore any Matter of Institution, only he was desirous of informing the People how their own admired *Prophets* had foretold his Coming, and that his *Appearance, Life, Doctrine, and Miracles, had fulfilled their Prophesies that Day, in their Ears,* to the End they might receive him, for he was the *Messiah* of the World; nor is there Instance of any such Sermons recorded by the Evangelists.

Fourthly, The *Apostles*, in their many Sermons recorded in the *Acts*, never practis'd any such Way, or form of Declaration of the Gospel to the People, though they often cited Passages as the Holy Spirit brought them to their Remembrance, which is not now denied but practised by us; and if such as had the Writings of the *Prophets* took no Text out of the *Prophets*, I ask the Man, Why he and his Brethren, having the Writing of the *Apostles*, take Texts out of the Writings of the *Apostles*? But if the *Apostles*, notwithstanding the Writings of the *Prophets*, spake as the Holy Spirit moved them, without any such Formality; *the present Ministers ought in Imitation of the Apostles* (since they are so precise at *Imitation* in lesser Matters) to do the like, but apprehensive of their little Ware and Trade, in Case they should abandon that profitable Practice of Merchandizing with the Saints Words, *they seem resolved to persevere in their ungodly Traffick*, and which is worse, endeavour to shew the Words of these Holy Men to vindicate their own corrupt Practices.

Fifthly, If they will have their Works to be the Superstructure that's built upon the Foundation of the Prophets and Apostles Writings, then such as is the Foundation, such must the Superstructure be; *but the Foundation is Revelation,* therefore the Superstructure cannot be Premeditation; for as Iron and Clay can never mix, by Reason of an Opposition and Inconsistency in their Natures, so is it equally impossible that Revelation, should be a Foundation, for the Invention and inexperienc'd premeditated Discourses of Men; they can never incorporate; the Building cannot subsist of such contrary and incoherent Matter; *The Souls that are built on that Foundation, must be as living as the Foundation they are built upon.* Nay, nothing can be more Irrational and Irreverent, than to make the Lord *Jesus Christ* the Chief Corner-stone of a Building contrived, and premeditated by Men, not inspired, the Foundation of which upon our Adversaries Concessions is very Revelation.

Sixthly, But if Christ's Example in this Case be of such Importance and must be inviolably observed, How comes it that the present Ministers have so exceeded it? Did *Christ* preach by an Hour-Glass? Did he put on *Ceremonial Garbs and Vestments, divide his Text into it may be twenty Particulars, raise Doctrines, draw Uses, and lastly make Applications, as the Priests now do, to the confounding and darkning of God's Counsel, and the People's Understanding, instead of opening the former, and informing the latter?*

Seventhly, Not that we think it is a Fault to use the Words of Scripture, when the same Spirit that gave them forth brings them to our Remembrance for present Service, but that which objects against that Practice, is their making Use of these Holy Men's Words, for a Subject to premeditate and build their dark Conceptions, and meer Imaginations upon; for we affirm, *that none ought to Preach in the Name of the Lord, but such as are impowered by the immediate Teachings, and Requirings* of his Holy Spirit; and that it's as suitable and necessary to this Age, as ever it was to any former Age; and from the Eternal God do I warn all the Hirelings that read me, to lay close to heart, that such as run and are not sent of him, and that say, the Lord saith, and he hath not spoken by them, but borrow the Words of those, by whom he spake in Ages past, and add thereto their own carnal Meanings and uninspired Interpretations, (and all for Gain too) the dreadful God of Heaven and Earth will reveal himself in Flames of consuming Fire to their Everlasting Destruction, for the Blood of Souls lies at their Door; but as for him that hath received the cleansing Word of Reconciliation, in the Power and Divine Authority of the same, let him declare it where-ever called; *and as he hath freely received, so freely let him give.*

To the Third and Fourth Objections, he says we make, namely, *Against their Praying before and after Sermons, and their observing of Days and Hours, to Preach in, and Pray in:* Thus he pretends to answer, *viz. That it is of good Report, and that Prayer sanctifieth all Things, and that the first Day was intituled* Sabbath *under the Gospel, from* David's *Words, this is the Day which the Lord hath made, and* Christ's *Resurrection, and Redemption of Man: And because the Ninth and Third Hours amongst the Jews were Times for Devotion, the like should be now:* But that it is no new Thing for the Man to mistake, I should wonder that he would dare to charge us with that in Print, which our known Practice in a great Measure vindicates us from: But how can I expect that he should not mistake our Principles, who does not know his own. However, I reply,

First, Prayer is of good Report, and we both own and practise it with all relative Circumstances of due Reverence: But is it of good Report for unregenerated and uninspired Men to pray? The Apostle says, *That Praying ought to be with the Spirit*; then not without Inspiration; and if so, such can never pray acceptably to God, that are so far from praying by the Impulses, Teachings, and Motions of that Divine Spirit, as that they deny with Vehemency the very Doctrine of Inspiration. And that this must be the Sense of the Apostle, and Holy Scriptures of Truth, (nay the Tendency of the Man himself, if he understands what he writes.) Consider the Word *Sanctify*. I ask what kind of Prayer can Sanctify? That which springs from any thing below the Inspiration of the Eternal Spirit of Truth? Are the most zealous Cries and passionate Supplications of Man, unassisted or unmov'd thereto, sufficient to sanctify any Action or Thing? The Scriptures resolve us, *I will pray with the Spirit and with Understanding also*; as if the Apostle would let us know, *That without the Spirit to enliven and assist, it were as impossible to pray acceptably to God, as without the Gift of* Tongues, *to pray intelligibly to the People*; and indeed more. And I can give no better Reason, nor can another be rendered, why those Heaps of Prayer, and daily Repetitions do so little Good, and are so ineffectual, than *their Proceeding from, and being offer'd by unclean Hearts and polluted Lips*, who are so far from praying by the Spirit, *that they furiously deny the Doctrine of Inspiration and Revelation*, (which are one) *as dangerous and diabolical.*

So that we do not deny true and proper Prayer at any Time, *but those formal, set, and pre-appointed Prayers, which shew themselves to be the Invention and Contrivance of Man's Spirit, and not of God's.*

That their *Prayers* are such, there needs no other Instance than their constant Practice, before and after Sermons, and upon Set Days, &c. For either they must make appear, that they have the Holy Spirit at their Beck, or else confess that they make and perform those Duties (as they falsely call them) in their own Will and Time, which, of the two, is most reasonable to believe.

Secondly, As to the Force of his Answer to our Fourth Objection, (as he stiles it) *That we are displeased that they observe set Times, Days, and Hours*, &c. namely, *That the First Day is the Gospel-Sabbath by divine Appointment, because called the Lord's-Day (which it is not by Creation) and that the Jews observed the Ninth and Third Hours, for their Devotion, and therefore Set-Days, Hours, and Times,* &c. *ought to be as well under the Gospel, as the Law.*

I briefly reply thus, It is greatly to be suspected, that most of those Objections he would have to be ours, are his own; or he would have proved them ours by Quotation, which he hath mostly omitted from the first. If by Set-times he means, *Days set apart* (not as more intrinsically sacred, or in themselves more Holy than others, but) only to assemble upon, to wait upon God, and receive of his Heavenly

Heavenly Benefits; *we are so far from being destitute of them, that as 'tis impossible for us to perform an Action without Time, so have we distinct Days and Times, we meet upon, well-known throughout the World, where any of us do inhabit:* In this Sense then we cannot be obnoxious; for it is perfect Matter of Fact, that in that Sense we allow of Days and Times; but as to Consecrated Days and Times, and the superstitious Observation of them; as if the Holiness of the Day called loudly on us for our particular Devotion, as being this or t'other Saint's, and not that our Devotion rather required a Time to be performed in: This we are displeased with, and boldly testify against, *as beggarly and Jewish:* What said the Apostle, (urged by his Godly Jealousy) to the *Galatians*? *But now after ye have known God, or rather are known of God, how turn ye again to the weak and beggarly Elements, whereunto ye desire again to be in Bondage; ye observe Days, and Months, and Times, and Years; I am afraid of you, lest I have bestowed upon you Labour in Vain, &c.* Which is Defence enough for us; for if the Apostle said it, the Holy Ghost said it; and we are sure, whoever require or practise any thing contrary to this Reproof, they are great Strangers to the Liberty of the Gospel, being yet in Bondage to the beggarly Elements of weak and Antichristian Dispensations; for such implicitly deny him to be come in the Flesh, that hath put an End to them all, who is the *Everlasting Day of Rest,* and *Sabbath* to his People.

Gal. 4. 9. 10. 11.

How ridiculous the *Parson* shews himself, in offering to maintain the moral Holiness of the first Day, is evident; since if it therefore was of Divine Appointment, because not the Lord's Day by Creation, then was not the seventh *Sabbath,* the Lord's Sabbath, because so by Creation; as if that it's being so from the Creation, hindred it's being so by Divine Appointment. But this Ribaldry well becomes the poor Priest; besides, how comes he to know that *John*'s being in the Spirit upon the Lord's Day, *was the first Day of the Week.* Or what Institution can be infer'd from it's being called the Lord's Day, in case *John* meant so? He certainly little deserves to be stiled an *Evangelical Minister, who instead of Preaching the End of all Holy Days, Feasts, new Moons, solemn Assemblies, and Sabbath-Days, is asserting and maintaining the absolute Necessity and Service of them under the Gospel.* Let no Man judge you in Meat, or Drink, or in *respect of an Holy Day, or New Moon, or of the Sabbath, which are Shadows of Things to come, but the Body is of Christ.* This Doctrine *Paul* preached and writ, how then it should be Evangelical to institute a second visible Sabbath in the Room or Place of the first, when the first was abrogated as shadowy, is absurd, and incongruous; for the Reason of the visible and external Rest, was the visible and external Creation; but becase the second Creation is *Invisible and Spiritual, by the invisible Word of his Power, viz. The Regeneration and Redemption of the Soul of Man* (begetting him anew to God) *therefore should the Gospel-Sabbath be also spiritual and invisible:* to which these Words refer, *Come unto Me, all ye that Labour, and are heavy Leaden, and I will give you Rest. We which have believed do enter into Rest: There remaineth a Rest for the People of God:* And had this poor Man known, what the Gospel-Sabbath means, he would have rested from this foolish (nay) wicked Work, his Ignorance and Malice have brought forth against the Owners and Professors of the true *Sabbath-Day.*

Col. 2. 16, 17.

Mat. 11. 2. 8.
Heb. 21. 3. 9.

He might have better learnt from the reformed Churches abroad (as they are called) and more particularly from their grand *Champion,* and most *Celebrated Founder, Calvin;* let the Priest first answer his Arguments against *a visible temporary Sabbath,* under the Gospel, before he attacks the *Quakers,* as heterodox in the Point.

And as to the Inference he makes, *viz.* That because there were set Times and Days under the *Jewish Constitution,* therefore should there be some under that of the Gospel also: Here can be nothing said by me which can render him more a *Jew* and an *Anti-Evangelical Minister* in the World; for the contrary is most true, *viz. That because they were Ceremonially or Typically used under the Law, therefore, and on set Purpose, they are not to be us'd under the Gospel, which is the End of the Law, as to those Things.*

In short, I do declare again, that though we utterly renounce all special and moral Holiness in Times and Days, yet we both believe it is requisit that Time be set apart for the Worship of the Almighty, and are also every where found in the diligent Practice of the same: And howbeit, we cannot own so strict an Institution, *as to Sabbatize the first Day,* nor that it has any Holiness, inherent to it;

1671.

Chap. III.
p. 114, 115.

yet as taking the Primitive Saints for an Example, *with Godly Reverence we constantly assemble upon it.*

His Charge of our denying Family-Duties is equally false, and Devilish, with all the rest; *for we know it is our Duty, and is also our Practice, to retire from our external Affairs, and wait upon the Lord every Day, that we may receive Strength from him, and feel his Heavenly Peace and Blessing to descend upon Us, at our rising up, and lying down; that so to him, over and above all visible Things, Honour and Praise may be returned, who is worthy for ever.*

Chap. IV.

CHAP. IV.

p. 116, 117, 118.

THE next Charge he brings against Us is this, *That we assert all outward Church-Polity, Church-Officers, and Church-Ordinances to be ceased since the Death of the Apostles*; for Confirmation of this, he quotes (a Thing he seldom does) One *Joseph Frice* who (says he) affirms, *that the true Church ceased since the Death of the Apostles, until the raising up of God's own Seed out of the Earth, to stand a Witness against wicked Murderers, and Persecutors of the Saints, and true Church of Christ*: but in what Chapter or Page we are to find this, I cannot tell, nor has he told Us, and if he has mistaken the matter quoted, and insisted on, as he hath the Name, we have little Reason to believe what he writes; for his Name was *Fuce*. But he proceeds, he thinks, upon clearer Evidences. *The Quakers Lancashire Queries* 115, 118. *To observe Ordinances, as sprinkling Infants, to tell the People of a Sacrament, and following outward Teachings, &c. Where did God Command it?*

This Doctrine he esteems heinous, and thus he undertakes to confute it.

First, says he, *God hath all along had a People, even under Antichrist's Reign, whom he calls his sealed Ones, that have been his faithful Witnesses; And as God in the Beginning instituted Church Offices and Ordinances, so hath he ingag'd his Word to continue them unto the World's End; of which Number were the* Waldenses, Albigenses, Hussites, Hugonites, Lutherans, and Protestants, ('tis well he hath left his *Independent, and Presbyterian* Brethren out) *these were some of those that did oppose Antichrist, before ever the vain-glorious boasting Sect of* Quakers *were heard of in the World, who are the very Synagogue of Satan, I dare affirm.*

His Confidence, Ignorance, and Envy, are Great Companions in this Paragraph, which none can think an hard Saying, but such as are dark, both to the Scriptures and the best Story; I shall not reflect upon his begging the Question, but attend the more substantial Part of his pretended Answer.

2 Thes. 2, 3.

To deny an *Apostacy* (which implies a falling away) is to deny the prophetick Testimonies of the Scriptures, for said the Apostle *Paul, Let no Man deceive you, by any Means; for that Day shall not come, except there come a falling away first; and that Man of Sin be revealed, the Son of Perdition, &c.* the like *John* in his Epistles, *Antichrist is already come*; and in his Revelation, he tells us, that the *Witnesses were slain, and the Beast, and the false Prophet, and the Dragon, and the Whore*, (Phrases to express a devilish and apostatized Church and Power) *Reigned and overcame the Saints, and none for a Time appeared to make war with the Beast.*

Rev. ch. 17, 18, 19.

That this began Immediately after the Death of the Apostles, is very evident, from that Account History gives Us *of the new Inventions and Additions that were successively brought into the* Church, insomuch, as *that the Worshipping of Angels was in the earlier Part of the second Century*; and though Persecution did much depress that Spirit of Apostacy and hinder it's growth, yet no sooner did *Constantine* begin to favour the Church, than she transported with the Apprehension of so sudden a Change (as from Persecution to an easie splendid Life) forgot the Simplicity of the Christian Life and Doctrine, and spur'd hard in the Pursuit of Men's Inventions, till through her multiplied Superstitions, *she had form'd up that Great Whore, who* (under all her Pretensions to be a Virgin, the Lamb's Bride and Apostolick Church) *has appeared an open Whore, having defiled the Nations, and made them Drunk with the Cup of her Fornications* (consisting of Pride, Empire, Idolatry, Error, Avarice, Persecution, and all other Abominations; and 'tis with the Strength of this Cup, that *Jenner* is intoxicated, and reels, and rails in his malicious Attempts against us) but this was not done at once, the Cup was some time in filling, and sometime in drinking, and the Nations were apostatizing, before they were apostatized.

Nor

Nor does this impeach God of Breach of Promise, for these Words, *I will be with you to the End, &c.* were first spoken to the Apostles, not only as Apostles, but as Believers, and the Promise is therefore extensive to all, and every individual Person of the Faithful.

And secondly, They are but conditionally said, ' If you do as I command you, ' but if you fall away, and apostatize through the subtil Devices of the Man of ' Sin, then I will not be with you, but give you up to believe a Lye, and be damned: And this was mostly the Case of the Apostacy: If any did dissent from the universally pressed Conformity to the *Papacy* (that about the Six hundredth Year had mounted the Chair, and rounded the Ears of Princes with an invisible Power, and unlimited Prerogative) ' It was after a wandring and sculking Manner, very ' destitute of that Church Order, and Ordinances, as the Man would suggest; ' their work being rather to testifie their Dissent, than positive Judgment of Things.

The *Waldenses*, the first, and oldest much, that he mentions, are very young comparatively with the prolix Night of Apostacy; for 'tis not Five Hundred and thirteen Years since *Peter Waldo* Citizen of *Lyons* in *France*, the first publick *Renouncer* of the *Romish Church*, for her new embrac'd Inventions (from whom they are call'd) began to publish his Dissent from the *Romish* Religion, and higher he durst not venture.

The *Albigenses*, from the Country *Albi*, were later, and the rest Successors to both: Besides, they were not in any Church Capacity, but tost and disperst up and down the World, diverted from all Establishment that could be thought the *Presbyterian Model of the Man in Hand*.

But that which is worthy of our Notice, is, That these very Men so much renowned by him, held those individual Principles, for which he violently condemns us. 1st, *They would not swear upon any Account.* 2d, *They declaim'd against a settled Priest-hood, or Ministry by Way of Distinction*; but what this Man says of *Singers*, that all good Christians are *Gospel Choristers*, and therefore they need none by Way of Distinction, as under the Law; so they say of Ministers, that all good Christians are Ministers, and have a right according to their Gift and Abilities given of God, to preach to others. 3d, *They exclaim'd against Tithes*; 4th, *They did perfectly disown all Universities as conducing to the making of a good Minister*; And lastly, *They were Enemies to, and Remonstrators against the Inhumanity of Persecution*, which is the best Character of Presbyterianism, and which it can no more live without, and be, than a Leopard can be such without his Spots. So that he writes against, and esteems Heterodox and Antichristian, those very Men that he at the same Time implicitly stiles Opposers of Antichrist, and such as Worship God in the Beauty of Holiness.

And though he would march away in Triumph over us, as imagining his Advantage sufficient to justify his Glorying, *That we should disown those People, that so long since dissented from the Idolatries of* Rome, *and narrow all Reformation to our selves*; yet we would have all to know, that (though we do confess it is our Faith, that so glorious a Vision, since the Primitive Days, has not happened to any, as to us in this our Day) the Praise and Honour of which is due only to the Lord, (Yet) *this Seed was rising in these* Waldenses, Albigenses, *&c. and by the Virtue and Life, and Power of it, were they quickned and enabled to cry out against the Abominations of those Times, and their Testimonies we own, their Memories we honour, and their Sufferings we have sweet Fellowship with*, knowing they were our Martyr'd Brethren, *and that we are rais'd by the Almighty Hand of the Lord, to bring forth more to the Light, and compleat that Work,* which was but dawning in that Day. And though our Appearance has not been long (perhaps twenty Years) yet *Truth is Everlasting*, and we are raised to declare it boldly to the Inhabitants of the Earth. And what is frequently objected against us, namely, our being but of Yesterday, is the same with that Spirit of Old, which *both ask'd Christ, how old he was; and that despised* Timothy's *Youth*; and that has objected to Protestants themselves their Revolt and Novelty. But Verity and Antiquity (as to present Appearances) are two Things; and if Antiquity shall be received for a sufficient Plea, then because the Papists were before the Presbyterians and Independents, they are therefore more Orthodox; if the Presbyterians and Independents shall say, *what they hold was before Pope or Popery*: So say we, 'Tis not therefore the Age of Men, or of a Dispensation, but the Reason and Truth of the Principle or Way that recommends; and in that Sense we are the *Apostolick Catholick Christians*.

1671.

Chap. IV.

Jo. Per. Hist. Wald. l. 2. c. 4. p. 77. 78, 79, 80, 81.

Vign. lib. Hist part 1. Sernag. c. 47: Chaff. l. 3. c. 7.

1671.

Chap. IV.

To conclude my Reply to this first Answer, What if it should be granted him, *that there was not such a falling away*, since the Matter in Debate is about *Church-Offices and Orders*, which will ye have? There is not one he has named, but has something different one from another, and all from the Scriptures, after his own Sense of it. O the miserable Confusion of this poor Man! I confess there is but little Reputation to be gotten by writing against one, whose Age must be an Excuse for his Folly.

1 Tim. 6. 13, 14.

His second great Reason, by which he does Essay to prove, *That there was no such Apostacy*; contrary to Scriptures, History, and his Learned Brother *Timothy, the Preface-Man,* (is drawn, as he thinks) from *Paul's* Words to *Timothy, That Commandment which* Paul *gave to* Timothy, *is to be kept, till the Coming of our Lord Jesus; but a Visible Church-Polity, or Church-Order, and Officers, is Part of that Commandment, therefore it is to endure to the End.*

How weak, how false, and scandalous to Sense and Scripture, is this Way of arguing; methinks it should be obvious to every Half-witted Man.

What was that Commandment? If he means the whole Epistle, as Page 119. I ask, *If a Distinct, Decimating, or Tything Priesthood be there? If Brawlers, Persecutors, and Swearers* (contrary to Christ's Commandment) *be there? If any Thing of the Sacrament; Humane Teachers; and that Toy, Foppery, and very Bauble and Abuse of Religion, Baby-Baptism, be there?* Read the Epistle well, and tell me, *If amongst all those Things, that* Paul *said, were able to make the Man of God Perfect* (and which I grant were enjoyn'd Timothy to follow as Apostolical Tradition) these recited Grounds of Controversy betwixt us, and this Man of Strife (with the rest of his angry Brethren) are to be seen or found?

1 Tim. 6. 6, 7, 8, 9, 10, 11, 12, 13, 14.

But if the Commandment was particular, then we may observe that the Apostle was treating of Covetousness, the Root of all Evil, and the Parson's Trade: *Godliness with Content* (says Paul) *is great Gain, for we brought nothing into this World, and it is certain we can carry nothing out: And having Food and Raiment, let us be therewith content; but they that will be Rich fall into Temptation; for the Love of Money is the Root of all Evil: But thou, O Man of God, flee these Things, and follow after Righteousness, Godliness, Faith, Love, Patience, and Meekness: I give the Charge, in the Sight of God, that thou keep this Commandment: (without Spot unrebukeable)* this the Priest left out, he had little mind to let us know Covetousness was reproved (the Sin of his Livery) and that the Ministers of Christ were by positive Precept to live irrebukeably; for that they think a most Damnable Error.

Let it suffice, that they who peruse the Epistles to *Timothy*, will find, *they mostly* (if not altogether) *consist of such Commands as tend to Holiness of Life and Conversation*, rather than to Discipline, and Shadowy Ordinances and Institutions. I would the Priests dare but to stand the Trial of all their Doctrines, and Ecclesiastical Government, by those very Epistles, the Controversy would soon end in their utter Confutation and Shame: And the truest Design and Use of their Academical Learning, is to learn Evasions, Equivocations, and dark Fetches, to secure themselves from the very Dint of Scripture and Reason, whose Nakedness God will make bare in the Sight of Nations, to the loathing of their Persons, and utter Abhorrence of their Sinister, Simonious Practices.

Pag. 120, 121, 122, 123, 124, 125.

He proceeds eagerly to vindicate the Church-Discipline asserted in *Paul's* Epistles to *Timothy*; and by his Way of Reasoning, would both perswade the World, That the *Quakers* absolutely deny it; and, if he can, confute them of that great Error.

But I may say of this poor Man, as the Apostle did of his Country-men, *That he is very unhappy in his Zeal, for it is by no Means according to Knowledge.* We not only own Pastors, Elders and Teachers in the Church of God, and ever did, (if that be his Church-Polity) and are perswaded 'twill last to the End; but are as ready to question, why he will not allow of Apostles, Prophets, and Evangelists now, as well as then: For he is earnest, whilst he abuses us with the Denial of all, to vindicate himself in the Denial of some, and (those I think the more material) his Defence of his Opinion is this; *That they were but for a Time, because Extraordinary*; as if they were not as much wanted now as then; but methinks the Reason they give to evince the Non-necessity of an immediate Mission, carries in it (like the *Trojan Horse*) such an Army, to the utter Ruin of the *Priest's Cause*, that were they not perfectly blinded, they would be ashamed to use, or urge it for their Defence.

For

For why should there not be the same Need for an extraordinary Ministry now, as was then? Is the World more truly Christian, than in the Time of those Churches, when they flourisht? And if the *Word of Reconciliation* is to last to the End, then that Office to whom it was more eminently committed; but that was the Apostleship; therefore I will read the Words thus, (and *Jenner* has taught me so to do) *Go teach all Nations, ye Disciples and Apostles (in the Name and Persons of all succeeding Disciples and Apostles) Baptizing them into the Name of the Father, Son and Holy Spirit; and lo I am with you (Disciples and Apostles successively) to the End of the World;* which because *Jenner* says, Page 131. *Is not to be restrain'd, or confin'd to that Age,* (as the Word sometimes signifies) *but to the End of the World;* and that it cannot Rationally be supposed, it was meant that they should personally live so long, I must conclude, that 'twas the Office and Calling of the Apostleship that should so indure, and which Christ would accompany to the End.

Secondly, The Scriptures expresly say and testify, (against these mumbling Hirelings of the World) *That in the Last Days God would pour out of his Spirit on all Flesh, and the Young Men should see Visions, and Old Men dream Dreams,* and the Apostle encouraged, nay, enjoyn'd the Churches to seek after Prophesie, for that was the most excellent Gift then in the Churches, which he would never have done, if Prophets had never been to succeed in the Christian Church: *Follow after Charity, and desire Spiritual Gifts, but rather that ye may Prophesie;* and if the End why Prophets were given, was, that they might readily unfold dark and mysterious Sayings, 'tis strange that there should be any Need for them in those Days of the Apostles, when such Great Fathers of Knowledge were living, and none now when the World is so fill'd with Contention and Dispute about the Abstrusity and Mysteriousness of many eminent Texts; and *Jenner* himself thinks there is no Apostle to decide it.

Thirdly, Since Evangelists were to assist the Apostles, and that it is evident the Apostleship is not terminated, by Consequence the Office of Evangelists is not ended; the Great Reason why the Mercenary Priests withstand that Ministry which is Supernatural, is, their Self-Consciousness of Insufficiency, and dreading the Misery of being dispossest of fat Benefices, who are like *Religious Janizaries,* that stick not to fight the Devil's Battle for Pay, against the True Powerful Gospel-Ministration.

He proceeds to charge us with Two Objections, that I think so nearly resemble the Honesty of our Principles, as we may very well venture to own them, and as readily confute his suppos'd Answer to them: They are these.

First, *That they use to go to* Oxford *and* Cambridge, *to learn the Gospel, whereas* Paul *said, He was not taught from Man, nor by Man,* &c.

Secondly, *That they are Hirelings, because they teach for Hire; and so no Gospel Ministers.*

We own the Charge, but let us hear his Answer.

The Israelites *had Schools of the Prophets at* Bethel, Jericho, &c. Elisha's *College was so fill'd, they enlarg'd it, and that in those Schools Prophets Prophesy'd not by immediate Revelation is manifest, in that* Samuel *was standing over them, as One appointed thereunto; Had they been immediately taught by God, why was* Samuel *appointed their Guide and Teacher; we only go to the Universities to learn Languages.*

'Tis granted the *Israelites* had Schools; but the Question will be, For what End and Purpose? To teach their Children the idle Stories of the *Heathen Pagan Schools,* which make up the present Body of the Learning of the Times, or the Sciences truly so called?

In short, either the End of those Schools was Instruction and Knowledge in Civil or Religious Affairs: If the first, We deny they exceeded Propriety of Speech, their own Stories, Writings, and such like common and useful Qualifications; and it rests on the *Priest's Part* to prove the contrary.

But if about Things of Religion, as the Instance of *Elisha* and *Samuel* seem to import, then let us examine the Texts; That relating to *Elisha* only says thus much, *That the Sons of the Prophets said to* Elisha, *Behold the Place where we do dwell, is too strait for us,* which does not answer the Reason of it's Quotation, nor the Context; but the other Instance of *Samuel* is most pat.

And Saul *sent Messengers to take* David, *and when they saw the Company of the Prophets Prophesying, and* Samuel *standing (as appointed over them) the Spirit of God was upon the Messengers of* Saul, *and they also Prophesy'd:* I appeal to all Im-

1671.

Chap. IV.

Joel 3.

1 Cor. 14. 1.

Page 27. 28, 29.

2 Kings 6. 1.

1 Sam. 19. 20.

1671.

Chap. IV.

partial Men, if this be not a *Prophesying upon an Inspiration*; and therefore nothing can be more incoherent with the Place, than that *Samuel* was their efficient, or so much as helping Cause to their Prophesying; for the Place expresly says, *That the Spirit of God was upon* Saul's *Messengers, and they Prophesy'd too*, implying, that the Company, or School of the Prophets, *Prophesy'd by no other Way*. This displeased *Saul*, for he sent Prophets three Times, and still was serv'd so; and at last went to *Ramah* himself, where he prophesy'd also; that it was a Proverb, *Is Saul also amongst the Prophets*. I cannot but here take Notice what a State *Jenner* and his Brethren would reduce the Christian Administration to, who do not allow it a *School of the Prophets* now, when there were many under the Law.

Read Mach. Disp.1.2.c.5. Card. de Sap. l. 2. Pet. Bel. Observ. l. 1. c. 35. Ouzel Animad. in Min. Felix, p. 25. Constit. Clem. Ran. l. 1. c. 6. Jac. Laur. de l. Gentil. p. 40, 41.

To end this Particular, I would have him tell me, if these Schools were fashion'd after those of *Athens*, and other *Greek Academies*? If the perplext Notions, and abstruse Metaphysicks of *Epicurus*, *Aristotle*, &c. were to be found in their Libraries? Nay, if the vain Quiddities, idle and gross Terms, and most sophistical Ways of Syllogizing, with the rest of that useless and injurious Pedantry (to Mankind, brought into the *Christian Religion* by Popish School-Men, and so eminently in Vogue in *Oxford* and *Cambridge*, and which above all Things fame their Students) were the Subject and Matter of their Study and Learning? He that runs, may read both the Purity and Simplicity of the Ancients Literature, and the Sophistry, Uselesness, and Affectation of the Science, falsly so call'd, now in Reputation in the World.

O how evidently from hence, may we observe the World's Declension from the Primitive Spirit! When for the first Hundred Years, scarce an Eminent Scholar was to be found amongst the *Christians*; and such as were, disclaim'd all Power in their vain Philosophy, to convince, or convert them to the Knowledge of the *Mysteries of the Christian Religion*. And that Men send their Sons, *One to be a Physician, and the other a Priest*, to the Academies of this Land, is such a Notorious Piece of Matter of Fact, as to deny it, were eminently to prove it: For who at Noon-Day, will say it's Midnight, but a Mad-Man: And in the World there are not Places of more Folly, Ignorance, and Impiety, and Fountains so impure, as their corrupt Streams, which alone, almost infect the whole Land with Debauchery, and at best Persecution, and Anti-Christian clumsy-witted Pedants, and useless Pragmaticks.

The Priests affirming, they only use those Places to Skill themselves in the Languages, is a downright Falsity; for Learning, as to the Philosophical Part of it they have maintain'd as absolutely necessary to the Qualification of a *Gospel-Minister*. Besides, I utterly deny, that *Tongues* themselves, are so much as Instrumental to open the mysterious Sense of the Gospel, albeit I acknowledge them very useful to correct wrong Translations; but that goes no farther than the Letter, in which the Life and Nature of the Gospel never stood.

Luke 10. 7.
2 Cor. 8.

His Answer to the remaining Objection, is briefly this: *That the Priests had a full Maintenance under the Law, by God's Appointment in Tythes, Offerings, and Suburbs*; *this* Micah *reproved not, but Men-Pleasers for Hire*; *the present Ministry are not blameable in this Particular: Besides*, Christ *and* Paul *warranted Wages, tho' not Tythes, and God would have it so*; *and furthermore the Law of the Land has given it to the Ministry*; *and the Tenths are as much theirs, as the Ninths are the People's*.

To all which I reply with a Good Heart; for no Employment is more pleasant to me, than uncovering the Wicked Avarice, and Horrid Deceit, of this *Decimating Simonious Priesthood*.

'Tis true, that the Maintenance of the *Priests* and *Levites* was out of the Tythes, Offerings, &c. But what then? Were they to maintain no more? (that the Priest was unwilling to instance) so horribly unjust is he, that he does lessen God's Appointment, to vindicate the Mercenary Appetites of his Brethren, or else he would have told us, that the poor Widows and Orphans were provided for out of them: But is he, or are they of *Aaron's Priesthood*? If they be, let him or them produce us good Evidence of it; and when they have done, we will have Scripture to prove that *England* was divided into Tribes, and the Land equally allotted them, only the Tenth for the Priesthood, the Widow, Poor, and Orphan, &c. If they are not of that Priesthood, but that the Priesthood is chang'd, how come they to demand a Maintenance, as peculiar to that Priesthood, and upheld by the same abolisht Law as the Priesthood, which was peculiar to the *Jewish Church*?

Next,

Next, he belies *Micah*, and the Holy Ghost too, for the Words are far from his Construction of them; yet, were they as he would have them, they are most True of him and his Brethren; for they will not undertake a Cure (as they call it) but upon such close-made Contracts, as Market-People truck or sell their Commodities; and such as most contribute, they most connive at, and indulge in their Impieties: This is Matter of Fact, that if a large Benefice or People is vacant, or be destitute of a *Minister*, they *(Courtier-like)* make Friends to such Persons in whose Power the Disposal of it is, and make no Scruple (upon Success) of leaving the Leaner (though perhaps honester People, or Parsonage) for the more Fat and Beneficial. O true, but most horrid Simony, Oppression and Cheat! *A Mountebank is an honest Man to a Parson.*

And for Christ and *Paul*, their Discourse of Wages, he mistakes the Matter: For that was only to take or accept (not all that an honest free Heart should give, for some would have pull'd out their Eyes, and others have sold all they had, to have accommodated the Apostles with a Footstool; but) so much only as was convenient, what was set before them, or they stood absolutely in need of: But not to hoard up out of set Stipends, and those extorted too, by inhumane Force, and meer Coercive Power. *Paul*'s taking Wages of other Churches to do the *Corinthians* Service, was no more but this, that the Church of *Corinth* being high, proud, boasting, and conceited of her Accurateness, Wisdom and Learning, the Apostle would not be so free as to accept of them, what would but defray his common Charges whilst with them, lest they should have taken Occasion to suspect he made Advantage to himself by them, and that thereby the Dignity of his Gospel should have been lessened; which, with the other confirmed Churches, he was not so much in fear about.

This I affirm (in a sound Understanding, by the same Spirit of Wisdom, that then guided *Paul*) that the only Cause of his not accepting what might have accommodated him with common Conveniencies, *Was his Tenderness and Care of, and Regard to the Reputation of the Blessed Gospel, having to do with a People Wise, and whose evil Eye was not so clos'd as that it would not be ready to make the worst of Things, and that would have thought him more oblig'd than it was fit for the Freedom of an Apostle to be in such Respect*; but Jenner *would not tell us that* Paul *work'd at* Rome *Two Years at his own hired House*. And as for the more modern Institution of *Tithes*, I am not to inform my self; but would tell *Jenner* (if he be ignorant of it) or any else, whose Desires after the Truth may engage them to peruse this Discourse, *That it was Antichristian every where, but more Devilish than ordinary in* England.

About the Years, three and four Hundred after Christ, *it was familiar with the Christians, to lay apart a Tenth of the Profit they made of their Estates, for the Maintenance of such Members and Ministers as wanted*, but this was not by Institution; for both they might have refused it, without any just Ground of Censure, (though not Charity) and when they did give it, *the how much and to whom*, was in their Election; for where they found them more or less wanting or deserving, there they gave, and exhibited of their Substance.

But in some Process of Time, the Insolency and Greatness of the *Roman Bishop*, obtain'd and enjoyn'd a Tenth from several *Countries*, to the Maintenance of a *Clergy*, by him calculated, to the Promotion and Security of his Antichristian Grandeur in the World, as a temporal, as well as spiritual Prince.

However, they could not readily get the English in the Humour, of parting with so considerable a Share of their Estates, seeing the *Priests* so *Proud, Rich, Deboyst* and *unthankful* already; (For *Austin the Monk*, was denied it by the King) till by a fatal Tragedy, it was introduc'd and confirm'd; namely *Murder* and *Adultery*; these were the *immediate Parents* of the *English* Decimation, or Tenths; for *Offa* killing *Ethelbert*, gave a Tenth of his Goods, to pacifie his Ghost; and *Edgar*, being greatly inamour'd of *Ethelwold*'s Wife, to obtain his impious End, struck not to imploy this infamous Means (*viz:*) His abominable *Murder*; the *Pope* (more doubtless out of Love to profit, than any Abhorrence to Sin) sends forth a *Thunderbolt* upon the Head of this Homicidious *Prince*, whom to appease, *Edgar* confirm'd to the Church, the Tenth of all the Fruits of his Field and Cattle, to them and their Successors: The greater the Sin, the dearer the Pardon; *The People's Wickedness is the Popes only Fair for costly Absolutions*; and the vilest Miscreants are his best, most constant (and to be sure) most welcome Customers.

1671.

Chap. IV.

Gratian. Cauf p. 16. r. c. decin.

Seld. c. 6. p. 80, 81.

Seld. p. 67.

1671.

Chap. IV.

Thus were *Tithes* inflituted; and Cuftom and Covetoufnefs have continued them to this very Day: But the Lord God Everlafting, having fhin'd in our Hearts, and given us to behold the *Myftery of Iniquity*, and that great *Apoftacy* which hath been over Nations; and amongft other Things, endued us with a true Underftanding, both of the *Miniftry*, and their ungodly Ways; which not only hath begotten in us an Abhorrence of their Ways, and a publick Denial of them; but an holy Zeal to teftifie againft their filthy Lucre, and horrid Coufenage of the World; and to the *Glorious Freedom that is now come from Heaven* to Mankind (if they will receive it) *from the oppreffing Yoak, of a Prieftly Tyranny, and Minifterial Bondage.*

To conclude, and fum up all; What has *Jenner* and his Gang to do with the *Levitical Prieft-hood* who fay they are no Jews? *(Vifible I mean, for Invifible and fpiritual I am fure they are not.)*

What have they to do to inftance *Chrift* and *Paul*, to vindicate his taking Wages, who is not contented with their Appointment? For the Evangelical Inftitution was this; No fooner had Chrift fpoke of Wages, than he explains his Meaning thus, *Whatever is fet before you that eat*; which fuppofes Election in the Man of the Houfe, no pofitive Obligation being farther upon him, than Chriftian-Charity (which indeed is the greateft in the World, in one Senfe) and content in the Receiver, without farther Demands, or Contract for larger Allowances.

And though I am well fatisfied that the Force of a Chriftian Miniftry is fuch, that many Hearts ftand ready to fupply the Wants of thofe that minifter. Yet I am as well affured that the Inconfiftency betwixt *Us* and the prefent *Priefts*, (in the Matter debated) lies more on the Side of Wages, than any other Thing, and whilft they pretend to the Vindication of a Chriftian Miniftry, it is in very Truth, but a Defence for their unreafonable *Incomes*, or that Miniftry, which proves them *dumb Dogs, that feek Gain from their Quarters, making War againft them that put not into their Mouths*, as moft experimentally we have known it, as well under the *Presbyterian* and *Independent*, as prefent *Epifcopal Government.*

Laftly, I will not ftand amaz'd at his *Impudency*, for I know it fuits the Perfon's Confcience, that a *Presbyterianized Independent* (or religious kind of *Hermaphrodite*, halting betwixt two) fhould offer to vindicate the Legality of *Tithes*, upon fuch an Abominable Inftitution; efpecially, when three Things more are duly confidered.

Firft, *That they were enjoyn'd by that Power, his learned Brother* Timothy, *calls the* Whore *in his Preface*, (which, however truly, was but faucily done of a Son) and to maintain her Antichriftian Bratts and Off-Spring; but whilft they difown her, they cunningly know themfelves concerned in her Care, *and as Men that love the Treafon, and hate the Traytor*; they hugg the Tithes, but fay they hate the Whore.

Ufh. de Ecl. Chr. Succefs. c. 6. p. 155. Acts and Monum. p. 435. 461. 536, 537.

Secondly, The *Waldenfes* and *Reformed Churches* Abroad; but particularly feveral of our Native *Martyrs*, teftified againft the Lawfulnefs of Paying or Receiving them; as *W. Thorp, &c.* not to particularize the Cloud of Ancients, (I mean the Fathers) as *Chryfoftom*, and others, that deteft them as now exacted.

Thirdly, His Impudence is manifefted, in *pleading for a Maintenance of a Miniftry that by his Principles he and his Brethren difown.*

But that I may remove the Objection of *Proportion*, namely, *That fuch as pay not Tenths act injurioufly, Becaufe they pay but for nine Parts in Rent, or Purchafe*; let the four Particulars be confider'd,

Firft, That they were extorted; and therefore it is moft reafonable that they fhould be returned to their firft Owners.

Secondly, That they have not only a Tenth of the Product of the Earth, but of the poor Country Man's Labour; which is wretchedly infamous, That becaufe King *Offa* committed Murder, and *Edgar* Adultery, the Farmer and his whole Family fhould toil and fweat to pay the Pope a Mulct, or Penitential and Expiatory Tax: It was the Countryman's before, and fhould be again.

Thirdly, If a poor Man plow up a Piece of Ground unfown, or manur'd in Man's Memory, and by his own Induftry obtain a Crop; *Is this the Increafe of the Earth, or the Farmer's Labour?*

Fourthly, Many Times they fcarce get their Seed, yet the Tithe of what paid Tithe before, muft be paid to the Prieft; for it, being but the Seed that comes again, which paid Tithe the precedent Year, that pays now, It follows that the fame pays twice, and fo the Prieft has Tithes, not becaufe the Earth brings forth her Increafe, *But becaufe fhe brings forth no Increafe.* O the unjuft, yet frequent

Practices, of the Ungodly Ministerial Mercenaries of this Age! Either let *Jenner* and *Tayler* own their Ministry, or disown their Tithes; since the Disowning the former, and defending the latter, is but an Instance of Avarice, and an Evasion of the Suffering that would attend that Testimony.

Fifthly, But above all, Consider that *Liberty of Conscience is* destroyed by it: For what if I in Conscience deny that Religion, to whose peculiar Use and Constitution I once allow'd Tithes? Can I in Honesty pay them? *Shall I contribute to a Religion, and the Ministers of it, which in Judgment I renounce?* But in Case I don't, *Is it rational to persecute me for not upholding a Religion I disown?* What would not these Mungril Independents own? For the Primitive of them deny'd and writ sharply against Tithes.

They disown a Ministry, and allow them Maintenance; and they are for Liberty of Conscience, and yet would have a Man persecuted for not paying to a Religion and Ministry, which he conscienciously disowns: O the Blindness and Folly of these Men! Certainly God has given them over to believe a Lye; and I observe, *as the Light shines brighter, they grow darker;* and be it known to them, that before the Glory of the *reproached Light within,* which we confess to, and they blaspheme against, *shall all their Religion vanish; as the Shadow of the Night doth fly before the insuing Brightness of the Sun;* and all People shall see an Emptiness and Insufficiency in their Ways, to obtain Everlasting Peace with God: Then shall the Nations walk in the Light of the Lamb and be saved. So much for *Tithes*.

CHAP. V.

HIS next Charge upon us is, *A Denial of Church-Ordinances, as useless to them that have receiv'd the Anointing; Whether Baptism, Lord's-Supper, Singing of Psalms, &c.* Which he undertakes to be of a Nature lasting and perpetual: First he says, *That there are Ordinances, because the Apostle commended the Corinthians for keeping the Ordinances, as he had delivered them unto them:* Then he says, *He shall endeavour* (though to no Purpose) *to prove the Continuance of them for ever.*

Baptism, and the Lord's Supper, are visible Church Ordinances: But they are to continue to the End of the World: Therefore for ever.

The *Assumption*, as he calls it, or *Minor Proposition, &c.* That they are to continue unto the End of the World, he proves out of Scripture, as he thinks, by defending the Perpetuity of that Mission, from the Endeavours of such as would stint the *Greek* Word, to that Age, for which I am his Debtor, it being a Work done to my Hand.

Go teach all Nations Baptizing them, &c. *and lo I am with you to the End of the World,* Mat. 28. (and here he shews himself not a little skilled in the Original, at least he fancies so) *for as often as ye eat this Bread, and drink this Cup, ye shew forth the Lord's Death 'till he come*: To all which I reply thus:

I conceive the Man is much beside his Mark; For that Hinge on which the whole Controversy turns, he seems on Purpose to avoid: What if the Apostle commended them for keeping the Ordinances committed to them? Does it therefore follow, that he meant the Priest's Idle *Baby-Baptism, their Kind of Supper, and canting of* David's *serious Psalms, in wretched Meeter?* Did he not as heartily recommend his *Godly Traditions and Ordinances to* Timothy, *as he commends the Corinthians?* And do we find any one of those now mentioned amongst them? 'Twas ridiculously done in the Priest, to endeavour to prove the Perpetuity *of Water-Infant-Baptism, &c.* Before he had prov'd it to be an Ordinance of Christ: First, Let him remember in his next to prove them such *Ordinances as he commended the Corinthians for keeping*: And which he charg'd *Timothy* solemnly to observe, before he sets about their Perpetuity.

Besides, What Man of Sense can think his Scriptures pertinent to his impertinent Matter?

First, Go teach, then Baptize, says the Text; upon which I urge thus: Were it a Water-Baby-Baptism, none were to be baptiz'd, but such as were first taught or discipled, *But Infants are not capable to be taught and discipled, in that ignorant Estate*: Therefore it could not be intended of Children.

Secondly, I deny that any Water is mention'd, or so much as intended: That there is none mention'd, is a Demonstration from the Text it self: That none can be intended, I prove thus:

First, The Mission we all agree is to the End of the World; but *Water-Baptism is not to the End of the World:* Therefore not intended in that Place.

Secondly, That Mission was as well *Paul's* as *Peter's*, *John's*, &c. for he came behind none, (as it is said) *but Paul deny'd it to be any Part of his Mission, in that great Expression, I was not sent to Baptize,* with Water, *But to preach*; Therefore *Water Baptism is not perpetual.*

Thirdly, If the Text intended Water Baptism, then could it Baptise, not only ἐν τῷ ὀνόματι, but εἰς τὸ ὄνομα, *not in the Name* (as falsly rendred) *But into the Name of the Father, Son, and Holy Spirit: But that Water can never do.* (For the Name stands for the Nature) Therefore not intended there.

Secondly, As to the *Lord's Supper*, we know, That Christ apprehending the Weakness of his Disciples, did think fit to leave them some figurative *Mark or Token* of Remembrance, for them to be in the Practice of, 'till he was better known to them, Mystically, or in Spirit; therefore He said, *Do this 'till I come, who am the Bread that came down from Heaven, that whosoever eats thereof shall never die. And the living Vine that affords the new Wine in this Kingdom.* In short, either the Bread and Wine are the Figure, or Substance; *Not the Substance say all (but Papists) therefore the Figure.* If a Figure, then of something; *but they cannot more properly figure to Us, any thing besides the Heavenly Bread and Wine*; therefore they so signify, *viz. Christ the Mystical Bread and Wine, that nourish the Soul to Eternal Life*; if so, (which as I think, none that own the Christian Religion denies) I argue thus:

Figures and Shadows are only of Force 'till the Substance come; but the Substance was then come in the Apostles Days: Therefore in Point of Institution, they were done away.

That the Substance was come is evident; for if the Heavenly Bread and Wine (the Things signified) were eat and drunk, then were they come, and the *Figure in Point of Institution and Duty, at an End: But they did eat and drink of the Heavenly Bread and Wine, consequently the Representations or Signs were at an End,* that they did so eat and drink, I prove thus:

If they had not eaten and drunk of the Mystical Bread and Wine, they had hungred and thirsted again, and died Eternally.

But they had Life, for they had Christ in them the Hope of Glory; and whosoever hath the Son, (the *Heavenly Bread and Wine*) *hath Life; therefore they did Eat and Drink thereof: and consequently the Substance was come, and the Shadow or Sign at an End; some that stand here* (saith Christ) *shall not taste of Death, 'till they see the Son of Man come in his Kingdom* (which is within; and there it is the true Spiritual (and not Historical, Notional) Believer should sit down with him at his Table, and drink of the New Wine, &c.) 'Tis true, both were practised, *but an Example or meer Practice is no Institution:* especially when in Point of Precept, and Institution, the Thing in Debate is absolutely abrogated, and at an End.

Besides, I have a Discourse on these very Subjects more at large, that may for the Sakes of honest-hearted *Enquirers,* come suddenly to publick View.

As to his *Musical Psalms,* they are utterly deny'd by us to have been a Primitive Practice, or so much as in Force upon any kind of Institution, either from Christ or his Apostles.

Spiritual Songs, or Psalms in Spirit, their Hearts making Melody to God, &c. are by us own'd, and us'd: *But that ever they Sung, made Tunes, and set Forms of Psalms by entire Assemblies, of another Man's various States and Conditions, whilst none of their own* (and mockt the Holy God to his Face, with down-right Lyes under a Notion of Devout Singing) we challenge this *Ballader* to prove: It is a very Shame that he and his Brethren should deny the *Common-Prayer-Book, because a Form, and yet have Forms of Singing:* Besides, I would in short observe, that *a Psalm* was not the State of all in the Primitive Assemblies; *some, nay the greatest Part might be in a Frame of Sorrow, Contrition, and Prayer for Remission, or Strength, Faith, Victory over Sin,* &c. *whilst a Spiritual Song was perhaps the Condition of some that had obtained Dominion over Sin, and were not so immediately in the Warfare and Battel as their Brethren:* But the present Singing and Praying of *Professors,* shews, that they are far from having a due Sense of the Weight of either,

ther *this Practise being so much in their own Wills, Forms and Appointments* (rather by Way of a Literal Imitation of the Primitive Saints, than from any true Sense, or Spiritual Motions in themselves.)

I shall here over-look his Charge against us, as Enemies to Magistracy, with his Design therein, referring it to another Chapter, because it has not so immediate Relation to the preceding and succeding Matter: That which next followeth is our Sixteenth Error, as he calls it, namely, *That we hold that the Spirits are not to be tried by the Scripture*; which, how true it is in our Sense, I shall proceed to make appear, and that as well from his own Propositions, as ours; for I am designed to make a short Work with them, believing he grew weary as he grew nearer to the End of his Book: It favours so rankly of meer Ribaldry and Dotage.

To confute us, he quotes this Scripture; *Dearly beloved, believe not every Spirit*, but try *whether they be of God, or no*: and says occasionally upon it in another Place, viz. *My Spirit that is upon thee, and my Words which I have put into thy Mouth shall not depart out of thy Mouth, nor out of the Mouth of thy Seed for ever*. That the Holy Ghost is not only the great Dictator of the Scriptures, but also our Guide to the right understanding of them.

Now I would be glad to know, if the Man sets not up a Trial of Spirits by the Spirit, rather than by the Letter of the Scriptures.

First, He cannot but acknowledge, they had then a Rule and Measure to try Things by; What was it not the old Testament? *For that could not be a Rule for* Paul *to deny Circumcision and overturn all the Ceremonies of the Law, as in his Epistle to the* Hebrews; with many other Things by Way of Variation, and Institution.

Nor could it be the new Testament, (as it's called) for *Jenner* says, that those *Scriptures were not then extant*, as in Page 102. Then it must needs be the Holy Spirit and Anointing that they had received; for it is not to be supposed they were without any; *and unless* Jenner *will not have the Spirit of Truth to be a more infallible Tryer of Spirits, than the dead Letter of the Scriptures, he must allow, that the true Christian Church has the same Guide and Rule, if he believes that God is as propitious, and careful, and good to us in these last Days* (of which the greatest Things were promis'd) *as to the Primitive Believers*.

But, *Secondly*, If the Scripture is to try, and yet not without the Interpretation and Sense of the Holy Spirit, I appeal to the whole World, *if the Holy Spirit be not most of all and principally the Rule and Guide*, as he himself contradictorily stiles it, Page 144.

Thirdly, To try Spirits by Letters, is most improper; the contrary being most rational and natural, viz. *To try Spirits by the Spirit*, and Writings by Writings, if there must be a Rule of Judgment.

Fourthly, That very Promise by him quoted out of Scripture, intimates the same, *for if the Reason of the Word's being in Christ's Mouth, was the Spirit's being upon him: and that the Words of God should not depart out of his Mouth, nor his Seed's Mouth forever* (who are his begotten Children.) Then must the same Holy Spirit, the Author of these Words, necessarily dwell and abide upon them for ever; and that's the Rule; though I would have the Man to think, we grant the Scriptures to be a Secondary Rule to the Holy Spirit; and to such as believe them, they are very edifying, and Confirmations, though still the intrinsick Ground of Faith, and Knowledge, be the Discoveries and Seals of the Holy Spirit of God; For, says *Jenner* himself, (to his evident Contradiction) *Though the Scriptures be the Touch-stone*, Page 142, 145.

For, if the Scriptures be not the Rule without the Spirit, the Spirit must needs have the greatest Share in that Office, *especially since he was a Rule before the Scriptures were ever given forth*; and certainly, since the Scriptures were *indicted* by him, so as that the dark Sentences and Mis-translations, are only to be interpreted and rectified by him: The Scriptures are so far from being our Rule, and he from being no Rule, that he is the very Scripture's Rule; restraining, transposing and enlarging the Sense of Words, Verses, and whole Chapters.

'Tis true, the Touch-Stone tries Gold, and that from an intrinsick Virtue, proper, and congenial to the Stone it self; but have the dead Letters of the Scripture that distinguishing Property and exertive Virtue? *Jenner* denies it, in the Words just now repeated, *For without the Spirit*, says he, *they are of no Value or Service* to us. Then, say I, *either God gave them for a compleat Rule, or he did not. If for a compleat Rule, there is no need of any additional Assistant, as the Spirit; If not, then he gave them for no Rule; because all his Gifts are perfect, and his Rule could not be deficient: And it is to be suppos'd, that in what Gift soever he should fail to us, he would not in a Rule of Life and Doctrine, the Capital, and most Eminent of all*: But methinks this our Demonstration should satisfie all; *when neither Man nor Scriptures are near us, yet there continually attends us that Spirit of Truth, that immediately informs us of our Thoughts, Words, and Deeds; and gives us True Directions what to do, and what to leave undone*; Is not this the Rule of Life? *If ye are led by the Spirit of God, then are ye Sons of God.* Let this suffice to vindicate our Sense of a true and unerring Rule, which we assert not in a Way of Derogation from those Holy Writings, which with Reverence we read, believe, and desire always to obey the Mind and Will of God therein contain'd; *and let that Doctrine be accurst that would overturn them.*

His next Cavil, *Is at the Plainness of our Deportment and Expression; He calls them our Principles*; and we are content as well to own them, as to confute his Folly in opposing them.

To our not saluting any, he opposeth that Scripture, *If you Salute your Brethren only, What do you more than others*: But the *Quakers*, says he, *Salute none but those of their own Sect, though the Apostles in their Epistles did.*

But neither is he just to the Sense of the Scripture quoted, nor the Practise of our Friends. (But I perceive the Man would be doing) though he does, he does not know what, or but very little) For Christ's Purpose in that Scripture, was to admonish them to Universal Love, as the Context manifests; *If ye love them that love you, What Reward have you?* He struck at the Revenge of those, then under the Law, *Who would have an Eye for an Eye, and a Tooth for a Tooth*; that made it a standing Maxim, *To love their Friends, but hate their Enemies*; and not that the Lord Jesus Christ design'd so much as to encourage People to imitate the vain and flattering Salutes, then, and now practis'd in the World; but did severely reprehend them, when Personally in the World, making the Salutations and Greetings of that Age, a great Mark of it's Apostacy; giving it in Charge to his Disciples, *That not only they should not Salute any Man, but also to avoid and beware of those that love Salutations; for they shall receive greater Damnation*: That he belies us, is as evident, as that he wrong'd Christ, and the Holy Scriptures; For not only do we take Notice of our Friends, but are, in our Accostings of such as are known to us, especially in Case of Intimacy or Business, ready to Salute them, so far as stands with an honest, plain, loving, *Christian* Mind, and that as well by Epistles as other Conversation: But it was ill done of him to urge the Apostles Epistles, that were only written to the Brethren, to prove we ought to Salute Strangers: I suppose there is no such Stuff, as, *My Lord, your Lordship's Most Obedient Servant, and My Most Humble Service to your Lordship*, &c. O the devilish Flattery, and vain respecting of Persons that is in this wicked World! Well, the God of our Plainness will judge for it all; and sweep these Things out of the Earth, which Pride, and Vanity have introduc'd.

He says, *Our second Principle is, to give no outward Token of Reverence to Magistrates, Parents, Masters, or any other Persons*: Upon which he makes this Reflection *(but we have learned otherwise) For* Abraham *bowed to* Heth's *Children;* Joseph's *Brethren to* Joseph; *so did* Abigail *to* David; and the Apostle says, *Render Honour to whom Honour is due*, &c.

To all which Slander and Ignorance, I give this short Reply, Read my Book, *No Cross, No Crown*, Chap. 1, 2. (for I have written largely of it in another Discourse) Reverence and Honour are substantial Things; and though in all Actions, there is an intrinsick and extrinsick Respect, yet 'tis as impossible that the Appearance and the Thing should be separated, as that the Resemblances of Bread and Wine should remain in the *Romish Eucharist*, and not the very Substance of both; so that we are for such Reverence and Honour as have a Service in it, to those to whom we shew it; for all other Honour is Deceit: And what the Apostle saith of Science and Philosophy, I may say here, *'Tis a vain Respect and Honour*, falsly so call'd; the *Centurion* was more honoured by his Servants and Soldiers, in their obeying his Commands, *when he said to One, go, and he went; to another, come, and he came; and to a third, do this, and he did it*, than by all the mimical Gates and deform'd Cringes, us'd in this *Frenchify'd* World; for did *Respects* lye in Hats, *Kirches*, and
Bowings,

Bowings, the vilest Miscreants, and debaucht Persons, and most void of True Reverence and Honour, would be the most expert and accomplish'd; which is a greater Sin to say, than for me not to Cap the old foppish Man in Hand.

The third Principle he charges upon us as some heinous Offence, is, *Our not giving Titles, especially that of Master, which Abraham was call'd seventeen Times in one Chapter*; David *call'd Saul Master, and one of the Sons of the Prophets, calls* Elisha *Master*, &c.

To which I must needs say, that People ought to be deeply in Love with those vain Customs, to practise them under no better Covert, Proof, nor Defence, than the Fig-Leaf Arguments and Quotations of this poor Man: We own and use that Expression, in the Sense the Scriptures do allow of it, namely to such as have Rule and Authority over us: *It was* Abraham's *Servant that fetch't* Rebecca *for his Son* Isaac; *But did* Rebecca, *or her Relations, ask for Master* Abraham, *or Master* Isaac? It seems the World knew less of Mastership, and Titular Honour at that Time of the Day, than in our Vain-glorious Age.

David call'd *Saul* so, as he was King, and in that he ow'd him a Subjection: But the Case is much alter'd; yet they are our Masters, whom we obey.

Elisha by his own Confession, *Was as an Overseer to the School of the Prophets*, and we never deny'd but Children ought to esteem, call, and obey them as Masters, who are their Instructors, in Trades, or Literature of any Kind, the like in Apprentices and Servants.

But it is easy to observe, of how little Force the Words of Christ are with a Priesthood, calculated to please and daub the World, instead of living in that *Cross*, which is an Offence, and very Death to the Proud, *Who are Pleasers of Men rather than God, and who have the Persons of Rich Mortals in Admiration for Reward:* Therefore it was, that this Beggarly Priest ran up and down (in *Ireland*) to Great Men's Houses, with his Books, that he might be gratify'd (as most did) Ten-fold more than they cost him; which he would not have done to the poor and unable to reward him, though their Souls are no whit inferior; but it may be of more Importance in God's Account, and greater Enquirers after Religion; but a Priest is too black to blush. *Well, the Day of the Calamity of this Cut-purse Generation of Priests, the dreadful God of Heaven and Earth is hastening, and none of them shall be able to escape the Stroak of his Fury; for his Controversie is against them; and Everlasting Woes will be their Portion for all their Avarice, Imposture, and Persecution in the World.*

Let such as are affected with Gaudy Titles, peruse the severe Character Christ gives the Scribes and Pharisees, in his Caution of them to his Disciples, *Wo unto them, for they love the uppermost Rooms at Feasts, and Chief Seats in the Synagogues, and Greetings in Market-Places, and to be called of Men Rabbi; neither be ye called Masters, for One is your Master, Christ; and all ye are Brethren; but he that is Greatest amongst you, shall be your Servant.*

There can be but three Significations of the Title *Master*.

First, That of being so as a Teacher or Grandee of a Sect, in which Sense the *Scribes* and *Pharisees* then, and *Jesuits* and *Friars* now, receive it; they are sometimes called *Master*, sometimes *Father*.

Secondly, The other, out of meer Formality, there being no Reality in it, because no Power nor Office that could require it.

Thirdly and Lastly, They may be called so, from some Office or Place, which they bear; this is a Reality and most Reasonable: Christ intends not this by his Prohibition, only the other two; for the first robs him of his Honour; *who is the alone Master and Father in Heavenly Matters*; and the second, *Is a downright lying Vanity, but the last a Reality.*

That which the Priest pleads for, was *Elihu's* Caution and Refusal, *I know not* (says he) *to give Flattering Titles: In so doing, my Maker would soon take me away.* He little thought of it, when he complemented the Lord and Lady *Donegal* with his Copper Rhetorick, Stuff so bald and wretched, as deserves first a *Peccavi* for his Sin; and then an Apology for Stile; Shreds of *Latin*, and superannuated Pedantry. It cannot be forgotten by the Priest, (if ever he did remember it) That the *Hebrew*, *Greek*, and *Roman* Universities call'd, saluted, and mentioned Persons and Authors by their bare Names, as *Adam*, *Enoch*, *Noah*, *Abraham*, &c. *Socrates*, *Plato*, *Antisthenes*, *Zeno*, &c. *Brutus*, *Scipio*, *Cato*, *Seneca*, *Epictetus*; and besides that, the Apostle *James* represents it as a Great Sin to respect Persons, whether by Titles or Places. *Marlorat* out of *Luther*, and *Calvin* says, *That it is repugnant to the*

the Light within them, insomuch, that those that follow such Things, are condemned within themselves.

Heed not thy Nobility, nor let it be a Reason for thee to take Place of any: Esteem not those of meaner Extraction thy Inferiors; *for our Religion admits of no Respect of Persons,* said *Jerom,* (and much more) to the Noble *Celantia.*

And said Learned *Casaubon,* in his Discourse of Use and Custom, *He is not counted a Civil Man, now of late Years amongst us, who thinketh much, or refuseth to subscribe himself Servant, though it be to his Equal or Inferior;* yet Sulpitius Severus *was very sharply chid by* Paulinus, *for subscribing himself* His Servant, *in a Letter of his,* saying, Take Heed hereafter, how thou being from a Servant called into Liberty, Dost Subscribe thy Self Servant unto one who is thy Brother and Fellow-Servant. 'Tis not a Testimony of Humility, To pay those Honours to a Man, which are due to the One Lord, One Master, and One God.

This was the Sense and Simplicity of those Times; but they are chang'd, and the Clergy now are as loose as they were then strict; and instead of binding the vain and foolish Appetites of Men, they rather daub and indulge them in those Things, whereof both Priests and People ought to be asham'd; but 'tis fit it should be so, that they may be manifested not to be of God, but Sworn Enemies to his Truth and Servants.

The last Principle he charges on us as Heterodox, is, *Our holding it to be a Duty to* (Thou) *all Men, because we* (Thou) *God*: And indeed it's Reason good enough, and a better than the Man is furnished with, to oppose or answer it, which is this.

We thereby are taught to own the Simplicity of the Essence of God, and to Men it's us'd only in Civility, as Sir, Master, Most Honourable, &c. A poor Shift. I grant it properly signifies One, and therefore is aptly us'd to God, because He is but One; but if that should be the Reason why we should use You (which implies more than One) to any single Man, because he is but One, I cannot fathom the Logick of it; if it be a Word fitted to the Singular Number, I say because but One; for if there were more, the Civility would be lessened by the Necessity of using it, if it be a Word fitted to the Singular Number, (and we have not another) Why should we not as well use it in Discourse to a Man, as to God? But above all, that he should urge the Civility of it, as a Reason for the Use of it to Men, and yet use *Thou* to the Most High GOD, is a Sauciness almost impardonable; for if *You* be therefore us'd in the Place of *Thou,* because more respectful; What follows? But since we say *You* to Men, and *Thou* to God, we express more Civility to our Fellow-Creatures, than to our Great Creator; this Man has ill learnt his Catechism: But for him to say, That 'tis equivalent with the Words, *Sir, Master,* &c. is an high Instance of his little Skill in Languages; for this relates not to Title, but Number: The Question is not, *Whether this Man ought to be Master?* But *whether One Man be Two Men?* Which, till the Man be able to prove, either let him use that Only Word, that denotes a Singular Number, or we shall think his Brains squint, and that he dreams of Two instead of One.

And though he scoffingly calls our Obedience in these Things, *The Cross,* and lyingly says, *We are otherwise ignorant and prophane Creatures, far from the Form, much more the Power of Godliness,* Yet this I lay upon him, by Way of Answer, *The Lord God rebuke thee*: We make not them to be the Best, or only Instances of *True Quakers,* knowing and declaring to the World, *That Salvation from Sin, and Justification with God, through the Operation of the Power and Spirit of Jesus Christ, is that which chiefly makes a* Good Christian, *Man, or Woman, and where that Existence is wanting, all Conformity to external Appearances of Self-Denial, will prove unavoidable at the Great Tribunal of God.* Yet I must tell the Man, *That he talks evilly of Things he knows not*: For we would have given all we had in this World, that we might have answer'd a Good Conscience to God, and have kept in the Customs and Friendship of this World; but when it was manifested to us, how much they pleas'd proud Flesh, and that they were of the Offspring of a vain, wanton, proud Mind, that pleas'd it self in Flatteries, *We were constrain'd by God's Spirit alone, to cross them in those very Particulars,* though it greatly crost our selves first; which was no sooner done, but we quickly came to see the Value they put upon them, by the Displeasure and sottish Rage that most have shown at our refusing to practise them: Mordecai *could not Bow to* Haman; *nor can we to the* Hamanites *of our Age; the Spirit is still the same on both Sides.*

CHAP. VI.

SINCE I had to do with any of the *Adversaries* of Truth, I have not met with one who lays himself more open to the severe Blows of her Defenders: But indeed, there is little Triumph over so feeble an Enemy; for had I not been told, the Man is not reputed in the general Mad (I mean distracted in his Naturals) I should have thought him fitter for *Bedlam*, than to discuss Controversies: His succeeding Matter, if any, is so confusedly huddled together; *such are his Repetitions, so many his Tautologies*, and interwoven with lying Stories (*most of them mill'd out of the Devil's Mint*) and aggravated by him, *with all his little Skill and great Envy*; that how to rally all into such an order, as may admit of an Answer (though little of it can be thought by sober Men to merit any) I have been greatly at a stand: And if he will owe me ill-will for my publick Refutation of his Errors, and Reprehension of his Slanders; at least, *He ought to think himself obliged to my Civility, in methodizing his otherwise most immethodical Discourse.*

I shall in this Chapter glean his lying Stories of the scattered Seed of false Doctrines, held by him, or undeservedly cast upon us; in my next following, *vindicate our Life and Doctrine from any Inconsistency with the Civil Government*; in my last *Justifie my Friends from all his Impostures and Calumnies.*

First, He takes up an whole Chapter in his Endeavours to prove that we deny the Lord that bought us, though very falsly and equally insuccessfull.

Because we deny that Person (the Son of God) that died at Jerusalem *to be our Redeemer.* p. 153, 154.

Which most horrid Imputation has been answer'd more (I believe) than a Thousand Times, by declaring that he that laid down his Life, and suffered his Body to be crucified by the *Jews*, without the Gates of *Jerusalem*, is Christ the only Son of the most High God: But that the outward Person which suffered was properly the Son of God, we utterly deny, and it is a perfect Contradiction to their own Principles; *A Body hast thou prepared me*, said the Son, then the Son was not the Body, *though the Body was the Son's*, this brings him more under the Charge of making him but a meer Man, than us, *who acknowledge him to be One with the Father, and of a nature Eternal and Immortal*; *for he was glorified with the Father before the World was.*

But I might invert, *that such as live in Sin and plead for it Term of Life, and who are of a persecuting Spirit and Teach for Hire, and Divine for Money, and maintain shadowy Practices in Opposition to the Substance and Nature of the second Spiritual Covenant, and Appearance of Christ without Sin to Salvation, they are the Deniers of Christ*; or *Anti-Christs*; but such is *Jenner* with his Brethren; therefore *Anti-Christs.*

Secondly, But he says, *That we deny Christ to be a distinct Person, therefore we deny the Lord that bought us.* p. 154.

In answer to this I shall make these three Offers. First, if he will but bring me One Scripture (for he calls it his Guide and Rule) that has directed him to such a Phrase, *as distinct Person*, or that says, *I and my Father are two*, instead of, *I and my Father are One*. Secondly, If he will but bring me one Piece of Antiquity *for the first two Hundred Years*, that us'd any such Expression. Thirdly, And if he can deny that the Popish School-men (through the Assistance of the *Aristotelian*) (*or Infidel*) *Philosophy*, were not the *Grand Fathers and Promoters of such like monstrous Terms, and uncouth Phrases*, I will be contented to take the Shame upon me of denying *proper, apt and significant Phrases*: But till then I will tell him, that if the Son of God did purchase our Salvation distinctly from the Father, *the Father was not concerned in our Salvation, but Christ only*; and if he did so purchase it, *as God the Son (distinct from the Father)* then God the Son, (by his Principles) *cannot be the same with God the Father*; and all the Earth, *with all their idle Sophisms and metaphysical Quiddities shall never be able to withstand the Conclusion to be*; two Gods; otherwise, if the Purchase was by God the Son, then God the Father was concern'd as well as God the Son, *because the same God*; if not, then either Christ's God-head was not concern'd in the Purchase, *or there must be two Gods*; so that which he calls, *a Personality distinct from the Essence*, could not do it; *and if the Divine Essence did it, then the Father and Spirit did it as well as the Son, because the same individual Eternal Essence*: O the fond dotage and

I

dark

dark Conceits of Men about that blessed Mystery! Let *Jenner* turn to the fifth Chapter of *John*'s first Epistle; *where he may find our Faith at large in the Point*; and if he is not satisfied therewith, his Refusal shall set the very Letter of the Scriptures (his pretended Rule) over his Head, that he would suggest we deny.

Thirdly, He saith, *That we own Christ to be but meer Man, and that he had his Failings in the World, therefore we deny him·* Indeed, if this were as true as it is false, his Consequence would be just; but Methinks he should have better study'd his own Reputation, than to assert any Thing so contradictory to his preceding Sense of us,

For no farther off, than the same Page, *he affirms we deny that Person to be Christ, that suffer'd without the Gates of* Jerusalem, and now he charges us with disowning him to be Christ on any other Account, than that *of meer Humanity*: So that his Charge is briefly this, *They own the true Christ not to be a Man; but however they own the true Christ to be only a meer Man; and they hold a Perfection, and yet say that Christ had his Failings*: Horrid Weakness and Contradiction!

Fourthly, That we hold, *All that Christ did in the World, was only as a Figure and Example; therefore we deny the Lord that bought us.*

This Language he cannot produce in any Author, that is an acknowledged true *Quaker*; for we affirm, he did many Things, *wherein he was neither a Figure nor Example*; though, in some Sense, he may be the *former*; and in many, the *latter*: For in him we have Life, and by Faith, Atonement in his Blood; yet 'twas the Language of the Apostle *Peter*, *For even hereunto were ye called, because Christ also suffer'd for us; leaving us an Example, that we should follow his Steps.* 1 Pet. 2. 21.

Fifthly, *That we deny Justification by the Righteousness which Christ hath fulfilled in his own Person for us (wholly without us) and therefore deny the Lord that bought us.* Pag. 155, 156, 157.

And indeed, this we deny, and boldly affirm it in the Name of the Lord, *To be the Doctrine of Devils*, and an Arm of the Sea of Corruption, *which does now deluge the whole World.*

I shall not much insist upon this, as I have not upon the other four Particulars; they having been irreconfutably consider'd, and answer'd, by my Friend and Partner in this Discourse, in his first Part of this Apology: Only this I shall observe and add.

First. No Man can be justified without Faith (says Jenner.)

No Man hath *Faith without Works* (any more than a Body can live without a Spirit (says *James*.)

Therefore the Works of Righteousness, by the Spirit of Christ Jesus, are necessary to Justification.

Secondly. If Men may be justified, whil'st Impure, *then God quits the Guilty*, contrary to the Scripture; which cannot be.

Thirdly. Death came by actual Sin, not imputative, in his Sense; *therefore Justification unto Life comes by actual Righteousness, and not imputative.*

Fourthly. This speaks Peace to the Wicked, whilst wicked; *but there is no Peace to the Wicked*, saith my God.

Fifthly. Men are dead and alive at the same Time, by this Doctrine; for they may be *dead in Sin*, and yet *alive in another's Righteousness, not inherent*, and consequently, Men may be damn'd actually, and sav'd imputatively.

Sixthly. But since Men are *to reap what they sow*; and that every one *shall be rewarded according to his Works*; and that *none are justified, but the Children of God*; and that *none are Children, but who are led by the Spirit of God*, and that *none are so led, but those that bring forth Fruits thereof*, which is *Holiness*; 'tis not the Oyl in another's Lamp, but in our own only, *which will serve our turns*; I mean, the Rejoycing must be in our selves, and not in another: Yet to Christ's Holy Power alone, do we ascribe it, *who works all our Works in us, and for us.*

To conclude this brief Account, I am constrain'd, for the sake of the simplehearted, to publish to the World, of our *Faith in God, Christ, and the Holy Spirit.*

We do believe in *One only Holy God Almighty*, who is an Eternal Spirit, the Creator of all Things.

And in *One Lord Jesus Christ*, his only Son, and *express Image of his Substance*, who took upon him Flesh, and was in the World; and in Life, Doctrine, Miracles, Death, Resurrection, Ascension, and Mediation, perfectly did, and does continue to do the Will of God; to whose holy *Life, Power, Mediation*, and *Blood, we only ascribe our Sanctification, Justification, Redemption and perfect Salvation.*

And we believe in *One Holy Spirit*, that proceeds and breaths from the Father and the Son, as the Life and Virtue of both the Father and the Son, a Measure of which is given to all to profit with; and *he that has one, has all; for those Three are One, who is the* Alpha *and* Omega, *the* First *and the* Last, *God over all, blessed for ever*, Amen.

1671.

Chap. VI.

Having thus fairly vindicated our Faith in *God, Christ*, and the *Eternal Spirit*, I shall end his following Reflections, which are just as true and rational, as the rest; but that which of all Things I find most perplexing in my Pursuit of him, is his interwoven Charges and numerous Repetitions, so like their Hour-glass way of Preaching. *That one would think he were giving us a Sermon, rather than a Dispute:* For instance, He takes up several Pages about our *Denying the Lord that bought us; and the Perniciousness of our Ways, and Blasphemies against God and Christ (under distinct Heads)* as if any Body should doubt that, who believes his precedent Doctrinal Charge against us; he might have much better imploy'd himself to pick Straws, than first to beg the Question, and then to tell the World those Consequences, that are as evident as a Man's Nose in his Face: But I proceed to Particulars.

In his Discourse of the Perniciousness of our Ways and Practices, he says, *We persecute the Truth, and it's Followers, with our bitter Railings and Reproachings.* O wretched Impudence! Could any but a Priest, brazened with Rage and Folly, ever pronounce so great a Lye? Who has most reviled, the *Quakers*, or *Jenner*? Is not his whole Discourse chequered with Marks of his deepest Envy, and blackest Blasphemies against God, his Truth, and People? Who says, ' They ' are of the Devil; their Light is an *Ignis Fatuus*, a Dim Light; the Spirit of ' the Devil; that we are possest, are Witches, and acted and moved by Satan; ' Enemies to God, Christ, the Spirit, Religion, and Humane Societies; with a- ' bundance more of the like Complexion. Do not those Expressions bespeak the Pit to be the Place from whence they came? But this is the natural Scent of the *Presbyterians* and *Independents* Breath; for it always stinks of Scurrility and Persecution.

p. 15, 4.

But suppose we had imploy'd our Tongues or Pens to declare the Rottenness and Hypocrisie of that crew of Men he belongs to; ' is that a greater Evil than ' to cast us into Goals? To whip our Bodies? and sometimes murder us by stink- ' ing Dungeons, and barbarous Beatings? Nay, the very Priests have betaken ' themselves to their Canes, and Fists, when they have had nothing to say in de- ' fence of their impious Cheat of the Poor: We have a red Catalogue that shall ' stand recorded against our *Presbyterian* and *Independent* Persecutors, that their ' Names, and Natures too, may stink to Posterity.

Seventhly, His next is a prophane Reflection upon our trembling, viz. *That our Quakings at silent Meetings are diabolical:* But we are not without precedent Precept in the Point; but I perceive that *Jenner* (for all his Boasts) is so far from making the Scripture his Rule, that he contemns and prophanes the very Examples and commands, that they most evidently hold forth.

p. 15, 8.

Moses was a *Quaker*; for 'tis said of him, *That he exceedingly Trembl'd and Quak'd:* Habakkuk said, That *his Lips Quiver'd, and Rottenness entred into his Bones, and he Trembled within himself, that he might have Rest in the Day of Trouble:* And did not the Apostle exhort the Churches, *That they should work out their Salvation with Fear and Trembling?* And did he not tell the *Hebrews*, That *God would shake both the Heavens and the Earth once more.* Read the Scriptures quoted.

Heb. 12. 21.
Hab. 3. 16.
1 Cor. 2. 3.
Ephe. 6, 5.
Phil. 2. 12.
Heb. 12. 26.

But perhaps it will be objected, *That we do not so Tremble.* To which I answer, and God bears us record;
' The Holy dreadful Power of the Lord God being upon us, and a deep Sense ' of our own Transgressions (and no Witchcraft or Possession, as he most wickedly ' suggests) were the first Ground and Cause of our Trembling; *and whether he re-* ' *pents, or no,* Terror shall seize on him for this Enterprize; and a Cup of Dread

' and

1671.

Chap. VI.
Pag. 164, 165, 166.

' and Trembling shall he receive at the Hand of the Lord God Almighty, before
' whom we Fear and Quake.

Eighthly, He proceeds to charge us *of a Confederacy with the* Papists, *by a fancy'd Unity of Doctrine.*

1. That *we with them, esteem the reform'd Ministers none of Christ's.*

But herein he shews himself void, both of Charity and Truth; for such as are truly reformed, we esteem Christ's: But the Question will be, *whether they be such?* Besides, If we esteem them not his Ministers, 'tis for those very Reasons, for which (in a larger Sense) we utterly disclaim and renounce the *Roman Catholicks*; Nay, *'Tis for that of* Popery, *and wherein they are as yet unreformed, that we disallow them the Title of* Christ's Ministers; so far are we from any *Truce* or *Confederacy* with *Papists*, or that black hellish Power which they abet and maintain.

2. That *we agree in the Justification of Man by his Works.*

But this is a meer Slander; since we disown any Share in such an Anti-christian Doctrine; we say, That *all Man's Self-righteousness is but as filthy Rags*; *and that even those Works, which are wrought by him, through the Assistance of the Spirit of Christ; and that Obedience which he yields thereunto, are not strictly meritorious*; only they have an *inducing, procuring, and obtaining Power and Virtue in them.* That is Merit where there is an Equality betwixt the Work and Wages; but all those Temporary *Acts of Righteousness, can never equal Everlasting Life, Joy, and Happiness,* (being of Grace, and not of Debt) and therefore strictly no Merit; but such good Works may be truly said to obtain Eternal Life and Peace with God, because without them there is no Salvation. But of this the *poor Priest* is ignorant.

3. Farther, he says, That *with them we deny the Reading of the Scriptures to ignorant and unlearned Men.*

But Men had Need to have an Over-stock of Charity, to believe (indeed not to reprove) him: Did he not in Pag. 136. accuse us, for *Objectors and Disputers against Learning, as useful to a* Christian? And does he now *make us to insist upon it, as a necessary Qualification to the Reading of the Scriptures:* Surely he has either mistaken us, or we are quickly chang'd: Wretched Folly and Contradiction! He wounds himself, not us: but we have spoken to this before.

4. That a Man may perfectly keep the Law, he charges as an Error in both; the Absurdity of which is best seen by the Consequence of his Apprehension, *viz.* That *the End of Christ's Coming, is not that through him we should fulfil the Law, but break it:* He that does not obey it, is under it; and *he only is redeemed from it, that keeps it*; David *kept it, and so did* Paul, *through the Law of the Spirit of Life in Christ Jesus.*

If this were the worst Principle held (not practised) by the *Papists* Anti-christ would be nearer to *Jenner*, and his Brethren, than them.

5. He says, We *both deny the imputative Righteousness of Christ.*

As for us, I answer, That in the Scripture-usage of the Word *Imputation*, we own it; but not the *lazy sophisticated Stretch, these Sin-pleasing Times have brought it to:* Christ's Righteousness actually and inherently made ours through Faith, is the great Ground of Justification, and another we own not.

6. He charges us with a *Denial of the Scripture to be the Supream Rule.*

And we do so, and have defended our Judgment in that Point, in several Places in this Discourse, and therefore omit Repetition; a dreaming Faculty, this Man is foully guilty of, in this latter Part of his Book.

7. That *we both pretend to Revelation and Miracles.*

This we have honestly explain'd and defended: That Revelation which is sober and true, according to Scripture, I have asserted in my second Chapter at large: And for Miracles, we confess they are not ceast; yet, to us, *we have a more sure Word of Prophesy.*

8. He tells the World, That *we do not know whether* Purgatory *be revealed in Scripture, or not.*

Which, besides that it's a bad Proof to convince People, that we are Papists, who are so doubtful of a Point, with them so undoubtedly believed and peremptorily asserted; we might defy the Devil himself to have invented any thing more improbable and void of all Appearance of Truth; for we know that *Purgatory* is neither in Scripture nor Reason: Well may I say, and indeed I do, *How long, Lord God,*

God, Holy and True, how long will it be e're thou rebukest the Lying Tongue, and smitest the Lips of those that are given to Leesing?

We utterly renounce all Concern in the Foppery of that Opinion; and I, my self, have within these two Months, publisht a Discourse against the *Papists*, wherein I do particularly refute that *Romish Phantasm*; and I dare say, by Reasons not borrowed from (nor usual in) the Discourses of their Enemies, as *Jenner* has done from ours.

1671.

Chap. VI.
See my Caveat against Popery, p. 27, 28.

9. He winds up his Charge of this Nature, with this farther Imputation, *That we claim an Infallibility*. To which I answer,

p. 175, 176.

The Spirit of Truth is infallible, therefore such as are led by it, fail neither in their Judgment nor in their Practise; for the Reason of Error and Uncertainty, is the not being conform'd to (nor guided by) it, as all the Children of the Lord are. We have not attributed an Infallibility to our selves, thereby to involve People more into Failures, as hath the Pope of *Rome*; but do ascribe all our In-errableness to God's Spirit, whose Manifestation is universal: And thus much for his Accusation of a Confederacy with the *Papists*.

His Answer to that Objection, *Of our writing against* Popery; is only taking with those that resolve not to be informed; for were they candid, *the Folly, Ignorance, and Malice* of it were enough to anticipate all our Answers: *For if we build up* Popery *by pulling it down, he ought to set us up by the Reason of Contraries, that he may pull us down; or that in the midst of our Endeavours to detect the Villainy of the Priests, and overthrow the Foundation of* Jenner's *Building, we are seeking the Prosperity of it*; but if this be ridiculous, the other cannot be rational.

Next, He has a Mind to lessen, first, *Our Troubles and Travels*, for the Promotion of the *Truth*; and next, *Our Constancy in Suffering*, at least the Ground of it; for he says, *The one is done by the Devil, the other by the* Jesuits.

But how sober or candid this is, let the Impartial judge: Because *Judas* was a Man, *therefore is every Man* Judas? Or, *because the Devil is a Spirit, and so is* Michael; *therefore is the Devil* Michael? Is it to touch the Merit of our Cause, to say, *The Devil or the* Jesuits *do so, and so*; prove that we have the same Principles and Ends, and then let us be coupled with them, not before: The End of our Travels has been to convert Men from the unfruitful Works of Darkness, and Power of Satan's Kingdom, and not to establish his Dominion. And for our Sufferings, we leave both our Reward and our cruel Adversaries with the Lord; but better had it been for poor *Jenner*, he had never been born, than thus to revile the Innocent and Persecuted Family of God.

10th. He would insinuate a Belief in People, *That we bear Witness to our selves, and therefore are not of God*. But that we are of God, I prove, *Because we have only born Witness to the Truth, and the Effects of our Travels and Labours only unto us*. (1st,) Our Doctrine against Priests and Professors, and our Sufferings from them, have all along resembled the Case of Christ himself. (2d,) As he foretold their Downfal, so *did we foretel the Downfal of Presbyterians and Independents, with all their Pride, Strength, and Self-Idolatry; and that is come to pass*. (3d,) We have been *Instrumental in checking Impiety; and many Thousands have and do confess and testify, that our Ministry is in Life and Power, and from God*: So that our *Sufferings, Self-denyal, the Priests and Professors Downfal, and the Success God hath given us* (or rather his blessed Truth) bear Witness that we are not of Man, but God.

p. 114.

Read Edw. Burrough & G. Fox, their Epist. to the Parliament and Army.

11. As to his idle Repetitions, by way of reiterated Accusations, *concerning the Trinity, God, Christ's Offices, and the Holy Spirit, with his Metaphysical* (to him unknown) *Personality*; they have been largely spoken to already, only these Two Particulars I cannot well omit.

p. 188, 189, 190.

1. That how lately soever it was, he accus'd us of Confederacy with the *Papists*, he takes Occasion in discoursing upon the *Trinity*, to charge us with the Denial of that, which they (he says) own; namely, *Three distinct Persons*: I wonder not that they own it; for they are the *Grand Patrons* of the Doctrine; nor do I more wonder that he does so suddenly disjoyn those he so lately put together, though others have Liberty to do it, who know him less than I do; for now he denies us to be *Papists*.

p. 198.

2. Amongst

1671.
Chap. VI.
p. 190.

2. Amongst his Lyes of us, relating to our Denial of the Holy Ghost, he wedges in this impious and ignorant Aspersion, viz. *That all the Murthers, Whoredoms, and flagitious Wickedness, that any of them* (Quakers) *commit at any Time, they father upon the Holy Ghost, who mov'd them thereunto* ; and thus he proves it, *Because we say a Measure of the Spirit is in every Man.*

But what he charges upon us, is most properly his own, for as he greatly injures us by saying that we commit any of those Impieties, whilst his Hearers live in them, and he pleads against an Impossibility of overcoming them ; and which is yet worst of all, in that he says, we father any (much more such) gross and foul Iniquities upon the Holy Spirit (which I am perswaded all but *Jenner* and his Crew will clear us from (who had rather we should be such, then they should want Matter against us) so is he guilty of the highest Blasphemy, in charging the Holy Ghost with a Consent to Sin, because present in Man, when Man sinneth ; for he that infers, because the Holy Ghost is in Man, when Man sins, *therefore the Holy Ghost sins, outstrips the whole Record of Scripture in point of President for horrid Ignorance and Blasphemy.*

Did not God give his good Spirit to *Israel*? And did not *Israel* rebel against it? Therefore did the Spirit rebel? Is the Blood of the Covenant in Fault, if a Man tread it under Foot? Shall a Third Man in a Room, where two seek each other's Blood (after all his Disswasions and Reproof) be accus'd for a Murderer, if one fall by the other's Hand, only for being present?

We say a Measure of Divine Light is in every Transgressor, even at the Instant of his committing the vilest Sin ; yet it consents not to it, but stands a Witness for the Lord God against the unrighteous Soul. *So let the Blasphemy lie at* Jenner's *Door.*

p. 192, 193.

12th. But he says we blaspheme the Ministry, and quotes *James Naylor*'s Expressions to his *Weathercock Brother* a *Demas Baxter*, which had they been Ten Thousand Times more significant, earnest and sharp against that cursed bitter Stock of Hirelings, they had but been enough, and I would then say not enough ; but that the Reverence I bear to the Holy Spirit would oblige me to acquiesce in whatever he should utter through any Prophet, or Servant of the Lord.

And we have nothing for them, but *Woes and Plagues, who have made drunk the Nations, and laid them to Sleep, on the Downy Beds of soft Sin-pleasing Principles, whilst they have cut their Purses, and pick'd their Pockets* ; Tophet's *prepar'd for them to act their Eternal Tragedy upon, whose Scenes will be the renew'd, direful, anguishing Woes of an Eternal Irreconcileable Justice.*

13th. As to his tedious Account of the Judgments of the Lord upon *Impostors* and *Ringleading Hereticks*, they may be true for ought he or I know, and yet I will never burn in the Assertion of their Verity : But this I say to him, that we are unconcern'd in the Recital of them, and 'tis but a meer Begging of the Question, *to say such Things shall inevitably fall on us.* First let us be truly and plainly proved these Hereticks, *and then let him leave our Doom to him whose alone Right it is to render it ; but the Parson would hang us first, and Try us afterwards.* But we expect better Dealings from the Lord, whose we are : Though we have no Reason but to expect worse from him : However, this let him know, that if he repent not his Portion will not be less from the Lord's Hand, than the hatefullest Heretick he has named ; nay, but the Measure his waspish *Spirit* does meet to us, will the just God of Vengeance recompence upon his Head, in Everlasting Burnings, which I could heartily desire might never be his Portion.

Nor are his Designs of farther Tendency than to scare the Simple-hearted by his swelling Words of Vanity, *being those raging Waves of the Sea that foam out their own Shame* ; or else by his idle Scribling to procure a Subsistence to himself, *his Books being saleable no where but at the Shop of more than treble Gain, and mostly bought by the Men of Charity.*

14th. His next Business is to shew, *how many have been deluded by immediate Revelation*, but I can find amongst them all but *One*, and he *One of the best Men of his Age* ; and to whom the *Non-Conformists* have been more beholden, than any of the Primitive Antiquity, and none so much admired by them ; I am sure by Dr. *J. O.* And that is, *famous and learned Tertullian* ; But what was his Crime? *Why the same that* Paul *and* John *were guilty of* : Namely, *the indwelling of the Holy Spirit, and Obedience to it's Holy Will and Motions:* Let him produce me any such
delu-

delusive Visions as he prates of, out of that honest Father, and we shall willingly quit our Assertion; 'till then I shall undertake his Vindication.

But O that ever a poor Man should so far err from his Creator, as to blaspheme the immediate Revelation of his Eternal Spirit. My Spirit's griev'd to think of the many Thousands that are destroy'd, *by such Soul-Murderers*, through their Industry to fill their Heads with the like *Darkness, Error and Prejudice*; *but thanks be to the Lord God for ever: His Power is known, and blessed Light risen, that will overturn, confound, and for ever scatter all before them.*

However, by the Way (for as the Proverb says, *give the Devil his Due*) we are obliged to him, that in Page 208, he confesses, *that in the second Century or Hundred Years from Christ, Revelations were in the Church*: And whether the seventeenth Hundred Years ought to impeach the Second, *So saucily as* Jenner *does* Tertullian, is a Question that may be ask'd without the Imputation of Impertinency, especially considering he denies Revelation.

And for his Invitation to us, *to quit the Table of Revelation, to feed at his hungry Ordinary, where every Dish we know is stolen*, I would have him to understand us better, we have arriv'd at the Fountain, and disdain the broken Cisterns. We have a better than the *Pharaonian Task-masters of* Egypt. *The Gospel is preached without Money and without Price: our first Love is God, and our first Works Righteousness, which we are doing*; but the *Priest's first Love, is Money,* (the Root of all Evil) *and their first Work's getting it* (though Religion be a Cloak to their Avarice) and this they will do as long as they can.

We therefore knowing the *Covetousness, Cruelty, Pedantry* and great *Ignorance* of those pretended *Physicians, do Call and Charge, and Warn all, in the Name of God* (*as having receiv'd Authority of the God of Life, Power and Dominion*) *to come out from amongst those Merchants of* Babylon; *that they may hearken to the Voice of Truth; that Leads to Life and Righteousness; for their Ways are Death, and their Paths Everlasting Destruction.*

15th. And since he hath undertaken to admonish the *Orthodox* (as he calls them) and particularly *Ministers*; I shall conclude this Chapter with a Word of Advice to both, that they may be truly *Orthodox*.

First, *Know that the Fear of the Lord, that is Wisdom; and to depart from Iniquity, that is a Good Understanding.*

Secondly, *To do this, Mind that Measure of Light and Grace which God hath placed in thy inmost Parts; and obey the same, for it leads into all Meekness and Righteousness.*

Thirdly, *Deny thy self all that which it would not have thee do, but is offended with thee for so doing, and thou shalt receive Power to become a Son of God.*

Fourthly, *This brings thee out of all the Fashions of the World, and fashions thee according to the New and Inward Man.*

Fifthly, *Then wilt thou know what Christ's Life, Death, Resurrection, Ascension, and Mediation mean; and what justifies and sanctifies; and finally saves from Sin here, and Wrath hereafter.*

Sixthly, *And this will beget holy Zeal in thee, to testify against all the unequal, persecuting, sin-pleasing Ways and Worships in the World; and give thee Fellowship with the Father, and with the Son, and with the Holy Spirit, and the Spirits of Just Men made perfect; and thy Portion shall be Blessedness for ever.*

And if thou art a Minister, consider these few Things:

1st. *Renounce thy Call as being of Man.*
2d. *Thy own Preachments, as being the Invention of thine or other Men's Brains, and not thine own Experience.*
3d. *Forbear all Persecution for Conscience.*
4th. *Bow to the Teachings of the Light, and become a Child and Scholar of it.*
5th. *Relinquish and testify against that Oppression of Tenths, as a Simonious and Anti-christian-Yoak; otherwise, thou shalt never receive the Reward of a Minister of Christ Jesus.*

These are Truths, that shall stand justified *at God's Tribunal, in that great and notable Day, when all shall receive their Reward according to their Works*, 1 Pet. 1. 17.

O the Calamity of such as say, *Thus saith the Lord, and he never spoke to them; and who run, and he never sent them, that have Taught for Hire, and Divin'd for Money, and prepar'd War against all that have not put into their Mouths!* Well, if any of them happen to read these Things, let them know, that they have been warn'd by a Servant of the Lord, who, in their Rebellion, is clear of their Blood, though the Blood of the whole World should lie at their Door.

CHAP. VII.

BUT the surest, and most crafty Fetch, the *Priest* has through his whole Discourse, is, *The Design of rendring us inconsistent with Government*; that what his Tribe has only Will enough to do, they might incense the Civil Magistrate, and imploy his Power, to accomplish and inflict upon us; and this he earnestly endeavours, by an odious Comparison of us to *John* of *Leiden, Becold, Knipperdolling*, &c. But since his Design is to expose us to the Hatred of Government, he would have nearer approach'd the Mark, by a Comparison of us to his Brother *Presbyters* and *Independents*, whose rank Enmity to all Government, and Scorns of Obedience to all Authority *(but their own)* have given later Evidence how well they love to Head the Stage of Usurpation, though at the Cost of Natural Rights, and Natural Privileges: Of which more anon.

He has not dealt with us like a Man, much less a *Christian*, and least of all like a *True Minister*; for he thinks it Reason enough, *To make us inherit their Miscarriages, that we might but inherit their Punishment*: For he has not instanc'd any one Fact, by us committed, that either paralleleth that Relation (be it True, or false) or in the least affronteth our Native Laws. But since some may expect that I should say something of our Judgment in Point of Civil Government, I proceed briefly thus.

First, We believe it is the Will of God, and Dictate of Nature and Reason, That Mankind should associate, or live in Society.

Secondly, That such Society, or Societies, should have Just and Righteous Laws.

Thirdly, That these Laws be either of a Nature Fundamental (and so indispensible) or Superficial (and so alterable.) By the first we understand the Determinations of Right Reason, concerning Moral and Just Living, with certain Privileges that in the first Constitution are agreed upon as Essentials in Government; as Metes, Bounds, and Land-Marks of Truth, Equity, and Righteousness; that as well confine Rulers, as People. By the *Second* we understand, certain Temporary Laws, Proclamations, or Customs, that relate to more trivial Matters, and that receive Alteration, with the Reason of them, according to that Maxim, *Cessante ratione Legis cessat Lex*, of which the People and Rulers are Judges.

Fourthly, We believe that all such Laws ought to be punctually kept, and neither the Innocent to be punish'd, nor the Guilty to go free; that no Respect be shew'd in Judgment.

Fifthly, That no Man be punish'd by a Law he never heard of, or doth not understand: For where there is no Law, there is no Transgression; and therefore it is Reasonable, that the Laws be both promulgated, and recorded in a Language intelligible by the meanest Rustick.

Sixthly, That no Delays should be upon any Pretence to Justice; nor that the Person of any Man should be had in Esteem for Reward.

Seventhly, That the Punishment never exceed the Offence.

Eighthly, That Magistrates be not allow'd to commit those Iniquities they chastize others for, lest they punish the Effect of their own Example.

Ninthly, As a wicked Magistrate is one that converts his Power to please his Passion, feed his Pride, and fill his Purse, rather than to the well-ordering of the People, over whom he is set: So do we esteem him a Godly and Just Magistrate, whose Mind is exercis'd in the Pure Law of God, to do equal Justice, and yet to love Mercy; whose Example teaches the People how to live, as not needing Laws whilst under them. *This is the Man that is worthy of double Honour.*

Tenthly, As all Magistracy was Originally instituted for the Good of the People, so ought all Magistrates to answer the End of their Office and Trust; namely, The Preservation of the People by their own Example, and the fair and equal Execution of the Laws: And the People stand as firmly oblig'd to obey the Magistrate, (Conscience only excepted) and diligently to seek the Well-being of that Government;

or else the Magistrate is excus'd in the Denial of the Law's Protection to them: For no People can justly claim the Benefit of that Government they seek to ruin.

Thus much and enough to confute the angry Priest, whose Personal, or Tribian Quarrel with us, he would make the whole World's; that the Number of our Adversaries might increase with the Degrees of his unjust Hate.

His Design in rendring of us Enemies to Government, being only to deprive us of the Protection of it: For, 'tis not without Cause, that these Malicious and Monopolizing Partisans of our Age, employ themselves so diligently, to raise their Dust of Lies and Slanders, to darken the Magistrate's Prospect of us; lest by a direct and clearer View of our Just Principles and Behaviour, their Pride, Avarice, and Cruelty, should come more to Light; and the Gallows, contriv'd to hang *Mordecai*, should be the last Stage for those proud *Hamans* to tread and act their Parts upon.

But this open Challenge I make to the *Old Man and his Fraternity*, That if amongst the many Plots that have been spoken of, and several have been hang'd for, One (known, and by us esteem'd a) *Quaker*, has been found amongst them? I shall confess so far to his Imputation, as that the Magistrate is excusable in a discreet Jealousie over us.

And in his next, let him challenge me (if he dare) to tell him, Whether they were not all, or most of them, either *Presbyterians* or *Independents* that were concern'd. I would have the Man to know, That I am not so void of Tenderness to all that go under those Denominations, as to expose their Reputation to the Scorn of every *Reader*, as his indiscreet and false Reflections upon us (in Point of Government) would lead me to; only I would be glad to know by the next, whether one *T. Jenner* was not Chaplain to the *Irish-Brigade*, that went over to *Rout* (him they called) Sir *George Booth* in *Cheshire*, 1659. I therefore return him his Distich thus,

Region, Estate, Rule, (Civil and Divine)
Religion, all, does Jenner *undermine*.

I shall conclude the Chapter with this One Question to the Man in Hand, *Whether those only are not the Men who least deserve Protection or Liberty from any Government, who whilst they angrily demand IT for themselves, are so penuriously Selfish and Unjust, as to deny it to other Men? And whether this Principle destroys not the Universal Empire of the Great God, and does not implicitly accuse him of His Impartial Raining upon both Just and Unjust, as well as that it destroys the greatest Part of Civil Society now in the World?* I am confident he must say, *Yes*.

And more truly dare I say to *Jenner*, Thou art the Man. For, lest the Magistrate should be too slow in his Pursuit of us, he sticks not to provoke him to a Persecution; that, when against themselves, they esteem most Unchristian: Nay, he plainly showeth, that how much soever he and his Brethren stand in need of a Toleration, he had rather there were none, than that the *Poor, Despis'd Quakers* should have any; as if Persecution were unlawful against none but themselves, or Unjustifiable against all but the *Quakers*.

But how ingenious it is to essay the Ruin of us, our Families, and Long-Labours in that Plantation, whether in getting or improving it, let the more Sober of all Perswasions judge; how Antichristian it is, I know; and heartily could wish, *The Lord would Convince him of the same, lest his End be Everlasting Destruction.*

CHAP. VIII.

THE Business of this my last Chapter, will be a Vindication of our Innocence, against the foul Lies, and scaring Characters the Devil's Friends have often put upon us, (though by the *Friends of* TRUTH they have as frequently been detected and return'd upon their Heads) and of which the Man in Hand has made a plentiful Collection, to the End that the Simple-hearted may be deter'd from embracing the Blessed Way of Everlasting Life, which the Lord God Almighty in Great Love and Faithfulness, hath brought to Light in these Last Ages of the World; a Way so even and plain, that (as the Prophet said) *The Wayfaring Man, though a Fool, cannot err therein*. In order to which, I shall premise Four Things.

First, That it has been very usual with the Lord, to suit his Dispensations to the Frame and Capacity of the World to receive them, as the Time before the Law, under the Law, and after the Coming of Christ, does evidently shew.

Secondly,

Secondly, That those more New and Heavenly Discoveries, have with the Person that God hath chosen to testifie of them to the World, constantly been wont to receive very cross Usage and inhumane Entertainment, being pursu'd by whole Armies of Lies, Slander, and Reproach, imputing their Success to Witchcraft, as if they had *Cast out Devils by* Beelzebub *the Prince of Devils* ; witness the Entertainment of the Ancients, as from *Abel's Day to the Primitive Persecutions* ; not to mention the many Instances of that Kind, which the *Protestants* Revolt from *Rome*, and divers Separations from them, might plentifully furnish us with.

Thirdly, That we are taught from hence, not to impute *Falshood or Error to any Religion, because disguis'd or vail'd from the common Eye by those Clouds of Slander and Reproach, her Enemies may have exhal'd, on Purpose to eclipse some more engaging Truth and Beauty in her than their own.*

Fourthly, This hath been more our Case, than any Society of People upon Earth ; for, as the *Papist* defam'd the *Protestant*, so did the degenerated *Protestant* the *Puritan*, who falling into a rigid *Presbyterian*, became as angry with the *Independents*, and both displeas'd with the *Baptists* ; but all enrag'd against the Appearance of the Blessed Truth; *Pilate* and *Caiaphas* combining by Civil Power, and Lying Accusations, to accomplish (if possible) a perfect Overthrow both of Her and Her Children.

Therefore how Good a Thing is it to embrace the Apostle's Exhortation, *Try all Things, and hold fast that which is Good?* Which leads me to the Examination of those Stories he frequently takes the Liberty to tell of us in his Discourse.

First, The first considerable *Lye* that falls within my Precinct, is in page 153. his Words are these, *That* Penn, *another of their Teachers, did boldly affirm to a Friend of mine in* Dublin, *That whosoever shall expect to be sav'd by that Jesus Christ that was Born in* Judea, *and suffer'd at* Jerusalem, *shall be deceiv'd.*

To which I answer : This is the very Off-spring of the Devil, the Father of Lies : For the Lord God, who is Righteous in all his Ways, and Just in all his Doings, to whom alone it belongs to search the Heart, and try the Reins, and to recompence every Man according to his Work, he knows, to whom I can make my solemn Appeal, *That those Words, or any other of that Tendency, did never proceed out of my Mouth.*

But if *Jenner* would have shew'd himself a Man (for Christian he is none) he should have told me who that Person is, that he calls his Friend, *that is so much mine and his own Enemy :* I doubt not but I have Witnesses of what I said ; and methinks nothing but the Fear of his Testimony, should have made *Jenner* to have conceal'd his Name : The Slander in general hath been answer'd already, and therefore I omit to enlarge here.

Secondly, His second Lye runs thus, William Spencer *lying in Bed with one of the* Quakers *three Nights, the last Night was very troublesome ; on a sudden he heard something hissing about the* Quaker's *Head, which affrighted him ; he endeavour'd to rise, but the* Quaker *perswaded him to lye still, and expect the Power to come ; the* Quaker *laid his Head on* Spencer's *Shoulder, and did blow like the Hissing of a Goose towards his Mouth, which made him cry for a Light. What is this but meer Sorcery and Wickedness?* Says Jenner.

But besides, that it is most ridiculous to infer Sorcery and Witchcraft from any such foolish Actions : It is utterly deny'd that there ever was such a Thing ; and because he tells this Tale by Rote, I will refer him to the Person most concern'd, who is named *John Lawson*, a Shopkeeper in *Lancaster*, who is known to be an Honest Man, and Sufficient Person, and able to give Satisfaction in this Point, to the Confusion of *Jenner* and his Author.

Thirdly, His next Falshood and Slander is this : *A Minister went with some Friends to a Meeting of* Quakers *in* Durham, *where he pray'd, but his Legs trembled ; whilst he pray'd to God as a Creature, there was little Disturbance ; but when in the Name of Christ, then the* Quakers *Roar'd, Howl'd, Squeak'd, Yelp'd, with a Humming Noise ; Half of them were so terribly shaken, that it was a Wonder they liv'd : One ask'd him if he were come to Torment them : And as he departed, one said, All the Plagues of God be upon thee. What could be more like the Devil?* Says *Jenner*.

I answer : Nothing but this Story, and him that made it, who was a *Malicious Anabaptist*, his Name was *Tilham*, one that by a deceitful Stratagem, made his Escape out of *Ipswich* Goal, and ran his Country for his *Roguery* (holding and practising

practising such immoral Principles, as made him detestable to all Moral and Sober Men.) It was not at *Durham*, but at *Derwentwater*, that he came into a *Quaker's Meeting*, where, if his *Legs Trembl'd*, it either was by a Good or Evil Power; if a *Good Power*, it would have bound the (suppos'd) Evil One in the *Quakers*; but if a Bad One, he was as Criminal as the Story would render them. But is it not preposterously foolish for any to think, That the *Quakers* should be so well satisfy'd with his Prayer to God, and yet so dissatisfied when in the Name of Christ, *Who is God over all, blessed for ever?*

But what will not Wicked and Ungodly Men do, to prosper their own Ends and Designs? But they shall never hurt that innocent People, who among the Churches of God are of Good Savour, for their Integrity, and Upright-walking with God.

Fourthly, The next Devilish Untruth runs thus, *That one in* Kent, *going to a* Quaker's *Meeting, was so wrought upon, that he fell a Dancing, and went Home distemper'd in his Mind, and soon after ended his Life.*

That this came out of *Hell*, he refers to a Book call'd, *Hell broke loose*; and I refer the Reader to the Answer, entitul'd, *The Mouth of the Pit Stopt*, written by that Judicious Friend, and Faithful Servant of the Lord, *Francis Howgill*, where he may receive ample Satisfaction.

Fifthly, The next Story he tells, is of a Woman in *Buckinghamshire*, *Who being at a* Quaker's *Meeting, was sudddenly transported with great Raptures; and after fell into grievous Cursing and Blaspheming, crying,* Fox a Devil, Fox a Devil, *until she dy'd.*

To which I need not give another Answer, than I did to the former, for it coming out of the same *Pit*, the same *Hand* hath stopt it: Yet that the *Reader* may be satisfied, as well of the Falseness of the Story, as of the Wickedness of the Maker, I must tell him I was lately in *Buckinghamshire*, and have made Enquiry, but can find no Footsteps towards any such impious Matter; but if any such a Thing were, the only Blasphemy I observe from *Jenner's* Relation, was against *George Fox*, in speaking evilly of the Lord's Servant.

Sixthly, The next Lye he would endeavour to confirm our Adversaries with, and delude simple People to the Belief of, is, *The Notorious Story, the* Sherburn *Witches, of which*, says he, *there were near Two Hundred at a Meeting, most of them* Quakers *and* Anabaptists; *but particularly three Men and two Women, who were formerly* Quakers; *they tormented Mr.* Liford, *Minister of* Sherburn, *to Death, and forc'd Mr.* Baulfeild, *his Successor, out of Town,* &c.

I need not go about to prove this to be a Lye, the whole Country will do it for me; for neither had they Power over our Friends, they being preserv'd by the Eternal Power of God; nor do his Words themselves imply they had; *For*, saith he, *three Men and two Women, formerly* Quakers, *were committed to* Dorsetshire *Goal*, &c. But if it were true, they were formerly *Quakers*, and were committed for *Witchcraft*, I can give no better Reason for it, *Than because they remain'd not* Quakers *still*: For had they continu'd in their Most Holy Faith, neither had the Priest had Ground to say, *They were formerly Quakers*; nor the Magistrates Occasion to commit them for Sorcery: And had their Ministers been Men chosen and sent of God, to Preach His Everlasting Gospel, and Faithful in their Places, those *Infernal Spirits would have had no Power over them*, which does clearly evidence on what Foundation that Kind of Priesthood stands.

But whilst the Man is belying us, he will not hear the Country tell that Story of his Brethren, let him enquire there, and he may be inform'd, *How many* Presbyterians *and* Independents *were clapt into* Dorsetshire *Goal on that Account: Nay, their Priests turn'd Wizards too, but that's no Wonder; since they have Bewitch't the People ever since they have been Priests*. I hope the *Baptists* will acquit us, if they will not *Jenner*, for his Story strikes at both: *But 'tis Impiety in Grain, first to be* Witches *themselves, and then lay it upon others*; like Jezebel *that Bloody Harlot, who first bely'd the Lord's People, and then Persecuted them*. But these Stories well become his Author, who being Conscious to himself of so much Villany, *thought it his Wisest Course to conceal his Name, and whom the Vengeance of the Almighty will one Day make to wish, that he also had conceal'd his Book*.

Seventhly, He farther adds out of *Higginson*, *That G.* Fox *was vehemently suspected for a Sorcerer; and this is one ground, that when Strangers were brought into his Company he would talk with them, and hold them by the Hand.*

But as this idle Suspicion, and ground for it, have been long since sent back to *Higginson* in the Answer to his Book; so may we easily infer from the Reason us'd to prove *George Fox* a Sorcerer, that *Jenner* is a Witch; for, if speaking to People, and taking them by the Hand, can bewitch them; who alive can fling the first Stone? *But no Lye is too great, nor Story too foul* (however confutable from within it self) *for an* Independent *or* Presbyterian *to embrace against the poor Despised* Quakers.

Eighthly, His eighth Story, is his eighth Lye, It is of one *Coppinger*, That affirm'd to an Ironmonger of *Bristol*, That he frequented all publick and private Meetings (and (himself being a *Franciscan*) said, That two of his Order were chief Speakers among the *Quakers*, and that he had spoken amongst them thirty Times in *London*: Henry Denn (says he) writes for them in his Book call'd (A *Quaker* no *Papist*) saying, That the present *Romish Church*, and no other, is the present Spouse of Christ, or else there hath been none in all Ages.

This ancient Imposture hath been twice roundly answer'd; first, by *John Audland*, (a Servant and Labourer of the Lord in those Parts, who hath receiv'd his Wages, and is at Rest) in Answer to *W. Prinn*; and the second Time, so effectually by *George Whitehead*, as *Prinn's* Courage fail'd in a *Rejoynder*, and whose Share in this Discourse may better acquaint *Jenner* with his manner of handling the Enemies of Truth.

We utterly deny the Story; and the just God, whose is Vengeance, will compleatly recompence this Wrong upon the Slanderer's Head.

But the Confusion of the Man may easily manifest, that a lying Spirit is his Companion; for, that *Henry Denn* should write for the *Quakers* to prove them no *Papists*, and yet conclude that the present *Romish Church is the only Spouse of Christ*, is such a Medley of Contradiction; as no Man of Sense, or in his Wits, could be guilty of.

But *Henry Denn* writing against *Smith* of *Cambridge*, in defence of us, as not being Popish, he hath either taken *Smith's* prejudiced Inference of *Denn's* matter, to be *Denn's*, or else mistaken *Smith's* Consequence as drawn by *Denn* to be his: For, what Man out of *Bedlam*, can apprehend that *Henry Denn* designed to prove the *Quakers*, *Papists*, by his Book entitul'd, *A Quaker no Papist*.

Ninthly, He says, that *Fox* and *Whitehead* (pretending Infallibility in all Points) *say, they know all the Fathers of the first Three Hundred Years were* Papists.

But certainly, He thinks we ought to believe himself infallible, or else he would not impose upon us the Credit of Stories unprov'd; nay, that never can be proved; they are both so far from the Ignorance of such an Assertion, that their better Skill in Antiquity is able to prove, not only the *Papists* had no Share in the first three Hundred Years, but that both *Presbyterianism* and *Independency* (notwithstanding their Boasts to Purity) received their Births in after Ages: However, that Instance was ill placed to prove the *Quakers Papists*. Besides, He is beholding to a couple of Libels, being the unsubscrib'd Spawns of some of the croaking Frogs of the University of *Cambridge*, which were long since refuted by the Persons concerned.

Tenthly, He saith, *An* English *Jesuit, bred in* Cambridge, *confest to a Gentleman in* London, *that there was a good honest People, called* Quakers *(whom he jeer'd at) that did their work at the second Hand.*

For this Lye he is beholding to a Book, call'd *The Quaker's Folly*; but by the Reply to it, proved to be *Danson's*. But if the *Papists* are as great Villains, as they represent them; Why may they not as well belie us, as they think they injure them: However, The *Jesuit* thought us to be honest, which he could not think his Design to be; since People know how little it costs *Jesuits* to lye, they ought not to believe them: For there is no Reason why *Jenner* should believe the *Papists* against us, and not against himself; since if they Lye of one, they may Lye of both.

Eleventhly, His eleventh Lye may well be termed the greatest, because he did it the most knowing (and like the Man, his Words (before he printed it) shew'd him to be, when he said, *I will be revenged of the* Quakers) it is concerning one *Ann Wright* of *Castle-Dermont* in the Nation of *Ireland*, now deceas'd; of whose upright walking, all that knew her (nay, *Jenner* himself) cannot but speak well: I shall not undertake the Answer of it, because it is so well done by her own Husband, who (though no *Quaker* (as he says himself) yet) would not have

Slanders

Slanders survive his Wife's Innocency; nor her Name be recorded for an Apostate, a Witch (and what not) without a Vindication both of Her and the Truth. The Defence follows.

I *William Wright* of *Castle-Dermont*, in the County of *Kildare* in *Ireland*, being desired to certifie the very Truth concerning my Wife (now deceased) whom *Thomas Jenner* belies in his Book intituled, *Quakerism Anatomized, and Confuted*; dated at *Catherlough*, *November* the 30th, 1670.

I do therefore truly and really certifie the real Truth, which I will maintain before the highest Powers in *Ireland* (if thereunto call'd) or elsewhere; and thus I proceed.

In pag. 126. of the said Book, the said Author *Thomas Jenner*, goes about to prove *George Fox* a Sorcerer by divers Instances in *England*, to which he farther adds; *saying*, The last Summer the said *G. F.* (as I am informed) came to the House of one Master *Wright*, near *Castle Dermont* here in *Ireland*; whose Wife had for a long Time refused to go to the *Quakers* Meetings, or to hear them; but as soon as the said *G. F.* came thither, and had spoken with her, taking her by the Hand, and she hearing of him, she, without any farther Arguments immediately turns an absolute profest *Quaker*.

But before I proceed farther, I shall clear this Page of his Book (162) his Book was dated *November* 9. 1670. he saith, *The last Summer G. F. came to my House, as he was informed*; and proves it in his Margent by John Taylor (*their Servant*, saith he) Now that this is most abominable false, will easily appear; for G. F. *was not in* Ireland *any Part of that Summer*. 1670. let any prove it if they can; and if it be denied, there may be Hundreds and Thousands brought in to prove the contrary, and to affirm where he was: And besides all this, the Witness *John Taylor* is a Carpenter, whom he brings to prove this Lye, an horrible Apostate from all Appearance of good; for he hath not only been a zealous and diligent Hearer of Sermons, and a Follower of the best and most able Ministers in and about the North Part of *Lancashire* for many Years; but one that writ most of their Sermons: But is some Years since turned a most wicked Swearer, and Blasphemer; insomuch as I and my Wife heard him say, ' That others had serv- ' ed God in Hypocrisie, when he served him in Sincerity; and he saw that God ' had rewarded them in this Life, and rewarded him not; and therefore he was ' resolv'd to set himself against God, as much as he could; (I and my Wife being by the Fire side, and he at Supper with the rest of my Servants) at which Words I stood a little amazed, not knowing what to say; and my Wife not hearing; or not fully understanding what he said, ask'd, *What is that he faith?* And when he understood that she heard him not fully, he repeated the self same Words again, purposely, as I suppose, to vex and grieve her tender Spirit. And another Time, He being a Suiter to a Widow, that liv'd upon *Castle-Dermont*, said, *I wish I may have her, though I renounce Heaven for her.* And at that Time he was a grievous Enemy to the said *Thomas Jenner*, who us'd sometimes to come to my House, and stay all Night (and was very welcome) but whenever the said *John Taylor* (being at work in or about my House) knew that the said *Thomas Jenner* was in my House, he would find out something or other to find Fault withal, that little concern'd him, that he might come Swearing and Cursing, purposely to vex the said *Tho. Jenner*; because he being a *Nonconformist*, and one that hated such Wickedness, he thought it would vex and grieve him, and my Wife.

The like he did in the Sight and hearing of my worthy Friend *John Price* of *Dublin* (a Man well known to most Men of publick Dealing in *Ireland*, to be a Man of Truth both in Word and Action) he, seeing of the said *John Taylor* before his Apostacy, to be in Want, lent him twenty Shillings, which he promis'd to pay him again, but never yet did; the said *John Price* being at my House; and this *John Taylor* knowing it (after his Apostacy) he came in Swearing and Staring, as if he had been possest; and I know and believe it was purposely to vex the said *John Price*, whom he knew hated such abominable Wickedness, and to grieve me and my poor Wife; whereupon the said *John Price* desir'd me to stop the said Twenty Shillings out of his Wages, and give it to some poor Body; but I never yet could do it conveniently: And this is one of *Thomas Jenner's Authors and Witnesses*

1671.
Chap. VIII.

Witnesses to his Book full of Lies; with whom also he sent the said Book to the Bishop of Laughlin *for his Approbation (and for ought I know Benediction upon it)* Now let any one judge, whether *Thomas Jenner* did refuse to conform to the setting up of the Bishops for pure Conscience-sake, or in hopes of a sudden Change, or a present discontinuing of them; for if they and their Way had been a Stumbling-Block in my Conscience, I would never have sought for Approbation, of any one of them, to any Thing I had writ. And though the said *John Taylor* did very much hate and envy the said *Thomas Jenner*, and would abuse him in my House (insomuch as I have been forced to put *Taylor* out of Doors) yet since *Taylor* knew *Jenner* was writing a Book against the *Quakers*, he hath been his great Friend, and hath told him all Things that have been done in and about my House, that was for his, and their Purpose: Besides, The said *Thomas Jenner* wrote not his Book impartially, and without Prejudice; but with Prejudice, Malice and Revenge; as appears by his Words to a Friend in *Dublin*, to whom he said, *He would be revenged of the* Quakers, *as* Sampson *on the* Philistines *for his two Eyes*, viz. Mr. Wright, *and* Mrs. Wright.

But to return to his Book (Pag. 162.) he saith, *As soon as* G. F. *had spoken with my Wife, taking her by the Hand, and she hearing of him; she, without any farther Arguments, immediately turn'd an absolute profest* Quaker.

Now that is an absolute Untruth, I do affirm, and can bring in Scores of honest Men to do the like; and thus is the Cause of my Knowledge, G. F. was at my House near *May-day* (as it is usually called) in 1669. (I think it was) but if not, I am sure it was not after the first Week in *June*; and my Wife was no more moved to be a *Quaker* by him, or at that Time, than she had been at any Time within eleven or twelve Years before; no, nor about three Months after.

For, the first that she heard publickly speak was *Robert Lodge, June* the 13th 1669. and there was little Appearance of a *Quaker* till about the End of *July* next; and yet *Thomas Jenner* saith, in the Margent of his Book, at the lower End of the Page 162. *(By her own Confession to my self and others.)* which is as false, as that the Sun is Darkness; for this she said at *Dublin*, her self, to be a Lye; and she might be believed by all that ever knew her: Besides, I know it my self to be false; for she was no such profest *Quaker*, nor any at all, until near three Months after. But now to the next page, 163.

He saith, Formerly she was esteemed of by the best Christians, to be a very Sober, Modest, and Religious good Woman; yet soon after G. F's meeting with her, &c. she was indefatigable Day and Night in the use of all possible Means she might by Word and Pen, yea, and by Gifts also.

Of this concerning Gifts, I did ask her in particular, which she deny'd; and I knew her to be of that Uprightness of Heart, that she durst not give away any Thing without my Knowledge and Consent.

Farther, he saith, *That of late she went to* Dublin *in a Frolick:* Which is very false; for those that go in a Frolick, are commonly Merry and Jocund; but the Lord knows, she parted from me with many Tears.

He farther saith, That she cover'd her self with Sack-cloth and Ashes (that is true) and in that Habit (saith he) she passing through the Streets in *Dublin* (that is false) She past through no Streets in *Dublin* in that Habit.

He saith, *She went into a publick Assembly, where she sate her down in the* Lord Arch-Bishop *of* Dublin's *Seat.* That she went into a publick Assembly is true, *but that she sate down in any* * *Seat whatsoever is a Devilish Lye*; as may be fully proved by the whole Assembly at *Patrick's Cathedral* in *Dublin*: The Time when it was done was upon the 17th Day of *April,* 1670. (being the Lord's-day, or first Day of the Week) I name the Time and Place, that all such as desire to know (and find out) very Truth in every Particular, may enquire and be satisfied.

---

* I under-nam'd do testifie that it was a great Mistake of *Thomas Jenner*, who said *Ann Wright* did go into my Lord Arch-Bishop's Throne or Seat in St. *Patrick's* in *Dublin*; and he quoteth me for his Witness in his Book, pag. 163. To what he said of me to witness, for to be true; I say, I cannot but say it was not true, but his great Mistake, as aforesaid; for she did not offer to come into his Seat, *but stood in the Alley Quietly.* Witness my Hand this 16th of *February,* 1670. in *Dublin,*

Robert Brady, *Verger.*

He farther proceeds, and faith, *Now laft of all, fhe is departed very lately for England, there* (as he faith) *to endeavour the converfion of the Higher Powers.*

Now that fhe went for *England* is true, but that fhe went to convert the higher Powers is falfe, and that fhe ever faid fo is alfo very falfe; for fhe was commanded by the Lord God of Heaven and Earth (no doubt) to go through the chief Streets in *London*, in Sack-cloth of Hair, and Afhes upon her head, to be a Sign of fome Judgment yet to come upon the City (except they repent) but after what Manner it was not reveal'd unto her, nor was fhe to enquire into it: But if *Thomas Jenner* had fuch a Command, he would make as much haft as fhe did; but it is not the Rich, the Honourable, the Scribe, nor the Wife, *that God hath chofen to do his extraordinary Work; but the contrary.*

He faith farther, *That fhe, with her Comrade, the Wife of* Maj. Bennet, *are bound for* Rome, *as 'tis faid*; I wonder he did not bring in his Blafphemous Witnefs, *John Taylor*, to prove this Lye alfo; for there was never Word, nor Sign for Motion of any fuch Thing.

And laftly, he faith pofitively, *Their going to* Rome *was to convert the Pope*; which is like all the reft; for no Doubt but that is altogether impoffible: For, *if Antichrift, the Man of Sin, or Son of Perdition, may be converted, then may the Pope; which is the fame Thing.*

There are many more Things in the Book, which he charges the *Quakers* with, which I know to be falfe, as any of thefe; but becaufe they do not concern me in Particular, I fay no more; knowing his Book is, and will be view'd and anfwer'd by thofe, whom God hath endued with more excellent Gifts and Graces, and alfo with a more excellent Pen, than is given to me: Yet what I have here fpoken is Real, Plain, and abfolute Truth. And though I cannot receive all Things, that thofe People call'd *Quakers* do hold; yet I judge and believe, that Living Praifes are amongft them; and that as Chrift Jefus, the true Corner-Stone, was a Stumbling-block and a Rock of Offence to the *Scribes* and *Pharifees*, who thought themfelves wifer than all; fo I believe the *Quakers* are appointed by God to be a Stumbling-block, and a Rock of Offence to the great Profeffors and Wifemen of this Age: And I pray God, I may not be one of them, that fhall ftumble and fall by them. And I wifh all in the true Fear of the Lord God Almighty, even the God of the Spirits of all Flefh, the True and Living God, to take Heed, and be careful of fpeaking more than they know concerning them.

And this is his Teftimony who defires Truth may be magnified above all Error.

Decem. *the* 11th, 1670.   William Wright.

Thus much from her Hufband (and no *Quaker*) in Vindication of his Wife and the Truth.

The Reference he made to the *Verger* of St. *Patrick*'s (as he calls it, and no fmall Favour too, being from a *Prefbyterianiz'd Independent*) we have accepted of, and accordingly enquired of him the Matter affirmed, *who under his Hand denies it, and charges* Jenner *with a manifeft Lye.*

Firft, *His Ingratitude* in bringing her upon the Stage, *to whom he was beholden, and at whofe Houfe he had lain fo often, and been fo Welcome; and that upon a Religious Account.*

Secondly, *His Folly*; in acknowledging fhe was of the beft *Chriftians, thereby intimating the worft ftaid behind.*

Thirdly, *His Infamy*; *in combining with an Apoftate, a Drunkard, a Blafphemer* (and what not) *to vilify our Friends.*

Fourthly, *His notorious Lying*; 1. In faying G. F. *was there in* 1670. 2. In charging A. W. *with bribing People to own her Judgment.* 3. In faying, *She paffed through* Dublin *Streets in Sackcloth.* 4. In faying, *She did it in a Frolick*, a profane and ingrateful Expreffion, as well as that it was a Lye. 5. In faying, *She fate down in the* Archbifhop's *Seat.* 6. In faying, *She went over for* England *to convert the Higher Powers.* 7. In faying, *She and Major* Bennet's *Wife defign'd for* Rome, *to convert the Pope.* 8. *That fhe immediately turn'd a profefs'd* Quaker *upon* G. F's *fpeaking to her, and taking her by the Hand.* In fhort, His whole Charge is but one whole great Lye.

Thus

1671.
Chap VIII.

Fifthly, But the last Thing I observe is, Jenner's *Temporizing with the Bishop of* Laughlin *and* Fernas, *about his Book*; he, whose Principles would lead him *to dye his Hoary Head in* Episcopal *Blood*, can (however) claw (with *their Lordships*) *to scratch and tear the* Quakers *to Pieces*; which may inform them what they themselves ought to expect, *from the Spirit of* Jenner *and his Brethren, had they a Power suitable to their* Scottish Directorian Will.

In short, Who can own him? Who can hear him? Who can possibly defend him? *Certainly so much Folly, Falseness, Ingratitude, and Envy, are not to be excus'd by any, that would not be esteem'd accessary to his Crimes, and a Party with him in his Guilt.*

12th. Lastly, I shall wind up his Lies with his most blasphemous Story against God, and abusive of us, viz. *Some blaspheme God, as that blasphemous Wretch, who ran into the Market-place stark Naked, and uttered these Words*, It is not I, but God that goeth Naked.

O the Devices of the envious Generation of Priests, to defame the righteous Heritage of the Lord! For, as we utterly deny any such Saying, ever to have proceeded out of the Mouth of a true Quaker, (nor know we of any under that Name that hath so said) so is it most contrary to our Principles, who admit not of God's Confinement to a Person, or visible local Being, or to consist of any visible Substance; but assert him to be the infinite Fulness and Eternal Spirit.

However, we deny not, but several have been mov'd of the Lord to go Naked into Steeple-houses, Markets, *and* Cities, *for a Sign to the People*; *but more especially to the Priests, of the* Nakedness *of their spiritual Conditions*; *and as stript as they were of their Clothes, would the Lord God strip them of their deceitful Garments, and those false Coverings, made of their own Will-worships and Carnal-performances*; *that whilst they thought themselves* Rich *and wanting* Nothing, *they should appear* Poor, Naked, *and wanting of the* Covering *of the Lord's Spirit*; *which is the true* Garment, *that gives Right to the Marriage-Supper of the Kingdom.*

One Thing I cannot omit to observe, That amongst all the Lyes and Slanders I have prov'd him to have cast upon us, he never offer'd any tolerable Testimony for our very Adversaries to believe the Truth of any one of them, which should be no small Testimony, for both our Friends and Enemies to disbelieve all of them.

But since that, Taylor and Jenner have taken so much Pains, to exasperate the Minds of People against us and our Principles, by their Collection of Lyes; it may not be improper to the Work in Hand, to tell a few of those many *true* (but most lamentable) *Stories, occasioned by the Cruelty and Oppression of their Brethren, the* Presbyterian *and* Independent Priests, *upon the Bodies and Estates of our dear Friends, during the Time they acted their ungodly Parts upon the late Stage of forsworn Government.* We shall not take them for our Example; for we shall both name the Persons *Suffering*, the *Reason why*, the *Places where*, with their several *Prosecutors*; being Facts committed in the Sight of the Sun, and presented to the then *Supream Authority*, as *our just Complaint* of *our unjust Grievances*; with ready Proof in Hand.

First, Temperance Hignel, of the City of *Bristol*, for speaking to *Jacob Brint* at *Temple Steeplehouse*, was struck down to the Ground by some of his Hearers, who were followed with many Blows upon her by the rude Multitude, to the Shedding of her Innocent Blood; swelling of her Eyes, and tearing off and taking away her Clothes: And in that barbarous and immodest Manner, they endeavour'd to have dragged her to a Pond, and thrown her in; but were prevented: Yet after all this Cruelty was she committed (by *J. Knight (that errant Persecutor)* to *Bridewell*, and from thence to *Newgate*, where her Illness dangerously increasing upon her, she was carried out; but within three Days died.

Secondly, Boniface Norris of *Cambridge*, being near *Eighty Years* old, broken and decay'd in *Body*; not able to travel on Foot, was riding to a Meeting on a First-day, about two Miles from his House, was stopt by Constables and others, who demanded Money of him for Riding that Day, which he refusing; *Dudly Pope*, call'd a Justice, caused him to be brought to the Sessions, and there fined him 10 s. which because he denied to pay, he was flung into Prison: And his old Wife for refusing the Payment of five Pounds, which the same Pope unjustly fined her, for

only

only speaking to the Priest of *Ower*: And so both kept from their poor Family; the old Man falling soon Sick, was only turned out of Prison to die.

Thirdly, *Richard Sale* of *Hole*, for declaring against the Wickedness of the *Priest* and *People* in *Chester*, and demanding *Justice* of the *Mayor* upon a rude Fellow of that City, one *Haman Kirks*, who had beaten and bruis'd him, and shed his Blood; was by the Command of that inhuman Mayor, *Peter Leight*, put five Times into a Murdering-press, which is a Hole hewn in a Rock, call'd *Little-Ease*; the first Time eight Hours, the second Time three Hours, the third Time four Hours, the fourth Time four Hours, and the fifth Time five Hours: And the said *Richard Sale* being a Man of a gross Body, could not be prest in under the Force and Strength of four Men, to thrust him; insomuch that two or three of the Times the bruised and crushed Blood gushed out of his Mouth and Nose: The last of the five Times was in the First Month, called *March*, 1657, and in the sixth Month, 1658, he left this Life; during which Time, he was never well in his Body: But those Bruises so mash'd his Body, and caused such un-natural Swellings, as on his Death-Bed he solemnly uttered these Words, *My Blood will be required of yonder Bloody City*; *for* Peter Leight *hath murdered me*.

Fourthly, *George Humble* of *Durham*, an aged Man, for reproving one *George Lilborne*, for persecuting some of his Neighbours for speaking to a Priest, was sent by him to Prison, and there kept a few Days, and died.

Fifthly, *Jane Ingrum*, for going to visit some of her Friends, who were cast into Prison in *Cornwall*, was, by *John Champion*, cast into Prison at *Exeter*, and there kept upon Straw 'till she died.

Sixthly, *Richard Ashburner* of *Gleaston* in *Lancashire*, an old Man, was cast into Prison by Priest *Shaw* of *Aldingham* in *Lancaster* Castle, for Tithes, where after almost two Years cruel Imprisonment, in the coldest of Winter, he died.

Seventhly, *Rebecca Barnes* and *Elizabeth Holme*, within a few Miles off *Armschurch* in *Lancashire*, in Company of divers others, met *David Ellison*, Priest, *and his Wife*, &c. to whom *Elizabeth Holme* speaking a few Words, the *Priest* set his *Wife* upon her, crying, *Down with her, down with* Jezebel; and they knocked her down for dead; and when Capt. *Barnes*, and Capt. *Cubbin*, with others, would have preserv'd her, the Priest's Party took Hedge-stakes, and fell heavily upon them, shedding much Blood; insomuch that *John Barnes* kept his Bed; and *Rebecca Barnes*, by Reason of many Bruises upon her Breast, and elsewhere, took her Bed, and within seven Days died.

Eighthly, *Thomas Broomby*, a poor old Man, and a *Thatcher*, was imprison'd by *Ralph Holingworth*, Priest of *Fillingham* in *Lancashire*, for about Six Shillings Eight Pence, *Tithes*; and because the Goaler finding him to be Meek and Harmless, allow'd him more Liberty than the Felons; the Priest first sent his Son, and then came himself, and charged the Goaler to keep him *Close Prisoner*: The Goaler's Mother asked the Priest, what he meant to do with the poor Man? Would he starve him? He answered, He owes me Money: She said, What is it? and I will pay it. But the Priest, instead of regarding her Proffer, petition'd the Judge of Assize to have the Goaler fined, for letting the poor Man have Liberty to work for his Family; saying, *He deserved to have Irons put on him, and that he would make him an Example*. The Goaler's Mother, who had kept the Goal Fifty Years, said, She never knew any use more Cruelty to a Prisoner, than this Priest did to this poor Man; whom he kept a Prisoner above one Year and five Weeks in the Pit, amongst the Felons, until he died.

Ninthly, *Edward Roberts*, at the Suit of *Lyonel Godrick* Priest, was kept close Prisoner for Tithes, one Year and near an half, during which Time, he was suffer'd to come forth but once, and then presently remanded; nor would they suffer his Friends to see him, not so much as his Wife or Children, above twice or thrice during the long Time, till he sickned: *The Priest threatned, he would make* Roberts *an Example to all, that should deny his Ministry*; saying, *he should lie and rot in Prison, and that it was Pity he, and such as he was, should live in a Common-Wealth*. Yet, notwithstanding, this Ungodly *Pharisee*, had the Man's Body in Prison, to shew himself a Thief, as well as a Murderer, *He took four Horses, worth twenty eight Pounds, for Tithes valu'd at three, and Priest-like, return'd nothing again*. (The like Trick he serv'd his Brother) and as if he had not given Evidence enough of his Unrighteous and Hireling Spirit, he farther adds, *That if there were not a Law to compel his Parish to pay him Tithes, he would chuse to be their Hogherd, rather*

1671.

Chap. VIII.

than their *Teacher*. At laſt, *The honeſt Man was thruſt into a cloſe Hole, where he fell Sick, and in few Days dy'd.*

Tenthly, *Elizabeth Fletcher*, a young Virgin, (by the World accounted of a great Family) *for ſpeaking the Word of the Lord, to the Scholars of* John's *Colledge in* Oxford, *was by them dragg'd to a Pump, where they held her Mouth to the Spout, and pumpt until they had almoſt ſtifl'd her to Death : Then they bound a Cord about her Knees, and ſet her upon her Head, and pumpt her again, uſing many brutiſh and obſcene Words, which 'twere a Shame for any modeſt Perſon to repeat; After this, they ty'd her to one* Elizabeth Levenſe's *Arm, and dragg'd them about the Colledge ; and as not content with this, drove them into a Pool: And to conclude the Tragedy, flung* Elizabeth Fletcher *with ſuch Violence againſt a Grave-Stone, as cauſ'd her to ſpit Blood, which Uſage ſhe complain'd of to her Death.*

It is worthy of our Obſervation, that this aggravated Inhumanity, (at which a gallant *Roman* would bluſh) was acted under the *Vice Chancellorſhip, of Doctor* John Owen, *and Headſhip of his Name-Sake, one* John Owen, *a great* Independent, *being, as I remember, then Head of* John's Colledge

Eleventhly, *John Ceſon,* was in Priſon in *Ipſwich* Goal, for not paying Tithes to one *John Paget* Prieſt of *Oldham*, and one Prieſt *Glanfield*; where being put into a cold, wide, open Room, (much annoy'd with Wind and Smoak) for about three Months, in the coldeſt of Winter, through this cruel Uſage, he dy'd.

Twelfthly, It would be almoſt endleſs to particularize the bloody Sufferings and Cruel Perſecutions, that have been inflicted upon the *Lord's Witneſſes, by that ungodly Generation of Prieſts and Profeſſors,* and therefore I ſhall end my Relation with that notorious, but moſt lamentable Piece of Cruelty, that was inflicted upon our dear deceaſ'd Friend and Brother James Parnel, *by the* Independent *Prieſts of* Great Cogſhall *in* Eſſex, *to the immortal Infamy of them, and the reſt of their Murdering Hypocritical Tribe.* The *Prieſts and People of* Cogſhall, keeping a Faſt, againſt the ſpreading of Error, *James Parnell* came into their Steeple-Houſe, and after they had ended, ſpoke a few Words, *and ſo went out again*; but one *Dionyſius Wakering* call'd a *Juſtice,* follow'd and clapt him on the Shoulder, ſaying, *I arreſt you (without any legal Proceſs)* and by the Inſtigation of divers *Prieſts,* the ſaid *Wakering,* with three more of his Brethren *Injuſtices,* committed him to *Colcheſter Caſtle*; where he was kept cloſe Priſoner in Irons and Chains, Hand and Feet, Day and Night, till brought to *Chelmſford Aſſizes,* at which Time they took off his Chains, to bring him to the Bar, but left his Hands in Irons as before : His Entertainment was like his Commitment, barbarouſly Unjuſt ; For Judge *Hill* did not only incenſe and over-aw the Jury, but partially deny'd him that Liberty of clearing himſelf to his Jury, contrary to *Engliſh Rights* and *Priviledges*; to the Pretence of maintaining of which, did theſe *Independent* Prieſts preach up, and abet the Neceſſity of the King's Beheading, and that Blood-ſhed, which went before and followed it : But the falſe Prophet hath ever been wont to ride on the Beaſt's Back, and therefore we do the leſs wonder, that *Pilate* ſhould be ſo ſubject to the *Jews.*

In ſhort, the Judge fin'd him *Forty Pounds,* and committed him cloſe Priſoner till Payment ; Requiring the Goaler not to admit any of his Friends to him, though they came with Relief: However, the Goaler deny'd not ſuch Entrance, as came to abuſe, Scorn, and beat him ; his Wife has ſet her Man upon him, nay, ſhe her ſelf has not ſpar'd to club him ſeveral Times, ſwearing ſhe would have his Blood : Sometimes they would not ſuffer Victuals to be brought to him ; at other Times they would ſet the Felons to take it from him : They would not ſuffer our Friends to bring him in ſo much as a Trundle-Bed, to lie on ; but cold Stones were his Bed and Pillow too, that in moiſt Weather, would be covered with Water ; and though they extorted four Pence a Night, yet did they threaten, if he did but walk in it ; and as if this were a Place too good for him, they put him into one call'd, *the Hole on the Wall,* which was ſo high, that the common Ladder was too ſhort by ſix Foot ; and when his Friends would have furniſht him with a Cord and Baſket, to receive his Victuals in, they would not ſuffer them ; ſo that he muſt either run the Hazard of his Life, by falling or by ſtarving : At laſt the Lord permitted their murdering Ends, to be in a great Meaſure anſwered ; for, after a long ſuffering in this *Hole,* where nothing preſented, but Miſery to his outward Man, there being neither Air nor Warmth, but a perpetual cold Damp (he being very much benummed in his Joynts) as he was climbing up the Ladder, with his Victuals in one Hand, and catching at the Rope with the other, he miſt the Rope, and fell a very great Diſtance upon the Stones; which Fall ſo exceedingly bruiſ'd and

wounded

wounded his Head, Arms and Body, that they took him up for dead: But the Way they took to cure him was this, They put him into a little low Hole, call'd the Oven (not so big, though something higher than some Baker's) where there was not the least Hole or Window, for any Air to refresh him; nor would they admit of a little Charcoal to warm him: And when he was in a likely Way to recover, (that they might twice murder the same Man) they would not let him take a little Air, to refresh his (almost suffocated) Body, though Bonds and Bodies were offered for his Security, to have him dead or alive, forth-coming: Nay, he did but once step into a close stinking Yard, belonging to the Castle; and for his Punishment, they shut him out all Night, being a cold Winter Season. Their Rage thus encreasing, his Sufferings being daily added to, by their insatiable and malicious Thirst, after his innocent Blood; and seeing his Life could not long continue in that Place and Condition, there was not a little Labour and Means, us'd to lay it before the highest in Authority; yea, more concerning that Man (that his Life might have been saved, and they kept from shedding innocent Blood) than ever was concerning any (if not all) that were imprison'd before him; but no Justice nor Compassion could be found; and though they were particularly told of his Wounds, Weakness, and evil Usage, yet such was the Devilish Instigations of the Priests, they believ'd not till his Death confirmed our Complaints; and then his Persecutors were as busie to cover themselves, as they had been to kill him, as if he had been accessory to his own Death, who, to clear himself of all Guilt, did, to a Couple of our Friends, that then stood by him (for before they admitted none) thus take his Leave of them and the whole World, HERE I DIE INNOCENTLY: This last Expression clos'd the Eyes and Mouth of that Valiant and Faithful Young Man of God, who like young *Habbakuk*, dy'd by the Hands of the Murdering Priests, for boldly declaring the Word of the Lord against their Hypocrisies and Abominations; as his own Book, call'd, *The Fruits of a Fast*, more particularly manifests.

O the Oppression, Envy, Hatred, and Persecution of that *Hypocritical Generation!* How have they stoned the Servants of the Lord, and murder'd his Prophets that he sent forth in his Power, to declare of his Love to the Nations? The Spoils and Robberies they have committed, and the Innocent Blood which they have shed, still cry, how long Lord God, Holy and True, and they yet remain as a dreadful Hand-writing upon the Wall against them.

This is that harmless Man, whom *Jenner*, in Page 157. Reports to have starv'd himself at *Colchester*; to whom did that wicked Crew deny, *What they treacherously pretended before God, Angels and Men, they only sought and fought for*; namely, *Liberty of Conscience, and the free Enjoyment of those Liberties and Priviledges, which are the undoubted Birth-Right of every* English-Man.

And what greater Testimony can any give, of their *Apostacy to the nethermost Pit of Blackest Hell*, than after all those *Vows, Declarations, Remonstrances, Solemn Oaths, Engagements*, and *Protestations* (that the then Rulers and Priests made to God and the poor People) among whom *Taylor* and *Jenner* had their Share) to keep no one Promise with him or them, *as if it had been both their Duty and their End to break them all.*

No Age ever produc't such *National Gigantick Treacheries*, as these; for, such as were once against Tithes, persecuted for them; and those who were for Liberty of Conscience shewed at last, *That they only intended it for themselves*: Thus have these poor Nations been the Stage on which the *Mountebank Priests and Apostatiz'd* Julians, *have acted their several Parts of Self-Interest, Oppression and Revenge.*

' O my Soul! Touch thou not their Secret, neither come within their Dwell-
' ing Place; for they wait, by the Way-Side, in Companies like Robbers, for thy
' Life; and they are fill'd with Cruelty, their Tongues are like Stings of Asps, and
' their Throats as open Sepulchers; they tear off Men's Flesh with their Teeth,
' and suck out the Marrow from their Bones, and chop them for the Caldron:
' Therefore it is, when they cry for Deliverance, the Lord God doth not hear them;
' and when they call upon him for outward Relief, that he hideth his Face from
' them: For, whilst they cry Peace, they bite with their Teeth, and against him
' that putteth not into their Mouths, they prepare War.

This farther I would observe, that the Lord God pursued several of these Persecutors, with his Vengeance, particularly *Wakering*; and they were *Spectacles of Astonishment* to the Countries about them: Nor does *Jenner's* Damnation slumber.

The Conclusion, *by Way of* Exhortation.

Therefore to all you Inhabitants of *Ireland*, or elsewhere, into whose Hands this Book may come, am I constrain'd by the Word of Eternal Life, to send this one short Exhortation, *Obey the Light, that leads out of Darkness: Stand in Awe and Sin not*; *for the Pure and Holy God is Light*; *and if thou wilt have Fellowship with him, thou must not walk in the unfruitful Ways of Darkness: For, to Fear God, that is Wisdom*; *and to depart from Iniquity, that is a good Understanding.* Your Notions of God and Christ will never save you: *It is the Power of an endless Life, that must redeem you*; and whoever are not by it ransom'd from the Power of Sin and Satan, *but rest in the Ways and Worships of this wicked bloody World, they have no Interest in* Christ Jesus, *the Light of the World*; *for he is the Power of God, in them that believe, unto Salvation.* And this I testify in the Name and Authority of the Lord God Almighty, *That another Way there is not to Eternal Peace, than through the powerful cleansing Operation of the Spirit of Truth in the inward Parts:* And blessed art thou, Man or Woman, who knowest Christ Jesus, *the Power, Wisdom, Virtue, and Life of the Father to dwell in thee, and thou in him.* This was *Abel*'s Faith, and *Enoch*'s Way, where the Translation is known, *from under Satan's Power unto God's.* This is the Day of the Revelation of the Mysteries of God's Kingdom; for the Spirit is pour'd forth, and the Anointing is come, and the Days of Refreshment from the Presence of the Lord are known: *Let the Mouth of the dumb Shepherd be stopt, and let the Hireling hold his Peace*; *neither go you out after his Voice any more, that makes a Prey upon you, and eats you as a Man eateth Bread*; *but know, that the Covenant of the Lord is with you, if you believe and obey*; *and your Iniquity shall be done away, and your Transgressions remembred no more*; *and Heavenly Bread will he give you in your Houses, and Living Waters will he cause to spring in your own Wells*; *and great will be your Peace.* But if you will not hearken to the Voice of the True Shepherd within you, that leads out of all Unrighteousness, nor to the Testimonies of the Sheep of his Pasture, whom he sends forth among the Wolves of this Generation, but withstand the Day of your Visitation, and Gathering into the Heavenly Fold, (*chusing rather to wander abroad upon the barren Hills and desert Mountains, as Sheep without a Shepherd (wherever the Wolf of Persecution comes) feeding upon Shadows, Notions, and Husky Professions, which give no Nourishment unto a Dominion over Sin, nor sensible Assurance of Life and Peace Everlasting*; *but under all which, Envy, Hatred, Backbiting, Lying, Swearing, Drunkenness, Uncleanness, the Love of this World, and slavish Fear of Men do live and reign*) your Portion shall be with them for ever, who said of Old unto God, *Depart from us, for we desire not the Knowledge of thy Ways*; *and in your Desires shall you cry, but the Lord will not answer*; *and though you seek him, yet will he not be found of you*; *in that Day shall your Peace-speaking Hirelings stand you in no Stead, and the Narrow Coverings of your empty Professions, never be able to hide your Nakedness from the All-seeing Eye of God, the Righteous Judge of Heaven and Earth, who will reward all according to their Deeds done in this Mortal Body.*

O my Friends! That it may never be your Lot to receive the direful Sentence of *Depart from me into Everlasting Burnings*; but that you may have the *Oil of Righteousness in your Lamps* (even the Anointing within you) that when the Bridegroom comes, though at Midnight, you may enter with him to the Marriage-Supper, fill'd with the Oil of Joy and Gladness for evermore.

And as for my own Part, whatever may be the Consequence of this Undertaking, I am resign'd to the Orderings of the Lord, having herein singly sought the Glory of His Name, by the Confutation of the *Adversaries of His Truth, and Information of the mis-led Souls of his Creatures*; that through all the Travels, Labours, and Tribulations, that may attend me, *He only, who made the Heavens and the Earth, and the Fountains of Water, even the God and Father of our Lord Jesus Christ, who hath Redeem'd me, whose Glory I behold, and with whom is my Fellowship in Spirit, may have the Honour, Praise, and Everlasting Dominion, who is God over all, God worthy to be Blessed for ever.* Amen.

From *Newgate* in *London*, where I am a Prisoner for the Word of GOD, and Testimony of JESUS, the 28th of the 4th Month, 1671.

By a Witness of His Eternal Power, against all the deceitful Priests, and Powers of Darkness,

W. P.

An Animadversory Postscript upon Tim. Taylor's Preface.

First, THO' it be no Wonder, that an Old Man should dote, or a *Presbyterianiz'd Independent* be Malicious and Ill-natur'd, yet that *Timothy Taylor* should turn Prefatorian to such an one, whose Politicks he would have us think seldom fail him in all his Actions, I confess a little startles me : *What, at this Time of the Day, when Co-Dissenters, and a whole Flood of prophane Impiety is deluging the Nations, to essay our utter Subversion, and what in him lies to render us the Young Cockatrices of the Country, who are only fit to be kill'd as soon as we are born:* But he gives us this for his Excuse (if it be any) *That whilst some are bending all their Forces against one Error, they ought to take Heed another more pernicious does not grow up* ; (for, saith he) *Little did the Religious Emperor* Constantine, *and his Godly Successors, together with the Holy Pastors, imagine, that while they were opposing the Heresies of* Arrius, Donatus, *&c. in the mean Time they were nursing up Antichrist.* [Preface, p. 1.]

But how this can justifie his Undertaking, or excuse the wretched Contradiction of his first and second Pages, I leave the sober Reader to determine.

'Tis strange to me, That the growing up of a New Error, should be a Reason for not Warring against the Old One, *On whose Legs and Shoulders the New One stands* ; and certainly the Man was not a little besides himself, when he says, *That Religious* Constantine, *and the Holy Pastors Nurst up Antichrist* ; for if they Nurst him with the Best of their Civil and Ecclesiastical Power, (as they most truly did) they can never deserve the Titles of *Religious and Holy from any that are so* ; tho' 'tis Good Reason, *That the Antichristian Off-spring should have kind Apprehensions of their Fathers Fosterers.*

Secondly, But above all Things, that *T. T.* should dare to reckon *Donatus* with the Hereticks of those Times, to whose very Separation from the then Christians, he and his Brethren mostly owe the Model of their *Independent Polity.* [Pag. 2.]

I shall not make it my Business to run through his whole Preface, nor needed he to have writ it, but that he would be busie, though about what was not to the Purpose ; only I shall observe the Intent of the whole, and such particular Passages therein, as more immediately concern us.

He writes a Preface to a Book (from Head to Tail, if it has either) against the *Quakers,* and two Thirds of it are wholly bent against the *Romanists,* in an Historical Way of the Rise and Growth of that *Monstrous Anti-Religion,* wherein he can design but two Things, *Either a shewing of himself that he can read, and is a little skill'd in knowing how to tell a Story* ; or else, *As an Induction to the Anatomizing of* Quakerism ; 'tis hard to say which most wounds his Reputation, for as the first shews him to be Conceited to no Purpose, so the other accuses him of gross Ignorance : For never yet was there a Religion profest, that so effectually struck at *the Root of the Superstitious Splendid Pageantry-Religion of Rome* in this World, as doth our Spiritual Profession. *And that the Jesuits should ever design any Thing so remote and averse from them, to bring People about to them, is a Piece of Ignorance only fit to be credited by such silly Women as* Taylor *and his Brethren lead Captive, who are given up to believe a Lye.* However he proceeds thus:

He says, *That to raise up a New Interest to weaken the rest, is the* Jesuit's *Master-Piece* ; *and that this was that Rapsody of the Heresies of the* Quakers, *which is a proper Medium to the Grand Design ; for they strike at the very Canon of Faith, the Charter of Government.*

I question not, but it is the Design of *Rome* to prosper *her Interest all the World over,* and particularly in these Countries ; but that she should endeavour it by *Mediums,* so opposite to her End, namely, *Conversion to Popery,* as to imploy a People about it, that are as much farther from *Popery,* than *Taylor* ; *as that they disown a settled Ministry, Tithes, Infant-Water-Baptism, Swearing, Steeple-Houses, External and Visible Signs under a Gospel-Administration, the Complements, Fashions, and Customs of the World* ; all highly own'd, venerated, and conform'd to, by *Taylor* and his Brethren. In short, if the Way to bring about *Popery,* be to remove farthest from it, and the high *Road to Papacy,* be to ride fastest from it, we are never like to come justly under his *Canting, Weak, and Beggarly Imputation.* [Pag. 19.]

And if we hold any Heresie, 'tis more than we know, *or than he has Wit and Truth enough to prove* ; but this we confess, *That after the Way which such as he call*

call *Heresie, do we, and will we, Worship the God of our Fathers*. But I would desire all sober Persons to take Notice of that one Pedantick, but Dangerous Phrase, *Of the Canon of Faith being the Charter of Government*; which, if I understand any thing, is this, *That T. T's. Faith only gives Right to Government, and consequently where there is not True Faith in* Taylor's *Sense, he wants but as much Power as such want Faith, to Convince them with the* Romish *Argument, of excluding them the Protection (though not the severest Punishments) of Government*. This one Doctrine is not only what *Jenner* charges upon us, pag. 136, but is that very Principle, *for the Promotion of which, the* Jesuits *are so indefatigable and infamous with most Princes*; for, if the Charter, Bond, and Right of Government stand not on the *Foundation of Common Justice, Reason and Property*, but upon certain abstruse Notions of Faith, *farewel the Security of all States, and Political Societies in the World*. And indeed, the Treacherous Actings of the latter Part of the late Times, did eminently evidence, *How much it was as well his, and his Brethren's Principles to practise, as believe, such Murdering Stabs, and Treacherous Steletto's unto Government*; else, *What meant that Hide-bound* Scottish *Covenant, and* Calviniz'd *Common-Prayer-Book, call'd by the New Name of the* Directory, *and that strait-laced Engagement, and Model of Faith, hatch'd and fledg'd in Eleven Days Time at the* Savoy, *That whoever refus'd Compliance therewith, and Conformity thereto, were to be esteem'd* Hereticks *to the Church, and* Delinquents, *(if no* Traytors*) to the State*; *to whose Door may the Nations lay the* Oliverian *Tyranny, and also that Oppression and Persecution, which Reign'd during his Usurpation of His Master's Authority:* When about Thirty of our Dear Friends were inhumanly murdered, either by Mortal Blows, or Nasty Poysoning Dungeons (not to speak of the Oppressions and Robberies that were then committed by *Taylor's* Brethren, upon many honest Families) for refusing to pay them Wages, that never served them, nor that they ever hired.

By what other Way was the *Republican Model* totally destroyed, than the Treacherous Combinations of the Priests, who feared that the Equity of their Designs that most befriended it, would question their Ministry, at least, abrogate, and finally destroy their *Tithes*, their *Belly*, their *God*? Therefore it was they, *Boniface* like, *assisted to the Murthering of the* Common-Wealth, *(they had so Solemnly Sworn to maintain the Interest of) that they might instal* Oliver *(the English Phocus) the mighty Monarch, that he in Gratitude might Establish them the Great* Dictators of Conscience *in his Territories*. This was their *Moses*, the *Light of their Eyes*, and *Breath of their Nostrils*; Immortal Oliver. *And his* Son, (when he was gone) *the* Good Joshua, *that was to lead them to the Holy Land* (whilst led by the Nose with every Priest-Pedant) *as if like* Solomon, *he were reserv'd from Blood, that he alone might build the Temple to God*. O the unheard of Hypocrisie of that Age! *Sycophants in Grain, enough to poison the whole World with their Flatteries*; *whose Interest was their Conscience, and Power their Religion*; *Devotion only serving to stalk their Stratagems to Promotion:* But the Just G O D hath swept them off the Stage, and their Sun is set, and shall never rise more. And here I shall insert his Distich.

> *He is a Tyrant dy'd in Grain,*
> *Who from the Dunghil comes to Reign.*

I Answer, *Presbyterians* and *Independents*.

> *If He's a Tyrant dy'd in Grain,*
> *That from the Dunghil comes to Reign;*
> *They must be* Traytors *that have been,*
> *So accessory to the Sin:*
> *A Title very fit for them,*
> *That have been False to God and Men,*
> *As* Taylor *and his* Brethren.

Pag. 20.

Fourthly, Yet he would have us think better of him, than to imagine that he should believe, *One* Quaker *in an Hundred is a Dogmatical Formal* Papist; but he believes, *Many* Jesuits *are stalking under them, and Plowing with their Heifers, that once more they may set the Pope's Chair above* Christ's *Throne, and his Mitre above the Crown*.

Here he affords us a little better Quarter than his worthy Brother *Jenner*, who, in pag. 164, and 165, accuses us of a Compliance with the *Papists*, which implying a Kind of Contract, or Confederacy, 'tis utterly impossible we should do it, *and yet not One in an Hundred of us know it*: But as *Taylor* presently after says, *Like* Absolom's *Two Hundred Men, we go out in our Simplicity, and we know not where.* 'Tis strange to me, that such a simple and in-expert People, should be able to manage the profoundest Stratagem of State, that was ever agitated in the World; namely, *The Reversion and Restoration of the Papacy*. Will People sell their Wits? or rather pay such Impostors for robbing them of their Understandings? Can any Thing in Nature be half so ridiculous? 'Tis strange, that Men have not Wit enough to shew their Malice; nor will we accept of his Apology; *we profess to know what we say and do, and utterly renounce his Fig-leaf Garments of our Ignorance*, he, more out of Disgrace than Friendship, would cast over us. These idle Dreams have ever attended any Revolution or Separation in these Nations, since the Reformation: and though Time hath worn them much away, yet *Taylor's* Reproaches upon us, are but the second or third Edition of those the ancient Prelates flung upon the first *Separatists*; so that he must declare himself, either a meer Prelatick; or else, *for shame relinquish their Abuses, and quit plowing our Backs with the Bishop's Heifers*. But I smile at the Man's Folly, That he cannot be contented to endeavour to lash others, but he must whip himself too: Who ever found the *Quakers* aspiring to either *Mitre* or *Crown*? But has not *Taylor's* restless Gang done both? *Were not the* Babylonish Tythes, *and* Antichristian Benefices, Pleasant, Good, *and* Christian Conveniencies, *when they got them; and that Crown, once of the fourth* Monarchy, *and Image, that was to be destroyed, a goodly Ornament upon the Head of a* Private Person *devoted to their Interest?*

Fifthly, He ventures to tell a Story of a Jesuit, *That was discovered to have preacht at the* Bull-and-Mouth *in* London, *as a* Quaker, *by a Person in company with his Friend that told it him; and that the Jesuit confest his Order to him, but conjur'd him Silence,* &c.

To which I shall say no more but this, That he should either have told us his Friend's Name, that we might have fairly enquired into the Matter; or else, have held his Tongue: It being neither Christian nor Manly to shoot People in the dark, to accuse, and not bring the Accuser forth; I therefore charge him to tell us who they were that made this great Lye, or I shall post him for a Lyar.

But because that scruple may be removed from the Minds of simple People, let them know, *That there is not one, who is in the Lord's Work, esteem'd by us a Minister of the Gospel, that we do not know him, his Family and Dwelling, which ought to satisfie all Minds in doubt concerning us.*

Sixthly, He says, *That one came from the* Pope, *with personal Unction, to preach Notions in* England, *who joyned with the* Antipedo-Baptists; *and in his preaching expounded* Luke 17. 21. *The Kingdom of Heaven is within you* (that is) *not without you in Forms and Ordinances*.

To which I answer, That (though I have reason enough to question the Story, because of the great Lye I saw under *Timothy Taylor's* own Hand, about the River *Band* in the North Part of *Ireland* (representing that as a *presaging Miracle of strange and prosperous Revolutions* (perhaps to his Dianian *Independency*) which was but an ordinary and customary Efflux of the River, as well as that the *Antipedo-Baptists* are high Denyers of the Doctrine preach'd by the *Jesuit*; and therefore far from complying with them.) I do not know that it is criminal to hear or receive Truth from any Body, and such I esteem that Doctrine: For, I boldly affirm, *That the Kingdom of God consists of what can never perish with the using, as all External Things must undeniably do:* And till T. T. has more *Sense, Judgment,* and Religion to confute me; I am like to rest in the same Opinion I have of him, and my own Belief.

Seventhly, But he is very angry with *Samuel Fisher,* For (says he) *I would fain know of any rational Man living, if any probable Reason can be rendred, why the* Pope *and his Cardinals, should be so indulgent to Mr.* Samuel Fisher, *the* Quaker, *(who was formerly a Man well esteemed of for his Gifts in his Country) he travelled to* Rome, *bore his Testimony there against them, and yet they would not suffer him to be medled with.*

This

1671.

This Story was coyn'd in Hell, by his learned conceited Mr. *Danson*; for tho' *S. F.* was at *Rome*, yet did he not only leave his own Country to deliver a Message there, (his Voyage extending much farther) and that he bore his Testimony at *Rome* is most true, which *Taylor* never did, nor dares to do; whilst he has not Arms for his Succour, or some Garrison to his Relief; a poor white-livered Chaplain, that rather knew how to flatter away the Booty of his Regiment after a Prey; and dissemble them out of the Tythes of their Hard-gotten Spoils, by his hired *Thanksgivings*.

But he adds, *Could a Protestant Minister have given his Testimony against the Pope in* Rome, *and escaped the Inquisition?* Which he supposes a great Discovery of our Confederacy.

To which I will only tell him, That perhaps the *Pope* was satisfied, we intended not his Temporal Kingdom; and he knew his Iniquities had so long since forfeited his Share in an Heavenly one, as he was not at all solicitous to mind that, or those that did; but having well experienced the killing Principle of the *Protestant*, and that therein he was a Pig of his own Sow, he seemed resolv'd not to fledge his Young with the Feathers pluck't out of his own Wings.

But I dare undertake, if there must be a Pope till *Taylor* and his Fraternity go to *Rome* to convert him or his, their Expectations of possessing the pleasant Gardens of *Italy*, will be certainly frustrated: No, They have better learnt Self-security; the *Inquisition must first be down, a good Stipend ingaged, and an Army for Security, before they will trust their Skins in a* Cardinal's *Clutches*. All the Difference I know betwixt them, is this, That *Taylor* and his Gang have the more seeming Religious Way of Cheating of the two; the former being grown almost out of Date.

In short, *S. F.* escaped their Prisons, as he did yours at home, by the Power and Providence of the Lord, that carried him over the Heads of *Pope, Cardinals, Presbyterians,* and *Independents* too: Had the *Quakers* been *Papists*, they had not been put to Death at *Paris* and *Rome*, as they were.

Eighthly, He says, Mr. *Fisher, in the Conference with learned Mr.* Danson, *affirm'd, That Good Works are the meritorious Cause of our Justification, which he calls, the Pope's Chappel Divinity, and a Cockatrice springing out of the Root of a* Romish *Serpent*.

But such is our Unhappiness, that whil'st we are despised for Idiots, and Men altogether ignorant and incult, we meet with such Cavilists, or down-right Pedants, as that the *very Words we use must not import their common Sense, lest they should miss of an Objection against our clearest Truths*.

I would have him know, that the *Learning, Honesty, and Christian Spirit of our dear Friend,* S. F. *are not to be added to, or diminished from, by all their utmost Endeavours* (neither of them being his Match in those very Things that did bespeak him exquisitly dextrous in their own Schools.)

The Word *Merit*, so much snarl'd at, allows a two-fold Signification; the first, *A Proportion or Equality betwixt the Work and Wages*, which is the strictest Sense, and that which he least of all intended; the second, *Something that may be said to procure*, and in some Sense *to deserve or obtain*, and so Good-works do: Since without them *there is no Acceptance with God, nor Title to Life Everlasting*.

Ninthly, As for his Comparison of us with his Country-man, *John Wilson* of *Cheshire*, about the Year 1646. *Who* (he says) *was bewitched, and after many Exorcisms*, particularly of his Reverend Brother *Samuel Eaton*, (whom God cut off soon after his Book of Lyes was printed against) his Partner by turns in the Duty of the Day) *was compleatly delivered, when he himself was calling upon God*.

But I have this Reason to give, why we are not under this Possession; *for neither are we guilty of those diabolical Instances of Rage and Fury, as he expresseth; nor is he able to deliver us (if possest) but rather turns Devil himself; at least, stands in need of the same Exorcism to eject that foul Spirit of slander, which pestilentially raigns in him*.

But to pass by his telling us how much more effectual his Prayer was than all the rest (nay than his very reverend Brother *Eaton's* too) which I have great Cause to question, whilst he remains possest with the filthy Spirit of pleading for Sin Term of Life, Persecution, Tythes, and the rest of that Complexion) I would gladly know the *English* and Sense of the Gifts of Tongues being the Gift of God, and

and yet the Gift of the Devil too, as in *Wilson*, &c. Have they the same Gift too? Are we denied by him to have the Gift of Tongues, because God will not work Miracles to confirm our Lyes? and yet can he say in the same Page, That *Wilson* spoke *Hebrew, Greek*, and *Latin* (though unlearned) *by Reason of a Diabolical Possession:* But besides, if the Devil has such Power over those Tongues *(the first called sacred, because the Jews; and the second not less esteemed so, because of the New Testament* (so called) I would gladly know how *Taylor* can tell when they are given of God, and when of the Devil; or whether the Scripture can give him such an immediate Power of discovering, or something more intrinsick and spiritual to distinguish; the Words are the same (that is, 'tis *Hebrew* and *Greek* still) of which the Scripture may judge; but by his own Confession, the Spirits are not: and who shall judge of their Differences? Certainly this overthrows all the Attempts those Men have made against *Inspiration* and *Revelation*; wherein they forgot, that 'tis a grand Charge that the *Friendly Debate* lays against their whole Tribe, as being both Assertors and Preachers of the same; and that it was that kind of Doctrine which first drew from the Church of *England*, into the present Novelisms and Incertainty: 'Tis strange, that what was a main Pillar in the *Independent* Building, should be a rotten Post in ours: But as the Things of God knows no Man, but the Spirit of God; so the Scriptures not being that Eternal Spirit, *the Spirit, and not the Scriptures, is the Rule of Knowledge in all Divine and Spiritual Things.*

Tenthly, He prays the Lord, *To anoint our Eyes with Eye-salve, that we may see our Heresie is but of Yesterday, they began in* Lancashire *in the Year* 1652. *whereas God hath had a Church and People to himself all along, during the Kingdom of the Dragon; and the Gates of Hell, as they have not, so shall they never prevail against it.*

But as the Hope of the Hypocrites shall perish, and the Prayer of the Wicked is an Abomination, so is his Prayer nothing but Lyes and Contradiction; for neither was our visible Beginning (or rather Restauration) in *Lancashire*, in fifty two: nor can he prove such a Church-Succession as he asserts; if there was, I ask what it was in *Constantine*'s Time, and his Successors? Not the Arrians, Donatists, &c. says *T. T.* Not *Constantine*, and his *Bishops*, say I (unless *Antichrist's Nurses were the Church of Christ and Heavenly Spouse)* let him in his next tell us how to reconcile so much Nonsense and Opposition.

But where did he find his diminutive *Independency?* How many Years before *Burton?* (whom I name with no Disreputation (*his Day considered*) Was there such a Church-Policy during the *Apostacy?* If not, I have Dr. *Owen* against Dr. *Caudery* (as they call them) *to prove all others were in the Apostacy: And where was this pure Primitive Church then?*

And if *T. T.* did not dread the civil Power, he would say (as he dares to think) *That the Gates of Hell have lately prevailed against his beloved* Independency.

Eleventhly, But he proceeds to pray, *That leaving our Idol, the Light within, we would try all Principles by the Scriptures; that so they may be built upon the Foundation of the Apostles and Prophets, Christ being the chief Corner-stone.*

But what can be more dark and stupid, than this Man's Request? (not to esteem the Scriptures, for those we respect, but the Idleness of the Man is most notorious) *If there be but one Foundation, and that be the Scriptures;* then what Foundation had Moses; the Prophets and Apostles, that were some before the Old, and others before the New Testament (so called) was writ? Besides, can Christ be the chief Corner-Stone of so many dead Letters, in which are no Stones at all, much less Living Stones? But *T. T. errs, not knowing the Scriptures, nor the Power of God.*

Twelfthly, Says he, *O That he that is the True Light, that lighteth every Man that cometh into the World* (that is, *Natural Men with Natural Light, and Spiritual Men with Spiritual Light*) *would enlighten these poor deluded Souls, to see that 'tis in vain for them to attempt the Subversion of Gospel Ministry and Ordinances, which, maugre all Opposition that Devils and* Quakers *can make, must remain.*

One would think he were very zealous, and I should believe so too, did but his Zeal run parallel with his Weakness: I am ashamed that any Man should quote Christ for a Natural Light; nay, I pity, whilst I must reprove, him for his Blasphemy; for if Christ, as the Light of the World, enlightens with a Natural Light, then *is He a Natural Light*; becaufe fuch as is the Effect, fuch muft the Caufe be, and no Fountain fends forth Streams of diftinct Waters: *In Him was Life:* What? Divine or Natural? Both I grant, as he was God, and as he took Flefh; yet as there underftood, It was a Divine Life; for it was his Life, as the Word and Godhead himfelf; therefore an Invifible, Spiritual and Intellectual Light: Thus the Words following fhew, *And that Life was the Light of Men*; which if faid properly of his Natural Life, were moft untrue; for he being vifibly withdrawn, all Natural Light would be withdrawn too: but if fpoken of his Divine Life (as moft truly and properly it was) then was the Light not Natural, but Divine. Nay, it ftands farther to Reafon; for the Difpenfation then to be erected was not a Natural, but a Spiritual one; and confequently the Light of that Difpenfation, not Natural, but Spiritual: Befides, I wonder with what Confidence any Man can impeach us of Neglect of Scripture, who in that very Reproach, ftrays from the fimple Phrafe of it: Does that Scripture fay, *That is, Natural Men with Natural Light, and Spiritual Men with Spiritual Light*, as he has additionally expreft? Let him know this, and we will ftand to it, That there is, properly but One Natural and One Spiritual Light; the latter is Chrift Jefus, the former the vifible Sun; all other ufes of the Word are borrow'd, and Metaphorical.

Thirteenthly, He concludes thus, *O that God would fill their Hearts with Trembling for their Scoffing at Chrift, as* Mr. Samuel Clark *did to me, I believe thy* Chrift *is above the Clouds*; *and as* Thomas Lawrech *faid to Mr.* Caffin.

Indeed I had thought thefe two Petulant Scriblers had agreed better in their Teftimony; for one fharply reproves us for Trembling, calling it by a Name no lefs offenfive that that of Witchcraft; and the other as earneft feems to pray, that we might fear and tremble.

As for *Caffin*'s Story, it has been anfwered again and again; though I wonder he fhould quote an *Antipedo-Baptift*; for ought he knows, the Man's a Jefuit (I am confident he has Malice, if he had but Wit enough to be one) befides, there is no fuch Man as *T. Lawrech*, his Name is miftaken.

And for *Samuel Clark*, he has told me himfelf, that no Man us'd more Craft to infinuate and work upon him, than *T. T.* and when he found he was no Fifh for his Net, but rebuk't his Hypocrifie, Envy, and Covetoufnefs; then 'twas, and not before, that he broke forth into his Wild and Hateful Accufations againft both him, and all that feemed never fo little inclined to the Ways of Truth.

Fourteenthly, To conclude, I wonder with what Confidence he dares to come out in Print againft us, who, being fairly challenged by Me, (with the Man in the tall black Cloak, and the reft that befpatter'd us of all Perfwafions, as holding damnable Errors;) avoided it, by refolving rather to run the hazard, of not proving their Calumnies, than Thin their Flocks, and lofe their own Reputation, by the dint and foyl of a fair and open Difputation: 'Tis true, that *T. T.* and his Brother *Maddir*, would have met me privately (at leaft, they talk't fo to me by Proxy) but till I thought it probable, That a Tradef-man would be difwaded from a full Cuftom, I had no Reafon to embrace it, and therefore wholly waved any private Conference; knowing how far, in their Reports, they would have fmother'd and over-lay'd the Truth, to their Advantage, and great Difcredit of her Friends.

But if he, or any elfe, will pleafe to give a fair, full, and free hearing of the Points in Controverfie; we never will baulk fuch an Appointment (though it be irkfome to us, as Men, to combat every inconfiderable Wrangler, that hath no more Wit than to abufe what he does not underftand) But through the Affiftance of the Lord's Power, we fhall maintain our fo much reproached Principles (to be the Truth, as it is in Jefus) againft the quainteft Stratagems, and fouleft Imputations of our Enemies. For, whatever fome are pleafed to think or fay of us, we are engaged in God's Caufe, and nothing but the *Zeal of his Houfe conftrains us* (beyond our natural Temper, or Regard to this World) *thus boldly to ftem the Tides of all Oppofition, and never to turn our Backs upon the Truth, or flee the fierceft of her Adverfaries*;

For our Reward is Life Everlafting.

Newgate in *London* the 29th of the 4th Month, 1661.

W. P.

THE
Spirit of TRUTH Vindicated;
Againſt that of
ERROR and ENVY;
Unſeaſonably Manifeſted in a late Malicious LIBEL intituled,

The Spirit of the Quakers *Tried,* &c.

By a Friend to Righteouſneſs and Peace, W. P.

Ever Learning, and never able to come to the Knowledge of the Truth.
But Evil Men and Seducers ſhall wax worſe and worſe, deceiving and being deceived, 2 Tim. 3. 7, 13.

But unto you that fear my Name, ſhall the Sun of Righteouſneſs ariſe, with Healing in his Wings : And ye ſhall tread down the Wicked ; for they ſhall be Aſhes under the Soles of your Feet, Mal. 4. 2, 3.

To the Impartial READER.

I *Have at laſt, with ſome Difficulty, obtained a ſmall Reſpite, from more ſerious Affairs, to the Examination of a late Diſcourſe, intituled,* The Spirit of the Quakers tried, *according to that Diſcovery it hath made of it ſelf in their great Prophet and Patriarch,* George Fox, &c. *And whilſt I was willing to inform my ſelf of the Deſign and Temper of the Author, by a very careful Peruſal of his Book, (at leaſt, expecting ſomething that might pretend to claim a Reputation in Controverſy, excelling all other of our Adverſaries, (who never ſtruck higher than at our Doctrines) whilſt this Man ventures to tell the World what Spirits we are of) I find him in Reality filled with nothing, but* diſingenious Reflection, empty *Stories, and* unprofitable Cavils, *about a few Scriptures, he moſtly confeſſeth, that but one of us hath miſ-cited, either in Reference to a diſorderly Quotation of the Words, or an unſuitable Application of them.*

My Judgment I then made of the Man, and ſtill continue in, is this : Had he not wonderfully loved being Somebody in Print, he needed not to have given himſelf or other People the Trouble of ſo many unſerviceable Sheets ; nor a ſmall trifling Solicitor for their kind Reception in the World, the Toil of ſo much Inſinuation, even to Nauſeating. *But I deſign not to be long, and therefore ſhall briefly contract my Exceptions againſt the Author, to the Reader, into theſe four Particulars.*

1672.

1. *Then*, *He hath behaved himself the most unjust of any that ever yet undertook to write against us*; which so ill becomes a Man that would reform others, that it rather incenseth all worthy Minds, and is Reason enough to beget a Jealousy, both of the Truth of his Cause, and his own Honesty: For who (truly Just) would draw a general Charge from a particular Failing (in Case it were so?) And what good Christian would stigmatize an entire Body for the Defects of any individual Member?

He finds Fault with George Fox, and, to be revenged of him, bespatters a whole Society; so that if I should grant him all he would have against that Person, (whom I doubt not to defend from his base Abuse) yet why he should place his Infirmities (suppose them such) to our Account, cannot be resolved me by any that is not willing to suffer for other Men's Faults.

George Fox, he thinks, has miscited a Scripture, Ergo, —— He is an Impostor, and the *Quakers* a Pack of Hereticks:

It is after this lofty Manner of Disputing, he undertakes our Overthrow; but if this be arguing, the Man is Orthodox with a Witness, and deserves the Chair, *Nemine Contradicente*.

2. *My Second Exception is*, That if he had been provoked to any hard Thoughts against George Fox, from the perusal of his Book, it had been handsome, and well-becoming a Christian to have visited that so much mistaken Person (in his Account) and have endeavoured, either a better Understanding of him, or his better Information in the Scripture; and not (at a Juncture, when he might understand him to be at so great a Distance as America) exhibit an angry Charge against him in England. But his Generosity here, is much like to his Reason elsewhere.

3. But why, above all *Times of the World*, does the Man chuse the present Season, to shower down his Displeasure against us; just when we should make the best of an unexpected Toleration, to the Refreshment of our afflicted Minds and Bodies, by the late Persecutions that have been? What! Is he angry that we have Liberty, or does he think that none deserve it but himself? I wonder what *Testimony* there had been, or how few to have received a *Liberty of Conscience*, if the *Quakers* had squared their Carriage in the Storm, according to his sordid creeping into Holes and Corners, or else, to publick Places of Protection.

And if he tells us, that he had no Mind to add to our Troubles, he deals deceitfully; for as it is almost impossible for him to write against us, but he must expressly or implicitly contradict the avow'd Principles of the Church, by his scatter'd Seeds of Socinianism, so knowing the Danger that would ensue such Undertakings, as well as the Difficulty of Printing, his Self-Safety, and not Charity to us, was the Hindrance.

4. *And Lastly*, But why was he asham'd of his Name? (I cannot but make his own Words good by such an Inquiry (without concluding him a Prophet) and great Reason there is that we should ask him a Reason for it, if we may lawfully ask that which his whole Discourse seems to character him a Stranger to; for since he tells us, That he declines all Ways of Controversy with us, but that of *Matter of Fact*; however able we may be to clear our selves from such Indictments, yet our Ignorance of his *Name* deprives us of that Scope we might otherwise have, for producing (perhaps) as large a Catalogue of Doctrinal Mistakes, in what he himself, or those to whom he adheres have writ, *as he hath of verbal Ones out of any Writings belonging to the People call'd* Quakers. And though he seems to excuse the Absence of his Name, by that Occasion he pretends we take to abuse our Adversaries: Yet the truest Reason is a Consciousness of a disingenious and unjustifiable Practice in himself; perhaps he also was afraid of such Truth as may be seasonably told of him, to the discrediting of his Enterprize: But 'till he had been so served by us, it had become him not to have reproached us, in the Vindication of other Men, in whose Opinions he will by no Means allow himself to be concerned otherwise than to explode them for Heretical: *Thus the Man's for any Game*; he cares not whom he defends, if he can but have his End upon the Party he designs to mischief; sometimes he will be a Church-man against a Non-conformist, and back again; sometimes either, against a Quaker; then for him, against them both; and lastly, a Socinian against them all: *His seeming Labours against us for common Principles, being but a ploughing our Backs with their Heifers*, for the Promotion of his Biddlean or Socinian Cause; which Owl-light Way of stabbing Men, or deceiving People under the Livery of every Perswasion (whilst for none of them) is very

remote

remote from being either *Christian* or *Manly*; nor will the Righteous God of Heaven and Earth bless or prosper such ignoble, clandestine Projects, and mask'd Attempts, as our Adversary, and his small Cabal, are plentifully guilty of.

'*Tis true, I cannot say all are equally concealed in their Endeavours against us*; for when the Man has writ and printed his Book, there is a small Cryer of his, that like an eager officious Broker, runs to and fro to disperse it, most commonly known by Smelling; his Breath smelling of such foul Epithets as, Knave, Puppy, Fool, Rascal, Loggerhead, Cheat; *which with much more of the same loathsome Scent he is pleased to bestow upon* George Fox, as a necessary Introduction to our Adversary's Confutation of his Book.

Certainly, Reader, we have little Cause to esteem these Men, the Restorers of Paths to dwell in, Defenders of the true Religion, and Tryers of other Men's Spirits, *who give such little Proof of the Knowledge of their own*, as to be wanting in the very Alphabet or first Principle of Common Civility.

But, Reader, I will not longer detain thee in an Epistle, whatever Variety of Matter I may have to invite me; hoping that the ensuing Discourse will abundantly satisfy thee in those very Things for which our Adversary thinks us most unfit of all to be believed.

I have not given my self the common Range that other Writers do; *few caring to buy, and fewer to read large Discourses*; but as the Matter did briefly and naturally rise upon every Head, without any other Artifice or Dress, it is presented to thee. I omit more than an Hundred Things, that would engage to personal Reflection; for my Soul hath no Pleasure in striving therein, as knowing the Inconsistency of that uncharitable virulent Temper with a Christian Spirit, which I am assured is quite another Thing, from what is Verbose, Abusive, Cavilling, Airy, and meerly Notional; which had our Adversary duly considered, he would have found it more his true Interest to have liv'd in a daily Subjection to the pure Grace that brings Salvation, and have kept his Mind diligently exercised therein, to the perfecting Holiness in the Fear of the Lord, than thus to exalt himself against an inoffensive People; but I leave all with God, whose Will be done; recommending thee (Reader) to his Holy Witness in thy Conscience, to be by that alone Condemned or Justified in this Apologetical Undertaking.

WILLIAM PENN.

The Spirit of Truth Vindicated, &c.

I Cannot but esteem it a peculiar Providence of Mercy, from the most High-God, *to us his most despised People*, though an Instance of great Unkindness in our Adversary; that after our several Years Pressure, *under the heavy Calumnies of being involved with a Socinian Confederacy*, he should so suffer it to come to pass, that without the least Provocation given on our Parts, *one of that Sort of Men, should become our Compurgator*, indeed our best Advocate in Pleading against us; for whilst he goes about to detect the *Quakers* of an erroneous Spirit, *it is to be supposed that he denies them any Share in his*; *and therefore no* Socinians. I hope whatever comes of this Debate, we shall no longer suffer for being what we are not; it would be hard, that we should both be condemned for *Socinians*, and then abused for refusing to be so: Let them not be offended with me; if I use the Word; *It's not from any Undervalue of the Man they take it from, nor out of any Reproach to them*; but only as a Word of Difference to distinguish Persons or Perswasions by.

And without any other Prologue or Introduction, I shall descend to the Book it self.

§. 1. First then, he is pleased to allow us, at least, a great many among us, *To be Honest-Hearted, yet wonderfully deluded, and very dangerous to Christian Religion.* I confess it is no Wonder, when Men will make themselves Work, and rather than want it, bestow their Cavils at the Truth it self, that they should fall into strange and impertinent Contradiction; but that any Man pretending so highly to Reason and Religion, should shew so little Understanding in either, as to conceive that a

Man

1672.

Man can be *properly Honest-Hearted*, and yet deluded, and dangerous to the *Christian Religion*; I confess is beyond my Skill to reconcile.

I desire, God knows, *to be the Honest-Hearted Man, and let him take the rest to himself*: For that which reduces Man (*fallen short of the Glory of God*) to an Honest Heart, and a Life good and laudable, as our Adversary speaks of us, *must be the Grace of God, through Jesus Christ our Lord, and not another Thing*; and consequently, *who has that, is not deluded, nor dangerous to the* Christian Religion.

Pag. 1.

§. 2. *If we excel in all Things*, as he confesseth; which is to say, that there are but few Things wherein we don't transcend all others; how possibly can we be dangerous and dishonourable to the *Christian Religion*, among the few Things, wherein we are supposed wanting, which is the main Thing of all? If so, *What are the many?*

Pag. 1. 2.

§. 3. It was ill done, and an Aggravation, not only of his Uncharitableness and Incivility, but his great Injustice and Deceit, to refuse us his Name, upon a Pretence of avoiding a Subject for our Personal Reflection, *whilst both his Beginning and End is an entire Abuse, against our Persons and Practices*.

And what he owns Praise-worthy in us, is not because he would be honest to us; but that he might by paying us our Due, in lesser Matters, *the more plausibly rob us of our Right, to what is of more weighty Importance*, namely, The true Life and Doctrine of Christianity, which shews how little a Share he has of either.

§. 4. Nor does he less, than palpably bely us, in telling the World, We condemn all Virtuous Persons whatsoever, if not of our own Perswasion; since we never held nor defended any other, than the Principle of Virtue (there is *none good but one, and that is God*) and *such as are in all Circumspection conformable to him, those we esteem our best Friends*; our Controversie with the World, not being about dark, abstruse, unprofitable Notions, nor Contests about Words; but *Men's being so rich in Profession, and so barren in Obedience*; they saying, they will go, and they do not; praying, thy Will be done, and they never set about to do it; which Will is their Sanctification, through the Eternal Spirit, if they would obey the convincing Light thereof, in their own Consciences; since it was given, that all might be convinced of Sin; and in being converted and led by it, *they might be adopted Children of God, and Heirs of his Glory*.

Pag. 2.

§. 5. Christ's Person (which he prejudicially says we deny) is (strictly considered) an unscriptural Expression; for that Place which seems most to countenance such a Way of Speaking, viz. 2. *Cor.* 2. 10. Is to be understood, and may and ought to be rendred, *for Christ, by Christ's Authority, instead of Christ, in Christ's Presence, on his Account*, or the like: and it ill becomes a Man to write against others, for perverting of Scriptures, whilst himself is manifestly guilty of the same Defect. We reverently confess to *Christs Appearance*, both in Flesh and Spirit; and when called to it, *shall be as ready, Hearty and Christian* (God assisting) *in our Confession of the same, as to the Beginning, Progress and End of that blessed Manifestation, as the Person who accuses us*. But we dare not say, *That the intire Christ was that visible Body that was crucified*; as believing (with the Scripture) most sincerely, *that he that took upon him the Seed of* Abraham, *according to the Flesh, was, and is, and is to come, God over all blessed for ever*: Which Perswasion, I know to be most Heretical in this Adversary's Apprehension, and no Part of his *Biddlean Creed*.

Pag. 2.

§. 6. His Darkness, *in reflecting upon our Heaven within us, denying us to have a due Regard to Things above on Christ's Right-Hand*, is as thick as *Egypt's*; for if God's Presence makes the Heaven, as we have been always taught, and all have believed and confest, then, since God vouchsafes to *Temple and Tabernacle in Men*, it follows, that his *Heaven is there also*: But certainly this Conceited Man fancies with Sottish *Reeve* and *Muggleton*, and the vain *Anthropomorphites* of old, *That God's in the Shape of a Man, and that Heaven is a Visible Place to be liv'd in*, bearing some Resemblance to this *Visible World*; which characters him more *Mahometan* than *Christian*; otherwise he could never be so stupid or malicious, as to conceive, that because we assert a Divine and Heavenly Enjoyment of God's Presence within us, *therefore we deny Christ the Dignity of his Father's Right-Hand above us*, or that there is no such Thing, *As setting our Affections on Things that are above*: What can be more dark and ignorant than this Man's Inference?

Pag. 2.

§. 7. But he farther tells us, *That though we are much to be commended for our Courage and Patience, yet we are highly to be discommended for our Superstition and gross Ignorance*. I dare warrant, the Man is highly opinionated of this fine gingling Phrase: But it's beyond the Ken of his greater Knowledge (as he thinks) to

vindicate

vindicate his own Expression from Folly and Inconsistence, as well as justifie his Abuse of us thereby: For I utterly deny, *That any Man can be much commendable for his Religious Courage and Patience* (Divine Gifts) *and yet be superstitious and grosly ignorant*; for the Day is not an Effect of Light, *more than Heat, Passion, Persecution, Frowardness and Precipitation, are the proper and natural Fruits of Superstition and gross Ignorance:* But such as have done the Will of God, have need of Patience: Why, because it works Experience, and that Hope which makes not ashamed, nor afraid; the want of which, made this Man, with the rest of his Serpentine Associates, creep and cringe to this and the other conforming Chaplain (friendly to their Faith) as the *Mountains and Rocks that were only able to cover in the gloomy Day of severe Inquisition after, and Persecution upon the despised* Quakers; this is the Meaning of his following Words, *Whereby you expose your selves in great Part to those Labours and Hazards you undergo*; to render which into better *English*, thus, That because you will walk in a *Way not conformable to the World, too severely press a* Christian Life, *as that without which you deny all Possibility of Salvation*, particularly in keeping your Meetings, *not forsaking the assembling of your selves together*; and refusing to acquiesce in the Obedience of those Laws about Oaths and Tithes, and sometimes going to hear a Sermon, to prevent Excommunication, and the Brand of Phanaticism, or Separation, with the like *Convenient Prudent Actions*, you do unnecessarily run your selves into Sufferings, and bring upon you what you might with Christian Policy and Discretion, secure your selves from.

And if he denies my Comment, I am able to prove it upon better Terms, than he can our Superstition and Ignorance; for with him and his Brethren, *to think Practice more necessary than Notion, is want of Discretion; and to be Plain in the Profession of our Faith, and Constant, is the Superstition and Headiness he chargeth us with.*

§. 8. But he promiseth for the future to decline this Way of Procedure, and withal, *To avoid the Use of both Scripture and Reason, in that our Leading-Men have so ordered the Matter, that we refuse our Ear to the most demonstrative Arguments against us, and embrace the weakest Reason on our Side.*

I will not give him the *Lye*, but I hope he will not say I am uncivil or unchristian, if I tell him, he has already contradicted himself, and broke his Word with us; for within eight Lines, he that Promised *To relinquish all Personal Reflection, and proceed to his Business, in the next Sentence lays to our Charge a greater and more unjustifiable Crime, than what he left off with before, by how much it is worse to refuse Information when clearly given, than to be so grosly ignorant as to need it:* What fair Dealing we may expect from a Man not just to us, no, not to himself eight Lines together, let the sober Reader judge.

§. 9. But when did any of our Leading-Men, as he is pleased to call them, refuse this *Idle Boaster*, indeed a *very Dreamer*, such Sober, Rational Conference, in Publick or Private, by Personal Discourse or Writing, as might be to Edification? They were never the Men that deny'd it on those Terms, wherein it might redound to such Christian Advantage, as should be principally aimed at in the like Exercises.

§. 10. And for accepting the *Weakest Reason that is on our Side*, I shall only say, That so very Grateful is the lowest Degree of Reason to us, wheresoever we find it, that we can no more deny it, or occasionally refuse our selves the Use of it, than the greatest, since it's being so does not unreason it, or render it no Reason in it self; though confessedly a less Degree of Reason: Nor is it possible that the meanest Appearance of Reason can withstand the greatest, since Reason always acknowledgeth and owneth her self in what Degree so ever she meets: *It is not Stature that makes a Man, nor Magnitude a Tree or Stone, but the Nature and Property of each.*

And truly we are well contented with our weak Reason (as he is pleased to call it) we know it to be *God's Light, Grace and Spirit of Truth*, that since we gave our Minds intirely to be governed and exercised by it, *We have found that Mortification of Sin and Corruption, that Renewing of Heavenly Divine Life, that Holy Courage and Patience, and it has brought us to so good an Understanding of the Mysteries of God's Eternal Kingdom, and Assurance (as we are faithful to the same) of Everlasting Blessedness*; that 'tis beyond the Power of the Ratling of these Leaves of Charge and Reproach, to scare us from our Standing, or beget the least Question in us us concerning the Certainty of this Pure Unchangeable Way of God, in which we walk; but is invisible to his Vulturous Eye, who so disdainfully writes against it.

I had some Hopes he had done with Personal Contest, at least against the Body; but I find him still in his Reflections, *For whilst you look upon your selves as led by an infallible Spirit (though it be indeed nothing but the Fancy of* G. Fox, *or some other of your Teachers) you must needs reject the clearest Light that God hath given to Men or Angels, when it opposes your Sentiments.*

Though he could scarce say any Thing of us more disingenious and scurrilous, rendring us such deluded Sots, and very Idiots, as to captivate our own Understandings (if he can think we ever had any) to the Dreams and Fancies of a few illiterate Men, *under an Apprehension of being led, not by them, but an infallible Spirit:* Yet since in this one Expression lies wrapt up, if not his great Undervalue of an Infallible Spirit, at least, his Disbelief of any such Thing, as the Guide of Men, and his unworthy Reflection upon us in crediting any such Doctrine, I am more than ordinarily engag'd to state and vindicate that one necessary Doctrine, (viz.) *Whether God's Holy and Infallible Spirit be the proper Rule of Faith, Judge of Controversies, and Guide of a Christian Life, or any other Thing:* This I reckon as the main Hinge on which all turns, and I now make it my Post, by which in God's Strength I am resolved to stand firm in it's Defence, and that by Scripture and Reason, hoping, whatever uncharitable Thoughts he entertains of us, that he is not so void of all Sense of either, as that they may not be used with Advantage to him under his present Ignorance and Presumption.

'Tis true, this deserves an intire Discourse of it self, as that which, above all other Subjects disputed on in the whole World, deserves Man's most weighty Consideration; and if the Lord make Way, it may be by some or other more distinctly and at large handled another Time, in a particular Tract; however, I shall state, and briefly defend the Question, I hope to present Satisfaction.

The QUESTION Stated.

Whether God's Holy and Unerring Spirit (for I am so Charitable as to think he believes God's Spirit to be so) *is, or should be the proper Judge of Truth, Rule of Faith, and Guide of Life among Men, especially under the Administration of the Blessed Gospel of our Lord and Saviour Jesus Christ, or not?* I affirm it, and proceed to prove it both by Scripture and Reason.

First, Gen. vi. 3. *And the Lord said, My Spirit shall not always strive with Man, for that he also is Flesh; yet his Days shall be an Hundred and Twenty Years,* &c.

If God's unerring Spirit has been wont to strive with Men, either to convince them of, and convert them from the Evil of their Thoughts, Words and Deeds; or else, to provoke them yet more fully to do the Will of God, so as to press on from one Degree of Glory to another, then Men have had an Unerring Spirit to be their Teacher, and Judge and Rule, and Guide of that Truth, concerning that Faith, and in that most Holy Way which leads to Eternal Life: But the Scripture proves the first Proposition, *That God's Spirit has frequently strove with Men,* and for the Ends before-mentioned; and consequently, *They have not been without an Holy Unerring Spirit to Teach, Judge, Regulate, and Guide them.*

Secondly, Neh. ix. 19, 20. *Yet thou in thy manifold Mercies forsookest them not in the Wilderness; the Pillar of the Cloud departed not from them by Day, to lead them in the Way; neither the Pillar of Fire by Night, to shew them Light, and the Way wherein they should go.*

Thou gavest also thy Good Spirit to instruct them, &c.

If under the Dispensation of the Law, God gave his good Spirit to instruct his People, which is to say, *that it should teach them, rule them, and guide them* in whatever was necessary for them to know or do; otherwise God's Spirit would have been lame and defective in his holy Instruction (which far be it from any sober Man to affirm) then will it follow, that *much more should the same Eternal Spirit be poured out under the glorious Dispensation of the Gospel:* But all that acknowledge the Divine Authority of the Scriptures must confess to God's Goodness to his People in the outward Wilderness, in the free Gift of his Eternal Spirit; *therefore the Eternal Spirit was and is the Teacher, Judge, Rule, and Guide of his People.*

Besides, that State was but Figurative of the Mystical Travel of the true Church in the Days of the Gospel; and how is God so propitious now as then,

if

if he be not as a Pillar of Cloud by Day, and of Fire by Night, I mean Spiritually and Invisibly, *so to illuminate his People concerning the Way he would have them to walk in.*

Thirdly, Job 32. 8. Prov. 2. 6. *But there is a Spirit in Man, and the Inspiration of the Almighty giveth them Understanding.*

For the Lord giveth Wisdom; out of his Mouth cometh Knowledge and Understanding.

If the Spirit in Man, *be not of Man,* as the foregoing Words shew, and therefore is that Divine Spirit, by and from which comes the Inspiration of the Almighty; and if the Understanding, mostly intended, be of Divine and Eternal Matters, as the whole Subject treated on in the preceding and following Chapters, as well as that in which the Words are, manifests; *then is it not from the Strength of Man's Reason, Memory, or utmost Creaturely Ability, that his Knowledge of Religious and Heavenly Things comes; but from the Revelation and Discovery of the Inspiration of the Almighty?* And if by such Divine Inspirings it be that the Will of God comes to be understood, *then certainly must God's unerring Spirit be the Judge of what is God's Will from what is not, and the Rule how, and in what we ought to believe unto Salvation, and that Guide which infallibly leads in the Way that is most acceptable with the Lord.* Nothing can be more Natural than these Consequences.

Fourthly, Psal. 139. 7. *Whither shall I go from thy Spirit, or whither shall I flee from thy Presence.*

If God's unerring Spirit be so nigh, and the Sense of it so certain, it must either be to reprove for Evil done, or to inform, uphold, lead, and preserve in Reference to all Good : Now in which of the two Senses it shall be taken, *the Presence of God's Eternal Spirit, and his being the Saints Instructor, Judge, Rule and Guide,* are evidently deduceable from the Words.

Fifthly, Psal. 143. 10. *Teach me to do thy Will; for thou art my God; thy Spirit is Good; lead me into the Land of Uprightness.*

The Question will be, Whether it was *David's* Intent, and the Scope of his Desire, that God should teach and lead him by his good Spirit, or some other Thing; but methinks it is resolvable in the Affirmative in two Respects,

1. In that *David* is so very frequent in his Desire to the Lord for the Assistance, Strength, Teaching, and Guidance of God's unerring Spirit; otherwise declaring, *How that the Word was hid in his Heart;* and largely speaking of the Force of that Internal Law, Word and Spirit of God, which plentifully shews, how much he was an *Enthusiast and Quaker,* in the Sense this Man esteems us most Heterodox.

2. The very Words imply the Thing we urge them for, and can import no other Sense, viz. *That God would please to teach him to do his Will, and lead him into the Land of Uprightness by his Good Spirit :* Else, what did that Clause do there, the Unerring Spirit being that by which God vouchsafes to discover his Divine Knowledge, and convey his most Spiritual Succour and Consolation to his People? And consequently his Saints have ever known, and do, more especially under the Gospel, *Enjoy an infallible Judge, Rule and Guide in and about Faith and Worship.*

Sixthly, Isa. 30. 1. *Wo to the Rebellious Children, saith the Lord, that take Counsel, but not of me, and that cover with a Covering, but not of my Spirit; that they may add Sin to Sin.*

From whence I plainly argue thus:

If they are Rebellious against God, and add Sin to Sin, who take not Counsel of him, and are not covered with his Holy Unerring Spirit, *that leads into all Truth, Innocence, Patience, Faith, Hope, Charity, and every good Word and Work.* Then

1. God's Children *have an immediate Councellor, and need not another; and are covered, or encompast about by the infallible Spirit of God to all Soundness of Mind, and Holiness of Life.* And

2. They must be Heinous Offenders, and obstinately Rebellious, and Adders of Sin to Sin with a Witness, that not only neglect, or refuse to be so counsel'd and cover'd; but dispute fervently against it, as a meer Whimsie, and Effect of an Ignorant, Erroneous Spirit; for besides that such deprive themselves and others of the unspeakable Benefit that comes thereby, they are most ingrateful to God, and do certainly incur his fierce Wrath, in their so wicked Requital of him for his Heavenly Gift.

Seventhly, Isa. 59. 21. *As for me, this is my Covenant with them, saith the Lord, My Spirit that is upon thee, and my Words which I have put in thy Mouth, shall not depart*

depart out of the Mouth of thy Seed's Seed, faith the Lord, from henceforth and for-ever.

I think it is granted by all that own the Christian Religion, that this remarkable Place refers to Christ, the true Seed and Heir of Promise, who bruiseth the Head of the Serpent, in whom alone all Nations of them that believe come to obtain the Blessing: But whether it will be allowed, or another Interpretation alloted (as that the Promise was to the Church) to be sure here is enough to maintain our Position, *viz.* That God, in the Days of the Gospel more particularly, has given his good Spirit for an Instructor, Judge, Rule and Guide, in all that concerns the Eternal Well-being of the Souls of Believers, as I proceed to prove.

If that very same Eternal, Holy and unerring Spirit, which God poured out upon his only begotten Son, *be in a Way of succession ordained to continue with and upon all the Faithful, his Seed, and Seed's Seed, begotten unto a lively Hope by the raising of Christ Jesus from the dead, and so become Members of his own Glorious Body, then are not the Children of God destitute of his unerring Spirit, nor left to their own frail, and fallible Judgments, to determine of what is Right or Wrong, what Men should believe, and what not, how they should walk, and how not.*

But so gracious is the Promise, and so certain is the Performance (as we livingly witness against all dry cavilling Letter-mongers in the World (who quarrel about the Holy Men's Words, and are Strangers to the Convictions, Judgments, Trials, Tribulations, Temptations and Travels they underwent, in order to that Knowledge they had (and which frets their serpentine Natures, whose vulturous Eye would in it's unregenerate State of Worldly Wisdom, that knows not God, fain (without the Death of the Cross) creep into the Knowledge of the Mystery of the Resurrection, which State alone knows the Things that are above, at the Right-Hand of God.

Therefore I conclude, That God's unerring Spirit under the Gospel, *does attend, assist, direct, and finally establish his Children in the Way of Truth*; and that his so doing is but the Answer or Accomplishment of the most eminent Prophesies, refering to the Transcendent Glory of the last Ages of the Church.

Eighthly, Ezek. 36. 27. *And I will put my Spirit within you, and cause you to walk in my Statutes, and ye shall keep my Judgments, and do them.*

Behold a most pregnant Instance in the express Language of the Holy Ghost, brought to the Proof of our Assertion, that (with Reverence we would say it) scarcely could it have been more exactly and emphatically worded, as I proceed to shew.

1. That this Passage has a relation to the Times of Reformation, or Coming of the Messiah, and Days of the Gospel Covenant; read the whole Chapter. I know not that it was ever doubted, or otherwise taken by any, *no not the very Rabbies themselves*, who from such Places have observed the Coming of a Messiah, and glorious Times that would ensue.

2. That if it be granted, then the *Unerring Spirit of God was to be placed within the Hearts and Consciences of his People*, and consequently they could not be properly and truly under the new Covenant, and be without it, since the having of that Eternal Spirit for the Ends and Purposes afore-mentioned, is the very Badge, Condition, and Mark of the New and Last Covenant.

3. It seems to be the Means under the Gospel, by which *God causes his Children to keep his Statutes,* &c. *I will put my Spirit within you, and cause you to walk in my Statutes; and ye shall keep my Judgments, and do them.*

To conclude (to speak strictly) If in the Days of the second Covenant, which began from Christ's visible Appearance, God put his Spirit within his People, as faith the Apostle to the *Hebrews*, and that it was thereby he did and doth cause them to walk in his Statutes and keep his Judgments; then *God's Children are not without an infallible Teacher and Leader in the Things that appertain to their Eternal Salvation:* But we plainly see and read from the very Letter of the Scriptures, that God gives his *Spirit; or Light within, to Judge, Lead and Guide*; and consequently, the opposite Doctrine is both false and very pernicious. I might farther argue thus, That if God's unerring Spirit only enables Men to walk in his Statutes, and keep his Judgments to do them, then *since all are required to walk therein, none are exempted from a sufficient Measure of that unerring Spirit in order to it.* Much might be argued hereon, but this shall suffice.

Ninthly, Joel 2. 28, 29. *And it shall come to pass afterward, that I will pour out my Spirit upon all Flesh, and your Sons and your Daughters shall Prophesie, your Old Men shall dream Dreams, your Young Men shall see Visions: And also upon the Servants and upon the Hand-maids in those Days will I pour out of my Spirit.*

That this is generally believed, and frequently quoted as a Proof of Gospel-Times, is well known to most who are inquisitive after Matters of Religion, and how hard it bears upon the Anti-spiritual Opinion of our cavilling Adversary, though very evident; yet we shall farther proceed to shew,

1. Here is God's Royal Engagement, to effuse or pour forth of his blessed Spirit in the Days of the New Covenant.

2. Here is on whom it is to be poured forth, exprest in two Words, *All Flesh*; in more Words, *Young and Old, Men and Women, Masters, and Servants*: Mark the Universality of God's Mercy and Grace. Now from hence I argue,

If God's Unerring Spirit be to be poured out on all under the New Covenant, and that this is the Time thereof, *then has God poured out of his Unerring Spirit*, as aforesaid; that the Spirit is to be poured out under the Administration of the Gospel the Text proves; that this is the Time he himself confesses, pag 1, 12, 13, 45. therefore the Conclusion is undeniable, *viz.* That God has poured forth of his Holy and Unerring Spirit.

Again, If the Spirit of God is that, without which none can obtain Prophesie and Vision, and that Prophesie and Vision are Christian-Church Gifts, then, *since the Church of Christ is not to be without Prophesies and Vision to the End of the World*; it follows, *she cannot be without an infallible Spirit to the End of the World.*

Or thus, If without having the Spirit none can have Prophesie and Vision, and that Prophesie and Vision are both to be and to continue in Christ's Church universally; then it will naturally follow, *that she cannot be without that Unerring Spirit*; and that such as are, cannot in that State be *Members of the true Church*; then consequently Hereticks, as concerning the true Faith.

Tenthly, Hag. 2. 5. *According to the Word that I Covenanted with you when ye came out of Egypt, so my Spirit remaineth among you, fear not.*

This Place doth very emphatically prove my Assertion, concerning the Judgship and Guidance of God's Spirit, two Things seem clear.

1. That it was a part of God's Old Covenant, to wit, That his Spirit should remain amongst them.

2. That the Spirit's so remaining was to some eminent Service; for said the Lord, *Fear not*; as much as to say, don't faint in your Minds, concerning the Work you have to do, neither be ye filled with Doubts or Scruples, who shall inform us, who direct us, or we want a Leader in this difficult Matter, some one to remove our Objections and Fears, and to preside or be as Judge among us, how to order and regulate us to the Doing of the Service expected from us; for thus faith the Lord, *My Spirit remains among you, fear not*; He is sufficient for you, He shall teach and counsel you, repair to Him, advise with Him, and you shall be supplied with all Things necessary for you: Don't rebel against my Good Spirit, and you are safe; it shall be well with you. In short,

If it was a Condition of the Old Covenant, That God should accompany his then Children with the Assistance and Presence of his good Spirit, and accordingly he testified by his Prophet, That his Holy Spirit remained among them, *then much more reasonable it is to believe, that the Presence of that Eternal Spirit should continually accompany his Children under the New and Last Testament:* The first part the Place proves, the second is made good by the plain Import of the following prophetick Verses, where he saith, *I will shake all Nations, and the Desire of all Nations shall come: And I will fill this House with Glory; and the Glory of this latter House shall be greater than of the former, saith the Lord of Hosts.*

How then can it possibly be, That God's Evangelical House and Tabernacle should be a dry, empty, barren erroneous Man, always enquiring, but never coming to the infallible Knowledge of the only True God, and Jesus Christ whom he hath sent, whom to know by the Revelation of the Eternal Spirit is Life Everlasting?

Nay, who so great, who so pernicious Enemies to the transcendent Glory of the latter House, and Temple of God, *as the cavilling Anti-spiritual Men of our Age*, who are so angry with those that own a *Conviction, Faith and Worship grounded*

1672.

upon an *infallible Inspiration*, that their Rage leads them (becauſe they feel it not) to the utter denying of any ſuch Things: but I will aſſure them, they ſhall yet grope in the dark, till they come into the daily Obedience of the Light, *and there reſt contented to know only as they Experience*; and not from a ravening comprehending Brain, that would in it's unregenerated State, graſp at the clear Myſteries of the Kingdom; into which, fleſhly Comprehenſions and Notions can never enter: but all muſt be unlearned from their firſt Birth, Education and traditional read Knowledge, as well as unmanned, that is, again become a little Child, before the Secrets of God's Work come to be made known; therefore ſaid our Lord Jeſus Chriſt, *I thank thee, O Father, Lord of Heaven and Earth, that thou haſt hid theſe Things from the Prudent, and revealed them unto Babes.*

Eleventhly, John 3. 5. *Jeſus anſwered, Verily, verily I ſay unto thee; Except a Man be born of Water and of the Spirit he cannot enter into the Kingdom of God.*

This moſt weighty Scripture, containing the very Work of Regeneration, and, *ſine quâ non*, or that only certain Means, and Condition Requiſit, without which there can be no obtaining of Eternal Life and Salvation; requires our beſt Notice and Conſideration: in order to which I ſhall divide the Place into theſe two Heads, and briefly raiſe my Argument thereon.

1. Chriſt's moſt poſitive Excluſion of all from any Portion in God's Kingdom who were not born again (in anſwer to *Nicodemus* his carnal Conceit of the Impoſſibility of an old Man's entring a ſecond Time into his Mother's Womb.)

2. That the Birth which all ſuch as would inherit God's Kingdom ſhould be Witneſſes of, *was and is the Birth of Water and the Spirit*; upon which I thus proceed to argue,

If none can Inherit God's Holy Kingdom, but thoſe who are regenerated of Water and the Spirit, *then none can inherit God's Holy Kingdom, but ſuch as are cleanſed by Water, and taught, led and guided by God's Holy Spirit.*

The firſt none can deny that own the Scripture, it being a Part of the very verſe quoted; the ſecond I evidently prove thus.

If Water and Spirit be the only operative to Regeneration, and Regeneration the alone Way to the Kingdom of God, *then can no Man inherit God's Kingdom, that is not regenerated*; neither can any Man be regenerated, that is not *waſhed by the Water of Life, begotten, wrought, formed, inſpired and acted by that Eternal Spirit to Newneſs of Life.*

That to be begotten, is to be principally guided and acted by that by which any is ſo begotten, I prove.

No Man can live, move, be ſenſible, or act, but from the original Heat, Life, Motion and Action of that which did beget him; becauſe the Nature of that which begets, being conveyed to the begotten, truly renders him begotten, or elſe there were no ſuch Thing; *but every regenerate Man is the Begotten of the Eternal Spirit, ſo far as concerns his Renovation or Regeneration; therefore every ſuch regenerated Man was and is led, motion'd and acted by that Eternal Spirit which begot him*; and conſequently, the Saints which are the regenerated, are not left deſtitute of an infallible Teacher, Judge, Rule and Guide amongſt them.

In ſhort, We look upon being born of Water and the Spirit to be, *Our being cleanſed from all Filthineſs, and quickned, informed, ruled and guided by the moſt pure and perfect Dictates and Operations of God's Eternal Spirit*; And how a regenerated Man can be made or continued ſuch, without the daily Guidance of that infallible Spirit, *and the Scriptures kept clear from the Reflection of Contradiction, if not groſs Error*, is a Riddle too hard for me to explain, and a Task I may without Preſumption ſay too great for our trifling Antagoniſts to perform.

Twelfthly, John 14. 16, 17, 18, 20. and 16. 13. *And I will pray the Father, and he ſhall give you another Comforter, that he may abide with you for ever: Even the Spirit of Truth, whom the World cannot receive, becauſe it ſeeth Him not, neither knoweth Him; but ye know him; for he dwelleth with you, and ſhall be in you. I will not leave you comfortleſs, I will come to you; at that Day ye ſhall know, that I am in my Father, and you in me, and I in you.*

Again, *Howbeit, when he the Spirit of Truth is come, he will guide you into all Truth.*

Upon theſe Divine Paſſages, thus particularly expreſt by the Holy Ghoſt, I offer theſe ſhort Arguments,

1. If the Spirit of Truth, or most Infallible Spirit, be God's Gift to his Servants, in Gospel Times, to abide with them for ever; then *are they accompanied with an Infallible Spirit*. but we see the plain Text proves, that God gives his Spirit of Truth to his Servants, that they might be assisted in all their Wants; and therefore they are not without such an Infallible Spirit. And our Adversary is more to blame to reflect upon the Guidance of an Infallible Spirit, which is so consonant with the express Letter of a Multitude of Scripture-Passages, than *we are because we credit G. F. upon Conviction.*

And if he tells us, That unless we believe what our Eyes see of Contradictions (as he pretends) by him collected out of G. F's Book, that he will not believe whatever we shall say or affirm; we may on much better Grounds conclude, never to believe what he asserts, and wholly to decline Writing or Speaking to him (to use his own Words) if hereafter he will dare to continue in the Belief of so Antiscriptural and Anti-gospel an Apprehension, as that there *is no Infallible Spirit to guide Men in the Way of Salvation*; which is as expresly evident from many naked Texts of Scripture, as that *God is Truth*; else never did any Writing more delude Mankind, because none could be more particular and plain in the Promise and Allowance of it: But *let God and his Written Will be true, and our Unspiritual Adversary in his confest Fallible Judgment of us a very Lyar.*

2. If the not seeing and knowing of the Spirit of Truth be the Reason rendred by our Lord Jesus, why the World receives it not, then may we most justly infer, that they never saw it, neither know it; but are of the World, who cannot receive it, but write against it, in Reference to it's greatest Office, *viz. Of being the Saints Teacher, Leader and Comforter.* And indeed, because the Spirit is not some visible Elementary Thing, that may be seen by their outward Eyes, and be comprehended by their dark confused and disputative Brains (which is contrary to the Decree and Way of God's manifesting of his Will from the Conviction of the least Sin, to the Enjoyment of the highest Glory) therefore *they dis-regard it as contemptible, and dis-believe it as incredible.*

3. If the Ground of the Saints Knowledge of that Infallible Spirit, be the *Spirit's inhabiting them* (for, *He dwelleth with you, and shall be in you*) then *were they not without that Spirit*; and consequently they were attended with an Infallible Guide within them.

4. If the Lord Jesus would not leave them comfortless, but though visibly withdrawn, yet in a more Spiritual and Invisible Manner, would come to them again; and that *at that Day they should know, that he was in his Father, they in him, and he in them*: Then were *his Servants not destitute of an infallible Judge, Leader and Guide, because they had him, that was the Way, Truth and Life, to whom all Power and Judgment were committed.*

5. If both the Spirit of Truth, was promised to come, and when come, to guide into all Truth; that is to say, that whatever they scrupled, were ignorant in, or ought to know and practise, with what they were obliged to reject and testifie against, should be by that Eternal Spirit discovered unto them, then *undoubtedly they were not without an infallible Spirit, to Judge, Regulate and Guide them, in all that concerned Faith, Worship and Conversation*: But the first Proposition is purely Scriptural, and therefore the Consequent not deniable by such as own the Divine Truths contained in those Writings.

Nor is the Dint of this to be avoided by Saying, that these Promises were only to the Apostles, and no Body denies them to have had all this; *for if we are to walk, as having them for our Examples; we are to have the like Sufficiency and Guide.* Nor does Christ leave the Matter there; for in his most solemn Prayer to his Father, he thus speaks, *Neither pray I for these alone, but for all them that shall believe on me, through their Word, that they all may be one, as thou Father art in me, and I in thee, that they may all be one in me*: Which, how it is possible for those, who then believed, and us of after Generations to be, *without being born of and baptized, and drinking into the same one Eternal Spirit*, I know not how to believe, neither can any Man, that gives himself the Use of his own Understanding.

Thirteenth. Rom. 8. 1. 9. 14. *There is therefore, now no Condemnation to them which are in Christ Jesus, who walk not after the Flesh, but after the Spirit, but you are not in the Flesh, but in the Spirit, if so be that the Spirit of God dwell in you: Now if any Man have not the Spirit of Christ, he is none of his. For as many as are led by the Spirit of God, they are the Sons of God.*

1672.

1. If to be brought and kept out of Condemnation, Men must walk according to the Leadings and Guidings of the Spirit of God, and that it is a State unto which Christian Men should come, then *are they not without God's infallible Spirit, to lead and direct them, in what Way they ought to walk*, and consequently, *the contrary Opinion is perniciously false*; since such much needs live ever under Condemnation, who are so far from walking after the *Leadings of God's unerring Spirit, that they deny Men to have any such Thing*. Again.

2. If to have the Spirit of Christ dwelling (that is, *ruling*) in us, be to live no more after the Flesh; and not to have that infallible Spirit of Christ, ruling in us, be to be none of Christ's; then *both Christian Men should not be without Christ's Spirit dwelling in them; and such as are without that Spirit are none of Christ's:* But we plainly see, that the *Apostle* asserts, that every Man that walks not after the Flesh, has that Spirit dwelling in him, and is guided thereby; and that such as have not the holy Spirit of Christ, are none of Christ's; therefore it follows, That Christian Men are led by an infallible Spirit. But,

3. If as many as are led by the Spirit of God, are the Sons of God, as faith the Apostle, then *both God's Children are led by an infallible Spirit, and such as are not we utterly deny to have any Part or Portion in him, notwithstanding their Praying, Preaching, Writing, Reading and Disputing:* But the plain unalterable Words of Scripture testifie, that both God has given his good Spirit to lead Men into that holy Life, Nature and Conversation, by which they truly become his Image and Children; and that such (and we may say only such) are his own begotten Children, and Heirs of Eternal Glory.

Fourteenth, 1 Cor. 2. 10, 11, 12, 14, 15. *But God hath revealed them unto us by his Spirit; for the Spirit teacheth all Things, yea, the deep Things of God.*

For what Man knoweth the Things of a Man, save the Spirit of a Man, which is in him; even so the Things of God, knows no Man but the Spirit of God.

Now we have received not the Spirit of this World, but the Spirit which is of God, that we might know the Things that are freely given to us of God.

But the natural Man, receiveth not the Things of the Spirit of God; for they are Foolishness unto him; neither can he know them, because they are spiritually discerned.

But he that is spiritual judgeth (or discerneth) *all Things, yet he himself is judged* (or discerned) *of no Man.*

Methinks the bare Recital of these Pathetical Sayings of the holy Ghost; on the Matter in Controversie, might be sufficient Proof for the Affirmative of the Question, did not our Adversary, under all his Pretences of honouring the Scriptures, either implicitly, deny them their just Authority, or by false Glosses disguise and pervert them, to his sinister Perswasions, and so I proceed, as before, to offer my Argument upon them.

1. If the blessed Things which God hath prepared for them that love him, are not revealable, but by his Spirit, and were then thereby revealed, as says the Scripture quoted, and Context, then *since there were those at that Time who loved God, and that there be many now who love God, it will naturally follow, That both then and now, the Things that God has laid up for such, both then were, and now are revealed by his Eternal Spirit*; and consequently, *God's People are not without a familiar Communion with the holy Spirit of God.*

2. If the Spirit of a Man, or humane intelligent Spirit, be that by which Man comes to an Understanding of those Things, that strictly and properly concern him, in an humane Capacity; and that the Spirit of God is that only by which Man comes to know the Things of God, because the Things of God knoweth no Man, but the Spirit of God; then *it is utterly impossible for our Adversary himself, or any else to obtain the Knowledge of the Things of God, or his Kingdom, (but by the pure unmixt Revelation of God's Eternal Spirit) from all the Comprehensions, Conceivings, or Imaginations of Man's utmost Strength or Science (For* (as faith the Apostle) *the Spirit searcheth all Things, yea the deep Things of God.*

3. If the Knowledge of those Things that are freely given of God, is only to be had from the Revelation of his holy Spirit; then since in every Age, from the most primitive Times, it has behoved every Christian Man to understand those Good and Heavenly Things, it follows, *That it has behoved them, and still does all, to wait for the Knowledge and Enjoyment of those blessed Advantages which only are revealed by the Eternal Spirit:* And is not that Science infallible? Which the Spirit of this World ever was, and will be a Stranger too, under all its disguised Shews of Religious Worship, with which it has deceitfully adorned it self, in a Way of Scorn of

and Opposition, to the most *Spiritual Appearance of God*, making good the Apostle's Saying, *For they are but Foolishness unto them.* To conclude,

4. If the spiritual Man, or that Man in whom dwelleth the Spirit of God, and who is led by it, discerneth and judgeth all Things, and is not judged, or cannot be seen or discerned (he being in the Light, and the natural Man in the Dark) then *is or should God's holy Spirit be the right Judge, Leader and Guide of all, because it alone gives true Discerning, sound Judgment, and leads in the Path of Life Eternal:* For it searcheth the deep Things of God, which all natural Understanding can never fathom, because they are spiritually to be discerned.

Fifteenth, 1 Cor. 6. 19. *What? know you not that your Body is the Temple of the Holy Ghost which is in you, which ye have of God? and ye are not your own.*

The Apostle treating of the great nearness that every Believer stands in to the Lord, and that blessed Union, which the Dispensation of the Gospel brings to, by putting away the Filthiness of the Flesh and Spirit, and by the Answer of a good Conscience before God; in winding up this Subject, he thus smartly; and as if his Query were enough, to clear up all that he had to say to them, as to their Duty, and his Exhortation, asks, *What? know ye not that your Body is the Temple of the Holy Ghost, which is in you*: From whence I draw this Argument,

If Believers be the Temple, in which the holy Ghost dwells, as evidently speaks the Scripture, *then are they not left without an infallible Spirit, as Judge, Rule, and Guide to repair to*; but it is apparent to Sense, that the holy Ghost is, by the Apostle affirmed, to inhabit, or take up his Abode in Believers; therefore they must needs be attended with an infallible Spirit; and for what? if not the End before mentioned.

Sixteenth, 1 Cor. 12, 13. *For by one Spirit are we all baptized into one Body, whether we be* Jews *or* Gentiles, *whether we be* Bond *or* Free; *and have been all made to drink into one Spirit.*

By which Divine Sense of the Apostle, we cannot but allow, that if they were both baptized by one Spirit, into one Body, and made to drink into the same Spirit, that the *Saints were not without an infallible Spirit*; since such Baptizing and Drinking, do emphatically imply the whole Work of the Spirit in their Regeneration, and their daily Union with, and intimate Enjoyment of it, the whole Course of their Lives. And certainly, if by that Eternal Spirit, they were baptized into that one Body Christ, *It was as impossible for them, as Members thereof to live without the Life, Virtue and Spirit of Christ their Head, as for any natural Body to live without the same Life, Blood, Heat and Motion, which belongs to it's Head.* And how this Man can be esteemed a good *Christian*, who would render Christ Jesus the Head of a fallible Body, by divesting Christians of an infallible Spirit, I leave to Persons of better Judgment, more honesty, and greater Moderation than himself to judge.

Seventeenth, 2. Cor. 3. 18. *But we all with open Face, beholding as in a Glass the Glory of the Lord, are changed into the same Image, from Glory to Glory, even as by the Spirit of the Lord.*

This whole Chapter is an admirable Account of the Super-Excellency of the Gospel Administration of Life, to that of the Law, how far it did transcend it, as to all Spiritual Knowledge, Privilege and Enjoyment, which I desire the Reader seriously to read, as well as to consider what is offered from the Verse cited.

If a Christian's Change into God's Image, from Glory to Glory, be the Work of the Eternal Spirit in Men, it follows necessarily, *That* Christians *can no more be without the Discoveries, Leadings and Orderings of God's Spirit, than they can be his Children without his Image,* (since whatever they think, say or do, in Reference to Religion, should bear a near Relation to that Resemblance of God, which above all Things they ought to act correspondently with) but we see how very expresly and profoundly the Apostle describes the exceeding Blessedness of the New Covenant, namely, *A being changed into the Image of God, from Glory to Glory*; not by our own Notions or Comprehensions, from the Strength of our Natural Reason, or any Book without us; but by the Spirit of the Lord operating in us; therefore God's Children *are not without an infallible Spirit*, unless he should deny God's Spirit to be such, which methinks I cannot believe him to do.

Gal. 3. 3. *Are ye so foolish, having begun in the Spirit, are ye now made perfect in the Flesh?*

If Christians are both to begin and end in the Spirit, or if a Christian throughout the whole Course of his Life, from the first Step or Measure to the Fulness and Perfection of his Stature, is to be informed, regulated and guided by the infallible

1672.

fallible Spirit of God, as the Apostle's Reproof of the *Galatians*, for their declining to be ordered thereby, evidently proves; *then* Christians *ought to begin and end in the Strength, Knowledge, Wisdom and Guidance of an Infallible Spirit*; and consequently, that Doctrine which denies such an unerring Spirit to be the Judge, Rule and Guide of Christians, is Anti-christian.

Gal. 4. 6. *Because ye are Sons, God hath sent forth the Spirit of his Son into your Hearts.*

If God sends forth his Spirit into the Hearts of his Children, *then are they not without an Infallible Spirit*; but the express Letter of the Scripture affirms it: And consequently, our Adversary's Reflection upon us, for making it Part of our Belief, is unsound, and condemnable.

Gal. 5. 16. 18. *This I say then, Walk in the Spirit, and ye shall not fulfil the Lusts of the Flesh.*

They that walk by the Spirit, *must first have it*; and next, *be led by it*: But the Apostle exhorted the Church so to walk; therefore *the Church had, and* Christians *have the Spirit, and should walk in or by it*; that is, according to the Motions, Leadings, and Rule of it.

Eph. 1. 17. *That the God of our Lord Jesus Christ, the Father of Glory, may give unto you the Spirit of Wisdom and Revelation in the Knowledge of Him.*

If the Heavenly Wisdom, and Revelation in the Knowledge of God, be through the Spirit; then, *as without Revelation, there is no Knowledge of God, so without the Spirit there is no Divine Wisdom and Revelation*: And if the Church was attended with that Wisdom and Revelation, *then with that Spirit from whence they came*; and consequently *Christ's Church is not without that Eternal Unerring Spirit*; as saith the Apostle in the 5th Chapter, *Be not drunk with Wine, wherein is Excess; but be filled with the Spirit*: Which signifies the Apostle's Mind to be quite another Thing, from the Judgment of our Adversary, who thinks, *All Men ought to be empty of it*; esteeming such as are filled therewith, *as the Jews did* Paul, *Drunk with New Wine.*

1. Thess. 15. 19. *Quench not the Spirit.*

If those could not quench the Spirit, who had it not, *then those to whom he gave that Caution had the Spirit, consequently the Primitive Churches were not without an Unerring Spirit*; because they were not without the Spirit of God, which is Unerring.

1 John 2. 27. *But the Anointing which ye have received of him, abideth in you; and ye need not that any Man teach you, but as the same Anointing teacheth you of all Things, and is Truth, and is no Lye; and even as it hath taught you, ye shall abide in him.*

If the Judge of Truth from Falshood, the Rule of what ought to be received and embraced, and the Guide of Life, be the Anointing, which none denies (that I know of) to be the Spirit of God, *then both the only Way to be taught all Things necessary to be believed and performed, is the Anointing, and that Anointing is in Believers respectively*; but the Scripture so asserts: And consequently, the right *Christian* is not without that Infallible Spirit, to teach and lead him into all Truth.

1 John 3. 24. *And he that keepeth his Commandments dwelleth in him, and he in him; and hereby we know that he abideth in us, by the Spirit which he hath given us.*

If the Union betwixt Christ and his Children be, that they dwell in him, and he in them; and that they thereby know it, *by the Spirit that he hath given them*; which implies, that they had the Unerring Spirit of Christ: then *true believers are not without Christ and his Spirit dwelling in them, to Guide, Rule and Instruct them in all Things necessary to Eternal Life and Salvation*: He that denies the first, denies the Scripture; and he that rejects the second Proposition, had as good deny that Day is an Effect of Light.

Jude 5. 19, 20. *These be they who separate themselves, sensual, having not the Spirit. But, ye Beloved, building up your selves in your most Holy Faith, praying in the Holy Ghost,* &c.

If such as have not the Spirit are sensual, *then, because the true Children of God are not sensual, it follows, that they have the Spirit*; and that those who have it not, are not the Children of God, because such are sensual.

This the Apostle farther manifests to be his Mind, because, leaving the Sensualists, he addresses himself to the Sanctified of God, exhorting them, *To build up one another in their most holy Faith, Praying in the Holy Ghost*: Which shews, that they

they performed their Worship to God in the Motion of the Eternal Spirit; and consequently, they could not be destitute of an Unerring Spirit in what concerned them, either towards God or Men.

Thus have I briefly run through the Scriptures of Truth, and doubt not but I have made it appear, That God has afforded his People in all Ages such a Measure of his Eternal Spirit, as hath been sufficient to *Inform, Rule and Guide them*, infallibly, in and about those Things which are absolutely necessary to be known or done unto Eternal Life.

It remains, That I evidence the Truth of my Assertion by Reason also, which I shall endeavour with what convenient Brevity I can.

That Christian Men *have an* Infallible Principle *to* Judge, Rule, *and* Guide them, *I prove by* REASON.

First, I Shall take it for granted, That no Man, whom either Education or Conviction gives to believe there is a God, can be so unreasonable as to think, That any Man may be farther able to understand what this God is, and his Divine Pleasure concerning him, *than the same is discovered to him by some external or internal Operation from the same infinite Being:* This then must either be by the visible Creation, or *that invisible Taste or Relish the Soul has by Virtue of the Divine Touches, Influences and Discoveries, that the Almighty Invisible God is pleased to approach his Creatures by,* as the next clearest Way to communicate unto them the Knowledge of himself.

Secondly, And as I know not any, who professeth Religion, that makes the least Scruple of this; so how is it possible, that such Discoveries as God himself is pleased to make, should be fallible, or subject to any Defect in themselves; for, were that admitted (as must be, upon the Principles of our Adversary) then must we conclude an imperfect Knowledge; nay, *an uncertain* (not to say erroneous) *Knowledge of, and Faith in God,* to be from God's own defective Manifestations of himself; which however truly deduced from his Positions, *is a most Unworthy and False Reflection upon the Mercy and Goodness of God.*

Thirdly, There is an absolute Necessity, That what it is convenient for Man to know, should be certainly and infallibly discovered to him, because of that great Corruption, Idolatry and Superstition, *which through that misty and uncertain Prospect they say Man has of the Divine Will, he may be subject to fall into;* and like the vain Worshippers of old, conceit an *Ape, Serpent, or Crocodile to be a Deity,* or some other Beings, or Fancies, though less Gross, yet too gross for a Christian Man.

Fourthly, Upon our Adversary's Principles, there can be no assured Ground of Comfort; for when a Man shall think he hath wrought out his Salvation in the Way he conceives most acceptable with God, perhaps he hath followed an erroneous Judgment, and unsubjected Affection, and when Repentance may be too late, he is to be fobbed off with such an Award as this, *You had no Infallible Knowledge, and having lived in an erroneous Sense of your own, you must inherit the Displeasure that follows:* thereby making well or ill believing or doing, *a meer Lottery, or doing of Things by Chance,* and not from any certain Knowledge in themselves of what God required of them: *A Conceit worthy to be disdained by every sober Man.*

Fifthly, And were I as our Adversary, I would never beat my Brain about what is True or False; since upon his Principles, when Truth meets me, *I know her not from Error;* and after I should have writ Volumes, *I am as certain of the Truth of what I oppose, as of what I assert;* so that the *Quakers* may be in the Right for ought he knows; nor have they any certain Grounds from him on which to alter, or believe the contrary.

Sixthly, Nor does this Opinion of our Adversary *(that there is no such Thing, as Man's being now led by an Infallible Spirit)* end there; for it rendereth the Almighty more unjust than the worst of Men; since first he seems to offer Men the clearest Discoveries of so much of his Will as he requires them to live conformable unto; yet, *means nothing less, by leaving Mankind to labour under the Perplexi-*

ty of an uncertain Knowledge: And secondly, Concludes him, notwithstanding, *under the greatest Certainty of Eternal Punishment.*

Methinks then, If these Things seem unreasonable, (though the genuine Effects of a Fallible Guide) our Adversary should by this Time think fit to allow us,

1. That God cannot be known, *but by the Discoveries he makes of himself through his Eternal Power and Spirit unto Mankind.*
2. That though such Discoveries may be imperfect in Degree, yet *not in Kind.*
3. That such Revelation, Discovery or Instruction is infallibly true, and that there is nothing wanting on God's Part, *to accommodate Man with a Spiritual, Certain, Infallible Discovery and Knowledge of Almighty God his Creator; and therefore Man has to rectify and assist his Fallible Judgment, an Unerring, Certain, Infallible Spirit, Power, or Principle; which as Man listens unto, and follows, his Understanding becomes illuminated, his Reason purified, and a sound Judgment restored;* and in all Things is he made a fit Tabernacle for the Glorious God to live in: Thus is he *King of Saints, and will he be King of Nations, who is God over all, Heaven and Earth, blessed for ever,* Amen.

There be two Objections, which I foresee may be made by some to the Way I have taken to prove, That a *Christian's* Judge, Rule and Guide is the Unerring Spirit of God; which I shall endeavour to answer.

Obj. 1. *Though you have said a great deal to prove, that* Christians *should have an Infallible Spirit in general; yet you prove nothing distinctly; but confound a Judge, Rule and Guide together.* To which I answer,

Answ. 1. That to me there is no more Difference, than essentially there can be in the *Wisdom, Justice and Holiness of God,* which are but so many Words, that agree to express the Perfection of one and the same Being; and so that as the one cannot be without the other; but the same Eternal Godhead is all, and *that in all:* for he is truly *Wise, in being Just,* and both, *in being Holy;* and back again, they are so interwoven, that the one goes not without the other; thus it is in being a *Judge, Rule and Guide:* for that which gives me a right Sense or Judgment of Truth from Error, is as well to me *a Rule, what I should believe, or disbelieve; and a Guide, what I should practice, or not practice; as at first it was my Judge, of what was Truth from what was Error.* So that the same Informing Convincing Spirit, is that *Ruling and Guiding Spirit* (and not a distinct Spirit, or Medium) by which such as are convinced through the Illumination and Reproof of it, are to be ruled and guided in all they believe and practice, about Matters relating to God and his Worship.

Obj. 2. But at this Rate, *you utterly contemn and seclude the Scriptures, as having no Part nor Portion in being a Judge, Rule or Guide to* Christians.

Answ. 2. By no Means; for though we acknowledge it to be our Principle, That the Eternal Spirit, who in several Generations hath revealed a great Part of the Things contained in the Scriptures, is superior to these Writings; yet far be it from us for ever, *to deny the absolute Necessity of our Conformity to such weighty Christian Truths and Principles, as are therein expressed, and urged upon the Churches, as what are indispensable to Eternal Salvation:* So that we plead not, that the Spirit of God should be a Judge, Rule and Guide contrary to the Truth declared in Scripture, *not yet exclusive of the Scripture;* but as the Holy Men of old Time were ordered, ruled and guided by that Eternal Spirit, in Reference to those weighty Things, which the Prophets and Apostles were moved to exhort those of that Time to press after; so that it is impossible for Men now to come into a right Christian Frame, and keep therein, *but by the Spirit's being their Judge, Rule and Guide, as he was to the Ancients, who trusted in God, and obtained a good Report.*

In short, The Scripture is much like the Shadow of the True Rule, which may give us some Ground to guess what the Rule it self is; *as a Chart, or Map of a Country, how it lies, yet not be the very Place it self:* and in this Respect it may be a Kind of Secondary Rule, carrying with it a Testimonial Confirmation, that what we are led by is the *True Spirit,* because the People of God, in old Time, enjoyed

enjoyed the fame, as the Eternal Spirit first of all confirms the Divine Authority of the Scriptures unquestionably to us, That they are a Declaration of the Will and Pleasure of Almighty God to the Sons of Men in several Ages of the World.

He that is so inward with a Prince, as to know, *vivâ voce* what his Mind is, heeds not so much the same when he meets it in Print (because in Print) *as because he has received a more living Touch and sensible Impression from the Prince himself, to whose Secrets he is privy.* And this the Scriptures teach us to believe is a right Christian's State and Privilege; for said the Apostle, *We have the Mind of Christ; and the Secrets of God are with them that fear Him; and guide me by thy Counsel, and bring me to thy Glory.*

To Conclude; The Scriptures we own, and the Divine Truths therein contained, we reverence and esteem, as the Mind and Will of God to Men; and we believe that they ought to be conformed to, according to the true Intent of the Holy Spirit therein; and we know, that all good People will respect them, read them, believe and endeavour to fulfil or obey them: And those who trade either *Ministerially* or *Controversially* with them, and are out of that Cleansed, Holy and Self-denying State they testify of, and believe it not attainable, *the Plagues therein declared of shall be their Portion for ever.*

I know that *Authorities* are of no great force with him, but since I write more out of an Expectation of Benefit to others, on whom this Libel has taken any Hold, perhaps it may not be unseasonable to subjoin a few, and the rather since we have not only the Suffrage of some, who are called *Socinians*, whom he pretends to follow; but thereby we may justly take Occasion to detect him of Contradiction to their Sentiments, whilst one of them.

1. Then first, Upon that remarkable Place in *John*, where Christ promised to send his Holy Spirit, *Howbeit, when the Spirit of Truth is come, he will guide you into all Truth*, &c. Those two famous Commentators (I mean so accounted by the *Romanists*) *Tolletus* and *Maldonatus*, and the last very frequently, and with great Respect commemorated and quoted by *Crellius*, one of the most redoubted of the *Socinian Party*. [1 John 26. 13.]

Tollet thus, " He shall, when he is come, manifest all those Things which ye are not able to bear, and discover to you all that Doctrine, that is fit for my Church to believe and practise. He shall teach you the compleat Truth; and to this End God gives it to the Faithful, and to his Church, that in Doctrine, Life, and Government, she may inerrably be guided. [Tol. in 16. c. Joan. com.]

Maldonat. Shall lead you into all Truth: that is, says he, " Discover unto them, and to the Church of God, all that Truth which is convenient or fit for them to know concerning Salvation. Thus says *Cyril. Theophylact, Augustine*, and *Beda* too. [Mald. in 16. cap. Joan. comm.]

Beza tells us, " That *Protestants* believe God to have given his Spirit, not only to his Apostles, but to his Church, that by her Testimony the World may be convinced of Sin, that many Consciences may be compelled to confess, that they have sinned in not believing on him, *&c.* [Bez. in 16. c. 9. comm.]

Dr. *Hammond* thus: " But when the Holy Ghost comes, whose Title is the Spirit of Truth, he shall instruct you what is to be done, which he shall reveal to you. And I will ask my Father, and he shall send you the Holy Ghost, to Interceed, Exhort and Comfort; and when he is come, he shall abide with you; that is, all that shall succeed you in the Faith for ever. As in his Comment on the 28th Chapter of *Matthew*, upon these Words, *I am with you always, even unto the End of the World*. " And though I shall now shortly part with you, yet I will, by sending the Spirit upon you, to lead you into all Truth, and by my perpetual Presence and Assistance afforded you, and by that Authority that I have received of my Father, and now commit unto you, *John* 20. 21, 22. continue with you and your Successors unto the End of the World. [D. H. H. Parap. on Evang.]

Now, If we read that Scripture he quotes, as an Interpretation of what he understands by Christ's being with them and their Successors to the End of the World, we shall find it to be this: *Then said Jesus to them again, Peace be unto you: As my Father hath sent me, even so send I you: And when he had said this, he breathed on them, and saith unto them, Receive ye the Holy Ghost.* What can be fuller

1672. fuller, than that in his Apprehension, *Not only the Apostles, but their Successors in the Faith, were to have continued unto them the perpetual Presence and Assistance of the Holy Ghost.*

Hutc. comm. on John.

And says no mean *Protestant* upon the Place, and very truly: "It is by the Spirit only, that Men who do not profit under outward Means, will be enabled to profit; who, when he cometh, reveals Truths clearly, and bears them in with Life and Power upon the Heart, and doth renew Men's Spirits to embrace and submit to them. *And on the 14th Chapter thus:* "The Spirit of God in Believers is not only a Comforter, to apply and bear in the Consolations of God, purchased by Christ upon their Hearts, but is their Advocate also, who pleads their Cause with God, by furnishing them with Prayers and Groans that cannot be uttered.

I shall now produce the Sense of several Persons so Great in the *Socinian Way*, conformable to what has been asserted concerning the Holy Spirit, that one would think our Adversary ought to be concluded by it.

Socin. Explic. loc. Script. p. 101.

And the first shall be *Socinus* himself, who in his Explication of the first Verse of the 8th Chapter to the *Romans*, speaks in short thus: "Neque enim jam carni sed spiritui obsequuntur; spiritus namq; vitalis imperium, cui & ego, & omnes qui Christi sunt subduntur, nos a jugo peccati & mortis asseruit: *For neither do they now follow, or live after the Flesh, but the Spirit; for the Power of the Living Spirit (to which, both I and all who are Christ's, are subdued) hath freed us from the Yoak of Sin and Death.*

Slicht. in Joan. Evang. comm. c. 16.

Slichtingius, who in his Comment upon the Passage already mentioned, especially that Part, *He shall lead you into all Truth*, gives us his Mind thus,

"Quando autem veniet ille, nempe Paracletus, spiritus ille veritatis, ducet vos, nempè, internâ illuminatione, in omnem veritatem, nempè, ad salutem æternam pertinentem, ita ut omnia sciatis, & intelligatis quæ vera sunt & ad salutem pertinent. That is, *When the Paraclet, to wit, the Spirit of Truth shall come, by his internal Illumination, or inward Enlightening, he will lead into all Truth, and to the Knowledge and Understanding of all those Things which are True and Necessary, and do pertain to Eternal Life.*

Now, since all are concerned in the End, namely, *Eternal Life*, methinks it is most Reasonable, that all should Share in the Means to it; I mean, *The Teachings and Guidings of that Unerring Spirit.* Thus much for this Place: I will instance one Place more, and the Thoughts of these Men upon it, I mean this last cited, and one not less Famous in the same Way.

Crell. in Epist. Paul. ad Rom.

Crellius, in his Comment upon the *Romans*, Chap. viii. Vers. 14, and 15. *For as many as are led by the Spirit of God, are Sons of God, for ye have not received the Spirit of Bondage*, &c. says, "Etenim quotquot spiritui illi divino se regendos tradunt, ejusq; ductum sequuntur, quemadmodum sanè faciunt ij, qui ejus ope carnis opera in se perimunt, eaq; non admittunt, illi Dei ipsius sunt Filij: qui quemadmodum jam naturæ ipsius sunt quodammodo participes; ejusq; similes; Ita etiam vicissim Deo filiorum loco habentur, ab eoq; sunt adoptati, & in Filiorum jus adsciti. Eos autem qui a Deo instar Filiorum diliguntur, vitæ sempiternæ fore participes, quanquam per se unicuique videtur patere, mox tamen planum faciam. Certainly then our Adversary, if he hath any Regard for *Crellius*, will not oppose himself to the Necessity of *Christians* being accompanied by an infallible Spirit, when this Author plainly tells us, *That without that Spirit of God, and the Operation of it to a Regeneration of Soul, there is no being a True Child of God, and Heir to the Possession of Glory,* as he farther speaks upon the 17th Verse.

Slicht. in Ep. ad Rom. com. c. 8.

Slichtingius gives us the same Interpretation, differing only in the Expression, *says he,* "Probant illos victuros esse, si spiritu actiones corporis mortificent. *Again,* "Spiritu Dei agi, ferri, impelli, regi, & spiritu actiones corporis perimere. *They prove themselves to be Conquerers, if by the Spirit they mortifie the Deeds of the Body.* Again, *To be acted, led, moved, perswaded, governed, ruled and directed, and to overthrow and destroy the Works of the Flesh, by the Spirit of God, this is to be a True Child of God.*

Crell. in prior Epist. ad com. cap. 2. v. 12.

Crellius is most express upon the 12th Verse of the second Chapter of *Paul's* First Epistle to the *Corinthians*, "Sed spiritum qui est ex Deo, id est, qui ex Deo proficiscitur seu derivatur in homines, ideoq; Dei Spiritus merito vocatur. *But the Spirit which is of God, that is, which proceedeth from God, or is derived from God into Men, and therefore is deservedly called the Spirit of God.*

Crellius,

Crellius, upon that remarkable Passage of the same Apostle, and in the same Chapter, *But the Spiritual Man judgeth all Things*, &c. speaks thus, "Opponit "animali homini spiritualem, Spiritualis autem homo ille est, qui non solum spi-"ritu Dei præditus est, sed etiam ejus ductum sequitur, & a spiritu ipso totus "pendet.

1672.
Crell. Epist. ad Cor. com. cap. 2. v. 15.

Says he, The Apostle opposeth the Spiritual to the Natural Man; that is, the Spiritual Man who is not only endued with God's Spirit, *but is also under the Spirit's Conduct, and wholly depends upon it.*

What Man speaks more pathetically for Inspiration, than *Crellius* doth, in whom our Adversary pretends to believe.

Nor is *Slichtingius* much behind him, who on the same Place gives us his Mind thus: "Spiritualis autem, id est, homo divino spiritu non tantum præditus, sed "illi etiam totus deditus.

Slicht. inter' Epist. ad Cor. comm. c. 2.

But the Spiritual Man, that is *(faith he)* not only the Man, who is endued with (and guided as by his Good Angel,) the Holy Spirit; *but who is also rendered or yielded wholly to his Government.*

"Dijudicat quidem omnia; id est, omnia quæ dicuntur cognoscit, qualia sint, "an divina sint, an prophana; de omnibus judicandi habet facultatem.

Judgeth all Things, that is, says *Slichtingius*, *He measureth and knoweth all Things that are spoken, of what Sort soever they may be, whether they be Divine or Prophane, because he has the Faculty or Gift of Right Judgment concerning all Things.* Thus far *Slichtingius* concerning this Place: I shall mention one more of this Kind, and then I shall conclude.

Crellius, upon that Passage to the *Galatians*, *God hath sent forth the Spirit of his Son into your Hearts*, farther observes, "Quia in cordibus hominum vim suam "exserat. *Again*, Spiritus istius operationis est, ut nos ex paterno Dei in nos amore "certos reddat, & filialem erga eum fiduciam nobis ingeneret.

Crell. in Ep. Paul ad Gal. comm.

What can we desire beyond this against our Adversary in this Point, to prove, that the *Primitive Socinians*, as they are called, believed God to have given, and still to give his Good Spirit unto Believers, as without which they could not, neither can be Children of God? *It is God's displaying his Power in the Hearts of Men, and it is by the Operation of his Spirit, that he makes us acquainted with his Fatherly Love to us, who begets in us a Filial, or Son-like Faithfulness towards him.*

Slichtingius, on that notable Saying of the Apostle *John*, in his first Epistle and second Chapter, *But the Anointing which ye have received of him, abideth in you; and ye need not that any Man teach you, but as the same Anointing teacheth you*, commenteth,

Slicht. in prim Epist. Joan. c. 2. v. 27.

"Unctio, pro eo quo facta est unctio, id est, pro oleo cœlesti, qui spiritus est "sanctus. *Again*, Hic enim erat spiritus istius sancti Effectus, qui eo fine daba-"tur, ut esset internus doctor veritatis, & in omnem deduceret veritatem. *Again*, "Unctio, id est spiritus sanctus, vos de omnibus docet, nempe ad salutem perti-"nentibus. In *English* thus, *Unction stands for Heavenly Oil*, that is, *the Holy Ghost or Spirit:* And to this End was the Holy Spirit given, *That it might become an internal Doctor, or Teacher of Truth, and lead into all Truth. Again, The Unction is the Holy Ghost, which teaches you all Things*, to wit, *what pertains to Eternal Salvation.*

Certainly, either our Adversary ought to relinquish his great Opinion of these Men, or else conclude, That *Enthusiasm, or Spiritual Motions, Revelations, Teachings, Rulings*, and *Guidings*, are not Things absurd, fantastical, or inconsistent with Christianity; *but most agreeable with, and suitable to the Nature of it, as that without which no Man can possibly be a Right Christian.*

But neither is *Crellius* of this Mind in his Commentaries only, where the Weight of Scripture tends him to these Interpretations; but in his Book of *One God the Father*, he frequently takes Occasion to declare himself, I think most plainly; I wish he had been as Sound and Clear in his Understanding of all other Points: "The Holy Spirit is the Power or Efficacy of God; namely (that we may explain "it) which proceedeth from God, and issuing unto Men, doth Sanctifie and Con-"secrate them, and produce various and admirable Effects in them; which Power "and Efficacy of God they are wont to call Divine Inspiration. *Again*, That the "Holy Spirit is given to Men by God, and that Men obtain, receive, and have "Him from God by Prayers, as numberless Places of the Holy Scripture shew, out "of which it is sufficient to have looked into but these few, *Luke* 11. 13. *John* 7. "39. and 14. 16, 17. (a Place by me quoted to the same Purpose) *Acts* 5. 32. and "15. 8.

Crell. of One God the Father, p. 197.

1672.

Pag. 205.

Pag. 208.

Pag. 218, 219.

Pag. 221.

Pag. 222, 223, 224, 235.

Curcell. adverſ. Mareſ. differt. prim. pag. 114.

"15. 8. Cor. 6. 19. By the Holy Spirit in theſe Places, is underſtood, *Some Divine and Holy Inſpiration, or ſome Power flowing from God, which is as it were breathed into Man.* Again, The Holy Spirit is properly given unto Men, and not Metonymically nor Metaleptically; *that is*, the Gift of the Holy Ghoſt, is ſimply and plainly to be taken as expreſt: Which (*ſays Crellius*) was not unknown even to the *Gentiles* themſelves; although in the mean Time, they did moſt grievouſly err in the Thing, taking a Falſe Inſpiration for a True One, a Deviliſh for a Divine. It would be tedious to inſtance a fourth Part of what he argumentatively writes on this; only I will produce a few of thoſe Scriptures which he ſo underſtands, and applies, 2 *Cor.* 1. 22. and 5. 5. — *Epheſ.* 1. 14. here a Pledge and Earneſt are mentioned. "Next, *ſays he*, all thoſe Places, where the Holy Spirit is ſaid to be poured out on Men, as *Iſa.* 44. 3. *Joel* (by us cited) chap. 2. 28, 29. *Zachariah* 12. 10. *Tit.* 3. 6. Where (*ſays he*) Men are ſaid to be *Baptized in, or with it.* Again, agrees to it that of Chriſt, who in *John*, inviting Men to the Participation of ſo excellent a Gift, thus ſaith, *If any Man thirſt, let him come to me and drink:* Underſtand it (*ſays Crellius*) of that Living Water, which, it is manifeſt, is the Holy Spirit: Let thoſe Places be added (*ſays he*) in which Chriſt himſelf is ſaid to be *Anointed*, or others are ſignified to be *Anointed with the Holy Spirit*, *John* 7. 37. *Iſa.* 61. 1. *Luke* 4. 18. *Acts* 8. 38. *Heb.* 1. 9. *Pſal.* 51. 8. 2 *Cor.* 1. 21. 1 *John* 2. 20, 21, 27. He proceeds to ſeveral Arguments upon divers other Scripture-Heads, as all Scriptures touching Divine Participation, not quenching the Spirit, the Holy Spirit being ſent, The Spirit ſearching all Things, &c. But above all, I ſhall conclude his whole Diſcourſe with this one Expreſſion, *viz.* "In this we know that we dwell in him, and he in us, becauſe he hath given us his Spirit, which we have expreſſed, is both perfect, and plainly expreſſeth the Thing given, and ſuch indeed, as may demonſtrate moſt clearly that God dwells in us, in ſome moſt Singular and Divine Manner, and we in him, and that there is a moſt ſtreight Bond of Love and Conjunction betwixt us and him; for how could we be more ſtreightly joyned with him, or he with us, than when he hath imparted to us of his Holy Spirit.

Curcellæus ſhall conclude theſe Teſtimonies: "Nec enim definunt fideles eſſe Templum ſpiritus ſancti; nimium quia Deus in ipſis per ſpiritum ſuum habitat: *That is*, Neither do the Faithful ceaſe to be the Temple of the Holy Ghoſt: Why? *Becauſe God by his Spirit dwells in them.*

Thus much for the Firſt Part of this Diſcourſe, I ſhall now apply my ſelf to the Second, which concerns a Vindication of *George Fox, and his Citation of Scripture*, from the Reproach and unworthy Dealing of our Adverſary.

A Vindication of *George Fox*, and the Truth by him Vindicated; particularly his *Quotation of Scripture*, from the Calumny and Cavil of this Libeller.

WE ſhall ſay nothing here of the Diſingenuity of the Man, in writing againſt a particular Perſon, to prove a Charge againſt a People, having already pointed at it in another Place; but ſhall fall to the Charge it ſelf, which I will faithfully lay down in his own Words, and the rather, ſince it is one main Part of his Proof aginſt G. F. *That he is an Impoſtor*, becauſe he renders not the very Words of Scripture, though Words importing the ſame Senſe.

Pag. 3. *If you will but allow us Competent Witneſſes to prove that* G. Fox *killed a Man, ſuppoſing we have ſeen him at Noon-Day thruſt him through the Heart with a Sword; Or if you will grant that we can read* Engliſh, *and know that* A. B, *is not* C. O. *then upon theſe Conceſſions we will undertake to prove, that* G. Fox *is a Falſe Prophet, a Lyar, or Impoſtor.*

This *Reader* is the Charge: And doſt thou not think it is rarely drawn up? Well may I ſay rarely, for I dare ſay, it is the firſt of the Sort that is extant in the World.

I muſt confeſs I am at a Stand what he intends with his ſuppoſitory Introduction to it; for I as little underſtand what the Man means by *allowing Us Competent Witneſſes,*

Witnesses, (when the *Us* are to see the Thing done) as he can pretend Difficulty in the obscurest Passage in *G. Fox*'s Writings: For either he should have said, *If you will but allow Us* (to be) *Competent Witnesses*, supposing we have seen him at Noon-Day, &c. or if, as by him already phras'd, viz. *If you will but allow Us Competent Witnesses* (leaving out *to be*) then say I, it should be, supposing They, (and not We) have seen him at Noon-Day, &c. for as expreft, they are Competent Witnesses: But if this be so trivial, as that our Time might have been better spent, and our Charity have overlookt it, as a Slip of the Man's Pen, or in the Compositor's Setting: Methinks he was as lavish of his Time as Penurious in his Charity, that, without any Just Provocation, he should trouble the World with an entire Book, containing little else but a Collection of such slender (at moft) Omissions, enlarg'd with his own *Malicious Comments*.

Well, but it is now Time, that we should see this wonderful Discovery he has made of *George Fox*, and that so plain, as killing a Man at Noon-Day (which unhandsom Comparison is no mean Instance of his own vexed, base, and murdering Spirit) or as his Mathematical Demonftration, that *A. B.* is not *C. O.* for which peculiar and easie Way of well-expressing of a Charge, we remain his Debtors.

To prove this Charge (the only Thing we want, for of false Accusers and Accusations we have enough) he thus goes about it, to use his own Words.

If G. Fox, in Matters of Concernment, not only to Men's Bodies and Estates, but also to their Souls and Eternal Estates, affirm that to be True, which to your own Eyes is manifestly False, or that to be False, which is True. Again, If G. F. doth belye not an ordinary Person, a mortal Man or Prince, but God Almighty, our Lord Jesus Christ, and the Holy Ghost. Moreover, If he deal thus through Design and Purpose, then he is what I have said, viz. a False Prophet, Lyar, and Impostor with a Witness.

This is but *Petitio Principii*, or a meer begging of the Question, nothing more is proved here than in the Charge it self; nay, it is but the Repetition of the Charge, expressed in other Terms; yet to it so expressed, I return in short thus much.

F. St., I deny *George Fox*'s affirming Things to be True which are False, and False which are True, to be obvious to our Eyes or Senses; for we can see no such Thing: And since we are so to see them, in order to the Conclusion, it follows, that *He is no False Prophet, Lyar, or Impostor, by his own Rule*.

But *Secondly*, I utterly deny, that *George Fox*'s so affirming or asserting, supposing as our Adversary says of him, renders him either a *False Prophet or Impostor*; since he only is a False Prophet, that either runs to inftruct or teach People, and is not sent of God, but speaks other Men's Words, not his own Visions; or who prophesies such Things to come, as never come to pass, but happen quite contrary, in neither of which Acceptations is *George Fox* proved a *False Prophet*; therefore none. The like may be urged to clear him from Imposture, since he only is an *Impostor*, that assumes to himself the Dignity of an *Extraordinary Ambassador* from God, and proves a *Cheat*, as *Simon Magus among the Samaritans and Romans, Mahomet among the Turks, and the late Jew in Italy*. So that if *George Fox* had singly affirm'd that to be True which were False, it prov'd him *No False Prophet or Impostor*; and therefore our Adversary shews himself a raw Disputant, and meer Novice, in the sound framing of an Argument; For what Man that understands an Horse from a Cow, would thus argue? *If G. Fox, in Matters of Concernment, not only to Men's Bodies and Estates* (then in Matters of Concernment, in Part to Men's Bodies and Estates) *affirm that to be True which is False, he is a False Prophet and Impostor*; He might as well have said, *If George Fox affirms he gave Ten Pound for an Horse, when he gave but Five, then G. Fox is a False Prophet and Impostor with a witness*: But I think it will not hurt us, to let him have to himself the whole Reputation of this Kind of proving to People's Senses the Truth of his Charge, who, had he not been void of all Sense himself, and Reason too, would never have suffer'd so much Weakness and Untruth to pass the Press without Correction.

Nay, though he could make it appear (which neither his Wickedness nor Prejudice will ever be able to do) that *George Fox* has designedly, and on Purpose belied the Almighty God, the Lord Jesus Christ, and the Holy Ghost, as he chargeth him to have done; yet still I affirm, that he could not properly and strictly be term'd a *False Prophet or Impostor*, though all, but such, would justly conclude him as Wicked as our Adversary is malicious: For might not a deboist Fellow, that mocks at God and Godliness, when he kills, lyes, or commits Adultery, say in his

Defence,

Defence, as the Apostle did, on a more serious Account, in another Case, that his Spirit was willing to have avoided such Things, but the Flesh was weak, and that it was not he which did those Things, but Sin in him, hereby belying the Holy Ghost, which in the Apostle intended quite another Thing: Yet I hope, none in their Wits, would count such a Fellow a *False Prophet or Impostor, though very impious and prophane.*

And that there are too many, who from *Nathan*'s Words to *David*, in the Case of *Uriah*'s Wife, and from the Liberty taken by some of the Ancients, have interpreted and concluded, that their boundless Lusts are by Scripture irreprehensible; *thereby making at first Sight, the Holy Ghost an Accessory to their Licentious Practices*, who was the Author of the Truth therein contained, (which is belying him with a Witness) I suppose, our Adversaries Observation in the World cannot but give him to understand: Yet how we can properly Character such *Libidinoso's*, or inordinate Persons, *False Prophets, or Impostors*, is left with the ingenious Reader to consider.

I hope by this Time, the Way he takes to prove *George Fox* what he wickedly says him to be, is evidently detected of Insufficiency, and that upon his own Positions, *George Fox* cannot be concluded either an *Impostor or False Prophet*. I shall now make it appear, that he is as well mistaken in the Proof of the Truth of his Charge, as in the Way he took to state it, and that no Man in that Compass, could well have manifested more Weakness, Folly, Malice, and Untruth (as well in defending of his own, as in opposing our Principles) than this our Adversary we have in Hand.

To follow him into every Absurdity, would not only be more than he deserves at our Hands, or any Man's that loves Time better than to lose it; but it would needlesly swell the Discourse, beyond both my Intention, and the Service it is designed to; I shall therefore contract and divide his Exceptions to *George Fox*'s Quotation of Scriptures, into these three Sorts.

1. Such as may refer to Doctrinal Difference, I mean wherein he opposeth us.

2. Such as refer to his *Socinian* Interpretation of the Scriptures, wherein Christ's Divinity is asserted, where we oppose him.

3. Such as are meerly trivial, in which there can be no Pretence for accusing *George Fox* of any Alteration, as to what himself judges generally to be the Sense of the Places, only perhaps a transposing of the Words, or the using of a Word of equal Force, but not the same, no ways detracting or varying from the Mind of the Scripture.

But that a Man should make fifty Doctrinal Cavils, to no solid Purpose, befits no Man that loves to be profitably employed; but it therefore suits him, that is so over-run with the Lazy, as I am really perswaded, he busies not himself in one serviceable Work in a Week together; only sits upon his own Saturnal Dreams till he has with Difficulty hatcht them into some seeming Consistency, and then they are to flutter abroad upon his Paper Wings (scarce Good enough for Waste) to the Shop, which trafficks in such Kind of Ware) till Persecution comes, with the Scorch of which they are wont to singe and wrap up like a Scrole: But enough of this. Now for his Doctrinal Exceptions.

He begins with what we confess to God's Glory to be our Beginning, and stumbles at it, as much as did the *Jews* of Old; *I mean Christ Jesus the Great Sun of Righteousness, and Light of the Invisible and Spiritual World, by which the Invisible Souls and Spirits of Men come to obtain the Saving Knowledge of God, and what is required from them, in order to their Eternal Salvation.* What can we expect then but Darkness, from him that seeketh to disparage the Light. But let us hear him.

The first Scripture which I shall pitch upon as misrecited (in his Language (that is *George Fox*'s, perverted and corrupted) shall be that in *John* 1. 9. He cites it almost as often Wrong as Right. The Scripture runs thus in our Translation, *That was the True Light that lighteth every Man that cometh into the World.* A long Porch, where's the House) says he, *in* the Greek *it is coming, (not that cometh) and so it may refer to Light as well as Man.* But *George Fox* hath it thus, *John* said, *Every Man that cometh into the World is Enlightned*, and several Sayings of the like Tendency. But now hath he observed that Exactness, which he requires in others? *May there be no Difference between Lighteth and Enlightneth; Must every Man of Necessity be Enlightned, because the Light lighteth him?*

Wonderful

Wonderful Distinction! Certainly this Man sets up for a *New Class of Criticks*: I wonder into what Labyrinth he hath travell'd for this Notable Gloss! A Body would think he had left his Wits (if ever he had any) behind in Exchange. But I answer,

I look upon it as Conceited and Presumptuous, for any Man to undertake what he cannot prove, and not less base, to affirm a Man miscites, perverts, and corrupts Scripture, when he renders the Genuine Sense of it. And this I briefly prove,

If I grant to this *Pseudo-Linguist* that ἐρχόμενον is a Participle, and not a Verb, as our *English* renders it, What then? Must it needs follow, that it refers to τὸ φῶς and not to πάντα ἄνθρωπον? Has he made no better Use of his *Greek Grammar*? 'Tis strange that any Man so mean in that Tongue, should undertake to thwart the current of all indifferent Translators, whom he sticks not to make Use of at other Times.

I have taken a View of the most and best Editions, both of *Greek, Syriack, Arabick, Æthiopick,* and *Latin,* I could at present find; besides, several other Languages, amongst others, a *Gothick* and *Anglo-Saxonick Testament,* which I suppose I understand as much as he doth *Greek,* or thereabouts, which I shall also produce for his Satisfaction.

The Greek.
Ἦν τὸ φῶς τὸ ἀληθινὸν ὃ φωτίζει πάντα ἄνθρωπον ἐρχόμενον εἰς τὸν κόσμον.

He was the True Light, which enlighteneth every Man coming into the World.

The *Syriack* Version has it, Omnem venientem in mundum; *All coming into the World*: Which, says *Drusius,* is sufficient.

The *Arabick* hath it thus, *That was the True Light, which Enlightens every Man;* making *Coming* to begin the next Verse, which I suppose was a Mistake in the Version of it; however, it gives no Force to our Adversary, since he is said, *To Enlighten all Men before his Coming, or being come into the World, is mention'd by the Evangelist,* In Him was Life, and that Life was the Light of Men; He was the Light of Men.

In the *Æthiopick* Version we find it thus, *And He is the Light of Righteousness, which Enlightens all Men coming into the World.*

Which Luther *renders thus.*
Erat lux illa, lux vera, quæ illuminat omnem hominem venientem in mundum.

Luther.
He was the True Light, which enlightens every Man that comes into the World.

Which Erasmus *renders thus.*
Erat lux illa, lux vera, quæ illuminat omnem hominem venientem in mundum.

Erasmus.
That Light was the True Light, which enlightneth every Man that comes into the World.

Which Beza *renders thus.*
Hic erat lux illa vera, quæ illuminat omnem hominem venientem in mundum.

Beza.
This was the True Light, which enlightens every Man that comes into the World.

Montanus *thus.*
Erat lux vera, quæ illuminat omnem hominem venientem in hunc mundum

He was the True Light, which enlightens every Man that comes into this World.

The Italian *Version thus.*
La vera Luce, era quellach, illumina ogni huomo che viene all mondo.

Italian.
The True Light was that which enlightens all Men which come into the World.

The Spanish *thus.*
Aquella Palabra era la luz verdadera que a lumbra a todo hobre, que viene en este mundo.

Spanish.
Which Word was the True Light, that giveth Light to all Men that come into this World.

The French *thus.*
Ceſte lumiere la eſtoit la veritable, qui illumine tout homme venant au monde.

French.
The ſame Light is the True Light, which enlightens all Mankind coming into the World.

Thus a Tranſlation in 1631.
La vraye lumiere eſtoit celle qui illumine tout homme, venant au monde.

The Tranſlation in 1631.
The true Light is that which enlightens all Mankind coming into the World.

Thus a later Tranſlation 1658.
Elle eſtoit la lumiere veritable, qui illumine tout homme, venant au monde.

The Tranſlation in 1658.
That was the true Light which enlightens all Mankind coming into the World.

High-Dutch, *or* German, *thus.*
Das war das Warhafftige Licht, welches alle Menſchen erleuchtet, die in dieſe Welt kommen.

German.
That was the true Light, which enlightens all Men that come into this World.

The Low-Dutch *thus.*
Dat wareachtige Licht was deſe die allen Menſchen verlicht komende in de Werelt.

Low-Dutch.
This was the true Light, which enlightens all Men coming into the World.

Anglo-Saxonick.
Soth leoht wæs that onlyht ælcne cumendne man on thiſne Middan-eard.

Anglo-Saxonick *verbatim.*
It was the true Light, which enlightens every Man coming (or coming Man) into this World.

I know not any Verſions or Copies extant but what are of the ſame Import with theſe already cited. That which ſeems farther neceſſary is, what hath been the Judgment of Ancient and Modern Writers in the Point.

Gregorius Nazianzenus, concione de Baptiſmate, is very expreſs in this particular, τῦ ἀληθινῦ φωτὸς τῦ φωτίζοντος πάντα ἄνθρωπον ἐρχόμενον εἰς τὸν κόσμον.

Chryſoſtom largely and earneſtly diſcuſſes this Thing, and concludes, that ἐρχόμενον ought to be joyned to ἄνθρωπον and not to Φῶς and in explicating this Queſtion, *Whether then is not every one* (ſavingly) *enlightened?* he very truly and to purpoſe ſaith, It is not any defect in the Light, but their Fault who will not admit of it, and yield to it; Ἡ μὲν γὰρ χάρις ἐκκέχυται, πάντας μετὰ τῆς ἴσης καλοῦσα τιμῆς, οἱ δὲ ἐκ ἐθέλοντες ἀπολαῦσαι τῆς δωρεᾶς, ἑαυτοῖς δίκαιοι ταύτην ἂν εἶεν λογίσασθαι τὴν πήρωσιν which is as much as to ſay, The Grace is impartially ſhed abroad (or held forth) unto all; but who wilfully refuſe that Heavenly Gift, muſt impute their Blindneſs to themſelves.

Thus alſo *Lactantius* taught, withal, not only applying the Participle ἐρχόμενον to ἄνθρωπον; but in Honour of that *Light,* aſſerts it to have an ἐνέργειαν, an Efficacy, or effectual Operation in all ſuch as believe in it, and walk up to it.

I ſhall now briefly touch upon the Opinion of ſome approved Men of Learning in this Point.

Eraſmus gives this paraphraſtical Account upon the Place, ' Non erat *Johannes* ' lumen illud de quo loquor, nam lumen hoc, de quo loquor, erat lumen verum ' quod illuminat omnem hominem venientem in hunc mundum. Making the Evangeliſt thus to ſpeak, John *was not that true Light, of which I ſpeak; for this Light I ſpeak of, was the true Light, which enlightens every Man that comes into this World:* And anſwering the ſame Objection (as our Adverſary maketh) *Ambiguitatem ſuſtuliſſet additus articulus* τὸν ἐρχόμενον: that is, The τὸν *not being in the* Greek, *renders the Senſe too ambiguous.*

Beza is peremptory in the Matter, for making the Objection our Adverſary doth, he anſwereth; ' Venientem in mundum, ἐρχόμενον εἰς τὸν κόσμον, id eſt, naſ' centem, ut explicat Chriſtus ipſe hoc dicendi genus infra 18. 37. Et additum ' eſt iſtud partim emphatico Pleonaſmo, partim ut tollatur Judæorum et Gentium
' diſcri-

' discrimen. *Act.* 10. 35. *Rom.* 11. 25. *& Gal.* 13: 26. Quod autem nonnulli Parti-
' cipium ἐρχόμενον putant posse ad τὸ φῶς referri, ut ita convertas; Hæc erat illa Lux
' vera, quæ, veniens in mundum, illuminat omnem hominem: id, inquam, vide-
' tur violentum, & tractationem hujus argumenti, id est, manifestationes Christi
' confundere; Malo igitur significari, nullum hominem nasci hujus Lucis expertem.
*Coming into the World, that is, being born, as Christ himself explains this Manner of
speaking below in the 18th Chap. 37 verf. And that is added partly by an emphatical
redundancy, partly to remove that Distinction which was between* Jews *and* Gentiles.
Acts 10. 35. Rom. 11. 25. & Gal. 3. 26. *But because some think the Participle*
ἐρχόμενον *may be transposed to* τὸ φῶς *to be construed thus; This is the true Light,
which coming into the World, enlightens every Man: which with me seems to confound
the handling of this Argument (that is of Christ's Manifestation) as unnatural and
extorted; I had much rather it should signifie, that no Man is born void of this
Light.*

' *Maldonatus*, whom *Crellius* often cites with great respect, says; ' Quem sensum
' *Cyrillus* et alij quidam secuti sunt, estq; non falsus, non absurdus, sed meâ sen-
' tentiâ non proprius. Nam ut alia non esset ratio, nomen hominis proxime ad-
' hærens jure sibi hoc participium vendicaret. Et Christus non solum in hunc
' mundum veniens, sed et postquam venit, et antequam veniret, erat Lux vera
' quæ illuminabat omnem hominem venientem in hunc mundum. Et alii Aucto-
' res omnes ita intellexerunt, ut non Christus veniens, sed Christus omnem homi-
' nem venientem in hunc mundum dicatur illuminasse, *August. Chrysost. Beda, The-
' ophylact. Euthym.* That is to say: Which Opinion *Cyrillus* and some others fol-
' lowed, and it is neither false nor absurd, but in my Judgment not proper: For,
' though there should be no other Reason, *Man*, being the next Noun, should of
' right challenge this Participle to himself. And *Christ* was, not only *when he came
' into this World, but before and after he came, the true Light, that enlightneth
' every Man that cometh into the World*, And all other Authors, as *Augustin, Chry-
' sostom, Beda, Theophylact,* and *Euthymius, &c.* understood it thus; It can not be
' said, that Christ coming into the World enlightens all Men, but *that Christ en-
' lightens all Men coming into the World.*

And of this Mind also is *Drusius*, upon the text, ' *omnem hominem venientem in
' mundum*; Satis erat omnes venientes in mundum. Sed homo dicitur antequam
' in mundum venit: in mundum venit cum nascitur. Igitur homo veniens in
' mundum, non est homo simpliciter, sed homo natus, aut qui nascitur. *Ebræi
' tamen* באי עולם vocant omnes homines. *Lib. Musar. c.* 5. Si congregarentur
' omnes venientes in mundum, ad creationem pulicis & ad infundendam animam,
' non possent. In *Munere novo* (Liber est ejus nominis) videbunt omnes venientes
' mundi, i. e. in mundum, 78. 2. & alibi sæpe. *Phesictha* 2. 1. Testimonio sunt
' omnibus venientibus in mundum, quod inter eos sit Divinitas. That is to say:
' *Every Man coming into the World,* says he, *All coming into the World, had been
sufficient. But he may be called Man before he comes into the World: he comes into
the World when he is born; Therefore Man coming into the World is not simply a
Man, but a Man born. But the* Hebrews *call all Men* באי עולם *that is, coming or
being born into the World.* Lib. Musar. c. 5. *If all that come into the World, should
meet to make a Flea, and to infuse a Soul, they could not do it: In* Munere novo
(a Book so called) *All coming of the World, that is, into the World shall see,* 78. 2.
and often elsewhere. Phesictha 2. 1. ' All coming into the World have a Testimo-
' ny, that there is a Deity among them. Thus much concerning the Sense of
Learned Men upon the Place controverted, which if it doth no good, will I hope
do no hurt, though a Man would think that so many able to teach him *Greek*,
might conclude him, unless he has more to tell us, than in his Libel.

Overlooking then some other Authors, I shall, as I am able, give my own Reasons, why ἐρχόμενον more properly belongs to Man than Light.

First, If Christ be that true Light by way of Eminency, which not only the
Scriptures most plainly character him to be, but all Criticks and Interpreters agree
to be the import of the Place, then will it necessarily follow upon their Notion,
who generally make *coming* the Participle of *Light* rather than *Man, that true
Light never saw the World, or rather the World true Light, till the Messiah's visible
coming, and that consequently all Antecedent Livers to his External Appearance,
however good and holy Men, were destitute of the true or saving Light, as having
never rose upon them, nor they been illuminated or refresht with the Divine Light*

and Heat thereof; which, as it is a most irreverent Thought of God, and uncharitable towards many deceased Generations, so it is for ever to be exploded for false, and inconsistent with the Impressions incident to every Man, as well as the Testimonies of the Scripture. For who living can believe, that before the *Messiah*'s Coming there was not a sufficient Light given to those Holy Patriarchs and Prophets, which if true, Christ as that true Light, by way of Eminency, must have been before such Manifestation. We shall easily grant, that in reference to the Trascendency of it's Appearance, *as to what had been it might be said more eminently to come at that Time*, but to exclude all lesser Degrees of Illumination by the same saving Light, *antecedent to it's brighter Discoveries in that Day*, we can never do; but do and shall maintain the contrary, knowing, that it is not a distinct, or other Light that saves now, than formerly did; but a more large Discovery of the same.

To which agrees that of Christ himself, Job. 8. 56, 58. *before* Abraham *was I am*; Abraham *saw my Day, and was glad*; And that of the Apostle 1 Cor. 10. 4. for they drank of that Spiritual *Rock that followed them, and that Rock was Christ. The Way of the Just is a shining Light.*

2. Besides, what shall we say upon their Transposition of the Words, as to the Time then present? I mean when the Light after their Sense, *was coming into the World*; for that the Scriptures will be most false, methinks they themselves should see; since it is notorious, *that neither whilst he was coming, nor come, one quarter of Mankind was any whit extraordinarily enlightned, much less savingly by him*; but they remained Infidels as before.

3. Nor is this all, for at this rate, *We*, since his Departure, are left as destitute as they before his Coming, and as they who heard not of him, when he was come were wholly ignorant; for how is it possible, upon their Interpretation, that we should have any saving Light? Christ, in whom was that excellent Light and Power, is gone, say they: The Scriptures in many Points are left dubious, as *Peter* testifies of *Paul*'s Epistles, say I: neither is there any unerring Interpreter or Guide to be obtained at this Time, say they again: *Certainly then, there can be but little true Knowledge, sound Faith, or well-grounded Comfort in so ill-founded a Religion, whose Belief is a kind of Fiction, and their Hope but a better Sort of Despair.* To conclude.

4. We therefore think it a wrong done to the Text, because of the Participle's unsuitableness to Light, and it's natural Agreement to Man; for Men are continually coming into the World, and *as such enlightned*, which cannot be said of Light in their Sense. The Messiah don't visibly appear as formerly; That Light is eclipst, as he himself said it was convenient to be, or the Comforter would not come; *but that Divine intellectual Light, which was most excellent, he promised should endure with his to the End*; by a Degree of which also the Holy Patriarchs of old saw the Glory of his Day, and Evangelical Dispensation, though as to the then State of the World, it was altogether unfit for it; wherefore it is said, that they desired to see his Day and saw it not; How? *Did they not see it as to themselves? By no Means*; for many of them saw it, *but they never saw it break forth as God's Dispensation to the World* (though they much desired it) because of the World's Incapacity to receive it.

What shall I farther say? If *coming* cannot so properly be said of Light in their Sense, as of Man in ours, (since so every Man in all Ages comes to have the Benefit of that Light offer'd unto him, which in the other Sense must be lost to Thousands, or they lose the Advantage of it (being not then born in that Age, in which that Sun (though for a little Season) was pleased to visit the World) then let it not be *Light coming*, but *Man coming into the World*. In short, take it in their Sense, *and one Age is hardly befitted*, take it in ours, *and all Mankind is illuminated*.

As to the Drift of our Adversary in his Transposition of the Participle, *viz. The Divesting Christ of all Right to Eternal Divinity,* (which is the *Snake in the Grass*) I shall anon sufficiently, I hope, vindicate that great Truth; though I cannot but wonder, since we without damage can allow him, that the Words may be true both Ways, as I have already, and may yet farther demonstrate, that he would desire only to receive them in one, as if on purpose he had a mind *to dethrone Christ from the Seat of his Eternal Majesty*; For what if *John* had chiefly intended a Description of the Heavenly Structure of the New World, and Christ to have been the

Enlighner of all that come into it; and farther, that the Messiah, then coming, was Author of that most excellent Creation; must it needs therefore follow, that he was not antecedent to that Work, that he never enlightned the Fathers and holy Men of Old, with a sufficient Measure of that same Light, which, without Measure, appeared in him, and far greater than before, to the Sons of Men? *I appeal to any modest intelligent Man, if this be not Ingratitude, nay Sacrilege in the highest Degree.* Certainly, therefore it can be no Injury to the Scripture, if we say, that He who enlightned the Patriarchs and Prophets of old, *hath, in a more excellent Manner and suitable to the Spirituality of his own Divine Nature, revealed himself in this Gospel-Administration,* the which may aptly be compared to a well-built Temple, which has been of old begun, but left to these latter Days of Christ's more eminent Manifestation, to superstruct, compleat, adorn and fit for him the eternal Light of Life and Righteousness to be worshipped in; so that there is a great Difference, as *Grotius* in other Words doth well observe, between the Beginning of an Administration, and of the Author of it, *That might be the Beginning of those large Discoveries, but not the Light that gave them*; and consequently, notwithstanding *John* should have intended a Divine Creation, yet it will not necessarily follow, that the Light, which is that Creator, *was not in being antecedently to that Divine Creation*; and so God, both by *Pre-existence*, and *Omnipotency*. But I shall say no more of this, I mean the Transposition of the Participle ἐρχόμενον, till our Adversary says more to the contrary, if we may then think it worth our Notice.

But it may be fit to observe, that the Man shows a wavering in his own Judgment, which is not only manifest from his Saying, *it may as well be referred to Light as Man*, but in a Manuscript to a Friend of ours, he affirmed it to be unreasonable, to refer *Coming* to *Man*, and not to the true *Light*; all we can say is this, that though it show him to be unsettled in his own Thoughts, yet he was willing to be a little more modest in Print, than in his Manuscript.

For his Distinction between *Lighteth*, and *Enlightneth*, I confess my Self troubled, not at his great Skill, but Folly; It shows, he would say something, if he could tell what, and to use a familiar Proverb, The poor Man will be playing at small Game, rather than stand out. Then, let's to the Word, since he would be thought a *Critick* Φωτίζει we read in the *Greek*, in the *Latin* Illuminat, and should in the *English* Enlightneth; the Defect is not in the *Original*, or *Latin Versions*, but our *English* only, I perceive, whether it be Original, or Translation, which makes most for him, that is the infallible *Text*, till it happens to contradict him, and then, *if in the Original, the Word is foisted in, or thus to be transposed, or rendred*; if in any of the *Versions*, then *it is not so in the Original, it is lamely rendred*, and the like. But this Challenge I make to the Man, that if he can find one Version in three, (and three to one that's odds) which renders it different from what we understand by it, I shall acknowledge him a *Critick*, and our selves ignorant in Words. All the Greek Copies and Latin Translations, I ever saw or heard of, import no other thing than *Illumination or Enlightning*. All that I have hitherto mention'd, so give it us, *quæ illuminat omnem Hominem*, &c.

1 Sam. 14.22.

That this is the constant Use of the Word, throughout both the Old and New Testament (so called) is evident: It is said, of *Jonathan*, that *after he had tasted a little of that honey, into which he put his Rod, his Eyes were enlightned*, פִּי־אֹרוּ עֵינָי, quia illuminati sunt Oculi mei. See, *faith* Jonathan, *I pray you, how mine Eyes have been enlightned*. The *Chaldee* Version hath it, illuxerunt Oculi mei, *how my Eyes shined*; The *Syriack* thus, *my Eyes have received Light*: The *Arabick* thus, quomodo illustrata est Acies mea, *how is my Eye-Sight clear'd*; but the *Septuagint* expresseth it thus; Ἰδὲ διότι εἶδον οἱ ὀφθαλμοί μου, *Behold how my Eyes have seen*; which in a mystical Sense is the same now, for that eternal Light or Word of Life, *is that Honey out of the true Rock, and Milk that the Prophet exhorteth the Jews to buy without Money, and without Price*; And who taste of that in Faith, receive that blessed Effect, namely, true Illumination, Thus *Job, to bring his Soul from the Pit*, that is from Darkness, Death and Sin, לְאוֹר ad Lucendum in Luce viventium, to be enlightned with the Light of the Living, The *Chaldee* has it after this Manner, *that my Soul may shine by the Light of the Living*: The *Syriack* and *Arabick*, *that it may see the Light of Life*; Job. 33. 30. and upon v. 28. which speaks to the same Purpose, says *Vatablus*, De Luce illâ Cœlesti intelligit, fruetur Dei conspectu, which is, *He means by that heavenly Light, he shall enjoy the Presence of God*. Likewise *David* most emphatically useth the same Verb, and that to our Purpose undeniably.

כִּי־אַתָּה תָּאִיר נֵרִי וחוה אֱלֹהַי יַגִּיהַּ חָשְׁכִּי

Psal. 18. 28. 29.

Quoniam tu illuminabis Lucernam meam, Deus meus illuminabit Tenebrositatem meam: *For thou wilt light my Candle; the Lord my God will enlighten my Darkness.* The *Chaldee* has it thus, *because thou wilt enlighten the Candle of Israel: The Lord my God will bring me out of Darkness into Light:* A notable Addition, at least Explanation of the Place, yet this is in the *Chaldee Version.* The *Syriack, Æthiopick* and *Septuagint* are the same; the *Arabick* differs only in Tenses, thou dost enlighten, for wilt enlighten, and he hath enlightned my Darkness, for he will enlighten my Darkness. And if the Spirit of Man, be the Candle of the Lord, and that God only can light it, then certainly, since Man's Spirit is within him, it is not more unsound, nor any more violating the Scripture Sense, to say, *that God enlightens,* than that he lightens every Man within, by communicating of his own Light to Man's Spirit, which receiving it, becomes lighted by it, to all right Knowledge and good Works. Farther, if *David's* Darkness was within him, in his Soul and Understanding, as certainly he meant it so, when he speaks of it, *then must that Light which was to shine there, shine in* David's *Soul and Understanding.* And what false Doctrine or English it is, or Perversion of Scripture, to say that Man is then enlightned, let sober People judge.

Ep. 1. 18.
Bez. in nov. fæd.

It is thus exprest in the Greek Copies of the new Testament also, and the Latin Versions of them, witness the Apostle *Paul* to the *Ephesians,* πεφωτισμένους τοὺς ὀφθαλμοὺς τῆς καρδίας ὑμῶν &c. *Illuminatos Oculos Cordis Vestri.* Beza has it in his Copy and Version, πεφωτισμένους τοὺς ὀφθαλμοὺς τῆς διανοίας μοῦ illuminatos Oculos Mentis meæ, The *Syriack* has it, *that the Eyes of your Hearts may be enlightned,* The *Arabick* thus, *enlightning the Eyes of your Hearts:* The *Æthiopick* thus, *and may enlighten the Eyes of your Hearts;* all agreeing in the Word *Illuminating* or *enlightning,* only one says of the Heart, and the other of the Mind, τῆς διανοίας, from διὰ & νοὸς νοῦς that is, *Mens,* or the *Mind of Man,* which indeed are but so many Words to the same Purpose; certainly then this Word, *Enlighten,* is not of so dangerous Consequence nor inconsonant to Scripture Language, as this idle and ignorant Person would render it.

Heb. 6. 4.

The like we find in the Epistle to the *Hebrews, for it is impossible for those being once* φωτισθέντας, *Illustratos,* or *inshined·* But, sayes *Beza,* Illuminati, *Enlightned,* if they fall away to renew them again, &c. they change in their Cases and Words, but not Sense; for to shine in the Understanding, or lighten the Understanding, or enlighten it, are the same with me, that love Time better, and my own Reputation, than to lose both by vain conceited Distinctions, that only show the Emptiness of the Head from whence they come.

Heb. 10. 32.

The like we may read in the tenth Chapter of the same Epistle, but call to Remembrance the former Days, ἐν αἷς φωτισθέντες, *in quibus illuminati,* in which ye were enlightned, says *Montanus,* quibus postquam illustrati fuissetis, by which ye were shined into, says *Beza,* that is, *enlightned, say I.* To which, agree most of the Versions, made Use of in this Discourse, whether Oriental, or any other; Also *Zegerus, Drusius, Grotius* and others, are wont to give this Interpretation upon it, both in their Places before mentioned, and else where, that φωτίζειν imports as much, as to *enlighten the Eyes of Men's Understandings unto the Knowledge of Christ,* also to *indoctrinate or baptize* them into the Knowledge of Evangelical Truths.

Crell. in Epist. ad Heb. c. 10. verse. 32. comm.

Crellius shall conclude the Matter, who in his Comment upon that Place of the *Hebrews,* saith, ' *Illuminati:* Luce nimirum Evangelicâ, per quam, ut Apostolus " loquitur, Vitam & Incorruptibilitatem Christus illuminavit, per quam omnes er- " rores, omnem mentis caliginem & cæcitatem expulit. The *English* Construction is, *Enlightned,* that is to say, *with the Gospel Light, by which (as saith the Apostle) Christ brought Life and Immortality to Light, and by which he expelled all Error and all Darkness and Blindness of Mind.* Certainly he was for Illumination, and such too as is infallible, (a Stumbling-block to our *Erroneous* Adversary, and his Brawling Associate, *T. F.*)

By which it evidently appears, that not only the word φωτίζει in the Text controverted, whether as *Verb, Adjective,* or *Participle,* signifies, and is used to express what *We* understand by *Illumination* or *Enlightning,* and so rendred by *Translators* and *Commentators;* but also the Holy Pen-men have employed it to that very Purpose, in most of those Places throughout the New Testament, (so called) wherein they have treated of Divine *Enlightnings, Inspirings* or *Illuminations*. But after what hath been urged in Defence of our Use of the Word, and for which he impertinently reflects upon G. F. What, if I should grant him his two empty Exceptions, (that are like Wasps without Stings) viz. *Coming* to refer to *Light*, and that *Lighteth* and *Enlightneth* are different Terms. First, As for *Coming*, it's referring to *Light*, it would amount to no more than this, that being to give an Account of the Evangelical Testament, and Gospel Administration, he might tell us, *that the breaking forth, Appearance or Coming thereof gave Light to, or illuminated all Men*; or, God was now fulfilling his Promise by his Son; namely, *that he would pour out his Spirit upon all Flesh*, that is, *every one should be enlightned with that blessed Sun of Righteousness, who then rose in a more extraordinary Manner than before*. Now, this being the best Use that could be made of referring *Coming* to *Light*, and not to Man; What great Matter should *We* lose by it. O, say these Followers of *Biddle*, and Mungrel *Socinians, but We should get by it*; *for We would thereby be in Hopes of shutting Christ out of all Pretences to an Eternal Divinity*, by restraining *his Beginning to Christ's being born of the Virgin*. By being with God, We should have it, *that he was bodily taken up into the highest Heavens, and there personally taught by God, upon solemn Conference betwixt them, what He should do on Earth, where He received his Verbal Commission, and descended*.

And by the Words, being God, *that upon his doing what was commanded him, here in the World* (for his Faithfulness) *he was godded*, that is, *not a God by Nature, but by Office, by Favour, and Acquisition*. O strange Imagination! Be these the Men that are not for *Meanings, Allegories,* and *strained Glosses*, but the *Punctual, Literal, Rational Scripturists*, whose Maxim is, *Non credimus quia non legimus*, We don't believe because we don't read it. If G. F. or any *Quaker* in *England*, had undertaken to have imposed such an Interpretation upon the World, in Favour of his Belief, how inflamed would our *Adversaries* have been against us? and *that this Fancy should be the first Corner and Foundation-Stone of their Building*, is very unhappy: And I heartily pity some of the first Inventers of this Notion, (indeed a very Fiction) that being so very rational in some other Principles, especially against *Infidels, Jews, Papists,* and *Atheists, they should notwithstanding draw a Cloud over the Brightness of their other Labours*, by the unjustifiable Scandal *this one Conceit brings upon them*, which I verily believe to be *buoy'd up* in the Opinions of several, by the Reputation that may be due to some other more scriptural and truly rational Doctrines.

Secondly, What if it should, contrary to the Current of almost all Versions, be allowed, that Φωτίει is *Lighteth*, and not *Enlightneth*? For my Part, I see no other Loss in it, than that it is not so forcibly exprest; For Man being composed of Soul and Body, the Soul is the Interior, the Body is the Exterior Part of Man; so that when the Body is lightned by the Sun, or, any other Fire, we may say the External Part is lighted about it's Business or Occasions; and when the Internal Part, the Soul, is lighted, *We may in Reference to the whole Man say, He is enlightned or lightned within*, because the Soul may properly be said to be *Internal* or *Within, or the most hidden and Spiritual Part of Man*. Behold then the Redoubtableness of this *Adversary*, his Will is *good*, I mean bad, as the Apostle saith in a more serious Case, *To will Mischief to us was present with the Man, but how to perform he knew not*; yet this pedling Controvertist will be doing, though as little to Purpose as need be: Witness one material Part of his Observation against G. F. *if it hath any Matter at all in it*, viz. that he changed the Phrase, and Tense or Time. Alas, poor Man! And what then? *Ergo*, saith he, G. F. is a *False Prophet, a Lyar*, and *an Impostor*: Boldly said; but prove it, who can, or will, for him. But what then will become of the Man that would have the Text controverted thus rendred, *Hæc est Lux illa vera quæ venientem in mundum illuminat omnem hominem*: This were as ingrammatical altogether, but we spare him, though we must remember him; for we cannot esteem it Doctrinal Error for a Man to miss a Tense, and would have him and all Men know, that *our Religion stands not in Grammatical Tenses*, but *the Fear of God, and Faith in Christ Jesus, whose Blood cleanseth from all Sin, such as walk in his Light*. Nor did the *Prophets* and *Apostles* stand upon Tenses, especially *Jeremiah* and *John*, whose *Hebrew* and *Greek* don't much exceed the *Quakers English*. G. F. was not sent to preach up Propriety of Speech, *the World is but too curious and proud in such Human Science* and Acquisition; *But like a Faithful Minister of God, by his Eternal Spirit and Power to turn People from Darkness*

Darkness to the Light (in which the Ransomed walk, with Everlasting Joy upon their Heads) and from the Power and Kingdom of Satan, which stand in the Lust of the Eye, Lust of the Flesh, and Pride of Life, unto God, and his Holy Kingdom, which stands in Righteousness and Peace, and Joy in the Holy Ghost, Rom. 14. 17. And as such it is that *G. F.* is owned and respected with other publick Labourers amongst us, *who seek not Honour from Men, as our Adversary and most of the rest of Men do; but that which is from God and his Wisdom, which is first pure, then Peaceable, Gentle, and easy to be entreated;* which is not of this World, but by the Children thereof esteemed *Foolishness* and meer *Enthusiasm, and that in a Way of Derision:* and we know that we are of God, and the Generality of the World lies in Wickedness, either of Flesh or Spirit.

Having, I hope, sufficiently prov'd, that the Participle ἐρχόμενον, *Venientem,* or *Coming,* is to be referred to *Men,* and not to *Light*; and that Φωτίζει is properly *Illuminat,* and that *Enlighten:* Nay, in Case they were not so, that it would prove little prejudicial to our Sense (as the Difference hath been already explained) I am now willing to make appear, that the Light, of which we have been so treating, is no natural nor created Light; but, *a Supernatural and Eternal Light,* which done, we shall conclude, at least on this Subject, the Controversy.

1. If Man be enlightned by that Word, which *was with God, and was God, and that before the World was;* then Man is enlightned by a *Supernatural* and *Eternal Light:* but the Scripture in the first, second, and third Verses of *John*'s first Chapter, proves Man to be so enlightned, and that Light to be such, as before said; *therefore Man is illuminated by a Supernatural Eternal Light.*

If he object another Sense of these Verses, than the Words simply and nakedly seem to import; for Instance, that the Beginning, there mentioned, relates not to the World, and visible elementary Creation, but the invisible Creation, as I know is their common Refuge. I reply,

2. If all things were made by him, and without him nothing made that was made; then, either *John* spake Equivocatingly, not meaning what he said; or else, plainly and properly, and consequently all Things (of which the World is the greatest Part) were made by him; and therefore *He must needs have been before all created Things.*

3. If he were that true Light, *by Way of Exemption to all others,* (as the *Socinians* are wont to interpret *God* to be *true God, John* 17. 3. and there is no Reason to the contrary) *then was he Light in himself;* and consequently, did not illuminate by a receiv'd or borrow'd Light, from another; *but ex se, out of himself, and from himself only,* and therefore God; as saith *John* in his first Epistle, *This then is the Message which we have heard from him, That God is Light,* &c. The first Proposition is Scriptural, and needs no Proof; and the second I prove thus,

4. If the Divine Life of this creating Word be that True Light by Way of Excellency and Exclusion of all others, *with which he enlightens every Man, coming into this World,* then must he be Light in Himself, and from Himself; unless he can be Himself without that Divine Life which is in Him; which because he cannot, it will follow, that he is such a true Light as hath been asserted; and consequently, must be God, *inasmuch as he, who is the Fountain of true Life, is God.* Which I farther prove thus,

5. If he, who is eminently that true Light, by whom only all Mankind is enlightned, neither is, nor can be that Light, as any Part of Mankind, however immaculate *(since so he would be a light unto himself,* which is both absurd and impossible) then that Creating Word, which is that Divine Life, which is evidently that true Light, by which all Men are enlightned, neither is nor could be a *Mortal Man, however Holy; and properly therefore it was not Christ, as Man, but as God, that was and is eminently the Light of Men.* Which I farther prove.

If that Light, *in which all Men ought indispensibly to believe for Salvation,* be the Light, with which Men are enlightned; *then are all Men savingly and supernaturally enlightned:* But the Scripture here quoted proves the Light in which all should believe, and which illuminates all, to be the same; and consequently, the Light, wherewith Men are enlightned, is Saving and Supernatural.

7. If that World was made by him, in which he was, and which knew him not; then, because this *Elementary World was the World in which he was*, and *Mankind then in it, those that knew him not*, it follows, that this *visible Elementary World, and Mankind in it, were made by him*; and if made by him, *then necessarily he must have been before them*: and since this Word is that Light, by which Men are enlightned, it followeth, that they are illuminated by a Supernatural and Eternal Light.

8. If to as many as receive him, (the true Light enlightning all) to them he gives Power to become the Sons of God; then the Way to be a Son of God is, *to obey the Light*, or to receive and obey the Light is the Way to be a Child of God; *not born of Blood, nor of the Will of the Flesh, nor of the Will of Man, but of God*; but the Scripture plainly testifies that to be the Way: *therefore the Light is Saving and Supernatural*.

Thus much in short from Scripture: I have a few Arguments to offer from Reason.

It is, I think, granted on all Hands, That God has enlightned Mankind with some Light or other; the Question then will be this, What Nature this Light is of, Saving or Insufficient, Natural or Supernatural? I prove it to be Supernatural and Saving thus:

1. If the Light, with which God has enlightned Men, were natural, then could it inform Men only in and about natural Affairs; but we see that Men do thereby in Measure *know and discern Things that are Supernatural*; therefore this Light is not Natural, but is Supernatural, and consequently Saving.

2. That it gives Men some Knowledge of Divine Things, I suppose all believe; however, I thus prove it: God gave it for some End, or no End; for no End we cannot, we dare not suppose; if for some End, then not in Reference to Natural Things, because they are knowable by the Spirit of Man as such; *consequently it must be in and about Things relating to Man's Duty to God and his Neighbour*, in which consists the Salvation of his own Soul: If so, then I prove it's Sufficiency thus:

3. Whatever God gives to any Man for any End, *is sufficient for that End for which he gives it him*: But God has given his Light unto Men, in order to their Duty to Him and their Neighbour, in which consists the Salvation of their Souls; and consequently that Light is sufficient to that End.

That what God Gives to any End is sufficient to compass it, I thus prove;

4. God requires all Men strictly to serve and obey him, and to work out their Salvation with Fear and Trembling; or else, their End shall be Destruction: But this the Almighty (with Reverence I say it) could not justly do, unless the Light with which he enlightens Men, were sufficient and saving; *therefore, unless our Adversary will impeach him of manifest Injustice, or deny that he thus requires Men to fear him, and work out their own Salvation, he must grant, that not only God hath illuminated all Men, but that the Light, wherewith he hath illuminated them to that great End, is Saving and Supernatural*.

Object. I know the Objection that is on these Occasions frequently started, *viz. How cometh it then that all Men have not a clearer View of this Light whereof you speak?*

But Men must have a Care of concluding the Light ever the less Divine in it self, because of that dim and imperfect Sight their own Infirmities cause them to have of it; perhaps some are as incapable to behold the Light as it is, as an Infant to make a true Prospect by the Natural Day: Others are grievously infested with *Rheums, Bloodshed*, and many other Distempers; whilst not a few either wilfully close their Eyes, are blinded with Motes and Beams, run into obscure Places, or by their continued Obstinacy in Wickedness, come at last wholly to lose both the Light, and their Capacity of seeing it. Such are those on whom the Night comes, in which none can work; and this was impenitent *Jerusalem's* Case, which is too too frequently and lamentably parallelled in our Days. Men must not think to see all at once; and because their inquisitive, impatient and wand'ring Mind is not answered by whole Heaps of glittering Discoveries; *therefore, in a*

brittle

brittle unsubject Nature, fling off all Regard to the Light of God, and vainly think to compass Salvation in their own unwarrantable Strivings.

Let Men consider seriously their own dark State, how long the Light hath shined there uncomprehended; and since it has pleased the Eternal God to visit them with such a Ministry and Testimony as turns them unto that blessed and unchangeable Light, diligently adhere to it, and be humbly contented to Practise what they know, (for, to that only End and Purpose does God cause it to shine in their Hearts) before they look after other Discoveries, *from that grasping, ravenous, comprehending Spirit in Man, which would know the End before it practiseth the Beginning*, which is cursed of God, and is for Eternal Judgment; this lost *Adam* his *Paradise*, and obstructs Thousands from entring into the Way of God at this very Day.

Wherefore blessed are they, who knowing their own Weakness, wait diligently upon the Lord, for such daily Dawnings of his own saving Light, as suit their own States, *as to their daily Temptation, Preservation and Increase, in the Experimental Knowledge of the Way of God*: Such are not wise above what's written in their Hearts, by the Finger of God; and speak and declare of God, and his unchangeable Way, according as they have felt and handled; I mean, *as he hath revealed himself both in Judgment and Mercy*, through the In-shining Light of his Son.

And this I publish to the whole World, *That I never knew God truly and heartily, to be of purer Eyes than to behold Iniquity, I was never conscientiously convinced of any Evil, I never was brought into true Repentance, I never experienced real Atonement, I never had right Faith in Christ*, nor did I ever inwardly come to feel a Cleansing from any Sin, and a being justified by his Blood, by which to know him my Mediator, Saviour and Redeemer, but by the Reproofs of that Light, wherewith Christ has enlightned me, and by turning to it, and walking in it with all Godly Fear and Subjection, according to it's Blessed Discoveries and Requirings. Wherefore I boldly call it, *A Sufficient, Saving and Supernatural Light*: And according to the Truth of this, *so let my Soul find Mercy with my God by Jesus Christ.*

I shall sum up my Sense briefly thus:

All Mankind have been *Benighted*,
All Men have *Degenerated*;
In that State, *all are Ignorant*;
In that State, *all are Corrupted*;
And in that State, *all are Damned*:
    And this Certainly.

God would have *all Men be saved*;
But they can *never be Saved*,
'Till they be Regenerated:
To be that, *they must be Washed*;
To be Washed, *they must Believe*;
And to Believe, *they must Repent*;
And to Repent, *they must see why*,
And to do this, *they must have Light*:
    And all this Certainly.

This *Light* must give true and *right Sight*;
This *Light* must be *sufficient*;
Then this *Light* is *infallible*;
Then this *Light* must needs be *Saving*:
    And all this is True.

This, by their own Principle, cannot be deny'd, as well as that it is true in it self.

I conclude, therefore, That all Men of themselves want Light; that God, since he would have all be saved, has given all Light; that this Light must give a certain Discerning; and that such as are guided by it are consequently certainly led. In short, The Light is both Universal, Supernatural, and Infallible.

That this is not our Judgment only, I shall mention a few of many, that assert it to be a SAVING LIGHT.

1. Thus believed *Origen.* Φῶς δὲ Ἐθνῶν ἐν τῷ Ἡσαΐᾳ ὡς προείπομεν παρατιθέμενοι τὸ Ἰδὲ τέθεικά σε εἰς φῶς Ἐθνῶν, τοῦ εἶναί σε εἰς σωτηρίαν ἕως ἐσχάτου τῆς γῆς —— ὁ δὲ σωτὴρ ἐλάμπων τοῖς λογικοῖς, κ̀ ἡγεμονικοῖς, ἵνα αὐτῶν ὁ νοῦς τὰ ἴδια ὁρατὰ βλέπῃ, τῷ νῷ τοῦ κόσμου ἐστὶ φῶς. He is truly called the Light of Nations, or the *Gentiles*, by *Isaiah*; *I have given thee for a Light, to lighten the* Gentiles, *and for my Salvation to the uttermost Parts of the Earth* — But truly, our Saviour is the great Light of the intelligible World, enlightning those in the most excellent Parts of their Souls, who are capable of Reason, that the Mind may discern and perceive to it self those Things that are most proper and worthy of Men's Pursuit after. Orig. in Joan. c. 1. v. 9.

2. *Chrysostom* positively declared his Judgment in the Matter, as we have observed before.

3. *Erasmus*, upon the same Place tells us, "That it's Import, so far as concerned "the Nature of the Light, lies here; Illa lux, erat Fons Luminis, unde ipsi quoq; "Johanni suum fluxit Lumen: That Light was the Fountain of Light, *from whence* John *himself received that Light he had.* If so, then a *supernatural and saving Light*, then *God*, and consequently *more than a Man*; because as such, John *was before him*, and could not be enlightned by him. Erasm. in prim. cap. Joan. comm.

4. *Beza*, though he restraineth that Light to a particular Number, which is not the Point in Controversie, yet he confesseth it to be a *Saving Light*, at least, to as many as God hath destinated it: "Quasi de regenerationis gratiâ hic agitur, "quæ Filiis Dei peculiariter est destinata. Bez. in nov. fæd.

5. *Tollet* speaks very notably on this Occasion: "Sunt vero tres illius lucis "proprietates: antiquitas, veritas, & communitas, quæ cum Johanni non insint, "rectè conclusitur illum lucem illam non esse — quæ illuminat omnem hominem "venientem in Mundum; non in Judæos solum, sed et in omnes gentes Lumen "suum diffundit — Dicitur autem Lux illa omnem hominem illuminare, sicut & "Sol, qui sufficiens lumen expandit, & omnes illuminat & omnibus propositus est, "ut videant: quod si qui non vident, defectus Solis non est; sic *Christus* in hoc "Mundo, omnibus quidem hominibus, quantum est in se, & ex efficaciâ Lucis "suæ lucet. *That is*, There be three Properties which are peculiar to the Light; *Antiquity*, which (says he elsewhere) is Eternity; *Truth*, by Way of Excellency; and *Community*, in that all Men who are born into the World partake of it, or are enlightned by it. — *But that Light, like unto the Sun, is said to enlighten all Men; who streams forth Light sufficient, that it may give Light to all; and He is set before all, that all may see. Thus doth Christ on his Part, illuminate all Men with His Efficacious Light.* Toll. in prim. cap. Joan. com. pag. 39.

6. *Maldonatus*, to the same Purpose thus: "Nonnulli hoc de naturali rationis "lumine intellexerunt. Sed minime dubium est de spirituali lumine intelligendum, "de doctrinâ, de fide, de gratiâ, de vita illâ de quâ dixerat; & vita erat Lux ho- "minum, *Cypri.* lib. 1. & *Christus* non solum in hunc Mundum veniens, sed & post- "quam & antequam veniret erat Lux vera quæ illuminabat omnem hominem ve- nientem in hunc Mundum. *Which is to say*, "Some have understood this Place "as treating of the Light of Nature or Reason; but, *says he*, there is little Doubt, "*But it is to be understood of a Spiritual Light, of Doctrine, of Faith, of Grace, "and of that Life, concerning which he* (viz. John) *had said, and that Life was the "Light of Men*, as says Cyprian, lib. 1. — *And not only at Christ's coming, but both "before and after he came, He was the True Light, which enlightens every Man "coming into the World.* Maldon. in prim. Joan. cap. comm. p. 411, 412.

7. *Vatablus* has it in the same Sense with *Erasmus*, He was the Fountain of Light it self, "Unde etiam Johannes quicquid habebat Lucis. *From whence* John *received what Light he had.* Vat. in prim. cap. Joan. comm.

Zegerus, though not on these very Words, yet to the Context, *In him was Life*, &c. speaks thus: "Et Vita erat Lux hominum, & Lux in tenebris lucet; illa in- "quit, vita per quam condita sunt omnia, illa vita quæ est Verbum, imo quæ "Deus omnis Vitæ Fons, ipsa semper fuit, & est Lux omnium hominum, quæ om- "nibus impertit naturalis luminis & gratiæ beneficium: & hæc Lux in tenebris "animarum nostrarum lucet, quas animas obscurârat Princeps iste tenebrarum Di- abolus. *And that Life was the Light of Men, and the Light shines in Darkness*, &c *That Life*, says he, *by which all Things were made; that Life which is the Word,* Zeg. in prim. cap. Joan com.

yea,

1672.

yea, which *is God, the Fountain of all Life*; *that very Life ever was, and is the Light of Men, which furnisheth all both with the Advantage of Natural (or Worldly) Light, and the Light of God's Grace*: And this Light shineth in the Clouds, or dark Places of our Hearts, which the Devil, that Prince of Darkness, hath vailed.

Com. in Joan. cap. 1. com.

Cameron also is not foreign in his Exposition, but seems to conceive the same Thing: " Etsi verum est omnem humanæ mentis Lucem esse ab illo Sole, attamen " intelligendum est præcipuè de illa Luce quæ est ad salutem, & quâ fit ut tenebris " peccati & mortis liberemur. *And though it be True, that what Light Man hath, it proceeds from that Sun, yet it is chiefly to be understood of that Light which leads to Salvation, and by which we may be freed from the Darkness, or Grave of Sin and Death.*

Thus much as to the Judgment of these *Grandees* (in the World's Account) as to their concurrent Exposition of this Place, by which it may be seen, that Men famous for acute Learning, have had that Sense of the Truth of the Letter of the Scripture, *which we have been reputed Hereticks, indeed what not, for maintaining as an Article of Christian Faith*: It is to be hoped, that People will accept of Truth from them, if their Prejudice will not admit them to embrace it from us; but since it is not our own Praise we seek, but the Glory of Him that made us, and the Salvation of others, *We shall not be displeased if they receive the Truth at any Hand, so they receive it as it is in* JESUS.

Here I would fain break off, but that I feel my self somewhat prest with a few Passages which refer to the *Light*, towards the Conclusion of the Libel, that may not improperly be considered under this Head.

Certainly it would be thought very strange, and that I have spent my Time as unprofitably as the Emperor that would be all Day a killing of Flies, if at last I should make this Man speak the *Language of the Light*, nay, to be a *Defender of it too*, against whom I have been all this While defending it; but who can help it, if Men will self-contradict, and put Weapons into their Opposer's Hands, to disarm and conquer themselves?

Tho' in one Page he tauntingly says, *He is perswaded that some of us have such an Opinion of the Light, our Great Fundamental, that though an Angel from Heaven should Preach any other Doctrine, than that which* G. F. *hath preached, they could not give Ear to it* (which saying one would think abusive enough of the Light) yet he makes amends in the next, where he thus addresseth himself to us, *Or rather that so much reproached Light*; *I appeal to the Light in every one of you, whether he is not guilty himself in a much higher Degree of such Things as he condemns in others.* Monstrum horrendum! What Man of tolerable Sense would thus write his own Reproof, and in less than two Pages give himself the Lye? But it is Just with God that such Men should be strongly infatuated. Is it not strange that he should mock at our desiring to be informed by the Light at the Bottom of one Page, and make his own Appeal unto it at the Top of the very next? Is it fit to direct us in, and about what he writes, and not concerning the Writings of other Men? Or, Is it a true and approved Light when it concurs with him, and *but a weak, delusive, and what not Light, when it leads us to oppose him?* But out of his own Mouth let him be judged. I shall therefore contract the Benefit I make of his own Appeal into these Two Arguments.

1. That unto which he makes an Appeal must be capable of giving an infallible Judgment, and so *A True Judge, or else he appeals foolishly*. But the Light within, is that unto which he makes his Appeal, and we would not think him to do it to a Thing not fit to give to a certain Judgment; *therefore the Light is an infallible Judge by his own Appeal.*

2. If it be appealed to by him as competent Judge; nay, that by which we should satisfie our own Consciences, touching the Things he lays to G. F's Charge, namely, *Impostor*, &c. and since those Things are of the highest Nature in Religion, or against it, then will it follow, *That the Light is to be the Judge of* George Fox, *and not only of him, but concerning those weighty Points of Religion wherein he is abusively charged by the Libeller*: And if so, I would both tell him, That G. F. *is pronounced not Guilty by the Verdict of that* Light, *from which there is no Appeal*; *and himself first Guilty of charging him with what he has not proved*; *and secondly, of abusing, degrading, and contemning the Light*; and then, contradictorily to himself, *of making his Solemn Reference and Appeal to the* Light, *as the most Impartial and Unerring Judge*,

Tell

Tell me now, what could we have said more in Praise of the Light, so far as meer Words go? And what could he have said more against himself?

He farther adds, *That 'tis the* Protestant *Principle, as well as ours; that it is evident by their Dissent from the Church of* Rome, *who pretends to be the Infallible Guide in Religion. No, says the Protestant, Every Man is Judge for himself.* Farther, *That God has for that End, endued every Man with such a Light of Common and Certain Principles, written in every Man's Heart, that if a Prophet should come, and give them a Sign or Wonder, to draw them away from the Observation of that Light, and those Principles, they ought not to adhere to that* Prophet (see Deut. 12. 1, 2, 3.) *Moreover, God, they say, has promised His Holy Spirit to those that humbly implore it, in the Obedience of that* Light. Farther, *That we have entertained it under New Names; that the Contention between us and our Adversaries, is about Words*; *Natural Light,* say they, quoting that of the *Romans,* For when the *Gentiles*, that have not the Law, do by Nature the Things contained in the Law, they having not the Law, are a Law unto themselves. *Divine Light, say you,* John 1. 9. *Is not the Difference betwixt you and others about Names; for whether God hath given it Men by Nature or not, it is of God in respect of it's proceeding from Him, and tending to Him.* Thus an eminent Preacher, in a great Assembly of late upon the Text, " And so far the Quakers *are in the Right, That every Man* " *hath the Motions of Good and Evil within him; which, in plain Cases of Good* " *and Evil, Right and Wrong, will tell him what he ought to do, and what he ought* " *to avoid, by which he ought to be directed; and that his Conscience will acquit and* " *excuse if he do the one, and accuse and condemn him if he do the other.* Thus far our Adversary and his Eminent Preacher.

To the first I shall say, that taking it for granted, he is as *Orthodox as a* Protestant, whose Cause he would seem to vindicate, yet he grosly contradicts himself, compared with his several lessening Expressions of the *Light:* But I hope, now he has told us that both the Protestants and himself receive and assert the *Light* to be the right Judge and Guide, *that both will never more be angry with the poor* Quakers *for being of that Mind*; And that our Adversary will particularly retract his Manuscript to G. W. in Defence of the Scriptures being the Judge, Rule, and Guide, or to that Effect.

As for his refusing us the Reputation of having shown them the Way to such Belief, saying, *It was always theirs*; We are contented to sit down without the Glory of being so much as Instrumental to such Convictions. In short, *If the Light within be a more certain Ground than very Signs and Wonders*; Nay, *that excellent Gift, with which God has endu'd Man in order to the safe Conduct of his Life,* as our Adversary hath plentifully confest, then have we obtained our Post *(viz.* that the Light is an Infallible Guide) and need no more contend about what is so exprefly yielded to us, and the accord *confirmed by the Concessions of an Eminent Preacher too,* whom I wish as Eminent a Practitioner, and not less found in his Life than Pulpit. But alas! such is our Man's Uncertainty to himself as well as others, that it seems Impossible with him, to write two Pages, and they not quarrel with each other, *and both Mutiny against their Author*; for after his Elogies bestowed upon the Light, he is once more come to unbespeak them, like the Sullen Cow, that spills the Milk she gives.

And that which is more to be wondred at, this miserable Man begins to except against the Sufficiency of the *Light*, from those very Reasons, for which he seems to have asserted it in an high rate, thus; *And this helps me to shew in the third Place, that you extend the Doctrine of the Light in every Man farther than you ought; for it is not to be extended to all Cases whatever, as if every Man that attends to the Light in him, did certainly know, what is good, what is Evil, Right or Wrong in every Case.*

I heartily pity the Man, and am really afraid he has overcharged the Strength of his Brain, for with me such manifest Contradiction is but a smaller Degree of Distraction; I would fain have a rational Answer from him, if he be yet capable of one. How can the Light be *Judge of Good and Evil,* and yet *not be so,* and all within the Space of ten Lines? If the Light, as by him acknowledged, be a Judge of Good from Evil, and the contrary, *then in all Cases, where Good and Evil, Right and Wrong make up the Question, the Light cannot be secluded as wanting in true Judgment, because Good and Evil are part of the Question, in the granted Proposition*; Deny that the *Light* is sufficient in any Case of Right or Wrong, and deny all. But to me it seems very strange, that the very same Light, which was at t'other Side of the Leaf the great Judge of Doctrinal Truth, and with which God had endu'd Men to their singular Benefit, *should at last be denied the Ability of giving Right Judgment in Matters that strictly belong to Good and Evil.* What is this but to say, it is a Judge of Good and Evil; *But is not a Judge of Good and Evil* God's Gift, to guide us, yet in many Things it may err? Well, but what are all these Things of Moment into which this Light is unable to wade? O! many Difficulties, *even Good Men differ in their Judgments about them, so we see among the Saints at* Rome, *to whom* Paul *wrote,* One (faith he) *believes that he may eat all Things, another who is weak eats Herbs ; One Man esteemeth one Day above another, another esteemeth every Day alike,* Rom. 14. 2, 5. O stupendious Folly! This Way of Reasoning well becomes him; for what is it but to say, This Light of which I speak, hath Sufficiency in it to discover the Nature of Things of greatest Concernment, but not these minute and trivial Matters, she can judge of Doctrines, but not of Ceremonies, and can try Spirits but not Infirmities, whether they be such or not. But I hope that Men in their Wits, and I write to no other, will never abandon their Reason so far, as to think those Persons not being as yet so clearly disentangled from the *Jewish* Ceremonies and needless Observations of that exterior Worship, shall be interpreted a defect in the *Light* about difficult Matters; for neither are such Things difficult, but discerned to be sometimes the needless Scruples of Weakness, sometimes the Dotage of Superstition, many Times Will-Worship : nor can any Blame be cast more upon the *Light,* or the *Light* justly suffer the Imputation of Deficiency, than the External Sun, *because some People have such sore Eyes that they cannot strongly behold the Light.*

'Tis true, perhaps Abstinence may be both best, and often enjoyned some Persons, either by Way of Testimony against Excess in others, or having been too apt to give themselves an undue Liberty, and *on all, that they may eat and drink in fear,* as faith the Apostle ; *I keep under my Body, and bring it into Subjection, lest having preacht to others, I my self should become a Cast-away.* But what then? Must the *Light* be no whit concerned therein because of the great Difficulty in the Point? By no Means, the *Light* dictates and requires these Things in their Times and Seasons; for whatever our Adversary does, no sober Man can believe that the *Light* is sufficient to the most weighty Things that concern Man's Salvation, and yet unable to judge of those Differences mentioned by the Apostle, *which were such Weaknesses as needed Christian Charity to bear with them.*

Nay, it was by the *Light* that their Weakness was seen, neither could it have been born, or they ever have grown stronger than to Place Dissents in those trivial Things, *but by walking up to the Light,* which was alone able to give them Right Discerning in the Case. I conclude therefore that in the Instance made by our Adversary, there could be no Difficulty too great for the *Light,* nay that *the Instance is so trivial in Comparison of the excellent Knowledge, and Judgment, which are received by the Light,* that it makes but the more for us to the Disparagement of him that hath alledged it.

And thus much (though a Knock to himself, even whilst he thinks us under his blow) when he says, *And where is the Infallibility you speak of in particular Persons, in all Cases? I am perswaded if you consider this well, you will perceive that the Light in every Man (especially in those whose Judgments have been prepossess'd into false Notions, as many of you have been before you were* Quakers) *doth not teach him all Things whatsoever, but all Things that are necessary for him to know in order to an Holy Trust in God, and sincere Obedience in the general Course of his Life.* Well! before I would undertake Controversies, and thus give away my Cause, nay so wofully, yea, frequently contradict my self, I would never write while I live. But to make my Advantage of this too ;

Infallibility of Persons, any farther than as they are joyned, and conformed to the Light of God, we never affirmed; and *Fallibility of the Light, because of the Fallibility of Persons, We never owned,* and now deny as a most Ridiculous and False Consequence.

He tells us of Contrary Judgments in our Assemblies of Business, and from thence queries, Where is the Infallibility of Persons? What then, in Case that were true, as we disclaim it? *Why I am perswaded the Light in every Man doth not teach him all Things.* This New Way of Demonstration I am a Stranger to; What is it but to say? *You sometimes differ, therefore the Light is fallible ;* or thus, Every Man

Man that sins is enlightned, *therefore the Light in every Man sins*; If this be Absurd and Wicked, let our Adversary purge himself if he can.

Well, *but Infallibility in all Cases* doth suppose, that though not in all, yet in many, at least in some Cases, Man may be infallible; If so, I ask, in what? Surely in those *wherein they walk conformably to the Light*: If so, then what's the Consequence but this; *When Men live up in all Things to the Light, they are Infallible*, but when they go from it, they are not. Surely then the Man has but hitherto beat the Air.

And why may We not make the most of what he says for us, and infer, If that before We were *Quakers*, and come to live under the Holy Conduct of this *Light*, we were possess'd with false Notions, he means (or at least the Expression will bear it) that since we *were Quakers we came to be possess'd with true ones*. Well, but the extent of the *Light* is not to all Things, yet, (says he) what is it to, say I? Why only to *all that is necessary for him to know, in order to an Holy Trust in God, and sincere Obedience in the general Course of his Life*. Very well, I would now fain understand the Difference, *of knowing all, or Right or Wrong, in all Cases wherein a Man is concerned*; and knowing all Things necessary for him to *know*, unless he will confess, when he said the *Light* was not sufficient to determine the Right and Wrong of all Cases, *that he meant of Cases that did not concern Men to know*; and then we will with him conclude so too. But if the *Light* be sufficient to discover unto Man all that is fit for him to know, in reference to God, and his own Soul, *and yet in some Case it cannot determine the Right from the Wrong, in which Man's Good is concerned*, it is manifest to all the World, that this will be the direct Consequence, the *Light* is not sufficient to give Men the Knowledge of all that is fit for them to know, but *the Light is sufficient to discover unto them all that which is necessary for them to know*.

But he is wonderful Jealous that We neglect the Means the *Light* doth dictate unto us the great need and use of; namely, *the Scriptures, and other diligent Study*, and here he falls down right upon us: *Must God be bound with his Divine Light and Inspiration to supply the Defects of our Idleness and Pride? for when other Men count it great Mercy in God, that he is pleased through the vilest Means that may be, and through their earnest Study and Diligence, to grant them the Knowledge of his Will, enlightening their Mind by his Holy Spirit*; *You must have it like the Angels that always behold his Face by immediate Revelation, and without Labour and Industry*.

Methinks he is both Angry, Uncivil, and Irreverent. *Angry*, that others should enjoy through their *unfeigned Repentance*, and humble constant walking with that *Holy Light*, which convinced them, through daily Discoveries from the Lord, of their Duty towards him, and all Men, with renewed Refreshment and Consolation, *which he by all his poring, beating of his Brains, and daily striving can never obtain*; But the Scriptures are herein fulfilled, *the Holy Way the Vulturous Eye did never see*. Some would have the Kingdom of God by Violence, and many strove to enter, but could not; And that same Ravenous Spirit after Knowledge, our Adversary must come to know judged, and cast out of himself, *as what rob'd Man of Paradise at first, and keeps Thousands out at this Day*, and see himself to be Low, and Empty, and Poor, and Naked, *before he be exalted as Full, Rich, and wanting nothing*.

Uncivil, that he should fall in that rough and reflecting Manner upon us (who neither knows us to be Idle, or Proud, and least of all in any Thing which concerns him) but if our diligent waiting to receive from God Strength, Knowledge and Comfort *(and not running in our Own Wills)* be Idleness, *in that Sense We evermore desire to be Idle*. It is by the same Figure that we are Proud, namely, We rejoyce with Boldness in the God of our Salvation, declaring to the World what God hath done for us, not flinching in Times of Tempest, *neither suffering such Creeping Spirits as his to be owned by us, as Men walking in the Light, and ransomed from this Ungodly World by the precious Blood of the Lamb of God that takes away the Sin thereof*.

Irreverent, in that he makes God to convey the Knowledge of himself *through the vilest Means*, Vile had been more than enough, *he might have kept Vilest to himself*. I have not read in all the Scriptures of Truth any such Expression; 'Tis true, *David* in answer to those who counted his serving of God a Vile Thing, *said then, He would be Vile still*: but that is no Warrant. And God's Judgment pronounced upon *Eli's* House, much less, *because his Sons made themselves Vile, and he restrained them not*; *therefore have I sworn to the House of* Eli, *that the Iniquity* ty of *Eli's House shall not be purged with Sacrifice nor Offering for ever.* And the Apostle *Paul* useth the same Word in the same Sense, *For this Cause God gave them up to vile Affections, &c.* Now for any Man to expect that God by vilest ways should make himself known is an unscriptural and irreverent Saying: but this may show how dark and vile the Man is in the use of such unsuitable and unsavory Expressions.

However, He once more hopes to make amends, *if his last Will and Testament may stand*; I mean his last Account of his wavering Belief of the Light, then the Light is what we have said it to be, viz. *Supernatural and Saving.* Hear him:

So now my Friends, I deny not that there is a Light in every Man, which he is obliged, under Pain of the displeasure of the Almighty, diligently to eye and follow; that so doing, it will lead him by Degrees into all necessary Truth, and at length to Eternal Life.

A large Confession to the Light, and as large a Contradiction to pag. 38, 40, 41. which because we have already observed and improved to the Benefit of our own Belief; let this suffice, that at last we have obtained what we have sought for, viz. *That the Light is a Saving Light:* I shall conclude this Subject with this friendly Caution, That they will ever hereafter do exceedingly well to remain constant to their own Grants, and not through any disgust at the use we have made thereof, *in re-handling the same Controversie, like Children, first give and then take away again.*

And now let none be displeased that I have been so particular in handling this Point of the Controversie, which concerns the Light, since I confess it to be the most eminent Article of our Faith, *Christ the true Light enlightening every Man that comes into the World with saving Light,* and therefore deserves of such as so believe, *to be defended with all the Circumspection and Advantage they are capable of;* and I am not conscious to my self of any neglect in the Case. For what concerns the remainder, though I esteem it less worthy, yet not wholly unworthy our Notice, and therefore shall briefly consider it, I hope to Satisfaction.

His second *Doctrinal Cavil*, or that part of our Faith which he seems to single out for Combat is, *Not Swearing*, and that upon Occasion of *G. F*'s Complaint of the Translators in those Words. G. F. saith, 1 Cor. 15. 31. *I protest by your Rejoycing, &c.* now *I protest* is added, for there is nothing for it in the Greek, καθ ἡμέραν ἀποθνήσκω: To which, that I may pass by his Reflections upon G. F's Greek, or rather the Oversight of some Transcribers, to be sure no Doctrinal Error, and therefore might have escaped so much insulting Reproof: He thus answereth, *My* Greek *Grammar saith, that* Μὰ *ma and* νὴ *ne, are Adverbs of Swearing, &* Scapula's *Lexicon saith,* νὴ *is a Participle of Granting and Affirming, and with an Oath.* The *Grammar gives for Example,* νὴ Διά, *so it is, by* Jupiter; *neither may any one excuse him by saying, that* ne *signifies* by, *and not* I protest; *for* νὴ *being a Participle that imports Swearing; and* by *is sometimes used when there is no Swearing, it seems to have been necessary for the Translators to put in* I protest, *or some other Word equivalent:* How very trivial this Objection is, and with what Weakness and Deceit he manageth it, I hope very evidently to make appear.

'Tis granted to him what his Grammar tells him, that Μὰ & νὴ both are Adverbs of Swearing, or have been frequently used among the *Greeks* in their Oaths; though νὴ had been enough for him to instance, *unless he would have us think him learned in Adverbs*, at least, such as concern Right Swearing; also *Scapula* intimates as much; but what then? Because *by* is often used to express an Oath, must it necessarily follow, that whereever *by* is used it is to import an Oath, or *Swearing is implyed?* And herein he dealt unfairly with us; for, though out of his own Words we might well infer as much, viz. that νὴ is a Participle of Granting or Affirming, *and with an Oath*; yet that is, both beside and with, not always with an Oath; he should have told what *Scapula* said a little lower, Νὴ *particula est, interdum indirectè ponitur, nullâ præcedente interrogatione, pro utique, equidem, profectò:* Νὴ, says *Scapula*, is a Particle, and is sometimes placed indirectly, with never an Interrogation before, for *verily, indeed, truly, &c.* I will not insist upon the suitableness of such a Signification in this Place; but shall tell the Man, that allowing it to be anciently in the best Copies (which Chrysostom, *if not* Theophylact, *does more than doubt*) yet it can have no other Force or use in this Place than

than to render the Verse thus (viz.) *Upon the Account of your Joy, or for the Sake of your Encrease in Christ, which is the Ground of our Joy, I dye daily*, or rather, *I am daily ready to be offered up:* And indeed unless Men by Zeal or Prejudice have vailed their own Understandings, the Place it self, and context plainly intimates so much. For first, it is absurd to suppose, that the Apostle should Swear by what is not a *real Ens* or *Existence*; and should we grant, that all Swearing was not by Christ prohibited, (as we never can) yet our Adversaries conclude, *That all Swearing by any other Thing than God Himself is prohibited*: now the *Corinthians* rejoycing was not Almighty God, by whom alone they say *Men should swear*. Besides, let the Context be weighed, and it has reference to the *Glorious Kingdom, which all Men, who are Partakers of the first Resurrection, come to inherit*; of which says *Paul*, If there were any doubt, *why are any baptized for the Dead, and why stand we in Jeopardy every Moment?* But as if he should have said, So far am I from doubting or fearing, that upon the Account of your farther Sufficiency or increase (in Christ the Ground of Rejoycing) *I dye, or am ready to dye daily*; that is, *I am ready to seal it with my Blood:* an hearty Encouragement to the *Corinthians* to go on, *and not that they should think there was no Reward for all their Faith and Tribulation*. Let this be well weighed with our common *English* Version, and I perswade my self, that not only this will seem very Consonant, but the Vulgar very abrupt and incoherent; and however improper the Man is pleased to be himself, I caution him hereafter of rendring the Apostle so.

See Orig. in Mat. p. 487.

Now for the Right Sense of the *Greek* COPY, with the Confirmation of some other Versions, and Judgment of both Ancient Fathers and Modern Criticks.

Καθ' ἡμέραν ἀποθνήσκω, νὴ τὴν ὑμετέραν καύχησιν, ἣν ἔχω ἐν Χριστῷ Ἰησοῦ τῷ Κυρίῳ ἡμῶν.

It is vulgarly rendred thus, *Per diem morior, Per vestram gloriationem quam habeo in* Christo Jesu *Domino nostro*.

That is,
I dye every Day, through (or *upon the Account of*) your Joy, which I have in Christ Jesus our Lord.

In the Latin Interpretation of the *Arabick Version*, it is thus render'd.
Et ego quidem singulis diebus morior per realitatem Gloriæ vestræ, quam habeo in Jesu Christo Domino nostro.

In English *thus.*
And I indeed dye every Day, through (or *by Means of*) the Reality or Truth of your Joy, which I have in Christ Jesus our Lord.

The *Æthiopick Version* thus Latined; wherein *I dye daily*, is omitted.
Et quare igitur nos laboramus, omni hora & trucidamur? & propter gloriationem nostram, Fratres nostri, quæ in Domino nostro Jesu Christo *est.*

In English *thus.*
And wherefore do we labour, and are slain every Hour? even (*our Brethren*) for our Rejoycing, which is in our Lord Jesus Christ.

This last seems to carry with it something of Difference from the *Greek Copy*, and other Versions; yet if the Sense I have given of the Place be received, the Alteration will be only, the Omission of *I dye daily*, and *our* for *your Rejoycing*; Which is not much to Purpose, it being truly the Joy of both: For, Whether *your Rejoycing* relates to the preceding Queries, or *I dye daily*, it still remains firm, that all those *Jeopardies, Sufferings and Deaths*, were on the Account of that Truth, Hope, Rejoycing and Glory mentioned, or implyed in the Text; where let it be observed, that *slain*, and *dye daily*, which strictly would signifie a Time past, as well as present, are to be accepted in this Sense, *That they were daily in Hazard of their Lives through grievous Sufferings; and were freely and daily given up for their Testimony unto Death it self*.

I forbear to instance in many of the present used Languages, designing to be short; and shall therefore hasten to give the Sense of some of the Ancient and Modern Writers in the Point.

Jerom, who lived about the Year 383, thus rendreth the Words in Controversie, *Propter vestram salutem*; not through your Rejoycing, but for your Salvation; which is yet more emphatical than I have rendered it, though to the same Purpose.

Jerom. on the Place.

Chrysostom

1672.

Chryſ. on the Place.

Chryſoſtom obſerves upon this Paſſage to the *Corinthians*, "Profectum ideo dic "gloriam, ne videretur exprobrare quod tam aſpera paſſus eſſet ob Evangelium, "cum ob hæc non ſolum non doleret, ſed duplici nomine gauderet, & quod ea "paſſus eſſet ob Evangelium Chriſti, & quod ea quæ paſſus erat ceſſerant in pro-"fectum *Corinthiorum*; That is, *Chryſoſtom* believes *Profit* therefore to be called *Rejoycing*, that he might not ſeem to upbraid for ſo hard Things as he ſuffered for the Goſpel, *Who was not only not troubled, but in a double Senſe rejoyced, both that he had ſuffered thoſe Things for the Goſpel of Chriſt*; and that thoſe Things which he did ſuffer, *turned to the Profit, or Spiritual Benefit of the* Corinthians. He therefore accounts, *Per veſtram Gloriam mendoſè ſcriptam*, not ſo expreſſed in the ancient Copy, but corruptly written.

Amb. on the Place.

Ambroſe alſo took it in that ſame Senſe with *Chryſoſtom*, not Νὴ, or by; but διὰ *propter*, or for the Sake of your Joy.

Theophy. on the Place.

Theophylact is more peremptory and clear in the Matter, that is, Διὰ ὑμετέραν καύχησιν, *Propter veſtram Gloriationem*; or rather thus, *Veſtri profectûs gratiâ*; for the Cauſe of your profiting, or on the Account of your Increaſe in the Knowledge of the Truth, which adminiſters True Joy.

Zeg. in 1 Cor. c. 15. v. 31. Ann.

Zegerus is of this Mind upon the Place, and takes not a little Pains to confute the other Notion.

Grot. in prim. Epiſt. ad Cor. c. 15. Ann.

Grotius, although he does not altogether ſeem to acquieſce in that which I have already urged, yet is he very remote from the common Tranſlation, and ſo near to it, that it may not be amiſs to offer him: "Quam verè (*ſays he, in the Perſon of the Apoſtle*) "ego gaudeo de veſtro profectu in Chriſto, ita verum eſt me quotidie "paratum mori. *As I truly rejoyce at your profiting in Chriſt, ſo True it is that I am daily ready to dye* (for *it* is wanting, but may be underſtood.) To this of *Grotius*, a conſiderable, but nameleſs *Engliſh Annotator*, does agree.

Var. Lect.

And let me farther add, that the various Lections have it by Way of Correction, *propter*, not *per*; *for*, and not *by*.

And now it may be Time for me to tell our *Adverſary* in general, and *mine in particular*, that though I don't bluſh to read his Impertinencies, (perhaps I am not ingenious enough, for ſuch he ſays will) *he ought at leaſt to be aſhamed of writing them*: And I am truly in Pain for him, that he ſhould both afflict himſelf, (*for the poor Man has an irkſome Way of telling his Tale, and is fain to Churn long before any Thing comes*) and alſo diſturb others with any Thing ſo meanly inviting, and little profiting the People.

To Conclude, If any would in ſhort know the plain and honeſt Reaſon of our refuſing to *Swear*, (to omit the many Arguments that might be urged (what Gloſſes might be given, or Authorities produced) 'tis this, *That as Chriſt Jeſus is the Author of ſo perfect a Religion, that the leaſt Affirmative or Negative, be it but Yea or Nay, is compleatly and unqueſtionably True; ſo it is below His Evangelical Righteouſneſs, and ſuch as are gathered not only to the Belief, but Poſſeſſion of it, to ſo much as admit of an Oath, as being fitter to be enjoyned equivocating Phariſees, than Honeſt-Hearted Diſciples, with whom it is the ſame Thing to Lye as to Forſwear* For, an Oath having been made from the Diſtruſt of Honeſty in Him that was to take it, where the Cauſe is removed (Lyes, Equivocations, Mental Reſerves, &c.) the Effect, or that extraordinary and ſcrupulous Way of Evidence would ceaſe. And if any object the Law of the Land, or the Ignorance of Magiſtrates of our Truth and Innocency, I anſwer, *The Law is either anſwered by Truth being ſpoken, or ſatiſfied by an Infliction of the ſame Penalty upon the Lyar that is incurred by a Perjured Perſon*; we need no Fines, Racks, nor heavy Imprecations, to ſcare us into Truthſpeaking, who Believe in, Fear and Worſhip the God of all Truth, and that in Spirit and Truth.

Pag. 31. Mat. 23.

The next abuſe of us, ſo far as concerns our Belief, belongs to reſpecting of Perſons; he calls it, our *Great Doctrine*, in a Way of Reproach, and often cavilling, not without his wonted Folly, at G. F's *Wo unto them that are called of Men Maſter* (in which he only ſays what is certainly imply'd in Chriſt's Prohibition (which he ſhould have firſt confuted) he undertakes the Refutation of it thus:

True indeed, ſays Chriſt, *Be not ye called Rabbi; for one is your Maſter, even Chriſt, and all ye are Brethren*, &c. Now I will take the Liberty to argue a little, becauſe the Text ſeems to be ſo plain on your Side: *Firſt*, You do reſtrain it from excluding all Men from being called *Maſter*, whilſt you allow your Servants to call you *Maſters*, becauſe you are their *Maſters* (which Exception is not in the Text) why may not another call you Maſters, becauſe you have Servants, and are Maſters?

I Anſwer,

I answer, First then, he has broke his Word with us, which in plainer *English* is, he has told us a Lye, in assuring us at the Beginning, He would deal with us neither from Scripture nor Reason, and yet undertakes both: Certainly he is ill able to maintain Right Swearing, that is wanting in True Speaking, or writing at least. We may well suppose his Evidence, so much boasted of, has left him now, that he betakes himself to Scripture and Reason for Defence; but considering how little they will prove friendly to his Cause, he is no otherwise to be complained of for Breach of Word, *than that the Will may be accepted for the Deed*.

But next, The Text also must be blam'd; Why? May an honest-hearted Man say, *Because upon our Adversary's Principles it seems to be against Men's being call'd* Rabbi, *and yet is not*: Strange Irreverence to Holy Writ. What, make it say one Thing in most express Terms, as much as, *Thou shalt not Steal*, and yet mean the quite contrary: Who makes it their Rule now, We or our Adversary? But let's examine his Meaning: and he is so absurd, that I am confident I have heard a better Argument out of *Bedlam*; however, let us once more repeat it, *If you call Men Masters, that are really your Masters, why may you not call your very Servants Masters, if they have Servants?* which is as much as to say, *If you call Men Masters that are really your Masters, why should not you call other Men Masters, tho' they are not really your Masters?* O! but they are other Men's Masters; Are they? *Then let other Men call them so*: For there is no more Reason that we should call other Men Masters, that are not our Masters, because they are really some bodies Masters, then that *we should call other Men Fathers, and Servants, and other Women Wives, that are not our Fathers, Servants, nor Wives, because they are really Fathers, Servants, and Wives to other Persons*.

We can call *Him* Master, Father, Servant, or *Her* Wife, who really is so to us; but in doing it otherwise, we believe we should Err. A Master and Father, of Old, I confess to have signified a *Religious as well as Civil Honour* (I mean, *Sect-Masters*) *among the Jews*; but since both are as well repugnant to common Truth, as the Christian Religion, we renounce the Title; and are the rather so to do, because of that great Thirst, which this Age, as well as that in which our Lord so severely reproved it, has after that very Vanity, Deceit and Wickedness; and this simple honest Practice, and Zeal for it, we are not asham'd to have weighed in the Ballance of God's Sanctuary, against all the flattering, cringing Customs of Personal Respect, whether by Word or Gesture, now practised in the World.

Well, But he is of the Mind, that the Scripture is not a little for him, *since the Apostle, both in his Epistle to the* Ephesians, *and in that to the* Colossians, *exhorts Fathers not to provoke their Children, and Masters to give what was equal to their Servants*: In which the poor Man is as much beside himself, at least the Matter, as in all the rest; for, he might as well argue against what he takes for granted, *viz. That we refuse not to call such Masters, as really are our Masters*; as to suppose we deny, that an *Apostle or Minister of Christ might exhort the Fathers of Children to be tender to them, and Masters of Servants to be just to them*. Certainly none can be so stupid as to imagine, that the Apostle called them *Fathers and Masters in a Way of Title, or upon singular Respect*: We may as well suppose, that because he doth reciprocally exhort *Children and Servants*, that therefore he stiled them so *in a singular Respect*. Either let our Adversary deny that particular Homage and Respect intended by the vulgar Titles of *Master, Lord, &c.* or else prove, *That the Apostle had the same Intention with these of our Times, in their Titles of Respect to one another, when He wrote to* Fathers, Children, Masters, *and* Servants.

But let it suffice, that he was laying down a general Rule for both, as in Reference to such Relations, without having any particular Persons or Titles in his Eye; and unless he had known and mentioned all the Names of those that then were, and hereafter should be *Fathers and Children, Masters and Servants*, he could not otherwise have expressed his Mind.

But why should I farther contend with so much Weakness! yet he seems to have a little *Greek* for his Ignorance; let's hear what it says, Κύριος, Διδάσκαλος, Ραββι, Ἐπιστάτης, Καθηγητής, Δεσπότης, are all rendred *Master*: But that which is used by *Christ in this Text*, Mat. 23. 10. *is*, Καθηγητής, Katheegeetees, *which signifies (as the Learned tell us) a Leader of the Way, or Guide*; but as for the Word Κύριος, Kyrios, *which the Apostle* Paul *useth to the* Ephesians *and* Colossians, *and is translated sometimes* Master, *and sometimes* Sir, *most often* Lord; *we find that the Apostles, both singularly and plurally suffered themselves to be called by it, as the* Greeks *called* Philip, Sir, we would see Jesus, *John* 12. 21. *and the Jaylor came Trembling, and fell down before* Paul *and* Silas, *and said,* Sirs, *or* Masters, *what must I do to be saved?* I Answer,

This makes nothing for the Business, though it makes Business; for none questions the Use of several Words upon several Occasions in Scripture, as the Apostle to the *Ephesians* and *Colossians* doth, *Father, Master,* &c. which I have already explained, and proved nothing to the Matter in Hand. Κύριος may signify a *Lord* or *Master* thus, because it properly imports Authority, or One having Power, a Governour, or the like; But this makes for us; *such as are our Governours we do distinguish by Titles that plainly express their Authority, though not with all those gaudy Flatteries, that Men in Deceitfulness invent, and use to gratify the Proud Part in any Man.* But what is this to calling Men Master; since we deny not the Use of *Master, Father, Son, Servant,* &c. where they are significantly, and not improperly and Sycophantly used? And for the *Greeks,* that desired *to see Jesus;* and the *Jaylor,* that tremblingly cry'd out, *Sirs, What shall I do to be saved?* They are no Instances of Advantage to him; unless we should be so very ridiculous as to think, that *because any Man customarily calls me* Master, *therefore I must call him or other Men* Master, *And that I thought it well done in him to call me so*; or, because any Man commits an Evil, and our Adversary does not immediately reprove him, therefore *it is no Evil in it self,* and he commits the like: So, What if *Philip, Paul* and *Silas* were called *Sirs,* (not either to *Tempt, Jeer,* or *Flatter* them, but in a customary Manner, in which many scarce think what they say) must it follow, that the Practice was not after the Proud Fashions of the *Gentile* Nations; or that they were guilty of the same Practice, because they did not just then reprove it, when the *poor Greeks* look'd for a Saviour; and God's heavy Judgments had taken hold on the *Jaylor,* causing him to possess the Sins of his Youth, which made him a *Quaker* indeed (for he came fearing and trembling unto them) No, no, the Matter was then of greater Moment, the *Salvation of Souls:* had they talked to them of the Title Master, or Masters, that would have been no Answer to their weighty Question, nor any Allay to that earnest Enquiry and deep Agony the Queriers were under, *Shew us the Saviour; O! what must I do to be saved?* So that how Reproveable soever that had been in it self, or at another Time, yet it did not seem then to the Holy Ghost to be the Time; the Matter in Hand was how to bring them to the Light and Knowledge of that Jesus which was given for a Saviour; and when they had found him, and he had discipled them, *to call no man Master, nor to look for it, because One was their Master,* would all naturally follow, as relative to that Evangelical Religion?

Well, but says he, *Mary Magdalen called Jesus Sir,* (*supposing he had been the Gard'ner*) *and you will not say that Jesus suffered her to Sin in his Presence without reproving her* (which I abhor to think.) Yet this won't serve his Turn; for first, that *Sir* was not of that Force and Emphasis, which *Master* was (the Title mostly insisted on) the next Verse tells us, where Jesus said unto her *Mary, and she turned her self, and said unto him* Rabboni, *which is to say* Master, as if she had first recalled her self, and then *styled him by a more reverent Title than she gave him as the supposed Gard'ner.* Next, We know that 'till the pouring out of the Holy Spirit (*which was to bring all Things to their Remembrance, that Jesus had at Times said unto them,* and to lead them into all Truth) the *Disciples,* among whom she was not the *least,* were in the Practice of more Customs than that, which after they grew up in a more mature Knowledge of Christ and his invisible Kingdom, they declined and finally rejected. Nor doth it follow that she therefore did well, because she was not reproved of Jesus (where the Stress seems to lie) or did that which in the true State of Christianity was so much as allowable: for Christ never particularly check'd Peter *for denying him,* that we read of, and I suppose all grant Peter did amiss; yet by our *Adversary's* inconsequent Way of arguing, *he either would make* Peter *not to have done ill in denying the Lord, or Jesus so, in not reproving for doing it,* which let me tell him, we also abhor to think.

But now he doubtless pleas'd himself with the Conceit of having irrecoverably caught us in that Passage of *Stephen's,* where he saith, *That He, a Man full of Faith and Power, said to the Council of the Jews,* Men, Brethren and Fathers, *They were not his Fathers, but they were Fathers.* In which his Good-will is seen, but how to effect what he would have, is as difficult as before; for the *Jews* being a
People

People peculiarly separated from all other Nations in Comparison of others, might not unfitly be called a great Family, as being lineally descended of Twelve Brethren, so that it was frequent among them, instead of *Ancestors*, to say, our *Fathers did so and so*; And this Way of Speech *Christ* himself used, when he said, *Your Fathers eat Manna in the Wilderness*; wherefore what Stephen said, might be both allowable and true. They were *Men*, that is not disputed; They were *Brethren*, as being of the same Blood, and *Fathers*, as Elders of the Tribes under that particular Constitution. Besides, both his own and (if Married) his Wife's Fathers and Grandfathers might be then living, and either of the Council, or concurring with it.

In short, We therefore refuse the Style of *Master*, and are very Cautious of being in the least lavish in Titles of Worldly Honour, because We with Lamentation behold, through the *Illumination* of God's blessed Light, the Spoil, Cruelty and manifold Evils that *Proud, Flattering, Honour-seeking and Honour-giving Spirit has made amongst the Sons of Men*, which to compass unjust Dominion, *hath sacrificed the Blood, Wealth, and Peace of Nations to it's ambitious Aims, and esteem'd it no small Accession to the Magnificence of her Exploits, that almost in all Ages she hath led the Rights, Properties, and Persons too, of Millions as Captives in Triumph after her, and through the Gulph of Rapine and Blood lanch'd into the vast Ocean of unlimited Power,* What Impiety is there in the World that may not in some Sense be resolv'd into that of Pride or Covetousness after Honour, as it's proper Center; *Men's over-value of themselves, and their Displeasure against such as have not the like Thoughts of them, beget Revenge,* which taking it's Opportunity, *breaks forth into Blood and Murder:* O! let Men learn to dread the Living God, and fear all their Days before him, and that will sweep the Mind of these vain Thoughts, and bring it from such exalted Conceits, and it's insatiable Thirst after Honour, *and will establish it in the Humility and Lovely Plainness of a Meek and Quiet Spirit, which is of great Price in the Sight of the Almighty God*; which because the World is not adorn'd with, but doth both seek and give worldly Honour, and Personal Respect, whilst perhaps such entertain deadly Hatred against each other, and resolve one another's Ruin for outward Ends, *we are constrained by the Meek and Lowly Spirit of Christ Jesus our Lord to testify against the World's Vain Honours, and to hold forth an Example to them, what they must all expect to come to, before they can receive that Honour which is from God.* And this is that honest Reason, why We of this Age, do with *Elihu* say, We know not (how) to give flattering Titles, for in so doing, our Maker would soon take us away. Thus much in Answer to his Cavils, whose Emptiness might have been enough to found out their own indesert of any: but for the Sake of the Honest-Hearted I have said something, enough for the Place and Occasion; If any desire farther Satisfaction, they may please to peruse a Book entituled, *No Cross, No Crown*, and the *Serious Apology for the Principles and Practices of the People call'd Quakers, Page* 139, 140, 141, 142. which with several others, sufficiently vindicate both our Principle and Practice in this particular, as also others of the same Nature and Tendency.

His fourth *Fling* at us is about *Women's Speaking in the Church*, in which Point he would seem to Triumph not a little over G. F. *Let your Women keep Silence in the Churches, for it is not permitted unto them to speak; but they are commanded to be under Obedience, as also saith the Law. And if they will learn any Thing, let them ask their Husbands at Home; for it is a Shame for Women to speak in the Church,* 1 Cor. 14. 34, 35. Here if the Apostle (says he) *doth not command Silence to Women by Sex, in those Cases, wherein he allows Men by Sex to speak, I understand nothing that is written*; But G. F. Page 380, says, —— ' Now the Woman ' here hath an Husband to ask, and not usurp Authority over the Man; but Christ ' in the Male, as in the Female, who redeems from under the Law, and makes ' free from the Law, that Man may speak, &c. *Now if we may take Liberty to expound the Scripture thus, it will be a Nose of Wax, that may be turned which Way we please: Besides, it seems to be built upon a Mis-reading of Husband for Husbands, because Christ, who is but One, is made the Husbands that must be asked at Home.* So one of your Authors saith, " But what Husbands have Widows to " learn of but Christ? And was not Christ the Husband of *Philip's* Four Daugh- " ters? And may not they that learn of their Husbands speak then?

But before I go any farther it may be observed, how very slight his Return is to G. F's Sense of the Place; and especially, that though he quotes another

Friend's

1672. *Friend's* Query on the Matter, he never offers to give it any Anfwer, and I am really perfwaded, he was confounded by it.

However, Why is it fo abufive of the Scripture, to fay that which the Scripture faith it felf? Are not the Spirits of Believers properly the Lamb's Bride, as being the True Church, to which he is a Bridegroom, and of which he is the Head? Methinks he muft never have read, or at leaft have forgot what he read in the Scriptures of Truth, who denies this: If fo then, Why is it improper or abufive as he calls it, to fay, that when Men's Spirits of themfelves, efpecially in the unlearned State, fpeak, *it is that Woman, which is forbidden to fpeak of her felf,* fince the Context faith, that though they may all fpeak one by one, yet it is if any thing be revealed to them, which becaufe that cannot be without Chrift reveal it, whom the Father hath ordained to be his Eternal Word, by which to declare to Man the invifible Things of his Kingdom; *it follows, that it is Chrift the Bridegroom and Husband of his People, who by his Power fpeaks through his People, to the Edification of his Body?* And as the Woman is the Weaker Veffel, fo is Man in Comparifon of Chrift; and therefore may not unfitly be accounted a Woman, from his *comparative Imbecillity*: So that as Chrift Prefides or Governs in the Affemblies of his People, it may be rather faid, *the Man, that is, the Bridegroom and Husband of his People fpeaks in them, and by them, than they themfelves,* who without him, *are but as the Strength of a Woman,* and it being her Place to yield to the Sovereignty of her Lord and Hufband, to whom is ordained the Rule, *fhe ought to receive the Law from his Mouth,* who is the Everlafting High-Prieft, and Prophet of his People.

But now, Suppofe I fhould yield it to him that the Apoftle chiefly intended the Words in a literal Senfe, and not fo myftically, as we have already difcours'd, will it therefore be untrue myftically? By no Means; *it is frequent to find both a myftical and literal Senfe in the fame Paffage,* as when the Evangelift alludes to *Ifaiah's* Prophecy, *Chap.* 5. 3. proving it to be fulfilled by Chrift's bodily Cures; which is true in that Senfe, yet hath one more inward and myftical. But to be fhort, I utterly deny from the literal Text, that Women are prohibited to preach, *fingly as Women, or of that Sex,* and for no other Reafon, and confequently that fome Women may preach, I prove thus:

Mat. 8. 17.

If the Apoftle had Companions and Fellow-Labourers in the Gofpel that were Women, then we ought to believe, that all Women, as Women only, were not by him denied to fpeak in the Church: But the Apoftles had Female Fellow-Labourers in the Gofpel; therefore not all Women, but fome Women only, are excluded. That he had fuch Companions, he himfelf is Witnefs; I commend unto you, (*Romans*) *Phebe, our Sifter, which is a Servant of the Church which is at Cenchrea. Greet Prifcilla and Aquila, my Helpers in Chrift Jefus.* Again, *Salute Tryphena and Tryphofa, who labour in the Lord: Salute the Beloved Perfis, which labour'd much in the Lord:* who were all Women, *Aquila* excepted.

Rom. 16. 1.3.

Next, If the Prophecy of *Joel* refer to the Times of the Gofpel, in which God promifed, *To pour out of his Spirit on all Flefh; and your Sons and your Daughters fhall Prophecy, &c.* as is remembred, and fo applied by *Peter,* when the Holy Ghoft was poured forth at *Jerufalem; then Women were not exempted, as Women, from the Gift of the Holy Ghoft, and Prophecy thereby:* But it was never yet queftion'd by any that I know; and therefore *Women, as Women,* are fo far from being excluded, *that they are to partake of the Promife as well as Men.*

Joel 2. 21.

Again, If *Anna* preached to the People in the Temple at *Jerufalem,* the Glorious Day of Ifrael's Redemption; as may be read in *Luke:* and *if* Philip's *four Daughters were Prophetefjes: and if* Prifcilla *expounded to* Apollos, *as well as her Husband, the Way of God more perfectly,* even at that Time, *when he was a Preacher among the People,* as may be read at large in the *Acts*; then, fay I, with good Reafon, *Women, as Women, are not denied by the Apoftle to teach and inftruct in the Ways of God.* But the Scripture evidently proveth, That fuch Women there have been; and confequently, *Women, as Women, are not prohibited.*

And methinks the Place, urged by him, againft it, clearly intimates as much; For, the Apoftle is not treating in that Chapter, who, or what Sex fhall prophefie, and what not; *but of that Order and Decency, which fuch as prophefie ought to obferve:* For when he faid, *You may all prophefie one by one,* if it had been afked, *Who, Men or Women?* Doubtlefs he would have anfwered, *All, or every one, provided any Thing be revealed to you:* So that then this Prohibition of the Apoftle, extends only to their Diforder in the Church, *occafioned by their Ignorance, which*

put

put them upon the proposing of their Doubts, and Scruples unseasonably; that is, such of them as were unlearned, and not an *Anna*, a *Priscilla*, a *Tryphena*, a *Tryphosa*, or a Beloved *Persis*, *who preached Israel's Redemption, and expounded the Way of the Lord, and were Fellow-Labourers in the Work and Gospel of Christ*; So then the Words are to be read thus, *I permit not an unlearned, or Ignorant Woman, to speak in the Church; and if she will learn any Thing, let it be at Home of her Husband; for 'tis a Shame, that such a Person should be suffered to trouble the Church with her unseasonable and unlearned Questions.*

And to this Sense, *Grotius* himself does more than incline, as may be read in his *Annotations* upon this very Place; says he, Intelligendum verò cum Exceptione afflatus Prophetici, ut diximus supra: It is always to be understood with an *Exception to Prophetick Motions or Inspirations*, as we said before, which implies a plain Contradiction to the Opinion of our Adversary, who vainly supposeth, *That Women, as Women, are exempted.* Again he tells us, *That such Women are the Subjects of the Apostle's Discourse, who being Ignorant, and not well understanding what may have been spoken by the Teacher in the Congregation; were not to interrupt the Speakers:* Ne interrumpant Loquentes, sed Mares Domus suæ interrogent, qui aut respondebunt ex se, aut consulent Peritiores: *But ask their Husbands at Home, who will either answer themselves, or consult those who may be more experienced.*

Thus much on this particular, and I believe enough to reconcile all sober Minds to the serious Exhortations and Reproofs, *as well of good and holy Women as Men*; who are also Witnesses of his Resurrection, *who was dead, but is alive; and lives for ever.*

Scriptures Socinianiz'd.

I Shall not attend his Sophistication of several Scriptures, in which his Displeasure against G. F. comes not from his ardent Love to any common Principles, which he has hitherto seem'd to militate for; but his great Regard to *Socinianism*, both against G. F. and them.

The first is, his Exception to G. F's Citation of that Scripture, *And have put on the New Man, which is renewed in Knowledge after the Image of him that created him*; where G. F. puts *Them* for *Him*, making the Saints the antecedent to *Them*, whereas the *New-Man* is the antecedent to *Him*, and shows, that the New Man is created, *which* G. F. *is not willing to allow; for he corrects his Adversary for saying*, The Light is a Creature, which is to say, *Christ, who is called the Light, is here called, a New Man, and such a one as is created; and consequently is not God, but a Creature:* A Doctrine that well becomes our *Adversary*.

To which I answer, That the New Man, who is there said to be created, is put in Opposition to the old Man, mention'd in the Verse before, who is thus described by the Apostle, *But now you also put off all these, Anger, Wrath, Malice, Blasphemy, filthy Communication out of your Mouth: Lye not one to another, seeing that ye have put off the old Man.* Which shews, he meant by the Old Man, those Habits and Customs of Evil (which were almost become natural) that they were before addicted to; and consequently, that the New Man was the inward Regeneration, or New Creation of the Soul, Mind and Spirit, with the Inclinations and Affections thereof; so that the Image of the New Man, may be created or begotten in Believers, and on that Account be call'd the New Man; but not that Christ Jesus is the created New Man: For, it is he, by their own *Principle*, *That creates all Things in the Heavenly World of the Gospel*, who having all Power, begets his People into a new State, *renewing them in all Divine Knowledge after the Image (or that they may be the Likeness) of him that created him*; that is, *that Image*: For nothing can be renewed that was not lost; but Christ was never lost (to speak properly) in our Adversary's Sense, as well as ours; but the Image of Christ has been lost, almost from the Foundation of the World; *Therefore it is not Christ, but his Image, that is renewed, and anew created*; So that if G. F. did put *Them* for *Him*, it is not false; *for to create them anew in his Image, or a new Image in them, is all one*; and the Words will bear it, that Christ creates new Men after his own Image; in which Sense, *the Image of Christ is by him renewed and created in right Believers*, and they made new Creatures by bearing his Image.

His next Perversion of Scripture is that in *John*, which he saith, G. F. often useth, and always abuseth, as he remembers: I doubt his Memory much; but let's hear it, *And now, O Father, glorifie thou me with thine own self, with the Glory which I had with thee before the World was.* Thus the Scripture, but G. F. thus, *Christ, who was glorified before the World began.* On which read his Comment. *You will say perhaps, his Words and Christ's are the same in Sense;* but doth God give G. F. his *Infallible Spirit to correct his Son Christ's Words.* Sottish Ignorance, and Enmity with a Witness! What, is every Variation of a Word or Syllable, a *Wrong done to the Meaning of the Scripture?* And did ever Christ, his Apostles or any sober Man living, chide or reprove a Person, if through *Defect of Memory*, or for *Brevity*, or in a Way of *Paraphrase* he did leave out, or put in, or change a Word, not in the least perverting the *Sense?* So uncharitable a Person I know not ever to have heard of, fitter to be severely reproved, than answered: And to whom Silence had been the best Confutation, had it not been more for the Sake of others than his: To dare to conclude a Man a *Lyar, Impostor, False Prophet, and I know not what more, because he expresses the same Matter with a small Variation in the Words:* But I shall say more of this else-where.

He proceeds, ' Nay doth' not G. F. take his Phrase in a divers Sense, from what
' Christ intended by his; for (says he) it is manifest that Jesus prayed now to
' be glorified with the Glory, wherewith he was not then glorified, but God was
' glorious before the World was, therefore Jesus intended by the Glory he had
' with the Father before the World was, the Glory he had given him in Decree
' before the World was.

The Clinch is foolish, and his Consequence false and pernicious. For what if Christ was not then glorified, *must it therefore follow, that he was not in being, much less glorified before the World was?* Can he be so great a Stranger to the Apostle's Doctrine, delivered in his Epistle to the *Philippians*, where we find him first *Equal with God*, as being in his very *Form* or *Essence*; next, making himself of *no Reputation*; then appearing in the *Fashion* or *Likeness of Men*, and lastly, that he *humbled himself, and became obedient unto Death, even the Death of the Cross,* which shews that he was in an exalted and glorified Estate, before he humbled himself, *else how was he humbled?* And it is a Piece of Sacrilege and Ingratitude, I almost tremble to think on, that because he was pleased to descend in the Likeness of Men, in Order to the Salvation of Mankind (in which *our Adversary may also have his Share, if he unfeignedly repent*) he should unworthily rob him of all *Pre-existence in the Form of God*, whilst he himself thought it *no Robbery to be equal with God*; So that though in his humble Estate and Fashion of a Man, *He could not properly be said to be glorified, and therefore prayed to be so*, yet it is no right Consequence, that therefore he never was before; For that would be to say, because an Earthly *Prince*, may for a certain Time debase himself, and take upon him the Condition of an Inferior Person, for some great Benefit, that he thereby designs to do his Country, if after having affected it, he desires to be received again, into that Glory and Splendor he enjoyed before, *that therefore he never had any before, only in Decree*; if this would be both false and absurd, the other is much more. This is the great Mystery of the *Socinians*, indeed the Rock on which they split; they do not distinguish betwixt the *Form of God* and *Likeness of Men*, that which came into the World, *to do the Will of God*, and the Body *he took*, in which to perform it.

Nor does this Scripture at all make for his Opinion; *for Jesus was not yet glorified*, since it might as well have been said, he has not yet died the Death of the Cross, neither is risen and ascended, which *was the Period of that State, unto which he has from the Form of God Humbled Himself*, even to the being of no Reputation, which he thus expresseth himself: *I have glorified thee on Earth, I have finished the Work thou gavest me to do*: And in another Place thus, *I came forth from the Father, and am come into the World.*

Again, *I leave the World, and go to the Father*: Where is the same Reason that we should believe he was with the Father before he came into the World, *as that he did come into the World, and afterwards go to the Father again*; else, why is it *again going to the Father.* But now let me ask him, if he can be so brazen'd as to think, that God allows him, not only to correct *his Son Christ's Words*, but the very *Substance* of his Prayer? Was it so great a Crime (in his Account) for G. F. to

say

say * *who was glorified before the World began*, instead of, *glorifie thou me with thy own self, with the Glory which I had with thee, before the World was?* And is it no Ways reprovable in him, instead of the last Clause, to turn it thus, *Glorifie thou me with thy own self, with the Glory which I had with thee, not actually, but in Decree only, before the World began?* That ever any Man should undertake to correct others in that, which doth not deserve it, *whilst the Beam is in his own Eye*, and he is himself most guilty! My Soul blesseth God, that our Religion is above these flight *Shifts*, and pitiful starting Holes: I would tell the Man in his own Words of us, though more seriously, that he, whom G. F. and all of us call Christ, by Way of Excellency, was, in the Sense aforementioned, glorified before the World began: And if what he calls Christ, was not, it is to us a Proof, that he was not that True Christ, which both appeared to the Fathers of old (for the Rock followed them, and that Rock was Christ) and in the Fashion of a Man in these latter Times, humbling himself to the Death of the Cross. Thus much in the clearing of this Place.

3dly He is very angry with G. F. that he makes Christ speak these Words by the Prophet *Amos*, *Behold I am pressed under you, as a Cart is pressed with Sheaves*, which says he, *belongs to the Lord* * or *Jehovah*. Grant it, does it not therefore belong unto Christ, *who is God over all blessed for ever*; that said, *before Abraham was I am?* But he gives us no Reason to the contrary; and till he does let this suffice, that as Christ has been a Lamb slain through Sin and Iniquity, so also has he been pressed thereby, as a Cart is with Sheaves, and that since the Foundation of the World. [Page 15.]

4thly, He quotes G. F. thus, ' The Promise is to the Seed; the Seed is Christ; ' and Christ is all: *To which he says, the Apostle has it thus*, And when all Things ' shall be subdued unto him, that God (*not Christ*) may be all in all He could ' not have done a greater Injury to the holy Spirit's Words, than to put Christ ' for God. [Page 15.]

It will not be hard to clear this Mistake in our Adversary, and that to his great Shame; For who will think him fit to manage Controversies, that is ignorant in the very Letter of the Scripture? It is evident, that he denies Christ to be all, and in all; and that G. F's so asserting him to be, is the Cause of his Cavil at him: Now hear what the Apostle says in the Matter, Col. 3. 11. *Where there is neither* Greek *nor* Jew, *Circumcision nor Uncircumcision*, Barbarian Scythian, *Bond nor Free*; *but Christ is all and in all*: And if Christ be all, and in all, and he that is all, and in all, be the true and Living God; then, *because Christ is all, and in all, Christ is the true and living God*.

Now, who has done the Injury to the Holy Writ, G. F. or this obstinate and peevish *Adversary* to Jesus Christ, the only Lord of Glory?

5thly, His next *Socinian* Clash at G. F's Citation of Scripture, is in the same Page with the former, and it is at his Saying *God is the Word*, instead of, *the Word was God*, adding, *That though the Word was made Flesh, (or was Flesh) yet no considerate Man will say, that Flesh is the Word.* A great Deal of do, for Fear Christ should be God; but from this notable Distinction of his, we are not without a Relief: If the Word was God, and the Word be God, *then God must needs be the Word*; that is, if he that is called God, be the same Being with him that is called the Word, as the Word may be called God; for Instance, if Christ and Jesus agree equally to one and the same Being, what is the Difference betwixt saying, *Jesus* was *Christ, or Christ* was *Jesus?* Certainly we may justly say of him, what he in a Way of Reflection says of G. F. Methinks he is more Nice than Wise. And for his Instance about the Word's being made Flesh, that is, (says he) *was Flesh*: I deny his Paraphrase; for it is neither properly to be read, was made Flesh, nor was Flesh; but rather, *The Word took Flesh, and pitcht his Tent or Tabernacle in us*: Thus *Clarius*, and almost all agree it to import a more spiritual Signification; so *Erasmus* and *Grotius* especially; and for the Ancients, they were positive, *Ireneus, Justinus, Tertullianus, Origen, &c.* but above the rest, *Tertullian adv. Praxeam*; but this is not so very material to the Point. However, if the very Word had become very Flesh, I mean visible to carnal Eyes, it would not be inconsiderate in [Page 15.]

---

* *Remember the Prophet* Micah, *Chap.* 15. 2. *But thou* Bethlehem Ephratah, *though thou be little among the Thousands of* Judah, *yet out of thee shall he come forth unto me, that is to be a Ruler in* Israel; *whose Goings forth have been from of Old, from Everlasting.*
* *Read Mal.* 3. 1. & 4. 5. *and observe that Christ is called Lord by Way of Excellency.*

any Man to say, the Flesh is or was the Word: And if our Adversary understood himself, he would perceive, that there would be only a Transposition of Words, and no material Alteration: *For that which is now Flesh*, or (as the *Hebrews* have it) *Man, is the Word*; as that which is God, *is also the Word*. But enough for this, only we may observe by the Way, that the Man is not so hearty an Enemy to Transubstantiation as he would have us believe, pag. 44. who can think the Word was properly made Flesh.

6thly, His Objection against G. F. for joyning Christ with God, saying, *His Father and He are greater than all*, is Irreverent and frivolous; For, who dares deny it? and what abuse is it to Scripture? Sure I am his saying so, and that without any Reason, shews him to be a Man of unreasonable Confidence.

7thly, He is angry that when G. F. mentions this Passage, *To whom every Knee must bow, and Tongue confess to the Glory of God*, that he adds not *Father*. I could not have believed, that any Man, who loves Seriousness, should bestow his Time so idly: *Is this the earnest and deep Study he talkt of, by which he hopes to obtain Divine Knowledge?* But, says he, Why did he not add the Term Father to God, nor insert, that *Jesus Christ is Lord?* But the Truth of this Scripture, that the Father and Son are one, consists not with their Doctrine. I confess it is somewhat hard to understand what he would be at; but let it suffice, that he who is called God, is called Lord above an Hundred Times, therefore one; to which Christ Himself bears Record, *I and my Father are one, my Father worketh hitherto, and I work*; *for, whatsoever Things he doth, those doth the Son. To us a Child is born, to us a Son is given, and the Government shall be upon His Shoulders; and his Name shall be called Wonderful, Counsellor, the Mighty God, the Everlasting Father, the Prince of Peace*; the same Power, Spirit, Light, Life, Wisdom and Being for ever.

8thly, His next Antichristian Cavil is at G. F's making the Holy Spirit as well to proceed from the Son, as from the Father: The Scripture runs thus, ' But when the Comforter is come, the Spirit of Truth, whom I will send unto you ' from the Father [*even*] the Spirit of Truth, which proceeds from the Father, ' He shall testifie of Me: *But, says he, according to* G. F. *thus*, Christ is in the Fa- ' ther and the Father in Him, and He will send them the Comforter, that proceeds ' from the Father and the Son: And for this quotes an Epistle writ by G. F. and J. S. and prefixt to G. W's Book of the Divinity of Christ. It is past my Skill to understand the Difference, unless it be this, That he makes the Spirit to proceed as well from the Son as from the Father, and so it doth if I understand Scripture; for the Place it self saith it: But when the Comforter is come, *whom I will send unto you from the Father*; which shews, *that not only God, but Christ also, sends forth the Holy Spirit into the Faithful*. Also, *But if I depart, I will send Him unto you: He shall not speak of Himself, but whatsoever He shall hear— He shall glorifie me and shall shew it unto you*—And when he had said this (Peace be unto you; my Father hath sent me, even so send I you) *He breathed on them, and said unto them, Receive ye the Holy Ghost*. In short, If the *Holy Spirit be sent by Christ*, and *received of Christ*, and *is breathed on His by Christ*, then the Spirit must needs proceed or come from Christ; and consequently, what G. F. said is found and scriptural, and our Adversary's Clamours are Vain and Envious: For, whilst he quotes G. F's calling upon *Vincent, Danson*, and others, for plain Scripture, and would suggest, because *doth proceed* is mentioned instead of *is sent*, that he himself is unscriptural. He omits to tell the World what it was G. F. made that Demand for, viz. to prove *Three Distinct and Separate Persons in the Godhead*. Now whether there is the same Reason for the one as for the other, I leave to all sober Men to judge, yea, to our Adversary himself, if he dare be just.

9thly, His last *Socinian* Objection to G. F's Citation and Application of Scripture, is this, That whereas the Scripture says, ' For this End Christ both dyed and rose, ' and revived, that He might be Lord both of the Dead and Living: He says, *That he might be God both of the Dead and Living*. Also, where the Scripture says, *Let the Word of Christ dwell in you richly*: G. F. has it, *Let the Word of God dwell richly in you*: By all which it is easie to observe, how averse he is from allowing Christ the least Share in an Eternal Divinity, making it his Business to abstract from every Scripture that may in the least Favour such a Thing, and imperiously rant it over us in the abusiveft Terms, as *Impostor, Lyar, False Prophet, Forger, void of all Reason*, with abundance of the like Complexion, the proper Language of Brutish Malice, and not a True Disciple.]

But

But let us answer to his Objection, If Christ be God over all, as saith the Apostle, then why not *God both of the Dead and of the Living*, as well as *Lord both of the Dead and Living*; and likewise, why not, let the Word of God, as well as let the Word of Christ dwell in you richly; for if the Word of Christ *be the Word of God*, and if God be the Lord, and the Lord, God, then why not *God in both Places as well as Lord?* First, I am well assured that God is called Judge of Quick and Dead, and if so, *then because Christ is Lord of Quick and Dead, Christ the Lord is God of both Quick and Dead*, unless there be more Lords of the Living, and the Dead, than the One Almighty God and Lord of Heaven and Earth.

Besides, methinks this Critick might have consider'd, that it is not expresly in the Greek, *that he might be Lord*, but that he might *Reign over the Dead and the Living*, so saith the *Arabick*; but the *Æthiopick* has it, *That he might judge both the Dead and the Living*. In short, Christ is called both God, Lord and Judge; and since there is but one only True God, Lord and Judge of right Christians, we therefore believe, *Christ to be that only True God, Lord, and Judge of both Quick and Dead.*

And here let me caution the Man of his eager Opposition to Christ's Divinity, since supposing it should not be true, *there can be no Detraction*; and if it should prove true, as he may one Day know, he will be guilty of robbing Christ of that, for which he thought it no robbery himself to be equal with God; that is, to be the *only True God Himself*.

A Summary Consideration of such Scripture Citations, as he trivially Objects against; not so much about Matter of Doctrine, as in Point of imperfect Quotation and Transposition of Words.

First, GEorge Fox, in answer to a Priest thus ' Contrary to *John's* Doctrine and ' Christ's, who saith, The Light that doth enlighten every Man that ' cometh into the World, is the true Light, that Man through the Light might ' believe. Our Adversary answers, *That it is through Him, that is,* John Baptist. Now granting it to be so; yet *John* was no more Instrumental than as by the Light fitted to be so; as *Erasmus* well said, and others, Whatsoever Light *John* had, *he received it from Christ the Fountain of Life:* So that still the Light was that *Medium* or *Instrument*. Besides, he does not positively charge G. F. with referring those Words to that Verse; and to be sure that is no Doctrinal Mistake, since most true in it self.

Secondly, His next Criticism is this, whereas the Scripture runs thus, ' For God, ' who commanded Light to shine out of Darkness, hath shined in our Hearts, to ' give the Knowledge of the Glory of God in the Face of Jesus Christ. *He brings* ' *in G. F. citing it thus,* The Light which shined in their Hearts to give the Know- ' ledge of the Glory of God in the Face of Jesus Christ. *Again,* Which was the ' Work of the true Apostles, to bring People to the Light within, that shined in ' their Hearts, to give, &c. *Again, he says,* The Light, that which gives the ' Knowledge'. But, says he, if he had recited it right, it would then have appeared, *not only that God was the Giver, but also, that it is the Light of Knowledge, and created; for God causeth Light to shine out of Darkness by creating it,* Gen. 1. 3, 4. Thus far this impertinent Man.

To all which I say, that first he obtrudes an arrant Lye upon our very Senses, to say, that G. F. has not rightly cited it, for so much as he did cite; For God caused the Light to shine, where? in their Hearts: So says G. F. But for what? to give of the Knowledge of the Glory of God in the Face of Jesus Christ: And doth not G. F. say the same? Wretched Scribler! How Idle, how Frivolous, and how very Troublesom is he with his ridiculous Remarks?

Thirdly, That the Knowledge comes by the Light, all but such Bats as himself must needs see; For why did God give his outward Light, if not to give External Sight, and Discerning? And to what purpose did He cause his Invisible Spiritual Light to shine, *if not to give an Internal Knowledge of the Glory of God in the Face of Jesus Christ?* Besides, God himself is Light, He is that Great Supernatural Sun, that shines throughout the Intellectual World, offering unto Men the Knowledge of his Divine Glory, and that in the Face of Jesus Christ. This is our Message, as it was the true Messengers of Old; And who talk of the Creation of this Light, because it gives Knowledge, may as well say, *God who was the Fountain of it was created too,* because He gives Knowledge; I would have him give us one Scripture that therefore calls the Light created, because it gives Divine Knowledge; *or if he can, but one Reason*; who fools himself, and would others, with the Conceit that he is a great Master of it: For what grosser Darkness can be, than to assert the Creation of the Light upon that very Account, for which we ought most truly to believe it Spiritual and Eternal; But enough for this.

Fourthly, G. F. saith, *But the Word is nigh thee in thy Heart.* Deut. 30. *Moses* saith our Adversary, *says, But the Word is very nigh thee in thy Mouth, and in thy Heart, that thou mayst do it*; Where observe, that the only Difference lies, in leaving out, *in his Mouth*, though it be imply'd; for where it is in the Heart, it will be in the Mouth. But Reader, dost thou not think this a New Way of proving a Man an Impostor, Lyar, False Prophet, and what not? But I dare tell him, that he will not grow over-rich with the Spoils he is like to gain by such Conquests, though his Fancy be strong, which is the Disease that follows him.

Fifthly, However he is resolved to proceed, that what each Cavil wants of Strength in it self, shall be supply'd by the loud Suffrage of their Number, G. F. says, *And the Angel said unto them that went to the Grave without, Why seek ye the Living among the Dead? He is risen*; which our Adversary corrects thus, Now the Angels Words runs thus; *Why seek ye the Living among the Dead? He is not here, but is risen:* So G. F. leaves out, *He is not here,* out of the middle of the Citation, for that would have overthrown his Opinion of Christ within. I still intreat the Reader to observe what Slight Grounds he hath to build his infamous Charge upon: But what will not Envy do? but, he greatly errs, if he thinks that the putting in, or leaving out of those Words doth overthrow our Hearty Belief of Christ's manifesting of Himself within; For if the Angel chiefly intended the Resurrection of that Visible Body which was slain a few Days before, will it therefore follow, that the Place may not also be very aptly used to express the Mystical Resurrection of the Divine Life (which for many Ages hath as well by *Jews* as *Pilates, Circumcision as Uncircumcision, Professors as Prophane,* been crucified, laid as in a Grave, and a Stone rowl'd over it, yea and guarded too, by Bands of Soldiers, left that which is so destructive of the Pride, Glory, Pleasures, and Religions of this World should rise again to testifie against them all) which has been the Cause why Truth hath ever met with rugged Entertainment from the Men of the World? And it is evident that the Angel's Reproof imply'd an Instruction of them concerning what Faith they ought to have had in the Promise of his Resurrection, which did direct them to an inward Power, whereby they might have had a more Heavenly Sense of a Resurrection and Life in themselves, far more beneficial to them, than coming thither in an affectionate haste after his Visible Appearance, which it was expedient for them should be with-drawn.

Sixthly, G. F. *He is risen, and the Saints sits with Him in Heavenly Places.* Our Adversary adds *(we must take no Notice of the Failure in Syntax, for that's frequent) Now Paul says* Ephes. 2. 6. *And made us sit together in Heavenly Places in Christ Jesus.* Now there may be a different Sense of sitting with Christ, and sitting in Him; *For the People of a State may be said to sit in their Ambassadour when He is seated,* but scarcely *with him,* I answer, First, he wrongs G. F. in saying he has abused the Scripture by putting *with* for *in,* since there is no Difference at all in what he would Fantastically have to be *one*; for if the People are in the Ambassadour, and the Ambassadour sits, *then the People sit, or I don't understand Words*: for who can the Ambassadour represent but the People? If then the Ambassadour sits, *certainly the People sit representatively.* Now though the Similitude be lame, yet it plainly refutes him as to the Use for which he brought it: I conclude therefore that such as sit in the Heavenly Places in Christ Jesus, *can't be said to stand with Him, if He be there seated, and consequently they sit with Him,* suitable to that Expression of his, *Ye are they which have continued with me in my Temptations, and I appoint unto you a Kingdom as my Father has appointed unto me, that ye may eat and drink at my Table in my Kingdom, and sit on Thrones, judging the Twelve Tribes of* Israel. Secondly, He tells us a plain Lye, for finding Fault with G. F's Syntax, viz. *Sits* for *Sit,* he says, that he must take no Notice of that which at the same Time he flings in his Dish, and almost continually; but with such Disdain of him, as if he

were

were the only *Master of the Sentences, Doctor of the Chair, or Grand Critick of the Age*; who to speak Truth, shews himself a Scholar, much at the same Rate, and by the same Figure that *Pedlars are called Merchants.*

Seventhly, But now he thinks he has enough against G. F. and manages it, not with a little Triumph; *And so to the Word Christ Jesus, Him by whom the World was made, before it was made.* This he thinks stabs our Cause to the very Heart, and proves that good Man *an Impostor, Lyar, False Prophet, Deceitful Chapman, and what else you will, without controul.* But let not his frothy Spirit boast so much saying he despairs of Information, *&c.* since if so, it was foolishly done of him to solicit for an Answer, and would not have been much wiser in us to have gratified him, if a Benefit to others had not invited us to it.

But is there no Allowance to be had for *Curt Expressions, Escapes of the Pen, Oversight in Compositors, and Errors in the Press?* Doth he deal candidly, or as he would be dealt by? But suppose the worst that may be *(for we would not indebt our selves to his Favour)* can we make no Sense of it? Suppose a Comma at the first *made,* and read it thus, *Christ Jesus, Him by whom the World was made, before it was made;* where, *and,* being understood, explaineth the Sense, *was,* maketh it more clear: And how frequent are such Words, nay, of more Moment, left to be understood? Read the Scriptures, and how many Words are there that have none in the Original, *and read but the other Words once without them,* and G. F's. Expression will not seem absurd or paradoxal. Besides, it is allow'd by all, if the Transposing of the Words will make out the Sense intended, that it removes of right, the Exception: Now read the Words thus, *And so to the Word Christ Jesus, before the World was made, Him by whom it was made,* and then let our Adversary quarrel his Fill.

However, we have one Way of reading these Words, yet, and that by Figure he hath taught us, *viz. Christ Jesus, Him by whom the World was made* in Decree, *before it was actually made;* for so he says, Christ had of his Father's Glory before the World began, not actually, *but by Decree only,* which if it seem Ridiculous, I hope he may have a better Understanding both of himself and the Place. But to proceed:

[*Seventhly,*] G. F. answering a Priest that denies Conscience can justifie, says, *which is contrary to plain Scripture, where the Apostle saith, their Consciences either accusing or excusing.* But hear our peevish Adversary, *who would think that G. F. should have either so little Wit or Conscience as to write in this Manner?* For the Scripture Words are these, *their Consciences also bearing Witness, and their Thoughts the mean while accusing or excusing one another.* The Difference (I mean Doctrinal) in this Place I don't see; It becomes a Man of his Wit and larger Conscience to perceive it, *who can make and fling Dirt for the Alteration or Omission of a Word not absolutely necessary:* for how can we suppose he meant those good Gentiles that became a Law unto themselves, to have *Thoughts* different from their *Conscience,* so far as concerned Evil or Good, and the Peace or Trouble that followed the doing of the one, or the committing of the other? For to what did their Conscience bear them Witness, if not to their Doing Well or Ill, and consequently to acquit or accuse? *Therefore their Conscience did bear Witness to the Accusing or Excusing as well as their Thoughts, for that their Thoughts and Opinion of one another's Innocency or Guilt are squared by the Witness that their Conscience did give,* the Place strongly implies. In short, they could not make that Judgment of one another without a certain Knowledge of the same Thing in themselves, and they must have received that only by the Testimony of their own Conscience; which is no more but this, *the Judgment of a Man concerning his own Good or Ill State, by the In-shining and Discoveries of God's Holy Light:* and this the Gentiles had in Measure, and our Adversary granteth it, as well as his Eminent Preacher, Page 40.

Eighthly, G. F. says, in answer to the Priest, that denied him to be perfect who bridled his Tongue, *which is contrary to the Apostle* James, *who saith he is*; which our Adversary calls belying the Apostle, who says, *If any Man offend not in Word, the same is perfect.* And what difference is there now? One says, *He that bridles or rules the Tongue,* and the other saith, *He that offends not in Word is the perfect Man:* Unless a Man's Tongue can be said to be bridled or ruled when it offends (which cannot be supposed by any, but Persons of this Man's Ignorance.) In short, *Not to offend in Word, or bridle that which would utter it, is one and the same*

same Thing; for that which bridles the Tongue bridles the Body, which is the perfect Man that offends not in Word.

Ninthly, G. F. says, *That God works all in us and for us*; for which he reflects upon him as at other Times, saying, He knows no such Place; but it is strange that he never heard or read, *And there are Diversities of Operations, but it is the same God which worketh all in all——according to the Power that worketh in us; for it is God that worketh in you both to will and to do.* Now, unless when God works all in all, &c. we are to exempt his working in us, *(and so give the Scripture the Lye)* or, if wrought in us, *yet not for us;* which is to give our Understanding the Lye; it will follow, and doth follow, That God, who worketh all in all, — according to his Power in us, both to Will and to Do, does work it both in us, and for us. But, O the Vanity of this poor Man! that thinks by these Paper-Pellets his Malice casts at us, either to wound us in our selves, or in the Minds of sober People.

Tenthly, But he thinks he has done G. F's Business for him now, where bringing him in, saying, *through the Power of God the Gospel*; Again, *the Gospel is the Power of God:* He thus adventures to correct him, The Apostle saith, *I am not ashamed of the Gospel of Christ, for it is the Power of God unto Salvation,* &c.

Now where to find out that Difference, which this *Quick-sighted Man* abuses G. F. for (saying, it proceeds *from the same bitter Root in him that perverts the Sense of Scripture*) is past my Skill; for, *if the Gospel be God's Power, then is God's Power the Gospel:* In one of the Passages it is as he would have it, which may show, that G. F. meant by the other Transposition of the Word: *No New Sense or Doctrine*; Gross Folly, Incharity, and Carping.

Eleventhly, But if he stiffly charges him with Mis-citation in this Passage, G. F. *And so deny Christ the Lord that bought them.* Peter saith only, *Denying the Lord that bought them.* Which, says he, may as well agree *to God the Father, as Christ the Son.*

We may guess at his Meaning without an Interpretation; But must Christ be Lord, and not Lord, at every Turn, when this presumptuous Person will? If the foregoing Chapter be consider'd, it will appear, That *Christ is that Lord that some should deny, after they had made Profession of him.* In short, If a Man's believing Christ to be that Lord, must conclude him an *Impostor, &c. who is true*; let all the World read, and observe of what Ungodly Stuff and very Trash his Libel doth consist,

Twelfthly, the Scripture (saith our Adversary, and his own) runs thus, *He that believeth on Christ, out of his Belly shall flow Rivers of Living Water;* where *His Belly* is plainly spoken of *Him that believeth:* But G. F. applies it to the Light *Christ, out of whose Belly flowed Rivers of Living Water, the Light, the Light must be magnified by G. F.*

To which I shall only say, That it is no improper Sense at all; *for no Man's Belly can be filled, but from Him; therefore He is the Fountain of Living Water Himself, from whose Belly ours come to be filled.* Besides, If a Scripture will admit of two distinct Senses, without Contradiction, it may be used in both those Senses, upon Occasion: So Christ the Light (whom we will magnify above our Adversary's Darkness) is that Belly and Fountain; and such as believe in Him, shall have their *Bellies* filled with the Rivers of Living Water, that come from him: He is the *Fountain that is set open for* Judah *and* Jerusalem, *and the River that makes glad the City of God.*

Thirteenth, G. F. *The Church is the Pillar and Ground of Truth, without Spot or Wrinkle, or Blemish, or any such Thing.* Our Adversary thus, And the Apostle saith, *That He might present it unto Himself a glorious Church, not having Spot or Wrinkle, or any such Thing.* He saith, that *might* and *should,* not that *it is*; but this is the old devilish Distinction of Sin-pleasers, that would never have the *Church Compleat:*

Two Things follow hence: *First,* A Disbelief of the Perfection of the present *Mystical Church, by which Christ is rendred the Head of a spotted Body. Secondly,* That he is himself in a spotted and wrinkled Condition, and every such Thing; and therefore *an unfit Person to maintain the Faith of the true unspotted Church of Christ.*

Fourteenth, G. F. True Christians *are Flesh of His Flesh, and Bone of his Bone.* But the Apostle, says our Adversary, has it thus, *For we are Members of his Body, of his Flesh, and of his Bones.* The Fault is this, that he left out, *For we are Members*; hoping that it sufficiently proves Christ to be in Heaven, absent from his Church;

Church; not considering, that *a Body can be no more without it's Head, than Flesh*; nay, *it can better dispense with the Loss of much Flesh and many Bones, than the Head*; for, if that be absent, the Body quickly dies: *Christ is the Head, Root, and Life of his Church, without which she can never live one Comfortable Day*. Besides, it contradicts positive Scripture, *I will not leave you Comfortless, I will come to you; I will be with you to the End of the World: because I live you live also. He that is with you shall be in you,* &c.

_{John 14. 18, 19. Mat. 28.}

Fifteenth, G. F. and the Apostle said, *The deep Things of God was revealed by the Spirit of God.* But the Apostle, saith our Adversary, speaketh not so, *But God hath revealed them unto us by his Spirit; for the Spirit searcheth all Things, yea, the deep Things of God.*

_{P. 20. 1 Cor. 2. 10.}

Let all sober People judge, whether this Man does not groundlesly cavil at us: For, if God reveals his deep Things by his Spirit, *then does the Spirit give unto us the Revelation of the deep Things of God.* Could he blush, he might be asham'd to shew himself such a frivolous Busy-body.

Sixteenth, G. F. *And so, who is in Christ is a New Creature, old Things pass away.* Our Adversary, The Apostle thus, *Therefore if any be in Christ, he is a New Creature, old Things are passed away, behold all Things are become New,* 2 Cor. 15, 17. The Apostle speaks of the *New Creation, as done*; G. F. *as a Thing doing*; but with great Patience (for a little would be tired.) I answer, Where old Things are done away, and all Things become New, there the New Creation is done; *But in such as he, that believes the Church of Christ to be spotted, wrinkled,* &c. all Things are far from being made New, since old Things are not passed away; and in such there can be no New Creation as yet.

_{P. 21.}

Seventeenth, G. F. For it is the Savour of Death to the Death, and Life to the Life. The Apostle, saith our Adversary, thus, *To the one the Savour of Death unto Death, to the other the Savour of Life unto Life.* Thus, that he may be true to his Way, he undertakes the Confutation of G. F. and Proof of him to be an *Impostor*: The Difference between the Apostle's Saying, and G. F's Citation, is, in putting *the* before Death and Life, which is the same in Sense and Intention. But again,

_{P. 21. 2 Cor. 16.}

Eighteenth, The Scripture quoted by our Adversary thus, *Of this Sort are they which* Creep *into Houses, and lead captive silly Women, laden with Sins, and led away with divers Lusts, ever learning, but never able to come to the Knowledge of the Truth:* But G. F. saith, "Of such as have got the Words, &c. who are Repro-"bates concerning the Faith; which crept into Houses before the Apostle's De-"cease; which have kept always Learning, and never able to come to the Know-"ledge of the Truth; led away with divers Lusts. Very well; and what's the Error or Perversion here? Why, the *Apostle does not attribute to these false Teachers, that they kept People always learning, but they led captive such as were so*. And what then? therefore is it not true in the Sense in which G. F. quotes it? What Wrong is there done to the Text, or such Teachers either? For who knows not that false Teachers do keep People always learning, but never bring them to the Knowledge of the Truth? And certainly they cannot be false Teachers that are not led away of divers Lusts; therefore they are both led away of divers Lusts, and they lead others too. But it is worth our Notice, that he who has so frequently, and with such Derision, reflected upon 'G. F's *Syntax* and *false English*, is so far from being Unblameable himself as to make that Elegant Apostle guilty; for in the Epistle it is, They which Creep; in his Quotation, *They which* CREEPS. But we delight not to spend our Time so unprofitably; such are his Contests about the *Hebrew, Greek,* and *Latin*, *being set over Christ's Head by his Crucifiers*; for he would have it written as said in the Scriptures; and G. F. says, *Set atop of Christ*, that is, *over His Head*; and true it is what he observes, That *all Languages have crucified Him*; and those that have been most Learned, have been farthest from the Kingdom that is resembled to little Children: *I thank thee, O Father, Lord of Heaven and Earth, that thou hast hid these Things from the Wise and Prudent, and revealed them unto Babes.*

Nineteenth, G. F. says, the Gospel *is preached in every Creature*; Our Adversary says, *was preached to every Creature*; and both are true; for in Time past it was, and now I hope he will not deny but it is. *In every Creature,* or *To every Creature* may be the same; For when the Gospel of Repentance and Faith in God, are by his Light and Spirit secretly revealed and declared in every Heart, doubtless 'tis also to the Heart as well as in it; And though there may be outward Preaching

_{P. 22. 23.}

1672.

Preaching of the Gospel, yet that which is Effectual, comes from the Spirit and Power of the Gospel, and reacheth into the Innermost Parts, *and the same Spirit gives there the true Discerning and Sense, and makes the Effectual Application thereof, so that his Carping there is like all the rest, Malicious and Troublesome!* But he hath something to the same Purpose.

Page 23, 24.

XX. Again *G. F. If Christ be not within People, they are Reprobates.* The Apostle and Translators say, Know you not your own selves that Christ is in you, *except ye be Reprobates,* 2 Cor. 15. 5. as if *in you* could admit of no other Sense but *within you*. Let us see if the Words of Christ will always admit that Sense, *Mat.* 20. 26, 27. *But it shall not be so* within you, *but whosoever will be Great* within you, *let him be your Minister*, &c. thus far our Adversary. But certainly the Man can't think, that because 'Εν may sometimes signify *among,* that therefore in all Cases it must do so; for let us read the Verse cited so, *Know you not your own selves that Christ Jesus is* among you *except ye be Reprobates?* This, in his Opinion, of Christ's Residence, would be most false: Besides, if it should be read *within you,* it might be understood thus, *within your Precinct, Company, or Society*; and the Sense very good still. However, it shews he hath but little to do, who shall employ his Time in *within you* for *in you,* since whatever is in any Thing, *is within that in which it is,* or else I know nothing. But he tells us that G. F. is guilty of the like Fault in Relation to *John* 2. 27. where the Apostle speaketh of the *Anointing, which abides in you*; but he thus, *the Apostles brought the Saints to the Anointing within them*; To which I say, that He is guilty of the like Fault of Fooling as before; For a School-boy would be whipt for so much Ignorance and Ill-spent Time: He might have learn't better his Greek Grammar; but indeed, I have Cause to question his Proficiency: 'Εν δυσὶν ἢ τρισὶν ἡμέραις, says *Xenophon,* Intra duos vel tres dies, *within two or three Days,* where 'Εν is used to express *within*.

P. 24.

XXI. His Cavil at G. F's calling the *Kingdom of God,* the *Kingdom of Heaven,* and then saying it is the grossest Forgery, *is as solvable as the rest:* For first, the Kingdom of God and the Kingdom of Heaven are all one, unless when Men are in the Kingdom of Heaven, they are not in the Kingdom of God; and so contrary-wise.

Mat. 3. 2.

Thus *John* called that very Kingdom which in the Text is styled the Kingdom of God, *the Kingdom of Heaven*; The like may be read in the 10th of *Mark.* If then the Kingdom of God and Kingdom of Heaven be all one, *certainly if the Kingdom of God be confest to be within,* the Kingdom of Heaven must be there too. If this be the grossest Forgery, G. F. is far from an *Impostor*.

Luke 17. 20.

P. 24, 25.

XXII. He quotes *Isaiah, To the Law and to the Testimony, if they speak not according to this Word, it is because there is no Light in them,* Isaiah 8. 20. but G. F. thus; *For Isaiah bid them come to the Law and to the Testimony, and you that come not to that Rule, it is because you hate the Light in you*; where he is much displeased that it is *hate the Light*, and not rather, that *they have no Light*; But this proceeds from that ungodly narrow Spirit, that would not all should be Enlightned, and would rather lay the Blame of not Living up to the Law and Testimony *to God's not giving Men Light, than to his and other Men's hating of it*: but every one has Light, though every one hath not the Benefit of it through their own Disobedience to it.

P. 25.

XXIII. G. F. *The Letter was dead, and did not give Life*; but, says he, I am to seek for the Scripture, I find indeed the Apostle *Paul* saith, 2 Cor. 3. 6. *The Letter killeth.* But here he is not Just to his Promise, as in several other Places; he finds G. F. using some Scripture Words mixt with the like Matter, and presently says, *He knows not to what Place they do agree, if not to such a Saying of this or that Apostle,* making him to quote that which it may be was not in his Mind to quote. Next, the Literal Knowledge does kill, and not make alive; and the Letter may also be called Dead, because it makes Dead by Killing, as well as that in another Sense, there is no Life in it: But we know the strict Sense of the Place to relate to the Dispensation of the first Covenant.

P. 26.

XXIV. But now he thinks he has unveil'd all, and detected G. F. to the Purpose. G. F. *in Answer to a Priest about the Resurrection of the Body,* he says, answers thus, *Christ — is the Resurrection and the Life, and thy dead Body shall live with my dead Body*: This is Scripture; but he calls it the greatest Vanity, and Lightness, besides Forgery, that he has observed, in citing of Scripture. And behold his Refutation! Is not this Man a strange Kind of Champion, who, besides his Abuse, gives us no Knowledge that he takes any Notice of G. F. in the Matter. For my Part, I think the Answer is Good; for Christ is the Resurrection, and we do confess

fess to a Resurrection of the Dead out of the Graves in the Judgment-Day, by the Voice and Power of Christ Jesus our Lord, *that Men may be Fashion'd like unto His Glorious Body, which is Spiritual, and Glorious, and Immortal.*

XXV. But he chargeth G. F. with wrong Citation and Paraphrase, *Mat.* 5. 37. *But let your Communication be Yea, Yea, Nay, Nay; for whatsoever is more than this, cometh of Evil.* G. F. thus, He (Christ) says, *In all your Communication let your Yea be Yea, and your Nay Nay, for whatsoever is* contrary *is Evil:* Why not here as he has it afterwards? *Whatsoever is more is Evil,* charging us with calling God to Witness in Communication, *&c.*

Tis strange to me, that one, who not long ago was for *Swearing,* should now think the *Quakers,* that are against it, *go too far in calling God to Witness.* But let the Man know, that by *contrary* G. F. understands the Extraordinary Ways of Affirmations, as Oaths, and the like, especially in Cases of Evidence, wherein an *Evangelical Righteousness is more than ordinarily concerned:* This he might have collected from those Words he after cites; but he wanted that Candor, that Generous Adversaries shew.

XXVI. He is very angry with G. F. for putting *is* for *was*; *God is in Christ, reconciling the World unto himself,* 2 Cor. 5. But methinks, if he considers as he believes, that all Men are not actually reconcil'd, then Men are at most *but a reconciling,* and *that's the Time present:* Wherefore, if God in Christ only can reconcile the World unto himself, then since there is the greatest Part of the World unreconcil'd, though the Work be going on in some; it will follow, *That either none now can be reconcil'd,* or else God is as well (though not by so Visible an Appearance) in Christ *now reconciling the World unto himself as formerly;* therefore *is,* may be as proper as *was.*

XXVII. But he brings in G. F. answering a Priest about the Saints enjoying the Divine Nature thus: *Doth not the Apostle say, that the Divine Nature the Saints were made Partakers of:* But saith our Adversary, *Where doth any Apostle say so?* Peter saith, 2. Pet. 1. 4. *Whereby are given unto us exceeding Great and Precious Promises, that by these you might be Partakers of the Divine Nature;* in which I see no Difference at all, that would have given any Sober Person the least Scruple; for both import a *Participation of the Divine Nature.* Doubtless it griev'd the Man he had no more against God's People partaking of the Divine Nature; for he seems to desire to work out all himself, and to be as little indebted to God as he can; but, poor Man, his Works will be burnt.

XXVIII. G. F. quotes this Scripture, *Heb.* 10. 26, 27. *And he that sinneth after he hath received the Truth, there remaineth no more Sacrifice for Sin, but a fearful looking for of Judgment.* But saith our Adversary, *The Scripture hath it, For if we sin wilfully after that we have received the Knowledge of the Truth,* &c. so that the Difference, as he confesseth, lies in the Word *Wilfully.* But as all Men sin not of Compulsion, but wilfully, so it was never our Principle to make God an hard Master, or an unmerciful Judge, as he well knows; and methinks he should have had more Respect to the Just G O D, and his own Soul, than to insinuate what in his own Conscience he knows to be a plain Falshood, on Purpose to bring us into Suspicion and Disgrace. But I wish him Repentance and Remission for this *Wilful Sin.*

XXIX. Here he does not so much charge G. F. with corrupting Scripture, as with *Idleness and Ignorance* in making Use of it: Now let us see wherein; why G. F. will have the Scriptures to be the *Words,* but not the Word of God by Way of *Excellency,* as in *Luke* 1. *Acts* 1. *Rev.* 22. also Moses himself call'd them *Words;* to which our Adversary replies, *That in the Instance out of the* Acts, *that Word which is Englished* Treatise, *is the same with that in the first of* John, *which is called the* Word. But this is Weak; for the same Word may be used to several Ends; I mean, that the same Word which signifies the Word of God, as an Excellent Being, may be simply used at another Time for Discourse, Reason, Speaking, or the like; and great Care is to be taken in rendring of Words, that they may bear the Sense they are employed for in that Place. So in the *Acts,* it was an Historical Discourse, or Narrative of the Actions of the Apostles, and therefore would have been ill appropriated to another Signification. Thus ὡς may be taken simply for the Sun in the Firmament, or the Sun of Righteousness, and the Light of the invisible Word.

But that which is unanswerable is this, that the Word of God cannot be subject to those Corruptions by Translations, Fire, Water, Age, and abundance of Casualties, which the Scriptures are; therefore the Scriptures being subject to these Things

1672.

Things, *They cannot be eminently the Word of God, but Christ the Light only; yet the Words of God, or Treatise and Declaration of His Will, that is, so much of it, as was given forth by the Holy Ghost.* I am sorry the Man is so over-run with an envious Scurvy (who once promised better Things) as to employ his precious Time about Things of so little Moment, or Advantage to the World.

Pag. 32.

XXXI. I shall now conclude these Observations with his Conclusion; and I am very glad we are so near the End (of what has scarce either Head or Tail). But let's see what Leave he takes, and how he winds up his Criminal Animadversions upon *George Fox*, which he doth thus, G. F. *God justified* Job *and said,* Job *did not sin with his Mouth: But,* says he, *the Scripture has it thus,* Job *did not sin with his Lips;* which he says, *Is far from not sinning with his Mouth;* but which Way I know not: For *Lips* are often by *Synecdoche* put for *Mouth;* so that if the Lips did not sin, the *Mouth did not sin.* But after this Art of Evasion, a Man may say himself, or Faith, to be almost any Thing; and for his Defence urge, *It was not he* (reserving) *but his Lips that said so.* I would have the Man to know, *That we despise his Shuffles, and esteem him,* though not a less malicious, *yet a far less formidable Adversary, than some we have met with:* Neither have I been thus *Liberal* for his Libel's Sake, but having an Opportunity (after much Business on another Subject) to insist upon these Serious Doctrines herein handled, I found my self deeply engaged to do what I did effectually. But I have a few Things yet to offer, which done, we shall conclude this Controversie, at least for this Time.

First, I would desire all that read our Discourse, to observe, That what makes up the far greatest Part of the Libel, is the Author's Snarls at *G. F*'s imperfect, or defective Quotation of Scriptures; *mostly confessing, that the Alteration lies more in the Words, than Sense of the Places by him cited.* If therefore I shall make it appear, that both Christ and his Apostles have not observed such Exactness, as he so severely reproves *G. F.* for the Want of, it is to be hoped, that he will either retract his unworthy Abuse of that Innocent and Good Man; or else, not think it hard in us, to charge this Blasphemous Inference upon him, namely, *That he makes Christ Jesus and His Apostles, Perverters of Scripture, and what else he wickedly concludes against* G. Fox.

Scriptural Quotations of Scripture, not Verbatim, *by* JESUS CHRIST, *and* His APOSTLES.

For I say unto you, that this that is written, must yet be accomplished in me; and he was reckoned amongst the Transgressors: For the Things concerning me have an End. Luke 22. 37.

Therefore will I divide him a Portion with the Great, and He shall divide the Spoil with the Strong, because he hath poured forth his Soul unto Death; and he was numbred with the Transgressors, and he bare the Sins of many, and made Intercession for the Transgressors, Isa. 53. 12.

Observation 1. Where, take Notice, we have *reckoned* for *numbred*, and *amongst* instead of *with*; besides, abundance omitted and added, as the last Clause in *Luke*. And is not this as imperfect, as *Before the World began*, for *Before the World was?*

For this is He of whom it is written, Behold I send my Messenger before thy Face, which shall prepare thy Way before thee, Mat. 11. 10.

Behold I will send my Messenger, he shall prepare the Way before thee, and the Lord whom ye seek, shall suddenly come to his Temple, &c. Mal. 3. 1.

Observ. 2. Let it be remarkt, that *will* is left out before *send*, that *before thy Face* is added; and that we have *which shall*, for *and he shall*, with much not mention'd: Certainly this had been very heinous in *G. F.* when it was an Instance of his Imposture to cite Mouth for Lips. Thus much in Brief of Christ's Quotation of the Prophets; now for his Apostles, whether out of the Evangelists, or other Epistles.

That

That it might be fulfilled which was spoken by the Prophet, saying, I will open my Mouth in Parables, I will utter Things which have been kept Secret from the Foundation of the World, Mat. 13. 35.	There is no such Scripture in these Words, that I can find; only *David,* speaking of himself, saith thus, I *will open my Mouth in a Parable, I will utter dark Sayings of old,* Psal. 78. 2.
As it is written in the Book of the Words of Esaias *the Prophet, saying, The Voice of one crying in the Wilderness, Prepare ye the Way of the Lord;* make his *Paths straight,* Luke 3. 4.	*The Voice of one crying in the Wilderness, Prepare ye the Way of the Lord;* make straight in the Desert an High-way for our God, *Isa.* 40. 3.

Observ. 3. I hope this may a little shew the Man himself, and that G. F. is not such a bitter Enemy to Scriptures, and Perverter of the Text, as he would represent him; since we have, *make his Paths straight,* for, *make straight in the Desert an High-way for our God:* Certainly this must be a grosser Failure, I mean in our Adversary's Opinion, than G. F's saying, *enlightneth* for *lighteth,* or *Christ within you* for *Christ in you.*

For thus it is written by the Prophet, And *thou Bethlehem,* in the Land of *Judah,* art not the least among the Princes of *Judah*; for *out of thee shall come* a Governour, that shall Rule (or Feed) my People *Israel,* Mat. 2. 5, 6.	But *thou Bethlehem* Ephratah, though thou be little among the Thousands of *Judah,* yet *out of thee shall he come* forth unto me that is to be Ruler in *Israel,* whose Goings forth have been from of Old, from Everlasting (the *Hebrews* phrase it, from the Days of Eternity.) *Mic.* 5. 2.

Observ. 4. Where we have *and* for *but*; *Ephratah* not quoted; *though thou be little,* for, *thou art the least*; *among the Princes,* for, *among the Thousands*; *out forth, and shall come a Governor, that shall Rule my People Israel,* we have for, *shall he come unto me, that is to be Ruler in* Israel, *whose Goings forth have been from of Old, from Everlasting.*

For it is written in the Law of Moses, *Thou shalt not muzzle* the Mouth of *the Ox that treadeth out the Corn,* 1 Cor. 9. 9.	Thou shalt not muzzle the Ox when he treadeth out the Corn, *Deut.* 25. 4.

Observ. 5. In this Passage we also have an Addition and Alteration, *the Mouth of the Ox,* for *the Ox*; and *that treadeth,* for *when he treadeth, &c.* which tho' all one in Sense, yet had been Matter of Crime enough against G. F. had he but made the same Alteration.

Of this Man's Seed (that is, David, *the Son of* Jesse*) hath God, according to his Promise, raised unto* Israel *a Saviour* Jesus, Acts 13, 22.	And there shall come forth a Rod out of the Stem of Jesse, and a Branch shall grow out of his Roots, *Isa.* 11. 1.

Observ. 6. The great Difference of which, I mean as to Expression, one would think might sufficiently justifie G. F. and I believe will in the Judgment of all such as reverence the Scriptures of Truth; for I don't see that there be four Words alike, yet the Sense one.

Then shall be brought to pass the Saying that is written, Death is swallowed *up in Victory. O Death, where is thy Sting? O Grave, where is thy Victory?* 1 Cor. 15.	He will swallow *up Death in Victory,* Isa. 25. 8. *O Death,* I will be thy Plagues; *O Grave,* I will be thy Destruction, *Hos.* 13. 14.

Observ. 7. The Alteration here is manifest also, *Death is swallowed up,* for *He will swallow up Death*; and, *O Death, where is thy Sting,* for *O Death, I will be thy Plagues,* &c. We shall conclude with one more out of the Epistle to the *Hebrews.*

1672.

| But unto the Son he faith, Thy Throne, O God is for ever and ever; a Scepter of Righteoufnefs is the Scepter of thy Kingdom, *Heb.* 1. 8. | Thy Throne, O God, is for ever and ever; the Scepter of thy Kingdom is a Right Scepter; thou loveft Righteoufnefs, *Pfal.* 45. 6, 7. |

Obferv. 8. Here we have *A Scepter of Righteoufnefs is the Scepter of thy Kingdom*, for *The Scepter of thy Kingdom is a Right Scepter*.

Thus (befide many more Places, paft over for Brevity Sake) have I made it evidently appear, that G. F. cannot be accufed by any, *that would not accufe Chrift Jefus and his Apoftles themfelves, as to Mif-citation of Scriptures*; if their not Citing of thefe exprefs Words may be juftly fo reputed, which, though I utterly rejeƈt it, yet fince our Adverfary hath made a Crime fo capital in G. F. it may not be unfeafonable to offer, *That he doth inevitably conclude Chrift Jefus and his Apoftles under the fame Fault*, which how fuitable foever it may be to his Religion, *we have more Godly Fear and Reverence upon our Spirits, than fo much as to admit of any the leaft Detraƈtion from them any where*, and leaft of all would our Underftandings let us on this Occafion.

But what if we were unable to render thofe obvious Reafons already offered? Would it follow, that G. F. muft neceffarily be condemned as a Perverter of Scripture; and as having cenfured others for that, wherein he is as inexcufable himfelf? By no Means: For it is granted on all Hands, that what moft of all aggravates the Blame of any Difputant, is erring from, or falling fhort of, or contradiƈting his own *avow'd Principles*. This was the Cafe of the Priefts G. F. difputed againft, but not his. They fay, That the Scriptures, or Writings of the Holy Men of God, as they are tranfmitted to us, with every Point, Iota, or Parcel of them, *are fuch a Sufficient, Infallible, Perfpicuous and Conftant Rule, as that God hath not left, or given unto Men, any Thing more clear, certain*, &c. But G. F. and we who are called *Quakers*, although we heartily acknowledge the Scriptures fo given forth, to be a Declaration of the Mind of God, fo far as it pleafed him to difcover it; and that Men ought to believe, read, obey and fulfil them, as the Ancients did: Yet that the Eternal Spirit is by Way of Excellency, the Rule and Guide of Chriftians, *Who Convinceth the World of Sin, Reproves for, and Redeems from it, into the perfeƈt Liberty of the Sons of God, as received and obeyed*: And this only gives the Knowledge of the Truth of the Scriptures, and brings into thofe States of which the Scriptures are but a Godly Narrative: And that this Infallible, Living, Divine Spirit, is therefore the moft certain and unerring Rule, above and beyond the meer *Letter*, which hath been, and is fubjeƈt to many Mifcarriages: Wherefore G. F. had good Reafon to put the *Priefts* upon Scripture Proof, *and that fo Critically*, as that they might not foift in any Doƈtrines upon abftrufe and difputable Confequences of their own drawing, but grounded on exprefs Texts of Scripture: For, *if they defended the Scriptures in every Iota, to be the very Word of God, and only Standing Rule of Faith, Worfhip and Converfation under the Gofpel*; it was but Reafonable in him to tye them to their own Rule; whilft, on the contrary, G. F. not believing them to be that alone moft excellent ftanding Rule of *Chriftians*, (however he might otherwife efteem them) as rightly believing, That not a Law Engraven on Tables of Stone (much lefs writ on Paper) but an invifible Spiritual Law of Life, writ in the Hearts and Confciences of Men and Women, was, and is the Great, Living, Infallible, and Perfonal Gofpel-Rule; he was not confined to the very exprefs Words and Points thereof as his Rule.

So that there is not, there cannot be the fame Reafon for reproving G. F. of what they are moft deferving of fevere Cenfure. Nay, G. F. is very excufable, in what they by their own Principle are condemnable. And therefore he cannot be upon the fame Terms with them: For it would be to fay, *That becaufe I oblige a Man with Striƈtnefs to his own Rule, therefore I am an Impoftor if I do not as precifely fquare my felf by the fame*; which is to beg more than becomes a Modeft Man to afk, or a Reafonable Man to grant: For it is the very Thing controverted, *Whether that Light, Life, Power and Spirit, which gave forth the Scriptures at feveral Times, on feveral Occafions, be that only Infallible Rule of* Chriftians, *or the Letter, fo fubjeƈt to Variety of Corruptions, Additions, Diminutions, &c. either in it's Original, or the numerous Tranflations that are in the World, whereof fcarcely Two agree*. We fay, *Not the Letter, but the Life it felf is the Evangelical Rule*:

They

They say, not any such Divine Life, by any Internal Discoveries or Operations, but the *bare single Letter, or Scriptures containing so many express Words, Points,* &c. *are that only Gospel-Rule.*

Wherefore to make G. F. as condemnable as the *Priests*, they must first prove him to hold the same Principle that they do; which because he does not, he is not liable to the same Reproof with them, indeed to none at all. Where let it be farther considered, That they affirm the Scriptures to be their Rule, *wholly excluding the Spirit of God*: And we believe the Eternal Spirit to be our Rule, not excluding the Serious Use of Scriptures, suitable to that Saying, *They that are led by the Spirit of God, are the Sons of God*; and, *I will write my Law in their Hearts, and put my Fear in their inward Parts: The Scriptures testifie of me, but ye will not come unto me that ye may have Life.*

But before I conclude this Subject, I must needs tell the Man that he hath not only taken as well a New as Insufficient Way, to prove *G. F. an Impostor*, &c. but he has equally manifested his Ignorance, and Want of Candour in what he has done: For who is there that ever understood the Laws of Translation, that would revile a Man for giving the same Sense in Words, as forcible, though not the very same? Or, *Who would count a Man an Impostor, False Prophet*, &c. *because of a meer Verbal Alteration in a Sentence, where the Matter remains intire, and unviolated.* Certain I am, that the best Translators in the World, have endeavoured to make their Authors speak their Matter in the Phrase and Propriety of that Language, into which they have been rendered, which had been utterly impossible, if they had been turned *Verbatim*, and after the Genuine Phrase and Mode of their Original Tongues: Such Versions being like the wrong Side of the Cloth, or reading Words backward. Let our Adversary inform himself, after what Manner all the *Classick Authors, Great Philosophers, and Famous Historians, are made* French *by the Criticks of that Tongue, in their New Academy at* Paris: *Nor is our Country wholly void of Instances*: As the Translation of *Thucydides, Polybius, Justinus, Cæsar's Commentaries, Quintus Curtius, Livius, Seneca, Tacitus, Homer, Virgil, Ovid, Lucan, Council of Trent, Campanella, Du-Plessy, Grotius, Bocolini, Malvetzy, St. Amour,* and forty more Pieces, in which I dare affirm, that neither *Verbs, Nouns, Pronouns, Participles, Gerunds, Adjectives, Conjunctives, Copulates, Subjunctives, Prepositions, Adverbs, Tenses, Cases, Numbers,* &c. are so much as considered in their Translation, but only how the Matter so exprest in it's Original Tongue, may be most aptly rendered into our own: If then this Scope is both practised by, and allowed to all *Translators*, I would fain know why it should be so Criminal in G. F. to have given the Scope and whole Tendency of Scripture-Texts, in other Words than what are in our common Translations.

But certainly, this shews that Rank Enmity which lodgeth in the Man's Mind, and is to me a plain Demonstration of his implacable Malice, that *(like the Black Jaundice)* has so over-run him, as I fear it will almost be impossible that he should ever recover to any tolerable Moderation, though We could desire he might come to a Sight and Sense of his Folly, Ignorance, and Bitterness against us, and not longer continue to kick against the Pricks in himself, nor to endeavour (however he miss his Aim) to gore the Sides of an Innocent People, with his false Glosses and Calumnious Accusations; *for certainly the Righteous God of Heaven and Earth will effectually judge for these Things, by whose Eternal Power and Spirit, and for whose Cause on Earth we are what we are at this very Day*: And though the Contradiction of Obstinate Sinful Men, be truly Burthensome on their Account; and and this *continual Toil of Controversy very unpleasant to our selves*; yet for the alone Sake of God's unchangeable Truth, and Heavenly Way to Life Eternal, *we do cheerfully overlook our own Trouble, Weight and Exercise, counting it our Duty* (and therein our Satisfaction*) to be at all Times ready for the Service of it, let what will ensue.* And be it known to all the World, that as our Religion stands not in the Doctrines, Meanings, Preachings, or Notions of Men's devising or deducting from the Scriptures themselves, *but in the Living Quickning Power of the Eternal God, which plainly discovers Sin, and wounds deeply for it; and as obeyed, ransoms the Soul from Death, Hell, and the Grave, to serve the Living Lord God, in His New, Living, and Spiritual Way*: So do we proclaim it to the Nations, that all Religions short of this, are but the Form without the Power, and make up but that Whore with her Golden Cup, which has bewitched Tongues, and Kindreds, and People, *She that has a Name to Live as the Lamb's Bride, True Church,* &c. *whilst indeed She is but that Great Harlot, that has committed all manner of Abomination*

nation with whole Kingdoms, under the specious Shew of Religion: Wherefore every one of you, to whom this Book comes, search and examine in the Dread and Fear of Almighty God, how it stands with thee: *Hast thou ever been prickt to the Heart, and repented with that Repentance which sorrows for Sin past, and turns from Sin to come; which is never to be repented of? And dost thou feel the Living, Powerful Workings of God's Power and Spirit in thy Heart, regenerating thee, without which thou canst not be a Child of God, and Heir of Glory? I say, O Man! Unless thou comest to know the Work of thy Soul's Redemption from the Pit, and Deliverance of thy Mind from the Snares and Temptations of the Devil begun in thy self, by which to live to God, and to have the Testimony of His Eternal Spirit in thy Conscience, that thou hast turned at the Reproof of Instruction, and hast felt the Blood of Cleansing, and art now walking on in the strait and narrow Way of Life and Righteousness, which crucifies the Earthly Mind,* thy Praying, Preaching, Observations, and whole Religion are vain, and will prove all of none Effect, in the Day when the Lord God Eternal shall make strict Inquisition and Search after what Fruits have been by every one brought forth.

Wherefore be ye all awakened to the Fear of the Lord, and mind diligently that Blessed Light, which shines in your Hearts, and is able to give unto you the Knowledge of God in the Face of Jesus Christ, which is the True Knowledge and Wisdom that comes from above, that make Wise to Life Eternal: For, the Wisdom that is from below, *may study, carp, contend about Scriptures and Religion, and from thence frame and imagine how those Things are wrought, that are mentioned therein, and I know doth, but can never give True Unfeigned Repentance, nor Living Faith, by which to overcome the World, and to live unspotted in it, walking with God till the Time of Dissolution comes.* O! this is the Life of *Christians* indeed; and Blessed are they for ever, who having found that *Living Holy Light and Power,* abide with it; certainly it will never fail them in any Time of Streight, or Hour of Temptation; *but will always reveal it self to their Defence and Protection (as their Minds are circumspectly Eying the same) though whole Armies should besiege them, both within and without, to their utter Ruin and Destruction.* This is that Foundation which can never be moved, and that durable Rock which the Gates of Hell could never shake, nor prevail against them that built thereon in any Age; for which the Holy Host of Heaven, and we on Earth, Magnifie the Name of GOD, and return and ascribe to Him, by JESUS CHRIST, all Honour, Glory, Praise, Wisdom, Power, Strength, Majesty and Dominion, who alone is worthy, now and for ever.

THUS in the Fear of God, and in a Measure of Good Understanding, which I have received from Him, have I gone through what I promised in the Beginning, *And do believe the Lord will make my Labour effectual to the Vindication of His Righteous Truth and Servants in the Hearts of many,* which is the alone Mark I have in my Eye, and not to gratifie their Desire, or as esteeming my self (though they do) the *Single Man* that was best able to encounter them, which, tho' fawning enough, cannot but manifest the Contradiction of that Person from whom it came, who, a little after that creeping Invitation to answer him, says, *That if I do, he shall ever after have a better Opinion of the Popish Writers that defend Transubstantiation,* implying, *That I should be the absurdest of Men, by how much there is not a more ridiculous Position in any Religion than that.* But this Absurdity and Abuse I return upon himself, since no such Writer could spend his Time more unprofitably than our Adversary, in his trivial Objections against G. F. and perhaps scarce so scurriloufly.

I forgive him his small *Essays* at me, (for they pinch me not) only I will tell him, that the *Eighteen-Pence Apology* he would seem to lash both me and G. W. for, *contains that Truth, Reason and Evidence*, as are not refutable by a greater Man than himself; and will stand over the Heads of those peevish, perverse Spirits concerned in it, for ever.

And for the Excuse he makes, why he scruples to tell us who he is, I have already answered it, and therefore need not reiterate the same Things, only one Passage may be farther considered, and that is, where he says, *If you had my Name, it must be considered what Party I am of, whether* Episcopal, Presbyterian, Independent, *&c. And accordingly all that is odious, either in the Doctrine or Practice of the whole Party, or any* Particular *Person thereof, must be reckoned up against me;* or if

I should

I should chance to be an Old Man, as your Adversary Jenner, that would help to render me Doting at every Turn; or if I have been a Brasier, or a Taylor, the World must be told my Name, with Tinker and Taylor at the End on't; and if this won't do, you have a Way of suggesting (as G. Whitehead against Mr. Danson, that he was given to Gaming, Bowls, and Nine-Pins) and if it prove False, you may come off as he, by saying, You did but Query, &c.

To all which I say, *First*, That he horribly belies us, for we never charged the Infirmities of a Single Person farther, than upon that Guilty Person, unless he were connived at, or justified in his Wickedness by any whole Party. I charge him to give us one Instance to prove his Reflection. *Secondly*, We know him to be neither *Episcopal, Presbyterian*, nor *Independent*, but a *Vizarded Socinian*, either ashamed, or afraid of his Profession. *Thirdly*, In the worst Sense he is an Old Man, for *Malice, Slander, Pride and Enmity, reign in him, the Nature of the Old Man that is Accurst*. And, *if he be otherwise Young, he is so much the more blameable, that he should dote before he is old*. *Fourthly*, We never told the World Men's Trades in a Way of Detraction, or Reproach; our Souls abhor it; it is well known what we are our selves, not of the Great Tribes of the Earth, and therefore ought the less to despise others for being Mechanicks, whilst we are mostly such our selves; though were we what we are not, *It were a Token of Pride and Incivility, as the other would be of Insolency, to disdain either Poverty or Labour*. It may be indeed, that the Trade of some Man may more generally denote him, than his *Name*, because there may be many of the same Name, but not of the same Calling; as many *Bunnians*, but not many *Bunnians* that are *Tinkers*; and being generally so stiled, not in Reproach (that we know of) (*since that Title neither adds nor diminishes*) but in a Way of Distinction, *perhaps we may have so distinguished him*; but certainly if our *Adversary* were either of an honest Calling, or sought not after a Reputation in the World above it, he need not be ashamed of telling us who he is.

Lastly, his base Suggestion of *G. W.* is manifest; for who knows not that the Priests give themselves the Liberty of more than that, what Game (almost) do they scruple to play at: But indeed their Religious Game they are most constant and expert in, *which they get most by*; for in other Sports they sometimes lose, but *in that Game they always win, the poor People are the Losers:* And if *G. W.* to detect the Priest, since others gave themselves that loose, did therefore make that Query; must it therefore be taken for granted that he concluded him such? Would this malicious *Adversary* be so served in every Query that may be put by him? But I appeal to all the Reasonable Men that shall ever read us, if his Apprehension of our Calumniating him, be a Good Reason for him to refuse us his Name, *Whilst he takes his whole Fill in abusing of us, and that by Name too*; thereby condemning that in others, by Way of Anticipation, which he is actually Guilty of himself.

Well, but the Holy, and Just God, will certainly one Day avenge our Innocency, upon the Head of this malicious Slanderer, and all such as wilfully take Part with him to traduce it, unto whom we recommend our selves in all our Endeavours, for the *Promotion of His Holy Truth*, being freely resigned to do his Will in our Generation, knowing that He is a plentiful Rewarder of those that truly fear him, tho' the Time hastens that he will also take Vengeance upon the Ungodly; *and I doubt not but in that Day*, our Adversary will wish he had as well concealed his Book as His Name.

POSTSCRIPT.

I Am to advise the Man, if he intends any farther Controversie with us, That he should not lose his Time, nor trouble us in the Defence of any common Principles, wherein we are judged to Err, *For we have common Adversaries enough upon our Hands* (especially since he cannot but be Conscious of Hypocrisie to himself in such a Work, that not being the Ground of his Displeasure against us) but if he please to be so open with us, as to come forth in what we have some Ground to believe his Complexion, that is to say, If he will tell us, that Christ is but *Purus Homo*, purely a Man; that the Holy Spirit is a Creature; that Father, Son, and Spirit are Three distinct Essences and Persons; that God is in a Bodily Shape in Heaven, like a Man; a gross Conceit borrowed from the *Egyptian Monks* (therefore called *Anthropophormites*) that the Soul is Mortal, with some other the like Articles of his *Biddlean* Creed, then *I hope we shall endeavour to maintain the Truth as it is in JESUS, and to give a sufficient Reason of the Hope that is in us.*

THE
New Witnesses prov'd Old Hereticks:

OR,

Information to the Ignorant; in which the Doctrines of *John Reeve* and *Lodowick Muggleton*, which they stile, Mysteries never before known, revealed, or heard of from the Foundation of the World, are proved to be mostly ancient Whimsies, Blasphemies and Heresies, from the Evidence of *Scripture*, *Reason*, and several *Historians*.

ALSO

An Account of some Discourse betwixt *L M.* and my self, by which his Blasphemous, Ignorant and Unsavoury Spirit is clearly and truly manifested, in Love to the Immortal Souls of those Few, who are concern'd in the Belief of his Impostures.

By a Living True Witness to that One Eternal Way of God, revealed in the Light of Righteousness, W. Penn.

Now as Jannes *and* Jambres *withstood* Moses, *so do these* (Reeve *and* Muggleton) *also resist the Truth, Men of corrupt Minds, reprobate concerning the Faith. But they shall proceed no farther, for their Folly shall be manifest unto all Men, as theirs also was,* 2 Tim. 3. 8, 9.

To the READER.

READER,

Amongst the many strange Pretensions, that have been made to *Religion*, and the Authors and Abettors of variety of Sects, through every Generation, from the most primitive *Christian Times*, there has not appeared (though not a less formidable yet) a more compleat Monster on the Stage of Controversie and Opinion than this of *John Reeve* and *Lodowick Muggleton*, Brethren and Associates in the blackest Work that ever fallen Men or Angels could probably have set themselves upon: What many Ages singly were infested by, we are assaulted with at once; and as if the scattered Limbs of Heresie had rallied and re-enforced themselves for a new Combate; no sooner was the Glorious Truth appearing, than they were ready to make their utmost Opposition, either by their Enchantments, to delude the Souls of some; or through their unparallel'd sottish Folly, to scandalize the World in general against all Religion, as ridiculous; and amongst others, the true as also Fabulous: Yet the Lord God of Eternal Power, whose Thoughts and Ways are not as Mortal Men's, but Infinite and Almighty, like himself, having decreed the Redemption of the fallen Souls of Men, by the Illumination of their Understandings;

standings, and Quickening of their Minds, dead in Trespasses and Sins, by the living powerful Operation of his own Eternal Spirit of Holiness, did appear in so great Glory and Majesty, that those Fogs and Mists, which began to over-spread the Earth, were soon scattered, and the Everlasting Light arose, and hath effectually shined forth unto the Convincement and Conversion of Thousands from the Ungodliness of this present evil World, and the Fruitless Religions that are profest therein, to live a Sober, Heavenly, Righteous Life and Conversation.

But alas! Some few have strayed by the Way, one hither, and another thither, for want of that Subjection and Holy Watch they ought to have lived in, unto the Blessed Living Truth of God: And as many Snares have been presented to delude, so amongst others, their sottish Imaginations have not been without the Power of a Temptation, and too effectual upon some, the Lord knoweth, which though their Number be but very small, yet the Concernment of their Immortal Souls is great: For who living, that have tasted of the sure Mercies of God, and enjoyed of the Reward of Faithfulness to the Truth, but must needs Pity, Sorrow and Lament on their Behalf; some that might have run well, and would not; others that began to do it, and Satan hindred?

No sooner were *Adam* and *Eve* made sensible of the Blessedness of their Innocent State, than the Serpent endeavoured to beguile them; How? by preaching Righteousness, Holiness, Watchfulness and Godly Fear, as without which none should ever see the Lord? No, nothing less, but by *Idle Dreams, Luciferian Thoughts* and *Exalted Imaginations*, above the *lowly Awe* and *Fear, they ought to have lived in towards their Almighty Creator:* And thus in some Measure hath it fared with a few unhappy Souls, that have been beguiled by these Impostors.

I shall not altogether make it my Business to confute their Tenets; but since they more than once, with an intolerable Pride, boast of these Things, as New Revelations, and challenge the whole World to disprove them, and upon this single Credit it is *that their credulous Adherents are so mightily perswaded of their Patrons Sincerity and Infallibility* (it being their first Lesson at entrance, To abandon all Scripture or inward Witness) And that *Muggleton* to my Knowledge, in his Discourses, and otherwise, makes it his brag, That he not only knows more than all Men ever did or shall know to Eternity; but that the Doctrines *Reeve* and he say they are deputed to declare (by Virtue of an immediate oral Commission from God himself) are such divine Revelations, as were never known to Men or Angels before them.

And consequently, since their Followers have nothing for Proof besides their bare Assertion (which is most arrogant and false (for they deny all inward Witness) It will appear both reasonable and necessary, that by an external Judge and Witness they should be tryed; and if upon their Arraignment at the Bar, they be found only to have patcht up *old Phantasms* together, and published them under the Name of *Transcendent Spiritual Treatises, Divine Looking-Glasses,* and the like; *I hope they will be judg'd by every sober Person to be both horrible Impostors, and their Commission to be a meer Counterfeit.*

The New *Witnesses* Prov'd Old *Hereticks,* &c.

I now proceed to perform what has been promised by most Undeniable Proof.

First, **R**Eeve and *Muggleton* declare as a great Secret to the World, *That God is not an Infinite Spirit in every Place at all Times* (contrary to the Scriptures, which say, He measures out the Heavens with his Span, nor can the Heaven of Heavens contain him) *but against Men and Angels, and by Authority from the Holy Spirit* (to use their own Words) *God is but in the Shape of a Man; and that Man, in respect of his Body, is the Image of God.* Transf. Spirit. Treat. pag. 15. Div. Look. Glass pag. 3, 4.

That this is against Scripture we prove.

First, *There is none like to the God of* Jeshurun, *who rideth upon the Heaven in thy Help, and in his Excellency on the Sky: The Eternal God is thy Refuge, and underneath are the Everlasting Arms,* Deut. 33. 26, 27.

If the God of *Jeshurun* be the true God, and none be like to him, *then cannot Man's bodily Shape be the Likeness of the true God*; consequently, if *Muggleton's* God be in the Likeness of Man's bodily Shape, *he is not the True God*, because he is not that God of *Jeshurun*, which none is like unto.

Again, If the Almighty God were but of the Dimension of a middle statured Man, how could he be said to ride upon the Heavens and the Sky; and to have his Everlasting Arms under a People, many of whom are singly bigger than himself; for by *Muggleton's* Principles, We are still to keep to the Literal Sense.

Secondly, *But will God indeed dwell on the Earth? behold the Heaven and Heaven of Heavens cannot contain him*, 1 Kings 8. 27. 2 Chron. 2. 6. chap. 6. 18.

If the Earth, on which dwell so many Millions of Men, be not able to receive God, as he is, and in Comparison of limiting him to any Place, (suitable to such a Body as *Muggleton* saith he hath) the very Heaven and Heaven of Heavens cannot contain him; Certainly this immense and infinite Being must be of a larger extent, than the Proportion of a mortal Man, his own Creature.

Thirdly, *Who hath measured the Waters in the hollow of His Hand, and meted out the Heaven with a Span, and comprehended the Dust of the Earth in a Measure, and weighed the Mountains in Scales, and the Hills in a Balance,* Isa. 40. 12.

He that cannot measure the Waters in the hollow of his Hand and mete out the Heaven with his Span, and comprehend the Dust of the Earth in a Measure, and weigh the Mountains in Scales, and the Hills in a Balance, is not the true God; but a God of Man's Stature can never do that; *therefore the true God is not such an one, neither can such an one be the true God.*

Fourthly, *To whom then will ye liken God? What Likeness will ye compare unto Him? The Workman melteth a Graven Image, and the Gold-smith spreadeth it over with Gold: Have ye not known? have ye not heard? hath it not been told you from the Beginning? have ye not understood from the Foundations of the Earth? It is he that sits upon the Circle of the Earth, and the Inhabitants thereof are as Grass-Hoppers, that stretches out the Heavens as a Curtain, and spreads them out as a Tent to dwell in.* Isa. 40. 18, 19, 21. 22.

In this Passage is a most pregnant Overthrow of this vain Opinion.

1. That God of whom Man can make a Likeness, is not the true God; but such an one is *Muggleton's*, therefore not the true God.

2. If God was of Man's Figure and Stature, *then Gold-smiths were able to make His Likeness*; but this the Scriptures utterly deny, and ask, what likeness will ye compare unto Him? *Therefore God is not in the bodily Shape of a Man.*

3 God by his Prophet disdained all such vain Conceits, and lest any should think so meanly of Him, he gives his own Character, *Have ye not heard? hath it not been told you from the Beginning? It is he that sitteth on the Circle of the Earth, and to whom the Inhabitants thereof are as Grass-Hoppers; who stretches out the Heavens as a Curtain, and spreads them out as a Tent to dwell in.*

Fifthly, *God is a Spirit, and they that worship him must worship him in Spirit and in Truth,* John 4. 24.

If God be a Spirit, he is either a finite or an infinite Spirit; a finite he cannot be, and be God; therefore an *infinite one*.

If God be an infinite and immense Spirit (which are Terms reciprocal) *then not a Body of a little more than five Foot high*, as blasphemous, ignorant and sottish *Reeve* and *Muggleton* darkly imagine; *but the only wise and invisible God is that infinite Spirit, therefore not confin'd to any bodily Shape.*

Sixthly, *For what the Law could not do in that it was weak through the Flesh, God sending his own Son in the Likeness of sinful Flesh, for sin condemned sin in the Flesh,* Rom. 8. 3. *But made himself of no Reputation, and took upon him the Form of a Servant, and was made in the Likeness of Men,* Phil. 2. 7.

By the Likeness of sinful Flesh, and was made in the Likeness of Men, we understand and grant Christ's taking upon him not only the Shape of a Man, but the Flesh
and

and Blood of a Virgin; the Question will then be this, Whether Christ had this Shape before he took it? If he had, he took it after he had it, which is absurd; if not, he was before he had it; and if he was before he had it, either he was like his Father, or he was not; if not, then not his Son; if he was, then because the Scripture declares him to have taken upon him the Likeness of a Man, *which supposeth him to have had a Being before he took it:* God is not in the Likeness of sinful Flesh, nor made in the Likeness of Men; but is the Divine Immortal Substance, of which Christ was the express Image before he took upon him the Form of a Servant, or was made in the Likeness of Men, which take Notice are both joyned together, as Expressions of his Condescension, as the following Verse also shews; and in being found in the fashion of a Man (as being a new and uncouth Thing to him) he humbled himself, and became obedient unto Death, &c. This was in the Day he took upon him the Form of a Servant and likeness of Man, making himself of no Reputation; and not whilst he was in the Form of God, when he thought it no Robbery, to be equal with God.

In short, If that only makes equal with God, which is found in the Form of God; *then that which is in the Form of a Servant, and in the Likeness of Men, is not in that State equal to God*; and if that be so, as it is, if Scripture be true, certainly there is ground to believe, that Reeve and Muggleton are not a little out of the Way, in asserting, That God's Form is the Pattern or Image Man's body was made by.

But here I expect to meet with an Objection, that it may be fit to remove, as that only one which can carry any Colour of an Answer with it.

Object. *Most of those Scriptures, especially out of the Prophets, only intend to shew God's Sovereign Power, and not that he is not a Person, as I assert him to be.* Thus far Muggleton and his Company.

I Reply, All Scriptures either import a literal or a mystical Sense, and either would serve us against this false Witness; if he says they should be construed mystically, I will tell him, that he must give us the same Liberty in that Place to do the like, *Let us make Man after our own Image*; for they only collected from that Passage God's Image by Man's Likeness; but in many of the Places urged by me, those Members, which in a literal Sense denote a Body like to Man's, are particularly mention'd: We will never allow him to allegorize the more literal, and *literize the more allegorical*; if the one must be literal, let the other be so too, especially there being more ground for it.

To Conclude, if he will interpret God's *Hands*, and *Arms*, and *Span* to signifie his Power, as is most true; then will I also explain God's Image to be Holiness, which is also true. But if he will have it, that because God made Man after his Image, and that Man has an *Head, Eyes, Nose, Mouth, Ears, Hands, &c. Therefore God has such too*, I will infer, because the Scriptures say, *He span'd the Heavens with his Right Hand, and rid upon the Circle of the Earth*, That he really and bodily did so span the Heavens with a great Hand, and rid with a mighty Body upon the Circle of the Earth; which how ridiculous and false soever it is, is as true as *Reeve*'s or *Muggleton*'s Conceit: Thus far indeed they would be in the right, by such a Consequence, That Almighty God would have a Body, but they would grosly lye in the Dimensions of it, who say, *'Tis no bigger than a middle statured Man*. Thus much, if not too much upon this Piece of old vain Anthropomorphitism.

That this idle Opinion is against that Understanding which God has given Men to judge of the Difference of Things, we also prove.

First, If God were a Person of Man's Stature, it would destroy his Ubiquity or Omnipresence, which is one of his most Divine Properties, rightly attributed to him: For, how is it possible so inconsiderable a Body can be at all Places at one and the same Time, by which to see and understand all Things, or to administer Strength and Comfort to his scatter'd Flock throughout the World?

Secondly, If they would say, he is present by his Spirit (as read Reeve's Epistle to his *Divine Looking-Glass*) I affirm against all *Muggletonians* upon Earth, That then not that Body, but *that Omnipresent Spirit is the truly Infinite God*.

Thirdly,

Thirdly, But I would fain know how God and his Spirit can be divided or separated; Can any Man be truly such, whose Spirit is absent from him? What Body is a living Body without a Spirit, any more than Faith can be living without Works? How then can God's Body, no bigger than a Mortal Man's, be contained in *Reeve*'s and *Muggleton*'s conceited Heaven, *and his Spirit every where?* Where God's Spirit is, God is; he can never be divided from his own Life and Spirit; for God is that Spirit, or that Spirit is God; they are synonimously or equivalently to be taken. This the Apostle believed, when he told the *Athenians*, *That God was nigh to every one of them, and in him they lived, moved, and had their Being.*

Fourthly, How was it possible for *Reeve* to hear God speak with a Voice of Words from beyond the Stars, as one Body speaks to another, and no Body hear besides himself, *nor the visible Firmament or Air to receive any Alteration or Discomposure*, as ever was when Voices of Words have been uttered, whether to *Moses*, or of Christ, or otherwise?

If any say, *It was a spiritual Voice*, such talk sottishly; *no Carnal Ear can hear a Spiritual Voice*, as *Reeve* himself teacheth, p. 47. T. S. T. concerning which something may be fitly hinted else-where.

Fifthly, But I would add from their wicked Principles, That if Man be God's Image, in Reference to his Body, then, because *Reeve* and *Muggleton* declare that a select Number of Men's Bodies and Souls are pre-ordain'd to be eternally damned, therefore God has decreed his own Image to Everlasting Vengeance, and that to glorify himself too; which one Horrible Impiety I desire all to weigh, and then there needs no farther Undertaking to his Confutation.

That this is OLD, and also Exploded HERESY, I prove.

This wonderful dark Secret is to be read in *Theodorus* of Heresy, the 4th Book, and 10th Chapter, where he speaks of one *Audæus*, who liv'd in *Cœlosyria*, in the Time of *Constantius* the Emperor, and grounded his Conjecture upon these Words, *Let us make Man after our Image.* Also several Monks inhabiting *Ægypt* conceited the God that made Heaven and Earth to be no bigger than a Man. Of which Opinion, with *Muggleton*, was one *Theophilus* of *Alexandria*, and others, they were called *Anthropomorphites*, as may at large be seen in *Eusebius Pamphilus*'s 6th Book and 36th Chapter; also in *Socrates Scholasticus* in his 6th and 7th Books: This was about the Year after Christ 403, and One Thousand Two Hundred Sixty Nine Years since.

Secondly, THEIR second Secret is, *That God did not create the Heavens and Earth out of Nothing, but the Substance was with God from Eternity*, T. S. T. Page 12.

That this is also inconsistent with SCRIPTURE we prove.

First, *In the Beginning God created the Heavens and the Earth, and the Earth was without Form and void*, Gen. 1. 1, 2.

If they were created before they were formed, as saith the Place, then Creation and Formation are not one and the same Thing, as *Reeve* and *Muggleton* assert in their *Transcendent Spiritual Treatise*, p. 16. So that either the Authority of Scripture must be denied, or else Creation is first a bringing forth of the Chaos or rude Substance, and Formation the Disposition of it into such Parts, and Designation unto such Ends or Services, as that all-wise Creator might think most befitting his great Work. Enough might be said on this one Particular to confute all with whom the Scriptures remain of any Force.

Secondly, *Hearken unto me, O Jacob, and Israel my called; I am he, I am the first, I also am the last; my Hand also has laid the Foundation of the Earth*, Isaiah 48. 12, 13.

To be first, and to have laid the very Foundation of another's Being, supposeth that Thing neither to be before it, *nor so much as in Time equal with it*; and therefore denotes Priority and Superiority: Wherefore thus I argue, If God was before so much as the Foundation of the Earth was laid, then was neither the Earth, nor Foundation of it, from Eternity with God. But the Text affirms, That God was first, or before the very Foundation was ever laid; therefore neither the Earth, nor Superstructure, as to it's Form, nor yet it's Foundation or first material Principle was Co-eternal.

In short, Nothing can be said to create any Thing that is equal in Time with it, because such Creation supposeth the one to receive it's Being from the other: and since God gave it's Foundation, or first Bottom, the very material Principle, it follows, *there could be no Co-eternity betwixt them.*

Thirdly, ———— *And the Word was God: All Things were made by him,* John 1. 1. 3.

If all Things were made by him, *then both Heaven and Earth, because they are Part of all Things, were made by him*; but the Place says, all Things (or whatever has Being) were made by him; *therefore all Co-eternity of Earth or Heaven with the Everlasting God is excluded and refuted.*

To this answers that Passage of the Apostle *Paul* in the *Acts, God that made the World, and all Things therein,* &c.

Fourthly, To conclude this Head, *For by him were all Things created; and he is before all Things; and by him all Things consist,* Colos. 1. 16, 17. *And thou Lord in the Beginning hast laid the Foundation of the Earth, and the Heavens are the Works of thy Hands,* Heb. 1. 10.

That which had a Beginning, which was made, and which was and is upheld by another, *neither can have been contemporary nor co-eternal with that from which it received it's Being*; but that did the Heaven and the Earth, and from Almighty God, as the Place proves: Therefore not Co-eternal with him.

Nor can their idle Shift any Ways secure them from the Dint of these Scriptures, nor the Arguments built upon them, *viz.* making *is* fashioning, *so God made the Heavens and the Earth, as a Carpenter makes a Door or a Chest; he fashions it of Wood, but he does not make the Wood:* A Distinction fitter for *Bedlam,* than Men pretending to be in their Wits: Can any rationally think, that when God is said to lay the Foundation of the Earth, and to make the Heavens, and all that live therein, that he only fashion'd them up? *Who made the Trees, Plants, Beasts, Fowls, Fishes, and rational Creatures? Do they strain at a Gnat, and swallow a Camel?* Can they think that it was harder to Almighty God, to create out of Nothing the more inanimate or lifeless Part of Heaven and Earth, *than to compose that Variety of excellent Creatures, and to infuse that great Spirit and Soul, by which they are respectively instincted or acted.*

But how pertinent his Distinction is betwixt fashioning and making, we will manifest by that remarkable Passage to our Purpose in *Paul's* Epistle to the *Philippians,* Chap. 2. *And being found in Fashion as a Man, he humbled himself,* &c.

Was Christ a real Man, or not? If not, then *Reeve's* and *Muggleton's* Fleshly Mortal Notions, of the Immortal Son of God, fall to the Ground; *if a real Man, then to be fashion'd may import to be, and the Fashion of a Thing passeth for the Being of a Thing.*

Of what Value now their Distinction is, they may consider if they please.

But this Opinion is also against REASON.

First, It is the Nature of what is Eternal, or from all Everlasting to be *Infinite, Unalterable* and *Almighty*; for it oweth no Original or Preservation to another, and is equivalent in all other Properties to Eternity: Now where there is not Proportion, it is highly to be suspected, That there is no such Thing at all; but is a mere *Chimera,* and real only in a Fiction.

Secondly, That there is no Resemblance is manifest, the whole visible World is full of Time, *inconsistent with Eternity,* as having Beginning and End; the Heavens have their set Motions, the Earth her distinct Seasons, in which are various Revolutions, and both filled with divers Temporary Agitations and Motions: Therefore it is impossible that Heaven and Earth could have been from Eternity, which are so filled with and made up of all the Instances of Time and Mutation; for should they, *The Sun must always shine, the Rain descend, the Tide flow, the Winds blow, the Winter last, and every Alteration that is in Time be perpetual.*

Thirdly, It is utterly impossible, that Temporal Beings could receive their Sustenance and Growth from what is by Nature Eternal; there being as great Contrariety, at least, Difference between them, as there is betwixt visible and invisible, Spiritual and Carnal Things.

Fourthly,

Fourthly, Such as is the Food, such should the Life be; now if this visible World should be Eternal, *then the Food that springs from it should nourish to a Life as Eternal as that World which does produce it.* Nay, since Man's Body was made of the Earth, we might well infer, *That Man's Body, as so made, is Eternal;* and if Eternal, as such, not Mortal, which Experience tells us is an idle Tale. But let this suffice at present.

But that this Conjecture had other Founders than *Reeve* and *Muggleton*, I prove, and that by two Instances.

Augustine says, That there were several that affirmed, That the Water was not made by God, but was *Co-eternal*. Next, a certain Sect called *Seluciani* taught, That the Substance of the Creation, or whereof the World was made, was not made by God, *but Eternally* with God (then no Creature, and then God) as may at large be read in the said *Augustine*'s Book of Heresies; this Heresy reigned about *Anno* 300 after Christ. To say nothing of that known Philosopher *Aristotle*, who was sometimes Idolater, sometimes Atheist.

Thirdly, THE third Secret, which only was revealed to *Reeve* and *Muggleton*, if we will believe them, is, *That the Soul of Man is generated or got by the Man and Woman with the Body, and that the Body and Soul are inseparable.* T. S. T. p. 42.

That this is contrary to SCRIPTURE TESTIMONY, I prove.

First, *And the Spirit to God that gave it,* Eccl. 12. 7.
No Carnal Generation can bring forth a pure Spirit; External Matter producing only External Matter of it's own Kind.
But the Soul of Man is a Spirit, as the Words express it in *Reeve*'s and *Muggleton*'s own *T. S. T. p.* 44. Therefore no Man gets the Soul or Spirit of a Man when he generates the Body.
Secondly, That which returns to God came from God; *but the Soul of every Man returns to God, and consequently came from him.*
I omit mentioning more Scriptures, because the following Principle being a Consequence of this; what I prove there is proved here, namely, *The Immortality of the Soul*, against their Atheistical Assertion, of the Soul's Mortality with the Body: For where there is no Corruption, there could be no proper Generation; and if the Soul be Immortal, it was not descended of Mortal Race, or begotten of elementary visible Matter.

That this is against all Right UNDERSTANDING, I prove.

First, Such as is the Soul, such must that be which produceth it; *but it is Spiritual.* Now that which generates the Body of Man, *being only and meerly visible Matter, it cannot produce or generate an intellectual Soul or Spirit.*
Secondly, If Man got the Soul, then would that Soul be as well the Image of the Father as the Body, *and partake as intirely of the Father's Nature and Disposition in all Respects:* But Experience shews us, That Sober Parents have Wild Children, and Religious Children Debauched Parents; *therefore Parents do not generate the Soul.*
Thirdly, If Soul and Body be inseparably generated, *then the Sexes as well belong to Souls as Bodies*; the which as it is absurd, *so would there be Men and Women in that very Distinction to all Eternity:* And who ever read of She Souls or Female Souls?
Fourthly, If Soul and Body were intermixedly and inseparably generated by Man, *then in all Anatomies it were no more difficult to find out the Soul than any other Part:* and in Case of Opening or Dissecting of Living Men, as I have at the *University* seen living Beasts by Anatomists, it would not be impossible, but rational, that one should behold the very Thoughts, Purposes, and Intents of such Men's Hearts and Souls. But because this were most Vain, we shall conclude, The Soul is not generated with, nor inseparable from the Body, but of an immaterial Nature.

That this is no newer than the rest, and was esteemed *Heresy* in the Primitive Times, I will Evidence.

There was a Sect called *Luciferians*, from one *Lucifer* of *Sardinia*, and the *Tertullianists*, who held, That the Soul was transfused by Generation from the Parents to their Children, *and that the Soul is of the Flesh, and Substance of the Flesh*; of which read *Socrates Scholasticus*, in his 3d Book, and 7th Chapter; also *Augustine* of *Heresies*; and *Theodorus*, his 3d Book and 5th Chapter, about *Anno* 350.

Fourth, THE Fourth sublime Mystery of those Phantastick and Imaginary Persons is a Consequence of the former, namely, the Mortality of the Soul, *That the Soul and Body go to Dust, and rise together at a General Resurrection.* T. S. T. p. 43, 44.

That it is consistent with SCRIPTURE, I prove.

First, *And the Lord God formed Man of the Dust of the Ground, and breathed into his Nostrils the Breath of Life, and Man became a Living Soul,* Gen. 2. 7.

If the Breath of Life made a dead Body live, then the Privation of the Breath of Life, makes a living Body dead; *since the Life it has was from and is whilst that Breath inspired remains in it*; and if so, *then not the Soul, but the Body dies.*

2. This is farther prov'd thus, If it was living Breath before it entered into the Body, it must be living Breath after it is withdrawn from the Body; *since the Body makes no Alteration upon it, but it upon the Body*; as from a life-less Heap to a living Body, and from a living to a dead Body again.

3. Though some of those Things which are living may die, *because they live by the borrowed or lent Life of another*; yet every Life, *as Life,* cannot die; for since Life and Death are contrary, as Light and Darkness, *because very Light can never in it self be utterly extinguish'd by Darkness, so as to become very Darkness, nor Truth Untruth by Error,* it is impossible that the Breath of Life, or Soul of Man, can suffer Death, as here understood; for that were very Annihilation it self, *or being from an intelligent Something made Nothing.*

Secondly, *And he cried unto the Lord, and said, O Lord my God, hast thou also brought Evil upon the Widow with whom I sojourn, by slaying her Son? And he stretched himself over the Child Three Times, and cried and said, O Lord my God, I pray thee, Let this Child's Soul come into him again: And the Lord heard the Voice of Elijah, and the Soul of the Child came into him again, and he revived,* 1 Kings 17. 20, 21, 22.

If the Soul was withdrawn when the Body lay dead, as the Place proveth, *then the Soul lay not dead from all Motion, Life and Heat, in the Body, as one inseparable Lump.* But the Soul was separated, and when it did return, according to *Elijah's* Prayer, and had resumed it's forsaken dead Body, it revived the Body again; therefore the Soul died not with the Body, nor at all; inasmuch as if it had died, when separated, it could not have revived the dead Body, when returned.

In short, This Place most expresly proves, 1st, *The Bodie's Death, from the Soul's Separation:* 2dly, *The Soul's certain Departure from the Body:* 3dly, *The Soul's living after Separation.*

Thirdly, *Then shall the Dust return to the Dust, as it was; and the Spirit to God, that gave it,* Eccl. 12. 7.

This Place very evidently harmonizeth with the former, and is a pregnant Instance to the Confutation of that *Atheistical* Opinion, and as pertinent here, as where mentioned. For, as Man is composed of Body and Spirit, so they have two Originals; the one from below, *Dust*; the other from above, the *Breath of Life*; They have also two Dooms, *the Dust to the Dust, from whence it came*; *the Soul to God, from whence it came*, to be by him sentenced to the Blessed or Cursed State for ever, according to the End of that Chapter, *For God will bring every Secret Thing to Judgment*; from whence I argue,

1. That only can properly return to Earth that came from it, *that is, Dust*.

But the Soul never came from Dust nor Earth, as *Reeve* and *Muggleton* affirm, *p.* 45. T. S. T.

Therefore

Therefore it is impossible that the Soul can truly be said to *return to the Earth*.

2. That which returns to God is what more immediately and eminently came from him, and that cannot die.

But the Soul doth return to the End aforesaid.

Therefore the Soul came from him, and dieth not, neither can it with the Body return to Dust.

Fourthly, *Be not afraid of them that kill the Body, and after that have no more that they can do*, Luke 12. 4.

If *Reeve* and *Muggleton* speak Truth, then he that kills the Body kills the Soul too; for he cannot kill the one without the other.

But Christ Jesus, the Author of Truth and Salvation, saith, *The Body may be killed by Man, and the Soul remain alive*; therefore *Reeve* and *Muggleton* are Lyars against Christ and his Doctrine.

The Body's Death is Natural, the Soul's Spiritual; Man's Power extendeth but to one, and consequently the latter is independent of the former.

Fifthly, *For me to live is Christ, to die is Gain; but if I live in the Flesh, (or Body) this is the Fruit of my Labour: yet what I shall chuse, I wot not; for I am in a Streight betwixt two, having a Desire to depart, and be with Christ, which is far better*, Phil. 1. 21, 22, 23. From whence I plainly argue,

1. If to die was Gain, *then he was not to enjoy less of that Divine Consolation which he had living*, since to live was Christ. But he that has lain Body and Soul One Thousand Six Hundred Years in the Grave, and may for ought we know One Thousand Six Hundred more, *must needs have lost not only a little, but all that he enjoyed Living, instead of farther Gain*: Therefore I infer, *Their Principle of the Soul's Mortality is contrary to the Testimony of the Apostle*; for with him to die was Gain. That this was the Apostle's Sense, I proceed yet farther to make appear from his own Words.

2. The Reason of his Streight was, Whether to live to serve Christ, or die to enjoy him: *But this had been no Streight, if he was to lose what he had, and not to enjoy him after Departure in any Sense, as the Dead don't*; therefore it was not the Apostle's Judgment, though it is Wicked *Reeve's*, and Blasphemous *Muggleton's*, *That the Soul is deprived with the Body by Death, of all Divine Enjoyments of God, or Punishment from him, 'till the Day of Resurrection*. For the Apostle counted it far better, to depart, and be with Christ; which had been a Vain, if an In-obtainable Desire, as would follow from their Anti-Scriptural Opinion.

Sixthly, *And when he had opened the Fifth Seal, I saw under the Altar the Souls of them that were slain for the Word of God, and for the Testimony which they had held; and they cried with a loud Voice, saying, How long, O Lord, Holy and True, dost thou not Judge and Avenge our Blood on them that dwell on the Earth?* Revel. 6. 9. 10.

If their Souls liv'd after their Bodies were slain, then they did not die together; but the Scripture proves, their Souls lived after their Bodies were Slain: for they cried for Vengeance on the Blood-thirsty Inhabitants of the World; therefore Souls are not Mortal, as Bodies are.

In short, *Their Bodies were Slain*, their Souls were alive; *their Bodies were in the Grave*, their Souls under the Altar, *worshipping God Day and Night for ever and ever*.

That this is against REASON, I farther prove.

First, There is nothing Mortal that is not Elementary, or composed of visible Matter or Substance; but *the Body is that only Part of Man, which is so composed*.

And consequently, the Body is the only Mortal Part of Man.

Secondly, That only can be subject to visible and material Generations, Agitations, Motions, Privations, Diminutions, Increases, Alterations, Operations and Corruptions, which is of a Visible, Elementary, and Corporal Substance, (for an Invisible none ever saw subject to any one of them) but of such is the Body, and not the Soul (by *Reeve* and *Muggleton* their own Assertion, of Man's Nature *to be of the Faith which is God's Nature*.)

Therefore the *Body is subject only to Generation and Corruption*, and not the Soul,

That

That the Soul is not of the same Nature as the Body, I thus prove,

Thirdly, That which is intellectual, which in it's pure Nature knows, comprehends, governs and orders all visible, elementary and corporeal Beings, and yet is Invisible, Spiritual, Rational, and Internal (as is manifest from it's Heavenly Meditations, it's secret Thoughts, it's serious Reflections, acute Memory, and profound Reasonings about the Causes and Effects of all Things) *cannot but be of a Nature more refined, excellent and noble, than to fall under the same Generations, Revolutions, and Corruptions, those inferior visible Beings are subject to.* But such is the Nature of Man's Soul, as daily Experience manifests to all that will not wilfully Blind their Eyes; therefore though Man's Body be Mortal, as being of that grosser Substance and Elementary Nature, yet *his Soul is of an immortal Nature, and can receive no Alteration of Being by any that may or can happen to the Body, which is but a Well-Organiz'd and disposed Instrument for the Soul to exert or put forth her self by,* according to the good Pleasure of God, and that creaturely Prudence necessary to be eyed in and about all Worldly Concernments.

Thus much and enough to this Point.

That this is as Grey-headed as *Atheism*, we may suppose; and that it is not only their only Revelation I prove:

John the 22th Bishop of *Rome*, and some in the Countries of *Arabia*, held this very Doctrine, affirming, That Souls and Bodies dyed and rose together; of which read *Origen*, and *Eusebius Pamphilus*, lib. 6. chap. 36. nor can any be ignorant that converse with Story, that long before, since, and at this Day, where *Reeve* and *Muggleton* were never thought on, this wretched Opinion is but too rife, Anno 249. 1423. Years since.

Fifthly, BUT their most admirable Secret of all is, *That God descended with his Body in the Shape of a Man, and dissolved himself into the Virgin's Womb, and so brought forth himself a Man; who after he had lived to such an Age, was Crucified, and really dyed, or ceased to be either God or Man for Three Days and Nights*: T. S. T. p. 23 to 30.

That this is in three Particulars highly inconsistent with Scripture I prove.

First, God did not so transmute his Divine Nature into Fleshly Mortal Nature.

1. *Your Father* Abraham *rejoyced to see my Day: Then said the* Jews *unto him, Thou art not yet Fifty Years old, and hast thou seen* Abraham? *Jesus said unto them, Verily, Verily, I say unto you, Before* Abraham *was, I am,* John 8. 56, 57, 58.

If that which was before *Abraham*, and yet then in being the same, was God, as none that own the Scriptures do deny; *then because that outward visible Body was not before* Abraham, *that was not God:* The first all grant, the second none reasonably doubt; for Christ was crucified about the Three and Thirtieth Year of his Life: And then I hope none will believe the Eternal *Deity* was *Transmuted*, or *Transubstantiated* into that Visible Body; for so Christ's Answer would not have been true: for that mortal Body, which say *Reeve* and *Muggleton* was *the Eternal God*, had a Beginning, *and was of that Age the* Jews *said it to be*.

2. *Whose are the Fathers, and of whom as concerning the Flesh Christ came, who is over all, God blessed for ever,* Rom. 9. 5.

If Christ, as concerning the Flesh, was not God, as the Text manifestly implieth *(by a Distinction betwixt his Appearance in that Body of Flesh, and his Divine Essence or Being, with their Originals)* then that fleshly Body was not God, or the Eternal God was not Substantially Transmuted into that Fleshly Body.

Secondly, Neither could *Elias* be God's Deputy to transact in his stead the Affairs of Heaven, during that Journey which these Impostors affirm God to have taken, from any Scripture Evidence.

1. *For my Father is greater than I,* John 14. 28.

And he kneeled down and prayed, Father, if thou be willing, remove this Cup from Me; nevertheless, not my Will, but thine be done, Luke 22. 41, 42.

If *Elias* was that Father which Christ spake of, and prayed and cryed to, as *Reeve* and *Muggleton* assert; then either he that cryed to him was not God, *but* Elias *really God* (and so they both contradict their own Doctrine, who tells us, That he that was born of the Virgin, and dyed on the Cross, was the Everlasting Father) *or else, that which needeth and crieth for Help of another, was greater than that, which was able to succour and deliver it;* which how absurd it is, let all sober Men judge: Therefore he to whom he cry'd and pray'd in all Streights, and whom he had affirmed to have received all his Doctrine and Commission from, *and who was greater than all, was the only true God, and not any glorified Creature.* For God could not leave *Elias* his Deputy, and not leave him his Power, which if he did, *he left Himself*; since without his Almighty Power he were not God.

Secondly, *I thank thee, O Father, Lord of Heaven and Earth, because thou hast hid these Things from the Wise and the Prudent, and revealed them unto Babes.* Mat. 11. 25. *The Hour is come, glorifie thy Son, that thy Son also may glorifie thee. And this is Life Eternal, to know thee, the only True God, and Jesus Christ whom thou hast sent. And now Father, glorifie thou me with the Glory which I had with thee before the World was.* John 17. 1, 3, 5.

On this Place I raise these three brief Arguments;

1, If *Elias* was not the Father of our Lord Jesus Christ, nor Lord of Heaven and Earth, but a created Being, as all confess, *then it was not unto* Elias *that Jesus returned that Heavenly Thanks-giving, but to his own Father, greater than all, who is Lord of Heaven and Earth.*

2. If he to whom he prayed be that only true God, and that to know him, and Christ Jesus whom he hath sent, be Life Eternal, *then was it not* Elias *to whom he prayed, because all grant, that he is not the only true God, nor did he so love the World as to send his only begotten into the World, that through believing in him it might obtain Eternal Life.* This most plainly knocks down all Conceit of a Deputed God, that Christ should pray unto, because, supposing that such a Thing could be, *yet he could not be that only true God, whom to know were Life Eternal:* But this to whom Jesus prayed, who say *Reeve* and *Muggleton* was Elias, saith Christ Jesus, *was the only true God, whom to know is Life Eternal.*

3. This God to whom Christ prayed, that he would glorifie him, was the same Eternal God with whom he had Glory before the World began; *but* Elias *was Two Thousand Years or more after the World was made, instead of being before the World began; and consequently,* Elias *was not that God and Father, unto whom the Lord Jesus made his Supplications.*

Object. But *Muggleton* will tell me, *That* Elias *was enthroned with that God-like Power, Glory, Wisdom and Majesty, that rendred him all that which was needful to make able to answer all those Petitions, and what ever else was necessary.*

Answ. If the Majesty, Power, Wisdom and Glory of God were left with *Elias*, I would fain know what God had to dye with; for 'tis his Power, Glory and Divine Wisdom that makes him God; If *Elias* had them, *God left himself destitute of what made him God:* For how can a Man leave his Properties alive behind him that truly Man him, *and yet be said to dye in* Reeve *and* Muggleton's *Sense*, which is, That all those Faculties and Properties dye with a Man? Would one not rather say, that such an one does not dye, *because that which makes him a true Man lives;* So that their Conceit is spoiled in the over-turning of this one Thing; for, *shew the Impossibility of God's dying, and yet leaving his Power, Wisdom and Glory with* Elias, and the whole Fabrick, filled with their many Chambers of Imagery, will fall to the Ground; for, say they, *without a God's dying, and becoming from Immortal Mortal, and from Mortal, Immortal again, the whole Heaven and Earth would be out of order, and no Right Knowledge or Salvation can be procured or arrived at.*

Much might be urged from many other Scriptures, as that God raised him, and that he is set down on the Right-Hand of the Most High, but let this suffice.

Thirdly, Nor is there any Thing in the whole Scriptures of Truth, that so much as incourages any to believe the Mortality of the Immortal God.

1. *Even from Everlasting to Everlasting, thou art God*, Psal. 90. 2.

He that was from Everlasting, and is to Everlasting, never ceaseth to be, *as that which dyes doth*; but the true God was from Everlasting, and is to Everlasting; therefore *Reeve* and *Muggleton*'s Mortal God is not the true God; or, the true God never ceaseth to be.

2. *Hast thou not known, hast thou not heard, that the Everlasting God, the Lord, the Creator of the Ends of the Earth, fainteth not?* Isa. 40. 28.

He that could never faint, could never dye, because Death is more than a Degree beyond fainting (though fainting be a Temporary with-drawing of Life) *but the true God and Creator of the Ends of the Earth never could faint*; therefore the true God could never dye.

3. *And one of the Malefactors said, Lord, remember me when thou comest into thy Kingdom? And Jesus said, Verily, verily, I say unto thee, To day shalt thou be with me in Paradise,* Luke 23. 42, 43.

If Christ, the Author of all Truth, spake Truth, as most unquestionably he did; then both himself and the Malefactor were in Paradise that Day, and consequently, it was utterly impossible that they should both dye from all visible and invisible Life, Sense, Understanding and Enjoyment. But I hope, none are so impudent as to say, Christ spake not the very simple Truth, and *so would have deceived the poor Man*; and yet I know not how far *Muggleton* will go in this Matter, since he told me, that *Moses* in his Discourse of the Creation, *set the Cart before the Horse*; and that if *Paul* were alive, *he would reprove him*, and so censure that Holy Spirit by which he wrote.

Therefore it was not the Eternal Deity that suffered Death, *but the Body of outward Flesh, subjected to all those natural Passions of Heat, Cold, Hunger, Thirst, Life and Death* (as ours are, sin only excepted) *which the Eternal Infinite Creator had provided*, through which to manifest his Everlasting Wisdom, Counsel and Mercy for the Redemption of Mankind.

That these three Branches of this sottish Opinion are all of them greatly repugnant to that Understanding God has afforded Men to measure and distinguish Things by, I prove.

First, It was impossible for God to transubstantiate himself from an Immortal Deity to a mortal Man.

1. It must suppose God's begetting himself, which is absurd, and impossible: since being begotten, *supposeth him to have had a Beginning* (that gave Beginning to all) and to beget, *supposeth him to have been before he was begotten, and so before he was.*

2. Such as is the Begetter, such must the Begotten be: We see, Men get Men; Horses, Horses; Fish, Fish; and every Seed has it's own Body, as say *Reeve* and *Muggleton*; then, *by good Consequence, the Immortal God must have begotten himself an Immortal God, one that could not dye by the Hand or Cruelty of his own Creature.*

3. It is as impossible for God to become a Creature, or to dissolve his own Infinite, Immortal, Eternal Nature into a Finite, Mortal, Created or Generated Nature; *as for a Mortal Created Nature to be refined, preferred, and transmuted into an Infinite, Immortal, Creating Nature.* In short, It is as impossible for God, as God, to become a dying Man, *as for a dying Man to be changed into an Immortal Eternal God:* They are reciprocally impossible and Blasphemous.

Secondly, It is absurd, and untrue to affirm, that *Elias* was God's Deputy, and he to whom Christ prayed when in that Body of Flesh.

1. He that is Infinite, is every where, and circumscribed to no particular Place; but *Scripture, Reason*, and *Reeve* and *Muggleton* (yet they are seldom of one Mind) *own and declare the Infiniteness of God,* therefore God is every where, and if every where, then not excluded Heaven, the Habitation of his Throne, and consequently *Elias* was not God's Deputy, neither was it any ways needful that he should be.

2. That which in any Sense may be said to want, is not God, who is all in all to himself; *but who needed a Deputy, neither was Omnipresent, nor Almighty, and therefore not the only True God.*

3. Either Christ did not stand in need when on Earth, or he did; if not, *then he was not sincere in his Supplications*; if he did, *then the Omnipotency was with* Elias (he that supplies Wants is greater than he that is supplied) *and consequently, he that cried was not that Everlasting God and Father, but* Elias.

4. *Elias* was not so considerable as *Moses*, who was the first Grand Commissioner of God's Dispensations to the Sons of Men (as *Reeve* and *Muggleton* affirm) why then should *Elias* be preferred to *Moses*, a meek Man, *Israel's* Leader; and who said of Christ himself, *That a Prophet like unto me shall the Lord your God raise up unto you, him shall you hear in all Things* (then not *Reeve* and *Muggleton* in any new Thing) 'Tis strange therefore, that *Moses* was not rather of the two, elected to represent him in Heaven, who was a Figure of him on Earth. But though *Reeve* would not tell us so, I am of the Mind I know the Reason of it, namely, That Christ did not call, *Moses, Moses,* but Eli, Eli, *when upon the Cross*; and I am perswaded he had no other Ground for that Conceit, not considering that *Eli, Eli,* are Hebrew Words, importing no more *Elias, Elias,* than they do *Moses, Moses,* but *My God, My God,* as the Place expresly shews us.

Much more might be said, but let this serve.

Thirdly, That the Immortal God could never Dye, or cease to be, is manifest, and the contrary Blasphemously False.

1. If God was he that made all Things, and by whom they are upheld, as all believe, that believe there is a God at all, then had he ceased to be, the *Created had ceased to have been upheld*; and consequently all had fallen into it's first Chaos, or *else the World can subsist without Him.*

2. That he, whose Nature it was never to have Beginning, and ever to live without Variation, could never become so contrary to his own Nature and Being, *as to change, dye* or *cease to be*; but such was the true God, therefore he never dyed.

If Saints live, move, and have their being in God, as say *Reeve* and *Muggleton,* pag. 201. D. L. G. then either *God never dyed, or there were no Saints when the* Jews *Crucified Christ, or the Saints dyed too.* They deny them all; they say, God Died, and there were *Saints,* and they Lived, Moved and had their Being in God, *though Dead*; which how all, or any of them can hang together, let sober People judge.

4. If God died, *who lived, and by whom?* For nothing can live of it self, that had beginning from, or Dependence on another, as had all the visible World on God; *therefore because all lived, and was preserved, that had it's Being from God, He from whom they had their Being, could not be annihilated whilst they remained in Being.*

5. If God was raised by *Elias,* then either *Elias* was the True God, *or* Elias *the Creature was stronger than* Jehovah *the Great Creator.* Let this serve to confute, and for ever to overturn these idle Chimeras of those filthy Dreamers *Reeve* and *Muggleton.*

That this Blasphemous Conceit of the Immortal God's Mortality, is not new, I shall make appear.

First, *Valentinus* is said, openly to have published at *Rome, That Christ brought a Body down from Heaven, and that he after some Time passed through the Virgin's Body again.* Noetus affirmed, *That the Father, Son and Holy Ghost were Flesh, or that one Person of the Son of Man, or that Person so long since at* Jerusalem, *to be Father, Son, and Spirit; and that when he suffered on the Cross, the Father, Son and Holy Spirit died.* See *Euseb.* his 4th Book and 10th Chap. *Ireneus. Epiphanius Heres.* 31. & 57. about *Anno* 150. which is 1522. Years since. What Stange New Revelation this is!

Lastly, I May mention another of their Tenets, held at this Day by all *Calvinists* abroad, and of several Sects in these Nations; namely, *Predestination, or that God from all Eternity, without any other Inducement than his own Pleasure, hath decreed some for Salvation, and some for Damnation; contrary to which, all their Obedience or Rebellion shall be in vain, to alter his Determination.* D. L. G. p. 72, 73, 74.

That this Principle is Accurst by Scripture I prove.

First, The Righteousness of the Righteous shall be upon him, and the Wickedness of the Wicked shall be upon him; but if the Wicked will turn from all his Sins that he hath committed, and keep my Statutes, he shall surely live, he shall not dye, Ezek. 18. 20, 21.

1. If Righteousness or Wickedness are the Grounds of God's Rewarding or Punishing the Souls of Men, *then is there no Predestination previous, without Consideration had to their Works;* but the Text affirms this most plainly; therefore such Decrees are denied and disowned.

2. If Man may turn from his Righteousness and Wickedness, *then are the Means no more inevitably Predestinated for Men to use, than before-mentioned;* but Men may turn from either, and accordingly they will be rewarded; therefore no such Predestinated Damnation or Salvation.

Secondly, For it is good and acceptable in the Sight of God our Saviour, who will have all Men to be saved, and to come unto the Knowledge of the Truth, 1 Tim. 2. 3, 4.

If the Apostle writ by the Spirit of God, that gives to know the Mind of God; then it was the Good Will of God, that all Men, not excluding any upon a Predestination, should come to the Knowledge of the Truth, and be saved: And consequently, there is no Predestinated Restraint upon Men's Understandings, from knowing the Truth, nor fore-appointed Bar from their enjoying the End of such True Knowledge, *even the Salvation of their Souls.*

Thirdly, The Lord is not slack concerning his Promise (as some Men count Slackness) but is long-suffering to us-ward, not willing that any should perish, but that all should come to Repentance, 2 Pet. 3. 9.

The Long-suffering of God either related to the Elect, or Reprobate, or Neither.

Not to the Elect, *because there is no need of fearing their Perishing.*

Not to the Reprobate, *for there is no Possibility of their Repentance.*

Therefore to neither; and consequently, either the Place is spurious, or deceitful; *or else those Kinds of Elections and Reprobations are meer Phantasms.* Let these few Instances serve, of those Hundreds that might be mentioned, most expresly to confirm the same.

That this is highly inconsistent with REASON, I briefly prove.

First, it renders God most Unwise, to make so many Thousand Creatures on purpose to Rebel against him, *to Kill, Lye, Steal, Blaspheme, and commit all manner of outragious Wickedness, to the grieving of his own Spirit,* the making him Repent he had made the World, and obstructing of his Glorious Work of Reformation.

Secondly, It greatly disparageth his Justice, which consists in proportioning Rewards and Punishments to the Good and Evil Works of Men, and overturns both, *by making their Eternal States necessary and unavoidable upon a* Predestination, *without any Regard to their Works;* so that Man is damn'd for not doing what he can't do, any more than it is possible for him to break an Almighty Decree.

Thirdly, It quite destroys his *Mercy,* and renders him the most Cruel of all Beings; for instead of not being willing, or desiring the Death of a Sinner, *He is here made to desire, and take Pleasure in it too;* nay, so Essential is this unutterable Cruelty to his Glory (as say the Asserters of this Opinion) that it would be lessened or eclipsed without it: O infamous!

Fourthly, But above all Things, it strikes at the very Root of *God's Rectitude,* and Faithfulness, and makes him worse than the worst of Men and Devils: For whilst he says, *Your Sins have kept Good Things from you; as I live, I delight not in the Death of a Sinner; Repent, and Iniquity shall not be your Ruin; How long would I have gathered you, and ye would not? But now God commands all to Repent; God is no Respecter of Persons, but they that fear him in every Age shall be accepted,* &c. with many more. They make him but to complement with wicked Men, *and speak them fair in Words, meaning nothing less in his Heart, having Pre-Ordained them to Eternal Wrath.*

Fifthly, This Principle would defile his eternally inherent *Holiness,* by making him as well the Father of Sin, as of Destruction; for Men are either damned for something, or for nothing; if for nothing, that were most Wicked in these *Predestinarians*

destinarians Account, then for something: And what is that? *Sin:* Very well: And how came they to this Sin? *They committed it:* And how came they to do so? *They would do it.* Why? Could they have avoided it? *By no Means.* Where's the Difference then betwixt being Damn'd for not doing what they could not, and doing nothing? The Predestination was not, that all Evil Men, that wilfully withstood Mercy, should be Damned; *For they were Ordained never to receive it*; but that such a Number, consisting of such and such particular Persons, *should Unalterably and Unavoidably be Damned, only to Glorifie God.*

Sixthly, But this would stain the Glory of the Almighty, in that neither in himself, nor from the Redemption and Salvation of the Souls of Men, his Glory is great enough, *unless it be compleated in the Eternal Destruction of far the greatest Part of Mankind.*

Seventhly, This destroys all *Good Works*; for, may all say, *Neither can my Good nor Evil Works make one Hair white or black*, add, or diminish, in reference to God's unalterable Decree; *and therefore will I give my self unto the Liberty of the Flesh, and enjoy the Pleasures of this Life*, whilst I can have them.

Eighthly, It destroys all Government, since who cares how desperate he is, or what Injury he does, who conceiting to himself his Post is pitcht, his State set, and that unchangeably; but breaking all Laws, takes his Revenge on what would bring him to condign Punishment for his Exorbitancies.

To conclude, and come somewhat closer to the Persons concerned: What signifies their coming to call them to Repent, *that cannot be saved if they do?* Or to warn such to Repent that cannot be Damned? *What signifies their Commission?* Or *their Cursing, or Blessing? For can they Bless him to Life, that is Ordained beforehand to be Damned? Or can they Curse him to Death, who is Pre-ordained to Eternal Life?* If therefore Men are Pre-ordained to Salvation or Damnation, to what Purpose should any fear their Curse, or prize their Blessing, since neither can alter or change the Condition of any Person; and what more contrary to the Mind of the Merciful God, *who is willing that all should come unto the Knowledge of the Truth, and be saved?*

That Antiquity both knew, and abhorr'd this Opinion, is manifest.

Read *Josephus*, in his 18th Book of Antiquities, and second Chapter. Also *Epiphanius*, in his Preface to his first Book of Heresie. Again, *Eusebius*, in his fifth Book, Chap. 13. and *Socrates* in his first Book, and Chap. 17. and you will be fully informed of the Abettors of this dangerous and wicked Opinion, namely, a Sect of the *Pharisees*; also *Florinus* and *Blastus*, against whom *Ireneus*, Bishop of *Lyons* in *France*, wrote two Epistles, and a Book call'd *Ogdous*, wherein he tells *Florinus*, "That when himself was a Child, and with the famous *Christian Polycar-* "*pus*, who conversed with *John* that conversed with *Christ*, he remembred him to "be busie about the Emperor's Court; and farther tells him, *That had the Apostle* "*John but lived to have heard that Damnable Doctrine, which makes God the Author* "*of Evil, he would have said, Good God, unto what Times hast Thou reserved me!* "And tells him, *That in publishing so wicked an Opinion, he had declared that which* "*all the Hereticks before had never durst to pronounce plainly*, with much more to this Purpose, against him.

The Sect called *Manichees*, from one *Manes*, held, and promoted this Opinion of *Fatal Destiny*, who, *Muggleton-like*, is reported to have called himself *Christ* and the *Comforter*, and published the Work of one *Buddas* in his own Name, calling it, *A New Dispensation*; all which, *Reader*, I assure thee, Histories do inform us, to have been known in the 2d, 3d, 4th, 5th, and 600 Years after *Christ*, which is above a Thousand Years since: In which Time, many were the impudent Spirits that assum'd to themselves as great Authority as *Muggleton* in *Reeve's Absence doth at this Time*; namely, *Simon Magus*, who had so far possess'd the *Romans* with his Sorcery, of his (pretended) Divinity (calling himself to the *Samaritans* the Father; to the *Jews* the Son, to the *Gentiles*, the Holy Spirit) as that the Heathens erected a Statue or Image of him, in the Time of *Claudius* at *Rome*, having this Inscription, *Simoni Deo Sancto*, to the Holy God *Simon*. Next, one *Helen* a Woman, that accompanied him, whom he called the *Principal Understanding*, much like *Muggleton's* Daughter, who, *Reeve* said, *Should be the Chiefest of Women. Eusebius* in his 2d Book, and 12, 13, and 14th Chapters. After this, one *Menander*, said to have been a Sorcerer, and the Disciple of *Simon*, went up and down, deluding silly,

silly credulous People, by affirming to them, *He was the Great Power of God, come down from Heaven, and that all were to believe in, and be Baptized in his Manner, or they could not be saved, but those that did, should never dye.* Read *Eusebius* in his 3d Book, Chap. 23. *Ireneus*, Book 1. Chap. 21. *Epiphan. Haeres.* 22. Again, *Carpocrates* is reported to have (like *Reeve* and *Muggleton*) patch'd his Opinion (who was so Vain-Glorious as to affirm he knew all Things) out of *Simon, Menander, Nicholas*, (from whence came the *Nicolaitans* in the *Revelations*) *Saturninus, Basilides*, &c. and see *Epiphan. Haeres.* 27. also *Augustin* of Heresies. Again, we find that *Eusebius* tells us of one *Montanus* (whereof *Montanists*, or *Cartaphrygians* are called) who taught in *Phrygia*, that he was *the Holy Ghost*, as may be seen in the 5th Book of *Eusebius*, 13, 14, 15, 16, and 17th Chapters. Also that one *Buddas* affirm'd, *That he was born of a Virgin, (as true as* Muggleton's *being the Last Witness of God.)* This *Buddas* writ a Book, and in his swelling Pride, styl'd it *Mysteries*, much like the Whimsies of *Reeve* and *Muggleton*, in their *Transcendent Spiritual Treatise* ; next, he wrote a Book, called *The Gospel*, of the Nature of *Reeve* and *Muggleton's Divine Looking-Glass* : His End was to break his Neck : Tis to be fear'd that a worse will be miserable *Muggleton's*, even Torment of Spirit, as *Reeve* is said to have left the World in. To conclude, *Noetus*, the Ring-Leader of that Great Mystery, (never revealed till within these Twenty Years, says *Reeve* and *Muggleton)* namely, *the Godhead being a Man, and so absolutely Flesh and Blood, as that when the Body dyed, the Godhead ceased, and lay under Death's Power three Days and three Nights.* He, through the Height of his Imaginations, called himself *Moses*, and *Aaron* his Brother, as *Reeve* called himself and *Muggleton, T. S. T.* see *Epiphanius Haeres.* 57. By all which, Reader, I am not without Hopes, but it does appear, how falsly, and with what Treachery, these Persons have dealt with poor silly People, who not being satisfied in what they did know, have pin'd their Faith on the Sleeves of such as told them Things they did not know, and so have been given up to believe a Lye : For what is more evident, than that in this very Trial he, and his deceased Colleague, are found Guilty of Error, Treachery, and great Deceit : Therefore, *Reader*, delay not to pass the Just Sentence of Impostor and Counterfeit upon them, and their Commission, who would raise to themselves a New Sect out of the Ruins of *Old Heresies*, and that under the Pretence of *Choice Revelations*, wherein there is no Proof beyond their bare Assertions, and to make them pass, forge an Authority from Heaven (which loaths both them, and their Lyes) to back and recommend them as unheard of Mysteries.

O ! sell not thy Reason, whoever thou art, enslave not thy Judgment, nor rob *God's Light and Grace of it's Office*, to guide and teach thee in the Denial of those Evils that are to be forsaken, and in embracing whatsoever ought to be followed : Bring not thy self under the Power of an ignorant, arrogant, blasphemous, and sottish Man, but remember that God Almighty, who cannot lye, hath promised, *That in the last Days he would be the Teacher of his People by his Spirit of Truth, and where is the Habitation of the Most High, but in the Contrite and Humble Hearts of Men ? For whatsoever may, or can be known of God, is manifested within,* who having illuminated all, and given to every a Man a Talent, into it, *Reader*, have thy Mind retired, and wait to have it subject thereunto, and thou shalt come to know him *(whom to know aright is Life Eternal.)* But as I have plainly shown their abominable Cheat, *in obtruding Old Fables for New Revelations upon People* (whereby I have discharg'd the first Part of my Promise) so for a Confirmation of my Judgment concerning *Muggleton*, and to accomplish this abridg'd Discourse, take my following Relation, with the same Impartiality that I give it thee.

I Have been twice to visit *Lodowick Muggleton*, and at each Time I staid too long to repeat all, or the very Words which passed betwixt us ; yet shall I faithfully write something of the Matter and Words, as near as I at present do remember them.

    Penn. Art thou the last Witness that ever shall be ?
    Mug. *Yes ; and there shall never be another.*
    P. Who sent thee ?
    M. *God spoke to* John Reeve, *and he spoke to me.*
    P. Is that all thou hast to produce, only *J. R's* Word for it ? This he avoided.
    Again, P. Thou sayst God did not create the Earth and the Heavens, he only fashion'd them ; making them Co-eternal with God ; but *Moses* said he did : Let me see a Bible.

    M. Moses

1672.   *M.* Moses *put the Cart before the Horse.*
[This I bore for the next Question's Sake.]

P. Paul the Apostle, who also wrote, *by the Inspiration of the Holy Ghost,* saith *God created all Things,* or made them; and the World is a great Part of all Things: Besides, if it was before he made it, in this Sense, Must it not be God? Since nothing which is uncreated can be a Creature.

M. If Paul were living, I would have reproved him for that: Come not here to dispute, but believe, I say it, that's enough.

P. Canst thou reprove the Holy Ghost; for he spake by it?

M. Yes.

P. That's Blasphemy; besides, if thou sayst it, must I therefore believe it, because thou sayst it?

At this he grew inraged; and but for an Acquaintance by, and a Friend of his, I had doubtless been Curst at that Time.

The next Time I came (with a Friend in Company) I found him sitting by the Chimney-Corner, quaffing with some of his Followers and Benefactors, as what we saw before us did Evidence. My first Salute was thus:

P. How is it *Lodowick?* Methinks thou look'st with thy old thread-bare black Suit, like a sequester'd begging Priest.

M. I am a Priest.

P. Art thou? Of what Order?

M. The Order of Aaron.

P. Aaron! *Where be thy Bells then?*

M. I have them in the Mystery.

P. Mystery! For Shame, don't talk of a *Mystery;* for there was no such Thing that did belong to that *Order;* Things were altogether External, Typical, and Figurative: Methinks this were enough to show, that thou art no Ways concern'd in any *Christian Commission,* who art *not a Priest after the Order of* Melchisedeck, *but* Aaron, whose Priesthood is at an End, as said the Apostle to the *Hebrews,* ch. 7. so that thou hast Unchristian'd thy whole Commission, and brought it under the *Law of a Carnal Commandment;* and therefore hast no Part nor Portion *in the Power of an Endless Life,* as saith the same Apostle. He interrupted.

M. Have a Care, Life and Death's before thee; therefore chuse Life and live, &c.

P. But *Lodowick,* thou pretendest to know the Dimensions of God, how high may he be?

M. Betwixt your Height and his, (meaning a Friend then present.)

P. O Abominable! Well, *L. Muggleton,* God will blast thee for ever, thou Presumptuous and Blasphemous Wretch, If thou turnest not from thy Wickedness, with much more.

M. Thou shalt be Damned, God has decreed thou shalt be Damned; thou art of the Seed of the Serpent.

P. Why then didst thou set Life and Death before me just now, (saying thou hadst more Mind I should be saved, than any of the *Quakers)* if I am ordain'd to be damn'd? *Is it not great Deceit, to exhort a Man to chuse what he cannot have, though he bid for it, and to refuse that which he is unable to avoid?* But *Muggleton,* I will not say, that I serve such a God; no, my God never ordained thee to be damned, *whether thou dost well or ill*: This destroys all Rewards and Punishments, and makes Evil and Good unavoidable.

M. I would not give a Pin for that God which would save us both, now I have Damn'd thee.

P. Why dost thou talk of a God; for thou sayst, *Thy God can dye;* did the Immortal God ever cease to be?

M. I would not give a Rush for that God which can't dye.

P. I say, thou and thy God shall to the Pit, from whence ye came, where is Death and Darkness for ever: How can God cease to be, *and yet be God*; since if he ceast, every thing that remained in Being, must have been greater, since below ceasing to be is nothing? But suppose this Nonsense and Blasphemies; how rose he again?

M. God left Elias *with Power.*

P. Then *Elias* was greater than God; for that which raiseth, is greater than that which is raised; but if the Power never dyed, *the Power was God,* and that which dyed, not God: O, Hellish Impudence and Blasphemy! O, *Muggleton,* thy End will be Destruction.

M. W. P.

M. W. P. *I say thou art a Damned Devil; remember* Thomas Loe, *who was the wickedest Devil that ever I knew, who never went out of his Bed after I Curst him.*

P. Thy Curses are under my Feet; *Thomas Loe* was known to be an infirm Man in his Natural Constitution (as well as by his great Labours) for near these sixteen Years, who is gone to rest: But art thou not ashamed to say, he never went out of his Bed, who was as well as he used to be, and often after abroad? And when he fell sick, was often up, and changed his Lodging before he dyed, having been ill three Weeks. Is this thy infallible Spirit, that thus suggests Lyes to thy self and others?

M. *I heard so.*

P. Is that enough for one that pretends to be the last Witness of the High and Mighty God, to say for a Lye, *I heard so?* Cover thy Face for Shame.

M. *He w' it me a Curse, and he writ a very good Hand too; but for all that he was a Damned Devil, and thou W. P. art as arrant a Devil as he, and you shall be Damn'd together.*

P. *Lodowick*, in this thou hast told another Lye; for it was an Apprentice that writ it: Where is thy Unerring Spirit now, thou *Vile Impostor?* And for being Devils, and Damn'd together, God rebuke thee; only this know, that I am willing to go where he went, and whither thou canst not come, without great and unfeigned Repentance.

M. *Just so, many of you* Quakers *have dyed after my Curse, amongst others,* William Smith.

P. This is a notorious Lye; for the Man is yet Living: Well, *Muggleton*, God will reckon with thee for all thy Wickedness.

M. *Thou art a Cheat, and a Deceiver,* W. P. (my Friend spoke)

G. W. *Muggleton*, have a Care what thou sayst; for though it is our Religion to forgive Injuries; yet perhaps his Friends would question thee, and make thee prove it.

M. *I care not a Fart for him, nor his Friends, nor the Greatest Man in* England.

P. Thy black Mouth is no Slander; but know, *Muggleton*, That from my Youth I have sought God, and dared not willingly to abuse a Worm: And as my Friend has said, thou knowest there are Laws, other People make use of to vindicate their Credit by, but I forgive thee; thereby thou may'st know the Difference betwixt our Gods, and our Religions; thou revilest, and passest Curses upon me, I freely forgive thee.

M. *I care not a* Turd *for you, nor the Law neither.*

This, with many more unsavoury foul Expressions fell from his Mouth. He also affirmed, *That God never gave a Law but to Devils; and that* Moses *and the* Israelites *were so.* I askt him if he received a Law? He said, *Yes.* I askt him for whom? He said, *For the People of these Nations to whom he was sent.* I told him, *Then that render'd both himself, and those to whom he was sent, Devils by his own Assertion.*

In short, such Impertinency, such Blasphemy, such sottish Nonsense, and such unsavoury ill-bred Expressions, I don't remember to have heard from the Mouth of any Man, pretending to Religion. If this be your *Prophet*, (you that believe in him) your *Last Witness, the only Messenger of the Spiritual Dispensation, and Grand Commissioner of Heaven*, whom all must credit, or be damned: For Shame, own not so manifest an Impostor, so foul a Wretch, so ill an Example; *his Arrogancy, his Ignorance, his Sottish Life, his Cowardliness, and finally, his abominable Lying Spirit is far from the Holy, Patient, Suffering, Self-denying, and Heavenly Life of Christ and his Apostles, who being Reviled, Blessed.* I therefore intreat, nay, warn the *Reader* hereof; and to fear the Infinite Almighty God, whose mighty Judgments (for Sin in the Consciences of Men and Women) are come; and not to Worship this Beast, nor any Evil Thing, by bowing to his dark Imaginations: For know of a certain, the Time is at hand, *when every Word, Faith and Work shall be tryed*, that they who believe the Truth, and live in it, may have Rejoycing in themselves, and not in another; when *Muggleton*'s Airy Stories (which may perhaps swell and puff up the Minds of silly People) shall vanish; and such as have made his Lyes their Refuge, shall be swept away, and their Place not be found among the Living. Therefore mind the *Light*, the *Grace*, the *Gift of God* in your selves, which leads to Repentance, and all manner of Godly Conversation (*a Thing* Muggleton *meddles not with*) that by it your Hearts may be sanctified, and settled in the Belief of the Truth, as it is plainly revealed to every Particular in Christ Jesus, shall you obtain a sound Understanding, and possess the Habitations of true Peace, when *Muggleton* and his obstinate Brats shall howl in the Lake that burns with Brimstone and Fire for ever and evermore. W. P.

John Reeve *and* Lodowick Muggleton, *Contradicting Themselves, and One Another.*

IT can be no Wonder unto such as have impartially read thus far, that these Men should contradict themselves, and one another; who are filled in their Discourses (or rather Ravings) with nothing sober and consonant; but Confusion heap'd upon Confusion, to the astonishing of every Man that is in earnest about Religion, and has any due Fear and Reverence for God; but because they lay it down, as the Mark only of the True Commissioners of Heaven, in nothing to Jar or Contradict, I am the more induced to add to my own Pains and the Readers, a Comparison of their Contradictions.

Doth not this Demonstrate those to be the Commissionated Witnesses of the Unerring Spirit, that are endued with a Divine Gift, to write a Volume as large as the Bible, and as pure a Language as that is, with as much Variety of Matter, without looking in any Writing whatsoever, *or Having any Real Contradiction in it,* R. & M. Div. Look Glass, Page 112.

Contradiction I.

Therefore it is written, *Dust thou art, and unto Dust thou shalt return:* When the Lord spake those Words, he did not speak to the Flesh, or outward Form, or Body of the Man; *but he spake to the Inward Spirit or Soul, that understands the Words of a Spirit.* Look in his *Transc. Spiritual Treatise*, p. 44.

Wherefore it may be queried by some, What was that which entred into the Dust, and brought forth Angelical Bodies; was it any thing else, but the Divine Nature of God Himself?

Unto this Curious Query, from the true Light of Life I answer,

That neither the Spirit of Angels, nor any other Creatures were formed of the Divine Nature; *but the Souls of* Adam *and* Eve *only,* His Divine L. Glass, p. 8.

Animadversion I.

If that which returns to Dust, cannot be said to return to Dust, unless it first came from Dust; then, if the Soul returns to Dust, it consequently came from Dust; and if from Dust, then was it not formed of the Divine Nature, as on the other Side is affirmed, and therefore a Contradiction.

Contradiction II.

Again, I declare, That when the Elect are Glorified, *they are absolutely of the very same Glorious Nature, both in Spirit and Body, as God is.* T. S. T. p. 46.

Therefore the most Wise and Holy Creator created the Bodies of Angels Spiritual, and their Natures Rational; and he made the Body of the Man *Adam* Natural, and his Soul Spiritual: *For, if their Spirits and Bodies had been both of the Divine Nature, then it would have been impossible for them to have been capable of any Sin or Evil, any more than the Creator Himself; for what would have been formed, but Creators only, instead of Creatures?* D. L. G. page 9, 10.

Animadversion II.

If to be in Body and Spirit Spiritual, be to be Creators, then Gods; and if the Saints are to be of the same Body and Spirit, *then they are to be Creators, and consequently Gods;* which is absurd: For if the Reason, why Man was not at first made

made all Spiritual, but the Soul Spiritual, and the Body Natural, *was, because he had been a Creator*, as they say, which was impossible; then, if Man is to be of the same Body and Spirit that God is, as they affirm; *Man is to be a Creator in the next World.* Monstrum Horrendum!

Contradiction III.

If the very God-head had not died, (that is) *If the very Soul of Christ, which is the Eternal Father, had not died in the Body, or with the Body, to quiet or satisfy the Cry of the Guilt of Sin in Men's Spirits, all Men would have perished to Eternity: Thus the Father and the Son was but one unseparable Person in Immortal Glory, from all Eternity; and became, in Time, one unseparable Person in Mortality.* T. S. T. p. 25, 26.

If Angels and Men had been both of God's Divine Nature in their Creation, then instead of their being capable to be changed into an higher or lower Condition, at the Divine Pleasure of the Creator; *would they not rather have been Unchangeable Creators, than Changeable Creatures?* D. L. G. p. 9.

Animadversion III.

If the Reason why Men and Angels are not of the Divine Nature, be, That they are subject to Change, and that if they had been made of it, they would not have been capable of Mutation into lower or higher Degrees, at Divine Pleasure; then because God is of that Divine Nature, *it is consistent with his Nature to Change, or be Transmuted*, as they often speak, *from an higher State to a lower*; and so, their whole Conceit of the Deity's Mortality, is Vain, and by themselves Contradicted.

Contradiction IV.

Again, Many seeming wise Men do imagine the Lord to be a Vast Spirit. D. L. G. p. 16.

Others blasphemously say, that the Spirit of Man is God, and that the Body only dies: *These say also, God is an Infinite Spirit.* T. S. T. p. 44.

Is not that Infinite Spirit, and it's Glorious Properties, but only one Essence, or God-head Substance? D. L. G. p. 106.

You may know, that all things are possible and very easy for an Infinite Spirit to bring to pass. D. L. G. p. 114.

Animadversion. IV.

It can be no Crime, for any to believe, God to be an Infinite or Vast Spirit, as one while they would have it, whilst presently they call the *God-head Substance*, *an Infinite Spirit*, and confess *all Things to be possible unto an Infinite Spirit*. O Gross Contradiction!

Contradiction V.

I say, In the Great and Notable Day of the Lord, by his Decree, they shall every one of them rise out of the Dust together; not with the same Bodies that died, because there was somewhat of God in those Bodies. T. S. T. p. 11.

So likewise that Infinite Spirit abiding within the glorious Body of Christ, is so unspeakably fiery Glorious, *that no Created Spirit of Man nor Angel is able to bear the In-dwelling Essence of it.* D. L. G. p. 69.

Animadversion V.

If something of God dwells in this Life in the Souls and Bodies of Men, *then it is not so fiery Glorious, but it may abide in them, and they not be consumed*: For God's Nature or Essence is irreconcileable to nothing but Sin; the Righteous shall behold him Face to Face: So that one while, God dwells in Men; another while, if it should be so, Man would be consumed. Behold the Self-Opposition of these Miserable Witnesses.

Contradiction VI.

How can any Rational Wise Man possibly think, that Man, or any other Living Forms, should ever be without a Glorious Creator, to give them their Beings at first. D. L. G. p. 16.

This was the Creator's very Case in the Matter of *Creation*; and who dares speak against it? no Spiritual Wise Man, I am sure, only some Lustful Persons, may dispute against it, *though it be contrary to their own Reason, when it is sober.* D. L. G. p. 12.

I confess, it is not only contrary to Reason, but far above all Reason's Reach, truly to understand the Mysteries of the Creation. D. L. G.

Animadversion VI.

If an Appeal be made to rational Men, concerning the Creation by a God, and if it be contrary to sober Reason not to believe so, *then it is not far above, nor contrary to all Reason, to understand the Creation*; for else, why is it rendred by them so agreeable to Reason, and *an Appeal made unto Rational Men concerning it?*

Contradiction VII.

Again, *For your Information, in whose Persons, the Lord by his Holy Spirit Delights to dwell.* T. S. T. p. 22.

Whoever thou art, that boasteft of a God, and a Christ, and his Ordinances, and of a Glory to come without thee, in the Highest Heavens; if thou should'st be left to the Pride and Envy of thy Formal Spirit, *to condemn the Invisible Teachings of the Lord Jesus Christ in his Innocent People*, because they are contrary to thy Opinion; I say, from the Everlasting Emanuel, *That thou art also but a Reprobate.* D. L. G. p. 68, 69.

For in him dwelleth all the Fulness of the Godhead bodily, and from his Fulness we all receive, and Grace for Grace. *If Christ, or his Spirit, were within Men when they uttered those Words, all Faith or Hope, in Reference to Eternal Glory was vain.* D. L. G. p. 67, 68.

Animadversion VII.

If Christ delighteth to dwell in the Persons of his People, by his Eternal Spirit, and that he thereby teacheth their Souls what he requires from them, as say they; *then it is not in Vain to believe or hope, though Christ, or his Spirit, were within,* as they also say: nay, they affirm; *That the Souls of the Redeemed is the Throne of God, on which he now sits,* D. L. G. p. 46. And therefore, though Christ, or his Spirit were in Believers, yet that would not make their Faith and Hope Void; Why? Because they stand therein.

Contradiction VIII.

Is that Eternal Spirit, in it's Heavenly Virtues, any Thing else, *but Immortal Crowns of bright burning Glories?* Tho' the Eternal Spirit, *be that Invisible God, that by the Power of his Almighty Word hath created all Things*; and though all Power, Wisdom and Glory proceeds only *from an Invisible Eternal Spirit,* D. L. G. p. 106.

Can this Infinite Spiritual Glory, *be sensible of it's Divine Excellency, or be a perfect Blessedness, except he hath a distinct Body, suitable to his Eternal Spirit;* yet without a Body, Face, or Tongue, or a Majestical Person, like unto Earthly Monarchs, he could not possibly have spoken distinct Words, nor his Glory have been perfect. D. L. G. p. 106.

Animad-

Animadversion VIII.

If that which is requisite to define or render God truly such, be singly attributed to the Eternal Spirit, without the Mention of a Body, *then is the Eternal Spirit the Invisible God,* as they themselves prove. If the Eternal Spirit be nothing else than Crowns of Immortal Glory, and that it is the Invisible God, whose Power created all Things; *and if all Wisdom, Glory and Power proceed only from this Invisible Eternal Spirit,* as they say; *then not unto a Body, but unto that, who* alone *has all Power, Wisdom and Glory, is the Godhead to be ascribed*; but that is unto the Invisible Spirit: And if the Eternal Spirit be thus qualify'd, how possibly can it's Glory be eclipst for want of a Body, Face, or Tongue? Is the Eternal Spirit Crowns of Immortal Imperfect Glory? *And how can all Glory alone be given unto the Spirit, whose Glory is Imperfect, without a Body?* He should have said, From the Spirit and Body alone proceedeth all Glory, &c. But this Confusion is like the rest.

Contradiction IX.

Moreover, You may know, That those Men called, *Independents, Anabaptists, Presbyterians, are the Literal Apostolical Jews.* D. L. G. p. 191.

Furthermore, *Those* Anabaptist, Presbyterian *Men, which hold it lawful to persecute Men, in their Persons and Estates, upon a Spiritual Account; I say from the Eternal Spirit, That they are for the most Part, the Off-spring of those bloody-minded* Jews *that Crucified the Lord of Glory upon the Account of Blasphemy.* D. L. G. p. 192.

Animadversion IX.

That Exception should have been made before: for, if those that are called *Independents, Presbyterians,* and *Anabaptists,* are *Apostolical Jews,* and yet such as are for Persecution for Conscience, are of their Race that put Christ to Death, then they are not of the *Apostolical,* but *Mosaical Jews:* But how can they make that hold together? The *Apostolical Jew,* is one, not outward in the Letter, but in the Heart, and in the Spirit; if so, *either they are* Independents, Presbyterians, *or* Anabaptists; *or else those three Opinions are come to be of theirs,* since at the Distance they stand, they cannot be under the same Covenant and Circumcision. But to be short, By their declaring them (whilst not their Followers) *Apostolical Jews,* we may conclude, That *Reeve* and *Muggleton* count themselves none of them, but Men of another Dispensation; *and therefore not of the Circumcision in Heart, which is not according to the Letter, but the Spirit*; beyond which Dispensation, all other Pretensions are Imaginations and vain Exaltations.

Contradiction X.

It is not thy Natural or Allegorical Whimsies, that can blind the Elect, *nor pacify the Judge of Life and Death within thee.* D. L. G. p. 268.

And now I desire no other Witness, to bear Record in the Consciences of Men to this Epistle, whether it be Truth, or no, but the Everlasting *Jehovah,* or Eternal Spiritual Jesus himself. D. *L. G.* p. 208.

Again, *If every Man have the Spirit of Christ living in his Conscience, as many Men vainly imagine; What then is become of the Spiritual Body of that Jesus that ascended into the Throne of his Glory, in the visible Sight of Men and Angels?* D. L. G. p. 68.

Animadversion X.

If the Judge of Life and Death be in Man, *then Christ unto whom all Judgment is committed, is in Man, to justify or condemn him*; therefore Christ, or his Spirit, or both are in Man, and consequently, it is no Impediment to, nor Denial of Christ's Ascension with a Glorified Body: *Neither is it vain to believe, that the Spirit of Christ lives in the Consciences of Men.* Observe their Folly, The *Judge of*

1672.

Life and Death is within thee; Again, It is vain to imagine, that the Spirit of Christ lives in Men's Consciences: Thus they say and unsay almost in a Breath. But above all, That the Everlasting Jehovah, and Eternal Spiritual Jesus, should be in Men's Consciences the true Witness, and yet not be in Men: Who can understand this strange Riddle?

Contradiction XI.

But you may say, Did God the third Day arise from the Dead, by his own Power, or by the Power of his Deputy, *Elias?* To which I answer, *He by his own Decree, and Spiritual Compact, with* Elias, *and by that Spirit of Faith, in his Innocent Body, the which Faith died in his pure Body, and quickened immediately, and brought forth that Natural Innocent Body, out of the Grave, a pure Spiritual Body.* T. S. T. p. 32, 33.

Therefore whosoever saith, that any other Body ascended into Glory, but that very same Body of Flesh and Bones that suffered Death upon the Cross, he is an Antichrist, and in utter Spiritual Darkness. D. L. G. p. 15.

Animadversion XI.

If the Body died a Natural Body, and was brought forth, a Spiritual Body; then, unless that Spiritual Body laid down it self, and resum'd it's Natural Body, as at the first, it could not be the very same Body, of Flesh, Blood and Bones, that Died, which Ascended; but it must have been a Spiritual Body. In short, If Natural and Spiritual be not all one, as say they else-where in these Contradictions, then was it no more the same Body, than Natural is Spiritual, and Mortal Immortal, upon their own Principles; and consequently, Reeve *and* Muggleton *are the Antichrists, and in utter Darkness.*

As for the Three-fold Answer he gives to the Objection, it is wretchedly Blasphemous. 1. God's Decree. 2. His Compact with *Elias.* 3. His own Spirit of Faith. To the first I reply, What did the Decree avail, when the Power was in another, and when he that made it, was dead? To the second I return, *That God's Rising lay on the Side of* Elias's *Honesty, in performing Obligation, and keeping Covenant,* and not in any other Thing. 3. As to that Spirit of Faith, they confess it died, if so, *how did the Faith raise him?* Besides, In whom should God have Faith? In Himself? *He was dead*; In *Elias?* He could not exercise it, when in the Grave. Again, He that believes, enjoys not fully; and has Confidence in one Greater than Himself; *but God wants nothing, and can have no Object for Faith,* and therefore no Faith. O the Unparallelled Sottish Folly, and Raving Conceits of these Men!

Contradiction XII.

So likewise, I positively affirm, against all Gainsayers under Heaven, *That I John* Reeve *am the last commissionated* Prophet, *that ever shall declare Divine Secrets, according to the Foundation of Truth, until the Lord Jesus Christ appear on his Throne of Glory.* D. L. G. p. 119.

A True Interpretation of all the chief Texts and Mysterious Sayings, and Visions opened, of the whole Book of the *Revelations of St. John*; wherein is unfolded, and plainly declared, those wonderful deep Mysteries, and Visions interpreted, concerning the True God, the *Alpha* and *Omega*; with Variety of other Heavenly Secrets, *which hath never been opened, nor revealed to any Man, since the Creation of the World to this Day, until now:* By Lodowick Muggleton, *&c.*

Animadversion XII.

Who shall we believe of these two? they both pretend the same Commission, and yet contradict: But how can any Credit be given thereunto? when (though *Reeve* says, he was awake, at the receiving of it, yet presently after tells us, that) he knew not, *whether he was an Immortal God, or a Mortal Man:* What ground is there for any Belief, of what *Reeve* himself was so far from a clear Knowledge of, of, *as that he was not more unable to resolve, whether he was an Immortal God, or a Mortal Man:* than to know the Truth of all his Revelation? O, the Willingness in Men to be blind! Certainly if the Devil himself should, as a Devil, seek Proselytes, some would follow him.

A few *Additional Observations* upon some Passages, of *John Reeve* and *Lodowick Muggleton*, in the before-cited Books.

The Spirit of Faith and Love, infinitely in the Glorious Person of God, overfloweth as a Fountain, continually with Revelation of New Heavenly Wisdom, from whence flow New Joys, and Glory to Himself, T. S. T. p. 46.

Observation, That unto which any Thing may be added, cannot be said to be Perfect, and consequently cannot be God ; *but he unto whom Wisdom is renewed, wanted that Wisdom before he had it, and consequently was not Perfect, and therefore not the True God* ; unto whom there is no Encrease of Wisdom, Power or Strength; but was and is, and will be for ever the same Unalterable Being ; Infinite in Wisdom, Power, and all other Divine Excellencies, without any Diminution or Addition.

The Reason why Men's Bodies in Death, or after Death, do Rot or Stink, in the Grave, and come to Dust, is, because there was Sin in their Bodies; *whilst they lived*; *but on the contrary, if Men had no Sin in their Natures or Bodies, they might Live and Dye, and Naturally Rise again, by their own Power, in their own Time,* T. S. T. p. 33.

Observ. O the exceeding Folly and Blindness of this sottish Man! Why should Sin only cause the Body to Rot, Stink and go to Dust? Does not the Scripture, and *Reeve* himself, in his *T. S. T.* p. 44. give another Reason, namely, *That what came from Dust, is that which must go to Dust?* Besides, If the Flesh of Beasts, is capable of Dying, Rotting, and going to Dust, who never sinn'd, why should not Man have Dyed, and gone to Dust, though he had never sinn'd? For though there is a vast Difference betwixt Men and Beasts, in reference to their Souls, and Bodies too, so far as may concern the Distinction of Kinds; yet as to their being lyable to one and the same External Casualties, and Sufferings, by Hunger, Thirst, Sickness, Death and Corruption, *no Man can rationally contradict :* But above all, this deserves our Observation, That since *Reeve* is Dead, Rotten, and gone to Dust, he was not cleansed from Sin, as he is said to have pretended ; but by Reason of his Wickedness, Death holds him in the Grave, and consequently, he cannot have been God's last Witness, whose Witnesses he hath always cleansed from that, against which they were to Witness. And it is farther evident, That Sin is not the Cause of Men's Bodies crumbling into Dust, from *Reeve*'s own Words, who saith, *The Most High God, by his Unsearchable Wisdom, hath Decreed, that all Light of Life in Man, shall become Dead, Dust, or Earth,* D. L. G. p. 17. So that God's Decree, *and not Man's Sin*, in his own Sense, *must be the Reason of such Conversion and Corruption.*

Therefore you may know, that the Lord's Reasoning with the Jews, was only by his Prophets, which were Rational Men, like unto themselves, which were sent to Convince those stony-hearted Jews, by declaring the Glorious God, and his Spiritual Truth unto them, in the Balance of their own Reason, D. L. G. p. 117.

Observ. It is remarkable, with what unusual Nonsense, and Contradiction he proceeds, in his whole Affair, since herein he Contradicts one of his main Foundation Principles ; namely, *That God hath not in his Glorious Spirit, one Motion of Reason inherent, nor yet the Elect of God*, as may be seen, D. L. G. p. 18. and T. S. T p. 17. Whereas it's manifest unto all Men, who would not deny themselves the Use of their Understandings, That none can properly reason of any Subject, unto whom Reason cannot be, or is not inherent ; so that if God, did both Reason with the *Jews*, and his Prophets were Rational Men, then may we safely conclude, That Reason is Inherent, to God, and his Elect Children ; and that Pure Reason is not inconsistent with, or distinct from the Nature of Love and Faith; not only, because it is most rational to believe in, and love God most uprightly ; but because *John Reeve* himself (that great Enemy to all sober Reason) makes it the Balance,

1672.

in which the Prophets Declaration of the Glorious God, and his Spiritual Truth, should be weighed.

Again, I declare from the Holy Spirit, The Lord spake by Voice of Words to his Three Commissioners, which he hath sent unto the World; yea, I know God the Father spake unto Moses, as a Man speaks unto his Friend; and I know, that God spake unto the Apostles, in the Person of his Son, because I know the Lord God spake unto me in the Person of the Holy Ghost; *only the two former Witnesses, saw the Person of God, in Part Visibly, but I saw the Glory of his Person Invisibly, or within me, because I am the Messenger of the Holy Invisible Spirit,* T. S. T. p. 35.

Observ. Upon all this I make my following Observations, as regular as this Irregular Confused Matter, will permit me.

First, Then I would fain know, how he came to this Mighty Confidence in God's speaking to *Moses*; for it is in no part of his Commission; and *Muggleton* says, Moses *set the Cart before the Horse; and they both of them despise the Scripture, in Comparison of their own Writings.*

Secondly, Though God might speak in the Person of his Son to his Apostles, yet I utterly deny, upon *Reeve*'s Principles, that the Lord Jesus could speak unto him, in the Person of the Holy Ghost, because this would necessarily imply a Trinity of Persons, which is by him elsewhere absolutely denyed; therefore the Lord Jesus could speak to him in no other Person, than his own, if at all.

Thirdly, If God spake to *J. Reeve* by Voice of Words, because he affirms him to have so spoken to *Moses*, and the Apostles; then may we plainly infer, that God should as well have shewn his Person unto *J. R.* as he believes him to have done to *Moses*, and the Apostles, since if he did not decline to utter Words to the Carnal Ear, in this third Commission, as is pretended, any more than in the two former, there is no Reason in the World, why *John Reeve*'s Carnal Eye should not have had equal Priviledge with the former Commissioners, in visibly beholding God's Person also: but since he makes God so to differ in the one, we ought the less to believe him in the other; that is, If his Carnal Eye could never see Him, because of the Spirituality of the Commission, his Carnal Ear could never hear him, for one and the same Reason; therefore all a Counterfeit.

Fourthly, Suppose he had seen the Glory of God's Person within him, *yet that had been impossible, unless God's Person had been within him, since his Person and his Glory are inseparable*, as he largely affirms, D. L. G. p. 106. and if so, how manifest a Contradiction is it to several Places of his Writings? particularly this, 'The Spirit or Person of Christ, may fitly be compared unto the Face of the Na-'tural Sun; you may know, that the Natural Spirit of the Sun, is so exceedingly 'Fiery Glorious, that no created Thing, that hath Natural Life in it is capable of 'it's in-dwelling Brightness, but it's own Body or Face only: If this be true, then *Reeve* could not behold the Glory of God's Person within him.

Fifthly, But let us suppose, that by *Reeve*'s Principles, the Glory of God's Person, may be beheld, yet it is highly against them, that it should be beheld within; for if the Body and Soul of Man, are one individual and inseparable Substance, as he says they are, then can there be no Invisible Eye, distinct from that which is Carnal, to behold an Invisible Glory; and if so, then could *Reeve* never see God's Glory Invisibly within him; and consequently, he had no Commission: But out of his own Mouth he is prov'd a Lyar and Impostor. I shall conclude the whole with Queries to L. *Muggleton*, and his Companions.

Ten Queries Propounded.

I. IF *J. Reeve* and *L. Muggleton* were the two True Last Witnesses, mention'd in the *Revelations*; How comes it, that they bear not the same Testimony, when risen, that was born before the slaying of the Witnesses; since they were not other Witnesses, that rose, than those that were slain, and consequently, the Testimonies no more vary than the Witnesses themselves?

II. If they be the same Witnesses, should they not have Prophesied, 1260. Days, that is Years; and have been slain Three Days and an Half in spiritual *Sodom* and *Egypt*, where our Lord was crucified, and then have risen from the Dead?

III. How did they Prophesie so many Years? How were they (Visible Witnesses) slain in spiritual *Sodom* and *Egypt*, where Christ was crucified? Does not this show the Witnesses to be Spiritual and Mystical, like the Place in which they were slain, (the Hearts of Men) and their Death to be the same? And were they ever such Witnesses, so slain, so long slain, and in that Place, as in the *Revelation* exprest?

IV. If they be the same Witnesses, were they not to Live, and Dye, and Rise together? Has not *Reeve* been Dead many Years?

V. If they were the True Witnesses, When did they shut the Heavens, that it Rained not, turn Water into Blood, and Smite the Earth with Plagues?

VI. If *John Reeve* was the *Moses*, or Principal Understanding; and L. *Muggleton* the *Aaron*, or Mouth only, as says *Reeve*; then whether *Muggleton* be any Thing, but an Empty Mouth, now his Understanding, *Moses*, is gone?

VII. How can *Muggleton*, upon *Reeve's* Principle, be a Witness or Commissioner for God, who confesseth, He never had any Commission by Voice of Words, but from *Reeve* only, whom he trusted; though *Reeve* himself affirms, That there is no True Commission, but by Voice of Words to the Party sent?

VIII. Whether Men's Trusting upon *Muggleton* (who relied upon *Reeve*) without any Internal Convictions from the Eternal Spirit, be not as Sandy a Foundation as the darkest *Popery*.

IX. Whether, there ever was a Pope on Earth, that usurped, or exercised a more Arbitrary Enslaving Power over Men's Consciences, in Imposing his Faith upon Penalty of Immediate Curse, and Eternal Damnation, than *J. Reeve* and L. *Muggleton* have done, and the last remains to do; by affirming, That whom he Curseth, God Himself cannot Bless; and whom he Blesseth, God Himself cannot Curse: Though *Reeve* and *Muggleton* have Curst, and Blest, and Curst the same Person, and that more than once?

X. And lastly, Whether upon the whole, these Men, in their Commissions, Doctrines, Jurisdictions, Sentences, Lives and Conversations, are like unto the Last Witnesses of the Lord Jesus Christ; or those Ungodly, Proud Boasters; wandering Stars; Clouds without Rain; Raging Waves, Exalted above all that is called God; Perverters of the Truth, whose Belly is their God, who Glory in their Shame, whose End is Destruction and Perdition?

POSTSCRIPT.

Since the finishing of the fore-going Paper, it came into my Mind, that if I affixt a *Postscript*, touching the Commission it self, that might remove all Credit in the same, the rest would dye of it self. 'Tis true, this might have been better plac'd in the Front, as the best Preludium to the Discourse of it self; but it failing of that Place, I was rather willing it should go for a *Postscript*, than lose that Service, I am not without Hope, it may perform in Publication of it.

A Brief Examen of REEVE *his Commission.*

Saith he, ' I Declare from the Lord Jesus, That no Man can understand any ' Thing of those Things that are Invisible to our Natural Eyes, but by the Spirit ' of Revelation; therefore it is written, *That Faith is the Substance of Things* ' *hoped for, and the Evidence of Things not seen*: In his *Transcendent Spiritual Treatise*, as he calls it, pag. 16.

If these Things are Invisible to Natural Eyes, then are they Inaudible by Natural Ears, both being Capable and Natural alike: And if no Man ever can or could See them, no Man could or can ever Hear them; and if no Man could or can, then *Reeve* never did: And if he never heard with his Carnal Ears, *for He implies so much, that denies the Power of seeing such Spiritual and Invisible Things to natural Eyes*, then was his Commission a Counterfeit: For he affirmed, That the 3d, 4th, and 5th of *February*, 1651. *He Heard God resident above the Stars, speaking to Him then in Bed on Earth, by a Voice of Words, giving to him his Pretended Commission*, T. S. T. pag. 5.

In short, Four Things I recommend to the Serious Consideration of all Soberminded People, with a Story to conclude.

1. That a Commission should be given by a Voice of Words, *from the farthest Heaven to any Man upon Earth, and neither any other Hear the same, no, not so much as* Muggleton *Himself; nor yet the Heavens nor Air to receive any Impression or Alteration*, is an incredible Thing with all Persons that are in their Wits.

1672.

2. Not only in this doth his Commission strangely vary from that of *Moses*, but in the Consequence thereof most dangerously, in as much as no Man living is assured of the Verity of this Commission, *from any Convincing Testimony, either from without, or within him*; a Credulity God himself never exacted, or expected from his Creatures: For, the Reason of God's Complaint against a Rebellious People, *never was for not believing without Convictions*; but because the Creation without, and his Good Spirit within, *had so plentifully proved a God, and that Fear, Reverence and Obedience which were due to Him*, and yet that they were not delighted to retain the Most High in their Knowledge.

3. That this should beget an utter and perpetual Abhorrence in us of all such Impostures; do but call to mind, what an Overthrow this gives to all those famous Prophesies, *of God's Tabernacling in His People, His Teaching them, pouring out His Spirit upon them, and of their beholding Him Face to Face*; since in this one Conceit, all that believe it, are brought under the Verge of these Men's Imaginations, without the least convincing Ground for any such Belief, unless the Fear of their Insolent Curse.

4. To Conclude, if his Commission was after a Visible External Manner, like *Moses*, as he affirms, *He must needs have Visible and External Miracles to confirm such a Visible and External Commission*: For, to deny Visible Miracles to a Visible Commission, *is to deny that Commission*; and to pretend Invisible Ones, *is Improper, Unnatural and Untrue*.

My Story is this, and not Unknown to some of the *Creditors* of this *Counterfeit Commission*.

A Considerable Commander of the *English* Army, in *Ireland*; and but too stiff against Lay Preachers (esteemed *Presbyterian*) hearing in his Bed a still Voice, *Requiring Him to go Preach the Gospel to the* Indians, was so much amaz'd, that he question'd if he were not asleep, *as* Reeve *did, whether He was an Immortal God, or a Mortal Man*; and finding himself Awake (though he could rather have wisht it but a Dream) it greatly Terrified him; to leave his Family, Command and Station, to go Preach the Gospel (who scarcely ever adventur'd to Preach (whatever he did to Pray) in all his Life) was Matter of much Disquiet to him; till in the End, he rather inclin'd to incur the Curse that followed his Disobedience, than to leave his wonted Course of Life, and take up one so difficult to him, and in which he was so unable, as well as Unwilling to acquit himself: But it ended not so; for, I think, the next Night, or Morning, or in a little Time after, the same Voice came to him, with the same Command, which increased his Perplexity; but still, as I was inform'd, he continued averse from such a Voyage and Enterprize, till the Third Time of his being thus Alarum'd, and then, as the Story went, he gave (for ought I know, as Freely) up to Preach to the *Indians*, as *Reeve* did to go to *Muggleton*, and *J. Robins*, &c. and I am strongly of the Mind, the Authority may have been much alike, for it proved in the End, to be the Abuse of some of his Companions, in a way of Unjustifiable Waggery and Merriment, through a Trunk, or some such hollow Thing, placed with it's Mouth or Muzzle near the Commander's Bed. What shall we say then of *Reeve's* Voice of Words? A Man swelled with Conceits more ready and deserving to have been abused, than the Person concerned in this Story: And concerning whom *Muggleton* told me, *He thought Him Hot-brain'd, and Distemper'd in his Head*, and that he had told him so; a Thing not hardly to be credited by such as read his Folly, *Certainly God never gave a Commission yet, in that Way wherein Man's Wit or Malice could Equal it*. And I would know, what one Extraordinary Circumstance attended the giving of this Commission to *Reeve*, that may groundedly Engage any to the Belief of it? But indeed, it was notably done of Him, to pretend an Authority of which he was the sole Judge, and Witness; and a Power to Curse all such as Refus'd his Testimony, without his rendering a Reason for the Hope that was in him. Never did the Devil more befool himself, nor any of Mankind, than in his Divulging, and **their Believing of these Sottish Blasphemies.**

Plain-Dealing with a Traducing ANABAPTIST:

OR,

Three LETTERS writ upon Occasion of some Slanderous Reflections, given and promoted against *William Penn* by one *John Morse*.

Published for Common Benefit, that all Impartial People may be better acquainted with the Invective Spirit of some so called, and their ungodly sly Way of Defaming such as dissent from them, especially in their Restless Endeavours against the Poor QUAKERS.

By a Lover of Charity *and* Sincerity *in all,* W. Penn.

The PREFACE.

READER,

With what Regret of Spirit I behold the Controversies of our Time, and how unpleasant it is to me to be concern'd therein, God is Witness: And I think it cannot reasonably be hard for any to believe me, when meer Reputation would forbid a Man to subject his Religion or Good Name to the Folly and Malice of every inconsiderable Wrangler.

But so intolerable are many Separatists, and of them, some Anabaptists, in their Lyes, Slanders, Traducings, and what not, which may proceed from Wrath and Envy; that, lest some of the Dirt they throw should stick, we are necessitated to that Defence, we neither think the Truth (otherwise) wants, nor our Adversaries could deserve at our Hands, and least of all the Man concern'd in these Letters.

But we have the less Reason, I confess, to expect good Quarter from him, who denies it to his Church-Sister, or doubt that he should slyly suggest Evil against us, who basely goes to Law with her, and that before those who by his own Principles he accounts Unbelievers. Only we cannot but think it a strange Use that these Men make of Toleration, to persecute by Revilings those that have most suffered for want of it, as if they would walk Antipodes to the Government: For whilst that persecuted, they seem'd to pity us; but now that tolerates, they appear to envy us. What? Do they think it a Blemish to Toleration, That any should be quiet but themselves; and therefore will continue that as justifiable in them, which they accounted condemnable in the Powers? But this notably shows their Spirit, who thus adventure to persecute without Power: Let who will believe they would not do it if they had Power; for my own Part, I declare my self none of that Number; and think it the best Way, both to wish, and lawfully endeavour they may never have any to try.

Reader, I have nothing farther to say in this Epistle, but that the Person herein concern'd, unworthily reflecting upon me (for something in a Discourse I lately publisht against the close, but faint Endeavours of a vizarded Socinian) as that I was an Erroneous and Blasphemous Person (Terms the most hateful to a Christian Man) I writ him,

him, as in Conscience oblig'd, a kind of Challenge to make it good, which he vainly endeavour'd by his Answer, as my Reply will farther manifest. Perhaps their Publication may be seasonable, if not to some of their own Way (for which I greatly hope) at least to others; and I am confident to all who cordially love Truth, Righteousness and Peace, above charging God with Hardness, and impeaching that People as Erroneous, which most vigorously believe and assert the Universality of his Rectitude and Mercy.

WILLIAM PENN.

PLAIN-DEALING, &c.

John Morse,

Understanding that thou hast made use of my Name to so evil a Purpose, as to charge upon it Error, if not Blasphemy, upon Occasion of a Book lately writ by me, in Defence of the Light and Divinity of Christ; and not being unwilling to have such Reflections past unexamin'd; These are to let thee know, that I expect thy Proof, if any thou hast, that if it be true, I may take Shame to my self in the ingenuous Acknowledgment of my Fault; or else, that thou dost confess, thou hast unworthily traduc'd me.

Great is the Truth, and it shall prevail; I am therein a Friend to thee and all Men.

Rickmansworth, the 25th of the 10th Month, 1672.   W. P.

In Answer to which he sent me the following Letter, so writ and phras'd verbatim.

William Penn,

IN Answer to a Letter thee sents me; I shall acquaint thee how I came to speak of thee, and to have thy Book: A Friend of thine came to invite me to a Meeting of yours; I asked her, What moved her to invite me? She said, the Light in her: I asked her, What that Light was? She told me, It was Christ, and that the same Light was in me, and in every Man and Women, and if obeyed by me, was sufficient to save me: I asked her, What was that that came into the Room, when the Disciples were met together, the Doors being shut? She told me, It was a Spirit: I asked her, How she knew it was a Spirit? She told me, The Light, Christ, in her told her so: I asked her, Whether I should believe the Light, she said was Christ, or Christ's own Words, as thou mayst see in the 24th of Luke, verse 38, 39. Christ said, A Spirit hath not Flesh and Bones, as ye see me have? I shewed to her how grosly the Light in her had erred, therefore it could not be Christ; for Christ cannot err: I might be larger herein, but shall forbear. After this thy Friend brought me thy Book to read, and when perused it, returned it again, and did say, there was Error in it, and that thou contradicts thy self in that Book; see page 21. where thou sayst, That if God's unerring Spirit only enables Men to walk in his Statutes, and keep his Judgments to do them; then since all are required to walk therein, none are exempted from a sufficient Measure of that Unerring Spirit in order to it. And page 22. or thus, If without having the Spirit, none can have Prophesie and Vision, and both to be and to continue in Christ's Church universally; then it will naturally follow, that she cannot be without that Unerring Spirit; and that such as are, cannot in that State be Members of the true Church, then consequently, thou sayst, Hereticks. Pag. 25. thou sayst, The World cannot receive the Spirit of Truth. Again, pag. 34. Jude 19, 20. These be they who separate themselves, sensual, having not the Spirit. First thou sayst no Man is exempted from a sufficient Measure of the Unerring Spirit; and after thou sayst, Hereticks and Sensualists have it not, nor the World cannot receive the Spirit, this judge is Error, and Contradicting of thy self. See also page 71. where thou chargest God Foolishly; compare Romans 9. verse 17, 18. 19, 20, 21, 22. Nay, but, O Man, who art thou that repliest against God? Shall the

the Thing formed, say to him that formed it, Why hast thou made me thus? Hath not the Potter Power over the Clay of the same Lump, to make one Vessel unto Honour, and another unto Dishonour? *I hope these few Lines, although brokenly Pen'd, may prevail with thee, whereby thou may'st ingeniously acknowledge thy Error, and God shall have the Glory.* Farewel.

Watford, the 4th of the 11th Month, 1672.

John Morse.

To which I make this Reply.

Rickmansworth, the 9th of the 11th Month, 1672.

John Morse,

MY Religion teaches me no Respect to Persons nor Abilities, and therefore I shall willingly reply to thy Answer that Yesterday came to my Hand; and if thou knew'st my other Occasions, thou could'st not but esteem thy self *indebted to my Charity*; for indeed, I have no other Inducement to send these Lines. First then, I take Notice thou addressest thy self in the Stile of a *Quaker*, which for a Man so averse from him, *as an angry Anabaptist, to do*, with me relishes either of Jeer, or Hypocrisie; unless thou hadst this Tenderness upon thee, thou would'd not offend me; I hope the latter, tho' a Mistake; for I would have every Thing appear in it's proper Colour: *I love no Apes in Religion, and desire that Foxes should appear in their own Skins, and Lambs in theirs*.

Next, thou givest me an Account of a Passage that fell betwixt thee and one of *Anne Stoddard*'s * Maids, from whence thou collectest, *That great Error dwells in the Light.* I perceive how much more willing thou art the Light should be blamed, than the Lass. But what if so be that an *Anabaptist* should wickedly kill a Man, *within an Hour after he had been Dipt, would it be Reasonable, Charitable, or Christian, to charge that upon his Renouncing the Church of* England's *Baptism* (as they call it) *and receiving of another?* Would it have been good arguing, that because *some of the Children of* Israel *in the Wilderness Rebell'd against* Moses *unjustly, yet as a Tyrant, pretending to a better Way of Government, more easie and just, therefore the Spirit God had given them was Erroneous; though it was truly grieved thereat*. If all the *Quakers* in *England* should utter the grossest Errors, *the Light wherewith Christ, as the Word-God hath, and doth enlighten, ought not to be charged with such Defects, but rather they, for not bringing their Errors to the Light*. And I affirm, there is no true knowing either of Evil or Good, but in the Light, wherewith Christ hath illuminated Mankind; and if thou knowest any thing savingly, it is thereby; therefore kick not against it; neither fling thy Cavils at it, I warn thee from the Lord; for, if thou seekest to pervert the Right Way of the Lord, by thy *Night-Works against the Light*, it will certainly be one Day thy woful Condemnation.

* Whom thou hast deceitfully and obscurely endeavoured to ensnare.

That which concerns me, is called, *First*, Error and Contradiction; and, *Secondly*, Foolishly charging of God.

My Error and Contradiction is this, *That in one Place, I make all Men to have a Measure of the Spirit*; and in another I say, *That such as have it not are Hereticks concerning the Faith*; as also, that I quote these Passages, *John* 14. 16, 17, 18, 20: again, 16, 13. *where Christ promiseth to send that Spirit which the World cannot receive*; also that of *Jude*, *Sensual, not having the Spirit,* which thou judgest to be Error and Contradiction: Did I not know thy Meaning, I should take it for granted, that *what thou callest the Contradiction, was also the Error*, namely, *That all had not the Spirit:* But understanding by thy second Carp, the Narrowness of thy Soul (for it is *Predestinarian*) I will take it for granted, thou meanest quite contrary, namely, That God's Universal Love to Mankind, is the horrible Blasphemy thou in Words (I heard) dost charge me with, though thou art something more Modest in thy Letter, by calling it a *Foolish charging of God*.

In short, I answer to this first Cavil.

In Page 21. It is a Consequence drawn from the Place, *suited to my own Assertion*. In Page 22. it is a Consequence I make * *their Principle to speak that deny the Universality of the Light and Spirit*. In the one I say, all are illuminated, or have a Measure of that Spirit, because all are commanded to keep God's Statutes, *which it is impossible to do without such Divine Assistance:* In the other Place I make the Consequence to be, that to be sure, the Spirit is the Rule to Believers, *the Thing chiefly aim'd at in the Question*, because without it there would be no Vision or Prophesie,

*That is, such as shut Believers from the Guidance of God's Spirit.

1672.

phesie, which some Professors confess are to endure till Christ's second Coming personally, there, by their own Principle, *they must be Hereticks concerning the True Faith.* But again, it is not said, that such Hereticks have not the Spirit at all, because they have it not as their Rule; for [*Having*] has a twofold Use in Scripture, the one as a *Condemner*, in which Sense none is at one Time or another, without a Measure of the Divine Light and Spirit to reprove them; and, secondly, the so having it, as to enjoy and possess it as *A Rule, Guide, and Invisible Minister of Life, Comfort and Refreshment,* in which Sense *the World has it not*, that is, received it not, as faith the Text; yet the very next Chapter says, *That it should convince the World of Sin:* A Man may hear a Reproof and Instruction, yet not follow it; so that such as receive not the Spirit, that strives with them, may be truly said, *to be sensual, * not having the Spirit, because they receive it not to the Ends for which it was, or is sent.* I hope then I shall not be longer charged with Error or Contradiction in this Particular.

* It is not theirs by the Adoption of Believing.

The second Part of the Charge is, *That I should foolishly charge God* (which more hiddenly, I hear, has been styl'd *Blasphemy*) Let us hear my Book speak.

Spirit of Truth Vindicated, p. 71.

God Requires all Men strictly to serve and obey him, and to work out their Salvation with Fear and Trembling, or else their End shall be Destruction: But this the Almighty (with Reverence I say it) could not justly do, unless the Light, with which he enlightens Men, were Sufficient and Saving.

I own the Words expresly, and will abide their Defence before *Men and Angels*; and before I have done, I hope, *Blasphemy* shall not lie at my Door, in the Sense of every Man that is not principled *to make God an hard Master*.

First, I say, *That it is inconsistent with the Rectitude of God's Nature,* to esteem that naturally Just in himself to Man, which by his Law written in the Hearts of all Men, is adjudg'd most Unreasonable, Cruel, and Unjust among Men; for since whatever is Holy, Good and Upright, is deriv'd to us from God, and that we are to be Perfect, as our Heavenly Father is Perfect, it is utterly impossible that He should be Just in that which is most Unjust in Man: For Instance;

That it cannot be consistent with the Nature of God, that He should damn any Man, for not improving a Talent He never gave him: Because a Man commanding his Servant to go so many Miles within such a set Time upon Pain of Death on Foot, whilst he either fetters him in a dark Cellar, or cuts off his Legs, is Cruel, Unjust, and Impious.

Secondly, This Doctrine makes *God Partial,* which is Infirmity at best in a Man; nay, it makes him the worst of *Dissemblers,* which my Soul loaths to think, and my Hand almost trembles to write: For to what Purpose does he invite, saying, *Ezek.* 18. *He delights not in the Damnation of Sinners, but rather that they should Repent,* and yet never gives them any Ability whereby to do it. Nay, if thy Principle may be credited, has taken Order by an Eternal Provision of Decree that they should not.

What an Affront, nay, down-right Lye doth this Doctrine, opposite to what I asserted, give to the Scriptures which testifie, *God so loved the World, as to give and send his Son, that such as believed might have Life,* and yet from Eternity to provide by Decree that perhaps Nine Parts of Ten in the World should have no Light or Spirit to assist them, *But whether they did Well or Ill, should inevitably be Damned*; though God declares himself, to be a Rewarder of Men according to their Faith and Works, not according to such Decrees.

O Barbarous Cruelty, and most aggravated Injustice! What! Tell Men, that if they Believe they shall be Saved, and yet hinder them from Believing; *for if the Reprobate should believe,* God's Decree (as they call it) *would be broke, which is impossible.* Again, *Warn Men of Damnation, professing no Delight in their Destruction, and for Fear they should Repent and be Saved, determine by an irrevocable Decree that they should be Damn'd.* O Vile, Hideous, and Blasphemous Doctrine! It renders the most Merciful and Just God most Cruel and Unjust, and also *turns the Reins upon the Necks of the People,* to commit what they will; for indeed who will be bounded, that stands upon so good or bad Terms as an immutable Decree. This Doctrine may perhaps a little influence such affectionate Minds as conceive themselves interested in that Electionated Love of God: But do not the most of those who believe it *Buoy up themselves above the Daily Cross, and so live above the Holy Chastisements of God for Sin, because of this sure Bottom, as they vainly imagine it,* whilst the

the Generality are so far from being reclaim'd, who know themselves to be Prodigals, that being discourag'd through such a Kind of Predestination, they quit all Hope of returning for Mercy, whose Ends must needs be Destruction? *O merciless Faith, O injurious Assertion, both to God and Men! Let my Soul for ever beware of such Impiety.*

But because thou seem'st to charge the Scripture with having led thee into this Foolish Charging of God, I shall observe thy Quotation of 17, 18, 19, 20, 21, 22, of the 9th Chapter to the *Romans.*

The Apostle begins this Chapter, *Rom.* 9. (or else they that divided his Epistle into Chapters, made it to begin) with his great Sorrow for his Country-Men, the *Jews.* He enumerates their Privileges, and could wish himself accurst for their Sake; yet whilst he lamented, *that they to whom were the Covenants, Glory, Adoption, and whose were the Fathers, and of whom Christ himself came after the Flesh, being of the Seed of Abraham,* should thus barr themselves out of Christ's Kingdom, and not be of the *True Israel* and Circumcision in Spirit, read verse 6. *So that the being of the Seed of* Abraham, *after the Flesh, or* Isaac, *or any other Man ever so Righteous, rendered them not Children of Promise*; albeit it be said, *In* Isaac *shall thy Seed be called,* for then would all *Isaac*'s Seed have belonged to the Promise, which in *Esau* was not verifi'd, as testifies this very Scripture. Neither, because they are the Seed of *Abraham,* are they all Children, but in *Isaac shall thy Seed be called.* What is this [*Isaac*] and what is this [*Calling?*] that is, faith the Apostle, *They which are Children of the Flesh, these are not the Children of God*; that is, *They that are Carnally descended, are not the Seed*; *Isaac* is understood mystically, *as shewing forth One conceived by the extraordinary Power of God, in whom all Nations should be blessed with Freedom and Adoption, as they come to believe and obey*; wherefore adds the Apostle, *The Children of the Promise are counted for the Seed*; Who are they? *The Jews Inward, and the Circumcision in Heart.* So that here is only the Election of the True Seed, [Mystical Isaac] or [Isaac in Spirit] *such as through Repentance, Faith, and Good Works, come to be translated into the Pure Nature thereof, who have been refined in the Refiner's Fire, purged and cleansed, and so made Chosen Vessels of Honour*; which Word [*Chosen*] or [*Choice*] signifies a Thing more precious than ordinary, *and therefore Elected.*

So on the contrary Hand, when Men have sinned away their first Stock, God is not bound to recruit them again; He may proceed to determinative Judgment if he please. Here it is, *That he will have Mercy on whom he will have Mercy, and whom he will he hardeneth.* And though *Pharoah,* that wicked King, was at last hardened by the Lord, yet, if the 1, 2, 3, 4, 5, 6, 7, 8, and 9th Chapters of *Exodus* be but read, it will appear, *first that God did not harden* Pharaoh, *before* Pharaoh *had grievously imbondaged* Israel, *rejected his Counsel, despised his Visitations, and so hardened his own Heart*; and with an audacious Contempt asked Moses, *Who is the Lord that I should obey his Voice,* &c. Secondly, That God raising him up, was not from an innocent Child, to be a wicked King, as if God had infused a Cruel and Wicked Quality into his Heart; O God forbid! But he suffered him not to be quite wasted with the many Judgments that God brought upon him for his Rebellion, who after every Judgment, still increased in his Wickedness, but raised him yet up again, that he might renown his Name, and proclaim his Great Power, as well to punish obdurate Sinners, as ransom his own People. Thus God endured this Vessel of Wrath, to make his Wonders known. So, what if God did give over *Jerusalem* and her Children to Destruction, who resisted the Heavenly Invitations of his Son, and rather chose the *Gentiles,* Who could impeach him? Had he not waited long? Which of the Prophets had they not Slain? And did they not cry of Jesus himself, *Let his Blood be upon our Heads,* &c. Wherefore if God would harden them he might: *Since here He might have Mercy on whom he pleas'd to have Mercy, and whom he would of such Impenitents he might harden.* In short, Man was made a Chosen Vessel, a Right Plant; but through Degeneration, he became a Vessel of Dishonour, and a Plant of a strange Vine: *Those therefore who are Regenerated by the One Holy Seed, which Seed is Christ, Elect and Precious,* God makes *His Vessels of Honour for ever*; and they who have spent their Heavenly Portion, defil'd themselves, resisted the Heavenly Invitations, and are become One Spirit with the God of the World, who Rules in the Hearts of the Children of Disobedience, such Adulterated Ones God separates from him, as Vessels of Dishonour and Wrath, fitted for Destruction (but by themselves, not from the Lord.)

Thus

Thus much briefly at this Time, as to the Doctrine of *Predestination*, as it is destructively and extravagantly believed by too many Professors of Religion. And to this Ninth Chapter to the *Romans*, the Intention whereof borders not in the least upon that Ungodly Fancy of Personal Election. I shall sum up the whole of both Sides thus,

W. Penn's *Faith*.	J. Morse, *his Faith*.
1. I believe, God hath given unto all Men sufficient of his Light, Spirit, or Grace; which obeyed, will lead to Blessedness: *Because God would otherwise exhort Men to what he should not have given them Power to do*; which is unworthy of his Righteousness.	1. *I believe, That God requires all Men to hear and obey; or that all have the Gospel tendered; yet deny*, that all have Grace sufficient to embrace it, or to live up to it, *so as to be saved: For, God may bid Man believe, and be saved, and not give him Power to do so.*
2. I believe, That God hardens no Man to Sin, *till Man has first hardened himself against God by Sin*; or that Sin goes before Hardening.	2. *I believe, That God raised up Men, and hardens them on Purpose*, to Glorifie himself in their Destruction; *not considering Sin as the Main and Provocative Cause to that Hardening and Destruction.*

Upon the whole, I leave it with God, and his Witness in every Conscience, whether it be *William Penn*, or *John Morse*, that hath writ Error, Contradiction, and Blasphemy against God, Scripture, and Sound Reason?

So truly desiring thy better Information in these weighty Matters, that knowing the Truth, thou may'st obey it, and be saved; (for God would not that any Man should be Damned, but that all should come to the Knowledge of the Truth, and be saved.) I remain

Thy Well-Wisher, and all Men's, *W. P.*

An ACCOUNT *of some Discourse betwixt one* Sarah Lane, Quaker, *and* John Morse, Anabaptist; *for the clearing the* Truth *his Relation abuses with Forgery*.

S. L. *John Morse*, we are to have a Meeting to Day, and I had a Desire thou should'st know of it.

J. M. *I have heard your Friends formerly; they deny the Scriptures to be the Word of God.*

S. L. We own them to be the Words of God, given forth by the Spirit of God, and a Declaration of the Mind and Will of God; but *the Word it self is God*. Read the First of *John*, and there thou wilt find, *That the Word was in the Beginning, and all Things were made by it*; which cannot be said of the Scriptures.

J. M. *But you disown Baptism.*

S. L. What Force is there in it?

J. M. *There is little in it, only an Outward Ordinance, that we must do till Christ comes.*

S. L. Dost thou look for Christ to come again?

J. M. *As for that we must leave it, and not presume too far.*

S. L. I do witness him Spiritually come; and such as are come to the Substance want them not: But if there be little in the Ordinances, as thou say'st, What great Need is there of doing them? Christ came not to continue, but to put an End to Types and Figures. And for Water-Baptism, many of us have had it, and been among you that use it, and we that did so, are come farther, to see beyond that, to the Inward Baptism, which is the Substance, that ends the outward.

J. M. *The Scripture tells us it is an Ordinance.*

S. L. Dost thou own Two Baptisms to continue, contrary to the Scripture? *John* said, He should decrease, that Baptiz'd with Water; and that Christ should increase, who was to Baptize with the Holy Ghost, and with Fire.

J. M. *But you own the Light to be in every Man and Woman?*

S. L. I own and confess, that Christ has enlightned every Man and Woman.

J. M. *What,*

J. M. *What, Christ, the Fulness to be in every Man and Woman?*

S. L. No, not Christ's Fulness; but a Measure of his Light is given to Every One.

J. M. *Every one, What, has every Man a Measure?*

S. L. Yes.

J. M. *What then is the Reason that Drunkards and Lewd People live in their Wickedness, if they have that Light?*

S. L. The Reason is, because they do not obey it; there is something in them that shews them their Sin, when they have done amiss, and reproves them; for they will say, *Lord forgive them*, or the like; that must needs be good that shews them when they have done what they ought not to do.

J. M. *I confess, there is something that does shew Men Sin, but it is not sufficient.*

S. L. It is sufficient, if it be obeyed; but God said, His Spirit should not always strive with Man: yet every Man has a Day, or a Time to be tried; if they rebel, and won't obey, God then gives them over.

From this he fell to curious and unnecessary Questions; As the Devil did about the Body of *Moses*, so did he about the Body of Christ: But this he insisted on mostly the Second Time.

J. M. *What was that which appeared to the Disciples, when the Windows and Doors were shut, was it Flesh or Spirit?*

S. L. Spirit.

J. M. *Christ himself said, he had Flesh and Bones, when they doubted, thinking he might be a Spirit. But tell me, what became of the Body of Christ?*

S. L. I shall not meddle farther with such Matters, nor run into Things which I have no certain Knowledge of; neither would I have given thee that Advantage by my simple Answer, if I had been aware of thee. And if I have reply'd unadvisedly, that is nothing to our Friends.

J. M. *But, the Light was that which led you into this Mistake.*

S. L. The Light never leads into any Thing that is Wrong.

READER,

THIS *is the very Truth of the Matter, which I the rather add, that what Advantage he may think to have gained, and his Boast of it, may receive some Allay by a plain and true Relation of the whole, so far as could be remembred.*

Of what Force then her Mistake is against the Light, is to be learn'd from her own Ingenious Confession; and if John Morse *were Candid, he would have laid the Blame where it was proper, and not have charg'd it upon the Light within.*

And indeed, if we consider, first, that Christ's Coming in, the Doors being shut, is not mention'd in that Scripture, Luke 24. 38, 39. *as cited by him, but in* John 20. 19, 26. 2dly, *That he was not there without his Spirit.* 3dly. *Were it not unjust to say, the Light in the Disciples grosly erred, when they supposed they had seen a Spirit?* Luke 24. 37. 4thly, *That it was a Foolish and Unnecessary Question on his Part.* 5thly. *That he took base Advantage of it.* 6thly, *That the Maid so particularly Clear'd the Light from leading her into any, the least Mistake.* 7thly, *That I could ask him ten Questions for his one he put to her, of the like abstruse and obscure Matters, that I have Cause to believe he is wholly ignorant of, and the Knowledge of them not necessary to Salvation; I say, considering these Particulars, and that all arose from her loving Invitation of him to a Meeting, I cannot see but he is far more Condemnable than the Maid; and I believe, the Light in every unprejudiced Conscience will say the same.*

This was my POSTSCRIPT to my LETTER to him, which ends these present LETTERS.

IT comes into my Mind to express thus much farther concerning the Lass, that the Simplicity of her Answer is to be excused far sooner than thy *Un-Christian and Un-Charitable Spirit, that lay in Wait to betray*, and if such Watchings for Evil be uncondemned of thy Religion, *I pronounce it Anti-Christian and Devilish*, and that in the Name of the Lord; And as for our Light, *thou shalt never be justified, whilst that condemns thee*, and if it be insufficient as to thee, it is *because thou never yet didst give up thy self to the Holy Conduct thereof*, but unworthily disparagest that, *which I can make appear thou livest not up to*. Repent, therefore, and *be Baptized of Fire, (which consumes the Thorns and Briars with which you* Water-Baptists *scratch and rend at us) and know a Purging from dead Works in the Name of the Lord*, or Thou and They of thy Spirit, will be utterly lost in the Day of the Lord.

THE
Proposed Comprehension
Soberly, and Not Unseasonably, Consider'd.

ALthough the Benefits wherewith Almighty God has universally bless'd the whole Creation, are a sufficient Check to the Narrowness of their Spirits, who would unreasonably confine all Comforts of Life within the streight Compass of their own Party (as if to recede from their Apprehensions, whereof themselves deny any Infallible Assurance, were Reason good enough to deprive other Dissenters of Nature's Inheritance, and which is more peculiar, *England's Freedoms*.) Yet since it fares so meanly with those Excellent Examples, that many vainly think themselves then best to answer the End of their being born into the World, when by a *Severity*, which least of all resembles the *God of Love*, they rigorously prosecute the Extirpation of their Brethren: Let it not seem Unreasonable, or Ill-timed, that we offer to your more serious Thoughts, the great Partiality and Injustice, that seem to be the Companions of a *Comprehension*, since you only can be concerned at this Time, to prevent it, by a more Large and Generous Freedom.

First, then, *Liberty of Conscience* (by which we commonly understand the free Exercise of any Dissenting Perswasion) is but what has been generally pleaded for, even by the *Warmest Sticklers* for a *Comprehension*, and without which it would be utterly impossible they should be comprehended: The Question then will be this, *What Ground can there be, why Some, and not All, should be Tolerated?* It must either respect *Conscience* or *Government:* If it be upon Matter of mere *Religion*, What Reason is there that one Party should be Tolerated, and another Restrained; since all those Reasons, that may be urged by that Party, which is *Comprehended*, are every whit as proper to the Party *Excluded?* For if the Former say, *They are Orthodox*, so say the Latter too; If the one urge, *It is impossible they should believe without a Conviction; that the Understanding cannot be Forced; that Mildness gains most; that the True Religion never Persecuted; that Severity is most Unworthy of her; that Sound Reason is the only Weapon which can Disarm the Understanding; that Coercion doth rather Obdurate than Soften; and that they therefore chuse to be sincere Dissenters, rather than Hypocritical Conformists:* The other Party says the same. *In fine*, There can be nothing said for Liberty of Conscience,

upon

upon Pure Conscientious Grounds, by any one Party in *England*, that every one may not be interested in; unless *Any* will undertake to judge that of *Five Sorts of Dissenters*, Two are really such on Convictions, and Three upon meer Design. But if such Sentence would be lookt upon as most Arrogant and Unjust, how can it be Reasonable, that those whom some endeavour to exclude, should be thus prejudg'd, and such as are comprehended, be therefore so only from a strong Opinion of their Reality. We may conclude then, that since Liberty of Conscience is what in it self *Comprehenders* plead, and that it is evident, to affirm this, or that, or the other Party *Orthodox*, is but a meer Begging of the Question. What may be urged for one, is forceable for any other: *Conscience* (not moveable but upon Conviction) being what all pretend themselves alike concerned in.

But they say, that such as are like to be comprehended, are Persons, *not Essentially* Differing; that it were pity to exclude them whose *Difference* is rather in Minute Matters, than any Thing Substantial, whereas you err in Fundamentals. But how Paradoxal soever such may please to think it, that we should therefore plead the Justice of taking those in, Some unkindly would have left out, we know not; however, we believe it most reasonable to do so; For certainly the Reason for Liberty or Toleration, should hold Proportion with the weighty Cause of Dissent, and the Stress Conscience puts upon it. Where Matters are Trivial, they are more blameable that make them a Ground for Dissent, than those who perhaps (were that all the Difference) would never esteem them worth contending for, much less that they should rend from that Church, they otherwise confess to be a True One: So that whoever are Condemnable, certainly those who have been Authors and Promoters of Separation upon meer Toys and Niceties, are not most of all others to be justified. Had they conscientiously offer'd some Fundamental Discontent, and pleaded the Impossibility of reconciling some Doctrines with their Reason or Conscience, yet promising quiet Living, and all Due Subjection to Government, they might have been thus far more excusable, that People would have had Reason to have said; Certainly small Matters could not have induc'd these Men to this Disgraceful Separation, nor any thing of this Life have tempted them to this so Great and Troublesome Alteration: *But to take Pet at a Ceremony, then Rend from the Church, set up a New Name and Model, gather People, raise Animosity, and only make fit for Blows*, by a Furious Zeal kindled in their Heads, against a few *Ineptiæ*, meer Trifles; and being utterly vanquish'd from these Proceedings, to become most earnest Solicitors for a *Comprehension*; though at the same Time of hot Pursuit after this Privilege, to seek nothing more than to prevent others of Injoying the same Favour, under the Pretence of more *Fundamental Difference*; Certainly this shews, that had such Persons Power, they would as well Disallow of a *Comprehension* to those who are the Assertors of those Ceremonies they recede from, as that for meer Ceremonies they did at first Zealously Dissent, and ever since remain more Unjustifiably Fierce for such *Separation*. And truly, If there were no more in it than |this, it would be enough for us to say, That some in *England* never Rent themselves from the Church at all, much less for little Matters: that they never endeavour'd her Exile, but she found them upon her Return, which they opposed not, nor yet since have any Ways sought to install themselves in her Dignities, or enrich themselves by her Preferments. We appeal then to all Sober Men, if what is generally called the *Episcopal* Party of *England*, can with Good Conscience, and True Honour disinherit those of their Native Rights, Peace, and Protection, and leave them as Orphans to the wide World, indeed a Naked Prey to the Devourer, who from first to last have never been concerned, either to endeavour their Ruin, or any Ways withstand their Return, whilst it may be some of those, who have been the most Vigorous in both, and that for *Circumstantial*, and not *Essential Differences*, may be reputed more deserving of a *Comprehension*, than we are of a *Toleration*.

But it will be yet said, *You are Inconsistent with Government, They are not, therefore You are Excluded, not out of Partiality, but Necessity*. What Government besides their own they are consistent with, we leave on the Side of Story to tell, which can better speak their Mind than we are either able or willing to do: But this give us Leave to say in General, If any apprehend us to be such as merit not the Care of our Superiors, because supposed to be *Destructive* of the *Government*, let us be call'd forth by Name, and hear our Charge; and if we are not able to answer the Unbyast Reason of Mankind, in Reference to our Consistency with the

1672. Peace, Quiet, Trade, and Tribute of these Kingdoms, then, and not before, deny us all Protection. But that Men should be concluded before heard, and so sentenced for what they really are not, *is like beheading them before they are Born.* We do aver, and can make it appear, that there is no one Party more Quiet, Subject, Industrious, and in the Bottom of their very Souls, greater Lovers of the Good Old *English* Government and Prosperity of these Kingdoms among the *Comprehended,* than, for ought we yet see, may be found among those who are like to be unkindly *Excluded*; However, if such we were in any one Point, *Cure rather than Kill us*; and seek the Publick Good *some cheaper way than by our Destruction*; Is there no *Expedient* to prevent Ruin? Let *Reason qualify Zeal,* and *Conscience Opinion.*

To Conclude, If the Publick may be secured, and Conscience freely exercised by all, for the same Reasons, it may by some (and since Liberty of Conscience, is Liberty of Conscience, and the Reasons for it, equivalent) We see not in the whole World, why any should be depriv'd of That, which others for no better Reasons are like to enjoy.

Let it not then be unworthy of such to remember, that God affords his refreshing *Sun to all*; The Dung-hill is no more excepted than the most delightful Plain, and his *Rain falls alike* both upon the Just and Unjust: He strips not Mankind of, what suits their Creaturely Preservation; *Christians* themselves have no more peculiar Privilege in the Natural Benefits of Heaven, than *Turks* or *Indians*. Would it not then be strange, that *Infidels* themselves, much less any Sort of *Christians,* should be deprived of Natural Privileges for meer *Opinion,* by those who pretend to be the *Best Servants of* that *God,* who shews them quite another Example, by the Universality of his Goodness as Creator; And *Believers in that Christ,* who himself preacht the *Perfection of Love, both to Friends and Enemies*, and laid down his Life to confirm it when he had done. If Men should love their Enemies, doubtless they ought at least to forbear their Friends: And though some Differences in Judgment about *Religion* be a sufficient Reason to excommunicate a Man the Air Ecclesiastical, yet nothing certainly of that Sort ought to Dis-privilege Men of their Air Natural and Civil to breath freely in: And let that *Good* our Superiors have observed to be the *Fruit of our Toleration,* not be weakned or blasted by an Untimely *Comprehension* of some, to the *Exclusion* of the rest; since the Reason holds the same for the less formidable Separatists, that may not be however any whit less Conscientious.

We will omit to mention, how much more Suitable it were to *State-Matters,* that all Parties should be kept upon an equal Poize, a Thing most true in it self, and most secure to the *Publick Magistrate*; and will conclude at this Time, That though we no Ways design a *Mis-representing* of any, much less their *Exception,* and least of all their *Persecution*; yet, a *Comprehension* either respecting the *Persons* and their *Qualifications,* or their *Separation,* and the Grounds and Reasons of it, We seriously believe, can never be consistent with that *Conscience, Honor, Wisdom,* and *Safety,* that ought to be the *Mark,* those who are concerned in it, should take their Aim by. But if a *Comprehension* should at last be compass'd, it is not doubted by many wise Men, but it will be found as Impracticable as other *Acts* more seemingly *Severe* have been, and at last will necessitate to that well-order'd universal Toleration of all, who both profess and practise *Peace, Obedience, Industry,* and *Good Life,* which will best please Almighty God, and rejoyce the Hearts of all Good Men.

From Real Friends to KING *and* COUNTRY.

THE SPIRIT

OF

ALEXANDER the Copper-Smith Juftly REBUKED:

OR,

An ANSWER to a Late PAMPHLET, Intituled,

The Spirit of the HAT, *or the Government of the* QUAKERS.

In which the Confederacy is Broken, and the Devil's Champions defeated.

By a True Witnefs of the One Way of God, W. P.

Neverthelefs the Foundation of God ftandeth fure, 2 Tim. 2. 19.

SATAN, that Great Enemy to the Work of God, failing of his End in all thofe Attempts he hath made to hinder, pervert, or deftroy it, by the earneft Endeavours of fome of the moft Envious among the many *Sects* in this Nation, hath at laft pitcht upon an Old *Canker'd Apoftate* (the beft Spoke in his Wheel) and therefore call'd an *Ingenious Quaker* by the *Publifher*, becaufe he has endeavour'd to promote the Common Defign of our Overthrow in this World.

It is a manifeft Token to me, that the *Devil* is hard befet, his Affairs brought to a low Ebb, and his Condition Defperate, that he is fled to his laft Refuge of Falfe Brethren, and very *Apoftates*. A Treachery that fhall ever more infame this perverfe *Alexander* with Good Men, and encreafe his Account with the Great and Terrible Judge of Heaven and Earth.

But is it not ftrange to fee, that *Independents, Anabaptifts,* and *Socinians,* now in Arms againft the *Quakers,* fhould fo heartily hugg the Labours of one they efteem fuch, and which is more Remarkable, as a true and primitive One too; as if they had been all this While angry with us, *not for being* Quakers, *but for being not True Ones*; which is fuch a Thing, as would make a Body think them to be the only Right *Quakers,* at leaft Well-wifhers to them; and we but a Pack of Apoftates. O how Ingenuous is this Author of the *Spirit of the* HAT! A fit Title for it; in which there is fo little Head, or at leaft no more Brains than in an empty Hat; and as little Fear of God, and Honefty towards Men, as could be well found within fuch a Compafs. I fay, how ingenuous is he to rail againft Power, *and love it*; to decry Authority, and feek it; to accufe G. F. for Tyranny, and ufe fo much in doing fo; to be Angry, not that there is Rule, but that he has no Share in it; to repute our Cenfure of a Difturber about fuch Unprofitable

and

and Unseemly Customs, as to keep on the *Hat* in Publick Prayer, a Resemblance of the Church of *Rome*'s *Excommunications*, and to rebuke a Malapert Stickler against the Church's Peace, Usurpation and Oppression: But, which is rarest of all, *Independents, Anabaptists* and *Socinians*, are to fledge their naked Cause with this Man's *Feathers*, and his Lyes are to be their Refuge, and 'tis that very *Hat* we would have *off* in Prayer, they desire to cover their Head with in this Day of Battel against the *Quakers*.

Are they such Friends to that Token of Irreverence to God? Will they spit in our Faces for not pulling off our *Hats* to them, and yet glory in the *Envious Labours* of a Man that denies it to God himself, and therefore cannot be owned of us? Shall we be counted Conceited and Ignorant to forbear that Ceremony to Men; and this vile *Apostate* reputed Ingenious, *&c.* for making so bold with God? What! Is it become a Crime in the *Quaker* to perform that sincerely to his Creator, which is with so much Formality every Day done by his Opposers? O Partial! O Unreasonable and Down-right Impious Generation! who are not only ready to invent, pervert and misconstrue us about Matters of Religion; but can take Part with an *Apostate*, *a Clamourer*, *a meer Alexander*, *Phygellus*, *Hermogenes*, *Hymenæus, Philetus:* In short, *a very Mutineer* in Religion, to bespatter us and our Principles in the World; and that because we abhor, renounce, and rebuke with Severity that rude Imagination of the *Hat* on in Publick Prayer, which, did we use it, we should be but esteemed by you the worse, or you go from your own Principles. Nay, is it not unjust with a Witness, that we should be so vehemently decry'd by some, because we preach not with our Hats off; If yet we must be run thus furiously down for disowning a Person, *that in Praying keeps it on*; Certainly it must needs be manifest to all the Impartial World, that such Procedure is freighted with the very *Rancour of Malice*, *Fury and Revenge*; and, which is more, with Folly too: They have writ their own Answer in their base Accusation, for either they, I mean the *Professors*, that printed, buy and disperse the Pamphlet, own him for a *Quaker*, or they do not; if not, it is no Discredit to us, that he should pretend to be precisely one, and us to be *Apostates:* If he be one; then either a better or a worse; if a better, and that by better is understood, more separated from the several Sects of *Professors*; then behold, how much more kindly they receive a *True Quaker* in his first Principles and Practice, than such as they conceive to have Apostatiz'd: It would make one think, *that they are no Abettors of those Priests and Professors, that writ so sharply against them in their first Appearance:* If worse, and that by worse is understood Apostatized, or gone back; then is not his End answered, which he pretends was to testify against our Apostacy, that is, Our Running into *Forms, Methods*, and *Discipline*, like to other Professions; that is, *Presbyterians, Independents, Anabaptists, &c.* and if so, I wonder with what Confidence those Professors dare undertake our Disgrace by it, when at the same Time that he thinks to render us Odious, *he makes the Reason of it to be our becoming like unto them.* Certainly if our *Order, Discipline*, and *Church Authority be Apostacy*, we cannot be the only People that are concern'd in his Meaning. In short, the Matter is so ordered, that whatever they venture to urge against us, strikes them sorely. What then can the Professors do in all this Busle? Why thus much; a Turbulent Spirit is disown'd by the *Quakers:* He contemns their Church-Authority which so renounced him: For this he cries; *They are like* Rome, *and are quite Apostatized:* And if so, may the sober Professor say, then we are all *Apostates* too, it being but what we our selves do practise, and that frequently.

In short, There is nothing, that this *Alexander the Copper-Smith* hath said more Disgraceful of the *Quakers*, than that the most uncorrupted of them should despise Government *(his own notorious Fault*; and I know not why, unless because he is not our Dictator) who underwent, and still do all Hardships that befal our Testimony; that the Principle of Truth and Righteousness might govern not only *Individuals, but whole Societies.* We shall not think our selves nor Principles much put to it, to vindicate these Assertions: 1. That we are a Religious Body. 2. That we have, as such, a Power within our selves. 3. That by the Power and Spirit of the Eternal God, we have condemned, as well as justified many Practices. 4. That being in Holy Peace and Unity, and that Singular Spirit of the *Hat* getting Place with some, and Secret Rents, Divisions, and Animosities being like to ensue among us, as among the first *Christians*, we did, with such other Carriages, as were reputed unbecoming the Blessed Gospel, condemn that of keeping the *Hat* on in Time of Publick Prayer to Almighty God, (to whom alone from a sensible Mind

we

we perform that Holy and Due Reverence) as introduced by a Singular, Conceited, and Deceitful Spirit. 5. That the Author of the *Spirit of the Hat, &c.* hath resisted many *Loving Treaties, Serious Invitations, and abundance of good and wholesome Advice, for his own Good, and the Church's Peace,* and because he is not own'd in that Practice, which, should we do, God's Spirit would disown us in so doing; therefore, as a Man enraged beyond all Bounds of not only *Christianity*, but Manhood, with Folly, Madness, and desperate Revenge has he endeavoured our Ruin among Men. Now that herein he has not shown himself the *Primitive Quaker*, and great Lamenter of our Apostacy, as he pretendeth, may be clearly seen, in that he doth endeavour to render the Good as well as Bad among us suspected by those, who, he confesseth, cannot have that Discerning he hath; and consequently their Lives and Ministry ineffectual; Next, to do it at this Time of the Day; What greater Demonstration of Implacableness can there be, when so many are against us? And that as *Quakers* in any sense; yea, for owning those Principles, he himself asserts; their Hands are strengthned thereby. *Lamentation, Murder; Mercy, Revenge; our Recovery, our utter Destruction*; and nothing below it must have been sought by that Discourse; but it all retorts from our Impenetrable Armour upon himself, and he will prove at last only to have discovered his own Nakedness by this impious Attempt. Whence, if any Thing appears, it is this, that because he is indeed gone back from what he was, and we remain what we were, the World, that once persecuted him, and still doth us, count him now a very White Boy; and I am perswaded, let him but continue to write against us, though a pretended *Quaker*, I dare warrant, they will reckon him a very good *Christian*

It is this Sort of unruly Beast that the *Professors*, (who themselves would have cast him out an Hundred Times) maintain for an *Ingenious Quaker*, though their bare Entertainment of him against us, were Ground enough to suppose him either an Impostor or Renegade, as indeed he is little better; since first he pretends to be that in Religion which he is not: And secondly, that he is slipt from what he once was, or at least pretended to be. I will briefly observe the most weighty Things of his Libel, and which indeed comprehend the Whole, and so close this Animadversion.

First, That G. *Fox* should say, *No Liberty out of the Power*; which he compares with the *Papist*, thus: *No Liberty out of the Church. What! Liberty to the* Sectary? *No, What! Liberty to the* Heretick? *No.* And G. *Fox*, says he, thus: *What! Liberty to the* Presbyter? *No. What! Liberty to the* Independents *and* Baptists? *No; Liberty is in the Truth.*

Upon which he Comments at large: But had this Man but one Grain of that great Stock of *Righteousness* he unjustly pretends to, and seems to lament the Absence of among us, he would never have dared to suffer this to be so printed to the World. The Truth of the Matter is this: G. *Fox* having an Occasion to speak of *Liberty of Conscience*, said, He never liked the Word, as commonly us'd; for, *Conscience being an Inward and Spiritual Thing, no mortal Man could bind or inthrall it:* He meddled not at all with the Outward Exercise of Conscience, as to the Performance of Worship, commonly called, *Liberty of Conscience;* wherefore he proceeded, *No Liberty out of the Power*; that is, *The Power of God.* Nor in reality is there: For all Consciences that are defiled, or enslaved by Wicked Works, they are not truly free; the Power of God has not delivered such into the Glorious Liberty of the Sons of God: And since those Perswasions Deny Liberty from Sin on this side the Grave, at least the immediate *Light, Power* and *Spirit of God,* to work it in the Soul, he therefore said, What! Liberty to the *Presbyterians, Independents, Baptists? &c.* No: That is, *What Spiritual Liberty and Freedom of Conscience?* No, for then in vain are we become *Quakers,* as the World calls us: *And why should they deny a State of Freedom?* In short, He spoke, and meant it of an Inward Liberty of Conscience from Sin, which is call'd in Scripture, *Purging the Conscience from Dead Works,* and *If the Truth make you Free, &c.* and this *Alexander* the *Copper-Smith,* that Vile and Peevish Apostate, turns to an outward Exercise of Religious Worship, as if G. *F.* would have had *those Professors persecuted by the Civil Magistrate.* O Base and Wicked Perversion of an Innocent Man's true Words! But for all this shall the Eternal Just God bring him to Judgment.

His next great *Cavil* is about his *pulling off the HAT at Publick Prayer*, either upon Conviction, or the Judgment of the Body; wherein he tells us, *That not only some of us counsell'd, or requir'd him to yield, because the Body would have it; saying,*

saying, That was yielding to the Power: But his not so yielding, but persisting, is no Dissension; but our Disowning any Person for that Cause, is a Breach of the Great Gospel-Character of Liberty. Let him deny this to be the Strength of his Book if he can or dare; and which is as soon blown away, as the Chaff before the Wind.

There is either such a Thing as a *Christian Society*, sometimes call'd a *Visible Body*, or *Church*, or there is not: If there be not, all is at an End; and why Contend we at all? If there be; then this Church either has Power or not: If no Power, then no Church. If a *Body, Church* or *Society* (for the Word *Church* signifies no more, borrowed from the Assemblies of the *Athenians*) then there must be a *Power* within it self to determine; *an Anointing to lead into all Truth.* Deny this, and all falls of it self. Well, but this I suppose, will be confessed to. The Question then is this, *But, how far may this* Church *injoyn the Consciences of Individuals any Performance, supposing their Dis-like?* I answer, It would be first enquired into, Whether those Things have been once generally own'd by such a *Church* or not? Secondly, Or if it be about some superadded Ceremony, something over and above what each Member at first sat down contented with?

Now it is manifest, that this very perverse and Quarrelsom Man, when he at first came among us, and walkt with us, was not in any such Practice, *As keeping on his Hat in Time of Publick Prayer*; but believ'd, and in some Measure walked in the Way we profess, conformable as we are, and we hope, for Conscience-sake. He dare not also say, That he enjoy'd not some Comfort from those Prayers that came *through an Uncovered Head*, but acknowledgeth the contrary; and at that Time of Day all was well: *It was the Gospel, the Truth, the Way of God,* said he; and others, since of his Stamp, were zealous also to promote it. This now will be the Question, *Whether, If any Person that had given those Signal Testimonies for a Way and People, and so incorporated himself with them, finding afterwards Fault with a Practice so Innocent, so Reverent, as keeping off the Hat in Time of Publick Prayer to Almighty God, should step out of that comely Order, set up a New Mark and Standard, whereby some should have their Heads covered, others uncovered* (a most divided, confused and unseemly Sight) *the Church in this Case may not Admonish, and after her due Admonition, and the Parties tenacious, resolute, and captious Disputes for that unsuitable Practice, may not justly disown him as a Disputer about needless Questions, and one that is gone out of the compleat Union of the Body, and exercised by another Spirit?* Deny this, and Farewel to all *Christian Church-Order* and *Discipline*; yea, and Truth it self: For it is an absolute Inlet to *Ranterism*, and so to *Atheism*, near whose Borders this Author dwells. I say, If the Scripture is to be credited, this is sound Doctrine; If the several *Societies* or *Churches* then gathered were not to pass Judgment, till the *Hereticks* or *Schismaticks* were convinc'd of, and acknowledg'd their Mistake, they had never done it, since upon such Conviction and Acknowledgment they ceased to be such; unless we should believe, that notwithstanding they were convinced in their Consciences of their Errors or Dissensions, they still persisted in the Belief of them, which I will not affirm. If then a *Society* or *Church* so anointed, as aforesaid, have that *Power*, We do by Authority thereof, as a *Christian Society*, judge all Persons concern'd with the Spirit of this Author to be thus far led by a Delusive, Turbulent, Unchristian Spirit, which, if once given way to, there is no Imagination so sordid and scandalous, as it would not lead to; and by this will we stand in the Day of the Lord, when it will be proved no *Popery*, but *Gospel*, to do so with him, and this Novice appear a *Wretched Slanderer*.

His Objection, *Were I among you, could I Marry, if an whole Nation, since you deny it to Dissenters from you?* is childish in every Thing but the Malice of it. If all the World but he were Believers, he might ask the Apostle *Paul* that Question, who said, *Be ye not unequally yok'd together:* It is not the Fault of the Body that he dissents, but his own Imaginations and Whimsies. His Suggestion, *that we would then deny him a Burial, because we should deny it him always as one of us;* but especially our now usurping his Property in a burial Place, is a down-right Forgery.

That our *Friends require any Man to practise what they are not convinc'd of*, I utterly renounce in their Name, and that as an Infamous Slander. But that we will be well satisfied with any Member's Dispractice of an orderly Performance, once cheerfully own'd, is also true, and most reasonable and orderly.

That

That *we Exalt our selves* is a Calumny of his making; but we know our Places in the Body. And for his saying, *Every Member is Equal*; it is false: For though it belongs to the same Body, yet not to the same Service; some are in that Sense more Honourable than others. This shows an Aspiring, Discontented Mind in him, that where he can't be Superiour, he would be Equal.

He saith, *That with sorrow hath he seen pulling down, haling out, and thrusting forth of our Meetings, and that we went as far as our Power, and wanted only more to punish.* p. 29.

But could we do so, as he wickedly and falsly suggests, we should have been perhaps more formidable to our Insolent, Envious and Perverse Opposers, who come not for Conscience-sake, or to seek Satisfaction, which we shall never refuse, but to Disturb, introduce a Rabble, beget Laughter, or any Thing that might disquiet our Assemblies, and as much as in them lies, render them unprofitable to the People. If we ever so us'd any Conscientious Inquirer or Opposer, let us know them. It is Baseness it self to suggest our Ill-using of People in general, and none named: Perhaps we have refused and condemn'd the Bawling Opposition of such Apostate Slanderers as our Adversary; but we appeal to God's Holy Witness in all Consciences, if that has been, or is our Practice, which is insinuated against us, much less that his Uncharitable Expression, *If we had Power equal to our Will, we would Punish*, should have any Place; the Suggestion of the common Adversary.

For his saying, *That the Ministers are Ravening Wolves, that prey upon the Flock: and that if they commit a Fault, they are not to be judged by the Laity, but their Peers or Equals.* p. 29.

It is easie with him to Slander, but hard to prove. What one Minister ever made a Prey upon this Author's Person or Estate, let him give us his Name. *If Preaching the Everlasting Gospel in Season, and out of Season, Rising early, and lying down late, Suffering, Travelling, Spending and being spent in Body and Estate, Sacrificing the Joy, Strength, and Pleasure of their Youth, to the Service of the Living Eternal God, and the Salvation of People's Souls*, if all this makes them Ravenous Wolves of Prey, then hath he rightly denominated them; but if this be Love unfeign'd to God and Men, then will that Righteous Judge certainly reckon with this Apostate for all his Slanders and Calumnies against his Faithful and Painful Messengers.

For *not being judg'd by the Laity, but their Peers*, as he wickedly distinguishes; be it known to all, That if any such Person have committed an Injury against any of those, who are not exercised in the Ministry; then as well those as the Ministry are proper Judges: But in Cases that may more strictly concern the Exercise of his Gift, it is most equal and reasonable, that such other faithful publick Labourers as may be gotten together with some of the more approved among us, whom we can call Elders, should be Judges in the Case. But how? Only as they are upon serious Waiting to receive Counsel and Wisdom from God, directed of his Holy Spirit to speak, act, or determine. Now what great Matter of Evil, *Apostacy, Popery, Tyranny, Lordlings*, &c. can there be in so orderly a Practice? O this Libertine, Ranting Spirit! That therefore hateth us, because we would have it Ruled, Guided and Govern'd with the Curb of Truth; and not under a Pretence of Gospel-Liberty run out into all Excess, in which we have some Cause to fear this pretended Lamenter hath too deeply involv'd himself. True Liberty is not to Commit Sin *Innocently*, as some fancy, but to be freed from Sin, which is ever *Nocent*, and will prove destructive of all who are seduced by it.

Nor is he less untrue and unrighteous to us, when he says, *That as others err'd in setting up the Scriptures as the Standard, Trial, and Touch-stone of Doctrines and Spirits, so we do greatly err in setting up the Body above the Spirit.*

There is no such Doctrine as the Latter maintained among us: It is well known that the Former is by many Professors, yea those, who boast in his Treachery and Lyes; But this always hath been, and still is, and we hope, ever will be our Belief, that no meer Body of People, without the Guidance of God's Spirit, are capable of Determining in Matters of Religious Concernment: For it is not an Hundred Persons (singly void of the Holy Spirit) coming together, that makes them any whit more certain in their Judgment. The only and indispensible Qualification to that great Work being Discoveries and Assistance of the Holy Spirit: A Body then, without the Holy Spirit, can be no Touch-stone; but a Body, attended with the Holy Spirit, certainly is. The Question then is not, *If we prefer the Body above the Spirit?* For that is the Falfe Infinuation of this Apoftate, who is inraged, that we fhould fo feverely cenfure him, and fuch Contentious Perfons as he is; But, *Whether we, as a Believing Body have the Holy Spirit, or no?* Of which much hath been faid by Way of Vindication already in other Tracts; and we fhall leave it to God's Witnefs in the Confciences of thofe we are concern'd with in Matters of that Import, whether we are acted by that Holy Wifdom and Direction, which gives true and found Judgment. We know we are of God; and the World, whether Apoftates or others, that thus withftand our Teftimony, are in the Gall of Bitternefs, and Bond of Iniquity.

His Objection, *That the Hat on in Prayer is a Trifle, or of no fuch Moment, as juftly to occafion fuch a Bufle*, makes for us; fince he can't be other than a Trifler at beft, for all his high Pretences, who hazards the Church's Peace, gives this Difturbance, bears this Ill-will, and fhows that Revenge for a Trifle; 'Twere well if his Confcience were fo nice in Cafes of more Weight: I fear he is as well a *Demas* as an *Alexander*, and that *his Cries againft our Minifters decent and clean Apparel*, is but a better Sort of Cover for his own rufty pharifaical kind of Garb, the Effect perhaps of his fordid Avarice, It feems by his Letter, that the *Quakers mean Clothes made up much of his Convincement at firft.* Truly, that Faith which came in by the outfide, will go out by it too.

But it is a Wonder to me, that the Coftly Clothes, and Prodigal Feaft (to Excefs and Derifion) of that Exalted *J. Pennyman*, and his Beloved, *Mary Bateman*, (who in Token of her Self-Denial, and Attainment to a more excellent Adminiftration, exchanged her Cloth Wafte-Coat for a Silk Farendine Gown, her Blew Apron for one of Fine Holland, and her ordinary Bodice for Rich Sattin it felf; to fay little of her Riding in Fine Coaches, and feveral other Things *(once accounted by her Self-Righteoufnefs, Abominable Things)* did never offend this Author's Nice and Squeamifh Stomach: But we are they only, who muft be Condemned; and I perceive that muft be reputed a *Sin* in us, which is accounted a *Virtue* in them. Away with fuch Deceit for Shame.

Pag. 18. He fays, *That we defert the Light, for the Judgment of the Body*: A wretched begging of the Queftion: We do deny that to be Light in him, which oppofeth it. *He at other Times grants the Body has Light, though not fome Elders:* But the *Body* judgeth him: How will he do then? For him to fay, *He believes the Body to be in the Right, and yet fubject them to his own Conceits, is what deferves to be difdain'd of all Underftanding Men.* He fhould have gone to thofe Elders, and cleared himfelf, if he had ought againft them, and not place their Mifcarriages (as he thinks) to the Acoount of the *Whole Body.* Were he any Thing of a *True Quaker*, (and that he pretends to) he would have abhorred to add thus to their Endeavours, that ftrike at True as well as Falfe. And if by True, is underftood fomething more refined than we are, he may be faid to add to our Sufferings fo much the more. What, but a Dark, Envious, Inveterate Man, would have done fuch a Thing at any Time, but efpecially at this Juncture and Seafon?

Behold the Hat *now, and what a Notable Spirit it affords us, one Drop of which, by Antipathy, were enough, one would think, to Cure any one, not too far gone in Prejudice and Schifm!* O that all who profefs the Truth of the Living God, may be kept out of fuch Temptation, that they may never facrifice the *Peace of the Church*, and *Quiet of their own Souls*, to the Introduction, or Promotion of any Thing fo Unferviceable, Senfelefs, and Unprofitable, *both to Soul and Body*; but Eyeing the Bleffed TRUTH in their inward Parts, may by it be Exercifed in Body, Soul and Spirit, to all Godly Converfation among Men; fo will God be Glorified, and they preferved.

For his other Stories, fome Things are True, and hurt us not, but fhow our Care to preferve Unity and Order, though they will the 𝕵𝖚𝖉𝖆𝖘 that both reveal'd and augmented them. Other Paffages are greatly abufed, and down-right Lyes told, as before, three of which, I cannot forbear to mark out, with a Challenge to prove them, notwithftanding the following Teftimonies, *pag.* 22, 23, 43. Firft, *That our Miniftry is Vicious and Wanton, Guilty of Whoredom; and that Strumpets are among them.* This we do, in the Name of the Holy God deny, and defie any Man on Earth to prove any Part of this Ungodly, General Charge againft our Miniftry, to fo much as belong to any one Perfon by us accounted of it: If any fuch Thing be, let the Accufer, his Witneffes, and the Accufed be brought forth, and an Hearing fhall never be refufed. But let me afk this *Apoftate*, If ever he knew fuch an one?

If he admonish'd him? If upon Continuance in such Ungodly Living, he told it to the Church, before this Publication of his Ungodly Slanders to the World: If he says he did, he adds to his Lyes; be it then True or False in it self, he has done but like a *Treacherous Renegade*; I fasten an *Action of Defamation upon his Head*, and that in the High and Holy Court of Heaven, before God the Righteous Judge, who will avenge the Cause of the Innocent upon their false Accusers.

Next, *That we, with the* Papists, *prefer a loose Person before a Non-Conformist, or such like*, is an horrid Lye. We own, and cannot but cherish Sobriety, and a Conscientiousness to God in all, which we never could Prophaneness; but where Men, like the *Pharisees*, have a Shew of Religion, and their Fury hath eaten out their Moderation, insomuch, as that they are become Envious and Persecuting, such we say, *Are worse than Publicans*, as saith the Scripture, *Whoremongers and Adulterers shall enter the Kingdom of God before them*. But neither is this the Case in Hand; for he is far less excusable, who having walked with *Upright People*, deserts them, than those *Non-Conformists* that were never of them. *Non-Conformity* may be Ignorance, but *Apostacy* is wilful distorting, and erring from the Faith, Worship, and Discipline of the *True Church*: And, as a *Christian* turn'd *Turk*, is observ'd to be most Cruel to the Profession; so none so great Enemies to the *Poor Quakers*, as those who have been reputed of them. *The worst Enemies are those of a Man's own House*. 'Twas *Judas* the Disciple, that betray'd his Lord; and none we hear of, did *Paul* more Wrong, than *Alexander* the Copper-Smith.

Lastly, *His Judging their Recantations, that deny'd their former Acts of Dissension, and gave Testimony against them, to have been done in an Hour of Temptation*, is a Lye in it self, and in him high Incharity, and at most but a Begging of the Question: I challenge him to prove it; If he can't, he is a Belyer of God's Convictions upon the Soul: Their profest Sincerity, and Brokenness of Heart, and Contrition of Spirit, had been enough to have melted any Thing, but an *Adamantine Alexander, the Apostate*, who not only was *Bad*, but we never heard that he proved *Good* again; the Doom I fear of this Perverter of the Right Way of the Lord, who will certainly reward him according to his Works. But because I design not to be long, nor yet to give an Account to the World of our *Church-Procedure*, nor are we obliged to it for every Nameless Accuser, let this suffice to show the Baseness and Revenge both of the *Author* and his *Publisher*, and their great Inconsistency with the Designs of each other, and his with Sound Reason, Scripture, and himself.

God will bless the Horn of his Salvation above all their Opposition; he will Prosper his Truth, Bless His People, and Dissipate every Mist that Ignorance, Rage, or Malice of Ungodly Men, may for a Time cloud the Beauty of the One, or call in Question the Unspotted Reputation of the other by; and He shall have the Glory, whose it is, for ever.

I am a Servant to the TRUTH, *and to them that Love it,*

WILLIAM PENN.

Judas, and the Jews,

COMBINED AGAINST

CHRIST, and His Followers.

BEING

A Re-joynder to the late Nameless REPLY, call'd, *Tyranny and Hypocrisie Detected*, made against a Book, entituled, *The Spirit of Alexander the Copper-Smith, Rebuked*, &c, Which was an Answer to a Pamphlet, call'd, *The Spirit of the Hat*.

IN WHICH

TRUTH is cleared from Scandals, and the Church of CHRIST, in her Faith, Doctrine, and Just Power and Authority in Discipline, is clearly and fully Vindicated, against the Malicious Endeavours of a Confederacy of some Envious Professors, and *Vagabond, Apostate Quakers*.

By a Member and Servant of the Church of CHRIST, William Penn.

He that dippeth his Hand with me in the Dish, the same shall betray me, Mat. xxvi. 23. *They went out from us, but were not of us*, 1 John ii. 19. *In Perils among False Brethren*, 2 Cor. xi. 26. *Nevertheless, the Foundation of God stands sure*, 2 Tim. ii. 19.

The INTRODUCTION.

THE *Just Defence of our so much Reviled Principles and Persons, is so ill resented by our Enemies, that instead of publickly Recanting their Injustice, they repute us more Criminal for so doing, than themselves in first traducing us.* It is become a Sort of Petty Treason *to reprove them, they are grown almost incorrigible*; and to controul them, though in a Lye, *is hateful: So much more do they prefer our Destruction, than the* Truth *it self, or their own Reputation. Strange! That it should be reputed Innocency to accuse the Guiltless, and Guilt to defend them. Are we of God, then shall we stand, maugre your Assaults; if not, we shall fall without them. What need this* Clubbing *for Mischief, and* Caballing *to our Ruin? The* Jews, *I believe, never studied the* Crucifying of Christ *more vehemently, than you vigorously combine and plot the* Massacring of our Names, Credit *and* Principles *out of the World; yea, and we have Cause to suspect our Persons too, or else this* Socinian-Defender *of the Hat-Spirit, would never have told the World in almost so many Words,* That Blasphemers were to dye by the Law of God, and the Quakers are Blasphemers; *every Man can make the Conclusion, that understands what a Conclusion is.* See pag. 23. *It's a Work becomes Darkness; for such I call your* Nameless Pamphlet, *in which you have abused Virtuous and Good People by Name, not daring to stand the Test of putting your Names to your Abuses: against which can be no Fence but Innocency, and that remains unshaken by all your Blustering Epithets: That rests with God, who will quell your swelling Rage, and speedily*

speedily rebuke that great Hurricane your Envy has raised to over-set us in our Voyage to Eternal Rest. But he that *said to* Moses *in an Hour of Straight,* Stand still, and thou shalt see my Salvation, *has once and again comforted us under all these Discouragements: Neither are your Combinations Terrible ; No, though Evil* Spies *have been your Informers. Our greatest Trouble is your own Hardening, and we are sorry to see you make so much Haste to* Old Jerusalem's Portion. *For us, we know in whom we have believed : Who, as he feedeth the Fowls of the Air, and clotheth the Lillies of the Field, preserves us, so that your Buffettings may prove our Trials, but in the End your own Judgment. For, however you buoy your selves up, by the Acceptance you find with some Airy, or Prejudiced Spirits, God will certainly enter into Judgment with you for your Envious Proceedings, who not being able to carry on your own Controversies, now* Lift your selves Combatants *for a few* Stragling Apostates ; *not out of Love to* True Quakers, *but Hatred to such as are so. What Sense is there in believing you only intend a* False Quaker, *who have writ and abetted those Writings that are against us as* Quakers *at all ? But what shall I say ? It is an Age grown to that Degree of Impiety, that there is no Friendship so strait, no Relation so near, no Truth so evident, nor Life so innocent, that some Men are not hardy, and wicked enough to break, violate and slander, to avenge some supposed Wrong, or gratifie an Emulous Spirit.* Controversie Ended upon Socinian Principles, *&c.* is risen now in One, about the Hat on in Prayer. *What Variety of Shapes do our Adversaries put on, to compass their Ends ? It has been their Practice, first to abuse our Principles, and then rail at our Defences ; and for vindicating our Religion, to fall foul upon our Persons ; and those chiefly who are most active in that Service. There needs no other Demonstration of this, than the* Scurrilous Libel *now to be considered ; which with me carries so mischievous an Aspect, that the Parties concerned in these Undertakings, do by it proclaim, they only want as much as Power as Will,* To send us and our Principles to *New-England* for a Venture. *God deliver us from those Magistrates, that are as Angry in Government, as these Men are in Religion: But this is our Joy,* That these Enemies speak all Manner of Evil against us falsly, for our Lord and Saviour's Sake. *We maintain our Principles; that angers them ; Miscarriages joy them, whatever they pretend ; and if they can bring some Writers and Preachers out of Request, they think they do their Business. But we cannot believe that Sober and Judicious Persons will think the worse of us, or our Cause, for these Malicious Endeavours against it. We have only to do with some* Old Adversaries, *new Vampt, with the Slanderous Stories of some* Modern Apostates. Had not Judas helpt, the Jews had been to seek. A few Vagabond Quakers *are their Intelligencers ; it's all but a Piece of Treachery and Envy : And truly 'tis fit we should be tryed as well by False Friends as Professed Enemies, that in all Things we may approve our selves* Compleat Conquerors, *through the Invisible Power, and to the alone Honour of the* Eternal TRUTH, *professed by us. And so we enter upon the* Libel *it self.*

Judas and the Jews, &c.

WE are told in the Title Page of the *Libel,* that it was writ in Defence of a Letter, entituled, *The Spirit of the Hat ;* and, *Against the Deceitful, Invective, and Railing Answer,* called, *The Spirit of* Alexander, *&c.* Indeed it is wonderful strange, that to reprove an *Apostate* should be reputed Railing ; and that this *Secretary* to this *New-founded Cabal,* should practise it in censuring it. He cannot forbear it in his Title Page.

He begins with *Tyranny and Hypocrisy Detected ;* which four Words he explains to us thus : *Or, a farther Discovery of the Tyrannical Government, Popish Principles, and Vile Practices of the now* Leading Quakers. In all which, if there be no Reviling, there is no Thing in the World ; for these Words reach to the End of all Villany. Meek Man, that he would be thought ! Who seems to engross Railing into a Company, and seems not so angry at it in us, as that we use it *Unlicensed of his Cabal* ; for he exerciseth it at such a Rate in checking it, as if he might do it *Cum Privilegio.* But it right-well agrees with the Advocate of an *Apostate Cause.* I complain of nothing in this Kind more, than that we must not Rebuke ill Language

guage without being Guilty of it: Nay, such is the Peevishness of our *Adversaries*, that to mention *theirs*, is Criminal: But we shall run the Hazard of their Frowns, rather than be *False to the Truth*, or wanting to our selves in it's proper Place. Let it suffice that the *Title* manifestly speaks what the *Libel* vainly condemns.

This Secretary, (I suppose in the Name of the Cabal) begins his Libel thus, *How Dangerous a Thing it is, for a Man to engage himself publickly for any Single Party upon the Account of Religion, is greatly manifest in the* Leading Quakers, *and especially in* W. Penn, *from whose Parts and Education, one would expect more than ordinary Candour and Ingenuity.*

By which, I perceive, he is, from a *Raging Socinian*, become an *Universalian*. But why then so bitter against us? Sure he is of a Party in that ; and how dangerous a Thing it is, Time will more fully shew. However, he declares himself of *No Party*, by which I suppose he excludes the *Christian* ; for the Prophane of that Time reputed him a *Sectary*, and all must acknowledge him to be of a Party.

How I came to be of this Way, is best known to God ; but thus much I must say, that nothing short of the Divine Word of Life and Power, has wrought that Alteration upon me from what I once was, to what I now am. The *Trials, Travels, Tribulations, and Exercises, that from Fourteen Years of Age have attended me, but more especially since I was brought to own and abet this Holy Way I now profess, are too many to be related.* And from the Hour I was first Convinced of this Eternal TRUTH, to this of writing this Discourse, I can with Boldness declare to all the World, *I have had no other Aim nor End than God's Honour, the Good of others, and my own Salvation in the Day of the Lord.* In short, I have learned to turn my Back to the Smiter, and my Cheek to the Plucker off of the Hair: And it is not for any Adversary at this Time of Day, under any Pretence of Parts and Education, to dis-ingage my Affection from this Right Way of the Lord, Remembring, *My Lord made himself of no Reputation*, and, *that the Prophet was accounted Mad*, and *the Apostles Drunk.*

But he says, *I having imbarked my self amongst those People, and having obtained an high Repute among them, I betook my self to such pitiful Shifts, Scurrilities and Bravings* (he is pincht) *to uphold their Detected Cause and Tottering Kingdom*, ('twill stand for ever) *as one would think could not proceed from any Man professing* Christianity ; *witness my late Controversial Writings*, ibid.

But I cannot expect to be Well-spoken of by mine Enemies, especially when they declare themselves to be such, *because of that Way I so earnestly defend.* But this Man is not so ignorant surely, as to imagine I imbarkt my self among this People, to obtain Repute or Grandeur, who lost all with Men when I first came amongst them. I would have my implacable Enemies know, that had no more Durable and Eternal Things been in my Eye, I might have had my Share where more is to be got, than amongst this Despised People ; but Envy is Blind, and Rage Foolish. For my Controversial Writings, they stand unanswered, among the rest my *Spirit of Alexander*, &c. the Strength of it being foully over-looked, as we shall anon have Occasion to shew.

He tells the World, (pag. 4, 5.) *That notwithstanding we call the Spirit of the Hat, Lyes, Forgery, Defamation, with abundance of Terms of the like* Foxonian Leaven (a Scornful Nick-Name) *yet when we come to Particulars, we either first confess what we deny, with an idle Distinction, except some few Things ; or secondly, acknowledge them by Silence ; or thirdly, use some Deceitful Terms of Denial, which the Reader cannot discover ; or, fourthly, take an Occasion from some Circumstances, perhaps not rightly set down, to deny the whole Matter* ; which doubtless are very bad Things, if True.

He has hereby rendred us, not only *No Christians*, but the *Worst of Men*. All I can say at present is this, it has never been my Practice to palliate that which cannot be justified, or to treat any Adversary so deceitfully. But 'tis expected he should prove what he says, or else we must invert the Character upon himself.

He tells us (I suppose, in order to prove what he hath said,) *That W. P. doth in the Name of the* Quakers *acknowledge, That the Complaint made in the* Spirit of the Hat, *is True, namely,* " That we required him to yield [*to our Determination against his Conscience*] " because the Body would have it so ; saying, that was yield-
" ing to the Power: And that I undertake in Opposition to the Author, *That his*
" *not so yielding, but persisting, is Dissension* ; but our Disowning [*Excommuni-*
" *cating, and Depriving of a Liberty, of Marrying, Burying,* &c.] any Person for
" that Cause, is no Breach of the Great Gospel-Charter: This, he says *I labour to do*

do with the same Arguments Papists use against Protestants, who pretend to no such Power, and that they may be found every where answered in Protestant Writings. A mean Answer, but a Notable Go-by, in Case I had so exprest my self, but most forgedly does he deliver my Words, and Tendency of them.

Was this Man chosen for your prime Tool of Controversie, who can only tell *One Big Lye, and then run away?* My Argument (forsooth) are *Popish*, there's Confutation enough; But with whom? Ignorance and Prejudice? An easie Way to brand Reason, and render the clearest Truth suspected in a Nation as abhorrent of *Popery*, as this we live in; a shameful Injustice, that *Sectaries* should traduce us with that, which was once their own Suffering from others. But what if I had us'd any Argument for the *True Church*, which is employed by the *Papist* in Defence of a False One, Must *Truth not be Truth in it self*, because mis-applyed? And suppose the *Protestant* has answered the *Papist*, Is that any Answer to me? How great an Untruth has he told in his Title Page, when he calls his Pamphlet, *A Defence of the Spirit of the Hat, against the Spirit of* Alexander; who in four Pages after tells us, *He intends not to meddle with the Arguments of it.* But perhaps he will Fault me (for these People are very full of finding Fault, though they mend none in themselves) in that he has referred us to *Protestant-Writers*; a Defence boldly begged, but never to be accepted of by me. Does he think I must turn over *Melancthon, Chemnitius, Oecolampadius, Jewell, Whitaker, Reynolds*, and others, for an Answer to the *Spirit of* Alexander *the Copper Smith?* After this Rate, it were far easier to Answer than Accuse. I am of Opinion, that Dr. *Stillingfleet's* Adversaries would look upon their Cause as little injured by any bare Reference to *Ancient Protestant-Writers*, how excellently soever they acquitted themselves at that Time of Day; fresh Opposition requires fresh Vindication. If I had been *Popish*, the Man should have shewn me in what; and when he had done, have soundly confuted it, and not in the midst of his Exclamations against Shifters, give such just Occasion to say, thou art the Man. I am willing to forgive him at this Time; But let him be better instructed of his *Cabal* against the next, and see if he can learn more Truth, than to call his Libels Answers, whilst they prove themselves Evasions; For Truth will work through all odious Names: And it is not pinning the *Pope* upon our Tail, and crying, *Popery, Popery*, that will confute our Principles; However, till we are better known, it may disrepute our Persons.

But let his base Constructions be considered Our Reproving Men for going out of the decent Order and happy Unity of the Body, he calls *Requiring Men to set down by our Determination against their Conscience*; And our disowning that Breach upon Persistance, *Excommunication from Burying and Marrying.* They ejected themselves by their Novelties, and we are not ashamed to repute such as *Publicans and Heathens that will not hear the Church of Christ*, Mat. 18. Had they Faith? they might have kept it to themselves, and not have disturbed the Church's Peace with their new Practices, indeed Institutions; for what was it less than to require our not practising of the Hat off in Prayer, who called pulling it off a *Popish* Tradition, unless Men are not to leave of *Popish* Traditions: So that they, and not we were to blame, as the Sequel will farther prove; But I could not pass by this Part of the Disingenuity of this Libeller.

As the *Libel*, so our Discourse will consist, of Matter of Argument, and Matter of Fact. I shall begin with Matter of Argument, which shall consist of a farther Defence of what is asserted in my Book, entituled, *The Spirit of Alexander the Copper-Smith revived and rebuked.*

The grand Cause of that Dissension which was begun by *Jo. Perrot*, long since happily ended among our selves, though renewed, divulged and aggravated, for the Strengthening of the Hands of our common Enemy, by certain *Perverse Apostates*, as delivered in the *Spirit of the Hat*, and *Defence of the same*, they must with me grant to be this.

The Quakers teach that every Man is enlightned with a sufficient Light to Salvation, And that all Faith in, and Worship to God ought to stand upon the Convictions, and in the Leadings thereof; yet we are obliged by their Body unto that, which we have no Motion for, but rather against, and upon our Refusal of such Compliance as they expect, we are disowned as not of them: So that the Sufficiency, Convictions and Leadings of the Light must vail to the Body, and not the Body to the Light; wherefore not the Light, but the Body is become the Quakers Rule. Thus *Thomas Hicks's Con. Dial.* p. 63, 64, 65. *Spir. Hat.* p. 11, 12, 13. *Defence* of it, p. 5, 6, 7. Their
Common

Common Aggravations, especially of the two latter are these, *That they are denied Marrying, Burying, Trading, that they are distracted and so deprived of all both Ecclesiastical and Civil Privileges.* The Aggravations we shall consider in their Place; And first to their Objection or Argument, as I have fairly, fully and faithfully laid it down.

'Tis a Truth, and as true, that we urge, both the Universality and Sufficiency of the Light to Salvation; and that every Man ought to follow only the Teachings of it about Faith and Worship. This is granted on all Hands, even by the *Cabal* to credit their present Work, and obtain their envious Ends upon us and our Principles; Therefore no Part of the Question to be controverted. The Matter in Difference strictly lies here, that is, by resolving these four following Questions, the Objection will be fully and plainly answered.

2. *Whether Christ has given to his Church, consisting of faithful Believers, and obedient Walkers by the Light or Spirit within, such a Sense, Tast, Relish and Savour of the Nature of Spirits, as upon all Occasions the great Enemy of Christ and his People may take upon him (under never so seeming innocent Appearances and Transformations) to condemn any Thing by his Church practised, or innovate any Thing by the Church never practised, but condemned, Yea, or Nay?*

2. *Whether such a Society, Body or Church, after due Admonition given to any dissenting or innovating Person, may not Lawfully and Christianly deny their Communion in Testimony against that wrong Spirit, such Person or Persons may be acted by?*

3. *Whether such Person or Persons may not hold this granted fundamental Principle of the Light, &c. before recited, in the Understanding, and yet be acted by a wrong Spirit to Divisions, and then plead against the Church, under the Pretence of acting by the Light within; and consequently, whether he can, or ought to be judged by any for so doing, because every one ought to act according to the Light that is within them?* And lastly,

4. *Whether the Body of the* Quakers, *or their present Opposers be that Church, Yea, or Nay?*

The first is so evident in the Affirmative, That to reject it, is nothing less than to deny Scripture it self. It was the express Promise of Christ, to send the Comforter, *the Spirit of Truth to lead into all Truth*; which the Apostle *John* assures us, was made good, not only to the Disciples, but the then Churches of Christ, to whom he writ these unanswerable Passages, *Ye have an Unction from the Holy One, and Ye shall know all Things.* Again, *But the Anointing, which ye have received of him, abideth in you, and you need not that any Man teach you, but as the same Anointing teacheth you of All Things, and is Truth and is no Lye; And even as it hath taught you, ye shall abide in him.* By which it is evident, that the Church of Christ had an Infallible Spirit, by which to discern the Spirit of a Sheep, from the Spirit of a Wolf, though he came in *Sheep's Clothing.* This Doctrine Christ himself taught us, when he said, *Beware of False Prophets, which come to you in Sheep's Clothing.* Again, *Take heed that no Man deceive you; For many shall come in my Name, saying I am Christ, and shall deceive many.* Whence it follows, that there should be False Prophets, yet in *Sheep's Clothing*, which is a deceitful Spirit, acting under refined Appearances; and to compass it's Deceit the better, shall palliate it, with the Pretence of being led by the Spirit or Light of Christ within: So that as Deceitful Spirits were foretold, the Way to know them was both promised and enjoyed; *My Sheep hear my Voice*, said the great Shepherd, *and a Stranger will they not hear.* Who is this Stranger? Not always False Doctrine, but a False Spirit, covered with True Doctrine, *They shall come in my Name*, that is, pretending Authority from me, and speaking my Words, not having my Spirit: Christ's Spirit within, is his Voice within, and 'tis that alone gives to discern the Strange Voice, let it come with never such True Words. Had Christ left his Churches destitute of this Touch-Stone, they had been imposed upon by every False Spirit, and his Flock devoured by every Wolf in Sheep's Clothing. Sheep know Sheep, not only by Sight, but Instinct, and Wolves too; For if Shepherds be of Authority, they tell us, *that if a Wolf be near, though out of Sight, the Sheep will bleat their Antipathy:* So do the Sheep of Christ know each other by the Instinct of that Divine Nature they are mutually Partakers of, and by it do they discern the *Wolf within*, notwithstanding *the Sheep's clothing without.* It was for this End they were to have *Salt* in themselves, the Anointing and Spirit in themselves, that they might see, relish and discern

cern thereby, who were so Salted, Anointed and Spirited, which in the Ground could never be visibly discerned.

2dly. The second Question I also take in the Affirmative, and for which there is both express Scripture, and Unanswerable Reason. This is seen in the very Case of *Alexander the Copper-Smith,* who was denied and rejected, notwithstanding that he made Profession of Christianity; And there is cause to believe, that the Difference began *from his emulous Spirit's taking Occasion against the Apostles Authority,* and the Power of the Elders in the Church. It was doubtless for something not unlike to this, that *Paul* complained of him to *Timothy,* Alexander *the Copper-Smith did me much wrong, of whom be thou ware also; for he hath greatly withstood our Words.* Which is the very State and Character of the present Apostates, Who pretend with *Alexander,* not to withstand Truth or Christianity; but a Lordly *Paul, Timothy, or such like eminent Labourers:* They pretend to own the Churches, but deny some of their *Leading Ministers.* That this was *Alexander's* Disease, the next Verse proves; *At my first Answer no Man stood with me, but all Men forsook me. I pray God it may not be laid to their Charge.* Who was this People but the Church? For of the *Heathen* it could not be said. And what was *Alexander's* aim besides Ambition? I mean, to discredit the Apostle, that he might gain the Repute, and bring him down from that Authority God had given him in the Church, that he might usurp it to himself. What did the Apostle do in the like Case? shrink? No; hear him: *For though I should boast somewhat more of our Authority (which the Lord hath given us for Edification, and not for your Destruction) I should not be ashamed.* 2 Cor. 10. 8. But no more of this at present. That Christ as well gave his Church Power to reject as to try Spirits, is not hard to prove. That notable Passage, *Go, tell the Church,* does it to our Hand: For if in Case of private Offence betwixt Brethren, the Church is made absolute Judge, from whom there is no Appeal in this World; how much more in any the least Case that concerns the Nature, Being, Faith and Worship of the Church her self? The Judgment Christ passeth in the Matter, is sufficient to the Resolution of our Question; *But if he neglect to hear the Church, let him be unto thee as an* Heathen *and a Publican.* This I say on the Account of those *Apostates,* who pretend to be the Men they ever were; For this Man that works with their Tools, is upon his own Principle, as much an *Heathen* and a *Publican* as any Thing else, and tells us to boot, *that it is dangerous to be of any one Party;* Therefore not of the *true Church's Party.* I omit any particular recital of the Apostle *Paul's* frequent and earnest Dehortations from so much *as keeping Company with perverse Disputers about needless Questions,* or any that infested the Church, and disturbed her Peace, and that Practice, in which she was at first setled, with unprofitable Novelties, under what Pretence soever: They that can read, may find in his Epistles enough to this Purpose. 'Tis true, They used no corporal Violence, or any civil Power to punish such obstinate Dissenters; nor is that Unchristian Practice so much as any Part of the Question: But first, to reprove and admonish, and in Case of Persistance, then to disown and reject, which is a Part of the Question, and a Part of the Scripture too. And indeed it is most reasonable, that as a Civil, so a *Christian* Society should have this Power to preserve it self from the *Taints* and *Infections* of hurtful Spirits, for such tend not to farther Knowledge, Increase in Holiness, or Peace, but Strifes and Divisions, Animosities and Rents, Backbitings and Revenge, to the laying waste of God's Holy Heritage.

3dly, The *third* Question we also accept in the Affirmative. *That Men may believe, confess and subscribe to the Truth of the Doctrine of the Universality, Sufficiency, and immediate Teachings of the Light, as to Faith and Worship, and yet be declined from the Living Sense, Power and Ordering of it, so as to be acted by a wrong Spirit to Divisions, and notwithstanding plead his Following of the Light within against the Judgment of the Church, who reproves him for so doing.* In short, That a Man may follow a Wrong Spirit when he thinks he follows the Right; and though he ought to follow the Light and Spirit, *yet is to be judged when he does not act thereby (though he may think he doth) by such as walk thereby.* In this, the Scriptures of Truth are very positive. The *Jews* owned the Law at what Time they rebelled against it, and thought they acted according to Scripture, when by their Traditions they made it of none Effect. There was a certain Generation *that were pure in their own Eyes,* That is, believed themselves to be of a Right Spirit, whom the Holy Ghost reproved for being guided by a Wrong one. It was no other State than this that Christ spoke of, when he said, *If therefore the Light that is in thee, be Darkness, how great is that Darkness?* Some doubtless acted by Virtue of this Darkness, not as Darkness, but as Light; was it therefore Light, because they thought so? when it is manifest, that they were against Christ, the true Light, as you are now. Or, would the Plea of such an one be so valid against the Body of a Church, walking in the true Light, as to disengage any from her Judgment? Or, must we therefore conclude, that the Light is not a Rule for Men to walk by, because some mistake, or swerve from it? Or, that he who calls his dark Imagination, a Motion of Light, is therefore not to be condemned, because 'tis every Man's Duty, to follow the true Light? Shall this Position, I say, that all Men ought to follow the Light in themselves, deprive the Church of the Power of judging that for a dark Imagination, which from the Savour and Sense of God's Light and Truth, she feels to be so, because some Person or Persons, plead that they therein follow the Light? This opens a Door to all Licentiousness, and furnisheth every *Libertine* with a Plea. What might have been said in this Case against the ancient *Christians?* Every Man ought to walk in the Spirit and to be led by the Spirit; shall therefore any Man's Pretence to be led by the Spirit, that is not, secure him from the Judgment of those that are really led by the Spirit? Or, shall the Judgments of those, who are led by the Spirit, against him that pretends to be so led, be reputed *Tyranny*, and a going from the Leadings and Judgment of the Spirit, to the Leadings and Judgment of Men? Or, because of granting the Light to be obey'd in all it's Leadings; And it's Leadings to be waited for, in Order to Faith and Worship; that therefore, there is no Way left to judge, which are in the Wrong of the two, that equally say, *they are led by the same Light?* For if Men would come to the Salt, Grace, Truth, and faithful Witness in themselves, which only gives to discern and savour true Spirits from false Ones, they would hereby arrive at certain Knowledge in the Matter, but where People stand, they can never distinguish, because they are from under the Conduct of that Spirit, which alone reveals the deep Things of God. In short, as no Man's Saying, *he is in the Right*, ought to conclude him to be in the Right; so neither can that hinder that he should not be found out by such as are in the right Spirit, to be in the Wrong, if in it. He that says, *he is ruled by the Scripture*, may err, as well as he that says, *he is led by the Light*; therefore is he not to be censured? Or, is there no certain Way of knowing him to be in the Wrong? It is the Spirit of Truth, that opens the Truth of Scripture; much more can it only give to relish Spirits. Which leads to the last Question.

Whether the People called Quakers, *or those few stragling Fellows of* John Perrot *are this True Church, and acted by this divine Light and Spirit, yea or nay?* To answer this Question, I shall keep very close to the Concessions of these present *Apostates*, for it is not so much my Business at this Time, to prove us a true Church to them, that had never any Relation to us, as against those who acknowledge themselves once to have been of us, but now decline us.

That God sent forth a spiritual Ministry, that many were gathered by it, and settled in the Way of Everlasting Peace, and called by the World, Quakers, the Author of *the Spirit of the Hat*, fully confesseth, *pag.* 9. That it was then the Church of God, four Lines after undeniably prove. *And the Lord did daily add unto the Church, and raised up many to go forth in the Power, to preach the Everlasting Gospel; whereby the Church multiplied and encreased, to the Astonishment of the Nations.* By this we see, it was then the Church in their Opinion, without Dispute; I would fain know how it comes now to be no Church? Has her refusing to conform to *John Perrot's* Innovation of the Hat on in Time of publick Prayer, unchurched her? I have hitherto thought, that a *Society's* going from, or adding to, what it was when truly called a *Church*, was that which only did unchurch it, and not continuing as it was; And if this be good arguing, the People called *Quakers*, remain still the same Church, *but their Adversaries are not the same Members*. In short, where the first Occasion of Offence was given, there was the first Breach of Unity. Had the Church imposed upon them, there would be some Reason for varying of her Character, and condemning her as fallen; But the Innovation being their own, she is not accountable unto them, but they to her, for such unwarrantable Novelties: So that the Question is not, whether the *Quakers* impose, but *whether they did not innovate?* All was well till this Imagination was hatched; *The Spirit of Judgment and Burning had it's Course, their Vessels were filled with Refreshment, Springs of Life broke out in their Bellies, and Bread of Life dwelt within them*;

they wanted no good Thing, as that Letter of the *Hat* relates. If this may be credited, how comes so sudden a Revolution, that in a Year's Time, *the Mighty should be fallen, the Stars ceased to give their Light, the Poor distressed, the Young ones bruised, and Conscience imposed upon by a Law?* which wretched Deceit, methinks, should be obvious to every Impartial Reader. There is no Wisdom to believe Men so inconstant to their own Apprehensions, and who, of all Times in which to prove this great Alteration, should make Choice of that, in which was so great a Persecution, and so noble a Testimony, born for the Truth, viz. 1662. But the Truth of the Matter is this. *John Perrot* (who if he had been as faithful as his Companion, might with him, have been hanged at *Rome*, (as we have been informed) to his own Comfort, the Truth's Honour, and the Church's Peace) came Home as filled with Conceit, as he pretended his Body had been oppressed with Sufferings, which kindling so great a Love in the Hearts of some Tender Friends, as that they unwarily became Incouragers of his Ambition, in their too high exalting and lamenting his Sufferings, which having rendred him *Master* of their Affections, they most of them easily became Embracers of his Invention. We had Reason to believe it had almost been impossible for him ever to have made one *Proselyte*, had not the Noise of his foreign Tryals disposed the Hearts of some affectionate People to receive his Impression; he that will please to consider the *improbable Account he vainly gave of his own Sufferings, saying*, that since Adam's Day, none had ever undergone the like; *his singular Style; Proverbial Chapters, in Imitation of* Solomon; *his toyish conceited Rythms; his Title Page of the* Wren *in the* Burning Bush, *waving her Wings of Contraction*, &c. *His peculiar Subscription, which was generally* John *(and could not be so, because there was no more of that Name among us, but because he would be the* John *of* Johns) and which is yet more ridiculous, in a Letter to several grave Women, *your tender* Sister John, *with his absurd new fangled bodily Greetings, his most papal Salutations to* G. Fox. E. Burroughs, *and others* (by them rejected, and himself reproved) as if he had spent his Time in learning all the superlative Complements of *Rome*: I say, he that pleases to consider these Things, must needs think, that the Man had lost his Guide, and was dangerously elevated above the holy Fear of God, and heavenly Life of the Truth; and his Standing being soon discerned by several weighty Friends, he was soberly, secretly, and frequently dealt withal: His Condition represented, his Danger shewn, and a Station of Safety pointed to him: It was the daily Travel of many, who sought his Welfare, and the Church's Peace, to bring him to a Sense of his own Condition; But no Argument or Entreaties could prevail, no Sighs or Tears could soften him, but resolved he was for a Sect-Master, and his Mark must be, *the Hat on in Time of publick Prayer*. That which yet whetted many simple Hearts to follow his Example, was with his Sufferings, his Pharisaical Pretences, to an higher Dispensation, but instead of shewing them a readier Way, to an higher State of Holiness, he diverted their Minds from the more weighty Things of the Law of the Spirit of Life in Christ Jesus, to contend for that rude and unprofitable Practice of the *Hat on in Time of Publick Prayer*; an Invention to no Edification, but to the great Disturbance of the Church: Thus began what Rent he sought to make amongst us. Before this, we were at Peace, our *Sion* prosperous; and these *Apostate Adversaries* allowed us to be God's Church, his chosen People. I appeal now to the whole World of moderate and impartial People, whether we acted herein, unlike *Christians*, sober and prudent Men? And if any of our publick Enemies, who pretend to own a Church-Authority (some of them also being Members and Leaders) would not have done the like? Must we suffer for that which they justifie? We rejected a Practice we had no Authority for, neither without, nor within: We saw who brought it in, and what acted him, with the Bent and Tendency of it; And it was as much our Duty to withstand the Entrance of that which was wrong, as to continue in the Practice, of that which was right, and settled in the Power of God long among us: We might invert their Plea much more truly; the Light within enjoyned us to disown them, had we not then sinned, to have declined? Or, is our Light, *Darkness*, because they call their Darkness, Light? In short, the *Church* never knew it, when so much admired by her present Enemies, and because when it came, she rejected it, therefore are they become her Enemies, which proves *Them*, and not the *Church* to be changed. But supposing we had nothing of this to our Defence, what is become of the once acknowledged blessed Church, and her powerful Ministry? If we have lost both, who has found them? If due to any Body, in Case our *Adversaries* be in the Right, it must be to them: But I

1673.

Spirit of the Hat. p. 10.

know of no *Church*, nor do I hear of any *Ministry* they have, nor the *Power* of God manifest among them, either for the Building up of themselves, or the Gathering of others. What! Is the *Church* already returned into the Wilderness? And is the *Power* lost, which they acknowledge, was once amongst us, and to God's Eternal Praise, we daily witness in City and Country to attend our Travels? But as they were not of God in their Dissensions; so neither have they stood. We suffer as we did; The World loves them more than it did; They are Friends, but both Enemies to us. Their *Sect-Master* return'd with the Dog to the Vomit, to *Swearing, Fighting, fine Cloaths, Cap and Knee to Men, who could sit on his B—— with his Hat on his Head, when he prayed to the Most High God. Some of his Followers ran into Looseness and Rantism; others into Enmity and Earthly Mindedness; but far the more considerable returned to their first Love and Works, whom God hath since frequently blest with his heavenly Presence, and sealed to them the Comfort of the Holy Communion of the Brethren.*

To sum up what we have been saying, *First*, The True Church of Christ, by the Gift of the Holy Spirit, from Christ, the Head, is enabled to try, savour and relish Wrong Spirits under never such Right Appearances, as that, without which she could never be preserved *from the Wolves that are in Sheep's Cloathing, nor the Deceivers that come with Christ's Words out of Christ's Power and Life. Secondly,* That this Church hath as well Power to reject the false Spirit, as to try it. *Thirdly*, That Men may be in the Words and not the Spirit of Truth; that notwithstanding it is the Duty of all Men, to act by the Light and Spirit within, that hinders not, that such as walk not according to the Light within, though they may pretend to do it, should be known and judged of them that really do so. *Fourthly*, That we were this True Church of God by our *Apostate Adversary's* own Confession: And we have proved, *that not we, but our Adversaries have altered (since the Time that large Confession mentions) by giving the Offence, and making the first Breach of Unity,* notwithstanding the many Christian Courses that were taken to restore them, and preserve Concord among Brethren: Therefore our Judgment of them is not that of a *Dark, Dead Body*, but a Living, Spiritual Society, and in the Gift, Discerning and Authority of God's Holy and Unerring Spirit, which they acknowledge we once had, and cannot prove, when, and by what we lost it. And blessed be the Lord God of Heaven and Earth, *his Living Power is with us, he owns our Ministry and Fellowship in the Hearts of Thousands, yea Ten Thousands have bowed to the Righteousness of his Scepter, since the Day that perverse Core first troubled our* Israel. *No Tryals have scattered us, nor Sufferings worn us out; but, to the Honour of the blessed Name of the Lord, we have been by it kept to this Day, whose Goodness renews with the Morning, and whose Mercies endure for ever. Blessed are they that fear him, such will he always keep in perfect Peace.*

But the Author of the *Spirit of the Hat*, and his Tyrannical and Hypocritical Defender in his *Libel*, call'd, *Tyranny and Hypocrisy Detected*, cry out, This is *Arrant Popery*. But I will tell such Licentious Spirits, That it is plainly Scriptural; What if a False Church assume the Privilege of a True One, does that make the True Church a False One, for pleading that Privilege? The *Papists* say, God ought to be worshipped; must we not therefore worship him, because they say so? 'Tis just as good as to say, That because one Man cheatingly calls himself by another Man's Name, therefore that other Man must renounce his own Name. Prove Discerning, and Judgment by the Holy Ghost, in any Body, or Society, to be the Mark of a False Church, and ye do your Business, otherwise you must acknowledge it to be the Privilege of a True Church; but deny it to be ours, as we do, that it is the Church of *Rome*'s. But we have prov'd out of your own *Pamphlets,* that you acknowledge us to have been the True Church, and in our own Discourse, that we have continued that, which we ever were: And that God's powerful convincing and converting Ministry remains amongst us; Therefore that Privilege upon your own Principles, does belong to us.

But perhaps they will endeavour to avoid the *Dint* of these convincing Arguments, thus, *We deny not the Body of the People called* Quakers, *nor as they act in the Light, that they have true Judgment: But we complain against your* Foxonian *Unity, which consists of certain Ministers and Elders, which lift up* G. Fox *for a Bishop, a Pope, and a King, making his Papers Edicts, and then entitling them, the Judgment of the Body; whereas indeed 'tis but the Mind of a Cabal of* Foxonians; *the Leaders are the Men we strike at.* See *Spirit of the Hat,* Page 11, 12, 13, 14, 15, 16. *Tyran. Defend.*

But should we allow this to be True, as we reject it for a Slander, 'tis granted to us, that the Body of the People, called *Quakers*, is not their Aim, but some few Particulars that make not up the hundredth Part of the Church (and who will in the Things objected, sufficiently clear themselves) so that the Judgment of the Body is not deny'd, because of the Judgment of some few Elders that displease them. The Question then will be, whether the Body in all Places concerned has given it's Judgment against that innovating Spirit of *John Perrot*, yea or nay? The Determination of which Question gives a great Insight into the present Controversy; In order to which I offer two Things to be considered: *First*, That in all Places where *Jo. Perrot*'s Spirit and Practice made any Appearance through the Churches in this or other Nations, there has been a two-fold Judgment given. 1. That of the Church, in the Fear and Presence of the Eternal God she worships, according to his free Spirit, and that Discerning which was given her of him, concerning which, if there be any Scruple, in the publick Canvas of this Matter, we can readily produce a Multitude of Certificates to verify it. 2. The Judgment of many considerable Persons against themselves and their own Practice, whose Simplicity was betray'd by that dissensious Spirit. But it so happens, that some of them, of how good Report soever, are now not to be credited, because it crosseth the Humour of those Envious Authors, and their prejudiced Adherents. What Name shall we call this Partiality by? Who praised their Honesty when they espoused the Hat, and now question their Conscience in declaring their Mistake: And such is the Fool-Hardiness and Vanity of this *Socinian Apologizer* in the Defence of the *Hat on in Prayer*, That in a great Marginal Note, he cries out, *What's become of* John Osgood's *Integrity, that he should put his Name among such Men as these?* As if we had committed all the Infamies prohibited in the first and second Table of God's Law, rather than seasonably given Check to the boundless Novelties of an Imaginary Innovator. This is your *Universalian*, that tells us *how dangerous it is to be of a Party*, who has bestow'd an whole *Pamphlet* in Defence of one, built upon no better Foundation *than the irreverent Practice of the Hat on in Time of Publick Prayer*. But his own Revilings and unjustifiable Officiousness have prov'd it dangerous to be of such a Party indeed.

But why must not the rest be credited? Are they deceived in Returning? Shew it. Was it imposed upon them, as they suggest? Prove it. *John Pennyman*, if he has not lost all Conscience and Memory, can tell them another Story; For, as became the People of God, for the Decision of this Controversy, a very great Meeting was desired and appointed, unto which both Sorts willingly resorted; So that it was not Imposition, but Choice: In which great and earnest were the Desires and Travels of those who had opposed the Spirit of *John Perrot*, that the Lord himself would please, in some signal Manner, to break forth amongst them, that the Judgment which should pass among them, in order to a Reconciliation, might not be accounted the Judgment of Man, but the Judgment of God. These faithful Cries entred the Ears of the God of Peace, whose Compassions fail not, That with an high Hand and an out-stretched Arm, he rent through the Meeting, that both Sorts were greatly broken, and humbled before the Lord. In which deep and tender Sense, *J. P. J. C.* (though never in the Practice of the Hat) *J. O. J. C. W. P. W. G. G. W.* and *John Pennyman* himself, with very many more (not now to be mentioned) in Fear and Trembling, and great Brokenness of Spirit, to the Astonishment of all Beholders, *plainly and fully testified against the Spirit and Practice of* J. Perrot, *as being out of the Life of the Truth, and Unity of the Body*. And who was more Express, Earnest, Frequent in the Judging that Spirit than this *Envious Apostatiz'd J. Pennyman?* Did he not say of those that opposed *J. Perrot*'s Spirit: *You are more Righteous than we? And if you had not stood we had perisht?* And did not he call that Spirit of *J. Perrot* that led to keep on the Hat in Publick Prayer, *The Spirit of Witchcraft and of the Devil*, and to that Purpose? And is he not now in Defence of that Spirit? What shall we say then upon his present Distance and Enmity? Hath he not pronounced his own Character and Sentence hereby? What Heed is to be given to such a Changeable Self-Contradicting Person? Now, that the Government of our Christian Body should be called *Tyranny*, and the Confessions of these Men *Hypocrisy*, tell me, tell me, thou, that art my impartial Reader, what Sort of Conscience our present Enemies have, thus to treat both the one and the other: How evident is it, that these great Enemies of Imposition would have been the Task-masters themselves, who are Insolent and Uncharitable enough to censure these Men in pulling off their Hats again, to be guilty of *Hypocrify*, who in Fear to God, and the Senfe of his Spirit, condemned the keeping of it on. Deceit! Oh, how unworthily have they dealt with us? and how ill an Ufe have they made of all wholefome Counfel to reclaim them? That little Yielding, that our Friends at firft fhewed to re-gain them, they made Ufe of to confirm them; and their Obftinacy leading us to more Severity, like Baftard Children, they ran away with open Mouth, *bauling into the very Ears of fome Envious and Bufy-body Profeffors, Impofition, Popery, Tyranny, Arbitrary Government*; and thefe are become Themes for fuch prejudiced Perfons as this *Adverfary*, to declaim againft the poor *Quakers* upon. Where it may not be unfeafonably obferv'd; *That if we fhould as ill beftow our Time in gathering up all the Villainous and Impious Mifcarriages of many profeffed Members of the feveral Religious Ways within this Kingdom, I doubt not but we might cut them out more Work than they would be willing to have.* Had we thus begun with them, How Condemnable would they have thought it? But it having been their Practice towards us, we muft not chide them for Injuftice, left we be reputed Railers; For fo big is the Beam in their own Eyes, that the vileft Abufes againft us pafs for Innocent and Juftifiable Things with them.

The *fecond* Thing I have to offer in order to a full Determination, is this; That either the whole Church, or that Part of it which never was concerned in thefe Debates, particularly the *North of* England, *remote from us, yet confifting of a very great Part of the Body of our Friends, both in Number and Solidity, and who have never varied from their firft Station*, upon any general Propofal the prefent *Hat-Men* fhall make for the Demand of their Judgment, provided it may be conclufive with them, (at leaft fo far as to clear Particulars from that high Charge of *Tyranny* and *Hypocrify*) will, we do believe, *freely declare themfelves, according to that Senfe and Underftanding they fhall receive of the Mind of Chrift therein*, from him alone, who is the Leader and Shepherd of his People. If none of all this will do, let them take their Courfe, and furnifh thefe *Ifhmaelites* and Uncircumcifed *Philiftines* with all they can, to our Trouble, God will bring us through it all; And for that Difhonour, they have hereby brought on the Way and People of the Lord in General, by putting their pretended Exceptions againft fome few Particulars into the Hands of thofe Men (who do not fo much ftudy the Difgrace of a few Publick Labourers, as the Overthrow of the whole People and Way, (improving all they can fcrape, how much foever interlined with Falfhood, to that very End) will God, the Righteous and Terrible Judge of Heaven and Earth, require an Account; *and Wo, Sorrow and Eternal Perplexity will be the fwift Recompence of your Treacherous Doings*, unlefs you find a Place for *Repentance*, and can yet wipe away all thefe Scores by true *Contrition*.

Some farther Ground of our Satisfaction in Proceeding againft *keeping on the Hat in Time of Publick Prayer*, efpecially, as we are now concerned with thefe Sort of *Apoftate-Adverfaries*; which is not to difpute, but farther to declare our Belief, and the Reafon of our Practice in the Matter, and fo leave all with the Lord.

I. AS Man confifts of Soul and Body, and as the Body is a Kind of Form to the Soul, fo, whilft Body and Soul remain unfeparated, there will and muft be fome Form fuited to the Body, whereby to exprefs the publick, Spiritual Worfhip performed by the Soul: Such are Places, Words, and Geftures; and, in the Performance of fuch Worfhip, the Body can no more be exempted from fome Form or Expreffion, than can the Soul in it's inward and fpiritual Station. To deny this, is to denote a Man void of Senfe and Reafon; fo that though we grant the Outward and Inward Coming of Chrift, to have abrogated fuch Types and Figures as forefhewed a farther Glory, yet Tokens and Demonftrations of prefent inward Reverence and Divine Honour to God in Publick Performance of Worfhip, we not only never denied, but do affirm them to be as adequate or proper to the Body, as are Reverence and Honour to the Soul.

II. It hath seemed Good to the Holy Ghost, and to us, in the solemn and publick Performance of Prayer unto the Lord, to pull off our Hats, to express the Unveiling of our Spirits, and that reverent Submission and Supplication, which becomes poor Petitioners to come in, and offer up their Desires with, to the Great King of Glory, and God of the Spirits of all Flesh. And God has made it a Token of inward Homage by the Requirings of his own Truth. And it is fit it should be observed, That these present Opposers not only acknowledged the People, called *Quakers*, to be a true Church whilst in this Practice (which I deny any Church to be that continues in the World's Rudiments) and that they have frequently suggested us on this Occasion to be Retainers of; But that they have received heavenly Refreshment by those *Prayers*, that have been offered up by uncover'd Heads: And that God should send forth such a Spiritual *Ministry*, so richly furnished, and rarely qualified, by the Divine Power and Wisdom of God a few Years before, as the Author of *The Spirit of the Hat* confesseth, and that in their Performance of Worship to God, they should be Worldly, and vainly Ceremonious, can be no Ways consistent. And I do here appeal to all sober Persons, if after so large a Testimony, given to the People called *Quakers*, as a True Church, and her Ministry and Worship as Powerful and Pure, before ever this Imagination came forth, it could be any Thing Solid, Seasonable, or Edifying to Introduce or Trouble the Church with that Practice, which they acknowledge She was Blest, and Prosperous without.

III. But again, It denotes and signifies the Difference that is between Worship to God, and Ministry to Man; there is not equal Homage, indeed none at all, in declaring God's Will to Man, but the other is all Matter of pure Homage, and to discover this Difference by some due and suitable Posture, is so far from being unlawful, that the contrary is very condemnable.

IV. It is never to be thought reasonable by People not out of their Senses, at least upon our *Adversary*'s Principles, that a Man should be mov'd to Pray, and yet in that Motion not moved to shew it. What! would they have a Man, when he is moved to Pray, wait for another Motion to be led to discover it? But above all the rest, How do they that stand with their Hats on, testify their Unity with him that prays (as they confess a Man may by the Spirit of the Lord) with his Hat off? I say, What greater Token do they give of their joining with such Prayers, than the *Publican or Pharisee*, who by that very Posture testify their Dislike. But yet farther, Suppose an *Hat-Man* be moved to pray with his Hat off, as they confess he may, What becomes of the rest of that Opinion in the Meeting? If they pull it off meerly as having Unity with his Prayer, then they are gone; for that is our Ground, who say, that Soul and Body, Prayer and Gesture must go together. If they say, it is upon them not to pull it off, Two Things will follow: *First*, The Spirit of the Lord moveth People in the same Meeting, at the same Instant of Time, and in one and the same Duty, unto two contrary Things. 2*dly*, That they may have Unity with the Prayer, and not with the Gesture; with one Motion, and not the other. That they have Unity with the Prayer, and give, and wrap up their Spirits in the present Sense that's stirring in the Assembly, with his that is the Mouth, without an extraordinary Impulse to pray with him in their own Spirits; yet require such a Motion to join with the Gesture; so that they can pray with the Man moved, but not pull of their Hat with the Man so moved. The Confusion, Contradiction and Absurdity of this Imagination, ought for ever to justify the *Quakers* Seasonable, Solid and *Christian* Proceedings against the Introducers and Abettors of it; for a Contradiction in Gesture, when Gesture stands upon Motion, is (proportionably) as real a Resistance against the Spirit, and committing of Disorder in *Christian* Assemblies, as in Matter of Doctrine, or any other essential Part of Worship.

V. The Generality of the Friends in the Nation renounced it; where I cannot but take an Opportunity to defend a Passage in a Private Letter writ by me, upon the Intreaty of one of *John Perrot*'s Disciples, in much Kindness, to satisfy and reclaim him, and cited by the Envious *Author of Tyranny and Hypocrisy Detected*, Page 25.

W. P. saith

1673.

* *W. P.* faith, that God hath given greater Judgment to his Church, than to the individual Members of it, is a true Position, and the Church of *Rome* errs not in that, but in accounting themselves a true Church: These are not my very Words; a Disingenuity, if I am not mistaken this *Author* wrote once almost a whole Book against; however, I abide by the Passage: For if Christ bid Individuals tell the Church, and yet the Church has no more Discerning or Judgment than they had in themselves before such Appeal, and which can't be better'd by it, away with Reason: If in the Multitude of Counsellors there be Safety, respecting Worldly Matters, why not respecting Spiritual Matters? Supposing, as we ever did, that God's Power, Spirit, and Presence preside in any such Church, Body, or Assembly. This is more than the Cavil deserves, but I was willing to express my Mind more fully for the Reader's Satisfaction.

VI. This Innovation brought with it Division, instead of Unity; Confusion, instead of Order; Heart Burnings, instead of Love; and diverted the Minds of some from the more weighty Things of God's Living and Spiritual Law.

VII. Had it been never so Innocent, it cost more than it was worth, and their insisting so much upon it, to the Disturbance of the *Church's Concord*, was no small Evidence of the Wrongness of that Spirit, which introduced and maintained it. This shall sufficiently rebuke and judge both it and them, that it added nothing to Life and Salvation, nor to the Edification of the Body of Christ, *which is the End of every True Motion*; for it carried neither interior, nor exterior Homage, Service or Benefit in the least, either to Persons in their own Particulars, or to the Church in General.

And whereas they frequently have accused the Body of our *Friends*, which still remains, as they once confest, the Body of Christ, of being Guilty of *Popish Customs*, in not being Guilty of their Irreverence; and that the Minds of People were not yet inwardly and spiritually exercised in Worship, it is evident, that their new-fangled Practice, Dissent about it, and continual Defence of it, did more draw out the Minds of some People, and exercise and perplex them about Postures and Gestures, than ever they were before: So that what they falsly charge upon the *Church*, is their own proper Character. Our *Friends* prudent Stop to this troublesom and endless Sort of Innovation, deserves none of those *Hard Names* these *Scurrilous Libels* give both them and their Proceedings.

But they object something *G. F.* and my self have writ against *Hat-Honour*, as, *That we should repute it an Earthly, Vain, and Mean Thing, minded only of Men in the Fall; that if pulling off the Hat were true Honouring or Respecting, Vile Persons would be the most Civil; Real Respect is a more Substantial Thing, manifested by Obedience.* This our *Adversary* quotes out of *G. F's* Book, called, *True Honour among the Jews*; and mine, entituled, *No Cross, No Crown*; but they forgot to be so ingenious, or on Purpose would not be so Just, as to tell People, *That we writ against the Fallen Honour of the Hat to Men*. Because we deny it to Men, must we therefore deny it to God? No: *But we therefore deny it to Men, because we give it only to God, as one of those Gestures, which outwardly distinguishes Worship to God, from Ministry to Man.* But this is their Drift and Ground of their citing those Passages, *That if it be so Mean and Earthly a Thing, to pull off the Hat to Man, how comes it so Eminent a Gesture in Worship, and why not esteemed as earthly and empty a Thing, in respect to Worship as Civil Honour?* I think I give the Force of their Objection, and shall as easily answer it.

That which gives *Weight to any Gesture*, is the *Reason inducing to it*, and *both the End and Frame of the Mind in using of it*. God's Spirit has required this before ever *J. Perrot* was born into so much as the Profession of our Living Way, as a Testimony against the *Ranting Spirits*, that were then very rife in this * Nation, and hath continued it amongst us a *Gospel, Decent, and Reverent Expression*, or *Token of the Unveiling of our Spirits to God in Prayer*. Now strip this Gesture, or

---

* How came this Letter into the Socinian's Hand? Doth not this prove a Cabal? And that *Quondam Quakers*, now Apostates, are their Spies? Was this my Reward for a Loving and Courteous Letter, which kindly invited him to my House, for farther Satisfaction? Treacherous Person! to give it up into proclaimed Enemies Hands, (such Baseness is like an Apostate) and not to grapple with one Part of it's Strength, so disingenuous an Adversary.

* As Dr. Gell and a certain Person of worldly Quality, said, " That had not the Quakers come, the " Ranters had over-run the Nation.

rather

or rather empty it of this solid Reason inducing, and both take away that End, and remove that Frame of Spirit, in which that Gesture is used; and truly we may then very well repute it, *A mean and beggarly Thing for the Sons of Men to bluster about.* To have it in the Sense it is given to God, they cannot: To have it without that Sense, is to have an empty, insignificant Gesture. And should we allow of it, what Distinction could be found to save us from performing that to Man which we do to God? Since the Gesture denotes none, neither can (and our *Adversary* denies a Way to judge the Meanings of an Inward Spirit by) besides Man's requiring, upon an earnest *Thirst* after Honour, that Posture which we only give to God, in his own pure Worship, makes the Doing of it Sinful, if there were nothing else in it; and therefore we deny it to Men, at what Time in the Reverence and deep Humility of our Spirits, we give it to God; out of which Sense it is nothing, but in it, acceptable and requisite. We also know that Men in the Fall, can give but *Fallen Honour*; and where Gestures are invented or practised by a Fallen and Earthly Spirit, the Respect they set upon them, is not the True Honour and Respect, *but Fallen and Earthly*; in this Sense it is we call it *Fallen, Earthly, and Vain*. More Substantial Things may be so reputed, as *Prayer*, &c. when not proceeding from a right Ground, much more a Gesture relating to it. Our *Adversaries* do ill, to conclude so generally; they should have weighed, that as we can give it to God only in the Restoration out of the fallen Ways and Worships of Men, so the Use of it in that Estate, must needs render it a Fallen, Mean, Earthly, and Empty Thing, as indeed are all their Worships, who stand not in the Power and Spirit of God; much more, when any the like Practice is used to Mortal Man. But they farther object a Passage in a Letter to *J. Perrot*, from *R. Hubberthorn*, (ibid. p. 24.) *Then no such Reasonings had we had, if so be the Free Spirit of the Lord had been minded, which is not to be limited, neither to the keeping on the Hat, nor putting off the Hat in Time of Prayer.* But what adds this to their Cause, in Defence of which they brought it, who go about to limit the Spirit, and not we, as *R. H.* also says, for our Business is to be limited by the Spirit, and not to limit it, or, to out-run it. I hope, none will infer from thence, that Men ought to keep their *Hats on:* Or, that the same Spirit would lead to those contrary Gestures, as say some of *J. Perrot*'s Followers: For *R. H.* meant nothing less; but he was sure, if they had kept to that Free Spirit (that had already limited to, and confirmed the pulling it off) *there would not have been such Reasonings about keeping of it on, or off*; And why? Because they would have felt a Pre-conclusion, which would have settled them out of the Reach of the Bondage that Spirit of Delusion had brought them into: For the Liberty of the Spirit stands not in being moved to contrary Things, that is *Ranterism*; but in being freed from every high Thought, and exalted Imagination, to abide in the Order of the Gospel. But our *Adversary*, who can at Times, and for his own Ends engage for any Cause, tells us in *J. Perrot*'s Defence, *That he did not enjoyn the Practice; for he left all to the Free, Universal Spirit,* pag. 24. But after this, our *Adversary*, if he would have defended *J. P.* to Purpose, he should not have told us *Pag.* 32, 33, *that* J. Perrot *had received Command against it from the Lord God of Heaven and Earth in his Captivity at* Rome, *to testify against the Custom and Tradition of Taking off the Hat by Men, when they go to pray to God:* And the Truth is, he did at other Times call it a *Romish Tradition*. But what follows from these two Passages that so greatly justle at one another? Does not the first imply, that a Man may lawfully pull off the Hat in Prayer; and the latter expresly judge it as a Tradition of Men? Either his Command was false, or he was Deceitful in his Answer to our Friends; For that a Man may be left to his Liberty, whether he shall practise the Traditions of Men in the Worship of God (upon *J. Perrot*'s Pretences to Divine Motions altogether in Worship) is the Height of all Contradiction; yet this is the Doctrine of *J. Perrot*, as we have it delivered to us by his *Apologizer*: To give Liberty to pull it off or put it on, as it was with People to do, and yet that he was commanded of God to testify against it positively and generally, as a Tradition of Man; As if People might use, nay, be moved of God, to perform in his Worship any of the Traditions of Men, which God himself had given express Sentence against. It is not short of *Blasphemy* it self. And for our Friends, that is, *G. F. G. W.* and others, which this Man says, owned *J. Perrot*'s Motion for *Rome*, and counted him a good Friend, p. 32. They do aver that they denied that Motion, and never so reputed him. However it be, this *Apologist*, vowed to our Disgrace, bestirs himself not a little in Defence of *J. Perrot* and his Followers, as if *first* he lov'd the Hat on in Time of

Prayer, which he denies in it self; *Secondly*, As if he believed and allow'd of Motions, which he both denies and scorns; *Thirdly*, As if he liked a true *Quaker*, and was not so much displeased at the Light, as at People's Leaving or Confining it in it's Leadings and Requirings; Who by his great Envy to our Persons, shews his Hate to true *Quakers*; and by his base Conclusion from the Pretences of both Parties to have been led to a contrary Thing by the Light within, That the Light is a Kind of Miserable, Uncertain Thing; and waiting to be ordered by it, a very dubious Piece of Business, to the Disgrace of Christ's Light; Reviling then, as well the one Sort as the other, and bringing his Blow well-nigh as hard upon the *Hat-Men* as upon us, see *Page* 23, 24, 25, 71, and *ult*. In which the Drift of his Business is to drive People off from the Leadings of the Light, instead of pleading on the Behalf of these *Apostates* being led into that Practice by it, as he vainly doth, *Page* 32, 33. Let Disingenuous *W. M.* and Furious *J. Pennyman* see to what Pass they have brought their Affairs, who, under the Pretence of proving the *Quakers* Apostacy from the Teachings of the Light, have furnisht a Man with Complaints against us, who could so little dissemble his Dislike against the *Principle* it self, as to conclude *Uncertainty*, *Confusion* and *Blasphemy* to attend that very Assertion about the Light's Teaching, which the People, called *Quakers*, in the Beginning made, and is by this Adversary, in other Places, on these *Apostates* Account seemingly pleaded for. Let them glory in this Man's Endeavours, if they will; Their wicked *Hypocrisy* and great *Treachery* are herein manifest beyond what may at this Time be said by us: They loved the Motions of the Principle at an odd Rate that set a Man to defend them that is an Enemy to them. His Conclusions prove what I said in mine Introduction, that it was against the *True* Quakers *and their ancient confest Principle he chiefly levelled his Scoffs, Nick-Names, Reflections and gross Perversions, and not meerly against us as False* Quakers, *or Persons gone from our first Principle.*

To prove this, behold how, and why he triumphs! *That our Principle admits of no Means whereby to discern one immediate Teaching from another.* Perrot *says one Thing, and* Fox *another; Who is in the Right?* or to that Purpose.

It would have done well if *W. M.* and *J. P.* had answered this Objection, before they furnisht him to plead their Cause and defend them to be in the Right, from those Motions their own *Apologist* denies any Certainty to; and I may now take Occasion to ask him, why he is so peremptory in his Censures of us to be in the Wrong, who denies any Certainty of Judgment of either Side? How comes he so certain in Condemning and Justifying? Partial Man! But no greater Evidence can well be given of the Wrongness of *J. Perrot*'s Spirit, than has been already related, viz. *The Disturbance of the Church; The Unprofitableness of the Thing; The scandalous Lapse and Apostacy of himself and several of his Followers, and the Judgment others zealously past against themselves whose Simplicity had been betrayed.* The Fruits testify what Spirit it was, though, upon our Adversary's saying, that there is no inward Test or Trial of Spirits, at least implying so much, he contradicts Scripture, and undervalues the Gift of God; For he had as good say, *That a wrong Spirit, covered with fair and undeniable Pretences, is not discernable by the Light and Spirit of God within; A Man may be wrong within, and Right without, have the exact Form, but not the Power of Godliness.* What can try Spirits, but the Spirit? No Writing can tell me a Wrong from a Right Spirit in the Ground, though it may describe good and bad Fruits, and from such Actions Men may by a Writing describe the Right from the Wrong; But what gives to relish, taste, favour, a Wrong Spirit in Sheep's Clothing, beside the Heavenly Instinct of the Divine Nature? As People are turned to that they can discern, as saith the Apostle, *The Spiritual Man judgeth all Things*, (that is, of Right he may) *and is judged of no Man* (that is, not discerningly of the meer Natural Man) And as the Spiritual Man's Discerning is from the Spirit that searcheth out the deep Things of God, so is God the Judge and Law-giver to his People under this Dispensation. If the Gospel-Fellowship be in Spirit, True *Christians* must have an Inward Taste and Sense of one another's Spirits; and what gives to favour a right, *at the same Time, gives to relish a Wrong Spirit.* The same *Objection* he makes against the Light may be made against the *Spirit*, (which is but another Name for the same Principle) and I hope, he will not dare to say that any Confusion can follow upon holding that *Men under the Gospel ought to be led by it:* Yet, this granted, suppose Men pretending to be led by the Spirit, to be gone from the Spirit, or that Men equally pretending to be guided by it, differ, as *Paul* and *Barnabas* and *Peter*, what should

should determine? No *Writings* of the Old Testament could, at least without *Meanings*; and the same Difficulty lies about the Meanings of *Scripture*, as about being led by the Spirit. In this Case what shall be done? Surely the Spirit must not be upbraided nor branded: Neither will it follow, *That there is no Judge*; for Christ is the great Judge, appointed of God, the Spiritual great Prophet that speaks from Heaven, and in his own Time will give Judgment to the View of all Men. In the mean while he satisfies the Minds of those who are truly led by his Spirit; and Withering, Decay, Murmuring, Complaining, and finally Apostacy will follow upon the Pretenders, as is fulfilled in the present *Judasses*. This hath been largely argued elsewhere, yet I was not willing to let this Passage of our Enemy's pass unconsider'd, which indeed is the Strength of his Book, and what the ablest of our *Adversaries* can say against us on this Account.

I have proceeded thus far more particularly in Defence of the Church, against the *Apostate Adversaries* and their *Apologist*, about the Argument by them made about the *Hat*, and those Discords that ensued; In which I hope, I have not exceeded the Bounds of Truth and Moderation.

For the latter *Objection*, which is directed not so much against the *Body* of our Friends, as *a select Number of Ministers and Elders devoted*, as he falsly and scoffingly suggests, *to the Promotion of G. F's Authority and Interest*, I can with all Clearness and Sincerity, and that in the Name of many Brethren, give this following Testimony.

G. F. I would have all to know, *seeks not Himself*, but Christ, and as becomes a true Apostle, and Servant of his Lord and Master, Jesus Christ, Early and Late, in Season and out of Season, with incessant Pains and Care, (not being Burthensome unto any) endeavours to promote the Work of God in the Earth; and is so *far from Lording it over any*, that he daily serves all for the Truth's Sake, thinking no *Labour* too great, nor *Condescension* too mean, whereby he may be serviceable to any, in what concerns their eternal Well-fare; and this some of these *Apostates* must needs know He has approved himself, and still doth among us, to be *a Man of God*, and *a True Prophet of the Lord*; and as such, we do value him, and the Rage of Men shall not Dis-settle us from our Sense and Regard of him, who seeks not himself, nor his own Things, but the Things of God, that Christ, and his Power alone may be exalted in the Hearts of all People, and all Flesh humbled; and for this alone are all publick Labourers of Value with our Friends, and no otherwise Respected or Regarded than in the Lord, which is not *Tyranny*, but *Duty*: Wherefore those Terms, of *Foxonian*, *King George Fox*, *Foxonian Leaven*, G. Fox *and his Party* or *Adherents*, are with many more, Words of Scorn and Abuse; he has no such intended Lordship, nor are we of his Party, but *God's Free-Men*, and True *Christians*, being with him Baptized *by One Spirit into One Body*; the Unity of which these smiting *Apostates* and their abusive *Libeller* can never break.

I shall touch upon their Aggravations about not *Marrying*, *Burying*, &c. before I come to those other Reflections made against G. F. our *Ministry*, and *My self*, and all before I end my Share in this Re-joinder.

First, He is pleased to say, *That we deny Trading, Marrying, Burying, and all Ecclesiastical and Civil Privileges to those that dissent from us*, p. 7. These were the Aggravations I before promised to observe.

But alas! What shall we say to a Man thus hardy, and resolv'd to be Wicked, that he may render us so? Did we ever forbid Men *Trading*, or endeavour to take People off from Trading with them? *J. Pennyman* can say no such Thing without Lying; for several have lovingly frequented his Shop, since he enviously visited and disturbed our Meetings: And how many do we daily trade with, that are not of us, in Love and full Assurance of their Honesty.

For *Marrying*, I referred the Author of the *Spirit of the Hat* to the Apostle's Dehortation, *Be ye not unequally Yoked together*. It seems, if we cannot own Persons to be of us, that are not of us, we must be abused. This made the present *Apologizer* (if I am not out of my Guess) Angry and Enraged with us at first. 'Tis not meer Talking of Christ, and hammering out a few Notions in the meer Strength of Man's Will and Wisdom, that makes a *True Christian*; therefore we could not receive him for our *Sect-Master*, that angers him. And for *Marriage*,

1673.

we cannot have Unity with any in that Solemn Performance of Marrying, who are acted by a Wrong Spirit, and so gone out of the Union of the Body of Friends: We do not deny them that are so Married, to be Married at all, as this Enemy would conclude, though to be Married in the Unity we can never own them.

As to our denying of *Burial* unto such *Apostates*, my Words in the Book, called, *The Spirit of Alexander the Copper-smith Rebuked*, carry no such unnatural Sense. Two Things I denied (1.) *That we therefore denyed them a Burial, because we should always refuse it as of us, whilst they continued in that Dissenting Spirit from us.* (2.) *That we Usurped their Property.* To the first, says our Adversary, *They* (Quakers) *would not suffer such to stink above Ground, but he should be buried, not among the Catholicks; but as Hereticks in Spain or Italy*, p. 19.

Behold the Candor of this Interpreter! What a strange Improvement has he made of my Sayings? much more resembling the Carriage of that Sort of *Catholicks* (he likens us to) against such pretended *Hereticks*, as the poor *Waldenses*, than we do in the Case of Burial.

I say again, That as our Friends intended upon their first Purchase of a *Burying Place*, that their Dead Bodies should lie together from the People of distinct Ways, which is warrantable from *Abraham's* Practice in *Genesis*; so do they not desire, that such as have been of them, and have afterwards run out, should lie among them, unless it be the Desire of the Deceasing Parties, or that they declare their Unity with Friends: yet we would not by any Means be thought to deny any Person whatever, a *Burying-Place*, though we could never allow it to them as one of us, since that were most unnatural. I would fain know, if this *Adversary* would observe no Distinction in this Case? or what Injury there is done, in making that Difference, *when Dead*, which was observed by the deceast Party himself, *when Alive?* For the Property that he says some of them have, 'tis true, and was never denyed; but that we usurpt it, we did and do reject as a Slander: They never desired their Part of the Collection that bought it, nor did we ever refuse to repay it, but are ready to be quit with them when they will; a Perverse Apostatized Generation! For *Ecclesiastical Privileges*, I know not what he means; and those Scoffs ill become a Man that pretends to Religion: Such Privileges, as are the peculiar Right of every true Member of Christ's Church, it must be confest, that such Starters aside from the Primitive Fellowship of it, *do deprive themselves of Church-Privileges*; we don't. But this, says he, *is more than any beside the* Papist *dare pretend to; the* Protestant, *or Church of England challenges no such Power*, p. 5. But he that has ventured to tell so many false Things of us, may dare to bestow one upon her, especially when it is considered, that he is a *Concealed Person*, and may be *False and Base with Security*. Does not the *Church of England*, both Excommunicate, and stir up the Civil Magistrate against such as dissent from her in meer Circumstances? Does not the long Difference between her and the ancient *Puritans, Presbyterians and Independents, Baptists*, and Us more particularly, sufficiently Disprove that bold Assertion? But we pretend not to imitate any; but really act according to that Understanding and Sense which God has given us in these Things, and in which we commend our selves to him, being herein willing to abide his Judgment.

To the Rest of those Cruelties he makes us guilty of, he doth, with the Author of the *Spirit of the Hat*, charge us *with Pulling down, Haling out of our Meetings, and consequently wanted only Power to punish them*; adding, *That my Appeal to God's Witness in all Consciences, for our Vindication, shows me greatly to be lamented, as either Blind or Impudent; That we have also Pusht, Pincht, Kickt and Trod upon Feet and Toes*, sending us to *Francis Chadwell* for Proof thereof.

But, to say nothing of his Ill-Language, my Appeal stands as it did; and as before, so now I will put it between Impartial and Moderate Men, if ever we so used any Consciencious Inquirer, or Opposer? No, nor any else after that Manner represented by our Adversary; and God will plead our Innocency against him, in the Hour of his Righteous Judgments, he shall not go Uncondemned down to his Grave.

For *Francis Chadwell*, he is a Man of no Conscience, nor Credit, in what relates to us; I my self have known him grosly guilty both of *Lying* and *Tipling*: No frothy Stager is less to be regarded in Religion, than this Man's Witness, *a Light, Scoffing, Taunting, Tumultuous Person*; who after an Hundred Solid Confutations, One of which had been enough to strike an ingenuous Man to the Heart, has continued

tinued to Bawl and Disquiet our Meetings, Time after Time: His Aim hath been to raise up an Envious and Scoffing Spirit in People against us, Jeering, Laughing, Houting, with such unseemly Carriage, as wholly unbefit him for a Witness against us; He had as good as confest, that he has been Hired by some Professors to disturb us; and told me, *If I would give him Five Hundred Pounds he would be a* Quaker *too*; yet, this is our *Socinian Adversary's Serious, Conscientious Inquirer, or Opposer.*

He also brings in one *William King*, whom he says, *We Haled out of our Gallery in* Grace-Church-Street, *with such Violence, that he hath scarce felt the Stairs, but that he hath often felt our Cruel Hands, witness* G. Whitehead's *Pinching him in the Arm, at* Jer. Clark's *House; and that We would not suffer him a Prisoner among us, though for the same Cause, and all this for some Disagreement in Judgment.*

I confess, I have no great Acquaintance with the Man; but *first*, deny that ever he was haled out of *Grace-Church-Street*, or any where else; but it may so happen, that he offering to keep the Meeting when ended by our Friends, the People pressing out, and he speaking, might bear him away with a Croud, which hath fallen out to many that have been Speakers, and not Opposers: Perhaps some disturbed and hindred of Hearing, may on their own Account have shov'd him, or put him by; what's that to us?

For G. *Whitehead*'s Pinching him, it is like the rest, full of Slander; He is known to be a Man of more Temperance and Command of himself, if he had been provoked. 'Tis true, He took him by the Sleeve to turn him to a Looking-Glass, that he might behold his Envious and Passionate Countenance, as *G. W.* avers, and others present: But had it been true, how one Pinch can prove that he had Often felt our Cruel Hands; Unbyassed Readers may best judge.

That he was a Prisoner is confessed; that we Refused him to be among us, is denied: But that we were not in Unity with him, we are not afraid to own. I know not that I ever spoke to him but once, and that was in *Newgate*, being a Prisoner my self; and if he will speak Truth, he can say nothing bad of me. For G. *Whitehead's Charging* Henry Pawson *not to entertain him*, it is false; For what is it but to suggest, that we would Refuse him common Hospitality? 'Tis true, that *G. W.* as in Conscience-bound, warned them of him, as one of the Ancient Creepers into Houses, Disaffected to the Brethren, and Prone to Discords (as by his frequent Disturbances in our Meetings is evident) therefore not to entertain him as one in Unity with us; but if he, or any of them want (supposing first their Lawful Endeavours to procure sufficient Maintenance) I know not one among us, who would not readily Administer to their Necessities.

But we gave out a Paper against John Pennyman *when he was in Prison, and would not spare that grave, ancient Gentle-Woman* Ann Mud, *who being Moved to speak a few Words,* T. Matthews *pulled her away by Violence, and that we were the People in former Days that vexed, and disquieted all Sorts of Religious Assemblies, and clamoured against those as Persecutors, that obtained their Peace by Thrusting and Carrying us out.*

But I will tell him *first*, that our Paper against *John Pennyman* was as necessary to clear us from that Instigation of the *Devil* that led him to give up to burn the Scriptures of Truth, and the Writings of Friends (which were some of those Papers) this Apologizer (fitted for all turns of Deceitful Evasion) calleth *Wast*, p. 37. under the Pretence of the Motion of God's Spirit, as for an Innocent Man, in Sight of a Murder, to clear himself from being guilty of so heinous a Fact. We delighted not at his Imprisonment, for we were wounded by the Cause of it; and had great Reason to deny that Action, which brought a Reproach upon our Principle and Practice, that never belonged to either. God's Spirit hath hitherto led us to Read, Believe, Obey and Witness the Scriptures, and not to tear them, as did our Adversary's Orthodox *Elizabeth Barnes* (p. 52.) in the Height of Rage before mine Eyes; and offer to burn them, as did his so much *Commended and Defended* John Pennyman. I perceive, this *Socinian* Author denies our Testimony by his Dislike of it, and consequently owns that Wicked Position, *That the Spirit of God may lead a Man to burn the Scriptures of God*; against which our Testimony was mainly directed.

For his *ancient, grave Gentle-Woman* (as he calls her) she hath been so Unhappy as through her Excess of Affection to *J. Pennyman*, to be a Sharer with him in his perverse Out-cries against us; yet I can scarcely think that she will attest any such Thing:

Thing: But if it were true, as I believe it to be false, it can be no valid Argument against the *Faith, Worship or Actions of the Body of the* Quakers. But, why Moved? Methinks, here and in *J. P*'s Case, he hath learned to pronounce *Moved*, as if he believed the Spirit in these Days used any such Thing. Is he angry with us for resisting *Ann Mud*'s Motion, who himself, p. 32, 33, 71. denies the Certainty of any such Thing? but Envy blinds Men. We shall also grant that we are the Men whom the Eternal God from Time to Time raised to testifie against the *Hireling Teachers* that took Money for that which was not Bread, but were like Wolves in Sheep's Clothing, devoured the Flock, and made a Prey of the People; and God hath blessed us in that Service, for before a Gathering, there was to be a Scattering: And God made us Instrumental to turn People from Darkness to Light, from the Power of Satan unto God, *by directing their Minds to the Gift of His Holy Light and Spirit, which discovers the Deeds of Darkness, convinceth the World of Sin, revealeth the Mind and Will of God, and gives Power to the Creature that believes in it, to obey and do it.*

For this Testimony in the Hirelings Synagogues, *did the False* Jew, *or* Christian, *Hale, Tear, Beat, Bruise, Knock down, Stock, Whip, Imprison,* with many such like Horrid and Inhuman Actions, which became not our Adversary's Interest (had he been an Impartial *Historian*) to mention: But, have we been no otherwise disturbed? or have we so used our Disturbers? Our Faithful Chronicles of the Bloody Tragedies of that Professing Generation will tell future Ages other Things. O the Partiality of this *Socinian* Apologizer for our Disturbers! But to close this. Either our Adversary condemns our former Testimonies against the *Priests* in their *Steeple-Houses*, or he does not; if he does, he cannot justifie the Senseless Bawlings of Proud and Envious *J. Pennyman, Francis Chadwel* and the like Disturbers of our Assemblies, upon his own Comparison. If he justifies their Disturbances of us, especially those given by his *Prime and Singular Witness*, F. Chadwel, with what Face can he censure our Serious and Solemn Admonitions, or Reproofs in the *National Synagogues*: Let it be as it will with him, we expect an higher Judgment, and to that shall we gladly yield.

And for those Two or Three Stories of the Wantonness and Uncleanness of some particular Persons among us, though it is spoken to in some following Testimonies, yet I have thus much to say; *J. W*'s Name is Basely and Falsly used by the Libeller, though he could not have mentioned it but upon Information from some of these Defaming *Apostates*, whom God will judge, for endeavouring to Murder the Reputation of an Ancient, Solid, Faithful Labourer in God's Work. Shall *Ifs* and *may be's* conclude Men Guilty? It is not the first Mistake *W. M.* if he be their Informer, hath committed, whose Jealous Surmising Soul can scarce do any Thing else in Cases relating unto us, as I have experienced: His *Worth* is lighter to the Man, his Name is brought in to slander, than the Chaff to the Wheat.

For *the two Young Women,* concerning whom *M. T*'s Information is cited, they were examined; Childish, Toyish, and unseemly Carriages were with much Contrition confest: but for any such gross Wickedness, as was and is suggested by these Men, they said it was false, if there was a God in Heaven. For *M. T.* we shall say no more till we have a more express Account of his Concernment in that *Libel*, or Information mentioned therein: We see no Name to it, and might as well suspect that with other Things; however, our Friends behaved themselves in that Matter as became God's People to do.

For *T. M.* One Story is cleared by the Woman's Testimony, and *W. M*'s Malice discovered. For his common Uncleanness under Pretence of Physick, *&c.* We know not how to allow it for Truth, as exprest: But this is certain, that he has been several Years since dealt withal by our Friends, and in particular by a *Physician* about it; and in what there was any just Ground to Condemn him for, he was judged, his other Unwatchful Carriages denied, and his Conversation turned from by our Friends.

Lastly, Suppose these Enemies of God, and his Work, and People, could Say and Prove Ten Times as much; shall those Miscarriages bring many Thousands of People out of Request, and go for an utter Blast upon their Faith, or Way? Vain Men! Should we tell the Stories of the Abominable Practices of both such Apostates, and some envious *Professors*; what of Sin could we not find several that have profest their Way guilty of? But we will make no *Musick* for the *Atheist.*

Has

Has not every Miscarriage, as Known, been Reproved? Yes; Every Unfruitful Work of Darkness, as by the Light within, when known only by the Party Offending, so by the Light in our Friends, as a Church, when known to them. Is not this Gospel-Order? Or must some raw Slips of Unwatchful Persons Antichristian our whole Society?

Reader, These Things and Persons objected, have been several Years since examined; who were Innocent, Acquitted; and who were Guilty, Condemned, according to the Righteous Law of God: And upon this old Condemned Stuff our Enemies feed, with this they Arm themselves against us, and upon this Quagmire, as their best Foundation, they stand. In short, They have been False to God, Abusive to his People, Hurtful to the Moderate, and basely Treacherous to their Ancient Friends. If being Base to God and Men can render Men *Christian*, then they deserve to be so accounted of: But till *Religion* cometh to be read Backwards, let them go for Enemies to *Christianity*, and Murderers of Natural Affection.

To conclude, Our *Ministry* is of God; it stands in the Power of the Living Spiritual Gift of God, to testifie against all Ungodliness: And if any Particular has ever slipt, and brought Dishonour to the Truth, such hath been Reproved in Righteousness, and only Received upon Unfeigned Repentance; which is God's Way. But to Publish, Proclaim and Aggravate Miscarriages of Any to the World, who profess Religion, committed many Years ago, Examin'd, Judg'd, and they Forgiven, upon Repentance, by the Lord, and therefore Received again by us; and all this done with Design to blast our Credit, Disgrace the Way we profess (tho' they were no way concerned to meddle or interpose) To do all this, I say, is not to be acted by the Spirit of God, but That, of an Accursed *Ham*, and Treacherous *Judas*; and the Lord will avenge our Cause, we doubt not, in due Time.

But an Heinous *Blasphemy* is laid to the Memory of *Josiah Coale*, by this Angry Agent, in Behalf of these *Apostates*; and that is, a Passage in a Letter writ anciently by him, in his Life-time to G. *Fox*, viz.

That G. F. *was the Father of many Nations*.

But what *Blasphemy* is in this? Is it any more than to say, That by him, as an Instrument in the Hand of God, People of many Nations have been begotten to God? Was not *Paul* a Father of many Nations, who begot the *Corinthians*, that were *Greeks*, and the *Romans*, that were *Latins*? But farther,

Whose Life hath reached through us thy Children, even to the Isles afar off, to the begetting of many again unto a lively Hope, for which Generations to come shall call thee Blessed.

Very well; And what *Blasphemy* lodges in these Words? Is not that which is the Life of one Good Man the Life of another? Were not the *Christians* of old by One Spirit baptized into One Body? What Life G. F. had was from Christ Jesus and it was no other Life J. *Coale* writ of: And I hope, *The Life of Christ is one in All*; and who can limit it? And *Josiah Coale*, with others, were Children in the Sense afore-mentioned; and that Life through those Children, by him (instrumentally) begotten, did reach to those *Isles* afar off, unto which he and others went to preach the Everlasting Gospel. *Paul* reached to the Churches, though afar off, 2 *Cor*. 13. 10. He was Present in Spirit, though Absent in Body; for, *I verily, as Absent in Body, But Present In Spirit, have judged already, as though I were present——In the Name of our Lord Jesus Christ, when ye are gathered, and My Spirit in the Power of the Lord Jesus Christ, cast forth* (and taken in too upon Repentance, without going to the Lord Mayor and Alderman) 1 *Cor*. 5. 3, 4. His Life and Hope was through *Timothy*, *Titus*, and others, extended unto many. And why shall not Generations to come *call an* Apostle *Blessed*; and bless the Name of the Lord for him, respecting the Benefit any such one might be in God's Power to a People? Is not the Memory of the Just Blessed? *Prov*. 10. 7. And did not the Lord by his Prophet say of *Israel* his People, *I will make thee an Eternal Excellency, and the Joy of many Generations?* Isa. 60. 57. What if J. *Coale* had so spoke of G. F. and God's *Israel* now? Would it have been *Blasphemy*? But these Err, not knowing the Scriptures, nor the Power of God, like the *Jews* of old.

But yet again, *whose Being and Habitation is in the Power of the Highest.*

And so is the Being and Habitation of every Child of God, or else he is in the Power of the *Lowest*, *the God of the World, whose Habitation is in Darkness*. Are we not to turn away from such as stand not in the Power of Godliness? And did not the Apostle go, to turn People from the Power of *Satan* unto the Power of God,

1673.

God, which is the Power of the Highest? And is it notwithstanding *Blasphemy* to stand in it, or testifie of one that doth stand in it, that he doth so stand? O the Idle Opposition! but great Envy of our Enemies! They seek nothing less than the Blood of this Upright Man, as the next Words, and their Aggravation of them prove.

In which Thou Rulest and Governest in Righteousness, and thy Kingdom is establisht in Peace, and the Increase thereof is without End.

Upon this our *Adversary* takes frequent Occasion scoffingly to call him, *King George*; suggesting him to be so vile an *Impostor*, as to assume unto himself *the Compleat and Peculiar Dignity, Dominion and Authority due to Christ*. See *Pag.* 53, 54, 55. Which *Blasphemy*, I am of the Mind, our *Adversary* thinks deservedly Punishable *after the Severest Sort of Death*. But he unworthily traduceth that Good Man, and lays the Harmless Scripture-Expressions of a departed Servant of the Lord, upon the *Tenters* or *Rack*, that he may stretch them to his own Vile and Bloody Purposes. Hath this Man forgot that there were ever such Passages writ, as these? *The Good Seed are the Children of the* Kingdom, Mat. 13. 28. *The* Kingdom *of God is within*, Luke 17. 20. *The Saints shall judge the World*, 1 Cor. 6. 2, 3. *But ye are a* Royal *Priesthood*, 1 Pet. 9. 2. *And thou* (the Lamb) *hast made us unto our God* Kings *and* Priests, *and we shall* Reign *on the Earth*, Rev. 5. 10. *And I appoint unto you a* Kingdom, *as my Father hath appointed unto me, that ye may Eat and Drink at my Table in my Kingdom, and* Judge *on Thrones the Twelve Tribes of* Israel, Luke 22. 29, 30. *It is the Father's good Pleasure to give you a* Kingdom, Luke 12. 23. *who hath translated us into the* Kingdom *of his dear Son*, 1 Col. 13. [the Untranslated therefore Rage] *Wherefore we have received a* Kingdom *that cannot be shaken*, Hebr. 12. 28. [they then had it] *I beheld, and the same Horn made War with the Saints, and prevailed against them, until the Ancient of Days came, and* Judgment *was given to the* Saints *of the Most High; and the Time came that the* Saints possessed the Kingdom, *whose Kingdom is an everlasting Kingdom*, Dan. 7. 21, 22, 27. By all which it is manifest, that it is the Privilege of every Saint and Child of God to be a *King*, a *Royal Priest*, to have a *Kingdom*, and to *Rule, Govern, and Reign in Righteousness and Peace without End*. So that *Josiah Coale*, and every *Heir* and *Co-heir with Christ*, Rom. 8. 17. doth as well reign in an Everlasting Kingdom of Righteousness as *G. F.* doth, or shall do; for we have One Faith, One Baptism, One Power, One Lord, One Kingdom. Where let it be noted, that by all these Titles and Privileges, we only mean and understand, *Dominion over, Not Bodies nor Souls, Not Flesh nor Blood*; but in the Sense of the Apostle, *Ephes.* 6. 12. *Principalities and Powers, the Rulers of the Darkness of this World, and Spiritual Wickednesses in High Places*, which center in the Invisible, Dark Power of the God of the World, that since the Beginning hath drawn and acted Man out of God's Counsel and Power, in which the Kingdom stands: *For though we walk in the Flesh or Body, we do not War after the Flesh; for the Weapons of our Warfare are not Carnal, but Mighty through God, to the pulling down strong Holds, casting down Imaginations, and every high Thing, that exalts it self against the Knowledge of God*, 1 Cor. 10. 4, 5. And as our *War* and *Weapons*, so our *Kingdom* is not Carnal, but Spiritual; not of this World, but that which is without End; and of this we are not asham'd

It may not be unseasonable to take Notice of that Passage in his Book so often mention'd, eagerly insisted upon, and aggravated to the Height of *Ananias*'s Belying the Holy Ghost, viz. That G. Fox, *this Great Prophet* (as he in Abuse calls him) *should break open and alter the Contents of* John Whitehead's *Letter, which (as he said) was writ in the Name of the Lord, and that to a quite contrary Sense; making the Letter to judge those that kept the Hat on, whereas J. W. therein justified both, those that kept it off, or on*. Thus, saith our Adversary, doth G. Fox *bely both* John Whitehead *and the Holy Spirit of God, and that knowingly*. He proceeds, *O prodigious Impudence! He that counterfeits any Man's Name in a Matter of any Concernment deserves to be exposed on the* Pillory, *and to lose his Ears; How much greater * Punishment doth he deserve that Counterfeits both the Name of God and Man, in a Matter of Religious Concern*. This, says he, *is the Course that* G. F. *took to make his Injunctions to be observed*.

But this is the Course more truly to make the Impiety of this Adversary more Notorious. For first, *G. Fox* never opened his Letter, nor made any Alteration in it at all, that I dare affirm in so many Words; much less did he belie the Holy Spirit; and, least of all, do it willingly. I perceive by his Conclusion, fion, he acknowledges that the Holy Ghoſt as really mov'd in *J. Whitehead* as in *Peter*, contrary to his own Principle. Any Thing will they all grant, that they may Slander or Injure us in the Minds of the People. How knows he it was a true Motion? Doth he not deny it may be known? If ſo then, How dare he be ſo poſitive in the Cenſure of *G. Fox*? Will he make the Motion uncertain, and yet certainly judge *G. F.* for a *Forger*, who was yet Innocent? I leave it to the *Reader*, what to call this Part of his Tale. Secondly, *J. Whitehead* gave Power by Letter at that Time to the Brethren of London, *to ſupervife and alter it, as they ſhould ſee convenient*: and no otherwiſe was *G. F.* concerned in it, than as one aſſenting with other of our Friends, that, according to Power given and their beſt Underſtanding, did alter it for the better, and herein did *J. W.* teſtifie his Unity and Fellowſhip; *for the Spirits of the Prophets are ſubject to the Prophets*: So that what was done, was no more than what *J. Whitehead* left Power to do, and which the Scripture juſtifies. Wherefore Prodigious Impudence belongs not to *G. F.* but this hardy Adverſary; and Prodigious Cruelty, Perſecution, if not Murder too, is he guilty of that would have him not only *Pillory'd, and loſe his Ears, but his Life too*, or ſomething very near a-kin to it. This is confirmed pag. 33. where he charges us to be *Blaſphemers*, and that ſuch ought to Dye by the Law of God in former Times; The Conſequence is plainer than his Power to execute it. *O the Miſeries! O the Forgiveneſs of theſe exceeding Meek, Suffering, Bruiſed Little Ones!* As they would have us think: *But, O Deceitful and Blood-thirſty Generation!* Who have endeavoured what in you lies, to betray with your *Treacherous Kiſs of pretended Love to our Souls*, our Faith, Reputations and Lives too, into the Hands of ſome Bloody-minded *Jews*, who are not of the Circumciſion in Spirit, but luſt againſt thoſe that are, that they may be ſtirred up againſt us; But God will reckon with you and them too, for theſe Things.

This Adverſary takes an Occaſion to faſten a Lye upon a Paper ſet forth in the Name of the *Quakers*; but he ſays, writ chiefly by *G. F.* and *G. W.* in ſaying, *That we have paid our Taxes and other Dues more than any People, according to our Abilities.* When (ſays our Adverſary) *their Neighbours know all over* England *there are (at leaſt) ſome Taxes or Aſſeſſments, which they have peremptorily refuſed.* But why muſt we be branded for Lyars becauſe of that Saying, or our Adverſary's baſe Aggravation? I do affirm, *That we have been overſet more than any*; and Paying thoſe Extream Aſſeſſments gives good Ground for Saying what we did. But indeed, ſome *Hat-Spirits* perhaps could not ſay ſo; but why? *Becauſe ſome of them are ſo leavened into another Spirit, that they almoſt queſtion the Payment of any, as* M. Boreman, *now called* M. Pennyman, *did*.

I muſt not be plainer, leſt the *Cabal* farther repreſent me as one that expoſes Perſons to the Laſh of * Government. Wherein we can pay we do, what ever they come for, and in ſome Caſes, wherein we cannot anſwer their Demands for Chriſt's Peaceable Goſpel-ſake, They commonly Take Three Times the Value, ſeldom, if ever, Returning any again; But this our Adverſary calls no *Paying*: Sure I am, it is Loſing more than our Adverſary dare adventure; for if I miſtake not, he can ſend out all thoſe Things rather than ſuffer, though perhaps againſt his Conſcience alſo.

Well, *but*, if we will believe him, *there is ſuch an Arrogant, Imperious and Audacious Paper given forth by* R. Farnſworth, A. Parker, G. Whitehead, J. Coale, J. Whitehead, T. Loe, S. Criſp, T. Green, T. Moon, *and* J. Parks, *as he thinks was never given forth by Mortals*. A Charge ſo great, and a Reflection ſo ſharp, that it had need be one of the worſt Papers that was ever writ. Now let us hear what it is.

1. *They allow not ſuch to have Dominion in the Church, who exalt themſelves above the Body of Good and Ancient Friends.*

Now, what hateful Thing did they deliver in this wholeſome Chriſtian Saying? It ſeems, this Enemy of God, and true Righteouſneſs, would have liked us better, *if Bad Friends had been ſuffered to exerciſe the Dominion over the Body of Good and Ancient Friends.* But he ſtarts out thus, *That by the Body of Good and*

---

* But is not this to render us Obnoxious to the Government? I abhor that Practice: But baſe and ſelf-ended Spirits are to be humbled, and not think themſelves fit to cry down other People's Religion, that have by Treachery, Perſecution and Falſeneſs too much reproacht all Religion; Let them leave Scribling and Snarling with their Writings, and Repent.

Ancient Friends is meant G. Fox *and his Adherents*; which Sort of Interpretation well becomes such a *Cabalistick Writer*; for after those Allowances, I could misrender the best Cause, Pretences or Actions in the World. It is an arrant Falshood: He was then far from them; Neither had they him in their Eye in doing it, but God's Honour, and the Church's Peace.

2. *That such as are not in the Unity with the Ministry and Body, have no Gospel-Authority to be Judges in the Church: And that it is abominable Pride, when any Particular will not yield* To the Witness of God in Friends.

But what is the Matter with our Adversary? Hath he lost his Wits that he makes this so Criminal? Are any to be Judges in that Church they have no Unity with? and amongst the Ministry they deny, or are at Distance from? Strange Contradiction!

But why is it so Heinous, to call such Proud or Self-willed, *who resist the Witness of God in Friends?* Certainly the Expressions are sound, unless Scripture be defective: He that can see any Thing in them, that deserveth such hard Words, as this *Billingf-gate Rhetorician* bestoweth upon us, has better Eyes than I.

3dly, *But they say, That the Church (without Dissenters) has Power to Determine Controversies.*

Very well; and is it not true? Are the Dissenters from the Church Part of the Church they dissent from? For Shame! Thou Learned, and talk so Idly? Scripture declares, That God has given the Power of Determination to his Church: All the World knows, That Dissenters are not of that Church they dissent from; therefore the Church without Dissenters, has that Power of Determination.

4ly, and 5ly, *But they add, That such disapproved Ministers, ought to leave off Ministring till they are Reconciled to the Church: And If approved Ministers degenerate to Division, the Church has Authority to deal with them in the same Manner; and that no such Persons Writings should be publisht with Consent,* &c.

What of all this? He that can call this *Imperious, Audacious, &c.* can call any Thing. To allow, that Dissensious Preachers and Writers are by the Church they dissent from to be approved of in the Course of that Ministry and Writing, is such a *Bedlam, Boundless* Piece of Stuff, that none but one, who thinks it Dangerous to be of any Party, would be the Author of such a Wild Expression.

6ly, *But they advise, That such whom the Holy Ghost had made Over-seers should not admit of the Weak to that Trust, nor such as seek not the Good of all:* Which *All* this Disingenuous Wrester interprets, The great Body of George Fox and his Party; But Men of Wisdom and Moderation will not, I am confident, so spoil the Text with his Comment.

This is the *seventh Time* in two Pages that G. *Fox* is brought in, as to the Explanation of the Word *Body*, who was then close Prisoner at *Scarbrough*, where no Letter was suffered to come to him, *and who never knew of any Paper till some Time after it's being out.* O the Implacable Envy of these Men! I have hitherto waited for that *Arrogant, Imperious* and *Audacious* Passage, which might have raised up our Adversary's Choler, and whetted him to this Degree of Scolding; but find no worse than what I have transcribed and justified, this *last* excepted, and I think it justifies it self: such as seek the Good of all are certainly Fittest. If he dare tell us his Name, and meet me by Day *(as he can post up his Scurrilous Title Pages on the City Posts, with Flambeaux or Links, and a Guard by Night)* I will any where, and in any sober Auditory maintain the Truth of all these Particulars, and their clear Consistency with Scripture and Reason, on whom he has bestowed so many hard Names.

But 'tis to be lamented of his *Cabal*, that he should with his Passion and Hate divulge so much Ignorance, as to cry out, *That* (he thinks) *the* Pope *himself hath never taken such Power as to determine in Matters of this Nature and Manner, but in a general Council.* Poor Man! Brand us he would one way or other: Has he never read the *Council of Trent*, nor considered, among many others, *the Life of* Paul *the Third?* Is he to be informed of that Controversie long on foot between the *Jesuits and the Doctors of* Sorbon, *and the Followers of* Jansenius? I thought Councils had sometimes been as meer Cyphers in *Italy*, as Parliaments are in *France*.

But

But this Man is as Kind to *Elizabeth Barns*, one of that Backsliding Spirit, as he represents me elsewhere Unjust to *M. Boreman* that was; For though she has *Torn the Bible* (calling it in my hearing, the *Pope's* Idol, the *Professor's* Idol, and the *Quaker's* Idol (an incredible Thing with *J. Faldo* and *T. Hicks*) and committed more than a small History of shameful Miscarriages since; yet is he pleased to tell us, *That she, seeing the Ministers exalted themselves, cried out, while R. Farnsworth was preaching,* You have whored from the Lord. *Farnsworth* (says our Adversary) *replied, Thou art a Whore*; but for fear of being too great a Forger, he brings it afterwards thus in a Parenthesis, *or the Whore*; This Michael Stanclift *called* Unsavoury: For which, says this Secretary, *he was cast out, as calling the Spirit of Truth Unsavoury.*

O the wretched Work these People make! Will our Adversary justifie her Interruption of *R. F.* in Preaching, who condemned it in us, that did it after a more seasonable and justifiable Manner, a little before? Yes, that he will. But does he think *R. F*'s Reply Unsavoury, and not *E. Barns* Out-Cry, who only returned her own Word to her self? Yes, that he does. Strange! But does he take *E. Barns*'s Word, *Whore*, in a spiritual Sense, as Degenerating; and will he seem to understand *R. F*'s Word, *Whore*, only in a *Common* and *Proper Acceptation, as a Dishonest Woman?* Yes, that he does. Well, but was it *Unsavoury* so to reply, and not in *E. Barns*, so to interrupt and speak? *Yes, that it was,* implies this present Apologist, both of himself and *M. S.* O Monstrous! O Partial! But perhaps *M. S.* apprehended that *R. F.* meant by *Whore*, an Unclean or Dishonest Woman in the Sense before-mentioned, and then there might have been some Ground for his Answer; but if *M. S.* took *R. F.* in the Sense in which he spoke it, to wit, that *she was gone out of her Habitation* (that is, the Truth) *turned Harlot in Spirit, and so was become Clamorous* (as speaks the Wise Man) and should notwithstanding call that *Unsavoury*, it was a Sign, that he had more Unity with that *Unclean, Ranting, and Envious* Spirit in E. B. *than the Friends of Truth, that generally judged her*: And truly in that Case it was Time for them to tell that *Angry Old Man* their Mind of him; In which, they did but that, which I dare answer for, before the great and Terrible Judge of Heaven and Earth.

Mine own DEFENCE from the most Considerable Reflections, made by this *Libeller* against Me.

§. 1. HE is pleased both to Jeer and be Prophane, upon this Passage in the *Spirit of Alexander the Copper-Smith Rebuked*, *We require not Men to practise what they are not convinc'd of; but we will be well satisfied with any Member's Dispractice of an Orderly Performance, once Chearfully owned.* For this he calls me *a Deep-studied Man,* and the Passage, *a Learned Distinction. Let the Learned* (says he) *vail to* W. *Penn; but* (as one recalling himself) *probably he writ by Revelation.*

But what Answer do all these Words give? O, but 'tis all one; *for two Negatives* (says he) *make an Affirmative in English.* What, if there be but one, for two I cannot find? But he at last, like a Dim-sighted Man, has fumbled out the Matter, as he thinks, to wit, *That we require not Men to leave off to practise what they have practised,* Cujus Contrarium verum. For shame! What! no more Understanding, and yet pretend to write Books? Are not my Words expresly otherwise? But I say again, 'Tis one Thing to introduce a Practice not at first known, when our Adversaries spoke such Glorious Things of our *Faith, Worship, Order* and *Ministry,* and require the Conformity of any of the Church to it; and quite another Business, for any of the Church to dispractise, as a *Romish* Tradition, and Tradition of Men, or leave off any orderly Custom God brought his Church first forth in, and which all once own'd and were in the Practice of. But I begin to despair of making this *Cabalistick Libeller* any honester towards the poor *Quakers*.

§. 2. But the Author of this *Libel* hath so little Conscience, as yet to say, *That the* Quakers *allow no Liberty to* Presbyterians, Independents *and* Baptists, *because they are not in the Power of Truth*: but says he, W. P. *never wants a Salvo for* George, *let him say what he will*; *he meant it, says* W. P. *not of Outward, but of Inward*

1673.

Inward Liberty, and yet W. P. *knew it was spoken to one who pleaded for Liberty of Conscience about his Hat.*

But, thou *Libeller*, was he a *Presbyterian, Independent*, or *Baptist?* Or does this prove that I would defend G. F. *Let him say what he will?* Art thou a Man pretending to Truth or Honesty, that art so untrue and dishonest to thy Opposer? But I know no such Thing that it was spoken of a *Hat-Man*; this I know from G. F's own Mouth, and what I have frequently heard him say on this Subject, *That the Conscience was within, and nothing could give it Liberty from the Thraldom of Sin, but the Power of God within.* He thus distinguisht from the common Use of the Word, which is the publick Exercise of Conscience; so that what he meant of the Inward State of the Conscience to God, *they pervert to the outward Exercise of publick Worship.* Now, because the *Presbyterian, Independent* and *Baptist* generally deny, that ever the *Conscience* can be *Free*, or at *Liberty from Sin*, he queried, *What! Liberty to the* Presbyter, *&c.* and answered thus, *No Liberty out of the Power of God, Christ Jesus; and such as have Liberty, but not in Christ Jesus, the Power of God, it is in Old Adam, and are to be turned from.* No Man that is not eaten up with Prejudice, and a *Party* with these Traducers, can think that G. F. ever intended any other Liberty than what was internal, as the Conscience is. I could define that both Sides in this very Instance, might be the Measure of the Truth, or Dishonesty of either; for I am in no one Thing of this Kind better satisfied, *than in the wilful Abuse of our Adversaries, and our own unblemisht Innocence.* God will reward all according to their Works. Amen.

§. 3. He tells us, *There was a Complaint against me of divers Lyes, Calumnies and Abuses, committed by me, in my Book* (pag. 43.) *entituled*, The Spirit of Truth, &c. *carried to the* Bull and Mouth, *to the Body of the* Quakers *then sitting there, by Half a Score of Citizens and others, but they were not admitted.*

Answ. 'Tis true that I writ such a Book, and that they came with such a Complaint; but a *Lye*, a *Calumny* and *Abuse*, that God will Revenge, if not Repented of, to call any Part or Parcel of it either *Lyes, Calumnies*, or *Abuses*. H. Hedworth was nipt for his Nameless, Scurrilous Letter; Dull and Angry Man! He could never answer it, therefore strove how he could defame it's Author. Notable Controvertists indeed! First write Books against Persons, and instead of answering, cry out for Justice, as if I had committed some enormous Fact in confuting his *Libel:* But what Nonsense is it for People to come to a Body for Justice, which they so manifestly disown, and these nameless Authors constantly vilifie? Indeed they are grown so angry at our honest and quick Defences, that some are fallen to Personal Criminations, and others to downright menacing us with *Judges, Courts of Justice, and Corporal Punishments; A Crew of Petulant Disputants, and Bloody-minded Adversaries.* Well, but what Reception found they? G. Whitehead, says he, *told them, He would shew it to* W. Penn, *if they would set their Hands to it.* And was not this Reasonable? Should Men complain and not Subscribe the Complaint? *Such Dark-Lanthorn Acts become not Good Men.* But *it was shewn to* Stephen Crisp *also, and left Signed in his Hands, who told them, that he had shewn it to me, and that I had answered it in Print.* And was not that the best Way, that what came by *Print*, should go by *Print?* They know their Malice is ready, and they think their *Wits* are so too; and all know, they have their Presses open. What! Must we not defend our selves without being brought upon *Tryals?* Before what *Court* did we endeavour to bring them for beginning with us? The World may by this see, what a Way such Peevish Persons would take to be uncontrouled in their Writings, had they so much *Power* as they have *Pride* and *Passion*. But this is not all; for upon my Saying in my *Winding-Sheet, That* Anabaptists *came to* Bull and Mouth *to demand Judgment against* W. P. *for* All *being in the Place of* Many, *and asking, whether they were not well imployed*; at which he cries out in the Strain of some Great *Don.* What Penn. *Is this the Custom of* G. Fox's *Court, to jeer the Poor Petitioners?* No, *Libeller*, 'tis neither G. Fox's *Court* (as thou scoffingly callest it) nor did I *jeer*; nor were they that came, *Petitioners:* We neither scorn nor bely them, as is falsely charged upon us. And though there were more Particulars, yet that the Printers putting All *instead of* Many, *was one of them is granted; and that I never said,* They came with no more, *what I did say will sufficiently clear*; therefore this Libeller hath both scorned and bely'd me, and abus'd and jeer'd G. Fox, &c. *which indeed is most Times the Work of a concealed Author.* Well, but 'tis for this he is pleased to confer upon me the *Knighthood of the Post*, which I thus far accept of, *that I stood my Post when he ran away*; but be it as it will, his Reeling upon it hath broken his own Head against it, whether I would or no. But one Reason why he so entitles me, is, my *Swearing the Truth of what I either know to be False, or do not know to be True*. This, I suppose, may startle every *Reader* that remembers I am called a *Quaker*, and have writ against Swearing: But the Man had a notable Way to come off, in which he is singular. 1. *In Case our Words go for Oaths:* 2dly, *In that our Appealing to God is an Oath*, pag. 49. But before his Charge will teach us, he must first prove, That we ever broke our Words so solemnly given, as he pretends; and *secondly*, That an Appeal to any Thing is a *Swearing* by that unto which the Appeal is made: But the Man being of late Years turned *Scholar*, may be forgiven his Ignorance in Definitions, as I heartily do his Malice.

§. 4. In Page 44. he tells me, *That since I love not to be called bare* William, *as the* Quakers *do, but do almost beg my due Title of* J. Morse, *he thinks it to be equal that he calls me Mr.* Penn. But I could wish he would let us know what to call him, who scarcely studies our Destruction more, then to conceal himself in compassing it? I am contented to be called by my Name; but this *scornful Libeller*, besides his Nick-Names, often robs me of *Half* of it, and that after this very Passage, which shews how little Heed is to be given to his Words. But because he quotes us a Book to prove my Ambition, I will give the *Reader* an Account of the Matter. Some Letters past betwixt *J. M.* and me; on his Part he used *Thou and Thee*, conforming himself to that Language to me, which I knew he practised not to other People: *I told him it ill became one as angry with the* Quakers *as himself, to imitate them in Using that Distinction in Language, which he otherwise denied*, saying, *I loved Foxes should appear in their own Skins*. This is the Substance of that Petition, this present *Adversary* represents me to have made for Titles of Honour, against which he knows I have writ, and blamed me for so doing; but what Twigs will not such drowning Causes and Defenders catch at, to endeavour to save an irrecoverable Life.

See Plain-Dealing, p. 7.

§. 5. I am now come to what our *Adversary* takes high Advantage at, as if he had enough to blow us all away at one Breath: *That I should exclaim for Proof of that Passage in the* Spirit of the Hat, *that our Ministry was Vicious and Wanton, and that Strumpets were amongst them. And that* John Pennyman *was willing, as he publickly declared in* Gracious-Street, *to answer my Challenge, and that I should come with* J. Osgood, J. Claypole, *and* William Brand, *to his House next Day for a particular Charge, which* (says this Adversary) *he soon drew up and sent to* W. Penn, *to which* (he says) *according to my wonted Modesty; I replied*, That we wondred to see so empty an Account, after so great a Charge publickly exhibited, that before we met about it, we would know if this were all he intended; for we would not have our Charge by Piece-Meal. *Thus*, saith this Libeller, *These great Champions evaded*, &c.

Pag. 48, 58, 59.

To all which, *Reader*, take this faithful Answer. A Challenge I made to prove that infamous Charge; and it is as True that *J. Pennyman* made us believe some such Thing as is said (to say nothing of his insolent Carriage) But this I boldly affirm, for I have his Letter by me, there was scarce one of these twenty four Particulars that so much as related to that infamous Charge, upon which my Challenge was grounded. To accept my Challenge upon one Thing, and to offer to answer it with another, shows their own Shortness, and not our Cowardice. What he said to the Purpose, was no more than the Charge it self contained, and that in a Way of Postscript too: He gave us this General Answer, *He could say this, and he could say that, but he cared not to meddle with such dirty Matters*. Is this to answer our Challenge? Unjust Men! That in your *Nameless Pamphlets* would Rape us of our Reputation, which you have never yet dared to our Faces to Question. God can best rejoyn to such Replies, and with him we leave both our Cause and Innocency. O, but says our Adversary, *we will come to a Trial with you before Twelve Judges, Six of each Side, equally disinterested, and in Case we fail of such a Number of Persons, we are willing in Case of Difference about them, to refer the Umpirage to the Lord Mayor of* London, *or any Aldermen or Common-Council-Men*. But as great *Knaves* as ye would make us, I hope, ye do not think us such *Fools*, as to accept a Challenge from no Body; for such I call an hidden Author: Let us see who he is, and what he would be at? Can any Wise Man think, that if such Infirmities were, this scurrilous and blindfold Way of using us ought to prevail with us? No, as we deny far the greatest Part of his Stories, especially as aggravated, so shall we not debase our Christian Authority so far, as to be accountable to every *Fleering, Scoffing, Busy-Body Adversary*: We can Reprove and Exhort, and Exercise Church-Discipline

Church-Discipline in the Power of Christ Jesus, without running to *Twelve Judges*, Let these *Nameless and Shameless Adversaries first go with the Ungodly, Numerous Miscarriages of their own Parties, and make them Judges in that Respect*. We need none to give us Discerning or Judgment; Christ has furnisht us already, and doth in all Occasions. But had these Things been all True, as represented, yet not being injurious to any of our Adversaries, it no Ways concerneth them to be satisfied in our Proceedings; nor are we accountable to them by any Law of God or Man, upon their Envious Requirings. *Renegados Informations are no Proofs*. Hath any Wronged them, they shall be Righted so far as we are able; But have any slipt, must we therefore divulge it? Or are we therefore no Body of Christians? Though the Principle be never so Perfect, Men are no longer so than in Conformity to it. The Ancient Christian Churches had the Spirit of Truth; yet some Failures attended some of their Members for want of keeping that Watch they ought, must the whole *Church of Christ* therefore be defiled or condemned, and the Eminent, and Laborious Servants of God therefore discredited? Or should the Apostles have gratified the *Inquisitive Jews, Heathens, or Backsliders*, about any Miscarriages within themselves, who were too apt to charge them with far more Vile Practices than any instanced in either of these *Two Malicious Pamphlets*. There is no Church, or Religious Society whatever, that thinks it self obliged to inform every Envious *Busy-Body* with the Infirmities of any accounted Members, which is to publish it in *Gath*, and tell it in *Askalon*: Or the Time, Manner, and Matter of any of her Censures, unless the Facts themselves have been Notorious, or are Injurious to those without: Let any of them give me an Instance to the contrary if they can. It is *Prejudice to Religion it self*, to divulge Censures beyond the Reach of Offences, since it is to divulge the Offence it self; We shall therefore give no such ill President, by gratifying the *Minds of our Clamorous Adversaries, and some Vagabond, Treacherous Quakers*. The Church is neither accountable to her publick Enemies, nor her Apostate and disowned Friends. *J. Pennyman* and *William Mucklow*, with the rest of the *Corish* Company, first cry out of Evils committed, and next, against the Order establisht to prevent and judge them. The one must be called, *The Camp Defiled*, and the next, *Tyranny*, or, *Arbitrary Government*. This hath been judged Years since, and they now feed upon. In short, the *Libel* is hereby answered: What is Right is Defended, and what is Wrong, was long since, and in the Order of the Gospel, Condemned. And if this will not satisfie, we recommend our Cause and Persons to God, who is hastening to bring forth that Fatal and Unanswerable *Argument* of Astonishing Judgment upon the Inhabitants of the Earth, which will prove us to be the People which God hath gathered by the Power of the Resurrection of Jesus Christ from the Dead, who is become our Light and Life, the Head of our Body, in whom we stand, and for whom we now suffer upon the Earth, to whom be *Glory and Dominion for ever*.

§. 6. But to render me yet farther Odious, and as a great Testimony for *G. Fox*'s being accounted King of the *Quakers*, and that Lordliness we exercise, he tells the World, (pag. 55.) *That William Penn did not speak unadvisedly, when he writes of his Membership in the Quaker's Body. That it is an Honour more desirable than to be a Companion of Kings*.

Reader, his wresting lies here; whereas I, in the Humiliation of my Soul, preferred that Living and Spiritual Membership, Almighty God in his Rich Mercy hath given me among this People *(whose Portion outwardly, hath been Suffering of all Sorts)* abundantly before the visible Pomp, Grandeur and Pleasure, of being the Companion of Earthly Kings, he turns it *to the being a Companion to King G. Fox, as he mockingly calls him*; besides the Absurdity which follows such a Construction: For what is it but to say, *That I prefer my being a Companion of a King, before being the Companion of Kings, and that of such an one too (if he must be one) as hath not One to a Thousand, if to Ten Thousand with other Kings*. This is to render me Foolish and not Ambitious. But I never understood that *Membership* in any Body, was to have a Principality before, especially as I placed the Comparisor. I am perswaded, if he thought one so easily obtainable, he would not long decline being of some one Party or other, though now upon his present Principles, a very Stragler; every Thing and Nothing.

Well, though what I am, is far enough from being either *Prince*, or *Prince*'s *Fellow*, in our *Adversary*'s Sense; yet I have found such a Station, in which is that *Peace*, which I justly prefer before all Worldly Dominion.

§. 7. But

§. 7. But this *Libeller* angrily proceeds; *For ought I see* W. P. *calls all of us that are Married, Rogues, our Wives Whores, and our Children Bastards.* But the Drift of this Scurrilous Consequence is to bring me and my Relations under these hateful Epithets. This is like a Man, that would tell a Lye of himself to fasten an ill Thing upon another; But he will not be thought to be without a Reason for this Unreasonable Consequence; *For he will not call her,* says he, *by his, but her Widow's Name, consequently, she is a Whore, and her Child a Bastard.* Such dirty Names become so dirty a Pamphlet. I administred no just Occasion for such *Reflection:* I called her not by that Name to fasten Dishonesty upon her; for I never intended any Thing so gross, but to denote who she was, being better known in her Singularities by her old, than by her new Name. But if this Man had travelled no farther than *Holland* it self, he might have learned, *that Women are seldom, if ever, called by their Husband's Name: Are their Husband's therefore Rogues, their Wives Whores, and their Children Bastards?*

But that he may stoutly vindicate them, and wreak his Displeasure upon me, he proceeds. *Is it because they were not married by the Law of the Land? that is as strong against himself; therefore the true Reason of his abusing them, must be their not being married in the Way of the* Quakers?

Answ. Suppose us neither to have been married by the Law of the Land, this officious Apologist might have saved the Comparison 'till I and my Wife had proved our selves *as great Bedlams as they shewed themselves at* Merchant Taylor's Hall, *to the great Scandal of Religion, the Trouble of Wise and Sober Men, and the Derision of the Multitude.* Is that which was once by you improv'd to the Disgrace of the *Quakers*, now vindicated against them? It seems it had been ill done in the *Quakers,* but *is very defensible in* John Pennyman. We are contented with the Distinction, and the Apology for it. No Wonder their Books are printed for *Francis Smith* the *Anabaptist* to vend, *who* (as I am informed) *was one of the Orderers of the Disorderly Feast, being seen with several others of that Sect, that Day, as busy among the many Pasties, as he hath been since in selling their Libels*; who, by the Way, promised in my Hearing, *Never to get Printed, or Sell any Books that contained Personal Reflections*; but Gain with such is Godliness. All I can say, is, We are not deceived in him. There is a certain Harmony amongst them, that very well suits the Cause they promote.

But he says, *I am not singular in judging so hardly concerning Persons not married after our Way*; *For,* says he, *other Foxonians* (a Scoff) *have done the like in their Writings.*

This *Author* will by no Means pass for either *Lyar* or *Reviler,* who, as in other Passages, so in this, hath proved himself both: We deny not those to be *Marriages* which are not according to our Way, but we should unjustifiably differ from the Common Way, *if we did not believe our own to be most according to the Example of the Holy Men and Women of Old.* We countenance no Clandestine Marriages, as we have Reason to believe *John Pennyman*'s was: for he came not to *Merchant-Taylor's Hall to be Married, but to declare he had taken* Mary Boreman *to be his Wife,* whose Consent was only guessed at by her Silence; but when, how, and before whom he did it, is known to few, if any: We could ask Questions, that would put them very hard to it, but we delight not in meddling with such Stuff. *To conclude,* We therefore call her his Wife, because he confesseth her to be such; but not upon those plain, publick and orderly Proceedings towards God, Relations and Friends, which are owned and practised by us the People of God, called *Quakers.*

But he hath not done with me yet; *for he counts it special Malice, that I so described* Mary Pennyman *in her Apparel, as if,* saith he, W. P. *were as intimate with her, as he is said to be with* Gulielma Maria: *But* M. Pennyman *is better known for an Honest Woman, than* W. P. *is for a Man.*

There is little Reason that I should believe, that this Man hath Courage enough to question my Honesty to my Face, who was afraid to put his Name to his Slander. I envy not *M. Pennyman* her Honesty, and am very well contented with mine own; however it may be represented by mine Enemies, who are too Partial to be Judges, and instead of Confuting, can only Revile me, which shews no great Store of Honesty in this Slanderer. My Reflection upon *M. Pennyman*'s Apparel was Just and Righteous; I struck her own Spirit with her own Weapon. *Were our Ministers*

Ministers degenerated because they wore better Clothes? And was M. Pennyman more regenerated in leaving off her mean ones? Yes, for she says, *that having come through her Sorrow, the Outside is little to her.* Would not the same Excuse serve us? It seems it is no hard Matter for her to endure Richer Apparel, that is, on her own Back, *but not upon another's*; Ranterism is lodged under this Liberty, which leads to what she once judged as unbecoming Truth. But methinks her higher Attainments might allow her *Equals* and *Betters* to wear Camlet, whilst she wears Silk; they are all, I know, good in their Places; but *Hypocritical, Self-Righteous Pretences are not to pass without Rebuke.* But I cannot imagine, what should induce this *Libeller* to reflect upon my Intimacy with *Gulielma Maria*, and that in such suspected Terms, *as if she were another than the Party he represented me to be married to a little before*; for he presently reflects Dishonesty upon that said Intimacy, telling us at the Tail of it, That *M. P.* is better known for Honesty than I am; as if that Intimacy rendred me as culpable, as if it had happened between *M. Pennyman* and my self. It were well, if he had been so cautious elsewhere in telling of Lyes, as he is here in speaking the Truth; But do what we can, the Folk of this Man's Strain will make that a Ground of Reflection upon a *Quaker*, which is very allowable in themselves. He tells you above, I was married, and had a Child, and a little below that, I was said *to be* Intimate *with G. M.* that is, *with the Person that is my Wife*, as if it were to render a Man suspect to be intimate with one's own Wife. Whether there be most of *Folly* exprest, or Slander intended in this Way of Writing, let the Moderate *Reader* judge. But because the Reflection as well extends it self to her as to me, I will only say thus much in her Defence, *She needs none*; and to be questioned from so foul a Mouth, is a great Addition to her *Credit*, but his own *Guilt*. His Comparison of her with *M. Pennyman*, that formal Piece of *Hypocrisy*, giveth but such as know both, the better Means to judge of either; The well-known *Innocence, Meekness* and *Faithfulness* of the one, more lively setting out the *Deceitfulness, Pride* and *Treacherous Apostasy* of the other.

In short; Who would be well spoken of by such that chuse *Virtuous Persons* to speak *Evil* of, and *Apostates* to *Commend*? But all this, and many more Rude and Defaming Speeches must I and mine expect from this Perverse Generation, who have rewarded us Evil for Good. What Scurrility, Railing, Nick-Names, Mocks and Jeers are vented against us, with other Servants of the Lord? But in all these Things our Eye is to him, for whose Sake alone (he is our Record) we are become *Marks* for Furious Men to shoot their Arrows at; But the Lord is our Pavilion, and his Strength our Fortress: He covers our Heads in these and all other *Battels* (at what Time these Creeping *Judasses* and Envious *Libellers* lurk and hide) so that we are not moved. We recommend our selves to his peculiar Care and Providence, that in his Holy Truth we may live, and rather than relapse, for it constantly die, that, whether we live, or whether we die, God may be magnified in the Earth, and that shall be our exceeding great Recompence of Reward.

And for these Apostates, *who once dipt with us into the same Dish, and fed at the same Table, who have tasted of the Word of God, and the Power of the World to come*; but have betrayed the Spirit of Truth to the Spirit of Delusion in themselves, and given him and his Motions into the Hands of the False *Christian* of this Day, to *Deride and Scorn*, and who have had so *little Regard to the Profession*, as to bring it under Reproach, and to the *Common Law of Friendship*, as Treacherously to divulge the Secrets of some of their ancient Acquaintance; and finally, who have endeavoured the Disgrace and Hazard of the *Lives and Liberties* of some of the Servants of God, because of their Faithful Testimony against their Apostasy; I must tell them, and do in the Counsel of God, *Their Bands shall be made strong*, and that Eternal Power at which they strike, reigns over their Dark, Dividing Envious Spirit, in the Hearts of that People, they have called by so many Scoffing Names; and more than a Mill-stone will it be about their Necks, and the Weight of all these Wicked and Treacherous Doings, will God bring upon them, in a Day, and an Hour, when they shall not be able to escape the Rod of his Fury. *Ah! Poor Men! What have ye been doing?* Verily, your Damnation *slumbers not; and the God, whose Name you have caused to be blasphemed amongst the Heathen, will one Day require these Things at your Hands, and Recompense Vengeance in Flames of Fire, for all your Hard Speeches and Sinful Contradictions against the Holy Spirit of Truth, and those who are led by it.* I am not in any Rage, God knows

knows; but *I am grieved for you.* I could wish a Place of Repentance might be found, if the Lord saw Good, though I rather fear, your many and grievous Provocations have shut the Door against you: For as *Core* and his Associates were outwardly swallowed up of the Earth, so hath the Earthly, Sensual and Devilish Spirit of the World received you into the Bowels of it, and you are become as really One against our Lord and his Anointed in this Generation, as ever *Pilate, Herod, Judas* and the *Jews* were combined against Him and His in the Days of his Flesh; *Who have strengthned the Hands of the Mocker and Scoffer; greatned the Envy of the Professors, and made the Atheist glad.* But may this Lamentable Course your Disobedient, Watching-for-Evil, Slippery, Backbiting and Exalted Spirit hath brought you into, with the sad Consequence of being hardned therein, be a perpetual Warning upon the Minds of all, who make Profession of God's Eternal Truth, *that they be not High-minded, but fear*; minding their own Conditions, and their Growth and Increase in the Work of the Lord, that so Love and Unity may be preserv'd, and all *Watchings for Evil, Distrusts, Surmisings, Emulations*, and whatever makes for Discord or Dis-affection, may be judged out, and the *Sourness* of that Spirit that leads thereunto, turned from, and rebuk'd in the Power and Authority of God, who is able to keep us and preserve us unto his Heavenly Kingdom, to whom be everlasting Glory and Dominion, *Amen.*

Now, *The Just shall live by Faith; but if any Man draw back, my Soul shall have no Pleasure in him,* Hebr. 10. 38.

And because Iniquity shall abound, the Love of many shall wax cold. But he that shall endure unto the End, the same shall be saved. Matth. 24. 12, 13.

And THIS GOSPEL *of the Kingdom shall be preached in all the World, for a Witness unto all Nations, and then shall the End come.* Ver. 14.

WILLIAM PENN.

Note, Several *Testimonies* printed at the End of this *Treatise*, are here Omitted, not being penn'd by this *Author.*

A POSTSCRIPT to the READER,

Concerning the UNITY of our Adversaries against us, amidst the great Discord they are at amongst themselves.

HOW hearty these Men are in their Envy against Us, and Hatred to the Way we profess, is very discernable from their close Confederacy and strict Union, who are as remote, and differing from, and absolutely contradictory to one another in their Faith, Worship and Discipline, as to the Quakers themselves, against whom they have Combined. They are made up of some Presbyterians, Independents, Anabaptists, Socinians, *and* Apostates from Us. *A strange Medley of Adversaries, and stranger, that there should be such Union to Mischief! But let us view some of their Principles.*

First, *The* Presbyterians, Independents, *and* Anabaptists, *believe that the* Father, the Son, *and the* Spirit, *(though three Names, denoting Three Personalities or Subsistences) are One, Infinite, Eternal and Omnipotent God, At which the Modern* Socinian *cries,* Blasphemy and Idolatry; *For,* says he, Christ is but purely a Man, and the Spirit but a Creature. *Now come in these Apostates against the Presbyterians, Independents, Anabaptists.* We deny your Personalities and Subsistences; *And to the Socinians,* We own Christ and the Spirit to be of one Nature and Being with God the Father; And it is Blasphemy to say, that Christ and the Spirit are Creatures. *Here's the first Discord or* Jumble *between our Adversaries.*

Secondly, *The* Presbyterians, Independents, Anabaptists, *and these Apostates,* assert God to be a Spirit, *At which these Socinianiz'd Followers of* John Bidle, *say,* There's no such Thing; *but, with* J. Reeve *and* L. Muggleton, That he has a Body like to a Man, and inhabits a certain Place.

1673.

Thirdly, *The Presbyterians, Independents, and Anabaptists, concerned chiefly against us, hold,* That God from all Eternity elected a certain Number to Salvation, and reprobated the Residue to Eternal Damnation, without respect to any Condition of Obedience or Disobedience, thereby to illustrate his own Sovereignty and Glory; *which Principle these Apostates have so much Understanding yet left, as to repute pernicious and damnable. The like do some of these* Socinians *we have to do with*; *others of them having* wheel'd off a few Years since to the *Geneva* Predestinarian Side.

Fourthly, *The Presbyterians, Independents, and Anabaptists believe,* That by Christ's Life and Sufferings wholly without, God's Justice was satisfied for Sins, and Justification compleatly wrought for the Elect, not only by forgiving Sins past, but reputing them really Just and Righteous whilst actually Sinful; *which Kind of Doctrine these Apostates deny, as also doth the* Socinian, *affirming,* That God needed no such rigid Satisfaction; that this is not to make him Righteous, but Revengeful; and that Christ cannot so properly be said to be the Cause as the Effect of the Father's Love; *For God so loved the World, that he gave his only begotten Son,* &c. *And though such are forgiven who truly Repent, and that Remission was sealed by Christ's Blood, as a Sacrifice; yet Men are not made really Righteous within, by any Imputation from another's Righteousness without, while they are really Unrighteous within. This is the 4th Contradiction.*

Fifthly, *Presbyterians, Independents, and Anabaptists,* believe Christ to have now in Heaven an Human Body, or one of Flesh, Blood and Bones. *The Socinian and these Apostates say,* he hath no such Body, but that which he hath is more Spiritual and Glorified.

Sixthly, *The Presbyterians, Independents, Anabaptists, and these Apostates, affirm* the Immortality of the Soul. The *Socinians* deny it.

Seventhly, *The Presbyterians, Independents, Anabaptists and Socinians,* deny the Light that shines within, to be Christ in his Spiritual Appearance. *These Apostates, though erred from it, yet* affirm it to be such.

Eighthly, *The Presbyterians, Independents, Anabaptists,* deny that it can lead Men that obey it unto Salvation. *The Socinian, with these Apostates, affirm,* that it is able to lead such as follow it to Eternal Life.

Ninthly, *The Presbyterian, Independent, Anabaptist and Socinian,* deny the Spirit to be poured out in these, as former Ages; or that Men ought to wait for the Motions of it to Preach, Pray, or Praise God. *These Apostates, in Words,* confess to maintain the contrary.

Tenthly, *The Presbyterian, Independent, Anabaptist and Socinian, affirm,* That the Scriptures are the only standing Rule, to measure and try Doctrines, and Spirits by, under the Gospel: *These Apostates believe no such Thing.*

Eleventhly, *The Presbyterians, Independents, Anabaptists and Socinians,* disown the Practice of keeping on the Hat in Time of Publick Prayer; *These Apostates call the Pulling of it off,* a Tradition of Men, a Romish Tradition, &c.

Yet, Reader, for our seasonable and due Proceeding against them, as Innovators upon the Church of Christ, and Disturbers of our Peace, by this new, unprofitable, and irreverent Practice, denying them in their Persistence, and rejecting their Motions, as not coming from the Spirit of God, are we furiously fallen upon by some of each of those fore-mentioned Parties; (who as Men forgetting their own Essential Differences, and that Persecution they have followed one another with for Years) like the ancient Scribes, Sadducees, *and* Pharisees, *unanimously endeavour our Disgrace and Overthrow in the World; as if they were all of one Faith in Doctrine, who scarcely in any two most weighty Points hit: which shews, that Men under divers Fundamental Differences, may be acted by one and the same Spirit of Envy and Bitterness against the Truth, and them that live therein. What else can I call that which has given these Apostates that Place in their Hearts, (that while Faithful, hated them, as they still do us) who* Judas *like have run away from us, to inform our Enemies which Way they may take us at an Advantage?*

These Men they hug, commend and vindicate at so high a Rate, as if they were the only great Patrons on Earth for Righteousness, (as much as they differ) and us, as a Crew of Tyrants *and* Hypocrites. *Their* Innovation *must be called* Gospel-Liberty; *but our* Religious Government, Tyranny: *They justify the Motions of these Apostates, and condemn Us for refusing them, whom themselves both deny Motions, and the Way to know them. They put me in Mind of the* Jews *of old, who*

who were seldom wanting in the Promotion of the Christians Sufferings by the Heathen; nay, they were glad, and improved the least Occasion to set the Infidels upon their Backs: Always the Jew and Heathen *said* Amen *to the Destruction of the Christians*; yea, *that very Thing for which the* Jew *in his Time suffered from the* Heathen, *to wit*, That they worshipped an Asse's Head, *was after abusively made the Reproach of* Christians, *both by* Jew *and* Heathen. *What other have we received from the Separatists of this Age? Who make us to inherit that Sort of Suffering which they once thought Ungodly in their Adversaries.* How welcome was a *Renegado Christian* to the *Heathen*, or a *Backslider* to the *Jew*? *How chary were they of such an one's Intelligence? And how apt to aggravate it to the Wrong of Christianity? But if that was nevertheless* True, *because of the Unfaithfulness and Treachery of it's Professors; neither is our Way to be concluded False, nor our Society Criminal, because a few stragling Renegadoes have in their Discontents, furnisht some common Enemies with a broken and imperfect Account of our* Church Proceedings: *But as this will turn little to their Credit, with Wise and Just Men, so have we Confidence in God, that having brought us through many Difficulties, he will continue to preserve us through the Peril of* False Brethren, *and all other Tribulations, which do, and will but work a far more exceeding Weight of Glory, yea of that Glory which was with the Father before the World began; and in the Possession of which, the now despised Flock of God shall rest with him in that World which never had Beginning, and is without End.*

W. PENN.

QUAKERISM

A New *Nick-Name* for Old CHRISTIANITY:

BEING

An *Answer* to a Book, Entituled, *Quakerism No Christianity*; Subscribed by *J. Faldo*.

IN WHICH

The *Rise*, *Doctrine* and *Practice* of the Abused *Quakers*, are Truly, Briefly and Fully, Declared and Vindicated, from the False Charges, Wicked Insinuations, and utmost Opposition made by that Adversary.

By one of them, and a Sufferer with them in all their Sufferings, W. PENN.

Behold, I will make them of the Synagogue of Satan, who say they are Jews, *and are not, but do Lye: Behold, I will make them to come and Worship before thy Feet; and to know, that I have loved thee*, Rev. 3. 9.

To the READER.

However our many Sorts of Enemies may please themselves, with their brisk Endeavours against us, and the Expectation they thence have of our Utter Overthrow especially some Independents, Anabaptists, and Socinians; Be it known to the whole World, Professor and Prophane, our Confidence is in God, for whose

1673.

Holy Truth-fake we are as Men killed all the Day long; and it is our Perswasion, that many Thousands in these Nations have that Sense of us in their own Consciences, which it is as impossible for the utmost Power or Artifice of our angry Adversaries to extinguish, as the Sun in the Firmament. We matter not their Flourish, Number, Threat or Force, though Gog and Magog are combin'd to seek our Ruin; God that made the Heavens and the Earth, the Sea and Fountains of Water hath them all in Derision, *and will not be wanting to assist us*, otherwise forlorn upon Earth, *in this juncture of close Attack (we waiting on him) with that Divine Courage, Wisdom, and Patience, which may enable us to surmount the Difficulty of the Work*, and through the Tribulations of our Day, bring us to the Recompence of that Peace which is Eternal. And indeed, this is our Joy above all worldly Things, that the Lord is our Light, and our Salvation, *we know it, we experience it*; therefore whom should we fear? Though all *Sects seem met in one*, as a mighty Man of War, to our Overthrow, *the despised Stripling (by this great* Goliah*) has a* Sling and a Stone, *that (however contemptible, yet) coming in the Name of the Lord, will give this* Giant's Head a Victim to his Faith. *We know in whom we have believed, and cannot be Cudgel'd, Jeer'd, Rail'd or Smooth'd out of our most Holy Faith, which has God for it's Father, and Victory for it's Off-spring. A Birth unknown to the Bawling* Pharisees *of the Age; nor can any but a Conquerour inherit.*

Reader, *their Cries for* Scripture, Christ, Fundamentals, *and the like, are meer Pretences that make but up a Cloak to cover the Avaricious and Ambitious Ends of those leading Men in every Party, that as deeply and vigorously prosecute our Ruin, as a* Jew *doth Riches; but the Reason is known to Almighty God. Because the* Quakers *having been taught that Inward, Heavenly, Straight and Narrow Way to Life by an* Internal Living Teacher; *they would*, say they, *frustrate all Hope of farther Advantage,* the Ignorance of People in the Things of God has hitherto benefited us withal, *by their most vehement Declaration to the World, that* no Man can be a Child of God, who is not begotten of God; and that no Man can be so begotten, but by the Internal Operation of his Spirit to Wash, Cleanse and Inliven the Mind to Godward; that this is the Deepest and most Excellent End for which Man was made, the Law was given, Prophets raised, and Christ Came, Lived, Died, Rose and Ascended: That who know him not thus let into the Conscience, in order to purge it from Dead Works, by the Destruction of that Power which produc'd them, to lead Captivity captive, and Reign as King, Lord, Judge and Lawgiver, are Enemies to the Cross of Christ, and are at best but *Carnal, Historical,* and meerly Outside-Christians. *And this we standing by, and they knowing full well, with the fatal Consequence to their Designs that would attend the Universal Reception of this Kind of Doctrine, they seek to divert the Minds of Tender and Enquiring People by all the* Hideous, Devilish Falsities, Satan's utmost Interest can furnish them withal; *deforming us with what Mire they can either borrow or invent, hoping by such Besmearings to make the Dogs fasten us for some Monstrous Beasts, and chusing rather to* Solemnize *our Funeral, with the Merriment of the Vulgar, than suffer them to know us truly as we are, lest their sober Conscience should enquire or be toucht with any the least Pity for our so hard Dealing at their Cruel Hands.*

Well! but for your Sakes, O Impartial People! Am I at this Time engaged in Spirit to concern my self, otherwise against my Will, to take an Angry, Scoffing Independent Priest in Hand; *a Man I know not, but by his Book, and certainly an Ignorant, Malicious and Scurrilous one too. I perceive how unknown soever he is to me, I am not to him, and he has taken great Care to tell me so:* But mine own Concern would have suggested Silence to me for an Answer to his Uncivil Reflections (for Arguments I cannot call them) had not my earnest Desires been for the Vindication of that Truth, Living, upon all Occasions offer'd, *which the Grave will prevent me doing. It is my Satisfaction God has made it my Lot; and that of suffering from Detractors, I esteem not the least Part of my Crown: For whose Holy Service, he is my Witness, I have long since chearfully sacrific'd my All of Contentment in this World; and yet am not without a Share from his peculiar Providence.*

But let us see if the Quakers *are those Miserably Deluded Wretches, this taunting Priest would represent us, whose* Trifling Quirks *show the Emptiness of the Head, and Airiness of the Mind from whence they came. If we are what he asserts, we are the worst of Men, by how much we pretend to greater Things; but if it shall appear, we are Scripturally* Orthodox, *in some of those very Points for which he represents us* Heterodox, *and mistaken by him in the rest; I hope it will not be without Good*

Good Reason, that I have entitul'd this short Discourse Quakerism a New Nick-Name for Old Christianity.

Reader, *The whole of what I have to desire from thee is an* Impartial Mind *in the Perusal of this Defence and Just Explanation of our so much mis-represented Faith and Doctrine; with that we dare adventure our Cause, and without it there is no Truth so clear, that* Prejudice *may not question it. Let not the Multitude of our Adversaries be an Argument against our Cause; Their Reviling ought not to pass for Reason, nor Noise for Conquest. With God Almighty and his Holy Witness in thy Conscience, do I leave the Issue of this Endeavour: Be Serious, be Considerate. Farewel.*

Thy Friend, very ready to serve thee with all Sincerity for the Truth's Sake, as it is in *Jesus*,

WILLIAM PENN.

QUAKERISM
A New *Nick-Name* for Old CHRISTIANITY, &c.

CHAP. I.

The Introduction. Our Adversary's Definition of Christianity *Defective. True Christianity Stated.* Quakerism *Mistaken by him. It is proved True Christianity, and a Quaker a Right Christian*

§. 1. Among many other Persons, that have of late Industriously essayed the Mis-representing the *Quakers*, and their Religion (overcasting the Sincerity of the One, and darkning the Excellent Beauty of the Other, by their *Mists of Ignorance and Prejudice*) *John Faldo*, though the *Last*, has not been the *Least* concern'd.

§. 2. I am truly Sorry to see, that among the several Arguments, some Men's Prudence render'd, for Toleration, *that of giving Dissenters Liberty, and they would War within themselves*, should be so amply verified by their Unchristian Irruption upon us (disturbing those by Slanderous Pamphlets, who would not be concern'd in their Heats.) But this Folly and Uncharitableness, I am to tell the World, lies not at the *Quaker's* Door, who seek Peace with all Men; but some Restless Spirits among other Perswasions, whose whole Food seems to turn into Contest, and shew they can no more live without it, than the Air they breath in. What shall we do then? Suffer their Slanders, Detractions, Additions, and Down-right Abuses of us to pass Unanswer'd? No: for then we shall be concluded, either *Guilty* or *Vanquisht*. What then? Why we will defend our selves with Truth and Moderation; and that I hope, with God's Assistance, to do in this short Treatise, to the Confusion of our Enemies, and Renowning the Truth, and Clearing our Innocence to the World.

§. 3. The Author is pleas'd to call his Book, *Quakerism no Christianity*. A Title of more Reproach and Infamy, than became a *Christian* Man to give. But let's hear what he means by *Christianity*.

§. 4. By Christianity, *we are not to understand all those Matters of Faith and Practice, which* Christianity *doth oblige us unto*.

A strange Definition of true *Christianity*: For, if to Believe, and Do all *Christianity* requireth, be not *Christianity*, then there is something beyond all that *Christianity* requires to be believ'd and done *that is Christianity*; else I understand nothing. But saith he, *It takes in whatever is worthy in those Religions, it hath superseded, yea, the very Heathens*. What then? Is it not therefore *Christianity*? Egregious Weakness! What an Hair has he split? but it flies in his Eyes: Is it not therefore *Christianity, because* Christianity *takes it in*? If *Christianity* takes in whatever is worthy in other Religions; then, since *Christianity* is Worthiness it self, Comprehensive of whatever was in any Degree Excellent among *Jews* or *Heathens;*

Heathens; will it not follow, That, to Believe and Practife all that *Chriftianity* requires, *is Chriftianity*; unlefs we are to underftand, That *Chriftianity* does not require what was Worthy and Commendable among *Jews* or *Heathens*, which he fays, we are.

§. 5. This then does not make *Chriftianity* a Diftinct Thing in kind, from what was Worthy, as he calls it, that is, Godly, among either *Jews* or *Heathen*. but that Chrift did by his Vifible Appearance benefit the World with a more glorious Manifeftion of the fame Divine Power, Purity, Truth, Wifdom and Righteoufnefs, than former Ages were either capable of, or attended with. To exclude then all Antecedent Times from any fhare in *Chriftianity*, is both Weak, and Cruel; fince it plainly fhuts them out of all Hopes of Eternal Salvation: For if no Name be given but the Name of Chrift, under the whole Heaven, by which Men can be faved; then, *either Chrift was always in fome Meafure or other a Saviour, and fuch as were faved, in fome Degree or other, Chriftians*; or there was one Saviour before Chrift's outward Coming, and another fince; or laftly, *all that were antecedent to that Appearance, were damn'd*.

§. 6. I appeal then to the Confciences and Underftandings of all impartial People, if our Belief be not the moft Juft, Merciful and True; that however it pleafed God to fend his Son a Light into the World at that Time more eminently than before, yet that he was fo far Spiritually manifefted in all Ages, as the Word of God nigh in the Heart, and great Commandment in the Confciences of Men, as who believed and obey'd, obtain'd Remiffion of Sins and Eternal Salvation. This is clear; for if no Man could ever fee, or know the Father but the Son, and he to whom the Son reveals him, then becaufe many of the Holy Ancients both fpiritually faw and knew God (otherwife they could never be faved) it follows, *that Chrift did in all Ages reveal God*, who being Light, and that it is Light alone which can Reveal or Manifeft; it was a Light within, that he communicated unto the Soul of Man, which is within Man, the Knowledge of the Pure God: *Whatever may be known of God is manifeft within Man, for God hath fhewed it unto him*: So that the Contradiction and Error of the Man's Definition of *Chriftianity* is evident.

§. 7. But yet a little farther: He plainly *Heathenizes* that notable *Chriftian* Paffage of the Apoftle, refufing it all Privilege within the Bounds of *Chriftianity*, viz. *Whatfoever Things are True, Honeft, Juft, Pure, Lovely, of Good Report*; *if there be any Virtue, if there be any Praife, think on thefe Things*. Now if this Religious Chymift fhall once extract all Things that are *Honeft, Juft, Pure, Lovely, and of Good Report*, from *Chriftianity* (which the Apoftle maketh the Sum of what he had been writing (unlefs it is not a Chriftian Epiftle) and therefore ends with a *Finally, my Brethren*) tell me, *O fober Reader*, what a kind of *Chriftianity* there would be in the World! O Monftrous Impiety! Is this Man fit to write of *Chriftianity* that places it beneath the loweft Step of Purity; making manifeft Difference betwixt being *a Child of God, and a Chriftian*? True, the outward Hiftory of Chrift's exceeding Love to Mankind, deferves all humble and reverent Credit as a Godly Tradition, and it fhould for ever bind Men to receive and fear and worfhip him: Yet I boldly affirm, that though the Manifeftation was clearer; *yet Salvation was Salvation, and a Child of God, a Child of God in all Ages*. For what is it but to fay, *that Pure Religion and Undefiled, which is to keep our felves unfpotted from the World, belongs not ftrictly to the Chriftian, but Jewifh or Pagan Religion*; *and that James was but a moral Man in the Matter, and not writing on a Chriftian Subject*. What an empty Trunk, *a Vox, & præterea nihil*, a founding Brafs and Tinkling Cymbal would this Man make of true *Chriftianity*! Yet thus far we may force him to fpeak Truth, though in double Contradiction to himfelf; that fince *Chriftianity* takes in all that was worthy in all Ages (not as Alien then, but related to her felf) *fomething of the Nature of true* Chriftianity *was in the World before that more Vifible and Glorious Manifeftation of it*; *unlefs Chriftianity be fuppofed to take into it felf what is not of it's own Nature*: Thus was Chrift the Rock the Ancients built on before *Abraham* was, whofe Day he had a Sight and Senfe of, and from it rejoyced greatly.

§. 8. *Chriftianity* then is not an *Hiftorical Belief of the Exterior Acts*, the true Chrift did in that bodily Appearance, *which is but Hiftorical Chriftianity*, as our Adverfary weakly argues; for that was the leaft Part of it, fince *Chriftianity* is that which brings to God, which Thoufands that believe only the other will never arrive at: but a *firm Belief in him that fo Appeared, Lived, Died, Rofe and Afcended*

cended, both *as testified of in the Scriptures of Truth, and more especially as he breaks in upon the Soul by his Divine Discoveries, as the True Light enlightning every Man,* this I call Christianity; and *that Man is a Child of Light, who obeys that Light; a true Christian, who is Christ-like; a Child of God, and Heir of the Promise, who is inwardly renewed and begot anew of the Incorruptible Seed, and Word of God:* For those who were Christians of old, were such as came to know Christ, *no more after the Flesh, but as the second Adam, the Lord from Heaven, the Quickning Spirit,* who said, *I am the Resurrection and the Life*; really witnessing him to be that in themselves, wherefore they *Believed,* and upon Repentance, received Remission of Sins and Eternal Salvation. And I do affirm, that Christianity stands in the Manifestation of a Measure of that Righteous *Power, Wisdom, Truth* and *Life* in the Soul, which appear'd so largely and gloriously in that Body at *Jerusalem,* to work Repentance, then give Remission, so Renew, Redeem, and finally Save: And who came to be made sensible of that Heavenly Treasure in their mortal Bodies, and to improve it as good Stewards, were Possessors of true *Christianity,* and therefore *Right Christians.* The Distinction betwixt Moral and Christian, the making Holy Life Legal, and Faith in the History of Christ's outward Manifestation only, *have been a deadly Poyson these latter Ages have been infected with,* to the Destruction of Godly Living, and *Apostatizing* of those Churches, in whom there might once have been begotten, some *Earnest, Living Thirst* after the Inward Life of Righteousness.

§. 9. By this, I think it may be pretty well known, what we mean by *Christianity,* and a *True Christian:* How far this will agree with his Definition of *Quakerism,* and a *Quaker,* I will proceed to examine.

Quakerism *is an heap of Tenets, with the usurped Names of true Christian Principles, which are yet really no such Thing, but subverting both Foundation and Fabrick of true Christianity;* And I call him a Quaker *that professes the Light within every Man to be the Lord, and Saviour, and very God:* So that then I *say* Quakerism *is no Christianity.*

§. 10. Indeed, if *Quakerism,* respecting us, were this, I would say so too: But because it is justly a Stranger to any such Imputation, I rightly fasten that of Ignorance or great Malice upon our *Adversary.* I have already exprest our Judgment of *Christianity,* which I suppose to be the *Quakerism* struck at, whatever may be pretended, at least, what is our *Quakerism,* or *Christianity* rather: And we leave our Belief with that God who made it so, to justifie it, and us, who thus stedfastly hold, and daily, yet patiently suffer for it, by his own Discoveries in the Consciences of Men. But this I will add, That since he has rendred us to be one Thing in Shew, and another in Reality, our Appeal is to the God that made Heaven and Earth, to right us in the Minds of all.

§. 11. We dare not Believe or Practise what comes not in by True Conviction (Things meerly Historical excepted, and yet there is a Conviction for them too) The *Devils* who knew Christ and trembled, were more sensible than those who know him only by Hear-say, and make a Mock of that Trembling, which seizeth the Contrite Souls of Men for Sin. We declare in the Presence of the Eternal God, that it was the Strivings of the Holy Spirit in us, that first moved us to solid Repentance, and as we came to be judged by it, and reconciled unto God in our Minds, so have we appear'd before all Men; *therefore it is utterly False, that We cover our Tenets with the Names of Christian Principles,* since these following, which are ours, are truly *Christian* and *Scriptural* (1.) *God created Man Innocent, in his own Image created He him.* (2.) *That Man or all Mankind has faln short of the Glory of God through Disobedience.* (3.) *That in the Seed promised Redemption can only be had.* (4.) *That this Seed is He that in Time was called* Christ. (5.) *That by this Holy Seed, both before and since that Coming, the Serpent's Head hath been perticularly bruised in all who have been redeemed or saved, as the Holy Men and Women of Old, and such in every Age as have known a Sanctification.* (6.) *That this Seed appeared in the Fulness and Stature of a Man in that Outward Body prepared of God above* 1660. *Years since, and in it encounter'd and conquer'd Satan, and trod him under His Feet.* (7.) *That he bore the Sin of the World.* (8.) *That he laid down his Life a Ransom for all.* (9.) *That such as Believ'd and Follow'd him as he then appear'd, receiv'd Remission of Sins, and Eternal Life.* (10.) *That what was then outwardly done, did still refer and had Relation to an Inward Work in the Souls of Men: The Holy Life put forth it self to work Inward Conviction, and drive the*

Mind

1673.

Chap. I.

Mind into a Measure of the same in it self; for the whole End of it was, to draw the Minds of Men more Inward, to a Manifestation of that same Life, Virtue, Power, Wisdom, and Righteousness in each Particular, which appeared in that Body in General, and qualified it to that great Work, and sustain'd it under all it's Sufferings, and put that Great Value upon them, which really was in them: Wherefore, to the Divine Power first, and to the Holy Manhood next, do we ascribe that Grace and Wonderful Benefit that thereby came unto the World.

§. 12. But next, we must deny his *Quaker*, as well as his *Quakerism*: Indeed, they go together; who misseth one, it is unlikely he should hit the other. We never said, *That the Light in every Man was the only Lord, and Saviour, and very God.* Let him but show us any such Passage of any one acknowledg'd to be a *Quaker*, and he will say something: But methinks he that has quoted so many Passages out of our *Friends Books*, to so little Purpose, should not have neglected to instance in some one of us, that hath so exprest our selves; it shows, that either he thinks to be believ'd Hand over Head, or really there is no such Doctrine by us asserted, and consequently he knew no such Place to cite. But for the Uprighthearted in all Forms, who are desirous of the Substance, that will give Life to the Soul, and who stand only at a Distance from us, on the Account of the many frightful Characters their Teachers give of us, I shall briefly open our Faith in this Matter.

§. 13. *First*, We assert, *That all Men are enlightned* (let it be *Lighted* in their Souls or Understandings, if our *Adversaries* will) This is prov'd from *John* 1. 9. Also, *Whatever may be known of God, is manifest within, for God has shewn it unto them.* Again, *Whatever is reproved, is made manifest by the Light; for whatever makes manifest, is Light.* All Knowledge of God comes by the Light he gives into the Soul, as well as that all have that Light, though few obey it.

§. 14. *Secondly*, This Light is Divine, *because it is the very Life of the Word, which is God*; not an Effect of it's Power, as a Created Light, which some vainly fancy; but in *Him*, or *It*, the *Word*, was *Life*, and that *Life* (Numerical) was the *Light* of Men: *What is Life in the Word, is Light in Men, and who follow that Light as a Reprover of the Deeds of Darkness, shall be made Children of Light, and have the Light of Life.*

§. 15. *Thirdly*, Though we say, *that all are enlightned by it*, or receive Light from it, yet far be it from us to assert, *Every such Illumination is the only Lord, and Saviour, and very God.* By no Means, but rather thus, *That the only Lord, and Saviour, and very God, is the Great Sun and Light of Righteousness to the Invisible World of Souls and Spirits* (if I may so speak) who manifests unto every Particular, that which concerns the State of every Individual; but not that every such Enlightning should be the *Intire Lord, Saviour, God*; so that this Priest is already found deficient in his Work: He should better have understood us before he had given an Account of us, and discovered his Opposition to us. What Superstructure can we expect from so infirm a Foundation; how shall *J. Faldo* prove *Quakerism No Christianity*, who is defective in his Definition of both? Certainly the *Quaker* may be the *Best of Christians* for ought he has groundedly opposed to him: I am sure he would have thought such a Mistake in us most heinous; to say nothing of that Advantage he would have taken to shew his little Wit, and great Prejudice in aggravating our Ignorance to the World.

Chap. II.

CHAP. II.

How Christianity *was introduc'd, hurts not the* Quakers. *The Question is not of* Christ's Visible Coming; *that is owned by them. Nor is their Religion a New One from that of* Christianity; *but the Recovery of Lost Primitive Christianity, since the Reign of Anti-Christ in the World. That* Quakerism, *as call'd, made its Way by Purity, Sorrow and Rejoycing, as well as* Christianity. *The Priests Vilifying Expressions Rebuk'd. That the Distinct Times of their Appearance, is no Argument against their Harmony, or being but Two Words for the same Thing, since the same Truth may appear at Two Distinct Ages of the World. It would strike out* J. Faldo *as well as the* Quakers, *if the contrary were admitted. That he grosly contradicts himself as to Time.* Christianity *hath more or less been in the World where Godly Men and Women have been, as well before as since that Appearance. We intend no New Dispensation, but the Renewed Revelation of the same Power, which is the True Gospel.*

§. 1. THE next Mis-Representation, is of the Manner of our Appearance, and the Time of it, by Way of Comparison with that of *Christianity*, little to his Purpose, and in my Judgment, much against him.

§. 2. *Christianity was introduc'd by Preaching the* Promised Messias, *and Pointing at His Human Person: But* Quakerism *by Preaching a Light within.*

I answer, that this is nothing injurious to the *Quakers* at all, but highly on their Side; for had they preach'd Christ now coming in the Flesh, *they had deny'd his True and only great Visible Appearance,* at Jerusalem, *which all True Quakers own.* Since then they believe that Appearance, and therefore need not preach what is not to be again; and that the whole Christian World besides, have so long and lazily depended on it, without their thirsting after His Inward Holy Appearance in the Conscience, to bind the Strong Man, Spoil his Goods, and Cast him out; in short, to discover Sin, Wound for it, and make an End of it by the Brightness of his Spiritual Coming into the Souls of all such as wait for him, and will receive him (in which Sense he was revealed in such, and became in the Saints of Old the Hope of their Glory) I say, since he has been so much talk'd of, and depended on, as to his then Visible Manifestation of himself, and so little, if at all, desired after, as to his Spiritual and Invisible Coming into the Hearts of Men, to finish Transgression and bring in Everlasting Righteousness: Therefore God raised us up, and we are now gone forth into the World to declare, *That He is Spiritually Manifested; as then fully in that Body, so now measurably in the Consciences of all People, a Divine Light, Reproving every Unfruitful Work of Darkness:* So that here is the Mischief, the Malice and Ignorance of our Enemies do us in the World, that because we Speak so much of, and Preach up, and Write for *Christ's Inward* and Spiritual Appearance, as a Light to Mankind, therefore they conclude with a mighty Confidence, *That we deny his outward Coming, Life, Death, Resurrection, and Ascension, and the Benefits thereof.* O Darkness it self! We have our Witness with the Lord of Heaven and Earth, *that we own him to be the Saviour General of the whole World, as to that Appearance, and that he obtained Precious Gifts for Men*; but we say (and our Adversaries have not wherewith reasonably to unsay it) that *first the Divine Light, Life, or Power, that shined through that Blessed Manhood, was excellently the Saviour, and the Manhood but Instrumentally:* Thus the Scripture, *There is no Saviour besides me, saith God; a Body hast thou prepared me: He* then was greater than *his Body*; for it is call'd a *Veil*, and very properly; *for it veil'd much of that Divine Life, which when it was withdrawn* (as he himself said, it was expedient) *the Saints did witness inwardly Reveal'd, Christ in them, their Hope of Glory.* And *secondly,* No Man or Woman in the World, is savingly benefited by his then appearing as a Saviour, and obtaining precious Gifts for Men, but as every such Individual Person comes to experience his Internal Manifestation, to *Convince, Condemn, Wound, Heal, Break, Bind up, Slay, make Alive, in the Newness of the Spirit:* This is the State of Right Redemption and Salvation, and thus is he particularly a Saviour, and every such one is greatly benefited by him, as he was in that former Appearance the General Saviour of Mankind. Behold then, *O you that are Impartial!* How unworthily he hath injur'd us? To make People believe, *That we testifie to Christ's Inward Appearance in Opposition to, and Denial of his Outward*; which is far from our Hearts so much as to conceive.

§. 3. But again he tells us, (Pag. 9, 10, 11.) *That Christianity made it's Way by the Purity of it's Doctrine, the Gracious Words that Christ spoke, by Signs and Wonders; but* Quakerism *by Blasphemies against the Lord Jesus Christ*; and quotes E. B. saying, *Your imagin'd God above the Stars*; and G. Fox, *There are Miracles among Believers in the Spirit,* &c. frothily querying, *Whether it smells more of the* Fox, *or the* Goose.

'Tis true, the Purity of it's Doctrine was, and is, an admirable Enforcement it had, and hath above all other: Nor can he fasten justly any Impurity upon what we profess, though he endeavours to detract from it by base Aspersions, for indeed it is the same. *Sweet were the Words of Christ, I grant,* but altogether Severe and Terrible, to *Pharisaical Hypocrites,* who were both the *greatest Scripturians,* and *Haters of Him, in that Age.*

1673.
Chap. II.

§. 4. Nor is it true that E. *Burrough* fo expreft himfelf in *Derifion of God's Prefence above the Stars*; but of People's imagining him to be in the *Likeness of Man*, and fo denying his *Omniprefence*, that He fhould not be as well below as above.

§. 5. But *Wonders and Miracles* were wrought. What then? Are not the *Quakers* True *Chriftians without them*? See the Wickednefs of this Spirit that works againft us; *unlefs we will work Miracles to confirm that Doctrine in this Generation, which was confirmed by Miracles Sixteen Hundred Years ago, either it is not True, or we have no Right to it.* But by the Way, obferve their Folly, *for they Unchriftian at once Chriftianity and themfelves too*; *fince Chriftianity muft either be no longer fuch, nor they Chriftians, whilft they cannot work Wonders to prove it, or themfelves to be fuch*; or elfe the Quakers *are never the lefs True Chriftians, for not working thofe Wonders they boldly require from us*. We pretend not to a New Miniftration, and fince the Queftion is not about the Vifible Coming of the *Meffiah*, which call'd for Vifible *Miracles* (for that's granted on all Hands in *Europe*) but the Spiritual Appearance of the *Meffiah* in the Hearts and Confciences of his People, that he might not have a bare and empty Title when he was call'd J E S U S, *but really fave his People (now as then) from their Sins*; the Cafe is plainly alter'd *as to obvious Miracles to our Carnal Senfes*; *the prefent Work being to open the blind Eye, and unftop the deaf Ear of the Mind*; blinded and ftopt by the God of this World. And thefe are greater Things, of more Weight, and the Confequence of them of far greater Importance. And judge you, how Vain, Light, and unbecoming a Minifter of the Gofpel of Chrift Jefus, that requires an Account for every idle Word, was it in *J. Faldo*, when treating of *Chriftianity*, to fay, *Whether it fmells more like the* Fox *or the* Goofe? *Vain and Frothy?*

§. 6. But once more, (Pag. 11, 12.) *Chriftianity entred the World with Ravifhing Songs, and Hallelujahs of the Angels, Healing all Difeafes, Cafting out Devils, Preaching Peace*: But Quakerifm *entred the World, as if Hell had broke loofe, and Poffeffions by Satan had made Way, and fitted Souls for the* Quaker's *Spirit.* ——— *O the Hell-dark Expreffions of the* Quaker's *Spirit, Frightful, and Amazing Words, Bitter Curfes, Howlings and Roarings!* And what elfe J. Faldo's *Devil pleafeth, by which to render the* Quakers *Odious.* Well! But to Anfwer him.

It was a Time of Joy, and a Time of Sorrow; the Spirits of the Juft rejoyced that he was born forth into the World, and that Sun of Righteoufnefs rifen, whofe Difcovering Light, and Refrefhing Beams would renew the World, that had been in great Meafure bewilder'd, fince it's firft innocent State: *But therefore was it not a Time of Wo, Sorrow, Terror, and Grievous Diftrefs to all the Workers of Iniquity? Did not Chrift come to bring War as well as Peace*; *a Sword, a Fire upon Earth? Did not his Fore-runner come in an Aftonifhing Manner, in differing Attire, of another Diet, and from a Defolate Place to Preach Repentance, and to Warn them,* With an O Generation of Vipers, to flee the Wrath to come? *Did he not fay, that an* Ax, (a fharp and tetrible Inftrument) *fhould be laid to every Unfruitful Tree?* And did not the Apoftles Preach *to the Pricking of the Hearts of Thoufands*; and *Paul* by Name, *that* Felix *himfelf trembled?* And all, *as knowing the Terrors of the Lord themfelves, they warn'd others? Wherefore Judgment is faid to have begun at the Houfe of God*. Finally, Did not the Devils Howl, Roar, and Tremble, *forefeeing they fhould be diflodg'd by One Stronger than themfelves*, Chrift, the Son of the Living God? *And was there no Terror, Dread and Amazement in all this? I perceive it may be a Virtue in the* Primitive Chriftians, *but a Vice in the* Quakers, at leaft in J. Faldo's *Account*.

But this know, O impartial People, the *Quakers* were overtaken by the mighty Hand of God, *and great were their Travels and Pangs of Sorrow, under the Righteous Terrors of the Lord*, whofe Hour of Juft Judgments was come; and being thereby made Witneffes of his Handy Work, and redeem'd through Judgment, *they became Minifters of Judgment unto others*; and the Terror of it ftruck Thoufands; *the Devils trembled,* and all Flefh (at leaft in fome) *was as Grafs, and the Beauty of their Carnal, Outfide Religion, but as the Flower of the Field*; which, in the Name of the Lord we teftify, fell, and wither'd before the Brightnefs of his Appearance to us; *who put on Strength like a Giant that was to run his Race, and girded himfelf with Power*; *and who was able to ftand before him? The Hills melted at his Prefence, and the Mountains fled before him into the Sea.*

And art thou given up, *J. Faldo*, to call *Light*, Darknefs; and *Darknefs*, Light; the Terrors of God, the Poffeffions of Satan; and Remorfe of Confcience, Hell broke Loofe? O Unhappy Man! The Lord will reckon with thee for this Blafphemous

phemous Impiety: And this I say to thee, and all thy Associates, *That Eternal Misery will be the End of you, for all your sweet Notions of Religion, unless you obtain Mercy through the Fire; the fiery Judgments of the Lord revealed in your Consciences.* For that End is Christ now, as formerly, manifested, that *Judgment might be laid to the Line, and Righteousness to the Plummet in all*: And because we earnestly contend for the *Inward Work of Christ*, as the most Beneficial to Mankind, therefore it is that you *Priests* have us in Hatred, Scorn, and Derision, all the Day long; and indeed, we are grievously wronged by your Wickedness and Cruelty; *But the Lord is our Strength, of whom therefore should we be afraid? And why do you Rage, and imagine a Vain Thing concerning us?*

§. 7. Now for the Time when *Christianity* and *Quakerism* came (as he is pleas'd to distinguish them) Pag. 13. 14, 15. Some, says he, *date Christianity from the Birth of Christ*. Others, *With much more Reason, from the Resurrection of Christ*, witness that Place, *All Power is given unto me in Heaven and in Earth.*

The Consequence of this Assertion is thus much, *That Christ taught not Christianity*; *That his Disciples who believed in him, were but a better Kind of* Carnal Jews: *That Christ's Life, Doctrine and Miracles, were not perform'd under a State of Christianity*; *That he had not all Power before his Resurrection*, contrary *to the Scripture.* In short, *That* Christ and Christianity *did not go together*; and if you will, *That Christ was not Christ, but a Good Extraordinary* Jew, *before his* Resurrection; for I am sure his Notion of the Beginning of Christianity, warrants the Consequence. O the Orthodoxality of this Whiffling-Priest, Busy-Body, and Conceited enough.

Well, but this is not all, we have Contradiction to add to his Burden; *Christianity made it's Way by many Signs and Wonders wrought before Multitudes, and that not only by Christ himself, but also by his Disciples and Servants*, Both Before, And After His Death. If this be not Giving and Taking, Granting and Denying, there is no such Thing in the World: *For here is Christianity before Christ's Death, and yet with much more Reason, here is a Denial of that Assertion*, and Affirming that it took it's Rise after His Resurrection. Truly, we need not much fear the Consequence of such Encounters, when our Adversary puts Weapons into our Hands to his own Shame and Overthrow.

§. 8. But that he may be farther kind to us, he proceeds, *The Disciples were called Christians at* Antioch, Acts 11. 26. *But the Thing Christian, might well be before the Name Christian.* Enough for us, sober Reader, to defend our First Chapter (but a woful Contradiction to himself) where we say, that what was call'd Christ, *was before the Name*, and something of the Excellent Nature of Truth, Purity, Holiness, which leads to *Salvation*, &c. which the Word *Christianity* with us imports at large (unless they should be excluded as any Parts thereof, which supposeth a Christianity Destitute of Truth, Purity, Holiness, *&c.* like that of this Age) though in no Appearance so clear, as in that, in which Christ visibly manifested himself.

§. 9. But upon *Peter*'s Words, *If any Man suffer as a Christian, let him not be ashamed*, 1. Pet. 4. He observes, *here Christianity is distinguisht both from* Judaism *and* Heathenism. *Both the* Gentiles *and the* Jews *were bitter Enemies to the* Christian *Name; and that not for the* Name, *but the* Thing's *Sake.*

This must either regard the *Apostate Jew and Gentile*, and so we close; or the *Jew and Gentile* upon their Inward Knowledge of God, and Obedience to Him; and here we recede, and must deny his Assertion (nay, it would be a Contradiction to that Justice, Purity, and Worth he allows them to have had, since it were to say, that such Qualifications could be Ignorant of Christianity, the Perfection of them) for the *Good* among them became Disciples, at least Lovers of the Christian Religion, then not Haters of either Name or Thing: For where among *Jews* or *Gentiles*, their Hearts were Upright to God, according to that Discovery he made of himself to them, and that they kept to the Divine Sense and Relish which they had of the Love, Purity, Justice, Mercy, Goodness, and Recompence of God (for such as in any Age could come to God, did *first know that God was, and that He was a Rewarder of all those that did draw nigh unto Him*, to obtain which Knowledge, God had manifested it in Man; for he had shewn it *there* unto him) I say, those who so retained the Sense of God in their Knowledge, were not aggriev'd, *Christianity* should take Place; for they measuring Things as they inwardly felt them, were proper Judges of God's Rising and Breaking forth among the Sons of Men; they could feel Him leading out of, and beyond the Use of those Elements which were once added because of Weakness, and now became Beggarly by a brighter

Glory.

Glory: An inward Sense being that they kept to, as the more sure Word, as they felt a with-drawing of the Divine Life, Power, Spirit, out of those inferiour Institutions, they followed it, not staying in any outward Dispensation, because God had been there, if he had once left it: But such as were Literal, Formal, Exact, Critical, *they were the Persons*, who having least of the Divine Sight and Sense of God's Goings among the Sons of Men, they contended for God's Exterior Appointments; as that they were signally given; Good Men had practised them, and are we Wiser then our Fathers? No, we will have our Reasons *(indeed Darkness)* satisfied in the Matter. Behold the *Pharisee and Greek of Old*, to whom Christ's outward Appearance was to the one a *Stumbling Block*, and to the other *Foolishness*; and the many-headed Professor now, who esteems no better of his *Spiritual Manifestation* in the Hearts of the Children of Men. O! What will the End be, of the Gaudy, Obstinate Hypocrites of this Age, who resist so great Salvation? Tribulation and Anguish for ever, unless they Repent; *for what Men Sow, that shall they Reap*; and, *who have improved their Talent, shall enter into the Joy of their Lord*.

§. 10. Well, But when came this *Quakerism* into the World? He tells us, (Pag. 15. 16, 17.) about the Year 1651. quoting E. B's *Epistle* before G. F's *Great Mystery*; also a small Treatise writ by *J. Whitehead*, and *J. Pennington*; from whence he infers, *That Quakerism is a late Dispensation, therefore not that of Christianity*. But certainly this Man hath taken a very quick Course to Unchristian himself and all the *Presbyterians, Independents,* and *Anabaptists* in the World, as well as the *Quakers*. For I would ask him, if there was not a Time since the Primitive Age, wherein Darkness had overspread the Earth, the Beast did Reign, and the Pure Religion was wholly Wilderness? If so, consequently the Resurrection of Truth is no more a New Dispensation, or not that of Christianity, than a Man that is exiled his Country, is not essentially the same Man, when he returns, that he was before. And so far is my Argument for those *Separatists*, that though I take them to be short of the True Evangelical Faith and Righteousness, yet I acknowledge them to have a Reformation unknown in that thick Apostacy, which had cover'd the World, and eclipst the Blessed Light of the Glorious Gospel that shin'd in the first Ages after Christ: But since we are of another Religion by his Account, than the *Christian*, because we cannot say, that we were always successively from the Apostle's Time, I will argue, that the *Presbyterians, Independents,* and *Anabaptists,* are not *Christians*, nor is what they profess, to be esteem'd *Christianity*, because they cannot prove a Regular Succession from the Apostle's Times, their Date also being of later Years. What will they say then? The *Church* was fled into the *Wilderness*; *Truth* exil'd; *God* as a Stranger in the Earth; yet *Truth* still the same in it self. Very well, so say we: God was pleas'd to renew the Right Christian Dispensation to us, and by us, according to *John's* Vision, *That the Everlasting Gospel was preacht again*, intimating, *That there had been a Time wherein it was not preacht*. If this be not a New Gospel, because a-new, or again, preacht, neither is that which *J. Faldo* calls *Quakerism*, a New Dispensation, because it is *Preaching a-new the Everlasting Gospel* to the Sons of Men; which is God's Power inwardly manifested for the Conviction, Conversion, Redemption, and Salvation of the Souls of such as believe it.

§. 11. And tho' he particularly seems to triumph over *Isaac Pennington's* distinguishing between the Dispensation of *Moses, Christ,* and *His Apostles,* and *This* of our Day, as if they had been Three several Dispensations, and consequently, if Christ's was not that of *Moses*, because it swallow'd it up; neither this the Dispensation of Christ, which *J. Pennington* saith, it swallows up; yet to me it seems a pitiful Catch; and shows, he knows not how to take Things with that Candor they are writ. *J. P.* means not a Distinct Administration in Kind, but Dispensation of one and the same Light, Life, and Power by Nature, at several Times, and sundry Manners to the World: *Christ* was before the Law, under the Law, with the Prophets, but never so revealed as in that *Holy Manhood*; will it therefore follow, he was not Antecedent to that Appearance, or He, that appeared then more Gloriously, had never shown himself before? Or, because of a Difference in Manifestation, therefore *not* the same H E (through all those several Manifestations) in Himself? Certainly this Man is very Unjust to *J. P.* especially, when the Words above quoted, that speak of a Dispensation he experienced a little before God broke forth by us called *Quakers*, could have informed him, that he meant the divers Breakings forth of God's Light and Truth, in order to the full Discovery, and Recovery of *Lost Primitive Christianity*. So that this present Appearance swallow-

swallowing up all going before it (had he so term'd it, as he doth not, and is therefore wrong'd) is no more than God's Retrieving to us the Ancient Gospel, with additional Blessings and Assistances, giving us the same Life and Foundation they had, and what else He pleased by Way of Improvement; which alters not the Nature, no more than a Child in Christ is not that Numerical Creature, but another Distinct Being, when a Man. And if this Account of Things will not satisfie him, he may chuse: I have thus far cleared the TRUTH, and those who sincerely profess it, and therein my own Conscience, both to God and the World.

CHAP. III.

J. Faldo's Charge. That the Scriptures are not the Word of God, Reasons for it. The Scriptures by him urg'd against us, clear'd, and prov'd to be for us. They are the Words of the Word, a Declaration of the Great Law, Word, or Commandment, but not that Law, Word, or Commandment.

§. 1. THIS Chapter will concern the Scriptures more directly, in which we hope to prove, that not we, but our *Adversary*, is mistaken with respect to what he chargeth upon us.

§. 2. (Pag. 18. 19, 20.) He intitles his Chapter thus: *That the* Quakers *Deny the Scriptures.*

I was almost astonisht at it, because he pretended to prove all out of our own Books, and none such had ever yet come to my Hand: But upon my sober Perusal of the Matter, I found this to be the Upshot, *That the* Quakers *Deny them to be the Word of God*; therefore they deny them altogether: Whence I take good Heart to show his Ignorance, or great Dishonesty.

§. 3. I will allow to him, without going any farther, that the People called *Quakers, do deny the Scriptures to be the Word of God*, and therefore shall take for granted, what he quotes out of *J. N. F. Howgil, J. Parnel*, and *W. Smith*. But that we do consequently deny the Scriptures, we shall oppose, we hope, to the Death.

§. 4. I do declare to the whole World, that *We believe the Scriptures to contain a Declaration of the Mind and Will of God*, in and to those Ages in which they were written, being given forth by the Holy Ghost, moving in the Hearts of Holy Men of God; That they ought also to be Believed, Read, and Fulfill'd in our Day, being Useful for Reproof and Instruction, that the Man of God may be perfect: And that they have been, and are Instrumental to great Good upon the Spirits of People, by the secret Power of God, which often strikes, and presseth home to the very Conscience, the weighty Truths declar'd therein; yet *We do deny them to be the Word of God, ascribing that alone to* Christ Himself, *and that not without Scripture and Reason.*

§. 5. *First*, It is granted on all Hands, that *CHRIST* is expresly called in Scripture *The Word of GOD*, but no where, that the Scriptures are so stiled.

Secondly, That tho' I should allow it to be a Figurative Expression, and therefore says our *Adversary*, *improper*, yet because a Word among Men, conveys the Mind of one unto another, and that *Christ is the Great Word of God*, that in all Ages hath convey'd, or spoken the Mind of God unto Mankind (and so the Author of all Good Works) He only may by Way of Right and Excellency, be so stil'd of us.

Thirdly, I shall easily grant to him, that one Word may stand Representative of many; and that the Ten Words were not Ten Numerical Words, because each Word contained many: Yet this I will say, that *Word* in Scripture is taken for *Commandment*, and they have an equivalent Signification, as in *Deuteronomy* may be seen. And since that was the Import of the Ten Words, *to wit*, Ten Commandments, each Word has it's own Commandment; Therefore it is no more against us, to allow those Ten Words, to be more than Ten Words, than Ten Commandments, to have more than Ten Words.

And whatever our *Adversaries* may say, or think of us, we therefore decline to call the Scriptures the *Word of God*, because *we believe it to be a Title only due to that Living, Quickning Word, by which God vouchsafes to disclose His Mind and Will unto Mankind,* Christ, *the Way to the Father.*

§. 6. But says our *Adversary* to this *Argument*, The Word was God, therefore the Scriptures cannot be the Word, because they are not God: *Let me tell you, that the Scripture may be the Word, and Christ the Word also; and yet though Christ be*

the

the Word of God, the Scriptures the Word may be quite another Thing. Certain I am, this is quite another Thing than good Doctrine: How can the Scriptures be the Word of God, and Chrift the Word of God too? Are there two Diftinct Words of God, the one quite another Thing from the other? O fhameful Arguing! If he had faid, Chrift is *the* Word of God, and the Scriptures *a* Word of God, he would have hit the Mark a little better: But to affert *Two General Comprehenfive Words of God*, founds harfh and inconfiftent. I would fain know, in Cafe we fhould admit this abfurd Affertion, how he would diftinguifh between thefe Two General Comprehenfive Words? For my Part; I think it as good Senfe, to call a *King's Letters*, King; or an *Ambaffador's Credential's* Ambaffador. *O no, fays our Adverfary, you miftake; Chrift is called a Light, a Rock, a Lyon, will it thence follow, that there are no other Lights, Rocks, or Lyons.* I anfwer, There is no other *Light, Rock* or *Lyon* than Chrift, with refpect to *That* for which *He* is fo called; Neither is there any other *Word* than *Chrift*, with refpect to *that* for which he is fo ftyl'd, to wit, *God's Living, Powerful Word*: And this decides the Controverfy, and plainly adjudges us the Matter againft the utmoft Force of our Adverfary, to the Contrary: For if he is therefore a Light, becaufe he only can, and doth difcover the unfruitful Works of Darknefs; *a Rock*, becaufe whoever build on him, is fafe; and a *Lyon*, becaufe the *King* of all, whofe Utterings are able to terrify all Deftruction from his Walks, but what he brings upon his Adverfaries, and therefore there is not another *Light to inlighten Man's Soul*, or *Rock for Chrift's Church to be built on*, neither *any other Lyon to fecure them from the Devourer*: confequently, becaufe he is the Living, Spiritual, Powerful *Word* of God, *there is not another, that's the Word of God.*

§. 7. But he farther fays, That the *Word of God* is fo expreft in Scripture, as it muft needs be underftood not of *Chrift*, but the *Scriptures*. *He that regardeth not the Word of the Lord. He that feared the Word of the Lord. Stand thou ftill a While, that I may fhew thee the Word of God, the Sword of the Spirit, which is the Word of God.* And *the Cares of the World — choak the Word, and it becometh Unfruitful*, Mark 4. 19. *which*, faith he, *cannot be underftood of* Chrift *or* God, *and that a little Skill in the Original would free us from thofe Miftakes*, and to that Purpofe.

To which I anfwer, That the *Word of the Lord* mention'd in *Exodus* and *Samuel* are properly to be underftood of the Living, Spiritual *Word of God*, which fpoke to the People through thofe Servants of the Lord; For who received or rejected the *Mind of that Word*, expreft in many Words, received the Word, and it had a Place in their Hearts; or elfe rejected it, and it had no Place in them: This makes nothing againft us in the leaft. For that Paffage in the *Ephefians, Beza*, whom he quotes, I fuppofe as embracing his Judgment, has determin'd the Matter; for he has it, *the Spiritual Sword*. Then let us read the Word thus, *The Spiritual Sword is the Word of God*, or *The Word of God is the Spiritual Sword*. For Chrift is as truly a Sword, an Axe, a Fire, which the Word of God is called, as a Lyon, a Rock, a Door. And for the laft Paffage of *Mark*, which feems to carry moft of Weight in it for our Adverfary, it may rightly be underftood of that *Truth, which Chrift, the Word, livingly fows in the Hearts of Men and Women, the Word of Advice, Reproof, Inftruction*, and the like: But of the Scriptures it cannot be underftood, as neither can any of the other Places.

For *Firft*, Thofe two Paffages in *Exodus* and *Samuel* concern only particular Cafes, at a Time, when not a third Part of the Scriptures were written, as our Adverfary will confefs. And for that in the *Ephefians*, 'tis manifeft that the Scriptures, which are fubject to fo many Cafualties as they are, are not the Spiritual Sword, or Sword of the Spirit, therefore not the Word of God, whofe Edge never blunts; For as is the Spirit, fuch is the Sword, and fuch the Word, to wit, Living, Spiritual, Powerful, which the Scriptures of themfelves (I think; all will, or fhould acknowledge) are not. I will not ftick to confefs alfo, that a Word of Advice, a Word of Counfel, a Word of Reproof, and a Word of Comfort lodge in the Scripture; or the Scriptures, with Refpect to the Times, wherein they were given forth, (and now daily, as brought Home to the Confcience by the *One Word of God*, who gave them firft forth) are Words of Truth, Knowledge, Wifdom, Love, Reproof, Exhortation, Edification, *&c.* yet never can we be brought to attribute unto the Declaration *that Title, which is peculiarly due to Him, whofe Declaration it is.* A Prince may exprefs his Mind in Words, but thofe Words are not that Prince; neither can any one of his Titles, as a living Prince, be properly

given

given to his said Declaration. Nor have we any other Way to distinguish between the *Word* and *Words, Commandment* and *Commandments,* the *Thing It self,* and *those Expressions* by which it doth declare it self, than *the Word of God,* and the *Words of the Word,* which are the Words of God, or *Holy Writings:* Holy with Respect to the Matter or Truth they treat of.

§. 8. But here *J. Faldo* steps in, and seems to offer an Expedient in this Streight; Says he, *Though you say they are not the* Word of God *eminently, and I believe so too; for the* Scriptures *cannot be the Word of God in that Sense wherein* Christ *is, yet you may call them the Written Word of God, for so we distinguish them.*

Truly, this seems pretty modest, though here we must part too, unless he will come a little nearer; For neither can the Word of God properly be said to be written: The Words by which the Mind or Will of the Word is exprest, may be recorded, and, as such, a True Declaration; but it is as impossible for the Word of God to be written, as it would be for a *Prince,* or *Senate* to be *written,* or contained in Letters, though their Will and Pleasure may be largely declared by a Writing; because it would be to say, that the *Word of God could grow Old, Decay, be Lost, Mis-rendred, Corrupted, Transcribed, Re-printed, Corrected, and be Subjected to Fire, Water, Vermin,* &c. which were impossible. So would it be an absolute Derogation from the Dignity peculiarly Due to the Living Word of God, to give that which is it's proper Title to any Thing beneath it's Living, Powerful, Quickning Self. He has a Scripture or two for us; I have written to him the great Things of my Law; *A sharp Rebuke,* says he, *to the Objectors against the Written Word of God,* but I don't see it for my Share. The great Things of the Law, Word, or Commandment, which are required, may be written, but that doth not follow, that the Eternal Law, Word, or Commandment Requiring, is a written Law, Word, or Commandment, but the Contrary; And for *Moses's Writings,* of which Christ spoke, 'tis manifest, they were not called the Word of God, but *the Word of God himself called them Writings.*

§. 9. But *J. Faldo* objects on t'other Hand, that he much feareth, *the Scriptures will lose of their Authority with People, in case they should not be so acknowledged;* and at last he falls so downright upon us, that he boldly, but weakly concludes, *who deny the Scriptures to be the Word of God, deny them in every Respect: For who denies them that Title, denies what they have been generally known by, distinguisht from, and lifted up above all other Writings; and that Appellation, on which is grounded their Authority, and which puts an Awe upon the Consciences of Men.* How weak and vain this is, I could freely leave to the *Reader,* without any farther Consideration; But that it might not be thought by any therefore Unanswerable, I will say, *That to call them the Words of God, and declared Mind and Will of God to Mankind, is no such Diminutive Title,* but altogether Worthy of them.

§. 10. If we do deny to them what has been wrongly attributed, that no Ways lessens their Authority, but corrects the Mistake of those who thought of them beyond what they really are; It is a poor begging of the Question, to say, We deny them, that which many have ascrib'd to them. Their Authority is grounded upon the Living Word of God, and who comes to that, Honours the Scripture aright; and who err from the Holy Conduct of it, their Verbal Praises of the Scripture, are but like the Pharisees Painting the Prophets Sepulchres, whilst they were Persecutors of One greater than the Prophets: And who knows not, how much the Shell hath had ascrib'd unto it the Honour, only due to it's Substance, by those Watchmen of the Night, whose Dark Minds could see no farther?

§. 11. And for the Awe they have upon Men, this is my Judgment, and I am not asham'd of it, that attributing so much to the Letter of the Scriptures, and declining that Regard Men ought to have had unto the Holy Living *Word of God,* that alone creates all Things New, and was the Author of, and Rule to those found Words themselves, *hath robbed the Living Word of God of it's True and Rightful Honour, and rendred Men's Hearts more formal, and less Awful than they would otherwise have been;* So that the only Way for People to come to a True Sight of, Sincere Respect for, and Grounded Belief in the Holy Scriptures, is, *to be turned to the Voice of the Living, Powerful Word of God, from whom they came, which is nigh unto every one, to direct, and order, and Discipline to, and in that Way of Holiness,* they testify of, *and which leads to Eternal Happiness.*

CHAP.

CHAP. IV.

His Charge. *What he quotes proves it not.* Revelation, Infallibility, *and* Inspiration *considered.* The Priest prov'd uncertain of his own Faith. *Our Friends debase not the* Scriptures, *but lift them up.* His Objection *against our Books Titles answer'd.* The Use of Scripture asserted. The Light *vindicated from Insufficiency.* Something of the True Light.

§. 1. **H**IS Fourth and next Chapter to be examined, endeavours to prove, *That we equal our Writings and Sayings to the Scriptures, and prefer them before the Scriptures.*

In this Undertaking, he must either prove, what he asserts, from our own Writings expresly, or Consequentially. To run through every Quotation he makes, would be as Tedious, as Impertinent; But a few of what make most to his Purpose, I will faithfully observe with his Inferences.

§. 2. He begins with a Book, intituled, *Love to the Lost*; (and so will I) *The Things following which I have declared of, are not the Things of Man, nor by Man did I receive them, but by the Revelation of Jesus Christ*: W. Dewsberry thus, *The Word of the Lord to his Beloved City, through your Brother and Companion in the Tribulation and Kingdom of Patience in the Lord Jesus Christ.*

Now what to say here in their Defence, when he lays nothing to their Charge, but what hath been generally exprest, I know not; Certain it is, that *No Man knows the Father but the Son, and Him to whom the Son* Reveals *him. The Inspiration of the Almighty giveth Understanding*; and, *No Man can know the Things of God but by the Spirit of God.* Well may we conclude then, that *J. Faldo* knows God no better than I do *Terra Incognita*; for he denies all Knowledge of him by any Internal Discoveries: What he knows, is by Man, and from Man.

What Offence, or Undervalue, I would fain know, can it be to the Scriptures, that Men should know God that only Way, by which they testify, God can be known of Men? Or, Why should he be angry at this Author, for Confessing to have known God that very Way, by which the Scriptures declare him only to be known? But indeed, it happens ill to the Priest, for all this is to prove too, *that We deny the Scriptures, though hereby we fulfil them.*

§. 3. For *W. D*'s Words, *they are also firm*; for God promised the Re-pouring out of his Spirit, and the Re-preaching of his Everlasting Gospel: And since the Question is not, whether we have it; but, *whether it be an Invalidating the Scriptures, for any, under the Plentiful Pourings out of the Spirit, and Power of God, to say, This is the Word of the Lord*; I say, it is firm, that so saying may therefore be in the Latter as well as Former Days allowable, and no Detraction at all from the Scriptures: And for the Conclusion of his *Epistle*, it is what every good Christian Man can say. What Folly, what Impudence is it in *J. Faldo*, to make that an Equaling our Writings to Scripture, or Preferring them before it, which both his own Tribe (I am able to make appear) hath frequently used, though by them irreproveably? And which indeed is the Condition of every good *Christian-Man*, namely, *to be a Brother, and Companion to the Children and Family of God, in the Tribulation and Kingdom of Patience in the Lord Jesus.* Well! If this Man's manifest Weakness make not for our Cause, I should very greatly wonder.

§. 4. And therefore, says he, *Pennington prays seriously, My Upright Desire to the Lord for you is — That he would strip you of your Knowledge of the Scriptures, according to the Flesh*; By *Flesh*, says he, their Sense is, *the Use of our Understandings* (though Sanctified) *as will appear in the Key, &c.*

But this Expression serves for a *Notable Key* to open his Ignorance and Dishonesty: His *Ignorance* is evident in Reputing it a Slight of the Scriptures, to desire that Men might be stript of their Fleshly Knowledge of them. I do affirm it to be both Seasonable and Serious; and did not *J. Faldo* stand upon a tottering Basis, he would not so declaim against us for Undermining it. But let all behold his *Dishonesty*, to say, that we desire *to be stript of the Knowledge of the Scriptures after our Sanctified Understanding, and that Flesh* which can never inherit the Kingdom of God, to wit, the *Carnal,* Dead, Dark, Unregenerated *Understanding* to be all one. O Disingenuous Man! Art thou fit to be a *Gospel-Minister*, who hast not learnt to do as thou wouldst be done by? I leave it with the Conscience of the

Reader,

Reader, how juftly or unjuftly thou haft dealt with us in this Matter, and what all or any of it concerns the Scriptures; For if Men will not underftand them as they are, is it the Fault of the Scriptures? No, furely; fhall then *Ifaac Pennington*'s Defire, that they might be ftript of their wrong Knowledge of thofe weighty and holy Writings, be interpreted a Difrefpect to them, and a preferring our own Writings before them, which fo heartily feeks their Right Knowledge of them? If this be the Way to prove *Quakerifm no Chriftianity*, we need not much fear the Iffue of his Attempt.

§. 5. But he proceeds to prove our Equaling of the Scriptures two Ways: *Firft*, From our pretending to *Infallibility*. *Secondly*, Our Plea for the Neceffity of *Infpiration*. He quotes G. *Whitehead*'s Letter to him, *Whether Infallibility be attainable by any in thefe Days? Which we affirm, is to true Believers; which if thou denieft, we queftion thy Call*. Of *Infpiration* he cites *J. Story*'s fhort Difcovery thus, *Therefore may I fay, much more, it is not in the Power of that little Book, either to throw down Self-will in any, in whom it is not yet fubdued, or to exalt the Truth in general, becaufe it is only* Queries *gather'd by the Author* from the Letter *of the Scriptures without, and no Meffage of Heavenly Prophefy, Doctrine or Exhortation receiv'd by the Author from the Lord through the Divine Infpiration of his Light and Spirit within*; Therefore I fay, *It is a very Vain and Idolatrous Exhortation*. To all which fober Matter I have no other Anfwer from him, than that the Quakers Writings are full to this Purpofe. Indeed I am glad of it, or we had little Reafon to fuffer what we do for our Diffent from the Carnal Profeffors of Religion in the World: But I have this to fay to him; He that doth not infallibly know what he knows of God or Religion, *knows nothing certainly, which concerns either*. Now if Men cannot attain to any fuch Certainty, Farewel all Religion; For, *That a Man fhould affirm, and not know whereof*; That he fhould profefs God and Religion, yet be uncertain of both: But that *J. Faldo* fhould Preach of both, *and profefs himfelf Errable in all fuch Doctrine*; Who ought to believe him? Why fpends he his Breath at a Venture? Rather let him eat, drink, for to Morrow he fhall Dye; for Death is certain. This is your *Independent*, *Fallible*, *Errable*, *Uncertain* J. Faldo, *Preacher to a People at* Barnet, *and*, God knows, *a Lamentable one too*. What Reafon have any to Believe him againft Us, who is Uncertain of the Truth of what he fays againft us, by his own Principle?

§. 6. For *Infpiration*, the Scriptures are not more exprefs in any one Thing. No Man can know the Things of God by the bare Spirit of a Man: But, the Spirit of a Man, or a Man diftinctly confidered from the Infpiration of the Almighty, can read *Scripture*, and form *Queries*, and call them *Chriftian* too; yet, *who will dare affirm this Man's Queries to be Chriftian?* Can they beat down *Self-will?* They may talk of it, or exalt the *Living Truth*, that came not from it. This is the Scope of *J. Story*'s Anfwer to the Queftioner; For, what is this but Stealing the Prophets and Apoftles Words, when they are made Ufe of out of that Senfe in which they were given forth, and to another End, than that for which they were given forth, which proves to us, that the Senfe, and not the Words, fhews the End of their being fo given forth. The Scriptures are a Sealed Book to all, but thofe who know them by the fame Hand, which Originally gave them. So that however common they may be in the World, they are Strangers to them that underftand them not: And though Old, refpecting the Time, when they were revealed to the Saints, yet New to every Age; fo that we affert not a Revelation of new Things, but renewed Revelation of thofe Things God made former Ages Witneffes of; otherwife Men are no more benefited by them; And to be benefited, they muft be made ours by the Spirit, which made them the Holy Ancients.

§. 7. In fhort, No Man can underftand Spiritual Things, but the Spiritually Difcerning; None can fo be without the Infpiration of the Almighty, or Spirit of God. This is Scripture. Now the Author of thofe Queries, and *J. Faldo* alfo, denying Infpiration, *they confequently deny themfelves to be Spiritually Difcerning*; and for Men *not Spiritual*, to Judge of Religious and Spiritual Matters, much lefs to write of them, and bid their Writings go, and *throw down Self-will, and exalt the Truth*, is Vain and Idolatrous; For, the Scriptures themfelves, confider'd meerly as fuch, are unable, much lefs Writings founded on the Authority of *Self-will*; for it is the alone Privilege of God's Power and Spirit, and no Writing whatever, diftinct from it, can perform that Great and Mighty Work in Man.

§. 8. And, for *Equaling our Writings* with the Scriptures, because we assert Inspiration, and that what we have received, and do declare of the Things of God, is from the Revelation of his Spirit in our Hearts, it is a foolish Inference: Truth was and is Truth all the World over, and there was and is but one Way to come to it in all Ages, I mean Inspiration. The Scriptures are True, and our Writings are True; but will it therefore follow, that we bring them upon a Vie? Is this your Disputant? But to determine this Case, He should first have prov'd, if he could, what Power God gave to the Ancients, and what to Us. How much of his Spirit to those Ages, and what to this; or else he loseth himself. If he can Experimentally tell, what were their Discoveries and Experiences, and what are Ours, he would be a proper Judge: But to think to run us down by Exalting them, or to lessen what we are, by Increasing their Praise, is an Old Artifice of the Devil; and Sober Men will be more true to themselves, and just to the Matter, than so to censure us. *Cannot one Man be another Man's Brother, and not the Elder Brother?* Doth it follow, that because God has made what we know our own, by his Holy Inspirations and Operations, that therefore we put our selves *upon the Comparison with the Ancients?* If true Christianity fill up, or add to Christ's Sufferings, yet behind, why should their *Writings be shuffled out of all Relation to the Scriptures?* There may be a Relation, *where there is not an Equality, much less a Preference,* and that we do assert against all Opposers.

§. 9. But now let us see what he says of our setting the Scriptures beneath our own Writings; and I will take his own Way to do it.

The Characters of the Scriptures, given by the Quakers, *as says* J. Faldo.	*Characters of their own* Teachers *Writings, and Sayings, given by them.*
Feeding Death with Death. The Letter which Killeth. [Declar. from the Minist. of the Word, p. 7.]	*The Voice of the Son of God was utter'd forth by him, by which the Dead was rais'd.* [F. H. Life of E. B. p. 20.]
Seeking the Living among the Dead [J. Parn. Shield.]	*His Words Ministred Grace to the Hearers* [Fox jun. Life E. B.] A Mistake, for he dy'd before E. B.

Reconciled: Death is a State without the Living Experimental Knowledge of God, and his Work in the Heart; And that State will talk of the Fame of Wisdom, as saith the Scripture, and that from the Scripture, that is, from, or in the Words of Scripture, being Ignorant of the true Sense of the Scripture, thinking there to have Life; which Literal Knowledge it feeds upon, and contents it self with, where Nations have lain Apostatized from the Life of God, and Power of Godliness. *The Letter Killeth*, that is, the Literal Knowledge (or rather their Imaginations from the Letter, not being Divinely Inspir'd, so as to understand it) by which Men buoy and lift up themselves as *Christians* in the World, and yet are Strangers to the inward sensible Work of God: And it does *Kill* the Soul, with respect to that true Life the Spirit and Power of God begets in all right *Christians*, through whom the Voice of the Son of God has, does, and will utter it self, to the Ends of the Earth, for the Raising the Dead in Trespasses and Sins, as that *worthy* Servant of God did, who is now with his Lord. This disreputes not the Scriptures, but those who make a wrong Use of them; nor is there any Comparison betwixt Reading what God's Spirit requires, and immediate Hearing his Voice, and being sensible of his present living Touches upon the Soul: Writings are but Holy Things at second Hand; a Living Ministry is the very Life, Power and Spirit present, and more immediate In short, the Testimony of *F. H.* we prefer not before the Testimony *Luke* gives of Holy *Stephen*. We prefer the Scriptures before all Writings, but before God's immediate Power we dare not.

Paper, Ink, and Writing the same, pag. 7.	*A Shield of the Truth,* [Title *J. F's* Book.]

Reconcil. What's this to the Purpose? We say that the *Scriptures*, or the Writings, not the Things written of (mark that) are Paper, Ink and Writing, which was spoken abstractively, and upon a Comparison of them with the Word of God (that was with God, and was, and is God over all, blessed for ever) Doth any
Man

Man think, that we believe greater Things of *J. Parnel*'s Book? By no Means, He call'd not his Book, consisting of so much Writing, Ink, and Paper, a *Shield of Truth*; but that of which it treated, was the *Truth*, and with respect to the Controversial Part of it, as it was writ in Defence of the Truth, it might be term'd a *Shield*; in which Sense the *Scriptures* by him urged, have the upperhand of his Writing, by whose greater Authority with Men, he abets and maintains the Doctrine contended for.

Shews you (I suppose the Light) *your own Faces, which the Scriptures cannot do* [Scorned Quak. Account, p. 20.]

A Spiritual Glass opened [Smith's Catech. &c. & Morn. Watch.]

Reconcil. This can be no way hard to reconcile; For, when we say, the Scriptures cannot shew Men at all Times, and in all States, their Conditions, but the Secret In-shining Light of God alone, we are not so unworthy as to intend, that any Book of ours can; No, but with Respect to that *Principle* which it directs to, and is able to tell a Man All that ever he did, *The only Spiritual Glass*, and which the best of Writings fall short of.

Precepts and Traditions of Men [Morn. Watch, p. 18.]

Truth's Principles [Title of *Crook*'s Book.]

Reconcil. It is deny'd that ever any such Words were ever spoken, or written of the Holy Scriptures, as *Precepts and Traditions of Men*; for they contain the Holy Precepts and Traditions of the *Word of God*, who is God himself; it is base and unworthy, thus to mince and mis-represent our Writings. For *Truth's Principles* signifies no more, than the Declaration of what we believe, as the very Beginning of the Book expresly proves.

That Light is in the Scriptures, prove that; or tell me what one Scripture hath Light in it [Lip of Truth, p. 7.]

Light risen out of Darkness. Title of *Farnsworth*'s Book.

Reconcil. There is not Light in the Scriptures, that is, there is not Living, Spiritual, Essential Light in the Scriptures, or by Way of Excellency; *but a descriptive and declarative Light they carry with them of the true Light*, the Author of those excellent Things therein mentioned; In which Sense alone do we understand *Richard Farnsworth*'s Title. God having caused his Light to spring out of Darkness, and he being then the Witness of it, testified to the Truth thereof, by a Declaration to the World of what he knew in the Matter. He did not say, That *Book* was that *Light*; for so it had never been before him that writ it, *and the Writings of it*; and what Casualties the Book was, or is liable to, would fall upon the *Light*, though he bears Record to an *Everlasting Spiritual Light*, that shines Within, *where his Book cannot be*. But rather, that he knew and witnessed the *Visitation of the Day-spring of God's Eternal Light of Life to the World*, he writ his *Book*, to give *Notice thereof*, calling it by that *Name*, because his *Subject* treated on, doth manifestly import so much; not that the *Book* was that Holy and Eternal *Light*.

§. 10. Let it suffice to all impartial People, that we only desire to make Difference betwixt the *Writings*, and the *Thing written of*; and to the Eternal Overthrow of our Adversaries (not wholly without their own Help) since they think, the *Titles* we give our Books (very Glorious in themselves) most unworthy of them, but proper to the Scriptures, which they say, we slight. Let it be consider'd that not one of those Books is destitute of Scripture; but is either generally in a Scripture Stile, or particularly defended by Plenty of express Scriptures cited; *therefore of Necessity, they, the Scriptures, must also partake with them in Common of those famous Titles*: And thus far have they the Preference, that they are quoted on Purpose, to give the Truth we write of, greater Credit; what is that greater Credit, but to be exactly agreeable with themselves? So that our Adversaries Argument amounts to thus much; *They therefore prefer their own Writings before the Scriptures, because they in all their Writings earnestly endeavour by numerous Quotations to prove, what they write, to be according to the Scriptures.* Behold Reader, how at one blow we fall! The whole Chapter of this *Fallible, Errable, Uncertain, Busie Priest*, with respect to his Charge of our preferring our own Writings before the Scriptures.

§. 11. But there remain two Things to be considered before we close this Chapter. *First*, his untrue Inferences; *Secondly*, his base Comparison of us with the *Papists*, with Design to render us Odious to all that abominate their *Idolatry*.

First, *That the Scriptures both are, and ever were Superfluous; for, the Light within (as they pretend) was always fitted to Inspire every Man and Woman in the same Manner, and to all Intents and Purposes, as they were inspired, and written.*

Which, how just and true it is, we do reserve the Examination of to God's Witness in the Conscience of the *Reader*. Only, thus much I will say; that tho' all Ability was, and is in Him, whom we declare to be the Light of all Mankind, to Reveal the whole Mind of God, yet, inasmuch as very few in all Ages were so resigned up to the Holy Conduct of it, as they ought to have been, the Lord hath put it into the Hearts of Many, to stir up the Negligent and Slothful, by a Reminding them with that Counsel, in outward Writings or other Verbal Testimonies, which they had long slighted in themselves, that it might Instrumentally work upon them unfeigned Repentance and Conversion to God. Therefore went God's Messengers forth, Line upon Line, and Precept upon Precept; here a little, and there a little; But this I affirm, and that in the Name of the Lord, against the uttermost Strength of this Busie *Priest*, that, had those *Prodigals* in all Ages lived up to that Measure of Divine Light (the Talent God gave to every Individual) there had not been any such need for those Messages: Wherefore the Occasion of them was not for want of any sufficient Gift from God, but because of their own Rebellion. Nay, they were the *Testimonies of the very Light of Christ* (in the Prophets and Apostles, who were Heirs and Children of Light) which they gave forth at divers Times in their several Ages, as God pleased to move upon their Spirits with respect to Mankind; so that still it was the Light within, which so reproved and exhorted. But, suppose that the World had not been so Rebellious, neither will it follow, but that a slow Improvement of the Heavenly Gift, might have occasioned many Divine Exhortations; yea, the Exercises of Men's Spirits, as *David*'s for Instance, in reference to the Spiritual Travel, might for the Benefit of others have been written. Let us suppose the highest State of Deliverance, and Praise, Men are capable of arriving at in this World; yet Epistles of Divine Love, Experience, heavenly Praises, *&c.* might have been transmitted from Church to Church, as of the Flock and Family of God. Therefore I utterly deny, that the Perfection of Light's Teachings make the Scriptures superfluous, much less the general best Attainments that have been, and now are in the World.

§. 12. But that any Man, so conceited of his Abilities, as *J. Faldo*, should so basely mistake Reason, and abuse his Reader, as to infer from the Ability of the Light in It self, *whether obey'd, or not obey'd*, the Uselessness of the Scriptures, or Testimonies of Holy Men to the World, is Ground for just Censure and severe Rebuke; for it were to say, that because a Master is of himself able enough, therefore all Books are superfluous. The Scripture don't argue the Insufficiency of the Light, since so, the Instrument would rise against it's Principal; but the Insufficiency of the Creature, in which Condition Line upon Line, and Precept upon Precept may, by the Light within good Men, be given forth *to invite and encourage Man to yield Obedience to the Conviction of the Light within every such Rebellious Person*; in which the Love of God is marvellously expressed, who by his Holy Light within, and it's Testimonies without, endeavours the Conviction and Reformation of the Children of Men.

§. 13. But hear him in his second and last Inference; *upon the same Ground, the Tenets and Assertions of all the Heathens are to be received as of equal Authority with the Scriptures; for they resulted from their Light Within, improved much more orderly and to the Purpose than the Quakers do theirs. Yea, the bitter Scoffs of Lucian, and Julian the Apostate must be admitted into the same Order, for if it be admitted, they did not Vilifie, and Scorn, and Deride the Scripture and Christianity, according to the Dictates of their Consciences;* it cannot be denied, that they therein acted from the Power within, which whether it were the Power of Darkness, or not, the Quakers having no Rule to judge it by, but their own Sentiments, it *is left by them undetermined*; And I know not hardly any Worse they said of Jesus of

Nazareth, *the Scripture, and* Christianity, *than the* Quakers *have done under other Names.*

This Passage Impertinent enough to the Purpose, and as Black as Hell it self in Malice against that despised Remnant of People called *Quakers*, by God's Assistance, I will effectually answer, to the shame of this ungodly Slanderer.

The *Gentiles* Light was one in Nature with that, which the *Evangelist* saith, *enlightneth all Men* (a Text, whose Plainness and Expressness yields that Advantage to us, against the utmost Force of all our *Adversaries*, which they are Angry at, but can never Invalidate) I say, one in Nature with that Divine Being; and as such, transcending all Writings whatever: Yet that the *Gentiles* had that Light in a more excellent Degree, than that in which the *Prophets* and *Apostles* enjoyed it, whence came those excellent Writings, I utterly deny, and that in the Name of all true *Quakers*. I say again, that, though the least Measure of Pure *Light it self*, is to be preferred before all the Writings in the World, *as meer Writings*; yet that it may not be comparable to that Degree and farther Discovery of Light, which was witnessed by those who gave forth those Writings, I grant: So that to bring the Sayings and the Assertions of the *Heathens* upon an Equality with the Writings of the Holy *Prophets* and *Apostles*, we dare not assent to; but vehemently oppose any such Inference made to be the Product of our Belief. For though, as I said before, any measure of *Light it self* is beyond the most excellent *meer Writings* of a far greater; yet the Writings or Sayings given forth by that lesser Appearance, are not to be brought into Comparison with those of a greater Discovery, *no more than the Degrees of Discovery, or Manifestation of the Light it self*. This the Apostle *Paul* practised; who, notwithstanding that he rightly knew that Administration to supersede, and transcend what went before, stuck not to remind the *Heathens* of their own Authors, as *Aratus, Menander*, &c. *by an apt Application of them to this Purpose, in Defence of his Doctrine*. And if Those who became a Law unto themselves, Doing the Things contained in the Law, were to be preferred before the Circumcision, who kept not the Law, and that, who lived without Law outward——yet according to Law inward, should be judged by Law inward, which was substantially the same (as testifies the Apostle) with what was required by the Law outward; *Then their Law within Substantially consider'd, did not fall short of that Law without, nor they who kept it of the Circumcision themselves*; which most clearly overturns that Ignorant or Malicious Cavil, to wit, *that the* Quakers *have no Mean by which to judge of the Ground of Wrong and Right Actions*; For if the *Scriptures* be that only Judge, then there could have been no Knowledge of right or wrong Actions, Spirits or Powers, before they were given forth: Which because the *Patriarchs*, and *Gentiles* had an evident Sight and true Sense of, by that Internal Law of Light in the Heart and Conscience, without Scripture, it follows, that the *Quakers* owning the same Light, and that, in a more eminent Discovery, cannot be guilty of such an Ignorance.

§. 14. But a little farther to inspect his Argument: If the having no Outward Rule was to be without all Rule, whereby to Try a Right from a Wrong Power; I would gladly know, how the *Prophets* themselves were assured of the Truth of their Motions, being without any outward Touch-Stone; and by what Means the *Apostles* knew, that the Spirit or Power which acted them to reject and decry the whole Service of the *Jews*, which God had so peculiarly Instituted (Circumcision for Instance, that was given for a Sign FOR EVER) was the right Spirit or Power? I ask, *Was it the Scripture without, or the Son of God, otherwise called the Light or Word of God, revealed in them?* But I will yet proceed; Suppose any Man who is call'd an *Independent*, and owns the Scripture to be that which *J. Faldo* reputes them, should pretend a *Vision* of very strange and unwonted Things, should imitate a Trance, and personate some Extraordinary Inspired Person, by what Place of Scripture would *J. Faldo* assure himself or others, of the Sincerity or Imposture of such a Person? His Rationals being otherwise Sound; his Life Sober, and his Pretences no way anti-Scriptural? *O Weak Man!* Is thy Religion without a secret *Light, Life, Power, Virtue, Sight or Relish* of the Root and Ground of Things; or rather dost thou conclude, that all Mankind, however Christian, are left *Destitute of any Inward Power to Try or Discern Spirits*, because it is thine own State of Darkness? I affirm to thee and all the World, that in this Case, no outward Mean whatsoever decides the Matter, or clears the Doubt; only the invisible Light, Power or Spirit of God: Yea, and that in far less Cases too.

1673.
Chap. IV.

In which Sense chiefly, it is the Dispensation of the Gospel, so call'd, and justly preferr'd before all other.

And this I leave with him; that nothing can judge of the Root and Ground of Evil, but the Root and Ground of Good. The Works of Evil, the Scriptures tell us, are abominable; But the Question is, *How do I know, what they declare to be Evil, is so?* What works the Conviction in me? And where an Evil Spirit brings it self not forth into those Works, what shall discern him, except it be the Good Spirit? It is the Power of God within, that crusheth the Power of the Devil within. The Scriptures without Reprove his Works without; But since the Things contained in the Scriptures were such in themselves, and true, and experienc'd before they were written: Will it not follow, that the inward Power was both a sufficient Judge, and their Author too, and consequently Greater.

§. 15. But above all, the Impudence of his Wickedness; both to charge the Impiety of *Julian* and *Lucian* upon the Light within, by placing them in the same Order with the best of *Heathens*, and *Quakers*, walking up to the Light within; and to affirm, for all that the *Quakers* have to judge to the contrary, they acted by a Divine Power; *Ranking the* Quakers *Faith in Christ, upon an Equality in Evil, with their horrid Blasphemies.* The Top of all Uncharitableness, and a very Lye; for this is to say, *That the best and worst of* Heathens *were all alike:* That they wanting Scriptures, could not rightly discern the Difference between the Bad and Good; that those who live up to that Light (As he cannot deny the *Quakers* to do in a great Measure) are but in *Julian* the Apostate, and scoffing *Lucian*'s Rank; In short, that the *Quakers* Believing *in one God; that he has Enlightned all Men; that he has Striven by his Light and Spirit in the Consciences of Men through all Ages, and by it, in the Hearts and Mouths of his Prophets; and above all, by that blessed Appearance of Christ Jesus, who Tabernacl'd among Men in that Body prepared for that purpose; who therein preach'd the Heavenly Kingdom within; wrought Miracles; laid down his Life for the World, rose again, and ascended to the Father; leading Captivity captive, and gave Gifts for Men;* that who believes in him, and takes up his Cross, shall be his Disciple, and presevering, have Everlasting Life: That the *Quaker*'s Faith, (I say) in this Solemn and Conscientious Manner, upon which they Place the Eternal Happiness of their Souls, should scarcely be a Jot better, than the *Apostacy of* Julian, *and the Impiety of* Lucian; *and but only serve, to render us as Great Despisers and Contemners of Christ and all his Religion, as they were.* O strange Comparison! Well, they tell us of a Book coming out of our Hard Sayings to our Opposers; But match this, impartial *Reader*! But however the Devil blinds and hardens this *J. Faldo*; sure I am, the *Devil* himself knows better. What shall I say? Truly nothing more; but leave it with the Righteous God of Heaven and Earth, to plead our Cause in the Hearts of all People, and avenge himself upon his Adversaries, to whom Vengeance belongs.

§. 16. For his Comparison of us with the *Papists*, we little heed it. He tells the World, the *Papists* own Revelation (which he proves at large) and the *Quakers* hold Revelation also; Therefore *the* Quakers *are Papists*, or very near them, as his Story, indeed an arrant Lye (either in him or the *Papist*) will inform us; where he says, (Pag. 55.) *That a Papist upon being askt, which of all Sects in* England *approach'd them most? Replied, The Qua—* How near we are to the *Papists*, in Faith, Worship, and Discipline, shall ⸺ left to them that know, and have seen more than this Conceited *Priest*. But *Argumentum ad hominem*. Thus, the *Papists* own a *God*, and a *Trinity of Persons*, &c. and *J. Faldo* owns a *God*, and a *Trinity of Persons* also; therefore *J. Faldo is a Papist*, or very near a-Kin to one. Would this be Just? If not, neither is his Conclusion of Force against us. What is Truth, is not discommendable, where-ever, and by whomsoever held. It is high Weakness to exclaim against *True Christians*, for holding any Truth in common with the very *Turks*, and much more condemnable to conclude them *Turks*. But we must be run down if they can, and therefore no Matter what *Ugly Skin* they cast over us, *so the Dogs will but fasten.* The Lord God plead our Cause on Earth.

CHAP.

CHAP. V.

The Charge Stated, not Proved. The Scriptures *not the Most Excellent, or Only General Rule. God may speak by Instruments. The Instruments not the Rule, but that which useth them. That the* Scriptures *being Obligatory, does not conclude it the General Rule under the Gospel. The Disingenuity of our Adversary, in citing the Apostle's* Words, *Reprehended. The* Scriptures *no Judge in that Sense wherein they are not the General Rule. The Scriptures confest to.*

§. 1. HIS Fifth Chapter designs to Prove, *That we Deny the Scriptures to be a Rule of Faith, and Judge of Controversies;* (Pag. 65, 66.) And that he may sufficiently prejudice his *Reader* against us, and our Most Holy Faith, he not only tells him, that to deny them to be the *Word of God,* is a good Reason, why he should conclude us to deny them to be a Rule (though at the same Time, it manifestly shows, that we would acknowledge them to be such, were they the Word of God, and that therefore the Word of God is our Rule) but he suggests, that we believe a Conformity to their Guidance, *cannot render a Prophane Man less Prophane.* To prove this, he quotes *James Parnel* thus : *And he also that saith, The Letter is the Rule and Guide of the People of God, is without, feeding upon the Husks, and is ignorant of the True Light, which was before the Letter was.* Shield of Truth, pag. 10.

William Smith thus : *And if thou lookest upon the Scripture to be for a Rule, and for Trying, thou givest that unto them, which is due unto Christ ; for He is the Rule, and leads His People ; and He alone searches the Hearts, and tries the Reins, and not the Scripture.* Again, But if you will see a Mouth full of Blasphemies against the Authority of the Scripture, read with Horror and Amazement, the following Words. *God is at Liberty to speak to His People by them, if he please, and where they are given by Inspiration, he doth so ;* but says *J. Faldo,* The Sting is behind, and in the Tail of this Non-such Sentence : *And so He is at Liberty to speak by any other created Thing, as to* Balaam *by his Ass.* Naylor's Light of Christ, &c. pag. 19.

In Answer to all which, he says just nothing ; but thinks it is enough to have cited these Passages, and seems to triumph, as Reasonably, as the Man which dreamt he did Eat, but Awake and Hungry, delighteth himself in his Sleeping Feast. Let us try to rouse him out of this Lethargy of Ignorance and Conceit.

§. 2. I shall freely confess, that for the same Reasons, that we deny the Scriptures to be the Word of God, we cannot own them as the General Rule of Faith. But also, as we acknowledge them to be the Words of the Holy, Living, and Powerful Word of God ; so that they express and declare unto us many Holy Rules for Godliness : And I declare in the Name of all the *Right-Born Quakers* in the World, *That we utterly reject all such, as Deny the Scriptures to be Profitable for Reprehension, Instruction, Exhortation, and Edification.* How Vain then is this Man's Impeachment of us, as Persons void of all True Respect for them ?

§. 3. In short, as the Scriptures are not the Word of God, *but a Declaration of the Word of God,* so the Scriptures are not the General Rule, *but a Declaration of the True General Rule ;* which I prove thus.

That which always was, and is a more General Rule than the Scriptures, must needs be, and is most properly *The General Rule,* and not the Scriptures ; but that was, and is the Light of God in the Hearts of Men ; consequently not the Scriptures, but the Light was, and is most properly, *The General Rule.* The Middle Proposition only to be accepted against is clear, in that before the Scriptures were writ, and since, where they have not been known, Men have been, and are Convinc'd, Reprov'd, Inclined, Taught, Order'd and Ruled by the inward Appearance of God's Light in the Conscience. And among those who are called *Christians,* let them be just to God and their own Souls, *and they must confess, that there is something very near them, when the Scriptures are quite remote,* both from their Persons, and their Thoughts, which upon any Miscarriage is a swift Witness, to smite : And upon the Approach of Temptation is as quick to warn, and disswade the Mind from falling into the Foulness of it. Is not this then more Living, Immediate and General, that neither Sea nor Land, Day nor Night, nor any Condition, *but a Seared Conscience,* can exempt People, or deliver them from the Secret, Living, and Sensible Touches of this Holy Witness, whether they be to Counsel, Justifie, or Condemn?

demn? This searcheth the Heart, this tryeth the Reins; of which *David* said, *It had made him Wiser than his Teachers*, who read and expounded the outward Law unto him.

§. 4. And indeed, it is unworthy of the Excellency of the Administration of Life it self, more Glorious than that of Condemnation, the State of the Law, that an outward Book, though Declaratory of never so much Good, and not the Good it self, should be the Sole General Rule of such as are under it. What is it, but to subject the Spirituality of the Gospel to the Letter of the Law? And thus much worse, that then they had either the Daily Living Voice of God, or a Law Engraven on Stone, whilst the Scriptures, which they call the present Gospel Rule, are but on Paper. But can any True Christian think, that God is so wanting to his Promise, who promised *to Write a Law in the Hearts of his People*, as to bound them by meer *Literal Prescripts*? No surely, but much rather, that the Law of the Spirit of Life in Christ Jesus, which he promised to write in the Hearts of Men and Women, should be the Rule of this Administration, *which is a Living, Powerful Rule*, present upon all Occasions, and in all Straights, and ready to assist with Counsel, Wisdom, and Knowledge, all who act agreeably to the Mind of God, who will reward every Man according to his Works: So that *J. Parnel*, and *W. S.* their Expressions are clear'd. For *J. N*'s, the Last of the Three, it was not written in Derision of Scripture, as is unworthily suggested; but to prove, that God is not limited to Instruments. God, whose Holy Spirit is the Living, Substantial Rule, may appear after divers Manners, either by bringing into the very Conscience the Truth of some weighty Passage in the Scripture, or by a Ministry, or any other Way; yea, by *Balaam's* Ass to *Balaam*, and that without Blasphemy or Prophaneness; For by whom, or what, may not the Almighty direct the Sons of Men? Still it was not so mean a Creature as an Ass (which God spoke by, to aggravate the Stupidity of *Balaam*, and Greaten the Miracle) No; Nor the Apostles themselves, much less their Writings; *But the Word of the Lord, that was as a Fire, to the Workers of Iniquity, and Sanctification, and Reconciliation to them that believe it.* That was the *True Rule*; wherefore said the Prophet, *Hear the Word of the Lord*. What Word? *That, nigh in the Heart, which* Moses *and* Paul *Preach'd*. Still the outward Instrument is not the Rule; the *Prophet* is not the Rule; the *Apostle* is not the Rule, much less are their Writings, seeing they are all but External Instruments: And this I will abide by, against all the Instruments of our Enemies by God's Assistance, both that they are but such Instruments, and that such Instruments are not the Gospel-Rule, *but that Light, Life, Power or Spirit, which useth them*. And who attributes that Honour to the Instrument, which is due to the Chief Mover in it, or by it, commits down-right Idolatry; therefore what is flung upon the *Quakers* by their *Adversaries*, is more justly chargeable upon their *Adversaries*. But we cannot help it, if that People will not work through the Outward to the Inward; the Writings or Persons, to the *Light, Life, and Power*, that employ them for any Use or Service in the World! Nor shall we ever be condemned of God, that we therefore decline to attribute those Titles to the Scriptures (otherwise worthy above all Books) which are only due to that which gave them forth; especially, since what we believe in the Matter, is with an Holy Fear and Reverence towards our God, and Good-Will towards all Men.

§. 5. But he objects, (Pag. 68, 59, 70, 71.) (1.) *That what is therein affirmed by the Lord, we ought to believe*; proved from Christ's Words, *O Fools, and slow of Heart, to believe all that the Prophets have spoken!* Luke 24. 25. (2.) *That what is thereby commanded (not being repeal'd by the Coming of Christ) it is our Duty to obey*, Deut. 5. 34. (3.) *That the Holy Scriptures do in their Kind determine, or discover to us, whether we believe and walk, or practice aright or not*, proved hence; *All Scripture is given by Inspiration of God, and is profitable for Doctrine, for Reproof, for Correction, for Instruction in Righteousness, that the Man of God may be Perfect, throughly furnished unto all Good Works*; and herein [all Things which are written in the Law and the Prophets] *do I exercise my self to have a Conscience void of Offence*. 2 Tim. 3. 16, 17. Acts 24. 16.

To all which I say, we do with him acknowledge, that, whatever the Lord hath by his *Prophets* and *Apostles*, who writ the Scripture, *affirmed*, and *required* (taking in his Exception about *Christ's Coming*) it is our Duty both to Believe and Obey; so that there is no Difficulty in that Matter. For the last Passage, there is some sober Scruple in our Minds about it; for there are manifest Contests in the World, both about *Faith and Practice*. They result not from the Scriptures, I grant;

grant; but that they proceed from Men's wrong Apprehensions of *Scripture* in a great Measure, that I affirm; and I know no Man so stupid, as to deny. Now, I would fain know, which Way those wrong Apprehensions are to be rectified: He says, *By Scripture*. I say, *Not*; for the Key is wanting. What is that *Key*, may some say? *The Spirit of Truth, who gave them forth*. Who can explain any Man's Mind so well as himself, in a Matter, wherein he is not rightly understood; or it is hard to understand him? And if none but what is endued with Reason, is capable of understanding a Rational Proposition, neither can any Man whatever understand Spiritual Propositions, or Propositions about Spiritual Matters in the Scriptures, *but by the Illumination of the Holy Spirit in some Degree or other*. This is so clear, that the Sun is not more obvious at Noon-Day, in a clear Sky, than this must be to all Discerning Minds; so that the Scriptures, though professedly own'd by us to be Instrumental to the Knowledge of that Doctrine of Reproof and Instruction in Righteousness (weightily mention'd by the Apostle *Paul*, (for certainly they do declare to us very excellent Precepts and Rules) yet, they are so far from being THE General and Absolute Rule, that *the very Light or Spirit of Christ is, and ought to be our Rule, how far, which Way, and to what End, we are to believe and practise them*. And I cannot forbear at this Time (though I have done so) to shew the horrible Perversion of Scripture, this Man is guilty of in the last of these Two Scriptures, by him quoted for Proof of the Third Head. The Apostle in his Defence against the Publick Orator of the *Jews*, tells the Governour then present, among other Passages, that though he was no Disturber, as accused; yet, said he, I confess, *that after the Way which they call* Heresie, *do I worship the God of my Fathers, Believing all Things which are written in the Law and the Prophets, and have Hope towards God, which they themselves also allow, that there shall be a Resurrection of the Dead, both of the Just and the Unjust*.

§. 6. Now brings in *J. Faldo* these Words [*all Things which are written in the Law and the Prophets*] do I exercise my self to have a Conscience void of Offence towards God and toward Men. I do say, this is a Perversion of Scripture; for he hath *First*, left out that which is more applicable to the Words, and put that only in, which is least so: And *Next*, he has done it in the same *Character*, by which common Readers may be mistakenly strengthned against us; this is plain: And for the former, I affirm, that it could not be so proper in the Apostle to say, *He was exercised in his Belief of the Law and the Prophets*, as in that Way of Worship, *they call'd* Heresie, *and his Hope of a Resurrection*; both left out by our *Adversary*. Nor is such an Use of his Words suitable to the Condition *Paul* was in: For he having out-stript both the Law and Prophets, and *being brought to a Brighter Day, and more Excellent Dispensation*, he cannot be so rightly said to have been exercised in that he had left behind him, *as in the Work of his own Day, which fulfill'd and swallow'd up the other Dispensations*, as but Fore-runners of it; which was but that Spiritual Worship Christ set up, and he worshipp'd the God of his Fathers in, and endeavour'd to gather others to, though they reputed it *Heresie*, and that Hope of the Resurrection of both Just and Unjust, which they themselves pretended to own. What then could be *Paul's* Meaning in that Confession to the *Law* and *Prophets?* I answer, what is ours to the World, before whom we stand charg'd by the *Professors Tertullus, J. Faldo*, at this Day; namely, that though he preach'd a farther Glory, and they therefore accused him of Undervaluing the Law and the Prophets, becoming an Heretick, Seducer, and what not; as this Man doth us: He then (as we are now) *made his Defence, confest to the Law and the Prophets, yet testified to a more Spiritual Worship, but unto which they prophetically tended*. Whence we observe (1.) The greatest Enemies to the Spirituality of that Evangelical Dispensation, *were the greatest Professors of a Literal Religion, the only seeming Admirers of the Scriptures, and earnest Contenders for the Faith and Religion once delivered to the Fathers*, at least as they pretended. (2.) That they were wont to account such as were eminent Promoters of the Gospel, *Contemners, at least Slighters of the Law and the Prophets*. What need I say any more: Behold a Parallel, as plain as Light it self; *The Literal* Jews *then, the Literal* Christians *now*; *the Spiritual* Jews *then, the Spiritual* Christians *now*.

§. 7. But one Passage more. (Pag. 71.) *The Holy Scriptures determine according to their Kind, or as much as a* WRITING *can do, whether we believe or practise aright or not*; For, says he, *Those who come under the Executive Determination of Laws, do find, that Process in Writing doth not lose it's Force, for the Decrees and Sentences being put into that Form*

To his Assertion, and the Instance he brings to prove it, I will return this Answer.

To say the Scriptures determine as far as a WRITING CAN, does our *Adversaries* Business, I mean, for us; since it manifestly implies, *That it is no so determinative of all Cases, as some Thing else may be, which is a more Living, Immediate and Infallible Judge than a WRITING is, or can be*; and we will grant, that the Scriptures do determine, as much as any Writing in the World can do, unless God would please immediately, and more fully, to Reveal something, less clearly laid down in the Scriptures, *and then should require that Revelation to be written*, for Men must have a Care of limiting either his Power or Will. If *J. Faldo* had at the Beginning of his Opposition to the *Quaker's* Belief in the Scriptures, well considered this, I am of Opinion, that either he would have never given himself and us the Trouble of so much needless Discourse; or have been so careful of his Cause, as never to have wounded it with this fatal Blow, *that the Scriptures can determine as far as a Writing will go:* Nothing to the Question at all, which lyes here, *Whether any the best Writing, or the Spirit of Truth, that gave it forth, is Judge*; and as far from his Purpose, as quite losing of his Cause amounts to. Again,

§. 8. His Instance about the Law is lame, for the Good Laws of any Land, are but *Reason written*, or rather declared by Writing, which is obliging against the Corruption of a *Judge*, but not the Reason of the Judge. Neither is the *Law the Judge*, but there is a Judge, who interprets, and speaks from the fresh Discoveries of his own Reason, the Meaning and Intendment of those written Laws. If the Laws be sufficient without a Judge, why is there a Judge? If then they are *Dark, Obscure*, and *Doubtful* in many Cases, so as to need a Judge and Interpreter, which I call *Living and Immediate Reason*, then since the Scriptures are Writings, in which are many Things very difficult to be understood, it follows, *that there must be an immediate Living Judge*; which must be therefore the Spirit of Truth that gave them forth; because, *None knows the Things of God, save the Spirit of God*; and that those who are the Makers of Laws, are the only Persons who are fit to to judge and determine in Case of Difficulty, by a Declaration of their Mind or Intention in any such obscure Passage. So that if *J. Faldo* should write a Thousand Years against the *Quakers*, he would never be able to weather this one Passage, *in which he has most evidently subjected the Scriptures to a more Living, Spiritual, and Immediate Judge, then any meer Writing possibly can be*, which he makes them but to be.

§. 9. In short, either the Scriptures are not obscure (a Thing we daily see) or if so, yet sufficient, which is impossible, or they must have a Judge, which is most True and Necessary; and what Judge, but the Spirit of Truth, which leads into all Truth? And so far are Decrees from determining, because written, that they are therefore Determinative of Controversie, because of that Conviction, the Power from whence they came, works upon the Conscience. So that, though what is True in it self, is not the less so, because written; yet is not the Writing (subject to an hundred Casualties) nor Matter therein declared, as there, eminently the *Rule*, much less the *Judge*, after our Adversaries Notion of a *Judge*; but that Living, Powerful Spirit, which gave it forth, and who are made Spiritual Men by it: For the Spiritual Man judges all Things. Such Writings may be Declaratory of the Mind and Determination of the Living *Rule* or *Judge*, I grant; but also I utterly deny, that the Writings themselves are that Rule, how People are to believe them; and a Judge, how to determine of the Difficulties and Obscurities within themselves. A meer begging of the Question, and a Thing altogether absurd.

We cannot end this Chapter without an Acknowledgment of the Goodness of God, in opening Things so clearly, to the making known *His Divine Light and Truth*, and manifestly discovering the Great Darkness and Blindness of it's Opposers.

CHAP. VI.

We deny the Charge. *His Proof, no Proof; but against himself. We own, Believe, and desire to Obey the* Scriptures; *they afford Comfort, and are as* Lights *in the* World; *but not that* True Light. *The Light and Spirit Superior to them.*

§. 1. THE next Charge he brings against us, is a Consequence of his already mistaken Judgment, and untrue Assertions concerning us, viz. (pag. 78.) *That we take People off from Reading the Scriptures, and Looking into them for Instruction*

struction and *Comfort*; to prove which, as he thinks (for none else can, that is not either as deeply ignorant of us, or as malicious against us, as *J. Faldo* shows himself in almost every Particular) he brings out *W. Smith*, speaking thus in his *Catechism*, pag. 95. *And this is the Meaning of our Doctrine, to bring People to the Everlasting Word of God in themselves.* O Ungodly Man! What Evil Spirit hath possest *J. Faldo* into this wretched and impious Consequence? Certainly he is grosly blind, or he has sinned against the Light of his own Conscience, if he hath Conscience enough to think it a Sin, which I profess, I doubt, when the *Malignity, Frothiness, Envy,* and *Impious Injustice* of the Man are set before me. For (1.) let any tell me, if it be a Sin, to bring People to the Everlasting Word of God in themselves; though he *Dirts* us not a little for so doing. (2.) If we do hereby take Men off from Reading and Looking into the Scriptures, I do affirm against this Ungodly Priest, and that by Authority from God, the Scriptures, Reason, and the first Reformers too, that no Man on Earth can understand them, but by being first brought to the Everlasting Word of God nigh in the Heart, by which the Lord speaks forth his Will to the Creature; and the Scriptures themselves direct to this, and never said that of themselves, some *Overdoing Priests* assert concerning them; whose whole End is this, that by Exalting the Letter, and Excluding the Spirit, they may lock up all Knowledge in their own *Arcanum*, and plead the Impossibility of knowing the Things of God any other Way, than by their Literal Ministration; for should Men but be turned to the Certain Witness of God in their own Consciences, there placed of the Lord, their whole *Trade, Power* and *Reputation*, would fall, and their Deceits be made manifest in the View of the World; which God, the Righteous Judge of Heaven and Earth, is now accomplishing.

See Calv. Inst. Eras. in Nov. Test. 1 Cor. 2. 2 Pet. 1. 19. Bez. ibid.

§. 2. But he says, (pag. 79.) *That J. Parnel censures such that draw People's Minds from the Light within to the Light without, putting the Letter for the Light*, Shield of Tr. pag. 10. And what then? Because we say, *That he who Enlightens all Men, GOD, that is the Sun, and Fountain of all Divine Light, and in whom there is no Darkness at all, is Greater than the Scriptures*; therefore will it follow, that we take People off from Reading, or Looking in them. Behold your *Priest*, you that hear him! *Is this Man to be accounted of as a Minister of the Gospel, that thus unrighteously deals with us?* But God will recompense upon his Head in the Day of his Terrible Vengeance, for all his Hard and Ungodly Sayings against us.

We do say, and that rightly, *Whoever puts the Letter in Opposition to, or above the Spirit, is an Idolater*; For there can be no Comparison rightly made between them; the Heavens don't excel the Earth more, than the Spirit does the Letter, and the Power the Form: But if we do not therefore deny the *Form of Godliness*, because we prefer, and press more earnestly *the Power*; neither do we exclude the Scriptures, because we prefer, and press the *Everlasting Word of God nigh in the Heart*: And this I will tell him, *That, to busie the Minds of Men with the Depth of those Truths the Scriptures declare of by Reading, and Exercising their Minds, in Meditating thereon, before they have been turned unto the Measure of the Light, or Grace of God in the Heart, to believe and obey that in it's Secret Discoveries, Reproofs and Strivings, is, to set Men about Images, to conceive a God, a Christ, a Salvation, a Damnation, an Heaven, an Hell; by which the inward Work of God is over lookt, and they become Rich in Notion, whilst most Barren in Obedience, and of all People that live upon the Earth,* the Greatest Idolaters; *because they bow down to their own Imaginations for Real Truths:* And this is the State of every Opposer to the Sacred Light within, how full so ever of the meer Literal Knowledge of the very Scriptures themselves: For indeed, who knows the *New Birth*, though the Scriptures declare of it, but who really experience it?

§. 3. But *J. Story* he thinks, has contributed much to prove his Assertion in this Passage. *And although the Holy Scripture without, and the Saint's Practices are as* Lights in the World; *yet, far be it from all True Christian Men, so to Idolize them, as to set them in Esteem above the* Light, *which is sufficient to guide, or to esteem them equal with the Light and Spirit of God within.* J. S's Short Discourse. p. 2. To this he objects, That J. S. *confesses them to be as Lights, but not a Light, and that our Commendations of that Idol the Light within, are such, that if they were True, he were a stark Fool, that would direct his Eyes to the Scripture.*

But here the *Priest* fails egregiously: For if the Scriptures are as Lights, I cannot see how they should be denied to be as in the Nature of a Light; unless to acknowledge their Testimonies to be as *Lights*, be to deny them to have *any Light at all.* Is this the *Great Originalian, Linguist, Critick, Philosopher,* and what else his own Conceit will have him? What is it but to say, *That Six Burning Candles are Six Lights*? But not that they give a Light, either joyntly or separately; But 'tis below us to pursue every Advantage his Ignorance gives us: I find him more in Words than Matter, a great Deal, and I suppose, more are of that Mind, or else what means his great Pains to be made Waste Paper of already? *Quakerism No Christianity,* has exchang'd the Book-Seller's Stalls for the Tobacco-Shops. Poor Man! Perhaps he will write another Book, to complain of the Deadness of Professor's Hearts, that they make so ill Use of the Labours of Painful Ministers. I am confident, nothing but his Fear of losing by it, could divert him from such a *Lamentation.*

But to his Reflection upon the *Light, as our Idol; and their Folly, who attend upon the Scriptures, when they have so excellent a Light in their own Bosoms;* the Substance of the rest of the Chapter, I thus return. God is that Light which hath Enlightned Mankind, and to have the highest Reverence for him, and believe in him, can be therefore no Idolatry: And for the Scriptures all grant, that there is a State above them; for I hope, the Man does not think, that People shall have Bibles in Heaven, and the more any approach to the Heavenly Life, and Glory, the less Need there will be, and yet not the less Value of them. But this we also say, *That they are profitable for Instruction, and Comfort in this World:* And God hath spoke, does, and yet will by the Scriptures, speak to the Consciences of Men: For being given forth by the Spirit of God, they do declare that *Reproof, Exhortation,* and those *Promises,* which being felt in some Sense of the same Divine Light, *do administer Knowledge and Refreshment.* But we do also and again declare it as our Faith, *That the Pouring out of the Spirit, is a Gospel-Privilege,* yea, the very proper and peculiar Promise and Blessing of the Father in that State; and that, as the Spirit is superior to the Letter, so we earnestly contend not against the Scriptures, *but for that Living, Experimental Knowledge of them,* which all witness, who are truly taught and led by the Spirit, *and which can't be obtained by any meer Writings whatsoever.* Nor does it follow, (p. 81.) that because God has given a sufficient Light, therefore all other Means should be superfluous. Certain I am, this Argument is fitter for *Bedlam,* than one who more than once Vaunts himself to be a *Critick (indeed a Quibler)* For what is it but to say, that though every Man has Reason enough in him to know, that Intemperance is below a very Brute, yet because he is Intemperate, his Reason is not sufficient to inform him better; Or, if it be sufficient, he ought to despise another's Admonitions however seasonable, his Reason being enough to his Information: Was *Nathan* of no Use to *David,* who had so secret, and sufficient a Teacher? And here I do observe, that all our Opposers split themselves, and will for ever, unless better inform'd: *They ignorantly, or basely infer a Fallibility, or Insufficiency to be in the Light, from the Fallibility and Rebellion of those Persons, who, we say, are Lightned by it:* And on the contrary Hand, *That all should be necessarily Infallible, who are Enlightned by an Infallible Light,* not considering, *that neither is the Grace of God Insufficient to Save, because Men refuse to be Saved by it; nor, though it be Sufficient, and Infallible in it self, that therefore all those to whom it is tender'd, are sav'd; or therefore are Infallible, without any Consideration had to their Obedience.* How False? How Injurious? How (almost) Unpardonable is this Priest then? Who seems to charge us with believing, (pag. 81.) *That all Power in Heaven and in Earth, is in every Particular Man,* because, says he, *This Light in every One is God, Christ, Spirit,* &c. For, though we confess, that as to every individual Person, all the Power, which is required to redeem that Soul from the Pollutions of the World, unto the *Pure and Undefiled Religion,* is in that *Divine Principle,* which, with Respect to the Great Darkness of the World, is very aptly denominated *Light,* yet that therefore the whole Light and Power of it should be comprehended by, or contained in every individual Soul, I utterly Renounce as no Consequence of our Doctrine; for that were to say, *In every Room where the Sun shines, there is a distinct Sun.* These are but some of the *Priests Old Bulbeggars,* to scare the Simple, and they will at last do as much for their Inventors. It shall suffice us (1.) that though the Light shines not alike into all Habitable Places, yet the same Light, by Nature, shines into all such Places. For Illustration only; if a Man has Six Rooms expos'd to the Sun, there may be more Light in some one than another, yet not therefore another Sun or Light. (2.) If People refuse to see by it, it implies no Deficiency in the Light, but argues manifest Rebellion in the Party. (3.) That, whatever Means

it

it may please God to use, to stir up Men to observe and obey the Light they withstand, they ought not to be thought superfluous, or the Light thereof Insufficient. (4.) That all such Means as can be effectual, proceed from that Divine Principle in *others*, and with Design of turning the *Rebellious* to the Grace which they resist in themselves. So notwithstanding the *Quakers* do own, and assert the Spirit to be Superior to the Scriptures, especially in this Administration, yet they by no Means deny the Scripture all Service or Benefit, but Believe, it ought to be Read, Believ'd, Honour'd, and Obey'd, as that, by which God has, doth, and may yet reach to the Hearts and Consciences of People. *And to the Righteous Lord God of Heaven and Earth, who is the Searcher of the Hearts of all Men, do we make our Appeal in this Matter, against the Unrighteous Dealing of this Traducing Priest.*

CHAP. VII.

Commands *upon Conviction to be obey'd.* All General Commands *Obligatory*; Particular Not, *but upon Particular Commission.* Our Adversaries *Disingenuity.* The Scriptures *a Means, by which God may be known*; *but* Not the Principle.

§. 1. THO' indeed we need not concern our selves any farther in this Subject, after the Dispute of his Premisses, namely, *That because the* Quakers *Deny the Scriptures to be the Word of God, therefore they Deny them to all Intents and Purposes*, much less, that we should esteem our selves obliged to consider what remains after such plentiful Confutation, being but Consequences of the *Priest's* drawing from his own False Assertions already enervated; or a mistaken Understanding of ours, plainly discover'd, and which indeed seems both to resemble, and follow the Old Way of *Two and Twentiethly, Beloved,* to spin out the Hour-Glass, I mean, saying over the same Things in other Words; yet, that we may remove all Ground of Scruple, I will lay down the several Charges of the remaining Chapters, concerning the *Scriptures,* and the best Proofs he brings for them, and briefly examine both.

§. 2. (Pag. 87.) *The* Quakers *affirm, the Doctrines, Commands, Promises, Holy Examples expressed in the Scriptures, as such, not at all to be binding to us. This,* says he, *is a Denying of the Scriptures, and the Authority of the God of the Scriptures.* For the Proof of this, he brings out E. Burrough's speaking thus: *That is no Command of God to me, what he Commanded to another; neither did any of the Saints which we read of in the Scripture, act by that Command, which was to another, not having the Command to themselves; I challenge to find an Example to it.*

To this I answer briefly, and plainly. *Edward Burroughs's* Expression may be taken Two Ways, and both Safe enough, to the Honour and Credit of the Scriptures, though not to the Charity or Honesty of *J. Faldo.* No Command in the Scripture is any farther obliging upon any Man, than as he finds a Conviction upon his Conscience; otherwise Men should be engaged without, if not against Conviction; a Thing Unreasonable in a Man. Therefore the *Apostle,* when he wrote to the Churches, exhorted them, *Not to do those Things whereof they were ashamed, to shun what was manifested to be Evil*; and affirms, *That whatever might be known of God, was manifested Within*; *for God had shown it unto them.* So that Conviction can only oblige to Obedience; and since what works that Conviction, *is the Manifesting Light, Universal Grace, or Quickning Spirit in the Heart of Mankind,* it follows, *that the Principal Ground for our Faith in the Scriptures, and Reason of our Obedience to the Holy Precepts therein contained, is the Manifestation, Conviction, and Secret Drawings of the Light, or Spirit of God in the Conscience:* And thus *E. B*'s Words are Sound and Scriptural; for the Scriptures are chiefly believed to be True upon Conviction, therefore every Practice therein. And when any Man is Convinced, that what was Commanded another, is required of him, then, and not till then, he is rightly authoriz'd to perform it. Again,

§. 3. Such Commands are either relating to *Ordinary* or *Extraordinary Cases*: By *Ordinary Cases,* I mean, such as chiefly concern *Faith and Holy Life,* which are General, Permanent, and Indispensible; and then I deny his Consequence. By *Extraordinary Cases,* I understand, Moses's *going to* Pharaoh; *the Prophets several Manners of Appearance to the Kings, Priests, and People of* Israel, *with other Temporary Commands relating to Outward Services,* &c. And so we do say, that what is Commanded one Man, *is not binding, as such, upon another.* But when the Lord shall say, *If thou Sinnest thou shalt Dye*; *If thou keepest my Commands, thou shalt Live*;

1673.
Chap. III.
1 Pet. 2. 21.
Heb. 13. 7.
2 Thef. 3.

Live ; *Be ye Holy, for I the Lord your God am Holy.* Alfo in Cafe of Example, as the Prieft cites, *Whofe Faith follow, confidering the End of their Converfation. Leaving us an Example, that we fhould follow his Steps. For your felves know you not, how you ought to follow us. For after this Manner in the Old Time, the Holy Women alfo, who trufted in God, adorn'd themfelves.* I fay, thefe Precepts and Examples are obliging upon all : Why ? Becaufe they more or lefs meet with a Conviction in the Confciences of all : For I am perfwaded, none that have a Reafonable Soul, who have not out-lived their Day, and on whom the Night is not come, among the *Indians* themfelves, but would readily fay, *Thefe are True and Weighty Sayings* ; *for Faith in God, and an Holy Self-denying Life, are neceffary, both to Temporal and Eternal Happinefs.* Thus then are we clear from his Ungodly Confequence, indeed Afperfion, to wit, *That the* Quakers *affirm the Doctrines, Commands, Promifes, Holy Examples, expreffed in Scripture, as fuch, not to be Binding.* But let's hear another of his Confequences, by Way of Charge, and fee if he will acquit himfelf better than before.

§. 4. (pag. 96, 97.) *The* (Quakers) *deny the Scriptures to be any Means by which we may come to know God, Chrift, and our felves.* To prove this, he quotes *W. Smith's* Primmer, p. 2.

" Q. Is there not another Way, by which we may come to know God ?

" A. Nay, Child; there is not another Way, *for Chrift is the Way.* To which he replies,

Chrift faith, I am the Way, no Man can come to the Father, but by me ; *but he doth not fay, that there is no Coming to the Knowledge of God but by Chrift* ; *For, fome Knowledge of God may be attained, not only without Chrift, as the Means, but without the Scriptures alfo* ; Quoting that Paffage in the firft of the *Romans* : *For the Invifible Things of him are clearly feen, being underftood by the Things that are made,* &c.

To all which I fay, (1.) That greater Untruth, Irreverence, and Impertinency could not well have been expreft, than in his faying, *That no Man can come to the Father, but by Chrift, and no Man can come to the Knowledge of God, but by Chrift,* are Two different Things : For it manifeftly implies, that Men may know God without Chrift, either inwardly or outwardly, *(though no other Name be given) and that to know the Father, was to know fome other Kind of Being, than to know God* : Or, *That when they did know the One, they did not know the other.* (2.) That it was never denied by any *Quaker*, that God might, and fometimes does reach into the the very Heart and Confcience by the Scriptures : Shall I allow, that a Man may be convinced of his Evil by reading one of our Books ; and fhall I deny it to be as poffible for any to be Convinced by reading fome in the Holy Scriptures ? God forbid. Neither did *William Smith* ever mean, that Chrift was fo the only Way to the Father, as thereby to exclude all Inftruments ; *for thereby he had both cut off all Benefits that could accrue to People by his Books, and alfo from that Miniftry God had given him to profit others with*, which was far from his Thoughts, we may be fure. So that the great Wickednefs of this *Prieft* is herein manifeft, without farther Coft to know him ; for he argues from our denying that there is any other Way to the Father, but Chrift, *to our excluding the Scriptures, and confequently our own Books, and Miniftry with them, from being any Way Inftrumental of Good.* Reader, what can be faid to fuch a Man ; but that he is either Ignorance or Malice it felf ? I wifh it were the former, but his Book makes me fear the latter.

§. 5. In fhort, through all Inftruments, *He,* who in Time, and with refpect to that Manifeftation, was call'd CHRIST, was, is, and ever will be the *Alone Way to the Father.* And though he may difcover himfelf by divers Inftruments, yet it is but in order to incline Man *to his Holy Voice in Man* ; Some Hear and Obey and Live ; Others refift the Grace, grieve the Spirit, turn from the Way of the Light, and are in a State of Death.

God hath been frequently pleafed to move in the Hearts of the Obedient, to vifit the Rebellious, that the Inward Strivings of the Holy Spirit might be the more Efficacious by it's Strivings, through fome outward Inftruments ; but ftill it is the fame Light, Grace, or Spirit of God : Nor is the *Light Within,* any Whit the more Infufficient to reclaim the Rebellious, if minded ; for it is the fame Light with that, which moves in the Hearts of the Obedient to bear Record for God, againft their Ungodly Deeds. Only Men's Minds being far ftrayed from that Holy Light, or Word in the Heart, and gone abroad into the wide World of Lufts and Vanities, it hath pleafed God to vifit Mankind fo degenerated, by thofe who have

been

been Obedient Children, to the End they might be the more easily gained to a Subjection unto the Holy Light in themselves: So that all Conviction and Conversion, are to be ascribed to the Light, Grace, and Spirit of God, whether immediately in the Creature, or mediately by any Instrument. Only take this by the Way, that whatsoever is Efficacious mediately, is not to be understood simply of another Man's Measure of Light or Grace, but in Conjunction with what God hath given, and may be at work in the Party convicted and converting; for every Mediate Conviction gives an Addition of Life, and Strength to the Immediate Conviction that is wrought by the Operation of that so long neglected Measure of Light, Grace, or Truth, in the particular Conscience: We appeal then to every Impartial Person that reads us, if we own not the Scriptures in that very Sense he would have People believe, that we deny them, to wit, *That God may, and doth speak to People through the Writings of the Holy Prophets and Apostles, which are commonly call'd Scriptures; and consequently we do not deny the Scriptures to be any Means by which we may come to know God, Christ, and our selves, so often as it shall please the Eternal God to reach into the Hearts of Men, by any of those* TRUTHS *therein declared of.*

CHAP. VIII.

His Charge of our denying the Scriptures any Means by which God does enable Men to resist Temptations; and that we say, they are Dangerous to be read; rejected. His Proofs Lame. The Scriptures are believ'd to be a Means, &c. *The true Knowledge of them Divine. No Knowledge of Divine Things, but upon Experience. It does not Destroy Faith. W. Penn's Words safe and sound. The Priest a meer Shuffler. Learning, a Servant to Truth. Christ, the Word of God. Faith by our Adversary, prefer'd before Scripture. The Scripture ought to be Read, Believ'd and Obey'd.*

§. 1. HE farther charges us, *with denying the Scriptures to be any Means, whereby to resist Temptation; and that we say, That they are Dangerous to be read.* For Proof of which he quotes a Book, called, *Love to the Lost*; and mine, Entituled, *The Spirit of Truth Vindicated.* The first is this, *For, those only are Children of God, who are led by the Spirit of God, to whom they who were led by the Letter, were Enemies:* From whence he concludes, *That we account it a very dangerous Thing to Read the* Scriptures. Now if this Passage hath any Relation to his Charge or Conclusion, no Man ever saw the like; the whole Scope of which is but this. That there are Children of the Fleshly, Literal and Historical Knowledge of the Scriptures and Religion, who are Strangers to, and therefore Persecutors of the Children born of the Spirit: And that in all Ages there hath been more or less of this among Inward and Outward *Jews* and *Christians*: and let *J. Faldo* deny it if he dare. How Wicked then is he to extort (indeed invent) an Inference so foreign to the Matter, and then charge it upon the *Quakers* in general; as if it were prov'd by that Passage in particular, which can no ways be concern'd in any such Unrighteous Doctrine. I perceive, it is as impossible for our Adversaries to do any Thing against us, without they have the Making of our Consequences, as we are sure to find them mishapen enough, by that Time they get clear of their Hands; but blessed be the Name of our God, who has given us an Understanding, and Boldness both to search the Reins of our Enemies Cause, and defend his, which he has put into our Hands in this our Day.

§. 2. But hear him farther, if it may be worth while: *That this Abominable Tenet is the* Quakers, *Take one Instance more out of their Famous Author,* W. P. *or* William Penn.

' But I will assure them, they shall grope in the Dark, till they come into the
' daily Obedience of the Light, and there rest contented to know only as they
' experience; and not from a ravening comprehending Brain, that would in it's
' Unregenerated State, grasp at the clear Mysteries of the Kingdom, into which
' Fleshly Comprehensions and Notions can never enter: but all must be as Unlearned from their first Birth, Education, and Traditional read Knowledge, as
' he is unman'd that is again become a little Child, before the Secrets of God's
' Work come to be made known. *Spir. Truth Vind.* p. 23. Upon which hear his Comment.

That W. P. (of all others) should talk at this rate, is most Ridiculous. What! Know only as they experience, know what God is no farther than they experience: Can we experience his Omnipotency? What! Know the Death of the Man Christ Jesus, the Life to come, and judging of all Men by the Lord Jesus, only by Experience? Where is Faith all the while? If none but Believers are Saints, such as W. P. are professedly none.

If *Reader*, we are got beside the Matter charg'd against the *Quakers*, to wit, *that they deny the Scriptures to be any Means whereby to resist Temptation*, our wandring *Adversary*, who led me thither, is only to be blam'd; But since I am here, I shall endeavour to clear the Truth and My self, before we return to the Point in Hand.

It cannot be so ridiculous in *W. P.* to assert the Impossibility of any Man's Knowing God, or the Things belonging to his Everlasting Kingdom, but by Experience, or, as God hath been pleased, by the Inspiration or Illumination of his Light or Spirit to demonstrate, or discover unto Mankind, as it is Impious and Antichristian in *J. Faldo*, to assert the Right Knowledge of God obtainable any other Way, than by Experience. And this, *Reader*, choaks *J. Faldo*, and the rest of his Partners more than they are willing their Followers should know: who, for all their Cries against us, *as Overturners of a Gospel, and Establishers of a Legal Righteousness*, dread the Consequence of having their own *Strivings, Runnings Willings, and Literal Knowledge laid aside*, in which their Life, Faith, Worship, and whole Religion mostly stand, and of being reduced to the very Alphabet of Inward and Experimental Religion, *where the Righteous Judgments of God are known* for Sin, which they shake off, on another (mistaken) Account; and in this Mystery the Devil works most subtilly, and vigorously against the Light of Christ within, and it's True and Holy Birth.

§. 3. But says he, *How! Know God's Omnipotency experimentally?* Very well! say I, against the Folly of this *cavilling Priest*. Experience is Demonstration; and the World without, and the Redemption I know within, which no Power, but what is Almighty, could ever have effected, *make up that Demonstration; which is that Experience*, therefore I only know God's *Omnipotency* by *Experience*.

§. 4. *But is it thus, that you know Christ died, that there shall be a Judgment, and an Immortality?* I answer, not altogether thus; One Part is Matter of Story, and is believed, *first*, Historically, upon the Credit of History; and *then* upon the Account of Inward Conviction too: The other is Knowable only upon Experience; For we feel in our selves Rewards and Punishments for Good and Evil in this Life, and receive them as Earnests of what will attend Mankind in the next: And we have an inward Sense of a never dying Life; which, as we are Gather'd into, and Grow up in, we shall Inherit Eternal Felicity; and as there is an Erring from that Holy Spirit of Life, the Wages of such Rebellion will be the direful Portion of Death and Misery to every Soul for ever.

§. 5. Nor does this clash with *Faith*, whatever the *Priest* would suggest. For *Faith is a believing in, or relying upon God, with Respect to a farther Knowledge and Enjoyment of him*; which no ways impugns or withstands a Knowledge of God upon Experience, so far as Men do experience: wherein they simply believe, *they do not yet so perfectly experience, which ends Faith*; yet it abides certain, that when they do experience, that farther Revelation of the Goodness, and Mercy, and Riches of the Love of God, as the End of their Faith, *then, and not before, they may be said to know those Things*. Why then should we be denied to conclude, and that most rightly, that to *Know*, and to *Experience*, are equivalent Terms? No *Knowledge* without *Experience*; no *Experience* without *Knowledge*. And tho' Men may believe in a farther Enjoyment of what they now have but an Earnest of, yet *that*, as such, they know not, consequently they experience it not. And so much this insolent *Vilifier* of that serious Expression, confesseth to us, and disputes for (as he thinks against) us, when he says, *where is Faith all the while? And if none but Believers be Saints, such as* W. P. *are professedly* none. Since then my Affirming no *Knowledge* of God without *Experience*, strikes not at *Faith*, because *Faith*, says our Adversary, *is not a clear knowing, but believing or relying upon God, as to Things not yet clearly known and enjoyed*; what has the Man been a doing all the while? But here was his shameful Mistake and Contradiction; That *Knowing* and *Believing* are *one and the same Thing*; and this I will make appear from his own Words, and a Contradiction to himself, at the End of it.

§. 6. He

§. 6. He quarrels my affirming all Knowledge to rest upon Experience, and opposes to it this Question, *Can we experience his Omnipotency?* as much as to say, *yet we know it;* else he queries impertinently. If so then, that God's *Omnipotency* may be known, and not experienced (the purport of his Query) it must be only by *Faith;* and if by *Faith, then a Man may certainly know any Thing to be what it is, and yet at the same Time only believe it to be so:* which he as earnestly withstands, when he asks, *Where is Faith all the while?* &c. I would then fain be resolv'd, whether that Man, suppose *J. Faldo,* who says, that Knowing and Believing are One, and Knowing and Experience are Contraries, be more ridiculous; or *W. P.* who affirms, that *Faith* (which strictly taken, is but an Evidence of Things, not yet *clearly seen, experienc'd or known*) and *Knowing* are not one and the same Thing; and that *experiencing* and *knowing* can never be Contraries?

§. 7. I would advise this *Priest* to be less conceited, and better grounded the next Time he has to do with us; for even in those Places, where he seems most *Insulting,* he appears most *Weak.* Reader, what we experience, we know; and from hence are taught to believe that Fulness to be in God, which we can never comprehensively Know; so that our Knowing God from *Experience,* does not weaken *Faith,* but as Enjoyment is the End of Faith, so from thence great Encouragement is to be taken, to press on from *Faith to Faith;* till there is an Arriving, *at the Measure of the Stature, of the Fulness of Christ.* But he leaves not off here.

§. 8. *I shall not Comment on his* ravening comprehending Brain (a most *affected Pharisee among the Quakers) nor his* clear Mysteries, *as clear a Contradiction as it is;* nor Fleshly Comprehensions *as much Untruth, and Non-sense, as (according to their Meaning of it) it Comprehends;* for I have not Room to spread all his *Rubbish.* I wonder not at his Course Usage of me; 'tis like a Man of his *Breeding, Fury* and *Profession;* there is abundantly more yet behind, some of which will be observ'd in a more proper Place.

But to reply; *Ravening,* is a most proper Word, and due to *J. Faldo,* with his whole Tribe of *Priests* (and, if he will, *Raving too;* some few more moderate ones excepted) for we commonly understand by a *Ravenous Dog,* one that is *Greedy, Sharp-set, that hunts hard for Prey, that snatches and catches at every Thing he likes, or may answer his hungry Appetite.* Now whether this may relate *to that greedy pursuit of the* Priests *after Hire, the Bason, the Box, the Purse;* or that insatiable Thirst they have after Knowledge of those Religious Matters, which were the *dear-bought Experiences of ancient Saints,* whilst Strangers to the *Fiery and Refining Judgments of the Lord;* through which alone it is obtained; certain it is, that the Word is most aptly used by the *Quakers* against that *Ravenous Generation.*

§. 9. *Comprehending Brain,* is compassing, or mastering of any Thing in the Understanding; and where People are more studious to fill their *Heads with Knowledge, than to adorn their Hearts with Righteousness,* we use those Words in a way of Reproof: Since having learnt of God, what we know of him, through the Operation of his Light in our Consciences, it is our Testimony, and our work in the World, *to beat down that Thirsting Spirit after much Head-Knowledge, and press all to the continual Observance of an humble and constant Obedience to the Grace of God manifested in their Hearts, that teacheth to deny all Ungodliness, and Worldly Lusts, and to live Soberly, Righteously, and Godlily in this present Evil World,* which is the *Undefiled Religion.*

Nor his Clear Mysteries; as clear a Contradiction, as it is. It was not Clear, but Clean in my Copy, which I suppose I can produce, and has been so corrected by me. Ingenuous Men would allow *some Grains* for ill-Printing, to us especially, who have not the Press open, nor those Advantages for Well-Printing, which our Adversaries Enjoy; that Day is not yet come to us: *J. Faldo's* Title is *Imprimatur* enough; *we swim against the Stream, such as he, with it:* But God can, and will turn the Rivers of Waters, and make the Sea Dry-Land. *Vincit qui patitur.*

§. 10. But once more hear him. *What is to my present Purpose is in the last Part of his Saying,* ' All must be as unlearned from their Traditional read Know-
' ledge as he is unman'd, *&c.* Where he falls out of all Bounds upon us; and draws this Consequence, and asks these Questions: *Sure the Scripture-Knowledge being Read-Knowledge, or Knowledge that comes by reading (as one Means) is a most hateful Thing to God. That he will impart none of his Secrets to those, that will understand any Thing by his written Word. How came God to fall out with his own*

1673.
Chap. VIII.

Off-spring? Did he write, and cause it to be written, and yet never intended we should read it; or reading it, that we should not believe a Word of it? Shall they be judged by the Law, who live under it, and yet the Knowledge of God thereby be a Sin, and Hindrance to their Salvation? To what an Height of Wickedness and Folly do they quickly go, who are poysoned with that Abomination of holding the Light in every Man's Conscience to be God, Father, Son, Spirit, Christ, Scripture, all? W. P. what means your Latin, Greek, Authors, Logick, Scripture-Quotations? Did you learn all those Things by Immediate Inspiration? But I smell your Design; you would have us throw away all the Knowledge we have by Reading, or Tradition, till we come to be regenerate, that is, Quakers. *But in the mean Time, you would have us without the Armour of Light* (For whatsoever makes manifest is Light) *that we may not be able to defend our selves against the most Ignorant Non-sense, that the meanest of your Votaries can attempt us with. But God Above, and the Scripture without, have taught us better Things. I am not unwilling to quote a few Scriptures.* Put on the Armour of Light, Rom. 13. 12. The Word of God is quick and powerful sharper then any two-edged Sword, Heb. 4. 12. Above all, taking the Shield of Faith, wherewith ye shall be able to quench, &c. and the Sword of the Spirit, which is the Word of God. *Observe, Faith in the 16th Verse is preferred above the Word of God in the 17th Verse; therefore it is not Christ the Word, but the Scriptures the Word: For Faith is not above Christ;* Jesus Christ, *who had less need of Scripture than any of us all, resisted Satan's Temptation by Scriptures,* It is written, It is written, Mat. 4.

I have, Reader, given his Mind at large, and the rather, that the Inconsistency of it, with the Charge he begun his Chapter upon, and the Contradiction of it to himself, might more evidently appear. My Meaning is too fouly conceal'd, and disingenuously evaded by the Man. How could he think, that I should speak so reverently of the Scriptures, and quote them diligently, and very often to the Proof of my Assertions, and yet mean nothing less abusive of them, than his untrue Consequences? I intended no more than this; That Men in a State of Degeneracy from God, may have a Profession of God, and Religion, taken up from the Words of Scripture, and outward Practice of the Saints; not being so much as sensible of the *Remorse, Convictions and Judgments, God brings upon every Soul for Sin, which is the Beginning of his Work of Redemption:* And that many are Rich in Notion, and a Shew of Religion; who never begun right, but must know a being stript of all their Knowledge, and those wrongly apply'd Promises they have taken as to themselves out of the Scriptures, and those Imaginations they have raised thence, towards a Fabrick of Religion; *and so become Poor and Naked, and Hungry and Thirsty, as a little Child, or new Bottle fitted for the new Wine of the Spirit; and to which the Scriptures testifie.* Many can talk of Christ from the Scriptures, which crucifie him in themselves by wicked Works, and do render Praises to him, as the Seed that hath bruised the Serpent's Head, while the Serpent may be yet reigning in them. All such Knowledge and Profession of Religion from the meer Letter of the Scriptures, distinct from the Revelation and Operation of the Eternal Spirit within, must be Unlearnt, Unravell'd, Unbottom'd; one Stone must not be left standing upon another, that there may be a Beginning upon a right Foundation. But far be it from me, to say, *That a Man must unlearn that Knowledge he has had of the Scriptures from the Key of* David, *the Living Word of God, when it has opened the Mysteries therein declared of;* By no Means; *for such Knowledge is Right, Natural, Sanctified from God, and to be esteem'd very Excellent and Divine.*

§. 11. My *Latin, Greek, Authors, Logick, Scripture-Quotations,* I therefore us'd, and urg'd, with plainness and brevity, to prove and recommend the Truth I defended to the World; that lying under great Discredit with too many, they might see that ready to it's Confirmation, which they perhaps would not otherwise have thought upon: But the *Priest* has been as Uncandid with me here, as with my Friends and Self abundantly elsewhere; for he infers general Affirmatives or Negatives from particular Propositions: because I affirm'd, that Unregenerate Men must begin again, that their Religion must be unlearn'd, as to their Way of acquiring it, the Priest concludes, the *Quakers deny all Knowledge which comes from reading, Meditation, or any such Means, however sanctified;* than which, there can be nothing of that kind more Untrue; since it were to say, *because we deny an erroneous Understanding, therefore we deny all Understanding;* or, inasmuch as we condemn all ill-acquired or wrong-gotten Knowledge, for that Cause we *we are to be concluded Enemies to all true and well gotten Knowledge.* But we must bear this, and a great deal more; and the rather, since he does so seasonably assist to his own Confutation, by acknowledging *that the Scriptures without, and God above, has taught him better Things.* Now what is this *Teaching of God above?* If it be in the Scripture, it was impertinent to say any more than that the Scriptures have taught them better Things: But if he meant that God taught by his immediate Discoveries; with and beside the Scriptures; then wherein do we differ? Why has he taken so much Pains, and flung so much Dirt? He bids us also *to put on the Armour of Light:* If he means that of the Scriptures, he errs egregiously; for no Man can put them on, neither are they *that Light which manifests every Thought, Word or Deed*; but that Light which we assert to have been before the Scriptures were, and now is, where they are not, or at least, when they are not thought upon, which is something more Immediate, Living, Spiritual and Inward, and that brings Thoughts, Words and Deeds to Light, savours, relishes, discovers, and accepts or condemns. In short, thus; if whatever makes manifest, is Light, then because the Thoughts, Words and Deeds of Men and Women have been manifested unto them in all Ages, as well before Scriptures were, and where they have not been, as since they were, and where they have been; it follows that they had Light, and that the same Light cannot be the Scriptures, though the Matter written, called Scriptures, was manifested by that Light to the Holy *Pen-men* before they were written, which still makes for the Authority of the Light within. The *Priest* exhorts us to that he endeavours to overthrow, and with which Holy Armour we have fairly foyl'd him in his own Field. The same may be said of the Word of God, though not of the Scriptures any farther, than the sharp-Word of God may speak, or pierce through them into the Consciences: for with good Reason do we affirm, that the *Scriptures* or Writings, *are not that Sword, but that from whence they came.* The Word was a *Fire,* an *Hammer,* a *Sword,* in the *Prophets:* But the Words or Writings it spoke by, were not that Fire, Hammer, nor Sword; *neither had they any other Edge than what the Word put upon them.* To the same Purpose may I argue against their being the Off-spring of God, properly; for, as such, they could not be subject to Casualty. God's Off-spring is more Living and Eternal; that Word is too high, for, properly taken, I mean as Writings, they were the Off-spring of the Writers only; but the Truth they declare of, is of God, and that will abide for ever.

§. 12. But upon the *Shield of Faith, and the Sword of the Spirit,* which *is the Word of God* he has a pretty Fetch. *Faith in the 16th Verse, is preferred above the Word in the 17th Verse; Therefore it is not Christ the Word, but the Scriptures the Word; for Faith is not above Christ.* But neither will this do his Business; and a Shame it is, that this Man should bring these Places to prove that the *Scriptures are Means, whereby to resist Temptation,* which concern them not, especially this in Hand; unless he would have Faith to be the Scriptures, or Word of God, in his Sense, which as it is absurd, so it will by him be denied, since he allows the Faith to be preferred above the Word of God, therefore distinct from it, and not consequently the same with it. And should we grant to him, That Christ is not understood by the Word of God, but the Scriptures, yet observe, the fatal Blow his Cause receives at his own Hand; Every true Christian hath Faith, that Faith is above the Scriptures, *therefore every true Christian hath something in him above the Scriptures.* Every true Faith overcomes the World, and quenches the fiery Darts of Satan, consequently Temptations; therefore it is not so properly the Scriptures, *but true Faith which is preferred above them, and resists Temptations, and overcomes the World.* The Just live by Faith, *but Faith is above the Scriptures; Therefore the Just live by that which is above the Scriptures,* and of Course the Scriptures are not the Rule of Faith; for how can any thing be ruled by that which is inferior to it? Thus much we get, granting to him that the Scriptures are *that Word of God.* But we deny that Gloss too. For the Spiritual Sword, as he says *Beza* renders it, which is that Word of God, must be at least of the Nature of that rest of the Armour mentioned in that Chapter, *I mean of an Invisible Spiritual Nature, which the Bible, as a meer Writing is not.* If any should say, *but the Truth it declares of*; I say so too; and the very Words, when by the living Word brought into the Conscience, do *Pinch, Prick and Wound*; but then that Operation comes from the Power of the Word, which through them reacheth into the Heart of the Creature, and so the Words without, and the Word within, carry a double Conviction with them. But, said Christ to the Devil, *it is written*;

what then? *Therefore must the Quakers needs deny the Scriptures to be any Means to resist Temptation.* Or rather are they not such Means, when God is pleased to use them, which I am sure, no right *Quaker* ever denied. Besides, it was reasonable that Christ should so answer, (set that Power aside which filled up those Words, and chained Satan) because the Devil used Scripture to prevail upon him, as the Place proves. However, we deny not, but confess, that where-ever God is pleased to speak by any Place of Scripture to a tempted Soul, the Scripture may be very well acknowledged to be a Means by which God scatters such Doubts and Despondencies, and gives Power over such Temptations; and that it may often so occur: Yet we would not have People fly to them, as what of themselves may be sufficient, but rather have Recourse to that Divine Faith, which the Scriptures testify *is able to quench the fiery Darts, and overcome the Temptations of this World*; and which *J. Faldo* has largely confest, *is to be preferred above the Scriptures themselves.*

§. 13. The other Part of his Charge, to wit, *That they are dangerous to be read*, has been answered again and again. We say, Let them that *read, understand, fear, believe and obey*; and then they will read worthily; otherwise, *Men read their own Condemnation and Destruction.* For the Holy Truths they declare of, are not to be seen, known, or enjoy'd by every prophane, nor yet professing Person that reads them; they are a sealed Book to all who err from, and despise that Word of God nigh in the Heart, which originally gave them forth, and now bears living Record to them. Blessed are they that rightly Understand and Do them, to such they are of great Price.

CHAP. IX.

That we do not put the Scripture, and Holy Spirit in Opposition. The Wickedness of the Priest, in his Proof. They accord, and we acquiesce in their Testimony. We do not say, that they are not to be obey'd without extraordinary Apostolical Revelation, as basely suggested. His Proof fictitious and forg'd. Such only are by us deny'd, as are only Literal Formal Christians. *The Scriptures own'd and believ'd in, by us, according as they testify of themselves.*

§. 1. TO close up his false *Charges* against us *about the Scriptures*, though I thought not to bestow so much Time about him, be pleased to hear him, and his Testimonies, which he thinks sufficient to prove what he says of us to be true.

§. 2. *That the* Quakers *put the Scriptures and the Spirit of God in Opposition to each other.* To make this good, he quotes *W. Smith*, thus, "Traditions of Men, "Earthly Root; Darkness, and Confusion; *Nebuchadnezzar's* Image; Putrefaction, "and Corruption; Rotten, and Deceitful; all out of the Life and Power of God; "Apostacy; the Whore's Cup; the Mark of the Beast; *Babylon* the Mother; "Bastards brought forth of Flesh and Blood; the Birth that persecutes the Son, "and Heir; Graven Images, *Morning Watch*, p. 22, 23. *It would amaze*, says he, *a* Christian *to read what is contained in the two Pages quoted, of vilifying Reproach to the Scriptures, and the Doctrines from them received: If this be not Opposing the Spirit of God to the Scriptures, and rendring them adverse to each other, the Devil himself must despair of Inventing Words to express it by.*

And now, *Reader*, it is Time for me, with a Soul full of Grief, to make my Appeal to the Righteous Lord God of Heaven and Earth, and his equal Witness in thy Conscience, if ever *Quakers* writ, or said any such Thing of the *Holy Scriptures*. O far be it from us! and very great and heavy will the Damnation of *J. Faldo* be in the Day of the Lord, unless he shall unfeignedly Repent, because of these detestable Lyes, that he seems wilfully to fasten upon our Writings. What *William Smith* said, reflected not in the least upon the Scriptures, nor yet those Doctrines, which were truly received thence. No such Words can be produced by our Adversaries: had *W. S.* written any such Thing, he that adds so much, that was not, we are to suppose would not have omitted mentioning of that, if it had been. But *W. Smith* addrest himself to that Adulterated Spirit, which had defiled Nations, that nevertheless were under the Profession of God, Scriptures and Religious Worship, though in Works they denied God; and as concerning Scripture and true Worship, grosly err'd, not knowing the Power of God, nor how to Worship him in Spirit, and in Truth: not that he ever durst to entertain so Blasphemous

phemous an Apprehenfion of thofe Holy Writings, or thofe Doctrines that are truly received thence, as is fuggefted by our moſt unfair Adverſary. And is it not the Height of all Unrighteouſneſs to his Neighbour, that when he condemns the Degenerated Spirit, Knowledge and Worſhip of any People, however profeſſing the Scriptures, and it may be pretending to believe accordingly, as *W. Smith* does all Apoſtate Chriſtians, *J. Faldo* ſhould infer, *that his Neighbour calls the Scriptures themſelves, and not a wrong Knowledge of them, Will-Worſhip, Corruption, Rottenneſs, Deceitful, Whore's-Cup, Apoſtacy, Earthly Root, Graven Images, &c.* and that he ſhould intend nothing leſs than *Oppoſition betwixt the Spirit and it's own Scriptures?* There needs no farther Confutation than the groſs and black Envy of our *Adverſary* about this one Paſſage. Be it known to all, we do affirm the Scriptures never did jar with the Spirit, nor the Spirit oppoſe himſelf againſt the Scriptures; and thus much our Writings can plentifully prove to all ſober Enquirers.

§. 3. But he offers another, and the laſt Proof of his Charge, from *J. Naylor*, " That of this Sort are they falſe Prophets (as I ſuppoſe he means) who have their " Preaching from Study, and other Men's Mouths, and not from the Mouth of the " Lord. From which he infers, that what we have in the Scriptures, is not from the Mouth of the Lord; and queries: *I would know* (faith he) *of the* Quakers, *what they will make of the Mouth of the Lord? It was ſaid to* Jeremiah, Jer. 15. 19. Thou ſhalt be as my Mouth.

Our Meaning is ſtill over-look'd by this diſingenuous Adverſary, and a quite contrary Thing ſubſtituted. The natural Purport of the Words can be no more than this: That though the Things declared of in the Scriptures, were the Word of the Lord to the Holy *Ancients*, and *Jeremiah*, as God's Mouth (not his Mouth therefore) to the People of *Iſrael*; yea, and much of it the Word of the Lord to us too; yet, for Men to ſay any Part thereof by rote, eſpecially if they add their own Comments and Gloſſes, fram'd from Study to any Part of the Scriptures, and cry, *Thus ſaith the Lord*; or *Hear the Word of the Lord*; *and not in the ſame living Senſe, nor upon the like Commiſſion, every ſuch one doth Rob his Neighbour, and ſteal his Words:* And he is no more a True Prophet for ſo doing, than a *Parrot* is a *Man*, becauſe he can talk. If then no ſuch Creature is therefore to be reputed Rational, nor what he ſays, Reaſon, as to him, though ſo in it ſelf, becauſe it proceeds not from the Root and Principle of Reaſon, but by meer Imitation, and conſequently a Prater, in no Caſe to be minded: Neither is he a *true Prophet, nor that the Word of the Lord, with reſpect to that Prophet, who has not received what he delivers, from the immediate Word of God himſelf, but by Hear-ſay, or meer Imitation.* No, he is but a very Babbler, and begets People no farther than into meer Words, and Imaginary Gloſſes, which is the Ground of that Uncertainty that is in the World about Religion.

The Scriptures then are to us obliging, as the Things they declare of were the Word of the Lord to ſeveral Ages (Temporal Commands excepted) and they are not without a Mouth; yet they, and *Jeremiah* too, are inferior to the Mouth of the Eternal Word, which ſpeaks in this Evangelical Diſpenſation the Will of God unto Mankind after a more living and immediate Manner, as was propheſied of old. And I may thus far gratify our *Adverſary's* Curioſity about *God's Mouth*, and tell him, that the Word of God, is from the Mouth of God; *and the true Prophets and Apoſtles in all Ages have been the Mouth of the Word of God, and the Scriptures are the Writings of thoſe Holy Prophets and Apoſtles, as they were the Mouth of the Eternal Word*, revealing God's Will in their Hearts, that they might declare it, whether by Word of Mouth, or Writing to the People; and this is the true Order and Deſcent of Things.

§. 4. But he has one Kick more at us, before he gives up the Ghoſt, in his Miſ-repreſentation of us concerning the Scriptures. *The* Quakers *hold it is a Sin, and the Sin of Idolatry, to believe and live according to the Inſtructions and Holy Examples expreſſed in, and by the Scriptures, except we have them by immediate Inſpiration, and at firſt Hand, as the Apoſtles received them: And now* (ſays he) *I am come to the higheſt Round of their Ladder.*

Indeed, thoſe Rounds of Ladders are very dangerous Places: I will not ſay how often, nor for what, an Army-Chaplain might deſerve to be ſo high exalted, but ſince his eager Purſuit after an Innocent People has brought him actually thither, and it falls to my Lot to be his Executioner; I ſhall take all the Care I can to acquit my ſelf well of my Employment; I will warrant him for ever coming down the

the same Way he went up. In order to which, let us first hear what Kind of Speech he will make us, to the Point in Hand.

William Dewsbury in his Discovery of Man's Return, p. 21. " All People may "search the Scriptures, and see how you have been deceived by your Teachers, "who have caused you to seek your lost God in Carnal and Dead Observations; "which they have not any Scriptures for. What this is to his Purpose, I cannot understand; to be sure it is for ours. For *W. D.* is so far from making it Idolatry to live up to the Scriptures, that he condemns their seeking for the true God, where he was not to be found, which, says he, they HAVE NO SCRIPTURE FOR. *As much as to say, that they seek after God not according to Scripture*, and therefore are both Deceivers and Deceived. Certainly this is a miserable Farewel he takes of the *first of his Book*, and the *Quakers* Denial of the Scriptures; that they should therefore affirm a Practice according to Scripture, without immediate Inspiration, Idolatrous, *because they assert such to be deceived, who seek after God, not according to the Scriptures*; If so much Impertinency should fall from a poor *Quaker*'s Pen, *what Reproach, Insolence, and Triumph* would there be. But he has another Witness, that 'by the Mouths of two Witnesses, his Charge against us, may be (not establish'd, but) evidently disprov'd.

§. 5. *And this is Babylon, the Mother of Harlots, viz.* [to read and practise, as the Saints did, and the Apostles of the Scriptures of the New Testament] *and the Abomination of all Uncleanness. W. Smith's* Morning Watch, p. 23.

Forgery in the Abstract, as base, black, and dishonest as Man can be to Man. What! rob him of Truth, of a good Conscience; foist in, put out, alter, gloss, pervert, and what he pleaseth. What! make us lye against God, his Servants, Scriptures, the Light within, and our own Souls? But I have the less Need to make our Defence, where his manifest Corruption of our Words accuse him, and my Answer to the *first Part* of his Charge in this Chapter has done it at large; Only thus much give me Leave to say, That *if Words urg'd upon one Subject, shall be apply'd to another of a different Nature;* and that our Adversary *can never prove his Charge against us, but by abusing, corrupting, mis-rendering and interlineating our Words*; There is no Reason that we should much concern our selves in the Consequence of such Debates; that Way of Demonstration will save us the Labour of a Vindication with all Sober Persons. But he has not done with us yet.

§. 6. *I am e'en tired with searching the sulphureous Veins of the Pit and Mire of* Quakerism, *the Root of all which, is the Deified Light Within: if you have not enough of this Smoak to satisfy you it is the Bottomless Pit it rises out of, I will give you two Ebullitions more, and then leave you satisfied, or to get better Senses.*

" So amongst the Words you find, how the Saints in some Things walked, and "what they practised, and then you strive to make that Thing to your selves, "and observe and do it as near as you can: and here you are found Transgressors "of the Just Law of God, who saith, *Thou shalt not make to thy self any Graven* "*Image, nor the Likeness of any Thing*. And, says *J. Faldo*, it follows now, what Difference is there in the Ground betwixt you and the *Pope*? though in the Appearance there seems to be such a great Space.

I have been the more punctual in the Recital of this, that I might shew to my *Adversary*, I will be just to him, though he be most egregiously Unmanly with us. He says, *That he is e'en tired*; indeed he has Reason for it, though for nothing else: For, who ever got any Thing by beating the Air, or Spitting against the Heavens?

The Sulphureous Pit of Quakerism, we can in one Sense allow, and *J. F.* may be better acquainted with it; For the Plagues which the never-dying Worm, the sharp reproving, condemning Light within, will inflict upon the Spirits of them who resist and gainsay the Truth, are aptly resembled to a Sulphureous Bottomless Pit: *Sulphureous*, because of the Insufferableness of the Smoak: *A Bottomless Pit*, by Reason of a Dismal, Endless State and Condition of Wo. And I doubt not, but *J. Faldo* has an Earnest of this, for his Attempts against the Light, and the Children of it.

This long Discourse is no more to us than the rest of his Trash, that we have already rejected as his own Invention and base Perversion of our real Meanings. Take *W. Smith* in his own Sense and Belief, and all is well: But receive him in *J. Faldo*'s Disguise, and truly we should not know him our selves. He intended, that all those real Experiments of other Persons (of which the Scriptures are full)

talks

talkt un-experimentally over, by Un-regenerated Spirits, can be no Ways beneficial; Nay, that what Ideas or Notions they may have to themselves *of the Holy Ancients Enjoyments,* while altogether unacquainted with them, *are but a Kind of Images;* which their believing in, and bowing to, as indispensable Gospel-Truths, is to be *reputed nothing below Idolatry it self:* Yet far be it from us to say, that to believe the Truth, as declared in the Scriptures, *is Idolatry,* as well as that it is manifest Folly in any so to say or think of us; when not only we are most careful and desirous of rendring what we believe *purely Scriptural;* But, I do declare, that as no Man can live the Life of the Scriptures without the Operation of that Spirit which gave them forth, so to live up to what they do *exhort and declare, is the highest Pitch of Purity Man's Nature is capable of aiming at, and attaining to.*

§. 7. He now intends to wind up his Discourse on the present Subject with a retrospective and contracted Argument of all those particular distinct Charges, *viz. They who deny the Scripture to be the Word of God; equal their own Writings and Sayings; deny them to be a Rule of Faith and Life, a Judge of Religious Controversies; take Men off from Reading them; deny the Scripture to be any Means whereby we may come to know God, or Christ, or our selves; affirm them to be no Means whereby to resist Temptation, and are dangerous to be read; deny them to be Profitable, but as Experienced; put Scripture and Spirit in Opposition; affirm the Doctrines, Commands and Holy Examples expressed in the Scriptures (as such) to be not at all binding to us; hold it as the Sin of Idolatry to believe and live according to the Instructions and Holy Examples expressed in, and by the Scriptures, except we have them by immediate Revelation, as the Apostles: They who do all these Things, mentioned in the foregoing Particulars, Deny the Scriptures.*

But the Quakers do all these Things; therefore they deny the Scriptures.

To which I return this Argument.

If to Deny the *Scriptures* to be the *Word of God*; to make what Writings are given forth by the same Spirit relative of the Scriptures; if not to prefer any Writings before the Scriptures, nor equal them to the Scriptures; if to deny the Scriptures to be most properly the general Rule of Faith and Life, and Judge of Controversy, and not the Spirit rather; if not to take Men off from Reading the Scriptures for Instruction, *&c.* if not to deny them to be any Means, whereby Men may come to know God, Christ or our selves; if to affirm them to be a Means whereby to resist Temptation; not Dangerous to be read; if to deny them to be read to any Profit, without the Assistance of the Spirit, especially by such as know them not, who are in a Rebellious and Unregenerate State; If never to dare to put the Scriptures and Spirit in Opposition to each other; if not to affirm the Doctrines, Expressions and Holy Examples, as such, not to be binding (Temporary Services excepted) if to hold it as no Sin of Idolatry, nor any other, to Believe and Live according to the Instructions and Holy Examples expressed in, and by the Scriptures: If to do all these Things, so mention'd, *be not to deny, contemn and Undervalue, but rather to honour, rightly instate and recommend the Scriptures;* then the Quakers, *who believe and do all this, are not Denyers, but Owners, Asserters and Defenders of the Scriptures,* so far as they themselves desire to be defended. But we have largely prov'd, that so to do, is not to deny them, and that the *Quakers* so hold; therefore the *Quakers* are no Deniers, but Maintainers of the True and Divine Authority of the Scriptures.

§. 8. For his Comparison of us with the Papists, (though he has been so Cunning, or Unjust rather, as to quote their *Authors* and not ours, and some Passages we justly doubt) it is Ridiculous, and every Way Unworthy of our Notice. A meer begging of the Question; and, by what we can guess, design'd only to bring an Odium upon us. He puts the *Scriptures* in the Middle, and the *Quakers* and *Papists,* like the two Thieves upon the Cross, on each side, to discover their Harmonious Agreement against them; which of them he makes to be him that should go to Paradise, I know not; but we have the upper Hand.

But we can never allow of the Comparison, *since the* Papists *place the Rule and Judgship, in a* Pope, *or General Council, and the* Quakers *in the Eternal, Unerrable, Holy Spirit of God,* and consequently, our Adversary is basely Irreverent to God, that brings the *Pope, or a Council of Fallible Men* upon a Comparison with his Infallible Spirit. Nor, if it were true, would it be any Thing against us; since *Protestants* will not allow themselves to be therefore *Papists,* because in several Things they agree; *as about God, Eternity, Christ, his Life, Death, Sufferings, Resurrection, Last Judgment, and Eternal Recompence.*

§. 9. To

§. 9. To conclude; We dare leave it with God, and all sober Men, to judge, how far *J. Faldo* hath abused us, in giving in so black a Charge against us, and traducing our Persons, and perverting our Writings to prove it, by base Characters fastned upon the one, and false Inferences charg'd upon the other; Which of themselves conspire the Overthrow of their Inventer; and thus is he fairly turned off *from the highest Round of the Ladder*, which he hath so unadvisedly *adventured to mount*. And as it fares with some Notorious *Malefactors*, he remains there *Pendent, as a Monument of his own Rash and Dishonest Undertakings, to the Terror of all Passengers, who shall happen to travel by this Way of Controversy to the Land of Truth*.

CHAP. X.

He chargeth us with a Denial of all the Ordinances of the Gospel. First in General, then in Particular. His Proof of the First Invalid. His great Disingenuity in resting our Words, especially J. Pennington's.

§. 1. THE *Second Part* of his Book begins *with the* Quakers *Denial of all the Ordinances of the Gospel*, as he will have it. (Pag. 1, 2, 3, 4, 5.) It is more than possible that we shall prove him, e'er we part, not only to be a Denier of the True Gospel Ordinances, but indeed, an Introducer of another *Gospel*, if such a Thing may be: But to his Charge; *First* in General, then in Particular, The Quakers *deny the Ordinances of the Gospel in General, by which*, says he, *I understand not those of Nature's Book, nor what was revealed by* Moses, *but those Ordinances which were commanded by Precept, or prescribed by Example in the New Testament*. Now to prove what he says of the *Quakers*, he cites *G. Fox* thus; " And we say, He, Christ, hath triumphed over the Ordinances, and blotted them " out, and they are not to be touched, and the Saints have Christ in them, who " is the End of outward Forms, *G. Myst.* p. 52.

In all which I find no Denial of *Gospel Ordinances*; Nor were they so much as meant by him: His Language is Scriptural; For Christ did *blot out the Hand-Writing of Ordinances, and he was to the Saints then, and is to those now, who rightly believe in him*, the End of *all Meats, Drinks, Washings, Days, or any other Temporal, Elementary or Figurative Worship*; for *J. Faldo then* to charge a Denial of all *Gospel Ordinances* upon these Words, *is to plead for a legal Dispensation, and Bondage to the Shadows of the good Things to come*; thereby making Christ's Coming of none Effect; *and consequently introducing of another Gospel*, as speaks the *Apostle*; besides that he basely wrests our Words.

§. 2. Again, *But* Pennington *is so Cruel, by that Time he arrives to* P. 38, *of Unity*, that he says, " Such of the People of God, as do not follow the Lord " perfectly out of the City of Abomination [VISIBLE WORSHIP] but be " found in any Part thereof when the Lord cometh to judge her, the Lord will not " spare them.

I perceive, that unless we will allow *J. Faldo* the Liberty of telling the World *our Meaning, or rather making his own to be ours*, his *Essays* come to nothing. What Words can be sounder of their Kind, [*Visible Worship*] being left out, and which our Adversary unworthily puts in? Are not People to follow God fully? Strange Doctrine that he teacheth! But grant him his *Gloss*, aliàs, *gross Comment*, without Distinction, and I know he does his Work. But we are not so easily to be *overlaid*. We do declare, that while Men have *Bodies*, which are the visible Parts of Men, and the Bodies of Men are conversably concern'd in Religious Worship as well as the Soul, *there will be, there must be, and there ought to be a Visible Worship*; Therefore most false is *J. Faldo's Paraphrase*; yet thus far we could go; That *Visible Worship (as such) without a due Regard to what Kind of Worship it may be, and what is the Root from whence it came, cannot be well-pleasing to God*; For then, that so *Splendid Whore, and Deceitful Prophet*, at large described in the *Revelation of St. John*, would be therefore true Worshippers, because *their Worship was Visible*: But I do perceive, that here it pincheth, with almost all Professions; *The* Quakers *would put us off our own Strivings, Willings, Runnings in our own Wisdom, Contrivance, Appointment; whereby we must take up such a Cross to self, as is insupportable to Flesh and Blood*: And indeed it is so; which all must come to know a Crucifying of, or they enter not into the Kingdom of God here, nor

hereafter:

hereafter: *The Old Leaven muſt be purged out, and the New Wine have a New Bottle: Men muſt become Children, and Religion, taken up not upon Conviction, muſt be abandoned for the leaſt Appearance of God's Light breaking in upon the Heart and Conſcience, reproving the unfruitful Works of Darkneſs.*

CHAP. XI.

The Firſt of the Particular Ordinances, he ſays we Deny, is the Miniſtry. *His Proof Lame. W. P. and his Friends defended. J. F. and his Gang Reproveable. We own a Goſpel One; but not his. The Calling abuſed by ſuch Pretenders.*

§. 1. HE now deſcends to ſhow our *Denial of the Ordinances of the Goſpel in Particular*; and we, to examine what he ſays; wherein, if he ſucceed no better than in his Endeavours to manifeſt our Denial of them in General, I think the *Reader* will have Reaſon to think, we ſhall not ſit down by the Loſs. But hear him.

§. 2. *They Deny all Miniſtry that hath a Mediate Call to that Office*; quoting *J. Parnel's Shield,* &c. p. 16. " And their Call to the Miniſtry we deny, which " is *Mediate.* Alſo *G. Fox,* in his *Great Myſtery,* pag. 45. " But who can wit-" neſs an *Immediate* Call from God, and ſpeak as they are moved by the Holy " Ghoſt, and ſuch Travel from Place to Place, having no certain Dwelling-Place, " *this Miniſtry we own and witneſs.*

The Charge againſt the *Prieſts* I eſteem Sound, but not *J. Faldo's* againſt the *Quakers.* We do for ſeveral Reaſons already urg'd, deny that any Man can be a *True Miniſter, who is not immediately Call'd*; for it's not, *Go ye forth into all the World, and Preach the Goſpel,* that belongs unto all Men, no more than becauſe Princes ſend Ambaſſadors to Princes with their Credentials, *therefore every Man ought to do the like in Imitation, without conſidering thoſe neceſſary Qualifications that belong to ſuch an Action.* Peter, John, &c. were a great While Diſciples, not at Academies, but in *Chriſt's School,* which taught *the Mortification of Luſts, and an Holy Self-Denying Life*; to ſuch it was that the Commiſſion came; but neither was their Commiſſion of Force, till they had received *that Anointing, which was to enable them to act by it.* If then every Holy Man as ſuch, is not fitly Gifted and Impower'd to be a Miniſter, but that it depends upon a more Immediate, and Extraordinary Thing; certainly thoſe, who take upon them the Miniſtry, that have neither learnt by True Mortification to be Holy, nor receiv'd any Power from Heaven to be Miniſters, but explode both as to the preſent Age, and *Teach for Hire, and Divine for Money,* are not of Chriſt's making, but their own; and therefore to be denied. And thus much *J. Faldo,* to his own apparent Overthrow grants us, where he ſays, (Pag. 9.) *We acknowledge that all True Miniſters of Chriſt ought to have an Immediate Call, ſuch as conſiſts in Grace and Gifts: And ſuch as have not this Immediate Call, we account unworthy of the Thing and Name.*

What more has any *Quaker* ſaid? Why is *James Parnel* quoted to prove that what he charges upon the *Quakers,* as to their Denying the Miniſtry of the Goſpel, is a Truth, when it is become no Crime at all in *J. Faldo* to aſſert, *That who are not Immediately Call'd, are Unworthy both of the Name and Thing?* Is he become an Enemy himſelf to that Goſpel-Ordinance? If Immediate, then not Mediate; and if not Mediate, then J. Parnel and G. Fox *writ Orthodoxally*; conſequently, we are not to be reputed *Deniers of the Miniſtry of the Goſpel, becauſe we aſſert that no Man is a Goſpel-Miniſter, who is not Immediately call'd thereto.* So that his mincing of the Matter in the next Page, will no Ways qualifie it, viz. *That Motions by the Holy Ghoſt he allows, yet he affirms, that thoſe who are moved by the Commands of the Spirit in the Scripture, are mov'd by the Holy Ghoſt:* For if any Holy Man reading the Apoſtle's Commiſſion, ſhall at that Inſtant of Time receive an Heavenly Power to make it his, laying that ſame Injunction upon him, and enduing him with ſuch a Meaſure of that Divine Power, as they received, *We ſhall cheerfully grant him to be truly call'd*; yet not becauſe *Go ye into all Nations and Preach the Goſpel, is there written,* but becauſe *God reſpoke thoſe Words by the ſame Living and Eternal Power, immediately to that Particular Perſon, which made, what otherwiſe was but the Commiſſion of the Apoſtles, his Commiſſion alſo.*

§. 3. But there is a Word or Two, which having lain hard upon his Stomach, he vomits up thus: (Pag. 10.) *As for having no Certain Dwelling-Place, and leaving Houſes, Lands and Poſſeſſions, let them repair to* William Penn, *and others of their Miniſters,*

Ministers, for an Answer to it, who have large Possessions and brave Habitations, such as few Ministers as they disclaim (especially the Non-Conformists) *enjoy.*

What Answer this is to that Part of G. *Fox*'s Words, which it pretends to refute, is obvious to the meanest Capacity that is not prejudic'd; For my Part, I know not what induc'd him to any Answer at all, being Scripture Words, unless it were, that he might reflect upon the Plenty God hath given some of us. *What! Doth he envy Men the Blessings of Heaven, upon their Industry? Or the Love of Parents to their Children? Is his Eye Evil, because God's Eye is Good? Doth his Mouth water after the* Quaker's *Possessions, now the Government hath justly and seasonably prevented him of a Fat Benefice?* But, why must *William Penn's* Name be question'd about Houses and Possessions? *Is he angry that an Enmity like his own, in his deceas'd Father, depriv'd him not of that Estate for Conscience Sake, he now begrudges him the Enjoyment of? But he dyed a better Man, a more Natural Father, and Sincere Christian, than a Man of* J. Faldo's *Sordid Conscience will ever do.* But let me tell the Man (if yet he be worthy of that Name) that *W. Penn first lost his Estate before he got it, and sacrific'd it, the Comfort of his Father's House, and whatever was dear of this World, to the Quiet of a Conscience void of Offence, before it pleas'd Almighty God to make all his.* Such as have known him better then *J. Faldo's* Informers, of the most Eminent both of *Presbyterians, Independents,* and *Anabaptists,* could tell him, *He hath had a Conscience* (whatever they believe now) *that was not to be caught by the Bait of Pleasure, Estate, Preferment, or Esteem in this World; as well as that no Severity us'd to bow or balk it, could prevail to renounce what it had believ'd upon Pure Convictions.* To conclude his Defence in this Place, *He got not what he hath, by Preaching* (as perhaps Mercenary *J. Faldo,* and many of his Coat have done) but having it, by God's Providence and Faithfulness, can notwithstanding (through the continued Love of God) *freely bestow his Strength, Labour, Estate, and Life too, for the Promotion of the Unchangeable Pure Way of God, in which he has believ'd, from whom he received, and to whom he owes all that he hath.*

But why *Poor Non-Conformists,* after all their preacht up *Battles, Spoils, Plunders, Sacrileges, Decimations,* &c. Rich, and Covetous as ever: As Rich, *because the Bason walks, and takes its Rounds Two to One of which it did;* and Covetous, *because they remain as discontented, as if they were Starving;* witness a late Begging Book from a *Non-Conformist's* Hand, *which conjures their Hearers into larger Benevolence,* though by the Stile one would think *it were their Just Due.* I am perswaded, *their Preachings, Christnings, Burials, Churchings,* alias, *Lying-in Visits, Exhortations, Thanksgivings, and Prayers, have cheated People of more Gold and Silver, than ever they did dare to make the least Pretence to* (though they always dar'd to take what they could get) *in their former Days of Power.* But this is nothing to me farther, than that it is less dishonourable to *William Penn,* or any other *Quaker,* whom God hath blessed with a plentiful Subsistence, that having Estates, *they notwithstanding should sustain the Labour, and Suffering, of Preaching the Gospel, and that at all Seasons, than in* J. Faldo *and his Brethren,* who (it's greatly to be feared) preach, what they call the *Gospel,* that they might get Estates, at least Livelihoods by it, let him or them say what they will. I could give him a long List of more *Exacting Jocky, Hawking, Mercenary Bargains of* Presbyterians, Independents, *and* Anabaptists, *than can readily be parallel'd by Parish-Priests:* A Thing once denied by them, and ought still to be detested of all others.

§. 4. But he ends not here concerning the *Ministry:* For, says he, *The Quakers Deny our Ministry, because we Preach from the Scripture.* A wicked Lye, minted out of Hell it self: We have laid down no such Proposition, nor tending to it. But he supposeth *J. Farnel* helps him to prove this Assertion. " And here is the Dif-
" ference of the Ministers of the World, and the Ministers of Christ —The One of
" the Letter, the other of the Spirit.

Strange Impudence, to call this a Proof. It is a Proof indeed, but against him; for if a False or *Worldly Ministry,* under the Form of Godliness may not be, Farewel Scripture. But if such a Thing will be allow'd us, then since the Letter or Scriptures *are not by them rejected, but in Shew most highly admired, and that they pretend to collect all they believe or know from thence* (though indeed they understand them not) we have great Reason to say, *That those who are Ministers only from the Letter, with what they imaginarily comment upon it, are not Christ's Ministers.* We are so far from making it a Reason why we deny your *Ministry,* who are under that Qualification, that we utterly deny you to have that Knowledge

from

from the Scripture which we except against, but your own Inventions, and Groundless Conceits alone: For though *J. Faldo* thinks it very *Heterodox* to say, that unless we are immediately assured from the Light within, of the Truth of what we hold, and that all Belief, not so discover'd, is a Lye, deriding at *Samuel Fisher's* Answer in that Case, (Pag. 14. 15.) *Those who Swore, as the Lord lived, Swore falsly because they knew him not to Live*; affirming to us, *That they were such as did not believe him to live at all, and therefore* S. Fisher *erred (in his Construction)* I say, though it be so, yet we are not forlorn of Reason as well as Scripture to our Defence. For no Truth is such to me, which I either do not know to be True, or have not some real Ground to believe to be such, *however True it may be in it self*. And that *Samuel Fisher* urg'd that Scripture pertinently, and consequently his Return upon it is impertinent, He himself has provided us with an Argument; for if he will not have it, that they therefore lyed, in saying *As the Lord liveth*, because they knew him not to Live, we must see what was the Reason that God gave their Asseveration the Lye. Says *J. Faldo, they did not believe him to Live at all*. Very well, then the Narrow of the Difference lyes here, That we say, *They knew him not to Live*; And *J. Faldo* says, *That they believ'd him not to Live*, Now I would fain know which are most excusable? One says, they *who said, as sure as the Lord Liveth, lyed*, because they knew not God to Live; and the other, *that they believ'd Him not to Live*. If any Thing be to be gotten, it is this, *That they who knew him not to Live, might believe him however to Live, whilst those who believ'd him not to Live, would not believe a Thing they had no Ground or Knowledge inducing them to*. But he has led us to a quick Expedient, *They did know God to Live*; because *he that lives, may know from thence that God Lives, who holds every Soul in Life that lives*. To which I return, *That they did believe God to Live, because they lived; for how could they doubt of His Living, who held them in Life*: But enough of this. To conclude: *A Living Spiritual Ministry we own, that Preaches the Everlasting Gospel in it's own Power, and that freely, to the Raising of People Dead in Trespasses and Sin, to turn them from Darkness to Light, that they might serve the Living Lord God of Heaven and Earth, in the Newness of the Spirit, who is worthy of all Honour and Glory for ever*.

CHAP. XII.

The Second Particular Ordinance is a Gospel-Church. *His Definition for us, by it's gross Contrariety to the Scripture. His base Inference of our Denial of Religious Societies, and Outward Gifts, from our Friends asserting of but One Catholick Church, and that it is in God. A Gospel-Church own'd. Our Adversary prov'd Heterodox about Apostolical Preaching. Inward Sense preferr'd before Intelligence.*

§. 1. THE next Gospel-Ordinance he says we deny, is a *Gospel-Church*; not to spend Time about his Way of Phrasing it, though uncouth enough; *We shall attend his Proof*.

Pag. 16. 17, 18. " And the Church so gathered into God, is the Pillar and " Ground of Truth, where the Spirit alone is Teacher. *J. N's Love to the Lost*, Pag. 17.

Upon which he argues thus, *The Gospel-Church is a Church which hath other Teachers, and not the Spirit alone; whereas the Apostles gave themselves to Preaching of the Word, and Elders were Ordained; therefore the* Quakers *Deny a Gospel-Church, and they contradict themselves, for they have more Teachers than all others*. A Lye to be sure.

There is greatly wanting to this *Priest* a better Understanding, or more Honesty in using what he has; for who is not blinded with Prejudice, may discern, that from our speaking of the *Universal Church of God*, which says the Apostle, as well the Quakers, *Is in God*; he infers, *That we deny all Visible Religious Societies, commonly called by the Ancients, the Churches of* Asia, Thessalonica, Ephesus, Corinth, *&c*. And from our asserting the Spirit to be the Only Gospel-Teacher of all who believe, he concludes, *That we Deny all Preaching of Men, though by the Spirit*. O Blind, or else most Disingenuous Man! What? Charge that upon us, *which our Practice gives the Lye to every Day*. But when we urge this against him, and such like *Adversaries*, then it is not that he hath mis-represented us, *but that we have contradicted our selves*.

1673
Chap. XII.

But to clear the Point, if it can yet be doubtful: We do believe, *There is One, and but One Universal Church, the Ground and Pillar of Truth, and that it is in God*; anchor'd, establisht, and built upon him, *the Rock of Ages, and Foundation of many Generations*: And as such, neither is every Visible Society, making Profession of Religion, nor are all of them together *That Church*; but such alone, *who are washed in the Blood of the Lamb, and ingrafted into the True Vine, bringing forth the Fruits of Holiness, to the Eternal Honour, Glory, and Renown of Christ the Head, who is over all, God Blessed for evermore.* And though there be a Mediate Preaching, which is to say, that the Spirit speaks by such whom he hath anointed to Preach; yet it cannot be strictly said, *That Man Preaches*, or it is *Man's Ministry*, but rather, *the Spirit by Man*, and that it is *the Spirit's Ministry*, and Man only a *Mean*, or *Instrument*, through which the Teaching is convey'd, or *Direction* rather to the *True Teacher, the Light in the Conscience*: Not that the Lord doth not sometimes plentifully Teach his Children without any such Means too, who are turned to the Grace in the Heart, and believe and walk in His Holy Light, where God is to be found, and an Access to this Holy, Blessed Presence administred; for he hath both promised *It* of Old, and perform'd *It* in our Days. Thus the *Apostles* were *Preachers*, not from Man, nor by Man, but by the Revelation of the Son of God, declaring of the Mysteries of God's Everlasting Kingdom, as they were moved by the Holy Ghost: And so none are exempted; *for all may Prophesie One by One, that the Church may be Edified*, 1 Cor. 14. 31. Yet I cannot but observe, that (1.) the Man implicitly denies *that to be a True Church, which is the Ground and Pillar of Truth*, for such *the Quakers* stile *A Gospel-Church*. (2.) That he affirms, *The True Church to have other Teachers than the Spirit*; which is to say, *That the Primitive Churches were not led, guided, and taught by the Spirit of God only, but by some other Teachers also*; contrary to express Scripture, the Promise of God, and very End of the Blessed Gospel. If he says, that he meant the *Apostles* that were Inspired, I answer, that was never deny'd by us, *because that was the Teaching of the Spirit by them*, which was very little less, than if it had been immediately in them: So that one of these Two Things must follow from his Kind of Arguing; *Either the Apostles Preacht without the Motions of the Eternal Spirit*; Or, *Preaching, as they were moved of God's Spirit, was their Preaching, and not the Holy Spirit's, that so plentifully dictated to them what they were to say*: But in as much as neither can be reputed True, by True Christian Men, I conclude *the Quakers Sound*, and their Boasting *Adversary*, Heretical.

§. 2. But he thinks he hath clearly got the Point of us, about a *Quaker's* telling him, *They knew, that One of the Dutch Nation Spoke by the Spirit in a Meeting of ours, though in that Language which was not understood by the Meeting, because they all found Refreshings.*

I will be Faithful in giving his Observation upon it: Of the unknown Language he says, *This was Orderly according to the Popish Mass, who Read Prayers in an Unknown Tongue to the People*; but herein he wrongs us, for though we do acknowledge, that the Pure and Single Power of the Almighty, may both strike Astonishment, and give Refreshment, where the Words utter'd are not always understood; since he doth both frequently without them; and that Understanding and Sense are Two Things; for the *Devil* may speak the best Words in the *Bible*, and be an *Undiscover'd Devil still*, except by this Divine Light, Power, or Spirit, he be inwardly manifested; consequently a *Right Sense* may be had, where Words may not be understood, which is the *One Tongue to the Children of the Light*. Yet we not only decry all design'd Obscurity by Praying and Preaching in unknown Languages, but with the *Apostle* say, that we chuse rather by far to speak in a Known Tongue, that the People may understand our Words, as well as have a Sense of our Spirits: Nor did ever any *Quaker* yet pretend to be moved to Pray in an Unknown Language, whilst he was Master of that which was well known to the People: Since then we don't affect such Obscurity, the Case of all those *Papists*, who Pray in *Latin*, rather than in their Native and Vulgar Tongue, he is very disingenious in that Reflection.

§. 3. Upon the *Quakers Reason*, why they knew that Declaration was from the Spirit of God, viz. *Because they found Refreshings*, he bestows this Confutation, *So have Children many a Time At Puppet-Plays. What a Pass are these People come to, who yet deny all Teachings of Man?*

But what a Pass, may I rather say, hath this Man's implacable Spirit against the Truth of God, brought him to? Who, to his Dishonesty before, adds Prophaneness,

ness, joyn'd with Scoff and Impudence, when he denies all Refreshment that comes not by Sound of Words, in a Known Tongue, *to be of any more Certainty from God's Spirit, than the Pleasure Children take at* Puppet-Plays, though he could not but think the Person that spoke to him, meant by *Refreshings, what came from God,* and *that there can be no Proportion, or Comparison, betwixt that Pious Answer, and the Ungodly Sport of* Puppet-Plays. *Ben. Johnson's* ALCHYMIST, which all Good Men detest, and, *himself dying, abhorr'd,* hath nothing in it *Half so Gross in Abuse of Religion.* I even tremble at the Thoughts of that *Hand-Writing upon the Wall,* which this Man's Impiety is writing (I fear with indelible Characters) against him, who will receive a just and certain Recompence at the Hand of the Righteous Judge of Heaven and Earth, for all his hard Speeches against the Holy Way of the Lord.

§. 4. But let me not omit to show the Blow he gives his own Cause in this Expression; since by the same Reason that we know no *Refreshment* to be any more of God, without known Words, than that of a *Puppet-Play: He knows not any more the Teachings of the God above,* p. 113. *nor the Motions of the Holy Ghost, or Dictates of the Grace of God Within,* Part II. p. 9, 10. (known Words being excepted) *to be of God, than that Refreshment Little Children have in a Puppet-Play;* the Consequence of which Diabolical Comparison is nothing less, than to overthrow all Inward Sense of God's Presence, or that Refreshment which comes from it: And then indeed, we must confess, we should be necessitated either to deny all Teaching, or conclude with this Antichristian Priest, *That Man's Teaching, or Ministry, ought to be adhered to.* Where, if *Puppet-Plays* be meer Imitations of Real Things, as I have been credibly told, we know not but our Ignorance of an Inward Sense, might render us very fit to judge in Favour of the Priest, and his *Puppet-Play Doctrine;* till when, we leave imitating *J. Faldo,* and the *Puppets* together, who alike fainedly represent Life, Power and Spirit, but in Reality are empty Sounds, and meer Wind ratling through Lifeless Trunks.

CHAP. XIII.

But we Deny Preaching, *says he. His Disingenuity in stating our Principles. We hold and practise* True Gospel-Preaching. *No Difference between what the* Light *Teacheth and the Scripture. Our Gospel is* Peace; *Our Adversary's is War,* &c. True Preaching *Converts, our Adversary's not.*

§. 1. ANother of those Ordinances he falsly affirms us to Deny, is *Preaching,* of which he speaks thus, (Pag. 20.) *They will allow an Hearing the Word Preach'd, and that must be the Light Within; but the Mind of God contained in the Scripture, they must by no Means hear Preached; for (as I hinted from* G. Fox) *we must not hear Man; for the Prophets bid cease from Man.*

This is so far from making against us, that it makes for us, at an high Rate; For who preaches without that *Light of Christ,* that the *Quakers* affirm all True Preaching proceeds from, Preaches not from the Discoveries and Leadings of the Light, and consequently all such Preaching *is in the Darkness,* where God's Counsel cannot be known. Nay, how is it possible that People can be turn'd from Darkness to the Light, (the End of Preaching) by those, *who Deny, that Men ought to Preach from the Revelations and Guidings of the Light?*

§. 2. He hath also with manifest Baseness, brought us in, as putting a Difference betwixt our Preaching by the Light within, and that Doctrine of God, which is contained in the Scriptures; whereas we Read, Believe, Practise, and Preach no other Doctrine for Truth, than what is explicitly or implicitly there held forth, and testified unto: Though we confess, that we don't so Believe, Practise, and Preach it, because there written; *but from an Inward Living Power or Spirit, which both opens the Mysteries thereof to our Understanding, begets right Belief of them, and at sundry Times moves upon our Hearts, to declare afresh those Ancient, Blessed Truths therein exprest.* And this is what G. F. meant, and *we* All *understand by ceasing from Man,* to wit, *meer Man, not Man Inspir'd,* or so Divinely qualified.

But he has a Scripture, and a Passage out of *W. Smith,* to justifie his Charge, at least he thinks so, Rom. 10. 15, 18. *And how shall they Preach, except they be sent? As it is written, How Beautiful are the Feet of them that Preach the Gospel of Peace?* &c. We say so too; and did we mean the same, 'twere happy for *J. Faldo.* By being sent, we understand by the Light within, and the Scripture without, a

being

being anointed by the immediate Power of God, without which the Disciples themselves, who had so many Advantages above us, were not to budge: They could have told most of what *Jesus* had done and suffer'd, which, though Truth in it self, and they able to relate it; yet bare Truth, and all they had seen or known, *without a Living Immediate Power and Commission within* (the Baptism of the Holy Spirit) *qualified them not to budge on God's Account*. If *J. Faldo* could give us as good Evidence of his being so call'd, as he hath done of a False and Enrag'd Spirit against the TRUTH, we should acknowledge him for a *Gospel-Minister*; but since he dif-acknowledges all Share in any such Mission, we justly refuse him any Part in a *Gospel-Ministry*.

§. 3. In short, if none can Preach without being sent, then since he and his Tribe were never so sent, they ought not to Preach, nor any to hear them; For Right Faith can never come by such a Ministry: No; They are Right Gospel-Ministers, and their Feet truly Beautiful, *whose Gospel is Peace on Earth, and Good-Will towards Men*; *Not Garments roll'd in the Blood of Kings, Princes, Rulers, and People*: *No Worldly Armies, Battles, Victories, Trophies, Spoils, Sequestrations, Decimations, and the like Blood-thirsty and Tyrannical Projects*: In which *J. Faldo*, and his *Poor Non-Conforming Ministers*, have had their Hands almost over Head and Ears, till they had well nigh lost their Ears, and their Heads too.

Such Covenant-breaking, Self-seeking, Proud, Covetous, Tyrannical, Club-law, Persecuting Priests, we could never own; but ever did, and ever shall, earnestly bear our faithful Testimony against them, as the Locusts, Catterpillars, Serpents, and Dragons of the Earth, whose Cruelty, Self-seeking, and Falseness, hath griev'd Good Men, and caused the Wicked to Blaspheme the Name of the God of Heaven, whose Damnation slumbers not, if by unfeigned Contrition not prevented.

§. 4. Well, but we are to hear what Strength *William Smith's Primmer* can give to his Charge.

" Quest. *Is there something of God in my Conscience, that will give me the Know-*
" *ledge of Him?*
" Answ. There is not any Thing else that can do it.

That is, principally there is no other Teacher, no other Revealer, or Discoverer of the Mind and Will of God to us, than *Christ the Light*, as saith the Scripture, *No Man knows the Father but the Son, the True Light, and He, to whom the Son reveals him*: *And whatever makes manifest is Light*. Now, unless a Man may know God without any Manifestation, it is impossible that he should be known without Light, that only gives it; especially when it shall be considered, *That HE is Light it self*: If then there is no knowing of God, but that which we know must first be manifested, and that whatever makes manifest the Things of God, *is Light*, it evidently follows, *That the Light is the Alone Author of those Discoveries Men receive of the Mind of God*. And whatever Knowledge may be given, or rightly obtained through the Scriptures, is not to be imputed to the Scripture as such, but that Divine Light, which gives inward Conviction of the Truth of what is outwardly read, or writ in that excellent Book called Scripture. So that still to Christ the True Light, as the chiefest Cause (in which Sense he is most properly so called) do we rightly ascribe all the Knowledge we have of GOD, and His Everlasting Kingdom.

CHAP. XIV.

His Charge of our Denial of Gospel-Prayer, inverted. The Prayer he pleads for, Anti-Gospel. True Prayer stated, asserted and defended, with Plainness from Scripture and Reason. Meer Formal Prayer, as well in Families as Meetings, and at Meals, as both False Worship, detestable to God. All False, wherein God's Spirit is not the First and Chief Mover and Assister. The Subtilty of Satan, in putting upon Unacceptable Prayer, to prevent True Prayer.

§. 1. BUT we Deny Prayer *as well as Preaching*, (Pag. 23. 24, 26.) if he may be Credited; and indeed we do so by the same Figure, or contrary Way of Speaking, *That we Deny them*, that is, as *John Faldo* owns them; but not that therefore we should deny them at all. His Charge lies in Three Parts.

First, *That we Contemn True Gospel-Prayer*; to prove which, he cites *W. Smith's Catechism*, p. 107. " Though some may not speak in such formal composed Words,
" yet

" yet in the same Wisdom their Words are formal; they can set their own Time
" to begin and end, and when they will they can utter Words, and when they will
" they can be silent; and this is the unclean Part, which offers to God, which he
" doth not accept. Very well, and what is this to the denying of Gospel-Prayer?
It seems then, that what Prayer this Passage reflects upon, is Gospel; consequently,
if I understand any Thing, formal, Wise Words, in Man's Time, and Will, which
is Unclean, is Gospel-Prayer, in *J. Faldo's* Account; otherwise it is utterly false to
say, *That* W. Smith's *Words prove the* Quakers *to contemn Gospel-Prayer*. But
what can be more clear to the View of every Impartial Reader, than that *J. Faldo's*
making that Prayer only which he is capable of himself, that stands in his own
Time, Will, Wisdom, and Invention to be Gospel, rather than to deny it, and
seek after one more truly Evangelical, is not so much to maintain the Truth as
himself.

§. 2. Secondly, he says, (Pag. 27. 30.) *That we own no Prayer that is not by immediate Inspiration, and Motion of the Spirit, and without the Use of our Conception and Direction of our Understanding.* His Third I will add to this, because to the same Purpose, viz. *That we own no Prayer, but what is by, and in the Light within*; and here he brings three or four Testimonies which are to the same Purpose. I grant what he says of us in this Particular *To be our Faith*, and shall prove it to be Sound Doctrine from the Scriptures of Truth. *The Worship of God is in the Spirit and in the Truth*, John iv. 24. Now unless Men may perform Gospel-Worship without the Spirit and the Truth, or if in the Spirit and the Truth, yet not by the Motion of either, a Thing absurd, it must needs be, that Men ought only to Pray or Preach, by the Motion of the Spirit, and of the Truth.

If such only are Children of God, who are led by the Spirit of God, and walk in the Light, as Christ is Light, and that therein Access alone may be had to God, who is Light, and in whom is no Darkness at all; then with good Reason may we say, *That no Prayer that ascends to God without the Leading of God's Spirit, and which is not by, and in the Light, can be acceptable with him*; consequently, *Gospel-Prayer is only from the Motions of the Spirit of God, and by and in the Light of Christ*. Again,

If no Prophecy or Preaching was to be of old, *but by the immediate Revelation or Motion of the Spirit*, though it was but to Men; of far greater Reason, should not any Prayer be made without a Motion of the same Spirit, which is to the Eternal, only Wise God.

§. 3. Nay, the Creature considered from under the Leadings of God's Spirit in all Religious Actions, is unable to think a good Thought, much less, to perform one good Work; and as the Professors say, *from the Crown of the Head to the Sole of the Foot, is altogether unclean*; it will follow then, *that either such corrupt and sinful Duties are Gospel-Prayer, and an Ordinance of God:* or else, that what we assert of Praying by the Motions of the Spirit, and in, and by the Light of Christ in our Hearts, *must be the only Gospel-Worship*, which we are yet farther inclined to believe.

For it is said in Scripture, *That the Word and Prayer sanctifieth all Things*: Now if we take this *Word* in our Sense, to wit, *the Word of God*; then we are to consider, whether the *Word* derives it's Sanctifying Vertue from the *Prayer*, or the *Prayer* from this *Word*? Not the former to be sure; If then it be allowed to be the latter, since this Prayer (which to be sure is Gospel, or the Apostle would not have owned it) *hath a Sanctifying Vertue in it*; and that no Prayer begun or carried on by meer Man, can sanctifie, because we are of our selves unable to think one good Thought, it evidently follows, *That this Word of God, which gives Prayer that Sanctifying Power, doth begin or move first to that Sanctifying, Acceptable, Truly Gospel-Prayer.*

§. 4. But now suppose by *Word* is meant the Words, either of Scripture, or Preachings, yet are we safe; For, since nothing can sanctifie, but it must be from it self, or something else, and that meer Man in Preaching or Praying cannot; and that God is that alone Power, Wisdom, and Eternal Spirit, that is able to sanctifie; it will follow also, That God's Spirit, or Power, moving in the Heart, is that alone which renders the Words, or Prayers of any sanctifying. Nor is this all; The *Pool of Bethesda* is a Notable Figure of the Matter in Hand; where the Certainty of being Cured upon stepping into the *Pool*, so soon as ever the *Angel* had moved the Waters, doth very lively represent to us, that what Benefit we may ever expect to receive from the Lord, comes not from an hasty Rushing into any Religious Performance

formance in our own Time, but our patient Waiting, till the Lord's Holy Angel stirs and moves the Waters, and then to lay all aside to imbrace so Blessed an Opportunity. *Farther,*

§. 5. *The Gospel-State is an Eternal Sabbath.* He that prays in his own Will, Time, Wisdom, Invention, is picking Sticks, and kindling a Fire, and compassing himself about with the Sparks of the Fire of his own kindling: This Man hath not *Ceast from his own Works*, he will suffer Loss in the Day of God, and his Bed will be made in Sorrow.

§. 6. Nor is this the utmost of our Force; for whatever God hath not required, just will it be with him to say, *Who hath required these Things at your Hands?* 'Tis true, God loves that his People should pray, and Christ enjoyns it; *but he also bids all Watch unto Prayer*; that is, Wait to feel that Spirit of Life to stir, which gives Life to Prayer, the *Key of David*, by which Heaven's Door is opened, and the Soul comes to receive True and Heavenly Refreshment. The Want of which maketh so much Complaint among some, *That their Duties are Unholy Things, they want Power, they have prayed long, but to little Purpose;* whereas had they Pray'd aright, that had never been. Much more might be said to this, but my Conscience is clear in the Matter, and I shall conclude this Point with a General Confession and Caution.

§. 7. *We do acknowledge,* That God is; That He ought to be Worshipped; That Worshipping of God is strictly a Bowing down before Him, in Fear and Holy Reverence, according as he makes himself known to the Creature; That Prayer is a Gospel-Ordinance; That it is not only Good, but Necessary to be used; That God only can give us to Pray aright, as well as to Pray at all; That therefore his Assistance is necessary; *to have which,* There ought to be a Waiting out of all Conceivings, Inventions, or Forms, to receive a Living Touch, and Sense from His Pure, Living, and Eternal Spirit, whereby to set our Spirits at work. This is that Oil, which makes the Chariot Wheels go smoothly, and without which they grate and jarr. Those who have not Words, especially in Publick Places, have Sighs and Groans, and a deep and silent Exercise of Spirit God-wards: In which Blessed Communion is joyned, and Refreshments that out-do all Worldly Satisfaction. That it is the Duty of all to wait upon God, and that not only at Publick Meetings, but at their own Houses also, and therein as well at their Meals, as at all other Times for Worship. If any have the Motion of God's Eternal Spirit upon their Hearts, let it be answer'd to God's Praise, and the Edification of others; if not, let none offer up an *Unsanctified, Dead Sacrifice to the Lord,* as all that comes from meer Man is, for it will be their Burden: Neither prodigally spend their own Portion, or that Bread upon others, God has bestowed for their own Use. *Thus, whether such Eat, Drink, Sleep, or otherwise enjoy of God's Benefits, let all be done with Holy Awe, and to the Glory of God our Father:* As it will certainly be, *If there be but a Still and Reverent Waiting in Spirit upon the Lord, in the Light of Christ, to be made Sensible of His Goodness, and Blessings upon us, and Unity with us in our Undertakings and Enjoyments.* And let this be a *Warning* unto all, in the Name and Fear of the Jealous God of Heaven and Earth, that they do not offer up to God their *Halt, and Lame, and Blind Sacrifices,* which my God abhors; especially you *Professors,* whose Leaves are large, *but your Fruit little:* Think not to be heard by your Multitude of Words, nor Variety of Duties; God regards the Root, the Life, the Power, the Spirit that begets them, and whose Life it is that animates them; if they arise from God's Holy Spirit, and Seed of Life, they can, they will intercede and prevail; but if not, God will say to you one Day, *Who has required these Things at your Hands?* O! For the Love of God, and your own Souls, offer not God a Worship out of His own Spirit, much less contend for it; for you strengthen *Satan's Bonds in so doing,* and *feed the Mystery of Iniquity, the Painted* Jezebel, *the Mother of Harlots,* from whom these false, accursed Births have come; who, under outward Imitations and Performances, holds People in Death and Darkness, and perfect Enmity against God, and His Living, Spiritual, Holy Seed in them, and others, that is able to bruise the Serpent's Head; which is the Pure Way of God, and in whom is the Blessing for ever: For the *Devil,* the subtil Serpent, having got into those Outward Courts of Religion, Signs and Shadows of the Good Things, which God had given Credit to by his Appearing once in them, he pleads their Divine Institution, against the very Life and Substance, that like Old Garments it hath put off; and so all are deceived by his Transformations and subtil Twinings, who come not to that Inward Sense of Life and Power, which relish the very Spirit, and

and can try the Inside: Servants are not Masters, because they wear their old Clothes; neither is the Devil an Angel of Light, because he puts on the Pure Ware, the *Spirits* old Clothes. God once appeared at the Mountain, and *Jerusalem*, therefore was either Worship to continue? No; God disappeared, that he might set up a more Spiritual Worship, where Meats and Drinks, and all outward Services, figurative of the Good Things, come to an End.

§. 8. Let it not be evilly taken by any of you, neither be ye offended in me, or the Doctrine I here defend; *For all Preachings, Prayings, Graces* (as they are called) *with the rest of the Worship of the Day, which arise not from the Holy Power and Spirit of God,* it is at this Time laid upon me, and I am bold to declare, in the Name of the Eternal Holy God, *A Blast, an utter Blast is coming upon them all, and they shall be found amongst the Chaff, and not the Wheat, in the Day of God's Terrible Tempest, where nothing, but the solid and weighty Seed, shall remain Stable and Unshaken.* O bow, bow, ye tall Cedars, and sturdy Oaks! Come out, and be ye saparated by the Power of my God, from all your Inventions, self-Contrivances, self-Runnings and Willings, ye Children of the Night, and Lovers of your own Works, more than Lovers of God's; who out of the Living, Pure Eternal Spirit of Life, are holding forth Faith, Worship, Prayers, and Ordinances, and contending for them, against the very Life it self, that in a more plain Appearance is risen and departed from them; and come to know the one True Faith, Worship, and Great Ordinance of God, by the Operation of his Spirit in all your Hearts and Consciences; else you will dye in your Sins, and *Christ shall profit you nothing,* but your Dreams of Salvation shall vanish, and utter Destruction will be your Portion for evermore.

CHAP. XV.

His Charge of our Denial of Baptism *and the* Sacraments, *introduc'd with a Discourse of positive Commands, Destructive of the Foundation of Religion. The Priest against God, Scripture and Reason. He confounds himself. Baptism of Water prov'd John's; and not to continue.* Mat. 28. 19. 1 Cor. 1. 17. Ephes. 4. 5. *cleared and vindicated. The One Spiritual Baptism defended.*

§. 1. I Am now come to the two last Particulars of this Charge. *Baptism,* and the *Lord's Supper,* which he introduceth with a short Discourse of the Nature of God's Commands, respecting *Gospel-Ordinances,* which he says, we deny. I shall only take Notice of this Passage, where he tells us, *That the Ordinances, hitherto consider'd, are called* Moral, *from their natural Obligation, although respecting the Substance, they deserve a more Evangelical Denomination, without which we cannot* (says he) *call them* Christian Ordinances. *But these two I come now to consider, are purely positive, and depend meerly upon divinely reveal'd Institution, and God has so express'd his Jealousie over this Right of his, that when Sins not only against natural Light, but superadded Precepts to confirm and strengthen it's Doubtfulness and Decays, have been passed by without any special Expressions of his Provocation; Sins committed against his positive Laws (as* Circumcision, *and all Ceremonial Laws, as well as Water-Baptism, and what is generally call'd the Lord's Supper) have been avenged with an high Hand.*

To all I return these short Heads of Matter. First, That a Ministry, grounded Internally upon the Grace and Gifts of God; externally upon the Scriptures of Truth; A well order'd Church, consisting of Religious Members; *Preaching, Praying, and that Scripturally too* (by him call'd *Christian-Ordinances*) are by him made *Natural to all Nations,* antecedent to Christ's outward Coming, and consequently, there was the *Thing Christianity,* before the *Name Christianity:* which pleads our Cause against his first Chapter; and a gross Self-Contradiction. Next, that those he calls *Natural Ordinances,* and of Universal Obligation, are far more *Substantial and Necessary to Salvation,* than those two of *Water-Baptism,* and the *Lord's Supper,* upon which he more peculiarly bestows the Title of *Christian;* since no Man can ever be saved without the one, I mean those *Natural Ordinances,* as he calls them; *and any Man may be certainly saved without the other,* that he so peculiarly calls *Christian Ordinances;* which how Unreasonable, and Preposterous it is, let the Impartial Judge.

1673.
Ch. XV.

Yet again, his great Ignorance, and Abuse of God, and true Religion, appears in this, that not only he himself egregiously errs in such a Construction, but confidently affirms *God to be more concern'd to vindicate the former, and take Vengeance for the Breach of his positive and exterior Precepts,* as the *Ceremonial Part of the Jews Worship, and the Bread, Wine, and Water* Sacramentally us'd now a-days (if yet as such, they may be accounted Precepts) which the *Devil* himself can creep into the Profession of, and cannot cleanse as concerning the Conscience, than of his fundamental natural and substantial Laws and Ordinances, without which God cannot be worshipped, nor one Soul saved; in plain Contradiction to that notable Passage of the Prophet, *Bring no more Vain Oblations, Incense is Abomination unto me, the Sabbaths, the Calling of Assemblies I cannot away with, it is Iniquity, even the Solemn Meeting. And when you spread forth your Hands, I will hide mine Eyes from you; yea, when ye make* (or multiply) *many Prayers, I will not hear; your Hands are full of Blood: Wash ye, make you clean, put away the Evil of your Doings from before Mine Eyes; cease to do Evil, learn to do well, seek Judgment, Relieve the Oppressed, Judge the Fatherless, plead for the Widow;* where the Cause is determin'd against him. For here we have an Account of their Exactness in many Outward Ceremonial Laws, standing in figurative Things, and a most severe Reproof of them, for their great Degeneracy and Corruption, as to their Morals, or Rebellion against God's Natural Ordinances, as *J. Faldo* calls them.

God himself brings the natural and positive Ordinances (as by this *Priest* distinguisht) into the Scales, and gives the Weight against the latter. Let him shew us whenever there was a Man washt and clean'd that was reprov'd for omitting any of those positive and Ceremonial Laws, as I have produc'd a plain Scripture, that expresses God's Detestation and Abhorrence of those of his Elected Nation the *Jews*, that erred from the Eternal Law of Righteousness writ in the Hearts of the very *Heathens*, though they were never so punctual as to their Observance of Outward Institutions; and he will do something; otherwise, as it is manifest, what a Kind of *Christianity* this Man would make, that any *Celsus* or *Porphyry* would blow away with a Breath; so it is most clear, that God lays a far greater Stress upon Men's walking up to those Immutable Ordinances (by our Adversary called Natural, which we can accept of, as being proper to Mankind) than those Temporary and Shadowy Services that must vanish upon the Appearance of the Substance it self.

And lastly, It is no less than *Blasphemy* in our Adversary, and an evident Contradiction to himself, to assert, That the Light he grants those Immutable Ordinances to result from, may be doubtful, or decay, respecting it self: Since it were to say, That God the Fountain of that Rivulet of Light, from whence those excellent Streams Come, is Doubtful, and lyable to decay; for whatever is naturally incident to any Measure of Light; is so to the whole: Nay, it is to affirm, That from a doubtful and decayable Light may and do issue forth Clear, Divine and Eternal Precepts of Righteousness. I would not have *J. Faldo* lay the Blame of his own Doubts or Decays upon the Light; but upon his own Rebellion against it. He has too too largely vilified that blessed Manifestation, to receive much Benefit by it. But O the Injustice of Men, *that impute all Incapacity to see, which is truly from themselves, to the Light Within,* which yet they refuse to be ruled by! Let the sober Reader be seriously warned, that he believe in no such Pestiferous Doctrine, which in short, tends to no more nor less, than an Exalting and Preferring the Exterior Coat, or Shell of Religion (and that most of their own making too) above and beyond that Eternal Light, which is the Law of God in the Heart, that leads to perform our Duty uprightly both to God and Man. For I had rather be *Moral Socrates* in the Day of God's Terrible Judgment, than *Out-side-Christian* J. Faldo, *with all his Jeer and Enmity against Christ's Light within.* But let's hear what he says to these *Christian Ordinances* in particular, though we have no Reason to expect much to his own Purpose, whatever he may say for ours, when we consider, how shamefully he has introduced them.

§. 2. *I shall begin with* Water-Baptism, *it being the first in order of the two, both in it's Institution and Practice; which the* Quakers *deny (in these Words)* ' Baptism ' we own, which is the Baptism of Christ with the Holy Ghost, and with Fire; ' but we deny all others. *J. Parnel's Shield of Truth,* pag. 11.

To

To which I say, that we have great Reason so to do; for first, Christ never was *Administrator of Water-Baptism, but that of Fire and the Holy Ghost*. Water-Baptism was *John*'s, the Fore-runner, figuratively, and used to that Preparation, necessary to receive the visible Coming of the *Messiah*; were the *Messiah* now visibly to come, and *John Baptist* alive, it would be Indisputable: But that Time being past, and it being *John*'s Visible Administration, which is over, and not *Christ*'s; and lastly, that the Fore-runner is not to continue, but give way to Him, and his Administration, that was so fore-run, which was Christ, and his Baptism; we do conclude, that there is no such *Baptism*, as J. *Faldo* charges us with the Denial of, that can plead any Continuance in the *Christian Church*: Which *John* himself was not unsensible of, when he said, *I shall Decrease, but he will Increase*; and who (like the Morning-Star) accordingly Decreast, and became Eclipst by the Encrease of the Brighter Glory of Christ, who was and is Lord of all.

§. 3. If any should say, that it is not meant of *John*'s Baptism; but a New Water-Baptism instituted by Christ, because of those Words only on which they ground their Commission, *Go teach all Nations, Baptizing them, &c.* J. *Faldo* answers for me, that it is a Mistake; He means *not another Water-Baptism from John's*, when he tells us, *that the Water-Baptism (which he calls the Christian Ordinance, and renders the Quakers a sort of Heathens for denying) is that Baptism which was in Point of Order and Justification, before the Bread and Wine were instituted:* which how well soever it may square with the *Episcopalians, Presbyterians, Independents,* and *Anabaptists* Notion of Baptism, (whom he says, he has no farther concern'd in his Book, than vindicated) and his own date of Christianity from Christ's Resurrection, it is manifest; first, *That no Commission was given by Christ, before he broke Bread with his Disciples*; Consequently he must intend John's only: And next, *That* John's *Commission it self is not extant*; much less any Commission to perpetuate *his, as generally obliging*: But above all, that the Disciples of Christ should not only use, but esteem for an Ordinance of Christ, a Baptism, *that had not their Lord for it's Administrator,* as saith the Scripture; *for Jesus baptized not*, is absurd, and altogether *Anti-Gospel*. If we will credit Christ's own saying, *The least in the Kingdom of Heaven is greater than* John; as if he should have said, *John*'s Administration was an Introduction, and a Kind of Preparation in order to my Coming, but no otherwise is it interested in my Kingdom, which is Spiritual, and that I am now about to set up in the Hearts and Consciences of Men; and the least of that Spiritual Kingdom is greater than the Children of *John*'s Watry Dispensation.

§. 4. That this is Truth I will farther prove even from that very Place, which they repute a sufficient Commission for Water-Baptism. *Go therefore and teach all Nations, Baptizing them in the Name of the Father, Son, and the Holy Ghost,* &c.

Mat. 28.

In discoursing of Things laid down by the *Evangelists*, it will not always suffice what some one *Evangelist* saith; as in the Passage Controverted. We have here a Commission, it is granted; but what it was with respect to the Baptism mentioned, and the Time when it was to take Place, will be the Question; To resolve which, we must have Recourse to another Place, without which this cannot be so clear to those, who seek after Scripture Demonstration. *Luke*, in his History of the *Acts* of the *Apostles*, soon after his Address to *Theophilus*, gives us an Account of some Farewel-Expressions, Christ used to his Disciples; not so fully exprest in his History; which he delivers to us after this Manner: *And being assembled together with them, he* (Christ) *commanded them, that they should not depart from* Jerusalem, *but wait for the Promise of the Father, which* (says he) *ye have heard of me. For John truly baptized with Water, but ye shall be baptized with the Holy Ghost not many Days hence.*

From whence nothing can be clearer, than first, that the Baptism mention'd in, *Go teach all Nations, baptizing them, &c.* was not the *Baptism of* John; but the *Baptism of the Holy Ghost,* call'd, *the Promise of the Father,* which they were to wait for, recorded by *Luke,* both in the 24th Chapter of his History of Christ, and the first Chapter of his History of the *Acts* of the *Apostles.* Nay, lest it should be thought, that he meant of another *Water-Baptism,* as some vainly imagine; to help their Understanding, and prevent all such Mistake, he distinguishes, *not betwixt* John's *Water-Baptism, and his own, but betwixt any Water-Baptism at all, and his own Baptism of the Holy Ghost. John* indeed baptized with Water, *but ye shall be baptized with the Holy Ghost.* Then you will be fitly qualified, and commissionated, after you shall have received the Promise of the Father, which you are to wait for, and then to go and teach all Nations, *baptizing them,* &c. Suitable to those Expressions of the *Baptist* himself; *I indeed baptize you with Water, but he shall baptize you with the Holy Ghost. His Fan is in his Hand, he will throughly purge his Floor. He that cometh after me is preferred before me.*

Besides, the very Words themselves taken in the *Original* Tongue, import in Point of Propriety nothing less. For the *Greek* knows no such Thing, as βαπτίζοντες αυτὲς ἐν τῷ ὀνόματι, &c. *baptizing them in the Name,* but βαπτίζοντες αυτὲς εἰς τὸ ὄνομα, *baptizing them into the Name of the Father, Son, and Holy Ghost,* which by the frequent Use of that Preposition, 'Εἰς, *Into,* it is impossible for Water-Baptism to do; no more, than for a Man by it to be baptiz'd with the same Baptism, wherewith *Christ was to be baptized;* to be *buried with him, Christ, to be baptized into Christ, and so to be baptized into his Death;* or by it, *and not by One Spirit, to be baptized into one Body.* Which because no *Water-Baptism* could ever do, it consequently follows, *that it was never intended of Water-Baptism,* since it would then have been, to ascribe that to meer *Water-Baptism,* which it is both utterly impossible for it ever to perform, and is really the alone Property of the *Spiritual Baptism* of Christ to effect.

§. 5. To our Objection of the Apostle's Answer, *Christ sent me not to Baptize, but to Preach;* he argues; *Because he did baptize some, therefore it was an Ordinance; and that he baptized so few, was but providential, not designed; and the Reason why it was not laid upon the Apostle Paul, was because his Call was Extraordinary and out of due Time.*

But the Confusion and the Weakness of this Reply, might save me the Labour of an Answer, with all, but those who might esteem it Unanswerable, because almost Unintelligible. For if every Practice was an Institution, then because the same *Apostle* Circumcised, it was a *Christian Ordinance. Practice* then, we see, and all the reasonable World knows, is not *Institution.* Many Things indifferent in their Nature may be practised and used, and yet never instituted or required.

That he had it not in his *Commission,* the *Priest* himself grants; but excuses that Defect by a greater, *viz. He was called extraordinarily, and out of due Time.* But as they were all extraordinarily call'd, or else the *Priest* contradicts himself, so if we may believe the *Apostle,* he was inferior to none of them; If not in his Works, I know no Reason, why he should be reputed so in his *Commission.* That his Commission was of God is granted on all Hands; And if it pleased God to make it none of *Paul's Commission,* we would be glad to see any of our Time produce one more large and effectual; 'till when, we are contented with no more Extent in the Point, than God pleased to give that *Great Apostle;* and believe, whatever *J. Faldo* says to the contrary, that he was a *Gospel-Christian-Apostle:* And if *Water Baptism* had been then reputed a *Gospel-Christian-Ordinance,* neither had God omitted that in his *Commission,* nor had the Apostle spoke so lightly of it.

§. 6. But *J. Parnel* offends him in these Words, at least he takes Offence at them; " They who would have one Baptism inward, another outward, would " have *Two Baptisms,* when the Scripture saith, *The Baptism is but one.* Shield of Truth, pag. LI. Which he would be thought to confute thus, and it seems more material, than any Thing he has writ on this Subject.

I must tell him by the Way, that he tells an Untruth wilfully. He uses, or rather abuses the Words of the Apostle just before repeated; one Lord, one Faith, one Baptism; *and there he adds* but, *which the Text has not.* And here the Scripture saith, the Baptism is but one: *Let him find me* (says *J. Faldo*) *such a Scripture, and I will be bound to turn* Quaker.

I perceive the Man thinks he can turn *Quaker* much at the Rate he can *Pray,* I mean when he will; but I will tell him so much, that it is as hard a Task for him to turn *True Quaker,* as to be a True Primitive *Christian,* a thing most difficult to be sure.

But to his Quibble about *But, J. Parnel* has told a wilful Untruth, in saying the Baptism is *but one:* I suppose it will be allow'd that there was one Baptism, in the same Sense that there was one Lord, one Faith. Now, if there is *but one Lord,* and *one* Faith, as it is to be supposed, *J. Faldo* believes, why should it be so Criminal to say, there is *but one Baptism?* If saying, there is one Lord, and one Faith, be *synonimous* or *equivalent,* with affirming that there is but one Lord, and one Faith; I cannot see how it should be an Untruth to say, *that there is one Baptism, is one and the same Thing with our saying, there is* (but) *One Baptism.* In short, if there is more than One Baptism, because the Apostle does not say, there is *but One Baptism*; then there are more Gospels, Lords, and Faiths, because the Apostle did not say, there was *but* one Gospel, *but* one Lord, and *but* one Faith; consequently there may be many *Gospels, Lords* and *Faiths*, as well as *Baptisms*.

§. 7. Enough of this Weakness; His Strength follows. *Water-Baptism is the Sign, the Baptism of the Spirit something.* (but not all) *signified. Now to call the Thing signifying and signified, by the same Name, doth not make them Two of that Name*, no more than there were two New Covenants, because both the Matter contained in it, Heb. 8. 10. *and Circumcision the Sign*, Gen. 17. 13. *are called the Covenant.*

I shall grant to him, that the Thing signifying, and signified, are sometimes called by one and the same Name; as *Baptism*: But when distinguisht by *Water* and *Holy Ghost*, I hope, nothing that is not as blind or hardned as *J. Faldo* (if yet he himself) will say, that therefore they are but one Baptism. Christ himself distinguishes betwixt *John and his Baptism*; and *himself and his Baptism*: And frequently his *Apostles*, yea the *Baptist* himself, seem'd to take all Occasions, whereby to let People know, that his *Baptism* was but that of Water, and that the Baptism of Christ *was not of Water, but of the Holy Ghost*, as the Scriptures in the *Margin* plainly prove.

So in the Word *Circumcision*, compounded of the same Letters, and Syllables, let it be used to express *that of the Body, or the Flesh*; or *that of the Heart in Spirit*: Yet it is to be hoped, that none will conclude, there were not *Two Circumcisions*, and so *Two Jews*; the one *Inward*, and the other *Outward*. Though now he is *no more a* Jew, *that is one Outwardly*; *neither is that Circumcision, which is outward in the Flesh*; *but he is a* Jew *which is one Inwardly, and Circumcision is that of the Heart, in the Spirit, and not in the Letter, whose Praise is not of Men, but of God.*

§. 8. And should we grant him what he desires, as to the same Name, being applicable to the *Sign* and the *Thing signified*; yet Weak and Wretched must his *Sophism* appear to all clear-sighted *Readers*; For if therefore the *Baptism of Water and of the Spirit are one*, because the same Word is applicable to the Sign, and the Thing signified, and in that Sense *they are both of them one Baptism*: Then by just Consequence, *must the Circumcision outwardly in the Flesh, and the Circumcision of the Heart in the Spirit, be One*; because the Word of it self is equally applicable to both; and Consequently they are *both* of them *One* Circumcision: What *Jew* living could have reason'd better for the Continuation and Perpetuity of *Circumcision?* But because he has said nothing here for Baptism, more than what may be said for Circumcision; and that Circumcision is utterly exploded of the Christian Religion, as a Sign, whose Signification is come, and therefore no more a Sign; our Assertion *of the One Spiritual Baptism of Fire and the Holy Ghost*, as only upon the same Foundation, proper to Christ's Kingdom, doth remain fixt and immoveable against all the *Batteries* of our *Adversary*.

CHAP. XVI.

The Supper *he says we deny, not deny'd but fulfill'd. The Scriptures Consulted. No Perpetuity prov'd. That it was a Sign. And that Signs were done away in Christ, demonstrated. The present Practice in the Case not Primitive. Our Faith left with God in the Matter.*

§. 1. BUT *the Quakers* (he says) *disown the Ordinance of the Lord's Supper to be now a Gospel-Ordinance*; for which he cites *J. Parnel*, a young Man now dead, often in his Eye, as he was grievously so to *J. Faldo's* Brethren the *Independents* at *Cogshall* in *Essex*, who by unparallel'd, and never to be forgotten Cruelties, murder'd him, as may be seen in my *Second Part of our Serious Apology*, pag. 185, 186, 187. His Words, as he quotes them, are these; " *For the Bread* " *which the World breaks, is Natural and Carnal*; *so also the Cup which they drink*; " *and here is no Communion, but what is Outward and Carnal.* Shield of Truth, pag. 13. Also *W. Smith* thus; They [Bread and Wine in the Lord's Supper] are the *Pope's* Invention. His Primm. pag. 39.

1673.
Chap. XVI.

To the first Citation, I answer, that the Bread and Wine, being of an Outward, Elementary Nature and Substance, may with respect to what they signify, be very properly termed Natural and Carnal, for so they are. And the World, that is, *those who are doing it upon meer Imitation, and not from any Heavenly Commission, they see no farther, and their Communion may well be said to be Natural, Outward, and Carnal.*

To the Second, I do challenge *J. Faldo* to make it good, and require it at his Hand in the View of the World, to produce any such Words out of *W. Smith*'s Books; and that he may not plead Mistake of *Authors*, I will give him the Scope of all our Books and Friends, to prove that we ever call'd *the Bread and Wine Christ blest, the Invention of the Pope.* O ungodly Man! What hast thou done, that God should thus give thee up, not only to believe Lyes thy self, but to endeavour to make others do the like! Thy Book shall be a Mill-stone about thy Neck in the Day of the righteous and terrible Judgments of Almighty God. We deny the Expression, and lay the Slander at *J. Faldo*'s Door.

§. 2. *But the* Quakers *main Objection* (says he) *is, that Christ is come in Spirit to them, and his Disciples were to do it in Remembrance of him 'till he came; therefore this Precept doth not bind them.* J. Faldo pretends thus to answer, *But who would think, that Christ in the Spirit was not come (either in shedding it Abroad miraculously as in the* 2d *of the Acts; or as a Sanctifier) in the Hearts of the People, when the Disciples and whole Church of* Jerusalem, *were so frequent in this Ordinance; and when the Apostle* Paul *tells us, to the* Corinthians; *The Bread which we break,* &c. *it was for those to whom Christ was come by a Spirit of Sanctification, not those in a State of Sin, unconverted to Christ.*

That I may briefly and fully reply, be pleas'd to observe (1) That we don't deny Bread and Wine to have been given, and that by Command of Christ to his Disciples. (2) That it was a Sign to them of that Life he would give for the World, and which at that Time they were weak in the Knowledge of. (3) We believe the Life most eminently meant, and which they were to do it in the Remembrance of, was that Flesh and Blood that in the 6th of *John* he said, *Who did not eat nor drink thereof, should have no Life in them;* and which, five Verses after, *he calls the Bread that came down from Heaven.* (4) 'Tis our Faith, that this heavenly *Bread and Wine, and Flesh and Blood,* which such were to eat of, that would have Life Eternal, for which he came (and of which the Disciples themselves were then so ignorant) was *the Thing signified by the Sign Christ gave* his Disciples. (5) That Sign is no longer of Force in Point of *Institution,* than 'till the Thing signified is come; so that who truly witness the *Coming of Christ into their Souls, and the Eternal Bread of Life, or Flesh and Blood, to nourish, are rightly come to an End of the Sign and Figure.* (6) That Christ did so come is evident from many Scriptures. *There be some standing here, that shall not taste of Death* (said he) *'till they see the Son of Man Coming in his Kingdom. I will not leave you Comfortless, I will come to you.* Implying, that he was the Comforter, that should come to them after the withdrawing of that Outward Appearance, which was expedient for them to be done: *He that is with you, shall be in you;* and Abundance to the same Purpose. (7) That the *Practice* of it after the Pouring forth of the Spirit, is not, neither can it be, any Institution, or so much as a Continuance of it upon an Institution, *any more than the Apostles forbearing several Things lawful in themselves, that were upon the Command of the* Jewish *Ceremonial Law forbidden; The Circumcision of many* Gentiles; *and above all, the Apostle* Paul's *purifying of himself at the Temple of* Jerusalem, *after he had been near thirty Years a Christian, or Gospel-Preacher, and consequently a Thrower-down and Demolisher both of the Temple, and all it's Ceremonial Worship.* (8) That every one who believ'd, and were in some Measure turned to the Christian Religion, and were accounted Members of the several Churches because of such Profession, *did not presently come to know Christ after the Spirit, or discern his spiritual Manifestation, and whilst they were as yet Weak and Carnal in their Conceptions of Christ, believing in him, and accounting of him but after the Flesh,* (a Knowledge of him, the Apostle himself confesseth once but to have had) *the Outward Bread and Wine might be suitable to that Sort of Belief, and a Sign shewing forth a more Spiritual, Internal Bread and Cup,* which the Apostle in the same foregoing Chapter to the *Corinthians,* expresseth thus; *For we being many are one Bread, and one Body; for we are all Partakers of that one Bread; The Cup of Blessing which we bless, is it not the Communion of the Blood of Christ? The Bread which we break, is it not the Communion of the Body of Christ? I speak as to wise Men:*

Men: Judge ye what I say. Which evidently imports a more Inward Heavenly Bread, *Fellowship* and *Communion*, both with Chrift, and one another. (9) It ought not to ftumble any, that it fhould laft *to that Day* and yet be laid afide *Now*; For, *Cuftoms*, when once *introduc'd and receiv'd, are not eafy to be relinquifht or left off*; and it having been the *Token* Chrift gave to his Difciples in the Time of their great Weaknefs, Fear and Unbelief concerning him, it was quickly embrac'd and imitated, by fuch as believ'd, efpecially *Jews*, who juft coming out of a Multitude of *External Services*, were ready to make Part of their Religion confift therein: But as fuch came to grow into the true *Jews* State, they faw beyond all Exterior Signs and Services, *And that things which could be tafted or handled, and that perifht with the Ufing, and that could never cleanfe the Confcience from dark Works, but were Shadows only of Chrift the Living Eternal Subftance and Bread of Life, could not be ftanding Ordinances of the Everlafting Gofpel.*

§. 3. And truly, when I have fometimes confider'd the Apoftle *Paul*'s infpir'd Epiftles to his *beloved Timothy*, and that among the many weighty, plain and neceffary Things therein declared, and recommended for the Increafe of Godlinefs, and good Order in the Church of Chrift, he fhould be wanting to exprefs fomething about thefe two Points, of *Water-Baptifm*, and the *Lord's-Supper*, fo call'd, and infifted upon, *as the moft weighty Ordinances of the Gofpel* (in Comparifon of which *Praying, Preaching, good Life, and fuch like* (the great Subjects of thofe Epiftles) *J. Faldo reputes meer Heathenifm*) I have concluded with my felf, that that had his Value of them been equal, with what fome now put upon them, he would not, or rather the Holy Spirit, *have omitted a very peculiar Recommendation of them.* But though this be fufficient to dull the Edge of their Spirits, who daily cut and hack at us for our (not Denial, but) affirming the fulfilling of them by the Coming of a more living Bread; Yet our fo knowing and witneffing a more Heavenly Table fpread, and the Prefence of the Eternal God withdrawn out of that Practice, fo abufed by the Idolatries, Superftitions and Perverfions of feveral Ages; and that Revenge, Blood-fhed and Deftruction, which have followed the feveral Contenders for it, all without Commiffion, as well as out of the Primitive Order, is the Chief Ground, not of denying it ever to have been in Ufe before it's Abufe, as is before expreft, but of our letting fall any farther Practice of it. And this I hope, will be accounted a Modeft, Sober, and Chriftian Account of our Faith, which we leave with God to weigh againft the *Chaffy Flurts* and *vilifying Epithets J. Faldo* ufes againft us; and which for Brevity Sake I omit to tranfcribe.

CHAP. XVII.

His Charge *of our Denying Chrift's Tranfactions to influence into our Juftification confidered. His* Proofs *not for him. His* Abufe *of our Friends Words.* Juftification *diftinguifht upon, as* Remiffion, *and as daily* Acceptance. *The Tranfactions of Chrift largely own'd by us. The Scriptures confirm our Faith in Chrift, as a general and particular Saviour. No Works of Man Meritorious.*

§. 1. I Am now come to that Part of his Charge, which affirms *our Denial of the Tranfactions of Jefus Chrift in the Flefh to have any Influence into our Juftification* (an uncouth Phrafe) *before God, and our Salvation.* To prove which he brings forth three Paffages of our Friends; " All that are called *Presbyterians,* " and *Independents,* with their feeding upon a Report of a Thing done many " Hundred Years ago. *E. Burroughs's Trump.* p. 17. Which *J. Faldo* wickedly conftrues, thus; *This he faith by Way of Reproach againft all that act Faith on, and receive Comfort from the Bleffed Effects of Chrift's Righteoufnefs and Sufferings by him wrought and fuffered, when he was in the World:* Whereas in Honefty and Truth (which *J. Faldo* fhews himfelf wholly unacquainted with) he meant no more, *than their Exceffive Admiration of, and the Regard to what Chrift did without, whilft they neglected, undervalued and decry'd for Blafphemy and* Enthufiafm *the Appearance, Work and Righteoufnefs of Chrift within.* But he thinks, we have miftaken him, and that he is better arm'd for us, than we are aware of: *What Righteoufnefs Chrift performed without me, was not my Juftification, neither was I faved by it:* R. *Farnfworth* he quotes for *Author*, but no *Book*; which is very unfair. However, this may be faid in Defence of *R. F.* that what gives daily Accefs and Acceptance to, and with the Lord, is that Preparation of Clean, and Righteous

Righteous Adornment the Soul actually receives from Christ, who is the Lord her Righteousness. And take Justification in this Sense, and not for Remission, in which he meant it, if ever he said it. And we do all own and acknowledge the same, and let our Adversary do his worst: Only I desire him to tell us the *Book* next Time, which affords that Expression.

§. 2. But *I. Pennington,* he thinks, he has made his own. *Can Outward Blood cleanse the Conscience? Can Outward Water wash the Soul clean?* Quest. p. 25. I beseech you that read me, hear his Comment, ' A plain Denial of the Efficacy of ' the Blood of Christ shed on the Cross to cleanse the Soul from the Guilt of Sin, ' by it's Satisfaction to the Justice of God.

I have had to do with many Enemies to God's Truth; But I must profess to the whole World, I never yet saw, spoke to, or read of a more disingenuous Man: To pervert our Words, alter Sentences, draw Generals from Particulars, and then call them Ours, is Base and Unmanly. I would fain have an impartial Man answer me. Doth *I. P.* deny, or any way meddle with the *Outward Blood* concerning the Guilt of Sin past, how far it had an Influence into Justification, *taking Justification in that Sense?* But does he not treat of the Outward Blood, with respect to *Purgation and Sanctification of the Soul from the present Acts and Habits of Sin, that lodge therein?* Is he so Sottish, as to make no Distinction betwixt being pardon'd Sin past, and the Ground of it; and being renewed and regenerated in Mind and Spirit, and the Ground of that Conversion? Or else is he so impiously Unjust, that because we do deny, that Outward Blood can be brought into the Conscience to perform that Inward Work (which they themselves dare not, nay, do not hold) *Therefore* I. Pennington, *denies any Efficacy to be in that Outward Offering and Blood towards Justification,* as it respects meer Remission of former Sins, and Iniquities? This may give the sober-minded some Relish of his Rancour: We do say, that Outward Blood can no more cleanse, then Outward Water; But we also say, *That Christ's Blood had an Influence into Justification (as he praseth it)* which I shall presently show.

§. 3. He undertakes the Defence, of what he falsly says we deny, but so confusedly, as ought to shame a modest Man, and a Pretender to Controversy.

His first Scripture is this. *And he received the Sign of Circumcision, a Seal of the Righteousness of Faith, which he had yet being uncircumcised, that he might be the Father of all them, that believe, though they be not circumcised, that Righteousness might be imputed to them,* Rom. 4. 11. His Observation and Inference run thus, *that Imputation is a Reckoning that to any, which they have not from themselves, nor actually from another, otherwise it could not be Grace, therefore it was the Righteousness of another, not his own.*

This is so base a Perversion and Mis-using of the Word, that Imputation *both in Scripture, and Common Discourse is always taken and used in the contrary Sense;* Let him produce me one Scripture that countenanceth his Notion. This imputed *Righteousness is best understood by the Context:* Even as David also describeth the Blessedness of the Man unto whom God imputes Righteousness without Works, *saying,* Blessed are they, whose Iniquities are forgiven, and whose Sins are covered; Blessed is the Man, unto whom the Lord will not impute Sin. Cometh this Blessedness then upon the Circumcision only, or Uncircumcision also? *For we say,* that Faith was reckoned to *Abraham* for Righteousness. How was it then reckoned? when he was in Circumcision, or Uncircumcision? And he received the Sign of Circumcision, a Seal of the Righteousness of the Faith, which he had yet being Uncircumcised, that he might be the Father of all them that believe, though they be not Circumcised; *that Righteousness might be imputed unto them also.* Verse 6, 7, 8, 9, 10, 11.

In which we may perceive, *First,* that the Righteousness was by the *Apostle* inferr'd from *David's* Words of the Blessedness of that Man, *unto whom God imputed not Sin.* As much as if he had said, *Whom God forgives, he imputes not Sin to*; and to whom he imputes not Sin, *such he looks upon as Righteous,* that is, to be as clear of the Guilt of former Sin by Remission, as if it had never been committed. *Secondly,* that not Works of our own, no, though assisted by the Holy Spirit to perform them, strictly consider'd, can justifie in this Sense, but Faith only in the Goodness, Mercy, and Promise of God to Pardon, Remit, and show Favour unto all such, who, distrusting their own Weakness, and Repenting of their former Miscarriages, humbly, yet firmly put their Confidence in him. This being *Abraham's* Case, with respect to himself and Posterity, God no more lookt upon him as a

Stranger

Stranger at a Distance from him, but one, who by Faith was brought nigh, and became thus justified, not by Works of Righteousness that he wrought, *but by Faith in God*, which was accounted unto him for Righteousness, and that really too; since he could not believe without an inward Act of Righteousness; but not of his own.

§. 4. In short, *Justification* bears a Twofold Sense in the Scripture; and because we are frequently mistaken about it, by such as understand not the Extent and Use of the Word, I will explain it. *Justification is sometimes to be understood of Remission, or Non-Imputation of Sin upon Repentance, and Faith in the Promise of God.* In which Sense we say, That all the Righteous Works Man is capable of, either from himself, if such can be; or from the Assistance of the Holy Spirit, strictly as such, can never move one Jot to Justification, that is, *to the Blotting out of former Iniquities*; for if Men could do more a Thousand-fold than they do, and that it were never so acceptable, *it is but their present Duty*, and cannot have Virtue enough in it to answer a present Obligation, and cancel the old Debt of Disobedience too: God only upon Faith in his Goodness, Mercy, and Holy Promise, can give Remission, Pardon, or make Free from the heavy Debt Transgression hath brought upon us; and that not as thereby meriting, but as obtaining such Remission from God, upon his own Free Tender. This is Evangelical Faith, and Righteousness too, of which *Abraham* was a Partaker, as well before as after Circumcision, that he might be the Father of all.

§. 5. But *Justification* is not only taken for *Remission of former Sins, and Accounting of Believers, as if they had never Transgrest*, that is *Righteous*; but for that Regenerate and Clean State of Soul, and that Access to, and Acceptance with God respecting Daily Duty; In which Sense, no Man, nor Woman ever was, or ever will be Justified another Way, *than by Inward and Real Righteousness*. Nor in this Sense can any be farther *Justified and Accepted*, than as they are thus *Purified and Regenerated*; since it would be to say, not only that God upon Repentance of former Sins, and Belief in his Promise, has blotted out their Iniquities, which may be, *whilst Habitual Sin is yet but a working out, and not quite overcome*; for that is True enough: But that God accepts such as Purified, Sanctified, and Regenerated (the other Sense of Justification) *while they are actually Impure, and Unregenerated*; this we abominate, and than which nothing can be affirm'd more Reproachful to, and Destructive of His Eternal Holiness.

§. 6. Having thus explained, and exprest what we understand by the Word *Justification*, I shall declare, how far we believe *CHRIST JESUS our Lord*, respecting his Coming both in the Flesh, and Spirit, influenceth into our Justification (as the *Priest* terms it) *The Seed*, afterwards call'd *Christ, was, and is God's Free Gift, Promise, and Covenant of Light, by whom alone, Remission, Justification, and Eternal Salvation did, or can come to Mankind: That in the Fulness of Time, a Body was prepared, in which he came to fulfil the Father's Good Pleasure; That He Preacht the Promise of Remission of Sin, and Salvation, to as many as believed in him, and took up his Cross and followed him; confirming the same by many Miracles*. For this Doctrine of Redemption, and asserting himself to be the Off-spring of God, One with God, to whom all Power in Heaven and Earth was committed, the *Jews* persecuted him, stigmatizing him with the Name of *Blasphemer*, and at last apprehended and crucified him. We do say then, That Faith in the same Christ, who then appeared, who so Preached, wrought Miracles, and laid down his Life for the World, and not in another, does give Remission of Sins; and as follow'd, as becomes all True Disciples, Eternal Salvation: Yea, That Outward Blood was then, and is now, to be Reverently believed in, as a Seal, Ratification, and strong Confirmation of that Glad Tidings of Remission of Sin, and Eternal Salvation, which he held forth in the Name of the Father, to those who would take up the Cross and follow him. And therefore with Good Reason, was Remission of Sins preached in *His Blood*, because it was the most Visible Eminent Act of his Life, both fittest to recommend his Great Concernment for poor Man, and confirm the Truth of that Blessed Gospel he preached to him in the World.

§. 7. And as for *Satisfaction*, tho' we deny any strict and rigid Purchase, as Carnally understood, and irreverently held by many; yet that the Offering up his Innocent Life did, and doth, turn to Account, to as many as truly receive him, we faithfully believe; yea, that he did bear that for Man, (I mean his Iniquity) *He could not for himself*; and has by that Suffering obtained Precious Gifts, that is, *That Victory Man could never have obtained*; yet still we do ascribe all that was done,

done, but instrumentally to the Bodily Sufferings, and principally to the *Will of that Divine Life, whose Body it was, which offer'd it up, and by the which Will it was Sanctified, and so acceptable with God:* Otherwise more, nay, all would be ascrib'd to the Body, which I affirm to be Blasphemy it self; for it was not the Body eminently, which saved the People from their Sins, but that which dwelt in it, whose it was; *So that though the Body bore the Name of the Whole, yet was it not the Whole;* but by *Synecdoche*, a Part for the Whole, which is very familiar in the Scriptures.

§. 8. To his Spiritual Coming into the Soul, do we ascribe the *Inward Righteousness*. We say, *That Christ as He is the Light, Power and Righteousness of God, being received into the Soul, and diligently obey'd, and Communed with, He doth first Convince of Sin; then brings Trouble for Sin; and Sin thus becoming a Load to the Soul, he administers Strength to shake off every such Load and Burthen, and to conquer and subdue the Power of Sin and Satan in the Soul.* In which Sense he is more properly and particularly *a Saviour, when he binds the Strong Man, spoils his Goods, casts him out, destroys the Works of the Devil, finishes Transgression, and brings in Everlasting Righteousness:* Otherwise, in vain would he have that Title, *And thou shalt call His Name* JESUS, *for He shall save His People from their Sins;* not the Effect, *Eternal Death, without the* Cause, *Sin: For the Wages of Sin is Death: As Men Sow, so shall they Reap.* And a dreadful Disappointment will it be to the *Hypocritical Professors of this Day*, that dream of *Justification, Redemption and Salvation*, and are yet carried away with the Temptations of *Satan*, at his Will; being ignorant of the inward Power of Christ, to bruise the Serpent's Head. To conclude, that Righteousness, which Christ, as God's True Light, Power and Righteousness works in us (therefore is not of us) is that which alone brings into True Union with God, and Membership with his unspotted Church; consequently, no Man without that Qualification, can be so accepted with him, or have Access to him; *For God is of Purer Eyes than to behold Iniquity; and without Holiness no Man shall ever see the Lord*. But let none mistake me, I do not intend, that who is not quite Perfect, is altogether to be Condemned; by no Means: But that Man is only so far accepted of God, *as he is really Regenerated, and Beautified by the Internal Righteousness of Christ.*

And to this Purpose, is that other Scripture, he quotes against us, *That as Sin has reigned unto Death, even so might Grace reign through Righteousness unto Eternal Life, by Jesus Christ our Lord:* For all Men having actually sinned, and Sin so becoming inherent; Grace *(that teacheth to deny all Ungodliness, and Worldly Lusts, and to live Soberly, Righteously and Godly,* which is that Righteousness) should also Reign in all by Jesus Christ. Now unless it be an Evil for us to say, that Men are accepted with God upon *Christ's Inward Righteousness*, when the Scriptures say, That the Reign of Grace through Righteousness (where Sin reigned, which was within Man certainly, and therefore *Inward)* is unto Eternal Life (as full a Word, as being accepted with God) I cannot see, *but in our holding forth Christ's Righteousness to be made ours, by the Operation of his Holy Spirit in the Heart, as the Efficient or Principal, if not only Cause of our daily Acceptance with God, we are Scripturally Orthodox.*

§. 9. We would also provide against the Malice of those Tongues, who, because we do allow Good Works or Fruits to be well pleasing to God, and necessary to Life Eternal, do therefore rank us among the *Papists, as pleading for the Merit of Good Works:* For we lay not this *Second Sort of Justification*, and much less the *First*, upon any Exterior Works, that the very Spirit of Truth leads into, *as meerly Exterior, be they Acts of Justice, Mercy, Charity, or such like:* But upon the Holy Working of GOD's Power and Spirit in the Heart, and the Creature's believing in, and resigning himself up unto God, to be by him renewed, ordered, led, and disposed: So that the Creature has no farther Share, than as he bows to the Requirings of God, and contentedly acquiesceth, in what it pleaseth Almighty God to do with him. So our Wills being daily submitted to the Holy Will of God, which is Sanctification, is the Ground of our Daily Acceptance with God, and being received (not just by the *Non-Imputation* of Sins formerly committed, for that alone depends upon Repentance, and Faith in God's Free Love to remit; but) as just, by being actually and really made so, through the Participation of the Just and Righteous Nature of Christ, who is to all such, *Wisdom and Righteousness, and Sanctification and plenteous Redemption;* and here we will end this Argument, leaving our Faith therein with God and Men.

I shall

I shall not here, as well as elsewhere, taking any Notice of his base Revilings, and sordid Idantry, unworthy of a Good Christian, or Man of Learning and Civility, and endavour, as God shall enable me, to acquit my self of the Remainder of his Book, wh the same Honesty, Truth, Reason and Brevity, that I hope, I have done, in wha I have hitherto undertaken and dispatcht.

CHAP. XVIII.

He says we disown the True Christ. It is proved, that He denies in Contradiction to himself what we deny; and that we are Scriptural and Sound in our Belief: And though we cannot exclude that Divinity from the True Christ, yet we also own, that the True Christ tok Flesh; that he appeared for the Salvation of Mankind, and that his Bodily Appearance was Instrumental in the Point. Christ owned according to Scriptures.

§. 1. HE is now arrivl at the *Root-Error of the Quakers*, as he is pleased to Name it, whois a Man of Names, and such as are Beastly enough too sometimes; but they ma pass perhaps for Gospel-Zeal, or a pretty Sort of Wit, amongst some of his smal Companions, *whose Disease is to be mistaken*; but let's hear him patiently.

(Pag. 70, 71.) *The Quakers disown, and deny the Christ of God, and set up a False Christ in his Room nd Stead; and attribute all to that False Christ, which is due and peculiar to the True Christ. This is that Non-such Lye, which travels to bring forth that Babel, wherewith their Religion abounds.* His Proof is at Hand. " This " we certainly know, nd can never call the Bodily Garment Christ, but that " which appeared and dwelt in the Body, *Pennington's Quest.* 23. 32. To which he says, *They do not deny, that there was such a Man as* Jesus, *the Son of* Mary; *and that God, or rather Christ was in him: But this is no more than they profess of themselves, that Christ as God, is in them; yet that Body of the Man* Jesus, *which he calls here the Bodily Garment, he tells us they can never call Christ.* This Quotation he offers at explaining by another from the same *Author and Book*, p. 20. " For that which he took upon him was our Garment, even the Flesh and Blood " of our Nature (VERY RIGHT; but what followeth, is wofully false) which " is of an Earthly, Perishing Nature; but He is of an Heavenly Nature. From whence *J. Faldo* infers against us, *That the Body, Christ took upon himself of our Nature, is not the Christ.*

But before we give him off, we hope, through the Help of our God to prove, the contrary to be highly against Christ, Scriptures, and sound Reason: He has done us Right in Two Respects, which may a little answer for the ill Language he giveth us in our Charge. *First*, That he acknowledgeth, we own, that there was such a Man as *Jesus, the Son of* Mary, (in Contradiction to Abundance of our Adversaries) *and that God was in Him*, which makes up our Christ. *Secondly*, That He whom we call *Christ*, is not *J. Faldo's* Christ; *for He was that Body only that dyed*; else what mean those Words inferred by Way of Proof against us, in Defence of the Charge; *The Body which Christ took on him of our Nature*, &c. And therefore they can never call that Christ, *intimating he doth*, as the following Paragraph tells us. *This is a plain denying the Man Christ Jesus:* Yet behold the *Babel* of the Matter, who after this dare say, (VERY RIGHT) to this Part of *J. Pennington's* Words; *For that which he took upon him, was our Garment, even the Flesh and Blood of our Nature:* Where he manifestly implies, that what he just now accounted the *Whole Christ*, and reproaches us for denying to be such, is not the *Christ Himself*, but his Garment only; *unless there be no Difference between Christ and his Garment*; or that *Christ was but the Garment of that more Excellent Soul, or Divine Being, that dwelt therein*, which is Unscriptural, and very Carnal. If this Man has not charged us with what he cannot prove; nay, if he has not manifestly contradicted himself in his Endeavours to do it, no Man was ever Guilty in those Respects. But that none may be stumbled by his *Untrue Character of us*; We do believe, and plainly declare, and that with Holy Reverence and Fear, that we cannot, we dare not call the *Meer Body, The Christ*, but the *Body of Christ*: That he was after the Flesh, Born of the Virgin, like unto us in all Things, *Sin only excepted*; and consequently, that Body must have been of the same Nature with ours; or else it had not been a Real, but Phantastical Body, is most True; and if it had not been so, neither could it have been a Garment of the Nature of our Flesh, which is so, and to which *J. Faldo* said just now VERY RIHT; nor could the Cruel Instruments have prevail'd against his Life, as they did.

And now, Whether it be most against *Christ, Scripture, and Reason*, to say that that Body, which was Nailed upon the Cross, *Was the Christ*, or, *the Body of Christ only*, I leave with *Christ, Scripture and Reason to determine?* Certain I am, that this Principle must center in that *Senseless Dream* of *J. Reeve* and *L. Mugleton*, as well as that it makes a perfect Difference betwixt *Him that was before Abraham*, and *Him* that said so: *Him*, that told his Disciples. *I will not leave you Comfortless*, and *Him* that said, *I will come to you again*. Nay, Why should Christ say to his Disciples, *It was expedient he should go away*, since certainly if some more Excellent and Profitable Appearance of himself had not been to succeed, at least as to them; it had been far more Expedient, he should in that Manner have remained amongst them. And why did the Apostle spek, *of no more knowing Christ after the Flesh, and of his being Revealed in him, and in the Saints, as their Hope of Glory, and that he was the Quickning Spirit, an Lord from Heaven*; if that Body was the Intire Christ, and not rather the Body prepared for that Divine Power, Wisdom, and Righteousness to transact in, and appear by, to the Sons of Men; which, with respect to that great Manifestation, was denominated *Christ*, or Anointed, shall we dare think that He, who so spoke, and of whom the Apostle so testified, was not the *True Christ* (which to be sure, was before that *Visible Body*) God forbid. Let that Sin lie at *J. Faldo's* Door.

§. 2. But he offers to us Scripture, (Luke 2. 26, 27. *And it was reveal'd to him* (Simeon) *by the Holy Ghost, that he should not see death, before he had seen the Lord's Christ. And he came by the Spirit into the Temple, and when the Parents brought in the Child Jesus, then took he him up in his Arms, and said, Lord, now lettest thou thy Servant depart in Peace, for mine Eyes have seen thy Salvation, a Light to lighten the Gentiles*, &c. And it is, and will be granted, that *Simeon* saw the Lord's Christ: But I hope, *J. Faldo* will not deny unto that Good Man, who waited for *Israel's* Consolation, that he had as well a Spiritual, as Natural, an Inward, as Outward Sight of Christ: For can he think, that the *Word* which took Flesh, was nothing of that Saviour, and that the *True Light* which then appeared, is to be excluded any Share therein? Will *J. Faldo*, or any Man that owns Scripture, dare to affirm, there was not something belonging to the *True and Compleat Christ*, beyond what his outward Eyes could possibly see? Certainly this Allegation from *Luke* 2. 26. will never prove the *Body of Jesus*, which the Father prepared for him, to be the *Whole Intire Christ, Saviour, Light, Salvation, and Glory of Israel*, unless Christ under all these Considerations consisted, or was made up of the meer Outward Body, that only was obvious to the Outward Eyes; which to affirm, were both to deny His Divinity, and to conclude *Simeon* void of any Spiritual Sight, or Intendment in these Words, of the *Lord's Christ, as a Light Enlightning the Gentiles, and God's Salvation to the Ends of the Earth*. Though still be it understood, that we confess that Child, as seen and understood by *Simeon*, with Respect to that great End of his Appearance, to be the *Lord's Christ*. Nay, *J. Faldo* says as much, pag. 70. otherwise there would be an exalting the Body above the Divinity; nay, an utter Exclusion of the Divinity with respect to the *True Christ*. Let none then be so Ungodly and Unjust to us, as to infer we deny the *Lord's Christ*, because we rather chuse to say, *The Body of Christ*, than *Christ*: For, says he, *Christ is God manifest in the Flesh*. See *J. F.* p. 72, 77, 84, 85, 93.

§. 3. And lest any should think, that therein I contradict the Inspired Saying of that Just Man, when he said, *Mine Eyes have beheld thy Salvation:* The Words import no more than this, Mine Eyes have beholden the Manifestation and Breaking forth of thy Seed and Heir, who is come to visit the World, and bruise the Serpent's Head: Mine Eyes have seen him by whom thy Salvation shall be declared; through whom thou wilt put forth thine Arm, and work mightily for the Salvation of Man.

And this his other Scriptures prove at large for me, the most Considerable of which I take to be this; (Pag. 7.) *The God of our Fathers raised up* Jesus, *whom ye slew, and hanged on a Tree; Him hath God exalted with his Right Hand, to be a Prince and a Saviour, for to give Repentance to* Israel, *and Forgiveness of Sin*, Acts 5. 31. Which can no more be understood expresly, strictly, and intirely so, than it would be Reasonable for a Man to say, *That when* Samuel *died, the Soul and Body which was call'd* Samuel, *died*; and not rather, *The Body of him who was called* Samuel: And this is the Ground and Reason why the *Socinians*, *Muggletonians*, and

several

several *Anabaptists*, hold the *Mortality of the Soul*, because otherwise those Words, which speak of the Death of Christ, could not be taken properly, as they take and defend them. I say then, and that with Force of Reason, and which at this Time may be more to the Conviction of some, the Suffrage of our malignant Adversary, *J. Faldo* himself, however contradicting to his fore-mentioned Sense, the Words are thus to be understood: *The God of our Fathers, who raised up* (the Body of) *Jesus from the Dead, which ye slew and hung upon a Tree; Him,* whose Body you so cruelly used, *hath God exalted with his Right Hand, to be a Prince, and a Saviour for to give Repentance to* Israel, *and Forgiveness of Sin.* To put this out of doubt, hear *J. Faldo* his own self.

Let not these Blasphemers of the Lord of Life, and Glory, delude People with a Fancy, as if we believe and preach the Flesh and Blood of Christ, *to be Christ, Separated from his Soul, of the Nature of Man's Soul (but Undefiled) or that we take His Man's Nature to be Christ, Separated from His Eternal and Divine Nature.*

One would think I had spent my Time in vain, when I set about to prove, that the *Divine Light, Life, Power, Wisdom, and Righteousness* were not unconcerned in the *True Christ*, and consequently that the *Body* which only died, was not the *Entire Jesus or Saviour*, since our *Adversary* calls us *Blasphemers and Deluders*, (and I know not for what, except it be) for Teaching that Doctrine he recommends in the same Paragraph, wherein he calls us those *Hateful Names*.

§. 4. But that his great Inconsistency with himself may be farther manifest, hear him again, (Pag. 75.) *If Men be so Blind as not to see the Error of Disowning* Jesus of Nazareth, *the Son of* Mary, *who was hanged on a Tree, put into the Sepulchre of* Joseph *of* Arimathea, *to be yet alive, and the Christ of God by all these Scriptures* (the most considerable whereof are consider'd) *it is a Blindness, wherewith never any before the* Quakers, *who professed the Scriptures to be a True Testimony, were smitten; surely God hath given them up for their Pride, Giddiness, or Idle Ignorance, and that Injustice, and the Devil hath blinded their Minds.*

Enough of him at this Time, in Contradiction to himself, and of his Ungodly Censure of us. But we hope it may not be improper to observe, *That though before he recommended to us the* Lord's Christ, *as consisting of a Divine and Human Nature, that is, God and Man, and that he would not be thought to call the Flesh and Blood, and Man's Soul, intirely Christ, in Dis-junction from the Divinity; Yet now, all those who say, That Body which was Born of* Mary, *hanged on a Tree, laid in the Sepulchre of* Joseph *of* Arimathea, *was not, and is not the Living Christ of God, are smitten for their Pride, Giddiness, or Idle Ignorance, and the Devil hath blinded their Minds with a Witness*: From whence Three Things result: (1.) That the *Divinity is no Ways concern'd in the Lord's Christ*: A manifest Contradiction to himself; or else, with *Noetus* of Old, and *J. Reeve* and *L. Muggleton*, of our Age, *the Godhead dyed in Company with the Manhood*: Blasphemy it self. (2.) *That the meer Body was the Only and Intire Christ*, whatever he pretends, *and not so much as the Man's Soul in Conjunction with it, unless the Soul was of such a material gross Nature, as that it could be hang'd on a Tree, Dye, and be laid in a Sepulchre (which is to assert the Mortality of the Soul)* all which happen'd to the *Lord's Christ*, says *J. Faldo*: But because the Man's Soul was not Mortal, and could not be hanged on a Tree, and put into a Sepulchre, it follows, that it was the Visible Body which could only be hang'd on a Tree, and laid in a Sepulchre, that was, and is, the Only and Intire Lord, and Saviour *Jesus Christ* in *J. Faldo's* Sense: Which, how impious it is against him, that truly is so; how grosly abusive of all People; and how Contradictory to himself, let the whole World of Reason judge. Is this the Man that must be thought fit to Rant it over us with such impudent Scurrility, Ungodly, as well as Unmmannerly Reflections? But in the Earth there is not any Thing so Fantastical, Conceited, Proud, Railing, Busie-Body, and sometimes Ignorant, as a Sort of Priests to me not unknown (among whom our *Adversary* is not the least) who think their Coat will bear out their worst Expressions, for Religion, and Practice an haughty Reviling for Christ, as one of the greatest Demonstrations of their Zeal; an ill-bred and Pedantick Crew, the *Bane of Reason, and Pest of the World*; the old Incendiaries to Mischief, and the best to be *spar'd of Mankind*; against whom the boiling Vengeance of an irritated God is ready to be poured out to the Destruction of such, if they repent not, *and turn from their Abominable Deceits*.

1673.
Ch. XVIII.

§. 5. If to excuse the Matter, he, or any else shall say, the Body is only *Synecdochically* or *Metonymically* taken, *a Part for the Whole, or Representatively*; I answer, that such a Distinction overthrows him for ever: For if the *Body*, which was called *Jesus*, and *Christ*, and *Lord*, &c. be by him allow'd as Representative of the *whole Jesus*, then was not that distinctly the Christ; nay, what has he been opposing all this While? We will as truly, and honestly say, as it is possible for him to do, *that it was the Body of the Lord Jesus Christ* (which sometime bore the Name of the whole Lord Jesus Christ, as the Saviour of Men) *that was born of* Mary, *was hanged on a Tree, and laid in the Sepulchre of* Joseph *of* Arimathea. And if he will adventure to say more, the Consequences *of Excluding the Divinity, and Man's Soul, from being any Part of the True Christ, or their Mortality with the Body* (which are Immortal) and not capable of being hanged on a Tree (much less buried for dead in the Sepulchre of *Joseph of Arimathea*) *will inevitably fall upon him, and dash him and his Carnal Notions into Peices:* Thus have I clear'd my Conscience in clearing up the Consistency of our Belief of the Bodily Appearance of the True Christ, with Scripture, and sound Reason; and I hope, to the plain Overthrow of our Adversary, and that with what Brevity was convenient.

Ch. XIX.

C H A P. XIX.

Our Adversary's Three proposed Scripture-Places *are by us rightly applied, and his* Charge *is found Untrue. Christ is proved the true Light, Comforter, Creator and Redeemer. Our Adversary's Objections examined and refuted. His Triumph turned to his Shame. The true Signification of the Word,* Φωτίζει *and* Ἐρχόμενον *confirmed.*

§. 1. BUT he undertakes a more particular Enervation of our Understanding of Three Places of Scripture, which he says, we grosly abuse. It will be worth our while, to hear, and stop him a little, for he makes great haft to Triumph.

That was the true Light, which lighteth every Man that cometh into the World; Our Business is to know three Things of him. (1.) *What Light it is?* (2) *In what Sense it enlightneth?* (3.) *How he understands every Man*; and this *Line* compasseth the Matter.

That, (says he) *Hath for it's antecedent, and is to be understood* of the Word, *which was in the Beginning with God, which was God, by whom all Things were made, the Light of Men, &c.* Light is taken properly for that which doth *Manifest* or *Discover any Thing: so Christ is Light*; but is now made manifest by the Appearing of our Saviour Jesus Christ, who hath abolished Death, and hath brought Life and Immortality to Light through the Gospel. *The Meaning is,* said he, *that Salvation Eternal, which God hath proposed to give to his People, which could not be seen in the Purpose of God, as such, is by the Appearing of* Christ in the Flesh, *and therein transacting and declaring this Salvation and Eternal Life, abundantly discovered: and as Light properly is that which makes Manifest, so* metaphorically *it is that which Comforts and Rejoyceth.* I do not in the least doubt, but *Christ the Word here is call'd Light in both respects; And this I take to be the Import of the 4th Verse;* In him was Life, and the Life the Light of Men, that is, *The Salvation and Life Eternal of poor Sinners was wrapt up in Christ, as God; the Consideration of God manifest in the Flesh for those Ends, is matter of Strong Consolation.*

In his First Part about the Scriptures he told us, that he was got to the highest Round of the Ladder; in this Place he has twisted himself Rope enough to answer the End of his climbing thither; for if I do not from hence irrefutably prove, (1) That the meer Body was not the Intire Saviour: (2) That the Light within is of a saving Nature; I shall be ready to allow all our Adversaries Detrectations from the Light within, but just Epithets, and a true Character of our Principles.

If Christ be the Light, which is that Word, which made all Things, and therefore God (as faith *J. Faldo*) then Christ was before his Appearance, and consequently our former Chapter is justified on our part against his Notions of the Lord's Christ: For it was impossible; That the Visible Body taken from the Virgin, should have made all Things, which was hung upon a Tree, and buried, &c. But *J. Faldo* expresly says, *As the Word is the Light of Men, so, or in that Manner is Christ the Light of Men:* Nay, he calls it, Christ's Appearing in the Flesh, therein

therein transacting and declaring Salvation, &c. intimating, That Christ was before he took that Flesh, or appeared in that Body; and that he therefore took it, and appeared in it, to transact, work, declare and bring to pass by and thro' it as a peculiar Vessel, and prepared Holy Instrument, the great Salvation, &c. and consequently Christ was, and is that Word which was with God, and is God, and the Light of Men, &c. And lest we should yet mistake him; he calls it *God manifested in the Flesh*, for those Ends, to wit, Salvation and Eternal Life: And that he might speak *all for us in a little*, and give the Death's-wound to his own Cause, he tells us in so many Words, *That the Salvation and Life Eternal of poor Sinners was wrapt up in Christ, as God*. Is not this pretty fair for an Adversary, as ill-willing to us and to the Truth, as *J. Faldo*, one of Ten Thousand in his Displeasure against us? Certainly, if the *Quakers* are condemnable for believing, It was and is Christ, as the Word in whom was Life, and that Life the Light of Men, that he was, and is a Saviour, *J. Faldo* must not be the Man, that shall give the Sentence, who, I know not how, nor why, but that God and his Truth may be glorified by his Self-overthrow, hath asserted the *Quakers* Principle, and that at an high Rate; and if it can be an Honour to him, that he has assisted to the Conquest of himself, he ought to have it without any Envy.

§. 2. But he is as serviceable to us altogether in Defence of the Light, however undesigned, which I prove thus: If Christ be properly that Light, which manifests or discovers any Thing (the Terms of his Concession) and therefore it doth manifest the Purpose and Grace of God, which was given in Christ before the World was, whereby Death comes to be abolished, and Life and Immortality brought to Light; Then must Christ Jesus, this manifesting Light, *be a Divine and Saving Light without all Dispute*: Now, *J. Faldo* affirms Christ to be that Word, and proper Light, that so manifesteth, and discovereth, as exprest; consequently, that Light, which doth so manifest and Discover, *is a Saving Light*.

Again, If the Light, be not only a Manifesting Light (which is to take it Properly) but a Comforting Light also (which is to take it Metaphorically, as saith *J. Faldo*) Then this Light, as the Word Creator, is not therefore call'd Light from a bare Act of Discovery; *but is a Principle of Life, Power, Virtue,* &c. by which such as obey it are consolated, and by the Reason of Contraries, who rebel against it are condemned: Which make up those two States of Light and Darkness; and their Rewards, Consolation and Misery.

And thus much our Adversary farther proves for us; *In him was Life, and the Life was the Light of Men*, that is, *the Salvation and Eternal Life of poor Sinners was wrapt up in Christ, as God:* Which is to say; That the Life of the Word was, and is the proper Light of Men, and unto all such poor Sinners as did and do believe in it, *that Light is unto them Salvation and Eternal Life*; than which, *nothing can be more Orthodox in the Point*. Who would think that *J. Faldo* should ever undertake the *Quakers*, so little understanding their Principles? And if he did know them, What should ail the Man to be so much our Friend to write against himself, under Pretence of writing against us? One would think, he did it by the same Figure *Irony*, that some call Fools, Wits: Yet he would fain distinguish Christ the Light, as *Creator* and *Redeemer*, making the first Common, the other Peculiar, and that spoils all. To which I shall briefly answer, for he only starts it himself: There is but one Kind of Light, which results from the Life of the Word, and because it cannot be such, but it must be Divine and Sufficient, as well to Redemption as Conviction; it will unanswerably follow, that the manifesting Light of the Word *J. Faldo* confesseth all Mankind more or less to be lighted with, is of a Divine and Saving Nature; and that which strengthens this Conclusion, is, *that Christ, as God, is by our Adversary made the Saviour*; and unless he would deny him that he calls God, to have been before that Manifestation in Flesh, a Redeemer to the Ancients (which were to conclude the Damnation of all that died antecedent) Christ, the Word, *as that Light was the proper Redeemer through all Generations*; Though I will grant to him, and that in the Name of all that People call'd *Quakers*, the Discoveries made by Christ, *or God manifested in the Flesh, transcended all former Manifestations*, and as in my *Spirit of Truth Vindicated* it is largely confest (had this Adversary been Ingenuous enough to have weigh'd it) So again I declare, that eminently whatever was before, or hath been since, might in a Sense be said of that Manifestation; because he that then appeared, was the Fulness of that Light, Life and Power which measurably was, is, is, and may be difpenfed to the Sons of Men; wherefore in that Senfe he was, both before and after, the fame Convincer, Converter, Redeemer and Saviour to the Souls of Men.

§. 3. But he is much ftumbl'd, and not a little abufive, becaufe I would have Φωτίζει render'd *Enlightneth*, rather than *Lighteth*, in my *Spir. of Truth Vindc.* faying of me, *I perceive he is as very ——— as thofe Phyficians, who impofe fevere Abftinence on others, but they themfelves will take their Cups off, and their good Chear to Wantonnefs and Giddinefs.*

How far this Character may be by any thought to refemble *William Penn* (a Man he often ftrikes at) I know not; but dare fay for him, he never was fo Difingenuous as to deferve it, and leaft of all from *J. Faldo*, with whom he never had to do, and who muft needs make a Random-guefs in the Matter. But this is not the only Scurrility, *William Penn*, however unconcerned he be, has received at the Hands of that Rude *Prieft*, nor that he is able to bear. He takes it for granted that *W. P*'s *Paffive Religion*, is like to be a Protection to his bafe Tongue, and fo long the *Prieft* fleeps in a whole Skin. I cannot imagine what his dafhoe——fhould fignifie; But it is ill done of a *Prieft* to quarrel his next Order, and one too, which, if I am not miftaken, the *Non-conforming Priefts* have fwarm'd after, as the next Way of Maintenance to their difplaced *Carcaffes*; infomuch, that we have almoft as many *Phyficians* as *Patients*. One would have thought *J. Faldo* had been looking that way by his *Ebullitions*, a Term of Art in pag. 127. But that is one of their laft Refuges: For it requires Pains, which Men of his Function can't abide. They are for the Land of *Milk and Honey*, whoever toils; and *that* they will make the Labours of others yield them *in a Land of Briars and Thorns*. But it happened unluckily, that he fhould charge fo much Epicurifm upon *Phyficians*, whilft they impofe fuch Abftinence on their Sick, to whofe way of Life fo many of his Friends are devoted. Shall I infer, it is *to have thofe Cups and that Cheer, their Ill-Preaching could not give*, and that *J. Faldo* is therefore as very a —— as thofe *Pharifees, that bound heavy Burdens, and lay'd them upon the People, but themfelves would not put their Fingers to fupport them.* Does he live to what he requires from others? if not (and the Courfe he takes, I know not how he fhould) let him take his *as very a*—— to himfelf, which much better becomes Him, than any Body I have to beftow it upon.

But to the Point controverted. I faid then, and do now again, that the Light muft be in the Soul, or Intelligent Place of Man; and with refpect to the Inward Parts, I faw no Difference between faying, the *Light of Chrift lighteth the Soul, or inward Parts of Man*, and that *the Light inlightneth Man*: Only fometimes I granted, that *Enlightning* did import *a Belief in the Light, and fome Divine Attainments* thereby; both which are fober, and true, and granted by *J. Faldo*, if I underftand what he fays when he confefleth, that moft Tranflators render it *enlightneth*.

§. 4. The laft of what concerns his pretended Defeat of our Conftruction of that Verfe; That was the true Light, *&c.* is *Every Man*: hear him; *If this Phrafe be taken ftrictly in it's full latitude* (a Phrafe I do as little underftand, as many of his other uncouth and contradictory Terms) *Intending every Individual without Exception; Chrift's Enlightning, muft be underftood, fo doing as Creator, not as Redeemer; this is the Opinion of many Superiors to me in Judgment by far* (It may be fo, though I am apt to think *J. Faldo* fcarce thinks fo.)

But this hath been fo effectually confider'd already, that it would be needlefs Repetition, a Fault I would not be guilty of (efpecially at this Time) to fay much to it: Let it fuffice, that the Light Naturally and Immediately refulting from the Word, which was and is the Life of the Word, *is the fame in Kind, both before that Manifeftation of God (who is Light) in that Holy Manhood, then, and fince;* though not the fame with refpect to the Degree of it's Difcoveries. But he tells us, though he can allow it univerfally *as Creator, yet not as Redeemer*; and brings us thefe Scriptures; *Whom we preach, warning every Man, and teaching every Man, &c. Commending our felves to every Man's Confcience, &c. The Lord upholdeth all that fall, and raifeth up all thofe that are bowed down* (The laft an old Objection (Now fays he, *the Apoftle could not warn all, nor recommend himfelf to every Man, it muft be then, all that he preacht to, and who heard him. So, who were upheld, God upheld; and who were raifed up, are raifed by him.*

But this is too mean to invalid the Force of the Place, and our plain and inextorted Underftanding of it. The Reafon of this Miftake lies here: If it be his

Light,

Light, says *J. Faldo*, as Creator, then it hurts us not; if as Redeemer; *why are not all redeemed?* putting no Difference *betwixt the Sufficiency of the Light to save, and the Salvation, that may be wrought by it upon the Obedience of the Creature.* A Doctrine accurst from God, and detested of all Men not mad, or abused by the Suggestions of others; for the *Calviniz'd Predestination* is at the Bottom of it. Let it suffice, and so we will venture it, (1) *That Christ died for all Men*, though all Men receive not the Benefit intended by it; The Neglect of Men don't render God's Love, *no Love*, or that it is not Universal, and least of all that it should be Insufficient in it self. (2) If God has not lightned the Soul of all Mankind with a sufficient Light to Salvation, the Damnation of Men can never lye at their own Door; neither will they be left without Excuse. (3) The Light with which he enlightens, being the Life of the Word, must be Saving; call it the Light of the *Creator*, or *Redeemer*, *for He is one in himself, and so is his Light*. (4) *All Mankind*, in all Copies and Translations, and from the Reason of the Thing, must be confest to be the Subjects of this Illumination; Neither let it be hard for our Adversary to grant; *since it may be the Light of Christ as Redeemer, and yet Men may not be redeemed thereby, through their own Disobedience.* And inevitable Redemption then not following upon Men's being thus lighted, *but upon their Receiving of it*, I cannot see but it may be allow'd us, *that all Mankind not being redeemed, is no Argument, why all Mankind should not be enlightned*; consequently *(for all the Force our Adversary brings to the contrary) Every Man in our Sense is lighted with a Light Saving in it self.* I omit to mention many ancient, great and learned Authorities, some of which are, and more may elsewhere shortly be produc'd in Defence of our Assertion.

Let my *Spir. of Truth Vind.* be perused, from p. 53. to p. 73.

§. 5. Now as to his Scripture-Quotations, they are no whit to his Purpose: For the Warning and Commendation were Universal, there is not one Soul exempted. And should I grant him his Desire, what could it avail? For if the Apostle had a particular Regard to those among whom he laboured, neither doth that hinder the Universality of the Truth of the Thing in it self, for the Warning is to all, or the Scripture is not binding to all, contrary to our Adversary's Judgment of it.

Nor is the Case parallel with the Relation given of the Divinity of the Word, it's Creating Power and peculiar Benefit of Light from it's own Life universally extended to Mankind, unless that in the Places where the Word *All* or *Every* is used without any Exception, an Exception should be made, because some one particular Case may admit of an Exception: For neither doth God raise up *all who fall*: Nor is it to be understood, that all who are raised up in all Cases, God doth immediately raise, but rather thus; the Lord alone is able to uphold all who fall, and raise up all that be bowed down, as to a Spiritual State, the Purport of the Words: So that the Universal, I mean *All*, remains entire, and the contrary Opinion, respecting the Light, ends in an absolute Denial of a Saving Light to the greatest Part of Mankind; which dreadful Consequence I had much rather should result from *J. Faldo*'s Opinions, than *W. Penn*'s Faith, as ill a Christian, as he is pleased to repute him, though it be for Vindicating the *Pure Christian Religion*, as it was once delivered to the Saints.

§. 6. But to shut up this Discourse, let us take notice of an Expression or two, that this *Critick* lets fall in the close of this Paraphrase, and this, Concerning Ἐρχόμενον or *Coming*, it being more properly referable to *Light*, than *Man*. *That was the true Light, which coming into the World lighteth every Man*, rather than *that was the true Light, which lighteth every Man coming into the World*. If, says he, *it should refer to Man, every Man, in the very instant of, or before his Birth, Christ enlightneth*; it must be meant of created Faculties —— *For Experience and Sense (without any one Instance to controul it) will tell us, that none can believe without Hearing, nor hear without a Preacher.*

He might much better have said of himself, than of the *Quakers*-Meeting, that he was but a *Puppet* indeed, who knows nothing but by Hear-say or meer Imitation: If Man have not some more inward Teacher, farewell to the Truth of all Revelation, the Scriptures, and whatever comes by, or from the Inspiration of the Almighty. This Man, if yet he ben't too much besotted to deserve so excellent a Name, at once destroys all Ways, or Means, whereby to know, and that not only to the *Quakers*, but himself too; For the Scriptures themselves being grounded upon Revelation, and his Knowledge, upon them, as he pretends: Take away Revelation, and ye take away the Scriptures; and consequently what

Knowledge *J. Faldo* pretends to have from them, falls to the Ground. To pass by what might be offered from the Ancient *Puritans*, *Brownists*, and *Independents*, on our Behalf, who were once reputed warm Sticklers, for that *J. F.* proudly esteems *Enthusiasm*, for which they became the Derision of Carnalists. He forgets to whom *Phanatick* belongs, and cuts off his pretended Preaching from the God above, &c. p. 113. Thus is this blind Leader fallen into the Ditch of his own digging.

But must it be absurd, because Children, at the Instant of their Coming into the World, can't be said to be so enlightned. Very well; and what thinks he of the Instant of Christ's Coming into the World, out of the Virgin's Womb? Did he enlighten all who should savingly be enlightned at that Instant? A Mad Disputant, indeed. What was it enlightned *Simeon*? Who told and revealed to him the Lord's Christ? For Shame quit all Pretence to Dispute.

§. 7. But let's hear him farther: *There is a Reason in the Text, gives such a Countenance to referring it to the Light, as will never be found for the contrary. That was the true Light, not This, or This is; not as Christ is now in Heaven, nor as present with the Evangelist John, and the then Saints; but it points at Christ's Appearance in the Flesh.* Very notable indeed, and we will not let it slip our Observation.

If the *Word* that made all Things, which was with God, and was God, was that true Light, as saith *J. Faldo* himself, p. 84, then can it never be restrained to that Appearance as the Beginning or End of it. Nay, the Evangelist is not yet come so much as to mention any thing of his Manifestation in the Flesh; and if we will believe *J. Faldo*, the Verse concerns the *Word* as *Creator*, and not as *Redeemer*, which he stints to his Coming in the Flesh. *See pag.* 89. But by his Interpretation, *that* is not relative to his Appearance in the Flesh, but rather to the *Word*, which was with God, and was God, as p. 84, and so the *Spanish* Translation has it, *That Word was the true Light*, &c. so that either the *Word* was not before that Appearance; or if it were, being that true Light, that true Light was before that Appearance; And Mankind being also antecedent to that Manifestation, may very well be said always to have been enlightned by that Light. For that the *Word* should be before that Appearance, and that true Light, which is the very Life of the *Word*, or *Word it self*, should be stinted to that Appearance, is as absurd, as any thing well can be. Again, that we should take *It* to deny Christ now to be the true Light, that enlightens all, because he was so, is a strange Impertinency, and gross Falshood; for then by good Reason ought we to infer, that because the Word was with God, and was God, therefore he is not now either with God, or God. Is this your *Tertullus*? Besides, if we had nothing of this to offer, the Evangelist might very well refer to that Appearance without any Denial at all of an antecedent Illumination: It being the most excellent breaking forth of the divine Light. And this is largely acknowledg'd and prov'd, in my *Spirit of Truth Vindicated*; which had he consider'd but half as much as he importunes us to do his own, he might have sav'd us the Labour of this Animadversion. But God knoweth, it is our Portion from many such like base and unworthy *Adversaries*. Every Thing is a Fault in a *Quaker*, and nothing in them. We have great Reason to despair of any Good upon the most of them, whose Spirits are so leaven'd into Prejudice and Revenge, that, not to bear their Lies, and to rebuke their Slanders, is accounted scarce so tolerable as Railing; But with God the righteous Judge of Heaven and Earth do we leave our Cause, to be by him pleaded upon the Necks of that Crooked and Perverse Generation.

§. 8. Upon the Second Scripture, (p. 94.) which he pretends we abuse, to wit, *But what saith it? The Word is nigh thee, even in thy Mouth, and in thy Heart; That is the Word of Faith which we preach:* and which, he saith, we join with the first of *John*, *In the Beginning was the Word, &c.* He observes thus much in short. *The Apostle alludes to the Words of* Moses *in* Deuteronomy: But the Word is very nigh unto thee, in thy Mouth, and in thy Heart, that thou mightest do it; *that is* (saith he) *the Laws, Statutes, and Commandments written in the Book of the Law, making the having the Word in the Heart to be an having them without Book, or by rote*, as he expresseth it.

But none of the most mistaken of our modern *Socinians*, (the greatest Contra-Spiritualist Men of our Time) I am perswaded, could have given us a more dark and carnal Interpretation of the Place; for the *Word of Faith*, is the Word which gives *Faith*, and in which Faith should be: It is called the *Word of Reconciliation and Regeneration*; which can be no other *Word*, than that which was in the Beginning with God; That, by which God utter'd and declar'd his Mind to the Sons and Daughters of Men in all Ages; That *Word*, whose Life was, and is the Light of Men: To make the *Apostle* to have preacht another Word, is as much as in him lies, to render him no Gospel-Preacher.

Besides, that *Word* mentioned by *Moses*, could not be the outward Commandments and Statutes; For the Question was not about them, but about the *Commandment* of Commandments, and *Word* of Words, which he resolves thus: *Let none say, Who shall ascend, descend, or go beyond the Seas, to fetch the Great Word and Commandment*; But the Word is very nigh thee קרב, קדוב, signifies the *Innermost of Men*. Whereinto the Outward Commandments could never come. Nay, I do affirm, and that with Holy Boldness, in the Spirit, Power and Illumination, of the Blessed Gospel, that all the by rote Learning of the Letter, of either Law or Gospel, as they are contra-distinguisht, is of no more Value to the true Knowledge or Worship of God, than the cutting off a Dog's Neck, either to God's Honour or Man's Profit, without the Inward Living Word should powerfully write, and engrave upon the Soul it's Holy Precepts; neither could there be any Conviction in the Conscience, concerning the Truth of those Statutes; nor indeed any Conscience at all; since *Conscience is no other, than that manifest Judgment Man makes of the Truth or Falshood of Things, with respect to his own Soul, from the Word or Light of God in his Heart*, according to the Practice of the Apostle, *who was manifest, and desir'd to commend himself to the Consciences of Men*: Not as to a blind unsensible Thing; but that Judgment in Man, though not from him, which was right, and not learned of Men, but received of God. Whereas *J. Faldo* scoffs at such kind of Knowledge, the Perniciousness of which Doctrine, ought to *antidote* all sober Persons from ever adhering to it, or him that preacheth it: For I will be bound to make it appear, that by his own Principles, he is assured of nothing, and must set down under the extremest *Scepticism* in the World: Or if concludable by any Thing, it must be by the Way *Rome* takes to resolve all Scruples, and that is Plurality of Votes, however directed; and this too, rather for Peace Sake, than any Certainty there can be in it. For who bear out all *Inward Sense*, Motions, Revelations, Inspirations or Enlightnings, resolving only to insist upon what may arrive to them from meer Books, because of the Fallibility of Man and Difficulty of the Matter they do contain; which Way can there be to compass any tolerable Certainty to rest Men's Souls upon? This is your once *Phanatical*, t'other Day *Enthusiastical*, now *Pragmatical* and *Scoffing J. Faldo*. The first in the very Beginning of *Independency* in the World, the best Part that belong'd to it, I mean *Enthusiasm*; but now deserted, by many as much as the true Religion is by the Church of *Rome*.

§. 9. The Third and last Scripture he undertakes to secure us from all Share in, (Page 98.) is that of *Peter*, *We have also a more sure Word of Prophecy, whereunto ye do well to take Heed, as unto a Light that shineth in a dark Place, until the Day dawn, and the Day-Star arise in your Hearts*. By this *more sure Word of Prophecy* (says *J. Faldo*) is meant *those Prophecies written in the Old Testament: which are call'd* (Verse 20.) *Prophecy of Scripture, and are called, the Light that shineth in a dark Place*.

I hope it will be always foreign to me, to detract from the Holy Scriptures; But the Truth I will take Liberty to defend. The whole Chapter is a very weighty and zealous Recommendation of the *Gospel* to the Churches, pressing them to call to Mind the Love of God unto them, and to Mind their Duty to him, who had so lov'd them; And as a great Ground, both of their Faith, Love and Duty, the Apostle in the 16th Verse tells them, *For we have not followed cunningly devised Fables, when we made known unto you, the Power and Coming of our Lord Jesus Christ; But were Eye-Witnesses of his Majesty; for he receiv'd from God the Father Honour and Glory, when there came such a Voice to him from the Excellent Glory, This is my Beloved Son, in whom I am well-pleased. And this Voice, which came from Heaven, we heard, when we were with him in the Holy Mount; We have also a more sure Word of Prophecy, &c.* Now that this cannot be meant of the Scriptures

tures (and take in the Comparison) I thus prove. If the Reason of their Assurance, that what they delivered to the Churches, was not Fabulous, but true, *was their being Eye-Witnesses of his Majesty, and Eye and Ear-Witnesses of that Testimony God gave of his Son in the Mount, by that Honour, Glory and Voice of Words, which were there uttered, and did in that Place appear*; then the Scriptures not only were not a surer Word of Prophecy, but not so sure, because they never heard nor saw them so delivered; nor yet had any of the Prophets, so Glorious, so Transcendent, and unquestionable a Testimony to their outward Eyes and Ears that we read of (*J. Faldo's* most infallible Way of true Knowledge (see Pag. 91.) as was that which God gave to his Disciples, when he testified, *This is my beloved Son, in whom I am well-pleased*; But we may inform our selves from the Verses recited, that they were a more eminent Ground for their Knowledge, Assurance, and Belief, than the meer Scriptures; And consequently the Scriptures are not *the more sure Word of Prophecy*. Again, The written Account of another's Revelation cannot be more sure to me than that Revelation which I do immediately receive from God; suppose it be from God: But this was a Revelation to the Disciples, and they were sure it was from God; Consequently the written Account of another's Revelation, as were the Prophecies of the Old Testament (so called) to the Disciples, could not be *a more sure Word of Prophecy*. For it were to say, that they were more sure, that he among them who was called *Jesus*, was the Son of God from *Isaiah's* Testimony, *That he would give him for a Light to lighten the Gentiles, &c.* than the immediate Voice of God, when he pointed so clearly at him, *This is my beloved Son*; He that is amongst you, whom you have followed, *This is my beloved Son, in whom I am well-pleased:* Than which, What could be more demonstrable on God's Part, and incredulous on their Side, who should yet subject that living Testimony, to any the best Tradition? Let me not forget to add, That what the Disciples then saw and heard from God, and the Epistle, *Peter* wrote by the Holy Ghost, being made Part of the New Testament-Writings, and they accounted more eminent by far than the Old, with respect to the more eminent Pouring forth of the Holy Ghost, in that Day, which the Prophets foresaw, and they enjoyed, the Old cannot in any wise be reputed a more sure Word of Prophecy, as *J. Faldo* asserts; therefore this more sure Word of Prophesy must be another Thing.

§. 10. What that is which may be reputed a more sure word of Prophesy, will much deserve our serious Consideration. If it was not the Voice in the Mount, which we have invincibly prov'd, to be more *Immediate, Living, Fresh, Convincing and Confirming* to the Disciples, than any the best written Prophecies they had; It will follow, that it was meant of the *Holy Anointing, that Spirit,* and *Measure of the Grace, or blessed Light of Christ*, which is Internal, and out of the Reach of all Visible Things, to *sophisticate, corrupt, mis-represent, mis-render,* or *mis-translate*, all which have greatly befallen the Scriptures: For I do affirm, that Sense it self is not so certain as Reason, and what clearly and fully occurs to the Understanding Part of Man, is a more solid Ground for Faith and Knowledge, than those External Sights and Visions, which Man might be attended with to Confirmation. For what shall be the Rule for trying the Certainty and Truth of any such Visions and Prophecies? It must be some Measure of that Anointing, which was afterwards given more largely to them, in order to try Spirits, and in all other Cases, which concern the Gospel; otherwise they should not have believ'd with any Certainty, or upon Spiritual Conviction as to themselves; For if a Man has not something Divine to direct and inform his Understanding as to the true Relish, Judgment, and Application of what he may read in any Book, or externally might appear to his Senses in the Way of Extraordinary Vision, there could be no probable, much less certain Ground for his Belief in, or Knowledge of the Truth of that Thing, however true in it self. In short, *That which is Truth it self, which is able to teach all Things, to try all Things, and to lead into all Truth* (which the Scriptures (though Truth) cannot do; for then, they would be Clear, Plain, Perfect, uncapable of Additions, Diminutions, Corruptions, Mistranslations, &c.) *must be this more sure Word of Prophecy*; But that the Anointing which the Saints had received of him was able to do, as faith the Apostle *John, but the Anointing which ye have received of him abideth in you, and ye need not that any Man teach you; but as the same Anointing teacheth you of all Things, and is Truth, and is no Lye: And even as it hath taught you, ye shall abide in him*; Therefore this Anointing, thus able to do all Things, must needs be *that more sure Word of Prophecy:*

Prophecy; if *more* shall be allow'd. In short, *The Law written in the Heart*, is a more sure *Covenant, Law and Word* than the *Law written upon Stones*, or the *Outward Book of the Law*; else, *the Dispensation of the Law of Life within, the Gospel-State*, would be *less Sure*, and therefore *less Noble*, than the *Law without*, and the Prophesies of the Old Testament (so call'd) *more Certain*, than the *Scriptures of the New, that belong to a more excellent Dispensation, and are an Account of the fulfilling of those very Prophesies*: Nay, it would be to assert, that the Words of both Scriptures are more sure and certain, and our Regard ought to be more eminently after them, *than the very Spirit from whence they came*; which (at least in the Church of God) every one has receiv'd a Measure to profit with, and so perfectly subvert the very State of the Gospel, which was and is the time of the Pouring out of the Spirit upon all Flesh, and bringing Mankind to a more near, sure and living Word of Prophecy, than any Outward Writings whatever can possibly be.

§. 11. But because he tells us in another Place, that a little Skill in the Original, would free us from many Absurdities; we shall a little examine both what the Original Text will make for the Clearing the Point in Controversy, and what may be the Sense of some Men of Learning (a Thing he pretends to) and Impartiality (which I hope, he has not Confidence enough to pretend to) I will suppose then the *Prophesies* of the Ancients to be intended, but deny any *Comparison* at all to have been made between them, and that Voice in the Mount.

2 Pet. i. 19. Καὶ ἔχομεν βεβαιότερον τ̃ προφητικὸν λόγον, &c. *We also have a More sure Word of Prophecy* as by our late Translation render'd. I cannot perceive that Comparison in the *Greek*, so hugg'd by the *Priests*, and insisted upon by our *Adversary*, with manifest Design to prefer the *Writings before the Spirit that gave them forth*, the great Evangelical *Word of Prophesy*, for the Words without any Wrong, not only may, which were enough, but ought to be rendred thus: *Also we have a very sure Word of Prophecy*; which neither questions the Certainty of the Voice, nor so much as intends any the least Comparison at all with it; which I take to be the very Ground of that Opposition which is made against us. The Reason why I so render it, is ready: Καὶ, *Also*, I know our Translation hath, *but*, and it is commonly understood by our Adversaries for Δὲ, *But*, which is a great Injury to the Sense; for Καὶ, *Also*, is conjunctive, and signifies only another Confirmatory Testimony, whereas Δὲ, or *But*, is a Word that mostly doth, and to be sure in that Place would signify a Comparison and *Opposition*: *Also* then, not being taken in the same Sense with *But*, there is nothing therein that can make for the *Comparison*, or any *Opposition* whatsoever; Now the *Comparison* it self Βεβαιότερον, lately render'd *more sure*, is in the ancient Translations more truly interpreted, *sure*, and *very sure*; in which there is no Room for any Comparison, or Opposition in the least: And if *J. Faldo* has but Greek and Honesty enough, he must needs acknowledge, that Positives, Comparatives, and Superlatives are used promiscuously in the Greek. See *Acts* 25. 10. where ὡς καὶ σὺ κάλλιον ἐπιγινώσκεις, is rendred, *as thou very well know'st*; whereas in *J. Faldo*'s Sense, κάλλιον would be interpreted, *as thou knowest better than I*; which certainly the Apostle *Paul* never intended, when he spoke to *Festus*. And as Καὶ, *Also*, is connective, and joins the 19th Verse to the 18th Verse, so τ̃, the expositive and distinctive Article, doth not precede, but follow Βεβαιότερον. The *Syriack*, one of the most approv'd Versions by learned Men, has it thus, *We have over and above a true or sure Word of Prophecy*. The *Arabick*, *We have beside, a very true Prophetick Word*. The *Æthiopick* has a Comparison, not respecting the Sureness, but the Antiquity of the Voices: *We have over and above an ancienter Word, or Testimony*, which is so respecting Time: The *French, German, Low-Dutch, Swedish*, and several of our ancient *English* Translations run thus; *We have also the sure Prophetick Word*; *We have also the right sure Word of Prophesy*: *We have also the very sure Word of the Prophets*. All which imports no more, than that they had over and above their own particular Assurances of the Truth of the *Christian* Religion, *the Testimony of the Prophets*, whose Prophesies were fulfilled by the Coming of *Christ*, and the Pouring out of the Holy Spirit; but if it were more, it was only so in Point of Authority, with their *Adversaries*: Not that the Voice the Disciples heard in the Mount, was less sure in it self, or that Knowledge of *God* and *Christ*, through the Operation of the Power of the Gospel in the Hearts of those Believers, than the ancient Prophecies of the *Prophets*; But perhaps they were not so effectual to perswade, as the Words of the ancient undoubted Prophets to confirm their Allegations. Thus Christ

Chrift, in our Tranflation, *Search the Scriptures*, not that they were a more fure Teftimony than what he himfelf livingly and immediately gave forth; But they fo reputing them, whilft they oppofed him, his Direction, to fearch the Scriptures, was for Confirmation of the Truth, they feemed to gain-fay from the Scriptures. What then? Shall we fay that the Prophets are a more fure Teftimony, than what Chrift the Living Word of God himfelf declared, or the Saints became Witneffes of? By no Means; But rather, that the Old *Prophecies* are alfo a true Prophetical Teftimony, like a fmall Light in a dark Night, they do fhew forth a Prophetick Light, 'till the Day-ftar of fulfilling them (which fome then knew, and others preft after) *fhould arife in their Hearts*, which is that Bleffed State of *Witneffing*, *J. Faldo*, and *T. Hicks* have beftow'd fo many impious Scoffs upon.

* Parap. in Epift. 2 Pet. c. 1. v. 19.

To this agree many Learned Men. I will begin with * *Erafmus*; " If fo be that
" the Prophet's plain Oracles be in great and weighty Eftimation among you,
" which prophecy by figurative dark Shadows of Chrift, *of much more Gravity*
" *or Weight, ought fo evident a Declaration by the Father himfelf of his Son to be.*
" *They, with their Prophefies, prepare the Minds of Men to the Truth of his Gof-*
" *pel*; In that they fhadow and covertly point out the Thing that the Gofpel
" doth preach. The *Prophets* agree with the *Father's Voice*, if a Man do rightly
" interpret them; *The Thing that Men fet forth by Man's Device, may be perceiv'd*
" *by Man's Wit*; But *the Thing that is fet forth by the Infpiration of the Holy Ghoft*
" *requires an Interpreter infpir'd by the like Spirit.* A fevere Check to the Contra-Spirituality of *J. Faldo*, and thofe other of the Carnal and Apoftate Profeffors of Religion in our Time, who have forgot the Ground of their Fore-fathers Revolt from the Idolatry of *Rome*, and Superftitions of a degenerated Prelacy; as well as that it fhows how much more *Erafmus* inclines to give the Preference, if any there be, to the Voice of God than to the ancient Prophecies. He alfo quotes *Auguft.* to his Defence.

Bez. in loc.

Beza not only renders it, " *we have alfo a very firm Word of Prophecy*, fhutting
" out all Comparifon, (the *Priefts Break-neck)* but affirms, if it fhould be accepted,
" as a *firmer Word* of Prophecy, it can only relate to fuch, *who might have enter-*
" *tained fuch an Extraordinary Belief of the Writings of the Prophets*; and not that
" in themfelves they were a *furer Word* of Prophecy.

Vat. & Clar. in loc.

" *Vatablus* in fhort tells us, that Βεβαιότερον, or *more fure*, is a Comparifon for a
" *Pofitive, more fure*, for *fure*; ufual with the *Greeks*. So fays *Clarius*.

Grot. in loc.

And *Grotius*, that Great Man, thus renders this " Part of the Verfe [Καὶ ἔχομεν
" βεβαιότερον ἢ προφητικὸν λόγον] that is, fays he, the Writings of the Prophets have
" been always in Credit and of Force with us: But now much more, becaufe we
" have feen the Fulfilling of them by the *Meffiah*, and their Agreement with him.
Certainly then, others, befides the *Quakers*, muft needs have been Perverters of this Place of the Scripture, in *J. Faldo's* Senfe: But he may hear from *Grotius*, that the Scriptures are neverthelefs valuable by thofe who witnefs their Accomplifhment; but the more: A Notion very rife in *J. Faldo's* Head.

Let it fuffice, that we have Stated and Vindicated the *True Chrift*, to wit, *God manifeft in the Flefh*. That we have attributed to God, manifefted in that vifible Body, *what we believe to be congruous, and according to Scripture and found Reafon.* And laftly that thofe Scriptures, which he thought to difintereft us in, *are fully and clearly vindicated from his falfe Gloffes*; proving their exprefs Defign perfectly deftructive of thofe Ends, our *Adverfary* endeavour'd to bend them to, which were his own, and not the Truth's.

CHAP. XX.

Our Adverfaries Charges *deny'd. His Proofs fail him. The* Quakers *are True* Chriftians; *and* Quakerifm True *Chriftianity. We own and profefs the only True God that made Heaven and Earth.*

§. 1. HE has hitherto charged us, one would think, as home as ever Man did, for what is beyond *Denying the Lord's Chrift, and that Love he manifefted in the World for the Salvation of Mankind*: But it is our Happinefs, that his *Proofs* have been always found as weak, as his *Charge* Defperate, and the little Quarter promifed us by the one, more than made up by the faint Performances of the other; elfe, how terrible would this Grim Character be to our felves, and much

more

more, to others, who do, and yet will, we hope, believe better Things of us, *viz.* (Page 12, 13, 14.) *The Quakers are grofs Idolaters, and Quakerifm grofs Idolatry.* And he affures us, *if there be any fuch Thing as* Idolatry *in the World, he will prove us guilty in the highest Degree.*

The Way he takes to prove this heavy Charge is this. *Thofe which own and profefs that to be God, which is not, are grofs Idolaters; but the* Quakers *do fo.* The fecond Propofition (the firft being granted by all) he endeavours to prove thus. *Who own and profefs the Light within, and the Soul of every Man to be God, own and profefs that to be God, which is not God. But the* Quakers *do fo; therefore Idolaters.* The making good this Charge, will lie upon the Teftimony he brings out of our Friends Writings, fince he pretends to no lefs Demonftration, for every Thing he has to lay againft us. I deny in the Name of all that abufed People; *firft,* that we ever own'd or profefs'd *the Light within every Man to be God,* (tho' we fay, it is of God) much lefs that we worfhip it as fuch: And, *fecondly,* we do for ever renounce any fuch Principle, *As that the Soul of Man, fimply as fuch, is the very Effence or Being of God:* If he fails in his Proofs, he muft fall with Infamy to the Ground. The firft Man he hopes to make fure with, (pag. 119.) is G. *Fox the Younger:* The Words, as he quotes them, are thefe; " I will make " you know, that I the Light which lighteth every Man that cometh into the " World, that all through me fhould believe, am the True Eternal God, which " created all Things; that by me (the Light) all Things are upheld; and that " there is not another befide me can fave. *Fox* Young. p. 53. *Although,* fays he, *in this Paffage, he doth not call it the Light within,* Pag. 50. " You fcorn me the " Light in you, p. 54. which will not own me the Light in them. *They,* he fays, *that cannot from hence read the* Quakers *own and profefs the Light within to be God, are not like to be much the wifer, for what they read.* (p. 120.) This cuts off all Hopes of *J. Faldo's* being wifer; for I fuppofe he read what he writ, as blind as he is: However, for the fake of others, I will endeavour to reconcile this feeming Contrariety.

In the firft Paffage he grants, that *within Man* was not mentioned; and by his Silence, I fuppofe, I may conclude it *Orthodox.* For no Man that believes Scripture, will dare to deny that God is *Light;* That every Man is enlightned by *Him;* and that by *Him,* who is call'd *Light,* all Things are upheld, and that *He alone is Saviour:* A Doctrine *J. Faldo* teaches, Pag. 84. 85, 89. To the other Scraps of Matter I anfwer, That we never did, do, nor fhall affert, the God that made Heaven and Earth, to be comprehenfible within the Soul of Man: No, it is more impoffible, than that the Sun in the Firmament fhould be contain'd within the Body of any individual Perfon. *But that God, who is the Great Sun of Righteoufnefs, doth as truly caufe his Light Spiritual to arife upon the Souls of Men, as his Sun Natural upon their Bodies;* and as what Knowledge we have of the Natural Sun, is by it's Light, Operations and Effects upon the World, fo our Knowledge of the Eternal Sun of Righteoufnefs, *God (who is Light, and in whom is no Darknefs at all)* is only and alone, by His Divine Light, Operations, and Effects in, and upon our Underftandings and Confciences: So that when we fay, *That the Light is within any,* we do not intend the *Whole Being of Light,* nor was it in this grofs Senfe, that G. *Fox* the Younger ever meant it. But, *That He, who is the Eternal Fountain of all Life, and Sun of Light, caufeth his Light to vifit the Hearts, and fhine into the Confciences of all Mankind, as well of fuch as Rebel againft it, and fcorn it, to reprove them, as thofe who Receive it, and gladly fubmit to it, to direct and juftifie them.* Wherefore we utterly deny, that the Manifeftation in Man, ftrictly confider'd, *Is the Moft High God,* but a Manifeftation of, or from God, *By the Infhinings of His Bleffed Light.* And we cannot be faid to Worfhip the Manifeftation, but that *Eternal God, which is Light, that is thereby manifefted;* and all Worfhip otherwife founded, is not of God, nor pleafing to him, but of the Invention of Men, which he will confound; and this, Scripture and Reafon are ready to defend. *Scorning the Light in them, and not owning the Light in them,* by our *Adverfary* fo ftrongly infifted upon, is no more than *fcorning and difowning him who is the Light that fhines in them, and that gives Light to them.* What very Vanity then, is all his Boaft? And how does his Charge retort upon himfelf? But that we may fend it quite back, to the Pit from whence it came, let's hear how he proves our Belief of the Soul, to be God, which he begins to do, with no fmall Shew of Affurance, that he fhall clearly compafs his End.

§. 2. (Pag.

1673. Chap. XX.

§. 2. (Pag. 122. 123.) "Every Man has that which is One in Union, and like, "the Spirit of Chrift; even as Good as the Spirit of Chrift, according to it's "Meafure. *E. Burroughs's True Faith*, &c.

And what's this to the Purpofe? Can any Man be fo ftupid, as to think *E. Burroughs* ever intended the Soul of Man, that purely and fimply conftitutes him fuch? For he is fpeaking of that *Univerfal Grace, Light and Spirit*, which God has given unto all, whereby they may be led to Eternal Felicity. And unlefs he will fay, *That a Meafure of the Holy Spirit*, (a Scripture-Phrafe) *which God hath given every Man to Profit with*, is not in Union with Chrift, nor as Good in Kind, as the Spirit of Chrift (which our *Adverfary* fays, *Is God*) it will evidently follow, that what *E. B.* writes, is Sound and Scriptural; however this makes nothing for our *Adverfary's* prefent Charge. But he ends not with him.

(Pag. 123. " Now my Soul and Spirit is center'd in it's own Being with God, and "this Form of Perfon muft return from whence it was taken. *F. Howgil's Teftimony of E. B.*

This Expreffion is deliver'd to us by *Francis Howgil*, as *Edward Burroughs's*, a little before his Departure, in that Senfible Teftimony he gave to the late Life, Labours and Death, of that Worthy, Painful, and Effectual Labourer, and his *Companion in the Gofpel of JESUS*.

But to help *J. Faldo's* Intellects, that they may no more look afquint upon such Weighty, Dying Words, let him know, that *E. B.* fpoke not of God as his Soul's being by Nature, or as of that very Being (for fo the Soul would be God indeed, and yet fubject to all thofe Pollutions and Punifhments, which do, and will attend Wicked Men *(Blafphemy with a Witnefs)* but God, as that Being, which by Regeneration, the New Nature, and Spirit of Adoption, all the Righteous Souls are gather'd to, and center'd in, as their Everlafting Habitation, and Eternal Life. The World may perceive with Eafe, at what Rate, and what Terms, *J. Faldo* fwaggers over the *Quakers*: But let him boaft that puts off his Armour.

§. 3. (Pag. 123.) The next Perfon he fingles out, is *G. Fox*, thus anfwering a Prieft. "*But God and Chrift is in the Saints, and dwells in them, and he,* (the Prieft) "*is a Reprobate, and out of the Apoftle's Doctrine.* Great Myftery, pag. 16.

I perceive, *J. Faldo* will rather quarrel Scripture, when he meets it in a *Quaker's* Book, than not have fomething againft them: But certainly if that be the Way to prove that we believe, the Soul is God, to wit, that God and Chrift are in the Saints; What will become of the Scriptures? Will they efcape *J. Faldo's* heavy Cenfures? Which fay, *That Chrift is in his Saints, the Hope of Glory. I in them, and they in me. The Tabernacle of God is with Men, and he will dwell in them.* Muft every Thing, that is in another, be neceffarily of that in which it is? But I hope, his Heat being abated, he may difcern the Weaknefs of his Attempts againft us. To proceed:

I. Pennington he alfo brings in, to make Good his Charge: How ferviceable he may prove, will better appear, when we have examin'd the Paffage. "That "which the Lord from Heaven begetteth of his own Image and Likenefs, of his "own [Subftance] of his own Seed, of his own Spirit and Pure Life. Queft. 27. But *J. Faldo* has mift his Aim, and miftaken his Man; for *I. P.* is not now fpeaking of the Soul of Man, fimply confider'd, *but of that Divine Life, Nature, Image, and Birth, that God by his Word of Life, creates, or begets in the Souls of thofe who once lived not to God, but themfelves, bearing the Image of the Earthly; and do turn at his Reproof, to walk in the Way of Life.* This will not move the Bufinefs one Jot farther, on the Behalf of our Enemies Charge.

§. 4. (Pag. 127.) We will clofe this Point, with a Paffage out of *Samuel Fifher's Velata quædam Revelata*, Pag. 13. of which he is very Chary: "As to the Spirit "of Man, which concurs to the conftituting of Man in his Primitive Perfection; "it is the Breath of Life, which God breathed into his Soul, after he had formed "him, as to his Body, of the Duft of the Earth; whereby he came to be a Living "Soul, a Soul, that did partake fomething of God's own Life,——This (Spirit of "Man) is that Living Principle of the Divine Nature, which Man did before his "Degeneration, and fhall again after his Regeneration partake of.

This Charge, fays our Adverfary, *being of fo black and horrid a Nature, I did judge it meet to prove it by abounding Inftances; and now Reader, put on the largeft Charity, and give me thy Verdict, if I have not made appear, that the* Quakers *are grofs Idolaters*, &c.

To answer which briefly, and to Purpose, and to close this Chapter, with a contrary Conclusion, I say, *That the Spirit of Man is not to be taken, as of, or from Man, or that it is any Part of Man's Nature, taking Man in an Abstractive Sense.* And had he been so fair, as to give us *S. Fisher's* Words at large, they would have prov'd of Age enough to answer for themselves. *S. Fisher* is to be understood of that Spirit, or Breath of Life, not that made Man simply a Living Creature, of a meer Reasonable Capacity, *but that Divine Life or Breath, which makes alive to God, and gives a kind of Heavenly Animation, Motion, or Life, to live to him, which constituted* Adam, *not a meer Man, but a Blessed, Holy, Heavenly-minded Man, before his Degeneration.* And that *S. Fisher* did never intend it of the Natural Soul of Man, but rather of the Divine Life of the Soul, without which the Soul is destitute of the Knowledge of the True and Living God, his own Words very plainly show: For if *S. Fisher* intended that Spirit, which is the Divine Principle, that Man did partake of before his Degeneration; certain and clear it is, that since Man did, under that Degeneration, partake of his own Soul, or else he could not have been a Man, *S. Fisher never meant the meer Soul of Man, but the Life of that Divine Principle which regenerates and renews the Soul unto a Life of Purity and Blessedness.*

So that we conclude, the *Quakers* not believing any such Strange and Unscriptural Doctrine, *As that the Soul of Man, is the God that made the Heavens and the Earth* (for so it would make it self, and what is greater than it self) *They are not those* Idolaters *they have been represented, and foully Characteriz'd by* J. Faldo: *But are Innocent and Free of all such Imputation; and he their Accuser, most of all Condemnable; yea, and that for* Idolatry *too, who professeth no Knowledge of God, but from Outward Sense, by Hearing, Reading,* &c. pag. 91. So that being destitute of the *Revelation of the Son*, that only can make known the Living Father, what Apprehensions he has of God, are not Experimental, but Imaginary; and Worshipping such an *Idea*, he Worshippeth not the True God, but the *Images of his own Brain*; therefore an *Idolater*. See Bishop *Andrews* upon the *Commandments*, and *Pagnin* upon the Word ירון.

CHAP. XXI.

Our Adversary *at a Loss to prove his Charge. We own so much of the* Resurrection *as the Scriptures express; more Curiosity Dangerous and Condemnable. Eternal Rewards own'd by us.* J. Faldo's *Book will prove it to Him, and our Tribulations to Us.*

§. 1. p. 132, 135. THE two last Charges, of this Second Part of his Discourse, *are our Denial of the Resurrection of the Dead* (that is, Dead Bodies) *and future Rewards:*

To the First; he brings in *I. Pennington* thus: " We say, that Christ is the Re-
" surrection, to raise up that which *Adam* lost, and to destroy him who deceiv'd
" him, *(viz. Adam)* so Christ is the Resurrection unto Life, of Body, Soul and
" Spirit, and so renews Man, &c. *Princip. Elem. People call'd* Quakers, p. 134. Upon which he comments, *What is this Resurrection, but what they call Regeneration?* (it seems he does not) *and the Resurrection of the Body is but in the same Sense, as the Soul and Spirit is raised.*

I can't help it, if *J. Faldo* has made a Quotation out of *I. P.* so unapplicable to his Business. I hope, none are so blind or partial, as to be angry, that *I. P.* did not write to his Purpose; it was sufficient that he spake to his own, or rather to the Truth's. Our *Adversary* falls downright upon us, with a Charge of Denying the Resurrection of the Body, and is angry that the Place he produces, helps not his Design. Certainly, with sober Men, the Blame will not lye at our Doors for not making good his Charge, but at his own, that he exhibited one he could not prove. But will he deny the Resurrection in *I P's* Words? If he does, I pronounce him no *Christian*; nor indeed will a bare Confessing to it render him One: And where he stands, I fear, he is but too far from both. Let it suffice, that those Words are a modest, serious, and full Answer to this *Caviller*, since he does plainly acknowledge *All* that the *first* Adam *lost to be restor'd by Christ the second* Adam; and all that the Sin of one incurred, *the Righteousness of the other Redeem'd from*. Now let his Notions of the Way and Method of Effecting this be what they will,

1673.
Chap. XXI

we desire not to be wise beyond what the Lord sees convenient for us, as this busy Intruder into sacred Mysteries hath done, that lives in the Land, not of Light, but gross Darkness within, and whose very borrowed, made, framed Light, from Reading, Art, Study and his own Conceptions, is the very Blackness of Darkness.

§. 2. (Page 136.) But he affirms, that *George Whitehead* should say, being prest in the Matter, that *he did not believe his Body should rise again after it's Death*, which he can prove by many Witnesses.

I know not if ever G. *Whitehead* did so express himself; But I see, every Expression must be treasured up to defend a decrepid Cause: Truth stands in no need of such Watchings, that would make a Man an Offender for a Word. But what if he did say so, and I should second him, would it follow that we deny a Resurrection? I am sure I will deny all such Consequences. Doth not the Apostle say expresly, 1 Cor. 15. 36, 37, *Thou Fool —— thou sowest not that Body that shall be.* Is Scripture grown into such mean Request with *J. Faldo*; or doth his Rage against the *Quakers* so transport him, that he knows not Scripture, when he meets it from a *Quaker*?

But says our *Adversary*, upon a like Place, and to this Purpose, (p. 139.) viz. *We shall all be changed: I would ask, if they would be content to be refused their Debts, if contracted before* Quakers, *and demanded when* Quakers; *I suppose they would believe that the Change in a Person, is not the Change of a Person; and that they are the same still to whom the Money was and is due.* But how clever soever any may think this *Simile*, we will prove it Lame and Defective; For the Change was not of the Body any farther, than as the Soul govern'd it after a new Way of Living. I cannot think that *J. Faldo* will dare to say, *that a Man's Body is rendred ever the less Corruptible by any the best Change the Soul can make in this World.* The Question is about what that Change must be which makes a Corruptible an Incorruptible Body? I mean not by Corrupt, *Sinful*, but that gross Elementary *Matter, which is subject to those Impressions, Influences, Mutations, and Passions which we see all Sublunary Bodies are subject to.* Either the Resurrection of the Body must be without that Matter, or it must not? If it must, *then is it not that same Numerical Body*; and so, their proper and strict taking of the Word *Resurrection*, they must let go. If it must not be without that same gross Matter it died with, then I affirm, it cannot be *Incorruptible*, because it will carry with it that which will render it Corruptible *ad Infinitum*.

And what can be more Unreasonable, than that Bodies compounded of this Elementary World, which, says our *Adversary, shall, and must by Nature have an End*, should out live their own Matter, and which is more, never End; I say, we cannot see how that which is of *Dust* should be Eternal, whilst that from whence it came, is by Nature but Temporal. And that which is yet most of all Irreconcileable with Scripture and right Reason, is, *that the Loss and Change of Nature from Corruptible to Incorruptible, Natural to Spiritual, should not make it another Body*. In vain do such dispute against the *Popish Transubstantiation* as an Absurd and Impossible Thing, who themselves are guilty in a Case of the like Nature. The *Romanists* affirm a Change in the Sacrament, though our Senses tell us it is the same Thing that ever it was.

Our *Adversaries* in the Point of the *Resurrection* boldly affirm, that it is the same Body, and yet Transubstantiated from Natural to Spiritual, or chang'd from what it was, to something it never was. For my Part, I think the Last not less Impertinent, and the Former more expresly Scriptural.

But because such Things run Men into *Unprofitable Questions, various Searches, and a Philosophical Way of Discoursing*, no Ways tending to God's Honour, nor the Soul's Profit and Comfort, I will conclude this Head with our Confession, *That every Seed shall have it's own Body, and that such an one, as it will please Almighty God to give*; and Thou Fool, belongs most rightfully to him, who acquiesceth not in an humble Contentedness with the Good-will of God, and that Manner of Body he shall give. And I think it would make more for Love, Peace, and Good-will, if our Enemies would leave those Things with God, *quicquid supra nos, nihil ad nos*, whose Will be done in Earth, as it is in Heaven.

§. 3. (Page 141, 142.) The Second Head of the Charge to be consider'd in this Chapter; to wit, *Our not Professing of Eternal Rewards*, needs no other Answer, than, That none ever read so; He quotes no such Thing, nay, he says, that *he has searcht, but to no Purpose;* And I challenge him to name one Person reputed by us, to be of us, *that has ever affirmed so gross a Thing* Well then may I call this the *Last great Lye of his Second Part of Lyes,* and *Slanders too*; such as he will be found much too weak to defend before the Tribunal of our God, where we have whereof both to answer, and justly accuse him before Angels, as well as that we have now plainly refuted him before Men.

But he makes this a Consequence of Denying the Resurrection, which is obviously weak; since whatever we have scrupled of the common gross Notion of the Resurrection of this Corruptible Body, we have ever held an Eternal State of Recompence.

But so mean are his Proofs for this Conjecture, if I may give them that Name, that they show far more of his Ignorance and Malice, than our Faith, in that *Atheistical Opinion:* However hear them. R. *Farnsworth,* said he, *was not saved by what Christ did at* Jerusalem; therefore, says he, *already saved:* But can any in their Wits think, he meant saved from Sin here, *to be the whole of Salvation and Blessedness?* O weak Man! Well, but *I. Pennington* says, *Who forget God are to be turn'd into Hell. What Hell?* says *J. Faldo, only in this Life.* A very Lye, and Infamous Slander: *J. Faldo's* Book against us, unrepented of, *will prove, we believe, that Eternal Wo and Vengeance shall be the Wages of that Hellish Work.* We say, That in this Life, Men have an *Earnest of Heaven and Hell,* and some Sense of both States, *as they are Good or Bad*; but never did we affirm *Men to enjoy that full Measure of Joy, or Torment, they shall have as their Eternal Reward or Recompence hereafter.*

But E. *Burroughs, the Day he died,* said, *he was now putting off this Manner of Person, and returning to his own Being.* Those are not his very Words; but what then? Is this to prove we deny an Eternal Recompence, to produce his own Testimony to an Everlasting State of Blessedness, that he Himself was just entring into? But *W. Penn* vindicates an Heaven within after his Fashion, against the Author of the *Spirit of the* Quakers *tried.* And what is this to denying an Eternal Heaven for the Righteous? Did not the Saints enjoy *Heavenly Places* in Spirit, when on Earth? O Carnal Man! Benighted by the Power of Darkness, whose Understanding the thick Fogs and Mists of Ignorance, Malice and Revenge, have overcast; *that thou call'st Good Evil, and Evil Good; Light Darkness, and Darkness Light.*

§. 4. I shall here, after his Example, resume the Question, and collect all that has been said, and made evidently to appear on the Behalf of *True Christianity,* and the Apostolical Professors of it, (I mean the People of God call'd *Quakers*) and so end this Discourse, respecting the Main of the Book.

If QUAKERISM *(so call'd) be not another Dispensation than that of Christ, preached and settled by the Apostles.*

If it deny not the Scriptures.

If it deny not all, nor any of the Ordinances of the Gospel.

If it deny not any Influence of Christ's Transactions, above 1600 *Years since, unto our Justification, and Salvation,* as he phrases it.

If it deny not Jesus *the Son of* Mary, *(after the Flesh) otherwise God over all, to be the Christ of God.*

If it own not false Gods, and be not Idolatry.

If it deny not the true Resurrection of the Dead.

If it doth affect *(an affected Expression of our Adversary's) or rather hold forth a future Blessedness or Misery in another World, according to the Deeds done in this*;

Then Quakerism, *in our Adversary's Account, must be* Christianity:

But *all these Things are true, and have been proved of* Quakerism *(so called) Therefore Quakerism, so call'd, is true Apostolical, or Primitive Christianity.* And this shall close our Chapter, and my honest and clear Answer to the Second Part of his Discourse, which makes up more than three Parts of Four of his Uncharitable and Disingenuous Treatise.

AN APPENDIX:

BEING

A REPLY to that last PART of his BOOK, which pretends to answer the First of my *Spirit of Truth Vindicated*, Entituled, *An Examination of the First Part of W. P's Spirit of Truth*, &c. *with a Rebuke of his Exorbiancies*.

§. 1. Though there has been no *Adversary* which has fallen to my Share, that has shewn more Incivility, and less Learning, (a Thing he pretends to) in Answer to any of my Books, than *J. Faldo* has done in this last Part of his *Quakerism no Christianity*; yet how little soever I have, at least to bestow upon him, I desire to manifest more Temper, Truth and Civility, than to recompence him with that ill-bred Language, those School-puns, and loose, irreverent, if not prophane Sayings, amidst the most weighty Matters, it hath pleased him to give me, for a great Share of his Answer to the *first Part of my Book*. I will rather betake my self to single out the Strength of his Objections, if any there be, and bestow my Time in Vindication of the Truth, than to rail, revile, undervalue and stigmatize with I know not how many disgraceful Epithets, a Way that never yet reacht into any Man's Conscience. And this Ken I have of *J. Faldo*, That all his Discourse of Christianity, interlin'd with so much Babling, Prattle, and base Abuse, would never move a sober Turk; and a *Banian* is a Saint to a Congregation of such Kind of *Christians*.

§. 2. He tells me (p. 2.) *he expected great Things, when first he set about to read my Book, and began to stagger in his Mind, as to that Ingenious Piece*, call'd, *The Spirit of the Quakers tried*, or to that Purpose: But knowing himself better, I hope he will excuse me, if I do not believe him. He never had that Opinion of any Thing writ in Defence of a People he testifies such irreconcileable Hatred to, which is none of the meanest Blots in his 'Scutcheon. *Penn, the Answerer, if he were not furnisht with Fore-head and Tales beyond Measure, his Pamphlet would have had nothing remarkable in it*; Whether this be most a Lye or an Abuse, I know not, perhaps the *Reader* may; but sure I am, there is more of both than stands with true *Christianity*, to give a Comprehensive Undervalue of what he can never answer, which perhaps goes for one among such as have Faith in him, or know no better.

§. 3. But he is angry at my stating the *Question*, thus, (p. 3.) *Whether God's Holy and Unerring Spirit is or should be the proper Judge of Truth, Rule of Faith, and Guide of Life, among Men, especially under the Administration of the Blessed Gospel of our Lord and Saviour Jesus Christ, or no?* I affirm it, and proceed to prove it by Scripture and Reason. Upon which be pleased to hear his Reflection, and from Hence make a Judgment, what that Spirit must be that should so pretend to answer my *Spirit of Truth*, &c. Considering his Words foregoing (which are too many and too worthless to transcribe) And what he drives at in the handling of this Question, I never read one so lame and deformed in my Life come forth with such State and Confidence, and such a Train and Rout of Mediums as deformed as it self; *There is in it neither Logick nor Honesty*: Certainly if he had not turned Quaker, and in that Fall put all out of Joint, he could not likely after such good Nursing have been thus lamentably cripled in his Intellects, and somewhat besides.

One would think the Strain of this Comment were Answer to it self: Why so much flourish, and little done? Must Noise supply the Absence of Reason? and base Reviling go for Confutation? Shallow Man! What Lameness is there in the Question? I profess I see none, nor has he so much as pointed at one Limb that is defective in all this Rabble of Reflection. [*I have neither Logick nor Honesty*] It had been to be wish'd that he had shown more of both in saying so, or held his Tongue. [*But my turning Quaker has put something out of Joynt*] But what, I know not, unless the good Opinion I once undeservedly had of such Mountebank *Priests*. But give him his due, he is the first Man that ever acquainted me with the Ground of Cripling. I was never yet wise enough to think it a Natural Effect of Ill-nursing; but Carelesness in Nurses, Falls and the like have brought it. I perceive he is not only a Well-wisher to *Physick* by his hard Word, *Ebullitions*, but a small Pretender to *Chyrurgery*, by his Term, out of joynt; when he has given better Proof of his well-setting to rights his own dis-joynted, or, if he will, dislocated Cause with that of Christianity, he may better set up for a Religious Bonesetter, and in the mean Time he can pass but for a Quack.

[*But I have no Logick*] And why? [Because I say, pag. 37. there is no more Difference to me between a Judge, Rule and Guide, than essentially there can be in the Wisdom, Justice and Holiness of God; he should have added, says *J. Faldo*, nor between Truth, Faith and Life amongst Men.]

I would know of any Man that can think himself capable of judging in the plainest Case; if this be an Answer to mine Argument; I said then; I do again, that there is no more Difference in them respecting the Principle, than essentially there can be *in the Wisdom, Justice, and Holiness of God*, which are but so many Words to express the Perfection of one and the same Being, for he is all, and that in all. Wise in being Just, and both in being Holy; They are inseparable, for *That* which gives me a right Sense or Judgment of Truth from Error, is as well to me a Rule what I should believe or disbelieve, and a Guide what I should practise or not practise, as at first it was my Judge of what was Truth from what was Error; All which sober, and indeed unanswerable Arguing he thought fit to overlook, which is very Disingenuous. I say, that *the same Spirit, which is a Judge, is a Rule and Guide, even in that very Act, wherein it is a Judge,* and that unavoidably; Therefore to distinguish them is frivolous, and to maintain one to be a Rule, and the other a Judge, is absurd and heterodox.

For *his Addition*, it is not hard to answer, *That there is more Difference between Truth, Faith and Life*; for one may be without the other two, I mean Truth abstractly: But if it shall be understood of Truth received into the Heart, I say, that there is so great an Affinity between Truth, true Faith, and an Heavenly Life, that they follow each other almost at an instant, and cannot be separated from each other.

§. 4. But *he is Angry that I should use those Words of Lord and Saviour in my Question*. I thought them sober; and I am sure I meant them of him that was before *Abraham*, that in Time appeared for the Salvation of his People, however he would disinterest us in them; but indeed the Way he takes to do it will do us no harm: For that he may insinuate we mean another Thing, he calls it *Playing at Blind-Man's-Buff*, which is worse than a *Buffle-headed Expression*. Is this your Gospel-Minister? Let him go wrestle at *Morefields*, play Foot-ball Matches, turn Ringer, a Practice he pleads for in his Book, and leave off Prophaning the Holy Name of God with such an unhallowed Mouth and unbridled Tongue. Some of my Scripture-Arguments he pretends to refute, I shall mention, and what he objects, that both may be weighed in an equal Ballance.

§. 5. The first Scripture by me urged is that in *Genesis* 6. 3. *My Spirit shall not always strive with Man,* &c. From whence I infer, that God's unerring Spirit both did so strive either for Conviction and Conversion, or to prompt to farther Attainments, and that they were not at that Time of the World without an Infallible Spirit to Teach, Rule, Judge, &c. To which he says, *My Argument is a Thicket of Impertinencies, that a Body had need of good Arithmetick to number the Terms, that I am a none-such for Diving, if I can fetch up from this Scripture what is mention'd in this Proposition.*

What need there is of this little Wit, a better Word for Pedantry, I know not, and I believe more are of my Mind; but if my Consequences are so Impertinent, and so Numerous that ordinary Arithmetick will not serve to reckon them, and lastly, so unnatural as that the Scripture will afford me not one of them, I am greatly to be blamed. But because what he says for me may be of more Force than all that I can offer, let this Passage be weighed [*It is more than probable that the Spirit did strive with them to make them better than they were, yet none of these Ends are expressed in the Text*] An eminent Contradiction to him, and which is more, to it self; For if the Spirit strove to make them better, then since that better consisted in a Discovery of Good and Evil, with an Election of the Good, and a Denial of the Evil, I would fain know of *J. Faldo*, how that could be, and the Spirit of Truth not be what I have instanced in my Argument. Was it not then a Judge of what was Good from Evil? A *Rule* how to chuse one and refuse the other? A *Guide*, to lead, direct, enable to the Choice, and preserve in it? O Weak Man! Is this the Upshot of all thy poor Insults? But why may not *William Penn* express the Scope of any Scripture in his Argument, though he find not the very Words in the Text, if it will bear them, especially since *J. Faldo* himself allows it, both in granting that the Spirit strove to make them better, which is not verbally exprest, and by his Weekly Practice of Preaching, where nothing is more frequent than his Exposition, and after a sort too which the Text many Times will not bear.

But he tells me that *my Question is, to prove the Spirit's Teaching indefinitely, or without Difference of Persons; and my Proof speaks of the Spirit's Striving with Wicked Men.* For this he cries out, that *I wander from Truth and Reason, and am Infatuated,* questioning, *if my Conscience have any Eyes*; and has Impudence enough to tell me, that *I am beholden to him for giving no farther Discovery of my Vanity and Folly,* &c.

How groundless his Cavil and Reflection are, and with what rude and unhandsom Terms he is pleased to give them, I need not trouble my self to shew; But certainly if God affords Bad Men his Spirit to strive with them; then Good Men, who cannot be such without it, but Sensual and Devilish rather, must needs have this Holy Spirit, as well to preserve them, as that it made them such; if so, then may we conclude our *Adversary* Weak, as well as Envious, who from that *Text* denies my Proof of the Universality of God's Spirit. For what is it but to say, that though all Wicked Men have the Spirit striving, Good Men have it not? Whose Conscience wants Eyes at this Time, will not be hard to determine; but sure I am, it was his Wisdom to leave off where he did, since his reputing my Sober Scriptural Argument Infatuation, Folly, &c. was the most evident Mark of his own he could well have given us.

§. 6. The Second Scripture I urge, and which he perverts, is that in *Neh.* 3. 20. *Thou gavest also thy Good Spirit to instruct them*; which, *says he*, without being so ingenuous as to mention, much less consider, and answer my Argument upon it, *is mainly the Spirit of God, which he put upon* Moses *and* Joshua, for which he quotes *Numb.* 11. 17. & 27. 18. *Psal.* 77. 20. But does he think us so Credulous, as to receive this Stuff for Gospel? Certainly we must commit the greatest Cruelty upon our Understandings to strain them to such a Fiction. He might with as good Reason have said, that the Pillar of Cloud by Day, and Fire by Night were seen of none but *Moses* and *Joshua*, as to grant, they had the immediate and general Benefit of them, and at the same Time deny them to have had the immediate Benefit of the Spirit's Teachings. Besides, had they not had some Measure of the Spirit of God, they could never have known that *Moses* had been so inspired, nor have so willingly bowed under *Moses* as they did, and have shewn themselves so well assured of his Conduct. Nor can the Objection of their Rebellion at Times invalidate our Reason, since it were to say, that they sinned not against the Spirit of God in themselves, but in *Moses* only. But because they did sin against the Holy Ghost in themselves, and that it was the greatest Ground for the Charging of Rebellion against them, we may well conclude that they had the Spirit, that is, the Conviction of it.

The Scriptures he brings, are no more to his Purpose, than the Story of *Tobit* and his Dog: For though there was the Gift of the Spirit poured out upon *Moses*, *Joshua*, and others, that was not common to the People; yet this proves not that they were not without a Measure of the Unerring Spirit to teach them what was acceptable with God; The Difference was not, that *Moses*, &c. had the Spirit, and the People had it not, but that he and some others had the Spirit of Government, and the People had it not: But what is this for him? *Doth not the same Eternal Spirit that teacheth to Rule, also teach People to be ruled?* Nay, I affirm,
that

that as God did gift several by his Holy Spirit to Govern, and consequently they had the Spirit; so did he bestow of his Holy Spirit upon the People, to enable them to live according to the Government, and consequently they had as truly their Measure of the Holy Unerring Spirit, as had *Moses, Joshua*, &c. theirs.

§. 7. The Third Scripture he would unconcern me in, is this, *And the Inspiration of the Almighty giveth them Understanding.* Upon this *he asks* me this Question.

But doth this encourage Men to cast off all External Means, and the Use of their Reason? Nothing less, says he; *Nothing less,* say I too: And who can help it, if he understands me so; But that he may be as base, as base can be, he asks this Question as the Result of my Argument upon the Place, and yet never answers it at all: But I cannot help it, if *J. Faldo* will render me a Fool, that he may shew himself Wise, I confess he wants some such Fool for his Work, and his own Weakness may tempt him to that Dishonesty. Only I would have the *Reader* know, that Reason, Memory and Understanding are all useful Servants; we deny them not a Place in the Heavenly Work, but as Instruments, not Agents; which should not move of themselves to Religious Worship, but in and by the Motions of the Holy Spirit of God.

§. 8. The next Scripture he thinks I abuse, is this; *Whither shall I go from thy Spirit; or Whither shall I flee from thy Presence?* From whence (*says he*) you can scribble thus. *If God's unerring Spirit be so nigh, and the Sense of it so certain, it must be either to Reprove for Evil done, or to Inform, Uphold, Lead and Preserve, in Reference to all Good: Now, in which of the two Senses it shall be taken, the Presence of God's Eternal Spirit, and his being the Saints Instructor, Judge, Rule and Guide, are evidently deduceable from the Words*——*rudis indigestaq; moles,* worse than ever Bear brought forth her Cubbs, says *J. Faldo*: But this is not all; hear him farther, *which with her Licking may be brought into some Shape, but your Products are so defective, both in Truth, right Reason, Syntax, and Sense, that it is no Dis-reputation to your Adversary to be confounded by them.* A notable Excuse for no Answer but Silence, which is always counted Answer enough by him, when he hath never another to give. Again,

It is an effectual (but an impudent) Course, to Silence all the World from Opposing you, by writing such confident confused Non-sense: We may suppose then that there is such a Thing as confused Sense. Yet again,

Were it not for the Sake of many who conceit your Infallibility, which you are here so blindly pleading for, I would as soon abandon my Time (Non-sense) *to dispute with a distracted Man in his Raving Fits, as with* W. Penn, *till he come better to himself, than I find him in his Pamphlet.*

And *Reader*, Canst thou think that my Adversary has taken a fair or probable Way to bring me to my self again, whose best Arguments are sordid, ill-bred Names, down-right Lyes and Slanders? I challenge any Man that can soberly pretend to Religion, to so much as abet this Manner of Proceeding against me, and the Way I profess: If this were to be *Christian, as it is Antichristian*; were I a *Turk*, I should take great Care I came not within the very Suburbs of so base a Profession. Where's *J. Faldo*'s Reading, Learning, Conscience, in this one Passage? I will not so much as attempt the Defence of my Argument; for it were to say, it needed my Assistance, or that my Adversary had done something to assayl its Security, who has so pleaded the Insobriety and Truth of it, by an Opposition that could become none but a Creature as forlorn of all Honesty as himself, that it is a Credit to my Cause, almost equal with our Clearness, that so much Rancour and Ignorance set themselves against it. This is no less Man than your Vaunting, Strutting, *J. Faldo* his own self, who thinks as well of himself, and deserves as little of it from other Men, as any Person that has come within my Ken a long Time. In short, whether I am out of my Wits, or he out of all Bounds of good Sense or Manners, shall be left with the *Reader* to determine. For my part; if this be the Way he intends to take to confute his Opposers, he is like to answer himself; And to give him his due, he is as good at it as most Men I know; and 'tis to be hop'd he may increase in that Science.

§. 9. But he tells me, that my main Fallacies are these two; First, *from an Infallible Spirit-Teaching, to the Infallibility of the Subjects in which the Spirit dwells as a Teacher.* Next, *from the Spirit's Teaching, to it's Immediate and Peculiar Teaching.* If the *First* be true, without any Consideration had to the Obedience of the Creature, and his being guided by the Holy Spirit, I will yield it to him that I have mistaken, though not fallaciously, that implying a Design to do so, which I had not: And for the *Second* I am content to stand by the Charge, not of a *Fallacy*, but *our Faith*, and such as is Defensible both from Scripture and Reason.

But if the Truth of no *Argument* I have made, nor any Expression that has fallen from me, doth so much as imply his Charge, let him not be angry with me, that I say, *He is one of the basest Perverters among Men*: And if that very Passage by which he hopes to prove this great Deceit of mine, is found mute in the Case, I hope no *Reader* will be so unjust to refuse me the Censure of his being *an Unfair Adversary*.

§. 10. The first Place he thinks to make for him, is this; *Quench not the Spirit:* On which I argu'd thus; Those to which he gave the Caution had the Spirit, if those could not quench it, that had it not, consequently the Primitive Churches were not without an Unerring Spirit. To which he says, *but suppose they had the Spirit, it is a miserable erroneous and weak Conclusion, that they were Infallible.* How far this makes for him, or rather how greatly he has mistaken me is evident, if it may be considered that there is not one Word of any Man's being Infallible in all my Argument; only that the Primitive Churches had an infallible Spirit, not of their own, or from themselves, but from God; and that they were only so in their Knowledge or Determinations from the unerring Guidance of God's Spirit; unless they either were without the Anointing, or the Anointing was Fallible, both which are contradicted by the Apostle *John* in the noted Passage, 1 *John* 2. 27. So that my *Adversary* is manifestly guilty of that Fault He doth with no small Aggravation charge upon me, *viz.* That from my Arguing the Certainty of the Primitive Churches having the Holy Spirit of God to direct them, from the Impossibility of their Quenching what they had not, he makes me to conclude *the Infallibility of the Churches, whether they were led by it or no*; As if I intended to plead the Infallibility of private Spirits, and not rather of the Holy Spirit of God, and such only as were conformable to it.

§. 11. His other Cavil confirms the Truth of my former Argument, and his own great Ignorance or Baseness. My Words are these, *If God sends forth his Spirit into the Hearts of his Children, then are they not without an Infallible Spirit*, grounded upon that Scripture, *Because ye are Sons, God hath sent forth the Spirit of his Son into your Hearts*, Gal. 4. 6. To which he says; *Your Adversaries have not so little Knowledge of the Spirit of God, as to say the Spirit of God is Fallible, nor yet are so Ignorant of your Spirits and of the Scripture, as to say, you are Infallible.* Now I have two Things to desire of the Ingenuous *Reader*; *First*, to find me out so much as one Syllable in my Argument, that infers or concludes the Spirits of such to be infallible, into whose Hearts God has shed abroad his infallible Spirit, whether they are led by it or not; or that I could intend a concluding of the Spirit of Man infallible, because God has given his own unto Men, that is unquestionably so. I am sure such a Thought never entred my Mind, as fruitful of them as our *Adversary* may be; *Adversary* I may well say, not only because he is one, but that he acknowledges to me as much, which let him know however, I am not such to him.

The *Second* Thing I have to desire of the Candid *Reader*, is, that he would weigh with himself, how Unjust this Man is to me, to infer Infallibility to Men, from my Affirming it to belong only to the Spirit of God; And as if he fear'd, I should not be as Heterodox as his Envy would have me, to conclude on my Account from what I urged to prove, *That God's Children in all Ages had an Infallible Spirit to Judge, Rule, and Guide them;* the Affirmative of the very Question debated (that is, God's Spirit) That every such one was Infallible in and from his own private Spirit. O Monstrous Perversion! I would impute it to his Mistake of me, it being far better to be ignorant than dishonest, but he will not let me, who a little below has Impudence enough to write; but we are Not Ignorant, *that your Principles make no Difference, or Distinction between the Spirits of God's People and the Spirit of God;* manifestly intending, (not that they are at variance, for so we should esteem his Charge a Piece of Justice, but) that the Spirit of the Creature and the Spirit of God are but one Spirit; An Absurdity that never fell from us. How many Times hath *J. Faldo* been guilty in his Discourse of plain Forgery and Dis-

Dishonesty against us. So certain as there is a God in Heaven, terrible will his Judgment be in that Great Day of Inquest, if he repent not.

§. 12. (Pag. 21, 22, 23,) He makes a great Stir about my checking the late *Socinian*, for making Christ the Head of a Fallible Body, saying, *If Christ be Head to none but the Infallible, Wo to the Poor Saints, who have trusted hitherto they had an Head in Heaven, who hath Pity on the Ignorant, and those that are out of the Way ; and I am sure Christ is then none of your Head.*

We have enough, and leave his very ill Language out. (1.) It is granted to us, that Christ is Head to a Fallible Body, or at least to Fallible as well as Infallible. I charge him to give us one Scripture for this, or he is gone, for all his Idle Puns, Shifts, and scoffing Flings at us. (2.) That a Man may be a Saint, which if we take it strictly, is one of that Number the Apostle prayed, *The Churches might be of* ; I mean those which were sanctified throughout, in Body, Soul and Spirit : I say, *That a Man may be such a Saint, and yet be Fallible or Erring.* (3.) That the Saints are ignorant and out of the Way : Truly this Doctrine very well becomes *J. Faldo*, I had rather it should be his than mine ; I will venture then in the Scale of Truth, without thinking I am on Hazard in the Matter, especially when, if I err, *That hinders not from being a Saint and Member of Christ :* But *J. Faldo, Can a Man be a Saint, and yet ignorant of so much of God, as is requisit to constitute him such? Or can he be such, and yet out of the Way which renders him a True Saint ?* It is the first Time that I ever heard in so many Words, *That a Man might be a Saint, and out of God's Way.* O Doctrine of Devils ! No Marvel so many Unclean Fowls flock to this Carcass. What ! *Saints*, and err from God's Way ? *Strange !* Saints, and ignorant of God's Mind ? It seems then, that neither Ignorance, nor Erring from God's Way, indispose any to be Saints. If this be not a plain Contradiction to the whole Record of Scripture, none ever was, is, or shall be esteemed such to the End of the World : How many, how grievous, and how sharp have God's Complaints been against those who have left the Right Way of the Lord, which has been the *Way of Light and Righteousness, the Just Man's Path through every Generation ?* No Wonder that such Doctrines are both greedily received and seriously maintained, that sooth up People in the Belief of such pernicious Soul-murdering Doctrines. And the Truth is, and I do boldly affirm it, and that in the Counsel of the Eternal God, *It is our striking so constantly and earnestly at this and such like Sin-pleasing Principles, that makes the Devil thus bestir himself in his ready Agents, to raise up, and bespatter us with such heavy Calumnies, as almost every one produceth against us.* But we lose not an Inch of Ground, nor a Dram of Courage ; our Godly Resolution redoubles with our *Adversaries* On-sets ; and whatever may befall us here, as our Hope, so our Reward, is from God, in that High and Heavenly Place, which is above the Reach of Time, and every Assault of our implacable Adversaries.

§. 13. (Pag. 24.) He tells me, *He might proceed to my fallacious Arguing from the Spirit's Teaching indefinitely expressed* (that is, by Scripture, Visions, Providences, &c. means our Adversary) *to it's Teaching peculiarly, frequently in my Pamphlet,* Pag. 18, 29, &c. that is, to the Spirit's Teaching Men and Women by it's daily and inward Discoveries, Motions and Operations. *But he will not* ; the Reason is, he dare not ; For if the Spirit be not an immediate Living Teacher, and works not as such, to the Information, Conviction, and Conversion of Men to God in these Days, let him for Shame relinquish all Pretence to Gospel, or an Evangelical Dispensation, of which it is the peculiar Promise and Priviledge.

§. 14. (Pag. 27.) Though for want of better Language, he is pleased to bestow upon this Godly Profession, the Term of *Beetle-headed Saying*, and affirms, *That the Scripture knows nothing of it* ; For which I may more reasonably affirm, *That He knows nothing of it :* For can this Man be so besotted, as to think, that when a Measure of the Spirit was given to all to profit with ; and that the Children of God were led by the Spirit of God, and the Spirit that was sent into the Hearts of the Sons of God, and the Anointing that was in the Saints that was able to teach them all Things, was any Measure, Part, or Parcel, of the Prophets or Apostles Writings ? I cannot yet think him so Blinded, as Ignorant or Envious as he is. Either these Passages are no Scripture, or that gross Absurdity must follow.

§. 15. (Pag. 27.) But he tells us, *That we may be mistaken, ever since some of us thought* Paul Hobson's *Mumbling through a Trunk, and an Hole in the Wall, to be the Voice of the Lord.* But were it as True, as it is in many Things false, it shews the Prophaneness of that *Anabaptist*, who dar'd to take the Lord's Name in his Mouth, and counterfeit a Solemn Commission to a poor whimsical Wretch ; and as it happened,

pened, out of a Spirit of Covetousness and Inhospitality, for he had no Mind to give him longer Entertainment; so that not knowing how better to be rid of him, than to forge a Commission, he wickedly contrived a Passage into the Chamber where the Man lay, and through a Trunk prophanely uttered a Kind of Commission, to go to a certain Place, where, I cannot tell; but I am sure, as the Story goes, out of his House, to whom his little Victuals had been a Burden; A Practice for the Avarice, Prophaneness and Abuse of it, to be abhorred and detested of all Sober Men. And I think the Man more excusable under his Mistake than Major *Hobson*, who ventur'd into so much Wickedness, and that with Design to bring him into it. 'Tis true, that such a Man there was, that he went to Major *Hobson*'s House, that he dealt so wickedly by the Man to be rid of him, that the Man had been among us; but as his Practice shew'd him to be none of us, so were not any of his Imaginations countenanced by us, but sharply rebuk'd; and therefore that Part of *J. Faldo*'s Reflection, a Lye: Yet, since he has gotten this Story by the End, I will see how much better grounded *J. Faldo* would be upon his Principles against a *Quaker*, should he be so impious as to put the same prophane Abuse upon him. Suppose *J. Faldo*, either by a Trunk, or Hole through a Wall, or one of the New-invented Trumpets, that carry a Voice a Mile, should have as far as Words go, a very Solemn Commission to go Preach the Gospel in any other Place than *Barnet*, (where I hear, he now lives) within this Isle, or some more remote Part of the World, and that not only once or twice, but many Times joyn'd with Threats and Promises, I will suppose his Inclinations will lie at Home, unless more be to be gotten (an infallible Ground of Motion with many of his Tribe) But I would know of him, which Way, or upon what Foot he would receive or reject such a Commission? The Scripture makes no Mention of any such Thing in Particular; in General it will not reach it, because this is no other Gospel, that he should be required to Preach, than that which he pretends to be according to Scripture. I say, with what would he relish, favour, or try this Voice? Would he reject it, because the Scripture did not particularly own it? There is the same Reason why he should embrace it, because it does not particularly deny it. How will he do then? Why, perhaps he will go, because there is no General-Rule in Scripture that withstands it. But how does he know, that so many good Words in themselves were spoken from God, and not to deceive, tempt, or abuse him? 'Tis true, the Scripture has general Denials to False Spirits, and general Testimonies to the Motions of the True One, but still here's but a begging of the Question; For how shall I know that the Voice or Spirit be True or False? It is not Unscriptural, Unreasonable, nor Improbable. Alas for *John Faldo*! Have all his Preaching, Praying, Writing, &c. no better Foundation than Hear say, Imitation, strong Fancy and external Sense? *Can he not favour and relish Spirits as well as Words?* If not, he may be truly stiled a Man of Words, but void of that Spirit which tries Spirits, and gives Right Discerning of those Things that may concern them, to all that believe in it, and are led by it. I might say much upon this Theme, but let this suffice to detect the weak Foundation of *J. Faldo*'s Faith, Knowledge and Practice; and that such as he, though pretendedly two or three Degrees more refined than the present Protestants, are miserably apostatized from the First Revolters from *Rome*'s Idolatries, who asserted, *None could understand the Scriptures themselves, much less benefit by them, who had not the same Spirit that gave them forth*; consequently, *the Spirit, and not the Scriptures, were the Principal Cause of Right Knowledge, and the Rule, for our very Understanding of them.* And truly, though *J. Faldo* would have the World think he both understands the *Quaker's Principles* very well, and has refuted them very clearly, yet whether he will give me Leave or no, I will make him speak the Language of the *Quakers* passing well in this Particular of the Spirit's being the Judge, Rule and Guide of Faith, Worship and Conversation, the Thing aim'd at in that First Part of my *Spirit of Truth Vindicated*, by him so much quarrell'd at, perverted and scurrilously abused, or else I greatly mistake his Mind. And, which will be much to my Defence, he must likewise have done so himself. Hear him,

§. 16. (Pag. 15.) *But Mr. Penn, do you deal fairly and honestly with your Adversaries, to imply in your Question that we deny the Spirit of God to be a proper Rule of Faith, Guide of Life, Judge of Truth? You know that we own it to be such; and that it doth both in the Conscience, and by the Scripture, Creation and Providence, perform such Acts,* &c. *and is to such Purposes, and that of Right. What can we say more? Has he not strangely mis-understood us? Again, Only we deny that the Spirit always performs these Acts without the Use of the Scripture, or any External Means.*

Truly and so do we; for we daily enjoy the Benefit both of God's Spirit by the Scripture, and publick Worship, as Means. If this be the Grindstone my Nose is to be held at, and by not mentioning of which (as he falsly says of me) I abuse and trifle with him and my *Unwary Reader*, I am contented to abide here while I live, as my Discourse at large upon the Scriptures must needs have informed those who have read it. But I am of the Mind that *J. Faldo* will find it too hot for him, and I am assured, that so much Concession overturns him for ever, as to his present *Basis*; For that he should oppose my Discourse that intended nothing more than to prove God's Spirit to be the Great Rule to Believers, and yet himself, after much Opposition, to give it away, and accord as far as any Man need to do, that would be of one Mind with us in the Point, favours of great Weakness and Inadvertency; not, that he now speaks Truth, but that he should so eagerly oppose it before.

§. 17. (Pag. 30.) There is one Passage more, which being to this Purpose, I will mention: *We value not the Sense (of the Scripture) for the Print's Sake, but the Print for the Sense's Sake, and the Blessings that attend that Way of Conveying the Holy and Revealed Will of God, and so much as to correct your Vapour.*

This he speaks upon my Words, that the Intimate of a *Prince* needs not so much an Edict because in Print, as because of his living and more immediate Touches he may have had from his *Prince*. Now let any tell me, if the *Quakers* have put the Scriptures into any Degree below that, wherein *J. Faldo* himself has plac'd them. Do the *Quakers* say, *That True Christians have the Spirit*; so says *J. Faldo* too. Do the Quakers *affirm that the Spirit of God is a Judge, Rule and Guide, and speaks forth the Mind of God into the very Conscience;* Does *J. Faldo* come one Jot behind them? But do they say, *That it is the Sense of the Truth declared of in the Scripture, that puts a Value upon the Declaration? And that Written or Printed Words, are Valu'd for the Matters Sake they treat of, rather than their own? Yea, that the Scripture of it self can do little?* It is *J. Faldo*'s own Doctrine! Very well! But does *J. Faldo* say, *That God doth not always speak in the Conscience immediately by his Spirit, but sometimes by the Spirit, through the Use of Means, as the Scriptures, Preaching, Praying, Creation, Providence,* &c. *and that by such Ways he reacheth into the Consciences of Men?* So say the *Quakers* too. Would the Man but be certain to himself, we needed no other Advocate; but his Ignorance of our Principles, or Prejudice to mis-represent them, makes him at once oppose us, and contradict himself.

And now we are come to the Conclusion of the Matter, which he says, *Is, to shew me my self in the Glass of Sense, if I think my Eyes worth an Using.* Indeed I do, and am willing to behold all he hath to shew me: *Reader,* hear him soberly.

§. 18. (Pag. 30.) *Foul Epithets; as Knave, Puppy, Fool, Rascal, Loggerhead, Cheat; This you say, was the Language of our Adversaries small Crier, but as you call it, of a loathsome Scent.* It seems *J. Faldo*'s Nose calls it no such Thing; A long Experienced *Chaplain,* a Kind of a Religious Gentleman-Usher, should have learned better Manners.

So, says he, *You blow it on the Author of the Book within five Lines. — Tryers of other Men's Spirits, who have (it should be give) so little Proof of the Knowledge of their own, as to be wanting in the first Principles of Civility. This is not fair* (says J. Faldo) *to charge him with another's Faults.*

It is some Justice to us, that he will account such Language to a *Quaker* a Fault. But I would have him know, that I never intended any such Thing as he basely infers, that is, to make *H. Hedworth* in the least Guilty of usually calling *G. Fox* those scurrilous Names; for though I think him Envious enough against *G. F.* in particular, as appears by another Sort of Language, and the *Quakers* in general, yet I believe him to have more Civility and Regard to his Way, whatsoever he thinks of me, than to dirt it with any Thing so gross. But for as much as *T. Firman,* the Author of that foul Language, was his great Intimate and Associate, that they have in common the same Creed, are joyntly interested against us, thereby earnestly endeavouring to promote their *Beloved Socinianism,* or *Biddleism* in the World, and Men acted not by two distinct Spirits, though one might launch forth more extravagantly than the other: And lastly, that *H. H.* had shewn other Sorts of Rudeness and Injustice to us in general, and many by Name, in *His Spirit of the Quakers Tryed.* I did say, *These Men,* and continue there still, the Method of their Proceeding then and since, especially that restless Calumniator, *Thomas Firman,* be-

1673.

ing such as must needs offend every Good Man; *Knave* and *Fool* being more in his Mouth still, than becometh any Man, that is not more of both than such he very frequently calls so. Some think it a Shame, that so ill a Tongue should go unrebuk'd of those whose Principles and Interest give them the Liberty of d[o]ing it in a Way, that if they know the Man, might be more effectual then all the Moderation and Reason that can easily be shewn him. But says *John Faldo* in his, or their Defence (for they love to claw one another) *Compare this Civility of yours with your own.*

To all this I say, *He obtrudes an arrant Lye upon our very Senses; Wretched Scribler* —— *How Idle, how Frivolous, and how very Troublesome is he, with his Ridiculous Remarks!* Very well: And *is this the Great Blow threatned? I fall not from one Tittle of it*: 'Tis all True, all his Due, I could not well have spoken more plain and pertinent Words: No *Knave, Puppy, Fool, Rascal, Logger-head, Cheat,* &c. No *Impostor, False-Prophet, Lyars, Trapans,* and what not did we accost them with. What! Must not we fling off the Dirt they cast upon us? Shall it be accounted Well-Phrasing, to call *us* all to Naught, and our earnest Refusal of such base Epithets, and severe Censure of such Scurrility, be reputed *Railery*? O Unreasonable Men! Ought People therefore to be kill'd, because they cry Murder? Or lose their Reputation, because they are Zealous to maintain it? But it was notably done of J. Faldo to provide for himself, whose ill Language he thought might meet with as sharp Rebukes, as that of our Enemies had done. Nor indeed will *we* let slip this Opportunity of Collecting and Publishing to the World, after what Manner he has *us*'d us, throughout his Discourse, and my self in particular, who never had any Thing to do with him in all my Life. If he has not said Worse of us, with whom we have had so little, if any Thing at all, to do, than he pretends I have against those Men that gave such Provocation, let me fall in the Good Opinion of the Reader, and the Just Witness in his Conscience condemn me: But if it appear, that this unprovoked Person is far more Guilty, than he can possibly render us, by vilifying Expressions against our Persons and Principles, I hope, and expect so much Justice from the Reader, as that the Innocent may go free, and the Guilty only be Condemned. That *J. Faldo* has not shewn himself that Man of Moderation, Civility or Religion, he pretends himself to be, and which I hear, some few have hitherto reputed, let the following Faithful, and True Collection, of but some of his many Unchristian Reflections, Names and Epithets, upon our Faith and Principles, be duly weighed by the *Impartial Reader.*

§. 19. *Penn furnished with Forehead and Tales beyond Measure.*] I am assured that's a Lye. I think my Forehead and Tales are like other Men's; if not, I have this Satisfaction, they are unlike *J. Faldo's.*

His Post is the Quakers *conceited Strong-hold of the Infallible Guidance of the Spirit of God.*] A *Post,* his *Post* can never stand long by, and such *Hold,* as all his Assaults can never enter or force; and we are glad it is ours indeed: For as above all People we need it most, so are we the only Sufferers in Defence thereof: Satan's Bulwarks shall be broken down before it.

§. 20. (Pag. 3.) *In debating of which, he waves and tosses like a Man in a confus'd troublesome Dream; I thought meet to give some Account of his Forces, considering him to be a Man of Noise, and no small Prop to the* Quaker's *Cause, in their own Esteem.*

I tost not beyond the Bounds of Scripture and Truth; my Arguments were short and plain, and what I writ was in Conscience and Seriousness, little meriting such rough and flashy Reflection from any Person pretending to Seriousness, and least of all, one that I never had to do with in my Life. *Dreams* I have none, they lie on *J. Faldo's* Side; He that calls Christ, Lord, and not by the Holy Ghost; He that says, He is his Redeemer, Saviour, &c. and knows not the Internal Operation of his Saving Power, nor that Virtue and Life to quicken to God, which comes therefrom, dreams of all these Things, and that is *J. Faldo's* Condition, who scoffs at Internal Knowledge without External Means, though to his own Confusion he sometimes reads another Lecture. *I am no Man of Noise, farther than your Noise makes me.* The Profession of the Way I am in, I came to through Sorrow for Sin, Circumcision from the World, Desires after God, and Life that is Everlasting; and ever since God has enabled me to His Service, (and here I hope to stand while I live) My Life, Spirit, Power and Principle wars against all yours that are embattell'd against us; and no Quarter I proclaim, in the Name of the Lord, to that wicked Spirit that acts you all against us; though to you Peace and Salvation, *if ye Repent.* Do you

you leave off your Envious Endeavours againſt us, or elſe blame your ſelves, and not us, for appearing on the Stage againſt you.

§. 21. *Deformed Confidence*; *neither Logick, nor Honeſty*: Certainly, if he had *not turn'd* Quaker, *and in that Fall put all out of Joynt, he could not likely after ſuch Good Nurſing, have been thus lamentably cripled in his Intellects*: *Ranknefs of* Quakeriſm. *The latter Part of the Queſtion, which expreſſes the Adminiſtration of our Lord and Saviour Jeſus Chriſt, is* Playing at Blind Man's Buff, — *your Guilt*, &c. *Baſenefs, confuſed Thicket of Impertinencies* — *if your Conſcience have any Eyes*; *Infatuated*; *I have ſhewed your Vanity, and made your Folly a Spectacle to the World*; *you talk at a miſerable lame Rate — worſe than ever Bear brought forth her Cubs — confident confuſed Nonſenſe*; *I would as ſoon abandon my Time to diſpute with a diſtracted Man in his Raving Fits, as with* W. Penn, *till he come better to himſelf*, &c. — *your pitiful Scribbling*, (yet *Wretched Scribbler*, was my hardeſt Word to H. Hedworth, he has obſerved againſt me) *not worth while to trace ſuch a Trifler in all his Vagaries — intangled Bottom, Beetle-headed Saying, Audacious Lines — he will daub his Adverſary*, per fas, per nefas, *Right or Wrong, and he that ſhall ſay the contrary, you will chaſtiſe him with Sarcaſms as keen as a* Badger's Teeth. *The next Book you write, let the Title be*, The Spirit of Babel, *from whence* Babble *in* Engliſh.

This, *Reader*, is a ſhort Account of ſome of that unhandſome Entertainment, I, a Stranger to *J. Faldo*, have received at his Hands. May my Soul never come within his Habitation; Prejudice, Envy and Cruelty lodge with him; Vanity, Frothineſs and Incivility, are like Veins through his Book, and ſerve to convey what Life it has, to ſuch as pleaſe themſelves with that baſe *Kind of Satyr*. Strange, that it ſhould be reputed ſo Criminal by *J. Faldo*, to check my *Adverſary* for abuſing me and my Friends by Name, when yet he excels in his Reflections upon us, and that without any ſuch Occaſion given! But, if we were Condemnable, ſure I am, it belongs not to *J. Faldo* to fling the firſt Stone. I am very willing to leave it with all *Sober Readers*, our Circumſtances conſidered, which of us ought to be accounted the *Unfair Adverſary*. O, When will it fall to my Share, to engage a ſober modeſt *Adverſary*! But why do I wiſh for that, ſince ſuch are our Friends. Well, it will greatly become me to be contented with my Lot; Faith I have, theſe Things will not laſt long; and Patience will give to ſee the End of that Belief. A little foul Weather, and our Enemies are for their Creeks again: 'Tis Natural with Inſects to Sting and, Frogs to croak, in Summer; and therefore it is, that our beſt Actions are Evil in the Sight of theſe *Carping Zoilus*'s. If a Man be one of them, then a Saint, though a Devil: If gone from them, then a Devil, tho' a Saint. Such is his Farewel to me, who in three Lines tells me, *He is a little pleaſant, he cannot Sweat about Cracking of Nuts, and yet that he has had ſome Heart-akes for me.* Miſerable Man! Does Levity and Seriouſneſs go together? Froth and Sorrow keep Company? What would any Man give for ſuch Heart-akes, that bring True Ones upon a Serious Mind? But what are his Heart-akes? Why, he bewails, that a Man of my Hopes ſhould be thus left of God (he fears for Pride and Giddineſs) *as to be made a Pillar of Salt*, &c. It ſeems then that there were once Hopes: But to what? To a Party. I know you very well, you will few of you ſtand by all that I could ſay, and prove of ſome of you: I would adviſe ſuch *Oppoſers to be quiet, enjoy their Toleration, a Kindneſs as Great as they deſerve*, and mind their own Concerns, and now their Hands are tyed againſt the Powers, not employ them upon our Shoulders.

But why ſhould God leave me, a *Sufferer*, from Fourteen Years of Age for *Conſcience-Sake* (he fears) for Pride and Giddineſs? But the Cauſe of my leaving you, was that of my once frequenting you, I mean *Conſcience*; when ſome I then diſſented from, had as hard Names to give, for that *Non-Conformity*. But the Truth is, when the *King* came firſt in, at what Time you were a little dejected, there was ſomething more Serious and Tender than ordinary revived among ſome of you, which did begin to gather out of the National Pollution, and fit for a farther Thing, but taking up a Reſt, growing hard, gaping after Changes, looking back, like *Lot's* Wife, upon your *Old Sodom*, for ſworn Government, Kings and Biſhops-Lands, Rich Benefices, Full and Stately Livings, many of you grew dry again, *were turned to Pillars of Salt*, my Soul wandered for Reſt, and at laſt found it, in that Tender, Holy, Pure Principle of Life and Righteouſneſs, which had been wont from a Youth to attend me, mollifie my Heart, allay my Affections, and preſerve me out of groſs Pollutions, which, whilſt ſuch of you in ſome Meaſure kept, that

1673.
are now manifestly gone from it, there was another Kind of Spirit that rul'd in you; And 'tis to this First Love and Works we desire your Return, such of you whose Day is not utterly past over your Head: And what any shall think of me, as this uncharitable *Adversary* hath expressed himself, as that I should seek Credit, a Party, *&c.* I heed not, for what I am at this Day I am by, through, and to God Almighty the Righteous Lord of Heaven and Earth alone. It is basely done of any Man, that is a Professor, who pretends to some Acquaintance with tender Conscience, and those Trials that attend it, to censure another Man's Change and Afflictions for Counterfeit and meer Design. O! The Righteous God will reckon with such Uncharitable, Disingenuous, Perverse Spirits in the Day that hastneth to Try all, and then will he recompense this ungodly Censurer of an Innocent Stranger to him, who, were I upon my Trial at the Bar of his own Party, there be of them enough to give Evidence of another Spirit than that of Vain Glory or Self; For where none of these Things have induced, but Sharpness and Severities have met me, there has been a faithful Answering of Convictions, to some of their Knowledge, who I believe, to be better Men than to refuse me a full Testimonial, if sought for. But as I shall not think my self so deeply engag'd, or my Reputation so shaken in the Minds of Thousands, as to need or desire it by any Power or Force *J. Faldo* can attack me with; so shall I leave the Concern of God's Truth, the Innocency of his People in General, and my own in Particular, to his Holy Wisdom and Providence, who, we are well satisfied, will plead our Cause in the Consciences of Ten Thousands to the Shame and utter Confusion of all our Obstinate *Adversaries*.

J. FALDO's KEY Prov'd Defective.

I Was not willing *J. Faldo*'s *Key* should go wholly Unconsider'd; the greatest Part of which I here publickly acknowledge to have done us such Right, that if his Explanation of many of our Words be not True, I am not asham'd to pronounce that the Scriptures must be False; so agreeable to, and consonant with Scripture has he spoken on our Behalf: And not only with Scripture, but that Sense of it too, which the Best, Wisest and most Learned both of the Fathers, and first Reformers have unanimously had; and on which Foundation, in some Measure, both *Puritans* and *Brownists* began their Building; Low, Meek, Spiritual and Plain, as is yet well remembred. But how grosly he has mis-represented us in other Parts, and that the True may not give Credit to the False with any, I will observe a few, with what Brevity I may.

J. Faldo, p. 62. *ASSEMBLING*, says he, *Meeting in Spirit*.

W. Penn. This is not Ingenuous; For with such as know us not, nor our Practice, it insinuates a Denial of Publick Worship, which we ever own'd, and hope, shall to the End; It is well known who have most shrunk from that Testimony: And if *J. Faldo* means, that they do not worship in Spirit, because he makes it Criminal in us, we have Reason to say, He and They are no Gospel-Worshippers: For People must either worship in, or out of God's Spirit; *If out of his Spirit*, then no Worship in Spirit and Truth, but the Device of their own Hearts; *If in the Spirit*, then the *Quakers* assemble as they should do, and *J. Faldo* is to be rebuk'd for little better than an Upstart Scoffer at Assembling in Spirit: The once avow'd Principle of the ancient *Brownists*, now call'd *Independents*.

J. F. Pag. 69. *The Will of the Flesh*, says he, *All that is chosen by Man, though he be thereby disposed by the Will of God revealed in the Scripture*.

W. P. This is false; Many Things may be, and are daily chosen by Man, that is not in the Will of the Flesh, nor by his own Will; much less, when any should be disposed thereto by the Will of God revealed in the Scripture: An Abominable Untruth, and so Notorious, that I need say no more; only Challenge him to produce any of us in Proof of his Exposition, if he can; otherwise he hath Slander'd us and our Principles: For the Will of the Flesh is that, which is quite contrary to God, and inconsistent with the Good of the Creature.

J. F.

J. F. Pag. 69. *State of Glory*, says he, *The State of Peace and Joy resulting from the Witness of the Light within in this Life.*

W. P. It is true, That Glory is revealed, from Faith to Faith, in this Life: But to stint the State of Glory to the Peace and Joy of this Life only, may justify his wrong Opinion of us, that we deny Rewards to come; but it cuts off from our stedfast Faith in an Everlasting Mansion of Glory and Blessedness, which (from the Light within, to all who obey it) shall spring as a River, and flow as an Inexhaustible Fountain: And *J. Faldo* shall never know true Peace another Way; That is the Word of the Lord to him.

J. F. Pag. 70. *Preaching for Hire, Hirelings*, says he, *to have a Provision for the Outward Man, as a Maintenance for Preaching, though no Bargain be made; yea, though such who receive it, would Preach, if they had never a Penny Reward in this World from those they Preach to.*

W. P. This is done like the Fox indeed. He would suggest, because we deny Hirelings, that is, Bargainers, Men that make it their Trade, that have no other, will seek no other, and yet preach, perhaps, but once a Week, if then; and bestow the Six Days, that might be otherwise employ'd, to study for that Day, instead of Preaching most of those Days, that therefore we are such Cruel, Hardhearted People, that such as Preach, and are Poor, either through a numerous Family, low Estate, many Losses, or a continual Attendance, from Day to Day, upon the Ministry they have receiv'd of God, we will not minister to their Necessities; for such as so receive any Assistance are Hirelings, and we should contribute to make them so. No, no, *J. Faldo*, the *Quakers* are no such People; but for all that, they can, do, and will renounce Thee, and such as Thou art, for Hirelings: *First*, In that you have not receiv'd the Living Heavenly Gift of the Ministry: And, *Secondly*, Because you do generally bargain, will not preach without it; and can basely leave an honester People, for a better Allowance; This is Notorious; therefore stop thy Mouth.

J. F. Pag. 72. *The Lust*, says he, *All Desires that accord not to the Light within, and proceed not from thence.*

W. P. What accords not with the Light within, is not of God; and so far we own his Explanation: but to say, that all Desires about such ordinary Things, as are left to the common Understanding, Prudence, and Liberty of Man to do, or not to do, are Lust, if they come not from the immediate Impulse of the Light within, is his own Notion, and not the *Quakers*: We do not subject that heavenly Principle to, nor concern it with, every Inferior and Frivolous Thing belonging to this World.

J. F. Pag. 75. *Christ, the Offering*, says he, *the Light within.*

W. P. This is no *Quaker's* Expression; and unless we are to answer for *J. Faldo's* Mistakes, we are unconcern'd in it: Only his Malice is manifest, for he would by this insinuate, that we deny Christ to be an Offering, as in the Flesh, and the Body then offered up to be concern'd in our Belief of the Offering: But I do declare it, to have been an holy Offering, and such an one too, as was to be once for all: Therefore let none receive his Abuse of us for our Faith.

J. F. Pag. 79. *Men-Pleasers*, says he, *They who comply with Men, though in Things not only lawful, but also to Edification.*

W. P. We charge this upon him as an Arrant Lye. We are so far from reputing such *Men-pleasers*, that we account them Sober, Courteous, and Commendable Persons: provided, he means by *Lawful*, and to *Edification*, what we do; otherwise he is not Honest, to obtrude Matters in Question for our Meanings.

J. F. Pag. 81. *Ravening Brain*, says he, *Studying and following after Divine Knowledge.*

W. P. This is not fair; The Word, studying, and following, we own in a Sense. Studying, that is, Meditating: Following, that is, Obeying the Light and Spirit of God: But because we deny the Dark and *Heathenish Metaphysicks*, the prolix and abstruse *Niceties* of the School-men, and affirm, There is no Way to become vers'd in the Things of God, but by being an humble Student, and diligent Disciple in the School of Christ, that is, to be taught of his Light, Grace, or Holy Spirit; Therefore we must be charg'd with the Denial of all right Study, and all right Ways to come to the Knowledge of Divine Things: Disingenuous Man!

J. F.

J. F. Pag. 86. *Traditions of Men, that is*, says he, *The Scripture, or Written Word.*

W. P. Shew us that in any Book, that is subscrib'd by an acknowledg'd *Quaker*, Tradition is a Delivering any thing down from one Generation to another; and as such, the Word is Inoffensive: but to say, They are the Traditions of Men, in the Sense Christ reproved the *Pharisaical Religion*, God forbid: I had rather my Tongue were cut out of my Head. O base Man! To abuse an innocent People thus grosly. The Scripture is a Godly Tradition, or Writing, given forth by Inspiration, and preserv'd through Generations, which we read, believe, and desire to fulfil through the Power of God.

J. F. Pag. 63, 82, 83, 87. *Babylon; Shadows, Spirit of Anti-Christ, Outward Court;* that is, says he, *all Ordinances, Worship, Faith, Obedience that have any Form, though Christ's and Gospel Forms,* being (with them) *the Worship of Heathens, not of Christians.*

W. P. This *Key* opens into as many Forgeries as ever I knew one *Key* do in my Life. Certainly, were not this Man left of God for his Enmity, he could never run into such extravagant Dishonesty. What! Bely us in the Sight of all? Indeed it turns upon himself: For Visible Worship, the Form of Godliness, Faith and Obedience to every Ordinance of God we own, profess, and practise daily and publickly through the Power of our God; in whose Name we renounce his Constructions, and trample upon all his Malice, black and enrag'd as it is.

J. F. Pag. 89. *The Vail is over them*, that is, says J. Faldo, *the Belief of the Man* Christ Jesus, *which was of our Nature, to be the Christ,* &c.

W. P. Let this be the Last (though several more might be observ'd) which at this Time shall be considered, in which we shall see that *J. Faldo* has done like himself, and the Man we have all along taken him to be. *The Vail is over them,* it is a Scripture Phrase, 2 *Cor.* 3. 15. used by the Apostle to express the Darkness and Ignorance that to that Time remain'd over the Understanding of the *Jews* in reading the Law, and this Vail he makes us to interpret after this gross and absurd Manner, namely, That the *Vail* is the *Man* Christ. Wicked Man! Did ever *Quaker* so irreverently express himself? Give us his Name, or tell us in what Book we may find it. What greater Malice couldst thou have shewn, than thus unjustly to pervert the Scripture in our Name, belying and abusing both? As if, because *Christ's Flesh* is called a Vail, and the Ignorance of the *Jews* a Vail, that therefore the *Quakers* must of Necessity mean by Vail in the first Sense, Vail in the second Sense; as if the Way to have the Vail rent, were to deny the Man Christ Jesus; which were to make Christ rend and destroy himself, who, as the Quickning Spirit, alone rends all Vails off the Hearts of Unbelievers. Nor indeed have I met with one Term absurd, or un-intelligible, unless the Scripture use such; therefore 'tis an Untruth to stile them absurd, and a Contradiction in him to offer at Explaining any thing, that is truly un-intelligible.

And that all the World may behold the Spirit of *J. Faldo,* how ill he governs himself against the *Quakers* (which makes not a little for them) let his following Epithets and Expressions be well weighed. I think they are so naked they want no *Key*; and glad we are he found no such Subjects from us to treat upon in his.
' *Horrid Imposture*; Ditch of Grossest Delusion; Subverting *Christianity*; their
' feigned Christ; Folly, Madness; It began in Blasphemies against Christ; grati-
' fying *Pride, Idleness, Giddiness*; In Professors Prophane; Vanity, Folly, Non-
' sense, Error. Whether it smell more of the *Fox* or the *Goose*. Imposture, Bab-
' ble, Blockish Person. Quakerism *entered the World as if Satan broke loose, and*
' *Possessions by Satan were to make Way and fit Souls for the* Quakers *Spirit*; O the
' Hell-Dark Expressions of the *Quakers* Teachers! What bitter Curses and Execra-
' tions. *Dismal Howling; Horrible Roaring.* Blasphemy; Wretch, Vain Fictions,
' *Quakers* Glow-worm, Deck their Idol, Real Non sense; *But 'tis Pity not to lash*
' *a little*; Idiots, Stark Blind, Steel Hard, Your Crooked, Unholy Principles.
' Their Light grows wiser and wiser. Opium of *Quakerism*; The *Quakers* Divine
' Spirit Dumb. Refreshments at *Quakers* Meetings, so there is at *Puppet-Plays*.
' Impudent Foreheads, Nonesuch Ignorance, Proud, Dreaming, Intolerable Noti-
' ons; Ignorance and Delusion. Out-strip all in the Crooked Way. Blasphemers
' of the Lord of Life and Glory. Surely God has given them up for their *Pride*,
' *Giddiness*, or *Idle Ignorance*, and that in Justice; and the *Devil* hath blinded
' their

'their Minds with a Witness, Horrible Abomination, Gross and Dark Conceits; 'The Rankness of *Quakerism*.

This *Reader* is a Taste of the Spirit of the Man, and since he contends for the *Scripture* to be his Rule, I would fain have the *Chapter* and *Verse* that will abet this Proceeding. Is this *J. Faldo*'s *Religion, Gospel, Preaching, Praying, Learning, Civility*, or whatever may be reputed Sober and Commendable? Away, Away for Shame! It would stumble a *Turk* to hear such Language from one that calls himself a *Christian* and a *Minister* too.

But is it after so great Abuse, so manifest Injury done us and the Truth too, that thou darest say, as thou dost, *I have the Witness in my Conscience* (who hast been thus long Under-valuing it for a *Glow-Worm*, an *Idol*, a poor Creature, Uncertain, Fallible, Errable, and what not) *that I have not in this Key in any Measure abused, or wronged the* Quakers.

Hadst thou been half so *Moral*, as thou pretendest to be *Christian*, I doubt not, but to have seen more Truth and Moderation. To belie any, is a great Evil; but to do it with a Shew of Religion, to call God's Witness, to palliate such Injustice, is the height of Blasphemy against God, and Wrong to thy Neighbour. Never more abuse Religion with a Pretence to it, nor for Shame profess *Christianity*, who art Inferior to a Thousand *Heathens*, and rather than not compass our Disgrace, wilt endeavour it *per fas, per nefas*, Right or Wrong: I am sure the Witness of God in thy own Conscience never suggested this Unrighteous Procedure; though wonder we must, that one, who has said so many detracting Things of him, should now appeal to him. Certainly, if the Witness of God be *J. Faldo*'s Rule and Judge, as his own Appeal makes him, the *Quakers* are the less to be blam'd for Believing in him, and desiring to be led by him; but we are well assured, that a Spirit of deep Prejudice hath animated him to, and through this Work, and not the Holy Witness of God, as both the Stile and Matter have abundantly testified. My Desire is, that before the Evil One precipitate him into farther Enmity against us, he may, by a serious Retirement of Mind to the Holy Witness of God, that gives a good Understanding, and brings just Reproof for every Unrighteous Thought, Word, and Deed, come to a Sight of his present Undertaking to be contrary to the Mind of God, and know true Repentance for it, and find Mercy of the Lord God: Which I heartily desire, and it is my Return to him for all his Hard Speeches utter'd by him either against us in general, or my self (though unknown to him) in particular,

God forbid, that I should Justifie (him) I will not leave my Innocency, 'till I Die. Job. 27. 5.

Who am a Lover of all Men; for I seek the Salvation of my Enemies,

WILLIAM PENN.

THE INVALIDITY

OF

John Faldo's Vindication of his Book,

CALLED,

QUAKERISM No CHRISTIANITY.

BEING A

REJOYNDER

In DEFENCE of the ANSWER, Intituled,

QUAKERISM a New *Nick-Name* for Old CHRISTIANITY.

Wherein many Weighty GOSPEL-TRUTHS are handled, and the Disingenuous Carriage of our Adversary is observ'd, for the better Information of all Moderate Enquirers.

In Two PARTS.

By W. Penn. *Who loves not Controversy for Controversy's Sake.*

Every Day they wrest my Words, all their Thoughts are against me for Evil, Ps. 56. 5.
— *But he that doth Wrong shall receive for the Wrong which he has done*, Col. 3. 23.

To all that Seriously Profess RELIGION, Among those called *Episcopalians, Presbyterians, Independents, Anabaptists, Socinians* and *Latitudinarians*.

THE Duty I owe to Almighty God, and the Respect I bear to his Truth, with that great Concern which lives in my Mind for your better Information about us (a poor People, traduced by some, despised by others) and our Principles (mis-given here, perverted there) are the only Inducements I have to pursue this tedious and unpleasant Controversy.

And that you might be undeceived of those false Apprehensions, vulgar Stories, or the Insinuations of more prevalent Agents have imprest you with, I could (God knows) be contented, that even Sufferings were added to my Labours. What would I not cheerfully undergo to win you into a serious View and impartial Consideration of our Case! Truly, I have a Belief of many of you, that were the Prejudice of Education and common Vogue of the World set aside, you would do us some Justice.

And

And I beseech you, weigh how much it becomes you, you, the serious Professors of Religion, *to give us a fair Hearing for our Principles and Reputations, before you finally determine any thing against us.* To Try all Things *was an Apostolical Exhortation: Nor can you escape the Censure of Dis-regarding it, if you decline a fair Inquiry after us:* Let not Education *be dearer to you than* Truth; *and see if more be not to be known by you than yet you know.* Objected Novelty *ought to have no Force with a* Christian, *since had that prevailed, he had never been one: Nor should the Offence, that Formality, or worldly Learning takes at us, stave you off from a serious Search, much less the* Crucify, Crucify, *of the Vulgar, because the God of Truth, when manifested in the Flesh, was not exempted from more of that than ever yet attended us;* Indeed *it should rather be an Argument for us.*

Believe us, we intreat you, when we tell you, that Religion, Pure and Undefiled Religion, *we greatly love;* 'Tis that we desire as well to Live as Defend: God *knows, we have long made it the Bent of our Hearts, and the whole Aim of our Lives; without it we were the Miserablest of Men: Yet how are we Defamed, Undervalued, Contemned and set at Nought, for a Company of* Seducers, Blasphemers, Idolaters, *and what not? But why? Because we are not understood, and as cunningly (by some) hindred from being so. But therefore is this Discourse more particularly* Dedicated *to you, that you may be both acquainted with the Foulest* Charges *one of our greatest Enemies hath exhibited against us, his Kind of Witnesses produced to convince them, and his Management of the whole Debate; with our Plain and Honest Vindication. If we shall be found guilty, then let us be Condemned for such as he hath represented us to be; but if innocent, suffer us not any longer to Groan under the Heavy Pressure of such Infamous Accusations; for in omitting to Right us for these Grievous Wrongs, you will make your selves Accessaries to an Injustice that must needs be detested of all Virtuous and Good Men.* I leave this Rejoynder *with you, containing the* True Meanings *of our Wrested Principles, and those confirmed by* express *Scriptures, many Reasons, and a Cloud of Testimonies: And shall conclude with a Passage out of* * Jerome, *well-becoming all Honest Writers, and fit to be observed of every impartial Reader.* Quæso, Lector, ut memor Tribunalis Domini, & de judicio tuo te intelligens judicandum, nec mihi, nec Adversario meo faveas, neve Personas Loquentium, sed causam consideres.
" *I beseech thee,* Reader, *that remembring the Judgment-Seat of the Lord, and un-*
" *derstanding that as thou dost judge, so thou shalt be judged, thou favourest*
" *neither me, nor mine Adversary that writes against me, and that thou regardest*
" *not the Persons, but the Cause only.*

I am a real Valuer of whatsoever is Worthy in any of you, and an Hearty Wisher of your Improvement in the Knowledge of those things that lead to Eternal Peace, which are only to be found in the Light and Life of Righteousness.

W. PENN.

The *Invalidity* of *J. Faldo*'s Vindication, &c.

The INTRODUCTION.

THIS *Controversie*, not of Choice, but absolute Necessity, thus continued, (and which hath swell'd this *Rejoynder* beyond both my Desire and Expectation, through such great Provocations and multiplied Wrongs, as are utterly inconsistent with the Honour of Truth to put up, and which require our serious Notice in it's Defence) was begun by *J. Faldo*, a *Non-conforming Minister* at *Barnet*, (disgusted, as I have heard, at the coming over of some of his Hearers to the Way we profess) in a large Discourse, entituled, *Quakerism no Christianity*; in which he not only accused us of the blackest Errors, but pretended to prove every Charge out of our own Writings; an *Essay* none had ever yet fallen on besides himself. At what Rate soever he proved them, certain it is, he charged us home, and managed it with Equal Disingenuity. This, it was my Lot to answer, which I did in a Book, call'd, Quakerism *a New Nick-Name for Old* Christianity, &c. Chiefly intending

1673.
Part I.

tending by it to difcover, how grofly he had miftaken our Principles, and unworthily perverted thofe Words we had employed to maintain them; and finally, to confirm our true Senfe with the Authority of holy Scriptures: Unto which he has ventured to give us a Reply, doubtlefs that he might not be thought to have nothing to fay, fo little hath he faid to the Purpofe, *which is already become the Difcourfe of the Moderate, and Regret of his Party*; But what he wants of *Solidity*, he fills up with *Air*, and places his *Reflections* to the Account of *Arguments*; and when he comes to a Pinch, he gives us *Confidence* for *Evidence*, attended moft commonly with a Rout of *hard Names*, to drive it more forcibly home. And truly herein he has deceiv'd me; for I muft needs fay, I did not take him to be one that would withftand fuch manifeft Conviction, and that with no other than Froth, Rant, and very Obftinacy: I hop'd that when I had given him a ferious Anfwer to his Book, he would either have ingenuoufly acknowledged his Miftake of our Writings, with this Satisfaction, that he found us not fo *Heterodox* as he apprended us to be; or elfe have beftowed upon us fuch a fober and convincing *Reply*, as might have fufficiently proved our Error, and juftified his own Undertaking: But inftead thereof, behold a *Pamphlet ftuffed with Rage and fcornful Abufe!* by him entituled, *A Vindication*; but is indeed *his Condemnation with God and all Good Men*.

He feems to have deferted the Matter, as giving that for gone; and under Pretence of anfwering my Book, fully pays himfelf of my Perfon. Of that he has no Mercy; I am all that a Man fwelled with Paffion, Prejudice and Revenge, can character me to be.

He complains much, *yet himfelf is the Injurer*; *Forgery* he lays at my Door, and 'tis *his own beloved Crime*; He fays I boaft of Victory, *yet John Faldo is the great Crack*; Where I rebuke his Froth, he returns me *Railing*; and if I improve his own *Similes* againft him, then *Difingenuous W. P.* Devotion he fleers at, as if it were *an old fafhioned Thing*; My Reprehenfion of his ill-Language he counts intolerable; *Is this your Meek Chriftian*, fays he? making it a greater Sin in me to Defend my felf, *than in him to Accufe me*; Perfonal and Principal Reflections run fluently through his firft Book; *My Reproof* of that unprovok'd Afperity, *he ftorms at*, and will needs have it to be *Reviling*; and inftead of Repenting of his ill Beginning with us, he hath greatly encreafed his Score, by a more *Scurrilous Reply*; as if the Man's Bufinefs were not to make us Better, *but prove and juftifie his own being Worfe*. He would make us in Love with our Errors, if fuch we held, that ufes fo ill a Way to reclaim us. Does he think we are to be *Jeered* or *Railed* out of our Religion? No, No. In his *firft*, he went too far; in his *fecond* he has done little elfe. What fhall we fay of thofe, whofe Pride has brought them to fuch a Pitch of Paffion, that *Rage* muft follow *Reproof*, and *Revenge* a *Confutation?* Without breaking one Part of the Law of Modefty, I may fay (for I know) he is irrecoverably gone in my Anfwer. *Not one Charge can he prove*, nor one Friend of ours can he make to fpeak to his Purpofe. He was for having us to *affaffinate our felves*; our Friends he would fain have *to turn Executioners to their own Principles*: This *Fool's Paradife* pleafed him; but the Difcreet know and think better: Some were ftartled at the Pretences of the firft, wherein nothing lefs than our *own Books* were to bear Witnefs againft us, who are now great Abominators of his Injuftice and Railing. Bleffed be God for that Good Succefs; we hope the like of our following Endeavours. I have for the Sake of fuch as expect an Anfwer, fent forth this *Rejoynder*; wherein feveral weighty Points are as clearly handled, as Time, Place, and other Occafions would permit. It greatly concerns all to be fully fatisfied therein: And I hope, there is enough faid for all Impartial Readers to reap that Benefit. I feek no Revenge, I aim not at Reputation, God is Record: Neither has he done enough to raife up the One, or queftion the Other; yet he has done doubtlefs what he could, and I muft take the *Will for the Deed*. I fhall not fhow my felf fo Perfonally concerned in this *Rejoynder*, as his Perfonal Reflections would make me; 'tis below the Spirit of a *Chriftian* Man to be difturbed by fuch Barks of Malice; Curs yelping at the Moon neither queftions nor eclipfes her Light: 'Tis a Sort of *Suffering I muft expect to undergo*; and the beft is, I find little Difficulty in it. And though I fhall not cite all his Injuftice towards me, for that were well nigh to transfcribe his Book; yet that which may be requifite, to give a farther Relifh of this pretended *Chriftian*, may be done in it's proper Place. In the mean Time I fhall betake my felf to the Confideration of fuch Paffages in his Reply, as may be thought to call for my *Rejoynder*, and that without thofe

infolent

infolent Checks, frequent Abuses, and very vain and gingling Taunts he has cramb'd his Pamphlet with: For I can suffer that my self, I cannot let the Truth suffer. Nor can I think my Silence to his Revilings the worst Answer, especially when *my Religion will not allow of a like Return in Vindication:* For though Scoffs and Abusive Reflections may discredit an *Adversary* with the Weak or Prejudiced, yet with a Serious *Reader,* they rather pollute, than defend a Cause. I will leave the whole Honour of that Way of Confutation to my *Adversary,* not being in such Necessity for Conquest, as to take that Dishonourable and Dishonest Way of procuring it: If I can make my *Rejoynder* a little more intelligible, than he has done his *Reply,* defend the Truth I own and honour, so as to answer my *Reader's* Conscience, I shall have obtain'd my whole End; and maugre the Impetuous and blustering Humour of a few *Enraged Adversaries, my Mind will sweetly rest in Peace with God,* in whom I have believed, and for whose Cause only I am thus warmly concerned in the World.

CHAP. I.

Of Christianity in General.

John Faldo, in his Book, entituled, *Quakerism No Christianity,* begins with his Account of *Christianity, What it is?* As I honestly observed in my Answer, called, *Quakerism a New Nick-Name for Old Christianity.* What he laid down was this, *By Christianity we are not to understand all those Matters of Faith and Practice which Christianity doth oblige us unto; for Christianity is a large and noble Thing, and takes in all that's worthy in those Religions which it hath out-stript:* To which I gave this Answer, (though disingenuously mangled and transposed by my Adversary) *A strange Definition of true* Christianity: *For, if to Believe, and do all* Christianity *requireth, be not* Christianity; *then there is something beyond all that* Christianity *requireth to be believed and done that is* Christianity; *else I understand nothing.* This is all he brings of my Answer to ground his *Reply* upon, omitting that Part of his Definition, and my Return to it, which in Honesty stood him most upon to consider. But *first* let us hear his Reply to what he has quoted (for *Reply* and *Rejoynder* distinguish our Matter.)

Reply, *You may as well affirm a Finger to be a Man, when separated from the rest of the Man, as common Justice, Truth, &c. to be* Christianity.

Rejoynder, Though the Finger be not the Man, yet it is Part of the Man, therefore common *Justice, Truth, &c.* by his own Instance, are a Part of *Christianity;* but if no Part of *Christianity,* then may *Christianity* be without Justice or Truth. My Drift was in my Answer, and is in my Rejoynder, That something of what was at *Antioch* called *Christianity,* was in the World before Christ's Visible Appearance at *Jerusalem.* And that his Coming was but to bring the World to a more improved Knowledge and large Enjoyment of that Divine Power, Wisdom, Life, and Righteousness, which former Ages had comparatively but an obscure Sight, and imperfect Sense of; and this was my Reason, because the contrary Opinion excludes all antecedent Times from any Share in *Christianity;* and plainly shuts them out of all Hope of Eternal Salvation, which my *Adversary* takes a little Notice of in these Words.

Rep. *If the Scripture had any where said, that none but* Christians *shall be saved, his Consequences had been grounded.* But he might have found asserted in my Book, *That Salvation depends on a Right Belief and Acceptance of the Covenant of Grace.*

Rejoyn. The Scripture saith (as I instanced for Proof of that little Part of my Answer by him considered) *For there is no other Name under Heaven given among Men, whereby we must be Saved, neither is there Salvation in any other.* Now how to distinguish betwixt a Man's being saved by Christ, and his being a true *Christian,* I must declare my Ignorance: Nay, *J. Faldo,* though in Contradiction to himself, tells us, *That Salvation depends on a right Belief and Acceptance of the Covenant of Grace.* Let him either show how a Man may rightly believe and accept of the Covenant of Grace, *and yet be no Christian,* or else he does nothing to his own Purpose, whatever he does for ours. Christ is called, *God's Covenant;* The New Covenant stands in him. How a Man may believe in the Covenant, and not in Christ, How in Christ, and not be a *Christian,* concerns J. Faldo *to reconcile;* only, Reader, let

1673.

Part I.
Chap. 1.

let me tell thee, that of about Six Pages concerning *Christianity*, this Man has not undertaken Eight Lines to reply to, neither are those the Strength of my Discourse.

To conclude, I dare not repute *Enoch* to be no Christian, *who walked with God*; *Abraham* no Christian, *who saw Christ's Day, and rejoyced*; *David* no Christian, *who was a Man after God's own Heart*: Neither can I believe with him, that the Apostle's Exhortation, Phil. 4. *Whatsoever Things are True, Honest, Just, Pure, Lovely, of Good Report, if there be any Praise, think on these Things*, is no Part of *Christianity*; or, *that a Child of God is not a Good* Christian; or, *that* James *was mistaken*, who said, *That the Pure and Undefiled Religion was to keep our selves unspotted of the World*; which strange kind of Consequences unavoidably follow from *J. Faldo's* Assertion and Definition. For our Parts, As we think it no Wrong to *Christianity*, so no Discredit to our Case, that it should be reported that we believe the *Word nigh in the Heart* (the Apostle *Paul* calls the Word of Faith and Reconciliation) to have been preached by *Moses*; that Christ, the Promised Seed, bruised the Serpent's Head, as well before, as at, and since his Visible Appearance; That *Enoch* when he walked with God, walked in the Light, in which he felt the Blood of Christ cleansing from all Sin; That the Spirit of God strove with Men as well before Christ's Coming as since; and that some were led by it before as well as since; and therefore *Children of God*; *and if Children, then Heirs*; *Heirs of God, and Joynt-Heirs with Christ*. Not that we deny a Pre-eminence to Christ's Visible Coming, and the greater Benefits that came into the World thereby; we would not be thought so to mean, at any Hand: only this, that something of that Divine Life, Power, Wisdom and Righteousness, that then so super-excellently appeared and broke forth, was revealed in all former Ages, as Mankind was in a Capacity to receive it; wherefore the Difference lay in the Manifestations of the *One Thing necessary*, and not in several Things: So that the *Law* is, as it were, the Gospel begun, and the *Gospel* the Law finished; or as *Augustine* expresses it, *Lex est Evangelium absconditum, & Evangelium est lex revelata*. The Law is the *Gospel obscured*, the Gospel the *Law revealed*; That is, suited to the Capacity of Ages.

Qua. no *Chr.*
pag. 13.:

But *J. Faldo* is Angry, that in my Recital of these Words out of his former Discourse, *But the Thing Christianity might well be before the Name Christian*, that I left out these following Words, *so short a Space*. Saying, *I am a Man of a seared Conscience, and that it is pity any Reader should be so tame to be thus imposed on*.

Rejoyn. I know not what he means by these last Words, unless he would have every Man that reads me, beat me. I have always thought it becoming a Minister of the Gospel to make People *Tame* and not *Wild*; Sufferers, not Hectors; but such Expressions very well suit with *J. Faldo's* Religion: For my *Conscience*, it is not so seared, but I can feel and resent *J. Faldo's* Injustice. God knows I left out no Words designedly; nor could the Insertion of them have disappointed me: For if the Thing *Christianity* may be before the Name a Day, then a Year, and so an Age, till we shall come to the first Man that ever God saved. All Men must be saved by either Law or Gospel; Now the *Law* strictly considered, *could never save*, it gives Life to none: So imports the Scripture, and so asserts B. *Usher*, B. *Sanderson*, *Allen*, and others; then it must have been by the *Gospel*, which is by the Apostle called the *Power of God unto Salvation*: and if all Men that were ever saved, were saved by the Gospel, then *True Christians*; unless Men may believe the Gospel, be saved by the Life and Power of it, and yet be *no Christians*, that is, not the Men, the Term *Christians* (given first at *Antioch*) doth signifie. I shall offer this short *Argument* to the Reader's Consideration. *If He that is born again, be a Christian, and such*, as enter into the Kingdom of God, *be born again*, then *because* Abraham, Isaac, Jacob, Samuel, David, *&c. entred into God's Kingdom*, it follows, *that they were born again*, and consequently *Christians*. How pernicious is that Principle, which denies the *New Birth* to be so much as any Part of *Christianity*, when, indeed, the greatest, as Christ's own Saying proves.

The Truth of the Matter is, *The very Life, Power and Spirit* of the Gospel, or *Christianity*, which to other exterior Performances, is as the Soul to the Body, *John Faldo would fain exclude from any Share in Christianity*; and for our preferring and pressing *That*, as the most important Matter, he over-runs us with all the Vilifying, Scornful Epithets, a *Lucian* could bestow upon a *Christian*: Indeed, *his Frothiness* is such, that were it not for their Sakes, who may yet be ensnared by his Adventrous

trous and Imperious Assertions and Reflections, I should not think *his Vindication* worth one Minute of my Time. But he proceeds.

Rep. *I undertook to prove* Quakerism No Christianity *from the confessed Newness of it by their own Party.* Penn *tells us,* p. 21. *the first Letters of the Names of some, the bare Names of others, whose Words I quoted, but dare not transcribe their Words, being so far to my Purpose. Only a Part of* Pennington's, *who saith of the* Quakers *Dispensation, that it swallowed up that of Christ and the Apostles: which* Penn *would take off by telling me, I have no Candour in so Construing the Words; as if* Pennington, *who was a Scholar, could not express his Mind congruously, but must have* Penn *to be his Interpreter.*

Rejoyn. Now what any can make of this *Cloudy Paragraph*, that has not read our former Books (indeed of the greatest Part of *his Vindication*) if then, I know not: But sure I am, he ignorantly or willingly puts the *Lye* upon himself, and greatly bewrays his own *Weakness.* Is this your Combatant, you, that blow him with Pride and Rage, that he may only have Wind to Crack out against the *Quakers*? What Reply is this wretched, disingenuous Section to my Answer? If I quoted not *E. Burrough's* and *J. Whitehead's* Words at length, and but a few they were, I quoted that for which the rest left out were quoted. He would fix the Beginning of *Quakerism* about the Year 1651. this was the Drift of his Quotations, from whence he concluded *Quakerism No Christianity.* Hear my Answer, and by that it will appear how suitable or sufficient his *Reply* is. 'Well, But
' when came this *Quakerism* into the World? He tells us, about the Year 1651.
' quoting *E. B's Epistle* before *G. F's Great Mystery*, also a small Treatise writ by
' *John Whitehead* and *Isaac Pennington*; from whence he infers, that *Quakerism*
' *is a late Dispensation*, therefore not *that of Christianity.* But certainly, this Man
' hath taken a very Quick Course to *Unchristian* himself, and all the *Presbyterians*,
' *Independents* and *Anabaptists* in the World, as well as the *Quakers:* For I would
' ask him, if there was not a Time since the Primitive Age, wherein Darkness hath
' overspread the Earth, the Beast did Reign, and the pure Religion was wholly
' Wilderness'd? If so, consequently the *Resurrection of Truth* is no more a New
' Dispensation, or other than that of *Christianity, than a Man that is exiled his Country,*
' *is not essentially the same Man, when he returns, that he was before*—But since we
' are of another *Religion* by his Account, than the *Christian*, because we cannot
' say that we were always successively from the Apostles Times, their date also
' being of later Years. What will they say then? The Church was fled into the
' Wilderness; *Truth* exiled; *God* as a Stranger in Earth; yet *Truth* still the same
' in it self: Very well, so say we. God was pleased to renew the Right *Christian*
' Dispensation to us, and by us, according to *John's* Vision, that the Everlasting
' Gospel was preached *again*, intimating, *that there had been a Time wherein it was*
' *not preached.* If this be not a New Gospel, because anew or again preached;
' neither is that which *J. Faldo* calls *Quakerism* a New Dispensation, because it
' is *preaching a-new the Everlasting Gospel* to the Sons of Men; which is God's
' Power inwardly manifested for the Conviction, Conversion, Redemption and Sal-
' vation of the Souls of such as believe in it.

In which, *First*, I take in that Part of the Quotation which was material to the proving of *Quakerism No Christianity*, at least in my Adversary's Apprehension. *Secondly*, I have Answered that *Objection*, both by showing that the *Presbyterians, Independents* and *Anabaptists*, whom he owns to be *Christians*, were novel; and that the Everlasting Gospel was to be preached *again*; which implied, that a Time there was in which it was not preached; consequently, that his *Objection* could not be therefore of any Force, as levelled at us: To all which he says nothing, only asks a Question concerning my Reproof for his want of Candor in explaining *I. Pennington's* Words, viz. As if *Pennington*, who was a Scholar, could not express his Mind Congruously, but must have *Penn* to be his Interpreter. Let us see if this be any solid Confutation of what I said. Reader hear me.

" And though he particularly seems to triumph over *Isaac Pennington's* distin-
" guishing between the Dispensation of *Moses, Christ, and His Apostles*, and THIS
" *of our Day*, as if they had been three several Dispensations, and consequently, if
" *Christ's* was not that of *Moses*, because it swallowed it up; neither this the Dis-
" pensation of Christ, which *Isaac Pennington* saith, it swallows up: Yet to me it
" seems a pitiful Catch; and shows, he knows not how to take Things with that
" Candor they are writ. *I. P.* means not a Distinct Administration in Kind, but a
" Dispen-

"Dispensation of one and the same Light, Life and Power by Nature, at several
"Times, and sundry Manners to the World: *Christ was before the Law, under the
"Law, with the Prophets, but never so revealed as in that Holy Manhood*; Will it
"therefore follow, He was not Antecedent to that Appearance? Or He, that appeared then more Gloriously, had never shown himself before? Or because of a
"Difference in Manifestation, therefore *Not the same* HE (through all those several Manifestations) in himself? Certainly, this Man is very unjust to *I. P.*
"especially, when the Words above quoted, that speak of a Dispensation he experienced a little before God broke forth by us called *Quakers*, could have informed him, that he meant the Divine Breakings forth of God's Light and Truth, in
"order to the full Discovery and Recovery of *Lost Primitive Christianity*. So that
"this present Appearance swallowing up all going before it (had he so termed it,
"as he doth not, and is therefore wronged) *Is no more than God's Retrieving to us
"the Ancient Gospel, with Additional Blessings and Assistances, giving us the same
"Life and Foundation they had*, and what else he pleased by Way of Improvement,
"which alters not the Nature, no more than a *Child in Christ*, is not that Numerical Creature, but another Distinct Being, when a Man.

Now can any Understanding Man account my Adversary's *Idle Shifting Question, a Pertinent Reply?* What if *I. P.* was a Scholar, might he not therefore be abused, or misunderstood? Is Scholarship a Protection against Wresting? Must *I. P.* intend what *J. F.* will have him, and not what really he did? But that it should be so Offensive to him, for *W. P.* to clear and defend the Passage, is delighting rather to have us Wrong than Right. But the *Quakers* must be Heterodox, though it be but to save *J. F.* from the Disrepute of Lying. 'Tis clear that *I. P.* intended no New Administration, *but the Restauration of Pure and Uncorrupted Religion*; that he never so worded it, as by *J. F.* cited, that I charge him with, but he thought it best to give it the Slip, or else I must impute it to his Carelessness.

Any unbyast Reader may perceive, *My Adversary has enough of the Controversie,* or he would never write so mean a Reply to such an Answer.

To wind up this, which more particularly concerns Christianity, I say, *That there never was but One True Foundation from Adam's Day to this, upon which the Holy Ancients built, and that was* Christ Jesus, *the Lord from Heaven, called the* Second Adam, *and Quickning Spirit.* To deny this, were to overturn the Chief Corner-Stone of the Christian Religion; and how Men could build on this Foundation, and not be *Christians*, I know not.

The *Christians* of the First Three Hundred Years after Christ, were then by the *Jews* and *Heathens*, as we are by certain Professors and Prophane in this Age, accused of affecting and following Novelties, as we learn out of *Eusebius Pamphilus, Præparat. Evang. lib.* 1. and *Theophilus Antiochenus, lib.* 3. *pag* 119. *Arnobius, lib.* 2. *pag.* 40. *Tertull. ad Nation. lib.* 1. *cap.* 10. with several other Writers. The Account, some of them give us, of what the Christians said in their Defence, was this, *That the Christian Religion was for Substance, the same with that of the Ancient* Jews, *whose Religion claimed the Precedency of all others in the World.*

That the Religion was in Substance the same, is expresly asserted and proved by *Eusebius.* The *Ancient Patriarchs* were the Christians of the Old World, who had the same Faith, Religion and Worship common with us, nay, the same Name too; Touch not mine *Anointed,* Τῶν χρίσων μȣ *my Christ's*; or *Christians.* Thus Dr. *Cave,* in his *Primitive Christianity,* out of *Eusebius Præpar. Evang. l.* 1. *c.* 5. *p.* 9. *Clemens Alexandrinus admonit. ad Gent. p.* 57. about this old Objection, queries thus, Τί δὴ ἐχὶ τῇ πρώτῃ τροφῇ γαλακῖι χρώμεθα, &c. Why do we not use our Mother's Milk for Food, to which we were accustomed when we came first into the World. And why do we increase our Estates our Fathers left us, *&c.* intimating that the Difference between what we call *Law and Gospel*, or that *Religion* which the Holy Ancients professed before Christ's Coming in the Flesh, and that which Christ Jesus and His Apostles taught, *Was not in Kind, but in Degree only*, the Ceremonial Part excepted; which the same *Clemens* calls *Childish and Trifling*; and the Apostle *Paul, Beggarly Elements, serving only the Non-age of the World in Religion, and therefore to be laid aside upon a more improved Knowledge, and full Enjoyment of it.* And this Christ's own Sermon upon the Mount clearly evinceth, who runs the *Sin of Adultery* as far beyond the Act, as the first Lustful Desire conceived in the Mind: And from *True Swearing*, to *Yea, Yea,* and *Nay, Nay*; and from *Loving our Friends*, to *Loving our Enemies*; and from *Self-saving to Suffering*. I say, unless we should with the uncertain and irreverent *J. Faldo*, exclude the Life, Doctrine and Miracles of Christ from any Share in *Christianity*, because, says he, it's dated, with more Reason, *from Christ's Resurrection* (and consequently *Christ Jesus* before but an extraordinary Kind of *Jew*) we must needs conclude, that as the Tendency of Christ's Life and Miracles was to Preach, Live, and Confirm His Divine Doctrine, so the very Bent of that Doctrine, *Was the Improvement and Perfection of that Righteousness*, which in former Ages was but begun, and more imperfectly manifested: So that *to be under Grace,* is not to live in the Breach of God's Law Uncondemned through Christ's Personal Obedience wrought wholly without us, *but to be led to deny all that Ungodliness, and those Worldly Lusts,* for which the Law takes hold upon the World, according to the Apostle to the *Romans*, Rom. 8. 1, 2, 3, 4. *There is no Condemnation to them that are in Christ Jesus, who walk not after the Flesh, but after the Spirit*, (implying, that who walked after the Flesh, were so long not under Grace, but under Condemnation:) Again, *For the Law of the Spirit of Life in Christ Jesus, hath made me free from the Law of Sin and Death* (that is, not only from *Death*, the Wages, but from *Sin*, the Work that leads to it:) Yet farther, *For what the Law could not do in that it was weak through the Flesh, God sending his own Son in the Likeness of Sinful Flesh, and for Sin Condemned Sin in the Flesh, that the Righteousness of the Law might be fulfilled in us, who walk not after the Flesh, but after the Spirit.* So that to be under Grace, is to be under the Government and Leadings of it; and to enjoy that Divine Power, which fulfills the Law, and redeems from those Corruptions, which prove Men rather to be alive without Law, than under Grace that fulfills it. Upon the whole; since some in all Ages have been taught, *(Tit.* 2. 12.*) To deny Ungodliness; and to Live Godly*, and that they could not so have done, without the Grace that brings Salvation; And since the Seed of the Serpent has been bruised in them, and that it could not be without Christ, the *Promised Seed*; and since such were then *Turned from Darkness to Light, and from Satan's Power unto God*; and that all this is purely Gospel and Christian; something of Christianity was in the World before that Visible Appearance of Christ, from whose Name the *True Religion* was so called: For though there have been Diversities of Gifts, yet the same Spirit; though Difference of Administrations, yet the same Lord. And though God, *Who at sundry Times, and in divers Manners, spake in Times past to the Fathers by the Prophets, hath in these Last Days spoken unto us by His Son*, yet he was the same God, who spoke by the Prophets, that spoke by the Son; though it is always confest, not in so plain, express, and excellent a Manner: The Difference therefore lay in the Manifestation, rather than in the Thing manifested. For through all Generations, there has been but one Seed, Truth, Grace, Word, Life, Power, or Spirit, by which any of the Sons and Daughters of Men were ever saved; and consequently *J. Faldo* has greatly wrong'd the *True Christian Religion*, as well as contradicted the *Ancient Writers*, and abused us, in Dating Christianity from the Time of Christ's Bodily Resurrection, and so bitterly reflecting upon them *That Conform not to his Narrow and False Apprehensions*.

CHAP. II.

Of Quakerism, *as this* Independent *Priest scoffingly calls our Holy Religion.*

IN my Defence of *the Truth we profess,* shewing not only the Consistency of it with *Christianity*, but proving it to be *Christianity*, there are four Passages he takes an abrupt Notice of. His Words concerning the first run thus.

Rep. *To purge away the Character I give of a* Quaker, *he tells you,* pag. 9. We never said, That the Light within every Man was the only Lord and Saviour, and Very God; let him shew us any such Passage, of any One acknowledged *Quaker*, and he will say something.

Now Reader observe his Reply. *The Man cannot see Wood for Trees. I quoted him Forty Places in my Book, that will prove it.* For Instance: *All Power in Heaven and Earth is in it*; Smith's Primmer, pag. 14. Again, *I will make you know, that I the Light, which lighteth every Man that comes into the World — am the True, Eternal God,* G. Fox, Jun. &c. These I quoted in my Book, yet could Penn say, *I thought to be believed Hand over-head.*

Rejoyn. That this *Adversary* is base with a Witness, remember, *Reader*, that there is not One Testimony, much less Forty, in that Place I quoted, and unto which my Answer was made. Next, observe how he suggests my smothering of those

1673.

Part I.
Chap. II.
See my Answer, p. 193.

ṫhofe Teſtimonies he brings, whereas I have particularly anſwered the *latter*, which includes the Force or Tendency of the *former, and Five more of his falſly pretended Forty.* But to the Point: *That I cannot ſee Wood for Trees,* is a very mean and *Wooden Reply*; what I have ſaid in my former Book, ſtands *Unanſwered*, and indeed is *Unanſwerable.* I ſhall contract it thus: " *No Man that believes* " *Scripture, will dare to deny that God is Light; That every Man is Enlightned by* " *Him*; And, *that by Him who is called Light, all Things are upheld: And that He* " *alone is Saviour:* A Doctrine that *J. Faldo* teaches, pag. 84, 85, 89. *That we* " *never did aſſert, That the God that made Heaven and Earth, was Comprehenſible* " *within the Soul of Man; yet that he gives Light to the Soul of Man.* To which, with much more, he returns us *Not One Word of Anſwer*, but would make People believe, it has been the Courſe I have taken with him. To conclude, *He muſt either deny Chriſt to have all Power in Heaven and Earth, to be the True Eternal God, or, That He who has that Power, and is that God, is not that True Light that Enlightneth every Man that cometh into the World*; or his Labour is but very Vanity, whoſe Wages will be Vexation of Spirit. But thus far we are well-aſſured, that *J. Faldo*, for all his Shews of Reverence to the Scripture, overturns the moſt evident Teſtimonies therein contained, by this one Aſſertion, *That God, who is Light, ſhines not in the Heart of any Man on Earth, nor ever did*; For what elſe can be the Conſequence of his decrying our Principle, that aſſerts, *Chriſt to be the Univerſal Light, Enlightning every Man that comes into the World*; Or, *That the Light wherewith every Man is Enlightned is Chriſt, or God?* I affirm, that which quarrels this Principle, would not in the very Ground, have *Chriſt to be God,* indeed, *Not God to be God*; ſeeing it is an utter Denial of His Omnipreſence, ſince God is not manifeſted but by His own Light; and He being every where, His Light cannot be limited, becauſe it cannot be diſtinguiſhed from himſelf. But what our *Adverſary* would be at, by this Kind of Reaſoning, he helps us in his next Particular to underſtand.

Rep. *He attempts to excuſe* Burroughs'*s Phraſe from Blaſphemy, viz. Your imagined God beyond the Stars. But how? They were expreſſed of People's imagining Him to be in the Likeneſs of Man, and ſo denying his Omnipreſence, that he ſhould not be below, as well as above.* To which he replies thus: *A rare Excuſe that denies* Chriſt'*s Manhood, and making the Manhood of* Chriſt, *in whom the Fulneſs of the Godhead dwells Bodily, to be a Popiſh Ubiquitary.*

Rejoyn. Muſt this paſs for my Confutation? A rare Excuſe indeed. But for what? Not *W. Penn*'s Denial of Chriſt's Manhood; but *J. Faldo*'s baſe Perverſion of *E. B*'s Words. The Queſtion was not about *Chriſt's Manhood*, but of *God Himſelf*, who prepared it in Time; A pitiful Shift, to infer *from God*, who is a Spirit, *to Chriſt's Body:* We know, that's not every where; But the *Word that was with God, and was God*, is not confinable. Though if the Truth were known, *J. Faldo's* Zeal for Chriſt's not being a Popiſh Ubiquitary, centers in his Belief of meer *Anthropomorphiſm,* I mean, that God is confined to a Body, and that Body to a certain Place; elſe why ſhould he oppoſe to my aſſerting of God's Univerſal Preſence, Chriſt's Manhood, the Fulneſs of the Godhead dwelling Bodily in that Manhood, and Chriſt's being Reſident in ſome particular Place? But it is after this lame, crabbed, and inſignificant Way of Writing, that he vindicates his firſt Piece of Forgery, and wicked miſ-giving of our poor Friends Meanings. But to proceed.

Rep. (Pag. 7.) *He tells you of the Companions I rendred* Quakeriſm *to be attended into the World with, and adds what elſe* J. Faldo'*s Devil pleaſes; yet inſtead of denying what I ſaid (except the Epithets) he thus excuſeth it. Finally, did not the Devils howl and roar, and tremble, when ſeeing they ſhould be diſlodged by One ſtronger than themſelves —— And was there no Terror in all this? Yes verily. And moreover, whereas People have taken the* Quakers *to be poſſeſſed of the Devil when ſo behaving themſelves, Mr.* Penn *hath here confeſſed they were not miſtaken: And more than that too, that they themſelves were* Devils, *for it was they that roared.*

Rejoyn. If this be to be a fair *Adverſary*, there is no ſuch Thing in the World. I will tranſcribe for thy Sake, *Reader*, what I excepted againſt in his firſt Book, and how I anſwered it.

" *But once more*; Chriſtianity *entred the World with Raviſhing Songs, and Hal-*
" *lelujahs of the Angels,* (Pag. 15, 16.) *Healing all Diſeaſes, Caſting out* Devils,
" *Preaching Peace: But* Quakeriſm *entred the World, as if Hell had broke looſe,*
" *and Poſſeſſion by* Satan *had made Way, and fitted Souls for the* Quaker'*s Spirit* —
" *O the*

"*O the Hell-dark Expressions of the* Quaker's Spirit, *frightful and amazing Words,*
"*bitter Curses, Howlings and Roarings;* And what else J. Faldo's Devil *pleaseth,*
"*by which to render the* Quakers *Odious.* Well! But to answer him.

"It was a Time of *Joy,* and a Time of *Sorrow;* the Spirits of the Just rejoy-
"ced that he was born forth into the World, and that Sun of Righteousness risen,
"whose Discovering Light, and Refreshing Beams, would renew the World, that
"had in great Measure been bewildred, since it's first innocent State: *But there-*
"*fore was it not a Time of Wo, Sorrow, Terror, and Grievous Distress, to all the*
"*Workers of Iniquity?* Did not Christ come to bring War as well as Peace, a
"a Sword, a Fire upon Earth? Did not his Fore-runner come *in an astonishing*
"*Manner, in differing Attire, of another Diet, and from a Desolate Place to Preach*
"*Repentance,* and to warn them with an *O Generation of Vipers, to flee the Wrath*
"*to come?* Did he not say, *That an Ax (a sharp and Terrible Instrument) should*
"*be laid to every Unfruitful Tree?* And did not the Apostles Preach to the *Prick-*
"*ing of the Hearts of Thousands,* and *Paul* by Name, *That Felix himself trembled;*
"and All, as knowing the *Terrors of the Lord themselves,* they warned others;
"*wherefore Judgment is said to have begun at the House of God.* Finally, did not
"the *Devils Howl, Roar and Tremble,* foreseeing they should be dislodged by one
"stronger than themselves, *Christ, the Son of the Living God?* And was there no
"*Terror, Dread and Amazement in all this?* I perceive it may be a Virtue in the
"Primitive Christians, but a Vice in the *Quakers,* at least in *J. Faldo's* Account.

"But this know, O Impartial People! the *Quakers* were over-taken by the
"mighty Hand of God, and great were their *Travels, and Pangs of Sorrow, under*
"*the Righteous Terrors of the Lord,* whose Hour of Just Judgments was come;
"and being thereby made Witnesses of His Heavenly Work, and redeemed through
"Judgment, *they became Ministers of Judgment unto others;* and the Terror of it
"struck Thousands, *the Devils trembled,* &c. And art thou given up, *J. Faldo,*
"to call *Light,* Darkness, and *Darkness,* Light? *The Terrors of God,* the *Possessi-*
"*ons of Satan,* and *Remorse of Conscience,* Hell broke loose? *O Unhappy*
"*Man!*

Reader, this was my Answer; how much of it he concerned himself with, I have already observed. What Use he made of that little cited is very obvious, viz. *To conclude us Devils.* What a False and Frothy Reflection is that, for one that would be accounted a *Divine?* To call this a *Reply,* is to abuse Controversie. 'Tis manifest, that *Quakerism* was not attended with more amazing Sights and Symptoms, than what our *Adversary* must needs confess to have been the *Companions of Christianity:* And as they agree in the Manner of their Appearance, so do *J. Faldo* and the *Pharisees* in their Judgment of both. Does *John Faldo* conclude us little better than *Devils?* The *Pharisees* called our Lord and Master, *Beelzebub,* the *Prince of Devils.*

Thus has TRUTH been ever accounted *Heresie* by the Priests and Rabbies of that Age in which it has appeared; we do the less wonder that *John Faldo* should not understand of what Spirit we are, who is yet ignorant of his own, and scoffs at the Revelation of that Eternal Spirit, which can alone give him to relish either. For the *Epithets* he bestows upon *Quakerism,* they stink too much to be medled with: *If they be* Christian, *there is nothing* Antichristian *in the World.* To rebuke his *Reviling,* he counts *Railing;* and it is come to that pass with his scolding Adherents, that for the *Quakers* not to pass by his unworthiest Reflections, however unprovoked, without any Reproof, is to merit their sharpest Retorts in the most vilifying Terms; I know not what to infer from such an humoursome Carriage, but that it is expected from the *Quaker's Religion* it should bear that, which *John Faldo's Vindication* tells us, his cannot; a great Credit to our Cause, against his Will.

Thus far of *Christianity* and *Quakerism,* as they are contra-distinguished by our Adversary.

CHAP. III.

Of the SCRIPTURES.

MY *Adversary* begun his first Chapter in his former Discourse, upon this General Charge, *The* Quakers *deny the Scriptures.* The Proof he offered was this, *The* Quakers *deny the Scriptures of the Old and New Testament to be the of God, and therefore they Deny the Scriptures.* Upon this account I thus delivered my self, He entitules his Chapter. "*That the* Quakers *Deny the Scriptures.* I "was almost astonished at it, because he pretended to prove all out of our own "Books, and none such had ever come to my Hand; but upon Perusal I found "this to be the Upshot, *That the* Quakers *Deny the Scriptures to be the Word of* "*God.* My *Adversary's Reply is,*

Rep. (Pag. 13.) *This is not the first Cordial you have made of a Wilful Untruth, nor yet the last by a great many. And you who summoned up Nine Arguments of mine more, which were the Contents of the Nine Chapters next following, should have been ashamed of calling this One, which was the First of Ten, the Upshot, and then insult. But I shall try how you break this single Cord, this One of Ten.*

Rejoyn. I will not say he has wilfully wronged me, but wronged me he has. I did not say, that it was the Upshot of his whole Discourse concerning the Scriptures, but of that single Chapter; for had I reputed his *Nine following Arguments* undeserving of any Notice, I might have called this single One the Upshot; but having singly refuted his subsequent Arguments, I could not in good Sense call the First the Upshot. 'Twas not therefore the Upshot of the whole, but of that Chapter in which the Word is used. I had good Reason so to term it, since the Proof was too particular for the Charge; it was not my wilful Untruth, but his Mistake. His suggesting, as if I only encountred that single Cord, is very disingenuous; for I throughly considered Nine following Chapters. Hear him farther.

Rep. *That you deny the Scriptures to be the Word of God you grant: But you say,* (Pag. 25.) *I declare to the World, that we own them to be the Declaration of the Mind and Will of God, with many other Things, which I shewed to be short of the main Ends of the Scriptures.*

Rejoyn. Whether those other Things left out, are short of the main Ends of the Scripture, or no, will best be seen by considering what those Things are.

I do declare to the whole World, *That we believe the* Scriptures *to contain a Declaration of the Mind and Will of God, in, and to those Ages in which they were written, being given forth by the Holy Ghost moving in the Hearts of Holy Men of God: That they ought also to be Read, Believed, and fulfilled in our Day, being Useful for Reproof and Instruction, that the Man of God may be Perfect.* Now if this belongs not to the main Ends of Scriptures, either they are none, or they are unknown. However, it was not so much the End, as Name of Scripture, that was then controverted. Again, he goes on thus:

Rep. (Pag. 25.) *I shall easily grant, that one Word stands Representative of many. An odd Phrase that represents him not able to express himself congruously. I have heard of Persons as Parliament-Men, but never of a Representative Word before.*

Rejoyn. He might have pardoned me an incongruous Phrase, if such it had been; for I have twenty Times over been so kind to him: But I must tell him, *it is not less proper,* though less used *in Words* than in *Persons.* He shews Ignorance in that *Philosophy* he pretends to be a *Master* of, where there are many single Words or Terms, that are significative of entire Sentences; but *(argumentum ad hominem)* granting to the *Scriptures,* that they are *the Word of God,* does not our Adversary repute that Title *Representative* as well as *Expressive* of those many thousand Words contained therein, if so, then there is a *Representative Word*; If not, it can never be so called in our *Adversary's* Sense. Again, he brings me in thus, *I think it is as good Sense to call a King's Letters King, as the Scriptures the Word of God.*

Rep. *But by your Favour, Mr.* Penn, *It is neither Non-sense nor Bad-sense to call a King's Letter the Word of a King.*

Rejoyn. This is nothing to the Purpose; the Stress lies here, *The Word of God being a Title given to Christ,* as the Title *King* is to a *supreme Magistrate,* whether it be Reverent or Significant to call the *Declaration,* Christ, the Word of God, any more than to call the Declaration of a King by the *Title* of King? For we therefore decline to give that Title to any Thing below Christ himself, to whom the Scriptures most emphatically ascribe it.

Because I said that it might be the Word of Advice, Reproof, Instruction, which Christ the Great Word of God livingly sows in the Hearts of Men and Women, that Christ spoke of, when he said, *The Cares of the World choak the Word,* and it becomes Unfruitful. He replies,

Rep. *Here you have yielded the Cause to save Christ from being the choaked and unfruitful Word.*

Rejoyn.

Rejoyn. I need not have done so for any such Reason, since Christ may in a Sense as well be Choaked, as by Sin afresh Crucified, and the Spirit Quenched. Nor could *Unfruitful* oblige me to give away the Cause, since the Word is *always Unfruitful, where rebelled against.* But is there no Difference, *J. Faldo,* between a Word of Advice Spiritually, livingly and powerfully sown in the Heart, by Christ the Great Word of God, and that Advice, Reproof, or Instruction declared by Writing?

This brings to the Point, *Whether the Scriptures or Christ may most deservedly be stiled the Word of God?*

Christ is God's living Oracle, and rightly called the *Word of God,* because that which livingly speaks forth the Will of God to the Souls of Men; The *Scriptures* are but that *Revelation declared and recorded*; consequently they can have no Right to that Title which is so suitably ascribed to the Author of that Revelation. To be sure *J. Faldo* acknowledges that they are not the Living, Powerful, Self-sufficient Word of God; Nor does he pretend to dispute for them to be such a Word of God as the *Quakers* deny them to be. Though it seems very strange to me, that there should be *Two Words of* God; the one quite differing from the other; or that any Word of God, if two there were, should be of it self Impotent or Insufficient, as he seems to allow in his *first Book,* pag. 20. 27. *Vind.* page 14, 16.

That the Word of God cannot grow old, decay, be lost, mis-rendred, corrupted, transcribed, re-printed. (p. 30.) But hear what he says to me.

Rep. Did we hold as you, that it is to be Understood of no other but Christ, it would be an Absurdity, but upon our Principles, none at all. Would you say, that the Scripture is absurd; For we are not as many that corrupt the Word of God, 2 Cor. 2. 17. *Many did so, and many do so still, of whom you are a Ring-Leader.*

Rejoyn. Truly if I am, I would be glad to know it, that I might be sorry for it. I would not willingly deceive my self and others, both of the Joys of this Life, and that to come. But I would desire *J. Faldo* to consider, if his *Greek Testament* will allow his *Translation,* and least of all, his *Argument,* which is this: *If Christ cannot be corrupted, somewhat else besides Christ is in Scripture call'd the Word of God.* I am not so lean with my Learning but I will spare him a Little. I find *Valla, Erasmus, Vatablus, Castalio, Clarius, Zegerus,* and *Grotius* say, the Greek Word there καπηλεύοντες signifies not *adulterantes,* but *cauponantes, vel abutentes re quapiam ad quæstum,* that is, *We are not as many who* Merchandize *with the Word of God, or use it to self Ends,* making a Trade of it, or as several of our Old *English* Translations have it, *chop and change,* which more sorely reflects upon my *Adversary's Profession,* than mine: For though I am a Corrupter of Scripture in his Sense, I am sure he is a Trader with it, in it's own Sense. I might instance to my Defence, in several other Languages, particularly the *Italian, Spanish,* and ancient *French* Translations, but I will be brief. Now, unless it be absurd to assert, that some Men have and may make worldly *Advantage to themselves* from that Place, the Living Eternal Word of God hath ministerially given them in the Hearts of People, and *false* to affirm, that the Scriptures of the *New Testament* were not then all written, nor gathered or compiled, as now they are, or made Canonical and Publick, 'till the Council of *Laodicea,* about the Time of *Julian the Apostate,* Anno 364. I cannot see how any may justly blame me, *for denying the Scriptures to be the Word of God,* from the Passage cited by my Adversary; that Men may make so ill an Use of the Living Word of God none dare deny. Now, that the *Scriptures* were at that Time Imperfect and Scattered, is clear: They were *Imperfect,* in as much as but Five of Twenty One Epistles were then writ, besides *John's* History of the Gospel, and his Revelation, and *Luke's* Acts of the Apostles. *J. F.* may hence see what a lame Imperfect kind of Word of God he disputes for. But I would query, Was there not a Word of God before them? *What was that Word of God that grew and multiplied before any New-Testament Writings were in Being?* Did not the Apostles preach it? Therefore I rather take it to be such a Word of God as attended the Prophets before them in an inferior Ministration, namely, the *Living, Powerful, Quickning Word,* who from it's various Operations is said to be as a *Fire,* an *Ax,* an *Hammer,* a *Sword,* a *Word of Reconciliation,* of *Patience,* of *inward Washing,* of *Faith* that overcomes the World in true Believers, that was *with God* in the Beginning, and *was God,* which at sundry Times and in divers Manners spoke ἐν τοῖς προφήταις, in and by the Prophets and Apostles, which was the *Author* of the Scriptures, and therefore before them.

Act 12. 24.

So that the *Scriptures* are no more than the *Mind* of the Living Word of God declared by Writing upon several Occasions; consequently to call them an *Holy Declaration of the Word of God*, is a more Evangelical and suitable Title than the Word of God, whose Declaration they are.

That they were scattered, and several Centuries or Ages uncollected, *History* tells us; particularly we find it in the *Council of Trent*, which is given us by he Learned and Judicious *Pietro Soane Polano*: They could not run their Canon higher than the *Council* of *Laodicea*, which, as we said before, was about 364 Years after Christ; at what Time, says a great Author, *Ambition prevailed with the Doctors of the Church, and they began to think* de piis fraudibus *of Holy Cheats, and would have their Doctrines pass* pro legibus, non pro consilio, *for Laws, not Counsel.* I prove as much and more out of several *Independent Authors*, who seem to give all for gone before the End of the third Century, though if some of them should now stand to the purest Tradition, they must needs give their present Practice for gone.

I cannot but observe after what a suspected Rate the *Scriptures* have been both first collected, and then convey'd through the several succeeding Ages; 'twas well said of my former Author, *Dubium igitur non est, quin Testamenta, vetus & novum, monumenta vera sint earum rerum, quæ dictæ & factæ sint a Prophetis & Apostolis.* Where though he calls them not the *Word of God*, yet allows them to be *Monuments* of those Things which were said and done by the Prophets and Apostles. But as he, and others, so I may well object, *Are we sure that the Judgment of those who collected them was sufficient to determine what was right, and what not?* For that which gives Scripture it's Canon, is not Plurality of Voices, but that Word of God which gave it forth; If that Divine Counsellor presided not, what Assurance have our *Anti-revelation Adversaries* of their Doctor's Choice? And granting that they have not rejected any Writing given forth by the Holy Ghost (which is a great Question) and that what they have given us was in the main writ by Inspiration (which I believe) yet how we shall be assured, that in above three hundred Years, so many hundred Copies as were doubtless taken, should be pure and uncorrupted? Considering the private Dissensions, the Readiness of each Party to bend Things to their own Belief, with the growing and succeeding Faults of leaving out, adding, transposing, *&c.* which Transcribers might be guilty of, perhaps more through Carelesness than Design, is beyond *J. Faldo's* Skill upon his Principles to inform us. From hence we may observe the *Uncertainty of* J. Faldo's *Word of God*, who by Authorities can never prove the Scriptures to be given forth by Inspiration, nor that they are truly collected; neither could those Persons, who first made them Canonical, be assured of the Exactness of those Copies they then found extant, nor was the Collector's Judgment Infallible; and to come nearer to our Times, Learned Men tell us of little less than Three Thousand *several Readings in the Scriptures of the New Testament in* Greek.

Far be it from me to write this in any the least *Undervalue* of that Holy Record: It's only to shew the weak *Foundation* my Adversary's *Faith stands upon*; I believe great and good Things of them, and that from no less Evidence than the Eternal Word that gave them forth, which hath oftentimes given my Soul a deep Savour of those blessed Truths it declares of; only we cannot allow them to be *The Word*, though the Words of God; and the rather, for as much as we see the great and general Neglect that People are guilty of towards that Living, Powerful, Regenerating Word of Life, by whom alone all right Knowledge and lasting Peace is deriv'd to the Soul of Man, through this Apprehension, that in having the *Writings* they have *the Word of God*, and therefore look no farther, the very State of the professing Jews of old, who thought better of the Scriptures than of Christ, believing to have Life in them, at what Time they crucified the Lord of Life and Glory. From whose Proceedings we learn thus much, That the worst Enemies to the invisible Word of Life, may carry the greatest seeming Respect to, and bestow the highest Titles upon the *Scriptures* that were given forth from it.

In short, It was when Men turned from the *Power* of Godliness to the *Form* only, that they did Canonize and lay so vast a Stress upon them. In the first and second hundred Years after Christ, they were so scattered, that very few had all of them; and it is not unreasonable for us to believe, that many had none of them, especially those of the New Testament: Were they therefore without *the Word of God*, and a sufficient Rule for Faith and Practice? Surely not; *It was an Administration*

ministration of Life and Power, of writing the Law in the Heart, and putting the Spirit in the inward Parts. From whence came that *Christian* Answer to the Heathen concerning Swearing, Fighting, and such Contra-Evangelical Practices, They could not do so because of God in their Consciences. At that Time of Day *the Anointing led them into all Truth.* But in Process of Time, when *Christians* grew Careless and Worldly, whereby they *lost the Power of Godliness*, then they began to set up an outward Pompous Religion, ascribing that to the Letter and Form, which was only due to the Spirit and Power; And as thus entered the *Apostacy* into the World, so where Men are not turned and conformed to that Eternal Spirit, and Divine Immortal Power, the *Apostacy* still remains. And our End in pressing People unto the *Eternal Word of Life* is, that they may be brought out of Death and Darkness, which the *Scriptures* can never do. They are a *Declaration* and *Testimony* of Heavenly Things, but not the *Heavenly Things themselves*; and as such, we carry an high Respect unto them: We accept them as the Words of God himself; and by the Assistance of his Spirit, they are read with great Instruction and Comfort. I esteem them the best of Writings, and desire nothing more frequently, than that I may lead the Life they exhort to; and whatever slight Apprehensions my disingenuous *Adversary* is pleas'd to have of these Kind of Acknowledgments, I write the naked Truth of my Heart, knowing I must give an Account to God.

CHAP. IV.

His Pretence of our Equalling our own Writings and Sayings with the Scriptures.

Without any flourishing Reflections, most commonly the Head and Tail, and sometimes Middle too, of my *Adversary*'s Reply, I shall lay down his Words.

Rep. The Means I used for confirming the first Part of this Charge were two. First, Their pretending them to be from Immediate Inspiration: This he is so far from denying, that he pleads for it; but after such a rude, impertinent Manner, that I should but injure you, and shew my self idle to transcribe and animadvert upon it.

Rejoyn. In how rude and impertinent a Manner I pleaded for it, the *Reader* may best judge by perusing something of the Passage.

" For *Inspiration*, the Scriptures are not more express in any one Thing. (P. 36, 37.) *No Man can know the Things of God by the bare Spirit of a Man.*

" The *Scriptures* are a Sealed Book to all but those who know them by the
" same Hand that originally gave them; so that however *common* they may be in
" the World, they are Strangers to them that understand them not: And though
" *Old*, respecting the Time, when they were revealed to the Saints, yet *New* to
" every Age. So that we assert not a Revelation of New Things, but a renewed
" Revelation of those Things God made former Ages Witnesses of; otherwise
" Men are no more benefited by them; And to be benefited, they must be made
" ours by the Spirit, which made them the Holy Ancients.

" In short, No man can understand Spiritual Things but the Spiritually Discern-
" ing, nor can he so be without the Inspiration of the Almighty; This is Scrip-
" ture.

" Now the Author of those Queries, and *J. Faldo* also denying Inspiration,
" *they consequently deny themselves to be Spiritually Discerning*; And for Men *not*
" *Spiritual* to judge of Spiritual Matters, much less to write of them, and bid
" their Writings go, and *throw down Self-will and exalt the Truth*, is Vain and Ido-
" latrous: For, the Scriptures themselves, considered meerly as such, are unable;
" much more Writings founded on *Self-will*; For it's the alone Privilege of God's
" Power and Spirit, and no Writing whatever, distinct from it, can perform that
" Great and Mighty Work in Man.

Now as Rude and Impertinent as this *Answer* may be in *J. Faldo*'s Eyes, his *Reply* has not afforded me Light enough to see it. He would prove us guilty of holding *Inspiration*, as if to do so were a Crime; From a Passage of *John Story's*, who rejected certain Queries, exhibited against the *Quakers*, because meerly grounded upon the Author's Imagination of certain Passages in Scripture, and not any certain Knowledge or Experience received from the Revelation of the
Spirit.

Spirit. It must be left to the *Reader* to judge how pertinently I returned upon my Adversary. Sure I am, that *Self-willed Queries* can never throw down *Self-will*: And to urge Scripture not experienced, is *to steal the Words of Truth from our Neighbour*. Inspiration was in Request after Scriptures were in the World; And indeed they are unintelligible without it. The New Birth is never the more known for Christ's Saying to *Nicodemus*, though thereby we are taught, that without it no Man shall enter into the Kingdom of God: It is the Spirit alone that reveals the Mysteries of Re-generation; therefore to deny *Inspiration* or *Revelation*, is to overthrow the only and Evangelical Way to Divine Knowledge. *Erasmus* himself could tell us, *What Men set forth by Man's Device, may be perceiv'd by Man's Wit*: But the Thing that is set forth by the Inspiration of the Holy Ghost, requireth an Interpreter inspired with the like Spirit; And without the Inspiration of it, the Secrets of God cannot be known; which is also the Substance of the fourth Article exhibited against the *Lutherans* in the *Council of Trent*, as an Erroneous Doctrine they held, That *to understand the Scripture neither Gloss nor Comment is necessary, but only to have the Spirit of a Sheep of Christ's Pasture*. *Vatablus*, on this Passage in *Job*, But there is a Spirit in Man, and the Inspiration of the Almighty giveth him Understanding, saith, *There is no Man, that doth not partake of the Spirit, and from Almighty God and his Spirit, Understanding and Wisdom is to be sought*. Adds *Clarius*, there is *no Understanding in Men*, nisi ab altissimo afflentur, *unless they be inspired from the Most High*. *Drusius* is yet clearer, *Our Eternal Help is from God, who illuminates our Minds, without whom we are unable to understand any thing in Divine Matters, and that inspires Men with that Understanding, which neither Age, nor Industry, nor Doctrine of any Man can possibly give*. *Cradock*, a famous *Independent* Preacher, tells us, That *if Men had all the Sermons, that ever they heard recorded, in their Memory, though some may think them very knowing, yet truly they might be miserable, confused and blind. For that it is the Spirit of God alone in the Heart, clears, orders, assures, and settles Things*; yea, *that the Scripture is a dead and speechless Thing without the Spirit of God*. This, says he, *is the exceeding Greatness of the Power of the Spirit of God*; And *it is a wonderful Thing to see how quickly the Spirit of God will make a Scholar ripe*. In short, as to him, he greatly extols the *Dispensation of the Spirit*; and, p. 210, ventures at a Kind of *Prophecy*, That *in these latter Times God will exalt his Spirit, and throw down every thing that exalts it self against the Spirit, and stands in his Light*. He affirms *the Spirit to be within, that the Children of God are taught by it*; *for*, says he, *If thou be a Saint, thou hast the Spirit of God as truly dwelling in thee as in the Lord Jesus Christ* (now Blasphemy) and that *the Way to know this Spirit to be in us, is from it's own Evidence, and that it is the Way to know it in others too*; from whence he draws such Kind of Conclusions, *That the Lord Jesus is anointed, and so are they; we have the same Unction with Christ; we have the same Offices with Christ; we have the same Love of God, the same Spirit, and the same Kingdom with Christ. The Church is the Fulness of Jesus Christ. It is said of the Oil that was poured on* Aaron, *It ran upon the Skirts of his Garments: so Christ being anointed, that Oil runs on us. Nay, the least Saint is as real a Prophet, Priest and King, as the Lord Jesus was (for he dwells in him) only in all things he must have the Preheminence*.

William Dell, no small Man in the Account of many who profess not themselves to be *Quakers*, positively saith in Answer to this Objection, That Men now are not to receive the Spirit in that immediate Way to understand the Scriptures, in which it was given to them who wrote the Scriptures (the very Point depending between *J. Faldo* and me) *Surely Mr. Simpson will not deny that the Spirit is given to that whole Church which is the Body of Christ*, seeing Paul saith, If any Man have not Christ's Spirit he is none of his, he is no Member of his. Now the Spirit is always given, to whomsoever it is given by the Father and the Son, as Christ taught his Disciples, promising them that *the Father would send the Spirit to them in his Name*; And also that *he himself would send it to them from the Father*; and was this Promise only made to them, and not to all the Faithful also? Doth not *Paul* say, Rom. 12. 13. of the whole Church, that *by one Spirit we are all baptized into one Body*, and are all made to drink into one Spirit; *because ye are Sons, God hath sent the Spirit of his Son into your Hearts, crying, Abba Father?* Gal. cap. 4 And do they not receive it alike immediately from God? Who can give the Spirit of God to Man, but God himself? When God promised to pour out his Spirit in the last

last Days upon all Flesh, did he Name any *Difference* in the pouring of it out, saying, some shall receive it immediately, and some mediately? No; But all who receive it, receive it alike immediately from him. And *by this Spirit* (saith *W. Dell*) *did Holy Men speak the Scripture, and by this only do Holy Men of God understand the Scripture.*

To this *Objection*, that Men now are to get Knowledge, to wit of the Scripture, by Studies and humane Learning, and not by Inspiration (still the very Matter betwixt us) he boldly, briefly and smartly answers, *This Doctrine carries the visible Mark of Antichrist upon it. For it is only the Inspiration of God, that enables a Man to know the Things of God, and not a Man's Study or humane Learning.* It is not in this Case in him that wills and runs, but in God that sheweth Mercy. Wherefore Christ hath said, *No Man knoweth the Father but the Son, and he to whomsoever the Son will reveal him.* Wherefore *Paul* prays for the *Ephesians*, that *God would give them the Spirit of Wisdom and Revelation in the Knowledge of Christ*, without which Spirit of Revelation Christ and the Father can never be known. Wherefore to *deny the Inspiration* of God's Spirit now, is the most gross and palpable *Doctrine of Antichrist and his Prophets.* To confirm what he writes, He brings several *Testimonies* out of *Chrysostom, Wickliff, Tindall, Zwinglius, Luther, Latimer* and *Calvin.* I will transcribe but two of them. Of the Knowledge of the Gospel *Zwinglius* speaks thus, *We must needs be taught of God, not of Men; for this is the Saying of the Eternal Truth, which knows not how to Lye,* John 6. *Luther* gives us his Mind thus, *The Scriptures are not to be understood, but by that very Spirit by which they were writ.* No Man sees one jot or tittle in the Scriptures but he that hath the Spirit of God; For all Men have a darkened Heart in such sort, that if they could speak and know how to bring forth all Things of the Scripture, yet have they not any true Sense or right Knowledge of them. For (saith *Luther*) *The Spirit is required to the Understanding of the whole Scripture, and of every Part thereof.* To this I am willing to add the Testimony of a Famous, English, Godly, and Learned, *Martyr, John Philpot*, in a Conference with *Bishop Bonner*, in his eleventh Examination before him and several other Bishops. *B. Bonner* asking, what meanest thou by writing in the Beginning of thy Bible, *Spiritus est vicarius Christi in terris*, The Spirit is Christ's Vicar on Earth? *Philpot* gave him Answer after this Manner, That *Christ since his Ascension worketh all Things in us by his Spirit, and by his Spirit doth dwell in us.* Again, in Answer to one *Morgan*, who mockingly queried, *Have you alone the Spirit of God, and not we?* he thus answered, *I say not, that I alone have the Spirit of God; But as many as abide in the true Faith of Christ have the Spirit of God as well as I.* Again, by way of Defence of his severe Rebuke of this insolent and scoffing *Adversary* (like mine) when he told him, that he *Raged*, he thus replied. *Thy foolish Blasphemies have compelled the Spirit of God that is in me to speak that which I have said to thee, thou Enemy of all Righteousness. I tell thee plainly, thou art not able to answer that Spirit of Truth which speaketh in me for the Defence of Christ's true Religion.*

Of this Judgment were the most eminent *Martyrs.* I shall conclude with *John Bradford*'s plain Assertion to the Arch-Bishop of *York. We do believe and know the Scriptures as Christ's Sheep, not because the Church saith, they are the Scriptures, but because they be so, being thereof assured by the same Spirit which wrote and spake them.*

How all these *Testimonies* can be True, and yet *Inspiration* Untrue, I shall leave with the sober *Reader* to judge. And if my *Arguments* are still *Irrational*, and my *Testimonies Insufficient* or *Erroneous* in his Account, it will become his Pretences to Divinity, not with Squibs and Railing, but by Reason, Scripture and better Authorities to discover it.

The second Way he took to prove *our Equalling our Writings to, and preferring them before the Scriptures*, is our Pretence to Infallibility. Hear what he says.

Rep. *Infallibility W. P. does not deny to be their Pretence, but would make it very necessary, and casts the contrary Opinion again, and again, and again too, as Dirt in my Face.* This is your Fallible, Errable, Uncertain *J. Faldo.*

Rejoyn. It is ill done of my *Adversary* to call my Answer *Dirt*, which is so serious, and to which he has replied little else but Dirt.

I perceive all along, notwithstanding the vast Difference he represents us to be at, as to a Worldly Condition, this *Priest* is ten Times more enraged, at the Just Consequences I draw from his own *fallible Doctrines*, than he thinks a *Quaker*

1673.

Part I.
Chap. IV.

My Anſ. p. 36

ought to be diplcaſed with him, for his numerous and ſcurrilous Provocations. But if it be *Dirt*, it ſticks faſt ſtill, for I find none of it wiped off. And how dirty it is the Reader may judge by peruſing it.

'He that doth *not Infallibly* know, what he pretends to know of God or Reli-
' gion, *knows nothing certainly* which concerns either. Now if Men cannot attain
' to any ſuch Certainty, farewel all Religion: For, *that a Man ſhould affirm, and*
' *not know whereof*; That he ſhould profeſs God and Religion, yet be uncertain of
' both; But that *J. Faldo* ſhould preach up, and *profeſs himſelf Errable in all ſuch*
' *Doctrine.* Who ought to believe him? Why ſpends he his Breath at a venture?
' What Reaſon have any to believe him againſt us, who is Uncertain of what he
' ſays againſt us by his own Principle. This is your *Independent, Errable, Fallible,*
' *Uncertain* J. Faldo.

Reader, this is by much the greateſt Part of that *Dirt*, he ſays, *I caſt in his Face*. But I muſt tell him, that greater *Ignominy* no Man can well bring upon the *Goſ-pel*, than that thoſe who are converted by it are both *Uncertain* of the Truth of it, and their own Converſion; he either ſeems to have forgot, or never to have underſtood the Meaning of thoſe Words delivered by the Apoſtle *Paul*, That *their*

Col. 2. 2.

Hearts might be comforted, and being knit together in Love, and unto all Riches of the full Aſſurance of Underſtanding, to the Acknowledgment of the Myſtery of God. Again, And *we deſire that every one of you do ſhew the ſame Diligence to the full Aſ-ſurance of Hope unto the End, Let us draw near with a true Heart in full Aſſurance of Faith.* And the Apoſtle *John* tells us, *He that believeth on the Son of God, hath the Witneſs in himſelf.* That *they knew that they were of God, and the whole World lay in Wickedneſs*. And that *the Son of God was come, and had given them an Underſtanding, that they knew him that was True, and were in him that is True, even in his Son Jeſus Chriſt*. And *this is the Record that God has given to us Eternal Life, and this Life is in his Son. He that hath the Son hath Life,* 1 John 5. 10, 11, 12, 19, 20.

If theſe prove not *Certainty in Faith, Hope* and *Eternal Life*, there is no Truth proved in Scripture; for that People ſhould have full Aſſurance, Chriſt in them their Hope, and Life, and Witneſs of theſe Things in themſelves, knowing him that's true; and yet be Uncertain of their Faith, Hope and Life, and doubtful of their Inward Witneſs, and the Evidence and Knowledge that is given by him, cannot be leſs contradictory, than to affirm Men ignorant of what they know, or guilty of what they are Innocent. To be *infallibly aſſured* of what we believe, is no Error in the Opinion of *John Philpot* and Biſhop *Latimer*, whatever uſe is made of it now to diſcriminate a *Quaker*. The firſt to the Biſhop of *Chicheſter*, who reflected upon him, as conceiting himſelf better learned than the Biſhop and the reſt of his Brethren (a Flout my lordly Adverſary has more than once beſtowed on

Book of Mart.
p. 577.

me) anſwered, *I take upon me the Name of no Learning; I boaſt of no Knowledge, but of Faith and of Chriſt, and that I am bound undoubtedly* (or infallibly) *to know, as I am ſure I do.* The Biſhop replies, *Theſe Hereticks take upon them to be ſure of all Things they ſtand in; you ſhould ſay rather, with Humility, I truſt I know Chriſt, than that I be ſure thereof;* which is ſo like *J. Faldo*, that he ſeems to be the Biſhop revived, proudly catechiſing and reproving the poor *Quakers*. But hear *John Philpot's* bold and ſmart Anſwer; *Let him doubt of his Faith that liſteth*, ſaith he, *God give me always to believe that I am ſure of True Faith and Favour in Chriſt*. Biſhop *Latimer* in his ſecond Letter directed to Sr. *Edward Bainton*, a Favourer of him that little Time he lived in Queen *Maries* Reign, who through his Deſire to preſerve him, was willing to allay the honeſt Man's Zeal for the Truth from the great Uncertainty that is in the World about Truth; ſays he, *Firſt ye miſlike, that I ſay I am ſure that I preach the Truth,* ſaying, in Reproof of the ſame, *that God knoweth certain Truth; Indeed God alone knoweth all certain Truth, and God alone knoweth it as of himſelf, and none knoweth certain Truth but God, and thoſe that be taught of God, as ſaith St. Paul, For God hath ſhewed it unto them; And Chriſt himſelf, They ſhall be all taught of God. And your Friends deny not but that certain Truth is communicated to us, according to Capacity. But as to my Preſumption and Arrogancy, either I am Certain or Uncertain that it is Truth that I preach: If it be Truth, why may not I ſay ſo? If I be Uncertain, why dare I be ſo bold to preach it? And if your Friends be Preachers themſelves, after their Sermon, I pray you aſk them, whether they be certain and ſure they preach you the Truth or no, and ſend me Word what they ſay, that I may learn to ſpeak after them. If they ſay, they be Sure, ye know what followeth: If they ſay, they be Unſure, when ſhall ye be ſure*

that

that have so doubtful and unsure Teachers? Thus much of *Infallibility*; when he has answer'd this we may give him some more; mean Time we shall proceed.

Rep. But farther, says W. P. *Cannot one Man be another Man's Brother, and not the Eldest Brother? This hath done your Work, or all Hope is lost.* It seems the Scriptures and your Writings may without Offence call one another Brother, yet not be thought to aspire to Equality. But why? Because forsooth you do not say, they are the Scriptures Elder Brother. I thought till now that Brethren had been a Term of Equality. And though in Humane Births there is a Natural Right to the Firstborn above the Rest, yet not in the Productions of Scripture; for the New Excelleth the Old Testament in Glory.

Rejoyn. In *Similes* there is some Allowance with honest Men, but none to be hoped for from *J. Faldo.* But if it be so hard for him to bear I cannot help it. Several Writings may be given forth from the same Spirit without coming upon the Vie. If we must needs equal some of our Writings to the Scriptures, because given forth by the same Spirit, then must every the least True *Christian* be equal to the greatest Apostle, because endued with the same Spirit.

The *Pouring forth of the Spirit,* which was the Promise of the Father, we have proved the very Substance of the Gospel, and *Inspiration* as necessary as Divine Knowledge, because the only Way to it. Whatever therefore hath been writ from *Adam's* Day to this, or shall yet be to the End of the World, from the Motion of God's Spirit in the Hearts of any of his Children, stands as nearly related to the Scriptures, as his several Manifestations of his Spirit in his Servants Writings. The Ancient *Christians* were Brethren, having one Father; Were they therefore equally dignified in Degree of Fellowship? And that was the Meaning of my former *Simile,* disingenuously taken by my Adversary: For as there is a Degree in natural, so in spiritual Births; The Dignity of the first lies in Priority of Time, the Dignity of the last in a more full Discovery of Immortality and Eternal Life. Thus the Scriptures of the New exceed those of the Old Testament. Where there is the first and most ample Declaration, there must be the Pre-eminence. Now alas, what can we boast of, that was not formerly testified unto; *we exalt no singular Spirit, neither walk we in an untroden Path*; 'tis the Everlasting Gospel we bear witness unto, and to the Revival and Breakings forth of that ancient Life, Truth, Spirit and Power, which according unto divers Dispensations, hath made People true Children of God. What do you esteem *your own Meanings* and Interpretations? Do you not intitle them to a very near relation, the *Text Interpreted?* We never intended to bring our Writings upon the Vie, and dispute, with the Scriptures, for the Preheminence: But *our Writings* farther *declaring of the same Truth from the same Spirit,* are related to them. If to testifie and exhort to the same Truth the Scriptures declare of, and that in the same Spirit of Christ by which they were given forth, be offensively to equal or prefer such Testimonies, we are indeed guilty of great Presumption. But if it be Scripturally True, *That as many as are led by the Spirit of God are the Sons of God*; and that such as are so led, may by that Spirit farther be drawn forth to fresh Testimonies to any ancient Truth or Truths declared of in the Holy Scriptures (whether by way of Prophecy, Information, Exhortation, Reproof or Comfort to Believer or Unbeliever (as must not be denied, since *God cannot be limited)* it cannot be Presumptuous or Arrogant, to affirm any Kindred or Relation between any such Writing or Writings of the Scriptures of Truth.

In short, Either there are never to be more Inspirations after the Apostles Decease, and consequently no more Testimonies nor Prophecies to be than what the remaining Scriptures give us, or *the Pouring out of the Holy Ghost belongs as well to after Ages* as to that (as hath been abundantly proved) and *therefore fresh Testimonies and Prophesies by Way of farther opening or pressing the ancient Truth, recorded in the Scriptures of the Old and New Testament, may in after Ages be given forth,* unless God and his Spirit should be limited, and many Parts of the Scripture remain unfulfilled.

If any shall object, *'Tis Adding,* according to *Revel.* 22. 18. I would have them know, that *the Addition intended was not of other Writings, but other Doctrines.* I will conclude this with a very notable Passage, delivered in a Book entituled, *An Examen of the late Assembly of Divines Confession of Faith presented to the Parliament,* Anno 1659. pag. 8, 10. *It is evident that the Lord will have Prophets in all Ages, and especially when he is about to bring extraordinary Judgments upon the World in general, and upon the Church in special; and that the Last Times shall a-*

bound most of all with the Prophetical Spirit. So that these extraordinary Ways of God's revealing himself, neither are ceased, nor shall determine in the militant Church.

Thirdly, whereas you say in the sixth Section, that nothing at any Time is to be added to the Scriptures of the Old and New Testament, whether by new Revelations of the Spirit, or Traditions of Men; We desire to know what Warrant you have thus to determine. If you say that in *Rev.* 22. 18. it is written, *That if any Man shall add unto these Things, God shall add unto him the Plagues that are written in this Book.* We answer, That so much in effect was forbidden long before, as Prov. 30. 6. *Add thou not unto his Words, lest he reprove thee, and thou be found a Lyar:* Yet many Books of the Holy Prophets and Apostles have been added since the written Word of those Times. Yea, the same Inhibition was given by *Moses*, Deut. 4. 2. and 12. 32. Ye shall not add to the Word which I command you, neither shall you diminish ought from it: Therefore this Addition thus prohibited must necessarily be understood of any new Doctrine in substance differing from the Old, even that of *Moses*; But that there should be a Vindication of the same when mis-understood, or a more full and free Publication of the same, by the Prophets of the Old Testament, or inspired Men of the New.

Rep. My Adversary *tells me a Blind Story, of preferring our Writings above the Scriptures, as being from God essentially in us;* But this, saith he, W. P. *has not one Word to.*

Rejoyn. I had little Reason for it. He confesseth, pag. 43. of his former Discourse, that he expected not to find any such Word as *Essentially* in our *Authors*. Doth he think I was to play the Fool in answering of him, a Thing he begs Excuse for in Replying to me? We affirm with the Scripture, that *God tabernacles in his Children*, that *Christ dwells in his People*, and that *the Holy Spirit Temples in his Saints*. *He was full of all Grace and Truth, and of his Fulness have we received* a Measure of Grace and Truth; and *he that sanctifieth, and they that are sanctified are all of one*; *After this Way that he calls* Heresie, *know we, worship we, and enjoy we the God of our Fathers*. But what was the second Argument by which he endeavoureth to prove we prefer our Writings and Sayings above the Scriptures.

Rep. My second is their Characters they give of them: concerning the Scriptures; *Feeding Death with Death, the Letter which killeth. Of their own Sayings, The Voice of the Son of God was utter'd forth by him,* &c:

Rejoyn. I told him before, ' That Death is a State without the living experimen- ' tal Knowledge of God, and his Work in the Heart. And that State, I said, will ' talk of the Fame of Wisdom, as saith the Scripture. At this he Scoffs, and makes as merry with it, as would some prophane Stager. And in the midst of his Desires to be thought *Meek*, to this little of a large and sober Answer, basely cropt, he gives the hard Names of *Non-sense, Folly* and *Impious*. The Scripture justifies me in what I said. For Men dead in Trespasses and Sins talk of God, and that perhaps according to the Letter of Scripture too; why may it not be then said, That Death talks of Wisdom, as well as Dead Men. But this he calls *arriving at as perfect Non-sense as* G. Fox *himself.* He would have done better not only to have answered, but considered my following Words, ' Death or dead Men's ' talking or feeding upon the Words of Scripture, being ignorant of the true Sense of the Scripture; But it had been vain to have expected this Candor from him.

In short, *The Scripture without the Spirit is Dead*, say some *Independents* as well as *Quakers*. Men Unregenerate are dead in Sins, say all. What can such Men's Feeding upon the Scriptures be, but one dead Thing feeding upon another. Remember it was Christ that said, *It was the Spirit alone that quickens*.

But that *this Man* may shew himself almost *irrecoverably gone in Dishonesty*, because I said, ' There is no Comparison betwixt what God requires, and an im- ' mediate hearing of his Voice, and being sensible of his living Touches upon the ' Soul: Writings are but holy Things at second Hand. He implies and replies thus.

Rep. Their Writings and Sayings they pretend to be perfectly immediate from the Spirit of God; *But the Scriptures handed through many Ages: And therefore there is no Comparison, because he affirms theirs to be more immediate.*

Rejoyn. Reader, Right me in this Matter: Was the Comparison betwixt our Writings and Sayings with the Scriptures, or any Writings or Sayings, and the
Imme-

Immediate Voice and Living Touches upon the Soul? Do not I expresly say, *Writings are but Holy Things at second Hand*: If so, how do I make our Writings holy Things at the first Hand? Do not I prefer the Voice of God to the Soul, and his Immediate Touches upon it, as well before our own Writings and Sayings, as the Holy Scriptures of Truth? And who dare deny that heavenly Enjoyment of God, to be the blessed End of Writings and Sayings too?

It is after a Manner not less Perverting, though much more Scoffing, that he deals with my Answer about our Friends *Denying Light to be in Scripture*, That is, said I, There is not living, spiritual, essential Light in the Scriptures. Now hear him.

Rep. *Did he not intend his Writings for the View of those only who understand no more right Reason than a Horse doth Hebrew; He could not expect any Success in such pitiful Attempts. Whatsoever makes manifest is Light, saith the Scripture: But if there be no Light, but according to the Character he gives; Candles, Stars, Moon, Sun, Reason, W. P's Writings also, are gross and perfect Darkness.*

Rejoynd. This Man would pass both for Just and Rational; *Just he is not*, who has left out those very Words which remove all Pretence to Scruple, viz. (*Answ.* Pag. 42.) " *That the Scriptures carried a Descriptive and Declarative Light with them*, that is, a Declaration from and of the Divine Light. Dares he affirm more? Or does this deny all other Lights besides the Living, Spiritual and Essential Light? Unjust Man! to leave out that which only could right his *Adversary*, and oppose his infamous Ends.

Besides, he abuseth Scripture; the Light mentioned in that Passage is the *Living Spiritual Light of God in the Conscience*, Ephes. 5. 13, as the Verse at length proves, viz. That *all Things that are reproved are made manifest by the Light*; *for whatsoever makes manifest is Light*. Again, Hear what he says to the same Matter.

Rep. (P. 22.) *And yet W. P. tells you of the Author of the Quakers Book, he writ to give Notice, of the Day-spring of God's Eternal Light of Life to the World, i.e. the Light within, that needeth the Light of Farnsworth's Book to be seen by: What cannot such a Reconciler do?*

Rejoyn. But what cannot such a Scoffer do, who dare affront God, and be Injust to Men in the View of the World? which is manifested thus; *First*, As I deny'd a Living, Spiritual and Essential Light to be in the Scriptures, or any other Writings; so did I acknowledge *a Descriptive and Declarative Light to be in them*, and measurably in other Writings, as well as the Scriptures, which he hides from the Reader, and then triumphs over a false Consequence, *Secondly*, If the Light within needs *Rich. Farnsworth's* Book, as a Light without, to be seen by, because it is by it testified to; the same upon his Argument may be said of *God himself, who is Light*, that he needed the Light of the Scriptures to be seen by. But what shall I say? The Man is desperate in his Ventures.

From my concluding upon his Accusation, and my own Answer, so that our *Adversary's* Argument amounts to thus much. * *We therefore prefer our own Writings before the Scriptures, because in all our Writings we earnestly endeavour, by numerous Quotations, to prove what we write to be according to Scripture*; For this he flyes out into this following Reply.

* Which concerns him, if he would have what he writes to be according to Scripture.

Rep. (Pag. 22.) *I leave it to my Reader* (says *J. Faldo*) *to give a Name to this Passage, the like to which for a daring Untruth the World hath scarcely been ever acquainted with; yet the Man pretends besides all other Graces to Infallibility. In many a large Libel I could produce where there is not one Quotation of Scripture:* W. Smith, *often quoted in* Quakerism no Christianity, *in his Directory for Religious Principles, consisting of above Two Hundred Pages, hath not one Scripture quoted, not one Exhortation to read the Scriptures; But as his main Scope, denies and throws Dirt upon them.*

Rejoyn. Reader, right a poor People once; Never, I think, did Man so slander Persons and Principles: Dwell a while here, then give thy Judgment of both. My *Answer*, unencountred by him, lay thus.

" Let it suffice to all impartial People, that we only desire to make a Difference
" between the Writings and the Thing written of; And to the Eternal Overthrow
" of our *Adversaries* (not wholly without their own Help) since they think the
" *Titles* we give our Books (very glorious in themselves) most unworthy of them,
" but proper to the Scriptures, which they say we slight: Let it be considered,
" that not one of those Books is destitute of Scripture; but is either generally in

My Answ. Pag. 42.

1673.

Part I.
Chap. IV.

" a Scripture Stile, (this Diſtinction I fear my *Adverſary* wilfully omitted) or par-
" ticularly defended by Plenty of expreſs Scriptures cited. *Therefore of Neceſſity*
" *they, the Scriptures, muſt alſo partake with them in common of thoſe famous Titles.*
" And thus far have they the Preference, that they are quoted on Purpoſe to give
" the Truth we write greater Credit. What is that *Greater Credit*, but to be ex-
" actly agreeable with them.

Now, Reader, *firſt* conſider; I did not ſay, that *not one Book is not without Plenty of expreſs Scripture cited*, as my Anſwer clears; but that every one of them is in a Scripture Stile, or particularly defended by expreſs Scripture cited.

W. Smith's Catechiſm belongs to the firſt; and if he would have faſtened the Lye deſervedly upon me, he ſhould have made it appear, that he treated not on the Truth declared of in Scripture, *ſcripturally*, which is as much the contrary, as any thing can be; For his *Catechiſm* contains nothing elſe; neither is it managed any other Way.

Secondly, If he can produce one Book, endeavouring to defend, or prove our Principle to be true, without ſuch Quotation, (for to ſuch Books the Paſſage by him cited relates) I will confeſs his *Ranting Abuſe* to be a Juſt Rebuke: But I make this Challenge to him, *To give me one Book out of a Scripture Stile, that is not Controverſial; or any Controverſial Book without expreſs Scripture cited?* If he cannot, his *vain Inſults* fall thick upon his own Head: But let us ſee if the Deſign of *W. Smith*'s Catechiſm be *to deny and throw Dirt upon the Scriptures*: In the thirteenth Page of *William Smith*'s Catechiſm, printed *Anno* 1667, we have this Queſtion and Anſwer *concerning the Scriptures*.

Q. Of what Service are the Scriptures, as they are given forth and recorded without?

A. Much every Way, unto thoſe that have received the ſame Spirit from which they were given forth; for unto ſuch they are Profitable, and make Wiſe unto Salvation, and are unto them of Service for Inſtruction, Edification and Comfort: The ſame Spirit in them receiving the Teſtimony of the Spirit, as it is declared in the Scripture; And there is an Agreement and Union in the Spirit within, and alſo in the Words without; And ſo there is Inſtruction, Edification and Comfort by the Scriptures unto all that are in the ſame Spirit that gave them forth.

Now, in my *Adverſary*'s Words, I leave it to my Reader to give a Name to his Paſſage, both againſt me, our Books, and particularly *William Smith*: The like to which, *for a daring Truth*, is not commonly told.

For if to confeſs to the Scriptures, to believe, to read, and to fulfil them, as what by the right Spirit makes Wiſe, through Faith, to Salvation, being full of Inſtruction, Edification and Comfort; *If this*, I ſay, *be to deny and throw Dirt upon them*, *William Smith* is deeply guilty; but I leave it with God, and my Reader's Conſcience, whether *J. Faldo* hath not denied all Honeſty in throwing ſo much Dirt undeſervedly upon *W. Smith*: But let us ſee what *Reply* he makes to my Anſwer in his Inferences, and indeed there is need of Patience in having to do with ſo much unworthy Shifting and ill Language; His firſt Inference was this: *If the Light within was always ſufficient, the Scriptures and other Means were ever ſuperfluous*. His Second, *By the ſame Ground the Writings of the* Gentiles, *yea, the bitter Scoffs of* Lucian *and* Julian *the Apoſtate, are of equal Authority with the Scriptures; for they reſulted from their Light within*.

Quak. noChr.
Pag. 59.

To all which, (as my full Anſwer) only thus much I will ſay, That though all Ability was and is in him the Light, whom we declare to be the Light of all Mankind to reveal the whole Mind of God. (Here he leaves off, and takes the reſt from the Beginning of another Paragraph, about a Page off, to clap to it) Yet that he ſo baſely miſtakes Reaſon, and abuſes his Reader, as to infer from the Ability of the Light (whether obey'd or diſobey'd) the Uſeleſneſs of the Scripture. Now hear his Reply.

Rep. (Pag. 23.) *Obey'd or Diſobey'd, were no Words of mine. But how can we know any thing the better for* W. P's *hard Names he puts upon it, ſeeing there is nothing that pinches him, but he hath preſently an hard Name for it. And ſo impertinently and ſlovenly impoſed, that a Man might learn far more genteel Railing under an Hedge; As baſe Compariſon,* p. 43. *Black as Hell in Malice,* p. 46. *The Impudence of his Wickedneſs,* p. 49.

Rejoyn.

Rejoyn. Whatever pincht me before, I hope the Reader will bear Witness for him, he has been more merciful in this Reply. He first brings little or nothing out of my Answer, and says just nothing to what he brought. He did not say *obey'd* or *Disobey'd*; The more the Shame; As my Answer to the Inference will sufficiently manifest, the Substance of which was this, " That if the Light had been " obeyed, and God's Spirit not rebelled against, there had not been so much Need " of *Line upon Line,* and *Precept upon Precept.* Therefore was the Light or Spirit " in it self insufficient; or Line upon Line superfluous. Is the Ability of a Master " questioned by the Use of Books ? or the Use of Books superfluous, because of " his Ability ? *Insufficiency belongs not unto the Light, but to the Creature that can-* " *not receive it as it is in it self.* A Condescension to such Ways and Means as " suit the great Weakness and Distance of degenerated Man from God, can no " more conclude the Light insufficient, than God, Christ and the Holy Spirit. To which let me add, that as the Law, so very much of Scripture, was added, because of Transgression; that makes it not superfluous, no more than the successless Strivings of the Spirit to bring out of Transgression (because of Man's obstinate Rebellion) renders the Spirit not sufficient.

To the *second Inference* he drew, I gave a large Answer, which I shall contract; " That the Light of the *Jews* and *Gentiles* was one in it self; That as either writ " by that Degree of Light they had, they might both be said to write by the same " Light, and yet the Writings be no more equal than the Degrees of Manifesta- " tion: That the Writings of the *Jews* greatly transcended those of the *Gentiles*, " from that greater Discovery God vouchsafed to them. That his bringing *Lu-* " *cian* and the best *Gentiles* upon an Equality, was wicked. That nothing lies " heavier against the Light within in that blasphemous Saying, than against the " Spirit in the Prophets, Apostles, and every good *Christian*, who by his *infatua-* " *ted Way of Arguing*, would make us believe that *Lucian* and *Julian* acted from " the Light within, *because they acted from something within,* and that *there is no* " *Distinction to be made between their Writings and the Scriptures themselves, upon* " *our Principle, because they writ according to the Light that was in them*; as he " says. What is this but to deny all Testimony within, or at least it allows but of such an one, as gives equal Evidence to *Apostates* and *Christians*, Men acted by the Power of Darkness, and the Principle of Light ? It shall now rest with my Reader to point where the Pinch was, For the *Ill Language* he says I gave him, to wit, a Line and an Half made up out of six Pages given on distinct Provocations; Let us examine [*Base Comparison,* Page 42.] This fell out upon his *comparing us with the* Papists (which we shall anon consider) *How slovenly* I was in doing so, I will not be mine own Judge [*Black as Hell it self in Malice,* Page 46.) fell from me on this Occasion; says *J. Faldo: I know not hardly any worse Lucian and* Julian *said of Jesus of* Nazareth, *the Scripture and* Christianity, *than the* Quakers *have done under other Names.* Now, Reader, if thus to Unchristian, Unscripture, *in fine,* Unreligion, Prophane, yea, Atheize a whole Body of People, bringing them into parallel with loose and heathenish Scoffers and Persecutors of the *Christian* Religion, who all this While reverently believe in Christ Jesus the Saviour of the World, in his Life, Death, Resurrection, Ascension, Doctrine and Miracles: I say, if thus to use us, is not *as black as Hell in Malice against us,* there can be nothing Black, Hellish, or Malicious. For the last Piece of Railing (as he calls it) [*The Impudence of his Wickedness,* p. 49.] What could it be else, to charge the Impiety of *Julian* and *Lucian* upon the Light within, and tell the World, *That upon the* Quakers *Principle, they may conclude their Writings as Canonical as the Scriptures of Truth.* But this Man studied Personal Reflection more than the Cause, or he would not have given but five Lines of nine Pages of my Answer, and never have considered that, as he ought. I could be glad to read one Page of his *Vindication,* without unnecessary Reflection, who for a Line and an half of pertinent Rebuke, by him out of six Pages of my Answer hardly pickt, (and by me fully defended) cries out of my *impertinent slovenly hard Names,* and that *genteeler Railing may be learned under an Hedge,* where I leave him to be better taught.

But he is very angry I contract his Comparison of us with the *Papists* in the Matter of Infallibility and Inspiration thus, " He tells the World, the *Papists* own " Revelation, and the *Quakers* hold Revelation also; therefore the *Quakers* are " *Papists*, or very near them. Hear his Reply.

Rep.

Rep. (Pag. 24.) *How can I guide* W. P's *Pen, to write Truth in Matter of Fact? If he find such an Argument in my Book, I will be content to be his Bond-slave. Can you believe that a Man can be bless'd with Apostolical immediate Revelations, for every Thing in Religion, that is not so honest, as to use the very Eyes in his Head?*

Rejoyn. By this we may perceive, it is high Tide with *J. Faldo*. First, Reader, I deliver not the Words in a different Character from my own, because I did not pretend to quote him: But that it was the Drift of the Comparison, and so no Wrong to his Intention, the Thing it self abundantly proves. *The Papists hold Revelation,* and *the* Quakers *own Revelation;* what's the Meaning of these two Propositions, unless it be the Conclusion I drew? But left the Man should be believ'd, hear what he says himself in his first Book, (Pag. 63.) *It is no little Absurdity in the* Quakers *to make Out-cry against* Popery, *while they plant and hug the Root in their own Bosoms.* Again, in the same Page, *It were no hard Matter to prove an Agreement in a Multitude of Particulars between the* Papists *and* Quakers.

Besides all this he brings in a Story (Page 55.) of a certain *Romanist*, who coming into *England*, and being ask'd, which of the multitude of Sects came nearest unto the *Roman Church?* reply'd, *The Quakers*. And this *J. Faldo* says, *he remembers*. How then he should forget, to that Degree of Abuse, that there is any Argument in his Book to prove the *Quakers very near to the* Papists, who in his Story uses that very Word to make People believe it, I cannot tell, unless his great Desire to bedirt *William Penn* transported him beyond all Remembrance of what he had writ. I might now demand his Promise, *of being my Bond-slave:* But, alas! Proud Man and Insolent, he is too high for that Office, if such I could accept of: Though I know not how he can come off, unless with this Passage, Page 57, *The* Quakers *out-go the* Papists *Far*; therefore *the* Quakers *are not* Papists, *nor Near them*. He thought I made him abuse us beyond his Intention, and he both intended and abused us beyond what I represented. If in that I wronged him, he has more Reason to Forgive than Revile me.

But how comes it to pass, that he says nothing of my *argumentum ad hominem*; *The* Papists *own a God, a Trinity of Persons,* &c. And J. Faldo *owns a God and a Trinity of Person, therefore* J. Faldo *is a* Papist, *or near a kin to one*. Would this be Just? If not, neither is his Conclusion of Force against us. *J. Faldo* holds something in common with *Jews, Turks, Heathens* and *Papists;* he would not take it kindly, if we should therefore conclude him, to be all or any of them? But he gave this the Go-by, which shews, he seeks not the Promotion of Truth, but Disgrace of his *Adversary*, indeed his very good Friend, though his own Indeserts will not let him believe it.

CHAP. V.

Of the Scriptures being the Rule of Faith and Life, and Judge of Controversy.

THE first Thing in this Chapter he chargeth me with, is *Forgery*; Let us see how he proves it.

Rep. Pag. 25, 26.) *The Charge in my fifth Chapter is, That the* Quakers *deny the Scriptures to be a Rule of Faith and Life, or a Judge and Determiner of Religious Controversies;* but P. as if he had sworn not to repeat my Words faithfully, transcribes them, *That we deny the Scriptures to be a Rule of Faith, and Judge of Controversies.*

Rejoyn. Reader, observe the *Forgery* lies here, that I left out *Life*, after *Faith*; and *Determiner*, after *Judge*; and *Religious* before *Controversies*: But because that which is the Rule of Faith, is the Rule of Life; and that Judge and Determiner are all one; and that the *Controversies* intended, were not about Questions in *Mathematicks, Philosophy, Trade,* or *Law*, common or civil, but purely about *Religion*, I thought it no Forgery to leave out Words not necessary, or what from the Nature of the Rule and Controversy on foot were manifestly implied; especially when I made no Advantage to my self by it. But every such little Thing must be called by an hard Name, or *J. Faldo* would have little to write, and but a few to believe his Books.

But to the Point, (avoiding many Occasions for severe Reflection) Perhaps he grants us what we can desire. For upon my asserting, that what was and is more general than the Scriptures, is most properly the General Rule, he replies,

Rep.

Rep. (Ibid. p. 26.) *I never affirmed them to be a general Rule, nor is it that I charge the Quakers for denying ; but I charge them with denying them to be any Rule at all of Faith and Life ; he mistakes the Question, and yields my Charge to be their Principle, and pleads for it,* p. 54.

Rejoyn. If that be not the *Question,* how have I granted the Question ? Do I plead for his Charge because I plead against the Scriptures being the General Rule, Pag. 54. which he says is no Part of the Charge, and what himself undertakes not to condemn ? But sure I am, *if the Scriptures be not the General* Rule (as he implies (and thereby cuts his own Throat, and grants to the *Quakers* the Question, as largely as needs to be) They are not *The Rule* by Way of Excellency, or the Rule by which God's People in all Ages have walked ; for that was and is General : So that the Scripture, upon his own Concession, is but a particular Rule, and therefore must be subservient to *the Spirit (who is the great Evangelical Rule)* as are many other Instruments, that have been made Use of upon several Occasions.

He might have learn'd thus much in Pag. 53. of my Answer, where I say that *we acknowledge the* Scriptures *to contain many Holy Rules for Godliness.* I would know of him how that could be, and yet deny them to be a Rule in any Sense. But we have good Reason to deny them to be *the Rule of Faith and Judge of Controversies, which can neither give nor govern Faith, nor Judge of Controversies,* as the many different Perswasions in the World fully prove ; for then all that have the Scriptures would be of one Perswasion, as it is most certain, those are, who have, and walk by, the One Spirit.

Wherefore since *the Scriptures themselves testify to the Spirit, as the great Judge, Rule and Leader,* especially under the New Covenant, where the Law is not written on Tables of Stone (much less Paper) but of Flesh, to wit, the Hearts of the Sons and Daughters of Men, the Spirit, and not the Scripture must be the Rule of Faith and Judge of Controversy.

In short, The Scripture cannot try a present Motion or Prophecy. Bad Spirits are wholly hid from it. For Instance, *Paul* reproved not the Spirit that cried, *These are the Servants of the Most High God, that shew unto us the Way of Eternal Life,* from the Scriptures; neither did *Peter,* Deceitful *Ananias,* but *from the Heavenly Instinct and Savour, Relish, or Discerning they received from the Spirit of God within them.* 'Twas in a Case of such Difficulty, that some in these late Times have writ, That the Scripture gave no general standing Rule (for all particular Cases) *in fleeing or standing in Times of Persecution, but that it was the Frame of the Spirits of the People of God to retire at that Season*; which whether it be true or false, that the Spirit of God did so influence them, two Things are undeniable ; *First,* That it was the *Frame of their Spirits,* witness their Practice ; *Secondly,* That the *Scripture was not sufficient* for them to square themselves by on that Occasion ; And what else do Professors mean, when they advise People *to seek the Lord* in this or the other Case ? Why do they not go seek the Scriptures rather? Doth not such a Practice manifestly detect the Scriptures of Insufficiency, and evidently prove their Acknowledgment both of Revelation, and their Recourse to a more Living, Spiritual, Immediate and Sufficient Rule ? Why else do they seek God's Mind (say they) by Prayers not Formal, but by the Spirit ? But this is become despised *Heresy* with *J. Faldo.* For Faith in his Sense, rises no higher, *than so many Articles, laid down* (suppose truly) *according to the bare Letter* of the *Scriptures,* which the Devil can believe as well as he : *This Faith* I call meerly *Verbal* and *Historical,* of which the Scripture may be a Rule, but *not of Saving Faith ;* for of that *Faith only the Spirit can be the Rule ;* and why ? because the Spirit of God alone reveals him to the Soul, who is the Object of Faith, and works Faith in the Soul upon that Object ; and as this only begets Faith, so it increases, *enlivens, rules, governs* and *strengthens* Faith unto Dominion. This alone unfolds those Mysteries spoke of in the Scriptures, Wherefore answered the *Eunuch* unto *Philip,* when he queried, Understandest thou what thou readest ? *How should I, unless* Τἱς ὁδηγήσοι *I had a Guide,* as says our *old* English Translation, which implies, That the Things declared of by the Scriptures are not to be understood from the Scriptures, but a more Living, Spiritual and Certain Guide. Wherefore we affirm, That *Repentance, Faith, Sanctification, Justification, Redemption, Regeneration,* &c. *are all a Mystery never to be disclosed, but by the Revelation and Operation of the Spirit of God in Man ;* the Scripture can only testify to such Things, that they are ; but it is *the Spirit alone that works them, and illuminates,*

Acts 8. 30,31

guides, governs and rules the Soul in and about such Things. 'Tis true, all the Spirit leads to is according to the Scriptures; it over-turns them not; for they declare of most of these Operations; yet because we believe, know and witness them from the Conviction and Operation of the Spirit, before we can possibly understand them in Scripture; therefore the Scripture is but a Declaration, and not the Rule of Faith, &c. And the only best Way to determine any Controversy on foot about *Repentance, Faith, Sanctification, Justification, &c.* is the Judgment of that Spirit which works them; For how can the *Scripture,* that has so many Meanings put upon it, *determine which of those Meanings is the true?* Let them shew me that Scripture that plainly and uninterpretedly tells me, such a Proposition is True, and such an one is False, that consists only of their additional Meanings; such a new Nick-named People right, and such wrong; and they do their Business; if they cannot, as it is impossible they should, they must have recourse to something else to rule and determine; and what can that be besides that *Eternal Spirit,* which wrought the true Faith, and ruled the Holy Life of those Ancients, who gave forth this Declaration of Faith and Life?

Can any Man tell another's Mind better than himself? or resolve any Doubt, or clear up any Mis-understanding concerning what is deliver'd, better than he that spoke it? *To understand those Holy Men's Mind, and disprove them that mistake it, there is an unavoidable Necessity of coming to that Spirit which made it theirs.* 'Tis granted, that all true Doctrine is according to Scripture; but the Question is, *What is true Doctrine?* Scripture is a strong Testimony; but what enlightens the Mind, resolves Doubts, and works Faith, and informs, guides and helps the Soul through the whole Work of Conversion, and without which the Testimony of Scripture it self is truly an unintelligible and an incredible Thing? This must be nothing less than *the Spirit it self.*

In short, *The Scripture* is not the Rule, but *Declaration of Faith and Knowledge;* That only must be the Rule of Faith, which gave and ruled the Faith of those that gave forth Scripture. And because none can give or work Faith now, but what did give and work Faith then; 'tis not the Scripture, but that which was before the Scripture, even *the Spirit of Truth,* which was the Author, Rule and Finisher of their Faith. And if our Faith in this Age be the same with the Holy Men's of Old, that gave forth the Scriptures; they are no more our Rule now than they were theirs then, who had a Rule and a Faith before them: But as it was a Declaration of what they believed, knew and witnessed; so it is a Declaration of what we now believe and desire to know and witness. *John*'s Epistle was not writ to be the Saints Rule; for he directed them to the Anointing; yet their Faith and Life of which the Anointing was the Rule, was according to *John*'s Epistle. Again, The Declaration in Time was after the Faith declared of; but where there was Faith there was a Rule, consequently that Declaration which was after that Faith and Rule, *was not that Rule*; so that the most that can be said against us is this: The Scriptures cannot be a Declaration of your Faith, 'till you come to such a Belief of the Truths thereby expressed, as they had who writ them; and a great Truth it is. But then say we, *The Spirit must work that Faith, before the Scriptures can be accounted a Declaration of our Faith, or we interested in them*; And because that *Faith has a Rule so soon as it has a Being,* it must needs follow, that the Declaration of that Faith cannot be either the Author or Rule of it. Here lies the Mistake of my Adversary and many more, that because what a Man does is according or agreeable to a Thing, therefore that is the Rule of the Thing done. To proceed:

For this Reason it is, a Constraint lies upon us from God to direct and exhort all People diligently *to mind that Measure of the Holy Spirit, which God hath given them to profit with,* as that alone by which Man comes to a certain Knowledge of his Mind and Will, and to do the good and acceptable Thing in his Sight, and that by which his poor labouring Mind is brought out of the Incertainties, numerous Interpretations and vain Janglings Men have pester'd the World withal; who have darkned Counsel, and bewildred many in their Conscientious Enquiries after God, drawing out their Minds from the seasoning Principle of Life, instead of bringing them nearer to the Lord; for which great and heavy Plagues hang over the Head of this Generation, who make War against the Spirit, with the Letter, instead of confirming it's Appearance from the Letter; and under Pretence of calling the Scriptures the Word of God, and Rule of Faith and Life, divert People from waiting for the *Word nigh unto themselves,* which is *the Word of Faith, and*

and gives Life to all that believe and obey it; decrying us as *Seducers*, and deriding us as *Enthusiastick Canters*, because we prefer and turn *all to the Spirit of Life within*: An Out-side, Carnal, Envious and Hypocritical Generation, they are.

I will conclude this Head with a Passage out of some certain Authors, that were never professed nor reputed *Quakers*.

Wherefore they who are true Believers (says the first) 'and have received Christ's
' Spirit, their Judgment is to be preferred in the Tryal of Spirits, *before an whole*
' *Council of Clergy-Men*. And they only who can try Spirits by the Spirit of God,
' and Doctrines by the *Word of God written in their Hearts, by the Spirit can in*
' *Measure discern all Spirits in the World*. And the Spirit of Christ, which dwells
' in all *true Christians*, cannot deceive, or be deceived, in the Tryal of Spirits.
' With abundance more to the same Purpose.

Dell's Tryal of Spirits. p. 10.

The other brings in *Two Objections*, frequently made against us, and by him pertinently answered for us.

Object. 1. ' *It is said* Isa. 8. 20. *To the Law and to the Testimony, if any Man*
' *speak not according to this Word, it is because there's no Light in him.*
' *Answ.* Truth; there is the Law and Testimony in the *Spirit*, as well as in the
' Letter; *The Law of God is in the Heart, there it is written*, and there it testifies
' the Truth of God; and if any Man speak not according to *this Rule*, it is be-
' cause there is *no Light* or *Morning risen in him*. The spiritual Man judgeth all
' Things, yet he himself is judged of no Man.

Collier Gen. Epist. page 246. c. 10. pag. 258. c. 12.

Object. 2. ' *It is said*, Gal. 6. 16. *That whoso walketh according to this Rule*
' *Peace upon him.*
' *Answ.* True; but that is not the Rule of the Letter, but of the Spirit, even,
' the Rule of the *New Man, which after God is created in Righteousness and true*
' *Holiness*. Read the Words before, and you shall see it: *There is nothing of any*
' *Value, but the new Creature*: And whosoever walketh according to *this Rule*,
' Peace shall be upon him, *&c.* * And truly, my Brethren, it is my earnest Desire,
' to see Souls *to live* more in *the Spirit*, and less in the Letter, and then they will
' see that we *judge of the Letter by the Spirit, and not of the Spirit by the Letter*,
' which occasions so much Ignorance amongst us; and those, who profess them-
' selves to be our Teachers, are chief in this Trespass: Observe this *J. Faldo.*
' Again, *The Spirit of God*, who is God, *is the* Alone Rule *of a Spiritual Christian*,
' *&c.* Farther declaring, *That some setting the Scriptures in the Room of the Spi-*
' *rit, they make them an* Idol, Ibid. Page 248.

Let him either discard these Men from being *Christians*, that were reputed great and refined Professors, before the breaking forth of the People called *Quakers*; or leave off censuring this Part of our Doctrine, as no Part of *Christianity*.

Nor have we any Ground to believe, that they were intended for the Rule at first, since they were not given forth all at one Time, (and yet every Age stood in Need of such a Rule) but on divers Occasions, as *Miscarriages in the Churches, threatning of Judgments, Prophecies, Histories, and Comfortings under Afflictions,* &c. required: Nor do they carry the least Method or Designment of the great Rule with them; here they are *Proper*, there *Figurative*; in one Thing *Literal*, in another *Allegorical*; without all Definition of Terms, framing of Articles, such Plainness and Coherence in Matter, and Intelligibleness of Language to all Nations, which may render them such a Rule. Besides, it is more than probable, *that much of the Writings of the New Testament are lost, from* Luke's *Words, in the Beginning of his History*, where he tells us, *He was but One of the Many, who did set forth a Declaration of those Things, which were most surely believed amongst them; even,* says he, *as they delivered them unto us, which from the Beginning, were Eye-Witnesses and Ministers of the Word.* For it must be considered, when *Luke* writ his *Narrative*, that *John's* History was not in being; and some will have it,

---

* Those Famous, Poor, Suffering *Christians*, the *Waldenses*, in the purer Times, besides many other weighty Points, wherein they symbolized with us, in this very Matter are not foreign, who in a Confession, about Five Hundred and Fifty Years old, laid this down as a Peice of their Creed, *that the Discoveries and Testimonies of the Holy Spirit in them, were the most convincing Evidence, and infallible Proof of the Divine Authority of the Scriptures.* Consequently the Spirit must have been their Judge and Rule concerning their Understanding the Truths testified by them; as *I. P. Perrin* their *Historian*, in so many Words, assures us concerning them, in the Beginning of his notable History of their *Rise, Doctrine, Sufferings and Progress*.

1673.
Chap. V.

that *Luke* wrote before *Mark*: But whether it be fo or no, certain it is, that *Mark* and *Matthew*, could not make up *thofe Many*, that took that Work in Hand; neither can we think, he fhould call *Matthew* and *Mark* Πολλοί, which fignifies with the *Athenians*, a *Multitude*; for a certain Learned Man will have it, that no better *Greek* was fpoken, than that wherein *Luke* wrote his Hiftory.

That thofe *Narratives* were not *Apocryphal*, but at leaft of equal Authority, with his Dedicated to *Theophilus*, his own Words tells us: For thofe that writ were fuch as related *what they received from Eye-Witneffes, and the firft Minifters of the Word*. Befides which, there were in the *Apoftle's Age*, and the two following *Centuries*, feveral Writings, (reputed genuine) Which either dyed out of the World, through that Neglect brought upon them, by the Advantage fome accounted *Hereticks* might make of them in Defence of their Opinions; or ftifled by the Subtilty of the *Romifh Church*, being more exprefly oppofite to her growing Superftition and Grandeur: And for fuch Writings as ftill remain among us, methinks, it fhould not be unknown to a Man of *J. Faldo's* Pretences to Learning, how much the *Authority of feveral of them has been queftioned*, by fome, and exploded by others, though never by any of us; particularly the *Epiftle to the Hebrews*, the *Epiftle of James*, fecond and third of *John*, fecond of *Peter*, *Jude*, the *Revelations*; and with fome, *Matthew's Hiftory* it felf, has not efcaped the like Cenfure. Of which, Reader, thou haft an Account at large, in that *Notable French Man* Dallæus *De ufu Patrum*, and a late Difcourfe mainly directed againft the *Roman Church*, entituled *Chriftophori Sandy Nucleas Hiftoriæ Ecclefiafticæ*. I would not any from hence fhould repute me fo Impious, as to endeavour to weaken the Teftimony of Scripture, or beget any the leaft Doubt of the Doctrine thereby declared; only upon our Adverfary's Principles, which fo ftrongly oppugn'd the Doctrine of Revelation or Infpiration, I muft take leave to conclude in his Name, and upon his Principles, *that the Word of God is imperfect, and a great Part of the Rule of Faith and Life, and Judge of Controverfie, is loft*; and that he has no more Reafon to believe the Truth of thofe great Things related in that Part of the Scriptures yet remaining, than any *Legend of Rome*: For exclude *Revelation*, and what Ground has he for his Faith befides Tradition? And what Evidence can he give us, upon his Principles, of the Truth of the former, and the Falfhood of the latter? Thefe *Councils* and *Synods*, who collected and cannonized them, he accepts for one Part, and rejects for the other. Again, he trufts their Judgment in picking and chufing, and yet rejects their Interpretation; as if it were not fo difficult to relifh the Genuine from Spurious Scriptures; as (when rightly difcerning them to be fuch) to underftand them; which is an abfolute Contradiction; *For how fhould they know True from Falfe, and not underftand the True?* That *Council* which made the Writings of the *New Teftament*, Canonical, left out the *Revelations* as *Apocryphal*; yet I hope *J. Faldo* accepts that as heartily and unqueftionably as the reft: And that *Council* which took in the *Revelations*, and made it firft *Canonical*, brought in with it the Books of *Tobit*, *Judith*, &c. which *J. Faldo* I fuppofe; with all his Brethren, rejects, as *Apocryphal*. Thus are *meer Men*, and the Judgments of fuch *Councils*, as he otherwife rejects, his Rule for believing the *Scriptures* that remain to be Canonical (if it be proper to fay, the firft is a Rule of his Canon, which is too fhort, and the other which is fuperfluous, as by his Account) My next Queftion is, *What was his Rule for believing thefe Councils?* I am fure he muft have been without all other, than a *Willingnefs to believe fo, becaufe they faid fo*; which, how like this is to his *Papift*, unto whom he would refemble us, let all fober *Proteftants* confider. I cannot fee how he is able to oppugn any Thing they fay upon Tradition, who mounts no higher for his Affurance than *Tradition*, and fuch too, as refts moftly within their Hands. But if it fhould be granted us, that to know Scripture to have been given forth upon * *Infpiration*, Men muft have Recourfe to Infpiration, then

Pag. 23, 24, 25, 26, 27.

Concil. Tom. 1. p. 481. can. 60. Anno 364. and p. 549. can. 27. Anno 417. after Chrift.

not

---

* I find *John Faldo* often fcorning *Infpiration*, and bringing it into Odium, under the Word *Enthufiafm*, ufed of late to fignifie Whimfical Pates, or Heads troubled with a Religious Kind of Frenzy; as if he had abandoned the Plea, Enjoyment and Practice of the beft *Separatifts*, whofe Names he emptily honours, and refolved to fet up for a *Coffee-Houfe Droll*, or a *Play-Prophanift*. To cool his *Courage* and ftop his *Career*, I commend two or three late Difcourfes to his Perufal, writ by Men of undoubted Learning, and pretendedly defended by *J. F.* in his *Quakerifm no Chriftianity*, againft the People called *Quakers*. The firft is *D. Patrick*, *His Friendly Debates*. 2d. *Fowler, his Defign of Chriftianity* (never to be anfwered by that angry Man that defigned it) And *W. Sherlock* his late Difcourfe of Jefus Chrift, &c. If both *Prefbyterians and Independents* are not throughly and truly charged to be *Enthufiafts*; Men

holding

not so much *Councils* and *Synods*, as the *Inspiration of the Almighty*, which gives certain Understanding, *is our Rule* in this Case; as well saith the *Assembly of Divines*, in their Confession of Faith. Chap. 1.

§. 4. *The Authority of the Holy Scripture, for which it ought to be believ'd and obey'd, depends not on the Testimony of any Man or Church, but only upon God (who is Truth it self) the Author thereof,* And since *J. Faldo* himself confesseth, *the Spirit necessary to the Understanding of the Scripture,* which implies the Insufficiency of the Scripture, to give that Understanding of it self, *The Spirit must be the Rule of our understanding the Scripture,* as it was before the Rule of our Faith, concerning the *Divine Authority* of Scripture; for the *Light of the Interpreter,* and not the Thing interpreted, *is the Rule both of Faith and Practice*; which is undeniably evident from the reconciling of seeming Contradictions: If the meer Letter of the Scripture were to be followed, no Man could ever make them meet in the same Truth; the many *Different Perswasions at this Day about Religion,* prove this, whose respective Authors and Abettors think it no mean Advantage to their Cause, that they hold the Scriptures to be their Rule.

But such as come unto the Spirit of God, know and believe the Truth, *as it is in Jesus, David's Key, that opens and none shuts,* is given unto them; and *the Secrets of their God remain with them.* This reconciles those seeming Contradictions, and leads through the greatest and deepest Truths mentioned in Scripture, without the least Doubt or Stumble: This is the super-excellent Benefit of the *New-Covenant Administration,* the *Promise* of the *Father,* the *Instructer, Leader,* and *Comforter* of all *God's Children*; And for a farther Account of which, I refer the Reader to my Book, entituled, *The Spirit of Truth Vindicated,* from Page 16. to Page 47. and *Reason against Railing,* from Page 24. to Page 46.

To prove his *former Charge,* he produces this Passage out of *James Nailor, God is at Liberty to speak to his People by the Scriptures, if he please, and so he is at Liberty to speak by another created Thing, as to* Balaam, *by his Ass*; and because I returned in Answer, To all which (said I) he *says just nothing*; he replies, *As if* (says he) *I were to answer the Proofs of my own Affirmation.* But that was not all; for, beside that; *it was no Proof*; He should have proved it *Erroneous* or *Contemptible,* as he stiles it, or else he doth nothing; To cite, and not to prove the Citation apt to the End, for which it was cited; that is, the *Doctrine* it contained or abetted, to be *Erroneous,* is impertinent. What! Is it false Doctrine to assert, *That God is at Liberty to speak by the Scriptures or without them?* Or is it to contemn the Scriptures, to say, as *John Faldo* cites *J. N,* that God doth speak to People by those Scriptures that were given forth by Inspiration? Or, is it no Proof, that God is at Liberty to speak by any other created Thing, to instance the Case of *Balaam's Ass?* But he will by all means have it, that according to *J. N.* to take an *Ass or Bible to be our Instructer, is of equal Prudence,* adding, *These Notions,* says he, *being by the* Quakers *sucked in*; *I wonder not that they leave the Teachings of God by the Scriptures, to attend on the Ministry of Asses.* But this indirect Reflection, and unsavoury Abuse, both shews the Vanity and Envy of the Man, and must needs beget an Abhorrence of his Proceedings against us, in the Heart of every solid Reader. It had much better become the *Author of poor Robin's Almanack,* or the *Cobler of Glocester,* than a Turn'd out Non-conforming Minister. *J. N*'s Words I fully vindicated in my Answer; his Drift was, to drive off People from this pernicious Apprehension, that God's Voice was only to be heard from the Scripture, thereby justling the Spirit out of Doors, and confining the Almighty to a certain Instrument; *and not that he intended to repute a very Ass of equal Value with the Scriptures*; though I do not doubt but the Voice of *Balaam's* Ass, was a more immediate and forcible Rebuke with him, than any Scripture then written.

But let this characterize our *Adversary* with every Just knowing Reader, that he brings *J. N*'s Words that allow such Scripture, as God shall please to speak to any by, *to be so far a Rule,* to those to whom it's directed, in order to prove, *That the*

---

holding what *J. F.* condemns us for owning, though less justifiably; and if more ridiculous Interpretations are not to be found among them, than was ever yet read in any *Quaker's Book,* I am content to suffer *J. F*'s Reproach as just (who does not do as he would be done by, his great Scab or Leprosie, and of some other of his Fraternity too) for alas, it is at best but a Piece of *Heathenism* with him; and a Man may be a very good *Christian* forsooth, by a New Art of Imputation, found out and accommodated to the Ease of Hypocrites, without the Streight and Legal Way of *Just* and *Holy* Living.

Quakers

1673.
Part I.
Chap. V.

Quakers *deny the Scripture to be in any Case any Rule at all:* But we must not expect better Usage from a Man, who is more perplext at our proving of our selves consistent with Truth, because it contradicts his Apprehensions and Charges exhibited against us in Print, than that we should be in the Wrong, though for that Cause he pretends to write against us. Strange! That he should rather desire we might be mistaken, than himself be thought to have mistaken us.

Pag. 28, 29

But he thinks I have greatly wrong'd St. *Paul,* and I know not why, unless it were in showing him to have been guilty of that Fault; for to prove *the Scriptures to be the Rule,* he brought this Saying of his; *And herein, that is,* faith our Adversary, [*all Things that are written in the Law and the Prophets*] *do I exercise my self, to have a Conscience void of Offence towards God and towards Men.*

Pag. 58, 59

My Answer then was, that he left out that which was more applicable to the Words, as the Place it self evidently proves; [*But this I confess to thee,* (that is, Fælix) *that after the Way which they call* Heresie, *so worship I the God of my Fathers, believing all Things that are written in the Law and the Prophets, and have Hope towards God, which they themselves also allow, that there shall be a Resurrection of the Dead, both of the Just and the Unjust; and herein,* faith the Apostle, *do I exercise my self, &c.*] Where it's evident, that believing all Things that are written in the Law and the Prophets, was not that wherein he said (so properly) that he exercised himself, as *in worshipping the God of his Fathers, not after their Way, and having Hope towards God of the Resurrection, &c.* there lay the Stress, as is evident from their calling that Worship *Heresie,* and afflicting him for that *Hope* which they otherwise allowed of. Nay, that very Passage he makes the whole Place to bear upon, comes in rather in the Nature of a *Parenthesis,* than a Principal Matter; His thus dealing with us and the Scripture I call'd a *Perversion,* at which he very vainly taunts, as if *it could not be a Perversion, because I confess that it somewhat relates to the Verses cited,* crying out, *This is his Mouse his Mountain travelled to bring forth:* But if to *clip a Text* be not a Perversion, or to *stretch it* to what it can never reach, nor ever intended, be not to *pervert and abuse Scripture,* certainly there is no such Thing. That he clipped it, is proved; that he misapplied it, is not less evident: For to believe a Thing, is not necessarily to make it a Rule; besides, if the Law and the Prophets were a Rule, because he was exercised in them, *then must his Worship and Hope also be a Rule, because he was exercised in them;* but that were improper and untrue. *He is Angry* that I said, the Apostle had out-stript the Law and the Prophets, therefore they could not be his Rule, replying, *If St.* Paul *had undertaken a Reply to this Gentleman, he would have undoubtedly lasht him severely for this Wrong done to him and the Truth.* But I am not of that Mind; for if he did not out-strip the Dispensation of the Law and Prophets, *how could he arrive at that State which witnessed the Fulfilling of the Law and the Prophets;* To deny this, is to deny the farther Illumination and Enjoyment of the Day; and according to *J. Faldo*'s own unhappy way of Reasoning, *the Apostle must not be a Christian;* for in denying the *Prophets* to be *Christian,* because they were before Christ's visible Appearance, and preferring *Christianity* so much above other fore-going Dispensations, as he doth, in not allowing the Apostle to have out-stript them, *he makes the Apostle to be no* Christian; *For which,* I will not say, *he would have Lasht, but Reproved this ignorant* Priest, *as one that knows not whereof he affirms.* But hear him yet farther.

Rep. *I said, the holy Scriptures determine, according to their kind, as much as a Writing can do. From whence* W. P. *infers, that it is not so determinative of all Cases as something else may be, which is a more living, immediate and infallible Judge than a Writing is or can be; an inference worthy of a poor Scholar, and a conceited Pedant. Is he gone beyond* Belshazzar, *who trembled at such a rate at the Writing* * *on the Wall. Did ever any Man in his Wits affirm the Scriptures to supply the Room of Eyes, Skill to read, Understanding, Conscience, and the Assistance of the Spirit of God, are not these in my Book all made necessary to render the Scriptures such a Rule and Determiner?*

* At whose Hand-Writing.

Rejoyn. But why such a trivial Rant for a Reply? and why such hard Words from a Man of his Circumstances? one on many Accounts so near what he represents me to be. Is it not true, that if something be *more firm than Writing,* that which is more firm, and not the Writing, *is the Judge and Determiner?* Suppose a Scripture for every Case that ever did or may happen (which we know, there is not,

not, and therefore not The Rule) yet if such Scripture need an Exposition, who is most truly the Judge and Determiner, the obscure Text or the clear Expositor? Certainly where the Stress lies, the Power of Determination must be, and there the Judgeship rests, but that is always in the Interpretation, since the Difficulty is not about believing the Text, but the *Exposition* given of it; therefore the *Expositor is both Judge and Rule, and not the Text expounded.*

And since *J. Faldo* has granted to us *the Assistance of the Spirit* for knowing the Scriptures, *the Spirit*, then, which gives us how to understand and believe, and enables us to fulfil them, *must needs be the Rule and Judge, and no Writing whatever.* I shall conclude this Point with my Rejoynder to this following Passage in his Reply,

Rep. But *W. P.* hath *not done trifling yet*, ' neither is the Law the Judge, but ' there is a Judge who interprets and speaks from the fresh Discoveries of his own ' Reason the Meaning and Intendment of those written Laws. But *Mr.* Penn, *The Judge is the Mouth of the Law, and subject to the Law, and prescribed in his Judgment to that Sense of the Law which is expressed by the Letter of it. If some of the Judges had the handling of you, for imposing your canting fresh Discoveries of his Reason upon them, they would tell you, they give Judgment from a Deep Study and Weighty Consideration of the Letter of the Law, and moreover give you some hard Names, or worse, for your canting Law added to your canting Gospel,* * *and yet the Light in their Consciences not give them the least rebuke for so doing.*

* His Blasphemy against the Light.

Rejoyn. I perceive he measures the Judges Displeasure by his own; Indeed they would be very *Unfit Persons* to sit for our Judges, that should be like him; Men that would *call hard Names*, and *do worse* to any Man, for allowing them to be guided by a Living Reason, would greatly evidence they had little or none, and therein indeed that we mischaractered them. But who most dishonours them? I that suppose them to judge and explain *Written Reason* by the Living Principle of Reason in themselves, or he that renders them so many *Posts* or *Pillars* that are to be moved by insensible Letters, without relation to any Reason inherent to themselves, and not otherwise. But hear my former Answer before I farther rejoyn.

pag. 61. ' His Instance about the Law is lame; For the good Laws of any Land ' are but *Reason written*, or rather declar'd by Writing, which is obliging against ' the * *Corruption of a Judge*, but not the Reason of the Judge; neither is the *Law* ' the *Judge*; but there is a Judge who interprets and speaks from the fresh Dis- ' coveries of his own Reason, the Meaning and Intendment of those written Laws, ' If the Laws be sufficient without a Judge, why is there a Judge? If then they ' are *Dark, Obscure* and *Doubtful* in many Cases, so as to need a Judge and *Inter-* ' *preter*, which I call living and *immediate Reason*, since the Scriptures are Writings, ' in which are many Things difficult to be understood, it follows that there must be ' an *Immediate Living Judge*, which must be therefore the *Spirit of Truth* that ' gave them forth, because *none knows the Things of God save the Spirit of God.* ' And that those who are the Makers of Laws, are the only Persons who are fit to ' judge and determine in Case of Difficulty, by a Declaration of their Mind and ' Intention in any such obscure Passage. In short, *Either the Scriptures are not ob-* ' *scure* (a Thing we daily see) or if so, yet sufficient, which is impossible, *or* ' *they must have a Judge*, which is most true and necessary; and what Judge, but ' *the Spirit of Truth, which leads into all Truth?* p. 61, 62.

Now one would have thought, that *an Answer so sober and reasonable* might have deserved a *Reply more civil and pertinent*, than my *Adversary* gave me: But I do the less wonder at it, since he makes it his Practice to give *hard Words instead of solid Answers.* But to his *Reply* as it is.

---

* I would desire the Reader to take Notice, that the first Reformers never intended by their great respect to the Scriptures, to establish them their Rule exclusive of the Spirit, as most do now, *W. Kiffin* for instance; only they did on all Occasions prefer them, as God's Tradition, to the Place of a Rule, beyond Popish Doctors or Councils, which they who know any Thing in these Matters are well assured to be the Truth of the Case. So that they were but a Rule comparatively, as we also hold; but by no Means can we allow that they prefer'd the Scriptures to that great Office exclusive of the Spirit; or that Men were not to have their Immediate Dependence upon it's Instruction, Discoveries, and Revelation, towards Faith and Good Life, So much at this Time.

Rejoyn.

Rejoyn. He tells me, * *the Judge is the Mouth of the Law, and Subject to the Law.* But I would have him confider two Things; *First,* that the Scriptures of Truth were never given forth after that formal regular Courfe that the Laws of *England* were; but to particular Perfons or Churches on particular Cafes, though together with hearty refpect I acknowledge and enjoy the Benefit of them. *Secondly,* The Queftion is not about Things obvious, but obfcure; and herein the Judge is not only the Mouth, but Inrerpreter of the hidden Meaning of the Law; This our *Adverfary's* own Words import; For if the *Law* were fo plain, as only to *need a Mouth,* what need would there be of *deep Study* and *Weighty Confideration,* which he makes neceffary to a Judge? the bare reading of the Law would be fufficient to determine all Cafes; Nay, it would end all going to Law: But inafmuch as the Laws are both numerous and intricate, as the Vexatious Cafes and Difputes of our Times fully prove, 'tis manifeft, that fome *other Judge and Determiner* muft be found out, one that underftands, compares and rightly applies Law, whofe Judgment muft decide and determine the Controverfie. Now though every fuch Judge may be faid to determine according to the Mind of the Law, yet his *Interpretation,* and not the bare Letter, is recorded for the *Determination of the Cafe* depending, from whence come our *Book-Cafes*; Nor indeed is this only referable to any certain Perfon, explaining the obfcure Paffages of Law, but the *Application of the Law to the Fact,* in which not only the whole living Reafon of the Judge is deeply and circumfpectly exercifed, but the Underftanding and Confcience of the Jury, refpecting the Nature of the Law, the Evidence of the Witnefs, the Heinoufnefs of the Fact, and Variety of Circumftances, wherein the obnoxioufnefs to Error lies (according to the *Greek* Proverb, Περὶ τῶν περιςασέων πλάνυ, i. *Error is about the Circumftances*) all in order to a definitive Sentence or Determination about the Point handled. Now for any Man to call the written Law the *Judge,* and not *Synterefis,* or living found Reafon and Confcience, in the Judge and Jury, to me feems very abfurd.

Befides, Let it be confidered, *Firft,* that *the Law is added becaufe of Tranfgreffion;* and fuch as live up to that Noble Principle from whence all good Laws come, have an higher Judge and Rule, than any of thofe written Laws, or any Interpretations of Men upon them; fo that if *J. Faldo* compares the Scripture to the written Laws, they who are led by the Spirit have an higher Rule than the Scripture: and as he that lives up according to written Laws, by the Rule of his *Synterefis,* or Law of Laws, the juft Principle in himfelf, does not deftroy but fulfil thofe written Laws: fo *they that live according to the Rule of the Spirit, do not invalidate, but fulfil the Scriptures.* There is no need of *Swearing* for a Remedy againft that Man's Falfenefs, who is come to the *Truth-fpeaking* of Chrift's Righteoufnefs; he that is come up to the greater, does not fleight, but anfwer, the leffer. *Secondly,* I befeech the Reader to obferve, that thefe written Laws had once a beginning, and that thofe that made them were not without a Rule and Judge in themfelves, both before, and in the making of thofe Laws (neither is that peculiar to them, the Law-makers) I ftill mean *Synterefis,* of which many Lawyers fpeak great Things, particularly a good old Law-Book, called, *Doctor and Student,* which is not leffened by thofe Laws, *nor ought any Law to be made, or take hold on any Perfon farther then he acts contrary to that juft Principle in himfelf*; which is called, the *Law of Laws,* the *Immutable Law,* by *Chief Juftice Hobart,* in his Reports, pag. 87. So that both the Law was made according to this *Synterefis,* which *Synterefis* or *Law of Righteoufnefs,* has not left us with a meer Declaration of it's Mind, fubject to many Cafualties and Difficulties, but remains in the Heart of Man to inform his Underftanding and correct his Life; confequently is the *Judge of Controverfie,* refpecting the *written Law* (about which, and the Application of

---

* *Note,* I have not made any confiderable Diftinction between the Rule, and the Judge, from thy Judgment of that little (if any) Difference that is between them. And my Adverfary to his own Confufion feemeth of the fame Mind; for notwithftanding he feverely and tauntingly reflects on that Paffage upon me in my former Book, yet in making the Scripture both Rule and Judge, he fhows to us that the Judge and the Rule are not at fo great a Diftance, as his little Skill in *Philofophy* would have rendered it. And herein he thwarts Dr. *Stillingfleet,* and Dr. *Tillotfon,* who againft the *Papifts* affert not the Scripture to be the Judge, but Right Reafon; And to fpeak the Truth of it, Nothing can be more abfurd, next to Tranfubftantiation, than that the Scripture fhould be the Judge of a Man's Meaning of any part of it felf, that is, if it be applied as a Right Rule; fince in fuch Cafes of Difference no Scripture ever yet fpoke clearer than it's firft Text; and the Queftion lies not about that, but the juft Interpretation.

it, many Times arises the Controversie) must not be the *written*, but this *Immutable Law in Judge and Jury*, from whence all good Laws proceed. It is a very depraved State indeed that knows no farther Obligation than a Written Law, whereas a great Part of Mankind is free from those Enormities the Law forbids and punishes, who yet know not the Letter of the Law; like unto the *Gentiles* of old, who *having not the Law, became a Law unto themselves, shewing the Work of the Law written in their Hearts*; which Law *Cicero*, in his Books of *the Commonwealth*, cited by *Lactant.* 6. Institut. 8 calls " *Right Reason*, agreeable to Nature, " given to all, constant and eternal, which calls to Duty by commanding, and by " Dissuasion deters from Deceit—No other Law may be put instead of this; nei- " ther is it lawful to derogate any Thing from it; neither can it be wholly abrogat- " ed; neither can we be loosed from this Law by *Senate* or People; *There is no* " *other Explainer or Interpreter of it to be sought*; neither will there be one Law " at *Rome*, another at *Athens*; one now, another hereafter; but being *one Law*, " *Everlasting and Immortal, should hold all Nations at every Time*: And there will " be one, as it were, Master and Commander of all, God, that Inventor, Disposer, " and Maker of this Law, to whom he that will not be obedient, must fly him- " self, and even in this Thing, must suffer very great Penalty, though he should " escape other Punishments. An excellent Place, which clearly explains the Nature and Virtue of this *innate Light*, says *Rob. Sanderson*, late Bishop of *Lincoln*, in his *Oxford Lectures*, concerning the *adæquate Rule of Conscience*, prol. 4. where he also calls it from *Calvin*, *A Spark of the Light of God, that he might have Preachers of his Will in our very Bosoms*; and that all other Laws are but *subservient to this* in the *Synteresis*, the very Thing that we assert *concerning the Scriptures being a Rule*. Thirdly, I would intreat the Reader to consider, that *cessante ratione legis, cessat lex*, i. e. the Reason of the Law ceasing, the Law ceases, is *an old Law-Maxim*. Now who shall be Judge of that, the *written Law*? By no Means. Yet that preposterous Answer only can suit our *Adversary*'s Principle. We say, *Living Reason must be the Judge*. In like Manner did the Spirit of God give his Servants an Understanding in past Ages, how to behave themselves with respect to those Laws, which were but Temporary, for whose Abrogation there was no express Scripture, which the *Scribes* and *Pharisees* by neglecting and grieving that Spiritual Leader, and sticking in the Letter of the Scripture, only continued and maintained against Christ himself, who fulfilled them.

To conclude, That which makes *Law*; That which explains *Law*; That, contrary unto which no Law ought to be made or obeyed; That which gives to know what is contrary or according to just Law; That which gives to apply and execute Law rightly, must be the Judge and Superior Rule; But that is this *Synteresis*, *Law of Laws*, says *Chief Justice Hobart*; *Right Reason*, says *M. T. Cicero*; *Innate Light*, says *B. Sanderson*; *The Law of God writ in the Heart*, says *Doct. and Stud*. *Spark of God's Light*, says *Calvin*; *A Living Rule and Everlasting Foundation of Virtue, planted in all Reasonable Souls*, says *Plutarch*; *God within*, says *Seneca* and *Epictetus*. Consequently, not any meer *written Law* can be the Judge and Determiner of Controversies in *Law*. This, Reader, holds almost all along the same with the Scriptures. That the *Law* is not Judge of the Doubts that arise about it self, but another, is already prov'd; and that the Scriptures can no more determine *Cases of Difficulty within themselves*, is as evident by the same Argument; and that Judge must either be some Man endued with the Spirit of God, as in Law Cases some Judge with Right Reason, or else the Eternal Spirit, as he is universally manifested in Men. The first I suppose our *Adversary* will think too fair a Pretence for *Popery* to be allowed, and the last he can never avoid, unless Man without the Spirit of God be able to determine of the Things of God; which were to deny the Scriptures of Truth, the Faith of the Ancients, the Doctrine of the Reformers, and Right Reason.

Thus, Reader, I conclude this Point, and could have been willing to have done so long before, had not the great Necessity of People's better Information, drawn me into a more free and large Discourse than my *Adversary's* very empty Replies could have deserved at my Hands.

CHAP. VI.

Of our dehorting People from Reading the Scriptures, &c. as charged by this Adversary.

Though I have said enough to persuade all sober Persons of *our reverend Esteem of the Scriptures*, yet am I willing to remove any the least Ground of Scruple by a brief Consideration of his four following Chapters, in which he would fain maintain his former *False and Unadvised Charges* of our holding those Holy Writings in great Contempt. He begins thus,

Rep. My Charge in my Sixth Chapter was, That the Quakers *take Men off from reading the Scriptures for Instruction and Comfort.* Penn *objects against my first Proof, as not having any such Consequence,* Pag. 63. And this is the Meaning of our Doctrine, to bring People to the Everlasting Word of God in themselves, Smith. Cat. Pag. 95. bestowing on me within Eight Lines, (P. 30, 31.) *Deeply Ignorant, Malicious, Ungodly, Possessed by an Evil Spirit, Wretched, Impious, grosly blind, Malignity, Frothiness, Envy, Impious, Injustice.*

Rejoyn. If ever Man had to do with an *Unjust Adversary*, it is my Lot; And let this very Passage be the Measure. *First,* What are those Words cited out of *William Smith,* that prove, *we take Men off from Reading the Scriptures?* What Reason has he urged, or Argument attempted, that were by me employ'd in Defence of the Passage, and Illustration of our Innocency? Shall this pass for my Confutation? Must my Book be no better answer'd? and yet led captive by *J. Faldo's* meer Pretences, to Wit, Reason, Religion and Learning. It's a Shame to Professors of Religion to countenance his Attempts, that maintains his Controversy with so much Weakness and silly Evasion. He tells you of my Rebukes, but is as true in that, as Just in the rest; For neither has he given all those Words, which abate that Harshness they seem now to carry with them, nor do they lie within the Compass of Eight Lines, as he would have you believe; But be they as they are, what Man, not *possessed with a Malicious Spirit*, would charge Untruths upon a Body of People, and then lay found Expressions upon the Rack, if possible to extort a Confession of them? Who but one deeply ignorant would repute it an Undervalue of Scripture, *to bring People to the Everlasting Word of God that gave them forth, that only gives to understand rightly and esteem them?* And can he be less than *Impious and Frothy,* that sports himself with our serious Belief, as well as very *Unjust,* that draws Conclusions our Premises will not bear, and then calls them, *Charges proved out of the* Quakers *own Writings.*

To give the greater Authority to what I said, I urged the Testimonies of *Calvin, Erasmus* and *Beza,* concerning which hear him.

Rep. But (Pag. 64.) *he fathers his Error on* Calvin, Erasmus, *and* Beza. *He directs precisely only to* Erasmus *and* Beza; *in* Nov. Test. 2 Pet. 1. 19. Beza's *Words on the Place which I have examined are these,* " So it may be taken for the Doctrine " of the Prophets; which was to those to whom *Peter* wrote more without Ex- " ception, to whom he may be said to have a Respect in this Passage. *Thus this Man can abuse Scripture, Reason, Reformers all at once.*

Rejoyn. If it be an Error, *Calvin, Beza* and *Erasmus* held it, as I will briefly prove. But why must *Beza*'s Words be cited, and *Calvin* not deny'd so to have writ, neither *Erasmus* by him consider'd, who of the rest I most *precisely* cited? But it made not for his Turn. He seems to adventure at my *Dishonesty,* provided it may bring Disgrace or Weakness to the *Quakers* Cause. But to make good my Quotations.

J. Calvin expresly tells us, *Idem spiritus qui per os Prophetarum loquutus est, in corda nostra penetret necesse est, ut persuadeat fideliter protulisse quod divinitus erat mandatum,* Calv. Institut. lib. 1. cap. 8. That is, " It is necessary, the *same Spirit* " that spake by the Mouth of the Prophets, *should pierce into our Hearts to per-* " *swade us,* that they faithfully delivered that which was committed to them of " God. What says *J. Faldo* to this?

Now let's to *Beza.* Our Adversary seems resolv'd to mistake me, that he may render me mistaken. I cited him to one Part of the Chapter and Verse, and he to another; For my Purpose was to prove, that *Beza* held it to be the *Right Way of understanding the Scriptures, to have Recourse to the Everlasting Word;* and he takes a Piece of the Nineteenth Verse, which related to the Comparison, Βεβαιότερον,

or

or *more sure Word of Prophesy* (which is sufficiently cleared in my Answer to his first Book.) But to pass by this Part of his Disingenuity, I will set down *Beza's* Words on the 19th Verse it self thus: *Imo quid si φωσφόρον vocavit solem ipsum,* i. e. *christum ipsum exhibitum, qui simul & ipsa lux est, & veram lucem mundo intulit?* That is, " Yea, What if he called the Day-Star the Sun himself, that is, Christ " himself exhibited, which both is the Light it self, and brought the True Light " into the World. Then *He* was to arise in the Heart, if *He* was the Day-Star in the Heart. And on the 20th Verse of the same Chapter, thus: *Ut prophetiarum intelligendarum & ad verum scopum referendarum rationem sciant ab ipso spiritu petendam qui prophetis ipsis illas dictavit:* That is, " (It was required) that they " might know the Way of understanding Prophesies, and referring them to the " right Scope, must be sought or fetcht from the same Spirit, which dictated " them to the Prophets themselves, and more to that Purpose.

Now let us come to *Erasmus*, by him willingly passed over, who on that Place says thus in his Paraphrase, " The Thing that is set forth by Man's Device may " be perceived by Man's Wit; but the Thing that is set forth by the Inspiration " of the Holy Ghost) *requireth an Interpreter inspired with the like Spirit.* Farther rendring the Scripture so mystical and allegorical, as not to be understood without it.

Nor shall this serve me; I will yet add Two or Three Testimonies more, and begin with *Luther*.

Scripturæ non nisi eo spiritu intelligendæ sunt quo scriptæ sunt: i. " The Scrip- " tures are not to be understood but by *that Spirit* by which they were written,

Peter Martyr, that famous *Italian Protestant*, teacheth thus, " The Spirit is the " Arbiter, by whom we must assure our selves for understanding of the Scriptures, " that thereby we must discern between Christ's Word, and a Stranger's quoting " Christ's Words; *My Sheep know my Voice, and follow not a Stranger's:* And among many other Scriptures he cites these, *The Spirit searcheth out the deep things of God.—The Comforter shall declare all Things that I have said unto you.—The Spiritual Unction shall shew you all Things.* — Again, *The Spirit of God reveals the Truth in the Holy Scriptures.*

Lastly, I find him expressing himself, in his *Oration to the University of* Strasburgh, thus, concerning the Scriptures, " *The School of this Philosophy is Heaven;* Moreover, faith he, " *We must remember, that the Teacher hereof is the Holy* " *Ghost.*

And Dr. *Ames*, a great Father of the *Independents*, and both a Learned and Good Man (his Day considered) in his Disputations against *Bellarmine*, takes this Advantage upon *Bellarmine's* Acknowledgment, that the Unction, 1 *John* 2. taught, though not all Things, yet all those Doctrines which they had already received of the Apostles, " *We require no more*, says Dr. Ames; *the Anointing of the Holy* " *Spirit doth teach the Faithful to understand those Things which they received of* " *the Apostles, therefore to understand the Scriptures in those Things which are* " *necessary to Salvation*; *for those Things those Believers had received of the Apo-* " *stles:* With much to the same Purpose in that Chapter.

I could produce many more *Testimonies* from Great and Famous Modern *Writers*, besides the Pathetical Expressions of a multitude of *Martyrs*, both *English* and Foreign, as well Famous for their Learning, as great Fidelity, that express themselves fully in Defence of our Assertion, " That to bring Men and Women to the " *Obedience of the Everlasting Word, nigh in the Heart, is so far from being re-* " *pugnant to, or undervaluing of the Holy Scriptures, as without their Acquain-* " *tance with it, and Conformity to it, they can never be read by any with Instruction* " *and Comfort.* But, if God please, there may be a Time, for our more full Disquisition of this Point.

But he thinks to supply his *Wilful Omission* and *Disingenuous Carriage*, about my Answer to the ill Use he made of my other Proof, by *reflecting upon my Honesty*, in transcribing his Second, taken out of our Friend *James Parnell's* Book, entituled, *The Shield of the Truth*, p. 10. because I added not these Words, *Seeking the Living among the Dead*, at the End of this Sentence, " By the same Light do we di- " scern him to be in Darkness, who putteth the Letter for the Light, and so draw " People's Minds from the Light within them to the *Light* without them. And as if he had fully obtain'd his Will upon us, by making us speak what he untruly says we own and practice, he goes on, *This needs no Comment to render it's Proof valid; and is out of the Reach of the utmost Stretch of* Penn's *Wit and Confidence,*

1673.
Part I.
Chap. VI

Luth. Tom. 2. Fol. 309. a.

Pet. Mart. com. loc. part.1. cap.6.

Part 2. c. 18.

Lib. 1. cap. 5. Thes. 32.

to put any *Appearance of another Construction upon it*. But methinks this Sound renders him very Empty. It must be a very plain Case, if not so much as the *Appearance of another Construction* can be made upon it, than what he would have it to import; but I am wholly of another Mind, and that there is no Difficulty in making a very free and sufficient Defence for the Passage; I ought to take it for granted, that the whole of his Objection lies against the Words I omitted, inasmuch as he pretends not to reply to my Vindication of the former Part of the Sentence, which was to this Purpose, That *by turning People to the Light of Christ we did not teach them to undervalue, but how they should most truly understand and value the Scriptures ; that the Spirit was more excellent than the Letter, the Power than the Form of Godliness, yet both Letter and Form to be respected in their Place, and that we only took our Aim against such as put the Letter in the Place of the Spirit, thereby keeping People from the Holy Spirit, by which alone the Scriptures are read and understood unto Edification and Comfort*. My Adversary, I say, taking no Notice of this, I must think, he had nothing to say, saving his Charge of the fore-mention'd Omission. To which thus much; I was not design'd; I took and defended the Substance of the Passage: For I would fain know, what Life is to be had in the Letter, without the Assistance of the Light or Spirit of Christ: If then the Letter is dead without the Spirit, which is *Old Protestant Doctrine*; Can it be any thing else than *seeking the Living among the Dead*, to draw People from the Light and Spirit of Christ within, to seek for *Life* in the meer *Letter* without; for so the Question ran. This was the State of the *Jewish Church* in her Apostacy, and is the Condition of Thousands at this very Day, who under Pretence of *Honouring the Scriptures*, despise, grieve, and in a Sense quench the Spirit that gave them forth, for which God is wroth with the *false Christian*, and his Religion and Worship is an Abomination in his Sight: and great and sudden will be their Distress; for his Indignation is kindled, and his Fury ready to be revealed; and in that Day shall such lofty Boasters as my Adversary be brought low, their Spirits faint, and Hearts fail within them; at what Time the Light, Spirit and Life of *Jesus* shall be unto all that trust therein, a Rock of Everlasting Strength, an immoveable Foundation and Sanctuary full of Comfort, Peace and Joy for ever. And indeed this Thing doth so deeply affect my Soul, that I cannot refrain from crying. *Wo, Wo, Wo, against all such Watchmen of the Night*, who rack their Wits for Tales and Stories, to scare well-meaning and devout People from the Enjoyment of the Life, Virtue and Substance of the Scriptures, Nick-naming that only Way by which so great and heavenly Benefit can ever be procured (I mean the *Inspiration of the Almighty*) with such hateful Terms, as *Enthusiasm*, *Quakerism*, *Familism*, a more refined Sort of *Ranterism*, &c. and what else may keep them in their Snare, stop their Enquiry, and render the Living Eternal Truth of God odious in their Sight; better were it for such that they had never been born, than *under Pretence of being Ministers of the Gospel, to murder the Life and Spirit of it*, estranging the Minds of People from that unchangeable Covenant, instead of interesting them in it, thereby manifestly depriving their Souls of Blessed and Eternal Privileges. They are like *Troops of Robbers* indeed, as the Prophet anciently said, *they murder'd by Consent*, most of them combining against the indwelling Life of Jesus, and immediate Springings and Flowings forth of his Spirit in the Hearts of his Children: Let it never be forgotten, that *the first Murderer was a Sacrificer*, and the deadliest Persecutor a *Pharisee*. Nor has there been a more Venomous, Enrag'd, Blood-thirsty Generation of Men, than the Formal Literal Professor, who ever call'd *God Father*, and *Christ Beelzebub*, who crucified his Son, and persecuted the Apostles, reputing them *Mad-Men*, that is, *Phanaticks* or *Enthusiasts*, *Seditious Fellows*, *Sect-Masters*, *Introducers of New Doctrines, Innovators upon the Church*, *Turners of the World up-side down*, in fine, *Despisers of the Writings of the Law and the Prophets*, while they themselves *thought to have Eternal Life therein*, being of the *Circumcision*, Sons of *Abraham*, and *Children of the Promise*. O! that these of our Day might repent, which those of that Day did not, lest neglecting God's present Visitation, (neither entring themselves, nor suffering others to enter into the blessed Rest) the miserable Doom of that Hard-hearted Generation overtake them, and that speedily.

CHAP

CHAP. VII.

Of Scripture-Commands, what are binding, and what not. Our Adversary's Disingenuity observ'd.

BUT however, he has fail'd in his last Chapter, doubtless he thinks he has done my Business in this; he begins like himself. *Pag.* 34.

Rep. My Charge and Argument in this Chapter is, The Quakers *affirm the Doctrines, Commands, Promises, Holy Examples expressed in Scripture, as such, not to be at all binding to us; such an Argument, and so proved by me* (mark Reader) *as a Thousand* Penns *can never invalid it*.

Rejoyn. What can there be more conceited than this? He must live very lonely and far from Neighbours, that proclaims so much Praise to himself, and has the wonderful Confidence to bid Defiance so vainly to others.

Reader, I beseech thee, for the Truth's Sake, on whose Side soever thou shalt find it to be, to examine with all Impartiality his *Charge*, our *Answer*; his *Reply*, and our *Rejoynder*: If his Honesty, Reason and Justice hold any Proportion to his great Confidence, we yield; But if upon an Impartial Consideration he shall be found to clip and pervert our Matter, and to shuffle with us in his own, once do a poor People Right, in giving Judgment against his horrible Injustice.

The *Charge* thou hast heard; the *Proof* was this, *That is no Command of God to me, what he commanded to another: Did any of the Saints which we read of, act by that Command which was to another, not having the Command to themselves,* &c.

Now before I give my Answer, as it was set down in my Book, I shall insert his Quotation of my Answer.

Rep. (Pag. 34, 35.) *To this saith* P. *I answer briefly and plainly, and he is as good as his Word. No Commands, saith he, in the Scripture, are any farther obliging upon any Man, than as he finds a Conviction upon his Conscience, otherwise Men should be engaged without, if not against, Conviction; a Thing unreasonable in a Man*.

Rejoyn. He has a notable Way of contracting his Adversary's Answers; I will set down what I writ, faithfully, plainly and briefly.

(Pag. 71, 72, 73.) " *Edward Burroughs's* Expression may be taken two Ways,
" and both safe enough to the Honour and Credit of the Scripture, though not
" to the Charity or Honesty of *J. Faldo*. Now follows that Part he cited. " No
" Command in the Scripture is any farther obliging upon any Man, than as he
" finds a Conviction upon his Conscience, otherwise Men should be engag'd with-
" out, if not against, Conviction, a Thing unreasonable in a Man; Therefore the
" *Apostle*, when he wrote to the Churches, exhorted them, not to do those things
" whereof they were asham'd, to shun what was manifested to be Evil; and
" affirms, *that whatever might be known of God was manifested within, for God
" had shewn it unto them*. So that Conviction can only oblige Obedience: and
" since what works that Conviction is the *manifesting Light, universal Grace, or
" quickning Spirit in the Hearts of Mankind*, it follows, that *the principal Ground
" for our Faith in the Scriptures, and Reason of our Obedience to the Holy Precepts
" therein contained, is the Manifestation, Conviction, and secret Drawings of the
" Light or Spirit of God in the Conscience*. And thus E. B's Words are found and
" scriptural. Again, Such Commands either relate to *Ordinary* or *Extraordinary*
" *Cases*. By *Ordinary Cases*, I mean such as chiefly concern *Faith* and *Holy Life*,
" which are general, permanent and indispensible: and then I deny his Conse-
" quence. By *Extraordinary Cases*, I understand *Moses's Going to* Pharoah, *the*
" *Prophets several Manners of Appearance to the Kings, Priests and People of* Israel,
" *with other Temporary Commands relating to outward Services*, &c. And so we say,
" that what is commanded *One* Man, *is not binding, as such, upon another*: But
" when the Lord shall say, *If thou sinnest thou shalt die; If thou keepest my Com-
" mandments thou shalt live; Be ye Holy, for I the Lord thy God am Holy;* ——For
" *your selves know ye not how ye ought to follow us,* &c. I say, these Precepts and
" Examples are obliging upon all; why? Because they more or less meet with a
" Conviction in the Consciences of all; For I am perswaded, none that has a rea-
" sonable Soul, who has not out-liv'd his Day, but would readily say, These are
" true

Ed. Bur.

1673.
Part I.
Chap. VII.

" true and weighty Sayings; For *Faith in God, and a holy self-denying Life, are*
" *necessary both to Temporal and Eternal Happiness.*

It was, Reader, to this sober Answer he flung out his fore-going *Rant*, and makes this following Comment and Reply, *viz.* says *J. Faldo,*

Rep. They *are no Commands unless we think so.* 'Tis *no Sin to break all the Commands in the Bible, if our Consciences can be so blind, dead or hardned, as not to tell us,* 'tis *a Sin. They who thought they did God good Service in killing his Servants did not sin in the least, because they were not convinced of a Command to the contrary. To vindicate my whole Chapter concerning the Scriptures.* 'Tis *a Principle that hath all Iniquity in the Womb of it. Who can find Names for such Impious Principles?* Penn *hath opposed, scorned the Truth, vilified it's Teachers and Defenders, so as scarce ever Man did; vented the most pernicious Errors,* told *abundance of those Things that are known to himself to be false.*

Rejoyn. Reader, This is all the Justice and Reason I can have, from this pretended *meek and suffering Non-conforming Parson.* What would such Men do, had they as much Power as Anger? But I shall leave him with his Pride and Passion. Is there any Thing more clear than that he extends the Words of *E. Burroughs,* to *Ordinary Cases,* which were wholly writ about *Extraordinary*; and that he takes no more Notice of my *Distinction*, than if there had been none made? As if it had been formerly an equal Sin, for any not to be *Circumcised,* and to *murder his Father or Prince*; or that there was the same Conviction universally upon the Consciences of all Men, *not to wear Linsey Wolsey, as to do by others, as they would have others do to them.*

Levit. 19. 18, 19

That what we say, was *E. Burroughs's* Meaning, his own Words undeniably prove. ' One, says he, was sent to Baptize, and another to Preach the Gospel: Which were particular and extraordinary Commands. He clearly shuffles and evades the Dint of my Answer, and would run us within the Borders of *Rantism.* The Question is not, *Are God's Commands no Commands, unless we think so, and therefore no Sin to break all the Commands in the Bible* (which is the Comment he bestows upon us) but whether this or that special Injunction, to any particular Person or Persons, to this or that particular End, be warrantably imitable, without sufficient Conviction and Commission: Must *J. F.* baptize, because *John* baptized? or turn *Preacher* because *Peter* was one. *E. B.* Only denied Imitation of Ancient Times, in Temporary and Shadowy Services, and all those Preachings, Prayers, Ordinances and Churches, that have not (as *Peter Martyr* well expresses) *the holy Spirit for their Root.* So that instead of his holding a Principle, that hath all Iniquity in the Womb of it, *John Faldo* first perverts his Words, and then to confute them, both implies a Denial of the holy Spirit to be the only right Leader to the Performance of Gospel-Prayer, Preaching and Ordinances, and of gathering of Evangelical Churches, and does as good as tell us, that God's Commandments are such to him, not because of any Conviction in himself, of the Justness of them, but from the Testimony of the Scriptures, which for all his high *Boasts* of *Christianity,* is a State far beneath those *noble Gentiles,* who *not having an outward Law,* were a *Law unto themselves,* having the Effect of it written *in their Hearts,* their Consciences, *bearing Witness,* &c.

And this we may boldly say, *that such as ever acted from that inward Sense, never thought they did God good Service, in killing his Servants*; whilst great Admirers of the Letter of the Scriptures, and who, as concerning this Commandment, *Thou shalt not Murder,* thought themselves most unblameable, believed, *they did God good Service in killing his Servants.*

Nor can I think it so great a *Disgrace* to our Cause, that we ingeniously profess the Reason, why we desire to fear God, and keep his Commandments, doing unto others, as we would have them do unto us, *not so much to be from the Letter of the Scripture, as the Convictions of the Eternal Light and Spirit of God in our Consciences*; As it ought to be unto *John Faldo* and his *Adherents,* who ground their Obedience upon the Letter of the Scripture; and not upon such internal Convictions. What is it but to say, They could *Lye, Swear, Steal, Kill, &c.* without any Remorse, did they not find such Injunctions and Prohibitions upon Record? A Consequence so detestable, yet so natural to their Principles, that if this render them not able Guides to the very Confines of *Rantism* and *Atheism,* I shall gladly ask an Excuse for my Ignorance, but that I may leave nothing undone, that may compleat the Satisfaction of every moderate Inquirer, I shall farther weigh and rejoyn to these Words of his,

They

They who thought they did God good Service, in killing his Servants, did not sin in the least, because they were not convinced of a Command to the contrary; nor the Idolaters in the Case of Baal, *because they thought* Baal *to be a God indeed.*

Now *Reader,* observe the Evasion: This Passage relates not to Men's practising *what God commands,* or our Tenderness in imitating other Saints without Commission, for Fear we should offer strange Fire, which is our Question; but their doing that which *God never commanded,* yea, *which Mankind in all Ages hath adjudged impious,* and which to be sure, his Holy Spirit, that *E. B.* said, All Men should wait to be convinced, assisted and led by in fulfilling God's Commandments, never moved any to. He unworthily draws a general Conclusion against us from meer particular Premises. It seems Men are to act without, if not against Conviction, upon his Principle; and it is the same Thing with him, to commit moral Enormities, from an hardned Heart, and to be tender of taking up an external Practice, or performing some Religious Duty, without the Convictions and Leadings of the Holy Spirit. The Apostle said to such, as had not as yet so full Clearness as others; *That if any were otherwise minded, God would reveal it.* He did not injoyn them, during that Scruple, to believe or practise the Thing doubted; but did Persecutors therefore act inexcusably in their fiery Zeal, because their blind Consciences checkt them not. Again, if *Blindness* came from *Education,* it is (though Blindness still, and therefore it was basely done of *J. Faldo,* to say in our Name, that it is not Sin in the least, *&c.*) more excusable: for in the Days of such Ignorance God winks: But if it be a Blindness, proceeding from long Disobedience and Rebellion, against Convictions and Strivings of the good Spirit of God, as his Word *Hardned* implies, then, I say, it is not only very heinous in God's Sight; but those Persons can never be excused, neither from great Guilt, nor the Sense of it in themselves, let them or *J. F.* talk never so much of Conscience.

Besides, the most Essential, and universally necessary Commands of God, were through all Ages confest to; both before there was any of those Writings, we rightly call the *Scriptures of Truth,* from the *Law of Nature,* as many stile it, or rather, *the Law God placed in Man's Nature,* and since, where they have never been; Therefore, whatever *particular hardned and seared Consciences* may say, we have the Consent of Mankind, and their own Rebellion and Lewdness against them. But the Words of *J. Faldo* in plain Terms import, as if, 1*st.* Men were not generally convinced of the Righteousness of the moral Commands of God; but that Men keep them because they are in the Bible only, which runs against the Testimony of Scripture, the Consent of Ages, and the Writings and Judgment of the most Honest and Learned *Protestants.* 2d*ly* As if it were a like Evil, Conscientiously to forbear Running, Willing and Striving in Matters of Worship, without the Spirit's Conduct, *and searedly to plead for the Commission of Murder and Idolatry,* because Men of such Consciences boggle not at it, (though that is more, than *J. F.* can prove; I mean, that they have no Stroak or Remorse) 3*ly,* As if we could *Worship, Preach, gather Churches,* and administer *Gospel-Ordinances* aright, without the *Spirit.* 4*ly,* That he is not Convinced by any other Testimony, than the Scripture without, of any Transgression against God's Law. 5*ly,* It supposes, that if Men stay'd till the Spirit mov'd, they should stay long enough (who vainly prate of praying by the Spirit, notwithstanding) never considering that the Spirit standeth ready, to reveal it self to their Assistance and Assurance who wait for it; and that all the *Children of God are led by the Spirit of God;* which being our Position, had it been but weighed by this Adversary, he could not (methinks) be so unjust in his Aggravations.

'Tis true, should we believe as he doth, *the Spirit is not to be waited for now a-days to lead us,* or that, *it is not ready to our Information, when we wait for it's Discoveries and Leadings,* our Assertion would look very absurd and loose; for it were to let fall all Worship, but not upon our own Principle, as I said before; for *first,* all Worship to God ought to be performed by the Assistance of his holy Spirit; for of our selves we can do nothing that is Good: And *Secondly,* God's Spirit is ready to assist, instruct and comfort those that wait diligently and patiently for it; yea, God has given it to the Rebellious, that it may judge them, if it don't lead them. It is such *Protestant Doctrine,* that I wonder Men should not know their admired Ancestor's Faith, when they meet it: O great Degeneration into Hardness and Ignorance! *Lastly,* There is the same to be said against Him, that pretends to ground all upon the Scripture, that he objects against us, who plead for the Conviction of Conscience, which the Instance of the *Jews Murder of our Lord Jesus Christ,* unanswerably proves; There was a Law, that *Blasphemers should be be put to Death*; By this Law they apprehended Jesus, adjudged, and got him to be executed: These Men above any Age exalted the Scripture as the only Rule. Where lies the Mistake? Not in the Scripture, *but in their blind and envious Application of it*. Now I ask, if the only Way for them to have come to the true Sense and Knowledge of him, and escaped that Wicked Murder, and the deplorable Consequences of it, had not been *to have waited upon God, for the Convictions Discoveries and Guidance of his Holy Spirit*; since Flesh and Blood, and the utmost Wit of Man, with the Exactness of the meer Letter of the Scriptures, could never give unto that Generation, the certain Discerning, Knowledge and Savour of him, whose very Words themselves were Spirit and Life? It was by a Divine Touch, Sense and Knowledge given from above, that he was truly discern'd, own'd and follow'd of those that believed in him, and cleav'd to him; therefore said Christ, *No Man cometh to me, but whom my Father draweth*: Where was that Drawing but within. Again, *Simon Peter, Flesh and Blood hath not revealed*, (what? Who I am) *but my Father that is in Heaven*. So that at last, *Men must come to this Spiritual Sense in themselves, to understand and apply the very Commands of Scripture*; otherwise not Justice, but detestable Murder, may under the Name of it, be confidently perpetrated; wherefore we exhort all, *to have Recourse to God's Spirit*, that illuminates certainly, and gives to act unblameably, *by which the Scriptures are only understood as they should be, and People brought into the Possession of that Life of Righteousness, they plentifully declare of*. Had it not been for this *inward Discerning*, there had been no *Ground for the Abolishment of the whole* Jewish *Service*, which follow'd some Years after Christ's Ascension. And it is the same Eternal *Spirit* that is the great *Rule* and *Judge* now, which *God promised* more particularly *to shed abroad in the latter Days*; and is the great Privilege inseparable from the New and Everlasting Covenant.

But to conclude, why should it seem so *Heterodox* in *J. Faldo's* Judgment, since if Men believe the Scripture, upon the Testimony of the Spirit, they practice it, by the Knowledge and Power of the same; How else could *Paul* have decry'd *Jewish* Ceremonies; or we know what to take and what to leave? Or why do we admit any Command therein mentioned? *They Circumcised, therefore must I Circumcise? They Baptized, must I therefore Baptize?* With forty more particular Cases, wherein nothing can secure any from the Imitation of them, *set Conviction and spiritual Discerning aside*. I will offer two or three *Testimonies* from approved Men in our Defence.

William Tindal, that ancient faithful *Protestant Martyr*, whom *J. Fox*, that writ the Books of Martyrs, calls, *The English Apostle*, speaks thus, *That it is impossible to understand in the Scripture more than a* Turk, *for whosoever* (or any that) *hath not the Law of God writ in his Heart to fulfil it*. Again, *Without the Spirit it is impossible to understand them*.

W. Tindal's Works, pag. 319, p. 80.

John Jewel, Bishop of *Salisbury*, in his excellent Book against the *Papists*, writ above One Hundred Years ago, says thus to our Purpose, ' The Spirit of God is ' bound neither to Sharpness of Wit, nor to abundance of Learning: Oftentimes ' the Unlearned see that Thing, that the Learned cannot see. Christ saith, *I thank* ' *thee, O Father, Lord of Heaven and Earth, that thou hast hid these Things from* ' *the Wise and the Politick, and hast revealed them unto the Little Ones*. Therefore *Epiphanius* saith, ' *Only to the Children of the Holy Ghost all the Holy Scriptures are* ' *plain and clear*. Again, ' Flesh and Blood is not able to understand the Holy ' Will of God, without *Special Revelation*. Therefore Christ gave Thanks unto his ' Father, and likewise opened the Hearts of his Disciples, that they might under- ' stand the Scriptures. *Without this special Help and* Prompting *of God's Holy* ' *Spirit*, the Word of God is unto the Reader, be he never so wise or well learned, ' *as the Vision of a Sealed Book*.

Bish. Jewel contr. Hard. p. 532, 534.

Now unless Men are bound to do what they do not understand how to do, then only are they to do them when they are *Revealed* or Discovered to them, which being by the Spirit only, according to their Doctrine, the Testimony and Discoveries of the Spirit are required to our understanding of the Scriptures, which implies and comprehends a Discriminating Knowledge, or certain Discerning of what we should practise, from what is not obliging upon us to practise, and consequently, that we ought not to run head-long without such Knowledge.

T. Collier, an Ancient and Eminent Man among the Western-Separatists of our Nation, writeth thus: ' *For me to speak of God, because another speaks of him,* ' *and to be able to talk much of God, as I read of him in Scripture*, Not being made

T. Collier's Works 247.

One

' One in the same Truth, *I see and speak* But what another hath spoken; *and so may speak truly sometimes of God, but it is by Hear-say*, Another Man's Truth, ' but not mine: *So, I doubt, many a Soul* Boasts in another Man's Light. — — Again, ' *I see that external Acting, according to a Rule without, is nothing, if not flowing from a Principle of Life and Love within.* Which is more than E. B. said, of whom *J. Faldo* (with unworthy Reflection and base Wrestings) hath said so much.

Thus much of *Sober Rejoynder*, and much more than my *Adversary's Scurrilous Reply* deserves; but the Concern I have for the *Information* of others, drew this from me. I shall pass by his *Ranting Strain* against us at the Top of his 36th Page, desiring to keep close to the Business; and where I may, without breaking his Matter, avoid troubling the World with a Transcript of them, I am very careful to do it: But this next Particular (as many more) being little else; and since he suggests thereby an Untruth with great Confidence against me, I should wrong both the Truth and my self in omitting it.

He charged us with *Denying the Scriptures to be any Means to know God, Christ, or our selves*; for which he quoted *W. Smith's* Primmer, pag. 2. because he there tells the Questioner, *That Christ is the Only Way*; to which *J. Faldo* answered, *That though Christ said, No Man can come to the Father but by me, yet he did not say, that there is no coming to the Knowledge of God but by Christ*; ' thereby making, as ' I observed in my Return to him, a *Difference between coming to the Father by the* ' *Son, and to God by Christ, though no other Name be given under Heaven, than* ' *the Name of Jesus Christ*, &c. *That we never deny'd the Scriptures to be a* ' *Means in God's Hand to Convince, Instruct, or Confirm*; nor could this be *W. Smith's* ' Meaning, since he would thereby have Cut off all Benefit from accruing to People ' by his Books, and also that Ministry he had receiv'd of God. In short, from our *Denying that there is any other Way to the Father but Christ*, he concludes, that we exclude the Scriptures, and consequently our own Books and Ministry with them, from being any Way *Instrumental* of Good: However, if I have err'd, it was in good Company, and that *J. F.* must acknowledge; for worthy *W. Tindal*, p. 80. of his Works, and *H. Bullenger*, a Learned and Famous *Reformer*, in *Switzerland*, in his fourth *Decad.* and eighth Sermon, dedicated to King *Edward* the Sixth, accord with me in the Matter. The former thus; *Without the Spirit it is impossible to understand them:* Then say I, *They are not a Means to know God Savingly without the Spirit.* The other says plainly, *Men fetch the understanding of Heavenly Things, and Knowledge of the Holy Ghost* from no where else than from the same Spirit. This hits the Mark: But to proceed. Of all this, and Two whole Pages more, he cites but two Lines and an half, included in what I re-cited, on which he bestows this Notable Reply.

Rep. (Pag. 36.) *This might look like an Argument for his Meaning, if it concerned almost any but the Quakers, who assert nothing almost but with a Contradiction. I should think it as hard a Task to reconcile the Quakers to themselves, as to make the Poles to meet, or to dig through the Earth with a Spade to the Antipodes.*

Rejoyn. Yes, *J. Faldo*, it concerns W. *Tindal* and H. *Bullenger*, thou seest, as well as the *Quakers*. But did ever any Man not miserably baffled, put off such serious Matter with such vain Reflections and Pedantick Similes? Will nothing serve the Man's Fancy besides *Poles* and *Antipodes*? Must the *Quakers* needs contradict, to save him from the Discredit of foully belying them? They are there, it seems, to oppose one another, where they will not harmonize to his End. Certainly this Reflection can never be consistent with *J. Faldo's* own Practice, who in a Book of nigh thirty Sheets, writ wholly against the *Quakers*, pretends to confirm his many infamous Charges by Scores of Testimonies, cull'd out of many of their own Books, which must be Unanimous, or they prove not his Charges, as he calls it; nay, he has again and again brag'd of their Harmony to his Purpose. Thus are we in highest Concord, when he thinks it makes for his Designs; and when against them, *as opposite as the Poles*. But blessed be the Lord, we have receiv'd that One, Eternal Spirit, by which we have been Baptiz'd into One Living Body, and are of One Heart, One Mind, and One Sense, concerning the Mysteries of God's Everlasting Kingdom: But as our *Adversary* has said nothing Sober or Rational to what I answer'd in Defence of *W. Smith's* Words, so would he make the World believe I dared not to encounter with one of his Testimonies. Hear him.

Rep. *I produced many Testimonies to prove my Charge, which* Penn *dares not deal with, nor bring to Light; take two of them:* " *Matthew, Mark, Luke* and *John* are " not

1673.

Part I.
Chap. VII.

" not the Gospel, but the Letter. The next, *Hebrew*, *Greek* and *Latin*, is nothing
" worth, as pertaining to the Knowledge of God, *J. Higgens's Warning*, pag. 7.

Rejoyn. That he so suggests, as I said, his own Words prove; yet that I did examine some of his Testimonies is undeniable; and to let him see I dare handle these without fearing they should bite me, I say, and that not without very good Seconds, *They are not the Gospel:* I mean, *Matthew*, *Mark*, *Luke* and *John*, or their Histories; for, *the Gospel of Christ is the Power of God unto Salvation*, so are not the Scriptures. *The Gospel is Everlasting*, so are not the Scriptures. *John saw the Angel flying in the Midst of Heaven, having the Everlasting Gospel to Preach*, which could not be the Scriptures. *The Gospel was Preached before the Scriptures were written*; therefore the Scriptures cannot be the Gospel. *The Gospel is but One*; but after this Man's Reckoning there should be Four; therefore they cannot be the Gospel: Which is farther proved from the Signification of the Word *Gospel*, to wit, *Glad-Tidings*, which are to be understood of the Coming of HIM, that was the Saviour of the World, of whose Blessed Appearance and wonderful Transactions, these *Scriptures are but the Narratives*. Besides, one of their Authors *(Luke)* expresly calls them a *Declaration*, consequently not the Gospel thereby declared of; which Definition *Peter Martyr*, that Superintendent Reformer in *England*, chuseth of all other, *Part 1. Chap. 6. of his Common Places*. *Tertullian* calls the Scriptures, *Instrumenta Doctrinæ*, i. e. Instruments of Doctrine. And the New-Testament Writings, *Evangelicum Instrumentum*, i. e. An Evangelical Instrument. And *Matthew* he calls, *A Faithful Commentator of the Gospel*. *Chrysostom* being requir'd to Swear upon the Gospel, both *denied those Histories to be the Gospel*, and *to Swear at all*. And Dr. *Featly* * will not acknowledge the *English Bible* to be the Authentick Word of God, because of Corruption, consequently not Authentick Gospel, therefore not the Gospel, for that is Authentick. I hope then I may without Offence, in Defence of the Truth, and that Honest Man (now at Peace, yet) so severely reflected upon, conclude, that *Matthew*, *Mark*, *Luke* and *John are not the Gospel, but the Letter, or Declaration of the Gospel.*

Dæ Præscr. Hæretic. adver. Marcion. lib. 4. De carne Christi.

* Against the *Anabaptists*. p. 1.

For his second Proof, viz. " That *Hebrew*, *Greek*, and *Latine* is nothing worth
" as pertaining to the Knowledge of God; I see no Error nor Blasphemy in so Innocent an Assertion. This is so like the catching at Twigs by drowned Men for Safety, that no Man, not as Destitute of Succour, would boast of the Evidence of so Speechless a Witness. There is not One Word it can *Speak* on the Behalf of his Charge. He is fled from the Scriptures to meer *Language*, and makes that a Letter indeed, which one would think he took just now for all Spirit, perhaps with this Distinction though, *That the Scriptures may be the Gospel in* Hebrew, Greek *and* Latin, *but by no Means in the* English: What becomes of the Vulgar then? But what can there be more Sottish, than for a *Protestant* at this Time of Day, to talk of *Knowing God by Hebrew, Greek, and Latin*; but above all, 'tis unpardonable in an *Independent Priest*, to write at this Rate, whose Folk for these Threescore Years, have *Totidem Verbis*, in express Terms, *Deny'd the Knowledge of all, or either, of those Tongues to be necessary to the Knowledge of God.*

Alas! Who once pretended more to the Spirit, and was more derided for doing so, than some of the Predecessors of these *Very Independents and Anabaptists*, now so hot against us? What else were the Invectives cast abroad against Ancient Separatists, as the *Alchymist*, *Assembly-Men*, *Hudibrass*, with abundance of more serious Declamations against them, under the Names of *Tub-Preachers*, *Gifted-Brethren*, &c.

But if Language learn Men to know God, which Christ himself said, *Was Life Eternal*, how comes it that *Scholars* are such *Ill Christians*, and that *Jews*, the *Natural Hebrews*, were such *Persecutors* in Christ's Time, and that they remain *Infidels* to this very Day? Methinks at this Rate the *Greeks*, when God condescended to speak forth the Gospel in their Language, should not have counted it *Foolishness*, nor have mocked at his Embassador, when he came on no less Errand, *Than that of Salvation*; and least of all, since they believ'd, should they have degenerated into so much Superstition. But why the *Latin* must be brought in, I cannot conceive, unless it be the better to enable People to understand the *Romish Translation*, for we never yet heard of so much as any Part of the Scripture that was Originally writ in that Tongue. 'Tis strange to me, he should so much despise the People whose Language he so much extols; and count the one serviceable to the Knowledge of God, whilst with more Reason he reputes the other such gross Idolaters.

Luther

Luther jerks the *Papists* for their laying that Stress *J. F.* doth upon Humane Learning. *W. Tindal* rejects it. *W. Dell* and *T. Collier* write expresly and unanswerably against the Necessity of it, or that it can give Man the Knowledge of God.

In short, common Experience, and the Christian Spirit and Conversation of Thousands that understand not One Sentence of *Hebrew, Greek,* or *Latin,* make Good the Assertion of our Honest Friend, *And is a sufficient Rebuke to this Vapouring Adversary, whose Defiance to me to encounter his Proofs, returns Weakness with Shame upon his Head.* For though he thought to fling me to the Dogs, or give me a Prey to Fierce and Lyonly Seconds, behold they are my Friends, and unanimously turn with me against himself, who had designed them upon such ill Service; a Recompence may he ever find, at what Time he shall endeavour to abuse our *Friends,* and pervert their Writings.

And so I shall end this Chapter, wishing for his Sake, as well as mine own, that I may meet, if not with more Reason, yet with more Moderation, in the Remainder of his Discourse.

CHAP. VIII.

That we do not deny the Scriptures to be any Means whereby to resist Temptation, in Opposition to, and Denial of our Adversary's Charge.

THE Charge by him endeavour'd to be defended, in his Eighth Chapter, is this, *That the* Quakers *affirm the Scriptures to be no Means whereby to resist Temptation*: I will set down his Words.

Rep. (Pag. 37.) *He passes over no less than Six Testimonies, without a Word to invalidate them; among the rest this, If you use any other Weapon than [the Light Within] in this Spiritual Warfare, you cannot prevail against him, that is, the Devil, So I more than proved my Assertion.*

Rejoyn. I therefore avoided considering *every Testimony* he brought, *first,* because many of them were so foreign, that there could be no Pretence for bringing them. *And next,* that I might not be prolix, I thought it sufficient to examine Three in Six, and with good Conscience I can assure my *Reader, I took,* as I thought, *those he Built most upon*. If he doubted of any he should not have brought them, I have answer'd the Law in the Case.

For this now recited, *'tis as weak as Water, to this Purpose,* though a strong Truth in it self; for the Intent of the Words, could be no other than this, that the *Armour of Light,* the Apostle exhorteth the *Church* at *Rome* to put on, *was sufficient to encounter the Power of Darkness; and that such as would overcome, should not neglect or exchange that Armour for other Weapons*; thereby not in the least excluding other such Instruments, as this spiritual Light might arm, or give Strength, and invigorate to our Help. And I am so far from doubting, that I firmly believe, *that God's Spirit, not only in Times past, hath made this Use of the Holy Scriptures, to Instruction and Comfort; but doth even yet to them, who read them in his Holy Fear and Wisdom.*

Reader, I am truly weary; not because I find my Way difficult, from the great Perspicuity and Reason, that are on the Side of my *Adversary;* no, nothing less in this World. But I know not which Way to turn my self, but I meet, either with *School-Boy Jeers, Insolent Language, Equivocations, or horrible Perversions*: God is Record between *J. Faldo* and *Me,* who of us two hath behav'd himself with most *Ingenuity* in encountring the strongest and fullest Arguments, and shown most *Reason* and *Moderation* in confuting them; two or three Instances of *his Failure in both Respects,* this Chapter presents thee with.

Rep. *The first Thing,* W. P. *deals with, is a Passage of* James Nailor's; " For " those only are the Children of God, who are led by the Spirit of God, to whom " they who were led by the Letter were ever Enemies. *From whence saith* Penn, " He concludes, that we account it a very dangerous Thing to read the Scriptures. " Now if this Passage hath any Relation to his Charge or Conclusion, No Man e" ver saw the like. *He should have added, that was always stark blind.*

Rejoyn. Here he has given my Reflection upon his ill Application of the Passage, omitting both my Exposition and Argument; An Injustice I do affirm every Page of his Book, to be guilty of.

What I said to explain the Sentence, was this; " That there are Children of " the Fleshly, Literal, and Historical Knowledge of the Scriptures and Religion, " who are Strangers to, and therefore Persecutors of the Children born of the Spi" rit; and that in all Ages there hath been more or less of this among *Outward* " *Jews and Christians*. And let *J. Faldo* deny this if he dare.

To all which, and much more, he says nothing; but to his blind Squib before-mentioned, he adds this *Wresting of the Passage*, by me so clearly expounded.

Rep. It is a Sign his Judgment is very feeble, that could not, or would not know, that it is dangerous to be led by the Letter, if they that were so led, were ever Enemies to the Children of God.

Rejoyn. What is this but to make us *Enemies to the very Scriptures*, who, without any Distinction, gives so *Wretched a Meaning* to Words so far from bearing it, whose True Sense was, as I observ'd already; to which I may add for farther Explanation, thus, That those who have Confidence in the Letter, Erring from, and Grieving the Holy Spirit, are notwithstanding Enemies to the Children of God, who are led by the Spirit, according to the True Meaning of Scripture, which the meer Letter-Professor, as such, can never attain to: So that the Danger lies here, *to be led by the Letter, without the True Meaning of the Letter*, or rather by his own dark Apprehensions concerning the Mind of it, instead of it; *As the Jews when they Crucified Christ by the Law of God against Blasphemers.* This is the Genuine Sense of our Friend's Words; For had they been writ in the Sense in which *John Faldo* takes them, we had then as greatly detested them, as he has now wrong'd them.

A second Passage is, in his first Book, pag. 109. his Words these, Isaac Pennington, who *speaking of Knowledge gain'd by the Letter of the Scriptures, writes thus,* "Making him Wise and Able in his Head, to oppose Truth, and so bringing him "into a State of Condemnation, Wrath and Misery beyond the *Heathen*, and mak- "ing him harder to be wrought upon, by the Light and Power of Truth, than the "very *Heathen*. Upon which *J. Faldo* bestows this Comment; *If reading the Scriptures, and getting Knowledge from them, puts us into a bad Condition beyond the* Heathen, *I scarce know what is more dangerous than reading the Scriptures.*

Reader, 'Tis worth our While to see, if *I. Pennington* be as bad a Man as *John Faldo* represents him; in order to which I ask, *First, May a Man, that reads and pretends to value the Scriptures, form up an Understanding of them, and yet be absolutely mistaken, for want of the true Interpreter, the Spirit of Truth?* I cannot think but *J. Faldo* himself will say, that such a Thing may be; I am sure I believe so; for it hath often been so already, and *J. Faldo*'s present Writings are an Unanswerable Instance for the Point. The next Question I would ask is this; *Whether such Persons so mistaken, are not very apt in Defence of their own Conceivings, to oppose the Truth it self?* Methinks the whole *Jewish Church*, at the Time of Christ's Visible Appearance in the World, in disputing against him, and decrying of his Religion, while they magnified the Scriptures, as the only great Doctors of them, should without farther Labour answer that Question in the Affirmative. *Next*, Let me ask *J. Faldo*, *If the high Conceit the* Jews *had of their Knowledge in the Commands, Doctrines and Prophesies of Scripture (however Erroneous for Want of the True Interpreter) did not render them more captious and obdurate than the* Heathen *themselves?* If he can read the Scriptures of the New Testament, he may answer this Question to our Mind, and his own Shame. *Lastly, Was not this State more dangerous than that of the* Gentiles? God himself long since resolv'd this Question, when he brought such heavy Judgments upon the *Jews*, and turn'd the Stream of his Love to the *Gentiles*. It was not for nought those Words were left upon Record; *He came to his own, and his own received him not*: That is, He came to the Nation and People of all others God had *selected* for his Service, to whom he had been propitious beyond Measure, whom he redeem'd by *wonderful Miracles*, and blessed with *Holy Leaders, Just Judges*, a *Righteous Law*, *True* and *Faithful Prophets*; whose were the *Covenants* and *Scriptures, who were the Seed of* Abraham, *and of whom Christ came as concerning the Flesh*; yet they received him not as God over all, blessed for ever, manifested in Flesh, in the Fulness of Time, for their Deliverance; but vehemently rejected him, under the Title of *Beelzebub, Prince of Devils*. By this Time, I hope, *Isaac Pennington*'s Passage is vindicated from the Malignity of our Adversary's Comment, whose Perversion must needs be open and conspicuous to all that read him; *First*, In charging him, *to have made this Reflection upon the Knowledge gain'd by the Letter of the Scriptures*; which are none of *I. P*'s Words: *Next*, in concluding, That by *I. P*'s Doctrine, *nothing can well be more dangerous than reading the Scriptures* (who always was, and yet is, a great Respecter and Reader of them) making the Stress of *I. P*'s Saying to lie in a Dislike and Contempt of the Scriptures absolutely, instead of their

dark

dark Interpretations upon, and Carnal Deductions from the Scriptures, which he only levelled his Discourse against.

Thus have we been serv'd in every pretended Proof he has brought out of our Friends Writings, to prop and enforce his feeble and incredible Charges; For where we reprove *Men's forming unto themselves Religion from the Letter of the Scriptures, according to their own Conceptions of it,* and give a Check to their great Eagerness to comprehend the most weighty Mysteries therein expressed, and their continual Questioning, Cavilling and Contending concerning them, whilst they themselves are ignorant of the very first Principles of Religion, being yet Strangers to Unfeigned Repentance from Dead Works, and Fear towards the Living God, *with loud Voices and Clamorous Tongues they thus exclaim against us,* after this Unruly as well as Unjust Manner, The Quakers *deny the Scriptures*; The Quakers *say they are not binding upon them*; The Quakers *say, it is dangerous to read them*; but I say in their Name, *Blessed are they, who reading, truly understand them, and live according to them.* I might here break off, but I intreat my Reader to peruse two notable Testimonies given by University-Men, and such as were reputed famous Thirty Years ago.

The first is out of *Joshua Sprigg's* Book, entituled, *A Testimony to an Approaching Glory,* Pag. 96. "Christ desires that his Disciples may be sanctified, not by "planting the Knowledge of the Literal *Word in their Minds,* but by ingrafting "the Nature of the Divine *Word in their Hearts.* Again, In Pag. 107, Christ "may offer himself long enough in the Letter in the History of the Gospel, but "if he appear not in the Spirit, and sit in our Consciences, to quiet them, we "shall never have any true Understanding of the Word aright. And, in Pag. 79 "and 80, We may see what is to be done by looking upon the History of Christ; "but *'till we find the same Things done in us in some Measure in the* Mystery, *we* "*can find little Comfort* ——— The whole *History* of Christ will profit you nothing, "nor all that you know, *except you find* Experimentally *the same Things done in* "*you by the Spirit.*

The Second is afforded us by *Christopher Goad,* stiled *Batchelor of Divinity,* and *Fellow of King's Colledge in* Cambridge, in his Book, entituled, *Refreshing Drops,* &c. Pag. 12. "There is no Knowledge of Christ, nor of the Scripture, but by "*Revelation*; it is that the Apostle prays for, *That God would give unto us the* "*Spirit of Revelation.* ——— Again, in Pag. 18, It is neither *Moses, nor the Scrip-* "*tures, nor Christ's Works,* can settle our Hearts, unless the Father be in them, "*&c.* Also, in Pag. 89, "To go forth in Man's Power, *in the Power of a Letter* "*of the Scripture only,* is not safe. Yet again, Pag. 87, upon *Acts* 17, Here they "hold *Paul* play in Reasoning and Disputing; *Paul* holds up Christ out of the "Scriptures, *and the* Jews *do dispute against Christ by the Scriptures*; And this is "that that all the Learning of Man doth, *all his Knowledge in the Scripture doth* "*but serve him, to oppose the Spirit.* The *greater Knowledge in the Scriptures,* "and the more Learning (if it be only of Man) *the greater Opposition unto Christ,* "*and unto the Spirit.* These *Jews* had Learning and Knowledge in the Scriptures, "meerly to oppose the Truth, the Power and Life of the Scriptures. And lastly, that we may not be too prolix, we shall content our selves (in the over-looking many more) with this Passage, in his last Testimony, Pag. 71, upon *Esa.* 25. "There are that have devoted themselves to the Law, and the *Letter* of Scrip- "ture; There are others that have their Life in the Creature; *God will shortly* "*draw all Life unto himself, and all they that run after other Gods, shall starve* "*and famish, they and their Gods.*

These Passages, Reader, speak for themselves; and, which is more, so much for us, that 'till *J. Faldo* and his Fellow-Separatists have publickly renounced them, and their Authors, we have great Cause to say, that such as themselves have hitherto reputed their Spiritual and Learned Ministers, do defend and rather out-word us in Testimony to the Truth: But before *J. Faldo* proceeds to any such Excommunication, let him remember that he cannot do it without Disturbance to the Grave, and Injury to the Memory of *Joseph Caryl,* that Famous and Ancient *Independent Pastor,* who Licensed *J. Sprigg's* Book, *Ann.* 1647, and consequently entituled himself to the Doctrine therein exprest.

And

And for *Chriſtopher Goad's*, not only *J. Sprigg* performed the Friendly Office of Publiſher after his Deceaſe, but himſelf was a Paſtor of a very eminent Congregation of *Independents* in his Life-time: Strange! that the Men of theſe Days ſhould not know the Principles of their Admir'd Fathers and Teachers, when they meet them; but that worthy Witneſs *C. Goad*, in his Concluſion of his laſt Teſtimony, Pag. 74 and 77, gives a good Reaſon for it; He that hath Ears to hear, let him hear; he that hath not, it may be will cry, *Whimſy, Fancy, and turning the Scripture into an Allegory* — and whilſt the Vail is over, *Error, Hereſy, Blaſphemy*.

I had thoughts of adding no farther Teſtimony, but a moſt remarkable Paſſage of that *Chriſtian* and Learned Martyr, Dr. *Barnes*, burnt for his Faith in King *Henry* the Eighth's Days, (after having been his Ambaſſador, and in high repute) preſſed hard upon me; and I know not but his greater Diſtance from us than thoſe before cited may carry more Authority, and obtain greater Favour with our Enemies, who will at leaſt make ſhew of Reverence to his *Antiquity* and *Martyrdom*; his Words are theſe.

" That Man's Will, Reaſon, Wiſdom, Heart, Soul, or whatſoever Thing is in
" Man *(without the Spirit of God)* is but the *Wiſdom of the Fleſh*; let him intend
" his beſt, do all that lieth in him, with all his Might, and all his Power, and
" yet can it not pleaſe God; *for it is all but Fleſh.* —— Again, " It is the Spirit
" of Chriſt that maketh him Chriſt's, and the Spirit of God giveth Witneſs to
" our Spirit, that we be the Children of God. Our Spirit giveth no Witneſs to
" himſelf, that he is Chriſt's; for then were the Spirit of God fruſtrate; where-
" fore, *let our Spirit, as well as he can, ſtudy his beſt, to apply himſelf to Goodneſs,*
" *or to the uttermoſt of his Power, and yet it is but* Wiſdom of the Fleſh, and
" hath no Witneſs of God; yea, it is but an *Enemy*, and it muſt needs be *Sin*, as
" St. *Auſtin* ſaith, *He that feedeth without me, feedeth againſt me.*

Thus far Dr. *Barnes*, which is but a little of the great deal he writes, to the ſame Purpoſe, againſt the *Papiſts*, about their Doctrine of *Free-will*. And indeed he cleaves the Hair, and hits the Mark above moſt Ancient Writers; for as he unanſwerably argues in that very Smart Diſcourſe, that Man's cleaving to his own Power, brought him into Tranſgreſſion, and conſequently could never redeem him out of it. So doth he expreſs the abſolute Neceſſity of Man's having Recourſe to the Spirit of God in himſelf, for Counſel and Aſſiſtance, in order to underſtand and fulfil the Good-will of God; which implies, that all thoſe who call it, *oppoſing the Spirit to the Scripture*, and *vilifying the Knowledge of Scripture*, to preſs the Underſtanding of it, and a witneſſing the Truths therein declared of from the Revelation and Operation of the Eternal Spirit only, *are upon the rankeſt Strain of Free-will*, that was ever yet broached among Men, and there we leave our bitter Enemy *J. Faldo*.

I am now come to a *Paſſage* more immediately concerning my ſelf, *which he thinks, touches me to the Quick*; but I know not why, unleſs he meaſures me by himſelf, being a Man ſo quick to be touched, that at the ſobereſt and ſolideſt Anſwer which I could give him, he doth ſo gaul and fret, that there is no coming near him, without being kick'd and abus'd. His Carriage towards me in this Particular, amongſt many Inſtances already paſt, and yet to come, proves what I ſay.

In a Book of mine called, *The Spirit of Truth Vindicated*, &c. in anſwer to a *Socinian*, who ſeem'd to deride the *Quakers* aſſerting a Neceſſity of having a Right Faith in God, and Knowledge of the Scriptures, from the Revelation and Operation of the Eternal Spirit, I uſed theſe Words. " But I aſſure them, they ſhall
" grope in the Dark, 'till they come into the Daily Obedience of the Light, and
" there reſt contented to know only as they Experience. At this he ſcoffed; *What know God only as they experience? Can we experience his Omnipotency? That W. P. of all others, ſhould talk at this Rate, is moſt Ridiculous.* To which he brings me in, thus anſwering, " 'Tis Unchriſtian in *J. Faldo* to aſſert the right Knowledge of
" God, obtainable any other Way than by Experience. Here's my *Reflection* by Way of Conſequence, but where's my *Argument*? That he left behind, as being better able to jeer it, than confute it; ſome ſhort Account of it I will give.
" That it is the Light or Spirit of God, that by it's Illumination giveth the right
" Knowledge of God, that ſuch Knowledge never goes without Experience. Again,
The

" The World without in it's Make, Order, Preservation, Providences, and his Power-
" ful Work of Redemption within prove what I writ: But of this he takes no
Notice. Now *his Dis-ingenuity* thus far is two-fold, *First*, His stretching the
Word *Experience* to all Cases; when the Scope and End of my Words went no
farther than *every Man's particular Saving Knowledge of God*, with Respect to his
Repentance, Conversion, and Eternal Salvation. 2*dly*, He not only has taken no
Notice of my Argument, but has abused the Consequence, *viz. That the Right or
Saving Knowledge of God is not obtainable but by Experience*; after this Manner.

Rep. Reader, *you have his Character of asserting, that Reason, Faith, Scripture, yea, the Spirit of God too (all which are not one and the same Thing with Experience) are not any Means by which to obtain the right Knowledge of God.*

Rejoyn. How like a Disputant or an Honest Man he deals with me, may be seen, *First,* In that *no Man can have Experience without Reason,* because Reason is that Part of a Man, which is eminently concern'd in receiving that Experience, therefore not the Giver of it, nor yet it without Reason. *Secondly,* The Work of Faith is one great Thing experienced. *Thirdly,* The Scripture is oftentimes an Instrument to that Experience. *Lastly,* The Spirit of God is the efficient Cause or Worker of Experience, in the reasonable Soul. For must not *He* be very blind or Malicious, that can suppose, I meant by the Knowledge of Experience, *such an one, as God's Spirit brings not to,* who have been all this while pleading for *that Knowledge and Experience, which the Spirit of God can only give,* and abused with a Witness by *J. Faldo* for doing so; but that he should suppose me to exclude Reason, from Men in their Experiences, which is to render them Brutes, and because therefore unreasonable, to be sure most uncapable of Experience (unless Men may experience without their Reasonable or Understanding Part) is a Wrong that would have drawn a whole Chapter of Railing from him, had he been so serv'd by a *Quaker.* And for Faith, How can a Man have it, and not know he hath it; and which Way may he possibly know it and not experience it? As to the *Scriptures,* they may both be instrumental to Experience, and with Respect to what they declare of, be also experienced.

(Pag. 39.) Two Places more, and we leave this Chapter, in which it will appear, that his Courage is as much upon the Ebb, as his Envy was before upon the Float. In his former Book he was so unhappy in his Cause, as to let fall this Expression, That *God above, and the Scripture without, have taught us better Things.* The Use I made of it in my Answer, he takes a little Notice of, I mean to recite, not confute it.

' Now what is the Teaching of the God above, said I? If it be in the Scrip-
' tures, it was impertinent to say any more, than that the Scriptures have taught
' them better Things. But if he meant that God taught by his immediate Disco-
' veries with and beside the Scriptures, then wherein do we differ?

To which I will faithfully set down his *Reply*, that, if there be any Reason in it, I may lose none of it in Transcription.

Rep. W. P. *thinks* (now) *he has me upon the hip; this Phrase he calls assisting to my own Confutation. If joyning the Teachings of God and the Scriptures always together be Self-Confutation, let me be ever so Confuted.*

Rejoyn. This is both Evasion and False Doctrine. Evasion in putting *always together* in the Reply, which was not in the first Passage; and very much alters the Case, since to say, that *God above and the Scriptures without have taught us better Things,* and to say, *if joyning the Teachings of God, and the Scriptures always together, &c.* are vastly differing. For the first Saying or Passage is general, and leaves God at Liberty to speak beside, with, or above the Scriptures; but the *Reply* ties God always to the Scriptures; that he cannot speak otherwise than by them, nor the Scriptures be without him, which makes up the *False Doctrine* I charged upon him. But if he means that God speaks nothing contrary to his Mind declared in Scripture, and the Scriptures nothing contradictory to the Mind of God, I acquiesce; yet this Concession not only brings him upon the *Hip,* but upon the bare *Ground* too; for it confutes him without controul, inasmuch as he grants, *that the Scriptures without are not sufficient to teach without the God above,* the

very

very Thing in Controversie almost from the Beginning betwixt us; so that I return his own Words upon himself, pag. 40. of his Reply. *All this ado is to make the Scriptures nothing without immediate Inspiration*; implying that we hold them to be profitable as God is pleased to discover unto us, and breath into our Hearts the true Meaning and Virtue of them, for our Instruction and Comfort; and what short of this doth *J. Faldo*'s Expression import, that makes the Teachings of the God above necessary to render the Scriptures truly profitable unto any: And what is this but to say with us, that they are of *no value* (not in themselves, but) to us, unless the God above unfold them, and brings our Souls into a Sense of those States and Truths they declare of. I leave my sober Reader to make his Judgment of this, and so proceed to the next Particular, which will end this Chapter. I will set down his Words.

Rep. *He quarrels with my Management of* Ephes. 6. 16, 17. *thus*, 'And a Shame 'it is that this Man should bring these Places to prove that the Scriptures are 'Means whereby to resist Temptation. *The Words are*, Wherefore take unto you the whole Armour of God; *And among the rest is reckoned* the Sword of the Spirit, which is the Word of God. *Why doth he not say, it is a Shame I produce any Scripture at all? which is like a* Quaker *throughly*; *but the Matter is, it is a Shame to call the Scriptures the Word of God, or a Spiritual Sword.*

Rejoyn. No such Matter. The Shame was, that *J. Faldo* perverted and mis-apply'd Scripture; and the Shame still is, that he should so bungle and boggle in the Business, as of Two Pages to take Two Lines, that concern'd not either the Exposition or the Argument, and when he has done, say nothing to it. Is this Man like to acquit himself with Advantage against the vain Attempts of *W. P.* as he is pleas'd to call them? *Reader*, I have often complain'd, and yet shall have Cause enough of my Adversary's unfair Dealing, in not reporting the fortieth part of what I urge, and that he is sure to take not what is most, but least material to my Cause, and then bestows a Squib or two upon it, instead of taking my Strength, or giving a sage Reply; and that I complain not without Just Cause; be pleas'd to consider my former Answer with what he first writ to occasion it; by which his *Honesty* in reciting, and *Reason* in replying may be most impartially judged of. Thus he, pag. 113. *Above all take the Shield of Faith, which is able to quench, &c. and the Sword of the Spirit, which is the Word of God.* Observe said J. Faldo, *Faith in the 16th verse is preferred above the Word of God in the 17th verse; therefore it is not Christ the Word, but the Scriptures the Word; for Faith is not above Christ. Jesus Christ, who had less need of Scripture than any of us all, resisted Satan's Temptation by Scripture, It is written, it is written,* Mat. 4. To which I gave this following Answer; ' But neither will this do his Business, and a Shame ' it is that this Man should bring these Places to prove that *the Scriptures are* ' *Means whereby to resist Temptation* (which Rebuke was the whole he recited) that ' concerned them not, especially this in Hand, unless he would have *Faith* to be ' the *Scriptures*, or Word of God in his Sense, which as it is absurd, so it will by ' him be deny'd, since he allows Faith to be preferr'd before the Word of God, ' therefore distinct from it, and consequently not the same with it. And should ' we grant to him, that *Christ* is not understood by the Word of God, but the ' Scriptures; yet observe the fatal Blow his Cause receives at his own Hand. ' Every true *Christian* hath Faith; that Faith is above the Scriptures, therefore *eve-* ' *ry true* Christian *hath something in him above the Scriptures.* Again, ' True Faith ' overcometh the World, and quenches the fiery Darts of Satan, consequently ' Temptations; therefore not so properly the Scriptures, as *true Faith, which is* ' *preferred above them,* (by *John Faldo* himself) *and which resists Temptation, and* ' *overcomes the World,* is, &c. Once more, the Just live by Faith, but *Faith* ' *is above the Scriptures,* saith *J. F. Therefore the Just live by that which is above* ' *the Scriptures,* and consequently, the Scriptures are not the Rule of Faith, for ' how can any Thing be ruled by that which is inferior to it? Thus much we get, ' granting to him, that the Scriptures are the Word of God in the Text. Now, Reader, tell me, of this Argumentation what has he taken, *what has he replied to?* Yet this Man is deem'd worthy by the Professors of our Times, to act the *Tertullus* against the poor *Quakers*.

For those Words, *The Sword of the Spirit, which is the Word of God,* I told him then, ' We rejected his Gloss; for the *spiritual Sword,* as he says, *Beza* renders ' it, must be of the Nature of the rest of the *Armour* mention'd in that Chap-
' ter,

'ter, that is, invisible and Spiritual, which the Bible or meer Writings we know 'are not. To which let me add; that I know no Reason *why the Shield of Faith should be preferred before the Sword of the Spirit*, unless it be because that's in the Verse before this, if we consider them in an abstract Sense, or as they are in themselves. For *Above all*, is not a preferring the *Shield of Faith* in Dignity before the Sword of the Spirit, respecting their own Nature and Quality, but with regard to the Creature: For, *if Unbelief enters, how can the Loins be girt with Truth, the Breast arm'd with Righteousness, the Feet shod with the Preparation of the Gospel of Peace, the Head covered with the Helmet of Salvation*, or the Enemy encounter'd with the Sword of the Spirit? So that respecting *Man*, not respecting the Dignity of the several Parts of the Armour, *Faith* is above all, or first necessary; for tho' God, Christ, the Holy Spirit, Eternal Salvation, be all, or either of them greater than Faith, as in themselves, yet without Faith no interest can he had in them. Wherefore our Adversary's *Preference* vanisheth, and his *Consequence* about the Scriptures being the Word of God falls to the Ground.

Concerning Christ's Answer to the Devil, *It is written, it is written*, I shall desire the Reader to observe in my Adversary's Reply, what of my Answer he transscribes, which I gave to the use he made of that Scripture; and what Sort of Treatment he affords me. These are his Words.

Rep. *Once more and I have done with this Chapter. But said Christ to the Devil, It is written*; What then, *says W. P. Therefore must the Quakers needs deny the Scriptures to be any Means to resist Temptation? pag.* 90. *You may fear the Man is craz'd, or was almost asleep when he wrote this. I produced the Example of Christ to prove that the Scripture is a Means for resisting Temptation, he resisting so effectually with* it's written, it's Written. *But Penn would make you believe I intended it to prove, that the* Quakers *deny the Scriptures to be such a Means. Can you think such a Man to be sinless, yea, Infallible.*

Rejoyn. His Froth and Reflection I am no otherwise concern'd at, than that it ill becomes a Pretender to Divinity. It is enough for me to shew, that he has willingly conceal'd my Answer, and hath made a Reply as if he had taken in all that was fit to be consider'd; my Answer lay thus, ' But said Christ to the Devil, *It is* 'written; What then? *Therefore must the* Quakers *needs deny the Scriptures to be* 'any Means to resist Temptation; (Here *J. F.* leaves me, but I go on) or rather are 'they not such Means, which I am sure no right *Quaker* ever deny'd. (Now '*Reader* mark) Besides, it was reasonable that Christ should so answer (set that 'Power aside, which filled up those Words, and chain'd *Satan*) *because the Devil* 'used Scripture to prevail upon him, as the Place proves. However we deny not, 'but confess that where-ever God is pleased to speak by any Place of Scripture to 'a Tempted Soul, it may very well be acknowledg'd to be a Means, by which God 'scatters such Doubts and Despondencies, and gives Power over Temptations, and 'that it may often so occur, yet we would not have People fly to them, as what 'of *themselves* may be sufficient: but rather have Recourse to that Divine Faith, 'which the Scriptures testifie *is able to Quench the fiery Darts*, and which, *J. F.* 'himself has largely confest, *is to be preferred above the Scriptures themselves.*

Now I desire the *Reader* to consider, *First*, That he gave not the 10th Part of my Answer in any respect. *Secondly*, That what of it would have prevented his reflecting upon me, he wholly omitted. He seems displeased that I made such a Question upon his citing Christ's Words to the Devil as this, *therefore must the* Quakers *needs deny the Scriptures to be any Means to resist Temptation?* telling Folks, *They may fear I was craz'd or asleep when I wrote it*; asking, *If they think such a Man to be sinless or infallible?* as thinking it improper to his Quotation, and yet would take no Notice of these Words, that were directed immediately to it, viz. *it was (therefore) reasonable that Christ should so answer, because the Devil used Scripture to prevail upon him*; the very Answer in his pretended Reply was wanting: With what Face then can our Adversary, over and above his other ill Words, charge me with *designing to render him impertinent*, by making him endeavour to prove that the *Quakers* deny the Scriptures to be such a Means, by the Question I ask'd, as if I had wrong'd him, and that he never intended any such Thing through the bent of the Chapter? And what can be clearer, than that he on Purpose avoided the Shock, and took Notice only of that Part of my Answer, which being torn from the rest, he thought fittest for him to play upon. But I see no Wrong

Wrong I did him in so asking what I did; for I am sure it was one End for which the Scripture was quoted by him; and the *Jeers* he bestows upon me and it, besides his wilful Neglect of the rest of my honest Return, and yet complaining for want of it when he had done so, is a pitiful come off for a Man of his Pretence to Controversie.

CHAP. IX.

Not we, but our Adversary opposeth the Teachings of the Spirit to the Doctrines of the Scriptures. The Testimonies brought by him cleared and delivered from his Application. Our Doctrine proved from Scripture and several Testimonies. His frequent and gross Perversions of our Words and Writings discovered and justly rebuked.

WE are now got to his last Chapter, relating to the *Scriptures*, in which he pretends to justifie his Charge, by farther evidencing a Consistency between it and *William Smith*'s Doctrine, which I utterly deny'd to have been *William Smith*'s Words or Meaning. The Charge was, That *the* Quakers *put the Spirit of God and the Scriptures in Opposition to each other*; His Proof of the Charge lies in these Words, *Traditions of Men, Earthly Root, Darkness and Confusion, Apostacy, the Whore's Cup, the Mark of the Beast, Bastards brought forth of Flesh and Blood*, &c. which says *J. Faldo*, in his first Book, *would amaze a Christian to read, what is contained in the two Pages quoted of vilifying Reproach to the Scriptures: If this be not opposing the Spirit of God to the Scriptures, the Devil himself must despair of inventing Words to express it by.* Thus far *J. Faldo*. And indeed I must confess, If all or any of these Things were ever said or published by *William Smith*, there is great Cause for Amazement, and Abhorrence too. But what said I to this? Truly enough; but that *J. Faldo* was careful to conceal: He brings in a small Limb of my Answer, and then scares it with hard Words. Take Notice of his *Reply*, to what he ventures to transcribe of my Answer.

Rep. Penn *saith*, W. Smith (pag. 41.) reflected not in the least upon the Scriptures, nor those Doctrines which were truly received thence. No such Words can be produc'd by our Adversary. *No Jesuit in the World did ever out-do* W. P. *in Equivocations and Subterfuges. His Stress lies on the Words* TRULY *received thence.*

Rejoyn. Suppose them to be my *Stress*, what *Subterfuge* lies there? Are there not Doctrines falsly deduced through Men's Ignorance of the true Intendment of Scripture? And do not such as confidently think them to be truly received from Scripture, as if they really were so. But the Stress lies here with *J. Faldo*; His Religion cannot bear a Scrutiny; and is as well nigh as shy of a Search as *Mahometism* it self. Though had *J. Faldo* and the rest of his Gang continu'd where they were, the poor *Quakers* might have had an Inquisition with a Witness at their Heels by this Time. But he has a farther Comment for us.

Rep. *The* Quakers *allow no Doctrine to be truly received from the Scriptures, but such as is received by immediate Inspiration, and not from the Authority of the Written Word.*

Rejoyn. Where's the Opposition now? Doth not he set the Authority of the Scriptures against the Inspiration of the Holy Ghost, at least exclude the Holy Inspiration from any share in that Authority, and so do what he can to shuffle out *the Spirit from being concerned in the Authority of the Scriptures*; which is, if not the only, yet the greatest Proof of their Authority, since it is chiefly by [*the Testimony of the Spirit in our selves that we know them to have been given forth by the Inspiration of the Holy Ghost in others*, as held both by the Primitive *Christians*, our Famous *Martyrs*, and most Considerable *Protestants*. He speaks as if he affected Obscurity, and aim'd only at jumbling and intricating, instead of explaining the Matter. But had we put the Spirit in Opposition to the Letter, it is no more than what the Scripture hath done before us, as *H. Bullenger*, that notable Reformer observes upon *Rom.* 2. 29. ' The Spirit, saith he, is opposed to the Letter, ' as when *Paul* saith, *The Circumcision of the Heart is the Circumcision that consist-*

'eth in Spirit, not in the Letter; And again, *The Lord hath made us able Ministers of the New Testament, not of the Letter, but of the Spirit; for the Letter killeth, but the Spirit giveth Life,* 4 Dec. 8 Serm. A notable Application to our Purpose; but while we only so oppose them, as to give the Preference to the Holy Spirit, *J. Faldo* falls foul of us for a Pack of *Enthusiasts*, shutting out the Spirit, at least setting it aside to exalt the Letter. But what doth he mean by these Terms, *Immediate Inspiration?* for a *Mediate Inspiration* I never heard of. Sure I am, that *Inspiration* is God's own Breathing into the Soul, by which it hath Understanding given it, whether it be of Things written, or not written; and how that can be done, and *not immediately*, I know not. If he will exchange his impertinent Distinction of *Mediate* and *Immediate* for *Ordinary* and *Extraordinary*, we shall allow him more than we can upon the other; for by *Ordinary Inspiration* or Revelation I understand such daily and common Vision and Discovery to the Soul, as concerns it in its general Station, respecting God and Men: By *Extraordinary*, such as great Fore-sights, or Divine Prospects, which give to fore-tell or prophesie Things to come, or decide some signal Controversies, or very special Case of Difficulty: The *first* is what I speak of; and do affirm, that neither can the Scriptures be understood, our Souls fed and comforted, nor our Duties to God rightly perform'd without it: The *last* is a Case so peculiar, that all along it is plain, I never intended it. But if by *Immediate Inspiration*, respecting us, he understands, *that from thence forwards we cast off all Scripture, as an antiquated, or insignificant Piece of Business* (which are yet Words too modest for his Malice to father upon us, as I shall anon make appear) then doth he wrong us and our Doctrine to an high Degree. And no Matter what he thinks of me, or what Names he may please to call me (who is too far gone in his present *splenetick* Disease, to think any better of such as I am) I shall plainly set down what was my Meaning by the Words he cavils at, viz. TRULY *received thence*, I hope, to their Satisfaction, who will be more dis-interested in their Judgment.

By *Doctrines* TRULY *owned and received from Scripture*, we mean such Holy Truths, as God by his Spirit (inlightning our Understandings) hath given us a *true Discerning* of to be such, and those are they which we put in Opposition to Men's *Carnal Interpretations* upon, and *Imaginary Deductions* from the Scriptures, and not that we clash the *Spirit's Inspiration* against the Scripture; for they harmonize, and bear reciprocal Testimonies to each other: And this God, that knows all Hearts, both knows to be our true Sense in the Matter controverted, and will one Day abundantly prove to our *Adversary's* Eternal Conviction. This, I fear, *J. Faldo* will never swallow; and why? because it would choak him: Perhaps I must be a *Jesuit*, an *Equivocator*, and what else he pleaseth; but wherefore? because it strikes at his Honesty, indeed Dishonesty; for he had rather we were, what he says we are, than receive a Contradiction by finding us otherwise, than he hath so confidently represented us to be. So much dearer is *Humor*, *Pride* and *Worldly Credit* to him, than our being not so mistaken as he thought for. Is this Man like to make Converts, that first maims my Answers, and then either pelts what he doth take with Dirt; or if one Sense worse than another may be had, that (usher'd in with a *Rant*, and wound up with a *Quibble*) must be given for an apt and irrefutable Reply: This hath hitherto been his Practice, and we now go upon both a Proof of it, and yet more evidently to clear the Truth.

In that little Piece of my Answer he cropt off from the rest, (for after his wonted Manner, he thought it not best for him to encounter it at large, but a snap and away) I told him, that he could produce no such Words, as, *Traditions of Men, Earthly Root, Darkness, Confusion, Corruption, Deceitful, Whore's Cup, &c.* as said of the Scriptures, out of *W. Smith's* Book, which was one Part of my Stress, he was willing to shake off, but it will not so easily acquit him. Observe his *Reply*.

Rep. And whereas W. P. *saith*, 'No such Words can be produced; *he intends no other, but that* Smith *doth not accuse himself in so many Words of Blaspheming the Spirit of God in the Scriptures, and the Doctrines from thence received.*

Rejoyn. His first Words bely me; nor can any Man be so sottish, as to think I intended any such Thing, as he would have his *Reader* believe; for that were no Answer to the Objection, but an arrant, yet fond, Cheat and Illusion. My Meaning went with my Words, and my Words meant as I just now explain'd them, the

Substance of which was in my *Answer*, though evaded by his *Reply*, and perhaps my *Rejoynder* will meet with no better Usage.

For his Phrase of *Blaspheming the Spirit of God in the Scriptures*, I will tell him, and that upon very good Authority, that he now plays the *Canter* with us, and that shamefully, *The Spirit of God* in *the Scriptures!* a Scripture for that, I intreat him. You may see what a Doctor he is, you that believe in him, that thinks, *he can clasp up the Spirit with his Bible*. It seems thus far *J. Faldo* and *Simon Magus* agree; for the *one thought he could buy it of* Peter, and the *other implies he may have it of his Bookseller*. Indeed if I thought *J. Faldo* could believe what he says, I should be the tenderer of him; for Ignorance is to be pity'd: But when he shall shut the *Spirit of God out of Men, and shut him up in the Scripture, though it call Men the Temples or Tabernacles of God and his Spirit, whilst it never calls it self so, but Holy Writings, or a Declaration of Things certainly believed*, he is to be censur'd for his improper and ambiguous Terms, and the rather, because his Charity is so small to others in Cases more excusable, and that no Man acts the *Doctor of the Sentences* to others more snappishly and imperiously than himself; however, I shall be so favourable as to take his Words in this Sense (else I know not which Way he will turn himself) *viz. The Spirit of God speaking* (when it pleaseth) *by the Scriptures*, which brings him and his Cause unavoidably over to us.

But let us see if *J. F.* can honestly fasten any of those fore-cited *Epithets* upon *W. Smith*'s Book; If he can, we will condemn the Book as heartily, as *J. F.* traduceth us in his. But if he shall be found to have wrong'd *W. S.* God that lives for ever will avenge our Innocency upon him; which we desire may extend no farther than to work him into true Repentance, and effectually to vindicate us in the Understandings of the Mis-informed. His Words are these:

Rep. (Pag. 41, 42.) *But that all that Inventory of execrable Names* W. Smith *doth intend of the Scriptures, and the Holy Doctrines grounded on the Authority of the written Word, take these Testimonies,* John 1. 9. ' He [that is *John*] beheld him, ' and his Glory, and felt his Power, and what his Power took away, then he de-' clared him as he knew him, and not from any Tradition or Writing before him; ' why then do you teach for Doctrines Men's Traditions? —— running into the ' Lines of what others have written, *Morn. Watch*, Pag. 6.

Rejoyn. These Passages from whence the particular *Epithets* are taken shall be considered anon.

This is one of those Testimonies he brings to prove he rightly cited and apply'd his former Testimonies out of the same Author; which had he intended in reality, he should as well have inserted the one as the other; to help such as had not seen his other Book, into a true Judgment of this; but then may he say, I should not make the best of my Case, which, to do him no Wrong, he studies more than the Truth, or any Thing else, next to his making the worst of ours. And now, *Reader*, that this Proof is as lame as his former, and wholly as silent to his wicked Purposes, consider I intreat thee, the Drift of this Man, as his Discourse at large manifests. Two Things he had in his Eye, *First, To beat People off from the Doctrines and Traditions of Men*, in the Sense Christ once spoke those Words, to wit, *not the Scriptures, but Men's human Interpretations of them*, with such Forms and Worships as they had invented in the Apostacy from the true Spirit of *Christianity*, as these Words by *J. F.* purposely omitted, notwithstanding they lay between the two first Sentences, which therefore make an absolute Break, though he makes none, do undeniably evince, to wit, *Weigh this Truth all ye Priests and Professors, and ponder it in your Hearts; have you beheld Christ, and seen his Glory? Have you felt his Power to take away your Sin? If yea, then why do ye teach for Doctrine Men's Traditions?* Again, Pag. 16. *For they being from the Life that gave forth Scriptures, their Understandings are darkned, and they err, and know not the Scriptures nor the Power of God.* Lastly, In the 14th Page he hath these Words, *All the vain Worships and Customs, which People at this Day are in, who yet abide in Forms and Traditions, are all come up since the Days of the Apostles, and are after Men's Traditions, and not after Christ. And the Conception of all hath been in Man's Imagination, and hath been brought forth in his own Will and Wisdom.*

By all which, Reader, it appears, that he distinguisheth between *Men's Traditions* and *God's Tradition*. For, *first*, How can he mean the *Scriptures* in the *first Passage*, (the Middle of which our Adversary so wilfully dropt) when he implies, that from feeling the Power of Christ to take away Sin, Men would leave off Teaching for Doctrine the Traditions of Men; making them thereby sinful, and a Sin to teach them; when *J. Faldo* confesses, that upon the Spirit's moving and giving us the Understanding of Scripture we do allow the Doctrines therein delivered to be rightly preached. In the *Second Passage*, he undeniably distinguishes between the *Scriptures rightly understood*, and their *Mistake of them to whom he wrote*; Not knowing, says he, *the Scriptures, nor the Power of God*, being darkned; which imports, that truly to know and teach *according to the Sense of Holy Scripture*, is a quite differing Thing from *Teaching for Doctrine the Traditions of Men*. Nor is his *Third Passage* less clear in the Point, p. 14. since he explains what he means by those offensive Words to *J. Faldo*'s Ear, by *such Customs, Worships, and Traditions as were not of Christ*, and that took their Rise since the Time of the Apostles, and proceeded from the Imagination, Will and Wisdom of Man; therefore not the Writings of either Prophets or Apostles, that were before such Apostacy, and which were given forth as they were mov'd of the Holy Ghost.

The *Second Thing* greatly in the Author's Eye, and with which his Spirit seems to be prest through the whole Book, is this; *Men ought to teach and preach to others no farther than they have a living Sense or Experience of what they so teach or preach*: that this was his Meaning, by those Words, *Running into the Lines of what others have written*; hear the following Words in his Defence. *How dare any of you*, saith he, *make mention of his Name, or speak of his Glory, or of his Power, seeing you have not beheld him yet made manifest in your selves?* Again thus, *For John testified, that the giving forth of the Law was by* Moses, *but Grace and Truth came by Jesus Christ*, John 1. 17. *Mark*, says he, *Grace and Truth were come unto* John *by Jesus Christ, and he had felt the Virtue of it, by which* Moses's *Administration was fulfilled in him*. I say, Reader, his whole Scope was to inforce the Necessity of coming into the Enjoyments of the Holy Ancients, and an Experiencing of the Truth of those Doctrines they declared, before Men are fit to teach them unto others. And as this is the Tendency of his Words, so does Holy Scripture strongly warrant the same; Particularly *Jeremiah*, and the Apostle *Paul* to the *Corinthians*; in *Jeremiah* thus; *He that hath my Word, let him speak my Word faithfully; What is the Chaff to the Wheat, saith the Lord? Is not my Word like a* Fire, *saith the Lord, and like a* Hammer, *that breaketh the Rock in Pieces? Therefore I am against the Prophets, saith the Lord, that steal my Word every one from his Neighbour*, Chap. 23. Verse 28, 29, 30. The Meaning of which notable Place is plainly this; Such as have God's Word to declare (which is known from all False Pretenders, who steal the Word from their Neighbour, and then cry, he saith, as the 31st Verse expresseth, by the Resemblance it bears to Fire, (a Thing easily to be felt) let them faithfully speak it.

But those who steal and preach the Word or Testimony that came from the Lord by and through another, as if the Lord spake the same by them, unto whom the Lord never spoke it; such Prophets the Lord is against, which strikes *J. Faldo* dead, respecting his Pretence for Preaching, who abundantly proves it to be his Belief, that such are as *Good Ministers* as any, yea, the only *Orthodox*, and the other but a Pack of Giddy-headed *Enthusiasts*.

The next Place is in the Apostle's 2d Epist. to the *Corinthians*, Chap. 10. Verse 15, 16. *Not boasting of Things beyond our Measure, that is, of other Men's Labours, but having Hope, that when your Faith is encreased, that we shall be enlarged by you, according to our Rule abundantly, to preach the Gospel in the Regions beyond you, and not to boast in another Man's Line of Things made ready to our Hands*. Of this Sort of Boasters is *John Faldo*, who hath nothing for his Religion, but the meer Bible, and but an usurpt Title to that.

Reader, take Notice, that all along *J. F.* hath made no Difference between the *Truths* the Scriptures truly declare of, and *Man's dark and unregenerated Conceptions upon Scripture about Truth and Error*. Thereby confounding that which in it self is most clearly different, to the End he may bring all those Blows we give at Men's Traditions and Doctrines, (which they pretend to be rightly deduced from Scripture, but in Reality, are their own Imaginations) *To bear hard upon the Scriptures themselves, and those Doctrines and Traditions that are truly delivered by them*; which is a wretched begging of the Question, that was not about the Scriptures, to which he would turn it, but his and their Way of underſtanding them, as if it were the ſame Thing to decry the *Scriptures,* as to diſclaim againſt *J. F*'s falſe Opinions concerning them.

But he thinks he has quite done our Buſineſs, and ſav'd himſelf from the black Blemiſh of Forgery, by another Teſtimony produced to the ſame Purpoſe, which is this: *And reading in the Scriptures, that there were ſome who met together, and exhorted one another, they obſerve and do as near as they can what they read of the Saints Practice, and ſo conceive a Birth in the ſame Womb, and bring it forth in the ſame Strength that others do, and in the Ground it differs not,* W. S. Pag. 22. But what of all this, *J. Faldo?* Can this Saying riſe higher than a Reproof of thoſe who are but in the *Form of Godlineſs,* whom the Scriptures exhort us *to turn away from:* But why was he ſo Diſingenuous as to refuſe us our Friends Words at large, thereby making People believe, that the Imitation reprov'd by *W. S.* concerns the Holy Life and Converſation of the Saints. For it's not two Lines before, that he tells us expreſly what Sort of Practice he means, when he writes thus, *And becauſe they* (Baptiſts) *read of ſome that went into the Water, and were baptized, they do the ſame.* In ſhort, The Zeal of his Spirit runs againſt all Apiſh Religions, and thoſe Perſons, who take unto themſelves the Name and Form of what they are Strangers to the Nature and Power of, being not led by the Eternal Spirit to worſhip God, but with an Unregenerate Mind and Ambitious Will, eagerly ruſh into thoſe Things for which they have neither Commiſſion nor Qualification.

I could urge ſeveral Teſtimonies out of Authors that neither liv'd nor dy'd in Fellowſhip with the *Quakers,* as a farther Vindication of their Senſe in this Particular; but Three ſhall ſuffice at this Time.

The firſt is given us by *Jo. Canne,* ſtiled by *Parſon Ball,* (an Eminent and Early *Presbyter*) The *Leader* of the *Engliſh Browniſts* or *Independents* at *Amſterdam,* more than 30 Years ago, *viz. Labour to Experience the Power and Leading of the Spirit: It is very dangerous to reſt in any thing that comes from the Creature, 'till you have the Witneſs of the Spirit, which is not fleſhly, heady, or empty; but powerful, inward, and abides, and ſettles the Soul.* In the Light ſhall we ſee Light, *and no where elſe, let them pretend never ſo high Attainments.* A Knock to *J. Faldo.*

The Second is a Paſſage in *W. Dell*'s *Trial of Spirits,* writ, as I take it, while he was *Maſter of Caius College* in *Cambridge.* 'They, ſays he, who want Chriſt's Spi-
' rit, which is the Spirit of Prophecy, though they preach the *Exact Letter* of
' the Word, yet are *Falſe Prophets,* and not to be heard by the Sheep. And one Reaſon among many for this Aſſertion, was this, ' *Under the New Teſtament we*
' *are not to regard the Letter without the Spirit, but the Spirit as well as the Let-*
' *ter, yea, the Spirit more than the Letter.* And therefore *Paul* ſaith, That *Chriſt*
' *ſhall deſtroy Antichriſt with the Spirit of his Mouth, and the Brightneſs of his*
' *Coming.* He ſcarce (ſaith this Author) takes any Notice of the *Letter,* but calls
' the true Preaching of the Goſpel, the Spirit of Chriſt's Mouth, or *the Miniſtra-*
' *tion of the Spirit.* His next Reaſon is this, ' *They that preach only the outward*
' *Letter of the Word, without the true Spirit, they make all Things outward in the*
' *Church, and ſo carry the People with whom they prevail, only to outward Things,*
' *to an outward Word, to outward Worſhip, outward Ordinances, outward Church,*
' *outward Government,* &c. *whereas in the true Kingdom of Chriſt, all Things are*
' *inward and ſpiritual; and all the true Religion of Chriſt is written in the Soul and*
' *the Spirit of Man, and the Believer is the only Book, in which God himſelf writes*
' *his New Teſtament,* Pag. 19, 20.

The third Teſtimony is out of *T. Collier*'s Works, p. 249. ' How can they teach
' others, who know not Truth themſelves, as they ſay, *but as they read it without*
' *themſelves?* And ſo at the beſt, *ſpeak but other Men's Light.* And if they miſ-
' underſtand what other Men have written, then they ſpeak Falſhood inſtead of
' Truth.

Thus much in Countenance of *W. Smith*'s Expreſſion, from Three Men of great Note among our *Engliſh Separatiſts.*

But let us hear what Uſe *J. Faldo* makes of the Teſtimony he brought, and which we have thus clear'd and confirm'd.

Rep. (Pag. 42.) *Then follows in this, and Page* 23. *all that Rabble of vilifying Expressions of both their Practices and Authority, quoted by me in* Quakerism no Christianity, *p.* 119.

Rejoyn. If this be true, *W. Smith*'s Book shall yet be blamed, as much as *J. Faldo* will otherwise have abused him. I will set down his Words faithfully, ' They, said he, hope to be saved after this Life is ended by Christ, *though they be* ' *Sinners,* and so are set down in a *Carnal Security,* and rest at Ease in the *For-* ' *mality,* and are *Strangers to the Quick'ning Spirit, and the Faith that they have* ' *made is not held in a Pure Conscience,* but is conceived in *the Heart that is De-* ' *generated and Corrupted.*

I Query of my *Reader,* if this was meant of the Scripture, upon whom *J. F.* makes *W. S.* bestow the Word *Corrupted?* Again, ' And what was, by the Saints ' given forth, and appears in Writings without them, that their Life is in, and ' that they contend about, and all strive to set up *their own Conceivings, and* ' *teach for Doctrines Men's Traditions.* Mark that, *Reader.* He speaks not against the *Scriptures,* nor of them, but their *Blindness* in using them, ' *and mind not the* ' *Measure of God in themselves;* that is, *Reader,* God's Measure, or the *Grace of God, which teacheth to deny those Sins* he told them a little before they liv'd in with Carnal Security. ' But, says he, stretch'd beyond it in the Comprehen- ' sion, *and run into other Men's Lines and Labours.* That is, They out-run their own *Experiences,* and intrude themselves into those Things, which were beyond their own Growth, which *W. S.* rebukes them for, making it his Business to turn them to *that Grace, which obeyed, teaches them not to vilify the Scriptures, but brings them into the right Possession of them, and Title to them:* which he makes appear to be more to their Advantage, than to dispute and contend about them, whilst *in Sinful Security, Formality, Estrangedness from the Quick'ning Spirit, Human Faith, Impure Conscience, and in a Degenerated and Corrupted Heart;* All which is in his 22d Page, and gives Light enough (to any Man, that has not, like *J. F.* put out his Eyes of Reason and Candour) unto these following Words, which can no more relate to the Holy Scriptures, than that Spirit from whom they came, to wit, ' They are all upon the Earthly Root, and in Darkness and Confusion in ' their Practice and Worship. Now, *Reader,* What does the Scripture practise, and whom, and how doth the Scripture worship; if the Word *(they)* relate to the Scriptures, and not those several Ranks of Professors to whom he expresly dedicated his Book? Yet farther, That from the Crown of the Head to the Sole of ' the Feet, the Image (that is, the several Sects) hath no whole Part in it, but is ' full of Putrefaction and Corruption, and every Branch rotten and deceitful, and ' no good Fruit is found; *for the bringing forth of all is from the Heart that is de-* ' *ceitful and corrupted,* which lies fal'n and degenerated from God. What Man, Reader, that ever thought to have his Proofs examined, would have dar'd to apply in the Author's Name, these Terms to the Scripture, that so particularly and plainly relate to Man in his fallen State. But please to consider what better Authority he has for the rest, *viz.* ' And are all found Wanderers in the Night of ' Apostacy, and in the Darkness have taken the Whore's Cup, and do drink it; ' And unto all those is the Cup of God's Indignation poured out, because they ' are Bastards, and not Sons. Upon which I query with *J. F.* who are the Wanderers? If the People, then the foregoing Word, *They,* of which the Word *Wanderers* must be the Relative, concerns Professors; and then all those Terms beforementioned belong not to the Scripture, and consequently are misapply'd by our Enemy. But if he says *W. S.* meant the *Scriptures,* how could they be said to wander, or drink the Whore's Cup? And if the *Whore's Cup* be the Scriptures, (as *J. F.* makes *W. S.* mean) either the People drank up the Scriptures in the Apostacy, or the Scriptures drank up themselves.

Next, Who are those *Bastards,* to whom the Cup of God's Indignation is pour'd forth? Certainly they are *Disobedient Children,* and not as *J. Faldo* would have it, *the Scriptures and Holy Doctrines deduced from thence.*

Reader, Doubtless the Man is desperate, and to me he seems to have laid Violent Hands upon himself, to the destroying of his Reputation among Men, and his Soul in the Eye of God; since after all this Injury to our *Deceased Friend,* he dares yet appear in so impudent a Strain, as this following Passage makes him Guilty of.

All this Penn *KNEW to be True, when he dared to make such Hypocritical Appeals to Delude the World, Save the* Quaker's *Credit, and Abuse me as a Forger.*

The Righteous God judge between us, Whether I writ otherwise than I knew, or he in affirming it, more than he knew. My Appeals were Solemn, in the Grief of my Spirit, to see a Man arriv'd at that Pitch of Falseness, as to pervert and forge about Sacred Things, even while himself would pass for a Minister of them; and I can scarce think any Man so prejudic'd against us, as not to conclude with me, that his Aim in this untrue Passage (to say no more) was to bear People down, as to the Honesty of his Quotation, by the mighty Vehemence and Confidence of his positive Charge against me, *To have known, what in Reality I never knew, and to have appeal'd hypocritically to God concerning our Innocency, who did it in the Humility and Sincerity of my Soul*, because the Man had no other Way left him, to secure himself from the deserv'd Imputation of Forgery, or wilful Perversion, scarce a Remove from it. But that by which he would clear himself from it, fastens it inevitably upon him, *and renders him One of the daring'st and most harden'd Perverters I have ever yet met with in all my Life.*

The next *Testimony* he brought to prove our *Opposition of the Spirit to the Scriptures,* and which he pretends to justifie against my Explanation, was this, *Of this Sort are the False Prophets, who have their Preaching from Study, and other Men's Mouths,* charging me, *That I treacherously left out, or from the Letter, and not from the Mouth of the Lord.* But as I us'd no Treachery, neither omitted it in Design, nor thought it Prejudicial to his Cause, since my Answer, as himself hath transcrib'd it, shews, that I understood it to be the Letter of the Scripture, that was meant, from whence they stole their Preaching, and not that they receiv'd it from the Mouth of the Lord; so in the End, it will prove more my own Disadvantage to have omitted it, than any Bodies else. I shall set down my Answer, as he has transcrib'd it, and his Reply, the equall'st Way of Judging.

' The Natural Purport of the Words, said I, can be no more than this: That
' though the Things declar'd of in the Scriptures, were the Word of the Lord to
' the *Holy Ancients and Jeremiah,* as God's Mouth (not his Mouth therefore) to
' the People of *Israel*; yea, much of it (mark) the Mouth of the Lord to us also;
' yet for Men to say any Part of it by Rote, especially if they add (mark) *their own*
' *Comments and Glosses, framed from Study,* OF any Part of the Scripture, and say,
' *Thus saith the Lord,* or *Hear the Word of the Lord, and not in the same Living*
' *Sense, nor upon the like Commission, every such One doth rob his Neighbour, and*
' *steal his Words.*

This is so much of my *Answer* as he transcribes, which seems thus far ingenious, that in three Times a larger *Answer,* he has not transcrib'd one Third of this; perhaps he thought it not so much for his Turn. But before I set down his *Reply,* I shall find *Two Faults* with this Recital; *First,* That he has (I will not say *treacherously,* or that I knew he did designedly misgive my Words, as he is frequently pleas'd to charge me) falsly set down one Part of my Answer; for in my Book it is, *If they add their own Comments and Glosses framed from Study,* TO *any Part of the Scripture,* and he transcribes it, *Framed from Study* OF *any Part of the Scripture*; as if *the Studying* OF *the Scripture,* and adding Men's own Glosses TO the Scriptures, *were one and the same Thing.* All I shall say of it is this, *'Tis a scurvy Mistake, and looks very suspiciously.* The *Second* is, That he has left out the most material Part of my Answer; The Stress of which in Brief lay here, ' *Parrots imi-*
' *tate Men*; But if such Creatures are not therefore to be reputed Reasonable,
' though the Sentence be Rational in it self, because it proceeds from *meer Imita-*
' *tion,* and not a Principle of Reason; neither is *He* a True Prophet, nor *That* the
' Word of the Lord, *with respect to that Prophet,* who has not receiv'd what he de-
' livers from the immediate Word of God himself, but by *Hear-say,* or *meer Imi-*
' *tation.* But of all this Part he takes no Notice. I now come to his *Reply,* which I will faithfully set down, and, I hope, as clearly enervate.

Rep. (Pag. 43.) *The Errors, Self-Contradictions, and Absurdities of* W. P. *I shall express briefly. First, What he saith they mean, I say they mean also, viz. The Scriptures are not the Mouth of God.*

Rejoyn. The Mouth of God is a most *uncouth Expression,* for which he has not One Scripture, from *Genesis* to the *Revelation*; nor do I see how he should, since it it is unfound, if not Blasphemous; for, by calling them not *A Mouth,* but THE *Mouth,* it renders them the most constant, necessary, and excellent Mouth, by which God, who is a Spirit, utters forth his Mind to his Children, thereby excluding

ding the *Word of God Nigh in the Heart, and His Spirit in their Inward Parts.* But to proceed:

What does he mean by *Mouth*, or how does he take it, *Properly* or *Metaphorically*? If the first, I deny it: If the last, I thus far concede, That the Scriptures, as other Things, may be in a Sense so stiled, when God pleaseth livingly to speak by them, otherwise I chuse to express my self, as in my Answer, by him also omitted.

'The *Eternal Word of God is the Mouth of God, and the True Prophets and
' Apostles in all Ages, have been as the Mouth of the Word of God,* declaring the
' Mind of it, either by Word of Mouth, or Writing, to the People, and the *Scrip-*
' *tures are the Writings of those Inspir'd Prophets and Apostles.* What more would he have?

Nay, there is not only no such Negative, as he charges upon us, in my Answer; but I do expresly say, *The Scriptures are not in a Sense without a Mouth,* and that *for God too,* being a Declaration of much of his Will and Works, though I cannot allow them to be *The Mouth of God in the Sense my Adversary throughout his whole Book tugs hard to get;* for by that Means we should with him shut up the Mouth of *the Eternal Word, which is* God's Living Oracle *to the Souls of his People.* But he proceeds.

Rep. W. P. *saith, The Things spoken of were the Word of the Lord. Then the Word of the Lord is, or was more than One, a Contradiction to himself.*

Rejoyn. Reader, take Notice that there is no such Thing as he pretends to reply to, in this Part of my Answer he brings into his Book; it seems he has left it behind him, and I must go back to look for it: My Words were these, *The Scriptures then are to us obliging, as the Thing they declare of was the Word of the Lord to several Ages, Temporary Commands excepted.*

Which import no more than this, That the Word of the Lord declared the Mind of the Lord by the Holy Prophets; and the Mind of the Lord is not distinct from the Word of the Lord, though the Declaration be different from the Thing declar'd of. I cannot see any *Contradiction* in what I writ. Sure I am, I meant not by the Thing they Declare of, the Declaration, either by Word of Mouth or Writing, *but the Wisdom, Will, Glory and Power of the Eternal Word, as they are Eternally One with, and in the Word, before so declared.* He was a little too nimble in the Business; but if I should let him make the worst Construction he is able, it can rise no higher than this, I should mean by the *Word of the Lord, the Living Command of the Lord in the Hearts of his Prophets,* afterwards declared by Word of Mouth, or Writing; For *Word* sometimes signifies *Command,* as thus, *This is the Word of the Lord,* or this is *the Command, or Mind of the Lord,* which are equivalent.

Rep. Thirdly, *That God hath a Mouth in a proper Sense.*

Rejoyn. This is untruly charg'd upon me. My Adversary's Reason for this indirect Consequence was, my saying, *That Jeremiah was as God's Mouth* (not his Mouth therefore) which to me is a Good Reason why he ought to have inferr'd the quite contrary, since *as his Mouth,* signifying no more than something *in lieu* of a Mouth, *and not His Mouth therefore,* was on Purpose brought in by me, to prevent that very Construction which my *Adversary* hath notwithstanding hit upon.

But to the next Part of his *Reply,* which is still by Way of Consequence, as he thinks from my Principles.

Rep. Fourthly, *What the Scriptures say, the Lord doth not say, unless he that utters them, hath the like Commission from God, as* Jeremy.

Rejoyn. A meer Tale of *J. Faldo's* making: *They are the Words of the Lord,* let who will speak them, or say them over. But they are not the Words of God, by, or through *that Person that is dead to them.* And instead of hearing and receiving them from such *Intruders and False Pretenders,* they ought to be flung back into their Faces, and they reprov'd for *False Prophets: What hast thou to do to take my Name into thy Mouth,* saith God, *that hatest to be reformed?* And how is he Reform'd, that is not Renew'd into that *Life, Power and Wisdom, that Man was indu'd with, before he came to be through Transgression deform'd.* The Drift of our *Adversary* is, *To prop and maintain a Company of dry, senseless, and Unregenerate Talkers for Worldly Maintenance.* They are of their Race, *Who Taught for Hire, and Divined for Money,* the *Chemarims,* or *Black-Coats, of Old Times.* The plain *English* of all *J. F's* Jeers and Railings at us, is this, *We deny him to be a Minister of the Gospel, who Preaches or Teaches what he has not experienced of God's Work in his own Heart,* viz. *Who Preaches of* David's *Languishings, and never was in them;*

of the Terrors the Apostles knew, and never felt them: In fine, the whole Exercise that attends the Soul of Man, from the Beginning of his Repentance, to the Compleating of his Salvation, and never have Experimentally trod that Path, and pass'd through those divers States. He is an ill Guide that never went the Way himself, and an unskilful Physician, who is ignorant both of the Disease and Cure. His Fifth Consequence is this.

Rep. *That all that call them by that Name, and tender them to others, are Thieves and Robbers.*

Rejoyn. This is a Piece of Gibberish I do not understand. *When did we call any Thieves or Robbers, for a Name given to the Scriptures*, if them he mean? On what Part of my Answer can he fasten these Words? 'Tis true, I said then, and I say again, *They are all Thieves and Robbers, that steal other Men's Experiences, and then Preach them for Advantage*. For, they that stole of old, were such as spoke *other Men's Words, without their Sense*. And as the *False Prophets* stole the True Prophets Words, which was one of their Marks; so the *True Prophets* did not speak in Imitation of one another; but as the Word of the Lord came upon their Spirits, so they declar'd it, which is prov'd thus: *First*, If it had been the Words or Writings of the True Prophets themselves, then it could not have been said, *Let the Prophet that hath a Dream, tell a Dream; and he that hath* My Word, *speak* My Word *faithfully*, since most, if not every one of them, had the Words, or Writings of the True Prophets by them. So that after *J. F*'s Conceit, every one of them might have spoken it, and then too when it pleas'd him; which being utterly inconsistent with the very Words and Nature of the Text, I conclude, it was an *Invisible, Immediate, and Spiritual Word the True Prophets spoke by, as they were moved of it*. *Secondly*, It was a *Fire and Hammer*, and that the Scriptures were not: *Thirdly*, It came at certain Times to them who had so much of the Scripture as was then extant always by them; therefore not the Scripture, but an *Immediate Word*. *Fourthly*, Otherwise there had been no more Scripture upon Inspiration, but a continual descanting upon those they had; therefore still an Immediate Word, and not the Words and Writings of others. *Lastly*, if the Difference then between a True and a False Prophet, *was the declaring faithfully the Word of the Lord, when, and as, they felt the Operation and Motion of it in themselves*, and a borrowing, or rather stealing those Words, and so without either the Operation or Motion of the same Eternal Spirit, which was before the Coming of Christ; much more then ought the True Prophets in these Evangelical Times (to whom was promised a more large Effusion of the Holy Spirit) *to wait for the Operation and Motion of God's Eternal Power, Word or Spirit of Life, in order to instruct others*. And more Reason have we to repute them *False Prophets*, that in these Days of greater Light, should prop up themselves as God's Ministers, with the old Cheat of *Stealing their Neighbour's Words*. Certainly they are less sufferable now, than at that Time; and if that Dispensation renounce them, this ought much more. But *J. F.* thinks he saith something, when he flings this Consequence upon me as ridiculous.

Rep. *That* Jeremy *and the Prophets are our Neighbours, though Dead Two or Three Thousand Years since*.

Rejoyn. I never said they were *John Faldo*'s Neighbours, nor does he deserve so Good Company, though he needs it. But let it suffice, that *J. F. steals as bad as* Jeremiah's *Neighbours did*; and thus far more boldly and notoriously, in that they perhaps got the True Prophets Words so soon, that some might not know who had them first; whereas *J. F.* runs back Two or Three Thousand Years a pilfering for his *Hackney Sermons* out of them, which are so well known to be *other Men's Lines and Labours*. Methinks People should not suffer themselves to be so miserably gul'd, nor lie at the Expence of *maintaining a Priest to tell his Tales*, who may buy each of them a Bible, containing the Writings of the Holy Prophets and Apostles, for Five Shillings, more to their Edification, since their Ministers, or Masters rather, deny Inspiration, and consequently all inward Certainty to their own Conceptions and Glosses, hugging *Fallibility as a necessary Article*, and flinging it more than once in our Teeth, as arrogant Heresie to say, *We are certain of what we Teach*. Truly, *my Soul magnifies the Lord, and I rejoyce in God my Saviour*, that he has disvail'd this *Mystery of Iniquity*, and dispoil'd that Painted Jezabel, and splendid *Whore of* Babylon, *who hath long sate upon the many Waters, and hath discover'd her Merchants, her Wares, her Witchcrafts, whereby her Abominations are known, and her darkest Stratagems and deepest Subtilties found out*. It's not her saying, *She's a Bride, a Church; nor her Merchants and People, that they are Ministers and Christians*

Chriſtians, that will ſerve their Turn ; for their Conception is known, their Original, their Number, their Power, their Devices and utmoſt Extent, and they are all found to be out of the Redeeming Power, Life, and Spirit of the Lamb. And for this Cauſe am I engag'd on Earth, and the Reproaches that attend me on that Account are unutterably more grateful to me, than the gaudieſt Titles, and ſweeteſt Entertainments this Temporal World can beſtow. It's for God, againſt the Devil ; his Power and Spirit, againſt Satan's ; the Spiritual, againſt the Formal Man ; and the Real Life of JESUS, and Heavenly Experience of his Salvation within, whereby the Doctrine of the Goſpel is accompliſh'd in Men, againſt all Transformation into Likeneſſes, and but meer Verbal Imitations and Outſides of Religion ; *For every Plant that the Heavenly Father hath not Planted, will he root up in this the Day of his Power*, in which the Lord will make his People a Willing People, and that not by indulging, but rebuking, and taking Men off from their own Willing and Running : For the Lord has decreed to over-throw the Banks, which the *Falſe Prophets* of the Nations have caſt up in the Night of Darkneſs, whereby all Refreſhment has been damm'd up from them, and the Nations have been like a parched Heath and deſolate Wilderneſs, that his Life, Power, and Spirit, may flow over every Kindred, Nation and People under the whole Heaven ; *and they ſhall be all taught of God, and in Righteouſneſs will he eſtabliſh them, and there ſhall be one Sheep-fold and one Shepherd* ; and the Idol Shepherds, who have no Viſion, neither have any Bread of Life wherewith to feed the Flock, God will utterly ſcatter and make an End of, and his Name ſhall be Famous and Renowned through all Generations. *Amen*.

But *Reader*, my Adverſary is not yet willing to leave me, he proceeds to tell us, *That the* Quakers *charge him, and ſuch others, with the Sin of Idolatry, to believe and live according to the Inſtructions and Holy Examples expreſſed in, and by the Scriptures, except they have them by Immediate Inſpiration* ; and though the Subſtance of it hath been already conſider'd by me, yet I ſhall not grudge my Pains, if the *Reader* will beſtow his Peruſal, and perhaps he may find ſomething not unſerviceable to the farther Clearing of our Senſe, and Detection of our Adverſary's Dis-ingenuity : He writes thus in his Reply.

Rep. (Pag. 45.) *I produced among others Two Teſtimonies which* W. P. *takes Notice of* ; *My firſt is out of* Morning Watch, *Pag.* 23. ' And this is *Babylon*, the ' Mother of Harlots, and the Abomination of all Uncleanneſs.

Rej. I need ſay the leſs to this, becauſe I have ſo clearly and lately defended W. S. in that Book and Page, from any ſuch wretched Meanings and Applications, which J. F. has employ'd his Wits to rack his Words to. Only *Reader*, obſerve *his Fallacy* ; that he ſets not down what Examples, and what Inſtructions, but confounds Moral with Ceremonial Precepts, on Purpoſe to make us at one Blow cut off all Regard to Scripture indifferently. * Next, mark *His Antichriſtianiſm*, in that he maketh the Mind of God, and Doctrines and Lives of the Holy Ancients in Scriptures, capable of being underſtood and follow'd, without the Inſpiration of God's Holy Spirit, thereby giving the Lye to the moſt expreſs Texts of Holy Scripture, and the plaineſt Aſſertions of the pureſt Fathers, moſt Famous Reformers, and conſtant Martyrs. I will ſay no more to this, than that our Adverſary himſelf, hath in the ſame Page cited ſo much of W. S. as declares his Perverſion of the other Part of his Book, viz. *And are all out of the Life and Power of God* ; that is, Thoſe that ſay they have God to their Father, ſpeak high Things of Holy Scripture, and bedeck themſelves with the Paſſages thereof, and notwithſtanding are out of the *Life and Power of God*, are not *True Jews or Chriſtians* ; but are of the Synagogue of Satan, the Abomination of all Uncleanneſs, and which help to make up *Babylon*, the Mother of Harlots.

For the *other Proof* he brought, which indeed was *his Firſt*, though in his Reply he tells us, *it was his Laſt*, he was afraid to meddle with it, and there was great Reaſon for it ; For he knew not which Way to handle it, but it would bite his

---

* But *J. F.* Is not that *Babylon*, or the *Antichriſtian Church*, which has the Shew and Outſide, but not the Life and Power of Godlineſs ? May not Antichriſt adorn himſelf with the Literal Profeſſion of the Goſpel ? Certainly all *Proteſtants* have accorded to this. I am ſure *J. Sprig, C. Goad, W. Dell, J. Saltmarſh, T. Collier*, yea, *J. Fox, Bp. Jewel, J. Reynolds, Dr. Willet, R. Abbot*, and a Nameleſs Worthy Author about Queen *Elizabeth's* Time, in his *Voice out of the Wilderneſs*, &c. allow of *W. Smith's* Doctrine, viz. That the meerly Literal, Formal, and Fleſhly-wiſe Church, not Regenerated into the Image and Life of the Son of GOD, is *Babylon* ; and ſome of them are moſt expreſs in the Matter, which I omit for Haſte.

1673.
Part I.
Chap. IX.

Fingers. I will set it down with my *Answer* contracted, that I may help the *Reader* to another Instance, by which he may take his just Measures of the Man in Hand, respecting his Sort of *Fair Dealing*, or *Strength of Argument*.

W. Dewsbury he cites thus in his *Discovery of Man's Return*, pag. 21. *All People may search the Scriptures, and see how you have been deceived by your Teachers, who have caused you to seek your lost God in Carnal and Dead Observations, Which they have not any Scripture for.*

Now, *Reader*, was not this an extraordinary Passage to prove *J. Faldo*'s Charge, viz. *That it was Idolatry to act according to Scripture, &c.* which is given by our Friend as a Reason why People ought not to follow their Blind Teachers: But be pleased to read my Defence, as I then writ it.

' *W. Dewsbury* is so far from making it *Idolatry to live up to the Scriptures*, that
' he condemns the seeking for the True God where he was not to be found, which,
' saith he, *they have no Scripture for*; As much as to say, that such seek after God,
' not according to Scripture: And therefore are both Deceivers and Deceived.
Unto which *J. F.* reply'd nothing, or perhaps *had nothing to Reply*, except an Acknowledgment, which he thought would not make for his present Sort of Credit.

He winds up this Chapter with a Justification of his Comparison of our Doctrine about the *Scriptures* with that of *Jesuits* and *Papists*. I will set him down at large.

Rep. Concerning my Parallel between the Jesuits *and the* Papists *in the venom Spit against the Scriptures*, W. P. *hath thus little to say, pag.* 101. It is Ridiculous, and every way unworthy our Notice, a meer begging of the Question; We can never allow of the Comparison. *But why all this Contempt?*

Rejoyn. Contempt pinches his proud Stomach. But, Courteous Reader, ask *J. F.* why he left out the Words immediately proceeding, viz. *He has been so Cunning or Unjust rather, as to quote their Authors and not ours ; and some Passages we justly doubt.* What *base Juggling* is this with his Reader, and *Abuse* of his Adversary. It concern'd him more *to be just* in this than to ask, *Why all this Contempt?* And had he not *less Honesty* than *Stomach*, we might have expected that Justice, the Want of which brings *greater Contempt* upon him, than my sober Reflection upon such unfair Dealing.

But he proceeds to cite these Words as the whole Reason, why we disallow the Comparison, ' Since the *Papists* place the Rule and Judgship in a *Pope*, and Gene-
' ral Council; and the *Quakers* in the Eternal, Unerrable, Holy Spirit of God. To which he replies thus.

Rep. The first is as I said ; the second is Blasphemously False ; for the Quakers *call their Light within the Spirit of God, which I have sufficiently proved to be a Blasphemer of the Spirit of God, a Sordid, Sinful, Corrupt and Ridiculous Thing.*

Rejoyn. What he means by *his first*, I know not, unless that he said *true of the Papists*. And if any of them have writ or spoke unworthily of the Scriptures, we utterly detest their Actions. For *his second*, I confess, I am greatly at a stand, I have travelled several Nations, convers'd with Men of most Ways of Religion, read a great many Books for my Time, but never yet did I meet with such an *Insolent, Blasphemous* and *Scornful Expression*, as this I now transcrib'd Word for Word out of his Reply. 'Tis true, there was an * Old Peevish Priest in *Ireland*,

---

* *T. Jenner, a Presbyter-Independent Priest of Ireland, writ a Book against us for Gain ; for he went from House to House of many sufficient, and some great Men, to present them ; some gave him a Crown, some two Crowns, some a Piece: Among others, he had the Confidence and Avarice to give one to the* Lord Lievt. *of that Kingdom: His* Secretary *carried it to him; he turning it over observed many black Charges, of foulest and most pernicious Errors to Religion and Civil Government: The* Parson *still stayed ; The* Secr. *thought he had favoured him sufficiently : But not understanding the Priests Aim, that is,* Lucre *(the Old Priests Sin) was prest to tell his Lord, that he waited for his Excellencies Answer. The* Secretary *was so civil as to answer his Desire : But when the* Lord Lievt. *understood his Drift, he returned the Book to the* Parson, *with this Account, That he was sorry to hear that the* Quakers *held such ill Principles ; but the* Tares *and the* Wheat *must grow together till the Day of Judgment. So the* Parson *was corrected for his Baseness, and disappointed of the great Bone he crept thither for.*

who *to get a little Money* (as clearly appear'd) writ an Envious Book againſt us, in which he called the Light within an *Ignis Fatuus*, a Dim Light, &c. who lived long enough to vex himſelf to Death with our Anſwer, as we are credibly informed, not long ſurviving it's Arrival, and general Acceptance of moſt Sorts of People in thoſe Parts; But never yet have I heard or read of ſuch *hard Names* from the worſt of our Adverſaries; For *Tho. Hicks* himſelf, in his *Dialogues* againſt us, acknowledges, that *the Light within checketh for many Evils, and excites to many good Things*, &c.

It were too large to go over the Praiſes given it by the beſt *Jews, Gentiles* and *Chriſtians*. *Philo* the *Jew* calls it an *Immortal Precept*. *Plotin*, a *Gentile*, ſays, it is *the Root or Life of the Soul: That this Divine Principle in Man makes a true and good Man*. *Clemens Alexandrinus* a *Chriſtian-Father*, ſpeaks of it thus, *The Light will ſhine out of Darkneſs, therefore it ſhines in the hidden Part of Mankind, in the Heart*. Again, *Man cannot be void of Divine Knowledge, who naturally, or as he cometh into the World, partaketh of Divine Inſpiration*, &c. Thus *Munſter, Vatablus, Clarius, Caſtellio, Druſius*, and *Codurcus* upon this Paſſage in *Job*, *And upon whom doth not his Light ariſe?* acknowledge both its *Univerſality* and *Sufficiency* too, where obey'd.

I could produce a Multitude of approved *Proteſtants*, without being beholding to one *Papiſt* (whatever *J. Faldo* ſays of us) in Commendation of the Univerſal Light within; but will conclude with *J. Caryl*, one of the moſt ancient and eminent Paſtors of the *Independent* Way, in his Expoſition on *Job*; and *J. Owen*, that great Doctor of *Independency*, in his *Latin Exercitations*, formerly writ againſt the *Quakers*, under the Name of *Phanaticks*, a Term ſince beſtowed and improved, by he knows who, upon ſuch as need no pointing at.

J. Caryl on *Job* 32. 8. ſays, that *Wiſdom and Knowledge in the Things of God, come from the Inſpiration, or in-ſhining, of the Light or Spirit from above*. And on Chap. 24. 13. *That Light there mentioned ſhined in Wicked Men's Hearts, as well as Good*, or to that Purpoſe; And *that it is not a Natural or Proper Light, as the Sun in the Firmament, but ſuch as reproved them for their Iniquity, and comes from Above*, &c.

J. O. abundantly confeſſeth to the *Morality and Univerſality of the Light*, calling it alſo a *Supernatural and Spiritual* as well as *Moral Light*, as he frequently phraſes it. Good Uſe of which hath been made by our Chriſtian and Learned Friend, *Samuel Fiſher*, in Anſwer to *Him, Rich. Baxter, J. Tombs*, and *T. Danſon*, unto which they have never attempted any the leaſt Reply that we hear of, tho' it greatly concerns their Cauſe and Credit to do ſomething in it. For my own part, I ſhall ſay no more to *J. Faldo*'s Refutation than that he calls the *Light within* us (by which it hath pleaſed God to redeem us from our Vain Converſation) againſt the Judgment of many Good and Learned Men in ſeveral Ages, *A Blaſphemer of the Spirit of God, A Sordid, Sinful, Corrupt and Ridiculous Thing*; for which God rebuke him.

But there yet remains a notable *Teſtimony* of our Friends to be conſidered, which *J. Faldo* produceth, to prove our *great Affinity with the Papiſts*.

Rep. *If any pretend to be of us, and in Caſe of Controverſy will not admit to be tried by the Church of Chriſt Jeſus, nor ſubmit to the Judgment given by the Spirit in the Elders and Members of the Church, but kick againſt it, ſuch, we teſtifie, ought to be rejected as* Heathens.

Rejoyn. Nothing but Rank *Ranteriſm* can call this *Popery* in ſuch Diſgrace, or reject it as unſound, as I will make appear.

The Church of Chriſt, endued with his Spirit, hath a Judgment; This Chriſt allows her, and that every Individual ought to reſt ſatisfied in it, in Caſe of Difference; therefore ſaid Chriſt, *Tell the Church, and if he refuſe to hear the Church, then let him be as an Heathen and* Publican. *The Saints ſhall judge the World*; and much more by their Judgment determine, or reconcile Things among themſelves.

No Caution or Reſolution could be more ſoundly and ſcripturally laid down; *Firſt*, It is the Church of Chriſt that judges. *Secondly*, It muſt be the Judgment of the Church by the *Holy Spirit*, or rather the *Holy Spirit in the Church*, not conſiſting fifting of Elders only, but *Elders* and *Members*, which make the whole Church. *Laftly*, The Perfons rejected are fuch as firft *kick* or fpurn againft the Admonitions of the Church of Chrift. What Man not bereaved of his Senfes, or as Irreligious as a *Ranter*, can fo fcornfully upbraid us with this Serious, Chriftian and Neceffary Difcipline? Yes! *J. Faldo* (who pretends both to his Wits and Religion) dares offer fomething againft it.

Rep. *O the Charity of the* Quakers *Leaders! All that will not fubmit to their little* Juncto, *are with them numbred with* Heathens *and* Infidels. *Here the poor* Quakers *may fee the Image of the Beaft among themfelves.*

Rejoyn. It were well if *J. Faldo* would fhow more *Charity* in pretending to rebuke us for the want of it; But will he allow of thofe Aggravations the *Epifcopalians* and *Prefbyterians* made upon, and againft, the firft * *Brownifts* about gathered Churches? Did not they draw as large Conclufions? And had they not as much Ground for doing it, as our Paffage can give to *J. Faldo*; fince they deny'd in moft harfh Terms *The Church of* England *to be the Church of Chrift?* The fame did the People call'd *Anabaptifts* both of the Church of *England*, and National *Prefbytery*. But why our *little Juncto*, otherwife call'd the *Spirit of* G. Fox, *and his Miniftry, or Reprefentative Body?* Is not this caft out on purpofe to infinuate, as if G. F. with other publick Travellers in the Service of the Church, were Lordly or Domineering, (as *J. Faldo* a little farther calls it,) who rarely meddle with thofe Things, leaving every Meeting to their own Power? But what Occafion had he for this Reflection on our Friends Paper, even as by himfelf given us? Doth it not mention the *whole Church*, and afterwards explain *who that Church* is, by thofe two Words, *Elders* and *Members*? But fuch is the Practice of *J. F.* in his pretended Difcovery of us.

Nor is there any Reafon, why *J. F.* fhould fo much ftomach the Word *Heathen*, fince he thinks it a Priviledge to be fo to us, at leaft to call us fo: Befides, we own every fuch one to have a *Saving Light*, which he denies to us, therefore lefs Charitable, nay Unjuft to the Light; for he efteems us only fit Company for the worft Sort of *Heathens*, fuch as *Julian* and *Lucian*.

It feems we muft be viler than *Heathens* and *Mahometans* with *J. F.* witnefs his firft Book: But we ought not by any Means to repute fuch as he is, that denies us and our Principles with Abhorrence, as to us, either *Heathen* or *Infidel*; What fhall we call him then? But hath the Man forgot that the drift of his Book is to *Unchriftian* us? That the Title of it is *Quakerifm no Chriftianity?* And that the Cry of his Affociates for thefe Twenty Years has been *Heathenifm, Gentiles, Moral*, but *not Chriftian Men*, and therefore *have excommunicated, beaten, imprifoned, and that to Death*, and yet by no means muft we deny thefe *Folks* to be true *Chriftians, that have fo long proved themfelves to be none:* Though this might fuffice, that fuch as that Paper concerned thought us *Chrift's Church*, therefore it was juft to them, whatever it may be to others for whom it was not intended: A Man may abufe the higheft Truths, taking to himfelf the Liberty he doth, to pervert our Words and Sayings: His *two Books*, in God's Day, will prove to his great Shame and Condemnation this one Charge, that I have often in other Words upon occafion faid concerning him, viz. J. Faldo's *Charge againft the* Quakers *are not their Principles, but his own Confequences falfly drawn from them*.

To conclude, If fuch inoffenfive, nay Chriftian and neceffary Refolutions for the right Difciplining the Church of Chrift in the Ways of Peace and Righteoufnefs, cannot efcape *J. Faldo's* Cruel Hands, inftead of rendring us *Papifts*, I fhall not wonder if from a *Non-Conforming Prieft* he turns *a Spanifh Inquifitor*, or any Thing elfe that can be worfe: But it is Pity he fhould leave us, and not fee his Face before he goes. I will acquaint him therefore (if yet a ftranger) with an *Excommunication* drawn up and pronounc'd by an *Independent* of great Note, being in the Parliament's Time *Mafter of Pembrook Hall in Cambridge, and Paftor of a Church in* London.

---

* See Dr. *Bilfon* and the Heads and Doctors of *Oxford* againft the *Brownifts* —— *Gifford* againft *H. Barrow, R. Bernard* againft *Brownifm*, anfwered by *I. Robinfon*; and —— *Ball* againft *I. Cann*, &c.

Svdrach

Sydrach Sympson's EXCOMMUNICATION of Capt. Richard Norwood.

> 'I do in the Name of the Lord Jesus and his People declare Mr. *Norwood* one that hath lifted up his Tongue and Heart against the Lord Jesus Christ, and God the Father, one that from henceforward we have no more to do withall till he repent, but shall continually pray that his Nights may not be quiet for the Thoughts of his Sin, but that his Bed may be filled with Tears. I charge all you both of the Church, and all other that are *Christians*, that you should look upon him as *one that God would have thus severely used, until that he* * *buckle under his Sins*, and then our Souls shall rejoyce. In the Name of our Lord Jesus Christ *we deliver him unto Satan for the Destruction of the Flesh*, that his Soul may be saved.

Rob. Nor. his Ans. to Syd. Sym. Excom. pag. 8.

* An odd and unsound Phrase.

To prove this Authority by Example, he produceth this Piece of Antiquity, however ill it befits an *Independent* Church-Man.

> 'The Church of *Pallemnis*, as *Semetius* reports, excommunicates *Andronicus* in these Words: *Let no Man account* Andronicus *a Christian, but look upon him as one whom God execrates; have no Company with him, but what is necessary.*

This Reader is the Moderation and Charity of such as *J. Faldo* accounts both a true Minister and a Christian Society; much of this have we found at the Hands of the same Sort of *Separatists*. But first observe (according as *J. F.* would have us understand it by his Censure of us in a Case less obnoxious) the absolute Authority personally assumed, and how much *S. S.* acted the Pope (in *J. F*'s Language) or arbitrary Prelate in this Matter, that had been an earnest Decryer of the same Spirit in a more national Clergy. 2ly, It is worth our Notice, that the Matter *First* charged was, a (pretended) Untruth, relating to Civil Commerce, from which he cleared himself to his Adversaries publick Confusion: But this was but the Preface, the Business is behind; for he denied *the Locality of Heaven and Hell*, that is, looked upon them as void of outward Place, and to have a more spiritual Signification, and that the other was too carnal, indeed *Mahometan*; and that he believed the Soul to have been *breathed from God*, thereby assigning to it something more of Divinity than the usual Opinion doth. For this and no more (as the Pamphlet informs me, which recites the Reasons of the Excommunication) do they excommunicate him; yet to colour the Business the better, like as *J. Faldo* does with us, *S. S.* expells him their Society, *for denying an Heaven and Hell at all, and as rendring the Soul God himself*; crying out, *Satanical Devices, Atheism and Blasphemy*. There is one Passage this Captain took Notice of, not unfit to be observed by us, with Respect to the Use *J. F.* makes of our Paper. *S. S.* in his Proem or Introduction to his Excommunication used among other these Words, *That though Men may withdraw themselves from the People of God, they cannot from the Ordinances of God*, meaning, as I suppose, that his pastoral Power could or should reach beyond *Constantinople* or a farther Place, to excommunicate, *Anathema, Maranatha*, an Offender, &c. But to this the Person so dealt with, answers, and for ought I know more justifiably than *J. F.* can pretend to do to us (for we allow no such personal and pastoral Dignity and prerogative Power to any Man, nor do we use any such Forms of Excommunication) says he, *Have I therefore withdrawn my self from the People of God, because I have withdrawn from you, Are none the People of God but your selves? What are all those you are withdrawn from, All Damned?*

This is such an *Argumentum ad hominem*, as I am of the Mind ought to trouble *J. F.* if the least Grain of Modesty be in him, what he chargeth upon us is outdone by themselves, and the Aggravations he would render us odious by, are made the natural Consequences of their own Excommunications.

I will conclude this with telling my Reader, that for no other Cause than what is exprest, namely *Opinion* (and that not very offensive) this Person once accounted greatly of among them, being a Member of their *high Court of Justice*, was first traduced, then excommunicated, after this, complained of to the Powers, by them, therefore deprived of his civil Employ; and though they were his Debtors, both

both for Money lent, and his Services done them (if we may credit his printed Narrative) the *Priesthood* so prevailed, that the Lord *Mayor Andrews* sent a Warrant for him, had him brought rudely and violently to the Sessions at the *Old-baily*, and there placed among Thieves and Murderers, in Order to his Trial for Blasphemy.

These were the *meek* and *hearty Pretenders to, and Fighters for Liberty of Conscience*, that when they had the Power in their Hand proved abundantly they intended it only for themselves; not unlike to their great *Geneva* Doctor, that made *Servetus* keep Company with his Books, or rather had him burnt by them (as if it had been to save Wood) for Exceeding their *Presbyterian* Reformation, and instead of repenting, defended it in Writing, when he had done, at what Time the said *Doctor and that whole City* were persecuted themselves with the *Anathema's of Rome*; and 'tis not to be doubted, but they thought them unchristian. It would fill a Volumn to tell the Tragical Excommunications and other notable Feats done by some of this Tribe of Men, for the Maintenance of their Church, Power and Dignity, oftentimes saving the civil Magistrate the Trouble of abusing such poor Dissenters from them, as we are, by a licentious Usurpation and Practice of his Power upon their Backs: We well know it; yet has this Man the Confidence to fall hard on us for censuring such as recede from what they once own'd, and because we can never allow them, as such, to be of us, he cries out, *O the Charity of the Quakers, the Quakers may see the Image of the Beast among themselves, &c.* But on better Grounds may every ingenious Reader return this Exclamation, *O the Incharity of J. F. and his Adherents, whose very Mercies are Cruelties.* Let him pack up his Pipes, and play us no more of these Envious and Hypocritical Notes, and hold himself contented, that whether we be the Image or no, to be sure he has made *Sydrach Sympson and his Church the Beast* in great Letters, *cum multis aliis*, not forgetting nor excluding his own railing and excommunicating self.

The CONCLUSION of the First Part.

WE have now run through his Nine Chapters, Seven of which concerned the Scriptures, doubtless writ to vindicate his former Discourse; but with what Success, I leave with Thee, Courteous Reader, to judge. And before I sum up our Sense, for a *Farewel* to this Part of his *Pamphlet*, I request thee, when thou next fall'st into Company with *J. Faldo* or any of that Tribe of Men (the pretended *Admirers of the Scripture*; and one would almost think, the devoutest *Observers of those Precepts*, and precisest *Imitators of those Examples* expressed therein) to ask in good Earnest, *Whether it be the whole, and every Part of Scripture they call the Word of God, and Rule of Faith and Life, or No?* If they say, *All and every Part of it*, then the Words of *Wicked Kings, False Prophets, Persecutors, &c.* yea, the *Devil himself*, therein at large declared, with the whole Jewish *History*, and *Ceremonial and Judicial Law (containing the Government, Sacrifices, Priesthood, and all other Jewish Rights)* will necessarily make up a great Part of the Word of God, and their Rule of Faith and Life. But if they shall answer *Negatively, that they are not in the whole and every Part of them the Word of God, and Rule of Faith and Life*; Then ask them, *Which are those Places, Precepts and Examples, that particularly concern us under this Administration?* And if they answer this Enquiry, and are not grown too hot and angry by this Time, entreat them to tell thee, *By what they discern and distinguish in this weighty Matter?* For if they either set aside what they should receive, or continue what should be laid aside, they *Add or Diminish* to what themselves acknowledge to be *the Word of God*: If they say, the *Harmony of Scriptures*, the same Question holds, *How, and by what doth it appear so Harmonious?* since there are very deep and obscure Places, and sometimes seeming Contradictions, and that in highest Points. If they say, *by the Spirit and Understanding of meer Man*; the Apostle *Paul* directly opposes himself to every such Answer, 1 *Cor.* 2. But if (thus driven) they answer in the Words of *J. Owen*, 'That the only *Publick, Authentick, and Infallible Interpreter* of the Holy Scripture is HE, *who is the* AUTHOR *of them, from the Breathing of whose Spirit it derives all it's Verity, Perspicuity, and Authority,* Exerc. 2, 7, 9. against the *Quakers:* Entreat their Patience to stand one *Question*

stion more, and thou haft done, *viz.* If the *Verity, Perspicuity* and *Authority* of the Scriptures depend upon the *Breathing of the Holy Spirit*; or as he expresses it a little farther, the *Infusing a Spiritual Light into our Hearts*; Then, *Whether People ought not to have Recourse unto the Holy Spirit and Light, as the only Interpreter, Judge and Rule, what Scripture remains of Force to our Day; and how, and which Way such Scripture is to be understood?* When thou haft obtained such sober Answers as thy Questions deserve at their Hands, I should be very glad to have the Perusal of them. In the mean Time we own, and with our whole Hearts confess,

First, *That the Scriptures* (given forth by Inspiration) *are a true and faithful Narrative or Declaration of the Mind of God towards the Sons and Daughters of Men, and his various Dealings with them, respecting Precepts, Prophesies, Threatnings, Promises, Providences, Rewards, Punishments, Deliverances, Doctrines, Examples and Practices.*

Secondly, *That they are Profitable for Reproof, Instruction, Edification and Comfort.*

Thirdly, *That it is the Spirit of God, which only gives Men to read, understand, and use them to Advantage,* as *Thomas Collier* hath well express'd it about Twenty Five Years ago *viz.* ' And truly, Brethren, it is my earnest Desire, to see Souls ' to live more in the Spirit, and less in the Letter; and then they will see, That we ' judge of the Letter by the Spirit, and not of the Spirit by the Letter, *which oc-* ' *casions so much Ignorance amongst us*; *And they who profess themselves to be our* ' *Teachers, are chief in this Trespass.*

Fourthly, *That the Holy Spirit is the New Covenant, Rule and Judge*; it being the Promise of the Father, and Ministry and Dispensation of the latter Days, as these Scriptures abundantly prove, *Neh.* 9. 19, 20. *Job* 32. 8. *Isa.* 59. 21. *Joel* 2. 28, 29. *Hag.* 2. 25. *Mat.* 16. 17. *Jo.* 14. 17, 18, 19. Chap. 16. 7, 8, 9, 10, 11, 12, 13, 14, 15. *Rom.* 8. 1, 9, 14. 1 *Cor.* 2. 9, 10, 11, 12, 13, 14, 15, 16. *Gal.* 5. 16, 18. *Eph.* 1. 17. 1 *Jo.* 2. 20, 27. Yet we deny not but the Lord hath and yet may make the Holy Scripture a Mean to several in the Hand of his Spirit, of Understanding and Comfort; and so far they may be a particular Rule: Yea, I do believe they have been, and yet are, next to a Living and Powerful Ministry, a more ordinary Mean, than many, if not any other whatever. Howbeit, we are not to center here, but press on forward to the Life, Power and Spirit it self, of which they declare; for into that God hath determined to bring, and (as it were) wind up his People, by which they come to be fulfilled; whereas those that stick in the Letter of them, and pass not through and beyond it, into the Life and Virtue they bear Record of, know but as the *Scribes* and *Pharisees* did, and cannot as such be true and faithful Witnesses for the true and living God.

Fifthly, *We have proved our Doctrine of the Scriptures and the Holy Spirit (as by us distinguisht and cleared from* J. F's *Perversions) by Abundance of such Authorities*, as, I think, he dares not gain-say. So that we cannot be longer *Hereticks*, and those continue *Orthodox*; shewing thereby, that we are but pressing more intirely, plainly and effectually what the best *Protestants* and *Separatists* have, at Times, not only let drop from their Mouths and Pens, but insisted on, and prophesied also the Increase and Enlargement of in the Hearts of Men, however forgot or denied by their Dry and Degenerated Posterity.

Lastly, *That we do not therefore exhort People to hearken unto the Voice and Leadings of the Holy Spirit, which strive with them* (as that by which God, who is a Spirit, comes truly to be known, and the Scriptures themselves only to be read with a right Understanding, and true Benefit) *with any the least Design, to justle the Scriptures out of their Place and Authority (No,* God knows it is not our Purpose*) but for this very End do we so write and speak, that People do come to possess what they declare of, and witness them fulfilled in themselves, instead of contending about what they do not understand, and which can never be revealed to that dead, dark and unregenerate State in which they live*; for the Lord is at Work (as I said before) to gather People more and more into the Spirit and Life of his Son, accomplishing his Glorious Promises in these latter Days, and bringing People to the good Things themselves, by which Out-sides are daily wearing off more and more, and the Testimonies of Holy Scripture witnessed and fulfilled in them that believe: Which is not to Overthrow, but to answer the great End of their first Publication and Preservation unto this very Day; Whereas the contrary is not truly to esteem them, but under the very vain Pretence of it, to withstand,

and as much as in them lieth, *to bar out the Great Gospel-Ministration, which stands in the Convictions, Instructions, Leadings and Orderings of the Holy Spirit:* And unto that must all come, who in this Life would witness a Translation into Christ's Kingdom, that is not of this World, and know a Being made free of that *Jerusalem* which comes down from above, the Mother of the Free-born, which they only are that have been born again by the Regenerating Word; to whom the Formal and Literal Professors are but as Hagar, and her Off-spring; unto Sarah and the Seed of the Promise. And this is the Word of the God of Heaven and Earth unto all those that are yet unacquainted with this *Convincing, Baptizing, Reconciling, Ingrafting and Regenerating Word, Power, or Spirit within.* And so I am thus far clear of your Blood, and am at Peace with the God of my Salvation.

THE SECOND PART.

CHAP. I.

Of Gospel-Ordinances in General, such truly embraced.

THIS Second Part of my *Rejoynder* is a Consideration of his Defence of his Charge, *of our Denying Gospel-Ordinances, the True Christ, with his Transactions at* Jerusalem; also, *that we are guilty of Idolatry, and own not the Resurrection of the Dead.* The Work of this Chapter will be to see, how he will make good our Denial of Gospel-Ordinances in General. Be pleased to hear how he handleth both me and the Matter.

Rep. Pag. 49, 50. *The first Proof is out of* Fox, Myst. p. 2. ' He hath triumph-
' ed over the Ordinances, and blotted them out, and they are not to be touched, and
' the Saints of Christ in them, who is the End of outward Forms. *This faith*
W. P. *Pag.* 103, *is Scripture Language. But why so? Because some Scripture Words are in it, although the Text be mangled, corrupted, and abused to the Contradiction of Scripture-Truth. Thus they apply sinfully enough* False Prophets, Dogs, Serpents, Hypocrites, Devil, Lyar, &c. *But if I should call* W. P. *Thou Child of the Devil, Thou Enemy of all Righteousness, he would not therefore allow it to be all very true, though so applied, it looks much more like Truth than* G. *Fox's Scriptural Language, who hath these Words about Baptism and the Lord's Supper.*

Rejoyn. For his Proof as he calls it, it is not in Pag. 52 of G. F's Book, which were Answer enough to so shuffling an Adversary. I confess, in Page 16, I find it, but it is so far from being immediately directed to either *Baptism* or *Supper*, that there is no such Thing mentioned, much less insisted on from the Beginning of G. F's Answer to *J. Timson's* Book, to the very Place wherein the Words are found: Now, What to call this Piece of Invention, is left with every Reader's Discretion. But it is not less worth our Notice, that of all my Explanation of G. F's Words, he only reports these three, *viz. is Scripture Language*, who farther told him, ' Christ did blot out the Hand-writing of Ordinances, *Colos.* 2. 14.
' That he was to the Saints then, and is to those now, who rightly believe in him,
' the End of all Meats, Drinks, Washings, Days, or any other Temporal Ele-
' mentary or Figurative Worship, according to Verse 16, 17. By this it will appear, whether of us two have most honestly and most truly applied Scripture; I in thus expounding and vindicating G. F's Passage, or *J. Faldo* in calling me (by Implication) *a Child of the Devil, and an Enemy of all Righteousness.* But again,

Rep. Pag. 50. *I also told Mr. Penn, That if the Saints having Christ in them, were the Consideration, for which the Ordinances were not to be touched, then not only we, but even all other Saints under the Mosaical Administration sinned in their Practices of God's Ordinances also; for they had Christ in them in those Days in the same Sense as the Saints in these.*

Rejoyn.

Rejoyn. This Saying carries with it a large Conceſſion to Chriſt's Manifeſtation in the Hearts of his People, as well under the Moſaical Adminiſtration, as that which we call, for Diſtinction, *Evangelical*; Indeed larger, than true, if *by the ſame Senſe*, he underſtands, that all that he was to his Apoſtles, and the Churches by them planted, he was to the People of *Iſrael* under the Conduct of *Moſes*; for, *firſt*, it is manifeſt they were not capable of ſuch Diſcoveries, being weak-ſighted, carnal, and greatly addicted to embrace the Fopperies of the *Heathen:* *Secondly*, There would have been no need of ſhewing forth a farther Glory by Types and Figures, or to entertain Minds ſo enlighted and heavenly with ſuch low, and as the Apoſtle phraſeth them, beggarly Things; had they enjoy'd Chriſt under the Adminiſtration of *Moſes*, as in more Goſpel-Times. But above all, that *J. Faldo* ſhould plead for the Continuance of Ordinances after Chriſt had blotted them out, and *ſuch Meats and Drinks, &c.* as Chriſt ended, (being the Subſtance of them) becauſe Chriſt might be in ſome Meaſure known to the Saints of old, at what Time ſuch Ordinances were given forth, and ſuch Meats and Drinks obſerv'd, is *Jewiſh*, and, as I ſaid in my Anſwer, to plead for a Legal Diſpenſation and Bondage to the Shadows of the good Things to come, thereby making Chriſt's Coming of none Effect. But to proceed,

Rep. Page 50. *Yet though P. gives me bad Words to ſtrengthen his Argument, he grants what I ſay to be true in his Anger*; for (ſays he) Chriſt is to the Saints now, who rightly believe in him, the End of all Meats, Drinks, Waſhings, Days; *Here Lord's-Supper, Baptiſm, Chriſtian Sabbath, or Day of Holy Reſt, are all deny'd in Four Words.*

Rejoyn. If they be, it is his own Fault; for inſtead of my granting what he ſays to be true, I never mentioned them; and indeed he hath ſo manifeſtly given away his Cauſe by this unadviſed Expreſſion, as we need no more againſt him on this Occaſion: For thoſe *four Words* by which he makes me to deny the *Lord's-Supper, Baptiſm*, and the * *Chriſtian Sabbath*, are ſuch as we muſt reject, or we turn the Goſpel-Miniſtration out of Doors; They are the Apoſtle's own Words to the *Coloſſians*, (Col. 2. 16, 17.) *Let no Man therefore judge you in Meat or in Drink, or in Reſpect of an Holy Day, or of the Sabbath Days, which are a Shadow of Things to come*, but the Body is of Chriſt; and to the *Hebrews*, Chap. 9. Verſe 10. *which ſtood only in Meats, Drinks, and divers Waſhings, and Carnal Ordinances, impoſed on them until the Time of Reformation.* I ſay, here the four Words are denied to be Evangelical, viz. Meats, Drinks, Waſhings, Days; and ſince *John Faldo* will have the *Supper* to be conſider'd under *Meats* and *Drinks, Baptiſm* under *Waſhings*, and the Chriſtian *Sabbath* under *Days*, either He muſt with us, Deny them, as *Meats, Drinks, Waſhings* and *Days*, that are aboliſh'd, and therefore not fit to be continu'd under the Evangelical Adminiſtration; or maintain the Continuance of *Meats, Drinks, Waſhings* and *Days*, to keep up the *Supper, Baptiſm*, and

---

* To call any Day of the Week a *Chriſtian-Sabbath*, is not *Chriſtian* but *Jewiſh*; give us one Scripture for it; I will give two againſt it. Gal. 4. 9, 10, 11, 12. where the Apoſtle makes their Obſervation, or Preference, of Days, to be no leſs than a Token of their Turning from the Goſpel. Alſo Col. 2. 16. An outward Sabbath, or keeping of a Day, to be but a *Shadow*; and that Chriſtians ought not to be judged for rejecting ſuch Cuſtoms; for this very Reaſon the Proteſtant-Churches beyond the Seas *generally deny the Morality of the Firſt Day*, counting all Days alike in themſelves, only they have Reſpect to the Firſt Day, as an *Apoſtolical Cuſtom*, and think it convenient to give One Day of Reſt from Labour to Man and Beaſt each Week. Of this Mind ſeveral *Learned Proteſtants* of our own Country have declared themſelves to be; So that neither our *Engliſh Epiſcopalians*, nor *French Presbyterians*, can eſcape *J. Faldo's* Conſequence any more than the *Quakers*; for if thoſe that deny the *Supper, Baptiſm, and the Firſt Day of the Week to be the* Chriſtian *Sabbath*, deny *Goſpel Ordinances*, then thoſe who deny the Firſt Day of the Week (J. F's Chriſtian Sabbath) to be the *Chriſtian Sabbath*, muſt needs deny a *Goſpel Ordinance*, but that do many *Engliſh Epiſcopalians*, and moſt *French Presbyterians*, therefore both ſeveral *Engliſh Epiſcopalians*, and the generality of the *French Presbyterians*, are Deniers of a *Goſpel-Ordinance*: Conſequently J. F. told an Untruth in his Preface, when he aſſured both *Epiſcopalians* and *Presbyterians*, that they were *no farther concerned in his Diſcourſe than vindicated*. In ſhort, Though we aſſert but one Chriſtian Sabbath, and believe that to be the Everlaſting Day of Reſt from all our own Works, to Worſhip and Enjoy God in the Newneſs of the Spirit; yet 'tis well known that we both meet upon the Firſt Day in the Week, and behave our ſelves with as inoffenſive a Converſation as any of our *Sabbatharian Adverſaries*. The Honour is God's, by whom we are what we are; but this Teſtimony I record for God, His Goſpel and Right-begotten children, that the *Meats, Drinks, Waſhings* and *Days-obſerving Chriſtians are not come ſo far, as thoſe fooliſh* Galatians, *for whom the Apoſtle travelled again, until Chriſt were formed in them*, Gal. 4. 19. *being yet Strangers to the Life, Power, Spirit, and Subſtance of the Goſpel.*

Sabbath, and thereby espouse the *Jews* Quarrel against the *Christians*, and defend the most Rank, Childish and Carnal Part of *Judaism* against Christianity it self.

My Reader may by this perceive what a Gospel it is *J. Faldo* would have, who pleads for the Use of those Things under the Gospel which are repugnant to the Nature of it; for in one Place the Apostle calls them *Shadows*, and in another, *such Figures as could not make such as used them perfect, as pertaining to the Conscience*, Hebr. 9. 9. which the Gospel doth not continue, but make an utter End of, by the bringing in a more excellent Covenant, Hope and Service.

His saying I was Angry, and gave him bad Words, is like the rest: What shall I say to a Man that dares say any Thing, be it never so far from Truth, provided it may cast an Odium upon me, where he can't confute me? The hardest Words I gave, were, that he *basely wrested our Words*; of which let the Reader judge: And for Anger, God knows I had none; I pity him. But he goes on.

Rep. Page 50. W. P. *to make a full End*, adds, ' or any other Elementary, Temporary, or Figurative Worship. *Now if he can shew us any Gospel-Worship, considered entirely and formally, that is not Temporal Worship, he will do more than ever Man yet did; but in the mean Time he hath confirmed my Charge.*

Rejoyn. I have confirmed it by the Rule of Contraries, or by the same Figure our Friends Writings use to maintain his Accusations: Certainly *J. F.* can never mean as he writes, and be Knowing and Honest too. If to confute his Charge be to establish it, I hope my *Reader* will say, *I have done it effectually*; I know not whether to impute it to his Vanity or Laziness; for at every Turn we must prove his Charges, give Evidence against our selves, and *Dye by our own Hands*, while it is to be remembred, that amidst all this Folly, *J. Faldo* must have the Liberty of Tampering with his Witnesses, that is, *Resting, Patching, Adding, Diminishing, Transposing, Mis-interpreting our Words and Meanings*, or else he would be wholly at a Loss. Many Instances I have given of his Skill herein; and his pretty Sort of wresting the Word *Temporal* in this very Sentence, doth make up another; for I mean by *Temporal*, as the Words *Elementary* and *Figurative* immediately following do fully explain, no other than such a Worship, *as is instituted for a set Time, till something more excellent and durable comes in the Room of it, as the Typical Worship of the Jews, that served it's Season, and then gave Place to the Spiritual and Eternal Worship of the New and Everlasting Covenant:* And this Man takes me, *as if I understood it of a Worship performed within Time in any Sense*, thereby making me to deny the Performing of Worship to Almighty God, the Time Men live in the World, because it may be called from the Word *Time*, or Tempus, *Temporal*, restraining that to the Nature of *Worship*, which only relates to the *Act* of Worship: As thus, The *Act* or Performance of Worship may be to Day, the Nature of that Worship, *Eternal*; so that Worship may be performed within *Time*, and yet not be by Nature *Temporal:* But the Worship of the *Jews*, respecting those Exteriour and Shadowy Things, was by *Nature Temporal*.

Reply, (Pag. 50.) W. P's next Fault he finds, is with my saying, *That* Pennington *meant by the* City of Abomination, *Visible Worship*. *If the Worship which he acknowledgeth God to be found in, and which Professors, about the Years* 43, 44, 45, 46, *used, were Visible Worship, or any Part of it Visible Worship, then* Pennington *said it of Visible Worship.*

Rejoyn. A Fault so palpable is soon found; Who not stark Blind with Envy, would make so ill a Construction of so sound an Expression? *J. P.* said, *The Lord would not spare such as do not come out of the City of Abomination*, that is, saith *J. Faldo*, *Visible Worship*, as if they were Synonimous, or Terms of equal Signification; *City of Abomination*, that is, *Visible Worship*; back again, *Visible Worship*, that is, *City of Abomination*. Is this Man fit to write of Religion, that adventures so boldly to pervert Men's Writings? But he thinks this will excuse him, that *I. P.* meant such Worship as God was found in, and which Professors used about 43, 44, *&c.* but this is too boldly obtruded; for, what Man can think *I. P.* so brutish, as to call that Worship, in which himself confesseth God to be found, *the City of Abomination?* *I. P.* spoke of the Nature of, and not the Visibility of Worship; for there is not a Word of it in his Writings, so that he endeavours to maintain One Falshood by another. But that his Charge is yet True against the *Quakers*, he produceth a Testimony out of G. F's *Mystery*, pag. 65. " *Paul* brought the Saints " off from the Things that are seen, and Water is seen, and it's Baptism; adding, *Now unless* W. P. *will say, That Things seen are not Visible*, G. F. *hath certainly failed* W. P. But this Shift will not serve *J. Faldo*'s Turn, since G. F. meant a *Visible*

Visible Changeable, and not a *Visible Permanent Worship*; This Passage relates to *Figurative and Temporary Services*, standing in those Things which were but Signs of the Substance to come, and which are finished by it: So that the Apostle did indeed labour to bring the *Jews*, and other weak *Christians*, off from their *Visible*, *Typical*, or *Legal*, to the more *Spiritual Worship of the Gospel*; not that they should be debarred from expressing that Worship; for while Bodies * and Souls are together, there is (as I writ at large in my Answer) a Necessity of some Bodily Demonstration. I will yet give one Relish more of the Man's disingenuous Spirit, before I conclude this Chapter.

* See Judas and the Jews combin'd against Christ.

Rep. (Pag. 50.) *Before W. P. parts from this Argument he grows kind, and shews the Power of Condescension to have place in him* (by these Words) " Yet thus far we " could go, That Visible Worship (as such) without a due Regard to what Kind of " Worship it may be, and what is the Root from whence it came, cannot be well-" pleasing to God : *A great Compliance indeed, which is thus much Just, and no more, a Man's filling a Dung-Cart, or W. P's acting on the Stage, or the Table in their Meeting-Place, as like a Fencer as ever was seen, are not Worship because seen, though they should by some be so called; for every Thing that is seen, is not therefore Worship.*

Rejoyn. His acknowledgment of my Condescension, is a small Artifice to insinuate my yielding him the Cause. But what Reason he had to commend me, would be better seen, by considering how aptly and honestly he hath replied to that little Piece of my Answer he found in his Heart to give us. He thinks to fling us off with his dirty and vain Similitudes; I writ of Visible Worship, as *Praying, Speaking*, &c. on a Religious Account, he turns it to any Visible Thing, as *Filling a Dung-Cart, Acting on a Stage or Table as a Fencer* (Similes right-well suiting his Disposition) as if I denied that to be Worship, which was seen, *because seen*, which was the farthest Thing from my Thoughts, and is not at all deduceable from my Words, yet hath this Man the Confidence to tell his Reader, *That they signify just thus much and no more.*

But in good Conscience, *Courteous Reader*, can this Man think to escape the Hands of God, that acts with so much wilful Baseness against me, as to make no Difference between my Saying, *That Visible Worship, as such, unless proceeding from a Right Root, cannot be well-pleasing to God*; and saying, *That Visible Worship is not Worship, because Visible, though it should proceed from never so True a Ground*, which he makes my Answer to speak, at least he infers so from it, though a direct Contradiction? Is it one and the same Thing to say, *Visible Worship is not therefore True Worship, because Visible*, and concluding *filling a Dung-Cart is not True Worship, because Visible?* Is it honestly done to apply that to Acting upon *Stages* and *Fencing*, which by me was joyned to Worship? If I had said *Visible Fencing*, as such, is not Worship, because seen, *his silly Shift might have had something in it*; but to make no Difference betwixt saying, that Visible Prayer is not True Worship because seen, and *Fencing, or filling a Dung-Cart is not True Worship because seen* (thereby turning what I said of Worship, to every *Trivial or Common Action among Men*) is unworthy of an ingenious Disputant, much more an *Humble Christian*, and least of all a *Christian Minister*. In short, I spoke against Visible Worship, not *Rightly Grounded*, (a Position as True as Scripture it self; for it is Scripture twenty Times over) and he twisteth it, *to my Denial of Worship because Visible, be it grounded as it will*, as his last Words in the Chapter tell us, *For every Thing* (says he, as the Sense of my Answer) *that is seen, is not therefore Worship*; instead of this, *Every Worship that is seen, is not therefore True Worship*. But his extending the Major Proposition to *every Visible Thing*, and not to *Visible Worship only*, opens a Gap for his wild and extravagant Similes. I will lay down our Propositions, that the whole World may see his unjust Way of dealing with us.

My Proposition lay in Form thus.

That Visible Worship, which ariseth not from a Right Ground, is not acceptable with God.

But John Faldo's *Visible Worship (say) ariseth not from a Right Ground.* Therefore,

John Faldo's *Visible Worship is not Acceptable with God.*

The Argument, as he gives it in my Name, formed, lies thus.

That which is seen, is not Worship.

But a Man's filling a Dung-Cart, &c. *is seen.* Therefore,
Filling a Dung-Cart, &c. *is not Worship.*

Which Argument makes nothing Worship that is seen, or visible, however truly grounded, because *Visible*, instead of making such Visible Worship not True, which doth not proceed from a right Root.

Now be pleased *Friendly Reader*, to observe whither this Evasion drives the Matter.

If that which is seen be not therefore Worship (as says *J. F.* in my Name) *then publick Praying or Preaching, though of never so True a Kind, or arising from never so Right a Ground, because seen, is not Worship, much less True Worship:*

By this it undeniably appears, that my Adversary hath at best mistaken my Answer, which abundantly confesseth (as he himself hath observed in his *Reply*, p. 50.) *That there will be, there must be, and there ought to be a Visible Worship*; and that such Visible Worship only is rejected, *which ariseth not from a Right Ground in the Heart* : But how can this be, if publick Praying and Preaching, *springing from never so Spiritual a Root, because seen, must be no Worship* (which *J. F.* tells the World in my Name) How can these so grand Opposites meet ? Or how is it possible to reconcile Things as contrary as this ; William Penn *owns Visible Worship :* William Penn *denies Visible Worship ?* For it is no less than to make me renounce Visible Worship for Visibility's Sake, who by my Principles and * Writings hold and maintain such *Visible Worship*, as is of a True Nature, or springs from a Good and Spiritual Ground : So that it is not the Visibility, but the Ground or Nature (not being as it should be) that is the Reason of our Exception.

* See Judas and the Jews combin'd against Christ.

Dr. Everard's *Sermons.*

' Beloved, I would have you ponder these Things well : If ye set up Ordinan-
' ces, &c. *so as to build and rest in them, ye do make Idols of them, or at best, you
' play the Babes and Children with them, by resting always on such Crutches and Go-
' bies, and never come to be Young Men, much less as Fathers in Christ*, pag. 562. And
' truly, with some Men herein lies the Top, or Quintessence of their Religion,
' *making such ado about Shadows and Figures, and Resemblances, and they let the
' Truth, the Substance, the Thing pass, and regard it not ; forasmuch as they are
' so zealous and hot about Forms.* But if they are by any drawn up to speak of the
' *Substance, they are as Men lost, cold and heartless* ; which is a plain Evidence to
' me, *That they prefer the Shadow before the Substance, being meerly exercised about
' Childish Things, and are not willing to come up to the Truth, to the Excellencies and
' Glories, of what Baptism, and other Ordinances signifie,* &c. p. 560.

C. Goad's *Last Testimony*, p. 76.

' Ordinances are Vails, Man's Ministry is a Vail ; if we see God in it, it is but
' darkly.

C. Goad's *Secret and Safe Chamber*, p. 72.

' The Carnal *Jew* looks for the fulfilling of the Letter, the Spiritual *Jew* looks
' for the Spirit : *Abraham, Isaac* and *Jacob sought a Country, not an Earthly One,
' but an Heavenly :* We pitch upon Figures and Vails, *and enter not within the Vail.*
' These outward Things are a Vail, *a Table made a Snare* ; but when we are *turned
' to the Lord, the Vail shall be taken away.* All Man's Teaching, Wisdom, &c.
' makes the Vail the thicker : Those that only feed upon the Vail, upon Outward
' Things, in which God may appear, *their Life shall be destroyed, when others are
' fed and feasted.*

Joshua Sprig, *Pag.* 142, 143, 144, 147, 148.

' The Design is to couple the Lord and Ordinances together ; and we cannot en-
' dure to hear of the parting of them. Swear by the Lord, and Swear by *Malcham*,
' so we have but Ordinances we are well ; something from the Fleshly Form and
' Appearance we do promise our selves, and so, like the *Israelites*, hanker after
' the Flesh-Pots of *Egypt*, though they had as good Meat in the Wilderness : So,
' though

'though God offer himself, and *Christians* tell you, they cannot find God in such
'Forms, but find Him abundantly Good in the Spirit; and though he be gone out
'of the Temple, yet they find Him in their Hearts, they press you to wait till
'God appear to you in the Spirit: O, say you, I can never believe it, that God
'should do it without an Ordinance. This is to say, *That the Fleshly Form doth
'add something to God, who being All in All, is sufficient without it* — You are like
'a Man that is kept up with Cordials, not to be compared with him that is in a
'Way of Recovery, when you want the Physician it is as much as your Life is
'worth; and if the Cordial be long a fetching, you begin to faint; you have
'not your Strength within you, but in Cordials without you: So is the Case be-
'tween you that live upon Ordinances, and they that live upon Christ in the Spi-
'rit; Christ is never in a Journey, or to fetch a great Way off.

T. Collier's *Works*, p. 46.

'The *Christians* Privileges under the Gospel, they are all *Spiritual*, and *so are
'their Ordinances*.

T. Collier's *Works*, p. 241.

'God was in Christ reconciling Men to himself; yet this Dispensation of the
'Father was but a Fleshly Dispensation, comparatively with a more Spiritual, this
'Fleshly Righteousness answering a Fleshly Transgression. Thus likewise hath he
'given *Ordinances answerable to this Fleshly Dispensation*, wherein, when he plea-
'seth, he appears in, and through, these Ordinances; yet note, *That God never
'appears in any Fleshly Dispensation to keep them in the Flesh, but that through
'these he might bring up Souls to himself in that Spirit*.

Sprig's *Testimony to the approaching Glory*, p. 55.

'Ordinances are but the Shadow as it were of the Image, therefore take heed of
'*Idolizing Forms*: Your Interest lieth *in knowing the Father, not in knowing of any
'Form whatsoever*; and take heed of censuring and judging Spiritual Discoveries.

CHAP. II.

Of True and False MINISTRY.

OUR *Adversary* endeavours to strengthen his General Charge considered in the former Chapter, by proving our Denial of each Ordinance in particular. He begins in his other Book with the *Ministry:* His Proofs, as he calls them, were these; 'And their Call to the Ministry we deny, which is Mediate, *J. Parnel's Shield*, p. 16. Also G. *Fox*, in his *Great Mystery*, p. 45. 'But who can witness 'an immediate Call from God, and speak as they are moved from the Holy Ghost, 'and such Travel from Place to Place, having no certain Dwelling-Place. *This Ministry we own and witness*.

Now, without reporting one Word of my Answer, he concludeth his first Paragraph, concerning *J. Parnel's* Words, thus: *Having this Charge confessed, there needs no farther Debate*. O disingenuous Man! What! Only repeat the Charge, and the pretended Proof out of *J. P.* without inserting any Thing of my Defence, or Explanation, and then cry, *Having this Charge confessed, there needs no farther Debate*. Poor Brag! Yet nimble and notable Way of contracting Controversie indeed: What is this but saying the same Thing over again. But as a Man that hath forgot himself, in his next Section he thus recollects.

Rep. p. 51. *To my Proof of a Call by Men, W. P. says nothing; but that he may not seem to have nothing to say, he tells us,* 'It is not, *Go ye forth into all the 'World and Preach the Gospel*, that belongs unto all Men, no more than because 'Princes send Ambassadors to Princes with their Credentials, that therefore every 'Man ought to do the like in Imitation, without considering necessary Qualifica-'tions; (thus far *W. P.*) *Did you ever meet with so ignorant and impertinent an Answer? Did ever any of us take those Words for our Only Call? Or pretend we had a Call thereby, to Preach to all Nations?*

Rejoyn. Why so much Contempt? I have hitherto thought that *Christ's Commission to his Apostles,* had been pretended by you, to be a *Successive Commission;* if
neither

neither the *Spirit of God Within*, nor the *Scriptures Without*, give that Call, What doth? It had much more concerned *J. F.* to declare what he meant by his *Mediate Call*, and not to ask, *If ever any met with so ignorant and impertinent an Answer*. But let this suffice, *That he denies that any of them pretended a Call, or Authority from Christ's Commission to his Disciples to Preach*, &c. Next, that he can only mean by a *Mediate Call*, that of the People, since he had excluded a *Call by the Spirit within, and the Scriptures without*: But because the Call of a People is neither that which qualifieth, nor authorizeth any Man in himself, without the Commission of God's Spirit in a Man's self, it is the Commission immediately received from God's Spirit, and proper Qualifications, that make the *Minister*, and not the Desire of the People; that is an Invention hatcht in *Babylon*, whereby as well blind Pharisees as True Disciples; base *Hirelings*, as Godly Shepherds, may be made Ministers. There is this farther *Lazy End* in it, that being once called by any People, they think themselves only obliged to reside there, where they may take their Ease, unless a *Fatter Benefit* present it self, at which they have been always wont to catch with Greediness, still with this Design, that they might Live with more Worldly Peace and Fatness. This was one of those Doors by which the Apostacy crept in; for the whole World is God's Field or Vineyard, and such as he calls to Labour, neither will, nor ought to be limited by Men, but alone by the Good Husbandman, who has called them into his Vineyard. But he proceeds,

Rep. p. 52. *Did we ever say*, It belonged to all Men *to Ordain Ministers, and without considering Qualifications.*

Rej. Did I ever say you did? What *Trifling* is this? But did not *J. F.* charge my Answer just now with Impertinence and Ignorance, for making them to ground their Call upon the Apostles Commission only, and does he not now make me to accuse them with holding, *That all Men may Ordain Ministers?* What Agreement can there be in this? Especially when there are no such Words in my Answer? But it shows the poor Man is hardly put to it: For his inferring, *that not only it belongs to all Men to Ordain Ministers, but also without considering Qualifications*, is utterly false; for *J. Faldo*, to his apparent Overthrow, *Pag.* 9. as I have observed in my Answer, p. 106. grants us in so many Words, *That all True Ministers of Christ ought to have an immediate Call, such as consists in Grace and Gifts; and such as have not this immediate Call, we account unworthy of the Thing and Name*. Thus hath he given away his Cause, yet still he swaggers like a Conqueror: But may I ever be thus overcome? For if this *immediate Call* constitutes both the THING and NAME, then a *Mediate Call* (let him understand what he will by it) neither worthily gives *Thing* or *Name*, else what means his reputing *such as have not this immediate Call, unworthy of the Thing and Name*: It is to say, if I understand any Thing, and that in so many Words, *Mediate Ministry, and Ministers, are unworthy of being called Ministry and Ministers, because the immediate Call only makes worthy of both Thing and Name*.

Rep. p. ead. *But W. P's Comparison exceeds*, because Princes send Ambassadors to Princes, *That is, Gods send Ministers to Gods*, therefore every Man ought to do the like; *a rare Similitude-Maker*.

Rejoyn. A rare Similitude-Taker! *Reader*, I would not have diverted thy Eye from the Controversie, but that he forceth me to shew, how much more like a *Vain Whiffler*, than a Grave Divine, he Governs himself; I have hitherto learnt, that *Similes run not always upon Four Feet*; should they, what Havock might we make in Holy Scripture? *Similes* ought to be taken where the Similitude lyeth; It had been but leaving out two Words, that is, *to Princes*, and he had lost his Quibble; for all sober Readers will discern, that the Force lay, *upon Private Persons imitating Princes in sending out Ambassadors*; that is, because Christ sent forth his Disciples, and Princes their Ambassadors, *therefore every Man must turn Disciple and Ambassador*, which we call acting without a Commission, and which *J. F.* hath sufficiently rated us for; and what is worse, forged in our Names, that *without an immediate Commission we deny Obedience to all the Commands in the Bible*; but that we have already considered in our Chapter of Commands.

Rep. p. 53. *In W. P's Answer his Passion so blinded him, that he tells me, I therefore pretend to refute G.* Fox, *and therefore was impertinent, and that the Words were Scripture Words; whereas I quoted J.* Parnel *for those Words, not G.* Fox. But for *W. P.* to call them Scripture-Words, *which are neither in that Order, nor so much as relating to such a Subject, much less to the same End in any Place of the Scripture, is such an impertinent Whimsie, as becomes one, who is resolved to say something, no matter what.*
Rejoyn.

Rejoyn. If any *Paſſion* I had, he was unfit to ſee that *Mote* in my Eye, who diſcovers ſo great a Beam in his own. The Miſtake was inconſiderable, for it was not in any Alteration about Words or Matter, but the Perſon that ſhould write them, which ſo long as he was one that J. F. *calls a Quaker*, was altogether as much to his Purpoſe. But I have this farther to ſay, he led me into that Miſtake by putting *G. Fox. Myſt.* p. 45. right againſt *J. P*'s Paſſage, and ſo connected them without any Mark of Diſtinction, that he rather deſerves to be blamed for Negligence, than I to be reflected upon for *Paſſion* or *Blindneſs*. But be it *J. Parnel's* Saying and not *G. F's*, ſure I am *J. Faldo* hath very untruly cited it. Thus it begins; ' But who can witneſs an Immediate Call from God (leaving what follows in a differing Character quite out) ' *from the Outward Callings and Countries, Lands,* ' *Livings and Poſſeſſions, into ſeveral Countries to preach the free Goſpel as they have* ' *received it by the immediate Inſpiration of the Spirit* (now comes in another Piece of *J. Faldo's* citing) ' *and ſpeak it forth as they are moved from the Holy Ghoſt* (here he lets fall again) *And as the Spirit gives them Utterance, freely, as they* ' *have received it freely*; *by which Miniſtry many are convinced; and as they abide* ' *in it are converted, as Many in the Nation who are now new Creatures, can wit-* ' *neſs to the Honour and Glory of God*; *and this Call we own and witneſs, and this Mi-* ' *niſtry we own and witneſs, which is immediate and ſtands in the Will of God*; *And* ' *ſuch covet no Man's Silver nor Gold, neither could be hired to a certain Place* (now comes in another Piece of *J. Faldo's* Citation) ' *but travel from Place to Place and* ' *have no certain Dwelling Place* (here he drops again) ' *and ſuch are the true Mi-* ' *niſters of Jeſus Chriſt, who make the Goſpel free and without Charge* (now comes the laſt Parcel of his Citation) ' *and this (Miniſtry) we own and witneſs*.

This Reader was *J. Parnel's* Doctrine, which, if it be contrary to a *Goſpel-Miniſtry*, there is no Goſpel-Miniſtry can be proved by Scripture; read theſe Scriptures, *Iſa.* 35. 2. *Mark* 16. 25. *Amos* 3. 7, 8. *Amos* 7. 14, 15. *Gal.* 1. 11, 12. 1 *Cor.* 1. 17, 18, 19. chap. 2. 10, 11, 12, 13, 14, *&c.* 2 *Pet.* 1. 21. *Acts* 2. 4. *Acts* 20. 23. 1 *Theſ.* 9. 6. *J. F.* ſhould have proceeded, and have given us four Lines more of this young Man's Diſcourſe; but as he left out what bore moſt cloſely and hardly upon *Hirelings* before, ſo would it not have been for the Intereſt of himſelf and his Brethren to have brought in this little of a great deal that immediately follows, *viz.*

[' And for the Teſtimony of this true Miniſtry, ſome of us are *impriſoned, ſome* ' *ſtoned, ſome ſtocked, whipped, and ſhamefully intreated as Vagabonds, and Deluders,* ' *and Wanderers, and Raiſers of Sedition, and peſtilent Fellows,* and eſteemed not ' worthy to live in the Nation, both by Prieſts, People, and Rulers.]

A Shame to *Independents* that then ruled, and which is worſe, the Guilt of the Blood of this Innocent Man lyeth at the Door but of too many of them, about *Coggeſhal* and *Colcheſter* in *Eſſex*, who by their cruel Impriſonment (ſcarce to be parallelled by any Story) brought this godly young Man to an untimely Death. I need not tell you why, he hath done it to my Hand; becauſe, ſays he, ' *We de-* ' *clare againſt all who come not in by the Door, but ſeek to climb up another Way by* ' *their Study, Inventions, and Serpentine Wiſdom and Knowledge, and ſo are Thieves* ' *and Robbers*— *Such Miniſters and their Miniſtry we deny*; *for the Hand of the* ' *Lord is againſt them,* &c. Great and true Words; No Man can miniſter that which he hath not; no Man can have thoſe Things which qualifie him *a true Miniſter*, but *by the Inſpiration of the Almighty, and the effectual Operation of his Power and Spirit*: God's Meſſengers were ever led, taught and furniſht by God's Spirit, not by *human Invention and Acquiſition,* which *Paul* counted *Droſs and Dung in Compariſon of the Excellency of the Knowledge of his Lord Chriſt Jeſus, through the Revelation of the Eternal Spirit.* But that *J. Faldo* may be the better uuderſtood about the Miniſtry he pleads for, take, Reader, a Paſſage he cites out of *G. F's* Book, called *Gr. Myſt.* which doubtleſs he reputes very heterodox, or he would never bring it to prove a Charge containing ſuch Matter as he counts ſo. ' *Thou* ' [*the Prieſt*] *art corrected by the Scripture, and the Apoſtle corrects thee, who ſaid,* ' *I have not received it of Man, nor by Man, and bid others look at Jeſus, the Au-* ' *thor of their* Faith; *Their Writings*, ſaith *J. Faldo*, *are abounding with Matter of this Nature*; So much the better ſay I; for it is old Scripture Doctrine, and *J. Faldo* gives us plainly to infer by his Diſlike of this Paſſage, that he maintains a Miniſtry received *of Man and by Man*, and that People ought to look unto them, and not to Jeſus the Author of their Faith. If this be one of *J. F's* Chriſtian Ordinances, as his Diſcourſe evidently makes it, I hope, my Reader will the leſs wonder

der at those hard Charges against us in it; for the plain English of his Charge against us is this, *The Quakers deny the Ministry that is of Man, or by Man, therefore they deny the Gospel-Ministry.* Poor Man! what a pass hath he brought his Affairs to? Indeed I pity him, and fear the Consequence of his Disappointment, since a Man of his Stomach, to charge so *high* and make so *little* of it, may, with the Loss of his Honesty, for ought I know, hazard his Wits too.

To wind up this Chapter and prove to all the World I have not mistaken him, hear him.

Reply, p. 55. W. P. *produceth one of my Testimonies out of* J. Parnel, *yet but by halves,* ' And here is the Difference of the Ministers of the World and the Mini-' sters of Christ— The one of the Letter, the other of the Spirit. *To which he replies,* Strange Impudence to call this a Proof; *But I cannot help it, if* P. *will say the Sun is Darkness: Before I part with him here, I will furnish my Reader with that Part of the same Testimony he treacherously leaves out;* ' for they are meer Deceiv-' ers, and Witches, bewitch People from the Truth, holding forth the Shadow ' for the Substance; and what is the Chaff to the Wheat? *Add this to the other (as it was in my Book) and I dare trust my Reader that is willing to speak Truth to pass his Censure; It follows in the same Author before quoted:* ' And so the Devil ' takes Scripture to maintain his Kingdom, and this he delivers by the Mouth of ' his Ministers, which he sends abroad to deceive the Nations leading People in ' Blindness.

Rejoyn. Let the Reader observe, that what he here pretends to quote out of *J. P.* follows as himself said, what we have just before transcribed. Three Things contain my Rejoynder.

First, He reports not my Answer which was to this Purpose. ' It is a Proof in-' deed, but against him; for if a false or worldly *Ministry* under the Form of God-' liness may not be, farewell Scripture; But if such a Thing will be allowed us, ' then since the Letter or Scriptures *are not by such rejected, but in Shew most highly* ' *admired, and that they pretend to collect all they believe or know from thence* (tho' ' indeed they understand them not*) we have great Reason to say, That *those who* ' *are Ministers only from the Letter, with what they imaginarily comment upon it,* ' *they are not Christ's Ministers,* p. 110. Of which and much more he hath not given us a Word; how can he reply honestly, and intelligible, who neither gives nor takes Notice of the Answer he should reply to. *J. Parnel's* Words plainly relate to a Ministry not gifted nor qualified by the Holy Ghost; and *J. Faldo* tells us in so many Words, *that without it none are worthy of the Name or Thing;* Yet doth he make it as unreasonable for me to say *J. Parnel's* Words prove not our Denial of a Gospel-Ministry (which so obviously own it) as for him to assert the *Sun is Darkness.*

Secondly, I did not leave out that which he chargeth me to have done *Treacherously,* the best Word he can afford me on the like Occasions; he must be quite bereaved of his Senses, that thinks I should fear defending *J. P.* in calling such *Deceivers* and *Witches* (as bewitching the People from the Truth) who are made *Ministers by the Will of Man, without the Inspiration of the Spirit, Gift of the Holy Ghost, Will of God, and are Coveters of Men's Silver or Gold, Preachers of their own Inventions, Persecutors, Revilers, stirring up of the Magistrates to stone, stock, whip, imprison, &c.* all which *J. P.* gives as the Character of the Ministry he writ against; for if this be the Gospel-Ministry, the Devil is a Saint: The Truth is, *John Faldo's* Book is generally to be read backward.

Lastly, There is no such Passage of the *false Ministry,* much less of the true, in page 15, 16, or 17. of *J. Parnel's Shield,* as *J. F.* suggests; however I believe the Devil useth sometimes Scripture, and that he hath had, and hath many Ministers whom he sends abroad to deceive the Nations, leading and keeping People in Blindness, under a Pretence of Christianity and Conformity to the Doctrine of the Scriptures, in order to maintain his *Anti-christian Kingdom;* all true *Protestants* were of that Mind; but *J. F.* is none of that Number. Doubtless the poor Man is brought to a low Ebb, that brings this to prove we deny Gospel-Ministry, which the honest Martyrs, primitive Reformers, and what is more to our Purpose, the Scriptures themselves say again and again; The contrary will unavoidably prove, *the Ministry of the Church of* Rome to have been *not Anti-christ's* but Christ's true Ministers, since they both *use Scripture, preach Scripture, and call themselves the Ministers of the Gospel by Apostolical Institution and Succession,* In this disarmed Condition we leave him and the Chapter, confessing to all the World, that such a

Ministry

Ministry as hath effectually known the Operation of the Spirit of God in themselves, as to those Things which concern Redemption and Eternal Salvation; and that he draws forth by his Holy Spirit, indues with his Heavenly Power, *for the turning of Men from Darkness to Light, from the Power of Satan unto God*, we own, honour and love, and only deny and reject that Ministry which is *by the Will, Study or Acquisition of Man* in his unregenerated State, who not being acquainted with the Effectual Operation of the Word of God in themselves, are wholly dark as to those Things which relate to the true Ministry, not knowing what they deny nor whereof they affirm; which doth not edifie, but hazard the immortal Souls of Men: And as they want the Inspiration of the Almighty, to instruct them, so (being Strangers to the Work of God in themselves, and not waiting to feel an Endowment with Divine Power from on high) there proceeds no spiritual Life or divine Virtue from them, to make their Ministry effectual, which is the Cause of that Lamentable Decay of Holy Living that is in the World, and great Increase of all manner of Unsavoury and Irreligious Conversation. I will conclude with two or three Testimonies given by Men once in request with Separatists.

Christopher Goad's *Invalidity of Church-Censures*, pag. 64, 65.

' It is the Spirit that makes Ministers, and those Ministers that remain by the
' Spirit do minister the Spirit, and that is ministring of the Gospel, *when we mi-*
' *nister the Spirit.*
' I am a Minister of the new Testament *so far as the Spirit speaks in me and*
' *by me.*
' In whomsoever the Spirit stands up and speaks, *that Person for the Time is a*
' *true Minister.* The Spirit doth not regard *Sexes, the Spirit regards not Age,*
' *Learned or Unlearned:* 'Tis not Age nor Sex, nor any major Part can minister
' Spirit, but whom the Spirit pleaseth.

Christopher Goad. *Right Spir. &c.* pag. 21, 22.

' The Ministry that is calling us off from Man, from the Glow-worm Light of
' this Creation, from Man's Parts and Gifts, into the Spirit, that is the Ministry
' we should look after.
' The Truth is, there is no true Prophet, no true Testimony given of Christ,
' *but by those that see him*, and the nearer to him the clearer Sight of him, *the*
' *more clear and Powerful is the Testimony given of him:* That Testimony that is
' given to him by those that do not see him present and come, is not in deed a
' Testimony to Christ, *but to Anti-Christ*; he is such a Prophet as *Balaam* was,
' *that had nothing but Notion.*
' All true Prophets that prophesied of Christ saw him, *and he was in them.*

Christopher Goad's *Paraphrase upon* Act. 17. pag. 28.

' We know *no other Guide but the Spirit:* There is not any Minister in the World
' that is our Guide, or any Company of Ministers, *but the Spirit, if he speaks in*
' *them and by them*; We have but one Master, that is Christ.

T. Collier *in his Works*, p. 47, 48, *and* p. 430.

' Upon that Scripture, *Mal.* 27. *The Priest's Lips should preserve Knowledge, and*
' *they should seek the Law at his Mouth; for he is the Messenger of the Lord of*
' *Hosts.* Now this usually is applyed to the Ministers, who have given themselves
' the Title of Priests, and that the People should seek the Knowledge at their
' Mouths, and indeed they themselves have done what in them lies, not only to
' bring People into this Error and Ignorance, but to keep them in it, whereas
' Christ is indeed *the alone Priest*, the Substance of the *Jews* Type, *and the People*
' *are to seek the Law at his Mouth*; but he is the Messenger of the Lord of Hosts;
' he is called the Messenger of the Covenant, *Mal.* 3. 1. the alone Prophet and
' Teacher of his People.
' The Spirit being lost, Anti-christ sets the Wisdom of the Flesh (*human Industry,*
' *Tongues and Arts*) in room of it, it is the Anointing of Anti-christ; for in all
' Things

'Things Anti-chrift feeks to imitate Chrift, as well in the Flefh as in the Spirit.
'Again, *The Saints are made Partakers of the fame Spirit the Apoftles were.*

W. Dell's *Sermons*, pag. 16, 17, 18.

'There is a Neceffity of this *Power of the Holy Spirit* for Minifters. For *firft*, If they have not this Power of the Holy Spirit, they have no Power at all; for *Chrift fent them only as his Father fent him.* Without this Power they are infufficient for the Miniftry; for no Man is fufficient for the Work of the Miniftry by any natural Parts and Abilities of his own— but only by this Power of the Spirit; and till he be endued with this, notwithftanding all his other Accomplifhments, he is altogether infufficient— but only by the Power of the Holy Spirit coming upon them.

'He cannot fpeak the Word of God but by the Power of God.

'Chrift himfelf without this Power of God could not have fpoke one Word of God.

W. Dell. *Stumbling Stone*, pag. 8.

'The Miniftry of the new Teftament is a common Miniftry, belonging equally and alike to all the Seed of Chrift.

W. Dell: *Trial of Spirits*, pag. 17, 18.

'The true Prophets fpeaking the Word of God by and in the Spirit, as *Paul* fays of himfelf, and other Believers who had received the Spirit, *We have the Mind of Chrift*; But the falfe Prophets, *though they fpeak the Word of the Letter exactly, and that to the very Original and Curiofity of Criticifms,* yet fpeaking it without the Spirit, *they are falfe Prophets before God and his True Church;* feeing all right Prophecy hath *proceeded from the Spirit in all Ages of the World;* but efpecially it muft fo proceed *in the Days of the New-Teftament,* wherein God hath promifed *the largeft Effufion of his Spirit.*

Greenham, *Serm.* 1. pag. 51.

'Without this Spirit of God, *no Holy Exercife can have it's full Effect;* for the Word works not where the Spirit of God is wanting— when we have not *the Spirit of God to teach us, fpeak of the Law or the Gofpel, &c. we are little affected therewith,* unlefs God give us of his *good Spirit* to profit by the fame.

CHAP. III.

That we own a Gofpel-Church, contrary to our Adverfary's Charge.

THE next Thing our Adverfary charged us with a Denial of, is a *Gofpel-Church;* one of his Proofs, as he will have them called, was in *J. N's Love to the Loft*, pag. 17. 'And the Church fo gathered into God is the Pillar and Ground of Truth, where the Spirit alone is Teacher. Upon which he argued thus, *The* Gofpel-Church *is a Church which had other Teachers, and not the Spirit alone; Therefore the* Quakers *deny a* Gofpel-Church, *and they contradict themfelves; for they have more Teachers than all others:* Thus his firft Book, pag. 16. To which I returned, That fuch as are not blinded with Prejudice, may difcern that from our fpeaking of the Univerfal Church of God, which (fays the Apoftle as well as the *Quakers*) *is in God;* he infers, 'That we deny all Vifible Religious Societies, commonly called by the Ancients, *Afia, Theffalonica, Ephefus, Corinth, &c.* Now obferve this Reply.

Reply, pag. 59. *Not one Word of this in all my Book; My Charge was, That they deny a* Gofpel-Church, *not Vifible Religious Societies.*

Rejoyn. Confidently faid; but if all the Words be not there, doth it follow the Matter they import is not there? If he doth not mean, That we deny a *Vifible Religious Society* to be a Church, what makes him to infer our Denial of a *Gofpel-Church,* from our afferting it to be *Invifible.* Two Things muft follow from this Reply: Either a Gofpel-Church is *not vifible,* and then he breaks his own Neck; or *not a Religious Society,* and fo he is impious: If then a Gofpel-Church is a Vifible Religious Society, and we deny a Gofpel-Church, it muft follow, that we deny ny a Visible Religious Society, which in *John Faldo*'s Opinion makes up a Gospel-Church. To conclude, a Gospel-Church and a Visible Religious Society he makes to be quite differing Things: But perhaps, he will come off thus; *I did not say, ye denied the visible religious Societies, called the Churches of* Asia, *&c. but that you deny them, or such as they are, to be Churches:* But neither will this serve his turn; for we both own them to have been Gospel-Churches, and are taught by *J. F.* to believe, That a Gospel-Church is not only not invisible, but another Thing than a visible religious Society too; It is worth our while to hear his Reason for it.

Reply, p. 59. *Religious Societies may be as far from a Gospel-Church, as half a dozen Christian Friends associated together to eat a good Dinner, or carry on a Trade; yet he dirts me with want of Honesty to grace his Forgery.*

Rejoyn. He might as well have said to the *Ale-House* or *Tavern*, whither he invited a Friend of ours after disputing with him, doubtless not out of Love to our Friend, but the good Liquor, a Sort of Liberty once counted *Scandalous* by many of his Pretensions, especially when just after so serious an Exercise; but it is grown familiar with Men of his Coat, to fall *from the Bible to the Pot*, and so back again. But, *Friendly Reader*, what sayst thou of this Man's Evasion? Who will have me to mean by *visible religious Societies*, visible civil Societies; for such I count *good Men at an Ordinary, or a Committee of Trade*; Vain and Shallow Man! Did I not give Intimation enough what *Religious Societies* I meant, when I instanced the *Churches of Asia, Thessalonica, &c.* to explain what I meant thereby? Whether I did play the *Forger*, or my *Adversary* the *Dishonest Shifter*, let the impartial Reader judge. Again,

Reply. W. P. *proceeds*, p. 113. *in the same Evil*, ' And from our asserting the ' Spirit to be the only Gospel-Teacher, he concludes that we deny all Preaching of ' Men though by the Spirit ; *the four last Words* though by the Spirit *are added by him, and meerly forged.*

Rejoyn. They may be added, but not forged; One would think it is only then, when without the Holy Ghost, that we deny it by his Words, and that hurts us not; but I take it the other Way, and the Truth is, it is a Mistake he commits against us, where-ever the like Subjects fall in his Way; for this implies, as if we denied *Preaching by Inspiration*, and that he all along had maintained it : A Doctrine he every now and then flings in our Dish, scorns and derides: Thus can this Man's Conscience sail by any Wind to gain the Shore; and after all these Shuffles dares to conclude, *That we* in Terminis *deny all Preachings of Men*, because *G. F.* said, *cease from Man*, when there is nothing more palpable, than that *G. F.* meant *Man* considered *in his own meer Ability*; that is, from such as the Prophet forbid, not from true Prophets ; but our Adversary the Preachings of Men, *though by the Spirit of God*; for how can he make us to contradict our selves in saying, *Man is the Spirit's Instrument* (which he understands to be the Preaching of Men by the Spirit) if he doth not make us deny all *Preaching though by the Spirit.* In short, I hope my *Reader* will think it no Forgery, whatever my Adversary may, (who ever and anon would hide his own Weakness by a hard Word flung upon me to amuse the credulous Reader) to say that from our Asserting, *The Spirit to be the only Gospel-Teacher* of all who believe, he concludes, That we deny *all Preaching of Men, though by the Spirit*; else there would be no Sense in his charging us with a *Contradiction*, because we say, *The Spirit is the only Teacher*, and yet that the *Spirit teacheth by Men*, if he did not understand our Ceasing from Men, or Denying Man's Ministry, *to be our Denial of Man's Preaching by the Holy Spirit.* But he will not give over yet: These Words, *The Spirit the only Teacher*, he often flings up as Words indigestible by his foul and phlegmatick Stomach; for upon my saying, That such as preach by the Holy Spirit are rather the Instruments than the Teacher, or Man is that by which the Spirit conveyeth his Teaching unto others, he replies thus.

Reply, pag. 58. *So that after* W. P's *own strict Account he allows their Practice*, viz. Preaching of Men, *to give the Lie every Day to their Tenets.*

Rejoyn. If Preachings of Men by the Spirit be the Preachings of Men, such Preachings we shall always allow, and think it no Lye or Contradiction to our Tenets ; But if he that dictates a Letter of Intelligence be the Informer, and not the Scribe, the Holy Spirit must be the Teacher, and Man but the Instrument. True Teachings are not only Words, but Matter, and that accompanied with Divine Power, which flow from the Eternal Spirit ; Men give them but the simple Covering of Expression, and that by the Spirit's Appointment ; therefore not so properly the *Teachings of Men* by the Holy Spirit, *as the Teachings of the Holy Spirit by and through Men*; consequently not Man's Teachings, but the Spirit's.

Again, Because we charge him with bringing in *other Teachers than the Holy Spirit*, contrary to express Scripture, the Promise of God, and the very End of the Blessed Gospel, he replies.

Rep. Pag. 58, 59. *Can you think this Man worth disputing with, who rambles and talks he cares not how?* If what P. said be true, the Exhortations to do the Work of an Evangelist, feed the Flock over which the Holy Ghost had made them Overseers, *were not intended of Man's Teaching*; but the Spirit of God only exhorted the Spirit of God to these Actions, and Man had not, hath not any Agency in Teaching.

Rejoyn. But did we ever say, *Man had no Share in being taught*, whatever we have said against the utmost of *Man's Natural Ability*, considered separately *from God's Spirit* about his Teaching? We never yet said, That Man was not to be taught: Is there no Difference betwixt *Men's Teaching without God's Spirit*, and *Men's being taught of God's Spirit*? At whose Door then should we lay this Absurdity, *The Spirit of God exhorted the Spirit of God?* What an idle *Non sequitur* is this?

Nor do we deny all Agency in Man, when managed by the Holy Ghost; A Man might as well argue (following *J. Faldo*'s Steps) against the Apostle *Paul*, when he said, *It is no more I that live, but Christ in me*, that is, The Apostle had *no Life in him in any Sense*; Would this be good Doctrine? But more openly do the Words of Christ lay to the Exception of such Cavillers, *'Tis not I that speak, but the Father in me*; Again, *It is not you that speak, but the Holy Ghost in you*; For, after *J. Faldo*'s Paraphrase, we must either deny that Christ or his Apostles spoke those Words, *or* confess that they contracted themselves in saying, they did not speak when they did; or, *Lastly*, He must acknowledge to us, That *such Teachings and Speakings are not the Teachings and Speakings of Men, but of God by and through Men*. Let him first see if he can reconcile himself to these Scripture-Passages so pertinent to our Purpose, and leave off his silly Shifts, as easily confuted as discovered.

Upon my saying, That ' we do believe that there is One, and but One Universal
' Church, the Ground and Pillar of Truth, and that is in God, and that the Mem-
' bers of it *are washed in the Blood of the Lamb, and grafted into the True Vine,*
' *bringing forth Fruit unto Holiness,* p. 113. he thus replies (and I beseech my Reader to consider it.)

Rep. Pag. 59. *If he own no other Church but this, which is the Character of the invisible Church, he owns not a Gospel-Church, whose Order and Frame is according to the Doctrine of the Apostles, and Practice of the Saints in the New Testament.*

Rejoyn. We are beholden to him for this; May we ever meet with such Adversaries! It seems then my *Definition* hath nothing to do with the *Gospel Church*, What is it but to say, that the *Gospel-Church is not the Pillar of Truth*, The Gospel Church is *not washed in the Blood of the Lamb*, The Gospel Church is *not grafted into the True Vine*; and that Men may be *in the Truth, washed in the Blood of the Lamb, grafted into the true Vine, and bring forth Fruit unto Holiness*, and yet no Ways concerned in the Gospel Church; in short the *Gospel Church is not the Universal Church, nor the Invisible Church a Gospel Church*; and what is his Reason, if any there can be, for all this pernicious and Anti-christian Doctrine? Because a *Gospel Church is one whose Order and Frame is according to the Doctrine of the Apostle and Practice of the Saints*. Worse and worse it seems then in *J. F*'s Sense, that the Order and Frame the Doctrine of the Apostles brought the Church of Christ to, and the Practice of the Saints in the New Testament, had nothing to do with *the Pillar of Truth, dwelling in God, being washed in the Blood of the Lamb, grafted in the true Vine, and bringing forth Fruit unto Holiness.* What Sort of *impious Gibberish* is this? For according to his Notion of the Gospel Church, the *most Satanical Crew may as well be of that Church as the best of Christians*; since the External Order (at most but the Form of Godliness) was, and is, imitable and imitated by arrant *Hypocrites*.

By this Argument, *Elias*, and the Seven Hundred who had not bowed their Knees to *Baal* (so invisible as *Elias* himself knew not of them) were *Schismaticks* or *Infidels* to the then *Jewish* Church, being *without all Visible Church, Policy or Order*; and the *Jews* that had it, though Apostatiz'd, must have been *God's Legal Church*. It will also follow, that for above 1200 Years together, since Christ's Time, there hath

hath been *no Gospel Church, yet Gospellers*, as their Enemies have called them, which were to grant to the *Roman Catholicks* all they desire. *What was that Church that fled into the Wilderness?* It must either be the Gospel Church, or not the Gospel Church; *If not the Gospel Church, then not the Christian*, and consequently the *Anti-Christian Church*; But that could not be, because she fled from *Antichrist*: If the Gospel Church, then may a Church be Gospel without Punctuality in visible Order; for it is notorious by all Story, the Remnant of the Woman's Seed, who have born a faithful Testimony against the Spirit of Antichrist in their Sack-cloth and Wilderness Estate, have been destitute of that visible Order. Indeed I hitherto thought, that a *Gospel Church constituted* necessary External *Order*, and *not* that meer external *Order* constitutes the *Church Gospel or Evangelical*; But *J. Faldo* says *No*, who seems not to scruple at the Word *Church*, but to play upon the Word *Gospel*, as if external Order and Government were synonymous, or of equal Force; whereas the *Gospel* is called in Scripture *The Power of God to Salvation*, from that Spiritual Redemption it efficaciously worketh in them that receive it, from the Bondage of Corruption, under which they have fruitlesly laboured; which is the Reason, and a good one too, why it signifieth *glad Tidings*; since nothing can be more joyous to a weary and heavy-laden Sinner, than to be eased of his former Iniquities, by Remission, and purged from the Nature and Habits of it in the Soul, by the Operation of this Heavenly and Everlasting Gospel; which worthy *Christopher Goad (Right Spirit of Christ*, Pag. 17.) calls, *the forming or bringing forth of Christ in us.* What is all our *Adversary* hath said, but to make Remedies against, or Condescension to the Weakness of the Church's Infancy, as says *Honest W. Tindal* in his *Works*, p. 9, 436, 438. *the only great Constitutes of a Gospel Church?* By which he denies a Gospel Church to have been antecedent to that External Order, and consequently that the Believers were not a Gospel Church, when met together on the Day of *Pentecost*, nor long after: since the Gospel had been many Years preached, Multitudes converted, and many baptized by the One Spirit into the One Body of true Gospel Fellowship, before ever those Epistles were written by the Apostle *Paul* either to the Church at Corinth, or to *Timothy*, in which only External Order is mention'd: Nay, at this Rate, he hath Unchurched every Part in *England* but one, if yet one may be excepted; for if *External Order only constitutes a Gospel Church*, every Part in *England* differing greatly in their External Order, it must follow, that none but one, if any one, can have any just Pretence to a compleat Gospel Church, consequently *Mungrils*. He still forgets what he promised, that *None of them were farther concerned against the Quakers than Vindicated.* Howbeit, Herein they may hold him excused, that he hath equally unchurched Himself and those he preacheth to, in Company with all other Parties in *England*, being out of that Order.

But I intreat the *Reader* to consider, what a Monster he hath made of *Christ*, who describeth him with *two such Bodies to one Head*, one *Invisible*, the other *Visible*; one washed in the Blood of the Lamb, grafted into the true Vine, bringing forth Fruit unto Holiness, Qualifications hid from the Eye of the World, as worthy *John Bradford* told *T. Weston*, as in *B. Martyr*, p. 104, 312, *That the Church of Christ is Invisible to him that hath not a Spiritual Eye*; The other constituted of People, (no Matter how *Unregenerated if*) submitted to *an External Structure of Order and Discipline*; A Cover for all the Wolves, Antichrists and Hypocrites, that have been, are, or shall be to the End of the World. In short, No Position can be more destructive to the Power of Godliness, the Fellowship of the True Church that lives in God, and pernicious to the Souls of Men, by securing them in their Fancied Relation to a Gospel Church, whilst in an Un-gospel Spirit, estranged from the Power of the true Gospel, and unacquainted with the Congregation of the Faithful, who through Faith overcome the World, and know a Washing in the Blood of the Lamb, and a being grafted into the true Vine, and made to drink into the one Spirit, bringing forth Fruits unto Holiness. To conclude, After this Sort of Doctrine, *Men may be Members of a Gospel Church, and not of the True Church*; Members of a Gospel Church, and *not good Christians*, no, *nor good Men* it self. Indeed *such a Pastor*, as our Adversary, *suits such a Church, and such a Church exactly fits such a Pastor*; from whom God deliver me and all People, and them from themselves, I mean the Power and Prevalency of that pernicious Doctrine and Spirit that now infects them. He proceeds however, with what Success we shall see.

Rep. Pag. 59, 60. *To this of their* Invisible Church, *I told* W. P. *of their Officers very suitable to a conceited Nothing.* Fox Myst. p. 2. 'The Holy Ghost made 'the Officers of the Church Overseers; The Overseers to be Invisible, for they 'saw with an Invisible Eye, and so were in the Spirit, which is invisible, and not 'in the Flesh. *But* W. Penn *meddled not with this, which I dare say (as much as he hath of the* Quakers *Spirit) he cannot tell the Meaning of himself.*

Rejoin. I had no Reason to meddle with what I could not, nor cannot yet find; I intreat my Reader to consider the Unreasonableness of his Taunts; In his *first Book* he sent me to *Pag.* 8. where no such Thing was to be found, yet did I not place it to the Account of his Treachery, the best Construction he can make of any Innocent Omission on my Part; In his *Reply* he sends me to *Pag.* 2. and there I am as wise as I was before, no such Words or Matter appearing: What shall I say of such an *Adversary?* Was I then to be blamed for *not meddling with what was not to be found?* Or deserve I not better Terms at his Hands, who made no hard Use of it in my Answer? Or, Lastly, Is he not worthy of double Blame, that adds to his first Mistake a second, and then abuseth me, as if on Purpose I had avoided the Dint of an Authentick Testimony, hitherto not produced? But suppose G. F. hath ever written any such Passage, doubtless by *Invisible Overseers* he only meant, *Spiritual,* not *Carnal-minded Men, who by the Invisible Eye, which the true God hath opened, might watch over the Flock, as to their inward and spiritual Conditions:* This the following Words make good, '*for they saw with an invisible* '*Eye, and so were in the Spirit, which is invisible, and not in the Flesh.* In short, they were not meer outward Officers, exercising an Outward Rule and Dominion about Outward Things, but Men qualified by the Holy Ghost, with an inward Discerning to Oversee the Spiritual State of the Church; not that their Persons were invisible, or their Actions towards the Church, but that *Heavenly Faculty* given them of the Holy Spirit, which *rendred them Overseers,* or Men able to see or discern the State and Condition of the Church, was of an Invisible Nature.

He fell very foul upon us in his first Book, because of a *Dutch Woman's speaking in one of our Meetings in her own Tongue;* charging upon us, That *we did orderly, according to the Popish Mass, which was to pray in an Unknown Tongue.* To which I made a large, and I hope, sufficient Answer, of which he reports but these two or three Parcels: First, That *I called it a Disingenuous Reflection;* Next, That *we do not affect such Obscurity?* Lastly, *The Divine Light, Power or Spirit inwardly manifested, is the one Tongue to the Children of Light.* This he calls *Foolish, Antiscriptural, Ridiculous;* But if it be so, I owe it to him alone, who hath made so Foolish and False a Citation of my Words; Howbeit, he saith nothing to what he hath cited, his hard Words set aside. His *Reflection* was *Disingenuous,* because such a Practice is not *common* or *usual* with us; Nay, that was accidental. Therefore to charge it upon us as *conformable to the Orderliness of the* Popish *Mass, as if it were a Principle with us to teach, as with* Romanists *to pray in an unknown Tongue,* was more than *Disingenuous;* for it was *False* and *Malicious,* being thrown out by him on Purpose to defame and disgrace us.

That we do not affect such *Obscurity* I affirmed, and our Practice evidenceth it, being rather jeer'd for our too much Rusticity and Plainness, and our frequent decrying of dark School Phrases, and Rhetorick, by which great Writers wrap up their Matter from the Understanding of the Vulgar. That the *Divine Light, Power or Spirit inwardly manifested* are none of my Words; I will report my Answer, both more largely and truly, and leave it with the Conscience of my Reader, thus:

'The single Power of the Almighty may both strike Astonishment and give Re-
'freshment where the Words uttered are not always understood; since he frequent-
'ly doth both without them: Understanding and inward Sense are two Things;
'for the Devil may speak the best Words in the Bible, and be an Undiscovered
'Devil still, except by this Divine Light, Power and Spirit he be inwardly mani-
'fested, consequently a right Sense may be had, where Words may not be under-
'stood, which [Sense] is the *one Tongue to the Children of Light;* yet we do not
'only decry all designed Obscurity, by Praying and Preaching in Unknown Langu-
'ages, but with the Apostle say, That *we chuse rather by far to speak in a Known*
'*Tongue,* as well as have the Sense of our Spirits: Nor did ever any *Quaker* yet
'pretend to be moved to pray in an Unknown Language whilst he was Master of
'that which was well known to the People. Since then we do not affect Obscu-

'rity

' rity, the Case of the *Papists*, (who pray in *Latin* rather than in their Native or
' Vulgar Tongue) he is very Disingenuous in that Reflection,

But in Reply to all this, he only gives us thus much.

Reply, Page 60. *Sure I am, that the Spirit of God, by whom the Apostle* Paul *was directed, is not the* Quakers *Spirit, nor it's Doctrine the same with theirs in the same Case:* I shall be to him that speaketh a *Barbarian,* and be that speaketh shall be a *Barbarian* to me, 1 *Cor.* 14. 11.

Rejoyn. I would fain know by what Means *J.* Faldo hath that Discerning between the Spirit of the Apostle, and the Spirit of the *Quakers*. Is it because the *Dutch Woman* spoke in an *English Meeting?* Do we hold, teach or Practice any such Thing? Besides, the Apostle tells us, That *though an Unknown Tongue might render him as a* Barbarian *to him that understandeth him not,* will it therefore follow, *that he was a* Barbarian, or that he *had not the Spirit of Christ dwelling in him?* By no Means; for he might *speak Mysteries in the Spirit,* as saith the Apostle, Verse 2. *Men may also pray in the Spirit in an Unknown Tongue,* Verse 14. *A Man may bless, praise and give Thanks to God in an Unknown Tongue,* Verse 14, 15, 16, 17. Nay, the Apostle saith of such an one, *Verily, thou givest Thanks well.* Now, how all this can be, and yet that such a Person should be acted by another Spirit than the Spirit of God and the Apostle, for my own Part I cannot see. In short, The Apostle tells us, That *Tongues are for them that believe not,* Verse 22. But our Friend spoke among them that believed; and though they did not all know what her bare Words imported, yet they might be and were sensible of the Divine Power in which she spoke, which gave a general Refreshment unto them of that Assembly, that were acquainted with it; otherwise all Fellowship in Spirit must be renounced: But 'tis to be any thing *J. F's* Froth will have it, because it's unknown to his thick and carnal Understanding. However, the Want of a known *Tongue* may render one *less Profitable,* but not less a *Christian;* for a Time should come, the same Apostle said, that *Tongues should cease,* but never that *Christian,* or *having the Spirit of Christ* should cease; therefore to repute all that cannot speak in a Known Tongue *Antichristian,* or of *another Spirit than the Spirit of God and his Apostle,* is unworthy of any Man that makes any the least Pretence to the *Christian* Religion, indeed to common Sense.

One Passage more, and then we conclude this Chapter.

Reply, Pag. 60. *To my Reflection upon their affirming* she spake by the Spirit, because they all found Refreshings, *viz. So have Children many a time at Puppet-Plays,* W. P. *calls me all to naught, especially because* I could not (as he saith) but think it meant by *Refreshings,* what came from God. *But let not* Penn *think we take our selves bound to reverence such Fooleries.*

Rejoyn. That it was a *Reflection* he confesseth; whether it were not an unseemly one I refer to every Man of Conscience. I did not intend to oblige *J.* Faldo to believe what we say, but reprove his prophane Scoffs at what we believe. I would have so much Regard to any People seriously professing Religion, as not to explain what they mean by their *Refreshment,* by the Pleasure some irreligious People take at the vain and frothy Sport of *Puppet-Play;* And the worst Word I gave him and his Comparison, was *Prophaneness;* farther adding, ' that it outdid *Ben Johnson's Alchymist* (a Play made in Scorn of *Puritans*) which all good Men detest, and himself dying abhorred.

But why may not People be refresht in their Souls from that divine Power, which may attend a Person speaking in a Language unknown? Suppose a Godly Assembly of *English* People and an *English* Preacher endued with God's holy Spirit, and there happen into such a Congregation some serious Foreigners of the same Judgment, is it absurd to say, That notwithstanding their Ignorance of the Signification of the Words spoken, *they may have an Inward and Spiritual Sense of the Zeal, Power, and Spirit that eminently attends the Preacher?* if it be, how much more ridiculous is it then for People to say, It gladded their Hearts to see such a Godly Countenance, or to hear the Voice or Sound of this or the other good Man, though they had no distinct Understanding of his Words? I am in this Case a more allowable Witness than *John* Faldo, who have seen Sinners struck, the Weak strengthned, and the Strong confirmed, at the hearing of the Truth of God declared in a Language they could not understand; The Divine Power and Virtue went forth, and they were judged, comforted or confirmed in themselves, and they no Fools (though *J. Faldo calls such Things Fooleries* and *Puppet-Plays*) To deny this is to overthrow *Spiritual Fellowship in the Ground of it;* and *to center in this Atheistical*

cal Notion, That all our Knowledge of God comes in by our carnal Eyes and Ears; that is, What others have written, and what others have told me, that I believe, and therefore I believe, and not from the Testimony of that infallible Spirit of God in my self; which Credulity renders him more like *Rome* in that, wherein she is condemnable, than any thing he can truly suggest of us; but this gross Doctrine being so obviously taught by our Adversary in his first Book, second Part, p. 91, we have the less Reason to wonder that *Fooleries* and *Puppet-Plays* are the best Words he can bestow upon the *Divine Consolation, Refreshment and Communion of the Holy Spirit within Men.*

We will add these Testimonies, as the Conclusion of this Chapter.

W. Tindal, *in his Works*, p. 250.

' *Church,* the Elect, in whose Hearts God hath written his Law with his Holy
' Spirit, and given them a feeling Faith of the Mercy that is in Christ Jesus our
' Lord.

D. Barnes's *Works*, p. 244.

' The Holy *Church of Christ* is nothing else but that Congregation that is sanc-
' tified in Spirit, Redeemed with Christ's Blood, and sticketh fast and sure, alone-
' ly to the Promises that he made therein.
' So that the *Church is a Spiritual Thing,* and no exterior Thing, but invisible
' from Carnal Eyes (I say, not that they be invisible that be of the Church, but
' that holy *Church in her self is invisible)* as Faith is; and her Pureness and
' Cleanness is before Christ only, and not before the World; for the World hath
' no Judgment nor Knowledge of her, but all her Honour and Cleanness is be-
' fore Christ sure and fast.

Peter Martyr. *fourth Part of* Common Places, Cap. 1. Pag. 1.

' The Name of a *Church* is derived of the *Greek* Καλεῖν, that is, *to call*; for none
' can be Partakers thereof, which come not thereunto by the *Calling of God.* And
' to define it, we say, that it is *a Company of Believers and regenerate Persons,*
' *whom God gathereth together in Christ by the Word and the Holy Ghost* —— It is
' every where called the *Body of Christ,* because all the Members thereof have him
' for their Head, of whom by the Joints and Sinews they take their growing, and
' attain unto Life by the Inspiration of the Holy Ghost.

Christoph. Goad, Page 37.

' 'Tis a sad Thing that there are *Churches*——that think it is enough there is a
' Form of Godliness, that we are in Church-Fellowship, and so lie down together
' and sleep; I have no Quarrel with Churches, or any Form, but *such as have*
' *not the Spirit in them*; here are all asleep, asleep in Death.

T. Collier's *Works*, Page 42.

' The *Church of Christ,* under the Gospel, are the *Spiritual Seed,* the Seed ac-
' cording to the Promise.

T. Collier, Page 102.

' The *Church,* which is Christ's Kingdom, are a People *(Saints chosen)* called
' out of the World; they are not of this World, as he is not of this World.

W. Dell's *Sermons*, Pag. 152, 156. 186.

' The *Church* is a *Spiritual Invisible Fellowship,* gathered together in the Unity
' of the Faith, Hope and Love.
' Christ and the Spirit are the only Officers.

CHAP. IV.

His Charge, of our denying to hear the Word of God examined: True Preaching acknowledged.

HE hath maintained this Charge againſt our Anſwer, with the ſame Sort of Jeers and Flouriſh (but manifeſt Inſucceſs too) that he hath done what went before. His Words are theſe.

Rep. p. 61. *Concerning denying the Ordinance of hearing the Word Preached, to my Proof from* G. F. *We muſt not hear Man, &c.* W. P. *ſaith, That is ſo far from making againſt us, that it makes for us at an high Rate. Much like the Mad-man of* Athens, *who called all the Ships that came into the Port his own, while he was for all that, but a poor Thred-bare Gentleman. I proved, that they aſſerted the Light to be only Preached, to be the only Preacher, and only preached to; yea, and the only Obeyer.*

Rejoyn. If this be done, *Erit hic mihi magnus Apollo*; *If to ceaſe from Man be not falſe Doctrine*, then *not to hear Man is no falſe Doctrine*; for Man is taken in the ſame Senſe in both Places; for as God never intended by *ceaſing from Man,* that they ſhould not regard his *Prophets,* who were Men, when they came to declare His Will; ſo neither did G. F. intend that Man ought not to be heard when he comes on God's Errand, or Meſſage, in the Name of the Lord, but *meer Man,* Man in his Natural Capacity and Ability, without the Holy Spirit and Power of God, which is but a Carnal, Humane, and Worldly Miniſtry.

To ſay we only *Preach the Light,* is no more than to report, *The* Quakers *Preach Chriſt*; for our Doctrine directs People to the Knocks of Chriſt, the True Light, at the Door of the Soul, who is the Saviour, Redeemer, and Preſerver of them that believe in him, and keep his Commandments. But that we ever ſaid, *That it was only Preached to; yea, and the only Obeyer of ſuch Preaching,* is as falſe as any Thing that can be ſaid. He tells us he proved it; I will give the ſtrongeſt Paſſage he brought, *J. Parnel's Shield,* &c. Epiſt. " *To the Light of God in all your Con-* " *ſciences I ſpeak.* Very well; And what then? Is the Light therefore preach'd to, taught or inſtructed, when he only *appealed to the Light in all their Conſciences,* concerning the Truth of what he ſaid, as the Apoſtles did? *To the Light I ſpeak,* that is, *To the Light I direct my ſelf*; *To that I make my Appeal, if what I write be not True? For whatſoever is reproveable is made manifeſt by it,* Epheſ. 5. 13. This Conſtruction is Natural, our Adverſary's forced; for nothing is more common with us in General, and that Author in particular, than to turn People to the Light, preſſing their Conformity to the Reproofs and Inſtructions of it, always reſpecting it as given us of God, to be our True, certain and conſtant Teacher, and always have we been reproach'd by ſuch as J. Faldo, for doing ſo. But above all, that this Paſſage ſhould be brought to prove *the Light is the Obeyer* of ſuch Doctrines and Inſtructions, who is the Author of them, is an Abſurdity that reflects *great Ignorance,* or *ſomething worſe, upon our Adverſary.*

We have already declared our Faith ſo freely and plainly in this Matter, beſides the Teſtimony of our daily Practice, that we need ſay no more than this: A True, Living Goſpel-Miniſtry we own; and the Service and Benefit of ſuch an one we have enjoyed; and *Beautiful are their Feet, who come in the Power and Demonſtrati- on of the Spirit, that open the blind Eye, turn People from Darkneſs to Light, and from the Power of Satan unto God,* Acts 26. 18. that He may be their Inſtructor, according to that Promiſe, *They ſhall be all Taught of Me,* which is the chiefeſt End of all External, Inſtrumental Miniſtry. To prove our Senſe of True Preaching, we may add theſe Two following Teſtimonies out of that Renowned *Independent,* Dr. Everard.

Dr. J. Everard's *Sermon,* Militia Cœleſtis.

" Truth it is, many toſs and tumble the Letter ——— and make you believe they
" expound it, and give you the Senſe and Virtue; Yet how ſhallow, how literal,
" how humane, how low, how ſenſual and carnal do they make the World to be?
" Even your Rabbies, your Doctors, your great Scholars; which ſhews, if God
" Himſelf, if the Lion of the Tribe of *Juda,* if the Root of *David* do not open the
" Seals, 'tis not all the Learning, or all the Univerſities in the World can help us
" to the Myſtery, and the Mind of Chriſt, as the Apoſtle calls it, Shadows vaniſh-
" ing, &c. pag. 326.

" I dare

"I dare not offer at any Method in the whole, nor at any Connection in the
"Parts: For I find that all the *Curious Dichotomizers* do but dream and play with
"the Scriptures, feeding themselves with Fancies, and not Truth; for, sure I am,
"the only Method that Holy Men of old observed, was to speak as they were
"moved by the Holy Spirit — There be many Expositions on this Place, which I
"will not trouble you withal, for Men speak according to Men; but the Scrip-
"tures were written by God's Spirit, dictated by his own Finger: We must there-
"fore labour to find out what is God's Mind in the Scriptures, whatever Men say,
"pag. 369, 370.

CHAP. V.

Of True and False PRAYER.

HE pretends in this Chapter, which containeth not a Page, to refute several Pages in my Book, relating to *Gospel-Prayer*, in which, if I mistake not, he hath done Me, and the TRUTH I defend, the greatest Service that a Reasonable Man would desire at the Hands of his Adversary; for the Truth of the Matter is, the Man hath shrunk from his Post, and deserted his Colours, which we shall make appear, by comparing his first Book with his Reply.

Rep. W. P. *according to my Charge, disowns Man's Will, and the Use of his Conceptions, to have any Thing to do in* Gospel-Prayer, p. 122. *and disowns all Prayer that is not By, and In, the Light Within, The* Quakers *Christ. The Reasons he gives, are as Witless, as his Assertion Truthless.* Thus: 'Now, unless Men may 'perform Gospel-Worship, without the Spirit and the Truth; or if in the Spirit 'and the Truth, yet not by the Motion of either, a Thing absurd, it must needs be 'that Men ought only to Preach and Pray by the Motion of the Spirit and of the 'Truth. *How absurd is* W. P's *Reasoning here? As if the Understanding, Conceptions, Will of Man in Prayer, must needs exclude the Motions of the Spirit, or the Motions of the Spirit exclude them.*

Rejoyn. The first Thing our *Adversary* charged upon us in his former Book, was our *Denial of Gospel-Prayer*, to prove which, he cited *W. Smith*, who in his *Catechism*, p. 107. spoke against Prayers of Man's forming, in his own unclean Wisdom, to be performed at his own Time, and in his own Will; which I answered thus.

It seems then, that what Prayer *W. Smith's* Passage reflects upon, is *Gospel-Prayer* in *J. Faldo's* Account: Of this he takes no Notice; he might think it is his *Interest*, but I am sure it was not his Honesty to omit it; for it was to entitle Prayers hateful to God, *Gospel*, that he might have his Will of us, in making the World believe that we deny *Gospel Prayer*; he was far from the Carriage of a Worthy and Generous Adversary in this, that knowing how apt many are to receive any Charge against us, would have acted deliberately and faithfully, as one concerned by the Constraint of Conscience, when he (alas) sent his many Charges as false as black, to incense the Ignorant and Credulous against us; Revenge for the Loss of some Hearers, and that which follows, animating to this *Unchristian Essay*.

But he proceeded thus; That *we own no Prayer that is not by immediate Inspiration and Motion of the Spirit, and without the Use of our Conception and Direction of our Understanding.* He brought two or three Testimonies to confirm this Limb of his Charge; I avoid reporting them by confessing the Matter; my Business was therefore to maintain our Assertion, in order to which, I produced *John* 4. 24. *The Worship of God is in the Spirit and the Truth*, which he left out, and from thence I gave the Argument by him repeated, which he is pleased to call *Witless and Truthless, as if,* says he, *the Understanding, Conceptions, and Will of Man in Prayer, must needs exclude the Motions of the Spirit, or the Motions of the Spirit exclude them.* But this, Reader, we will easily scatter, for if a Man offer up his own Conceptions, he cannot be said to offer up what is injected by the Holy Ghost, by whom alone God's Children cry, *Abba Father*; for by Man's own Conceptions, I mean what simply proceeds from Man, and where any Man prays such Conceptions, he must needs exclude the Injections and Motions of the Holy Spirit, and offer up an Unclean Sacrifice; else there would be no Difference between the Prayers of the Righteous and the Wicked.

The *Will of Man in Prayer* was not mentioned in the first Book: But if by *Will*, he means *Man's Praying in his own Power, and how, and when he pleaseth*, we also deny that; for how can he be said *To Pray with the Spirit, and Worship in the Spirit,* who acts without the Will, Guidance, and Motions, of the Spirit: And if he means the *Will of Man subjected to the Will of God, and Rule of the Spirit*, then we say, *Such Prayer is not in the Will of Man properly, but in his Will, to whom the Will of Man is subjected:* That is properly done in the Will of Man, which is done at Man's Disposal, or is in Man's Power to perform ; but it is not within the Compass of Man's Will to offer up a Spiritual Prayer, consequently, it belongs to the Holy Spirit to furnish Man with that Capacity : So that by the *Will of Man*, we do not understand the *Will subjected*, but the *Will absolute*, and that we exclude. The Will of Man in that Case is swallowed up in the Will of the Spirit, as the Apostle *Paul*'s Life was swallowed up in Christ ; *It is not I* Paul *that live, but* Christ *in me* ; *It is not I* Paul *that Pray, but the Spirit that prayeth in me,* that is, *I* Paul *live by, and through the Life of Christ Jesus, and in Subjection to him* ; *and I* Paul *Pray by, and through the Spirit, and in Subjection to it's Holy Motions.* I distinguish between Things being done *contrary* to the Will of Man, and *not according* to the Will of Man ; for *Paul* might pray not according to his own Will, but the Mind of the Holy Spirit, and yet not pray *contrary* to his own Will, because resigning of his own Will unto the Power and Leadings of the Holy Spirit (to be acted by that, whereby he receives a New Will, even the Will of the Holy Spirit) he does not resist, or act contrary to the Will of the Spirit, though not according to his own Will.

But for our *Adversary* to say, *We deny the Use of our Understanding in Prayer*, is a great Mistake, if not a Slander ; That which I objected against, was another Word by him carelesly, or designedly omitted, to wit, the *Direction of our Understanding* ; for *there is as much Difference between the Use of our Understanding, and Direction of our Understanding*, as between a *Master and a Servant*, as to *Command and Obey :* Understanding is always made Use of by the Holy Spirit in Prayer ; for without it, there would be no Subject for the Spirit to act or work upon, But the *Direction of our Understanding in Prayer*, is perfectly exclusive of the *Direction of the Holy Spirit* ; for there cannot be *Two Directors* ; besides, if the *Direction in Prayer* be ascribed to the Understanding, there is nothing left that may be attributed to the Spirit, wherefore say we, *The Understanding is not to direct, but to be directed in Prayer to Almighty God, by His own Holy Spirit*, according to that Notable Passage, Rom. 8. 26, 27. *The Spirit also helpeth our Infirmities, for we know not what we should pray for as we ought, but the Spirit it self makes Intercession for us, with Groanings which cannot be uttered, and he that searcheth the Heart, knoweth what is the Mind of the Spirit, because he maketh Intercession for the Saints according to the Will of God.*

I offered Eight Arguments in Defence of this Doctrine, whereof he cited but' One, and said no more to it than I have reported ; for that Little he added, was but an Aggravation of his fore-mentioned Consequence. Seven then of my Arguments remain unmedled with ; I will hint at Three, to show, not my Reason, but my Adversary's Shuffle.

If the Children of God are led by the Spirit of God, (and not by their own Wills, Conceptions and Directions) *then no Access to God without it*, consequently, *Prayer without the Leadings of God's Spirit, is not acceptable with him.*

Again, *If no Prophecy or Preaching was to be of Old, but by the Revelation or Motion of the Spirit, though but to Mortal Men, of far greater Reason should not any Prayer be made to the Eternal Only Wise God, without the Motion of the Holy Spirit.*

Lastly, *Man of himself is unable to think a Good Thought*, and as the Professors say, *from the Crown of the Head to the Sole of the Foot, altogether Unclean* ; therefore *he canno perform Gospel-Prayer by the Direction of his own Understanding, Use of his own Conceptions, and Strength of his own Will.*

To this Purpose was my Fourth Argument, which, with those that went before, and follow after it, my Adversary unmanfully declined. I will conclude this Chapter with Six Testimonies ; the first out of a Venerable Author (with almost all Non-Conformists) *J. Calvin.*

In one of His Sermons upon Job 32. 8.

It is the Spirit of God who dwells in Men, *&c.* ' Man (says he) cannot discern
' any Whit of God's Secrets till he be enlightned ; we can never by our *Will reach*
' *so high as to know God, we must put our Reason from us, and renounce it utterly*
' (what says *J. Faldo* to this Doctrine of his Father *Calvin*) Again, if we will have
' our Lord to fill us with his Wisdom, it behoveth us to *become Fools* ; that is to
' say,

See my Answer, p. 133. Rom. 13. 14.

'say, *We must not bring any Thing of our own*, for that were the shutting of the
'Door against God.

H. Bullenger's 4th Decad. Serm. 5. p. 665.

'The Spirit of Man praying in this World, being enlightned with the Spirit of
'God, groaneth and maketh Intercession for the Saints.

W. Perkins, *the* English Calvin, *in the same Men's Thoughts*, p. 336. 21. *writes thus.*

'All Exercises of Christian Religion *are to be in the Spirit. The Inward Moti-
'ons of the Spirit, are of themselves the Worship of God*, whereas our Words and
'Deeds are not simply, *but so far forth, as they are found in the renewed Moti-
'ons of the Heart.*

Gualt. Cradock *upon* Ephes. 3. p. 169.

'That you may see the Greatness of his Power, what a World of Prayers doth
'the Spirit of God put into thy Heart, that thou art never able to utter with thy
'Mouth. All the Wisdom of the World cannot make one Spiritual Petition. We
'may make Forms of Prayer, but now the Spirit of God, that knows the Mind of
'God, *That* makes Prayers according to the Will of God, and *He* (Spirit) prays
'with Sighing and Groaning unutterably: I speak to them that know the Work-
'ing of the Spirit. If the Lord should only hear the Prayers thou mak'st with
'thy Mouth, thou wouldst be a Poor Man, but the Lord respects the Prayer of
'thy Heart.

W. Dell's *Sermon*, Christ's *Spirit*, &c. p. 35.

'When God hath a Mind to give us the Spirit, he puts us in Mind to ask it;
'yea, God gives us the Spirit, that by it we may ask the Spirit, seeing no Man
'can ask the Spirit but by the Spirit, *Acts* 1. 14.

Dr. J. Everard, *the Great Spiritual Separatist, in King* James *and* Charles *the First's Time.*

'Be assured whatever Prayers, whatever Sighs, whatever Groans thou puttest
'up to him, *he loaths all but what His SON makes*; but all his Requests are heard
'and granted, *Pag.* 225. —— Be sure that your Prayers be such as become God's
'Ear to hear; for all the Prayer of *All Flesh* through the whole World, is dis-
'pleasing to God, *Pag.* 243. —— Not the *Best Duties* you can perform, will please
'him, except they be Salted and Seasoned by His own Son, *Pag.* 9. —— Never
'think that all your Prayers, your Tears, your Alms, *&c.* please Him, *but only
'that which is His Son's own Actions and Work in you*, Pag. 355. But know, He
'(God) regards none of these Prayers: But when *His Son, in whom He is well-
'pleased*, when he prays, He hears Him always; but if any other prays, he regards
'not, *Pag.* 438, 442.

'*Again*, 'It must be His Son's Work in us, else he loaths all, even the *Best of the
'Sacrifices*; if it be not Jesus Christ in us that doth all, *viz.* that loves God, and
'fears God, and obeys God, and believes in God, *&c.* His Father regards it not.

But what thinks *J. Faldo* of all these Things ? *J. Calvin, W. Perkins, H. Bullenger, Gualt. Cradock,* are unquestionable, *W. Dell,* Master of *Cajus Colledge* in late
Times; and for Dr. *J. Everard,* his Works were Licensed, *Decemb.* 6, 1652, by
no less Man than *J. Caryl,* and approved by *Thomas Brooks* and *Matthew Parker,*
all Three *Independent Pastors*; the First lately deceased, the other Two not many
Days ago Living, who, I hope, are able to justifie their Kindness to that Notable,
and doubtless very Religious Man.

Perhaps the TRUTH may find better Quarter for these Great Authors Sake,
therefore I bring them, though indeed it is truly lamentable, that the *Professors* of
our Age will not know the Doctrines of Men they hold in great Admiration, when
they meet with them in the *Poor Quaker's Writings*; but instead of acknowledging,
miserably brow-beat them with opprobrious Language, thereby bringing the Greatest Truths into Suspicion with the Vulgar. *But, O Lord God of Truth, This hath
been the Portion of thy People, and Lot of thy Children, whom Thou hast Gathered
out of the World in all Ages, at the Hands of those, who boast themselves in other*

Men's Labours, and have a Name to Live, but are Dead to that Life in which they should Live to Thee: They seem to Honour the Prophets, and Garnish the Sepulchres of Thy Servants that are at Rest; but having erred from the Conduct of Thy Spirit, and resisted the Holy Motions of it, they are become the greatest Persecutors, Resisters, and Vilifiers of Thy Holy, Living, Pure, and Spiritual Way. O Lord God arise for Thy Great Names Sake, seize upon their Consciences by thy Invisible Word of Power; lay Judgment to the Line, and Righteousness to the Plummet; dash their Fine Carved Images in Peices, and let thy Consuming Fire take hold on their Chaff and Stubble, and bring them to Thy Righteous Ballance, that they may see themselves and their Religion to be lighter than Vanity; that they may Witness thy Mighty Work of Redemption and Salvation, before they depart hence and are never seen more, through Jesus Christ, *the Alone Advocate and Mediator, Intercessor, Redeemer, and Saviour of all Thy Dear Children, who have Believed in His Heavenly Appearance, by whom be Everlasting Honour, Glory and Dominion.* Amen.

CHAP. VI.

Of Positive Ordinances, as our Adversary calls them, to wit, BAPTISM, *and the* SUPPER.

HE introduced his Discourse of *Baptism*, and the *Supper*, with an Account of the *Nature of these Ordinances*, distinguishing them by Natural and Positive. He excepts against my reporting of One Part of his Doctrine, calling it by no milder a Name than *Forgery*. I will give both our Quotations, that my *Reader* may the better see what Ground he hath for such severe Reflection: I cited him thus,

'The Ordinances hitherto considered, are called Moral, from their Natural Ob-
'ligation, although respecting their Substance, they deserve a more Evangelical
'Denomination, without which we cannot call them Christian Ordinances. This he calls *Forging, Corrupting his Words, and that he that hath the Conscience to deal with such an Adversary, may make him say what he lists.* Reply, p. 56.

I will now punctually transcribe his Words, as himself hath quoted them, and a plain Self-Defeat will lye at the Bottom of all this Displeasure.

Rep. pag. 66. *My Words were these to a Letter; The Ordinances I have hitherto considered, are called Moral, from their Natural Obligation; although that Substantial and Essential Part and Qualification of them, their Respect to a Mediator, will require a Denomination more Evangelical, and without which we cannot call them Gospel, or Christian Ordinances. Let* W. P. *make the best Advantage for his Cause these Words will afford him; and spare not.*

Rejoyn. Having his Leave, I hope he will not be angry if I take him at his Word; but before I proceed, I cannot but declare my Amazement, in his calling this Circumstantial Omission by no milder Term than *Forgery*, who, God is Record between us, of Fifty Testimonies, which he hath pretended to take out of our Friends Writings, hath miscited, or misreported One Half of them, and imposed False Glosses upon the other.

Now let's see wherein I have wronged him: I will observe every Variation; The *First* lyeth between the *Ordinances hitherto considered*, and *the Ordinances I have hitherto considered*; it seems *I have* was left out, but this is not one Step to Forgery. The *next* lyeth between these Two Passages, *although respecting their Substance, they deserve a more Evangelical Denomination*; and his Saying, *although that Substantial and Essential Part and Qualification of them, and their Respect to a Mediator, will require a Denomination more Evangelical*, the Difference lyeth here; first, that I have put but the Word *Substance*, in the Room of *Substantial, Essential Qualification, their Respect to a Mediator*; wherein I conceive I have not wrong'd his Matter, for the Substance of the Moral Ordinances, and the Substantial or Essential Part or Qualification of the Moral Ordinances are *equivalent*: The Difference only lieth that I did not repeat his *Four Terms*, when *One* would serve, but used the Word *Substance*, as carrying in it the Import of the rest; For the Moral Ordinances *Respect to a Mediator*, I say, they either respect the Mediator from the Substance or Circumstance of them, not the Circumstance to be sure, therefore the *Substance*, and that Word I used in the Place of *Substantial* or *Essential*, as before. I cannot yet see where the Forgery lyeth; but let us proceed; The *next* Variation lyeth between *will require* and *deserve*. Now I know not any Wrong I did him, in saying, *those Moral Ordinances deserve*, instead of *those Moral Ordinances will require:*

quire: The harsher Word of the Two is in his own Quotation. There be yet *Two Faults* more that I have committed, that help to the Forgery in my Adversary's Opinion; The *One* is this, I cited it *a more Evangelical Denomination*, instead of *a Denomination more Evangelical*; The other was this, instead of *Gospel or Christian Ordinances*, I did only set down *Christian Ordinances*. All these Things considered, I cannot believe these Omissions are able to stain my *Credit* in the Judgment of any *Sober Reader*, though *J. Faldo* tells me, *They are enough to stain any Man, which is not all Black already*.

This miserable Shift, and causeless Cry of *Forgery*, designed to amaze and divert the *Reader* from calling upon him for a more *Serious Reply* to the Use I made of his own Doctrine against himself, cannot take me off from pursuing my Advantage; for I think those Omissions so little to his Prejudice, that the inserting what I left out, would, if possible, have made more to my Purpose. The Use I made of it was this:

First, *That a Ministry is grounded internally upon the (Special) Grace and Gifts of God, externally upon the Scriptures of Truth.* Secondly, *That a Well-ordered Church consisting of Religious Members, Preaching, Praying, and that Scripturally too, are by him called* Christian Ordinances, *and made Natural to all Nations before Christ's Visible Coming; and consequently,* there was the Thing Christianity, before the Name of Christianity; *which pleads our Cause against his First Chapter, and his gross Contradiction to himself.* Thirdly, *Those he calls* Natural Ordinances, *and that are of Universal Obligation, are far more Substantial and Necessary to Salvation, than those* Two of Water-Baptism and the Lord's Supper, *upon which he more peculiarly bestoweth the* Title of Christian: *Since no Man can ever be Saved without the One, I mean those* Natural Ordinances, *as he calls them, grounded internally upon the Grace and Gifts of God, and any Man may be certainly Saved, without the other that he so peculiarly calls* Christian Ordinances, *viz.* Water-Baptism *and the* Supper.

I say, his Citation hinders me no more of this Advantage, than mine he excepteth against; for if the *Substantial and Essential Part and Qualification of them, and the Respect to a Mediator,* will require them to be Christian Ordinances (that Part I left out, and for which he quarrel'd me) what Reason can there be for his counting me a *Forger*, and telling the World, That *I first cut off his Matter, and then tell him of Self-Contradiction,* when the Words omitted give a farther Weight to my Consequences, and justifie them beyond all Opposition: For if these Ordinances be Moral, naturally obliging *with all*, Gospel and Christian from their Substantial and Essential Qualification, and the Respect to a Mediator, then there must needs have been *Christian or Gospel-Ordinances from the Beginning of the World*. In short, since he denies not my Consequence upon that Citation I made: and that we have shown the Difference to be little, and what there was to make for me, I think I may well conclude, that my former Argumentation was found. Thus much for this Cavil. He goeth on,

Rep. Pag. 66. *A Passage*, Pag. 133. (*in* W. P.) *I cannot perswade my self to let pass*: W. P. *thus*, It is no less than Blaspheming in our Adversary, and an evident Contradiction to himself, to assert, That the Light he grants those immutable Ordinances to result from, may be doubtful or decay, respecting it self, since it were to say, that God —— were doubtful, and liable to decay. (Thus far *W. P.*) The Light *I spoke of was Natural Light, or the Light of Nature in express Terms, which we dare not, nor the* Quakers *do not say is God, but an Human Faculty.*

Rejoyn He might very well have *perswaded himself to have let this Passage pass*, unless he had given it a better *Reply*: He is willing to bring us in for Stars, but we reject his Kindness.

The *Quakers* say, That *God is the Great Sun of Righteousness, and Fountain of all Light; That he enlightens all with a Measure of his own Divine Light, and that from thence proceed these Moral, General, and Obligatory Ordinances,* which *J. F.* himself confesseth to be *Gospel and Christian;* and therefore it is both a *Contradiction*, and little less than *Blasphemy*, to call the Light a *Sinful, Sordid, and Ridiculous Thing*, as p. 47. of his *Reply*, and yet say so much in Praise of these Natural and Universal Ordinances.

But above all, that he should say, *The* Quakers *Deny the Light to be God*, and own it but for an Humane Faculty, who imploys many Pages to prove the contrary, and not above Two Pages off, expresly calls it the *Quaker's Christ*, shows him either to have been very careless, or not well himself, when he writ so extravagantly.

We are now come to consider the Ordinances themselves, and first that of Baptism.

Rep. pag. 67. *Water-Baptism* W. P. *disowns to be a Gospel-Ordinance, his Reasons I shall answer briefly.* Christ never was Administrator of Water Baptism, pag. 133. *It is Christ's Command, and not his being immediate Administrator, that constitutes an Ordinance.*

Rejoyn. He should have given my first Reason before he had pretended to answer it. I farther told him, 'That *Water-Baptism was* John's *the Fore-runner, used
' figuratively and preparatively to the Visible Coming of the* Messiah, *which being past,
' that Preparatory Dispensation is gone with it ; and lastly, that the Fore-runner is
' not to continue, but give Way to him and his Administration that was so fore-run,
' which were* Christ and His Baptism. *That* John *was to decrease, that is,* Water-
' Baptism, *and Christ to increase,* that is, *His Evangelical and Spiritual Admini-
' stration.* To all this *J. Faldo* says nothing : So that he speaks Truth but by Halves, that is, what he said was *No Answer,* yet it was briefly said. However, I do affirm, that *Water-Baptism* is therefore *Legal,* because Christ is not it's Administrator ; for the Legal Dispensation came by *Moses,* but the Evangelical by *Christ,* not his Disciples ; and this not coming by Christ, it cannot be Evangelical, consequently no *Gospel-Ordinance.* Besides, I deny that it is Evangelical, because He is not Administrator ; for Christ is the alone Administrator of all Things relating to his own Kingdom ; the Temple, Worship, Altar, Circumcision, Baptism, &c. are invisible, answerable to the Nature of his Priesthood and Kingdom. Again,

It is said of *John,* That *the least in the Kingdom of God is greater than he, yet that a greater Prophet hath not risen than* John *the Baptist,* Mat. 11. 11. Now his could never be understood of *John's* particular Condition, but of his Water-Administration ; therefore *Water-Baptism* is not Evangelical. I might tell him in short, That he has given away his Cause in this Particular, by ranking *Water-Baptism* among the *divers Washings,* pag. 50. The Apostle *(Heb. 9.)* accounts Legal, and abrogated, by bringing in of a better Covenant, the great Evangelical Ordinance. Next, let him tell me, *where it is that Christ commands Water-Baptism :* But this perhaps he thinks he hath done, in his Answer to my Second Reason, as by him reported.

Rep. pag. 67. *Again,* W. P. *pag.* 136, faith, That Baptism mentioned *Mat.* 28. was not the Baptism of *John,* but Baptism of the *Holy Ghost,* called the Promise of the Father — He distinguisheth not between *John's* Water Baptism and his own, but betwixt any Water-Baptism at all, and his own Baptism of the Holy Ghost. *Baptism with the Holy Ghost, was not in a proper, but Analogical and Metaphorical Sense.*

Rejoyn. J. Faldo hath done ill to drop my Answer, and render it so obscure, if not impertinent ; for by making that Gap in the middle, to whom can we refer that Word HE ? To *John ?* That cannot be ; how can the after Sentence relate to the former, or be understood as it is ? But thus hath he dealt with me from Time to Time, which I will not call *Forgery,* but *Disingenuity* I am sure it is. I said, as he reports me, That *Water was not understood in that Text :* He shifts it off with saying, That *the Baptism of the Holy Ghost is not a Proper but Metaphorical Baptism.* But what is this to his proving, That *the Baptism in the Text was that of Water, and not that of the Holy Ghost,* which was, and is the Question between us ? I told him, ' That Christ in all Likelihood Commissionated them to Baptize with that
' Baptism wherewith *they were to be Baptized themselves* ; my *Reasons* were three :
' *First,* Because His Baptism was that of the Holy Ghost ; and we are to suppose,
' that he commanded them to Baptize with his own Baptism ; therefore not with
' Water. *Next,* Because these Words, *Go, Teach, Baptizing,* being some of the
' last Words *Matthew* reports him to have spoken while in the World, they must
' need have Relation to that Saying which *Luke* recordeth in *Acts* 1. to have fallen
' from him immediately before his Ascension, *viz. And being assembled together
' with them, he commanded, that they should not depart from* Jerusalem, *but wait
' for the Promise of the Father, which,* saith he, *ye have heard of me* ; For John
' *truly Baptized with Water, but ye shall be Baptized with the Holy Ghost not many
' Days hence.* I say, the other Passage in *Matthew* must needs have Relation to
' these Words, inasmuch as they are by *Two Evangelists* recorded to have been spo-
' ken before His Ascension, it being within four Verses of this Passage, that *Luke*
' tells us, *He was taken up out of their Sight.* For in this Part of *Luke's* Narra-
' tive, the Commission given us by *Matthew* is wholly omitted, which doubtless

1673.

Part II.
Chap. VI.

'was spoken at the same Time; for we frequently find, That *what One Evangelist*
'omits, *the other supplieth*; Therefore I read the Words thus, John *indeed Bapti-*
'*zed with Water, but ye shall be Baptized with the Holy Ghost*; *Then Go, Teach all*
'*Nations, Baptizing them,* &c. Unto all this he is so Silent, as if there had been
no such Thing observed. My *Third Exception* against Water-Baptism, respecting
this Text, *Matthew* 28, 'That the Preposition εἰς or *into* the Name, &c. could
'not be said of Water, therefore no Water-Baptism; which he takes a little No-
'tice of, thus replying.

Rep. pag. 67. *Baptism with Water was into the Name,* &c. *as a Sign*; *and Baptism with the Holy Ghost, which is the Gifts of the Holy Ghost, might also be where
the Persons so Gifted, were not really ingrafted into Christ, or sanctified.*

Rejoyn. That *Baptism with Water* may be *into the Name of the Father*, is not
found, unless it could *Baptize into the Nature of the Father*; for nothing less than
Regeneration is wrapt up in the Text: Besides, that is unworthy of the Spirituality
of Christ's Ministration and Kingdom, that He should make Water-Baptism Two
Thirds of his Commission, which Men may be Baptized with, and yet be as great
Strangers, yea, Enemies to Father, Son and Holy Ghost, as the most impious of
Men. And admitting, that by the *Holy Ghost* is to be understood the *Gifts of the
Holy Ghost*, yet is it *Heterodox* with a Witness, to say, That *a Man may be Baptized
into them, and yet remain unsanctified, and ungrafted into Christ*; for what is it but
to say, *That to be Baptized by the Holy Ghost, is not to Sanctifie Men, nor Graft
them into Christ*; for such hath been his Carelesness in this Expression, that he hath
not particularized what Gift Men may have, and not be Sanctified or Grafted into
Christ, but plainly denies in General Terms, *the Baptism of the Holy Ghost to be the
same Thing with Sanctifying and Grafting Men into Christ*: *So many as were Baptized into Jesus Christ, were Baptized into His Death*: Was this done by Water?
Where is *J. F*'s Figure now he cast to abuse the Text, *Mat.* 28. Again, As many as
have been Baptized into Christ, *have put on Christ, Gal.* 3. 27. I would fain know
by what Figure *J. Faldo* makes Water-Baptism a putting on of Christ; such easie
putting on of Christ, will fall hard one Day upon such as he, and the like Christians. But why should I expect a better Account of these Divine Mysteries from a
Man that knows so little of them, and sets so slight by them? But let us hear him
a little farther.

Rep. pag. 67. *Many Things are expressed by the Word* Baptism, *yet but* One Proper Baptism, *which is Water*.

Rejoyn. If he had said *One Shadowy Baptism*, it had been better expressed, for
that he himself elsewhere acknowledges it to be; however his *One Proper Baptism*
is not the *Apostle's One Baptism*, Eph. 4. 5. unless he will make the Baptism of
Water, and the Baptism of the Holy Ghost, to be but one and the same Baptism;
if he can, he will perform an Impossibility; if he cannot, there will be Two Baptisms, *John's Proper Baptism, Christ's Improper Baptism*, as *J. F.* will have them
contradistinguish'd.

Now which of these *Two is the Evangelical and Durable Baptism*, the One the
Figure, the Other the *Substance*; the One the *Fore-runner*, the Other the *Thing
Fore-runned*? May we not ask of *Water-Baptism* as Christ askt concerning *John*?
What went ye forth to see? One that said of His Dispensation, *I must Decrease,
Christ Increase.* I will not allow of *J. Faldo's* Word *Proper* at this Time, though
allowable enough among *School-Men*, because the Philosophical Sense of it is not
known to the Vulgar; The Word *Proper* now bearing a different Signification; and
in the after common Usage of the Word, *Christ's Baptism of the Holy Ghost is the
Only Proper Baptism*, and, *that of Water but Shadowy and Figurative*. I will give
him a like Case upon his Use of the Word *Proper*, and leave it with my *Reader* what
to call this Part of his *Reply*: There was but *One Proper Paschal Lamb*, and that
was a Beast with four Legs: Also, there was but *One Proper Circumcision*, and that
was the Circumcision of the Flesh; therefore are they Evangelical, or to continue?
But doth not he know that they are notwithstanding abrogated by *That Lamb and
Circumcision*, which according to his Language, are not *Properly but Metaphorically
so*? Insomuch, that after the Apostle's Speech, *that is no more that Lamb, nor the
Circumcision, that is outward, neither Baptism,* &c. *but that which is not in the Letter, but in the Spirit*, Rom. 28. 29.

I more than hinted pag. 138, 139, of my Answer at this very Thing, upon his
making the Baptism the *Sign, and Thing signified, but One Baptism*, as a True Exposition of that Passage of the Apostle to the *Ephesians, One Lord, One Faith, One
Baptism*;

Baptism; But he is afraid to meddle with that; for indeed never Man more over-shot himself, opening such a Gap to *Judaism*, as I suppose no Man pretending to be a *Christian*, ever ventured at.

But he faintly goes on in these Words.

Rep. pag. 67. *W. P. tells me*, p. 137, *of the Apostle* Paul's *Practice. Practice then we see (and all the Reasonable World knows) is not Institution. This is not a very Sound Expression in it self. I do not say, that Practice is Institution, but the Practice of the Apostles, in Pursuance of an Institution, is a Proof of it's Continuance.*

Rejoyn. The Expression is Sounder than he is *Ingenuous*: He neither sets down his own *Passage* nor my *Answer*; how then can he honestly or intelligibly reply: However, he tells us, that he can beg the Question, that is, *That the Apostles practised upon an Institution*; thus he defends his Assertion, by repeating his Assertion. We have great Reason to suppose him pincht, or else we should not find him so tame; here a Man may handle him without Knocks. But why did he take no Notice of the rest of my Answer, and say so little to this; and which is worse, an Untruth too? For he positively lays down in the Second Part of his First Book, pag. 39, this Argument; *Because* Paul *did Baptize some, therefore it was an Ordinance.* Now what can we call this, but a Contradiction to himself, who manifestly infers Institution from the Apostle's Practice, and yet says, He doth not say that Practice is an Institution; unless he will shroud himself under the doubtful Signification of the Word *Practice*, which may as well be used about one Thing as another; but as I meant it of an Apostolical Religious Practice, so he ought to mean in his Use of the Word *Practice*, or else he equivocates.

He also told us before, That the Reason why *Water-Baptism* was not laid upon the Apostle *Paul*, 1 Cor. 1. was, because *His Call was Extraordinary, and out of Due Time.* To which I answered, 'That if he *was inferior to no Apostle in his Works*, 'why should he be reputed so in his Commission? That the Priests generally allow 'them to have been all extraordinarily called (it has been their Plea against our 'Call in these Days) That no Man in our Days has a larger Commission in the 'Point; and lastly, That since he was a Gospel-Christian-Apostle, if Water- 'Baptism had been then reputed a Gospel-Christian-Ordinance, neither had God 'omitted that in his Commission, nor had the Apostle spoke so slightly of it, as he 'doth, when *He 'thanks God that he Baptized so few*; *for*, says he, *I was* NOT 'SENT *to Baptize, but to Preach the Gospel*, 1 Cor. 1. 14, 17. Acts 26. 18.

But to all this, and abundance more, he was willing to be silent: Yet, that he may not be thought to say nothing, although he gives not the *Reader* that Part of my Answer unto which he replies (I conceive lest his Weakness should be too nakedly exposed) he doth at a Venture bestow thus much at Random upon me.

Rep. pag. 68. *If W. P. intended by the Thing Signified, Saving Grace, then it was come to many before Baptism at all was instituted, and Faith in Jesus Christ was required in all before Baptism was offered*; *If of the Gifts of the Holy Ghost, the Apostle* Peter *was so far from Arguing after his Fashion, that he makes it the Ground of Baptizing them.* Can any Man forbid Water that these should not be Baptized, who have received the Holy Ghost as well as we? *But if W. Penn had been there, he would have reproved* Peter *of Ignorance and Sin.*

Rejoyn. No such Matter; But I may well reprove *J. Faldo*, as guilty of both, who is so ignorant as not yet to know the Thing signified; and so sinful, as to charge the Apostle *Peter* with that which his own Words will not bear; for here is no more of an *Institution* than there is in *Paul's* Words to the *Corinthians, As often as you do this, &c.* Christ's Baptism is the inward Washing by the Word of Regeneration, which makes perfect as pertaining to the Conscience, of which Water-Baptism was but a Figure. I grant that the Sign ended not so soon as the Thing signified began, in Point of *Practice*; but I affirm it did in Point of *Institution*. It is not bright Day as soon as it is Day-break; *Shadows vanish gradually*; and Customs (especially if grateful, as were Signs and Ceremonies to *Jewish-Christians*) are not easily left. Water-baptism was the *Prologue* to Christ's Visible Appearance, and when he was come, *a kind of outward Testimonial or Signification of their Belief in the Visible Appearance of the then so much denied, so cruelly derided, and crucified Jesus*: Wherefore I say, it was not Evangelical, but an Introductory Ceremony, suited to the external State of Things in that Day, which in some competent Time so varied, that there could be no Pretence of *Christian*-Prudence for perpetuating the Practice of it, much less any Reason for it's *Institution*; for as the Christian Power and Spirit then brightned, and Christ came to be more and more formed in the Hearts of his People, *Water* gave way to the Holy Ghost and Fire; *John* to Christ; *and their Carnal Historical Faith of Christ* to the Revelation of the Son of God in them, the *one Thing necessary*, even the *Eternal Substance*, that, as He grew up, and put forth himself gradually, wore off all Shadowy and Figurative Observations. Thus did God restore the Kingdom to *Israel*, and bring back the Captivity of his People; having laid Help upon one that is Mighty, *the Son of his Love*, who always was the Baptizer of all them that believe in him, into his own pure Nature, which is that Regeneration, without which, *no Man shall ever enter into the Kingdom of God.*

CHAP. VII.

Of the Bread and Wine, which Christ gave to his Disciples after Supper, commonly called the Lord's Supper.

OUR Adversary begins his Sixteenth Chapter thus.

Reply, pag. 69. W. P. *having little to any Purpose to say upon the Point of the Lord's Supper, hath recourse to his old Shifts; First he charges the* Independents *with the Death of* J. Parnel, p. 141. *But what is that to the Question? and I believe as little to the Truth, as my Hand in the Blood of Kings and Princes.*

Rejoyn. Then is *J. Faldo* deeply guilty of the Blood of Kings and Princes; for certain Persons of that Way apprehended, imprisoned, and hardly used him to Death; *Doubtless, no Murderer, no Traitor was ever handled at that inhumane rate by English-men, as was this poor Young Man by those pretended Saints.* I refer my Reader to the second Part of our *Serious Apology*, p. 185, 186, 187. for farther Satisfaction. Nor have I used *any Shifts* to avoid the Strength of *J. Faldo*'s Charges or Proofs. I am glad when he meddles with Matter; for I find more Trouble, Chaff, Froth and Pedantry, than when I encounter any Thing more solid; But if this be not crying out—first, there is no such Thing, as I will make appear in this very Chapter. I brought several Reasons to justifie our Discontinuance of the Supper, soberly discoursed in four or five Pages: He takes no more Notice thereof, than if there had been no such Thing, saving that he tells us, He *neglects them because they bespeak the Emptiness of their Author*: Such a Way of Replying, that had I loved Shifts more than honest Answers, and could put off my Conscience at that easie but unjust Rate, it would have saved me the Troubl of having to do with *J. Faldo*'s Essays against the *Quakers*. He bestows his Time in making good two Proofs he pretended to bring out of our Friends Writings; how well he acquits himself we will examine.

J. Parnel it seems said [The Bread that People broke in that Observation, was Outward, Natural and Carnal]. This he counted most Heinous. I told him, That the Bread and Wine being of an Outward Elementary Nature and Substance, may in Comparison of what they signifie, be very properly termed Natural and Carnal. Upon which he bestows this Reply, after his wonted Modesty.

Reply, pag. 69, 70. *Very well becoming* Penn's *knowing Divinity and Philosophy; Fire and Air are of an Elementary Nature; are Fire and Air therefore Carnal?*

Rejoyn. We would not that any should think that we intend by Natural and Carnal the worst Sense that may attend these Words; for sometimes they import a Wicked and Accursed State; but simply as they are opposed to Things supernatural and spiritual, and in this Sense all parts of this visible World may fall under their Signification.

Outward relates to the same Thing, and so doth *Elementary*, as vulgarly understood, and by me appropriated. I was not making a Philosophical Lecture, but writing of plain and Evangelical Doctrine; I know that Words in Philosophy do carry a quite other Sense than what they bear in common Conversation. I opposed *Natural* to *Supernatural*; *Carnal* to *Spiritual*; *Outward* to *Inward*; and *Elementary*, which relates to any of these Worlds Elements, to *the Nature of that Food which comes down from above*; and I think *Bish. Wilkins*'s *Real Character* will vindicate me from the Crowing Charge of this pretended Divine and Philosopher.

His next Testimony was out of *W. Smith*'s *Primmer* They [Bread and Wine in the Lord's Supper] are the Pope's Invention. This I utterly denied to have been
delivered

delivered by *W. Smith*, and did require him in the View of the World to produce any such Words out of the Books of *W. Smith*, or any other of our Friends. His Reply is this.

Reply, p. 70. *What W. P. insinuates I charged them with, viz. calling the Bread and Wine Christ blessed, the Invention of the Pope; I am as little concerned to make Proof of, as he is honest to make report of; for my Book lays no such Thing to their Charge.*

Rejoyn. What a silly Evasion is this? Did he not charge us with calling the Bread and Wine of the Lord's Supper *the Pope's Invention?* And doth he now tax my Honesty in saying, *That he makes us to call the Bread and Wine Christ blessed, the Invention of the Pope?* I would fain know what is the Difference between these two Expressions; were not the Bread and Wine Christ blessed, the Lord's Supper? If not, he knows what follows; and if they were the Lord's Supper, then to call the *Bread and Wine Christ blessed*, or *the Lord's Supper the Invention of the Pope, is equivalent*; therefore he ought to think himself greatly concerned to make us Satisfaction for having cast so great a Scandal upon us and our Doctrine. But he hopes to help one Shift by another. Hear him.

Reply, p. 70. *But you are to take Notice that W. P's Words import that very same Bread and Wine which Christ and his Disciples eat and drank together at* Jerusalem.

Rejoyn. O *J. Faldo*, leave of these *horrible Falshoods*: Hath neither Christianity, nor thy Profession, nor common Reputation, Power enough to influence thee into more Justice towards thy Adversary? What Man of Sense can think I meant only that *very same Bread and Wine which Christ and his Disciples eat and drank together?* There is no Foundation for this ill Comment; And I dare appeal to my Reader's Conscience in this Matter: And so meanly hast thou managed this Matter, that thy very next Words show the slightness of thy Reply.

Reply, p. 70. *Whereas my Charge is of the Bread and Wine used in the Ordinance of the Lord's Supper after his Death among God's People and his Churches.*

Rejoyn. What Difference was there in Point of Time between Christ's eating the Supper with his Disciples *just before* his Death, and their breaking Bread together *soon after his Death?* Not a Year; whereas the *Pope* showed not himself till near six hundred Years after. I cannot see, Friendly Reader, how much more criminal I made my Adversary by charging him with saying in our Name, *The Bread and Wine Christ blessed is the Invention of the Pope*, than he hath made himself by his own Saying, *That we call the Lord's Supper eaten soon after his Death, the Pope's Invention*; unless he should deny the Latter to be the same Sort of Supper with the former. In short, We cannot but repute this an Injury too apparent for *J. Faldo's* utmost Invention to cover. But that he may not suffer the Imputation of Forgery, at least a very gross *Perversion*, he thus braveth me.

Reply, p. 70. *If* Penn *dare deny it to be in* W. Smith's *Book which I quoted three or four Times over in* pag. 29. *I shall prove him a Deceiver to all that will but read it,* W. S. *answers to this Question,* ' I would know, Father, how it is concerning ' these Things called Ordinances, as Baptism, Bread and Wine, which are much ' used in their Worship? *Answ.* Why Child, as for those Things they rose from ' the Pope's Invention.

Rejoyn. This Citation, as rankly and partially as he hath put it down, doth not prove that we account the Lord's Supper, either as it was eaten by Christ and his Disciples before his Death, or by his Disciples after his Death, *to be the Pope's Invention*. How can it, since we know the *Pope's* Date to have been so many Hundred Years after that Practice; His Citation must therefore be understood of such a *Baptism* and such a *Supper* as the *Apostate Church* hath presumed to Practise; and that I put not a fairer Gloss than his own Answer will allow, observe these Words; ' and the whole *Practice of those Things*, As They *use them, had their Institution by* ' *the Pope, and were never So ordained of Christ:* strongly implying, that what was of Christ's Ordination was not of the *Pope's* Invention and Institution; consequently, That the *Lord's Supper was neither a Popish Invention nor Institution*; which is yet plainer from his following Words: ' *For he did not ordain sprinkling Water* ' *in a Child's Face, or to make a Sign of the Cross in his Forehead, nor God-Fathers* ' *and God-Mothers to undertake for it*; *Neither did he ordain Bread and Wine to be* ' *SO* (or after that Manner) *used and received*. So that nothing can be plainer than that his Reflection lies against their Manner of practising and using them, and not against the Things themselves, as at any Time practised by Christ or his Disciples and Followers: Therefore he is quite beside the Truth, in telling the World

World that he doth but apply thefe Words *Pope's Invention* to the Name, that is, *Lord's Supper*, which the *Quakers* apply to the Thing; fince we fo clearly diftinguifh between *Baptifm* and the *Lord's Supper* (Name and Thing) and thefe Practices and Ufages of them, which have rifen fince the Apoftacy; Now it refts with thee, Friendly Reader, to pafs Judgment, which of us two hath acted the *Deceiver* (to leave out a great many more of his hard Words) he that affirmed *W. Smith* called that *Baptifm* and *Lord's Supper*, which was in Ufe fome Time as well after Chrift's Death and Afcenfion as before, *the Pope's Invention*, or I that affirmed, and from *W. Smith*'s own Book have exprefly proved, that there was no fuch Thing faid, as *primitively* practifed, but only as they have been fince abufed by the Apoftate Church. For the Supper it felf I refer the Reader to the fixteenth Chapter of my Anfwer, and fhall only fay at this Time, that as it was a Commemoration or Remembrance of Chrift to the Difciples, who were at that Day fo weak in Faith, as *Luke* 24. 11. *Mary Magdalen*'s news about Chrift's Refurrection feemed to them as idle Tales; yet that the Service and confequently the Inftitution of it were void, as they came to witnefs him the Evangelical Supper or Paffover to their Souls, and that we therefore difcontinue it. *Firft*, Becaufe the falfe Church hath made a Market with her imitating that primitive Practice, drawn the Minds of People abroad from the Heavenly Bread of Life, which is only to be received within, and hath been fhedding fo much Blood about it, rendring it and Water-Baptifm the *Seals* of Chriftianity, thereby puffing up People to believe that of themfelves which they are not; Next, we have the Teftimony of God's Spirit, that he is withdrawn from fuch Obfervations that have been fo much infifted on and magnified in the World; Laftly and eminently, we difcontinue it, becaufe Chrift is become unto our Souls that very Thing, which it was moft truly and properly the Sign of, to wit, the Heavenly Bread and Paffover, which nourifheth the Soul unto Eternal Life. Where by the Way it muft not be forgotten how perverfly he wrongs Chrift and Holy Scripture, who turns this Paffage, *Do this till I come*, after this ftrange Manner; *The Lord's Supper is a Remembrance of Chrift's Death paft*, NOT TO COME, Rep. p. 71. wherein *firft*, he makes as if there were a Death to come; Next, Inftead of exhorting People to look for his Coming, until which he bid his Difciples practife it, he turns back their Eyes from that Expectation, and makes the Sign wholly to have Reference to what was paft, and not what was *to come*, thereby feeking to perpetuate his Abfence, and bar out his Appearance (implied in thefe Words, *till I come*) which ends the Abfence, during which the Inftitution lafteth; For the plain Englifh of it framed into an Argument is this: *The Supper is to remember Chrift's Death that is paft, but that will be always paft, therefore it ought to be always fo remembred*. The like may be faid upon the Word *Remembrance*, for if it ought to be practifed becaufe of remembring Chrift's Death, then *for ever*; becaufe his Death ought *never* to be forgotten. Thus it perverts the Text, in that it makes not the outward Supper to ceafe upon his Coming, as *John* 14. 23: *Rev.* 3. 20. (which is the Evangelical Supper) till whofe Coming Chrift bid his Difciples do it: But to continue it upon the Score of remembring Chrift's Death only (which as I faid before, ought never to be forgotten) is confequently to continue it upon Inftitution for ever.

I fhall only leave two Things with my Reader, and fo proceed to the next Chapter; *firft*, That from our difcontinuing the Practice of thefe Outward and Temporary Obfervances, *J. Faldo* concludes, *our abfolute and general Denial of them*. *Secondly*, Becaufe fome of our Friends have denied, rejected and termed *Popifh*, the long Abufe of thefe Things, he makes no Difficulty of charging us in fo many Words with calling Water-Baptifm and the Lord's Supper, as laid down in Scripture and primitively practifed, *Popifh Inventions*, &c. God if he pleafe make this Man fenfible of his notorious Injuftice towards us.

CHAP. VIII.

Of the Doctrine of JUSTIFICATION.

HE introduceth his Chapter of Juftification in thefe Words.

Reply, *pag,* 71. *Upon the Point of Juftification I cited* 18 *Proofs to my Charge, To three of which* W. P. *anfwers by Way of Evafion and Railing, being filent to the Reft.*

Rejoyn.

Rejoyn. I cited but three, and thought them as sufficient as threescore, sure I am, they carried the Sense of the other fifteen, if not, he did ill to produce them. I have answered the Law in the Point. And for Evasion and Railing, if ever I used either, it was not in this Chapter, where I have bestowed ten Pages of Sober and Christian Discourse; unto which he returns me but three Pages in Defence of his former Application of our Friends Writings, for Maintenance of his Charge; and what his Carriage in this particular is, I will leave with my Reader.

His Charge was, *that we denied the Transactions of Jesus Christ in the Flesh to have any Influence into our Justification before God.* Three of his Proofs I considered, and rescued from his Tyranny. The first was this: ' All that are called *Presbyterians* and *Independents*, with their Feeding upon a Report of a Thing done ' many hundred Years ago, *E. Bur. Trump.* Pag. 17. This *J. Faldo* called *Reproaching such as act Faith on Christ's Righteousness and Sufferings by him wrought and suffered when he was in the World*: An Answer that suits all Hypocrites at what Time their Historical Faith is struck at; but what said I? why thus he brings me in. ' *E. B.* meant no more than their excessive Admiration of and Regard to what ' Christ did without; Thus far *J. Faldo* quotes me, and then replieth.

Reply, *pag.* 72. *Then* W. P. *thinks to salve all with his Meanings which are well nigh as corrupt as the* Quakers *Text; for the Admiration of what Christ then did, will admit of no Excess.*

Rejoyn. There is much more Reason that we should give our Meanings of our own Writings than *J. Faldo* for us, since he is always sure to make them against us; if he will not allow us to explain our own Minds, but make it the Priviledge of an Adversary, we are sure to be worsted, be it right or wrong, nor can he escape by his own Practice: But why is my Meaning corrupt, or the Text either? May not, nay, do not People rely upon those External Transactions of Christ, (as recorded in Scripture Story) so as to neglect the whole Work of Redemption and Sanctification by the Power of Christ within? Or is it false Doctrine to affirm that those who hold the whole Work of Man's Salvation to have been throughly wrought by Christ's visible Transactions in the World (thereby excluding the most necessary Operation of his Power and Spirit for the Redemption of such as have been imbondaged by Satan, are *Excessive* in their Apprehensions of what Christ did for Mankind, when visibly in the World? If it be, we must ingenuously confess, we are Holders and Maintainers of corrupt Doctrine. But whilst Scripture is of any Value, that denies Heaven to *wicked Workers* (though fair *Professors*) that says, *without Holiness no Man shall see the Lord; and without being born again no Man shall enter the Kingdom of God; That Men shall reap what they sow; and that Men are sanctified before they are compleatly justified;* We need not much fear to say, That such as attribute all unto Christ's visible Transactions, when he was in the World, are *Excessive* in so doing. And if this be true, how unfair was my Adversary in leaving out that Part of my Answer, which would have farther explained my Mind, and prevented his making so ill an Use of that which he did report; but perhaps, this might be one Reason for his Omission, which ought to have been a Reason against it; for to these Words *E. B.* meant their Excessive *Regard to what Christ did without;* I added, *whilst they neglected, undervalued and decry'd for Blasphemy and Enthusiasm the Appearance, Work and Righteousness of Christ within*, p. 148.

Mat. 7. 23, 27.
Heb. 12. 14.
John 3. 3, 5.
Gal. 6. 7, 8, 9.

To be short, friendly Reader, *J. Faldo*, either design'd to drop this Part of my Answer, that he might the better rack the other to his own End and our Disgrace, (which if he did, it was unmanly, much more unchristianly, done) or, he intended his Reply for my whole Answer; and then his Doctrine will lie thus: *Whoever so regards Christ's Transactions without as to neglect, undervalue and decry for Blasphemy and Enthusiasm, the Appearance, Work and Righteousness of Christ within, are not Excessive or out of the Way in their Apprehension of Christ's Transactions; But* J. Faldo *hath that Regard to the History of Christ's Transactions, whilst he neglects, undervalues and decrys for Blasphemy and Enthusiasm the Appearance, Work and Righteousness of Christ within; Therefore* J. Faldo's *Regard to Christ's Transactions, whilst he so neglects, undervalues,* &c. *is not Excessive or out of the Way.* Thus it lyeth for him; Let us now see how his Reply formeth it for us.

Such as say, We ought not so intirely to regard, or rest upon Christ's visible Transactions in the World, as to neglect, undervalue and decry for Blasphemy and Enthusiasm the Appearance, Work and Righteousness of Christ within, *hold and maintain*

tain corrupt Doctrine; But *so say* E. Burroughs *and* W. Penn; *Therefore* E. B. *and* W. P. *maintain corrupt Doctrine.*

These Arguments are the Natural Import of *J. F*'s Reply; how sound and consistent with Scripture and Reason, is left to the Judgment of Impartial Men. Had E. Burroughs's Works been more ingenuously weigh'd, he would have seen them to have been no witness for his Turn; *for may not Men feed upon a Report of good Things, and for want of unfeigned Repentance, true Faith and humble Obedience, never be benefited by them?* If *J. F.* denies it, he consequently excludes the inward Work of Faith and Repentance from being necessary (says he and all such Professors) to apply Christ's Transactions beneficially; and if he confesseth Repentance and Faith to be requisite for the right and profitable Application of Christ's Transactions, then is not feeding upon a Report of them sufficient (for at that Rate all the *Hypocrites and Lord-Lord-cryers in the World*, however impious, would be certainly saved) doth *E. B*'s Reproof of such who vainly hope thereby to be justified and saved in the Sight of God deserve to be stiled *corrupt Doctrine*. I could here produce many solid Testimonies out of the Writings of several ancient and worthy *Protestants*, but shall confine my self within the Compass of a Passage given us by a present Writer, quoted by our Adversary in his first Book, p. 58, and that is Dr. *Stillingfleet*, in a Discourse called his Six Sermons, ' If they ' did believe Christ came into the World to reform it, that the Wrath of God is ' now revealed from Heaven against all Unrighteousness, that his Love which is ' shewn to the World is to deliver them from the Hand of their Enemies, that ' they might serve him in Righteousness and Holiness all the Days of their Lives, ' *they could never imagine that Salvation is intailed upon the Gospel on a mighty* ' *Confidence or vehement Perswasion of what Christ hath done for them*, p. 160. Thus teacheth Dr. *Patrick*, Dr. *Tillotson*, Dr. *Craddock*, W. *Shirlock*, and others, call'd *Episcopalians*, (to say nothing of the general *Independents* and *Baptists*) How will this agree with *J. F*? But above all, how *Episcopalians are no farther concerned in his Book than vindicated*, a Story he hath the Confidence to tell *in his Preface*, whilst they are so manifestly contradicted in the Great Point of Justification, every common Capacity will see without farther Pointing. And so we proceed to the next Exception he makes against my Defence of a Saying charged by him upon R. *Farnsworth*, as fit for his Turn.

Reply, Pag. 72. *To the second Citation*, (viz. What Righteousness Christ performed without me, was not my Justification, neither was I saved by it) W. P. *seeks to mend one Error by another, much akin to it, thus*, (What gives daily Access and Acceptance to and with the Lord, is that Preparation of Clean and Righteous Adornment the Soul actually receives from Christ, &c. Take Justification in this Sense, and not for Remission—and let our Adversary do his Worst. *There needs a Diver of Delos to make very good Sense of these Words. I am so well acquainted with the Quakers Meanings, as well as their Sayings, that I dare affirm he intends by all this no other Righteousness for Access and Acceptance than what is subjected in Men, and is therefore their own Righteousness.*

Rejoyn. The Words he charged upon R. *Farsworth*, I defended conditionally, that is, That if ever he spoke or writ them, he did not intend any Benefit that came by Christ's Offering of himself by the Eternal Spirit a Sacrifice for all, for the Remission of Sins that are past through the Forbearance of God, which is the first Part of Justification; But that the Justification and Salvation he understood, were not from the Guilt of Sin past by Christ's Offering, *&c. But from the Root, Nature and Power of In-dwelling Sin, through the Powerful Operation of Christ's Spirit in the Inward Parts, in the Heart and Conscience*.

But first let it be remembred, that he cited no Book, a Fault I found with him before, and desired him, just where he leaves off, that the next Time he would let us know what was the Book that afforded that Expression, which he hath not done; next, That he dares affirm we intended our own Righteousness to be that which gives us Acceptance with God; whereas in so many Words I said, that the Clean and Righteous Adornment, which gives the Soul Admittance into God's holy Courts, must actually be received from Christ, *the Lord her Righteousness*, which four Words, with a great many more, he disingenuously skipt. For those Words of his, *subjected in Man*, I know not what he means by them, unless it be a Righteousness within the Power and Ability of Man to bring forth; (for I know no other Righteousness that can be subjected in Men) and that this was not my Meaning (notwithstanding his obtrusive Confidence) my own Words plainly evidence.

dence. He might as properly say, that a Child's *being washed clean by it's Father, is it's own Cleanness, or that it made it self clean*; or, because a poor Man in Rags intreats some better Raiment at the Charity of a great Man, and that he would please to take him into the Capacity of a menial Servant; *therefore that Livery or Apparel bestowed upon him, by which he is denoted, and hath the Access proper to one of his Family, was of his own proper Cost or Working; and not the Gift of his Lord and Master.* If this be absurd, *John Faldo*'s Consequence cannot be Rational.

In short, The Everlasting Righteousness which Christ brings into his People, by which he fits them for his Father's Communion, is not the less *of him*, nor the more of or from us, because *in us*.

But that I may not trouble my self to challenge him to prove this Pernicious Meaning to be ours, he says he will prevent me with a Citation out of *W. Smith*'s *Cat*. p. 74. '*Quest.* What is the Righteousness that justifies in the Sight of God? *Answ.* For we have Life, before we have Motion, to act or do any thing that is pleasing to God, and in that Life we have Salvation, and so Life and Salvation is freely given us from God.

Rep. Pag. 72. *This Citation Mr. Penn had to consider in this Chapter he pretends to answer, but he forbears it among many other, which say more for my Purpose than he dare transcribe.*

Rejoyn. If there were others more to his Purpose than this, he is to blame to conceal them; but believe him that will, I cannot; And we have Cause to think, that if he hath misapply'd this, he would not have been very faithful in the rest; I do seriously profess, I never met yet with his Peer for quoting.

First, There is no such Question either in Page 74, or in several Pages before or after that, if in the whole Catechism.

Secondly, He hath left out five Words of the Answer, which stood us most upon to be cited, and altogether the true Question, which was this:

' *Quest.* But whether do you not depend upon the Things ye do for Life and
' Salvation?

' *Answ.* Nay, we do not so; for we have Life, before we have Motion, to act
' or do any thing that is pleasing unto God.

What, Reader, can be clearer, first, than his Denial of our Dependence upon Good Works for Life and Salvation? Next, What plainer, than that he excludes Action, and consequently Works, as in the Creature, from so much as pleasing God; unless God vouchsafe to breathe the Breath of his own Life, and thereby impower him to bring forth Fruits of Holiness? Lastly, That the Reason of Man's Acceptance is not his own Works or Actions, but his being found acting and working in the Living Faith, which is the Gift of God, by and through which Access to, and Holy Fellowship with God, are enjoyed by his Children —— And thus much *W. Smith*'s following Words tell us; ' and so Life and Salvation is freely
' given us from God, and by his Grace we are saved through the Faith which
' we have in him, and that puts us upon Motion and Action to do his Will in all
' Things, *and yet not to depend upon what we do for Life*—— But do all Things
' which he commands us from the Motion (or first setting on Work) of his Life;
' and this is *Life* before Action, which moves us to Action, and not *Action* before
' *Life*, thereby to attain Life, *Catechism*, Page 73, 74.

Now, Reader, this considered, give us thy Judgment of *J. Faldo*'s daring Proof; Doth it not to a Tittle make good his Charge, *That the Quakers are for Justification by their own Works?* What sort of Conscience must he have, that dares look the World in the Face, and obtrude such *arrant Untruths* upon it? Doth this Scandalous Perversion become a Man who two Pages off tells us *of his abhorring to Mis-cite, Mis-render or Mis-apply our Writings?*

To conclude: He seems to write at all Adventures, supplying his Weakness with Confidence, and drowning the Noise of his own Forgeries by his vehement Clamours against such imaginary ones as he hath provided for me, to go under my Name, which is his greatest of all. I heartily pray to God, that he may be stopt in this Unconscionable Course, and come to find true Repentance, that Eternal Anguish do not irrecoverably over-take him, as the Just Recompence of such Unjust Dealing with us.

His third Citation was out of *I. Penington*; 'Can outward Blood cleanse the Conscience? Can outward Water wash the Soul clean? His Comment upon it is this, *A plain Denial of the Efficacy of the Blood of Christ shed on the Cross to cleanse the Soul from the Guilt of Sin, by it's Satisfaction to the Justice of God.* To which I answered, 'Doth *I. P.* deny or any Way meddle with the outward Blood concerning the Guilt of Sin past, how far it had an Influence into Justification, taking Justification in that Sense. But doth not *I. P.* treat of the outward Blood with respect to Purgation and Sanctification of the Soul from the present (Nature) Acts and Habits of Sin that lodge therein? Is there no Difference betwixt being pardon'd Sin past, *and the Ground of it*, and being renewed and regenerated in Mind and Spirit, *and the Ground of that Conversion?* His Reply to this, though he gives not two Lines of what I now repeated out of my Answer, lies thus:

Rep. Pag. 74. *And if we allow Penn's Construction, that he denied the Blood of Christ, which he calls outward, to have an Influence into Sanctification, he commits a foul Error; for cleansing the Conscience by Sanctification is the Effect of the Blood of Christ, as well as the other. The New Testament or Covenant is by Christ said to be the Cup of the New Testament in his Blood, wherein all the Promises and Mercies of the New Covenant are asserted, of which, I think, Cleansing by Sanctification is none of the least.*

Rejoyn. If *by the Promise of Sanctification to be asserted in the Blood of Christ,* he understands that both the Promise of Sanctification, and all other Promises relating to the Dispensation of the Gospel, *were asserted, ratified and sealed to them that believe, in and by the Blood of Christ,* I shall heartily and cheerfully submit; But if he mean that the Blood of Christ, shed so many Hundred Years ago by the Hands of Ungodly Men, is the inherent real Purger of the Conscience from Dead Works, I must deny what he says; *for the Scripture attributes Sanctification to the Eternal Spirit*; It is one Article of the common Creed of the called *Christians,* viz. the *Laver of Regeneration, which is by the Spirit.* But what is all this to *J. Faldo's* defending himself from abusing *I. Penington's* Words? to wit, that by asking, *Can outward Blood Cleanse? Can outward Water wash the Soul?* He would make him to deny Christ's sacrificing of himself upon the Cross to have any Influence towards the Remitting of the Guilt of Sin past, which is quite another Thing; as this Argument manifests, which naturally expresseth *J. Faldo's* wresting of *I. P's* Words,

He that denies outward Blood can cleanse the Conscience, denies that outward Blood may be a Sacrifice whereby to declare the Remission of the Guilt of Sin past, which is so absolutely and obviously false, that it may be seen of every mean Capacity; Yet hitherto *J. Faldo's* Reasoning runs. Once again, before we leave him, thus:

He that is pardoned the Guilt of Sin that is past, by the Blood of Christ, as a Sacrifice declaring Remission to all that believe, is by the same Blood washed, cleansed, renewed and regenerated in his inward Man from the very Nature, Power and indwelling of Sin; which is as untrue as the other; yet both these Arguments follow upon *J. F's* mis-rendering of *I. Penington's* Words; But his Credit in this Particular is not at all blemisht by his Comment upon *I. P's* Words, if we will believe him; for he thinks it may be justified by a Passage out of *W. Smith.*

Rep. Catech. Pag. 64. 'We believe that Christ in us doth offer up himself a Living Sacrifice to God for us, by which the Wrath of God is appeased to us. *This Passage I cited, which Penn among many others takes no Notice of*; And if this *can be the Blood of Christ shed at* Jerusalem, *on the Cross of Wood, it is a most incredible Mystery.*

Rejoyn. There is no Difficulty, Friendly Reader, in unfolding his pretended *Mystery,* if the Question unto which the Answer was made be considered, which was this, *What is your Faith concerning Christ in you, as a Redeemer?* which relates not to the Blood of Christ shed on the Cross of Wood; wherefore to make the Answer deny Remission of Sins to be declared by Christ's sacrificing of his Body the Cross (which was no Part of the Question to be answered) is like all the rest of his Injustice towards us; If the Answer had rejected that Sacrifice, we should have condemned it, as much as he hath abused it; But unless he denies that Christ offers himself in his Children in the Nature of a Mediating 'Sacrifice, *W. Smith's* Words are so far from denying the Blood of Christ shed upon the Cross of Wood, that he must allow them to be found in themselves; *for Christ is a Mediator*

ator and an Atoner in the Consciences of his People, at what time they shall fall under any Miscarriage, if they unfeignedly Repent, according to 1 *John* 2. 1, 2. as allowably as that he prays in his People, as their Head, which *A. Sadeel* faith out of *Augustine*, and *D. Everard*, as anon. So that upon the whole, this is as strong and clear a Proof, as others that he hath hitherto brought; for as they, so this (in Question and Answer) wholly concerns what Christ is to Man *in Man*, (which was no Part of the Question) and not what he was to any in his Visible Appearance, which was the only Question.

Before I leave this Particular, I must again declare, That we are led by the Light and Spirit of Christ with Holy Reverence to confess unto the *Blood of Christ shed at* Jerusalem, *as that by which a Propitiation was held forth to the Remission of the Sins that were past through the Forbearance of God unto all that believed:* And we do embrace it as such; and do firmly believe, that thereby God declared his great Love unto the World; for by it is the Consciousness of Sin declared to be taken away, or Remission sealed to all that have known *true Repentance and Faith in his Appearance.* But because of the Condition, I mean *Faith* and *Repentance*, therefore do we exhort all to *turn their Minds to the Light and Spirit of Christ within, that by seeing their Conditions, and being by the same brought both into true Contrition and Holy Confidence in God's Mercy, they may come to receive the Benefit thereof*; for without that necessary Condition, it will be impossible to obtain Remission of Sins, though it be so generally promulgated thereby.

To conclude; As in my Answer at large, so here, in short, I say, Justification may be taken in a two-fold Sense; Compleatly, and Incompleatly; or rather thus, compleat Justification hath two Parts; the first is, *not imputing past Sins, or accounting a true Penitent, as Righteous,* (or clear from the Guilt of past Sin) *as if he had never sinned, through the Remission which God declared and sealed up to all such in the Blood of his Son*; and thus far Righteousness as imputed goes, and is the first Part, or Justification begun. The Compleat, or last Part of Compleat Justification, *is the Cleansing of the Conscience, and regenerating the Mind from the Nature, Power, and In-dwelling of Sin, by the effectual working of the heavenly Power of Christ, and bringing into the Heart, and establishing, his Everlasting Righteousness in the Room thereof.*

Some Scriptures Considered relating to this Doctrine.

To the first Part belong such Scriptures as these; *Isa.* 53. 11. *He shall bear their Iniquities* וסבל septuagint ὄισει that is, *He shall bear away their Iniquities,* as did the *Scape Goat* figuratively under the Law; or, *That God would declare his Remitting or Passing over the Sin that was past, and that he would be in Christ reconciling the World unto himself, not imputing their trespasses unto them.* Rom. 3. 25. 2 Cor. 5. 19, 20.

Also Rom. 4. 5. *But to him that worketh not, but believeth on him that justifieth the Ungodly, his Faith is counted for Righteousness*; that is, God acquitteth upon Repentance, and Faith in his Promise, such as have lived in a Course of Ungodliness. For no present Work, how good soever, can justify any Man from the Condemnation which is due for the Guilt of Sin that is past. So that justifying the Ungodly in this Place is *pardoning* the Ungodly; and being so pardoned, upon Faith in the Promise of God, *is accounted for Righteousness*, or as if the Person pardoned had never sinned; and this appears from the 7th and 8th Verses, *Blessed are they whose Sins are forgiven, and whose Iniquities are Covered.*

Again, Chap. 5. 6. *For when we were yet without Strength, Christ in due Time died for the Ungodly*; and, Verse 8, But *God commended his Love towards us, in that while we were yet Sinners Christ died for us*; That is, Christ laid down his Life to reclaim Sinners, and to declare the Righteousness of God for the Forgiveness of the Sin that is past, to all Ungodly and Sinful Men, that turn from the Evil of their Ways by unfeigned Repentance; it was done in and by Christ for all Ungodly Men, but not to the Benefit of any without Repentance Not that People should go on in Sin, but by so recommending of his Love, and sealing such Glad Tidings with his own Blood, to allure and engage them from their present Course of Sin, 1 *John* 4. 19.

He first loved us; Men must not therefore continue in Sin, that Grace (that is Forgiveness) *may abound*; God forbid, Rom. 6. 1.

The last confiderable Place is in the second Epistle to the *Corinthians*, Chap. 5. 21. *For he hath made him Sin for us, who knew no Sin*; That is, *He was made a Sacrifice*

Sacrifice for the remitting or passing over of the Sin that was past, for such as repent and believe; that they might be made the Righteousness of God, or rather accounted Righteous in the Sight of God, as if they had never committed Sin, by not imputing, or forgiving, the Sin that was past.

This Sense the two foregoing Verses confirm, to wit, *that God was in Christ reconciling the World unto himself, not imputing their Trespasses unto them, and hath committed unto them the Word of Reconciliation. Now then we are Ambassadors for Christ, as though God did beseech you through us, We pray you in Christ's Stead, that you would be reconciled to God,* Verse 19, 20. agreeing with Rom. 3. 25. *Whom God hath set forth to be a Propitiation through Faith in his Blood to declare his Righteousness for the Remission* (or passing over) *of Sins that are past, through the Forbearance of God*; which is neither a *rigid Satisfaction for,* nor a *Justification from Sins that are past, present, and to come,* as a late shallow Writer in his *Preface* to the *Hartford self-confuting Pamphlet* idly and falsly call'd the *Quaker converted,* would have us believe, but an *acquitting from or remitting of past Sin upon Faith and Amendment of Life,* which makes up that only imputative Righteousness, that the Scripture holds forth, or we can allow of.

The Scriptures that belong to the second Part of this Doctrine, which makes up compleat Justification, are such as these: *Keep thee far from a false Matter, and the Innocent and Righteous slay thou not, for I will not justify the Wicked,* Exod. 23. 1. *Lord who shall* abide *in thy* Tabernacle, *who shall* dwell *in thy* Holy Hill? *He that* walketh uprightly, *and* worketh Righteousness, *and* speaketh the Truth in his Heart, Psalm. 15. 1, 2. *When a Righteous Man turns away from his Righteousness, for his Iniquity that he has done, shall he die:* Again, *when the wicked Man turneth away from his Wickedness, and doth that which is Lawful or Right, he shall save his Soul,* Ezek. 18. 26, 27. *Not every one that saith unto me, Lord, Lord, shall enter into the Kingdom of Heaven, but he that* Doth *the Will of my Father which is in Heaven,* Matt. 7. 21. *Unless a Man be born again, he cannot enter into the Kingdom of God,* John 3. 3, 5. *If ye keep my Commandment, ye shall abide in my Love,* John 15. 10. *For not the Hearers of the Law are justified, but the Doers of the Law shall be justified,* Rom. 2. 13. *If ye live after the Flesh ye shall die; but if ye through the Spirit do mortify the Deeds of the Body ye shall live, for as many as are led by the Spirit of God are the Sons of God,* Rom. 18. 13, 14. *That the Offering of the Gentiles might be acceptable being sanctified by the Holy Ghost,* Rom. 14. 16. *But this is the Will of God, even your Sanctification,* 1 Thes. 4. 3. *Because God hath from the Beginning chosen you to Salvation through Sanctification of the Spirit, and Belief of the Truth,* 2 Thes. 2. 13. *Was not* Abraham *our Father* Justified by Works, *when he offered* Isaac *his Son upon the Altar? Ye see then how that by Works a Man is justified, and not by Faith only,* Jam. 2. 22, 24.

In all these weighty Passages there is nothing more clear than that Sanctification both ushers in, and compleats Justification. *First,* In that no Man can have Right to Remission of Sins, but upon *Unfeigned Repentance* and *True Faith* begotten in the Heart, which is as well the Beginning of Sanctification, as Introduction to Justification. 2*dly,* That (though we grant as before at large, *Remission of Sins,* not to be the Effect or Purchase of inward Righteousness and Holiness, for it's impossible; but the free Love and Mercy of God, yet) without the Holy Sanctifying or Regenerating Work of God in the Heart, by the Operation of his Eternal Spirit, whereby to do the Will of God, as it is in Heaven, it is impossible to have Access *into God's Tabernacle and Holy Hill,* much less to be justified by him. And indeed, as true Repentance, which is the Beginning of the Work of Sanctification, opens the Way *for the Remission of Sins that are past,* which I call the first Part of Justification; so is Regeneration or Sanctification throughout, in Body, Soul and Spirit, as well the *compleating* of Justification, as Sanctification, consequently *it is that second Part of Justification;* because it is a making Man *just by Nature,* who was before Just but by Imputation; that is, he that was accounted just by not having Sin imputed through Repentance and Faith in the Love of God, declared in and by Christ, *is now inwardly made more just, because made Holy, as God is Holy,* Levit. 20. 7. *Perfect, as his Heavenly Father is perfect,* Matt. 5. 48. *Righteous, even as God is Righteous,* 1 John 3. 7. *through the effectual Working of the Holy Ghost.*

There are Two Scriptures which prove this.

The one is, 1 Cor. 1 30. *But of him are ye in Christ Jesus, who of God is made unto us Wisdom and Righteousness, and Sanctification and Redemption*; where the Word

Word *Justification* is left out, and yet the *Thing Justification* doubtless included and implied.

The other is, Rom. 8. 30. *Moreover, whom he did predestinate, them he also called; and whom he called, them he also justified, and whom he justified, them he also glorified*; where *Sanctification* is left out, yet without Dispute the *word Justification* includes *it*. Nor are we alone in this Judgment, since both Ancient and Modern Writers avouch the same.

Irenæus, adv. Heref. lib. 4. cap. 30.

Irenæus, Disciple to *Polycarpus*, who was Disciple to *John* the Divine Apostle, ' says, *Justi autem Patres virtute Decalogi conscriptam habentes in cordibus suis* ' *legem*. The Patriarchs, says he, were justified by virtue of the Law written in ' their Hearts.

Again, (*Lib.* 3. *cap.* 4.) ' He speaks of many Nations of the *Barbarians* of whom ' they that believe in Christ have Salvation written in their Hearts by the Spirit, ' without Paper or Ink.

Clemens Alexandrinus, Strom. lib. 7.

And says *Clemens Alexandrinus*, who lived in the same Century; ' Ye are made ' of him to be Righteous, as he is Righteous, and leavened of the Holy Ghost.

Orig. Epist. ad Rom. L. 4. c. 4.

And *Origen* also tells us, ' Therefore Christ Justified them only, who have be' taken themselves to a New Life by the Example of his Resurrection, and have ' cast away the Old Garments of Unrighteousness and Iniquity, as the Cause of ' Death. Thus far the *Fathers*.

Of the Reformers from Popery.
H. Bullenger, Decad. 1. Serm, 6 de Justif.

H. Bullenger thus; ' To justifie signifieth to remit Offences (that is, as I distin' guisht the first part; but hear what followeth) ' to cleanse, to sanctifie, and to ' give Entrance of Life Everlasting. Again, ' Justification is taken in this present ' Treatise for the Absolution *and Remission of Sins, for Sanctification and Adoption* ' into the Number of the Sons of God.

D. Barnes's Works, pag. 243, 244, 245.

To him I will add *D. Barnes*, Burnt in *Henry* the Eighth's Days who in his *Discourse of the True Church against the* Romish *Bishops*, asserts in full and pathetical Expressions; ' That what gives her Acceptance in the Sight of God, is her being ' presented to God by Christ her Head, without Spot, *through the Washing of Re*' *generation*.

B. Downam. of Justif. chap. 1.

So *Bishop Downam* of *Justification* distinguisheth and determineth this Point almost in the very same Terms.

I will conclude with some Passages out of *J. Sprigg*'s Book, entituled, *A Testimony to an Approaching Glory*.

J. Sprig. Test. p. 81, 82, 83, 84, 85, 88, 89.

' We may be bold to say after Christ, That *Flesh profiteth nothing*. If you on' ly know Christ's Dying and Rising *without you*, it will profit you nothing, *ex*' *cept* you have him Dying and Rising *within you*. Error in this *is the Root of the* ' *Dead Faith, whereof the World is full* —— *Paul* doth not say, that the Hearing ' that Christ died for the Sins of Men, doth make them free; No, there was the ' Spirit of Life in Christ *Jesus*——Here is that which puts a Difference, *when the* ' *Spirit of Jesus Christ brings the Covenant to the Heart of a poor Creature, when* ' *the Spirit of Adoption and Sonship revealing us God as our Father, revealeth God* ' *in Union with us, our Righteousness and our Strength*, he doth indeed seal us to ' the Day of Redemption; He sets apart Christ's Sheep, this distinguisheth them ' from the other. So that if you lay your Salvation upon an * *Historical Christ*, ' ye will be deceived, If you will have that in which you may confide, you must ' have *Christ revealed in you* in the Spirit.

' This is the Sum of all I desire to commend unto you, that we are not justi' fied, we are not sanctified by Christ's dying, *by Christ's suffering in the Flesh on*' *ly, That is not the compleat Ministration of our Salvation* (There indeed we see our ' Salvation as in a Glass, and it is transacted as in a Figure, as in the History) but
' then

* What says J. F. to this? Is it not beyond what E. B. said of a Report of Christ.

'then are we actually sanctified, *when as God doth send that same Spirit of Adoption into our Hearts*, revealing unto us the Love of the Father, and revealing unto us our Reconciliation, that Reconciliation that was held forth to us on the Cross, but which is dispensed unto us, *by our being offered up upon the Cross, as Christ was*.

All these Persons put great value upon the Inward Work of God and Christ in the Heart, and plainly determine Sanctification and Justification to be one and the same Thing; but if any one have the Preference, the Scripture it self gives it to Sanctification, 1 Cor. 6. 11. *Know ye not that the Unrighteous shall not inherit the Kingdom of God; Be not deceived, neither Fornicators, nor Idolaters, nor Adulterers, nor Effeminate, nor Abusers of themselves with Mankind, nor Thieves, nor Covetous, nor Drunkards, nor Revilers, nor Extortioners shall inherit the Kingdom of God; and such were some of you; but ye are washed, but ye are* sanctified ἐδικαιώθητε *ye are justified in the Name of the Lord Jesus, and the Spirit of our God.* H. Grotius expounds the Word *sanctified* Ἡγιάσθητε accepistis spiritum sanctum, *ye have received the Holy Ghost*, and the Word *Justified*, majores quotidie in justitiâ fecistis progressus, *ye have made daily greater progress in Righteousness*. And D. Hammond, in his Annotations upon the fifth Chapter of the second Epistle to the *Corinthians*, interprets Δικαιοσύνη or *Righteousness*, a being *first sanctified*, and then justified.

To end this Chapter, serious Reader, It is our Faith, that Christ, to conform us to his Heavenly Image, who have by wicked Works degenerated into the Earthly, and thereby rendered our selves Aliens, yea, Rebels to his pure Law of Life, first declares or holds forth Forgiveness of Sins past, upon true Repentance, by the laying down of his Life; and then works out, by his Holy Power and Spirit in our Consciences, the Sin that is inherent, and in the Room thereof brings in his own Everlasting Righteousness. So that our being accounted *Righteous*, is as Christ was accounted a *Sinner*; That is, he was not a Sinner *by Commission or Guilt*, neither were we as of our selves Righteous *by Innocency or Non-commission of Sin*; for then there had been no need of Remission to have been declared by his publick Offering up of himself: But he was so reputed, from *bearing away the Sins that were past through the Forbearance of God*; and we are accounted as Righteous (upon Repentance and true Faith) *because of that Remission and perfect Acquittance of Sins that are past, as if we had never committed them*. Therefore wofully will they be mistaken, that shut out the inward Work of God in the Heart, and stretch this to Sins past, present and to come, without any regard thereto; when as the Benefit of Christ's Suffering, can in no Sense be known or enjoyed, without the true *Faith* and *unfeigned Repentance*, which must precede Remission it self (and by whom, or where is that wrought, if not by Christ within) much more must they go before compleat Justification, which compriseth Sanctification and Redemption, we cannot but pronounce it a Dangerous Doctrine; since it flatters People with that being compleated, that is not; thereby deluding their poor Souls into a Perishing Security.

CHAP. IX.

Of the True Christ. We own, and our Adversary prov'd to deny, him.

THE sixteenth Chapter of his first Book charged us with the *Denial of the Christ of God*; Among other Testimonies that he brought out of our Friends Books; to maintain it, I did effectually consider two; viz. 'This we certainly 'know, and can never call the Bodily Garment Christ, but that which appeared 'and dwelt in the Body. Again, 'For that which he took upon him was but a 'Garment, even the Flesh and Blood of our Nature, I *Pennington* Quest. p. 20, 23, 32. To introduce my Answer, I observed at the same Time, and in the very same Page, *He confest, That we don't deny there was such a Man as Jesus, the Son of Mary, and that God, or rather Christ, was in him*, which I then said makes up our Christ; I meant, God manifested in the Flesh. He replieth thus.

Reply, Pag. 76, 77. *But this I told W. P. was no more than the Quakers profess themselves*; We witness (*faith* Fox) *the same Christ that ever was, now manifested in the Flesh*.

Rejoyn. He should have given us the Book and Page, where G. F. hath so expressed himself; however, we deny not that Doctrine; *for God doth dwell and walk in his Children, who are called his Temples and Tabernacles in Holy Scripture,*
2 Cor.

2 Cor. 6. 16. Rev. 21. 3. But we must for ever reject *J. Faldo*'s ignorant or worse Consequence; That because *we own*, that God dwells in his Children, therefore *he dwelt no more in that Body of Flesh he prepared to manifest himself by than he doth in his People*; Or, that our asserting, that God appeared and *dwelt* in that Holy Body eminently prepared by him, is to be understood in no larger Sense, than that in which we understand him to dwell in his Children. I might as well argue against the Scripture as *J. Faldo* doth against us; Christ was full of Grace and Truth; therefore when he fills his Children with Grace and Truth, *they have as much Grace and Truth in them as their Lord and Master*. Or thus, God was in Christ, and God was in *Paul*; therefore *he was as much in* Paul *as he was in Christ*. It is after this Rate, Reader, our Adversary essays to confute us, as if we made no Distinction between the *Fulness* and the *Measure*, the *Treasury* and the *Gift*; He was full of Grace and Truth, and of his Fulness have we received and Grace for Grace, *John* 1. 14, 16.

The next Thing I observed from what he gave as our Confession of the true Christ, was this, *That he whom we call Christ, is not* John Faldo's *Christ; for he was that Body only that dyed*; here he cuts my Answer off short and bestoweth this Reply upon it.

Rep. Pag. 75. *Here the Word*, only, W. P. *forgeth; he makes my allowing Christ's Body to be his Garment, to imply, it is not Christ himself.*

Rejoin. Why did he not give my Words; who knows by what he quoted of my Answer that he had ever been so kind? the Man knew it pincht him, and seem'd resolved to conceal it. It was this: ' In the midst of his second Proof, ' he inserts these two Words, VERY RIGHT, as his Assent to that Part of it, ' which to me seems as inconsistent with his Purpose as may be, to wit, *that which* ' *Christ took upon him was our Garment, even the Flesh and Blood of our Nature*; ' therefore said I, *John Faldo* as well as we acknowledgeth, That the *Garment* is ' not Christ, unless there be no Difference betwixt *Christ* and his *Garment*; Or, ' that *Christ* was but the *Garment* of that divine Being that dwells therein; which ' were unscriptural and very carnal; and I still say, That Christ's *Garment* can never constitute him Christ. And that, as he darkly calls it the (intire) Christ (as I shall make appear) so hath he in this Concession contradicted himself, and utterly given away the Cause. But he is of another Mind as his Reply will inform us.

Reply, *Pag*. 76. *The Apostle* Paul *calls his and the Saints Bodies their Clothing*, 1 Cor. 5. *yet they were never the less a part of themselves*.

Rejoyn. A meer Rattle for Children. Did the Body God prepar'd for his Son to do his Will in, help to constitute him Christ, as much as the Apostle's Body did help to constitute him *Paul*? If it did, why may we not as well say that *Paul* was among the Fathers in the Wilderness so many hundred Years before he was born, as the same Apostle doth assert, *Christ by Name to have been the spiritual Rock of which the Fathers drank in the Wilderness*, 1 Cor. 10. 4. for if the Body constitute him Christ, as says *J. F.* then he could no more be Christ before he had that Body, than *Paul* could be *Paul* before he had his Body; and consequently, There is no more Absurdity in affirming, That *Paul* was *Paul* so many hundred Years before he was born, than that Christ was Christ so many hundred Years before he was born.

Again, If *Paul*'s Body were but a Clothing, how much more remote doth *J. F*'s Comparison make Christ's Body to be from his Divinity? Since *Paul* did not preexist, Christ did; but he that took that Body, and that Body that was taken, were not of equal Date; for the Body was taken in the Fulness of Time; but he that took it, and manifested himself by it, was from Everlasting. In short, Christ qualified that Body for his Service, but that Body did not constitute Christ; He is invisible, and ever was so to the ungodly World; (that was not his Body) as honest *J. Bradford* told *Arch-Deacon Hapsfield.* B. Mart. 3 Vol. p. 293. and so much the Word χειστος or *anointed* signifieth, which was not outward after the *Jewish* Ceremony, but by the Spirit and invisible Power of God.

Lastly, I will leave it with my Reader to consider what better Terms than *Earthly and Perishing*, *J. F*'s Comparison implieth to Christ's Body; for such was the Apostle's and the Bodies of those Saints he writ to. But he will by no Means have himself concerned with a great Part of my following Discourse, which was, he thinks, in Opposition to no Body; because I argued that the meer Body of Christ could not be the *intire Christ* (though he makes our Denial of it to be a disowning of the true Christ) producing a Passage out of his Book to my Purpose in Contradiction to himself, *viz*. p. 72. *The Flesh and Blood of Christ we do not believe to*

be

be Chriſt, ſeparated from his, Man's Soul, or that to be Chriſt ſeparated from his Divine and Eternal Nature; beſtowing upon me for ſo ill employing of my Time, theſe Terms, *Vain Trifler—Pedantick Magiſterialneſs, Forger, and that it is a greater Wickedneſs than being a Thief*; to make him aſſert the meer Body to be the intire Chriſt; adding, *but this is Penn's high-way and beaten Road*. One would think after all this, that I had wronged him with all imaginable Baſeneſs, in faſtning upon him any ſuch Concluſion; yet if I make it not appear by his Reply (which one would think, he ſhould have penned a little more cautiouſly after he had given ſuch Occaſion by his former Diſcourſe) and that too in his very next Page, let my Reader ſay, I merit all thoſe hard Words that *J. Faldo* flingeth ſo angrily upon me.

He produceth ſeveral Scriptures to prove (as I underſtood him) the Manhood to be the Chriſt of God or (elſe he did nothing) for without ſo believing and arguing, it was impoſſible for him to prove our Denial of the true Chriſt, becauſe we aſſerted Chriſt to have been before that Body, conſequently that it was not the intire Chriſt which I explained and reſcued. He omits giving the Reader any Account of it, only in general Terms, and that not without Perverſion; His Reply unto which will make good my Conſtruction of his Words, or I am greatly miſtaken.

Rep. Pag. 77. *Whereas I produced Abundance of Scriptures to prove that the Man Jeſus is the Chriſt*, W. P. *will by no means allow them to have that Senſe; no, not that in* Luke 2. 26. *And it was revealed to him (Simeon) by the Holy Ghoſt, that he ſhould not ſee Death before he had ſeen the Lord's Chriſt, neither that the Child Jeſus whom* Simeon *took up in his Arms, was the Chriſt*; Certainly, (ſays W. P. Pag. 161.) This Allegation from *Luke* 2. 26. will never prove the Body of Jeſus, which the Father prepared for him, to be the *whole intire* Chriſt, &c. *Neither did I produce it to prove the Body to be ſuch; what Diſputing can there be with a Man that keeps neither to my Words, nor to the Queſtion.*

Rejoyn. But is this the great Enemy to Forgery, the expreſs Quoter, one that cites to a Tittle, and ſcorns, as to Ignore his own Conceſſions, ſo to render his own Concluſions for his Enemies Aſſertions? Who charges me with denying this Paſſage among others, as any whit proving the Man Jeſus to be the Chriſt, whilſt he quotes my own Concluſion upon it to have been no other than *the Body of Jeſus*, to have been the *whole and intire Chriſt*. Now he can't compaſs his End, he produced not thoſe Scriptures to prove any ſuch Thing; but what is clearer than that it is the ſame Thing with *J. Faldo*, to deny the Body of Jeſus to be the intire Chriſt of God, *and to deny the Chriſt of God*; conſequently, that by the Chriſt of God he underſtands with L. Muggleton only the Body that died? So that he did but evade, when he ſaid that I argued againſt no Body, in affirming and proving that the Body taken in that Time was not the whole Chriſt of God; and that he produced thoſe Scriptures to that very End, notwithſtanding what he ſays to the contrary; for what elſe can any infer, when he ſo obviouſly makes no Difference between ſaying, The Man Jeſus is not Chriſt, and *the viſible Body of Jeſus is not the whole intire Chriſt*.; Thus, Reader, he Faulters at the Entrance. I will give a brief Account of near two Pages of Anſwer by him omitted.

' It is and will be granted that *Simeon* ſaw the Lord's Chriſt; but I hope *J. F.*
' will not deny unto that good Man who waited for *Iſrael's* Conſolation, that he
' had as well a ſpiritual as natural, an inward as outward, Sight of Chriſt; for it
' were both to deny Chriſt's Divinity, and to conclude *Simeon* void of any ſpiritu-
' al Sight or Intendment in theſe Words of the Lord's Chriſt, *as a Light enlight-*
' *ning the Gentiles,* &c. though ſtill be it underſtood, *that we confeſs that Child as*
' *ſeen and underſtood by* Simeon, *with reſpect to that great End of his Appearance, to*
' *be the Lord's Chriſt*; Let none then be ſo unjuſt as to infer we deny the Lord's
' Chriſt, becauſe we rather chuſe to ſay the Body of Chriſt, than Chriſt; for ſays
' *J. Faldo* as well as we elſewhere, *Chriſt is God* manifeſt in Fleſh; See my *An-*
ſwer, Page 161.

Nothing can be clearer than that I only argued in Oppoſition to his carnal Doctrine, againſt the meer Body's being the Chriſt of God, Now, ſince he makes me hereby to deny the Man Chriſt Jeſus, I muſt conclude, that by the *Man Jeſus* he underſtands no more than the *meer Body of Jeſus*, otherwiſe, how do I deny the Man Jeſus to be the Chriſt of God, in only ſcrupling to call the *meer and only Body of Jeſus the Chriſt of God*. His next Animadverſion was this.

Reply,

Rep. Pag. 78. *Let us observe how* W. P. *abuses that Scripture,* Acts 5. 30, 31. *The Words (says he) are thus to be understood, The God of our Fathers (who raised up (the Body of) Jesus from the Dead, which ye slew, and hung upon a Tree, him (whose Body you so cruelly used) hath God exalted at his Right Hand,* &c. *Beside this Construction, which renders it not to be Christ, but only his Body which suffered, and so Christ never suffered nor died, nor rose, he* (W. P.) *puts instead of* whom he slew, which he slew, *that it may intend only the Body, and not the Person of Christ.*

Rejoyn. I appeal to my *Reader's* Understanding and Conscience, if *J. Faldo* doth not in this Sentence, make the *meer Body of Christ to be the Christ of God* ; for one Reason why he denies my Interpretation, is my making the *meer Body* only to have dyed, which not being the *intire Christ of God*, it was not He, but his Body only that dyed: So that either *J. Faldo* holds the *meer Body to be the Christ*, or else, *that something more dyed than the meer Body*: But because he acknowledgeth the *Deity* could not dye, nor that the *Soul did dye*, it must follow that the *Body* only dyed: And since he will strictly have it, *That the Christ of God dyed, the meer Body must be the Christ of God*.

His Second Exception is very trivial, and what in it can be thought to deserve an Answer, is included in what was said before ; for *whom* might be attributed to the Body, as it represented the whole or intire Christ, that is Metonymically spoken, the *Thing containing*, for the *Thing contained*, which is very frequent in Scripture ; for many times that is ascribed to the Body of *Jesus*, *which belongs to the Whole Christ*. This, with abundance more of pertinent Answer, he takes no more Notice of than if it had never been written. But a little to give *J. F.* his Humour, and to see if the Upshot rises higher than *which*. What doth he understand by the Person slain? (according to *J. F*'s own Distinctions) Was it the Godhead? That he denies, *Book the First, Part* 2, *pag:* 73. Was it the Man's Soul? No. Reply, *pag.* 78. *Must it not be the Body then?* And if so? What corrupting of Scripture is it to say, *which ye slew*, instead of *whom ye slew*? 'Tis at this slender trifling Rate he hath dealt with us throughout the Controversie. Two Passages more before we conclude this Chapter.

Upon my recollecting the Whole of this Argumentation, and concluding thus, *Since the Divinity could not dye, and the Man's Soul was not Mortal, much less could be hanged on a Tree, or put into a Sepulchre,* it follows, *That it was the Visible Body only that dyed,* &c. *and that it is therefore the Intire Lord and Saviour Jesus Christ,* in *J. F*'s, as well as Blasphemous *L. Muggleton's* Sense ; he makes this Reply Word for Word.

Rep. 78. *But if it follows upon my Sense, it follows upon the Words and Scope of the Scripture, which saith the same in so many Words, and in Sense an hundred times. But there is no such Absurdity follows upon either ; The Soul can't dye, cannot therefore the Man dye? If not, there is no such Thing, as killing of Men, or Mortal Men.*

Rejoyn. Man cannot properly be said to dye whilst his Soul lives, but he may be said *to cease to be in this Visible World, or to depart out of it, and to lay down his Mortal Body* ; so that the Body dyes but not the Man ; I know it is a common Phrase, but synecdochically spoken, where that is ascribed to the whole Man, which only belongeth to the Mortal Part of Man. This brings the Business no nearer than it was before ; for if I understand any Thing, *the Comparison makes the Death of Christ to be the Death of his Body only*, and that it is call'd the Death of Christ, instead of the Death of the Body of Christ, from that familiar Usage in Speech, the *Thing contained*, for the *Thing containing*, that is, *Christ*, instead of the *Body of Christ*. In short, because such Murderers, who are said to kill Men, kill only the Bodies of Men ; those *Jews* who crucified Christ, properly crucified the Body of Christ only, though in a more Mystical Sense, they may be also said in that very Action, to have murdered the *Prince of Life and Glory,* 1 Cor. 2.

His other Passage, containeth a Reflection upon my Saying, *That Souls could not be Hanged on a Tree.*

Rep. pag. 79. *I had thought that the Soul being United with the Body till Death, where-ever the Body was disposed, the Soul was also ; and therefore the Body so long as it liveth, hanging on a Tree, the Soul hangs there too ; also many a poor Wretch can tell him at the Torment of Execution, that his Doctrine is false ; for were but their Souls separated from their Bodies, they would feel no Pain, nor cry out of their Torment.*

Rejoyn. A very Shuffle, and nothing to the Purpose. The Soul is in the Body so long as the Body is alive upon the Tree, and yet it self not strictly hanged on the Tree; for if it were, then would it be as impossible for the Soul as Body to free it self, whilst the Soul by his own Allowance is incomparable and impassible, because immaterial; whereas *Nails, Ropes,* or any other Instruments of Cruelty, can only fasten upon Material Things; for if the Soul could be properly hanged, She could as well be burnt, and laid into a Sepulchre. A Man might as well say, if *J. Faldo* were hanged on a Tree, his Watch in his Pocket would be hanged; or if he were put in the Stocks, his Understanding would be in the Stocks. Nor hath any poor Wretch Reason to complain of my Doctrine at his Execution; for I never denied, that Pain was a Sign of the Soul's not being separated, since it is an undeniable Reason, why it is not separated; however, it is not the Soul, but the Body (through that Sensibility the Soul, while unseparated, continues in it) which feels that Pain.

But I could tell *J. Faldo* of many Blessed Martyrs, that in the midst of Flames, were carried above the Sense of Pain; not because their Souls were not in their Bodies at the Stake, but from the exceeding Joy of the Holy Spirit, which by the Way may as well be said to be tied to the Stake, as the Soul, because in the Soul; for that is the Conclusion of *J. F*'s Argument; The Soul is in the Body, therefore the Soul is as well tied as the Body; the Holy Spirit and his Comforts are in the Soul, therefore tied as well to the Stake as either Body or Soul.

In short, Souls may be hanged upon Trees, as Souls in Scripture are said to die, or be slain, an *Hebrew* Phrase; not that Souls really did die or were slain, but that Man is called many Times by his nobler Part.

I shall conclude this Chapter with a few Reasons for the Hope that is in us, concerning the Subject Matter of this Chapter, and two or three Testimonies in Confirmation of them, which I offer with all Tenderness of Conscience unto my serious Reader.

First, This Opinion of our Adversary's renders Christ not to have been the Saviour of the World from *Abel*'s Day, contrary to Scripture, which teacheth us to believe, *That there was never another Name or Power by which Men could be saved, than the Name and Power of Jesus Christ,* Acts 4. 12.

Secondly, It makes Christ's Words either an *Equivocation* or a Contradiction, when he said unto the *Jews, Before* Abraham *was I am*; since it makes him that was before *Abraham,* and him that said so, not the same Person or Being rather.

Thirdly, Because χριϛὸς, or *Anointed,* hath a Relation to his being King, Priest, and Prophet, which are both of a more Spiritual Nature and Dignity, than the Flesh Christ took of the Seed of *Abraham*; for he was made the High Priest of the second Covenant, was without beginning of Days or End of Life.

Fourthly, Because Christ himself magnifieth the *Spirit above the Flesh*; They look not farther than his Body, or Flesh as it was visible to the World, and he appointed them to look farther, yea, to his Flesh and Blood Spiritually, which is Meat indeed, and Drink indeed, being that living Bread which came down from Heaven, that who eats thereof shall live for ever, *John* 6. 48, to 58, and 63. And those that see not through and beyond that visible Body or Flesh, which was the Vail which the Eternal Word took to transact and represent as in a common Person, that which every Child of God ought measurably to witness in his own Particular, unto the beholding and partaking of the Divine Wisdom, Power and Righteousness that dwelt therein, which are Meat indeed and Drink indeed unto every hungry and thirsty Soul, they are not yet come to the Chief *Corner-Stone that is Elect and Precious,* but are carnal, not knowing the Scriptures nor the Power of God, *Matt.* 22 29.

Fifthly, Christ Jesus laid far more Weight upon the Coming of the Comforter, or himself, in his second and spiritual Appearance in them, among whom he bodily conversed, than upon the Continuance of his bodily Presence, *John* 16. 7. intimating that he intended a more spiritual Communion with them, *they in him, and he in them, even as he was in his Father, and his Father in him,* Chap. 17. 21, 23, a Fellowship beyond what they had already known, how could it otherwise have been *expedient* as the Text expresseth it, if the Change from his visible to invisible Presence, had not been both more glorious and advantagious: His Disciples believed him for the Words he spoke, Chap. 16. 30. But Ver. 31, 32, Jesus answered them, *Do you now believe? Behold, the Hour cometh, yea, is now come, that ye shall be scattered every Man to his own*; as much as if he had said, You shall then know me, and believe in me upon a more clear and certain Ground, when you shall have received thus of my Fulness, *and Grace for Grace*, John 1. 16. and be scattered to it, which is hard to be done while I stay in this Capacity among you; therefore it is *expedient* that I go away, as to my bodily Presence, *John* 16. 7. (on which you have such great Dependence) but I, *(Christ)* will not leave you Comfortless, *I will come a Comforter unto you*, Chap. 14. 3, 18, 19, 20. *For lo I am with you always, even to the End of the World*, Matt. 28. 20. this is the Christ of God.

Sixthly, Because the Apostle *Paul* desired not, thenceforth to know Christ after the Flesh, but spiritually, as he was the Son of God revealed in himself, 2 *Cor.* 5. 16. *Gal.* 1. 15, 16. And as the Apostle counted all other Knowledge Dross and Dung to that of the Glory of God in the Face of Jesus Christ revealed in him; so was he not contented that the *Galatians* should rest in a fleshly Knowledge of Jesus Christ, *but travelled in Birth with them* (like a faithful Witness of the inward Work of God) *a second Time until Christ was formed in them*, Gal. 4. 19. who doubtless was the true Christ.

Seventhly, Because that Flesh of Christ is called a *Vail*, but he himself is *within* the Vail, which is the Holy of Holies, *whereinto* Christ Jesus our High Priest hath *entred*, Hebr. 10. 20, 21. And as he descended into, and pass'd through a Suffering State in his fleshly Appearance, and returned into that State of Immortality and Eternal Life and Glory from whence he humbled himself, which was and is the Holy of Holies (then obscur'd or hid by his Flesh or Body within the Vail) while in the World) so must all know a Death to their Fleshly Ways and Religions, yea their Knowledge of Christ himself after the Flesh, or they stick in the Vail, and never enter into the Holy of Holies, nor come to know him in any Spiritual Relation, as their High and Holy Priest that abides therein.

Eighthly, Because that Christ lives and dwells in the Hearts of his Children, *John* 14. 23. Chap. 15. 5. Chap. 17. 21. *Colos.* 1. 27. which cannot be said of the Outward Body of Christ.

Therefore I cannot by any Means believe that the meer visible Flesh and Body constitutes Christ; though I shall confess, that respecting the Administration, and the Service of that Holy Body (fitted and qualified of God as an Instrument to usher, introduce and bring it forth into the World) it may very well have attributed to it the Name *Christ*, being so nearly related; But rather that Divine Nature, Wisdom, Power, Righteousness, Grace and Truth, of which he is the Fulness, (whose transcending Glory was vailed by that Body of Flesh he wore, and was only let forth in that Day as any were capable of beholding and receiving it) which dwelt therein. And those who at this Day do feed upon the History of the Bodily Appearance (yet honourable in it's Place) and know not a Breaking through the Vail, by witnessing a Measure of the same Divine Wisdom, Power, Righteousness, Grace and Truth revealed and born forth in themselves, they are but carnal and fleshly *Christians*, being unacquainted with the Formation of the Christ of God in themselves, which is the opening of the Mystery of Christ, God manifested in the Flesh, and Christ abiding the Hope of Glory in the Souls of his People.

This distinction, friendly Reader, of *Christ* and his *Body*, is very unpleasant to me; but I am thrust into it by the loud Clamours of our Adversary against us, and as too short, he wrests our Words so as to rebuke his fond Absurdities, I hope sufficiently detected, and which was more in my Eye, and indeed lay hardest upon my Spirit, to oppose and defeat his Carnal Objections against the Glorious Christ of God; for, by his vehement Out-cries at us, as Persons denying the Christ of God, because we rather chuse to call that Body that was prepared of God, the *Body of Christ*, than *Christ himself*, to beat People off at once from hearkening after our Doctrine of the spiritual Second Coming of Christ into the Souls of Men; for if his Doctrine be true, Christ doth not really dwell in his Children; thereby depriving the Children of Men from the most Heavenly Enjoyment and Privilege God hath laid up for them that Fear him: For I am bold to affirm, and that in the Name of the only True and Wise God, *The True Church is become Christ's Body, and he* (the Divine Wisdom, Power, and Righteousness) *lives, reigns, and puts forth himself in and by her*; *and that all those who come not thus to experience the Christ of God to dwell in them, their King, Prophet and High Priest*, (who is without Beginning of Days and End of Life) *they are ignorant of God's Christ, do stick in the Vail, and know not any Entrance into the Holy of Holies, where the*

Divine Unction from the High Priest is received, and the Blessed, Holy, Spiritual Fellowship of the Gospel is witnessed; for which Glorious Dispensation we contend through all Difficulties, making it our Business to promote it in the World; and though it be now but as a Cloud of a Span long, yet it shall spread and cover the Heavens, from whence the Inhabitants of the Earth shall receive Refreshment, being bedewed and covered with the Virtue and Righteousness thereof, for want of which the World is as a Wilderness, being over-run with all Manner of Impiety under a specious Shew of Religion, making up that Whore of *Babylon* and Mother of Harlots, and City filled with all Sorts of Abomination, against which the Wrath of God is now, and will yet be more and more revealed. O! Compassion to the Souls of Men, our Brethren in the Flesh, opens our Mouths with frequent Cries, that they would come out of her, lest they be Partakers of her Plagues; *for, knowing the Terrors of the Lord, we therefore perswade them to a diligent Search after the one Thing necessary, which shall never be taken from them,* I mean, *the Testimony of Jesus in themselves, that they are his by the Washing of Regeneration:* For with great Sorrow I write it, God knows; Unspeakable and Irreparable is the Loss Multitudes have sustained by such Carnal Conceits, as their Preachers through Blindness have begot a Belief in them of, and a Zeal for, as sufficient to Salvation, to the suspecting and open decrying under the hateful Names of *Error, Heresy* and *Blasphemy*, the very Soul or Substance of *True Christian* Religion, which only brings to the Inheritance of it.

For us, our Appeal is to God, and that Impartial Generation he is now bringing forth, who will have an Ear to hear, and a Palate to favour and taste the Truth of this Ancient Mystery, *Christ in them the Hope of Glory*, at what Time these Testimonies shall be of value, however dis-regarded by the false *Jew* and Carnal *Christian* of the present Age.

I will end my Part herein with our most solemn Confession in the Holy Fear of God, *That we believe in no other Lord Jesus Christ than he who appeared to the Fathers of old at sundry Times and in divers Manners, and in the Fulness of Time took Flesh of the Seed of* Abraham, *and Stock of* David, *became* Immanuel, God manifest in Flesh, *through which he conversed in the World, preached his Everlasting Gospel, and by his Divine Power gathered faithful Witnesses; and when his Hour was come, was taken of cruel Men, his Body wickedly slain, which Life he gave to proclaim, upon Faith and Repentance, a general Ransom to the World; the Third Day he rose again, and afterwards appeared among his Disciples, in whose View he was received up into Glory,* but returned again, *fulfilling those Scriptures,* He that is with you, shall be in you; I will not leave you comfortless, I will come to you again, and receive you unto my self, *John* 14. 3, 17, 18. and *that he did come and abide as really in them, and doth now in his Children by Measure, as without Measure in that Body prepared to perform the Will of God in; That he is their King, Prophet and High Priest, and intercedes and mediates on their Behalf, bringing in Everlasting Righteousness, Peace and Assurance for ever into all their Hearts and Consciences; to whom be Everlasting Honour and Dominion,* Amen.

A few Testimonies in Defence of our Sense.

B. Jewel's *Sermon upon* Jos. 6. 1, 2, 3.

My first Testimony is out of that great *English* Author and worthy Man Bp. *Jewel*, who speaking of what Christ was to the Jews in the Wilderness, says thus; 'Christ had not yet taken upon him a Natural Body, *yet they did eat his* 'Body; He had not yet shed his Blood, *yet they drank his Blood.* St. *Paul* saith, '*all did eat the same Spiritual Meat*, that is, the Body of Christ: *All did drink of* '*the same Spiritual Drink,*that is,the Blood of Christ; and that as *Verily and truly as* '*we do now*; and whosoever then did so eat *lived for ever.* I think a pregnant and apt Testimony to Christ's being the Christ of God before his Coming in the Flesh. But this being the Language of a Bishop, though more than an Hundred Years old, perhaps his Stomach will not digest it, and therefore let's hear what some considerable Separatists will tell us.

Joshua Sprig. *Test. to an Approaching Glory,* p. 80, 81, 86.

' I beseech you, therefore, be not offended, when, as we say, That Christ, ac-
' cording to the *History* of him, only, and according to his Ministration in the
Flesh,

' Flesh, is but a Form, in which God doth appear to us; and in which God doth
' give us a *Map* of Salvation; Thou knowest it not to be thy real Salvation, *ex-*
' *cept it be revealed in thee by the Spirit* —— *A Map serves until a Man knows the*
' *Country*—— There is Christ in the Flesh and Christ in the Spirit; Christ in the
' Flesh is the Witness, the common Person in whom our Salvation is transacted as
' in a Figure; Christ in the Spirit, *is the real Truth and Principle of Righteousness,*
' *and of Life*; *he is the real Salvation within us.* Again, in his Preface, he saith,
' That in that Degree that the Spiritual Administration takes Place, *the Fleshly*
' *Administration gives place*; in that Measure that Christ's Second Appearance
' draws on us, *we are drawn from under his first Appearance.*

Thus far *Joshua Sprig*, whose Book was licensed, as we have formerly said, by *Joseph Caryl*, a reverend Minister among the Independents.

C. Goad's *Last Testimony*, p. 76, 77.

' Destroy the Vail, and destroy Death; the taking away of the Vail is the ta-
' king away of Death; Death, upon a true Account, is nothing but a Vail upon
' God who is our Life, even Christ's Flesh was a Vail. Ordinances are Vails. If
' God be our Life, *the less we are in these Things, the more we are in Life.*

T. Collier's *Discovery of the New Creation*, Page 399.

' We have had very narrow Apprehensions of Christ, and the Manifestation of
' the Glory of Christ, *limiting it to the one Man,* when the Truth is, *that Christ*
' *and all the Saints make up but one Christ,* 1 Cor. 12. 12. And God as *truly ma-*
' *nifesteth himself in the Flesh of all his, as he did in Christ,* although the Measure
' of that Manifestation is different.

What says *J. Faldo* to these Things? Are not we out-done in our Expressions by professed Ministers, and those of the *Independent* and *Baptist* Way? Shall we be stiled Blasphemers, that more modestly utter our Belief, whilst these Men, notwithstanding, pass for Orthodox? I hope *J. Faldo* has more Reverence for *J. Caryl*, than to question his Judgment in the License of the first; and not so little Respect for the two last, as to cry out *Heresy, Blasphemy, &c.*

CHAP. X.

Three Scriptures rescued from the False Glosses of our Adversary; John 1. 9. Rom. 10. 3. 2 Pet. 1. 19.

OUR Adversary employs his 19th Chapter in Defence of his Exposition of three Passages in Scripture against what I offered in my Answer to be the true Scope and Intendment of them; But what shall I say? So lamely doth he cite me, so constantly overlook me, that unless he had hoped to be believed, write what he would, or that what he writ would pass for a Reply, whether it deserved to be called so or no: I can see no Pretence for continuing the Controversy; for either he grants what we say by contradicting himself, or says nothing to what we deny, that may strictly merit our Notice. But let him speak for himself.

Rep. p. 80. *Upon my Exposition of* John 1. 9. That was the true Light, &c. W. P. *makes an huge Brag of the Advantage I give his Cause; and thus he argues from my Words:* If Christ made all Things, then Christ was before his Appearance, p. 168. and consequently, Christ was and is the Word, which was with God, and is God, and the Light of Men, &c.

Rejoyn. If he saith nothing, as nothing he says to what he cites, blame not me, for I would have reported it: But whether I had any Advantage, or having it, bragged of it, will be best seen by giving my Answer as it lay.

' If Christ be that Light, which is that Word which made all Things, and
' therefore God (as faith *J. Faldo*) then Christ was before his bodily Appearance,
' and consequently our former Chapter is justified on our Part against his Notions
' of the Lord's Christ; but *J. Faldo* expresly says, p. 84, 85, *as the Word is the*
' *Light of Men, so, or in that Manner, is Christ the Light of Men*; nay, he calls it,
' *Christ appearing in the Flesh,* consequently, Christ was before he took that Flesh,
' or appeared in that Body (not to constitute him or make him Christ, but to
' transact, work, declare and bring to pass by and through it, as a peculiar Vessel,
' and

' and prepared holy Inſtrument) therefore Chriſt was and is that Word which was with God, and is God, and the Light of Men.

This was my Argument grounded upon his Conceſſions; What Advantage it is to our Cauſe, let it anſwer for it ſelf; what Brag I made I know not, unleſs it was my calling his Acknowledgments a Juſtification of our foregoing Chapter. I leave the Meaning of his Silence to my Reader, and inſert his Reply to another Part of my Anſwer, which was this: 'And leſt we ſhould yet miſtake him, he calls it ' *God manifeſted in the Fleſh*; and that he might ſpeak all for us in a little, and ' give the Death's Wound to his own Cauſe, he tells us in ſo many Words, That ' the *Salvation and Life Eternal of poor Sinners was wrapt up in Chriſt as God*. Mark his Reply.

Rep. p. 80. *Yea, and as Man too; yet as this excludes not his Divinity as neceſſary to our Salvation; neither doth his Divinity exclude his Humanity as neceſſary.*

Rejoyn. Theſe Words, *Yea, and Man too*, are added; but with this woful Impertinency, that they wholly contradict his Saying, *Salvation of poor Sinners was wrapt up in Chriſt as God*; for they imply a Denial of Man's Salvation, being wrapt up in Chriſt as Man; and that this was his Meaning, take his own Words, as they lie in his own Book, *Part* 2, *Pag.* 85.

And this I take to be the Import of the 4th Ver (John 1.) In him was Life and the Life was the Light of Men, *That is, the Salvation and Life Eternal of poor Sinners was wrapt up in Chriſt as God, who being ſo qualify'd was capable of working in it.*

I ſay again, and all reaſonable Men muſt acknowledge, I did not wrong his Meaning, but gave his Senſe and not mine: To be ſure, there are no ſuch Words as theſe, *yea and as Man too*, which is juſt as if I ſhould ſay, *The Underſtanding of a Man is wrapt up in him, as he is a reaſonable Creature*, and being charged with a Self-Contradiction, ſhould abſurdly add, *yea, and as an Animal too*, There needs no Pointing at ſo much palpable Weakneſs.

His other Words about the *Divinity's not excluding the Manhood of Chriſt as neceſſary to Salvation*, is no Part of the Queſtion, but a meer Go-by or Slip to the Buſineſs; for all was neceſſary that God thought neceſſary, that is, inſtrumentally: But will it therefore follow that the Salvation and Life-Eternal of poor Sinners was wrapt up in *Inſtruments*?

But let us ſee what he ſays at the Defence I made for my rendring of the Word φωτίζει *enlightned* in my Book entituled, *The Spirit of Truth Vindicated*. Hear him.

Rep. p. 81. *I know not any Cauſe he hath to think me ſtumbled at his rendring* φωτίζει, *enlightned, unleſs for rebuking him for waſting ſo many Pages in quoting Authorities for that which would be granted eaſily.*

Rejoyn. He and his Friend *H. H.* are the more to be blamed that they put me to ſo much Expence, to make good what at leaſt he intended to grant me; but his *eaſy granting* is of thoſe Things that are too hard to be kept; however I accept his Acknowledgment, as alſo of his Silence to what I writ in Defence of our Underſtanding the following Words (ſo much controverted by ſome) *Every Man coming into the World*: However, there is one Paſſage that muſt not ſlip: It is this:

Rep. p. 81. *The laſt Part of my Expoſition, viz. That the That was the true Light points at Chriſt's Appearance in the Fleſh, I added, in his State of Humiliation*, This ſaith *W. P.* p. 178, ſtints Chriſt to that Appearance, denies Chriſt now to be that true Light that enlightens all, and he might as well infer, that becauſe the Word was with God and was God, therefore he is not now with God or God.' But to blaſt all in a Breath, ſays he, Is this your *Tertullus? I would have Mr.* Penn *more ſolid and pertinent, or leave his ſcribling Humour, which at this Rate is fit to write to none but thoſe that can find Refreſhment by a* Dutch *Woman's Babbling, (though underſtanding not one Syllable) upon the Conceit it comes all from the Spirit.*

Rejoyn. Whether my *Anſwer* or his *Reply* be *more ſolid and pertinent*, I ſhall leave with my Readers to judge. O how ready are Men to condemn in others what they indulge in themſelves? It is ſtrange to me if my Adverſary be not guilty in cenſuring; But that hurts him more than me. I ſay again that his Drift was to unconcern, *That was the true Light*, in any other Time than Chriſt's Coming in the Fleſh; to which I oppoſed about a Page and an half, of which he hath reported not above four Lines, and thoſe not as they lay. Take it, Reader, briefly thus: 'If the Word that made all Things, which was with God and was God, ' was that true Light, as ſays *J. Faldo* himſelf, p. 84. then can it never be re-
' ſtrained

'ſtrained to that Appearance as the Beginning or End of it; nay the Evangeliſt
'is not yet come ſo much as to mention any thing of his Manifeſtation in Fleſh;
'and if we will believe *John Faldo*, the Verſe concerns the Word *Creator* and not
'*Redeemer*, which he ſtints to his coming in the Fleſh, ſee Page 89. But by his
'Interpretation *that* is not relative to his Appearance in the Fleſh, but to the
'*Word*, which was with God and was God, as p. 84. and ſo the *Spaniſh Tranſlation*
'hath it, That Word *was the true Light*, &c. ſo that either the *Word* was not be-
'fore that Appearance; or if it were, being that true Light, *that true Light was*
'*before that Appearance*. Therefore Mankind may very well be ſaid, to have al-
'ways been enlighten'd by that Light, for that the Word ſhould be before that
'Appearance, and that true Light, which is the very Life of the Word, or Word
'it ſelf, ſhould be ſtinted to that Appearance, is as abſurd as any thing well can
'be. Now, Reader, comes that Part which he cited, but more regularly; 'That
'we ſhould take *That was the true Light*, &c. to deny Chriſt now to be the true
'Light that enlightens all, becauſe he was ſo, is a ſtrange Impertinency and groſs
'Falſhood.

In Reply to all which next to what I have already tranſcribed, he ſays no more than this:

Reply, Page 82. *W. P. ſhould have undertaken to prove that Chriſt was before that Time, and is now God manifeſt in Fleſh, as he was then, and to thoſe Ends.*

Rejoyn. I did abundantly prove it in our Senſe, and nothing ſolid hath been offered to invalidate what I alledged; but let it ſuffice that he hath granted my Charge. Firſt, In denying Chriſt to have been *either Chriſt or the true Light before that Time*, a manifeſt Contradiction to himſelf, p. 84, 85, 86, 87, 88, 89, of his firſt Book, ſecond Part. *Next*, He therefore denies, that Chriſt is now the true Light, becauſe, *he is not at this Day God manifeſted in Fleſh in the ſame Manner as he was then*, and thus much farther, that he was the true Light before that Appearance *(Socinianiſm* in the Abſtract*)* I do not ſay ſo in Diſgrace, but becauſe he pretends to diſown it. For his ſaying, I ſhould have undertaken to prove them is abſurd, unleſs I had denied them. This, with me, is Matter enough to impeach my Adverſary of blackeſt Sacrilege. I need add no more, nor no more will I add, than this, The Queſtion was not, whether we affirm Chriſt to be that Light by his viſible and bodily Appearance, Life, Doctrine, Miracles, Death, Reſurrection, &c. in this Day, which he was in that. But whether theſe Words *that was the true Light*, did not relate to the Life of the Word which was with God and was God (and conſequently if he did not enlighten Men) before he took Fleſh, in the Fleſh, and after his Reſurrection and Aſcenſion by his Eternal Power and Godhead, as the Great *Sun* of Righteouſneſs and *Spiritual Luminary* of the Inviſible and Intelligible World? Unto which his Words bear no Relation, unleſs it be any to deny the Queſtion.

In ſhort, I told him the very next Words to thoſe he cited, That ſhould we grant the Evangeliſt to refer to that Appearance, *John* 1. 9. yet it would conclude no Denial of Chriſt's being the true Light that enlightens every Man that cometh into the World both before and ſince that Appearance, becauſe it was the moſt eminent breaking forth of the Divine Light; which doubtleſs had been enough to ſatisfy any moderate or modeſt Man, but not ſatisfying him, I muſt infer as before, that his Diſpleaſure is againſt our believing Chriſt to have enlightned before, and ſince that viſible Coming, which if I underſtand any thing, is in ſo many Words to deny his Divinity.

The next Scripture by him expounded and by me reſcued, was *Rom.* 10. 3. *The Word is nigh thee*, &c. he doth but touch upon it, and gives ſo little of my Anſwer, that there is ſcarce Head or Tail to be made of his Paragraph. I will contract my Anſwer, and give his Reply.

He made the *Word* to be the *written Laws, Statutes, and Commandments given by* Moſes, his firſt Book, p. 94. I anſwered, 'It could not be ſo underſtood, for
'the Queſtion was not about them, but about the Commandment of Command
'ments, and Word of Words, which he reſolves thus: *Let none ſay, who ſhall*
'*aſcend, deſcend, or go beyond the Seas to fetch the Great Word and Commandment,*
'*but the Word is very nigh thee* קרוב of קרב ſignifies the innermoſt Parts of Men,
'whereinto the outward Commandments could never come. Beſides, without
'the Word nigh in the Heart, there could be no Conviction upon the Conſcience,
'&c.

Rep.

1673.
Part II.
Chap. X.

Rep. p. 82, 83. W. P. *puts* to fetch the great Word and Commandment, *in the Letter of the Text, as the very Words of* Moses, *A Crime to be abhorred, yet frequent with him that pretends a sacred Esteem of the Scriptures. In few Words to answer all*; Moses *said of this Word*, Verse 12. It is not in Heaven, *which may be said of the Book of the Law, or written Word, but not of Christ the Word — also as I told him before, 'tis such a Word as uses to be in the Mouth, which is the Organ and Instrument of speaking — the* Greek *Word for the* Word *is* ῥῆμα, *which is never to be understood of Christ*; not λόγος, *which is sometimes intended of Christ the Word*.

Rejoyn. This looks more like a Reply than any thing we have had a great while, yet that it only looks so, will lie on our Part to show. First, He charges me with Forgery; Let's see what it was. I said, to fetch the Great Word or Commandment, and the Scripture says, to bring the Word or Commandment. Now I know no Difference betwixt fetching and bringing; 'tis true, I added Great, which if God's Word or Commandment be not, I did amiss; If it be, he is an idle Caviller, fitter to kill Flies all Day with the foolish Emperor than to write Books of Religious Controversie. It is called *Commandment*, Deut. 30. 11. and *Word*, Verse 14.

But *it is not in Heaven*, therefore it is *not Christ*, says our Adversary: I believe *J. Faldo* knew in his own Conscience, that those Words were spoken on Purpose to prevent the Excuse of being without a Commandment, and that so nigh as their own Hearts or innermost Parts, and not to exclude the Word Heaven, but rather thus: *The Word is not so in Heaven as that it is excluded your Consciences, or that ye need to say, who shall go up to fetch it down, for it is in your Hearts to instruct you that you may do it, and reprove you if you do it not.* God was never the less in Heaven for being nigh unto the Consciences of the *Athenians*, which was *Paul*'s Doctrine, *Acts* 17. 27, 28. for, says he, in the Name of one of their own Prophets, *In him we live, move, and have our Being*; for we are also of his Offspring.

Erasmus, in *Deut.* saith, *non* supra *te sed* intra te *est sermo valdè*, i. e. The Word is not *above thee*, but *very within thee*.

The *Samaritan* Copy hath it (not the Word, but) the *Thing is in thee*, according to the *Hebrew* Word דבר which is often so translated.

Fagius, upon the Place in *Deuter.* thus: In Corde *dicit, quia Legem cordibus Judæorum inscripserat Dominus priusquam in Tabulis illis lapideis Decalogum insculpsisset,* i. e. In the Heart, saith he; because the Lord *had written the Law in the Hearts of the* Jews, before he had graven the Decalogue in the Tables of Stones.

For it's being *such a Word as useth to be in the Mouth*, I must tell him, that is such a Word *as useth to be in the Heart too*; which he takes no Notice of in my Answer; and I am sure it is not so impossible for the Eternal Word to express it self by the Mouth of a Man, and so may be said to be in the Mouth, as it is for the Book of written Laws and Statutes *to be in the Heart*. Besides, the *Commandments* are mention'd, Verse 10. but this *Commandment* or *Word*, Verses 11. 14. which cannot in good Sense be called the same, but rather that *Law, Word*, or *Commandment* mention'd by the Apostle, *Rom.* 2. 14, 15. which he acknowledged, the good Gentiles both to have had written in their Hearts, and to have lived up to in good Measure; unless we can suppose that God hath been less propitious to the *Jews* than the *Gentiles*; I mean, that God gave the *Gentiles* an *inward* and the Jews *only an outward Law*. But suppose, what our Adversary says of the Word in *Deuteronomy* to be true, he hath confounded himself in this, That he makes the Word, *Rom.* 10. 8. the same with the Word mentioned, *Deut.* 13, 14. The one is (as says *J. F.*) the *Word of* Jewish *Statutes*, among whom is the *Hand-writing of Ordinances, the ceremonial and judicial* (as well as moral) *Law*; The other is the *Word of Faith, which blots out the Hand-writing of Ordinances, and ends the Ceremonial and Judicial Law*: But because these two Laws or Words cannot be one and the same, and yet that the Apostle alludes to the Word in *Deuteronomy* to be *Christ* himself; for if that be one with the Word of Faith the Apostle writes of to the *Romans*, then because the Word of Faith, *Rom.* 10. 8. is Christ, the *Word* mentioned in *Deuteronomy*, must also be Christ; that they are one and the same Word the Apostle's Allusion proves, and *J. F. confesseth*, and that the Word of Faith, *Rom.* 10. 8. is Christ, let the two foregoing Verses of the Text be consulted. *But the Righteousness of Faith speaketh on this wise, Say not in thine Heart,*

Heart, who shall ascend into Heaven, that is, to bring Christ *down from above, or who shall descend into the deep, that is, to bring up* Christ *again from the Dead; but what saith it, The Word is nigh thee, even in thy Mouth and in thy Heart, that is the Word of Faith which we preach,* verse 6, 7, 8. where nothing is more clear, than that the *Word* nigh in the Heart, is *Christ the Word*; for the Question here is, how they shall get the Word. The Apostle answers it, though not under the Name of Christ, yet under a Name attributed to Christ; If our Adversary count Christ and the Word of Faith two differing Things, by the same Reason may we say, that the Word in *Deuteronomy,* concerning which none needeth to ask who shall go up into Heaven to bring it down, and the *Word nigh* are two Words; but if that Question be needless, *Who shall go up into Heaven to fetch it down unto us,* ver. 12. be answered in ver. 14. viz. *but the Word is very nigh unto thee,* and consequently, that it is but *one Word or Commandment* that is understood in the Question and the Answer, then may we with good Reason conclude that *Christ* in the 6th and 7th Verses, and the *Word of Faith* in the 8th Verse are one and the same Thing under two Names, else there can be no Sense or Coherence in the Apostle's Words; for what Answer is this? *But what says it, The Word is nigh thee in thy Mouth and in thy Heart, that is the Word of Faith which we preach,* to this Question, *Who shall ascend to bring Christ down? Who shall descend to bring Christ up.* If Christ and the Word of Faith are not Synonymous or equivalent Terms? The Question the Apostle makes the Righteousness of Faith to forbid, is about Christ's Absence or Remoteness from the Heart; *Say not in thy Heart,* and it is answered and resolved *with the Nearness of the Word in the Heart,* which could be no answer or Solution in case *that Word was not Christ, or Christ that Word;* for the Reason why the Righteousness of Faith saith on this wise, *Say not in thy Heart, who shall ascend to fetch Christ down,* implies, that he is not shut up in some remote Place, *but that he is nigh,* and needs no fetching; and if nigh, *then not another from the Word nigh,* which is the Answer to the Question.

To make it yet plainer and detect my Adversary, I will parallel the Case, *Jacob* being ancient, desired to see *Joseph* before he died; suppose him to have askt, *how shall I do to see* Joseph? And that some-body answered, *Do not ask how thou shalt see* Joseph, *for thou seest* Reuben; Tell me if this would be thought a fit Answer to *Jacob's* Question; yet this must be the Case of those who deny *Christ* and the *Word* to be *one* in this Place: But if some-body should have said to him, *Do not ask who shall show thee thy Son* Joseph, *for the Ruler of all* Egypt *standeth nigh thee:* Would not every Body think the Person meant *Joseph* that was so. This is so plain to our Purpose that every common Understanding may discern the Reasonableness of our Interpretation.

For the Greek being ῥῆμα, and not λόγος, it makes nothing against us, in that ῥῆμα hath the same Signification with λόγος, as *Scapula* informs us out of *Plato.*

Clemens Alexandrinus Admon. ad Gent. on *Isa.* 2. 3. הדבר ומוה calls it the Word of the Lord λόγος οὐράνιος, γνήσιος ἀγωνιστὴς, ἐπὶ τῷ παντὸς κόσμῳ θεάτρῳ στεφανούμενος i. e. the HEAVENLY WORD, *the true Contender for Mastery, crowned in the Theater of the whole World;* and in his *Strom. l.* 2. speaking of the same Place (*Rom.* 10.) faith, ὁ θεῖος λόγος κέκραγεν πάντας συλλήβδην καλῶν. *The DIVINE WORD cries, calling all Men without Distinction,* which must needs be Christ the Living Word of God.

Besides, there is but one Word in the *Hebrew* רבד most commonly used to signify a Word; and though ῥῆμα & λόγος are two Words, yet they both are under this one Word in the Hebrew רבד as in *E. Hutter's* Translation, *John* 1. 1. *Rom.* 10. 8. 2 *Pet.* 1. 19. But the Weakness of our Adversary in this Particular must needs be obvious to all that consider how poorly he begs the Question, in saying that ῥῆμα doth not signifie Christ the Word, which is the Matter disputed; he appeals to the use of the Word, which helps him not; for sometimes ῥῆμα signifies as well Christ as λόγος and sometimes λόγος doth not signify Christ as well as ῥῆμα; his Reply confesseth the latter, and the Text and Context of this Place, with *J. F's* Interpretation *Rom* 10. 8. make good the former, I do but herein make use of *J. Faldo's* own Rule, *The Construction of Words of various Significations is to be made as most suits with the Context,* Rep. pag. 83. and so we leave him in this Particular.

The Third Scripture was, 2 *Pet.* 19. καὶ ἔχομεν βεβαιότερον τὸν προφητικὸν λόγον. This Scripture was effectually rescued in my Answer from the ill use many have made thereof against us and the Truth; He says little, if any Thing, besides meer Cavil,

1673.

Part II.
Chap. X.

vil, leaving the moſt conſiderable Part of the Defence of our Tranſlation of the Text behind him. After four Pages eſcaped, he begins with me thus.

Reply, Pag. 83. W. P. *tells me,* 'That though our Tranſlation hath it καὶ *(alſo)* 'yet it is commonly underſtood by δὲ *(but)* it ſignifies a Compariſon, Pag. 186. If 'J. F. hath but *Greek* and *Honeſty* enough, he muſt needs acknowledge that Po-'ſitives, Comparatives and Superlatives are uſed promiſcuouſly in the Greek. *This I ſhall ſhew is little to Purpoſe, except his Oſtentation,* &c. *If* Stephanus, Paſtor, Schrevelius, Scapula *and* Leigh *underſtand* Greek, καὶ *ſignifies* And, Alſo, For *and* If, Although *and many more, yea, and very often* But, *and is an Adverſative Particle,* καὶ ἐκ ἐγνώκατε αὐτόν, John 8. 55. *Yet or but ye have not known him.*

Rejoyn. Oſtentation belongs (with Emptineſs) to this Reply; firſt, I never ſaid καὶ did ſignifie *but* in no Place, next, I only ſaid, it was commonly by our Adverſaries underſtood ſo here, and conſequently made an Adverſative Particle, contrary to the Nature of the Text, and all Tranſlations that I have ever ſeen or heard of: It had been to his Purpoſe if he had brought *Stephanus, Paſtor, Schrevelius, Scapula* and *Leigh* to prove that καὶ ought to be rendred *But* in this Text in order to make good his Adverſative Particle, thereby quarrelling the Tranſlation, and continuing a Compariſon not well conſiſtent with the Text. Again.

Reply, Pag. 83, 84. But that βεβαιότερον *ſhould be rendred in the poſitive Degree, not comparative,* W. P. *produceth ſome authorities. The* Syriack *and* Ethiopick *Verſions, which give him little Countenance by we have over and above a ſure Word.*

Rejoyn. I told our Adverſary in my Anſwer, That if the Tranſlation were *more ſure Word of Prophecy,* we muſt either underſtand it of the Eternal Word, or conclude that the Writings of the Prophets were more ſure to the Apoſtles, *than the Voice they heard from God himſelf in the Mount.* I produced ſeveral Authorities (as he well ſaid) to exclude the Compariſon of *more ſure*; ſome he hath taken Notice of, as the *Syriack* and *Ethiopick* Verſions; but that they give little Countenance to my Attempt is vain and falſe, unleſs there be no difference between ſaying, *We have over and above a ſure Word* (which is but an additional Teſtimony) and *We have a More ſure Word.* The Caſe may be parallelled thus; I have alſo *another* Witneſs, which I deſire may be called and heard: Is there no Difference to be found here? Another ſure Witneſs, another more ſure Witneſs; Is not all Preference ſhut out of the firſt, and brought in by the laſt? J. Faldo muſt needs be guilty of great Ignorance or Immodeſty in this Particular.

Reply, Pag. 94. W. P. *tells me,* The *French, German, Low-Dutch, Swediſh,* have it in the poſitive (or ſure Word) *but I not having his* Polyglot *Bible cannot eaſily examine them all, if he doth not wrong them.*

Rejoyn. But if this great Linguiſt had it, he would find none of thoſe Languages in it; I know not what he means by *examining them eaſily in it,* without it; but he ſpoke more Truth than he is aware of; for if he will go to *E. Hutter,* he may find them without the *Polyglot,* though perhaps *not eaſily,* as he well ſays; for I ſcarcely think he maſters Twelve Languages. To conclude, This I will aſſure him, They all ſpeak for me, and I am ready to think they were tranſlated by as able Men as himſelf, at leaſt, let him and them diſpute that.

Reply, Pag. 84. He adds Eraſmus's *Paraphraſe, and* Beza's, *both of whom he abuſes.* Eraſmus *renders it by* firmiorem, Beza *by* firmiſſimum; *the one a moſt firm, the other more firm; in the old Latine it is moſt ſure, in the new Latine more ſure,* So D. Hammond, Arias Montanus, *and* Piſcator.

Rejoyn. This looks like ſomething, ſo do Bubbles; but they eaſily vaniſh. *Eraſmus* I quoted in his Paraphraſe, not in his Tranſlation; but *J. Faldo* after his old wont, obſerves not the Difference, but ſets *Eraſmus* againſt *Eraſmus*; or rather, to put the Trick upon me, would have Folks think, that *Eraſmus's* rendring it by *firmiorem,* was not in his Tranſlation, but Paraphraſe, which I quoted; for he is ſo far from allowing *firmiorem,* or more ſure to be the Word of the Prophets, according to the common Acceptation, at leaſt, that againſt which we object, that he expreſly ſays, 'If ſo be that the Prophets plain Oracles be in great Eſtimation 'among you, which Propheſie by Figurative Dark Shadows of Chriſt, *of much* '*more Gravity or Weight ought ſo evident a Declaration by the Father himſelf of* '*the Son be*; which turns the Text upſide down, as to the Vulgar Senſe of it. This I cited out of his Paraphraſe upon this Epiſtle, *J. Faldo* ſhuffles from the Paraphraſe to his bare Tranſlation, which he explains in his Note in *Criticis Sacris* thus; *Verum Græcis mos eſt ſubinde comparativum pro poſitivo uſurpari:* That is, 'It is the 'Cuſtom

Cuſtom of the *Greeks, ſometimes to uſe the Comparative for the Poſitive.* And if he underſtands *Latine* he may know, that *Senior* is alſo uſed for *Senex*.

'Tis true, *Beza* tranſlates it *firmiſſimum* (moſt ſure) or very ſure) which alſo excludes Compariſon, as *Ipſiſſimus* (the very ſame he, not the moſt ſame he) If *J. Faldo* denies this, it will ſhow him ignorant in the *Latine* Tongue; for the Superlative or *firmiſſimum* exceeds the poſitive or *firmum* by *valdè* (very) as well as by *maximè* (moſt) However, had we nothing of this to urge, yet his own uſe of the Compariſon, as his Conceſſion to what I ſaid in my Anſwer, and *Eraſmus* and *Beza* confirmed there at large, gives us all we deſire; for he acknowledges, That *the Writings of the Prophets are not* MORE *true in themſelves than any other Revelation of the Mind of God*; but more certain, with reſpect to the *Jews,* who had a greater Eſteem for, and Teſtimony of the Writings of the Prophets to be of God, and not a Deluſion, than of *Peter's* Revelation: So that we ſee from *J. Faldo* himſelf the Scripture is not ſet above the Spirit, as the more ſure Word, the Thing promoted of old by our Enemies, and which we only oppoſe; for, I doubt not but the Scriptures were more ſure to the *Jews* than Chriſt himſelf, elſe they would never have thought to find Eternal Life in them, whilſt they neglected, yea, perſecuted him, which whether it was their Perfection or Imperfection ſo to do, I leave with the Judgment of my ſerious Reader; yet doth the poor Man vainly call this his *defending theſe three Paſſages from my Corruption and the* Quakers *Service.* May my Adverſaries always defend themſelves at this rate, and I ſhall never fear any loſs to the Cauſe; For what with his miſrendering of our Writings, unfair Quotations, plain Wreſtings, pitiful Evaſions, and at beſt weak Replies, *never did Cauſe receive more Advantage at the Hand of an Enemy,* than ours hath from *J. Faldo.*

I will give one Proof more before we leave this Chapter.

Rep. pag. 84. *My Expoſition of* Coloſſ. 1. 25. Chriſt in you, &c. *(though the moſt oppoſite to the* Quakers *Chriſt within)* W. P. *hath not one Word of Anſwer to.*

Rejoyn. I know not whether he means the Text, or his Expoſition to be moſt oppoſite to our Chriſt within. The Text is *Coloſſ.* 1. 27. not 25. and is thus, *To whom God would make known what is the Riches of the Glory of the Myſtery among the* Gentiles, *which is Chriſt* IN *you the Hope of Glory:* In which I find not one Word that oppoſeth Chriſt's Dwelling in his People; One would think our Adverſary ſpoke *Ironically,* or by Contraries, if he meant it of the Text; for it ſeems an impoſſible Thing to me, that a Text ſo plainly expreſſing Chriſt to be *in* Men, ſhould notwithſtanding prove *Chriſt not to be in Men.* If he underſtood it of his Expoſition, how can that truly expound the Text, which expounds it quite to another Senſe than it will bear? At leaſt, he ſhould call this a begging of the Queſtion. Let us hear what he offers.

Firſt Book, Part 2. p. 100, 101. *For Chriſt to be in the* Gentiles *(rightly underſtood would be no ſuch hard Matter for the* Gentiles *to believe, as to believe ſuch a Glory to be attained by Faith in and Obedience to the Laws of a Man who dyed as a Malefactor, and that this Death of his ſhould reconcile God to Man with the Addition of ſuch a Purchaſe.*

This Sort of Doctrine well becomes *J. Faldo;* I perceive I have not miſtaken him. What Carnaliſt in the World could have let drop a more pernicious Sentence to the Doctrine and Kingdom of Chriſt, than to render it more difficult to believe, and lay a greater Streſs upon the External, than the Internal Work of Chriſt. We muſt read the moſt weighty Scriptures backwards upon this Man's Principles: He hath helped us to a New Way of rendring the Text; not, *this Myſtery among the* Gentiles *is Chriſt* IN *you the Hope of Glory*; but *this Myſtery among the* Gentiles, *is a Man who dyed as as a Malefactor, by His Death reconciled to God,* &c. Behold your Expoſitor! I dare warrant this Comment will never trouble the next Collection of Criticks. At this Rate, the *Lord-Lord-Cryer is highly privileged,* and the *Galatians* had paſſed the moſt difficult Birth, *before they had known Chriſt to be formed in them*; Regeneration is a ſlight Thing, in Compariſon of the Knowledge of Chriſt after the Fleſh.

This Doctrine brings not Men *to Chriſt in them the Hope of Glory,* but inticeth them into the Vain Hope of the Hypocrite, which periſheth. The Hiſtory is made the greateſt Myſtery, and to believe the one Matter of greater Difficulty, than to experience the other. Beſides, Why ſhould his Dying as a Malefactor, render him unfit to be believed; ſince his Virtue was moſt Exemplary, his Miracles ſtupendious, his Doctrine Spiritual and Powerful, his whole Deportment amongſt the *Jews*

Innocent and Heavenly? Did not *Tiberius* himself move to the *Roman Senate* his being *taken into the Number of their Gods*, upon the Report of his mighty Works? 'Tis strange that should be reputed most Mysterious, which was the Introduction to the Mystery; and those Transactions counted most difficult, that were by the Divine Wisdom of God ordained as so many facile Representations of what was to be accomplished in Man. In short, it is to lessen, if not totally to exclude the True Mystery of Godliness, *which is Christ manifested in his Children, their Hope of Glory*. But he proceeds thus:

The Man Christ that was Nailed on the Cross, the Quakers *do not believe to be in them; for the God-head of Christ, that is every-where, and every-where alike — He is in every Thing at all Times, and nothing can be void of his Presence. So that if this be it you mean, the Saints have no more Privilege than any other Creature whatsoever.*

The second New and Living Man, who is the Lord from Heaven, the Quickening Spirit, the Anointed Saviour, whose Body was Nailed to the Cross, we confess before Men to be the Christ; and do by Virtue and Authority of Scripture assert him to dwell in his Children; and we see nothing offered by *J. Faldo*, that can induce the weakest of us to desert this Faith, having with the Testimony of Scripture, *that of Christ in our selves:* But let it be considered with what Confidence this Man excludeth Christ from the Souls of his People, as well with respect to his Godhead as Manhood; but if in any Sense he may be said to be in them as God, it is no more *than He is in Cats and Dogs:* O Irreverent, O Prophane Man! *Are Beasts and Birds as properly the Temples of the Living God, as sanctified Men?* How can God be said *to dwell and walk in his People*, if so remote from them as *J. Faldo* represents him to be? The Apostle is much to be blamed, according to our Adversary's Doctrine, for letting fall this Passage, *I live, yet not I, but Christ liveth in me*, Gal. 2. 20. The Upshot of this Sort of Doctrine is downright *Atheism*; for as they that know not God from the Manifestation of God Within, are ignorant of him, if *Rom.* 1. 19, says true. So those who teach that God is no more in his Saints than in any other Creature, endeavour to invalidate the most convincing Testimony Man can have of a Deity, and to principle Men for the *Rankest Atheism* that ever was: Yet such a Sort of a Doctor *J. Faldo* is become, and of all other Texts in the Bible, from which to preach it, hath chosen this, *Col.* 1. 27. *This Mystery among the* Gentiles, *is Christ in you, the Hope of Glory*, which indeed of all other doth most oppose and subvert it. Once more, and he hath done with us upon this Passage, for this Time.

—— *Christ is in his People by his Graces, wrought by His Spirit, which is His Image and Likeness — by the Manifestation of His Love and Glory, His Works and Image in and on the Soul — and do as effectually possess the Soul for Christ His Use and Interest, as a Faithful Friend can do, according to that Text*, That Christ may dwell in your Hearts by Faith, *Eph.* 3. 17.

But I would fain know of *J. Faldo, How Christ's Graces, Works and Image can be there, and Christ the Workman excluded?* If Christ be not actually there, they can never actually be wrought there; for none can work them but Christ by His Spirit. In short, either they may be wrought without Christ's Spirit, which *J. Faldo* disallows; or Christ's Spirit may work them, and yet not be where it works them; or if the Spirit may be where it worketh them, yet Christ cannot be where it works them, and consequently divided from his own Spirit, *though indeed the Lord Christ is that Quickening Spirit, which only makes alive again to God, who is the Resurrection and the Life*. O the dreadful Darkness that yet over-spreads the Hearts of (called) *Christians*! It may be as truly said of them as it was of the *Jews, The Vail is yet over them, and Christ Jesus, the Anointed Saviour, is unknown to them by that Redemption, which he effectually worketh in all those that hearken to his Voice, and are conformed to His Holy Government. They are Witnesses of his Graces, Works and Image, through believing in his Appearance, and giving up* (like the Clay in the Hand of the Potter) *to be ordered and disposed by him*. Nor doth the Scripture he quotes, impugn the *Real Presence of Christ in His People*; for, *By Faith Christ dwelleth in the Hearts of His Children;* that is, *by believing in Christ, he cometh to live and dwell in us, who, through the Unbelief of Men, is shut out from being Head and Ruler in them*. Our Adversary would make *Faith and Christ's Real Presence incomparable or inconsistent*, whereas the one cannot possibly be enjoyed without the other; Faith being as the opening of the Door of the Heart to receive Christ in, to be Lord and King; and if this be not *J. Faldo's* Faith, he is void of the Faith of God's Elect,

See Rom. 8. 9, 10, 11. *where the Spirit of Christ and Christ are equivalently taken.*

Elect, which purifieth the Heart, and gives to see God, according to *Mat.* 5. 8. *Blessed are the Pure in Heart, for they shall see God.* This Doctrine is the Overthrow of *Christianity*, a turning back of the whole Stream of the New Covenant, a cutting off the Spiritual Union; for the *Christian Dispensation* is IMMANUEL, *God with us*; the Word is not stinted to Christ as the Head, but *concerns the Body also*; and God is manifested measurably in his People, as he was in Fulness, by and through that Holy Body; nay, some Eminent Professors have gone so far as to say, *They make up but one* χριςὸς, or *Anointed*; *for the Oil runs from the Head to the lowermost Part of the Garment*, which takes in all. It gives the Lye to Christ's own Words, who said, *He would come and receive them to himself, he would not leave them Orphans*; which implies a Real Presence.

TESTIMONIES.

Good Old *Apostolical Ignatius*, was not of *J. Faldo's* Mind, who in his Epistles produced, and endeavoured to be proved Genuine by Bishop *Usher*, *Isaac Vossius*, and Dr. *Pearson*, says in that to the *Ephesians*, pag. 26. Πάντα ἓν ποιῶμεν ὡς αὐτῶ ἐν ἡμῖν κατοικοῦντος, ἵνα ὦμεν αὐτῶ ναοὶ καὶ αὐτὸς ἦ ἐν ἡμῖν θεὸς ἡμῶν. i. e. *Let us do all Things, he so dwelling in us, that we be His Temples, and He our God In us.* Οἰκοφθόροι βασιλίαν θεοῦ ὐ κληρονομήσουσιν. *The Corrupters of his House shall not inherit the Kingdom of God.*

Justin Martyr, Expos. Tid. p. 375. Βλέπετε πῶς τὴν οἰκοδομὴν τὴν ἐν χριστῷ διδάσκων, δἰ ἧς ναοὶ χριστοῦ γινόμεθα κατὰ τὸν γεγραμμένον, ἥσω ἐν αὐτοῖς, καὶ ἐμπεριπατήσω, καὶ ἔσομαι αὐτῶν Θεός. i. e. *See*, faith he, *how he* (Paul) *is teaching the Edification that is in Christ, whence we are the Temple of Christ, according to what is written*, I will dwell in them, and walk in them, and I will be their God.

The Story of *Richard Woodman* in the Book of *Martyrs*, affordeth thus much to our Purpose in Answer to the Bishop of *Winchester: I believe verily that I have the Spirit of God —— No Man can believe aright without the Spirit of God ——— It is impossible to believe in God, unless God Dwell in us.*

C. *Goad* defends our Faith in these Words: *The Gospel is nothing else but the bringing forth of Christ In us: It calls us from Conformity to the World, and from walking as Men unto the Life of God*, Right Spirit of Christ, pag. 17.

T. *Collier, God is a Mystery*, Col. 22. *and it is by the Appearance of God In Us, we come to know God, who is a Mystery. The Truth is, that we have had, and still have low and carnal Thoughts of God, judging him to be a God Afar off, and not a God nigh at Hand. This is that Antichrist which denies Christ to be come in the Flesh.* See his Works, p. 399.—— Again, *God who is in himself, and in the Son, not only by Union, but also by a Dispensation of Grace to Men, is likewise in the Saints, and that not as in the Creatures, or other Men,* But He is in the Saints as He was in Christ. *The Saints are Truly made Partakers of His Nature, hence called Christians; they are* Christed, *and indeed,* Christ and Christians make but One Christ, One Anointed, One God fills them both. *See his Works, pag.* 241, 242.

J. Sprig in his Preface faith thus: *Those that know Christ in them only* mediatione virtutis, *not* suppositi, *know not so Full and Glorious a Proportion in him to their End. It is and must be confessed, that God is, and subsists otherwise in Himself than in Men*; but this hinders not the Immediateness of his Presence, and Dwelling in Men —— *If you confine Christ's Dwelling to a Local Heaven, you are ignorant of that which is the greatest Joy that can be*; Christ dwells in the Heart. *Sprig's Testimony*, pag. 87.

Thus *Martin Finch*, who stiles himself, *Preacher of the Gospel*, in his Little Treatise, entituled, *Animadversions upon Sir* Henry Vane's Book, pag. 81. *The Word of God abode and dwelt in them* (1 John 2. 14.) *If we take it for Christ, they had him* (Christ) *Abiding in them; and surely, they that abide in Christ, and have Christ abiding in them, they are True Saints.*

Thus, *Reader*, we take Leave of this Chapter, and proceed to examine his next.

CHAP. XI.

That we are not Guilty of Idolatry, as charged by our Adversary. True Worshippers. The Charge inverted.

IN his former Book, he charged us with the *Sin of Idolatry*; his Argument lay thus, *Those who own and profess that to be God which is not God, are gross Idolaters*; *But the* Quakers *do so, in professing the Light Within, and the Soul of every Man to be God*; *therefore Idolaters.* The Testimonies upon which he insisted, I faithfully and fully considered, in above Seven Pages of Sober Answer; he returns me about Three in Defence of his Charge, not giving above a Dozen Lines of what I writ, and those made up of Scraps, rather contracting what he said before, then making any substantial Reply to them: But however, I will be just to him. Thus he begins.

Rep. pag. 84, 85. *To my Charge of Idolatry, he answers as one that intended to confirm, not confute it: His very Denials implying a large Grant of the Question,* p. 192, 193. We do for ever renounce any such Principle, as that the Soul of Man, simply as such, is the very Essence and Being of God. *Then it is with him the very Essence or Being of God, though not because it is the Soul of Man.*

Rejoyn. No such Matter; but it is plain how much the Man is upon the Catches. His Argument led me to such an Answer, for he calls it, *The Soul or Spirit of a Man, which is a* Constitutive *Part of a Man,* pag. 114. I was therefore led by him to write in that *Abstract Sense*, which thus far makes for him (in case he can maintain his Charge) that the Idolatry would be the grosser; Besides, *God is the Soul, or Life of the Soul,* therefore there was a Necessity for such a Distinction.

Rep. p. 85. W. P. *pag.* 193. We never did, do, nor shall assert the God that made Heaven or Earth, to be comprehensible within the Soul of Man — so that when we say the Light is within any, we do not intend the whole Being of Light. *All that* W. P. *denies here, is but God's being so in the Soul of Man, as that He is no where else, or nothing else, yet allowing the Soul and Light Within to be God Essential.*

Rejoyn. It were heartily to be wished, we had nothing but Ignorance to charge him with in this Passage; but methinks he would not have us to take him for a Man of so little Understanding, as he must needs have, that writes so much Falshood, and does not know it.

First, He hath dropt the most Substantial Part of my Answer in the Middle.

Secondly, These Passages relate not to the Soul, but to the Light, upon Occasion of a Place he cited out of G. *Fox* the Younger, therefore not applicable to the Soul, yet by him as well applied to the Soul as to the Light.

Thirdly, He says, All that I deny in those Words, he quoted out of my Answer, *is only God's being so in the Soul of Man, as that He is no where or nothing else,* which if he had only said it of the Light, it would be no Contradiction to my Principle or the Truth; for the Light is as well on the Earth as in the Heavens, and in my Chamber as in the Firmament, without any Error in Physicks, and so may God, whom in my Answer I called the *Great Sun of Righteousness,* that caused his Spiritual Light to arise and shine into the Souls of Men, be God as well within as without the Soul; for where-ever Divine Light is, God is; and where God is, Divine Light is: Howbeit, we do not call the Manifestation of Light, *God,* though the Manifestation of God.

Fourthly, His saying, That I yet allow the Soul and Light within to be God Essential, is a down-right Falshood, as with Respect to the Soul; it is nigh Two Pages before that I considered his Charge against us about the Soul; What shall I call then his thrusting of it in here, which cannot be concerned in the very Nature of the Answer? As thus appears, If the Soul be God, God is comprehended within the Soul, and is no where, or nothing else but Soul, and where the Soul is; An Absurdity, yea, a Blasphemy, never rightly to be inferred from any Thing I ever said or writ, thus scandalously flung upon my Answer by *J.* Faldo, for want of a better Reply; I cannot think that ever Man adventured (under his Pretences of Religion) so knowingly to pervert, wrest, and misapply Men's Words about Doctrines of the greatest Importance. This shows he values Credit more than Conscience, who undertakes to fasten a Blasphemous Consequence untruly on my Words, lest he should be thought to have charged us beyond what he could prove; but his Weakness

ness bewrays his Malice: For if the Soul may be God, and yet I deny that God may be nothing else (his very Words in my Name) then may the Soul be God, and God the Soul, and yet God something else, and that something else God. When or where did I ever give Occasion for such *Blasphemous Gibberish?* Yet this is the Result of what he dares tell the World is my Meaning. I may say the same respecting Locality or Place; for what Man not stark Mad, would say the Soul is God, yet deny not but that God may be else-where, which *J. Faldo* also makes (though an express Contradiction to his Wrests) a Piece of my Meaning; for, unless God may be divided from God, where-ever he is, the Soul is, if the Soul be God; and so one Man is in another, and every Man *Ubiquitary,* or every where at the same Time.

Friendly Reader, none of this Blasphemy and Nonsense belongeth to me, therefore I return it to the True Parent, to maintain it as he is able.

But he would have the World believe, that of *Twenty Three Citations* out of acknowledged *Quakers, I did but nibble a little at Five of them.* I think him not worth proving a L——, that have already so many Times done it upon unquestionable Ground in this Discourse; besides, I should be necessitated to transcribe my whole Answer; but I beseech this Kindness of the *Reader,* that he would not think his Time lost in perusing the 20th Chapter of my Answer, where he may see himself if I have only nibled, perhaps he will have a better Opinion of my Endeavours. I shall have Occasion here to touch upon some of them, and no more, yet enough to show my Adversary's unfair Dealing.

Rep. *To Fox Junior's, who calls the Light,* The Eternal God which Created all Things. *In his continued Discourse (personating the Light) he calls it,* The Light in you, me the Light in them; *which P. would evade, by saying, I granted that in the First Part* Within Man *was not mentioned.*

Rejoyn. Had I said no more than this, it might have past for an Evasion; but to pass over a Page and an Half of pertinent Answer to his Application of both Passages out of G. F. and then say I evaded them by urging his Grant, that *Within Man* was not mentioned in the first Passage, is to act the Shifter with a Witness; especially when the little Part he quotes, was not said by me concerning the last Passage, in which lay the Difficulty (to wit, *Me the Light in them*) but the first on which he very little insisted himself, viz. That the *Light is the Eternal God,* &c. This transposing of my Answer, and exchanging it, was not ingenuous. This, *Reader,* in short, I offered as the Explanation of *G. F*'s Expression, and the Conclusion of a great deal more, too large to be recited, viz. " That He who is the Eternal
" Fountain of all Life, and Sun of Light, causeth His Light to visit the Heart, and
" shine in the Consciences of all Mankind, as well of such as rebel against it, and
" scorn it, to reprove them, as of those who receive it, and gladly submit to it,
" to direct and justifie them; wherefore we utterly deny that the *Manifestation* in
" Man strictly considered, *Is the Most High God,* but a Manifestation of God, and
" from God, by the *In-shining of His Blessed Light*; and we cannot be said to wor-
" ship the Manifestation, but that Eternal God (who is Light) that is thereby ma-
" nifested, pag. 194.

The next Testimony brought by him, and examined by us, was out of *E. Burrough's True Faith,* &c. for Page he gave us none, neither then nor now; but supposing True Citation, a Thing most unusual with him, I will set down his Words as they lye.

Rep. p. 85. *The next* W. P. *brings off as clearly:* " Every Man hath that which
" is One in Union with the Spirit of Christ, even as Good as the Spirit of Christ,
" according to his Measure, *E. Burroughs.* Can any Man, *saith W. P.* be so stupid as to think that *E. B.* ever intended the Soul of Man, that purely and simply constitutes him such; for he is speaking of that Universal Grace, Light, Spirit, which God hath given unto all, *&c. His* purely and simply constitutes, *is pure Learned Nonsense. If what every Man hath, be as Good in Kind as the Spirit of Christ, which* E. B. *confesseth, it must be God and Christ.*

Rejoyn. He should either have past the Manner of my Expression, or have corrected it better; but I had rather be guilty of Nonsense than horrible Perversion, *J. F*'s Crime; for he applies that to the *meer Soul* of Man which *E. B.* not only intended, *but expressed of the Light of Christ Within Man.* I will set down some of his Words, that it may be an indelible Brand upon *J. F.* a **Notorious** Abuser of our Writings.

E. Bur-

E. Burroughs in his Answer to *J. Bunnion* and this Passage [*Heathens, Turks, Jews, Atheists have that that doth convince of Sin, yet are so far from having the Spirit of Christ in them, that they delight to serve their Lust.*] Thus expresseth himself. ' Do they serve Sin or Lusts because Christ hath not given them Light to dis-
' cover their Sin? or because they *hate the Light that is given them?* Tell me, is
' not the Light or Spirit of Christ the only Thing that doth convince of Sin, *Or*
' *doth any Thing convince of Sin contrary, or besides, or without the Spirit of Christ?*
' If nay, then it must needs be that it is from, or by, or *something of the Nature*
' of the Spirit of Christ which is in the *Heathens, E. B.* argues and about five or six Lines lower thus concludes: ' Till thou provest the Light of Christ, which
' thou confessest every Man hath, to be contrary to the Spirit of Christ, I shall say,
' *Every Man hath that which is one in union with and like the Spirit of Christ, even*
' *as good as the Spirit of Christ, according to it's Measure.* Now let *J. Faldo* blush if he can. Certainly, Reader, greater Injustice could not well have been acted towards any Man's Writings, than he hath acted in this Particular; for what is clearer, than that the Soul is no farther concerned in *E. B*'s Words, than that *it ought to obey the Light and Spirit he writes of.* I told him this before, as that Part of my *Answer* he hath transcribed into his *Reply* shows, to wit, *that* E. B. *was speaking of the Universal Grace, Light or Spirit which God hath given unto all, &c.* of which he takes no Notice, but thinks an Epitome of his first Book of Accusation and Wresting Reply enough to my Answer. But which is yet baser; he hath the Confidence for all this, *to cry out against Shifting and Evasion.* But to make it yet plainer, I will set it down more distinctly.

E. B. Every Man hath that which is as good and like the Spirit of Christ.

J. F. *Then every Man's Soul is as good and like the Spirit of Christ, which is God; therefore the Soul is God.*

W. P. answers, *E. B.* understood it not of the *Soul*, but the *Universal Grace, Light or Spirit*, therefore no Proof.

J. F. If what every Man hath be as good in kind as the Spirit of God, which *E. B.* confesseth, it must be God and Christ.

W. P. That which *E. B.* confesseth is of the Light or Spirit, and not the Soul, therefore *J. F*'s Charge is false.

Now Reader, what shall we call this but *Petitio principii*, a begging of the Question, a repeating of his Perversion, It is so, because I will have it so, as much as if he should say, I have charged them higher than any; more than that, I pretend to bring their own Books for Evidences. If I yield to have perverted them, my Credit is gone, my Books are despised, and which is worst of all, my Gain is lost. But to the next.

Reply, Pag. 86. *That of* Fox *he deals treacherously in leaving out the Proposition to which the Answer is made, and thereby it's Sense also.* F. brings in the Priest *saying*, It is an Expression of a dark Mind to say, that God is not distinguished from his Saints. *To which he replies,* He is a Reprobate and out of the Apostles Doctrine. *What can be better proved? If God be not distinct from them, not only their Souls, but the Composition of the Saints, Souls and Bodies are God: But if this Passage do not prove P. a designed Deluder, none in the World will.*

Rejoyn. The Substance of my Answer took in the Priest's Assertion, but that *J. Faldo* almost always takes Care to conceal. G. F. writ not like a Philosopher, but an honest, plain, Christian Man; Nor is it any Disadvantage to our Cause, that either willingly or through Unskilfulness he neglects them; for he meant by not being *distinct*, that they were not at a Distance in Point of Place, by Reason of the dwelling of God and Christ in his People; It is apparent G. F. intended no more by his Answer, which our Adversary in his first Book gave in these Words. *But God and Christ is in the Saints, and dwells in them, and he* (the Priest) *is a Reprobate, and out of the Apostles Doctrine.* We see by this that the Question was not, whether the Soul be God and Christ; *but whether God and Christ are at a Distance from or dwell in the Saints*, yea or nay? I leave it with my Reader's Conscience, who hath shown himself the designed Deluder of us two.

Reply, W. P. *tells me,* p. 197. *That Fisher did not mean the Spirit of Man that is any Part of Man's Nature whereas his very Words are,* ' The Spirit of Man
' which concurs to the constituting Man in his *primitive* Perfection. *I told him also that* Fisher *allowed no Man in his degenerate Estate to have any Spirit at all as Constitutive of Man.*

Rejoyn. 'Tis true, if he puts *primitive Perfection* to it; * for nothing can reduce Man to his primitive Perfection, but that *Holy Spirit* which he may be said to have lost (that is all, Interest in) by his Transgression; but to say *he told me that* S. F. *allowed no Man in his degenerate Estate to have any Spirit at all, as constitutive of Man* meerly, is to tell his Reader an impious Falshood twice over, and not to essay the enervating of one of those Reasons by me urged to prove it so: S. *Fisher's* Words were briefly these: ' As to the Spirit of Man, which concurs to the con-
' stituting of Man in his *Primitive Perfection*, it is the *Breath of Life which God*
' *breathed into his Soul*—whereby he became a Soul, *that did partake something of*
' *God's own Life.* This is *that living Principle of the Divine Nature*, which Man
' did before his Degeneration, and shall again after his Regeneration, partake of.
' I told him that S. *Fisher* did never intend it of the *Natural Soul of Man*, but
' rather of the Divine Life of the Soul, without which the Soul is destitute of the
' Knowledge of the true and Living God, his own Words very plainly shew; for if
' S. *Fisher* intended that Spirit which is the Divine Principle that Man did partake
' of before his Degeneration; certain and clear it is, that since Man did under that
' Degeneration partake of his own Soul, or else he could not have been a Man,
' S. Fisher *never meant the meer Soul of Man, but the Life of that Divine Principle*
' *which regenerates and renews the Soul unto a Life of Purity and Blessedness.* Unto which and much more he affords me no other Reply than what I have already
inserted, to wit, *I told him that* Fisher *allowed no Man in his degenerate Estate to*
have any Spirit at all as constitutive of Man; as if his meer *tell him* were Convincement enough to his Reader, that S. *Fisher* held *all sinful Men to have no Soul*, and
he knows the Consequence; If no Souls, then no Punishment; for to be constituted a perfect Man to God, and a meer Man, is not one and the same Thing; neither
can partaking of the Divine Life or Nature be so understood, *as that the Soul is*
that Divine Life or Nature it self; or that such as partake not of it, *have no Souls.*
Such Doctrine better becomes *J. Faldo's* Adventurous Abuses than the Writings of
that honest and Christian Man.

He tells us of some other Quotations which I medled not with, particularly, that G. *Fox* in his Book called the *Great Mystery*, &c: should say, *The Soul was Equal with God, that it was without beginning, infinite in it self and a Part of God*; for which he assigns us no Page in his Reply, in his first Book, the 16th; I have diligently perused it and find no such Thing; however should he have ever written these Words, I dare say for him, he understood no more by *Equality* than *Unity*; for God is greater than all; by *Infinite* no more than something *that is not finite*, or which comes not to an End; *and by the Soul's being without Beginning, and a Part of God*, no other than *that Divine Breath of Life*, which is as the Soul or Life of the Soul, that came out from God, and therefore is of God; that Cause is much to be suspected that props it self with such shallow Cavils; he observes no Nicety of Expression in his Writings, and it is therefore disingenuously done of any to make this ill Use of his plain and vulgar Phrases.

But lest all this should fail, and he had Reason to suspect it, he brings us out a Piece of a Letter, formerly written by *Josiah Coale* (who lived and died a faithful Servant of God, and is now at Rest with him) put into his Hands, I suppose, by his *Gentleman*, Pag. 94. as he received it at the Hand, I suppose, of some *Vagabond-Quaker.*

First, That he should call George Fox *the Father of many Nations*; but what is this more than to say, that Men of several Nations have been begot unto Christ through him; Thus Paul *was a Father to the* Romans, Corinthians, &c. 1 Cor. 4. 15. *for though ye have Ten Thousand Instructors, yet ye have not many Fathers; for in Christ have I begotten you.*

Secondly, *That his Life hath reached through his Children to the Isles afar off, to the begetting of many again unto a lively Hope.* But what of all this? The Life of God is one in all; *Paul* lived by the Life of Christ, and so did *Peter*; Paul *was present in Spirit, though absent in Body*, 1 Cor. 5. 3, 4.

Thirdly, *That Generations to come should call him blessed*: But is not the Memory of the Just blessed? *Prov.* 10. 7, and did not God by *Isaiah* Promise concerning

---

* *Homo rationabilis factus, irrationabiliter vivens, amisit rationem; tradidit se terreno spiritui*, Psal. 48. 21. vide *Irenæus*, p. 336. i. e. A Man who is made reasonable, living unreasonably, hath lost his Reason, having given himself up to an Earthly Spirit.

Israel, I will make thee an Eternal Excellency, and the Joy of many Generations, Isa. 6c. 37. This belongs to *G. Fox, Josiah Coale,* and every *Child of God*; yea, and *J. Faldo* too, if he were so good as he should be.

4thly, *That his Being and Habitation was in the Power of the Highest.* And so it should be; for that is the Habitation of every Child of God; for others dwell in the Power of the World. In short, we are exhorted to stand fast in the Power of Godliness; and we read that it was the End of the Evangelical Ministry *to turn People from the Power of Satan unto the Power of God,* which is the Power of the Highest.

5thly, *That he ruled and governed in Righteousness:* This is but what *Paul* exhorts *Timothy* to do in the Church of Christ, as both his Epistles inform us at large; Every Elder, Overseer or Pastor in the Church of Christ is bound to do so; If *J. F.* can prove he doth otherwise, he may then charge him with uncomely walking, but not *J. Coal* with Blasphemy for saying, *that a good Man governs in Righteousness.*

Lastly, *That his Kingdom is established in Peace, and the Increase thereof is without End:* So is the Kingdom of the Saints of God. That they have a Kingdom and Dominion is clear from several Scriptures: *It is the Father's good Pleasure to give you a* Kingdom, Luke 12. 23. *Wherefore we have received a* Kingdom *which cannot be shaken,* Heb. 12. 28. *The Saints shall judge the World,* 1 Cor. 6. 3. The Nature of this Kingdom is declared. Luke 17. 12. *The Kingdom of God is within.* John 18. 36. *My Kingdom is not of this World.* Rom. 14. 17. *For the Kingdom of God is not Meat and Drink, but Righteousness, Peace and Joy in the Holy Ghost.* The Durableness of this Kingdom is laid down by *Daniel,* and the Time came that the Saints possessed the Kingdom, *whose Kingdom is an Everlasting Kingdom,* Dan. 7. 22. 27.

Yet these so innocent Expressions, so scriptural, and therefore so easily defensible, doth this Adversary of ours call an *Evidence of the blasphemous unheard of Passages and Principles among our Ministry conceived, vented and allowed, which did the World know, it would make their Ears tingle, and their Hearts ake.* But we will see if these Words belong not of more Right to a Passage, that fell from the Mouth of a Court-Chaplain, in the Golden Age of *Independency,* not in a private Letter, but a publick Auditory, that we may help him to a clearer Sight of his own Folks, and that his severe Exclamation better suits them than us.

After the Death of *O. C.* that all due Acknowledgments might be paid to his Memory for the noble Acts he did, *of breaking all Oaths he made to God and Men, to advance his own Family and Interest, though to the Scandal of Religion and Loss of the Cause,* a certain Chaplain of his broke forth with this Extatical and Elegiack Assertion, *that if that were the Word of God* (meaning the Bible in his Hand) *then as certainly, that blessed Spirit* (the Protector) *was with Christ at the Right Hand of the Father; and if he be there, what may his Family expect from him? for if he were so useful and helpful, and so much Good influenced from him to them, when he was in a mortal State; how much more Influence will they have from him now he is in Heaven?* The Father, Son and Spirit, through him, bestowing Gifts and Graces upon them.

I will omit naming the Party, he is dead, I give the Fact, and it speaks so much Idolatry, that nothing Ranker can be produced of the most Extravagant Votaries of *Rome.*

God, if it pleaseth him of his Great Mercy, give this poor Man Repentance, before that Hour overtake him in which it will be hid from his Eyes, which ends my Return to these hard and Evil Speeches.

I shall, as my Manner hath been, produce the Testimonies of certain considerable Men in defence of what we believe, concerning the Light within; and others relating to the Soul of Man, for their Sakes, whom Tradition hath abused, and the frequent Clamours and Invectives of many against us blinded, so as to think we are the *Sink of Error and Off-scouring of all Heresy*; to the End that they may see our so much decry'd Doctrine, clearly and abundantly approv'd by such as are of general Reputation among them.

Of the Light shining in Man.

Vatablus and *Drusius* upon *Job* 24: 13. They are of those that rebelled against the Light, say, *that it is the Light of God, and that it is God himself.* I suppose, none

none will doubt that this Light shined in the Consciences of those that rebelled against it, consequently, the Light that shines in the Conscience is the Light of God, as he is the great Sun of Light.

Munsterius and *Clarius* upon *Job*, Chap. 25. 3. Upon whom doth not his Light arise? Ask, *Who is there in whom the Light of the Divine Wisdom doth not shine?*

Codurcus is of the same Mind, saying, *he enlightneth all Men,* referring us to *John*'s Testimony.

Drusius upon the same Place queries, *Who receiveth not his Light, and is not illuminated by his Light?*

Erasmus and *Vatablus*, on *John* 1. 9. calls it the *Fountain of Light, whence the Light also flowed to* John *himself.* Now if this Light be in Men, and of the Fountain of Light, which, say they, is God, I hope none will deny then the Light that shines in Men, is Divine Light, and consequently God, 1 *John* 1. 5.

Zegerus on *John* 1, ver. 4, 5. *In him was Life, and the Life was the Light of Men, &c.* expresseth himself thus: *That Life by which all Things were made, that which is the Word, yea, which is God the Fountain of all Life, that always was and is the Light of all Men — and it shineth in the Darkness of our Souls, which the Prince of Darkness had darkned.*

Cameron on the Place saith, *It is to be understood especially of that Light which is unto Salvation, and whereby it comes to pass that we are freed from the Darkness of Sin and Death.*

All which is to say, that the Light which shineth in Man's Heart is Divine and Saving, therefore God manifesting himself in Man.

Dr. *H. Moor,* in his *Philosophick Cabal,* Page 27, says, *The Light purs'd* Adam, *and upbraided unto him his Case after his Transgression, and that it was the* Divine Light; *wherefore he was asham'd, and hid himself at the Approach of the Divine Light, manifesting himself to him to the Reprehension and Rebuke of him*———*And the* Divine Light *charged all this Misery and Confusion upon the Eating of the Forbidden Fruit, and Luscious Dictates of his own Will*———*And the Divine Light spoke in* Adam, *concerning the Woman: What Work hath she made here?*

Thus doth he make the *Light that reproves in the Conscience* to be the *Divine Light,* and consequently of the *Nature of God, who is the great Fountain of Divine Light*; Nay, to put it out of Doubt, he reads those Words, which in *Genesis* say, *It was God himself that reproved* Adam, after the Manner before expressed, to wit, the Divine Light in *Adam* reproved him; thereby making the Divine Light in *Adam* and *GOD* to be ONE and the same Being.

Of the SOUL.

Justin Martyr brings *Tryphon* questioning thus concerning the Soul, and himself allowing it.

Ἡ ψυχὴ θεία καὶ ἀθάνατός ἐστι, καὶ αὐτῆ ἐκείνε βασιλικῆ μέρος, &c. That is, Is the Soul Divine and Immortal? Is it a Particle of that Commander himself, and as it seeth God, so is it also permitted to contain Divinity in our Mind, and thereby even now to be happy? *Yea, altogether, said I.*

Tertullian. de Anima, Pag. 297, asserts the Immortality and Divinity of the Soul.

P. Fagius in Gen. 2. 7. Rabbi Nehamanides *hath observ'd, That he that breatheth on any, contributes something of his own to it; whence Christ our Saviour, when he would communicate the Holy Spirit to his Disciples, he did it by breathing upon them, signifying that he contributed to them something of his own that was Divine.* The Word נשמת *signifyeth something* Divine *and* Heavenly; *some think* שמים *because the Immortal Soul of Man is a certain* Divine Thing *come from Heaven. And the* Poets *call the Soul of Man a* Particle of Divine Breath נשמת חיים, *a* Breath *or* Spiritus, Divine, Heavenly, Vital, Immortal, *and enduring for ever. The* Soul of Man Divine *and* Heavenly, *consists in a* Divine *and* Heavenly Spirit. *The Author* Hiskuni *understands it to be an Inspiration from the Holy Spirit of God.*

Peter Martyr speaks of the Soul thus in Psalm 94. *We are taught not to withdraw from the Divine Nature those Things that are perfect and absolute in us,* p. 12. and in p. 122. *They say* (says he) נשמה *doth chiefly signify that which is* Divine *and* Reasonable *that God doth give unto us.*

H. Bullen.

H. Bullenger faith, *The Soul is a Spiritual Substance poured of God into Man's Body*; in his 4th Decad. 10 Serm.

Augustine faith, *It is felt in the Life——it is unutterable,—breathed into Man's Body by God of his own Essence and Nature——from the secret Power of God.*

In short, Very various have been the Opinions of the Ancients concerning the Soul : *Plato* divided it into Two Parts ; *Zeno* into Three ; *Panætius* into Five or Six ; *Soranus* into Seven ; *Chrysippus* into Eight ; *Apollophanes* into Nine ; some of the *Stoicks* into Ten ; *Possidonius* into Twelve, as *Tertullian* reports in his Book *de Anima*, p. 273. and *H. Bullenger* tells us, *That hardly two say one and the same Thing concerning it.*

Seeing then that Men of such excellent Abilities, and nicest Disquisitions both in Nature and Theology, rather prove their own Contradiction and Confusion, than give us any certain Account of the Soul, what she is ; and that the Scripture mentions it so rarely and obscurely, and that *J. Faldo denies all immediate Inspiration*, (as he calls it) which is the only Way left us to understand it, he hath not shewn himself a *Charitable Divine*, but an *Impious Wrangler* in falling so heavily upon us with the opprobrious Name of *Idolaters* for assigning something more of Divinity unto the Soul in it's Primitive Perfection, than his Opinion will allow us.

CHAP. XII.

Of the Resurrection of Dead Bodies, and Eternal Recompence. Our Doctrine maintained by Scripture, Reason and Authorities.

IN his former Book he charged us with the *Denial of the Resurrection of the Dead, and Eternal Recompence*. The Testimonies he brought for Proof were such as render'd him very weak, or something worse, I hope they were sufficiently disengag'd from his Service, unto which, according to his old Custom, he hath not thought fit to reply : He only takes Notice of two or three short Passages out of six or seven Passages of Answer, on which he bestows a few Squibs, and concludes with that Contempt and Rudeness no Man pretending to *Religion* or *Humanity* would have vented, especially against a Man that he provok'd to answer him, by beginning to abuse his Friends in general, and him in particular ; considering withal, that his Profession is to suffer, not to insult. Strange ! that my *Religion* and *Conscience* should subject me to so much Contempt, with a Man that pretends to both. But *W. P.* I dare say, had not been thus treated by *J. F.* could he threaten the Law, and Flant and Swagger at the Rate *J. F.* doth. But it is like such Folk, to insult where they may do it safely.

One of his Testimonies was this, *Christ is the Resurrection, to raise up that which Adam lost, and to destroy him who deceiv'd him* ; *So Christ is the Resurrection unto Life of Body, Soul and Spirit, and so renews Man*, Princ. pap. call. Quak. p. 34. I will not trouble my self, nor spend my Reader's Time in transcribing what I said in Defence of this Passage, as to the End he design'd it ; Nothing can be clearer, than that this concerns *Regeneration*, so says *J. F.* himself, pag. 132. consequently the *Resurrection of Dead Bodies is not concerned in it*.

His second Testimony fell from *G. Whitehead* in these Words, if we may believe him ; *I do not believe this Body shall rise again after it is Dead*. I told him of this Disingenuous Catching, and put him in Mind of the Apostle's own Expression that justifies the Saying, if it was ever said——*Thou Fool—Thou Sowest not that Body that shall be*. But unto whatever I urged for the clearing of our Friends Words and Writings from his ill Constructions, like an unfair, if not a fearful Adversary, he makes no Return.

I will now set down what he thought fit to give us.

Rep. p. 88. *Take W. P's own Words (acknowledging the Truth of my Charge)* Either the Resurrection of the Body must be without the Matter, or it must not ; If it must, then it is not the same numerical Body, and so their proper and strict Resurrection they must let go ; *although this allows my Charge true, and so enough to it's Vindication*; yet *I shall answer P's Arguments against the Resurrection, wherein he opposes Philosophical Conclusions to the express Doctrine of the Scriptures.*

Rejoyn.

Rejoyn. If I have herein vindicated his Charge, it muſt follow that he charged us with denying the Reſurrection of the Body *without any Allowance of Change as to that Matter and Corruptibility it was buried with*; conſequently, *That* J. Faldo *believes a Reſurrection of the ſame Carnal Bodies that are interred without any Alteration whatever*; for that allowed, *they cannot riſe properly and ſtrictly the ſame Bodies.* If our rejecting this Carnal Dream of his, is that horrid Principle he charged us with denying, we have no Reaſon to be much concerned abont the Succeſs. But he proceeds.

Rep. p. 88, 89. *The latter Part of* W. P's *Dilemma is the Horn with which he puſhes at the Reſurrection,* viz. *If it muſt not be without that ſame groſs Matter it died with, then I affirm it cannot be incorruptible, becauſe it will carry with it that which will render it corruptible ad infinitum.*

The Body muſt neceſſarily be the ſame Matter is allowed, but W. P. *calls it in his Aſſumption of the ſecond Part of his* Dilemma, *the ſame groſs Matter, which makes his Argument Fallacious in the Form of it. But to let that paſs, it ſhall be the ſame Matter and numerical, though not of the ſame Groſneſs; and ſhall have the ſame Subſtance and Eſſential Form, though not the ſame Accidents.*

Rejoyn. Is this the Scripture-Doctrine, he ſays, *I oppoſe with Philoſophical Concluſions?* Would he would give us but one Scripture that looks but favourably towards this Reply; I never read one yet *of a Body's having the ſame Matter, and not the ſame Groſneſs, the ſame Subſtance and Eſſence, and not the ſame Accidents.* For Shame; muſt our Denial of *Phyſical Niceties,* or rather *J. Faldo's* Abſurdities, be branded for *horrid Doctrine.* 'Tis true, in *Philoſophy,* that a *Subſtance* may loſe it's *Accidents* and yet remain the ſame Subſtance. Things may be diſcolour'd, yet the ſame Beings they were before: But that Matter ſhould be ſuch, and not groſs, is incongruous with Scripture and *Philoſophy.* Matter and Groſneſs, or Corruption, are *Synonymous* in *Philoſophy* and common Speech: But that Groſneſs, or the *Subſtantial Part* of any Man's Body ſhould be but an *Accident,* that the *Accidence* teaches all Boys in a *Noun-Subſtantive,* deſerves a Laſh at leaſt. Are Fleſh, Blood and Bones *Accidents,* or that of them which is groſs and corruptible an *Accident?* I wonder what a fearful Sort of a Noun-Subſtantive *J. F.* would be in caſe he were *condens'd* and *rarified* of ſuch *groſs* and *corruptible Accidents*; Indeed one would think his Head, if not all the reſt, had been near akin to them, when he writ this Piece of *New Philoſophy.* But this abundantly proveth upon what Foot his Reſurrection ſtandeth, if it may be ſaid to have any, or ſtand at all.

Fallacious is but one of his hard Words; for if the Body riſeth with the ſame Matter it carried to the Grave, it riſeth with groſs Matter, unleſs it carried no groſs Matter thither. Let him chuſe of the two, which to deny. But is this to Anſwer my Argument, to tell us with ſo much unwarranted Confidence, that the Body ſhall be the ſame Matter, Subſtance, and Eſſence, &c. the very Queſtion? What is this but to ſay, It ſhall be ſo, becauſe it *ſhall be ſo?* If he would have done any thing, *he ſhould have demonſtrated how Matter can be without Groſneſs, and the moſt groſs and material Par. of the Body to be but the Accidents.* But he thinks he hath ſaid ſomething to the Point.

Rep. p. 89. *To talk that it* (the Body) *cannot be incorruptible becauſe beyond the Nature of Matter it ſelf, is to talk like an* Atheiſt, *making Nature to be God, and not acknowledging the God of Nature.*

Rejoyn. Did I dare ſport in Religion, ſcarce ever Man gave a fairer Occaſion in his Compaſs; But he practiſes it, and I abhor it. This is ſuch a *riddle me, riddle me,* as I never heard of before.

W. P. ſays, *The Nature of Matter admits not of Incorruptibility,* ergo, W. P. *is an Atheiſt,* ergo, *he makes Nature to be God,* and ergo, *he acknowledges not the God of Nature.*

This is the very Man, that not a Page off, reflects Ignorance upon my Philoſophy: Doubtleſs a Peerleſs Diſputant, one Way or other. May he evermore thus confute me? which is all I will ſay to ſuch ſubtle Reaſoning and lofty Argumentation in this Place. Yet he has not done.

Rep. p. 89. *If God be Omnipotent, (which he is, or he is not God) he is able* (as the Apoſtle ſpeaks) *to ſubdue all Things to himſelf, with which Words he anſwers all Cavils from Impoſſibility in Nature.*

Rejoyn. The Queſtion was not about God's Power; nor was it ſo much as any Part of the Queſtion; But *whether Matter is not by Nature corruptible, and how that which is corruptible by Nature, may be by Nature incorruptible.* This Scripture

he

he urges to prove his Carnal Resurrection, will as well prove the *Popish* Transubstantiation, or any the most unreasonable Conceit in the World; for it is but saying, *All Things are possible with God, and God is able to subdue all things unto himself*; and the Business is done at *J. Faldo*'s Rate of arguing. But the Question is not about what God can do, but what *he hath done, and has declared he will do*.

I know there are Impossibilities in Nature, which God's *Omnipotency* makes possible; but if *J. Faldo* doth not know that there is a Difference between Impossibility in Nature, and *Contrariety to Nature*, I now tell him there is one, and that so wide, as though Almighty God frequently supplies Nature's Want of Power, yet he rarely, if ever, acts contrary to and inconsistent with the Nature of his own Creatures; What is Spiritual, remains *Spiritual*; what is Material, *Material*; and what is Corruptible, *Corruptible*. But let us see how much better he acquits himself of another Passage, which he ventures to cite, and in my Opinion doth no more.

Rep. p. 89. W. P. *proceeds farther in this vain Reasoning, and wicked too,* p. 202. *I say, we cannot see how that which is of the Dust should be eternal, whilst that from whence it came, is by Nature but temporal; and that which is yet most of all irreconcileable with Scripture and right Reason, is, that the Loss and Change of Nature from Corruptible to Incorruptible, Natural to Spiritual, should not make it another Body. That it is according to Scripture I have given large Proofs in my Book, to no one of which he replieth, as also how unreasonable it is to call that a Resurrection, which is not of the same Numerical Body.*

Rejoyn. We may guess how well he prov'd it in his first Book by the Strength he hath employ'd to maintain it in his second. But let all sober Men judge if this Reply be pertinent to this Part of my Answer; yet he promised he would answer my Arguments. For the Scripture, it is clear, *That Corruption shall not inherit Incorruption; neither can Flesh and Blood inherit the Kingdom of God*, 1 Cor. 15. 50. Thus *Annota. cert. Div. Anno* 1645, upon the Place; and if he will know the *true Resurrection*, let him learn to understand this weighty Passage: *For we know, that if our Earthly House of this Tabernacle were dissolved, we have a Building of God, an House not made with Hands, Eternal in the Heavens*, 2 Cor. 5. 1. And I cannot but wonder, my Adversary's Understanding should be so benighted, as that contrary to express Scripture, he should assert a Resurrection of the same Body that is buried, *properly and strictly so*; the Apostle teaches us to believe that it is not that *same Body that is sown that shall be*; for though we shall be chang'd from Mortality to Immortality, Corruption to Incorruption, 2 *Cor*. 5. 1: and 1 *Cor*. 15. 37, 50. yet (Men's Bodies of) *Flesh and Blood shall not inherit the Kingdom of God:* For the Word *Resurrection*, Ἀνάστασις doth not strictly imply a taking up of the same Numerical Body, as he would have us believe from his new found Relative IT, (first Book, 2d Part, p. 103.) for which *Beza* shall give him a Release both from the *Latin* and original *(Greek)* there being no Word in either for (his *Relative*) IT, on which he and his factious Brother *Hicks* have so *relatively* insisted; Indeed as their last and best Refuge. The Text lyeth thus:

Σπείρεται σῶμα Ψυχικὸν, ἐγείρεται σῶμα πνευματικὸν. *Seritur corpus animale, resuscitatur corpus spirituale,* i. e. *A natural Body is sown, a spiritual Body is raised*; that is, They lay down a natural, and take up a spiritual Body, or in Lieu of a Natural, receive a spiritual Body; not that the Natural Body shall be *transubstantiated* into a Spiritual Body, or that admitting of such an Exchange, that the Spiritual is the same Numerical Body, that was *the Natural*; for so the Natural and Spiritual Body would be one and the same; but suppose *J. Faldo*'s *Relative* IT to hold, I do utterly deny that this Text is concerned in the Resurrection of Man's Carnal Body at all. I will recite it with the five following Verses as they lie in our *English* Translation.

It is sown a Natural Body, it is raised a Spiritual Body; *There is a Natural Body and there is a Spiritual Body*; *and so it is written, The first Man Adam was made a Living Soul, the last Adam was made a Quickning Spirit*; *howbeit, that was not first which is Spiritual, but that which is Natural, and afterward, that which is Spiritual*; *The first Man is of the Earth Earthy, the second Adam is the Lord from Heaven*; *As is the Earthy, so are they that are Earthy*; *and as is the Heavenly, so are they also which are Heavenly*; *and as we have born the Image of the Earthy, we shall also bear the Image of the Heavenly*, v. 44, 45, 46, 47, 48, 49. I say this doth not concern the Resurrection of Carnal Bodies, but the *two States* of Men under the first and second *Adam*, Men are sown into the World Naturally, and so

they

they are the Sons of the first *Adam*; but they are raised Spiritually, through him who is the Resurrection and the Life, and so they are the Sons of the *second Adam*, the Lord from Heaven, the Quickning Spirit. The very Words of the Apostle undeniably prove this to be the Scope; how else could the first *Adam*'s being made a *living Soul*, and the second *Adam* a *Quickning Spirit*, be a pertinent Instance to prove Natural and Spiritual Bodies; upon which follows, that the Natural was first, that is, *the first* Adam, *and then that which is* Spiritual, *which is the second Adam*, the Quickning Spirit, the Lord from Heaven, who came to raise up the Sons of the first *Adam*, from their *Dead* to his *Living*, their *Natural* to his *Spiritual Estate*.

But perhaps it will be objected, that the 47th Verse, *The first Man is of the Earth Earthy*, and Part of the 9th Verse, *We shall also bear the Image of the Heavenly*, seem to imply a bodily Resurrection; But let the whole Verses be considered, and we shall find no such Thing. The first Man is of the *Earth Earthy, the second Man is the Lord from Heaven*; who sees not that this is rather spoken of the *Earthy-Mindedness*, than of the Earthy Body of *Adam*? It was mentioned to shew the great Disparity that is between the Nature and Qualification of the first and second *Adam*; the following Verse puts this Interpretation out of Doubt, *as is the Earthy, such are they that are Earthy; and as is the Heavenly, such are they also that are Heavenly*.

For those Words, *We shall also bear the Image of the Heavenly*. I cannot see how they should relate to the Resurrection of the Carnal Bodies of Men; for the *Image of the Heavenly*, is a renewed State to God, through the Operation of the Spirit and Power of Christ, the first Part of the Verse clears it; *and as we have born the Image of the Earthy, we shall*, (or rather, *let us bear*) the Image of the Heavenly.) as *Ambrose* and *Theophylact* read it, and fix or seven Copies besides have it) which is as much as to say, *That as we have born the Image of the God of this World, by becoming his Children, so may we bear the Image of the True and Living God, by being redeemed from a vain Conversation, having our Consciences sprinkled from dead Works, and being born again of the incorruptible Seed, by the Word of God, which lives and abides for ever*. * Had this concerned the Resurrection in our Adversary's Sense, the *Image* would be changed wholly, (Accidents would not serve his Turn) therefore not the same Image, unless the *Earthy could be the Heavenly Image*, which were impossible; for we should lose our Earthly Bodies, at what Time we become *the Image of the Heavenly*, in this World, if this Conceit had any Truth in it, and if of the other, they to be sure must never enter; for another takes Place: But as it was never understood so by any that I know of, but evermore of that *Earthly Image*, which came by Transgression, and the *Heavenly Image* that comes in obeying the Truth by the Spirit, according to what the Apostle saith, Col. 3. 8, 9, 10. *But now you also put off all these, Anger, Wrath, Blasphemy, filthy Fornication, out of your Mouths, lye not one to another; seeing you have put off the old Man with his Deeds, and have put on the new Man, which is renewed in Knowledge after the Image of him that created him*: So, 'till the Natural Man that is sown, *comes to die to his own Image, Will and Affections, he can never be quickned into this Glorious Image of the second* Adam, *the quickning Spirit, who is the Lord from Heaven*.

But suppose it were to be understood rather of Bodies than Souls, the Text may be as well translated a *Living* as a *Natural Body is sown*; yea rather so, for the Word is not ἐυσικὸν but ψυχικὸν, or *Animale*, that imports as much as a *Soul's Body*, and such an one, I dare say, *J. Faldo* would not be willing to sow, except he had a Mind to be buried alive: So *Clarius* both translates it, and interprets it, *Corpus animale accipiendum est, cui anima vitam præstat ne intereat*. i. e. A *Souly* or Living Body is that, to whom the *Soul gives Life that it doth not die*.

Annot. cert. Divin. anno 1645.

---

* If it be objected, *that Adam is not mentioned as degenerated, but as created, and therefore this Interpretation will not do*. I answer; 'tis true, he is said to be made a living Soul; but first, this makes not for the Resurrection of dead Bodies, and so far our Adversary gets no Strength. 2dly, Though the Apostle begins with the first *Adam*'s Creation, yet he orderly comes to the Earthly Image, that the living Soul put on by Disobedience, which introduceth the Necessity of the Coming of the second *Adam*, and his Quickning Spirit to create anew, and bring into the Image of God. So there is *Adam*, as sown, and his Posterity representatively in him, and his and their Lapse, and then the Restoration by him that is the Resurrection and the Life, the second *Adam*, the Lord from Heaven however.

But

But to go farther; suppose the Apostle treated of a Natural Change, and not only of the Spiritual State of the Soul in this Life, yet can it be extended no farther than this; when good Men lay down this Earthly House, or Tabernacle of Clay, the Image that came to us from *Adam*'s Loyns, we shall be cloathed upon of Immortality, received into the Building that is Eternal, in the Heavens, and be made like unto his Glorious Body; 2 Cor. 5. 1. *Philip.* 2. 21. *We sow a Natural, we reap a Spiritual, and we sow not that Body which shall be; but God giveth it a Body as pleaseth him*, 1 Cor. 15. 37. 38.

I also parallelled my Adversary's *Change*, yet *Sameness*, of Bodies with the *Popish Transubstantiation*, shewing, that the Absurdity *Protestants* Charge upon this, is equally chargeable upon that; only with this Distinction, that the Papists *deny it to continue a Wafer after Consecration*; but *John Faldo* asserts, *the Spiritual Body to be the same Carnal Body after Mutation*, which is a Kind of *Consubstantiation*, and far more ridiculous: But of this he took no Notice, and his Silence is prudent: Things unanswerable are better unmedled with, than cited and not confuted; He knows who pass'd for wise Men by holding their Tongues; I wish that were his greatest Fault.

I will conclude this Head with a few Testimonies in Defence of what we have said against *J. Faldo*'s *Carnal Resurrection*, referring my Reader to my Chapters of the Resurrection both against him in my Answer, and my Book against *T. Hicks*, entituled, *Reason against Railing*; and particularly the second Part of a Discourse (that we hope will suddenly be publish'd) call'd, *The Christian Quaker*, for his fuller Satisfaction of our Scriptural Judgment, and our *Adversary's fleshly Apprehension* concerning the *Resurrection*.

H. More, *Myst.* God. Page 221, 224, 225.

Dr. *H. More*, the *Cantabrigian Philosopher*, begins his Discourse of the *Resurrection* with this Censure of *J. Faldo*'s. " We come now to the second Particu-
" lar propounded, the *Resurrection of the Dead*, which I dare say the *Atheist* will
" listen to, with more than ordinary Attention, *and greedily suck in the Doctrine,*
" *provided it be stated with the most curious Circumstances that the* RIGIDEST
" OF THEOLOGERS *will describe it by, that we shall have the same* NUMERI-
" CAL *Bodies, in which we lived here on Earth, and that those very Bodies* (the
" Mould being turned aside) *shall start out of the Grave*. This Doctrine the
" *Atheist very dearly hugs as a Pledge* in his bold Conceit of the *Falsness and*
" *Vanity of all the other Articles of Religion*; wherefore he fancying the Upshot
" of *Christianity* to be so groundless and incredible, he fairly quits himself of the
" Trouble of all, and yields himself up wholly to the Pleasures of this present
" World.

To the Objection of *Atheists*, who play hard upon *J. Faldo*'s Carnal Resurrection.

" First, *In that* Canibals *proper Bodies are made up of the Flesh of other Men,*
" *so as if every one had his own, he would have never a Body in the Resurrection.*

" Secondly, *That it implies that all Men are buried, when as* Myriads *are drown'd*
" *in the Sea, and eaten by Fishes.*

" Thirdly, *That Men's Bodies are passing like Rivers, consequently no more the*
" *same* Numerical *Bodies, than the Water that runs away is the same River; and*
" *upon this Score the Body of an Old Man must pay for the Sins of a Young Man,*
" *whose youthful Body felt the Pleasure, and is gone.*

' He thus answers out of the best Sort of Philosophers, That the Soul of every
' Man is his individual Person, and that She alone it is that *sees, hears, enjoys*
' *Pleasures, and undergoes Pain, and that the Body is not sensible of any Thing, no*
' *more then a Man's Doublet, when he is well Bastinado'd*; and this Answer (says he)
' *Takes away all the first and last Cavil* (he goes on) *and why do Men plead for the*
' *Consociation of the Soul's numerical Body in Reward or Punishment, but that they*
' *fancy the Body capable of Pleasure and Pain*; *but they err, not knowing the Nature*
' *of Things*; *the Body being utterly incapable of all Sense and Cogitation, as not only*
' *the* Best Platonists, *but also that excellent Philosopher* Des-Cartes *hath determined,*
' *and is abundantly demonstrated in my Treatise of the* Immortality of the Soul. See
' Book 2. Chap. 2. 4, 5, 6. To the second Cavil I answer, *That the Universal*
' *Expression of Men's Rising out of the Grave, is but a Prophetical Scheme of Speech,*

' the

'the more strongly to strike our Senses, as I have already intimated, in my Exposi-
'tion on 1 Cor. 15. against the Psychopannachites. See Book 1. c. 6. §. 3. This
'Succour, saith he, we have against the Atheists out of Philosophy; but I answer
'farther as concerning the Scripture it self, That I dare challenge him to produce any
'Place of Scripture, out of which he can make it appear, that the Mystery of the Re-
'surrection implies the Resuscitation (or raising up) of the same Numerical Body:
'The most Pregnant of all is, * Job 19. which late Interpreters are now so Wise,
'as not to understand at all of the Resurrection: And for 1 Cor. 15, that Chapter is
'so far from asserting this Curiosity, that it plainly says, it is not the same Body.
'But the Atheist will still hang on, and object farther, That the very Term Resur-
'rectio implies, that the same Body shall rise again; for that only that falls, can be
'said properly to rise again. (Where let the Reader take Notice, that D. More calls
John Faldo, Atheist, for it his Objection against me, Rep. p. 89.) But says D. More,
'The Answer will be easie, the Objection being grounded meerly upon a Mistake of the
'Sense of the Word, which is to be interpreted out of those Higher Originals, the
'Greek and Hebrew, and not out of the Latin, though the Word in Latin doth not
'always imply an individual Restitution of what is gone or fallen; as in that Verse in
'Ovid.

   Victa tamen vinces subversaq; Troja resurges.

'But this, saith he, is not so near to our Purpose (*yet it excludes the same Nu-
'merical Troja*) Let us rather consider the Greek Word ἀνάστασις, which *Resurrectio*
'supplies in Latin, and therefore must be made to be of as large a Sense as it.
'Now ἀνάστασις is so far from signifying (in some Places) the *Reproduction*, or
'*Recovery of the same Thing that was before*, that it bears no Sense at all of *Reite-
'ration in it*, as Mat. 22. 24. Καὶ ἀναστάσει σπέρμα τῷ ἀδελφῷ αὐτοῦ; *and shall raise up
'Seed unto his Brother.* Also Gen 7. 4. there ἐξαναστάσει, and ἀνάστημα signifies meer-
'ly a *Living Substance*, and therefore ἀνάστασις in an Active Signification, according
'to this Sense, will be nothing else *but a giving or continuing Life and Substance to
'a Thing.* The Word in the Hebrew, that answers to ἀνάστημα, is יקום which
'Translators translate a *Living Substance*; whence תקימה according to this Analo-
'gy, may very well bear the same Latitude of Sense that תחיה they being both
'Words that are rendred *Resurrectio*, but simply of themselves only *Vevification*,
'or *Erection unto Life*.

Thus far D. H. More, against J. Faldo's *Carnal Resurrection*, of whose Philosophy, Scripture-Challenge, and Criticisms, let him clear himself if he can. I shall
also produce a Testimony out of T. Collier.

   T. Collier's Works, Pag. 169.

'This Doctrine of the Resurrection of this Body, is by some denied, and by
'others *too Carnally looked upon*; some thinking, *that our Bodies of Flesh shall be raised
'in the same Form in which they dyed*; others, that they shall be Spiritual, yet question,
'Whether they shall be of the same Substance; therefore it will be necessary to con-
'sider Two Particulars for the clearing of it: *First*, By what Power we shall be
'raised. *Secondly*, With what Bodies.

   1. By what Power.

Answ. 'First, By the same Power by which Jesus Christ was raised, which was
'by the Power and Spirit of God. *Secondly*, By the same Power and Spirit that
'the Saints are raised from the Spiritual Death of Sin and Self, *Phil.* 3. 10. *Rom.* 8.
'11. This being a Truth, that they shall be raised by the same Power, it may
'somewhat direct us to the Form in which they shall be raised, which is the Se-
'cond Particular; that is, *In a Spiritual Form, not in a Fleshly*; for as the Spirit
'of Christ raiseth us up in the Spirit, while we are here, *so shall it raise up our
'Spirit in the Last Day*: It is sown a Natural Body, it is raised a Spiritual Body;
'*Our vile Bodies shall be changed, and made like His Glorious Body.*

D. H. Hammond also denies *a proper and strict Resurrection of Bodies*, and consequently is guilty of that horrid Principle, as J. Faldo calls it, which may be seen at
large in his Comment, 1 Cor. 15. Among other Things, he tells us of one *Synesius*

---

* Note, Reader, that our Translation is erroneous, *Job* 19. 32, *whom mine Eyes* shall behold. In the Hebrew thus, ועיני ראו ולא זר, i. e. *mine Eyes* have *seen*; the Septuagint ἑώρακε, videt, doth *see*, as *Drusius* and *Cadurcus* observe.

out of *Vossius*, who was made Bishop, *notwithstanding he refused to Subscribe the Article of the Resurrection of the Body*, which shows how much greater Charity they had for Dissenters, *than our rigid Adversary*, whilst a *Dissenter*; for indeed *it was very diversly thought on, and very obscurely laid down in the Beginning of the Third Century*, says P. D. Huetius in Origenianis, p. 132.

Farrellus, Calvin's Predecessor at *Geneva*, and one to whom that Eminent Reformer writ many *Loving and Respectful Epistles*, usually beginning with *Clarissime, Charissime*, and such like, did both deny the Resurrection of the same Numerical Body, but defended his Opinion, and disputed strenuously against the Vulgar Notion, which plainly opposeth *J. Faldo*'s, but more especially * *Thomas Vincent*'s gross Notion of the Resurrection, who hath taken upon him in a large Discourse, called, *Christ's Certain and Sudden Appearance to Judgment*, pag. 48, 49, to write the *History of it*, wherein he is so punctual, that he doth not only tell them what Bodies they shall have, but what Encounters and Dialogues are like to pass, even to Scolding, Railing, Scratching, and I know not what besides; so Vain and Ridiculous is that Author.

I will wrap up these Testimonies with two Passages out of *Origen* in *Jerom*, *Non easdem Carnes nec in ijs formis restituent quæ fuerunt Semina*, i. e. The Seed shall not restore the *same Flesh*, nor in the *same Form* ——— Again, *Non oculis videbimus*, &c. We shall not *see with Eyes, hear with Ears, act with Hands, walk with Feet*, in that Spiritual and Æthereal Body that is promised, that is not *subject to be toucht or seen with Eyes*, &c. This, and much more, is urged by *Jerome*, against *John of Jerusalem*, Epist. cap. 8.

These Testimonies I have produced, to shew the Arrogancy and Uncharitableness of *John Faldo, in counting it an horrid Thing to reject his Carnal Notion of the Resurrection of the Dead*, and that to such a Degree *destroys* (if you will believe him) *all Hope of Immortality*; most absurdly placing Eternal Felicity therein.

The *Resurrection* we own, and for the Manner of it, we are not inquisitive; and as I told him before, so again, ' Because these Things run Men into unprofitable
' Questions, and a Philosophical Way of Discoursing, no Ways tending to God's
' Honour, nor the Soul's Profit and Comfort; I shall decline any farther or nicer
' Disquisition, and content our selves with this, *That if we Live Holily, we shall Dye*
' *Happily; and if we walk in His Fear, we shall Depart in His Favour*; and at being
' *Unclothed of Mortality, we shall be Clothed on with Immortality and Eternal Life:*
' For God will raise such into Immortal Life and Glory, who truly *Dye in the*
' *Lord*. But we cannot but take Notice of the Subtilty of God's Enemy, who, by
' casting Curious, Intricate, and Unprofitable Questions, about what Bodies the
' Dead shall rise with, and bringing us under Vulgar Reflections by not consenting
' thereto, endeavours to divert the Minds of People *from our most frequent and*
' *fervent pressing a Part in the First Resurrection, that only Saves from the Power*
' *of the Second Eternal Death*; of which let my Reader receive this Friendly Warn-
' ing; for besides that it is a *Satanical Decoy*, *Thou Fool* belongs to none more, *than*
' *him, who acquiesces not with all humble and contented Submission in the Good Will*
' *of God, whose Will be done in Earth as it is in Heaven.*

To the Second Part of his Chapter, which concerneth *our Denial of Eternal Rewards*; although it deserves not our Notice, for the Folly and Falshood it contains; yet that he may not make my Silence to yield his Charge, and to show that in every Point he behaves himself dishonestly towards us, I shall consider that Little he says.

Rep. p. 89. *Concerning a Reward in the World to come, which I affirm they did not profess*, W. P. *opposes, rather because he would not be thought to subscribe to me, than that he believes not what I say to be True.*

Rejoyn. This Man pretends to judge Hearts, not only without Words, but also contrary to Words. I did most expresly tell him, *That though we own the Beginning of Heaven and Hell to be in this World* (who charged us with the Denial of them any where else) *yet that they were but Earnests of that Compleat Joy or Torment that Men should receive as their Eternal Reward or Recompence hereafter:* But this passes for Hypocrisie with *J. Faldo*'s present Sort of Conscience: And he proceeds,

---

* O the Angry Countenance the Wicked will have on that Day!——O the Angry Speeches!——It may be, from Words they fall to Blows, and tear one anothers Hair, and spurn at one anothers Bellies, bite one anothers Flesh, and even claw out one anothers Eyes.

Rep.

Rep. p. 89. *W. P. tells me,* pag. 203. None ever read so; *J. Faldo* quotes no such Thing; Nay, he says he hath searcht, but to no Purpose. *My Charge was not, that they deny a Reward in another World, but that they profess no such Thing; yet being Silent to it, hath a full Consequence that it is none of their Belief.*

Rejoyn. How could his Charge imply no such Thing, who makes our Silence (upon which he grounded it) to have this full Consequence, *That a future Heaven and Hell are none of their Belief,* and if not believed, denyed. However, it makes not a little for us, that he not only never read so, quotes no such Thing, and says, *He hath searcht to no Purpose,* but that he hath made no *Reply* to these Words, he recites out of my Answer, which hath this full Consequence, *That for* J. Faldo *to charge what he has never read, what he hath searcht for and could not find* (p. 141, 142,) *and therefore could not quote upon us to our Scandal) is unworthy of any Man pretending to Common Honesty.*

But what doth he mean by our not professing Eternal Rewards? Our not daring to enter into the Secret of the Almighty? What, how and by whom they are to be distributed? What other End have our Meetings, Writings and Sufferings? Must I always deny Eternal Recompence, where I do not expresly declare I own it? How many Times in Religious Discourses will *J. Faldo* come under the like Imputation? he cannot shew me one Book that was ever writ by any of us, in which it is not abundantly implied, if not most plainly expressed: Were there no such Thing, it would belong to us, above all other People, to use the Apostles Words, *We are of all Men most miserable;* but God hath fixed that Hope of Immortality and Eternal Life in our Souls, which all *J. Faldo's* Clamours will be too weak to shake. But were we darker in this Point (than whom none are clearer) we and our Books have *Moses,* the *Prophets* and their Writings to keep us Company, who mention it but obscurely, and not so frequently and unquestionably as we do. *J. Faldo* loves to hear talk of Heaven, but despises and shuns the Way which leads to it; and because our greatest Pains are imployed in bringing People into that streight and narrow Way that leads thither, rather than by *delicious Fables* to preach them into an Hope of Heaven, whilst in a State of Disobedience to God's Holy Spirit, therefore is it that he concludes us not to believe Eternal Rewards, that is, to deny them. Never did Man catch at such broken Reeds to save himself from the just Abhorrence of all sober People. We deny his *Carnal Resurrection,* therefore we must *needs deny Eternal Rewards.* Again, We do not believe Eternal Rewards (if he may be credited) *yet he never read so, much less found* it so by his own Confession; and therefore could never quote it so. If we speak of Salvation, unless we put *future* or *eternal* to it, he confines it to this World; he deals so with *Heaven* and *Hell;* boldly concluding, from what we say Men feel and know of those Things here, our dis-belief of any such Thing hereafter. I told him of *B. Hall* and *T. Brooks,* their Books entituled, *Heaven upon Earth,* but he says nothing to that. In short, he seems to have made it his Business to render us but as odious, as his Wits and worse would let him, but let him go with this Character, no Man *having charged so home, proved so weakly, and abused so grosly,* as this Adversary hath done.

Because I concluded my Answer to the two first Parts of his former Book, tho' contrarily to what he did, yet in the same Method, he is pleased thus to treat me.

Rep. pag. 90, 91. *See how good* W. P. *is at Aping my Logick. If Quakerism (so called) says* he, *be not another Dispensation than that of Christ preached and setled by the Apostles; If it deny not the Scriptures; if it deny not all nor any of the Ordinances of the Gospel,* &c. *And so he goes on with his Negatives; by the same good Logick I will prove Geometry, Logick or Philosophy to be Christianity. If Geometry,* &c. *deny none of these Things, Geometry is Christianity; but it doth not, therefore Christianity; yea, if we will pass to the Concrete, you may prove an* Horse *or a* Goose *a Christian by the same Argument; for they deny none of these Things.*

Rejoyn. Take away his idle Carps and Cavils, and he would have nothing to say, and he rarely says any thing, but something is against himself. Who any whit intelligent or candid, considering that I resumed the Argument in opposite Terms, could think I intended it not to opposite Ends? That is, when *J. Faldo* tells us *that we deny the Scriptures and all the Ordinances of the Gospel,* and we answer, *that we do not deny the Scriptures or any Ordinance of the Gospel,* that we thereby do not mean, or these Words do not imply, *an Acknowledging the Scriptures and every Ordinance of the Gospel;* for Instance: Suppose any Man charges

J. Faldo with a Denial of the Scriptures to be the Word of God, and Baptism and the Supper to be Ordinances of the Gospel, and he shall answer, *I do not deny the Scriptures to be the Word of God, nor Baptism nor the Supper to be Ordinances of the Gospel:* Are we to conclude, *that* J. Faldo *acknowledged the Scriptures to be the Word of God, and those Ordinances to be Gospel, no more than an Horse or Goose?* I will form it into an Argument for his Sake.

He that denies the Scriptures and Ordinances of the Gospel, is no true Christian; But *W. P.* (says *J. Faldo*) *denies the Scriptures and Gospel Ordinances;* Therefore *W. P. is no true Christian.*

I deny the *Minor*, or second Proposition; I query then, if I ought not to be understood, *to own the Scripture and Gospel Ordinances?* If not, there is no Disputation: If I ought to be so understood, was it ingenuous or just in him so to cavil? But that his Honesty and Logick may yet more clearly appear, I will give his Reply in this plain Argument, wherein I wrong him not one Title. *Whosoever denies not the Scriptures and Gospel Ordinances is a true Christian:* But *an* Horse *or a* Goose *doth not deny the Scriptures and Gospel Ordinances;* Therefore *an* Horse *or a* Goose, *according to* J. Faldo, *is a true* Christian. I know he would fling this Absurdity upon me; but he right well deserves it himself, who would extend the *Major* Proposition beyond it's Bounds; for it was not *Who* or *Whatsoever* did not deny Christianity, thereby including *all Sorts of Beings and Things* (which made a Gap for his *Horse* and his *Goose)* but if *Quakers* or *Quakerism*, so called, (of whom was the Controversy, and who must either deny or own) *do not deny the Scriptures,* &c. *it follows, they own the Scriptures,* &c. for by the same Rule that his owning the Scriptures includes no Denial of the Scriptures, it holds *è contra* that our not denying of the Scriptures, *includes an owning of the Scriptures,* or else his Argument proves nothing; for if it stands not upon the Rule of Contraries, it will follow, *that we may deny them, and yet own them;* for not denying them (though there be no *Medium*) is with him no owning them. But what Part is not that Man fitted to act, who can argue against his Adversary at such a Rate as this.

W. P. denies not the Scriptures, yet for all that, *he owns them no more than an Horse or a Goose;* and why? because they do not deny them.

Next to this Injustice, his *Logick* in these Attempts excels. But, above all the rest, that the first Piece of my Argument, as formal as any Thing can be, should not escape this Man's Abuse, *viz. If Quakerism* (so called) *be not another Dispensation than that of Christ, preached and settled by the Apostles, then the same,* said I; *though not another, yet not the same,* says he; Let the Reader judge in this Case: My Adversary, in his first Book, 2d Part, Page 144, begins thus: *If Quakerism be another Dispensation than that of Christ, settled and preached by the Apostles:* Now what is plainer, than that this is a *Negative*, as well as mine; *for another Dispensation is not the same.* Next doth it not imply, *that Quakerism* (so call'd) *is not Christianity, if another Dispensation?* And why may it not follow, If it be not another Dispensation, *that it is the same with that of Christianity?* Is not this implied as strongly and clearly as his Consequence in the contrary Proposition? Why should his *Negative* pass, and mine be stopt; or his Consequence hold, and not mine? He will have, That if Quakerism be another Dispensation, *then not the same;* but I must not be allow'd to infer, If Quakerism (so call'd) be not another Dispensation, *it is the same;* as if it were not alike to say, *If Quakerism* (so called) *be not another Dispensation, then the same:* Or thus; *If Quakerism* (so called) *be the same Dispensation, then not another.* Our Controversy lay upon *absolute Contraries*, not upon Things *only indifferent*, as *Geometry, &c.* for they are neither for, nor against Christianity, neither do they own or deny them. But if *J. Faldo* will be understood of his Saying, The Quakers deny the Scriptures, *that the Quakers do not own the Scriptures;* Why should not we be understood, when we say, we do not deny the Scriptures, *to mean that we do own the Scriptures.* His Objection is, we run upon Negatives, whose first Proposition, of Nine Parts, *hath Eight Negatives in it;* unless, *If the Quakers deny Scriptures, Ordinances, Christ, &c. and affect not a future Blessedness, &c.* are no Negatives; or that we must not thereby understand, *They do not own them;* for if he sets it not in Contradiction, but at the Distance of Geometry only, how can he conclude, *The Quakers deny the Scriptures;* yet so he concludes *per fas, per nefas?* What can be said to a Man of this hardy Stamp? whom neither *Logick, Reason*, nor *Modesty* can bound, yet a pretended Master of them all. Had I used him at this *toyish, gibing and*

and illogical Rate, I had been an *airy Sophister*, of no more serious Conscience or Religion than *Punchanello*; but being his Adversary, I must be a *Dunce*, an *Ignoramus*, and *something else* (he was so wise as to hide from us) which are the Epithets he is pleased out of his great Store-house of Ill Language to bestow upon me at Parting. But, which is stranger, if any thing be strange that he doth, after all the *Perversion, Addition, Diminution, Wresting, Misquotation, Evasion,* and *School-Boy Puns and Gibes*, he hath the Confidence thus to end this Chapter, and his Defence of the first and second Part of his Book:

Thus I have honestly and clearly vindicated every Charge in that Part of my Book which intends the Proof of Quakerism to be no Christianity.

How honestly and how clearly he hath vindicated his Charges belongs not to either of us to judge, whatever we think; but is left with every impartial Reader to determine; though, if it be as he saith, I am yet to learn what an *Honest and clear Vindication* meaneth; for, according to that Sense, I have had of him through this whole Controversy, and the most upright Observation I could make of his Management, it seems to me a moral Impossibility that he should not be conscious to himself, of exhibiting Charges he hath not prov'd; of abusing our Writings to endeavour it; of declining the Strength of our Answers, and vilifying of our Persons for writing them. To the Righteous God I recommend the whole, and according to our Truth and Honesty in this Matter, may we receive the Sentence of Well or Ill done, &c. I hope my Conscience will abide the Search; for God, that knoweth all Hearts, is Witness, I have not the least Guilt upon me for my Concern and Carriage in this Affair, having done to him, as I would all Men should do unto me, and therein fulfilled the Royal Law.

CHAP. XIII.

My Adversary declines meddling with my Appendix. *His Disingenuity great. His Perversions and Wrestings about his* Key, *pretending to open our Words, Detected.*

WE are now come to his Two and Twentieth and last Chapter, which for his Truth, Reason, Language and Carriage towards me, is an exact Representation of his intire *Reply*, which will not be hard for any serious Reader to observe, and make that use of it which may for ever discard *J. Faldo* in his Opinion from any future Pretence to honesty in Writing, till he hath publickly recanted this; but because I always desire he should speak for himself, be pleased to hear him this.

Reply, Pag. 91. *In W. P's Answer to the third Part of my Book, he says nothing to the Chapter of the Characters of Apostolical Persons and Inspirations, wherein (it consisting of Twenty four Pages) I agitated at large these Points, to the Overthrow of their pretended Apostolical Ministry, and Inspirations of the same kind with theirs, common to all Believers, on which Quakerism is founded.*

Rejoyn. This Complaint might have been very allowable in case I had not already sufficiently considered and answered whatsoever was of Moment in those Twenty Four Pages under the Head of *Inspiration*; and that himself had not been so shamefully unjust, as after having attackt the first Part of my Book, entituled, *The Spirit of Truth Vindicated*, with Thirty Four Pages, and I replied in an intire *Appendix* of Thirty Pages, he had not willfully neglected to give us one Word of Rejoynder: I beseech my Reader to take Notice of this one great Piece of Disingenuity; for if I must be chid, because I did not unnecessarily repeat Controversy, having already defended our Doctrine in this Point, under the Head of *Inspiration* and *Gospel-Ministry*, What shall be said to him, that unprovokedly fell foul of my fore-named Book, and after I had replied in it's Defence takes no more Notice, than if he were wholly unconcerned in any such Attempts? He must either think what he writ irrefutable or indefensible; If the first, then he need not have replied at all, since I am perswaded he believes one Part of what he writ to be as irrefutable as the other: if because indefensible, he is to be excused, *yet deservedly to be blamed for finding that Fault with others which he is much more guilty of himself*. To say nothing of his Pretence of Answering Two Hundred Fifty Four Pages within the Compass of Ninety Six, and that *Skip* he makes over my whole Key, consisting of *about half a score Pages*, added for the Opening our true Meaning from that perverted Sense, ignorant and malicious Persons have put upon our

Prin-

Principles: And laftly, his Vindication of his Key in not a page and an half againft Six or Seven Pages of my Anfwer, wherein, I hope, it was proved abundantly defective. But let us hear what he fays to remedy thofe defects I therein charged upon it.

Reply, Pag. 92. *In my Key of Two Hundred and Fifty Particulars, he excepts againft Ten; Five of which he farther explains, the other Five he oppofes.*

Rejoyn. This looks unfair on my Part, till my Reader be informed, that not one of thefe Two Hundred and Fifty Particulars had fo much as the Name of Man or Book, confequently no Page, how to find and read any of thofe Things he affirms to be our Senfe or Meaning, which is enough to difcredit an Honefter Writer than *J. Faldo*; fo that what I did, was more than could be juftly expected, much lefs challenged from me: However, I took Ten of the moft fufpicious. If he be difproved in thofe, there is great Reafon to fufpect him about the Reft, till he hath produced more unqueftionable Evidence. Of thefe he tells us, I explain one Five, and oppofe the other, Let us hear how he gives my Oppofition, and what is his Replication.

Reply. The firft of thefe is in pag. 247. The Will of the Flefh, i. e. *All that is chofen by Man, though he be thereto difpofed by the Will of God revealed in the Scriptures.* This W. P. *calls* Falfe, and an Abominable and Notorious Untruth. *I have proved at large their calling all Things of a Religious Nature by that Name which are not by Immediate Infpiration: Although the Scriptures have Precepts and Examples, commanding and prefcribing them.*

Rejoyn. If this be not to beg the Queftion, no Man ever did it fince the World was. He fays, he hath proved it at large: And I fay, I have refuted it at large; and what fays he to that? No more than this, *I have proved it at large,* &c. Doth this Man look like an able Difputant? That he is not an honeft one, take my Anfwer, by him omitted, with his own Words faithfully cited.

J. F. Page 69. The Will of the Flefh, i. e. *All that is chofen by Man, though he be thereto difpofed by the Will of God revealed in the Scripture.*

' W. P. This is Falfe; *Many* things may be and are *daily chofen by Man,* that is
' not in the Will of the Flefh, nor by his own Will, much lefs when any fhould
' be difpofed thereto by the Will of God revealed in the Scripture: An Abomina-
' ble Untruth, and fo Notorious, that I need fay no more; only challenge him
' to produce any of us (that is, any of our Sayings or Writings) in Proof of his
' Expofition, if he can; otherwife he hath flandered Us and Our Principles: For
' the *Will of the Flefh,* is that which is quite contrary to God, and inconfiftent with
' the Good of the Creature.

How well he hath acquitted himfelf in Point of Honefty, as well as Ability, firft, in fo maiming my Anfwer; and next, in faying nothing to it, is ftill referred to my Reader's Judgment, and fo we proceed.

Reply, Pag. 92. *The fecond is,* Pag. 249. Chrift the Offering, i. e. *the Light within.* W. P. *calls this* no Quakers Expreffion; *that it is, take this Proof.* We believe that Chrift in us doth offer himfelf up a Living Sacrifice to God for us, *Smith. Cat.* Page 64.

Rejoyn. I ftill fay, it is no *Quaker*'s Expreffion; Though the Light that fhineth in our Hearts be Chrift the true Light: But that which I moft infifted on, he hath (as he ufeth to do) quite left out; viz. *for he would by this infinuate, that we deny Chrift to be an Offering as in the Flefh, and that Body then offered up to be concerned in our Belief of the Offering; but I do declare it to have been an Holy Offering, and fuch an one too, as was to be once for all; therefore let none receive his Abufe of us for our Faith.*

He that hath half an Eye may fee, how poorly and meanly he hath fhifted off the Weight of my Anfwer. Again,

Reply, pag. 92. *The third,* Men-Pleafers.. *Senfe. They who comply with Men though in Things not only Lawful, but alfo to Edification.* This W. P. *calls* an arrant Lye; but the ground is, provided *J. F.* meaneth by 'Lawful, unto Edification, what we do. *I am not fo filly to put fuch Bonds on the Truth.*

Indeed I never took him to be fo Silly as Mifchievous in the Matter, not to ufe his own Phrafe more—— than *Ignoramus*; for inftead of putting Bonds on the Truth, he hath broken all Bonds of Truth; he pretends to give our Senfe of *Men-Pleafers,* and fubftitutes his own in the room of it; and when we tell him that if he means by Lawful and to Edification, what we do, he belies us; he confidently replies, *I am not fo filly to put fuch Bonds on the Truth*; as if in rendring

our

our Senſe of Words, *he were not bound to keep to our Senſe of them*; how is it our Senſe, *if it be his, and not ours*; and how truly ours, *if it be putting Bonds on the Truth to render ours truly?* But the Man's preſent Hardneſs is beyond wondring at. To the next.

Reply, page 92. Traditions of Men, i. e. *The Scriptures or written Word*, pag. 250. *To this* W. P. *adds*; But to ſay, they are the Traditions of Men, in the ſenſe Chriſt forbad the Phariſaical Religion, God forbid: I had rather my Tongue were cut out of my Head. O baſe Man, to abuſe an Innocent People thus groſly. *I have already proved the Phraſe to be the* Quakers, *viz.* Smith's *and* Naylor's.

Rejoyn. This anſwers it ſelf: If he had taken off the Force of my Words, I might have beſtowed a Rejoynder upon him; in the mean Time, I have diſproved his pretended Proof, where I met with it; and what I find here, is but a meer begging of the Queſtion. The fifth and laſt Particular he thus endeavours to vindicate, is this.

Reply, page 93. The Vail is over them, pag. 251. *Their Senſe I give of this, he preſents the greater half of* (which explains the other) *by an &c. to blind the Reader, and make the* Quakers *believe, I deſerve the Imputations of* Malice *and* wicked Man, *which it ſeems he is reſolved aforehand to beſtow on me.*

Rejoyn. The Man is weary of his Work, as we may ſee, by the great haſte he makes over every Particular. No Man living that hath not read both our Books can make any Senſe of this Hodge-Podge Section; that ever any Man ſhould touch with Religious Controverſy, that is ſo viſibly defective in it! My Anſwer ſhall be my Rejoynder: for, ſure I am, he hath overlookt it, and therefore yet to be replied to.

J. F. pag. 89. The vail is over them, *that is* ſays J. Faldo, *the Belief of the Man Chriſt Jeſus, which was of our Nature to be the Chriſt, &c.* pag. 251, 252.

' W. P. Let this be the laſt (though ſeveral more might be obſerved) which at
' this Time ſhall be conſidered, in which we ſhall ſee that *J. Faldo* has done like
' himſelf, and the Man we have all along taken him to be. *The Vail is over them*,
' it is a Scripture-Phraſe, 2 *Cor.* 3. 15. uſed by the Apoſtle to expreſs the Dark-
' neſs and Ignorance that to that Time remained over the Underſtandings of the
' *Jews* in reading the Law; and this Vail he makes us to interpret after this groſs
' and abſurd Manner; namely, *that the Vail is the Man Chriſt*. Wicked Man!
' Did ever *Quaker* ſo irreverently expreſs himſelf? Give us his *Name*, or tell us in
' what Book we may find it. What greater Malice couldſt thou have ſhown, than
' thus unjuſtly to pervert the Scripture in our Name? abuſing both, As if, becauſe
' *Chriſt's Fleſh* is called a Vail, and the Ignorance of the *Jews* a *Vail*, that there-
' fore the *Quakers* muſt of Neceſſity mean by *Vail* in the firſt Senſe, *Vail in the
' ſecond Senſe*; as if the Way to have the Vail rent, *were to deny the Man Chriſt
' Jeſus*.

All this my Adverſary thought fit to conceal, leſt his tranſcribing it unto his Reply, would have made that Diſcovery of his Baſeneſs, which he ſhould never have been able by all his Shifts to palliate. I think I did not *nick-name* this Chapter, when I called it a Repreſentation of his whole Reply: He ends as he began, *with Squibs, Puns, Evaſions and Ill Language*; for unleſs the Goodneſs of a Book be to be meaſured by the Paint of a Title-Page, or *bare Writing* reputed *Replying*, he might with more Senſe and Reaſon have called it *Froth, Folly and Fiction*, than *a Religious Vindication*, &c. No Man I ever read of hath exceeded the Bounds of Truth by obtruding Falſhoods, and wandred from the *Decorum* of a fair Adverſary, by unfair Citations and obvious Wreſtings, or betaken himſelf for Sanctuary to ſuch ſilly Shifts, and School-boy Jeers, at the rate this Adverſary hath done: And I have no Reaſon to Doubt of others being of the ſame Mind, ſince the World is not ſo deſtitute of Underſtanding, as to be cheated with his *hocus-pocus Tricks*, to take *Tin* for *Silver*, or *Copper* for *Gold*, or *Froth* for *Subſtance*, or *Inventions* for *Texts*, or *Wreſtings* for *Meanings*, or *Gibes* and *Taunts* for *pertinent Replies*. I have hitherto abundantly ſatisfied my ſelf concerning him, and I hope all that read me, both of him and his *Eſſays* againſt the People called *Quakers*: If not, it ought not to be charged upon me as wanting good Will to do it: I was never more ſedulous, and I think never more faithful in any ſuch Affair. And to the End my frequent Complaint of his *unfair Dealing* may be farther juſtified and confirmed, and his Deportment in the whole Controverſy more exactly related, I intreat my Reader to conſider what I have now to tell him.

CHAP.

CHAP. XIV.

Of Reflections on Persons and Things.

IF we will believe *J. Faldo* in his own behalf, he abhors that sordid Way of Writing, which some Practise, of *Reflecting, Nick-Naming, giving Ill-Language, &c.* either to his Adversary or his Doctrine. But as it fares with most Men, they condemn in others what they indulge in themselves; so truly, No Adversary in the midst of all his severe Censures of that unchristian Way of procedure, hath made more bold with his Reader, nor fallen more fouly upon his Adversary, yea, *Persons unconcerned*, than *J. Faldo* hath done.

We were as quiet, as Men that had scarcely known there was such a Person in the World, when our Peace was disturbed by a great Book, entituled with no more Modesty nor Mercy, than in plain Terms, *Quakerism no Christianity*. In this he chargeth us at once with whatever all our Adversaries put together had from Time to Time insisted upon to render us *Odious*; almost every Charge as scandalous and impious as rankest Blasphemy; and both rendred and called so (for ought I know) more than Twenty Times in that Discourse. This Book I thought I answered with more Moderation than either it deserved, or the Law of Retaliation would have granted: At the latter-end of it, I ran up a few of his many unworthy Reflections, Jeers and Scoffs together, that I might the better help my Reader to a true Relish of our Adversary's Spirit. He says nothing to them, which makes me conclude, I have not injured him, nor in one Word done him wrong; for had I, without doubt he had not past over my Collection with so deep Silence. I think it fit to transcribe them, that my Reader may see what Provocations I met with to draw Rebukes from me.

' *Horrid Imposture*; Ditch of Grossest Delusion; Subverting *Christianity*; Their
' Feigned Christ; Folly, Madness; it began in Blasphemies against Christ; Gra-
' tifying *Pride, Idleness, Giddiness*; In Professors Prophane, Vanity, Folly, Non-
' sense, Error: Whether it smell more of the *Fox* or the *Goose*; Imposture; Bab-
' ble, Blockish Person; *Quakerism entered the World as if Satan broke Loose*, and
' *Possessions by Satan were to make way and fit Souls for the* Quakers *Spirit*; O the
' Hell Dark Expressions of the *Quakers* Teachers! What bitter Curses and Exe-
' crations! *Dismal Howling*; Horrible Roaring; Blasphemy; Wretch; Vain Ficti-
' ons; *Quakers* Glow-worm; Deck their Idol; Real Non-sense; *But 'tis Pity
' not to lash a little*; Idiots, Stark Blind, Steel Hard; Your Crooked, Unholy
' Principles; Their Light grows Wiser and Wiser; Opium of *Quakerism*; The
' *Quakers* Divine Spirit Dumb; Refreshments at *Quakers* Meetings, so there is at
' *Puppet-Plays*; Impudent Fore-heads; Non-such Ignorance; Proud, Dreaming,
' Intolerable Notions; Ignorance and Delusion; Out-strip all in the Crooked
' Way; Blasphemers of the Lord of Life and Glory; Surely God has given them
' up for their *Pride, Giddiness*, or *Idle Ignorance*, and that in Justice; And the De-
' vil hath blinded their Minds with a Witness; Horrible Abomination; Gross
' and Dark Conceits; The Rankness of *Quakerism*.

And though I have carefully avoided his ill Example, yet such is my Unhappiness, that my Reproofs are stiled *Railing*; and Religious Censures, given forth from a grieved Spirit, counted *Ill-Language*. But what seems yet most insufferable, this very Man, that calls every sober Reprehension by an Hard Name, is most profuse in his black Epithets upon us; as if notwithstanding the Circumstances he mostly confesseth he is under in the World, as his Complaints tell us (which is no Fault laid to his Charge) he thinks it more intolerable that we should censure his Domineering, Scoffing Strain, against an intire People, be they what they will in Reputation, Merit, Honesty or Acceptance among Men, than that he should use it. What Blindness hath seized him, that he should not see this a Fault in himself? Is he fit to reprove, who out-does the Reproved in that for which the Reproof is given?

But before I reflect his Miscarriages of this Nature upon him, he hath something to say to me. It seems I have not behav'd my self towards him with that Subjection to his unprovok'd Abuses, which he thought became me to a Man of his Quality. Let us hear what hath stumbled him, and how patiently this pretended Enemy to Personal Reflections takes it. The first is this.

I hap-

I happened to let fall in my Answer, not material to the Point, this, but as a *passant* Expression, and so intended: *I find him more in Words than Matter, and I suppose more are of that Mind; or else what means his Pains to be made waste Paper of already*; Quakerism no Christianity *hath exchanged the Booksellers Stall for the Tobacco-Shops*.

This so harmless and true Saying hath given him great Offence, at least he hath taken it; what had become of me, had I been either as *petulant* or *vain-glorious*? I will give his Words, that my Reader may judge if the Man have any Vanity. After this Debate of serious Matter; *Now, Reader* (says he) *I am come to a Passage which makes me conclude it's Author desperate*.

As if all the Error and Blasphemy he laid at my Door in his foregoing five Chapters had been Toys and Trifles, but dark Conjectures and meer Guesses to this great *Discrimen* of my desperate Condition. O monstrous Vanity of Vanities! But he goes on.

A Passage (says he) *that renders* W. P. *careless how justly odious he becomes with Thousands, so he may but lessen the Reputation of my Book,*

Better and better, or worse and worse, which my Reader will. Doth my Reputation depend upon the Good-liking of *J. Faldo's* Ungodly Charges, propt with false Citations, Perversions, &c? I am miserable then. No Head, not empty, would make so great a Sound. It seems his Books have *Thousands of Votaries:* Hundreds are a Number *too diminutive* to vow Maintenance to his Labours. These Words show the great Vanity of the Author, *or the Debility of his Cause, that must have whole Regiments of Auxiliaries to his Protection*, chuse him whether. But that he may leave no part of his *Picture* undrawn by his own Hand; for who can (or will) do it so well? hear him yet farther.

The Acceptation my Book hath had in the World becomes not me to express.

A clever Way to tell us both his Book's Acceptance, and his own Modesty: Yet he so loves the *Theme* he can't give over.

The second Impression of above 1250 *may be abroad e're this comes to Hand.*

And how should they chuse, since the *New Cabal*, contriv'd to over-throw the *Quakers*, have taken a way of packing such Books into the Country as a new sort of *Manufacture*, where long before the second Impression came out, in several Parts of *England*, they lay so heavy upon hand by the peaceable Disposition of both Preachers and Hearers, that (as I have been credibly informed) some better affected to such Work than ordinary, have gone from House to House, offering, yea, pressing them upon the People, as if it had been an Alms to buy them. Yet he goes on still.

I cannot yet find by enquiring that any of W. P's *Answers to my Book have come to the Preferment to adventure that Passage.*

It seems he hath enquired; Strange Vanity! But what then? Therefore unworthy? So was *W. Tindal's* then in *Henry* the Eighth's Days; *H. Barrow* in Q. *Elizabeth's*; from whom descended those that are undeservedly called his Followers; I mean, *such* Independents *as* J. Faldo *is become*. Had it been a good Argument against *Luther's* Books, that they were not sold at *Rome*? Or *what Preferment had it been to despised Truth to lie upon the same Stall by Error and Imposture?* It's well our Books escape Burning, and our selves too, amidst such ill Neighbours as *J. F.* Conveniency to dispose of our Defences we like, and sometimes want. *His Attempt is a Licence to lye upon any Stall without fearing a Search:* But he should not insult over that low Condition God is pleased to exercise us in: Though we think it no Preferment to our Books to keep Company with *J. Faldo's* at any Time; nor should we desire it, but to disprove their black Charges.

But as if I had committed the most enormous of all Crimes, in saying, That his Book had exchanged the Book-seller's Stall for the Tobacco-shops, he cautions me, *not to pass yet a while by the Book-sellers Shops, for fear they should point at me, and do something else for a Non-such.*

I know not what, unless he had some private Intelligence, that they intended to break my Head with some of his Books, to prove to me by the Experience of *Battery*, that they had not left the Book-seller's Stall.

But this is not all; he tells me on this only Occasion, *I have not the Fear of God before mine Eyes; The Words of my Mouth are Iniquity and Deceit; That I left off to be wise and to do good; that I set my self in a Way that is not good, and abhor not Evil*, Psal. 36. 2, 3, 4.

Upon

Upon this Text he preaches my Infamy and Difgrace, but with an Abufe to the Text as well as to me, and all for that only Paffage. Nay, the Book-fellers, *J. Robinfon* at the Sign of the *Golden Lyon* in *Paul's-Yard*, and *R. Boulter* at the Sign of the *Turks-Head* in *Cornhill*, are brought forth with a *Fearful Whereas* againft *W. P.* upon no other fcore then to buoy up the Book's Sale and the Author's Credit; And by this pair of Book-fellers, whom I know not (and I fcarcely think ever heard of, efpecially the latter) much lefs had I ever harmed them; am I call'd all to naught, *unlefs Notorious, Falfe, Difhoneft, Impudent, Brazen-faced Detractor* are no fuch Thing, and this in one Page, and that in a *Certificate* too, as if they had not been giving meer Teftimony but *Sentence*, and that after a municipal Procedure of a *Billingf-gate* Judicature. But I forgive them; befides, the Words call neither of them Author.

Two Things I fhall obferve: Firft, *That his Book has had general Acceptance by Learned Divines, both of Conformifts and Non-conformifts.* Secondly, *That we have endeavoured to prevent the Sale of J. F's Book.*

To the firft I anfwer, *their Learned Divines* I know not; and how fhould I, their Names are concealed? But granting what thefe Men fay, it proves nothing: I could produce the Letters of Men, of known Honour, Learning and Quality, not only in *England*, but abroad in the World, to Balance the Scale, *who condemned his Enterprize of Weaknefs, Uncharitablenefs and Wickednefs*; heartily embracing the Anfwer as a Check but due to his Exorbitances. But let it be as it will in the Efteem of Men; we the poor traduced *Quakers* have a farther Appeal and expect an higher Judgment: In the mean Time, we reft in good Providence, and defire to purfue our Chriftian Duty.

In the fecond Paffage I do aver, they have wronged us; *for we never endeavoured any fuch Thing as to prevent the Sale of our Adverfaries Book, therefore in fo many Words they have certified an abfolute Untruth;* which ill becomes Men pretending to Confcience, as the latter of them doth, going under the Name (as I take it) of an *Anabaptift*, but I fuppofe fomewhat *Becalmed*.

This I thought to have prefixt in Form of a *Certificate* under feveral Hands, after their Example; but I had more Regard to the Weight and Gravity of my Difcourfe, than to feem fo concerned for my Reputation about a very *Trifle*, wherein, had they what they defire, *J. F's* Book would appear never the lefs impious, nor my Anfwer one Jot lefs formidable; and fo I end with him upon this Score.

His next Difturbance at me, is in pag. 43, 44, 45. of his Reply; on this Occafion: He would needs turn *Hangman* to us in his former Book, faying, *That now he was come to the higheft Round of the Ladder,* I prefume, in order to execute us: But I was fo modeft, as to ufe no Word fo grofs to him, only inverted the Allufion, and turned his Simile back upon him, thus: *I will not fay for what an Army-Chaplain might deferve to be fo highly exalted; but fince his eager Purfuit after an innocent People, hath brought him actually thither, and it falls to my Share to be his Executioner, I fhall take all the Care I can, to acquit my felf well of my Employment.* At this he rages beyond meafure, though he be only entangled in a Rope of his own providing. He muft needs be medling with *Ladders*, and *truffing* up the poor *Quakers* and their Principles, without all Civility, Mercy or Juftice; and becaufe I improved his own Similitude to the Difpatch of his Caufe, that he had defigned to illuftrate the Execution of us and ours by; He, as one befide himfelf, calls me *Hangman, Bungler, infallible Stager*, and in plain Terms *Fool.* But this is little to what is behind; for it feems, I am not enough for him to wreak his Difpleafure upon, and therefore of all others my *deceafed Father*, whofe Grave with *Heathens* had been a Guard from all Reflections (efpecially, when as unconcerned as what was never born, in the Controverfy) muft be fetcht up to anfwer for his Sons Mifcarriage (if fuch had been) his Words are thefe.

But why an Army-Chaplain deferves that Preferment more than a military Sea-Captain, his Father's Character.

Infolence and Pride! for fhame, *John Faldo*, fhall the moft barbarous Nations make it a ftanding Axiom, *De Mortuis nil nifi bonum*; And doth *J. Faldo*, a *Nonconforming Minifter*, that fhould be more humble from his Profeffion and Meannefs, break that laudable Saying by *De mortuis nil nifi malum*. Strange! But why my Father of all others? Did he ever wrong him? But had he; where is *J. Faldo's* Chriftianity in the Point? *Is this the Way to prove Quakerifm none?* One would have thought I had been enough to fatiate the revengeful Stomach of this *Canibal,*

bal, without haling him out of his Grave, whom Death hath freed from the Concerns of the Living, and the Earth intombed out of their Sight.

What kind of *Sea-Captain* he was, becomes not me to tell, nor need I; the World knows it: Neither shall I stomach his Comparison or diminutive Epithets. His Question I therefore refuse to answer, because every observing Person may easily satisfy himself, as to the vast Disparity that is between the Station and Service of *every such one* and an *Army-Chaplain*; for it is but to distinguish between the Preservation of a Man's Country from the Rapes and Spoils of Foreigners, *and the ruining it by turning Incendiary, kindling Animosities, and blowing them into Domestick Wars,* and the Question is fully answered. However, I would have J. F. be more careful how he meddles with the Men of that Element; for if they should know of his *base Reflections and Comparisons*, they would, I assure him, do more than point at him, as he said of *his Booksellers* to me.

The next Passages in my Answer which trouble him not a little, are these two, that I should say to these Words, *poor Non-Conformists*; ' but why poor Non- ' conformists, after all their preach'd up Battles, Spoils, Plunders, Sacrileges, De- ' cimations, &c. as Rich and Covetous as ever. Again, Upon the Description of the *True Ministry*, I said, ' No, they are true Gospel-Ministers, and their Feet ' truly beautiful, whose Gospel is Peace on Earth, and Good-will towards Men; ' and not Garments rolled in the Blood of Kings and Princes, Rulers and People. ' No Worldly Armies, Battles, Spoils, Sequestrations, Decimations, &c. in ' which *J. Faldo* and his poor Non-conforming Ministers have had their Hands, ' &c. *p.* 52, 53, 62.

This may perhaps sound harsh; but I shall easily take that off by declaring the Occasion. My Adversary must needs reflect upon me, and some other of my Friends, for our *Estates, Houses, and plentiful Subsistences*; and having first abused us by making it necessary to a True Minister after our Principle, *to have no House,* jeers at our Poverty, and envies our Prosperity; bidding such as had no dwelling Places, *to repair to* William Penn, *and such other* Quakers, *for an Answer, who have large Possessions and brave Habitations, such as few Ministers, especially the poor* Non-conformists *enjoy*. Upon this I depainted what some of their Ministry had been, and what it is; not varying one Tittle from the true Character of them, so far as I know it. *What had he to do with our Livings? What with our Ministry? Shall he rant uncontroulably? Has he a Privilege to make us Fools and Knaves at Pleasure without Contradiction? Is there no* Supersedeas *to such* Unchristian *Procedure? We must be abused if Poor, and jeered or envied if Rich*; and that by a Man, who is one of that Tribe which hath given the signallest Proof of a false Ministry, by the great Degeneracy of the late Times, whereinto they were not only fallen, but have been the Ring-leaders unto others corrupted by it. But I beseech my Reader to consider his *Reply* to what he thus drew upon his own Head.

1. *That my Accusations are false,* which is sooner said than prov'd; twenty Years have made them good.

2. That I have, like an *accursed* Ham, *discover'd by Father's Nakedness*. No such Matter, J. *Faldo*, That *Fig-leaf* will not cover thine. My Father was no Domestick Incendiary, much less an *Army-Chaplain* or *Parson*; of such I spoke. *He complotted none of those Tragedies*, nor was his Estate advanc'd by any of the consequential Gains: *His Family never saw Two-pence of any Sequestration or Decimation-Money, nor possest one Foot of King's, Queen's, or Church-Lands,* though perhaps some honest Men did. Accuse that can, provided he will prove, or else he had better hold his Tongue. I can say, and that with Sincerity to God and Man, that *after twenty five Years of publick and very eminent Sea and Land Employs (requiring much Time, Prudence, Care, Faithfulness, Government) and the many great Opportunities he had to swell his Estate to a very considerable Bulk, and that as laudably as any publick Officers raise themselves, he departed this World with a most clear Conscience in all those Respects, leaving not half that which many* London Shop-keepers *arrive at by their private Acquisitions*. Base then, and unworthy with a Witness, to bring him or me into your Society; We are unconcern'd in those Enormities, for which I justly made the Reflection.

3. But he says, that *I spit Defiance against the King's Gracious Laws, and Act of Oblivion; that if I be displeased, I will call for Fire from Heaven to devour the whole Stock and Kindred of one that offends me*.

God forbid, and forgive him. I would rather die my self than bring any such Damage upon any of you: But you are to be put in Mind of old Times, *to humble you*; *Some of you perk up so high, as if none were fit Guides for Heaven but your selves; would sit Inquisitors upon other Men's Religion without Contradiction, and yet have given such eminent Proofs of your Degeneracy, fresh in our Memory.* I have not said half so much as *John Cann,* the old *Independent Pastor,* left behind him in his little Treatise, called, *The Time of finding,* which is an entire Testimony against your *Apostacy,* for so the old Man calls it, and the *second* since his Day, preferring *the worst of the former Bishops* before you. See his *Epist. Dedicat.* Most sharp are his *Reprehensions* of you in the *Discourse* it self.

To talk of the *Act of Oblivion,* is not so pertinent, as to live that humble Life your former Miscarriages should in very Prudence engage you to. This were a better Use of the King's Clemency, than to trouble the World with such unnecessary Contests, especially when they expose other more harmless Dissenters to the Severity of the misinformed Magistrate, and rude Vulgar, and prejudice the Minds of sober Inquirers against them: This is to be as bad out of Power, as you were in it.

Neither would I be understood to have spoken of all Sorts of *Non-conformists,* (having always been one my self and a true Lover of the Honest of them) which *J. Faldo* takes great Pains to insinuate; No: Nor of all called *Ministers,* neither. I aim'd at such only *who remain in their Partial, Narrow, Bitter Spirit,* unfit for God and Men. 'Tis notorious to all inquisitive Minds, what Misery these Nations have been reduc'd to, through the pernicious Councils, horrid Flatteries, and most partial and ambitious Practices of many of the *Non-conforming* Clergy when Time was; They always stood in the Way of whatever tended to the true Freedom of this Mighty Nation from greatest Thraldom. I could particularize in twenty great Instances, and bring the Complaint of many considerable Persons against them. Many *Pamphlets* are extant that loudly speak the same, especially two, call'd, *The first and second Narrative of the late Parliament's Proceedings,* &c. Printed *Anno* 1658 and 1659, as I take it, in which the greatest *Hypocrisy,* the most detestable *Falseness* to God and Men, and a Sort of *Flattery* to their New *Monarchy,* exceeding all modern *Idolatry,* yea, *Blasphemy* it self, are brought to Light, and laid at the Doors chiefly of the Priesthood among all Perswasions, in any Power, at that Time; Out of which and several others, I have extracted about one Sheet, which I intended for the Press, but pure Tenderness to those that acted with Integrity and Conscience, stopt it's Publication: I was careful not to give any Occasion for them to be born hard upon by such as knew not well how to distinguish between Persons and Things that differ; though such as I meant, well deserve it from us, that when in Power persecuted us, contrary to their own Engagements, and now out of Power, malign and abuse us by slanderous Reports and invective Libels: Nor is it wholly laid aside, though *pro tempore* suspended; New Provocations may give Occasion for their History to come Abroad to the Nation more compendiously than ever. A Work I take no Pleasure in, but am heartily sorry, that such as have given that just Occasion for Rebuke, should (as not having their Fill of us before) fall so severely on us now about Religion, who have so eminently prov'd themselves false to God, Religion and the Kingdom; and thereby necessitated us to rip them up and shew how nauseous this Officiousness of theirs is; as if they thought to expiate old Crimes and prove themselves zealous for Religion, by perverting, abusing and gainsaying ours.

This is the present Plague that infects the Families of but too many, through the secret Instigations of their Ministers, yet too inward with them: And I know, that the most honourable left among the Dissenters, lament at this Day the Stinginess of their Clergy, whose Fierceness is rather encreased (than lessen'd) with their Loss of Power. But such generous Persons, as have acted truly upon Conscience, according to the best of their Understandings, and have ever continu'd immoveable for General and National Good, no Man holds in greater Value than my self; I wish for every such one, the King and Kingdom had a Thousand. It is an Abuse therefore in my Adversary to extend my Words to *all Non-conformists,* which only relate to the *Narrow-Spirited, Angry* and *Imperious among their Teachers.* And if it be for my plain Dealing with them, he (like himself and his Cause) threatens me *with the Punishment of the Judge, Law,* and I know not what beside, unless I repent me of my Saying (at what Time he pleads the King's Oblivion (showing himself more below him in Mercy, than he is in Dignity) Let him begin when he will, it will never lessen my Credit, nor greaten his. But that he

should

should, after so much Provocation, such Scurrilous Replies, Hard Names and Black Characters, given by him, say, I am turned Cavalier *and* Prelate *too, to satisfy my Lust of Anger*; adding *We see what a Change the* Quakers *Light can make when it acts the Part of Fire,* are Words very Indiscreet and Ungrateful, as well as Scoffing and Prophane; for they fling such Scurvy Reflections upon *Cavaliers* and *Prelates,* as become not one who got his *Oblivion* by the *former,* and his *present Liberty of Preaching and Licence for Printing* by the *latter*: For it is as much as to say, that both *Cavaliers* and *Prelates are a Sort of Revengeful, Angry and Fiery Persons* (to be sure bad enough, or he would not have rendred me either, when he went about to character me to Disgrace) So unthankful is he for his Oblivion and all other Benefits that he now enjoys at the Hands, and by the Moderation of either Cavaliers, that is, *Royalists*; or Prelates, that is, *Episcopal Protestants*; whom notwithstanding, he pretended to be no farther concerned in his Essays against us, than vindicated, as I have frequently observed.

But lastly he excepts against my Mention of one of his new *Benefactors.*

There is a Gentleman, Mr. T. F. *against whom Mr.* Penn *hath such a Spleen, that to my great Wonder I find him in all his Writings (I have read) attempting his Disgrace, who never wrote against him; and if my Information fail me not,* P. *hath been engaged by him to another Kind of Deportment.*

How black am I with *J. Faldo*'s Dirt? but none of it will stick. *Spleen* I never had to the Man; but once a Friendship, that had never been broken by me; but as it came, it went. At the Time of our Disputation with *T. D. T. V. T. D.* and *W. M.* at the *Spittle,* being engaged in the Negative concerning the common Doctrine of *distinct and separate Personality,* he and some others fell into great Intimacy with us; Who but we in his and their Thoughts? at what Time they were not quite discovered by us; But pulling off their Masks, at least we found them to have been the Followers of *J. Biddle,* in that which is commonly call'd the *Socinian* Way; and that their peculiar Regard to us came from an implicit Vindication of one of their Principles, for which we came under the Scandal and Odium of *Socinians*: Pulpits rang how the *Quakers* had unmask'd themselves on that Occasion; and their warm Disputes, in our Defence, did not a little strengthen the common Reports that went of us, and me in particular. When my Book intituled, *The Sandy Foundation Shaken,* came out, it being a farther Detection of what we call Errors, and it happening that *Socinians* did the same, as if I was a rank *Socinian* (who had never read any one *Socinian* Book in all my Life, if look't into one at that Time) so these Men, at least *T. F.* was ready to believe me nearer akin to them, than, God knows, I was; that is to say, *in Denying the Divinity of Christ,* At this Time, what would he not have done for me, if I might have believ'd him, and in Reality the Man was wonderfully taken; but, which was grievous, he was shamefully mistaken; and when he came to read my Confession to Christ's Eternal Godhead, in my little Book, intituled, *Innocency with her open Face,* (though he had another, call'd, *The Guide Mistaken,* that p. 28, abundantly doth the same, which was writ and read by him before the *Sandy Foundation* was thought of) he deserted me, broke all Bonds of Friendship and Rules of Civility, and his extreme Shews of Kindness, turned to continual excessive Reflections; he would have it a *Retraction,* rather than be thought to have been mistaken; He had built his Hopes too high for the Foundation, and then became Wrathful, that they fell. And though I sought his Friendly Behaviour, having no Thought in my Heart but Love and Friendship to him; yet so invincible was his Displeasure, that there was no Holding for me of his Good-will, *and believing Christ to be God*; They were with him as inconsistent, as Light and Darkness; I know no other Reason (if this be any) for his Sharpness to me; And God knows, this is the very Truth. I leave it with my Reader to satisfy his own Conscience concerning this Matter.

But *he never wrote against me*; Truly he needed not, who hath another Instrument so nimble, and so idle a Scribe as *J. Faldo* for the Purpose. But it calling me the basest Names, undervaluing, detracting and traducing me in almost all Companies behind my Back; and in a Garden at *Hoxton,* where I went to accompany some of my Relations, to affront me with opprobrious Names, as many can witness, who demean'd my self with all Gentleness towards him; and to act in the Quality of an incessant Agent against us by Informations, Reports, Books, *&c.* (*Who once did all these Things for us* (and we are no worse than we were) If these Things be no just Provocations to mention two Letters, I am to blame: Yet that I

name

name him in almost all my Writings, or all that he hath read, is false; for in the *Spirit of* Alexander *the Copperfmith, &c.* which J. F. quotes, he is not nam'd, and of above Twelve Books, he has mention'd but in Three, and that obscurely; this makes the Fourth against my Will. The Occasion, besides what hath been already touch'd upon, was this; H. H. one of his Friends, writes a Book against us, or rather to us, against G. F. J. Faldo's Master T. F. was the Promoter and Scatterer of these Pamphlets, especially upon the *Exchange*, where (and not in private Converse, as J. F. says, and makes to be the only Reason of my taking Notice of him, that he may render me Base to his Neighbours) before several, and those of divers Persuasions, he called G. Fox *Knave, Puppy, Loggarhead*, with such like unhandsome Terms, unworthy of a Man of T. F's Consideration in the World. This I would never have repeated, had not J. Faldo drawn, yea, compelled it from me, by suggesting an Untruth, and substituting it in the Room of the True Reason.

Well, *But if his Information fail him not, I have been engaged by* T. F. *to another Kind of Deportment.* And suppose all this, hath he not disingaged me sufficiently? I owe no Man any thing beyond Truth, nor will be fettered from my Testimony by any Obligations. But I never was engaged to him beyond what I have faithfully related, except it was his lending me (as he thought) by one that was my Servant at that Time of my Tower-Imprisonment, about Forty Pounds (he coming in my Name, counterfeiting both Messages and Letters, as I made appear to him afterwards) which, though mine Eyes never saw one Penny of it, nor was there a Penny employed in my Service, or to my Use, I did, when God enabled me, having then no Estate in my Hands, faithfully repay, as if I had really had every Penny; believing then, and still, that it was Kindness in him to me that was abused by a knavish Servant; and I would never let him suffer for it: If herein I have wrong'd him, he may forgive me.

But because in my Answer to *J. Faldo*, and what he said in his Behalf against us, I told him, that some thought it a Shame, that *so ill a Tongue should go unrebuk'd of those whose Principles and Interest give them the Liberty of doing it in a Way that might be more effectual than all the Moderation and Reason that can easily be shewn to him;* J. Faldo, exactly like himself, strains these Words, *all the Moderation and Reason*, which I intended, *of our bearing his Abuses, only shewing their Unreasonableness by Writing*, to nothing below some *Unjust and Violent Course to rid him out of the Way*; which are but softer Words for down-right *Murder*; and to countenance this Comment of his, I was told, I think, by one that had it at T. F's Mouth, *that he was advised to take the Law of me for his Security.*

But to put all this out of Doubt, those that thought it a Shame, he should so frequently, violently and publickly revile honest Men, bringing their Common Credit into Question by scurvy Names, meant by the Way that might be taken, only the Law, which was what some counselled him to use to secure himself against me. These Men had need have good Consciences, *that are thus afraid before they are hurt.*

Thus have I vindicated those Reflections *J. Faldo* laid such Foundation for; and if T. F. be troubled at this, I must tell him, so am I, but I cannot help it; Let him better advise his Scribe next Time; for I have nothing but hearty Love and good Wishes for him; nor have I said any Thing harsh or disgraceful in this Defence of my self, imputing much of what hath happened more to his Natural Haste, and sometimes ungoverned Speech, than a Premeditated Injustice; He knows how often I have caution'd him in those Respects, while we conversed together; Nor hath it been my only Observation and Admonition, but a great many others, and some of his own Friends too. Thus I leave T. F. in perfect Good-will, to see what Leave it is that *J. Faldo* is taking of us.

His *Epilogue* degenerates not one Jot from the Book it self; And as if he would do me a great deal of Mischief in a little Compass, and say whatever is rude and unjust, once for all, he tells his Reader, *That I have egregiously play'd the Forger; that I am a Cheat; that all Men understanding Controversy, will judge me worthy to be made a Proverb of, and when they would express an impudent Forger, to say no more than* W. PENN, *Rep.* pag. 95.

And that he may add Prophaneness to his Railing, he proceeds, *A Great Poet of their own hath these Words, worthy to begin all Mr.* Penn's *Books on that Subject as it ends this of mine.*

If a meer Scoff in Scripture-Phrase be prophaning Scripture, then I have not over-charg'd him in calling this Phrase, wherein he useth *Paul's* Words to the *Athenians*

nians (but with Scorn and Levity) against us, *Prophaneness.* But let us hear these so much derided Words.

' And they that would be satisfy'd concerning us any Way, they must find us
' and know us *in the Principle of Life,* where we are, and not in their own Reason,
' where we are not; and so let none Reason about us, for there they can never
' know us, nor come unto us, *W. Smith's Cat.* p. 94.

But why so much Contempt upon this Passage, unless it be to shew us, that he can still Scoff at that *Principle of Life,* which is the Strength and Habitation of God's Children, as he hath done already throughout both his Books. Did the Disciples of the Pharisees find out Christ's Meaning by their Reasoning about it, *John* 6, or would not either have relish'd the true Meaning of his Words, had they dwelt in the Divine Principle of Life? Why did Christ say, *I thank thee, O Father, Lord of Heaven and Earth, that thou hast hid these Things from the Wise and Prudent, and revealed them unto Babes,* if they were discoverable by human Reasoning? for *Babes* are ignorant of that Art; yet out of the *Mouth of Babes and Sucklings, &c.* The Apostle's Question, 1 *Cor.* 1. 20, was very impertinent, if *J. Faldo* may be of Authority, who said, *Where is the Wise? Where is the Scribe? Where is the Disputer, &c.* for this implies an Exclusion of all those Arts, Sciences, and natural Gifts from any Capacity to reveal the deep Things of God, shut up in the Divine Principle of Life. Besides, *W. S's* Words imply a *Clouded* Understanding and *degenerated,* and therefore Uncapable. *J. F.* must either intend by his *Derision,* that he thinks *W. S.* deserves to be hiss'd for denying the Knowledge of Divine Things to be attainable, by the Degenerated Understanding of Man, or sanctified: If the first, All may have Cause to abhor his False Doctrine: If the latter, I would know which Way that can be, without the Divine Principle of Life? * This abundantly manifests *J. Faldo's* unsavory Spirit, and proves him to be ignorant of the Way, Method and Work of God in his Children. When the Natural Man by his Reason can know Christ, he may know his Sheep, the Scriptures and the Power of God, and not before; but because it is impossible in Reasoning or Arguing, *pro* and *con,* by the utmost Strength and Search of Natural Abilities, to know Christ, but by the Revelation of the Spirit of God alone, as hath been abundantly prov'd; therefore *William Smith's* Words are sound and weighty, and *J. Faldo's* carnal and Prophane; shewing himself to be a Mocker of the Privileges and Mysteries of the Gospel; but what else may we expect from one that walks after the Lusts of his own vain Mind, having not the Spirit, *Jude* 18, 19. Yet that we may manifest how inconsistent he is with himself, as that he can't write against us, but he must write for us, take this Passage out of *Quakerism no Christianity* (which ought always to begin his Books against us upon this Subject, as it ends this Chapter of mine.)

' Those Gospel-Illuminations are beyond the utmost Reach of our Natural Fa-
' culties of the Mind (though sanctified) and therefore it is said to be 2 *Tim.* 3.
' 16. Divinely inspired; It is not produced in the Exercise of the Rational Facul-
' ties; the Soul is purely passive or receptive therein; and is to those Illuminations
' as the Wax is to the Seal.

CHAP. XV.

His several Gross Miscarriages summ'd and farther observed.

I. *Of his over-looking my Answer and Arguments.*

OF Twenty Two Chapters in his Reply, there is not one of them, in which he hath not wilfully declined inserting my Answer and Arguments, and only flutters about, pecks and scratches at some Part that is of least Moment to the Reason of the Point; perhaps some Rebuke or Reflection upon the ill Use he makes of our Friends Writings; particularly Pag. 9, 22, 23, 24, 30, 31, 35, 53, 56, 57, 71, 73, 82, 83, 85, 86, 90, 92, 93. How is it possible my Arguments should

---

* Dr. *Barnes, J. Bradford, J. Calvin,* Bp. *Jewel, W. Perkins, W. Green, J. Caryl,* Dr. *Owen,* with an Hundred more of this Mind, admir'd by such as *J. F.* yet that Doctrine derided by him in us, particularly *J. de Westphalia, No* Man can know the Mind of Christ, which he holds forth in his Words, but *he* alone. *Paradox in Fasc. Rer.* p. 163.

be conquered, when they were never encounter'd? I was never yet so unjustly dealt withal in this Particular by any Adversary of his Pretences.

II. *Of his drawing False Inferences.*

Where he ventures at any Time to insert any considerable Part of my Answer, he is sure to draw some Inference that may bring an Odium my Words never deserved. I could particularize at large, Pag. 6, 13, 17, 18, 31, 35, 41, 42, 47, 49, 71, 72, 73, 74, 75, 85, 86, 87, 88, 89, 90, 91, but take these following for the rest.

1. From *Edw. Burroughs* Reflecting upon People's imagining God to be confined to some Place beyond the Stars, he implies, *they deny Christ's Manhood*, Vindic. Page 6.

2. From our not stiling the Scriptures the Word (but Words) of God, he infers, *that we deny the Scriptures*, First Book, p. 18, 19.

3. From our Asserting the Doctrine of Inspiration, and Certainty of what we are inspired either to write or speak, he infers, *not only our Equalling with, but preferring what we speak and write before the Scriptures*, First Book, p. 40, Vind. p. 17.

4. From our condemning the Imitation of any of the Holy Men of God of former Ages in particular Cases, without they are thereunto required by the Spirit of the Lord, he infers, *that Commands of God in Scriptures are no Commands unless we think so; and that it is no Sin to break all Commands in the Bible, if our Consciences can but be so blinded as to tell us it is no Sin*, Vind. p. 34, 35.

5. From our asserting that there is no knowing of God but by the Spirit; and that Men's Apprehensions of God, and his Work in the Souls of his People, are but the Endeavours and Effects of the Wisdom of the Flesh, he infers, *that we oppose the Spirit and the Scriptures; nay, that we reject and scorn them*, Vind. p. 41, 42, 47.

6. From our denying a Carnal, Worldly, Mercenary Ministry, Lifeless Prayers, a meer formal Church, Preaching, and not by the Spirit; and *W. Smith*'s saying, that the present Use of Bread and Wine, and Water, called *Baptism* and the *Supper*, (as they are used at this Day) are no other than *Popish* and Human; he infers, *that the Quakers deny the Gospel-Ministry, Gospel-Prayer, Gospel-Church, Gospel-Preaching; and that we call* Baptism *and the* Lord's Supper, *as* Preached in the first Age after Christ, *the Pope's Inventions*, &c. Vind. from p. 49 to p. 71. O Injurious!

7. From our reproving People for feeding in an Unconverted State upon the meer Report of what Christ hath done without them and depending thereon, and from our asserting that Justification (taken for Remission) goes not before Repentance, which is an inward Work, much less that Men can be compleatly justified, or made inwardly *just*, but by the *washing of the Word of Regeneration and Sanctification of the Eternal Spirit*, this Man dares to infer *Our Denial*, yea our *Undervaluing*, and that to the Degree *of Blasphemous Contempt of the Transactions of Christ at* Jerusalem, Vind. p. 71, 72, 73, 74.

8. From *J. Pennington*, asking, *If outward Blood would cleanse the Conscience from Indwelling Sin*, he infers, *that we deny all Benefit by the Blood of Christ shed upon the Cross, for the declaring of Remission of Sins*, Rom. 3. 25. First Book, 2d Part, p. 46, 47. Vind. 77.

9. From our chusing to call that Body God prepared in which to do his Will, the Body of Christ, rather than the Christ of God; And from our asserting, God to be that Light which enlightens every Man; and that the Soul of Man had something of the Life of God in it's Primitive Perfection, he makes no more ado, but concludes, First, *That we deny the Christ of God*; 2dly, *That we make the Measure of Light in every Man the Eternal God, thereby confining him to Man's Soul*: And, lastly, *That the Soul of Man is God himself, and so God saves God, and God worships God*. This my Reader may find in his Vind. from p. 75 to 87, particularly this following of *E. B.* about the Soul.

10. From *E. Burroughs*'s affirming the Light of Christ in every Man to be one with the Spirit, and as good as the Spirit of Christ, (in order to prove it the same) *J. Faldo* infers, *he made the Soul of Man God; because that which is as good as the Spirit of God is God*, Book 1, Part 2, p. 122. Vind. p. 85, 86. As if *E. B.* had spoken it of the Soul of Man, and not the Light of Christ shining in the Soul of Man, as his Words express it.

11. Lastly,

11. Laſtly, from our Denial of his carnal Reſurrection, as inconſiſtent with Scripture and Reaſon, he takes Heart to tell all People, *that* W. P. *and all the through* Quakers, *deny the Reſurrection of the Dead, and are guilty of not believing a future Reward in another World*, with a Train of ill Language, too long to bring in, Vind. p. 88, 89, 91.

This, Friendly Reader, hath been the Entertainment we have received at *J. Faldo's* Hands; but all Things ſhall work together for good.

III. *Of his evading my Anſwer and Arguments.*

It is very frequent with him, next to leaving out what I ſay, or faſtning falſe Conſequences upon what he tranſcribes, to evade the Strength of mine Anſwer, either by pretending *to have ſaid enough in his firſt Book*, (as if that had foreſeen my Anſwer, and anticipated his Reply with a Refutation) *or by ſome one Word which will ſerve him to play at; or by being in haſte; or elſe my Anſwer deſerves no Reply at all*, &c. An Evidence of this Sort of Carriage, my Reader may find in his Reply, p. 5, 17, 18, 38, 51, 57, 58, 59, 69, 71, 76, 91, 93. One at large for all.

To my ſeveral Arguments in Defence of Immediate Revelation, Inſpiration (as he terms it) he returns three or four Lines.

This W. P. *is ſo far from denying, that he pleads for it; but after ſuch a Rude, Impertinent Manner, that I ſhould but injure you, and ſhew my ſelf idle to animadvert upon it,* p. 17. The cheapeſt Way that ever Man took to confute his Adverſary. Doth this become any Man of his Pretence to either Scholarſhip or *Chriſtianity*.

IV. *Of his Forgery or Perverſion.*

I am ſorry I have ſuch reiterated Occaſion to charge him with Forging, that is, foiſting in Words into our Writings and Sayings, that are wholly inconſiſtent with them, or perverting thoſe he delivers, to the End he may make them pronounce his Mind the more plainly. A few of many Places I have obſerv'd, as in Page 22, 25, 41, 42, 50, 51, 92, 93. Of which I ſhall give four Inſtances more particularly.

1. I. *Pennington* ſpeaking of Knowledge according to the Fleſh: By Fleſh, ſays, he, *The* Quakers *underſtand the Uſe of our Underſtanding* (though) *ſanctified*, Firſt Book, Pag. 41. Vind. Pag. 24, 25.

2. His ſecond is, *making* W. Smith *to call the Scriptures, Traditions of Men, Earthly Root, Darkneſs, Confuſion, Corruption, Rotten, Deceitful, the Whore's Cup, the Mark of the Beaſt, all out of the Life and Power of God*; and not that he meant them of thoſe *who had degenerated from the Power of Godlineſs, and had ſet up their own Imaginations in the Stead of God's Inſtitutions, teaching for Doctrine the Traditions of Men*, firſt Book, Pag. 117, 119. Vind. 41, 45.

3. The Third is, his making I. *Pennington* to call viſible Worſhip *the City of Abomination*, Vind. Pag. 50.

4. Laſtly, That he gives, in our Name, this Interpretation, of the Vail is over them; i.e. *the Belief of the Man Chriſt Jeſus, which was of our Nature to be the Chriſt*, &c. Vind. p. 93.

V. *Of his Grand Improbabilities and downright Untruths.*

This Charge, I know, muſt needs be very unpleaſant to a Man as Vain Glorious as many Places of his Book declare him to be, but I cannot help it; 'Tis Truth, if there be any Truth in the World, that he hath writ a great many unlikely and abſolute untrue Things. Let my Reader take the Pains to look over theſe following Pages of his Reply, and I am well aſſured, if impartial, he will not think that I have in a *Tittle* wrong'd him, Pag. 6, 7, 18, 21, 33, 35, 38, 39, 42, 46, 47, 48, 49, 55, 56, 65, 70, 72, 73, 89, 93. Of which I will only inſtance four.

1. Firſt he affirms, *that he quoted forty Places out of our Friends Books, that would prove the Light within* (as within us) *to be the only Lord, and Saviour, and very God*, p. 6, whereas he brought not any one that either proved the Terms or the Matter.

2. Secondly, *He confidently* accus'd us, *of charging the Miſcarriage of Men's Souls on the Knowledge the Letter of the Scriptures, by God's Bleſſing, doth convey*, Pag. 21.

3. Thirdly, Whereas I said that *W. Smith*'s Words reflected not in the least upon the Scriptures, nor those Doctrines truly received thence; neither that any such Words can be produced by our Adversary, he boldly tells his Reader; *I intended no other but that* Smith *doth not accuse himself in so many Words of Blaspheming, the Spirit of God in the Scriptures, and the Doctrines from thence received; as much as to say, We both knew it to be Blasphemy, but* W. Smith *did not call it so*, p. 4. There is no ingenuous Man that will not abhor the Falseness of this Passage.

4. Lastly, I opposing his Affirmation, that we did not profess or believe Eternal Rewards, thus pretends to confute me : W. P. *opposes me rather because he would not be thought to subscribe to me, than that he believes not what I say to be true*, p. 69. But if this be true, sure I am, there is no Truth in the World.

And indeed, there is no giving this Sort of Carriage at large, but by transcribing far the greatest Part of his Book.

VI. *Of his Idle Jeers and Frothy Expressions.*

I have not met with any Man writing upon so serious a Subject as Religion is, that gives himself the Liberty of so many vain Expressions, as if he had intended his Discourse for vulgar Merriment, and not for Christian Information. If my Reader please to trouble himself with the Perusal of these following Pages, he shall find enough to nauseate, p. 6, 22, 23, 26, 27, 29, 30, 34, 37, 40, 47, 50, 51, 53, 58, 60, 69, 71, 72, 95. Take two Instances : *He cackles like an Hen, when he has laid a worse Thing than an Egg*, p. 47.

Again, Because we said, God spoke once by *Balaam*'s *Ass*, thereby proving that he did not always speak by the Scriptures, he thus reflects, *I wonder not that they leave the Teachings of God by the Scriptures, to attend on the Ministry of Asses*, thereby calling us Asses, p. 27. Which, how witty soever he thinks such Sort of Sayings, to be sure, they are more Frothy and Irreligious, than becomes a Man professing Religion, much less writing of the weightiest Points of it.

VIII. *Of his Vain Glory and Self-Praise.*

At this he is excessive; So conceited is he of his own Abilities, and impatient after Praise, (the greatest Discovery of Pride and Weakness that any Man can make) which my Reader may find, p. 28, 32, 33, 34, 50, 52, 61, 63, 65, 84. I will give one Proof for all.

My Charge and Argument in this Chapter (says he) *is such an Argument, and so proved by me, as a* Thousand Penns *can never invalidate it*, p. 34.

The Truth of which, as also the Vanity of it, may be seen both in my Answer and Rejoynder; however, he stops his Reader's Mouth, and counts him *senseless and desperate that is not of the same Mind*, p. 36.

VIII. *Of Railing and Ill Names.*

No Man pretends to dislike, yet no Man practises these ill-bred, as well as unchristian Courses more than *J. Faldo*, where he wants Reason he imposes an hard Name ; and if he be rebuk'd, he calls it Railing, reflecting that upon us for reprehending it in him. If I call his Comparison base, that is so, and that he manages it maliciously against us, he replies, *that more genteel Railing may be learned under a Hedge, and that those Words are slovenly imposed* upon Him; as if he were too great to be reproved, or licensed to rail without Controul, at least against the *Quakers*; for if I tell him, he is unmannerly, he counts our own Practice a Dispensation ; inferring from our Dislike of vain and fruitless Complements, *a Liberty to treat us with what unseemly Language pleases him best* ; This my Reader may see at large, if it please him to look into these Pages of our Adversary's Reply, p. 5, 8, 16, 20, 27, 29, 33, 35, 45, 49, 50, 52, 54, 58, 62, 63, 64, 69, 72, 73, 77, 82, 87, 91, 95.

But to omit whole Sentences, and yet to give some Instances more at large than by bare Figures, my Adversary hath liberally bestowed out of his great Store of ill Language these following Epithets, as well upon our Religion and Friends, as my self for defending them. That *our Light is the second Anti-christ, the* Quakers *Idol, Pernicious Guide and Saviour, Fanciful Teacher* ; in fine, *a sordid, sinful, corrupt and ridiculous Thing* ; and our Religion and Practice *Blasphemy and Idolatry*,

P. 47,

p. 47, 85, 87. Our Friends (*Quakers*, so called) *benighted with palpable Knavery and Impudence*; *Absurd and Blasphemous Idiots*; *Out of their Knowledge and Wits also*; *prodigiously wicked*; *Speak the amazing Delusions of* Satan. And that I am a *presumptuous and blind Accuser*, a *Sophister*, an Haman, *an accursed* Ham, *a treacherous and wilful Deluder*, *a Mad-man, an Hangman, an infallible Stager, a Fool, an Ape, a Dunce, an impudent Forger*, and what not, that his Rage and Folly can foam out, p. 4, 53, 54, 59, 61, 63, 65, 90, 91, 95.

I desire my Reader would also take Notice, that besides his excessive ill-using of us, and reputing our Rebukes for doing so, Railing (which shows the *Beam to be in his own Eye*, and that his Nature is as proud to reject Reproof, as it is foul and rough to occasion it) he gave us the On-set; Had he not begun with us, we know not that ever we should have meddled with him; but having begun, and withal so miserably abused us by *foul Charges*, *false Citations* and *vilifying Language*, that it should be more unreasonable in us to censure him, than in him to deserve it, no impartial Man can ever think, What is *J. Faldo* for a Man, of what *Rank*, what *Quality*, what *eminent Office or Dignity* in the World, that we must be *kick'd* by him up and down four or five Hundred Pages, for whatever he pleaseth to count us, and not be told, *he wrongs us*? Is the Quality of this diminutive Priest so much above the whole Body of the People, called *Quakers*, that to stop him in his Career of Scoff, Jeer, Taunt, foul Names and Reflection is to deserve them? But over and above, that this shews his Disposition to be Imperious and Impatient, as well as Rude and Frothy, and therefore very inconsistent with his Pretences to Meekness and good Manners, but most of all with his Reprehension of others in Cases less offensive; it will neither confute my Arguments or damnify my Person, which makes me the less solicitous of making any other Rejoynder. I should here bring in my Conclusion to this whole Discourse, but left any may yet doubt of the Truth of these Things, as believing me to have made an ill Use and partial Relation of them, I shall yet offer for farther Confirmation of my Sense of the Man, and his Undertaking against us, this undeniable Evidence, to wit, that he hath dealt imperfectly and falsly with the World in his Account of our Writings, which he makes the Foundation on which every Charge is built, that he exhibits and aggravates against us. I have here and there, in my Book, touch'd already upon this great Failure; But I shall more particularly inform my Reader of it in this Place.

Of Imperfect and False Citations.

Forasmuch as *J. Faldo* would have all People believe, that he hath charged the People, called *Quakers*, with nothing that their own Books do not clearly and plentifully prove, (insomuch, as he counts those that think so, *senseless and desperate*) and that many who read him, may be ready to credit him, because they see Books, Names and Passages frequently cited, especially those who have not the Books by them, to examine how honestly he deals with us, I thought it requisite to end this Book with this farther Unanswerable Discovery of his Defective Foundation, that in many Places we find *Names without Book*, *Books without Parts, Chapters and Pages*, yea, *without Names*; and *Pages without Number or Figure*; *many falsly cited*; *some added to, others diminished from in the Beginning, middle, or End of Sentences*, thereby robbing them of their own Explanation, that he might the better fit them for his Purpose. Take these few Instances.

I. Names without Books.

G. Fox,	Book 1, Part 1. Pag. 47	C. A.	45
G. Fox,	48	R. Farnsworth,	46
J. Nailer,	90	G. Fox, jun.	83, 119
C. A.	Pt. 2. p. 7	R. Farnsworth,	142
W. Dewsbury	11	E. Burroughs,	143

Thus far of Names without Book, which is not fair in any Adversary. Now of Books without Pages, and Page without Number.

II. Books without Parts, Chapters, and Pages.

Morning Watch,	Book 1, Pt. 1, p. 37	W. P. Spir. of Truth,	32
Light out of Darkness	37	Love to the Lost,	39
Shield of Truth,	45	True Faith,	122
Love to the Lost,	45	F. H. Testimony,	123
Life of E. B.	45	Great Myst.	124, 125
Epistle of W. Dewsbury	47	Velata quædam revelata,	133
Velata quædam revelata,	53	Great Myst.	142
Morning Watch,	92	Some Principles of the Elect People,	142
Morning Watch,	Pt. 2, p. 19	Great Myst.	Vind. p. 86.

III. Books Falsly Cited.

G. F's Great Myst.	Book 1, Pt. 1, p. 41	J. Parnel's Shield of Truth,	22, 23
W. S's Primmer,	144	W. Smith's Cat.	27
Great Myst.	52	W. Smith's Prim.	37
Great Myst.	57	Love to the Lost,	40
Love to the Lost	118	W. Smith's Prim.	42
G. Fox's Great Myst.	Pt. 2, p. 10	W. Smith's Prim.	Pt. 3, p. 94
G. Fox's Great Myst.	12	W. Smith's Prim.	Vind. p. 8, 70

Thus much at present of False Citation, which, to say no more, makes any Book uncapable of being answered.

IV. Several Passages Clipt and Maim'd.

J. St. Short Disc.	Book 1, Pt. p. 42	J. N. Love to the Lost,	Pt. 2, p. 6
Short Discovery,	80	I. Pennington's Quest.	19, 23
W. Smith's Prim.	88	W. Smith's Cat.	26
J. N. Love to the Lost,	89	W. Smith's Prim.	37
E. B. Answ. to Choice Experience,	89	G. Fox's Gr. Myst.	40
J. Story's Short Discov.	89	J. N. Love to the Lost,	43
W. Smith's Prim.	114	W. Smith's Cat.	69
J. N. Love to the Lost,	120	Love to the Lost,	103

Reader, These are but a very few of what we could offer; for indeed there is scarcely one Passage that he hath not mangled on Purpose to make it speak the better on his Behalf, which given at Length, would have cleared it self.

V. Certain Places more particularly Perverted, by adding or Mis-applying.

I. Pennington's Quest	B. 1, Pt. 1, p. 41	W. Smith's Prim.	42
E. B's Answ. to Choice Exper.	89	I. Peningt. Quest.	46, 47
I. Peningt. Quest.	109	W. Smith's Morning Watch	48, 49
W. Smith's Morning Watch,	119	I. Peningt. Quest	70, 71
W. Smith's Morning Watch,	126	I. Peningt. Quest.	81
Love to the Lost	25	I. Peningt Quest.	126
J. N. Love to the Lost,	27	I. P. Quest.	129

These, Reader, are but some Hints I was willing to give thee of our Adversary's Disingenuous Carriage towards us, either in letting drop that which may be most material, at least might be more explanatory of our Friend's Intentions, foisting in Words wholly inconsistent with the Scope of our Passages, or mis-applying them in Favour of his black Charges, all which may clearly be seen by a Comparison of his Books with our Friends Writings, a great Part of which, I must confess, it will be difficult to procure, since to prove his Miscarriage in Citations, I have not been able to compass above one half of the Books he names; but that carries this woful Reflection with it, if his Use of 15 Books in Thirty affords us so many gross Instances of his unfair Dealing with us, what might we have expected upon our Examination of the rest? In the mean Time we shall without Leave suspect him, having so much Reason for it.

To compleat what I have done in this Particular, let me tell thee, Reader, that in his Comparison of us with the *Papists*, he sets down Twenty several Passages as our Doctrines and Opinions, *not producing so much as Person, Book or Page to avouch them*; a Piece of Justice he denies not to the *Papists* themselves at what Time he refuseth it to us, though not they, but we were the People against whom the Discourse was writ: which, though gross enough, yet nothing compared with his Disingenuity at the End of his First Book, where, under the Pretence of furnishing his Reader with a Key to understand the *Quakers* Meanings by, he sets down no less than about Two Hundred and Fifty Particulars in our Name, *without so much as the bare Mention of one Author, Book or Page, to countenance his Attempt*. Yet, after all this, he cannot bear to be told of his unfair Carriage, and his unjust Dealing towards us; His Quality, or his Pride, is so great, it will not bear a Reprehension; I never met with a Man of so much Falseness and Stomach together. He thinks it so great a Punishment to be told of his Miscarriages, that if we will not let him pass for *a Faithful, Sober, Meek, and Christian Author*, however he hath prov'd himself the Contrary, *we must expect all that his Scorn and Anger will cast upon us*: But such Vindications of his *Essays*, will be Hand-writing enough against themselves and their Author, who ought not to flatter himself after these great Evils, with the Hopes of Impunity; *for such as he hath sown against us, such shall he reap at the Hand of God, the Righteous Judge of all, who will reward every Man according to his Works*. But I desire with all my Soul, that God may shew him Mercy, that Repentance may yet over-take him, and this Iniquity be blotted out before he departs this World, and is no more seen. I would beseech him, in the Love of God, to fight no longer against the Truth, and for a Cause, his Conscience (might it speak) would tell him, is not the only true God's, *but the Honour and Interest of the God of this World*, whom the formal *Christian* is led and ordered by, that is so sharp against us. Let him not be afraid to take Shame for that which is shameful, lest vain Credit, brings Sorrow hereafter. I cannot be otherwise perswaded, but that *Reputation* prevailed more with him than *Conscience* in this Controversy; he tugs so hard to prop the one, and there is so little Savour of the other: God could never be in that Design, nor amidst those Thoughts, that were laid with so great Mistake, and which have been vented with so much Fury. I must needs say, There was neither Truth to inform us, nor Charity to gain us: It stumbled the Weak, grieved the Tender, and offended the Peaceable among those Professions he pretended to vindicate, gratifying only such as are of a *Litigious* and *Contentious* Nature, whose unreasonable Heat it had been his Duty rather to abate by sweet Perswasion and a meek Example. *I have this Comfort in my Conclusion of this Controversy, that I most heartily forgive him all the Injustice and Unkindness he hath shewn, at least so far as I am therein concerned, and that I think is more than any Man; And with the same Love that God hath loved me, I do with all my Soul fervently wish his solid and unfeigned Repentance, that he may receive the Love and Mercies of God in the Remission of his Sins, and Reconciliation of him by the Power and Spirit of Jesus Christ our Lord, that he may know the Excellency and Glory of the Truth in the inward Parts, and what are those good Things, no Carnal Eye, Ear, or Heart hath ever seen, heard or understood, that God hath laid up for them that truly fear him, and which he daily reveals unto all such by his Eternal Spirit.*

The CONCLUSION.

THUS, *Friendly Reader*, are we come to the End of our Task, wherein I hope, the Doctrines of that despised People, in Derision, called *Quakers*, their Worship and Church-Practice, are evidently and firmly vindicated against vulgar Mistakes and Reports, and more especially those many black Charges, so confidently exhibited by *J. Faldo*, in his First and Second Books, both by a fair Rescue of our Words from his gross Perversions, and indirect and unnatural Meanings, and the Confirmation of our real Sense, with Plenty of plain Scripture, many Reasons, and the unquestionable Testimonies of several Ancient and Modern considerable Authors. My Design hath not been Conquest, but Information, that by these Religious Wars we may at last arrive at Peace; And these Weapons be all beaten into Plough-shares, so as to learn War no more: That to fear God and work Righteousness (the Life of Jesus Christ our Lord, who hath left us his most Holy Exam-

Example, that we should follow his Steps) may be the very Bent of our Hearts, the Resolution of our Minds, and constant Practice of our Lives, which bring the Soul to the Inheritance of Substance, and establish the Heart for ever.

O that all who read this Discourse, may with me wind up their Spirits, and lodge their Souls, not in the Love of Controversy, but of that Divine Life, which stills, resolves, and fixes all, and gives such Heavenly Waiters to feel and enjoy Immortality! To see and possess something that is beyond Time, and these painful Exercises that are within it. O! this makes Men Weighty, Serious, Loving, Meek, Holy, Forbearing, and Constant, the Image and Delight of God! Such become Livers of *Pure and Undefiled Religion*, who have been hitherto but so many vain and verbal Contenders for Religion; so shall this Scripture be fulfilled to our un-utterable Rejoycing: Psal. 85, 9, 10. *Surely his Salvation is nigh them that fear him, that Glory may dwell in our Land; Mercy and Truth are met together; Righteousness and Peace have kissed one another.*

The God of Everlasting Strength bless and prosper this Glorious Work in the Earth, to the Praise of his Holy and Blessed Name, *Amen.*

WILLIAM PENN.

Wisdom Justified of her Children,

From the

Ignorance and Calumny of H. Hallywell,

In his BOOK, Called,

An Account of FAMILISM, *as it is Revived and Propagated by the* QUAKERS.

By WILLIAM PENN.

But all these Things will they do unto you for my Name's Sake: Yea, the Time cometh, that whosoever killeth you, shall think he doth God Service. But be of good Cheer, I have overcome the World. John xv. 21. and xvi. Ver. 2. 33.

TO THE

Justices of the Peace in the County of *Sussex*.

A Certain Person in your Parts hath lately troubled himself and the World with a Book, entituled, An Account of Familism, as it is reviv'd and propagated by the Quakers; *and this dedicated to Sir* J. Covert, *Knight and Baronet, &c. How ill he spent his Time in Writing it, and how unadvised he was in publishing it, an impartial Perusal of this small Discourse will briefly yet abundantly manifest.*

I come not to you for Protection (a Thing he and his Cause wanted) but for Impartiality and Justice; Truth *is sufficient to patronize and defend her own Cause from the Lash of* Envy, *without the weak Auxiliaries of Human Force; She gives* Sanctuary *to all that take to her for Refuge, but is all-sufficient to her own Relief from the deepest Pressure, and most inveterate Prosecutions of her implacable Enemies.*
And

And though the Evil Disposition of the World to receive her Apologies, seems to conspire with the Indefatigable Endeavours of Her Adversaries to traduce Her; yet her own purest Innocency and Unwearied Patience hath ever in the End broke forth to that clear Conviction of it's Opposers, as hath prov'd at once both their Confutation and their Shame.

And let it seem no Riddle to you, that I write so assured of Truth on our Side, There is no Objection our Adversary has made to the contrary, we shall not easily remove. Our Meanness in Quality, Breeding, Literature and Fortunes in the World (badges of Reproach with him) will receive an ample Parallel from the best Persons and Times, and is so far from making to Overthrow, that if the Scripture and other Story be to be credited, they tell us, that not many Wise, Learned or Noble; *Not that they are excluded, but as Persons* stumbled at the Cross of Christ, and the Simplicity of the Gospel, *through the Power that Greatness and Pleasure have with them, they exclude themselves.*

But since Great and Rich Men have Souls to be saved as well as Poor, it is equally their Concern to inform themselves of that Way which most assuredly leads to the rest that is Eternal. I confess the Variety of Sects in the World *to be a great Discouragement, especially when we consider with what Confidence each Party pleads the Truth and Divine Original of his own Perswasion;* But Men are not to be satisfied with Pretence but Evidence: Education *is too short, nor will* Tradition *reach far enough, to ascertain any Man of the Verity of his Perswasion.*

Could the two first have done, there had been no Need of Relinquishing the Roman Church, *who was neither wanting in Pretences, nor an Education prejudic'd enough against all Reformation;* And if Tradition had been all-sufficient, *the Direction of God's Unerring Grace, and the necessary Conviction of Men's Reasons, might have been spared.*

For if Men are to believe what is recommended for true, because Recommended, and not because True, we are to believe we know not what, and shall be to seek so far for a Reason for the Hope that is in us, that in Reality we can have no other Answer to give, than that such or such told us so, and therefore we believe it: But if the Ground of our Faith ought to be more sure and better founded, it will stand us greatly upon to examine, What is the Reason we have to render for our Faith and Hope in God, and that Belief we have of Holy Scripture? If we err here our Building is insecure; and the Danger is, that we shall not only one Day lose our Faith, but, which is worse, our Souls too. This necessarily brings a Man to a more Inward Search and Testimony, some Divine Principle *in Man, planted by God himself, which gives to believe* that God is, and that he is a Rewarder of them that fear him.

This the best Heathens, as well as Jews and Christians, *have highly venerated, and many are the Testimonies they have left upon Record, to the Divine Original, and excellent Use of it, both to know God, and our selves; And truly it was this Holy* Principle *in all Ages that hath attended Mankind with those* Checks, Reproofs and Directions, *by which he hath had any Discerning of what should, from what should not be done. This is that which has given him the certain Sound and true Relish of what God has ever required at his Hand, as said the* Prophet Micah, God hath shewed thee, O Man, what is Good, and what he requires from thee; to do Justice, love Mercy, and walk humbly with thy God, *Mic.* 6. 8. *In the* Psalms *thus,* Thou givest thy Mouth to Evil, and thy Tongue frameth Deceit: Thou sittest and speakest against thy Brother; These Things hast thou done, and I kept Silence; Thou thoughtest I was altogether such an one as thy self, but I will Reprove thee, and set them in order before thine Eyes, *saith the Lord. And the Apostle* Paul *tells us,* Whatever may be known of God is manifested within. *And what can that be by which God so manifesteth himself, but what* Moses *called the* Word nigh, in the Heart, *that the* Children of Israel *were to obey; That* Job *calls* Light, *which the* Wicked rebel against, not loving the Ways thereof: *The like doth Christ in* John, *when he complained,* that Men would not bring their Deeds to be examined by it. *In all Ages hath the Almighty more or less pleaded his own Cause in the Consciences of all People by this* Divine Principle of Light, *however variously denominated; And whatever* Faith *or* Hope *Man has, not grounded upon the Discoveries, Convictions and Directions of* This, *it is a* by-rote Faith, Hope, and Religion.

Therefore I beseech you to whom this Discourse is more particularly dedicated, to consider of us, not by Tradition, Education, Religions *establisht by Humane Laws, or Imperial Decrees, but by that Understanding this* Immortal Law and Ever-

Everlasting Foundation of Virtue (*as Heathen* Plutarch *calls it*) *will afford you to judge us by.*

It has been Man's Venturing to wade into the Holy Scriptures without this Divine Principle, that has caused so many fearful Miscarriages about Religion. Something *in Man prompts him to Religion, but Man being not wholly guided by that which so inspires him with Religious Desires, hastily spoils all with the Intermixture of his own Fancies and Conceits; and because He is assured that What first inclined him was Right, he sticks not to stile his own Inventions* Orthodox; *and then impatient of Contradiction, with a Fury, as great as his Ignorance, endeavours the Overthrow of whetever stands in his Way, and refuses to receive his Mark in his Forehead, or in his Right Hand This has occasioned so much Trumpery in Religion;* Ceremonies, Shew, and meer Formality have swallowed up the greatest part of it: *Now were Men brought to God's Heavenly* Gift in themselves, it would reclaim and leaven the Mind, chain the Affections, and bring Religion into Holy and Self-denying Living, and erect an Holy Regiment *in the Heart and Soul, by which the Heavenly* Image *would be renewed, and Man become as one born again, without which Translation, there can be no entring into God's Heavenly Kingdom.*

This the first Protestants *made to be their Reason of their Revolt from* Rome: *For though 'tis true, that they charged the* Papists *with making God's* Tradition *(the Holy Scriptures)* void *by their numerous dark Traditions; yet That which begot that Holy Loathing of* Rome's *Superstitions, Idolatries and Will-Worship, was God's* Grace *in the Hearts; and their best Argument against* Rome's *Assaults was this,* The Scripture which I believe from the Testimony of the Spirit of God in me, and which I can only understand from the Illumination thereof, owns no such Thing, and therefore I reject it.

Such as converse with Luther *and his Followers,* Zuinglius *and his Followers, will find this to have been the Foundation of their whole Work.* And our own Martyrology *is full to our Purpose, particularly* Tindal, Tims *and* Philpot.

I omit to mention a whole Cloud of Witnesses, because I intend not to dwell here, only this I would be at, and I intreat you all to weigh it, If any Thing can give to understand aright, and enable to practise those Things of God, which it is necessary for Man both to know and do, but God's Light, Grace or Word in the Heart; *What else can give us to relish the Divine Authority of the Scriptures themselves, or to believe the Things therein treated of to be undeniable Truths? Indeed, the Want of This has been a great Occasion of Atheism; Man making, practising and enacting That for Religion, of which People have had no Assurance in themselves: But if they should speak their Hearts, 'tis more probable, They do not believe it, but instead thereof deride it, and so under a Shew of Religion, live as Men without God in the World.*

To prevent which, and to bring Men to the true Understanding of what God expects from them, in order to that great Account they are to give unto Him at the Revelation of his Righteous Judgments (when he will judge the Secrets of all Men by Jesus Christ) we do exhort all to Christ's Pure, Unerring Light in the Conscience, (John 8. 12. 1 John 1. 5, 6, 7.) *which is sufficient to daily Understanding and Duty, that what they believe and profess in Matters of so high Importance, They may be convinced in their very Conscience, by the good Understanding the Inspiration of the Almighty gives, of the Truth and Necessity thereof; and not suffer themselves to be carried away with the Torrent of* Fathers, Councils, Synods, Doctors, Scholars, National Constitutions, &c. *(big and most Times untrue, and too often empty Words)* without that inward Conviction and Testimony of God's Good Spirit in Your Own Consciences, the old Protestant, and only primitive Ground of True Faith and Obedience.

I know, and shall always acknowledge, that in the Time of Ignorance the Almighty winked, and that in every Age he has expressed his Regard to those under the various Forms of Religion ever in the World, who have been Sincere-hearted and of Sober and Conscientious Conversation; But I must also tell you, that by how much the more, needless and unwarrantable Customs, Will-Worship and Human Religion built upon the dark and uncertain Conjectures of Men, are receded from, *and the Minds of People engaged in a diligent Attendance upon that* Divine Principle which only can clear up their Understandings, and give them an experimental Knowledge of the True God, and that Way of Worship and Service which may be most acceptable with him, *by so much more certain will they be of the Truth of their Religion, in as much as they have over and above all external Record, the Assurance of* Unquestionable Convictions *in their own* Consciences.

Thus

Thus God, that made Heaven and Earth, knows, we came to receive that Knowledge of him, Which we now expose our selves to all Hardships, to maintain.

We profess God; but like our Neighbours, in Works we denied him. We worshipp'd him after Man's Conceivings, insomuch that I may say, we worshipp'd the Unknown God in a False Way. No doubt but we were stockt with the Common Talk of Religion, but the Cross of Christ we were Strangers to. His Blood we extolled, whilst by Wicked Works we trod it under Foot; And believed our selves saved by it, Who were uncleansed from Sin. The whole End of his Coming we esteemed the Top of all Love; but never knew enough of it, truly kindled in our Hearts, whereby to work such Faith and Resignation, as could give us Victory over the World. Thus were we Jews-like Children of God whilst we crucified the Son of God; and of the Seed of Abraham, whilst the Serpents Seed reign'd; Heirs of the Kingdom, yet not born again; Free, yet the Bondslaves of Vanity. O! at this Time of Day it was that God found us out, and broke in upon our Souls with his Righteous Judgments for Sin, and laid Judgment to the Line, and Righteousness to the Plummet, within us; the Book of Conscience was opened, and great Fear surprised us, and deep Sorrow fell upon us, which brought that sudden and Strange Change, that made us both the Derision of Prophane, and Wonder of Sober Men.

The Author of the Account of Familism, for want of more Skill, and Seriousness, calls it the Hypochondria, as if it had been only a Flux of Melancholy overpowering the Strength of Reason, and carrying the Understanding captive at the Impetuosity of it's Fancies. But having been thus made sensible of the Terrors of the Lord for Sin, and being brought into a True Understanding of that Religion and Worship which most please God, some of us were constrained, and in Conscience bound, to go forth into the World, and publish these Tidings of Judgment for Sin, and Conversion through Righteousness, wrought by the mighty Power of God in the Conscience, that all might be awakened to try their Works, Faiths, Worships and whole Religions, whether they were of God or Men; or they had been doing their own Wills, or the Will of God; that so they might be brought to experience God to be a God nigh at hand, reconciled in Christ, blotting out Sin, and renewing a Right Spirit within, by which their Religion might not longer stand in the Traditions of Men, or on the Education of Parents, but upon the Convictions and Operations of God's Grace in the Conscience. And thus is all that Christ did without brought nigh and home to the very Soul. The Seed of the Woman is known to Bruise the Head of the Serpent; Christ, the Light, and Lamb that taketh away the Sins of the World, not only to take away Sins past through Remission, but Cleanse from the Nature, Root and Ground of Sin, by His Holy Blood, which sprinkles all Consciences that wait and walk in the Light (the Just Man's Path) from Dead Works, to serve the Living Lord God in Uprightness for ever.

For this Cause are We brought out into the World; and behold the Vessel we are embark'd in, our Lading and the Country we make for! The Vessel, Truth; the Lading, Faith and Good Works; Our Souls, the Passengers; and the Country, the Land of Everlasting Rest.

This I could not but present you with, that no Endeavours of our Enemies may be able to lodge a false Character of us and our Principles with you; Though I must faithfully tell you, that I should wrong my own Reason, as well as your Judgment, and speak against my Conscience too, if I should let in one Thought of this Man's Ability to do us any great Mischief with you: for, out of no Insult, but in Real Truth, I take Him for a very Unskilful Pilot on our Coast, a Man unacquainted with our Concerns; and a most Incompetent Person for an Antagonist.

Accept (for I can ask no Excuse for) my Plainness, I have not fawned, I never could, and now much less: These Matters not only deserve, but require greatest Plainness. And Men that believe they shall have to do with God, after they have left having to do with Men, ought to act with greatest Circumspection and Sincerity. Remember your Original; remember your End; and know assuredly that but Breath is in your Nostrils; and for every Deed done in this Mortal Body, whether it be good or whether it be evil, will God, the Righteous Judge, require an Account from You before his great Tribunal, where may you all be able to answer with Joy,

I am Your Faithful Friend,

WILLIAM PENN.

Wisdom Justified of her Children, from the *Ignorance* and *Calumny* of *H. Hallywell.*

CHAP. I.

His EPISTLE Considered.

THE *Adversary* we have to do withal begins his Dedicatory Epistle thus, *The daily and Numerous Encrease of the Heretical Generation of* Quakers *in these Parts made me a little more then ordinarily inquisitive into their Doctrines and Perswasions; which I found not only Destructive of Civil Government, but of Religion it self.*

'Tis natural with Ignorance to be Proud, and Envy to slander. His Enquiry has been at our *Adversaries* Doors, not ours. They that read him, and those Books that lately came out, may know his Informers without farther Cost: But *Book-Robbery*, though to Untruth, is an old *Priest-trick*.

If his Sort of rendring us inconsistent with Government could incense the Civil Magistrate to our Destruction, we know very well Traducers would not be wanting. *Truth* has never been persecuted under it's own Name: *Heresy* is an old *Blot* the *Devil* has cast upon it, that it may become suspected with the Simple; And *Christians* were of old worried in Beast-Skins: Such Coverings the present *Heathen* Spirit has provided for us. But as we cannot but bless the Name of Almighty God, that he has brought us to the Knowledge of his *good old Way of Truth in the Inward Parts*; So do we affirm it to be neither averse from Government, nor destructive of Religion; right *Government* being according to it; and pure *Religion* being to keep our selves *Unspotted from the World*, and to do or suffer, which we have ever done: and God knows, to that is the Tendency of our Holy Principle, to wit, *Moderation, Justice, Industry, Temperance and Upright Conversation*. But the true *English* of this wicked Suggestion is no more than this; The *Quakers* and their Perswasion are inconsistent with *Will-Worshippers, Hirelings, Men-Pleasers, Persecutors* and *Oppressors*; They give the World an *Alarm* for these Things, and Round their Ears with the Necessity of walking in so streight and narrow a Way, *as gives great Disquiet to the Libertine, and brings the Priests Qualification into great Question, and his Trade into absolute Danger.*

No wonder then, so many hard Names are cast upon us, to deter such as are unacquainted with us; and beget Scruples in them that are Well-disposed to us. However, this Contentment this Paragraph gives, that notwithstanding all this Opposition, *we daily and numerously encrease*, for which my Soul is greatly glad, and my Knees bow to the God and Father of our Lord Jesus Christ, that he would continue to prosper and speed his own great Work of Redemption in the Earth. But he goes on.

For what else can be expected from them who deny the Scripture to be the Word of God, and Rule and Guide in Matters of Salvation.

Answ. We do not deny the Scriptures to be the Word of God, and Rule and Guide in Matters of Salvation, out of any Undervalue of them; but from that reverent Regard we have to Christ the Great and Eminent Word, *who was with God, and was God, by whom all Things were made, Who is the Way, Truth and Life, the great Prophet, Judge, Law-giver and Priest to his People, whose Lips preserve Knowledge*. He is the New Covenant, Rule and Judge, and without him we can neither understand nor believe the Scriptures as we should do; Nay, so far are they from being a Rule, *&c.* that a Thousand Cases may happen wherein they cannot be a Direction to us. Nay, *they may be burned, drowned, torn, lost, mistranslated, added to, diminisht, Men may be robbed of them, imprisoned from them*; but none of all this can or ought to be said of the *Great Gospel-Rule*: God has ever been Sufficient to his People in every Age; And since they only are Children of God, *who are led by the Spirit of God, and that it is the Spirit of God alone which leads into all Truth*, It follows that the Law of the Spirit of Life, writ in the Heart,

and

and not a Law writ on Paper (a State less excellent than the *Jews*, whose Law was written upon Stone) *is the great Evangelical Rule of Living*; Yet are the Scriptures an Holy Declaration of the Word of God, and of the Rule and Guide in Matters of Salvation: And we reject for ever that Spirit which leads into those Principles and Practices, that in the least contradict *the standing and permanent Truths therein mentioned*; For they were written by Holy Men of God, being inspired thereto, and contain *Godly Reproof, Admonition, Exhortation and Prophecies, for the Edification of the Church, and perfecting the Man of God to every good Word and Work*, through Faith in Christ Jesus; and as such, many Directions, Precepts and Rules are therein laid down, yet they all refer to the *Grace, Light, Spirit, Word or Anointing within*, as That by which Man ought to be *Ruled, Governed and Ordered to God's Glory and his own Comfort*, as they first were who gave them forth; for they were *Witnesses of the Truth of what they writ*. So that they are an Holy Declaration of the Way of God, and that Holy Principle which leads to it, and in it, without which the Book is sealed, the Scriptures are unknown; and consequently not the Scriptures, *but that Holy Key of David is the Rule, how far, and which Way we are both to understand, interpret, believe and practise them.*

This may be enough to shew the Disingenuity of our Adversary in representing us to his *Knight*; For because We cannot give that Title and Office due to Christ himself from him to his bare Declaration, he would insinuate *that we refuse all Conformity to the Holy Examples and Testimonies therein related and exprest, as if we were a most dissolute Crew of Libertines*.

But he tells us, that this Person (whose Name I suppose we shall prove he has made too bold with) *so well knowing our obstinate and perverse Humour, in the Discharge of his Trusts committed to him under his* Most Sacred Majesty, *he could do no less than present him with this Treatise, that going under the Name and Protection of so worthy and accomplisht a Person, it may in some measure obtain it's desired Effect, by putting a Stop to the growing Evil, and confirming those who are not seduced in the Truth of their Profession*. A most non-sensical Expression.

Answ. But I am willing to hope better Things of him, than that he should go upon the *Priest's Message*, or turn their *Knight Errand*. But what's the Matter that the *Quakers* are so Perverse? They cannot say *right Worshipful*, because they think that of right belongs to God; nor *most sacred Majesty*, that being fit for no mortal Man: Neither can they lie and flatter with *Your most obliged and affectionate Servant*, for they are more obliged to God than Man, and to one Man more than another. He either knew not, forgot, or slighted the Rebuke of *Paulinus* to *Sulpitius Severus*, who said, *It becometh not Christ's Free-men to subscribe themselves Servant*, &c. But it is nothing with such as our Adversary to *Cog, Lie and Flatter*; 'Tis one Part of his Manners.

I would fain know what Rule he had for all this? Did the Holy Prophets and Apostles teach him any such Trash? Will he prate of Scripture for a Rule, and yet *bridle his Flattering Tongue no better?* The Customs of the *Heathens* have entred the Profession of *Christianity*, and that Old Spirit under this New Trim goes off for a very *Good Christian*.

O, but *the* Quakers *are obstinate in other Cases for all this!*

Answ. Why so? Because they will by all Means stand to their Principles; They will not play the *Sycophants*; Threats do not fright them, nor Promises gain them; They love their Conscience above their Conveniency, and seek to please God rather than Men. Perhaps, *this Sort of Men* the *Knight* has found them, but could have wisht them more pliant to the Laws, it may be, that he might have some colour to be kind: Must therefore this *Busy-Body* entitle his Name to all his own Follies, Lyes and Slanders against us? What can any moderate Person think, but that the Patron of such a Discourse has been an eminent *Persecutor*, whose Protection is so plainly called for to a Book that without doubt would have him so? For my Part, I think the *Knight* ought to repute that Ignorant and Disingenuous Discourse so far from being a Testimony how much the Author is his most obliged and affectionate Servant, that for Interesting his Name and Power therein, he should hereafter look upon him as an Enemy to him, his Name and Family.

Before I conclude, give me leave to ask him, why he sought for Protection? Is his national Cause defended by *Princes, Parliaments, Navies, Armies, the Learned, Rich and Powerful Clergy*, both *Universities*, the *Generality of the Gentry and Commonalty*, so weak and gasping; or are the poor despised, traduced and trodden down *Quakers* so potent and terrible, that a Book of eight Sheets dare not peep

---

1673.

Chap. I.

Tit. 2. 11, 12
John 3. 19, 20, 21.
Rom. 8. 13, 14.
1 John 2. 27.
Read *Quakerism* a New Nick-Name for old Christianity, *from* pag. 24. to p. 202. *Also* Reason against Railing. *from* p. 24. to p. 47.

out against them, but a big Title must be got to recommend and patronize it. But how *Worthy* soever the *Knight* be, that will not hinder my Proceeding to shew the *Unworthiness* of the Book, and therein of the Author, as well to his Patron as the despised *Quakers*.

CHAP. II.

Containing an Answer to his first Chapter, in which he pretends an Agreement to be between the Quakers *and other* Ancient *and* Modern Hereticks.

The Comparison Examined and Proved Defective.

OUR Adversary, that he may the better Prejudice his Reader against us, introduceth his Discourse with a Comparison of us, to the most noted and odious of the reputed ancient and modern *Hereticks*, doubtless hoping, that what he wants of Argument to render us such, may be supplied by that ill Opinion, Men have of those he brings us into parallel with. The first Man he thought fit to pitch upon is *Simon Magus*, a Man famous for his infamous Sorceries, with whom he wickedly yoaks that faithful Minister of God, *George Fox*, because, saith he, Simon Magus *gave out that he was God the Father*; *And* George Fox *before the Justices at* Lancaster, *that he was equal with God*.

Ans. There is no believing a decimating, persecuting *Priest*, against a *Quaker* till he makes more Conscience of telling Lyes, who hath given too many Demonstrations of his Desire to have us run down at any rate, to be credited by those who love Truth more than Partiality.

George Fox denies the Words, they were never so spoken by him, much less were they ever intended in that Way our Adversary takes and improves them; For though there be not an Equality, yet there is an Unity, as testifieth the Scripture; *Let the same Mind be in you, that was also in Christ Jesus, who being in the Form of God, thought it not Robbery to be equal with God.* And *He that sanctifieth, and they that are sanctified are all of One*; *for which Cause he is not ashamed to call them Brethren.* Again, *They that are joyned to the Lord are One Spirit*; and, *He that doth Righteousness is Righteous, even as He is Righteous.* To deny this is to deny the most Heavenly Benefit we have by Christ, namely, that *Unity* and *Fellowship* we have with the Father and with the Son, That it was an Unity, not an Equality, especially in the Sense he takes the Word, the faithful *Narrative* of that Proceeding, printed in the Year 1654. will farther testify.

How great then must this Man's Miscarriage be, who, to render a good Man an *Impostor*, turns Forger himself? But God will reward him.

The next Pair he pitches upon to prove his Assertion, is *Menander* and *James Naylor*. (pag. 3.) *The one for affirming Himself to be sent from the invisible Regions to be the Saviour of Mankind.* And James Nailor *for asserting himself to be Christ, and accepting Hosannahs and Divine Worship in the Streets of* Bristol.

Ans. What *Menander* was I know not, and it is hard believing a Character of any Man, when it is given by his Enemy: But sure I am that *James Naylor* never asserted himself to be the Christ of God; Neither did he ever deny Him that appeared at *Jerusalem* to be the Lord's Christ, as his Writings plentifully declare, especially one Paper written by him to the then *Parliament, when a Prisoner in* Bridewel.

" Christ Jesus the Emmanuel (of whose Sufferings the Scriptures declare) Him
" Alone I confess before Men, for whose sake I have deny'd whatever was
" dear to me in this World, that I might win him, and be found in him and not
" in my self, whom alone I seek to serve in Body, Soul and Spirit, Night and Day,
" according to the Measure of Grace working in me; *even to that Eternal Spirit*
" *be Glory, and to the Lamb for ever.* But to ascribe this Power and Virtue to
" James Naylor, *or for that to be exalted or worshipped*, To me is great Idolatry.
" So having an Opportunity given (with Readiness) I am willing, in *the Fear of*
" *God the Father, in Honour to Christ Jesus*, and to take off all Offences from e-
" very Simple Heart, without Guile or Deceit.

His third Comparison lies betwixt *Photinus* who is said *to have denied the Trinity*, and *G. Fox*, as guilty of the same Error in his Account. *pag.* 4.

Ans. I can find no such Place in the Book so called; Either our *Adversary* sets up for a New Controvertist, or he dishonestly shunned giving us the Page: But I am willing to believe, that he took it as he found it in some other *Adversary*;

for any Thing reported or printed against a *Quaker*, is ground enough for an envious Priest to accuse him.

But what if *G. Fox* denyed the Unscriptural Expressions, viz. *The Trinity of distinct and separate Persons*? must it necessarily follow that he denyed the *Three* that bear Record in Heaven, the *Father, Word* and *Spirit*? We justly renounce those Barbarous-School Terms, as not suited to God's Heavenly Manifestations, but the dark Conceits of some *Popish Doctors*.

His fourth Comparison is made between *Socinus* and *James Naylor*, in that the one denyed the *Satisfaction of Jesus Christ, and look'd upon his Passion only as an Example*.

The other in that he affirmed, the End for which Christ did suffer, was to be a living Example to all Generations, Love to the lost. p. 50.

Answ. He has not truly delivered the Opinion of *Socinus*, whose Books shew, (however mistaken about Christ's Divinity) that he ever esteemed his Death and Passion to have more in it, than a bare Example: Nor has he faithfully dealt with *J. Naylor* in this Quotation; For *first* I find not the Words as cited: and *next*, the Word (O N L Y) is by himself omitted, which alone renders the Passage *Heterodox*. Suppose then that *J. Naylor* writ, *that Christ was in his Suffering a Living Example to all Generations*; Is there no Difference between *Christ's being in his Death and Passion only our Example*, which he charges upon *Socinus*, and Christ's being *our living Example in Suffering*, which he attributes to *J. Naylor*? How can there be a Comparison, where there is so great a Disparity? The *First* is denyed by all that own Christ: The *Last* is owned by all that do not deny *Peter*, who thus writ to the scattered Brethren, *For even hereunto were ye called, because Christ also suffered for us, leaving us an Example that ye should follow his Steps*. 1 Pet. 2. 21.

His fifth Comparison he makes between the *Valentinians* and the *Quakers*. The Former, *he says, arrogated to themselves a Knowledge beyond Christ and his Apostles*; The Latter, *impudently throw away the written Word of God, and delude the credulous Vulgar, with new fangled Revelations*; which he thinks he has prov'd by two Instances. 1. That *Tho. Hollbrow* a *Quaker, to one that urged Scripture, answered*, " What dost thou tell me of Scripture, which is no more to me than an old " Almanack. 2. *That Fox and Hubberthorn in a Book, called Truth's Defence, say*, " The Scriptures are no standing Rule, and it is dangerous for ignorant People to " read them.

Answ. To the *first* I say, there is great Difference between one that was *no Quaker*, and one that was or is a *Quaker*; We have examined the Matter, and by all we can find, both that Saying is not true as charged, and it is of an ancienter Date than the Coming of any of our Friends into those Parts, therefore not the Saying of a *true Quaker*. To the *Second* I return thus much, 'Tis true there is such a Book, and it was written by *G. Fox*, and *R. Hubberthorn*; but he has not given us so much as one Page to direct us to the Passage: So that either People must read till they find it, or else take his Perversion for our Assertion. Unworthy Man! does he think us such Wretches, that we deserve not common Justice? Methinks Justice should not be denyed where so little Mercy is shewn.

But to answer the Instance. Our Judgment about the *Scriptures being the Rule*, we have already delivered; And in what Sense *it is dangerous to read them*, their own Book will declare.

" 'Tis dangerous, say *G. Fox*. and *R. Hubberthorn*, to read the Scripture in Or- " der to make *War against the Saints, to give carnal Expositions upon them, and* " *Meanings contrary to them, and to make a Trade of them; but blessed is he that* " *doth read and doth understand them*. If this prove that Slight to Scripture, our *Adversary* would suggest them to be guilty of, then let us be condemned: But God's Witness in every unseared Conscience will acquit them, and judge him for corrupt Citation, and hard Speeches, who dares to cry thereupon, *Are not these as Impudent Hereticks, as the Valentinians* (whom he represents to have arrogated to themselves a Knowledge above Christ and his Apostles) which, how true soever it may be of them, I am sure is false enough of us; for those hideous Consequences he makes, are not deducible from any unperverted Saying to be cited out of *Truth's Defence*.

And lest any should think, we deny, with the *Papists*, the Perusal of the Scriptures to Ignorant People, from what our Adversary says, know that they spoke of such *Ignorant and Unlearned Persons*, as in reading, *wrested them to their own Destruction;*

ſtruction; now unleſs it be not dangerous to read to *Deſtruction*, they are not chargeable with Blame in that Matter.

But who are the Knowing and Learned? The *Jewiſh Doctors?* and *Greek Philoſophers?* No, but *Fiſhermen and poor Mechanicks diſcipled in Chriſt's School*, for the Excellency of whoſe Knowledge *Paul reputed his Gamaliel-Acquiſitions, but Droſs and Dung*: So that their *Knowing* and *Learned* are many Times the *Ignorant and Unlearned* we ſpeak of, whoſe Wiſdom God will confound, and whoſe Underſtanding he will bring to nought.

His laſt Compariſon of us in this Chapter is, with *Marcus, an old Heretick*. The Agreement he makes betwixt us *lyes in our mutual Pretences to Inſpiration and Prophecy*. For as he reports him *to have abuſed many ſilly Women, under Colour of conferring on them the Gift of Propheſying, and that he had a familiar Spirit by which he brought himſelf into Credit with his deluded Followers*; So he tells us that he has had it confidently affirmed, *that about the firſt Riſe of the Quakers, in the North of England, ſeveral Perſons by Gloves and Ribbands and divers Charms were really bewitched by them. And doubtleſs many of their Quaking Fits were real Poſſeſſions by the Devil*.

Anſw. What *Marcus* was is nothing to us; If he has done amiſs, he has anſwered for it by this Time. I confeſs, I am not over fond of the Characters left us of ancient *Hereticks*, knowing what Kind of Creatures the beſt *Proteſtants* are with *Papiſts*; and what fearful Monſters ſeveral ſober Separatiſts are reputed among ſome Proteſtants: But this I know, if what he hath ſaid of ſeveral *Ancients* be no truer than what he hath ſaid of us, he has groſly abuſed their Doctrines and their Memories.

For the Witchcraft of *Gloves, Ribbands* and *Charms*, 'tis ſcarce worth my Notice; his Folly in mentioning it, being a ſufficient Reproof and Confutation to himſelf. A Story fit for none at this Time of Day, to report or believe, but a Man of his Size. I thought they had been worn out by this Time.

But let the ſober Reader judge, which Savours moſt of Satan's Deſign, this idle, yet Scandalous, Story, *or our fearing and trembling at the Word of the Lord, and thoſe Terrors that broke in upon our Souls, becauſe of Sin and Iniquity?* 'Tis but the old Spirit of Mockery, that acted the *Jews* and *Heathens* againſt the *Chriſtians*, and *Papiſts* againſt *Proteſtants*, and too many *Proteſtants* of ſeveral Sorts, againſt ſome more reformed Seperatiſts:

For had the Reverend Fear of God poſſeſſed our *Adverſary*'s Heart, in the writing of this Diſcourſe, there had been no Room for ſuch irreligious Scoffs againſt an inoffenſive People. But the Devil, becauſe he would be God, calls God the Devil, and Chriſt Beelzebub; Light, Darkneſs; and the Power of God, the Power of Satan; and the Fear and Trembling brought by the one, the Poſſeſſions and Witchcrafts of the other. Certainly ſuch Men live in a dry Land, they ſee not when Good cometh. But what will not an enraged Tything Prieſt do to deſtroy us, who (he knows) are Diſcoverers of ſuch Deluders?

C H A P. III.

His pretended Agreement between the Authors of Familiſm and the Quakers conſidered. His Objections anſwered.

I Now come to conſider the Reaſon of the Title of his Book, and what Ground he had to name us, the *Revivers* and *Propagators* of *Familiſm*, with the moſt weighty Objections he makes againſt us, (if in Truth I may repute the ſtrongeſt of them ſuch) and that with what Brevity, Truth and Faithfulneſs I can.

The great Authors of this Doctrine of Familiſm, he ſays, *were David George and Henry Nicholas, but more eſpecially the latter, as having more improved and diſſeminated the pernicious Errors introduced by the former*. He beſtows many ſevere Expreſſions upon them, more, I think, than becomes a Man of any Charity to give. I am not their Advocate; but ſo much Spleen and ſo little Reaſon, againſt Dead Men, can be neither Chriſtian nor Manly. What he ſays they held, and how far we are concerned in it, it is our Buſineſs to enquire.

§. 1. *Of Chriſt's Miniſtration.*

And firſt he tells us, that *H. N.* ſhould ſay, " that not only the Law of *Moſes* " but the Miniſtration of *Chriſt*, and his *Apoſtles*, were only temporary Things in- " ſtituted to bring Men to the perfect Reign of the Spirit; *and then, like Horn-*
Books

Books and Primmers to grown Understandings, to be thrown away, p. 10, 11. And that *this is the full Sense of the Quakers*, says our *Adversary*, p. 10, 11, 12, 13, 14. *Hear* John Crook *a Quaker*; " We believe by the same Gift of Grace, that there " are several Ministrations, and several Operations, according to 1 Cor. 12. And " all by the same Spirit, as before and after the Law by *Moses*, and after by *John* " the Baptist, and *Christ* and his *Apostles*. And by this Spirit were the Scriptures " given forth, and the Holy Men of God did speak, prophecy, preach and pray, " as they were Moved; and to answer the Service God had for them to do, they " were to wait, as Christ commanded his Disciples, to receive the Promise of the " Father ——— And therefore as it was the Practice of the People of God in old " Time, to wait for the Moving of this Spirit, that they might speak as it gave " them Utterance in the Evidence and Demonstration thereof; so do this People, " called *Quakers*, now. Upon which our *Adversary* dares to observe, *that we, with the* Familists, *deny the Ministration of Christ to be the Ministration of the Spirit, and consequently charges us with a Blasphemous Derogation from the Honour of our Blessed Saviour, who said to his Apostles*, John 16. 14. *He shall receive of mine, and shew it unto you.*

Answ. If our *Adversary*'s Weakness has run him into this strange Parallel, he is to be pity'd; but if his Envy, he is severely to be rebuked. Will any Man that has Sense or Honesty say, it is all one to affirm that Christ's Ministration is *an Horn-book that Time casts off with Infancy*; and that it is a Waiting to receive the same Spirit Christ commanded his *Apostles* to wait for, as the Promise of the Father, and the peculiar Gift and Privilege of his own Ministration? Does not *J. Crook* expresly draw a Parallel between the Holy Men of God of old, *and the* Quakers *of our Time; that as they then, so the* Quakers *now wait to be taught, moved and ordered by the same Eternal Spirit, through which all come to be baptized into One Body?* How was that then no Spiritual Ministration, when we desire to be conformed *unto the Spirit* and *Holy Example thereof*, not making this a new, but reviving that old and durable Ministration of the Spirit? Therefore *Blasphemous Derogations* will return to our *Adversary*, as unduly charged upon us, with a Charge upon him of base Derogation from the Truth of our Belief.

But he thinks that *Humph. Smith* has made much for him in thus Querying; p. 15. " Whether should People be led in these Days by *Moses*, according to his " Outward Ministration, or the Person of Christ, *(limiting him to his Visible Ap-* " *pearance)* or the Spirit of Truth, which he promised to pour out after his " Ascension; which contains the Substance of what he quotes out of *Humph. Smith*, and to which he thus answers, *There is no sober Christian can read this Passage without Anger and Disdain to see such wicked Wretches scoff, and fleeringly insult upon the sacred Person of our Lord Jesus*; *The whole History of whose Life and Death, in the Letter of it, they esteem no better than one of* Æsop's *Fables*.

Answ. But our *Adversary* will not so easily escape the Hands of the Just God, (whose is Vengeance) for these Ungodly Defamations, as he well knows he may do ours: Anger, Disdain, and Lies, become him, and it is little to be wonder'd that he should be guilty of them all against a *Quaker*. If *H. Smith* had asserted *that* Moses *could not be our Leader, neither the Visible Person of Christ, but the Spirit of Truth*, he had not exceeded the Warrant of Scripture, nor the very Judgment of this Reviler. It is not two Pages off that he quoted John 16. 14. *He shall receive of mine, and shall shew it unto you*: Which, if I understand any thing, imports thus much; *That those Things which they knew not whilst Christ was with them, after his Ascension the Holy Ghost should reveal unto them*, as these two preceding Verses fully prove. *I have yet many Things to say unto you, but ye cannot bear them now*; *Howbeit, when the Spirit of Truth is come, he will guide you into all Truth, and he will shew you Things to come.* Nay, Christ himself says in the 7th Verse, *Nevertheless I tell you the Truth, It is expedient for you that I go away*; *For if I go not away the Comforter will not come unto you*. And in the 14th Chap. Verse 16, 17, 18, 19, 20, he speaks thus, *I will pray the Father, and he will give you another Comforter, and will abide with you for ever, even the Spirit of Truth*: So that the *personal Ministration* was manifestly *transient* and *temporary*; but *That* of the Spirit was to abide for ever. But I would not any should think it to be less Christ's Ministration, because the Ministration of the Spirit; for the Lord is that Spirit, as his own Words manifest: Again, *I will not leave you Comfortless, I will come to you. Yet a little while, and the World seeth me no more, but ye see me: Because I live, ye shall live also*; *For he that dwelleth with you, shall be in you*. At

that

1673.
Chap. III.

that Day you shall know that I am in my Father, and you in me, and I in you. And that this Comforter is Christ in his Spiritual Coming and Appearance, let it be farther observ'd, that the same Word for *Comforter* (Παράκλητος) in *John* 16. 7. is the Word used by the same Apostle in the first Verse of the 2d Chapter of his first Epistle, for *Advocate*, when he says, *We have an Advocate with the Father, Jesus Christ the Righteous.*

In short, the Dispensation of his Visible Appearance was but Temporary: *It is expedient for you that I go away.* But his *Ministration*, who so appeared, then disappeared, and after re-appeared in a Spiritual and unalterable Ministration, *Lo, I am with you to the End of the World*, Mat. 28. 20. And truly thus much our *Adversary* (p. 13.) in Contradiction to himself, grants us, that *the Ministration of Christ was indeed the Ministration of the Spirit.* Now what Scoffs, Fleerings or Insults against the sacred Person of our Lord Jesus any can see in this Doctrine, to incite a sober Christian to Anger and Disdain, I leave to any but such an Angry Disdainful Enemy to judge?

I cannot forget this horrible Lye of us, concerning the *Scripture*, stolen probably out of an *Anabaptists* lying *Dialogue* lately printed against us. *Prelaticks* and *Sectaries* can sometimes agree against *Quakers*, *Æsop's Fables* have more Worth in them than all the *Books* that ever were written against the *Quakers*; I do not at all doubt but there are twenty Fables in *Æsop*, that, well considered, would have taught them more Discretion and (it should have been their own Fault if not) more Honesty too, than any or all of them have shewn in their utmost Endeavours against us. *But that we have no more Regard to, nor Belief in the Holy Scriptures of Truth, than in Æsop's Fables*, is a Story more prophane and fabulous than any Fable in *Æsop*; and God will recompence with a Vengeance this *Defamer* of an Innocent People, unless diverted by his unfeigned Repentance.

§. 2. *Of Revelation.*

He tells us, the second Thing wherein the *Familists* and *Quakers* are all one, *is the Pretence of Immediate Revelation.* Dav. Geo. and H. N. *both pretended to receive their Doctrine from the Angel* Gabriel. *And* W. Gibson, *the* Quaker, *says*, p. 16. *that the Gospel which they preach they have not received it from Men, nor from Books, nor from Writings, but by the Revelation of Jesus Christ in them, and then denies the Scriptures of the Old and New Testament to be the revealed Will of God.*

Answ. After what Manner D. G. and H. N. received their Commission I know not, but sure I am that *W. Gibson's* Assertion is sound. Take away *Revelation* and the Gospel ceases of Course; Christ is put beside the Dignity of his Prophetical and Priestly Office; the Promises of God will be broken; and the most excellent Part of the Scriptures, God's Traditions, made void. Who was it said, *A Prophet shall the Lord your God raise up like unto me*, Deut. 18. 18. *Him shall ye hear in all Things. There is a Spirit in Man; and the Inspiration of the Almighty giveth Understanding*, Job 32. 8. *As for me, This is my Covenant with him, saith the Lord, My Spirit that is upon thee, and my Words which I have put in thy Mouth, shall not depart out of thy Mouth, nor out of the Mouth of thy Seed, nor out of the Mouth of thy Seed's Seed, saith the Lord, from henceforth and for ever*, Isa 59. 21. *I will Reveal unto them the Abundance of Peace and Truth—*, Jer. 33. 6. *I thank thee, O Father, Lord of Heaven and Earth, because thou hast hid these Things from the Wise and Prudent, and hast* Revealed *them unto Babes—— And no Man knoweth the Father but the Son, and he to whom the Son will* Reveal *him*, Matt. 11. 25, 27. *No Man can come unto me, except the Father which hath sent me, draw him.* John 6. 44. *But God hath Revealed them unto us by his Spirit. For the Spirit searcheth all things yea, the deep things of God. For the Things of God knoweth no Man but the Spirit of God*, 1 Cor. 2. 10, 11. Chap. 14. 30, *If any Thing be revealed to another that sitteth by, let the first hold his Peace. For when it pleased God to* Reveal *his Son in me. For I neither received the Gospel of Man, neither was I taught it, but by the* Revelation *of Jesus Christ*, Gal. 1. 12. 16. *If any be otherwise minded, God will* Reveal *it to him*, Phil. 3. 15. As I said before, so again, Who uttered these excellent Sayings, and for what End? If no *Inspiration*, no *Understanding*; If no *Revelation*, no *Knowledge*; And if the Spirit cease to teach, (as it can never teach, but by Inspiration or Revelation) then the Administration of Christ and his Apostles is ceased indeed; And so, not the *Quakers*, but their *Adversary* overturns the Gospel-Ministration, as begun and preached by Christ and his Apostles. And be it known to all the World, we think *Revelation* no Disgrace to our Cause. *Parrots* may learn Scripture, but can never experience it; And those know little better who

who know not by Experience: They are unprofitable *Canters* indeed, who confidently talk of what they never felt, and idle Boasters who buoy up themselves unto the Reputation of Ministers and Christians, with a loud Talk of their Travels, Tryals, Inspirations, and Experiences, whom they plainly mock in their Posterity, concluding all blind because themselves cannot see. In short, Let it be the Character of the despised *Quakers*, (and we glory in it) that all the *Councils, Synods, Universities, Doctors, Scholars, and the most Unanimous Decrees, Learned Books*, and whatever the Power and Art of the Spirit of Man can produce, will never be able to give, or rule that true Faith which overcomes the World; For *that which may be known of God is manifested within Man*: And though outward Records may testify of and direct to that Unerring *Light* and *Spirit*, by which Man comes both to know God, and to be made Conformable to his Heavenly Image; yet nothing below the Discoveries, Convictions, and Effectual Operations of the Eternal Spirit, can give Man the certain Knowledge of God, nor that daily Ability by which alone he may be enabled to obey him.

Pag. 16, 17, 18. But he opposeth to us Miracles and Reason, insinuating that we have no more of the last than the first, and therefore not to be believed. To the first, I say, we pretend to no other Religion, than what was professed and practised by the Apostles, and therefore need no new Miracles after that Manner to confirm that which has been confirmed by Miracles already; especially to those who believe those Miracles: And to deny Revelation where there are no Miracles, is to discard many of the Prophets, and to deny the Pouring forth of the Spirit upon the Primitive Christians. But above all, hear the Man's Interpretation of Deut. 18. 22. *When a Prophet speaks in the Name of the Lord, if the Thing follow not, nor come to pass; that is,* saith this horrible Perverter of holy Scripture, *if he do no Miracle*; whereas the *Verse* intends no such Thing. Is this to rant over the *Quakers* for Idiots, as if he were some Doctor of the Chair, that where the Scripture speaks of *Prophecy*, he should render it *Miracle*; as if he that is a Prophet, is a Worker of Miracles, and that Miracles and Prophecy are equivalent? But (*Argumentum ad hominem*) let us see how it will hold. He that is a true Prophet must necessarily work Miracles; *But the Priests of* England *cannot work Miracles*; therefore, *the Priests of* England *are all False Prophets*. A true Conclusion, yet false Premises; A Paradox. Now for the Reasonableness of our Doctrine: 'He 'thinks a very mean Capacity can find none in it; for how should there be any 'Reason in what they teach, when they themselves, *says he*, deny the Use of 'Reason. (pag. 18.) But none have less than they which pretend to so much. This Man dares swagger for Reason, and yet cries out, *Heresy*, as soon as he sees it. His Reason is, *the Authority of his Church*, The Say-so *of some University Doctor*, finally, *The Works of some learned Men*; and offer never so much Reason and Conscience against them; and your Reason is Sophistry, and Conscience, *Enthusiasm*. The justest Separation in the World is with such but *Schism*, and which is the last Stratagem, such Persons must be Enemies to *Cæsar*. But I may say of those Men, as *Heraclitus* said of their Fore-Fathers, *If blind Men were to judge of Sight, they would say Blindness were Sight*. 'God is the Fountain as well of Reason as Light: And we assert our Principle not to be without Reason, but most Reasonable; Whence it is frequent with us in our Reproof of Cruel Men, to say, *they are Unreasonable*, whether it be to Man or Beast, making good what the Prophet saith, *For his God doth instruct him to Discretion, and doth teach them*. Again, *Come and let us Reason together*. And *Tertullian* will have the first Verse of *John* thus rendred; *In the Beginning was Reason, and that Reason was with God, and that Reason was God; by that were all Things made, &c*. And this seems no foreign Interpretation, for in the 10th Verse of *Jude* we have sensual Men not having the Spirit, called ἄλογα ζῶα, *Unreasonable Creatures*, according to which the Apostle *Peter* speaks, ἕτοιμοι πρὸς ἀπολογίαν αἰτοῦντι λόγον, *to him that asks Reason ready to give it*.

Thus much (to overlook our own Translation in *Paul's* second Epistle to the *Thessalonians*, where he calls such *Unreasonable Men that have not Faith*) concerning Reason: So that it is very evident by our Adversary's denying, and the *Quakers* asserting an unerrable Principle to be in Man, and the Refusal of the one, and the Readiness of the other to be governed thereby, that not the *Quakers*, but their Enemies are Unreasonable both in their Faith and Practice.

§. 3. *Of Forms of Prayer.*

Our Adversary spends two or three Pages in proving the Necessity of *Bodily Worship*, and he doth it so lamely, that if it were so much my Judgment to deny it, as it is to practise it, I know nothing he has said, to incline me to it. This he makes an Introduction to that Agreement, he says, there is between *D. G. H. H.* and the *Quakers, in their mutual Renouncing both Bodily Worship and Visible Ordinances.* For Bodily Worship, I need say no more, than that our publick Meetings judge him guilty of great Dishonesty. For his *Visible Ordinances*, we shall proceed to consider them. The first is concerning *a Form of Prayer*, hear him.

With the like silly and weak Confidence they exclaim against Forms of Prayer, when as our blessed Saviour taught his Disciples a Form. Matt. 6. 9. *After this Manner therefore* pray ye, *&c.* And lest, says he, *we should think that this was only a Pattern,* Saint Luke Chap. 11. *expresses it, when ye pray, say,* Our Father, *&c. that is, do it in these Words. Moreover* John *taught his Disciples; and one of Christ's Disciples desired that he would teach them: where we are told,* first *that* John *delivered a Form of Prayer to his Disciples.* 2. *That Christ's Disciples besought him that he would also give them some Form of his making.*

Ans. But can this Man have the Vanity to plead the Necessity of the Use of this Form, much less of those that are of Mens Invention and Appointment from those Quotations? Has his Religion brought him no farther? Can he believe that *Matthew* writ by the Holy Ghost, and yet imply an absolute Reproof in his so much more commending *Luke's* Account, which, he thinks, requires the express Words, and not others like them? But let it be considered, that this was a Time of Infancy; and that it was before the more full pouring out of the Spirit, is certain; and that they knew not *Gospel-Prayer* as afterward, is undeniable. Besides, It is either Sufficient, or it is not; If *Insufficient*, it reflects on Christ, beside, who can supply it's Defect? If *Sufficient*, why do you use any other? What ever it is upon our Principles, you must confess it to be a setting of your Posts by God's Posts; your Invention by his Institution. It is meer Deceit to attempt the Defence of the *Popish English Mass-Book* from Christ's Prayer. Prove your Forms to be of Divine Institution, and that God by his Spirit now requires them, and the Debate will end; otherwise we reject the Allusion as improper and incoherent. The Spirit is not confinable to set Forms, though in Times of Ignorance he hath administred Comfort in them to those who were sincere, and knew no better: But Forms are not therefore to be perpetuated; for that were to obstruct the more free Operation of the Spirit, and our Expression by it: It is at best but a State of Weakness to be condescended to, but never to be pleaded for; God's Spirit will be unlimited, as well as the Words, he prompts us to, must never by another be confined.

§. 4. *Of Baptism.*

He says, *we both Deny Baptism* (by which I understand *Water*) *because Christ finding it among the* Jews *adopted it into his Religion; a Ceremony neither burthensome nor offensive, and the only Door set open under the Gospel for Salvation.* For which he brings three Scriptures, *Matt.* 28. 19. *Go, and teach all Nations baptizing them in the Name of the Father, &c.* To the same Purpose by *Mark*, chap. 16. ver. 15, 16. *And Christ's Saying,* John 3. 5. *Except a Man be born of Water and of the Spirit, he cannot enter into the Kingdom of God.*

Ans. If Baptism was ever *Jewish* as our *Adversary* grants, then because Christ came to end all *Jewish* Ceremonies, Water-Baptism can bear no Evangelical Perpetuity. And if it should be objected, that *it was used after the Pouring forth of the Holy Ghost,* I answer, so were *Circumcision, Vows, Purification, Forbearing to eat Things strangled and Blood*; And the common Practice of *Christendom*, so called, sufficiently tells us, what is become of those Observations. Using and Instituting are two Things. The Apostles condescended where they never commanded.

In the two first Scriptures, which contain a Commission, there is no Water mentioned; That there is a *Baptism of the Holy Ghost*, I hope, all will grant; That such a Baptism admits of no outward Water is plainly implied: And that it was the Baptism of the Holy Ghost (and therefore not of Water) which Christ intended, I will briefly prove.

First, This Commission was some of the last Words Christ spoke; that it is to be fulfilled is certain; that they could not do it without Power is clear; that neither of those Chapters mentions any such Endowment must be granted. Whither then must we go to fetch that Account here omitted? I would desire my *Reader* to turn to the first Chapter of *Luke's Acts of the Apostles*, where we shall find Christ's last Words to his constant Followers thus left upon Record; *And being assembled together with them, he commanded them that they should not depart from* Jerusalem, *but wait for the Promise of the Father, which, saith he, ye have heard of me. For* John *truly baptized with Water, but ye shall be baptized with the Holy Ghost not many Days hence. When they therefore were come together, they asked of him, saying, Lord, wilt thou at this Time restore again the Kingdom to* Israel? *And he said unto them, It is not for you to know the Times or Seasons which the Father has put into his own Power*; *But ye shall receive Power, after that the Holy Ghost is come upon you, and ye shall be Witnesses unto me, both in* Jerusalem, *and in all* Judea, *and in* Samaria, *and unto the uttermost Part of the Earth. And when he had spoken these Things, while they beheld he was taken up, and a Cloud received him out of their Sight.* Now if the Promise of the Father was the Pouring out of the Holy Ghost, and if the Pouring out of the Holy Ghost be the Baptism of the Holy Ghost, and that the Baptism of the Holy Ghost was that which qualified them to be his Witnesses, as the whole Place fully proves; *Then, Go, and teach all Nations,* &c. in *Matthew,* and, *Go ye into all the World,* in *Mark,* must not have been spoken before these Words in the Acts, *at least not to take Place till they themselves had been baptized with the Holy Ghost*; and consequently the Baptism mentioned in that Commission, must not have been a *Water-Baptism,* as *John's* was, *but that of the Holy Ghost which they were to be baptized with*: So that the Order of the Words, *at least in Execution,* if not in Expression, must have been this, *John indeed baptized with Water, but ye shall be baptized with the Holy Ghost not many Days hence*; *Then go ye and teach all Nations, baptizing them in* (or rather into) *the Name of the Father, Son and Holy Ghost*; *And lo, I am with you always unto the End of the World.* Nor is this incredible, when we consider, that without their so baptizing, it had been utterly Impossible for them *to have turned them from Darkness to Light, and from the Power of Satan unto God.* And doubtless they might as well baptize with the Holy Ghost, *as reconcile by the Word*; For where the one was, the Power of the other could not be wanting.

For the third Scripture, though *Water* be mentioned, yet what *Water* will be the Question. That it is not meant of outward Water, I offer several Reasons. 1. To be born of Water and of the Spirit is no more, *than to be born of Water,* or *of the Spirit,* καὶ being here explicative; For were it otherwise, and that by Water were understood *External Water,* this Absurdity would inevitably follow, that the Soul of Man which is Spiritual and Internal, could in part be regenerated by *Water External and Elementary:* But this Place is excellently unfolded, by that notable Passage of the Apostle *Paul* in his Epistle to *Titus,* chap. 3. 5. *Not by Works of Righteousness which we have done, but according to his Mercy he saved us, by the Washing of Regeneration and Renewing of the Holy Ghost*; where we not only have the Washing of *Regeneration* to parallel being *born again of Water* (which say we, must be as Spiritual as the New Birth it produceth) but also *the Renewing of the Holy Ghost* to answer *being born again of the Spirit,* That as the washing of Regeneration, or Renewing of the Holy Ghost, are Synonymous, or Expressions to the same Purpose; so being born again of *Water,* or being born again of the *Spirit,* are equivalent.

But if our *Adversary* will have this *Water* to be material in Honour of his Baptism, Let him never refuse the like Liberty to us in Construction of that great Water-Baptist's own Words: *But he shall baptize you with the Holy Ghost and with Fire,* that is, *material Fire.* Mat. 3. 11. My Judgment is, if that were the Church of *England's* Baptism, he had never been her Son, though such Sons are ready to *Christen many with that Fiery Baptism.* But if such an Interpretation be absurd, let him not esteem his own Rational: And if it must be the *Holy Ghost,* or *Fire,* then let it be *Water,* or *Spirit*; for indeed they are but so many Words, intimating the various Operations of one Divine Power.

In short, *John* was but a Forerunner, therefore not to be perpetuated: *He was the Water (but Christ the great Spiritual) Baptist*; The former to decrease, the Latter to increase: *And the least in Christ's Kingdom, which is not of this World, is greater than John*; not than his private State, *but outward Administration.*

Paul (whose Commission was larger than any Priest's in *England*) tells us, *He was not sent to baptize* (with Water) *but to Preach*; And instead of enjoyning the Practice of it upon others, *he thanks God that he baptized but very few himself,* which surely he had never done, if it had been Part of his Commission, or the durable Baptism of the Gospel; For he had just Reason to suspect some disaffected would make that ill Use of his Liberty, *that it was to ingratiate and set up himself, being conscious that he had no Authority for what he did.* This he farther gives us to believe in that pertinent Passage to our Purpose; *There is One Body,*

One Spirit, One Lord, One Faith, One Baptism, One God and Father of all. If more Baptisms than one, then more *Bodies, Spirits, Lords, Faiths, Gods,* and *Fathers of all, who were above all, and through all, and in them all,* unto whom *Paul* wrote. If this be absurd, and that there is but one Baptism, I hope, it will not be denied to be *that of the Holy Ghost*, which is both most suitable to the Evangelical Ministration, *and the peculiar Baptism of Christ Jesus our Lord.* I shall touch upon one Passage more.

The like Figure whereunto even Baptism also doth now save us; as our modern Translation has it, From which, though our Adversary would infer *that Water-Baptism is to be used, as co-assistant with the Answer of a good Conscience, to Salvation,* (pag. 28, 29,) I doubt not unanswerably to maintain our foregoing Assertion.

This Verse admits of various Readings in ancient Copies, and diverse Interpretations by learned Men. We shall a little disquisite the Matter, that he may see we shall not refuse *Learning* where it may perform the Office of an honest Servant, not an Usurper. Ω (some have it ο or ὅ; the Modern *Greek* ὁμοίον καὶ ἡμᾶς (*Augustin* has it *Vos*, and our old Books, saith *Zegerus*) ἀντίτυπον (which *Vatablus* makes the Truth relative to the Type *Flood*. And saith *Grotius*, "Vox ἀντίτυπος est communis "utrique relato, i. tam Figuræ tribuitur quam Rei per Figuram significatæ; signify- "ing *Type* and *Antitype*, or the Thing signified by the *Type*) *Erasmus* hath it, cui "nunc simile sive respondens Baptisma, so that Baptism may answer as the Thing "typified, not another Type) Ἀντίτυπον, says Dr. *Hammond*, (a famous Man of "the English Church) is certainly best renderd *Antitype*; yet there be two diffe- "rent Senses, sometimes Contradictious; thus *Zenephon* and *Hesychius*. Then "Destruction was by outward Water, *now Salvation by Inward*; otherwise *pro* or "*in lieu of another*, as ἀνθύπατος, he that supplies the Consul's Place, so ἀντίτυπον "βάπτισμα (as in an old Copy in *Oxford*) is the *Ark inward,* supplying the Place "of the *Ark outward*. Νῦν σώζει βάπτισμα, which *Capellus* understands to be *Baptis-* "*mum internum, quo fimus Mortis & Resurrectionis Christi participes. Hujus in-* "*terni Baptismi Typos aliquot habemus in V. T. imprimis autem Arcam diluvii, et* "*Arcam Noæ.* By Inward Baptism we are made Partakers of Christ's Death and Resurrection. Of this Inward Baptism we have several Types in the old Testament, of which *Noah's Ark* was one. *Grotius* refers us to these Scriptures for an Apostolical Exposition, *Rom.* 6. 3, 4. *Ephes.* 4. 5. *Gal.* 3. 27. *Col.* 2. 12. all which refer to Man's being *baptized into Christ's Death, his putting on of Christ,* and to *the one Lord, one Faith, one Baptism.* And indeed *Beza* shewed them the Way, who will have it, that the Baptism which answered to *Noah's Ark, was not material Water,* but the Power *of Christ within,* which preserves us cleansed, and enables us to call on God with a good Conscience. Nor is Dr. *Hammond* of a different Judgment in this Case, who not only will have ἀντίτυπον rendred *Antitype*, but the *Baptism* that is that *Antitype,* answering to *Noah's Ark, to be the inward Washing of Men's Consciences from Pollution, and delivering them from the Deluge of Sin and Destruction.*

Not only from all this do I conclude, the *Baptism* mentioned in that Place, to be the *Antitype*. or Truth answering to the outward and typical Salvation of *Noah's Ark*; but for those Reasons which were with me, before my Perusal of these Authors, and which I shall now briefly offer. *First,* If ἀντίτυπον βάπτισμα were but a Type or Figure, one Type would answer another, which is not proper. *2dly,* It were both to suppose, that the Gospel were a State of Figures (which is the Substance of all) and of such Figures too, as are less demonstrative or significant; for, what is that Sprinkling, Baby-Baptism (for Dipper or dipped I suppose our *Adversary* to be neither) to the Words *Deluge* and *Noah's Ark*. *3dly,* The Baptism in the Text, must be such an one as hath Efficacy enough in it *to save,* which outward Water can't do; Besides the Word σώζει, or saveth, hath Relation to *Noah's Ark,* wherein the eight Souls were saved; therefore the Antitype, or Truth answering to that, as Type. *4ly,* It is such a Baptism *as saves by the Power of Christ's Resurrection.* answerable to *Rom.* 6. 3, 4. *Know ye not that so many of us, as were baptized into Jesus Christ, were baptized into his Death? that like as Christ was raised up from the Dead, by the Glory of the Father; even so we also should walk in Newness of Life.* *5ly,* And this the *Parenthesis* in the Verse undeniably proves, being an illustration of the Baptism intended, *not the putting away of the Filth of the Flesh, but the Answer of a good Conscience towards God,* or as some have it, interrogatio, ἐπερώτημα Inquisition or Enquiry, alluding to the Oracle *U R I M* and

T H U M M I M,

THUMMIM, by which Men have Boldness and Access to God; so as to render the Verse, "Cui etiam ex adverso oppositus, nos servat Baptismus, non is quo carnis sordes abjiciuntur, sed is quo fit ut bona conscientia Deum interroget per resurrectionem Christi, *i. e.* To which the directly Opposite Baptism also now saveth us, *not That by which the Filth of the Flesh is cast off, but That by which it is effected*, that a good Conscience may ask God by the Resurrection of Jesus Christ. From all which, two Things result; *First*, that the Verse ought to be thus rendred, *Answerable to which Figure Baptism now also saveth us, not the putting away of the Filth of the Flesh, but the Account of a good Conscience to God, by the Resurrection of Jesus Christ*. And indeed the most disputable Part of this Verse is abundantly confirmed on our side, by the Simplicity of the Ancient *English, French* and *Spanish* *Translators*. And I wonder that any Man of common Sense, not greatly abused by Prejudice or Custom, can think, that the Baptism mentioned, should be that of Water, when the middle of the Verse provides this material Distinction, *not the putting away of the Filth of the Flesh* (the Effect of outward Water) *but the Answer of a Good Conscience to God* (the Fruits of the Holy Ghost alone) to that very End that People should not think so; I mean, that it was a Water-Baptism.

Secondly, It may not be improper for us to observe, That if one Verse hath such Variety of Copies, Readings, Transpositions and Senses, as hath been noted, beside what we could yet produce, that they are at a miserable pass for an Universal, Living, Constant and Unerring Rule, who esteem the present Scripture such, exclusive of the Spirit, which Time, Variety of Transcribers, Translators, Interpreters and Expositors, have rendred so Uncertain. But if we had been unprovided of all this to our Defence, what has our Adversary to do to charge us with a Discontinuance of Water-Baptism, till he had first clear'd his own Opinion from Popish Innovation and Invention? What Scripture or pure Antiquity has he for *Infant-Baptism*, one of the *Unscriptural and Senseless Ceremonies of his* Religion, about which such as he make more stir than about that of the Holy Ghost? A Man may guess what a Christian he is, and how well he is versed in Christ's Doctrine, who can call a little Water shed by a Priest's Hand *the Door into God's Kingdom*. How much is this short of the Romish Priest's making his God, who says, *the Bread is Christ after Consecration*, since Christ, who is God over all, Blessed for ever, saith, *He is that Door*; which H. Hallywell *will have his Infant-Water-Baptism to be*.

§. 5. *Of the Supper.*

But he saith of us and the Familists, *By the same Diabolical Spirit, wherewith they are possessed, they lay aside the Sacrament of the Lord's Supper as a Thing too Carnal.* (pag. 30, 31.) In Opposition to which he produceth *Matt.* 26. 26, 27. How that *Christ took Bread and blessed it, and brake it, and gave it to his Disciples, and said, take, eat, this is my Body;* Then he took the Cup and gave Thanks, and gave it to them, saying, drink ye all of it. St. Mark, *chap.* 14. *repeats the very same, and says, they all drank of it;* But St. Luke Chap. 22. 19. *and* St. Paul 1 Cor. 11. 24. *added these Words* [do this in Remembrance of me] *which import both a Commission and Direction to use and continue them.*

Ans. 'Tis granted, that Christ, eating the Passover with his Disciples, did Familiarly represent that Flesh and Blood, which he gave for the World, that whoever eat thereof should have Life Eternal abiding in them. Nor is this strange; for it was his Familiar Way of opening his deepest Mysteries, and recommending the most excellent of all his Commandments; witness his Discourse concerning the Blessed Unity of Christ and his Members, by the Similtude of a Vine and it's Branches; And both his *Washing his Disciples Feet, and requiring them to follow his Example*. John 13. 5, 14.

That this Practice was enjoyned his Disciples, is not warranted from *Matthew, Mark*, or *in Remembrance of me*, as our Adversary observes: But that they should be *Paul's* also, as he affirms, is both an abuse of the Scriptures, and them that read them; For these are the Apostle's Words, *as often as ye eat this Bread and drink this Cup, &c.* which amounts to no more than this, when ye do eat this Supper, do it worthily; so that there is no Command to do it, though as often as they did do it, they were exhorted to do it discerningly: *As often as you do it;* and *Do it often*, are differing Sayings.

And that *Luke's* Words do not perpetuate it, especially as now used, I shall prove. First, if it be but a *Sacrament or Sign*, as saith our Adversary, then can it not of right continue longer than till the *Thing signified* shall come. *Do this till*, that is, when that

that is come, till the coming of which, the Sign was to be used; there remains no longer any Institution.

Now between all Types and Antitypes, Shadows and Substances, Parables and Morals, there must needs be some Resemblance, or else the End of their being used will be lost to them, for whose Sakes they were appointed: For instance, Christ is called a Door, because no Man comes to the Father, *but through him*; A *Lyon*, from his Strength and Dominion; A *Lamb*, because of his Innocency; A *Vine* because of that Excellent Fruit he brings forth; and lastly, he calls himself by the Name of *Bread*, because of that inward *Strength* and *Nourishment* such receive that feed Spiritually upon him: Wherefore the Substance shadowed out, by this outward Bread and Wine, is no other than *Christ, as the Bread that came down from above, and that Flesh and Blood which all were to eat and drink of* that would have Eternal Life; mentioned at large *John* 6. So that admitting of a Command, it must be thus read, *Do this till I come, who am the Heavenly Bread, and Flesh and Blood, that give Eternal Life to them that feed thereon*; which Bread the Apostle very well understood, when in the foregoing Chapter to the *Corinthians* he thus delivered himself, *I speak as to wise Men, Judge ye what I say, The Cup of Blessing which we bless, is it not the Communion of the Blood of Christ? For we being many are* One Bread, *and* One Body, *for we are all* Partakers *of that* One Bread, 1 Cor. 10. 15, 16, 17. And this Christ himself intimated in the following Verse to that Passage out of *Matthew*, *But I say unto you, I will not drink henceforth of this Fruit of the Vine, until that Day when I drink it new with you in my Father's Kingdom.* And I query if that was not made good, on the Day of *Pentecost*, when scoffing, yet truly (like *Caiaphas* in another Case) several Spectators said of the Disciples, *They were full of New Wine*: Acts 2. 13. Which was the Beginning of the Restoration of that Kingdom of God to *Israel*, that the Disciples a little before so weakly queried after.

In short, The Father's *Kingdom* is *within*, Luke 17. 20. What was that Fruit then that was to be drunk anew in that Kingdom? Certainly it came from himself, the true Vine, and must be of a Spiritual and Inward Nature, like to the Kingdom.

To conclude, If Bread and Wine be but a Sign; And if Things signified ought to resemble their Signs; And if Spiritual Bread and Wine mostly answer those Visible Signs; And if they are to be had in the Kingdom of God; And if the Kingdom of God be within; And that who eat not that Bread, and drink not that Wine, have no Life in them; Then because the Apostles had Life Eternal in them, and we a Measure of the same in us, Christ, the Heavenly *Bread and Flesh, and Wine and Blood*, was then and is now come, and consequently, the Shadows of those good Things (as to any Institution) were and are at an End: And as there is but One Spirit, and One Lord, One Faith, One Baptism, One God and Father, One Heavenly Kingdom, One Holy Body; So but *One Bread, and but One Cup, and but One Communion and Fellowship, and that is with the Father and the Son, by the Holy Ghost*.

But here, as in the Case of Water-Baptism, it will be objected, why were they then afterwards used?

Ans. The Practices of good Men, though in Things temporary, are many Times too greedily received, and too long doted upon by those who desire to be reputed their Followers. Any thing once becoming customary is hard to be left; Several *Jewish* Ceremonies the Holy Ghost thought fit to be dispensed with for a Season, that were never to be perpetuated. But what has our Adversary and the several Sorts of *Protestants* in the World to do with *Baptism and the Supper*, and deny that Qualification and Commission the Apostles had? They will never stand our Enquiry about their Call, which they know, we have great Cause to scruple, indeed to deny; For all must or should know that was either *Immediate*, or *Mediate* and *Successive*. If Immediate, then they must necessarily confess to a Commission upon Inspiration, and then *Quakers*. If Mediate and Successive, then either *beside* the Church of *Rome*, or *through* the Church of *Rome*; *Not beside* the Church of *Rome*, because she cannot prove any regular Ordination, or uninterrupted Succession, either as to Faith or Discipline. If *through* the Church of *Rome, then they own the Ordination of a Church they renounce, and grant Her the Keys, whom they have writ against for these six score Years, under the Name of Whore of* Babylon, *and Mother of Harlots, and all Abominations of the Earth*. Can that which you account a corrupt Fountain, bring forth clean Streams? Will Men seek Ordination at the Hands of that Church, they resolve to employ it against? *Has she forfeited her Religion, and*

and not her Power? When did ever God make over his Authority by such an Entail? If Mens Errors and Vices do not un-minister them, It will follow, that they may be *Ill Christians*, but very good Ministers. For Shame never renounce the *Roman Church* as False, if her Ordination must be True; For what has Power to make a Minister, must be allowed to have Power both to instruct and conclude him in what he is to minister: Wherefore never let any own her to have Heaven's Keys of Church Authority, and then deny her as Heretical; For where-ever any Church or People are truly such, that Church or People have thereby forfeited all Right thereunto: And as the contrary Opinion has long enricht the *Pope's Coffers*, so the Unwary Concessions of some certain *Protestants* thereto, have too evidently given away a great Share of that good old Cause.

I have dwelt longer upon these Particulars, than my Adversary's Weakness could deserve at my Hands, but their Information hath induced me to it, who are assaulted by the envious Endeavours of our several *Adversaries*, that daily seek, how to *mis-represent us*, *and our most Evangelical Principles*.

CHAP. IV.

His Third Chapter examined, which consists of the Holiness of Times, Places, Things and Persons under the Gospel.

§. 1. *Of the Sabbath-Day.*

HIS Accusation is, that *the Familists and Quakers put no Difference between one Day and another, the Sabbath no more than another Day; That many Times they follow their usual Trades on a Sunday.* pag. 34. 37, 38, 39.

Ans. What the *Familists* did is nothing to us (if they did so) But sure I am he has abused the *Quakers*; For 'tis well known, that in what Country soever they live, they follow the Practice of the Apostles, in Assembling together on the first Day of the Week: They do it constantly and reverently. Who most prophane that Day, the *Quakers*, or the *Sons and Daughters of the Church of* England, Their *Feasts, Drunkenness, Wantonness, Gaming*, and other Recreations, as they call them, are so many Demonstrations, to help every common Understanding to a Resolution in the Point. And to say, *That we many times follows our usual Trades* on that Day, is a plain Untruth, the whole World knows better, though we do not Judaize; For Worship was not made for Time, but Time for Worship: Nor is there any Day Holy of it self, though Holy Things may be performed upon a Day.

But he tells us, yes; *For the fourth Commandment being as Moral as the rest, and that requiring a Sabbath-Day, the Sabbath-Day is perpetuated also.*

Ans. But this hurts us not, since the *Jewish-Sabbath* is not observed by the Church of *England:* But if a Sabbath-Day be Moral, because mentioned in the fourth Commandment; Then because the *Jews* seventh-day Sabbath is there particularly mentioned, *Their Sabbath must be only Moral*, and consequently Unalterable.

But says he, ' No; For that the Apostles and succeeding Church of God, may
' very reasonably dispose of us in Matters of this Nature; And it is obligatory
' from the Ten Commandments, every one of which is moral, and binds all Chri-
' stians still; and therefore the Church of *England* (though these rebellious *Qua-
' kers* disown their Mother) doth make it Part of her Liturgy.

Ans. If it be as Moral as all the rest, as it must be if it be Moral, because of it's being there, they could no more dispense with it, than with any other Commandment: To call that Day Moral, and make it Alterable, is Ridiculous. 'Tis true, the Apostles met upon the First Day, and not on the Seventh; but as that released us from any pretended Morality of the *Seventh*, so neither did it confer any Morality upon the *First*; yea, so far were they from it, that not one speaks any such Thing; but *Paul* much the contrary: *Let no Man judge you in Meats or in Drinks, or in respect of an Holy-Day, or of New Moons, or of the Sabbath-Days, which are a Shadow of Things to come, but the Body is of Christ*. Col. 2. 17, 18. The outward Sabbath was Typical, of the great Rest of the Gospel, which such come to, who cease from their own Work, and in whom the Works of God's new Creation come to be accomplisht.

And though I should acknowledge the other Commands to be Moral, yea, and Times too, both respecting God's Worship, and the Creatures Rest; yet there is no more Reason for the Morality of that Day, because amongst those Commandments, than for the Ceremoniousness and Abrogation of several Moral Precepts, because scattered up and down among the Ceremonial Laws, recorded in *Leviticus*.

I grant, the Apostles met on that Day; But must it therefore be Moral? Certainly, the Scriptures Silence in this Particular must either conclude a great Neglect against those Holy Men, in not recommending and enjoyning more expresly *both Water, Bread, Wine and Holy-Days, in their several Epistles to the Churches*; or warrant us in our Belief concerning the Temporariness of those Things. Let not our Adversary reproach us for not believing that to be durable, which was weaning off and vanishing in those Days; but soberly consider, that the Practise of the best Men, especially in such Cases, is no Institution, though sometimes it may be an Example. But I perceive he makes bold, like an Irreverent Son, with his Ghostly Fathers, who through his Reflections upon us, severely rebukes them. Has he so quickly forgot the *Book of Sports, and who put it out*; when not to prophane this Sabbath with Dancings, Riots and Revels, had been enough to render a Man an Enemy to Cæsar, and a schismatical Puritan to the Church? If he be not satisfy'd with this, I refer him to *Calvin's Institutes*, Bp. *Ironside*, and Dr. *Peter Heylin*, concerning the *Non-morality* of the Sabbath; and a great Wonder it is, that *John Calvin* and *Peter Heylin* should be of one Opinion in any Thing.

§. 2. *Place of God's Worship.*

He is very angry with us for denying a more than ordinary Sanctity to Places, and says, *that we esteem a Church no more than a Stable; That the* Jews, Heathens, *and* Turks *have their Synagogues, Temples and Moschs to pray in: That Christ went to a Prayer-House*, Luke 6. 12. *and* Acts 16. 13. *Where* Paul *and others went out to a River's Side, where an Oratory was reported to be.*

Answ. We value the true Church more than a Stable, but we value a good Stable before a false Church, as such. But I suppose he means by Church, an *House*; and then I must tell him, that I prefer a Stable better than no House, but a good House better than a Stable. But why is a Stable such an ill-favoured Place? Has he forgot *that the Head of the true Church first lodged in one*, when there was no Room for him in a whole Synagogue, yet Room enough for a Company of Cavilling Murdering Scribes and Pharisees? There is no doubt but the *Jews* had Synagogues enough, *for it was out of them the Apostles were to be haled*, because of their Testimony against those that were in them. 'Tis true, the *Heathens* had *Temples*, and the *Turks* have their *Moschs*: I like the Comparison and the Proof very well. For I take some of your *Steeple-House-Guests* to be as good Christians, as some of the worst Sort of them. It was the old *Heathenish* Spirit which under the Cloak of *Christianity* both erected those stately Edifices, instituted that Pompous Worship, and exacted those vast Revenues, that have burthened the World these many Ages; *whilst the pure Apostolical Spirit, and Religion, have been as driven into a Sack-cloth and Wilderness Estate.*

That *Christ* went to a Prayer-House, and that *Paul* and the Church met in an *Oratory* by the River Side, is a pretty *Rattle* for Children, and may pass as unquestionably with those who are willing to be cheated, as the Story of St. *Dennis*'s Body, that went a Mile without his Head, and St. *Winifred*'s Head a great Way without her Body, to a Papist.

But he affirms, *that the first Christians had distinct Places to meet in, and that they called them Churches.* Pag. 47, 48, 49.

Answ. Christ went not to the Synagogue or the Temple to eat the Passover; 'Tis certain that the Twelve met *in an Upper Room*, upon their Return from Christ's Ascension; and it is said, when the Day of Pentecost was fully come, *they were all with one Accord in one Place*, (Acts 2. 1, 2, 3, 4.) at what Time that excellent Glory appeared; but here is no Mention made of either *Temple* or *Synagogue*: One would have thought those *Conventicles* (for so they were then called and since) should not have born away the Glory and Honour of that Holy Solemnity from those Cathedral and Canonical Places: What sullen Separation did the false *Jew* then repute it, as well as the false *Christian* now the like Practice. Certainly this ran retrograde to the Grain and Humour of that Age; And the poor Apostles were therefore esteemed as great *Phanaticks*, and as much reproached as any of the *Quakers* in this. I must also confess, they continued daily with one Accord in the Temple Acts 2. 46. but they broke not Bread there, that was done κατ' οἶκον, that is, *in the House*, if he will have it so, instead of *from House to House*; to be sure, it was

not

not *from Church to Church*, as he would have the House called; for then we should understand the following Verse thus, and the Lord added to the Church daily such as should be saved, that is, *to the House.*

But I see no Reason why he should fall so hard with his Criticisms upon κατ' οἶκον, and let καθ' ἡμέραν in the same Verse alone; For, as *Valla* and *Erasmus* well observe, κατ' οἶκον is as well rendered *per singulas domos*, or *domesticatim*, i.e. *from House to House*, as καθ' ἡμέραν per singulos dies, sive quotidie, i.e. *daily*, *or from Day to Day*.

But he will needs have it that the Apostle * 1 *Cor.* 11. meant by *Church* the *House*, when he said *have ye not Houses to eat and drink in, or despise ye the Church of God?* His Reason is, if it may be thought one, *because the Apostle in the 18th Verse says, when ye come in the Church; and in the 20th Verse, when ye come together into one Place*; So that the *Word Church signifies the Place*.

Answ. When ye come together in the Church, signifies no more than in the Congregation or Assembly, or among your selves as a Church, (observe well the Margin) And to make the *Church* allude to Place in the 20th Verse, is a base wresting of our *Adversaries*; for there is no Greek Word there for *Place*.

But he thinks he has one Argument more, from *Paul's Greeting* Priscilla *and* Aquila, *and the House that is in their House*, Rom. 16. 3, 5. And again, *sending Salutation from them*; Aquila *and* Priscilla *salute you much in the Lord, with the Church in their House*, 1 Cor. 16. 29.

Answ. If this be to prove an House to be a Church, I never saw the like. It seems we must read, after his Dialect thus, *Greet* Priscilla *and* Aquila, *and the House that is in their House*. But in Contradiction to all this, he tells us in the next Page, *By the Church, at such a Man's House, must be meant the whole Congregation of the Saints assembled at such a Man's House*; and truly, Reader, I think so too. But if the Saints met to make the Church, *then the House is not the Church*, nor indeed can an House meet together in an House.

But now I will tell this Defamer of us, that though we have no stately *Basilicos*, or *Palace-Churches*, as some call them, *beautify'd with Painting, Images, Flags, carved and engraved Work, and built to the East, in Imitation of the* Heathen Idolatrous Temples; yet, like unto the Apostles and Primitive Christians, *we assemble from House to House*, and if he will have it so, *there are several convenient Publick Places on purpose to meet and perform divine Worship in.*

§. 3. *Of Tythes.*

His next Section, and as became a careful greedy Hireling, by much the largest of any in his Book, is employ'd in the Defence of the *Priests* Maintenance, the *sine quâ non* of their *Calling*. From Page 51 *to* 69, His first Argument is, *That God will have a Rent and Tribute paid him. That thus he dealt with the Children of* Israel, *from whom he reserv'd a Tythe to himself, and that in* Abraham's *Time Tythes to* Melchizedeck *were paid, after whose Order Christ was made a Priest.*

Answ. The Tythes that were paid *Melchizedeck*, were but of the Spoils *Abraham* took from his Enemies; and that not by Compulsion but Choice. *Melchizedeck* was King of *Salem*. King of Peace, Priest of the most high God: He freely administred Bread and Wine to *Abraham* to refresh him; and when he had done, prayed and praised God for him without Bargain or Hire: Whereupon *Abraham* gave him the Tythe of all, as a Token of his Thankfulness.

Now let *the Priests of* England *prove themselves to be of* Melchizedeck's *Offspring, Men of Peace, Priests of the most high God, and let them but minister to us of the Living Bread and Wine, and wrap up all with such Prayers and Praises to God for us, as he will accept*; and when all this is done, if we refuse them the Tythe of our Spoils, let us be recorded for Ungrateful Men: But whilst *Priests are Men of Contention, Hirelings, that seek Gain from their Quarter, prepare War against them that put not into their Mouths*, are not Priests of the most high God's

---

* *Vetabl.* Ecclesiam vel congregationem.
  Clarius, Ille conventus in Ecclesiam non eâ causâ fit: hoc quod facitis in contemptum Ecclesiæ Dei redundat, & eorum pudorem qui minus habent.
  Zeger, Confunditis eos qui non habent quod offerant & manducent.
  Cameron. Dei Ecclesia hic privatis ædibus non opponitur. Dei Ecclesiam contemnere est pudore afficere tenuiores, qui magnam Ecclesiæ partem constituebant.
  Locus loco opponitur grammaticè, non logicè. i. e. *Church or Congregation. The Church is not opposed to private Houses. To despise the Church, is to make ashamed the Poor of it.*

Anointing, and who inſtead of giving us Bread and Wine, oppreſs us unto Death for a Four-penny Eaſter-Reckoning, and in Lieu of Prayers and Praiſes to God for us, Anathematize, Whip, Impriſon and Baniſh us for Impoſtors, Hereticks, Men inſpir'ed by Satan, and ſuch like, let it not be wondred at that a poor *Quaker* hath a Teſtimony againſt ſuch a Prieſt; and that he rather chuſeth do die (unjuſtly his Priſoner) than pay Tythes to him, that is an Uſurper of the Name, Authority and Office of a True Evangelical Miniſter.

And for his Inſtance of the Land of *Canaan*, it brings no Obligation upon us, *England* is no *Canaan*, neither as to it's Acquiſition, nor Diſtribution; When the *Saxons* came into *England*, God reſerved no ſuch Rents. And if it be well argued of the Apoſtle, (*Heb.* 7. 12.) that becauſe the Law is changed the Prieſthood is alſo; Then certainly it is no ill Conſequence, that the *Way of Maintenance* muſt be changed too, at leaſt as to Inſtitution.

But, ſays our *Adverſary*, in the Apoſtle's Words, 1 Cor. 9. 14, *The Lord hath ordained, That they which preach the Goſpel ſhould live of the Goſpel.*

Anſw. We are contented with this, but the Prieſts are not. They cannot prove themſelves Miniſters of the Goſpel, unleſs by that never-failing Argument of human Law and Force, if yet that can prove them ſuch. Beſides, Here is no Stint or Method; *What or How?* It is left to God's Witneſs; but that they dare not leave themſelves with; Earthly Powers muſt firſt make them Miniſters, and then get them Maintenance. But there's not a Word *of Paul's working with his own Hands,* nor Chriſt's Explanation of *the Labourer is worthy of his Hire*, to wit, that he *ſhould eat what is ſet before him, and,* Melchizedeck *like, bleſs the Houſe, if worthy;* Nor do I hear of ſo much as one *Itinerary-Preacher*, who to be ſure carried no Tythes upon his Back, as the Prieſts of our Days do into their Barn; *they ſued, excommunicated, impriſoned none unto Death for Hire's Sake.*

He that Minds God more than his Belly, ſhall never want for his Belly; for the Authority of Him in whoſe Name he goes, makes ſufficient Way for his Subſiſtence, without the Force of Imperial Decrees; *The Cattle upon a Thouſand Hills are the Lord's.* The Primitive *Chriſtians* paid no *Tythes* that we read of, yet they forbore not to adminiſter freely to the Neceſſities of thoſe who were faithful Labourers and Travellers amongſt them. The Law that ſettled that Maintenance, *was the Law in the Heart, and the Witneſs of God in the Conſcience, to which* Paul *particularly deſired to be made manifeſt.* 'Tis true, about Four Hundred Years after Chriſt, the then *Chriſtians* began to lay up the *Tythe* of their Subſtance, towards the Maintenance of ſuch Members and Miniſters of the Church as wanted. But this was out of their own *free Will, not as ſettled Maintenance, nor by Compulſion*, as our Countryman, *Jo. Selden*, a learned Antiquary, tells us.

<small>Gratian. Cauſ. p. 16. R. C. Dec. Selden. c. 6, p. 80, 81.</small>

But our *Adverſary* ſays, that *Chriſtian Emperors, Kings, Princes, and other Nobles, by the all-wiſe Providence, inſpiring their Hearts, have given Houſes, Lands and Tithes for the Maintenance of the Miniſters of the Goſpel, and ſecured ſuch Poſſeſſions. And therefore, ſuch are Sacrilegious and Robbers of God, who with-hold them; Such Tenths being as much the Miniſters as the Ninths are the People's.*

Anſw. I perceive the Prieſt allows *Inſpiration for Tythes*, though we are *Familiſts, Quakers and Fanaticks* for abetting the Doctrine of Inſpiration in the Worſhip of God. O Mercenary, O Hireling and Irreverent Saying! that God ſhould be more concerned for Carnal than Spiritual Things, and inſpire Men about Tythes, and not about Divine Worſhip. Who but a Dark and Mercenary Prieſt could have uttered ſo impious an Expreſſion?

I grant, that when *Auſtin* came into *England*, he deſired Tythes of *Ethelbert*, as I take it, King of *Kent*; But the King's Care of his People, and the Averſion of their Humour to all Encroachments, diſappointed the Monk. However, *Time bringing forth Murder and Adultery, They brought forth Tythes.* For *Offa* killing *Ethelbert*, gave a Tenth of his Goods to pacify his Ghoſt. And *Edgar* being greatly in Love with *Ethelwald's* Wife, to obtain his End, murdered him; upon which the Pope ſending forth his Bull, *Edgar*, to appeaſe him, confirm'd to the Church the Tenth of all the Fruit of his Field and Cattle, to them and their Succeſſors. And as Murder and Whoredom introduced them, ſo the Cunning and Covetouſneſs of the Clergy have continued them; *For when the Heptarchy became a Monarchy, the Prieſts evermore would thruſt in for a Share with the Conqueror*; and this Wrong Way came Tythes to be the Prieſts Right, as he calls it.

<small>Selden, p. 67.</small>

But let this pretended Proteſtant anſwer me, if he dare.

Was

Was the Church then degenerated or no? Was it not a Time of Popery? Did not the first Martyrs except against her? Was it lawful for Princes to give away other Men's Goods upon the Account and for the pretended Expiation of their Sins?

Could the giving of them atone? Is it not an acknowledging of the Pope's Power to absolve? Is it not a Buying or Bribing off the Guilt of Sin against Almighty God, by Gifts to a Mortal Man, and those extorted from poor People too? Is this Protestant Doctrine? But above all, *is this instituting Tythes upon Inspiration?* Hell her own self was the Foundress of these Things. He may remember that there is better Antiquity for that *Voice*, which the Ancients report to have been heard that Day *Constantine* conferred those large Endowments upon the Church, than for the Institution of Tythes and Rich Benefices; I mean that Voice through the Heavens, *This Day is Poyson poured into the Church.* Since which Time it has been observ'd by the best Princes, Wisest Counsellors, and most moderate Clergymen, *that the Enrichment and Impowering of Church-Officers, has been the Canker of the Church, and the Moth of the State.*

'Tis not my Business to write an History; but I recommend to the Inquisitive Reader, *Wickliff's Remonstrance, The Plowman's Complaint, Chaucer's Plowman's Tale, Walter Brute,* and *W. Thorpe's Examination, in the Martyrology; Pareus: History of the Waldenses,* and *Jo. Selden,* Men that ought not to pass for, or be reputed *Phanaticks*, especially by such who call themselves *Protestants*.

I shall only say, first, That they were the People's wholly. 2dly, It is now the People's Labour, more than the Priest's Land, that brings the Increase: And Men ought not to be constrained to pay those they never hired; nor to labour for those that profit them not. 3dly, They were given to *expiate Murder and Adultery, and uphold an Idolatrous Clergy,* upon Protestant Principles, and therefore to be remov'd, as were the high Places and Groves, Idolatrous, dedicated among the *Jews.* 4thly, Because it is most reasonable for a Man to believe according to his own Conscience, and not according to another Man's Conscience; " It is Unrigh-
" teous to prosecute a Man for not maintaining that Religion, which in his Con-
" science he believes to be false; as well as that it is the Badge of a False Religion to persecute for Maintenance. 5thly, Though they may be confirmed by some Princes, yet, considering the End to which they were given, to wit, for the Maintainance of a certain Sort of Religious Order, now exploded, whose Successors these are not, (and so the ancient Constitution broken) we can't see any Reason why they should remain, unless any thing commanded is to be obeyed, because Commanded, and not because in it self Lawful. Two Things I cannot but observe. *First,* That he affirms, *The Clergy of England have not a Tenth,* much complaining that every one Snips from them; *cujus contrarium verum*; For they not only snip, but slice from every Body else. I commend to his Perusal a Pamphlet, entituled, *Omnia comesta a Belo,* where he will find a very particular Account of the Revenues of *Archbishops, Bishops, Archdeacons, Deans, Canons, Prebends, Parsons, Vicars, Petty-Canons, Singing-men, Choiristers, Organists, Gospellers, Epistlers, Vergers, Chancellors and their Attendants, Delegates, Registers and their Clerks. Gentlemen-Apparitors, Inferior Apparitors, Proctors, &c.* I doubt not but *Fifteen Hundred Thousand* Pounds a Year, will be the modestest Accompt that Computation will admit of, *which is but double the Revenue that former Monarchs have had for the Maintenance of their Family, Crown and Dignity, their Civil Justice, Armies, Navies, and costly Embassies.* If all this be to resemble Christ Jesus and his Apostles, the Scripture has given us a very wrong Account of him and them.

The *second* Thing I would observe is this, That he has the Ignorance and Confidence to argue from the Super-excellency of Christ's Ministration to that of *Moses; That the Maintenance of the Ministers of the Gospel should proportionably exceed the Maintenance of the Priests under the Law.*

Answ. But certainly he is one of the first Men that made this wild Interpretation of the Glory of the latter House excelling the Glory of the former; as if Christ's House were outward, or his Glory either. Would he have one outward Temple figure out another? as if Christ should bring in another *Levitical* Law to excel that of *Moses.* Certainly *the New Jerusalem, after this Man's Rate of Disputing, must be an outward Structure of material Sapphires, Emeraulds, Jaspers, &c.* But there is a *Pope* and a *Mahomet* in his Belly, whether he knows it or no; For these Fleshly Conceits first set them to work upon their Pompous Worship, neglecting the Holy, Pure, Self-denying and Spiritual Religion of Christ Jesus and his Apostles, who neither practised nor set up any Shadowy and Ceremonial Wor-

---

Bp. Jewel on Hagg Hodie venenum infusum in Eccl.

Cobham, Bernard, Tindal, Frith, Charl. V. Emp.

ship, not settling themselves in Splendid Livings, to lead Easy, Quiet and Voluptuous Lives, Freely they received, freely they gave; not as our *Adversary* ridiculously understands it, *that they gave their Miracles, but sold their Preaching:* Indeed the Spirit of a Pompous Antichrist, who pleads for *State* under a Self-denying Gospel. Christ's Kingdom is not of this World; and yet our Adversary pleads for the Grandeur of a Worldly Worship, Ministry and Maintenance; we may allow him therefore and his Tribe to be Worldly Christians, *but not true Followers of that Jesus, who said, when he was in the World, I am not of the World*; which leads me to the next Section concerning the *Ministry*.

§. 4. *Of Ministers of the Gospel.*

In Defence of the Church of *England*'s Ministry he tells us, (p. 70, 71, 73, 74.) *that they have first the Testimony of their own Conscience, that they are furnished to that Office.* 2dly, *The outward Call of the Church by Imposition of Hands and Prayers.*

Answ. If the Ministers of the Church of *England* have the Testimony of their Conscience, it must be either a true or a false Testimony. *If a False*, then not truly called, upon our *Adversary's* Principles; *If True*, then infallibly so, and consequently, both every Man hath an *Infallible Witness in his own Conscience, and the Preparation and Call of this Witness is the inward Call to the Ministry*; Now how this can be without Revelation and Inspiration I know not. But it seems, Ministerial Qualification must be judged of by the Witness in the Conscience, which is the *Overthrow* of the Priest's Cause and Doctrine: But I deny that the Priests Act upon this inward Testimony; for they are afraid of being made manifest to the Conscience: And when we urge this Inward Manifestation, they cry out with our Adversary, *Enthusiasm, Familism, Quakerism!* But if this must be the alone Judge of Qualification, let him for Shame give over Vilifying our publick Labourers, and Incensing our Superiors against us, who honestly plead Conscience in the Case, and us for Refusing the National Priesthood, which we believe in the Presence of God, Angels and Men, *to be not so qualified.* For *Covetousness, Bargaining, Stealing their Neighbours Words, Preaching their Experiences, not their own, not knowing experimentally whereof they affirm, nor turning People to Righteousness, but persecuting them that love it, and daubing Sinners with untempered Mortar*, are altogether inconsistent with it.

For the *Laying on of Hands*, it is well known to be a *Jewish* Ceremony; And we read that *Saul* and *Barnabas* preached before the Apostles laid Hands upon them. Besides, it is not every Body's Hands will serve; they must be Men inspired upon our Enemies Concessions, and not every *Foul Fist:* Nor did it give Authority, but as many other *Jewish* Ceremonies, *it was made Use of to express that Mission which had a more Inward and Spiritual Ground.* They were named Apostles from one of the meanest Offices that belonged to the Temple; *not Lord Primates, Lord Archbishops, Lord Bishops, May it please your Grace, May it please your Lordship, Right Reverend Fathers in God, &c.* These Things came from the *Pope*, and thither they will and must return.

To Conclude: Because our Adversary tells us, that the Church, from the Days of the Apostles, has had a successive Apostleship and Ministry to confer; whether he will or no, he must imply, *that there has been a true Apostolical Church ever since*, which is to give the Lye to the Holy Ghost that prophesied of a falling away and a great Apostacy. 2 *Thes.* 2.

2dly. That, if the Ministry of the Church of *England* be lawfully descended, and are Successors of the Apostles, and so primitive Ministers, they must be Apostolically qualified; but they are not so Apostolically qualified either as to the *Work of God in themselves, the Gift of the Holy Spirit, daily Information, the Effect of their Ministry, that Patience, Meekness, Plain-dealing, Perseverance, Godly Hospitality, continual Labour, and Self-denying Conversation:* consequently not lawfully descended, nor true Successors of the Apostles and primitive Ministers.

Nor do we think it *such an intolerable Presumption, for Mechanicks and Tradesmen to preach the Gospel*, as he would have it: For we well remember, that those who believed and followed the Son of God, were reproached by the *Scribes* and *Pharisees*, the Learned and National Teachers *of the Jews, for illiterate Persons*, crying out in that Day, Have any of the Rulers or of the Pharisees believed on him, but this People, who know not the Law, are accursed? It was that

Generation that called him and his Disciples so often, *This Fellow, Away with this Fellow, This Pestilent Fellow*, after the Rate our *Adversary* doth treat us, as we may have Occasion anon to observe. In short, *Peter* and *John* were found unlearned. *Ouzelius*, in his *Animadversions* on *Minutius Felix*, saith, "that as the *Gentiles* "did object to the *Christians* their *Rude Style, Ill-bred Language*, and *destitute of* "*all Address or Civil Salutation*, calling them *Rusticks* and *Clowns*; so did the "*Christians* by Way of Irony and Contempt, *term them the Well-bred, the Eloquent* "*and the Knowing*; This he proves by ample Testimonies out of *Arnobius, Lactantius, Isidorus, Pelusiota, Theodoret,* and others.

In the Constitutions of *Clemens Romanus* (as supposed) it is enjoyned, "*abstain* "*from all the Books of the Gentiles.* Also the *Council of Carthage* had an express Canon against *Reading* Heathen *Authors*, then *Aristotle*, and all that Philosophy, which fits Priests at both Universities.

Gratian hath also such like Passages as these, by Way of Complaint. "*We see* "*that the Priests of the Lord, neglecting the Gospels and the Prophets, read Comedies or Play-Books, and sing Love-Verses,* &c.

Cardan tells, "that *Gregory*, though a Pope, burnt several Lascivious *Latin Authors*, as *Cæcilianus Affranius, Nævius Licinius,* &c. Nor had *Plautus, Martial* "and *Terence*, now School-Books, escaped him, could he have helped it. In "like Manner *Gregory Nazianzen*, the Father, suppressed several *Greek* Authors, "as *Diphilus, Apollodorus, Philemon, Alexis, Sappho,* &c.

"And *Petrus Bellonius*, that inquisitive Traveller, when at *Mount Athos*, where "lived 6000 Καλοίερoι in *Monasteries*, did not so much as find (no nor in all "*Greece*) one Man acquainted with the Conversation of these Poets; For though "they had several *Manuscripts of Divinity in their Libraries, yet not one Poet,* "*Historian or Philosopher. That they anathematized such Priests as studied Poesy, or* "*transcribed Books not treating of Religion.*

"And *Dominicus a Soto*, strongly pleads not only the Liberty of every Man's "Teaching any Good that he knows, *but that it is his Duty to teach it.*

"*Machiavel* assures us, the first Promoters of Christianity, *commanded all Poets* "*and Historians which treated of the* Gentiles *vain Conversation and Worship, to be* "*burned.*

Farther, concerning the *Illiterateness, Meanness* and *Novelty*, the *Gentiles* did object against the *Christians*, *see Dr.* Cave's *Primitive Christianity*.

By all which it appears, that the *Quaker*-Preachers are nevertheless *Orthodox* for being ignorant in Human Science, since the most Orthodox Preachers have been generally such, and that both before and after the Coming of Christ.

In short, that *Ministry which is Experimental and Powerful, for the turning of many from Darkness to Light, and from the Power of Satan unto God,* is the only True and Evangelical Ministry; and such an one we both own and enjoy, blessed be the Name of our God for ever.

CHAP. V.

His fourth Chapter considered: Quakery (*as he calls it*) *no Sadducism, as he would suggest. His Measures of us wrong.*

HIS great Ill-will to the *Quakers* puts him upon flinging any thing upon them that he thinks will stick; at least that he would have to do so. We must this Turn be, with all, *Familists, Sadducees*; but the fierce Will of the Man has precipitated him into a strange Mistake: Hear him.

H. N. *owns No other Immortality than the Continuance of his Doctrine, nor Judgment-Seat of Christ, nor Heaven, nor Hell, but what are in this Life.* The Quakers (says he) *do the like*; for T. Foster *says, in a Book,* called, *A Guide to the Blind,* "*that the Second Appearance of Christ is in Spirit, to end Sin and finish Trans-* "*gression.*

Now if this proves the Agreement, I never saw the like (taking for granted what he represents *H. N* to have held, in which I know he belies him.) Is there no Difference between saying, *that Christ's second Appearance is in Spirit, and denying Immortality, Eternal Judgment, Heaven and Hell?* O Hideous Consequence and Comparison! But why is it such false Doctrine to say, that Christ's second Coming is Spiritual; shall he ever come so Fleshly as before? Is not he glorified? After what Manner was it he promised to come, when he said, *some standing here shall not taste of Death 'till they see the Son of Man come in his Kingdom.* Mat. 16. 28. *I will not leave you Comfortless, I will come to you; yet a little while and the World sees me no more; but ye see me, because I live ye live also. He that is with you shall be in you,* John 14. 17, 18. And when the Apostle *Paul* said, *Tho' I have known Christ after the Flesh, yet henceforth I know him so no more; When it pleased God to reveal his Son in me.* I ask, if this was not both a Second and a Spiritual Appearance? Certainly it must be another Appearance from the former, therefore a *Second*; and it must be a Spiritual one, because it is Unreasonable to believe that Christ, as to his bodily Appearance, could be all this to his Disciples and Followers; therefore, *His Second Appearance is Spiritual.*

And for *Judgment, Immortality, Heaven and Hell in this Life,* were not our *Adversary* a Senseless Novice in these Matters, his own *Doctors* would teach him, *That there shall be no other Judgment, Immortality, Heaven or Hell hereafter, than what every one has some measurable Sense or earnest of in this Life.* From hence he is so unjust to us, and *H. N.* too, as to give out to the World, *We both deny all future Immortality, Judgment, Heaven or Hell.* I have declared the utmost of the Thing, and doubt not but Time will make him greatly ashamed of his Undertakings.

Pag. 82. But G. Fox, *the* Sadducee, (says he) *holds, the Soul is a Part of the Essence and Being of God; therefore his Conclusion is unquestionable*; or to that Purpose.

I am very ready to think the *Devil* grievously angry with that *good Man,* and indeed he has Reason for it, (if I may say, That the *Devil* can have Reason for any thing he does) for he hath shrewdly *brow-beaten* his Cause in the World, and a great Instrument has God made him of *Noble, and Valiant, and Durable Acts among the Sons of Men:* And we shall so much the more respect and Honour him, by how much Untoward Spirits seek to bear him down in the Minds of People. But to answer our *Adversary:* How comes it he never quotes when he cites, I mean *page his References?* Does he think we are bound to peruse a *Folio* to defend any *Passage* from his Random Reflections? What is he for a Man, that he treats us so *a la neglegence*; with this contemptuous Neglect? Does he conceit People beholden to him for his Slanders without Proof, or that any Thing against a *Quaker* is Evidence enough? But I will tell the Man, he mistakes G. F. for the Purport of his Words are to shew, *That the Life God breathes into the Soul of Man, by which Man comes to live to God, is something of the Divine Being*; not that the Soul, as a Created Capacity, without that Inspiration, is Part of God, or of his Divine Being, and so far *Candor* (that keeps the Eye clear) would have let him see, had not Prejudice and a Desire of Mis-representing, and running us down, hurried him beyond the Bounds of all Moderation: Nor is he alone in the Matter? For many Learned *Rabbies* and modern Orthodox *Divines* (as they are called and reputed) have affirmed the same. Let it be Truth for their Sakes, if not for his.

In short, Were we of the Mind he would have People to think we are, of all Men none would be so Miserable: What! Suffer in this World, because of our Faith and Hope, in the Life of the other, and yet deny the very End of that Hope, Faith and Eternal Life, which alone bears us over the Troubles of this Temporal One? I am persuaded all moderate Persons will think better of us.

CHAP. VI.

He endeavours in his Fifth Chapter, to prove us Inconsistent with the Good of Civil Magistracy. *Our Adversary's Reason too short for his Envy:* Swearing *not Lawful.*

HAD not this Chapter been found among the rest, I might perhaps have taken him for some Zealous Church-man, vexed only at the Increase of the poor p. 90, 91, 92. *Quakers,* on a mere Religious Score. But when I see him wilfully Mistaken, and purposely Characterizing them Enemies to Government, and that to the Insecurity of Civil Magistrates, I perceive what he would be at, and that nothing will serve him below our Throats. He has multiplied Words unnecessarily; these two, *hang them,* would have both explain'd and perhaps gratified his Mind better.

He delivers it as a Fundamental of the *Quakers* Religion, *That they testify against Proud and Lofty Magistrates, who Rule not for God, but themselves*; to which, as a dangerous Doctrine, he opposeth the Apostle *Peter's* Exhortation; *Submit your*

your selves to every Ordinance of Man for the Lord's Sake, whether to the King, as Supream, or unto Governors, that are sent by him for the Punishment of Evil-Doers, and for the Praise of them that do well; crying out, *Is not this a Doctrine fitted to stir up Sedition and Rebellion; and that such are only Magistrates in our Account that are Righteous in our Esteem. If a Magistrate be wicked, Obedience,* says he, *is still due to him.*

Ans. True, but not to that which is Wicked; for that were to open a Door to all the Impiety a *Nero* could be guilty of. But what Contradiction is there betwixt the Apostles Language and the *Quakers?* Can any sober Person think, the Apostle *Peter* exhorted the Churches to believe Evil Magistrates to be Good ones? or prove Lofty Magistrates who rule not for God fit to be obeyed *therein?* This were to understand, as if the Apostle meant, *That such as rule not for God, Punish Evil-Doers, and Praise them that do well;* A Contradiction. If our Faith be Dangerous, the Scripture must be in Question. *Must a Reproving of Evil be a disowning of Magistracy? It seems then that Magistrates are not to be reproved, let their Practices be never so exorbitant. Is there no Difference between our Dislike of the unjust Act of a* Julian*; and our Rebellion against Just Authority? If shewing Men their Evils, be Disrespect, and a Reprehension of them as Unchristian, be Rebellion; we must read Religion backwards.* But God deliver all Magistrates from such Counsellors, and us from such Enemies.

But that which is very remarkable, is the Contradiction he gives himself, and the Injustice he shews to us; who in one Page says, ' we would destroy all Magi-' strates, not of our own Opinion: And in the very next gives it for our Judgment, though with great Dislike, *that Magistrates ought not to impose Opinions in Matters of Religion,* as if we were such Wretches, as to deny that Power unto Magistrates, which we would tyrannically use our selves.

But he thinks he has enough against us in this Expression, " All Governours " ought to be accountable to the People, and to the next succeeding Rulers, for " all their Actions which may be enquired into upon Occasion. This (says our Adversary with a great Rant) *borders upon Treason, respecting his Majesty, the King of* England.

Ans. But what if he was not then in *England,* but a Sort of People that held this very Principle, and who had sworn to God, before Angels and Men, to maintain it, and broke their solemn Oaths? Was it not, *Argumentum ad hominem,* to such a Generation? And does not our Adversary know, that there are Elective Governments in the World, and annual Choice of Officers in our own Country, that are accountable both to the People and their Successors?

But since he has brought the King of *England*'s Name on the Stage, upon this Occasion, I shall briefly tell him and the World, two Things, and let Men relish them as they please. *First,* That it is not for the Interest, or Honour of his Government, For any to be over officious in the enlarging his Prerogative beyond those bounds, the excellent fundamental Laws of *England* have circumscribed the whole Government with. No Princes Crown in *Europe* stands more firm than his, upon *English* Law; The Law gives both Right and Might. It has been the Part of such as dare not trust their Lives and Actions with the Law, to whisper unlimited Power into the Ears of Princes; but their ultimate Aim was not their Soveraigns Greatness, but their own Protection. We are no Sycophants, yet we fear God, and honour the King. *Secondly,* It is not our Business to meddle with Government; but to obey or suffer for Conscience-sake: Can our Adversary ask more? Several of us have been the faithful Servants both of Him and his Father, and God knows, our Kindness is not changed with our Religion, though it admits not of our former Way of shewing it. And this I may truly say in general, That not only our Principle leads to no such Nice and busy Medlings, but we are actually unconcerned in any such Things: We speak not this out of Fear or Flattery; the Truth has placed us far above both; but knowing the World will never be good till every one mends one; and that God's Grace has therefore universally appeared, and yet doth in the Hearts of Men, It's both our Desire, Duty and Practice to endeavour after that Holy, Righteous and Innocent Life it leads to, and that as well for others as our selves.

Of SWEARING.

But he says, (pag. 93.) *Inasmuch as we refuse to swear before a Lawful Magistrate, we contradict the Word of God, and throw away the greatest Tye any Prince hath upon his Subjects,* Infinuating, *as if we had been dabbling with the* Jesuits *in this Matter.*

Ans.

Anf. 'Tis strange that such an illiterate Sort of *Mechanicks, and Rustick Rabbies* (as he is pleased to call us) should hold such Correspondence with one of the most learned *Classes* in the World: But as there is more Difference between us and the *Papists,* than the *Protestants* and the *Papists,* by how much the *Protestants* have many Things that are *Popish,* and we have not; so have I ever found these silly thred-bare Slanders, to be the Refuge of Shallow Heads, and Weak Causes. But I would have all know, as I have else-where said, *The Ground of Swearing is either through Distrust of Honesty in Him that swears, or Weakness in Him to whom the Oath is made.* The *first* takes in all the Swearing that is now in the World; the *last* those Oaths God condescended to make to the *Jews.* So that it *is either an extraordinary Way of Evidence to awe Witnesses into Truth, or an extraordinary Way of Promising to work Belief in the Incredulous.* Now Incredulity and Dishonesty are both Unchristian; For as none are *Christians,* but those *who are buried with Christ by Baptism, and are raised up unto Newness of Life*; so in that pure Law of the Spirit of Life, *Swear not at all,* is recorded. And so far is this from Contradicting the Word of God, that the great Word of God hath so enjoyned us, for all our Adversary's Paraphrase upon it, to wit, *Swearing in Communication*; for the Swearing prohibited was such as the Law allowed, as *Bp. Sanderson* well observes, *It was not needful that Christ should forbid, what was forbidden in it self, or was always Unlawful,* which Swearing in Communication was and is, as by the *third Commandment,* Thou shalt not take the Name of the Lord thy God in vain.

Christ brought forth a Righteousness that needed it not; for that Grace, Faith and Truth, which came by Jesus Christ, take away the Necessity of an Oath. Consequently so far as any are in that Incredulity or Dishonesty which needs it, so far they are not the Followers and Disciples of Christ, nor qualified with his Evangelical Righteousness. Indeed 'tis a shameful Thing, and very dishonourable to the Christian Religion, that they who pretend themselves to be of a Christian Society, should be so un-Christ-like, *to want and use the scareing and affrighting Asseverations dispensed with in some of the weakest Times of Knowledge, by which to assure one another of their Faith and Truth.* In such Cases where is their Evangelical Link and Tye of Unity? Certainly a true Christian's *Yea* should be *Yea,* and his *Nay, Nay*; that is, in Answer to all Questions, whether it relate to matter of Evidence or Promise, they should speak the Truth, and mean and do what they say; which is enough.

This Truth is so natural, that it is familiar with some to say, *I had rather take his* * *Word than the other's Oath*; which shews, how much Honesty is more credible than Swearing. This made the primitive *Christians* not only Refuse to Swear by the Fortune of *Cæsar,* but to swear at all, telling their Judges in their Answers, *It was unlawful for a Christian to swear.* And Bp. *Gauden* himself assures us, *that they were so strict and exact, that there was no need of an Oath among them*; *Yea, they so kept up the Sanctity and Credit of their Profession among Unbelievers, that it was Security enough in all Cases to say,* Christianus sum, *I am a Christian*; And that if any urged them farther, *they repeated this as the only Satisfaction they would give:* The Veracity of their Word. And that he might farther shew, how dishonourable and needless a Thing it was for Good and Holy Men, and true Christians to Swear, he brings in the Whole Body of the *Essæans,* several wise *Heathen, and Christian Fathers*; Indeed it was a Primitive Maxim, *Non oportet, ut vir qui Evangelicè vivit, juret omnino.* It behoves not that a Man of an Evangelical Life should swear in any Case. And this Doctrine was closely follow'd by *Chrysostom, Theophylact,* and several other ancient *Christian* Doctors. Nor were the *Heathen* wholly insensible of the Truth of this Matter, as Bp. *Gauden* farther informs us out of *Polybius* " That the better and simpler Ages of the World rarely used any Oaths at all, no " not so much as in Judicature; but after Perfidy and Lyes encreased, Oaths en- " creased, as a Remedy to restrain those Mischiefs. To which let me add, That some of the ancient Sages, *Socrates* and *Xenocrates,* knew, urg'd, and also practised a Life beyond an Oath.

---

* As the Thief in *Essex,* who robbing a *Quaker* in company with another, and using them fairly, desired them not to stir, till they were got clear of the Road; upon which said the other Man, I'll swear; *you swear, you'l swear through an Anvil and back again*; *will the other promise?* Thieves know Honesty, though they do not practise it.

So that if those who are truly discipled, redeemed and renewed by the Power and Spirit of Christ Jesus, need no Oath (Nay, that it is a Questioning of their Veracity, and an Affronting of their Profession, to offer them one) *and if the Lying, familiar Swearing, Forswearing, and fraudulent Dealing of Wicked Men make their Oaths of little or no Credit* (as saith the Bishop out of Lactantius *and* Austin) *certainly it will be much better to prevent Swearing, and punish Lying with the Penalty due to Forswearing:* which suggests an unanswerable Return to that familiar Objection, *But how do we know that ye are those Honest Men?* For we have not only the same Answer the ancient *Christians* had to give, with this severe Rebuke, *That ye are the Reproach of* Christianity, *who under that good Name act those vile Impieties the nobler* Heathen *judged, and the loosest have not out-done*; but we have this farther to offer: *Dispense with our Consciences in not-Swearing, and punish our Untruth when ye find it, as severely as ye do their Perjury.* What more can be desired, *since Truth-speaking fulfils the Law, and Punishing False-speaking satisfies it?*

CHAP. VII.

Of the Light Within.

IT is Matter of sad Complaint, that a Man should write of so excellent a Subject as the *Light Within*, and shew so much Darkness in treating of it. p. 99, 101, 102, 103.

But lest he should say, That our uncertain and various Expressions, for such he esteems them, put him besides all Faith in it, we shall endeavour to make their Consistency both with themselves, and the Scriptures of Truth appear,

He quotes *Tho. Foster*, in his *Guide to the Blind*, p. 1. thus, " God is the Light. p. 7. *as a Man forgetting himself,* " Christ Within is Man's true Light to walk by; And in p. 9. *As doubting whether that would hold Water*; says, " The Spirit of " Christ in Man is the true Light and Guide, and this Light enlightens every Man " that comes into the World. *But* (says he) *if* James Naylor *may be Judge, our Friend* Thomas (he was so, though thou art an Enemy, and a Mocker of his Memory) *is very much mistaken*; *for in his Book, called,* A Door opened to the Imprisoned, p. 2, 3, *he says,* " That the Light of the Word is God's Love to the " World; and this Light is not given to any till they come out of the World. *And that* George Whitehead *in the Seed of* Israel's Redemption, p. 20. *says,* " That " the Light Within, is a Measure of the Lord's Life and Light.

Ans. To the first Quotation, there can be no Cavil; for 'tis plain Scripture, *God is Light*, 1 John 1. 5. And it was the Apostolical Message so to preach, *That God is Light, and in him is no Darkness at all.* John 1. 9.

The second is also most true; for Christ is Man's true Light, *that was the true Light which enlightens every Man, &c.* And that it was for Man to walk by, both Christ and his Apostles prove. *I am the Light of the World, he that followeth me shall not walk in Darkness, but shall have the Light of Life.* Joh. 8. 12. Again, *If ye walk in the Light, as He is in the Light, &c.* 1 Joh. 1. 7. God is Light, and Christ is Light; and since there is no knowing of God or Christ but by the Manifestation of Light; and that none know the Father but those to whom Christ, the Light, reveals him; therefore Christ is Man's true Light, without which Man can never know either God or Christ.

For his third Quotation, I see no Contradiction in it to the two former, unless Christ can be without his Spirit; for if the Spirit of Christ dwell in any Man, *Christ dwells in that Man.* This Language the Apostle used to the *Romans*, Chap. 8. 9, 10, 11. *If the Spirit of God be in you.* Again, *If the Spirit of Christ be in you*; yet again, *If the Spirit of Him that raised up Jesus dwell in you*; all which are *Synonymous*, or to one and the same Purpose. For Shame, thou a *Scholar*, a *Grœcian*, a *Disputant*, that makest such sorry Cavils; might not the *Jews* and *Heathens* have made the same Exceptions against the Apostle? But 'tis an old *Devil-Trick* to be-saint and extol the Holy Ancients, *whilst they hugg the Spirit that murdered them, and with it persecute the Truth in this Age*; so cunning is the Devil, and so blind is the World. But let us see how much more Honest he is in his next Quotation, than Rational in the three former.

That *the Light of the World is God's Love to the World*, I find in *James Naylor's* Book; But that *the Light is not given to any till they come out of the World*, is a direct

1673.

Chap. VII.

direct *Lye to our Principle*, and a putting an absolute *Forgery upon his Book*; For he says, That God has given his Light to the World, that therein is his Love manifested, that such as follow it in it's Leadings out of the World, have the Nature of Sons: But Sonship is that which cannot be had whilst in the World's Nature; therefore they are to come out of the World's Ways, to follow the Light, which visits Man in the World's Ways, in order to bring him out of them, and here the true Sonship is received; so that the Sonship and not the Light, is that which cannot be had in the World. Now what Contradiction can this be to our Dishonest Adversary's honest Friend *Thomas*, who said, *that the Light enlightened every Man that comes into the World?* Sure I am it is a plain Instance of our Adversary's Disingenuous and Injurious Practice.

For *G. Whitehead's* Words, The Substance of them is to be found in *Joh*. 1. 14, 16. *The Word was full of Grace and Truth, and of his Fulness have all we received, and Grace for Grace.*

But he says. *H. N. teaches that every Godly Man is God incarnate, and Christ incarnate*, and that this is the Doctrine of the *Quakers* (says he) I prove. First, because *T. Foster* in his *Guide to the Blind*, pag. 13. saith, " The Light which is " Christ within, is not Natural, but Sufficient to Salvation. Now I appeal to the whole World, What Affinity there can be between *H N's* Words and *Tho. Foster's*. Is God incarnate or Christ incarnate, to be found in his Assertion? Nor will I pass my Word for his right Quotation of *H. N.* What he quarrels at here I know not. Would he not have Christ manifested within? Or would he have him Natural, in Opposition to Spiritual? Or would he have his Light and Spirit insufficient to Salvation? If he intends any of these, he crosses express Scripture, blasphemes against God, and frustrates the very End of the Gospel; If none of them, why was this Passage cited? But he thinks *G F.* has made much for his Purpose, who in his *Great Mystery*, p. 207, 201. saith, *Christ is not distinct from the Saints, and he that eats the Flesh of Christ hath it within him.* And what of all this? Is Christ divided from his Saints, *Was he not in them of Old the Hope of Glory? He that's with you, shall be in you. And at that Day ye shall know, that I am in my Father, and you in me, and I in you.* For the other Part, I wonder he cited it: Certain it is, *That unless Men eat the Flesh of Christ, they have no Life in them.* Now how a Man can be said to eat any Thing, and not have it within him, is a Distinction past my Understanding.

Col. 1. 27.
Joh. 14. 17.
.20
John 6. 53.
54.

But *Geo. Fox* saith, p. 206. *If there be any Christ but He that was crucified within, he is a false Christ; and he that hath him not within, is a Reprobate.*

Answ. Our Return to this will be very short. 1st. By Christ *crucified within*, he does not deny that he was once *crucified without* (as the same Page proveth) as our *Adversary* would insinuate. 2dly. There can be no False Doctrine in it, unless the owning of Christ being crucified within, through Wicked Works, necessarily should imply our Denying *that he was ever crucified without*; from the Danger of which Consequence the Scriptures of Truth sufficiently secure us. *Heb.* 6. 6. *Seeing they crucify to themselves the Son of God afresh.* Also *Rev.* 11. 18. 3dly. And that such are Reprobates in whom he lives not; remember that unanswerable Passage, 2 Cor. 13. 5. *Examine your selves. whether you be in the Faith; prove your own selves: know you not your own selves, how that Jesus Christ is in you, except you be Reprobates?*

But says our Adversary, *Ric. Stubbs*, a Quaker, told *Eliz. Wetherly*, That *the Jesus who was born of the Virgin, and dyed at* Jerusalem, *was a false Christ and an Antichrist.* But this needs no long Answer; for it is an absolute Untruth, raised by the *Devil* within, and his envious Emissaries without, to bring us, the poor despised People of God, into Infamy with all who have any Reverence for the Name of Christ; And God will plead our Innocency in this Man's Conscience, by that Holy Light which he blasphemously saith, *leads down to Hell and the Devil, carrying Man, like an* Ignis fatuus, *into Bogs and Ditches, causing him at last to fall into the Pit of Everlasting Destruction.* For this I would have all the World to know,

Psal. 7. 9.
Jer. 11. 20.
Amos 4. 13.

That God, *Who is the Searcher of the Heart, and the Tryer of the Reins, who alone sheweth unto Man his Thoughts*, is the great Spiritual *Light, John.* 1. 1. And 'tis as such, that he setteth Man's Sins before him, as faith the Apostle, *Whatsoever makes manifest is Light*, Ephes. 5. 13. And faith the same Apostle, *Whatsoever may be known of God, is made manifest within Men*; for God hath shewed it unto

John. 3. 21.

them, *Rom.* 1. 19. Such as bring their Deeds unto this Light, *may know whether they are wrought in God or no.* And for this End hath the Eternal Word enlight-

ned

ned every Man that cometh into the World, that he may come to the Light, and walk and grow up in it: For as all have given unto them out of his Fulness Grace for Grace, *so from his Fulness of Light, hath he given all Men Light for Light*; not a meer natural Capacity or creaturely Understanding, but *that Divine Light or Grace, which is able to teach, sanctifie and govern the Soul to God's Glory, and it's own Everlasting Happiness*: In the Word by whom all Things were made was Life, *and that Life was the Light of Men*; And as it was then, so is it now the Condemnation of the World, *that Men love Darkness rather than Light, because their Deeds are Evil*. Some, with the *Pharisee*, prefer their Formal, Literal and Ceremonial Religion; and others, their Pleasures, Pastimes and Worldly Honour and Profit, before this Inward, Pure Light, and Law of the Spirit of Life, the Leaven of the Kingdom, and Truth in the Inward Parts, which frees from Sin, and brings into the Heavenly Liberty of the Sons of God. And we do testifie in the Name of God, that it is only by this Measure of that Divine Fulness, which above One Thousand Six Hundred Years ago was manifested in the Flesh, that any Man or Woman can ever come to a right *Sight, Sense, Relish and Enjoyment of the Blessed Ends and Effects of his Gracious Appearance, Heavenly-Gospel, Mighty Miracles, Holy Life, Death and Sufferings, his Powerful Resurrection, Glorious Ascension, and constant Mediation and Intercession*. And that all Knowledge, Faith, and Worship, not grounded upon this internal Sight, Sense and Operation of this Divine Measure of Grace, Light and Truth in the inward Parts, are but Historical and Pharisaical; *making up but the* Jew *outward, and* Christian *outward*, who are not Children of the Free Woman, nor Heirs according to the Promise. And if for this blessed Testimony we must be thus abused, defamed, and set at nought by the Black-robed-Rabbies of this World, as the Prophets, and Christ, himself, were, God will be our abundant Recompence, who is the Author of that good Reformation begun, and will, I hope, be the Finisher of it, to his own Immortal Honour, and our unutterable Rejoycing, World without End.

CHAP. VIII.

Of some of our Adversary's Lyes and Slanders.

HIS next Chapter containing a short Account of the *Quaker's* Pretences to immediate Revelation, hath been already effectually considered; only I shall take Notice of two or three Particulars.

First, *That he would have the Sadness and Dejection of those that turn Quakers, and the Zeal and Fluency of those that Preach among them, to be the Effect of the Hypochondria.*

Answ. This shews what an easie Religion our *Adversary* lives in, who yet knows not the Terrors of the Lord: How unfit is he to Warn Men? Had he ever known God's Word to be as a Sword, an Hammer, an Ax, a Consuming Fire and Everlasting Burnings against Sin and Iniquity, the Pangs of a New Birth, and how hard it is to become a true Disciple through the daily Cross, he would never have made such a frothy, dark and envious Construction of our Serious Convictions: But God's Fire will one Day burn up his peaceable Habitation; and in that Day of *Alarm*, he and the rest of his *Jovial Crew*, shall know the Meaning of these Words, *They that pierced him shall see him, and all the Kindreds of the Earth shall wail because of him.*

But whatever Disease we have, his frequent and senseless Scoffs at us, and our Holy Way, shew that the Spleen is very prevalent in him.

For his Reflection on *Edw. Burroughs*, it will do him no Harm; his Soul is with God, and his Memory shall out-live his Enemies Hate. And for this *Ranting Scribbler*, he is not worthy to carry his Books after him.

For his Gentle-man of *New-Castle*, who affirmed, *Some* Quakers *came to* Kendal *Church, and said, they had a Commission from the Lord to pull down the Steeple-House; And another in Sermon Time to pull down the Hour-Glass*, I must tell him, that we know no such Thing, and if it were a fair *Adversary*, he would have told us, who this Gentle-man was, and who the *Quakers*, that we might have informed our selves of the Truth of the Matter; though we have great Cause to conclude it a down right Forgery. For the other, it is altogether as likely to come of the same Stock; but if such a Thing ever were, I dare say, the *Priest* was in a worse Taking than the *Quaker*; however, it was no Theft, because they all saw for what End

1673.

Chap. VIII

it was done: And every Body knows, the *Prieſt* can tell how to call for another Glaſs; for the Truth is, ſome of that Profeſſion can hardly preach without them; for they elevate them above his *Quaker's Hypochondria*.

That *the Wife of one* Williamſon, *ſhould call* Ja. Milner, *the Eternal Son of God, at* Appleby, is an arrant Falſhood; for we have particularly enquired, and can find no ſuch Thing.

That a *Woman at* Weighton *in* York-ſhire, of that *Goatiſh Herd* (as he is pleaſed to call them) *went naked up to another Woman's Huſband's Bed, and bid him open his Bed to her, for the Father had ſent her,* is a Slander hatcht in Darkneſs: We deny it in the Name of the Lord God; And I charge this diſingenuous Man, if he has any Regard to his Reputation, or thoſe he belongs to, to prove, if he can, the Truth of this Story.

And that he ſhould at laſt call this, *A Taſte of the* Quakers *deluded Dreams, melancholick Fancies, Impoſtures, Injections, everlaſting Errors and Deceits,* is the Top of what Impudence and Forgery Man can well be guilty of againſt his Neighbour. But why our *Goatiſh Herd* above all others? Unjuſt and Uncivil Man! Look at Home for Shame. How often are *Quakers* brought to Eccleſiaſtical Courts for Uncleanneſs? We know they are too often ſummoned there for Tythes: It would be almoſt endleſs to tell the Stories of both Prieſts and People's Wickedneſs that follow them; one would think that no Church of *England Man*, that knew any thing of the preſent Age, or that thought we did, could believe that forging one unclean Lye againſt the *Quakers*, ſhould invalidate their Religion, who believes his own to be true, notwithſtanding thoſe numerous Inceſts, Adulteries, Fornications, Concupiſcences, Murders, Lyes, Perjuries, Diſſimulations, Thefts, Injuries, and ſuch like, that have been, and daily are committed by his *Dear Fellow-Communicants, The Sons and Daughters of the Church of* England. Let him therefore draw in his Horns, and leave off puſhing at us with his Forgeries and Defamations; and repent of this ungodly Way of dealing with us, that he may find Mercy to his Soul.

Chap. IX.

CHAP. IX.

Of PERFECTION.

I Perceive, the Man would fain ſay ſomething of every Controverted Head, held by the *Quakers*, though as little to Purpoſe as may be. There is but one Thing commendable in his whole Chapter, and that is it's Brevity. He ſtumbles at the very Entrance, and never recovers himſelf to the End.

The Quakers *talk much of Perfection from Sin, in this Life, and that they have already attained to it.* Quote, he ſcorns, his *Word* is Credit enough, at leaſt he would have it ſo; but to let him go on. This, ſays he, is the *Phariſee*'s *Litany*, God, I thank thee! I am not as other Men are. *The* Antinomian *Litany, the Doctrine of* Dell, Saltmarſh, Town, *and all* Antinomians *and* Familiſts; *And that Malice and Railing perpetually make up the greateſt Part of the* Quakers *Speaking to the People*. But what of Argument can be found in ſuch meer Aſſertion and Reflection, I leave with ſober Men to judge. He neither underſtands, *Antinomians, Familiſts,* nor *Quakers*. And truly I am ready to think him ſome raw, unfledged, ungraduate, who by this Eſſay aims at that Proof of his Abilities, as may induct him to ſome Fat Benefice; or elſe One that thought we deſerved no larger Teſtimony of his Ability, Honeſty, and Diſcretion, in his Endeavours againſt us.

In ſhort, A perfect Principle we plead for, and preſs the Neceſſity and Benefit of Man's Conformity to it; That though it be a *little Leaven, it is able to leaven the whole Lump*; That this Grace brings Salvation from Sin, by the Power it gives them that obey it, to mortify Sin; elſe what a Riddle would thoſe Scriptures make, *That ſpeak of Sanctification throughout in Body, Soul and Spirit. That He that's born of God, ſins not. Old things are done away, behold all things are become new: I write unto you Young Men, becauſe ye have overcome the Wicked One. Be ye perfect, as your heavenly Father is perfect. Unto a perfect Man. Let us cleanſe our ſelves from all Filthineſs of Fleſh and Spirit, perfecting Holineſs in the Fear of the Lord. The God of all Grace make you perfect,* &c. Wherein not only a *Perfection from Sin,* but the going forward to a *perfect Man in Chriſt,* is exhorted to, and prayed for; therefore not inobtainable.

1 Theſ. 5. 23.
1 John 5. 18.
Cap. 2. 13.
Mat. 5. 48.
Eph. 4. 13.
2 Cor. 7. 1.
1 Pet. 5. 10.

To

To conclude: We do not teach People the Perfection of our Persons, but the Principle of God, and our Experience of it's Converting and Translating Power, *Christ* is stronger than the *Devil*; And for this, was, and is he manifested, *To end Sin, and destroy the Works of the Devil*; a Doctrine the Church of *England* teaches in her Baptism. Nor do we say, That every Man is perfect from Sin as soon as he is convinc'd of Sin: No, there is a great War, a long Wilderness to travel through, many Enemies to subdue, and difficulties to surmount; and those Enemies are mostly those of a Man's own House. We therefore exhort all to wait for God's Arising, that his Enemies may be scattered, that witnessing a victorious State over Hell and Death, by the Power of Christ Jesus, *such may obtain the New Name which is written in the Lamb's Book of Life*, and promised to all that Over-come: Which is far from that Ungodly *Ranterism* he would fasten upon us and our Principles; And I doubt not but Time, Patience, and our Blameless Conversation, shall dispel those Mists, Malice and Ignorance may have raised to darken and blemish the Reputation of our Practice, Persons and Principles in the World.

CHAP. X.

His Ninth and Tenth Chapter of the Ways and Arts that the Quakers *use in gaining Proselytes, with the Advantage their Way has over other* Heresies, *honestly considered, and briefly confuted.*

Pag. 117. THE first Artifice, he says, we use, is, *To come in Sheep's Clothing. Now what is this Sheep's Clothing* (says he) *but only the Innocence and Purity of the* Christian *Doctrine; when as their main Purpose is to devour credulous Souls.*

Answ. If we have the Sheep's Clothing, and if the Sheep's Clothing be the Purity and Innocence of *Christian* Doctrine, then is our Doctrine Innocent, Pure, and *Christian*. And since he avers the Doctrine of the Church of *England* to be so remote and opposite, this Character must necessarily imply, that her Doctrine is Hurtful, Impure, and Antichristian.

But what have we Seduced People to? *Drunkenness, Whoredom, Perjury, Wantonness, Idleness*, or any such Unseemly or Irreligious Practice? Let him tell me who of us are less Serious, less Moral, or worse Livers than we were before. But the Truth of the Matter is this: Our Way of Devouring People's Souls, as he calls it, *is that which hinders the Hireling Priests from Devouring the People's Pockets, and endangering their Souls too*, who teach for Hire and Divine for Money, and make Religion but a Stalk to Preferment, who have the Shell without the Substance, the Form without the Power; From such, in Obedience to God's Spirit, we have turned away; and because we have dared no longer to put into their Mouths, their Covetous Spirit has swelled, notwithstanding their Pretences, and their Sheep-skin burst, and an arrant Wolf has come forth; no true Sheep, but a Sheep-Fleecer, and a Sheep-sucker, of their Blood, whose Innocency and Patience have plainly proved them such. But the Wolf's and the Fox's Skin have been always good enough for us; any thing to disguise, and make the Dogs fasten and worry to Death. *Our Conscience they call* Enthusiasm; *and our solemn Confession, Collusion, and Equivocation; our Perseverance is reputed Obstinacy; our Plainness, Singularity; our Industry, Worldly-mindedness; and our Retired Living, Penuriousness; our Rebukes of Evil, they will have to be Censoriousness; and our Disregard of Company, Pride and Sullenness*. Whatever God by his Light has made Conscience to us, there are a Sort of Men, that have so little Conscience, as to constue it all backwards, rendring us instead of Honest Conscientious Men, *A Pack of Fraudulent, Cheating Fellows*: But we cannot help it, if Men will rage, they must; Their Shame, and our Patience, will the more appear.

He says, *Our Second Stratagem is, to bring the People out of Love with their Pastors, who have the Care of them*.

Answ. I know not a *Quaker* in the World that would not administer both Food and Rayment, to the worst Persecutor, as a necessitous Creature: But I hope, they would suffer, unto Death, before they would contribute either to him as a Priest; No, God's Witness in our Consciences never said *Amen* to their Ministry. They have the Scriptures, true; But the Word of Reconciliation, that brings to God, and of which they declare, they want. I know that some of them can talk well; so can some *Mountebanks* and *Comedians*. Do they witness the Truth of what they

they speak? Their Heads know, but do their Hearts feel the Operation of that Truth they will sometimes in Words declare? Have they travelled the Way, and traced the many anxious Steps of *that new Birth*, which is the only Door into the Heavenly Kingdom? But, alas! *Oxford* and *Cambridge* make them, and their Parents and Patrons prefer them; a good round Maintenance is mostly their Aim on all Hands: Tell them of the Necessity of an Inward Work, that it is the Spirit of God that only makes a Man a Minister of God, and that the Anointing, which true Christian-men receive, is sufficient to their Instruction, and presently the Cry is, *Donatism, Pelagianism, Familism, Brownism, Jesuitism, Quakerism*, or any other Name that begets Jealousy, Undervalue and Hatred. In short, we do believe, that the settled Ministers of the World are so far from being Beneficial to People, that on the contrary, they exercise their Minds with a Sort of unexperienced, unauthoriz'd Preaching, *leading from the secret Strivings, Discoveries and Conduct of that Spiritual Minister, of the Everlasting Covenant, which is able to bring Man into that Way of Holiness, without which no Soul shall ever see the Lord*: And this is the true Reason why we are turned unto God's Minister, Christ Jesus, who says, *Learn of me*: Of whom God said, *this is my Beloved Son, hear him*; and reject the *Ministry of Man*.

Our Third Artifice *by which* he says, *we gain our Proselytes, is denying all Humane Learning, and Use of Reason: That we are the most sottish and ignorant Sect that ever appeared in the World*; Yet for our own Turn we will be nibling at it, as G. W. *in mentioning a Moth-eaten Manuscript mentioned by* Beza *in his Annotations*.

Ans. We have already said enough to defend Christianity, from the absolute Necessity of Humane Learning, either to understand or vindicate it; and so false is his Assertion, that since Prophecy has ceased in the Church, *secular Learning hath been of greatest Use and Benefit to Religion*, that there is nothing more true than the contrary, as it is commonly understood, promoted and practised in the World. I would fain know, how many *Rabbies, Greek* and *Latin Philosophers*, yielded themselves Proselytes to the Christian Religion, though they had his *Presence, Ministry, Miracles, Death and Resurrection amongst them*, who was and is the Author and Master of it? If such Learning be so great a Friend to Truth, how comes it that the greatest Things have fallen to the Share of Poor and Illiterate Men; And that such have been most apt to receive, and boldest to suffer for it? Why not *Rabbies* rather than *Fisher-Men*, which was before the Pouring out of the Spirit of Prophecy? And for what Reason should so many learned *Academies*, since the pretended, * Ceasing of it, be overrun with such foul Idolatries, Gross Superstitions, and flagitious Living, as 1200 Years past will witness. Nay, on the Occasion of any Reformation, with whom is there more to do, and who harder to be brought to yield than *Universities* have been? Scripture and Story give it clear against him.

Not that I would be thought to oppose all Sorts of Learning neither; It has been Man's Erring from his Divine Guide, that has made Way for those numerous *Theses, Distinctions, Books* and *Controversies*, the World for Ages hath been infested with. Such are the obscure, unintelligible and unprofitable *Metaphysicks* of the *Heathen*, too greedily received and mischievously increased by *Fathers, Councils, School-Men*, and our modern *Universities*, to the corrupting of Christian Doctrine, and disputing away the Benefit of Christian Life. An unbounded *Curiosity* and *Fancy*, have been the Womb that hath brought forth so much troublesom and unprofitable Matter; which began with a Degeneration of Philosophers: True Philosophy in the Beginning of it being no more, than the Way of Holy Living, by the Mortification of Passions. But Learning, as Religion, failing by Corruption of Men, is now degenerated into quite another Thing. *Socrates* taught proper Speech and good Life, and such a Course of Learning as turned to daily Practice and Profit; severely forbidding all Curiosities and Niceties, as what turned not to Good Life, which he reputed the best Science; and *Plato* would have the *Poets* banished out of his Common-Wealth, as corrupting it with Fables: Thus was Learning, as Religi-

---

* *But why is it ceast? because* ceast *to, you, Sons of the Night? Did not Christ promise to be with his to the End; Either that is not so, or his being with them, endues them not with the Spirit of Prophecy; Was it not Apostolical, and in the first Churches? Why not now? Is it less wanted? Is* Christ *not that to his Church he was? A blind Argument indeed! because the Priests of Man's making have it not; therefore none have it.* I will pour out my Spirit upon Thee, and upon thy Seed, and thy Seed's Seed unto all Generations. *Isa.* 5. 9.

on, once Pure and Simple. * In short, all *Right Learning* is to be divided into these Two, *True Knowledge* and *Proper Language*. This *Knowledge* relates *First* to God, and that's only to be received from the Spirit of God; And, *Secondly*, the Things of this Life; and therein the Spirit of Man has a large Field to act in, to the Enlargement of it's own Understanding, and Benefit of the whole Creation as subject to God's Grace, as knowing the Nature and Order of Things in the Creation, Building, Improvement of Land, Medicine, Chirurgery, Traffick, Navigation, History, Government, with many other Honest, Useful, and Profitable Arts and Inventions, for the Help and Good of Mankind. And if Man had kept in God's Counsel, the many superfluous and unnecessary Arts and Inventions that are in the World, had never been brought forth by him; and Time will work them out, as it brought them in, so that what is Plain, Honest, Serviceable, and of good Report, shall be preserved for the Good of the Creation.

As for *Language*, it must be granted that there is a Propriety and Decency in Language: But as Men have followed the *Outside of Religion*, and left the *Substance* behind, so have they done with *Learning*: They have neglected *Matter*, the most Beneficial Part of Learning, and devoted themselves to an Excess of fine Speaking, of which Bishop *Wilkins* in his Real Character complains not without a Cause, when he says, *That this Grand Imposture of Phrasing hath eaten out all Solid Learning.*

Yet Language is very convenient for Men's Converse with Books and Nations of a different Tongue; however, we utterly deny them to be absolutely necessary to the True Knowledge of the Mysteries of God's Kingdom. So that the *True English of the Quakers* denying all Reason and Learning, is this; We refuse to commend or practise Unnecessary Studies, Nice Controversies, Voluminous and Intricate Disputations, Obscurity of Language, Affectedness of Stile, Excess of Elegancy, believing, that Learning as well as Religion, stands in need both of great purging, and reducing: And that those Subjects and Employments, which are most serviceable and beneficial to Mankind, and agreeable to God's Grace, digested into easy and familiar Methods, and treated on in the plain and ordinary Way of Speaking, best deserves Man's Time and Regard. And for his Reflection upon G. *Whitehead*, it no farther deserves our Notice, than that he flung a greater upon *Beza*, whose Learning he makes a little too bold with. To say no more of his *Moth-eaten-Manuscript* than this, That the best Copies he has had for his Rule, have been near a-kin to such *Moth-eaten Manuscripts*; and if such a Manuscript was the Holy Scripture, as I believe it was, he was too Bold, and Irreverent, as well as Unwary and Foolish, in calling it a *Moth eaten-Scripture*, thereby implying it to be a *Moth-eaten-Rule*; not that I take it to be his Rule, who has so fearfully erred and strayed from the Holy Precepts and Exhortations of it.

The fourth Thing by which he reports us to proselyte People, is, (Pag. 122, 133,) *To deceive and associate first with Women, therein imitating the Devil.*

Answ. First we deny it, as being like the rest of his idle Stories, and those that not only in the Primitive Times by the *Heathen*, but in several Ages since, and Degrees of breaking forth of Truth and Reformation from Apostate Generations, have been by them fastned upon the Sincere Professors thereof, as *Waldenses*, *Lollards*, *Hugonots*, and *Protestants* themselves, in their first Day, as well as more modern Dissenters. We must take our Share, it is no new nor strange Thing.

But supposing it to be True, that our Endeavours are first directed towards the *Women*, I see no Evil in our Beginning to undeceive, where the *Devil* began to deceive. If they are so easie to be perswaded, why not to Good as well as to Evil? But these idle Shifts and pitiful Reflections, deserve rather to be disdained then considered.

Lastly, (Pag. 125, 126, 127,) *For our pretending to higher Degrees of Holiness, and Cracks, and Boasts of Inspirations, with our* † *Bewitching Language, which is*

---

* These Men were only versed in their own Tongues; They were many of them Mechanicks and Tradesmen: Answering among the *Gentiles* to the Prophets, and Apostles among the *Jews* and *Christians* (though far short of them.) So that Learning and Philosophy, like to Religion, are now so changed, the Ancients would be at a Loss to know them: Another Thing has possest it self of the Name of each: For to be a Philosopher, or Lover of Wisdom, which was to eschew all Evil; and Learning, which was to unlearn every ill Thing, as *Socrates* said, are now turned to dark and Unprofitable *Contests*, Elaborate and Unserviceable Studies, to stuff Men's Heads.

† *Rainerius* the Monk, and a terrible Enemy to the poor *Waldenses*, made the same Complaints against them. They used, *says he*, to teach first what the Disciples of Christ ought to be, and that none are His Disciples, *But they that imitate His Life*. And that the Popes, Cardinals, &c. because they live in Pride, Avarice, and Luxury, &c. are not the Lawful Successors of Christ, in that they walk not up to His Commandments. Thus says the *Monk*, they win upon the People. *P. P. Pet. Hist. Wald.*

nothing

1673.

Chap. X.

nothing but *Canting, and Scripture Phrase fitted to Feminine Fancies* ; by which (he says) *we have the Advantage of all other Heresies*. I return thus much.

Answ. It is our Faith, that God, who made Heaven and Earth, will judge the Secrets of all Men by Jesus Christ; so that it is not only my Duty, but my Interest to speak the Truth of my Conscience in this Matter. We dare pretend to no higher Degree than we have attained; but we must make a Difference between what we were whilst under the Ministry of Man, and what we are, since our being turn'd to God's Powerful Word in the Heart, Christ's Ministry: We should be false to God, injurious to our Neighbour, and smother and belye our own Convictions, if we should not say, *That we have found our Judge near us, our Guide, Law-giver and Rule very nigh unto us* ; and those Infirmities, Temptations, and Corruptions, God has, by this Heavenly Grace, given us Power against (by which we have known that Mortification of Sin, and Conformity to the Will of God) which the utmost of our former Profession could never free us from. And if this Plain and Christian Confession must be called by all those hard Names our *Adversary* finds for our Honest Intentions, we must, as we have done, recommend our Cause to God, and His Holy Witness in all Consciences, and him to be judged by him to whom we desire to stand and fall in all we say, do, and take in Hand; to whom alone we owe the Honour of our Experiences and Preservations.

However, the Irreverence of the Man deserves both our Notice, and the Reproof of all that read him: *What! Is Scripture-Language become a Cant; and a Sober and Seasonable Use of it, Canting fitted to Feminine Fancies?* But we think it not more his Folly, Contradiction and Blasphemy, to speak with that Contempt of the Holy Scriptures, and his pretended Rule, than an Advantage he gives our Cause, to tell the World, *That of all others, the* Quakers *Speak and Preach the Scripture-Dialect*. But it is the Mother-Tongue of such frothy Minds so to prophane; and for all their pretended Respect to the Holy Scriptures, the Spirit and Life, that belong unto them, are made but Matter of Jeer and Mockage: They would not be thought to undervalue Christ, the Scripture, nor his Religion, but with the Height of Formality seem to Reverence and Applaud them all, *yet Persecute to the Death those that are His Holy Offspring, by the Spirit of Regeneration; which shows their Esteem of Christ, Scripture and Religion, to be but a Kind of Blindfold Respect; and that indeed their very Spirits turn within them against that which is, truly Christ-like, Scriptural and Religious*. The Devil ever understood his Interest better, than to persecute Truth under that Name; yet for all his fair Pretences to Saintship, he constantly became a fierce Devourer of those that have been the Children of the Truth: And I may truly say to this Opposer, *That for all his Religion, Learning, Church-Communion, and that Stir he maketh against us, as a Crew of* Hereticks, *and Impostors, he knows not what Spirit he is of, who has writ a Book, rather to Abuse, than Inform us, and instigate the Civil Magistrate to destroy us, than by solid Argument to Refute or Reclaim us*. He that has but Half an Eye may see his Aim was not so much our Conversion, as Disgrace, and, if possible, our utter Ruin; But 'till our Adversary's Labours prove as Dangerous to us as his Design (no doubt) was Wicked, we have little Cause to dread the Success of his Attempts.

And that he may see a little of himself, if he thinks himself worth looking upon, let him be pleased to take a View of some of those many Reviling, Scoffing, Rude and Contemptible Epithets he is pleas'd to bestow on us, an entire Body of People: *Heretical Generation of* Quakers; *Slaves to Pride, Covetousness, Lust; possest by the Devil, and a Diabolical Spirit; Apostates, Phanaticks, Spiritualists; Black, impure Hearts and Mouths; Bewitched with their Sorceries and Inchantments; Impertinent Cavilling Fellows, Rebellious* Quakers, *Cheats and Mountebanks; A Beastly and Quaking Generation; Juglers; Quaking and Impudent Hereticks; A Sottish Sect; Illuminado's, Inspirado's; Their Cheats and Impostures, Enthusiastical Hereticks, A Goatish Herd*.

Epistle, p. 6. 7, 29, 32, 33, 35, 40, 41, 53, 77, 94, 206, 111, 117, 121, 110, 109.

And of our Principle thus, *Their Light leads to Hell and the Devil, and carries a Man like an* Ignis Fatuus, *causing him to fall into the Pit of Everlasting Destruction; who are led by this, are made obnoxious to all the Impostures and Injections of the Devil, and to lye under Everlasting Errors and Deceits*.

* To all which I have no other Answer than what it is to itself; for it contains

---

* Bishop *Sanderson* highly honours and characterizes the *Light*; he calls it, The Eternal Law of Righteousness, and a Rule sufficient to Good Life. See his Book in *Latin*, entituled, *De Oblig. Jur. promiss*.

that Charge against it's Author, that I shall leave him to clear himself from, both to God and the whole World; only I cannot be so wanting of Civility to the Person he dedicated his Book to, as not to let him know, that it is unworthy of his *Quality and Repute* amongst Men, to have his Name used to the Protection of so much *Rudeness, Irreligion and Abuse.*

I cannot think so meanly of him, as that the Endeavours of so scurrilous an Author should excite him to any Severity against that poor People he has so basely wronged: For such a Thing were not only beneath that Place he holds amongst Men, but would be to intitle himself to all our *Adversary*'s Shameful Miscarriages, and encourage him to persist in what it greatly behoves him to Repent of: Which God grant for his Mercy-Sake; which is my whole Answer to his ill Treatment of us, and worst Wish I have for him.

A Conclusion *to those to whom the* Discourse *is Dedicated.*

SINCE then it is so evidently proved by Scripture, Reason, and Undoubted Presidents, that it is no new or unwonted Thing, for * *National Churches* to be deceived, notwithstanding they have been endowed with *Power, Learning, Nobility, Wealth, and Worldly Glory:* And that it hath pleased Almighty God in the most Signal Reformations that have been wrought upon the World, to employ a Sort of Plain, Simple, and Illiterate People: Let not our Meanness, Plainness and Simplicity, be any Argument with you against us, in the Mouths of that *Decimating Tribe*, whose Trade it is to oppose that Reformation, which in Conscience can neither own nor pay them; The Old Enemies of God's Appearance in the World, who therefore dread a Free and Universal Preaching, because the Ingrossment of it to themselves, has proved so profitable. Be *Gamaliels* at least, I beseech you, and Fight not their Battels: *If we are not of God, we cannot stand; And if of God, they must fall.* Leave us therefore with our Spiritual Weapons to decide this Controversie, without interposing your Worldly Power. 'Tis strange that we should be such *Ignorants*, and *Hereticks* too, whilst they Bless themselves with the *Name of Learned and Orthodox*, and yet dread the Consequence of being left by you to a *Fair Field* with us. Are not their *Universities, Bishops and Doctors*, enough to Silence such *Illiterate Whifflers*, as our *Adversary* is pleased to call us, without the Argument of your *Carnal Sword?* Certainly they ill deserve Fifteen Hundred Thousands Pounds a Year, if at last you must do the Business for them: What less can we expect from the worst of Persons and Causes? But as this Employment is below the Dignity of their Office, who are Publick Magistrates, and much too Narrow for that Universal Influence it should have for Publick Good, so remember that Great Saying of the late King, to the then Prince of *Wales.*

Always keep up Solid Piety, and those Fundamental Truths, which mend both Hearts and Lives of Men, with Impartial Favour and Justice. Your Prerogative is best shown and exercised in remitting, rather than exacting the Rigour of Laws, there being nothing worse than Legal Tyranny. Again, *A Charitable Connivance and Christian Toleration often dissipates what rougher Opposition fortifies:* Which had been the Saying and Counsel of King *James* before him. It is a sure Rule in Divinity, *That God never loves to Plant His Church by Violence and Bloodshed.* And in his Expositions on *Rev.* 20. he saith, *That Persecution is the Note of a False Church.*

Heresie must be cut off with the Sword of the Spirit, saith *Jerom. The Church doth not Persecute, but is Persecuted,* saith *Hilary. If you will, with Blood, with Evil, and with Torments defend your Worship, it shall not thereby be defended, but polluted,* said *Lactantius.* I will conclude with *Chrysostom; It is not* (saith he) *the Manner of the Children of God to Persecute about their Religion, but an evident Token of Antichrist.*

So let your Moderation be known unto all Men, the Lord is at Hand.

I am a Friend to all Men, who would have Vice *Punish'd,* Conscience *Tolerated, and* Righteousness *Establish'd, whose End is Peace and Assurance for ever.*

The 16th of the 5th Month, 1673.   William Penn.

Jer. Proæm. lib. 4.
Hilar. contr. Auxent.
Lact. lib. 5. cap. 10.
Relig. Urif. pag. 192.

* I intreat you to read a late Piece of Dr. *Cave's*, called *Primitive Christianity*, in which the Poverty, Simplicity, Meanness, Manner, and Place of Worship, Maintenance, Ministry, objected Novelty, &c. of the Ancient *Christians* are related.

REASON against RAILING,

AND

TRUTH against FICTION.

BEING AN

Answer to those Two late Pamphlets, Entituled, *A Dialogue between a* CHRISTIAN *and a* QUAKER, *and the Continuation of the Dialogue, &c.* By one *Thomas Hicks*, an *Anabaptist* Teacher.

IN WHICH

His { Dif Ingenuity, Prophaneness, Forgeries, Cavils } is/are { Represented, Rebuked, Detected, Confounded. }

AND

Thomas Hicks proved *No Christian*,

By several short ARGUMENTS raised from His Ungodly Way of Procedure against us.

By One that cannot but contend earnestly for the TRUE FAITH, *once delivered to the* SAINTS, William Penn.

Ye shall conceive Chaff; ye shall bring forth Stubble; your Breath as Fire shall devour you, Isa. xxxiii. 11.

To the READER.

Reader,

Of what Sort of People soever thou art, sure I am, that Almighty God hath placed a Witness for Himself in thy Conscience, unto whom thou must stand or fall in the Terrible Day of Account. Vain will all prove that enables not to abide the Test of that Day, when the Works of all Mankind shall assuredly come to Judgment: But blessed for ever will they be, who, not deluding themselves with Unprofitable Notions, shall appear with Consciences void of Offence before God, Angels and Men. And as I have been taught to seek that Happiness above all other, however mis-represented by Ungodly Men, so would I not for many Worlds hazard the Peace of that State, by any unjust Procedure against this Adversary now before me, however provok'd by his Exorbitances. I would give the Worst of Men their Due, and as I justly esteem him of that Number, so God forbid that I should in the least deprive him of his Right, a Robbery I would not (after his Example) be Guilty of.

Sorry I am, that so many Occasions are renewed to trouble both thee and my self with Books of Controversie; did I consult my own Ease, and the Common Peace of the several Religious Interests of this Land, Silence should have been my Choice.

God is my Record, these Things have deeply griev'd my very Soul, and made me cry, O when will Men rather press after Piety, than contend for Opinions; and de-

vote

vote themselves to the Sincere Practice of that True and Undefiled Religion, instead of pursuing the sinister Ends of what they falsely repute such! Shall Noise always go for Zeal, and implacable Contest constantly be esteem'd contending for the Faith once delivered to the Saints? *Miserable People!* Who know not that of all the Enemies Faith has to overcome, there is not a greater to be conquered? It is an old Fetch of the Devil's to besaint his own Off-spring, that he may beguile the Simple-hearted; and to think of doing God good Service in persecuting his Truth, was the Condition of the high-professing Jews of old.

Reader, It hath been our great Unhappiness, that we have not been hitherto known, as we are; for since we evermore desire to be unvail'd to God, there is no Reason why we should abscond our selves from Men; no, would we were known of Men, as we are known of the Lord: But such is the Impudence of this Adversary, that whilst we seek nothing more than to be understood, he would have the World believe, we glory in being Unintelligible, and seems to make the whole Drift of his Discourse to be a Discovery of us; who, instead of pulling our pretended Mask off, puts a frightful Vizard on, and then leads us up and down his Dialogues for a Sight; This is G. Fox, that G. Whitehead, and the other Edward Burroughs, or William Penn, &c. perverting, detracting, mis-construing, vilifying, slandering to the Height; and, which is worst of all, this villainous Practice is to pass for godly Zeal, and in Defence of the Gospel.

Reader, I have only this to request, be moderate, be impartial; and this grant for thy own Sake, that what Judgment thou shalt hereafter make of us, or our Enemies, may be such, as thou shalt not be ashamed of in the Day of the Lord God. Certainly it concerns us to beseech all to weigh these Things; For never were Men more innocent, and yet never any rendred more Nocent: Our Reputation here, and our Welfare hereafter, are brought into Question; we must be at once the Worst and most Imprudent Men, if what is charged, be True; and if False, our Adversary greatly both: For such is the Accusation, that nothing short of foulest Wickedness can lye at one of our Doors. And though I know many slight him, who yet are not of us, reputing him no better than a meer Janizary in Religion, one that fights for his Pay, and writes for his Living, a kind of Homily-Hireling, not worth our Notice; yet, since such is the Unhappiness of some, that they stick not to entertain more favourable Thoughts of his Endeavours against us; for their Sakes, and to detect his Envy, Error and Injustice to the World, am I now engaged. And if God give one Life, I hope to pursue this Undertaking effectually, let him get what Stock of Force and Ammunition he can.

Reader, I omit to say more here, but that I am (with all Sincerity)

15th 3d Month, 1673.   Thy True Friend,

WILLIAM PENN.

Reason against Railing, and *Truth against Fiction.*

CHAP. I.

The Introduction to the Discourse. Reasons why the Dialogue *was not answered before.*

IF it shall be wondered at by any, that we are so quick with our Return to *T. H.* upon his *Second Dialogue,* who seemed no more concerned for his *First:* 'Tis fit that such know the *Reasons* we have to give in our Defence.

First, We esteemed it a Fiction, calculated to the vain and scoffing Humour of the Vulgar, without all Savour of Mercy, Justice, Seriousness or Civility; worthy of no Man's Patronage, that would be in Earnest about Religion; To employ our Time about a large, compleat and distinct Book, had been to lose it.

2dly. *George Whitehead*, the Person most engaged, had given such an Account of it in brief to the World, that with many it seem'd sufficient; since the Contradictions, by him observ'd, are no Ways reconciled, nor so much as attempted by *T. H.* in his last Dialogue.

3dly. Because whatever might seem to carry any Force with it throughout that confident Piece of *Forgery*, we resolved to consider among many other *Adversaries* in one large Volume, which is accordingly done. And had it not been for other intervening Discourses, with the great Difficulty we have to print our just Defences, when we have made them (a Strait our Enemies are not put to) it had long e er this come to publick View.

4thly. Several other Adversaries were then before us, who, whether they said any thing more injurious or no, to be sure, pretended better Proof and Evidence for what they affirmed.

5thly. So just Complaint having met him, as well from several unconcerned in our Way, as our Friends, to wit, That he had charged the *Quaker with saying what he did not, at least to him, and in that Case, if ever he could prove it to have been either his Saying, or his Belief at any Time, or in any Case.* He now, to vindicate himself from such Injustice, hath given us a *Second Part*, wherein he hopes to make good what he charged upon us in his *First*, by Quotations out of our own Books, which, if faithfully done, I shall freely acknowledge, that a *Quaker* is quite another Thing than a *Christian*. And as this may suffice all, but such as are resolv'd never to be satisfied with any thing that comes from us, of the Reason of deferring our farther Answer; so having now that Ground to proceed upon, which we never had before, I shall, with God's Assistance, make the best of it I can, in Defence of the Truth, and the Innocency of them that profess it; only give me Leave to hint at a few Things, which may not be improper to the Matter in Hand, because they do not a little Discriminate and give to relish the Spirit of our *Adversary*.

CHAP. II.

Something of the Manner of his Dealing with us.

FIRST then, He has taken a very unequal Way to represent our Faith, Doctrine and Practice to the World, in that he hath rather delivered his own *Fury* than a true *Quaker*, and shews to the World, rather what he would have us to be, than what we are.

Can it be fairly done, to propose the most knotty Questions for himself, and *give the weakest Answers for us?* Had he but had the Generosity of a *Roman*, he would have given us fair Dealing for our Reputations: To make a *Fool* and an *Heretick* both, and then call him a *Quaker*, is no less than a *Rape*, because a violent Robbery committed upon those that go under that Name.

The best of Men can never escape, let their *Adversaries* have but the Characterizing of them. It had become *T. Hicks*, if he would have shewn himself a *Christian and a Champion too*; first to have set down our Principles and Arguments, as delivered and urged by us, and then have enervated both by his pretended greater Strength of Scripture and Reason, before he had made so many Trophies of Conquest; But because, had we been in the Wrong, this had been the Practice of a true *Christian*, and that this hath not been his Practice, we are taught to infer, that *T. Hicks* is thus far *Antichristian*.

Secondly, He has not only made us weak and Ridiculous by *Answers no Ways to the Purpose*, but to *bely our very Consciences and Principles*. For when he asks us, Do you believe the Scriptures to be true Sayings of God? he makes us to answer, *So far as they agree to the Light in me:* An Answer never so delivered by us. And when he queries, Will you be so liberal of your Revilings, whether your *Adversary* gives Occasion or not? He answereth for us, *It concerns us to render them as Ridiculous as we can, and to make our Friends believe they do nothing but contradict themselves, which is enough to us.*

Certainly these Things shew such premeditated and wilful Obstinacy to be wicked, that were we, what he represents us to be in this very Matter, the severest Plagues and Judgments of the Eternal God we might justly expect to be our Portion for ever. I fear *T. Hicks* measures us by himself; and that the Answer he feigns to the Second Part of his Dialogue, will be his Lot as truly, as he has there

feignedly

feignedly said it. It would take up too much Time to enlarge, only thus much let me say, That Man is hard put to it, and Unjust with a Witness, who not only invents Answers to dif-repute a Man or People, but such as are *very Lyes* too against their Faith and Practice.

Thirdly, Nor is this all, but he hath managed the whole of his *Dialogues in a Spirit of Prophanation,* by a taunting and inapplicable Use of many serious Words, that have at one Time or other been seasonably uttered by Sober, Simple and Religious People to the insnaring Questions of such Trepanners as himself. As for Instance, *Thou manifestest thy Darkness, that thou art still in thy Imagination; What dost thou witness in thy self? I see thou art a poor Dark Creature, as by thy talking is manifest; yea, it is manifest in the Light; yea verily: Alas! for thee, I bear Witness against thee: We are dead to Distinctions: Thou manifestest a Perverse Spirit.*

These, *Reader,* with the like Expressions, doth this Ungodly Scoffer give to the World in the Name of a true *Quaker,* as some of his best Answers; and that to such Questions, whose Matter hath been effectually considered and answered in many of our Books: However, his Spirit shews, to whomsoever those Answers are improper, in one Sense they are not so to him. But above all, that a Man pretending to Religion himself, and such an one too as next to us stands fairest for Reproach, should give our serious Language in a Jeer, as if we were fitter to be derided than Informed, is horridly wicked. Can his Conscience be so seared, as to handle Holy Things without Fear? Is Singularity grown so odious to an *Anabaptist Preacher,* that he should make it a Subject for his Scorn and Drollery? However this may resemble *T. Hicks,* he does not herein answer the first Love of the People who go under that Name, while he shews so much implacable Hatred to his Conscientious Neighbours, thereby not discountenancing the prophane Rabble in their frequent Scoffs at us, but furnishing them with such a Work of Darkness, as excites them farther to it, making us to inherit those cruel Mockings, which were once the Portion of his own Profession. We know, what Answers not God's Witness, shall never be able to abide the Trial, and therefore we are the less concerned in his Comical Abuses of us, more becoming a *Moorfield* or a *Smithfield* Stage-Play, than a *Christian* Treatise. Thus much and no more, *of the Spirit of the Man* in general, because more largely handled elsewhere.

CHAP. III.

The Question Stated, and accordingly Pursued. Our Adversary proved False and Weak.

WE shall now descend to the *main Question,* and that which is the Ground of his *Second Dialogue,* and without which there can be no Defence of his *First,* viz.

Whether those Doctrines and Expressions, charged upon the People called Quakers by Tho. Hicks *in both his Dialogues, be really the Doctrines and Sayings of that People, or not?* And afterwards, *Whether what we do own, and is by him charged with Error, is sufficiently opposed or proved such?*

He affirms, *they are; and undertakes to prove his Assertions out of their own Works,* which naturally leads me to consider, what are those Doctrines and Expressions he hath charged upon us to be ours; and what are those Proofs, by which he endeavours to make good that Charge. I shall first of all treat upon the more weighty Parts of Doctrine, and reserve the more trivial Matters to the latter End.

The first considerable Thing he endeavours to suggest against us, is, *Our making the Light in every Man to be God,* which he undertakes to prove from G. *Whitehead's* Discourse upon *John* 1. 4. *In him was Life, and the Life was the Light of Men;* That if the Life was the Divine Essence, the Light must be so also; for such as the Cause is, such the Effect must be. Upon which says *T. Hicks,* " From this " kind of reasoning we may conclude, not only the *Light within,* but every Crea- " ture both *Beasts* and *Trees* are God; these being Effects of infinite Wisdom and " Power. Dost thou not Tremble at this Consequence?

Ans. This very Thing shews great Disingenuity in *T. Hicks,* That from G. *Whiteheads* asserting & proving the Divine Nature of the Light within, he should insinuate, *that every Measure of Light in Man is whole God,* and which is yet more gross, to

conclude

conclude from *G. Whitehead*'s faying, Such as the Caufe is, fuch the Effect muft be; that *Beafts and Trees are God, becaufe the Effects of his Power*; whereas *G. Whitehead* did not intend it of a meer Potential, but Natural Effect, that is, fomething refulting from the Nature, and not the meer Power of the Divine Life. Men are the Natural Off-fpring and Product of Men, but fo are not all thofe other Things in the Creation, which are notwithftanding the Effects of their Art and Power, fo that there needs no Trembling at *G. W*'s Blafphemy, as he afterwards calls it but better Information to *T. Hicks*'s Ignorance, or Rebuke to his wilful Blindnefs. For this I refer the Reader to *G. W*'s Part of that larger Volume.

Again *G. W.* affirm'd it muft be God, becaufe to deny it fo to be, was to deny the Omniprefence of God, " Then it feems, fays *T. H.* that *the Light within, and* " *the Omniprefence of God is one and the fame Thing with him.* Is this your Cham- " pion? May we not conclude the Body of Man as well as the Light within to " be God by this Reafon?

Anf. By no means, and 'tis a Shame to hear that a Man pretending to Controverfy fhould ask fo ridiculous a Queftion. Is there no Difference betwixt a Man whofe Reins are on his Neck, following the Luft of the Flefh, the Luft of the Eye, and the Pride of Life, and the Light within, that *T. H.* himfelf acknowledgeth to convince of Sin, reprove for it, and unto which Man ought to give Attendance? Is there as clear a Proof of the Omniprefence of God in the one as in the other; I would know who is he that fearcheth the Hearts, and trieth the Reins, and telleth Man his Thoughts? Do not the Scriptures attribute this to God, and that as the moft convincing Proof of his Omniprefence? And if he doth fo fearch the Hearts and try the Reins, let us underftand, if it be not as the *Great Light*, that enlightneth every Man that cometh into the World, fince the Scriptures teftify that *God is Light*; that *every Man is enlightned*; that *God fearcheth all Hearts*, and that *whatever doth make manifeft is Light*: Now unlefs a Man may have his Heart fearched, his Reins tryed, his Deeds manifefted and judg'd without an inward Light, it muft neceffarily follow, that *the Light within, prefent with us every where*, is to us the *great Proof of Gods Omniprefence, and therefore of God.* And though every Meafure of Light diftinctly is not that Intire Eternal Being, yet we are bold to affert, that it is no other than God the Fulnefs of all Light, who fearcheth the Heart and tryeth the Reins, and telleth Man his Thoughts, that doth fhine into the Inward Parts of Man, and doth there convince of Sin, reprove for it, and lead out of it, *as believed and obeyed:* And 'tis by this Inward Difcovery chiefly Men come to know that God is, and that he is a Rewarder of them that fear him; whence, when Men are Innocent, it is frequent with them to fay, being unjuftly accufed, *my Heart mifgives me not, my Confcience doth not condemn me, I have good Courage to look my Accufer in the Face*; A State tranfcending the utmoft Stretch of all *T. H*'s imagined Chriftianity.

In fhort *T. Hicks*'s confident Conclufions againft us arife from thefe Miftakes. *Firft*, He infers from Man's being Ignorant of all he ought to know, *the Inability of the Light to inform him,* never confidering Man's Obedience or Religion. 2*ly*, From Chrifts being the Light that enlightens every Man, *every Man's having the whole Chrift in him*; And thirdly from our afferting God and Chrift to be one, *our Denial of Chrifts Outward Perfon and Bodily Appearance* at Jerufalem, fee pag. 3, 4, 5, 6, 7, and 14. of the *Dialog.* and 41. *Contin. of the Dial.* with much more of that fort: Than which, what can be more grofly Injurious to any People. Either let him leave of Writing, or underftand better what he writes againft us. In fhort, we are willing to let the Controverfy lye here; that the *Quakers* own, promote and affert, that *the Life of God which is the Light of Men, with which every Man is enlightned, is fufficient to Everlafting Salvation*; And *Thomas Hicks* afferts and promotes, that this Life of God, which is the Light of Men with which all Men are enlightned, *is not fufficient to Salvation.* I am not willing to break my Defign of following his Charge and Proofs by much controverting the Doctrine in it felf, fince 'tis enough for me to fhew, that the Doctrines and Sayings he faftens upon us, and the Proofs he brings to maintain them, are not ours: yet I am willing to mention one Paffage among feveral others, that if I underftand any Thing, is a grand Contradiction to his Opinion of the Light's Infufficiency.

He quotes *Stephen Crifp* thus, *If the Light ought to be obeyed, then it muft be fufficient.* To which *T. H.* returns this Anfwer. " But I appeal to the Light in " thee, whether this be not an Infufficient Proof. I grant it ought to be obeyed, " fo

" so ought the lawful Commands of Magistrates, Parents and Masters; yet who
" thence infers, that therefore they are a sufficient Rule to Salvation?

Answ. This cuts the Throat of his whole Design, For by the same Reason, that such who obey the lawful Command of Masters, Parents and Magistrates, are to be reputed good Servants, Children and Subjects, those who obey the *Light* are good Subjects, Children and Servants to God; And if those who so keep the Commandments of Parents, Masters and Magistrates, escape Punishment, and obtain their good Will, Favour and Recompence, which is an outward Salvation, then those who obey the *Light* by his Allusion, do obtain Favour, Love and Recompence of the Reward of Righteousness, which Righteousness, that it might be fulfilled in us, so obeying and walking after his Spirit, was the End of God's giving his Son a Light, condemning Sin, and that they that walk thereafter, might not have Condemnation, *minding the Things of the Spirit of God, the Spirit of him that raised Christ from the Dead, the Spirit of Christ, Christ in them, not minding the Things of the Flesh, which* φρόνημα, or *Minding*, as it may be render'd, cannot be subject to the Law of God, but they that are subject and are led by the Spirit of God, they are the Children of God, and Heirs according to the Promise. Most Ungodly then must *T. Hicks*'s Consequences be, that because we say, Christ enlightens every Man, *Saul persecuted the Church, and the* Heathens *multiplied their False Gods by the Light within.* Like unto which is his Arguing, p. 14. where he thus pretends to answer his feigned *Quaker*: *If indeed thou knowest not what I aim at in this Question, then thy Light cannot be God, as thou sayst it is; for God knows the Hearts and Intentions of all Men:* Thereby confounding the Light and Creature together, and concluding Imbecillity, Insufficiency and Ignorance in the Light, which are the Imperfections of the Creature. Was there ever any Thing more Scoffing, Prophane and Dark than this? Might not the *Gentiles* have treated the *Christians* after this Manner, that if they knew not all Things (whether it concerned them to know them, or not) the Christ and Spirit they pretended to be led by, were not God? This is so far from proving the Light not to be God, that admitting of it, it were to prove every Man a God. Is every Master as ignorant as his Scholar, because his Scholar knows not as much as his Master? *T. Hicks* knows not all Truth, nay *T. Hicks* may be led into many Mistakes? *Is his Bible, which he calls his Rule, therefore the Cause?* Certainly by his Way of Arguing against the Light, if he be not Perfect and Infallible, the Scriptures must needs be Insufficient and Errable: But if it be an Evil, to make the Scripture accessory to *T. H*'s Mistakes; of equal Reason it is *Impious* in him *to charge Men's Infirmities upon the Light, and repute that Insufficient, because they are Rebellious.* Education, Prejudice, Interest, Self-Righteousness, Evil Living, bring Vails over the Understanding, that, though the Light shine in Darkness, they comprehend it not.

When *Saul*'s Formality, and Pharisaical Righteousness became shaken by the *Law of Light* in the Conscience, then, and not till then he cries out, *O wretched Man that I am!* Whilst *Saul* gave more heed to his Outward Religion, than the Light in his Conscience, he did Persecute, and thought it a Duty; 'twas when the Light struck him, that he became awakened: But if he persecuted the Church by the Light within, why not by the Spirit too, since God gave the *Jews* his good Spirit? If *T. Hicks* will say, *But he resisted that*; so say I, as to the Light; Formality, Tradition, and many Superstitions (attended with an Ignorant and Harsh Zeal) darkened him, that he could not behold it. But it is a gross Contradiction in *T. H.* to say, *The Light ought to be obeyed*; and yet say, *That it led* Saul *to persecute the* Christians.

And he abuses many of the *Heathen-Philosophers*, as well as the Light, in saying, *That the Light within reproved them not for multiplying their Deities.* For all learned Men must needs know, as I have else-where at large proved, that by the Light within they have decried the *Heathen-Gods*, maintained *the Doctrine of the One only Wise God*, and for their Faith and Perseverance *they have been Taken, Imprisoned, Arraigned, Condemned and Executed*, though it went for Justice upon the Enemies of the Gods. Who knows not this, is a Stranger to Story.

But hear *T. Hicks*, ' *I demand an Instance, among the many Thousands of Mankind,*
' *that hath been convinced, or reproved for not believing* Jesus *to be the Christ by*
' *the meer Light within, before any Revelation was brought unto them; though I*
' *grant that the Light in thee may reprove for those Sins, the Common Light in all*
' *Mankind will not, because thou hast borrowed much Light from the Scriptures, which*
' *all have not.*

Ans.

Anf. I may well suppose, that as many have been reproved for not believing *Jesus to be the Christ,* by the Light within, as by the Scriptures; and my Reasons are; *First,* Because those who crucified him, were Admirers of the Scripture, and pretended to prove out of their own Law, that it was both lawful and necessary he should be put to Death; whereas had they *brought that Deed to the Light,* the Light would have shown it not to have been wrought in God; which the Scriptures without that Light could not so effectually do. 2*ly,* Those who by Scripture came to any Convincement, originally received it from the Revelation of the Light within, which both opened the Scriptures and their Understandings. 3*ly, Peter, Andrew, Matthew, Nathaniel,* the *Centurion, Ruler, Diseased Woman, &c.* confess'd him from the Illumination and Operation of the Light within, since whatever makes Manifest or works Conviction, is Light; They were not Disobeyers and Rebellers against it, who most readily received and followed Christ; They who waited for *Israel*'s Consolation, lived in the Just Man's Path, a *shining Light,* which shined brighter and brighter to the leading such as walked in it, to the great *Light of Israel,* when he appeared.

Farther, To say that *the Light we have, being much of it borrowed from Scripture, Reproves for those Sins, the Common Light in all Men will not,* is great Wickedness; for it is to say, that the Light wherewith Christ hath enlightened all Men, will not Reprove for all Sin; thereby placing the Defect manifestly upon the Light, as before, and not upon the thick and gross Darkness (through Disobedience of the People) as well as that he attributes to the Scripture that Conviction, which is chiefly due to the Light. For by what Way can Mankind arrive at true Sight, Discerning and Knowledge in the Understanding Part, but by the Light, and that as it shines into the Understanding; is it not the Light to which every Deed should be brought, to see if it be wrought in God, or no? What can any Man solidly and beneficially learn by the Scriptures, but through the Discoveries of that Inward Light? Are they not dark Sayings, or rather Man dark to those Sayings, if the Holy Light arise not to shine forth, and give to understand their Scope and Tendency? All Scripture but Prophecy, which was given forth by Inspiration, as *Reproof, Exhortation, Doctrine, &c.* were first experienced or witnessed, (by those at whom *T. Hicks* may equally cavil and Scoff, *(What's your Witnessing to me)* and that through walking in the Light of the Lord, the Just Man's Path; and were written for the sake of others, that they might be assisted and helpt to the same Experience, but not another Way, than through the same Steps they had trodden: So that the Ground of the Holy Ancients Experiences now written, and of the true Knowledge of the Scriptures, and Comfort from them, as an outward *Means,* and *whatever is to be obtained and enjoyned within, is originally and chiefly ascribable to the Discoveries, Convictions and Leadings of the blessed Light of Christ within, through every Generation,* however variously the Principle may have been denominated; as, the *Word of God nigh, Wisdom, Light, Spirit, &c.* under the Old Testament; and *Light, Grace, Truth, Christ, Spirit, Anointing, Gift of God, &c.* under the New Testament.

Two short Scripture Arguments spring in my Mind for the Divinity and Sufficiency of the Light, and then I shall consider his Objections:

I. If *God* be *Divine* and *sufficient to Salvation,* and the *Word* be *God,* and the *Life* of the *Word,* the *Light of Men,* then is the Light of Men *Divine and Sufficient to Salvation.*

But *God* is *Divine,* and *Sufficient to Salvation,* and the *Word* is God, and the *Life* of the *Word, One* with the *Word,* and the *Life* of the *Word,* the *Light of Men.*

Therefore I conclude, that *the Light of Men, which is the Life of the Word, which Word is God, is Divine and Sufficient to Eternal Salvation.*

II. That which was in all Ages the just Man's Path, and there where the Blood of Cleansing is known to cleanse, and by which Fellowship is enjoyed, and the Light of Eternal Life obtained, is, ever was, and ever will be a Divine, Sufficient and Saving Way; But such a Way is the Light as the several Scriptures in the Margin will testifie, *Consequently, the Light is Divine and Sufficient to Salvation.*

The only Cavil at these Arguments will be this; *I deny this Light to be the common Light in all Men.* To which I say, that there cannot be Two Spiritual Lights of the Life of the Word; and not the same, if Two could be; For whatever is of the same Nature, though not of the same Degree, is still the same in Kind. If there be another Light that is Saving, tell us from whence it comes; but first prove

this

this not Saving: And as these Things are too Difficult, I hope, for him to compass, so is it as *Ridiculous* and *Blasphemous* to think, that God should give Man an Insufficient Light. But why any, if not Sufficient?

I have heard and read often, *That all God's Gifts are Perfect.* 'Tis strange, that his Light to Men should be so Lame, Defective and Imperfect, as *T. H.* represents it. But suppose this Light to be so; Why an Insufficient Light, and a Saving Light both? The latter would have done our Business. It is Injurious to Man to let him have a Fallible Guide; For when he may think himself certain, he may be in the greatest Danger by mistaking one for the other; or thinking not of them as they are. But Thanks be to the God of Light, we know (for *We Witness*) better Things, how ill a Reason, and how offensive soever *Witnessing* is to *Thomas Hicks* an *Anabaptist-Teacher*; to whose Brethren *Experiences* once were the great Foundation of both their Knowledge and Comfort, though now mockt at by him with great Derision in a *Quaker*.

But to his Objections faithfully contracted:

1. *If this Light ever was and is Sufficient, how comes it, that Men have been and are so degenerated in Faith, Discipline and Worship? They have all this Light by your Principle.*

2ly, *If this Light had been Sufficient, wherefore should God have superadded so many other Ways and Means; they would be then needless?*

3ly, *Christ being the Only Saviour, who was born of a Virgin at* Bethlehem, *wrought Miracles, was Crucified, bore our Sins, &c. I query, how all this can be affirmed of the Light?*

4ly, *Are not all the Generations of* Christians *since Christ's Time till within these very few Years certainly Lost and Damned, forasmuch as they acknowledg'd not this Light within, as the True Christ?*

To the first I answer, There is nothing therein, which may be thought to reflect upon the Light, but what falls as heavily upon all other *Ways, Helps, Ordinances, Appointments*, yea the *Scriptures*, and which is more, upon *God*, and *Christ*, and the *Holy Spirit too*; For if the Degeneracy of Man, that is the sad Effect of his own Rebellion, shall be a valid Proof of the Insufficiency of the *Light within*, then must we conclude from the Degeneracy, that hath been among *Jews* and *Christians*, and which remains to this Day, *that all those Assistances, Ways and Helps which have been given, in reality were not Potent nor Sufficient to the End for which they were given*; The Consequences of which Opinion of our Adversary's are these Two, and sad enough. 1. That God *in his Ways must have been and is Insufficient*; and 2. That *Man never was, neither is in any wise faulty*. In short, that may be sufficient to Salvation, which if neglected, will never work Salvation, as in the *Parable of the Talents* may be seen.

To the Second I briefly say, That Man's Mind being so much abroad through unstable and vain Wandrings from God's Light, the Lord in Wisdom and Condecension to the Weakness of Man, and Darkness of that Carnal State, did accommodate both his Discoveries to Man, and that Worship he required from Man, according to his Capacity to receive the one, and perform the other. If God went into Outward Things to meet with Man's Mind that was abroad, to the End that gradually it might return Home, *shall we infer Weakness in the Light?* Man in that State was incapable; he must have been new-moulded, and as another Creation, to have then received that Testimony in all it's Plainness, which God hath brought forth in after Ages.

If any will undertake to charge Weakness upon Man, let him; But I warn all, how they conclude it against the Light, since the same falls on God and his good Spirit, who made Use of such Ways and Means in order to gain upon Man's Mind, and beget a right Understanding and Sense of what was his Will concerning him: Besides, not only did the Divine Light and Life appear unto Man in, and through, those Things as Vails; But that which gave Man true Discerning, Repentance, and to do the Thing that ever was acceptable with God in any Measure, and which was as the Soul, Life and Spirit of all the true and well-pleasing Sacrifices, *was a Measure of that Divine Light of Life in their Hearts at that Time*; though as *Samuel* in a like Case, they knew it not. Let none then charge the Weakness of the Administration upon the Light, but the Generation, to whom he that is the Light of and in Men, appeared, as Mankind has been able to receive the Knowledge of him: It was not Insufficiency in God, nor in his Light or Spirit, if Man's Eyes were not strong enough to behold the Brightness of what after Ages have beheld;

beheld; But it was his Mercy and Goodness, that he proportioned both his Discoveries and Requirings according to Man's Ability.

To conclude; The Light is still the same in it self through all Ages, and not a whit the less Sufficient, because through its Invisibility and Spirituality, and the Wandrings Abroad and great Carnality of Man's Mind, some External Means were used, suitable to Man's Weakness, through which to reach into Man, and raise up some farther Knowledge of the Spirituality of God's Worship: Nor because of the Light's Sufficiency as to it self, ought any to infer, that those Ways or Means were vain or needless; For as the Weakness of Men should not call the Ability of the Light in Question, nor their Carnality take off from the Light's Sufficiency, Spirituality or Divinity, so neither doth the Sufficiency of the Light render all Means accommodated to Man's Weakness vain or needless; especially when the Virtue that is in them, comes from the Light of Life.

To his *Third Objection*, which with most Opposers carrieth the greatest Weight, I have this in Plainness and Brevity to answer.

We *own* not, neither do we confess to another *Christ* than him, *who after the Flesh was born of the Virgin* Mary, *at the City of* Bethlehem, *in* Judea, *who preacht an Everlasting Gospel, wrought Miracles, bore our Iniquities, and was cut off, or dyed for the People.* But since *Thomas Hicks* would have us believe, that he is not yet *Socinian* enough to deny the Divinity or Godhead of Christ, and therefore that Christ was not only a Man; much less, that which was born of *Mary*, was crucified, and laid in the Sepulchre of *Joseph* of *Arimathea*, was the whole Christ; I must distinguish.

The *Word* that was with God in the Beginning, and was God, who in Time took Flesh, was and is the Light of the World; in the Fulness of Time he manifested himself in a more familiar and intimate Manner to Mankind, in order to which he prepared an Holy Body, in which he preached his Everlasting Gospel, wrought many Miracles, drew many after him: *He sustained grievous Weights, the Burden of the Iniquity of the whole World lay upon him, he travelled under it, and trod the Wine-Press alone, and was pressed as a Cart with Sheaves*; And so well did he love the World, that, to testify the same, he gave up his Life not only to recommend his Love, but to confirm his unchangeable Gospel of Remission of Sins, and Eternal Salvation to as many as believed, and followed him the Light of the World; that so Remission might not only be preached in his Name, but in his Blood also (for it was a Time of Blotting out; for God was in Christ reconciling the World unto himself.) In which Manifestation, he not only drew many to him, and gave Testimony of his Salvation to some Particulars, but he combated the Serpent, bruised his Head, and gave him an absolute Defeat in the General, scattering his Oracles, chasing his Infernal Spirits, causing his own Light more universally to clear up, and break forth into the World, insomuch that Thousands followed him: He qualified and deputed Ambassadors; Commissioned and impowered them from on high; whose Message was Powerful, and whose Ministry was Effectual; yet when all this is said, and believed most surely, as well as exprest most plainly, That which gave the *Life, Power, Virtue, Strength*, and *Efficacy* to all this, and to whom therefore eminently the *Work, Salvation, Power and Glory are most deservedly ascribable, is the Word that was in the Beginning with God, and was God, whose Life was, and is the Light of Men, who took Flesh, and was manifested therein.* Therefore *He* who is our Light, ought not to be denied, being the true Christ, and true Saviour; For no other Light and Life than appeared in that Body, that was then an Offering for Sin once for all, is the Life and Light that we assert and defend. And for that Holy Body, it was our Lord's, as the Scripture speaks, Joseph of Arimathea *begged the Body of* Jesus, Mat. 27. 58. Mark 15. 43. Luke 23. 52. *They found not the Body of the Lord Jesus*, Luke 24. 3. He prepared it, he took it, he was manifested in it and by it; how can we deny that Body which was our Lord's? By no Means. To conclude, Though the Divine Word of Life and Light died not (for Christ as God over all blessed for ever, could not die) yet his Body did; *and so his Fulness therein and thereby manifested, have we received, and Grace for Grace.* So that all those who are talking of the Body of Christ, and seeking to represent us to the World as Deniers and Despisers of his Appearance, are but in the Steps of the Persecuting Jews, who as they cried up the Prophets, but being Strangers to their Divine Life, relisht not, favour'd not, and therefore yielded not to Christ (the Rock who followed the Fathers in the Wilderness; the

Fountain

Fountain of all the Life and Refreshment of the Holy Ancients) but with their Proud, and Conceited, and indeed Mistaken Knowledge, not from, but of the Letter, and in a bitter Zeal for their Dying Forms and Traditions, did they war against the Breaking forth of that Day of Salvation, and that as *Heresy, Blasphemy*, and the like; so now, these Men seem busy and great Sticklers for the *Body of Christ*, (which they know not) and for *Bread, Wine, Water*, &c. and all in Opposition to a more Plain and Inward Manifestation of the Divine Light, Life and Substance shed abroad, as the Accomplishment of the Promise of the Father in this our Day and Generation. But as it fared with those of old, so shall it with these Opposers, their Visitation shall pass swiftly over their Heads, and their Temple shall be cast down, and not one Stone of their fair Edifice shall be left standing upon another.

To his *Last Objection* I must tell him, that we have not that Uncharitableness in our Principles, which our *Adversaries* are guilty of. He, like the Jews of old, is ready to think every Man damn'd, nay, by his Principle, it is not avoidable, who hath not heard of the Name *Christ*, or is not entred into some kind of Church-Fellowship upon common *Christian* Confessions, as they are called, and distinguished from meer Morality or Good Life: But for my Part, as God had a People among the *Gentiles* of old, *who became a Law unto themselves, doing the Things contained in the Law*, whom I believe to be at Rest and Peace (notwithstanding the severe and positive Censures I have heard from several Professors against them, and Millions more) so, though much Darkness hath prevailed in most Parts of the World, and still continueth, yet then, and where the Day of Ignorance remains, and where there hath been and is a Walking with Sincerity towards God, according to their Knowledge, I do believe the Lord did and doth wink, and had and hath Mercy on men, though great Strangers to that *Christian Profession* so much *boasted* of among too many in our Nation: And I doubt not, but that there may be found some Thousands both of *Turks* and *Indians*, who would not only have detested, in Point of Credit, but in Fear to God dreaded, doing a Tittle of what *Tho. Hicks* hath falsly and impudently said and done against our *Persons, Practices and Principles*.

In short, though God in every Age hath had a Regard to the Sincerity of People's Hearts, and their Upright Living, though subjected under gross Forms, and in the darkest Seasons of the World; yet, *God having now caused his Day-spring from on high to visit, whereby more certain Knowledge and sound Judgment is given of the Darkness that hath covered the Earth, the Superstition, Idolatries, human Inventions, Will-Worships, Violence, Cruelty, Wantonness, Intemperance, Avarice, and all Manner of Ungodliness*; all are required to hearken to the Lord's Voice, *to obey his Call, to let him in, and bring their Deeds unto the Light, that Christ, who is that true Light, may discover the Enemy, may bind him, spoil his Goods, and cast him out; that he may reign over Thoughts, Words and Deeds*; so shall such be able to say as *David* did, *O, all that is within me, praise his Holy Name!* For Christ will be known, as he is the Saviour of the Soul from Death, the Restorer of Paths to dwell in, who destroys the Works of the Devil, and brings in Everlasting Righteousness to the Soul. And though few observe it, That which is truly commendable in any People proceeds from the secret Power and Efficacy of that Inward Principle we so much testify of: *'Tis that convinces, discovers, reproves, restrains, tenders, humbles and affects the Soul*, and not their several *Outward Forms*, which, with Robbery to the Light or Grace within, they are apt to attribute it to, and whereby the Devil beguiles them into a Continuance of them. Wherefore let all our Opposers be dehorted from their vehement out-cries; for who withstand, revile, and set at nought this Blessed Appearance, God, the Lord of Heaven and Earth, will break them to Pieces, if they come not to timely Repentance for it.

CHAP. IV.

Of the True Evangelical RULE.

AND this for ever rases the Foundation of *T. H's* Building; as indeed *how can any thing so infirm long continue, built upon Forgery, and the Heighth of all Partiality*: who makes us *Hereticks*, that he may be found; and abusive, that he may either shew his own Patience, or colour his frequent base Revilings of us: I say this overthrows his whole Discourse about the Scriptures being the Rule of Faith and Practice under the New Covenant. For, whatever is *more Ancient,*

more

more Universal, and Able to Inform, Rule and Guide, that must eminently be the Rule; but that has been, and *is, the Light within:* consequently that has been, and ought to be *the Rule of Faith and Practice.* That it has been and ought still to be the Rule exprest, is proveable thus:

That which led those Holy Men into those Things, of which the Scripture is a Declaration, must needs have been the Rule; But that was the Principle of God within, by what Name soever denominated. That this is true, let it suffice to say, That who walked in the Light in any Age, so far walked in the Counsel of God. And that all Mankind had an Ability from God so to do, is our Belief, what Abridgment soever *T. Hicks*'s detestable Opinion of Reprobation may make of the Love of God.

That it ought still to continue *to be the Rule of Faith and Life,* I prove thus: That which is every where, which makes manifest that which is displeasing, and that which is acceptable to God, without which the Scriptures are unintelligible, and by living up to which, Men only may come to witness the Truth of those Things declared of in the Scriptures, must be, and ought to be the Rule of Faith, *&c.* But all this is true of the Light; which is farther proved thus:

The Light *Thomas Hicks* acknowledges all Men have. The Light *Thomas Hicks* acknowledges all Men ought to attend unto: (p. 7.) Now, unless some Man, who hath lived unblameably up to the Light, can give us a Demonstration of it's Insufficiency to shew, and teach him, that farther Thing, that God requires him to believe and do, there can be no valid *Argument* against the Light's Sufficiency. If *T. H.* dare be the Man, we shall join Issue with him in the Trial of the Matter: But if the Light be before-hand with Mankind, furnishing him still with Work enough to do, as it certainly ever hath done, and still doth, let it be known to *T. H. that such as would know more of Christ's Doctrines, must first do his Will according to what they do know;* And as it is the common *Method* of the Dealing of God towards the Sons of Men; So is it great Impiety in any Man to infer or conclude *Insufficiency to be in the Light to discover and teach Man what he ought to know and do, from Man's Ignorance of all that he ought to know and do;* since the Ground of that Ignorance is, his not doing, what the Light of God requires from him, as his present Duty to perform.

That *the Scriptures are Unintelligible without it,* is easily prov'd from the Variety of Judgments that are in the World about most of the Fundamental Doctrines contained therein; as about *God's Essence and Similitude, Christ and the Spirit,* their *Divinity, Predestination, Original Sin, Free-Will, Redemption, Satisfaction, Justification, Faith and Works. In short,* the *whole End of Christ's Coming, Living and Dying,* are strongly controverted: Now were the Scriptures so clearly capable to determine in these Matters, the Differences would quickly end; But since the utmost Ability they of themselves can give, is not enough to render those Things obvious, that are now doubtful and disputable; There is a Necessity of Man's Recourse to some other Thing, which is able to discover the Mind and Intention of the Holy Pen-Men. Now I would be glad to know of any sober Man, if any thing besides the Light shining into the Understanding is able to give true Sight, Discerning and Judgment, about the Points controverted? Would it not be reputed Madness to bid Men read, *that have no Eyes, or if they have Eyes, at least no Light to read?* The whole Scripture, as it relates to Man's Duty, is a Declaration of the woful State of Darkness, and the blessed State of Light and Life, with the Way of Translation out of the one into the other. And was this Knowledge *without* Experience, or *by and through* Experience? I hope no Man will say, the Holy Pen-Men were not Witnesses of the Things they wrote; and if they were, I would fain know, by what other Way they came to understand and comprehend the Darkness that was within, *than by the Light within;* And to know the Temptations and Subtleties of the Spirit of Darkness, the Discoveries, Reproofs and Leadings of the Light, the Tryals, Travels, Exercises, and finally the perfect Translation so frequently expressed in these Holy Writings, *but through the Manifestation of the Light of Christ in the Conscience, their Obedience to it, and it's Operation to their Redemption and Sanctification.* So that the State of *Judgment, Repentance, Remission, Regeneration,* called the New-Birth, and perfect *Justification,* were their Experiences (or Witnessings, for all *T. Hicks*) from the Inward Work of God's Light upon their Hearts and their Souls, which though the Scriptures declare of, they can never bring Man into, nor can any Man groundedly aver the Truth of those Things, 'till he comes through Obedience to the Light

Light in his own Conscience to experience the same *Judgment, Repentance, Remission, Regeneration*, called the New Birth, and perfect Justification before God; Since then the Scriptures can do none of these Things of themselves, however Instrumental they may be of Good, but the Holy Light in the Conscience, and that these Things are not knowable, though they may be read, talked and writ of, without being led by the same Spirit, and treading the same Steps of deep Experience the Holy Ancients trod in, and have left us for an Example, it must be granted, whether *T. Hicks* will or no, *That the Author of those Discoveries, Convictions, Judgments,* &c. *must be the Standing Immutable Rule to the Soul, what, how far, and which Way we are to deny or own, reject or embrace, relinquish or follow, with Respect to those Things that please God, or that please him not.*

His Objections I shall contract into these Four, urged by him for the *Scriptures*, and against the *Light's being the Rule of Faith and Practice*; and indeed they are the greatest Strength of his Book, if any it has.

First, *The Light Within cannot give a clear and distinct Account how Sin came to be*; *if we consult the* Wisest Philosophers, *we shall find a deep Silence touching this Point: They saw Sin did overflow, but could not by all the Improvements of the Light in them, find how Sin came to be.*

_{Dial. pag. 21, 22, 23.}

I am perswaded *T. Hicks* never consulted so much as the meanest of them, at least effectually; had he, *His Dialogue* would have favoured of more True Science and Morality; for I will make it appear that he has contradicted himself, abused the Philosophers, and blasphemed the Light in this one Passage.

Where there is no Law there is no Transgression; then where there is Trangression there is a Law. Now *T. Hicks* granting that the *Heathen* knew there was Sin, they must know it by Virtue of some Law that made it so. This Law was not written, but themselves declared, God had imprinted it upon their Hearts, as an Immutable and Infallible Guide to them in their Actions. If so, how could they be ignorant of Sin's coming into the World, who knew it to be a Deviation from God's Living Commandment in their own Conscience, and a committing quite contrary Things? If *T. Hicks* means, by clear and distinct Account, the History of *Moses*; that is, that *Adam* and *Eve* were beguiled by the *Serpent*, who tempted them with an *Apple*, &c. 'tis no Ways to his Purpose; For that which is sufficient to that Faith which concerns Salvation, is, to know that God is, that He is Pure and Holy, that He has given Man the Knowledge of himself, and His Will concerning Him, by some *Inward Law, Command, Light, Grace, or Spirit*; *and that who acts not correspondently to this Guide, is a Transgressor, and incurs the Penalty*; *and that the* Heathen *had this, their Books at large tell us:* Nor does *T. Hicks* deny it, so that he manifestly contradicts himself, and abuseth the *Philosophers*, in saying, They could not find out, how Sin came, since they expresly say, That God made all Good, and that Man's Erring from the Divine Law in him, brought Evil into the World. And I boldly affirm, and in the next Head will prove, that the meer History is not absolutely necessary to Salvation.

_{Pythag. Socrat. Cleant &c.}

Now that herein he has Blasphemed against the Light, is evident; since it is to say, That God gave Men a Law and Light not sufficient to let them see, how Sin entred the World; which is to say in plainer *English*, What is Sin; it will and must end there. Besides, suppose the *Philosophers* had been ignorant, must it needs follow, that the Fault and Want was in the Light, and not in them? Will *T. Hicks* become their Warrant in the Matter, *That they arrived as high as the Light could teach them, and that the Deficiency lay on the Side of the Teacher, and not on theirs?* Confident, yea, Impudent Man! Why should either the Darkness of any Age be charged upon the Light, or render it Insufficient; or the more clear Breaking forth of Light in a following Generation, be reputed another Light, because another Degree than what obscurely shined forth in the former; since it was not the obscurer in it self, but through the gross Blackness that might have over-cast that People because of Disobedience, it seemed so to them? But let us hear him farther.

2. *Nor can this* Light *give any Account of that Remedy which God in His Infinite Wisdom provided,* JESUS CHRIST, *that He should be Born of a Virgin, Dye for others, and Rise the Third Day:* This is the Pinch.

_{Dial. p. 33.}

But I answer, *First,* That the Prophets saw it by this Light, unless that they saw it without Light, or that the Light they saw it by, was not the Light of Christ, *as the Word that was with God, and was God*; which, I hope, *T. Hicks* upon serious Thinking, will not say; for of no other do we speak. *Secondly*, Those that believed Him, when he came, could never have received him, had they not seen

seen him by an *Inward Eye*, enlightned by that Light in Measure in themselves, which then so unmeasurably appeared in Him; For the *Jews* had the Scriptures, and according to their Understanding of them, they reputed him a *Blasphemer*; and both plotted, promoted, and obtained his Crucifixion. The *Question* will be, *Why did they not better understand them?* The *Answer* is, because they Rebelled against that Spirit which could only so inform them: *Had they brought their Deeds to the Light, they had received Sound Judgment, and a True Measure would have been given them, which they rejecting, that was both the Ground of their Ignorance, and the Just Reason of their Condemnation.* Hence we see, that Light, and not the Scriptures, was the higher Rule and Judge of Thoughts, Words and Deeds, yea, and which Way the Scriptures themselves were to be understood; And truly it is strange, that the *Light in Men* should not lead naturally to it's own Being and Fountain. 'Tis Proverbial among Men, *The Way to the Fountain-Head is to trace the Stream.* If the *Light in Man* leads not to *Christ, who gives that Light*, let us leave off all Talk of Religion; for to what, or whom else was it given to lead us?

But says *Tho. Hicks*, tell me, *Who, or what was Christ in that Manifestation it self, but that Divine Word, Life, or Light manifested in Flesh?* Will not then a Measure of the same in Man, lead him of Course to acknowledge the Fulness, or in following it's Leadings, bring to Eternal Salvation; Or can that Light resist that Manifestation, as thou dost elsewhere seem to affirm?

Dial. p. 38. 42. — *If Christ has enlightned Men with the Light of his own Life, and if they are required to bring their Deeds to be tryed by it, and if they are invited to follow it, and in following it, are promised, no more to abide in Darkness, but have the Light of Life, because of the Blood of Cleansing, that is therein met with, whereby such are cleansed from all Unrighteousness, and yet the Light neither a Rule nor Saving, then what else can be either a Rule or Saving?*

But this Light (says he) *could not tell any that* JESUS *should be Born of a Virgin, Dye for Sinners, and Rise again.* But this is so great a Mistake, that had he conversed with the *Sibylls*, or other *Heathen Writers*, he might in good Part have informed himself to the contrary. But here I distinguish of *Faith*, There is an *Historical and Saving Faith*, and there is an *Historical and Saving Rule*, as the Faiths, so the Rules differ. If *T. Hicks* says, *That 'tis the Scriptures that give the Knowledge of those Transactions*, I must then understand him to mean *Historically*, if I assent, *which is not Saving*; for then all who believe those Things to have been *must therefore be saved*; the contrary to which is daily seen with our Eyes; since who believes not that Report among those who are yet in great Wickedness? But if we are to penetrate deeper, and that *T. Hicks* should hold as he seems plainly to do, that what Faith we can have of the most weighty Truths declared of in the Scripture, is from it, and not from the *Light or Spirit within*, I must firmly deny it; For *Faith is God's Gift*, not the Scripture's Gift: No, so far are the Scriptures from giving Faith, *that it is God's Spirit alone, that gives both to understand and believe them.* The Scripture tells me of such *Prophecies, Histories*, and *Epistles*, and of such Men as *Moses, Job, David, Isaiah, Matthew, Paul* and *John*; But what is it that gives me to believe the Things they writ of to be True? Is it not the Testimony and most certain *Amen* in the Conscience? And what is that there, which Seals to those excellent Truths? Which Way then can the Scripture be a Rule to me, in believing the Scripture, when that Faith is begotten of God, by his Light and Spirit concerning the Scripture? If the meer Scripture could give me Faith, then it might be allowed to Rule my Faith; but when God by his Spirit alone begets Faith, without which I can neither understand nor believe the Scriptures, tell me, *If God's Spirit be not the Rule of my Faith; what, how far and which Way I am to believe them, or the Things believed?* Certainly they can never be my Rule, *How far, and which Way I am to believe themselves*, who of themselves cannot give me that Faith; but it must be wrought by another Thing; *so that what gives to believe, rules the Belief, and not the Thing believed:* Therefore the Scriptures cannot be the Rule of Faith.

Now as to this *of Christ's Outward Manifestation*, I say, so far as it is Historical, the Scripture is that which furnisheth me with a Belief; But I utterly deny, that they give to believe it in that deep Sense, *which may be truly called a Saving Faith.*

The *Pharisees* had the Scriptures, and they pretended to admire *Moses and the Prophets*; yet they *Crucified Christ*, and sought to countenance their Murder by Scripture. Now had they believed and esteemed the Writings of *Moses* and the *Prophets* from an Inward Sense of God's Spirit *(which the meer Scriptures could not*

not furnish them with) they had rightly understood them, and not made so ill an Use of their Historical Knowledge, as to *Crucifie the Lord of Life and Glory*. This shews that Men may have an Historical Faith, and yet not the *True Faith nor Knowledge of the Scriptures*, What then gives to believe aright now? Why truly that which did then, *the Light and Spirit of Truth*; no Man could call *JESUS* Lord without it, that is, truly so, or upon Good Ground. No Man could confess that Christ was come in the Flesh, *but whose Spirit was of God*, yet now nothing is more common, and yet nothing is more True, than that Thousands of them are not of God, but lye in Wickedness, alienated from the Life of God, *&c*. *What is the Matter then?* Why this, Those who then confest that *JESUS* was come in the Flesh, did it by Virtue of an Invisible Sight, and through a Divine Illumination in their Souls: For impossible had it otherwise been for them in any Measure to have seen through the Vail of his Flesh, *into that Divine Life, Power and Wisdom that unmeasurably filled it*, but having some inward Sense and Taste of that most Excellent Being, that was manifested in, and by that *Bodily Appearance*, therefore did they confess to it, and their Spirits were truly reputed by *John* to be of God.

And as in that Day it was impossible for any truly and acceptably to confess to Christ, without a Discerning given, and Faith wrought by the Light and Spirit of God in the Heart, *which was the Saving Faith*; so is it now equally impossible for any to believe that Christ appeared, and that he spake and did all these great Things, so as to be benefitted thereby, and any Ways accepted of God therein, but as the Light and Spirit of Truth open those Things to the Understanding, and from a Measure of that Divine Life which then immeasurably appeared (for we have all received of his Fulness and Grace for Grace) True Faith comes to be begotten in that Manifestation, and a Right Confession unto it. In short, *He that calleth Christ Lord*, must now, as then, do it by the Holy Ghost, that is, *from an Experience or Witnessing of his Dominion, and Rule*, which, through the Operation of the Holy Spirit, the Soul is to be subjected to; so that whoso believes more than Historically that Christ came in the Flesh, must do it by *Virtue of the Divine Light and Spirit*, which alone gives to relish and favour the Truth, Nature and End, of that Appearance.

And though it may be allowed, that the Scripture is a Rule, respecting the History, as it was to those of Old, in Reference to the particular Prophesies fulfilled in Christ's Coming; yet as there was then a more Inward and Heavenly Sense of Christ, which drew many after him, and begot deep Faith in him, so must there now be a more Inward, Spiritual, and deep grounded Faith of those Things recorded in Scripture, *of Christ's Appearance*, &c. *than the meer Letter is able to give*. And therefore that Light and Spirit which gives that discerning, and works that deep Sense and Faith, must needs be as well the Rule as the Author of it, and not the Scriptures; For if the Scriptures be the Rule, then either of Themselves or by Interpretation. *If of themselves*, then either in their Translations, or Originals. Not *in the Translations*, unless the *Translators* had been so Inspired, that they mist not a Tittle, which I am sure is not so; and consequently none but Scholars have a Rule, for the Unlearned are secluded; *and therefore the* English *Bible is not a Rule*.

If in the *Originals* of *Hebrew* and *Greek*, Query, In what Copies? There are various Lections in *Hebrew*: And for the New Testament, so called, there are no less than Thirty Copies, and all differing; *in fine*, there are many Thousands of various Readings.

Now let's Dialogue a little upon Supposition only.

Quaker. If by *Interpretation*, Who shall Interpret? Meer Man?
Anabaptist. *No.*
Q. The Light Within?
A. No.
Q. The Spirit?
A. No.
Q. The Church?
A. What Church?
Q. Shall Right Reason interpret?
A. Yes, says *T H.*
Q. I Query, *Which of them is the Rule?* And when that's found out and determined, then let *T. Hicks* prove that it is unquestionably True, and has remained
uncor-

uncorrupted through every Generation: And by that Time he has done all this, he shall have done a great Deal towards our Satisfaction. *But what is this Right Reason?*

A. *'Tis a Faculty in Man rectified.*
Q. Very well: *But who has this rectified Faculty?*
A. Thomas Hicks, *say.*
Q. Has none it but He?
A. *Yes.*
Q. Have none Right Reason but such?
A. *It was an Old Saying, Dip or Damn; but Interest has taught us more Discretion.*
Q. Well then; Others may have Right Reason that are not Dipped?
A. *We say so, whatever we think among our selves.*
Q. What's the peculiar Benefit of Dipping?
A. *Much every Way.*
Q. But which Way?
A. *We are brought into Church-Fellowship.*
Q. Are you brought into Fellowship with God by it?
A. *No; I cannot say so.*
Q. No! What's your Fellowship worth then? The Saints Fellowship was in the Light, and the True Church-Fellowship was in Spirit: What do you receive when you are Dipt?
A. *Nothing.*
Q. Are you no Better?
A. *No.*
Q. Why, I once thought you received the Holy Ghost out of Hand?
A. *I thought so too, but was mistaken.*
Q. Why wast thou Dipt then?
A. *To fulfil the Scripture.*
Q. But what led thee to it?
A. *My own Desire.*
Q. Is not that Will-Worship?
A. *What, to do as the Scripture exhorts?*
Q. How knowest thou it exhorted to it?
A. *I thought so.*
Q. Is that enough? Where's your being led by God's Spirit? But to our Business.
Q. How shall I know *Thomas Hicks* has this Reason before-mention'd?
A. *He loftily says so.*
Q. But is that sufficient? Well, but where is this Right Reason?
A. *In Men.*
Q. Is it so? Then it seems that which gives the True Knowledge of the Scripture, *is in Man.* But tell me honestly, Do ye believe this Right Reason may Err?
A. *No; For then it were not Right Reason, if it could be Wrong.*
Q. Well argued. But if a Man Errs, is it not the Fault of Right Reason?
A. *By no means.*
Q. Thou speakest honestly. But why then does *T. Hicks* charge the Light, the *Quakers* profess, with every short-sighted imperfect Saying or Action of this or any other Generation.
A. *Does he?*
Q. Yes; it is the great Drift of his Books.
A. *Truly that's not fair.*
Q. Honestly said. But if this Right Reason cannot Err, then cannot Man Err?
A. *No, that does not follow; for Man may not submit to it.*
Q. Why, may Man have something in him that cannot Err, and he not be Unerrable?
A. *Yes.*
Q. Rightly said. But why then does *T. Hicks* conclude so of us?
A. *It is unfairly done.*
Q. Very well. But you say, that this Right Reason is Part of Man's Soul, or I am mistaken; see *Dial.* pag. 32. If so, then Man's Soul must be Infallible?
A. *O, Infallible; that Word affrights us. What, Infallible? Pray what's Infallible?*
Q. Poor Man! I see it scares thee indeed. Why, Unerrable and Infallible are all one. Yea, Right Reason is Infallible by the same Reason, that it cannot be Wrong.

A. *But*

A. *But the* Popes *talk of being Infallible; are not you like them?*

Q. Never the more like them for that; Talking, and being so, are Two Things. Men should not deny the *True Christ* because of an Impostor; nor any fear Infallibility, because the Pope makes Market with such Pretences. If thou art not certain of what thou believest, thou hast not that Faith which was once delivered to the Saints; for that was Certain, and therefore Infallible.

A. *Why; Is Certain and Infallible all one?*

Q. Yes; Certainty and Infallibility is the same. But what think'st thou of the Light in this Case under Debate? For either it is the Rule, or it is given to understand and use the Rule, or else it's given for nothing?

A. *'Tis not the Rule we are taught to say; and yet we cannot conclude it to be given for nothing.*

Q. Very well; then it must be given in order to understand and use the Rule. Now supposing the Scriptures be the Rule, that which informs me of my Rule, and teaches me how to use it, must be greater than my Rule, *in that it teaches me to know and do that my Rule cannot do of it self:* I query then, *If this Light be not my Rule, how and which Way I come to understand and use this Rule.* So that it is eminently the Rule because of it's Present, Immediate and Certain Direction and Knowledge, and the *Scripture at most but a Kind of Declaratory and Secondary Rule,* and therefore subject to the Holy Spirit in the Apostles and Primitive Christians, who took not Measures by it, when it distinguish'd the Ceremonial from the Moral Precepts, so intermixed in the 19th of *Leviticus,* and other Places; but their Minds being exercised and guided by that Holy Living Rule, they left off, or continued for a Time several *Jewish Observations,* as there might be a Service therein signified to them from that Living Rule. *The Light and Spirit of God then is both* THE *Rule of Faith and Guide of Life, Superior to the Scriptures, and That by which only they can be rightly known, believed and fulfilled.* A Doctrine Evangelical, and not disowned by those first *Protestants,* who testified that no Man could understand the Scriptures given forth by Inspiration, *but by a Measure of the same Spirit.* To conclude, *Historical Faith Scripture is a Rule of, but Doctrinal and Saving Faith, the Light and Spirit of God, can only be the Rule of;* for that which giveth Faith, is only that which rules Faith.

3. But (says he) *how could you have known, that Swearing in any Case were Unlawful, if it had not been written,* Swear not at all; *Is not then that Scripture your Rule in this Case?* — Dial. p. 22.

But this shews both the Ignorance of T. *Hicks* in the Writings of the best *Gentiles,* and his Acknowledgment of the Light's Sufficiency, in Case we are able to prove *Swearing* disallowed and dispractised before Christ's coming in the Flesh.

The *Seven Wise Men* famous among the *Greeks,* and Contemporaries above Five Hundred Years before Christ came in the Flesh, esteemed *Swearing* but a Remedy against Corruption, in Evidence: To be sure, they both believ'd and exhorted People to that State which needed it not. — Stob. 28.

Socrates plainly says, *That there is a Life more Firm, and Unquestionable than an Oath:* Consequently Swearing not the best State. — Id. 114.

And *Xenocrates* was had in that Veneration in *Athens,* for his exceeding Virtue, that the Magistrates thought it a questioning of his Honesty to offer him any Oath, and therefore refused, implying, that Oaths were not made for the *Best of Men,* and that there is a State attainable, which is more Excellent than that in which Oaths are used. — Val. Max. 2. 10. Cic. pro Bal. Laert.

And thus was that Evangelical Precept, *Swear not at all,* arrived at, preferred, and honour'd by profest *Gentiles,* about Five Hundred Years before it was uttered by our Lord JESUS CHRIST; therefore the Light, from T. H's Objection answered, is proved sufficient.

4. *But here is an utter Insufficiency* (if we will believe him) *in this meer Light Within to direct us the Right Way of Worshipping God:* This, says he, *is manifest from the great Loss the Wisest among the Heathen have been, and are at, about this very Thing, the multiplying their Deities, Worshipping Devils,* &c. — Dial. pag. 35, 36.

He is an incompetent Witness against the Light's Sufficiency, that has never tryed the Extent of it's Ability by a Life conform'd to what it leads to: If T. *Hicks* walk'd without all Reproof, it were something; but for a Man to talk of it's Insufficiency, whilst it shews that which he is not come up to, as well as that it condemns for Daily Failings, is Arrogancy with a Witness.

1673.
Chap. IV

But why is it *Insufficient to direct him the Right Way of Worship*. Because *T Hicks* has not found it; Is it a good Argument against the Scripture, that because those who pretend to Square their Faith by it, manifestly Err, therefore it is Insufoficient to direct them Right? *Thomas Hicks* will never allow this against the *Scriptures*, and yet he calls us Names for not tacitly suffering his base Abuses against the *Lord's Light*, Rom. 1. 19, 20. What if any of the Heathen *became Vain in their Imaginations, who when they knew God, Worshipped Him not as God*, will it follow, that God's *Manifestation of himself* (as the Apostle plainly speaks) *in Man, was an Insufficient Manifestation?* The Jews *turned Idolaters, they Worshipp'd a Calf, and offer'd their Children to* Moloch, (Devotion made up of Murder and Idolatry) *was God's Light, Law, or Good Spirit, and the whole Series of Love and Mercy shown unto them, Insufficient, because of their Rebellion?* I affirm that *Thomas Hicks*, by this Argument, is the horrid'st Blasphemer that ever lived among Men: *For if the False Deities of the* Heathen, *and their Worshipping of Devils, with the horrid Idolatries of the* Jews, *were not the Effects of their own Erring from a Sufficient Light or Manifestation, to have better informed and directed them, but through the Insufficiency of the Light to discover the* True God, *and how to Worship Him,* T. H. *has evidently laid the Charge at God's Door*; for he could not Reap where he had not Sown: And thus far doth he render the Almighty accessory to those Impieties, *That He gave not Man a Sufficiency of Light to inform him better, that he might have escaped so gross Abomination*; which ends in that detestable Doctrine *of Eternal, Unconditional Reprobation*; *an Off-spring of Satan, a Murderer from the Beginning*.

In short, Christ is the Light of Men: The Way of the Just is a shining Light: He that is the Way, Truth and Life, is the Light; Therefore those who Worship God according to the Light, Worship him in the Spirit and in the Truth, and walk in the Just Man's Path: For that Men should walk up to the Light of Christ, *and yet be Ignorant of the Right Way of Worship, is gross Ignorance and Darkness*. For *Tho. Hicks* then to say, that God doth make more known, than is, *or can be known by the Light*, is false and contradictory; For unless there be two Distinct Divine Lights by Nature (which is an absurd Thing, so much as to conceive) or that God can manifest any Thing without Light, it will follow, *that both the Light is One, and that it is that One Light, whereby God hath revealed himself through all Ages*: And here I would be well understood; for I know one Age hath been attended with larger Discoveries, yet this argues no Deficiency to have been in the former Manifestation, though it implies Weakness in the People that they could not receive the same Light in a greater. The Light is therefore One in it self, however variously it may break forth in any Age and Generation; I know it hath arisen higher and higher; the Difference is in Degrees, not in Nature; and so *T. H.* in great Contradiction to himself acknowledges, *Dial.* p. 36. What hath been the Duty of every Age, it hath shewn, and the best Reason and Rule for the Obedience to any Thing superadded *hath been the Convictions and Leadings of the Light, according to that Manifestation, it gave before*; Those that went from the Light, and sat down, grew Rich in literal Knowledge, were the Opposers of the more glorious Breaking forth of Light, and not those who kept close to what was revealed. So 'tis at this Day; *Such as have kept to the Tendering Grace and Spirit among Professors, such are most moderate to us, and inclin'd after us*; The Hard, Dry and Cavilling amongst them, *as they are strongest in their Combatings, like the Pharisees of old, so are they most darkned from the Light, and most of all despise the Testimony of it, and set at nought and oppose, as to the Death, all those who are become Witnesses of the fresh Resurrection of Light and Life* (If I may so speak) *in the Hearts of People*. I know not what better to call them, than *Thieves* and *Robbers*, spoken of by Christ, who have gone aside from the tender Spirit of *Jesus Christ*, that in Days past strove with them, and with whose secret Voice they were in some measure affected, and have set up themselves in a Form, without Power, *Praying, Preaching, Dipping and all other Acts of Worship, Ordinances, &c.* without the Leadings of God's Spirit: Wherefore, said Christ, of the like People, *All that came before me are Thieves and Robbers, they climb over the Wall, they come not in at the Door*; which Door is that State of Witnessing, at which that light and frothy Prophanist, *T. H.* bestows so many foul Reflections; forgetting how much of the ancient *Puritan, Brownist* and *Baptist* Religion was made up of Experiences, which, with Men that understand Words, hath the same Signification, as well as that *Witnessing* is more Scriptural. And indeed, I wonder not at all at it; for where Men that have had some Inward Sense of Life Eternal,

give

give not way to the more full Breakings forth of the same, but run into Forms, and take up their Rest by the Way, and so come to withstand it, they lose what they had, and center, where those be who at first oppos'd them, emptying from one to the other till they arrive at *Rome* again, that so the Battel may be of *Michael* and the Devil, the *True Church* against *the False*, Power and Form of Godliness against Form without *Power, and the Traditions, Superstitions and Inventions of Men*; by which they have endeavoured to make void God's Law: For whoever have lost their Inward Sense of God, and withstand the Propagation of that Inward Religion, however their Form may be more Scriptural, the same Spirit enters them that reigned in their old Persecutors, and they at last run back, and end in that, from whence they at first reformed. So dangerous it is to rest satisfied with a finer Form, which in Truth is but a better Covering for the old Enemy of God's Spirit and Power to act more disguisedly and securely in.

But lest any should think that all this is said to justle the Scriptures out of all Use and Service, read these few lines following with Patience and Impartiality. Though we eminently account the Light or Spirit of Christ to be the Gospel, Living and Immediate Rule (as the great Promise of the Father (and that without being ruled and led or guided by it, there is no being a Child of God) yet we do not thereby intend an Exclusion of the Scriptures from being Obligatory, or as not Declaratory of those Heavenly Blessed Truths, that are fit to be read, believed and practised; God forbid, No, we know better and practise otherwise, and have good Satisfaction therein. Nor do we say that those essential Things relating to Faith and Godliness mentioned therein are by us to be slighted or contradicted; *or that the Light and Spirit we are led by, doth or can lead to any such Thing; for by it's Holy Discoveries and Convictions are we made acquainted with them*; and our *Faith concerning them is firm, and they are thereby made our Duty, and such is their Correspondence and Agreement, that from an* Inward Assent and Living Amen, from God's Light in our Consciences *do we testifie of their Truth, Use and Dignity*. And very vain is *T. Hicks*'s Objection, If your Light be Sufficient, why do you read them? since we may return to him the same; If the Scriptures be Sufficient, *why dost thou use other Means?* Though God's Grace be Sufficient of it self, therefore is the Creature always in that Condition, wherein he needs not Means? And notwithstanding it be the Dispensation of *Light and Life*, more Immediately than has been known to former Ages, yet we deny not the use of such Means, as may be used of God's Light and Spirit, as will be spoken more largely to elsewhere. Man's Mind being Carnal and abroad, Means in God's Power are us'd not as settl'd Teachers, but as Instrumental in God's Hand to testifie of and direct to that one *Great Prophet and Living Teacher* in the Hearts of Men, that all may come thither and be taught of him.

CHAP. V. *Of his Insinuations against us concerning the* Scriptures.

BUT *T. H.* that he may be true to his Ungodly Way of perverting our Principles, would insinuate, First, ' *That we esteem the Scriptures no farther, than as they were the Experiences of Ancient Saints, thereby rendring the many Prophesies and Promises therein recorded, not yet fulfilled, Unprofitable*. But to take off all Credit to this evil Suggestion, let our sober Readers know, that *by the Light of Christ in our own Hearts and Consciences, as to confirm what of the Scriptures we have experienced, and press after the Compleating of those Enjoyments therein expressed; so are we taught reverently to believe those Holy Prophecies and Promises yet unaccomplished to have been given forth by the Inspiration of the Almighty; and that they shall be as certainly fulfilled, as they are written*. Yet we dare boldly affirm, and that in the Name of the Lord (before whom we shall give an Account for every Deed done in the Body) *that the greatest Reason of our Belief concerning them, is not from any Outward Thing, but that Inward Testimony, Record and Heavenly Amen,* that we have frequently received from the Holy Light within us, to the Truth and Faithfulness of those Sayings. And if any *Quakers* there be that are not thus minded, they are to me unknown, and I publickly renounce, and protest against that Principle that would in the least derogate from those Holy Writings; which leads me to his Second Insinuation, viz. *As if because we do deny the Scriptures to be the Rule of Faith and Practice, in Honour to that Divine Light, which was the Author of them in the Holy Pen-men*, " *that we should therefore eny* " *all those Holy Precepts, Commandments and Rules relating to Life and Godliness,*
" *that*

"*that are therein contained:* A Consequence so foul, that God forbid any of us should ever give any Just Occasion for it; For we both believe Men ought to live up to them, and that they are highly Reproveable if they transgress against them. But the Reason why, is that Conviction they meet with from the Light in their own Consciences; wherefore the Scriptures are so far from being the great Rule of Faith and Practice, *that the Light of Christ within is both our Warrant and Rule for Faith in, and Obedience to them.* And let *T. H.* say if he can, that the *Waldenses, Albigenses, Lollards, Hussites, Lutherans, Calvinists* and other *Protestants* made not the Testimony of God in their Conscience the chief Ground of their Belief of the Scriptures; to say nothing of the primitive *Christians* and most *uncorrupted Fathers,* who are many and positive on our Behalf.

3*ly,* He insinuates, that *we equal, nay prefer our Books before the Scriptures, because of the Titles we give our own Books, viz.* The Voice of Wisdom, A Testimony for God, &c. *and what we give the Scripture,* namely, Letter, &c. This I have largely spoken to in my Answer to *J. Faldo,* but not knowing whether ever that may be where this probably may come, I shall say thus much, If at any Time we call the Scriptures the Letter, *it is not that we mean thereby, our Books are the Spirit,* or that we would irreverently set them below our Writings, but upon *a Comparison only betwixt the Scriptures and the Spirit* that gave them forth, and that, I hope, may be done without the least Disrespect, though such whose Religion stands in Letter and Time, and not in Spirit and Power, be angry at it. But that we should be thought to slight the Scriptures, because we bestow such Names upon our Books, is a strange kind of Consequence. Are not our Books mostly written in a plain, familiar and Scripture-stile? Do we not earnestly endeavour to confirm what we write *by Scripture,* which not only renders it a Part of our Book, but the most *Noble Part* too? And shall we notwithstanding be reputed Slighters of the Scriptures? Certainly if our Books are called, *The Voice of Wisdom,* and *A Testimony for God,* because from the Voice of Wisdom, and God's Witness in the Conscience; by good Reason must the Scriptures be interested therein, *which are also a Part of them, and such an one too unto whom our Quotation implies a Manifest Preference.*

His next Insinuation is, that *it is Dangerous for Ignorant People to read the Scriptures,* flinging those hateful Names of *Jesuit* and *Romanist* upon us. This Doctrine he lays to the Charge of *G. Fox* and *Rich. Hubberthorn,* in a Book called, *Truth's Defence,* pag. 101, But the Truth of the Matter I will relate out of that Book it self, which has been most partially and basely represented by him.

The Priest's Query lies thus, " *Whether the Scripture being Carnal, and the Letter Killing, as you say, we may read them without Danger?*

' *Ans.* The Letter which killeth, 2 *Cor.* 3. 6. is Dangerous; for thou takest it
' here to war withal against the Saints, *with thy Carnal Mind, giving out thy Carnal*
' *Expositions upon it:* And the Ministers of the Letter are Ministers of Death,
' which is to Condemnation, and *you take it to make a Trade with it,* and with
' what the Prophets, Christ and the Apostles said; so that some have Sixty,
' some an Hundred Pounds a Year: But Christ cried, *Wo unto such whited Walls.*
' And here *you read with Danger,* who speak of them, and speak a Lye, because
' you speak of your selves, and you wrest the Scriptures to your own Destruction,
' *and to you it is Dangerous to read or speak of it,* who know not the Life of it,
' as the *Pharisees,* who were learned in the Letter, but knew not Christ. But I
' say, *Blessed is he that doth read, and doth understand.*

This is the true Account in brief of their Answer to the Priest's Query: And I appeal to God's Witness in the Reader's Conscience, if any Thing of what that vile Man would suggest, is to be found in these Men's Words; who by Letter evidently mean the *Legal State of Condemnation*; by Dangerous, not what Edification was to be got with respect to reading, but that Aggravation of Punishment, which would be the Recompence of those who make *a Trade of them, and oppose them, Pharisee-like, to the Life and Spirit of Christ Jesus, wresting them to their own Destruction.* Reading to such End and Purpose, *will prove Dangerous with a Witness.* And that it was at such a sort of Reading they struck, consider this Passage, But I say, *Blessed is he that doth read and doth understand.*

Let this Forgery so obvious, ring through the Streets and Towns, where-ever his Book or Name is known; however this is little to what's Behind. For my Part I speak my Conscience in Sincerity; I had rather perish off the Earth, than live so great a Burden of foul Dishonesty, as I doubt not but a little Time will manifest him to be.

That the Baseness of his Intentions in this kind of Arguing may yet farther appear, let this gross Inference directly charged by him upon our Principle, of the Light's being our Rule, be diligently considered.

From our Asserting the Light Within to be our Rule, he tells the World, *That we mean the Holy Qualification, that is in us:* Which were it true, he would hit the Mark, when he says, *that Holiness, being a Conformity to the Rule, it cannot be the Rule.* But never yet certainly did any, but *Thomas Hicks,* so misrepresent the poor *Quaker:* Nay, he Confounds and Contradicts himself. How can we be said to make our Holiness the Rule, when we affirm it only to be a walking up to the Light within, which is Holy? He says that we assert the Light to be the Rule, how then is our Obedience to it the Rule; for that is true Holiness? *Is there no Difference between a Rule, and Obedience to it? Holy Life, and that which gives it, or makes it so?* What a Meeting here is of Ignorance, Malice and Lying? Any Thing to spoil the *Quakers*; but God will break the Bow and Spear of their Enemies.

Again, From his *Quaker's* telling him, 'Thou takest up the Saints Words; but 'if thou hast not the same Spirit, what are the Words to thee; he dares to suggest, *that our Opinion of the Light's Sufficiency in every Man cannot be true;* And all the Reason he gives us for his strange Conclusion, is this; *That those Words imply, that the Spirit or Light of God is not in all Men.*

Now what is more evident, than First, That it is not our Answer? 2. That it concerns not the Sufficiency, so much as the Universality of it? 3. By not having the Spirit, or Light, is not meant, that we believe that God has not given a Measure of his Good Spirit unto all to profit with, or that there be some, whom he never enlightned, but that they so have not the Spirit, as to walk by it, be benefitted by it, or come to enjoy it as their Teacher and Comforter; and that some may be said, not to be Enlightned, who are not through Faith in, and Obedience to the Light, come to be advantaged and made Children of Light by it. Let this suffice at present to shew the Man's Ignorance of our Principles, or his great Unrighteousness to pervert them.

I shall now attend the next Point by him handled, and that is *Christ's Person,* and *our Faith* in him, which, he says, we deny, and indeed he does but say it.

CHAP. VI. *Of our Faith in Christ.*

HIS next Cavil is at *our Belief in Christ,* and which is worse, he would be thought a *Christian* in doing so. The great Stress lies here, *Tho. Hicks* would have the World think, we Equivocate about our Faith in That *Christ* which after the Flesh appeared and dyed at *Jerusalem.* The Reason of all this Clamour and Injustice on the Part of our angry and restless Adversary is this; if I wrong him let him shew it me: *The* Quakers *say, that Christ is in them ; Christ is God, is God Man in them?* Again, *The* Quakers *say, that Christ is in them ; But since there is but One Christ, who was born of a Virgin, and that he suffered at* Jerusalem, *being there crucified, can that Christ be in Man?* The false Doctrine or Absurdity he would run us upon, is one of these two, *Either that we deny Christ's Manhood, or that He is actually in our Bodies with that Body he appeared in at* Jerusalem, *which is Impossible,* witness this one Passage, *If God be Christ, as* Penn *saith ; or, If the Light within you be the Christ, as* Naylor *and* Hubberthorn *affirm, is it proper or safe to say, God was Slain, or the Light in you was Crucified.*

To which I answer, That as in other Things, so in this, our Adversary has shewn his great Ignorance or Malice. For is it reasonable to infer from our Affirming in Scripture Language, Christ is in the Saints, *that we deny him as to his Visible and Bodily Appearance in the World*; and that because he is God, *therefore he was never Man*; *or that the Word took not Flesh*; Is this to understand us right, or give the World a true Measure of our Belief, who confess Christ to be every where, and if so, then in his People, see Cont. p. 34. Ah, God the Righteous Judge shall plead with thee in a Day that thou shalt not be able to escape his Terrible Recompence, if thou repentest not. Let it suffice to the sober *Reader* (for of himself I have little Hopes) that we do believe that *Christ, who is God over all, blessed for ever,* did come of Abraham's Seed according to the Flesh, that the Body prepared of that Line was his Body, that what Sufferings befel it were the Sufferings of Christ,

just

just as the Body is called *the Body of Christ:* Yet this we do say, and that not in any Undervalue to the Body, or Bodily Sufferings of Christ, *that the Divine Word, in whom was Life, and whose Life was the Light of Men* (who took that Flesh) *is eminently to be look't upon, and that to believe and obey the Light of his Life, wherewith he has enlightened us, is both the best Way to know the Sufferings of his Body, and to receive the Benefit of them.*

In short, unless Christ be not God, and unless the Light be not Christ, *I know no Hurt I have done, to assert him to be God,* nor any Reason our *Adversary* hath to infer, *therefore I, or any of us, deny him to have taken Flesh, or that he suffered without the Gates of* Jerusalem, *or that he is not as well Christ without as within us.*

Again I do affirm that by the same Reason the bodily Sufferings of the *Word*, whose *Life* was the *Light* of Men, are frequently attributed to the *Word* it self, as if the *Word* had immediately sustained them, and not the *Body*; the *Light* which shineth in the Consciences of Mankind, which is the very *Life* of the *Word*, or *Word* it self, is not unconcern'd in the bodily Sufferings, but both gives to believe them aright, and to receive Benefit by them, and that as the Sufferings of his own Body, by and through which his Glory, Grace and Truth, did shine forth, in the World : Which are now revealed afresh in the Hearts of all who believe in him. Let our *Adversaries* deal so fairly with us, as to distinguish between *Christ*, and the Body of *Christ, as before* Abraham *the Rock in the Wilderness*, and the Appearance of Christ in the Flesh, and not infer from our denying that the whole Christ could die; *that Christ,* that is, *the Body of Christ suffered or died not*; And when we say, he who took Flesh has appeared to, and in our Hearts, *that we exclude and deny his then Visible and Bodily Appearance, or that he is not now as well without us, as within us*; and we shall never doubt of a good Issue. But truly after the Rate we have been used by him, the most Scriptural Assertions can never escape being accounted false and unwarrantable. For because we are with godly Fear Jealous, lest the whole Christ should be thought to have been then crucified, when his Body was, which strikes at the Life of the immortal and Divine Being, we are represented by this Perverter of our right Meaning, *as Denyers of that Body, whilst he himself acknowledgeth that the meer Manhood was not the Christ, but the Word made Flesh, Emmanuel.* Page 44. Dialogue.

2. Because we assert that true Light, with which every Man is enlightned, to be in it self the Christ of God, and Saviour of the World ; *he infers that we deny the True Christ, because he dyed and rose again, &c.* Which the Light never did, never considering that if he makes what dyed and rose again, the entire Christ and Saviour, he excludes the Divinity or Godhead, *which he confesseth to be Christ, in Conjunction with the Manhood,* and which the Scripture calls *strictly the Saviour, besides whom there is none*; and which *J. Faldo* himself pag. 85. part 2. Acknowledges to be such. But if *T. Hicks* does allow, as indeed he doth, *that Christ is God,* as well as *Man,* there is nothing befalls us from his Inference, but what strikes himself equally ; for if the *Light,* with which Men are enlightened, be not *Christ*, because it cannot dye, *then Christ cannot be Christ as God, because God cannot dye.* Well ! But *T. Hicks* tells us, that Christ as God is also Christ, and that it was Christ's Body only that dyed: Therefore I conclude, *that to own Christ to be that true Light, which enlightneth all Men, or that true Light to be Christ, is no Derogation from Christ or Undervalue to his Bodily Sufferings.*

3. And because that one of us spoke of a twofold Appearance of Christ in the Soul, first, *as a Seed of Light in Man,* and next, *as perfect Day, or in a full grown State of Glory,* Therefore says he, *a Personal Coming in any Respect, is denyed by you,* Contin. page 45. which Conclusion is so horribly unjust, that no Impartial Man needs an *Answer* to it. And let the Partial know, that we have not only confessed to his Personal Appearance, But *T. H.* has so much faith for us. *Dial.* pag. 45. The Baseness and Self Contradiction of the Man is notorious enough as to this Point.

I shall proceed to the next Particular, and that is, *If Christ signifie Anointed, and Christ be God, as* Penn *saith, I would query,* (saith our Adversary) *whether God himself was anointed?* Contin. pag. 47.

But though this might have seem'd something from a *Socinian* Hand, yet from *T. Hicks*, it gives no Difficulty at all ; for since he acknowledgeth Christ to be as well God as Man, and that Christ was not anointed by Halves, but intirely, as the Word χριϛὸς Christ, from χρίω *to Anoint*, doth imply, I would fain be informed (*Argumentum ad Hominem*) Who anointed the Godhead, without which *T. Hicks* affirms

affirms again and again, *Christ was not Christ*, because (says he) *Christ is God manifest in the Flesh*. Dialog. pag 44. And since he is for Querying, let me ask him, who is understood in that Passage, *God, even thy God hath anointed thee with the Oyle of Gladness*, &c? Was that said of Christ or no? If not, say so; If it was, as most, or all believe, then, *whether the Divine Nature of Christ was unconcern'd in that Anointing*? And who it was that anointed him is evident from the Place? If *T. Hicks* will limit God to the Manner of his Manifestations and Operations respecting us, that is, that he is no otherwise to, and in himself, than what he appears to us to be; What will he make of that Place. *To us a Child is born, to us a Son is given, he shall be called Wonderful Counsellor, the mighty God, the everlasting Father, the Prince of Peace?* &c. Shall God's Condescensions to Man's Weak and depraved State, by personating, and representing Things to his Capacity, be an Argument that he is no otherwise in himself? Are we confused because we use his Words? or shall Man rise up against God's Way of uttering forth himself suitable to the Shortness of his Understanding? This Kind of Cavil might better become a *Carnal Pharisee, or Scoffing Heathen*, than a Man pretending to Christianity. Base Man that he is, who rewards the Almighty so ill for his Merciful Condescensions! But to the Blind all Things are dark.

But he thinks that he has caught me irrecoverably: Hear his Dialogue. Chr. *Was not Christ God's Gift?* Quak. Yea he was so. Chr. *To what End?* Quak. His Doctrine, Life, Miracles, Death and Sufferings to God is the Gift and Expression of God's Eternal Love for the Salvation of Men. *Penn*'s Sandy Foundation, Pag. 19. Chr. *Thou hast affirmed that God is Christ: If so, Did God die and suffer to God?*

To which I answer, That *T. Hicks*, as in other Places, so here is basely Unjust, and if he accounts me his Adversary or an Opposer of his Principles, though I never had to do with him in particular, nor any of that People in General; It behoved him to be honest, and give me my Due; Instead of which he leaves out some Words, and horribly perverts the rest. For, *first*, I did in that Book acknowledge and confess to *Christ's Bodily Appearance, and that he was born of the Virgin Mary after the Flesh*, and that largely and plainly, p. 36, which he wholly omits to mention. *Secondly*, I do not remember that I so express'd my self, that God was Christ, but whether I did or no, to insinuate a Denial of his Manifestation in Flesh is most perversly wicked and ungodly, as well as that it plainly shews, notwithstanding his feigned Confession to Christ's Divinity, that in Truth he owns him not to be God, or he has very ill express'd himself when he says, thou affirmest *God is Christ*, (or Christ is God) for it implies he does not; else what means his following Words, *did God himself die and suffer to God?* He thus queries to shew the Absurdity of believing *God to be Christ, (or Christ to be God)* and tells us that he believes what died was the Intire Christ. Certainly, he is either *Rank Socinian* in the Point, (which I mention not in Disgrace, unless it be to that Party that so impious a Person is of it) or he has not well given us his Mind. But this proves what elsewhere I observe of him, that from our asserting *Christ to be God or God Christ*, Tho. Hicks is ignorant or malicious enough to infer, that *we deny that ever he took Flesh*; whence he would fasten such like Absurdities upon us, *you say Christ died, Christ you say is God, did then God die?* &c.

But if he has represented us to deny the Bodily Appearance, why did he not also make us to *deny his Death and Sufferings too*, and then there had been no Room for that preposterous Conclusion; But to insinuate a Belief of our Denial of Christ's Coming in the Flesh, and not of his Death, that he might bring us upon this Pinch of Contradiction, to wit, *that God died, and not the Body in which he was manifested*, is such an invented Piece of Dishonesty as deserves nothing else than the Abhorrence of all Impartial Persons; In short, we say, *that God manifested in Flesh was the true Christ that then appeared, that the Flesh, and not God, died, and that the whole of the Appearance, whether in Life or Death, was for Man's Salvation* And if Tho. Hicks is not herewith contented, we cannot help it, but hope others are not so Unreasonable.

But he proceeds thus; *Give me Leave to ask you*, directing himself to his 'foresaid *Quaker, Whether one great End wherefore Christ was given, and came into the World, was not to seek and to save such as were lost.* Quak. Yea, he came to seek and save the Lost.

Christ. *But who, or what, is this that was lost?*

1673.
Chap. VI.

He wickedly and with an Aggravation, like the Enmity of his Spirit, thus makes G. *Keith* to answer, *That which is lost is still in Man,* That *Christ came to seek and save, and all his Ministers preached People to this,* the Lost in Man, a lost God, a Lost Christ, *&c.* To which says *T. H. Blush, O Heavens! and be astonished, O Earth! Was ever such a Thing as this heard of before, that* Jesus Christ *came to seek and save a Lost God, a Lost Christ?* &c. *Was ever God and Christ in a Lost Condition?* But the Heavens may blush, and the Earth be astonished indeed at such sordid and base Dealing. G. *Keith* means, *that Christ came to seek and to save,* by turning People to enquire after *a Lost God and a Lost Christ,* the Groat *within, the Pearl in the Field,* &c. that is, to God's Light in them, by which God and Christ are revealed to the Soul; *For whatever may be known of God is manifest within,* Rom. 1. which they rebelling against, had lost the Knowledge of the only true God, and Jesus Christ: And this unrighteous Person turns it that G. *Keith* meant, that Christ came to seek and save *a Lost God, and Lost Christ*; What Sense can there be in so horrible a Perversion, as well as that there is no Colour for it, who endeavours to insinuate that Christ *came to save God and Christ,* not the Soul, by turning it to *seek after God and Christ*; and to represent God and Christ's Condition Lost and Perilous, instead of theirs, who had or have lost God and Christ. In short, Lost, as taken by *T. H.* is meant of *Man's Lost Condition,* and as there used by G. *Keith,* is understood of God and Christ, *whom Man had and hath lost the Knowledge of, and Fellowship with.* But such sinister Practices favour of the Height of Dishonesty; The Inventor of *Baxter Baptized in Blood by Anabaptists* is nothing to this horrible kind of Perverter; And I doubt not, but *T. Hicks's* Recompence will be more terrible from the Hand of a just God, irritated by such Irreligious Proceedings. However, I will return upon *T. Hicks* what more concerns him than he is aware of: If Christ came to seek and to save that which was lost, *then because the whole World was Lost, he came to seek and to save the whole World*; And if so, then Reprobates, *because lost,* or else there can be no such Thing, *as Eternal Reprobation,* or Men from Eternity unalterably decreed to Eternal Destruction; How much more this confounds his own partial Opinion of *Predestination* than any thing he has said can the *Quakers* Principles, let the sober-minded judge.

Chap. VII.

CHAP. VII.

Of the Seed, *and Redemption of the* Seed.

HIS next Stumble, and gross Perversion of our Words, is concerning the *Seed,* from a Passage or two taken out of the Books of *J. N.* and *G. F. That the Seed is Christ, that the Seed wants Redemption, as being laden by Sinners as a Cart with Sheaves,* &c. He thus argues; *If then Redemption be of the Seed, and this Seed be Christ, either there must be more Christs than one, or else Christ came to redeem himself.* Again, *Christ without you esteem to be but a Creature*; *but the Seed within you say is God. Tell me seriously, whether a Creature can redeem the Creator. Can you pretend to be guided by an Infallible Spirit, and yet be guilty of such Gibberish and Folly as this?*

To which, before I make my Answer, I think fit to insert that which he gives in the Name of the *Quakers.*

Here thou shewest thy dark Mind, and that thou art still in thy Imagination, understanding neither the Redemption nor the Seed; which however feign'd by himself against himself, is so great a Truth, that there is scarcely one Passage in his Dialogue more allowable.

But to his Argument and Question. We do assert the Redemption of the Seed, for the Light and Life which has been as sown in the Heart of Mankind, has been loaded with Sin, *pressed down with Iniquity, grieved and almost quenched through Disobedience,* which Words are not *properly,* but *metaphorically* to be taken, as used by the *Holy Pen-men,* whereby to make Things the more plain and easy to common Capacities. It is said in Scripture, *Out of Ægypt have I called my Son,* a Place of *Bondage and grievous Weights, Burdens and Oppressions,* from all which the Seed was to be redeemed; and Christ came, or God was manifested in the Flesh, *that the Seed of Light, Truth and Righteousness might break through and arise over all Corruption, by which it had been grieved and pressed down.* And it is no Contradiction to say, *That God did rid himself of the Enemies that oppressed his own Righteous Life, or that he brought Salvation to himself*; for the Scriptures frequently

quently speak on that wise, especially in those two notable Passages of *Isaiah*, *And he saw that there was no Man, and wondered that there was no Intercessor, therefore his Arm brought Salvation to him, and his Righteousness sustained him,* Isa. 59. 16. Again, *The Year of my Redeemed is come; and I looked, and there was none to help; and I wondered there was none to uphold; therefore mine own Arm brought Salvation unto me, and my Fury it upheld me,* Isa. 63. 4, 4. Whence it is no Ways absurd that we affirm, that the End of God's manifesting himself in the Flesh, was for the Redemption or Deliverance of his Holy Life that was in Man, but as a small Seed, even the smallest of Seeds, that had been long vexed, grieved, bruised and pressed down by Sin and Iniquity; For the End of that Appearance was, that Sin might be destroyed, *and that Christ, who had been as a Lamb slain from the Foundation of the World,* might be exalted in the Hearts of Men and Women, *and his, and their Foes, made his and their Foot-stool*: For the Work is Inward, we do aver in the Name of the Lord; *for where the Devil hath Reigned, and had Dominion,* to wit, in Man, *there he must be defeated, and subdued*; and Christ alone, by whom that is brought to pass, ought and must have the Power and the Kingdom for ever. And if this be the *Folly* and *Gibberish* the *Quakers* must be charg'd with from this *Anabaptist Preacher,* we are content to use it, as well as patient to bear his insolent Scoff; only let all take Notice, that we understand not by the Seed's Redemption, its being redeemed from the *Pollution,* but *the Weight* of Sin and Iniquity; for it was and is pure for evermore.

Now, as to our calling *Christ without a Creature,* I must tell him, 'tis not our Language; but if he means by it the Body born of the *Virgin,* I suppose T. *Hicks* is far from believing that to be the *Creator,* though his Manner of Speaking shews a Dislike of us, that we don't, because he says that we esteem *the Christ without, or the Outward and Visible Part of Christ but a Creature,* as if he believed it to be the Creator. However, manifest it is, he believes, *that the Redemption wrought,* is not by that God, who in those foregoing Passages speaks so expresly to that Purpose, and who in Time manifested himself in the Flesh, *but the Flesh only,* by and through which he was so manifested.

CHAP. VIII.

Of the SOUL of Man.

HIS next Abuse of us, that I shall take Notice of is this, " That G. *Fox* and others hold the Soul to be a Part of God, of God's Being, and that it is " without Beginning: (*Dialog.* p. 1.) *All which* (says he) *is as much as to say, the Soul is God.* So that God sets up a Light in himself, which he himself is to obey, and in so doing God shall be saved.

Behold your *Anabaptist Preacher!* A *Man of Truth, Tender Conscience, of the first Form of* Christians, *a Contender for the Faith once delivered to the Saints,* and what else he falsly pretends, and in vain would have us think him to be. *What so Base? What so Irreligious as this Perversion? Men nor Devils could never study more our Wrong, than this pretended* Christian *has done:* If this be his *Christianity, The God of* Abraham, Isaac *and* Jacob *preserve my Soul from ever coming within the Borders of such Religion*; but *Christianity* is abused by such Traducers, and God's Spirit is grieved by such Injustice. I would not use the worst of Men, no not Devils themselves, at that unequal Rate he deals with us, who both mis-cites our Words, and abuses the true Meaning of what is truly cited. G. *Fox* says thus, *God breathed into Man the Breath of Life, and he became a Living Soul, and is not this of God, of his Being? &c. And is not this, that comes out from God, Part of God?* Where nothing can well be clearer than that G. F. intends that *Divine Life, Power* and *Virtue,* by which *Adam* in Soul and Body came to live to God. Can T. H. say, after all this, that he cited G. F. right, and ask the *Quaker* in his *Dialogue,* Darest thou say I have not quoted him truly? Hardned Man!

Breathed, that is *Inspired: Breathed* being the *English* Word, *Inspired* borrowed from the Latin *Inspirare*; the Greek has it ἐνεφύσησεν, as *John* 20. 22. hath *breathed into, enlivened, inspired, quickened*; the *Hebrew* ויפח *and he breathed or blowed:* on which R. *Nachmanni* and the Author *Hiskuni* in P. *Fagius*'s Comment on the Place, speak thus, *That God inspired Man with something of his own Substance; that he contributed something to him, and bestowed something of his own Divinity upon him, and that God did inspire Man with the Holy Ghost*; and that נשמה *is a proper*

proper Word for it. Which is as much as can be collected or justly concluded from what *G. Fox* hath said concerning Men. But this Ungodly Person would infer from our afferting that the *Breath* God breathed into *Adam*'s Soul, whereby it lived to God, was of God's own Divine Life, *that the Soul of Man, as a meer Creature, created Capacity, is of God's own Being and Substance*; and when he has done, with a *Taunt* becoming none but a *Prophane Person*, tells us, *that then God sets up a Light in himself, which being obey'd by him, he comes to be saved*; as if the Soul needed either a Light or Saviour, in Case it were God; or, that God could obey any thing, or needed Salvation. *O monstrous Blasphemy against God, and horrid Injustice to us!* For as God can obey none, nor need Salvation, neither in Sense can we be thought so to believe of the Soul, as by him represented; since our pleading for a Saving Light, the Necessity of Obedience to it, the Eternal Reward of Life or Death, Happiness or Misery, as it is conformed to, or rebelled against, prove our Faith in that Matter to be quite another Thing. If this be your *Champion*, I dare warrant his own Baseness shall be his own Overthrow; we need no more against him, than his own Ignorance, Malice, Lyes, Forgeries and Slanders to his utter Confutation in the Minds of all Impartial Persons.

CHAP. IX. *Of* Justification, *and something of* Satisfaction.

THE Doctrine of *Justification* is the next Particular that I am to take Notice of. He begins with the *Quaker* thus, *Pray what is your Opinion of Justification by that Righteousness of Christ, which He in his own Person fulfilled for us Wholly without us.* Quak. " Justification by the Righteousness which Christ fulfilled for us in his own Person, *Wholly without us*, we boldly affirm it to be a Doctrine of Devils, and an Arm of the Sea of Corruption, which doth now deluge " the World, *Will. Penn.* Apol. p. 148.

This *Apology* cited was written against a malicious *Priest* in *Ireland*, who in a Book by him published not long before, laid it down as Unscriptural, and a very heinous Thing in us to deny *Justification* (without any Distinction exprest) *by the Righteousness which Christ wrought in his own Person*, Wholly without * us. To whom I made the Answer given by *T. Hicks*; And if therein I have croft the express Testimony of the Scriptures, let any shew me; But if I have only thwarted a most Sin-pleasing (and therefore dangerous) Notion; let such as hold it look to that: He has not offered me one plain Scripture, nor the Shadow of a Reason, why this Passage ought to be reputed unsound or condemnable. If any Living will produce me but one Passage out of Scripture, that tells of a Justification by such a Righteousness as is *Wholly without us*, I shall fall under it's Authority; but if we only deny *Men's corrupt Conceits and Sin-pleasing Glosses*, and they offer us nothing to our Confutation, or better Information, we shall not think bare Quotations of our Books to be sufficient Answers. But to the End all may understand the Reason of my so answering that *Priest*, take those short Reasons then rendred, with any one of which I am to suppose *T. Hicks* desired not to meddle.

' *First*, No Man can be justified without Faith, (says *Jenner*.) No Man hath
' Faith without Works (any more than a Body can live without a Spirit (says *James*.
' Therefore the Works of *Righteousness*, by the Spirit of *Jesus Christ*, are neces-
' sary to *Justification*.

' *Second*, If Men may be justified, whilst impure; then God quits the Guilty,
' contrary to the Scripture; which canot be, I mean while in a Rebellious State.

' *Third*, Death came by actual Sin, not imputative, in his Sense; Therefore
' Justification unto Life comes by actual Righteousness, and not imputative.

' *Fourth*, This speaketh Peace to the Wicked, whilst wicked; but there is no
' Peace to the Wicked, faith my God.

' *Fifth*, Men are Dead and Alive at the same Time, faith this Doctrine; for
' they may be dead in Sin, *and yet alive in another's Righteousness*, not inherent;
' and consequently, Men may be damned actually, *and saved imputatively*.

' *Sixth*, But since Men are to reap what they sow, and that every one shall be
' rewarded according to his Works; *and that none are Justified but the Children*

---

* *If wholly without us, then none of it within us.*
It was such a Justification, as respected being made just by the Destruction of Sin inherent by the Spirit and Power of Christ Jesus, and not being accounted Just from the Guilt, and former Sins freely remitted in his Blood, as an Offering for Sin once for all to every one that truly repents.

'of God; and that none are Children but who are led by the Spirit of God, and that
'none are so led, but those that bring forth Fruits thereof, which is Holiness; is
'not the Oyl in another's Lamp, but in our own only, which will serve our Turns;
'I mean the Rejoycing must be in our selves, and not in another: Yet to Christ's
'holy Power alone do we ascribe it, who works all our Works in us. All which
'was not only not answered, but not cited by him.

 He brings me in again thus; *Justification is not from the Imputation of another's Righteousness; but from the actual Performing and Keeping God's Righteous Statutes*. Sand. Found. p. 25. To which, after this base and disingenuous Citation, he returns me only this Answer; *It is not written*, Rom. 5. 19. *By the Obedience of one many are made Righteous?* But before I explain the Truth of that Scripture, be pleased to hear my Argument, as it is laid down in my Book, and then give thy Judgment, *Reader*, upon the Man.

'*The Son shall not bear the Iniquity of his Father, the Righteousness of the Righ-
'teous shall be upon him, and the Wickedness of the Wicked shall be upon him, when
'a righteous Man turneth away from his Righteousness, for his Iniquity that he has
'done shall he dye*; Again, *when the wicked Man turneth away from his Wickedness,
'and doth that which is lawful and Right, he shall save his Soul alive*; yet saith the
'*House of* Israel, *The Ways of the Lord are not equal. Are not my Ways Equal?*
'If this was once equal, it's so still; for God is unchangeable; And therefore I
'shall draw this Argument, that the Condemnation or Justification of Persons is
'not from the Imputation of another's * Righteousness; but the actual Perfor-
'mance, or not keeping of God's righteous Statutes or Commandments, other-
'wise God should forget to be equal: Therefore how wickedly unequal are those,
'who not from Scripture Evidences, but their own dark Conjectures, and Interpretati-
'ons of Obscure Passages, *would frame a Doctrine, so manifestly inconsistent with God's
'most pure and equal Nature*; making him to condemn the Righteous to Death,
'and justifie the Wicked to Life, from the Imputation of another's Righteousness.
'—— A most unequal Way indeed.

 Where observe that the Answer he makes me give in his *Dialogue*, is delivered by me with an *If it be so*, fetcht expresly from the Text it self: So that the Scripture, and not *W. Penn* is most struck at by him. However it be, he has offered us no Opposition yet, but that Passage out of *Romans*, which will not be found inconsistent with *Ezekiel's* Testimony, on which my Argument was grounded.

 The whole Verse was thus, *For as by one Man's Disobedience many were made Sinners, so by the Obedience of one, shall many be made Righteous*; which if the whole Chapter be well considered, is no more than this; that as *Adam*, Representative of Mankind (from whence he had that Name) was he by whom Sin entred into the whole World; So *Christ* was *He*, by whose Coming, and Obedience, Righteousness had an Entrance to the Justification of many. In short, the Work Christ had to do was *two-fold*. 1st. *To remit, forgive, or justifie from the Imputation of Sin past, all such as truly repented, believed and obeyed him*. And 2ly, *by his Power and Spirit operating in the Hearts of such to destroy and remove the very Ground and Nature of Sin, whereby to make an End of Sin and finish Transgression present and to come*; that is, the *first* removes the *Guilt*, the *Second* the very *Cause* of it. Now I grant, that *his Obedience unto Death* was in Order to make Men righteous, because it was in the Nature of a *Sacrifice*, by which God testified unto the World his Desire of Reconciliation through the Remission of the Sins that are past, which was held forth, and came, and was confirmed by that Obedience, even to the Death of the Cross; In which Sense the *Just suffered for the Unjust, and whilst we were Sinners, Christ dyed*: He was made Sin, that is, *to take away Sin from us, (an Hebraism) and he justifieth the Ungodly*, that is, *remitteth the Ungodly upon Repentance*, and *bore our Iniquities*, or bore away our Iniquities, that is, *by this Offering for Sin, was Remission for Sins past, declared and affirmed and declared unto all, as an Universal Propitiation*; For God was in all these Sufferings, shewing forth his Love and reconciling the World unto himself, not imputing their Trespasses unto them. But still Repentance was that which brought Home the general Pardon promulgated, in and by that holy Offering up of his Body once for all, unto every particular Soul. Thus by the Obedience of that one Man, even to the Death of

---

* *As wholly without us*
It is to be understood of *a Righteousness wrought by Christ's Power within, when I speak of being justified; that is, made Just by it*.

1673.

Chap. IX.

the Cross, many come to be made Righteous, that is, *Justified from many Offences*, see *Rom.* 5. 6, 7, 9, 10, 11, 12, 13, 14, 15, 16, 17. But if this first Part of Justification, which is *Remission of Sin*, be not obtainable by any, however General it be in Christ, *without Repentance from Dead Works*, which implies *Faith, Contrition, and Amendment of Life*, how miserably is *T. Hicks* out, who brings this very Scripture we are upon, to prove that we are compleatly justified *(which takes in both Forgiveness of Sin past, and a being inwardly made Just through the casting out of Sin by the Just and Holy Power and Spirit of God appearing in the Heart and Conscience) by Christ's Righteousness*, Wholly Without Us.

I grant, that Forgiveness of Sin is God's free Love, meer Grace, and rich Mercy, declared in and by Christ Jesus to the World, and that this Grace abounded unto all ; *for He was a Propitiation, not only for the Sins of those that believe, but of the whole World* ; yet the whole Benefit thereof should never redound unto any, whilst alienated from God by wicked Works.

Peter preached another Doctrine : For though *Christ dyed for the Ungodly*, yet they were not thereby Justified, that is, pardon'd for Sin past, while Unrepentant. *Peter* says Acts 3. 38. *Repent, and then they should receive Remission of Sins*. Now I would fain know how this Repentance is wrought, by which, as a Condition, any come to have an Interest in that great Pardon held out to the whole World ; *Is the Spirit of Christ unconcern'd in it ? Can we think One Good Thought of our selves ? Are we not altogether degenerated Plants of a Strange Vine ? By Nature Children of Wrath*, &c. Is not this frequently confest by the Professors of Religion in our Times, and the most affected Piece of their Righteousness too ? Well then ! *If we cannot Repent of our selves, and that Repentance is a Condition, and that it is in the Soul, and that it cannot be there without the Spirit of Christ work it*, tell me plainly, *if something is not to be done Within, and therefore of the Nature of Inward Righteousness, before any Benefit be procured, deriv'd or receiv'd from Christ's Death and Sufferings to any particular Person*. This is close to the Point, for therefore it is that we affirm, *That such as go on to transgress against the Law of the Spirit of Life, and so disobey the Light, and grieve the Holy Spirit by wicked Works, are not in that State Justified* ; I mean now, that they are not so much as forgiven, and least of all, that they should be look'd upon as compleatly *Justified*, that is, by *Qualification and Participation of the Divine Nature, truly and inwardly made Just* ; since it would be to say, That by the Obedience of One, many shall be made Righteous, who notwithstanding remain Disobedient and Rebellious to God's Grace which has appeared unto them. We do say again, that such a Doctrine, so *speaking Peace to a State of Sin and Death, and shutting out an inward Work, many Ways necessary to the Forgiveness of Sin past, or Daily Acceptance with God*, Is no less than the Doctrine of Devils, *and the worst they have to propagate, to the Dishonour of God, and the Eternal State of People's Souls*. In short, here lyes the gross Mistake of our *Adversaries* ; they make the Sufferings of Christ which peculiarly relate to the first Part of Justification, *Remission of Sins past*, to be that which has answered, not only for Sins past, but present and to come, so as to acquit them from all Inward Work as necessary to Justification compleatly taken, contrary to express Scripture, *Rom.* 5. 25. and the Great End of Christ's Spiritual Manifestation in his People. There might be much more said in this Matter, but because he thinks I have not made a little for him, in my Book truly entituled, *The Sandy Foundation Shaken*, and that I am to be short, I shall proceed to dispatch what remains, as God shall enable me.

To that Answer he gave out of the *Romans, (By the Obedience of One,* &c.) already with other Scriptures explained and vindicated from his Abuse of them, he makes me thus to answer him.

Quaker. *It is a great Abomination to say, God shall condemn and punish his Innocent Son, that he having satisfied for our Sins, we might be justified by the Imputation of his perfect Righteousness. O why should this horrible Thing be contended for by Christians ?* Penn. ibid. p. 25. 30.

To which he returns, Chr. *How now Mr. Penn, Is the Doctrine of Christ's Suffering for Sinners, to make Satisfaction to Divine Justice, an horrible Thing, and an Abomination to you ? Do you consider what you say ?* And thus brings me in answering him. Qu. *This I do say, that the Consequences of such a Doctrine are both Irreligious and Irrational*. Penn, ibid. p. 16. Now that he has dealt Blasphemously with God, and Injuriously with me, as well as that he has given me no Account of

his

his Thoughts upon the Error he makes me guilty of, in Case I held it, besides that impertinent Question, plainly appears.

First, he has dealt Blasphemously with God, in calling *Christ's Suffering, God's Condemning and Punishing his Innocent Son*, &c. which his Censure of my so Phrasing their Opinion, manifestly implies. Now I appeal to all Impartial People, which of us Two is most to be blamed, I that confess to Christ's Sufferings as the Effect of God's Love, thereby not to satisfy himself as a Revenger, or as if he could not forgive (for none of that is in the Verse at all) which yet is in their *Sordid Opinion*, but as a God full of Mercy, Forgiveness and Pardon to all True Penitents, *to declare to the World His Free Remission of Sins, and that He would not impute their Iniquities unto them, if they would Repent, Believe, and Obey*; or T. Hicks, who holds that God Condemn'd and Punish'd His Innocent Son for other Folk's Sins, that He might be satisfied; for Pardon He neither could, nor would: And, which is most absurd, Christ being the same God, he at once makes him the Party satisfying, and the Party satisfied, which is absurd and impossible; besides, 'tis such a Satisfaction as hath paid all Debts, past, present, and to come, whereby all inward Righteousness, though of Christ's Working, is not necessary to Justification in any Kind.

Secondly, He has dealt *Injuriously* with me, and that in Two Respects. 1. In not stating the Doctrine truly, which I opposed, and my Words at length, that they might speak for themselves (But in that Case, perhaps he thought he should have been obliged to answer them, a Thing he every where seems afraid of, his Trade is Cavilling.) And 2dly, *In that he brings this Passage which opposed such a* Satisfaction, as is said, *to have paid for Sins past, present, and to come*, to answer a Scripture which concerns Justification, and that Part of it too, *which relates to Remission of Sins*; insinuating, that I make *Men's own Works sufficient to Justification* in the first Sense, I mean, *Remission*; and in the second Sense, I mean, *Daily Acceptance upon being made Just*; and lastly, *That I overturn all the Righteousness, Death and Sufferings of Christ*; whilst in Truth and Sincerity of Soul, 1 By Justification, not by another's Righteousness *Wholly Without*, I only meant, *That it was Christ's Righteousness wrought in us, and not our own, which made inwardly Just, and which gave Daily Acceptance, and brought into the Heavenly Fellowship with the Father and with the Son*; the Justification then intended by me. 2*dly*, Since God has made His Truth known to me, I have ever understood Christ's being offered up, *to signify the carrying away of Sin, the bearing away of Iniquity, that by which God declared Remission and Forgiveness of Sins past to all that Repented*. And this Justification, called *Rom.* 4. *ver.* 5. 6, 7, 8. *God's not Imputing Sin*, I have ever owned to be the Free Unmerited Love of God to the World; And was not that Justification by me spoken of in the Passage cited? 3*dly*, That which I opposed was so rigid a Satisfaction, *as made it absolutely unavoidable or necessary in God to require a Satisfaction*, thereby robbing Him of the Power of His Free Mercy and Loving-Kindness to remit and pass by, and that Christ did not answer or pay, by the Act of His Suffering, for Sins past, present, and to come; but as he declared Remission by His Blood for the Sins past of the whole World, the Beginning of His Work; *so that He doth by His Power and Spirit, subdue, destroy, and cast out Sin out of the Hearts of all who believe in Him, whereby their Consciences come to be made Pure, and they sanctified throughout in Body, Soul and Spirit*, which necessitates to Good Life, and speaks no Peace to the Wicked in their Wickedness, nor yet to the slothful, formal, and carnal Professor of Religion. Therefore such rage, and imagine a vain Thing against us.

That the Consequences of the common Notion of both Satisfaction and Justification are *Irreligious and Irrational*, though what has been said might suffice with Sober and Impartial Readers, yet I may anon have farther Occasion to prove it. In the mean Time, he tells the World, That *William Penn*, in Answer to this Question, *How did Christ fulfil the Law for Sinners?* says, *That Christ fulfilled the Law Only as our Pattern or Example*, Sand. Found. p. 26. In which he has done exactly like himself; for if he can find the Word *Only* there, or such an Answer to such a Question, or the Matter strictly contained in that Question, he has not wronged me; but sure I am there is no such Question, and as sure, that the Fulfilling of the *Law*, was not the Subject treated on, and very certain, that the Word *Only* was not there; therefore he is a Forger. That which I said, with the Scripture on which it was grounded, follows, *If ye keep my Commandments ye shall abide in my Love, even as I have kept my Father's Commandments and abide in His Love*.

' [From

1673.

Chap. IX.

'[From whence this Argument doth naturally arise; If none are truly Justified
'that abide not in Christ's Love, and that none abide in His Love that keep not
'His Commandments, *then consequently none are Justified but such as keep His
'Commandments*. Besides, here is the most palpable Opposition to an Imputative
'Righteousness that may be; For Christ is so far from telling them of such a Way
'of being Justified, as that he informeth them, the Reason why he abode in his
'Father's Love, *was his Obedience*; and is so far from telling them of their being
'Justified, whilst not abiding in his Love, *by Virtue of his Obedience imputed unto
'them, that unless they keep his Commands, and obey for themselves*, they shall be
'so remote from an Acceptance, as wholly to be cast out; *in all which Christ is
'but our Example*.] Now that this concerned not the *Whole Law* Christ came to
fulfil; *The whole * Law he fulfilled, the Place of Scripture quoted, the Nature and
Matter of the Argument clearly proves.* Next, If Christ had been other than our
Example in that Case, then he should have fulfilled his own Commandments in our
stead, who from Obeying his Father's, taught us, our Duty was to obey His. And
supposing that he could have kept his own Commandments, and obey'd himself
for us, or in our stead, it would have followed, (1.) That we needed not to have
kept them, unless they were to be observed twice over. And that (2ly.) in not
keeping of them, we had been notwithstanding justified from his alone Fulfilling
of them; unless his Answering them had been Insufficient. The first of which, if
I understand any Thing, *opens a Door to all Licentiousness* (however Upright some
may be in their Intentions to the contrary) And the last strikes dead their own
Opinion *of the Sufficiency of Christ's Personal Obedience, to perform all needful on our
Account*; From hence he undertakes to charge me with the *Merit of Works*. My
Words at length are these; which he thought good to conceal.

' Was not *Abraham* justified by Works when he offered *Isaac*? and by Works
' was Faith made perfect; and the Scripture was fulfilled, which saith, Abraham
' *believed God, and it was imputed to him for Righteousness*. By which we must
' not conceive, as do the dark *Imputarians* of this Age, that Abraham's *Offering
' Personally was not a Justifying Righteousness*, but that God was pleased to ac-
' count it so; since God never accounts a Thing that which it is not; nor was
' there any Imputation of another's Righteousness to *Abraham*; but on the con-
' trary, his Personal Obedience was the † Ground of that just Imputation; and
' therefore that any should be justified from the Imputation of another's Righte-
' ousness, not inherent, or actually possessed by them, is both Ridiculous and
' Dangerous.—*Ridiculous*, since it is to say, *A Man is Rich to the Value of a Thou-
' sand Pounds, whilst he is not really or personally worth a Groat*, from the Imputa-
' tion of another; who has it all in his Possession: *Dangerous, because it begets a
' confident Perswasion in many People of their being Justified, whilst in Captivity to
' those Lusts, whose Reward is Condemnation*; whence came that usual Saying a-
' mongst many *Professors of Religion, That God looks not on them as they are in *
' Themselves, but as they are in Christ*; not considering, that none can be in Christ,
' who are not *New Creatures*, which those cannot be reputed, who have not disro-
' bed themselves of their Old Garments, but are still immantled with the Cor-
' ruptions of the Old Man.

* That is, within them as to Qualification.

In all which I see nothing Unsober or Unsound. But he thinks he has caught
me fast in my *Caveat against Popery*, where in distinguishing betwixt *Grace* and
Merit, I say, *Grace is a Free Gift requiring nothing*; and *now ask*, says he, *was
not* Abraham *Justified by Works? and that Good Works may be said to procure, deserve or obtain*, Apol. 198. *Is this writ like an Infallible Dictator?* Thus far T. H.

Ibid.
p. 52, 53.

There is an old Proverb, *That some love the Treason, but hate the Traytor*. No
Man that writes, rants it more imperiously than *Tho. Hicks*. It is hard to say, whe-
ther his Dishonesty or his Impudence be the greater. I think, I never used *Thomas
Hicks* so ill, or any of his Way, as to deserve so many *Scoffing Taunts, Base De-
tractions*, and *Down-right Scurrilities* from his Hand; But let that pass. To the
Point. Hear what I have said in the *Caveat*. p. 12.

' *Grace* and *Merit*, as stated by *Calvinists* and *Papists*, are taken for *Faith without
' Works*; and *Works without Faith*; like the two *Poles*, Doctrines the most oppo-
' site: Now Rewardableness is neither, but something in the middle, and indeed

---

* He was our Example in Holiness, though not in his Ending Types and Shadows.
† God's Love is not excluded, nor his Power that so wrought in *Abraham's* Heart.

' the

'the most true; for *Grace* is a Free Gift, requiring nothing: *Merit* is a Work
'proportionable to the Wages: Rewardableness, is a Work without which God
'will not bestow his Favour, and yet not the Meritorious Cause; for that there
'is no Proportion betwixt the *Work* that is *finite*, and *temporary*, and the *Reward*
'which is *infinite* and *eternal*; in which Sense both the Creature obeys the Com-
'mands of God, *and does not Merit, but Obtain only*; and God rewards the Crea-
'ture, and yet so, *as that he freely gives too*.

Now what Contradiction is there in all this? I plainly distinguish the Word *Merit* in the strictest Acceptation of it, from that which is truly Scriptural, respecting us at least. That I did not mention *Merit* in my *Sandy Foundation shaken*, the Book proves. Is there no Difference between obtaining the Justifying Presence of God by the Fruits of the Spirit in our Heart and Lives, *and strictly meriting his Acceptance of us by Works, and those of our own making too, as what* T. H. *doth wickedly suggest*? I say, ' *Abraham* was justified in offering up his Son, because he
' had been condemned if he had disobeyed. But says *T. Hicks*, He was justified before. And why was not his whole Life mention'd to his Justification? But I must tell *T. H.* that as among Men the Will is taken for the Deed, so the Lord finding *Abraham* right in his Heart, that he believed, and would obey; he was as much justified therein, as if he had actually done it. We have cause to believe *T. Hicks* never knew what the Consequence of that working Faith, and offering up an *Isaac* to God is. Nor was it needful to recite the whole of his Life: Measures are frequently taken by some eminent Trial. If he was accepted, in that, Obedience being the Condition, where that was before, he was before accepted no doubt. But says he, see the *Caveat*, p. 12. and *Apol.* p. 198. How do they agree? Truly very well: For *Grace is free, requiring nothing.* How? Nothing at all? By no Means. *How then is it free?* Grace is free, because it was the good Pleasure of God both to give Remission of Sins, and Eternal Life to as many as should Repent, Believe and Obey to the End, and thereby come to be conformed to the Image of his Son. But may *T. Hicks* say; *Is Repenting nothing? Believing nothing? Obeying nothing?* No, *T H not one jot of Merit in all that*; It is the *Great Grace of God*, to give us Eternal Life upon so small Conditions. They obtain it; *but that is God's good Pleasure, and no Purchase*, therefore Grace still; All that is our Duty; *the Reward is Free*; God giveth it, but chuses a Way by which to do it. If *T. H.* will understand Grace, as my *Caveat* condemns it, I cannot help that; sure I am, I never writ such Doctrine as my Faith, and therefore no Contradiction to my self, whatever it may be to him. But says he, *Your* Apology *speaks that good Works may be said to procure, deserve, or obtain, &c.*

My *Apology* as my self, and other Books, are not *Apology enough* for me and my Friends against such Envious Perverters as *T. H.* though I doubt not but they may be effectually such with more moderate Persons; thus it speaks,

' The Word *Merit*, so much snarled at, allows a two fold Signification; the
' *First*, a Proposition or Equality betwixt the Work and Wages, which is the
' strictest Sense, and that which he (*S. Fisher*) least of all intended; The *Second*,
' something that may be said to procure, *And in some Sense* to deserve or obtain,
' and so good Works do; *since without them there is no Acceptance with God, nor*
' *Title to Eternal Life*.

Where it is observable, how basely he has left out, both *my absolute Denial of the strict Sense of the Word MERIT*, and those qualifying and distinguishing Words, which come after *Procure*, and before *Deserve*, namely, And in some Sense, *to deserve or obtain*, with the last Clause. Certain it is, that whatever Sense I had, *T. Hicks* took me in the worst he could invent, *yea in that very Sense, which all along I have most particularly refused and condemned*; A Baseness, and Piece of *Forgery*, unworthy of any Man pretending to Good Conscience!

But he proceeds still, and much after the same Manner; he would have People believe, *That we assert the Ground of our Rejoycing and Acceptance to be not in, and from the Righteousness of Christ imputed to us by Faith* (where observe, that *Wholly without us*, is omitted, to render us Deniers of Christ's Righteousness in any Sense) *but only in a Righteousness inherent in us, and done by us*; Which great Untruth he gives the Lye to, in his own Book. But because he pretends to fetch this out of my *S. F. Shaken*, p. 27. let's hear what I have said. *But let every Man prove his own Work, and then shall he have Rejoycing in himself alone, and not in another. Be not deceived, for whatsoever a Man soweth that shall he reap.*

'If Rejoycing, and Acceptance with God, or the contrary, are to be reaped
'from the Work that a Man soweth, either to the Flesh, or to the Spirit, *then
'is the Doctrine of Acceptance, and Ground of Rejoycing from the Works of another
'utterly excluded*; every Man reaping according to what He hath sown, and bear-
'ing His Own Burden.

The Question will now be, Whether I meant this of the Creature alone, or by the Assistance of God's Holy Spirit, by which his Children are led?

Concerning which I need say no more, than what that Book speaks in my Defence, yea, that very Page, from whence he fetches this pretended Dangerous Assertion. *For as many as are led by the Spirit of God, are the Sons of God.*

'How clearly will it appear to any but a Cavilling and Tenacious Spirit; that
'Man can be no farther * *Justified*, than as he becomes obedient to the Spirit's
'Leadings; For if none can be a Son of God, but He that's led by the Spirit of
'God, then none can be justified without being led by the Spirit of God; because
'none can be Justified but he that is a Son of God: so that the Way to Justifica-
'tion and Son-ship, is through Obedience to the Spirit's Leadings.

* Justification not as Remission, but as made Just.

By all which it appears, that I am not speaking of Remission of Sins, as if by our Conformity to the Spirit it self, we could so justifie our selves, No; but *that by being Led by the Spirit of God, and Fulfilling of his Royal Law, Men come to be accepted, as Children of God; and the Ground of their Joy is from their own Experience of the Work of God in them.* What was it made the *Faithful Servants* that improved their *Talents* be accepted; and gave an Entrance to the *Wise Virgins* into the Bride-groom's Chamber? Was it not the *Improvements* of the one, and the *Oyl* in the Lamps of the other? And if *T. Hicks* come not to know that Holy State, he shall never know Eternal Rejoycings, *that is the Word of Truth to him*; For such as he sows, such shall he reap, in God's Day of Account. Wherefore that Scripture by him brought out of *Isaiah* makes greatly for us; *Surely shall one say, in* (or from) *the Lord have I Righteousness*; that is, not in or from my self; *In the Lord shall all the Seed of* Israel *be justified, and shall Glory.* Is there no being in the Life, Power, Nature and Virtue of that Seed? then no Salvation. Also that of the Apostle *Paul* to the *Corinthians, Christ is made unto us Righteousness; wherefore let him that glorieth Glory in the Lord.* For this I affirm, and that with Boldness and Truth, that *Isaiah* and *Paul* speak of a Real and Inward Righteousness, not the less in the Creature, because not of the Creature, but of Christ.

Contin. p. 54.
Isa. 45. 24. 25

1 Cor. 1. 30, 31.

Was not *Paul's* Righteousness the Son of God revealed in him? that *everlasting Righteousness*, that Christ, binding and casting out of the Strong Man, making an End of Sin, and finishing of Transgression, he brought and brings into the Soul? For that their Righteousness should be *in* or *from* him, or that he should be made their Righteousness, *and they never know a being cloathed and made Righteous by it, were Absurd and Impossible.* In short, As we know no Righteousness out of Christ our Lord, so knowing his Appearance in us, and that Grace for Grace, received of his Fulness, in whom are hid the Treasures of Wisdom and Knowledge, and being obedient thereunto, we know and Witness a Participation of his Everlasting Righteousness, Holy Wisdom and Saving Knowledge, which qualifie and adorn the Soul for the Blessed Marriage of the Lamb, *who takes away the Sins of the World*; not only the *Guilt* of Sins past by Remission upon Repentance, but as a Redeemer from under the Power and Nature of Sin present and to come, through the Virtue of his Holy Life in the Soul, which is the *Compleating of Justification*, and the Thing now insisted on.

Lastly, he gives under the *Quakers* name, as a dangerous Doctrine, this Passage; *Justification goes not before, but is consequential to the mortifying of Lusts, and the Sanctification of the Soul.* Penn, Sand. Foun. Sh. p. 27. To which he answers. *Doth not this import that a Man must be formally just before he be justified? I would ask whether Remission of Sins be not one Part of Justification?* Qua. I suppose it may. Chr. *Can one be forgiven that is not Guilty? It looks like a Contradiction, to pardon one that is Innocent. Certainly he that is pardoned must be a Sinner.* To all which I return thus much; Were he True and honest in his Reasoning, I had been to blame for my Ignorance, and *T. Hicks* to be commended for his Answer; but he dodges basely. He would avoid my Argument about the *second Part of Justification*, by suggesting that I meant it of *the first*, to wit, *Remission of Sins*, as much as if he had said; *What, must all Sin be mortified before a Man be pardoned his old Score? and can a Man's own Good Works so remit, Cancel or Justifie?* But his Sleight will not do. I have often declared that upon Repentance God doth not impute past

Cont. p. 59.

Iniquity to any, therefore that Part of his Answer which seems most smart upon me, that is, *Can one be forgiven that is not Guilty?* &c. vanisheth of Course; for the Question is not, Whether Man in his natural Estate is Guilty before God, and such can be no otherwise so justified, that is, *Remitted*, than by the free Love of God, which is the first Part of Justification, as David speaks, *Blessed is the Man unto whom the Lord will not impute Sin*. But whether Men are *daily accepted as Children of God, redeemed, and saved of the Lord, and justified as such, in his Presence, farther than as they come to be led by his Holy Spirit, and know Victory over Sin? which is the second Part of Justification.* So that he did dishonestly with me, to suggest my Denial of Remission of Sins past, upon any other Score than the Mortification of Sin in the Party so pardoned: For though Sin may not be mortified, yet if there be a Foundation of true Repentance laid, *the Guilt of former Iniquities, I have often said, is not imputed.* It was therefore very unfairly done of him, from Asserting daily Acceptance, and Fellowship with God, to be the Consequence of a Self-denying and mortified Life through the powerful Working of the Spirit of Christ in Man, to infer, that *before this Work was done, there could be no Remission of Sins past*; as if it were the procuring Cause of Pardon, and not the free Love of God upon Repentance. In short, it is to say, that because I deny Men may be justified in the second Sense, without being made truly and really Just, that therefore *Men are to be made Just and Innocent before they are forgiven*; which is Justification in the first Sense. And thus has he dodg'd disingenuously with me throughout this Point: Where I meant by Justification, *Remission of Sins*, he has run it the other Way; And when I have understood it of a *State of Fellowship and daily Acceptance with God*, then he has taken it for *Remission*, with manifest Design, to render me as confus'd, contradictory and unscriptural, as he could; but all that lights upon himself, and I doubt not but in the end it will appear, that I have contended for the Justification of Life, whilst his Aims will have been at nothing more in all his Bustle, *than to promote a Justification in a State of Death, where the indwelling Life, Power and Virtue of Christ, which gives to live to God in the Nearness of Life, cannot be enjoyed nor known*: else, what Means his reputing that Assertion in my *Sandy Foundation shaken*, so Erroneous, namely, *without Good Works there is no Acceptance with God*, which, without any Wrong to him, causes me to believe, that it is his Faith, *that Men may be accepted with God without Good Works*; and *consequently that they are not necessary to Salvation.* I wish for his Sake, more than mine own, he had been no more Injurious to me, and the Truth I have defended, than I have been to him, in expressing but the Natural Result and Tendency of his Doctrine.

I shall now be as good as my Word, and that is, to produce an Argument or two against the Common Doctrines of rigid *Satisfaction* and *Justification*, as they have been opposed by me in this short Discourse, and that out of my Book called, *The Sandy Foundation Shaken*, because it has been most in this Adversary's Eye; That if he thinks fit to reply, he may have something else to employ his Mind about than to write Dialogues filled with *Lyes, Shifts, Forgeries, Scoffs, Impudence* and *Scurrility*.

Of SATISFACTION.

1. *Who is a God like unto thee, that pardoneth Iniquity, and passeth by the Transgression of the Remnant of his Heritage? He retaineth not his Anger for ever: because he delighteth in Mercy.* Micah. 7. 18. [Can there be a more express Passage to clear, not only the *Possibility*, but *real Inclinations* in God to pardon Sin, and *not retain his Anger for ever?* Since the Prophet seems to challenge all other Gods to try their Excellency by his God, herein describing the Supremacy of his Power and Super-Excellency of his Nature, *that he pardoneth Iniquity, and retaineth not his Anger for ever:* so that if the Satisfactionists should ask the Question, Who is a God like unto ours, that cannot pardon Iniquity, nor pass by Transgression, but retain his Anger until some-body make him Satisfaction? I answer, Many amongst the harsh and severe Rulers of the Nation; but as for my God, he is exalted above them all, upon the Throne of his Mercy, *who pardoneth Iniquity, and retaineth not his Anger for ever, but will have Compassion upon us.*]

2. *And forgive us our Debts, as we forgive our Debtors.* Mat. 6. 12. [Where nothing can be more obvious than that *which is forgiven, is not paid*: And if it is our Duty to forgive without a Satisfaction receiv'd, and that God is to forgive us as we forgive them, then is a Satisfaction totally excluded. Christ farther paraphrases

phrases upon that Part of his Prayer, v. 14. *For if you forgive their Trespasses, your Heavenly Father will also forgive you.* Where he as well argues the Equity of God's Forgiving them, from their Forgiving others, as he encourages them to forgive others, from the Example of God's Mercy in forgiving them; which is more amply exprest in *Chap.* 18. where the Kingdom of Heaven (that consists in Righteousness) is represented by a King; *Who upon his Debtor's Petition, had Compassion, and forgave him; but the same treating his Fellow-Servant without the least Forbearance, the King condemned his Unrighteousness, and delivered him over to the Tormenters.* But how had this been a Fault in the Servant, if his King's Mercy had not been proposed for his Example? How most unworthy therefore is it of God, and *Blasphemous* may I justly term it, for any Man to assert that Forgiveness impossible to God, which is not only possible, but enjoin'd to Men.]

Consequences Irreligious and Irrational.

1. That it's Unlawful and Impossible for God Almighty to be Gracious and Merciful, or to pardon Transgressors; than which, What's more Unworthy of God?

2. That God was inevitably compelled to this Way of saving Men; the highest Affront to his incontroulable Nature.

3. That it was Unworthy of God to Pardon, but not to inflict Punishment on the Innocent, or require a Satisfaction, where there was nothing due.

4. It doth not only dis-acknowledge the true Virtue, and real Intent of Christ's Life and Death, but intirely deprives God of that Praise which is owing to his greatest Love and Goodness.

5. It represents the Son more Kind and Compassionate than the Father; whereas if both be the same God, then either the Father is as loving as the Son, or the Son as angry as the Father.

6. It robs God of the Gift of his Son for our Redemption (which the Scriptures attribute to the unmerited Love he had for the World) in affirming the Son purchased that Redemption from the Father, by the Gift of himself to God, as our compleat Satisfaction.

7. Since Christ could not pay what was not his own, it follows that in the Payment of his own, the Case still remains equally grievous; Since the Debt is not hereby absolv'd or forgiven, but transferred only; and by consequence we are no better provided for Salvation than before, owing that now to the Son, which was once owing to the Father.

8. It no Way renders Men beholding, or in the least oblig'd to God; since by their Doctrine he would not have abated us, nor did he Christ, the last Farthing, so that the Acknowledgments are peculiarly the Son's: which destroys the whole Current of Scripture Testimony, for his Good will towards Men.—O the Infamous Portraiture this Doctrine draws of the Infinite Goodness! Is this your Retribution, O Injurious Satisfactionists?

9. That God's Justice is satisfied for Sins past, present, and to come, whereby God and Christ have lost both their Power of injoyning Godliness, and Prerogative of punishing Disobedience; for what is once paid, is not revocable; and if Punishment should arrest any for their Debts, it either argues a Breach on God's or Christ's Part, or else that it hath not been sufficiently solv'd, and the Penalty compleatly sustain'd by another; forgetting *that every one must appear before the Judgment-Seat of Christ, to receive according to the Things done in the Body,* Rom. 14. 12. 2 Cor. 15. 10. Yea, every one must give an Account of himself to God. But many more are the gross Absurdities and Blasphemies, that are the genuine Fruits of this so confidently believ'd Doctrine of Satisfaction.

Of JUSTIFICATION.

1. *Not every one that saith unto me Lord, Lord, shall enter into the Kingdom of Heaven; but he that doth the Will of my Father. Whosoever heareth these Sayings of mine, and doth them, I will liken him unto a Wise Man which built his House upon a Rock,* &c. Mat. 7. 21. 24, 25. [How very fruitful are the Scriptures of Truth in Testimonies against this absurd and dangerous Doctrine; these Words seem to import a two-fold Righteousness, the *first* consists in Sacrifice, the *last* in Obedience; the one makes a *Talking,* the other a *Doing Christian.* I, in short, argue thus: If none can enter into the Kingdom of Heaven, but they that do the Father's

ther's Will, then none are justified, but they who do the Father's Will, because none can enter into the Kingdom, but such as are justified. Since therefore there can be no Admittance had without *Performing* that Righteous Will, and *Doing* those Holy and Perfect Sayings, Alas! to what Value will an imputative Righteousness amount, when a poor Soul shall awake polluted in his Sin, by the hasty Calls of Death to make it's Appearance before the Judgment-Seat, where 'tis impossible to justify the Wicked, or that any should escape uncondemned, but such as do the Will of God]

2. *For not the Hearers of the Law are just before God, but the Doers of the Law shall be justified.* [From whence how unanswerably may I observe, unless we become *Doers* of that Law, which Christ came not to destroy, but, as our Example, to fulfil, we can never be justified before God; wherefore Obedience is so absolutely necessary, that short of it there can be no Acceptance; Nor let any Fancy that Christ hath so fulfilled it for them, as to exclude their Obedience from being requisite to their Acceptance, but only as their Pattern, *For unless ye follow me*, saith Christ, *ye cannot be my Disciples:* And it is not only repugnant to Reason, but in this Place particularly refuted; for if Christ had fulfilled it on our Behalf, and we not enabled to follow his Example, there would not be Doers, but *One* Doer only of the Law justified before God. In short, if without Obedience to the Righteous Law none can be justified, then all the *Hearing* of the Law, with but the meer Imputation of another's Righteousness, whilst actually a Breaker of it, is excluded as not justifying before God. *If you fulfil the Royal Law, ye do well; so speak ye, and so do, as they that shall be judged* thereby.]

3. *If ye live after the Flesh, ye shall die; but if ye through the Spirit do mortify the Deeds of the Body, ye shall live.* Rom. 8. 13. [No Man can be dead and justified before God, for so He may be justified that lives after the Flesh; therefore they only can be justified that are alive; from whence this follows, If the Living are justified and not the Dead, and that none can live to God, but such as have mortified the Deeds of the Body through the Spirit, then none can be justified but they who have mortified the Deeds of the Body through the Spirit; so that * Justification does not go before, but is subsequential to the Mortification of Lusts, and Sanctification of the Soul through the Spirit's Operation.]

* Justification is compleatly taken. Jam. 2. 21. 24

4. *Was not* Abraham *our Father justified by Works, when he had offered* Isaac *his Son upon the Altar? Ye see then how that by Works a Man is justified, and not by Faith only.* [He that will seriously peruse this Chapter, shall, doubtless, find some, to whom this Epistle was written, of the same Spirit with the Satisfactionists and Imputarians of our Time; they fain would have found out a Justification from Faith in, and the Imputation of, another's Righteousness; but *James*, an Apostle of the most High God, who experimentally knew what true Faith and Justification meant, gave them to understand from *Abraham's* Self-denying Example, that unless their Faith in the Purity and Power of God's Grace, had that effectual Operation to subdue every beloved Lust, wean from every *Delilah*, and intirely to resign and sacrifice *Isaac* himself, their Faith was a Fable, or as a Body without a Spirit; and as Righteousness therefore in one Person cannot justify another from Unrighteousness, so whoever now pretend to be justified by Faith, whilst not led and guided by the Spirit into all the Ways of Truth, and Works of Righteousness, their *Faith* they will find at last *Fiction*.]

Consequences Irreligious and Irrational.

1. It makes God guilty of what the Scriptures say is an Abomination, to wit, that he justifieth the Wicked.

2. It makes him look upon Persons as they are not, or with Respect, which is unworthy of his most Equal Nature.

3. He is hereby at Peace with the Wicked, (if justified whilst Sinners) who said, *There is no Peace to the Wicked.*

4. It does not only imply Communion with them here, in an Imperfect State, but so to all Eternity; *for whom he justifieth, them he also glorifieth*; Rom. 8. 30. Therefore whom he justified whilst Sinners, them he also glorified whilst Sinners.

5. It only secures from the Wages, not the Dominion of Sin, whereby something that is sinful becomes justified, and that which defileth, to enter God's Kingdom.

6. It renders a Man justified and condemn'd, dead and alive, redeemed and not redeemed at the same Time; the one by an Imputative Righteousness, the last by a Personal Unrighteousness.

7. It flatters Men whilst subject to the World's Lusts, with a State of Justification, and thereby invalids the very End of Christ's Appearance, which was to destroy the Works of the *Devil*, and take away the Sins of the World.

CHAP. X.

Of the Doctrine of Sanctification *and* Perfection. *The Ignorance or Malice of* T. Hicks *Detected.*

OF the Doctrine of *Sanctification* he has several *Unsanctified Passages*, though he bestows not much Time upon that Important Subject; some of which I take a little Notice of.

Christ. *Let us understand your Opinion of Sanctification. what it is?* Out of *Edw. Burroughs* he answereth himself thus. Quak. *'Tis Christ.* Hence we conclude, to *say Sanctification is Imperfect in this Life, is as much as to say, Christ is Imperfect.* To which he replies. Christ. *'Tis true, 'tis Jesus Christ by his Spirit is the Author and Worker of Sanctification ; but will it therefore follow, that the Work of Sanctification in us is Christ, or that this Work is perfect in all it's Degrees?.*

Now let any tell me wherein *T. Hicks* who frequently insults over the Grave and Labours of that Faithful Servant of the Lord, could have more grosly mistaken *E. Burroughs*, than he has done, on purpose, I doubt not, to insinuate his Belief of the contrary to what he opposed. But hear *Edw. Burroughs*'s Words at large in Answer to Priest *Eaton*.

" Thou sayst, *Sanctification is not Perfect in this Life*; And *the New Man, the* " *Spirit or Law of the Mind, is that Grace or Imperfect Sanctification :* Then Christ " is not Perfect in this Life; for He is made of God unto us Sanctification, 1 *Cor.* 1. 30.

In this it is evident, *First*, That the *Priest* did not so much strike at the Work done in the Creature, as at the Perfection of the Principle, by which the Work should be perfected in the Creature.

2*dly*. *E. Burroughs* did not in that Place meerly intend the Work of Sanctification, but the Author and Worker of it, who is oftentimes called by the Name of the Work it self, the *Cause by the Effect*, as is plain from the Scripture quoted, in which he used but *Paul*'s Words.

How basely done was it then, in *T. Hicks*, not only to leave out what the *Priest* asserted, but to mis-construe *E. B*'s Answer, and (that such Perversion might go the more Unquestioned) omit the Insertion of that Scripture, in which Christ is by the Apostle said *to be made Sanctification to the Saints*; the Mention of which would have given a clear Understanding of *E. Burroughs*'s Answer, and broke the Neck of his Ungodly Purpose to mis-represent him. • We say, and it was the Faith and Tendency of the Writings of that Just Man, 1. *To assert a Perfect Principle of Righteousness and Sanctification*, which is Sanctification and Perfection in the Abstract. 2. *The Possibility of being Perfectly Sanctified by it*. 3. *That such Sanctification, when taken for the Author of it,* (who is the Fountain of all Holiness and Purity) *is Compleat and Perfect*. 4. When taken for the Work of the Spirit in the Creature, *it is first Perfect in Degree only*; but as the Creature comes into perfect Subjection unto the Spirit and Power of him that raised up Jesus from the Dead, which hath wrought that Perfection in Degree, *he comes to experience that Sanctification throughout, in Body, Soul and Spirit*, which the Apostle otherwise minded than *T. Hicks*) prayed the Churches might *witness*, which is that blessed State, *wherein he that's born of God sins not ; Old Things are done away, all is become new; No more I, but Christ that liveth in me. I write unto you, Young Men, because ye have overcome the wicked one : Be ye perfect, as your heavenly Father is perfect— unto a perfect Man. That the Man of God may be perfect The God of Peace make you perfect in every good Work. The God of all Peace make you perfect. Let us cleanse our selves from all Filthiness of Flesh and Spirit ; Perfecting Holiness in the Fear of the Lord.* With many more Places of like Importance.

But he objects, *Why doth the Apostle exhort Sanctified Persons to put off the Old Man* (from *Colos.* 3. 5) *If where the Old Man, the Body of Sin remains, none are Sanctified, as saith* E. B.

This indeed is the Drift of the Man, he would be Sanctified whilst Unsanctified; as Dangerous, as it is Absurd: For what Thing can be and not be the same Thing, at one and the same Time? But I deny they were then Sanctified who stood in Need of that Reproof and Exhortation, to wit, that they should mortify such Lusts, as *Fornication, Uncleanness, Inordinate Affection, and Covetousness, which is Idolatry.* Sanctifying such are, who are Mortifying: but when Sin is not Mortifying, none are Sanctifying; and where Sin is not Mortified, no Man is Sanctified. We may easily see, what a *Church-Fellowship* T. H. *can allow of, and what a Gospel-Sanctification it is he pleads for.* Can Men be Sanctified, and yet so Corrupt? If they can, tell me in what Sense, and from what they are cleansed? Is this the End of pleading for Perfection in Degree, to allow these Abominable Enormities, as *Church-Infirmities?* Away, for Shame! But that a perfect Sanctification is no *Heresy,* suppose they had been Sanctified Persons to whom the Apostle wrote, (which could not be, Sanctifying was the most) yet, since he exhorted them, *to put off the Old Man,* which Old Man is *the Body of Sin, and that when he is off, he is not on, and that the Apostle exhorted them not to an Impossible Thing,* I conclude from his Question, that a State of perfect Sanctification is attainable. He pretended to correct E. B's Extravagancy; but whatever Face he puts upon it, this is the Mark he aims at. To conclude, and sum up his ungodly Method; E. B. speaks of a perfect Sanctification in Christ. T. H. infers, that same perfect Sanctification immediately to the Creature; not only confounding the *Worker* and *Work*, the *Cause* and the *Effect*, about which one Piece of Baseness he bestows not a little Pains; but suggesting thereby, that *we deny all Sanctification or Perfection in Degree,* and that we are as compleatly Perfect as Christ himself.

Next, He leaves out those Words that would best explain his Mind. And, *Lastly,* All his Opposition is, because the *Quakers* are for having Men Sanctify'd before they are accounted so, and New Creatures before they ought to be reputed Good *Christians;* which so directly *Un-churches* and *Un-christians* T. *Hicks,* that we may well believe it a main Reason for his Implacableness against them.

CHAP. XI.

Of COMMANDS, MOTIONS *and* MINISTRY. T. Hicks *proved Unjust to us, and an Enemy to God's Law, Gospel, the* Quakers, *and himself.*

HE has not less abused and bely'd us in these three Particulars, than in any thing he has written against us, which I shall briefly shew.

To this Passage in E. *Burroughs's* Works, " *That is no Command to me which is a Command to another, neither did any of the Saints act by a Command that was given to another,* he thus answers, *Then that Law which forbids Idolatry, Adultery, Murder, Theft and bearing false Witness, is no Law to you.* And after having made this indirect Consequence, he breaketh forth, *Impiously Horrid, Ungodly, Irreverent Patronizers of Blasphemy, Countenancers of such, Novices, Prophane Scribler,* and Abundance more.

Now though I have said something to this before, and have largely vindicated that Passage against J. *Faldo,* yet I cannot well omit touching here upon it, the Matter being so aggravated by this disingenuous Person.

These Commands must either relate to *Ordinary* or *Extraordinary Duty;* I mean, they must either be such Commands, as that of *Moses's going to* Pharaoh, Isaiah's *going Naked,* Jeremiah's *making Yoaks,* Amos's *going to the King's Chappel;* with many more: And here I do affirm with that faithful young Man of God, that the Command which came to them, not coming to another, that other Person is not only not warranted, *but condemnable, in an Imitation of any of them.* If then such Extraordinary Commands, as these before mentioned, must not be intended, then those that are Ordinary and Common to Mankind must, as *Fearing God and working Righteousness towards God, towards their Relations, both Natural and Civil.* Now I would ask T. H. if he believes that *Idolatry, Murder, Theft and bearing false Witness,* be not reproved by the *Common Light* in all Men? if not, T. H. gives the Lye to all Mankind, and his own Books too; Nay, what is it good for? But if they be; query, *If any can confess to one God, love his Neighbour, be Chaste, be Just, and speak Truth in his own and Neighbour's Cause, without being thereto obliged* ed *by that Light he hath?* Did the *Gentiles* of old the Things contained in the Law, without a *Word, Commandment, Law* or *Light* within, inducing them thereto? I perceive *T. Hicks owns no Command in himself against Idolatry, Aultery, Murder, Theft* and *bearing false Witness*; which is to say, if the Scripture did not restrain him, *he should be guilty of all.* Farewel *Grace, Spirit, Light,* and *all Inward Rule or Judge, by which to see, taste, relish,* and *determine of Things.* But in this Condition, how knows he that the Scriptures were writ by Inspiration? If he says he was told so; I ask how they knew it? If they say they were told so too, and so upwards; I ask what Assurance can any Man's *Say-so* or *Hearsay* be in a Matter of such Importance? Nay, Suppose I should grant them a true Tradition from the Apostles Times, I ask, *How knew they to whom they were writ, that they were the Fruits of Divine Inspiration?* In short, take away all Inward Testimony, or the Certainty and Sufficiency of it, and *Farewel* to all Right Belief of the Scriptures themselves. Behold the Strait he is run into! But if at last *T. H.* shall desire a little more Room, and acknowledge the *Spirit* must give the *Discerning,* and *Relish,* and *most Convincing Testimony*; will it not follow that he believeth the Scriptures, and performeth what may be his Duty therein, upon that *Conviction, and nor meerly because written or recommended by any Man whatever?*

But he proceeds to prove *E. B.* as he thinks, an *Enemy* to God's Commandments, and a very Lyar. The Thing he wickedly, but in vain aims at.

He quotes him thus: " *Quak.* You are not dead with Christ who are yet subject " to Ordinances, *E. B.* p. 105. To which hear him. Christ. *The Spirit of God in the Scriptures assures us, that they who are subject to, and keep the Commandments of God, are the Children of God, and they who do not are Lyars.* See the first Epistle of *John* 2. 3, 4. and Chap. 5. 2, 3. *Yet this Wicked Man saith, That they who are subject to Ordinances are not Dead with Christ.*

Edw. Burroughs's Words are those of the Scriptures of Truth, therefore true Words in themselves. But how does *E. B.* abolish what God perpetuates? I am sure I can plainly perceive that *T. Hicks* does call a *Conscientious, Departed Sufferer,* and *Prisoner unto Death for the Testimony of Jesus,* Wicked Man, *because he dared not be guilty of Will-worship, by going into any Practice of Worship, without the Leading of God's Spirit.* Six Particulars comprehend my Answer in Brief.

First, That *Edward Burroughs* only pleaded against such Performances, under the Name of Ordinances, as were but Shadowy, * Elementary and Perishable Things; and which they were not led to by God's Spirit, but took up unwarrantably, and by meer Imitation, and therefore *Will-Worship.*

2. That *Thomas Hicks* implies by calling him *Wicked Man,* that it is a Wickedness, *not to take up any Outward or Visible Part of Worship in a Man's own Will and Time, but to stay God's Time, and wait for the Leadings of God's Spirit:* From whence I infer, *He is no Child of God; for every such one is led by the Spirit of God*; therefore no better than an Ape, or Imitator of the Outsides of Religion. In short, *a Will-Worshipper, and not a Worshipper of God in the Spirit and in the Truth.*

3. Let it be observed, that there is not so much as the least Mention made in all the *Epistles* of that *Beloved Disciple,* of any of those Ordinances, *which stood in Visible and Corruptible Elements,* but the Scope and Tendency of them is the most Inward and Spiritual of any of the Apostolical Writings: *So that to bring in Things of a Temporary, Shadowy Nature, among the Spiritual and Durable Commands of Christ under the New Covenant State, without keeping of which Men incur Eternal Wrath, is an Abuse both of the Apostle's Words, and E. B's, which he intended by them to confute.*

4. *T. Hicks* does as good as tell us, *That the Commandments of God may be kept without the Spirit of God*; since he opposes the Necessity of doing God's Commandments, *to our doing them in the Time and Will, and by the Assistance, of God's Spirit*: O Irreligious Man, and Enemy to God's Spirit!

5. It plainly tells us, that *Thomas Hicks has no Command in himself for doing what he does*; that the bare Authority of the Scripture is all he has to induce him, which rases to the Ground *that old Protestant Doctrine of Believing the Scriptures from an Inward Testimony, and Worshipping God in Spirit and Truth.*

6. *Lastly,* If all are *Lyars* that keep not God's Commandments, and therefore none of his Children, as saith the Place, and as asserts *T. Hicks,* then either *T. H.* keeps God's Commandments, and so is Perfect, or he must be a Lyar, and so no Child of God.

That

That he keeps not God's Commands I prove.

Such as say that Man cannot *fulfil, obey or keep the Law, nor the Gospel; Pray, Preach, Dip, Eat Bread, and Drink Wine, nor live without Sin,* keep not God's Commandments; but so doth T. H. *expresly* or *implicitly*; therefore he keeps not God's Commandments, and consequently is a Lyar, and no Child of God ; *For the Lyar is for the Lake.*

To say, *We deny Obedience to God's Commands,* because we deny the present Necessity or Use of their *Water, Bread and Wine,* will never hurt us; For, *First,* we know, and they confess, that they were in the Beginning used as Figures and Shadows of a more Hidden and Spiritual Substance.

2. That they were to endure no longer than till the Substance was come : Now the Time of the *Baptism of the Holy Ghost, Christ's Only Baptism, therefore called the* One Baptism, *has been long since come :* Consequently the other, which was *John*'s was fulfilled, and as becomes a Fore-runner, ought to cease. The like may be said of the Bread and Wine; *for as there is but One Baptism, so there is but One Bread. The Least in the Kingdom was Greater than* John*'s Water-Baptism*; *He was to Decrease, Christ to Increase.* Jesus *Baptized not with Water :* 'Tis true, he bid his Apostles, *Go, Teach, Baptizing,* &c. but no Water is mentioned : But *Luke,* in the First of the *Acts,* says, that before Christ gave that Commission mention'd by *Matthew,* he said, John *Baptized with Water, but ye shall be Baptized with the Holy Ghost not many Days hence*; and then comes the Commission in Force, *Go, Teach, Baptizing,* &c. How ? *With the Holy Ghost* ; *turning People from Darkness to Light, and from the Power of Satan unto God.*

3. *They were but the more Noble among the Meats and Drinks, and divers Washings,* that the Apostle said, *Were but Shadows of the Good Things to come :* For I would not that any should be so Sottish as to think, that Christ came to abolish those Shadows of the *Jews,* and institute other in their Room ; by no Means : He came to remove, change, and abolish *the very Nature of such Ordinances,* and not the particular Ordinances only, to wit, *an Outward, Shadowy, or Figurative Worship and Religion.* For it was not because *they were Jewish Meats and Drinks, and divers Washings, but because they were Meats and Drinks, and divers outward Washings at all,* which never could, nor can, cleanse the Conscience from dead Works, nor give Eternal Life to the Soul ; else wherein would the Change be ? I affirm by that one Scripture, *Circumcision is as much in Force as Water-Baptism*; *and the Paschal Lamb as Bread and Wine :* They were both Shadows, and both *Elementary and Perishable.* And though the *Latter* were more immediately *fore-running and introductory of the Substance it self, yet not to be perpetuated* ; For a Continuance of them had been a *Judaizing of the Spiritual Evangelical Worship*; The Gospel would have been a *State of Figures, Types and Shadows,* which to assert or practise, is as much as in such lies, to pluck it up by the Roots ; The Appellation, *Ordinances of Christ,* I therefore renounce, as Unscriptural and Inevangelical : Besides, *a Spirit of Whoredom from God, gross Apostacy into Superstition and Idolatry, yea, a Spirit of Hypocrisie, Persecution and Murder, and all manner of Wickedness has got them, and covered it self with them,* Jezebel-like, *the old Enemy of God's Faithful Prophets and People.* And we can testifie from the same Spirit by which *Paul* renounced *Circumcision,* that they are to be rejected, as not now required ; neither have they, since the False Church espoused and exalted them, *ever been taken up afresh by God's Command, or in the Leading of His Eternal Spirit :* And the Lord will appear to gather People out of them ; but never to establish, or keep People in them, no ; they served their Time ; and now the *False Church* has got them ; yea, the *Whore* has made Merchandize with them, and under such *Historical, Shadowy, and Figurative Christianity, has she managed her Mystery of Iniquity, unto the beguiling of Thousands, whose Simplicity the Lord has, and will have tender Regard to.*

But they *Baptized after the Holy Ghost was poured out.* True ; and they also would not *Eat the Flesh of Things Strangled, nor Blood*; *They Circumcised and Purified themselves in the Temple, and had Vows after the Pouring forth of the Holy Ghost.* By which we may learn, that Condescension and Practice are quite differing Things from Institution ; else *Paul* would never have said, *He was not sent to Baptize* (i. e.) *with Water,* whose Commission doubtless, went as far as any of the rest.

But they brake Bread, and Paul *received it from God.* True ; But *Paul* never enjoyned it ; He said, *As often as ye do it,* &c. which is very wide of any Institution.

on. Again, Read the Chapter foregoing, 1 *Cor.* 10. where he tells the *Wise Men of another Bread than that he spoke to the Weak of, who Eat and Drank to Excess, not discerning the Lord's Body.*

Farther, Let it be confidered, that no other Apoftle recommends thefe Things, nor *Paul* himfelf, to either the *Romans*, the *Corinthians* (in his Firft Epiftle) the *Galatians, Ephefians, Philippians, Coloffians, Theffalonians, Hebrews* (it his) nor to *Timothy, Titus* and *Philemon*, when he fet down the Order of the Churches. What an Over-fight (might one then fay, according to *T. H.)* was it in him, not only not to prefs and charge, but not to mention the *Sacraments of the Church, Neceffary to Salvation*, as they are called and efteemed? Would it not have been accounted a great Neglect and Defect in *Calvin*, if he had been filent to any Church Inftitutions in his Time and Form; or to fay, *He thanked God he Baptized none but fuch and fuch?* Yet how full are his and their Epiftles of Divine Exhortation, Information, Reproof, Inftruction, and the like? Is it not very Wicked then in *Thomas Hicks*, to tell the World of our *Denying to keep God's Commandments in General*, becaufe we refufe to practife thefe *Shadowy, Temporary, Perifhing Things*, efpecially at this Time a Day, after fuch an Abufe of them, and that the *Gentile-Spirit* has troden them under Foot fo long, being Part of that Outward Court of Religion, given to them, which were left out *at the meafuring of the Evangelical Temple of God*, Rev. 21? Befides, what Authority have thefe Men for ufing them? To do as Men would be done to, concerns all, in all Ages; but to practife *Figures and Shadows* in Religion, we know does not. A Church cannot be without one, yet without the other. Would it not be Ridiculous in any Man to adorn himfelf either as fome Eminent Commander, or other Officer, becaufe it is required by Office or Place of every fuch one that really is fo? The *Apoftles* Baptized, therefore muft *T H?* The *Apoftles* Anointed with Oil, therefore fhould *T. H?* Nay, Chrift wafhed his Difciples Feet, telling them, they ought, or it was their Duty fo to do one to the other, therefore fhould *T. H?* The Believers Sold their Poffeffions, and had all Things Common; but will *T. H.* either imitate, or enjoyn this upon his Hearers? But fince *T. H.* and his *Adherents*, do not feveral fuch Things, once done and enjoyned too, as *Blood, Things Strangled, Anointing with Oil, Wafhing of Feet*, &c. Why are they not to be as much blamed, as we are for omitting that of *Bread and Wine?* Or why fhould not they rather defift Practifing of thofe with the reft, and that upon the fame Terms? I will warrant *T. H.* for going to *Synagogues, Decrying Hirelings, Preaching Freely, Expofing himfelf to all Hardfhip for the Gofpel's fake*, which the *Apoftles* did.

To conclude, God never condefcended to ufe fuch Things (to lead to, and hold forth the hidden Subftance) that People fhould reft there, and much lefs in a Way of Oppofition to the Subftance it felf; fuch an Ufe of them has caufed God to loath them, and enjoyn us to teftify againft them. Remember the Inftituted *Brazen-Serpent* of old, *&c.* what became of them in the like Cafe? We would be glad to fee more *Honefty, Meeknefs*, and *Godly-mindednefs* in our Oppofers, tho' there were lefs of this Imitation: They are for *fuch Commands*, as they call them, which *Hypocrites, Apoftates, the Falfe Church*, yea, *the Devil himfelf can come into*; but as for thofe that concern the *Daily Crofs, and Victory over Sin*, they can Wickedly plead a Kind of Liberty from, at leaft to, their unconquerable Infirmities, as they are willing to believe them. But we teftify againft the *Falfe Church*, whofe Faith and Worfhip ftands not in the Life, Power and Spirit of God, however deckt with the ancient Attire of the True; for her fineft Forms out of the Life and Power of God we renounce, and as becomes the *True Evangelical Church*, we affert, *That he is not a* Jew *or* Chriftian, *who is one outwardly, neither is that now the Circumcifion, Baptifm and Supper, which is Outward*; *but he is the* Jew *or* Chriftian, *that is one Inwardly*; *and that is the* Circumcifion *that is of the* Heart, *that the* Baptifm, *which is of the* Holy Ghoft *and* Fire, *and that the* Supper, *which is of the* Bread *that cometh down from* Above, *which gives Eternal Life to as many as Eat thereof, and that is the* Wine, *which is to be Drunk New with* Chrift *in the Kingdom of God Within*, Luke 17. 20.

Much might be faid in this Matter, but I refer the *Reader* to the Book entituled, *Quakerifm a New Nick-Name for Old Chriftianity.* However, let it be noted, that our *Adverfary* is for Will-Worfhip, and not the *Quakers*; for we affirm that no Sacrifice nor Performance can be acceptable with God, *to, and in which His Holy Spirit leads not*; by the which only, *Self* is abas'd, kept under, and in perfect Obedience to, and watchful Obfervance of, God's Holy Will. But *T. Hicks* makes this

a Strange

a Strange and Dangerous Doctrine, infinuating that we perform nothing but upon a Kind of Spiritual Compulsion, as if that God required Man to do all his Commandments without His Holy Spirit, always ready to incline and help them, either to begin or perform any such Duty; or that there were no Difference between waiting for the Natural Springs of Divine Power to assist, *and being compell'd to worship*. But this shews his great Ignorance of God's Spirit, in it's Daily Movings upon the Heart of Men, either as a Reprover, or Comforter for Good; for were he better acquainted with it's Dealings, it would not be so uncouth to him, to hear of our Waiting to feel the Holy Stirrings of it, in order to every Religious Performance: Wherefore let not his *Ignorance* be any *Argument* against our Holy Gospel-Practice. The Saints of Old had a Warrant in themselves for what they did: They were not wont to run into the Imitation of former Generations, as to any External Appointments because then commanded, and practised as proper, but consulted the Anointing they had receiv'd about the Continuation or Dis-use of such Figures or outward Services; and as they receiv'd Wisdom and Counsel therefrom, either to use or decline the Practice of them, they acted, and no otherwise; making Good the Apostle's Saying, *That as many as are led by the Spirit of God, are the Sons of God:* Are we led by it in *All Things*, then in, and about God's Things. Had it not been for this, how could the Apostles have preach'd down the whole *Ceremonial Worship of the Jews*? The *meer Letter of Scripture* could never have been their Rule in the Case. If any say, *They were extraordinarily Inspired*, I answer, *How did such as then Believ'd, know that, if not from an Inward Testimony?* Nay, *What Rule had the many Thousands then to Worship God by?* The Hebrew Bible *was little, or not at all known to the* Gentiles. The Scripture tells us, *that whole Churches were settled in the Faith before the Epistles were writ*; And it is hard to think, when they were writ, *that they could be suddenly collected*; and when collected, *that every Individual could get a Copy*, that, to be sure, *ought to have a Rule*; for Printing was not so early in the World, and Transcribing must needs have been too irksome for every Person to obtain a Copy for his, or her peculiar Benefit: But because we are taught to believe, *that they wanted not a True Rule of Faith and Practice, and that the Scriptures, especially of the New Testament, could not be all that to them*, our present Adversaries *conclude to make the Great Rule*, let them not be displeas'd if I infer from hence, *that a Measure of that Holy Spirit, which was given to every one to profit with, was their Rule*, and therefore ought to be, our Great Rule and Guide, in all Things relating to Faith and Worship. And let it be remembred, *that Christ promised to send the Spirit of Truth to lead into all Truth*; as much as to say, *None are led into the Truth, nor in the Truth, but by the Holy Spirit of Truth*; or, *that their Practice is a Lye, or they are led into a Lye, who are not led by the Spirit of Truth, that alone leads into all the Ways of Truth*: Whereby *Truth* is not to be understood the *meer Letter of the Scripture*, which notwithstanding is True, but the *Living, Powerful Truth*; *Christ the Way, the Truth, and the Life*, of which the Scripture is but a Record, or Declaration: Many may run into a Practice of several Outward Things mentioned in the Scriptures, to have been the Practice of the Saints of former Ages, and yet not be led into the Truth; for all that is but Will-Worship, Imitation, and Unwarrantable. To be led into the Truth, is to be led into God's Living Power, Wisdom and Righteousness, whose Fruits are Peace and Assurance for ever: This is the Truth, the Spirit leads, and is All-sufficient to.

Certainly, *Christ* intended This for the *Great Evangelical Leader, Rule, Judge, Law-giver and Guide through the whole Course of Regeneration, the only Way into the Everlasting Kingdom*. And all those who are not by this Holy Spirit prepared, moved and assisted to perform Divine Worship unto God, but run into that weighty Duty, or any other (supposed) Ordinance, without it's Pure Leadings, which makes it a *Spiritual and Living Worship*, they are but those anciently fore-told of, *Lord, Lord Cryers*, whose Portion shall be that dismal *Depart from me, I know you not, who has requir'd these Things at your Hands*. Let this therefore be a Warning unto all *Professors*, in the Name of the Lord, that they Run no longer *Unsent*, nor think to be accepted for their many Words; God regards the Heart that he has broken, and is made Contrite before Him, and which trembles at His Word: 'Tis not meer Worship, but *that which is Spiritual*, which He expects and accepts; and to perform that, Man must cease from his own *Spirit, Strength, Strivings and Imitations*, and become Dumb before the *Lord*, and as a Man Dead to *Self-Performance*, and then will he breath into him the Spirit of Supplication, and raise him up in the Newness of his own Divine Life; whereby (though but in Sighs and Groans) *a Spiritual and most Acceptable Worship shall be offered unto God*, in which his Soul will be well-pleased, and every such one come to be refresh'd and establish'd in Righteousness. For all *Offerers* and *Upholders of strange Fire*, of what Sort of People soever they may be, *in the Great and Notable Day of the Lord God, will he cause to lie down in Sorrow.*

And because he thinks his Advantage is not small, that he hath against us, by basely inferring and aggravating such Consequences as this, *What of Duty we neglect, we are to charge upon the Spirit's not moving us to it*; or because we must not obey without a Motion, *we are acquitted from all Fault till then*, &c. Let me tell him, that he striketh himself, and not the *Quakers*; For they hold, *that God's Spirit ought to be Daily waited for; And that it is always ready to inform and instruct Man's Soul, and to move it to those Thoughts, Words and Deeds, with respect to God and Man, as are Well-pleasing to the Almighty*: For we do not only teach, *that the Spirit of God is always present to Convince of Sin, but to lead out of it, and in that Way of Holy Living, which is well-pleasing unto God.* In short, God's Worship stands in the Spirit, and I testify from the Eternal God, all other Worship than what springs from a Mind touch'd, sanctify'd and mov'd of his Holy, Quickning Spirit, is abominable to Him; His Righteous Soul loaths it: And what else were their Sacrifices, as theirs were, who in my Hearing said, *Pray Brother will you Pray? No, Brother, I am not so well able as you are; Let Brother such a one Pray, he is better Gifted for the Work*, &c. Complementing, Shifting, and at last Praying, &c. in their own Wills, and *not in God's Motion* —— This God hates.

Next, since the Pouring forth of the Spirit is the Great Gospel Gift, and that the Children of God are to be led by it; in what should we more diligently wait for it's Heavenly Assistance, than in that Part of our Duty which we owe to God? Is his Worship Spiritual, and can we perform it out of the Motion of his own Spirit? For what then was His Spirit given? Again, If Men should Pray in a known Tongue, *much more with the Spirit*, as the Apostle speaks; No Wonder the Professors ask Pardon for their Prayers. Indeed God's Spirit gives them to see the Emptiness of their Righteousness, and condemns them for it, wherefore they are at Times dissatisfy'd in them; yet they will not learn of him, to be guided by him, who would cover them with Everlasting Righteousness. Blessed would they be, if their Minds were stayed in his Counsel; but instead thereof, *T. H.* does as good as say, *That if he should stay till the Spirit moved him, he might stay long enough*; rendring the Spirit *Wanting* in that for which he was shed abroad in the Heart: Because through his Enmity and Darkness, and hasty Running in his own Spirit, he feels it not to lead him; else he would never infer, from our asserting the Necessity of the Spirit's moving to Right and Acceptable Worship, *that we are acquitted from any Fault in omitting to do that which is Good, and the Blame must be laid upon the Spirit.* But let me ask him, *Can any Man do Good of himself?* Surely he will say, No. How then shall Man do that Good he ought to do, but by the Holy Ghost? *Canst thou call Jesus Lord by any other Power or Spirit?* Read the Scriptures. What greater Contradiction can there be, than to believe, Man of himself can do no Good; and yet to say, *He can do it without God's Spirit to incline and assist him thereunto?* But if the Spirit do not, what does? *Tell me, what can tender the Heart, prepare the Soul, raise the Affections, give True Feeling of Wants, and help to perform all in that Fear, Reverence, and deep Sense (which becomes all New Covenant, Spiritual Worshippers)* if this cannot, or do not? Nay, what an Affront is it to God; since it is to suppose, *that Man wants Him not, that his Spirit neither moves to Duty that ought to be performed, nor yet condemns for Duty omitted?* Behold the Impudence of the Man! He talks of *Gospel, Christ, the Mysteries of his Glorious Kingdom*, &c. What grosser Opposer of the New Covenant can there be, *who denies the very Life, Virtue and Soul of all True Gospel-Worship and Discipline*; and without which, the otherwise best Christian-Church that ever was, *would be worse than Legal?* For they that Worship not from the Motions of God's Spirit, *offer strange Fire, set up their own Worship, and are Image-Makers*; *such ask, but they receive not, because they ask not aright.* For if no Man can call *Jesus* Lord, but by the *Holy Ghost*, no Man can pray to the Lord, or in his Name, *without the Holy Ghost*; yet a Sigh or Groan from it's Holy Operation, that Sacrifice, though without Words, is manifold more engaging and effectual with the Lord, than the most excellent Performance of Man's own Spirit. 'Tis the Fear and Heavenly Sense of God in the Soul, that recommends the Performance, and that the Holy Spirit

begets:

begets: And as the Minds of Men and Women are exercised in the Law of this Pure and Quickening Spirit, as it appears in them, *they shall know the True Worship, which stands in Life and Power, whose End is Everlasting Peace*; *when the Lord, Lord, Cryers, that have Prayed and Preached in their own Wills and Wisdom, as well as to their own Ends and Advantages, shall be cast out for ever, with a Depart from me ye Workers of Iniquity.* But there is one *Objection* taken from my Book, called, *The Spirit of* Alexander *the Copper-Smith*, &c. which he thinks, splits us irrecoverably. It runs thus:

'Either there is such a Thing as a *Christian Church*, or there is not; if there be, 'then this Church either hath Power, or hath not? If no Power, then no Church, 'If a Body or a Church, then there must be a Power within it self to determine.

To which says *Tho. Hicks*; *For* Christians *to plead this, who own the Scriptures for their Rule, and not the meer Light within, the Argument may safely be allowed*; *But you cannot stand by this: For will you say, what a Man doth without an Inward Motion is accurst, and yet disown him for not doing what he is not moved unto?*

But though this be plausible, it is no more; For the Difficulty remains, in Case the Scriptures be admitted for the Rule; for Instance: The Church unto which *Tho. Hicks* belongs, own's the Scriptures to be the Rule: But suppose *Tho. Hicks* in some one Point believes the Scripture not to intend the same Thing, the rest of the Church understand it to mean, as in Case of *Free Will*; I query how this Matter will be reconciled? *They affirm the Scriptures to be the Rule*, and say, *This is the true Sense of the Scripture*, Tho. Hicks also affirms *the Scripture to be the Rule*, but that *his Sense is the Mind of the Scripture*: This occurs almost daily among those who believe the Sctipture to be the Rule of Faith. Now observe the Parallel.

The *Quakers* by the Light within them, *as their Rule*, judge that rude Imagination of keeping the Hat on in Time of publick Prayer.	The Anabaptists *by the Scripture*, as their Rule, *censure* Thomas Hicks *for upholding a contrary Sense to the Scripture.*
The Dissenter from the *Quakers* says, the *Light*, (which he calls his Rule) *manifests no such Thing to him*, nor doth he believe it to be the Mind of the Light to him.	Thomas Hicks *makes Answer to the Church, that by the Scripture he understands quite another Thing, and the Scripture is his Rule for what he says and maintains in the Matter.*

I would ask any Man of common Sense, if the *Scripture* is not as well set in Opposition to it self, by these two Pretenders, as the *Light within*? And if the Church of *Anabaptists* would not therefore doubt the Truth of their Interpretation, but proceed to censure *Thomas Hicks* a Disturber of their Church in it's Doctrine or Discipline by the Introduction of new and unprofitable Opinions? Neither are the Body of the *Quakers* to question their Judgment given by the *Light within as their Rule*, to be a true and unquestionable Determination against such *Alexanders* and Enemies to the Peace of their *Jerusalem*.

But I would farther tell *Tho. Hicks*, that though we renounce all Worship not led to by God's Spirit (his Reflection upon which shews it to be none of his Faith or Practice, *and so no Spiritual Worshipper*) Yet the Men testified against in that Book, were such as had been in Unity with us before, and in going from that into differing and opposite Practices, we imposed nothing upon them, *but they innovated unseemly Customs upon us*, so that which *Tho. Hicks*'s Conscience had no Mind to observe, lest he should lose the Force of his Cavil, removes it out of the Way.

Let *Tho. Hicks* tell me by what other Rule than God's Spirit, Men's Spirits, and the inside of their Religion can be tryed, relisht, or favoured, and he doth something: The *Devil* can transform into all outward Forms, and subscribe the best Methodiz'd true Articles that ever were written; Who, or what shall unmask him? God gave us the true Taste, Savour and Discerning of that Spirit that leads out several from the Heavenly Unity, and from thence we gave our Judgment. If Men become darkned, and led by a Delusive Spirit, and call that the Light, though it give the Lye to the Light, and strikes at the Life, they, whilst faithful, felt among us, they must look to that. You say, *Every Man ought to make the Scripture his Rule*, some that say, they do, you say do not; do you think your Judgment the less valid? By no Means; Neither do We. Will you not desist from censuring those that answer not the Scripture, though they fancy that they do? Why may not we also, by the Light of Christ, judge those to be deluded, who notwithstanding

standing pretend to be ruled by it? Ye turn People to the Scripture, and they mistake it; We direct People to the Light, but they mistake it: So that here is the *Difference* between our Saying, *that Men should do nothing but what the Spirit requires*; and your Teaching, *that Men ought to do nothing but what the* Scripture *requires*. For if we disown them for not doing what we know the *Spirit* requires, you daily disown such as do not some things you suppose the *Scriptures* do require: And as you think the Scripture to mean the same, you ever did, notwithstanding your Opposer's Suggestion, we are by you justified in maintaining our Judgment against those Pretenders to the Guidance of the Light.

To conclude, I see no Difference between *Tho. Hicks*'s saying to me, *William Penn, thou bidst me obey the Light within me, and because I do, thou disownest me*; and my saying to him, *Thomas Hicks, thou bidst me obey the Scriptures, and because I do, thou censurest me*. This drives unavoidably to an infallible Spirit, whereby to favour all Spirits, Words and Works; for the Anointing is Judge, and meer Pretenders weaken not its Judgment: And 'till Men come thither their best Duties are Unholy Things.

Let none fancy an *Impossibility of Trying Spirits* by that without which it is utterly impossible to try them. God's Spirit gives his Children to favour and discern Spiritual Bad, as well as Spiritual Good Things; It is not unknown to such as are led by God's Spirit, of what Nature and to what Tendency such Words or Actions may be. It was on this alone, and upon no other Foundation, the Spiritual Gospel, Sound and Heavenly Fellowship, stood of old; for by One Spirit were the true *Christians* baptized into One Body.

O You that are Professors of Religion, who in Days past, and Years that are gone over your Head, prayed loud and fervently for the Spirit, *rise not up against it* because it stains your Beauty, subjects your Wills, brings you out of Self, and overturns your dead Forms, where the Spirit of this World has had its Seat for Ages, and in a Mystery insnared and beguiled you; But wait upon God in deep Silence to all Fleshly Conceivings, and Will-Worships, so shall you come to feel *God's Pure and Quickning Spirit*, to Enliven, Tender and affect your Hearts; in which State one Sigh or Groan is more Valuable, than Years of unprepared and unsanctified Will-sacrifice.

The next Thing aimed at in this Cavil, attended with so much Bitterness and Rude Language, is this, that *T. Hicks* being desirous to represent the *Quakers* to great Disadvantage, takes not a little Pains to incense Parents, Magistrates, and Masters against them, as Neglecters of all Lawful Commands, without an Immediate and Extraordinary Impulse to perform them.

Were we such Wretches as he would render us, we should not deserve to live in Civil Societies. What I shall say in our Defence is briefly this.

1. The *Quakers* Principle and Practice have proved themselves consistent with Government, because they have encouraged to Good Life, Peace, and honest Industry. I shall not here seek an Eye for an Eye, nor tell any of those *Black and Horrible* Tragedies, *that go up and down the World, under great Authors Attestations, of the People called* Anabaptists. No, I have more Regard to the *Sincere* and *Moderate* among them; though 'tis a great Shame to the *Profession*, which lies more dangerously exposed to the Lash of Story than we do, that *T. H.* should be suffered among them, at least as a *Teacher*, after such *Forged, Prophane* and *Abusive Trash*. But for this Time I spare him; yet if he proceeds on this wife against us, perhaps he may hear farther of me, and so may that People to whom he belongs, if they take not some other Course with him.

2. As to the Commands of *Parents*, I have this to say, and that by good Experience of more than one, That those who have had Children of our Way, though with great Disquiet, and not a little Displeasure and Severity against them at first, have left the World with this Testimony of their Children, they never disobeyed them, but for Conscience Sake, and from Threatning them with the Loss of all, *have become so Affectionate towards them, and Confident in them, as to entrust them with the Whole of their Worldly Substance*. 'Tis true, here and there a Crooked Perverse Professor, whose Husbands, Wives, Children or Servants convinced, have the worst of Lives, through their extream Opposition, and Watching for Evil, may perhaps have 'spy'd *an Indiscretion*, which, though against his own Blood or Family, his Enmity has aggravated to an heinous Offence, *and then it must be given for a Demonstration of the Erroneousness of the* Quakers *Way*. But how Just, Natural or Conscientious such Proceeding is against such Dissenting Relations, or the

the People they associate with, let all Impartial Persons Judge. This is not doing as they would be dealt by; Liberty of Conscience! Tyranny, and *Egyptian* Oppressions. I ask, Would the *Anabaptists* be thus served concerning their own *Proselytes*? Did they never any of them suffer from their *Parents*? And have not their Parents complained of them? And has that been taken by their Church always for sufficient Proof.

And for the Story of the *Woman that went rambling from her Family and Husband, bidding him take another Woman*, &c. *with some pretending Revelations to refuse just Debts*, I shall say no more but thus, We know of no such Things, *and believe them to be downright Lyes*, as others that are gone before them; However, should they be as true, as we hope they are false, we can but judge them, and that we do by the Light of Christ Jesus to the Pit for ever. But if we should take this Course, of proving the *Anabaptists* those vile *Impostors*, he doth call and pretend to prove the poor despised *Quakers* to be, p. 69. How many Miscarriages might we collect and publish against the People that are called by that Name; but we do not desire that *Prophanists* should have any such *Themes* from us, to sport their Unclean Minds upon, notwithstanding T. *Hicks*'s Liberality to them: Is it not then wickedly done in him, to tell us in the same Page, *That if a Miscarriage be, it is improved by us to make the Truth Odious*, who without such *Arguments and his own Forgery*, would in Truth have nothing against us. But truly it is very hard, that we should suffer as we have done, for the Miscarriages of other Parties, and yet receive these gross Abuses at their Hands: But our Eye is to the Lord, and our Innocent Suffering Cause will he plead in his own Time, whose Will be done by us, and that will be our Everlasting Rejoycing.

3. For *Masters*, I must speak my own Experience; many have desired to retain us, and great Trusts have been reposed in us. *To whom were we False? Of whose Service were we Negligent? When did any of us say, I am not moved to do this or that, when so required thereto? Shall a Lying* Dialogue *be Demonstration enough to prove us what so invective an* Adversary *would have People believe us to be?* We do declare to all, that the *Light* whereby we are enlightned, always commands and strictly enjoyns us *Duty, Obedience, Love, Peace, Gentleness, Faithfulness, Industry, Holy Living*; And whatever is supposed to the contrary, we disclaim it in the Fear and Name of the Righteous God of Heaven and Earth to be no Product of our Holy Principle.

I shall now attend his Cavils about the *Ministry*, and give a short Taste of the Rancour of his Spirit therein. He asks, *What is the True Ministry?* To which he maketh G. W. answer. " *Quak.* In the New Covenant God is the Teacher of his " People himself immediately, by his Immediate Spirit, Power and Unction, *Christ Ascended*, p. 64. Christ. *If so, wherefore were Apostles, Prophets, Evangelists, Pastors, Teachers*, &c. *given, and set in the Church for the Work of the Ministry? And why do ye set up one among your selves, and appoint Ministers before-hand to speak in such a Place, and at such a Time.* From whence I plainly collect thus much.

1. That T. H. in so many Words denies *God's Immediate Teaching by his Spirit, Power and Unction under the Gospel*; And in that one Expression strikes out, what in him lies, *the whole Pourings out of the Holy Ghost, the great Promise of the Father; being led by the Spirit; no more I, but Christ that liveth in me; the Tabernacle of God is with Men, and he will dwell with them; the Anointing which ye have received of him abideth in you; and ye need not that any Man teach you*, or you need not Man's Teaching &c. In short, the very Dispensation of the Gospel, which is a *State of Power and Life immediately received of God*, is deny'd by him.

2. That in acknowledging such Officers to continue in the Church, he must confess to their Qualifications, or he does nothing. Now, that which qualified them, was the *Receiving of the Holy Ghost, and those Heavenly Gifts by it, which were necessary for the Discharge of those respective Services in the Church*; By this it appears, that either *Thomas Hicks* must now yield to Preaching and Praying by the Motion of the Holy Spirit, or in opposing of it, *acknowledge to his own Contradiction, that there are no such Apostles, Prophets*, &c. (*who ministred to the Church, as any thing was revealed to them, the great Evangelical Qualification to the Ministry*) in our Days.

3. But why should T. *Hicks* therefore degrade the Dispensation because the People are not yet fitted for *It*, or oppose the Means used to bring them to *It*, to the End for which the Means are employed; Besides, Is it Man's Teaching, or *Christ*

by and through Man? *God was in Christ; and Christ in his Ministers reconciling the World unto himself*, that he might be the Immediate *Priest, Prophet* and *King* to the Souls of People. Might not the same Objection be more colourably made against the Apostle *John*, (1 *John* 2. 27.) who at that Time wherein the Churches were so weak, and the Means so many, and lately established, said unto them, *But the Anointing which ye have received of him abideth in you, and ye need not that any Man teach you, but as the same Anointing teacheth you of all Things, and is Truth, and is no Lye; And even as it hath taught you, ye shall abide in him:* Where he is so far from meer Man's Teaching, (*T. Hicks's only Teaching*) that by his Words he would think, the Churches to whom he wrote, had as well been gathered without Means, as that he admonished them to abide in that Holy Unction, as Sufficient to their Instruction and Comfort: Therefore let him go ask the Apostle *John*, why Men were to attend upon the Holy Anointing as Sufficient; notwithstanding those Means then provided? And the Answer to that Question will be ours. But here is the Darkness of the Man from *our denying of empty unauthorized Imitations*, he infers our Denial of such Means as God's Power uses; and from our using such Means our Contradicting our selves, and Immediate Teaching; and because we use Means in God's Power to bring People to God, the Judge of all, that he may be their Judge and Law-giver, and that from his Immediate Hand they may receive Wisdom, Knowledge, and Comfort, he ignorantly concludes that Men, where they are, ought not to have Means used to bring them to this Blessed State; but that God should immediately teach them there.

4. I charge him with another *Lye*, in saying *that we appoint Ministers beforehand to speak in such a Place, at such a Time, and much less that the End of our Meeting is to decoy, trapan, and inveagle others*, as he scoffingly and falsely insinuates. We deny the Suggestion, and renounce, and judge such Practices by that pure Spirit that hath otherwise taught us; God preserve us from that *dry Hireling Custom*, and Practice of *Thomas Hicks*, and avenge our Cause upon the Head of this Ungodly Slanderer. But he thinks he has utterly foiled us in his Representation (indeed Perversion) of our Belief about the Seed, which tho' spoken to some Distance before, yet I am willing to say something to it, lest it be taken for granted, and his scurvy Names accounted due Titles to such miserable Wretches as he endeavours to render us. The Objection entirely is this.

You say, that the Work of the Ministry is to point People to this Seed; That to the Carnal Mind, which rules in any, the Commands of Christ are not given; And that the Spirit not only manifesteth the Promises, but exerciseth Faith in, and fulfils them; out of *E. B. G. K. G. W.* p. 106. Im. Rev. p. 77, 78. Chr. Asc. p. 10. Query, *Is nothing else taught but this Seed, then your Ministry is only God Preaching to himself?* &c. *Will your Prate of Infallibility, and Talk like Mad-men?* You are implacable Enemies to the Christian Religion; Men Inspired by *Satan*, and as vile Impostors as ever were. Here stop a While.

Certainly, Reader, No Man was ever given up to a Spirit of greater Injustice, Dishonesty, and bitter Rage against any People than *T. Hicks* seems to be against us: He does not so much prove us Bad, as he would make us so, that he may cover his Wickedness against us. What false Doctrine is it, to preach People to the *Seed* God has sown, in which is *Virtue, Life* and *Power*, to bring forth blessed Fruits to God? To suggest from thence, that there is nothing to be taught but the **Seed**, is great Darkness and Prejudice; For the *Ministry* is not to teach the *Seed*, but to bring down, and humble the Mind of Man to it, *that the Mind may be taught, and the Seed delivered from under the Pressure of Sin and Ignorance.* Strange Contradiction! *that the Seed should be sown in Man for it's own Salvation, and not for Man's?* What, but Wickedness it self, could thus write of us?

And that the Carnal Mind receives not the Things of God, because it perceives them not, is *according to Scripture*, if not according to *Thomas Hicks*. But it is not the first Time by many that Scripture in a *Quaker's* Book has been given, under that Name, for gross Error and Delusion. *That the Spirit manifests the Promises, exerciseth Faith in, and fulfils them*, cannot be false Doctrine, if it be allowed to give a true Understanding of them, and if it gives to exercise in them, and finally, to accomplish or fulfil them. But his Insinuation lies here, that the Spirit of God is that which believes in God, and exercises Faith for it self in God, which was never *G W*'s Intent. But as I have said, *the Spirit is that only which gives us Faith, and exerciseth that Faith it gives in the Promises of God, which are Yea and Amen*

Amen in that Seed, the *Quakers* preach People to believe and grow in; for which T. *Hicks* is pleased to call us *Praters, Canters, Enthusiasts, Mad-men, Idle, Non sensical, Blasphemous, Inspired of* Satan, *and as vile Impostors as ever were,* &c. For which God Almighty rebuke his Envious, Enraged and Unclean Spirit.

CHAP. XII. *Of Resurrection and Rewards.*

THE last Doctrine he insinuates our Denial of, is that of the *Resurrection from the Dead.* That which he brings under the *Quaker's* Name, as a sufficient Proof for that Suggestion I shall relate, that every Impartial *Reader* may be satisfy'd of the Man's Inconsistency with sound Doctrine, as well as the Common Justice of Doing as he would be done by.

In Answer to his Questions about the *Resurrection of the same Carnal Body that dies,* he brings in G. *Whitehead* thus:

Q. *Is it not written, Thou Fool, that which thou sowest is not the Body which shall be, but God gives a Body as pleaseth him?*

Thus (saith *Thomas Hicks*) *Whitehead* replied; and G. *Fox* the Younger speaks to the same Purpose. *To Fools that say, This Body of Natural Flesh and Bones shall rise; I say, The Body which is sown, is not the Body which shall be.* I query, *(saith he)* Whether both these Persons do not tacitly deny the Resurrection of the Body?

Now that T. H. hath shewn himself at once Dishonest and Erroneous too; Let it be observed, 1. That from our Denial of the Resurrection of the same Natural, Fleshly Body, he absolutely infers and concludes, *our Denial of the Resurrection of the Body in any Sense;* which is great Injustice to any Adversary. 2. Let it be well observed, that *he makes the Scripture it self to deny the Resurrection, and so Heterodox,* by Accounting G. *Whitehead* and G. *Fox* their Answers in Scripture Language, *to be a Denial of the Resurrection:* For if T. *Hicks* does not intend by his Arguing, That the same Body that died, without a Mutation, shall rise again, what makes him to quarrel the Apostle *Paul's* Saying, *Thou Fool, that which thou sowest is not the Body which shall be;* and repute us *Hereticks* for believing him?

Certainly his gross Belief of the *Resurrection* is inconsistent with Scripture, Reason, and the Belief of all Men right in their Wits in the Point. How can he have the Confidence to call the *Scripture his Rule,* and yet Contradict it so egregiously, as when the Apostle tells us, *It is not the same Body that is sown that shall be,* to assert, *that it is the same Body,* and that who says the Contrary, denies the Resurrection of the Dead, and Eternal Recompence? In short, We do acknowledge a Resurrection in order to Eternal Recompence, and that every Seed shall have its own Body, and rest contented with what Body it shall please God to give us; But as we are not such Fools as curiously to enquire *What?* so must we for ever deny the gross Conceits of T. H. and his *Adherents* concerning the *Resurrection.*

But T. *Hicks* would have us believe, that the Apostle said *Thou Fool,* to him *that denied, and not to him that owned the Resurrection;* But he must excuse us if we refuse to Credit him; for it was not, Whether every Seed should rise with its own Body, or that Bodies should rise, but, as taking that for granted, the Question was, *What Bodies they should be.* So that *Thou Fool* is most due to T. *Hicks* and his *Associates,* who are not, with us, satisfied to leave all with the Lord, but intrude and query, *What Bodies shall rise?* Wherefore no Answer can be more proper to him than, *Thou Fool,* (Thomas Hicks) *That which thou sowest is not the Body that shall be.*

But he thinks he is not without Reason; *For,* says he, *If the It in the Text be not the same Body, how can that be called a Resurrection; for that supposeth the same?*

I Answer, If a Thing can yet be the same, and notwithstanding changed, for Shame let us never make so much Stir against the Doctrine of *Transubstantiation*; for the Absurdity of that is rather out-done, than equalled, by this Carnal Resurrection.

The *Papists* say, That *the Bread and Wine after Consecration are very Christ, tho' the Accidents remain.* Tho. *Hicks,* and Abundance of that Sort of Men, hold, *That Man's Body in the Resurrection is the same with that Carnal Body buried, and yet that it is changed to a Spiritual Body:* How is it possible that I should be the same, and not the same? How that Body, and yet, as the Apostle says, *Thou sowest not that Body that shall be,* is very hard to reconcile.

And truly, that which is yet very strange, Those *Three Scriptures* peculiarly cited in Defence of his gross Conceit of the *Resurrection*, are either relative of another Matter, or directly opposite to, and inconsistent with his Assertion.

1. *And this Mortal shall put on Immortality, this Corruptible shall put on Incorruption*, 1 Cor. 15. 53.

I grant that this implies a Change; but I deny, that it so much as intimates, that Men shall rise with those very Carnal Bodies that were buried. No, the Apostle not only tells us, that the Body sown is not the Body that shall be, *but that Flesh and Blood cannot inherit the Kingdom of God*, ver. 50. If the Flesh and Blood be transmuted, or changed into no Flesh and Blood, I query, (and I think I may do it safely too) *Whether It be the same Flesh and Blood, that is changed into no Flesh and Blood, that is the Body raised?* O Absurd, Dark and Carnal Man!

Nor am I afraid to tell him, that the Scripture cannot rationally be taken strictly, as Translated (neither ought many more) for there are certain *Figures, Modes* and *Ways* proper to that Language in which this Epistle was written, which are to be understood with Allowances; for how can the *Mortal* (taken for *Mortality*, and not him who in Part is *Mortal*) put on Immortality; *Can Mortality be clothed with Immortality?* Then it seems that Mortality is the Person, and Immortality the Garment. If T. Hicks should tell me, No, it is meant that the *Mortal Body should be changed into an Immortal Body*, it follows that he is gone from the Letter of the Text into an Interpretation, as well as that it contradicts his absurd *Identity* or Sameness of Body: If so, it is as Lawful for me (and more, if in the Right) to construe it thus, *That we, who are Mortals respecting our Bodies, put off the Mortal Part, and put on instead thereof Immortality*; suitable to that weighty Passage of the Apostle *Paul*, 2 Cor. 5. 1. For, *We know that if our Earthly House of this Tabernacle were dissolved, we have a Building of God, an House not made with Hands, Eternal in the Heavens*; which as directly concludes the Change, not of Accidents, but Bodies, from an Earthly House or Tabernacle, to an Heavenly House or Building, as ever any Thing can be spoken by Men or Angels.

To conclude: Since *Mortality* cannot properly put on *Immortality*, but Man that is clothed with *Mortality*, may put off, or exchange *Mortality for Immortality*, because otherwise *Mortality would have Immortality for its Garment*; a Thing impossible and absurd; I do infer that this Place yields no Strength at all to T. *Hicks's* gross Apprehension of the *Resurrection*.

2. His next Scripture is that in the *Romans*, But *if the Spirit of him that raised up* Jesus *from the Dead, dwell in you, He that rais'd up* Christ *from the Dead, shall also quicken your Mortal Bodies by his Spirit that dwelleth in you*.

But this is nothing to T. H's Purpose in the least; for the Apostle treats not here of the *Resurrection of Dead Carnal Bodies* in our *Adversary's* Sense, as the whole Chapter seriously proves; but of the *Inward Work of the Spirit*, in order to the making Man's Body a fit Temple for the *Holy Ghost* to dwell in, as he writ to the *Corinthians*.

3. The third Place he brings, is out of the Epistle of *Paul*, writ to the *Philippians*: *He shall change our Vile Bodies*: Upon which he says, *This cannot be meant of a New Created Body, because such a Body cannot be said to be either Vile or Changed*.

But what makes this for his Conceit? Surely nothing: For if the *Vile Body* be changed, *then it is not that Vile Body*; therefore not the same Body. Again, to say, *that Scripture can't be meant of a New-Created Body, because such an one can't be said to be either Vile or Changed, makes much against him*: For, 1. It is to say that the Body that shall be, is Vile, else what means his Saying, *Because such a Body cannot be said To Be* (not to have been) *either Vile or Changed*. 2. Though the Body that shall be, may not be said to be either Vile or Changed, yet it may be given of God in Lieu of a Vile Body, and so the Vile Body Changed for One that is Glorious. It was either Ignorantly or Sophistically done in T. *Hicks*, to imply, *That Body that shall be, could not be said to be Changed*; since the Change lies on the Side of the Vile Body, that is exchanged for a more *Glorious Body*: Therefore all along we must conclude, *it is not the same, but another Body*. But how Disingenuous is T. *Hicks*, to repute G. W's Answer in the Apostle's Words, a pressing the *Metaphor* too far, and yet by so doing, runs himself into this Dark Imagination of a *Fleshly Resurrection*.

But T. *Hicks* thinks, *The Joys of Heaven Imperfect else*.

I answer. Is the Joy of the Ancients now in Glory, Imperfect? Or are they in Heaven but by Halves? If it be so unequitable that the Body which hath suffered should

should not partake of the Joys Cœlestial; Is it not in Measure unequal, that the Soul should be rewarded so long before the Body?

This Principle brings to the *Mortality of the Soul* (held by many *Baptists*) or I am mistaken: But why must the Felicity of the Soul depend upon that of the Body? Is it not to make the Soul a Kind of Widow, and so in a State of Mourning and Disconsolation, to be without its *Beloved Body*? Which State is but a better Sort of Purgatory. See *T. V.* and *T. D.*

What made the Apostle *willing to be absent from the Body, that he might be present with the Lord,* 2 Cor. 5. 8, 9. if such a Dissolution brought Sadness instead of Joy, as our *Adversaries* in the *Point of the Resurrection suggest,* if not boldly affirm? In short, If the Compleat Happiness of the Soul rests in a Re-Union to a Carnal Body, for such it is Sown, then never cry out upon the *Turks Alcoran*; for such an Heaven, and the Joys of it, suit admirably well with such a *Resurrection*. The Reasons I have to give against this Barbarous Conceit, I thus contract.

1. Because that the Scripture speaks of a Dissolution, and no Resurrection of that which is dissolved, being Earthly, and Unfit for a Cœlestial Paradice; and therefore holds forth a *Building of God, an House Eternal in the Heavens.*

2. If the Body be the same, it must have the same Nature, otherwise not the same Body: But if it have the same Nature, it will be Corruptible still: Mortal Seeds bring forth Mortal Natures, not Immortal; Neither can Mortal be Immortal, and yet the same Nature as before, for that Change made, tell me, What remains of the Old Earthly Body?

3. It makes the Soul uncapable of Compleat Happiness without a Fleshly Body, as if Heaven were an Earthly Place to see, walk in, and for all our Outward Senses to be enjoyed and exercised, as in this World, though in an higher Degree; which I call *Mahometism*: For what Spiritual Happiness the Body now can have, respecting God, is derived through the Soul to the Body, and not through the Body to the Soul. Besides, if so great a Change or Alteration pass upon the Body, how is it that Carnal and Sensible Body that suffered? And how can that same Body be equally Sensible of Cœlestial Delights? For the Flesh and Blood that suffered, is not to enter God's Kingdom; and if that very same Carnal Body enter not, which sustained any Part of the Tribulations, the great Knot is broken, and our *Adversary's* strongest, if not only Plea, is render'd Invalid: For if the same Natural Body, Parts and Senses, consisting of Living Flesh, Blood and Bones, that suffered and dyed, rise not, another is given in which the Children of the Resurrection (who have suffered in the Flesh) have their Recompence: And if they do so strictly Rise as they Dyed, then every Man is to Rise *Married, Low, High, Fat, Lean, Young, Old, Homely, Handsome,* and according to former Complexion and Sex: And which is yet more unreasonable, *This Body is to be Uncorruptible, Immortal, Spiritual, Fashioned like Christ's Glorious Body, and as the Angels of God.* May our Adversary blush at these dark Imaginations but here touch'd upon, because more largely handled elsewhere? Only I cannot but signify, that this Sort of *Resurrection* pleaded for, is renowned by some *Baptists,* and several other more Clearsighted *Professors.*

For our Parts, *A Resurrection* we believe, and of Bodies too, unto Eternal Life. What they shall not be, I have briefly said and proved; What they shall be, we leave with God, who will give every One a Body as pleaseth Him; and *Thou Fool* belongs to the *Unnecessary Medler.*

CHAP. XIII.

A Collection of some of T. Hicks's *many Contradictions, Perversions, Lyes, Forgeries, Railings and* Scoffs *at* Witnessing; *from all which, he is proved to be neither a* True Christian, *nor a* True Man.

His CONTRADICTIONS.

Argum. I. HE *that contradicts himself, is not led by God's Spirit, and consequently no Child of God, nor certain of his own Faith; but so doth* T. Hicks; *therefore* No Christian Man.

He tells us, *That the* True Light *hath Enlightned every Man, from* John 1. *and that* | *In Contradiction to which, he makes this Light to be but a* Part of the Soul, *by which*

1673.
Ch. XIII.

that it ought to be attended upon, making the Light to be distinct from the Soul, and not the Soul, *Dial.* 7. 22.

2. He acknowledges, *That the Light checketh within for many Evils, and exciteth to many Good Things, and that he ought to shun those Evils, and do that Good*, p. 8. In short, *That Christ is the Light and Life of Men*, p. 22.

3. But I do, and must bear Witness against thy Erroneous Opinion, *If true to the Light in me*, p. 8. *I am to do what the Light in my self directs me, and herein is my Comfort*, p. 91. Again, *Where a Rule is, there must be Light in the Subject, yielding Obedience*; otherwise *no Reasonable and Acceptable Service*, p. 14. *I grant it ought to be obeyed*, p. 7.

Again, he says, that 'tis no Disparagement to the Light within, to say, *that God doth make any Thing more known of his Will than is, or can be known by it*; for *'tis but to say*, that each Degree of Light is serviceable to it's End, p. 36.

which he falls into the same Confusion he falsly would fasten upon us, namely, *That if the Soul ought to obey the Light, it would it self, which is absurd, and cannot be*, Dial. p. 14. 32.

Yet he dares to tell us, that *this Light, in directing to it's Best Actions, swelleth Men but with Proud Conceits*, and that *it doth deceive and misguide such as follow it*, p. 3. and 37.

To Unsay which, he assures us, as his Judgment at least, *That the Light is Uncertain; in one Man it teaches one Thing, in another the directly contrary*; so that (*says he*) *there can be no Certainty of Truth or Error, Sin or Duty, by this*.

In direct Undervalue of, and Opposition to which, he tells us, within two Pages after, *that the Improvement of the Light within, subverts the Covenant of Grace, the only Way God hath Revealed for Salvation*; *And, that it directly opposeth it self to the Ends of the Covenant, and ought to be rejected*, p. 38.

From all which it is very observable, First, *That the Light is Christ's Light.* 2. *That it ought to be obeyed.* 3. *That it is not a Distinct Light from a Gospel Light, but in* Degree *only, and consequently, One and the same Light*; therefore *Saving in it's Nature.* But in Contradiction to all this, he says, 1. *That it is Part of the Soul.* 2. *That it will Misguide and Deceive.* 3. *That it is Repugnant to the Ends of the Covenant of Grace, and ought to be Rejected.* These are a few of his very many Self-Oppositions. Now if this be to argue *safely, prudently*, and like a *Disputant*, I am greatly mistaken: Sure I am, there is nothing of *Truth* or *Christianity* in such Confusion. For that Man should be obliged to obey a Light that does *misguide*, or that Thomas Hicks *should talk of acting according to the Light in him, making his Appeal thereto in others*; and yet *suggest that it may deceive and oppose the very Ends of the Covenant of Grace*, is with me the Top of all Impudence, and Self-Contradiction.

Of the Quakers Principles.

And Thomas Hicks's *Perversions*.

Argu. II. *Who Perverts and Misrepresents another Man's Principles, acts not like a* True Christian Man; *but so doth* T. Hicks, *therefore no* Christian-Man.

1. Because we hold, Christ is God, and God the Light, and that all Men are Enlightned by Him;

2. Because we assert it to be sufficient to save all from Sin; who are led by it, and walk in it;

3. From our Belief in the Light's Sufficiency to save, as that which was, and is given of God for Salvation, to as many as bring their Deeds to it, and are translated by it.

He concludes, *That every Man comprehends whole God, and whole Christ*, Dial. p. 2, 3, 4, 5.

He concludes *from the Ignorance and Wickedness of those that have it tendered to them, but obey it not, that the Light is Ignorant, Weak, and Deceivable*, Ib. p. 10, 32, 33, 34.

He infers, *That all other Means are needless, not considering it was not the Light's Insufficiency, but Man's Weakness, that has necessitated the Great Light to make Use of External Means to bring Men's Minds, from wandring abroad, to the Inward Light, which is the Just Man's Path*, Ib. 12, 36, 37

4. From our making the Illumination in Man to be a Natural Emanation, or Product of the Divine Word which made all Things.

He wickedly turns it to an Effect of God's Power, *and so would by that Argument make the Trees,* &c. *also Divine,* Ibid. p. 3. 4.

5. From our asserting that Christ shineth by his Light in the Heart of every Wicked Man, as well as every Good Man.

He tells People, that we hold Christ to be in every Wicked Man, as he is in his Saints, Cont. p. 45, 46. *though such Ungodly Persons partake not of his Holy Life and Power, neither are subject unto his Government.*

6. From our affirming God's Promise made Good, that he would be the Teacher of his People; and directing People to God's Light in them, as the Gospel-Instruction to the Way of Life.

He Wickedly infers against us, yet as our Meaning, that we deny all Ministry, all Visible Worship, &c. *though they stand in God's Power and Spirit;* Dial. p. 42, 43. *A Thing never believed nor intended.*

7. When we speak of Christ's Manhood, or Christ's Visible Appearance, and when we speak of his Eternal Godhead, or as he is now to his Saints and People, saying, he was never as such, Visible to Wicked Men.

He is not ashamed to tell the World in our Name, that Christ was never Visible to Wicked Men, as to that Bodily Appearance, and therefore that we deny any such Appearance at all. Cont. p. 37, 43. 41.

8. From our Believing Christ to be in his People, according to express Scripture, and our asserting that as such, he is Crucified by Wicked Men.

He infers, that we deny Christ to be as well without, as within; and that he was ever Crucified in the Flesh, Dial. p. 44. *O Wicked Man!*

9. From our Denial of their rigid Satisfaction, that is, that Christ was punished by his Father for our Sins; and that Sins past, present and to come, are answered for; and that Men may be Holy in Christ, by Virtue thereof, whilst not New, but Old Creatures, and so Unholy in themselves, their Consciences not being Purged from dead Works;

He unworthily concludes, that we disown Christ's Death and Sufferings as a Propitiation, that his Body was an Offering for Sin, that he bore the Weight of the Iniquity of the whole World, that he carry'd away Sins past, and sealed Remission in his Blood to as many as believe; and that we expect to be both forgiven and accepted, not for Christ's-fake, nor in his Sacrifice and Righteousness, but our own Works, Dial. p. 9. 10. Cont. 48, 49, 50, 51, 52, 52. *All which is an horrid Abuse of us.*

10. From our asserting the End of Christ's Coming to be not only the Forgiveness of Sin past upon Repentance, but the finishing of Transgression in the Creature by the Operation of his Power in his Inward and Spiritual Appearance;

He wickedly infers, that we make his Visible Appearance of no Value, and, deny the End of Christ's Sufferings. Dial. p. 10. Cont. p. 50, 51, 52, 53, 54, 55.

11. Because we say that Men are not accepted of God, but upon the Inward Work of the Holy Spirit in the Soul, as to daily Communion with God: And that there is not another Way to be saved from Sin present and to come, than by Christ's Inward Manifestation and Operation.

He Insinuateth as our Faith, that we purchase our Forgiveness by our own Good Works, and not that Christ was God's Propitiation, by whom Remission of Sins past came; *which is the meer Love and Mercy of God, declared then by him in the World more eminently, and now by the Light in the Conscience, to all that Repent.* Ibid. p. 51, 52, 53.

12. Because we make Obedience a Condition to Salvation.

He would have People believe, that we make it the Meritorious Cause, *and so Papists,* Dial. p. 2, 63.

13. Because we say that Christ is but our Example in his abiding in the Father's

So Wicked is he as to conclude, that we believe Christ to be in *All Things but*

1673.
Ch. XIII.

ther's Love by keeping his Commandments;

14. From our pleading for a Perfection from Sin, and a Growth to the Measure of the Fulness of the Stature of Christ in this Life.

15. From our asserting True Rejoycing to be the Result of God's Work in Man, and Man's Conformity to him, and what Man sows he reaps.

16. Because we say, that such Works as are wrought by the Holy Spirit in us, are necessary to Eternal Life, and may in a Sense be said to obtain it; since the Lord hath so freely offered it upon the Condition of Believing and Obeying, the Fruits of the Spirit of God in Man.

17. Because we say all True Spiritual Liberty stands in God's Power, that looses from *Satan*'s Snares.

18. From our asserting that the Breath of Life, which came from God, by which *Adam* became a Living Soul to God, was something of God himself.

19. From our Preaching the Redemption of the Seed from under the Weight and grievous Pressures of Sin, and calling it the Lost Groat, and Pearl in the Field, *&c.*

20. Because we say the Scriptures are not the great Gospel-Rule but the Spirit, because the Dispensation of the Spirit is that of the Gospel more peculiarly, and that without it we cannot understand, or savingly believe any Thing declared of in the Scripture; and therefore that it is our Rule for believing the Scriptures themselves;

21. From our asserting, that what was a Commandment to any Servant of God in old Times, is not so to us, because so to them; that is, such *as going to* Pharaoh, *going Naked, going to the King's Chappel, as* Moses, Isaiah *and* Amos *did*; as also those Elementary Types, Shadows and Figures appointed for a Season, and to pass off, That such are not Commandments to us unless required by the same Spirit anew;

an Example. Ibid. p. 54. *Behold this Wickedness!*

He confidently infers our Denial of a Perfection in Degrees, and our Belief of as high a State of Perfection of Glory in this World, as hereafter. *Dial.* p. 48, 49, 50, 51.

This Person basely infers our utter Denial of any Cause of Rejoycing from what Christ had done for us, when bodily in the World, or by his Righteousness now in us. *Ibid.* p. 53.

He Wickedly suggests in our Name, that we expect to Merit Eternal Life by Good Works, and those of our own working, as the Spider weaves his Webb out of his own Bowels. *Thus does he pervert and misconstrue our pure Faith.* Dial. p. 38. Cont. p. 51, 52.

He unrighteously infers, That who are not of our Way, should have no Liberty. *Cont.* p. 87. *O Impious Man! God will reckon for these Things with thee.*

That he may keep his old Wont, he falsly renders it as our Meaning, that the Soul is a Part of God; and then fastens all his hideous Consequences Dishonestly upon us. Dial. p. 45, 46.

He dares to give it our Faith, that we believe that Holy Seed to be in a Lost, Undone or Polluted State, *Dial.* p. 47. *Cont.* p. 49. *than which what can be more Wicked?*

He basely suggests, that *Quakers* cast off all Precepts in the Scriptures, and will not bound either their Doctrines or Lives thereby, and so will not bring their Cheats and Impostures to the Test thereof, counting them of no more Authority *than Æsop's Fables.* Dial: p. 20, 21, 22, 23, 24, 30, 31, 32, 33, 34, 35, 36. *Cont.* Epist. to the Reader. *Behold your* Anabaptist-*Preacher! Indeed an Ungodly Wrester to his own Destruction.*

It is not a little his Endeavour Unrighteously to infer, that those Moral, Perpetual, and Eternal, Holy Precepts, thou shalt have no other God but me; thou shalt not Murder; thou shalt not commit Adultery; thou shalt not Steal; thou shalt not bear false Witness, *&c.* are not binding upon us: But that we give our selves the loose of such horrid Principles, as the contrary; and are therefore inconsistent with Civil Government, *Cont.* pag. 59, 60. *As if that Eternal, Holy, Omnipresent Light, with which we are enlightned, did not continually declare and require these Just and Righteous Things at our Hands. God rebuke him.*

He

22. From our Use of the Scripture, and a Ministry with such like Means, though by the Assistance and Leadings of the Eternal Spirit, and for this End, that all may come by them, *as Helps*, to the Life and Power it self; the great End of all External Means;

He would insinuate the Insufficiency of the Light, and does prefer the very Beggarly Elements of the *Jewish* Religion before it, *which holds as well against* God, Christ *and his* Power, Grace *and Holy* Spirit, *because the like Means are used, notwithstanding, to reclaim and restore Men to a State of Happiness; but if that were Wicked, what can his Reflection be upon the Light?* Dial. p. 37, 41, 42, 49.

23. Because we say that no Man can rightly worship God, without the Preparation and Motion of his Holy Spirit, which we daily wait to feel, and accordingly are prepared and drawn forth to worship the Lord, whether in publick or private; for we never sought his Face in vain.

This Envious Man suggests, that we never wait to be so prepared or moved; But if the Spirit of God compels us not, God must go without his Worship, and not blame them, *with such like*, making as if the Spirit were as far off, as he would have Christ; and that to stay till Men were mov'd, were never to worship: *which sufficiently shews his Ignorance of that Spirit, whose alone Leadings make a Child of God, as well as the Wicked Use he makes of that Holy and Christian* Practice, Cont. p. 60, 61.

24. From our asserting, that every Man ought to be convinc'd of what he does, and that by the Light in him, as his Rule of Faith and Duty, before he sets about to do or perform it.

He insinuates, the Impossibility of our Renouncing and Rejecting any tenacious Disputer about unprofitable Questions, that may go out from us as a Religious Society, because such Person or Persons, may plead the Light within for it, *Cont.* p. 64, 65. *As if they might not as well plead the Scripture too, upon his Belief of a Rule, and give him the same Difficulty? Must every one use the Scripture right that pretends to it as their Rule? If not, then why may not several pretend to the Guidance of the Light, for that which the Light really condemns.*

25. From our denying the Resurrection of the Natural and Corruptible Body, and leaving it with the Lord to give us a Body as pleaseth him,

This Caviller and Foolish Intruder into Sacred Mysteries, endeavours to possess People with our being Shufflers about, and Denyers of the Resurrection of any Body to Life Eternal, however Spiritual or Glorified. *Dial.* p. 56, 57, 58, 59, 60, 61, 62.

26. And from our asserting the Unity of God and the Soul, and our Denial of their Carnal Resurrection,

He blindly concludes, that the Soul is part of God, and so no future Rewards or Punishments at all to be expected by any. *Dial.* p. 16, 17.

Thus much to give the World a Taste of the Man's Spirit. He that can thus far believe him to be an *Honest Man*, ought to be condemned for great *Ignorance* and *Dishonesty*, God that made Heaven and Earth, will Recompense it into *his Bosom with a Vengeance, if he Repent not.*

A Collection of a Few of his Many GREAT LYES.

Arg. III. *He that Lyes is not of God*; but Thomas Hicks *is a Lyar; therefore not of God, then* No Christian.

1. First, *That our owning of Christ Jesus is indeed no other than* A meer Mystical Romance, *and that the Christ we own is no other than a* Mystical Romance, Dial.

Dial. p. 10. *Contin.* p. 9. A Prophane Untruth; *Untruth*, in speaking so of us; and *Prophane* with a Witness, to call the Light a *Mystical Romance*, which he just now said, *ought to be obeyed.* Is this your Champion?

2. *That according to the* Quakers *Conceits, Scripture and Reason must not be made use of,* Ibid. p. 26. A Lye our Books and Practice plentifully prove.

3. *That the Light in us sees no Necessity of a Mediator,* Ibid. p. 35. When God knows we feel the daily Benefit of one.

4. *That the* Quakers *account the Blood of Jesus Christ no more than they do the Blood of a* Common Thief. Ibid. Pag. 38. An Ungodly Aspersion.

5. *That we deny his Visible Coming and Appearance in the World,* Cont. p. 37, 45. Though a Contradiction to himself.

6. *That the* Quakers *hold, they can work a Compleat Righteousness* Out of their Own Bowels, *Ibid.* Epist. *and* p. 53. *Dial.* p. 38. and yet a while since, all was to be done by the Motion and Operation of God's Spirit alone. O Confusion it self.

7. *They own Christ in all he did,* Only *as an Example,* Contin. p. 54, yet just now he made us deny his Coming at all. What strange Lying and Self contradicting is here?

8. *That the* Quakers *Dissemble when they tell People they own the Scriptures, and that they render them of no more Authority than* Æsop's *Fables,* Cont. Epist. That a *Quaker* should say, *That which troubles thee is thy* Puzling *thy self so much in that* Book the Bible, *thou wilt never be setled till thou throw that Book* Away, *Cont.* p. 76. A Wicked Lye. Also, *That a* Quaker *should say to one* T. Hollbrow, *What dost thou tell me of the Scriptures? they are no more to me than an old Almanack:* Which we renounce both as being a Lye, and an Irreverent Expression. For *J. Nobbs* on whom it is charged, was a *Ranter*; and if I mistake not, it was spoken before the People *Quakers* were known in the Southern Parts, if not before God's Breaking forth by them.

9. *That any* Thing *against our Ministry (though never so true) must be looked upon as the greatest Lye,* Ibid. Epist. But this is one to be sure; God will clear their Innocency and confound their bitter Enemies.

10. *That* Nicholas Lucas *said to one of* T. Hicks's *Acquaintance, that he might burn the Bible, and serve God as well without; and that he might write as good Scripture himself, if he would have any,* Ibid. pag. 5. A Lye, which he disowns.

11. *That they appoint their Ministers afore-hand, to speak in such a Place, and at such a Time; and that they go to Meetings only to encourage* (that is, *to decoy, trepan and inveigle) others,* Ibid. p. 66. Very Lyes, I testifie in God's Fear.

12. *That the* Quakers *bid People follow the Light within, and if they do so, then will they load such with most bitter Revilings,* Ibid. p. 68. A Lye, every tittle of it. What? Are they represented to be *Overturners of all Things to exalt the Light within,* and now revile People most bitterly if they obey it?

13. *That one of us should bid her Husband take another Woman,* Ibid. p. 63. We charge upon him for a Slander.

14. *That Motions of God's Spirit are pretended by* Quakers, *at least one of them, to refuse Just Debts, and that they may do so by their Principles,* Ibid. p. 69. is also a Story hatcht in Hell.

15. *That scarce a Man that reads* W. Penn, *but thinks him to be either* Distracted *or Worse,* Cont. p. 87.

16. *That such as ask us Questions we call Reprobates, in the Sorcery, Witchraft, polluted Beasts, Serpents, Sots, &c.* Ibid. p. 86.

17. *That one of us should say, of one that had writ against us, that if he writ any more against us, we would Print any Thing against him, that any would report,* Be it what it would. *Dial.* p. 73.

18. *If any Discourse with us, 'tis the Man, and not the Argument that we will be concerned with. And if we can fix any Thing that is Odious, it shall pass for an Answer, and a Confutation; And to fill up their Wickedness they will in their solemn Way of Prophaneness and Blasphemy, bless God that they have thus answered.*

But who has most medled with Persons may be seen, who unprovokedly has taken into Twelve Sheets about Twenty Persons, and all of them such as have been wholly unconcerned with him, and are Strangers to him; a Way I never took. How far we meddle with our Adversaries Strength, our Books will best declare

clare. Nor were his Dialogues with me lefs than a moſt undeniable Demonſtration of the higheſt *Forgery, Partiality, Cowardlineſs* and *Impudence* that ever was given by Man, who falls upon our Concluſions, and never concerns himſelf in our Premiſes: *A Principle obtained through many Arguments, he can tell how to crop, clip, pervert and diſguiſe, and then call it ours*; But to engage an Argument that leads to it, as by us defended, it is not in him ſo much as to adventure; *His Forgeries have been his Anſwers; And our Principles abuſed, he thought, Confutation enough to themſelves.* When he has given an Error, for a *Quaker's* Principle, truly all may believe it, if they will, for him, he has offered in no Place but little to the contrary, and in moſt Places nothing at all.

How Honeſtly or Worthily he has dealt with us is farther evident, who brings in five of us, *Fox, Dewsbury, Criſp, Whitehead, Penn,* under the Suſpicion of being Wilful Lyars, Fornicators and Adulterers: For though he ſays *but ſome of them*; yet not Naming *Who,* the Blemiſh lies againſt us all, every one being left to his Liberty to think, which are the Men.

Ah! the God of Vengeance will repay this Murdering, Wicked Spirit, that as greedily Hunts after our Ruin, as the Evening Wolf doth after the Prey. If theſe Defamations are to paſs unjudged of the *Anabaptiſts,* God's deſpiſed Light will judge them, when all their Profeſſion ſhall never relieve them from under the Burden of it.

Thus far of *Contradictions, Perverſions* and *Lyes.* Now for a few of his *Forgeries.*

Some of *Thomas Hicks*'s FORGERIES Detected.

I ſhall now endeavour to give ſome brief Account of his *Forgery*; and notwithſtanding the Hole he hopes to eſcape at, I doubt not to make it appear that he is guilty of it, and therefore a *Forger.* My Argument runs thus.

Argu. IV. *He that gives that for a Man's Anſwer to any Queſtion, that is not his Anſwer to that Queſtion, is a Forger; but that* T. *Hicks hath done, therefore a* Forger, *conſequently* no True Chriſtian.

He agrees to the Firſt Propoſition: the Second he denies, as I ſuppoſe, which I will prove.

T. H. Anabaptiſt, Is it Honeſt in you to deny the Scriptures to be a Rule to others, when at the ſame Time you make it a Rule to your ſelves? *Dial.* p. 24, 52.

Quak. Thou miſtakeſt us when we make Uſe of the Scriptures. 'tis only to quiet and ſtop their Clamours that plead for it as their Rule.

Anab. Did this Light within create the Heavens and the Earth, *&c.* it being proved that it ſelf is but a Creature?

Quak. Yes.

Anab. Is this Light within the Immediate Object of Divine Worſhip?

Quak. Yea.

Anab. Doth not this juſtifie that horrid Act of *James Naylor's* at *Briſtol,* in receiving *Hoſannah's* with Divine Worſhip, &c? *Dial.* p. 64, 65.

Quak. I think not meet to anſwer ſuch Enquiries. A wicked Lye; for we diſowned what was Condemnable, as himſelf afterwards did. Again,

Anab. If this Light be the Rule, who is the Subject capable of underſtanding it? *Ibid.* pag. 13, 14, 15.

Quak. Thou art Drunk with Words and Carnal Diſtinctions, I know not what thou wouldſt be at. A very Lye.

Anab. More the Pity, if thou ſo furiouſly Contendeſt for this Thing, and yet knoweſt not what I would be at, &c. *He makes us Bad that he may condemn us.*

Quak. Thou art a Wicked Creature; Blackneſs of Darkneſs is reſerved for thee. This is given in Deriſion.

Anab. Was not my Queſtion Plain and Familiar; but is this Anſwer pertinent? Is it not needful we ſhould be informed, who muſt obey this Light? &c.

Quak. Thou art a Serpent, and the Curſe of God is Eternally upon thee. A Queſtion never ſo anſwered that he can prove.

Anab. This Language is ſo Natural to you, that it is as difficult for you to leave it, as for the *Ethiopian* to change his Skin, &c. *Ungodly Man! Who ſees not that 'tis his Deſign not to be informed, nor inform us; but to Scoff and Deride us?*

Quak.

Quak. *Thou manifestest thy Darkness, and that thou art still in thy Imagination.*

Anab. What need these Impertinencies? *T. Hicks* *is the Father and Forger of them.*

Quak. *I comprehend thee, and see the Serpent's Subtilty in these Questions; thou art out of the Truth, and drunk with Words.* What is he that spues out these invented Answers?

Anab. Either thou canst, or thou canst not answer me; be so free and honest as to tell me so. If thou canst, pray let me know, whether the whole Person, or Part, or something else? *What is this but to incense People against us, and beget Derision?*

Thus Reader, does this Ungodly *Anabaptist* (the Scandal of his Profession) treat us. We charge it all with *Forgery* in the Name of God, the Lord of Heaven and Earth; and every Body that is not Blind, may see enough of *Scorn, Ignorance* and *Prophaneness*. But hear a little more.

Anab. Do you believe the Scriptures to be the true Sayings of God? *Ibid.* p. 25.
Quak. *Yea, so far as they agree with the Light within.* An Arrant Forgery.
Anab. How shall I know that?
Quak. *I Witness it.*
Anab. Must I believe thee upon thy own Words?
Quak. *I would have thee do so.* Abominable Forgery!
Anab. Was't thou never Mistaken about Persons and Things?
Quak. *This is an Ensnaring Question.*
Anab. Did the Primitive *Christians* use to answer thus?
Quak. *We deny Imitation; We are to speak as we are moved.* O Ungodly Mocker and Forger!

Here's your *Anabaptist*, a *Preacher*, a *Perverter*, a *Forger*, and a *Prophaner* of wholesome Words. Who moved him to this *Romance*, but the Father of Lyes? What *Quaker* can this be besides his; I mean, *that Unchristian* Thomas Hicks? God will avenge the *Quakers* Cause upon his Head, as sure as he is God, if he for these Things repent not. But yet a little more upon Perfection.

Anab. Will this convince me, or any other, of your Perfection? *Ibid.* p. 72, 73.
Quak. *Though it do not, yet thereby we shall render you so Odious to our Friends, that they will believe nothing that is spoken by you against us.*
Anab. Then may I not conclude, that the Reason why you so freely Rail against, and Reproach your Opposers, is only to secure your own Credit with your *Proselytes*?
Quak. *I cannot deny, but that there may be something of that in it.* O Unreasonable Man!
Anab. Will you be so Liberal of your Revilings, whether your *Adversaries* give Occasion or no?
Quak. *It concerns us to render them as Ridiculous as we can, and to make our Friends believe, they do nothing but contradict themselves: And if this fail, we will insinuate something by Way of Question, that may be Reproachful to them.* O Horrible Impiety! God, our God, vindicate our Innocency from these Hellish Slanders.
Anab. But doth not this signify a very Dishonest and Malicious Mind in you?
Quak. *We care not what you think, provided our* Friends *think not so.* Again, *We will give it out, that we have both Answered and Confuted our* Adversaries, *and our* Friends *will believe us, which is enough to us.*

Observe, *Reader*, what a very Villain this *Anabaptist* has made of a *Quaker*: But where will it light, *when the* Anabaptist *shall be known to be the Maker both of the* Quaker *and the* Villain *too*? If this be not Forgery, there is no such Thing in the World? O my Heart trembles within me, to think of this detestable Piece of Cheat. He writes as if he were hardned against God, desperate against us, and resolved to the Abuse of the poor People, to make them believe his *Fictions* to be *Truths*. But the *Devil* always spoils his own Business: For who (not quite distracted) can think it to be more our Interest, to please our Friends, *that we are already sure of*, than those who are not yet such, with Design to make them ours?

I charge these Things, with Abundance more, relating to both our Doctrine and Practice, upon him, as *Abominable Forgery*: And the Weight hereof shall lye upon his Soul in the Day of his Death. And the Righteous God of Heaven and Earth will terribly plead our Cause in his Conscience, to his great Amazement, and perpetual Anguish, if he repent him not of these Undertakings.

But

But he objects, what Fierce and Impertinent Language he has given in Answer to several Questions *E. B.* furnisheth him with, in his Answer to one *Philip Bennet*, a Priest; As these: *Thou art a Wicked Creature, Blackness of Darkness is reserv'd for thee. Thou art a Serpent, and the Curse of God is eternally upon thee. Thou Beast, to whom the Plagues of God are due*; with which he makes a great Boast in his *Continuation of his Dialogue*, written in Part, to prove the *First no Fiction*: But till it be better done, he will remain a *Forger* in the Minds of all Impartial People; for that is not the twentieth Part of what he has given under the *Quaker's Name*. Should that be admitted for a Proof so far as it extends, We have little Reason to believe that to be a sufficient Proof of the Reality of the first, whose very first Question and Answer is a downright Forgery in *G. Whitehead's* Name, and that *with no Quotation*, though he promis'd it; at once proving himself *Lyar and Forger too*. But in Defence of that worthy Sufferer, and deceased *Prophet* of the Lord, I have this to say.

1. *First,* God having raised him with others, by His Eternal Power, which was very Dreadful, and Lived as a Flaming Fire in the Bosom of them, against the *Formality, Hypocrisy, Covetousness, Persecution, and other Wickedness, of that Generation of Covenant-Breaking Professors, both with God and Man, from whom they underwent bitter Mockings, and cruel Sufferings,* He and They have been drawn forth of the Lord, *to check, rebuke, and strike Dumb, that Unclean, Unregenerate, and Serpentine Spirit and Nature, which was predominant, and that under the Shew of Worship, and Forms of Religion, acted in a Mystery against the Life and Power of Godliness.* Wherefore, when this *Priest,* in his Subtilty, and unclean Wisdom of the Tribe and Trade of the *Ungodly Pharisee,* proposed these *Deep and Weighty Queries* (not so much to be inform'd, as to ensnare; that's God's Word of Truth) *whose State was to come to Judgment for Sin, and into the deep Fear, Awe and Dread of Almighty God, because of Iniquity, that through God's Righteous Terrors and Judgments, he might learn the True and Experimental Knowledge of what was convenient for him to know* (For they that do the Will of God, can only know the Life and Truth of his Doctrine) I warrant it from God, and by the Sense of his Eternal Spirit do declare, that it was the Portion, *and only Fit Answer to be given to those Trepanning Questions*: And had *E.B.* gone into a familiar *Opening* of all the Deep Things of the Spirit of God, and Mysteries of his Holy Kingdom, to his Vultrous, Unclean, Serpentine Eye, who was in that Nature that Crucified the Lord of them, *E. B.* had brought upon himself, the Wrath of the Eternal, Allwise God, whose Righteous Judgments were come, and at that Time abroad in the Earth; And I do believe they struck the Priest home, or we had heard of him e're this; *For Hypocrites, and Disobedient Men, sometimes are sooner struck with Judgment than Argument.*

2. Nor did the *Priest* enquire so harmlesly, as *T. Hicks* would falsly insinuate. It is the Language of a *White Devil,* set on *to Carp, Cavil, Catch, and Ensnare the Innocent,* for the Promotion of the outside and formal Religion, then cryed up; and secretly to smite at, and withstand the Lord's Spiritual Appearance then breaking forth in the Nation. But the *Priest queries smoothly.* And what then? *Is it ever the farther from being Serpentine for that?* Was it not then the *Jews* sought to entrap Christ by their Questions, when they came with a seeming Veneration and Acknowledgment, calling Him *Master,* and the like? *Are sharp Words a greater Provocation, than a Subtil, Twining, and Deceitful Spirit?* If *Thomas Hicks* can no better discern Spirits, than to believe every Thing fairly spoken, to be True, his Judgment is like to be little minded; he is Dead to all Right Feeling. Every Spirit and Question is not to be answered; And can he so basely misconstrue our plainest and most upright Assertions, and yet put so high an Estimation upon every Thing writ against us? He shews he would have us misrepresented at any Rate. Let it suffice, that *E. Burrough* gave no harder Names than the Scripture by *Rule* allows, we read of *Dogs, Bears, Wolves, Swine, Serpents, Vipers, Foxes, Children of the Devil,* and such like; and as that Nature to whom they were then given, thought them hard, so does *Thomas Hicks* now; but the same Power that then gave them, has now us'd them, to the same End and Purpose; and I abide by it.

3. Whereas *Thomas Hicks* insinuates, that what *E. B.* said was to the Man, especially as to determining his Eternal State; I say, he has in a great Part mistaken both him and us; For it was not so much to the Person, *as that accursed Seed which was transformed in him, by whom the Soul was deceived, and the Heel of the True Seed bruised:* Therefore it was an Answer of Love to the *Priest,* though a sharp

sharp and heavy Answer of Judgment upon *that Mind in him*, which never did, nor never will, nor can please God in any.

4. 'Tis very hard and wicked with a Witness, in *Thomas Hicks*, that he should run away with two or three Leaves of a large Folio Book, of about Nine Hundred Pages, *consisting of so many Solid Testimonies, pertinent Answers, Heavenly Epistles; his Pleas of Liberty of Conscience, his Letters, Prophesies, and Messages to the Powers* (some of which his Party is concerned in) and overlook them all; yea, and like a most *Irreligious Miscreant* indeed (for 'tis but a Misbeliever) and with as much Hard-heartedness and Inhumanity, as could be shewn by one Man, *trample upon all his Valiant Acts, Tedious Labours, Great Sufferings, and Testimony unto Death it self, for the Free Exercise of a Good Conscience to God and all Men*: And as if it were not enough, to rob him of the Praise due to his Life, and to speak Evil of him now he is dead, *he endeavours what in him lyes, to invalidate his Reward, by rendring him unworthy of any Portion but what's to be had in Hell*. God is my Record this Day, I would not, to inherit more Worlds than there are Stars in the Firmament, have so violated the Law of Charity, against the most violent of our *Deceased Opposers*; and God is All-sufficient both to find out, question, and recompense this *Ungodly Traducer*, whose Envy, I doubt not, has Fire enough in it, to burn that Good Man's Bones with his Books, as the *Blood-thirsty Pope* did *Honest Wickliff's*; but Thanks be to Almighty God, 'tis not in his Power, nor any of his *Old Covenant-breaking, cankered Adherents*: God has swept them off the Stage; And I declare it to be both my *Faith and Prayers*, that they may never come on it more; For it is scarcely to be doubted, but if that Day were come, rather than not root out the *Quakers, Thomas Hicks* would first forge *Faults*, and then *Evidence* to prove them. No Man can be secure of him in common Converse, who, to compass his End, upon such as oppose him, will *Self-Contradict, Pervert, Lye, Forge*, beyond which, in this World, is nothing but direct Murder, and that's a Question, *Since in some Cases it were less irksome to Dye, than to be Defamed.*

Is this *Doing as Men would be done to*? Was D. *Patrick*'s *Friendly Debate*, betwixt the *Conformists* and *Non-Conformists*, so Unrighteous in the Account of the *Non-Conformists*, because he made their Answers? And doth *Thomas Hicks* pursue that Example; yea, to a *Continuation* also, as he did before him: Nay, did not *Thomas Hicks* once, upon a Time, condemn the Disingenuity of that Way of Writing? Yet himself the Man. Let us but consider the early and great Care of some called *Anabaptists*, to detect the *Forgery* of the *New-England Bloody-Baptism*, lately cryed and vended in this City. Could one think that a Chieftane of them should be so Guilty of the same Injustice? And which is worse, hardened in it too? And which is worst of all, at that very Instant, when they were testifying their great Abhorrence to all such Actions, and using all possible Means to check and interdict the Forgery? But we may learn from hence, how hard it is for *Thomas Hicks*, and some of his Abettors, in the Midst of all their pretended Zeal for the Christian-Religion, *to do as they would be done by*: They can fly to the *Council-Board* for an Order against it; to the *Lord Mayor* for a Prohibition of it's Sale; to the *Archbishop's Chaplain*, both to recal his License to the Forgery, and give them one to detect it. *What have they mist to clear themselves*? But this had been less suspected to be done meerly out of Reputation, if they had taken that Vile (yet their Brother) *Anabaptist, T. Hicks*, into hand, for his Envious, Lying *Pamphlets* against us; whose Greater Pretences to Religion, renders him far the worse *Forger* of the two: For the *Author of that Pamphlet* did not so much make it the Principle of those People to destroy, as to recount under the Relation of a *Brother* to the Party murdered, the *Lamentable Tragedy* acted by a Member or two of that People, which, if it had been True (as perhaps it is a Lye) the whole Body had not been concern'd to answer for the Passion and Fury of two or three particular Persons, farther than to renounce that Action. But *T. Hicks* hath publickly avowed *Lyes* against us, the grossest imaginable, rendring us *Inconsistent with Christianity*, and *Destructive of the Government* under which we live, and that by *our Principles too*; than which no greater *Charge* can be given, as well as no greater *Lyes told against us*. Well! God will be even with them for these Things; and will rid both Himself and us of that Generation of Vipers and Hypocrites, who make Lyes their Refuge, and glory in their Warfare against the Lamb, and His Followers; who will assuredly have the Victory: But the Tender-Hearted God will gather, and that speedily, I do believe, as well as that I do very greatly desire it:

To conclude, in both Books he has given those Answers in our Names, which never

never were our Answers at all; And that little he has quoted out of our own Books, he has given as those Answers to other Questions, and many Times to other Matter, therefore not our Answers, but his own: And consequently *Th. Hicks* is guilty of *Forgery*, and so a *Forger*. Thus much of this Subject, to his eternal Infamy, if not wip'd away by unfeigned Sorrow and Amendment of Life.

1673.

Chap. XIII

Of his Railing, Ill Language and Evil Treating our Friends in General, and my Self in Particular.

Arg. V. *He that rails, reviles, calls Names, &c. is no true* Christian; *but such is* T. Hick's, *therefore no true Christian.*

It seems a great Crime with *Tho. Hicks*, that the *Quakers* will not own the Scurvy Reflections of their *Adversaries* (which were the next Way to be thought *Guilty*) And which is stranger, he calls them Names for defending themselves. If we refuse their base *Epithets*, reject their Lyes, and lay their Slanders at their own Door; they report us a Sort of *Foul-Mouth'd People, Censorious and Judging*; and which is most intolerable, they account such Carriage towards us *Gospel-Zeal* and *Plain-Dealing*, which are only better Words for *Reviling and Railing*. But, whilst some have thus shewn themselves against us, upon close Encounters with our Books, *Tho. Hicks*, that he may be extraordinary (though in Wickedness) *forges ill Language under our Name, that he may the better practise Railing against the* Quakers, and insinuate with the Vulgar for a Reality, a *very Fiction*; but since the Answers, as they are, he pretends to condemn as bad, he is at once to be blamed for *Forgery*, *and forging that which is reproveable too.*

But that which deserves our Notice is, that *Tho. Hicks* should be the Man, of all others, that takes most upon him *to rail the* Quakers *for their sharp Dealing with their* Adversaries, who is not only Unjust in doing so, *but excessive in his Bitterness against them*, witness these Scurrilous invective Expressions.

A Dialogue between a Christian *and a* Quaker. *Their owning Christ, and the Christ they own, a meer Mystical Romance. Cheats and Impostures, Lyars, Malignant Errors. Their Hypocrisie, Deceit, Equivocations.* The Way, they arrived to that Degree of Perfection, *was by Quaking, foaming at the Mouth, with dreadful Roarings and Howlings, and this*, he says, *the Devil influenced us un o. Again, Delusions, Impertinent Canting, Non-Sense, Blasphemy.* The Devil's Slaves. *Paganism. Satan's Snares. Pernicious and Perilous Errors. They are inspired and influenced by that grand Impostor the Devil. Blasphemous and Ridiculous Canting. Enthusiastical. They decoy and trepan. Your Idle, Nonsensical and Blasphemous Prating. Inspired by* Satan. *You are as vile Impostors as ever were.*

Dial. p. 1. 10. 27. 28. 41. 43. 78. 79, 80, 81, 89. Cont. Tit. Pa. p. 50. 56. 58, 66, 68. 70.

Thus much of Us and our Way in General, besides his *Knaves, Cox-Combs, Impudent and Audacious Fellows*, that he has called our Friends in Religious Conferences. I think it not unseasonable to say something of that Entertainment I have had at his Hand. I am wholly a Stranger to him; I ever had an Esteem and tender Regard to the Tender-Hearted among that People with whom he walks; I know not that ever I had to do with them in general, and I am sure, nothing at all with *Tho. Hicks* in particular, as to Religious Controversie. I may farther say, that some of them have known me long, my *Temper, Education, early dissent from National Worships*, my *Sufferings* upon it; and if they will be true to me, they must say, I have had the keeping of a good Conscience above the one half of my Life in my Eye, being now about Twenty nine Years old. Now that *T. Hicks* in the midst of his severe Rebukes of us as abusive to our *Adversaries*, should treat me with such Unhandsome Reflections, as *Confident Dictates, intoxicated with Pride; Tinkling and Ridiculous Words; Arrogant and Conceited Man; Confident Dictator; Rash, inconsiderate and Opinionated; I appeal from W. Penn in his Rage and Fury; His Talk bewray'd his Arrogancy, transported with Pride and Error; Brazen'd with Impudence, Rage and Folly; Precipitate into Blasphemy.* I say, that he should thus vent his Passion and Displeasure upon me, who never had to do with him, is certainly very Unchristian, and altogether Unworthy of any Man that pretends to correct others.

Dial. p. 83, 84, 85, 92. 93, 94. Contin p. 87.

But why *Transported with Pride and Error*? only, because I said, in Defence of God's revealing his Will to Man, *that methinks this one Demonstration should satisfy all*, viz. *when neither Man nor Scriptures are near us, there continually attends us that Spirit that immediately informs us of our Words, Thoughts, and Deeds, and gives us true Directions what to do, and what to leave undone.*

And this is the whole Provocation, or Reason assigned by him, for such Rude and Unhandsome Expressions, *and that to a Man that never had to do with him.* God's Witness in all Consciences judge betwixt us, if so true an Expression deserves such Affronts; and if such an Answer ought to pass for a Confutation. Besides, it is basely done of any Man, to run down the Labours of any Man by *Shreds* and *Scraps* of Matter; or to fall upon a Conclusion without so much as encountring one of those many Arguments that lead to it. A Way, Tho. Hicks, of all Men, has proved himself most expert and most unjust in. But why *Confident Dictator, and brazened with Impudence, Rage, and Folly?* Because in my *Second Part of the Apology* in Answer to T. Jenner, a *Priest* in Ireland, who had published Scores of Lyes, Scandals, and Personal Defamations against many of our Friends, and particularly against my self, (that his Book seemed but an *Epitome of Lyes and Abuse*) I did say, *O wretched Impudence! Could any but a Priest brazen'd with Rage and Folly ever pronounce so great a Lye,* as that we should persecute the Truth and it's Followers, with bitter Revilings and Reproachings? when yet says T. Hicks, *that to which* Penn *thus replies, is such a Matter of Fact, that Thousands can bear Witness to the Truth of it.* But herein has he done foolishly; for it being yet disputable betwixt us, *what is Truth, and what is Persecuting, and what is Reviling,* Can he have so little Modesty in his Cries against Impudence, as to make our Accusers and Parties, either *Judges* or *Witnesses?* We shall submit it to an Impartial Judgment; but not to T. Hicks's Pride and Passion. However, this is most true, that to call Christ's Light an *Ignis Fatuus, a dim Light, the Spirit of the Devil, to say that we are of the Devil, that we are possess'd, are Witches, acted and moved by* Satan, *Enemies to God, Christ, the Spirit, Religion, human Societies*; with many Stories that we have offered to prove *Lyes* in the Sight of all Men, and particularly what he charged upon my self, viz. *That* Penn, *another of their Teachers, did boldly affirm to a Friend of mine in* Dublin, *that whosoever shall expect to be saved by that Jesus Christ that was born in* Judea, *and suffered at* Jerusalem, *shall be deceiv'd*; which I declare to be a Lye *in the whole, and every Part of it*: I say, this is certain, that so much Evil Treatment may well extort that sharp and just Rebuke from me: But if it be Criminal (I know in T. Hicks's Account it is) for me so to Characterize a *Priest* that has written an entire Book against us, in which he had most wickedly bely'd our Principles, and abused our Friends, and bespattered my self in particular; what can he think of himself, to say so much more of me, who never writ against the *Anabaptists* in general, nor Tho. Hicks in particular, *much less,* that I have *vented or aggravated so many horrible Lyes against either them, or him?* If his Conscience condemn him not of Baseness, Passion and Partiality, it is feared; and if the *Party* he belongs to, judge him not for such unjust Procedure, they will be condemned by God's Light, that will bring every unfruitful Word and Work into Judgment.

His insinuating *that I entitle* J. Naylor's *Blasphemy and Railing, wherewith he was charged at* Bristol *upon the Holy Spirit, and that neither he had, nor I have Words enough to signify our Venom and Malignity*; because I said of *James Naylor's* Book writ long before his being so charged, "That if he had treated that accursed Stock " of *Hirelings* ten thousand Times more sharply, it had been but enough; is like the rest of his ungodly Perversions already noted; For *first* I spoke against Hirelings; and I have said nothing of them, that the Holy Prophets have not exceeded, who called them *Dumb Dogs, Greedy Dogs, Wolves,* and such like. But T. Hicks's Concern for *Hirelings* shews both that he is one himself, (and indeed has been so a long Time) and next, that he is fallen, with many more, from the *first Love* and *Principle* of that People called *Anabaptists*.

2. From my Justifying *James* Naylor's Sharpness in a particular Controversy against a *Deceitful, Lying Priest*; he infers, that I defend him as to his publick Miscarriages at *Bristol*. Is this thy Conscience? Have all thy pretended Scriptural Doctrines, Knowledge, Study, Preachments, &c. brought thee no farther? God will blast it all; and bring thee to Judgment for these Things.

Well may I return the third Particular against thy self, *and warn all People how they adhere to a Man filled with so much Untruth, Slander, Perversion and Forgery*; who art alienated from God's Light, as near as it is to thee, and that Heavenly Life that is felt therein by all those who believe and obey the Light.

Reader, Let us not be esteemed *Railers* because we rebuke *Railn*; Nor our *Religious Censure* of their *Perversions, Forgeries* and *Prophaneness,* be accounted *Reviling?*

Reviling? 'Tis Trouble enough to us to be thus concerned in Controversy; We would find other Employment, if such Envious Spirits found not this for us. 'Tis not our Choice, but theirs; They began, and, which is worse, when the Powers left off. Their restless Spirit shows, it must have it's Vent some Way. *Policy* and *Enmity*, together, have turn'd it upon us; so that our *Peace* from the *Powers* proves a *Persecution* from some of the *Professors*, as the Experience of the *base Cowardise* of many among them gives us to remember, that the *Power's Persecution* was the Time of *their Peace*, who, *like Insects, lay dead during those Winter Seasons*; We were then their Mud-walls to flat the Shot, and Bulwarks to resist the Assaults; and the more *Moderate* prayed, that we might be enabled to stand; But no sooner were we come out of the Fiery Furnace, than we were saluted with an *Imposture from* Lincoln, *and a Lye from* Dover, both subscrib'd by *Anabaptist* Preachers, with several Clamorous Books since. An ill Recompence indeed for our Love and Sufferings: But from God is our *Reward*, therefore we are not moved; with whom we leave our Innocency; and he will Effectually plead our Cause with our *Adversaries*.

His SCOFFS, or slight ESTEEM of WITNESSING; With a *Word to Professors*; With a Conclusive *Supplication to the Lord*.

Argum. VI. *He that Slights and Scoffs at* Witnessing, *is no True Christian; but that doth* Tho. Hicks, *therefore no true Christian*.

IT was the Way of the True *Prophets*, *Apostles*, and *Churches of Christ*, to declare of what they had known *Experimentally* of God and his Work, otherwise they must have been uncertain of the Truth of those Things they have recommended to us: * And since the Times of *Reformation*, from the Thickness of *Popery*, *Experiences* have been very Excellent Things. I remember, tho' very young to Thousands, what a great Stir and Flocking there has been in my Time after such *Preachers*, who could by any *Experiences* approach the Consciences, and tell People upon Trial what *God* was, and what *Christ* was, and the *Holy Spirit*, with Respect to the Soul of Man, as to *Manifestation, Operation, Conviction, Faith, Temptation, Victory over Sin, Regeneration*, and the like. Indeed, it was the Want of this Preaching that gave such a Dif-relish to People of the National *Priests*, and they suffered not a little for their Change: Sure I am, some Forms, reputed less *Phanatical* than that in which *T. Hicks* is, prest closely after such a *Ministry*, and utterly decry'd all other to be Beneficial in the Church of Christ: But the Lord having appeared in a more Immediate and Spiritual Manner, and some having taken up their Rest by the Way, (thereby *losing their first Desire and Love*, and so the more Insensible of these farther Breakings forth of God's Power amongst them) under the more refined Form they have sat down in (and where the Lord in some Measure might have appeared to them) do they in this Day *set themselves to War against the Light and Life of Christ within*. For indeed it is a State too *Inward, Self-less*, and *Spiritual*, for their Carnal Minds, that can only perform an Outward and Formal Worship, to arrive at. Now such being closely beset in their Fading and Dying Forms, and many on all Hands, in whom there are any tender Desires

---

* The *Waldenses* accounted themselves Witnesses; their best Argument was their Conscience, P. P. Perrin, *Hist. Wald*.

Luther opposed the *Pope* and his Adherents, particularly about *Justification by Works*, upon Experience, He made it to stand in the Testimony of God in the Conscience, that he was accepted from an Inward Work of God's Spirit, and not any Outward Works, much less such as their Works were. *Wessel, & Luth. confer. Fox. Mart.* 2 *Tom.*

The *English Martyrs* laid the Stress of their Opposition to *Popery*, upon their Witnessing better Things. *Book of Mart.*

The *Brownists* call themselves God's *Sack-Cloth-Witnesses* in their *Apology* dedicated to *King James*, in the Beginning of his Reign, 1. yea, in that *Epistle Dedicatory*, they speak several Times to that Purpose, their being Witnesses, that they did Witness, &c. The Like often in the Preface and Book it self, with great Zeal and Honesty. 'Twas what they all in their several Days felt springing up in them, that gave them to relish Persons, Words, and Things; and as they favoured, so they testified. Their Experience was the Ground of their Knowledge: And their Inward Witnessing the Work and Will of God, the Reason of their outward witnessing for it unto Death it self.

after God's Invisible Presence, falling from them, (like Men that seek themselves, and not the Lord) they are labouring hard to prevent such a Separation from them; and indeed they are grown so Dry and Barren of all Good, by their Opposition to the Lord's Truth, as now revealed among us, that they come to lose (with their former good Desires) their very Doctrine; And that which above all Things was once most desirable to the better Sort of them) and applauded by all, is become a *Theme for Scorn and Derision*; I mean, WITNESSING.

T. *Hicks*, though an *Anabaptist-Preacher*, cannot abide to hear of *Witnessing*. He had as lieve meet with *the Lye*, as *Witnessing*, for an Answer. He commonly bestows *Ignorance*, *Folly*, or such like upon it for a Companion; And though another Return might be as easily found out by him, yet because it may not so well suit the *Scoffer* and *Prophane*, WE WITNESS IT is to go in it's Room. To which Kind of Answer he usually replies, *What is thy Witnessing to Me? Do not put us off with your Witnessings, which signify nothing to us. Thy Commands and Witnessing are much alike to me*, with more of this Kind.

My *Friends*, In the Love of God, that would have you redeemed and saved, I beseech you, *turn away from such blind Guides*, their Paths are Darkness, and the End thereof Death; If ever you will know and worship God aright, you must come *to the Measure of his Spirit in you*, that is given *to convince the World of Sin*, and you must know the Work thereof *Experimentally* in you, or your Souls perish for ever. My *Friends*, I have a great Stress upon me concerning you, would I could reach into every Soul of you, that you might be touched with this true Testimony; for I know not more truly that God is, *than that I feel him to be a Rewarder of every Man according to his Works; and such as Men sow they must reap.* And truly, *my Friends*, Time passeth away apace, and the Day makes haste over you, if your Visitation be shut up in God's withdrawing the Light of his Countenance, (inwardly to be felt and known by such as turn to it) *your Condition will be miserable for ever.* I beseech you, in the Bowels of the Love of *Christ Jesus*, unto whom this comes; Be still, cool, and moderate, *let him in, whose Right it is*; He will *affect your Hearts, purify your Souls, destroy your Enemies, and finally save you from Sin here, and Wrath to come*; for to that End was he given a *Light to lighten the* Gentiles, *and for Salvation to the Ends of the Earth*. And hold no Communion with such unsavoury Persons as *T. Hicks*, a Man turn'd, I testify, from the Grace of God into Dryness, and Wantonness, and Prejudice, who makes a *Mock at Experience*, and to whom *the Weighty Work of Witnessing is Matter of Derision*. O the Ill Use he has made of Religion, and the Lamentable End he is come and coming to! *My Friends*, get to *Experience*, get to *Witnessing* by all Means, and that with all Speed; *for those who cannot* witness God's *Work and Will done in them to their Sanctification, shall never see Heaven; That is the Word of the Lord God of Life and Power, and it is sealed for ever.* Ah! Life for your Souls, or you perish, which is only known in the Light; and you must be born again, or you enter not into the Kingdom of God. No splendid Shew, no Methodical Articles, no Outward Fellowships will serve Turn; *Friends*, They will all stay behind, when you must go away once and for ever. Therefore be not Opposers of God's Work in your selves, nor others; but seek after Invisible Life for your Souls, that will go with you; And if you will *believe in the Light, you shall not abide in Darkness, but shall have the Light of Life*; which, blessed be God, we do *Experience*, yea, Tho. Hicks, *we Witness it*. And though thou hast bestowed much Time to *Abuse Bely, Slander, and Traduce* our Friends in General, and my self (*a Stranger to thee*) in Particular, yet I can forgive thee, and the Lord is Record for me, I wish thy Salvation. O that these heavy Things might not be laid to thy Charge! For, so sure as God liveth, *Great will be the Wrath that shall follow:* yea, God will visit for these Unrighteous Dealings: And I testify to thee from God's Living Spirit, if thou desist not, and come not to deep Repentance, the Lord will make thee an Example of his Fury, and thy Head shall not go down to the Grave in Peace; and by this shalt thou know, that not a Lying, or Delusive, but a True and Infallible Spirit hath spoken by me; yea, the Light within will bear Witness to the Truth of these Things on thy Dying-Bed; and then remember me. I wish well to all; I seek the Good of all; I have nothing in my Eye, *but the Glory of my God, the Prosperity of his Truth, and the Salvation of all People*, through their Belief in it, and Obedience to it. Wherefore my Heart is not discomforted, but I have Peace with him, whose Presence I feel, in which is Life to my Soul, Strength towards my Labours, Support under Sufferings, and a plentiful Reward for them all.

A Conclusive Supplication.

O LORD God! Plead thy own Cause, and the Innocency of thy own poor People; O Lord! Reach into the Consciences of all thy Enemies; Breathe a Blast upon all their pleasant Shews; Strain the Glory of their Will-Worship; Bring them down, that thou mayst exalt them; Wound them, that thou mayst heal them; Break them, that thou mayst bind them up. O, that they may all hunger and thirst after thy Appearance; that thy Life, and Power, and Wisdom, they may come to Witness, that they may be all saved in this thy Day, O Lord, from every Barren Way, and from every Evil Work; that the Life of thy Pure Spirit may shine forth by them to thy Eternal Praise, who over all art worthy, who art God, Blessed for ever, Amen.

Magna est *Veritas*, & Prevalet.

Great is the Truth, *and it doth Prevail.*

A POSTSCRIPT *of Complaint against the Unfair Dealing of our* Publick Enemies.

SINCE God visited us by his glorious *Light*, and that he alarm'd, quicken'd and raised us by his Almighty *Power*, that broke in upon our Hearts and Consciences to discover Sin, wound for it, and redeem from under the Yoak of it, that our *Religion* might not stand in *Word* and in *Form* only, but in *Power* and *Life*: But specially since our *Outcry* against the Formality and Emptiness of the many *Religions* in the World, preaching the *Necessity of Obedience to the Daily Cross unto Salvation*; many have been our *Enemies*, and those of divers Sorts. What *Stratagems* they have used may be better known, when it shall be considered what they have not used to our Destruction; Indeed few, or none: For if *Lyes, Forgeries, Perversions, Mis-representations*, Aggravation of *Invented Miscarriages* would have done, we had not been now in the World: But God has preserved us to this Day, and the Points of their Arrows have retorted upon themselves, and the Hole they have digged for us, they have often fallen into themselves; and our Patience and Resolution will wear out their Envy and Cruelty.

Among other of their *Essays, Writing* hath not been the least in Practice and Request. But this we have publickly to declare of, and that in a Way of *Just Complaint*: Our *Enemies* multiply their Books against us; yet *never answer our Defences.* The utmost of their Endeavours towards it seems to end either in *Cavilling, Perverting, Mis-representing our Words and Meanings* (rather disguising than confuting our Principles) or else inventing *Error* and *Weakness* in our Name, that they may the more easily convict us of both; though guilty of neither.

Since therefore they afford us no Just Dealing, but instead of weighing our Reasons, in Vindication of our so much decryed *Way*, seek to defame it, through Ignorance or Malice, or both; We thought it fit to let them know, that we have several *Books* already out, which contain a large and effectual Defence *of our Principles* and *Practices, which we demand a serious Consideration of, and full Answer to* before we shall think our selves obliged to any farther *Tracts* in our Vindication, than what have been already writ, and which we are now in Hand withal. For that we should so often defend our selves, *and our Defences be neglected*; and instead of an effectual Consideration of them, that they should fall to their old, and so often repell'd Charges and Accusations, as if they writ, not to have us clear our selves, nor yet that they would justifie their Mis-representations of us, by confuting our *Apologies*, but to *bedirt and disguise us to the People*, is most Unreasonable on their Side, as well as that it would argue great Indiscretion on ours, to follow them into every repetitious Accusation. For our Parts, we can never think our selves obliged to justifie our Principles so many Times over, against the same Charges, till our Answers have been better weighed: For as such Trouble would be almost endless; so in Reality, *it looks more like making us Work, than Refuting us.* Besides, I must needs tell the World, the base Cowardice of this *Adversary* in hand; for we have offered him a freee Meeting with his Books in our Hands, proffering to refute them *vivâ voce* before the World; but instead thereof, or any other way (as several have been tendered) he disingenuously slinks away, and puts off by meer Shifts and Evasions: His Business is to write *Dialogues*, when he is sure to answer himself, and to back his Forgeries with Lyes.

But avoiding all *Party-Reflection*, or any farther Aggravation of this base Fear and Injustice too; we shall among the many Books writ by us in general *in Defence of our Way* we profess, lay these few upon the Heads of our several *Adversaries*, as containing much of what can be said in Behalf of our Principles and Practices.

1. *Priests and Professors Principles,* writ by G. *Fox.*
2. *Rusticus ad Academicos,* writ against *J.* Owen, *R.* Baxter, *J.* Tombs and *T.* Danson, by *S.* Fisher.
3. Ἐπίσκοπος Ἀπόσκοπος, writ against Bishop *Gauden,* by *Samuel Fisher.*
4. *Edward Burrough's* Works.
5. *The Divinity of Christ, &c.* writ against *J.* Owen, *T.* Danson, *T.* Vincent, *W.* Maddox, by G. W.
6. *Oaths no Gospel-Ordinance,* against *A.* Smallwood, writ by *Francis Howgil.*
7. *The Great Case of Tythes,* by *Francis Howgil.*
8. *Immediate Revelation, &c.* writ by G. *Keith.*
9. *The Serious Apology,* writ against *T.* Taylor and *T.* Jenner, by *G.* Whitehead and *W.* Penn.
10. *The Nature of Christianity, &c.* writ against *R.* Gorden, by G. *Whitehead.*
11. *Christ Ascended, &c.* writ against *J.* Newman, by G. *Whitehead.*
12. *The Light and Life of Christ within,* &c. writ against *W.* Burnet, by G. W.
13. *No Cross, no Crown,* &c. writ by *W.* Penn.
14. *The Spirit of Truth Vindicated,* &c. writ against the *Socinians,* by *W.* Penn.
15. *Quakerism a New Nick-Name for Old Christianity,* &c. writ against *J.* Faldo, by *W.* Penn.
16. *The Christian-Quaker,* &c. writ against the Strength of all our many *Adversaries* in general, and several of them in particular; divided into two Parts, the first by *W.* Penn, the second by G. *Whitehead.*

These, with our present Discourse, let them answer; and if they have any Thing that's new to offer, we shall, we hope, by God's Assistance, freely and faithfully consider it; otherwise let Shame cover the Face of our Enemies for their Unjust Out-cries and Base Forgeries against us, whom they cannot by Reason Silence, nor sober Argument confute.

THE
Counterfeit Christian detected; and the Real Quaker justified,
OF
God and Scripture, Reason and Antiquity.
AGAINST

The Vile *Forgeries,* Gross *Perversions,* Black *Slanders,* Plain *Contradictions,* and *Scurrilous Language* of T. *Hicks* an *Anabaptist* Preacher, in his Third *Dialogue* between a *Christian* and a *Quaker,* call'd, The Quaker Condemned, &c.

By way of *Appeal* to all sober People, especially those called *Anabaptists* in and about the City of *London.*

By a Lover of Truth and Peace W. P.

The PREFACE.

Reader,

IT was about a Month after the Publication of T. Hicks's *last* Dialogue, *e'er I knew there was such a* Pamphlet *in the World; I took great Care to get it, and then*
us'd

us'd no less Diligence to peruse it, which having done, I shall briefly and faithfully give thee my Sense, both of the Man and his Work, and, I hope, sufficient Proof to justifie that Account.

Some were of the Mind, our full and sober Answer to his other disingenuous Dialogues, with that Remembrance we gave him of his own former Dislike and Reprehension of that unfair Way of Writing Controversie, to some of his own Profession in *Wiltshire*, would have had some Place with him, and influence upon him, towards a more Just Procedure with us for the future; That instead of a Man of Straw, and a Fool and a Knave of his own creating (and therefore call'd by him a Quaker, that he might the better intitle us to his invented Error, Blasphemy and Immoralities, and bring us under the Odium that follows) we should have seen, if not a real Contrition for the Wrong done us, at least, if in the Wrong our selves, some Arguments more fairly given, and tenderly prest, in order to reclaim us: But in lieu of a solid and edifying Confutation (were we in the Wrong) the Man is become resolv'd and desperate; without all regard to God, Reason, Scripture, his own Credit, and the Repute of his Party (not a little weakned by his Carriage) for it seems no matter with him how black the Stratagem be, provided it renders but the Quakers and their Faith detestable. And so remote is he from the least Acknowledgment of his former Miscarriages, to wit, Forgeries, Perversions, Evasions, Lyes, Slanders and Railings, that with regret I speak it, he has presumptuously continued and advanced in that Ungodly Practice, as if he would maintain our Iniquity by the doubled Confidence of another; increasing, with the number of his Dialogues, the number of those Impieties, for which his other two were so frequently rejected of sober and well-disposed People. Now if the Man be so bad, and that in his Book too, how his Book can be good, is beyond the Skill of any Man to tell us. That he deserves no better Character at any Good Man's Hand, and that I write but the very Truth of the Matter, I shall proceed to manifest by such Instances and Evidences, as I think cannot be justly questioned of either Reason or Sense.

Reader, *be but intent and impartial in thy perusal, and I desire no more at thy Hands to our Vindication and our Adversary's utter Shame.* Farewel.

The *Counterfeit Christian* Detected, &c.

NOT long after *Tho. Hicks* had brought forth his Piece of *Fiction*, being charged by several, as well those that were not of our Way, as our own Friends, with having made a *Quaker* of his own (and no wonder then that he should confute him) he, as one concern'd to buoy up his Credit above those Assaults, writes the *Continuation*, or Second Part, endeavouring to make appear, that he had not wrong'd us in his first. I undertook to consider them, and that in a Spirit of Moderation, to the People of his Profession, and to him, at most, but in a Way of grave Rebuke of his Unchristian Practice. In this I represented his *Forgery*, with many other of his Unrighteous Dealings towards our Persons and Profession. At this he fumed and raged; and where he might safely do it, in City and Country, I was a *Knave*, and I know not how many more hard Names, that both suit his *Envy, predominant Passions*, and *sordid Practice*, to the Disgrace of his Religious Pretences. But it has so happened, that about a Year's Time after, he has thought it requisite to give us six Sheets, which are to advocate his Cause, and prove to the World that I am *an Arrogant, Abusive, Prophane, Impertinent Man*, with abundance of the like Dirt, out of his foul Pit, which he loads almost every Page withal.

The Intent of this last Undertaking, *is to condemn us out of our own Mouth*, and shew to the World, that we verify what before he had charged upon us, and we so confidently denied: But if upon Examination, it shall appear, that my Charges against him remain firm, and that by the Assistance of this last *Dialogue* it self, I hope, notwithstanding his high Rants, mighty Confidence, most positive and dogmatical *Say-so's*, and hard and scornful Names, with which he endeavours to over-bear us, he shall be reputed the Man we have describ'd him, and therefore unworthy of the Name of *Christian*, which he untruly gives himself in his *Dialogues*.

Sect. I. Tho. Hicks *proved guilty of Forgery.*

I Shall begin with an Account of his Title-Page, and what he promises his Reader there; *The* Quaker *condemned out of his own Mouth, or an Answer to* W. Penn's *Book, entituled,* Reason against Railing, *and* Truth against Fiction; *wherein* W. P. *hath confessed, That if those Things objected against the* Quakers *in two former Dialogues be true, then a* Quaker *is quite another Thing than a* Christian. *That those Matters heretofore objected were, and are, real Truths, and no Fictions, is fully cleared and evinced in this Third Dialogue between a* Christian *and a* Quaker *by* Thomas Hicks, Tit. Pag.

That a *Quaker* is Condemned out of *Tho. Hicks*'s Mouth, is no Wonder to me; but that he should be Condemned out of his own, would be strange, and is, we hope, a Task too difficult for him to surmount. However, he tells us, that what Things he objected against us in his former *Dialogues*, called *Fictions* by us, are cleared and evinced to be no Fictions, but *real Truths* by him: This is either true or false; if true, we are wrong; if false, *T. Hicks* is still to be reputed a *Forger*.

He that would clear himself from any Charge, must be sure to take into his Answer the Matter of that Charge, or he shuffles with his Adversary, and maketh no allowable Defence for himself. That this is *T. Hicks*'s Case, *instead of Condemning the* Quaker *out of his own Mouth*, and consequently that he is worthy to be condemned himself for his Enterprize, I shall briefly shew.

I charged him at the Entrance into my former Book, with having answer'd his own knottiest Questions in our Name, with the most weak and impertinent Returns he could well invent; and in many Pages there was not so much as a Quotation to be seen (a Practice to be detested of any that have learned but the very *Alphabet* of Common Honesty) to which the Man says nothing, yet would be thought a fair Disputant, yea, a *Christian* too, if any Body will believe him.

Next, I charged him with having given some Answers, we could acknowledge ours, joyned to their proper Questions, unto such Questions, as they were never returned to, therefore guilty of *Forgery*; though not in making them Answers at all, yet in giving them for Answers to those Questions unto which they never related, which is a manifest Misapplication of them; But of this neither do we hear one Word.

Again, Though what he has said in his Title-Page be enough for us, and we shall anon descend to use it, yet does not that contain or reach my Question, as in Honesty it ought to have done, which was this; *Whether those Doctrines and Expressions charged upon the People called* Quakers, *by* Tho. Hicks, *in both his Dialogues, be really the Doctrines and Sayings of that People, or not?* And afterwards, *Whether what we own, and is by him charged with Error, is sufficiently opposed or proved such?* Reason against Railing, p. 6. Which, Reader, takes in not only what *T. H.* objects against the *Quakers*, but what he invents and answers for *them, and under their Name, whether it be about Doctrine or Practice.* Nor is this all that may be learned of *T. Hicks* in his Title-page; For, to compleat his Baseness in that very Passage, observe, that as he only renders us concerned at his *Objections*, so does he confine these Words [*are real Truths and no Fictions*] unto them. Whereas it is notorious to all that have but turned over my Answer, that it was not only, nor indeed so much, his Objections against us, *as those Answers he gave for us, that I charged with Fiction*. But *T. Hicks*'s Policy in this Contrivance is not unworthy of our Notice, though always of our Approbation; for this is the plain Language of it, *If I use not these Stratagems to cloud the Question, and vary the Charge, I am a Forger,* &c. *there's no Help for it; and that discards me with all Men, even those of my own Party; wherefore I will so order the Matter, that I will only bring my self upon the* * *Proof of my own Objections, and overlook theirs.* But though this goes a great Way, yet this alone will not do; For I query, Dost thou intend by Objections, which thou say'st I call *Fictions*, all, or some; if but some of them, thou shouldst in Honesty have said so; if all, as thy Words imply, then hast thou farther abused us; for my State of the Question includes a grant of some of them in Point of Citation, though none as Errors.

But, Reader, this is *T. Hicks*'s Fetch (for without them he can do nothing against us) *If I can extend the Word Forgery or Fiction, as well to Things they do grant, as those they deny, by some such general Words, as Matters objected against the* Quakers, &c. Then by proving they acknowledge I have rightly quoted and

charged

* Not that I allow him to have rightly charged us in every Thing in that Sense neither.

charged them in some three or four Particulars, I will clear my self from the foul Imputation of *Forgery* in all the rest.

That this is the very Truth it self, and therefore *Forgery* in the Abstract, let the Reader know, that this has been his Practice, to wit, *Where we have never charged Forgery upon him, he has taken his Opportunity, and that with the Confidence of an Innocent*, to cry out, *Is this candid to call me a Forger, when you confess the Thing—Then I am not guilty of Forgery—this clears me from being a Forger—* Examine these Pages in his Third *Dialogue*, viz. p. 4, 5, 6, 9, 29, 36, 39. and mine to which he there refers, and which he pretends to answer, and thou wilt have such Evidence of the Truth of what I say to thy very Sense, as must needs render my Adversary's Carriage worthy of thy severe Censure.

But as he hath attempted the Proof of his Innocency in this Matter, by Places that never reflected any such Sort of Guilt upon him (therefore still the Man once charged to be) so has he wholly declined medling with the very *Head of Forgery*, under which I ranked near *Twenty Answers, set down by him in our Name, that were never given by us, in either Matter or Form, to those or any other Questions*, as a Demonstration of the Truth of my Accusation; some of which are so very gross, that had not his Envy over-powered his Wits, Credit with his sober Neighbours would have disswaded him, if the Apprehension of God's Judgments could not have deterred him.

Before I produce Particulars, I shall recite a Passage in his second *Dialogue*, p. 2. as a Proof of the unmeasurable Confidence, as well as Folly and Wickedness of the Man. *Quak.* Thou hast presented the World with a *Quaker* of thine own framing, making him to speak those Impertinencies and Falsehoods that were never uttered by any real *Quaker*; Therefore it is a Forgery. G. W. Epist to D. Pl. Anab. *You had done well, if you had produced some Instances wherein I made them speak what was never uttered by a real* Quaker: *But if I can prove that what is spoken under that Name is the Language of a real* Quaker; *then thou hast confessed that such may be guilty of Impertinencies and Falshood.*

But T. *Hicks* has made them speak what was never uttered by a *Real Quaker*, and has not so much as attempted to prove the contrary; Therefore *T. Hicks* by his own Argument is guilty *of Impertinencies and Falshoods*. This I made appear in my Answer to his former *Dialogues*; and therein *did well by his own Confession*; For I produced several Passages to make good my Charge of *Forgery*, unto which he is wholly silent. I shall instance in three or four of them, that my *Reader* may both perceive the Spirit of the Man, and see at what rate he has clear'd himself from my Imputations.

Anab. *Is it honest in you to deny the Scripture to be a Rule to others, when at the same Time you make it a Rule to your selves?* Dial. 1. pag. 24, 52.

Quak. Thou mistakest us; when we make use of the Scriptures, it is only to quiet and stop their Clamours, that plead for it as their Rule.

Anab. *Do you believe the Scriptures to be the true Sayings of God*, ibid. p. 25, 2.

Quak. Yea, so far as they agree with the Light within.

Anab. *May I not conclude, that the Reason why you so freely rail against and reproach your Opposers, is only to secure your Credit with your Proselytes*, ibid. page 72, 73.

Quak. I cannot deny but that there may be something of that in it.

Anab. *Will this convince me or any other of your Perfection?* ibid.

Quak. Though it do not, yet thereby we shall render you so Odious to our Friends, that they will believe nothing that is spoken by you against us.

Anab. *Will you be so liberal of your Revilings, whether your Adversaries give occasion or no?* ibid.

Quak. It concerns us to render them as ridiculous as we can, *and to make our Friends believe, they do nothing* but contradict themselves: And if this fail, *we will insinuate something by way of Question, that may be Reproachful to them.*

Anab. *But doth not this signifie a very Dishonest and Malicious Mind?* ibid.

Quak. We care not what you think, *provided our Friends think not so. We will give it out, that we have both answer'd and confuted our Adversaries, and our Friends will believe us, which is enough to us.*

What a Wicked and False *Quaker* this counterfeit *Christian* hath made, to abuse true ones? If this be not *Forgery, palpable Forgery*, and that not only against some one Person, but the People in general, personated by his *own made Quaker*,

1674.
Sect. I.

there is no such Thing as *Forgery* in the World. O you that seriously profess *Religion*, can you away with this?

But hath he vindicated himself from these base Courses, or honestly confessed them? *Neither*. How then can he justly call himself a *Christian*, or be thought to have answered my Book, that hath thus basely declined that Part of it, which stood him most upon to disprove? But how grossly soever he hath represented us, and how silently over-look'd our Charges, he wants not Confidence to write after this Strain; *I do affirm in Seriousness, that the Account I have now, and heretofore, given of the Quakers, is no other than the very Truth*, Epist. p. 5. How serious is this Man in his Lying? *Forge* first, and then *Lye* to prop it: Impudence in Grain!

For what he hath said heretofore, relating to this Particular, I have here briefly considered it. Let us see if he be any better now; In order to it, I have already shewn you the Shuffle of his *Title-Page*: I will now proceed to give you an Account of his Progress in this *Black Art of Forgery* and base *Abuse*.

Anabapt. *I am not conscious of having objected any thing against you in my former Dialogues, but what I am certainly persuaded to be true*, p. 1.

But is not T. *Hicks* conscious of first making us say that we never said, and then calling it, *A Dialogue between a* Christian *and a* Quaker? That T. *Hicks* was a *Forger* I have evidenced: That he is one still, his own Words shew; for instead of retracting, he pleads Innocency in being so: No wonder this Man can write against the Light within; whose Conscience, if we will believe him, is so seared, that it feels no Risings against the foulest *Forgeries*. But let's hear him a little farther.

Anabapt. *I am so confident of the Truth of those Allegations, that I doubt not to avouch them, to all impartial Men*, Ibid.

We never doubted his Confidence, but Honesty. His *Allegations* must either respect those Passages, which he book'd and pag'd, or else all that he alledges under the Name of *Quaker*: If the former, he is a *Forger* still; for more than Three Hundred in his *Dialogue* were neither book'd nor pag'd: If the latter, he tells a plain Untruth; for he has not so much as attempted to avouch them, unless it is to be understood of his Confidence.

Seven Instances I shall give of his Continuance in FORGERY.

I. T. *Hicks*'s first *Forgery* begins with his *Title-Page*, and in that very Passage, where he promiseth *an Evincement of his own Objections to be no Fictions, but real Truths*; to wit, that he doth not only content himself in making the Evincement of his own Objections against us (unfairly over-looking ours) to be all he is concerned in, but in so many Words tells the World, *That I confess, if those Things objected against the* Quakers *in the two former* Dialogues *be true, then a* Quaker *is quite another Thing than a* Christian; who never said or confessed any such Thing in all my Life: For I well knew, that the Controversy rose higher, and went farther than his meer Objections; I mean, *to all he gave under our Name*; as both the Question stated, and my Pursuit of it do evidently prove. So that he, to make the Clearing of his own Objections enough (yet more than he can ever do) brings me in with a Confession of a Thing I never thought on, much less ever writ; what shall I call this but *Forgery* upon *Forgery*?

II. His Second *Forgery* brings me in thus: Qua. *If the Quotations be true, I do freely acknowledge, that a* Quaker *is quite another Thing than a* Christian. Reason against Rail. p. 2.

There is no Passage so laid down by me; my Words are these, T. Hicks *hath given us a Second Part, wherein he hopes to make good what he charged upon us in his first by Quotations out of our own Books*; If faithfully done, *I shall freely acknowledge that a* Quaker *is quite another Thing than a* Christian. Where it is observable, that I do not lay the Hazard of a *Quaker*'s being a *Christian*, meerly upon the Truth of his Quotations, but the Use of and Application of them, *if they be faithfully done*: that is, if he can make those Quotations and his Charges meet against us, I shall concede; for a Quotation implies an Agreement. He hoped to creep out at a few right Citings, *and to be over-look'd all false Applying and Perverting*, by unnatural Consequences, to his Crooked Purpose. Though had I said, as he sets me down, I should have no Cause to fear the Issue; since if naming us may go for Quoting, he has done it an Hundred Times, where he has directed to no Particular Way of knowing the Truth thereof, consequently is a *Forger*; and where he

has

has been more punctual, I dare abide by every such one he ever made, well-knowing he cannot get one Letter to speak for him, but by his meer Sophistry and customary Wrests.

III. His Third *Forgery* in this Third *Dialogue*, is thus laid down by him. He begins with an Answer to the last Passage he quoted for mine.

Anab. Art thou well advised in what thou sayst? p. 1, 2.

Quak. Were we as thou representest us, the severest Plagues and Judgments of the Eternal God we might justly expect to be our Portion, *Reason against Railing,* page 4.

The Stress lies here, Whether this Answer were ever given by me to the Question 'tis now made an Answer to? I say, *No*; Therefore a *Forger*. Next, let us see if it was ever given to a Question of the like Tendency? *No*; Therefore the greater *Forger*. I will set down the two Passages unto which this hath been given twice for Answer, that my *Reader* may be helpt to a clearer Sight of the Man.

In this Third *Dialogue* he queries of me:

Anab. Art thou well advised in what thou sayst, in saying; If my Quotations be true, thou dost freely acknowledge that a Quaker *is quite another Thing than a* Christian. Dial. 3, p. 1.

Quak. Were we as thou representest us, the severest Plagues and Judgments of the Eternal God we might justly expect to be our Portion. *Reason against Railing,* Page 4.

Thus *T. H.* lays it down: But let us see how it is in my Book.

T. H. queries, *Will you be so liberal of your Revilings, whether your Adversary give Occasion or not?* He answereth for us: Quak. *It concerns us to render them as ridiculous as we can, and to make our Friends believe, They do nothing but contradict themselves, which is enough to us.* Upon which, Reader, I made this Reflection: *Certainly these Things shew such premeditated and wilful Obstinacy to be Wicked, that were we what he represents us to be,* in this very Matter, *the severest Plagues and Judgments of the Eternal God we might justly expect to be our Portion,* &c. p. 4. If only said in this very Matter, then not in every Matter *T*. Hicks pleaseth to wrest or twist it to: O gross Abuse! Shall this Man go for a *Christian*? But his Evil is greatly heighten'd, when we consider, that these Words were spoken of such a Passage, as to this Minute he never so much as attempted to clear from the Imputation of *Forgery*, though so much charged upon him, p. 67 of my Answer; because there was no Quotation for it, nor in Sense can be expected for so plain a Fiction: And yet he makes it a formal Answer to a Question about right and wrong Quotations, which were not there in Question; as if it were one and the same Thing, to say, The Plagues and Judgments of God we might expect, &c. *if so morally Evil as he brought us in speaking our selves to be,* for which he directed us to no particular Proof, neither could: And to say, We might justly expect the Plagues of God, &c. *if he represented us right, as to Quotations about Doctrines out of our own Books, which was never the Question.* He that can thus invent, add, diminish, and transpose, both Words and Sentences, may write *Dialogues* at Pleasure, and as easily abuse the Prophets and Apostles, yea, *Christ Jesus* himself, as the People called *Quakers*.

IV. His Fourth *Forgery* he makes, and that I think fit to remark, is this.

Anab. But dost thou indeed believe, that those Quotations in the former Dialogues are Forgeries?

Quak. *I do so.* Dial. 3, p. 2.

This is all false; I never thought so, much less writ so; nor was that the Question, taking *Quotations* for Places cited, as to Book and Page. And if generally accepted by him, he brings me in denying all, which was as much beside my Thoughts.

Thus he shuffles with me, and endeavours to delude simple People by the Word *Quotation*, (which taken strictly, does not reach the one Half of those Answers he made us to give) by getting a few Passages acknowledged, which he has punctually made, (though miserably perverted) to make them believe, all given under our Name, not so cited, are also allow'd under the same Term [*Quotations.*]

Besides, He has not referred us for any such Answer in any Book I ever wrote. This, *Reader*, is so far from proving and evincing former Charges against us, that it is to multiply more *Fictions*, and add to his other Score.

V. His Fifth *Forgery* is in Page 59, and consists of two Parts: The first is, The foisting in of the Word *only*; The second of mis-placing and mis-applying my Answer, that he may the better have his Ends upon me, which is but one of his many untruly *reigning* Sins. Observe, because I told him, that *E. B.* in saying, 'That was not a Command to him, which was a Command to another, *respected not those universal and eternal Precepts of fearing God, and working Righteousness* (as *T. H.* untruly inferred) *But more extraordinary and particular Injunctions; such as the Going of* Moses *to* Pharaoh, *with many more.* And because I explain another Passage out of *E. B.* by him cited and wrested, *viz.* 'You are not dead with Christ, who are yet subject to Ordinances; after this Manner, *E. B. pleads* only *against such Ordinances, as were but Shadowy, and to pass off*; He puts the Adverb *only*, by me mentioned in what I said to this last Citation out of *E. B.* in my Explanation of the first Citation, where I never mentioned it. And that he might fasten a Contradiction upon me, he omits this last Citation out of *E. B.* mentioned in his second *Dialogue*, and makes the Answer I gave to his Use of it, to belong to that which I gave to the Former about Commands, as if they had been but one entire Answer to one and the same Passage, which were really two.

The Advantage he hoped to gain, was this, that I should say, *E. B.* intended by Commands, only extraordinary Ones, as *Moses's* going to *Pharoah*, &c. and yet say, That *E. B. only meant such Ordinances as are Shadowy;* if *only* such extraordinary, then not *only* such Shadowy; if *only* such Shadowy, then not *only* such Extraordinary; as if they had been said of the same Passage, and on the same Occasion; whereas the first was in Page 47 of *E. B*'s Works, and the other in Page 105, as *Thomas Hicks* himself quotes them, in his second *Dialogue*, p. 59, 61.

But that which yet adds Blackness to this *Forgery* is, first, that at what Time he foisted [*only*] into my Explanation of the first Passage, he basely left out these three Words, [with many more] which were on Purpose to shew I did not stint *E. B*'s Use of the Word *Command*, to the extraordinary Cases instanced in my Answer. And next, that after all that premeditated Injustice, he flings these stinking Interrogatories at me, *Dost thou consult thy Credit in multiplying such Instances of thy Inadvertency and Folly? What Reason hath any Man to believe thee, either in what thou affirmest or denyest, that dost so apparently contradict thy self?* This is not only to be bad, but brazen withal. To contradict a Man's Self is reproveable; but to make Contradictions in another Man's Name, is detestable; To commit Injuries against any is ill done; but to brave the Wronged with insolent Reflections, must needs be a great Aggravation. What think the more sober among the *Baptists* of these Things?

VI. The Sixth *Forgery* I shall now mention, is the Answer *T. H.* makes *G. W.* to give in his second *Dialogue*, Page 1. The Question and Answer I will recite.

Anab. *I have formerly detected you of several pernicious Errors, concerning the Scriptures, Light within, Person of Christ and Resurrection,* &c. *What say you thereunto?*

Quak. I say the Plagues and Judgments of God will follow thee.

G. W. denies that this was ever his Answer to that Question, *Appendix, p.* 13. Though he at the same Time tells *T. H.* he no Ways doubts the Thing. *T. H.* that he may not lie under the Charge of *Forgery*, so fix'd upon him by *G. W.* has by his Legerdemain, p. 69, trapt in *Joh. Gladman*, to cloak his Fiction, thus; *Whereas G. W. denies that he said*, The Plagues and Judgments of God would follow *Tho. Hicks, these may certify, that G. W. and my self being in Discourse about the Dialogue* between a Christian and a Quaker, *he said*, The Plagues and Judgments of God would follow *T. Hicks*, and all that had an Hand in that *Dialogue*, or that dispersed it. *J. Gladman, Dial. p.* 8.

But the Meanness of the Shift aggravates the *Forgery*: Did *G. W.* ever deny that he had said so to *J. G.* or was that the Question? Vain Man! or tell us, Does *J. Gladman* certify, that *G. W.* said so to *T. H.* at what Time he controversially askt him that Question? Which is to come close to the Question: Or does he say, there ever was any such Question ask'd him? Clear 'tis, *G. W.* never deny'd that he had spoken those Words, or to the same Effect, to any Body at any Time, or upon any Occasion, (Therefore hath *J. G.* also manifestly wronged him in saying, *Whereas G. W. denies that he said, &c.* this is an Untruth, as is evident by *G. W*'s own Answer, *Appendix*, p. 13) and as evident it is, that the Substance of this Certificate goes no farther than to testify that which was never yet denied; *Therefore no Certificate to clear the Matter objected against* T. H. to wit, That he never receiv'd by Word or Writing any such Question from *T. H.* much less did he ever return him any such Answer; consequently *T. H.* is a *Forger* still.

I will briefly parallel the Case: Let us suppose a Dispute between *T. Hicks*, a *Predestinarian*, and *J. Ives*, an *Universalist*, both *Anabaptists*, about *Election and Reprobation*; And *J. Ives* using his Wits to depaint *T. H*'s Opinion to the greatest Disadvantage; which *T. H.* looking upon as Unfair, and thinking himself not to have been doctrinally, gravely, and justly dealt with, as by the Law of Sober Disputation should have been, falls upon *J. Ives*, with this Rebuke, *Thou art an Ungodly, Vain, and Captious Man; the Judgments of God will overtake thee, if thou Repent not, for thy daring Opposition to the Gospel, and unfair Dealing with me.* *J. Ives* immediately writes a *Dialogue*; the first Question suppos'd to be this:

J. Jves. What dost thou say, *T. H.* to those gross and blasphemous Absurdities I charged thy narrow and ill-natur'd Opinion with; *of damning Men unconditionally, from all Eternity, to glorify God*, thereby rendring God *more Cruel than Men and Beasts, that naturally take Care of their Off-spring*, representing him *partial and double-minded, as having a revealed Will that speaks of his Desire that all should be saved, and a secret Will notwithstanding that damns far the greatest Part, whether they Obey or Rebel?* with much more of the like Cruel and Black Aspect. I suppose thou hast considered them well; Hast thou any Reasons to offer in Countenance and Defence of this horrid Opinion? What sayst thou?

T. Hicks is made by *J. Ives* to answer thus:

T. H. *I say, thou art an Ungodly, Vain and Captious Man; The Judgments of God will overtake thee, if thou Repent not, for thy daring Opposition to the Gospel, and unfair Dealing with me.*

Now, I ask *T. Hicks*, if he thinks this Reflection, by him given upon the supposed disingenuous Carriage of *J. Ives*, to be a proper and suitable Answer for *J. Ives* to give in his Name to a *Doctrinal* Question, unto which it was never given as an Answer? If not, how injuriously has he dealt with *G. W.* Are our Rebukes of *T. Hicks*'s Unrighteous and Prophane Carriage in his *Dialogues*, the only Reasons we are able to render in Defence of our Belief, or against his Doctrinal Objections? Or may a Man honestly take another's Answer, and give it to his own Question, however impertinent, and that in the other Man's Name, with Design to render him so? If not, then certainly *T. H.* has not acted the *Christian* but the *Counterfeit* with us: And God will require this Wickedness at the Church's Hand to which he is related, if they indulge or connive at it.

VII. His Seventh *Forgery*, and the last which I will now mention, is this, and I intreat my *Reader's* Attention; for *He* or *I* must Needs be very guilty.

In his second Dialogue, p. 5. He thus brings me in:

Anab. *Be free and plain with me, how and in what Respect, is Christ said to fulfil the Law, and to dye for Sinners.*

Quak. He fulfil'd the Law *only* as our Pattern or Example: Christ is so far from telling us of such a Way of being *Justified*, as that he informs us the Reason why he abode in his Father's Love, was his *Obedience*: He is far from telling us of being Justified by *Virtue* of his *Obedience* imputed, unless we keep his Commands and obey for our selves; in all which Christ is but our Example, *Pen. Sand. Found. shak.* page 26.

To this, Reader, I return'd two Pages of Answer, in Defence of my Book, and to detect his *Forgery*, some of which he hath ventur'd to give, but with his wonted Disingenuity perverted: Let us hear him patiently.

Anab. *But forasmuch as thou seemest to grant that Christ's Death was in the Nature of a Sacrifice, how will this agree, with what thou hast formerly asserted? viz. That Christ fulfil'd the Law, only as our Pattern and Example, Dial. 3 Page 74.*

Quak. In this *Question* thou hast done exactly like thy self; for if thou canst find the Word *Only* there, or such an Answer to such a Question, thou hast not wronged me; But sure I am, there is no such Question, and as sure, the Fulfilling of the Law was not the Subject treated on, and very certain, the Word *Only* was not there; Therefore thou art a *Forger*. That which I said, with the Scripture on which it was grounded, was this: *If ye keep my Commandments, ye shall abide in my Love,* &c. *Reas against Rail.* p. 78. *Sand. Found.* p. 26.

Anab. Here *it is hard to say, whether thy Dishonesty or Impudence be the greater; for in this Answer thou art guilty of no less than three notorious Untruths: First, thou insinuatest*, as if the Text above named were the only Text from which thou didst argue in thy *Sand. Found.* p. 26. 2*dly*. Thou art sure, the Fulfilling of the Law was not the Subject treated on there. 3*dly*. Thou art very certain, the Word *Only*

Only is not there: *Thus hast thou aggravated thy Wickedness in adding Lye unto Lye, and all this knowingly,* Dial. 3 p. 74, 75.

Sect. I.

'Tis now Time for me to speak; and I beseech thee, *Reader*, hear me; for it is of great Moment to determine who is the *Forger*, who is the *Lyar*; T. H. or W. P.

First, he suggests by this Question, *If Christ's Death was in the Nature of a Sacrifice, as thou sayst, how will this agree with thy former Assertion, that Christ fulfil'd the Law*, only *as our Pattern*, as if the Death and Sufferings of Christ, as a Propitiation to declare God's Righteousness for the Forgiveness of Sins that are past, upon Repentance, had been Part of that Doctrine in that Part of my Book, unto which those Words relate, viz. *Christ fulfil'd the Law as our Pattern*, which really was no Part of that Doctrine, as may be seen. *pag*. 24. 26.

For because we assert him to have been our Example in fulfilling the Righteousness of the moral Law, T. H. would conclude from my Words, *that he was only our Example in ending Types, Shadows, Sacrifices, Propitiations,* &c. *of the Law*; Therefore 'tis great *Forgery* in him, to make me Answer two Questions, the one in p. 52. of his Second *Dialogue?* the other in p. 74 of his last *Dialogue*, which take in the Death and Sufferings of Christ, *that wholly related to but some Part of the personal Obedience of his Life.*

I cannot forbear one Instance more of his foul Miscarriage in this particular, *viz.*

Anab. *Are we no farther concerned in the Obedience and Sufferings of our Lord Jesus without us, than only as our Example or Pattern?*

Quak. What more wouldst thou have? I have told thee, that Christ fulfilled the Law; but *Only* as our Example.

Where there is nothing clearer than that he thrusts the *Sufferings of Christ* into the Question, which was no Part of the Question, making me to deny the Benefit thereof, because I assert him to be only our Example in that which is our daily Duty unto Acceptance with God; not in being a Sacrifice for Sin. Is this not to be *Guilty of Fiction?* Or is this to describe a real *Quaker*, and act the Part of a true *Christian?* O hateful Injuries!

But 2*dly*. In his Quotation of my Answer he hath omitted two Passages; for when I said, If he can find such an Answer to such a Question he has not wronged me, I placed the Words between, which he dropped, viz. *or the Matter strictly contained in that Question*, which I knew he could never compass, because his Question was, *in what Respect Christ died for Sinners*; and the Answer he made me give, truly related to the Fulfilling of the Righteousness of the Law in our selves. O injurious Man! Is this the *Christian?*.

His next Omission is this Part of my Answer, which followed from my Argument (by him cited for Proof of his Charge) upon *John* 15. 10. If you keep my Commandments &c. *Now* (said I) *that this concern'd not the whole Law, Christ came to fulfil; the Law he fulfilled, the Place of Scripture quoted, the Nature and Matter of the Argument clearly prove.* Again *He was our Example in Holiness, though not in his ending of Types and Shaddows,* Reas. against Rail. page 79. Which Passages *Reader*, plainly evidence, that if ever those Words were spoken by me, they never extended to Christ's being but our Example, in the Fulfilling *of the whole Law*, which T. *Hicks* by his Sophistry would insinuate.

For Answer to his *Three notorious Untruths* he charged on me, take what follows. 1. He says I insinuate as if *John* 15. 10. *were the only Text from whence I argued in* Sand. Found. pag, 26. Which Passage, *Reader*, is so far from Truth, that I only charg'd him with having argued from that Text in which no such Word or Matter was to be found, which he denies. 2*dly*, He says, *that I am sure the Fulfilling of the Law was not the Subject treated on there; and that I know therein I have spoken falsly*.

But sure I am, he hath told two *Tales* in charging one upon me: For, *First*, how could the Law, as he understands it, to wit, *the whole Law that Christ came to fulfil*, be intended, when the very Text and Argument upon it, shew, that it was the Keeping of *Christ's Commandments*, that they might abide in his *Love*, and without which they could not be accepted, that was insisted on.

2*dly*. He tells an *Untruth* in charging me with the *Knowledge* of that which was not: But as he declined this Scripture, so the Arguments by which I proved the Impossibility of Christ's keeping his own Commandments in our stead, with which I made good my Conclusion, *viz*. The Necessity of keeping his Commandments as he kept his Father's, In Order to Acceptance with him.

3*dly*, He says, *I am certain, the Word Only is not there, and so add Lye unto Lye knowingly*;

knowingly; which, Reader, makes other *Two Untruths* on my Adversaries Part: For *first*, there is no such Word in all that Argument and Paragraph out of which he made his Citation, as may appear. *Sand. Found. shak. page* 26. *Argum.* 5. *Dial.* 2. *page* 52. *Reas. against Rail. page* 79. 2*dly*, His Saying I shall know of a Thing that never was, makes up his other Falshood: But to the End he may acquaint all with my *Folly* and *Madness*, as he is pleased to term his own horrible Fiction, he tlles me, that he referred in his Citation not to *John* 15. 10, but *Rom.* 2. 13. *Not the Hearers of the Law are just before God, but the Doers of the Law shall be justified.* But do Men use to refer to Places they never cite, either as to *Words, Chapters,* or *Verse,* for they are not mention'd in his *Dialogues*: How then did he refer to them.

If he says, it was to my Argument, I make the same Demand. Do Men refer to *Arguments* they never mention? If to those they do mention, then I can easily prove, it was not this Scripture or Argument upon it, that *T. Hicks* referred to, Reader, peruse *Sand. Found.* p. 26. *Arg.* 5. *Dial.* 2. p. 52. *Reas. against Rail.* p. 78. 79. and thou shalt see his palpable Untruth.

But because he builds here upon this *Argument*, let's hear it: *Unless we be Doers of the Law, which Christ came not to destroy, but as our Example, to fulfil, we can never be just before God: Let not any Fancy, that Christ hath so fulfilled it for them, as to exclude their Obedience, from being requisite to their Acceptance; but Only as their Pattern.* Here *Only* is mentioned: But *first*, this was not the Place cited, but *another* that had it not, as before-express'd; Therefore I no *Lyar,* but *T. Hicks* a *Forger.* 2*dly.* This *Law* mentioned *Rom.* 2. 13. was the *Moral and Eternal Law of God*, and not that *Shadowy Law* containing *Ceremonies, Sacrifices, Propitiatories, Meats, Drinks,* and *divers Washings,* &c. which Christ by his Life, Death and Sufferings, fulfill'd and ended, in which *T. H.* would make me say, That Christ was *Only* our Example: That it was not the whole *Jewish Law*, the two next Verses prove; *For when the* Gentiles, *which have not the Law, do the Things contained in the Law, these having not the Law, are a Law unto themselves, which shew the Work of the Law written in their Hearts*: Therefore not the whole *Jewish Law*, for that they had not; consequently, I do not contradict or make void the Benefit of Christ's Death and Sufferings, by saying, He was only our Example in keeping that Law which the best *Jews* and *Gentiles* were to keep, and kept, and the Righteousness of which is to be fulfilled in us. Thus hath he unworthily *added, diminished, mis-rendred, transposed,* &c. from Time to Time. Certainly, the People called *Anabaptists* are deeply concerned to reckon with him for this *great Scandal* to their Profession.

But suppose I meant the *whole Law* of God in that Place, I see no worse Consequence from my Words than this, That so far as Man's Obedience to God's Law is requisite to his Acceptance, so far *only* Christ became our Example; For as he was not our Pattern in Things that more peculiarly related to him to perform and finish, so was he no more than our Pattern in that which is our constant Duty to do. Now let *T. H.* snap and catch what he can, with all his *Legerdemain,* p. 69. only take this along with him, That by his Reflection upon that Argument, *viz.* That Christ hath not so fulfilled the Law for us, as to exclude our Obedience from being requisite to our Acceptance, he implies *a Denial of the Necessity of obeying the Law of God to Acceptance with God*: A Doctrine suited to his Practice, contrived and continued to the Ease of Hypocrites; no wonder he struggles so hard for it; for without it, nothing but Horror would surround him, though at this Rate he must not always expect to escape the Blow (I mean not *assassinating* of him) a Trick that lives nearer his Complexion than mine, but that Vengeance which is the Recompence of every Soul that loveth and maketh a Lye.

With you, the People called *Anabaptists*, I leave this Section; Right us, Right your selves; Right our Profession of such an Unfair Adversary, and your selves of so scandalous an Advocate.

§. II. *That* T. Hicks *has grosly perverted our Writings.*

TO *Forge* is bad, but to *Pervert* may in a Sense be worse; since it is to mis-use true Words, and by Disguise twist them to a Sense never intended, when many Times that which is false is undiscernibly swallowed for the Sake of something that's true.

1674.
Sect. II.

This was another Charge I exhibited against *T. Hicks*, and an Argument by which I proved him no *Christian*. I frequently in my Book took Occasion to detect him of this Unworthy Practice, and more especially by six and twenty Instances under a distinct Head, containing ten Pages, our *Principles* in one Column, and his *Perversions* in another; but he seems dumb to the Charge. Shall I enter him Mute? that may alter, but not excuse the Punishment (*Assassinating* always excepted.) I shall, *Reader*, for thy Sake and the Truth's, produce some of them, that those to whom this may come, may have some Account of his Carriage in his former *Dialogues*.

I. From our Belief of the Light's Sufficiency to save, he infers, *That all other Means are needless*, Dial. 1. p. 36, 37. not considering it was not the Light's *Insufficiency*, but Man's Weakness, that occasion'd them. He might object Insufficiency as well against God, Christ, Spirit, Grace, &c.

II. From our making the Illumination in Man to be a natural *Emanation* or Product of the Divine Word which made all Things, he wickedly turns it to *An Effect of God's Power*, and so says, *we would make Beasts and Trees*, &c. also divine, Ibid. p. 4.

III. From our asserting that the Light of Christ shineth within the Hearts of Wicked as well as Good Men, He tells People (in our Name) *that he is in the Heart of every Wicked Man, as he is in his Saints*, Cont. p. 45, 46. Though through Rebellion they partake not of his Life, Power, &c.

IV. From our affirming, that God is the Teacher of his People, He infers, *That we deny all Ministry and Visible Worship*, though they stand in God's Power and Spirit, 1 *Dial.* p. 42, 43.

V. From our believing Christ to be in his People, according to express Scripture, and that as such he is crucified by Wicked Men, He infers, *That we deny Christ to be as well without as within; or that he was ever crucified in the Flesh*, 1 Dial. p. 44. Contin. p. 37, 40, 42.

VI. From our denying of their rigid Satisfaction, that is, that Christ was punished by his Father for our Sin; and that Sins past, present and to come, are answered for: And that Men may be Holy by Virtue thereof, tho' not new, but old Creatures, and so Unholy in themselves, He unworthily concludes, *That we disown Christ's Death and Sufferings, as a Propitiation, that it carried away Sins past, and sealed Remission in his Blood to as many as believe: And that we expect to be both forgiven and accepted, not for Christ's Sake, nor in his Sacrifice and Righteousness, but our own Works*, 1 Dial. p. 9, 10. Contin. 48, 49, 50, 51, 52, 53.

VII. From our pleading for a Perfection from Sin, and the Duty of growing to the Fulness of the Measure, &c. He infers, *Our Denial of Perfection in Degrees, and our Belief of as high a Degree of Perfection in this World, as hereafter*, Dial. 1. p. 48, 49, 50, 51.

VIII. Because we say, that such Works as are wrought by the Holy Spirit in us, are necessary to Eternal Life, and may in a Sense be said to obtain it, since the Lord hath so freely offered it upon the Condition of believing and obeying, which are the Fruits of the Spirit of God in Man; *T. Hicks* suggests in our Name, *That we expect to merit Eternal Life by our good Works, and those of our own Working, as the Spider weaves his Webb out of his own Bowels*, Dial. p. 38. Contin. p 51, 52.

IX. Because we say, All Spiritual Liberty stands in God's Power (that redeems from *Satan's* Snares) He inferreth, *That who are not of our Way, should have no Liberty*, Cont. pag. 85.

X. Because we say, The Scriptures are not the great Gospel-*Rule*, but the *Spirit*; The Dispensation of the Spirit being that of the Gospel more peculiarly; and that without it we cannot understand, or savingly believe any Thing declared of in the Scripture, and therefore that it is our Rule for believing the Scriptures themselves; He basely suggests, *That the Quakers cast of all Precepts in the Scriptures; and so will not bring their Cheats and Impostures to the Test thereof, counting them of no more Authority than Æsop's Fables*, Dial. 1. p. 20, 21, 22, 23, 24, 30, 31, 32, 33, 34, 35, 36. Contin. *Epist.* to the Reader. Behold your *Anabaptist-Preacher*!

XI. From our preaching Men to a lost God and Christ, to God and Christ whom they have lost Fellowship with, He perverts it to our Believing, *That God and Christ were in a lost or undone Condition*, Cont. p. 49.

XII. From our asserting, that what was a Command to any Servant of God in old Time, is not so to us, because so to them, that is, such as *Moses*'s going to
Pharoah

Pharoah, the Performance of *Types*, *Shadows* and *Figures* appointed for a Season, and to pass off, unless requir'd by the same Spirit anew, He falsly infers, *That those Moral and Eternal Precepts, Thou shalt have no other God but me, Thou shalt not Murder, Commit Adultery, Steal, Bear False Witness*, &c. *are not binding upon us, but that we give our selves the Liberty of such horrid Principles, as the contrary to those Principles, and are therefore inconsistent with Government*, Contin. pag. 59, 60. Who would have expected this from a profest *Baptist*, and Preacher too?

XIII. From our denying the Resurrection of the natural and corruptible Body, leaving it with the Lord to give us a Body as pleaseth him, as 1 *Cor.* 15. 36, 37, 38.

This Caviller endeavours to possess People with *our Denial of the Resurrection of any Body to Life Eternal, however spiritual or glorified*, Dial. p, 56 to 62.

And lastly, from our asserting the Unity of God and the Soul, and Denial of his carnal Resurrection; he concludes, *That the Soul is Part of God, and that no future Rewards or Punishments are to be expected*, Dial. 1. p. 16, 17.

These *Reader*, are some of the many Perversions this Ungodly Man is guilty of against our Principles. Is this to condemn the *Quaker* out of his own Mouth, and to evince his Objections against him to be real Truths? Is not *Counterfeit* a Name good enough for him that has thus counterfeited a *Quaker* and a *Christian* too? Will this bring Honour to his Brethren? Or can it be consistent with their Credit, to encourage such base Attempts, when but a midling *Heathen* would have abhorred to have been the Actor of half that Injury *T. H.* hath not only committed, but continues in, and boasts of.

And that he has taken himself to no better Refuge from the Pursuit of our Arguments, notwithstanding the Cautions of our former Book, I shall in a few Instances make evidently appear to all that dare trust, and will but impartially use, their Eyes.

1. From my saying, That those that crucified Christ were Admirers of the Scriptures, and pretended out of their own Law, that it was both lawful and necessary he should be put to Death: Whereas, had they brought that Deed to the Light, the Light would have shown it not to have been wrought in God; which the Scriptures without the Light could not effectually do: He makes no Conscience of inferring, *That I intimate an Insufficiency in the Scriptures to convince the* Jews *that Murder was a Sin*, Dial. 3. p. 13. Whereas the Question was not, whether Murder was a Sin; but whether the *Jews* thought *that* Murder, by the Scripture: if they did, give us an Instance; if they did not, then I have the End of my Allusion, to wit, If the Scriptures are not therefore insufficient in *T. H*'s Account, because the *Jews* were not convinced by them of Murder; neither ought the Light within to be reputed insufficient, because Men were not convinced of their Unbelief in Christ by it. I will answer him in setting down his own Words to me: *O Impious Man!* says he: *The Defect was not in the Scriptures, but in themselves, in not attending to what was therein delivered, wherein Murder is peremptorily forbidden*: Right; But, *O Impious Man!* say I, the Defect was not in the Light, but themselves, in not attending to it, whereby Murder is also forbidden. How much more sufficient now, *T. H.* is the Scripture than the Light? Vain Shuffler!

But this is not all his Perversion; for he farther infers in my Name, *That the Scriptures did rather countenance and justifie, than condemn them in that Fact*, Dial. 3. p. 13. Which, Reader, in plain Terms, is as much as to say, because the Scriptures do not *so effectually* discover evil Conceptions as the *Light within*; therefore the Scriptures *rather countenance and justifie them*: Monstrous Baseness! The Truth is, were his Endeavours against us but well weighed of all that see them, there were little need of our Labour in his Discovery, or our own Defence. But that which aggravates his Sin, is the hard Words he gives me after all; I know not why, unless to cover his own Guilt, or make his credulous Reader think me as hateful, as he would have me.

2. The second Perversion I shall instance, is this: Because I told him (in Answer to his Objection about the Light's Insufficiency, for it's not discovering to the *Heathen-Philosophers* how Sin came into the World) if he meant by that Discovery, a clear and distinct Account and particular History, how *Adam* and *Eve* were beguiled by the Serpent, it was no Ways to his Purpose (unless he can prove the Knowledge of it absolutely necessary to Salvation) He, according to his usual Baseness, makes me to say, *The Penning of that History was to no Purpose*, Dial. 34. thus interrogating of me, *Wilt thou dare to say, the Knowledge of this is to no Purpose?*

Why then did the sacred Penmen give such a full Account thereof? As if it were one and the same Thing for me to say, the Penning of that History is to no Purpose, and to say, *It is not to* T. Hicks's *Purpose?* Is this the Way to prove the *Quaker* no *Christian?* But since this full Account is made such a great Instance by T. H. for the Sufficiency of the Scripture, and Insufficiency of the Light, let him tell me, *What Paradise* Adam *was put in; and where it was? What was that Serpent that tempted* Eve, *if a fallen Spirit, or a Beast of the Field? And what was that Fruit and Tree God forbad, and the Serpent tempted the Woman to eat of? And what was the Voice* Adam *heard in the Garden? What were those Fig-Leaves he covered himself withal? And what was that Death that he dyed? And what were those Cherubims and the flaming Sword and the Tree of Life, all mentioned in that History.* If he takes the Account *Literally*, let him say so; but let him take this with him, that then *Adam* bodily dyed, before he begot his Sons and Daughters; and the History gives us no Account of his corporal Resurrection: But if he take the Account, in whole, or in Part, *mystically*, then how is it full, clear and distinct, not distinguishing Literal and Natural from Mystical and Spiritual Things: Is this the Way to prove the Insufficiency of the Light within, that sends all People to the Light within for a sufficient Account, which, says Dr. *Henry Moor* of *Cambridge*, *spoke in and reproved* Adam *for his Lapse from God*, Philosoph. Lab. p. 27.

However it be, this lies at T. *H*'s Door, that because I said, his Instance of *Moses*'s Writings *were nothing to his Purpose*, he makes me to conclude, *They were writ to no Purpose:* If he loved his Soul, he would hate these Courses, that need no Aggravation, their own Infamy is enough.

3. Again, from my acknowledging that the Scripture furnisheth me with the Knowledge of Christ's Visible Transactions; he infers thus, *which is as if thou shouldst say, God manifested in the Flesh could not have been known by thee, were it not revealed in the Scriptures, intimating, that thou couldst* NEVER *have known it by the meer Light in thee*, Dial. 3. p. 44, 48.

Which intimates, that *Thomas Hicks* is an arrant Perverter of my Sense. Is there no Difference between saying, I was informed of a certain Passage by A. B. and saying, *It was impossible I should have known it any other Way than by* A. B. But why all this wresting? Is it to conclude, *therefore the Light within is Insufficient?* which may as well be inferred against God, Christ and the Holy Spirit; for he makes me to exclude all other Ways of Discovery, than what is made by Scripture. If an Account were wanting, the Light of Christ is as sufficient now, as it was in the Time of *Moses* and the *Prophets*, who wrote both of Things past and to come: But a Relation being with us, the Light of Christ doth nothing unnecessarily. But T. H. 'tis like, degenerates not from his Ancestors; he can cry, *Come down and save thy self, &c.*

4. From our asserting the Works of the Spirit in us necessary to our compleat Justification or Acceptance with God, he insinuates, *Our making those Works the meritorious Cause of our Salvation*, Dial. 3. p. 69. which is manifestly denied and rejected by me, in my Answer, p. 72, 73, 82, 83, 86. which he no more regards, than if it never were: The Trick of an unfair and shuffling Adversary.

5. From my asserting the Necessity of an inward Work of Righteousness, by the Power of Christ in these Words of the Apostle to the *Galatians*, Let every Man prove his own Work, and then shall he have Rejoycing in himself, and not in another: He, to make his Ends upon me, infers, *That the Doctrine of Christ dying for Sinners, hath nothing in it, as the Ground of our Rejoycing: For our Rejoycing must be in our selves, not in another*, Dial. 3. p. 69, 70.

That, Reader, which aggravates this wretched Consequence by him charged upon me, is first, that he says, it is *plainly deducible*, which is so plain a Wrest: And next, that they are the Apostle's Words, and not mine, of which he makes so ill an Use.

Is this to make the Scripture his Rule, that is so unruly in his Abuse of them? I am sure, a lying and an abusive Spirit has been his Rule throughout his three *Dialogues*, which God rebuke.

6. The sixth Perversion is as follows: Being formerly assaulted by T. *Hicks*, Cont. p. 50. for having said in a Book entituled, *The Serious Apology*, &c. p. 148. That *Justification by a Righteousness wholly without us, is a Doctrine of Devils*; I undertook my Defence, and performed it in my Answer to his other *Dialogues*, from p. 66. to p 98: I distinguished upon the Word *Justification*, first, as it might be taken *barely for the Remission of Sins, or the acquitting Men of the Guilt and*

Punishment due to Sin, which was the free Love and Mercy of God upon Repentance (declared in Chrift's Death, as a Propitiation for the Sins of the whole World) and therefore not to be merited by the beft Works we can perform, 2dly, *As it imported a being made inwardly juft by the bringing in of Chrift's Everlafting Righteoufnefs to the Soul.* To leave out this latter, and make the former only fufficient (whereby Men are left in an unjuft and unrighteous State) I affirmed to be a *Doctrine of Devils*. But notwithftanding this plain and fcriptural Diftinction to fatisfie *T. Hicks* (would he but be fatisfied) what I meant by Juftification; He is fo unjuft to me, as to infer in my Name, ' That I account the Doctrine of Chrift's Death ' in the Nature of a Sacrifice, to declare the Righteoufnefs of God, for the Re-' miffion of Sins that are paft *(becaufe tranfacted* without us) a Doctrine of De-' vils, *Dial.* 3. p. 72, 73, 74.

Canft thou, *Reader*, in earneft think, this Man makes Confcience of his Endeavours againft us, who commits thefe frequent Abufes againft our Books, Perfons and Principles? As if becaufe I acknowledged Chrift's Death to be in the Nature of a Sacrifice, to declare God's Righteoufnefs, in the Remiffion of Sins that are paft, unto them that believe, *&c.* to be one Part of Juftification; and that this Tranfaction was, confeffedly, *without us*, even while we were Sinners, *&c.* that therefore, I fhould call this the Doctrine of Devils, *becaufe without us*, though the World *wholly* be not there, upon which lay the Strefs, and which was only faid by me of a Juftification, that *wholly* excludes Chrift's Righteoufnefs revealed within, to the making Man Juft, unworthily applying that Reflection to the Beginning of Juftification, that I have fo exprefly owned, which was made againft a Doctrine no ways concern'd in this true and Gofpel-Juftification. In fhort, If Juftification by Chrift's Righteoufnefs without us, be the fame, *with being juftified by Chrift's Righteoufnefs* wholly *without us*; then *T. H.* is not fo bad a Man, as I have reprefented him. But if there be any Difference, as undeniably there is, and a material One too; then *T. H's* Inference and Conclufion, in my Name, make a foul Perverfion.

7. The laft Perverfion I at this Time think fit to mention, is *his* laft, both in his Epiftle and Book, to wit, from my faying, upon a fad Confideration of his many Mifcarriages towards us, *That his Head fhould not go down into the Grave in Peace*; he thus interprets my Words: ' I muft take them either as a Prediction, or ' as a Menace, or fome Mifchief, he himfelf, or fome influenced by him intend ' to perpetrate upon me: The former I fear not, the latter is moft Probable: As if, *Reader*, his not fearing a Prediction, implies my not meaning a Prediction. But why is the former not feared, *and the latter more probable?* becaufe he would render me a *Murderer*, as his following Words fufficiently evidence. *Wherefore*, fays he, *I defire all, to whom this Book may come, that if at any Time they hear of any Violence offered me, or that I be* Affaffinated, *they would remember thefe Words of* W. Penn, *that my Head fhall not go down to the Grave in Peace, Epift.*

Now though this miferable Conftruction be ridiculous with wife Men, and rejected of feveral of his own Way, and fo unlikely a Thing in it felf, that I fhould proclaim that to be my Defign that leads to the *Gibbet*, viz. *Murder*; yet I was unwilling to pafs it by, fince *firft*, it rather renders him to be the Man he fuggefts me to be: And, *fecondly*, it aggravates the Sin of his falfe Conftruction; becaufe to infinuate it the better, he has left out all thofe Words going before and after, that had they been mentioned, would have detected his Malice, viz. *Though thou haft beftowed much Time to abufe our Friends in general, and my felf in particular, a Stranger to thee,* yet I *can forgive thee: O, that thefe heavy Things might not be laid to thy Charge: God will vifit for thefe Unrighteous Dealings, if thou defift not.*

Now, Reader, if I forgive, how can I *Affaffinate?* And if it be God's Vifiting Hand, how can it be *mine*, *or any influenced by me?* Again, thefe following Words were the next to thofe by him cited, viz. *Yea, the Light within will bear Witnefs to the Truth of thefe Things on thy* DYING BED, *and then remember me*. How comes this *T. H.* to be omitted? *Dying-Beds* do not ufe to be *Unnatural Daaths*; Nor will the Light within bear Witnefs for Murder: *Was all this left out to evince, that the* Fictions *I charged upon thee, were real Truths, and no Fictions; and that a* Quaker *is quite another Thing than a Chriftian?* Becaufe it is his Honour to be quite another Thing than fuch a *Chriftian* as thou art, that is a very *Counterfeit*.

Reader, Does not thy Soul rife againft thefe abominable Practices? Falfhood was ever hateful to Truth, and Bafenefs to an Honeft Mind, which *T. H.* being proved thus guilty of, I muft conclude him quite another Thing than a *Chriftian.*

Thus

Thus have I finished my Observations on his Perversions, leaving them also with the People called *Anabaptists*, upon whom I cannot chuse, but frequently call for Justice, against this their unjust Member; concluding my Complaint in this Section, in Honest *John Husse*'s, against the like Adversaries, on the same Occasion: *Some of these Propositions I did Write and Publish, other some mine Enemy did feign, now adding, then diminishing and taking away, now falsly ascribing and imputing the whole Proposition unto me.*

§. III. T. H. *Proved Guilty of* Lyes *and* Slanders.

Reader, in my Answer to his former *Dialogues*, I charg'd him with *Eighteen Lyes* and *Slanders*, under a distinct Head, *Pag.* 154, 155, 156. of which I find not that he hath taken any Notice, saving Two by Way of farther Affirmation, but no Proof. A few I shall mention to his utter Shame, with all Men loving Religion.

1. That *the* Quakers *owning of Christ Jesus, and the Christ they own, are a meer Mystical Romance*, Dial. p. 10. Cont. p. 9. A prophane Untruth!

2. That *the Light in the* Quakers, *sees no Necessity of a Mediator*, 1 Dial. p. 35. when, God knows, we feel the Daily Benefit of him.

3. That *the* Quakers *account the Blood of Christ no more than they do the Blood of a common Thief*, Ibid. p. 38. An Ungodly Aspersion!

4. That *we deny his Visible Coming and Appearance in the World*, Cont. p. 37. This he contradicts else-where.

5. That *the* Quakers *dissemble when they tell People they own the Scriptures; and that they render them of no more Authority than* Æsop's *Fables*, Cont. Epist. Both abominable Untruths.

6. That a Quaker *should say, The Thing that troubles thee, is thy puzling thy self in that Book the* Bible, Thou *wilt never be settled till thou* throw *that Book away*, Cont. p. 36. An arrant Slander.

7. That a Quaker *should say to one* J. Nobbs, *What dost thou tell me of the Scriptures, they are no more to me than an* Old Almanack (whereas *J. Nobbs*, if he be alive, and have but a little more Honesty than *T. H.* can't but confess that he was no *Quaker*; nor that there was one so call'd in that Country, when any Thing like those Words was spoken) As *T. Holbrow*, the Person charg'd by *J. N.* related it to me the last Summer, *Dial.*

8. That *the* Quakers *appoint their Ministers to speak in such a Place, and at such a Time: And they go to Meetings only to* Decoy, Trepan, *and* Inveigle, Cont. Pag. 66.

9. That *a* Woman-Quaker *should bid her Husband take another Woman*, Ib. p. 63.

10. That *the Motions of God's Spirit are pretended by* Quakers, *at least one of them, to* Refuse *Just Debts*, Cont. p. 69.

What Man that makes Conscience of *Lying*, would have told so many gross Untruths; and that cared for his own Reputation, would have pass'd over their Proof in such Silence?

Either he thinks it no Sin to render Men *Hereticks* and *Knaves* at Pleasure; or that there is no Obligation upon him to maintain his foul Imputations. But let's see how much better he is grown since his *Second Dialogue*.

1. The first *Great Lye* he tells in his *New Book*, is the very first Sentence that is writ in it, viz. *The* Quaker *Condemn'd out of his own Mouth*: For it is his foul Mouth that hath both Accused and Condemn'd him; as we have already prov'd, and shall yet have farther Occasion to do.

2. His *Second Untruth* is in the fourth Page of his Epistle, viz. That *there was a Person esteem'd by the* Quakers *a Friend, of whom* W. Penn *gave this Character, That he might be trusted with one's Life (notwithstanding* W. Penn's *Infallible Judgment) counterfeited (like an Ungrateful and Unworthy Wretch)* W. Penn's *Hand, took up a considerable Sum of Money in his Name, (pretending for his Use) which* W. Penn *in a little Time found (though to his Cost) to be a meer Cheat.*

Reader, He hath put the *Quaker* in this Man's Livery, that he might have the fairer Plea for abusing him. *Ungrateful and Unworthy Wretch* are Words not so much flung at the Fact, or the Man, as the *Quaker*: For were it the Temper of *Thomas Hicks* to be Grateful, and Worthy to them that oblige him, he would never be Injurious to them that never hurt him. But be that as it will, I have three Things to say to *T. Hicks*, *First*, That this Man was never a *Quaker*, unless such as sometimes come to *T. Hicks*'s Meeting, are to be reputed *Anabaptists*, having never come under any of those External Significations, by which they are differ'd from other People; and I think I that knew him, ought to be believ'd before *T. H.* who perhaps never saw him. *Secondly*, If he were an *Unworthy Wretch* for Counterfeiting my Hand in *Money-Matters*; how much more *Unworthy Wretch* is *T. Hicks, who hath Counterfeited the Faith, Doctrine and Practice of a great Body of People, to the rendring them Infamous with all Men,* were that Work as Really Believed, as it was Enviously Contrived. *Thirdly*, But for all my *Infallible Judgment I was Cheated*, says *T. H.* How plentiful, *Reader*, are the Instances *T. H.* gives us, to detect him: For besides the Baseness of his Taunt, he inferreth from our asserting an *Infallibility in the Principle*, our arrogating an *Infallibility to all our Persons*, as well in Civil as Religious Concerns, whether we obey it, or no. But to turn it back upon himself: Have no *Anabaptists* been cheated, notwithstanding they pretend the *Scriptures* to be their *Infallible Rule*? If they have, Shall I make one of *T. H*'s Conclusions, viz. That *they are Infallible, because they have an Infallible Rule;* Or, *That their Rule is Fallible, because they are Fallible themselves*? Or, in Case of being Cheated, should we tauntingly say, *Where is your Infallible Judgment, because you say, you have an Infallible Rule.*

3. I charge him with slandering our Friends, with saying, *That when it hath been demonstrated to them,* wherein (he thinks) I have erred, *What dost thou tell us of W. Penn; He is an heady, rash, Young Man, we take no Notice what he saith —— Yet acquaint them with the like Extravagancies in the Writings of the former,* G. F. &c. *They will either peremptorily deny them so written, or else tell us, We understand not their Meaning*, Epist. p. 5. This let him prove if he can.

4. That *the* Quakers *excuse some of their Villanies, by Pretences to the Innocent Life.* This we esteem an abominable Falshood, 3 *Dial. Epist.*

5. The next Slander is, That the *Quakers warn their Proselytes against reading their Adversaries Books, lest their Wickedness should be detected*, pag. 76. A very Falshood.

6. That W. Penn, *by the Sense of the Eternal Spirit, doth declare, that* Cursing, Railing *and* Lying, *were the only fit Answers to be given to the Priests trepanning Questions*, pag. 10, 80, 81, 82. O Ungodly Slander! The Lord rebuke thy foul Spirit.

7. That the *Quakers have discovered themselves to be no other than the Spawn of that wicked Brood, the* Ranters, *having lick'd up their Vomit*, p. 80. What say the *Baptists* to this? It is known, none so much opposed them.

8. The *Quakers say, they witness Innocent and Sober Enquirers after their Faith and Religion to be Beasts, Sots, in the Sorcery and Witchcraft,* p. 85. which manifest Slander, I suppose, proceeds from certain Names *Edw. Burrough* gave to a Priest, that by subtil Queries endeavoured to trepan some of our Friends, as they of old our Lord and Master, under the Censure of *Blasphemy*, and as was attempted upon some about that very Time. So that he was an *Innocent and Sober Enquirer*, by the same Figure that *Tho. Hicks* hath been an *Innocent and Sober Dialoguer*, who first invents *Lyes*, and then kicks them up and down for our Principles and Practices.

9. Another Notorious *Falshood* committed by *Tho. Hicks* against us, is in p. 88. to wit, *That some Overtures have of late been offered the* Quakers, *in order to a publick Meeting, to debate the Chief Things in Difference betwixt them and others; which the* Quakers *refused, under Pretence of being cautious not to run themselves voluntarily into Jeopardies, and therefore think it their best Way to Rail at their Adversaries.* It is to be hoped *Tho. Hicks* by this Time, hath sufficiently shewn and vented his Falshoods and Slanders, by the Frequency of them; and that for the future they will less need our Animadversion. That this is One, and a *Great One* too, take what follows.

W. Hayworth, an empty, but hot-headed *Preacher*, among the *Professors at Hartford*, often making a Kind of Challenge to some of our Friends to meet with any of their Teachers, and being answered that they would not refuse him a Meeting, he proceeded thereon, and proposed *Ware* for the Place; against which the Scruple was made, and not about a Meeting, as *Thomas Hicks* falsly relates: This our Friend's Answers to *W. Hayworth* prove. In *Th. Prior*'s first Answer to *W. H.* it is said, *I perceive they (the* Quakers*) are not intended to refuse thee a Meeting, at a convenient Time and Place agreed on by both Parties; and it is expected and intended, the Book authorized by thee, styl'd,* The Quaker Converted, *be the Subject of the Dispute.*

Dispute. And in the second Paper to *W. Hayworth*, it is proposed, That *the Meeting be at* Theobald's; *and that after the said Book be fully discoursed, if he had not Disputing enough, such other Questions as tend to Edification be propounded, and a farther Time taken to discourse them*: But he would no Ways consent that his *Book* should be the Subject; saying in his Letter, *That to undertake it, would narrow the Debate.*

Judge now, Reader, who evaded the *Meeting*; and if *Tho. Hicks* hath not falsly accused the *Quakers* with refusing it; yet doth he Rant, Revile, and add Lye unto Lye in that very Page where he told this, that he might make the most of his fancied Advantage against us, to our Disgrace, and his own Triumph. But he shall fail in his Endeavours, and God will advocate our Cause among Men, against these foul and provoking Imputations. One *Slander* more, and we end this Section.

10. That *the Tendency of all the* Quaker's *Reasoning about* Instituted Religion, *is to* Debauch Mankind, *to teach them how to live in Rebellion against God. Their Religion is a meer Cheat, calculated only to the Service of the Devil, and their own Lusts, and inconsistent with Government,* Dial. 1. pag. 62. Dial. 3. p. 65.

Here is a great Deal in a Little, all at once: This shews what the Man would be at, and makes Good what elsewhere he saith, *That we are inconsistent with Government,* Cont. pag. 69. The Consequence is plain; A *New-England* Antidote to rid *Old-England* of the Epidemical Disease of *Quakerism*: For it is a Maxim in Law, *That whosoever is inconsistent with Government, deserves not the Protection of Government.*

But that this Language should drop from the Pen of an *Anabaptist* to a *Quaker*, is justly surprizing; since a Multitude of his Profession stand charg'd on Record with so many gross Immoralities, erroneous Doctrines, and rebellious Practices, as have rendred them and their Profession, the Suspicion of the Weak, the Abhorrence of the Multitude, and at best the Dislike of many Good Men: But though *T. Hicks* hath invented Crimes to blacken us, I shall not so much as recriminate the People that go under that Name, having abundance more of Charity for them, than the softest Passage in *Tho. Hicks's Dialogue* can afford us. I am well satisfied, that I have thus far honestly represented him in his Inventions, Perversions, Slanders and Aggravations, so inconsistent with the Spirit, Language and Carriage of a *True Christian*; and therefore his Pretence of being such, renders him but the Greater COUNTERFEIT.

§. IV. *That* T. Hicks *is Guilty of* Plain Contradictions.

IT is inconsistent with the Credit of any Man that writes, to contradict himself: But for one who pretends himself a *Christian*, so to do, and that in Matters of Religion, is shamefully to make void his own Pretences. That *Thomas Hicks* is the Man, I produced several *Proofs* in my Answer to his former *Dialogues*: But they were equally disregarded with the rest, not having so much as attempted the reconciling of them.

I will briefly repeat some of them, and add more out of all *Three Dialogues*.

1. Contradiction. First, *I, T. Hicks, do acknowledge, that the Light within checketh for many Evils, and excites to many Good Things; and that I ought to shun those Evils, and do that Good,* 1 Dial. p. 8. ——— Yet in direct Contradiction he dares to tell us, *That this Light in us, directing to it's best Actions, swelleth Men with proud Conceits; and that it doth deceive and mis-guide such as follow it,* 1 Dial. p. 3, 37, 38.

2 Contr. I, Thomas Hicks, *do, and must bear Witness against thy Erroneous Opinion, if true to the Light in me,* Dial. p. 8. *I am to do what the Light in my self directs me, and herein is my Comfort,* p. 91. *I grant it ought to be obeyed,* p. 7. ——— Yet in direct Contradiction, and to unsay this, he tells us, *That the Light is uncertain; in one Man it teacheth one thing, and in another directly contrary; so that,* saith he, *there can be no Certainty of Truth or Error, Sin or Duty by this,* Dial. p. 42.

3 Contr. Again, *Thomas Hicks* says, *That it is no Disparagement to the Light within, to say, That God doth make any thing more known of his Will, than is, or can be known by it; For it is but to say, that* Each Degree of Light *is serviceable to its End,* 1 Dial. p. 36. ——— Yet in direct Contradiction to, and undervalue of this, he says within two Pages after, *The Improvement of the Light within subverts the Co-*

venant

venant of Grace, the only Way God hath Revealed for Salvation; and that it directly opposeth it self to the Ends of the Covenant, and ought to be rejected, pag. 38.

My *Animadversion* contracted, upon these *Contradictions*, I will give: If this be to argue safely, prudently, and like a Disputant, I am greatly mistaken; sure I am, there is nothing of Truth or Christianity in such Confusion: *For that a Man should be obliged to obey a Light that doth mis-guide, or that* T. Hicks *should talk of acting according to the* Light *in him, making his Appeal to it in others; and yet say, that it may deceive, and oppose the very Ends of the Covenant of Grace, is with me, the Top of all Impudence and Self-Contradiction.*

All this, Reader, he pass'd with his usual Silence.

How concern'd he was to consider it, I shall leave with thee to judge, having hereby so manifestly forfeited his Reputation, both as a *Christian* and a *Disputant*. But I will not leave him here; I shall greaten his Score e're we part, and yet evidence, that he hath said little against us, wherein he hath not said a great Deal in Contradiction to himself.

Contr. I. *I*, T. Hicks, *appeal to the Light in thee,* Stephen Crisp, *whether this be not an Insufficient Proof; for I grant the Light ought to be obeyed; It checks for Evil, and excites to good things,* Dial. 1. p. 7. 8.

Yet in Contradiction to this, hear what he says:

I deny not a Light to be in every Man; for the Understanding and Conscience being Parts of the Reasonable Soul, these do remain still in the Worst of Men, though the Rectitude be lost, Dial. 1. p. 32.

Observ. Is it not Madness in T. Hicks, to appeal to a *Light* that hath lost it's *Rectitude* (that is, Reader, which through Depravity is become *Darkness*) for an Evidence about Matters of the greatest Concern in *Religion?* Can such a *Light* check for Evil, and excite to Good, that T. H. says, hath lost it's *Rectitude?* And is it a *Crooked and Depraved Light,* that he grants, is to be obeyed and followed? Is this the Man fit to reprove the *Quakers*, for turning Men to a *Sufficient Light*, who himself confessedly follows a *Crooked and Depraved Light?* No Wonder if he cannot see the Truth and Streightness of our *Light*, who judgeth of it by a Light that hath lost it's *Rectitude*: For, saith he, *I do and must bear Witness against thy Opinion of the Sufficiency of the Light in every Man, if I be true to the Light in me, that hath lost it's Rectitude,* 1 Dial. p. 8, 32.

Contr. II. *It will be our Wisdom, yea, our Duty (also) to attend to the Light within,* 1 Dial. pag. 13. as the Place imports.

Yet in direct Contradiction he says, p. 38.

What intolerable Pride and Arrogancy have you Quakers *arrived to, and all this in following the Conduct of the Light within?*

What sayst thou to this, Reader? Is the Man like to make the *Quaker No Christian?* Is it not a Shame for those called *Anabaptists*, to suffer this Man as well in his manifest Weakness, as great Dishonesty, to manage the Controversie against us?

Contr. III. *That which any of you* Quakers *have said of the Light within, hath been no more than what the Apostle speaks of the Man of Sin. And what may as well prove* Mahomet *to be the* True Christ, *as the Light in you. Again, If thou sayst that the* Light in every Man is Christ, *I charge it with Blasphemy,* 1 Dial. p. 3. 11, 12.

Yet in direct Contradiction, T. H. faith,

How could you (Quakers) *call the* Light within Christ, *if some Scriptures had not mentioned* Christ in you, *and, that He is the Light and Life of Men,* 1 Dialog. pag. 22.

Observ. Does John 1. 4, 9, chap. 14, 20. 2 Cor. 4, 6. chap. 13, 5. Gal. 1. 16. which we are wont to offer, as well prove the Man of Sin, and *Mahomet*, to be Christ, as the *Light* which T. H. acknowledgeth to check for Evil, to excite to Good Things; and confesseth, as before, That *the Scriptures have given us to call the Light within Christ, and Christ the Life and Light of Men?* Wert thou aware of these Things, T. H. when thou wrotest them? Art thou fit to accuse me of *Inadvertency*, that committest it thy self. I will not say that any of thy Friends, being charg'd with thy Follies, replied, *What dost thou tell us of* T. Hicks? *He is a Heady, Rash Man, we take no Notice of what he faith.* But that thou hast proved thy self Rash and Heady, and that they ought to take no farther Notice of thee, than to check thee, thy wretched Management of the Controversy against us sufficiently proveth: But let us proceed.

1674.
Sect. IV.

IV. Contr. *You* Quakers, *since you have reprobated the Scriptures from being your Rule, and given up your selves to the immediate Motions and Government of the Light within, have arrived to this Degree of Wickedness, to deny Jesus Christ to be a distinct Person without you*, 3 Dial. p. 15, 16.

Yet in plain *Contradiction* he says, *That every Man hath a Light within him, is not denied; and that it ought to be obeyed is granted*, Ibid. p. 8.

Observ. The Consequence, *Reader*, which is this, *That Men ought to obey that Light, the Government of which leads to deny Jesus Christ, &c. and to persist in a Reprobation of the Scriptures.* Is this Doctrine like to *Christian* the Anabaptist, and *Unchristian* the Quaker?

Contr. V. *Verily, I much doubt, that you believe that Jesus Christ is the Son of God, and that as concerning the Flesh he was put to Death at* Jerusalem, 1 Dialog. p. 43, 44.

Again, *The* Quaker *denies that Christ was ever Visible to Wicked Men; and consequently that Person, called in the Scripture by this Name, who conversed in the World and suffered Death openly and visibly at* Jerusalem, *to be the Christ; So that a Personal Coming in any Respect is manifestly denied by you*, Contin. p. 37, 45.

Yet to un-say and contradict all this, he says, *I never charg'd you* Quakers *for denying that bodily Appearance*, 3 Dial. p. 26. *I no where accuse you for denying Christ's Bodily Appearance*, Ibid. p. 33. *Ye have confessed to* Christ's *Bodily Appearance*, Ibid. p. 31.

Which is as much as to say,

Observ. The *Quakers* do own Christ's Visible Appearance: The *Quakers* do not own Christ's Visible Appearance; yet I doubt whether they own Christ's Visible Appearance or no. Is this Man fit to write Controversy that is of three or four Minds in the writing of it? Confusion will be the End of all this, not our Confutation, but Vindication, in the Minds of impartial Men.

VI. Contr. His sixth Contradiction is this: *That the Religion of the* Quakers *is a Cheat, calculated only for the Service of the Devil and their own Lusts*, 1 Dial. p. 62. yet confesseth to us, *That every Man is enlightned, that this Light checks for Evil, and exciteth to Good; That it ought to be obeyed*, Dial. 1, p. 7, 8. Dial. 3. p. 8. *And that this is the* Quakers *first and grand Principle*, Dial. 1, p. 6.

Observ. Now, *Reader*, How our Religion can be *calculated* to the Service of the *Devil*, and our own Lusts; and yet the first and grand Principle of that *Religion* be unconcerned in that Hellish Service, is more than I can tell.

The plain *English* of his gross Contradiction is this: *That the Light within, which checks for Evil, and excites to Good, and ought to be attended upon and obeyed, is the first and grand Principle of that Religion, which is calculated to the Service of the Devil, and their Lusts that receive it.* For which detestable *Blasphemy*, with more Reason may I use T. H's Exclamation, *Blush, O Heaven! and be astonish'd, O Earth! Was ever such a Thing as this heard of before?* I must tell the People called *Anabaptists*, that the Attempts of T. *Hicks* will prove as great a Reproach to their Profession, and bring the Endeavours of our *Adversaries* into as utter Abhorrence with all honest-minded People as any Opposition ever made against us.

Contr. VII. The seventh Contradiction, and the last I shall here mention, is very well worth the Notice of my *Reader*, since it doth at once invalidate his whole Enterprize with Persons of Understanding. And that is this:

A Dialogue between a Christian *and a* Quaker, *wherein are faithfully represented some of the Chief and most Concerning Opinions of the Quakers*, 1 Dial. Title-page. Again,

A farther Account of their perilous Errors, clearly and plainly represented, Cont. Title-page. Again,

The Things objected against the Quakers *in the former Dialogues, are fully cleared and evinced*, 3 Dial. Title-page. Yet, as a Man infatuated with a Spirit of *Contradiction*, thus gives the Lye to his three *Title-pages*, and in them to his *Three Dialogues*.

The Doctrines delivered (by the Quakers) *are such, as neither themselves, nor any for them, can give us a distinct and intelligible Account of: And that the Tendency of all their Writings and Declarings, doth but lead People into the Thicket of Absurd, Inexcusable, and Unintelligible Dotages*, Contin. Epist. 3.

Observ. Now, *Reader*, If no Man can understand them, how can T. *Hicks* represent and evince them? Are they inexplicable by every Body, and yet explicated by him? Be they unintelligible to all People, and yet not only pretended to be understood

derstood by him, but by him made intelligible to others? How can he with Honesty or Sense pretend to give an Account of our Doctrines to the World, who confesseth not only that he has not, *but he cannot have from us or any other a distinct and intelligible Account of them?* Has he not then shot his Bow at Random? Is this the Way to evince and confute them? Never, certainly, *Reader*, did any Man, thought to be in his Wits, give greater Ground for People to believe him out of them: We have no Cause to fear what a Thousand such *Adversaries* can do against us, who thus manifestly help us against themselves, and fall by their own Weapons: Which leads me to conclude this Part of this Discourse; and that I shall do in this Argument:

He that pretends to be a Christian, *and yet commits* Forgery, *useth* Perversion, *tells* Lyes, *publisheth* Slanders, *and in his Endeavours* contradicts himself, *and that materially, must be a* Counterfeit, *and no* Christian: *But such a Man we have evidently prov'd* T. Hicks *to be*; Therefore, *I think I may be held excusable in concluding that* Th. Hicks *is a* Counterfeit *and no* Christian.

THE
Real QUAKER Justified:

In a DEFENCE of the DOCTRINES held by him against the *Mean Sophistry* and *Shuffling Opposition* of *Thomas Hicks* the COUNTERFEIT.

§. I. *Of the* Light *within*.

THO' it Matters not much what so ill a Man says of any *Religion*, yet, lest some should be so weak as to conclude from our Silence, our Doctrines indefensible; and that in having the last Word, he has the best Cause. I shall briefly consider his Oppposition.

Counterfeit. *I do say, that the* Quakers *affirm the Light in every Man to be God:* And W. Penn *asks*, Who of us did ever say, that the Light within is the whole entire God? Reason against Railing, p. 7. *when I no where express those Words*, 3 Dial. p. 4.

Quaker. Nor do I, T. H. in the Manner delivered, nor to any such Charge, as thou now makest them to answer: What I said, with the Ground of it, was this: G. W. inferring from Joh. 1. 4. *That if the Life was of the Divine Being, the Light must be the same:* (which was against T. H's calling it an Effect) *for as is the Cause, the Effect must be:* * Thou madest this unreasonable Conclusion, *that not only the Light within, but every Creature, as* Beasts *and* Trees *are* good, *because the Effects of God's Power and Wisdom.* I then charg'd thee with insinuating, that every Measure of Light in Man is whole God: So that thy not expressing those Words will not acquit thee from not *insinuating* them; since thou dost insinuate upon what G. W. said, not only every Measure of Light, but every *Tree* and every *Beast*, because an Effect of his Power, to be *God*.

C. Thou sayst the Light within is *not a* potential, *but a* natural *Effect, which thou illustratest thus:* Men are the natural Off-spring and Product of Men, *&c. Tho' this be true, yet a Son is a distinct Person from his Father: Is the Light within such an Effect? Is it another God?* Ibid. p. 5.

---

* Which was only admitted with Respect to it's Illumination or Measure of it's Appearance in Man; It was never G. W's Principle or Words, that the Life, which is the Light of Men, Jo. 1. 4. is but in it self a meer Effect; for he owns it in it's own Being to be no other than God himself, and values not the Counterfeit's Quarrel.

Q. I will answer thee in the Language of thy own Creed: The Son of God is the natural Off-spring of God, *is he therefore another God?* The Holy Ghost proceeds from the Father and the Son, *is he therefore another God?* Here is *Off-spring* and *Production*; What sayst thou, *T. H.* to this?

C. If *the Light within be a* natural *Effect, then it is a necessary Effect, and that from Eternity: But were Men from Eternity, in whom God had thus naturally shined? If not, How is the Light within a natural Effect? It is in vain to pretend to Infallibility, whilst thou talkest thus idly,* Ibid.

Q. Both thy silly Sophistry and Reflection are too weak for the Business. If the Light within had taken it's Beginning with Men, as *T. H.* asserts, *Dial* 1, *p.* 32, It were a good Consequence, *That the Light were not Eternal, and therefore not God;* or if the Light had necessarily been within from Eternity, that Men were from Eternity: But that Men were from Eternity, because the Light which shines in Men was from Eternity, is to say, the Word, as manifest in the Flesh, was from Eternity, *because the Word was from Eternity,* or that *Immanuel,* God with Men, was not from Eternity, *because he was not with Men, nor Men with him from Eternity.* In short, thy *Sophistry* plays upon the Word *within*; we speak of the Eternity of the Light's Nature, and thou turnest it to an Eternity of Manifestation; as if because we say, the Light within is Eternal, that therefore it must needs have been *Eternally within.* This is not to act the *Christian,* but play the *Jew* against the Son of God: For the Term *Effect,* it is variously spoken and taken among Men: The Light of the Sun is called an Effect of the Sun, and yet the Light of the Sun, *is not another Sun.* Howbeit, the Scripture holds forth the Life of the Word to be the Light of Men; Consequently, *The Life and Light are one.*

C. Though *thou wilt not affirm every Measure of the Light within to be the Eternal Being; yet thou wilt not deny, but that it is God. This clears me from Forgery.*

Q. Thy saying so, makes thee but the more Guilty, because the Passage thou pretendest to answer, has no such Charge in it; besides, thou hast perverted my Words as thy self hast given them, *viz.* 'Tho' every Measure of Light distinctly 'is not that entire Eternal Being, yet we are bold to assert, that it is no other 'than *God, the Fulness of all Light,* who searcheth the Heart, *&c.* that doth 'shine into the inward Parts of Man, and doth convince, reprove, *&c.* These latter Words were omitted by thee, on Purpose to make the Word *God* relate to the *Measure* of Light, which is joined by me to the *Fulness.* But this is frequent with thee; Proceed.

C. Either the Light within in the least Measure, is God, a Creature, or nothing: Thou wilt not say it is the entire God; thou darest not say it is a Creature; it must then be nothing: Might not thy Time and Abilities have been better improv'd, than in contending for that, which is neither God nor a Creature.

Q. This Reflection as well reaches thee for contending against nothing, as me in contending for nothing: But *(Argumentum ad hominem)* consider this; either the Spirit in the least Measure of it is God, a Creature, or nothing: I suppose *T. H.* will not say, that in the least Measure it is the *entire God*; *T. H.* dares not say it is a *Creature*; shall *W. P.* then say in *T. Hicks's* Name, it must be *nothing?* Thus, through Inadvertency, do Men intangle themselves in their own Net; we speak of a Measure of the Light and Spirit of God in Man, *T. H.* presently prophanely takes God into Parts and Pieces, as pag. 4, 5, 6, and then charges it upon us, as the Consequence of our Doctrine: Are not Measures and Degrees Scripture-Terms? Does it strike at God's *Immensity,* because he measures forth himself, in his inward Discoveries, according to Man's Capacity; It is called Measure, with Respect to Man, and not that God is divisible.

But the Truth is, *T. H.* Thou hast made it thy Business not soberly to argue, but vainly to quibble, manifestly aiming to take frothy Minds: A small Share of such *Sophistry* might easily obscure the clearest Truth, and seem to lead in Triumph the strongest Arguments given in it's Defence; but the best of it is, such Attempts are short-liv'd, and so are thine? not, I promise thee, that I intend to have thee *Assassinated.* But let us hear what farther thou hast to say upon this Passage.

C. For the other Part of thy Discourse, viz. That God searcheth the Heart, who denies it? But what is this to the main Point? Because God searcheth the Heart;

is therefore the Common Light *in every Man God? Surely, no Man, except under the Power of Delusion, would thus Reason,* p. 6.

Q. The Word *Common* is neither ours, nor the Scriptures, yet if that be the main Point, it will not be hard to prove, provided, by *Common*, thou meanest that which shines in all Men; for if God be the Searcher of all Men's Hearts, and he that shews unto Man his Thoughts (as we must believe, 'till *T. H.* can groundedly assign us some other more common Searcher of the Hearts. &c. than God) and if God doth this, *as he is Light, who is Light,* 1 Joh. 1. 5. and Ephes. 5. 13. Then this *Light* which *T. H.* calls *Common*, and which we from Scripture say, *enlightens all Men*, is God, as John 1. 4. *In him was Life, and that Life was the Light of Men:* And here is thy main Point concluded against thee. I shall add, Reader, to this, another Instance of his evasive Carriage, which I entreat thee to take particular Notice of, that thou mayst see at what Rate he shuffles with us.

In his first Dialogue, p. 7, he quotes *Stephen Crisp* thus, *If the Light be obey'd, then it must be sufficient*; and answers, *I grant it ought to be obey'd, so ought the lawful Commands of Masters,* &c. *Yet who will thence infer, that they are a sufficient Rule to Salvation?*

To this I reply'd, as he quotes me, *Dial.* 3, *p.* 8. By the same Reason, that such as obey the lawful Commands of Masters are reputed good Servants, *those who obey the Light, are good Servants to God:* And if those who so keep the Commandments of Masters, obtain their Favour and Recompence; then those who obey the Light, by *T. H's* Allusion, *obtain God's Favour and Reward of Righteousness*, unto which he makes this Answer:

C. This concludes not the Question *in Controversy, therefore it can be no Prejudice to me.*

Q. No, *Thomas Hicks*? Is it nothing to the Purpose, that those who obey the Light, *are saved from the Wrath, and receive the Favour and Reward of God*; as Servants which obey their Masters Commands, are saved from the Wrath, and receive the Favour and Recompence of their Masters? Let the Reader judge how much this concerns the Question.

C. I confess, the Light within ought to be obey'd, and so ought the lawful Commands of Masters, from whence thou boldly, like thy self, concludest to the Sufficiency of the meer Light within: *Such Extravagancies as these do ordinarily attend thy peculiar Genius*, Dial. 3, p. 9.

Q. Soft a little! If the Light ought to be obey'd, it is a sufficient Rule for that Obedience: To keep to thy own Parallel of a *Master* and a *Servant:* How can a Servant be condemned of his Master for not answering his Command, whilst the Master's Command is not a sufficient Rule for the Servant's Obedience. *The Command implies a sufficient Rule to the Performance of the Thing commanded.*

C. 'Tis true, that God approves of Servants that do sincerely obey the Commands of their Superiors; will it therefore follow, that their Commands are sufficient to guide us to Salvation, p. 9.

Q. What a wretched Shuffle is this? Was it ever the Question, *Whether the Commands of Masters were sufficient to guide us to Salvation?* Or are the Commands of the Light, about the Things of God, no more sufficient to Salvation, than the Commands of Masters (be they about what they will) are sufficient to Salvation? Is not this taking away the Comparison, by putting the Subject of it in the Room of that for which it was brought? making Salvation to be as natural a Consequence of following the Commands of Masters, as of following the Requirings of the Light. But we are not so to be shifted off; for by the same Reason, that the Civil Commands of a Master obey'd, are sufficient to the obtaining of a Civil Salvation from Man's Wrath; *The Spiritual Commands of the Light obey'd, are sufficient to the obtaining of a Spiritual Salvation;* that is, a being sav'd from the Wrath to come, which is and shall be farther revealed against all the Workers of Iniquity. Let me use thy own Words, fasly reflected upon me in this very Matter; *Where Proof is defective, thou beggest the Question,* (nay, I may say, changest it) *and triumphest in thy own Confidence, which a modest Man would not do:* Away with these poor Shuffles, for Shame! Is this to evince the Matters objected to be real Truths?

But what sayst thou to my Argument, p. 15, grounded on *Jo.* 1. 4? 'If God be 'Divine, and sufficient to Salvation, and the Word be God, and the Life of the 'Word, one with the Word, and that *Life* the *Light* of Men; then the Light of 'Men is Divine and Sufficient to Salvation.

C. O! What profound Divinity and exquisite Logick is this! I perceive thy Mind abounds with Ignorance, from the Arguments that spring thence. Thou huddlest the Principal Agent and Ordinary Means together, p. 18.

Q. A rare Excuse for *thine*—— or something worse. Ought they not to be together in an Argument designed to prove them one? *Ordinary Means* are thy own Words, and not mine. A meer Shift for an Answer. But to go on.

C. How can God himself be called a Means? p. 18.

Q. After the same Manner that his *Power* saveth us, and his Spirit sanctifieth us, and that *he becomes the Teacher of his People*; such a Means, if thou wilt call it so, my Argument was offered to prove the Light to be. Is this to act either the *Divine* or *Logician*, after all thy conceited high Rants, thus pitifully to beg the Question? But what follows?

C. Thy Argument is fallacious, because that which is spoken in the First should exactly be the Subject of the Second Proposition, p. 18.

Q. And so it is. See *Reas. against Rail*. p. 14.

C. If the Proposition were right, yet thy Conclusion doth not reach the plain Terms of the Question, viz. Therefore the common Light in every Man is God, and sufficient to Salvation.

Q. Though I told thee before, that the Word *Common* is none of ours, yet I am not offended with it: For the Love of God is never the worse for being common, whatever thy *Reprobation-Faith* thinks of it. But art thou willing, in Earnest, this should be the Question between us? For I perceive, when thou art put to a Pinch, it is frequent with thee to turn me off with such Expressions as these, *Prove this to be the Common Light within*; *What is this to the Common Light within Men?* Meer Evasions; and most Times attended with hard Words to cover them, as in Page 9, 14, 15, 17, 39, 42, 43, 52, 53, &c.

C. This is the Controversy between us, whether the Common Light in every Man be God, Christ, and sufficient to lead to Salvation, p. 8. *If thou couldst demonstrate this, it would put an Issue to a great Part of the Controversy between us*, Ibid. p. 17.

Q. Very well; Thou hast granted, *That in the Word was Life, and that Life the Light of Men*, as John 1. 4. on which I grounded my Argument; and that the *Life* and *Light* there mentioned, are one with the *Word*, (or of it's own Being) consequently God, and *sufficient to Salvation*. But that such a Conclusion reacheth not the Terms of the Question, to wit, the *Common Light in Men*; which thou denyest to be one with the *Life* of the *Word*, and therefore Insufficient to Salvation. Upon this I thus argue, for the bringing of the Controversy to an Issue.

If the Light of Men, *John* 1. 4. be the Light of *All* Men, then it is a Light *common* to all Men. Thou must deny one of these two, either that the Light of Men is the Light of all Men; or, that the Light of *All* Men is *common* to all Men; The latter I should think in Point of Reputation, thou wilt not be so Unreasonable as to deny: The former then I must suppose thee to reject, viz. *That the Light of Men is the Light of all Men*. This I shall maintain by the General Phrase of Scripture, *Ecclef*. 1. 13.—*This sore Travel hath God given to the Sons* Of Men, chap. 2. 3, 8. the same chap. 3. 10. *I have seen the Travail God hath given to the Sons* Of Men, ver. 18. 19. *That which befalleth the Sons* Of Men, *befalleth Beasts*; *as the one dyeth so dyeth the other*, Jer. 32. 19. *Thine Eyes are upon all the Ways of the Sons* Of Men, *to give every one according to his Ways*. Which prove, that *Of Men*, is meant *Of All Men*. I will add two Places more out of *Prov*. 8. 4. *Unto you, O Men!* I (Wisdom) *call, and my Voice is to the Sons* Of Men. and ver. 31. *My Delight is with the Sons* Of Men. This proves Matter and Phrase: For both *Of Men* signifieth *Of All Men*; and this Voice cometh from him, in whom are hid all the Treasures of Wisdom and Knowledge, even the *Eternal Word, in whom is Life, and this Life the Light of Men*. From all which I conclude, that the Light of Men is the Light of all Men, yea, *Every Man that cometh into the World*, John 1. 9. And that the Light of all Men, is a Light *Common* to all Men; and that the Light that is common to all Men, is a *common* Light. Now *T. H.* thou hadst done something, if thou hadst given us a plain Reason and Scripture for *thy Two Lights within*, Common and Special; and made Good that Distinction between Light and Light, in *Job* 24. 13. *John* 1. 4, 9. chap. 3. 20, 21. *Ephes*. 5. 13. 1 *John* 1. 5, 7. chap. 2. 8, 9, 10. and have told us, if thou couldst, *Where the common Light endeth*, and the *special Light begins*: And if the *Special* reprove for Evil, as well as the *Common* (which thou sayst, reveals much, and ought to be attended to) thou should'st have let

let us know how the Discoveries, Motions, Reproofs, and Commands of the one, might be discern'd and distinguish'd from the other: For we own but *One Real Spiritual Light* to the Sons of Men, though divers Manifestations and Operations of that one Light, suited to the Capacities of all Persons and Ages; and not to shuffle me off with asking me, *How canst thou infer with such presumptuous Confidence, wilt thou dare stand by this Consequence?* After thou T. H. hast made it as Ugly as thy Malice and Dishonesty could well contrive. Mean Artifices to bear thy *Weak Reader* in hand, that thou hast hit the Mark, when thou hast all along shot quite beside it; Practices unworthy of any fair Disputant, much more a Man of thy *Pretences to Religion*. Had'st thou truly regarded the Light of which thou hast writ so many slight Things, we should not have seen that *Envy, Passion, base Shuffling, Insolence*, &c. that thy Writings now abound withal. Therefore under all thy higher Conceits, thou standest Condemn'd of the Light: Be exhorted first to obey it, before thou undertakest to write of things thou vainly think'st beyond it.

TESTIMONIES concerning the *LIGHT Within*.

Munsterius, Castalio, Vatablus, Drusius, Clarius, Codurcus upon *Job* 24. 13. and chap. 25. 3. *They are of those who Rebel against the Light. Upon whom doth not his Light arise?* Say, that this *Light is of the Divine Wisdom and Fountain of Light,* alluding to the *Psalmist,* τὸ φῶς τῦ Ἰσραὴλ; and *Mat.* 4. 19. *The People that sat in Darkness saw Great Light.* Also see these Men, *Erasmus* and *Camero,* upon *Job* 1. 4, 9.

I shall for a farther Defence of the *Light*, produce some Testimonies from several *Gentiles* some Hundreds of Years before Christ.

Orpheus, His Hand reaches to the End of the Sea, his Right Hand is every where (then within) of him alone are all things, *Clem. Alex. Strom, lib.* 5.

Thales thus: There is but One God; He is Glorious for ever; He knows Hearts and tells Thoughts. He makes the Teller of his Thoughts God, as in *Amos* 4. 13.

Pythagoras thus: God resembleth *Light and Truth*; He is One; He is not *Out* of the World; He is the *Salt* of all Ages, *One Heavenly Light*, and Father of all things, only Wise, Invisible, yet Intelligible. *The very Language of the Apostle,* Jambl. Just. Mart.

Heraclitus thus: God is not made with Hands.

Pythagoras: What things are agreeable to God, cannot be known, unless a Man Hear God Himself.

Again, Having overcome thy Rebellious Appetite, thou shalt know the *Cohabitation* of the Immortal God, and Mortal Men; whose Work is Immortality, Eternal Life, *Tim. de Anim. Mund.*

Sophocles, speaking of the Precepts written in Man's Heart, *saith*, God is their Father, not Mortal Nature. Neither shall they ever be abrogated; for there is in them a Great GOD, that never waxeth Old. *Again, saith he,* This is with respect to Man's Conscience, a Divine, a Sacred Good, God the Overseer. *Oedip. Tyr. Cl. Alex, Str. l.* 5.

Socrates had the *Guide of his Life within him*, and Preach'd as he was moved by it, even in the Streets; And dyed for Reproving the Corruptions of the *Athenians* in Manners and Religion.

Plotin taught, That Man had a Divine Principle in him, which maketh a True and Good Man.

Hieron called it, *A Domestick God.*

They held Victory over their Sins, by the Power of it; witness *Chilon, Socrates, Plato, Zeno, Antipater,* and others; which Doctrine of Perfection, thou T. H. with all thy pretended *Super-added Light*, canst not tell how to swallow. As they prest Perfect Living, so they clearly laid down Eternal Rewards, *the Pure to God, the Impure to Chains,* said *Pythagoras,* as if he had read that Scripture writ Six Hundred Years after him, *The Pure in Heart shall see God.*

The Good, said Socrates, *shall be united to God in an inaccessible Place; the Wicked in convenient Places suffer due Punishment.*

And though they might not have the *Jewish* History and Chronicle, yet they had a sufficient Law and Light within to Salvation; and such as trusted in it, came to Salvation by it: And so much the Apostle says, *Rom.* 2.

And for the *Fathers*, that they confirm the *Testimonies of the Gentiles,* and speak not of another *Eternal Law and Light*; briefly thus.

Justin

1674.

Sect. I.

Justin Martyr in his *Apology* faith, *God has built to himself a Natural Temple in the Consciences of Men*, as the Place wherein he would be Worshipped, and there Men ought to look for his Appearance.

Clem. Alex. Admon. ad Gent. It is *the Voice of Truth that Light will shine out of Darkness.* Therefore does it shine in the hidden Part of Mankind.

Lactant. de Cult. ver. The Law of God is made known unto us, *whose Light clearly discovers the Path of Wisdom. That Law is Pure and unspotted Reason, diffused through all the World.*

Athanas. contr. Gent. *The Way to attain to the Knowledge of God*, is Within us; which is proved from Moses, *who faith*, The Word of God is Within thy Heart, *and from this Saying of Christ*, The Faith and Kingdom of God is Within you.

Sect. II.

§. II. *Concerning the* SOUL *of* MAN.

Counterfeit. I Affirm, that G. F. says, *The Soul of Man is Part of God's Being, without Beginning and Infinite*, which is to say, *The Soul is God*, Dialog. 3. p. 19.

Quaker. I have two Things to say First, That in Case G. F. so holds, thou haft done unworthily to conclude generally against the *Quakers*: In thy former *Dialogues* thou charged'st it upon the *Quakers*; and now thou layest it directly upon G. F. Are such Shiftings and Runnings from *Generals to Particulars*, allowable in Divinity? Is this equal Dealing? But *Secondly*, I deny that G. F. so holds; What sayst thou to that?

C. G. Fox *in his* Great Mystery, p. 90, in Answer to one that said, *There is a Kind of Infiniteness in the Soul; yet it cannot be Infiniteness it self, speaks thus: Is not the Soul without Beginning, coming from God, returning into God again? Hath this Beginning or Ending? And is not this Infinite in it self? Can any Thing be clearer, than that* G. F. *makes the Soul the Subject, and not the Divine Life?* Ibid. p. 20, 21.

Q. Yes, that there may: For it is clear enough that G. F. intends by the Soul and Breath coming out from God, *the Divine Breath, or Soul of the Soul*, as *Augustine* calls it; and as *Mach, Neshemah, Pneuma, Animus*, and *Spiritus* signify: 'Twas this made *Adam* a Living Soul to God. [Thou dealest unfairly with G. F. and us, in making his Questions about this, both his and our Affirmation, *That the Soul* (or Spirit) *of Man is God*. A manifest Falshood and Abuse.] And was not the *Death* threatned *Adam* upon Disobedience, the Loss of this? They that read G. F.'s Books with a more impartial Mind than thou doft, may see that sometimes he speaketh of the Soul, as of the Man, p. 91. where he says, *That such as receive the Light, receive Redemption, whereby their Spirits, Bodies and Souls are sanctified*; and sometimes he speaks of the Soul, as respecting that *Breath of Life*, by which it became a Living Soul to God, which is Man in the Heavenly Image. He that reads pag. 90, 91, 100. may discern the Truth of this. But why art thou not angry with the *Priest*, for talking of a *Kind of Infiniteness in the Soul*? 'Tis at the *Quaker*, and not the *Principle*, thy Gall is stirr'd: For a *Kind of Infiniteness must be an Infiniteness, and not a Finiteness*. Did G. F's Words at most rise higher? What farther doft thou object?

C. But G. F. *faith* pag. 100. God breathed into Man the Breath of Life, and he became a Living Soul; and is not this which cometh out from God, Part of God? Which Soul Christ is the Bishop of. *Can Fox here intend, that Christ is the Bishop of the Divine Life, &c? Yet is he as absurd in calling Christ the Bishop of the Soul: For if the Soul be Part of God's Being, and Christ be God, then one Part of God must be Bishop over another*, Ibid. p. 21, 22.

Q. Suppose this Cavil had any Thing in it, and that thou hadst herein faithfully represented our Belief, might not I retort upon thy own Creed, that *God is the Father of God*: And when Christ prayed, *God prayed to God*; since the One Nature could not pray without the other, and the *Spirit makes Intercession*, that is, *God intercedes with God*. What think'st thou of this T. Hicks? Besides, I told thee then, that God Inspired Man with something of his own Substance, in the Name of R. *Nahmanni, Hiskuni*, and P. *Fagius*, That God contributed something to him, and bestowed something of his own Divinity upon him, and that thou did'st manifest thy self an ungodly Person, for inferring that what is vulgarly call'd the *Soul of Man*, to wit, the meer Creature, is Part of God's own Substance, because we asserted,

serted, the *Life*, *Breath*, or *Soul*, as it may very well be term'd, *which God breathed into Man, was of his own Being and Substance*: What sayst thou to this?

C. If *G. F.* be understood to speak with Reference to the Soul, then my Inference is Natural and Proper, viz. That the Soul is of God's Substance, and Part of God's Being, Pag. 22.

Q. Are all thy Brags come to this? Take *Soul* as before expressed, and it is granted without any Damage to our Doctrine. For the Scriptures, that testifie, God communicated of *his own Breath, or Life unto Man, whereby he became a Living Soul*, do not confound Man and that Divine Life; no more doth *G. F.* he never affirmed Man to be God, his own Words distinguish them, viz. *God Breathed into Man*, &c. and consequently, that Man is not that Breath of God which he Inspired Man with. *Again*, *G. F.* in many of his Writings, speaks of the *Fallen and Degenerated State of Men, the great Pollution and Wickedness they lie and live in; and that heavy Wrath and Vengeance which will follow:* All which concerns *Man*; it was not *That*, but *Adam* which was beguiled: Had *Adam* liv'd in *that Life*, he had been preserved. But suppose what I said granted the Question, as it did not, Many Great and Learned Men have run in the same Line, and they escaped the *Cries of Blasphemy, Absurdity*, and the rest of thy Exclamatory Terms, from Millions: What maketh Thee then keep such a Barking at us? Is it that thou hast more *Authority*, or less *Candor*?

Before I conclude this Section, I would put thee in Mind of a double *Injustice* thou hast committed: The One was in making this False and Prophane Consequence, *That God sets up a Light in himself, which he himself is to obey; and in so doing, God shall be Saved*, to follow from *G. F's* Words forecited. The *Second is*, in my giving this sharp Rebuke for this Passage, as an *Answer* in thy *Dialogue*, *without so much as inserting one Word of it*, that thou might'st cover thy own Unrighteousness, and render me severe. These Tricks, *Thomas Hicks*, will never compass thy End, but greatly contribute to frustrate it.

§. III. *Concerning the* Redemption *of the* SEED.

Counterfeit. *Forasmuch as Christ came to seek and to save that which was lost, I did Query, Who, or what was that which was lost?* Ibid. p. 34.

Quaker. I know thou didst; and that thou mad'st *G. Keith* answer, *That which is lost is still in Man; that Christ came to seek and save, and all his Ministers Preached People to this, A Lost God, a Lost Christ*, &c. Upon which thou mad'st this Exclamation, *Blush O Heavens! And be Astonish'd O Earth*, &c. *Did Jesus Christ come to seek and save a Lost God, a Lost Christ? Was ever God and Christ in a Lost Condition?* I told thee then, and do still, that the *Heavens* and the *Earth* might blush at thy base Dealings with *G. K.* I also told thee, as thou hast cited me, that he intended no other than that Christ came to seek and to save, by turning People to enquire after a Lost God, and a Lost Christ? What say'st thou to this?

C. If by Lost, *we must not understand* Man's Lost Condition; *what less can be understood, but that* Jesus *came to seek and to save a Lost God*. 'Tis true, *G. K. speaks of People's Finding a Lost God, whom they had Lost, Ibid.* p. 35.

Q. If this be true, that *G. K.* so speaks, to wit, that by Lost God, he understood People's losing of God, what's become of thy *Blush O Heavens*, &c. Is God and Christ in a Lost Condition? It is well thou art drawn to confess this against thy self?

C. But still, *if* Lost *be meant only of God and Christ, how can Christ be said to seek and save a* Lost God? Ibid.

Q. No such Words ever fell from *G. K.* to any such Question, as thou makest them an Answer to. Thou hast unworthily perverted both his Words and Sense. Though *Lost* be said of God, yet the Loss is Man's; for every Man who hath Lost God, is truly in a *Lost Condition*. But to apply that *Lost Condition* to God, and not Man, because Man hath Lost God, and is admonished to seek after a Lost God, is to commit great Injury against us, as thou hast attempted with thy silly Insinuation, viz. *If Lost be meant Only of God and Christ*, &c. What poor begging Shifts art thou put to?

C. But, *to put the Reader out of Doubt, that what I infer is indeed your very Opinion*, G. F. *and* J. N. *tell us, that the Seed wants Redemption, and the Seed is Christ;*

1674. *Chriſt*; either then there muſt be more *Chriſts* than one, or *Chriſt* came to redeem himſelf, Ibid.

Sect. III. *Q.* Is it to put us out of Doubt, to leave it in Doubt whether G. F. and J. N. ever ſaid any ſuch Thing, or theſe Words, as laid down together? For thou referreſt to no Book.

But ſuppoſe it be true; will it bear thy Inference; *therefore God and Chriſt are in a loſt Condition?* Is it all one to ſay, that Chriſt is bruiſed and Oppreſſed, and crucified afreſh by wicked Men, and put to open Shame; and to ſay, *That Chriſt is in a loſt Condition?* If it be not, as every ordinary Capacity may eaſily ſee; how needleſs, as well as how falſe is this Rant of thine? p. 36, viz. *Wilt thou aſſert the very Thing which I infer from your Words, and yet ſay,. I pervert them; May we not juſtly eſteem of thee, as a heady, raſh and inconſiderate young Man,* &c. Thus, *Thomas Hicks*, where it is impoſſible for thee to make good thy Concluſions, thou telleſt me of granting the Charge, and then falleſt into thy uſual Inſults, the better to inſinuate a Credence of thy Ability and Honeſty with thy *Reader*.

C. But is it not abſurd, yea, blaſphemous, to talk of God's redeeming the Seed? Ibid.

Q. No more Blaſphemy than is in the Scripture, which ſays, *Out of Egypt have I called my Son, a Place of Burdens*. But I the leſs wonder at thy Ignorance in theſe Heavenly Things, who didſt never yet drink of his Cup, nor waſt baptized with his Baptiſm, nor knew'ſt the true Fellowſhip of his Death and Sufferings; but art now adding to them by as provoking Impieties, as any Man of this Age hath committed againſt him.

Give me thy Judgment of theſe Scriptures, and my Conſequence from them. *And God ſaw that there was no Man, and wondred that there was no Interceſſor; therefore his Arm brought Salvation to him, and his Righteouſneſs it ſuſtained him,* Iſaiah 59. 16. Again, *The Year of my Redeemed is come, and I looked, and there was none to help, and I wondred that there was none to uphold; therefore mine own Arm brought Salvation unto me, and my Fury it upheld me*, Chap. 53. 4, 5. Whence it is no Contradiction to ſay, That God did rid himſelf of the Enemies of his own Precious Life, or that he brought Salvation to himſelf.

C. I infer from your Words this horrid Abſurdity, That God Redeems himſelf, pag. 37. *This is thy Truth againſt Fiction.*

Q. It is not from our Words, but the Words of Scripture; and but that thou art become Shameleſs, I ſhould wonder that any Man pretending the Scriptures to be his Rule, ſhould charge plain Scripture with *Abſurdity and Blaſphemy*.

C. Thus Chriſt is at one and the ſame Time, at Liberty and in Bondage, Redeeming, and Redeemed, Conquering, and yet Preſſed down: And though this Kind of Language be Folly and Madneſs, yet thou telleſt us, thou art content to uſe it, p. 38.

Q. And it were well if thou would'ſt be contented not to abuſe it: *Is this thy Religion*, to vilifie the Language of other People's Religion; nay, of Holy Scripture it ſelf?

But how dark art thou, *Thomas Hicks*, to make both a Wonder and a Scoff at *Chriſt's Conquering, and yet being Preſſed down at the ſame Time*; when the Scripture ſo plainly holds forth, that *He is Crucified* by ſuch Counterfeit Chriſtians as thou art, at what Time *He Reigns in the Hearts of his Children?* And is not the Spirit ſaid to be *Quenched by ſome*, at what Time *it Lives in others?* And is he not grieved by the Rebellions of ſome, whilſt he is delighted in others? Was not God at Liberty at what Time he ſaid, *They made him ſerve with their Sins?* And was *He not Whole*, at what Time he ſaid, *He was Broken*, Ezek. 6. 9. * Canſt thou Reaſonably infer, becauſe of theſe Expreſſions, us'd after the Manner of Men, that it is *Abſurdity and Blaſphemy*, that God *heals* himſelf, *delivers* himſelf, and *eaſes* himſelf of his Enemies, Words of equal *Import?* Methinks thy unſavoury Carriage ſhould reflect Shame upon *W. Kiffin*, with his Elders, &c. to ſuffer ſuch irreverent Traſh to come out of their Congregation; if they value their Credit, they will not ſuffer thee any longer thus upon the *Ramble*.

But before I leave thee in this Section, I have One Thing more to charge thee with, and that is, not only the Abuſe of our Words, by concluding from Man's

---

* *Thomas Hicks* takes that Literally, which is Metaphorically ſpoken, both in Scripture and our Books, and makes Literal Conſequences upon Metaphorical Premiſes, as if God had Hands, Eyes, Head, Arms, could be imbondaged, broken, &c. after a Worldly Manner, or in a Strict and Proper Senſe, and not rather in a more Hidden, and Metaphorical Signification: He is herein either very Blind, or very Malicious.

being turned to seek after a lost God and Christ, that God and Christ are in a *lost Condition*, but that they only want Redemption, and that *Men and Women are not the Objects of Redemption*, as in 3 *Dial.* p. 37. Than which nothing can be more false, and consequently injurious to a People. But I have left wondering that thou shouldst be base.

§. IV. *Concerning our Belief in* Christ.

Qua. ANother Instance by which thou undertakest to prove the *Quaker* no *Christian*, is, *his Denial of Jesus Christ to be a distinct Person without him:* Is this true, or no?

Counterfeit. I accuse you for denying Jesus Christ to be a distinct Person without you, p. 25.

Q. I say that thou hast varied thy Charge, and given thy self an Answer to it out of my Book, which was never an Answer to any such Matter, viz. *Herein thou hast shown thy Ignorance and Malice;* nor is it so in my Book, but Ignorance or Malice: Thou also omittest the Ground of my so speaking, which is not fair, viz. *The* Quakers *say, that Christ is in them, Christ is God-man; is God-man in them?* Again, *there is but one Christ, born of a Virgin, that suffered at* Jerusalem: *Can that Christ be in Man?* In Defence of which strange Construction of our Belief, thou hast offered nothing to what I opposed. Howbeit, I desire my *Reader* to take Notice, that since thou pretendest to own but one Christ, and sayst, that it is impossible that Christ should be in Man, that thou both denyest the Scripture, and contradictest thy self; there is not any Doctrine clearer in holy Record, than that of Christ's indwelling with his Saints, *John* 14. 20, 23. chap. 15. 4, 5. chap. 17. 23. *Rom.* 8. 10. 2 *Cor.* 13. 5. *Gal.* 1. 29. *Col.* 1. 27. *Rev.* 3. 20.

The same Objection thou makest against us, holds good against them, 'tis thus, Christ is *God-man;* can *God-man* be in the *Corinthians?* What might not *T. Hicks* have cavilled against Christ and his Disciple, as well as against us. Is this the Way to prove the *Quaker* no *Christian*, that makes that Thing Error, which can only constitute Men right *Christians:* For if Christ be not there, no *Anointing* can be there, which *John* says, leads into all Truth: Besides, thou contradictest thy self, as thou mayst see, *Dial.* p. 22, 23. But to thy present Charge.

C. This I object against you, your denying Christ to be a distinct Person without you; to which thou speakest nothing, signifying thereby, that you are pinched, Ibid. p. 26.

Q. I told thee under the Head of Perversions, that this was not all thou mad'st us to deny; for thou didst untruly infer *Our Denial of Christ's Bodily Appearance*, concerning which thou speakest nothing, *signifying thereby, that thou art pinched,* unless it be to deny thou ever saidst so, as p. 26, 31. thereby adding a Lye to the Shuffle. But why are we pinched, because we say nothing to a Doctrine the Scripture says nothing of: Give me one Place that mentions Christ *to be a distinct Person without us;* art thou so destitute of common Sense, as to think of proving the *Quaker* no *Christian*, because he denies a Doctrine, not expressed in Scripture; and yet at that Instant to magnifie the Scripture, as thy sole Rule: Verily, thou makest thy self a Derision to all wise Men. But go on, make the best of thy Charge.

C. G. F. in his Great Mystery, p. 16. *writes thus*, Thou art deceived, who sayst Christ is distinct from the Saints: Can any Man eat the Flesh of Christ, if his Flesh be not in them?

Q. This probably thou mayst have found in thy Brother Faldo's *Book, and thou mightst have found it defended in mine.* Where is *Distinct* among *G. F*'s Words, which are these, ' But God and Christ are in his Saints, and dwell in them, and ' walk in them; and he, the Priest, is a Reprobate, and out of the Apostle's Do-' ctrine: Which plainly shews that *G. F.* only opposeth Christ's being *at a Distance*, as divided from the Saints, because they who know not Christ to be in them, the Apostle terms *Reprobates*; and not that Christ and his Saints are in distinct Beings. That Christ's Flesh must be in People if they eat it, is so far from being either Matter of Error, or any Proof for thee, that, till thou canst prove, how a Man may eat his Victuals without him, thou wilt but render thy self ridiculous in talking at such an idle rate. What else hast thou to offer?

C. G. Whitehead *faith*, Jesus Christ a Person without us, is not Scripture-Language, *Dip. pl.* p. 13—— We cannot own your Limitations and unscriptural Notions concerning Christ's Being, *R. against R.* 1. p. 22.

Q. But

1674.
Sect. IV.

Q. But (why dost thou leave out the Word *God-man,* which thou usedst at *first,* and was repeated by *G. W.*) what of all this *T. H?*

C. If these be your Words, wherein is my Ignorance or Malice manifest, in giving the World an Account of your Belief? Ibid. p. 26.

Q. Thou mightst as well have said of our Dis-belief of thy unscriptural Belief: Canst thou upon second Thoughts perswade thy self, that this is the way to prove the Quaker *no* Christian, *condemn him out of his own Mouth and evince his Errors to the World,* that wanderest from sound Doctrine and wholsome Words, to effect it. Howbeit, not so much for thy sake, who makest it thy Business to render us a Scorn and Reproach among Men, by the most injurious Practices upon our Persons and Principles; as for theirs, in whom there is some Tenderness and sober Enquiry, I shall endeavour to take away all Occasion of Stumbling, by this short and serious Account of our Belief.

'Tis granted, that Christ, who is God over all, blessed for ever, is a *distinct* Being (though not *at a Distance*) from the Saints; Otherwise, it would be all one indeed to say, as thou, *T. H.* wickedly concludest, p. 30. from thy own Invention of Man's being the Seed, which is God, that it is all one, whether we call God by the Name of *W. Penn* or call *W. Penn God* and *Christ*; a blasphemous Absurdity indeed, as thou sayst! But then, what art thou that madest it? Next, we never said, that Christ was not as well *without* us, as *within* us; for we cannot comprehend him, but are comprehended of him: We never set any Limitations to Christ's Presence; they are the false and hateful Inferences of our Enemies; And let the Reader beware, that he be not abused by them. For the Word *Person* (as thou usest it, in telling us of *Christ,* God-man, a distinct Person without thee) it is no Scripture-Phrase; for in *Heb.* 1. 3. Ὑπόστασις, *Hypostasis* signifies *Substance*; and in 2 *Cor.* 2. 10. ἐν τῷ προσώπῳ χριστοῦ, signifies *in Christ's Stead, Name, Sight or Authority, or for his Sake,* as *Grotius, Erasmus* and the Ancient Fathers have it. However, I hope for our Tenderness in this particular, considering that *T. H*'s Charge is no Scripture-Phrase, and that such like Expressions occasion People to retain mean and dark Apprehensions of God, and Christ, and his Place of Residence, we shall not suffer in the Mind of our sober *Reader,* as Men undeserving the Name of *Christians.* Hast thou *T. H.* any more to offer upon this Head?

C. If the Light be Jesus Christ, and a Measure of it in all Men, but more eminently in your selves; whether W. P. *and* G. W. *may not as properly be called Jesus Christ, as that Bodily Appearance or Outward Person? And why may not Divine Worship be given as well to you as to him?*

Q. That Jesus Christ is the *Light of Men,* the Scripture holds forth; but that *W. P.* or *G. W.* should be the *Proper Body* prepared of God, for himself to be manifested in (as was that in which God was manifested in the Flesh: in whom dwelt the Fulness of the God-head) is not scriptural, nor a Consequence from our Opinion; but a blasphemous Inference of thy making, to be abhorred of just Men. Are we Christ's Body, *as that was?* Did we ever say, that the Fulness of the God-head dwelt bodily in us? He is manifested in us measurably, to save us: But was he so manifested in that Manhood to save it? Or is either *G. W.* or *W. P.* as properly and peculiarly the Man-hood of the Saviour as that he took to manifest himself Saviour in? Thou shalt see whither thy *Sophistry* will lead thee: The Son of God appeared bodily and visibly at *Jerusalem:* The Son of God was revealed in *Paul*; therefore *Paul* might as well be called *Jesus Christ* as he, in that Appearance. Again, Divine Worship is to be given to Christ: but Christ was in *Paul*; *therefore Divine Worship was to be given to* Paul. Again, *T. H.* doubtless, at least many of the *Baptists,* believe they have the Spirit of God, and that the Spirit of God is God, and therefore to be worshipped; will it be a good Consequence, *That* T. H. *or those* Baptists *are to be worshipped?* These vain Cavils and Sophisms thou undertakest to entertain thy *Reader* with, and to abuse us by, are great Instances of a weak Cause and an evil Mind.

C. Be not angry if again I ask thee, if Christ *signifie Anointed, and God be Christ, as thou affirmest; whether God himself be Anointed,* Ibid. p. 32.

Q. It seems then, *Socinian*-like, thou dost not affirm that God is Christ; and yet it is but two Pages before that thou sayst, *The God-head of the Son, and the Man-hood conjunct, is the Christ.* And *Dial.* p. 44. Thou callest *God manifest in the Flesh,* Christ. Is not God then Christ by thy own Words? But what Answer did I give thee to thy Question about Anointing?

C. *Thou*

C. Thou sayst, Christ was not anointed by Halves, but entirely; *herein thou contradictest thy self, and overthrowest thy own Distinction between Christ and the Body of Christ.*

Q. No such Matter; for the Distinction came from thy insinuating, that the Man-hood of Christ was the Christ, because that only could be Anointed, upon which, knowing it was lately thy Opinion, that Christ was God as well as Man, I said, that he could not be anointed by Halves; *and therefore Christ was anointed as God as well as Man:* What sayst thou to this?

C. The Difficulty still remains: If God alone was that which was anointed, the Question returns upon thee, whether God did anoint himself, and with what, and to what End?

Q. Thou art mistaken, and miserably beggest the Question, and sendest it back again: For when thou (to prove the meer Manhood to be the Christ or Anointed) didst insinuate the Impossibility of Christ's being anointed as God: I did then, and now more largely return this to thee, since thou confessest Christ to be *God* as well as *Man,* and that *God manifest in the Flesh,* makes the true Christ or Anointed, and that it is absurd to think he should be anointed by Halves · Is not God or the Divine Nature also anointed? if so, *T. H. who is it that anointed the Godhead, and with what, and to what End?* These are thy own Words, and they belong to thy own Doctrine. Thou didst object against our Principle, and happenedst to contradict thy own Principle in it: I sent thee the Objection home again, for thee to disingage thy own Principle of it *First*; Thou growest angry, tell'st me of contradicting my self, and returnest me the Objection never considered; but back it must go, and when thou hast found the Way to clear thy own, that shall serve for thine and mine too. And thus I leave thee and thy Cavils in this Section.

§. V. *Concerning the Gospel-Rule.*

LET us hear what thou hast to say to the Arguments I gave about the Rule.

C. You deny the Scriptures to be the Rule of Faith and Practice unto Christians, pag. 38.

Q. Thou wouldst here insinuate, as if our Faith and Practice were not according to Scripture, because we do not assert them, but the Spirit that gave them forth, to be the Rule, especially, in new-Covenant Times: I grant the Scriptures are to be fulfilled, and that many Heavenly Exhortations, Reproofs and Instructions therein contained, are to be regarded by us; but that which is my Rule to direct my Understanding, what is fit for me to embrace, and what to reject, and how to understand that which is to be received, must be the Spirit of Truth, which alone gives true Discerning: Therefore let us hear what thou sayst to my Argument, *Reas. against Rail.* p. 25. as thou thy self hast cited it, *Dial.* 3. p. 38. *viz.* ' That ' which is more *Ancient,* more *Universal,* and more *Able* to inform, rule and guide, ' that must more *eminently* be the Rule: But that hath been, and is, the *Light* ' *within*; therefore that hath been, and ought to be the Rule of Faith and Practice: What dost thou offer to invalidate this Argument?

C. Then herein I have not misrepresented your Belief, p. 39.

Q. But is this the Way to confute our Belief? Or did we charge thee with misrepresenting it in this particular? Dost thou think thus to evince the Truth of thy Objections, by granting us the Matter objected: It seems, we are to take this for thy Answer; and consequently, that the *Light within is eminently the Rule,* for ought thou hast said against it. Proceed.

C. But forasmuch as you often say, you own the Scriptures, and the Holy Rules therein contained: In what Sense do you acknowledge them to be your Rule?

Q. Thou makest me to answer this Question thus, *The Scripture is the Rule of Historical Faith; the Spirit can only be the Rule of saving Faith,* Reas. against Rail. p. 40. But can any Man that hath the least Dram of Honesty or Justice, think this the Way to confute me, to skip over near Fifteen Pages, containing several Arguments made to evidence and confirm the Truth of the First?

Hadst thou not a Conscience, that dares do and say any Thing, thou couldst never have given me such an unhandsome Slip. But let us hear what thou sayst to that which thou hast cited.

C. If the Light within be more able to inform, rule and guide, and therefore more eminently the Rule; what need is there of an historical Rule? p. 39.

Q. Did

1674.
Sect. V.

Q. Did ever any Man, pretending to be in his Wits, talk so idly? What is it but to say, *If the Spirit of God was always more able than the Scripture, what need is there of having Scripture?* Is not this to infer from God's Condescension to Man's Imbecillity, that the Light and Spirit of God are Imbecil: Is not this to reprobate all external Means, and to conclude God, Christ, the Light and Spirit insufficient, because that any were ever used: Is it a good Argument, because the Light does not reveal such a Thing, therefore the Light *cannot* reveal such a Thing, which is the utmost Strength of thy Opposition. I farther told thee, that those who gave forth the Scripture, came to the Enjoyment of those Things through the Light and Spirit of God, or they could never have writ them; therefore the Light and Spirit, and not the Scriptures, were the Rule of their Faith. But of this, and abundance more to the same Purpose, thou takest no Notice: I farther told thee, that the Prophets saw him with this Light, unless they saw him without Light, and that those that believed him, when come, could not have received him, had they not beheld him with an inward Eye. Thus thou quotest me: What Reply makest thou to this?

C. *That the Prophets saw him by the Light of Divine Revelation, I grant: And that none do believe in him, that do not know him, is true; but that this Light or inward Eye is the* common Light *in every Man, that thou must prove,* p. 42.

Q. It was formerly, and is again prov'd to be the same Light, though not the same in Manifestation: Every one had the same Light, but not the *same Prophesies,* nor the same *Sights:* When thou hast proved *two inward Lights,* it will be Time for thee to talk at this Rate: Nothing did then, nor can now, lead truly to know and confess to the Word that took Flesh, in which Word was Life, and that Life the Light of Men, but such Discoveries as proceed from a Measure of the same Light, as hath been already proved. And should I admit of thy Construction, that the Light by which some had a true Sight of Christ before, and at his Coming, was not the common Light, as thou callest it, but that which thou thy self allowest to be Divine; yet wilt thou give me Leave to infer in thy Name, that the Divine Light was insufficient, before such Time as it reveal'd those Things to the Prophets, and gave those that were alive at Christ's Spiritual Coming, a Knowledge and a Sense of them, because they did not know them before they knew them? For at this Rate thou treatest us about the Light within; the Light within doth not do this, *therefore the Light within cannot do it,* presumptuously concluding it insufficient to discover those Things, that either do not need a Discovery, because they are already known, or that it seemeth Good to God in his Wisdom to conceal.

C. *If the Scriptures tell thee there was such a Man as* Moses, David *and* Matthew, &c. *without which thou couldst not have known any such Thing; so the Scripture tells thee what they spoke and wrote of; therefore the Scriptures must be the Rule of thy Belief, both concerning those Men and their Sayings,* p. 45.

Q. I grant the Scriptures tell me, there were such Men as *Moses, David* and *Matthew,* and that they wrote: But what is it that gives me to believe the Things they wrote to be true? The Rule of Saving Faith is that we speak of, and not that which is Historical? It is impossible for me to understand the Truth of those Things, 'till I come to that Spirit of Truth that gave them forth; for no Man can know the Things of God, save the Spirit of God. The Want of which hath been the Cause why so many have been bewildred about the Things there declared: * Spiritual and Heavenly Things are not discernible by carnal Men, they are

---

* I would ask him how he knows the Scriptures extant are perfect both as to Number, and Copy, and Transactions? Several Books are lost, that is certain; does the Scripture tell us what they contained? if not, the Rule is imperfect by T. H's Consequence. The *Copies* are above *Thirty in Number,* at least, in which there are *Thousands of different Readings;* the *Translators greatly differ,* and have *greatly corrupted.* Also T. H. is to look to prove the present Collection Canonical, If he pleads the Testimony of God within, *his Cause is gone;* if Tradition, I ask how? Is he assured the first *Canon* was rightly made? The Council, was either Fallible or Infallible; If the first, What Assurance has he? If the last, it grants Infallibility, since the Apostles, 360 Years; but begets the Question, How does T. H. know they were in the Right? And if in one Thing, why not in all? But those Councils contradicted; and none ever gave the Catalogue, as now it is; nor can T. H. give a Canon for it. And if he cannot assure us that it is exact with the *Original,* free from *Variation, Corruption, Mis-translation,* &c. as it is not, he can never prove it the Rule, as he endeavours, in Opposition to the Spirit, for that is always plain and perfect. But more of this in the *Christian Quaker;* not to lessen Scripture, but to confound such Cavillers.

hid

hid from their Eyes; and 'till the Light shine out of Darkness, to give them the Knowledge of the Scriptures; they are as a sealed Book, and they labour in a *Labyrinth* of Uncertainties. I do say again, the Light in all Ages hath made known *Doctrines* fit to be obeyed, though not the *Histories* and *Narratives* of other Men's Actions; which is thy silly *Objection* against the Light's Sufficiency. But one Thing I must not forget, on which thou didst not *a little* depend, as an Instance to prove thy Conceit, *viz*. *How could we have known, that Swearing in any Case were unlawful, if it had not been written in the 5th of* Mattoew, *Swear not all*, Dial. 1. p. 22. But this I proved to thee, to have been revealed above 400 Years before that was written; but what is the Reason thou over-lookest that Answer? *Clinias* was taught by it rather to suffer a great Fine, than swear; the *Essæans* had rather dye than swear, which was long before Christ came in the Flesh: Was not the Light then a sufficient Rule for their practising of an Evangelical Doctrine by thy own Argument? But *T. H.* art thou not greatly ashamed, that because I supposed upon thy Principle, *the Light and Rule to be two*, Reas. against Rail. p. 39, that therefore I contradict my self, and overthrow mine own Opinion, saying, *If Light be given to understand the Rule, then it self is not the Rule, much less greater than the Rule*; and as if thou hadst come rightly by this Consequence, falling into thy customary Insults, telling me, *This is so far from being Truth against Fiction, that it discovers me to be a rash, heady, confident and ignorant Man, one that neither cares what he says or affirms.* Hadst thou any Regard to God, thy own Conscience, thy Neighbour, or thy own Reputation, thou wouldst never commit, much less continue to practise, these horrid Wrongs against me. However, as I said before, so again: I affirm, that supposing the Scriptures were the Rule, that which informs me of the Rule, and teaches me how to use it, *must be greater than the Rule*, in that it teaches me to know, and do, what the Rule cannot do of it self: I query then, if this Light be not the Rule, how and which Way I come to understand and use the Scriptures? *&c.* therefore *eminently the Rule*, the Terms of my Argument; for the Question lay not upon particular Rules.

C. *The Primitive* Christians *took not their Measures from the* Light within, *but from the Will of God revealed to them*, p. 46.

Q. This is Confusion it self: Are the Light within and the Will of God revealed inconsistent Things? Who was it revealed to them (*Paul* turned from Darkness to Light) the Will of God, but the Light? And what was it taught them the Truth, when *John* said, *They had received an Anointing, which abode in them, and taught them all Things*; unto which he directed, and with which he left them, *John* 1. 2, 27. And doth not the same Apostle tell us, if we walk in the Light, we have Fellowship one with another? *&c.* Was not the Light then the Rule of their Obedience, and the Way in which they were to walk? For the Accomplishment of that Prophetick Speech, Isa. 2. 5. *O ye House of* Jacob, *come ye, and let us walk in the Light of the Lord!*

And is there any Thing plainer, than that the Apostle *Paul* describes the Children of God, to be such as are *led* by the Spirit of God, *Rom.* 8. 14. and that he exhorts the *Galatians* to *walk* in the Spirit, chap. 5. 16. and the *Ephesians* to *walk* circumspectly, which was according to the Manifestations of the Light, chap. 5. 14, 15, 16. Finally, Does not the same Apostle pronounce *Peace on as many as walk according to the Rule of the New Creature*, Gal. 6. 16.

I farther told thee, that the *Waldenses, Lutherans, Protestants, Calvinists, &c.* made the Testimony of God in their Consciences the chief Ground of the Scriptures, *Reas. against Rail.* p. 48.

C. *That the* Waldenses, &c. *made the Testimony of their Consciences the chief Ground of the Belief of the Scriptures, is confidently said, but more than ever* W. Penn *is able to prove.*

Q. But if *W. Penn* is able to prove that the *Waldenses, Lutherans, Protestants, Calvinists*, yea and *Independents*, and *Anabaptists* too, have made the Testimony of God in their Consciences, the Ground of their Belief of the Scriptures, wilt not thou then appear to have told a confident Untruth? Let us hear what they say.

That the *Waldenses* held so, thou mayst inform thy self if thou pleasest, out of their History, penn'd by *John Paul Perin* of *Lyons*, Lib. 1, Cap. 1, Cap. 11, Cap. 13.

Luther taught, *That the Spirit is required to the Understanding of the whole Scrip-*

Scripture and of every Part thereof. Again, *The Scriptures are not to be understood but by that very Spirit by which they were wrote*, Tom. 3, fol. 169.

John Bradford, a worthy Martyr, thus answered the *Archbishop of York*, who catechised him how he came to know the Scriptures? *We do believe and know*, said he, *the Scriptures, as Christ's Sheep, not because the Church faith they are the Scriptures, but because they be so, being thereof assured by the same Spirit that wrote and spake them*, Book Mart. Vol. 3, p. 298.

William Tindal, another faithful Martyr in *Hen.* VIII's Time, writes thus: *It is impossible to understand the Scriptures more than a* Turk, *for him that hath not the Law of God written in his Heart to fulfil it.* Again, *Without the Spirit it is impossible to understand them*, W. Tind. Work. p. 319 & 80.

B. Jewel against the *Papists* hath this Passage; *Flesh and Blood is not able to understand the Holy Will of God, without special Revelation, therefore Christ gave Thanks unto his Father; and likewise opened the Hearts of his Disciples, that they might understand the Scriptures: Without this special Help and Prompting of God's Holy Spirit, the Scriptures are unto the Reader, be he never so wise or well learned, as the Vision of a sealed Book.*

Calvin saith, *It is necessary that the same Spirit that spake by the Mouth of the Prophets should pierce into our Hearts, to perswade us of the Truth of what they delivered*, Instit. lib. 1, cap. 8.

Beza saith, *That the understanding of the Scriptures should be fetcht from the same Spirit that dictated them*, Bez. in Nov. Test. 2 Pet. 1. 19.

Pet. Martyr taught, *That it is the Spirit of God that reveals the Truth in the Holy Scriptures*, Com. loc. p. 2, cap. 18.

H. Bullinger asserted in his 4 Decad. & 8 Serm. dedicated to K. *Edw.* 6. *That Men fetch the Understanding of Heavenly Things, and Knowledge of the Holy Ghost, from no where else than from the same Spirit.*

What sayst thou to this, *T. H*? Can the Holy Ghost be this *Discoverer* and *Instructor*, and yet not *eminently the Rule*?

But inasmuch as thou chargest me with denying the Scripture's Authority, and then railest, p. 61, because I place it upon the Testimony of the Light and Spirit of God in the Conscience; Hear what Dr. *John Owen* says, *The only Publick, Authentick and Infallible Interpreter of the Holy Scripture, is He who is the Author of them, from the Breathing of whose Spirit it derives all it's* VERITY, PERSPICUITY *and* AUTHORITY, Exerc. 2. 7. 9. What would have become of me, *T. H.* if I had spoke so broad as this? This makes the Spirit *Interpreter, Judge* and *Rule* of our Knowledge, therefore *eminently the Rule*.

T. Collier, an ancient and confiderable *Baptist*, shall be my last Instance here; *There is the Law and Testimony in the Spirit*, saith he, *as well as in the Letter*.

The Law of God is in the Heart, there it is written; and there it testifies the Truth of God: And if any Man speak not according to this Rule, it is because there is no Light or Morning risen in him. See his Works, p. 294. Again,

Others know no other Touch-Stone nor Tryal, no other Light, by which they judge of Truth, than Scripture; thus putting it in the Room of the Spirit, which is Light, and the Greater Light: For they say, they cannot know Truth 'till they bring it to the Letter *for Tryal; thus making an* Idol *of the* Letter, *setting it up in the Room of God*, Ibid. p. 248.

I could produce a great Cloud of more Witnesses, both of Fathers and other Authors; But I hope I have discharged my self of my Engagement, and made appear, That what I asserted was not too hard for me to prove, and therefore thou *T. H.* wert too confident in saying so: but thy notorious Ignorance in these Things may a little excuse thee.

But thou chargest us with undervaluing the Scriptures, a Fault I abhor to be guilty of; Let me hear in what?

C. *You contemptibly call the Scriptures the* Letter, *whilst you intitle some of your own Pamphlets*, The Voice of Wisdom, A Message, *&c. wherein you manifestly prefer your own Writings before the Holy Scriptures*, p. 55.

Q. This Cavil has been answered again and again. I told thee before, and thou hast cited me thus: 'If at any Time we call the Scriptures Letter, it is not that we
'mean our Books are the Spirit, or that we irreverently set them (the Scriptures)
'below our own Writings, but upon a Comparison only between the Scriptures
'and the Spirit that gave them forth. What Return dost thou give to this?

C. It

C. It is to aggravate, not to excuse your Error.

Q. Is it an Error to call the Scriptures the *Letter* in a Comparison with the *Spirit*? And an Aggravation of that Error, to prefer the *Spirit* before the *Letter*? But is this all thou haft to say to the Matter?

C. Why have you not Respect to this Comparison when you entitle your own Books? But that you would have us to believe that your Writings are more eminently from the Spirit than the Scriptures?

Q. How do we prefer our *Writings* above the Scriptures, which we prove by the *Scriptures*? I perceive it is become almost impossible with thee to make any other Constructions, than what rather shew thine own Envy, than our Sense. Was there ever the same Reason for a Comparison between our Writings and the Spirit? Did we ever set them up for the *only Rule of Faith and Obedience*, and that in Opposition to the Spirit, as the *New-Covenant-Rule*, like those that maintain that Plea? If there were the same Occasion, thou shouldst quickly hear of the same Distinction and Comparison. But go on.

C. Hence it is, That when both stand in Competition you thus distinguish them; Letter, yea, dead Letter, *as the proper Term for the Scriptures;* but The Voice of Wisdom *to your Book: Art thou not ashamed of this Baseness and Prophaneness?* Page 56.

Q. Whatever I am, I perceive thou art not ashamed of making me *base* and *prophane* too, and printing a most horrid Untruth to render me so : There is not a Sentence in thy Book gives a clearer Testimony of the Injustice of thy Carriage than this in Hand. For nothing is more frequent with thee throughout thy *Dialogues*, than first to invent something odious in our Name, and then, as if none so Modest and Righteous as thy self, cry out, *Who would not be astonished at this Blasphemous Absurdity?* p. 30. *Art thou not ashamed of this Prophaneness and Baseness?* p. 59. *O Impious Man*, &c. p. 13. But let this determine this Point between us. Produce but one of our Friends, that ever brought his Writings in *Competition* with the Scriptures, calling the Scriptures the *Dead Letter*, and his own Books the *Voice of Wisdom*, &c. and I will yield thee to have written Truth : If thou can'st not, thou hast but fastned *Baseness, Prophaneness* and *Lying* upon thy self; With thee I leave them; for there thou oughtest to rest, 'till thou canst better clear thy self of them.

I charged thee with having wronged *Geo. Fox* and *Rich. Hubberthorn*, in making them to say, *It is dangerous for ignorant People to read the Scriptures*; and then fixing the Name of *Jesuit* and *Romanist* upon us; producing the Words at large, which thou hast basely contracted to thy own Ends, leaving out what might most make for their Innocency, and the Evincement of thy own Forgery.

Thou givest the Words thus, *The Letter killeth, is Dangerous :* In my Quotation and in their Book thus, *The Letter which killeth,* 2 Cor. 3. 6. *is Dangerous* [*for thou* (Priest) *takest it here to war withal against the Saints, with thy carnal Mind, giving out thy carnal Expositions upon it.*] All this, *T. H.* thou hast unworthily left out, that thou mightest the better fasten thy Fiction upon *G. F.* and *R. H.* I ask, Is it not dangerous to read the Scriptures to these Ends ? *And the Ministers of the Letter are the Ministers of Death;* here thou leavest out again [*which is to Condemnation, and you take it to make a Trade with it, and with what the Prophets, Christ and the Apostles said, so that some have* 60 *and some* 100 l. *a Year; but Christ cry'd Wo unto such Whited Walls*] having left out this Part, that concerned the Hireling thou puttest in again : *And here you read with Danger, who speak of them, and speak a Lye, because you speak of your selves :* Here again thou lettest drop [*and you wrest the Scriptures to your own Destruction*] (as the Unlearned and Unstable do; and is not this Dangerous in them ? Then thou bringest in this, *And to you it is dangerous to read or speak of them*; omitting all that here follows by me cited to clear them of thy Charge, viz. [*who know not the Life of them, as the* Pharisees*, who were learned in the Letter, but knew not Christ: But I say, Blessed is he that Readeth and doth understand*] All this so necessary to give the Understanding of their true Meaning thou hast designedly over-look'd : However, let us hear what Defence thou hast made for thy self.

C. The Question respects the whole Scripture, *which you say, is Dangerous and Killing; The Ministers of the Scriptures are Ministers of Death, and it is Dangerous for them to read them : What a shameless Man art thou, thus to confess what I accuse you of, and yet condemn me as a Forger?* p. 57.

Ffff *Q.* These

Q. These foul and confident Questions thou usest to ask me, with which thou wouldst insinuate thy *Innocency*, do but aggravate thy *Forgery*. For, *first*, How do I confess what thou accusest us of, when it is neither to be found in my Words, nor theirs upon whom thou chargest them, *viz. It is dangerous for Ignorant People to read the Scriptures.* 2*dly.* I told thee they meant by *Ministers of the Letter*, Ministers of the Law and Death, because of Transgression, and thou makest it Dangerous for such to read the Scriptures; Whereas G. F. and R. H. said, *It was Dangerous for Hirelings and Whited Walls to use them against the Saints with their carnal Expositions, opposing them,* Pharisee-*like, to the Life of them, wresting them to their own Destruction.* It is Dangerous for such to read them to such Uses and Purposes, not in any Sense, as thou untruly sayst; Of this thou takest no Notice. So that here the Reader may plainly see thy first *Forgery*; since it was not the Man of no Letters, but the *Men of Letters*, such as the *Scribes* and *Pharisees*, who used them against the right Heirs of them, of whom G. F. and R. H. spoke. And thy *second* is not less visible, in that thou hast imposed upon the Reader my Confession of thy Accusation, who never confessed any such Thing. These are some of thy wonted Tricks, ever and anon employ'd to cover thy Nakedness with, and to get off unsuspected, from encountering the Difficulty of our Charge, Proof or Argument. I appeal to God's Witness in my Reader's Conscience, to right us against the many Injurious Practices against us; And shall conclude with this Acknowledgment and Argument concerning the Scriptures.

We do receive and believe the *Scriptures* given forth by Holy Men of God, as they were moved of the Holy Ghost, *and that they are profitable for Doctrine, for Reproof, and for Instruction in Righteousness*; yet since they are Writings relating to the Things of God, no Man can understand them, or have an assured Testimony of them, but by the Spirit of God, 1 *Cor.* 2. which alone reveals the deep Things of God; It was not the Scripture, but the Father that revealed Christ to *Peter*, Mat. 16. 5.

Farther, The New Covenant Times are Times of Fulfilling the Scriptures, by the Pouring out of the Spirit, therefore People's Regard should be to the inward Drawings and Leadings of the Holy Spirit. The *Law* outward was a *Rule* to the *Jew*, though not eminently unto them (for the Lord gave them also of his good Spirit; and what for, if not to rule them?) But the *Law of the Spirit of Life* promised to be revealed within, under the New and Everlasting Covenant, was certainly to be the *Rule* under that Covenant, being a Time for the more immediate Flowings forth of Spirit and Life. We do not say that every one hath hereunto attained; But we affirm, that God hath given a Measure of his Spirit unto Men and Women, that they might receive the precious Promises, unto which we direct them for that End. I know that T. *Hicks*, according to his wonted Baseness, p. 49. interprets our Saying, that we deny the Scriptures to be the Rule of Faith and Practice in Honour to the Divine Light, *to be our denying and rejecting the revealed Will of God*, as if Men must hate their Parents, because they are to love Christ first, *Mat.* 10. This were to say, that *Paul*'s Regard to the Law of the Spirit of Life in him, as his *Rule*, was not to fulfil, but to *deny and reject the Law without*: If this Consequence be false against *Paul*, how can T. H's *Consequence* be good against us? Is it to reject and deny the Scriptures, to have the good Things they declare of brought in by the Eternal Spirit? And since the Scriptures cannot fulfil themselves in us, but the Spirit, is not the Spirit the *Rule* and *Guide* to our Divine Knowledge and Enjoyments. But from our asserting the Spirit to be the Rule, *T. H* infers, *That we deny to live according to the Scriptures*, a Mistake he fell into before, which I offer'd to help him out of in my Answer; for to own the Scriptures to be the Rule, and to live according to the Scriptures, are not one and the same Thing: For the *Gentiles* did the Things contained in the outward Law, and yet had not the outward Law for a Rule, *Rom.* 2. 14.

Nor is it to be doubted, but that *Paul* and the primitive *Christians* lived up to the outward Law (that is, the inward Law outwardly declared) by the Law of the Spirit of Life, which was the Rule of their Obedience: Yet can any infer, that the outward Law, and not the inward, was the *Rule* of their so living? And I must tell thee, *Thomas Hicks*, that thy exalting of the Scriptures, is but an Endeavour to throw down the Spirit; which *Sacrifice*, be it known unto thee, the Lord of Heaven loaths. And I will say to thee, as G. F. and R. H. said to the *Priest*, They are Dangerous to be read and used for those Evil Purposes thou employest them upon: But as they said, (though that also thou didst overlook) so say I, *Blessed is he that doth read, and understand them.*

TESTIMONIES concerning the RULE.

Irenæus, Pag. 242, 384, 389. *The Writing in the Heart is the Rule.* Again, l. 5. c. 8. *The Word giveth his Spirit to all, to some according to Condition.* And l. 4. c. 30. *The Fathers were justified by the Righteousness of the Law in them, therefore had no need of* Reproving Letters.

W. Perkins's Works, Vol. 3. p. 220. *The Light of Nature and Grace teacheth to do as we would be done to*, p. 221. *It is the Fulfilling of the Law, the* Rule *to judge Scripture. That (of God) made the Rule, Something in the Conscience* ; *Happy Times if Men would follow it.*

Bishop *R. Sanderson*, De Obligat. Conscient. pag. 127. *A Rule of Discerning without the Scriptures.* Regula discernendi extra Scripturam.

And *T. Collier* in plain Words saith, *The Spirit of God, who is God, is the* Alone Rule *of a Christian*, Gen. Epist. to the Saints, chap. 12. — *The Spiritual Man judgeth all Things by the* Rule of the Spirit, ibid. *The Law of the New Testament is written in the Heart*, ibid.

But what Need is there farther of my maintaining this Point, concerning *The Light being the Rule in all Ages*; since thou hast made such ample Confession, *That the Godly in all Ages, before Christ in the Flesh, were turned from the Darkness to the Light*, pag. 64. This Light must needs be within, because the Darkness is there: And it must needs be sufficient, because thou sayst it was that which *Paul* was sent to turn People to, p. 63, 64. And what could this Light be for, if not to Guide, Rule, and Lead them in the Ways of Godliness, and consequently the *Rule* of the Godly in all Ages? Therefore the more General Rule, because the Scripture was not in all Ages; and sufficient, because it was of God appointed for the Godly Man's Way; unless thou wilt suppose, that they were turned to an Insufficient Light.

§. VI. *Of Commands and Ordinances, particularly* Baptism *and the* Supper.

Quaker. I Have sufficiently shewn, under the *Section of Forgeries*, the horrid Abuse thou hast committed in thy last Book against *E. Burroughs*, concerning *Commands and Ordinances*; I shall here farther detect thy Miscarriage.

The Matter charged upon *E. B.* I shall set down with his Name before it.

E. B. You are not yet Dead with Christ, who are yet subject to Ordinances.

T. H. The Spirit of God in the Scriptures assures us, that they that keep the Commandments of God, are the Children of God, 1 John 2. 3, 4. *Yet this Wicked Man*, *E. B. saith*, That they who are subject to Ordinances, are not Dead with Christ. See *Coloss.* 2. 19, 21.

Q. E. B. pleads only against such Performances under the Name of *Ordinances*, as were but *Shadowy, Elementary and Perishing Things*, appointed for a Season, and to pass off. Thus thou thy self hast quoted me, *Dial*. 3. *p*. 59. *What sayst thou to this?*

C. If thus E. B. did plead, *Why dost thou say I belyed him?* ibid. p. 59.

Q. Because in thy former *Dialogue* thou madest him as well deny to continue Obedience to such Eternal Precepts of Righteousness, as thou thy self confessest the *Light Within* dictates, as to *Shadowy, Elementary, and Perishing Things.* For about his saying, *That was not a Command to him, which was a Command to another*, thou didst most unjustly infer, *That the Law which forbids Adultery, Murder, Theft, and bearing False Witness, is no Law to us*; breaking forth upon us, with *Impiously Horrid, Ungodly, Irreverent, Patronizers of Blasphemy, Countenancers of Novices, Prophane Scribler*, with Abundance more : Whereas pag. 47. of his Works, whence the Passage was taken, proves it to have been writ about extraordinary and particular Cases; as, *Thy Running to Preach, because* Peter *Preacht*; or, *Plunging People in the* Thames, *or elsewhere, because* John *Baptized many in* Jordan. *What sayst thou to this?*

C. Thou hast a strange Confidence! *If thou hadst examin'd the Place my Quotation refers to, thou must needs know I have not bely'd you: If thou hast not, how darest thou thus charge me?* Pag. 58.

Q. My Confidence is grounded upon Examination: And this *Ranting Answer* will not clear thee. And the greatest Kindness that can be shown thee, is, to believe, *thou took'st the Quotation first upon Trust.* But in this Dialogue thou art left without Excuse : For had *E. B.* intended *General Commands*, it would not have

1674.

Sect. VI.

have cost thee much more Trouble to prove it, than to say it; doubtless it would have been a Pleasure to thee. But as a Man Guilty, thou art wilfully Silent about those Horrid Constructions made upon his Words, as the Genuine Sense of the Place, and vainly thinkest to shift it off, with accusing me of strange Confidence: But I return thee thy own Words, *If thou, T. H. hast examined the Place thy Quotation refers to, thou must needs know, that thou hast belyed us; if thou hast not, how darest thou thus* (continue to) *charge us?* But what sayst thou concerning Shadowy Ordinances?

C. *Forasmuch as thou confessest, that* E. B. *did plead against such Ordinances as were but Shadows, appointed only for a Season, and to pass off, that such* (Ordinances) *are no Commands to us, how wilt thou prove this?*

Q. This is to grant, that thou art for continuing Shadows under a Gospel-Dispensation: My Reason against it is this: Shadows are Members of the Ceremonial Law, the Substance of which is the Gospel: The bringing in of the Gospel is the Ending of them; because Shadows give Way to, and End in their Substance. But let me see how thou bring'st me in to answer thy Question: " Let it be ob-" served, that there is not the least Mention in all the Epistles of *John*, of any of " those *Ordinances*, that stood in *Visible and Corrupt Elements*, so that to bring in " Things of a *Shadowy and Temporary Nature*, among the *Commands of Christ*, is to " abuse the Apostle. What's thy Return to this?

C. *Let it be observed what an arrogant, abusive, prophane, and impertinent Man, this* W. P. *is. Suppose none of the positive Institutions of Christ be expresly mentioned in his Epistles; Did he therefore deny them?* Pag. 60.

Q. To pass over thy hard Names, thou dost suggest to the *Reader*, as if this were my whole Strength, in Answer to thy First Query, viz. *How wilt thou prove Shadowy Ordinances to be no Commands to us?* Whereas it was never given by me to any such Question; nor indeed would it have been Proper to do so: But since thou hadst so little Sense, as to quote *John*'s Words, viz. *They that Love God keep his Commandments*, in Order to prove the Continuance of *Shadowy Ordinances*, I had so much Sense in me, as to make Use of thy own Citation against thee, where no such *Ordinances* are mentioned, upon which thou foolishly queriest, Did he therefore deny them? Which was not the Question: But whether that Place proves them. But this I am bold to infer, *That it was not* John's *Message to recommend and perpetuate them, as thou dost:* And it is strange to me, that they should be of such Weight in the *Christian Religion*, and not One Apostle mention them in all their *Epistles*, save *Paul* once, in denying *Baptism* a Share in his Commission; and another Time in Regulating the *Corinthians* about their Disorderly Use of the *Type*. If *Bodily Exercise profits little in Religion, much less Shadows.* If Men run into External Performances, without the *Leadings and Preparings of the Spirit*, such Duties cannot be acceptable to God; running into External Imitations, without Internal Qualifications, gives but to boast in another Man's Line; And such Oblations are so far from being accepted, that they are abominated. To this let us hear what *T. Collier* will say, a Man of greater Eminency and Antiquity than *T. Hicks* in the *Baptist's Way*; *I see*, saith he, *that External Acting, according to a Rule without, is nothing, if not flowing from a Principle of Love and Life within*, Works, p. 247. I perceive *T. H.* thou art not of that Mind, so far from it, as to account it Error: But let us hear what else thou hast to say, in Defence of thy formal, unwarranted Practice.

C. *We are certain, that our Lord did walk in the Observance of Positive Institutions; and he that abideth in Christ, ought to walk as he walked*, 1 John 2. 6. p. 61.

Q. What makes thee forge, pervert, lye, slander, and abuse us then? *If thou wouldst be a Christian, thou shouldst walk as he walked:* He was Loving, thou art Envious; He Meek, thou Passionate; He Long-Suffering, thou froward; He was Good to his Enemies, thou base to thy Neighbours. Surely thou hast forgot, that if thou walkest as he walked, thou must have to do with that dangerous Doctrine of Perfection, as thou elsewhere *reputest* it. But at thy Rate of quoting this Scripture, and following of *Christ*, thou may'st as well bring in *Circumcision and the Passover, as Baptism and the Supper*. Christ told his Disciples, *The Spirit should lead them into all Truth*, after his Ascension; and his Beloved Disciple *John* referred the Churches to the *Anointing*.

C. *You tell us these Ordinances were used as Figures and Shadows, no longer to endure, than till the Substance comes*, viz. The Baptism of the Holy Ghost. *The Reason can be no other than the vain Conceit of a deluded Mind*; for they are no

Figures

Figures of the Baptism of the Spirit; therefore this can be no Reason for the abolishing of them: Christ commands his Apostles to Teach and Baptize, promising to be with them to the End of the World.

Q. Who ever said, that Breaking of Bread was a Figure of the Spirit's Baptism? It's a meer Fiction of thy making, as Page 107. of *Reason against Railing* will shew. But if Water-Baptism, and Breaking of Bread are no Figures nor Shadows, they must be *Substances*; and what Difference then there is between thee and Popery in this Point, let the *Reader* judge. And for *Christ's* bidding his Disciples, *Go, Teach, Baptizing*, Mat. 28. I told thee, " *That no Water was mentioned*; and that Luke, " *in the First of the Acts, says, before the Commission mentioned by* Matthew *could* " *be given, at least executed*, John *Baptized with Water, but ye shall be Bapti-* " *zed with the Holy Ghost, not many Days hence. And then comes the Commission* " *in Force.* Go, Teach, Baptizing; How? *With the Holy Ghost, turning People* " *from Darkness to Light, from the Power of Satan, unto God.*

C. *If the Baptism of the Holy Ghost do put this Commission in Force, as thou say'st then the Obligation to those Duties signified in the Commission, cannot be taken off: If so thy Argument falls.*

Q. A poor Shuffle indeed! Does my Argument fall, because thou beggest the Question? Which is, *Whether their Baptism be with Water or the Holy Ghost?*

C. *If Baptism of Water be not intended, then none; Not the Baptism of Afflictions; for the Apostles were not to Persecute: Not the Baptism of the Holy Ghost; for that was a Promise, not a Commission,* p. 63.

Q. Thou dost but trifle with us still. Though *to be Baptized* was a Promise, yet *to Baptize* was a Commission. *To be Baptized not many Days hence,* was the Promise of Christ; but *Go and Baptize all Nations,* which followeth, was a Commission; and that it was with no other *Baptism, Christ's Distinction* sufficiently proves, viz. John *indeed Baptized with Water, but ye shall be Baptized with the Holy Ghost not many Days hence*; stay till then, and *Go, and Teach, Baptizing all Nations,* &c.

C. *To Baptize with the Holy Ghost, was none of their Duty, it being properly Christ's Work,* p. 63.

Q. It was both their Work and Duty, witness that *Simon Magus* would have bought that Gift of *Peter:* And that *Paul* Baptized with the *Holy Ghost,* Acts 19. Did he not therein do his Duty?

C. *Is it proper to say, I Baptize you with the Spirit into the Name of the Spirit?*

Q. Yes, if thou hast the Spirit; unless thou *wouldst make a Counterfeit Christian* of him, whom thou, without the Spirit, *Baptizest into the Name of the Spirit. Wouldst thou have a Man Baptized into the Name, and not into the Nature of the Spirit? Can a Man Baptize into Spirit and into Life, without Spirit and Life?* God did Convert, Reconcile, Baptize, Beget, and Build up Thousands to himself by them, unto whom the Word of Reconciliation was committed, and who were Embassadors in *Christ's* Stead.

Now, as for *Water-Baptism*, what *Paul* says of himself, I may say of his Commission, *It was not behind any of the Rest*; yet he denies *Water-Baptism* to be any Part of it, and it is as plainly rejected of him, in Point of Institution, as any Thing in Scripture. So that either *Water-Baptism* is none of *Christ's Institutions*; or else *Paul* had no Commission to perform *Christ's Institutions,* which were strange. T. Collier determines this, *The Baptism of Christ is the Baptism of the Spirit.*

But if any of you can shew a larger Commission than *Paul* had, let him produce it; if not, I must conclude, *They Run, and are not Sent.*

§. VII. *Of the Doctrine of* JUSTIFICATION.

I Perceive by what thou hast writ of *Justification,* thou intendest to end at the Rate thou hast manag'd the Controversie all along; I mean with the same *Shuffles and Injustice.* I will set down thy Charge, the Answer thou makest me give, and thy Reply.

C. *Thou hast boldly affirm'd, That Justification by that Righteousness Christ fulfilled for us, wholly without us, is a Doctrine of Devils, Apol.* pag. 148. *What say'st thou to this?*

Q. This Apology cited was written against a malicious Priest in *Ireland,* R. against R. p. 68. *If thy Position cannot be proved, it will be no Excuse to say, It was given*

given to a Malicious Priest; yea, thy Folly and Rashness is the more aggravated, &c. pag. 96.

Q. As if I had given that Answer, not to inform Persons against whom the Book was writ, and the Occasion of the Passage, but (as one unable to say any Thing in my Defence) to extenuate the Fact, and excuse my writing it. I perceive, rather than want Occasions to abuse me, thou wilt make them. But what sayst thou concerning Justification?

C. Thou supposest the Doctrine of Justification by that Righteousness which Christ fulfilled wholly without us, to be a Sin-pleasing and dangerous Notion: What Reason hast thou so to esteem it? Pag. 67.

Q. I do so; taking my Words in my Sense, and my Reasons are, *First*, Because *wholly without us*, is an Unscriptural Phrase. *Secondly*, It takes away the Necessity of all Inward Work. *Thirdly*, No Man is justified without Faith. No Man hath Faith without Sanctification and Works; therefore the Works of Righteousness, by the Spirit, are necessary to compleat Justification.

Q. Whether a sincere Faith is necessary to our Justification, is one Thing: But whether such a Faith be our sole Righteousness, by which we are Justified, is another, pag. 67.

Q. And whether *T. H.* be not an idle Shifter is another thing. Was it the Question, *Whether our Faith were the sole Righteousness to Justification*; or whether Justification were by a Righteousness *wholly without us and our Faith too?* If a Sincere Faith be necessary; then because Faith is not Faith without Works, Justification is not wrought wholly without. I told thee before, that this Doctrine of thine, *Speaks Peace to the Wicked*, whilst Wicked. But there is no Peace to the Wicked, saith my God.

C. It is horribly Wicked to conclude, that what Christ hath done and suffered without us, is to speak Peace to the Wicked whilst such.

Q. Right; but who is the Man? Not *W. P.* for opposing a Doctrine which leaves Men as Wicked as it found them; yea, encourages them in it. I appeal to the sober Reader, if it be all one, to say, That *Justification by the Righteousness of Christ wholly without, which leaves the Conscience as polluted as ever, is to speak Peace to the Wicked, whilst Wicked*; and to affirm, That *what Christ hath done and suffered without us, is to speak Peace to the Wicked, whilst Wicked*. Thy indirect Consequences *T. H.* are too obvious and numerous to deceive any ordinary Reader. But what sayst thou to my Distinction about Justification? " Christ's Work was " Twofold; *First*, To Remit, Forgive, or Justifie from the Imputation of Sins " past, such as truly Repent and Believe. *Secondly*, By his Power and Spirit work-" ing in the Hearts of such, to destroy and remove the very Nature of Sin, to " make an End of it, to finish Transgression present and to come: The First re-" moves the Guilt, the Second, the Cause of it: Methinks this should a little al-" lay thy Clamours.

C. This Distinction of the Work of Christ, proves not what thou hast asserted, viz. That Justification is not by Imputation of another's Righteousness; much less that such a Justification is a Doctrine of Devils, pag. 72.

Q. This shews thee weary of the Work, or else thou wouldst not so soon after my Distinction, continue in thy Mif-Construction of my Words, for the clearing of which, my Distinction was made: I grant, that such as Repent and Believe, receive Remission, or a Justifying from former Sins, through the Righteousness of God declared in, and by Jesus Christ. But is this *Compleat Justification?* Is this a making Inwardly Just, through a Purging out of Iniquity, and Mortifying of Corruption, and bringing in Christ's Everlasting Righteousness? If not, then to exclude this, and yet conclude Men compleatly Justified, by what Christ hath done *wholly without, is a Doctrine of Devils*; for it leaves Men in an impure State, and allows the Devil's Kingdom to continue in being. In short, it is as much to say, that *W. Penn* calls what Christ hath done for *Men without*, a Doctrine of Devils, because *W. P.* asserts that to be a Doctrine of Devils, which maketh all that is necessary for Man's compleat Justification before God, to have been wrought by Christ *wholly without*, thereby excluding the Necessity of the *Just-Working*, or *Just-Making* Power of Christ from Man to that Work. Well, but I also told thee, of the Necessity of Faith and Repentance, even to the First Part of Justification; consequently, that Men cannot be justified in any Sense, without Regard had to an Inward Work, viz: *Of Sanctification, without which there can be no True Believing.*

C. Though

C. Though this be more close to the Point than any Thing thou hast spoken, yet it is not so close as to prove thy Position: For if Repentance be but a Condition, then it is not the Sole Righteousness *for which we are justified*, pag. 73.

Q. Produce me but one Passage of ours that ever spoke that Language, and I will yet say thou hast not wronged us. Besides, this Answer is wide from thy Purpose, though it comes very close to mine: For from contending for Justification by a Righteousness *wholly without* (the Question) thou art come now to contend against a Justification by a Righteousness *wholly within*, which was not the Question.

C. But thou sayst Abraham's *Personal Obedience was the Ground of his being accounted Righteous*: If so, Then we are not made Just by a Righteousness perform'd without us, but by a Righteousness perform'd by our selves. But then, what wilt thou say to this Text; If Abraham were Justified by Works, he hath whereof to Glory, but not before God? Rom. 4. 2. p. 77, 78.

Q. The Apostle *James* bears me out in what I said; for if *Abraham* were Justified by Works, as said *James*, then his Obedience to God's Spirit, which makes up those Works, gave him Acceptance in God's Sight: And let *T. H.* say, if he dare, that *Abraham* was not Justified in God's Sight, in his resigning up *Isaac* for a Sacrifice; and if he were, how do I err?

But that I might not be thought to oppose one Apostle to another, know, *Reader*, that the Apostle *James* speaks of such Works, as were not performed in *Abraham*'s own Strength, but through Faith, and his Obedience to God's Spirit; and therefore *Evangelical*. And the Justification they lead to, was a Daily Acceptance with God. The Works, the Apostle *Paul* speaks of, were *meerly* Abraham's *in his own Power* (as those of the *Jews* from the Law) therefore not Justifying before God in any Sense; least of all could they merit Remission, or purchase *Abraham* those Great Blessings and peculiar Favours that it pleased Almighty God to bestow upon him above others. *Works* and *Justification*, thus distinguish'd and allow'd, prevent Men's setting one in Opposition to the other; and here *Paul* may come in without *Contradiction* to James: *If Abraham were justified by Works, he hath whereof to Glory, but not before God.* The whole Chapter concerns a Justifying by the Remission of Sins that are past, as the following Verses evidence: *Even as David also describeth the Blessedness of the Man unto whom God imputeth Righteousness without Works, saying, Blessed are they whose Unrighteousness is forgiven, and whose Sins are covered. Blessed is the Man to whom the Lord will not impute Sin*, Rom. 4. 6, 7, 8. So that the Righteousness not obtainable by the Works of the Law, Ver. 16. and the Justification (which *Abraham*'s own Works could not procure) which is obtain'd by Faith in the Love of God, is here explain'd to be, *the Forgiving of Iniquity, and the Covering of Sin.* But this is far from maintaining the *Compleatness* of Justification from a Righteousness *wholly without*.

TESTIMONIES concerning JUSTIFICATION.

Erasmus: *We grant to be Justified by Faith, that is, Hearts to be Purged.* See Fascicul. rerum expetend. pag. 129. De amabili Eccles. concord.

The Fathers were Just by the Righteousness of the Law in them, Iren. l. 4. c. 30.

Noah, Abraham, &c. Were Just by the Law Natural (that is Eternal) Tertullian Adv. Jud. p. 184.

Clem. Alex. saith, *That Abraham was Justified by Faith, but that Faith he calls*, τέλειον καθαρισμὸν, *a Perfect Purgation*, lib. 1. præd.

Justin Martyr. Defens. ad Anton. saith, Socrates *Lived with the Word, and that he knew Christ in Part*, Defens. ad Senat. That was by the Light Within: How could he know him otherwise.

Scultetus p. 38. of his Medulla saith, *There are some at this Day of his Opinion, and that do reckon* Melchizedeck, Abimelech, Ruth, Rachab, *the Queen of* Saba, Hiram, Naaman, *&c. among Christians.*

H. Bullinger Decad. 1. serm. 6. de Justif. *To Justifie, signifieth to remit Offences; to Cleanse, to Sanctify, and to give Entrance of Life Everlasting.* Again, *Justification is taken for Remission of Sins, for Sanctification and Adoption into the Number of the Sons of God.*

Sect. VIII. §. VIII. *Of Personal Reflections.* T. H's *Scurrilous Language.* The Conclusion.

THOU accusest me with defending and justifying E. B. in *Cursing, Railing and Lying, and that in the Name of the Lord,* Dial. 3. p. 10, 82, 83. where it is to be observed, that thou dost not only esteem it so thy self, but supposest me both to confess it to be such, and that notwithstanding I warrant it from the Lord. These are thy *black and odious Insinuations and Conclusions,* as may at large be seen in the Pages before-mentioned; as if to deny them to be such, were to affirm them such; for I know not by what other *Figure* I allow them such. But because this cannot appear less than an absurd and incredible *Lye,* to all that have their Senses, I shall the less heed it; But what Proof dost thou bring that E. B. *curses, lyes and rails?* To call what he says by such hard Names, concludes no such Thing. All I see is, that thou run'st to the Words by him utter'd, as if a Repetition were a Proof: Poor Man! This it is to be upon the Fret, Proud and Passionate: E. B. must *curse, lye and rail,* because *thou sayst so.* Is not this to act the Dictator with a witness? The Truth is, I scarce think there ever was a fouler. But thou stomach'st my saying *that the Scripture allows those Names,* and retort'st, *it seems you can make the Scripture your Rule for Lying, Cursing and Railing* But this is as irreverently said of the *Scripture* as abusively of us, and absurdly in it self; can any Man make them his Rule for that which is *impious?* I had thought that at what Time any act wickedly, they cease to make them their Rule. Shall I make one of thy Conclusions now against thee? *T. Hicks says, the Scripture may be a Rule for Lying, Cursing and Railing.* But is every Example a Rule? a Rule always relates to Duty; a President or Example not. Is it my Duty to call bad Men by all the Names mentioned in Scripture, because there are such Examples? What then should I call *Thee,* that art as bad a Man, every Jot, as the worst of them? This shews that the Scripture cannot be a Rule in an hundred such Cases, but the *particular Measure of Wisdom* from God, that is always present, and gives to understand and apply Things suitably, and not upon meer Imitation, where thy *Religion,* such as it is, stands. I say, that our justifying our Practice by the *Example* of Scripture, does not conclude it our Rule, or any Man's whatsoever, in so citing it: And therefore thy thread-bare Answer, *it seems you are forc'd to make Scripture your Rule to prove this or that,* is out of Doors and to be despised, as plausible as it looks: Again, if the Scriptures be our Rule in any particular Cases (and I think we live up to it more than thou dost, with thy *three impious Dialogues*) yet this concludes not the Matter in Question for thee; since it proves not the Scripture to be *eminently the Rule,* or the most *eminent or general Rule,* &c. But T. H. why has E. B. transgress'd more than either *Prophets* or *Apostles,* yea than *Christ* himself, when he (to such carnal Men as thy self) seemed so unkind and harsh in his Answer and Rebuke of *Peter*'s Love and Care of him, as to say, *Get thee behind me Satan?* The Priest that E. B. gave those Names (no one of which was harder than *Satan*) was never half so kind to him, as *Peter* was to Christ; Nay, they were entrapping Questions; such as they used to assault Christ with, when they sought Occasion against him, whom he called *Children of the Devil.* And we know that some of thy Race T. H. in the former Times when Power was in your Hands, diligently sought Matter against us: G. Fox was about the same Time indicted for *Blasphemy,* and great endeavours us'd in some of the old *Pharisaical* Stock, thy Brethren, to take away his Life, E. B. knew whom and what he answer'd: And I do say, that by thy Argument about the *Scriptures being the Rule,* without farther Regard, thou oughtest to stop thy Mouth, unless thou canst prove that E. B. had not the same Warrant the holy Men of old had, to name thy Predecessors by; to do which, thou must come to the discerning of Spirits: And by what wilt thou perform that Enquiry and Judgment? How canst thou tell, whether a Man using Christ's Words to *Peter,* to a loving Disswader of him from Sufferings, that only intends his Good, is well or ill done? The Scripture is no Rule for our discerning aright this Case; nor is it his Duty, in case he be in the right, because Christ's Words are there recorded, unless he be thereto prompted, of the same Power: Yet if he say so, and be reproved by any; 'tis and must be granted that there is an Example which shuts the Mouths, or should do, of all who respect the Scripture; which is our Case with thee. Well, but Christ had no Provocation by *Peter*'s Words, but the Spirit that lurkt in them, which favour'd not the Work of God then doing; To relish the like Case aright there must be the same Spirit; which *T. H.* rejecting

for

for the Rule of right Judgment, to be sure he can be no right Judge of *E. B.* But upon his own Opinion ought to be silent from farther Clamour against him, and repent of his *scurrilous reproachful Language,* with which he has so often run over his Grave.

But thou chargest p. 86. *Nicholas Lucas* with saying, *That if the Bible were burnt, as good an one might be writ,* and though he denies it, yet thou tellest us, *it is never the less a Lye for that* ; and that he knows his Accusers. But suppose it were true, had it not more become an *Anabaptist*, and a Preacher too, (especially, when one of the Scriptures in thy Title Page is, *A Man that is an Heretick, after the First and Second Admonition reject, who never dealt so with either him or us, that thou hast so publickly writ against as such)* first to have dealt with *N. L.* about it; and granting he had been so obstinate in a wicked Saying, as thou Dialoguest him to be, had this been a sufficient Ground for thee to charge it upon the Persons and Principles of the People called *Quakers?* But now thou hast given the World a Saying to measure us by, that is, *First*, of several Years standing, and but lately raked up, and might have been either at first *mis-apprehended*, or some Word *forgotten* or *mis-placed*. *Secondly*, That *N. L.* denies that he ever spake it, by a serious *Certificate* in *G. W*'s *Append.* confirm'd by *H. Stout*, appeal'd to by thy *Anabaptist* Informers, which thou hast not so much as attempted to invalidate. *Thirdly*, That he abhors the Matter contained in the Story, and that without all mental Reserves. And *Fourthly*, That it's charged upon, and made to be the Measure of *Us* and our *Principles* and *Motions*, thereby making us to blaspheme God's Spirit, as well as reprobate Scripture, (and that with no small Aggravation) who are innocent, by never speaking the Words, by never countenancing such Words, and by not holding the Matter directly or indirectly contained in them; and we do utterly renounce and abhor both the one and the other. Well, *T. Hicks!* God will plead our Cause against the Malignity of thy Slanderous Spirit: No Justice, no Discretion could ever have led thee to this monstrous pitch of Abuse: Thou shewest how glad thou art to bedirt us, by making other Folks *Lyes* thy *Charges*, and then insisting on them with as much Confidence, as if thou wert infallibly assured of every jot. But we have some Cause to suspect thee more than ever; thy Tale wears so many Dresses: One while it is, *Thou mayst burn thy Bible, and write as good an one thy self*, Contin p. 5. Another while, *We may burn our Bible, and make as good an one our selves*, Dial. 3. p. 3. And last of all, it is to go thus, *If the Bible were burnt, as good an one might be writ*, ibid. p. 86. Now, *T. H.* answer; thou that pretendest to such Punctuality, which of these are we to take? The *first* is unlikely, because what ever we think we could do, to be sure thou canst not think that a *Quaker* should have so good an Opinion of an *Anabaptist Woman*, *as that she could write another Bible as good as this*, that we are sure understands not this. If we must take thee in thy *Second* Account, then the Woman is out in her first Story: If in the *last* Relation of this *Fiction*, then it concerns the *Quakers* no more than the *Anabaptists*. For suppose the World were under one Emperor, and he so *impious* as to enjoyn the burning of all the Bibles, and all were burnt; I hope they are not so *irreligious* as to limit God's Power, who is Almighty, that he could not furnish us with one as good as this, especially, since *Christians* would else, as you must hold, be without a Rule: for I would have thee take Notice *T. H.* that thou hast so materially varied in thy Charge, that now it is not, whether, if the Bible were burnt, any Man could make as good an one; but whether, if it were by such Impiety burnt, *as good an one might not be writ*, which Words are general. Here, *T. H.* to give the———his due, thou hast helpt thy *Friend Quaker*, by bringing him in saying what *T. H.* unless he would question God's Omnipotency, dare not deny.

But to conclude, either these Mistakes proceed from the first Authors, or from *T. H.* If from the *first Authors*, why should they be credited at all, who show such Uncertainty? if from *T. Hicks*; what Reason has he to be so infallibly sure of their Memories, who is not sure of his own Books, much less of his own Memory, being found in such manifest *Variations?* But since every just Judge accounts that Accuser and Witness of little Credit, that are found diverse and inconsistent in their Stories; I hope my sober *Reader*, who is made judge betwixt us, will in Justice cashier *T. Hicks* from all Credit with him in these Attempts. But as against *N. L.* so against *S. Eccles*, *T. H.* has publisht a *foul Slander*, viz. *That he should say, the Scriptures are a Lye.* This *G. W.* Append. p. 12. reflected upon thee, as an abusive and false Charge; To which I cannot find that thou sayst any more than this, *that*

one

1674.

Sect. V.

one of thy *Witnesses against* N. L. *can testifie, that* S. E. *said, he used Scripture, only to satisfie him,* Dial. 3. p. 86. Doubtless that Witness has long Ears, thou hang'st so fast by them. But he *can* witness it. But why *does* he not? Is that *Put off* like to confirm the Charge? But granting thy Witness remembers better against *S. E.* than *N. L.* Does *E. S*'s Saying, that he us'd Scripture to satisfie his Opponent, prove, that he said, *the Scriptures were a Lye?* Do Men use to prove Truths by Lyes? Doth not this make *S. E.* imply the Lye to his own Principles, whilst he quoted Scripture to prove real Truths; What sayst thou *T. H.* Is this to evince the Truth of thy Objections and Charges against the *Quakers*, and secure thy Credit with thy own and other People, that carries with it what merits the Detestation and Rebuke of every honest Mind?

But that thou mayst go out with the same *braving Rant* thou camest in with, and the like Honesty, thou tellest thy Reader, *that* W. P. *is guilty of wilful Lying, in saying, that thou disingenuously slankedst from a publick Meeting, and evadedst the offer made thee by* G. W. *to that Purpose:* It is not unlikely but thou takest thy old Way of proving, which is in the End to detect thy self of that thou chargest me with the Guilt of. *First* thou sayst, *that long before my Book was out, thou didst desire to meet with me, and I refused.* But doth this prove me guilty of wilful Lying, in charging thee with evading the offer made for a publick Disputation? Are the Terms of a Meeting for a publick Disputation in thy Answer? If not, How does thy Answer reach the Question? Well, But I refus'd; to do what? *To meet a Man in* private *that had twice printed me a Knave, a Fool, an Heretick, a Blasphemer,* and I know not how much more, either in those Terms or in Circumlocution, to the World: No such Matter, *T. H.* I never intend to release thee from the Burden and Shame of so many publick and manifest Villanies as thou hast committed against me, a Stranger to thee in all respects, and my Friends in general, that, it may be, never heard of such a Man. Besides, let me tell thee, I look upon thee to be so base a Person, that as I shall always desire to have nothing to do with thee (for that Cause, and not thy Abilities) so I never intend to trust my self in such private Manner with any Man, that is detected of such notorious *Perversion, Lying and Forgery*; there being no Security to any one in common conversing with thee; save that thou deservest no Credit against any Man, who hast so publickly forfeited all Credit in thy numerous *Fictions against us.* But to prove thou hast not evaded the publick Meeting, thou tellest thy Reader, *that thou didst send six Questions to* G. W. *to debate them upon Notice in a convenient Time and Place; that he refus'd; therefore* G. W. *did both shuffle and lye*; which is the *great Shuffle* of thy Third. Dial. in *little*, or the *Evasion* of thy whole Book *Epitomized:* For as thou hast pretended in thy Third *Dial.* that the Evincement of thy own Objections was all that we required or stood upon for thee to do; so here thou makest as if the Discussing of those Objections (herein consider'd) had been all there was any Ground to dispute upon; which was for thee, who art the *Abuser, to chuse a Charge for the abused to insist upon.* But why didst thou not tell thy *Reader*, that G. W. *first sent thee a Charge in writing; and that he offered in a publick Auditory to prove thee guilty of* Forgeries, Self-Contradictions, *and* gross Errors, *from thy own Dialogues?* Instead of yielding to the Test, even about Matter of Fact, where thou hast grosly abused us, thou didst in plain Terms shuffle by a fresh Proposal of *Question*; as if thou wert to teach us where and what to charge our Enemies with; and then prescribe Rules (with many taunting Expressions, omitted in thy Third Dial.) how to behave our selves, on purpose to evade the Meeting. I would have thee know, it was our Right to make the *Complaint*; and hadst thou been a *Man of any Honesty,* thou wouldst readily have considered it, and joyn'd Issue upon our Charge.

This, in Reputation to thy self, as well as *Justice* to us, thou ought'st not to have declined: And yet to aggravate these Shuffles G. W. proffered in his 4th Paper to thee *a Note of the Particulars charg'd as Forgeries, &c. if thou desiredst it*; so willing was he and others to have seen thee in a publick Auditory. But seeing this would not do, he and I went to *John Gladman's,* desiring him to offer thee from us, *we would meet thee and any else to defend thee, in a publick Auditory, with thy* Dialogue *in one Hand and the Bible in the other*; the fairest of tenders; to make thy own Book the Subject; and the Scriptures, (thou sayst we reprobate) *A Rule.* But this thou canst not but know was also rejected: So that to conceal these *Shifts,* nay, to say thou art no *Shuffler,* and which is worse to charge *G. W.* with both *Shuffling and Lying, at what Time thou art so manifestly guilty of both, is to heighten thy Unworthiness to a monstrous Pitch.*   But

But as the *Matter* of thy Book is injurious, so thy *Language* insolent and scurrilous; entituling us *Cheats, Impostors, a mad, arrogant, abusive, prophane Man, Knave*, in Discourse [*Coxcomb*] *impious Cursers, Lyars, Blasphemers, most implacable Enemies to the Christian Religion, as vile Impostors as ever were, influenced and inspired by the grand Impostor the Devil*; calling our Religion, *malignant Errors, a mystical Romance, Satan's Snares, Blasphemy, blasphemous Absurdities,* I proclaim, to the World, that your Religion is a meer Cheat, calculated only to the Service of the Devil, and your own Lusts; and abusing our religious Language with such like Expressions as these; *Impertinent Canting; your idle non-sensical and blasphemous Praying*; Terms that as much unbecome thy Pretences, as they resemble the rest of thy Practices. Canst thou with good Conscience upbraid *E. B.* with rebuking a Priest in *Scripture-Language*, whilst thou hast taken the Liberty, throughout thy *Dialogues*, when and where thou wert never provok'd, of such foul and frothy Expressions, as becomes not any Man writing of Religion? Is this to make the Scripture thy *Rule*; or to act the *Christian* against the *Quaker?* and to prove the *Quaker* none? No such Matter *T. H.* but much the contrary, and that in the Minds of not a few, and those too, of thy own Way, though of a better Spirit, who have disown'd them, Root and Branch. I would not, after thy Example, *reprobate* all with thee, God forbid: That God has turned these ill design'd Attempts to our Advantage, remember what Sort of *Salute* was lately given thee, by a Religious and Ingenuous Person in *Bristol* (once a Preacher among the *Independents*) at thy reflecting upon his adhering to the Way we profess, viz. *That he read thy Dialogues before he ever read the* Quakers *Books (or Answers) and that the Disingenuity of that Dealing (he apprehending it to be no real* Dialogue) *was a Furtherance of his Inquiries, and so of his Convictions, grounded upon thy* Abuses; An Argument never to be answer'd by thee, *T. H.* if thou shouldst write Three *Dialogues* more, unless they were as remote from these as thou wert from Honesty when thou writ'st them; who dost first *Forge*, and then *Lye* and *Rail* to maintain it.

Think not with these *Comical* Courses to obtain thy Ends upon us, nor raze the Foundation of our *Religion* by thy abusive *Interludes*; in which thou hast not *imitated* Christ, but Ap'd the prophane Stager; writing a sort of *Mock-Religion* instead of solid Controversie; therein playing the Humourist with the Vulgar, like *Aristophanes* of old, (though with worse Malice, and less Wit) who sacrific'd the Virtue and Gravity of *Socrates* and his Friends, to please their Enemies, and profit himself; the Hinges on which thy *Dialogues* turn. The *First* is manifest, and so is the *Last* to the Value of 300 Books at an Impression [if some of thy Assistants do not wrong thee, as we suppose not] (ask the Bookseller else) besides *Perquisites;* hereby proving thy self, *one of those unruly Vain-Talkers, who writest Things thou oughtest not for filthy Lucre-sake*, applied to us in thy *Title-Page*, but due to thy Self.

And however *sweet* these Courses may relish to thy worldly Palate, thou wilt find them deadly *Poysonous* in the End; at what Time thy own *Dialogues*, and not I, nor any influenced by me, will prove so many *Assassinators* in thy own Bowels. God, if it please him, give thee Repentance, that thou mayst escape his fierce Wrath to come. *Amen.*

Now sober *Reader*, I shall address my self to thee, and God's righteous Witness in thy Conscience, whether I have acquitted my Self in this Controversie as becomes a *Christian-Man*, against the Violent and Unfair Assaults of my Adversary? and if I may not with very good Reason conclude, that he has all this while but *counterfeited* the *Christian*, and abused the *Quaker*; and consequently, that he (and not the real Quaker) *is quite another Thing than a Christian?* Let Righteous Judgment take Place.

23d of the 5th
Month 1674. *A True Lover, and hearty Wisher of thy Souls Felicity.*

W. P.

Not every one that saith unto me, Lord, Lord, shall enter into the Kingdom of Heaven; but he that doth the Will of my Father which is in Heaven, Mat. 7. 21.

For he is not a Jew which is one outward; neither is that Circumcision which is outward in the Flesh: But he is a Jew which is one inwardly, and Circumcision is that of the Heart in the Spirit; and not in the Letter, whose Praise is not of Men but of God, Rom. 2. 28, 29.

But as then he that was born after the Flesh persecuted him that was born after the Spirit, even so it is now, Gal. 4. 29.

But be of good chear, I have overcome the World, John 16. 33.

A JUST REBUKE

To One and Twenty Learned and Reverend

DIVINES (So called)

Being an ANSWER

To an ABUSIVE EPISTLE against the People called *Quakers*. Subscrib'd by Thomas Manton, Tho. Jacomb, John Yates, John Sheffield, Anthony Palmer, Tho. Cole, Tho. Doelittel, Rich. Baxter, Will. Cooper, Geo. Griffith, Matth. Barker, John Singleton, Andr. Parsons, Rich. Mayo, Tho. Gouge, Will. Jenkyn, Tho. Watson, Benjam. Needler, Will. Garslake, Stephen Ford, Samuel Smith.

By WILLIAM PENN.

Quid enim iniquius, quam ut oderint homines quod ignorant, etiamsi res meretur odium, Tertul. Apolog.

—— The Lord,—— Frustrateth the Tokens of the Lyars, and maketh Diviners mad, that turneth wise Men backward, and maketh their Knowledge foolish. *Isaiah* xliv. 24, 25.

THE CAUSE of the *GOD of TRUTH* hath rarely wanted the Endeavours of Men of greatest Power and Literature in almost every Age, to slander it, nor the constant *Adherers* to it, contumelious Treatment for their Integrity: No Virtue hath been so Conspicuous, no *Quality* so Great, no *Relation* so Near, as to protect them from the Fury of blind *Tradition* and prejudic'd *Education*. But as this ought not to discourage any that pursueth so *Good and Heavenly an Interest*, especially when the Invincible *Faith, Patience,* and *Hope of those Holy Ancients*, that so heartily espoused it, stand before us as so many bright Examples and Encouragements; so neither have the many and great Attempts of *Men of divers, yea opposite Interests*, to render us *Unfit for the Earth*, and (what in them lyeth) *to invalidate our Claim to Heaven*, abated one Grain of our Love to, Confidence in, and Zeal for, that worthy Cause: And Blessed be the God and Father of our Lord Jesus Christ, their Essays have been Insuccessful, their Designs frustrated, and not one of their Weapons form'd against our *Sion* hath yet prospered; But

—— *Crescit sub pondere Virtus.*

These very Sufferings God hath turned to our Enlargement, daily rewarding our Tribulations with Patience, and our Conflicts with Joy in the Holy Ghost; fulfilling to us that comfortable Saying of the Apostle, *All Things shall work together for good to them that love him.* Having this *Encouragement* from God, what *Injury* soever we sustain from Men, well may we say with that Kingly Prophet, *Whom should we fear? Of whom should we be afraid?*

With

With that Godly Resolution, which becometh the Justness of my Cause, I enter upon my present Work, and first of the Occasion.

We have been long threatn'd with a Report of the *joynt-Endeavours of many Ministers*, which rais'd several into an Expectation of some notable Piece, some grave and moderate Disquisition of what had been as frivolously as fouly managed by our other petulant *Adversaries*, that the *Controversy* so long depending, might terminate with some Advantage to such as had made any sober Enquiry after it; but we had no sooner received and lookt into the Book, than we saw our selves under a very great Disappointment; for instead of some New Essay, behold! An Old Discourse new vampt, or *a new Impression of a Book* twice largely consider'd, and some think, *effectually Answer'd*, I mean, John Faldo's *Quakerism no Christianity*, but *now recommended*, as the Title-page tells us, by the *Epistle of many Learned, and Worthy Divines*.

But since it hath pleased so many Persons under that *Character*, to fall in with his Discourse against us, *to Commend it so highly, Recommend it so earnestly, and bestow so liberal an Elogy on him that writ it*, I think I may without any the least Injustice, look upon them as *Authors of the Impression*, and consequently (by espousing his Endeavours) *Responsible to the* People call'd *Quakers*, for all those *Miscarriages* therein rightly chargeable by them upon him: And I no ways doubt, through God's Assistance, to evidence their *Concern* in this Affair to carry with it an utter *Inconsistency* with that Superbe *Title* they have either given themselves, or the Author or Bookseller conferr'd upon them, for the good Turn of their so seasonable *Epistle*, viz. *Learned, Reverend and Worthy Divines*; Words that make a fine jingle, and please and blow up Vain People at a strange rate.

The first Paragraph of their *Epistle* is a great Truth, both worthy of the Minds of good Men, and necessary to be consider'd at any Man's Entrance into the Judgment of another's Cause; It runs thus:

One and Twenty Divines. *That, as God is the Wise Distinguisher of Good and Evil; and so loveth the Good in any, as not to abate his Hatred of their Evil; and so hateth the Evil, as to love all that is Good; So is it no small Part of the Wisdom and Integrity of his Servants to Imitate him herein; and not like Men blinded by Partiality, to justifie all in those whom they like, and Villify all in those whom they dislike,* &c.

W. P. One would think by this that *you* had Imitated God in *your* Conduct towards the *Quakers*; and doubtless *you* writ it, that those that read it should think so: but why? I know not; unless because *you* looking upon *your* selves his Servants, such ought to do so, or else to give greater Credit to *your* Work than *your* selves perhaps believe it deserves: But let us hear what Use *you*, the great Men of *Uses*, make of this Introduction; I find it in the next Paragraph in these Words.

One and Twenty Divines. *This Justice we must and will observe towards this People, called* Quakers,—*The Fear of God and Love of Truth, forbids us to render them Worse or Better than they are.*

Better! there is little Fear you will: You may turn *Pelagians* in the Case, and exclude all Divine Assistance; for I hope none are so ignorant in this Age, as to think that Men of your Stamp need special Grace to keep you from the Sin of rendring the poor *Quakers better* than they are: How much *Worse* will be the Question? I confess, you say fair; but what if you break your Word with us? Must not your Censure of us fall upon your own Heads? And will it not be reasonable for us to interpret your Use of so true an Expression to be a Trick to decoy People into a Belief, that you had taken right Measures of us, whilst you have really dealt most unjustly with us.

Let me a little expostulate with you in this Matter. You have either read or not read the Book ye recommend: If you have not read it, certainly you have done very Ill to recommend it, since you know not what you recommend; which is not *to Imitate God*, or do the *Quakers* Justice: If you have read it, you manifestly entitle your selves to all the Evils of it. Again, since the Strength of the Book depends upon *Testimonies* out of our Writings: either you have compared his *Citations* with the Books themselves, or ye have not; if you have not (and I am apt to think that's your Case) you commend him, and condemn us by rote: If you have compared and considered them, you must needs have offered great Violence to your Understandings in giving your Approbation, which anon we shall so undeniably evidence, as it would have been comparatively your Virtue, to have recommended the Book without reading it or examining the Citations.

Besides,

1674.

Besides, the most of what he chargeth upon us to be our *Principles*, are not so laid down by any one of us, nor, say we, sayable by any of us upon real Principles; but are such *Consequences* as he through Ignorance or Malice hath indirectly drawn from our Words: For Instance, *That there is no other Judgment, Heaven or Hell, than what is within us in this Life:* Which is so far from being our *Principle* in *Our* Words, that it is as inconsistent with the Truth of our Creed, as Darkness is with Light: Charge this upon him, and he will tell you, I doubt not, *That this is not the* Quakers *Faith* in terminis, *but the Consequence of it*; but then it is to be observed, that he must have the making of it. I would fain know of you, if you would be so treated with Respect to the Articles of your own Creed? Would you esteem it just in me, to give my *Consequence for your Principle*, supposing I thought it a true Consequence, especially if you reject it? For Example; You are most, if not all of you, strict *Calvinists* in the Point of *Election* and *Reprobation*; would you take it for a candid Representation of your Judgment, that I should proclaim it to the World, T. Manton, T. Jacomb, &c. believe, *That God is the Author of Sin*; *That God's Secret Will crosseth his Revealed Will*; *That no Man is obliged by the Laws either of God or Men*; *That Men are not the Cause of their own Destruction*; *That there are neither Rewards nor Punishments*, &c. because perhaps I believe those *Consequences* to be deducible from the *Calvinistical Principle*? I am perswaded you would look upon me as an injurious Person in so doing; yet this hath been the Practice of your *Reverend Author* J. Faldo; and which is less to your Credit, you have notwithstanding commended him in it, which, how well it suits with *One and Twenty Learned and Reverend Divines* I leave to their Judgment who understand what Persons of such a Character ought to do and be. But I hope you do not think this to be *Imitating of God*; if you do, your Case is desperate.

But had your Carriage been less blameable in these Particulars, it had not only been your *Discretion* but *Duty*, to have enquired if ever any Thing had been writ in Answer to this Discourse you recommend, by any of that People that it was writ against; if there had, to have procured and perused it, before you had so freely spent your peremptory Judgment against us.

You generally fling *Infallibility* at us, though it be about Matters of highest Importance to Salvation, as if it were a Capital Sin to be assured of what a *Christian* ought not to make a Doubt of, and yet nothing below ascribing such an *Infallibility* to your *Reverend Author*, can excuse you in not examining him by our Discourses, before you confer'd so kind an *Epistle* upon his Book: I ask you, if the like Practice would please you in your own Case? you have prov'd, it doth in ours, which makes not for your Honour: Some of you are Writers your selves, and thereby have ascended to no small Degree of Fame for something or other; tell me honestly if you would think it a Piece of Justice in any *Class* of Men to recommend a Book most abusive of your Religion to the World, *for an Ingenuous Essay, an Exact Account of your Belief, a Tract that in* Matter, Proof *and* Style (your own Words) *merits the Notice of all such as desire an Information concerning your Principles of Religion*, whilst you both disown the Principles of Religion it calls yours, and in *Two large Answers* have detected him of several hundred *Miscarriages against your Persons and Principles*? I am perswaded you will provide better for your selves. But if you must needs be so liberal, methinks your *Recommendation* had been better bestow'd upon his *Vindication*, since his writing *That*, proveth, *This wanted it*, and if it wanted it then, it wants it still, and yet it seems the *Book Vindicated* must be the *Defence* of the *Vindication*, and all the Return I am like to have to my *Rejoynder*, bating *The Epistle of many Learned, Reverend and Worthy Divines*, in Praise of such a Book, and such an Author: May none of you, at least in this *Temper*, be *Inquisitors* when I am to be examin'd for my *Religion*!

I shall now fall more closely to the *Matter* of your *Epistle*.

One and Twenty Divines. *The Quakers preach another Gospel, and endeavour to seduce well-meaning Souls, to whom they speak in unintelligible Words, and from whom they hide the Poyson of their Antifundamental Doctrines.*

W. P. Here is a great deal in a little, and very sourly said: Were it as True as it is False, the Day were yours.

You say, *We preach another Gospel:* You do but *Say* it, and I thank God, *You can Do no more.* But doth it become *One and Twenty* Learned and Reverend *Divines*, to give so general and black a *Charge*, without making any the least Offer to Prove it? Is not this to *Calumniate* rather than to *Confute* us? If you say your

Reverend

Reverend Author, *John Faldo*, hath done it for you, I must tell you, that he is an *Irreverent* Abuser of God, the *Christian Religion* and the *Quakers*; and which is more to my Contentment, whatever it be to his and yours, Some, and *No Quakers too*, think, I have proved him such. And let me ask you, *If it be* Another Gospel, *To own Remission and Eternal Salvation by the Son of God, both as he appeared above* 1600 *Years ago in the Flesh, and as he reveals himself within in Power and Spirit?* What is the Gospel or Glad Tidings, but *Deliverance from Sin here, and Wrath to come?* And what can effect this, but the Powerful *Grace of God that bringeth Salvation*, which is dispensed to all Men by *Him, who is full of Grace and Truth?*

For the other Part of your Accusation, *That we should Say One Thing and Mean another*; it is by Consequence, to call us the *Worst Sort of Knaves*, by how much a Deception in Matters of Eternal Moment, is more Impious than any Cozenage about Things of this Life; and yet you would be thought *Charitable Men*, and say, *We want it:* Is this the Way to supply us? But I would willingly know of you, *By what Skill you arrive at the Knowledge of our Hearts?* *Inspiration* is one Part of our Heresy, if your *Reverend Author* is to be Credited: The Scripture cannot be your *Rule* in the Point; for that no where faith, *The* Quakers *say One Thing and mean another*; and if you measure us by our Words, you must grant, that either *you do not understand us*, or we mean very *Good Things*; for you elsewhere say, *That our Obnoxious Tenets we usually Mask under Expressions Doubtful, Unintelligible, or under Scripture and Orthodox Phrases.* If *Doubtful*, your Consequences cannot be certain; If *Unintelligible*, you infer that which you do not know; If *Scriptural and Orthodox*, you must either tell us, how you come to know our *Meanings to be Contradictory to our Phrases*, and prove them such, or you must acknowledge that we stand upon equal Terms with your selves; I do not say, *Upon no Better*, for as *Great Infidels* as you would have us to be, we have both *Discretion and Religion enough*, not to write such *Abusive and Contrary Things*, as so fluently drop from the *Pens of One and Twenty Learned and Reverend Divines*. But your *Incharity* far exceeds your *Indiscretion*; You make us to know *Poison*, and to hide *Poison*, given for *Antidotes, Destructive to the Souls of Men and Women*. I would fain know, why the Conscience of a *Quaker*, should not be as Good as the Conscience of a *Presbyterian or an Independent?* What Mischiefs have we made our selves Authors of to the World, that it should not be as Valid every Jot? Have we no Souls to be Sav'd? Is there no Desire in us that they may be Sav'd? No Honesty? No Conscience? No Fear of God? All animated to such Evil Purposes, *as the Wilful Damning of our selves, and the Proselyting others into Eternal Misery; and rather than not compass such an End, expose our selves to all Sort of Sufferings in this World?* O Bitter Invective! God, the Searcher of Hearts, will require this Injustice at your Hands: You have unworthyly traduc'd the Reputation of those who dare meet you with a Publick Test, to prove their Integrity to God and Men. Why will you give such Occasion to remind you of *Old Stories?* But of that anon. Had you judg'd us *Ignoramus's, you had been Kind to the Cruelty of making us Designed Murderers to our own and other Men's Souls*. God forgive you. But this I must tell you, that it is not We, *That say One Thing and think another*, but *You*, and such as *You* are, *That make us think another Thing than what we say*, and then entitle us to your own Inventions. I must farther tell you, *We make it not our Business, as you falsly insinuate, to decoy People into Antifundamental Principles:* For besides that we know none to be such that we hold, *We make not our Religion to stand in a Belief of so many Verbal Articles; but a Conformity of Soul to the Grace of God.* It is a great Part of our Duty, to dehort People from Curious Enquiry after *Notions and Opinions, be they never so True in themselves, knowing how much more Beneficial it is to Men, and Well-pleasing to God, to have an Honest Heart than a Full Head: Doing is degenerated into Talking, and the Life of Religion into Contention about the Notion of it*; Such Christians will not stand in God's Day: Besides, many of those, who are otherwise remote enough from saying any Thing in *Favour of the Quakers*, do frequently acknowledge, *That they generally Preach and Press Good Living*. It is our Desire to bring Men into a *Sense of God's Grace in their own Hearts, and to know the Effectual Operations of it, to the Renewing of their Mind to God: And, That Divine Assistance Within, and Right Use of the Holy Scriptures Without, are enough to inform them of what is fit to be Believed*. And though you would have People think very severe Things of us, *with Respect to the Scriptures of Truth*, by telling them, *The* Quakers *hold, that the Scriptures are not the Word of God, nor a Rule of Faith and Practice*; yea, *That we readily assert it in so many Words*;

Words; I must tell you, *You have acted with us herein far from Men of Common Ingenuity*; A Man might at this Rate, by Scripture prove, *There is no God*, if he would but leave out, *The Fool hath said in his Heart*. We deny the *Scriptures* in that Sense, *wherein you deny them, to be the Word of God*; that is to say, *The Word that was in the Beginning with God, and was God*, which you call the *Essential Word*; and, because we find in no Place, that it calls it self, *The Word of God*, we rather chuse to say, *The Scriptures given forth by Inspiration, are the Words of God*. The like Abuse you put upon us, about denying them to be a *Rule of Faith and Practice*; you leave what makes for us behind, that you may make your Advantage of what you take; *That the Scripture is not a Rule therein, in all Things exprest, you your selves confess, respecting the Dispensation of the* Jews, *and other Things*; and that there may be some Things wherein the Scriptures cannot be a *Rule*, I presume you will not deny; and that they are not a *Rule* in any Case, the Import of your Charge, we utterly deny; for we believe, and know, they contain many *Godly Rules*. I shall place this to the rest of your Account of *Calumnies*, and so proceed.

One and Twenty Divines. *Though the Reverend Author hath shewed you how much Infidelity is among them, and how many of the Very* Essentials *of* Christianity *their Leaders contradict, and how consequently they are indeed No* Christians; *yet it is not his Purpose (as he plainly premiseth) to fix this sad Character upon all those who pass under the Name of* Quakers — *There are divers of them, who are Honest, and Well-Meaning Persons* ——

W. P. Methinks you are got into a very kind Mood, of a sudden, but it holds not a whole Page; for you tell us soon after, *That the whole Body of this People seems to be Judicially deserted of God:* If so, then *No more Christians than their Leaders*, as you are pleased to call them; neither *Honest nor Well-Meaning*, unless God judicially deserts Honest and Well-Meaning People. In the next Page, you call them *Wasps of Satan's Hiving, who have Hives but no Honey, or Sweetness of Spirit, except for themselves*. The less we have, the more you have; and would not one think you *All Honey*, by your Writings? How can you expect that we should have any to spare, whom you make to have so little, if any at all? And what Need is there of giving to them, that think they have so much already? The Truth is, *We are* Wasps, *and you are* Bees, *by one and the same Figure*. We know that you have always a Good Name for your selves, and have long loved the *Honey Pot*; But where did you get it? Did you gather it? No such Matter. Of whom then? Of the People, no Doubt; *They Toil, and you Talk; they are the* Bees, *and you so many* Cunning Hivers, *at the Tinkling of whose Bells, the* Silly Bees *assemble, and when you have safely Hived them, your next Business is to take their* Honey *from them*. Howbeit, if we are *Wasps*, then not *Bees*, by which, I suppose, you intend *Christians*; if so, *Your Charity is at an End*, and those you *Christian'd* with J. Faldo *just now, you do here manifestly Unchristian*; unless *Wasps be Christians*; and that *Christians, while such, may be Judicially Deserted of God, and Hived by the Devil*. Methinks such Contradiction becometh not Men of your Stile and Pretences.

But tell me, *Why are we Judicially Deserted of God?* Is it not because we have *Judiciously* deserted you? And don't you therefore say, *We are Hived by the Devil*, because we will not let you Hive us? Speak Truth, fain would have it (according to the Old Proverb) *As your Bell Tinketh, the* Poor Quaker *Thinketh*. But blessed be God, His Grace has made us Wiser than *such Teachers*; we know the Heavenly Voice of our Spiritual Shepherd, and can no more suffer our selves to be carried away with a *Worldly Ministry*; and that I aver to be such, *which is not Founded upon the Revelations, and Internal Motions of God's Holy Spirit*; a Principle you do, in the Person of your *Reverend Author, J. Faldo*, not only deny, but deride; who is so far from shewing any *Infidelity* amongst us, that his Book is but a Proof of his *Own Injustice*; and not that our *Principles, but his Corrupt Consequences, contradict the Essentials of Christianity*. This is an Inadvertency in you, that well deserves, as my *Reproof, so your Repentance*. But to your next Passage.

One and Twenty Divines. *And the Truth is (excepting some* Jugling Socinianiz'd *Persons, or* Papists, *that assume their Name) there are few of them who are Men of so much Understanding, and Consistent Principles, as to be Able and Willing to give a Methodical and Intelligible Account what they themselves or their Party hold*.

W. P. A quick Way to do a *Quaker's* Business at once: He must either be an *Ignoramus*, a *Socinian*, or a *Papist*, chuse him whether; if an *Ignoramus*, he is laught at; if a *Socinian*, or *Papist*, he is hated. Doth this flow from the *Beeishness* of your

your Nature, *Jugling Socinians, Papists,* or *Ignoramus's?* These Expressions do not Quadrate with the Titles of *Learned and Reverend Divines.* What is it but to tell us, you resolve to render the *Quakers* odious, and if they have nothing of themselves, you will adapt any Thing that is hateful of other Persuasions, into theirs, that you may bring them into Suspicion, and Abhorrence with your People. However, you are so constant to contradict your selves, that you grant to some of us, *Both an Ability and Willingness, to render a Methodical and an Intelligible Account of what we and our Friends believe,* after having rated us, *For Designed Obscurities, and Affected Unintelligibleness.* But that I may not leave you so, let me tell you, first, that both *Socinians* and *Papists* have written, and that with Severity against us; next, The Labours of no Adversary have had more Grateful Acceptance in the Thoughts of your *Reverend Author,* J. Faldo, than a *Noted Socinian,* of whose Attempt he speaks thus, *I resent it as one of the Best, and most ingeniously managed, that ever I read against that Sort of People,* meaning the *Quakers.* He also, both in his *First Book,* and in *His Vindication,* as heartily advocates the Cause of a *Socinian* against me, as if he had been doubly Fee'd to the Work. Besides all this, we have been of late both publickly and vehemently, yet groundlesly, exclaimed upon, *For denying the Man Christ Jesus, and ascribing the Christship to the Divinity alone;* and you know the *Socinians* own Him to be but a *Bare Man;* and that some of our Eminentest Adversaries in that Controversy, were assisted by *Socinians,* I am able to prove. But to what a Pitch of Inconsistency may not the Pride, Passion, and Prejudice of Men raise them? You think it enough to do our Business, to *Pin the Pope at our Tail;* but you may remember how Unjust you thought such Suggestions from some of the former *Prelates of the English Church,* who made the same Use of your Separation; and as well as you *Presbyterians and Independents* agree against us, both of you have *Mutually Jesuited one another;* the Refuge of Malice, when driven to a Pinch. *To conclude;* I must tell you, we are neither *Socinians* nor *Papists;* and I do hereby require at your Hands, to produce One *Socinian* or *Papist* that goes under the *Name of a Quaker among us;* till when, you remain under the Just Imputation of *Slanderous Persons.* But let us see what is next.

One and Twenty Divines. *Diverse Honest, Well-Meaning, and Ignorant Persons, have fallen in with the* Quakers, *supposing them by their Plain Habit, Austerity, and Rude Deportment, to be the Strictest, and therefore the Holiest Sort of Professors. — And thus seeing no farther, they become* Quakers, *from the same Principles in the Main, and from the same Dispositions, as the more Ignorant Votaries among the* Papists, *are* Carthusians, Franciscans, *and other such like* Monks *and* Nuns.

W. P. I would fain ask you, if you can yet think your selves *Men of Charity?* You elsewhere say we want it; and at this Rate we may do so for all you. Behold the Brand you set on every Soul that leaves you! Can you satisfie your Consciences, that you have herein shown the *Justice* you promised us, in describing the *Quakers,* or imitated the Rectitude of God in the Measures you have taken of us? Truly if you can, they are greatly to be suspected: Give us one Instance of any Honest, or Well-meaning Person, *That for the Sake of those Outward Appearances became a* Quaker, which in other Terms is, to expose themselves to the *Bitter Anathema's* of such High Priests as your selves, the Severity of their Dearest Relations, the Penalties of Magistracy, and to the General Reproach of the Multitude. Methinks, upon second Thoughts, you should not have such *Good Ones of your selves,* and *such Bad Ones of your Neighbours;* But though you take so little Care of being Tender, nay, *Just to us,* yet you should be more Circumspect for your selves. You tell us in the Person of *J. Faldo, That the* Quakers *deny to perform any Thing Relative of Religion, but upon Inspiration, or Motion of the Spirit;* and you all know, or may know, the Papists *turn not* Carthusians, Franciscans, *&c. upon such Pretences, or as being so disposed:* You, or your People have affirmed, *That they by such Works, think to Merit Eternal Life;* Whether it be True or False, let them look to that; sure I am, that such as say, *Those Works are my Works, and that upon my Principle,* who otherwise tell the World, *That I admit of no Work in Religious Matters, but by the Impulse of God's Spirit,* contradict themselves to Purpose, and that you have done. *Popery* brought into Company with what you call *Quakerism,* doth your Work with some of your Vulgar; but your Comparison had shown less of Envy, if you had pleased to produce those Principles, and describe those Dispositions you unworthily insinuate *Quakers* and *Monks* in common to be acted by. But methinks your frequent frothy Reflections upon our *Deportment as Monkish and Cynical,* &c. look more than ordinarily ugly, from the Mouths of such as profess

fess themselves to be of the *Race and Stock of Ancient Puritans, whose Little Bands, Cropt Locks, Exceeding Plain Apparel, Severe Aspects*, with many more Instances of Precifeness and Austerity, (as you call it) were the Subjects frothy Minds play'd upon. You do not think *Ben Johnson* acted like a *Christian-Man* in his *Comical Representation of Puritans*, and yet your selves call'd, *Learned, and Reverend Divines*, have shown as much *Injustice*, tho' it may be, *One and Twenty more of you could not show so much Wit*.

It is known to God, with what Sincerity we are acted in Obedience to the Convictions of his own Spirit, and that it is not *Affected Singularity*, but *Real Conscience*, that engageth us to those Things you make the the Subject of your Mockage and Contempt ; *and God hath to reckon with you for the Liberty you give, and your People take*. To indulge them in that *Unchristian Latitude*, and fling *Monkish Austerities* upon us, who, through Fear of offending Almighty God, by giving Way to a Worldly Appetite, Conscientiously live under some more than ordinary Restriction, is to deal deceitfully with them, and injuriously with us ; and God will judge for these Things. The Truth of the Matter is, you are Angry the People can live without you, and rack your Wits to bring that Principle, People and Way, into Suspicion and Hatred, whose Self-Denial judgeth you and yours : Your Interest in People stands in that, which, when the Everlasting God shall terribly shake all Things, will fall ; and such as have vainly conceited themselves *Christians* upon your Character, will be found without their *Wedding-Garment*. But the Truth is, nothing is well with some Men that a *Quaker* doth ; If he be *Retired*, he is *Sullen* ; if *Plain* in his Apparel, *Cynical*; if Careless about Salutation, *Proud* ; His *Industry* must be *Worldly-Mindedness* ; His *Moderate Uses* of Enjoyments, *Penuriousness* ; His *Hospitality, Flesh-Pleasingness* ; His being *at a Word*, a *Decoy for Custom*, and a *New Way of Cheating* : If he refuse to answer any Questions relating to Religion, either he can *Give no Account of his Religion*, or, *He holds some Error he is afraid to discover* ; if he doth answer them, either it is *Nonsense* or *Equivocation :* In short, his *Virtues* must be *Vices* ; but this is his Resolution, if to be, as he is, be to be *Vile*, he will be more *Vile* ; and I doubt not but God will plead our Cause against you, and evidence to you and all Men, that we have not pursued *Cynical Singularities*, nor *Affected undue Separation* ; but with Holy Fear, and Sincerity of Soul, have been herein resign'd to the Good-Will of God, as he hath made it known by the Light of His Son in our own Consciences ; and this I affirm, that all those Endeavours many Vigorously employ to vilifie an Inward Principle, and dissuade Persons from believing in it, waiting upon it, and being guided by it, center in the *Rankest Atheism*, because the Sense and Influence upon the Mind, is the most Sensible, Express, and Constant Argument for God, and His Pure Religion, which lost, makes Way for Infidelity. But as in Point of Doctrine, so in Conversation, you believe we are not all alike ; your Words are these :

One and Twenty Divines. *And yet some of them being Rich, and grown into Estates in the World, can, and do Live in as Flesh-Pleasing Fulness, Splendor, and indulging to a Sensual Life, as others whom they have Condemned*.

W. P. I would willingly know these Persons, who they are, and where they Live : Did you love Truth, and your own Credit, ye would scarce be so lavish of your Words. You say, *We Condemn all but our selves* ; what is the Consequence but this, if you speak True, *That there is not a Person in the World that is not a* Profest Quaker, *who either hath more Ability to Live Flesh-Pleasing, or that actually doth indulge himself more to a Sensual Life, than some* Quakers *can, and do*. Which Way to save your Credit, I know not, unless you make it appear, that the *Quakers* are both as Rich as other Men, and as indulgent to themselves in all Sensual Pleasures. I perceive, rather than the *Quakers* shall want Faults, you will make some for them ; a Practice very unfit for *One and Twenty Learned and Reverend Divines !* But to do you Right, you are kind in your Cruelty ; you provide against believing what you say, by saying what is incredible of us.

I shall now consider your *Recommendation of his Book*.

One and Twenty Divines. *Wherein the* Quaker's Principles *are more throughly investigated than in any Book which we have seen* ; *and we judge it for Matter, Proof and Stile, to be especially useful for those who need, or desire Information concerning the* Quakers, *and their Principles*.

W. P. Had we no other Weapon, this were enough to Wound your Cause ncurably ; for, *First*, He hath laid down about *Twenty Principles* in the *Quaker's* Name, *Eighteen of which are not only none of theirs*, as so exprest, but not so much as by by *Confequence*. That they are *None* of ours, it is enough we fay fo, unlefs our Faith is not to be taken at our Mouths, but at our *Adverfary's*. He that tells me, *I believe that which I do not believe, is either Foolish or Dishonest, and his Confutation is not of me, but of himself.* That they are not our Principles by Confequence, I have abundantly proved, both in *My Anfwer and Rejoynder*: However, *Matter*, *Proof* and *Stile* you commend it for. The *Matter* of it lyeth in the *Proof of it*: What *Proof* and what *Stile*, I am willing to fhew you; and *First*, as to Proof: Who would not think it excellently performed, that hath fuch an *Epiftle*, and fo Subfcribed, on Purpofe to recommend it?

But that fo many Men, with fuch *Fine Titles*, may be Guilty of great Miftake and Abufe, I will produce you *Ten Inftances of Notorious Perverfion*, any One of which, were unworthy, even of fuch *Poor Heathen* as ye think us to be, referring you to *My Anfwer* and *Rejoynder*, for a more compleat Detection of his *Mifcarriages*.

1. *John Faldo* affirms, *That* W. Smith *had not One Exhortation to read the Scriptures; nay, that the Main Defign of the Book was to deny them, and throw Dirt upon them*; yet *J. F.* cites him concerning the Scriptures, thus:

    Child, Then the Scriptures are to be own'd, and believed, *&c.*

    Father, *Yes, They are to be* Own'd, *and* Believ'd, *and they that do not fo, are to be* Denied.

    Obferv. Can any Thing be more inconfiftent than your *Reverend Author*? Is it this *Sort of Proof* you commend? Can you think this the Way to Convert fuch *Infidels*, as you deem us to be?

    To this let me add another Notable Paffage in the fame Difcourfe, he faults with *Dirting and Denying the Scriptures.*

    Queft. Of what Service are the *Scriptures* as they are given forth, and recorded without?

    Anfw. *Much every Way, unto thofe that have receiv'd the fame Spirit from whom they were given forth*; for, unto fuch they are Profitable, *and* make Wife unto Salvation; *and are unto them of Service, for* Inftruction, Edification, and Comfort.

    Obferv. Is there *No Exhortation* lodg'd in thefe Words? And is this to *Deny, or throw Dirt upon the Scriptures*? If any Man fhall object *W. Smith*'s making the *Spirit neceffary to the Profitable Reading of the Scriptures*, let them go to *W. Tindal, J. Bradford,* Bifhop *Jewel, J. Philpot, Luther, Calvin, Peter Martyr,* and others, they will Preach them the fame Doctrine; which I have obferv'd in *My Rejoynder*, and may eafily be found in *My Catalogue of Authors.*

2. My Second Inftance fhall be this, That he maketh *W. Smith* call the Scriptures, *Traditions of Men, Earthly Root, Darknefs, Confufion, Corruption; All out of the Life and Power of God*; which he only afcribed to Degenerated Men, their Worfhip, Imaginations, and Traditions.

    Shall this be call'd *Proof* or *Perverfion*? Doubtlefs a *Proof of nothing, but of that Hateful Sort of Perverfion.*

3. That the *Quakers* underftand by Knowledge according to the Flefh, *the Ufe of the Underftanding though Sanctified*; which is alfo a grofs Abufe both of our Words and Senfe.

4. That *I. Pennington* fhould call *Vifible Worfhip*, as fuch, *the City of Abomination*. This is a downright *Forgery*; and *your Praife of his Proof makes you Acceffories*. Look on it as you will.

5. That by *Traditions of Men*, we underftand *the Scripture, or Written Word*. A bafe Abufe of our Words.

6. That the *Quakers* mean *by the Vail that is over the People, their Belief of the Man* Chrift Jefus, *Born of the Virgin* Mary, *to be now exifting in Heaven*. An Impiety of his own Inventing, and your Approving.

7. From *W. Smith*'s faying, that *the prefent Practice of the Sacraments, as* Baptizing with a Crofs, *and* counting the Bread and Wine the Flefh and Blood of Chrift, *arife from the* Pope's *Invention*, You in the Perfon of *John Faldo*, give out, *That* W. Smith *calls the Lord's Supper the* Pope's Invention.

    At this Rate, what will your *Teftimony* be worth? *Little*, certainly, with fuch as know good Coin from bad.

8. From *Edw. Burroughs*'s making the Light of Chrift within to be *One in Nature* with the Spirit of Chrift; *J. Faldo* infers, *That* the Quakers *hold the Soul to be*

Margin notes:

1674.

Quak. no Chri p. 45.

My Anfwer, Pag. 42. Rejoyn. p.60, 61, 62.

Rejoyn. ib.

Quak. no Chr. p. 117, 119. My Rejoynd. from p. 141, to 157.

Quak. no Chr. pag. 41. Anfw. p. 35. Rejoy. p. 424.

Vind. p. 50. Rejoy. p. 194, 195.

Quak. no Chr. Part 3. p. 88. Anfw. p. 250.

Quak. no Chr. p. 89. Anfw. p. 251, 252. Rejoyn. p. 395, 396.

Quak. no Chr. p. 163.

Vindic. from p. 75, to 87. Rejoy. p. 348, 349, 350.

be God: as if that had been said of the *Soul*, which was said of the *Light of Christ shining in the Soul*, or that they were *Synonymous*.

What cannot a Man of his Skill in *This* black Art do? Yet this is *your own Reverend Author*, who, for his Proof against the *Quakers*, is not a little in your Books.

Qua. no Chr. p. 9. 10.
Answ. p. 14.
Rejoyn. p. 420

9. Because G. F. rejected that carnal Notion that confines the Infinite Omnipresent God *to a Residence* only *above the Stars*, he makes no Difficulty of inferring, *That we deny the Manhood of Christ Jesus.* As Absurd as Base!

Qua. no Chr. p. 190.
Rejoyn. p. 126. 127. 425.

10. From our affirming that such a kind of *Reading of Scripture as the* Pharisees *used, and to those Ends,* makes Men harder to be wrought upon to true Conversation than the Heathen, *John Faldo* infers, *That reading the Scriptures, and getting Knowledge thence, puts Men into a worse Condition than the* Heathen; *and that there is scarcely any thing more Dangerous than reading the Scriptures:* Yea, he accuses us of *Charging the Miscarriages of Men's Souls on the Knowledge the Scripture,* by God's Blessing, *doth convey.*

Behold at what Rate your *Reverend Author* hath *investigated our Principles!* You have said truly in saying, *he did it throughly*; for he hath scarcely toucht any thing that he hath not *throughly abused*; yet this is the Man whose Attempts so obnoxious as you see you have adventur'd to commend. You say, *you judge* it (among other Things) for the *Proof of it, to be especially useful for those who desire Information concerning the* Quakers *and their Principles:* That ever Men of your *Age, Experience* and *Reputation,* should precipitate themselves into any thing so foul and scandalous! Can you believe this is *Imitating God, and being Just to the* Quakers? I hope your Condition is not yet so dangerous.

I think fit farther to add, for the Information of the Ignorant, that *J. F.* began with us in his Book, called, *Quakerism No Christianity*; I answered him in a Book, entituled, *Quakerism a New Nick-Name for Old Christianity*; against this he put forth his *Vindication,* unto which I made my *Rejoynder,* consisting of Twenty Three Chapters, in which I vindicated our Principles, stripping them of those frightful Vizards and hateful Disguises he put upon them, confirmed them *by many Scriptures and Reasons,* and to compleat our Defence, produced in Favour of the whole, above Two Hundred Testimonies out of both ancient and modern Authors. Besides all this, I faulted his Conduct and Behaviour in this Controversy, in above Four Hundred Particulars, and that under distinct Sections.

None of which hath he taken Notice of, how much soever it stood his Credit upon; but after his own Proof of his Books, wanting a *Vindication,* he *reprints* it to consummate the *Controversy.* To me it is a manifest Token that the Man hath gotten to a *Ne plus ultra, and* therefore goes back again, and doubtless, were not his Cause deeply sunk, it should never need the Help of *One and Twenty Divines,* and those term'd so *Learned* and *Reverend* as you are, to recover it, and yet you see at what a Rate you have perform'd your Task. We have Hopes you will be better advised the next Time; I am sure your Circumstances need it.

And that you have as well abused us in your *Style* as *Proof,* and therefore proportionably deserve the Censure of *Impartial Readers,* I shall produce *some Instances* out of your *Epistle* and his *Book* (I may say yours; for ye have made it so by adopting it:)

First, In your *Epistle,*

A *strange Sort of People, preach another Gospel, and endeavour to seduce well-meaning Souls; Poison of their Anti-fundamental Doctrines; Infidelity among them; Jugling, Socinianiz'd Persons; Papists; Carthusians; Franciscans, and other such like Monks and Nuns; Judicially deserted of God; arriv'd to Pride and Ignorance; seek Back-biting, Reviling and Reproaches; nauseous Conceitedness; Deluded Souls; Barbarous Language; Pitiful Ignorance; No Christians; subverting Christianity; Wasps of Satan's Hiving.*

This is the *Language* of your own *Epistle,* that do not love *Reflections* nor *Railing,* if we will believe you.

Now for the *Style* of your *Reverend Author* in his Books, whom you would have us believe a *Friendly Person* to the *Quakers.*

Of our LIGHT.

Ignis fatuus; *the second Anti-christ*; *the* Quakers *Idol*; *Pernicious Guide and Saviour*; *Fanciful Teacher:* And in his *Vindication, A Sordid, Sinful, Corrupt* and *Ridiculous Thing.*

Of our RELIGION and FRIENDS.

Quakerism made it's Way by, and began in, Blasphemies against the Lord Jesus Christ ; Quakerism *enter'd the World, as if Hell were broke loose, and Possessions of Satan were to make Way, and fit Souls for the* Quakers Spirit ; *Blasphemy and Idolatry.* Our Friends (*Quakers* so called) *Dark-Lanthorn-Men* ; *being fill'd with Palpable Knavery and Impudence* ; *Absurd and Blasphemous Idiots* ; *Prodigiously Wicked*; *O the Hell-Dark Expressions of the* Quakers Preachers *speak the amazing Delusions of Satan.* And in his *Vindication, A Presumptuous and Blind Accuser* ; *a Sophister*; *an* Haman ; *an Accursed* Ham ; *a Treacherous and Wilful Deluder* ; *a Madman* ; *an Hangman* ; *an Infallible Stager* ; *a Fool* ; *an Ape* ; *a Dunce* ; *an Impudent Forger*; and what not?

Is this to act like a FRIEND to the *Quakers*, or give *Testimony of a large Spirit and Principle,* as you (to make a foul Matter fair) have so untruly intimated? Doubtless, no Man hath taken more Pains to abuse a poor People, than *J. Faldo* hath to misrepresent the *Quakers* ; yet this very *Style* you more especially recommend: Can you yet think your selves *Learned, Reverend and Worthy Divines,* Men of *Conscience* and *Honour*? And the Truth is, you were very *hard put to it* to make up the *Recommendation* ; for in the Scope of four Pages, you *three Times* compare us to *Papists* and *Infidels* ; thrice charge and aggravate our designed Obscurity, with Abundance of *Impertinency* and *Contradiction* ; *four Times* go over our *Separation* from you ; and, *last of all,* you *five Times* charge us with *Singularities,* enlarge and grow Elegant upon it, *Repetitions, Tautology.*

And, by the Way, I must needs take this Notice of the *New Advertisement* in this *Impression.*

First, That the Advertiser most horribly abuseth us in saying, *We pretend all our Ministers to be Infallible.* More than ten Times over hath he both scornfully and untruly cast this at us: We ascribe not an *Infallibility* to Men, but to the *Grace of God,* and to Men so far as they are led by it ; for that it certainly teacheth what it doth teach.

Secondly, Whereas he insinuates, as if *I allowed of every Passage he cited, as of the Books and Authors themselves*: This is so great an Untruth, that many of them are *misquoted,* and almost every one of them *misapply'd* ; and this I have largely and frequently *complained* of in my *Answer,* and more particularly in my *Rejoynder.* I leave off *Wondering* at him ; for he seems to have prepared his *Conscience* for any thing that may countenance his Attempts against the *Quakers* ; which gives us Cause to suspect the Altering of the *Folio* of the *Old Book* in this *Impression,* is done on Purpose to hinder the *Reader* from finding his (in my *Answers* thereto referred) *Miscarriages.* But to you again.

Suppose we are as bad as you bespeak us ; how can you help it? Your Principle takes away all Liberty from our Wills, and tells us of being *ordained* to all these Mischiefs: Would you have us better than we can be? that is, to expect *Impossibilities* at our Hands? Or would you that we should attempt to *invalid God's Immutable* and *Absolute Decree,* which, besides that it cannot be done (allowing your *Notion*) were a great Impiety but to think of ; you should either change your Creed in this Particular, or seem less concern'd at the Event of Things confessedly *Irremediable.* I remember an Old Book published by *Three and Fifty Presbyterians,* some of whom help to make up your *One and Twenty Reverend Divines* ; it's call'd, *A Testimony to the Truth of Jesus Christ and our solemn League and Covenant,* (for you know they must go together) the Bent of it is to collect the then held *Errors,* and bitterly to exclaim on all that hold and plead for, or incline to favour a *Toleration* ; and such were *Episcopalians, Independents, Anabaptists,* &c. Among many other, these are brought in for capital Ones. 1. *HIERARCHY.* 2. *INDEPENDENCY.* 3. *An Opposition of the Doctrine of Election and Reprobation, as you hold it.* 4. *The Doctrine of the Freedom of Man's Will.* 5. *That Christ died for all Men, or that the Benefit of Christ's Death extended to all Men.* And some Leaves off, thus express themselves: ' Doubtless that old Serpent, call'd the ' *Devil,* hath been the grand Agent in propagating these *stupendious Errors,* all ' which *Errors, Heresies* and *Blasphemies,* we are confident we may *loath, execrate* ' *and abhor, and that without the least Breach of Charity.* O the Strength and Religion of this *Charity,* that can *loath, execrate, and abhor to think that Christ dyed for all Men, or that all Men may be sav'd!* as plain Scripture as any in Scripture. This they

they call the *Presbyterian Testimony*, which in plain *English* doth but *loath, execrate and abhor the Belief* of the Generality of *Christendom*. And that you may yet know your selves better, observe this Passage; *The Cursed Blasphemies; the General Looseness; the Spreading Heresies of our Times* have in a Manner *born down before them the Authority of the Sacred Scriptures, the Life and Power of Godliness, and our Solemn League and Covenant;* but above all, *Our Souls are wounded, to think with what Hope and Industry a* TOLERATION *of all these Evils is endeavoured.* Which in short amounts to this: 1. All that quadrate not with *Presbytery* is *Error, Heresy,* or *Blasphemy.* 2. That *above all Things it wounds them to think of having such tolerated as believe and maintain them.* This Doctrine (with some Allay) in the *Episcopacy*, you exploded for *Antichristian, Popish,* and *Tyrannical*. When through such *Pretences* you had mounted the Chair, by a notable Figure, call'd *Self-Interest,* it became an excellent Doctrine with you, yea a most necessary Part of your *Creed:* Pray tell me if this be imitating of God? Being Just to all Men? Doing as you would be done by? Can you yet be so blind as not to see your selves to be a great Way off from *Christian Charity,* and an universal *Communion of Christians*, that even make *Believing of plain Scripture*, a Reason *for your Abhorrence of their* Communion *that so believe;* unless they will subject such obnoxious Passages to *Calvinistical* Interpretations? Is not this like the *Egyptian Tyrant*, that stretch'd all longer that were shorter, and cut all *shorter* that were longer *than himself?* This shews, you *Cæsar-like*, would have had no *Equal,* and resolv'd to reign alone, come what will of those you now have learned to call *Christians:* It is but too manifest that the genuine Sense of your *Faithfulness* to promote *God's Cause and Interest, is* Your Selves.

But you are several Times angry with us for our *Separation*.

One and Twenty *Divines. They seek by Backbiting, Reviling and Reproaches, to disgrace the Doctrines, Practices and Persons of others, that they themselves may seem more excellent and glorious than all that have been excellent before them, and that they may not be thought unworthy of some Communion themselves, grow presently of Opinion, that all the rest of the World of profess'd* Christians, *are so ignorant, or so bad, as to be unworthy of Communion with them.*

W. P. Methinks that it is not only an ill Way to be thought more *Excellent* and *Glorious* than all that were *before* us; but that no Man that refuseth to captivate his Sense and Reason to serve the *Interest* of whatsoever you say or do, can believe that we should take such an improbable Way to *Glory:* Such juggling *Socinians* and *Papists,* as you make the chief of us to be, should better understand their Business, than to be guilty of so much broad and distastful Folly, in doing of it; but what cannot you say of the *Quakers,* who rather than not say enough will be impertinently *Tautological,* and say the same Thing in *four* Pages *five* Times over, to fix an *Odium* in the Minds of People against us: What is this but to do what you condemn?

But the Truth is, you have so well express'd the Matter for your selves, that an Unwary *Reader* would think you equally Enemies to *Separation,* and *Reviling* those you separate from. But of all Men this Language is most insufferable from you, who have transcended in the Guilt of those Things you seem so heartily to censure. You are made up of *Presbyterians* and *Independents;* let me a little Expostulate with you: *Argumentum ad hominem.*

I will begin with you who are called *Presbyterians;* Are you not *Separatists* from the Church of *England?* You know you are; And pray, what is the Ground of your *Separation?* Is it Difference in the *Essentials* of *Religion?* you know, you say, it to be only in some Matters of *Discipline;* for this you have divided your selves, and smartly vindicated your *Separation,* witness *Galaspee* in *Scotland,* and *Smectymnus* in *England*. Was it not a great Reason of the *Wars*, that divided so many *Families,* shed so much Blood, and exhausted so great a *Treasure?* Did it not lay *Episcopacy* in the Dust, and excite the *Parliament* in these very Terms? *Elijah opposed Idolatry and Oppression, so do ye: Down with* Baal's *Altars! Down with* Baal's *Priests! Do not, I beseech you, consent unto a Toleration of* Baal's *Worship in this Kingdom, upon any Politick Consideration whatsoever*. Which is as much as to say, Away with the *Archbishops, Bishops, the whole Ministry and Worship of the Church of* England. Again, *The Mouths of your Adversaries are opened against you, that so many Delinquents* (that is to say, Royalists) *are in Prison, and yet but very few of them brought to their Tryal* (Did he mean to release them?) And, saith another of your eminent Brethren before the Commons, *August* 28, 1644, *Ye cannot*

not *Preach* nor *Pray* them down *directly* and *immediately*—— *Well*, *That which the Word cannot do, the Sword shall:* To render which Saying authentick, the Apostle is brought in two Lines after. I could set out this Part of your Story to the Life, but at this Time shall forbear: Nor do I delight in this, but since I must needs mention *Your Separation*, how can I do it without telling who it was you separated from? And can I do it more candidly than *in your own Words*? I wish there had been no need for it: Only from hence you may observe your Sort of Dislike of *Separation*: and how notably *Presbyterians* revile even Men that are one with them in the Essentials of Religion.

Behold, a short Instance of your Carriage to the Church of *England* you separated from! Let us now take a short View of your Treatment of those that dissented from you: You shewed the *Independents* the Way, first to *separate* upon Conscience, and then to plead Conscience for *Separation*; and how reasonable it was that *Conscience* should be *Tolerated*. Are you constant to your selves? Do you give what you will take? No such Matter: But let us hear you. *Matters of Religion* (says Dr. *Corn. Burges* in his Sermon before the House of Commons, *Novemb.* 5. 1641.) *lye a Bleeding, all Government and Discipline of the Church is laid in her Grave; and all putredinous Vermin of old Schismaticks glory in her Ashes, making her Fall their own Rising to mount our Pulpits.* That the *Independents* are concern'd under the Term *Schismaticks*, Dr. *Cawdrey* bestows an whole Book upon it, which is Entituled, *Independency a great Schism*; yet some of these great *Schismaticks* are some of the *One and Twenty Reverend and Worthy Divines*. I find another of your Brethren, *Octob.* 22. 1644. that tells us of *Parliamentary Heresies*, saying, *You are the* Anabaptists, *and you are the* Antinomians; *these are your Errors, if they spread by your Connivance.* Was not this spoken like a Man of Charity, one that disdain'd not the *Communion* of other *Christians* that are not altogether of his Mind? A Virtue commended by you in your *Epistle*. Another eminent Person of your Way, before the Parliament, *Sept.* 12. 1644. *We are grown beyond* Arminianism, Brownism, Anabaptism; *we are come to the down-right* Libertinism, *that every Man is to be left to the Liberty of his own Religion: An Opinion most pernicious and destructive*, saith he. And another of your Brethren in his great *Zeal*, before the House of Commons, 1644. stiles them *Bastard Imps of the Whore of* Babylon: Though you know that many of you plead a *Romish Succession* for your *Ministry*, and consequently that you ministerially descend of what you call the *Whore*; think on't as you will. But all this is exceeded by a zealous *Presbyterian*, who in his Book, called, *The Gangrene*, &c. Part 1. p. 91. querieth thus; *Shall the* Presbyterians *Orthodox Godly Ministers be so cold, as to let* Anabaptism, Brownism, Antinomianism, Libertinism, Independency *come in upon us, and keep in a whole Skin, when Arch-Bishops, Bishops, &c. hazarded the loss of their Preferments to withstand the Toleration of Popery?* Where not only *Anabaptists* and *Independents* are rendred unworthy of a *Toleration* by this great *Presbyterian*; but their Perswasion rendred more intolerable than *Popery*. I would ask *G. Griffith*, *M. Barker*, *R. Mayo*, *M. Palmer*, *T. Cole* (who help to make up the *One and Twenty Learned and Reverend Divines*) if this Man was a *Wasp* or a *Bee*? one that had more of *Sting* or *Honey*? Well—what's his Resolution? *Let's therefore*, saith he, *fill all Presses, and cause all Pulpits to ring, and so possess Parliament, City and whole Kingdom against the Evil of Schism, and a Toleration, that we may no more hear of a Toleration, nor of separated Churches, being hateful Names in the Church of God*, Amen, Amen.

All I shall say of the Man is this; he was hearty in his Work, and what he did, he did with all his Might. Another of them runs so high, that he impeacheth *Gamaliel* for a *loose Naturalist*, *a Time-serving Politician*, *a second Achitophel*, and only because he was for *Toleration*; when you know, the rest of the *Jewish Council* were for *Persecution*: If you will not believe me, peruse *I. Ward's* Sermon before the Commons, 1645. How agrees this with your present *Desires of Indulgence, and Thanks for it*? Let me say, there is the same *Exception against you* upon this Doctrine, *as any other sort of Dissenters*: But, as ill as this Man thought of Worthy and Prudent *Gamaliel*, his Counsel hath been strong and seasonable, *even in Presbyterian Apologies*. But left you should reject these Evidences of your rank *Severity* to others, *though for minute Differences*, as being but the *Opinion of Three or Four Men*, I will conclude with the Judgment of the *Presbyterian* Ministers in the City of *London*, presented in a Letter to the Assembly of Divines sitting

ing at *Westminster*, 1645. INDEPENDENCY *is a Schism, they draw and seduce our Members from our Congregations; a Toleration of it will be followed with inevitable Mischiefs; They erect separate Congregations, under a separate and undiscover'd Government; They refuse Communion with our Churches in the Sacraments:* And are such Men fit to commend *Christian Communion* to others, who themselves break it, and impeach one another at this bitter Rate for doing so? But what follows? *The Godly, painful, Orthodox, Ministry will be discouraged and despised; the Life and Power of Godliness will be eaten out by frivolous Disputes and vain Janglings; it is too much to be doubted left the Power of the Magistrate, should not only be weakened, but even utterly overthrown, considering the Principles and Practices of* Independents, *together with their Compliance with other Sectaries, sufficiently known to be Anti-magistratical; Hereby we shall be involved in the Guilt of other Mens Sins, and thereby be endangered to receive of their Plagues; It seems utterly Impossible (if such Toleration should be granted) that the* Lord should be one, and his Name one, in the Three Kingdoms.

This seriously consider'd, let me ask you, if you did not think these *Independents* either so *Ignorant*, or so *Bad*, as to be unworthy of your *Communion with them*, or being so much as tolerated in their separated *Communion from you?* Certainly, if so small a Difference as that which remains between you and the *Independents*, finds not *Charity* enough with you to be tolerated, not only the *Quakers* have no Reason to expect *Toleration* from you, had you *Power* in your Hands; But there is great Need, that you should be ashamed of *Censuring others*, or being so *Narrow-spirited*, as not to *Commune with People of a different Perswasion in Matters confessedly of greater Moment*, than that upon which you have exercised so much *Gall*.

That You that are *Independents*, have thought the *Presbyterians* Unworthy of *your Communion*, it is needful only that we put you in Mind of your Separating from them, and sitting down in distinct Congregations under a different *Discipline and Administration of Ordinances*; The *Reason* of which, if we will believe the *Presbyterians* in the Account they gave to the *Parliament*, was, because you esteem them *Prelatical, Tyrannical and Anti-christian* in their Ministry: An ancient Acquaintance of mine, who had more Learning and Discretion than to be one of *your* Learned and Reverend Divines, in his Book against *D. Cawdrey*, doth affirm, *That Ministry that cometh through* Romish *Succession, and is no Ministry without it, can be no better than a* Romish *Ministry*; and the Truth is, I am of his Mind. *J. Cotton*, Brownists Apol. *J. Cann*, ancient *Independents*, also writ in Defence of *Separate* from *National Communion*.

From hence and that second great War between you and the *Presbyterians*, who should inherit what you had joyntly gotten from another Party, are none of the clearest Proofs to us of your Brotherly Love and Christian Communion, though a great Check to both of you for your turning Judges, who are such notorious *Criminals*; and yet I will not say but the *Presbyterians* Fury was your Provocation. In short; As the Reason you have both render'd of your Separation from the *Church of England*, and One from Another, is Greater Purity of Worship and Discipline; so *We* had never separated our selves from *you*, but upon the same Principle: And if this will not serve your Turn, when *You* that are *Presbyterians*, have given better Satisfaction to the *Church of England* for your separate Communion; and when *You* the *Independents*, have in the like Case answered the *Presbyterians*, and the *Anabaptists you*, *We* shall, we hope, not be wanting to our selves *in any necessary* Vindication *of Our Cause*.

I am sorry you have given me Occasion to remind you of your *Separation* among your selves: However, this deserves the Notice of all Impartial Readers, that though you were so *Bitter*, and all *Wasps* one against another for your Separation; yet that now you are Confederated against us without any other Provocation, than such as was the Cause your selves pretended for your own *Separation:* So that to use your own Words with better Reason, *You are the Men that have no Honey nor Sweetness of Spirit, except for your selves.* And I must needs say, that notwithstanding your *Reflection* upon us, as Destroyers of Christian-Communion, you have been so fond of your own Apprehensions, that many of your Way have lost the *Friendliness* so commendable in *Civil Society*; and some, no small Preachers neither, have vehemently *dehorted* their Hearers from so much as conversing with us, no not about the Lawful Things of this World, so far as may be avoided; nay, one of them was so extravagant as openly to profess, *He had rather his Hearers should go to a Baudy-House, than to a Quakers Meeting*: To such a Degree of Bitterness are some of you arriv'd, for all your Pretences to Charity. I am sure if you had had any Regard to those *Natural Truths*, you are forc'd to confess, make up Part of our Religion, viz. *To do as you would be done by; remembring that for all these Things God will bring you to Judgment*; you would never have dealt out such hard Measure to us; and it cannot be too much lamented, that Men will not make the best of their Accord, so far as they do accord; I mean what you do, if you mean what you write, viz. *That God so hateth the Evil, as yet to approve and love all that is Good; and that his Servants should not dispraise all in those whom they dislike:*

For, *We own ONE GOD; we fear him as well as own him; and through His GRACE are enabled to perform the Works of Righteousness, whose Fruit is Peace: We believe this Grace is communicated to us through Jesus Christ our Lord; that he is the Only and Compleat Saviour, as well from the Pollution as Guilt of Sin; that without his Holy Spirit we cannot please God; that therefore it is Reverently and Incessantly to be waited for, to inform, inable, and conduct, us through the whole Exercise of our Life, respecting our Duty towards God and Man; we also believe that there is an Eternal State for Sheep and Goats, Godly and Ungodly, and a Day in which God Almighty will judge the Secrets of all Men by Jesus Christ, rendring to every Man according to the Deeds done in the Body:* And this we do believe without any Mental Reservation whatever, and find daily Comfort both in Believing and Living accordingly; nor do I know that you in any Thing conrradict this, in Words, at least.

Now that your Zeal for your Way of Religion should transport you beyond all Natural Tenderness or Affection, as the Apostle renders it *(your Duty to every Man as he is God's Workmanship)* and then glory in so great a Vice, as a Christian Virtue, by terming it *Godly Zeal*, &c. which is no more but an Unwarrantable Heat for your particular Perswasions; I must needs say, is a great Way off from that Moderation that the Apostle exhorts us *to make known to all Men*. It is an ill Way of admiring Grace which destroys *Nature*, and such, I must needs say, some of yours is, or hath been, who have sacrificed *Universal Love, Natural Affection, Relation*, the *Liberties* and *Lives* of Men differently perswaded to the Promotion of your so much beloved Interests: Remember *T. Edwards's Gangrene*, and the *London-Ministers Petition*, and the *New-England* Tragedy. How exceeding short doth this fall of the Admirable Sweetness of his Nature, who is Lord of the *Christian Religion*, that was so far from Indulging Hatred to his Conscientious Friends, that he forbad it to his *greatest Enemies?* Can you call for Fire from Heaven upon *Dissenters*, and rather than not compass their Destruction, kindle *Fire on Earth* to devour them, and yet with any the least Pretence to Modesty check others for *Incharity* and *Separation?* But take this with you, that *good Notions* will signifie little to the Comfort of an *ill Soul* at God's Bar; it will not be *Well Held*, but *Well Done, Good and Faithful Servant*. Preferring Opinion before Piety hath filled the World with *Perplexing Controversies*, and *Men's Censures* have been according to Notion, not according to *Conversation*: It is not what *Works*, but what *Faith?* though *Works* best of all define and evidence what *Faith* is. But this Age hath no Kindness for *Good Works*; the more the Pity: Loose Men slight them in *Life*, and you in *Doctrine*; A Man cannot plead for them, but at the Hazard of being counted a *Papist*. Tell you, such an one is a *Virtuous Person*, and you answer us commonly, *He is a Good Moral Man, but he hath no Saving Grace*; as if *Grace* and *Morality* were at as great Distance as *London* and *Constantinople:* These Notions have abused *Religion*, and *greatly injured* the Souls of People; 1. By giving them to conceit themselves *Christians*, though *Unlike Christ*. 2. In Distinguishing between a *Good Man* and a *Christian*, from whence hath flown that Stinginess of Spirit, that denies any to have *Saving Grace* that fall not in with their *Principles*, and so divides *Grace* from *Virtue*, which God hath *Inseparably joyned*. This is the Doctrine that deceiveth Men, which makes them too great for the Rest of Mankind: *Moral Men* are no Company for them; they may be that, and go to *Hell* for their Pains, if what some of you say be true. It is the *Presbyterians* special Grace that saveth; for *Morality's Part*, alas! she is a poor *Heathen*, an *Alien*, an *Infidel, without the Pale of the Church, and Mercies of the Covenant*; but then it is to be understood of the *Scotch One*.

O! I beseech you for the Sake of Jesus Christ, by whom alone God will judge you and me in the *Dreadful Day of Account*; let the *Universal Principle* in your Consciences have Power with you; the Divine Fruit of which is, *first, A Discovery of Duty* to be done; and as closed with there, *next, Power and Ability to perform it*, which strips you of Self, and Glorying in it, and will work all necessary Works *In you* and *For you*: It will *first correct* and then *comfort* you; *It's Ways are Ways of Pleasantness, and all her Paths are Peace*; *To Faith it adds Virtue, to Virtue Knowledge, to Knowledge Temperance, and to Temperance Patience, and to Patience Godliness, to Godliness Brotherly-Kindness, and to Brotherly-Kindness* CHARITY. Contend not against it; your *Credit* is a *Temptation* to you; sacrifice it for the sake of your own and other Men's Souls upon the Altar of *Self-Denial*, and that Humble and Heavenly *Obedience* you owe to the God of the whole Earth; and think not *Repentance* a Work too *Mean* for you, because you have been so long Preachers of it to others; your Time hastens on, and in the Grave it will be too late: If it was *John*'s Honour to receive him when he came in Flesh; let it not be your *Judgment* to reject his Coming in *Spirit:* God knows I have no *Ill-will* but much Kindness for you; I wish you were as *truly taught* of him, as you are great *Teachers* of others: Could my Desires prevail, you should be such upon better Terms; but as *Wo* be unto them who are *sent* and don't *preach*; so *Wo be unto them who do preach and are not sent*; It is not hard in this Sense to be *Righteous overmuch*, to be too *Officious*, and to act *Thanklesly* for God.

O that we may all consider what we are *Building* with, and whether our *Works* will stand the Trial of God's Fire! whose *Terrible Day* hastens upon the World, in which he will severely plead with all Flesh that hath *corrupted it's Way* before him; as with the *Gentile*, so with the *Jew!* as with the *Prophane*, so with the *Professor*, Who hath had a Name to live, and yet will be found Dead, who calls himself a Jew, and yet *is not*; a Christian, and *is not*; who runs, and God hath not sent him; who cryeth, *thus saith the Lord*, and God hath never spoken by him: Let us therefore be perswaded into a Serious Examination of our selves, and Preparation for this Great and Notable Day of the Lord, that the Sound of the last Amazing Trump may not surprize us, nor any of us be overtaken at unawares, but in Godly Fear wait till our great Change comes, that with Holy *Habakkuk*, we may *all find Rest to our Souls in the Day of Trouble*, Amen.

Your Friend in much Sincerity,

WILLIAM PENN.

POSTSCRIPT.

AS for *his* Appendix, *it's an* arrant Cheat *obtruded upon the* Reader. *The* Title-Page *bespeaks it a* new Piece; *whereas it is no other in the* Matter, *and for a great Part of the Words of it, than what hath been answered by me again and again. It consists of two Parts*; 1. Two Letters *of our Friends, with his usual disingenuous* Discants; *which Letters are justified from his* Black Imputations *in my* Rejoynder, *and another Discourse, called* Judas and the Jews. *The second Part of the* Appendix *is a Collection of our* Principles, *which both in my* Answer *and* Rejoynder *I have prov'd to be his own Indirect and Foul* Consequences *from our Real Principles, which lye at his Door, or rather now at his* One and Twenty Learned and Reverend Divines, *that have so Imprudently espoused his Cause, and recommended his Endeavours.*

URIM

URIM and THUMMIM:

OR THE

Apoſtolical DOCTRINES

OF

Light and Perfection Maintained:

AGAINST

The Oppoſite Plea of *Samuel Grevill,* (a Pretended Miniſter of the Goſpel) in His Un-Goſpel-like Diſcourſe, againſt a Book, Entituled, *A Teſtimony of the Light Within,* Anciently Writ by *Alexander Parker.*

By WILLIAM PENN.

This then is the Meſſage which we have heard of Him, and declare unto you, that God is Light, *and in Him is no Darkneſs at all. If we ſay that we have Fellowſhip with Him, and walk in Darkneſs, we Lye, and do not the Truth: But if we walk in the* Light, *As He is in the Light, we have Fellowſhip one with another, and the Blood of* JESUS CHRIST *His Son, Cleanſeth us from all Sin,* 1 John i. 5, 6, 7.

The EPISTLE.

Candid Reader,

SINCE it hath pleaſed the Everlaſting God to viſit a poor deſpiſed People in this Nation, with a more direct, immediate and clear Sight, Senſe and Knowledge of *Him,* than heretofore they had, by the Shinings of His Eternal Life and Spirit in their Hearts, *thereby giving them a* True Diſcerning *of the* Ways and Worſhips *that have been in the World, which Gender towards meer* Outſide *and* Lifeleſs Formality; *and of that* Pure, Straight and Narrow Way, *that ſtands in the* Power of God, *and* Holy Life of Righteouſneſs, *many, very many, have been their* Trials, Exerciſes, *and* Deep Sufferings; *and that of* Slandering them, *and their* Moſt Precious Faith, *has not been the leaſt in their Eye; for by that* Practice, *hath the Enemy of* Chriſt's Kingdom *caſt ſuch* Miſts and Vails *over the* Truth, *as have obſcured the* Divine Beauty and Excellency *of it from the* Sight of People, *inſomuch that ſome have dreaded nothing more than the Reception of that* Principle, *which bears* True and Faithful Witneſs *for God in their own* Conſciences. *It is cryed down for* Inſufficient, *by ſuch as never tryed the Power and Efficacy of it, and termed a* Natural and Dim Light, *though It diſcovereth and inſtructeth Man, in, and about* Spiritual and Supernatural Things. *O that they would Obey this* Day of Small Things, *and remember,* That Obedience is far better than Sacrifice; *How much is there of the* Latter? *But how Little, O how very Little of the* Former! *What* Degeneracy *is there among all* Profeſſions? *Their* Tenderneſs *is withdrawing, their* Greenneſs *withering apace; and with the* Form *do they earneſtly contend, as the* Jews of Old, *againſt the* Very Power and Life of Godlineſs; *and ſee not that the* God of the World *has entred thoſe* Outſides of Religion, *wherein, perhaps, the* Lord *may formerly in* Condeſcenſion *have appeared, that he might lead them nearer to the* Subſtance it ſelf; *and for want of a* True Savouring Spirit *in this* Matter, Millions are deluded; *yea, ſo far, as therein, and therewith, to oppoſe a more* Clear and Heavenly Appearance *of God to the* Sons of Men; *thus do they reſiſt the* Viſitations of God's Love *to their* Souls, *and reject their own* Mercies. *O that an* Enquiring Tender Spirit *were more generally raised in the Hearts of People, that they would consider our Relation to the Latter Days, and how much it concerns them, in these* New-Covenant Times, *to be in Covenant with God ; which it is utterly impossible those should ever be, who rebel against the* Light, *by which he has Visited them with Daily Reproof and Instruction.* I have given Him, *said the Lord of his Son,* for a Light to lighten the Gentiles, and for my Salvation to the Ends of the Earth. This is that True Light, which enlightens the Souls of all, *as* John *testified,* 1 John 9. and the Nations of them that are saved, must walk therein. Come, let us walk in the Light of the Lord, *Isa.* 2. *This Measure of Light leads to God, who is* Light ; *and this* Measure of Grace and Truth, *guides the Soul unto Him, who is full of Grace and Truth, where Salvation is known, and* Plenteous Redemption *witnessed* ; *Blessings and Praises be to His Name for ever.*

Reader, *This Controversie, begun by* S. Grevil, *who calls himself a* Minister of the Gospel, *near* Banbury, *though briefly handled, is of great Weight* ; *for it consists of* Two Fundamental Doctrines of the Gospel, *and indeed the very Bottom of our Testimony, viz.* Christ's Manifestation of himself in the Hearts of His Children ; and the End of that Manifestation, *namely,* To make an End of Sin, destroy the Works of the Devil, finish Transgression, and bring in Everlasting Righteousness, *John* 1. 3. 5. 8. *Dan.* 9. 24. *These* Two Principles, *or rather* CHRIST JESUS Within, the Principle, and His Work, *compleat* Redemption, *are lately opposed by* S. G. *as laid down by* Alexander Parker, *in a Book by him set forth about Seventeen Years since. This is a* Sober Consideration, *and, I hope, a plain Enervation of his utmost Force, in* Defence of those Evangelical New-Covenant-Doctrines. *I recommend it to God's Witness in thy Conscience, who will Judge Righteous Judgment* ; *whose Servant I am, in Body, Soul, and Spirit, and whom I dare not but confess and vindicate before Men.*

WILLIAM PENN.

A General Defence of the LIGHT WITHIN, by Way of Introduction.

THO there be no Passage, or Proposition, to be found from one End of Holy Scripture to the other, more clearly laid down, than that in *John* 1. 9. *That was the True Light that Lighteth every Man that cometh into the World* ; yet so strong hath been the Envy, and so subtil the Endeavours of the Prince of Darkness, as scarcely any one Place hath been more wrested and abused, on purpose to hinder Mankind from minding the Manifestations of the Light, and yielding all ready Obedience to it, as the Way appointed of God to Eternal Life and Salvation.

Some will have it to be a *Natural Light*, though it be the *Very Life of that Word, which is God over All, Blessed for ever*, and wrapt up within those Verses, which only concern *His Eternal Power and Godhead*.

Others will have it read thus ; Not, that He Enlightens all Mankind, *but that all who are Enlightned, are Enlightned by Him* ; thereby, not only narrowing and wronging the Text, but rendring God so Partial and unjust to his Creatures, as to cause His Light of Righteousness to arise on some, without ever visiting the greatest Part of Mankind with so much as a Day of Salvation ; though he says, *He would not the Death of any, but rather that all should Repent, and come to the Knowledge of the Truth.*

There is a Third Sort, that will needs have it understood not of any Illumination by a Divine Light, or Spirit, but *the Life Christ lived, and the Doctrines He Preached, when Visibly in the World* ; which neither reacheth the Hundredth Part of Mankind, nor can be consistent with the Nature of that Part of *John's History*, which wholly relates to His Divinity, or what he was before he took Flesh.

'Tis true, Christ was the Light of the World in that very Appearance, and shined forth by His Heavenly Doctrine, and Self-Denying Life, a Most Holy Example ; yet not so, as to exclude himself from being that Spiritual Light, which shineth in the Hearts of the Sons and Daughters of Men. *He was full of Grace and Truth*, yet of his Grace hath Mankind received, *Grace for Grace*, which is that Grace of

God, that in all Ages hath appeared for Salvation; whose Nature and Property is so plainly described, and the Salvation it brings unfolded by the Apostle, 2 *Tit.* 11, 12. viz. *Teaching us, that denying Ungodliness, and Worldly Lusts, we should Live Godly, Righteously and Soberly, in this present World.* And so far is that Universal Light and Grace we testifie of, from leading us to undervalue Christ and the Scriptures, that we cannot but declare to all the World, in Pure Conscience towards God, and every Moderate Enquirer, that we never had any True Knowledge of God or Christ, any Right Sense of the Work of Conversion upon our Souls, nor any Right Sight or Relish of those Heavenly Truths declared in the Scriptures, till we came to know, and be Obedient to, the Manifestation of that *True Light,* which Enlightneth every Man; and the Appearance of *That Grace* which brings Salvation to our own Souls.

They are standing Truths: *That whatsoever may be known of God, is manifested in Man; for God hath shewed it unto him: That whatsoever is reproved, is made manifest by the Light; and that whatsoever doth make manifest, is Light,* Rom. 1. 19. Ephes. 5. 13. This cannot be *Natural,* unless of the *Divine Nature,* which reveals to Men *Divine Things.* 'Tis rare that we meet with any Adversary, who denieth it to reprove Evil, and to cherish that which is Good. And the Wise Man tells us, *That the Reproof of Instruction is the Way of Life,* Prov. 6. 23. If the Light reproves for that which is Evil, and that Reproof Seals up Instruction to Life Everlasting, how dare any call it a *Natural Light,* common to, yea, a Part of all Men in their Natural Estate, especially when the Apostle *Paul* hath so long since declared, *That the Natural Man receiveth not the Things of the Spirit of God; for they are Foolishness unto him; neither can he know them, because they are Spiritually discerned?* 1 Cor. 2. 14. Our very Case in Defence of the *Light Within,* against the *Wise Master-Builders of the Age.*

Nay, so far is Man in his Natural Estate from being acted and guided by this very Light, which our Enemies call Natural, that Christ himself saith, *He hateth the Light, neither cometh to the Light, lest his Deeds should be reproved:* But, on the other Hand, *He that doth Truth, cometh to the Light, that his Deeds may be made manifest that they are wrought in God,* John 3. 21. where it is evident, that the very Manifestation given, is Divine; much more the Nature of that Light that gives it. Indeed, how is it possible for Man to know Christ, who is Light, without Light? It was *John's* Message to Preach, *That God is Light,* 1 John 1. 5. The same Apostle testifies, *That the Blood of Cleansing is to be found of them that walk in the Light,* Ver. 7.

If any object, *That this is not that Light wherewith every Man is Enlightned,* The same Apostle in his History saith, *That in the Word was Life, and the Life was the Light of Men,* and that very Light *was the True Light that lighteth every Man that cometh into the World,* 1 John 4. 9. Let such give me as plain a Text against either the Sufficiency or Universality of the Light, if they can.

It's Properties and Effects prove it Divine, in that, First, *It manifests God,* Rom. 1. 19. Secondly, *It manifests Evil,* Ephes. 5. 13. Thirdly, *It is made the Rule of Walking by the Apostle.* See then that ye walk circumspectly, not as Fools, but as Wise, ver. 15. Fourthly, *It is made the Path to walk in,* John 8. 12. 1 John 1. 7. Isa. 2. 5. Come, let us walk in the Light of the Lord: And the Nations of them that are Saved, shall walk in the Light of the Lord, *Rev.* 21. 23. And so faith the Scripture of the Spirit of God. First, *In that it reproveth for Sin,* John 16. 8. Secondly, *In that it giveth Understanding, of the Things of God,* Job 32. 8. 1 Cor. 2. 10. Thirdly, *That it is a Rule for the Children of God to walk by,* Rom. 8. 14. For as many as are led by the Spirit of God, they are the Sons of God. Fourthly, *We are also to walk in the Spirit,* Gal. 5. 16. *This I say then, walk in the Spirit, and ye shall not fulfil the Lusts of the Flesh:* I hope none will deny that this Light, and this Spirit, must be of one and the same Nature.

But if any shall yet object, That this is to be understood of a Spiritual Light, and that ours is but a Natural one, I shall desire them to do Two Things, *First,* To prove that a Natural Light *doth manifest God, reprove for Evil, and cherish that which is Good,* since whatever is Part of Man in his Degeneration from God, is so far from giving one Good Thought, that it cannot rightly reprove an Evil One; and it is granted by our Adversaries, that what we call *Divine,* and they call *Natural Light,* can do both. Secondly, That in Case this Light be Natural, and can so manifest and reprove, that they would assign us some certain *Medium,* or Way, whereby we may truly discern, and distinguish, between the Manifestations and
Reproofs

Reproofs of the *Natural Light, from those of Divine Light*, since they allow the Manifestation of God, and Reproof of Evil, as well to the one as to the other. And I challenge them all to give us one Scripture that distinguishes between a *Natural and Spiritual Light Within*, reproving Evil, &c. They may with as much Reason talk of a Natural and Spiritual Darkness Within: 'Tis true, there is a Natural Darkness, to wit, the Night of the outward World; and there is a Spiritual Darkness, *viz.* the misty and clouded Understandings of Men, through Disobedience to the Light and Spirit of God: Let them assign us a third, or rather a second Darkness of the Understanding in the Things of God, if they can: Christ never distinguished between Darkness and Darkness, or Light and Light, in any *such* Sense, nor did any of his Disciples I ever read of; yet both have frequently spoken of Darkness and Light; what Difference doth the Scripture put, between Spiritual Darkness, and Darkness mentioned in these Places, *Luke* 1. 79. *Math.* 4. 16. *John* 1. 5. *Joh.* 3. 19. *Joh.* 8. 12, 35, 46. 1 *Thes.* 5. 4. 1 *Joh.* 1. 6. *Acts* 26. 18. *Rom.* 13. 12. 2 *Cor.* 6, 14. *Ephes.* 5. 8. *Col.* 1. 13. I find none; It is all one Spiritual Darkness: Neither is there so much as one Scripture that affords us a Distinction between *Light Within* and *Light Within*, that really are Light; peruse *Math.* 4. 16. *Luke* 2. 32. chap. 16. 8. *Joh.* 1. 4, 5, 7, 8, 9. chap. 3. 19. 20, 21. chap. 8. 12. *Acts* 26. 18. *Rom.* 13. 12. 2 *Cor.* 4. 6. chap. 6. 14. *Ephes.* 5. 8. 13. *Col.* 1. 12. 1 *Thes.* 5. 5. 1 *Tim.* 6. 16. 1 *Pet.* 2. 9. 1 *Joh.* 1. 5. 7. chap. 2. 8. *Rev.* 21. 23, 24. chap. 22. 5. And let the greatest Enemy to our Assertion do his utmost to sever Real Light from Light, or find out Two Lights in these Passages if he can; if he cannot, he is irrecoverably gone, and that upon his own Concession: For, as he yields to us, that the Light in Controversie manifesteth Evil, and reproveth for it; so doth Christ himself teach thus of the Light, John 3. 12. *For every one that doth Evil hateth the Light, neither cometh to the Light, lest his Deeds should be reproved:* And the Apostle *Paul* plainly saith, Ephes. 5. 13. *But all Things that are reproved, are made manifest by the Light*; Therefore not Two distinct Lights in Kind, but one and the same manifesting, reproving Light: And this the Apostle *John* proves beyond all Exception, to Wise and Considerate Men; *First*, In that he calls God *Light*, c. 1. 5. *Secondly*, In that he puts no *Medium*, or Third Thing, between that Light and Darkness, ver. 6. *If we say that we have Fellowship with him, and walk in Darkness, we lye*; intimating, that Men must walk either in Light or Darkness. I am sure, that which manifests and reproves for Darkness, cannot be Darkness; And so say our Adversaries of our Light. And as if the Apostle *John* would have anticipated their Objection, viz. 'Tis true, *your Light within reproves for Evil*; *but it is not therefore the Divine Light, which leads into higher Things, and which comes by the Gospel*; He thus expresseth himself, Chap. 2. *Darkness is past, and the True Light now shineth. He that saith, He is in the Light, and hates his Brother, is in Darkness even until now*, which is not another Light from God the Light, Chap. 1. For, as Light there is put in Opposition to Darkness, so Light here is put in Opposition to Darkness: The Darkness is one and the same, so the Light; Wherefore we may plainly see, that it is not another Light than that which reproveth a Man for hating his Brother, that brings a Man into Fellowship with God, and to the *Blood of Cleansing*, as the next Verse speaks: Therefore that Light which reproveth a Man for hating his Brother, is of a Divine Nature.

In short; That Light which is opposite to, and reproves spiritual Darkness, is a spiritual Light: But such a Light is that within, as our Adversaries themselves confess; therefore Spiritual. It is worth our Notice that the Apostle useth the same Manner of Expression here, Chap. 2. 8. *The* TRUE *Light* shineth, that he doth in his History, Chap. 1. 9. *That was the* TRUE *Light*, intimating the same Divine Word or *True* Light now shineth; and that it was that same *True* Light (for there is but one) that reproved such as hated their Brethren; consequently that Light, that so reproveth, is the True Divine Light.

And strange it is that Christ and his Disciples, but especially *John*, should so often make that very Light, which stoops to the lowest Step of Morality, to the Reproof of the grossest Evils, to be no other than the same Divine Light, that brings such as follow it to the Light of Life, and those who walk in it to the Blood of Cleansing, and to have Fellowship with God, &c. Nay, not only so, but make the very best of Man's being a Child of God, to depend upon his answering of the Light in a palpable moral Case, *viz. Not hating of his Brother*; And yet that our Adversaries should shut their Eyes from beholding it's Divinity, and

and conclude it therefore a meer Natural Light; This is both Unreasonable and Unscriptural.

But here is the very Ground of their Ignorance and slight Apprehension of the Light within, They have never known it farther than in the Capacity of a Reprover of Evil, (though that's enough with a considerate and tender-spirited Man to feel from whence it came) and so conclude it unable to give either farther Discoveries of God's Will, or Power and Virtue to enable to do it. But to all such as object against the Sufficiency of the Light of Christ within, either as to it's Knowledge or Power, I say, *Try it*; you are not proper Judges in the Case, 'till you have walked in it: If then you meet not with the Blood of Cleansing, and pure Fellowship with God, who is Light, it will be Time enough for you to object. Do not infer from the Discovery of small and great Things, two distinct Lights, instead of two Manifestations of one and the same Light; such as do the Will of God, so far as the Light in the Conscience enjoins them, shall know more of the Doctrine it teacheth all the Children of Light.

However, it hath pleased the Man we have now to deal with, to undertake a Refutation of a Book, entituled, a *A Testimony of the Light within*, written about Seventeen Years since, by *Alexander Parker*, a Servant of God in the Work of his Gospel: But I hope my Reader hath receiv'd that Satisfaction in what has been already hinted in Defence of the Light of Christ within, that he is in a very good Posture to hear what may be objected against it, by one that never yet knew the Power and Efficacy of it. It is the Advantage God hath given us over our Enemies, They fight us Blind-fold, and entangle themselves in their own Net: With Moderation, Plainness and Brevity, I have considered his Opposition, in Faithfulness to God, his Truth, and the Souls of all People.

Urim and *Thummim*, &c.

SAmuel Grevill, in his Rejoynder to *A. Parker*, p. 5, brings two Places against the Sufficiency of the Light within: The first is *Deut.* 31. 13. *That their Children which have not known* any thing *may hear and learn to fear the Lord your God, as long as ye live in the Land whither ye go over* Jordan *to possess it*. But this is answered without Difficulty; for *any thing* is not in the *Hebrew*: And it appears both from the Place it self, and Chap. 11. 2. that those many great and wonderful Works of Deliverance the Lord had wrought for them, and which their Children through *Non-age* knew not, were only intended; And because the Hearing of them might be a deep Engagement upon their Spirits to fear and worship the God of their Fathers, therefore were they to hear of those Noble Acts at the Mouths of their Parents, as the Place speaks. How this Instance proves the Insufficiency of the Shinings of Christ's Light in the Conscience, with Respect to their Duty to God and Man in that Day, is left with every Man of Sober Conscience to judge.

The other is 2 *Tim.* 3. 15. The Words, *Through Faith in Christ Jesus*, he omits: The Scriptures, *through* Faith, are able to make Wise, but not *without* Faith: This doth not prove that therefore Faith cannot make wise without the Scriptures; for that was before the Scriptures were written, as in *Abraham* and others.

To *John* 16. 2. They thought and apprehended, the Scripture commanded them to do God good Service, when they persecuted the Saints. Doth this set the Scriptures above the true Light, by which only we must rightly understand them? Not that we would exclude the Scriptures of that Service the Lord has appointed them to, but to maintain the true Light against vain Cavils; for God's superadding of Scripture, no more renders the Light Insufficient, *than the Spirit, Grace, yea, God or Christ*; Man being abroad from the Spirit, and not abiding in the Light, the Lord went forth into outward Means to bring him Home: *Is God's Condescension to Man's Weakness a Proof of his Insufficiency?* The Scriptures came from the Light, and testify of it, that the Nations of them that are saved must walk in it; This was the End of the Evangelical Ministry. And as for taking true Light from the Scriptures, without true Light within, how absurd and impossible it is, is obvious to all. That Light, that gives to understand the right Meaning of the Scriptures, must be true Light; else, how can it understand right? And how can it be put in us by the Scriptures, *when we must and do bring it with us to the Scriptures before we read them?* Doth the Bible send forth a Spirit to read it with? Or doth God send it from it? Or doth not he rather illuminate the Soul to understand it, as all the Ancient Fathers and Protestant Writers held? See what Testimony this Man gives for his pretended Light without, against the Light within; and after what Rate he disproves it, to satisfy his Neighbour: He manifestly sets the Scripture and the Light within that Harmonize at Variance.

But shall the *Evil, Envy, Pride, Passion, Murder and Darkness* then in the *Jews*, Discredit, Undervalue, or render Insufficient the blessed Light of the Lord, that at that Time shined in them (though their Blindness and Darkness comprehended it not) Why may I not as well say, they had no Scriptures, or that they did all those infamous, hardned Acts against Christ, by the Scriptures (since they thought so) as that *S. Grevill* should infer the one or the other against the Light within? Every Man hath Light from the Creating Word, and that is Divine, because the very Life of that Word; and by it, God, who is Light, is only truly known; and while Men hear, obey, and live in the Counsel of it, they walk in the Way of Truth and Path of Life, they feel the Light of Life, and experience the Blood of Jesus Christ to cleanse them from all Sin.

To his Answer about Perfection, *viz. That he pleads not for Sin, because he denies perfect Freedom from it, since he pleads for Sin, that telleth Men, they may Sin.* I say, If any hear an Advocate plead that such a Man must break the Law as long as he lives, will it not be understood, that he pleads for a Toleration of him in the same Evils after he hath been pardoned? But if any hear him plead, that the Law-makers say the same (that is, the Teachers) will they not conclude, that he makes them tolerate Injustice, that he blasphemes and slanders them, as the Word signifies? yet this is S. G's Case in Point of *Indulgence of Sin.*

To his other Comparison, p. 6, viz. *Who favours a Disease most, He that prescribes to his Patient to take Antidotes, or He that tells him, He has no Disease, nor needs to use any Means?*

I answer, He weakens a Man most, that perswades him, That his Disease is so rooted, that it is impossible for him to overcome it, yet prescribes Remedies, and puts the poor Man to Cost.

Nor doth Christ say, That all Men must offend, and that as long as Heaven and Earth endures; *but that one Jot or Tittle from the Law shall not pass, till all be fulfilled: And he that breaks one of the least of these Commandments, and teacheth Men so, shall be called Least in the Kingdom of Heaven*, Mat. 5. 19. And if the least be not to be broken, then all ought to be kept.

Because *A. P.* faith, *Where God is manifest within, he must needs be Light*; S. G. would make him to conclude, That *God, Christ and the Spirit are the Light within us.* It seems he dares not fasten his Consequences upon the Scriptures, but upon what *A. P.* alledgeth out of them: And doth not S. G. deny them by Consequence, as he denies the King that denies the King's Writ, since they hold forth that very Doctrine. If to reject Scripture be Erroneous, *S. G.* cannot be found, that makes that Consequence Matter of Error, which he himself acknowledges to be Scriptural: Hear him.

If *A. P.* intended not, that God and Christ are the Light within; to what Purpose did he alledge those Scriptures, which say, God *is* Light, and God *is in us*: Christ *is* Light, and Christ *is in us*? Which, Reader, if I understand any Thing, is to allow, that we have Scripture for our Assertion, and to give up the Cause as far as ever we contended for it, to wit, That God *is* Light, and Christ *is* Light, and as such, do *shine or appear in the Hearts of Men*, to give them the Knowledge of those Things which concern their Eternal Peace.

But S. G. says, *If Christ were the Light within, the Prophet would not have said, They have no Light in them.* That *Christ is the True Light*, John testifies, and that he was and is such a Light, *as was to enlighten the* Gentiles, the Prophet *Isaiah* tells *us*; and that *the Nations of them that were saved, were to walk in this Light*, *John the Divine*, in his Revelation, assures us. Now, unless the Soul of Man be not to be lighted with this Light, or that it is not to be understood of the Soul, but Body only, that was to walk in the Light of the Church; it will follow, that this Light must needs shine where the Soul of Man is, which is within; consequently, that Christ is that Light which shines within.

Paul,

Paul, that took Counsel to persecute Christ without, was struck at the Appearing and Shining of Christ within; *and when it pleased God to reveal his Son in him* (the true Light that enlightens all Mankind) *he consulted not with Flesh and Blood*, which is their State that reject and vilify his spiritual Appearance and Revelation of him in the Soul: But for all their vain Expectations and loud Boasts, in that State they shall never inherit the Kingdom of God; that is God's Word of Truth. As to the Prophet's Words, they are not to be understood, as if those wicked Men had no Light from God; but that they rebelling and blinding themselves against it, and following their own Imaginations for Truth, *They had no Light in all their Ways*; or, as S. G. well says, *Their conceited Light was Darkness*; *They walked in Darkness, and so participated or partook not of the Benefit and Blessing of the Light; but it shined in Darkness uncomprehended*: There was Light, *but it was not risen upon him, or no Morning risen in him*, as the Words may be rendred: Is there no Sun in the Firmament, because Men that are blind, or shut their Eyes, cannot, or will not see it? Or, Is a School-Master Unlearned or Insufficient, because any of his Lads play Truant, and neglect his Reproof and Instruction? Or, Is it reasonable for any of us to say, that such Scholars have no School-Master, because they are idle and regard not their Book, notwithstanding his daily Checks and Reprehensions of them? Or, Can they be said to have no Lesson, because they neglect to get it?

In short, Christ is the great Priest, Prophet, King, Judge and Law-giver under the New Covenant: He is the Shepherd that daily overlooks and feeds his Flock; and such as know not him so revealed in them, to be the very Hope of their Glory, are in a Reprobate Estate: And how he should be within, and not be Light, who is the true Light it self, from whom all they that have Divine Light, received it, will lye on S. G's Part to shew. And so far are we from lessening the Scriptures thereby, *That they are they which testify of Christ to be the true Light that enlightens all*: And with their Holy Record have we great Unity, and our Souls bless God for them, and the Benefit we have received, and yet do, in reading of them, through the Revelation of his Holy Spirit, without which they are but a sealed Book; as well said Learned Bishop *Jewel* against *Harding*, p. 532, 534.

In Page 7, he would set these as Contraries, *Great Light and No Light*, as without a *Medium*; and so argues, *Because Great Light was before deny'd to the* Ephesians, c. 2. 12. *therefore they had no Light*, and so make as if God had left himself without a Witness amongst them, which is a worse State than the *Lycaonians*, who had a Sense of his Wisdom, Power and Goodness from his visible Works, which outward Witness had been Insufficient, without an * inward Witness to join with it, and evidence it more closely unto them. No better Success had the Preaching of the Gospel had among the *Ephesians* without it, which because their Light in Time of their Ignorance of those Things, which then in due Time God revealed unto them in a greater Measure, did not teach (it being too high for their State) Therefore by his Consequence they had none, nor any before that Time: *For the † Mystery was hid from Ages and Generations, that then was made manifest to his Saints*; for if they had, as he seems to reason, *it would have taught them* Baptism, Supper, *&c.* Nay farther, as he argues, *All the Opinions that the* Episcopalians *and* Presbyterians *hold, Common Prayer or Directory, whether you will*; and not only to *Thou* and *Thee* Magistrates, as they did always, *but to stir up People for them or against them, as serves their own Interest*.

It is true indeed, an Outward Literal Knowledge of these Things, by the Help of Literature, as Men now have them, the *Jews* and *Gentiles* had not; for they were not written, as they are now, with Ink, but *with the Spirit in the Heart*, and they resisting that, could not know him * outwardly, because (though they knew

---

* *Paul* teaches, that whatever is reproved, is made manifest by the Light *Ephes.* 5. 13. And whatever may be known of God, is manifested in Man, *Rom.* 1. 19. And that which manifests is Light, as saith the same Apostle, *Ephes.* 5. 13. And he desired to be made manifest to the Conscience. Then there was Light; for Men were reproved, *Rom.* 2. 15. and they could not be reproved without it, *Ephes.* 5. 13.

† Was not that Mystery the great Work of Redemption? And were not Thousands redeemed before? If it was hid, it was to such as had lost it by Rebellion. It was the same Light, not the same Degree that ever saved.

* This proves not they had no Light; at most, it only shews to us, that it did not shine so clearly forth, which still implies, that it was the same in Nature. How could those in *Job* rebel against the Light,

1674

knew the Words and Sentences, yet) they knew not the Voices and Senses of the Prophets, but look'd for a Conqueror like *David*; as the Gentiles, like *Jupiter*, &c. And why may not Men now, with their Light he speaks of, mistake the Scriptures of the New, as they then did of the Old Testament, as he saith, *the* Quakers *may do with theirs*; unless he can prove, that his Light is the true one, because he says it is *Natural Reason*, and the *Quakers* false, because they maintain it to be of the *Divine Nature, Word, Reason* or *Wisdom*, that was in the Beginning with God, and was and is God, as say several Fathers in our Defence: For *Christ* that lightens every one that comes into the World, is call'd λόγ⊙, the *Word* or *Reason* of God, who as *Irenæus* saith, *Rationabiliter & sensibiliter Legem statuit*, established the Law reasonably and sensibly. And *Ardentius* interprets λόγο', in *Iren. Verbum, Sermo, Ratio*, Word or Reason. And saith *Irenæus*, p. 326. *Man, being made reasonable, lost Reason, and living unreasonably, gave himself over to the Earthly Spirit*, Psal. 48. 21. And *Justin Martyr* saith, that Christ was πᾶς λόγ⊙, *whole Reason*, as his Interpreter *Langius* renders it; and that which the Philosophers and Poets conformed to, was σπερματικὸς λόγε μέρ⊙ μετεσία, *a Part or Partaking of the Reason that was sown*; and he saith, *The Seed of the Word or Reason is sown or ingrafted in all kind of Men*, p. 46. And *Origen*, his Author, useth almost the same Words, *The Law sown in the Soul by common Notions, and the Word written in the Heart*. And *Justin*, in the Place quoted, makes ἔννοια and λόγ⊙, common Notion, and *Word or Reason*, and Nᾶς, or *Mind*, Synonymous, or of the same Signification, as *Origen* and *Irenæus* do; Almost the very Words of some of the Ancient Philosophers; For *Plotin* calls it *a Divine Principle, that makes the good Man, which* says he, is the *Root of the Soul*. And *Cleanthes, The Eternal Nature, sown and diffused through the Race of Man, and is the most sure and infallible Guide*, *Hieron* calls it a *Domestick God*; Seneca *diffused Reason*; Epictetus, *God within*; Plutarch, *a living Rule, interior Guide, and Everlasting Foundation of Virtue*; Philo, *The Immortal Law, engraven on the Minds of Men, no lifeless Precepts written on Paper, &c.* Nor do Modern Writers much, if at all, vary: *David Paræus*, another of his Authors, saith, in *Ursin*'s Body of Christian Doctrine, augmented, corrected and consummated by him, Quest. 6. *The Image of God contains all the Natural Notions of God, of his Will and Works, that is, perfect Wisdom in the Mind, perfect Righteousness and Holiness in the Heart, and all outward Actions. Perfect Wisdom is here said*, saith he, *not that which is ignorant of nothing; but that which is competent to a created Nature sufficient to it's Felicity*: So there is an Homonymy or double Signification of the Word *Perfect*. And in Quest. 92, he saith, *We were created, redeemed, and sanctified to this End, that we should* KEEP THE LAW MORAL AND NATURAL, BEING THE SAME IN THIS LIFE AND THE ETERNAL, IT NOT BEING ABROGATED AS TO OBEDIENCE. Now these Men, as *Irenæus* said of the Poets and Philosophers, *Every one seeing that which was connatural, from Part of the Divine-sown Reason, spoke excellently and where right, and consistent with themselves, they are ours*; so far *Irenæus*. And the Reader may take these quoted, better from us, than S. G's, from him, upon meer Trust.

Some Ancient Fathers and Protestant *Writers expound the Word* Nature *as I do*, says S. *Grevill*, if you will trust him: I say the like of my Exposition, and have already quoted them, and told him how far I credit them; and therefore in Pag. 8. he wrongs the *Quakers*; for they would not cite them if they gave no Credit to them, as he would have People to believe, as *Paul* would not have quoted the Greek Poet, if he had not believed that to be Truth that he said concerning God, *That we are his Off-spring*; which he brought to prove, that he is not far from every one. On which Place *Grotius* cites, *for the Essential Presence of God*, as he terms it, several *Heathens, Jews* and *Christians*, no fewer than Ten: I shall instance but in one. *Minutius Felix*, who says, *God is every where, not only very near us, but infused*; which because *A. P.* said not expresly, though S. G. charges him to say it by Consequence, he makes it *A. P*'s Principle, to shut it out of Men, (who charges it for an Error that he dwells in Men) and all that is not by Genera-

---

Light, if they had it not? *Codurcus, Drusius, Clarius, Vatablus* and others, are not of his Mind; for it is an invincible Truth, that such as rebelled against the Light, as *Job* 24. 13. and God's good Spirit, as *Nehem.* 9. 20. 26. (notwithstanding their Formality and External Preciseness) could not receive Christ Jesus; but crucified him when he came.

ration,

John 1. 9.
Prov. 8. 4. 31.
Iren. l. 5.
c. 18.

Justin Martyr
Apol. pro
Christianis,
p. 51.

Origen Commen. on *Rom.*
2. 14.
p. 428.

Stan. Vit. Philosop.

Ursin & Paræus Quest. 9.

Quest. 92.

Acts 17. 27.

Grot. on that Place.

Pag. 1.

tion, p. 8. And so not only many primitive and latter *Christian* Doctors, but also many others, that deny the rational Soul to be *ex traduce*, or by Generation, but infused, to be as great Blasphemers, as he would make the *Quakers*. And if he can produce neither Scripture (as I am sure he cannot) nor ancient nor modern Writers, for his Gift of the Spirit that comes by Generation, *He must be the Author of that new Doctrine*: A Gift or Grace is not one's Self, nor a Part of one's Self, nor one's own originally; but another's, freely conferred; χαρισθέντα, *Graces or Things freely given*.

1674.

Pag. 3.

He says, *To do as we would be done to, is sown in our Natures*; then the Seed of the Law and the Prophets contain'd what more eminently appeared, and was extended in the Gospel, even to the Love of Enemies, with the Reason of it; *for if you love them that love you, &c.* which the *Gentiles* had in them in Effect, tho' not in Letters. And *D. Paræus* saith, *In the State of Sin, a Man is not apt to do or think any Good of himself according to the Scriptures*, Ephes. 2. 9. and 2 Cor. 3. 5. &c. Then neither the Law, nor the Work of the Law, *was of themselves*, else how could they condemn them that had the Law, and transgressed it. And the Scripture saith, *That which may be known of God is manifest in Men*; *for God hath shewed it to them*; and *God hath shewed unto thee, O Man! what is good*, &c. Mic. 6. 8. which *S. G.* denies, calling it a Special Presence; from what Ground, he shews not, nor can he; for the Manifestation is common and universal, the Words therefore prove it; consequently, there is a common Presence; and indeed a special Manifestation implies a Common.

Luke 6. 31. 32.
Rom. 2. 14, 15.

David Paræus in his Epitome of Arminian. Artic. 3.

Rom. 1. 19.

He cavils about the Word *Perfect*, distinguished before out of *Paræus*, and tells of Darkness dwelling with Light, and Ignorance with Knowledge; I know not for what, unless it be to confess to us, That his Knowledge is not without Ignorance: But it seems he is afraid, lest his Kingdom of Darkness, Ignorance and Sin, should be destroy'd; therefore proceeds to write against a *Freedom from Sin in this Life*, and to oppose the Expositions of the Fathers and Protestant Doctors (which it seems are of less Credit with him than the *Quakers*) that hold, *That the Doctrine in Christ's Sermon, tends to a Righteousness beyond that of the Law*, charging them, as if they meant, that Christ set up a Righteousness or a Law, above his own Perfect, Everlasting, Spiritual Law, which some call Natural and Moral; " The same in " Nature, *saith Origen*, Entire, agreeing with the Eternal and Immoveable Rule " of Righteousness in God, abiding the same from the Beginning to the End " of the World; and therefore were we Redeemed and Regenerated by the Holy " Ghost, that we should keep this Law in this, and the Life Eternal, that is, Love " God and our Neighbour with all our Heart, not a New Doctrine, but the Old, " which was from the Beginning: Which Law Natural, *Noah* and *Abraham* kept " (*saith Tertullian*) and were Justified in it. *And farther*, In this Primordial and " General Law of God given to *Adam*, were all the Precepts of the latter Law gi- " ven forth in their Seasons; for, What Wonder, if he increase the Discipline " who Instituted it? And God at a certain Season exhibited a subsequent Law to " the *Gentiles*; and that which was promised again by the Prophets, Reformed " to the Better, that it should be kept.

Every Grace, or Gift of God, is Perfect, Jam. 1. 17.

Psal. 19. 7. 9.
Rom. 7. 14.
Ursin. Qu. 92. and Paræus.
Orig. Com. ad Rom. pag. 428.
1 John 2. 7.
Tertul. adverf. Judæos Sect. 2. & dr Coron, Sect 6. See Chrysostom To. 1 Hom. 17. Oecumen on Jam. 5. 12. Basil on Psal. 14. Hil. on Mat. cap. 4.
Gal. 3. 10. verf. 19.

These are their Words, which shew what Law was meant; namely, the Law of *Moses*, which was added because of Transgression, *till the Seed should come*; before which Time, many Things were winked at, and suffered, because of the Hardness of their Hearts, that from the Beginning were not so, which Christ brings to, that He might recover all that was Lost, and so give Power by His Spirit, to them that walk after it, that his Law might be fulfilled in them, in the Everlasting Righteousness of it, the very End of his Coming, " The Law being obscured by " the Fall, much obliterated and lost, lest the Relicks in the Minds of Men might " be thought to be an Opinion, GOD Prepared It, *saith Ursin*; which they that " walked after the Flesh could not keep, and the Knowledge of it did only condemn " them, and in that Manifestation and Capacity might be said to be Weak, and all " those Rites and Sacrifices added, ever unable to purifie the Conscience: *But they " that Love Him, keep His Commandments, and they are not Grievous*. So that it was the Relicks of the Law Natural repeated in the Decalogue, that Christ (as they say) came to set up a Righteousness beyond; and not only to repeat and confirm the Relicks, but restore the Whole in due Season, and bring on the Perfection, *to be Merciful* (as saith *Calvin* himself) *and Love Enemies*, " Beyond which *Remigius* saith (as *S. G.* cites) there can be no Love; and therefore having commanded this, " Christ saith, *Be ye Perfect*; this being the Perfection of Love. Perfect Love

Verf. 24, &c. Origen ut supra.
Rom. 8. 1, 2, 3, &c.
Mat. 18. 1.
Acts 3. 21.
1 John 3. 5. 8.
Titus 2. 14.
in loc. citat.
Bishop Sanderson de Conf. regul. prælect. 4. Sect. 31.
Heb. 9. 9.

1 John 5. 3.
Calvin.
Remigius.

casts

casts out Fear, and is the Fulfilling of the Law; And he that loveth God, keepeth His Commandments.

1 John 4. 18.
John 14. 15.
Rom. 13. 10.
Pag. 10.

But *S. G.* pag. 10. having taken away their Distinctions, by his Distinctions of the Moral Law, comprehending all Ceremonies, &c. relating to the Old Testament and New, under the Name of *Parker*, he tacitly chargeth not only *Remigius* and *Calvin*, but also *Chrysostom*, and many other *Fathers* and *Doctors* quoted, to be of the same Mind with the *Scribes* and *Pharisees*, in their Narrow Interpretations of the Law in some particular Precepts of it; for this he flings on *A. P.* for saying but the same Things; while indeed it is to be feared that *S. G.* is one of those who rest satisfied with a Partial and Outward Observation of Things, making void, or at least, declining the Weightier Matters of the Law, since he suggests, that an Endeavour is enough without keeping them.

But of the Difference of the Times and States under the Law and Gospel, in Manifestation and Power, he says nothing, whatever he knows; for that would cross his Interest grounded on this Kingdom of Sin, in putting an entire End to it: But how can he without Hypocrisie, say in the Lord's Prayer, *Thy Kingdom come, Thy Will be done in Earth as it is in Heaven*; whilst he is so far from believing it, and promoting it, that he sets himself to oppose it, and dispute against it? And how can the doing of God's Will in Earth, as it is in Heaven, stand with Praying for Forgiveness of Sins all their Life long? What doth this but over-turn the whole Condition of the Gospel: *Unless thou takest up my Cross, and follow me, thou canst not be my Disciple?*

He is not (I perceive) for being Baptized with the Baptism Christ was Baptized with; nor for Drinking of that Bitter Cup he drank of; He is rather for hushing himself and others asleep in this pernicious Hope, *That Christ hath taken up the Cross, been Baptized, and drank that Bitter Cup for them, and so they need not do it over again*; otherwise he would not dare to hold and maintain such a Continuance of Imperfection as he doth. He is not of the Apostle's Mind, that prayed for a Sanctification of the then Believers, not in Part, *but throughout, in Body, Soul and Spirit*. God will bring down this Kingdom, and it shakes already.

Pag. 11.

Pag. 11. As to his Reconciliation with God in his Continuation in Sin, they are inconsistent, considered in the same Degree: So that we may truly say, Whilst there is no Separation from Sin, there is no Reconciliation with God; but if there be Separation from Sin in some Measure, there is Reconciliation with God in some Measure: As Separated, so Reconciled; perfectly Separated, perfectly Reconciled: As we see in Natural Things, so full of Air, so empty of all else.

But he makes *A. P.* to say, *Till a Man be perfectly Separated from Sin, he is altogether out of Reconciliation with God*; but proves it not, nor indeed is such Doctrine proveable out of his Book.

Whereas he says, *God's Commandments do not shew Man's Power:* If he mean the Power that is given of God to Man, it is false; for that were to make God Unjust, and an Hard Master; for, where-ever God commands, it follows, that He hath given Power to do: And where He is not obeyed, it is a Sign that *that* Power is withstood, lost, or taken away, and Man hardened through Disobedience. And without that Principle of Faith and Love, by a meer Performance of Outward Observations, to think that a Man may be Justified, which only fulfills the Law, is as impossible and absurd, as if a Man should think one should rather live by Virtue of Outward Raiment or Apparel, than by Bread and Substantial Nourishment.

Gal. 3. 12.

God gave such a Measure of His Spirit to the *Israelites*, that if they had loved and followed it, and not been stiff-necked, they might have continued in the Obedience to all Things that were written in the Book of the Law to do them, (unless God commanded Impossibilities) and in that Way that they were commanded them, to wit, to separate them from the *Heathen:* And they, if they had been thankful, and glorified God by their Obedience to what they knew of Him, had not been given up to a *Reprobate Sense*; and if they had followed the Goodness of God, leading to Repentance from Time to Time, and had not had an impenitent Heart, they had received according to their Deeds, Glory, Honour, and Peace; for if it be given to the *Good Gentile*, then surely to the *Good Jew*. And if the *Jews* in Christ's Day had not brought forth Wild Grapes, and been like their Fore-Fathers, that rebell'd against *God's Good Spirit* (under Pretence of magnifying the Scriptures, and contending for the Faith of their Fathers) *they had not been blinded like them, nor the Vineyard taken from them, nor theirs laid Waste*.

Neh. 9. 10.

Rom. 1. 21.

Isa. 5. 3, 4, and 6. 9, 10, 11, 12.
John 12. 31, 42.
Mark 12. 9, 10.

As for *Phil.* 3. 12. *Not as though I had already attained, or were already Perfect:* It proves not that *Paul* was not clear from Sinning, *but that he had not yet perfected, or finished his Courſe, ſo as to have kept the Faith to the End,* to be out of Danger to miſs of the Reward, as he was afterwards, as appears plainly by the Compariſon he uſeth, *of a Courſe.* He doth not ſay (as this Man would have him) *That ſome that were Perfect, were otherwiſe minded;* But theſe that were Perfect, had a perfect Underſtanding of thoſe Things that were in Difference among them; of which he ſpeaks in that Chapter, about the *Conciſion,* as he terms it diminutively, *and the Righteouſneſs of the Law, and Preheminence ſought by it, without the Righteouſneſs of Chriſt,* which they had perverted and ſlighted, *being Dogs, making their Belly their God, and minding Earthly Things, and Glorying in their Shame, being Evil Workers, of whom he bid them beware.*

To his Sinning, through always needing more Grace; He that is capable of receiving more, and refuſeth and reſiſteth it, ſinneth; but to uſe his own Similitude, *A Little One* (as Chriſt calls ſome of His) that hath but a Little Heart, yet if he give it all to God, he can do no more, he ſinneth not, but fulfills the Law.

The *Hebrews* were chid becauſe they had not improved their Time; which if they had done, they had not ſinned. *Peter* and the Reſt of the Apoſtles, were in that Manner of Speech taught and inſtructed, *of the Power and Efficacy of Faith in it's Extent, which they ſhould receive after they were endued with Power from on High,* which they were commanded to wait for, that had they neglected, they had ſinned; and to expect it before the Time (as for a Child to aſpire to the Things of a Man) is the Part of much Heat and Confidence, and is Good to be diſcountenanced ſometimes, though not always to be diſliked. Not to be at preſent what they are exhorted to be for the future, to make that Tranſgreſſion, is to ſet Tranſgreſſion in Order of Time before the Law; whereas, where there is no Law, there is no Tranſgreſſion; for Sin is the Tranſgreſſion of the Law that is known: *To him that knoweth to do Good, and doth it not, to him it is Sin*; but in the Time of Ignorance God winks.

The *Corinthians* were exhorted to be in Underſtanding Perfect, as the Word τέλειοι ſignifies: To accuſe them of Imperfection, and ſo of Sin, becauſe then Children, and in their Minority (though Born of God in *John's* Senſe) were to accuſe not only the Saints departed, but all the Angels, of Sin, becauſe they have not attained to that Meaſure of Wiſdom that God is, upon his Principle; for his Argument implies as if there were no End of needing of Grace. I wonder he has forgotten his School-Diſtinction of *a quo & ad quem,* for Men may be Perfect from Sin, and not perfectly grown up to the Wiſdom and Knowledge of all the Weighty Myſteries of the Goſpel.

For his Notion of Sanctification and Purification, I ſay, Where the Conſcience is not defiled, it is purified; and Men are Sanctified, or dedicated to God by the Truth, and the Belief and Obedience of it, and there is no Sinning; elſe, how can they be Temples and Tabernacles for God to dwell and be Worſhipt in?

For the Place he brings that Men muſt Sin becauſe they are Men, he might better have given that Reaſon for the Devil's Sinning, becauſe he is a Devil; for Sinning is not Man's State, as Man, though in joyning with the Devil he may Sin, as the Word יחטא ſignifies, being Potential; and ſo *Paginus* renders it by *Peccet*; but he makes uſe of a bad Tranſlation, *His Holy Ghoſt,* as his Words imply, to countenance his bad Concluſion, That becauſe they may Sin, *therefore they muſt Sin.* See more in Dr. *Gell's* Eſſay to the Tranſlation of the Bible, pag. 762, 768, 772.

Becauſe *David, Pſal.* 19. thought it a hard Matter for him, or thoſe in his Condition at that Time, to underſtand their Errors from the Law of *Moſes,* thoſe Statutes and Precepts, *&c.* which through Neglect they might be ignorant of, and therefore there was a Sacrifice appointed for a Propitiation, and Prayers for Cleanſing from them, *ver.* 12. And becauſe the Pſalmiſt, *Pſal.* 130, being in the Deep by Reaſon of Iniquity, prayed for Forgiveneſs, ver. 3. 4. And becauſe the Apoſtle *James* ſaith, *In many Things we Sin all,* he concludes, *that not only David, but the Apoſtles too, in their beſt Condition, even to their Death, did ſin*; and that *James was a Curſer to his Death,* becauſe he ſaid, *With the Tongue Curſe we Men,* taking Advantage of theſe Holy Men, *to make them Offenders for their Words:* But what Good Man will believe him? No Wonder if he traduce the *Quakers,* and pervert their Words, when he is one of them that *David* ſpeaks of, *that wreſt his Words, and imagine Evil of him.* And for any Thing we know (for we cannot take his Words

---

1674.
Phil. 3. 12.
2 Tim. 4. 6, 7.

Verſ. 2.
Verſ. 9.
See Zegerus and Grotius, and Eraſmus on the Place. Pag. 12.

Heb. 5.

Mat. 14. 31.

See Grotius on the Place. John 7. 31.

1 Cor. 14. 20.

Ignatius Epiſt. to the Epheſians, ſaith, He that poſſeſſeth the Word of JESUS, can truly hear alſo his Silence, that he may be Perfect, pag. 26.

1 Kings 8. 46.
Eccl. 7. 20.

Pag. 13.

1674.

Words without Quotation) he may as much wrong, or wreſt thoſe Paſſages out of *Origen, Theophylact, Chryſoſtom, Ambroſe,* and the *Proteſtant Writers,* that he ſays he has read, about *Death's deſtroying of Sin,* which is for Deſtruction it ſelf; In my Mind the Devil may more fitly be ſaid to correct it: For if they that are Dead have ceaſed from Sin, then the Damned ſhall not Blaſpheme God, or elſe their Blaſphemy is not Sin; which *Proteſtant Writers* ſay not, nor the *Fathers* ever taught.

<small>Grotius on the Place. 1 Pet. 4. 1. Zegerus on the Place.</small>

But *Grotius* a *Famous Proteſtant Writer,* interprets it thus: *That as the Dead return not to their former Life, ſo neither He that is truly Dead to Sin, ought to return to his former Life again.* And *Zegerus,* another, ſaith, *That is, being looſed and freed from Sinning, ſo that he may not ſin, unleſs he will.* But this Man would have it, as if *Paul* meant, that *Bodily Death took away the Poſſibility of Sinning, and Life the Poſſibility of not Sinning.* However, he acknowledges, that by the Death of the Body of Sin, is meant, *the Separation of Sin from Man, and being freed from Sin, and ceaſed from Sinning*; yet ſays, that in *Rom.* 6. *there is not a Word to dehort them not to ſuffer any Sin to be in them*: But how can a Man let Sin be in him, and he not Sin? For it is not a Sin to be tempted, but to enter into the Temptation: He that ceaſes from ſinning, ceaſes from Sin; and whenſoever any yields to obey Sin, then he is the Servant of Sin: Can any Man commit a Sin, but he is captivated under the Power of it? And therefore in that Condition *Paul* cryed out, as a Diſtreſſed Captive, for Deliverance from the Body of Death, *not from the Natural Body*; for, before that was diſſolved, he ſaid, *I have finiſhed my Courſe, I have kept the Faith*; that is, He had endured to the End, and arrived at Perfection. *Eraſmus* ſaith, *It was in the Perſon of another,* which the Apoſtle ſpoke in *Rom.* 7. And *Grotius* on the ſame Place, will not have it *Paul*'s Condition when he wrote the Epiſtle to the *Romans*. *It is to be noted,* ſays he, *that* Paul *ſpeaks in the Firſt Perſon, not that he deals concerning himſelf, but for Modeſty's Sake, he had rather ſo expreſs odious Things, which he calls to transfer in a Figure,* 1 Cor. 4. 6. ſo in 1 Cor: 6. 12, 15. chap. 10. 29, 30. chap. 13. 2. Gal. 2. 18. *Chryſoſtom ad* 1 Cor. 12. ſays, *He takes heavy Things on his own Perſon. Hieron ad Daniel, Becauſe he is one of the People, he reckons their Sins in his own Perſon, which alſo we read, the Apoſtle did in the Epiſtle to the* Romans. But this Man interpreting it, *the Death of the Body,* inſtead of *the Body of Death,* firſt gives a Reaſon, why Sin muſt be deſtroyed by the Death of the Body, namely, *becauſe it entred by the Conjunction and Union of the Soul with the Body*; but that he proves not, and it were to diſprove himſelf in Pag. 8. For there he ſaith, *The Light is Reaſon, wherewith God hath endued Man's Soul, and is a Natural Gift, that comes by Generation:* How then, ſay I, is it conjoyned and united to it, if it be generated with it? For ſo 'tis one with it. Are there two Generations, one of the Body, and another of the Soul; one with Sin, and another without it; and the latter united to the former, that it may receive Sin, and ſay, *A Body haſt thou prepared me, O God, to do, not thy Will on Earth, as it is in Heaven, but the Will of the Devil, that at my firſt Entrance into it, and during my Continuance in it, I may always do thy Enemy ſome Service, who muſt have a Place allowed him in it as long as it lives?* Is not this Blaſphemous, and contrary to the Scriptures, which ſays, *He that defiles the Temple of God, him will God deſtroy.*

<small>Rom. 6. 18.</small>

<small>2 Tim. 4. 7.</small>

<small>Eraſmus and Grotius on Rom. 7.</small>

<small>Pag. 8.</small>

<small>1 Cor. 3: 17.</small>

I would fain know of *S. G.* how the Man of Sin got entrance to defile this Temple, if it was not through the Mind, by entring that with his Temptation, *of becoming as God, knowing Good and Evil,* which was ſome time after that God had breathed into Man the Breath of Life. If he ſays, it was, as inevitably he muſt, then will it follow, that Sin came not by Conjunction of Soul and Body, as he teaches, but after that Conjunction; and ſo his Reaſon for Death's deſtroying of Sin, which implies the Neceſſity of ſinning till Men dye, is quite overturned. Beſides, how can an Houſe of Clay, a lifeleſs Lump of Earth, be capable of Pollution any ways, but by him or them, that inhabit or enter it, as becoming his or their Organ, Inſtrument or Habitation?

Again, *S. G.* to prove that Death deſtroys Sin, brings *Rom.* 7. 24. as in the common Tranſlation, This Body of Death; whereas the *Greek* has it ἐκ τοῦ σώματος τοῦ θανάτου τούτου, who ſhall deliver me from the Body of this Death, which conſidered with the Context, ſhews it to be metaphorically and ſpiritually intended, which agrees with *Ambroſe*'s Interpretation, produced by *Zegerus* on that Place, and which he approves (viz.) *all Sins: J. Capellus* ſays, *It is the Maſs of Sin, not the Maſs of the viſible Body.* And *Druſius* ſays, ſome do underſtand it *turbam malorum,*

<small>Zegerus on Rom. 7. 24. J. Capellus and Druſius on Rom. 7. 24.</small>

a Mula Multitude of Evils. And as for *Chryſoſtom, Theodoret* and all thoſe *Proteſtant* Writers he has read (who knows who or where) you may either believe him upon truſt, or read all their Books, till you find his Interpretation; for particular Citation he affordeth us not.

But he asks, *how A. P. will prove that the Body of Sin is the ſame with the Law of Sin?* A Thing eaſily done after his way of proving Things; for *Grotius* ſaith, 'That *the Law of the Members* is the ſtrong Affections of the Fleſh, and the Law 'of Sin the Vehemency of Affections ariſing from the Fleſh, *and the Body of Sin,* 'ch. 6. 6. A Conjunction of many Members, that is *Vices, Col.* 3. 5. And indeed, the Scripture mentioned ſhews that one and the ſame Thing is intended: And it is but reaſonable for any to believe, that the Body of Sin gives *Law* to them that are under the Power of it.

Grotius on Rom. 7. 23 24.

Ibid. on Rom. 6. 6.

But *S. G.* from *Gal.* 5. 17. where 'tis tranſlated, *The Spirit luſteth againſt the Fleſh, ſo that ye cannot do the Things ye would,* ſeems thus to infer, *that therefore Men muſt of Neceſſity fulfil the Luſts of the Fleſh, and cannot do otherwiſe*: Whereas it ſhould be tranſlated, *ſo that ye* may not *do the Things that ye would*; which is thus interpreted by *D. Gell*, *That the Spirit hinders them that they may not do the Will of the Fleſh.*

But ſays *S. G. Paul* ſaith not, *Rom.* 6. 14. *No Sin ſhall be in you, but Sin ſhall not have Dominion over you.* I anſwer, Nor doth he ſay, that Sin ſhould be in them, and ſerve them: Where Men ſin, Sin hath Dominion. But tell me, *S. G.* Is not the ſtrong Man to be caſt forth, Sin taken away, and the Devil's Works deſtroyed?

See *D. Gell's* Eſſay, ſerm. 19. p. 775. pag. 15. *Mat.* 12. 26, 27, 28, 29. *Luke* 11.

Again, ſaith *S. G. Fleſh is the Root of Evil Affections and Luſts.* But if that Doctrine be true, ſay I, then God in giving Men Bodies of Fleſh is the Author of the Root of Evil Affections and Luſts; conſequently the Life of them is not a Bleſſing but a Curſe.

John 3. 5, 6.

Farther, *S. G.* tells us, *That the legal keeping of God's Commandments, is an univerſal and perpetual keeping of them; but the Evangelical is not ſo, but an Aim and Endeavour:* Which if I underſtand any Thing, is to make God in theſe New Covenant Times, to indulge in Man a ſlacking of Obedience to his Righteous Law. At this rate Chriſt came not that we ſhould fulfil the Law, but only that we ſhould endeavour it: Strange Goſpel! Are Men under a leſs Obligation to Holineſs, now they have more plentiful Aſſiſtances to compaſs it? Is this the Way to finiſh Sin, reſtore Man's Nature, and cloath it with Everlaſting Righteouſneſs? which is ſo far from deterring Man from not obſerving God's Law inviolably, that he teaches, *that an Endeavour to keep it, without exactly keeping it, is the Priviledge and Obedience of the Goſpel.*

Whether this Man writes like a Goſpel-Miniſter, or Servant of the God of this World, let the Conſcientious Reader judge. But he was not always of this Mind; for in pag. 10. he ſeems to plead for the higheſt and moſt exact Obedience, not only to the Law, as underſtood by the *Jews* in point of Moral Righteouſneſs, but as Chriſt wound it up to an higher Degree of Righteouſneſs. But let us hear what *Bp. Sanderſon* ſaith, in this Matter, a Man venerable I ſuppoſe, in *S. G's* Account.

'The Precepts of Chriſt in the new Law, as the Holy Fathers of the Church 'every where witneſs, are much more excellent as to ſome Things, than the Pre-'cepts of *Moſes* in the Old Law; not only in reſpect that they are propounded 'more fully, clearly and plainly; but alſo, inaſmuch as they *riſe higher, and call* '*up* Chriſtians *to a more eminent Degree of Perfection*, and that with more effica-'cious Allurements; namely, on the one Hand propounding the Example of Chriſt 'paſt; and on the other, the moſt ample Reward of the Kingdom of Heaven for 'the future. As in thoſe two great Duties of *Chriſtian-Life* moſtly appears, of 'loving Enemies, and taking up the Croſs, commanded in the new Law. And 'they are Commands univerſally obligatory; to the Obſervation whereof, all that 'profeſs the Faith and Name of Chriſt, *are bound* under Crime of moſt grievous 'Sin (namely, of denying Chriſt) and Penalty of Eternal Damnation, unleſs they 'repent. And he himſelf brings in *P. Andrews* thus, *That a Man moved by God's Spirit, out of Love to God, may be ſaid to fulfil the Law.* So that here are two Biſhops advancing Evangelical Obedience above that of the Law, in Point of Strictneſs and Purity, againſt this Man's libertine Undervalue, and dangerous Diminution of it.

B. R. Sand de conſc. reg. Prel. 4. Sect. 34. his Oxf. lect.

But this Adverſary thinks he ſays a great deal againſt us, in telling People, *That it is an Error to think, that any can be ſaved partly by their own Righteouſneſs.* And

1674.

And alas! whoever said it was not, that is rightly called a *Quaker?* We know better; and that it is by Grace we are saved; yet so, *As that we must be thereby taught to deny Ungodliness and Worldly Lusts, and to live Soberly, Righteously, and Godlily in this present World,* which is not our own Righteousness, but the Righteousness of God's Grace, *that is all-sufficient for so great Salvation:* And another Sort of Salvation, than that which comes by and in the Way of this Grace, is a *Satanical Delusion,* suited to the corrupt Minds of Men, that would be saved from Wrath, *the Wages,* but be indulged in Sin, *the Work.* However, 'tis plain by the Verses foregoing, That the Law there spoken of, is the Ceremonial Law, which not only they, but other Churches in those Times had, and made some Scruple of relinquishing, as may appear in his Epistles all along, wherein he dehorts them from any such Observation, which they inclined to, even upon an Opinion of Necessity; And which the said Bp. S. from *Gal.* 5. 2. observes, not only to be *dead,* but *deadly,* after *Augustin's* Distinction. But that Christians are held to the *Law moral,* not as given by *Moses*; but as declarative of the *Law Natural,* which before he had called *Divine*; He, the said *Bp. Sand.* doth with others agree, which as *Bp. Andrews* well says, *must be fulfilled with the Motion and Power of the Spirit of Christ,* who was sent, that the Righteousness of the Law might be fulfilled in us, by walking after the Spirit, whereas, the Flesh is weak, or a Man in his fleshly State being weakned, cannot perform it. *Bp. Sanderson* saith farther, ' The new ' Law, that is the Gospel, *binds all to whom it is preached to the Obedience, both of* ' *Faith and Life: To believe in Christ as a Redeemer, and obey him as Law-Giver,* ' *both which, unless they do, for their Duty neglected they shall suffer Everlasting* ' *Punishment.*

S. *Grevil* expounds 1 *John* 3. 9. *Whosoever is born of God, he cannot Sin,* that is, He cannot make a Trade of it, from *J. Leigh.*

Answ. H. *Grotius,* a Man, worthily of greater Authority, calls that *a pernicious* ' *Exposition, whereby,* says he, *they infer, that a Study and Endeavour to live well* ' *suffices for one to be accounted a Son of God, although the Things be not fulfilled,* ' *the Custom of Sin prevailing*; and he brings *Tertullian* in his Book, *De Pudicitiâ,* saying thus of Sin and Sinners ' *He that is born of God, will not at all commit these,* *and shall not be a Son of God if he shall commit them:* So a good Tree cannot bring ' forth evil Fruit; but it may become barren, rotten, vicious, and after it is so de- ' generated, it may be cut down; also an evil Tree may become good, and then ' consequently no more an evil Tree. And likewise *Chrysostom* on *Rom.* 8. hath the same Comparison. And *Jerom Didymus's Disciple,* l. 1. adv. Pel. saith, ' He ' that is born of God, sins not, as long as the Seed of God abides in him, vid. *lively.* And on *Matt.* 7. ' A Good Tree cannot bring forth Evil Fruit, *as long as it per-* ' *severes in the Study* of Goodness.

But, S. *Grevil* saith, *He hopes Parker will not say, God gives his People the Enjoyment of Heaven in this Life.*

I answer, *Bish. Hall* saith it, and entituleth his Book, *Heaven upon Earth,* acknowledging the same *in Nature,* though not in *Degree:* How ignorant is this Man of Scripture, or forgetful? Doth not *Paul* in the Epistle to the *Hebrews* (supposing he wrote it) speak of some *that may have tasted of the Powers of the World to come, and may fall from that Taste?*

But what means he by his always needing more and more Grace? If a Man be filled, he needs no more. And a Man needs no more in this State, than what he is capable of in this State. And for his Part, it seems he needs no more; *for he hath more than he useth,* though there is great need he should make more use of what he has. S. *Grevil* scoffingly comparing the *Quakers Speakers* with *Paul,* says, *If they could give that which they think is the Spirit, they would make more* Quakers; as much as to say, if *Paul* could have given the Spirit, more of his Hearers should have had the Spirit; and consequently, he was not a Minister of the Spirit in that Sense; as as if it had been *Paul's* Fault: But was not the Holy Ghost given by *Paul's* Hands? *Acts* 19. When he had laid his Hands upon them, *the Holy Ghost came upon them,* and they spake with Tongues and prophesied, What Gift was that *Timothy* receiv'd by the laying on of his Hands, called, the Gift of God? It plainly appears, that God by the Ministry of *Paul* did give the Spirit to several; and was he not at that Time a Minister of the Spirit? Was not he that ministred the Spirit to the *Galatians,* a Minister of the Spirit himself? It must follow undeniably; many Thousands were by his Ministry turn'd from Darkness to Light, and from the Power of Satan to the Power of God, to walk in the Spirit with God. And for all *S. G*'s unworthy Taunts; whether those that are now called forth, as they were, *not by Men, nor of Men,* to wit, the *Quakers Speakers*, as he is pleased to call them; or those that are made, called and upheld by Men, to minister the Letter, Writings or Declaration of the Gospel, after their own Imaginations, as *S. Grevil* and his Fraternity not unlike the false Prophets of old Time (which he calls, but falsely, *the Doctrine whereby the Spirit is conveyed*) do awaken more Consciences, and turn more to walk in the Spirit, to bring forth the Holy Fruits of the Spirit: Let the Fruits, that are brought forth in the World under both their Ministries, speak.

To prove that the Scripture or Writing is the Gospel; He saith, *The Scripture preached the Gospel to* Abraham; therein producing a Place against himself; for it plainly proves the Scripture is not the Gospel, since the Gospel was preached to *Abraham* by God, *before it was recorded or written by* Moses; That we chuse to call the Gospel, which the Scripture declares of, that is, The *Good-Will of God to Men, by his Mercy, Power and Goodness manifested to them*; and that may be resisted, as well in an inward Manifestation, as outward Declaration; for *Stephen* said to the *Jews, Ye do always resist the Holy Ghost, as your Fathers did*, &c. *Jonas* also disobeyed the immediate Call of God. — Acts 7.

And whereas he saith, *John Baptist* preached the Gospel? That is also clearly against himself; *for that was before the four Books*, which he maintains to be the Gospel, were written.

The Gospel is called a Mystery, hid from Ages and Generations, and is still hid from all the Rebellious and Disobedient, who walk not after the Spirit, but their own Lusts: But so are not those four Books, so call'd; neither are they the glorious Gospel, but that which they declare of. — Ephes. 6. 19. chap. 3. 3, 16. Col. 1. 26. 1 Tim. 1. 11.

None of those Fathers he speaks of, I dare say, if he quoted the Places, would be found to countenance his Definition: for he confesses, they say, *It forgives and justifies*, which the four Books do not; they only declare such Things to Believers. If *Matthew* and *John*, and *Paul* and *Peter* were not the Gospel, because they were Powerful Instruments to declare it; no more are their Books and Writings: They were not the glad-Tidings, but the Bringers and Publishers of it; their Books are no more, if so much, not being *vivâ voce*, as they say; the like Power not usually accompanying the meer or *dead Letter, as the living Voice*.

Where did ever any hear or read, that the Reading of *Peter*'s Sermon converted 3000. at one Time? *Ignatius* saith, The Gospel is ἀπαρτισμὸς ἀφθαρσίας, *the Perfection of Incorruption*; Paper and Ink are not so. And saith *Origen*, John *calleth the Gospel Everlasting, which may be properly called Spiritual*, that the Books are not, tho' they hold out Spiritual Things. *Clemens Alexandrinus* saith, *The Angel*, Exod. 32. *held forth the Evangelical and leading Power of the Word:* That Evangelical Power was not then of the Books, but of the Word, which was and is God blessed for ever. *Chrysostom* plainly saith, they are not the Gospel. R. *Allen* on the Gospel saith, *It is a Divine Message from God himself, that teacheth and assureth, &c.* How can it be Divine and work Assurance, if it be not a Spiritual and inward Work, which the Books are not, nor of themselves can work. *Peter Martyr* saith, *It is such a Doctrine as offered Christ unto us, and his Spirit and Grace, whereby is ministred Strength unto us to perform those Things that are commanded,* which the Books of themselves still cannot do, though they declare of that which can: Not that we would lessen them, as our ungodly Wresting Adversaries say; or that we would take off People from reading them; but if they of themselves could do, or had that Power which belongs to the Everlasting Gospel, how comes it that so many Studiers of them receive no clearer Knowledge and living Sense of God, Christ, the Holy Spirit, Scriptures, &c? We do teach, That to read them with a good Understanding, Men must come to that which gives it, *which is the Inspiration of the Almighty,* Job 32. 8. — Epist. ad Philadel. p. 44. Orig. Commen. on Joh. pag. 9. Clem. Alex. Pedagog. l. 1. p. 111. R. Allen on' the Gos. p. 1. P. Martyr. Com. Places, p. 3. c. 2.

But it is worth our while to consider what Work he makes of *A. P*'s saying, That *the Gospel is the Power of God to Salvation*; an absolute plain Scripture, as any in the Bible. *A. P.* doth *not deny that the Gospel was before all Time, consequently that it is the Essence of God, and he is a Disciple of the Heretick* Swingfield. Did ever Man pretending to Sense or Seriousness, make such wild, foreign and lame Conclusions? These are, it seems, to serve for *Bugbears*, to scare the People: He might as well have said, The *Quakers* believe the Life Everlasting, and conclude, *Therefore they make it the Essence of God*; which as reasonably proclaims the *Church of England* a Company of *Hereticks*; nay, all the World that believe that

Article, as he can brand *A. P.* for one, becaufe he faid, *The Gofpel is the Power of God, and Everlafting,* which the Scripture calls it.

In thefe Things he truly partakes with the *Falfe Brethren* he fpeaks of, mentioned *Acts* 15. 24. who did not only teach and eftablifh againft the abolifhing Power of the Gofpel, tranfient Obfervations, but their own vain Traditions for Doctrines, glorying in them, as did the *Jews,* crying, *The Temple, The Ordinances,* while they neglected the weightier Things, and made void the Commandment of God and Chrift, the Old Commandment and the New Commandment, the fame that was from the Beginning, the Firft and the Laft, even that which endures for ever.

Methinks thefe Hireling Minifters are like fome Mercenary Souldiers, or *Souldiers of Fortune,* as they are called, that cannot bear to think of the Enemy's being totally routed, left their War end, and their Pay with it: Such Perfons, inftead of purfuing the Enemy, turn about againft their valiant and faithful Followers, that cry, *They run, They run,* we fhall utterly rout and fubvert them: No! rather than heighten and purfue that Refolution, *they will bafely betray the Caufe, and it's moft fincere Abettors, into the Arms of the publick Enemy;* They make no Scruple of doing this Evil, not that Good, but *Gain* may come of it: They had rather the Devil were unfubdued, than they disbanded, that his being unconquered might be a Pretence for keeping fuch Mercenaries always on foot; who are therefore the greateft Enemies of Chrift's Kingdom in the Hearts of his Children.

Thefe are they that will flee, becaufe they are Hirelings, and care not for the Flock, *John* 10. And it fo falls out, that now we have not only the old Adverfaries, but thefe alfo betwixt them and us, who inftead of going on againft them, firft turn themfelves manifeftly againft us, and endeavour what they can to obftruct our March: *But the Lord God* Jehovah *is fufficient, our Pillar of Cloud by Day, and Fire by Night; he goes before us; Power and Might and Majefty are with him, whofe Holy Pure and Clear Voice we have certainly heard, and in whofe Bleffed Appearance we have firmly Believed; and it is fo well with us, who retain our firft Love to him and his precious Truth in the inward Parts, that we can fing for Joy, though in a weary Land, and in the midft of many Diftreffes.* And this we know affuredly, That he will fhake terribly the Nations, and bring Amazement upon the People; Their Confciences will be fuddenly awaken, and with terrible Judgment will he plead with all the Proud Profeffing, as well as Prophane, Flefh in this Land; it fhall wither as the Grafs, and the Beauty of it fade as the Flower of the Field: And in that Day fhall Obedience to, and Communion with the Light of Chrift within, be honourable and defirable in the Sight of Thoufands; and the Truth fhall have the Victory, and the Dominion fhall not be any longer the Devil's, but the Saints of the Moft High, over Hell, Death and the Grave; the Ancient of Days will bring it to pafs: Then fhall Babylon fall, and her Merchants howl; for the great Judgment will furprize them, as Travail a Woman with Child, and the Lord God will reckon with them for the Souls of his People. *O fear before the Lord, ye Priefts! and turn you unto him all ye Children of Men.*

W. PENN.

William Penn's *Juft Complaint againft,* and Solemn Offer *of a* Publick Meeting *to, the* Leading Baptifts *affembled at* Barbican, *the* 28*th of the* 6*th Month,* 1674.

On the Behalf of Himfelf, *George Whitehead,* and the reft of his Friends.

FOrafmuch as there is a very fcandalous Report raifed and propagated, both in City and Country, againft *George Whitehead* and my felf, as if " We had pur-
" pofely neglected to meet the Baptifts at their publick Affembly held in *Barbican*
" in *London,* the Day and Month aforefaid (to take Cognizance of *Thomas Hicks*'s
" Proceedings againft the People, called *Quakers,* according to our Appeal) not-
" withftanding that the faid *Baptifts* had given us Notice by Letters, dated the
" 15th of that Month, manifeftly difcovering thereby, that we were afraid to
" ftand by our printed Charges, and unable to make good what we had written a-
" gainft

" gainst him, in the Face of a publick Auditor (a Practice, if true, base and unworthy of *Christian* Men) I cannot with hold this brief Defence and Information from *City* and *Country*, thus horribly imposed upon, and grosly abused into a Misapprehension of the Matter.

I do say then, and most sincerely affirm, that I never had any Account of that Meeting, by either Letter, or Messenger, directly or indirectly, till about Ten that very Night after the Meeting had been: Nor did I receive any other during the Time of my Absence, from the 8th to the 28th of the said Month, at what Time came with it several Letters that had been sent after me in my Journey, which missing me, were returned. Moreover, the Letter directed to me, was not delivered to *Philip Ford* in order to be sent to me, though resident in the same City, till four Days after the Date thereof, who perusing and considering it's Contents, returned among other Things, this for Answer:

William Kiffin, H. Knolleys, &c. *These serve only to give you Notice, that W. P. was gone into the* East *of* England *about three Weeks ago, and I know not how to give him Notice hereof. This I thought good to let you know, and do judge that you ought to let others know it, that so vain Boasting may be prevented as much as in us lyeth*; Philip Ford.

And for *G. Whitehead*, I am also assured by his Letter from *Bristol*, that he received no Account of the Meeting till the 29th of the last Month, being the Day after it's Appointment; nor did his Wife know where to send to him before his Arrival at that City, as she affirms to me, and she told their Messenger when he brought the Letter to her, and thereupon immediately returned it: How then we could know of the Meeting, much more how we conld be justly thought on Purpose to decline the Meeting, is left with impartial Readers to judge.

However it seems very strange and unreasonable to us, that any Men should so absolutely take upon them to concern us in a Meeting without our Knowledge and Consent. They could not but think us Men of Occasions, and such too, as might as well call us to remote as adjacent Places: Wherefore to expect we should appear at their sole Appointment of Time and Place, without any the least Provision against such Emergencies, was to require Impossibilities at our Hands: But then to triumph over our undesigned Absence, what is that less than to aggravate their Injustice to us? To God's Witness in all Consciences we leave our Case.

And now be it known to all to whom this cometh, that I was so far from refusing a publick Meeting, whatever some have untruly reported, that I offered *John Gladman*, a Member of theirs, to meet the said **T.** *Hicks* with the *Bible* in one Hand, and his *Dialogue* in the other, which was rejected: And as I never refused a fair and publick Meeting, at any Time, to this People, whenever offered (and I have Reason to believe the same of G. *Whitehead*) so for him and my self, do I hereby give them a *Solemn Offer*, to meet us publickly at such Time and Place, as we and they shall mutually appoint, to prevent any Surprize to either Party: At what Time we shall be ready, with the Assistance of Almighty God, to maintain our Charge against *T. Hicks*, in his three *Dialogues*, which were and are the Subject Matter of the Controversy depending.

London, *the* 5th *of the* 7th Month, 1674.

W. PENN.

Naked Truth needs no SHIFT:

Or, An ANSWER to a LIBELLOUS SHEET, Entituled,

The Quaker's Last Shift Found Out.

IT is with no small Regret, *Sober Reader*, that I am thus necessitated to Vindicate my own and my Friends Innocency, against these unfair Assaults: I prefer Peace before War, and heartily desire loving Neighbourhood, rather than daily Contest; but this is our Satisfaction, we did not begin with them, but were begun with by them: And such great and general *Accusations* call for the like *Defences*;

since where *Charges* go unanswer'd, *Guilt* is most usually reflected, especially where WE are concerned; there being a Sort of Men *devoted to misconstrue* whatever we say or do, with whom it is become Criminal to defend our selves; and deserving to be chid for saying, *They wrong us*: Such continu'd unchristian Proceedings against us will, I hope, induce all Impartial People to hold me excused for publishing this *second Vindication*, which I intreat them in the Love of God to consider, that they may the better find out where the SHIFT lieth, whether in us, or this *Nameless Author* and his Abettors.

The Intent of my Paper was, to meet with the *Vox populi*, or common Fame, that as we might be defended, so the People disabused, by declaring, that *notwithstanding those Defamatory Reports City and Country had credited against us, we had not receiv'd their Information of the Meeting, much less designedly avoided it; That it was unfair to concern us in a Meeting without our Consent; and that we made them a solemn Offer of a Publick Meeting*, &c.

Now let us see how well he hath made good his *Title-Page*, in which he calls his Paper an *Answer* to mine.

He tells us, that *we made an Appeal to the* Baptists *against* T. Hicks, *and that upon this Appeal the Teachers and Elders among them desired* T. H. *that he would in a publick Meeting bring forth his Evidences and Witnesses: That Mr.* Kiffin *and Mr.* Knowls *wrot Letters the* 15th *of* Aug. *to* W. P. *and* G. W. *informing them of Time and Place*.

But what is all this, to prove that we receiv'd any *certain* Account from them of the Meeting; that we purposely avoided the Meeting; and that we were so far unconcern'd in it, as that our *Consent* to meet was unnecessary? The Ground of my Paper.

He says that G. W. *had Notice at the* Vizes, *having seen a Letter of* T. Hicks, *sent to one in that Town*: But suppose it to be true; what is that to me, the Person most of all concern'd in the Matter? Or, how doth this reach P. Ford's Letter, writ to inform them of my Absence, and to desire *the Meeting might be suspended, to prevent vain Boasting?* Was it suspended? *No*. And hath not vain Boasting followed? *Yes*. A Surreptitious Meeting! A vain Triumph! Doth not this Proceeding rather give cause to suspect a *Design* to meet in our Absence, that made it of no Moment to the Meeting, *after they heard of it*, though before they wrote for, desired and expected our Presence.

But, saith he, W. P. *was at Home the Night before*: Grant it: Must I therefore hear or know of any such Meeting, or my Concernment in it? *I received no Account*, I say again, of either the Meeting, or my Relation to it, directly or indirectly, 'till about Ten the Night after it was over. And for G. W's Knowledge of the Meeting, it is exprest with Injustice both to him and my self; for he had not that Account which belonged to him to have; Therefore *not His* Account. What was a *Rumour* to him; or T. *Hicks's Letter* to another Man, receiving no Account himself, much less any Account of his Concern in the Meeting, *'till the* 29th *of the last Month, which was the Day after the Meeting*. Besides, Must we take it for granted that G. W. was just then at Leisure to take Post for the Meeting; under both it had been well nigh impossible for him to reach it; for this *Author* tells us, that T. H. writ not 'till *the Tuesday before* the Friday (so called) on which the Meeting was appointed; which was to give him little above a Day to ride about Fourscore Miles: Moreover, He was then pre-engaged for *Bristol*; and so ignorant of his Concernment in the Meeting, that he writ afterwards to his Wife *to Know* if our Friends were concerned in it. This his Shift is too Thread-bare to palliate that unworthy Surprize.

But, *Others had Notice*, saith he. What then? say I. Were not we the Persons chiefly concerned? Could any Body else have answer'd for T. *Hicks* besides himself? Who then could fill up our Room, especially in Matters of Fact? If T. H. was thought fit to be there to explain and vindicate his *Dialogues*, then should we in Defence of our Answers: But, if our Absence might so easily be dispensed with, why should T. H's Presence have been so requisite? For T. H. and his Books, against our Books only, were unreasonable Odds. The Plea should have lain between Books and Books, the Controversy being written: And if it was needful that as well he as his *Dialogues* should be there, then that as well we as our Answers; though I cannot see with what Liberty we could have defended our selves, since *Such as offered to say any Thing in our Behalf were interrupted*; which

gives

gives us Cause enough to believe, that this Person was beside the Matter, when he tells us, that *the Baptists were glad to see any of us there.*

But he says, *That I Prevaricate,* in saying, The Baptists *concerned us in that Meeting, when we concern'd the* Baptists *in that Meeting*: A Shift to be sure, though not his *Last*. I would fain know, if we were not concern'd in that Meeting, because we concerned the *Baptists* in that Meeting; as I take it, we were reciprocally concerned in that Meeting, and therefore equally interested in the Appointment of Time and Place; for was there not the same Reason that we should be there, *vivâ voce* to make good the Charge in our Book, as that *T. H.* should be there, *vivâ voce* to endeavour to clear his Book from our Charge? Never can they defend themselves from that Injustice. It is not the Part of a just Judge, to hear and determine for one Party in the Absence of another. Besides, For what End did they pretend to give us Notice, if not that we should be there? It must not be forgot, that while *in their Letter to me they desire and expect it,* in the Letter to *J. Osgood they render it needless*; nay, it was asserted by one eminent among them in that Meeting, as I am credibly inform'd, *That neither* G. W. *nor* W. P. *were concerned to be present*: If so, Why was our undesigned Absence reputed and reported to be the Consequence of our Fears?

But the Man thinks he hath a stronger Argument than all this, in my Book (intituled, *The Spirit of Truth Vindicated,* &c. p. 78, " That to which an Appeal is " made, must be capable of giving an Infallible Judgment, and so a true Judge, " or else the Appeal is Foolish. He is so wise as to leave the Application to his Reader, for which Way he could make it bear to his Purpose, I know not: But let it suffice, *First,* That I made not the Appeal by him recited, as the *Postscript* of my Book proveth: *Next,* Nor can any sober Man think, we intended by our Appeal to the *Baptists,* our abiding by their Judgment, be it right or wrong; The very Words of it shew the Appeal to the *Baptists,* was not to try whether *T. H.* was guilty, but for Judgment against him, having proved him guilty; for that were to admit of their Judgment, to conclude us against our selves; they themselves will not think us so kind to them: Take the Appeal as this Person recites it; *Now, if you the Teachers and Elders, among the Baptized People, do not publickly clear your selves of* T. Hicks, *and these his unjust Proceedings against us; we may take it for granted, that you own his Work, and may justly deal with him as the* Baptists *great Champion, peculiar Agent or Representative,* &c. Now I would fain know which Way this binds us from all farther Meeting, upon the same Score? Nothing can be well clearer, than that this Appeal aim'd no farther, than to know *whether the* Baptists *did and would own or reject* T. H's *Proceedings, that we might the better understand whom to address our selves to next Time.* There is great Difference in the Nature of Appeals: And the Reason of my Writing, as he citeth me, was, to prove the *Light* capable of giving an infallible Judgment, from my Adversary's acknowledging it to be the *Gift of God,* and appealing to it, as a right Discerner, for Judgment about what is right, and what is wrong, which this Person, *T. H. like,* left out: Howbeit, thus far, what he cites reacheth our present Case; for, doubtless, they had Power to give Judgment against T. H. if they had been but as willing to use it, having such clear Evidences in our Books before them. Nevertheless, this doth not prove, *That we knew of the Meeting, that we were unconcerned in it, or that we designedly shunned it*: The Foundation of our Paper, no Ways shaken by this Libeller's Sheet. The Meeting was pretended for a *Church-Examination*; but almost every where, in and about *London,* noised by the *Baptists* themselves to have been for a *Disputation,* and our Absence accordingly interpreted: A manifest Injury to our Books, Persons and Professions.

For my Offer to *J. Gladman,* he meanly shifts it, and seems to creep out at the Word Formal; so that we are to read it thus, ' William Penn did offer, but *not* ' *formally Challenge,* to meet *T. Hicks* with the *Bible* in one Hand, and with his ' *Dialogue* in the other. Let it be so; I hope it is enough to satisfy the World, that *an Offer was made and rejected*: Nor is my printed one more Formal; for it was on Purpose made to remove all Obstruction to a Meeting, upon Terms formally proposed; for which I shall produce a Witness in convenient Time and Place. In the mean while it is to be considered, that the Person mistakes, when he makes *T. H. to have offered* W. P. *any such Meeting,* whatever he might do to *G. W.* as the very Page he refers to in *T. H's* Third *Dialogue* proves: Farther, That he never offered me any Meeting, *but in private,* and that too, not 'till after he had *twice publickly*

1674:
publickly wrong'd me, which was refused, not to decline a Meeting, but as reputing it too mean a Satisfaction.

For his reflective Commendation of my *Prudence*, because I did not, after their Example, appoint a Meeting without their Notice; it speaks so much the Justice of my Proceeding, that it reflects Folly upon the Mention of it, and not a little Falseness too, since a Meeting to be agreed upon by two Parties, cannot be said *to be lodged in any one of their Breasts*, without telling a manifest Untruth.

His black Menace of us and our Religion, with some *Hydrean* Piece, suddenly to be published, we are very little solicitous about; our Consciences are approv'd to God in this Matter, and we hope (through his Assistance (however mis-represented to the World) before we have done, to approve our Cause Just in the Minds of impartial People.

To conclude, since he tells us, *That the* Baptists *have received Satisfaction in* T. H*'s Proceedings against us* (and great Cause we have to believe, that some of them were not ignorant of his Libel) I do hereby soberly renew my *solemn Offer* to them, and expect from them a *Publick Meeting*, wherein we may have Leave too, *vivâ voce*, to repeat and defend our Charges, as *T. H.* manifestly had to read and vindicate his *Dialogues*. And be it known to all those *Baptists*, that though the Controversy fall in *T. Hicks*, by our Appeal to them, yet that it riseth in them by their Justification of him: Therefore, as we can never acquiesce in their Proceedings, which he calls a *Satisfaction*, that have prov'd thus plainly injurious; so from them do we yet expect that *Satisfaction*, which we are bold to ask, and in Honesty they are bound to give us, *in the Face of a sober Auditory*, at such Time and Place, as they and we, on Conference, shall mutually appoint.

The 11th of the 7th Month, 1674.

William Penn.

POSTSCRIPT.

OUR Inducement to the Publication of these two Papers was not *Vain Glory*, or *Worldly Reputation*, (which Christ Jesus our Lord and Saviour, hath taught us to die to) but singly the Glory of *God*, the Honour of his Truth, and the Rescuing of the Minds of *People*, from those false Reports they have been lately ensnared into the Belief of, to the Hurt of their Immortal Souls.

LIBELS No PROOFS.

WHereas I lately Published *A Just Complaint*, against the Partial Proceedings of several of those called *Anabaptists* against us, at their Meeting in *Barbican*, the 28th of the last Month, with a *Solemn Offer* for another, upon Just and Equal Terms, in Order to Debate such Matters of Difference as are now depending between us, it hath pleased *Some-Body* (but we know not who) to attempt the Answering of it, in a Sheet, called, *The* Quaker's *Last Shift Found Out.* And because I knew not but the *Baptists* might own it (a Defence of their Actions being thereby endeavoured) To the End the World might not be Abused, by *Shifts*, under the too common, but base, Disguise of *Reprehending them*, I replyed, shewing, that *Not One of the several Reasons inducing me to the Publication of my First Paper was enervated*; with a Renewal of my former *Solemn Offer for a Publick Meeting*, and much more, requisite to our Just Defence, and the People's farther Information.

Since when, I perceive a *Rejoynder* is abroad, made up of Folly, Falshood, and those mean Shifts his former would undeservedly have fastened upon us, and the Whole wrapt up in a Bungling Sort of Drollery. But I am to tell the Man and the World, *That I am not obliged to wait the Motion, or watch the Bark of every Libeller: Let Men shew their Faces, and tell their Names, or Fight with themselves.* Common Charity should protect every Man from the Attacks of a *Nameless Author*, especially, when against a People that are Innocent. Nothing but Malice, or Money, or some Evil Thing, can encourage any to such base Practices. *The Worthiest of Men and Actions*, have no Outward Fence against this *Flail*; but with the Worst must walk unprotected from such *Assassinates*. A Just Disdain is the Best Answer;

Answer; and that is what I now make him. *My Complaint is out, and my Solemn Offer abroad, and that with my Name at Length: It lyes at the Baptist's Door, and we wait for their Result.* And if this *Libeller* will dare to tell us *His Name,* who covereth his Untruths by concealing it, I do hereby offer, either in Print, or at that so much desired Meeting, to prove him Guilty of Folly, Lyes and Slanders, which now it can be of little Service to attempt, since, when that is done, at this Rate *No Body will appear Guilty.* These Unchristian and Unmanly Practices on all Hands against us, we patiently undergo, *having Full Confidence in GOD,* that He will yet give us an Opportunity, in which to prove our *Innocency,* and detect our many Adversaries of foul Injustice towards us.

The 21st of the 7th
Month, 1674.   WILLIAM PENN.

William Penn's RETURN TO *John Faldo's* REPLY,

CALLED

A Curb for W. Penn's Confidence, &c.

Writ in Defence of His ANSWER to *John Faldo's* PRINTED CHALLENGE.

MY Answer to *John Faldo's Challenge,* was in Terms so Modest, that no Man not bent to be Abusive, and resolv'd against all Candor and Moderation, could have taken such Pains as he hath done, to bedirt it. Would I so ill bestow my Time, I could nigh fill as great a Compass with the Hard Names he flings upon it; *The Refuge and Practice of Petulant and Empty Adversaries.* His Title charges it with *False Insinuations and Juglings:* I seriously profess, I never intended any Thing with more Truth, Plainness and Softness, than that short Answer. And truly, that which renders this Usage at any Time uneasie, is the fastning unjustly that *Character upon me and my Friends,* which is most deservedly their own, thereby concealing and securing the Offender, and substituting the *Innocent* in his Room, to the *Deceiving of the Simple, and exposing us to the Bait of the Rude and Ignorant Multitude:* But it is our Lot, and mine at this Time more particularly; I was treated at another Rate, whilst I could cry *Hosanna* to His Order.

But let us hear what he says to prove that my Answer contains *False Insinuations and Juglings.* I told him, *That it was unfairly done of him to chuse the* Barbican-Meeting, *to divulge his Challenge to me, which I had receiv'd no Notice of.* To this he replies, *That the Meeting was occasion'd by the* Quaker's *Appeal:* Which, beside that it is nothing to the Purpose, is a Great Untruth: Did we occasion any Meeting, wherein we were concerned to be present without our Notice and Consent, either as to Matter or Manner, Time or Place, taking the Word *Occasion* in the common Acceptation of it? No Body surely, but *J. Faldo,* and such Prejudgers can think so. For Shame be Just!

But he believes, *Such a Critical Season seldom happens, wherein both G. W. and I were before so long a Season out of the Reach of so Publick a Concern.* What then? Therefore were we not then out of Reach? What would he be at? Lamentable Weakness! Is this to justify *His Cowardly Braggs?* I will call them so now, since softer Terms far'd so ill at his Hands. But let *J. F.* know, *That for that Glorious Gospel of* JESUS CHRIST *our Lord,* he with as much Envy as Untruth,

truth, suggests us to deny, we are frequently engaged in remote Places, and that for Weeks, and sometimes Months, where no Letters can be sent to us with any previous Knowledge where to find us; insomuch as that our Nearest and Dearest Relations may have taken their *Leave of this World, and exchanged their Houses for Graves before our Return, or Knowledge of their Condition*, which might have been better considered by this *Stipendiary Resident*, who, though he gets more Money by it, is not exposed to that and many other Hardships.

But to palliate the Unjust Procedure of the *Baptists* against us, at their *First Barbican-Meeting*, he tells us, *A Tale of* G. Whitehead's *surprizing him with a Dispute upon Three Days Notice*, which he saith, *Was not according to the Agreement made betwixt him and some of our Friends*, to wit, *Mutual Consent*; which granted to him, neither helps the *Baptists*, nor hurts us: For, *First*, G. Whitehead went *principally to a Meeting of our Friends*, and if he might have Opportunity to allay the Heat of this Vapouring *Adversary*. *Secondly*, It was so far left with J. Faldo, either to *accept or reject*, as that it was most remote from the Thoughts of G. W. upon his Refusal, to assemble the Inhabitants of the Place, and in his Absence exclaim both against his Faith and Practice; our manifest Suffering from T. Hicks and his Confederates. *Thirdly*, There can be nothing well Falser, than his insinuating, *the Issue of that Meeting to have been his Quiet from the* Quakers; if by *Quiet*, he understands any Fear upon them from his Force of Argument to encounter him; since he could neither recover our *Half-Proselyte*, as he is pleased to call that Person, once an Hearer of him; nor did he rest one Month without a fair Offer of another *Meeting from some of our Friends*, *near the Place of his Residence*, which, as I am informed, he declined: I blame him not for so doing. But suppose G. W. was as culpable as he represents, who so little deserved his Reflection, how doth this excuse T. Hicks, or extenuate his *own Injustice*, who, without any Notice given to G. W. or my self, did so publickly at *Barbican*, in our Absence, abuse the one, and challenge forth the other, *in Defence of himself and Friends*, from a Charge then exhibited by him *against our Faith and Principles*, suggesting to the Auditory, as if what were in Reality but his own crooked Consequences (detested of us) had been the *Express Articles of our Creed*. If yet he can presume to believe himself Modest, Just, or Christian, his Case is desperate, and I heartily pity his Mistake.

But he faults me for saying, *He could not but know of my being at a great Distance*, telling me, *That I either make him an Extraordinary* Gnostick, *or my self such an Over-Lasher, as needs to have my Words well measured after me*. Truly, if J. Faldo hath the Doing of it, I am sure to be wronged, unless he hath changed his Wont. How near a-kin he is to the *Gnosticks* in other Respects, I will not undertake to determine; only if what *Epiphanius* writes of their Self-Conceit, be true, J. F. has printed himself one of the *Extraordinariest Gnosticks* of this Age: But I will stand to my Words, that he must needs know of my Absence, for they that gave him Notice of the Meeting, being some of the Persons concern'd, might also inform him, that I was at a great Distance, they receiving that Answer: But lest he should deny all this, as probable as it is, the *Prolocutor's* Gloss upon the Word *E A S T*, doth the Business to an Hair's Breadth; for unless J. Faldo's Ears happen like J. Ives's, to be all of a sudden thick of Hearing, or to have as great an Impediment as T. Hicks's Tongue (that is, in Cases unpleasant to them) he could not but observe, that W. K. insinuated, as if I had Voyag'd to the *East-Land*, or the *East-Indies*, too far for the Noise of J. Faldo's Charge to be heard, as *Empty* as it was. But I must not forget, and yet take no Delight to remember, that Grave Person purposely left out *England*, joyn'd to *East*, in the Letter, that he might better break his Jest.

But be it as it will, I cannot but return J. Faldo an *Allusion* in his first Book, it may be, not in the very Words, yet the same Sense, *viz.* That he doth with me in this, as nicely and unjustly, as some Physicians, who strictly prohibit that to their Patients, they Eat themselves with *Great Gusto*.

I farther told him, as he observes, *That I had twice Defended our Faith in Print against him, and that a considerable Book lay at his Door unanswer'd*. To this he gives me several Returns, worth noting, for something or other: One is this, *That he perfectly knows the contrary*, To what? *That I have twice Defended our Belief*. The Quibble is here; *I have twice Writ, but not twice Defended*; Notable! But he goes of late for a *Critick*. However, *Who says so? John Faldo*. Doth he prove as well as say? *No such Matter*. He would not be mistaken, yet in asserting he transcends; for he farther tells us, *That I have not Overthrown One Line of his Books*; in which, as he explicitly proves his own Impudence, and Ostentation, so implicitly he calls many, far from *Quakerism*, as he terms it, *Fools or Knaves, for their contrary Judgment*.

But to the next Reason; *My Prints have Confirmed him*; which, though no Evidence to others of the Reasonableness of his Belief, yet a great One to me, that *that* Scripture is fulfilling upon him, *Wicked Men shall wax worse and worse*. But this is not all:

He tells us, *That it is not a Considerable Book*: Who expected *J. Faldo* should say any other? But doth he not hold himself obliged to help others to the same Creed, if his Heat be any better than Mercenary? Should he not endeavour to disintangle those that are otherwise Opinionated of the Matter? Doubtless he thinks it not less deserving his Pains, than those his first Book pretended to refute: If he doth, he would have done well to point in what; if he doth not, why doth he not answer me as well as them? Or why did he begin at all, if he intended not to make Good what he said? *But I would not be thought to imitate* Pharaoh's *putting the People to make Brick without Straw, by urging him to Defend that which indeed is Indefensible*: Only, it is worth our Notice, *That the Book is not Considerable*; But prithee, Why? *I think so. Ergo, What? It is not considerable*. This Way of arguing calls *J. Faldo* an Idle Meddler, for ever Writing an Half Crown or Three Shilling Book, to terminate here, *My Adversary is not Considerable*. So much Wit, Folly, or Shuffle, call it what he will, would have saved him much *Brain-Work in the Beginning*; but it may do the Man some Good: *Folks say so of Experience Dear Bought*; and, *Better Repent Late than Never*; though it's commonly judg'd to be a Repentance *Per Force*.

Well, but there's more behind, *viz. Whatever Qualities my last Book had*, he tells me, *It is more than I knew, that ever he saw it*; *He is sure, I never laid it at his Door, by sending One of them to him*. If he had said, *By receiving One of them*, it had past him; for I might have sent it, and it might have many Ways miscarried: But I will not press him with this, nor talk either of *Gnosticks*, or *Over-Lashers*, to Lash him with. And that I may right my self, and shew him how willing I was it should lie at his Door, I did, *to the best of my Remembrance, order him One*, and if it came not to his Hand, it neither accuseth me, nor excuseth him. *John Faldo* sent me none of his, and I think I never gave that for a Reason, why either of them lay not at my Door.

But it seems *J. Faldo* hath lately been at *Bedlam*, and one would think so by the *Story* he tells; *An Impertinent One it is*; *Some-Body said something of W. P. &c. But who he knows not*; here is the Upshot. What I should say I know not; for he neither directs me to the Person, nor House: So I must be contented to leave it as I found it, with *J. Faldo* and *Bedlam*, a Place that suits the Relation.

He hath not yet done: *My Book is said to be Printed in* 1673, *and it stuck in the Birth till many Months were past of the Year* 1674. This hits the Book in the Head, provided the *Title-Page* may stand for one. But how doth *J. Faldo* know it stuck so many Months in 1674? Which Way came he so well acquainted with the Secrets of the Press? But let us see what this *Objection* amounts to. The *Title* is either printed first or last: If *first*, say in 73, would he have the Printer foresee all those Difficulties that may obstruct the coming forth of the Book till 74, in order to set down 73, 74? This were to make a *Gnostick* of him with a Witness; or if he doth not, his Book shall be charg'd with an *Untruth*: If the *Title* be printed *last* (which I suppose is common) say in 74, and he sets down 74, he tells an *Untruth* of the *Book*, though not of the *Title*: Should the Printer then have set it down 73, 74, because some of the *Book* was printed in 73, this had been an *Untruth*, respecting the *Title-Page*, for that was all, and only printed in 74.

That ever a Man that loves *Reputation* at the Rate they that know him say he doth, *Should be so Idle in Print!* Suppose his Observation True; Is the *Book* therefore not *Considerable*? Or doth it not lye at his Door? Or is *W. P.* to be blamed, which is the Business in Hand? What he would be at I know not; unless he design'd to shew that he is a *Critick*, and well skill'd in *Annals*. But I am of Opinion, *That* Baronius (after the Old Proverb) *may sleep in a whole Skin for all* John Faldo's *Attempts*.

His next Reason for not giving my *Rejoynder* any Return, is, as he says elsewhere, *Magnipotent. I have Two Thousand Pounds per Annum in Possession, as reported: I only waste Paper, but he* (Alas for him) *must write no more than is Deem'd Convenient and Satisfactory*.

M m m m

I perceive that *John Faldo* is govern'd much by *Reports*, and that may be *One Reason why the Man reports so much Untruth*: But if he will make that Report Good, I will give him a Years Rent, and let him waste Paper, or waste it in Paper, and then call it *An Answer to W. P.* if he pleaseth. I observe that his Want of it, is the Reason of his not being a better Friend to the Printer; for his Words, that *He must write no more than what is deemed Convenient*, imply, *That had he wherewithal, he might Write and Waste, and Waste and Write.* But what is the *True English* of this Apologetical Sentence? It is to be suspected this, viz. *I must write no more than can be Sold: The Booksellers do not deem more of my Writings Convenient and Satisfactory.* I cannot believe that *J. Faldo* could not write what he deems both Convenient and Satisfactory. But *what is become of that Greedy Appetite in Learned and Unlearned after his Books, not only Certified by the Booksellers, but with a most Nauseous Self-Glorying, proclaimed by himself in his Vindication?* For my Part, I know not what else to infer from all this, than that his Books are become a Drug; at least, they so far stick undigested in the People's Stomachs, if not unsold in the Booksellers Shops, as there is neither Appetite enough in the one, nor Room enough in the other, for more of the Labours of the Author of *Quakerism No Christianity*.

But he thanks me that I have put one Argument into his Mouth, viz. *Wherefore hath W. P. made such a Bustle against Mr. Hicks and me, seeing he hath not toucht, or much less answer'd, the far greater Part of my first Book?*

O that John Faldo *would but learn to write* Truth, *and not cover great Weakness and Baseness with so much* Untruth! *Have I not answered to every Charge in the first Book? Examin'd two, three, four or five of his Witnesses at a Time to each Charge;* that is, *Testimonies out of our* Friend's Books, *he brought to justifie it?* It seems then, that my not fully Answering of his *first* Book, is one Reason why he hath hitherto declin'd Publishing something against my *second*; but had the Man been of this Mind before, doubtless he would never have writ a *Second*.

But what saith *J. Faldo* to my *second Book*, wherein I charge him, *In Point of Fact, with so many horrid Abuses of our Principles and Writings?* Not one Word; *unless that it is a Considerable Book for Railing, Confidence, abusing Authors, Impertinencies, Falshoods, and unfaithful Citing what I pretend to Confute.* What Fence can be had against such a Flail? Is this through the Aboundings of the Mans Modesty? Am I not like to be Cur'd of my *Confidence, by a Curb made up of such Links?* Certainly, unless *J. Faldo* hath as little Brains as this Character of my Book shows him to have of *Honesty*, he cannot think this *Entertainment* should prevail with me to step over the Kennel to meet such *A ——*. If ever Man was wrong'd, I am in that Expression *though his Saying, and Not Proving, helps it a little*.

I will at present overlook all but the last ill Quality he fastens upon my *Rejoynder*, and that is, *Not fairly citing his Reply:* I think I may say, *I have quoted the Better Half of his* Reply *into my* Rejoynder, *and that with such Distinction, as any Capacity may discern his Matter from mine:* And where he hath quoted One Line of mine, I have quoted Three of his. But I cannot think this the Way to *Curb my Confidence;* or to *Act the Modest Man, To Charge and not Prove;* Nay, *to Overlook so much Charg'd and Prov'd against him* in My Rejoynder, That is, *Unfairly Citing us, grosly Perverting what is Cited, Adding, or Diminishing, as best answer'd his Ends; Overlooking my Matter and Arguments, and Evading the Strength of most of what he Cited; Charging Consequences unfairly drawn upon us for our Principles, and abusing our Writings to maintain that Abuse;* which is not only prov'd in the Body of the Discourse, but summ'd up at the End of *My Rejoynder*, to help the *Reader's Memory*. And so far hath the Man been from Defending himself Doctrinally, that he suffers himself to remain without all Defence against my Charges.

But he hath told us very seasonably, *His farther Writing is not deem'd Convenient or Satisfactory;* A great deal of Wisdom, believe me, in the *Deemers;* and a great Share of Submission in this Adversary. I confess it is no Argument to do Indiscreetly a third Time, because a Man hath done so twice before. Had I return'd him a *Scurrilous, Frothy, and Evasive Pamphlet* (like his *Reply*) *to his Great Book*, I should have blam'd *my self, not him;* but I did *Conscientiously consider it, and bestow'd a Large and Grave Discourse upon it, faithfully Citing, and* (I hope) *as fully Enervating it*. But to this he objects, and that seems the *Strength of his Sheet,* if there be any in it, that is, *That he made Twelve Citations out of our own Books, and brought Thirteen Texts of Scripture to prove* (One Point of many) *and that I took but Two of each;* which granted, makes nothing against me, but *Proves himself Weak,*

Weak, to say no worse: For either each of them he brought was *Pertinent*, or not; If not, then his urging them, calls him *Impertinent*; If *Pertinent*, I answer'd the *Law*, that saith, *In the Mouth of Two Witnesses*, &c. for I examin'd *Two*, I thought of his *Considerablest*, and found them nothing to his Purpose, but that he had aggravated his Evil, by grosly abusing our Books, to prove his Infamous Charge: Now I would fain know, if it became not *J. Faldo* rather to have shown how weakly I invalidated his Evidence, *and prov'd him an Abuser of our Words*, than to tell the World, *I took but Two into Consideration*; for if he be gone upon them, he is gone upon all; for they are not a Jot more to his Purpose, if so much, as those examin'd: And I did not hold my self obliged to answer every *Impertinent Line in his Book*: If I skipt the *Strength of his Evidence*, or that those I left, had something not exprest, or implyed in the other, it had been proper for him to have particularly and expresly excepted against me; all which he not doing, *His Objection is Frivolous*, and amounts to no more than a *Mean Shuffle*.

But he tells the World, *That also a whole Chapter of Apostolical Inspirations lye at my Door untouch'd, and that they may judge at what Rate I have answered his Book*.

Poor Man! Is this all he can do, after he hath thought fit to give us a second Book? Must his first be his *Asylum* still? Why did he not tell *T. H.* and *W. K.* so, to excuse his coming to *Barbican*? Is he for *Disputing* notwithstanding, and yet not for *Writing*? It seems then that *it is not deemed Inconvenient to Dispute, but Write*. Well! But why will *J. Faldo* drop Things against himself, and, as he terms it, *put Instances in my Mouth*, to prove him a most *Disingenuous and Impudent Person*? For did I tell him, *That what concern'd us upon the Point of* Inspiration, *I had treated on at large elsewhere, and there was no need of a Repetition?* Now hath he shewn or attempted an Enervation of that? *Nothing less*. Or that we were concerned in that more than in his 4th Chapter? *No such Matter*. Or hath he given us one Reason, why I ought to have considered it? Or dare he say, the other contain'd not the Matter of it? What more can we say to a Man of this Fore-head? I told him of *Scores of Passages given by him under our Name*, he had not so much as cited Person or Book for, as well as abundance wilfully abused by him, that he did cite: To all which he is as mute as if I had never accused him, or he had nothing to say in his own Vindication. Is his *Recrimination* (suppose a Reason for it in it's Place) a valid *Answer*? Would he have thought this enough to his two Books? How easily could we have told J. F. *Thou hast abused our Religion, Books, and Persons*; but would he have accepted this as a sufficient *Answer or Rejoynder*? He tells the World *of our denying the Man's Nature, or Man Christ Jesus*, and brings a Company of wrested and misapply'd Sentences to vail his Abuse from the Vulgar; when we most faithfully and honestly believe it, and never speak or write undervaluingly of it: But because we press and exalt his *Spiritual Appearance*, or *Christ*, as come in Spirit to the Soul for it's particular Redemption, the Work of our Day; the other being granted on all Hands; therefore Men of his Leaven infer, *That we make Void the outward Coming and Sufferings of Christ, and utterly deny and reject him, as he is the Man Christ Jesus*. I wish for their Sakes that thus traduce us, they were as far from drawing such *Consequences*, as our *Faith* is from countenancing them. Of this I have spoke largely both in my *Answer* and *Rejoynder*, disingenuously overlook'd by this Adversary.

But he faults me for saying, *That W. Smith's Catechism is scripturally written, &c.* but never takes Notice of his unworthy *Assertion*, nor my *Answer*, as he ought to have done. The Matter was this: *J. Faldo* making use of this Instance to prove we preferred our own Writings before the Scriptures, viz. *That we called our own Sayings and Books, The Voice of the Son of God as uttered forth by him*, &c. *Truth's Principles; Shield of Truth*, &c. I answered, that those Titles were given with Respect to that Divine Truth they declared of and testified unto; not in Comparison with the Scriptures: That not one of those Books were destitute of Scripture; but is either generally writ in a *Scriptural Style*, or particularly defended by express *Scripture cited*; therefore of Necessity the Scripture must also partake with them in common of those famous Titles: And thus far have they the *Preference*, that they are quoted on Purpose to give the Truth we write of greater Credit; What is that greater Credit than to be exactly agreeable with them?

This and more I gave for *Answer*; He replieth thus:

1674.

I leave it to my Reader to give a Name to this Passage, the like to which for a daring Untruth the World hath scarcely been acquainted with; yet the Man pretends, besides all other Graces, to * Infallibility.

Many a large Libel I could produce, where there is not one Quotation of Scripture. W. Smith, in his Directory for Religious Principles, consisting of about two hundred Pages, hath not one Scripture quoted, nor one Exhortation to read the Scriptures; but, as his main Scope, denies and throws Dirt upon them.

This was J. Faldo's Reply, I shall now contract the Substance of my Rejoynder to it.

First, I did not say that there was not one Book without Plenty of express Scripture, but that those Books (whose Titles he quoted) were either generally in a Scripture Style, or particularly defended by Plenty of express Scriptures.

Secondly, To confute me, he produceth one of those Books, wherein he saith, one Scripture was not quoted; as if that was sufficient to prove, it was not written generally in a Scripture Style, one half of the Question; Upon which I made him this Challenge, to give me one Book, out of a Scripture Style, that is not Controversial, or any Controversial Book without express Scripture cited: If he could not, his vain Insults should fall upon his own Head. In this Particular, though he has overlook'd all the rest of my Discourse in Defence of our *Faith, Writings and Principles*, he undertakes me in his pretended *Curb* to my Confidence, in these Words, To accept W. P's Challenge is no bold thing; and to shew his unparallelled Falsehood and Confidence, I shall need to give you but a few Instances out of W. Smith's Catechism and Primmer.

But, *John Faldo*, Do Three Instances, few enough to be sure, prove two hundred Pages *generally* unscriptural, the Terms of the Question? Methinks this shews more *Confidence* than a Man that undertakes to *Curb* another Man's *Confidence* ought to have; but all *J. Faldo's* Sayings are to be construed *cum grano salis*. But to the first Instance.

Child. I would know, Father, how it is concerning those Things call'd Ordinances, as Baptism, Bread and Wine, which are much used in their Worship?

Father. Why Child, as to those Things, they rose from the Pope's Invention—— And then the Priest gives it to the People, and tells them that it is the Blood of Christ shed for them, when it is Wine, and not Blood, Smith's Catech. p. 39.

I see nothing unscriptural in either Question or Answer; unless *J. Faldo* quibbles upon the *Pope*. 'Tis true, he rose not 'till several hundred Years after the Scriptures were written; but if there be an Use of those Things call'd Sacraments, invented by the Pope, after another Manner than they were ever practised by the ancient *Christians*, which is undeniable with *J. Faldo*, and that such an unscriptural Use may be called an Invention, and that the Pope be a Man, yea, the Man of Sin, as also *J. Faldo*, I suppose, and many more do conceive, and all this Scripturally; then, I hope, it cannot with any sober Pretence, be deny'd, but that *W. S*'s Answer is very Scriptural. But what makes this great *Pretender to Truth and Modesty* decline taking any Notice of that Charge I published against him upon Occasion of his most gross *Abuse* of *W. Smith* upon these Words? who would needs have it, that *W. Smith* calls the Lord's Supper the *Pope's Invention*, when I expresly prov'd out of the same Place, that *W. Smith* intended it of the present Practice of them, and not of any Primitive Institution? *W. Smith's* Words are these: *The whole Practice of those Things, as they use them, had their Institution by the Pope, and were never so ordained of Christ; for he did not ordain Sprinkling of Water in a Child's Face, or to make a Sign of a Cross in his Forehead, nor God-fathers and God-mothers to undertake for it; neither did he ordain Bread and Wine to be so* (or after that Manner) *used and received.* If this be to make *Baptism* and the *Supper Popish*, what becomes of his *Antipædobaptists* and all *Protestants*, that maintain the same respectively? But most evident it is, *W. Smith* intended not that *Baptism* and *Supper* used by the Ancient *Christians*; but most true it is, that *J. Faldo* made *W. Smith* to intend so. I leave the Reader to give a Name to this

---

* It is frequent with him, and that Sort of Adversaries, to fling Infallibility in our Teeth; and here he doth it with manifest Derision, as if it was a greater Evil to be Infallible, than to Err; but let the Reader know, that we do not so much as pretend to any such Thing, as meer Men; for as such, *Humanum est errare*; but in our Judgment of the Things of God, so far as we receive it from the Grace of God. And if this be a Piece of *Quakerism* in Opposition to Christianity, in *J. Faldo's* Account, the Scripture must answer for it; only I cannot but take Notice how he beats the Air, who either defends or proposes any Religion upon Fallible Grounds.

Carriage;

Carriage; the like to which, for a *Daring Perversion*, I yet know no Body guilty of, *J. Faldo* and *T. Hicks* excepted.

Now for the next Instance brought to prove our Books unscripturally written.

Child. 'Then the Scriptures are to be own'd and believed as a true Testimony 'of what the Saints were made Partakers of in that Day.

Father. Yes, they are to be own'd and believ'd, and they that do not so, they are to be denied.

An admirable Confession to the Scriptures: Is this the Way to prove *W. Smith's* Book unscripturally written? That there is not an Exhortation to read the Scriptures, and that the whole Scope of it is, to throw Dirt upon them, yea, to deny them, though *J. Faldo* himself tells us, that *W. Smith* teacheth, *that those ought to be deny'd that do not own them*; but the Truth is, *J. Faldo's* Proofs against the *Quakers* are like *Hebrew*, to be read backwards; He hath a Faculty, beyond the common Rate of Men, to facilitate his own Confutation. But he makes *W. Smith* farther to answer.

Thou must take Heed, Child, of giving more unto the Scriptures, than unto them belongs, lest in so doing thou diminishest from the Glory of Christ.

What of all this? May not People Idolize, as well as undervalue *the Scriptures*? Ought they to be put in the *Room of Christ*? Or is it ill done, to exhort People *to prefer* Christ *before the Scriptures*? How can *J. Faldo* call this Part of *W. Smith's* Answer Unscriptural, and yet believe those Words of Christ to be any Part of Scripture? *Search* (or rather, ye search) *the Scriptures, for in them ye think ye have Eternal Life, and they are they which testify of me, and ye will not come unto me that ye might have Life*, John 5. 39, 40. *I am the Way, the Truth and the Life*, John 14. 6. Christ himself here teacheth us, to give him the *Preference*; and implicitly rebuketh the *Jews* from expecting Eternal Life in the *Scriptures* rather than in *Him*, who is the Way, the Truth and the Life.

His last Instance is this:

Child. 'I am sensible that there is something in my Conscience that lets me 'see my secret Thoughts, and the Intents of my Heart; but I have not known 'what it hath been, nor hitherto have much regarded it.

Father. That is the True Light, &c.

Child. 'But if I should turn to it, and obey it when it reproveth me for Sin, 'is there Power in it to save me from Sin, and to deliver me from Iniquity?

Father. Yes, Child; All Power in Heaven and Earth is in it, &c.

Now judge, *Reader*, saith *J. F.* if all these Things are contain'd in the Scripture. But I will help the *Reader* to judge rightly in this Matter; and question not if by *Containing* he means as he ought, *the Substance of such Answers*, and not that they are so laid down, to prove them to be according to Scripture; and therefore Scriptural.

1. That it is *God, who searcheth the Heart, tryeth the Reins, and telleth unto Man his Thoughts*, the Prophet affirms; and I know no Body that pretends to *Christianity*, denyeth it.

2. The Apostle asserts, *That which may be known of God is manifest in Men; for God hath shewn it unto them*, Rom. i. 19.

3. That it was the Apostolical Message, *That God is Light*, 1 John 1. 5.

4. *That whatsoever doth make manifest is Light*, Ephes. 5. 13.

5. That *Christ*, who is God over all, blessed for ever, *is that True Light, which* (thus) *enlightneth every Man*.

6. *That all Power in Heaven and in Earth belongs to Christ, the true Light.*

Now unless he denies *Christ* to be *God*, or *Christ* to be *Light*, or, that He, the True Light, so searcheth, &c. or that all Power in Heaven and Earth belongs to *Him*, it will naturally follow, that to say, *All Power in Heaven and in Earth belongs to God*, *Christ* or the Light of the World, is *Equivalent*: For we do not assert, as some Ignorantly, and some Maliciously have printed and reported, *That all Power in Heaven and Earth is in the Manifestation*; but in him that gives the Manifestation. I have taken great Care, with several others, to explain our Belief in this Matter, if possible, to prevent such Evil-minded Men as this *Adversary*, from making so ill an Use of our Innocent Expressions, and giving their own Monstrous Consequences for our Scriptural Principles.

Thus much to evidence to my Reader, how groundlesly *J. F.* flung *Unparallel'd Falshood and Confidence* upon me for asserting, that those Books before-mention'd

were

were generally written in a Scripture Style; and with what Weakness he hath endeavoured to disprove me.

I shall, among a Multitude of Instances that might be given, produce Ten, to shew to my Reader with what Truth those Imputations belong to *J. Faldo*, and how exactly he character'd himself when he bestow'd that Reflection upon me.

1. *J. Faldo* affirms, that *W. Smith* not only quoted never a Scripture, and writ unscripturally, but *that he had not one Exhortation to read the Scriptures, nay, that the main Design of the Book was to deny them, and throw Dirt upon them*; yet *J. F.* thus cites him concerning the Scriptures:

Child. ' Then the Scriptures are to be own'd and believ'd, &c.

Father. *Yes, they are to be own'd and believ'd, and they that do not so are to be denied.*

To this let me add another notable Passage in the same Discourse, cited by me in that very Page of my *Rejoynder*, where my *Challenge* lay (which he thought no Boldness to accept) though he was so modest as not to be so bold with this Passage.

' *Quest.* Of what Service are the Scriptures as they are given forth and record-
' ed without?

Answ. Much every Way *unto those that have receiv'd the same Spirit from whom they were given forth; for unto such they are* Profitable, *and* make wise *unto Salvation; and are unto them of Service, for* Instruction, Edification *and* Comfort, Rejoynd. p. 61. Is there no *Exhortation* lodg'd in these Words? And is this to *Deny* or *throw Dirt* upon the Scriptures? If any shall object *W. Smith*'s making the Spirit necessary to the profitable Reading of the Scriptures, let them go to *W. Tindal, J. Bradford*, Bp. *Jewel, J. Philpot, Luther, Calvin, Peter Martyr* and others, they will preach them the same Doctrine; which I have observ'd in my *Rejoynder*, and may easily be found in my Catalogue of Authors.

2. My second Instance shall be this, That he makes *W. Smith* call the Scriptures *Traditions of Men, Earthly Root, Darkness, Confusion, Corruption*; And out of *the Light and Power of God*; which he only ascrib'd to degenerated Men, their Worship, Imaginations and Traditions. See *Quakerism no Christianity*, pag. 117, 119. Vind. p. 41, 45. My Rejoynder from pag. 141. to 157.

3. That the *Quakers* understand by Knowledge according to the Flesh, *the Use of the Understanding, though sanctified*, Qu. no Chr. p. 41. Vind. p. 24, 25. My Answer. p. 35. Rejoynd. p. 424.

4. That *I. Pennington* should call *Visible Worship as such, the City of Abomination*, Vind. p. 50. Rejoynd. p. 194, 195.

5. That by *Traditions of Men*, we understand *the Scripture, or written Word*, Qu. no Chr. Part 3. p. 86. My Answer, p. 250.

6. That the *Quakers* mean by the Vail that is over People, *their Belief of the Man Christ Jesus born of the Virgin Mary to be now existing in Heaven*, Ibid. p. 87. Vind. p. 93. My Answer, p. 251, 252. Rejoynd. p. 395, 396.

7. I take occasion to censure Men's adding their *Comments* and *Glosses* fram'd from Study to any Part of the Scripture; and *J. Faldo* cites me, as complaining of such as frame them from the Study of the *Scriptures*; as if Studying of the Scriptures, and Men's Adding their own Glosses to the Scriptures, were one and the same Thing, *Vind.* p. 42, 43. My *Rejoynd*. p. 159.

8. From *E. Burrough*'s making the Light of Christ within to be one in Nature with the Spirit of Christ; *J. Faldo* infers, *That the Quakers hold the Soul to be God*, as if that had been said of the Soul which was said of the Light of Christ shining in the Soul, or that they were Synonymous, *Vind.* from p. 75 to 87. *Rejoyn.* p. 348, 349, 350.

9. Because *E. B.* rejected that Carnal Notion that confines the Infinite, Omnipresent God, to a Residence only above the Stars, he makes no Difficulty of inferring *that we deny the Manhood of Christ Jesus*. As most absurd as base! *Q. no C.* p. 9, 10. My Answer, p. 14. Vind. p. 9. Rejoynd. p. 420.

10. From our affirming that such a kind of Reading of Scripture as the *Pharisees* used, and to those Ends, makes Men harder to be wrought upon to true Conversion than the Heathen, *J. Faldo* infers, *that reading the Scriptures, and getting Knowledge thence puts Men into a worse Condition than the* Heathen; *and that there's scarcely any Thing more Dangerous than reading the Scriptures*: Yea, he accuseth us of *Charging the Miscarriages of Men's Souls on the Knowledge the Scripture by God's Blessing doth convey*, Vind. p. 21, 37. Rejoyn. p. 126, 127, 325.

Thus

Thus much, and I wish there had been no Occasion for this, to evidence the false and unworthy Practice of *J. Faldo* against the Writings and Sayings of our Friends, in order to compass his Designs: I shall now give some touch upon his *Confidence*, since he hath entituled me to an unparallel'd Share, and counts himself the fit Person to *Curb* me for it.

J. Faldo began with us in a great Book called *Quakerism No Christianity*; I answered him in a Book, entituled *Quakerism a New Nickname for Old Christianity*; against this he put forth his *Vindication*, unto which I made my *Rejoynder* consisting of Twenty Three Chapters, in which I vindicated our Principles, stripping them of those frightful Vizards and hateful Disguises he put upon them, confirm'd them *by many Scriptures and Reasons*, and to compleat our Defence, produc'd in favour of the whole above *Two Hundred Testimonies* out of both ancient and modern Authors.

Besides all this I faulted his Conduct and Behaviour in this Controversy, in above *Four Hundred Particulars*, and that under distinct Sections, most of which were not less unworthy of a good *Christian*, yea, an honest *Heathen*, I will say, of any *fair Controvertist*, than the *Ten* I just now mention'd. Notwithstanding this great Obligation upon him, either to answer my Book, or enter Mute to any farther Proceed in this Debate; in my Absence at the first *Barbican* Meeting, before a great Concourse of People, after *T. Hicks* had won the Goal by running Alone, the Man, as one in Love with such *Romance-Trophies*, starts up like some *Herald at Arms*, bids Defiance to the *Quakers* and their Religion, gives forth his Challenge to *W. Penn*, to dispute him, ay, that he would; and instead of his *Glove*, flung a Paper to bind it, which when all came to all, *was but some of the Contents of his first Book twice largely answered*; and because no farther Notice was taken of this *Giant*, partly by not receiving his Paper so soon as he might expect, and partly by reason of these other Contests that claim Precedency; That he might not be thought *No-body*, when so many strove to be *Some-body* against us, he prints it, without all Consideration had to my *Rejoynder*, or so much as an *Apology* for his *Silence* to it, which, at least, had become a *Modest Person* to give: After all this can any Man think *J. Faldo Bashful*, or one that is so out of Love with *Confidence* in himself, as that he is fit to *Curb* it in others? Methinks he should not believe that repetitious *Farthing* or *Half-penny-Paper* feat enough to excuse him; or so sufficient to acquit him of old Debts, as that without any *Breach of Modesty* or *common Honesty*, he might encrease his former Score by fresh Charges: It is but reasonable that he should make good what he hath done first; and not, that we should gratifie every impertinent, tautological *Humour* of *J. F.*

But what saith *John Faldo*, to this Part of my Answer to his Challenge? viz. *But that I may acquit my self of that Duty incumbent on me for the Truth, I do hereby signifie, That in as much as the Controversy depending between T. Hicks, &c. and us, takes in the most of the Particulars of his Charge, we freely consent, that he should come in with them for a Share as Confederate in the same Work, and use his utmost Abilities to maintain his Accusations; And if in any Thing his Charge is singular, we shall be ready to hear and fairly debate it at the same Meeting or Meetings, to avoid fresh and unnecessary Contests as much as may be.* To this he thus replieth:

1. *I must fall into a Confederacy with the Antipædobaptists, in the same Work: Hold a little Mr. Penn! If I have my Option, I must deal with you singly; More confuse rather than assist: But it seems I must be wholly at your Appointment; for, although you had consented that in your Contest about Mr. Hicks's Dialogues there should Four of each Party have Liberty to speak; yet I no sooner began to oppose you (being desired to be one of the Four) but you told me, you were not to dispute with me, but Mr. Hicks, and call'd to T. Hicks, and were follow'd by the Quakers Clamours of Hicks, Hicks, which answer'd your End, and forc'd my Silence.*

Contradiction and *Falshood* make up his *Paragraph*. Was he not of the *Confederacy*, when he tells us himself, that he was not only a Party with them, but *One of the Four* pitcht upon to manage their Cause?

But if he have his *Option*, he must deal with me singly.

It is Time for him indeed, who hath been a double-dealing so long: But certainly, if the Man were not more than ordinarily fond of hearing himself talk, or extravagantly ambitious of a single Crown, he would be contented with a *Partner*; but this *Option* holds no Concord with his *Adoption* into *Confederacy*: He hath begun already as one of the four, what hinders that he should not continue so? But he thinks *that more than one confounds rather than assists*: If so, what

made

1674.

made *T. Hicks* have three to help him? And why did *J. Faldo* attempt it? Certainly he did not design to confound *T. Hicks*. To all this *Confusion* of his let me add his *Untruth*: He chargeth me with telling him at the *Barbican*-Meeting when he began to speak, *I was not there to dispute with him*, which is false to a Tittle; Either his *Ears* were as infirm, as his *Voice* was low, or else he saith this to serve his present Occasion: However, I said no such Thing; but understanding it to be him that spoke from some better acquainted with his * Person, I answered, *That the Noise of the Multitude was so great, We could not hear what he said*; Though had I given that Answer he made for me, I think it had been very reasonable, since he never told us, *That he was One of the four*; besides, more than that fixt Number had spoken before him. *That the* Quakers *should clamour*, Hicks, Hicks, *to answer my End, and force his Silence*, is as true as the rest; It was the Multitude that frequently and importunately cryed, *Hicks, Hicks, Hicks*; as looking upon it unreasonable that one who had shown himself so arch in abusing us, should pretend such Inability to answer our Charge, as that other Folks must mostly manage his Affair. But that to silence him was to answer my End, is both to tell A— and proclaim the good Opinion he has of himself, as if it stood our Cause so much upon, to have him silent, and *T. Hicks* speak: Poor *T. Hicks*! This was not kindly done of *J. F.* but perhaps he meant it of his better Elocution and Skill in stating the Question, recommended to us in his *Curb* to my *Confidence*: Modest Man that he would be thought!

But what saith he to this Part of my fair Offer, That *if in any Thing his Charge be singular, we should be ready to debate it at the same Meeting or Meetings with the* Baptists, *to avoid Unnecessary Contests*; since most of the Particulars of his Charge are taken in by the Controversy depending between us and the *Baptists: It is not only an Untruth* (says *J. F.*) *but a meer Shift*; for in the One and Twenty Proposals to be debated by them, there is not one of the Particulars of my Charge: Besides, in the Position to be disputed on, not only the Matter, but the Form, and each Term, is of great Consideration. Which is as much as to say, if I understand *J. Faldo*'s Meaning, that after we have disputed the Matter of the same Questions with *T. H.* and his Three Assistants, they must be disputed over again upon *J. Faldo*'s new Model, which one Nice and Humoursom Impertinency shall make Disputes both Endless and Useless: Let him bestow his Skill upon *T. Hicks*, his Cause wants it, and do their utmost together. But he would fasten an Untruth upon me, for saying, that most of the Particulars of his Charge are taken into that Controversy, affirming, *That in our One and Twenty Proposals there was not one of the Particulars of his Charge*: To which I need say no more but this, The Charge we exhibited against *T. Hicks* contain'd so many particular Charges: I grant they related to Matter of Fact, and in that sense the Particulars of *J. Faldo*'s Charge against us, were not explicitly there; yet they that please to read what follows the One and Twenty Particulars, as given into the *Baptists*, exhibited and read at *Barbican*, and since printed in our *first Account*, will find that we offer, after a full Consideration and Determination upon the foresaid Particulars, *to come to Doctrinal Points, which are chiefly in Controversy between us and them upon* T. Hicks's *Three Dialogues*; and I hope *J. Faldo* is not grown quite so desperate as to deny, that most, if not all the Particulars of his Charge, fall in with *T. Hicks*'s Attempts against us, and that materially too. I have heard as if such a Confession was one Part of his Speech at the first *Barbican*-Meeting: However, if he denies their Endeavours to have been so harmonious, I offer to prove them so; but could I not do it, yet I made Provision for him, wherein his Case is singular. Besides, I desire the *Reader* to take Notice, I did not say, the Particulars of *J. Faldo*'s Charge were exprest in the Catalogue of our Charge of Matter of Fact against *T. Hicks*, but that *they fell in with the Controversy*, which Word *Controversy* takes in both *Fact* and *Doctrine*: And since he could fall in with *T. Hicks* upon Matter of *Fact* at *Barbican*, wherein he was not concerned, there can be no just Pretence for him to refuse falling in with *T. H.* in Matter of Doctrine, wherein he is concerned: So that, in short, I am neither guilty of *Untruth*, who never said, that most of the Particulars of his Charge were concerned in the One and Twenty Particulars of Fact exhibited against *T. H.* but in the *Controversy*, which is most true; nor yet of *Shifting*, in referring him to our Meeting with *T. Hicks*, since I therein only

---

* I never saw him before; and he asserts in his printed Paper, that he never saw me till the *Barbican*-Meeting; yet several Months before in his printed *Vindication*, he saith, he had spoken with me.

offer what his own Words and Practice countenance me in, especially, since I farther add (as before said) That *if in any Thing his Charge was singular* from that Controversy, *we should be ready to hear and fairly debate at the same Meeting*, to avoid fresh and unnecessary Contests. One would think this were pretty fair to a Man under *J. Faldo's* Circumstances with us. I leave the *Reader* to say where the *Shift* and the *Untruth* lieth. Only let me add Two Passages more, that will not a little help him to make a true Judgment of the Man.

The one is his telling the World, *That by my Manuscript Letter to him, I do in effect unsay all again, that I said of accepting his Challenge in my Printed Answer*, and yet neither prints the Letter, though but short, nor that Passage he fastens his Consequence upon. It's true, I told him, that it was our present Resolution to stick to the Matter of Fact against *T. H.* and so much he prints; but what is that to the Purpose? Will any such Passage bear an *Ergo,* W. Penn *unsaith all he said of Accepting the Challenge, &c?* Or, *therefore* W. Penn *will never proceed to Matter of Doctrine, because he first resolves to stick to Matter of Fact,* the Method agreed upon?

The other Passage is this: *For my Part, though I shall not refuse any Opportunity offered to defend the Christian Religion from it's Adversaries; yet I expect that Mr.* Penn *shall undertake to defend the* Quakers *(and himself especially) from my Charge intire as it is exhibited, and until then I shall look on him as declining it.*

At what rate I decline a Meeting, and how well *J. Faldo* proves it, impartial Men may judge: But one would think by what he saith, as if he were another *Tertullian,* and the *Quakers* a pack of obstinate *Heathens*. He is unfit to defend *Christianity,* whose Works prove he doth not understand it, unless the *Jew* outward, with all his Envy, be the *Jew* inward; or a froward *Pharisee,* a good *Christian* : No, No. *J. Faldo,* we affirm, hath first charged impious Errors upon us, and then abused our Writings to countenance them with; And though this be largely and effectually discovered not only in my *Answer* (at which he let fly a *squibbing Reply*) but in my *Rejoynder* too (being a more particular Resumption of the whole Controversy, and unto which he never yet made any Return) we see he hath Forehead enough to insinuate as if the *Quakers* still remained undefended. This is the Man that undertakes to *Curb my Confidence,* who begs so unreasonably and importunately, and doth as good as threaten, if I refuse his Terms; and which aggravates the Matter, he would have People believe, that I shift defending the *Quakers,* whilst he is yet so manifest a Debtor to our Defences.

Well, but for all this, that it may sufficiently appear we neither did nor do decline a Meeting with him; Let it be observed, 1*st*, That I gave him timely Notice of our *Wheeler-street-Meeting,* with an Invitation to be there, and went more in Expectation of him than *T. Hicks,* from a Report that *T. H.* would not, but that *John Faldo* intended to be present, though both thought fit to be absent. 2*dly*, If he yet thinks it convenient to embrace that Offer already made, *viz. To be one of the four,* a Place he confesseth to have accepted at the *Barbican-*Meeting, even about another Man's Fact. Or *Lastly,* If through the Apprehension he hath of *T. H's ill Elocution,* and great Conceit he hath of his own Oratory, with his better Skill at *Forming* and *Terming* the Question, he can prevail with the *Baptists,* to be their Mouth in the present Controversy, we shall through God's Assistance be ready to embrace any convenient Time and Place for a free and publick Meeting.

And that he may not think himself unconcerned in this Proposal, nor want any Encouragement we can well give him to accept it, I do hereby offer at such a Meeting or Meetings, first, *To prove him, as well as* T: Hicks, *an Abuser of us and our Writings by Forgery and Perversion* ; And next, *to maintain those Doctrines which are indeed believed and asserted by us, to be Scriptural, and therefore* Christian. And if this will not please him I shall not think my self obliged to gratify every nice and critical Humour he is troubled with ; but leave him to tire himself with the Pain of his own manifest and merited Disquiet: Though my Soul beseecheth Almighty God, if it please him, to turn him and the Hearts of our Enemies, that they may see how much they wound *Christianity,* in pretending to defend it, and grieve that Holy *Spirit* which would lead them into *Holiness, Meekness, Patience* and *Love,* by these Tempestuous Assaults upon the *Faith, Practice* and *Persons* of their Harmless Neighbours.

I am a Real Friend in the Universal Principle of God to all Men, and therein seek Peace with all Men,

12th of the 9th
Month, 1674.

William Penn.

THE
SKIRMISHER Defeated,
AND
TRUTH Defended.

BEING

An ANSWER to a PAMPHLET, Entituled,
A Skirmish made upon Quakerism.

By WILLIAM PENN.

Jam iii. 13, 14, 16. *Who is a Wise Man, and endued with Knowledge among you? Let him shew out of a Good Conversation his Works with Meekness of Wisdom: But if ye have bitter Envying and Strife in your Hearts, Glory not, and Lye not against the* Truth: *For, where Envying and Strife is, there is Confusion, and every Evil Work.*

OF all the Evils that attend *Controversie about Religion*, there is none more Odious and Provoking, than that of *Mis-stating Principles*, and giving That *under Men's Names*, to the World, *for their Doctrine and Judgment*, *which they abhor to believe*, much more to assert and divulge to others. And this I hope, I may without Offence add, That to be Misrepresented hath mostly been the Lot of TRUTH in all Ages, *and Her peculiar Difficulty and Suffering from the World*: For, no sooner has Almighty God Blest Mankind with farther *Discoveries of His Heavenly Will*, and Divine Helps to perform it, than some or other, and those not a Few, have immediately opposed themselves to that Work, and the Lovers and Abettors of it: Nor have those Adversaries been of the Rabble, *Men of no Letters, Education, or Pretence to Religion*, by no Means, much the contrary, the Learned Crew, *the* Clergy, *that* Great Corporation of Religion ; *it hath been generally such, the* Chemarims, Men of the Black Robe, *that from a Pretence to Greater Knowledge than others, an Education in the Studies of Divinity, a Peculiar Warrant and Mission, with the Countenance of Worldly Authority, have used their Skill, and employed their Abilities to traduce* TRUTH, *and stigmatize* Her Followers ; *exposing Both to the Fury or Mockery of the World*: Tell me when this fell out otherwise, and allow me Scripture-Story but to be True and Sacred.

I pretend not now to write an *History*, no nor to Epitomize that which is already writ, nor need I, for the Case is evident ; but because Examples are so ready, I will instance in Him that said, *I am the Way, the Truth, and the Life*: One While the *Scribes* and *Pharisees* took hold of his *Nonconformity to their Customs*, and then He was a *Despiser of* Moses, *a Breaker of the Law*, One that made Void the Traditions of the Fathers : Another While, He was a Mean Fellow, but a *Carpenter's Son* ; And what Man of *Quality would follow* Him? Or who would make a Messiah of a *Mechanick?* Or a Saviour *of so Servile an Offspring?* But when this would not do, Then He was a Samaritan, *and had a Devil, and Cast out Devils by* Beelzebub *the Prince of Devils* ; thereby rendring His Person hateful to the *Jews*, that refus'd all Commerce with the *Samaritans*, and his Wonderful Works suspected of a Diabolical Power, lest the People should believe in Him. But this Trick failing, and the People believing, lest any of Note should be taken with him, they fling out, *That he was a very Idiot, one that knew not Letters* ; and that none followed him but

those

those that were Cursed, and knew not the Law, the Rabble, the Vulgar, and Illiterate People. But when this Stratagem succeeded not to lessen his Reputation, and question his Pretences, they bruited up and down, that for all his pretended Perfection, *He was a Loose Person, a Wine-Bibber, a Companion of Publicans and Sinners, not fit to be the Leader of a Strict Sect, nor qualified for so Glorious a Work as that of the* Messiah's. God still blasting their Designs, and the People flocking after Him, admiring His Doctrine, His Authority, His Wisdom, and His Miracles, the *Jewish* Council of Doctors and Rabbies roundly accuse Him of *Blasphemy*, and have the Confidence and Cruelty to seek his Life, telling *Pilate*, that *They have a Law, and by their Law he ought to Dye*; but *Pilate* scrupling the Matter, and finding their Proofs short, faints in their Business, which they perceiving, with one loud Cry, as it were Daring *Pilate* to deny them their *Murderous Ends*, tell him, *He is an Enemy to Cæsar*, hoping, though *Pilate* would not concern himself with their Laws and Customs, yet that being *Cæsar*'s Deputy and Officer, he would not suffer any Man to live that was a Declared Enemy to *Cæsar*'s Government; and they had their End.

Nor did his *Disciples* fare better, *who were accounted Enemies to the Law and Scriptures, Seducers, Deceivers of the People, Pestilent Fellows, Sowers of Sedition, Turners of the World upside down*, &c. But who were they that made this Lamentable Opposition? Were they *Literally Heathens*, or *Professedly Infidels*? No such Matter; for that might have in some Sense extenuated the Crime, at least have spoil'd our Parallel; *but they were the Offspring of* Abraham, *Great Scripturians, to whom pertain'd the Covenants, Promises, Adoption*, and if we will take their Word for it, *Children of God, in Bondage to None*; though it's not to be doubted but that they were by *Nature Heathens*, and for all their Great Profession, *Infidels in Spirit, and Great Slaves to Sin, and Children of the Evil One, all this While*. Now this has been our Case, who are in Reproach called *Quakers*.

In the First Place, we must honestly and plainly confess, before *Almighty God*, and all Men, that we have been of the Common Mass of Mankind, and had our Conversation in the Times past, in the Vanities, Pleasures, Sports and Lusts of this World, Living in some Respect, *Without God and Christ in the World* (though under a Profession both of God and Christ, as the most Part of *Christendom* (so called) do at this Day;) and in this dead Estate to the Living Sense and Enjoyment of God and Christ in our Souls, the Lord Visited us, and by *His own Convincing and Reproving Light, Power and Spirit, hath he awakened us, and brought us to behold Him, whom we, under all our Profession of Religion, had more or less grieved and pierced with our Vain Thoughts, Idle Words, and Unholy Actions*; and to Sorrow with True Godly Sorrow, and be in unfeigned Bitterness, as for our First-Born, or our Only Child; *the Lord thus Redeeming us through his Holy Rebukes and Judgments, from an Evil Conversation, and Converting us to Himself by His own Righteous Law in our Hearts*. And when it had pleased God thus to rouse us out of our Carnal Security, and Fire our House of Empty Profession about our Ears, and open the *Book of Conscience*, and call us to Judgment, kindling his Holy Terrors in our Hearts, because of our past Conversation, that had been in the Vain and Sinful Fashions and Customs of the World, calling *God our Father, and not Born of Him*, and *Christ Lord*, and not by *His Holy Spirit*, neither had taken up *His Daily Cross*, to the slaying of our own Wills and Carnal Affections, notwithstanding the great Profession that we in Words made of *Him*, and the *Christian Religion*, we came to see that *True Christianity* was another Thing than the World apprehended, and that *as he was no more a* Jew *that was one One outward, so neither was he a* Christian *that was one outward; but he was a* True Jew *and* Christian *that was one inward, whose Praise is not of Men, but of God*; in this Zeal that God had begotten in us for his Living Way, the Spiritual Circumcision, the *Right Christianity*, namely, *To be Christ-like, to do the Will of God in Earth as it is done in Heaven, to Live Unspotted from the World, and no more we to Live, Rule and Order, but Christ that Liveth in us, which is to have Eternal Life abiding in us*. In this Godly Zeal, I say, for this Pure and Living Way, we frequently testified to all People, *What GOD had done for us*, where *He* found us, what *He* Discovered to us, what *He* Condemned us for, what *He* Redeemed us from, and what *He* had brought us to, earnestly recommending the *Light of Christ Within, that manifests the Mind of Christ unto them*, vehemently decrying the Lifeless Profession they *Worshipped GOD the Eternal Spirit, in*; and shewing to them a more Excellent Way, because a more Pure and Spiritual Way; *manifesting to them how that they called* Christ *their Lord*,

Lord, *and did not obey Him*; their Saviour, *and were not saved from Sin by Him*; *yea, how they Magnify'd Him in the History, and Crucify'd Him in the Mystery, warning them of their Carnal Faith, Hope and Security they lived in, which cleansed not their Consciences from dead Works, nor overcame the Vain and Wicked Spirit of the World, particularly exhorting them to turn away from their* Hireling Teachers, *that had caused them to err*; *who, though they said,* Thus saith the Lord, *the Lord never spoke by them*; *and God said of Old,* Such should not profit the People, *who Fed and Clothed themselves of the Flock, but had no Heavenly Bread, no Green Pastures, no Pure Fountain to feed and refresh the Flock with*; *and that all should learn of the Lord, that Teacheth his People himself by* His own Good Spirit in their Inward Parts, *according to the Tenour of his Second and Everlasting Covenant,* That they turn not again unto Folly.

For this Testimony Sake hath the Devil raged, and plotted our Ruin ever since we have been a People, now like a Lion, then like a Lamb; one While in the Appearance of a Serpent, another While in the Shape of a Dove; but the *Lord God Jehovah* hath kept us hitherto, none of his Weapons have yet prospered, and 'tis our Faith none ever shall; for our Confidence is in him whom the Winds and Seas obey.

Sometimes they tell us of our Novelty, as the *Jews* did Christ; *Abraham was before thee*, say the *Jews*; *Before* Abraham *was, I am*, says *Christ*; the *Christians* were counted *Upstarts* both by *Jews and Gentiles*; yet their Way, and so ours, the Pure, Plain, Spiritual Religion and Worship, was before *Jew or Gentile* were; anon we are *Ignorant, Illiterate, Mechanical*; by and by we are *Subtil Jesuits, Crafty Deceivers*; then *Familists*, as quickly *Papists*; by some counted Enemies to *Cæsar*; by others *Temporizers*: Our Visage is continually marr'd in the Eyes of the *Outside Christians*, as was our Blessed Lord's and Master's in the Eyes of the *Outside Jews*; for what can escape their Censure; there is a Sort of Men nothing pleases; one says we are *Socinians*, owning Christ to be but *Meerly a Man*; another, that we are *Sabellians* and *Valentinians*, and *deny the Manhood of Christ*; starts up a Third, and says, *The* Quakers *expect to be Justified by their own Works*; a Fourth presently crys out, *They will do nothing unless the Spirit moves them* (how are the Works ours then?) *Some Imprison us, because for Conscience-Sake we cannot take up Arms*; Others, *For Fear we should*. Again, our *Plainness in Apparel* is concluded *Singularity*; Our *Proper Speech*, *Rudeness*; Our *Scripture-Dialect, Canting*; If we conscientiously refuse them our *Hat*, 'tis *Pride*; If out of Pure Tenderness we cannot *Swear*, *'tis Contempt of Authority*; and if we deny to *Pay the Parson Tythes*, 'tis reputed *Robbery*, though we have nothing for our Money of him: In fine, our *Silence* goes for *Sullenness*; our *Sobriety* for *Morosity*; our *Frugality* for *Covetousness*; and *for our Doctrines*, they are *only Antipodes to Truth*; for we are made to *Deny God, Christ, Spirit, the Immortality of the Soul* (yet that we hold our Souls to be God, Christ, and Holy Spirit too) *that we deny the Scriptures, Ministry, Church-Ordinances, Justification and Salvation by Christ, the Resurrection, Rewards and Punishments*; and which is yet farther observable, as it fared with our Dearest Master and His Followers then, The *Scribes, Pharisees, Sadducees, Galileans*, &c. ready before to devour one another, immediately united, and combined to oppose, traduce, trap, and ensnare them; so has it fallen out with us; for the Hand of every Party hath been lifted up against us; I scarcely know one that is under any *Considerable Notice in Christendom*, (however Violent and Irreconcileable among themselves) that hath refused that Common League and Confederacy, or that hath not by some or other of it's principal Agents, Vigorously, if not Scornfully and Persecutingly, decry'd and oppos'd us; yet we are Alive, and a *People*, Blessed be the Name of the L O R D. This leads me to ask the Question, *Why did they so use our Blessed Lord and His Disciples?* The Answer is easie, *Because they saw Him not, they knew Him not, nor His Followers as they were*; they *had lost their Divine Saviour, and professed the Words and Sayings of* Moses *and the Prophets, not in their Life and Spirit*; and I can give no other Reason why we are so little known to the World of *Christians* in our Age, than that they hold generally the *Christian Profession out of the Christian Nature, Life and Spirit*; for we are the most mis-understood and mistaken of any People, whence it follows, that our *Antagonists* of every Party, have charged us with Doctrines and Principles not of our owning, but their own Mistaking, if not Inventing, which is worse. 'Twere too tedious to enumerate all their Attempts there are not less, I believe, than One Hundred Books extant, Two Thirds of the most of them are Imagination, Romance,

mance, Fiction, and no Judgment, or Doctrine of ours. This is Notorious by our Answers; and I hope every Man's Word is to be taken about what his own Faith is, though not in the Proof of his Faith, to be a True Faith.

Of later Times, Two Persons have excelled in this Way of opposing us, *Thomas Hicks* and *John Faldo*; they are both Answered, according to their respective Tracts; and their farther Defence remaineth hitherto unattempted by any.

'Tis with a Passage in my Answer to *J. Faldo's* first Book, that this same *I. C.* stiled, *A Minister of the Gospel*, and a *Skirmisher* too, offers at an Encounter: I question not his Courage so much as his Skill; he shows Will enough, but his Abilities fail him: I am willing enough to perswade my self, *That he is more Novice than Soldier in this War*, and that this is rather a Spurt of Heat, then a Deliberate Action; for Wise Men count their Cost, Fools only invade without Force. I hope he will not be angry with me for this Opinion of him; I am sure he ought not, if he be *A Minister of the Gospel*; I know not how he will take it as a *Skirmisher*, an Employment of so different a Nature; but certain it is, that Mistake is more pardonable than Malice, and Ignorance excusable than Fiction: I would not willingly fall upon him with those severe Terms, and put him upon that Difficulty I have been constrained to treat others with, and reduce them to; I would chuse rather to inform, than chide him; only I must tell him, that he is fallen into the Road of as great and arch a Perverter of our Writings and Sayings, as any Enemy that ever appear'd against us, and improved his Mistake upon us, by as many Foul, Impious, and Detestable Consequences (*even to a Tautology*) as any other Adversary hath done, which would make one think, that there was more of Design than Accident, and Premeditation than Inadvertency in the Business. Be it as it will, the Man pretends to be offended at me, and endeavours to make others offended too. 'Tis highly fit as a *Christian-Man*, that I do my Best to remove the Reason of it, and that I shall, by the Help of Almighty God.

First then, I will set down that Passage of mine, which he makes the Reason of writing his Pamphlet, and annex some of the Consequences he draws from my Words, by which he would render them and me *Odious to his Reader*, and then fall to my Defence, which will not be difficult, and, I hope, not tedious to my ingenuous and inquiring Reader.

No Command in the Scripture is any farther obliging upon any Man, than as he finds a Conviction upon his Conscience — It is Conviction that can only oblige to Obedience — When any Man is Convinced, that what was commanded another, it required of him, then, and not till then, he is rightly Authorized to perform it.

These Parcels has he cull'd out of a Book of mine, called, *Quakerism a New Nick-Name for Old Christianity*, I writ in Answer to *John Faldo's* Book, Entituled, *Quakerism No Christianity*.

Quakerism a New Nick-Name for Old Christianity, pag. 71, 72.

Let's now see the Use he makes of them, and what Language he makes them to speak.

That this Position opens the Flood-Gate to all Error, Atheism, Impiety, and Wickedness; and that it is the Overthrow of all Law and Government, pag. 2. *That Sins of Ignorance are no Sins; for all Conviction is by Knowledge. — That this justifies* Paul's *Blasphemy and Persecution, and gross Sins against the Gospel, because he did it ignorantly*, pag. 3. *It justifies all Erroneous Doctrines, and Practical Misapprehensions, and whatever Vices lie in the Understandings of Men. —* Penn's *Position doth justifie the* Irish Rebellion, *the* French Massacre, *the* Marian Persecution, *the* Ten Persecutions of the Primitive Churches, *the* Gun-Powder Treason, Judaism, Mahometanism, Paganism, Popery, *and* all Erroneous Sects and Parties in the World, *with all their False Principles and Practices. Christ saith*, It is Life Eternal to know God and Jesus Christ, *Joh.* 17. 3. Penn's *Position saith, If you are Ignorant and Unconvinced, no Law can lay hold on you; if you be deluded, and practise according to the Conviction of your deluded Mind, you are warranted by the Commands of God, which do all center in Conviction,* pag. 4. *Again, If this Position be true, then* Conscience *and* Conviction *is God; and whatever* Conscience *says, must be done, be it Right or Wrong; and it lies in the Power of* Conscience, *to make void all the Laws of God, and do what it pleaseth. —— It will also follow, That he is the most free from Sin who hath the most Seared Conscience, and that the ready Way to Obedience and Salvation, is to Debauch and Sear the Conscience. —— If* Conviction *be the* Ground of Obedience, *and the* Authority of Scripture *depend upon the*

the Rectitude and Purity of Conscience, then all Rational Laws, Order and Government, both divine and human, are overturned, and a Stop is put to all Religion and Piety towards God, to all Conscience, Honesty and Charity towards Men——*So Princes and Rulers may command and make never so good Laws, Conscience may come and say, I deny all those Laws and the Makers of them; Children may refuse to obey Parents; Servants, Masters; and Inferiors, Superiors; if Conscience shall be unconvinced, and if it be deluded, Subjects may murder their Princes; Children, their Parents; Servants, their Masters; one Man another; there can be no Law, but Conscience; and whatsoever Conscience says, must stand, p. 5, 6.* —— *The* Quakers *Conscience says one Thing, the* Papists *another, the* Pagans, *the* Turks, *the* Jews, *the* Tyrants, *the* Traytors, *the* Hereticks, *the* Worldlings, *the* Hypocrites, *the* Proud, *the* Adulterers *Conscience, how many contrary Consciences are these? How many Gods shall we have, and contradictory Laws, if Conscience and Conviction be the only Thing which obligeth to Duty, p. 6, 7.* These, with abundance more of the like Nature, are the Consequences he rather bestows upon, than draws from my Words, as particularly he hath laid them down; pray hear his Farewel after such a violent and virulent Skirmish, *I would be glad to make the best of your Position, but I must profess my Conscience and Conviction, p. 13. I refer my self and what I have here writ, to impartial Censure, warning and entreating all People, as they love their Souls, to take Heed of* Quakerism ——— *Keep your Poison to your self, and none will perish by it but your self; but if you will needs vend it, and in the View of the Nation, and such at least as know the* English *Tongue, set up a Position subverting all Religion, Law and Government, and levelling all holy and profitable Rules and Commands to Men's Lusts, leaving no Man in the World under any Obligation, or any Duty to God or Man, farther than he is convinced in his Conscience; be it known to you, that Jesus Christ hath his Servants abroad, to bear Testimony for him against such* GOD-BLASPHEMING AND SOUL-DAMNING ERRORS; *and if you repent not, this that I have written shall rise up in Judgment against you, and shall be an Aggravation of your Misery in that Day.*

Prepare to answer the Righteous Judge, if your Conscience be blinded and seared now, it will be open and awaken then.

This, Reader, concludes his two Sheets of *Skirmish* upon me: But, by the Way, it ought to sound very strangely to my Reader, *that a Man should profess Conscience and Conviction for this long Anathema against Conscience and Conviction:* But by that Time he is as well acquainted with these Sort of Men as I am, he will leave off wondering that such Men contradict themselves; indeed they live by it.

But what shall I do or say to this *Goliah?* Behold the *Spoil* of his *Skirmish!* He has invaded my Body and Soul, Religion and Life; these he thinks he leads away in Triumph after him; for I am (if he may be believed) by my Doctrine, an *Heretick,* a *Blasphemer,* an *Atheist,* a *Traytor,* a *Regicide,* a *Parricide,* a *Murderer* of my *Kindred* and *Neighbours,* a *Destroyer of all Government, Divine and Human,* and a *common Enemy to Mankind, unfit for this World, and for Heaven in the next,* unless I repent, which ought to be very questionable to so dissolute and impious a Wretch, as this pretended Minister of the Gospel in his *Skirmish* hath been pleased to render me; what remains, but that the Dogs or the Lyons devour me, the Rabble or Government sacrifice me? I am only fit for *Prey,* if this be true; what now shall I do, revile him? *by no Means;* revenge my self by a bitter and invective Answer? *No such Matter;* but may not I be angry with him? *Not a Jot;* What then? *Pity and Inform him, though a Parson;* I think so too; wherefore overlooking all such Provocations, I begin and proceed in this Method.

First, I cannot but take it very ill, in Case I were unsound in any one Doctrine, not through Inadvertency, but knowingly and premeditately, that he, without any farther Search or unquestionable Proof, should fault and impeach the Way I profess, and upbraid an entire People with my Mistake; I ask if this be the Way to perswade me that he is a true Minister of the Gospel, one that is zealous to promote the Commandments of God, that in doing this hath broke *that* of loving his Neighbour as himself, and doing unto others as he would have them do unto him; *William Penn* holds a gross Error, *therefore the People called* Quakers, *and the Way they profess, must be skirmish'd upon with the foul Names of Murderers, Rebels, Traytors, Atheists, Heresy, Blasphemy, &c.* What Part of *Logick* or *Philosophy* is this? None, I think; I am sure there is neither Law nor Gospel for it;

but

but 'tis too frequent with many to live in the Transgression of those Commandments they verbally admire, even then when they are pleading for them.

In the next Place, I must needs observe to him his Disingenuity in telling me, *He would be glad to make the best of my Position,* after he had manifestly made the worst he could, his two Sheets being stuffed with the most abominable Consequences it had been possible for any Man to invent or aggravate against me; this seems to be a Degree beyond Ignorance, and looks very scurvily for a Man of his Function and Pretences, Skirmishing laid aside.

But that which weighs the most with me to suspect my present Adversary of unfair Dealing, (to let such Words as Forgery slip for this Time) is his taking my Matter to Pieces, clipping Sentences, and dropping that by the Way, which read with the rest, would, in my Apprehension, have defended the Passage from the Possibility of any reasonable Exception. Shall four Lines and an Half of a Book of above 250 Pages, and those cull'd too out of three several Places, reprobate the Book, the Author, his Religion, and the Body of People he relates to? I hope he has so much Conscience and Conviction left, upon second Thoughts, (if for my sake he is not out of Charity with both) as to condemn this Sort of Proceeding with us; but perhaps he will tell me, I make too much of it, and that it was but a Skirmish; if so, then no Battle or solid Encounter of both Armies, and if not, How came we and our Religion to be defeated, and taken, in his Apprehension; doubtless this must go but for a Vapour, and proves the Parson more a Man of his Words than of his Deeds.

Nor is this all the Ground of my Jealousy, for unless he had met with my Book by Accident, and had cast his Eye only on those three Places, not reading what went before, came between, or followed after, (a Thing scarcely possible) and upon that transient Notice had sally'd forth, and skirmish'd upon me, (a Rashness no Man in his Wits would be guilty of) or that when he had fallen so patly on those three Places, he resolv'd to see no more for fear of being better inform'd, a Disingenuity greatly unbecoming a Man of his Pretensions, it must and will follow, that he did knowingly and on Purpose omit both giving his Reader the Reason of this Part of the Controversy between me and *John Faldo,* and my Sense at large in Defence of our first Position; which done, would have sav'd him the Trouble and Danger of a *Skirmish,* and me the present Pains of giving him this *Repulse.* And here I intreat the *Reader's* Patience for a little Digression, if yet it be one.

John Faldo writes a Book, called, *Quakerism no Christianity*; in it he charges the People called *Quakers* with several erroneous Principles, whereof one is in general Terms, *That we deny the Scriptures,* upon this he bestows Nine Chapters; One of them is taken up with this Title, *That the* Quakers *affirm the Doctrines, Commands, Promises, and Holy Examples expressed in Scripture, as such, not to be at all Binding upon them.* To this Book I return'd my Answer, entituled, *Quakerism a New Nick-Name for Old Christianity*; I follow him Chapter by Chapter in my Course, I undertake him upon this Head. To prove his Charge, he produces a Passage out of *Edward Burroughs's* Writings, much at the same Rate that this *Adversary* quotes me, and such Harmony they hold, that they fall both upon the same Construction of us, as if they had compared Notes, or had abused us by Instinct. This I complain of in my Answer to *J. C.* how comes *J. C.* to make the same false Step, and yet have read that Answer; *E. Burroughs's* Words were these, as cited by *J. F. That is no Command of God to me, what he commanded to another*; *did any of the Saints which we read of act by the Command which was to another, not having the Command to themselves*——This *J. F.* improves at the same Rate that *J. C.* doth mine, to wit, *That it opens a Way to all Lewdness and Impiety, and hath all Iniquity in the Womb of it,* extending these Words to all Laws, which (as I make appear in my Answer, however overlook'd by this Man) were limited by *E. B.* and me, to *Temporary and extraordinary Cases.*

Had *J. F.* been quiet here, I could have hoped that he had both seen and sorrowed for his Mistake; but he persists in his horrid Abuse of *E. B.* and begins at the same Rate with me for defending him: This is in his *Vindication* of his former Book, to which I *Rejoyn* at large in Defence of my Answer, resume the Controversy entirely, distinguish of his Fallacies and Misrepresentations, and assert and maintain our own Principles, confirming them with some Hundreds of reputed Authorities, as well of former as more modern Ages. In this Discourse (hitherto unattempted by any) I make a farther Defence of *E. B's* and my own Sense from
J. F's

J. F's Misconstruction, which it had become this pretended Minister of the Gospel to have consulted, before he had engaged himself upon so strange a *Skirmish*.

That this Injury done me may more distinctly appear, I shall here set down once more (I hope without Offence to the Reader) the present Parson's Text, not his Sermon, that's too tedious.

—— *No Command in the Scripture is any farther obliging upon any Man, than as he finds a Conviction upon his Conscience——It is Conviction that can only oblige to Obedience——When any Man is convinced that what was commanded another is required of him, then, and not 'till then, he is rightly authoriz'd to perform it.*

I omit to mention his Comment; but every Thing that is vicious, prophane and diabolical he makes to follow upon these Premises.

That my Reader may the better see whether my Matter and Design, at large, merits any such Constructions, I chuse to insert, and that as the best and briefest Way, the 5th Chapter of my *Rejoynder* to *J. Faldo*, which contains his *Charge* and *Proof*, my *Answer* (thus pared and patched by *J. C.*) his *Reply*, and my *Rejoynder*, as a more compleat Defence of *E. B*'s and my Assertion against the vile Interpretations of *J. Faldo*, so dextrously followed by *J. C.* and therefore equally fit for him.

Here follows the 5th Chapter of my *Rejoynder* to *J. F.* containing a Vindication of my Doctrine from any such Evil Consequences as are by *I. C.* charged upon it, with this farther Advertisement, that the Reader observe, that those Lines of Capital Letters are the Passages quoted by *I.C.* and all the rest of my Answer in the Common Letter, with Comma's on the Sides, herein recited, and much more, is wilfully omitted by my Adversary; also the Reader is desired to consider of the Notes at the Bottom, by which he will be helped to understand the Disingenuity of *I. C.* against me, my Friends, and our holy Profession.

Of Scripture-Commands, what are binding, and what not. Our Adversary's Disingenuity observed.

p. 34. BUT however, he has fail'd in his last Chapter, doubtless he thinks he has done my Business in this; he begins like himself.

Rep. My *Charge* and *Argument* in this Chapter is, The Quakers *affirm the Doctrines, Commands, Promises, holy Examples expressed in Scripture, as such, not to be at all binding to us*; such an Argument, and so prov'd by me (mark Reader) *as a Thousand* Penns *can never invalid it.*

Rejoyn. What can there be more conceited than this? He must live very lonely, and far from Neighbours, that proclaims so much Praise to himself, and have wonderful Confidence to bid Defiance so vainly to others.

Reader, I beseech thee for the Truth's Sake, on whose Side soever thou shalt find it to be, to examine with all Impartiality his *Charge*, our *Answer*; his *Reply*, and our *Rejoynder*: If his Honesty, Reason and Justice hold any Proportion to his great Confidence, we yield: But if upon an impartial Consideration he shall be found to clip and pervert our Matter, and to shuffle with us in his own, once do a poor People Right, in giving Judgment against this horrible Injustice.

The *Charge* thou hast heard, the *Proof* was this, *That is no Command of God to me, what he commanded to another: Did any of the Saints, which we read of, act by that Command which was to another, not having the Command to themselves,* &c.

Now, before I give my Answer, as it was set down in my Book, I shall insert his Quotation of my Answer.

Rep. (p. 34, 35.) *To this, saith* P. *I answer briefly and plainly, and he is as good as his Word. No Commands, saith he, in the Scripture, are any farther obliging upon any* Man, *than as he finds a Conviction upon his Conscience, otherwise* Men *should be engaged without, if not against Conviction; a Thing unreasonable in a* Man.

Rejoyn. He has a notable Way of Contracting his Adversary's Answer; I will set down what I writ, faithfully, plainly, and briefly.

Page 71, 72, 73. " *Edward Burroughs*'s Expressions may be taken two Ways, and
" both safe enough to the Honour and Credit of the Scripture, though not to the
" Charity or Honesty of *J. Faldo.* Now follows that Part he cited. NO COM-
" MAND IN THE SCRIPTURE IS ANY FARTHER OBLIGING UPON ANY
" MAN, THAN AS HE FINDS A CONVICTION UPON HIS CONSCIENCE,

(*a*) other-

" (a) otherwise Men should be engaged without, if not against Conviction, a
" Thing unreasonable in a Man; Therefore the *Apostle*, when he wrote to the
" Church, exhorted them not to do those Things whereof they were (b) ashamed,
" to shun what was manifested to be Evil; and affirms, *that whatever might be
" known of God was manifested within, for God had shewn it unto them*. (c) SO
" THAT CONVICTION CAN ONLY OBLIGE TO OBEDIENCE; and since
" what works that Conviction is the *manifesting Light, universal Grace, or quick-
" ning Spirit in the Heart of Mankind*, it follows, that *the principal Ground for
" our Faith in the Scriptures, and Reason of our Obedience to the holy Precepts there-
" in contained, is the Manifestation, Conviction and secret Drawings of the Light
" or Spirit of God in the Conscience*: And thus E. B's Words are sound and scrip-
" tural, for the Scriptures are chiefly believ'd to be true upon Conviction, there-
" fore every Practice therein; AND WHEN ANY MAN IS CONVINCED,
" THAT WHAT WAS COMMANDED ANOTHER, IS REQUIRED OF
" HIM, THEN, AND NOT TILL THEN, HE IS RIGHTLY AUTHORIZED
" TO PERFORM IT. Again, Such Commands either relate to *Ordinary* or *Ex-
" traordinary Cases*; (d) By *Ordinary Cases*, I mean such as chiefly concern *Faith
" and Holy Life*, which are general, permanent and indispensible, and then I deny
" his Consequence. By *Extraordinary Cases*, I understand *Moses's going to Pha-
" raoh, the Prophets several Manners of Appearance to the Kings, Priests and Peo-
" ple of* Israel, *with other Temporary Commands, relating to outward Services*, &c.
" (e) And so we say, that what is commanded *One Man, is not binding, as such,
" upon another*: But when the Lord shall say, *If thou sinnest, thou shalt die*; *If
" thou keepest my Commands, thou shalt live*; *Be ye holy, for I the Lord your God
" am holy*; —— *For your selves KNOW YE NOT how ye ought to follow us?* &c.
" I say, these Precepts and Examples are obliging upon all; Why? Because they
" more or less meet with a Conviction in the Consciences of all: For I am perswa-
" ded, none that has a reasonable Soul, who has not (f) out-lived his Day, but
" would readily say, These are true and weighty Sayings; *For Faith in God, and
" an holy self-denying Life, are necessary both to Temporal and Eternal Happiness*.

It was, *Reader*, to this sober Answer he flung out his foregoing *Rant*, and makes this following Comment and *Reply*, viz. says *J. Faldo*.

Rep. *They are no Commands unless we think so. 'Tis no Sin to break all the Commands in the Bible, if our Consciences can be so blind, dead or hardened, as not to tell us 'tis a Sin. They who thought they did God good Service in killing his Servants did not sin in the least, because they were not convinced of a Command to the contrary. To vindicate my whole Chapter concerning the Scriptures. 'Tis a Principle that hath all* (g) *Iniquity in the Womb of it. Who can find Names for such Impious Principles? Penn hath opposed, scorned the Truth, vilified it's Teachers and Defenders, so as scarce ever Man did; vented the most pernicious Errors, told abundance of those Things that are known to himself to be false*.

Rejoyn. Reader, This is all the Justice and Reason I can have from this pretended *meek and suffering Non-conforming Parson*. What would such Men do, had they as much Power as Anger? But I shall leave him with his Pride and Pas-

---

(a) Ought any Man to obey what he does not know? and is not Knowledge *Conviction*? I provoke him or any to give me a Scripture for that. But more of this anon; observe what follows.

(b) The Apostle here does plainly exhort them to make their Conviction their Rule, for there was something in them that brought Shame over them for their Evil Deeds, the true Light and Spirit, that makes known what of God is to be known in Man.

(c) True still; for Man can't see without Eyes, nor act without Knowledge: But the Question is What Conviction this is; the Words prove that it is by the Light and Spirit of God; then the seared Conscience and debaucht Mind *I. C.* speaketh of are plainly excluded; here I mention the *Conviction* and that which works it; What Countenance doth either give *I. C.* to heap these foul and Impious Consequences upon me?

(d) This plain Distinction I made is left out by him, that he might the better have his Ends and conceal the Injustice of his Work.

(e) This is a direct *Contradiction* to his Inference and Allegation, who would have me to hold, that what is in any Case commanded one Man, is not binding upon another, when I limit it to Extraordinary Cases, and just after say, that the Moral Commands of God are obliging upon all. How is it then that I deny the Ten Commandments to belong to all Men, or that I hold, Men may kill, steal, &c. and not be culpable? O disingenuous Man!

(f) This Out-living their Day plainly shews, that I excluded seared Consciences; how then do I make a seared Conscience my Rule of Obedience, or the readiest Way to Salvation?

(g) Is not this the Language of *I. C*? Are they not Brethren in Abuse?

fion. Is there any Thing more clear, than that he extends the Words of *E. Burroughs* to *Ordinary Cafes*, which were wholly writ about *Extraordinary*; and that he takes no more Notice of my *Diftinction*, than if there had been none made? As if it had been formerly an equal Sin for any *not to be Circumcifed*, and *to (h) Murder his Father or Prince*; or that there was the fame Conviction univerfally upon the Confciences of all Men, *not to wear Linfey-Woolfey, as to do by others as they would have others do to them.* Levit. 19. 18, 19.

That what we fay was *E. Burrough's* Meaning his own Words undeniably prove: ' One, fays he, was fent to (*i.*) baptize, and another to preach the Gofpel: which were particular and extraordinary Commands. He clearly fhuffles and evades the dint of my Anfwer, and would run us within the Borders of *Ranterifm*. The (*k*) Queftion is not, *Are God's Commands no Commands, unlefs we think fo, and therefore no Sin to break all the Commands in the Bible*, which is the Comment he beftows) upon us) but whether this or that fpecial Injunction to any Particular Perfon or Perfons, to this or that peculiar End, be warrantably imitable, without fufficient Conviction and Commiffion: Muft *J. F.* Baptize becaufe *John* Baptized? or turn Preacher becaufe *Peter* was one? *E. B.* only denyed Imitation of Ancient Times in Temporary and Shadowy Services, and all thofe Preachings, Prayings, Ordinances and Churches, that have not (as *Peter Martyr* well expreffes it) *the Holy Spirit for their Root.* So that inftead of his holding a Principle that hath all Iniquity in the Womb of it, *John Faldo* firft perverts his Words, and then to confute them both implies a Denial of the Holy Spirit to be the only right Leader to the Performance of Gofpel Prayer, Preaching and Ordinances, and of gathering of Evangelical Churches, and does as good as tell us, that God's Commandments are fuch to him, not becaufe of any Conviction in himfelf of the Juftnefs of them, but from the Teftimony of the Scriptures, which for all his high *Boafts* of *Chriftianity*, is a State far beneath thofe *noble Gentiles*, who *not having an outward Law, were a Law unto themfelves, having the Effects of it written in their Hearts, their Confcience bearing witnefs, &c.*

And this we may boldly fay, That *fuch as ever acted from that inward Senfe, never thought they did God good Service in Killing his Servants*, whilft great Admirers of the Letter of the Scriptures, and who, as concerning this Commandment, *Thou fhalt not Murder*, thought themfelves moft unblameable, believed, *They did God good Service in killing his Servants*.

Nor can I think it fo great a *Difgrace* to our Caufe, that we ingenuoufly profefs the *Reafon* why we defire to fear God, and keep his Commandments, doing unto others as we would have them do unto us, *not fo much to be from the Letter of the Scripture, as the Convictions of the Eternal Light and Spirit of God in our Confciences*; as it ought to be unto *John Faldo* and his Adherents, who ground their Obedience upon the Letter of the Scripture, and not upon fuch internal Convictions. What is it but to fay, They could *Lye, Swear, Steal, Kill, &c.* (l) *without any Remorfe*, did they not find fuch Injunctions and Prohibitions upon record? A Confequence fo deteftable, yet fo natural to their Principles, that if this render them not able Guides to the very Confines of *Ranterifm* and *Atheifm*, I fhall gladly ask an Excufe for my Ignorance. But that I may Leave nothing undone that may compleat the Satisfaction of every moderate Inquirer, I fhall farther weigh and rejoyn to thefe Words of his.

They who thought they did God good Service in killing his Servants, did not fin in the leaft, becaufe they were not convinced of a Command to the contrary; nor the Idolaters in the Cafe of Baal, *becaufe they thought* Baal *to be a God indeed.*

Now, *Reader*, obferve the Evafion: (*m*) This Paffage relates not to Men's

---

(*h*) Is not this a plain Diftinction? What could be plainer againft any fuch Confequences as *J. C.* draws, and to prove that I underftood not what he renders me to have intended?

(*i*) How plentiful are the Evidences of our Innocency; and how diftinctly may the Reader fee that *E. B.* writ of Particular and Extraordinary Commands?

(*k*) Let me pray the Reader, and prevail with him to dwell a while upon this Paffage, and do an Innocent Man, yea, an Abufed People, Juftice. Does this plead for *Ranterifm, Atheifm, Blafphemy, Murder,* &c. as *J. C.* tells us?

(*l*) This is the Tendency of his Doctrine, who flies out upon Confcience and inward Conviction, as if they were the only great Enemies of his Salvation.

(*m*) This notable Claufe clears our Senfe more particularly, and gives a very plain Difcovery of our Enemy's Difingenuity. We fpeak of Pofitive, J. F. and J. C. conclude our Argument againft all moral Commands: Thefe are Minifters of the Gofpel all this while, if they may be believed.

practising *what God commands*, or our Tenderness in imitating other Saints without Commission, for fear we should offer strange Fire, which is our Question; but their doing that which *God never commanded*, yea, *which Mankind in all Ages hath adjudged impious*, and which to be sure, his Holy Spirit, that, E. B. said, All Men should wait to be convinced, assisted and led by, in fulfilling God's Commandments, never moved any to. He unworthily draws a general Conclusion against us from meer particular Premises. It seems Men are to act without, if not against Conviction, upon his Principle; and that it is the same Thing with him, to commit moral Enormities from an Hardned Heart, and to be tender of taking up an external Practice, or performing some Religious Duty, without the Convictions and Leadings of the Holy Spirit. The Apostle said to such as had not as yet so full clearness as others, That *if any were otherwise-minded, God would reveal it*. Phil. 3. 15. He did not injoyn them, during that Scruple, to believe or practise the Thing doubted; but therefore did Persecutors act inexcusably in their fiery Zeal, because their blind Consciences checkt them not: Again, If *Blindness* came from Education, it is, though Blindness still (and therefore it was basely done of J. Faldo to say in our Names, that it is not Sin in the least, &c.) more excusable: for in the Days of such Ignorance God winks: But if it be a (n) *Blindness, proceeding from long Disobedience and Rebellion against the Convictions and Strivings of the good Spirit of God*, as his word *Hardned* implies, then, I say, it is not only very heinous in God's Sight, but those Persons can never be excus'd either from great Guilt, or the Sense of it in themselves, let them or J. F. talk never so much of Conscience.

Besides, the most Essential, and Universally Necessary Commands of God were through all Ages confest; both before there was any of those Writings, we rightly call the *Scriptures of Truth*, from the *Law of Nature*, as many stile it, or rather the *Law of God placed in Man's Nature*, and since, where they have never been; Therefore, whatever *particular hardned and seared Consciences* may say, we have the Consent of Mankind, and their own Rebellion and Lewdness against them. But the Words of J. Faldo in plain Terms import, as if, 1*st*, Men were not generally convinced of the Righteousness of the Moral Commands of God; but that Men keep them because they are in the Bible only; which runs against the Testimony of Scripture, the Consent of Ages, and the Writings and Judgment of the most honest and learned *Protestants*. 2*ly*, As if it were a like Evil, Conscientiously to forbear Running, Willing and Striving in Matters of Worship without the Spirit's Conduct, and *fearedly to plead for the Commission of Murder and Idolatry*, because Men of such Consciences boggle not at it (though that is more than J. F. can prove, I mean that they have no Stroke or Remorse) 3*ly*, As if we could Worship, Preach, gather Churches, and administer Gospel-Ordinances aright without the Spirit. 4*ly*, That he is not convinced by any other Testimony than the Scripture without, of any Transgression against God's Law. 5*ly*, It supposes, that if Men stay'd till the Spirit mov'd, they should stay long enough (who vainly prate of Praying by the Spirit notwithstanding) never considering that the Spirit standeth ready to *Reveal* it self to their Assistance and Assurance, who wait for it, and that all the *Children of God are led by the Spirit of God*, which being our Position, had it but been weighed by this Adversary, he could not (methinks) have been so unjust in his Aggravations.

'Tis true, should we believe as he doth, *that the Spirit is not to be waited for now adays to lead us*, or that *it is not ready to our Information, when we wait for it's Discoveries and Leadings*, our Assertion would look very absurd and loose; for it were to let fall all Worship, but not upon our own Principle, as I said before; for *first*, all Worship to God ought to be performed by the Assistance of his Holy Spirit; for of our selves we can do nothing that is good! And *secondly*, God's Spirit is ready to assist, instruct and comfort those that wait diligently and patiently for it; yea, God hath given it to the Rebellious, that it may judge them, if it do not lead them. It is such *Protestant* Doctrine, that I wonder Men should not know their admired Ancestors Faith when they meet it: O great Degeneration into Hardness and Ignorance! *Lastly*, There is the same to be said against him that pretends

---

(n) What says my Reader to this Passage and plain Provision made by me, against blinded, deluded and hardened, Minds and Consciences? Does this agree well with my present Adversary's swaggering Consequences, especially that which makes me to deny Sins of wilful Ignorance? What Gospel can a Man so qualified be Minister of?

to ground all upon the Scripture, that he objects against us, who plead for the Conviction of Conscience, which the Instance of the *Jews Murder of our Lord Jesus Christ* unanswerably proves. There was a Law, that *Blasphemers should be put to Death*; by this Law they apprehended Jesus, adjudged and got him to be executed: These Men above any Age exalted the Scriptures as the Only Rule. Where lies the Mistake? Not in the Scripture, but in their blind and envious Application of it. Now I ask, if the only Way for them to have come to the true Sense and Knowledge of him, and escaped that Wicked Murder and the deplorable Consequences of it had not been *to have waited upon God for the* (o) *Conviction, Discoveries and Guidance of his Holy Spirit*, since Flesh and Blood and the utmost Wit of Man, with the Exactness of the *meer* Letter of the Scriptures, could never give unto that Generation, the certain Discerning, Knowledge and Savour, of him, whose very Words themselves were Spirit and Life? It was by a Divine Touch, Sense and Knowledge given from above, that he was truly discern'd, own'd and follow'd of those that believ'd in him, and cleaved to him; (p) therefore said Christ, *No Man cometh to me but whom my Father draweth*: Where was that Drawing but within. Again, *Simon Peter, Flesh and Blood hath not revealed* (what? who I am) *but my Father that is in Heaven*. So that at last, *Men must come to this Spiritual Sense in themselves, to understand and apply the very Commands of Scripture*; otherwise, not Justice, but detestable Murder, may under the Name of it be confidently perpetrated; Whererefore we Exhort all, *To have Recourse unto God's Spirit*, that illuminates certainly, and gives to act unblameably, *by which the Scriptures are only understood as they should be, and People brought into the Possession of that Life of Righteousness, they plentifully declare of*. Had it not been for this *inward Discerning*, there had been no *Ground for the Abolishment of the whole* Jewish *Service*, which followed some Years after Christ's Ascension. And it is the same Eternal *Spirit* that is the great *Rule* and *Judge* now, which *God promised* more particularly *to shed abroad in the latter Days*, and is the great inseparable Priviledge from the New and Everlasting Covenant.

But to conclude, Why should it seem so *Heterodox* in *J. Faldo*'s Judgment, since if Men believe the Scripture upon the Testimony of the Spirit, they practise it by the Knowledge and Power of the same; How else could *Paul* have decry'd *Jewish* Ceremonies; or we know, what to take, and what to leave? Or why do we omit any Command therein mentioned? *They Circumcised, therefore must I Circumcise? They Baptized, must I therefore Baptize?* With forty more particular Cases, wherein nothing can secure any from the Imitation of them, *set Conviction or Spiritual Discerning aside*. I will offer two or three *Testimonies* from approved Men in our Defence.

William Tindal, that ancient faithful *Protestant Martyr*, whom *J. Fox*, that writ the Books of Martyrs, calls, the *English Apostle*, speaks thus, That ' *it is impossible to understand in the Scripture more than a* Turk, *for whosoever* (or any that) ' *hath not the Law of God writ in his Heart to fulfil it*. Again, ' *Without the Spirit it is impossible to understand them*.

John Jewel, Bishop of Salisbury, in his excellent Book against the *Papists*, writ above One Hundred Years ago, says thus to our Purpose ' The Spirit of God ' is bound neither to Sharpness of Wit, nor to abundance of Learning: Oftentimes the Unlearned see that Thing, that the Learned cannot see. Christ saith, ' *I thank thee, O Father, Lord of Heaven and Earth, that thou hast hid these Things ' from the Wise and the Politick, and hast revealed them unto the Little Ones*. Therefore *Epiphanius* saith, ' *Only to the Children of the Holy Ghost all the Holy Scriptures ' are plain and clear*. Again, ' Flesh and Blood is not able to understand the Holy ' Will of God without *Special Revelation*. ' Therefore Christ gave Thanks unto ' his Father, and likewise opened the Hearts of his Disciples, that they might ' understand the Scriptures, *Without this special Help and* Promoting *of God's Holy ' Spirit*, the Word of God is unto the Reader, be he never so wise or well learned, ' *as the Vision of a sealed Book*.

(o) This farther proves what Conviction as well as what Commands I understood; and ought to shame my Adversary, if he has any Ingenuity in him, for that ill Use he has made of my Words about *Conscience* and *Conviction*.

(p) What says *I. C.* to this? Is the Conscience and Conviction I make so necessary, a blind, dark, seared Conscience? Do I leave it there? Is that the Language of my Doctrine? Is it not a *Conscience* convinced and taught by God's Holy Spirit? Let what follows, and the Three Testimonies be weighed.

Now

Now unless Men are bound to do what they do not understand how to do, then only are they to do them when they are *Revealed* or Discovered to them, which being by the Spirit only, according to their Doctrine, the Testimony and Discoveries of the Spirit are requisite to our understanding of the *Scriptures*, which implies, and comprehends a Discriminating Knowledge, or certain Discerning of what we should practise from what is not obliging upon us to practise, and consequently, that we ought not to run Head-long without such Knowledge.

T. Collier, an Ancient and Eminent Man among the *Western Separatists* of our Nation, writeth thus: " *For me to speak of God, because another speaks of Him;* " *and to be able to talk much of God, as I read of Him in Scripture,* Not Being " Made One In the Same Truth, *I see and speak* But What Another Hath " Spoken; *and so may speak truly sometimes of God, but it is by Hear-say,* " Another Man's Truth, But Not Mine; *so, I doubt, many a Soul,* Boasts In " Another Man's Light.'—— Again, *I see that External Actings according to a* " *Rule without, is nothing, if not flowing from a Principle of Life and Love within.* Which is more than *E. B.* said, of whom *J. Faldo* (with unworthy Reflection, and base Wrestings) hath said so much.

T. Collier's Works, pag. 247.

Thus far goes my *Rejoynder*, and, I hope, far enough to defeat our *Skirmisher*, and rout all his False Consequences in the plain Field; I will not abound in my own Sense, but shall leave every *Impartial Reader* to determine, whether *E. Burrough*, or *W. Penn* for him, understood, and intended, those Passages to all the Commandments of God, or those only that are of a peculiar and extraordinary Nature, which are both by *J. F.* and *J. C.* so odiously resented and improved, even to all *Atheism and Impiety*.

But for farther Satisfaction to my *Reader*, and to compleat this *Adversary's Defeat*, I will suppose him making this Acknowledgment and Objection, *viz.*

I grant that both J. F. *and my self, have unworthily wrong'd* E. B's *Words and Sense, and* W. Penn's *too, as to the Main Scope of the Controversie, believing they intended what they said, not of all the Commands of God, and I am willing to let go the Last of the Three Passages I cite in my Pamphlet, viz.* " When any Man is Con- " vinced that what is Commanded another, is required of him, then, and not " till then, he is rightly Authorized to perform it, *believing this related to Extra-* " *ordinary Cases*; *but I am yet dissatisfied with the other Two Passages still, viz.* " No " Command in the Scripture is any farther obliging upon any Man, than as he " finds a Conviction upon his Conscience. —— " It is Conviction that can only " oblige to Obedience. *I still believe that all those Horrid Consequences I Skirmisht him with, are due to that Doctrine.* What more can *J. C.* say for himself than this Objection imports? I shall now defend my Words, as he hath laid them down, from any such Inferences as he has given in their Name.

To make my *Answer* clear, it is to be consider'd; First, *What is that Conscience I mean*; next, *What the Conviction, and by whom given*; which understood, corrects his Folly (to say no worse) and ends the Debate with his Defeat.

To say nothing here of the *Various Definitions* that are of Conscience, nor is it so proper, for the Question is, *About what Conscience*, I shall keep to the Distinction in Scripture; the Scripture mentions Two Sorts of Conscience, a *Good and an Evil Conscience*; the Question will be, *Which I meant*; if the last, as says *J. C.* I am gone; if the former, he is routed; not the latter, say I, for Two Reasons, the One, *Because a Wicked Seared Conscience*, as such, rejects all *Conviction*; the other, because I have particularly declared against *J. F.* that I spoke not of any such *Conscience*; nay, I have excepted, and made Provision against any such Construction in my very *Answer*; so to take and render me then is Injurious. But if I meant it of a *Corrected, Rightly Qualified Conscience*, such as the Apostle speaks of, *Rom.* 2. 14, 15. *That bears Witness in the Gentiles to the Work of the Law of God writ in their Hearts*, then it will follow, that this *Skirmisher* is beside the Saddle, and hath Shoulder'd himself out of the Point.

But next, What is Conviction that obligeth? Is it Imagination only? Or, *A Diabolical Suggestion to Kill, Rob, Lye*, &c. as says *I. C.* No such Matter, but a Clear Understanding and Sound Judgment, and upon Right Conclusions, from the *Manifestation of the Light, Grace, or Spirit of God, that attends all People whose Day is not over for their Conviction and Conversion to God:* This I do Verbally provide for, in my *Answer* and *Rejoynder* to *J. Faldo*, yet hath *I. C.* so strangely render'd both me and my Assertions therein: Certainly this Man is the *Greatest of Novices* in our Controversie and Religion, or incomparably base; for either he supposeth

1676.

poseth that we do not hold, *That all Men are Enlightned with a Measure of Saving Light, so as that Men cannot plead Ignorance of what is fit for them to do*, which is our known Principle, and he confesseth it, *p. 13.* Or, that if he doth so know, he must admit that this *Divine Light is idle and insufficient to convince People*: Or, *Lastly*, believing neither, he doth very ill to tell the World in our Name, *That we make Debauched and Seared Consciences, our Rules of Obedience to Salvation*, and subject the Laws of God and Man to the Acknowledgment of such depraved Consciences.

Again, *Where there is no Law, there is no Transgression*, and where the Law is not known, there is no Law: Now *I. C.* would have us believe, p. 8. and 9. that the very Ten Commandments, as well as the Sayings of CHRIST, and Writings of *His Apostles*, are so Spiritual and Mysterious, that Carnal Men, as such, cannot know them, no, not so much as to understand what God means, when he says, *Thou shalt Not Kill:* Now, if this Tale be True, *What's become of* J. C. for if the Scripture says, *Where there is no Law, there is no Transgression*, and Reason assures us, *That where a Law is not known, there is no Law*, and that J. C. tells us, *That no Man that is not Spiritual, can know God's Laws and Commands, even when they are publish'd, and that the Spirit of God only gives the Spiritual Knowledge of them*; will it not unavoidably follow, *That no Command obligeth without Conviction*, since no Command tyes without Knowledge, which is Conviction, says J. C. p. 3. Yet again, the whole *Bible* J. C. receives for Truth, *either by Authority or Revelation*, both which Ways require Conviction; for if he goes upon the *Foot of Authority*, he must be satisfied in his Conscience, that those who Writ, divulged, preserved, and recommended it, have not put any *Trick or Abuse upon him*, which is Credit upon a Sort of Conviction; if he embraceth the *Bible* upon the Revelation and Testimony of the Spirit in himself *(the Old Protestant Plea)* that is not possible without Conviction, for Evidence is Knowledge, and Knowledge Conviction; and if I must have the Conviction of *God's Spirit for the Whole*, I must have it for the Parts; *and therefore no Command in Scripture is any farther obliging upon any Man, than as he finds a Conviction upon his Conscience*; the contrary makes God a very Hard Master; for 'tis to say, *That He Reaps where He hath not Sown; that His Laws are Binding where they are not known, and that He requires an Obedience, without giving Men the Understanding of their Duty.* Again, they are Christ's own Words, *I will send the Comforter*, or rather *Advocate unto you, and when He is come, he will convince the World of Sin.* I demand if the Conviction of the Spirit is here made the Rule of Judgment and Practice. Again, *If I had not done among them the Works that none other Man did, they had not had Sin:* Here Conviction goes before Sin, and that makes Death follow Sin: *For the Wrath of God is Revealed from Heaven against all Ungodliness and Unrighteousness of Men, who hold the Truth in Unrighteousness, because that which may be known of God, is Manifest in them, for God hath Shewed it unto them.* So the Prophet, *He hath shewed unto thee, O Man, what is Good. And upon whom doth not His Light arise? In Him was Life, and the Life the Light of Men, that was the True Light which Lighteth Every Man that cometh into the World. For it is a Shame to speak of those Things which are done of them in Secret; but All Things that are Reproved, are made Manifest by the Light. For the Grace of God that brings Salvation, hath Appeared unto All Men, teaching us, that denying Ungodliness, and Worldly Lusts, we should live Soberly, Righteously, and Godly in this present World. For if our Heart condemn us, God is greater, and knoweth all Things; Beloved, if our Heart condemn us not, then have we Confidence towards God:* Which Passages prove an Universal Principle, not Condemning without Requiring, nor Requiring without Manifesting and Convincing; therefore it is no *God-Blaspheming*, nor *Soul-Damning Error*, (as says J. C. pag. 14.) to affirm that there is no Obligation without Conviction, nor Duty without Knowledge; What would this *Skirmisher* make *Jews* of us, to act upon Zeal without Knowledge? Or, *Athenians*, to Worship and Dedicate Temples to an Unknown God? And lay it down for an Axiom of Divinity, *That Men stand oblig'd, not only without, but against Conviction:* Is he not like to give a rare Account of his Onset, that manages it at this Rate? The poor Man has mist his Blow, and is fallen down with striking at me; this appears by his manifest Mistakes, and gross Contradictions too, his Mistakes I have already shown: I shall now touch briefly upon his Contradictions, wherein he is as Kind as he was Cruel, and gives but all that he plundered from us, and so ends the *Skirmish*. His First Contradiction is this.

Job 16. 7, 8.
Chap. 15. 24.
Rom. 18. 19.

Mic. 6. 8.
John 1. 5. 9.

Eph. 5. 12, 13.

John 3. 20, 21.

Rom. 10. 2.
Acts 18. 22, 23.

I grant

I grant you, that no Man ſtands bound to obey any Command, which it is utterly impoſſible for him to know and be convinced of: But doth this aſſoil and clear him from yielding the Cauſe? — But where nothing hinders a Man from knowing his Duty, but his own Neglect and Wilful Careleſneſs, and where a Man ſhall by Sin debauch and ſear his Conſcience, will you excuſe this Man. — If indeed the Caſe were ſo, that no Conviction could be, or none that I could any Way compaſs, then I were in no Fault, but where it is my Fault if I be unconvinced — in ſuch Caſe God may juſtly charge me with the Omiſſion of Duty, and the Commiſſion of Evil — and by granting this, I aſſoyl and clear the Juſtice of God.

No doubt, in the leaſt, and a Seaſonable *Peccavi* for what he has done, for, how wide is this off what I have ſaid, of which J. C. has ſaid ſo very ill? I ſay, *No Command is obliging without Conviction*; J. C. faith, *No Command is obliging without Conviction, provided he doth not hinder his own Convincement*. As if I ſtated it, that *Let Men ſhut their Eyes, ſtop their Ears, rebel, blaſpheme, give themſelves up to all Superfluity of Naughtineſs, till Conſcience is Seared as with an hot Iron, yet without the Conſcience be convinced, or that God by Force make it to ſee, hear, and be ſenſible whether it will or no, Men are not obliged by any of his Commands*; for this is the very Way he ſtates the Caſe for me, though I do ſo particularly provide againſt any ſuch diſſolute and infamous Pretences. This is ſo plain, that when I ſay, that Conviction only obliges to Obedience, I add, that what works the Conviction, is the Manifeſting *Light*, Univerſal *Grace*, or Quickning *Spirit* in the Heart of Mankind; ſo that let us now ſee the real Difference betwixt this *Skirmiſher's* Grant at the End of the Day, and what he ſo furiouſly flew upon in the Beginning. Saith he, *I am bound to obey no Command, but what I am convinced of, provided I do not neglect or reject the Means of my Convincement*, p. 11. Say I, *No Command is farther obliging upon me, than as I find a Conviction in my Conſcience by the Light, Grace, or Spirit of God*, unto which all Men ſhould have regard; for that follows in my ſame Anſwer as an Explanation and Guard to that Aſſertion, moſt unworthily neglected by my *Adverſary*, only to make Room for this vain and fruitleſs *Skirmiſh*. Now, unleſs my Conviction, by the Grace of God, be neglecting the Means of Conviction, as moſt undoubtedly it is not (it being the only Way of True Conviction) What *Iota* of Difference is there between my Aſſertion, and his Conceſſion? For Inſtance, no Man is bound to anſwer a Queſtion he doth not hear, ſay I; No Man is bound to anſwer a Queſtion he does hear, *if he did not ſtop his Ears, or refuſe to hear*, ſaith he, as if I admitted, *that Men might ſtop their Ears, and yet be excuſable*, which is to read my Aſſertion thus, *No Man is bound to anſwer a Queſtion that he will not hear; and no Command is obliging upon a Man that will not be convinced*. The moſt contradictory to my Aſſertion that can well be, eſpecially when I neither lay the Obligation upon every Conviction, but that only which comes from the Holy Spirit of Truth, that is always preſent to convince all of their Duty; nor ſubject that Conviction to the corrupt Wills of Men.

I ſhall here ſum up all my Authorities into one, and that is *W. Perkins*, a Famous Man in his Time, whoſe Judgment may, perhaps, ſway a little to correct the Extravagancy of this *Young Skirmiſher*.

———— " Such Perſons as have not ſo much as heard of Chriſt, though they are
" apt and fit to be bound in Conſcience by the Goſpel, in as much as they are the
" Creatures of God, yet are they not indeed actually bound, till ſuch Time as the
" Goſpel be *Revealed*, or, at the leaſt, Means of Revelation offered. *Reaſon* I.
" Whatſoever Doctrine or Law doth bind Conſcience, muſt in ſome Part *Be Known*
" by Nature or by Grace, or by both; the Underſtanding muſt *Firſt of all conceive*,
" or, at the leaſt, have Means of conceiving, before Conſcience can conſtrain, becauſe
" it *Bindeth by Virtue of known Concluſions* in the Mind, therefore Things that are
" *Altogether Unknown, and unconceived of the Underſtanding*, do not bind in Con-
" ſcience. Now that the Goſpel is unknown of many, I have already proved,
" therefore it binds them not in Conſcience. II. *Paul* faith, *Rom.* ii. 12. *They which ſin without Law, ſhall be condemned without Law*. To this he brings *Auguſtine*, *Tract* 89, on John 15. 22. ſaying, *That the* Gentiles *may have an Excuſe for not believing in Chriſt*. Biſhop *Sanderſon* is of the ſame Judgment in his *Oxford* Lectures on Conſcience.

W. Perkins's Works of Conſcience, pag. 512.

Now for his next Contradiction, which is in ample Manner thus.

God and Conſcience will never ſmite for meer (p. 11.) *and total Impoſſibilities*; what are they J. C? *To obey a Command which it is utterly impoſſible to know or be convinced of*: Very well, enough of this before; but what's the Matter with Conſcience?

ence? How comes this strange Advance of a sudden from the Bar to the Bench? What, a *Regicide*, a *Parricide*, a *Murderer*, an *Adulterer*, a *Drunkard*, a *Thief*, a *Traytor*, a *Tyrant*, a *Blasphemer*, an *Atheist*, and now a *Judge*, and such a Judge too as takes Place next God himself in Judgment; *God and Conscience will never smite and condemn*, &c. O Powerful Conscience! And O Righteous Conscience too! What, a just Judge at last! Both able and equal? Certainly then it can be no Error to follow thy Dictates, nor make thy Convictions the Measures of our Obedience; but tell me, O Conscience, if Princes and Rulers make never so good Laws, wilt thou come and say, *I deny all these Laws, and the Makers of them; Children may murder their Parents; Subjects, their Princes; Servants, their Masters; one Man another?* pag. 5, 6.

Dost thou require Men to do all these Impieties *under Pain of Damnation?* If not, go to *I. C.* for Satisfaction, for he has grievously abused thee.

In short, Reader, so perplext is the Man in his *Skirmish*, that he seems to have scar'd no Body so much as himself; he has frightned himself with his own *Bulbeggar*, and, as it happens, with young *Hotspurs*, Conceit carries them on, but leaves them in the Fray, to get off as they can: So it has fallen out with *I. C.* he is in, and he knows not how to get out again.

One While he appeals to God and Conscience; *If God and Conscience approve me*, p. 2. Here he makes Conscience the Rule of his Writings, as well as God; another While, *We may do the most horrid Crimes, and yet Conscience stand to them, and not only not smite us, but approve us, and praise us*, p. 5. By and by, *God and Conscience will never smite and condemn for meer Impossibilities*; here again it is joyned with God in Righteous Judgment, *p.* 11.

Again, *If Conviction be the Ground of Obedience, and the Authority of Scripture depend upon the Rectitude and Purity of Conscience, then all Rational Law, Order and Government, Divine and Human, is overturned, and a Stop put to all Religion and Piety towards God, to all Conscience, Honesty and Charity toward Men. Let God command what he will, Conscience may come and say, I deny this Command, and him that commanded it*, p. 5.

I desire to know of this Man, by what Trope or Figure it is that he makes adhering to Conscience the Way *to overturn and stop Conscience*: That's the first Case of Conscience I have to ask of him.

The Second is this, How Conscience can be coupled with Honesty and Charity, nay, with God Himself, and yet have the Impudence to tell God, *I deny Thy Command, and Thee too*; Is not this strange Divinity? Surely this Man is but a Parson by the by, for he violates the common Rules of Theology, as their own Schools teach.

But once more in Honour of Conscience, and to make her Amends, as he began with the Leave of Conscience, he Ends, if we will believe him, with the Judgment of Conscience, hear him.

I would be glad to make the Best I can of your Position, but I must protest my Conscience and Conviction: Thus doth he make that his Guide his whole Pamphlet reprobates.

The next Contradiction is this, that Conscience is made by him to be *killed* with Sin, as if it were a Just Principle; and by and by he renders it the Seared Active Sinner, *p.* 5. Once more:

Lastly, he tells us, That *he grants that without the Light Within, we could not at all come to the Knowledge of the Scriptures,* p. 12. yet, *That the Light Within, gives the Drunkard Leave to be Drunk.*

Again, *The Light Within, which should be his* GUIDE, *like a Negligent, Drunken Coach-Man, sleeps, and the Horses run away, or he drives into Pits and Bogs; so doth the Light Within take Part with the Flesh and Satan against you*, p. 13.

These Contradictions speak for themselves, though against him; the Reader may easily judge at what a Pass this *Parson Skirmisher* hath reduced himself, that writes at this Random-Rate.

But what farther of his Elaborate Studies in Divinity? Why this, *If Scripture go* (says he) *farewel God, and Christ, and Heaven, and all Law, and Rule,* p. 13.

Now God forbid that the Scriptures should go; but since in telling a *Fib* of us (as if we slighted them) he has adventured such an *Axiom* abroad in the World, I think fit thus to animadvert: Doth God, Christ, Heaven, all Law and Rule depend upon Scripture? Strange Change! *The Creator depends upon the Creature; the Saviour upon his Message; Heaven upon the History of it?* Ridiculous, as well as Blasphemous. Well, but this is the worst Sense; let us see if we can find the Best, and that is this, *Farewel to our Knowledge and Enjoyment of God, Christ, Heaven,* &c. *if the Scriptures were lost*; but this is also Extravagant, since God hath not so tyed up himself to Scripture; the Scripture it self tells us, *Of a Law writ in the Heart*, and that this is not an Inferior State neither, but that of the *New and Everlasting Covenant*, Heb. 8. Again, Was there no God, Christ, or Heaven, Law or Rule before Scripture? The contrary is notorious, the World had enjoy'd many Ages before the Scriptures were in Being; Paradise needed them not; and *Abraham, Isaac* and *Jacob* had them not; and can this Parson think there was no Knowledge of God, Christ, Heaven, Law, or Rule in those Ages? Wonderful! What cross Prospects doth this Man take of Religion! But what becomes of his spiritual Laws writ in Man's Nature? Pag. 8, 9. if all would be lost with the Scriptures, (which God preserve) how cross is this to the Apostle's Sentence in this very Place, Rom. 2. *For the Gentiles, which have not the Law, do by Nature the Things contained in the Law, and are a Law unto themselves*: It seems here was God, Heaven, Law and Rule without Scripture.

Lastly, He would needs have it, *That Men may commit all Sorts of Impiety upon Conviction*; see p. 4, 5, 10, 11. Whereas all these Evils are committed against Conviction, says every Orthodox Man, be they Sins of *Wilfulness, Searedness* or *Ignorance*; for Wilfulness resists Conviction; Searedness overlays, smothers or kills it, if it be possible; and Ignorance is Darkness or Blindness, which is just opposite to Conviction.

Perhaps he thought any Thing would do against the *Quakers*, especially if *Skirmish* and *Imprimatur* began it; but can he in his Conscience think (for he now tells us he hath one, and he can appeal to it too) *that the Light within helps to the Understanding of Scripture, and ought to be our Guide*; and yet that it should be a *lewd, drunken, fleshly, satanical Principle, and a Rebel against God* that gave it for those excellent Ends *of knowing Scripture, and regulating our Conversation accordingly*? Shall I return him his own Saying? *Quis talia fando temperet a lachrymis?* Though we had all gone Astray, I ever thought our Guide had kept the Way, and that should be our Condemnation: but this Man teacheth other Doctrine, namely, that the *Guide God hath given us leads to be drunk, and takes Part with the Flesh and Satan against God*. What follows, but that every Man is discharged from adhering to such a Guide, especially since the People in the Coach are not to be blamed, if the Coach-man drive them into Pits or Bogs; but seriously, Parson, is there no *Soul-damning* or *God-blaspheming Error* in this Doctrine, that chargeth him with making so ill Provision for the Rule of Man's Life; *wouldst not thou take a better Coach-man, left thy Horses, with thy Wits, should run away?* And hath the Almighty so ill helped us with a Guide, and yet denounced so many heavy and eternal Punishments, in case I miss my Way? This false Step in Divinity drives me to observe three or four more, and so conclude.

Page 8, 9, 11. The next is this, *That the Indians have no Knowledge of Good or Evil*; which not only contradicts the Testimony of Travellers, and the Judgment of all Learned Men; and, which is more, the Scripture too, that demanded of old, *Upon whom does not his Light arise?* And tells us, *That every Man has a Measure of Light*, and *that the Grace of God appeareth to all Men*; but the Parson also contradicts himself; for he tells us of *Laws of God writ in Man's Nature*; which includes *Indians*, if *Indians* be Men.

His next Error expressed or implied by several Places of his Pamphlet is, *That all Men are not convinced, reproved or condemned, though they may have the Means of it.* (p. 9, 10.) I affirm that all Men are Convinced, though they lay it not to Heart; for Men see their Sin, unless they have sinned their Sight away, in case that can entirely be. *God hath shewed unto thee O Man what is good*: Mic. 6. 8. What Man is this? the *Jew*? yes, and the *Gentile* too: *O Man!* that is, Mankind; and can Man see the Good and not the Evil, or can he see either and not be convinced? *Monstrum Horrendum Ingens*: Pray how is Man left without Excuse, if God shows him not Good and Evil? and can he see, and not be convinced? Sight is Conviction.

But when all is done, granting the Man his black Opinion of Conscience and Conviction; what can he say of a *Quaker's* Conscience that I cannot say of a *Protestant's*? Will he bewray his own Nest, or mark his own Nose? What other Argument used *Luther, Melancthon, Zuinglius, Calvin* and *Beza*, &c. abroad; B. *Hooper*, J. *Bradford*, I. *Philpot*, B. *Jewel*, &c. at home? for their Separation from the Church of

Rome. Does not this Man know, that all those horrid Consequences he has heapt upon my Assertion, may be (and some of them have been) urged against the Men named and their Followers by the *Popish* Church, yea, and by one another too? Is this Man a *Protestant?* Why not a *Papist?* *Answ.* Because of Conscience and Conviction to the contrary; *Hold there,* says the Papist, *the Church is above a private Conscience;* and what know I but your Conscience will lie, steal, rebel against the Government, and at last cut Throats. O by no Means, *I. C.* may say, I am no such Man, my Conscience teaches me better Things: *Never tell me of that,* says the Papist, *whilst you make Conscience and Conviction the Rule of your Actions towards the Church, I have Cause to fear that will one Time or other pretend a Conviction to follow all Manner of Lusts, to overturn Law and Government, and to stop all Religion and Piety towards God, all Conscience, Honesty and Charity towards Men,* p. 15. But God and Conscience approve me, says *I. C.* p. 2. I cannot believe more than I can believe; nor do God and Conscience ever smite for meer Impossibilities, p. 11. and I must protest Conscience and Conviction for what I do, p. 13. And thus *I. C.* comes off with his *Papist.* Would one think then that this Man should fall so severely upon me for having any Regard to Conscience and Conviction? One would think he were beside himself, as well as the Truth: But I am not without Hopes of his Information and Repentance; till then I could advise the *Imprimatur-Man,* not to be so *Licentious;* and in the mean while, it can do him no harm to meditate well upon this Passage of Scripture, *And he causes all, both great and small, rich and poor, bond and free, to receive a Mark in their Right Hands or in their Foreheads; and that no Man might Buy or Sell, save he that had the Mark or the Name of the Beast,* Rev. 13. 16, 17.

I shall conclude with the Judgment of B. *Andrews,* W. *Perkins,* and B. *Wilkins,* upon Conscience, and that shall be my Contribution to the Parson's better Proficiency in Divinity; for I hear he is but lately and by Accident of the Trade.

Lanc. Andrews, Bp. of *Winton, on the Commandments,* chap. 6, saith, ' In the ' WORST of Men, when God puts the Bit in their Mouths, those *Sparks (viz.)* ' that he hath placed in Man, will fly out. N. 5. He calls Conscience, *God's De-* ' *puty or Vice-gerent.*

W. Perkins, Treatise of Conscience, in his Works *Theological,* vol. 1, pag. 17. London 1636. ' *Conscience* is a Part of the Understanding in all reasonable ' Creatures, determining of their particular Actions, either with them or against ' them.—— Understanding hath two Parts, *Theoretical* and *Practical;* under the ' latter is Conscience, because it's Property is to judge of the Goodness or Badness ' of Things, or Actions done —— Reason of the Name of Conscience, *scire* to ' know, is of one Man alone by himself; and *conscire* is when two at the Least ' know some one secret thing, either of them knowing it together with the other: ' Therefore the Name συνείδησις, or *conscientia,* Conscience, is that Thing that ' combines two together, and makes them Partners in the Knowledge of one and ' the same Secret. —— Man, by a Gift given him of God, knows, *together with* ' *God,* the same Things of himself: And this Gift is named *Conscience.* —— It is ' (as it were) *a little God, sitting in the middle of Men's Hearts, arraigning them* ' *in this Life, as they shall be at the Tribunal of God in the last Judgment.* ' —— Power in the Soul, the Property whereof is to take the Principles and Con- ' clusions of the Mind, and apply them, and by applying, either to *Accuse* or *Ex-* ' *cuse*———If Conscience be lost, it is only in Respect of the Use thereof, as ' Reason in a Drunkard, and not otherwise————Conscience is a Thing of a *di-* ' *vine Nature,* and is a Thing placed of God in the midst, between him and Man, ' as an *Arbitrator, to give Sentence, and to pronounce either with Man or against* ' *Man unto God.*

Bishop *Wilkins's Real Character,* Definition of Conscience, ' It's a Faculty where- ' by we apply general Principles to particular Cases, being a practical Judgment or ' Memory, relating to Matters of Duty. The Opposite to it, *Unconscionableness,* ' *Searedness, Profligateness,* &c.

These Testimonies give great Honour to *Conscience,* as the generality of Professions give to Men. By them it appears, that *Insensibility* is not *Conscience* or *Conviction;* and the Truth is, *unconscionable* implies that *conscionable* is *reasonable, just* and *good.*

For our Parts, we believe that God has placed his *Witness* in every Soul, Heart and Conscience; and that all Mankind shall be accused or excused by it; they that rebel against it, to them shall it be a Never-dying Worm; to them that love and obey it, an Everlasting Comforter.

By this hath God awakened and redeemed us from a vain Conversation: 'Tis his ancient Light and Spirit that strove with the old World, and strives with this. To no other Spirit is our Testimony, neither Conscience or Conviction, than that which is according to the Nature of it. And as I can make my Appeal to the Neighbours of *I. C.* and all other People else-where, if ever our Consciences or Convictions have led us to any such detestable Enormities, as he charges upon our Doctrines and Principle; and if we have not rather had our Conversation among them in *all Gentleness, Sobriety,* and *Honesty*; so do I warn all, to whom this comes, that they judge us not with unrighteous Judgment, nor readily receive the Reports and Suggestions of prejudiced Men against us and our Holy Way. It's no easy Thing to Flesh and Blood, for us to live uprightly in the Profession of it; meer Outside, Historical Faith, large Shews, much Talk for Religion, will not do the Matter, if the Heart remains unsubjected, the Affections unmortified, and no Peace with God sealed to the Soul; *Depart from me,* will be the last dismal Sentence.

Therefore my dear Countrymen, Grieve not God's Holy Spirit; encline your Hearts to his pure Word; 'tis nigh you, (*Rom.* 10.) that you should obey it and do it; it will reform and regenerate you; it will create all Things new, from an Hard to a Broken Heart, from a vain to a contrite Spirit; new Affections, new Desires, new Love, new Friendship, new Words, new Works, new Customs and Fashions, (not like the World's, that shall pass away, and Vexation of Spirit only remain in lieu of them for ever) Then shall the Peace of God flow into your Souls as a River, and nothing shall ever harm or make you afraid.

Truly, Friends, a Vain, Worldly, Unwatchful Conversation unrepented of, be your Profession and Church what they will, will one Day harm and make you afraid; for God will reward all People according to their Works: At that solemn Day it will not be, well talkt, or well profest, but *Well done good and faithful Servants*; Why? Because they have kept his Holy Sayings; Remember what Christ said, (by whom God will judge the Secrets of all Hearts in the Day of Account) that *for every idle Word which Man speaketh, shall he give an Account in the Day of Judgment.*

As one that knows the Terrors of the Lord, I would perswade all Men to turn to the living God; *For if the Righteous scarcely be saved, where shall the Ungodly and Sinner appear? For the Kingdom of God stands in Righteousness, Peace and Joy in the Holy Ghost*; and Sinners have nothing to do there: Neither think, that you are sav'd by Christ from Wrath, and not saved from Sin; or that he has saved you from the Guilt, though the Nature and Acts of Sin remain; no such can walk with God here; for they must be translated, changed, renewed; much less can they enjoy the Lord hereafter. Wherefore cast about, and see how it is with you; hearken while it is to Day; your faithful Monitor is in your own Bosom, and waits and knocks to be let into your most inward Affection, that he may be your Delight, the prime Object of your Love; and blessed are they that are not offended in him, but believe in him, and confess him before all Men; the *Outside Jew* despised him then, the *Outside Christian* slights him now; but blessed be God, this spiritual Appearance of Christ in the Soul, to the *Jews* (the Professors) a Stumbing-block, to the *Greeks* (the wise Men) Foolishness, is unto us, who have believed therein, the mighty Power of God to our Salvation; and the worst Desire I have for you is, That you also may sincerely believe, and when Time with you shall be no more, receive, with all those that in the Self-denying Life of Holy Jesus walk, and faint not, to the End of their Days, Glory, Honour and Eternal Life, *Amen*.

A BRIEF ANSWER TO A False and Foolish LIBEL, CALLED The QUAKERS OPINIONS.

For their Sakes that *Writ* it and *Read* it.

By WILLIAM PENN.

Being Defamed, *we Entreat*, 1 Cor. 4. 13.

The PREFACE.

Sober Reader,

THE End of Controversy with good Men, is the Advancement of Truth; with ill Men, of themselves and their base Interests; in all which God is Judge, who judgeth righteously, and will reward every one according to their Works, nor doth his Judgment slumber.

Most Parties in Europe boast themselves of being Christians, an excellent Character indeed; but the worst is, there is little more than a Boast in it. I am not uncharitable; I have first judged my self. Let none deceive themselves. To be like Christ, is to be a Christian, and not else; and Christians are in Concord; for Christ is not divided, neither is that Body, of which he is truly Head, at Variance; how much Discord, so much Degeneracy from God; for he is one, and so are those that are born of him; the Children of God are not divided, because one and the same Holy Spirit leads them.

That which is the Guide of one, is the Guide of all; and by this shall it be known who are God's Children, if they bring forth the Fruits of his Divine Spirit, which, saith the Apostle, are these, Love, Joy, Peace, Long-suffering, Gentleness, Goodness, Faith, Meekness, Temperance, against such there is no Law. And they, says he, that are Christ's, have crucified the Flesh, with the Affections and Lusts; this only will avail in the great Judgment of the Lord. Therefore I beseech all vain Contenders to consider of their own Standing, what their Work is, who Employs them, and what their Wages will be.

Tell me, thou vain Disputer and vitious Liver, what is Religion without Holy Love? what is Faith without Good Works? what is Worship without Godly Fear; and Christianity, without true Self-denial? It is not he that cries, Lord, Lord, but he that does the Will of my Father, said Christ, shall be accepted. There is a great talk of Man's Lapse in Adam, and Restoration in Christ, but they serve only for a sound with too many: For did People sincerely believe that they are fallen from true Love, Meekness, Patience, Humility, Mercy, Justice, Purity, &c. and did they but consider, that they are not restored to those Heavenly Qualifications, but that they live in fleshly Lusts of one sort or other, some in Voluptuousness, others in Envy; and therefore not really restored or redeemed by Christ, nor truly in a State of Salvation, but in

peril

peril of Eternal Misery, certainly they would not pass away their little Span of precious Time in so much worldly Pleasure, neglect of God, and Carelesness of the other World, if they have any the least hope of it.

Reader, the Petulancy of some Adversary or other has given occasion for this little Treatise: The Design of which is both to reprove him, and to hinder others from being abused by him, that so the Innocency of a People, whom God hath raised by his own Power and Wisdom to glorify him in their Bodies Souls and Spirits (which are his) may be delivered from the Mistakes of his Ignorance, and the Reflections of his Malice.

And truly, my fervent Prayers to Almighty God are, that he would yet more and more send forth his Light and his Truth to inform the Understandings, and overcome the Hearts of all People, that they may experimentally know the Redemption of their Souls from the Prevalency of Sin, and the Power of the God of this World's Lusts, by the Blood of Jesus, who is the Lamb of God that takes away the Sin of the World; then shall Love, Faith and Holiness increase and all Unrighteousness come to an End, Amen.

W. PENN.

An ANSWER to a *False* and *Foolish* Libel, &c.

OPINION I.

THE Quakers *deny the Authority of the Holy Scriptures, as the Rule of Faith and Practice unto* Christians.

Answer, This we flatly deny, and charge our Adversary to make it good *in terminis*, in so many Words, or retract his Charge. For the Authority of the Scriptures is the *Spirit* * *and Power of God*, which we say is our Rule and Guide, as it was the Rule of the Holy Men of God both before the Scriptures were written, and when they spoke and writ them. And to say we deny it to be our Rule, is to say we deny our own Principle, for owning of which you are angry with us. *Moses* is taken on all Hands to have been the first Penman of Sacred Story, and that we cannot rise higher than his Time for Scripture, consequently then the Scripture must take date; but who will deny that *Abel* had a Rule to worship God by, *Enoch* to walk with God by, *Noah* to preach by, *Abraham*, *Isaac* and *Jacob* to believe by? If they had none, say so; if they had, what was it, if not the *Spirit of Truth and Holiness*, that strove with the old World, but was resisted? And if the Spirit of God was the Rule of Faith, Worship and Practice, then, have we got another Rule in the room of it now? No such Matter; those that loved and feared God in all Ages were ruled and guided by the Spirit of God; and though many Helps have been afforded Men by the Father of Mercies and Lights, yet still the Spirit of Truth is the great Rule in and through them all. This is the Rule of all Rules, as God is the Light of all Lights; yea, this is that Rule of the New Creature; for the walking of the true Christian is in and after the Spirit; yea, 'tis the Mark of being a Child of God to be led and guided by the Spirit of God, this is the Scripture's Testimony. There is no Condemnation to those that walk not after the Flesh, but after the Spirit; and as many are led by the Spirit of God, are the Sons of God. The Argument is plain, and altogether as unanswerable; *That which is to* lead *Christians, is to* rule *Christians*; but *the* Spirit of Truth *is to* lead Christians, *consequently the* Spirit of Truth *is to* Rule Christians. So that to deny that the *Spirit of Truth* is the *Guide and Rule of Christians*, is to gainsay the Testimony of Scripture, and the very Tenour and Nature of the *second*, new and everlasting, *Covenant of Life* and Salvation; for in that State the *Law is writ in the*

Gal. 6. 15.
Rom. 1. 15.

Jer. 35. 33. 34.

---

* This was the Doctrine of Luther, Zuinglius, Calvin, Oecolampadius, Beza and Marlorat abroad; and of *W. Tindal, D. Barns, John Frith, John Bradford, J. Woodman, Philpot, Fox, Jewel, Whitaker*, &c. at home, that the Scriptures Authority to us stood in the inward Testimony of the Spirit of God. See my Quakerism a New Nick-Name for Old Christianity, and my *Rejoynder* in defence of the same, from pag. 24 to pag. 101. and from pag. 31 to pag. 186.

Heart.

Heart, *and the Fear and Spirit put in the* inward Part; and what for, if not to rule and guide the Soul in the Path of Life?

Heb. 8. 13.

To conclude, As the Spirit of Truth revealed to the Prophets Things to come, and was a Rule to them in discerning, receiving, declaring and writing those Things, so is the same Spirit of Truth the Rule and guide to all God's People in their reading and understanding of them now written: and blessed are they that read with a good Understanding,

And that the Simplicity of none may be abused, we declare, as we have frequently done, that the *Scriptures of Truth* were *given forth by the Holy Men of God, as they were moved by the Spirit of God*; and that they are a *Rule*, yea, an Excellent *Rule*, for *Instruction, Reproof* and *Doctrine*, and all true Christians ought to embrace and practice the *Holy Mind* and *Will of God* thereby declared. And they are those that truly and substantially *deny the Scriptures*, who in Words own them, but in Works deny them, and in their Conversations walk not according to the godly *Rules* therein contained; such are *Whoremongers, Fornicators, Drunkards, Lyars, Back-biters, Slanderers*, such as the Author or Authors of this Impious *Libel, Envious Persons, Rioters, Sporters, Vain Persons, Lovers of Pleasures more than Lovers of God:* These and such like are they that deny the Authority of holy Scripture; yet as the Devil used Scripture against Christ, so do his Children use *Scripture* at this Day against the Disciples of Christ.

2 Tim. 3. 15, 16, 17.
ch. 3. 1, 2, 3, 4, 5.
Gal. 5. 19, 20, 21.

OPINION. II. *The* Quakers *deny the Resurrection of the Body.*

Answ. The *Quakers* deny no Resurrection, that is according to Scripture; we own the Resurrection both of the Just and Unjust; and that our Adversaries shall know one Day to their Confusion, if they repent not. And as the Charge is laid down, we literally deny it, and require our Adversaries to prove it: For we declare to all People, we own the Resurrection of the Body according to the Pleasure of God: and every Seed shall have it's own Body; and Wo to the Wicked in that Day.

Luke 20. 35, 36, 37, 38.
John 11. 25.
1 Cor. 15. 34. 35, 36, 37, 38.
Rev. 20. 5.

OPINION III. *The* Quakers *deny the Person of Jesus Christ.*

Answ. If by Person of Christ is meant the Man Christ Jesus, we deny the Charge; for there is no other Name given under Heaven, by which Salvation can be obtained. 'Tis Christ alone that hath brought Life and Immortality to light: He is the Propitiation, the Mediator and Intercessor; and by him only can Man come to God: and no Man can come to him but such as come to his Spirit in their own Hearts. And such as have not the Spirit of Christ dwelling in them, are none of his. And these are they that deny Christ, that deny his Cross, break his Law, and live not according to his Example, who is meek and lowly, pure and undefiled, and separated from all Sinners. So that the Antichrists of our Days are those that live according to the Lusts of the Eye, the Lusts of the Flesh, and Pride of Life, without God in the World, that is, without a Sense of God upon their Hearts: but their Minds run after the Things that are seen, which are temporal, neglecting the Things that are eternal. And though such may profess Christ in Words, yet it shall be said unto them in the great Day of Account, *Depart from me ye that work Iniquity.*

Acts 4. 12.
2 Tim. 1. 10.
Rom. 3. 25.
1 John 2. 2.
1 Tim. 2. 5, 6
Heb. 8. 6.
ch. 12, 24.

Rom. 8. 34.
Heb. 7. 25.
1 John 2. 16.
Mat. 7. 23.

I would have our foolish and envious Adversaries look at home, and prepare for the Day of their Account to God, and leave off their Envy and Bitterness, and mind God's Fear, which will teach them to be meek and loving, sober and vertuous, that they may provide for their Latter End: For pure Religion stands not in accusing and slandering, reviling and persecuting, but in keeping unspotted of the World; for they who are of the World, are not of Christ; they who love the Pride, Pleasures, Honours and Lusts of this World *deny Christ*, they are the *Antichrists* indeed; for Christ saith, I am not of this World, neither is my Kingdom of this World, nor are his Followers of this World, therefore it is the World hates them; but not under the Name of Christ's Disciples, Christians or Children of God, by no Means; for such the World nominally owns; but as Hereticks, Blasphemers, and the like, which hath always been the Devil's Policy: For the Wolf with the Sheeps-skin on him has in every Age been worrying the Sheep that hath been covered with the Wolf's-skin; such have called Light Darkness, and Darkness Light.

James 1. 27.
John 8. 23.
ch. 15. 18, 19.
ch. 18. 36.
Mat. 5. 11.

1 Cor. 4. 10, 13.

OPINION IV. *The Quakers hold, that the Light in every Man is a sufficient Guide unto Salvation.*

Answ. This is unfairly laid down; but we say, that the Light of Christ in every Man is a sufficient Guide to Salvation; and who dares deny it? *I am the Light of the World,* faith Christ, *they that follow me shall not walk in Darkness, but have the Light of Life.* And faith *John*, *If we walk in the Light, the Blood of Jesus Christ shall cleanse us from all Unrighteousness.* And it was the Doctrine in old Time, *The Path of the Just is as the shining Light, that shines more and more unto the perfect Day.* And the Prophet *Isaiah* prophetically writes of the latter Days thus, *Come, let us walk in the Light of the Lord,* and by the same Prophet faith the Lord, *I will give thee* (Christ) *for a Light to the Gentiles, that thou may'st be my Salvation to the Ends of the Earth.* And the Apostle *Paul* had that good Opinion of the Light, that he advised the Saints of old, *to put on the Armour of Light, that they might walk honestly as in the Day, not in Rioting and Drunkenness, not in Chambering and Wantonness, not in Strife and Envy; but put ye on the Lord Jesus Christ, and make not Provision for the Flesh, to fulfil the Lusts thereof.* And it is nothing else, but the old *Jewish* Darkness, that spurns against the Light of Christ in our Day: for the same Spirit that rejected that Light, Grace and Truth, with which he was filled in the Day of his bodily Appearance, is the same that resists and slights that Light. Truth and Grace, which from his Fulness is distributed to the Children of Men but as it was then, so it is now the Condemnation of the World, that Light is come into the World, and that Men love Darkness rather than Light, and the Reason is plain, because their Deeds are Evil. Every Thing loves it's like.

John 8. 12.
1 John 1. 7.
Prov. 4. 18.
Isa. 2. 5.
ch. 49. 6.
Rom. 13. 12; 13, 14.
John 9, 14, 16
1 Cor. 12: 7.
John 3. 19.

OPINION V. *They hold that* Perfection *is attainable in this Life.*

Answ. This also is not fairly laid down, being without distinction; and did not Compassion to the well-minded incline me to deliver our Judgment in these Matters, I would have put our Adversary upon the Proof of his Assertions, without giving him the least help by a Sight of our true Principles, till he had first seen and acknowledged his own Ignorance and Inadvertency. We own Perfection according to the Scriptures; *Walk thou before me,* said God to Abraham, *and be thou perfect:* Who dare quibble this into an Imperfection? or who dare charge God with commanding what was impossible to be done? *Noah was a just Man, and perfect in his Generation, and Noah walked with God;* so did *Enoch. Job also was a perfect Man, and upright, one that feared God and eschewed Evil.* This Christ exhorted his Disciples to, *Be ye therefore* Perfect *even as your Father which is in Heaven is perfect.* This also the Apostle *Paul* prays for, *That they might be sanctified throughout, in Body, Soul and Spirit.* Again thus, *And the very God of Peace sanctifie you Wholely; and I pray God your Spirit, and Soul, and Body be preserved Blameless unto the Coming of our Lord Jesus Christ.* Yet farther, *Till we all come in the Unity of the Faith, and of the Knowledge of the Son of God unto a* Perfect *Man.* Again, *That the Man of God may be* Perfect. And to the *Hebrews* faith the Author of that Epistle, *Let us go on to* Perfection; and once more in the same Epistle he faith, *The God of Peace make you* Perfect *in every good Work to do his Will.* This also was the Apostle *Peter's* Prayer for the Holy Strangers scattered throughout *Pontus, Galatia, Cappadocia, Asia* and *Bythinia, The God of all Grace, who hath called us into his Eternal Glory by Christ Jesus, make you* Perfect. I will conclude with the Doctrine of the Beloved Disciple, that lay in the Lord's Bosom, and can give a better Account of his Mind and Doctrine than any of our Adversaries can do, thus, *If we walk in the Light as* (God) *is in the Light, we have Fellowship one with another, and the Blood of Jesus Christ his Son cleanseth us from all Sin.* Again, *I write unto you Young Men, because ye have overcome the Wicked One.* Again, *Whosoever abideth in Christ,* Sinneth *not; whosoever is born of God, doth* Not commit Sin; *for his Seed remaineth in him, and he* Cannot Sin, *because he is born of God.* Again, *If we love one another, God dwelleth in us, and his Love is* Perfected *in us; God is Love, and he that dwelleth in Love dwelleth in God, and God in him: Herein is our Love made* Perfect, *that we have Boldness in the Day of Judgment, because as he is, so are we in this World.* What say Rioters and Envious Persons to this, such as revile, waste and destroy their Neighbours for the Exercise of a peaceable Conscience?

Gen. 17. 1.
Gen. 5. 22. and 6. 9.
Job 1. 1.
Matt. 5. 48.
1 Thes. 5. 23.
Ephes. 4. 13.
1 Tim. 3. 17.
Heb. 6. 1. and 13. 21.
2 Pet. 5. 10.
1 John 1. 7. ch. 2. 13. ch. 3. 9.

science? Doth the Love of God abide in them? Are they like unto the God of Love in this World? Can they hope for his Mercies in that World which is to come, who are cruel and abusive to their honest Neighbours in this? But more of that another Time. Yet again, Whosoever is born of God *overcometh the World, and sinneth not*; but he that is begotten of God keepeth himself *that the Wicked One toucheth him not*. What think the Enemies of Perfection of this?

To conclude: They that deny Perfection from Sin, deny the End of Christ's Coming, if this Beloved Disciple may be Judge; for saith he, Christ was manifested *to take away our Sins*; and whosoever abideth in him, sinneth not: For this Purpose, the Son of God was manifested, that he might destroy the Works of the Devil; and whosoever is born of God, *doth not commit Sin*. And without Offence let me say, our Adversaries may better employ themselves, than to turn Advocates for the Devil and his Kingdom, as they seem to do, by charging the *Doctrine of Perfection* upon the *Quakers*, as an Evil Opinion; for no Man in his Wits, can believe they intend us any Reputation or Credit, when they set the *Mark of Perfection upon our Creed*. But is it not a Shame that Men, who profess themselves to be *Christians*, the Disciples of that Self-denying JESUS, should make their Lord's Office our Reproach, and the End of His Blessed Coming a *Mark of Heresy*? Why? Was He sent but to Save? And how does He Save, if People must necessarily live in Sin, that eternally loseth them, and to Save them from which He is come? *And thou shalt call His Name JESUS*, said the Angel, *because He shall Save His People from their Sins*: Alas! What have Men to be Saved from, if not from Sin? For Sin set aside, Man is Good, and All is Good; If then Sin loses Men Heaven and Happiness, Men must be Saved from it, or they will be eternally lost; for in that State *Christ* will profit them nothing.

To the Quotations *I shall make a* Brief Return.

The First Quotation: G. Whitehead *saith, That the Light Within must be God, because to deny it so to be, is to deny the Omnipresence of God.*

To what is here alledged, thus brought to disrepute our Holy Religion, I answer, That this Adversary has not told us whether they were Words spoken or written: If spoken, where be the Witnesses? If written, where is the Book or Paper? However, the Words are not Indefensible; *For God is Light, and in Him is no Darkness at all*; and He is Omnipresent, therefore in Man; and in Him we live, move, and have our Being, yea, more especially; for it is He that searcheth the Heart, and tryeth the Reins, and that telleth unto Man his Thoughts. Upon whom, said one of Old, *Doth not His Light arise?*

To the Second Quotation, viz. *It is Damnable Heresie to deny the Worshipping the Measure of Light in every Man. And that the Spirit which God breathed in Adam, was not Man's Spirit, but another; the Breath of our Nostrils, the Anointed Lord; this is that True Light which lighteth every Man that comes into the World:* See Robert West's Book, called *Damnable Heresies Discovered*, pag. 6.

I answer. *First*, That I have not the Book cited, or cannot find it. *Secondly*, That the Man is not entirely in Society with us, but there has been some Dissatisfaction in the Minds of our Friends about him in several Respects, and particularly this Book was not received or printed by us. Yet *Lastly*, I know not but many Good Things may be in it; but if in any Thing it be unsound, it will not lie at our Door: Nor do I believe that the Passage it self may not be Vindicated, and that by Authority of Reason, Scripture, and the Consent of Ancient and Modern Authors: I will only say, that every Appearance of God, is God; the Light that comes from God, is God; for God is Light, and cannot be divided from himself; and the Word *Measure of Light*, relates to our Capacity, that receive and know only by Measure, and not to God, who, properly speaking, *is Immeasurable*. And true it is, that the Breath God breathed into *Adam* was Divine, if the *Learned Rabbies*, Commentators on that Scripture, be of any Credit, as may be seen in *My Rejoynder to John Faldo*; for a meer Human Soul could not make *Adam* live to God, much less make him the Image of His Creator. And if it was the Divine Life, I hope none will question if that Life be Christ, who says expresly of himself, *I am the Way, the Truth, and the Life*; who also says, *I am the Light of the World*; and this is *John's* Testimony, *In the Word* (that made all Things) *was Life, and that Life is the Light of Men; And this* (says he) *is that True Light which enlightens every Man that comes into the World*. So much to that Passage.

To the Third Quotation out of *G. Fox* and *R. Hubberthorn*'s Book, called, *Truth's Defence*, pag. 101, I answer,

First, That the Quoter has wrong'd the Passage, and falsified the Book; for there is that quoted is not there. The Words are these, as given by our Adversary in the Name of *G. F.* and *R. H. We do deny the Scriptures to be the Word of God, and also to be a Standing Rule; and that it is dangerous for ignorant People to read them.* See *Fox* and *Hubberthorn*, in *Truth's Defence*, pag. 101.

I answer, All these Words [*We do deny the Scriptures to be the Word of God, and also to be a Standing Rule*] are not to be found there, they are added; which is a great Piece of Injustice; for the last Part, which lies as if we would deny that *ignorant People should read the Scriptures*, hear the Words themselves.

" Query. The Priest asks, *Whether the Scriptures being Carnal, and the Letter killing, as you* (Quakers) *say, we may read them without Danger?*

To this *G. Fox* and *R. Hubberthorn* answer:

" The Letter which killeth is dangerous; for thou takest it here to *War with*
" *against the Saints, with thy Carnal Mind and Expositions.* —— Again thus, Here
" you read with Danger, who speak of them, *and speak a Lye*; and it's Dange-
" rous to read that, and make a *Trade* of that, which the Prophets, Christ, and
" the Apostles spoke forth freely; and you wrest the Scriptures to your Destructi-
" on; *and to you 'tis Dangerous to read*, &c.

Now let all People of Candour, yea, common Sense judge, if this Sort of reading and using the Scripture be not dangerous: Thus the *Pharisees* and *Jews* used the Scripture against Christ. But does this give Ground to our Adversary to say, We hold it Dangerous for ignorant People to read the Scripture, because we say that a Covetous, Persecuting, or Malicious End, or Use of Scripture, is Dangerous? O the Perversion that is made of the Words and Sense of this Passage! The Lord forgive him, or them, that deal thus with us. Hear what the same Page says, But I say, *Blessed is he that doth read and doth understand*. This I have elsewhere observed more at large.

To the Fourth Passage, viz. That *J. N.* in *Answer* to the *Jews* says, *It is the the Devil that contends for the Scriptures to be the Word of God.*

I can say the less, because I have not the Book out of which it is pretended to be quoted: But certain it is, that the Devil, that loves not the very *Form of Godliness*, but to exalt it against the Power, and shelter himself for a Saint, has more than once, on the same Score, pleaded for the *Scripture* against *Christ*, and the *Letter* against the *Spirit*; not that he loveth the Scripture, or that the Scripture opposeth either Christ or the Spirit, but that he hath subtilly used the very Scripture, as little as he loves it, both to tempt and oppose even Christ himself. This is plain in his tempting Christ in Scripture-Language, and in the Persecutions of the *Jews* both against Christ and His Disciples, for which they urged Scripture; they relied upon them for Life Eternal, and not upon Christ; Him they set at Nought then, as much as the *False Christians* slight his Light now. And it was Christ's Complaint then, *In them you think* (said he) *to have Eternal Life, but you will not come unto me that you may Life.* Thus the outward *Jew* set up the *Scripture* against Christ in the Flesh, and thus the outward *Christian* sets up the *Scripture* against Christ in the Spirit, or, in *His Spiritual Appearance in the Soul*, insomuch that a Man runs the Hazard of being proclaimed a Blasphemer, that speaks but of *Christ Within*, yet it is express Scripture; and of being stigmatized for an *Heretick*, that calls Christ only that Word of God, to whom only that Name is given in the Evangelical Writings, though at the same Time a Man confess the Holy Scriptures to be given forth by *Divine Inspiration*, and that they are the *Words of God*. That *The Word* is His Name, *John* will be our Warrant in the Beginning of his History; and that His Name is called *The Word of God*, *John* also affirms in his *Revelation*. I will end with this, that *Luke* the Evangelist, in his Dedication of his History to his Excellent *Theophilus*, now Part of the Sacred Scripture, calls it, *A Declaration of those Things that were most surely believed among them*, and *not the Word of God*. We take him for our Pattern; when he is confuted, it will be Time enough for us to confess our Mistake.

Mat. 4. 6. 12. John 5, 9. and 19. 7. & 5. 39, 40.

John 1. 1. Revel. 19. 13.

Luke ch. 1.

To the Fifth Quotation, *viz.* That *G. Fox* says, *The Soul is Part of God, of His Being, without Beginning, and Infinite*. Great Mystery, pag. 68, 9, 29. I answer briefly:

That *G. F.* speaks of the Divine Soul, or Life of Man, that comes from God, by which Man liveth to God, so *Augustine* calls it *Anima Animæ*, the Soul of the Soul, or Life of Man's Soul; so *Rabbi Nunchmanni* and *Hiskuni*, in the Comment of *Paulus Fagius* take it, saying, *It's of the Being of God, His own Breath.* This is without Beginning, respecting God; and Infinite, or without End, respecting Man. Where is the Heresie of this?

To the Sixth Quotation out of the Works of G. F. Junior, viz. *We own the Scriptures as a True Declaration of the Saints Conditions.*

I answer: The Allegation is frivolous on the Side of our Adversary; for he doth not deny what G. F. asserts, nor does G. F. deny, but that there are many Scriptures which are *Promissory, Threatning, and Prophetick*: Does our owning the Scriptures to be an Account of the *Experiences of the Saints of Old Time*, exclude any farther Character? Or say that they are no more? What! Have People lost their Senses, or must any Thing serve to blemish *Quakers?* What Injustice is here! For Shame do as you would be done by.

To the Seventh Passage, alledged out of *George Whitehead's* Apology, p. 49. viz. *That what is spoken from the Spirit of Truth in any, is of as Great Authority as the Scriptures, yea, and greater.*

I answer in G. W's own Words, which are these, "That which was spoken from "the Spirit of Truth in any, is of as great Authority as the Scriptures or Chapters "are, and greater, as proceeding immediately from that Spirit, as Christ's Words "were of greater Authority, when he spoke, than the *Pharisees* reading the Letter; "and they and their Speaking we deny: This, *says he*, was my Answer.

Now I appeal to the Just Witness of God in every Conscience, if this Adversary was not very disingenuous, to take no Notice of this Distinction: For, in short, Two Things are in our *Friend's Words*; *First*, That what comes from the same Spirit of Truth, is of the same Authority; and who denies that? No Body that is in his Senses. *Next*, That what is spoken by the immediate Motion, Life and Power of the Spirit, is of more Authority, (that is, Force and Efficacy to move, quicken, enliven, or operate upon the Hearers) than the bare reading of a Chapter in the Scripture, especially by such as the *Pharisees* were, as a Letter cannot give that Impression which we may justly suppose the Lively Presence, Mind and Voice of the Person that writ it might. But the End of our Adversary plainly is this, to make us undervalue the Truth of the Scripture, and to debase the Authority of the Scripture with Relation to it's Verity; as if what was said now by the Spirit of Truth in any Godly Man, were more True than that which was spoken by the same Spirit in former Ages, which is a gross Suggestion. The Difference lying in these Two Things, *First*, Whether Christ's Words, spoken by his own Mouth, were not of greater Force, Vigour and Authority, to influence or quicken an Auditory, than the same Words written, and now read. *Secondly*, Whether the Words of Christ, when spoken by his own Mouth, were not of more Life and Authority than the Scriptures read by the *Pharisees.* The first is True, and much more the last; let this Adversary then be ashamed of his Injustice. Christ said of the Words that he spoke, *The Words that I speak, they are Spirit, and they are Life*; that is, as they proceeded from His Gracious Lips, and as they were uttered from that Divine Power, Glory and Authority, which dwelt in Him.

To the Eighth Quotation, That *Richard Stubbs*, a *Quaker*, should say, *That the Christ Born of the Virgin, and that dyed at* Jerusalem, *was a False Christ, and an Antichrist.*

I answer, There was never any such Man a *Quaker* that I know of, nor did ever any owned by us, utter so horrid a Blasphemy; we detest all such Impiety: Besides, the Story I suppose, came out of an idle Pamphlet, printed about Seven Years since, by a foolish Person in *London*, to get Money; a Fiction like to that of the *Island of Pines*, &c. But if True, Where's the Witnesses? *Shall the Say-so, or Authority of an Enemy prevail?* What must any Stuff serve to bedirt the *Quakers*, no Matter what, nor from whom? There is a Righteous God that will have the Judgment of these Things.

To the Ninth Passage, cited out of *G. F's Great Mystery*, pag. 206. viz. *If there be any other Christ than He that is Crucified Within, He is a False Christ.*

I answer, I have not the Book by me, but I will stand by the Passage; for either there is no such Thing as a *Christ Within*, or if there be, there must be *Two Christs*: Or, *Lastly*, it is the same *Christ* that suffered without, which is also crucified by Sin within. Now I leave our Adversary to chuse which of these Three he will accept of. Is there no Christ within? Or, Is there Two Christs, one within, and another without? Or, Is there but one Christ both without and within? Chuse him whether.

whether. But I would tell our *Adversary*, that a Christ was Revealed in *Paul*, and forming in the Hearts of the *Galatians*, and was in the Holy Ancients, the *Hope of Glory*, and so he is in his People in this Day, Blessed be the Name of the Lord. Yea, 'twas the Apostolical Exhortation: *Examine your selves whether ye be in the Faith, prove your own selves: Know ye not your own selves, how that Jesus Christ is in you, except ye be Reprobates.* So that such as deny Christ within, are out of the Apostolical Faith, and Reprobates. It was both Christ's Promise and Prayer, for says He to His Disciples, *Let not your Hearts be troubled; ye Believe in God, Believe also in me. I will not leave you Comfortless, I will come to you, I will come again. Yet a little While, and the World seeth me no more, but ye see me: Because I live, ye shall live also: At that Day ye shall know that I am in my Father, and you in me, and I in you.* That Christ prayed for this Fellowship is as clear: *Neither pray I for these alone, but for them also which shall believe on me through their Word; that they all may be one, as thou Father art in me, and I in thee, that they also may be one in us, that the World may believe that thou hast sent me; and the Glory which thou gavest me, I have given them, that they may be one even as we are one. I in them, and they in me, that they may be made Perfect in one: And that the World may know, that thou hast sent me, and hast loved them, as thou hast loved me. O Righteous Father! The World hath not known thee, but I have known thee, and these have known that thou hast sent me; and I have declared unto them thy Name, and will declare it, that the Love wherewith thou hast loved me, may be in them, and I in them.*

Gal. 1. 16. & 4. 19.
2 Cor. 13. 4.

John 14. 1. 3, 18, 19, 20.

Chap. 17. 20, 21, 22, 23, 25, 26.

This is the Blessedness of the Righteous, even in this World, the True Disciples of JESUS, *that forsake All for His Name, that take up His Cross Daily to their Vain Affections and Lusts, and boldly confess Him before all Men, by a Life of True Self-Denial.* O that all People would receive Him into their Hearts, that is, into their Love and Affections: *Behold, He stands at the Door and knocks;* shut not thy Door upon Him; let Him in, entertain Him in thy Soul, that He may wash thee, and cleanse thee by *His Own Spirit*, and by *His Own Water*, and by *His Own Blood*, that bear Witness for him on Earth, and these *Three are but One*: Then shall the Love of God abound in thy Soul, towards God, and towards thy Neighbour; this is *Christianity Indeed*: And the Truth is, 'tis want of Christ being known more within People, to purge their Hearts, and purifie their Consciences, that so much Vanity and Ungodliness are to be found among *Christians*: People can let the Devil be within them, but they will not allow Christ to be within them. But I would ask them and you, How the strong Man of Sin must be bound, that keeps the House (the Heart) and his Works destroyed, if Christ, the stronger than he, have no Entrance and Sway in the Conscience? For this know, that *from within proceed Evil Thoughts, Murders, Adulteries, Fornication, Thefts, False Witness, Blasphemies*; these, and such like, are the Things which defile the Man. Now, Who shall purge this Heart, and with what? Must not Christ do it, *He that Baptizes with Fire and with the Holy Ghost, whose Fan is in His Hand, and who will thorowly purge his Floor?* This was *John*'s Record, that was sent of God for that End. Now let those that call themselves *Christians*, consider Seriously, and in the Fear of God, if their Floors, *their Hearts*, be purged; if the Dirt and Chaff be swept away, if *Christ's Baptism of Fire*, has burnt up their Vain Thoughts, Lusts and Affections, or not; for by Fire will God plead with all Flesh. And let such consider, if they have been yet *Baptiz'd with the Holy Ghost*, that makes People Alive to God, and whether they live to God, and meditate in His Pure Law, or rather if they be not *Carnally-Minded*, which is Death, let them see if *Pride* don't profess *Christianity*, and if *Wantonness, Vanity, Covetousness, Fashion, Envy, Wrath, Malice, and such like*, don't make *Profession of Religion, Read, Pray, Preach, go to Church, and the like.* I say, in the Fear of Almighty God, let all that profess *Him*, and the *Christian Religion*, examine themselves, and prove themselves, *Whether Jesus Christ Live in them, and Rule in them, or another Nature, Principle and Spirit*; for God will not be mocked, *such as Men Sow, such must they Reap, in the Terrible Day of Judgment.*

Mat. 10. 38.
Chap. 16. 24.
Mark 8. 34.
Luke 9. 23.
Rev. 3. 20.

1 John 5. 8.

Mat. 12. 29.

Chap. 15: 19, 20.

Chap. 3. 11, 12.

To the Tenth Quotation out of *G. F's Way to the Kingdom*, viz. *That the Four Books of* Matthew, Mark, Luke *and* John, *are not the Gospel*.

I answer, If this be a Piece of Heresie, we have Good Company; for *Paul, Ignatius, Justin Martyr, Origen, Chrysostom*, and some of our *English Martyrs*, are of this Mind. *Paul* says, *The Gospel is the Power of God*; but it were Blasphemy with a Witness, to call these Four Narratives, or Declarations, the *Power of God*,

Rom. 1. 16.

1678.

in which there are the Sayings and Actions of the Devil, and *Wicked Jews* and Persecutors recorded, as well as the Expressions and Deeds of Christ and His Disciples.

Ignatius, in his Epistle to the *Philadelphians*, calleth it very near to *Paul's* Expression of the Gospel, ἀπαρτισμὸς ἀφθαρσίας, *The Perfection of Incorruption*, which these Four Books are not, that are composed of Paper and Letters, containing meer Reports and Records, though never so True; or the Consequence would be, that the Writings of the Prophets (because *Ignatius* saith in the same Epistle, *that the Prophets have announced and declared the Gospel*) are the Gospel in our Adversary's Account, if he believes *Ignatius*, that lived soon after. But it's clear that our Adversaries refuse the Prophets Writings that Title, and do not give it even to the Apostolical Epistles, yet are displeased with our Tenderness, in not Stiling these Four Books, or Histories, *The Gospel*.

When *Justin Martyr* speaks of these Four Books, especially when he citeth out of them *the Mocking of Christ*, prophesied of in the *Psalms*, and of Christ's Silence to *Pilate*, he saith, γέγραπται & δεδήλωται, *it is written and expressed*, not in the *Four Evangelists*, or in the *Four Evangelia*, or in the Gospel, or in the Writings of the *Four Evangelists*, as they do commonly now; But, saith he, ἐν τοῖς ἀπομνημονεύμασι τῶν Ἀποστόλων αὐτῶ, in the *Records* or *History* of his (Christ's) Apostles: Yea, he is so far from calling the Books of Scriptures either the Law or Gospel, that he saith, Christ Jesus is αἰώνιος νόμος ϰ καινὴ διαθήκη, *the Eternal Law and the New Testament*, which according to the *Prophesy should come forth to the Universal World*.

Eph. 6. 19.
& 3. 3.
Col. 2. 26.
1 Tim. 1. 11.

Chrysostom not only refused an Oath, but denied those *Four Books to be Evangile or Gospel*, though he refused not to call them, *The Writings of the Four Evangelists*. So said *William Thorp*, as may be seen in the *Book of Martyrs*. Besides, the Gospel is called, *A Mystery hid from Ages and Generations*, which Four Books were not; and it is still hid from all Envious, Proud, Lustful, Vain, and Evil-minded People.

To conclude: The Bible it self declares of the Gospel, but *is not that Gospel*; it declares of the Spirit, but *is not that Spirit*; it declares of the Light, but *is not that Light*; and it declares of the Eternal Power and Word, but *it is not that Eternal Power and Word of God*: Neither is the Light, Power and Spirit, in the Scripture, though they were in those that gave them forth, and live and abide for ever in Him, who is the Fulness of all Wisdom, Life and Truth, who is Lord and Author of the Holy Scriptures, given forth by Divine Inspiration.

To the last Citation and Exception, *viz.* that G. F. says, *That we ought not to Pray to God to give us a Sight of our Sins*.

I answer, That this Adversary misgives his Words, and suggests by those he cites, another Thing than is plainly and honestly intended by G. F. in his own Words; they are these, *And to you that Tempt God, and say, The Lord give us a Sight of our Sins*; mark, he speaks to those that Tempt God, and let me add, *Mock God too*; for to such he speaks, as what follows declares, *viz. Priests and People* (says G. F.) *does not the Light which Christ hath Enlightned you with, let you see your Sin? That Lying and Swearing, Cursed Speaking, Theft, Murder, Whoredom, Covetousness, Pride, Lust and Pleasures, all these Things to be the Works of the Flesh, and Fruits of Darkness? Mark now, this Light Within you lets you see it, so you need not Tempt God to give you a Sight of your Sins; for ye know enough, and waiting in the Light, Power and Strength will be given to you*.

Now, let the Impartial judge if the Consequence of these Words be, *That we must not Pray to God to give us a Sight of our Sins that we don't see*, which must be our Enemies Suggestion, or nothing, or not rather, *That we should not Tempt and Mock God, by Praying for a Sight of our Sins, whilst we see, and that there is not a forsaking of the Sins that we do already see*. I ask, Does it follow, that because we should not Tempt or Mock God, in Praying for a Sight of the Sins we have a Sight of, and yet don't forsake, that therefore we must not Pray to God for a Sight of those Sins that we have no Sight of, having first renounced those we have had a Sight of? Well, the Lord keep our Lives out of the Power of a Jury, that would take this Latitude of Construction.

The following Words of that good Man are these, and very savoury and Christian they are; ' For they that wait upon the Lord, their Strength shall be renew-
' ed (but for what, if not to forsake Sin, and serve the Lord God) ' and living in
' the Light, and walking up to God, it will bring you to true Hunger and Thirst
' after Righteousness, that you may receive the Blessing from God, and give over
' tempting of God to give you a Sight of your Sins. And why? Because you see

more

more than you forsake; forsake what you see, before you pray for more Sight; for all such Prayer in such Disobedience is a meer Mockery, and God will not be mocked: and be it known to all, that God has determined not to hear the Prayers of the Wicked; for they are, says the Prophet, an Abomination unto Him. This yet appears to be his Sense by the following Paragraph; 'And to all you that say, 'God give us Grace and we shall refrain from our Sin; there ye have got a tempt- 'ing customary Word; for the free Grace of God has appeared to all Men, and 'this is the Grace which shews you Ungodliness and Worldly Lusts: Now, thou 'that livest in Ungodliness, Lying, and Swearing, and Theft, and Murder, and 'Drunkenness, and Filthy Pleasures, and lusting after the World, thou art he that 'turns the free Grace of God into Wantonness, and casts his Laws behind thy 'Back, and walkest despightfully against the Spirit of Grace. O vain Man! yet 'thou canst say God is merciful, and live in thy Wickedness, passing on thy Time 'without the Fear of God, sporting thy self in thy Wickedness.

What think you now? Does this Man say, that People ought not to pray for a Sight of their Sins, which they see not, in order to Repentance, or can he mean so? let Candour speak. For that, as I said before, must be the Meaning of this Adversary, or he means nothing, because in the other Sense all must grant that Men ought not to tempt, provoke and mock God by praying for a Sight, when they have it and don't use it. What then is the Conclusion of this Matter? why plainly this, that from G. F. saying, that *those who say the Lord give us a Sight of our Sins, that have a Sight of them already and forsake them not, do therein tempt God*: This Enemy of ours, makes no Scruple of Conscience to infer and conclude that G. F. says, that *we ought not to pray to God to give us a Sight of our Sins at all*, without any regard to the Distinction of having the *Sight* already, be it that such have forsaken what God has given them a Sight of, or that they have Sins they have yet no Sight of, yet G. F. says, we must not pray for a Sight of our Sins, if this Adversary may be credited. Well, the Lord God Almighty, who is the Searcher of all Hearts, knows the End of this Person in writing and spreading these Calumnies and Perversions, and with him I leave him and his Work, but so, as that I sincerely desire, that he may have a Sight of his Sin against God and an harmless People, if he acts ignorantly; and that he may sincerely repent, and find Mercy with the Lord, if he acts maliciously, before he goes hence and be no more seen; for its not a slight Thing to mischarge, and that so peremptorily too, an entire People, about Matters of the World that is without End.

I shall conclude this Defence with these three Things, the first is, that most of the Opinions he calls ours are not so evinced, or so much as attempted to be proved, by the Author of the Libel against us. 2dly, Those that are endeavoured to be fastened on us, have not their due Proof, one Person it may be is produced to make good a Charge against a Body of People; would our Adversaries be thus used? would they be concluded by the Word or Act of any one Member of their numerous Communion? Certainly no: Besides, the Proofs that are brought, are some lame, others perverted, and some forged, which looks very dishonourable on the Part of our Accuser, first to mis-charge, then mis-cite, and lastly rack Words, well intended, to extort, if possible, a Confession of Guilt: But the Truth is, Error can only be maintained by Error, and therefore there is no wonder in the Case. This is the Usage we have mostly met with, but, Thanks be to God, we are neither surprized nor unprepared.

Lastly, I do hereby offer a fair and free Conference with the Author or Authors of the Libel, or any other that can soberly pretend to a Conscientious Dissatisfaction about our Faith or Practice, at such Time as shall be mutually agreed upon to be convenient.

And this I offer, not out of Vanity or Ostentation, but in Duty to God my great Lord and Master, and in good Will to all such Persons; and did not these Considerations prevail, to carry me to this Condescension, my manifold Affairs, and the many and large Books I have already writ on occasion of these and the like Imputations, would have disswaded me from any fresh undertaking of this Nature, and sufficiently guarded me against all Reflections upon my Silence.

I am a Friend to all Mankind,

WILLIAM PENN.

ENGLAND's

ENGLAND's *Great Interest, in the* CHOICE *of this* New PARLIAMENT: *Dedicated to* All Her Free-Holders *and* Electors.

SINCE it hath pleased *God* and the *King*, to begin to revive and restore to us our *Ancient Right of Frequent Parliaments*, it will greatly concern us, as to our present Interest, and therein the *Future Happiness of our Posterity*, to act at this Time with all the *Wisdom, Caution and Integrity we can.* For besides, that 'tis our own Business, and that if by a Neglect of this Singular Opportunity, we desert our Selves, and forsake our own Mercies, *We must expect to be Left of God, and Good Men too.* It may be there has never happened, not only in the Memory of the Living, but in the Records of the Dead, *so odd and so strange a Conjuncture as this we are under.* It is made up of so many unusual and important Circumstances (all affecting us to the very Heart) that whether we regard the Long Sitting of the *Late Parliament*, or it's abrupt and most unexpected *Dissolution*, or the *Prorogation* of the last, and it's surprising *Dissolution*, or the strong *Jealousies* of the People, and that *Universal Agitation* that is now upon the *Spirit of the Nation*, and the Reasons and Motives thereof (so far as we can reach them) *there seems never to have been a Time, wherein this Kingdom ought to show it self more Serious and Diligent in the Business of it's own Safety.*

To be plain with you, *All is at Stake*: And therefore I must tell you, That the Work of this Parliament is,

First, To pursue the Discovery and Punishment of the *Plot:* For that has been the *Old Snake in the Grass*, the *Trojan Horse*, with an Army in the Belly of it.

Secondly, To remove, and bring to Justice, those *Evil Counsellors, and Corrupt and Arbitrary Ministers of State*, that have been so Industrious to give the King Wrong Measures, to turn Things out of their Ancient and Legal Channel of Administration, and Alienate his Affections from his People.

Thirdly, To Detect and Punish the *Pensioners* of the former *Parliament*, in the Face of the Kingdom: This Breach of Trust, being Treason against the Fundamental Constitution of our Government.

Fourthly, To secure to us the Execution of our *Ancient Laws by New Ones*, and, among the rest, such as relate to *Frequent Parliaments*, the only True Check upon *Arbitrary Ministers*, and therefore feared, hated, and opposed by them.

Fifthly, That we be secur'd from Popery and Slavery, and that *Protestant-Dissenters* be eased.

Sixthly, That in Case this be done, the King be released from his *Burdensome Debts* to the Nation, and eas'd in the Business of his Revenue. And let me be free with you, if you intend to save *Poor England*, You must take this General Measure, viz. *To guide and fix your Choice upon Men, that you have Reason to believe are Well-Affected, Able and Bold, To Serve the Country in these Respects.*

The Words of the *Writ*, (at least, the *Import* of them) are, *To Chuse Wise Men, Fearing God, and Hating Covetousness*: And what to do? says the same Writ, *To Advise the King of the Weighty Matters of the Kingdom.* Let us not then play the Fools or Knaves, to *Neglect or Betray the Common Interest of our Country by a base Election:* Let neither *Fear, Flattery, nor Gain Bias us.* We must not make our Publick Choice, the Recompence of *Private Favours* from our Neighbours; they must excuse us for that: The Weight of the Matter will very well bear it. This is our Inheritance, *All* depends upon it: Men don't use to lend their Wives, or give their Children to satisfie *Personal Kindnesses*; nor must we make a *Swop of our Birth-Right*, (and that of our Posterity too) *for a Mess of Pottage, a Feast, or a Drinking-Bout*; there can be no Proportion here: And therefore none must take it ill, that we use our Freedom about that, which in it's Constitution, is the *Great Bulwark of all our Ancient English Liberties.* Truly, our not considering what it is to *Chuse a Parliament*, and how much *All* is upon the Hazard in it, may, at last, *Lose us Fatally by our own Choice.* For I must needs tell you, if we miscarry, it will be our *Own Fault*; we have no Body else to blame: For such is the Happiness of our Constitution, *That we cannot well be destroy'd, but by our selves: And what Man in his Wits, would Sacrifice his Throat to his own Hands?*

We, the *Commons of England*, are a great Part of the Fundamental Government of it; and *Three Rights* are so peculiar and inherent to us, that if we will not throw them away for *Fear* or *Favour*, for *Meat and Drink*, or those other little present Profits, *that Ill Men offer to tempt us with*, they cannot be altered or abrogated. And this I was willing to give you a brief Hint of, that you may know, *What Sort of Creatures you are, and what your Power is*, lest through Ignorance of your own Strength and Authority, you turn Slaves to the Humours of those, that properly and truly are but your Servants, and ought to be used so.

The *First of these Three Fundamentals is Property*, that is, *Right and Title to your own Lives, Liberties and Estates*: In this, every Man is a Sort of *Little Soveraign* to himself: No Man has Power over his *Person*, to Imprison or hurt it, or over his Estate to Invade or Usurp it: Only your own Transgression of the Laws, (and those of your own making too) lays you open to Loss; *which is but the Punishment due to your Offences*, and this but in Proportion to the Fault committed. So that the *Power of England* is a *Legal Power*, which truly merits the *Name of Government*. That which is not Legal, *is a Tyranny*, and not properly a *Government*. Now the Law is Umpire between *King, Lords and Commons*, and the *Right and Property is One in Kind through all Degrees and Qualities in the Kingdom*: Mark that.

The *Second Fundamental*, that is, *your Birthright and Inheritance, is Legislation*, or the Power of making Laws; *No Law can be made or abrogated* in England *without you*. Before *Henry* the Third's Time, your *Ancestors*, the *Freemen of England*, met in their own Persons, but their Numbers much increasing, the Vastness of them, and the Confusion that must needs attend them, making such Assemblies not practicable for Business, this Way of *Representatives* was first pitch'd upon as an Expedient, both to Maintain the *Common Right*, and to avoid the Confusion of those mighty Numbers. So that now, as well as then, *No Law can be made, no Money Levied, nor a Penny Legally Demanded* (even to defray the Charges of the Government) *without your own Consent*: Than which, tell me, what can be Freer, or what more Secure to any People?

Your *Third Great Fundamental Right and Priviledge is Executive*, and holds Proportion with the other Two, in Order to compleat both your *Freedom and Security*, and that is, *Your Share in the Judicatory Power, in the Execution and Application of those Laws, that you agree to be made*. Insomuch as *No Man*, according to the Ancient Laws of this Realm, can be adjudg'd in Matter of Life, Liberty, or Estate, but it must be by the Judgment of His Peers, that is, Twelve Men of the Neighbourhood, commonly called a JURY; though this hath been infringed by *Two Acts*, made in the late *Long Parliament*, One against the *Quakers* in Particular, and the Other against *Dissenters* in General, called, *An Act against Seditious Conventicles*, where Persons are adjudged Offenders, and Punishable without a *Jury*; which, 'tis hoped, this ensuing Parliament will think fit in their Wisdom to Repeal, though with less Severity, than one of the same Nature *(as to punishing Men without Juries)* was by *Henry* the Eighth, who, for Executing of it, Hang'd *Empson* and *Dudley*.

Consider with your selves, that there is nothing more your Interest, than for you to understand your *Right in the Government*, and to be constantly Jealous over it; for your *Well-Being* depends upon it's Preservation.

In all Ages there have been *Ill Men*, and we, to be sure, are not without them now, such as being conscious to themselves of ill Things, and dare not stand a *Parliament*, would put a *Final Dissolution* upon the very Constitution it self, to be safe, that so we might never see another.

But this being a Task too hard to compass, their next Expedient is, *To make them for their Turn*, by *Directing and Governing the Elections*; and herein they are very Artificial, and too often Successful: Which indeed is worse for us than if we had none. For thus the Constitution of *Parliaments* may be destroy'd by *Parliaments*, and we, who by Law are *Free*, may hereby come to be made *Slaves* by Law. If then you are *Free, and resolve to be so*, if you have any Regard to GOD's Providence, in giving you a *Claim to so Excellent a Constitution*, if you would not void *Your own Rights*, nor lay a *Foundation of Vassallage to your Unborn Followers, the Poor Posterity of your Loins*, for whom God and Nature, and the *Constitution of the Government*, have made you *Trustees*, then seriously weigh these following PARTICULARS.

I. In

I. In your present Election, *Receive no Man's Gift, or Bribe, to Chuse him*; but be assured, *That he will be False to you, that basely Tempts you to be False to your Country, your self, and your Children.* How can you hope to see GOD with Peace, *That turn Mercenaries in a Matter, on which depends the Well-Being of an Whole Kingdom, for present and future Times?* Since at a Pinch, *One Good Man Gains a Vote, and Saves a Kingdom*; And what does any *County*, or *Burgess-Town* in *England* know, but all may depend upon their making a *Good Choice?* But then to Sell the Providence of GOD, and the Dear-bought Purchase of your Painful Ancestors for a *Little Money*, (that after you have got it, *you know not how little a While you may be suffered to keep it*) is the *Mark of a Wretched Mind*. Truly, such ought not to have the Power of a *Freeman*, that would so abuse his own, and hazard other Men's Freedom by it: He deserves to be cast over Board, that would *Sink the Vessel*, and thereby drown the Company embark't with him.

Honest Gentlemen will think they give enough for the Choice, that pay their *Electors* in a constant, painful, and chargeable Attendance; But *Such as give Money to be Chosen, would get Money by being Chosen*; *they design not to serve you, but themselves of you; and then fare you well.* As you will answer it to Almighty GOD, I intreat you to shew your Abhorrence of this infamous Practice: It renders the very Constitution contemptible, that any should say, *I can be Chosen, if I will spend Money, or give them Drink enough*: And this is said not without Reason, *Elections*, that ought to be Serious Things, and Gravely and Reasonably perform'd, being generally made the Occasions of more Rudeness and Drunkenness, than any of the *Wild May-Games* in Use among us.

Thus by making *Men Law-Breakers*, they are it seems, made fit to *Chuse Law-Makers*, their *Choice being the Purchase of Excess*. But must we always owe our *Parliaments to Rioting and Drunkenness?* And must Men be made Uncapable of all *Choice*, before they chuse their *Legislators?* I would know of any of you all, if in a Difference about a Private Property, *an Horse or a Cow*, or any other Thing, you would be as easie, indifferent, and careless in chusing your *Arbitrators?* Certainly you would not: With what Reason then can you be unconcern'd in the Qualifications of Men, upon *whose Fitness and Integrity* depends all, you, and your Posterity may enjoy? Which leads me to the other PARTICULARS.

II. Chuse no Man that has been a *Reputed Pensioner*; 'tis not only against your *Interest*, but it is disgraceful to you, and the *Parliament* you chuse. The *Representative* of a Nation ought to consist of the Most Wise, Sober, and Valiant of the People; not Men of mean Spirits, or *Sordid Passions*, that would Sell the Interest of the People that chuse them, to advance their own, or be at the Beck of some Great Man, in Hopes of a *Lift to a Good Employ*: Pray beware of these. You need not be streightned, the Country is Wide, and the Gentry Numerous.

III. By no Means chuse a Man that is an *Officer at Court*, or whose Employment is *Durante bene placito*, that is, *At Will and Pleasure*; nor is this any Reflection upon the King, who being One Part of the Government, should leave the other Free, and without the least Awe or Influence, to bar, or hinder it's Proceedings. Besides, an *Officer* is under a Temptation to be *Byast*, and to say True, *An Office in a Parliament-Man*, is but a softer and safer Word for a *Pension*: The Pretence it has above the other, is the Danger of it.

IV. In the next Place, Chuse no *Indigent Person*, for those may be under a Temptation of abusing their Trust, to gain their own Ends: For such do not *Prefer you*, which should be the End of their *Choice*, but *Raise themselves by you*.

V. Have a Care of *Ambitious Men* and *Non-Residents*, such as live about Town, and not with their Estates, who seek Honours and Preferments *Above*, and little, or never, embetter the *Country* with their *Expences or Hospitality*, for they intend *themselves*, and not the Advantage of the *Country*.

VI. Chuse *No Prodigal or Voluptuous Persons*, for besides that they are not Regular enough to be *Law-Makers*, they are commonly *Idle*; and though they may wish well to *your Interest*, yet they will lose it, rather than their Pleasures; they will scarcely give their *Attendance*, they must not be relied on. So that such Persons are only to be preferred before those, *That are Sober to do Mischief*: Whose *Debauchery is of the Mind*: *Men of Unjust, Mercenary, and Sinister Principles*; *who, the Soberer they be to themselves, the Worse they are to you*.

VII. Review *the Members of the Last Parliaments, and their Inclinations and Votes, as near as you can learn them*, and the Conversation of the Gentlemen of your own Country, that were not Members, and take your Measures by both, by that

that which is your *True and Just Interest*, at this Critical Time of the Day, and you need not be divided or distracted in your Choice.

VIII. Rather take a *Stranger*, if recommended by an *Unquestionable Hand*, than a Neighbour *Ill Affected to your Interest*. 'Tis not pleasing a Neighbour, because Rich and Powerful, but *Saving England*, that you are to Eye: Neither Pay, or Return Private Obligations at the Cost of the Nation; let not such Engagements put you upon *Dangerous Elections*, as you love your Country.

IX. Be sure to have your Eye upon *Men of Industry and Improvement*. For those that are Ingenious, and Laborious to Propagate the *Growth of the Country*, will be very tender of weakning or impoverishing it: *You may trust such*.

X. Let not your Choice be flung upon *Men of Fearful Dispositions*, that will let *Good Sense*, *Truth*, and your *Real Interest* in any Point sink, rather than displease some one or other Great Man. If you are but Sensible of your *Own Real Great Power*, you will wisely chuse those, that will, by all Just and Legal Ways, firmly keep, and zealously promote it.

XI. Pray see, that you chuse *Sincere Protestants*; Men that don't play the *Protestant in Design*, and are indeed *Disguis'd Papists*, ready to pull off their Mask, when Time serves: You will know such by their *Laughing at the Plot, Disgracing the Evidence, Admiring the Traytor's Constancy*, that were forc'd to it, or their Religion and Party were gone beyond an *Excuse or an Equivocation*. The contrary, are Men that thank God for this Discovery, and in their Conversation Zealously direct themselves in an Opposition to the *Papal Interest*, which indeed is a Combination against *Good Sense, Reason and Conscience*, and to introduce a blind Obedience without (if not against) Conviction. And that Principle which introduces Implicit Faith and Blind Obedience in Religion, will also introduce Implicit Faith and Blind Obedience in *Government*. So that it is no more the Law in the one than in the other, but *the Will and Power of the Superior, that shall be the Rule and Bond of our Subjection*. This is that *Fatal Mischief Popery brings with it to Civil Society*, and for which such Societies ought to beware of it, and all those that are Friends to it.

XII. *Lastly*, Among these, be sure to find out, and cast your Favour, upon *Men of Large Principles*, such as will not Sacrifice *their Neighbour's Property* to the Frowardness of their own Party in Religion: *Pick out such Men, as will Inviolably Maintain Civil Rights, for all that will Live Soberly and Civilly under the Government*.

Christ did not Revile those that Reviled Him, much less did He Persecute those that did not Revile Him. He rebuk'd His Disciples, that would have destroyed those that did not follow, and conform to them, saying, *Ye know not what Spirit ye are of; I came not to Destroy Men's Lives, but to Save them*. Which made the Apostle to say, *That the Weapons of their Warfare, were not Carnal, but Spiritual*. This was the *Ancient Protestant Principle*, and where *Protestants* Persecute for Religion, *they are False to their own Profession, and Turn* Papists *even in the worst Sense*, against whom their Ancestors did so stoutly exclaim. Read the *Book of Martyrs* of all Countries in *Europe*, and you will find I say True: *Therefore beware also of that Popery*. Consider, that such Partial Men don't love *England*, but a *Sect*; and prefer *Imposed Uniformity, before Virtuous and Neighbourly Unity*. This is that Disturber of Kingdoms and States, and until the *Good Man*, and not the *Opinionative Man*, be the Christian in the Eye of the Government, to be sure, while Force is used to propagate or destroy *Faith*, and *the outward Comforts of the Widow and Fatherless, are made a Forfeit for the Peaceable Exercise of their Consciences to God*, He that Sits in Heaven, and Judgeth Righteously, whose Eye pities the Oppressed and Poor of the Earth, will with-hold His Blessings from us.

O lay to Heart, the *Grievous Spoils and Ruins* that have been made upon your harmless Neighbours, for near these Twenty Years, who have only desired to enjoy their Consciences to God, according to the Best of their Understandings, and to Eat the Bread of Honest Labour, and to have but a *Penny for a Penny's-Worth* among you: *Whose Ox or Ass have they taken? Whom have they wronged? Or when did any of them offer you Violence? Yet Sixty Pounds have been distrained for Twelve, Two Hundred Pounds for Sixty Pounds. The Flocks been taken out of the Fold, the Herd from the Stall; not a Cow left to give Milk to the Orphan, nor a Bed for the Widow to lie on; whole Barns of Corn swept away, and not a Penny return'd*; and thus bitterly prosecuted even by Laws made against *Papists*. And what is all this for? *Unless their Worshipping of God according to their Conscience; for they injure no Man, nor have they offered the least Molestation to the Government*.

Truly, I must take Liberty to tell you, If you will not endeavour to redress these Evils in your Choice, I fear God will suffer you to fall into great Calamity by those you hate. You are afraid of *Popery*, and yet many of you practise it; For why do you fear it, but for it's *Compulsion* and *Persecution*? And will you *compel* or *persecute* your selves, or chuse such as do? If you will, pray let me say, *You hate the Papists, but not Popery.* But God defend you from so doing, and direct you to do, as you would be done by; that chusing such as love *England*, her *People*, and their *Civil Rights*, Foundations may be laid for that Security and Tranquillity, which the Children unborn may have Cause to rise up and bless your *Names* and *Memories* for. Take it in good Part, I mean nothing but *Justice* and *Peace* to all; and so conclude my self,

Your Honest Monitor and Old England's *True Friend,*

PHILANGLUS.

ONE Project for the Good of *England*:

THAT IS,

Our CIVIL UNION is our CIVIL SAFETY.

Humbly Dedicated to the GREAT COUNCIL,

The Parliament of ENGLAND.

RELIGION, as it is the noblest End of Man's Life, so it were the best Bond of *Human Society*, provided Men did not err in the Meaning of that excellent Word. Scripture interprets it to be *Loving God above all, and our Neighbours as our selves*; but Practice teacheth us, that too many meerly resolve it into *Opinion* and *Form*; in which, not the *Text*, but the *Comment* too often prevails; whence it comes to pass, that those Bodies of Men, who have but one *Common Civil Interest*, are miserably distracted in Favour of their *adopted Notions*, upon which they are impatient to bestow an Earthly Crown. And this is the Reason of that Mischief and Uncertainty that attend Government. No sooner one Opinion prevails upon another, (though all hold the *Text* to be sacred) bnt *Human Society is shaken*, and the *Civil Government* must receive and suffer a *Revolution*; insomuch, that when we consider the Fury and Unnaturalness of some People for Religion, (which shews they have none that's True, (Religion making Men most Natural as well as Divine) we have Reason to bewail the *Mis-understanding* as well as *Mis-living* of that venerable Word.

But since 'tis so hard to disabuse Men of their wrong Apprehensions of Religion, and the true Nature and Life of it, and consequently as yet too early in the Day to fix such a Religion upon which Mankind will readily agree as a common *Basis* for Civil Society, we must recur to some lower but true, Principle for the Present, and I think there will be no Difficulty of Succeeding.

'Tis this, *That Civil Interest is the Foundation and End of Civil Government, and where it is not maintained entire, the Government must needs decline.* The Word INTEREST has a good and bad Acceptation; when it is taken in an ill Sense, it signifies *a Pursuit of Advantage without Regard to Truth or Justice*; which I mean not: The good Signification of the Word, and which I mean, *is a Legal Endeavour to keep Rights, or augment honest Profits*, whether it be in a private Person or a Society. By GOVERNMENT, I understand a *Just and Equal Constitution*, where *Might* is not *Right*, but *Laws* rule, and not the *Wills* or *Power* of Men; for that were plain *Tyranny*.

This Government must have a Supreme Authority in it self to Determine, and not be superseded or controuled by any other Power, for then it would not be a Government, but a Subjection, which is a plain Contradiction.

Having thus explained the Terms of the *Principle* I have laid down, I repeat it, *viz. That Civil Interest is the Foundation and End of Civil Government*, and prove it thus: The *Good* of the Whole is the *Rise* and *End* of Government; but the *Good* of the *Whole* must needs be the *Interest* of the *Whole*, and consequently the *Interest* of the *Whole*, is the Reason and End of Government. None can stumble at the Word *Good*, for every Man may easily and safely interpret that to himself, since he must needs believe, 'tis *Good for him to be preserv'd in an undisturb'd Possession of his Civil Rights*, according to the *Free* and *Just Laws of the Land*, and the Construction he makes for himself will serve his Neighbour, and so the whole Society.

But as the *Good* of the People is properly the *Civil Interest* of the People, and *that*, the Reason and End of Government; so is the Maintenance of that *Civil Interest entire*, the Preservation of Government. For where People are sure of their *Own*, and are protected from Violence or Injury, they cheerfully yield their Obedience, and pay their Contribution to the Support of that Government. But on the contrary, where Men are insecure of their Civil Rights, nay, where they are daily violated, and themselves in Danger of Ruin, and that for no Sin committed against the Nature of Civil Interest, (to preserve which, Government was instituted) we ought to suppose their Affections will flag, that they will grow dead-hearted, and that what they pay or do, may go against the Grain: And to say true, such Unkindness is ready to tempt them to believe they should not of Right contribute to the Maintenance of such Governments as yield them no Security or Civil Protection. Which unhappy *Flaw* in the Civil Interest, proves an untoward *Crack* in the Government; Men not being cordially devoted to the Prosperity of that Government that is exercised in their Destruction; and how far that Fraction upon the Common Interest of the People may affect the Government I cannot tell, but to be sure it is insecure to any Government, to have the People (it's Strength) divided, as they will be, where their Interest is so disjointed by the Government; One *Protected*, the Other *Expos'd*. Wherefore, Wise Governments have ever taken Care to preserve their People, as knowing they do thereby *preserve* their own *Interest*, and that how *Numerous* their People, so *large* their Interest. For not only *Solomon* has told us, *That the Honour of a Prince is in the Multitude of his People*, but Experience teaches, that *Plenty* of People is the Riches and Strength of a Wise and Good Government; as that is, where Vice is corrected and Virtue encouraged, and *All* taken in and secured in Civils, that have the same Civil Interest with the Government.

But as the *Good* and *Interest* of the *Whole* is the Rise and End of Government, so must it suppose, that the *Whole* (which takes in all Parties) concurs in seeking the *Good* of the Government; for the Reason of the Government will not suffer it to protect those that are Enemies to it's Constitution and Safety; for so it would admit of something dangerous to the Society, for the Security of which, *Government* was at first *Instituted*.

It will follow, that those that own another Temporal Power superior to the Government they properly belong to, make themselves Subjects not of the Government they are born under, but to that Authority which they avow to be superior to the Government of their own Country, and consequently Men of another Interest, because 'tis their Interest to pursue the Advantages of that Power they acknowledge to be sovereign; But those that own, embrace and obey the Government of their own Country as their temporal supreme Authority, and whose Interest is one and the same with that of their own proper Government, ought to be valued and protected by that Government.

The *Principle* thus far lies *General*, I will now bring it to our own Case.

ENGLAND is a Country *Populous* and *Protestant*, and though under some *Dissents* within it self, yet the *Civil Interest* is the *same*, and in some Sense the *Religious* too. For, *first*, all *English Protestants*, whether *Conformists* or *Nonconformists* agree in this, *that they only owe Allegiance and Subjection unto the Civil Government of* England, and offer any Security in their Power to give of their Truth in this Matter. And in the next Place, they do not only consequentially disclaim the *Pope's Supremacy*, and all Adhesion to *Foreign Authority* under any Pretence, but

there-

therewith deny and oppose the *Romish Religion*, as it stands degenerated from *Scripture*, and the *first* and *purest Ages* of the *Church*; which makes up a great *Negative Union*.

And it cannot be unknown to Men read in the Reasons of the *Reformation*, that a *Protestation* made by the *German Reformers* against the *Imperial Edicts of* Charles the Fifth, *imposing Romish Traditions*, gave Beginning to the Word *Protestant*.

In short, It is the *Interest* of the *Ruling*, or *Church-Protestants* of *England*, that the *Pope* should have no Claim or Power in *England*. It is also the *Interest* of the *Dissenting Protestants*, that the Pope should have no Claim or Power here in *England*, because they are subject to the same Mischiefs and Sufferings in their Civil and Religious Rights that the Church-Protestants are liable to; if then both are like to lose by *Pope* and *Foreign Authority*, their *Interest* must needs be *one* against *Pope* and *Foreign Authority*; and if they have but *one Interest*, it will follow, that the *Church-Protestant* cannot prejudice the *Dissenting-Protestant*, but he must *weaken and destroy his own Interest*.

The *Civil Interest* of English Protestants being thus the same, and their Religious Interest too, so far as concerns a *Negative to the Usurpation and Error of* Rome; I do humbly ask, if it be the Interest of the Government, to expose those to Misery that have *no other Civil Interest than* THAT *of the Government*? Or if it be just or equal that the *Weaker* should be prosecuted by the *more powerful* Protestants, whose Interest is *positively the same in Civils, and in Religion Negatively*? One would think 'twere reasonable that they should not suffer by *Protestants*, who if *Popery* have a Day, are likely to suffer with them, and that upon the same Principles. Experience tells us, That the wisest Architects lay their Foundations broad and strong, and raise their Squares and Structure by the most exact Rules of Art, that the Fabrick may be secure against the Violence of Storms; but if People must be destroy'd by those of the same Interest, truly that *Interest* will stand but Totteringly, and every Breath of Opposition will be ready to shake it.

'Twas the Inconfutable Answer *Christ* made to the *Blasphemers* of that Power by which he wrought Miracles; *A Kingdom divided against it self cannot stand*: what he said then, let me on another Occasion say now, an *Interest divided against it self must fall*.

I know some Men will take *Fire* at this, and by crying The C H U R C H, The C H U R C H, hope to silence all Arguments of this Nature; But they must excuse me, if I pay no Manner of Regard to their Zeal, and hold their Devotion both Ignorant and Dangerous at this Time. It is not the Way to fill the Church, to destroy the People. A Church without People is a Contradiction, especially when the Scripture tells us, that 'tis the People that makes the Church.

And 'tis not without an Appearance of Reason that some good and wise Men are apprehensive, that the greatest *Sticklers* for persecuting *Protestant Dissenters* in Favour of the *Church of* England, are Men addicted and devoted to the *Church of Rome*, or at least animated by such as are; who, despairing of doing any great Feats, if known, hide themselves under these Pretences; but the Meaning of it is to debilitate the *Protestant* Cause in general, by exciting the Church of *England*, to destroy all other *Protestant* Interests in these Kingdoms, that so nothing may remain for *Popery* to conflict with but the few Zealous *Abettors* of that Church.

And that this may not look disingenuous, or like a *Trick* of mine, I will enforce it by a Demonstration. It is plain Fact, that the *Church of Rome* hath ever since the Reformation practised the Restoration of her Religion and Power in these Kingdoms. It is as evident that *Religion* is with her a Word for *Civil Interest*, that is, that she may have the *Rule over Men both Body and Soul*. For 'tis Government *she aims at, to have the Reins of Power in her Hand, to give Law and weild the Scepter*.

To do this she must either have a greater Interest than the *Protestants* that are now in Possession, or else divide their Interest, and so weaken them by themselves, and make them Instruments to her Ends. That her own Force is Inconsiderable is clear: She has nothing within Doors to give her Hope but the *Discord* of *Protestants*. It follows then that she must of Necessity bestir her self, and use her Arts to enflame the Reckoning among *Protestants*, and carry their Dissents about *Religious* Matters to a *Division* in the *Civil Interest*. And it is the more to be fear'd, because whatever she has been to others, she has been ever true to her self.

If this then be the only Domestick Expedient left her, we are sure she will use it; and if so, it must needs be of great Importance with all *Protestants* to let fall their

their private Animosities, and take all possible Care that their *Dissents* about Faith or Worship, (which regard the other World) *divide* not their Affection and Judgment about the Common and Civil Interest of their Country: because if that be kept entire, it *equally frustrates* the Designs of *Rome*, as if you were of *one* Religion. For since, as I said before, *Religion*, with the great Men of that Church, is nothing else but a softer Word for *Civil Empire*, preserve you but your Civil Interest from Fraction, and you are in that Sense of *one Religion* too; and that such an one, as you need not fear the Temptation of *Smithfield*, if you will but be true to it.

This being the Case, I would take Leave to ask the *Zealous Gentlemen* of the *English* Church, *If Conformity to the Fashion of their Worship be dearer to them than* England's *Interest and the Cause of Protestancy?* If their Love to Church-Government be greater than to the Church and her Religion, and to their Country and her Laws? Or, lastly, Whether in Case they are sincere in their Allegations for the *Church*, (which, I confess ingenuously, I am apt to suspect) it is to be supposed that the present *Church-men* (Conformists I mean) are better able of themselves to secure *Protestancy* and our *Civil Interest* against the Attempts of *Rome*, than in *Conjunction with the Civil Interest of all Protestant Dissenters?* If they say, yes, I would have them at the same Time, for the same Reason, to give it under their Hands, that 'tis a standing Rule in *Arithmetick*, that ONE is more than SIX, and that hitherto we have been all mistaken in the Art of Numbers.

Being brought to this Pinch, I conceive they must say, that they had rather deliver up their *Church* to the *Power* and *Designs* of *Popery*, than suffer *Dissenters* to live freely among them, though *Protestants*, of one *Negative Religion*, and of the *same Civil Interest*; or else hasten to break those Bonds that are laid upon Dissenters of truly tender (and by Experience) of peaceable Consciences; and by Law establish the free Exercise of their Worship to Almighty God, that the *Fears, Jealousies, Disaffection* and *Distraction*, that now affect the one common Interest of *Protestants*, may be removed; for it seems impossible to preserve a distinct Interest from both. But to which of these they may incline, I must not determine; and yet I hope, they will not be of the Mind of a late Monk of *Cullen*, that in his publick Exercise exhorted the *Civil Magistrates* to chuse to have their City *Poor* and *Catholick*, that is *Popish*, rather than *Great* and *Opulent* by the Admission of *trading Hereticks*; but if they should, may our *Magistrates* have at least their Prudence; for the *Culleners* gave him the Hearing, but were as true to their Interest, as the *Monk* to his *Superstition*.

Under Favour, the *Civil Government* is greatly concern'd to discountenance such *Biggotry*; for it *Thins* the People, *Lessens* Trade, *Creates* Jealousies, and *Endangers* the Peace and Wealth of the Whole. And, with Submission, of what should the *Civil Magistrate* be more tender, than of suffering the *Civil Interest* of a Great People to be disturb'd and narrow'd for the *Humour* of any one *Party* of them? for since the *Civil Interest* lies as large, as the People of that Interest, *the People must be preserv'd in order to preserve that Common Interest*. Other Notions ever did divide and weaken *Empire*, and in the End they have rarely miss'd to pull the Old House about their Ears, that have govern'd themselves by such disproportionable Measures: By all Means, interest the Affections of the People in the Prosperity of the Government, by making the Government a SECURITY to their particular Rights and Properties.

I ask, if more Custom comes not to the King, and more Trade to the Kingdom, by encouraging the Labour and Traffick of an *Episcopalian, Presbyterion, Independent, Quaker* and *Anabaptist*, than by an *Episcopalian* only? If this be true, why should the rest be render'd uncapable of Trade, yea, of Living? What *Schism* or *Heresy* is there in the Labour and Commerce of the *Anabaptist, Quaker, Independent* and *Presbyterian*, more than in the Labour and Traffick of the *Episcopalian?*

I beseech you give me Leave, Is there ever a *Church-man* in *England*, that in Distress would refuse the Courtesy of one of these *Dissenters?* If one of them should happen to fall into a Pond or Ditch, would he deny to be helped out by a *Dissenter's* Hand? Is it to be supposed, he would in such a Pickle be Stomachful, and chuse to lie there, and be Smother'd or Drown'd, rather than owe Aid to the Good-will of a poor *Phanatick?* Or if his House were on Fire, may we think that he would have it rather burnt to the Ground than acknowledge it's Preservation to a *Non-conformist?* Would not the *Act* be *Orthodox*, whatever were the Man? So in Case of being *Sick, Imprison'd, Beset, Benighted, out of the Way, far from Kindred*

dred or *Acquaintance*, with an hundred other Cafes that may happen daily, can we think, that fuch Men would afk Queftions for Confcience Sake, or charge *Schifm* upon the *Relief* given them? No, no; *Self* will always be true to it's *Intereft*, let Superftition mutter what it will.

But fince the *Induftry*, *Rents* and *Taxes* of the *Diffenters* are as currant as their Neighbours, who lofes by fuch narrownefs more than *England*, than the Government and the Magiftracy? For till it be the *Intereft of the Farmer* to *deftroy* his *Flock, to ftarve the Horfe he rides, and the Cow that gives him Milk*, it cannot be the *Intereft* of *England* to let a great Part of her Sober and Ufeful Inhabitants be deftroy'd about Things that concern another World. And 'tis to be hoped, that the Wifdom and Charity of our *Governors* will better guide them both to their own real Intereft and their People's Prefervation, which are infeparable; that fo they may not *Starve them for Religion, that are as willing, as able, to work for the Good of King and Country*.

I befeech you, let *Nature* fpeak, who is fo much a better Friend to Human Society, than Falfe or Froward *Opinion*, that fhe often rectifies the Miftakes of a Prejudiced Education, that we may fay, how *Kind*, how *Gentle*, how *Helpful* does fhe teach us to be to each other, till that *Make-bate OPINION* (falfly called *Religion*) begins the Jangle, and Foments to Hatred.

All the Productions of Nature are by *Love, and fhall Religion propagate by Force?* If we confider the poor *Hen*, fhe will teach us Humanity. Nature does not only learn her to hatch, but to be tender over her Feeble Chickens, that they may not be a Prey to the *Kite*. All the *Seeds* and *Plants* that grow for the Ufe and Nourifhment of Man, are produced by the kind and warm Influences of the *Sun*. Nothing but *Kindnefs* keeps up *Human Race*: Men and Women don't get Children in *Spite*, but *Affection*. 'Tis wonderful to think by what friendly and gentle Ways Nature produces, and Matures the Creatures of the World; and that Religion fhould teach us to be *Froward* and *Cruel*, is Lamentable: This were to make her the *Enemy* inftead of the *Reftorer* of Nature. But I think, we may without Offence fay, That fince *True Religion* gives Men *Greater Mildnefs* and *Goodnefs* than they had before, that *Religion* which teaches them *lefs*, muft needs be *Falfe*. What fhall we fay then, but that even *Nature* is a truer Guide to Peace, and *better informs us to preferve Civil Intereft*, than Falfe Religion, and confequently, that we ought to be true to the Natural and Juft Principles of Society, and not fuffer one of them to be violated for *Humour* or *Opinion*.

Let us go together as *far as our Way lies*, and preferve our Unity in thofe Principles, which maintain our Civil Society. This is our Common and our Juft Intereft, all *Proteftant Diffenters* agree in this, and it is both Wife and Righteous to admit no Fraction upon this Pact, no Violence upon this Concord. For the Confequence of permitting any Thing to break in upon the Principles of Human Society, that is *Foreign* to the Nature of it, will diftract and weaken that Society.

We know, that in all *Plantations* the Wifdom of *Planters* is well aware of this: and let us but confider, that the *fame* Ways that plant Countries, *muft be kept to for preferving the Plantation*, elfe 'twill quickly be *Depopulated*.

That Country which is falfe to it's firft Principles of Government, and miftakes or divides it's *Common* and *Popular Intereft*, muft unavoidably decay. And let me fay, That had there been this Freedom granted Eighteen Years ago, *Proteftancy* had been too potent for the Enemies of it; nor had there been thofe Divifions for *Popery* to make it's Advantage by; at leaft, not in the *Civil Intereft* of the Nation. And where that has been preferv'd entire, it has been never able to prevail: Witnefs the careful Government of *Holland*, where the Prefervation of their Civil Intereft from Fraction hath fecured them againft the Growth of *Popery*, though it be almoft tolerated by them: So powerful are the Effects of an *United Civil Intereft* in Government. Now becaufe the *Civil Intereft* of this Nation is the *Prefervation of the Free and Legal Government of it from all Subjection to Foreign Claim*, and that the feveral Sorts of *Proteftants* are united, as in the Common *Proteftancy*, that is, a *General Renunciation of* Rome, fo in the Maintenance of this *Civil Government* as a Common Security, (for it ftrikes at both their Rights, Civil and Sacred; their Confcience, Religion and Law, to admit any Foreign Jurifdiction here) it muft follow, that had thefe feveral, as well *Englifh* as *Proteftant* Parties, been timely encouraged to this United Civil Intereft, they had fecured the Government from this Danger by rendring it too formidable for the Attempt.

But

But there is a two fold Mistake that I think fit to remove. *First*, That the Difference betwixt *Protestants* and their *Dissenters* is generally manag'd, as if it were Civil. *Secondly*, The Difference betwixt *Papist* and *Protestant* is carried on, as if it were chiefly Religious.

To the First, I say, 'Tis plausible, but false; it is an Artifice of ill Men to enflame the Government against good People, to make base Ends by other Mens Ruin; whereas they that dissent, are at a *Ne plus ultra* on the Behalf of the English Government, as well as themselves. They neither acknowledge nor submit to any other Authority. They *hold the one common Civil Head*, and not only acquiesce in the Distribution of Justice by Law; but embrace it as the best Part of their *Patrimony*. So that the Difference between *Protestants* and their Dissenters is purely Religious, and mostly about *Church-Government*, and some Forms of Worship, apprehended to be not so pure and Apostolical as could be desired; and here it is, that Tenderness should be exercis'd, if in any Case in the World, or St. *Paul* is Mistaken.

But as to the *Second*, under Correction, the Case is alter'd, for though it be mostly manag'd on the Side of *Religion*, The great Point is meerly *Civil*, and should never be otherwise admitted or understood. For want of this Caution *Protestants* suffer themselves to be drawn into tedious Controversies about Religion, and give occasion to the *Professors* and *Favourers* of that Way to exclaim against them, as *Persecutors* for Religion, who had reprobated such Severity in the *Papists* to their Ancestors (a most plausible, and very often a successful *Plea*) when in reality the Difference is not so much *Religious* as *Civil*. Not but that there is a vast *Contrariety* in Doctrine and Worship too; but this barely should not be the Cause of our so great Distance, and that Provision the Laws make against them; but rather that *Fundamental inconsistency* they carry with them to the Security of the *English Government* and *Constitution* unto which they belong, by acknowledging a Foreign Jurisdiction in these Kingdoms. So that drawing into Question and Danger the Constitution and Government, to which Scripture, and Nature, and *Civil Pact*, oblige their Fidelity and Obedience, there seems a Discharge upon the *Civil Government* from any farther Care of their Protection, that make it a *Piece of Conscience to seek it's Ruin* and which is worse, a *Principle, not to be informed of better Things*, for even here not Reason or Law, but the Pope must be Judge.

This being the Brief and modest State of the Case, I must return to my first great Principle, *That Civil Interest is the Foundation and End of Civil Government:* and that how much Men desert the Interest of a Kingdom, so much they *Wound* and *Subvert* the Government of it. I appeal to all Wise and Considerate Men of the Truth of this by the present Posture of Affairs and their proper Cause.

To come then to our Point, Shall English Men by *English Men*, and Protestants by *Protestants*, be Free or Opprest? This is, *Whether shall we receive as* Englishmen *and* Protestants, *those that have no other Civil Interest than that which is purely* English, *and who sincerely profess and embrace the same Protestation, for which the Ancient Reformers were stiled* Protestants, *or for the Sake of Humour or Base Ends disown them and expose them and their Families to utter Misery?*

I would hope bettter of our great Church-Men's Charity and Prudence; but if they should be so unhappy as to keep to their old Measures, and still play the Gawdy, but empty, Name of *Church* against the *Civil Interest and Religion of the Nation*, they will shew themselves deserted of God, and then how long it will be, before they will be seen and left of all sober Men, let them Judge. For to speak freely, after all this *Light* that is now in the World, no *Ignorance* can excuse such *Zeal*, nor will wise Men believe it to be either, but a Trick to weaken *Protestancy*, that her declared Enemy may with less hazard gain the Chair. And there is not so much reason to fear Profest *Roman Catholicks*, as those *Gentlemen*, who valuing themselves by their respects to the *Church* and Tenderness of it's *Independent* Honour, *have the Opportunity with less Suspicion of letting in* Popery *at the Back door*. These are Men that pay off the *Phanatick* in the Name of the Church, but for the good of the Pope, to whose Account those Endeavours must be placed.

But it will go a great Way to our Deliverance, if we are not Careless to observe the Secret Workings of those that have vow'd our Misery, and of them, such as are in *Masquerade*, and wear the Guise of Friends, are most Dangerous: But some Men are *Pur-blind*, they can see Danger as near as their Nose, but in a Difficulty, that is not a Foot from them, they are Presumptive, Rusty and not to be govern'd. Could some *Church-men* but see the Irreparable Mischiefs that will attend them (if sincere to their present Profession) unless prevented by a *Modest and Christian condescension to* Dissenting Protestant Christians, they would never suffer themselves to be Mis-guided by Stiff and Rigid Principles at this Time of Day.

If *Christianity*, that most Meek and Self-denying Religion, cannot prevail upon them, methinks the Power of Interest, and that *Self-interest* too, should have some Success, for in those Cases they use not to be obstinate.

But I expect it should be told me, *That this is the Way to Ruin the Church, and let in an Anarchy in Religion: Cujus contrarium verum.* I am glad to obviate this, before I leave you, seeing the Contrary is most true; for it leaves the Church and Church-men as they are, with this Distinction, that whereas now Conformity is Coercive, which is *Popish*, it will be then Perswasive, which is Christian. And there may be some hopes, when the *Parsons*, destitute of the Magistrates Sword, shall of necessity enforce their Religion by good Doctrine and Holy Living; nor ought they to murmur, for that which satisfied Christ and his Apostles should satisfy them: *His Kingdom is not of this World*, therefore they should not Fight for him, if they would be his Servants and the *Children* of his *Kingdom*, Christ, and not Civil Force, is the Rock his Church is built upon. Nor indeed has any Thing so Tarnisht the Cause of *Protestancy*, as the Professors of it betaking themselves to Worldly Arms to propagate their Religion. *David* could not wear *Saul's* Armour, and true *Protestants* cannot use *Popish* Weapons, *Imposition* and *Persecution*. In short; 'Tis the very Interest of the Church of *England*, to preserve the civil Interest entire, or else *Popery* will endanger all; but that cannot be unless all of that Civil Interest be preserved; therefore *Protestant Dissenters* should be indulg'd.

But some will say, *There is a Difference even among Dissenters; Some will give a Security to the Civil Government by taking the Oaths, others will not, and be it through Tenderness, how do we know, but Papists will shrow'd themselves under the Wings of such Dissenters, and so in Tolerating Protestant Dissenters to fortify Protestancy, in reality Popery will be hereby shelter'd* incognito.

I answer, *First*, That such Oaths are little or no Security to any Government, and though they may give some Allay to the Jealousy of Governours, they never had the Effect desired. For neither in private Cases, nor yet in Publick Transactions have Men adher'd to their Oaths, but their Interest. He that is a Knave, was never made Honest by an Oath: Nor is it an Oath, but Honesty, that keeps Honest Men such. Read Story and consult our Modern Times, tell me what Government stood the firmer or longer for them? Men may take them for their own Advantage, or to avoid Loss and Punishment: But the Question is, What real Benefit, or Security comes thereby to the Government? It is certain they have often *ensnared a Good Man*, but never *caught one Knave yet:* We ought not to put so great a Value upon Oaths, as to render the Security of our Government so low and hazardous.

God's Providence and the Wisdom of our Ancestors have found out a better Test for us to rest upon, and that is, our *Common Interest, and the Laws of the Land DULY executed:* These are the Security of our Government.

For Example, a Man Swears he will not Plot, yet Plots; pray what Security is this Oath to the Government? But though 'tis evident, that this be no Security; that Law which Hangs him for Plotting, is an *unquestionable one.* So that 'tis not for wise Governours, by Swearing Men to the Government to think to secure it; but all having agreed to the Laws, by which they are to be governed, *let any Man break them at his Peril.* Wherefore good Laws, and a Just Execution of them, and not Oaths, are the *Natural and Real Security of a Government.*

But next, though some may scruple the Oaths, 'tis not for the Sake of the Matter so much as Form, which you know is not the Case of *Roman Catholicks,* (pray distinguish) and those very Persons, whoever they be of *Protestant Dissenters,* I dare say, they will very cheerfully promise their Allegiance on the same Penalties, *and subscribe any Renunciation of Pope and Foreign Authority, which the Art of Man can Pen;* nor should it be hard for you to believe they should subscribe what they have always liv'd.

To that Part of the Objection, which mentions *the danger of* Papists *concealing themselves under the Character of* Protestant Dissenters; under Favour I say, it is most reasonable to believe, that those who will deny their Faith upon Record, as those that subscribe your Declaration do, will swallow the Oaths too; for the Declaration flatly denies the Religion, but the Oaths only the *Pope's Supremacy,* which even some of themselves pretend to reject. Therefore those that can sincerely subscribe the Declaration cannot be *Papists.*

If it be yet objected, that *Papists* may have Dispensations to subscribe the Test, or a Pardon, when they have done it; I answer, they may as well have *Dispensations* to take the Oaths, or Pardons when they have taken them, and these last six Months prove as much. There is no Fence against this Flail. At this rate they may as well be *Protestants*, as *Protestant-Dissenters*; *Ministers* or *Bishops* in *Churches*, as Speakers or Preachers in Meeting-houses: This Objection only shows the Weakness of both Oaths and Declaration for the Purpose intended, and not, that they can hide themselves more under one People than another. For they that can have a Dispensation or Pardon for one Act, can have it for another; especially when the Matter of the Declaration is of a more general weight to them, than that of the Oath; all which confirms my former Judgment of the Insecurity of such Oaths to any Government.

Give me leave then upon this to ask you, if you will bring a certain Ruin upon any Protestant *Dissenters* for the Sake of such an uncertain Security to your selves? for this is the Question; I beseech you to weigh it as becomes wise and good Men: shall they be Reprobated for tenderly refusing, what being perform'd, cannot save or secure you?

Consider, you have no Reason to believe, but those that are allow'd to subscribe the Declaration, or that will be pardon'd when they have done it, may be allow'd to take the Oaths, or will be *pardon'd* or *absolv'd*, when they have taken them: but you are certain on the other Side, that the Imposing of the Oaths will be a great *Snare* to many *Protestant-Dissenters*, that love the Government, and renounce both *Pope* and *Popery*; They will be ruin'd; which to me is of the Nature of an Argument for those People: For their not taking the Oaths, proves plainly, they have no Dispensations nor hopes of Absolution, and therefore no *Papists*; shall they then lie under the Severities intended against *Papists*, who have none of their Dispensations or Absolutions to deliver them from them? This is (with Submission but in plain Terms) to make the Case of the Kingdom worse; for it destroys those who are not Guilty, and whom, I believe, you would not destroy.

Having brought the Matter to this, I shall first offer you a new Test; Next, the Ways of taking it, with most Aggravation against the Party rejecting or breaking it; And lastly, how you may secure your selves from *Papists* disguising themselves among *Protestant-Dissenters*; that so nothing may remain a *Remora* in the Way, that shall not be removed, to leave you a plain and even Path to Peace and Safety.

The New TEST:

I A. B. do *solemnly and in good Conscience, in the Sight of God and Men, acknowledge and declare, that* King *Charles* the second is Lawful King of this Realm, and all the Dominions thereunto belonging. *And that neither the* Pope *nor* See *of* Rome, *nor any else by their Authority have* Right *in any Case to Depose the King, or Dispose of his Kingdom, or upon any Score whatever to* absolve *his* Subjects *of their Obedience, or to give leave to any of them to* Plot *or* Conspire *the Hurt of the* King's Person, *his* State *or* People; *and that all such Pretences and Power are* False, Pernicious *and* Damnable.

And I do farther sincerely profess, and in good Conscience declare, that I do not believe, that the Pope is Christ's Vicar, *or* Peter's Lawful Successor, *or that He or the* See of Rome, *severally or joyntly, are the* Rule of Faith *or* Judge of Controversy, *or that they can* absolve Sins: *Nor do I believe, there is a* Purgatory *after Death*; *or that* Saints *should be* pray'd to, *or* Images *in any Sense be* worship'd. *Nor do I believe, that there is any* Transubstantiation *in the* Lord's Supper, *or Elements of* Bread *and* Wine, *at or after the Consecration thereof by any Person whatsoever. But I do firmly believe, that the Present Communion of the* Roman-Catholick Church *is both* Superstitious *and* Idolatrous. *And all this I do* acknowledge, intend, profess *and* declare *without any* Equivocation, *or* reserv'd, *or other Sense, than the* plain *and* usual Signification *of these Words, according to the* real Intention *of the* Law-makers, *and the* common Acceptation *of all true Protestants.*

This is the *Test* I offer; large in Matter, because comprehensive of Oaths and Test too, yet brief in Words.

The next Thing is the Ways of taking it with most Aggravation upon the Refusers or Violaters of it.

1. That in all Cities and great Towns, Notice be given by the Magistrates thereof to the Inhabitants of every *Ward* or *Parish* to appear on such a Day, be it *New-Years-Day* or *Ash-Wednesday* rather (when the *Pope Curses all Protestants*) at their Publick Hall, or other Places of Commerce, where the *Magistrates* shall first openly *Read, Subscribe, and Seal the Test*. Then that it be read again by the proper Officer of the Place to the People, and that those that take it, *Do Audibly Pronounce* the Words after him that reads it; and when they have so done, that they Subscribe and Seal it. That such Subscriptions be *Register'd*, and Copies of each Parish's Subscription, transmitted to the *Parish*, and affixt upon some publick Place for all that will to see.

2. That in the Countries, the *Parishes of each Hundred or Rape*, may be likewise Summon'd to appear upon the Day aforesaid, *at the Head Market-Town in the said Hundred or Rape*, and, *that the Justices of the Peace within that Part of the Country, shall first Read, Subscribe, and Seal the said Test, in View of the People, and then that the People Say, Subscribe, and Seal the Test, as is before exprest*. Which being done, let the said *Subscriptions* be collected into One Volumn, and kept in the County Court as a *Book of Record*; and that to each Parish, be transmitted a Copy of the said *Parish's Subscription*, to be affixt upon some Publick Place within *the said Parish, for all to see*.

Lastly, Let this be done Annually, that is, upon every *New-Years-Day*, or *Ash-Wednesday*, as a *Perpetual Testimony of the People's Affection to the King and Government, and their Abhorrence of the Practices of* Rome.

The Abuse of this *Discrimination* should be very Penal; For '*tis a Great Lye upon a Man's own Conscience, and a Cheat put upon the Government*: Your Wisdom can best proportion and direct the Punishment; but it can scarcely be too severe, as our Business stands.

But as in Case of such Hypocrisie, a severe Penalty should be inflicted, so pray let Provision be made, that if any Person so subscribing, should be afterwards call'd by the *Name of Jesuit or Papist*, without very good Proof, it should be *deem'd* and *punish'd* in open Sessions, *for a Slander and Breach of Peace*, yet so, as that the Penalty may be remitted at the Request of the *Abused Party*.

I should think that this Business, carefully done, might render needless my Answer to the last Objection, viz. *Which Way shall we be able to prevent* Papists *from passing for* Protestant Dissenters, *that so the Security propounded to the Government, be not baffled by Disguise?* For no *Papist* can subscribe this, but he will Lye in the Face of the Government and Country, and that *Yearly*, and upon *Record* too; which is Ten Times more than a *Transient Oath*, mutter'd with *One Word spoken, and another dropt*. However, that we may carry it as far as Human Prudence can go, ——

I yet offer Two Expedients:

First, That upon Jealousie of any Person's being a *Papist*, or *Popishly Inclined*, who is known to frequent the Assemblies of *Protestant Dissenters*, Four of that Party, of most Note and Integrity, unto which he pretends to adhere, should be Summoned to appear before those *Justices of the Peace*, unto whom the Complaint is made, to testifie their Knowledge of the Person suspected, his *Education, Principles*, and *Manner of Life*; which Way of Inspection, as it goes as far as Man can reach, so can it scarcely fail; for those Persons will not only discover their own *Hypocrisie* if they conceal him, but expose themselves and their Friends to Ruin. So that to say True, *The Government has the Interest and Security of an Entire Party, for the Discovery of every such suspected Person*.

But if this will not do, then

Secondly, Be you pleased to refer the Discrimination of suspected Persons, to the Good Old Way of the Government, that is, *The Enquiry and Judgment of Twelve Men of the Neighbourhood*; to wit, *A Jury*, provided always, that they be such as have taken, or will themselves take the *Test*; else, that they may be *Excepted against by the Party suspected*.

Indeed a Good Expedient may be made out of both, for the *First* may be the *Evidence to the Last*, and I think you will hardly fail of your Ends.

I shall conclude with this Request, First, *to Almighty God, that He would please to make us truly and deeply sensible of His present Mercies to us, and to Reform our Hearts and Lives to improve them thankfully*. And, Secondly, *to you, that we may be Loving, Humble and Diligent, one to, and for another*; for as from such Amendments we may dare promise great and sudden Felicity to England, so if Loosness in Life,

Life, and Bitterness in Religion be not speedily Reprehended and Reform'd, and the Common Civil Interest maintained entire, God will, I justly fear, Repent He has begun to do us Good, Adjourn the Day of our Deliverance to that of our Repentance and Moderation, and Overcast these Happy Dawnings of His Favour, by a thick and dismal Cloud of Confusion and Misery: Which GOD Avert!

These Things that I have written, are no Wild Guesses, or May-Be's, but the Disease and Cure, the Danger and Safety of *England*; in treating of which, that God that made the World knows, I have not gratified any private Spleen or Interest (for I am sorry at the Occasion) but singly and conscientiously intended His Honour, and the Lasting Good of *England*, to which all Personal and Party Considerations ought ever to submit.

Amicus Plato, Amicus Aristoteles, sed magis Amica Veritas. i. e. *Anglia:*

Your own Faithful and Most Affectionate

PHILANGLUS.

A BRIEF EXAMINATION AND STATE of Liberty Spiritual,

BOTH

With Respect to Persons in their Private *Capacity*, and in their *Church Society* and *Communion*.

Written for the Establishment of the Faithful, Information of the Simple-Hearted, and Reproof of the Arrogant and High-minded, by a Lover of True Liberty, as it is in Jesus.

William Penn.

To go amongst the People of the Lord, called *Quakers*.

If the Son shall make you Free, *ye shall be Free indeed.* John 8. 36.
If we walk in the Light as he is in the Light, we have Fellowship *one with another, and the Blood of Jesus Christ his Son cleanseth us from all Sin,* 1 John 1. 7.

To the People of the Lord, called QUAKERS.

Dear Friends and Brethren,

IT hath of long Time rested with some pressure upon my Spirit, for Zion's Sake, and the Peace of Jerusalem, to write something of the Nature of True Spiritual Liberty; LIBERTY, one of the most Glorious Words and Things in the World, but little understood, and frequently abused by many. I beseech Almighty God to preserve you, his People, in the right Knowledge and Use of that Liberty, which Jesus Christ *the Captain of our Salvation, hath purchased for us, and is redeeming us into, who hath led Captivity captive, and is giving Gifts to them that truly believe in his Name. Christ's Liberty is obtain'd through Christ's Cross; they that would be his Free-men, must be his Bonds-men, and wear his blessed Yoke. His Liberty is from Sin, not to Sin; to do his Will, and not our own; no, not to speak an Idle Word. 'Tis not I that live (saith the Apostle) but Christ that liveth in me, who had set him Free from the Power of Sin, and brought Immortality to Light in him; whence he learned thus to triumph, O Death, where is thy Sting! O Grave, where is thy Victory! This is the Personal Freedom that comes by Jesus Christ, to as many as receive him in the Way, and for the End for which God hath given him, to wit, to be a Saviour and a Leader, to save us from our Corruptions, and guide us in the Narrow Way of his Holy Cross, and through the strait Gate of Self-denyal, which leads to Eternal Life. And as many as have enter'd at this Door, are come to have Unity with God, and one with another; To love him above all, and their Neighbours as themselves; yea, to prefer each other before themselves. Such will not violate the great Law of their Lord and Master; Love one another; the New, and yet the Old Commandment: These dwell in Love, and so they dwell in God; for God is Love. 'Twas the beloved Disciple's Testimony, and it comes up to what another Man of God hath said, namely, The Church that dwells in God, if she dwells in God, then in Love; consequently her Members are in Union, of one Mind in Church Matters, since she has but one Head to Rule her.*

Peruse this brief Discourse in this Love, and it may be to Edification. My Aim is to assert the Truth, detect Error, and point in true Brotherly Kindness at those Shoals and Sands some by Mistake, or Overboldness, have and may run upon. O Friends! I greatly desire, that the Spirit of Love, Wisdom, and a sound Understanding, of Meekness, Judgment and Mercy, may ever rest upon you, that blamelesly you may be kept, an Holy Family, at Unity with it self, to the Lord God your Redeemer, that he over all may in you, through you, and by you, be Exalted, Honoured and Praised, who is worthy and blessed for ever.

A Brief EXAMINATION, &c.

Quest. WHAT is *Spiritual Liberty?*

Answ. It is twofold; there is a true and a false Liberty, as a true and false Spirit, the right discerning of which concerns every one's Eternal Well-being.

Qu. *What is true Spiritual Liberty?*

Answ. Deliverance from Sin by the Perfect Law in the Heart, *The Perfect Law of Liberty* James 2. otherwise called, *The Law of the Spirit of Life in Christ Jesus, that makes free from the Law of Sin and Death;* else-where stiled, *The Law of Truth writ in the Heart,* which makes Free indeed, as saith Christ, *If the Son shall make you Free, ye shall be Free indeed.* So that the Liberty of Gods People stands *in the Truth, and their Communion in it,* and in the Perfect Spiritual Law of Christ Jesus, which delivers and preserves them from every Evil Thing that doth or would embondage. In this blessed Liberty, it is not the Will nor Wisdom of Man, neither the vain Affections and Lusts that rule, or give Law to the Soul; for the Minds of all such as are made Free by the Truth, are by the Truth conducted in doing and suffering through their Earthly Pilgrimage.

Qu. *What is False Liberty?*

Answ. A Departing from this blessed Spirit of Truth, and *a Rebelling against this Perfect Law of Liberty in the Heart,* and being at Liberty to do our own Wills; upon which cometh Reproof and Judgment.

Qu. *But are there not some Things wherein we ought to be left to our own Freedom?*

Answ. We are not our own, for we are bought with a Price; and in all Things ought we to glorify God with our Bodies, Souls and Spirits, which are the Lord's.

Qu. *But must we have a Motion or Command from the Spirit of Truth for all Things that we do?*

Answ. That may be according to the Truth, which may not be by the immediate Motion or Command of the Truth; for that is according to the Truth, that is not against the Mind of the Truth, either particularly or generally exprest. The

Truth commands me to *do all to the Praise and Glory of God*; but not that I should wait for a Motion to do every particular Thing. For *Example:* The variety of Actions in Trading, Commerce and Husbandry, the Variety of Flesh, Fish and Fowl for Food, with more of the same Nature, in all which there is a Choice and Liberty, but still according to the Truth, and within the Holy Bounds and Limits of it.

Qu. *Then it seems there are some Things left to our Freedom.*

Answ. Yes; but it must still be according to the Mind of God's Truth: There are Things enjoyned, such as relate to our Duty to God, to our Superiors, to the Houshold of Faith and to all Men and Creatures, these are *Indispensible*. There are also Things that may be done or left undone, which may be called *Indifferent*; as what sort of Meat I will eat to day, whether I will eat Flesh, Fish or Herbs, or what Hours I will eat my Meals at, with many such outward Things of Life and Converse; yet even in such Cases I ought to act according to the Truth, in the Temperance and Wisdom of it.

Qu. *But doth not Freedom extend farther than this; for since God hath given me a Manifestation of his Spirit to profit withal, and that I have the Gift of God in my self, should I not be left to act according as I am free and perswaded in my own Mind, in the Things that relate to God, left looking upon my self as obliged by what is revealed unto another, though it be not revealed unto me, I should be led out of my own Measure, and act upon another's Motion, and so offer a blind Sacrifice to God?*

Answ. This is true in a Sense, that is, if thou art such an one that canst do nothing against the Truth, but for the Truth, then mayst thou safely be left to thy Freedom in the Things of God, and the Reason is plain; because thy Freedom stands in the Perfect Law of Liberty, in the Law of the Spirit of Life in Christ Jesus, and in the Truth, which is Christ Jesus, which makes thee Free indeed, that is, perfectly Free from all that is Bad, and perfectly Free to all that is *Holy, Just, Lovely, Honest, Comely, and of good Report*; but if thou pleadest thy Freedom against such Things, yea, obstructest and slightest such *Good, Wholesome* and *Requisit* Things, thy Freedom is Naught, Dark, Perverse, out of the Truth, and against the perfect Law of Love and Liberty.

Qu. *But must I conform to Things whether I can receive them or no? Ought I not to be left to the Grace and Spirit of God in my own Heart?*

Answ. To the first Part of the Question, Nay; to the last, Yea. But now let us consider what is the Reason thou canst not receive them: Is the Fault in the Things themselves? Are they inconsistent with Truth, or will not the Truth own or assent unto them, or is the Fault in thee? that is to say, Is it thy Weakness, or thy Carelesness; If thy *Weakness*, it is to be born with, and to be informed; if thy *Carelesness*, thou ought'st to be admonished; for it is a dangerous Principle, and pernicious to true Religion, and which is worse, it is the *Root of Ranterism* to assert, *That nothing is a Duty incumbent upon thee, but what thou art perswaded is thy Duty*; for the Seared Conscience pleads his Liberty against all Duty, the *Dark* Conscience is here unconcerned, the *Dead* Conscience is here uncondemned, unless this Distinction be allowed of, that there may be an Ignorance or an Insensibility from *Inability* or *Incapacity*, or a Dark *Education*; and an Ignorance and Insensibility, from *Carelesness, Disobedience, Prejudice*, &c. So that though thou art not to conform to a Thing ignorantly, yet thou art seriously to consider, why thou art ignorant, and what the Cause of such Ignorance may be; certainly it can't be in God, nor in his Gift to thee; it must then needs be in thy self, who hast not yet received a Sense for or against the Matter, about which thou art in doubt. To the second Part of the Question; *Ought I not to be left to the Grace of God in my own Heart?* Ans. That is of all Things most desirable, since they are well left that are there left; for there is no Fear of want of Unity, where all are left with the one Spirit of Truth; they must be of one Mind, they can't be otherwise. So that to plead this against Unity, is to abuse the very Plea, and to commit the greatest Contradiction to that very Doctrine of Scripture, viz. *That all should be guided by the Grace and Spirit of God in themselves*; for the End of that Doctrine is certainty. *They shall all know me, saith the Lord, from the least to the greatest. And I will give them one Heart, and one Way, that they may fear me for ever, for the Good of them, and of their Children after them*, Jer. 32. 39. *And I will give them one Heart, and I will put a new Spirit within you; and I will take the Stony Heart out of their Flesh, and will give them an Heart of Flesh*, Ezekiel 11. 19. *And the Multitude of them that believed were of one Heart, and of one Soul,* Acts 4. 32. Is not this Unity too? *I will restore unto you a pure Language; they shall be of one Heart and of one Mind, and great shall be their Peace.* Therefore I must say to thee, Friend, What if thou wilt not be left with the Grace and Spirit of God in thy self, nor wait for it's Mind, nor be watchful to it's Revelations, nor humble and quiet till thou hast received such necessary Manifestations, but pleadest against the Counsel of the Spirit of the Lord in other faithful Persons, under the Pretence of being left to his Spirit in thy self; by which Means thou opposest the Spirit to the Spirit, and pleadest for Dis-unity, under the Name of *Liberty*; I ask thee, May not I exhort thee to the Practice of that I am moved to press thee to the Practice of? If not, thou art the Imposer, by restraining me from my *Christian Liberty*; and not only so, but away goeth Preaching, and with it the Scriptures, that are both appointed of God for *Exhortation, Reproof* and *Instruction.*

Quest. *But are there not various Measures, diversities of Gifts, and several Offices in the Body?*

Answ. True; but therefore are not the Members of one Mind, one Will, and one Judgment in common and universal Matters, especially relating to the Family and Church of God; And indeed there can't be a falser Reasoning than to conclude *Discord* from *Diversity, Contrariety* from *Variety.* Is there Contrariety of *Bloods, Lifes, Feelings, Seeings, Hearings, Tastings, Smellings,* in one and the same Body, at one and the same Time? No such Matter: Experience is a Demonstration against all such Insinuations. So that though it be granted, that there is Diversity of Gifts, yet there is no Disagreement in Sense; and though Variety of Offices, yet no Contrariety in Judgment concerning those Offices. Well, say the Holy Scriptures of Truth, *there is but one God; the Lord our God is but one Lord; there is but one God and Father of all Things; (that are good) and there is but one Lord, one Faith, and One Baptism;* and his Light, Life and Spirit is at Unity with it self in all; what comes from the Light, Life or Spirit in one, it is the same in Truth and Unity to the rest, as if it did rise in themselves: This is seen in our Assemblies every Day, and will be throughout all Generations in the Church of God, among those that live in the lowly Truth, in which the pure Sense and sound Judgment stands; *God is not the God of Confusion, but Order:* Every one in his Order is satisfied, hath Unity and true Fellowship with whatever comes from the Life of God in another; for this precious Life reacheth throughout the Heritage of God, and is the common Life that giveth the common Feeling and Sense to the Heritage of God. Degree or Measure in the same Life can never contradict or obstruct that which is from the same Life for the common Benefit of the Family of God. *The Lord is the Unmeasurable and Incomprehensible Glorious Being of Life,* yet have we Unity with him in all his Works, who are come to his Divine Measure of Light and Truth in our own Hearts, and live therein; and shall we not have Unity with that which proceeds from a Fellow Creature? In short, the Saints Way is in the Light, wherein there is neither Doubt nor Discord; yea, they are Children of the Light, and called *Light,* and *The Lights of the World*; and can it be supposed that such should disagree and contradict each other in their exterior Order and Practice in the Church before the World; O the blessed seamless Garment of Jesus! where that is known, these Things can never rise. But yet again, *The Just Man's Path* is not only a Light, *but a shining Light,* Brightness it self: Certainly there can be no Stumbling. It is also said, *That Light is sown for the Righteous*; then the Righteous shall never want Light upon any Occasion: And saith that beloved Evangelist and Apostle of our Lord Jesus Christ, *They that walk in the Light, have Fellowship one with another,* 1 John 1. Whence it is easy to conclude, they that go out of the Fellowship, go out of the Light; but if they that walk in the Light, have Fellowship one with another, what shall we say of those that plead being left to the Light to justify their not having Fellowship one with another? and, which is yet worse, who suppose People may conscientiously and Justifiably Dissent within themselves, and that by Reason of the Variety of the Degrees of the Spirit and Grace that are given of God unto them; as if the lesser Degree may dissent from the greater, because of it's not being able to comprehend it. And to make this Principle more Authentick, such tell us, *This is the Ancient Principle of Truth*; and object, *How will you else be able to maintain the* Quakers *Principles?* The Fallacy of all which, lieth (as I said before) in not rightly distinguishing between Diversity and Disagreement, Variety and Contrariety; for this Diversity hath Concord, and this Variety hath Unity? And it is a Blindness

that

that hath too much of late happened to some, by going from the one Life and Spirit of our Lord Jesus Christ, first to fall into Disagreements, and then plead for it, under the Notion of *Diversity of Measures*. I would ask all such Persons, who arrogate to themselves such a peculiar Knowledge of the Ancient Principles of Truth, or the *Quakers* first Principles; 1st, *Whether they believe there be a Christian Body?* 2dl., *Whether this Body hath an Head?* 3dly, *Whether Christ be not this Head?* 4thly, *Whether this Head be without Eyes, Ears, Smell and Taste, and this Body without Sense and Feeling?* If not, *Whether this Head Seeth, Heareth, Smelleth, Tasteth* DIFFERINGLY *and* CONTRARILY *to it self?* And whether this Body hath a contrary Feeling at the same Time about the same Thing? And if it be true, that the Church of Christ, redeemed by his most precious Blood to live to him, see with the same Eye, hear with the same Ear, speak with the same Mouth, live by the same Breath, and are led by the same Spirit, where is this *Disagreement, Contrariety* or *Dissent* about the Things of his *Church*?

Quest. *But the Members of Christ's Church in the Primitive Times had* different Apprehensions; *as the Apostles, and the People gathered by them.*

Answ. Pray let me know who they were, and in what Cases?

Quest. *The Persons were* PAUL *and* PETER, *and those* Christians *that differed about Meats; and the Scripture is plain in the Case.*

Answ. The *Difference* between *Peter* and *Paul* (in the *Acts*) testifies the Weakness of *Peter*, and the Place justifies *Paul*'s Reproof of his too great Compliance with the *Jews* in some of their *Rites*; which makes against *Liberty of various Practices*, in the Church of Christ, and not for indulging them. That Instance about the Difference of *Christians* as to *Meats*, &c. has nothing in it to the End for which it is alledged; for this related not to *Church-Order* or *Communion*, but *Private* and *Personal Freedoms*, what each might do with Respect to themselves; that is, they might make Laws to themselves, in Things that only concern'd private Persons, and it centred there; Here, *What I will eat, When I will eat*, Things to my self, and for my self, as a Man having Power over my own Appetite: The *Liberty* in Things Private, Personal, and Indifferent, makes nothing for *Dissenting about Church Matters in Things of Communion and Society*, and that also are not indifferent, as to *eat Fish*, or *eat Flesh*, or *eat Herbs*, plainly is: But necessary; As to be careful and orderly about the External Business of the Church: These are no *Jewish Rites*, nor *Shadowy Ceremonies*, no *Meats* nor *Drinks* that are Private and Personal, where Weakness is apt to mistake (That were an Unnecessary and an *Unchristian Yoke to bear*) but Things comely, orderly, and of good Report, that tend to Purity, Peace and Diligence in Things acceptable to God, and requisite among his People in their Temporal Christian Capacity. And herein the Apostle *Paul* exercised his Godly *Authority*; and we find that not only those that opposed themselves to it, as thinking, *he took too much upon him, (demanded a Mark of Christ's speaking in him)* are in Scripture branded with Contention. But the true Believers, that had in themselves a *Mark of Christ's speaking in him*, were of *One Mind, and avoided such as were given to Contention*; for it was not the Custom of the Churches of Christ. Thus were Christ's People of *One Heart*, in Things relating to their Communion. Yet a little farther; They that have the Mind of Christ, are of one Mind; for Christ is not divided: They that have Christ for their Head, have One Counsellor and Prophet, One Seer and Bishop, they disagree not in their Judgments in Things relating to him, and the Good of his Church; they have one and the same Guide; *For the one Spirit, into which they have all drank, and by it are baptized into one Body, leads them all.* Now to every Member is *a Measure of the same Spirit given to profit with*; and though every Member is not an *Eye*, nor an *Ear*, nor a *Mouth*, yet every Member hath Unity with the *Eye*, with the *Ear*, with the *Mouth*, in their proper and respective Acts, and they one with the other: The *Eye* sees for the *Mouth*, the *Mouth* speaks for the *Eye*, and the *Ear* hears for *both*; this Variety hath no Discord, but in this Diversity of Gifts and Offices, each Member is sensible of the other, and moves and Acts by one and the same Life, Spirit and Guidance, which is Omnipresent, proportionable to every Member in it's distinct Office. It must be granted, that there are Helps in the Church, as well as that there is a Church at all; and the Holy Ghost has compared those Helps (as is before-mentioned) to several Members and Senses of Man's Body, as an *Eye*, an *Hand*, a *Foot*, *Hearing*, *Smelling*, &c. All then cannot be the Eye, neither can all be the Hand, for then they would confound their Office, and act disagreeably to the Ordination of the great Orderer of his Church. And if I will not comply

1681.

with him that God hath made an *Eye*, because I am not that Eye, or an Hand, because I am not that Member my self, nor a Party to the Action, or Performance of that Member, I resist the Lord, though under Pretence of resisting Man for the Lord's Sake. And truly, this is the Rock that some of our own Time, as well as Persons of former Ages, have split upon, they have not been contented with their own Station in the Body, they have not kept to their own Gift, nor been taken up with the Duty of their own Place in the Church. If he that is a Foot would be an Hand, and the Hand covets to be an Eye, envying others their allotted Station, through Height of Mind, and walking loose from the Holy Cross, there can be no such Thing as Concord and Fellowship in the Church of Christ.

Farthermore, since the Spirit of the Lord is one in all, it ought to be obey'd through another, as well as in one's self; and this I affirm to you, That the same lowly Frame of Mind that receives and answers the Mind of the Spirit of the Lord in a Man's self, will receive and have Unity with the Mind of the same Spirit through another, and the Reason is plain; Because the same Self-evidencing Power and Virtue that ariseth from the Measure of the Spirit of Truth in one's self, and that convinceth a Man in his own Heart, doth also attend the Discovery of the Mind of the same Spirit, when delivered by another; for the Words of the *Second Adam, the quickning Spirit*, through another, are Spirit and Life, as well as in thy own Particular; this is discern'd by the Spiritual Man that judgeth all Things, although the Carnal Man pleadeth, *Being left to his Freedom*; and it may be talks of *being left to the Spirit in himself too*; the better to escape the Sense and Judgment of the Spiritual Man. It is my earnest Desire, that all that have any Knowledge of the Lord, would have a tender Care how they use that Plea against their faithful Brethren, that God put into their Mouths against the persecuting Priests and Hirelings of the World, namely, *I must mind the Spirit of God in my self*; for though it be a great Truth that all are to be left thereunto, yet it is as true, that he whose Soul is left with the Spirit of Truth in himself, differs not from his Brethren that are in the same Spirit; and as true it is, that those who err from the Spirit of Truth, may plead, *being left to the Spirit in themselves*, against the Motion and Command of the Spirit through another, when it pleaseth not his or her High Mind and perverse Will; for a Saying may be true or false, according to the subject Matter it is spoken upon, or applied to; We own the Assertion, we deny the Application: There lies the Snare. 'Tis true, the People of God ought to be left to the Guidings of the Spirit of God in themselves; but for this to be so applied, as to disregard the Preachings or Writings of Christ's enlightned Servants, because by them applied properly to the Preaching or Writing of false Prophets and Seducers, will by no Means follow. I say the Doctrine is true, but not exclusively of all external Counsel or Direction; therefore false in Application, where Men are allowed to have had the Fear of God, and the Mind of his Spirit, and are not prov'd to have acted in their own Wills and Wisdom, or without the Guidance of the Spirit of God, about the Things of his Church and Kingdom.

Quest. But though this be True, which hath been alledged for Heavenly Concord, yet what if I do not presently see that Service in a Thing, that the Rest of my Brethren agree in; In this Case, what is my Duty and theirs?

Answ. It is thy Duty to wait upon God in Silence and Patience, out of all Fleshly Consultations; and as thou abidest in the *Simplicity of the TRUTH*, thou wilt receive an Understanding with the Rest of thy Brethren, about the Thing doubted. And it is their Duty, whilst thou behavest thy self in Meekness and Humility, to bear with thee, and carry themselves tenderly and loving towards thee; but if on the contrary, thou disturbest their Godly Care and Practice, and growest Contentious, and exaltest thy Judgment against them, they have Power from God to Exhort, Admonish, and Reprove thee; and (if thou perseverest therein) in His Name to refuse any farther Fellowship with thee, till thou repentest of thy Evil.

Quest. But lest I should mistake, when thou speakest of True Liberty, that it *stands in being made Free by the Truth, from all Unrighteousness*, dost thou mean, That *no other Persons ought to have the Liberty of Exercising their Dissenting Consciences, but that Force may be Lawful to reduce such as are reputed Erroneously Conscientious?*

Answ. By no Means: It were a great Wickedness against God, who is Lord of the Souls and Spirits of Men, and ought to preside in all Consciences, who, as the Apostle saith, *Is the Only Potentate, and hath Immortality.* For though I give the **True Liberty of Soul and Conscience** to those only that are set Free by the Power of of Chrift, from the Bondage of Sin, and Captivity of Death, yet do I not intend, that any Perfon or Perfons fhould be in the leaft harm'd for the External Exercife of their Diffenting Confciences in Worfhip to God, though Erroneous; for though their Confciences be blind, yet they are not to be forced; fuch Compulfion giveth no Sight, neither do Corporal Punifhments produce Conviction: This we above all People, in our Day, have withftood, in Speaking, Writing and Suffering, and, bleffed be God, continue fo to do with Faithfulnefs. For *Faith is the Gift of God, and forced Sacrifices are not pleafing to the Lord*.

Queft. *But according to thy Argument, it may be my Fault, that I have not the Gift of Faith; and upon this Prefumption, it may be, thou wilt inflict fome Temporal Penalties upon me.*

Anfw. No fuch Matter; for fuch Kind of Faults are not to be punifhed with Temporal or Worldly Penalties; for whether the Errors be through Weaknefs or Wilfulnefs, not relating to Moral Practice, all External Coercion and Corporal Punifhment is excluded. *For the Weapons of our Warfare are not Carnal, but Spiritual.*

Queft. *But what then is the Extent of the Power of the Church of Chrift, in Cafe of Schifm or Herefy?*

Anfw. The Power that Chrift gave to his Church was this, *That Offenders, after the firft and fecond Admonition*, (not Repenting) *fhould be Rejected*: Not Imprifoned, Plundered, Banifhed, or put to Death; this belongs to the Whore and falfe Prophet: O! all thefe Things have come to pafs for Want of Humility, for Want of the ancient Fear, and keeping in the quiet Habitation of the Juft: The Truth in you all fhall anfwer me. And this I affirm, from the Underftanding I have received of God, not only that the Enemy is at work to fcatter the Minds of Friends, by that loofe Plea, *What haft thou to do with me? Leave me to my Freedom and to the Grace of God in my felf*, and the like; but this Propofition and Expreffion, as now underftood and alledged, is a Deviation from, and a Perverfion of the Ancient Principle of Truth; for this is the plain Confequence of this Plea, if any one (efpecially if they are but lately convinced) fhall fay, *I fee no Evil in paying Tythes to Hireling Priefts, in that they are not claimed by Divine Right, but by the Civil Laws of the Land. I fee no Evil in Marrying by the Prieft, for he is but a Witnefs.* Furthermore, *I fee no Evil in Declining a Publick Teftimony in Suffering Times, or hiding in Times of Perfecution, for I have* Chrift's *and* Paul's *Examples. I fee no Evil in Worfhipping and Refpecting the Perfons of Men; for whatever others do, I intend a fincere Notice that I take of thofe I know, and have a good Efteem for.* Laftly, *I fee no Evil in keeping my Shop fhut upon the World's Holidays and Mafsdays,* (as they call them) *though they are rather Lewdly and Superftitioufly than Religioufly kept; for I would not willingly give any Offence to my Neighbours.* And fince your Teftimony is againft Impofition, and for leaving every one to the Meafure of the Grace which God hath given him, not only, *No Man hath Power to reprove or judge me, but I may be as good a Friend as any of you, according to my Meafure.* And now, here is *Meafure fet up againft Meafure*, which is Confufion it felf——*Babel* indeed: This is that very Rock both Profeffors and Prophane would long fince have run us upon, namely, *That a Way is hereby opened to all the World's Libertines, to plead the Light within for their Exceffes*; Which indeed grieves the Spirit of God, and was feverely judged by our Friends in the Beginning, and is ftill reproved by them that keep their Habitation, though fome are become as wandring Stars through their own Pride, and the Prevalency of the Hour of Temptation that hath overtaken them; whereas had they kept in the Channel of Love and Life, in the Orb and Order of the Celeftial Power, they had fhined as fixed Stars in the Firmament of God for ever. And from the deep Senfe that I have of the Working of the Enemy of *Zion's* Peace, to rend and divide the Heritage of God, who under the Pretence of crying down *Man, Forms* and *Prefcriptions*, is crying down the *Heavenly Man Chrift Jefus, his bleffed Order and Government*, which he hath brought forth by his own Revelation and Power through his faithful Witneffes. This I farther teftify, *Firft*, That the Enemy, by thefe fair Pretences, ftrikes at the Godly Care and Travail that dwells upon the Spirits of many faithful Brethren, that all Things might be preferved Sweet, Comely, Virtuous, and of good Report in the Church of God. *Secondly*, That there never was greater Neceffity of this Godly Care than at this Day, fince we were a People, wherein the Crofs, by too many, is not fo clofely kept to as in Days paft, and in which there is not only a great Convincement, but a young Generation defcended of Friends, who though they retain the Form their Education hath led them into, yet many of them adorn not the Gofpel with that fenfible, weighty, and heavenly Converfation as becomes the Children of the Undefiled Religion, and the Seed of that precious Faith which works by the Love that overcomes the World. And the Lord God of Heaven and Earth, that hath fent his Son Chrift Jefus a Light into our Hearts and Confciences, to whofe Search and Judgment all ought to (and muft) bring their Deeds, and render up their Account, beareth Holy Record, that for this End hath he moved upon the Spirits of his Servants, and for this good End only have his Servants given forth, recommended, and put in Practice, thofe Things that are now in Godly Ufe among his People, whether in this or other Nations, relating to *Men's* and *Women's Meetings*, and their divers and weighty Services. And farther; in the Fear of the Almighty God, I fhall add, That Heavenly Peace and Profperity dwell with thofe who are found in an holy and zealous Practice of them; wherefore I warn all, that they take Heed of a flighting and obftinate Mind, and that they have a Care how they give Way to the Outcry of fome, falfly, entituled, *Liberty of Confcience againft Impofition*, &c. for the End thereof is to lead back again, and give Eafe to the Carnal Mind, which, at laft, will bring Death again upon the Soul to God, and the living Society of his Children. And indeed, it is a great Shame that any who have ever known the Truth of God in the inward Parts, and the fweet Society of Brethren, efpecially thofe who were early in the Work of this bleffed Day and heavenly Difpenfation, fhould fo far depart from the Fear and Awe of the Lord, as to ufe fuch Unfavoury, as well as Untrue Expreffions; this is very far from that meek Spirit of Jefus, and the firft Love, which they pretend to have fo fingularly kept in, which beareth all Things, fuffereth all Things, and endureth all Things, and teacheth to keep the Word of Patience in the Hour of Tribulation; Nay, but this is judging of Spiritual Things with a Carnal and Prejudiced Mind, ftumbling at the Matter, for the Sake of the Perfons through whom it comes, not eying nor weighing the Spirit the Thing arifes from, but the Perfon by whom it is fpoken, which darkens the Eye of the Underftanding, and blinds, by Prejudice, the Mind that fhould difcern, tafte and judge; from whence many Mifchiefs have fprung to the Church of Chrift in divers Ages: Nor is it the leaft Evil this Spirit of Strife is guilty of, even at this Day, that it ufeth the Words, *Liberty of Confcience* and *Impofition*, againft the Brethren, in the fame Manner as our fuffering Friends have been always accuftomed to intend them againft the perfecuting Priefts and Powers of the Earth, as if it were the fame Thing to admonifh and reprove Conceited, High-minded, Loofe or Contentious Perfons in the Church, as to compel Conformity in Matters of Faith and Worfhip, by Worldly Violence, upon the Perfons and Eftates of Confcientious Diffenters: O fuch Iniquity God will not leave unreproved!

This, *Dear Friends*, I fend amongft you, as a Token of my true Love, in the Revelation of the free Spirit of our God and Father, who have ever been a Friend to true Liberty, as in the State according to Law, fo in the Church according to Scripture, and as it ftandeth in the Truth of Jefus, that makes them who love it free indeed. Let us all keep low, and remember the Rock from whence we were hewn, and dwell in a tender and reverent Senfe of the daily Mercies and Providences of the Lord, looking well to our own Growth and Profperity in his heavenly Way and Work, then fhall the Defire of our Hearts be more and more after him, and the Remembrance of his Name; and with our Love to God, will our Love increafe one towards another, helping and aiding one another: And I no ways doubt, but God that has brought us out of the Land of *Ægypt*, and out of the Houfe of *Bondage*, and delivered us from the *Mouth* of the *Lyon* and the *Paw* of the *Bear*, will preferve his People from this Uncircumcifed Spirit that is not in Covenant with God, nor under the Yoke of his Holy Royal Law of *True Spiritual Liberty*; for they that keep and walk in the Light of Jefus, are fenced from the Power of this Crooked Serpent, that feeks whom he may betray; nor are any ftung by him but the Unwatchful, the Lifteners and Harkners after his jealous Whifpers, and detracting Infinuations: They are fuch as make their Dwelling in the Earth, where his Region is, and where he creeps and twifts, who is Earthly, Senfual and Devilifh, and fo is all the Wifdom that comes from him.

My Dear Friends: Keep, I pray you, in the Simplicity of the *Truth, and Crofs of JESUS*, and wait for your Daily Bread, and to be Daily Renewed from the Lord; look to your Increafe about Eternal Riches, *and be fure to lay up Treafure in Heaven that fadeth not away*, that your Faith and Hope may have Eternal Foundations

dations, which the cross Occurrences of Time, and Fears of Mortality cannot move: And beware of that Loose and Irreverent Spirit, which has not those in high Esteem among you, that are *Faithful in the Lord's Work, and that labour in His Blessed Word and Doctrine.* I plainly see a Coldness and Shortness on this Hand; and be the Pretence as it will, it is not pleasing to the Lord. They that love Christ, his Servants are dear to them, and they bear a tender Regard to their Trials, Travails, Spendings and Sufferings, who seek not yours, but you, that you may all be *Presented Blameless at the Coming of the Great God, and our Saviour Jesus Christ*; that so the Gospel-Ministry and Testimony may be held up with Holy Fervent Love, and Godly Esteem, to the keeping under every raw and exalted Mind, and whatever may slight and turn against it, lest God that has Richly Visited us with His Fatherly Visitations, and Day springing from on High, should remove His Blessing from amongst us, and place *His Candlestick* among other People. Be Wise therefore, O Friends! For behold He is at the Door that must have an Account of your Stewardship: Be watchful, keep to your First Love and Works, that so you may endure to the End, and be Saved. And having Overcome, you may have Right to Eat of the Tree of Life, which is in the Midst of the Paradise of God.

The God of Peace, who hath brought Our Dear Lord Jesus from the Dead, and us with Him, more abundantly enrich you all with Wisdom and Knowledge, in the Revelation of Himself, through Faith in His Son, by whom in these Last Days He hath spoken to us, who is the Blessed and Only Potentate, King of Kings, and Lord of Lords, who only hath Immortality; to whom be Honour and Power Everlasting. Amen.

Your Friend and Brother, in the Tribulation and Salvation of the Enduring Kingdom of our God,

Worminghurst in *Sussex*, the 20th of the 9th Month, 1681.

William Penn.

A LETTER *from* WILLIAM PENN, *Proprietary and Governour of* Pennsylvania *in* America, *to the* Committee *of the* Free Society of Traders *of that* Province, *Residing in* London. *Containing a General Description of the said* Province, *it's* Soil, Air, Water, Seasons *and* Produce, *both Natural and Artificial, and the* Good Increase *thereof. With an Account of the* Natives, *or* Aborigines.

My Kind Friends:

THE Kindness of yours by the Ship *Thomas* and *Anne*, doth much oblige me; for by it I perceive the Interest you take in my *Health and Reputation*, and the *Prosperous Beginning of this Province*, which you are so kind as to think may much depend upon them. In Return of which, I have sent you a long Letter, and yet containing as brief an Account of *My self, and the Affairs of this Province*, as I have been able to make.

In the first Place, I take Notice of the *News you sent me*, whereby I find some Persons have had so *little Wit*, and *so much Malice, as to Report my Death*, and to mend the Matter, *Dead a Jesuit too*. One might have Reasonably hop'd, that this *Distance, like Death*, would have been a *Protection against Spite and Envy*; and indeed, *Absence being a Kind of Death*, ought alike to secure the *Name of the Absent as the Dead*; because they are equally unable, as such, to defend themselves: But they that intend *Mischief*, do not use to follow *Good Rules* to effect it. However, to the Great Sorrow and Shame of the *Inventors*, I am *still Alive*, and *No Jesuit*, and I thank God, *Very Well*. And without Injustice to the Authors of this, I may venture to infer, *That they that wilfully and falsly Report, would have been glad it had been So.* But I perceive many frivolous and *Idle Stories* have been invented since my Departure from *England*, which, perhaps, at this Time, *are no more Alive than I am Dead*.

But if I have been *Unkindly used by some I left behind me*, I found Love and Respect enough where I came; *An Universal Kind Welcome*, every Sort in their Way. For here are some of several *Nations*, as well as divers *Judgments*: Nor were the *Natives* wanting in this, for their *Kings, Queens, and Great Men*, both visited and presented me; to whom I made suitable Returns, &c.

For the PROVINCE, the General Condition of it take as followeth.

I. The Country it self in it's *Soil, Air, Water, Seasons and Produce*, both Natural and Artificial, is not to be despised. The *Land* containeth divers Sorts of *Earth*, as *Sand* Yellow and Black, Poor and Rich: Also *Gravel* both Loomy and Dusty; and in some Places, *a fast fat Earth*, like to our *Best Vales in England*, especially by *Inland Brooks and Rivers*, GOD in His Wisdom having ordered it so, that the *Advantages of the Country* are divided, the *Back-Lands* being generally *Three to One* Richer, *than those that lye by Navigable Waters*. We have much of another *Soil*, and that is a *Black Hasel-Mould*, upon a *Stony or Rocky Bottom*.

II. The *Air* is Sweet and Clear, the Heavens Serene, like the *South-Parts of France*, rarely *Overcast*; and as the *Woods* come by *Numbers of People to be more clear'd*, that it self will Refine.

III. The *Waters* are generally *Good*, for the *Rivers and Brooks* have mostly *Gravel* and *Stony Bottoms*, and in Number hardly Credible. We have also *Mineral Waters*, that operate in the same Manner with *Barnet* and *North-Hall*, not Two Miles from *Philadelphia*.

IV. For the *Seasons* of the Year, having by God's Goodness now lived over the *Coldest and Hottest*, that the *Oldest Liver in the Province can remember*, I can say something to an *English Understanding*.

First, Of the *Fall*, for then I came in: I found it from the 24th of *October*, to the Beginning of *December*, as we have it usually in *England* in *September*, or rather like an *English mild Spring*. From *December*, to the Beginning of the Month called *March*, we had *sharp frosty Weather*; not foul, thick, black Weather, as our *North-East-Winds* bring with them in *England*; but a Sky as clear as in *Summer*, and the Air dry, cold, piercing and hungry; yet I remember not, that I wore more *Clothes* than in *England*. The Reason of this *Cold* is given, from the *Great Lakes* that are fed by the *Fountains of Canada*. The *Winter* before was as *mild*, scarce any *Ice* at all; while this, for *a few Days, Froze up our great River Delaware*. From that Month, to the Month called *June*, we enjoy'd a *Sweet Spring*, no *Gusts*, but *gentle Showers*, and a fine Sky. Yet this I observe, that the *Winds* here, as there, are more Inconstant *Spring and Fall*, upon that Turn of Nature, than in *Summer or Winter*. From thence, to this present Month, which endeth the *Summer*, (commonly speaking) we have had *extraordinary Heats*, yet mitigated sometimes by *Cool Breezes*. The *Wind* that Ruleth the *Summer-Season*, is the *South-West*; but *Spring, Fall and Winter*, 'tis rare to want the *Wholesome North-Western* seven Days together: And whatever *Mists, Fogs or Vapours*, foul the Heavens by *Easterly or Southerly Winds*, in Two Hours Time are blown away; the One is followed by the *Other*: A Remedy that seems to have a peculiar Providence in it to the Inhabitants; the *Multitude of Trees* yet standing, being liable to retain *Mists and Vapours*, and yet not one Quarter so thick as I expected.

V. The *Natural Produce of the Country*, of *Vegetables*, is *Trees, Fruits, Plants, Flowers*. The *Trees* of most Note, are the *Black Walnut, Cedar, Cyprus, Chesnut, Poplar, Gumwood, Hickery, Sassafrax, Ash, Beech* and *Oak* of divers Sorts, as *Red, White and Black*; *Spanish Chesnut and Swamp*, the most Durable of all: Of *All* which, there is Plenty for the Use of Man.

The *Fruits* that I find in the *Woods*, are the *White and Black Mulberry, Chesnut, Wallnut, Plumbs, Strawberries, Cranberries, Hurtleberries, and Grapes of divers Sorts*. The *Great Red Grape* (now Ripe) called by Ignorance, *The Fox-Grape*, (because of the Relish it hath with unskilful Palates) is in it self an *Extraordinary Grape*, and by Art, doubtless, may be Cultivated to an *Excellent Wine*, if not so Sweet, yet little inferior to the *Frontiniack*, as it is not much unlike in Taste, Ruddiness set aside, which in such Things, as well as Mankind, differs the Case much: There is a *White Kind of Muskadel*, and a *Little Black Grape*, like the *Cluster-Grape of England*, not yet so Ripe as the other; but they tell me, when Ripe, sweeter, and that they only want *Skilful Vinerons* to make good Use of them: I intend to venture on it with my *Frenchman* this Season, who shews some Knowledge in those Things.

Things. Here are also *Peaches*, and very Good, and in Great Quantities, not an *Indian Plantation* without them; but whether Naturally here at first, I know not, however one may have them by *Bushels* for little; they make a *Pleasant Drink*, and I think not inferiour to any *Peach* you have in *England*, except the *True Newington*. 'Tis disputable with me, whether it be Best to fall to *Fining the Fruits of the Country*, especially the *Grape*, by the Care and Skill of Art, or send for *Foreign Stems and Sets*, already Good and approved. It seems most Reasonable to believe, that not only a Thing groweth Best, where it naturally grows; but will hardly be equalled by another *Species* of the same Kind, that doth not naturally grow there. But to solve the Doubt, I intend, if God give me Life, to try *Both*, and hope the Consequence will be as *Good Wine, as any* European *Countries, of the same Latitude*, do yield.

VI. * The *Artificial Produce of the Country*, is *Wheat, Barley, Oats, Rye, Pease, Beans, Squashes, Pumpkins, Water-Melons, Musk-Melons*, and all Herbs and Roots that our Gardens in *England* usually bring forth.

VII. Of Living Creatures; *Fish, Fowl*, and the *Beasts of the Woods*, here are divers Sorts, some for Food and Profit, and some for Profit only: For Food, as well as Profit, the *Elk*, as big as a small *Ox, Deer* bigger than ours, *Beaver, Racoon, Rabbits, Squirrels*, and some eat *Young Bear*, and commend it. *Of Fowl of the Land*, there is the *Turkey*, (Forty and Fifty Pound Weight) which is very great; *Pheasants, Heath-Birds, Pigeons*, and *Partridges* in Abundance. *Of the Water*, the *Swan, Goose*, White and Gray; *Brands, Ducks, Teal*, also the *Snipe* and *Curloe*, and that in Great Numbers; but the *Duck* and *Teal* excel, nor so Good have I ever eat in other Countries. *Of Fish*, there is the *Sturgeon, Herring, Rock, Shad, Catshead, Sheepshead, Eel, Smelt, Pearch, Roach*; and in Inland Rivers, *Trout*, some say, *Salmon*, above the Falls. *Of Shell-Fish*, we have *Oysters, Crabs, Cockles, Conchs*, and *Muscles*; some *Oysters* Six Inches long; and one Sort of *Cockles* as big as the *Stewing-Oysters*, they make a Rich Broth. *The Creatures for Profit only, by Skin or Fur*, and that are Natural to these Parts, are the *Wild Cat, Panther, Otter, Wolf, Fox, Fisher, Minx, Musk-Rat*: And, *Of the Water*, the *Whale for Oil*, of which we have good Store, and *Two Companies of Whalers*, whose Boats are Built, will soon begin their Work, which hath the Appearance of a Considerable Improvement. To say nothing of our Reasonable Hopes of *Good Cod* in the Bay.

VIII. We have no Want of *Horses*, and some are very Good and Shapely enough; Two Ships have been Freighted to *Barbadoes* with *Horses* and *Pipe-Staves*, since my coming in. Here is also Plenty of *Cow-Cattle*, and some *Sheep*; the People Plow mostly with Oxen.

IX. There are divers *Plants*, that not only the *Indians* tell us, but we have had Occasion to prove by *Swellings, Burnings, Cuts*, &c. that they are of great Virtue, suddenly Curing the Patient: And for *Smell*, I have observed several, especially one, the *Wild Myrtle*; the other I know not what to call, but are most Fragrant.

X. The *Woods* are adorned with *Lovely Flowers*, for *Colour, Greatness, Figure* and *Variety*: I have seen the *Gardens of London* best stored with that Sort of Beauty, but think they may be improved by our *Woods*: I have sent a few to a Person of Quality this Year for a Tryal.

Thus much of the *Country*, next of the *Natives, or Aborigines*.

XI. The NATIVES I shall consider in their *Persons, Language, Manners, Religion and Government*, with my Sense of their Original. For their *Persons*, they are generally Tall, Streight, Well-built, and of singular Proportion; they tread strong and clever, and mostly walk with a Lofty Chin: Of Complexion, *Black*, but by Design, as the *Gypsies in England*. They grease themselves with Bears-Fat Clarified, and using no Defence against *Sun or Weather*, their Skins must needs be Swarthy. Their *Eye* is little and black, not unlike *A straight-look'd Jew*. The *thick Lip* and *flat Nose*, so frequent with the *East-Indians* and *Blacks*, are not common to them; for I have seen as *Comely European-like Faces* among them of both, as on your Side the Sea; and truly an *Italian Complexion* hath not much more of the *White*, and the *Noses* of several of them have as much of the *Roman*.

---

* Note, That *Edward Jones*, Son-in-Law to *Thomas Wynn*, Living on the *Schulkil*, had with Ordinary Cultivation, for One Grain of *English* Barley, Seventy Stalks and Ears of Barley: And 'tis common in this Country, from One Bushel Sown, to Reap Forty, often Fifty, and sometimes Sixty: And Three Pecks of Wheat Sows an Acre here.

1683.

XII. Their *Language* is lofty, yet narrow, but like the *Hebrew*; in Signification full, like *Short-Hand* in Writing; *One Word serveth in the Place of Three*, and the Rest are supplied by the *Understanding of the Hearer:* Imperfect in their *Tenses*, wanting in their *Moods, Participles, Adverbs, Conjunctions, Interjections:* I have made it my Business to understand it, that I might not want an Interpreter on any Occasion: And I must say, that I know not a Language spoken in *Europe*, that hath Words of more Sweetness or Greatness, in *Accent* and *Emphasis*, than theirs: For Instance, *Octockon, Rancocas, Oriclon, Shak, Marian, Poquesien*, all which are Names of Places, and have Grandeur in them. Of Words of Sweetness, *Anna*, is *Mother, Issimus*, a *Brother, Netcap*, Friend, *Usque Oret*, Very Good, *Pane*, Bread, *Metse*, Eat, *Matta*, No, *Hatta*, To Have, *Payo, To Come*; Sepassen, Passijon, the Names of Places; *Tamane, Secane, Menanse, Secatcreus*, are the Names of Persons. If one ask them for any Thing they have not, they will answer, *Mattá ne Hattá*, which to Translate is, *Not I have*, instead of *I have not*.

XIII. Of their *Customs and Manners*, there is much to be said, I will begin with *Children:* So soon as they are Born, they wash them in *Water*, and while very Young, and in cold Weather to chuse, they *Plunge* them in the Rivers, to harden and embolden them. Having wrapt them in a Clout, they lay them on a straight thin Board, a little more than the Length and Breadth of the Child, and swadle it fast upon the Board to make it straight; wherefore all *Indians* have flat Heads; and thus they carry them at their Backs. The Children will go very *Young*, at *Nine Months* commonly; they wear only a small Clout round their Waste, till they are big; if *Boys*, they go a Fishing till Ripe for the Woods, which is about *Fifteen*; then they Hunt, and after having given some Proofs of their Manhood, by a Good Return of *Skins*, they may *Marry*, else it is a Shame to think of a *Wife*. The *Girls* stay with their Mothers, and help to Hoe the Ground, Plant Corn, and carry Burthens; and they do well to use them to that *Young*, they must do when they are *Old*; for the *Wives are the True Servants of the Husbands*; otherwise the Men are very Affectionate to them.

XIV. When the *Young Women* are fit for *Marriage*, they wear something upon their Heads for an Advertisement, but so as their Faces are hardly to be seen, but when they please: The *Age* they *Marry* at, if *Women*, is about *Thirteen and Fourteen*, if *Men, Seventeen and Eighteen*; they are rarely Elder.

XV. Their *Houses* are *Mats*, or *Barks of Trees*, set on Poles, in the Fashion of an *English Barn*, but out of the Power of the Winds, for they are hardly higher than a Man; they lye on *Reeds* or *Grass*. In *Travel*, they lodge in the *Woods* about a Great Fire, with the *Mantle of Duffills* they wear by Day, wrapt about them, and a few Boughs stuck round them.

XVI. Their *Diet* is *Maze*, or *Indian Corn*, divers Ways prepared; sometimes *Roasted* in the Ashes, sometimes beaten and boiled with *Water*, which they call *Homine*; they also make *Cakes*, not unpleasant to Eat: They have likewise several Sorts of *Beans and Pease*, that are good Nourishment; *and the Woods and Rivers are their Larder*.

XVII. If an *European* comes to see them, or calls for Lodging at their House, or *Wigwam*, they give him the best Place, and first Cut. If they come to Visit us, they Salute us with an *Itah*, which is as much as to say, *Good be to you*, and set them down, which is mostly on the Ground, close to their Heels, their Legs upright; it may be they speak not a Word, but observe all Passages: If you give them any Thing to Eat or Drink, Well, for they will not ask; and be it Little or Much, if it be with Kindness, they are well-pleased, else they go away Sullen, but say nothing.

XVIII. They are *Great Concealers* of their own *Resentments*, brought to it, I believe, by the *Revenge* that hath been practised among them; in either of these, they are not exceeded by the *Italians*. A *Tragical Instance* fell out since I came into the Country: A *King's Daughter* thinking herself slighted by her Husband, in suffering another *Woman* to lye down between them, rose up, went out, pluck'd a Root out of the Ground, and Eat it, upon which she immediately dyed; and for which, last Week, he made an *Offering* to *Her Kindred, for Atonement, and Liberty of Marriage*; as Two others did to the *Kindred of their Wives, that dyed a Natural Death:* For till *Widowers* have done so, they must not *Marry* again. Some of the *Young Women* are said to take undue Liberty before *Marriage*, for a Portion; but when *Married*, Chaste: When with Child, they know their Husbands no more, till delivered; and during their Month, they touch no *Meat* they Eat, but with a

Stick,

Stick, left they should defile it; nor do their Husbands frequent them, till that Time be expired.

XIX. But in *Liberality* they excell, nothing is too Good for their Friend; give them a *Fine Gun, Coat*, or other Thing, *it may pass Twenty Hands before it sticks*; *Light of Heart, Strong Affections*, but soon spent; *the most Merry Creatures that Live, Feast and Dance perpetually*; they never have much, nor *want* much: *Wealth Circulateth like the Blood, all Parts partake*; and though none *shall want what another hath, yet exact Observers of Property.* Some *Kings* have Sold, others presented me with several *Parcels of Land*; the Pay, or Presents I made them, were *Not Hoarded* by the particular Owners, but the *Neighbouring Kings and their Clans* being present when the Goods were brought out, the Parties chiefly concerned, consulted what, and to whom they should give them. To every *King* then, by the Hands of a Person for that Work appointed, is a Proportion sent, so Sorted and Folded, and with that *Gravity, that is admirable*. Then that *King* sub-divideth it in like Manner among *His Dependents*, they hardly leaving themselves an *Equal Share with One of their Subjects*: And be it on such Occasions as *Festivals*, or at their *Common Meals*, the *Kings distribute, and to themselves last*. They care for *Little*, because they want but *Little*, and the Reason is, *A Little contents them*: In this they are sufficiently revenged on us; if they are Ignorant of our *Pleasures*, they are also Free from our *Pains*. They are not disquieted with *Bills of Lading and Exchange*, nor perplexed with *Chancery-Suits and Exchequer-Reckonings*. We *Sweat and Toil to Live*; their *Pleasure feeds them*; I mean, *their Hunting, Fishing and Fowling*, and this Table is spread every where: *They Eat twice a Day, Morning and Evening*; *their Seats and Table are the Ground.* Since the *Europeans* came into these Parts, they are grown great Lovers of *Strong Liquors, Rum* especially; and for it exchange the *Richest of their Skins and Furs.* If they are heated with *Liquors*, they are restless till they have enough to Sleep; that is their Cry, *Some more, and I will go to Sleep*; but, *when Drunk, one of the most Wretchedest Spectacles in the World*.

XX. In *Sickness*, impatient to be Cured, and for it give any Thing, especially for their *Children*, to whom they are extremely Natural: They drink at those Times, *a Teran, or Decoction of some Roots in Spring-Water*; and if they Eat any Flesh, *it must be of the Female of any Creature.* If they dye, they *Bury them with their Apparel, be they Man or Woman*, and *the Nearest of Kin fling in something Precious with them, as a Token of their Love*: Their *Mourning is Blacking of their Faces, which they continue for a Year*: They *are Choice of the Graves of their Dead*; for lest they should be lost by Time, and fall to common Use, *they pick off the Grass that grows upon them, and heap up the Fallen Earth with great Care and Exactness*.

XXI. These poor People are under a dark Night in Things relating to *Religion*, to be sure, the *Tradition* of it; yet they believe a *GOD and Immortality*, without the Help of *Metaphysicks*; for they say, *There is a Great King that made them, who dwells in a Glorious Country to the Southward of them*, and, *that the Souls of the Good shall go thither, where they shall Live again.* Their *Worship* consists of Two Parts, *Sacrifice and Cantico*: Their *Sacrifice* is their *First Fruits*; the First and Fattest *Buck* they kill, *goeth to the Fire*, where he is all Burnt, with a *Mournful Ditty* of him that performeth the *Ceremony*, but *with such Marvellous Fervency, and Labour of Body*, that he will even *Sweat to a Foam.* The other Part is their *Cantico*, performed by *Round-Dances*, sometimes *Words*, sometimes *Songs*, then *Shouts*, Two being in the Middle that Begin, and by Singing and Drumming on a Board, *direct the Chorus*: Their Postures in the *Dance* are very *Antick*, and differing, but all *keep Measure*. This is done with equal Earnestness and Labour, but great Appearance of *Joy*. In the *Fall*, when the *Corn* cometh in, they begin to *Feast* one another; there have been *Two Great Festivals already*, to which all come that will: I was at one my self; their Entertainment was a *Great Seat by a Spring*, under some *Shady Trees*, and *Twenty Bucks, with hot Cakes of New Corn, both Wheat and Beans*, which they make up in a square Form, in the Leaves of the Stem, and bake them in the Ashes; and after that they fell to *Dance*. But they that go, must carry a *Small-Present in their Money, it may be Six-Pence*, which is made of the *Bone of a Fish*; the *Black* is with them as *Gold*, the *White, Silver*; they call it all *Wampum*.

XXII. Their *Government* is by *Kings*, which they call *Sachema*, and those by *Succession*, but always of the *Mother's Side*: For Instance, the *Children* of him that

1683.

is now King, will not succeed, but his Brother by the *Mother*, or the Children of his *Sister*, whose *Sons* (and after them the *Children* of her *Daughters*) will reign; for no *Woman* inherits; the Reason they render for this way of *Descent*, is, that their Issue may not be *spurious*.

XXIII. Every *King* hath his *Council*, and that consists of all the *Old* and *Wise Men* of his *Nation*, which perhaps is *Two Hundred People*: Nothing of Moment is undertaken, be it *War*, *Peace*, *Selling of Land or Traffick*, without advising with them; and which is more, with the *Young Men* too. 'Tis admirable to consider, how *Powerful the Kings are*, and yet how they move by the *Breath of their People*. I have had occasion to be in Council with them upon Treaties for Land, and to adjust the Terms of Trade; their Order is thus: The *King* sits in the Middle of an half Moon, and hath his *Council*, the *Old and Wise* on each Hand; behind them, or at a little distance, sit the younger *Fry*, in the same Figure. Having consulted and resolved their Business, the King ordered one of them to speak to me; he stood up, came to me, and in the Name of his King saluted me, then took me by the Hand, and told me, *He was ordered by his King to speak to me, and that now it was not he, but the King that spoke, because what he should say, was the King's Mind.* He first pray'd me, *To excuse them that they had not complied with me the last Time*; *he feared, there might be some fault in the Interpreter, being neither* Indian *nor* English; *besides, it was the* Indian *Custom to deliberate, and take up much Time in Council, before they resolve*; *and that if the Young People and Owners of the Land had been as ready as he, I had not met with so much delay*. Having thus introduced his Matter, he fell to the Bounds of the Land they had agreed to dispose of, and the Price, (which now is little and dear, that which would have bought *twenty Miles*, not buying now *two*.) During the Time that this Person spoke, not a Man of them was observed to whisper or smile; the *Old Grave*, the *Young Reverend in their Deportment*; they do speak little, but *fervently*, and with Elegancy: I have never seen more *natural Sagacity*, considering them without the Help, (I was going to say, the *Spoil*) *of Tradition*; and he will deserve the Name of *Wise*, that out-wits them in any Treaty about a Thing they understand. When the Purchase was agreed, great Promises past between us *of Kindness and good Neighbourhood, and that the* Indians, *and* English *must live in Love, as long as the Sun gave Light*. Which done, another made a Speech to the *Indians*, in the Name of all the *Sachamakers* or *Kings*, first to tell them what was done; next, to charge and command them, *To Love the* Christians, *and particularly live in Peace with me, and the People under my Government*: *That many Governours had been in the River, but that no Governour had come himself to live and stay here before*; *and having now such an one that had treated them well, they should never do him or his any wrong*. At every Sentence of which they shouted, and said, *Amen*, in their Way.

XXIV. The *Justice* they have is *Pecuniary*: In Case of any Wrong or evil Fact, be it Murther it self, they Atone by Feasts and Presents of their *Wampum*, which is proportioned to the Quality of the Offence or Person injured, or of the Sex they are of: For in case they kill a Woman, they pay double, and the Reason they render, is, *That she breedeth Children, which Men cannot do*. 'Tis rare that they fall out, if Sober; and if Drunk, they forgive it, saying, *It was the Drink, and not the Man, that abused them*.

XXV. We have agreed, that in all Differences between us, Six of each Side shall end the Matter: Don't abuse them, but let them have Justice, and you win them: The worst is, that they are the worse for the *Christians*, who have propagated their Vices, and yielded them *Tradition* for *ill*, and not for *good Things*. But as low an Ebb as these People are at, and as glorious as their own Condition looks, the *Christians* have not out-liv'd their Sight with all their Pretensions to an *higher Manifestation*: What good then might not a good People graft, where there is so *distinct a Knowledge* left between *Good* and *Evil*? I beseech God to incline the Hearts of all that come into these Parts, to *out-live the Knowledge of the Natives*, by a *fixt Obedience* to their greater Knowledge of the *Will of God*; for it were *miserable* indeed for us to fall under the just Censure of the poor *Indian Conscience*, while we make Profession of Things so far *transcending*.

XXVI. For their Original, I am ready to believe them of the *Jewish* Race, I mean, of the Stock of the *Ten Tribes*, and that for the following Reasons; *first*, They were to go to a *Land not planted or known*, which to be sure *Asia* and *Africa* were, if not *Europe*; and he that intended that extraordinary Judgment upon them, might make the Passage not uneasy to them, as it is not impossible in it self, from the

Easter-most Parts of *Asia*, to the *Wester-most* of *America*. In the next place, I find them of like *Countenance*, and their Children of so *lively Resemblance*, that a Man would think himself in *Dukes-place* or *Berry-street* in *London*, when he seeth them. But this is not all; they agree in *Rites*, they reckon by *Moons*; they offer their *first Fruits*, they have a kind of *Feast of Tabernacles*; they are said to lay their *Altar* upon *Twelve Stones*; their *Mourning a Year*, *Customs of Women*, with many Things that do not now occur.

So much for the Natives, next the *Old Planters* will be considered in this Relation, before I come to our *Colony*, and the Concerns of it.

XXVII. The *first Planters* in these Parts were the *Dutch*, and soon after them the *Sweeds* and *Finns*. The *Dutch* applied themselves to *Traffick*, the *Swedes* and *Finns* to *Husbandry*. There were some Disputes between them some Years, the *Dutch* looking upon them as *Intruders* upon their Purchase and Possession, which was finally ended in the *Surrender* made by *John Rizeing*, the *Swedish* Governour, to *Peter Styresant*, Governour for the *States of Holland*, Anno 1655.

XXVIII. The *Dutch* inhabit mostly those Parts of the *Province*, that lie upon or near to the Bay, and the *Swedes* the Freshes of the River *Delaware*. There is no need of giving any Description of them, who are better known there than here; but they are a *plain, strong, industrious People*, yet have made no great Progress in *Culture* or *Propagation* of *fruit Trees*, as if they desired rather to have enough, than *Plenty* or *Traffick*. But I presume, the *Indians* made them the more careless, by furnishing them with the Means of *Profit*, to wit, *Skins* and *Furs*, for *Rum*, and such *strong Liquors*. They kindly received me, as well as the *English*, who were few, before the People concerned with me came among them: I must needs commend their *Respect* to *Authority*, and *kind Behaviour* to the *English*; they do not degenerate from the *Old Friendship* between *both Kingdoms*. As they are People *proper* and *strong* of *Body*, so they have *fine Children*, and almost every House full; rare to find one of them without *three* or *four Boys*, and as many *Girls*; some *six, seven* and *eight Sons*: And I must do them that Right, I see few *Young Men* more *sober* and *laborious*.

XXIX. The *Dutch* have a *Meeting-place* for Religious Worship at *New-Castle*, and the *Swedes*, *three*, one at *Christina*, one at *Tenecum*, and one at *Wicoco*, within half a Mile of this Town.

XXX. There rests, that I speak of the *Condition* we are in, and what *Settlement* we have made, in which I will be as short as I can; for I fear, and not without Reason, that I have tried your Patience with this long Story. The Country lieth bounded on the East, by the River and Bay of *Delaware*, and *Eastern Sea*; it hath the Advantage of many *Creeks*, or *Rivers* rather, that run into the main River or Bay; some Navigable for great Ships, some for small Craft: Those of most Eminency are *Christina, Brandywine, Skilpot* and *Skulkill*; any one of which have room to lay up the *Royal Navy* of *England*, there being from four to eight *Fathom* Water.

XXXI. The lesser Creeks or Rivers, yet convenient for Sloops and Ketches of good Burthen, are *Lewis, Mespilion, Cedar, Dover, Cranbrook, Feversham,* and *Georges* below, and *Chichester, Chester, Toacawny, Pemmapecka, Portquessin, Neshimenck* and *Pennberry* in the Freshes; many lesser that admit Boats and Shallops. Our People are mostly settled upon the upper Rivers, which are pleasant and sweet, and generally bounded with good Land. The Planted Part of the Province and Territories is cast into six Counties, *Philadelphia, Buckingham, Chester, Newcastle, Kent* and *Sussex*, containing about *Four Thousand Souls*. Two General Assemblies have been held, and with such Concord and Dispatch, that they sate but *Three Weeks*, and at least *seventy Laws* were past without one Dissent in any material Thing. But of this more hereafter, being yet Raw and New in our Geer: However, I cannot forget their singular Respect to me in this Infancy of Things, who by their own private *Expences* so early consider'd *Mine* for the *Publick*, as to present me with an *Impost* upon certain Goods Imported and Exported: Which after my Acknowledgments of their Affection, I did as freely Remit to the *Province* and the *Traders* to it. And for the well Government of the said Counties, *Courts of Justice* are establisht in every County, with proper Officers, as *Justices, Sheriffs, Clerks, Constables*, &c. which Courts are held every *two Months*: But to prevent Law-Suits, there are *three Peace-makers* chosen by every County-Court, in the Nature of common *Arbitrators*, to hear and end Differences betwixt Man and Man; and *Spring* and *Fall* there is an *Orphan's Court* in each County, to inspect and regulate the Affairs of *Orphans* and *Widows*.

1683.

XXXII. Philadelphia, the Expectation of those that are concern'd in this *Province*, is at last *laid out*, to the great Content of those here, that are any ways Interested therein: The Situation is a Neck of Land, and lieth between two Navigable Rivers, *Delaware* and *Skulkill*, whereby it hath two Fronts upon the Water, each a Mile, and *two* from River to River. *Delaware* is a glorious River, but the *Skulkill* being an *Hundred Miles* Boatable above the Falls, and it's Course *North-East* toward the Fountain of *Susquahannah* (that tends to the Heart of the Province, and both Sides our own) it is like to be a great Part of the Settlement of this Age. I say little of the Town it self, because a *Plat-Form* will be shewn you by my Agent, in which those who are Purchasers of me, will find their Names and Interests: But this I will say for the good Providence of God, that of all the many Places I have seen in the World, I remember not one better seated; so that it seems to me to have been appointed for a Town, whether we regard the Rivers, or the Conveniency of the Coves, Docks, Springs, the loftiness and soundness of the Land and the Air, held by the People of these Parts to be very good. It is advanced within less than a Year to about Four-score Houses and Cottages, such as they are, where Merchants and Handicrafts are following their Vocations as fast as they can, while the Country-men are close at their Farms: Some of them got a little Winter-Corn in the Ground last Season, and the generality have had an handsom Summer-Crop, and are preparing for their Winter-Corn. They reaped their Barley this Year in the Month called *May*; the Wheat in the Month following; so that their is Time in these Parts for another Crop of divers Things before the Winter-Season. We are daily in hopes of Shipping to add to our Number; for blessed be God, here is both Room and Accomodation for them; the Stories of our Necessity being either the Fear of our Friends, or the Scare-crows of our Enemies; for the greatest hardship we have suffered, hath been Salt-Meat, which by Fowl in Winter, and Fish in Summer, together with some Poultry, Lamb, Mutton, Veal, and Plenty of Venison the best Part of the Year, hath been made very passable. I bless God, I am fully satisfied with the Country and Entertainment I can get in it; for I find that particular Content which hath always attended me, where God in his Providence hath made it my Place and Service to reside. You cannot imagine, my Station can be at present free of more than ordinary Business, and as such, I may say, *It is a troublesom Work*; but the Method Things are putting in will facilitate the Charge, and give an easier Motion to the Administration of Affairs, However, as it is some Mens Duty to plow, some to sow, some to water, and some to reap; so it is the Wisdom as well as Duty of a Man, to yield to the Mind of Providence, and chearfully, as well as carefully, imbrace and follow the Guidance of it.

XXXIII. For your particular Concern, I might entirely refer you to the Letters of the President of the Society; but this I will venture to say, Your Provincial Settlements both within and without the Town, for Situation and Soil, are without Exception: Your City-Lot is an whole Street, and one side of a Street, from River to River, containing near one hundred Acres, not easily valued, which is besides your Four Hundred Acres in the City-Liberties, part of your Twenty Thousand Acres in the Country. Your Tannery hath such Plenty of Bark; the Saw-Mill for Timber, and the Place of the Glass-house are so conveniently posted for Water-carriage, the City-Lot for a Dock, and the Whalery for a sound and fruitful Bank, and the Town *Lewis* by it to help your People, that by God's Blessing the Affairs of the Society will naturally grow in their Reputation and Profit. I am sure I have not turned my back upon any Offer that tended to it's Prosperity; and though I am ill at Projects, I have sometimes put in for a Share with her Officers, to countenance and advance her Interest. You are already informed what is fit for you farther to do, whatsoever tends to the Promotion of Wine, and to the Manufacture of Linnen in these Parts, I cannot but wish you to promote it; and the *French* People are most likely in both Respects to answer that Design: To that end, I would advise you to send for some Thousands of Plants out of *France*, with some able Vinerons, and People of the other Vocation: But because I believe you have been entertained with this and some other profitable Subjects by your President, I shall add no more, but to assure you, that I am heartily inclined to advance your just Interest, and that you will always find me,

Your Kind Cordial Friend,

W. PENN.

Philadelphia, the 16th of the 6th
Month, called *August*, 1683.

An EPISTLE to the People of GOD called Quakers, in the Province of *Pennsylvania*, and the Territories *thereunto belonging*.

Dear Friends,

THE Salutation of my Love is unto you that make a Profession of the blessed Way of Truth in the inward Parts, desiring both Night and Day, with tender and fervent Supplication to the God of the Light that hath sprung upon us in a living and powerful Visitation, that we may all answer the Love and Mercy of the Lord to us, so plenteously manifested.

Friends, It is upon me, and long hath been, from the God of Truth and Righteousness, to communicate to you a short Word of Counsel and Advice: God hath brought us hither, and we are yet among the Living; He hath a Work for us to do here, tho' the Spiteful and Envious will not believe us: O! that we may be faithful to the Measure of Grace received, that the Evil-minded may be disappointed. Friends, keep in the Sense of that which first visited you, and kept you, and he that was with you to bless you in your native Country, will be with you and bless you and yours, and make you a Blessing to them that you are come among, that know him not, in this Wilderness also; for the Earth is the Lord's, and his Presence fills it, and his Power upholds it, and it is a precious Thing to enjoy and use it in the Sense and Feeling of the same; truly this Honour have all the Saints, to whom he will give it for a quiet Habitation: Have a Care of Cumber, and the Love and Care of the World: 'Tis the Temptation that lieth nearest to those that are redeemed from Loosness, or not addicted to it. The Moon, the Figure of the changeable World, is under the Foot of the true Woman, whose Seed —— we ought to approve our selves, God hath ordained it for a Footstool, and we must not make a Throne of it, nor doth it become them who seek Heavenly Places in Christ Jesus. O! shew forth a blessed Example, for the Lord's Sake; and truly, blessed is that Man and Woman, who in the invisible Power rule their Affections about the visible Things, and that use the World as true Travellers and Pilgrims, whose Home is not here below; such do not extort, grind or oppress their Neighbours in their Dealings, but are content with moderate Gain, looking to the Blessing that follows, knowing right-well, that they that over-value and over-care, fall into divers Snares and Sorrows, that hurt and pierce the Soul's Peace. And in like Manner, Dear Friends, have a Care of Loosness, for it becometh us to be watchful, and gird up the Loyns of our Minds, and be sober, and hope to the End. Are we from under outward Sufferings and Tryals that once we knew, and that carry an Humiliation with them upon the Spirits of People? Let us be more Circumspect, that we forget not the Lord nor his tender Mercies towards us; for he is God, and he can find us out, and Trouble, and Vex, and plague the Disobedient and Careless here, as well as in other Lands. Be zealous, therefore, for the Lord, for he is a Jealous God, and especially over those that have betrothed themselves unto him by the Profession of his Holy Truth, yea, he will be avenged of the Hypocrite and Rebellious, but the Obedient he will bless, which my Soul prayeth you may be, that so I may never have an Occasion to exercise any other Power than that of Love and Brotherly Kindness. And, Dear Friends, remember who it was that said to his Children and Followers, Ye are Brethren, have a Care of Unnaturalness in the Profession of the Truth: To be without Natural Affection to one another in the Truth, is a Mark of Apostacy, wherefore love one another, and help, and assist, and comfort one another; this was the new and living Commandment of our blessed Lord and Master, which if you keep, then can you not fall out, backbite, slander, go to Law, or hate one another in the Sight of the World, and that for the Things that perish; verily, if any do these Things, the Wrath of God will overtake them.

O, Friends! Let us call to Mind the Day that hath dawned upon us, and what Manner of Persons we ought to be: Besides, you know that the Eyes of the Inhabitants of the Lands, and those of neighbouring Countries, yea, the People of remote Regions are upon us, and our Doings, how we Live, how we Rule, and how we Obey, and Joy would it be to some to see us halt, hear evil Tidings of our Proceedings, as it would be an heavy, and an unspeakable Grief to those that wish well to our Zion. Friends, God requireth great Watchfulness from you, especially Elders and Teachers in the Church of Christ, that they watch over their own and other's Families, that whatever appears in any, contrary to the Testimony and Mind of Truth, may be brought to Judgment, and disowned, that the Camp of the Lord may be kept clean of the Uncircumcised that resist the Spirit.

My Friends, Remember that the Lord hath brought you upon the Stage, he hath now tryed you with Liberty, yea, and with Power too; he hath now put precious Opportunities into your Hands, have a Care of a perverse Spirit, and do not provoke the Lord by doing those Things, by which the Inhabitants of the Land grieved his Spirit, that were before you, but sanctify God, the living God in your Hearts, that his Blessings may fall and rest as the Dew of Heaven upon you, and your Off-spring; then shall it be seen to the Nations, that there is no Inchantment against Jacob, nor Divination against Israel, but your Tents shall be goodly, and your Dwellings glorious: Which is the daily humble Supplication of my Soul to my God and your God, and to my Father, and your Father; that am, with unfeigned Love, in that lasting Relation,

Your tender faithful Friend and Brother,

WILLIAM PENN.

A DEFENCE OF THE Duke of Buckingham's BOOK OF RELIGION and WORSHIP, FROM THE EXCEPTIONS of a Nameless AUTHOR.

Deceit is in the Heart of them that imagine Evil; But to the Counsellors of Peace is Joy. Prov. 12. 20.

To the READER.

IT pleas'd me so well to see any Thing in Defence of Religion, under the Name of the Duke of Buckingham, that I was quite of another Mind to the Gentleman that troubled himself with an Answer; And thought if he had said less to his Point, it shew'd, to his greatest Honour, by his own Sense, the Force of his Convictions, and how Little serv'd him to the Belief of a Deity.

That

That *so much* Wit *and* Quality, *that have made so Great Figure in the World, should give this Onset to* Atheism, *that had so long stol'n the* Credit *of both, to give her self Value with* Men *of Highest Rank, might have escap'd a* Reprimand *from the* Deist *or* Christian; *And This was enough to send the* Atheist *a Challenge.*

That his Discourse was not labour'd with Repetitious Thought, nor writ in the Language of the Schools, *is owing to his better* Genius, *and more* Sensible *Education. It needs no* Apology, *and is it's own* Encomium; *To be sure it is like Himself, and That is an* Original.

In this Evening of his Time, I heartily wish him the Felicity of living the Irreproveable Life of his Admir'd Instinct, especially, since He believes it is not out of his Power, and that such extraordinary Rewards follow it. And This will add a Demonstration to his Probabilities for Religion.

I would then press the Nobility *and* Gentry *of* England, *to the Imitation of so Illustrious an Example, and that those Virtues might be recovered, that once made the Discipline of their Ancestors so much the Honour of their* King, *the Safety of their* Country, *and the just Fear and Admiration of all Foreigners.*

For the Person that undertook to answer the Duke's Discourse, in my Opinion, he has, with the Duke, abus'd his Time; *As all do, that* Mistake, *write loosly, beg the* Question, *pervert the* Sense; *And, to Crown their Work,* Contradict *themselves.*

I bear the Noble Peer *this Friendship, and his Essay may Challenge it for a Duty: But I am particularly* Interested *in a* Reply, *by a Reflection the Author gives me in his Answer.* 'Twere Justice *to vindicate a less Man, when assaulted in my Name. But there is another Reason*; His *Arguments were too low an Entertainment for the* Duke, *and therefore fit for a Man of my inferior Talents. While I Reprehend his Performance, I must not be too confident in my own, especially when I have not his* Six Hours Haste *to offer in Excuse of my self*; For, *to my* Dulness *I must own, it has cost me the best Part of* Six Days, *and therefore Time for me to rest. Such as it is,* Friendly Reader, *Take, Read, and Judge. I am no* Sceptick, *for I believe what I write. If I err, I am to be informed: The Way must be* Reason, *as it is with all reasonable Men, and as I profess my self such, so from them I expect the Mercy that all Men need and desire, when it comes to their Turn to be where I am, I mean upon the Stage of* Censure. Farewel,

Just Reader, Thine of long standing,

WILLIAM PENN.

A DEFENCE, &c.

HIS first Paragraph contains his Wonder, *that the Duke should espouse the Cause of* Whiggism *in her old Age, when a cast Mistress, and scorn'd of all.* And all that know the D's Humour would wonder too, if the Thing were true; and if not, the Wonder turns upon the Man's Confidence. It has been the D's Fault to love fresher Game; But This is as much below his Wit, as the other against his Inclination. But if the Story cou'd be true, I am not of the Answerer's Mind; it was not his Pity but Policy, to entertain her; perhaps, to know the Secrets of his *Great Peer*, p. 1, for so *Cecil* serv'd *Essex*.

But what is *Whiggism*? He tells us very briefly, 'tis *Toleration* and *Persecution*; and that those *Qualities* made her *so amiable to the Associating Lords*. How this affects the D. that was not of their Knot, is unaccountable, and how those *Lds.* lov'd the persecuting Part of her, is as hard to understand; unless he means it of the *Exclusion*, and Prosecution of the *Popish Plot*; and if that be it, He does Ill to rail at the *Rom. Cath.* and their Religion too, p. 15, 21. *as able to ruin the whole Earth, and lay the Foundation of Eternal Mischiefs to Mankind.* But if *Toleration* be a Part of *Whiggism*, it may touch the D. in general: Only in this the Man is mistaken, she came not last to his Hands, he was the first of all the Peers of *England* that had her: And to his Credit be it spoken, in This he is constant, and more the same *George* D. of *B.* than this Author fancies him, p. 8.

But

But must the D's Book of the weightiest Matters, be disgrac'd with *Whiggism?* "Is it *Whiggish* to assert a God, his Providence of the World, the Immortality of the Soul, the Duty of Divine Adoration, Freedom of our Wills from *Absolute Predestination*, the Unreasonableness of one Man's forcing another Man's Conscience in *Religion*, the Necessity of good Works, and Rewards and Punishments?"

Must so noble a Design be blasted with so odious a Name? And his Essay branded without Distinction? Don't we all know that the *State-Dissenter* was esteem'd the *Whig*, and the great Offence of *Whiggism* the *Interruption of the Line?* Which must be the Persecuting Part of *Whiggism* in this Man's Account, or none. And can the Duke be guilty of this, for writing a Discourse against Persecution of any Body for Religion? If *Indulgence* be *Whiggism*, let him remember who it was that lately wanted it. And if Persecution be *Whiggism* too, who it is that he makes *Whigs* now: Himself a great One to be sure, p. 28, 29, & 30. In the mean Time, the Duke of *Buckingham*, it seems, *Has enter'd the Lists, is become a Champion, and a Glorious Protector of* Whiggism, alias, *Toleration of Dissenting Christians*; A greater Honour, I think, he could hardly have done him: And in this I am of his Mind.

His second *Paragraph* begins with a Question every Body may answer, to wit, *If it was not boldly done of him to answer a Peer of his High Rank*, p. 2. And for my Part, I think so, and something worse; considering the Abuse, Slightness, Untruth and Contradiction with which he has perform'd it. For the Duke cannot think it ill done of him to answer, but to answer ill, no Body can think well done, and that's his Case.

But to fight this Noble Peer with Success, he unhappily tells us, *He has armed himself with an Invulnerable Conscience*; And I am afraid so, because he shews himself insensible of his Injustice and Indecency to a Peer, that himself says, *Is of the Highest Rank*, in the Beginning of his Answer, and flies to the *Penal Laws* to support himself at the latter End of it.

But he would have us believe, *His Nature and Education are most soft and obliging*; and, if we may trust him, it is pity. his Religion should have spoiled him, or that a Man should be the worse for that which should have made him better.

He says, *Though in approaching so near his Grace, he cannot be* procul a Jove, *he will be sure to be* procul a Fulmine. This, I presume, was to pass for Wit, but he is somewhat unlucky in it, and either jeers the Duke, or Himself; For this is to tell us the Duke's Arguments have no Force; or if they have, he has Wit enough to keep out of their Way. I might add a Third, perhaps he presumes upon his Goodness, which I perceive is more than *Jupiter* himself must hope for in some Countries, from the *Malitia* of the Pulpit. But, now I think of it, who knows but he meant *Scandalum Magnatum*, and that by concealing his Name, he should escape the *Thunderbolt*; lest that might happen to turn the *Wine of his Hopes into the Vinegar of Despair*; his own sweet Metaphor.

He ends this *Paragraph*, p. 4, with bespeaking his own Impunity, *And professing a profound Veneration for his Grace's High Character.* He more than once labours to perswade the Duke to let him abuse him *Gratis*: To be sure, I shan't oppose the Charity, but advise him to prove himself the better Christian by exercising it. But methinks it shews the Man's Fear, and that, his Guilt; as his Hope, the Duke's Goodness, and his Diffidence in the *Invulnerableness* of his own Conscience. He would have something else to trust too.

It is an odd Thing to bespeak a Man's Sanctuary where he intends the Wrong, and presume upon the Goodness of the Person to abuse him safely. He profoundly respects the Duke, and yet makes him to keep, and be the Champion of *Whiggism*; and then too, *When every Body else, for Fear or Shame, has forsaken her.* I will end with this, That he that intitles a Man to the Sin, does his best to intitle him to the Punishment too: Which, in my Judgment, shews a *wild* and an *ill* Conscience in the Answerer.

His third *Paragraph*, p. 4, declares, *His own Belief is unavoidable*, and his Book, *That they that don't avoid their own Belief, to believe as he believes. are justly punishable*; and why? *Because he believes as the Church believes, that is, by Law Establish'd.* Here's the Reason of his *Creed*: And they that offer to have any better, are dangerous to the Government, p. 19, 22 and 23. I think I don't wrong him with Consequences; the Places import him as much. There is little else in this *Paragraph*, but that he has a Mind to shew his Affectation and Ignorance of
French,

French, by *Opinionatre*, instead of *Opiniatreté*, and cautions us to take Heed of him, for he does not know, *But he may be Mad before he has done, at least, Freakish and Unruly.* He would place it to the Infection of the Duke's Wit; but his Book proves he has escap'd the Contagion.

But in his fourth *Paragraph*, p. 5 & 6, It wants, *Temperamentum ad pondus.* If so, it shews the Man *Light-headed*; for that which has *pondus*, will not be taken with that which has none. All true Wit has Weight; for Wit is an apt and strong Expression of a Thing, such as strikes our Understanding *Truly* and *Lively*. I should take his Praise and Pleasure to be the best Argument in his Book, against the Duke, but that they are Dissembled. 'Tis a kind of a civil Way of taking Leave, to be Rude, (all Abuse is such:) For to tell us, *of his Grace's Facetious Pen, taking Air, Pleasant and Witty Reasonings*; In fine, *The* Tarantula *of his Paper* (which is a Fly, that makes Folks Dance and Caper,) as if the Duke had written a *Farce*, is Idle. It may be the *Encomium of a Play*, but it makes an ill Character for a Religious Essay.

But this sticks in his Stomach too, *That Noble Cavaliers should trouble their Heads with Religion*; And who knows but he has Reason, for 'twere the Way to make *Chaplains* necessarily Learned, or unnecessary and useless to their Masters. *He wonders as much at Noble Cavaliers writing of Religion, as to see a Blew-Apron Knight correcting* Euclid's Elements. And yet I think they use to wear Green ones that Teach them. I thought he would allow it to Nobles after Mechanicks; But this shews he is of the Tribe of ———, and has no Charity for those that han't enough to believe *in Verbum Ministri*. I expect in the next Book, the Gentleman will plead his *Charter* against such *Interlopers*. But the Duke hates *Ingrossers*, and is too Old to mend: 'Tis Labour lost; *He is and will be the same D. of* Buckingham *he was Forty Years ago*, in the Point Controverted. Arguments drawn from Selfish Topicks, and private Interests, move slowly with Men of large and Generous Minds.

This is worse by half *than Praying in Latin*, (which he is against, p. 15.) if I were to be Judge; For Men may learn that, but our Nobility must not meddle in Religion, though it seems They helpt to make *His*. However, he graciously allows this Noble Peer's *Notions to be fine, and many of them Natural and True*, yet in a Breath, *His Conceptions are greatly to the Disadvantage of Religion*, and why? *Because the Duke* (poor Man) *had not attended their Consequences*; of which, in Things Natural and True, I had always thought there had been no Danger.

He concludes with a Story of an *Airy Gentleman* of his Acquaintance (for he's of that Element) that being pressed with the Consequences of his odd Opinions, would cry, *A Pox upon Consequences, I hate these Consequences*: Who the Story belongs to, the Reader must Judge: But if the Answerer be not more Inconsequent than the Duke; I will share in the Blame, that for all him, had no Share in the Fault.

In his next Period, p. 6, 7, he looks like a Man of the *White Apron*; and I think it is as Lawful for a *Blue* one to talk of *Euclid's Elements*, as for that to meddle with Religion; and, of the Two, that spots least: He says, *He will not read us an Anatomical Lecture upon his Grace's Paper, nor curiously dissect every Nerve and Muscle.* This is, belike, to excuse both his Skill and Courseness; he was for shorter Work, though it favoured somewhat more of the *Butcher*. From hence he shifts Callings and turns *Cook*, Cousin *German* to t'other; and without so much as washing his Hands, falls to talk of *Hashing of Books, and serving them up with* Lemon *and* Anchovies. Men use the Metaphors of their Calling and Genius; but he shews ill Judgment: For an *Ass* in a *Chair* were as true Painting, as this Wit: That Sauce, in my Opinion, had done much better with a *Calve's Head*. And now he promises us his Matter in a Lump; and, to say true, it looks as if it came out of the Mine of Confusion, Gross enough.

He first salutes the Duke's *Method to confute the Atheist*, p. 8, and will not have the *Mutation of Things in the World a Reason against the Eternity of it, no more than the Duke's to render him not the same* George *Duke of* Buckingham *he was Forty Year ago*. But in this the Gentleman is short, and beside the Cushion: For though I fancy the Duke would say him many kind Things to be the same he was Forty Years ago, yet because he is the same *Personality* under Mutations, to conclude, The World may be Eternal, notwithstanding it's proper Revolutions, is a mighty *Non-sequitur*. For it is to say, because a Thing is, it must always be. I should rather think, that because the Duke is a Being of Time, and once was not,

and

and again will not be, that *George* Duke of *Buckingham* he is, and therefore he suffers those Mutations, we see him under: It is a good Argument, that the Revolutions we daily see the World subject to, makes it, at least probable, that it is a Being of Time, that once was not, and again will not be the World it is.

In Truth, there is no Parity in his Allusion, and therefore his Argument is fallacious; For how does this follow, that the World may be *Eternal* for all it's Changes, *because* George D. of B. *is the same he was Forty Years since, notwithstanding his Bodily Mutations.* I must return him his Complement, which he, with less Reason makes the Duke, that his Argument is not too Logical. A Thing's being the same, does not necessarily conclude it never had a Beginning, and to be sure it's *Mutation*, be it of Accidents only, does not make it's *Eternity* more credible.

If the Duke were Eternal, for all his Change, it were a good Argument that the World might be so too, under all it's Revolutions; But that the Duke's being that *Individual* he was Forty Years ago, for all his Mutations of Body, should prove the World Eternal, notwithstanding the Changes of it, is as unaccountable as his Poison of Wit, p. 4.

I take it to be a better Way of Arguing, that if the Duke was born, grows old, and must die, though he be the same Duke of *Buckingham* he was Forty Years ago, the World, that feeds him, had a Beginning, grows old, and will have an End, though it be the same in Nature that it was Five Thousand Years ago. And of this, the daily Mutations, we see it subject to, are almost a Demonstration.

For all the Productions of the World *Die*, and all that are nourish'd of it End: It can neither give nor feed a Life *beyond Time*. And that it self should yet be *Immortal*, that neither makes nor keeps any thing else so, is against that Parity of Reason, which we observe about all other Things, and cannot refuse here. All Productions are of the Nature of the Thing Producing: And tho' it may reasonably be ordained by some Superior Being, to entertain and nourish many Generations of Mankind, 'tis *Incomprehensible* that it self should be Eternal, whose Nature and Powers we see so short and finite by the *Revolutions* and *Mortality* of the Creatures they exert and feed. Plain it is, upon our Notion of *Creation*, this *Dilemma* vanishes, but upon *Production*, it will remain.

If it should be objected: *But the World out-lives Man, and the Creatures it produces; and if the Absurdity of the World's being Eternal, is taken from it's Productions not being like it Self, why does not the World, such as it is, produce or feed a Life as durable as it's own?* I answer, That it differs mightily, Men beget Lives longer and shorter than their own; *are they not therefore Mortal? Or did they not beget them?* It is one Thing to talk of *Mortal Production* out of an *Eternal Being*, and another Thing to say that a *Temporal Being* should produce or nourish another less durable than it self: Besides, the Objection granting the Question of the Non-Eternity of the World, it is easy to conceive that the *Supreme Agent*, whose Wisdom and Power made it, contriv'd that excellent Fabrick, House or Stage of Life, more durable than that of any Man or Age, to entertain so many Generations of Mankind, as he designed to inhabit and subsist in it. It lies much in the Frame and Constitution of the Subject. Men make Clocks that go a Week, a Month, a Year, Seven Years, and are out-liv'd by the Works of their own Hands. They may allow it to those of the *Supreme Agent* to survive them, without the Necessity of their being Eternal.

But, *Argumentum ad hominem*, the World cannot to him be mutable and Eternal; For 'tis plain, that he allows *Impassibility* (which he knows, with *Philosophers*, takes with it Immutability) *to be an Attribute of God, and that God only is Eternal*, p. 9. Now I cannot apprehend why he refuses *Mutability* to be an Argument against *Eternity*, or how the World may be *Eternal* tho' *Mutable*, when he argues that God is only *Impassible* or *Immutable*, because he is *Eternal*. Let him have a Care of his Airy Gentleman's Fate, p. 6. And yet if he be as much a *School-man* as he would have us believe, he must know that the Argument the Duke has advanc'd against the *Atheists*, is celebrated by the *Schools*. And tho' the *Apostle's* Testimony is a Begging of the Question to an *Atheist*, 'tis doubtless *Orthodox* with this Person; and he tells us, *That the Things that are seen are Temporal, and the Fashion of this World passeth away.*

But for all this, he fancies the Duke has done little, and that he could do Wonders against the *Atheist*, and therefore, *If he were to discourse him, he would press him with this* Dilemma. *If the World be Eternal, it must be the Cause of it's own Existence,*

Exiftence, p. 9. And this he urges without Mercy upon his *Atheift*, and runs thro' all the Confequences of it, with as much Confidence and Vanity as if he had firft obliged the World with the Knowledge of the Secret; and when all is done, it is better faid by the Duke, and with lefs Exception, in the main Queftion, p. 5. And to fay true, it grows upon every Common in the Country. But with his Leave, I take the Duke's Argument of the *Non-Eternity* of the World, from the *Mutability* of it, to be much the Better of the Two; for the Abfurdity of any Thing being the *Caufe or Effect of it's own Exiftence*, which this Man fays, *Is the Confequence of the World's being Eternal*, being perhaps as applicable to one *Eternal* as another, is no Credit to his better Way of difcourfing an *Atheift*, and proving a *Deity*. For a Thing to be the Caufe or Effect of it felf, is, in my poor Opinion, not too *Logical*, and, I am afraid, too near a-Kin to Nonfenfe. His making the Duke to hint at nothing elfe in Proof of a God, is dif-ingenious; for there is one Thing mentioned, he takes no Notice of, p. 5. *For*, fays the Duke, *Whether the World has been Created out of Nothing is not Material to our Purpofe, becaufe, if a* Supreme Intelligent Agent *has fram'd the World to be what it is, and has made us to be what we are, we ought as much to ftand in Awe of it, as if it had made both us and the World out of nothing.* Which plainly imports thus much; That though the Matter of the World were *Eternal*, the Wifdom and Power, of that Being which difpos'd and fram'd it into the Glorious and Regular Thing we all fee it is, fhew Him to be what we call G O D, and *Us* that we fhould fear Him; which is beft done by a Sober and Regular Life, becaufe that is moft fuitable to the Law of our Nature, and confequently the Mind of the *Great Workman*.

The Built and Skill then of the World thus proving the *Supreme Intelligence*, and at the fame Time, that He is the Object of the Adoration of His Creatures, we are naturally brought to the Duke's next Point, too weakly oppofed by his Unwary Anfwerer, *viz. That Man only, of all other Creatures, having had Conceptions, at leaft, Sufpicions of a* Deity, *and another World*; *It is probable there is* fomething nearer a Kin to the Nature of God in Man, *than in any other Animal whatfoever*; *and that* Inftinct *of a Deity, ought to be our Guide and Director, in chufing the Beft Way for our Religious Worfhip of God.* This is the Paffage the Gentleman falls upon, and tells us, p. 11, 12. *That that is as fair a Plea for the* Alcoran, *as the* New Teftament; *for* Pythagoras's *Golden Verfes, as St.* Paul's *Epiftles.* But which Way, he leaves us to guefs? And yet we fhall not guefs, to fay, That *Pythagoras's Golden Verfes are much nearer a Kin to St.* Paul's *Epiftles, than the* Alcoran *to the* New Teftament. For the one has Great and Excellent Truths, without Impofture; the other not. And tho' lefs Nobly defcended, and of inferior Authority, fo far as they are Right, it is no Difhonour to St. *Paul's Epiftles*, that *Pythagoras* writ Truth, nor to the *Inftinct* that his Verfes are fo far approved by it. And if this Gentleman would but allow the Duke the Law, which is yet lefs than the Courtefy, of the Learned, he knows how Fruitful the *Doctrine of Idea* is, to the Defence of the Duke's Inftinct.

To fay True, it were enough to refer the *Reader* to the Duke's Paper, and that of his *Anfwerer*. The Natural, Plain, and eafie Deduction of the one, from p. 11. to p. 19. the Difingenious Citation, Perverfion, and Confufion of the other throughout, will make him think I might have fpar'd my felf the Pains of following him here. But that it may appear beyond all Doubt, let us hear him at large, how well he grounds his Exceptions.

He fays, *If he be not miftaken*, (and that is modeftly condition'd) *His* Grace *muft mean Humane Reafon, not Regulated by any Publick and Politick Reafon of a Community, but as every Private Man's Reafon dictates to him*. And that then the Duke has this Confequence, *That it is one of the greateft Crimes a Man can be Guilty of, to force us to act or fin againft that Inftinct of Religion, and fomething a-Kin to the Sin againft the* Holy Ghoft. For this Doctrine, thus hafh'd and dreft by himfelf, he is angry with me; *And but that His* Grace *is no Minor, he fhould fufpect the* Pennfylvanian *had Tutor'd him with his Quakeriftical Doctrine:* Mighty Civil to the Duke, and very Juft to me. I am forry the Duke pays fo dear for my Acquaintance, and that I cannot have the Honour to have fuch a *Pupil* without a Jeer upon his. The Man might have Nam'd me plainer if he had pleas'd, without Fear of the fatal and murdering Blow of *Scandalum Magnatum*, though not without Great Scandal. But in this we are both Debtors to his fingular Goodnefs, that whofoever got the Child, he refolves to be Goffip; and for that Purpofe has provided Four Names, which are thefe Four enfuing Confequences.

Firft,

First, *That Reason is the* Sole *Guide of every Man's Religion,* tho' neither *Sole* nor *Reason* are any Terms of the Duke's Doctrine, and that the Duke excuses the Omission of Scripture, because of the Qualifications of the Men his Discourse was design'd to, that he might come close to their own Natures, and not beg the Question. But in it's due Place he recommends *Christianity* as the *Best Religion,* p. 18. and then to be sure he cannot neglect the Scripture.

His Second Consequence he pins upon the Duke, is as Just as the former, *That Divine Revelation is not Necessary to Salvation*; when it is evidently the Meaning of that Part of the Duke's Discourse, *That People use the* Light *that God has given them, to chuse a Religion by, and recommends the* Christian *for the Best.* Is it the Way to deny *Reveal'd Religion,* to press Men to chuse, with the Best Skill they have, *The Christian,* that is the *Truest Revelation?* Certainly this Man must be beside himself a little, or he could hardly be so much beside the Matter.

His Third Consequence is yet more disingenious than the other, for he makes the Duke to say, *That it is a most horrid Sin to lead Men out of the Errors Natural Religion, and Bare Reason, of Necessity lead Men to, whose very* Essay *was on Purpose to lead Natural Men, by the Way of First Principles, to embrace* Revealed Religion. But is it, in Good Earnest, a Sin to *lead* Men out of Errors, because it is a Sin to *force* Men against their Consciences? What Man can have an Happier Talent than this: The very Gift of Consequences. To shift *Force* for *Lead,* and *Conscience* for *Error,* shews his to be Invulnerable with a Witness. In one he forges, and begs the Question in the other: No Man could be more dextrous at it: Doubtless he will in a While, be as much out of Humour with Consequences, as his Airy Gallant; for no Man can make more. *I must not persuade a Man, because I must not* Force *him; I must not* Lead *a Man, because I must not drag and whip him: In fine, I must not Inform a Man, because I must not knock him on the Head.* If this be the Gentleman's *Leading,* I shall have a Care how I take him for a Guide. There's a Sort of Men, whose *Mercies are Cruelties,* and who, with all their Pretence to *Reveal'd Religion,* have not the Justice and Mercy of a poor *Benighted Pagan.*

His Last Consequence he draws from the Duke's Position and Deductions, is this, *That Men who believe a God, and follow the Dictates of Reason in his Worship, may be Saved in any, in all Religions, provided they know no Better.*

But how this Consequence can with any Justice be charged upon the Duke, that so expresly, p. 18. prefers the *Christian Religion,* is past my Skill. For unless he will make the Duke to say, *That no Religion is necessary to Salvation,* when he writes to perswade People to have one, he must confess, *He makes the Christian to be It,* because he recommends *That* to our Belief and Practice, confirming it to himself from the Agreeableness of it's *Doctrine,* with what he is prompted by his *Pious Instinct* to believe to be True. Can any Man then say with any Conscience, that is Just, *That the Duke of* Buckingham *thinks Men may be Saved in any, and in all Religions,* when he first makes Religion necessary, and then tells us, *That in his Conscience he believes the Christian to be the True:* As if his Business had been to Prophane, and not advance the *True Religion.*

And I cannot but wonder how this wild Conception came in his Head, so disagreeable to the *Duke's Reason, Instinct and Deductions.* If he had said, *In any, or all Perswasions,* he had Magnify'd the *Duke's Charity,* with this Distinction, *That Men of Sincerity in all Perswasions may be Saved,* and not that Men may shift Perswasions for Interest, and yet go to Heaven: Tho' if it were so, perhaps this *Doctor* might have the Better of the Two by the Notion; *Hypocrisy* being none of the Duke's Vice. But to say, *That Men may be Saved in any, or in all Religions,* is somewhat harsh upon the *Duke*; and yet if in all these Religions a Man must be, a Man that *believes in God, and lives Virtuously,* and in Modes of Worship *knows no Better* than the Tradition of his Fathers, it is hard to Damn him; And this Gentleman must produce better Authorities for his Severity, before it will have Credit with Men of Sense and Bowels,

Now, though this does not touch the Duke's Discourse any more than his Charity, to admit that a *Dissenter,* a *Roman-Catholick,* a *Jew,* a *Turk,* an *Indian may be Saved,* let us see how well it may be supported. St. *Peter* seems to have been of this Man's Mind in the Preamble to the Story of *Cornelius, Acts* 10. till better taught; and who knows what this Man may be in Time. *Of a Truth I perceive* (says Peter) *that God is no Respecter of Persons, but in every Nation he that feareth him, and worketh Righteousness, is accepted of him.* This was a *Gentile,* a

Roman,

Roman, neither *Jew* nor *Christian*, yet Devout, a Just Man, One Fearing God, And as such, with all, of all Nations of the same Quality, declared by this Great Apostle, *accepted with God*. So that it seems here is (greatly doubtless against this Gentleman's Mind) some Acceptance for the poor Men of the Duke's Instinct. Well, but let us suppose them to be *Comparatively Benighted*, Was not *Cornelius* so too? Yet we see the Consequence, *He was accepted as he was*; and why, but because Sincere, and he knew no Better? He stood the fairer for *Revealed Religion*, this prepared him for it: Nay, we are told by the same unquestionable Authority, *That in the Times of Ignorance, God winked*. And such to be sure, he thinks theirs are, and I think are like to be, for all him: For if I mistake not, the Man is for the Promise at Home, let what will betide them abroad. If he can but Sit under his *Own Vine*, let the *Boar*, the *Devil*, take the *Turk*, and all the rest for him. Extraordinary Calls are ceas'd; for there's Extraordinary Pains and Perils in the Case, and though he may love Souls well, yet who shall Pay him.

Well, but if *God Winks at the Ignorant*, must this Man be so prying? And if the Judge of the whole Earth will not be strict, Ought he to turn *Inquisitor*? Or must it be an Heinous Error because he says it, *That Men that Fear God, and follow the Dictates of Reason in Religion, and know no better, may be Saved?* Most Unjust then is his Clamour, *against the Divinity of* Calvinists, *as Inhuman*, p. 4. *That Damns Men*, p. 13. for not being better than they know how to be.

But the Man builds the Things he destroys; For he more than any Body believes One of these Three Things; *First*, That there is no such Thing as Salvation, or that Men may be Sav'd in the Religion as it is by *Law Establish'd*, in all Countries: Or that Men are bound to submit to the *Religion Established by Law*, let the Issue in t'other World be what it will: For that Power he gives absolutely into the Magistrate's Hands; And who can be judge upon him? The *English* of all which, I take to be this, that Men may be of any, or all Religions, but not in the same Country, for fear of suffering for it; But, *Cum fueris Romæ Romano vivito more*. One after another, at *Rome* a *Papist*, at *London* a *Protestant*, at *Constantinople* a *Mahometan*. This Principle, so Naturally his own, is the Consequence of his Malice upon the Duke; for he would have the Duke's Deduction of the Reasonableness of Men's choosing their Religion, by the Direction of that which in themselves is nearest a-kin to the Nature of God, to imply, that for all that, *Men may be of any, and of all Religions*, a pretty Way to shift with all Winds, and Sail the Compass round: But in this he has more than avenged the Duke's Quarrel upon himself; for he cannot make himself more Ridiculous, than in attempting to make the Duke so Unreasonable.

And he is just as fair to *Reason*, as he has been to the Duke: For if he says True, *A Man may follow the Dictates of it, and be of all Religions too*: Such a Gypsie is Reason with him. And if you ask him, *Why* Reason *is so prostitute a Thing, that nothing comes amiss to her*; His Answer is extraordinary, *For* (says he) *it can never lead Men to the Knowledge of the Belief of a Trinity, the Incarnation, Death Passion, Resurrection, Ascension, or Divinity of Christ*. Ergo What? Ergo, It will bow to any else, though it be never so Idle and Extravagant. Is not this sad Work for a *Doctor*?

But if the *Dictates of Reason* will fall in with any Religion, they may embrace the *Christian* as well as another, and then he's gone again. He will certainly hate Consequences too, when he has but thought of his own, *that so inevitably attended his Conceptions, to the Disadvantage of Religion*. But the Duke's Instinct, or that which God has placed in our Hearts, so near a-kin to the Nature of God, he says, must be Reason, and that Reason he makes an arrant Strumpet; for he assures us, *She is a Prolifick Parent of Idolatry, Superstition, Will-Worship, and a Thousand Absurdities more in Religion*, and *quotes All Times, Places, and Ages for Proof*, p. 14. But as it happens, names not one of them to the Point asserted.

Now the little Skill I have in Books, tells me quite other Things to the Tale of this Answerer: *That* Superstition *and* Idolatry *are the most Unreasonable Things in the World*; *that they could never Bribe Her at any Time*; *and 'till Sensuality had darkened and overlaid Men's Reason, It was impossible for* Superstition *and* Idolatry *to obtain that Empire, that in Prejudice of Reason, they have at any Time got upon the Belief of any Part of Mankind*. And if we will be just to *Ethnick* Ages, we find Men among them of extraordinary Light; That, *As having no Law, became a Law unto themselves, and that were of the Uncircumcision that kept the Law*, as the Apostle of the *Gentiles* speaks. Such were *Pythagoras, Anaxagoras, Socrates, Plato, Xenocrates,*

Xenocrates, Plotin, Antipater, Zeno, Epictetus, Seneca, Plutarch, Cato, Cicero, and others. And to be free with the Duke's Undertaker, I take Old *Plutarch* to be much a *Better Christian,* who calls this Instinct, *The Everlasting Foundation of Virtue: A Law written, not in Pillars of Wood or Stone, but in the Hearts of Men.* But that he may meet with some Rebuke, for much is owing him on this Account, I shall take upon me to examine his Imputations, be it upon this *Instinct,* or be that *Reason,* I will not quarrel the Word.

I do say then, *That he must either deny that God hath plac'd any such Thing in Man, to distinguish him from other Animals; or if that be True, He is to chuse his Religion without consulting it.* If the *First,* he makes us all *Beasts,* and himself an *Atheist*; If the *Last,* our Religion is in-evident, we know not what, for we are not to take the Judgment of the Divine Gift in our Election: What a Religion must that be? If his Argument were True, here would be indeed as fair a Plea for the *Alcoran* as the *New Testament.* But it were Blasphemous so to speak of the *Duke's Instinct,* For it is that Notion of God which is innate, and, as it were, Congenial to us: We bring it with us into the World. The peculiar Seal and Mark of Divinity: A kind of Counter-part of himself in Man; his Picture in little: The Attributes that are Infinite in him, being here Epitomiz'd and Resembled in Man, that by It he may have a Right Knowledge of his Creator, and Sense of his Duty. Antiquity offers a Cloud of Witnesses, both *Pagan* and *Christian. Justin Martyr, Clemens Alexandrinus* and *Origen,* exceed. But the Opposition is too mean to draw out so great an *Artillery*; It will be Time enough when a greater Force appears to assault so Venerable a Truth: And in the mean Time I will attend him in his Exceptions, such as they are. But perhaps he will excuse himself, because he does not *certainly know* what the Duke means by that Part of us, which is nearest a kin to the Nature of God. For he says, *If he be not mistaken, it must be Reason.* But if I be not mistaken, he had better have known first, and not have drawn positive Conclusions from doubted Premisses. But suppose the Duke understands *Reason* by that *Instinct,* rather than a *Divine Gift* to guide our Reason and Understanding, Will Reason plead the Cause of the Alcoran, as soon as that of the New Testament? What has God done then to make us Reasonable? I had thought that the *New Testament* had been a more Reasonable Book, and that God Almighty had not made Man so deceivable a Creature, or fram'd him with such false Intellects; and submitted him to such dangerous Errors. And though he might have made him Feeble, yet not so squint-ey'd or tender sighted that he could not see straight, or tell Colours, or distinguish an *Alcoran* from the *New Testament.*

I pray, is the *Alcoran* as Credible as *Christ's Sermons upon the Mount, to the Multitude, to His Disciples?* Wherein we find the *Most Excellent Morality, Piety,* and *Purity of Discipline*; so suitable to our Understandings, that they seem to answer the Perfection of Reason? I know he will tell us, he means it of Revealed Religion, as he does, p. 13. *Reason* (says he) *can never lead us to the Knowledge of the Belief of the Trinity, Resurrection, Ascension, or Divinity of the Son of God.* To be led to the Knowledge of the Belief of any Thing, is odly said; but let it pass: However, there is a Difference between Miracles and Fables; Arrant Fopperies and Fictions; so ill counterfeited too, that a Man of small Sight must needs discern them.

Tradition, and prejudic'd Education, indeed give Credit often to such Things; but Reason does not chuse, but is overborn: Besides, we have as good Authority for our Saviour's Miracles, as for any Thing we did not see: Of *Mahomet's* we have not the like; And this is farther to be said, *If Reason cannot work them, it never opposed them:* On the contrary, it leads us to believe them, and Revealed Religion for their Sakes; For a Man must be an Hog to oppose himself to so overcoming an Evidence, in Lieu of a Man that is led by Reason.

It seems to me, as if this Gentleman dare not venture his Religion with Reason, that opposes Reason to Religion. The *New Testament* is so far from refusing Reason any Share in our *Christianity,* that it is made a Duty to us to give a *Reason of our Christian Hope,* 1 Pet. 3. 15. And it were absurd to give a Reason for that which a Man receives without Reason, and is impossible to Receive by it, or for Reason to apprehend; and if it could, it judges so ill, that it will as soon prostrate it self to the *Alcoran* as to the *New Testament.*

But this is not all the Duke's Fault, perhaps he would go a great Way to yield him his Point; if he did but mean *Political Reason, or Reason regulated by a Community.* This he explains, p. 19. For his Community is the Government: But had not this been a fine Receipt to keep Christianity out of all Countries? For had this Reason of Community prevailed, there had been neither *Christians nor Protestants.* Without racking a Syllable of his excellent Argument, I think I may say, *It pleads as much for the* Alcoran *as the* New Testament, *and more in* Turkey: For if the Political Reason of the Community of a Country, is still to conclude those that dwell in it, *Turks,* must be *Turks*; *Infidels,* must be *Infidels*; *Idolaters,* must be *Idolaters* still: In which also I perceive he is a *Republican,* after all his Railing at *Common-Wealth's Men:* For the *Community over all Causes, with him, judges.* I don't know but it may run as far as *Exclusion* too: To be sure it would, if all had agreed; for all Measures of Right or Wrong, True or False, are by *my Man* humbly submitted to the Political Reason of the Community; What is this but to say, *That every Religion is best where it is Establish'd, though the most disagreeing among themselves, and any, or all of them, with the True?*

Nor is this the Extent of the Duke's Error, He is not only for Reason, *guiding and chusing,* but he would have *every private Man's Reason dictate for himself.* This is a Pestiferous Doctrine in the Answerer's Account; and yet should a Man chuse without himself, for himself, he must certainly be beside himself. Who should chuse for a Man but himself, if he must answer for himself? It would certainly be most unreasonable to judge a Man for a Thing he is not allow'd the Liberty of his Choice in: Nor do I think a Man can have any Reason to render for his Religion, that receives his *Religion without the Suffrage of his own Reason.*

Have our Bodies Eyes, and our Souls none? Shall our Temporal Part act upon Sight, and our Eternal upon Trust, and That not of God, but of Man? That when the poor Labourer will be Judge of his Pay, and not trust his very Minister about the Currentness of a *Groat,* we should be left without Distinction about that Treasure, which is of Eternal Moment to us: Surely then, Understandings are of no Use in Heaven: But I know not how to believe it. To be a Child in Malice is excellent; But under Favour, in Understanding, not. To trust out our Souls upon *Human Say-so's,* is to go into Coats again; *And to be sure, a Child's Coat, is a Fool, upon a Man's Back.* Let them wear Bibs that *Slabber,* and the *Blind* follow the *Dog and the Bell.* In Religion, Authority concludes Minors; but Conviction determines Men.

That this Gentleman should pretend to *Protestancy,* and rail at a Man's Judging for himself, is absurd. If the Reason of the Community must guide, let him not be so angry with the *Romanists,* for saying, *Believe as the Church Believes;* when he says, *Believe as the State requires:* The One presses Conformity *as by the* Catholick Church *Establish'd*; the other crys, *As by Law Establish'd:* A Doctrine Calculated to all Meridians.

I fear he grants too much for the Quarrel, but let Him look to that? For the one pre-supposes the *Holy Ghost* to conduct, to justify the Determination; The other scorns her Words, but won't bate one Jot of Conformity. I shall only tell him, that taking the *Translation of the Bible* to have been an Appeal to the People, made by the first Reformers, against the Church they Dissented from; If, as this Man suggests, the *English* of reading it now, be, that we must not make any Judgment to our selves of what we read, the Appeal cannot be determined, and our Case is not mended; On the contrary, it is made a Temptation of Trouble and Mischief to Us: For, whereas the Inspir'd *Doctor* tells us, that in Religious Matters, *We are to be perswaded in our own Minds, That they commended Themselves and Doctrines to Men's Consciences,* so making Them Judges for Themselves. *That Conscience Accuses and Excuses, ay, our own Hearts, that all are to walk as they have Received, and not usurp a Judging Power over our fellow Christians Faith or Liberty*; We are told now, that all our Faith and Worship must be submitted to the Political Reason of the Community, we are of, *hit or miss.* I take this to be leaping blind fold into t'other World in Matters of Salvation.

But it may be, he will tell me, that he has nothing to say against *Reason* consider'd in it's *Purity,* and *un-deprav'd,* only, *That it cannot lead us to the Knowledge of Revealed Religion*; and he says as much, *p.* 13. But this will not do, or else do worse than before; For if by Reason he means a *Reasonable Capacity,* he does not mean as the Duke means, and says, and then *he is mistaken indeed in what his Grace calls that Part of us that is nearest a-kin to the Nature of God,* to wit, His Instinct in Us, and is understood by this Noble PEER to be the *Guide and Director* of our Understandings in our Choice, and which gives the Rectitude and True Judgment.

On the other Hand, if he understands *Reason* abstractly, and as the Principle it self; It can no more be deprav'd, than the *Sun* darkn'd by the Mists and Vapours of the Earth. And truly it is just as reasonable to accuse the Law of *Moses* with the Death of our Saviour, and the *Gospel* with the Errors and Impieties of *Christians*, as to charge to the Account of Reason all the ill Things, that Men pretending to it, have committed. And yet to do the worst of them right, the most Idolatrous, Unnatural and Senseless, Rites the darkest Ages of the World ever had, they have discharg'd their Reason, and plac'd them, in all Times, to the unaccountable Tradition and Authority of their Priesthood: Where, for this Time, I will leave them too: Only I must needs say, I wish the *Dust* this Man has so vehemently rais'd upon Reason, be not to put out our Eyes too, that we may be less Resty, and lead better. For if such Men once get us out of our Depth, we are gone. Trust thick and three-fold; And the more Un-Intelligible, the more Venerable; this will be the Maxim.

But if I may, I would wonder for all that, how after all, He can so expresly contradict himself, as *p*. 14. to allow *Reason to Judge*, and *p*. 36. To send his Readers thither to convince others of their Duty both in their Spiritual and Civil Capacity. He must have relented him mightily, or having been in a Fit, is come to himself, or else his own Reason has had the Wind, and is too many for his Prejudices, or he could not have given himself so quickly so great a Reprimand; But this shews the Nature and Power of Reason, that it will rise to it's own Evidence and Vindication, even in the most Unreasonable Men.

But this Author tells the World, *That granting the Duke to have carried his Postulatum of the Being of a Supreme and Perfect Power, he would have followed his Blow at another Rate, and sent his Reader another Road*, which shews the Duke's little, and his better, Skill and Courage; tho he might have been so modest as to let us have been the Judges of that: *He did not catch this of his Grace's Pen*. And pray what would he have done? why, after a Flood of Words (and this is all.) he tells us; *That he would have sent them to the Scriptures*. And by this, one would think that the Man had never read the Book he pretends to Answer; For that Noble Peer expresly tells us in the Beginning of his Discourse, that he has to do with Men that deny their Authority, and therefore to use it to prove what he asserts, were to beg the Question. And I do assure him, so soon as he had *Gain'd the* Postulatum *of the being of a Supreme and Perfect Power*, he recommends them to the Christian Religion, of which I had always understood till now, the Scriptures had been the *Creed*.

Well, but in case of doubtful places he has an Interpreter, a Judge for Him at hand too, *and That is the Society of Christians*; why could not he as well have said the Church; and then have told us which *Church*; for there is not one of a dozen that don't alledge the Text for their Authority. But to do him Right, he has given us a Rule to know her by; he takes it, *(Good Protestant)* from *Vincentius Lirinensis*, and a Golden one it is, he assures us; But for all that, I fancy it has an Iron Rod at the Tail for him.

'Tis this, *Quod ubiq; quod semper, quod ab omnibus, id verè quidem Catholicum est*, and *that this would have shewn the Duke a Thousand Errors*, p. 15. Now, methinks, out of meer Pity, I am not willing to allow his Rule; For if I should, first this *shewing Rule*, will infallibly *shew* him, that the *Duke's Instinct* and the *Pensilvanian*'s *Doctrine*, (to his unspeakable Grief,) has the Hope to be Establish'd by it. For there is nothing more Ancient, more Universal, more constantly credited, at all Times, in all Places, by all Nations, than a *Divine Instinct in the Natures of Men*: And then, if this attempt upon the Duke has not been Unreasonable, as to the *Pensilvanian*, an Honour as much above his Hope, as his Adversary's Intentions, let Him Judge.

My second Reason of Unwillingness is this, he says, p. 16. *This Rule would have taught the Duke to avoid the cruel Divinity of* Calvinists *which his* Grace *lashes with so much Truth and Justice:* Where, besides the Non-sense of teaching a Man to dislike a Thing, he already is allow'd to have lasht with Justice, he confirms the Judgment of his Instinct, by which, he was led to lash the Doctrine, for a *Golden Rule*.

But lastly, as he has Establish'd the Thing he would overthrow, so it's to be fear'd, he has overthrown the Thing he would Establish, And would not a well-natur'd Man be sorry for that.

For

For most evident it is that the *Church* of *England* is not *every where*, there's for His *Ubique*: And some tell us, that She was not always what she is, there's for His *Semper*: And that every Body is not of Her Communion, this Gentleman's Invectives against *Dissenters* prove; the *Roman* Church charges Novelty; She flies to Scripture; The *Roman* Church disputes the *Sense*, the Church of *England* appeals to the *first Doctors* of the Church; the Romanists to the *Sense* of the Church upon the *Doctors*. Now says He, *The Society of Christians must be Judge*, p. 15. Not the *Few* that separate from the *Many*; For then they will be Judge in their own Cause, and the *Dissenters* at Home will expect the same Priviledge; If the Church they Dissent from, they are gone; If the *Scripture*, 'tis the Subject to be Judged. This must issue therefore, either in no Judge, or in an External Judge, or in an Internal Judge. If no Judge, we are left without Decision till the last Judgment. If an External Judge, it must either be the *Church* or *Civil Government*. If the *Church*, the *Romanists* think they carry it. If the *Civil Government*, to be sure the *Church of England* has it there. If lastly, an Internal Judge, that every Man should try, fasten and examine for himself, the *Duke's* Instinct (much against this Gentleman's Mind) will come in for a Share in the Choice of a Man's own Religion, and that within the Rule too.

The next Point he falls upon, is the *Duke's* Maxim about Perfecution, he does not think it *Antichristian* at Home, *but the Duke under a Mistake of the Reason, Nature, and Necessity of those Humane Laws* Dissenters *are prosecuted by* p. 17. And upon this he bestows eight Pages, which in a *Lump*, comes to thus much. *That though he allows, that punishing the Professors of a True Religion, purely for Religion, (living otherwise inoffensively to the* Civil Government) *is* Perfecution, *and truly* Antichristian, *which was the Primitive* Christians *case under the Heathen Emperours of* Rome; *yet the Laws against* Papists *and* Dissenters *are out of a* Political, *not* Religious *Necessity, to secure the Peace and Safety of the Government*; And if this be Antichristian, *the whole World, all Ages, Times, Governments, and Governours must have been*, and are Antichristian, *and it turns his Admiration into Wonder, that his Grace should be of this Mind that had his Share in passing those Laws.* I perceive his dis-ingenuity continues to the *Duke*. For besides that, he loves Wondring, he might know that the *Duke's* Share was to Vote against them, and so that he did not espouse *Toleration*, a cast Mistress; The *Duke's* Discourse relates to Men of *Conscience*, not *Rebellion*; And to conclude, more or less than the Question contains, is not fair or found.

The Duke says, 'tis *Antichristian to perfecute*: His *Answerer* says, *'Tis truly so of the true Religion*; And pray where does the Duke say it, of the false? But I am ready to think that if Perfecution, in all the World, were stopt, till that were determin'd, we should at least gain one Age of Peace: And to have any of it before, is, at least in this Author, unaccountable, and a begging of the Question.

But he would not have Danger ensue to Government, and therefore draws upon the Duke this unnatural Consequence; *That the whole World, and all Governments and Governours are Antichristian*; whilst that Noble Peer meddles not with Government, nor Solicits Freedom for them that disturb it. He declares himself *for Men's having Liberty to Worship God according to their Perswasion, and the Reason of it*. If Men will mis-call Conscience, his Plea is no Shelter; *Currat Lex*, His Argument is safe: The Consequence is the partial Application of his Answerer. The Duke thinks perhaps, 'twere more easie and Honourable to let ill Men not have that to say against good Government, *You trouble us for our Consciences*, since in it's self, there is no Real and Proper Overt-Act of Sedition, meetly in performing a differing Sort of Worship; and that there are, or may be Laws enough provided to secure the State from those civil diforders, that any such Man might attempt under that Pretence. Here, such People would not only justly suffer, but without a cover too: The Disgrace and Odium, in the Opinion of all, as well as Penalty, falling only upon the Criminals Head. I do with the last Duty and Deference a Man can bear to his King and Country, Wish and Pray for their Prosperity: I would by no Means that any Man should be indulg'd to their Detriment: I should, besides my civil Obligations, cancel those of Conscience before Almighty God, if I thought it; But I cannot prevail with my self, to believe that the Government may not be safe, by some civil Provision, with the most suspected *Dissenter*: Else 'twere past a scruple with me that his Liberty should at all Times purchase the publick Safety.

This Gentleman allows *all Dissenters may not be Guilty*; if so, it must be a dangerous Execution; especially when the Justice of our humane Laws *had rather an hundred Criminals should escape, than that one Innocent should perish*. But he says, *he has not* Momus's *Windows to see, and know them by*. I am sure he has too much of his Mind, or he had not troubled the World with such a Bundle of Exceptions: But if he can't distinguish them, will that excuse his destroying them? I am sorry this Gentleman's Divinity has no more Bowels, nor better Sense; for if Mankind be left without the Knowledge of *Guilt* from *Innocence*, They must punish in the Lump; They must be unjust.

This is Judging without *Overt-acts*; by Guess and Jealousy. A Way that may make an *Innocent Guilty*, and a *Guilty* Person *Innocent*. To be cast without Evidence is wrong, and what Witness is there of that which is only in *foro Conscientiæ?* then what Judge? A Piece of cruel *Enthusiasm*. I know not what to call it. Not only *Christianity*, but *Gamaliel*; ay, our owns Laws would have taught Him a better way of finding out Criminals, yet His excels.

Well, *But the Laws against Papists*, (He says) *are occasioned from their Unchristian Machinations and King-killing Doctrine, able to ruin the whole Earth, and lay the Foundations of Eternal Mischief to Mankind*; And for those against Dissenters, *They were made, because of their Rebellious, Excluding, Covenanting, Associating, Murdering Principles*. p. 15. 16. 21. 22.

Now though this Man would think it imprudent in me, and I, that it is none of my Business, to vindicate the Persons charged upon His Imputations; yet I have so much Justice, I confess, as not to condemn Parties by Particulars, and Charity as to be satisfied with their solemn disclaiming of such Practices: For I did never love that one Man should have the making of another Man's Faith or Confession, especially if He were His *Adversary*.

I must tell Him also, I cannot admire His *Wisdom, Manners*, or *Justice*, in his Reflection upon the *Roman Catholicks*, after the Assurances that so great an One of their Communion has given Him and His Friends of their Security and Protection: For if they are a People *able to ruin the whole Earth, and lay the Foundation of Eternal Mischief to Mankind*; believe me, *England* is in an ill pickle, and though I am an ill Judge, He has in it put but a *Scurvy Complement* upon the King. But if by the King's Promise *p.* 33. He means that the King is to destroy the Men of His own Faith, to support and secure Theirs; I shall only admire, first His Understanding, and next His Charity.

For *Dissenters*, I shall say no more, than that it may be, the Wars made Them, rather than They made the Wars, and that Things, *older than the Act of Oblivion*, are in Law, buried by it. And with Submission, this Gentleman's *Conscience*, for ought I know, might have done as well to let Them alone.

For the late Occasion He takes, let him be just, and He will find the *Excluders*, almost, every *Sunday* at their Parish Churches: And if three Quarters of them were to pray for their Lives, it may be they could better Read their Clergy, than say their Prayers without the *Publick Liturgy*. What follows? Shall I recriminate the Usage of the late King about the Declaration of *Indulgence?* And say, that some Men lov'd Him well for their own Ends? And that when they were not humour'd exactly, *They would pout, slack their Loyalty, and grow passive, let Things go as they will for them:* A Thing almost threatn'd by this *Loyal Gentleman*, p. 33. May not this be aggravated, and with as many harsh Words, by a Man of Words and no Charity? But I would be modest, and that not of Prudence, but Choice, for I hope He would give His *Replicant* the Liberty He expects, and takes with the Great Peer he answers.

And I must say I cannot but extreamly admire, that less than twelve Lines, so softly dropt by the Duke in Favour of *Liberty of Conscience*, should have almost as many Leaves of little Invectives to answer them. Believe me, it impeaches His Pretences to Christianity, and renders Him to have more of the *Fire-brand* than of the *Loyal Subject*.

I should end here; but there are two Things more I think must be mentioned, that nothing carrying any Pretence to Weight may be omitted.

First, *That the Reason of the Penal Laws is purely Political and not Spiritual, to obviate the Overacts, Acts of Treason and Rebellion; for a Man may be of any Religion to himself, and privately exercise it too, not exceeding such a number above their Families.*

Secondly,

Secondly, *That Toleration is the way to overthrow Religion, and with it the Government, especially as now Established; and is a fatal Enemy to Monarchy.*

To the first, I say, *Fact* must Rule us; I would desire to know if the *Act of Uniformity*, Printed with the *Liturgy*, be purely Political and not Spiritual? I hope, without Offence I may say, it is not. The Laws of the 23d and 28th of the Queen, *Requiring People to come to Church*, will not let People be of any Religion to themselves; for unless they are, at least once a Month, at *Divine Service*, and show, to joyn in the Publick Worship, by Law Establish'd, they pay twenty Pounds Monthly, and have two Thirds of their Real Estate expos'd to Sequestration. And this is done in one Place or another every Day. So that it is not true in Fact, *That People may have any Religion to themselves*; because, both those that keep at home, and within the number allow'd by the Act against *Conventicles*, and those that exceed it, are notwithstanding presented upon the Statutes of the Queen; Nay, I have known some Persons prosecuted by them all, at one and the same Time.

And, with all due Respect to the Wisdom of our former *Legislators*, if this Gentleman's Gloss be true, I think Improprieties should no more have been Enacted, than Impossibilities or Contradictions. To make a Man *Dangerous* to the State, for not going to Church; or a *Breaker of the Peace*, for being at a Meeting of an hundred People, when their Persons were *Naked*, their Entertainment meer *Devotion*, and their Behaviour very *quiet* and *Innoffensive*, sounds in the Use of Words, very harsh. It puts me in Mind of a Witty Passage of the *Lord Chancellor Hyde*, when the Bill prohibiting the Importation of *Irish Cattle* was read in the *Lord's-House*, hearing it stiled a *Nusance*; *Pray*, (says he) *let it for this Time be called* Adultery, *for one Word is just as fit as t'other.* Inadequate and unsuited Expressions are oftentimes of dangerous consequence. No Man knows where the Practice may stop. Religion should sweeten and humble the Spirits of Men, abate their Passions, and excite their Obedience to their Superiors. And it is one of the strangest Things in the World that greater Numbers may meet on Twenty other Occasions every Day, with less fear of the Breach of the Peace. As that Religion cannot be good that makes any Man the worse for having it: So I am not for beheading any Thing before it is born, or punishing People for fear of what they may do. I would hope the best, and that if they had that Freedom they desire in the Exercise of their Religious Perswasion, their Condition would teach their Wit, it were too good to hazard, that if their Duty or Gratitude did not oblige them, their very *Interest* must; and there is hardly one of them so stupid, as not to understand and pursue the Ways that preserve it.

For that of *Toleration*, it is my Opinion, he does ill to distinguish it from *Liberty of Conscience*; For if he mean the same Thing, it needed not have had a fresh Head with other Consequences; nor was requisite that I did farther consider it.

And I am heartily sorry, I must say, that to the End of his Answer he hardly fails of his usual Way of Construction: For after having made *Toleration* as ill a Thing as he could, and as such, the Duke to be the *Patron* of it; He falls on with a whole Volley of hard Words, asking the Duke, *p. 27, 28, 29.* *If he would give* Toleration *to a Rebellious, Associating, Sanguinary, Inhumane, Blasphemous, Murdering Conscience, such as that of Calvinists, that Decrees Damnation without free Conditions, Kill'd his Master, Father and Brother, and that particularly used him so ill.* But this is so far from determining, that in ill Language it miserably begs the Question, by the Reflection of false and Scandalous Consequences, upon what the Duke said in favour of *Indulgence*.

Is there no such Thing as *Conscience*, because it may be falsly pretended? Or shall a sober and Moral Conscience be deny'd *Indulgence*, because some or other may, or do misuse it? And that He may have something to think on; I ask if those Calamities were the Effects of a *Toleration?* If so, pray when was there one to do us so much Mischief? The Difficulty, I know, he will have to find one, makes me ask him another Question: If *Ease* to Men in that Respect, were not the Way of greatest Safety to the Publick, at least, fit to be tried. I must say, this Gentle-Man takes too many Things for granted, and needs a very merciful Adversary: One that will do less than not exact the uttermost Farthing, though he himself will reap where he hath not Sown, and Compel Conformity where he cannot convince. *The very Point*, he says, *His Grace has with so much Justice lasht the* Calvinists *for*, and that he himself did but just now call *Inhumane* and *Blasphemous*.

Good Nature, with all that little Prudence that falls to my Share, makes it easier to me to believe that a *Christian Toleration* were the best Way to prevent the

Mischiefs that are said to be the Effects of it. I say, by all Means *Secure the Government*; But withal, pray let us see if that may not be done, by some other and easier Method; It is Pity that it should cost the *Liberties or Estates* of so vast a People as do dissent, and, I would hope, without so much as an ill Thought to the King or his Government.

But he is so in love with the *Chase*, that without any more to do, he sends us to the *French King*, p. 29. *To take Measures for* England *in point of Religion*: Which is pretty well for an *Englishman* and a *Protestant*, and perhaps a *Doctor* too.

This in any Man had not been well, but in an *English Protestant*, with his Leave, is Impious, since it is to draw that *King's Severity* into Example, and render it a Prudence to be imitated here. A Notion, he has taught me to call, in him, *Atheistical*, because it cannot be done by a *Protestant, Whose Conscience*, as he says, *will not let him be of any, and of all Religions*. This yields little Consolation to the *French Protestants*: And if he would but think well upon it, not too much to the *English Church*; For, if he says true, *That* Lewis *the Fourteenth does well to compel an Union of his Subjects in his own Religion*; He has recommended a Policy that goes a great Way to discharge the King of his Promise, and make us all of his: I don't know whether *Coleman's* Letters say so much as this, that we made the Proof of the *Plot*. This may make *Roman Catholicks* amends for *Page* 27, 28, 29.

To conclude: He is so fond of the Instance, that he appeals to Crown'd Heads in General; *If a Toleration be not inconsistent with their Safety*. A Man had need be well assured, at least as far as an *Invulnerable Conscience*, to try his Appeal, but that I am, and therefore join Issue with him; submitting with all my Heart, to their *Royal Evidence* in the Decision of the Point: But because it requires more Room than agrees with the Success of this Reply, in an Age that loves not length, I have chosen to make it a Discourse of it self, and refer him thither: The Title, *A Persuasive to Moderation*: And shall conclude this with the *Wise* and *Christian* Judgment of King CHARLES the First, in his Advice to the late King.

" Take Heed (says he) of abetting any Factions, your *Partial* Adhering to any
" one Side, gains you not so great Advantages in some Men's Hearts, *Who are prone*
" *to be of their King's Religion, as it loseth you in Others*; Who think themselves
" and their Profession, first Despised, and then Persecuted by You. A *Christian*
" *Toleration* often Dissipates their Strength, whom Rougher Opposition Fortifies.
This was the Counsel of a *Crowned Head*: The Judgment of his Adversity: Always the Soundest: Resentments could not *Blind* it, nor Revenge of Wrongs, *Precipitate* it. In which, he acted the *Christian Prince*, and not the *Amilcar*.

Let us then remember his Counsel with his Afflictions, and the one the more endear the other to us; lest we despise some of the best Fruits of the *Autumn* of his Life, to wit, his *Wisdom and Goodness*, that the Gusts of Time and Troubles he lay under did not shake; and which he has recommended to us for a Guide in Future Times, to prevent them.

ANIMADVERSIONS on the APOLOGY of the *Clamorous Squire*, against the Duke of *Buckingham's* SECONDS, as Men of no Conscience.

The INTRODUCTION.

IT is a Judgment upon some Men, not only to mistake, but to refuse to be informed; as it is the worst of Natures to be afraid that other Men should be in the Right.

All Dissenters *must be in the Wrong*, whether they be or no: *And they must not mean any Thing that is Good, by good Words*, whether they do or no. Though it

were

were that they should say, they would not have the Government or National Church destroy'd, and only pray for a little Room to exercise their own Way quietly, and that they will pray for, and pay Tribute cheerfully to their Auspicious Cæsar.

And why all this Unkindness and Injustice, but for fear such Men of Wrath and Interest should want a Pretence to destroy them? Which, in my Opinion, shews them ill Sons of the Church, that unwillingly believe well of others, and had rather they were in the Wrong than in the Right.

For in all the late Pamphlets against Liberty of Conscience, there's not one Word of winning one poor Dissenter to the Church, no more than of Tolerating them out of the Church. But how peaceable soever he be, he is cast out for a Vessel of Wrath, good for nothing but to be Hang'd here, and Damn'd hereafter.

It is a Melancholy Prospect for him, but not without Instruction, and some Hope: For Extremes do the Authors of them no Good: And these Flashes may be but a Lightning before Death, I mean, of Severity.

It is always darkest before Day: Ease and Liberty of Conscience, for all this, may yet dawn under the Government of our Brave King.

And who would not hope a little longer, that has staid all this While? Will other Princes give better Terms in their Countries, or keep them better? Let's then be Patient and Humble, and pray God to mollify the Hearts, even of them that hate us. *Vincit qui patitur*. And so I come to the severe Gentleman against the Duke of BUCKINGHAM and his SECONDS, for Men of No Conscience; in which we shall have a Measure of his, of his own giving, and that will shew it to be none of the best.

Animadversions on the Apology, &c.

HE begins, Page 3, with the *Loyalty* of the *House of Commons*, and the Reason of his Judgment, to wit, *If we consider, Who has chosen them, and Who are chosen*. Now, no Body doubts their *Loyalty*, without this lucky Reason given by the *Squire*, of *Who chose them, and Who are chosen*. The Case is plain, and needed not his officious Note upon the House, for Spectacles to the People.

But if it be so, *The Dissenters Insolence is insufferable in their Pleas for Liberty of Conscience*. Which I take to be a Reflection upon that Great Assembly; it prejudges their Wisdom and Goodness. What knows he which Way Reason of State may incline their Judgment; or what Motives may induce their Debates and Resolves. Is it *Insolence*, and that unsufferable too, for Men humbly to pray, they may have Leave to say their Prayers in another Way than that which is common?

If any Man has done Ill, must the Principle suffer, and the Party pay the Reckoning, especially if neither be in the Fault? Here's a *Loyal* Parliament, *Ergo*, *A Million of People must be Ruin'd*. A fine *Christian*, and as good a *Statesman*. I hope, there's *Preference* of one, without *Destruction* of the rest, and *Rebuke* without *Ruin*. The Dissenter may *live*, though the Church-man only be *preferr'd*. And only let him be *preferr'd*, so that t'other may not be *confounded*.

He says, Pag. 3, 4, *Liberty of Conscience has embroil'd three Nations in Blood, and yet the Patrons of it allow'd it not to one another, as* Presbyterians, Independents, &c. *Nor did they to King* Charles *the First, the* Church of England, *or* Roman Catholicks. He might have added the *Quakers* too, that suffered more Cruelties than any other Party, under them.

But I pray, How does this shake the Reasonableness of *Liberty of Conscience*? For, *First*, That was not any Part of the stated Quarrel between the K. and Parliament. *Secondly*, If they that made the War, *disown'd* it, and *deny'd* it, How were they Patrons of it? Or how did that Principle come to lay three Kingdoms in Blood? It seems then that *Liberty of Conscience* must pay the Reckoning of the Men that are against it; or that because those Men were against it (and therein doubtless did very Ill) therefore the *Church of England* would do ill to give it. Make this good, and he shall be my Oracle.

But why? For Fear they should be undone by giving it, because they were undone that did not give it. Mighty well argued! This Gentleman bids for the first Doctor next ACT at *Oxford*.

You would not give it to me, that you wou'd not, and therefore why should I give it to you? No such Matter; Truly, I don't intend it. This is pretty *Logick!* 'tis Demonstration, backward. But *Passion*, though it rules Women, it should not rule in the Church. Wise and Good Men consider the Right and Prudence of a Thing, to which private Passions are made to submit.

Page 5. But the *Protestant Dissenters deserve no Liberty, because in* Seventy Two *they were for Liberty with the* Papists, *in* Eighty *without them, and now in* Eighty Five *it is not only lawful, but necessary, that the* Roman Catholicks *have their Liberty too.*

Granting this to be so, What's that to *Liberty of Conscience?* It only shews the *Partiality* of the Men, and perhaps that would have been granted him for a Word's asking. This Proves nothing against the Principle, though the *Squire* upon this so fiercely concludes *all the Villanies in the World against Liberty of Conscience.* But when he has done all he can, they were not *Dissenters*, under Correction, that in *Eighty* prosecuted the *Roman Catholicks*, and refused them *Liberty*, but *Church of England-men*, and such of them too, as would not allow it to some *Protestant Dissenters*, for Fear that *Papists* should hide themselves amongst them, and they therefore must swallow the most severe *Tests* that could be fram'd to shew themselves not Friends to that Communion. And, to tell Truth, and I beseech the *Gentleman* not to take it amiss, that I say, the *Dissenters* were invited to the Share they had in Opposition to *Popery*, by Church-men, ay, they were for a *Comprehension*, to make the Church stand broader, the better to receive the Assaults of *Rome* without Hazard. And had the *Dissenter* been more modest to his Mistress, and not so Malepert and officious, he had doubtless been upon better Terms with her now. However, her Anger must not endure for ever, nor destroy her Servant for being too busy or eager in the Service she call'd him to.

Well, *But the Duke of* Buckingham's *Seconds are Men of no Conscience, because they charge the Exclusion upon the Members of the Church of* England. This is so bitterly resented, that we are told, *That an honest* Turk *would have scorn'd so base a Practice, within five Years after the Fact, and in a Case wherein the whole Nation knows the contrary.*

If Exclusion, or no Exclusion, be to determine the true from the false *Church of England-men*, as Page 7, the Proposition will be doubly false; For there are Men that were not for Exclusion, that were not Members of the *Church of England*, and there are Members of the *Church of England*, that were for the Exclusion. And to this Charge in the *Reply* and the *Defence*, he gives no Answer but Anger, which for a Man to avoid, when the Question lies upon it, and that grounded upon Matter of Fact, shews his Fear of Success, and that, the Weakness of his Cause. But since the *Dissenters* by Wholesale are to bear the Blame, I do affirm the *Excluders* were *Conformists*, and are yet *Communicants of your Church*, and the greatest Part of them upon Education and constant Practice too. And that this is Truth, and no Slander, read the List, and 'tis a Demonstration. Nay, I challenge the *Gentleman* to name *six* Persons of all the *Excluders*, that dissent from the Establish'd Church.

Nor is this of Yesterday; for if we look back, we shall see the most celebrated Bishops of your Church barring the Succession in the Law of the 13th and 27th of Q. *Eliz.* and when that Queen pleaded Conscience in not assenting to a Law to put our King's Great-Grandmother, *Mary* Queen of *Scots* to Death, the same Reverend Bishops undertook to remove the Scruple; yet nothing but, *Away with these Disloyal Dissenters.*

Own them then ingenuously, that they are Members of your own Church, and that their Defection began within your selves; and that, for all your Invectives, and turning them over now to the Dissenters, because you are ashamed of them, they are in Communion with you still, and daily *Conformists* to the Worship, and as such, are admitted to the accustomed *Rites* and *Privileges* of your Church. Page 7. *To charge all Addresses, and the* Oxford *Parliament, to the Account of Dissenters, is not wise, any more than true, for it is to give the greater Numbers to the Dissenting Party, since it is plain, how unequal they were that fell in with that Excluding Humour in the Kingdom.*

But this is not all he has said, to prevent the *Legislative* Goodness to *Dissenters.* They must not have Liberty, *lest it be charged upon the Government as a Design to bring in Popery and Arbitrary Power.*

I remember a Story of *Harry Martin*, that when *Cromwell* came to diffolve the *Rump*, to juftify his Action, among other Things, he accufed fome of their Members of an *Evil Life*, faying, *Here fits a Drunkard, and there* (pointing to him) *fits an Whore-mafter*; *Harry Martin* fitting between two fober grave Men, jogg'd them, faying, *Which of you Two does he mean?* The *Diffenters* muft be blam'd by thofe that are Guilty. 'Tis hard to fuffer for Faults, and be chid by them that did them.

No, 'twas the Gentlemen of that Communion that impeach'd the Prerogative, in the Declaration of *Indulgence*, and fet the *Political Capacity of the King in Oppofition to his National*, and to make their Bufinefs more popular, beftowed that Comment upon it, of *a Defign in the Court to let in Popery and Arbitrary Government*.

Upon the whole Matter, 'tis not unworthy of fome Thought, that this Way of making *Whigs* and *Fanaticks* of all, that in every Point come not up to an Hair, though otherwife Men of *Virtue, Piety, Wifdom*, and perfectly Church-men, may prove of ill Confequence; for it narrows, where it is *Wifdom* to enlarge, and greatens, where *Prudence* enclines to leffen. I mean the Credit of Number.

This makes me the more admire one Expreffion, viz. pag. 8, *That the Members of the* Church of England *have turn'd over to the* Diffenters *all the Excluders, and laid the Bill of Exclufion at their Doors, and wafh'd her Hands of them, as* Pilate *did of our Saviour's Blood*. Where, befides the falfe Politicks of making fo many Thoufand *Diffenters* in two Lines, and that without all Hope of Recovery, he unhappily makes the Church of *England-men cowardly Pilate*, and the Excluders to anfwer the Place of our bleffed Saviour. A pretty Allufion to credit the Church, and difgrace Excluders.

This is not the happieft Part of his *Apology*.

But I would have hoped, that a Man who fhews not to want a Share of Wit and Expreffion, fhould be fo difingenuous, as from the Author's of the Defenfive Sheet faying, "Take off the Thing that Pinches, and fee then whether the " *Church-men* or the *Fanaticks* and *Catholicks* will be moft governable. To infer, *Perfecute the Church-men, beftow the Bifhopricks and Church-Revenues amongft the* Catholicks *and* Fanaticks, *and fee which will be the beft qualified, and moft dutiful Subjects. A rare Expedient*.

May I not better fay, a rare Confequence? As if eafing *Diffenters*, and not wringing their Backs, were ftripping the *Church*, and clothing *Diffenters* in Velvet, than which, nothing lefs was thought of. This Incharity and Injuftice ruin all. Such Men cannot hope to efcape the Judgment of God, that are fo Injurious in their Judgment to Men.

But he is angry with his Grace the Duke of *Buckingham*, for leading the Dance, and if a Dance it muft be, it is an old Country One, at which he has been Excellent of long Time, And who would not Dance to fuch a Fidler? But how *Tranfubftantiation* comes to be beholding to the Duke, whofe Conclufion excludes it utterly, of which a Boy of Seven Years Old is Judge, let the *Gentleman* confider once more.

However, his Grace may happen to afk this *Gentleman* once in his Life, *If he be the Man that charges him with leading the Dance to Men of* No Honour, No Confcience, No Honefty, *and that advocates a Caufe of fo much Treafon and Impiety, as is laid to the Charge of Liberty of Confcience*.

To the *Diffenter's Objection*, Pag. 10. he fays, in their Name, *That all the ill Things they have done, is becaufe there are Laws made againft them, and that they would be quiet, if they might have their Liberty*; and tells us, *That their ill and difloyal Practices in Queen* Elizabeth's *Time, drew the firft Law upon them, and that was the 35th of the Queen*. But that is no Anfwer to the Objection, for they were made Dangerous, as Conventicles are now, by Sufpicion and Prevention, not that they did any ill Thing deferving that Severity; but Church Refractorinefs, Bifhop *Whitgift* was pleafed to Tranflate into *Sedition*: The Old Way, *Indeed my Lord, they are Enemies to* Cæfar, *and Exalters of another King*, One JESUS. So that 'tis begging the Queftion, to ground this Law on the Seditious Practice of the *Diffenters*; and we are to learn when any of our Time had a *Toleration* to abufe, or when any fuch Thing was in being, to charge our Political, or Ecclefiaftical Calamities upon. I only pray to be informed, I fay, *When, Where*, and *How*? For I am intirely of his Mind, pag. 10. *That Wife Men will try as few Conclufions in Government (if fettled) as is poffible*; *and yet when only One Conclufion is left to be tryed,*

tryed, and that so necessarily prayed and prest, methinks 'tis not unwise to make the Experiment, when Mercy, Goodness and Charity are on that Side.

But alas! the Author of this *Apology* is not contented to fasten upon an Occasion given, and improve it with all the Aggravation of an unkind Nature, but turns *Fortune-Teller*, and reads us a Lecture by the flying of his *Jackdaw*, of our own Insides and future Devices: A downright Divination and Enthusiasm, as if he had been on an Errand to *Delphos*. Hear him, pag. 11. *That we were all thunder-struck, dreaded a Prince we had offended, and that had so much Diligence and Courage to repay us, and therefore turned* Trimmers, *went to Church, took the Sacrament, gave up the Game, set up for Loyal: And that in this Melancholy Frame, it was his Grace found us when he publish'd his Essay, and that no meaner Person durst do it though enough follow him.*

Now the first Part of the Story is false, and the last silly and saucy, as well as Untrue. *I see Dissenters Vertues (as few as they are) must be their Vices for a Need: Their Quietness is from the Stroke of Guilt, and their Conformity only Hypocrisie for Safety:* They have a fine Time of it, and are mightily oblig'd to this Gentleman's Goodness and Justice, much Good may it do them. But the Duke out of Measure, is made Brave in a bad Cause, a *Cataline* at least, or if you will, a *Corah,* that is, leading them back to *Egypt* again: A mighty Charge; and but that it is not True, 'twere an Impeachable Business; and because it is not, let this Gentleman take Heed of a *Scandalum Magnatum*.

But this Cry for Liberty here, is to break out with *Argyle*'s Plot in *Scotland*. This is shrewdly hit. Politick every bit of it. I thought *Argyle*'s *Presbyterians* and Liberty had not agreed so well together: I have heard such Folks hold as ill an Opinion of it, as this *Gentleman*, for his Ears.

But besides all this, he tells us, *Our Time is short, we must in pure Despair do Feats; and what are they but to maul and disgrace the Church Party at any Rate?* But if they will give us as good Quarter as they have receiv'd from the three or four *Pamphlets* for Liberty, I dare make the Bargain, that the *Dissenters* shall look no farther after Bishopricks, nor Church-Livings, and I would to God it might rest there.

What a Stir is here, that Men *pray to be quiet?* O! but we know you won't be quiet, and therefore you shan't be quiet: There is nothing so idle, as being very Cunning, and making every Thing a Plot. So *Tacitus* makes *Tiberius* to have a deep one, *in going to the House of Office:* To be sure it was a necessary one.

His Conclusion is hard upon us, that Advocate, the Cause of tender Consciences, saying, *We are Men of no Honour, no Conscience, nor Honesty*, but leaves the Proof to be understood.

Certainly he cannot have too much of those good Qualities, that advocates *Tertullus*-like, against tender Consciences, and to give him his Due, he is sensible of it; for he presently acknowledges *his Sharpness*, but excuses it with the Baseness of those that *dare affirm the Excluders were Church of* England-men. But for all that, it falls out to be true, and nothing but *Truth* pinches any Body.

He concludes in Defence of the *Church of England's* Severity, and says, *Tell me how Christ can be Head of opposite Bodies?* But what then? Must you persecute where your Head forbids it? Though he is not Head of opposite Bodies, he does not destroy the Bodies of which he is not Head. But what does this Man think of an opposite Head and Body, the Head of one Mind, and the Body of another? An Head and no Member. *Riddle me, Riddle me, What's this?*

He bids us, *Consider this following Place of Scripture, and bless the World with a Comment*, Rev. 11. 20.

Notwithstanding I have a few Things against thee, because thou sufferest (or tolerate*st) that Woman,* Jezebel, *which calleth her self a Prophetess,* (a godly Woman) *to teach and seduce my Servants to commit Fornication, and to eat Things sacrificed to Idols. Now*, says he, *I would fain know how long Toleration has been a Christian Virtue*, Rev. 11.

By this, never trust me, one would think him a Divine, every Inch of him, that can so cleverly take *Not Tolerating* IN Communion, for *Not Tolerating* OUT *of Communion*.

But is this the *Dissenters* Case? Have they ask'd for the Churches, or do they usurp the Pulpits? Or out of your Communion either, do they teach the Use of *Fornication* and *Idolatrous Food?* What Stuff is this for a Man of some Wit and Words? Besides, *Jezebel* was a *Persecutor*, and believ'd a *Whore*, which, with all the

the Manners I have, I would fain know to whose Church it is the most Part of our *English Jezebel's* go?

For his Query, *How long Toleration has been a Christian Virtue?* 'Tis plain, ever since Christ came, *That bid the Tares should grow with the Wheat 'till the Harvest*, which his own blessed Comment says, *Is the End of the World*, where I should be glad to meet this Gentleman, upon my Word. 'Till then, I would fain have him and his Friends let us alone, and then do their Worst.

Luke 9. 54, 55, 56, *They said, Lord, wilt thou that we command that Fire come down from Heaven, and consume them, even as* Elias *did? But Jesus turned about, and rebuked them, and said, Ye know not what Spirit ye are of: For the Son of Man is not come to destroy Men's Lives, but to save them.*

An Exposition upon which, because the Question is perfectly in the Text, is humbly begg'd,

Of His, to Command,

With Liberty *of* Conscience.

A PERSWASIVE to Moderation to *Church-Dissenters*, in Prudence and Conscience: *Humbly submitted to the* KING *and His Great Council.*

The EPISTLE.

HAVING of late Time observ'd the *Heat, Aversion* and *Scorn* with which some Men have treated all Thoughts of Ease to *Church Dissenters*, I confess I had a more than ordinary Curiosity to examine the Grounds those Gentlemen went upon: For I could not tell how to think Moderation should be a Vice, where Christianity was a Virtue, when the Great Doctor of that Religion commands, that *Our Moderaton be known unto all Men*; and why? *For the Lord is at Hand*: And what to do? but to judge our *Rancor*, and retaliate and punish our *Bitterness* of Spirit. And, to say true, 'tis a severe Reflection we draw upon our selves, that though *Pagan Emperors* could endure the *Addresses* of *Primitive Christians*, and *Christian Cæsars* receive the *Apologies* of *Infidels*, for Indulgence, yet it should be thought, of some Men, an Offence to seek it, or have it of a Christian Prince; whose Interest I dare say it is, and who himself so lately wanted it: But the Consideration of the Reason of this Offence, will increase our Admiration; for they tell us, *'tis dangerous to the Prince to suffer it*, while the Prince is himself a *Dissenter*: This Difficulty is beyond all Skill to remove, that it should be against the Interest of a *Dissenting* Prince to indulge *Dissent*. For though it will be granted there are Dissenters on differing Principles from those of the Prince, yet they are still Dissenters, and *Dissent* being the Prince's Interest, it will naturally follow, that those Dissenters are in the Interest of the Prince, whether they think on it or no.

Interest will not lye: Men embark'd in the same Vessel, seek the Safety of the *Whole* in their *Own*, whatever other Differences they may have. And *Self-Safety* is the highest worldly Security a Prince can have; for though all Parties would rejoyce their own Principles prevailed, yet every one is more solicitous about it's own Safety, than the other's Verity. Wherefore it cannot be unwise, by the Security of All, to make it the Interest as well as Duty of All, to advance that of the Publick.

Angry

Angry Things, then, set aside, As Matters now are, *What is best to be done?* This I take to be the Wise Man's Question, as to consider and answer it, will be his Business. *Moderation* is a Christian Duty, and it has ever been the Prudent Man's Practice. For those *Governments* that have used it in their Conduct, have succeeded best in all Ages.

I remember it is made in *Livy* the Wisdom of the *Romans*, that they relaxed their Hand to the *Privernates*, and thereby made them most faithful to their Interest. And it prevailed so much with the *Petilians*, that they would endure any Extremity from *Hannibal*, rather than desert their Friendship, even then, when the *Romans* discharged their Fidelity, and sent them the Despair of knowing they could not relieve them. So did one Act of *Humanity* overcome the *Falisci* above Arms: Which confirms that noble Saying of *Seneca, Mitius imperanti Melius paretur,* the mildest Conduct is best obeyed. A Truth Celebrated by *Grotius* and *Campanella*: Practised, doubtless, by the bravest Princes: For CYRUS exceeded, when he built the Jews a Temple, and himself no Jew: ALEXANDER astonished the Princes of his Train with the profound Veneration he paid the High Priest of that People: And AUGUSTUS was so far from suppressing the *Jewish Worship*, that he sent *Hecatombs* to *Jerusalem* to increase their Devotion. *Moderation* fill'd the Reigns of the most Renowned *Cæsars*: And Story says, they were *Neros* and *Caligulas* that loved Cruelty.

But others tell us that Dissenters are mostly *Antimonarchical*, and so not to be indulged, and that the Agreement of the Church of *England* and *Rome* in *Monarchy* and *Hierarchy*, with their Nearness in other Things should oblige her to grant the *Roman* Catholicks a special Ease, exclusive of the other Dissenters. But with the Leave of those Worthy Gentlemen, I would say, no Body is against that which is for him: And that the Aversion apprehended to be in some against the *Monarchy*, rather comes from Interest than Principle: For Governments were never destroy'd by the Interests they preserve.

In the next Place, it is as plain, that there is a *Fundamental* Difference between those Churches in Religion and Interest. In *Religion*, it appears by a Comparison of the *Thirty Nine Articles* with the Doctrine of the *Council* of *Trent*. In *Interest*, they differ; Fundamentally, because our Church is in the Actual Possession of the Churches and Livings that the other Church claims. What better Mixture then can these two Churches make than that of *Iron* and *Clay*? Nor do I think it well judged, or wise, in any that pretend to be Sons of the Church of *England*, to seek an Accommodation from the Topick of *Affinity*, since 'tis that some of her Dissenters have always objected, and she as constantly deny'd to be true.

I say, this Way of Reconciling or Indulging *Roman Catholicks* stumbles far greater Numbers of People of nearer Creeds, and gives the Church of *England* the Lye. But suppose the Trick took, and they only of all Dissenters had Indulgence, yet Their *Paucity* considered, I am sure, a Pair of Sir *Kenelm Digby*'s Breeches would set with as good a Grace upon the late Lord *Rochester*'s Dwarf. Upon the whole Matter, Let Men have *Ease*, and they will keep it; For those that might plot to get it, would *not plot to lose it*. Men love the Bridge they need and pass: And that Prince who has his People fast by Interest, holds them by the strongest human Tye; for other Courses have failed as often as they have been tried. Let us then once try a True Liberty: Never did the Circumstances of any Kingdom lye more open and fair to so blessed an Accommodation than we do at this Time.

But we are told, *The King has promised to maintain the Church of England*: I grant it: But if the *Church of England* claims the *King's Promise of Protection*, her *Dissenters* cannot forget *That* of his *Clemency*: And as they were both great, and admirably distinguished, so by no Means are they inconsistent or impracticable.

Will not his Justice let him be wanting in the *One*? And can his Greatness of Mind let him leave the *Other* behind him in the Storm, *unpity'd* and *unhelp'd*? Pardon me, we have not to do with an insensible Prince, but one that has been *Touch'd with our Infirmities*: More than any Body fit to judge our Cause, by the Share he once had in it. Who should give *Ease like the Prince that has wanted it*? To suffer for his own Conscience, looked Great; but to deliver other Men's, were Glorious. It is a Sort of paying the Vows of his Adversity, and it cannot therefore be done by any one else, with so much *Justice* and *Example*.

Far be it from me to solicite any Thing in Diminution of the Just Rights of the *Church of England*: Let her rest protected where she is. But I hope, none will be thought to intend her Wrong, for refusing to understand the *King's Promise* to her, in a *Ruinous Senfe* to all Others; and I am sure she would underſtand her own Intereſt better, if she were of the same Mind. For it is morally impoſſible that a *Conſcientious Prince* can be thought to have ty'd himſelf to compel others to a Communion, that himſelf cannot tell how to be of; or that any thing can oblige him to ſhake the Firmneſs of thoſe he has confirmed by his own *Royal Example*.

Having then ſo Illuſtrious an Inſtance of *Integrity*, as the Hazard of the Loſs of *Three Crowns* for *Conſcience*. Let it at leaſt excuſe Diſſenters *Conſtancy*, and provoke the Friends of the *Succeſſion* to *Moderation*, that no Man may loſe his *Birth-Right* for his *Perſwaſion*, and us to live *Dutifully*, and ſo *Peaceably* under our own Vine, and under our own Fig-Tree, with *Glory to God on High*, to the *King Honour*, and *Good-will to all Men*.

A PERSWASIVE to *Moderation,* &c.

MOderation, the Subject of this Diſcourſe, is in plainer *Engliſh*, *Liberty of Conſcience to* Church *Diſſenters*: A Cauſe I have, with all Humility, undertaken to plead, againſt the Prejudices of the Times.

That there is ſuch a Thing as *Conſcience*, and the *Liberty* of it, in Reference to *Faith* and *Worſhip* towards God, muſt not be denied, even by thoſe, that are moſt ſcandal'd at the *Ill* Uſe ſome ſeem to have made of ſuch Pretences. But to ſettle the Terms: By *Conſcience*, I underſtand *the Apprehenſion and Perſwaſion a Man has of his Duty to God*: By *Liberty of Conſcience*, I mean, *A Free and Open Profeſſion and Exerciſe of that Duty*; eſpecially in *Worſhip*: But I always premiſe this *Conſcience* to keep within the Bounds of *Morality*, and that it be neither *Frantick* nor *Miſchievous*, but a *Good Subject*, a *Good Child*, a *Good Servant*, in all the Affairs of Life: As exact to yield to *Cæſar* the Things that are *Cæſar's*, as jealous of withholding from God the Thing that is *God's*.

In brief, he that acknowledges the civil *Government* under which he lives, and that maintains no Principle hurtful to his Neighbour in his Civil Property.

For he that in any Thing violates his Duty to theſe Relations, cannot be ſaid to obſerve it to God, who ought to have his Tribute out of it. Such do not reject their *Prince*, *Parent*, *Maſter* or *Neighbour*, but God who enjoyns that Duty to them. Thoſe Pathetick Words of Chriſt will naturally enough reach the Caſe, *In that ye did it not to them, ye did it not to me*; for Duty to ſuch Relations hath a Divine Stamp: And Divine Right runs through more Things of the World, and Acts of our Lives, than we are aware of: And Sacrilege may be committed againſt more than the Church. Nor will a Dedication to God, of the Robbery from Man, expiate the Guilt of Diſobedience: For though Zeal could turn *Goſſip* to Theft, his Altars would renounce the Sacrifice.

The *Conſcience* then that I ſtate, and the *Liberty* I pray, carrying ſo great a *Salvo* and Deference to publick and private Relations, no ill Deſign can, with any Juſtice, be fix'd upon the Author, or Reflection upon the Subject, which by this Time, I think, I may venture to call a *Toleration*.

But to this ſo much craved, as well as needed, *Toleration*, I meet with two Objections of weight, the ſolving of which will make Way for it in this Kingdom. And the firſt is a Diſbelief of the Poſſibility of the Thing. *Toleration of Diſſenting Worſhips from that eſtabliſh'd, is not practicable* (ſay ſome) *without Danger to the State, with which it is interwoven.* This is Political. The other Objection is, *That admitting Diſſenters to be in the Wrong, (which is always premiſed by the National Church) ſuch Latitude were the Way to keep up the Diſ-union, and inſtead of compelling them into a better Way, leave them in the Poſſeſſion and Purſuit of their old Errors,* This is *Religious*. I think I have given the Objections fairly, 'twill be my next Buſineſs to anſwer them as fully.

The Strength of the firſt Objection againſt this Liberty, is the *Danger* ſuggeſted to the *State*; the Reaſon is, the National Form being *interwoven* with the Frame of the Government. But this ſeems to me only ſaid, and not only (with Submiſſion) not prov'd, but not true: For the Eſtabliſh'd Religion and Worſhip are no other Ways interwoven with the Government, than that the Government makes

Profession of them, and by divers Laws has made them the *Currant Religion*, and required all the Members of the State to conform to it.

This is nothing but what may as well be done by the Government, for any other Perswasion, as that. 'Tis true, 'tis not easy to change an Established Religion, nor is that the Question we are upon; but *State Religions* have been chang'd without the Change of the *States*. We see this in the Governments of *Germany* and *Denmark* upon the *Reformation*: But more clearly and near our selves, in the Case of *Henry the Eighth*, *Edward the Sixth*, *Queen Mary* and *Elizabeth*; for the Monarchy *stood*, the Family *remained* and *succeeded* under all the Revolutions of State-Religion, which could not have been, had the Proposition been generally true.

The Change of Religion then, does not *necessarily* change the Government, or alter the State; and if so, *a fortiori*, Indulgence of Church-Dissenters, does not *necessarily* hazard a Change of the State, where the present State-Religion or Church remains the same; for That I premise.

Some may say, *That it were more facile to change from one National Religion to another, than to maintain the Monarchy and Church, against the Ambition and Faction of divers Dissenting Parties.* But this is improbable at least. For it were to say, That it is an easier Thing to change a whole Kingdom, than with the Sovereign Power, followed with *Armies, Navies, Judges, Clergy*, and all the *Conformists* of the Kingdom, to secure the Government from the Ambition and Faction of *Dissenters*, as differing in their Interests within themselves, as in their Perswasions; and were they united, have neither Power to awe, nor Rewards to allure to their Party. They can only be formidable, when headed by the Sovereign. They may stop a *Gap*, or make, by his *Accession*, a Ballance: Otherwise, 'till 'tis harder to fight broken and divided Troops, than an entire Body of an Army, it will be always *easier* to maintain the Government under a Toleration of Dissenters, than in a total Change of Religion, and even then it self has not fail'd to have been preserved. But whether it be more or less easy, is not our Point; if they are many, the Danger is of Exasperating, not of making them easy; for the Force of our Question is, Whether such Indulgence be safe to the State? And here we have the first and last, the best and greatest Evidence for us, which is *Fact* and *Experience*, the Journal and Resolves of Time, and Treasure of the Sage.

For, *First*, The *Jews*, that had most to say for their Religion, and whose Religion was *Twin* to their State, (both being joined, and sent with Wonders from Heaven) *Indulged* Strangers in their Religious Dissents. They required but the Belief of the *Noachical* Principles, which were common to the World: No *Idolater*, and but a *Moral Man*, and he had his *Liberty*, ay, and some *Privileges* too; for he had an Apartment in the Temple, and this without Danger to the Government. Thus *Maimonides*, and others of their own Rabbies, and *Grotius* out of them.

The *Wisdom* of the *Gentiles* was very admirable in this, that though they had many Sects of Philosophers among them, each dissenting from the other in their Principles, as well as Discipline, and that not only in Physical Things, but Points *Metaphysical*, in which some of the Fathers were not *free*, the School-men *deeply engaged*, and our present Academies but too much *perplexed*; yet they *indulged* them and the best Livers with singular Kindness: The greatest Statesmen and Captains often becoming *Patrons* of the Sects they best affected, honouring their *Readings* with their Presence and Applause. So far were those Ages, which we have made as the Original of Wisdom and Politeness, from thinking *Toleration* an Error of State, or dangerous to the Government. Thus *Plutarch, Strabo, Laertius*, and others.

To these Instances I may add the Latitude of Old *Rome*, that had almost as many Deities as Houses: For *Varro* tells us of no less than *Thirty Thousand* several *Sacra*, or Religious Rites among her People, and yet without a Quarrel: Unhappy Fate of *Christianity!* the best of Religions, and yet her Professors maintain less Charity than Idolaters, while it should be peculiar to them. I fear, it shews us to have but little of it at Heart.

But nearer Home, and in our own Time, we see the Effects of a discreet *Indulgence*, even to Emulation. *Holland*, that *Bog* of the World, neither Sea nor dry Land, now the *Rival* of tallest Monarchs; not by *Conquests, Marriages*, or Accession of *Royal Blood*, the usual Ways to Empire, but by her own superlative *Clemency* and *Industry*; for the one was the Effect of the other: She cherished her People, whatsoever were their *Opinions*, as the reasonable Stock of the Country, the Heads and Hands of her Trade and Wealth; and making them eafy in the main Point, their *Confcience*, fhe became Great by them; This made her fill with *People*, and they filled her with *Riches* and *Strength*.

And if it fhould be faid, *She is upon her Declenfion for all that*. I anfwer, All States muft know it, nothing is here *Immortal*. Where are the *Babylonian*, *Perfian*, and *Grecian* Empires? And are not *Lacedæmon*, *Athens*, *Rome* and *Carthage* gone before her? Kingdoms and Commonwealths have their *Births* and *Growths*, their *Declenfions* and *Deaths*, as well as private Families and Perfons; But 'tis owing neither to the *Armies* of *France*, nor *Navies* of *England*, but her own *Domeftick* Troubles.

Seventy Two fticks in her Bones yet: The growing Power of the Prince of *Orange*, muft, in fome Degree, be an *Ebb* to that State's Strength; for they are not fo unanimous and vigorous in their Intereft as formerly: But were they fecure againft the Danger of their own Ambition and Jealoufy, any Body might infure their Glory at *five per Cent*. But fome of their greateft Men apprehending they are in their *Climacterical Juncture*, give up the Ghoft, and care not, if they muft fall, by what Hand it is.

Others chufe a *Stranger*, and think one afar off will give the beft Terms, and leaft annoy them: Whilft a confiderable Party have chofen a *Domeftick* Prince, *Kin* to their early Succeffes by the *Fore-father's Side* (the Gallantry of his Anceftors) And that his own Greatnefs and Security are wrapt up in theirs, and therefore modeftly hope to find their Account in his Profperity. But this is a Kind of Digreffion, only before I leave it, I dare venture to add, that if the Prince of *Orange* changes not the Policies of that State, he will not change her Fortune, and he will mightily add to his own.

But perhaps I fhall be told, *That no Body doubts that* Toleration *is an* agreeable *Thing to a Commonwealth, where every one thinks he has a Share in the Government; ay, that the one is the Confequence of the other, and therefore moft carefully to be avoided by all Monarchical States*. This indeed were fhrewdly to the Purpofe, in *England*, if it were but true. But I don't fee how there can be one true Reafon advanc'd in Favour of this Objection: *Monarchies*, as well as *Commonwealths*, fubfifting by the Prefervation of the People under them.

But, *Firft*, if this were true, it would follow, by the *Rule of Contraries*, that a *Republick* could not fubfift with *Unity* and *Hierarchy*, which is *Monarchy* in the Church; but it muft, from fuch *Monarchy* in *Church*, come to *Monarchy* in *State* too. But *Venice*, *Genoa*, *Lucca*, feven of the *Cantons of Switzerland*, (and *Rome* her felf, for fhe is an *Ariftocracy*) all under the loftieft *Hierarchy* in Church, and where is no *Toleration*, fhew in Fact, that the contrary is true.

But, *Secondly*, This Objection makes a Commonwealth the better Government of the Two, and fo overthrows the Thing it would eftablifh. This is effectually done, if I know any thing, fince a Commonwealth is hereby rendred a more copious, powerful and beneficial Government to Mankind, and is made better to anfwer Contingencies and Emergencies of State, becaufe this fubfifts *either* Way, but *Monarchy* not, if the Objection be true. The one profpers by *Union* in Worfhip and Difcipline, and by *Toleration* of Diffenting Churches from the National. The other only by an *Univerfal Conformity* to a National Church. I fay, this makes *Monarchy* (in it felf, doubtlefs, an admirable Government) *lefs Powerful, lefs Extended, lefs Propitious*, and finally *lefs Safe* to the People under it, than a *Commonwealth*; In that *no Security* is left to *Monarchy* under Diverfity of Worfhips, which yet no Man can defend or forbid, but may often arrive, as it hath in *England*, more than five Times, in the Two Laft Ages. And truly 'tis natural for Men to chufe to fettle where they may be fafeft from the *Power* and *Mifchief* of fuch Accidents of State.

Upon the whole Matter, it is to reflect the *laft Mifchief* upon *Monarchy*, the worft Enemies it has could hope to difgrace, or endanger it by; fince it is to tell the People under it, that they muft either *conform*, or be *deftroy'd*, or to fave themfelves, turn *Hypocrites*, or *change* the Frame of the Government they live under. A Perplexity both to *Monarch* and *People*, that nothing can be greater, but the Comfort of knowing the Objection is *Falfe*. And that which ought to make every reafonable Man of this Opinion, is the Cloud of Witneffes that almoft every Age of *Monarchy* affords us.

I will begin with that of *Ifrael*, the moft exact and facred Pattern of *Monarchy*, begun by a valiant Man, tranflated to the beft, and improv'd by the wifeft of Kings, whose Ministers were neither *Fools*, nor *Fanaticks*: Here we shall find Provision for Dissenters: Their *Proselyti Domicilii* were so far from being compelled to their National Rites, that they were expresly forbid to observe them. Such were the *Egyptians* that came with them out of *Egypt*, the *Gibeonites* and *Canaanites*, a great People, that after their several Forms, worshipt in an *Apartment* of the same Temple. The *Jews* with a Liturgy, they without one: The *Jews* had *Priests*, but these none: The *Jews* had Variety of Oblations, these People burnt Offerings only. All that was required of them was the natural Religion of *Noah*, in which the Acknowledgment and Worship of the true God, was, and it still ought to be, the main Point; nay, so far were they from Coercive Conformity, that they did not so much as oblige them to observe their *Sabbath*, though one of the Ten Commandments: *Grotius* and *Selden* say more. Certainly this was great Indulgence, since so unsuitable an Usage lookt like *prophaning* their Devotion, and a common *Nusance* to their National Religion. One would think by this, that their Care lay on the Side of preserving their Cult from the *Touch* or *Accession* of Dissenters, and not of *forcing* them, by *undoing* Penalties, to conform. This must needs be evident: For if God's *Religion* and *Monarchy* (for so we are taught to believe it) did not, and would not, at a Time when Religion lay *less* in the Mind, and *more* in Ceremony, compel Conformity from Dissenters, we hope we have got the best Presidents on our side.

But if this Instance be of most Authority, we have another very exemplary, and to our Point Pertinent; for it shews what *Monarchy* may do: It is yielded us from the famous Story of *Mordecai*. He, with his *Jews*, were in a bad plight with the King *Ahasuerus*, by the ill Offices *Haman* did them: The Arguments he used were drawn from the common Topicks of *Faction* and *Sedition*, That they were an odd and dangerous People, under differing Laws of their own, and refused Obedience to his; So denying his *Supremacy*. Dissenters with a witness: Things most tender to any Government.

The King thus incensed, commands the Laws to be put in Execution, and decrees the Ruin of *Mordecai* with all the *Jews*: But the King is timely intreated, his Heart softens, the Decree is revok'd, and *Mordecai* and his Friends saved. The Consequence was, as extream Joy to the *Jews*, so Peace and Blessings to the King. And that which heightens the Example, is the *Greatness* and *Infidelity* of the Prince: Had the Instance been in a *Jew*, it might have been placed to his *greater Light*, or *Piety*: In a petty Prince, to the *Paucity* or *Intireness* of his Territories: But that an *Heathen*, and King of One Hundred and seven and twenty Provinces, should *throughout* his vast Dominions not fear, but *practise Toleration* with good Success, has something admirable in it.

If we please to remember the Tranquility, and Success of those Heathen *Roman* Emperours, that allowed *Indulgence*; that *Augustus* sent *Hecatombs* to *Jerusalem*, and the wisest honoured the *Jews*, and at least spared the divers Sects of *Christians*, it will certainly oblige us to think, that Princes, whose Religions are *nearer of kin*, to those of the Dissenters of our Times, may not unreasonably hope for quiet from a discreet Toleration, especially when there is nothing peculiar in *Christianity* to render Princes unsafe in such an *Indulgence*. The admirable Prudence of the Emperour *Jovianus*, in a quite contrary Method to those of the Reigns of his Predecessors, settled the most *Imbroiled* Time of the Christian World, *almost to a Miracle*; for though he found the Heats of the *Arrians* and *Orthodox* carried to a barbarous Height, (to say nothing of the *Novatians*, and other dissenting Interests) the Emperour esteeming those Calamities the Effect of Coercing Conformity to the Prince's or State's Religion, and that this Course did not only waste *Christians*, but expose *Christians* to the Scorn of *Heathens*, and so scandal those whom they should convert, he resolutely declared, *That he would have none* molested *for the different Exercise of their Religious Worship*; which (and that in a trice (for he reigned but seven Months) calm'd the impetuous Storms of Dissention, and reduced the Empire, before agitated with the most uncharitable Contests) to a wonderful *Security* and *Peace*; Thus a *kindly Amity* brought a *Civil Unity* to the *State*; which endeavours for a forc'd Unity never did to the Church, but had formerly filled the Government with incomparable *Miseries*, as well as the Church with Incharity: And which is sad, I must needs say, that those *Leaders* of the *Church* that should have been the *Teachers* and *Examples* of Peace, in so singular a Juncture of the *Churches* ferment, did, more than any, *blow the Trumpet, and kindle the Fire,*

Fire of Division. So dangerous is it to *Super-fine* upon the Text, and then *Impose* it upon Penalty, for Faith.

Valentinian the Emperour (we are told by *Socrates Scholasticus*) was a great Honourer of those that favoured his own Faith; but so, as he *molested not the* Arrians at all. And *Marcellinus* farther adds in his Honour, *That he was much Renown'd for his Moderate Carriage during his Reign*; insomuch, that amongst sundry Sects of Religion, he troubled *no Man for his Conscience*, imposing neither This nor That to be *observed*; much less, with menacing Edicts and Injunctions, did he compel others, *his Subjects, to bow the Neck*, or conform *to that which himself Worshipped, but left such Points as clear and untouched as he found them.*

Gratianus, and *Theodosius* the Great, Indulg'd divers Sorts of *Christians*; but the *Novatians* of all the Dissenters were prefer'd: Which was so far from *Insecuring*, that it preserv'd the *Tranquility* of the *Empire*. Nor till the Time of *Celestine* Bishop of *Rome*, were the *Novatians* disturbed; And the *Persecution* of them, and the Assumption of the *secular Power*, began much at the same Time. But the *Novatians* at *Constantinople* were not dealt withal; for the *Greek* Bishops continued to permit them the quiet Enjoyment of their dissenting Assemblies; as *Socrates* tells us in his fifth and seventh Books of Ecclesiastical Story.

I shall descend nearer our own Times; for notwithstanding no Age has been more furiously moved, than that which *Jovianus* found, and therefore the Experiment of Indulgence *was never better made*, yet to speak more in View of this Time of Day, we find our Contemporaries, of remoter Judgments in Religion, under no manner of Difficulty in this Point. The *Grand Seignior, Great Mogul, Czars* of *Muscovia, King* of *Persia*; the Great *Monarchs* of the *East* have *long allow'd and prosper'd with a Toleration:* And who does not know that this gave Great *Tamerlane* his mighty Victories? In these Western Countries we see the same Thing.

Cardinal d'Ossat in his 92d Letter to *Villeroy*, Secretary to *Henry* the Fourth of *France*, gives us Doctrine and Example for the Subject in hand; " Besides (says he)
" that Necessity has no Law, be it in what Case it will; our *Lord Jesus Christ* in-
" structs us by his Gospel, *To let the Tares alone, lest removing them may endanger*
" *the Wheat*. That other *Catholick* Princes have allow'd it without *Rebuke*. That
" particularly the Duke of *Savoy*, who (as great a Zealot as he would be thought
" for the Catholick Religion) Tolerates the Hereticks in three of his Provinces,
" namely, *Angroyne, Lucerne* and *Perone*. That the King of *Poland* does as much,
" not only in *Sweedland*, but in *Poland* it self. That all the Princes of the *Austrian*
" Family, that are celebrated as Pillars of the *Catholick Church*, do the like, not
" only in the Towns of the Empire, but in their proper Territories, as in *Austria*
" it self, from whence they take the Name of their Honour. In *Hungary, Bohe-*
" *mia, Moravia, Lusatia, Stirria, Camiolia* and *Croatia* the like. That *Charles* the
" Fifth, Father of the King of *Spain*, was the Person that taught the King of
" *France*, and other *Princes*, how to yield to such Emergencies. That his Son, the
" present King of *Spain*, who is esteemed *Arch Catholick*, and that is, as the *Atlas*
" of the *Catholick Church*, *Tolerates* notwithstanding, at this Day, in his Kingdoms
" of *Valentia* and *Granada*, the *Moors* themselves in their *Mahometism*, and has
" offered to those of *Zealand, Holland*, and other *Hereticks* of the Low Countries,
" the *free Exercise* of their pretended Religion, so that they will but *acknowledge*
" and *Obey* him in *Civil Matters*. It was of those Letters of this extraordinary Man, for so he was (whether we regard him in his Ecclesiastical Dignity, or his greater Christian and Civil Prudence) that the great Lord *Fulkland* said, *A Minister of State should no more be without* Cardinal d' Ossat's *Letters, than a Parson without his Bible.* And indeed, if we look into *France*, we shall find the Indulgence of those Protestants, hath been a flourishing to that Kingdom, as their *Arms* a Succour to their King. 'Tis true, that since they helpt the Ministers of his Greatness to Success, that haughty Monarch has chang'd his Measures, and resolves their Conformity to his own Religion, or their Ruin; but no Man can give another Reason for it, than that he thinks it for his Turn to please that Part of his own Church, which are the present necessary and unwearied Instruments of his absolute Glory. But let us see the End of this Conduct, it will require more Time to approve the Experiment.

As it was the Royal Saying of *Stephen, King* of *Poland*, That he was a *King* of Men, *and not of* Conscience; *a Commander of* Bodies, and not of Souls. So we see a *Toleration* has been practised in that Country of a long Time, with no ill Success to the State; the Cities of *Cracovia, Racovia*, and many other Towns of

Note, almost wholly dissenting from the common *Religion of the Kingdom*, which is *Roman Catholick*, as the others are *Socinian* and *Calvinist*, mighty opposite to that, as well as to themselves.

The King of *Denmark*, in his large Town of *Altona*, but about a Mile from *Hamburgh*, and therefore called so, that is, *All-to-near*, is a pregnant Proof to our Point. For though his Seat be so remote from that Place, another strong and insinuating State so near, yet under his *Indulgence* of divers Persuasions, they enjoy their *Peace*, and he that *Security*, that he is not upon better Terms in any of his more *immediate* and *Uniform* Dominions. I leave it to the thinking Reader, if it be not much owing to this *Freedom*, and if a contrary Course were not the Way for him to furnish his Neighbours with Means to Depopulate that Place, or make it uneasie and chargeable to him to keep?

If we look into other Parts of *Germany*, where we find a Stout and Warlike People, fierce for the Thing they opine, or believe, we shall find, the Prince *Palatine* of the *Rhine* has been safe, and more potent by his *Indulgence*, witness his *Improvements* at *Manheim*: And as (believe me) he acted the Prince to his People in other Things, so in this to the Empire; for he made bold with the Constitution of it in the Latitude he gave his Subjects in this Affair.

The *Elector* of *Brandenburg* is himself a *Calvinist*, his People mostly *Lutheran*, yet in Part of his *Dominions*, the *Roman Catholicks* enjoy their Churches quietly.

The Duke of *Newburg*, and a *strict Roman Catholick*, Brother-in-Law to the present Emperor, in his Province of *Juliers*, has, not only at *Dewsburg*, *Mulheim*, and other Places, but in *Duseldorp* it self, where the Court resides, *Lutheran*, and *Calvinist*, as well as *Roman Catholick*, Assemblies.

The Elector of *Saxony*, by Religion a *Lutheran*, in his City of *Budissin*, has both *Lutherans* and *Roman Catholicks* in the same Church, parted only by a Grate.

In *Ausburg*, they have two chief Magistrates, as their *Duumvirat*, one must always be a *Roman Catholick*, and the other a *Lutheran*.

The Bishop of *Osnabrug* is himself a *Lutheran*, and in the Town of his Title, the *Roman Catholicks*, as well as *Lutherans*, have their Churches: And which is more, the next Bishop must be a *Catholick* too: For like the Buckets in the Well, they take turns: One way to be sure, so that one be but in the Right.

From hence we will go to *Sultzbach*, a small Territory, but has a great Prince, I mean, in his own *extraordinary* Qualities; for, among other Things, we shall find him act the Moderator among his People. By Profession he is a *Roman Catholick*, but has *Simultaneum Religionis Exercitium*, not only *Lutherans* and *Roman Catholicks* enjoy their different Worships, but *alternatively* in one and the same Place, the same Day; so ballancing his Affection by his Wisdom, that there appears neither Partiality in him, nor Envy in them, though of such opposite Persuasions.

I will end these Foreign Instances with a Prince and Bishop, all in one, and he a *Roman Catholick* too, and that is the Bishop of *Mentz*; who admits, with a very peaceable Success such *Lutherans*, with his *Catholicks*, to enjoy their Churches, as live in his Town of *Erford*. Thus doth Practice tell us, that neither *Monarchy* nor *Hierarchy* are in danger from a Toleration. On the contrary, the Laws of the Empire, which are the Acts of the *Emperour*, and the *Soveraign Princes* of it, have Tolerated these three Religious Persuasions, *viz.* The *Roman Catholick*, *Lutheran* and *Calvinist*, and they may as well tolerate three more, for the same Reasons, and with the same Success. For it is not their *greater Nearness* or consistency in Doctrine, or in Worship; on the contrary, they differ much, and by that, and other Circumstances, are sometimes engaged in great Controversies, yet is a Toleration practicable, and the Way of Peace with them.

And which is closest to our Point, at home it self, we see that a *Toleration* of the *Jews*, *French* and *Dutch* in *England*, all *Dissenters* from the *National Way*: And the Connivance that has been in *Ireland*: and the down-right *Toleration* in most of the Kings *Plantations* abroad, prove the Assertion, *That Toleration is not dangerous to Monarchy*. For Experience tells us, where it is in any Degree admitted, the King's Affairs prosper most; *People*, *Wealth* and *Strength* being sure to follow such *Indulgence*.

But after all that I have said in Reason and Fact, why *Toleration* is safe to *Monarchy*, Story tells us that worse Things have befallen Princes in Countries under *Ecclesiastical Union*, than in Places under divided Forms of Worship; and so Tolerating Countries stand to the Prince, upon more than equal Terms with *Conforming*

ing ones. And where Princes have been exposed to hardship in tolerating Countries, they have as often come from the Conforming, as Non-conforming Party; and so the *Dissenter* is upon equal Terms, to the Prince or State, with the *Conformist*.

The first is evident in the *Jews*, under the Conduct of *Moses*; their Dissention came from the Men of their own Tribes, such as *Corah, Dathan* and *Abiram*, with their Partakers. To say nothing of the *Gentiles*.

The Miseries and Slaughters of *Mauritius* the Emperor, prove my Point, who by the greatest *Church-men* of his Time was withstood, and his Servant that perpetrated the *Wickedness, by them*, substituted in his Room, because more officious to their Grandure. What Power but that of the *Church*, dethroned *Childerick*, King of *France*, and set *Pepin* in his Place? The Miseries of the Emperours, *Henry* the fourth and fifth, Father and Son, from their rebellious Subjects, raised and animated by the Power of *Conformists*, dethroning both, as much as they could, are notorious. 'Tis alledg'd, that *Sigismund* King of *Sweedland*, was rejected by that *Lutheran* Country, because he was a *Roman Catholick*.

If we come nearer home, which is most suitable to the Reasons of the *Discourse*, we find the *Church-men* take part with *William Rufus*, and *Henry* the first, against *Robert* their elder Brother; and after that, we see some of the greatest of them *made Head* against their King, namely *Anselm* Arch-Bishop of *Canterbury*, and his Party, as did his Successor *Thomas* of *Becket* to the second *Henry*. *Stephen* usurp'd the Crown when there was a *Church Union*: And King *John* lived *miserable* for all that, and at last died *by one of his own Religion too*. The Dissentions that agitated the Reign of his Son *Henry* the third, and the *Barons* War, with Bishop *Grosteeds* Blessing to *Mumford* their General: The *Deposition* and *Murther* of the second *Edward*, and *Richard*, and sixth *Henry*, and his Son the Prince. The Usurpation of *Richard* the Third, and the Murther of the Sons of *Edward* the fourth, in the Tower of *London*. The *civil War* that followed between him and the Earl of *Richmond*, afterwards our Wife *Henry* the seventh, were all perpetrated in a Country of *one Religion*, and by the Hands of *Conformists*. In short, if we will but look upon the civil War that so long raged in this Kingdom, between the Houses of *York* and *Lancaster*, and consider that they professed but one and the same Religion, and both back't with Numbers of Church-men too (to say nothing of the Miserable end of many of our Kings princely Ancestors in *Scotland*, especially the first and third *James*) we shall find Cause to say, *That Church-Uniformity is not a Security for Princes to depend upon*.

If we will look next into Countries where *Dissenters* from the National Church are *Tolerated*, we shall find the *Conformist* not less Culpable than the *Dissenter*.

The Disorders among the *Jews*, after they were settled in the Land that God had given them, came not from those they tolerated, but themselves. They *cast off Samuel*, and the Government of the *Judges*. 'Twas the Children of the *National* Church, that fell in with the Ambition of *Absolom*, and animated the Rebellion against their Father *David*. They were the same that revolted from *Solomon's* Son, and cryed in behalf of *Jeroboam, To your Tents, O Israel!*

Not two Ages ago, the Church of *France*, too generally fell in with the Family of *Guise*, against their lawful Soveraign, *Henry* the Fourth: Nor were they without Countenance of the greatest of their Belief, who stiled it an *Holy War:* At that Time, fearing (not without Cause) the *Defection* of that Kingdom from the *Roman* See. In this Conjuncture, the *Dissenters* made up the best Part of that King's Armies, and by their *Loyalty* and *Blood*, preserv'd the *Blood Royal* of *France*, and set the Crown on the Head of that Prince. That King was twice Assassinated, and the last Time Murdered, as was *Henry* the third, his Predecessor; but they fell, one by the Hand of a *Churchman*, the other, at least by a *Conformist*.

'Tis true, that the next civil War was between the *Catholicks* and the *Huguenots*, under the Conduct of *Cardinal Richlieu*, and the *Duke of Rohan*: But as I will not justifie the Action, so their *Liberties* and *Cautions* so solemnly settled by *Henry* the Fourth, as the Reward of their singular Merit, being by the Ministry of that *Cardinal* invaded, they say, they did but defend their Security, and that rather against the *Cardinal*, than the *King*, whose Softness suffered him to become a Property to the great *Wit* and *Ambition* of that Person: And there is this Reason to believe them, that if it had been otherwise, we are sure that King *Charles* the First would not in the least have countenanced the Quarrel.

However,

However, the *Cardinal*, like himself, wisely knew when to stop: For though he thought it the Interest of the Crown, to moderate their Greatness, and check their Growth, yet having fresh in Memory the Story of the foregoing Age, he saw, *'Twas Wise to have a Ballance upon Occasion*. But this was more than recompenc'd in their fixt Adhesion to the Crown of *France*, under the Ministry and Direction of the succeeding *Cardinal*, when their Perswasion had not only Number, and many good Officers to value it self upon, but yielded their *King* the ablest Captain of the Age, namely, *Turene*: It was an *Huguenot* then, at the Head of almost an *Huguenot* Army, that fell in with a *Cardinal* himself (see the Union Interest makes) to maintain the Imperial Crown of *France*, and that on a *Roman-Catholick*'s Head: And together *with their own Indulgence, that Religion, as National too*, against the Pretences of a *Roman-Catholick Army*, headed by a Prince Brave and Learned of the same Religion.

I mention not this, to prefer one Party to another; for contrary Instances may be given else-where, as Interests have varied. In *Sweedland* a Prince was rejected by *Protestants*; And in *England* and *Holland*, and many of the *Principalities of Germany*, *Roman-Catholicks* have approv'd themselves Loyal to their *Kings, Princes and States*. But this suffices to us that we gain the Point; for it is evident in Countries where *Dissenters* are Tolerated, the *Insecurity of the Prince and Government may as well come from the Conforming, as Dissenting Party*, and that it comes not from Dissenters, *because such*.

But how Happy and Admirable was this Civil Union between the *Cardinal* and *Turene*? Two most opposite Religions, both follow'd by People of their own Perswasion: One says his *Mass*, t'other his *Directory*: Both invoke *One Deity*, by several Ways, for *One Success*, and it followed with Glory, and a Peace to this Day. O why should it be otherwise now! What has been may be: Methinks Wisdom and Charity are on that Side still.

It will doubtless be objected, *That the Dissenting Party of England, fell in with the State-Dissenter in our late Civil, but Unnatural War*: And this seems to be against us, yet Three Things must be confessed: *First*, That the War rather made the *Dissenters*, than the *Dissenters* made the War. *Secondly*, That those that were then in being, were not Tolerated, as in *France*, but prosecuted. And, *Lastly*, That they did not lead, but follow great Numbers of *Church-Goers*, of all Qualities, in that unhappy Controversie; and which began upon other Topicks than Liberty for *Church-Dissenters*. And though they were herein blameable, Reason is Reason, in all Climates and Latitudes. This does not affect the Question: Such Calamities are no *necessary Consequences of Church-Dissent*, because they would then follow in all Places where *Dissenters* are *Tolerated*, which we see they do not: But these may sometimes indeed be the Effects of a violent Endeavour of *Uniformity, and that under all Forms of Government*, as I fear they were partly here under our Monarchy. But then, this teaches us to conclude, that a *Toleration* of those, that a contrary Course makes uneasie and desperate, may prevent or cure *Intestine Troubles*; as *Anno Forty Eight*; it ended the Strife, and settled the Peace of *Germany*. For 'tis not now the Question, *How far Men may be provoked, or ought to resent it*; but, *Whether Government is Safe in a Toleration, especially Monarchy*: And to this Issue we come in Fact, *That 'tis Safe, and that Conformists* (generally speaking) *have, for their Interests, as rarely known their Duty to their Prince, as Dissenters for their Consciences*. So that the Danger seems to lye on this Side, of *forcing Uniformity* against Faith, upon severe Penalties, rather than of a discreet *Toleration*.

In the next Place, I shall endeavour to shew the *Prudence* and *Reasonableness* of a *Toleration*, by the great Benefits that follow it.

Toleration, which is an Admission of *Dissenting Worships, with Impunity to the Dissenters, secures Property*, which is *Civil Right*, and *That Eminently the Line and Power of the Monarchy*: For if no Man suffer in his *Civil Right* for the Sake of such *Dissent*, the Point of *Succession* is settled without *a Civil War, or a Recantation*; since it were an absurd Thing to imagine, that a Man born to *Five Pounds a Year*, should not be liable to forfeit his Inheritance for *Non-Conformity*, and yet a *Prince of the Blood, and an Heir to the Imperial Crown, should be made incapable of Inheritance for his Church-Dissent*.

The Security then of *Property, or Civil Right*, from being forfeitable for Religious Dissent, becomes a Security to the *Royal Family*, against the Difficulties lately labour'd under in the Business of the *Succession*. And though I have no Commission for it, besides the great Reason and Equity of the Thing it self, I dare say, there can hardly be a *Dissenter* at this Time of Day so void of Sense and Justice, as well as Duty and Loyalty, as not to be of the same Mind. Else it were to deny that to the *Prince*, which he needs, and prays for from him. Let us not forget the Story of *Sigismund* of *Sweedland*, of *Henry the Fourth* of *France*, and especially of our *Own Queen Mary*. Had *Property* been fix't, the Line of those Royal Families could not have met with any Let or Interruption. 'Twas this Consideration that prevail'd with Judge *Hales*, though a strong *Protestant*, after King *Edward*'s Death, to give his Opinion for *Queen Mary*'s Succession, against that of all the Rest of the Judges to the contrary: Which Noble President, was recompenc'd in the Loyalty of *Archbishop* Heath, *a Roman Catholick*, in favour of the Succession of *Queen Elizabeth*: And the same Thing would be done again, in the like Case, by Men of the same Integrity.

I know it may be said, *That there is little Reason now for the Prince to regard this Argument in Favour of Dissenters, when it was so little heeded in the Case of the* Presumptive Heir *to the Crown*. But as this was the Act and Heat of Conforming Men within Doors, so if it were, in Counsel or Desire, the Folly and Injustice of any Dissenters without Doors, shall many entire Parties pay the Reckoning of the few busie Offenders? They would humbly hope, that the singular Mildness and Clemency, which make up so great a Part of the King's publick Assurances, will not leave him in his Reflection here.

'Tis the Mercies of Princes, that above all their Works, give them the nearest Resemblance to Divinity in their Administration. Besides, it is their Glory to measure their Actions by the Reason and Consequence of Things, and not by the Passions that possess and animate private Breasts: For it were fatal to the Interest of a Prince, *that the Folly or Undutifulness of any of his Subjects*, should put him out of the Way, or tempt him *to be unsteady to his Principle and Interest:* And yet, with Submission, I must say, it would be the Consequence of Coercion: For, by exposing *Property for Opinion*, the Prince exposes the Consciences and Property of his own Family, and plainly *Disarms* them of all Defence, *upon any Alteration of Judgment*. Let us remember, *That several of the same Gentlemen, who at first Sacrificed Civil Rights for Non-Conformity in common Dissenters, fell at last to make the Succession of the Crown the Price of Dissent in the next Heir of the Royal Blood.* So dangerous a Thing it is to hazard Property to serve a Turn for any Party, or suffer such Examples in the Case of the meanest Person in a Kingdom.

Nor is this all the Benefit that attends the Crown by the Preservation of Civil Rights; for the Power of the Monarchy is kept more Entire by it. The King has the Benefit of his whole People, and the Reason of their Safety is owing to their Civil, and not Ecclesiastical Obedience: *Their Loyalty to* Cæsar, *and not Conformity to the Church*. Whereas the other Opinion would have it, *That no Conformity to the Church, No Property in the State:* Which is to clog and narrow the Civil Power, for at this Rate, *No Church-Man, No English-Man*; and, *No Conformist, No Subject*. A Way to *alien* the King's People, and practise an *Exclusion* upon him, from, it may be, a Fourth Part of his Dominions. Thus it may happen, that the ablest Statesman, the bravest Captain, and the best Citizen may be disabled, and the Prince forbid their Employment to his Service.

Some Instances of this we have had since the late King's Restoration: For upon the first *Dutch-War*, Sir *William Penn* being commanded to give in a List of the ablest Sea-Officers in the Kingdom, to serve in that Expedition, I do very well remember he presented our present King with a Catalogue of the knowingest and bravest Officers the Age had bred, with this Subscrib'd, *These Men, if his Majesty will please to admit of their Perswasions, I will answer for their Skill, Courage and Integrity*. He pickt them by their Ability, not their Opinions; and he was in the Right; for that was the best Way of doing the King's Business. And of my own Knowledge, *Conformity robb'd the King at that Time of Ten Men, whose greater Knowledge and Valour, than any One Ten of that Fleet, had in their Room, been able to have saved a Battel, or perfected a Victory*. I will Name Three of them: The *First* was Old Vice Admiral *Goodson*, than whom, No-body was more Stout, or a Seaman. The *Second*, Captain *Hill*, that in the *Saphire*, beat Admiral *Everson* Hand to Hand, that came to the Relief of *Old Trump*. The *Third*, was Captain *Potter*, that in the *Constant Warwick*, took Captain *Beach*, after Eight Hours smart *Dispute*. And as evident it is, *That if a War had proceeded between this Kingdom and* France *Seven Years ago, the Business of* Conformity *had deprived the King of* many *Land-Officers*, whose Share in the late Wars of *Europe*, had made knowing and able.

But which is worst of all, such are not Safe, with their *Dissent*, under their own Extraordinary Prince. For, *though a Man were a Great Honourer of his* King, *a Lover of his* Country, *an Admirer of the* Government: *In the Course of his Life, Sober, Wise, Industrious and Useful*; if *a* Dissenter *from the Establisht Form of Worship, in that Condition there is no* Liberty *for his Person, nor* Security *to his Estate:* As *Useless* to the Publick, so *Ruin'd* in himself. For this *Net catches the Best.* Men True to their Conscience, and who indulged, are most like to be so to their Prince; whilst the rest are left to *cozen* him by their Change; for that is the *Unhappy End of Forc'd Conformity in the Poor Spirited Compliers*. And this must always be the Consequence of *necessitating the Prince to put more and other Tests upon his People, than are requisite to secure him of their Loyalty*.

And when we shall be so Happy in our Measures, as to consider this Mischief to the *Monarchy*, it is to be hop'd, it will be thought expedient to dis-intangle *Property from Opinion*, and cut the untoward Knot some Men have tyed, that hath so long hamper'd and gaul'd the Prince as well as People. It will be then, when Civil Punishments shall no more follow Church Faults, that the *Civil Tenure* will be recover'd to the Government, and the *Natures* of Acts, Rewards and Punishments, so distinguish'd, as *Loyalty* shall be the Safety of *Dissent*, and the whole People made useful to the Government.

It will, perhaps, be objected, *That Dissenters can hardly be obliged to be True to the* Crown, *and so the* Crown *unsafe in their very Services; for they may easily turn the Power given them to serve it, against it, to Greaten themselves.* I am willing to obviate every Thing, that may with any Pretence be offerr'd against our intreated Indulgence. I say *No*, and appeal to the *King* himself (against whom the Prejudices of our late Times ran highest, and who therefore has most Reason to Resent) If ever He was better Lov'd or Serv'd, than by the *Old Round-headed Seamen*, the Earl of *Sandwich*, Sir *William Penn*, Sir *J. Lawson*, Sir *G. Ascue*, Sir *R. Stanier*, Sir *J. Smith*, Sir *J. Jordan*, Sir *J. Harmon*, Sir *Christopher Minns*, Captain *Sansum, Cuttins, Clark, Robinson, Molton, Wager, Tern, Parker, Haward, Hubbard, Fen, Langhorn, Daws, Earl, White*; to say nothing of many yet Living, of Real Merit, and many Inferior Officers, Expert and Brave. And to do our *Prince* Justice, He *deserv'd* it from them, by his Humility, Plainness and Courage, and the Care and Affection that he always shew'd them.

If any say, *That most of these Men were Conformists*, I presume to tell them, I know as well as any Man, they Serv'd the King never the Better for that: On the contrary, 'twas all the Strife that some of them had in themselves, in the doing that Service, that they must not serve the King without it; and if in that they could have been Indulged, they had perform'd it with the greatest Alacrity. *Interest* will not lye. Where People find their Reckoning, they are sure to be *True*. For 'tis Want of Wit that makes any Man false to himself. 'Twas he that knew all Men's Hearts, that said, *Where the Treasure is, there will the Heart be also*. Let Men be easie, safe, and upon their Preferment with the Prince, and they will be Dutiful, Loyal, and most Affectionate.

Mankind by Nature fears Power, and melts at Goodness. Pardon my Zeal, I would not be thought to plead for *Dissenters Preferment*; 'tis enough they keep what they have, and may live at their own Charges. Only I am for having the *Prince have Room for his Choice*, and not be crampt and stinted by Opinion; but imploy those who are best able to serve him: And, *I think out of Six Parties, 'tis better picking, than out of One*, and therefore the Prince's Interest is to be Head of all of them, which a *Toleration effects in a Moment*, since those *Six* (divided Interests, within themselves) having but *One Civil Head*, become one intire *Civil Body to the Prince*. And I am sure, I have *Monarchy* on my Side, if *Solomon* and his Wisdom may stand for it, who tells us, *That the Glory of a King is in the Multitude of his People*.

Nor is this all, *for the Consequences of such an Universal Content, would be of infinite Moment to the Security of the* Monarchy, *both at Home and Abroad*. At *Home*, for it would Behead the Factions without Blood, and Banish the Ringleaders without going abroad. When the Great Bodies of *Dissenters* see the Care of the Government for their Safety, they have no Need of their Captains, nor these any Ground for their Pretences: For as they us'd the People to value themselves, and raise their Fortunes with the *Prince*, so the People follow'd their Leaders to get that
Ease,

Eafe, they fee their Heads promifed, but could not, and the *Government* can, and does give them.

Multitudes cannot Plot, they are too many, and have not Conduct for it, they move by another Spring. *Safety is the Pretence of their Leaders :* If once they fee they enjoy it, they have yet Wit enough not to hazard it for any Body : For the Endeavours of Bufie Men are then difcernable ; but a State of Severity gives them a Pretence, by which the Multitude is eafily taken. Men may indifcreetly Plot to get what they would never Plot to lofe. *So that Eafe is not only their Content, but the Prince's Security.*

This I fay, upon a Suppofition, *That the Diffenters could agree againft the Government* ; which is a begging of the Queftion : For it is improbable (if not impoffible without *Conformifts*) fince, befides the *Diftance they are at in their Perfwafions and Affections, they dare not hope for fo Good Terms from one another, as the Government gives :* And that Fear, with Emulation, would draw them into that Duty, that they muft all fall into a Natural Dependence, which I call, *Holding of the Prince, as the Great Head of the State.*

From Abroad, we are as Safe as from within our felves : For if *Leading Men at Home* are thus difappointed of their Intereft in the People, Foreigners will find here no *Interpreters of their* dividing Language, *nor Matter (if they could) to work upon* For the Point is gain'd, the People they would deal in, are at their Eafe, and cannot be bribed ; and thofe that would, can't deferve it.

It is this that makes *Princes* live *Independent* of their Neighbours : And, to be loved at Home, is be feared Abroad : One follows neceffarily the other. Where Princes are driven to feek a foreign Affiftance, the Iffue either muft be the *Ruin* of the *Prince,* or the abfolute *Subjection* of the *People*; not without the Hazard of becoming a Province to the Power of that Neighbour that turns the Scale. Thefe *Confequences* have on either Hand an *ill Look,* and fhould rebate Extremes.

The *Greatnefs* of *France* carries thofe *Threats* to all her Neighbours, that, politically fpeaking, 'tis the *Melancholieft* Profpect *England* has had to make fince *Eighty Eight* : The *Spaniard* at that Time, being fhorter in all Things but his *Pride* and *Hope,* than the *French* King is now, of the fame *Univerfal Monarchy.* This Greatnefs, begun with the *Eleventh Lewis,* fome will have it, has not been fo much advanced by the Wifdom of *Richlieu,* and Craft of *Mazarene,* no, nor the *Arms* of the prefent *Monarch,* as by the *Affiftance* or *Connivance* of *England,* that has moft to lofe by him.

O. Cromwell began, and gave him the Scale againft the *Spaniard.* The Reafon of State he went upon, was the Support of Ufurp'd Dominion : And he was not out in it ; for the *Exile* of the *Royal Family* was a great Part of the Price of that Aid : In which we fee, how much *Intereft* prevails above *Nature.* It was not *Royal Kindred* could fhelter a King againft the Solicitations of an *Ufurper* with the *Son* of his *Mother's Brother.*

But it will be told us by fome People, *We have not degenerated,* but exactly followed the fame Steps ever fince, which has given fuch an Increafe to thofe Beginnings, that the *French Monarchy* is almoft above our Reach. But fuppofe it were true, What's the Caufe of it ? It has not been old Friendfhip, or nearnefs of Blood, or Neighbourhood. Nor could it be from an Inclination in our Minifters, to bring Things here to a like Iffue, as fome have fuggefted ; for then we fhould have clogged his Succeffes, inftead of helping them in any Kind, left in fo doing, we fhould have put it into his Power to hinder our own.

But perhaps our *Crofs* Accidents of State may fometimes have compelled us into his Friendfhip, and his Councils have carefully improved the one, and hufbanded the other to great Advantages, and that this was more than made for our *Englifh* Intereft : And yet 'tis but too true, that the *extreme Heats* of fome Men, that moft inveighed againft it, went too far to ftrengthen that Underftanding, by not taking what would have been granted, and creating an Intereft at Home, that might naturally have diffolv'd that Correfpondence Abroad.

I love not to revive Things that are uneafily remembred, but in Points moft tender to the late King, he thought himfelf fometimes too clofely preffed, and hardly held ; and we are all wife enough now to fay, a milder Conduct had fucceeded better : For if reafonable Things may be reafonably preft, and with fuch private Intentions, as induce a Denial, Heats about Things doubtful, unwife or unjuft, muft needs harden and prejudice.

Let us then create an Interest for the Prince at *Home*, and *Foreign Friendships* (at best, uncertain and dangerous) will fall of Course; for if it be allowed to *Private Men*, shall it be forbid to *Princes* only, to know and to be true to their own Support?

It is no more than what every Age makes us to see in all Parties of Men. The Parliaments of *England*, *since the Reformation*, giving no *Quarter to Roman Catholicks*, have forc'd them to the *Crown for Shelter*. And to induce the *Monarchy to yield them the Protection they have needed*, they have with mighty Address and Skill, recommended themselves as the *Great Friends of the Prerogative*, and so successfully too, that it were not below the Wisdom of that Constitution, to reflect what they have lost by that Costiveness of theirs to *Catholicks*. On the other Hand, the *Crown* having treated the *Protestant Dissenters* with the Severity of the Laws that affected them, suffering the Sharpest of them to fall upon their Persons and Estates, they have been driven successively to *Parliaments for Succour*, whose Priviledges, with equal Skill and Zeal, they have abetted: And our late Unhappy Wars are too plain a Proof, how much their Accession gave the Scale against the Power and Courage of both *Conformists and Catholicks*, that adhered to the *Crown*.

Nor must this *Contrary Adhesion be imputed to Love or Hatred*, but *Necessary Interest*: Refusal in one Place, makes Way for Address in another. If the Scene be changed, the Parts must follow; for as well before, as after *Cromwell's Usurpation*, the *Roman Catholicks* did not only promise, *The most ready Obedience to that Government, in their Printed Apologies for Liberty of Conscience*; but actually treated by some of their Greatest Men, with the Ministers of those Times, for Indulgence, upon the Assurances they offer'd to give of their Good Behaviour to the Government, as then Established.

On the other Hand, we see the *Presbyterians*, That in *Scotland* began the War, and in *England* promoted and upheld it to *Forty Seven*, when ready to be supplanted by the *Independents*, wheel to the King. In *Scotland* they Crown him, and come into *England* with an Army to restore him, where their Brethren joyn them; but being defeated, *They Help, by Private Collections*, to support him Abroad; and after the Overthrow of Sir *George Booth's* Attempt, to almost a Miracle, restore him. And which is more, a Great Part of that Army too, whose *Victories* came from the *Ruin* of the Prince they restored.

But to give the last Proofs our Age has of the Power of *Interest*, against the Notion oppos'd by this Discourse. First, the *Independents* themselves, held the *Greatest Republicans* of all Parties, were the most Lavish and Superstitious Adorers of Monarchy in *Oliver Cromwell*, because of the Regard he had to them; allowing him, and his Son after him, to be *Custos Utriusq; Tabulæ*, over all Causes, as well Ecclesiastical as Civil, *Supreme Governour*. And next, the *Conformists* in Parliament, reputed the most *Loyal and Monarchical Men*, did more than any Body question and oppose the late King's *Declaration of Indulgence*; even They themselves would not allow so much Prerogative to the Crown, but pleaded and opposed his Political Capacity.

This proves the *Power of Interest*, and that *All Persuasions center with it*: And when they see the *Government* engaging them with a *Fix'd Liberty of Conscience*, they must for their own Sakes seek the Support of it, by which it is maintained. This *Union*, directed under the Prince's Conduct, would Awe the Greatness of our Neighbours, and soon restore *Europe* to its Ancient Ballance, and that into his Hand too: So that *He may be the Great Arbiter of the Christian World*. But if the Policy of the Government, places the Security of it's Interest in the *Destruction of the Civil Interest of the Dissenters*, it is not to be wondred at, if they are less found in the Praises of it's Conduct, than others, to whom they are offered up a Sacrifice by it.

I know it will be insinuated, *That there is Danger in Building upon the Union of divers Interests*; and this will be aggravated to the *Prince*, by such as would engross *His Bounty*, and intercept *His Grace* from a great Part of his People. But I will only oppose to that meer Suggestion, Three Examples to the contrary, with this Challenge, That if after Rummaging the Records of all Time, they find one Instance to contradict me, I shall submit the Question to their Authority.

The *First*, is given by those *Christian Emperors*, who admitted all Sorts of *Dissenters* into their Armies, Courts and Senates. This, the Ecclesiastical Story of those Times, assures us, and particularly *Socrates*, *Evagrius*, and *Onuphrius*.

The

The next Instance, is that of *Prince* William *of* Orange, who by a timely *Indulgence*, united the scattered Strength of *Holland*, and, all animated by the *Clemency*, as well as *Valour* of their Captain, crown'd his Attempts with an extraordinary Glory; and, what makes, continues Great,

The *last*; is given us by *Livy*, in his Account of *Hannibal's* Army; "That they consisted of divers *Nations, Languages, Customs* and *Religions*: That under all "their Successes of War and Peace, for *Thirteen Years together*, they never muti- "ny'd against their General, nor fell out among themselves. What *Livy* relates for a Wonder, the Marquis *Virgilio Malvetzy* gives the Reason of, to wit, their *Variety* and Difference, *well managed by their General*; for, said he, "It was im- "possible for so many *Nations, Customs* and *Religions* to combine, especially when "the General's equal Hand gave him more Reverence with them, than they had "of Affection for one another. This (says he) some would wholly impute to "*Hannibal*; but however great he was, I attribute it to the Variety of People in "the Army: For (adds he) *Rome's* Army was ever less given to Mutiny, when "ballanced with Auxiliary Legions, than when intirely *Roman*. Thus much in his Discourse upon *Cornelius Tacitus*.

And they are neither few, nor of the weakest Sort of Men, that have thought the *Concord* of *Discords* a firm Basis for Government to be built upon. The Business is to *Tune* them well, and that must be the Skill of the *Musician*.

In Nature we see all Heat *consumes*, all Cold *kills*: That three Degrees of Cold to two of Heat, allays the Heat, but introduces the contrary Quality, and overcools by a Degree; but *two Degrees of Cold to two of Heat*, makes a *Poize* in Elements, and a *Ballance* in Nature. And in those Families where the evenest Hand is carried, the Work is best done, and the Master is most reverenced.

This brings me to another Benefit, which accrues to the *Monarchy* by a *Toleration*, and that is a *Ballance at Home*: For though it be improbable, it may so happen, that either the Conforming or Non-conforming Party may be undutiful; the one is then a Ballance of the other. *This might have prevented much Mischief to our second and third* Henry, King John, *the second* Edward, *and* Richard, *and unhappy* Henry *the Sixth, as it undeniably saved the* Royal Family *of* France, *and secured* Holland, *and kept it from Truckling under the* Spanish Monarchy. While all hold of the Government, 'tis that which gives the Scale to the most Dutiful; but still, no farther than to shew it's Power, and awe the Disorderly into Obedience, not to destroy the *Ballance*, lest it should afterwards want the Means of *Overpoizing Faction*.

That this is more than Fancy, plain it is, that the *Dissenter* must firmly adhere to the Government for his *Being*, while the *Church-man* is provided for. The one subsists by it's *Mercy*, the other by it's *Bounty*. This is tied by *Plenty*, but that by *Necessity*, which being the last of Tyes, and strongest Obligation, the Security is greatest from him, that it is fancy'd most unsafe to *Tolerate*.

But besides this, the *Tranquility* which it gives at Home, will both oblige those that are upon the Wing for *Foreign Parts*, to *pitch here again*; and at a Time when our Neighbouring Monarch is wasting his People, excite those Sufferers into the King's Dominions, whose Number will encrease that of his Subjects, and their Labour and Consumption, the Trade and Wealth of his Territories.

For what are all *Conquests*, but of People? And if the Government may by *Indulgence* add the Inhabitants of Ten Cities to those of it's own, it obtains a *Victory* without Charge. The Ancient Persecution of *France* and the *Low Countries*, has furnish'd us with an invincible Instance; for of those that came hither on that Account, we were instructed in most useful *Manufactures*, as by Courses of the like Nature, we lost a great Part of our *Woollen Trade*. And as Men, in Times of Danger, draw in their Stock, and either transmit it to other Banks, or bury their Talent at Home for Security (that being out of Sight, it may be, out of Reach too (and either is fatal to a Kingdom) so this Mildness obtained, setting every Man's Heart at rest, every Man will be at Work, and the Stock of the Kingdom employ'd: which, like the Blood, that hath it's due Passage, will give Life and Vigour to every Member in the publick Body.

And here give me Leave to mention the Experiment made at Home by the late King, in his *Declaration of Indulgence*. No Matter how well or ill built that Act of State was, 'tis no Part of the Business in Hand, but what Effect the *Liberty of it* had upon the *Peace* and *Wealth* of the Kingdom, may have Instruction in it to

our

our present Condition. 'Twas evident, that all Men laboured cheerfully, and traded boldly, when they had the *Royal Word* to keep what they got, and the *King* himself became the *Universal Insurer* of Dissenters Estates. *Whitehall*, then, and St. *James's*, were as much visited and courted by their respective Agents, as if they had been of the *Family:* For that which eclipsed the *Royal Goodness*, being by his *own Hand* thus remov'd, his benign Influences drew the Returns of Sweetness and Duty from that Part of his Subjects, that the Want of those Influences had made barren before. Then it was that we look'd like the Members of one Family, and Children of one Parent. Nor did we envy our eldest Brother, *Episcopacy*, his Inheritance, so that we had but a Child's Portion: For not only *Discontents vanish'd*, but no Matter was left for ill Spirits, foreign or domestick, to *brood* upon, or hatch to Mischief. Which was a plain Proof, that it is the *Union* of *Interests*, and not of *Opinions*, that gives Peace to Kingdoms.

And with all Deference to Authority, I would speak it, the *Liberty* of the Declaration seems to be our *English Amomum* at last: The *Sovereign Remedy* to our *English* Constitution. And, to say true, we shifted Luck (as they call it) as soon as we had lost it; *like those that lose their Royal Gold, their Evil Returns*. For all Dissenters seemed then united in their Affection to the *Government*, and followed their Affairs without Fear or Distraction. *Projects*, then, were stale and unmerchantable, and no Body cared for them, because no Body wanted any: That gentle *Opiate*, at the Prince's Hand, laid the most Busy and Turbulent to Sleep: But when the Loss of that *Indulgence* made them uncertain, and that uneasy; Their Persons and Estates being again exposed to pay the Reckoning of their *Dissent*, no doubt but every Party shifted then as they could: Most grew selfish, at least, jealous, fearing one should make Bargains apart, or exclusive of the other. This was the fatal Part *Dissenters* acted to their common Ruin: And I take this Partiality to have had too great a Share in our late Animosities; which, by fresh Accidents falling in, have swelled to a mighty Deluge, such an one as hath overwhelmed our former civil Concord and Serenity. And pardon me, if I say, I cannot see that those *Waters* are like to *asswage*, 'till this *Olive-Branch* of *Indulgence* be some Way or other restored: The *Waves* will still cover our Earth, and a Spot of Ground will hardly be found in this glorious Isle, for a great Number of useful People to set a quiet Foot upon. And, to pursue the Allegory, What was the *Ark* it self, *but the most apt and lively* Emblem *of* Toleration? A Kind of *Natural Temple of Indulgence*. In which we find *two of every* living Creature dwelling together, of *both* Sexes too, that they might *propagate*; and that as well of the *unclean* as *clean* Kind: So that the *baser* and less useful Sort were saved. Creatures never like to change their Nature, and so far from being whipt and punish'd to the Altar, that they were expresly forbid. *These were Saved, these were Fed and Restored to their Ancient Pastures*. Shall we be so mannerly as to complement the *Conformists* with the Stile of *Clean*, and so humble as to take the *Unclean* Kind, to our selves, who are the less Noble, and more Clownish Sort of People? I think verily we may do it, if we may but be saved too by the *Commander* of our *English Ark*. And this the *Peaceable* and *Virtuous Dissenter* has the less Reason to fear, since *Sacred Text* tells us, *'Twas Vice*, and *Not Opinion*, that brought the Deluge upon the rest. And here (to drop our Allegory) I must take Leave to hope, that though the Declaration be gone, if the Reason of it remain, I mean the *Interest of the Monarchy*, the *King* and His *Great Council* will graciously please to think a *Toleration*, no Dangerous nor Obsolete Thing.

But as it has many *Arguments* for it, that are drawn from the Advantages that have and would come to the Publick by it, so there are divers *Mischiefs* that must unavoidably follow the *Persecution* of *Dissenters*, that may reasonably disswade from such Severity. For they must either be *ruined*, *fly*, or *conform*; and perhaps the last is not the *Safest*. If they are *Ruin'd* in their Estates, and their Persons *Imprisoned*, modestly computing, a *Fourth* of the *Trade* and *Manufactury* of the Kingdom *sinks*; and those that have helped to maintain the Poor, must come upon the *Poor's Book* for *Maintenance*. This seems to be an *Impoverishing* of the Publick. But if to avoid this, they transport themselves, with their *Estates*, into other Governments; nay, though it were to any of the King's Plantations, the Number were far too great to be spared from Home. So much principal Stock wanting to turn the yearly Traffick, and so many People too, to consume our yearly Growth, must

muſt iſſue *fatally* to the *Trade* one Way, and to the *Lands* and *Rents* of the Kingdom the other Way.

And laſtly, If they ſhould reſolve, neither to *ſuffer* nor *fly*, but *conform* to prevent both. It is to be enquired, if this *Cure* of *Church-Diviſion* be *ſafe* to the State; or not rather, a raking up *Coals under Aſhes*, for a future Miſchief? He whom Fear or Policy hath made *Treacherous* to his own Conſcience, ought not to be held *True* to any thing but his own *Safety* and *Revenge*. His Conformity gives him the firſt, and his Reſentment of the Force that compels it, will on no Occaſion let him want the laſt. So that *Conformity cozens* no Body but the Government: For the *State Fanatick* (which is the *unſafe* Thing to the State) being *chriſten'd* by Conformity, he is eligible every where, with Perſons the moſt devoted to the Prince: And all Men will hold themſelves *protected* in their Votes by it.

A Receipt to make *Faction keep, and preſerve Diſloyalty againſt all Weathers*. For whereas the Nature of *Teſts* is to *diſcover*, this is the Way to *conceal* the Inclinations of Men from the Government. *Plain Diſſent* is the *Prince with a Candle in his Hand :* He ſees the *Where* and *What* of Perſons and Things : He diſcriminates, and makes that a Rule of Conduct : But forc'd *Conformity* is the *Prince in the Dark:* It blows out his Candle, and leaves him without Diſtinction. Such Subjects are like *Figures in Sand*, when Water is flapt upon them, they run together, and are indiſcernible : Or *written Tradition*, made *illegible* by writing the *Oaths* and *Canons* upon it : *The ſafeſt Way of blotting out Danger.*

I know not how to forbear ſaying, that this *neceſſary Conformity* makes the Church dangerous to the State : For even the *Hypocriſy* that follows, makes the Church both *conceal* and *protect* the *Hypocrites*, which, together with their *Liberality* to the *Parſon, Charity to the Poor, and Hoſpitality to their Neighbours*, recommends them to the firſt Favour they have to beſtow. That *Fort is unſafe*, where a Party of the *Garriſon* conſiſts of *diſguiſed Enemies*; for when they take their Turns at the *Watch*, the *Danger* is hardly evitable. It would then certainly be for the *Safety* of the *Fort*, that ſuch Friends in *Maſquerade* were induſtriouſly *kept out*, inſtead of being *whipt in*.

And it was ſomething of this, I remember, that was made an Argument for the *Declaration of Indulgence*, in the Preamble, to wit, *the greater Safety of the Government, from* Open *and* Publick, *than Private, diſſenting Meetings of Worſhip*; as indeed the reſt bear the ſame Reſemblance. For theſe were the Topicks, *Quieting* the People, *Encouraging* Strangers to come and live among us, and *Trade* by it; and laſtly, *Preventing* the Danger that might ariſe to the *Government* by *Private Meetings :* Of greater Reaſon then from *Private Men*, not leſs diſcontented, but more concealed and ſecure by the Great *Brake* of Church Conformity. It is this will make a *Comprehenſion* of the next Diſſenters to the Church *dangerous*, tho' it were practicable, of which Side ſoever it be. For in an Age, the *preſent Frame of Government* ſhall feel the Art and Induſtry of the Comprehended. So that a *Toleration* is in Reaſon of State to be prefer'd. And if the Reaſons of the *Declaration* were ever good, they are ſo ſtill, becauſe the Emergencies of State that made them ſo, remain; and our Neighbours are not leſs powerful to improve them to our Detriment.

But it will be now ſaid, *Though the Government ſhould find it's Account in what has been laſt alledged, this were the Way to overthrow the Church, and encourage Diſſenters to continue in their Errors.* Which is that ſecond main Objection I propoſed at firſt, to anſwer in it's proper Place, and that I think is this:

I humbly ſay, if it prove the Intereſt of the three conſiderable *Church-Intereſts* in this Kingdom, a *Relaxation*, at leaſt, can hardly fail us. The three *Church Intereſts* are, That of the *Church of England*; That of the *Roman Catholick Diſſenter*; and, That of the *Proteſtant Diſſenter*.

That the *Church of England* ought *in Conſcience and Prudence* to conſent to the Eaſe deſired.

I pray, firſt, that it be conſidered, how great a Reflection it will be upon her Honour, that from a *Perſecuted*, ſhe ſhould be accounted a *Perſecuting Church :* An Overthrow none of her *Enemies* have been able to give to her many *excellent Apologies*. Nor will it be excuſed, by her ſaying, *She is in the Right*, which her Perſecutors were not; ſince this is a Confidence not wanting in any of them, or her *Diſſenters :* And the Truth is, it is but the Begging of a Queſtion, that will by no Means be granted.

No body ought to know more than *Churchmen*, that *Conscience cannot be forced*. That Offerings against *Conscience*, are as *odious* to God, as *uneasie* to them that make them. That God loves a *free Sacrifice*. That Christ *forbad Fire*, though from Heaven (it self) to punish *Dissenters*; and commanded that the *Tares should grow with the Wheat till the Harvest*. In fine, that we should *love Enemies* themselves: And to exclude worldly Strife for Religion; *That his Kingdom is not of this World*. This was the Doctrine of the *Blessed Saviour* of the *World*.

Saint *Paul* pursues the same Course: Is glad Christ is Preached, be it of *Envy*; the worst Ground for *Dissent* that can be. It was he that ask't that hard, but just Question, *Who art thou that judgest another Man's Servant? To his own Lord he standeth or falleth*. He allows the Church a Warfare, and Weapons to perform it, but they are not *Carnal*, but *Spiritual*. Therefore it was so advised, that every Man in Matters of Religion, should be *fully perswaded in his own Mind*, and if any were short or mistaken, God would, in his Time, Inform them better.

He tells us of *Schismaticks* and *Hereticks* too, and their Punishment, which is to the Point in Hand: He directs to a *first* and *second Admonition*, and if that prevail not, *reject them*: That is, *refuse* them Church Fellowship, *disown* their Relation, and *deny them Communion*. But in all this there is not a Word of *Fines* or *Imprisonments*, nor is it an excuse to any Church, that the *Civil Magistrate* executes the Severity, while they are *Members of her Communion, that make or execute the Laws*.

But if the Church could gain her Point, I mean *Conformity*, unless she could gain *Consent* too, 'twere but *Constraint* at last. A Rape upon the Mind, which may encrease her Number, *not her Devotion*. On the contrary, the rest of her Sons are in danger by their Hypocrisie. The most close, but watchful and Revengeful Thing in the World. Besides, the Scandal can hardly be removed: To *over value Coin*, and *Rate Brass to Silver*, Beggars any Country; and to own them for *Sons* she *never begat*, debases and destroys any Church. 'Twere better to *indulge* foreign Coin of *intrinsick Value*, and let it pass for it's Weight. 'Tis not Number, but *Quality*: Two or three sincere Christians, that *form* an Evangelical Church: And though the Church were *less, more Charity* on the one Hand, and *Piety* on the other, with exact Church-Censure, and less *civil Coercion*, would give her Credit with Conscience in all Sects; without which, their Accession it self would be no Benefit, but disgrace, and hazard to her Constitution.

And to speak prudently in this Affair, 'tis the *Interest* of the *Church of England*, not to suffer the Extinction of *Dissenters*, that she may have a *Counter-Ballance* to the *Roman Catholicks*, who, though few in Number, are great in *Quality*, and greater in their foreign Friendships and Assistance. On the other Hand, it is her Interest to Indulge the *Roman Catholick*, that by his Accession, she may at all Times have the *Ballance* in her own Hand, against the *Protestant Dissenter*, leaning to either, as she finds her *Doctrine* undermined by the one, or her *Discipline* by the other; or lastly, her *Civil Interest* endangered from either of them.

And it is certainly the *Interest* of both those *Extremes* of *Dissent*, that *She*, rather than either of them should hold the *Scale*. For as the *Protestant Dissenter* cannot hope for any Tenderness, exclusive of *Roman Catholicks*, but almost the *same Reasons* may be advanced against him. So on the other Hand, it would look imprudent, as well as unjust, in the *Roman Catholicks*, to solicite any Indulgence *exclusive* of *Protestant Dissenters*. For besides that, it keeps up the Animosity, which it is their Interest to bury; the Consequence will be, to take the Advantage of Time, to snatch it from one another, when an united *Request* for *Liberty*, once granted, will oblige both Parties, in all Times, for Example-sake, to have it Equally preserved. Thus are all Church Interests of *Conformists* and *Dissenters* rendered consistent and safe in their Civil Interest one with the other.

But it will last of all, doubtless, be objected, *That tho' a Toleration were never so desirable in it self, and in it's Consequence beneficial to the Publick, yet the Government cannot allow it, without Ruin to the Church of* England, *which it is obliged to maintain*.

But I think this will not affect the Question at all, unless by maintaining the *Church of England*, it is understood that he should force whole Parties to be of her Communion, or knock them on the Head: Let us call to mind, that the Religion that is true, allows no Man to do Wrong, that Right may come of it. And that nothing has lessen'd the Credit of any Religion more, than declining to support it self by it's *own Charity* and *Piety*, and taking Sanctuary in the Arms, *rather than*

than the *Understandings of Men*. *Violences* are ill Pillars for Truth to rest upon. The *Church of England* must be maintain'd: Right, but can't that be done without the *Dissenter* be destroyed? In vain then did Christ command *Peter* to put up his Sword, with this Rebuke, *They that take the Sword, shall perish with the Sword*, if his Followers are to draw it again. He makes killing for *Religion*, Murder, and deserving Death: Was he then in the Right, Not to call Legions to his Assistance? And are not his Followers of these Times in the Wrong, to seek to uphold their Religion by any Methods of Force. The *Church of England* must be maintain'd, therefore the *Dissenters*, that hold almost the same Doctrine, must be Ruin'd. A Consequence most unnatural, as it is almost impossible. For besides that, the *Drudgery* would unbecome the civil Magistrate, who is the Image of divine Justice and Clemency, and that it would fasten the Character of a *False* Church, upon one that desires to be esteemed a *True One*; she puts the Government upon a Task that is hard to be performed. *Kings can no more make Brick without Straw, than Slaves:* The Condition of our Affairs is much chang'd, and the Circumstances our Government are under, differ mightily from those of our Ancestors. They had not the same Dissents to deal with, nor those Dissents the like Bodies of People to render them formidable, and their Prosecution mischievous to the State. Nor did this come of the *Prince's* Neglect or Indulgence: There are other Reasons to be assigned, of which, the Opportunities Domestick Troubles gave to their Increase and Power, and the Severities used to suppress them, may go for none of the least. So that it was as *involuntary* in the *Prince*, as to the *Church* Anxious. And under this Necessity to tye the Magistrate to old Measures, is to be regardless of Time, whose *fresh* Circumstances give *Aim* to the Conduct of Wise Men in their present Actions. Governments, as well as Courts, *change* their Fashions: The *same Clothes* will not always serve: And Politicks made *Obsolete* by new Accidents, are as *unsafe* to follow, as antiquated Dresses are ridiculous to wear.

Thus *Sea-men* know, and teach us in their daily Practice: They *humour the Winds*, though they will *lie* as near as they can, and *trim* their Sails by their Compass: And by Patience under these constrained and uneven Courses, they gain their Port at last. This justifies the Government's change of Measures from the change of Things; for *res nolunt malè Administrari*.

And to be free, it looks more than Partial, to Elect and Reprobate too. That That the *Church of England* is prefer'd, and has the *Fat of the Earth, the Authority of the Magistrate, and the Power of the Sword in her Sons Hands, which comprehend all the Honours, Places, Profits, and Powers of the Kingdom*, must not be repined at: Let her have it, and keep it all, and let none dare seek or accept an Office that is not of her. But to ruin *Dissenters* to compleat her Happiness, (pardon the Allusion) is *Calvinism* in the worst Sense; for this is that *Horrendum Decretum* reduc'd to Practice: And to pursue that ill natur'd Principle, *Men are civilly Damn'd for that they cannot help*, since Faith is not in Man's Power, though it sometimes exposes one to it.

It is a severe Dilemma, that a Man must either renounce *That* of which he makes Conscience in the Sight of God, or be *Civilly* and *Ecclesiastically Reprobated*. There was a Time, when the *Church of England* her self stood in need of Indulgence, and made up a great Part of the *Non-Conformists* of this Kingdom, and what she then wanted, she pleaded for, I mean a *Toleration*, and that in a general Style, as divers of the Writings of her Doctors tell us: Of which let it be enough but to mention that excellent Discourse of Dr. *Taylor*, *Bishop of Down*, entituled, *Liberty of Prophecy*.

And that which makes *Severity* look the worse in the Members of the *Church of England*, is the Modesty she professes about the Truth of the Things she believes: For though perhaps it were indefensible in any Church to compel a Man to that which she were infallibly assured to be true, unless she superseded his Ignorance by *Conviction, rather than Authority*, it must, doubtless, look rude, to punish Men into Conformity to that, of the Truth of which, the Church her self pretends no Certainty.

Not that I would less believe a Church so cautious, than one more confident; but I know not how to help thinking Persecution harsh, *when they Ruin People for not believing that, which they have not in themselves the Power of believing*, and which she *cannot give them*, and of which her self is *not infallibly assured*. The Drift of this is *Moderation*, which well becomes us poor Mortals, *That for every*

Idle Word we speak, must give an Account at the Day of Judgment, if our Saviour's Doctrine have any credit with us.

It would much mitigate the Severity, if the Dissent were *Sullen, or in Contempt:* But if Men can't help or hinder their Belief, they are rather *Unhappy* than *Guilty*, and more to be *pitied* than *blamed*. However they are of the reasonable Stock of the Country, and tho' they were unworthy of *Favour*, they may not be unfit to live. 'Tis Capital, at Law, to destroy *Bastards*, and *By-blows* are laid to the Parish to keep: They must maintain them at last: And shall not these natural Sons, at least, be laid at the Door of the Kingdom? Unhappy Fate of *Dissenters!* to be less heeded, and more destitute than any Body. If this should ever happen to be the Effect of their own Folly, with Submission, it can never be the Consequence of the *Government's Engagements*.

Election does not necessarily imply a *Reprobation* of the rest. If God hath elected some to Salvation, it will not follow of course, that he hath absolutely rejected all the rest. For tho' he was God of the *Jews*, he was God of the *Gentiles* too, and they were his People, tho' the *Jews* were his peculiar People. *God respects not Persons,* says St. *Peter,* the good of all Nations are accepted. The Difference at last, will not be of *Opinion,* but *Works: Sheep* or *Goats,* All, of all Judgments will be found: And *Come, Well done;* or *Go ye Workers of Iniquity,* will conclude their Eternal State: Let us be careful therefore of an *Opinion-Reprobation* of one another.

We see the God of Nature hath taught us softer Doctrine in his great Book of the World: His *Sun shines,* and his *Rain falls upon all.* All the Productions of Nature are by *Love,* and shall it be proper to *Religion* only to propagate by *Force?* The poor *Hen* instructs us in Humanity, who, to defend her feeble Young, refuses no Danger. All the *Seeds* and *Plants* that grow for the use of Man, are produc'd by the kind and warm Influences of the Sun. 'Tis *Kindness* that upholds Humane Race. People don't *Multiply in Spight:* And if it be by *gentle* and *friendly* Ways, that Nature produces and matures the Creatures of the World, certainly *Religion* should teach us to be *Mild* and *Bearing.*

Let your Moderation be known to all Men, was the saying of a great Doctor of the Christian Faith, and his Reason for that Command *Cogent, For the Lord is at Hand.* As if he had said, Have a care what you do, be not *bitter* nor *violent,* for the *Judge is at the Door:* Do as you would be done to, lest what you deny to others, God should *refuse to you.*

And after all this, shall the *Church of England* be less tender of Men's *Consciences,* than our *common Law* is of their *Lives,* which had rather a *Thousand Criminals* should escape, than that *One Innocent* should perish? Give me leave to say, that there are many *Innocents* (Conscience excepted) now exposed, Men honest, peaceable and useful; free of ill Designs; that pray for *Cæsar,* and pay their Tribute to *Cæsar.*

If any tell us, *They have, or may, ill use their Toleration.* I say, this must be look't to, and not Liberty therefore refused; for the *English Church* cannot so much forget her own Maxim to Dissenters, That *Propter abusum non est Tollendus usus.* It suffices to our *Argument,* 'tis no *necessary* Consequence, and that *Fact* and *Time* are for us. And if any misuse such Freedom, and entitle *Conscience* to *Misbehaviour,* we have other Laws enough to catch and punish the Offenders, without *treating* One Party *with the Spoils of* Six. And when Religion becomes no Man's Interest, it will hardly ever be any Man's Hypocrisy. Men will chuse by Conscience, which at least preserves Integrity, though it were mistaken: And if not in the wrong, Truth recompences Inquiry, and Light makes amends for Dissent.

And since a plain Method offers it self, from the Circumstances of our case, I take the Freedom to present it for the *Model* of the *intreated Toleration.*

Much has been desired, said and prest, in Reference to the late King's being *Head* of a *Protestant League,* which takes in but a Part of the Christian World; the *Roman* and *Grecian* Christians being excluded. But I most humbly offer, that our Wise Men would please to think of another Title for our *King,* and that is *Head* of a *Christian League,* and give the Experiment here at Home in his own Dominions.

The *Christian Religion is admired of All in the Text,* and by *All* acknowledged in the *Apostle's Creed.* Here every Party of *Christians* meet, and center as in a General. The several *Species of Christians,* that this *Genus* divideth it self into, are those divers Perswasions we have within this Kingdom; The *Church of England, Roman-*

Roman-Catholicks, Grecians, Lutherans, Presbyterians, Independents, Anabaptists, Quakers, Socinians: These I call so many Orders of Christians, that unite in the Text, and differ only in the *Comment*; All owning *One Deity, Saviour and Judge, Good Works, Rewards and Punishments*: Which Bodies once Regulated, and holding of the Prince as *Head of the Government, Maintaining Charity, and Pressing Piety, will be an Honour to Christianity, a Strength to the Prince, and a Benefit to the Publick*: For in Lieu of an unattainable, (at best an unsincere) *Uniformity*, we shall have in *Civils Unity, and Amity in Faith*.

The *Jews* before, and in the Time of *Herod*, were divided into divers Sects. There were *Pharisees, Sadducees, Herodians,* and *Essenes*. They maintain'd their Dissent without Ruin to the Government: And the Magistrates fell under no Censure from Christ for that *Toleration*.

The *Gentiles*, as already has been observed, had their *Divers Orders of Philosophers*, as Disagreeing as ever Christians were, and that without Danger to the Peace of the State.

The *Turks* themselves shew us, that both other Religions, and divers Sects of their own, are very Tolerable, with Security to their Government.

The *Roman Church* is a considerable Instance to our Point; for She is made up of divers *Orders* of both Sexes, of very differing Principles, fomented sometimes to great Feuds and Controversies; as between *Franciscans, Dominicans, Jesuits,* and *Sorbonists*; yet without Danger to the Political State of the Church. On the contrary, She therefore cast her self into that Method, *That She might safely give Vent to Opinion and Zeal, and suffer both without Danger of Schism*. And these Regulars are, by the Pope's Grants, priviledg'd with an Exemption from Episcopal Visitation and Jurisdiction.

GOD Almighty inspire the *King's Heart, and the Hearts of His Great Council, to be the Glorious Instruments of this Blessing to the Kingdom*.

I shall conclude this PERSWASIVE, with the Judgment of some *Pious Fathers,* and *Renowned Princes*.

Quadratus and *Aristides* wrote *Two Apologies* to *Adrian*, for the Christian Faith, and against the Persecution of it.

Justin Martyr, an Excellent Philosopher and Christian, writ Two Learned *Disswasives* against Persecution, which he Dedicated (as I take it) to *Antoninus Pius,* and *Marcus Aurelius Antoninus*.

Melito, Bishop of *Sardis*, a Good and Learned Man, writ a smart Defence for the *Christian Religion,* and a *Toleration*, Dedicated to *Verus*.

Tertullian, in his most sharp and excellent Apology for the Christians, fastens Persecution upon the *Gentiles*, as an inseparable Mark of *Superstition* and *Error*, as he makes the *Christian Patience a Sign of Truth*. In his Discourse to *Scapula*, he says, *'Tis not the Property of Religion to Persecute for Religion; She should be received for Her self, not Force*.

Hilary, an early and learned Father, against *Auxentius*, saith, *The Christian Church does not persecute, but is persecuted*.

Atticus, Bishop of *Constantinople*, would by no Means have the Minister of *Nice* to respect any Opinion or Sect whatsoever, in the Distribution of the Money sent by him for the Relief of Christians; and by no Means to prejudice those that practise a contrary Doctrine and Faith to theirs: That he should be sure to relieve those that Hunger and Thirst, and have not wherewith to help themselves, and make that the Rule of his Consideration. In short, he made the *Hereticks* to have his Wisdom in Admiration, in that he would by no Means trouble or molest them.

Proclus (another Bishop of *Constantinople*) was of this Opinion, *That it was far easier by fair Means to allure unto the Church, than by Force to compel*: He determined to vex no Sect whatever, but restored to the Church the Renowned Virtue of *Meekness*, required in Christian Ministers.

If we will next hear the *Historian's* own Judgment upon a Toleration, *I am of Opinion* says he) *that he is a Persecutor, that in any Kind of Way, molesteth such Men as lead a Quiet and Peaceable Life:* Thus *Socrates* in his Third Book: In his Seventh he tells us, *That the Bishop of* Sinada, *indeed, did banish the Hereticks, but neither did he this* (says he) *according to the Rule of the* Catholick Church, *which is not accustomed to persecute,* lib. 7.

Lactantius tells the angry Men of his Time, thus, *If you will with Blood, Evil and Torments, defend your Worship, it shall not thereby be defended, but polluted.*

Chrysostom saith expresly, *That it is not the Manner of the Children of God, to persecute about their Religion, but an evident Token of Antichrist.*

Thus the *Fathers* and *Doctors* of the first Ages. That *Emperors* and *Princes* have thus believed, let us hear some of Greatest Note, and most pressing to us.

Jerom, a Good and Learned Father, saith, *That Heresie must be Cut off with the Sword of the Spirit.*

Constantius, the Father of *Constantine the Great*, laid this down for a Principle, *That those that were Disloyal to God, would never be Trusty to their Prince.* And which is more, he liv'd thus, and so dy'd, as his Great Speech to his Great Son, on his Death-Bed, amply evidences.

Constantine the Great, in his Speech to the *Roman Senate*, tells them, *There is this Difference between Humane and Divine Homage and Service, that the one is compell'd, and the other ought to be free.*

Eusebius Pamphilus, in the Life of *Constantine*, tells us, that in his Prayer to God, he said, *Let thy People, I beseech thee, desire and maintain Peace, Living free from Sedition to the common Good and Benefit of all the World; and those that are led away with Error, let them desire to live in Peace and Tranquility with the Faithful: For Friendly Humane Society and Commerce with them, will very much avail to bring them to the Right Way. Let no Man molest another, but let every one follow the Perswasion of their own Conscience: But let those that have a True Opinion concerning God, be perswaded, that such as regulate their Lives by God's Holy Laws, do lead an Holy and Upright Life: But those that will not conform thereunto, may have Liberty to erect and set up Altars. But we will Maintain the Church and True Religion, which thou hast committed to our Defence. Moreover, we desire that they may Joyfully receive and welcome this General Offer of Peace and Concord.*

This was the Judgment of the Most Celebrated Emperor that ever professed the *Christian Faith*. I have cited other Emperors in the Body of this Discourse; but because the Worst are to be commended when they do well, *Valens* himself, charm'd with the Sweetness and Strength of the Philosopher *Themistius*, in his Elegant Oration, grew Moderate towards the Orthodox, whom a little before he had severely treated: Of which these were the Heads; *That he Persecuted without Reason People of Good Lives: That it was no Crime to think or believe otherwise than the Prince believed: That he ought not to be troubled at the Diversity of Opinions: That the Gentiles were much more divided in their Judgment than the Christians: That it sufficeth, that every Sect aimed at the Truth, and lived virtuously.* We have had Modern Royal Examples too.

Stephen, King of *Poland*, declared his Mind in the Point controverted, thus, *I am King of Men, and not of Conscience; a Commander of Bodies, and not of Souls.*

The King of *Bohemia* was of Opinion, *That Mens Consciences ought in no Sort to be violated, urged, or constrained.*

And *Lastly*, let me add (as what is, or should be of more Force) the Sense of King *James* and King *Charles* the First, Men, as of Supreme Dignity, so famed for their Great Natural Abilities and acquired Learning; *It is a sure Rule in Divinity* (said King *James*) *that God never loves to Plant his Church by Violence and Bloodshed:* And in his Exposition on the Twentieth of the *Revelations*, he saith, *That Persecution is the Note of a False Church.*

And in the Advice of King *Charles* the First, to the late King, he says, *Take Heed of abetting any Factions; your Partial adhering to any one Side, gains you not so great Advantages in some Men's Hearts, (who are Prone to be of their King's Religion) as it loseth you in others, who think themselves, and their Profession, first despised, then persecuted by you.*

Again, *Beware of Exasperating any Factions, by the Crosness and Asperity of some Men's Passions, Humours, or Private Opinions, imployed by you, grounded only upon their Difference, in lesser Matters, which are but the Skirts and Suburbs of Religion; wherein a Charitable Connivence and Christian Toleration, often dissipates their Strength, whom rougher Opposition fortifies, and puts the despised and oppressed Party into such Combinations, as may most enable them to get a full Revenge on those they count their Persecutors, who are commonly assisted by that Vulgar Commiseration that attends all that are said to suffer under the Notion of Religion.*

Always

Always keep up Solid Piety, *and those* Fundamental Truths *(which mend both Hearts and Lives of Men) with* impartial Favour and Justice. *Your Prerogative is best shown and exercised in* Remitting, *rather than* Exacting *the* Rigour of Laws; *there being nothing worse than* Legal Tyranny.

Good ADVICE to the *Church of England*, *Roman-Catholick*, and *Protestant Dissenter*: In which it is endeavoured to be made appear, that it is their Duty, Principle, and Interest, to abolish the Penal LAWS and TESTS. *Beati Pacifici.*

To the READER.

Reader,

NO *Matter* Who, *but* What; *and yet if thou wouldst know the Author, he is an English-Man, and therefore obliged to this Country, and the Laws that made him Free.*

That Single Consideration were enough to command this Undertaking; for 'tis to perswade his Country-Men to be delivered of the greatest Yoak a Nation can well suffer under; Penal Laws for Religion, *I mean.*

And now thou hast both the Who, *and* What: *If thou art* Wise and Good, *Thou art above my* Epithets, *and more my* Flatteries; *If not, I am in the Right to let 'em alone.* Read, Think, *and* Judge. Liberty, English *and* Christian, *is all that is sought in the ensuing Discourse.*

Adieu.

GOOD ADVICE, &c.

PART I.

I Must own, it is my Aversion at this Time, to meddle with *Publick Matters*, and yet my Duty to the *Publick* will not let me be Silent. They that move by Principles, must not regard Times nor Factions, *but what is Just, and what is Honourable;* and *That* no Man ought to scruple, nor no Time or Interest to Contest.

The Single Question I go upon, and which does immediately concern and exercise the Minds of the Thinking, as well as Talking Men of this Kingdom, is, *Whether it be fit to Repeal the Penal Laws and Tests, in Matters of Religion, or not?* I take the Affirmative of the Question, and humbly submit my Reasons to every Reasonable Conscience. I say Reasonable, because *That* which knows not it's own Duty, Principle and Interest, is not so, and *That which is not willing to do to others as it would be done by*, less deserves to be thought so.

Now there are Three Sorts of People that will find themselves concerned in this Question, *The Church of England, the Roman Catholick*, and *the Protestant Dissenter*, and these make up the whole Body of the Kingdom; If it appear to be their Duty, Principle and Interest, the Question is gain'd, and no Body is left to complain; and if I am mistaken, it is with so great an Inclination to serve them all, that their Good Nature cannot but plead my Excuse, especially when they consider I am neither mov'd by Hopes nor Fears. Private Loss or Gain being farther from my Thought, than I hope they are from a Good Understanding.

I say, *First*, then it is the Duty of all of them, because they all profess that Religion which makes it their common Duty to do it; *Christianity* I mean: For no Christian ought to deprive any Man of his Native Right for Matters of Faith and Worship towards God, in the Way that he thinks most agreeable to the Will of
God;

God; becaufe it is neceffary to a Chriftian to believe, *That Faith is the Gift of God alone, and that He only is Lord of Confcience, and is able truly to Enlighten, Perfwade, and Eftablifh it*; and confequently that prejudicing Men in their Perfons or Eftates, or depriving them of any Station in the Government, they might otherwife, in their Turn, be capable to ferve the Publick in, is contrary to the *Tendernefs and Equity of that Religion*; which will yet farther appear, if we confider that Chriftianity is the *Sole Religion of the World, that is Built on the Principles of Love*; which brought with it the greateft *Evidences of Truth: Equally convincing our Underftandings with it's Light, and bearing down our Senfes with it's Miracles: Which filenc'd the Oracles of the Heathens by the Divine Power prefent with it, and vanquifht their Hearts, that had left nothing elfe to conquer, leading Kings and Emperors with their Courts and Armies in Triumph, after the* Defpifed Crofs of Him, who was the Holy and Bleffed Author of it.

It was He that laid not his Religion in Worldly Empire, nor ufed the Methods of Worldly Princes to Propagate it; as it came from Heaven, fo *That* only fhould have the Honour of protecting and promoting it. His whole Bufinefs to Mankind, from firft to laft, was *Love*. 'Twas firft Love in his Father to fend Him (as Saint *John* teaches) *God fo loved the World, that He fent His Son*, &c. It was Love in Jefus Chrift to come on that Errand; that He, *who thought it no Robbery to be Equal with God, fhould take the Form of a Servant to adopt us Children, and make himfelf of no Reputation with the World, that he might make us of Reputation with God His Father*.

And he did not only come in much Love, but preach'd it and preft it both to Friends and Foes; *Love one another*; *Love Enemies*; *Do Good to them that Hate you*; *Forgive them that Trefpafs againft you*; *What you would that other Men fhould do unto you, do that unto them*: *By thefe Things fhall all Men know you are my Difciples*; *for I came not to deftroy Men's Lives, no, not for Religion it felf*; *for my Kingdom, Power, Force, Weapons, and Victory, are not of this World*. In all this, Love prevails: It was His Great, His New, His Laft Commandment; of all his Difciples, the moft purfued by *His Beloved One*, that in his Bofom had learn'd His Heart, as his Divine Doctrine of Love in his Epiftles tells us.

As He Liv'd in Love, fo He Died in Love, with us, and for us, *and that while we were Rebellious too*; ay, He Pray'd and Dy'd for them who put Him to Death, fhewing us (fays St. *Peter*) *an Example that we fhould follow His Steps*. And what are they? Doubtlefs the Steps of Love, the Path he trod: *To do Good to Mankind, Enemies as well as Friends, that we may be like our Heavenly Father, that caufes His Sun to fhine, and His Rain to fall upon the Juft and Unjuft*. This muft be the Apoftle's Meaning, for the Reft of His Paffion was inimitable.

Now if this be *the Doctrine of Chrift, the Nature of Chriftianity, the Practice of the Primitive Church*, that like *Adam*, was *Created in full Strength, Beauty and Wifdom*, and fo an Example to fucceeding Ages of Religion, and to which we fo often refer as our Original; with what Pretence to a Chriftian Confcience, can any one ftickle to keep *Imprifoning, Banifhing, Impoverifhing, Hanging and Quartering Laws on Foot for Religion Sake*, but efpecially againft fuch as are by Creed Profeffors of Chriftianity as well as themfelves.

I know the Cafe is put hard by thofe that have the Laws on their Side, *We do this to fave our felves*; but an harder Cafe than Chrift's can never be put, whofe Anfwer in his, ought to refolve theirs fully.

Chrift is fent by his Father for the Salvation of the World: He introduces and proves his Miffion by Miracles, and the Great Authority of his Word and Doctrine: His Followers fully fatisfied who He was, whence He came, what He taught, and how eminently confirm'd, grew impatient at Contradiction; they could not bear the leaft Diffent; for when fome of the *Samaritans* refufed to entertain their Lord, becaufe they thought he was going for *Jerufalem*, the Place of their greateft Averfion, thefe Difciples were for having but the Word from his Mouth, and they would, in Imitation of *Elijah, have called for Fire from Heaven to have deftroy'd them*. But He turned and rebuked them, and faid, *Ye know not what Manner of Spirit ye are of, for the Son of Man is not come to Deftroy Men's Lives, but to Save them*. This Anfwer is to Purpofe, and for all Times, to be fure Chriftian Ones; and the higher the Pretenfions of any Party are to Chriftianity, the more inexcufable if they practife the contrary. Would not Chrift then hurt them that refufed him, and can we hurt our Neighbours for not receiving us? He condemned that *Spirit* in *His Difciples*, and fhall we uphold the *fame Spirit*, and that by

Law

Law too, which He condemned by his Gospel? *This is Killing for God's Sake, expresly charg'd by Christ with Impiety.* *They shall think,* says he to his Disciples, *they do God good Service to kill you;* Who should think so? *Why the Christian Persecutors.* Is it their Property to do so? Yes; What shall one think then of those Christians that profess it.

The *Jews* were grievously punished of God, for that Abomination of Sacrificing their Children to *Moloch*, but these Laws, though they change the Object, they have not lessen'd the Sin; *for they offer up Man, Woman and Child,* and tho' they say, *'Tis to God,* no Matter for that, since it makes their Case worse, for 'tis to imagine that so Good, so Just, so Sensible, so merciful a Being, can take Pleasure in so much Cruelty. Well, *But if we must not knock Folks on the Head, what must we do with them?* Take an Answer at the Mouth of Truth and Wisdom: *Let the Tares and Wheat grow together till the Harvest*; What's that? He tells you, *'Tis the End of the World*; so that whatever the Church of *England* is, 'tis certain Christ is for a Toleration, and His Doctrine is always in Fashion: What He was, He is, and will be; He went not by Reasons of State, or Customs of Countries; His Judgment was better Built, who came to give Law, and not to receive it, and 'tis *A Light and Rule to all Times*. *And He that Loves Father, or Mother, or Wife, or Children, or House, or Land, better than H I M,* that is, *His Doctrine* (of which this is so great a Part) *is not worthy of Him;* and I fear no other Reason induces the Church of *England* to decline it.

To confirm what has been said, tho' I design Brevity, let me not lose another Passage very pregnant to our Purpose; when His Disciples had accomplish'd their First Mission, at their Return they gave Him the *History of their Travels:* Among the rest, they tell Him of One they met with, *That in His Name Cast out Devils,* but because He would not follow with them, *They forbad Him:* Here is at least a *Dissenting Christian,* tho' *a Believer,* yet it seems not One of that closer Congregation; we also see their Zeal and Sentence. But what says the Master yet alive, and with them, *the Infallible Doctor, in whose Mouth was no Guile, who had not the Spirit by Measure, and was the Great Wisdom of God to His People,* Was He of the same Mind, or did He leave them without Rule in the Point? His Answer is this: *And JESUS said to them,* Forbid Him not, *for he that is not against us is for us.* The Prohibition is taken off, and their Judgment revers'd; and from His, to be sure, there lies no Appeal. For tho' a Power of Decision were allow'd to some One or more on Earth, in Matters obscure and undetermin'd, *Yet in Cases already adjudged by the Son of God Himself, who had the Chair, and could not Err,* there can be no Room for another Judge.

Now to apply it, I must first say, I find no such Disciples among those that are of the Side of keeping up the Penal Laws; God knows, the Disparity is but too unequal. But next, if they were all *Twelve in Westminster-Abby,* and should be of the Side of upholding the *Penal Laws* (which is the wrong Side they were of before) I should beg their Pardon, if I were of their Master's Mind, and objected his Wisdom to their Zeal, and his Gentle Rule to their harsh and narrow Judgment. And I beseech the *Church of England* to consider, that no Pretence can excuse Her Dissent, and less Her cross Practice to the Judgment of Her Saviour: *A Judgment that seems given and settled for the Conduct of the Church on the like Occasions, in succeeding Times:* And 'tis pity any Worldly Thing should have Place with Her to divert Her Obedience. Did *Christ* then come to *Save Men's Lives, and not to Destroy them?* And should She (She I say that pretends to be a Reformed Church) uphold those Laws that do destroy them? H E, Alas! went to another Village instead of Burning them, or theirs, for refusing Him. And She forbids any, that belongs to any other, to lodge in Her's, upon Pain of losing Life or Estate: *This may make Her a* Samaritan Indeed, *but* Not the Good One, *whose Example would have taught Her, instead of these sharp and ruder Remedies, to have poured the Oil of Peace and Gladness into those Chops and Wounds, that Time, and Heats of all Hands, had made in every Religious Party of Men.* Nor does She lose any Thing by Repealing those Laws, but the Power of Persecuting, and a Good Church would never have the Temptation. Come, Some-Body must begin to Forgive, let Her not leave that Honour to another, nor draw upon Her self the Guilt and Mischief of refusing it. She pretends to fear the *Strokes of the Romanists,* but I would fain know of Her, if following their Example will Convert them, or Secure Her? Does She hope to keep them out by the Weapons that have fail'd in their Hands, or can She Honourably censure Persecution in them, and yet use it Her self?

But

But she is extremely scandal'd and scared *at the Severity upon Protestants in France*. 'Tis certainly very ill; but do not the Laws she is so fond of point at the same Work, *Conformity*, or *Ruin*. And don't we know, that in some Places, and upon some Parties, her Magistrates have plow'd as deep Furrows, especially within these six and Twenty Years. *Husbands separated from their Wives, Parents from their Children, the Widow's Bed and the Orphans Milk made a Prize for Religion, Houses stript, Barns and Fields swept clean, Prisons crowded without Regard to Sex or Age, and some of both Sorts dungeon'd to Death, and all for Religion.* If she says they were *peevish Men, Bigots*, or mov'd by *private Interest*, she still made the Laws, and says no more for her self than the *French* say for their King, which yet she refuses to take for an Answer. Perhaps I could parallel some of the severest Passages in that Kingdom out of the Actions of some Members of the Church of *England* in *cool Blood*, that are even yet for continuing the *Penal Laws* upon their plundered Neighbours; so that this Reflection of hers upon *France*, is more popular than just from her. But I beseech her to look upon a Country four Times bigger than *France, Germany* I mean, and she will there see both Religions practis'd with great Ease and Amity, yet of this we must not hear one Word: I hope it is not for Fear of imitating it. However, 'tis disingenuous to object the Mischiefs of Popery to a general Ease, when we see it is the Way to prevent them. This is but in the Name of Popery *to keep all to her self*, as well from Protestant Dissenters as Roman Catholicks. How Christian, how equal, how Safe, that narrow Method is, becomes her well to consider, and methinks she ought not to be long about it.

I know she flatters her self, and others too believe, she is a *Bulwark* against Popery; and with that, without any farther Security to other Protestants, wipes her Mouth of all old Scores, and makes her present Court for Assistance. But when that Word *Bulwark* is examin'd, I fear it appears to mean no more than this, *That she would keep out Popery for that Reason, for which she apprehends Popery would turn her out*, viz. *Temporal Interest*. But may I without Offence ask her, when she kept Persecution out? Or if she keeps out Popery for any Body's Sake but her own? Nay, if it be not to hold the Power she has in her Hands, that she would frighten other Parties (now she has done her Worst) with what Mischief Popery would do them when it has Power. But to speak freely, can she be a Bulwark in the Case, that has been bringing the worst Part of Popery in these six and twenty Years, if *Persecution* be so as she says it is. This would be called *Canting* to the World in others. But I hear *she begins to see her Fault, is heartily sorry for it, and promises to do so no more*: And why may not Popery be as wise, that has also burnt her Fingers with the same Work? Their praying for Ease by *Law*, looks as if they chose That, rather than Power, for Security; and if so, Why may not the Papists Live as well as she Reign? I am none of their Advocate, I am no Papist, but I would be just and merciful too. However, I must tell her, that keeping the Laws on Foot, by which she did the Mischief, is none of the plainest Evidences of her Repentance: They that can believe it, have little Reason to quarrel at the Unaccountableness of Transubstantiation. It is unjust in Popery to invade her Privileges, and can it be just in her to provoke it, by denying a Christian Liberty? Or can she expect what she will not give? Or not do as she would be done by, because she fears others will not observe the same Rule to her? Is not this *doing Evil that Good may come of it*, and that uncertain too, against an express Command as well as common Charity? But to speak freely, whether we regard the Circumstances of the King, the Religion of his Children the Inequality of the Number and Strength of those of each of their Communions, we must conclude, that the Aversion of the Church of *England* to this intreated Liberty, cannot reasonably be thought to come from the Fear she has of the Prevalency of Popery, but the Loss of that Power the Law gives her to domineer over all Dissenters. And is not this a *Rare Motive* for a Christian Church to continue Penal Laws for Religion? If her Piety be not able to maintain her upon equal Terms, methinks her having so much the whip Hand and Start of all others, should satisfy her Ambition, and quiet her Fears; for 'tis possible for her to keep the Churches if the Laws were abolished; all the Difference is, she could not Force: She might persuade and convince what she could: And pray, Is not that enough for a true Church, without *Goals, Whips, Halters* and *Gibbets*? O what Corruption is this that has prevail'd over Men of such Pretensions to Light and Conscience? that they do not, or will not, see nor feel their own Principles one Remove from themselves; but sacrifice

the

the noblest Part of the Reformation to Ambition, and compel Men to truckle their tender Consciences to the Grandure and Dominion of their Doctors.

But because the Sons of the Church of *England* keep, at this Time, such a Stir in her Favour, and fix her Excellency in her Opposition to Popery, it is worth while to consider a little farther, if really the most feared and disagreeable Part of Popery, in her own Opinion, does not belong to her, and if it does, should we not be in a fine Condition, to be in Love with our Fetters, and to Court our Misery?

That Part of *Popery* which the Church of *England* with most Success objects against, is her *Violence*. This is that only she can pretend to fear: Her Doctrines she partly professes, or thinks she can easily refute. No Body counts her Doctors *Conjurers* for their *Transubstantiation*, or *dangerous* to the State for their *Beads*, or their *Purgatory*. But *forcing others to their Faith, or ruining them for refusing it, is the terrible Thing we are taught by her to apprehend*. Now granting this to be the Case, in Reference to the Roman Religion, where it is in the Chair. I ask, if the Church of *England*, with her better Doctrines, has not been guilty of this Impiety, and for that Cause more blameable than the Church she opposes so much? If we look into her Acts of State, we find them many, and bitter, against all Sorts of Dissenters. There is nigh twenty Laws made, and yet in Force, to constrain Conformity, and they have been executed too, as far and as often as she thought it fit for her Interest to let them. *Some have been Hang'd, many Banish'd, more Imprison'd, and some to Death; and abundance Impoverish'd*; and all this merely for Religion: Though, by a base and barbarous Use of Words, it has been call'd *Treason, Sedition, Routs and Riots*; the worst of Aggravations, since they are not contented to make People unhappy for their Dissent, but rob them of all they had left, *their Innocency*. This has been her State Act, to coin Guilt, and make Men dangerous, to have her Ends upon them. But that Way of Palliating Persecution, by rendering a Thing that it is not, and punishing Men for Crimes they never committed, shews but little Conscience in the Projectors. The Church of *England* cries out against Transubstantiation, because of the Invisibility of the Change. She don't see Christ there, and therefore he is not there, and yet her Sons do the same Thing. For though all the Tokens of a Riot are as invisible in a Dissenter's Meeting, as that in the Transubstantiation, yet it must be a Riot without any more to do; the English of which is, 'tis a Riot to pray to God in the humblest and peaceablest Manner in a Conventicle.

I know it is said, *The Blood-shed in the foregoing Reign, and the Plots of the Papists against Queen* Elizabeth, *drew those Laws from the Church of* England. But this was no Reason why she should do ill because they had done so: Besides, it may be answered, that that Religion having so long intermixt it self with worldly Power, it gave Way to take the Revenges of it. And certainly the Great Men of the Church of *England* endeavouring *to intercept Queen* Mary, *by proclaiming the Lady* Jane Gray, *and the Apprehension the Papists had of the better Title of* Mary *Queen of* Scots, *together with a long Possession*, were scurvy Temptations to kindle ill Designs against that extraordinary Queen. But tho' nothing can excuse and less justify those cruel Proceedings, yet if there were any Reason for the Laws, it is plainly remov'd, for the Interests are joined, and have been since King *James* the first came to the Crown. However, 'tis certain there were Laws enough, or they might have had them, to punish all civil Enormities, without the Necessity of making any against them as Papists. And so the civil Government had stood upon it's own Legs, and Vices only against it had been punishable by it. In short, it was the falsest Step that was made in all that great Queen's Reign, and the most dishonourable to the Principles of the first Reformers, and therefore I know no better Reason why it should be continued, than that which made the *Cardinal* in the History of the *Council of Trent* oppose the Reformation at *Rome*. That tho' it was true that they were in the Wrong, yet the admitting of it *approv'd the Judgment of their Enemies, and so good-night to Infallibility*. Let not this be the Practice of the Church of *England*, and the rather, because she does not pretend to it: But let her reflect, that she has lost her King from her Religion, and they that have got him, naturally hope for Ease for theirs by him, that 'tis the End they laboured, and the great Use they have for him, and I would fain wonder that she never saw it before; but whether she did or no, why should she begrudge it, at least refuse it now? since 'tis plain, that there is nothing we esteem dangerous in Popery that other Laws are not sufficient to secure us from: Have we not enough of them? let Her think of more, and do the best she can to *discover Plotters, punish Traytors, suppress the Seditious, and keep the Peace better* than those we have can enable us to do. But, for God's Sake, let us never direct Laws against Men for the Cause of Religion, or punish them before they have otherwise done amiss. Let Men's Works, not their Opinions, turn the Edge of the Magistrate's Sword against them, else 'tis beheading them before they are born.

By the Common Law of this Kingdom there must be some *real and proper Overt-act* that proves Treason; some *Malice* that proves Sedition; and some *violent Action* that proves a Rout or Riot. If so, to call *any Sort of Religious Orders*, the one, or *praying to God in any Way out of Fashion*, the other, is preposterous, and punishing People for it, down right *Murder* or *Breach of the Peace*, according to the true Use of Words and the old Law of *England*.

If the Church of *England* fears the Growth of Popery, let her be truer to the Religion she owns, and betake her self to *Faith*, rather than *Force*, by a *Pious*, *Humble*, and a *Good Example*: To *convince* and *perswade*, which is the highest Honour to any Church, and the greatest Victory over Men. I am for a National Church as well as she, so it be by *Consent*, and not by *Constraint*. But coercive Churches have the *same Principle*, though not the same *Interest*. A Church, *by Law Establish'd*, is a State Church, and that is no Argument of Verity, unless the State that makes her so be infallible; and because that will not be asserted, the other can never oblige the Conscience, and consequently the Compulsion she uses, is unreasonable. This very Principle *justifies the King of* France, *and the Inquisition*. For Laws being equally of Force in all Countries where they are made, it must be as much a Fault in the Church of *England*'s Judgment to be *a Protestant at* Rome, *or a Calvinist at* Paris, as to be a *Papist at* London: Then where is Truth or Conscience but in the Laws of Countries! which renders her an *Hobbist*, notwithstanding her long and loud Clamours against the *Leviathan*.

I beg her, for the Love of Christ, that she would think of these Things, and not esteem me her Enemy for performing the Part of so good a Friend. Plain-dealing becomes that Character; no Matter whether the Way be agreeable, so it be right: We are all to do our Duty, and leave the rest to God: He can best answer for our Obedience, that Commands it; and our Dependence upon his Word will be our Security in our Conduct. What Weight is it to a Church, that she is *the Church by Law Establish'd*, when no human Law can make a true Church? A True Church is of *Christ's making*, and is by Gospel Establish'd. 'Tis a Reflection to a Church that would be thought true, to *stoop* to human Laws for her Establishment. I have been often scandal'd at that Expression from the Sons of the Church of *England*, especially those of the Robe, *what do you talk for? our Religion is by Law Establish'd*, as if that determined the Question of it's Truth against all other Perswasions.

The *Jews* had this to say against our Saviour, *We have a Law, and by our Law he ought to Dye*. The Primitive Christians, and some of our first Reformers, died *as by Law Established*, if that would mend the Matter; but does that make it lawful to a Christian Conscience? we must ever demur to this Plea. No greater Argument of a Church's Defection from Christianity than turning Persecutor. 'Tis true, the Scripture says, *The Earth shall help the Woman*, but that was to save her self, *not to destroy others*: For 'tis the Token that is given by the Holy Ghost of a false Church; *That none must Buy or Sell in her Dominions that will not receive her Mark in their Forehead, or Right Hand*. That is, by going to Church against Conscience, or bribing lustily to stay at Home.

Things don't change tho' Men do. Persecution is still the same, let the Hand alter never so often; But the Sin may not: For doubtless it is greatest in those that make the highest Claim to Reformation. For while they plead their own Light for doing so, they hereby endeavour to *extinguish* another's Light that can't concur. What a Man can't do, *it is not his Fault he don't do, nor should he be compelled to do it, and least of all punish'd for not doing it*. No Church can give Faith, and therefore can't force it; for what is Constrain'd is not Believ'd; since Faith is in that Sense free, and Constraint gives no Time to assent; I say, what I don't will is not I, and what I don't chuse is none of mine, and another's Faith can't save me tho' it should save him. So that this Method never obtains the End designed, since it saves no body, because it converts no body; it may breed *Hypocrisy*, but that is quite another Thing than *Salvation*.

What

What then is the Use of Penal Laws? only to shew the Sincerity of them that Suffer, *and Cruelty of those that make and execute them.* And all Time tells us they have ever fail'd those that have leaned upon them; They have always been Losers at last; Besides, it is a most unaccountable Obstinacy in the Church of *England* to stickle to uphold them, for after having made it a Matter of Religion and Conscience to address the late King in Behalf of This, to think he should leave Conscience behind him in *Flanders*, or when they waited on him to the Crown, that he should send it thither upon a Pilgrimage, is want of Wit at best, pardon the Censure. Could they Conscientiously oppose his Exclusion for his Religion, and now his Religion because he will not leave it? Or can they reasonably maintain those *Tests* that excluded him when *Duke of York*, while they endured none to *hinder him from the Crown?* I heartily beg the Church of *England*'s Excuse, if I say I can't apprehend her: Perhaps the Fault is mine, but sure I am she is extremely dark. How could she hope for this King without his Conscience? or conceive that his Honour or Conscience would let him leave the Members of his Communion under the Lash of so many Destroying Laws? Would she be so serv'd by a Prince of her own Religion, and she in the like Circumstances? She would not, let her talk 'till *Doom's-day.*

To object the King's Promise, when he came to the Crown, against the Repeal of the Penal Laws, shews not his Insincerity, but her Uncharitableness, or that really she has a very weak Place: For it is plain the King *first declared his own Religion*, and then *promised to maintain her's*; but was that to be without, or together with his own? His Words shews he intended that his own should *Live*, tho' t'other might *Reign*. I say again, it is not credible that a Prince of any Sincerity can refuse a Being to his own Religion, when he continues another in it's well-being. This were to act upon *State* not *Conscience*, and to make more Conscience to uphold a Religion he cannot be of, *than of giving Ease to one his Conscience obliges him to be of.* I cannot imagine how *this Thought* could enter into any Head that had Brains, or Heart that had Honesty. And, to say true, they must be a Sort of State Consciences, *Consciences as by Law Established*, that can follow the Law against their Convictions.

But this is not all I have to observe from that Objection: It implies too evidently, first, that she thinks her self *shaken*, if the Penal Laws be repealed; then by Law Establish'd she must mean, *Established by those Penal Laws.* Secondly, That the King having promised to maintain her, as by Law Established, *he ought not to endeavour their Repeal by which she is established.* I confess this is very close arguing, but then she must not take it ill, if all Men think her ill founded; for any thing must be so, that is established by destroying Laws? Laws, that *Time* and *Practice* have declared Enemies to *Property* and *Conscience.* O let her not hold by that Charter, nor point thither for her Establishment and Defence, if she would be thought a Christian Church.

Plutarch had rather one should think there never was such a Man in the World, than that *Plutarch* was an ill Man. Shall the Church of *England*, that glories in a greater Light, *be more concerned for her Power than her Credit?* To be, than to be that which she should be? I would say, far be it from her, for her own Sake, and which is of much more Moment, for the Sake of the general Cause of Religion.

Let us see therefore if there be not another Way of understanding those Words more decent to the King, and more honourable for her, viz. that she is in the *National Chair, has the Churches and Revenues, and is Mother of those that do not adhere to any separate Communion, and that the King has promised to maintain her in this Post from the Invasions of any other Perswasion that would wrest these Privileges out of her Hands:* This he promised formerly; this he has very particularly repeated in his gracious Declaration: But to ruin Men that would not conform, while himself was so great a Dissenter, and came such, to her Knowledge, to the Crown, can be no Part of his Promises in the Opinion of Common Sense and Charity. Is there no Difference to be observed between not turning her out, and Destroying all others not of her Communion: He will not turn her out, there's his Promise, and he has not done it; There's his Performance: Nor will he do it, I am confident, if she pleases. But there's no Manner of Necessity from this Engagement that all Parties else are to be confounded. Tho' if it were so, 'tis ill Divinity to press such Promises upon a Prince's Conscience, that can't be performed with a good One by Any Body.

Let us remember how often she has upbraided her Dissenters with this, *Render to Cæsar the Things that are Cæsar's*, whilst they have returned upon her t'other half of the Text, *and render unto God the Things that are God's*. It happens now that *God* and *Cæsar* are both of a Mind, which perhaps does not always fall out, at least about the Point in Hand. Will she dissent from both now? Her Case, believe me, will be doubtful then. I beg her to be Considerate. 'Tis the greatest Time of Trial she has met with since she was a Church. To acquit her self like a Member of Christ's Universal One, let her keep nothing that voids her Pretensions. The *Babylonish* Garment will undo her. Practices inconsistent with her Reformation will ruin her. The *Martyr*'s Blood won the Day, and her Severity has almost lost it. They suffered by Law, she makes Laws *for Suffering*. Is this an Imitation of their Practice, *to uphold the Weapons of their Destruction?* I must tell her, 'tis being a *Martyr* for Persecution, and not by it. Another Path than that the Holy Ancients, and our humble Ancestors trod, and which will lead her to be deserted and contemned of every Body that counts it safer to follow the blessed Rule and practise of Christ and his inspired Messengers, than her narrow and worldly Policies. But that which heightens the Reproach, is the Offer of the Romanists themselves to make a perpetual Civil Peace with her, and that she refuses. Would the Martyrs have done this? surely no. Let her remember the first Argument honest old *Fox* advances against that Church, is the Church of *England*'s present Darling, viz. Penal Laws for Religion; as she may see at the Beginning of his first Volume: Doubtless he was much in the Right, which makes her extremely in the Wrong. Nothing, says the Prophet, must harm in God's Holy Mountain, and that's the Church, says *Fox*, and therefore he says, Christ's Church never Persecutes. Leave then God with his own Work, and Christ with his own Kingdom. As it is not of the World, let not the World touch it; no, *not to uphold it*, though they that bear it should trip by the Way. Remember *Uzzah*, he would needs support the Ark *when the Oxen* Stumbled; *but was struck Dead for his Pains*. The Presumption is more than parallel. Christ promised *to be present with his Church to the End of the World*. He bids them *fear not*, and told them, *that sufficient was the Day for the Evil thereof*. How? with Penal Laws? no such Matter; but his Divine Presence. Therefore it was, He called not for *Legions* to fight for him, because his Work needed it not. They that want them have another Sort of Work to do: And 'tis too plain, that *Empire*, and not Religion, has been too much the Business. But, O let it not be so any more! To be a *True* Church is better than to be a *National* One; especially as so upheld. *Press Virtue, Punish Vice, Dispense with Opinion; Perswade, but don't Impose.* Are there *Tares* in Opinion? let them alone; you heard *they are to grow with the Wheat 'till Harvest*, that is, *the End of the World*. *Should they not be plucked up before?* No; and 'tis *Angels* Work at last too. Christ, that knew all Men, saw no Hand on Earth fit for that Business. Let us not then usurp their Office. Besides, *we are to love Enemies*; this is the Great Law of our Religion; *by what Law then are we to Persecute them?* and if not Enemies, not Friends and Neighbours certainly.

The Apostle rejoyced *that Christ was Preached out of Envy*, If so, I am sure we ought not to envy Christians the Enjoyment of the Liberty of their Consciences. Christianity should be propagated by the Spirit of Christianity, and not by Violence or Persecution, for that's the Spirit of Antichristianity. Nor for Fear of it, should we, of Christians, become Antichristians. Where is Faith in God? Where is Trust in Providence? Let us do our Duty, and leave the rest with Him; *and not do Evil that Good may come of it*; for that shews a Distrust in God, and a Confidence in our own Inventions for Security. No Reason of State can excuse our Disobedience to his *Rule*; and we desert the Principles of our Heavenly Master when we decline it. The Question is about Conscience, about this we can none of us be too tender, nor exemplary. 'Tis in right doing that Christians can hope for Success; and for true Victory only through Faith and Patience. But if to avoid what we fear, we contradict our Principles, we may justly apprehend *that God will desert us in an unlawful Way of maintaining them*. Perhaps this may be God's Time of trying all Parties, what we will do; whether we will rely upon him or our own feeble Provisions; whether we will allow what we our selves, in our Turn, *have all of us desired*; if not, may we not expect to suffer the Thing we would inflict? for our Penal Laws cannot secure us from the Turns of Providence, and less support us under them. Let us consider the true Ground of the Difficulty that is made, if it be not partial and light in God's Scale; for to that Tryal all Things

must

must come, and his Judgment is inevitable as well as infallible. Besides, if we have not tried all other Methods, we are inexcusable in being so tenacious for this. I do therefore, in all Humility, beseech all Sorts of Professors of Christianity in these Kingdoms, to abstract themselves from those Jealousies which worldly Motives are apt to kindle in their Minds, and with an even and undisturbed Soul pursue their Christian Duty in this great Conjuncture: Considering *the Race is not to the Swift, nor the Battle to the Strong*, and that for all our Watchmen, *'tis God alone* (at last) *that keeps the City*. Not that I would decline a fitting, but an unchristian Provision: For though the Foundation were never so true, yet if our Superstructure be *Hay* and *Stubble*, (our own narrow Devices) the Fire will consume it, and our Labour will be worse than in vain. Let us not therefore *Sow what we would not Reap, because we must Reap what we Sow*: And remember who told us, *what we measure to others shall be measured to us again*. Let us therefore do unto all Parties of Men, *as we would be done unto by them in their Turn of Power*: Lest our Fear of their Undutifulness, *should tempt us out of our Duty*, and so draw upon our selves the Mischiefs we are afraid of. Sacred Writ is full of this, in the Doctrine of both Testaments; and, as we profess to believe it, we are inexcusable if we do not practise it. Let the Spirit then of Christian Religion prevail: Let our Policies give Way to our Duty, and our Fears will be overcome of our Hopes, which will not make us ashamed at the last and great Judgment: where, O God! let us all appear with Comfort.

I could yet enlarge upon this Subject; for nothing can be more fruitful. I could say, that a Church that *Denies* Infallibility, cannot *force*, because she cannot be *certain*, and so *Penal Laws* (tho' it were possible that they could be lawful in others) in her, *would be Unjust*. That Scripture leaves Men to *Conviction* and *Persuasion*. That the true Church-Weapons are *Light* and *Grace*; and her Punishments, *Censure* and *Excommunication*. That *Goals* and *Gibbets* are Inadequate Methods for Conversion, and that they never succeeded. That this forbids all farther Light to come into the World, and so limits the Holy One, which in Scripture is made a great Sin. And, lastly, That such ensnare their own Posterity that may be of another Mind, and forfeit by it the Estates they have so carefully transmitted to them. Thus far against Imposition. And against Compliance, I could say, that it's to betray God's Sovereignty over Conscience; To defy Men; Gratify Presumption; Soil and Extinguish Truth in the Mind; Obey Blindfold; make over the Soul without Security; turn Hypocrite, and abundance more; each of which Heads might well merit an whole Chapter. But this having been well and seasonably considered elsewhere, I shall now proceed to the second Part of this Discourse, in which I will be as brief, and yet as full as I can.

PART II. *That 'tis the Principle of Men of Note of all Parties.*

BUT what Need Is there of this, may some say, when all Parties profess to be of the same Judgment, *That Conscience ought not to be forced, nor Religion imposed upon Men at their Civil Peril?* I own they are all of that Mind, at one Time or other, and therefore, that I may purge my self of any Animosity to the Doctrine of the Church of *England*, I will ingenuously confess the severe Conduct I have argued against is not to be imputed to her Principles; but then her Evil will be the greater, that in Fact has so notoriously contradicted them. I know some of her Defenders will hardly allow that too; tho' the more candid give us their Silence or Confession: For they tell us, *'tis not the Church that has done it;* which, unless they mean, the Laws were not made at Church, must needs be false, since those that made and executed them were of her own Communion, and are that great Body of Members that constitute her a Church; but, by her shifting them off, 'tis but reasonable to conclude that she tacitly condemns what she publickly disowns. One would think then it should not be so hard to perswade her to quit them, in the Way she made them, or to enjoyn her Sons to do it, if that Language be too harsh for her. This she must hear of some Way, and I pray God she may endeavour to do her Duty in it. She is not alone; for every Party in Power has too evidently lapsed into this Evil; tho' under the Prevalency and Persecution of another Interest they have ever writ against Club-Law for Religion. And to the End that I may do the *Reformation* Right, and the Principles of the Church of
England

England Juftice, I muft fay, that hardly one Perfon of any note, died in the Time of Queen *Mary*, that did not pafs Sentence upon Perfecution as Antichriftian, particularly *Latimer, Philpot, Bradford, Rogers*, very Eminent Reformers. The Apologies that were writ in thofe Times, are of the fame Strain, as may be feen in *Jewel, Haddon, Reynolds, &c.* and the Papifts were with reafon thought much in the wrong by thofe Primitive Proteftants, for the Perfecution that they raifed againft them, for Matters of pure Religion. But what need we go fo far back? Is it not recent in Memory, that Bifhop *Ufher* was Employ'd to *O. Cromwell* by fome of the Clergy of the Church of *England* for Liberty of Confcience? Dr. *Parr*, in the Life of Dr. *Ufher* Primate of *Armagh*, fol, 75. has that Paffage thus.

'*Cromwell* forbidding the Clergy, under great Penalties, to teach Schools, or to
' perform any Part of their minifterial Function; fome of the moft confiderable
' Epifcopal Clergy in and about *London*, defired my Lord *Primate* that he would
' ufe his Intereft with *Cromwell*, (fince they heard he pretended a great Refpect for
' him) that as he granted Liberty of Confcience to almoft all Sorts of Religions,
' fo the Epifcopal Divines might have the fame Freedom of ferving God in their
' private Congregations (fince they were not permitted the publick Churches) ac-
' cording to the Liturgy of the Church of *England*; and that neither the Minifters,
' nor thofe that frequented that Service, might be any more hindered, or difturbed
' by his Soldiers: So according to their Defire, he went and ufed his utmoft En-
' deavours with *Cromwell*, for the taking off this Reftraint, which was at laft pro-
' mifed (though with fome Difficulty) and that they fhould not be molefted, pro
' vided they meddled not with any Matters relating to his Government.

Certainly thofe Gentlemen were of my Mind, And to give Dr. *Hammond* his due, who I underftand was one of them, he left it to the Witneffes of his End, as his dying Counfel to the Church of *England*, That they difplaced no Man out of the Univerfity or prefent Church, but that by Love, and an Holy Life they fhould prevail upon thofe in Poffeffion to come into their Church. But this lookt fo little like the Policy and Ambition of the Living, that they refolved it fhould be Buried with him. This I had from an eminent Hand in *Oxford*, a Year or two after his Death. An older Man out liv'd him, and one of the moft Learned and Pious of that Communion, Bifhop *Sanderfon* I mean: They were the two great Men of their Sort that was of the Party. Let us fee what this Reverend Man fays to our Point.

' The Word of God doth exprefly forbid us to fubject our Confciences to the
' Judgment of any other, or to ufurp a Dominion over the Confciences of any
' One. *Several Cafes of Confcience difcuffed in Ten Lectures in the Divinity School*
' *at* Oxford, 3 Lect. 30 Sect. pag. 163. printed 1660.

' He is not worthy to be Chrift's Difciple, who is not the Difciple of Chrift
' *alone*. The Simplicity and Sincerity of the Chriftian Faith, hath fuffered a great
' Prejudice fince we have been divided into Parties, neither is there any Hope that
' Religion fhould be reftored to her former Original and Purity, until the Wounds
' that were made wider by our daily Quarrels and Diffentions, being anointed with
' the *Oyl of Brotherly Love*, as with a Balfam, fhall begin to clofe again, and to
' grow entire into the fame Unity of Faith and Charity, *ibid. Sect. 29.*

' The Obligation of Confcience doth not fignify any Compulfion, for, to fpeak
' properly, the Confcience can no more be compelled than the Free-will. *ibid 4.*
Lecture Sect. 5. pag. 109.

' The exprefs Commandment of God doth oblige the Confcience properly by
' it felf and by it's own Force; and this Obligation is abfolute, becaufe it doth di-
' rectly and always oblige, and becaufe it obligeth all Perfons, and the Obligation
' of it is never to be cancelled. *None but God alone* hath Power to impofe a Law
' upon the Confcience of any Man, to which it ought to be fubjected, as obliging
' by it felf, —— This Conclufion is prov'd by the Words of the Apoftle, *There is*
' *but one Law-giver, who can both fave and deftroy.* In which Words two Argu-
' ments do offer themfelves to our Obfervation; In the firft place they affert
' there is but one Legiflator; not one picked out amongft many; not one above
' many; but one exclufively, that is to fay, One, and but one only. The Apoftle
' otherwife had made ufe of a very ineffectual Argument, to prove what he had
' propounded; for he rebuketh thofe who unadvifedly did pafs their Judgment
' either on the Perfons, or the Deeds of other Men, as the Invaders of their Rights.
' *Who art Thou* (faith he) *who doft judge another?* As if he fhould have faid, doft
' thou know thy felf, what thou art, and what thou doft? It doth not belong to
Thee

'Thee to thrust thy sawcy Sickle into the harvest of another Man, *much less boldly to fling thy self into the Throne of Almighty God*. If already Thou art Ignorant of it, then know, that it belongeth to him *alone* to judge of the Consciences of Men, *to whom alone it doth belong to impose Laws upon the Consciences of Men*, which none can do but God alone. *ibid pag.* 111, 112, 113.

'The Condition and Natural Estate of the Conscience itself is so placed as it were in the middle *betwixt* God and the will of Man, as that which is usually and truly spoken of Kings and Emperours, may as truly be verified of the Conscience of every Man, *Solo Deo minores esse, nec aliquem in Terris superiorem agnoscere*; They are *less than God only, and on Earth do acknowledge no Superior*. That Speech of the Emperour *Maximilian* the first is very memorable, *Conscientiis Dominari velle, est Arcem Cœli invadere*; To *exercise a Domination over Consciences, is to invade the Tower of Heaven*. He is a Plunderer of the Glory of God, and a *nefarious Invader* of the Power that is due unto him, whosoever he is that shall claim a right to the Consciences of Men, or practice an Usurpation over them. *ibid. Sect.* 11. *pag.* 115.

And yet this is the sad Consequence of imposing Religion upon Conscience, and punishing Non-conformity with worldly Penalties.

Let us now hear what the late *Bishop of Down* says in his *Lib. of Prophesy* to our Point, 'I am very much displeased that so many Opinions and new Doctrines are commenced amongst us, but more troubled, that every Man that hath an Opinion thinks his own and other Men's Salvation is concerned in it's maintenance, but most of all, that Men should be Persecuted and Afflicted for disagreeing in such Opinions, which they cannot with sufficient Grounds obtrude upon others necessarily, because they cannot propound them Infallibly, and because they have no Warrant from Scripture so to do; for if I shall tye other Men to believe my Opinion, because I think I have a Place of Scripture which seems to warrant it to my Understanding; why may he not serve up another Dish to me in the same Dress, and exact the same Task of me to believe the contradictory? *Liberty of Prophesy*, Epist. Dedicat. p. 8, 9.

'The Experience which Christendom hath had in this last Age is Argument enough that *Toleration of differing Opinions* is so far from disturbing the Publick Peace, or destroying the Interest of Princes and Common-wealths, that it does advantage to the Publick, it secures Peace, because there is not so much as the *Pretence of Religion* left to such Persons to contend for, it being already indulged to them. *ibid.* pag. 21.

It is a proverbial saying, *Quod nimia familiaritas servorum est conspiratio adversus Dominum*, and they who for their Security run into Grots and Cellars, and Retirements, think that they being upon the defensive, those Princes and those Laws that drive them to it are their Enemies, and therefore they cannot be secure, unless the Power of the one, and the Obligation of the other be lessened and rescinded; and then the being restrained, and made miserable, endears the discontented Persons mutually, and makes more hearty and dangerous Confederations, *ibid.* Page 23.

'No Man speaks more unreasonably, than he that *denies to Men the Use of their Reason in Choice of their Religion*. ibid. pag. 169.

'*No Christian is to be put to Death, Dismembred, or otherwise directly Persecuted for his Opinion, which does not teach Impiety or Blasphemy*, ibid. pag. 190.

'There is a popular Pity that follows all Persons in Misery, and that Compassion breeds likeness of Affections, and that very often produces Likeness of Perswasions; and so much the rather, because there arises a Jealousie and pregnant Suspicion that they who Persecute an Opinion are destitute of sufficient Arguments to confute it, and that the Hangman is the best Disputant. *ibid.* Page 197, 198.

'If a Man cannot change his Opinion when he lists, nor ever does heartily or resolutely, but when he cannot do otherwise, then to use Force, may make him an Hypocrite, but never to be a right Believer, and so instead of erecting a Trophy to God and true Religion, *we build a Monument for the Devil.* ibid. p. 200.

'The Trick of giving Persons differing in Opinion over to the secular Power, at the best is no better than *Hypocrisy*, removing Envy from themselves, and laying it upon others, a refusing to do that in external Act, *which they do in Counsel and Approbation.* ibid. pag. 209.

Thus

1687.
Part II.

Thus far *Bishop Taylor*, and one of the most Learned Men of the Church of *England* in his Time.

Let me add another Bishop, held Learned by all, and in great Reputation with the Men of his Communion, and among them *the Lords Spiritual and Temporal in Parliament assembled,* who have sufficiently declared against this persecuting Spirit on the Account of Religion, by their full Approbation of, and *Thanks returned to the Bishop of S. Asaph for his Sermon Preached before them* November *the 5th,* 1680. *and their Desire that he would Print and Publish that Sermon.* The Bishop says, that,

' They who are most given to Hate and to Destroy others, especially those others
' who differ from them in Religion, they are not the *Church of God,* or at least
' they are so far corrupt in that particular. *pag.* 8.

Again he says, ' That, of Societies of Men, Christians, of all others, are most
' averse from Ways of Violence and Blood; especially from using any such Ways
' upon the Account of Religion: And among Christian Churches, where they dif-
' fer among themselves, if either of them use those Ways upon the Account of
' Religion, they give a strong Presumption against themselves that they are not
' truly Christians. *ibid. pag.* 9.

' There is reason for this, because, we know that Christ gave Love for the Cha-
' racter by which his Disciples were to be known. *John* 13. 35. *By this shall all
' Men know that you are my Disciples, if you have love to one another.* And lest
' Men should unchristen others first, that they may Hate them, and Destroy them
' afterwards, Christ enlarged his Precept of Love, and extended it even to Ene-
' mies, and not only to ours, but to the Enemies of our Religion, *Matt.* 5. 43, 44.
ibid. Pag. 9.

' As our Holy Religion excells all others in this admirable temper, so by this we
' may usually judge who they are that excel among Christian Churches, when there
' happens any Difference between them, whether touching the Faith, or the Terms
' of Communion. They that were the more Fierce, they generally had the worst
' Cause. *ibid. pag.* 12, 13.

' The Council of *Nice* suppressed the *Arrians* by no other Force, but putting
' *Arrians* out of their Bishopricks; they could not think Hereticks fit to be trusted
' with cure of Souls; but otherwise, as to *Temporal Things,* I do not find that
' they inflicted any kind of Punishments; but when the *Arrians* came to have the
' *Power* in their Hands, when theirs was come to be the *Imperial Religion,* then
' Depriving was nothing, Banishment was the least that they inflicted. *ibid. pag.* 14.

' Neither our Religion, nor our Church, is of a *persecuting* Spirit. I know not
' how it may be in particular Persons; but I say again, it is not in the *Genius* of
' our Church: She hath no Doctrine that *teacheth Persecution. ibid.* p. 20.

' I would have no Man punished for his Religion, no not them that destroy Men
for Religion. *ibid. pag.* 37.

Dr. *Stillingfleet* comes short of none of them on this Subject. * Our Saviour,
' says he, never *pressed* Followers as Men do *Soldiers,* but said, *If any Man will
' come after me, let him take up his Cross* (not his Sword) *and follow me.* His was
' ἥμερος καὶ φιλάνθρωπος νομοθεσία, his very Commands shewed his Meekness; his Laws
' were sweet and gentle Laws; not like *Draco*'s that were writ in Blood, unless
' it were his own that gave them. His Design was to ease Men of their former
' Burdens, and not lay on more; the Duties he required were no other but such
' as were necessary, and withal very just and reasonable. He that came to take a-
' way the insupportable Yoke of Jewish Ceremonies, certainly did never intend to
' gall the Necks of his Disciples with another instead of it. And it would be
' strange the Church should require more than Christ himself did; and make other
' Conditions of her Communion, *than our Saviour did of Discipleship.* What
' possible reason can be assigned or given why such Things should not be sufficient
' for Communion with a Church, *which are sufficient for Eternal Salvation?* And
' certainly those Things are sufficient for that, which are laid down as necessary
' Duties of Christianity by our Lord and Saviour in his Word. *What Ground can
' there be why Christians should not stand upon the same Terms now which they did in
' the Time of Christ and his Apostles?* Was not Religion sufficiently guarded and
' fenced in them? Was there ever more true and cordial Reverence in the Worship
' of God? What *Charter* hath Christ given the Church to *bind Men up to more than
' himself hath done?* or to exclude those from her Society who may be admitted
' into Heaven? Will Christ ever thank Men at the great Day for keeping such out
' from Communion with his Church, when he will vouchsafe not only Crowns of
' Glory

* *Irenicum,* a Weapon-Salve for the Churches Wounds, by *E. Stillingfleet* Rector of *Sutton* in *Bedfordshire,* in Preface to the Reader.

' Glory to them, but it may be *Aureolæ* too, if there be any such Things there? The
' Grand Commission the Apostles were sent out with, was only to *teach what Christ*
' *had commanded them.* Not the least Intimation of any Power given them to im-
' pose or require any Thing beyond what himself had spoken to them, or they
' were directed to by the Immediate Guidance of the Spirit of God.

' Without all Controversy, the main Inlet of all the Distractions, Confusions and
' Divisions of the Christian World, hath been by adding other Conditions of Church
' Communion than Christ hath done.

' There is nothing the *Primitive Church* deserves greater Imitation by us in, than
' in that admirable Temper, Moderation and Condescension which was used in it
' towards all the Members of it.

' This admirable Temper in the Primitive Church might be largely cleared from
' that Liberty they allowed freely to Dissenters from them in Matters of Practice
' and Opinion; as might be cleared from *Cyprian, Austin, Jerome,* and others.—
' Leaving the Men to be won by observing the true decency and order of Churches,
' whereby those who act upon a true Principle of Christian Ingenuity may be
' sooner drawn to a Compliance in all lawful Things, than by Force and rigorous
' Impositions, which make Men suspect the Weight of the Thing it self, when
' such Force is used to make it enter. *In the Preface.*

The same is in effect declared by the *House of Commons,* when they returned their Thanks to Dr. *Tillotson, Dean of Canterbury,* for his Sermon Preached before them
' *November* the 5th, 1678. *desiring him to Print that Sermon,* where he says, upon our Saviour's Words, ' *Ye know not what Manner of Spirit ye are of,* Ye own your
' selves to be my Disciples, but do you consider what Spirit now Acts and Governs
' you? not that surely which my Doctrine designs to mould and fashion you into,
' which is not a *Furious and Persecuting,* and *Destructive Spirit,* but Mild and
' Gentle, and Saving; tender of the Lives and Interests of Men, even of those
' who are our greatest Enemies *pag.* 6, 7.

' No Difference of Religion, no Pretence of Zeal for God and Christ can warrant
' and justifie this Passionate and Fierce, this Vindictive and Exterminating Spirit.
ibid. pag. 7.

' He (*i. e.* Christ) came to introduce a Religion, which consults not only the E-
' ternal Salvation of Men's Souls, but their Temporal Peace and Security, their
' Comfort and Happiness in this World. *ibid. pag.* 8.

' It seemed good to the Author of this Institution to compel no Man to it by
' Temporal Punishment. *ibid. pag.* 13.

' To *separate* Goodness and Mercy From God, Compassion and Charity from
' Religion, is to make the two best Things in the World, God and Religion, good
' for nothing. *ibid. pag.* 9.

' True Christianity is not only the best, but the best natured Institution in the
' World; and so far as any Church is departed from good Nature, and become
' Cruel and Barbarous, so far it is degenerated from Christianity. *ibid. pag.* 30.

Thus far Dr. *Tillotson,* who, to be sure, deserves not to be thought the least Eminent in the present Church of *England.* Let us hear what Dr. *Burnet* says to it.

' Men are not Masters of their own Perswasions, and cannot change their Thoughts
' as they please; he that believes any Thing concerning Religion, *cannot turn as*
' *the Prince commands him, or accommodate himself to the Law, or his present Inte-*
' *rests,* unless he arrive at that *Pitch of Atheism,* as to look on Religion only as
' a Matter of Policy, and an Engine for Civil Government: Dr. Burnet's *History*
of the Rights of Princes, &c. in his Preface, pag. 49.

'Tis to this Doctor's Pains, She owes the very *History of Her Reformation*; and, as by it he has perpetuated his Name with Her's, certainly he must have Credit with Her, or She can deserve none with any Body else; for no Man could well go farther to oblige Her.

Let me here bring in a Lay Member of the *Church of England,* Sir Robert Pointz, in *His Vindication of Monarchy,* who yields us an excellent Testimony to the Matter in Hand: ' The Sword *availeth little* with the Souls of Men, unless to *destroy*
' them together with their Bodies, and to make Men *Desperate,* or *Dissemblers in*
' *Religion,* and when they find Opportunity, to fall into *Rebellion,* as there are
' many Examples, *pag.* 27.

' In the Ancient Times of Christianity, such Means were not used as might *make*
' *Hereticks and Schismaticks more obstinate than docible, through the preposterous*

'Proceedings of the Magistrates and Ministers of Justice, in the Execution of Penal
'Laws, used rather as *Snares* for Gaining of Money, and Pecuniary Mulcts im-
'pos'd, rather as *Prices* set upon Offences, than as Punishments for the Reformati-
'on of Manners, *ibid. pag.* 28.

'The *Ancient Christians* were forbidden by the *Imperial Law*, as also by the
'Laws of other Christian Nations, under a great Penalty, *To meddle with the Goods
'of* Jews, *or* Pagans, *living Peaceably, ibid. pag.* 29.

'For, the Goods of the *Jews*, although Enemies to the Christian Religion, *can-
'not for the Cause of Religion come by Escheat unto Christian Princes*, under whom
'they live. *Ibid. pag.* 29.

'It is truly said, that *Peace*, a Messenger whereof an *Angel* hath been chosen
'to be, *is scarce Established by the Sword*; and the *Gospel*, the *Blessed Peace*, can-
'not be published by the *Sound of Cannon*, neither the *Sacred Word* be convey'd
'unto us, by the *Impious Hands of Soldiers*; neither *Tranquillity* be brought to the
'*Persons and Consciences of Men, by that which bringeth Ruin unto Nations*,
ibid. pag. 70.

He has said Much in a Little; the Talent and Honour of Men truly Great. I give this still to the *Church of England's Principles*, which yet makes it harder for Her, to Justifie Her Practice in Her Use of Power. But let us hear a King speak, and One the *Church of England* is bound to hear by many Obligations.

King *Charles* the First, out of his *Tender and Princely Sense of the sad and bleeding Condition of the Kingdom*, and his unwearied Desires to apply such Remedies, as by the Blessing of Almighty God, might settle it in Peace, by the Advice of his Lords and Commons of Parliament, Assembled at *Oxford*, propounded and desired, *That all the Members of Both Houses might securely Meet in a Full and Free Convention of Parliament, there to Treat, Consult, and Agree upon such Things, as may conduce to the Maintenance and Defence of the* Reformed Protestant Religion, *with due Consideration to all Just and Reasonable Ease to Tender Consciences.* The King's Message of a Treaty, *March* 3. 1643. from *Oxford*, Superscribed to the Lords and Commons of Parliament Assembled at *Westminster*.

In the King's Twentieth Message for Peace, *January* 29, 1645, he has these Words, *That by the Liberty offered in his Message of the* 15th *present, for the Ease of their Consciences who will not Communicate in the Service already Established by Act of Parliament in this Kingdom, He intends that all other Protestants, behaving themselves Peaceable in, and towards the Civil Government, shall have the Free Exercise of their Religion, according to their own Way.*

In the Thirty Third Message for Peace, *November* 14, 1647, there are these Words, *His Majesty considering the great present Distempers concerning* Church-Discipline *and that the* Presbyterian Government *is now in Practice, His Majesty to eschew Confusion, as much as may be, and for the Satisfaction of His Two Houses, is content that the said Government be Legally permitted to stand in the same Condition it now is, for Three Years; Provided, that His Majesty, and those of his Judgment (or any other who cannot in* Conscience *submit thereunto) be not obliged to comply with the* Presbyterial Government, *but have Free Practice of their own Profession, without receiving any Prejudice thereby.* From the Isle of *Wight*.

In his Declaration to all his People, *January* 18, 1645, from *Carisbrook* Castle, after the Votes of no Address, He says, *I have Sacrificed to My Two Houses of Parliament, for the Peace of the Kingdom, All but what is much more dear to me than my Life, my* Conscience *and my* Honour.

In his Letter to the Lords, Gentlemen and Committee of the *Scotch* Parliament, together with the Officers of the Army, *July* 3, 1648, from *Carisbrook* Castle —— *As the Best Foundation of Loyalty is Christianity, so True Christianity is Perfect Loyalty.*

ΕΙΚΩΝ ΒΑΣΙΛΙΚΗ. Ch. 6. Upon His Majesty's Retirement from *Westminster*.—— *Sure it ceases to be Counsel, when not* Reason *is used, as to Men to* Perswade, *but* Force and Terror, *as to Beasts, to drive and compel Men to whatever Tumultuary Patrons shall Project. He deserves to be a* Slave *without Pity or Redemption, that is content to have* his Rational Sovereignty of his Soul, *and Liberty of his* Will *and* Words *so captivated.* —— Again, Ibid. *Sure that Man cannot be blameable to God or Man, who seriously endeavours to* See the Best Reason of Things, *and faithfully follows what he takes for* Reason; *the* Uprightness *of his Intentions will excuse the possible Failing of his* Understanding. —— Again, Ibid. *I know no Resolutions*

tions more worthy a Christian King, *than to prefer his* Conscience *before his* Kingdoms.

Chap. 12. Upon the Rebellion and Troubles in *Ireland.*—*Some Kind of Zeal counts All Merciful Moderation,* Lukewarmness, *and had rather be* Cruel, *than accounted* Cold, *and is not seldom more greedy to Kill the Bear for his Skin, than for any Harm he hath done.* —— Ib. O my GOD, Thou seest how much Cruelty among Christians is acted under the Colour of Religion, as if we could not be Christians, unless we Crucify one another.

Chap. 13. Upon the calling the *Scots*, and their coming—*Sure, in Matters of* Religion, *those* Truths *gain most on* Men's Judgments *and* Consciences, *which are least urged with* Secular Violence, *which weakens* Truth *with Prejudices ; and is unreasonable to be used, till such Means of Rational Conviction hath been applied, as leaving no Excuse for Ignorance, condemns Men's Obstinacy to deserv'd Penalties.* —— *Violent Motions are neither* Manly, Christian, *nor* Loyal. —— *The proper Engine of* Faction *is* Force ; *the Arbitrator of Beasts, not of* Reasonable Men, *much less of* Humble Christians *and* Loyal Subjects, *in Matters of Religion.*

Chap. 14. Upon the Covenant. —— *Religion requires* Charity *and* Candor *to others of different Opinions* —— *Nothing Violent and Injurious can be Religious.*

Chap. 15. Upon the many Jealousies raised, and Scandals cast upon the King, to stir up the People against him. —— *In Point of True Conscientious Tenderness (attended with Humility and Meekness, not with proud or arrogant Activity, which seeks to hatch every Egg of indifferent Opinion to Faction or Schism) I have oft declared how little I desire* My Laws *and* Scepter *should intrench over God's Soveraignty, who is the Only King of Men's Consciences.*

Chap. 27. To the Prince of *Wales.*——*Take Heed of abetting to any Factions ; your* Partial *adhering to any* One Side, *gains you not so great* Advantages *in some Men's Hearts, (who are* Prone *to be of their King's Religion) as it loseth you in others, who think themselves, and their Profession, first despised, then persecuted by you.* —— *My Counsel and Charge to you is, That you seriously consider the former Real or Objected Miscarriages, which might occasion my Troubles, that you may avoid them.* —— *A* Charitable Connivence, *and* Christian Toleration, *often dissipates their Strength, whom* Rougher Opposition *fortifies.* —— *Always keep up* Sound Piety, *and those* Fundamental Truths *(which mend both Hearts and Lives of Men) with Impartial Favour and Justice.* —— *Your Prerogative is best shewed and exercised in* Remitting, *rather than exacting the Rigour of the Law, there being nothing worse than Legal Tyranny:*

And as this was the Sense and Judgment of a King, that Time, and the greatest Troubles had inform'd with a Superior Judgment, (and which to be sure highly justifies the Measures that are now taken) So Dr. *Hudson*, His *Plain Dealing Chaplain*, must not be forgotten by us on this Occasion, who took the Freedom to tell His Royal Master, *That he look'd upon the Calamities he labour'd under, to be the Hand of GOD upon Him, for not having given GOD His Due over Conscience.*

One can easily imagine this to be *Reformation Language*, and then it is not hard to think, how low that Church must be fallen, that from so Free and Excellent a Principle, is come to make, execute, and uphold *Penal Laws for Religion, against Her Conscientious Neighbours* ; but it is to be hoped, *That like* Nebuchadnezzar's Image, *whose Feet was a Mixture of* Iron *and* Clay, *and therefore could not stand for ever,* Persecution *will not be able to mix so with the Seed of Men, but that* Humanity *will overcome it, and* Mankind *One Day be delivered from that Iron, Hard, and Fierce Nature.*

I have done with my *Church of England's Evidences against Persecution*: And for the *Judgment of all Sorts of Dissenters in That Point*, let their Practice have been what it will, nothing is clearer, *than that they disallow of Persecution*, of which their Daily Addresses of Thanks to the KING, for His General Ease, by His Excellent Declaration, are an undoubted Proof.

Thus then we see, it is evident, that it is not only the *Duty of all Parties, as they would be thought Christians, to Repeal Penal Laws for Religion*, but upon a Fair Enquiry, *We see it is the avowed Principle of every Party, at one Time or other, that* Conscience *ought not to be compell'd, nor* Religion *impos'd upon Worldly Penalties.* And so I come to the Third and Last Part of this Discourse.

PART III. *It is the Interest of all Parties, and especially the Church of* ENGLAND.

AS I take all Men to be unwillingly separated from their Interests, and consequently ought only to be sought and discours'd in them, so it must be granted me on all Hands, *That Interests change as well as Times, and 'tis the Wisdom of a Man to observe the Courses, and humour the Motions of his Interest, as the Best Way to preserve it.* And lest any ill-natur'd, or mistaken Person, should call it *Temporizing*, I make this early Provision; *That I mean, no immoral, or corrupt Compliance:* A *Temporizing*, deservedly base with Men of Vertue, and which in all Times, my Practice, as well as Judgment, hath shown the last Aversion to. For upon the Principle I now go, and which I lay down, as common and granted in Reason and Fact, with all Parties concern'd in this Discourse, that Man does not change, that *Morally* follows his Interest under all it's Revolutions, because to be True to his Interest, is his First Civil Principle. I premise this, to introduce what I have to offer, with Respect to the Interests to be now treated upon.

And first, I say, *I take it to be the Interest of the Church of* England, *to abolish the Penal Laws, because it never was Her Interest to make them.* My Reasons for that Opinion are these, *First,* They have been an Argument to invalidate the Sufferings of the *Reformers,* because if it be unlawful to disobey Government about Matters of Religion, they were in the wrong. And if they say, *O but they were in Error that punish'd their Non-Conformity*; I answer, How can She prove that She is Infallibly in the Right? And if this cannot be done, She compels to an Uncertainty upon the same Terms. *Secondly,* She has overthrown the Principles upon which She separated from *Rome :* For if it be Unlawful to plead Scripture and Conscience, to vindicate Dissent from Her Communion, it was Unlawful for Her upon the same Plea, *To Dissent from the Church of Rome*; unless She will say again, *That She was in the Right, but the other in the Wrong*; and She knows this is no Answer, but a begging of the Question; *For they that Separate from Her, think themselves as Serious, Devout, and as much in the Right as She could do.* If then *Conscience and Scripture,* interpreted with the *Best Light* She had, were the Ground of Her Reformation, She must allow the Liberty She takes, *Or She Eats Her Words, and Subverts Her Foundation*; than which nothing can be more Destructive to the Interest of any Being, Civil or Ecclesiastical. *Thirdly,* The *Penal Laws* have been the *Great Make-Bate* in the Kingdom from the Beginning: For if I should grant that She had been once truly the *Church of England*, I mean, consisting of all the *People of England,* (which She was not, for there were divers Parties Dissenting from the First of Her Establishment) yet since it afterwards appear'd She was but One Party, tho' the biggest, She ought not to have made Her Power more National than Her Faith, nor Her Faith so by the Force of Temporal Authority. 'Tis true, She got the Magistrate of Her Side, but She engaged him too far: For She knew, *Christ did not leave Cæsar Executor to His Last Will and Testament,* and, that *That* should be the Reason why She did so, was none of the *Best Ornaments to Her Reformation.* That She was but a Party, tho' the biggest, by the Advantages that Temporal Power brought Her, I shall easily prove, but I will introduce it with a short Account of our State-Reformation here in *England.*

Henry the Eighth, was a Kind of *Hermaphrodite* in Religion, or in the Language of the Times, a *Trimmer* ; being a *Medly of Papist and Protestant,* and that Part he acted to the Life, or to the Death rather ; Sacrificing on the same Day Men of Both Religions, because one was not *Protestant enough*, and t'other *Papist enough for him.* In this Time were some *Anabaptists*, for the Distinction of *Church of England,* and *Calvinist,* was not then known.

Edward the Sixth succeeded, a Prince that promised Virtues, that might more than ballance the Excesses of his Father, and yet by Archbishop *Cranmer,* was compell'd to Sign a Warrant to Burn *Poor Joan of Kent,* a Famous Woman, but counted an *Enthusiast :* But to prove what I said of him, 'twas not without frequent Denials and Tears, and the Bishop taking upon him to answer for it at God's Judgment, of which I hope his Soul was discharg'd, tho' his Body, by the same Law, suffer'd the same Punishment in the succeeding Reign. Thus even the *Protestants began with Blood for Meer Religion,* and taught the *Romanists,* in succeeding Times, how to deal with them.

At

At this Time the Controversie grew warm between the *Church of England* and the *Calvinists*, that were the Abler Preachers and the Better Livers. The Bishops being mostly Men of State, and some of them looking rather backward than forward, Witness the Difficulty the King had to get *Hooper* Consecrated Bishop, without Conformity to the Reserved Ceremonies.

Queen Mary came in, and ended the Quarrel at the Stake. Now *Ridley* and *Hooper* hug, and are the Dearest Brethren, and Best Friends in the World. *Hooper* keeps his Ground, and *Ridley* stoops with his Ceremonies to t'others farther Reformation. But this Light and Union *flow'd* from their Persecution: For those abroad at *Frankfort*, and other Places, were not upon so good Terms: Their Feuds grew so great, that the one refused Communion with the other; many Endeavours were used to quench the Fire, but they were ineffectual; at best it lay under the *Ashes of their Affliction for another Time*; for no sooner was *Queen Elizabeth* upon Her Throne, than they returned, and their Difference with them. They managed it civilly for a While, but Ambition in some, and Covetousness in others on the one Hand, and Discretion giving Way to Resentment on the other, they first ply the *Queen* and *Her Ministers*, and when that ended in *Favour of the Men of Ceremony*, the others arraign'd them before the First Reformers abroad, at *Geneva, Basil, Zurich*, &c. The Leading Prelates by their Letters, as Dr. *Burnet* lately tells us, in his Printed Relation of his Travels, clear themselves to those first Doctors of any such Imputation, and lay all upon the *Queen*, who, for Reasons of State, would not be brought to so Inceremonious a Way of Worship, as that of the *Calvinists*.

At this Time there were *Papists, Protestants, Evangelists, Precisians, Ubiquitists, Familists*, or *Enthusiasts*, and *Anabaptists* in England; when the very First Year of Her Reign, *A Law for Uniformity in Worship and Discipline was Enacted*, and more followed of the severest Nature, and sometimes executed. Thus then we see that there never was such a Thing as a *Church of England* since the Days of *Popery*, that is, *A Church or Communion, containing all the People of the Kingdom*, and so cannot be said to be so much as *a Twin of the Reformation*; nevertheless, She got the Blessing of the Civil Magistrate: She made Him Great, to be Great by Him: If She might be the *Church*, He should be the *Head*. Much Good may the *Bargain* do her. Now is the Time for Her to stand to Her Principle. I never knew any Body exceed their Bounds, *that were not met with at last*. If we could escape Men, God we cannot, *His Providence* will overtake us, and find us out.

By all this then it appearing, that the *Church of England* was not the Nation, the Case is plain, *That the Penal Laws were a Make-Bate*, for they Sacrificed every Sort of People whose Consciences differed from the *Church of England*; which first put the *Romanists* upon flattering Prerogative, and courting it's Shelter from the Wrath of those Laws. The Address could not be unpleasant to Princes; and we see it was not; for King *James*, that came in with Invectives against *Popery*, entring the *Lists with the Learned of that Church*, and charging Her with all the Marks the *Revelation* gives to that of *Antichrist*, grew at last so tame and easie towards the *Romanists*, that our own Story tells us of the Fears of the Increase of *Popery* in the latter Parliament of his Reign.

In *King Charles* the First's Time, no Body can doubt of the Complaint, because that was in great Measure the Drift of every Parliament, and at last One Reason of the War. On the other Hand, *the Severity of the Bishops*, against Men of their own Principles, and in the Main, of their own Communion, either because they were more Zealous in Preaching, more follow'd of the People, or could not wear some odd Garment, and less, lead the Dance on a *Lord's Day* at a Maypole, (the Relick of *Flora*, the *Roman Strumpet*) or perhaps for Rubbing upon the Ambition, Covetousness, and Laziness of the Dignified, and Ignorance and Looseness of the *Ordinary Clergy of the Church*, (of which I could produce Five Hundred Gross Instances) I say these Things bred bad Blood, and in Part, gave Beginning to those Animosities, that at last broke forth, with some other Pretences, into all those National Troubles that agitated this poor Kingdom for Ten Years together, in which the *Church of* England *became the Greatest Loser, Her Clergy turn'd out, Her Nobility and Gentry Sequester'd, Decimated, Imprisoned,* &c. And whatever She is pleas'd to think, nothing is Truer, *than that Her Penal Laws, and Conduct in the Star-Chamber, and High Commission Court in Matters of Religion, was Her Overthrow*.

'Tis

'Tis as evident, the same Humour, *since the Restoration of the late King,* has had almost the same Effect. For nothing was grown so little and contemptible, as the *Church of England* in this Kingdom, She now intitles Her self *The Church of:* Witness the Elections of the Last Three Parliaments before this. I know it may be said, *The Persons Chosen were Church-Goers;* I confess it, for the Law would have them so. But no Body were more averse to the Politicks of the Clergy; insomuch that the Parson and the Parish almost every where divided upon the Question of their Election. In Truth, it has been the *Favour and Countenance of the Crown,* and not Her intrinsick Interest or Value, that has kept Her up to this Day; else *Her Penal Laws,* the *Bulwark of the Church of England,* by the same Figure, that She is One *against Popery,* had sunk her long since.

I hope I may, by this Time, conclude, without Offence, that the *Penal-Laws* have been a *Make-Bate* in the Great Family of the Kingdom, setting the Father against his Children, and Brethren against Brethren; not only giving the Empire to one, but endeavouring to extinguish the rest, and that for this, the *Church of England* has once paid a severe Reckoning. I apply it thus: Is it not Her Interest to be careful She does it not a second Time? She has a fair Opportunity to prevent it, and keep Her self where She is; that is, *The Publick Religion of the Country, with the Real Maintenance of it;* which is a plain Preference to all the rest.

Violence and Tyranny are no Natural Consequences of *Popery,* for then they would follow every where, and in all Places and Times alike. But we see in Twenty Governments in *Germany,* there is none for Religion, nor was for an Age in *France*; and in *Poland,* the Popish Cantons of *Switzerland, Venice, Lucca, Colonia,* &c. where that Religion is Dominant, the People enjoy their Ancient and Civil Rights, a little more steadily then they have of late Times done in some *Protestant Countries nearer Home,* almost ever since the Reformation. *Is this against Protestancy? No; but very much against Protestants.* For had they been True to their Principles, we had been upon better Terms. So that the *Reformation was not the Fault,* but not keeping to it better than some have done; For whereas they were *Papists* that both obtain'd the *Great Charter,* and *Charter of Forests,* and in the successive Reigns of the Kings of their Religion, industriously labour'd the Confirmation of them, as the *Great Text of their Liberties and Properties,* by above Thirty other Laws; we find almost an equal Number to destroy them, and but One made in their Favour since the *Reformation,* and that shrewdly against the *Will of the High Church-Men too*; I mean, *The Petition of Right,* in the Third Year of *Charles* the First. In short, They desire a Legal Security with us, and we are afraid of it, lest it should Insecure us; when nothing can do it so certainly as their Insecurity; *For Safety makes no Man Desperate.* And he that seeks Ease by Law, therefore does it, because he would not attempt it by Force. Are we afraid of their Power, and yet provoke it? If this Jealousie and Aversion prevail, it may drive Her to a Bargain with the Kingdom for such General Redemption of Property, as may *Dissolve our Great Corporation of Conscience,* and then She will think, *That Half a Loaf had been Better than No Bread*; and that it had been more advisable to have *parted with Penal Laws,* that only serv'd to Dress Her in Satyr, than have lost *All* for keeping them; especially when it was but parting with *Spurs, Claws and Bills, that made Her look more like a* Vultur *than a* Dove, *and a Lion than a* Lamb.

But I proceed to my next Reason, why it is Her Interest to Repeal those Penal Laws, (tho' a greater cannot be advanc'd to Men than Self-Preservation) and That is, *That She else breaks with a King heartily inclin'd to preserve Her by any Way that is not Persecuting, and whose Interest She once pursu'd at all Adventures, when more than She sees was suggested to Her by the Men of the Interest She opposed, in Favour of His Claim.* What then has befallen Her, that She changes the Course She took with such Resolutions of Perseverance? For bringing Him to the Crown with this Religion, could not be more Her Duty to His Title, or Her Interest to support Her own, than it is still, *To be fair with Him.* If She ow'd the One to Him, and to Christianity, She is not less indebted to Her self the other. Does He seek to impose His own Religion upon Her? By no Means. There is no Body would abhor the Attempt, or, at all Adventures, condemn it more than my self. What then is the Matter? *Why, He desires Ease for His Religion*; She does not think fit to consider Him in this, (No, not the King She brought with this Objection to the Crown) Certainly She is much in the Wrong, and shows Her self an *Ill Courtier,* (tho' it was become Her Calling) first, *To give Him Roast-Meat,*

then

then beat Him with the Spit. Is not this to quit those High Principles of Loyalty and Christianity She valu'd Her self once upon, and what She can, provoke the Mischiefs She fears? Certainly this is dividing in Judgment from Him, that She has acknowledged to be *Her Ecclesiastical Head.*

My *Fifth Reason* is, That as the *Making* and *Executing* the *Penal Laws* for *Religion* affects all the several Parties of *Protestant Dissenters* as well as the *Papists* (the Judges in *Vaughan's* Time, and he at the Head of them, giving it as their Opinion, they were equally exposed to those Laws) and that they are thereby naturally driven into an Interest with them; so it is at this Time greatly the Prudence of the *Church of England* to repeal them, for by so doing She divides that *Interest* that *Self-preservation* allows all Men to pursue, that are united by Danger: And since She is assured the *Papists* shall not have the less Ease, in this King's Time than if the Laws were Repealed, and that her Fears are not of the succeeding Reigns, how is their Repeal a greater Insecurity, especially, when by that, she draws into her Interest all the *Protestant Dissenters,* that are abundantly more considerable than the *Papists,* and that are as unwilling that *Popery* should be *National* as her self. For if this be not granted, see what Reputation follows to the *Church of England.* She tells the King she does not desire his Friends should be Persecuted, yet the Forbearance must not be by *Declaration,* to save the *Government,* nor by *Law,* to save her: and without one of these Warrants, every Civil Magistrate and Officer in *England* is Perjur'd that suffers them in that *Liberty against Law.* How can she be sincerely willing that should be done, that she is not willing should be done *Legally?*

But, *Sixthly,* the *Church of England* does not know but they or some other Party may at one Time or other prevail. It seems to me her *Interest* to set a good Example, and so to bespeak easy Terms for her self. I know of none intended, and believe no Body but her self can place her so low, yet if it were her Unhappiness, I think to have *Civil Property* secured out of the Question of Religion, and *Constraint* upon *Conscience* prevented by a Glorious *Magna Charta for the Liberty of it,* were not a Thing of ill *Consequence* to her *Interest.* Let us but consider what other Princes did for their own *Religion,* within the last *Seven Reigns,* when they came to the Crown, and we cannot think so soft and equal a Thing as an *Impartial Liberty of Conscience,* after all that has been said of a *Popish Successor,* an ordinary *Character* of a *Prince,* or a mean *Assurance* to us: This ought not to slip her Reflection. Besides, there is some Care due to Posterity: Tho' the present Members of her *Communion* may escape the *Temptation,* their Children may not: They may *change* the Religion of their Education, and Conscientiously chuse some other *Communion.* Would they submit the *Fortunes* they leave them to the *Rape* of Hungry *Courtiers, Bigots* and *indigent Informers,* or have their Posterity *Impoverish'd, Banish'd* or *Executed* for Sober and Religious *Dissent?* God knows into whose Hands these Laws at last may fall, what Mischief they may do, and to whom. Believe me, a King of the Humour of Sir *J. K.* of the *West,* or Sir *W. A.* of *Reading,* or Sir *R. B.* or Sir *S. S.* of *London,* would, with such *Vouchers,* quickly make a *Golgotha* of the *Kingdom.* If She thinks her self considerable in *Number* or *Estate,* She will have the more to lose. Let her not therefore Establish that in the Prejudice of others, that may in the Hands of others turn to her Prejudice.

Lastly, I would not have her miss the Advantage that is designed her by those that perhaps she thinks worst of. I dare say no body would willingly see the *Presbyterian* in her *Chair,* and yet that may happen to be the Consequence of her Tenaciousness in a little Time. For if the Aversion her Sons promote by wholesale against *Popery* should prevail, the Remains of it in her self are not like to escape that Reformation. I mean, her *Episcopal Government,* and the *Ceremonies* of her Worship, for which she has vex'd the most Conscientious People of this Kingdom above an Age past. And the *Presbyterian* being a Rich, Industrious and Numerous Party, as well among the Nobility and Gentry, as Trading and Country People, I cannot see but the next Motion, naturally speaking, is like to tend that Way; for other Parties, however well esteemed, may seem too great a Step of Reformation at once, and methinks she has tasted enough of that *Regiment,* to be once wise, and keep the *Ballance* in her own Hands. And certain it is, that nothing will so effectually do this, as the entreated Liberty of Conscience; for then there will be four Parties of Dissenters besides her self, to *Ballance* against any Designs that may *warp* or *byass* Things to their *Advancement.* And that which ought to induce the Church of *England* not a little to hasten as well as do the Thing,

Thing, is this; She is now a Sort of National Church by *Power*, she will then be the Publick Church by Concurrence of all Parties. Instead of Enemies to invade or undermine her, they that should do it are made the Friends of her Safety by the Happiness they enjoy through her *Complacency*: And if any should be so unnatural or ungrateful to her, the Interest of the rest will oblige them to be her *Spies* and *Security* against the Ambition of any such *Party*. I do heartily pray to *God* that he would *enlighten the Eyes of her Leaders*, and give them good Hearts too, that *Faction may not prevail against Charity*, in the Name of Religion: And, above all, that she would not be proud of her Numbers, or stand off upon that Reflection; for that alone will quickly lessen them in a Nation loving Freedom as much as this we live in: And what appears in the Town is an ill Glass to take a Prospect of the Country by: There are Parishes that have Fifteen Thousand Souls in them, and if two come to Church it is Matter of Brag, tho' half the rest be sown among the several *Dissenting Congregations* of their Judgment. I would not have her mistaken, though *Popery* be an unpopular Thing, 'tis as certain she of a long Time has not been Popular, and on that Principle never can be: And if she should Plow with that Heifer now, and gain a little by the Aversion to Popery; when it is discerned that Popery does return to the civil Interest of the Kingdom they will quickly be Friends. For besides that, we are the easiest and best-natur'd People in the World to be appeased: There are those Charms in Liberty and Property to *English Nature*, that no Endeavours can resist or disappoint. And can we reasonably think the *Romanists* will be wanting in that, when they see it is their own (and perhaps their only) Interest to do so? These are the Arguments which, I confess, have prevailed with me to importune the Church of England to yield to the *Repeal of all the Penal Statutes*, and I should be glad to see them either well *refuted* or *submitted to*.

I shall now address my self to those of the *Roman Church*, and hope to make it appear it is their *Interest* to sit down thankfully with the *Liberty of Conscience* herein desired, and that a *Toleration and no more*, is that which all *Romanists* ought to be satisfied with. My *Reasons* are these: *First*, The *Opposition* that *Popery* every where finds: For in *Nothing* is the Kingdom so much of a Mind as in this *Aversion*: 'Tis no News, and so may be the better said and taken. I say then this *Unity*, this *Universality*, and this *Visibility* against *Popery*, make the *Attempt*, for more than *Liberty of Conscience*, too great and dangerous. I believe there may be some poor *silly Bigots* that hope bigger, and talk farther, but who can help that? there are weak People of all Sides, and they will be making a *Pudder*: But what's the *Language of their true Interest*, the Infallible Guide of the wiser Men? *Safety* certainly; and that in succeeding Reigns to chuse: And if so, their Steps must be modest, for they are *Watch'd* and *Number'd*. And tho' their Prudence should submit to their Zeal, both must yield to *Necessity*, whether they like it or no, What they convert upon the Square, *Perswasion* I mean, is their own, and much Good may it do them. But the Fear is not of this, and for compelling the averse *Genius* of the Kingdom, *they have not the Means*, whatever they would do if they had them: Which is my *Second Reason*. I say *they have not the Power*, and that is what we apprehend most. There are three Things that prove this in my *Opinion*. First, *their Want of Hands*, next, *Want of Time*, and lastly, *their Intestine Division*; which, whatever we think, is not Inconsiderable. They are *few*, we must all agree, to the Kingdom, upon the best Computation that could be made: Out of *Eighty Millions of People*, they are not *Thirty Thousand*, and those but thinly sown up and down the Nation; by which it appears that the Disproportion of the *Natural Strength* is not less than *Two Hundred and Seventy Persons to One*. So that Popery in *England* is like a *Spirit without a Body*, or, *a General without an Army*. It can hurt *no more, than Bullets without Powder*, or, *a Sword and no Hand to use it*. I dare say, there is not of that Communion, enough at once, to make all the Coal-Fires in *London*, and yet we are apprehensive they are able to consume *the whole Kingdom*. I am still more *afraid of her Fears* than of them; for tho' they seem high, she thinks their *Religion* in no Reign has appeared much lower.

O, but they have the King of their Side, and he has the Executive Power in his Hands! True, and this I call the *Artificial Strength of the Kingdom*. But I say, first we have his Word to bind him. And tho' some may think our Kings cannot be tyed by their People, certainly they may be tyed by themselves. What if I don't look upon the Act of both Houses to oblige the King, *his own Concession must*; and that may be given in an *Act of State*. I take the King to be as well obliged in *Honour* and *Conscience* to what he promises his People in another Method, as if it had been by his *Royal Assent in Parliament*; for an honest Man's Word is good every where, and why a King's should not I can't tell. 'Tis true, the Place differs, and the Voice comes with greater Solemnity, but why it should with greater Truth I know not. And if the *Church of* England will but be advised to give him the Opportunity of keeping his repeated Word with her, and not deprive her self of that Advantage by *Jealousies* and *Distances* that make her suspected, and may force him into another Conduct, I cannot help believing that the King will to a Tittle let her feel the Assurance and Benefit of his *Promises*.

But next, *we have his Age for our Security*, which is the *Second Proof, of the Second Reason*, why the *Papists* should look no farther than a *Toleration*. This is the Want of Time I mentioned. They have but *one Life in the Lease*, and 'tis out of their Power *to Renew*; and this Life has lived fast too, and is got within *Seven of Threescore*; A greater Age than most of his Ancestors ever attained. *Well, but he has an Army, and many Officers of his own Religion.* And if it be so, *What can it do?* It may suppress an *Insurrection*, but upon the Attempts we foolishly fear, they were hardly a Breakfast to the Quarters they live in. For if they were together, all the Confines or remote Parts of the Nation would rise like Grass upon them; and, if dispersed, to be sure they have not Strength for such an Attempt.

But if they are not sufficient, there is a Potent Prince not far off can help the Design, who is not angry with Protestancy at Home only. Suppose this, Is there not as potent *Naval Powers* to assist the *Constitution* of the *Kingdom* from such *Invasions? Yes, and Land One's too.* And as the *Protestant Governments* have more Ships than the other, so an equal *Land Force*, when by such Attempts to make *Popery* Universal, they are awakened to the Use of them: But certainly we must be very Silly to think the King should suffer so great a Shock to his own Interest, as admitting an Army of Foreigners to enter his Kingdom on any Pretence, must necessarily occasion. These *Bull Beggars*, and *Raw-heads and Bloody-Bones*, are the Malice of some and Weakness of others. But Time, that informs Children, will tell the *World the Meaning of the Fright*.

The *Third Proof* of my *Second Reason*, is, *The Intestine Division among themselves*. That *Division*, weakens a great *Body*, and renders a small one *harmless*, all will agree. Now, that there is such a Thing as *Division* among them is Town-talk. The *Seculars* and *Regulars* have ever been two *Interests* all the *Roman Church over*, and they are not only so here, but the *Regulars* differ among themselves. There is not a *Coffee-House* in Town that does not freely tell us that the *Jesuits* and *Benedictines* are at Variance, that Count *Da*, the Pope's Nuncio, and Bishop *Lyborn*, Dissent mightily from the *Politicks* of the first; Nay, t'other Day the Story was, *that they had prevailed entirely over them*. The Lords and Gentlemen of her *Communion* have as warmly contested about the *Lengths* they ought to go, *Moderation* seems to be the *Conclusion*. Together they are *little*, and can do little; and, divided, they are *Contemptible* instead of Terrible.

Lastly, The *Roman Church* ought to be *Discreet*, and think of nothing farther than the entreated general Ease, because it would be an Extreme that must beget another in the succeeding Reign. For, as I can never think her so weak as well as base, that after all her Arguments for the *Jus Divinum* of Succession, she should, in the Face of the World, attempt to violate it in the Wrong of One of another *Perswasion*, (for that were an Eternal Loss of her with Mankind.) So, if she does not, and yet is Extravagant, she only rises higher to fall lower than all others in another Reign. This were provoking their own Ruin. And, to say true, either Way would, as the *Second Letter has it, Discredit her for ever, and make true Prophets of those they had taken such Pains to prove false Witnesses*. And supposing her to reckon upon the Just Succession, nothing can recommend her, or continue her Happiness in a Reign of another Judgment, but this *Liberty equally maintained*, that other Perswasions, more numerous, for that Reason as well as for their own Sakes, are obliged to insure her. Here the Foundation is broad and strong, and what is built upon it has the Looks of *long Life*. The *Indenture* will at least be *quinque-partite*, and Parties are not so mortal as Men. And as this joyns, so it preserves Interest entire, which amounts to a *Religious Amity* and a *Civil Unity* at the worst.

Upon the whole Matter, I advise the Members of the *Roman Communion* in this Kingdom, to be moderate, 'tis their Duty, and it belongs to all Men to see it and feel

feel it from them, and it behoves them mightily they should; for the first Part of this *Discourse* belongs to their *Hopes*, as well as to the *Church of England's Fears*, viz. *The Duty and Spirit of Christianity*. Next, Let them do *good Offices* between the King and his Excellent Children, for as that will be well taken by so affectionate a Father, so it gives the Lye to their Enemies Suggestions, and recommends them to the Grace and Favour of the Successors. And having said this, I have said all that belongs to them in particular. There is left only my Address to the *Protestant Dissenters*, and a General *Conclusion* to finish this *Discourse*.

Your Case, that are called *Protestant Dissenters*, differs mightily from that of the *Church of England and Rome*. For the first hath the *Laws* for her, the last the *Prince*. Those Laws are *against* you, and she is not willing they should be Repealed: The *Prince* offers to be kind to you if you please; Your *Interest*, in this *Conjuncture*, is the *Question*. I think none ought to be made, that it is the *Liberty of Conscience* desired, because you have much more Need of it, having neither *Laws* nor *Prince* of your Side, nor a Successor of any of your *Perswasions*. The *Fears* of *Popery* I know reach you; but it is to be remembred also, that if the Laws are not Repealed, there wants no *New Ones* to Destroy you, of the *Papists* making; so that every Fear you are taught to have of their Repeal, is against your selves. Suppose your *Apprehensions well grounded*, you can but be Destroy'd; Which is most comfortable for you to suffer, by *Law* or *without it?* The *Church of England*, by her *Penal Laws*, *and the Doctrine of Headship*, has Armed that *Religion* (as it falls out) to Destroy you. Nay, has made it a Duty in the King to do it, from which (he says) nothing but *an Act of Parliament* can absolve him, and that she is not willing to allow. And is it not as reasonable that you should seek their Repeal, that if you suffer from the *Papists*, it may be without *Human Law*, as well as against *Christ's Law*, as for the *Church of England* to keep them in Force, because if she suffers, it shall be against the *Laws* made to uphold her? For not repealing them, brings you an inevitable Mischief, and her, at most, but an uncertain Safety; tho' 'tis certain, she at the same Time will sacrifice you to it. And yet if I were in her Case, it would please me better to remove *Laws* that might reproach me, and stop my Mouth when turn'd against me, and be content; that if I suffer for my *Religion*, it is against the *Law of God*, *Christianity*, and the *Fundamentals* of the Old and True *Civil Government of my Country*, before such Laws helpt to spoil it. In short, you must either *go to Church*, or *Meet*, or *let fall your Worshipping of God* in the Way you believe. If the first, you are *Hypocrites*, and give away the Cause, and reproach your dead Brethren's Sincerity, and gratify the old Accusation of *Schism, Ambition*, &c. and finally lose the Hope and Reward of all your Sufferings. If the second, *viz.* that you *meet against Law*, you run into the Mouth of the *Government*, whose Teeth are to meet in you and Destroy you, *as by Law Established*. If the last, you deny your *Faith*, *overthrow your own Arguments, fall away from the Apostolical Doctrine of assembling together, and so must fall into the Hands of God, and under the Troubles of your own Consciences and Woundings of his Spirit, of which 'tis said*, who can bear them. So that nothing is plainer than that *Protestant Dissenters* are not oblig'd to govern themselves after such *Church of England Measures*, supposing her *Fears* and *Jealousies* better Bottom'd than they are: For they are neither in this King's Time in the same Condition, with her, if the *Penal Laws* remain in Force, nor like to be so, if she can help it, in the next Reign, if they are not repealed in this; so that they are to be certainly Persecuted now, in Hopes of an *uncertain Liberty* then. Uncertain both whether it will be in her *Power*, and whether she will do it if it be. The *Language* of *Fear* and *Assurance* are two Things, *Affliction* promises what *Prosperity* rarely performs. Of this the Promises made to induce the late King's *Restoration*, and the Cancelling of the former *Declaration*, and what followed upon both are a plain Proof. And tho' the last *Westminster Parliament* inclin'd to it; no Body so much opposed it as the *Clergy*, and the most *Zealous Sons of that Church:* And if they could or would not then see it to be reasonable, I can't see why one should trust to People so selfish and short-sighted. But if she will stoop to all those *Dissenting Interests* that are *Protestant*, it must either be by a *Comprehension*, and then she must part with her *Bishops*, her *Common-Prayer*, her *Ceremonies*, and this it self is but *Presbyterian*; (and she must go lower yet, if she will comprehend the rest) or, if not, she must *Persecute*, or give this *Liberty of Conscience* at last; which, that she will ever yield to uncompel'd, and at a Time too, when there is none to do it, while she refuses it under her present pressing

Circumstances, I confess I cannot apprehend. But there is yet one Argument that can never fail to oblige your Compliance with the General Ease intreated, *viz. That the Penal Laws are against our Great Law of Property, and so void in themselves.* This has been the *Language* of every *Apology*, and that which, to say true, is not to be answered: How then can you decline to help their Repeal, that in *Conscience, Reason* and *Law*, you think void in their own Nature?

Lastly, There is nothing that can put you in a Condition to help your selves, or the *Church of England*, against the *Domination* of *Popery*, but that which she weakly thinks the Way to hurt you both, *viz. The Repeal of the Penal Laws.* For, as you are, you are *tyed* Hand and Foot, you are not your own Men, you can neither serve her nor your selves, you are fast in the Stocks of her Laws, and the Course she would have you take, is to turn *Martyrs* under them to support them: If you like the *Bargain* you are the best natur'd People in the World, and something more. And since *Begging* is in Fashion, I should desire no other *Boon*; for upon so plain a Loss of your Wits, your Estates will of Course fall a Stray to the Government, so that without the Help of a *Penal Law*, you make an admirable Prize.

I have no Mind to end so pleasantly with you, I have a sincere and Christian Regard to you and yours. *Be not Cozened, nor Captious, at this Juncture.* I know some of you are told, if you lose this Liberty, *you Introduce Idolatry*, and for *Conscience Sake* you cannot do it. But that's a pure Mistake, and improved, I fear, by those that know it so, which makes us the worse; for it is not *Introducing Idolatry, (taking for granted that Popery is so)* but saving the People from being Destroy'd that profess that *Religion*. If *Christ* and his *Apostles* had taken this Course with the World, they must have *Killed* them instead of *Converting* them. 'Tis your Mistake to think the *Jewish* rigorous *Constitution* is adequate to the *Christian Dispensation*; by no Means: That one Conceit of *Judaising Christianity* in our Politicks, has filled the World with *Misery*, of which this poor Kingdom has had it's Share. *Idolaters* are to be *Enlightned* and *Perswaded*, as St. *Paul* did the *Athenians* and *Romans*, and not *knocked on the Head*, which mends no Body. And, to say a *Christian Magistrate* is to do that, that a *Christian* can't do, is ridiculous; unless, like the *Bishop of Munster*, who goes like a Bishop one Part of the Day, and a Soldier the other, he is to be *a Christian in the Morning, and a Magistrate in the Afternoon*. Besides, 'tis one Thing to enact a *Religion National*, and *Compel Obedience to it*, (which would make this Case abominable indeed) and another Thing to take off *Christian Penalties* for the Sake of such Mistakes, since that is to give them Power to hurt others, and this only to save you from being hurt for *meer Religion*.

To conclude my Address to you, of all People, it would look the most disingenuous in you, and give you an Air, the least Sensible, Charitable and Christian, not to endeavour such an Ease, that have so much wanted it, and so often and so earnestly pressed it, even to Clamour. But that you should do it for their Sakes who have used you so, and that the Instruments of their Cruelty, the Penal Laws, should from a Common Grievance become a Darling to any among you, will be such a Reproach to your Understandings and Consciences, that no Time or Argument can wipe off, and which I beseech God and you to prevent.

The CONCLUSION.

I Shall conclude with one Argument, that equally concerns you all, and that is this; You claim the *Character* of *Englishmen*. Now, to be an *Englishman*, in the Sense of the Government, is to be a *Freeman*, whether *Lord* or *Commoner*, to hold his Liberty and Possessions *by Laws of his own consenting unto*, and not to forfeit them upon Facts made Faults, by Humour, Faction, or Partial Interest prevailing in the Governing Part against the Constitution of the Kingdom; but for Faults only, that are such in the Nature of Civil Government; to wit, *Breaches of those Laws that are made by the whole, in Pursuance of common Right, for the Good of the Whole.*

This Regard must at no Time be neglected, or violated towards any one Interest; for the Moment we concede to such a Breach upon our *General Liberty*, be it from an Aversion we carry to the Principles of those we expose, or some little sinister and temporary Benefit of our own, we Sacrifice our selves in the Prejudices we draw upon others, or suffer them to fall under; for our Interest in this Respect is common. If then as *Englishmen*, we are as mutually interested in the inviolable Conservation of each other's Civil Rights, as Men embark'd in the same Vessel are to save the Ship they are in for their own Sakes, we ought to Watch, Serve and Secure the Interest of one another, because it is our own to do so; and not by any Means endure that to be done to please some narrow Regard of any one Party, *which may be drawn in Example at some other Turn of Power to our own utter Ruin.*

Had this Honest, Just, Wise and English Consideration prevail'd with our Ancestors of all Opinions from the Days of *Richard* the Second, there had been less Blood, Imprisonment, Plunder, and Beggary for the *Government of this Kingdom* to answer for. Shall I speak within our own Knowledge, and that without Offence, there has been Ruin'd, since the late King's Restoration, above *Fifteen Thousand Families*, and more than *Five Thousand Persons* Dead under Bonds for Matters of *meer Conscience* to God: But who hath laid it to Heart? It is high Time now we should, especially when our King, with so much Grace and Goodness leads us the Way.

I beseech you all, if you have any Reverence towards God, and Value for the Excellent Constitution of this Kingdom, any Tenderness for your Posterity, any Love for your Selves, you would embrace this happy Conjuncture, and pursue a common Expedient; That since we cannot agree to meet in one *Profession of Religion*, we may entirely do it in this common civil Interest where we are all equally engaged; and therefore we ought for our own Sakes to seek one another's Security, that if we cannot be the Better, we may not be the worse for our Perswasions, in Things, that bear no relation to them, and in which, it is impossible we should Suffer, and the Government escape, that is so much concern'd in the civil Support and Prosperity of every Party and Person that belongs to it.

Let us not therefore uphold *Penal Laws* against any of our Religious Perswasions, nor make *Tests* out of each others Faiths, to exclude one another our civil Rights; for by the same Reason that denying *Transubstantiation* is made One to exclude a *Papist*, to own it, may be made one to exclude a *Church of England Man*, a *Presbyterian*, an *Independent*, a *Quaker*, and *Anabaptist*: For the Question is not who is in the right in Opinion, but whether he is not in Practice *in the wrong*, that for such an Opinion deprives his Neighbour of his common Right? Now 'tis certain there is not one of any Party, that would willingly have a Test made out of his Belief, to abridge him of his native Priviledge; and therefore neither the Opinion of *Transubstantiation* in the Papists, *Episcopacy* in the Church of *England* Man, *Free-will* in the Arminian, *Predestination* in the Presbyterian, *Particular Churches* in the Independent, *Dipping of adult People* in the Anabaptist, nor *not swearing* in the Quaker, ought to be made a *Test* of, to deprive him of the Comforts of his Life, or render him incapable of the Service of his Country, to which by a natural Obligation he is indebted, and from which, no Opinion can discharge him, and for that Reason, much less should any other Party think it fit, or in their Power to exclude him.

And indeed it were ridiculous to talk of giving Liberty of Conscience (which yet few have now the fore-head to oppose) and at the same Time imagine those *Tests* that do exclude Men that Service and Reward, ought to be continued: For though it does not immediately concern me, being neither *Officer* nor *Papist*, yet the Consequence is general, and every party, even the Church of *England*, will find her self concern'd upon Reflection; For she cannot assure her self it may not come to be her turn.

But, Is it not an odd Thing, that by leaving them on foot, every Body shall have Liberty of Conscience *but the Government*? For while a Man is out of Office, he is *Test*-free, but the Hour he is chosen to any Station, be it in the *Legislation* or *Administration*, he must *wiredraw* his Conscience to hold it, or be excluded with the Brand of Dissent: And can this be equal or wise? Is this the Way to employ Men for the good of the Publick, where *Opinion prevails above Virtue*, and *Abilities are submitted to the Humour of a Party*; surely none can think this a *Cure* for Division, or that Animosities are like to be prevented by the only Ways in the World that beget and heighten them. Nor is it possible that the ease that should be granted can continue long, when the *Party* in whose Favour they are not repeal'd, may thereby be enabled to turn the Point of the Sword again upon Dissenters.

I know *Holland* is given in Objection to this Extent of Freedom, where only one *Perswasion has the Government*, though the rest their Liberty: But they don't consider, first, *how much more* Holland *is under the Power of Necessity than we are.* Next, *That our Constitutions differ greatly.* For the first, 'tis plain, in the little compass they live in; the Uncertainty and Precariousness of the Means of their Subsistence: That as they are in more Danger of Drowning, so nearer ruin by any Commotion in the State, than other Countries are. *Trading* is their Support, *This*, keeps them busy, *That*, makes them Rich; and *Wealth*, naturally gives them *Caution* of the Disorders that may spoil them of it. This makes the governing Party wary how they use their Power, and the other Interests tender how they resist it; for upon it, they have Reason to fear a *Publick Desolation*; since *Holland* has not a natural and *Domestick Fund* to rely upon, or return to, from such National Disorders.

The next Consideration is as clear and cogent; our *Constitutions differ mightily*: For though they have the Name of a *Republick*, yet in their Choice, in order to the Legislature, they are much less free then we are: And since the *Freeholders* of all the Parties in *England* may Elect, which in *Holland* they can no more do than they can be chosen, there is good reason why all may be elected to serve their King and Country here, that in *Holland* cannot be chosen or serve. And if our Power to chuse be larger than theirs in *Holland*, we are certainly then a freer People, and so ought not to be confin'd, as they are, about what Person it is that must be chosen: Methinks it bears no Proportion, and therefore the Instance and Objection are improper to our Purpose.

But it is said by some, *That there cannot be two predominant Religions, and if the* Church of England *be not that,* Popery *by the King's Favour is like to be so.* It is certain that *two predominant Religions*, would be two Uppermosts at once, which is nonsense every where: But as I cannot see what need there is for the Church of *England* to lose her Churches or Revenues, so while she has them, Believe me, she is *Predominant* in the Thing of the World that lies nearest her Guides. But if I were to speak my Inclination, I cannot apprehend the Necessity of any *Predominant* Religion, understanding the Word with *Penal Laws* in the tail of it: The Mischief of it, in a Country of so many powerful Interests as this, I can easily understand, having had the Opportunity of seeing and feeling it too: And because nothing can keep up the Ball of Vengeance like such a *Predominant Religion*, and that *Penal Laws* and *Tests* are the Means of the Domination, I, for that Reason, think them fit to be Repeal'd, and let English Mankind say, *Amen*.

I do not love Quibling, but 'tis true, to a Lamentation, that there is little of the *Power of Religion* seen where there is such a predominant one, unless among those it Domineers over.

I conclude, they that are so *Predominant*, and they that seek to be so (be they who they will) move by the same Spirit and Principle, and however differing their Pretensions and Ends may be, the odds are very little to me, by which it is I must certainly be Opprest.

Dare we then *do* (for once) *as we would be done by*, and show the World, we are not Religious *without Justice*, nor Christians *without Charity*: That *False self* shall not govern us against *True self*; nor *Opportunity* make us Thieves to our Neighbours, for Gods Sake? The End of *Testing* and *Persecuting* under every Revolution of Government. If this we can find in our Hearts to do, and yet as Men, and as Christians, as English Men, we do but do our Duty, let the *Penal Laws* and *Tests* be Repeal'd; and in order to it, *Let us now take those Measures of Men and Things*, that may give our Wishes and Endeavours the best Success for the publick Good, that our *Posterity* may have more Reason to bless our Memories for their *Freedom* and *Security*, than for their *Nature* and *Inheritance*.

JUST MEASURES, in an *Epistle* of *Peace* and *Love*, to such *Professors* of *Truth*, as are under any Dissatisfaction, about the present Order practis'd in the *Church of Christ*.

Friends,

I Have, with a deep Sense and Sorrow, often beheld the Distance and Dissatisfaction you are under in Reference to your ancient and faithful Brethren, and that Fellowship, which, I am sure, was once very dear and valuable with you, and I would have the Charity to hope, is what many of you desire still: And, for your Sakes that would not willingly think amiss, nor differ, nor divide from those that otherwise you have an Esteem for and are in Judgment one with, as to the *Worship* and *Doctrines of Truth*, I desire to open my Mind, both with Tenderness and Plainness; and if what I say has the Voice and Matter of Peace and Love in it, and may be helpful to you, in closing with your Brethren again, I shall greatly rejoyce: In which, know this, I seek you not in the Words of *Man's Wisdom*, nor to raise *Controversy*, nor for *Victory*, nor any *By-ends*, but for the Sake of that *precious Fellowship* and *seamless Garment*, in which the *Truth* clothed us all in the Beginning, and with which it will clothe and comfort all its faithful Servants and true Friends to the End. First, *I shall begin with the Difference, and what you have both in Conference and Writing alledged for the Ground of your Dissatisfaction and Dissent*: Next, *I shall consider the Nature and Merit of it*; and last of all, *give my Sense upon the whole Matter, in order to a better Understanding for the Future*.

That there is a *Difference*, is but too plain, for it has in some Parts proceeded to a *Separation*, as well to Places of Worship as in Matters of Discipline. The Ground of this Dissatisfaction, upon which so great a Distance has been raised, you say is, *Requiring your Compliance with some Practices relating to Discipline*, particularly Women's *Meetings about Marriages, before they are admitted to be solemnized among us*; some of you thinking, *that there is no Service for* Women's *Meetings at all*; others, *no Service in their being distinct from Men's Meetings*, at least, *no Necessity for either, and therefore no necessary Compliance to be required and insisted upon, but every one left to their Liberty in Christ, lest Imposition and Formality should prevail among us, as they have done in other Religious Societies*. In this, I think, I have truly and fairly stated the Case on your Part, and given your Objection to our Practice, and the reason why you dissent from it.

Now *Friends*, I shall consider the Nature and Merit of this Dissatisfaction and Dissent, wherein I beseech your Attention, Patience, and Candour, and I hope you will find, that we are clear of the Imposition and Formality you object or fear.

In the first Place, I do not find that you have any just Cause to fear, in general, an infringement on your Christian Liberty, since it has been, and is most sincerely declared by the Brethren, chiefly concerned in the good Order and Service of the Church, that they have no Thought or Design of imposing any Thing upon the *Consciences of Friends*; or, that Friends ought to have now, any more than at the Beginning, any other Reason or Measure of Compliance or Conformity in Matters relating to God, than the *Conviction of the Light and Spirit of Christ in every Conscience*. But there is this Distinction to be considered well of, That the Matters in Difference are not such as require such an Exercise and Conviction of Conscience as is pleaded, because they relate not to *Faith or Worship*. Did they require *Faith*, or did they appertain to *Worship*, as if you were obliged to worship God only in such a *Place, Time, Gesture, Raiment, with such Words and Forms of Speech*, &c. which has been the Case of the *Dissenters* from the *National Church*, your Objection and Plea were good: But this about which your Dissatisfaction arises, is purely *Discipline in Government, and not in Worship*; *Formality in Order, and not in Religion*: It is about Methods of regulating our selves, as to the Civil or Outward

Part

Part of the Church, as we are a *Society*; how we may avoid Disorder, and preserve the Credit of our Society from Censure and Scandal.

For Instance, *To keep the Necessitous*; as *Poor, Aged, Sick,* and *Orphans*: *To reconcile Differences*: *To take Care of Births, Marriages,* and *Burials*: In fine, *To prevent, rebuke and restore disorderly Walkers*. To all which, I conceive, there is no Need of an *Act of Faith*, or other *Exercise of Conscience*, than as the Apostle exhorts, *To be ready to every Good Word and Work*: I mean, Here is nothing required to be believed as an Article of Faith; here is no *Novelty or Formality in Worship introduc'd*, or any Thing proposed as an End or Service for our *Men and Women's Meetings*, that can reasonably admit of the raising of such a Scruple of Conscience, since the Things proposed are Duties, that all Civil Societies, as well as Church-Fellowships, agree in, as requisite to the Support of the *Reputation of Fellowships and Societies*.

Now this being the *Great and True End, Use and Service of our Men and Women's Meetings*, and that 'tis the *End* that always denotes and constitutes the Nature of the Means, it cannot justly be thought to be of the *Nature of Imposition and Formality*, as the Words are commonly taken in an ill Sense, to expect the Compliance of Members of a Society, to such Methods of Order as the *Elders* thereof have exhorted to, and the Generality of the People have embraced, and which the most considerable Part of those that Dissent, declare they Dissent from, rather for Fear of suffering an Infringment of their *Christian Liberty*, than any Dislike to the Practice it self: I say, this cannot be called, or accounted such an Imposition upon Conscience, because *they are Expedients of Order, and Methods of Rule about Things universally agreed upon*. The *Thing* will not bear the Word; For Instance, Because I may say it is against my Conscience to confess to such an Article or Doctrine of Faith, or to worship God after such a prescribed Form, that therefore it would sound Reasonable for me to say, *It is against my Conscience to submit to the Counsel of the Church for ending of Differences; and it is against my Conscience, after having once told the Brethren I intend to Marry such a Woman, to come again a Fortnight, or a Month after, to ask if they have informed themselves of mine and the Woman's Clearness, both towards Parents and other Persons, before we Solemnize it*: Surely this would look to Reasonable People, *an Over-tender, or an Over-Righteous, or rather, indeed, an Over-free and large Conscience, that would scruple*, at Twice or Thrice publishing the Banns, *to prevent Undutifulness to Parents, and Injury to Pre-engagements, when those, we profess to exceed, require in their Communion that it be Thrice done*. In like Manner it would look very strange in me, to call a *Church-Care of circumspect Walking up to the Religious Principles of the Society that I have voluntarily embraced*, An imposing, or over-driving me.

But you object, *Why must we go before Women*, and, *Why Women apart from Men?* This still, Friends, can be no Imposition, as is before expressed, *because it is no Matter of Faith, nor Practice of Worship*, but *a referring still to our External Order of Life*: And we say, *Women as well as Men*, because they are concerned, for they are Part of the Church of Christ; and the *Common Banns* that are published in *Churches* (so called) *or Markets*, exclude not *Women* to make their Exception any more than *Men*. But why *Women apart*, say you? We think for a very Good Reason; the Church increaseth, which increases the Business of the Church, and Women, whose Bashfulness will not permit them to say, or do much as to Church-Affairs before the Men, when by themselves, may exercise their Gifts, of Wisdom and Understanding, in a discreet Care for their own Sex, at least; which makes up not the least Part of the Business of the Church, and this while the *Men* are upon their proper Business also. So that as *Men and Women* make up the Church, *Men and Women* make up the Business of the Church; and therefore it is very Reasonable they should be *Helpers together*, in doing the Church's Business. This Way Women are made Useful and Serviceable in, and to the Church, as were the *Holy Women of Old*, that were so much commended by the Apostle, for *Deaconnesses* indeed. And, as I said before, their Businesses being hereby distinct, *Two Businesses are doing at one and the same Time*, and consequently, there must needs be a greater Dispatch; which in Country-Places, and Winter-Seasons, where *Friends* come *Ten or Fifteen Miles to Meetings*, must needs be very convenient and comfortable. I may add, that there are divers Things that seem peculiar to *Women*, that were not fit for *Men*, and in which *Men* did, and would find themselves often at a Loss, which renders their distinct Meetings farther convenient.

These

1692.

These are the Reasons and Motives to the present Practice of the Church of Christ, without infringing Christian Liberty, *by compelling Conscience to any Matter of Faith or Practice, relating to Women*; we meaning, by our whole Order and Government, *no other Thing than a Careful Eye, and Check upon Practice; an Expediency against Irregularity in Conversation, whether towards them that are without, or those that are within the same Communion, to which the* Strong *will submit for the Sake of the* Weak.

My own Sense upon this whole Matter is, That *a misapprehending the Intention of the Brethren, and an undistinguishing Zeal against Impositions on the one Hand, and a Fear on the other Side, that those who so mistook and misrendered the Design of the Brethren, were either High-minded and unruly, or prone to undue Liberty, or that they not being the first Promoters of this Discipline in Government, detracted from them that were, and so would lessen the Credit and Authority of their Endeavours, with such as were peculiar Favourers; and that, in fine, their Dissent tended to the Breach of Brotherly Love and Unity in the Church*. I say my Sense is, *That this on each Side, with the Heats that followed, perhaps much worse than the Thing it self, gave Life to the Division that those that fear the Lord, have truly Mourned for.* And since I have hinted the Heats that may have attended the Management of this Difference, be not offended that I say, the *Difference, through those Heats, is now more in Spirit than Fact, in Mind than Matter*: It is come in Fact to this, *Whether the Care of Conversation should belong to* Women *as well as* Men, *especially relating to their own Sex, the* Women *being so great a Part of the Church*: And over this, I think, you are got for the most Part. 2. *Whether the* Women *may meet separately from the* Men? And for Answer to this, be pleased to take Notice of your own unavoidable Concessions: *You allow Meetings of Care in General, and do not deny Women absolutely their Share among the Men, and that particular Members must be accountable to the Society they are of, in Point of Conversation, according to the Rules embraced by the said Society.* I say, You own the End, you allow the Means, you refer the Choice of your Means to the Society, and you, as well as we, expect a Compliance with those Rules. Then the Question is, *Whether in Fact*, Women's Meetings *be a Part of that Discipline the Church admits of?* And it is evident, that the Church of God does, generally speaking, receive and practise it, with Satisfaction and Advantage. I would therefore beseech you, *Friends*, to ponder in your Minds, upon what a narrow Point your Distance stands, and that the main and tender Point is allowed you, *viz. Conscience is Free*, and unconcern'd in the Question; and the Visible Ground of Distance being so small, weigh with your selves by what has been, what may be the Consequence of this lamentable Breach.

I am as much for *Liberty* as any Man; I ever was so, and hope I ever shall be for it; but we must refer it to a proper Object, or we shall abuse what we do so much prize, and pervert one of the greatest Priviledges we can pretend to. I do not mean, by the Liberty, that we are to resign to the Benefit of *Society* That which is Private or Personal; No, this does not enter into Private or Personal Liberty, concerning which, the Apostles taught us to bear, and not offend one another; as about Meats and Drinks: I may add Clothes, Houses, Trades, *&c.* so as there be no Excess, for that is every where Wrong: These Things regard not Society, but a Man's Self, and his private Liberty alone. What is it to the *Society*, what or when I eat, what Sort of Clothing I wear, or House I live in, or Trade I will be of, so as Excess or Uncomeliness be avoided? This is still in my own Power, and many like Things, hard to be numbred, about which *Society* is not in the least concerned, nor in which any Member of it is interrupted, or called in Question. In the next Place, we do also all agree, that Faith must not be forced, nor Worship constrained, for that grates upon *Conscience*, which God only can effectually enlighten or rightly perswade. But that bears not upon our Question, as I said before; for the Compliance desired in it, is about *Order*, not *Faith*, and that not about *Worship*, but *Conversation*, in which if you submit your Liberty, it is for the *Good of Society*, and you have the Returns of it in the Benefit and Comfort thereof. Do you serve, or take Care of others, that before were free of that Engagement? Others also are tied by the same Rules, to serve and be concerned for you, that formerly owed you no Obligation; and if you are under the Notice and Reproof of others, as to your Personal Conduct, they are equally under yours upon Occasion; so that you lose nothing but what you get, nor give nothing but what you receive again, and to a right Spirit and a good Mind, this mutual Service will appear Reasonable, Christian, and Requisite. And as in no Age, the Resister and

Gain-

Gainsayers of *Care and Order*, in any of the *Lord's Eminent Servants*, have passed without the *Mark of God's Rebuke*, so those that have contested and opposed the *Wisdom of God in His Faithful Servants*, have ever failed of their Purpose, and been finally manifested to have been led by a wrong Spirit. And as observable it is, that those by whom the Lord has eminently appeared, and who were the first Instruments of his several Dispensations to the Sons of Men, have always exercised that Authority among the People they have gathered, and have been constantly preserved from falling away, though some or other have risen against them with that Clamour, as if they had set up themselves, and were gone from what they taught or were, and took too much upon them. *But what have they all come to? Read, and Judge.*

Nor was it ever heard of, in the *Dealings of GOD with the Sons of Men*, that He varied, or changed his Dispensations in the Life-time of the Instruments of any of them, as some have been ready to imagine, nor yet in that Age in which He has brought them forth: Which engages me to beseech you, in the Bowels of the Love of CHRIST, our Only Root of Life and Light, and Love and Peace, *that you be like minded with your Friends and Brethren*, and see that the Life and the Fellowship of the Truth be preserved in the Enjoyment and Practice of Fellowship; which will be, if the Love of God, which first made us Love one another, be kept in, for that is a Sovereign Antidote against all the Poison of Discontent, Evil Jealousie, and the Divisions that are wont to follow. And instead of reproaching our *Elders and Brethren*, whom God has Honoured, and whom we have Honoured, and could have laid down our Lives for, and who know nothing by themselves, but that they are as True to the Lord, and in as good a Condition in the Truth as ever they were, and have done, and intended in what they have done, as much the Benefit of the *Lord's People*. I say, *instead of reproaching them with Usurping Authority, and taking too much upon them*, let us consider, that those whom we have received with so much Reverent Love, and as worthy of double Honour in the Greater Things, are not unworthy to be heard and followed by us in *Lesser Matters*. Let us regard and value their Care, and Love them for it. So True is that Saying among Men, *That is Well Spoken which is Well Taken*, that the Bent and Purpose of a Man's Spirit, is that which gives the Just Reason of Acceptance or Rejection.

You have, *Dear Friends, judged too much after an Outward Appearance*, and, you may see, not truly there neither. *Open therefore your Hearts, your Souls and Spirits, and taste, with the Divine Sense of the Tender and Meek Truth, the Aim and End of Brethren:* Herein be a little more truly free and universal in your Minds, and you will perceive this Care has a large and long Prospect for Good. The due Exercise of your Spiritual Senses, will answer all your Objections, and satisfie every Upright Soul among you; *but if you look out, mistake Liberty, mistake Imposition, mistake Formality, mistake the Nature and End of Things, and the Intention of your Ancient Friends and Brethren in them*, you will judge carnally, and be ready to think, as if outward Rule and Lordliness were aimed at, and a departing from the Truth, even whilst our Care, in the Sight of the Lord, is for the Honour of it, in *Reference to the Young, the Weak, and such as may be Careless, and ready to fall asleep*; for such some yet are, and such are yet like to be; and for their Sakes a *Discipline*, as to Conversation, must be, as well as that there are Natural Infirmities, as *Sickness, Age*, &c. that unavoidably call for it. Nor did, or can ever any Community subsist without it; and the Heats, Prejudice, and Rents, that have arisen about the *How or Manner of it*, shew the Opposition not to be Right, nor of a Good Tendency; the End of that Order, in the Minds and Hands of those from whom we Joyfully received the Testimony of the Truth, being the Glory of God, and Good of His People, as a *Primitive Christian Society*.

To conclude: *As this is not a Plea for Imposition, nor Forms of Worship*, but *Forms of Discipline*, as to the Government and Behaviour of our selves in our Converse, both with those that are without, and those that are within, and that there is no Visible Communion, or Society in this World of Bodies, but what is subject to them, and must in some Sort subsist by them; I beseech you, that We, as becomes a Reasonable and Modest People, and as *Dear Children, may be of One Heart, and One Mind, and walk together as those that have been Partakers of One Life, and that have Drank into One Spirit*; for, *It is a Comely Thing to see Brethren walk together in Love.*

O Friends, Let us labour againſt ſecret Animoſities, Watchings for Evil, Detractation, *the Sin that flung the Angels out of their Heavenly Station*: Let us ſee to our own Spirits, how they are, if *Meek, Lowly, Humble, Tender*, by which the True and Preſerving Judgment is only known and felt; or, if not *High, Fierce, Hard, and Prejudiced*; for a Man may come to loſe a Good Frame of Spirit upon very Trifles. It is not always what the Matter is the Diſpute ariſes upon, but *how far the Thing is eſpouſed*, and what Place a Man ſuffers it to have in his Mind: If Jealouſy, Reputation, Revenge, or Contradiction, prevail, Diviſion muſt follow: Some are apt to reſent Things too ſoon, and carry it too far, even to Obſtinacy, through the Workings of the Evil One in a Myſtery; ſo that though the Pretence of the Quarrel may be ſome Fact or other, yet that has the leaſt Share oftentimes in the Difference, it being enflam'd and encreaſed by the *Myſterious Workings of the Spirit of Strife and Variance in the Mind*, according to an old Saying, *The greateſt Feuds oftentimes ariſe from the ſlighteſt Cauſes*. Let me beſeech and prevail with you to read and weigh the Bent and Force of the Apoſtle's Spirit in *Rom.* 12. alſo 14. 19. & 15. 4, 5, 6. and eſpecially 16. 16, 17, 18, 19, 20 Verſes. Likewiſe 1 *Cor.* 14. 32, 33. weighty places indeed. 2 *Cor.* 13. *Epheſ.* 4. 1, 2, 3, 4. *Phil.* 3. 16, 17, 18. ch. 4. 8, 9. *Col.* 3. 12, 14, 15, 16. 1 *Theſ.* 5. 12, 13, 14. 2 *Theſ.* 3. 4, 5, 6. He often commands Order and Obedience to the Apoſtolick Tradition in this Epiſtle, *Tit.* 1. 15. ch. 2. 1, 2, 3, 4, 5, 6, 7. *Heb.* 13. 1. And, 1 *Pet.* 4. 8. All which *exhort to Peace, Brotherly Kindneſs, to be of one Mind, to ſtudy one Thing. O follow the Things that make for Peace, and do not contend, diſpute, and ſtrive one with another.* A bleſſed Doctrine, and it has a bleſſed Reward. The Lord God Almighty diſpoſe your Minds, *my Friends*, to a tender returning State, and frighten not your ſelves with Deſigns (of the Brethren) that *have no Being, but in Jealouſy and Miſapprehenſion*: I beſeech you, in the Lord, lay down every *Mark* or *Enſign* of Difference or Separation, and behold our Arms as open as ever, to receive you, and *let your Heart be as our Heart*, and then our Meetings your Meetings: Let the *Fear* and *Awe* of the Lord, the becoming *Love* of his precious Truth, *which is* Chriſt *in us, the Hope of our Glory*, who gave himſelf for us, to redeem us from the Enmity, Death, and Curſe Diſobedience had laid us under, *melt* and *cement* us as one Lump; Fleſh of Fleſh, and Bone of Bone; ſo ſhall our Joy exceed our Sorrow, and Tears be wiped from our Eyes on this Occaſion; and GOD, our exceeding Great and Glorious Rewarder, be our Crown, Portion, and Diadem for ever.

Yours, In and for the Truth,

W. PENN.

A KEY, opening the Way to every CAPACITY; How to diſtinguiſh the *Religion* Profeſſed by the People called QUAKERS, from the *Perverſions* and *Miſrepreſentations* of their *Adverſaries*. With a Brief Exhortation to all Sorts of People to Examine their *Ways*, and *their Hearts*, and *turn* ſpeedily to the Lord.

The INTRODUCTION.

Reader,

OBſerving the prevailing Power of Prejudice, and the too great Eaſineſs of Mankind to be impoſed upon by deſigning Perſons, and eſpecially on the Side of Uncharitableneſs, (ſo depraved is the Nature of Man) and conſidering alſo what Miſchievous

chievous Effects that Evil hath produced among too many of all Sorts of People, to the Hurt of Civil as well as Religious Society, by the Coldness, Jealousy, Uncharitableness and Animosity, even to Hatred and Persecution, (the very Contraries and Reverse of the true Christian Religion) that have thereby abounded, we have the less wondred at the hard Treatment we, as a People, have suffered from other Perswasions, almost all of them having in their Turn, some, I hope, Ignorantly; others, I fear, wilfully; Misrepresented our Principles, Misgiven our plain Meanings, and called their own strained Interpretations, ay and their down-right Perversions too, our Faith and Religion: And thus dressing us in the Bear's Skin, the Credulous have been excited to look upon and treat us as Hereticks, Seducers, Blasphemers, and what not, while (blessed be God) our Aim and Bent have been the very Power and Work of Religion upon our Souls, that we might be God's Workmanship through Christ Jesus, his blessed Son and Heavenly Agent; taking this to be the very Life and Soul of true Religion; the Effect and Fruit of the Divine Nature, which makes us Christians indeed here, and fits us for Glory hereafter. And because we have chosen Retirement, Moderation, Self-denial, which to be sure are the Solids and Inwards, the Spirit and Substance of Religion, and have therefore waved and sequestred our selves from more Outward and Pompous Communions, Offence has been taken at us, and we have been disingenuously represented to the World; On which Account I have published this little Treatise, for the Sake of others, as well as in our own Vindication, but theirs especially that are under Prejudices from Vulgar Abuses. I would intreat such to consider, that if it be an Evil to judge rashly or untruly of any single Man, how much a greater Sin it is to condemn an whole People: And if the Matter about which the Judgment is made, renders it more or less Evil, certainly to condemn the Religion of an whole People in the Lump, which at once comprehends their Faith, Worship and Morals also, must be, if false or mistaken, as great an Injustice as can well be committed, and the Almighty will not hold them guiltless that have been so Uncharitable and Injurious to their Neighbours. And this we have frequently lamented as our great Unhappiness, above all that our Enemies have been able Argumentatively to urge against us, that we are yet unknown of those that stick not to condemn us. But they must certainly be inexcusable with Just Minds, that will take our Belief at our Enemies rather than at our Own Hands, who best ought to know what we Believe. But it will be the Business of this Little KEY to explain the pretended Obscurity, and shew the Difference between our Principles, and the Vulgar Account and Apprehensions, and thereby Open a Way into so clear and plain an Understanding of our true Principles, from our Enemies Perversions, that we hope, with God's Blessing, all Impartial Enquirers will be satisfied of our Holy and Christian Profession; And this we also earnestly desire for their Good, that as we have been call'd of God, out of the Evil of the World, to be a People to his Praise, through his Grace, so none may stumble or be offended at the Truth we testify of; but seeing the Excellency of it, by the Peace and Purity it leads into, They may embrace it, and walk in it; which is the best Way to end Controversy, and obtain the Great and True End of Religion, the Salvation of the Soul.

A KEY Opening the Way to every Capacity, &c.

SECT I.

Of the Light within, what it is, and the Virtue and Benefit of it to MAN.

Perversion 1. THE Quakers hold, *That the Natural Light in the Conscience of every Man in the World, is sufficient to save all that follow it; and so they overthrow Salvation by* Christ. A mighty Error indeed, if it were *True*:

Principle. But it is at best a great Mistake: For their Belief and Assertion is, *That* Christ, *who is the Word, that was with God, and was God;* (and is so for ever) *hath lightned every Man that cometh into the World, with his own Light,* as he is *That true* Light, or *such* a Light, as there is no other to be compared with him; which is the Meaning of the Emphasis *True* in the Text, *Joh.* 1. 9. And that such as follow the Reproofs, Convictions and Leadings of that Light, with which he enlightens

John 1. 1. 9.

1692.

See Isa. 49.6.
John 1. 4, 9.
c. 3. 21.
c. 5. 40. c. 8.
12. c. 10. 10.

enlightens the Understandings and Consciences of Men, *shall not walk in Darkness*, that is, in *Evil* and *Ignorance* of God, *but shall have the Light of Life*; that is, be in a *Holy* and *Living* State or Condition towards God: *A State of Acceptance and Salvation, which is from* Sin *here, as well as from* Wrath *hereafter:* And for which End Christ was given of God. So that they assert the *Light of Christ*, to be *sufficient* to save, that is, to *Convince* of Sin, *Lead out of* it, and *Quicken* the Soul in the Ways of Holiness; and not to be a *Natural* Light, otherwise than as *all Men, born* into the World, have a Measure of Christ's Light, and so it may, in a Sense, be said to be *Natural* to all Men, because all Men have it coming into the World. For this Light is *something else* than the bare Understanding Man hath as a Rational Creature: Since, as such, Man cannot be a Light to himself; but has only a *Capacity* of seeing, by means of the Light with which Christ, the Word, Enlightneth him. For we can no more be a *Mental* or *Intellectual* Light to our selves, than we are an *External* and *Corporeal* Light to our selves: But as the *Sun* in the Firmament is the *Light* of our Bodies, so the *Light* of the Divine Word is the *Sun* of our Souls; the glorious *Luminary* of the *Intellectual* World, and they that walk in it, will by it be led to Blessedness.

Rev. 21. 24.

Perverf. 2. *The* Quakers *hold, That the Light within them is* God, Christ, *and the* Holy Spirit; *so that every* Quaker *has whole God, Christ and Holy Spirit in him, which is gross Blasphemy*.

Princip. This is also a Mistake of their Belief: They never said that *every divine Illumination* or *Manifestation* of Christ, in the Hearts of Men, was *whole God, Christ*, or the *Spirit*, which might render them guilty of that gross and blasphemous *Absurdity* some would fasten upon them: But that *God*, who is *Light*, or the Word *Christ*, who is *Light*, stiled the *second Adam, the Lord from Heaven*, and the *Quickning Spirit, who is God over all blessed for ever*, hath *enlightned Mankind* with a *Measure* of Saving Light; who said, *I am the Light of the World, and they that follow me, shall not abide in Darkness, but have the Light of Life*. So that the Illumination is from God, or Christ, the *Divine Word*; but not therefore that whole God or Christ is in every Man, any more than the *whole Sun* or *Air* is in every House or Chamber. There are no such harsh and unscriptural Words in their Writings. It is only a *Frightful Perversion* of some of their Enemies, to bring an *Odium* upon their Holy Faith. Yet in a Sense the Scriptures say it, and that is their Sense, in which only, they say the same Thing. *I will walk in them and dwell in them. He that dwelleth with you, shall be in you: I will not leave you Comfortless*, I will come to you: *I in them and They in me: Christ in us, the Hope of Glory. Unless Christ be in* you, ye are Reprobates. *Little Children, of whom I travail again in Birth, until Christ be formed* in you. Now if they who denied his Coming in the Flesh, tho' high professing Jews, were to be accounted *Antichrists*, because Enemies to that Appearance and Dispensation of God to Men; what must they be reputed, who as *stiffly* disown his *Inward, Nearer* and *more Spiritual Coming, Formation* and *Dominion* in the Soul; which, is to be sure, the Higher and Nobler Knowledge of Christ? Yea, the *Mystery hid from Ages*, and now revealed to God's People: The *Riches of the Glory* of the Mystery which God reserved to be made known to the Gentiles, of whose Stock we are. Certainly tho' they are called Christians, they must be no whit *less Antichrists* than those obstinate Jews of old, that opposed his more visible and bodily Appearance.

John 1. 4, 8.
12.
1 Cor. 15. 45,
47.

John 14. 3,
17, 18, 20.
Col. 1. 26, 27.
2 Cor. 13. 5.
Gal. 4. 19.

Col: 1. 27.

Perverf. 3. *By the* Quakers *Doctrine every Man must be saved, for every Man, they say, is* Savingly Enlightned.

Princip. Not so neither: For tho' the *Light* or *Grace* of God hath and doth more or less appear to all Men, and that it brings Salvation to as many as are *taught by it to deny Ungodliness and Worldly Lusts, and to live Soberly, and Righteously, and Godly in this present World*, as the Scripture teacheth; yet it no Way follows that Men must obey, and learn so to do, *whether they will or not*. God tenders *Saving* Light *or* Grace to *All*, and by it calls All, and strives and pleads with All, according to the Measure and Manifestation of it; but if they will not hearken to it, he is clear of their Blood. His Light is *Saving* that lighteth them, but it cannot be said to save them, *while they rebel against it*. In short, tho' Men are lightned or visited with a *Saving* Light or Grace, yet the *Quakers* never concluded, nor can it rightly be concluded from their Testimony, that such Men must Necessarily and Absolutely be saved, whether they obey, or rebel.

Job 3. 20. 21.
Tit. 2. 11, 12.
Gen. 6. 5.
Ezek. 18. 21,
22, 23, 24.
Mic. 6. 8.
1 Tim. 2. 4.
2 Pet. 3. 9.
Job 7. 17, 18.
ch. 21. 17.
ch. 24. 13.

Perverf. 4.

Perverf. 4. *By the* Quakers *Light or Spirit, they may be moved to* Murder, Adultery, Treason, Theft, *or any such like Wickedness, because they say that such as are so led, have the Light within them.*

Princip. This never was their Doctrine, nor is it consequent of it: For tho' they hold that all have Light, they never said that all obey'd it, or that Evil Men, *as such, or in such Things,* were led by it: Much less could the Light be chargeable with the Sins of those that refused to be led by it. For herein they know the Spirit of God, and the Motions of it, from the Spirit of this World, and it's Fruits, That the Spirit of God *Condemns all Ungodliness,* and moves and inclines *to Purity, Mercy, Righteousness, which are of God.*

Joh. 3. 20, 21.
Gal. 5. 16-26.

They deny and abominate that Loose and Ranting Mind, which would charge the Spirit of God with their *unholy Liberty.* God's Spirit makes People free from Sin, and *not to commit sin.* Neither do they distinguish, as such loose People wickedly do, between the *Act,* and the *Evil* of it. Wherefore they say, that as the *Tree* is *known and denominated by it's Fruits, so Spirits are by their Influences, Motions and Inclinations:* And the Spirit of God never did incline any one to Evil. And for that Cause they renounce this Construction of the Ranters, *that Evil is no Evil when they are led to it by God's Spirit.* For that Grosly implies, As if the Spirit of God led Man at any Time to that which is Evil in it self, or that it were possible to *be sinless* in the Commission of Sin, as *Murder, Theft, Adultery, Revenge, &c.* For that never was nor can be the Way and Method of God's Spirit, which is *Pure* and *Holy* for ever; and brings all that regard the Convictions and Motions of it, into a *Sense* and *Sorrow* for Sin, and so leads them into a State of *Reformation,* without which, all Profession of Religion is meer *Formality,* and *Hypocrisy.* So that Man's Sin and Destruction are of himself, but his Help is in God alone, through Jesus Christ, our blessed *Sacrifice,* and *Sanctifier.*

SECT. II. *Of Infallibility and Perfection.*

Perverf. 5. *The* Quakers *must be all* Infallible *and* Perfect, *if they have such an* Infallible *Light in them.*

Princip. No such Matter: This is also a great Abuse of their true Meaning. They say the Principle is *Pure, Perfect, Unerrable* in it self, or else it were very unfit to lead Men out of Error and Impurity. But they never did assert themselves such, merely because it was within them: By no Means. But that all who are led by it, and live according to it's Manifestation, are so far Perfect, and *so far infallible in the right Way,* as they are led by it, and not a Jot farther. For it is not *Opinion,* or *Speculation,* or *Notions* of what is *true;* or *Assent* to, or the Subscription of Articles, or Propositions, tho' never so soundly worded, that according to their Sense, makes a Man a *True* Believer, or a *True* Christian. But it is a *Conformity* of Mind and Practice to the *Will of God,* in all Holiness of Conversation, according to the Dictates of this Divine Principle of Light and Life in the Soul, which denotes a Person *truly* a Child of God. *For the Children of God are led by the Spirit of God, but if any Man have not the Spirit of Christ, he is none of his.* And let it be noted, that tho' this Spiritual Principle be in Man, yet, *it is not of Man but of God,* through Jesus Christ. Who can lay down a more *Independent Doctrine* upon *Self,* and a more depending one upon the Grace or Gift of God? Let us not, I pray, be mistaken, nor suffer for such Misapprehensions, nor be made to hold what we don't, on Purpose to disrepute us with sober People, or to support the Mistaken Charges of our Enemies. Yet to shew that a State of Perfection from Sin (tho' not in Fulness of Wisdom and Glory) is attainable in this Life; they, among others, refer them to these Scriptures, which for Brevity's Sake, are not set down at large, but the Reader is desired to turn to them.

Rom. 8. 4.

Rom. 8. 9. 14.

Gen. 17. 1. Deut. 18. 13. Job 1. 1, 8. ch. 2, 3, &c. 8. 20. Psal. 18. 32. Ps. 37. 37. and 119. 1. Prov. 2. 21. Matth. 5. 48. Luke 6. 40. 1 Cor. 2. 6. 2 Cor. 13. 9. 11. Eph. 4. 13. 1 Thes. 3. 10. 2 Tim. 3. 17. Jam. 1. 4. 1 Pet. 5. 10. Heb. 6. 1. 1 Jo. 6, 7, 8, 9. Ch. 2. 20. 27. Ch. 3. 5, 6, 7, 8. Ch. 4. 17.

SECT. III. *Of the Scriptures, their Truth, Authority, and Service.*

Perverf. 6. *The* Quakers *deny Scripture, for they deny them to be the* Word of God.

Princ. They own and stile the Scriptures, as They own and stile themselves; viz. *A Declaration of those Things most truly believed, given forth in former Ages,*

1692.
Luke 1. 1.
2 Tim. 3. 16. 17.
Joh. 1. 4, 14.
Rev. 19. 13.

by the *Inspiration of the Holy Spirit*; consequently that they are *profitable for Doctrine, for Reproof, for Correction, for Instruction in Righteousness, that the Man of God may be perfect, throughly furnished unto all good Works*. They are the *Form* of *Sound Words*. We profess to believe them, and read them, and say, it is the Work we have to do in this World, and the earnest Desire of our Souls to Almighty God, that we may *Feel* and *Witness the Fulfilling of them* in and upon our selves; that so God's *Will may be done in Earth, as it is in Heaven*. But to call them the *Word of God*, (the Ground of the Charge) which they never call themselves, but which they peculiarly Denominate and Call Christ by; In Reverence to Christ, and in no slight to them (which they believe to be of *Divine Authority*, and embrace as the *best of Books*, and allow to be as much the *Word of God*, as a Book can be) They do, as in Duty and Reason bound, attribute that Title to *Christ* only.

And yet as the Word of God may, in some Sense, signify the *Command of God*, referring to the Thing or Matter commanded, as the *Mind of God*, it may be called *the Word of the Lord*, or *Word of God*: As, on particular Occasions, the *Prophets* had the *Word of the Lord* to Persons and Places; that is to say the *Mind* or *Will* of God, or that which was commanded them of the Lord to declare or do.

Mark 7. 13.

So Christ uses it, when he tells the *Pharisees, that they had made the Word* (or Command) *of God of none effect, by their Traditions*. But because People are so apt to think, if they have the Scriptures they have all (for that they account them the *only* Word of God, and so look no farther; that is, to no other Word, from whence those good Words came) therefore this People have been constrained, and they believe, by God's Good Spirit, once and again to Point them to the great *Word*

John 1. 4.

of Words, *Christ Jesus, in whom is Life, and that Life the Light of Men*; that they might feel something *nearer* to them than the Scriptures, to wit, the *Word in the Heart*, from whence all Holy Scripture came, which is *Christ within them the Hope of their Glory*. And to be sure He is the *only* right *Expounder* as well as the

Deut. 30. 14.
Rom. 10. 6, 7, 8.

Author of *Holy Scripture*, and without whose *Light, Spirit*, or *Grace*, they cannot be Profitably read by those that read them.

Pervers. 7. *They deny them to be any Means whereby to resist Temptation.*

Princ. This is a very Uncharitable Aspersion. True it is, that they deny the Scriptures *merely*, or of themselves, to be *Sufficient* to resist Temptations; for then all that have them and read them, would be sure to be preserved by them against Temptations: But that they should deny them to be any *Means* or *Instrument* in God's Hand, is either great Ignorance or Injustice in their Adversaries, *God hath made use of the Scriptures, and daily doth and will make use of them for Instruction, Reproof, Comfort and Edification, through the Spirit, to those that read them as they ought to do*. Thus they say, they have felt them, and so they have been and are made unto them, through the good Spirit of God, coming in upon their Spirits, in the Reading and Considering of them; and wish heartily They were more in Request with the Professors of Christianity.

SECT. IV. *Of the Holy Spirit of God, and it's Office, with respect to Man, and of* MINISTRY, &c.

Pervers. 8. *The Quakers assert the Spirit of God to be the Immediate Teacher, and that there is no other Means now to be used, as* Ministry, Ordinances, *&c.*

Princ. They never spoke such Language, and their *Daily Practice* confutes the Reflection. But herein we perceive the great Subtilty of Satan, as well as in other Things, to darken the Appearance of the Truth, and *Prepossess* Peoples Minds against it. For since he cannot hinder the *Exaltation* of the Spirit above all visible Instruments, nor the Necessity of its Manifestations, Convictions, Motions and Operations, to be known in the Hearts of Men, and the great Suitableness thereof to the Gospel-Administration, he would spoil all by over-doing the Matter, and carrying our Assertions beyond Bounds; For they never denied the Use of *Means*, but to this Day, from the Beginning, they have been in the Practise of them. But then they are such Means as are used in the *Life* and *Power* of God, and not in and from Man's *meer Wit, Will*, or *Carnal Innovation* or *Imitation*; the only Thing they strike at. For Instance, they cannot own that to be a *Gospel-Ministry*, that is without a *Gospel-Spirit*, or that such can be sent of God, that are not *taught* of God, or that they are fit to teach others what *Regeneration* and the Way to Heaven are, *that have never been Born Again Themselves*; or that such can ever bring Souls to God, that are themselves *Strangers* (like those in the *Acts* 19. 21.)

to the Baptism of *Fire, and the Holy Ghost*; Never having been *Circumcised* with the Circumcision *of the Heart in the Spirit*, Rom. 2. 29. Which is so absolutely necessary to make a *True Jew*, or a *Real Christian*, and much more the requisit qualification of a *Gospel-Ministry*.

1692.

This *Unexperienced* and *Lifeless Ministry*, is the only Ministry, and such the only Ministers, that the People called *Quakers, cannot Own and Receive*, and therefore *cannot maintain*. For the *Ministry* and the *Ministers* that are according to Scripture, they both own, Respect, and *delight* in, and are ready to Assist and Support in their Service for God.

Jo. 14. 16, 17
26 ch. 16. 13
Acts 1. 8.
Gal. 1. 1, 15, 16.

It is strange, because they deny all false Means, or Means not sanctified, or used in the *Openings* and *Leadings* of God's Power and Spirit, that therefore they must deny *All Means*, however *Rightly used* or *employed*. This is an Injustice to their *Profession and Practice*. Wherefore all are desired to take Notice, That *Evangelical Means* and *Order* they love and desire to keep: For they diligently assemble themselves together to wait upon God, to inable them to Worship him; where they both *Pray and Prophesy*, one by one, as *Prepared* and *Moved* in their Hearts by his Spirit, and as any Thing is revealed to them, according to *Primitive Practice*; otherwise they are silent before the Lord. Nor are they without *Spiritual Songs, making Melody in their Hearts* to God their Redeemer, by the same Holy Ghost, as often as they are comforted and moved by it, as was the *Primitive Practice*.

See 1 Cor. 14
15. 29, 30, 31
Joh. 16. 7. 20
22.
Eph. 5. 19.
Col. 3. 16.

SECT. V. *Of the Holy Three, or Scripture* TRINITY.

Perverf. 9. *The* Quakers *deny the Trinity.*

Princ. Nothing less: They believe in the *Holy Three*, or *Trinity* of *Father, Word* and *Spirit*, according to Scripture. And that these Three are Truly and Properly One: Of *One Nature* as well as Will. But they are very tender of quitting *Scripture Terms* and *Phrases* for *Schoolmen*'s; such as *distinct and separate Persons* and *Subsistences*, &c. are; from whence People are apt to entertain gross Ideas and Notions of the Father, Son, and Holy Ghost. And they judge, that a *Curious* Enquiry into those High and Divine Relations, and other speculative Subjects, though never so great Truths in themselves, tend little to Godliness, and less to Peace; which should be the chief Aim of true Christians. And therefore they cannot gratify that Curosity in themselves, or others: *Speculative* Truths being, in their Judgment, to be sparingly and tenderly declared, and never to be made the Measure and Condition of Christian Communion. For besides that Christ Jesus hath taught them other Things, the sad Consequence, in all Times, of *Superfining* upon Scripture-Texts, do sufficiently Caution and Forbid them. Men are too apt to let their Heads outrun their Hearts, and their *Notion* Exceed their Obedience, and their Passion support their Conceits; instead of a *Daily Cross*, a *Constant Watch*, and an *Holy Practice*. The despised *Quakers* desire this may be their *Care*. and the Text their Creed in *This*, as in all other Points: Preferring *Self-denial* to Opinion, and *Charity* to Knowledge, according to that great Christian Doctrine, 1 *Cor.* 13.

John 1. 1.
c. 14 c.
Rom. 9. 5.
1 Joh. 5 7.
1 Cor. 1 18.
31.
ch. 2. —
Col. 2. 8.

SECT. VI. *Of the* DIVINITY *of* CHRIST.

Perverf. 10. *The* Quakers *deny Christ to be God*.

Princ. A most Untrue and Unreasonable Censure: For their Great and *Characteristick* Principle being this, That *Christ, as the Divine Word, Lighteth the Souls of all Men that come into the World, with a Spiritual and Saving Light*, according to *John* 1. 9. *ch.* 8. 12. (which nothing but the Creator of Souls can do) it does sufficiently shew they believe him to be God, for they *truly* and *expresly* own him to be so, according to Scripture; *viz. In him was Life, and that Life the Light of Men; and he is God over all, blessed for ever.*

John 1. 1.
Rom. 9. 5.

SECT. VII. *Of the Manhood of* CHRIST.

Perverf. 11. *The* Quakers *deny the Humane Nature of Christ.*

Princ. We never Taught, said, or held so gross a Thing, if by *Humane Nature* be understood the *Manhood* of Christ Jesus. For as we believe him to be *God over all blessed for ever*, so we do as truly believe him to be of the Seed of *Abraham* and *David* after the *Flesh*, and therefore Truly and Properly *Man, like us in all Things* (and once subject to all Things for our Sakes) *Sin only excepted*.

Isa. 7. 14.
Mat. 1. 23.
Luke 1. 31.

SECT. VIII. *Of Chrift Jefus, His Death, and Sufferings.*

Perverf. 12. *The Quakers expect to be Juftified and Saved by the Light within them, and not by the Death and Sufferings of Chrift.*

Princ. This is both unfairly and untruly ftated and charged upon us. But the various Senfe of the Word *Juftification*, obliges me here to diftinguifh the Ufe of it; for in the natural and proper Senfe, it plainly implies, making Men Juft, that were Unjuft; Godly, that were Ungodly; Upright, that were Depraved; as the Apoftle expreffeth himfelf, 1 *Cor.* 6. 11. *And fuch were fome of You, but ye are wafhed, but Ye are Sanctified, but Ye are Juftified in the Name of our Lord Jefus, and by the Spirit of our God.* In the other ufe of the Word, which fome call a Law-fenfe, it refers to Chrift, as a Sacrifice and Propitiation for Sin, as in *Rom.* 5. 9. *Much more then being now juftified by his Blood, we fhall be faved from Wrath through him:* and 1 *John* 2. *If any Man fin, we have an Advocate with the Father, Jefus Chrift the Righteous; and He is the Propitiation for our Sins; and not for ours only, but alfo for the Sins of the whole World.* Which tho' a great Truth and moft firmly believed by us; yet no Man can be entituled to the Benefit thereof but as they come to believe and repent of the Evil of their Ways; and then it may be truly faid, That God Juftifieth even the Ungodly, and looks upon them through Chrift, as if they had never Sinned; becaufe their Sins are forgiven them for his Beloved Son's Sake.

Not that God looks on People to be in Chrift, that are *not in Chrift*; that is, that are not in the *Faith, Obedience* and *Self-denial* of Chrift; nor *Sanctified*, nor led by his Spirit, but *rebel* againft it; and inftead of *dying* to Sin, through a *true* and *unfeigned Repentance, Live* and *Indulge* themfelves daily in it; *for they that are in Chrift, become new Creatures; Old Things are paft away, and all Things, with them, become new.* Wherefore we fay, that whatever Chrift then did, both *Living* and *Dying*, was of great Benefit to the Salvation of All that have believed, and now do, and that hereafter fhall, believe in him unto *Juftification* and *Acceptance* with God: But the way to come to that Faith, is to Receive and Obey the *Manifeftation* of his Divine Light and Grace in their Confciences, which leads Men to believe and value, and not to difown or undervalue Chrift, as the *common Sacrifice* and *Mediator.* For we do affirm, that to follow this Holy *Light in the Confcience*, and to turn our Minds, and bring all our Deeds and Thoughts to it, is the Readieft, nay, the *Only right Way* to have *true living* and *fanctified Faith* in Chrift, as he appeared in the Flefh, and *to difcern the Lord's Body, Coming and Sufferings a-right*, and to receive any *Real Benefit* by him, as their *only Sacrifice* and *Mediator*: According to the Beloved Difciples Emphatical Paffages, *If we walk in the Light, as* (God) *is in the Light, we have Fellowfhip one with another, and the Blood of Jefus Chrift his Son cleanfeth us from all Sin.* And becaufe this People fay, that Chrift's *outward Coming* and *Sufferings Profit not* to their Salvation, that *Live in Sin*, and rebel againft this Divine Light, fome have untruly and uncharitably concluded, that they deny the Virtue and Benefit of Chrift's Coming and Sufferings in the Flefh, as a *Sacrifice for Sin.* Whereas we only deny and oppofe a falfe and dangerous Application of them in and to a difobedient State. For we believe Chrift came not to fave Men in their Sins, but *from* their Sins; and that thofe that open the Door of their Hearts at his *Inward* and *Spiritual Knocks*; [to wit, the Reproofs and Convictions of his Light and Grace] have *their Confciences fprinkled with his Blood* (that is difcharg'd from the Guilt of them) *from dead Works, to ferve the Living God:* And that fo far only as Men come by Faith, Repentance and Amendment to be Chrift's, Chrift is theirs, and as he has an Intereft *in their Hearts*, they have an Intereft *in his Love and Salvation.* That is, fo far as they are Obedient to his Grace, and *take up his Crofs, and follow him* in the Ways of *Meeknefs, Holinefs* and *Self-denial*, fo far they have an Intereft in Chrift, and no farther. And here *there is no Condemnation* indeed *to them that are in Chrift Jefus*, becaufe fuch *walk not after the Flefh, but after the Spirit*; for we have feen a *Shoal* or *Sand* here, that we fear many Thoufands have Split upon, which we defire to avoid, and are earneft that others may beware of it alfo; *viz.* that becaufe Chrift died a *Sacrifice for the Sins of the whole World*, by which he put Mankind into a Capacity of Salvation, and has given every one a *Talent of Grace* to work it out by; they prefume upon the Sacrifice, and Sin on, without a through Repentance, Reformation and Converfion to God, *not Dying* with Chrift to the World, but Living

ing in it, according to the Lusts and Spirit of it. Such as these may be assured that *where Christ is gone, they shall never come*; for says the blessed Apostle, *God sent his Son to bless us, by turning every one of us from the Evil of our Way*. So that the Contrite, Humble, Meek, and Self-denying People, are those that have the true and full Benefit of Christ's *Coming, Suffering* and *Mediation*, and of all those Holy Ends for which God his Father *Anointed* and *Gave* him to the World, *viz.* To be the *Way, Truth* and *Life*; *Light, Leader* and *Saviour*, to be a *King, Priest, Prophet, Sacrifice, Sanctifier* and *Mediator*. Being sensibly felt of all such to *Reign* over their *Hearts*, *Teach* them God's Royal *Law*, *Give* them *saving* Knowledge, and to *Mediate, Atone for, Sanctify* and *Justify* them in the Sight of God his Father, for ever.

By all which it is evident to any moderate Enquirer, that we acknowledge Christ in his Double Appearance as in the Flesh, *of the Seed of Abraham*, so in the Spirit, *as he is God over all, blessed for ever*. Wherein is a full Confession both to him as a Blessed Person, and as a Divine Principle of Light and Life in the Soul; the Want of which Necessary and Evident Distinction occasions our Adversaries frequent Mistakes about our Belief and Application of the Scriptures of Truth concerning Christ, in that twofold Capacity.

For it is not another than that Eternal *Word, Light, Power, Wisdom* and *Righteousness*, which then took Flesh, and appeared in that Holy Body, by whom they have received, or can receive any true Spiritual Benefit. They holding, *Light* is Only *from Him*, *Forgiveness* Only *through Him, and Sanctification* Only *by him*. So that their ascribing Salvation from Sin, and Death Eternal, to him in this Age, who now appears by His Holy Spirit to their Souls, as before expressed, cannot render him *no Saviour* in that Age, or make *void* the End and Benefit of his Blessed Appearance then in the Flesh on Earth, or his Mediation now in Glory, for those that believe in him in this Age. Whose *Doctrine Pierced*, whose *Life Preached*, whose *Miracles Astonished*, whose *Blood Atoned*, and whose *Death, Resurrection* and *Ascension, Confirmed* that Blessed Manifestation to be no less than that of the *Word God* (the *Life* and *Light* of Men) *manifested in the Flesh*, according to the Apostle *Paul*, for the Salvation of the World: And therefore *Properly* and *Truly* was the Son of Man on Earth, and is now as truly the Son of Man in Glory, as the *Head* of our Manhood, which shall also be glorified, if we now *Receive him into our Hearts*, as the *true Light*, that leads in the Way of Life Eternal, and *Continue in well-doing to the End*.

John 1. 4, 9.
1 Tim. 3. 16.

SECT. IX. Of Good WORKS.

Perverf. 13. *Thus it is the* Quakers *set up Works, and Meriting by Works, like the Papists; whereby Justification by Faith in Christ is laid aside.*

Princ. By no Means: But They say with the Apostle *James*, c. 2. That true *Faith in Christ cannot be without Works, any more than a Body can live without a Spirit*; and that where there is Life, there is Motion, and where there is no Divine Life and Motion, there can be no True Faith; Believing being a *Fruit of Divine Life*. Nay, by the Comparison, if they were separable, Works being compared to the Spirit, they would have the better. The very *Believing* is an Act of the Mind, *concurring* with God's working in or upon the Mind, and therefore a *godly Work*. And no sooner is True Faith begotten in a Soul, but it falls to working; which is both the *Nature*, and in some respect, the End of it.

Nor yet do we say, that our very *Best* Works, proceeding from the True Faith it self, can Merit; no, nor Faith joyned with them, because *Eternal Life is the Gift of God*. All that Man is capable of believing or performing can never properly be said to Merit everlasting Blessedness, because there can be no *Proportion* (as there must be in Case of Merit) between the best Works that can be performed in the Life of Man, and an Eternal Felicity. Wherefore all that Man can do, *even with the Assistance of the Holy Spirit*, can never be said strictly to Merit, as a Debt due to the Creature: But on the other Hand, That *Right Faith*, and *Good Works*, which arise out of it, or will follow it, may and do *Obtain* the Blessed Immortality, [which it pleaseth Almighty God to give, and priviledge the Sons of Men with, who perform that necessary Condition] is a Gospel and Necessary Truth. And this the *Quakers* ground upon, and therefore boldly affirm to the World.

So that they deny *all Merit* from the best of Works, especially by such as some *Papists* may conceive to be Meritorious. But as they on the one Hand, deny the Meritoriousness of Works, so on the other Hand, neither can they joyn with that

1692.

Phil. 2. 12.

Mat. 7.

Pf. 17.

Lazy Faith which *works not out the Salvation of the Soul with Fear and Trembling*. Pray let not *good Works* make Men Papifts, becaufe they make Men Chriftians. I am fure *believing and not working*, and imagining a Salvation from Wrath, *where there is no Salvation or cleanfing from Sin*, which is the Caufe of it, is no whit lefs Unfcriptural, and abundantly more pernicious to the Soul. *Bleffed is he that hears Chrift's Words, and does them.* The Doer is only accepted. Wherefore it fhall be faid at the laft Day, not well profeft, *But well done good and faithful Servant, enter thou into the Joy of thy Lord. Thou Holy, Humble, Patient and Meek Liver: Thou that lovedft Me above all, and thy Neighbour as thy Self: Enter thou. For, for Thee and fuch as Thou art, was it Prepared from the Foundation of the World.* Which Recompence of his Faithfulnefs, is the Infinite Love of God, revealed

Rom. 6. 23.

and given to Man, through Chrift. For though *Death be the Wages of Sin*, yet the *Gift of God is Eternal Life to fuch*. So that as the People called *Quakers* do not hold that their good Works *Merit*, neither believe they that their good Works *Juftify* them: For though none are *Juftified* that are not in Meafure *Sanctified*, yet

Ifa. 26. 12.

all that Man does, is *Duty*, and therefore cannot Blot out old Scores: For that is mere *Grace* and *Favour*, upon Repentance, through Chrift the *Sacrifice* and *Mediator*; our *Great Scape-Goat*. So that Men are not Juftified, becaufe they are Sanctified, but *for his Sake* that Sanctifies them, and works all their good Works in

1 Cor. 1. 30, 31.

them and for them, and prefents them blamelefs; to wit, Chrift Jefus, who is made unto them, as he was to the Saints of old, *Wifdom, Righteoufnefs, Sanctification and Redemption*; *that he that glorieth, might glory in the Lord.*

SECT. X. *Of Water-Baptifm and the Supper.*

Perverf. 14. *The* Quakers *deny the two great Sacraments or Ordinances of the Gofpel*, Baptifm, *and the* Supper.

Princip. Whatever is truly and properly a Gofpel Ordinance, they defire to own and practife: But they obferve no fuch Language in the Scripture as in the Reflection. They do confefs the *Practice* of *John*'s *Baptifm*, and the *Supper*, is to be found there; but Practice *only* is no *Inftitution*, or fufficient Reafon of Continuation. That they were then proper, they believe, it being a Time of great Infancy, and when the Myfteries of Truth lay yet Couched and Folded up in *Figures* and *Shadows*, as is acknowledged by Proteftants: But it is their Belief, that *no Figures* or *Signs* are *Perpetual*, or of Inftitution, under the Gofpel-Adminiftration, when Chrift, who is the Subftance of them, is come: Though their Ufe might have been Indulged to young Converts in Primitive Times, becaufe of the Condefcenfion of former Practices.

It were to *overthrow* the whole Gofpel Difpenfation, and to make the Coming of Chrift of none Effect, to render *Signs* and *Figures* of the *Nature* of the Gofpel, which is *Inward, Spiritual,* and *Eternal*. If it be faid, *But they were ufed after the Coming of Chrift, and his Afcenfion too.* They Anfwer, So were many Jewifh Ceremonies, not eafily abolifhed, as Circumcifion, &c. It is fufficient to them, That Water-Baptifm was *John*'s, and not Chrift's, See *Matt.* 3. 11. *Acts* 1. 5. That Jefus never ufed it, *John* 4. 2. That it was *no Part* of *Paul*'s Commiffion, which if it were Evangelical, and of Duration, would certainly have been. 1 Cor. 4. 15, 16, 17. And that there is but *One Baptifm*, as well as *One Faith*, and *One Lord*, *Eph.* 5. 4. And that Baptifm ought to be of the *fame* Nature with the Kingdom of which it is an Ordinance, and that is Spiritual. The fame holds alfo as to the Supper, both alluding to *Old Jewifh Practices*, and ufed as a Signification of a near and accomplifhing Work, *viz*. The *Subftance* they reprefented.

If any fay, *But Chrift commanded that One of them fhould* continue *in Remembrance of him*; which the Apoftle to the Church of *Corinth* explains thus; *That*

Luke 22. 19.
1 Cor. 11. 26.
Mat. 16. 28.
John 14. 17.
Mat. 26. 29.
Mark 14. 25.

thereby they do fhew forth the Lord's Death 'till he comes. We alledge, that he that faid fo, told his Difciples alfo, *that he would come to them again: That fome fhould not tafte of Death 'till they faw Him coming in the Kingdom: And that he that dwelleth with them, fhould be* in them: *And that he would drink no more of this Fruit of the Vine, 'till he fhould drink it* New *with them in the Kingdom of God.* Which is the *New Wine*, that was to be put into the *new Bottles*, and is the Wine

Luke 5. 37.
Luke 17. 20.
John 6. 53 to 63.

of the *Kingdom*; as he expreffeth it in the fame Place: Which Kingdom is *within*, as may be read in *Luke*. He was the Heavenly Bread that they had not yet known, nor his Flefh and Blood, as they were to know them; as may be feen *John* 6. So that though Chrift was came to *End* all Signs, yet, 'till he was known to be the

Sub-

Substance to the Soul, as the *great Bread of Life from Heaven*, Signs had their Service with them, to *Shew Forth*, and *Hold in Hand*, and in *Remembrance* of Christ: Especially to the People of that Day, whose Religion was attended with a Multitude of the like Types, Shadows, and Signs of the One good Thing and Substance of all, *Christ* manifested in his People. And that great Apostle *Paul* says expresly of the Jewish Observations, *That they were Shadows of the good Things to come, but the Substance was of Christ*. Hence it is, that the People called *Quakers* cannot be said to Deny Them; that is *too hard* a Word: But they truly feeling in themselves the very Thing, which outward Water, Bread and Wine do signify, or point forth [to say nothing here of their Abuse, and what in that Case may be argued, from the Instance of *Hezekiah's* taking away the *Brazen Serpent* by God's Command] they leave them off, as fulfilled in Christ, who is *in them the Hope of their Glory*: And henceforth they have but *One Lord, One Faith, One Baptism, One Bread, and but One Cup of Blessings*, and that is the *New Wine* of the Kingdom of God, which is within.

2 King. 18. 4.
Mark 14. 25.
1 Cor. 10. 15, 16, 17.
Luke 17. 20. 27.

SECT. XI. *Of the Resurrection, and Eternal Recompence.*

Perverf. 15. *They acknowledge no Resurrection of the Dead, nor Rewards to come.*

Princ. In this also we are greatly abused. We deny not, but believe the *Resurrection* according to the Scripture; not only from *Sin*, but also from *Death and the Grave*: But are *Conscientiously* Cautious in expressing the Manner of the Resurrection intended in the Charge, because 'tis left a *Secret* by the Holy Ghost in the Scripture. Should People be angry with them for not expressing or asserting what is hidden, and which is *more curious* than necessary to be known, and in which the Objectors themselves cannot be positive? *Thou Fool*, is to the curious Enquirer, as says the Apostle: Which makes the *Quakers* contented with *that Body*, which God shall please to give them hereafter: Being assured *that their Corruptible shall put on Incorruption, and their Mortal shall put on Immortality*, but in such a Manner as pleaseth God. And in the mean Time they esteem it their Duty, as well as Wisdom, to *Acquiesce* in his Holy Will. It is enough they believe a *Resurrection*, and that with a *Glorious* and *Incorruptible Body*, without farther Niceties; for to that was the *ancient* Hope.

1 Cor. 15. 36 to 54.

Now as to *Eternal Rewards*, they not only believe them, but as the Apostle says of old, *above all People*, have the greatest Reason so to do; for otherwise, who is so miserable? Do they inherit the Reproach and Suffering of all that have separated from Time to Time from National Churches? That is to say, Are the *Outcries* that have been against the *Protestants* by the *Papists*, and those of the Church of *England* against the *Puritans, Brownists*, and *Separatists*, fallen so thick upon them, and shall They hold Principles inconsistent with an Eternal Recompence of Reward? By no Means. It is their *Faith*, their *Hope*, their *Interest*, and what they wait and have Suffered for, and press, as an Encouragement to Faithfulness, upon one another. And the contrary therefore must be both an *Unjust*, and an *Improbable* Suggestion of their Adversaries.

1 Cor. 15. 19.

SECT. XII. *Of Civil Honour and Respect.*

Perverf. 16. *The* Quakers *deny All Civil Honour and Respect, but what is Relative or Equal between Men.*

Princ. We *Honour all Men in the Lord*, but not in the Spirit and Fashion of this World that passes away. And tho' we do not pull off our *Hats*, or make *Curchings*, or give *flattering Titles*, or use *Complements*, because we believe there is no true Honour, but *Flattery* and *Sin* in the using of them; yet we treat all Men with *Seriousness* and *Gentleness*, tho' it be with Plainness, and our Superiors with a *modest* and *awful Distance*; and are ready to do them any reasonable Benefit or Service, in which we think real Honour consisteth. Whereas those that thus reproach us, are often *Proud, Peevish, Snappish, Abusive* and *Oppressive* one to another; tho' at the same Time they can give one another the *Cap* and *Knee*, with smooth Words, which [too generally] they never mean: Which is far from true Civility, or Honouring all Men in the Sense that they are exhorted to by the Apostle.

1 Pet. 2. 17.
ch. 3. 9.
Rom. 12. 2.
Job 32. 21, 22
1 Pet. 1. 14.

And as for expressing our Respect to our Superiors in all Countries, we think it best done by obeying all Just Laws under their Government, according to the Say-

1692.
Luke 7. 8, 9.

ing of the *Centurion* unto Chrift, and which Chrift fo much approved of, *viz.* When he faid to one, *come, and he came ; to another go, and he went ; to a Third, do this, and he did it.* Reafonable Commands, and Ready Obedience. This is *honouring* of Government and Governours, and not *Empty* Titles, and *Servile* and *Fantaftick* Geftures, and drinking of their Healths 'till they drink away their own: The vain and evil Cuftoms of the World, taken from the *Heathen*'s Practices, and *Adopted* by loofe *Chriftians* in their Converfation, and fo become the Fafhion of the Times. And if to diffent from thefe Things, be to be vile, we are contented

2 Sam. 6. 22.

to be accounted more Vile, having *Chrift's Commands, Primitive Example,* and our own Convictions on our Side.

SECT. XIII. *Of Civil Government.*

Perverf. 17. *The* Quakers *are Enemies to all Government. Firft,* In that every one acteth according to his own Conceit. *Secondly,* Becaufe they won't *Support* Civil Government, *Thirdly,* Becaufe They *Refuse* to give Evidence upon Oath, as the Law requires.

Principle. That this is a Calumny, their Lives and Converfations fufficiently fhew ; for no People give the Magiftrates *Lefs* Trouble, or caufe that Charge or Burden to Sit lighter upon their Shoulders than thefe People do. And for their Principle, *They believe Magiftracy to be an Ordinance of God, and that He that Ruleth Well, is worthy of Double Honour, and deferves to be much Valued and Efteemed :*

Rom. 13. 1, 2, 3.

As fuch certainly do, *Who are a Terror to Evil Doers, and a Praife to them that do Well.* And farther, to fhew that they are a People that love *Order and Good Government*, they carefully practife it among themfelves: For if there be Twenty Meetings of Worfhip in a County, They, peradventure, *make Three or Four Monthly Meetings of Bufinefs,* and thefe *Monthly Meetings* are refolved into a *Quarterly*

Acts 6.

Meeting for the County, by fuch Members as they feverally appoint to conftitute it. And all the *Quarterly Meetings in the Nation,* by chofen Men out of themfelves, do conftitute *One General Yearly Meeting ;* unto which, the Meetings of thofe People, in all Parts of the World, have their Recourfe, *by Chofen Meffengers, or by Epiftles.* The Bufinefs of which Meetings, in their feveral Degrees, *is to promote Virtue and Charity, Peace and Unity.*

The Quakers *will not fupport Civil Government, and fo are ufelefs, if not dangerous to Government.*

This alfo is untrue, upon Experience: For what People is more induftrious under Government, or pay their Taxes better to it than they do ? And, *Tribute from the People, and Juftice from the Rulers, are the Support of Government in all Countries.* It is true indeed, that they cannot kill, or flay their own Kind, and fo are not fit

Mat. 5. 38---45.
ch. 26. 51, 52.

for Warriors with Carnal Weapons of Deftruction, becaufe they believe their *Bleffed Lord* forbad the Ufe of them to His Followers, when He faid, *They that take the Sword, fhall perifh with the Sword ;* and that the Ufe of the Sword in War, was one of thofe Things that God fuffered *for the Hardnefs of Men's Hearts, and that from the Beginning it was not fo:* In fine, that it came in with the Fall, and muft go out with it alfo. And as Chrift the *Repairer of Breaches,* and *Reftorer of Paths to dwell in,* comes to be known to Rule in the Heart, *Love will take Place of Wrath, and Forgivenefs overcome Injury and Revenge :* So the *Lamb* will be preferr'd before

Ifa: 11. 6.
2 Cor. 10. 3. 5.

the *Lion,* and *the Lion refign to, and lye down with the Lamb,* and Deftruction come to a perpetual End. For which Caufe, the *Weapons* of this People's Warfare are not Carnal, *but Mighty through God, to the pulling down the Strong Holds of Sin and Satan,* according to the Apoftle's Doctrine : Which is the *Holy War* indeed, ftiled by the *Holy Ghoft, The Saints Warfare.* And fince fo Holy, Lamb-like, and Peaceable a State, is both Prophefied of, and promifed, as the *Happinefs of the latter Times ;* and that It and They take their Beginning in Chrift, the *Beginning* and the *End* of all True Chriftians ; let not this People be thought Ufelefs, or Inconfiftent with Government, for introducing that Harmlefs Glorious Way to this diftracted World (for fome Body muft begin it) but rather Adore the Providence, *Embrace the Principle, and Cherifh and Follow the Example.* Believing with them, that Chrift, the Bleffed Shepherd of His Flock, will ever preferve the Faithful Followers of his Meeknefs, and Difciples of His Peaceable and Forgiving Doctrine.

The Quakers *refufe to give Evidence,* &c.

It cannot be their Fault, which is fo much their Defire, *viz. To be able to give Evidence upon all Occafions.* Nor, with Juftice, can it be reputed their Stubbornnefs, ness, but their Tenderness, since they cannot *Swear at all* and that the Law requires an *Oath* in Evidence. Now Christ having commanded His Followers *Not to Swear at all*, and that instead of an Oath, or in Cases where Oaths are allowed under the Law, their *Yea, Yea*, and *Nay, Nay*, should serve instead of *Swearing*; and that for this Reason, because *What is more than Yea, Yea, and Nay, Nay, cometh of Evil*; and for that Christians are commanded to avoid the very Appearance of Evil, much more that which cometh of Evil: Upon this Account they dare not *Swear at all*. So that it is *for Christ's Sake*, and the tender Respect they bear to his *Evangelical, Positive* and *General Precept*, that they cannot swear, who is the *Truth*, and has taught them to speak the *Truth* without an Oath.

1692.

Mat. 5. 35. 37.
Jam. 5. 12.

Now if this would be admitted [and often they have prayed that it might be, and, for Want of it, are not only less serviceable to their Neighbours than otherwise they could be, but are *great Sufferers in their Persons and Estates*] and that the Government would be pleased to accept their *Yea Yea*, and *Nay Nay*, instead of an Oath, as other Countries do in the like Cases, they would be ready to submit to the *same Punishment in Case of Untruth, that is due by Law to Perjury*: And upon all Occasions would be glad to help and serve their Neighbours with all their Hearts. Wherefore let not that be made their *Fault*, that is so much *against* their Will, and their Great *Unhappiness* and *Affliction*.

Thus, sober Reader, thou hast a brief Account of this *People*, their *Principles* and *Practice*, and therefore thou may'st see, if thou pleasest, with how little Reason they are *Despised* by some, and *Abused* by others; which hath been their Lot, in a large Measure, ever since they have been a People: Tho' the whole Bent of their Spirits and Testimony, since God, by his Grace, hath distinguish'd them, has been to *Promote the Experimental and saving Knowledge of Jesus Christ* in the World, *by turning the Minds of all People from the Darkness that is in them, to the Light of Christ which is in them*, as the *Great, Singular*, and *Necessary Agent* and *Principle*, by which *only Man* is enlightned and enabled to see and do the Will of God. For, 'till Men receive and are *Quickned* by this Divine Principle, they are *Hypocrites* and not *Christians*; *Bastards* and not *Sons*.

2 Cor. 13. 5.
Acts 26. 18.
1 John 1. 7.
ch. 2. 20. 27.
Rom. 8. 1---12.
John. 1. 5. 4.

Neither can they have true and living Faith, whatsoever they profess; nor can they truly and acceptably Worship God, whatsoever they perform. O then, let the poor *Quakers*, and their *abused* Principles have better Entertainment with Thee, *Reader*: And do not conclude because they direct People to the Light of *Christ* in them, that therefore it is a Mere *Natural* and Not a *Divine* Light; Or because they assert Christ to be the *Word of God*, and that he is revealed *in the Heart*, according to the Scripture, and that the *Scripture*, in that excellent Sense, is not so; that therefore *they deny the divine Authority of the Scriptures*, and that the Mind and Truth thereof, as declared by them, is not in *any* Sense the *Word of the Lord to Men*: Or because they don't receive the *Schoolmen's Trinity*, that therefore they deny the Scripture-Trinity of *Father, Word* and *Spirit*: Or that therefore they deny the *Divinity* of Christ the *Word*: Or that they deny Christ *without them*, who was the *Son of Man*, in a suffering State on Earth, and is now the *Son of Man in Glory*, because *They* Exalt *and* Press *an experimental Knowledge of Christ* within, *as the Truth, Substance, and Excellency of the* Hope of the Glory *that hereafter shall be revealed, as being the Riches of the Glory of the Mystery revealed, and to be revealed in these latter Days, according to the Scriptures of Truth*. Neither do thou say, they hope to be saved by their *Own Works*, because they press the Necessity of well-doing toward Acceptance with God; since they maintain, that *no Works that are not wrought by the Spirit of God are acceptable with him*; or that they hold even such Works to be *Meritorious*, because they say, Good Works are *Necessary* and *Rewardable*: Or that they are forgiven for what they do, and not for what Christ did: Or that they deny the *Use of Means*, because they reject Ungospel Ones: Or that they deny *Baptism* and the *Supper*, because they say, they are but Signs of the Spiritual Grace, and that they served but for a Time, and that they Experience their Accomplishment. Neither say that they are *Uncivil*, and Honour no Man, because they forbear such *Titles* and *Ceremonies*, in which true Honour and Civility do not consist: Or that they are against *Government*, because they cannot out of Tenderness, and not Obstinacy, conform to it in Matters relating to *Religion* and *Conscience*; in which Christ only is *Lord* and *King*: Since, *Reader*, thou plainly seest, That they believe the Light to be *Divine*, and the Scriptures to be of *Divine Authority*: That they own the *Scripture-Trinity*, or Holy Three, of *Father, Word* and *Spirit*, to be *truly* and *properly* One: That

Col. 1. 26, 27, 28, 29.
2 Cor. 13. 5.

Christ

1692.

Chrift is *God*, and that Chrift is *Man:* That he came in the *Flefh, Died, Rofe again, Afcended,* and fits on God's Right Hand, the *only Sacrifice and Mediator,* for Man's Happinefs: That truly *Gofpel-Means* and *Ordinances* are requifite, and to be reverently practifed: That good Works are Neceffary and Rewardable: That all Men are to be *honoured in the Lord,* according to their *Degrees:* And that *Government* in Church and State is *God's Ordinance,* and both Requifite and very Beneficial.

Now Reader, that which remains, is to recommend Thee to this *Divine Principle* of *Light* and *Life,* which they make the *Root* and *Spring* of all true Senfe of God, and Religion in Man: Even the *Light Within* which they began with, and comes from Chrift, and indeed is Chrift the Eternal Word, and which brings all that follow the Convictions and Leadings of it, to Chrift; that is, to his *Nature,* which is *Meek, Patient, Loving, Humble, Harmlefs, Self-denying* and *Holy;* and hereby to know him in themfelves according to Scripture, *to be the Hope of their Eternal Glory.* Who, as he is of *Abraham* after the Flefh, *fo is he God, the true Light, over all Bleffed for ever;* and *Lighteth all,* in order to Life and Bleffednefs. Unto the Manifeftation of whofe moft Holy and Bleffed *Light* within, Thou *Reader,* art earneftly exhorted. Bring thy Deeds to it, and Love it, and *Walk* in it, and thou wilt affuredly have the *Light of Life;* and *thy Fellowfhip fhall be with God, and with his Son and Saints, and the Blood of Jefus Chrift his Son fhall cleanfe thee from all Sin.* And *whatfoever Things are True, whatfoever Things are Honeft, whatfoever Things are Juft, whatfoever Things are Pure, whatfoever Things are of Good Report, if there be any Virtue, and if there be any Praife, think on thefe Things.* Which *Reader,* is, I know, moft earneftly defired on thy Behalf, by this defpifed and moft abufed People, call'd *Quakers.* So be it. *Amen.*

1 John 5, 6, 7.
Phil. 4. 8.

POSTSCRIPT.

Being an Exhortation to all People, to turn fpeedily to the Lord, and feek him while he may be found, whatever Perfwafion they are of, or Forms they are under, before the Dreadful Day of God's Vengeance overtake them.

1 Cor. 12. 7.
Tit. 2. 11, 12,
Rom. 5. 10,
12, 18, 19, 22
Mar. 3. 17.
ch. 17. 5.
Mat. 11. 29.
Ifa. 57. 21.

O Ye Inhabitants of the World, but more efpecially you that know this People, and among whom the *Teftimony,* which they bear, hath been held forth; Hear, and be intreated for your Soul's Sake! O that ye knew God your Creator, to be alfo your *Redeemer!* Who does as certainly *Vifit* you by the Spirit of the *Second Adam,* as ever he *Created* you in the *Nature* of the *firft Adam:* That as in one you fell, in the other you may *arife* out of your fallen and foul Eftate, and become a *Reform'd, Regenerate* and *Chofen* People to God. *This is my beloved Son, in whom I am well pleafed, hear ye him,* faid God the Father. And what fays Chrift, the Son? *Learn of me, for I am Meek and Lowly in Heart, and ye fhall find Reft unto your Souls.* For out of Chrift; out of his Spirit and Nature, verily we cannot have Peace. *No Peace to the Wicked,* no Peace to the *Proud* and *Ungodly,* faith the Lord. O Friends, you muft *take up your Crofs daily and follow him, or ye cannot be his Difciples,* his Followers, his People, his Friends; thofe in whom he is well pleafed. Whofe Doctrine is not fo much the good Words you read in Creeds and Catechifms, as it is the *Living Teaching* of his *Spirit in your own Hearts;* and whofe Religion is not Opinion, but *Experience;* not Notion, but *Enjoyment: Life from Death, Converfion, Regeneration:* In fhort, *Undefilednefs,* and *Holinefs, without which no Man fhall fee the Lord.*

Rom. 8. 1, 2, 5, 7, 8, 9, 13, 14.
2 Cor. 13. 5.
Gal. 5. 24.
1 Joh. 3. 3.
3 ch. 5. 4.
Jam. 1. 27.
Rom. 6. 19, 20.
2 Cor. 6. 17, 18.
ch. 7. 7.
Eph. 4. 34.
1 Thef. 3. 13.
Heb. 12. 14.
1 John 5. 4.
2 Cor. 10. 5.
Jam. 2. 19, 20
Gal. 6. 7, 8.
ch. 5. 22.

ch. 2. 8. 9.

Here is the Faith of Jefus: A Faith that *overcomes the World,* and *works by Love,* not Violence: Where Zeal and Charity are Companions, and Knowledge doth not puff up, but lives and works by *Obedience,* This is the *Faith* and *Religion* of Jefus: All others are the Faith and Religion of *Hypocrites and Devils;* which they may have, and be *Hypocrites* and Devils ftill: For tho' they believe, their Faith works not by Love; and though they know the Truth, they obey it not.

Wherefore Friends, it ftands you much upon to fee what Faith and Religion you have; and not flatter your felves on to *Perdition.* If it be the *True,* the *Pure,* the *Undefiled,* according to the Apoftle, *James* 1. 27. then you will have Light Hearts, and Eafy Confciences, *and an Hope that will not make you Afhamed:* Elfe, believe it, *Heavinefs, Anguifh* and *Tribulation* will (*whatever* be your *Profeffion*) overwhelm you, in the Day that God fhall enter into Judgment with you. For which caufe, O my dear Country Folks, and People, be intreated *while it is to Day,* to turn unto the Lord with all your Hearts, *and hearken to his Voice,* in your own Confciences,

Pfal. 95. 7.
Heb. 3. 7, 8.
13.

that calls you to Holiness, and *Harden* not your Hearts against his Reproof, *for the Reproof of Instruction is the Way to Life; Endless Life.* Did you but see that *God sees you* every-where, and in every Thing, and that *continually,* it would abundantly alter the Case with you. Then would you say as one of old, *The Lord was here and I knew it not.* Certainly, *Fear, Holy Fear* would take hold of you, an *Awe of the Omnipresent* Majesty would seize you, and you would not do that before God, which you would be ashamed Men should see you do. For no Place is secret to him: The *Light and Darkness are alike*: His Witness is with you as much alone, as in Company; and may perhaps be better heard by you.

Sin not then in the Face of God, in Contempt of his Witness, in Despight of his Spirit that is in you; but hear it, receive it, and love it, and you will be born of it, and become the Children of him whose Eye *Penetrates* the darkest Coverts, and Findeth out the secretest Corners. *Even he that Searches the Heart, and tries the Reins of Man, and sets his Sins in order before him, and telleth unto him his most inward Thoughts.*

This being the Case, what Manner of Persons ought you to be, O ye Children of Men! Do not satisfie your selves with *out-sides,* with a *Name,* a *Profession,* a *Church-membership,* &c. For 'tis not what you say, but what you do. But *Turn In,* and examine your own Hearts, see how they stand affected towards God and his Law and Truth in your inward Parts. Be Strict and True in the Search, as you would save your Souls. If your Minds be set on *Heavenly* Things, and that *Holiness* and *Charity* be the zealous *Bent* thereof, well will it be with you for ever: *To live then will be Christ, and to die will be your Eternal Gain.* For *blessed is that People and Nation whose God is the Lord.* But if the Love and Spirit of the World prevail; If *Pride, Covetousness* and *Luxury, Envy, Bitterness* and *Vainglory,* that are so very opposite to the Will and Nature of God, and his Holy Lamb; if these Things have Power over you, Flatter not your selves, you cannot be true Christians, nor in Favour with God, for you take his Name in vain: And your very *Prayers* and *Oblations* are an *Abomination* to the Lord, in that State. God calls for the Heart: *My Son give me thy Heart:* He has given Man the rest; but *That,* God will have for himself, if Man will have him for his God and Friend. Cozen not your selves therefore, O ye Sons and Daughters of *Adam!* for believe it, *such as you Sow, such you must Reap,* and *there is no Repentance in the Grave.* And a short, but great Work will God do in the Earth; and great Judgments, of divers kinds, will begin it, and they are at the Door. Yea, they are begun, if ye could but see them.

O Awake then, Awake out of the sleep of this World! Behold the Judge is at Hand, and the *Mid-night-Cry* is coming upon you as a Thief in the Night. Prepare, prepare, or you are excluded for ever! And remember, Salvation is from *Sin,* or it will never be from *Wrath;* so said the Angel, *Thou shalt call his Name Jesus, for he shall save his People from their Sins:* For it is the *Pure in Heart that see God,* and nothing *unlike* him can please him, and *less* live with him for ever.

The Eternal God *Reach* unto you by his Powerful Spirit, *Break* your Peace in the Broad Way, *Touch* you deeply with a Sense of your Disobedience to him, Give you true Contrition and Repentance, and *Create in you a Clean Heart, and Renew a Right Spirit with you*: To Conclude, Make you Holy, make you Zealous, and make you Charitable; that you may *Do,* as well as *Say,* and not only *Profess,* but *Possess* the Truth of the Living God in your *Inward Parts*: That *Pearl of Price, That Hidden and Eternal Treasure.* So shall you know that *the Times of Refreshing are come from the Presence of the Lord, and that the Kingdom is again Restored, unto* Israel! *ISRAEL,* the Prince of *Eternal Peace,* who hath prevailed with God for Man; *whose Scepter is a Scepter of Righteousness, and of whose Dominion there shall be no End.* So come Lord *Jesus*; come quickly. Amen.

Writ, in behalf of the said People, for the Information and Good of all, by

WILLIAM PENN.

The New Athenians no Noble Bereans: Being an Answer to the Athenian Mercury of the 7th Instant, in Behalf of the People called *QUAKERS*.

I AM heartily sorry to see Men, professing so much Ingenuity, fall so much below their *Pretensions*. Your *Design*, at first, carried the Face of Instruction, and gave us Hopes of a general Improvement of useful Learning; and for that Reason your Papers were as welcome to us as any other People; especially those that referred to *Natural Philosophy, Mathematicks*, and *History*; insomuch, that some of us collected them as they came out, and others bought them as they were compleated into Volumes; being much concern'd if at any Time trivial or light Questions were considered, as an unworthy Diversion from the End by you in the Beginning proposed. But you have not only been led, upon such Occasions, to exceed too often the Bounds of Modesty, but you have taken Occasion also to violate those of *Christianity*, in falling upon People's Opinions in *Religion*, instead of giving your own Impartially; and, upon their Persons likewise, and at last the *Society* it self; as if your Business were to expose them instead of informing them, and to increase Animosities rather than to take up their Time with more peaceable and profitable Subjects. What if you were led to speak of any Principle held by the People called *Quakers*? Could not that have been done as indifferent Persons, which you by your very Design would bespeak your selves to all Perswasions, and not as Party-Disputants and angry Antagonists? Might not the Intention of the People have past for good and sincere, tho' any Part of their Doctrine had, in your Opinion, been unsound; but you must use hard Words and Names for both Things and Persons? A sober and unconcerned Answer, upon any Question that might be sent you relating to their Belief, would have taken better with every Body that deserved your Pains, and have brought us sooner to reflect upon our Mistakes, if such they were: But, in Earnest, it looks as if you were almost aground, and wanted Matter, that so specious a Design as this first shewed it self, should dwindle away into Froward Controversy and Personal Invectives about *Religion*; or that you are not sufficient for your Work, that can so easily be moved out of your Province.

I beseech you leave this preposterous Digression, and pursue your own Business with more Care and Exactness; and, before you go, suffer your selves first to see a little better inform'd of what you have so irregularly and undeservedly censur'd.

You take Occasion at these Words, *Truth is always persecuted*, to say, *that will indifferently serve* Turk, Jew, Heathen, *or* Heretick, *as well as the* Quakers. This is harsh and unchristian. Are none worse than we? And we as great *Hereticks* as any? You judge before you convict us: 'Tis too gross Partiality, and false in every Degree. But whatever the Persecuted be, the *Persecutor*, to be sure, is always in the Wrong, which is your Case against the *Quakers*: But you recriminate, and will prove us *Persecutors*. That were to the Purpose indeed. Let us hear it. *You excommunicate such as will not be subject to your Injunctions*: And good Reason too, if they are Injunctions of Civil Order. He that joins himself to any Society, is oblig'd to the Rules of that Society; and every Society has, and must have that Power upon the Members that constitute it, or Confusion follows, and the Society dissolves. For instance, Injunctions about *Civil Controversies, Care of poor Orphans, due and orderly Proceedings relating to Marriages*, &c. are to be comply'd with, without the Reproach of *Persecution*: And yet farther too; look upon what Principles of Communion any Person enters into any Society, if he leave them, or any of them, it is no Persecution to disown him in that Thing wherein he alters; so that it touches not Person or Estate: for that is Persecution in a proper Sense; which is not our Case. But we *Imprison such as disturb our Meetings*. How this will be proved, is hard to tell; and yet if it be Persecution, it will light hardest elsewhere, even upon those, perhaps, that you account us Hereticks for separating from. But, Thanks be to God, we can and do deny the Charge. *See*, say you, *Francis Bugg's one Blow more*: But if this be *Athenian*, it is not *Berean*, to condemn an whole People upon another Man's Authority, that you are not assured was well grounded. Besides, it is a Book we have answered, which

you

you take no Notice of, and that is unfair, if you knew of it; and if you did not, you ought to have asked, before you had espoused another Man's Allegations. This is not answerable to that Candor you profess; and we must tell you, that *Francis Bugg* is an *Apostate Quaker*, an angry, unreasonable and clamorous Man; often and again detected and proved inconsistent with himself; and you will find, in the Issue, of no Reputation to your Charge against us. But did you ever read our *Orders of Discipline*, or have you been ever an Eye or Ear-witness of our *Injunctions upon Conscience?* If you have, you should have mentioned them, and shewn us our Fault; but your Evidence here, is what a discontented Man says, who speaks *ex parte*, and is Judge in his own Cause, against a Body of People he was once among, and zealous for; who, upon a private Controversy, because he had not his own Will, tooks Pet at those that could not be brought to humour him; and from thence, ran out from the very Profession of a *Quaker*; which shews the Foundation wrong, that quits a Principle for being displeased in a Man or Men. What will become of Society, if such Humours are uncontroulable, or they must give the Rule or Law to the whole?

Your next Proof of our being Persecutors, is from a Passage of *Geo. Fox* and *Geo. Roff*, in their Letters to *O. Cr.* by which we perceive your new Acquaintance, and with what *Tools* you work, which we are sorry for, both for your Sakes and theirs. But those Passages are plainly wrested by you; for they advise *O. Cr.* to go on in the Work he was called to; and what was that, pray? Is there one Word of *imposing* Religion upon the People of those Countries, or *forcing* them to abjure or renounce their own? No, not a Tittle of it. Where then is the Persecution? But inasmuch as they were Countries that did persecute, by which Means the Truth of God had not a free Entrance or Passage, but Inquisitions in Popish and Consistories in Protestant Governments suppress all that conformed not to their respective Establishments; therefore he should have made it his Business to open the Way for *a true Liberty of Conscience*, that Truth might not suffer under Violence, nor Persecution for Conscience Sake oppress it's Professors. This is the Upshot of those Passages, their very Scope and Tendency, as will appear to any impartial Reader, that will please to weigh them with what goes before and follows. But if you call this Persecution, to be sure it must be so to fight for Religion: And if it was unlawful for *O. Cr.* to fight for *Liberty of Conscience*, who was of a fighting Principle, what think you of punishing People because of their Conscience, that would not fight with you? You are very tender of a sudden, if it may but brush at us, while you do not consider the Blow you give your selves and your own Friends, that have but too signally appeared in that Spirit and Practice. *The Lord inform and forgive them.*

You justify calling us *silly Enthusiasts*, for believing *it is not lawful to Swear*, and say, *you are of the same Mind, because we, without Reason, by the Dictates of our own Fancy, which we call God's Spirit, oppose the Saints Practice of old, of which it was prophesy'd it should be used under the Gospel; was so by the Apostles and Primitive Christians, nay, by God himself, therefore the* Quakers *are silly Enthusiasts* Thus you.

Now we think this will nor prove us *Enthusiasts*, nor *Silly*, for we argue from a Text, and not our own Dreams or Fancies. Had we only pretended the Authority of a private Revelation for this Assertion, and that not true, then it had been *Enthusiasm*, and we *Enthusiasts*, in the worst Sense: It is *silly indeed*, to call an Opinion, grounded upon an express Text of Scripture, either *Enthusiasm* or *Silly*, when there is not a plainer Text for One God than this of our Saviour's against *Swearing*, Matth. 5. 34. *Swear not at all.* But if we had overstrained it, Where's the Silliness of it? Is it *Enthusiasm*, or *Silly*, to shut out all vain *Swearing*, by shutting out all *Swearing?* The Advantage of that exceeds the Disadvantage of Lying in Evidence, when that Lying is made as punishable as *Forswearing*. What *Silliness* or *Enthusiasm* is in this, pray you? *Scotland* and *Holland* think no such Thing, that have indulged that Tenderness.

And if the Text be but seriously considered, the Inference we make is beyond Exception.

First, The Tendency of that *Sermon upon the Mount*, is to shew, that the Righteousness of the *Gospel* excels that of the *Law*; as in the Case of *Adultery, Divorce, Revenge*, &c. But the Law forbad *false and vain Swearing*, therefore this must refer to that which was not forbidden under the Law. This is acknowledged by many learned Men, and in particular one of our own Nation, *Bishop Sanderson*,

1692.

in his *Latin Lectures, of the Obligation of an Oath:* But we, for another Reason, that shall anon be mentioned, think he yet narrows the Extent of that *Evangelical Precept,* for he refers to *Vows* only, and not swearing in any Case; but we, to *Swearing at all.* And our Reasons are, *First,* If it had been *Vows* only, there had been no Need of substituting any Way of Speaking in the Room of it. And, *Secondly,* If the Text cannot therefore refer to *Vows* in particular, *Swearing at all* must be intended; or nothing is forbidden, that was not forbidden under the Law. *Thirdly,* Christ's prohibiting Swearing, and substituting something in the Room of it, and that Something purely referring to the Way and Manner of Christians declaring the Truth, it is, to us, evident, that he comprehended all Cases wherein the Truth of a Thing is in Doubt, and consequently the End of Swearing: So, says Christ, *Let your* ὁ λόγος, *your Speech,* or *your Word, be Yea, Yea; or Nay, Nay.* It is rendred *Communication* in our Translations, that it might refer only to common Discourse, that Word being sometimes so understood; and yet *Communication* comprehends all Acts of Justice as well as other Parts of Life: For if it comprehends Discourse in Dealing, it also comprehends the Evidence of that Dealing, and the Laws of just Dealing; and consequently the Word *Communication* cannot lessen the real Force of our Sense of the Text; but the Words of the Text do plainly express a *Degree,* if not a *Form* of declaring Truth, be it *Yea* or *Nay.* And since Truth-speaking takes in and relates to Controversies amongst Men, as well as other Parts of Human Converse, this *Text* is a *Measure* of Truth-speaking on all those Occasions also. *Fourthly,* Now how far Christian Men may go in declaring the Truth, or where they are to be bounded, the *Text* is plain, *viz.* a *double,* but *bare Averment,* or *Denial:* Let your Word or Speech be *Yea, Yea; Nay, Nay;* That is, let your Answers, whenever you are asked the Truth of a Matter, go no farther than a *simple Affirmation,* or *Negation,* which you may double if you please. *Fifthly,* The Reason Christ gives for bounding his Followers within *Yea, Yea,* and *Nay, Nay,* excludes all Oaths, yea, all that is more than *Yea, Yea;* and *Nay, Nay;* to wit, that *they come of Evil,* because they proceed from Distrust, Infidelity and Impatience: A simple Assertion declares Truth; more, is a *Straining* of the Mind, and but to stoop to unreasonable Incredulity, which hath an evil Rise. Now what is more than *Yea, Yea;* and *Nay, Nay?* Why *Imprecations* are more, an outward Sign denoting an Oath is more, than *Yea, Yea;* and *Nay, Nay;* and consequently *cometh of Evil,* because below a Christian's Truth and Sincerity to gratify. *Sixthly,* And truly the Text is so far from excluding Judicial Cases, that it serves chiefly to relate to Evidence upon Differences. 1. Because it is in the *Room* of the swearing the Law allowed, which was *true* swearing: And, 2. Because of *doubling* the Assertion *Yea, Yea;* for a single *Yea* is enough for a Christian in ordinary Cases. Well, but you oppose to this, the Prophecy, 19 *Isaiah, v.* 18. to which, if you please, we will add two more, *ch.* 45. *v.* 23. and *Jer.* 4. 2. and make your Best of them: For besides, that it begs the Question, that the Prophet treated of Gospel-times, and not of some happy Time before the Period of their Dispensation, God might speak to them in the Language of their Time to be interpreted in a more spiritual Sense; and this the Place quoted by you shews: For, *Vers.* 21, Mention is made of *Oblation and Sacrifice,* that shall be offered in that Day, which, in a Jewish Sense, is not true of Gospel-times, but in a Gospel-sense, to wit, *Prayers* and *Praisings,* with *Heart* and *Voice,* is true. So it is in the Case of *Swearing,* they shall swear in that Day, as they sacrifice in that Day; that is, a Christian's Oath shall be his *Solemn Word;* and the Difference is not greater between them, than between the Sacrifices and Oblations of *Beasts* and *Birds* under the Law, and the Spiritual Sacrifices and Oblations of the *Hearts, Wills* and *Affections* of People under the Gospel: And thus you see, that Prophecy stands you in little Stead.

But you object the Practice of the Apostle, *Rom.* 1. 9. *God is my Witness.* 2 Cor. 11. 31. *God knoweth I lye not.* Gal. 1. 20. *Before God I lye not.* And you add, *If these are not formal Oaths, you would fain know what are?* In which, if you will not be offended, we will say as well as think, you have not been Ingenuous, to be so hard upon us, before ye had first stated and agreed with us what an Oath is; for if that be disputable, as it may be for what you have done to settle it, you argue at Random. Premises must ever be agreed by Disputants, or nothing can follow clearly and satisfactorily. We may say the same Thing you say, without allowing it the same Force and Extent; nay swear perhaps, in your Opinion, tho' not in our own; the same Words being an Oath, and not an Oath, as they may be

used

used and applied in different Manners. For if you should think that an Oath, which we think none, and you argue for Swearing by Proofs, that for that Reason are none to us; how do you prove Swearing *lawful*, or convince us that not Swearing at all is *Silly* and *Enthusiastical*, when you have not yet adjusted *what is Swearing at all?* This had been well worth your *Mercury*, for it had been informing, and shown good Reading.

But you put it off thus, after citing the Apostle's Words, *God is my Witness*, &c. *If these are not formal Oaths, we'd fain know what are.* In which you shift your Post, and turn *Querist*, instead of answering Questions.

But having such supposed able Men to deal with, we are not willing to put it off so; and therefore return it upon you, to state what an Oath is, which you so zealously recommend; denying, on our Part, any of those Texts to be an Oath,

As did *Basil the Great*, upon *Psalm* 15. And *Gregory Nazianzen*, in his Dialogue against *Swearing*: And Bishop *Sanderson*, in his Defence of *Joseph*, in his *Oxford* Lectures; which will much better defend the Apostle from your Imputation.

For what you say of *Tertullian*, you wrong him extremely, and your Reader also, by not telling him where to find it: For in his Apology, *Chap.* 32, whence, we suppose, your Objection is taken, he does equivocally and improperly own *Swearing*, *That they Swore, tho' not by the Genius of* Cæsar, *yet, for the Health and Safety of* Cæsar, just as they did Sacrifice. *Hoc salvum esse volumus, & pro magno id juramento habemus.* ' Our wishing well to *Cæsar* we have or account for an ' Oath, or instead of an Oath. And, as the *Pythagoreans* say, *There is in all reasonable Creatures an Oath or Tye,* viz. *A Mind, not to transgress the Law of God:* And, as *Clemens Alexandrinus* speaks, *That a good Man Swears by his Deeds.* So *Tertullian* urged upon them, That the Christians sacrificed *for the Health of* Cæsar as well as they, but it was in the Christian Way, by *pure Prayers.* So that as he was for *Sacrifice*, he was for *Swearing*. Thus to *Scapula*, C. 1. 2.

And in his Book of Idolatry, *Chap.* 11, *I speak not of Perjury,* says he, *because it is not lawful to Swear.* And, *Cap.* 31, *He that signs a Bill of Security, containing an Oath, is guilty of Swearing, and transgresses Christ's Command, who hath commanded not to Swear.* And speaking of the Temptations Christians were exposed to, if they should lanch into the Traffick of the World, he adds, *Not to speak of Forswearing, seeing it is not lawful so much as to Swear.*

We are the longer upon this, because he is one of your Authorities. Your other is *Athanasius*, *That he purged himself by an Oath, pleading the Apostle's Example.* Which, by the Way, looks like an Excuse for doing it, and as if in other Cases he did not allow it. But pray take the Pains to read his Annotations upon *Christ's Passion*, and you will find, first, That he denies all Swearing; and upon our Grounds. *The Evangelical Sentence,* says he, *of the Lord is,* Let your Yea be Yea, and your Nay, Nay: Thus far we, who are in Christ, may confirm our Words with Asseverations, but come no nearer to an Oath.

To this he objects himself the common Opinion, *That God Swore.* He answers it, *That God did not properly and formally Swear, nor could not; for the Nature of an Oath is to Swear by that which is Greater and Better than one's self,* Heb. 6. 16. But, if any Thing, says he, *this must be said, His Word is an Oath to Man for Verity, because of his Faithfulness and Truth.* And he will not have the Apostle to have Sworn, nor the most celebrated Fathers of and before his Time. So that we return it upon you, that if at any Time they used those Expressions of the Apostle, it was in Church-Matters, and because they did not think it an Oath. And if you will please to turn to *Justin Martyr's* Second Apology, *p.* 63, you will find he is of the same Mind; *We should speak, but not swear the Truth,* and vouches Christ's Authority, *Mat.* 5. for it. *Clemens Alexandrinus*, lib. 7. and *Tertullian's* Contemporary, *Cyprian, Hilary, Greg. Nyssen, Cæsarius, Epiphanius, Ambrose,* and *Chrysostom* above all the rest, styled the *Golden Doctor* or Father, out of whose Discourse, upon this Subject, we observe these five Things:

1. *That Oaths are not lawful under the Gospel.*

2. *The Reason of it, that their Evangelical Verity is the Christian, and a better Security.*

3. *That the Rise of an Oath is Infidelity and Distrust, which are from Evil, and that is below a Christian State; for he that dare not Swear, which once was permitted, dare not Lye, which never was permitted; and therefore his Yea is Yea, and his Nay, Nay.*

1692.

4. *That Swearing was a Condescension to a weak and low State of the World, to divert People from Swearing by false Gods, which was the Evil Custom of those Times;* as if God should say, I will suffer you to Swear, if you will Swear by me that am the true God, and not by their false Gods: And that from hence came his Command to Swear by him, not for the Sake of Swearing, but to avoid Idolatry.

5. *That this Principle is the only Means of rooting out all Evil Swearing out of the World.* Take the Cure for this most Pernicious and Epidemical Distemper, in the Words of *Basil the Great*.

The Remedy consisteth in a twofold Admonition: First, not to Swear at all: Secondly, to suppress the Form of Oaths. I will close with what the Institutions say, that go under the Name of *Clemens Romanus. Our Master hath commanded that we should not Swear, no not by the true God; but that our Word should be more credible than an Oath.* This *Clemens* was very ancient, you know, since the Apostle *Paul* mentions him, and that to him some of the Ancients ascribe the Epistle to the *Hebrews*.

We hope, after you have considered the Authorities that support this Doctrine, you will be so charitable at least to allow that we are neither *Silly* nor *Enthusiasts* for asserting it. This comprehending your Answers and Exceptions to the Queries upon this Subject (for against a Command so plainly proved, they must fall of Course) we are under no Obligation to consider them, and yet they shall not pass our Notice, tho' it were but to let you see how little they deserve it.

The first Query is, *If Christ's Coming did not supersede Oaths, since it was to end Sin, the Occasion of Oaths?* The Second, *If man, improving the Means given him to answer that End, may not obtain it?* I put them together because you give the same Answer to both, which is Negative; and for the same Reason, *viz. Because Christ did not come to end Sin*: And your Reason for that is, *That if Christ intended to have ended Sin by his Coming, it had been ended, which is not so, and therefore it was not the End of his Coming.* This opposes as plain a Text as is in the Bible, 1 *Joh.* 3. 5, 6. *And ye know he was manifest to take away our Sins. Whosoever abideth in him sinneth not; Whosoever is born of God doth not commit Sin.* The Angel thus declared the End of his Coming, *Mat.* 1. 21. Christ commands Perfection, *Ch.* 5. 48. *Be ye perfect, as your Heavenly Father is perfect.* The Heavenly Leaven was given to Leaven the whole Lump, *Chap.* 13. 33. The Apostle desired, That the Christians of his Time might be sanctified throughout in Body, Soul and Spirit; which leaves out no Part of Man, nor no Part of any Part unsanctified, 1 *Thes.* 5. 23. and exhorted them to press forward to the Mark, which was a perfect Man, even to the Measure of the Fulness of Christ. *Phil.* 3. 14, 15. *Eph.* 4. 13. In which Passages the End of Christ's Coming, and the Work and Blessing of the Gospel, *was to end Sin*, both as to the Guilt and Nature of it; and to sanctify and regenerate the Soul. Read *Phil.* 1. 10. 1 *Cor.* 6. 11. *Tit.* 3. 5. *Heb.* 2. 11.

2. Your Reason is both weak and dangerous: For if all comes to pass that Christ intends, then he intended not the Conversion of *Jerusalem*, notwithstanding he lamented it so, because it came not to pass. Again, If Christ intended to take away the *Guilt* and *Power* of Sin, it should accordingly be taken away: but in whole Nations or Believers, how very few can say it, or can you say it of? Nor know you but that there are some that walk *blamelesly* now as well as then. Your Ignorance is no Argument to the contrary: A Principle may be true for all Men's Practices, and God's End for Good to Man, though Man may frustrate it to himself.

3. The Scriptures you urge are against you, *Jam.* 3. 2. Here we will joyn Issue with you, this Chapter being a strong Proof of our Point; yea this very Verse: For it supposes a *perfect Man*, which you deny, and by the Similes of a *Bridle* and an *Helm*, it shews how a Man can come to be so. But, say you, in the Name of the Apostle, *In many Things we offend all*: Yet consider, pray, that the Apostle included himself no more there than Verse 9, where speaking of the Tongue, he also saith, *Therewith bless we God, and therewith curse we Men.* You cannot therefore think, I hope, that the Apostle was a *Curser*; but it was a Way of speaking to fetch in the Guilty, and the better to reach them, by personating them or involving himself among them.

Hear again the same Apostle, in this very Chapter, Verf. 11. 12. *Doth a Fountain send forth at the same Place sweet Water and bitter? Can the Fig-Tree, my Brethren, bear Olives?* Yes, say the *Athenians*, No, say the *Quakers*. Pray who keeps closest to the Text? Hear him farther, Verse 17. and Chap. 1. 27. he tells you the

Nature and End of their Religion. In few Words, *Humanity* and *Purity*, *Bowels* and *Holiness*, they are the pure Religion and *undefiled* in God's Sight, in his Account; not *Creeds* but *Practice*, not *Profession* tho' of true Words, but *Experience* and *good Living*. And, without Offence, had you been of this Religion, you would have been less Exceptious at us and ours. Your next Scripture is as unhappily chosen as the former, 1 *John* 1. 8. *If we say we have no Sin, we deceive our selves, and the Truth is not in us.* Now if you please but to read the Verse foregoing and following, perhaps you will see it is not to your Purpose.

If we walk in the Light as (God) is in the Light, we have Fellowship one with another, and the Blood of Jesus Christ his Son cleanseth us from all Sin. Now follows your Text, *If we say we have no Sin,* (that is, no Sin to be cleansed from, no Need of Christ to take away our Sins) *we deceive our selves and the Truth is not in us.* Observe now what follows, we desire you; *If we confess our Sins, he is faithful and just to forgive us our Sins, and to cleanse us from all Unrighteousness;* which comprehends both the *Guilt* and *Nature* of Sin. And that we have not misinterpreted your Text, the next and last Verse proves our Sense genuine; *If we say that we have not sinned we make him a Lyar, and his Word is not in us:* That is, if we say we have not sinned, and so have no Need of a Propitiation for Sins past, or to be cleansed from the Sin that is present, we make God a Lyar, that says we are Sinners, and therefore sent us his Son to redeem us from Sin. But now we will suppose your Answers good to the Two Queries; Pray what does that lessen the *Validity* of *not Swearing at all?* Though Men are not in all Things perfect, may they not tell Truth, and be believed, without the *Force* and *Strain* of an Oath? Must all Men be Lyars that are not sinless? Look about you *Athenians:* If this be not the Case, *Swear not at all,* is both good Doctrine and practicable, for all that you have said to the contrary.

Your Answer to the Third Query, *If there be a plainer Precept than this of Swear not at all,* is a *Jest* at us, but it turns in Earnest upon your selves. *Show us,* say you, *a more positive Command than that, He that hath Two Coats let him impart to him that has none, which if we followed in Winter Time,* you say, *we should look worse than we do.* But we tell you it is to be followed both *Winter* and *Summer* by all that will follow Christ; and however ill they look for it here to Scoffers, Christ will look very well upon them for it another Day. But you think you pinch us by urging the Text upon us literally, which alas is your Mistake; for so that we do not *Swear*, we answer that Precept though by other Words than *Yea* and *Nay*; and if we give of our Abundance to them that want, we answer this, though not exactly in a literal Sense; And now you see your *Jest* upon the Looks of the *Quakers*, makes you look no better than you should do. And thus much for your first Paper; what remains being but Heads insisted upon in your following *Mercuries*, where I shall find them, and in my next consider them particularly as they lye.

The Second Part of the New ATHENIANS no Noble BEREANS: Being an Answer to the ATHENIAN MERCURY of the 11th of the Fourth Month, called *June*, in Behalf of the People called *QUAKERS*.

YOU were certainly very much in Haste when you poured out such a *Mouthful of Charges* upon a poor People, that one Half of them, made good, must needs lay them as low as you wish; But they that count so quick, usually reckon without their Host, and must count again; as indeed you do; for in an after *Mercury,* you retract some of your Charges; which shews, by the Way, you went without Book in making them. To spare you, and save Paper, we will not repeat them here together, but as we answer them; for they are both foul and fully given.

Your first Charge is, *We speak contemptibly of the Bible:* But we hope not. Your Assumption has four Parts of Proof. 1. *We own it not,* you say, *as an adequate Rule of Faith and Manners.* For this you cite R. B's *Apology,* p. 25, & 43. And
what

what you cite is true; but you cite not all, and so leave what you cite more open to Exception, which is by no Means fair. Love but Truth and Ingenuity more than you love your own Credit, or slight ours, and we shall not doubt the Issue, even in your own Thoughts. *R. B.* tells you wherein the Scripture is not a Rule in all Cases and Circumstances, *viz.* It was not *Paul's* to go to *Jerusalem*, to be shut up there, rather than go back to preach to the Churches in *Greece:* Nor the Rule of *Paul's* Call, nor of any Minister of Christ to the Ministry; Nor with Reference to their going to this or that Nation to preach the Gospel rather than any others. It is not a Rule to *Prophesie*, as to when or what, at one Time or Place, more than another; for though it says, 1 *Cor.* 14. *That all may prophesie one after another, as it is revealed to them*, which authorizes the Practice, yet it is not the Rule of those Motions of the Spirit; neither to the Party moved to speak, nor to those that hear to judge aright: for no Scripture can tell me if I am moved by the Spirit of God or my own Spirit, or a transformed Spirit; nor can those that hear, judge of it, but by the Spirit of Truth. So that though the *Scripture* be a Rule of Words, it is the *Spirit only* that is a Rule to Men's Spirits concerning the Rise of true Prophecy in any. Again, By what Chapter or verse can you tell you are Believers? For tho' there are divers can tell what a Believer is, yet how do you know that you are such? By what Rule do you apply Scripture, nay, by what Rule do you believe Scripture? for the Scripture cannot be the Rule of your Belief of it self: And therefore it is that *R. B.* in our Name, says, they are not the principal Ground of all Truth and Knowledge, nor yet the primary adequate Rule of Faith and Manners: *But*, says he, *being a faithful Testimony of the first Foundation, they may be well esteemed a secondary Rule, and subordinate to the Spirit, from whence they have their Excellency and Certainty*, p. 38. And can you call this contemning of the Scriptures, without speaking contemptibly of the Holy Spirit that gave them forth? He argues thus: *If the Spirit only give the Knowledge of God, and by the Spirit we be to be led into all Truth, then the Spirit and not the Scripture is the Foundation of all Truth, and the primary Rule: But the first is true; therefore also the last. Again, That which is not the Rule of Faith to believe the Scriptures, is not the primary adequate Rule of Faith and Manners: But the Scripture is not, nor cannot be, that Rule; therefore*, &c. p. 38. 41, 42. You shew your selves too *Mercurial*, and ride Post over our Arguments, leaving them and the Matter behind you. The Scripture you oppose to all this, 1 *Tim.* 3. 17. and which is all you answer, and enough too were it but to your Purpose, proves only, *that all Scripture by Inspiration from God is profitable*; but it does not say, it is sufficient of it self for the accomplishing of the Man of God to every good Work; so is *Preaching, Praying* and *Meditating* profitable: but it does not say, that it is the *Fountain* of all true Knowledge, and the *only Rule* of Christians, or a Rule in *all particular Cases* that may occur to Men: And it is plain the Apostle referr'd to the Care of a Pastor, and to all particular Occasions. Less does he say, that the Spirit is not the Rule of Christians; and if it be a Rule at all, it cannot be a subordinate one to the Scriptures that came from it: No doubt but they are profitable, very profitable; and blessed be God for them; but must we contemn them *unless we prefer them to the Spirit of God?* The great and most excellent Rule of *Christians*, Joh. 14. 26. *The Comforter shall teach you all Things.* Ch. 16. 13. *The Spirit of Truth will guide you into all Truth.* The Apostle commended the Church *to the Word of God's Grace*, which is inward *Acts* 20. 32. See 1 *Cor.* 2. 9, 10, 11, 12. which Place attributes all Divine Knowledge to the Spirit of God, it's Searchings and Revelations. Again, *Tit.* 2. 11, 12. & 1 *Joh.* 2. 20, 21. *Ye have an Unction from the Holy One, and ye know all Things. It abideth in you; and ye need not that any Man teach you, but as the same anointing teacheth you all Things, and is Truth and is no Lye: and even as he hath taught you, ye shall abide in him.* We will close with the Words of Christ, whom all are to hear and prefer. *Joh.* 5. 37, 40. *Search the Scriptures* (or ye search the Scriptures) *for in them ye think ye have Eternal Life; and they are they which testifie of me. And* (for all that) *ye will not come unto me, that ye may have Life.* A most severe Rebuke to the better *Jews* of his Time; and as great a one to the Christians of that stamp now. They valued the Scriptures, but undervalued the Messiah when he came, that, from Scripture, they lookt for: What Blindness was theirs, that knew him not by so many Marks as they gave of him, but turned the Scripture against him, that testified of him? This is the Case of our Opposers with us at this Day: They oppose the Scriptures to Christ the Word, that shines in the Heart, and will not come to him,

the

the quickning Spirit, in themselves, that they might have Life; but think, by them, to have Eternal Life, and they are they that testifie of him. *Know ye not your own selves*, says the Apostle, *how that Jesus Christ is in you, except ye be reprobates*, 2 Cor. 13. 5.

This is the Doctrine that is our *Crime*, our *Enthusiasm*, our *Error*; and we are *Seducers*, *Deceivers*, and what not, for asserting, recommending and pressing it. But if this be to be *vile*, we are like to be *more vile*; for we must bear witness to that which the Scripture testifies of, *viz. the Spirit*, and prefer it before the Scripture, when the Scripture does so to it self. No Man's Letter is himself, nor so noble as himself. The Scripture is as the Letter or Epistle of the Holy Ghost to Men; but for that Reason 'tis not the Holy Ghost, nor to be instead of the Holy Ghost to us; nor, to be sure, to be preferred before the Holy Ghost. We bless God for the Scriptures: we read them with Comfort and Advantage; and they are profitable to the perfecting of the Man of God through the Assistance of the Spirit: The Scriptures declare the Things of God; but cannot work them in the Man: The Spirit only can do that; for which Cause we *honour, exalt* and *prefer* the Spirit, as that which fulfils the Scripture, and invite all to receive it, that it may make People spiritual; for *to be spiritually minded is Life and Peace*. Wherefore, as often as any of our Expressions are construed to lessen the Holy Scriptures, we ask it as a Piece of Justice from all our Readers, to take this Caution with them, we speak comparatively, not with our Books, or with Men, *but with Christ, his Light and Spirit*, from whence the Scriptures came. And in this Sense it is that R. B. and others, on the like Occasion, express themselves, when supposed to abate of the common Opinion of the Scriptures. For as *Face answers Face in a Glass*, so we say, and know, the Spirit and Scripture answer each other. And therefore the comfortable Evidence of a Christian Man, *is the Testimony of the Spirit of God within him, and the Scriptures of Truth without him*. Let it not then be any more a Fault in us to direct People to the Spirit of God, by which only they can come to the Possession of the Good Things the Scriptures speak of; for tho' they Exhort, Rebuke, Instruct, &c. yet without that great Agent, the *Spirit*, *influencing* and *enabling* the Creature, he shall never Experience the Truth of the Scriptures to himself in the most relative and excellent Parts of it.

2. The second Part of your Assumption is, *That we deny the Scriptures to be Necessary*; for which you cite S. *Fisher*, *Rust*, p. 112. and R. B. *Ap.* p. 68. It looks gross, as you lay it down; but pray take it altogether: They cannot be absolutely necessary to Salvation, where God has not made it necessary that they should be at all; for then that would be necessary which is not; and People, for ever miserable, for want of that which is not their Fault, that they have not. Again, It is allowed among Protestants, that where the Scriptures or Sacraments are withheld from People, as under Confinement, or providentially in Infidel Countries, there an upright Desire or Intention answers and supplies that want; then they are not absolutely necessary: So every where, by Consequence, where they cannot be had, they cannot be absolutely necessary to Salvation. This is not to render the Scriptures useless or needless, or to raise an Indifferency to them where they are enjoyed, by no Means; they are a great Blessing, and, as such, to be highly prized; and no Man, that has any Fear of God, or the least Taste of his Goodness, but must be of that Mind; but to vindicate God's Mercy and Goodness from leaving so great a Part of the World without the Means of Salvation, as they must be that want the Scriptures, if they are absolutely necessary to Salvation. To end this Head, consider, 1*st*, How long the World was without them. 2*dly*, How few and particular the first Books were: and, at last, in how narrow a Compass all the Old Testament Writings lay, compared with the whole World. And, lastly, How many Churches were gathered by the Apostles before the New-Testament Scripture was all in being, which is so much more beneficial, proper and advantagious to Christians, both as to Faith and Worship, than that of the Old Testament: And yet without that, for several Years, in which Time, doubtless, many fell asleep, they lacked no Rule: They had that which was *sufficient*, *viz*. the *Grace of God*, which taught them and led them in the Way to Blessedness.

Your third Proof, *Is our equalling* Apocrypha *with Scripture*, and quote S. F. *Rust.* p. 77, But if we don't equal Scripture with *Apocrypha*, it does not shew we slight the Scripture, to have more of it than ye allow that Title to: Did we make the Scripture *Apocryphal*, you had hit the Mark, in your Sense thereof.

However, firſt, your Communion frequently uſe it to conform their Doctrine, both in Pulpit and in Writing; and particularly the preſent Archbiſhop in his late Sermon before the Queen, upon *Pſal.* 73. 25. and that with a more than common Emphaſis. And if it were Spurious and a *By-blow*, as you are pleaſed to call us in reſpect of Religion, why ſhould ſo many eminent Poets of your own chooſe to vouch the Truth of Religion from thoſe Books, rather than *Plato*, *Philo*, &c.

3. Remember, if you pleaſe, that they were firſt left out by the Council of *Laodicea*, which was Three Hundred Sixty Four Years after Chriſt, and received again by the Council of *Carthage*, Anno 399, which at the Beſt, is but an indifferent Foundation for your Exception. Alſo pray take along with you, the Complaints of *Jerom* and *Epiphanius*, among others, of the *Partialities* that had been, even by the *Orthodox*, committed upon the New Teſtament, under Pretence of the ill Uſe ſome Hereticks (real or ſuppoſed) made, or might make of them, *Jer. ad Luc. Epiſt.* 28. *Epip. in Anc.* 7. 2.

4. Your fourth Part of the Aſſumption to prove your Charge, *Is, that we equal our own Writings unto the Scripture, and that it is the ready Way to make it both Blaſphemy and Nonſenſe:* And from thence you are pleaſed to call us *God's Ape*. Waving all your Reflections, that edifies very little, and cannot honour you, pray obſerve your Proofs. *G. Fox, Myſtery, pag.* 12. and *Francis Howgil, Anti. Volunt.* defeated, without a Page, *affirm the Neceſſity of an Infallible Spirit for Goſpel-Miniſters.* O Friends! Whither would you drive Things? What, make that *Hereſy*, which is the Root of all *True Religion*, as well as *True Miniſtry*? Can a fallible Spirit bring People into the Truth, or turn them to God? Is not the Spirit of God an Infallible Spirit? And are not the Children of God led by it? *Rom.* 8. 14. And we are not aſhamed to ſay, *That by that Holy Spirit, we are often conſtrained to Exhort, Rebuke, and inſtruct, as it giveth Utterance; and that God has owned our Labours with a comfortable Harveſt, bleſſed be His Name:* But for equalling our Writings with Scripture, we have no ſuch Expreſſions or Thoughts: It is a Word of your own, and a Conceit and Inference of our old Adverſaries. There are Degrees as well as Diverſity of Manifeſtatsons and Operations, but the *ſame Lord, and the ſame Spirit:* Yet if it will ſatisfy you, we have ever preferred the Bible to all Books and Writings of Saints and Good Men. You have other Proofs: You ſay, that *G. Roff writ to* O. C. Thus ſaith the Lord, *And that Branded Blaſphemer* Nayler *(whom we, you ſay, to this Day imitate, defend and admire) ſays in his Love to the Loſt. The Word of the Lord to His Beloved City; tho' the Holy Scripture muſt not have that Honour.* Now, know ye, if ye pleaſe, that we own the Style, and bleſs God His Word is among us, and when it lays a Neceſſity upon us, we can ſay in Truth, *The Word of the Lord:* And it is, or ought to be well known to this Nation, that we have ſpoken it in Truth; it having been fulfilled more than once upon thoſe to whom we have been ſent with it. And it is a Blindneſs and a thick Apoſtacy, that has overtaken ſuch as count it monſtrous to have a Viſion, or to know the Word of the Lord in Goſpel-Days; The Days of Light and Life, the Diſpenſation of Spirit and Power, and of the Word of the Lord, according to the Notable Paſſage, *Iſa.* 9. 21. *As for me, this is my Covenant with them ſaith the Lord, my Spirit that is upon thee* (ſpeaking of Chriſt) *and my Words which I have put into thy Mouth, ſhall not depart out of the Mouth of thy Seed, nor out of the Mouth of thy Seeds Seed, ſaith the Lord, from henceforth and for ever.* Alſo that of *Joel* 2. 28. *In the latter Days I will pour out my Spirit upon all Fleſh;* without Reſpect to Nation, Age or Sex. But you are very diſingenuous to thruſt into your Citation of *J. Nayler's* Words, by Parentheſis, whom you ſay we imitate, defend and admire; thereby ſuggeſting, that we defend him in Blaſphemy; which is more than you can prove by any Warrantable Authority: However, hereby you juſtify that Piece of Cruelty, done in that unhappy Age, and uſurped Power (as you ſuggeſt) which many Eminent and Sober People were grieved at: This is abuſive, and out of all Bounds of equal Dealing, and we wiſh you may repent of it: For we are ſo far from imitating, defending and admiring him in that Reſpect, wherein he gave Occaſion of Offence and ſtumbling, that we did not only at that Time diſown his Proceedings, but he very Solemnly condemned them himſelf, which was printed to the World; and he lived an humble, contrite and exemplary Life, and dyed, we believe, in Peace.

That we read our own Epiſtles in our Meetings, and not the Scriptures, is not from Diſreſpect to the Scripture; but becauſe of a particular Occaſion, and a Word of Exhortation thereby communicated. If it were Cuſtomary to read our Friends Writings,

Writings, as the Scriptures are in the publick Places of Worship, and yet did not read the Scriptures, we should deserve your Reproof; but that is not the Case, far be it from us.

The last Part of your Assumption, by which you would prove us to contemn the Scripture, *is our using, with the* Papists, *detracting Expressions, as a dead Letter, a Nose of Wax,* a Lesbian *Rule;* and for this you quote *S. F. p.* 48. It is low with you, that you have no more Evidence. But now be ingenious, Can you think we call the Scriptures so, or that we say Men make them so, or use them so? Lay your Hands upon your Hearts and think again, Is there any Thing more Proverbial, than to say, *That Men make a Nose of Wax of the Scripture?* But herein to joyn us with the *Papists,* is still more uncandid; for the very Place you cite, makes an Exception to the *Papist's Practice,* who use such Speeches Tauntingly, that is, in Slight, in Contempt of the Scripture. Then *S. F.* doth it not in any such Sense; Why then should you make him do it Tauntingly, and with *Papists,* when he so particularly provides against them both? You'd make ill Jury-Men with such Latitudes. The Scripture of it self is a *Dead Letter,* for all Letters are so in themselves, and you grant as much in speaking of the *Word of God*; but if they are made Alive to any Soul, by the Application of God's Holy and Quickning Spirit, they become Living to that Soul, as much as if the Holy Penman had spoke them in his Ear; and indeed no Words are Living to any Man, whether writ or spoken, but as they are made so by the Spirit, in the Heart of such a Man. But *Greg. Naz.* That we suppose you reverence, speaking of the Bible, said, *Is Religion placed in a Leaf? Fearest thou* (Paper or) *Parchment more than God?* This had been Heinous in us, and yet it is True. A *Lesbian Rule* he stiled it, ad Hominem. The Truth they declare is stable and certain, but Men twist, shift, and wring them, and so they become like the *Lesbian Rule,* that served all Turns; and for that Reason he urged, That Men should come to the Spirit of God, to receive the Mind of the Spirit in the Matter therein doubted or controverted.

Your Second Charge is, *That the* Quakers *will by no Means allow the Scripture to be the Word of God.* If you had said in *No Sense* too, you would have gone too fast; and yet your Intention in your Words looks that Way. Let us not differ, pray you, more than needs must, to support the Credit of your Charge. *You confess Christ is called the Word of God, but so is the Scripture.* And we say Christ is, but so is not the Scripture: You produce, *Jer.* 36. 4, 10, 12. We say, at that Rate, there are an *Hundred Words of God,* because it was the Style the Prophets used for every Message. But you go, I confess, a great Way to help out the Matter, when you allow, *That it is Ridiculous to say the very Letters are the Word of God, but the Sense and Divine Truths therein contained, and conveyed to us by the Co-operation of God's Spirit:* For in that Sense, every Passage thereof, given forth by Divine Inspiration, is the Will, Mind, Command, and if you please, so far the *Word of the Lord*; and so we do not, as you say, contradict our selves in using the same Phrase to our own Writings. But nevertheless primarily, and excellently, we attribute that Style to *Christ the Word, that was with God, and was God, and made All Things:* And we do not see but you yield it to us.

For your Third Charge, *Of turning the Sacred Truths of Scripture into Jejune Allegories,* since you refer your Proof to another Place, we also do our Answer.

Your Fourth Charge is, *That we speak not very Honourably of our Saviour.* But how does that appear? Do we say He is *No Saviour,* or that *He is a Deficient Saviour,* and leaves Men as Bad as he finds them, as too many shew that call Him so? And which is worse, plead to be so as long as they live, because, say they, *He did not come to take away the Nature of Sin,* which must be left for their Probation, and to shew forth God's Mercy to forgive; as if Sin were Serviceable? We have not thus dishonoured Him I hope. How is it, pray you, that we dishonour Him? Why, *First,* You say, *We make him a Monster:* That's bad indeed, or you are very Irreverent, as well as Unjust in your Expression. *Robert Barclay,* p. 306. you tell us, says, *He has Two Bodies.* Suppose so; one you grant; The other *R. B.* calls *Vehiculum Dei.* Not Two Bodies of the Virgin *Mary:* How is it a Monster then? You are more *Mercurial* than exact. But pray consider, and *Better Late than Never:* Did not all the Fathers Feed of Christ, as well as Drink of Him, do you think? Read 1 *Cor.* 3 4. *They did Eat the same Spiritual Meat, and did all Drink the same Spiritual Drink: (For they drank of that Spiritual Rock that followed them, and that was Christ.)* Now the Word *Body* is Figuratively used, as it imports a *Substance,* that is, *the Food of the Saints, their Spiritual Nourishment and*

Subsistence. You should be more deliberate, and not so wild and adventurous in your Censures. Your Reason is, *That we say Christ is actually present in every one of our own Bodies*; which you say, *Is a greater Degradation to Him than lying in a Manger.* But still we see you don't read the Bible, or remember what you read. Peruse 2 *Cor.* 13. 5. *Examine your selves, whether ye be in the Faith; prove your own selves: Know ye not your own selves, how that Jesus Christ is in you, except ye be Reprobates:* So that what you make a Dishonour to Christ, the Apostle makes an Evidence of being in the Faith. But this is not the only Point in which you Two differ. Yet know that Christ being in our Body, is none of our Phrase, and shews, as in other Charges (and which you ingeniously own in your *Third Mercury*) that you imperfectly know our Principles, tho' you boldly censure them. But were it so, yet the Apostle had defended the Expression, who speaking of the Divine Manifestation of Christ, and God in Christ, in the Creature, saith, *And this Treasure have we in Earthen Vessels, that the Excellency of the Power may be of God, and not of us,* 2 Cor. 4. 6, 7. To this add that of Christ's Prayer, *John* 17. 23. *I in them, and they in Me*; and it is to be hoped you will think a Man a little Better than a *Manger,* and yet it is no Degrading of Christ, *To say He is where He says He is,* and *where it is Antiscriptural to say, He is not.* Your last Reason for our Dishonouring of our Saviour, *Is our denying Him to be distinct from the Father.* But suppose this were True, Why do you strain so hard to depress us? Pray what were the Dishonour of it? It might, on our Parts, not look so Coherent; but to make the Son the Father, is Dishonouring the Father, rather than the Son. You had better not be medling, and let this Work alone; it is not your Talent, and ill becomes you. Howbeit know, if you please, we do think the Son *Distinct* from the Father; for Fatherhood and Sonship are certainly not the same. And the very Place you cite of *R. B.* p. 87, 88, you produced to prove your *First Reason,* tells you enough of that.

Now for the Citations out of *E. Burrough*'s *Trumpet,* p. 17. and *J. Parnel*'s *Shield,* p. 30. they mean no more than this, That we should not satisfy our selves only with what Christ did, and the Saints enjoyed, so long ago, *But that we should know and feel Him by His Light and Spirit nearer to us, that we might evidence His Work in our Hearts, and be Partakers of the Experiences of those Blessed Saints in Light:* And not that we denyed or slighted that Blessed Manifestation of the Son of God in the Flesh. This we have said again and again upon Occasion. *Isaac Pennington*'s Words, *Quest.* p. 33. is defended by express Scripture. See *Heb.* 10. 5. 7. *A Body hast thou prepared me. Then said I, Lo, I come (in the Volume of the Book it is written of me) to do thy Will, O God.* The Body, was not He, but His; and if Christ dwells in His People, as many Scriptures express, *the Body cannot be Christ, in a Strict Sense, because it cannot dwell in them.* And therefore the Absurdity that is flung at us, in Reference to our Use of that Expression, returns upon them that have so gross a Conception of Christ, and His dwelling in His People. You will have us confound God and His Saints, from a Passage in *G. F's Mystery. He is deceived, that saith, Christ is Distinct from His Saints.* The *Page* is not quoted, but we know the Place: We suppose it is a Mis-printing gives you that Apprehension; *Distinct* for *Divided*; they are *Distinct,* but not *Divided.* And this is that which was intended. You are too ready to catch and mistake also, when you oppose *G. F. Jun.* to *R. B.* One calling *The Light, God,* the other, *The Spiritual Body of Christ.* For, *He who is the Light, is God, and the Light is the Appearance and Manifestation of God.* You take it ill, that we should allow the *Light Within to be Christ,* and not the Man that Died at *Jerusalem,* to be *God or Christ,* in a proper Sense; they are your own Words.

Indeed, you are very unguarded in your Expressions. *Nor,* say you, *so much as Christ in a proper Sense.* We don't understand you. Would you have any Thing die but the Body? You deny the *Soul's Sleeping,* and falsly make it a Principle of ours, with the Addition of a *Socinian Dream.* If not, then ye say, *Christ Died,* as we say, since that was the Body of Christ that Died. *You Dream of our Idolizing one another from this Principle of Christ being in Men.* But take it from us, as you ought in Justice, what we believe, *and not from Enemies, that seek Advantages, and screw, wring, and pervert our Words, that we abhor such Practices.* But you have Three Evidences, that, as you think, cannot fail you.

1. *That many of us Worship'd* Naylor. Just as much as we Worship *Francis Bugg,* or *You.* But this we know, *That your Many, were a Few, and yet too many, giddy Men and Women, and that their Actions were denied by us, and by themselves at last.*

Your

Your Second Proof, as you pretend, is *J. Coal*'s Words in a Letter to *G. F.* And your last Proof, which doubtless you think your Best, is a Passage in a Letter of *J. Audland*'s to *G. Fox*. But *First*, where these Letters are, you do not tell us, nor give us any sufficient Authority for them, nor for the Truth of your Copies; which, upon so high a Charge, should, in common Justice, have been done.

2. Besides, they are given us in *Fractions*, and *&c*'s, as appears by your Breaks, and that is also unfair. For might not they write to *G. F.* and yet fall to pray and praise God occasionally also? A Thing frequent in Religious Correspondencies.

3. But if it were a Fault, must it include an whole People? Was it writ to them, or printed by them? Be just.

4. Is it their Practice? if not, you are to blame; and if it be, you must certainly have more Instances, and fresher than *J. A.* who has been deceast almost thirty Years. But this shews your Uncharitableness, that any Thing, at any Time, or at any Hand, shall serve you to back your unwary and unreasonable Charges against us.

5. And we believe *J. A.* was too good a Man to intend *G. F.* in that Sense you take it, and *G. F.* to accept it, whose Labour was to turn the Eyes of People from Man to Christ, which lays the Ax to all human and creaturely Exaltation. And *G. F.* lived a true Example of Humility, and abominated all such Appearances of Evil. And they that ever saw or heard him Pray, would not think he should like being any One's *Idol*, since above all Men, he appeared to express the *profoundest Reverence to God and Christ in Prayer*; as Strangers, to him and us, have occasionally observed and declared. And as he lived he died, in Care for nothing but the Glory of God, and the Exaltation of the Kingdom of his Son in his People; and, as it was said of *David*, he left us in a *good Old Age, full of Days, and of durable Riches and Honour*.

The Third Part of the New ATHENIANS no Noble BEREANS: Being an Answer to the ATHENIAN MERCURY of the 14th of the 4th Month, call'd *June*, in Behalf of the People called *QUAKERS*.

THE first Part of your *Third Mercury* finds an Answer in the Conclusion of ours to your Second; yet since you make such a Voluminous Puther about *R. B*'s Words of the Body of Christ, as well as of the Letter to *G. F.* taking up, in their Aggravation, more than the Room of seven other Charges, we shall consider what you say: Which is this. *If the Nature of this Eternal Light, Substance or Spiritual Body that is in all of them, be Material, as it must be, because, according to them, a divisible Substance, then there's plain Penetration of Dimensions, and every* Quaker *carries about all Transubstantiation in his Belly.* But why, pray you, must it be a material Substance? Do you find it in the First of *John*, 4 and 9, for there is our Light asserted and described. The *Life* of the *Word* is our *Light*, and your Light, *if you please. In the Word was Life, and that Life the Light of Men; and that was the true Light, that lighteth every Man that comes into the World.* Is that Life no Substance? And if it be, Is it a Material or Spiritual One? And if it be a Spiritual one, is it, or is it needful it should be, a Divisible One? Consider well, Is the Sun divided because all see by it? No more is Christ: So that Divisibility is your own Conceit, and not our Opinion or Consequence of it, but of your mistaking it: And all the *Transubstantiation* you thought was in our *Belly*, proves, at last, to be in your own *Heads*; and 'tis hoped this will help to get it out for you.

Again; you say, *If Immaterial, let 'em make Sense of it if they can, for to us 'tis pure Quakerism.* How now, *Athenians!* Have you never met with *Immaterial Substances* in your Reading? Then surely you have Travelled but a little Way in the Commonwealth of Letters. Both the New and Old Philosophy must be Strangers to you; and, which is worse, you are so to the *Bible*. Wash your Eyes, therefore, I pray, and turn to *John* 6, from 48 to 63, and tell us, if you will or can, Who is the Living Bread there that comes down from Heaven, and what is that Flesh and Blood Christians must feed upon if they would be saved? Here is an *Immaterial Substance or Body* for you, one of God's providing, that you in Derision call

pure

pure *Quakerism*; but very glad we are of it, and should be more, that you were better acquainted with it. We pity your extream Ignorance of Heavenly Things; for nothing else could make you so gross or abusive, upon so Essential a Part of Religion, and us for asserting it. Take not that strictly which is spoken with Construction, nor that properly or literally, which is figuratively and mystically express'd or to be understood, and we shall neither appear so monstrous, nor you so much mistaken. You may wring as great Inconsistency out of Scripture as any other Book, if you take that Course to expound it. Be therefore just to us, and shew you would inform us, or be informed by us, as sometimes you would have us to believe; but do not jeer at what you do not understand, nor charge what you do not know. For your Aggravation of the Letter to G. F. and the confident Conclusions you make of our *Idolatry*, they are both untrue and abusive; It is not our Principle, it was never our Practice; abhorring utterly that extravagant as well as unchristian Imputation; no People or Testimony, since the World began, laying Men lower than we have done, even to a Fault in our Adversaries Apprehension. For we have not only opposed an *Idolatry* to Creatures or Works of Men's Hands, which is the grosser Sort, but that of the Mind also: The Worship Men too generally and too zealously pay to their own *Imaginations*, or the *Ideas* they have fram'd to themselves of God and Christ, and will at any Rate make others do so too, if they can. A refined *Idolatry* too many are guilty of, that exclaim against the other; and very pernicious to the Soul's true Knowledge and Enjoyment of God and Christ.

Your Fifth Charge is, *That we deny the Trinity*. But you should in Justice, have added, of *Persons*, with all the *School-Niceties* and *Distinctions* that belong to that Sort of Explication of Scripture; for to that only it is your first Proof refers, *viz.* W. P's Sandy Foundation, p. 12. *For the Scripture no where calls God the Holy Three of* Israel, *but Holy One of* Israel. And if he had said *Imagined Trinity*, p. 16, as you cite, which he does not in the Copy we have, it ought not to be so heinous with you, since *Three Persons* are not to be found in the *Bible*, which you exalt for the only *Rule of Faith*. And if you will not allow that Council to be Infallible that formed that Article above 300 Years after Christ's Ascension, as to be sure you will not, I hope it must be their *Imagination of the Text*, if not *a Divine Inspiration*. Your Proof 1 *John* 5. 7. *There are Three that bear Record in Heaven, the Father, the Word, and the Holy Ghost, and these Three are one*, will not support your Charge, because it contains not the Matter controverted in it, *viz.* Three *Persons*, for that is the Point in Controversy. Let it suffice, if you please, that we believe the Scripture, tho' we reject that Interpretation; and that we own Three Witnesses, and that those Three are One; without allowing the Intricacy and Confusion of the Schools.

Your Second Proof is from *Sweet Sips*: But that's no *Quaker*'s Book, and so no Proof upon us. Be more Cautious another Time, and know better what you do.

Your Sixth Charge, *That we hold, the Soul Sleeps*, you your selves retract, but would have it a Fruit of your *Ingenuity*; and because we would encourage a Thing so rare with you, we will at this Time spare your Disingenuity in making it. But, as if you were more troubled at our being Clear than Guilty, and at your selves for missing the Blow at us, than for abusing us, to recover that Slip, and to make us Amends, your *Ingenuous Retraction* ends in two other Charges.

1. *That we Deny the Resurrection of the Body.* 2. *The Distinct Existence of the Soul after Death*. Your Proof for the *First* is G. *Whitehead's* Saying, *That he did not believe his Body should rise again after Death*: (But G. W. denies that to be his Answer:) And *William Penn's* not denying it to *John Faldo*. Whereas they answer no otherwise than what the Apostle said to the *Corinthians*, *Thou sowest not that Body which shall be*, 1 Cor. 15. 37. How is it then a Crime to deny your gross Conceit of the Resurrection? For in all Scriptural Respects we reverently and joyfully own the Resurrection, as we have good Cause to do of all People. And if you believe that *Death* came by *Sin*, that Innocent, Wise, and Upright Man, *J. Pennington*, 2 Prin. p. 34. was not out of the Way; to say, *that what we lost in the first* Adam *we regained in the second*; and the *Resurrection*, to be sure, is not the least Part; which is alone through him that was himself *the first begotten from the Dead*. And for *Sweet Sips*, tho' none of ours, yet no Proof for you, for the very *Quotation* owns the *Resurrection*. But curious Questions we avoid, and count them the *Foolish and Unlearned Ones* that the Apostle forbad, 1 *Tim*. 6. 4, 5. 2 *Tim*.

2 *Tim.* 2. 22, 23. being more folicitous that we appear accepted with God, than with what Bodies we shall appear.

2. That we *Deny the Distinct Existence of the Soul*, is as falfe as that we affert the *Soul sleeps*; but, perhaps, you think that *Sweet Sips* will help you out, *Ch* 26. but for that very Proof you owe us another *Retraction*; and we wifh you may do it more *ingenuously* than you did your laft.

Your Seventh Charge is, *That we have been lookt upon as Fly-blows of the Jefuits*. If fo, upon what Church, pray you, did they beget us? But out of the Abundance of your Hearts your Mouths fpeak, and that foully, and falfly too, too often. But your Proofs for this? *Why, most Writers say so.* Do they fo? where are they pray, and for what Reafons? but you fay not a Word of that. This you cannot think a Fruit of your Ingenuity; but it feems, if we would perufe Ignatius's *Life*, we'd think him *as Arrant a* Quaker *as* William Penn *himfelf*. So that while you take it ill of us to refer you, for our Belief, to our own Books, and don't write new ones to tell you our Religion, you take upon you to fend us to other People's Books to learn our own, and that with Reflections alfo. In this whatever you think, you are not over modeft or reafonable. But if *Infide*, be *Outfide*; if *Spirit*, be *Forms*; *Plainnefs*, *Pomp*; *Conviction*, *Implicit Faith*; and *Chrift's Kingdom be of this World*, you are in the Right, or elfe you abufe us.

Your Eighth Charge makes us *to deny the Plenary Satisfaction of Chrift, and to reft upon our own Merits*. 'Tis fome Comfort to us, that there is not one Charge that is a Text of Scripture, or delivered in Scripture-phrafe. Where do you find Plenary Satisfaction in the Bible? Or what do you mean by it? You that would have it the only Rule, fhould make it yours. You cite *J. N's Love to the loft*, p, 7. his *Righteoufnefs imputed, or put into the Creature*; and this you *fquib* at, not confidering that *Abraham* was really Righteous, when his Faith was *imputed, or accounted to him for Righteoufnefs*; or you will charge the Holy Ghoft with wrong Reckonings. But any Thing rather than have Chrift's Righteoufnefs within Men. Pray read 1 *Sam.* 22. 15. *Pfal.* 32. 2. and you will find *impute* or *imputeth* fo applied. Your fecond Proof is *R. B.* p. (no where) faying, *we are juftified by Chrift formed in us*. And fo we are in the compleat Senfe of the Word: for the Word comprehends *Remiffion of Sins that are paft upon Repentance*, and *Sanctification*, or being made Holy and Juft *inwardly*. And to be plain with you, we do believe, 1ft, *That Chrift died for all, and is a Propitiation for the Sins of the World*, 1 Jo. 2, 1, 2. 2dly, *That he was herein the Effect rather than Caufe of the Fathers love*; as Jo. 3. 16. & 1 Jo. 4. 9, 10. *God fo loved the World*, &c. 3dly, That *Juftification*, as taken *for Remiffion of Sin, accounting Penitents as juft as if they had not finned*, refers to Chrift as a *Propitiation*. *He was our common Offering for Sin*; and as the Word is taken for Man's being made *inherently* juft and holy, it refers to Chrift as the *Sanctifier* of his People; fo that 'tis *Chrift ftill, every Way, by which we hope for Salvation*. And for our *Works*, even the beft, fuch as *James* meant, *Jam.* 2. they are *rewardable*, but not *meritorious*; becaufe there is no proportion between the Work and Wages; *for the Wages of Sin is Death, but the Gift of God is Eternal Life, through Jefus Chrift our Lord*, Rom 6. 23.

Your Ninth Charge is, That we *deny the Divinity of Chrift*, (but your Reafons fhame your Charge) *and this they do with a witnefs*, fay you, *if they make him nothing but themfelves*: But if we don't, what have you made of your felves, think you? Who of us ever faid fo? Are we the *Light that lighteth all that come into the World*? or did we make the World? Indeed you are very grofs. Your other Proof is as lame; you fay, *we deny him to be God*; but not a Word of ours cited to that Purpofe, for we believe, that Chrift was God manifefted in the Flefh; as *Jo.* 1. 14. 1 *Tim.* 3. 16.

Your Tenth Charge is *Antartick* to your Ninth: For now you fay *we more plainly deny his Humanity*. Thus you make us fhift and take turns at Faith, till you have left us none: But what are your Proofs? G. F. Myft. p. 71. " Chrift is not *Humane*; where doth the Scripture fpeak of *Humane*? We deny the Word *Humane*. But that all Readers may deny you, till you deny your felves the Pleafure of Abufing us, we'll repeat the Place as it lies.

Prieft faith *Chrift's Humane Nature*, &c.

G. Fox Anf. " Where doth the Scripture fpeak of *Humane*? The Word *Humane*, " where is it written? tell us, that we may fearch for it? *Now we do not deny, that* " *Chrift according to the Flefh was of* Abraham, but not the Word Humane; and " Chrift's Nature is not Humane which is earthly, for that is the firft *Adam*. Now

1692.

Athenians, if you can, blush! What; make us deny that Christ came of the Seed of *Abraham* after the Flesh, by a Place that owns it, and that owns it fully, scripturally, and as it should be owned and worded by Christians, that use the Form of sound Words given them by the Holy Ghost, denying only a *School-Term* borrowed from the Ground: This is hard.

Thus you serve us also in your last Charge, where you will have us to deny *Angels*, *Spirits*, *Heaven*, and *Hell*, and so make an end of us and our Religion. And to prove it, you bring a Book, that is none of ours; and not without Injury to the Author neither; and then conclude us a *Compendium* of all *Heresies*; naming Twenty Two of them in rank and file, and a *cum multis aliis* at the tail of them. But if they had as foul play from their Judges as we have had from you, they will deserve a better Name. However, you are obliged to us, that we have abbreviated Heresy for you, and yet you have not convicted us of any one Point that deserves that black Name. We must say, we are sorry to see you act as if you thought us exempted from the common Claims of Humanity; to be dealt with as you please, and as if Injuries could not be committed upon such Wretches as we are in your esteem: For you *add, diminish, pervert*, and that boldly; and when you have shap't and drest up the *Monster*, you are pleased to write *Quaker* upon him, and then lead him about the Streets in your *Mercuries* for a Show, at a Penny a Piece: God Almighty shew you Mercy, that allow us none, but refuse to be just: For after all your black Charges, you fall to asking what our Faith is, which should have been first done.

You objected upon us, of turning the other Cheek: saying, it was Patience *per Force*.

But you are Mistaken in Fact, we have put up legal Advantages many Times, and endured and forgiven innumerable personal Injuries from those out of Office as well as from those that have been in Government, nay, often-times dared Cruelties and Oppression with a literal Conformity to the Text. Speak not so peremptorily what you do not know, you expect better Things from our Religion, than your own, and yet would have ours to be worse.

2. You say, It was not Conscience, but an unaccountable, not to say brutal Stubbornness. You have endeavoured to rob us of our Religion, will you now rob us of our Suffering, and the good Intention of it too? for that Word of yours, authorizes all the Imprisonments, Plunders, Banishments, and Murders we have suffered since a People, and if we should strain consequences, intitles you as arrant Persecutors as *B. Bonner*, or Dr. *Story*.

But, 3*dly*, You say we give hard Words; Do we? such as the Things call for, doubtless; I hope no personal Reflections? Yes, *Whitehead* complains of a new Persecution; and with very good Reason, when the old is justified by you, and you proclaim us a *Compendium* of Two and Twenty Heresies, with *multis aliis* at the End of it; which, in other Words, is saying, *Take them Dr.* Pinfold.

Again, You take it ill, he says, you make Beasts, and Devils, of us; but what else, pray, do you make of us, when you cannot make worse of us than you have?

You add, That we call you Impertinent; and pertinently, we think, to ramble as you have done, from your Province, to spread Invectives upon us. Wicked; what can you think it less, to abuse an whole People in the tenderest Point? Followers of blind Guides; how else could you have miss'd your way so much? for 'tis plain nothing can be more mistaken: 'Tis a wonder, say you, dumb Dogs don't come in too, though we have no silent Meetings. We can't think why you should wonder at that, since you know how much you have Barkt at us. There is no danger of your being dumb, but deaf. And since you brought in this to introduce your prophane Jest at our silent Meetings, we must tell you, you may see in your selves the use of Silence, by your abuse of Speech; and therein a Defence of us, and a Reproof to you. In short, we recommend silence to you, as *Pythagoras* did to his Scholars, till you have learnt to speak better than you do.

The next Thing is your ten Questions, an unreasonable as well as an unsuitable Conclusion; for you first Judge; and then Query; and after charging us home, you ask, What's our Belief? It shews too great a Levity for Men of your Claim to Sense; and, tho' not Enthusiastical, yet, if you will not be angry, it looks very silly: But because for that Reason it does not look malicious, you may have an Answer, tho' least of all for your Sakes, by another Hand. But, before we part, pray take this along with you: Our Religion, and the True Religion, which makes

People

People truly Religious, is the Fear of God planted in the Soul by the Grace of God, which sanctifies and rules the Heart and Affections, and not Creeds of Words, tho' never so True; for the Devils have Knowledge and Faith, but their Knowledge does not work by Obedience, nor their Faith by Love; and therefore they are never the Better for it: Nor are Wicked Men, as the World shews. Religion then is a Divine Experience and Work in the Soul, by the Divine Spirit. It is Regeneration, and that a New Creature, *Gal.* 6. 15, 16. And as the *Jew* Inward is the Circumcision of the Heart, so is that the Character of a True Christian. A short Creed of Words served of Old with an Upright Heart. *Thou art the Son of God, Thou art the King of Israel,* was *Nathaniel's Confession. My Lord and my God,* was all *Thomas* his Retraction and Creed, *John* 20. 28. And *Peter's* Confession of Faith is little larger, *Mat.* 16. 18. Thus also the Blind, Lame, and Sick, that came believingly to Him.

To be a Christian then, was to be like Christ, Meek, Humble, Holy, Loving, Patient; and this His Light and Spirit maketh those that embrace it. Unto which we refer and exhort you, and all to whom these Papers may come, as the Great Agent of Man's Happiness; desiring earnestly that our Care may be about our Conformity to our Saviour, rather than Controversies about Him; since the *True Religion is to be like Christ,* 1 *Pet.* 2. 21. *Chap.* 3. 10, 11, 12. 1 *John* 2. 6. Say not then, *That we Value our Title to Christianity by Human Laws*; you wrong us much: Ours hath an *Higher Claim,* and so must yours, if you expect to be Saved by it. We spoke not of being therefore Christians in God's Account, but of being esteemed enough, to Live quieter than your Invectives seem to let us, among Men. But it is not the least Part of the Cross we bear, to be, in almost every Thing, so much misunderstood, and by some so evilly represented. One While they will have us *Deny the Divinity of Christ,* another While, *The Humanity.* Sometimes we must be *Socinians,* then *Sabellians.* Very often we are told, *That we expect to be Saved by our own Works*; and as often, *That we will do nothing unless the Spirit move us.* Again, Sometimes we are said to send All to Hell but our selves; and presently, *We deny any such Thing.* Ay, we are accused with Idolatry to *Men's Persons,* and yet Scorn'd for denying all Honours or Respects to the Persons of Men. Just thus we are made *To disown all Ministry,* and by and by accused, *That every one among us is a Minister, or may be so.* It would be tedious to repeat the *Contradictions and absurd Dilemma's* Men have brought themselves into, by their rash and unjust Attempts against us; which they will easily perceive, that please to peruse some of our Controversial Tracts, as, *Rusticus ad Academicos,* the *Christian Quaker,* in Two Parts; R. B's *Apology and Defence; Quakerism a New Nick-Name for Old Christianity,* and the *Rejoynder* in it's Defence; *The Way Cast up; Reason against Railing,* and *Wisdom Justified of Her Children,* &c. In which our Belief is distinguished and defended, against the Abuses, Men, through Ignorance or Prejudice, have put upon it. God Almighty enlighten and forgive them; *that is the Worst of our Wishes,* for their many hard Speeches against us, and our Holy Profession: Concluding, *Your Well-Wishing Friends,* after all your Unfriendly Usage.

A REPLY to a *Pretended Answer,* by a *Nameless Author,* to W. PENN's KEY: In which the PRINCIPLES of the People called QUAKERS, are farther Explain'd and Confirm'd. By *William Penn.*

THO' I submit to Controversie as my *Drudgery,* not my *Pleasure,* otherwise than as it is my Duty, yet, I cannot but say, I am glad that the Publick Contradiction of a *Nameless Author,* to a small Treatise of mine, called, *A Key,* clearing our Principles from Vulgar Apprehensions, gives me farther Occasion to declare and justify them to the World: In the doing of which, I shall endeavour, with God's Assistance, so to Govern my self, that my *Antagonist* shall see it has not been in his Power, with all his scornful and abusive Treatment of me, my Friends, and our Holy Religion, to provoke me to any other towards

1695.

him in my *Reply*, than what is suitable to *Christianity*; whilst with great Levity and Prejudice, *He will by no Means allow us to be Christians.*

My *Reply* will be short, but I hope Clear and Satisfactory; in order to which, I shall observe this Method.

I. *His Mistakes in Point of Fact, and the Use he would make of them.* II. *His Insinuations and Insincerity.* III. *His Abusive Terms and Taunts upon us.* IV. *His pretended Answers and Interpretations of Scripture.* And, *Our Principles, so far as declared, and by Scripture defended in the KEY, maintained, against the Attempts of this Author, and farther Explained and Confirmed for a Publick Good.*

I. *His Mistakes in Point of Fact, and the Use he would make of them.*

He begins his Answer with a Passage meerly Personal, and not at all Relative to the Nature of the Discourse, *viz.* about a Pamphlet, writ in Defence of the *Bill for excluding the Duke of* York, *entituled*, A few Words about the Touchy Point of Succession: *Teaching the Parliament, That when they had made first an Address to the Duke to relinquish his Right to the Crown; if he refused, then (but not before) they might not only Justly, but Civilly exclude him by Act* —— When (says he) *I had perused this Piece, without judging the Merits of the Cause, or the Wittiness of the Argument, I concluded that* W. P. *was then a Man Principled for the Civil Liberties of his Country.*

Answer. But if I may be so bold with this Author, Pray, Why then Principl'd for Civil Liberties, and not afterwards? And why this upon me at all? But why at this Time, and upon this Occasion, of so differing a Nature, to be brought in by *Head and Shoulders*, as the Proverb is? But what if I never writ such a Pamphlet? (*as to be sure I did not*) What's to be said to, and of such an Author in such a Case, and in such a Time, and to a Man under *My Circumstances?* Let him know then, That I did not only never write such a Pamphlet, but I am sure that I do not remember I ever read one of such a Title, or heard of it; Nor was I of that Principle, and therefore I return the Civility of his Conclusion to him again; for I thank God I was always so much for *Civil Liberties,* that *I thought no Man ought to lose them for his Religious Principles.* And farther, *That they were never to be secured by this or that Man, but by a Good and Equal Constitution of Government, as some Papers by me, which I writ at that Time, as well as divers Persons yet Living, of Good Reputation, can evidence for me.*

But his next Paragraph explains the Matter, wherein he speaks thus: *I could no otherwise reconcile the Folly of his Prevarication in the late Reign, than by imputing them to his intemperate Zeal for a boundless Liberty of Conscience (according to the Doctrine of King* James's *Declaration.*)

In this he would be Charitable, but let him first be Just: If there were no Prevarications, then there is no Need of an intemperate Zeal for Liberty to shadow or reconcile them to my former Principles. And I am so much a Friend to him and his Brethren, *That I wish them free from all Intemperance and Prevarications too, and that in all Reigns.* And if it be possible, or worth While to reconcile him better to my Conduct, let him peruse my *Great Case of Liberty of Conscience,* printed 1671, and my *Letter to the Estates of* Embden, 1672, and my *Present State of* England, 1675. and he will find I was the same Man then, and acted by the same Principles. Not more intemperate in the Reign that favoured it, than in the Reign I contended with, that did not favour it: *And no Man but a Persecutor, which I count a Beast of Prey, and a declared Enemy to Mankind, can, without great Injustice or Ingratitude, Reproach that Part I had in King* James's *Court:* For I think I may say, without Vanity, upon this Provocation, *I endeavoured at least to do some Good at my own Cost, and would have been glad to have done more: I am very sure I intended, and I think I did Harm to none, neither Parties nor Private Persons,* my own Family excepted: *For which I doubt not this* Author's Pardon, *since he shews himself so little concerned for the Master of it.*

Page 8. Our Adversary misses again notoriously in Point of Fact, when he charges me, *Of Revenging my self upon* J. Faldo *and* T. Hicks, *for baffling of me Twenty Years ago.*

Answer. I had no Revenge in my Eye when I writ that *KEY*; for 'twas writ in Pity, not in Anger; to inform, and not to be revenged. I must beg my *Reader* to peruse it, who then can best judge if it tastes of that rank Spirit, and what

Spirit this Man is of, that shews such Indignation at it; as well as see how meanly he has performed his Pretence of an Answer, that meddles not with the Twentieth Part of it, tho' of different Subjects.

It is not in my Nature to remember Injuries Twenty Years ago, tho' this Man commits them unprovoked: Nor had I any Temptation to it, since I had all the Satisfaction I could desire but their *Conversion*. Concerning the first, I must refer my self to *Impartial Readers*; and of the last, the *Famous Barbican* and *Wheeler-Street Publick Disputes* do give this Man the Lye. For at the last, *T. H.* did not appear, and at the first he shrunk away. And if ever any such Publick Dispute determined with a visible Advantage on either Side, the *Impartial*, not of our Communion, gave it us. And for the *Encomium* he bestows upon them, with the *Poor Indian*, that desired not to go to Heaven, if the *Cruel Spaniard* went thither, I must say, *Let not my Soul go where their Souls are gone, if they did not heartily Repent of their Great Wickedness, against the People of God called* Quakers, *and their Holy Profession, before they dyed.*

Page 9. He saith, *The Light Within is no Scripture Expression, and the Nation had called nothing the Light Within, but the Effects of the Perceptive Powers of our Minds, that is, our* Thoughts.

Answer. By Nation, he must either understand a Parliament or Synod, for I presume he has not spoke with all the Nation. But if the *Common-Prayer*, Established by Act of Parliament, have any Share in the Sense of the Nation, or the *Synod*, or *Assembly of Divines*, that Sat between the Years of Forty and Fifty at *Westminster*, he will find another Light owned by them, than *Man's own Thoughts:* Which being all the Light Within that is owned by this Opposer, I may well return upon him that Scripture, misquoted by him, pag. 43. *If the Light that is in thee be Darkness, how great is that Darkness ———— Take Heed that the Light in thee be not Darkness.*

I shall consider his Abuse of Scripture in another Place, and shall say no more upon it at this Time, than that this Darkness being our Author's Light, he cannot comprehend the True Light; but with it opposes the True Light, and the Children of it. But that the *Light Within* should not be a Scripture Expression, is very strange: Pray, *What is Enlightning, but Light Within?* Can a Man's Mind be lighted, and have no Light there? *The Light is said to Shine in our Hearts:* Can that be, and *Not Within?* But more of this when I come to consider his Oppositions to the Light.

Page 15, 18, 19. *Notwithstanding their empty Pretence, the* Quakers *learn their Religion not from the* Light Within, *but from one another. They cannot Name one that was a* Quaker, *that was not made so by hearing them, or reading their Books. That* Quakerism *is erected by Art, Method and Management; by Consults and Clubs; all subordinate to a General Assembly, and not from the Sufficiency of any Principle in themselves, either of Natural, or Supernatural Donation.*

Answer. This is also False in Fact, there being many that came in a good Measure ripe to the *Communion of that People*, having for the most Part the same Sentiment, as all did from their own Convictions by the same Principle, tho' mediately or ministerially. But if this Man had considered well, he would have spared this Absurdity, for who did the *First Quaker* hear? He will surely allow us a *Beginning*. However, I would have him know, No Man can see Divine Truth by another Man's Speaking or Writing, but through Divine Light, that Shines in himself, giving him the Understanding thereof: *For tho' the Spirit of Man knows the Things of a Man, yet the Things of God knows no Man, but the Spirit of God*: And therefore it is upon Conviction, and not Human Authority, that our Religion is built. And 'tis great Uncharitableness in this Opponent, as well as Injustice, to charge a whole People with a Confederacy against themselves, to their Temporal Wo, and Eternal Destruction. That so much Sobriety, Patience, Self-denial, Suffering, Constancy through all Times and Conditions, *should be interpreted Trick, Jugling, Legerdemain, on Purpose to cozen the World, and their own Souls*; as this Author is pleased to render them. But to inform him a little Better, if yet he needs it; those Clubs, as he is pleased to term them, that are subordinate to a General Assembly, *are not Meetings to define and enjoyn Faith or Uniformity of Worship*, wherein Conscience is more immediately exercised; But Meetings of Order and Discipline, to take *Care of the Poor, of Fatherless and Widows, and all that walk up to the Holy Profession they make:* Which, I hope, is no Argument against

1695.

us, as if we embraced our Religion by Rote, and not by the *Illuminations* and *Convictions* of the Light and Spirit of Christ Jesus.

Page 52. *And W. P. thinks it consistent with the Honour that is due to the Scripture to compare it with* Roman *Legends.*

Answer. He would have done well to have cited the Place where I had done so ill. I must leave it to my Reader to do me Justice against this gross Writer, who says one of the worst Things without the least Proof. I am sure I could no more have been guilty of such an Expression than of renouncing my own Belief; I pray God forgive him: But I would have him remember *that he is* one Day to be judged for this Abuse.

I come to the Second Head of my Reply, *viz:*

II. *His Insinuations and Insincerity.*

Page 4. *W. P.* asserting *in sundry Pieces,* Liberty of Conscience, *to be* ex Jure Naturali, *has destroyed all Morality, confounded Blessings and Curses, Good and Evil, somewhat worse than* Hobbs *himself; for he only asserts a Natural Liberty, but this a Divine Privilege to do Wickedness in the Name of the Lord.*

Answer. He has not quoted any one Book, less the Place, where he makes me capable of being guilty of so dangerous a Principle; which, I hope, without being partial, I may say, is very disingenuous. If he can point me to any Part of my Writings, in Defence of that Noble Principle of Liberty, that has not in it a sufficient *Saving* to Morality, I will ask him and the World Forgiveness; and if it has, I hope he knows whose Part it is to cry *Peccavi.* But to insinuate I write for Liberty of Conscience, as a natural Right for those that should plead Conscience to overthrow it, because I did maintain it in Favour of those that kept within the Bounds of Morality, is to shew none towards me.

Page 6. *He very weakly, as well as unworthily insinuates, a near Relation betwixt me and the* Jesuits. *First, Some one of the Society may have at one Time or other had a Title-Page with the Words,* Misrepresented *and* Represented *in it, which makes up a Part of mine, with which he is so angry; as if Title-Pages were Confessions of Faith, or that the same Words might not be used by Men of different Perswasions. It is to say, because Misrepresented may be misapply'd, therefore 'tis not to be used. Any Man may be misrepresented, must he not therefore represent himself aright, for Fear of being a* Jesuit? *This, to be sure, gives a very ill Representation of him.*

In the next Place he says, *W. P. imping the Jesuit again, he represents his own Religion as like ours as may be, by the new softning Method of* Meaux.

Truly, I don't know what Religion he is of; for he has no more told us that, than his Name; but a Protestant, I suppose, at large: And yet I am ready to think I can subscribe as many of the Doctrines of the *Reformation* as himself. But if our *Religion* be so like it, Why does he labour in his whole *Treatise* to render ours so grosly contrary to theirs? Contrary Things don't look alike, for then they cannot properly be said to be contrary. And if we are of so softning a Disposition, does he well to be so very hard? But truly I think it no Fault to have a Religion unlike his, unless it had more of *Sobriety* and *Charity* in it. However, the *Jesuits* are much beholding to him, whatever I am, it being the first Time I have heard their Methods esteemed so soft: Nor had they now had, I believe, that Complement from him, but to render us *Jesuitical*, or *Popish* at least.

Page 7. He adds, *For W. P's Scheme is, first to give the Perversion of* Quakerism, *and then to represent it in Equivocal Terms, after his own Way.*

By which he would have the *Reader* think we are *insincere* as well as mistaken, and that we have a Design *upon our selves*, to cozen our selves as well as the World, in the great Business of Salvation. But what must that Man be that can have such a Design? Certainly, a Fool to himself, and a Devil to others: But then what must They be who render Men so absurd and impious, only to have their Evil Ends upon their *Character* and *Religion?* Doubtless they must be as bad every Jot. I must needs tell him, That little Treatise was not intended for Criticks, but plain and ordinary Understandings; to remove common and vulgar Prejudices, and in a familiar Style, and not after the Bishop of *Meaux's* Copy, which was performed with much Address and Exactness.

He says, My Terms are *Equivocal.* I am sure I have mostly expressed my self in those of the Holy Scripture: 'Tis a singular and unjust Reflection, to say I did it in my own Way, for it is in that Way which is common to the Writers of our Perswasion, and according to the Language of the Holy Ghost. And it's plain

from

from more Places than this of his Book, as *p.* 23, 41, *&c.* That he would have that little Piece of mine the Fruit of great Contrivance and Design: I know not why, unless that he might raise the greater Reputation to his own Undertaking; as he tells us *p.* 5. But that will depend upon the Conclusion, which will best shew how well he has acquitted himself.

Page 11, 12. He farther insinuates, *That we make the Light within the Rule, not only to direct our Belief and Practice of the Christian Religion, but to discover to Men the History of the Coming and Performances of Jesus of* Nazareth, *and that he is Christ the Lord; and this without the Help of the Scriptures.*

Answer. Now this is very insincere on his Part: For tho' the Light of the Eternal Word be without Doubt sufficient to reveal or discover those Facts where they are not known, if God pleaseth, yet we never said the Light was our Rule to that Purpose, but to judge of that which is revealed; or that the Discoveries it made, were of Things past and *Historical,* but of Things immediate and practical, as of Sin, in *Thought, Word* and *Deed,* and to be daily assisted to live *Soberly, Righteously,* and *Godly* in this World: To *Pray* and *Preach,* and *Worship* God; which relating to the *Service* of Jesus, and the Service of Jesus being by him allowed to be the *Christian Religion,* the asserting of that *Divine Light* to be the *Holy Rule* of our *Christian Conduct* to perform those Things, deserves not such abusive *Insinuations* and *Innuendo's* as this Author makes upon us.

Page 14. *He would have his Reader believe, as if there were not one Passage in all my Part of that Book called,* The Christian Quaker, *he can cite before it be corrected, both Style and Matter, because he only cites one which he thinks fit to correct; calling me for it a Lewd Author, and what else he pleases:* But according to his usual Practice, he has inserted no Page to direct us where to find this Assertion. If to me he has thought it not needful, I must tell him, His Amendment is as needless; for when I speak of *Christ,* I say He; and when of his Body, I say It: Notwithstanding, he charges me with other Things: But, I think, through the many Books I have written, it will never be found my Practice or Mistake, whatever may be the Printer's.

Page 23. *Since the Quakers will have their Light to be common to all Men, and not natural, there is no such Thing in the Universe.*

Answer. By which he insinuates, That a *Divine Light* cannot be communicated to every Man, and be Divine. Would he have shewn himself a candid Author, one that desired to have informed and not abused us, he would have first instructed himself what we have said on this Occasion. By Natural we mean mere Man; His *Compositum* or Make; that is of the Nature of Man, as he is Man: By *Divine,* what is *above* Man, and from God, to direct Man in all well-pleasingness to him. Yet if by *Natural* may be meant, that every Man that's born into the World has a Portion of this Light or Illuminating Principle to direct him in the Way to Blessedness, I should not very much quarrel at the Word, it being in a Sort natural to all Men to have it, because all Men that are born (from whence the Word *Nature* springs) as certainly have it, as that they are born into the World. See *John* 1. 4. 19. 1 *Cor.* 12.

These few Instances I thought fit to give of the unjust Insinuations and Insincerity of this Author; which brings me to my Third Head, *viz.*

III. *His Abusive Terms and Taunts upon us.*

Indeed almost every Page is fraighted with them. My *Key* is a *Picklock,* and we are *Imps* of the *Jesuits:* Our Writings are *Apocryphal,* our Phrases like *Gypsy-Gibberish* and *Beggars Cant,* our Arguments *Putid Sophisms,* our Leading Men a Pack of *Juglers, Sophistical,* of *Suborned* Sense: Men of *Trick* and *Leger-de-main,* abusing honest-meaning Men as *Juglers* do plain Country People: *Ranting Cant,* and that I debauch the *Scriptures;* with much more of this Strain and Style; besides that *Scorn* and *Levity,* which very much unbecomes one that pretends to correct others in Matters of Religion. I would fain have this Author to consider whether he has acted like one that has any Reverence towards God, or Compassion to a mistaken People, supposing us to be such. Certainly, whether we are in the Right or no, he must needs be in the Wrong, and his Religion vain, that has no better Bridle to his Tongue or Pen; Which said, I shall betake my self to my Fourth Head.

IV. *His Pretended Answers and Interpretations of Scripture considered.*

The first Perversion, mentioned in my *Key*, is *p.* 1, *viz. The Quakers hold, That the Natural Light in the Conscience of every Man in the World is sufficient to save all that follow it*: Which, by the Way, after the Flourish of an *Answer* to the *Key*, (at least as to our Doctrine of the *Light*) is all that's cited by him, so that my Explanations of our Principle, in Answer to this, and three other Perversions upon this Doctrine at the same Time, are not so much as taken Notice of by this Man, that pretends to have considered them all. But let us hear what he says upon this *Perversion*.

Page 7. *This is no Perversion, unless an Objection made against a Tenet be a Perversion of a Tenet, which no Body thinks besides W. P. for we only say, That the Quakers believe that a Natural Light is Supernatural and Saving: We mistake not their Meaning, but oppose it as an Error.*

Answer. He that changes the Terms of a *Question* abuses his *Antagonist*, and perverts the *Argument*, which is the Case: For the People called *Quakers* never said, That a *Natural* Light was *Supernatural* or sufficient to *Salvation*; and if *Natural* be not their Term, then it's a *Perversion* of their *Principle*. For whether they are mistaken in their Principle, or no, is not the Question; but whether their Principle is not misgiven by their Enemies. This Author seems to make it *Natural* in another Place, because we affirm 'tis *Common* to all, or that All are Enlightned: But this begs the *Question* in Point of *Argument*, and will not rectify or defend a Matter that is in Fact false: For besides, that it is not fair in any to charge their Consequences upon others for Principles, it is plain what any People say is their Principle, is the Rule for us to know whether what their Adversaries say is so, be their Principle or not. Suppose it were true, that what is Common is Natural, yet if we do not say so, it is a *Perversion* of what we say; and as such I give it in my *Key*. For, as I said before, What any People declare is their Principle, is the Rule for others to know whether what their Adversaries give for their Principle be theirs or not: Now whether the *Light* we call *Divine* be natural or no, shall be considered in it's Place; but that a Natural Light should be *Supernatural* and *Saving*, is not our *Principle*, but their *Perversion* and *Contradiction*. Waving then any more of my *Key*, which he pretends to answer, he undertakes to state our *Religion* and *Controversy* between us, in his own Terms and not ours; which I will not say is a *Lewd*, but Foul Way of treating any People or Opponent, in my Judgment; and I think I am not mistaken —— His Words are these.

Page 8. *If any Thing they say deserves Consideration, this is the Point; and of this they say,* 1. *That the Light within is the Rule of the Christian Religion.* 2. *That it is God and Christ.* 3. *That Quakerism is taught them by it.*

Answer. I could be glad this Author said any Thing that deserved the Consideration of good and Wise Men; I am sure he deserves their Reproof, that will not let us confess our Faith in our own Words, nor express our Religion in our own Way. However, I will observe what he says, as disingenuous as it is, and not write Forty Pages upon Four Lines, as he has partially cited out of my *Key*, and then call it an *Answer*. It is not our Way of Speaking to say the Light within is the *Rule of the Christian Religion*; but that the Light of Christ within us is the *Rule of true Christians*, so that it is not our Light but Christ's Light that is our Rule. *For in him was Life, and that Life the Light of Men*, John 1. 4. 9. c. 8. 12. *Life in the Word, Light in Men, and Life (too) where it is obeyed.* For Christ promises *the Light of Life to all that follow Him, the True Light that enlightens every Man that cometh into the World.* Christ himself hath made it the Rule of his Followers: *But he that doth Truth, cometh to the Light, that his Deeds may be made manifest that they are wrought in God.* So that Christians are to square their Lives by the Light of Jesus, therefore it is their Rule. It is the Christian Path to Blessedness. Christ exhorts his Followers to walk in the Light. The beloved Disciple begins his Epistles, as he does his History of the Gospel, with the Divinity and Doctrine of the Light; telling us, *That God is Light; that if we would have Fellowship with God, we must walk in this Light; and that the Blood of Jesus Christ cleanseth those only that walk in this Light, and that Religion without it is a Lye*, 1 John 1. To which let me add, That in his Book of *Revelations*, consonant thereunto, he saith, That the Nations of them that are saved shall walk in the Light. (of the Lamb, *Rev.* 21. 23, 24.) The Apostle *Paul* makes it Universal fal and Effectual, in his Epistle to the *Ephesians*, chap. 5. 13. *But all Things that are reproved* (or discovered) *are made manifest by the Light ; for whatsoever doth make manifest is Light.* Now All being reproved, All have Light ; and since that Light manifests every Thing that is to be known, Christ himself was known by it, and the Religion he taught, discovered by it, to be of God ; and such only received him and it, as obeyed this Light in their Consciences. The same Light is by the same Apostle rendred the *Christian's Armour* ; *And let us put on the Armour of Light,* says he, *let us walk honestly as in the Day, not in Rioting and Drunkenness, not in Chambering and Wantonness, not in Strife and Envying ; but put ye on the Lord Jesus Christ, and make no Provision for the Flesh, to fulfil the Lusts thereof :* Making it the same Thing to put on the *Armour of Light,* and to put on the *Lord Jesus Christ* ; certainly then Christ must be that Light, and that Light must be Christ. But he objects to this Doctrine.

Page 11. *The Christian Religion is nothing but the Service of Jesus of* Nazareth —— *Nothing then can be the Rule of this Religion but what discovers to us that there is one Jesus of* Nazareth, *and that he is Christ the Lord. But never was any one Man instructed by that Light that is in the Conscience of every Man, that there ever was such an one as Jesus of* Nazareth, *much less that he was the Lord,* and least of all *what he required of his Servants, therefore no Light within, common to all Mankind, can be the Rule of the Christian Religion, since it was never possible for any Man to learn the least Part of the Christian Religion by the Light that is in every Man's Conscience.*

To the first Part of what he says, *That the Christian Religion is nothing but the Service of Jesus of* Nazareth, I shall easily agree : For the Service of Jesus of *Nazareth,* is the Service of the God and Father of Jesus of *Nazareth* ; and that is to *fear God and keep his Commandments ; and to love God above all, and our Neighbours as our selves ; this is the whole Duty of Man,* Eccl. 12. 13. Matt. 22. 37. 39. That which Man has to do in the World for Salvation.

To the Second Part of his Proposition, viz. *That nothing can be the Rule of this Religion but what discovers to us that there is one Jesus of* Nazareth, *and that he is Christ the Lord* ; I shall likewise agree upon Distinction. I distinguish then between an *Historical* and *Spiritual* Discovery of *Jesus of* Nazareth ; and so of the Rule by which he and his Service are to be known. The Scriptures tell us of the Birth, Life, Ministry, Death, Resurrection, and Ascension of *Jesus of* Nazareth, and in brief of the Ministry and Sufferings of his blessed Followers and Apostles, and it must be acknowledged to be a great Mercy and Privilege to us, that we have them ; but they cannot savingly reveal Christ to a Soul ; neither can they give us the Soul and Substance of those Things that are thereby declared. They are an exact Map, or Picture of Things, but not the Things themselves. It is the Office of the Divine Light and Spirit of Christ to shew Men these Secrets ; and to none are they, or can they be known, but those that walk according to the Convictions of it : First, *In ceasing to do Evil, and denying all Ungodliness and the World's Lusts* ; and then, *in learning to do well, and living soberly, righteously, and godly in this present World.* So that those that read the Scriptures of Truth, by which they have an historical Knowledge of the Coming of Christ, and so are a Rule to that Knowledge, as also to the Doctrines therein expresly declared, they must come to the Light of the Eternal Word to understand them, and, to see the Glory of the only begotten of the Father, as those of old beheld it, else the Scripture is as a Sealed Book. Who knows God by reading of him, or Christ by reading of him, or Regeneration by reading of it, unless God is pleased by the Light of his Son, the true *Key of David,* to come in upon the Soul, and open to it the deep Things of God, viz. the New Creation, or the Regeneration of Man. Wherefore the Light or Spirit of Christ, which are the same, is the first Great Rule ; even the Rule of understanding the Scriptures, which we own to be the Secondary Rule : And we say, That a Measure thereof is given to all to profit with ; to lighten all, and search and lead all in the Way of Holiness, which is the Way of Eternal Happiness. His minor Proposition I must deny, viz. *But never was any one Man instructed by that Light that is in the Conscience of every Man, That there ever was such an one as Jesus of* Nazareth, *much less that he was the Lord, and least of all what he required of his Servants.*

In this I must dissent from him, especially as to the latter Part ; for though, as I have already said, the Scriptures are an Historical Rule, and Doctrinal too, so far as they are Plain and Express, yet the truest and most powerful Evidence to authorize

authorize our Belief of them, is the Testimony of the Light and Spirit of the Eternal Word, from whence they came, and that answers to it's own. This the Martyrs asserted, as *Hooper, Bradford, Smith, Saunders, Rogers,* &c. also *Calvin, Beza, Peter Martyr,* and *Erasmus* himself, refer to it in Proof of the Divine Authority of them; as may be seen in the Book of *Martyrs,* as also in the Writings of these Authors upon the Authority of the Scriptures. But if the Light we contend for does not *ordinarily* reveal the History of Jesus Christ, who dare say it cannot do so? Is it not more reasonable to suppose that there may be no absolute Necessity of it, since then God would have left much the greatest Part of the World without the Means of Salvation? Yet if it reveal that which he commanded his Servants, both to practise and preach, it overthrows his Proposition, and plainly proves that the Soul and Substance of what Christ commanded his Followers, is revealed, more or less, to all People, in all Nations, by this despised Light within. And besides Experience, which I shall anon come to, the Holy Scriptures speak as much; for, says the Prophet *Micah,* (Micah 6. 8.) *God hath shewn to thee, O Man, what is good; and what doth the Lord require of thee, but to do justly, and love Mercy, and to walk humbly with thy God?* Here is both Duty and the Way to understand it. Now this Duty and Service is the Service of God, and so of Jesus of *Nazareth,* who came to teach Men so to do, *viz. To do Justly, love Mercy, and walk humbly with God.* The Way to know and do this, is God's Illumination of Man. GOD HAS shewn unto thee, O Man! How does God shew Man? *Whatsoever makes manifest is Light,* says the Apostle *Paul* to the *Ephesians, Eph.* 5. 13, 14. So that 'tis by the Light of the Word, by which he made all Things, that he shews unto Man all Things necessary to Salvation, *viz. What is good, and what he requires of him:* What Service, Homage and Obedience he expects. So that here we have both the Universality and Sufficiency of the Light. Corresponding herewith is that great Saying of the same Apostle, to the *Romans,* Rom. 1. 19. *For that which may be known of God is manifest in them, for God hath shewn it unto them,* Which Way, I pray, does God manifest the Knowledge of himself in Men, but by the Light of the blessed Word, by whom he made Man, and without whom nothing was made that is made? *In him was Life, and that Life the Light of Men, and this is the true Light that enlightens every Man that cometh into the World,* John 1. 4. 9.

Now that the Christian Religion is this Duty, Service and Knowledge of God, we may satisfy our selves, from that blessed Sermon of Blessings, preached by Christ upon the Mount, *Matth.* 5. *Blessed are the poor in Spirit; blessed are they that Mourn;* (for their Sins, and for want of feeling Peace with God) *blessed are the Meek; blessed are they that hunger and thirst after Righteousness; blessed are the Merciful; blessed are the Poor in Heart; blessed are the Peace-makers;* and *blessed are they which are persecuted for Righteousness Sake.* If these States were blessed, and those under these blessed Qualifications, then to be sure such were in the Service of *Jesus* of *Nazareth,* tho' he was not then offered up, and that they knew not his History. Now that all have a Light to shew them the Happiness of these States, the Universal Testimony of all Ages and Nations assures us; and, to deny it, is to say the Sun did never Shine, since there was a Man in the World.

The same may be said of the rest of his excellent Sermon: *As that we should seek God, in the first Place, and trust Providence for the rest, and live by Faith in his Goodness: Be Charitable and Devout without Ostentation: Not so much as Lust in the Mind, and speak Truth without an Oath; bear Abuses, forgive Enemies, be sparing of censuring others, and finally do, as Well as hear, the Word of God, and to all Men as we would be done to.* These excellent Things, more naturally, and excellently exprest in that Sermon, than in the Writings of the most enlightned *Gentiles,* are yet to be found up and down in the Account given us of their Lives and Doctrines by *Strabo, Laertius, Herbert, Stanly, Cudworth,* and my Part of the *Christian Quaker.* By all which it may be seen, that the Blessed Word, who did himself preach so plainly and fully, yet concisely, this admirable Doctrine, had enlightned those Gentiles with great Knowledge, and instructed them therein, and that, several Hundred Years before he came in the Flesh. I hope the keeping of these Commands, and obeying the Precepts of Jesus of *Nazareth,* will be allowed to be the *Service* of Jesus of *Nazareth,* or else nothing is; and if so, then I must conclude, he may be served and obeyed of those that are not acquainted with his Coming in the Flesh, and becoming personally an

holy

Holy *Minister among the Jews*, and, in Conclusion, an *Holy Offering for the World*. For it is very possible that a Man may receive Benefit by a Medicine, of whose Composition he may be ignorant. And in General Pardons, it is not commonly known by those that sensibly have the Advantage thereof, by whose Favour and Advice the Prince was influenc'd to grant it.

Since then Humility, Mercy, Patience, Purity, Brotherly Kindness, Faith in God, Hope of Life Eternal, Charity to Men, Doing as a Man would be done to, and that with a distinct and Religious Reference and Regard to him, that must finally judge all Men, must necessarily belong to the *Service of Jesus of Nazareth*, since 'tis the *Substance of what Jesus of Nazareth Preached*, and the End of the Labour, Travels and Writings of *His Blessed Apostles*, (and that these Things were in a Measure in the World before the Coming of *Jesus of Nazareth* in the Flesh, and that even those that knew Him, and received Him when He did come, were those that walked up to the *Light of the Word*, by which alone His Inward Beauty and Glory were seen) we may reasonably conclude, against this Author, *That the Light with which the Word-God Enlightned Men, was a Divine, Spiritual, and Saving Light, because it Revealed these Truths to* Gentiles *as well as* Jews, *that had an immediate Tendency to Salvation ; and that in all Ages*. And that whosoever have walked according to it's Righteous Dictates, as well before, as since the Coming of Christ *(the Eternal Word)* in the Flesh, did so far perform the *Service of Jesus of Nazareth*, as they thereby served the *God and Father of Jesus of Nazareth*; for says Christ himself, *He that doth the Will of my Father, the same is my Mother, my Brother, and my Sister*.

To sum up this, once more, I say, We never said the *Light Within* is given to all Mankind, to reveal Facts done, or Historical Accounts of Persons and Actions, tho' we cannot say it is not able to do it, but ordinarily the Nature of Things, *as to Truth and Falshood, Obligation and Duty, Commission and Omission*; and therefore we say, That tho' all did not foresee the Coming of Christ, with the Circumstances that attended him, as some of the Prophets did, *That*, being an extraordinary Manifestation of this Light, yet all had the ordinary Manifestation of it, to do justly, love Mercy, and walk humbly with the Lord: And so they have now, tho' they have not the extraordinary Revelation of the *History of* JESUS *of Nazareth*; in which respect we confess the Scriptures to be a Secondary Rule, an Historical Rule, and a Rule of the Form of Sound Words in Doctrinal Truths: But the First and Great Rule is the Light and Spirit of God, as that was the Rule to them, by whom the Scriptures were given forth, in their giving them forth: And we also affirm, The Light and Spirit of God a Rule to Read and Understand the Scriptures by; and this was plainly seen in Christ's Time: For the *Jews* that rebelled against the Light, had the Veil over their Understandings, so that they could not see his Glory, but judged of Him according to outward Appearance, which was not Righteous Judgment; but those that loved the Light in that Day, the truly Conscientious to God, they brought their Deeds to the Light: They knew Him to be the Eternal Word, manifested in the Flesh, and thereby saw his inward Glory, *to be that of the Only Begotten of the Father, full of Grace, and full of Truth*.

If he object, *If all had this Light, Why did not all know him, as indeed that is the Weight of his Objection, and other Adversaries Oppositions*.

I answer, All have Reason, but all are not Reasonable; all don't use it: So all have Light, but all don't obey it. It is not the Light's Insufficiency, but Man's Disobedience, that renders him uncapable of the Knowledge of Divine Truth. Christ told the *Jews*, *If you do my Will, you shall know of my Doctrine, whether it be of God or no*. Obeying the Convictions and first Motions of this Divine Light, will increase our Light and Knowledge. Disobedience makes an unfruitful Ground, tho' the Seed be Good that is Sown in it: So that the Ignorance of those that have the Light, is not chargeable upon the Light, but their own Darkness, which comprehends it not, through Unbelief and Disobedience. The Scriptures then are the Rule to us, of the *History of JESUS of Nazareth*, and necessary to be believed where they are known; but the Divine Light and Spirit, the First and Great Rule by which they are to be truly and profitably read and believed, and without which Christ could not have been savingly known when He was in the World; nor can He be known now, nor the Scriptures that declare of Him: He is the common Rule to Mankind, who by His Light reveals Common and Essential Truths, relating to the Fear of God, and working of Righteousness: And it will be hard for this Man to Name one Nation or Person in the World, that knows not the Reproofs

proofs of this Principle, in Evil-doing; and in doing that which is Right, has not a Reference to the pleasing of Him, who is the great Rewarder and Preserver of Men, notwithstanding his Cavil to the contrary, pag. 12, 13. But I shall attend his further Exceptions.

Page 13. *They affirm the Light Within is Christ; and I say then it is nothing else but* Jesus *of Nazareth. If they make the Light Within to be Christ, and not* Jesus *of Nazareth, they make it* Antichrist; *and because they Worship God in this Appearance* (as they speak) *they are* Antichristian Idolaters.

Answer. This Way of arguing is very dark, as well as injurious. If by *Jesus of Nazareth* he only means what he took of the Virgin *Mary*, and will not consider him as the Eternal Word, but as Man, like to us in all Things, Sin excepted, He is not the Light Within, that we declare of, and Worship God in.

But this Author at the same Time declares not to believe that *Christ is the Eternal Word*, for he seems to deny his Pre-existence, *much more, that the World, and all that is therein, was made by Him.* And how Orthodox that is, let the Impartial judge. If he owns *Christ to be the Word, God manifested in the Flesh*, then I say, *The Light is Christ, as much as Christ can be called the Light*; and so not only *John* calls Him, *John* 1. 4, 9. but he calls himself so, *John* 8. 12.

This Antagonist seems too eager and rash, or he would have reflected better upon the *Way of the Holy Ghost's speaking in Scripture*; for sometimes Christ is so called, with Relation to his Divine Nature, and sometimes with Respect to his Manhood. *As he was of the Seed of* Abraham, *he is not God over All, Blessed for ever; he is not the Eternal Word, in whom is Life, and that Life is the Light of Men.* And as *he hungred, thirsted, sorrowed, wept, dyed, he was not the Divine Light, that lighteth every Man that cometh into the World:* Yet is alternatively called *Christ*, sometimes *Christ without Man*, sometimes *Christ in Man, the Hope of his Glory*; according to the double Respect he stood and stands in. Let not Men separate what God has joyned, which has been too much the Practice of our Opposers, to draw a Line of Reflection over our Religion, *as if it denied Jesus of Nazareth to be Christ the Lord, because we asserted him the Light of the World, and as such to be in Man:* Whereas they who consider him but in one Capacity, are too strict with the Text, to wrong us, and so in the End draw the Reflection upon themselves. But to run this Abuse of the *Holy Ghost*, as well as us, so high, as therefore to style us *Antichristian Idolaters*, shews a Bitterness as well as Mistake, that by no Means becomes a Critick upon other Men's Religion.

But that he may apply this Injustice home, he is pleased that it should light upon me, and therefore he quotes a Passage out of my Part of the *Christian Quaker*, tho' not the Page. I wave the Scurrility of his Introduction to it, pag. 14, 15. This is the Passage, as he gives it: " *The Power, Life and Light which inhabited* " *that Holy Person, which (or who) was Born at* Bethlehem, *was, and is chiefly* " *and eminently the Saviour, as prepared for the Work which Christ had to do in him.* *By which* (says he) *he makes the Light Within to be their Christ, and* Jesus *of Nazareth, the prepared Instrument of this Christ.*

Now by this, the *Reader* will have a clear Taste of the Justice of this Writer.

My Words are thus laid down by me, (*Christian Quaker*) pag. 104. chap. 21.) " *We confess, that though the Eternal Power, Life, Light, which inhabited that* " *Holy Person, which was Born at* Nazareth, *was, and is chiefly and eminently the* " *Saviour*, Hos. 13. 4. (For there is no Saviour besides me, *saith God*, (this he left " out) *yet that it was instrumentally a Saviour, as prepared and chosen for the Work* " *which Christ had then to do in it, which was actually to the Salvation of some, and* " *intentionally of the whole World, then, and in Ages to come; suitable to that Scrip-* " *ture*, Heb. 10. 5. 6. Lo I come, in the Volume of the Book it is written of me, " to do Thy Will, O God! A Body Thou hast prepared me." By which it is plain with what Unfairness he gave my Words before: First, he left out my Quotation out of *Hosea*, *For there is no Saviour besides me*, saith God, whereby it appears that the Eternal Power, Life and Light, was eminently concern'd in Man's Salvation. Secondly, He concealed that Scripture in the Conclusion of the Paragraph, out of the *Hebrews*, *A Body hast Thou prepared me*, &c. which plainly interprets what I mean by *Person*, and by *which*, and *it*, that he is pleased to change for *who*, and *He* and *Him*, to render me at once Absurd and Erroneous, and about which he calls me a *Lewd Author*, and all to Naught. This was done of Malice, doubtless, the better to have his evil End of me, by wringing my Words to the Sense he designed they should bear. Making me to divide, as well as distinguish, between

between *Christ*, and *Jesus of Nazareth*, and *Christ* and him that was Born of the *Virgin Mary*, reading *It, He,* and *Him*, which referred to the Body; so making me to intend *Jesus of Nazareth*, compleatly considered, when I plainly intended, from the Nature of the Words of the Text, and those Words, and the Scripture cited by me, in Proof and Illustration of what I meant by them, *the Body of Christ Jesus of Nazareth*.

Thus much of his Construction of the Words he quotes out of the *Christian Quaker*, before cited: But if he will allow us to speak our own Mind, in our own Words, and had rather we were in the Right, than in the Wrong, which does but become an ingenious Author (tho' it thereby appear that we are not what he had said us to be) then let him know, *We do not Divide*, or *Distinguish between Christ, and Jesus of Nazareth*. Nor did we ever say, that *Jesus of Nazareth* is Christ's Instrument to appear in, and by, for Man's Salvation; but that the *Word took Flesh*, and *this is the Christ, or Anointed of God:* And tho' sometimes the Term *Christ* is given to the *Word*, sometimes to the *Prepared Body he took*, as when he is said *To Dye, and be Buried, and Raised again*, &c. yet *God manifest in the Flesh, and Immanuel*; God with us in our Nature, *is that Christ of God, or Christ the Lord, that God hath, and will exalt*; *the Enlightener, Redeemer, Saviour of the World: Both an Offering for All, and the Mediator, and Sanctifier, of All that desire to come to God by Him*.

But he farther urges against us, and our Doctrine of the Light Within, as what is Fallacious on our Part, to draw in Proselytes, and which he terms a *Putid Sophism*, pag. 21, 22. viz. *Is there not a Light in every Man's Conscience? You experience one in your own. And is God Light? And Christ Light? And is not God within, and Christ within? Now this is all very true: But when from hence they infer, God is the Light Within, it is* Putid Sophism. *God being Light, and being within Men, proves not that God is a Light within Men. God is Light, and God is within other Things as well as Men: Is then God a Light within to every Tree, every Beast, every Star? If this be absurd, then God's being Light, and being within, proves but sophistically that He is the Light Within. And yet this is the constant Method the* Quakers *use, to teach their People the Divinity of the Light Within*.

Answer. I hope he will find no Cause to blame me for Imperfect, and less for Perverted Quotations: I cite him fairly and fully. Now, for *Answer*, I say, I never saw or heard of that Way of Reasoning or Tampering, as he stiles it, that he charges upon us to make *Proselytes by*. And I think I ought to be at least as well versed in our Way and Writings as himself. All Reasonable People will readily allow, they have such a Light, and in reading the Holy Scriptures, they find the *Enlightned Pen-Men* call *God Light, and Christ Light*, and are naturally led to believe, *That their Light is from God the Fountain of all Light*, especially when they read the first Chapter of *John*, and that of his First Epistle also. And it is granted by this Man, *That God is in Men, and that God is a Light within Men*. Indeed his Argument does not prove it, for it is not regularly formed to make such a Conclusion, which is his Fault, because it is of his own making: But neither is it a *Sophism*, or *Sophistical* in us, nor is the Reason Good that he gives against it, viz. Because it is absurd to say, *That God is a Light within Trees, Beasts, and Stars*, because God is within them, and God is Light; therefore it is so to say, that God is a Light within Men. For *Trees, Beasts,* and *Stars*, &c. are not of Man's Nature and Capacity, they are not capable of such a Manifestation of the Light of God, as Man is: God is in them after another and lower Manner, and to other Ends and Purposes. But why God, who is confest to be Light, and in Man, should not be *A Light then to Man*, I cannot comprehend. I do not say that it strictly follows in the Argument, but the Reason given against it is no Reason; and Reason and Scripture judge for us. For Man being a Reasonable Creature, 'tis his Duty, and the End of his Being, to know and serve God the Author of it; but this he cannot do, unless God manifest himself unto him: And since this Man grants, *That God is Light, and in some Sort in Man*, to what better Purpose, or which Way more properly and beneficially, *Can He be said to be in Man, than as a Light Shining there, to give him the Knowledge of God?* So that He is not only there as the Creator and Supporter of his Being, but as *His Illuminator and Instructor to his Well-Being*. The Scriptures already cited sufficiently prove, *That God is Light, and Christ is Light*, and, *that All Men are Enlightned by Him:* And to be sure it must be with His own Light. Now, tho' with a Fair Adversary, one might say, without Offence, *That God or Christ is the Light within Man*, yet it is not the common Way of our expressing our selves.

To be sure we have no such Meaning in that Way of Speaking, as some Adversaries strain our Words to, as if God and Christ were Comprehensible in, and by Man, to render us Absurd and Blasphemous. But we rather chuse to say, that God, or Christ, who is Light, hath *lighted Man*, and by the Light of Christ in Man, Man comes to know God and Christ: And that the Light in Man, is the *Light of God, or of Christ*, and not that God, or Christ, is the Light in Man. The Light in a Room at Noon-Day, is the Light of the Sun, but the Sun cannot so properly be said to be in the Room, because it's Light is there; for the Glorious, Unapproachable Body of it is elsewhere. I hope this will not pass with the Sober Reader for a *Putid Sophism*.

He farther says, p. 24. *I may not now adays, therefore, tell* Quakers *their own Religion is false, without telling them what is the Truth; lest I should Tempt them to leave* Quakerism *for Impiety and Irreligion, and not for the Service of* Jesus Christ.

Answer. We are beholding to him, that he thinks our Religion a Bar to Impiety and Irreligion; and, I wish neither had appeared in his opposing of it. The Truth he has a Mind to tell us, lyeth in a few Words, upon which he bestows no less than fifteen Pages, *(viz.)* That the Light which God hath given to Man for Salvation, generally speaking, is, besides Creation and Providence, the Writings of the Inspired Men of the Old and New Testament, which we call the *Scriptures of Truth*; no Light, Spirit or Grace, commonly or ordinarily opening and assisting our Understandings in the reading of them, but that the Light which is in Men, is the Effects of the Perceptive Faculties of our Minds, that is, our Thoughts, as he also tells us, *pag. 9*. So that what we Read and Hear with our outward Eyes and Ears, is thereby reported to our Mind or Judgment, whose Conclusion thereupon is this Man's Light Within. But, methinks, before he had been so positive and Voluminous in his own Notion, (where he'll find very few Abettors, I believe) he should have been so fair as to have consider'd what I have said in my *Key, p. 1, 2*. That seems to me to have more materially referred to another Light Within, than he has yet brought himself to. I will give the Passage at large as it lyeth, that it may speak for it self. " *The* Quaker's *Belief and Assertion is*, That Christ,
" who is the Word, that was with God, and was God (John 1. 4, 9. and is so for
" ever) hath enlightned every Man that cometh into the World, with his *own*
" Light; *as He is that True Light, or such a Light, as there is no other to be*
" *compared to him: Which is the Meaning of the Emphasis* True *in the Text. And*
" *that such as follow the Reproofs, Convictions and Leadings of that Light, with*
" *which he enlightens the Understandings and Consciences of Men*, shall not walk
" in Darkness : *That is, in Evil and Ignorance of God*; but shall have the Light of
" Life : *That is, be in an Holy and Living State or Condition towards God : A State*
" *of Acceptance and Salvation*, which is from *Sin* as well as from *Wrath*; (See
" *Isa.* 49. 6. *John* 1. 4. 9. c. 3. 21. c. 5. 40. c. 8. 12. c. 10. 10.) *And for which End*
" *Christ was given of God. So that they assert the* Light of Christ, *to be sufficient*
" *to Save; that is, to Convince of Sin, lead out of it, and quicken the Soul in the*
" *Ways of Holiness : And not a* Natural Light, *otherwise than as* All Men, *born*
" *into the World, have a Measure of Christ's Light, and so it may, in a Sense, be*
" *said to be* Natural to all Men, *because all Men have it. For this Light is* some-
" thing else *than the bare Understanding Man hath as a Rational Creature : For as*
" *such, Man cannot be a Light to himself*; *but has only a Capacity of seeing, by*
" *Means of the* Light with which Christ, the Word, enlightneth him. *For we can*
" *no more be a* Mental *or* Intellectual Light *to our selves, than we are an* External
" *and* Corporeal Light to our selves : *But as the* Sun *in the Firmament is the Light*
" *of our Bodies, so the* Light *of the Divine Word, is the* Sun *of our Souls; the*
" *Glorious Luminary of the Intellectual World; and they that walk in it, will, by*
" *it, be led to Blessedness*, Rev. 21. 24." Of all which, he takes this imperfect Notice, *The Concurrence of many Causes being requisite to produce Faith, the* Quakers *confound these Inspirations with the Light, and attribute the Efficiency of one Cause to another, which must needs Pervert all Sound Judgment of Things, and make them speak Inconsistences : As when W. P. says, Man cannot be a Light to himself, as if the Denial of the Divinity of the Light Within, implied any such Thing*; and Man has only a Capacity to see, *as if the Defect was in God's Works in Nature, and in the Scripture, and not in Man's seeing Faculty. Now such Expressions shew his Apprehensions are much Perverted about these Things.*

Answer.

Anſw. But this ſhews my Opponent to be either ſhallow, or worſe. I would be ſo Charitable as to think he miſtakes me, and in the Concluſion abuſeth himſelf. For why do the *Quakers* confound thoſe Inſpirations with the Light? We never limited all Divine Inſpirations and Operations to the Light, meerly as it is Light, as Phyſically, and by his Natural Philoſophy he ſeems to explain it. We ever meant a Principle in Man, that is not of Man, that is variouſly denominated by it's various Operations: *Light* from Deſcerning and Diſtinction: *Spirit* from Life and Power: *Word*, as it ſpeaks forth God's Mind to Man: *Truth*, in the Inward Parts, as it deals truly with Man, and would redeem him from lying Vanities: And *Grace*, as it is God's Gift, and not Man's Underſtanding, or Man's Merit. I ſhall not therefore quarrel with his Natural Philoſophy, p. 37, when he ſays, *The Sun Generates all Life, and it's Faculties in Bodies*, but not by it's Light; for we never ſaid it did, with Reference to the Light Within: Elſe all Men would have Divine Life as well as Light, which was never our Aſſertion, nor a Juſt Concluſion from that which is, it being Scripture, viz. *John* 1. 4. *In Him, the Word, is Life, and that Life the Light of Men*, not the Life of Men, but as they obey it: According to that clear and full Expreſſion of our Bleſſed Lord, *John* 8. 12. *I am the Light of the World, he that followeth me ſhall not walk in Darkneſs, but ſhall have the Light of Life*; that is, Life as well as Light. They that read him, will ſee who keeps neareſt to the Text, and who walks cloſeſt to the Rule and Form of Sound Words; which we hope neither he, nor any of his Abettors, ſhall ever be able to draw or drive us from.

For the Uſe he makes of thoſe Words of mine: *And Man has only a Capacity to ſee* (viz.) *As if the Defect was in God's Works in Nature and in the Scriptures, and not in Man's ſeeing Faculties*; he utterly miſtakes me: I will not ſay wilfully; but upon that he makes a great Pother, and depends the Strength of his Concluſion: For I ſpeak of Man in his Creation, and he of Man in his Fall. The Concluſion cannot be Right that is drawn from wrong Premiſes, and I hope he, when he thinks again, will think ſo too; and that his Pains, p. 36, 37. might have been ſpared. For I hope he will not think there was any Defect in Paradiſe, as there muſt have been, if Man had been defective in his Seeing Faculty; for even there he was but Man, and, as ſuch, he could not be his own Light; which is plain, in that when he Erred, he Erred from ſomething elſe than himſelf, himſelf Erring; Therefore that ſomething elſe muſt be the Divine Light he Erred from; in which if he had kept, the Subtil Inſinuations of the Serpent had never prevailed.

Man then had only the Capacity of ſeeing all Divine Objects; as Truth, Wiſdom, Goodneſs, Mercy, Juſtice, Power, &c. which were only diſcernible by the Inſhinings of this Divine Light of the Word of God. And ſince he alludes ſo ſtrictly in his Inſtances from the Creation and Natural Philoſophy, I hope he will allow me to ſay, That as the Eye of Man, though never ſo capable of ſeeing, cannot ſee any Object before it, in the Dark, unleſs an outward Light give it the Sight thereof; ſo no Man's Soul can ſee Divine Objects, though it's Eye, or Seeing Faculty were ever ſo capable, unleſs the Divine Light ſhined in it, to give unto it the Knowledge of the Glory of God therein. And I have not only my own Experience, but that of *Good Men* in all Ages of the World, according to the Degree of the Manifeſtation of the Divine Light, wherein they agree, and cannot err: Humility, Obedience, Love, Patience, Meekneſs, Purity, Charity, &c. are ſenſibly wrought in Men by this Divine Principle. Senſibly I ſay, for all his *Inſenſible Dogmas, pag.* 37, 38, 39. as that Man is not ſenſible of the Divine Agency or Inſpiration of the Almighty. For we know (*ſays he*) by Reaſoning, but not by Senſe or Conſcience: Abuſing that Scripture to countenance his inſenſible Aſſertion, *The Wind bloweth where it liſteth, and we hear the Sound thereof, but know not whence it comes, nor whither it goes*; which is not ſpoken of the Regenerate Man's not knowing how he is Regenerated, but that other Men know it not with all their Wiſdom and Knowledge, that are not Spiritually illuminated and experienced in the ſame Work: Anſwerable to that Place in the *Revelations of John, That he that overcomes, ſhall have a White Stone, and a New Name, that none ſhall know but he that has it*, that is, *but ſuch Conquerors*: For they that are overcome of the World, can never taſte or judge of the Rewards of thoſe that do overcome it.

And very ſorry I am for this *Oppoſer*, that he allows Man no Spiritual Senſes, or that which anſwers to our Outward Senſes; and if he does, ſurely they are to See, Hear, Smell, Taſte and Feel ſomething elſe than himſelf. How groſs then is his Position, *p. 37. But this I may say, that neither is the Illuminating, or Renewing, or Regenerating, or any other Divine Inspiration, immediately perceptible to any Sense, inward or outward, in Human Nature*; and if so, 'tis certain none of these can be a Light within us. But why it is not so, he has not told us, he cannot tell us, nor any Man else. To all which I shall oppose a few Scriptures, and then attend his Abuse of (those I cited in my Key, and) me, for the Application of them.

That there is another Light and Spirit that attend Men, than the *Effects of the Perceptive Faculties of their own Minds, as this Man calls it*, I urge that Passage in *Genesis, 6. 3 My Spirit shall not always strive with Men.* A plain Proof that God strove with the Old World by his Holy Spirit, which could not be if they had it not, or were unsensible of any such Thing, *Nehemiah 9. 20.* It is said, That God *gave them his good Spirit, but they rebelled against it*, therefore they had it. *David* prays that God *would not take his Holy Spirit from him*, which shews it was with him, and that not as a Prophet, but ordinarily speaking; for his Transgression was too heinous for that Dignity without a Course of Repentance, and a Restoration to his former State, which in the same Psalm he prays for: But 'tis evident, as bad as he was, he had yet the Holy Spirit in that Sense, in which we assert a *Measure of it to be given to all to profit with*, as the Apostle speaks, 1 *Cor.* 12. 7. Else he could not have said, *And take not thy Holy Spirit from me*; as much as to say, for if thou dost utterly deprive me of it, I shall grow Dark, Hard and Impenitent, and be undone for ever.

The Lord, by the Prophet *Isaiah*, proves, That his Spirit should successively attend his People; These are his Words. *And for me, this is my Covenant with them, saith the Lord, my Spirit that is upon thee*, (Christ) *and my Words which I have put in thy Mouth, shall not depart out of thy Mouth, nor out of the Mouth of thy Seed's Seed, saith the Lord, from henceforth and for ever*, Ch. 59. 21. And, I pray, who are Christ's Seed, and Off-spring, but true Christians? and, as such, they are intituled to this Promise, and therefore have the Spirit of God, and the fresh and living Revelation of it, whose Words are Spirit and Life.

Thus the Prophet, *Chap.* 44. 3. *I will pour Water upon him that is Thirsty, and Floods upon the dry Ground: I will pour my Spirit upon thy Seed, and my Blessing upon thine Off-spring.* A most ample and close Proof to my Point, That God gives his Spirit to Men, and that there is something more than the Light of Reading and Hearing of Men and Books, or the *Perceptive Faculty of the Mind, to instruct Men.* And that, not only in extraordinary Cases, and on singular and eminent Occasions, which our Opponent allows, as to *Moses*, the *Prophets* and *Apostles*, but ordinarily, commonly, successively: For to that the Text plainly reaches.

The Prophet *Joel* is yet more comprehensive, ch. 2. 28. *And it shall come to pass afterwards, that I will pour out my Spirit upon all Flesh*; Young and Old, Hand-Maids and Servants: No Age, no Sex, no Degree shall be exempted. The Apostle *Peter* apply'd this very Text to the Dawning of the Primitive Christian Days, as then begun to be accomplished, *Acts* 2. 17. Not that that which befel the Apostles and Disciples of Jesus in that Time, was the compleat Answering of that Prophecy, for that was not *all Flesh*. Besides, the very same Apostle, in the same Sermon, Ver. 39, tells his Auditors, that were made up of no less than *Fourteen* several Nations, *That the Promise was to them and to their Children, and to all that were afar off, whom the Lord should call*; So that the Gifts of the Spirit were the Fulfilling of the Gospel-Promise, and consequently the Great Gospel-Privilege and Qualification.

The Apostle *Paul* tells us, *Rom.* 8, That there is an absolute Necessity that People should have the Spirit of God *dwelling in them*, and that they should be *led* and *conducted* by it, or they cannot be the Children of God. Ver. 1, *There is no Condemnation to them that are in Christ Jesus, who walk not after the Flesh but after the Spirit.* Here it is the Christian Rule.

Again, Ver. 12. *But if the Spirit of him that raised Jesus from the Dead,* DWELL IN YOU, *he that raised up Christ from the Dead, shall also quicken your Mortal Bodies, by his Spirit, that* dwelleth in you: So that the Indwelling of the Spirit did quicken and comfort the Ancient Christians, and was Apostolical Doctrine.

Again, Ver. 14, 15, 16. *For as many as are led by the Spirit of God, they are the Sons of God*; which they cannot be if they have it not: *For ye have not received*

ceived the *Spirit of Bondage again to Fear*, but the *Spirit of Adoption, whereby we cry Abba Father*. The Spirit it self beareth Witness with our Spirit, that we are the Children of God, so that it is plain they had the Spirit. And I wonder what Witness Christians must have now, that they are the Children of God, if not the same Spirit, since if this Adversary say true, there is no such Gift common to Christians now, but only the *Notices God has given to all, of his Thoughts and Mind, by Creation and Scripture*. But, alas! too apparent it is that this Man knows little of the Working of God's Spirit, that so unspiritually speaks of it. Did not our blessed Lord say, *John* 3. 5, That unless Man be born of the Spirit, he could not enter into the Kingdom of God. Was this only for the Primitive Times? Then Men ever since have not been saveable, for they have wanted the Means of Salvation, to wit, REGENERATION. And if Regeneration be necessary to all, how can a Man be rationally said to be born of the Spirit, and not to have the Spirit he is born of; or be (as *Peter* phraseth it) a *Partaker of the* DIVINE *Nature*, 2 Pet. 1. 4. But more than this, Christ told his Disciples, That the *Spirit of Truth* he would send them, though it should be a Comforter to them that believed in him, and followed him, yet it should *Reprove* the World of Sin; which could not be, if the World had not such a Measure of the Spirit, as to reprove them in their Evil-doing. And indeed all that will be serious and reflect, must confess, from Experience, they have enough of it to reprove them for that which is Evil, and to bear a true and faithful Witness against every Evil Way.

Memorable is that Second Chapter of the Apostle, in his first Epistle to the *Corinthians*, a worldly-wise People, whose Faculties were as perceptive as our Opponent's, I doubt not, concerning the Office, Efficacy and Necessity of the Holy Spirit, to know God and our Duty to Him, in order to Salvation.

And what has been said of the Holy Spirit, may be said of the Divine Light: As one of the earliest Books in Scripture tells us: *Job* 24. 13. *They are of those*, says *Job*, speaking of the Wicked, *that rebel against the Light*. Then they had it: And if They had it, all had it: For to be sure the Righteous were not without it.

Again, *The Spirit of Man is the Candle of the Lord*, Prov. 20. 27, but it must be lighted by that Light we speak of, or it is a dark Candle. Now God lights the Candle of the Wicked, much more is he the Light of the Candle of the Righteous.

Again, he says, *How often is the Candle of the Wicked put out:* Job 21. 17. Prov. 13. 9. Which shews it is often lighted; and if *They* have the Light, the Righteous, to be sure, are not without it: For, *The Way of the Just is a shining Light, which shines more and more to the perfect Day*. Obedience to Light received, encreases Light. Now, if the Way of the Just be a shining Light, to be sure the Light is Saving, or is the Way to Salvation: And so the beloved Disciple has it, *Revel*. 21. The Nations of them that are saved shall walk in the Light.

David says also, in Proof of our Point, *The Lord is my Light and my Salvation*, Psal. 27. 1. Then he had an higher and clearer Light than his own perceptive Faculties.

Again, *Thy Word is a Light to my Feet, and a Lanthorn to my Paths*, Psal. 119. 105. Which was an Inward and Spiritual Word, for it was such an one as he could *find* in his Heart, according to *Moses, Deut*. 3. and the Apostle, *Rom*. 10.

David also, *Psal*. 42, prayed, that the Lord would *send forth his Light and his Truth*, which were the same Thing, *that it might lead and bring People to his Holy Hill and Tabernacle*. This was more than Man, or what was of Man's Constitution or Composition: More than the Perceptive Faculties of the Mind.

Moreover, God declared by the Prophet *Isaiah*, That he had given Christ *for a Light to lighten the Gentiles*; which was more than Man's Wit or Understanding, to be sure. And tho' Christ was a Light in his *Doctrine, Miracles* and *Example*, yet he was and is a Light within also, to enlighten the Mind, as *John* 1. 4. 9. with many more, before observed. And this Light and Spirit are of the same Principle, or the same Principle that is both Spirit and Light, tho' it may be, strictly speaking, not both in one and the same Act or Operation, as has been already noted. Nevertheless, the Scripture makes them to have one Operation, comparing *John* 16. 7. with *Eph*. 5. 13. For the first makes it the Office of the Spirit to *convince the World of Sin*, and the latter Place tells us, That whatever is reproved is made manifest by the Light: And the Apostle gives this for the Reason,

because,

because, says he, *whatever makes manifest is Light:* An Assertion that can never be denied. And as true it is that it must be a Divine Light, that reveals Divine Truths. And because it is necessary that all should know them for their Salvation, since God would have all come to the Knowledge of the Truth, and be saved, the Consequence must be good, that all have this Divine Light, more or less, for Salvation, tho' all don't obey it.

I might proceed to enumerate Scriptures through the *Prophets*, *Evangelists* and *Epistles*; but I think what I have said is a double Portion: And therefore I recommend it to the candid Reader's serious Perusal and Observation; and I doubt not but he will discern the Verity and Charity of our Principles, and the unjust Exceptions of our Opponent to them.

I come next to consider his Cavils against our Citations of Scripture, and indeed against the Scripture it self, which will not be hard to evince.

Page 41. He is angry, because I say that Christ has enlightned Men with his *own* Light; calls this very hard Names, and says, 'tis the Quakers *Apocrypha*: But we abide by it; and are taught so to do by the Scriptures, that he would have the World believe we deny, and make Apocryphal. *John* 1. 4. *In him* (Christ) *was Life, and the Life the Light of Men.* Now if this be not Man's Light, and if this Light, which is the Life of the Word, be not the Light of the Word, let me be blamed: If it be, how preposterous must this Man be to use me so harshly for a Truth so plain as well as important?

The next Scripture is that in *Prov.* 20. 27. *The Spirit of Man is the Candle of the Lord, searching all the inward Parts of the Belly:* That is, says he, *the Spirit of Man, which God hath made, hath in it's Nature a Consciousness of all his Thoughts, Purposes and Counsels within him.* But this Word Consciousness supposes a Knowledge, together with something else, that gives us that Knowledge: It is the very Import of the Words: And what is that, but that Divine Light which gives Light to the Candle: For a Candle cannot light it self, and by the Repetition of Sin, is said to be often blown out. For tho' it cannot blow that Light out, it blows out it's Enlightnings. Thus Sin quenches the Spirit; that is, the Enlivenings and Quicknings of it, for the Spirit it self cannot be quenched. Now this Note of his is so far from overthrowing our Use of this Scripture, that it establishes it, and defeats him of the End he proposed in opposing us.

Thus he abuses us and that Passage of our Saviour Christ, *If the Light that is in you be Darkness, how great is that Darkness?* As if Christ meant any Light but that of Man's Mistake and Presumption, or that we could assert God to be that Light in us, which Christ said might be Darkness: For this Man says, If the Light in us here mentioned was the Light that is good, the Supposal that it might possibly be Darkness, would be a blasphemous Supposition. He is to be pity'd as well as reproved, that can rave after this Manner.

The Use I make of that Scripture, 2 *Cor.* 4. 6. *God, that commanded the Light to shine out of Darkness, hath shined in our Hearts, to give the Light of the Knowledge of the Glory of God, in the Face of Jesus Christ,* was thus: That God had lighted the Hearts of Men, by breaking through the Darkness there, with his Divine Light. This Author, *p.* 43. limits this Light to the Apostles and Fellow-Labourers; and all the rest are to see with their Eyes, and without that Divine Light in themselves: In fine, to be concluded by their Authority, and not their own Conviction; for what he says centers there. Whereas the Apostle's Mission and Business, was *to turn People from the Darkness* (that was in themselves) *to the Light* that had shined there uncomprehended: Also to be made manifest in their *Preaching* to the *Consciences* of People; which could not be in Divine Truths without a *Divine Light*. I must leave this Way of our *Opponent's* treating of *Scripture* to my *Reader's Consideration*.

Page 45 *to* 57. His next Abuse is, that of *John* 1. 9. about which he bestows Room for Reason, being no less than twelve Pages. He that can make more of them than these Three following Heads, has a better Understanding than mine.

1. That the Life that is come by Christ is, that we shall *out-live the Grave*; not that the Soul is made Spiritually alive to God, while in this World, by Divine Quicknings, to the Use of her Spiritual Sensations, that Sin had taken away, by bringing her under a Spiritual Lethargy or Death: Which, how agreeable it is to that Saying of Christ, *John* 8. 12. *That they that follow him should have the Light of Life*; and, *John* 6. *unless you eat my Flesh and drink my Blood, you have no Life in you:* (Which implies an Inward and Living State of the Mind towards God

God on this Side the Grave) I muſt alſo leave with my Confiderate *Reader*, that has any Reliſh or Taſte of Divine Things.

2. The ſecond Thing he objects upon our Uſe of this Scripture, (*John* 1. 9.) is our making *Coming into the World* to refer to *Man*, and not to *Chriſt*; which, ſays he, is firſt *a Redundancy of Speech*, and next *dangerous*; *for it is as if a Man came from another World into this.* Now I would have this *Critick* know, if he can be ignorant of it, That divers Learned *Proteſtant Commentators* have taken that Way, as have ſome of the *Fathers*, and all the *Tranſlators* that I can compaſs, be it into the *Latin Verſions*, or our Vulgar *European* Tongues; as my Reader may pleaſe to ſee at large, in a Book of mine, called, *The Spirit of Truth Vindicated*, from *p.* 52 *to p.* 62. ſo that he muſt allow we are in good Company, if miſtaken; ſince ſo many *Criticks* and *Commentators* are with us; as Singular and Erroneous as he is pleaſed to repreſent us. But where is the *Redundancy?* Why, it is, that *every Man* would have ſerved without the Words *coming into the World*, which follow them. No Wonder he is ſo Churliſh to our *Writings*, that affords the *Holy Scripture* no more Reſpect. If he will read ſeveral Chapters of that belov'd *Diſciple's Writings*, and, indeed of many other of the Holy Penmen's, he may, if he pleaſe, make the like Exceptions. Thus that Saying of *Job*, uſed in the *Liturgy*, in the Office for the Dead, *Man that is born of a Woman, &c.* for, according to this *Critick's Learning, Man* had been enough, and the Addition, *That is born of a Woman*, dangerous; for that it implies there are Men that are not born of Women: Which I think would not mightily recommend his Skill or Judgment, as his Exception cannot juſtly impeach the Propriety of the Holy Scriptures. And if this Adverſary did believe that Chriſt made Man, he would believe he *Enlightens* him, as well as made him; and that the firſt Ten Verſes of that Chapter refer to his *Divinity:* What he was in himſelf, and what he was and is to Man, as the *Word-God*, by whom the whole World was made, and Man, in an excellent Manner, *Enlightned*, and this before any Mention is made of his Taking Fleſh, or coming of the Seed of *Abraham*.

3. But he would have *Lighteth* limited to *Chriſt's Coming in the Fleſh*, and that all were enlightned then by him: Now, I will not ſay, he was not a glorious *Light* in his *Miniſtry* and *Miracles*, in his *Life* and *Sufferings*; for if his *Diſciples* were by him called the *Lights of the World*, doubtleſs it may be better ſaid of him, their Lord and Original, *That he was the Light of the World*. But this hinders not that he ſhould be the *Light* of the World, in a more proper and immediate Manner, by his ſhining in the Underſtandings of Men, and giving them thereby the Knowledge of their Duty to God, and one to another. I muſt refer him to what I have ſaid in my former Book, upon this Head alſo; in Anſwer to one that deny'd the Pre-exiſtence of Chriſt, or that he had a Being before he was born of the *Virgin Mary*; in whoſe Steps this Man ſeems to tread. If he will read from *Page* 62 *to* 86, and the Reaſons and numerous Authorities, theſe may perhaps perſwade him that the 9th Verſe of the firſt of *John*, wholly relates to the *Word* before he took Fleſh, and as he is the immediate Enlightner of the Souls of Men. *In him was Life, and the Life the Light of Men*, Verſe 4. This was neither Sun, Moon, nor Stars; nor yet the Effect of the *Perceptive Faculties* of our Souls, nor yet any *Outward* and *Miniſterial Light* whatever; of all which I leave the ſober Reader to judge.

Page 52, 53. As for the groſs Abſurdity that he would run us into, of being *Be-Godded* and *Be-Chriſted*, according to our Principle, he has ſhewn ſufficiently he does not underſtand it, and therefore no Matter for his wild Conſequences, by which he would diſgrace it: But if by being Be-Chriſted, we are to underſtand *Divine Kindred* and *Memberſhip*, through *true Chriſtening*, which is the *Anoynting*, I *John* 2. 20, 27. we ſhall not ſhrink from the Word, becauſe of his Out-cries at us for it. I have already declared what we intend by being Enlightned, and that our Principle is not capable of any of the wild Inferences, this Man, through great Ignorance or Malice, charges upon it. But before I leave this Head, I muſt obſerve one *Diſtinction* of his, *Page* 54, 55, 56. That to himſelf, doubtleſs, looks very apt and determining, *viz. That we are not enlightned by what God is, but what God does*. This is upon my ſaying, *That God enlightens Men with his own Light*; calling me all to Naught for that Phraſe, as Unſcriptural, and of a *meditated Temperament*, to amuſe my Readers with: Rendring the *Light*, which we ſay true *Chriſtians* ought to walk by, to be *no otherwiſe God's own Light, than the Sun and the Rain are his own Sun and Rain:* Not of his Nature, but of his Creation

tion only; that I take to be his Meaning, a little Plainer than he has expressed it. To which I reply, in that famous and suitable Text of the beloved Disciple, 1 *Joh.* 1. 5, 6, 7. *This then is the Message which we have heard of him, and declare unto you,* That God is Light, *and in him is no Darkness at all; if we say that we have Fellowship with him, and walk in Darkness, we lye and do not the Truth: But if we walk in the Light as he is in the Light, we have Fellowship one with another, and the Blood of Jesus Christ his Son cleanseth us from all Sin.* Here I leave him to consider of this *Light;* whether it be a Created One: Such an One, as is not what God is, but what God does; and shall attend his Perversion of my present Use, and our Common Sense of several Scriptures, cited in Favour of our *Inward Principle*: And then shall conclude my *Reply* to his pretended *Answer,* to that Part of my *Key,* which relates to the *Light within.*

That I may make the Point plainer to the *Reader,* I shall first lay down the *Perversion* mentioned in my *Key,* then our *Principle upon it,* with those *Scriptures,* he takes Occasion to twist and turn from our true Sense and End in citing them, and of which he is so conscious to himself, that to anticipate my Reply, he gives it for me, as I shall anon observe, and not a great Way from our true Sense.

Perverf. *The* Quakers *hold, That the Light within them is* God, Christ, *and the* Holy Spirit; *so that every* Quaker *has* whole God, Christ *and* Holy Spirit *in him; which is gross Blasphemy.* Key, *p.* 2, 3.

By this my *Reader* will see what we except against, viz. The *Blasphemy* of making every *Quaker* comprehend whole God and Christ, and Holy Spirit in him. Now I must desire him to observe what our *Principle* says to this Suggestion.

Principle. " This is also a Mistake of their Belief: They never said, That
" every *Divine Illumination* or *Manifestation* of Christ, in the Hearts of Men, was
" *whole God, Christ,* or the *Spirit*; whereby to be guilty of that Gross and Blas-
" phemous Absurdity, some would fasten upon them: But that God, who is
" *Light,* or the *Word-Christ,* who is *Light,* the *Quickning Spirit,* and God over
" all, blessed for ever, hath enlightened Mankind *with a Measure of Saving*
" *Light :* So that the *Illumination* is from *Christ,* the *Divine Word*; but not there-
" fore whole God or Christ, in every Man, any more than the *whole Sun or Air is*
" *in every House or Chamber.* There are no such harsh and unscriptural Words
" in their *Writings*: It is only a frightful *Perversion* of some of their *Enemies,* to
" bring a Scandal upon their Holy Faith. Yet, *in a Sense,* the Scriptures say it,
" and that is their (the *Quakers*) Sense, in which they only say the same Thing.
" *He that is with you shall be in you: I will not leave you Comfortless, I will come*
" *to you: I in them, and they in us: Christ in us, the Hope of Glory: Unless*
" *Christ be in you, ye are Reprobates. Little Children, of whom I travail in Birth*
" *again, until Christ be formed in you.*

This is my Explanation of our Principle, about the Light, from the *Perversions* of our Adversaries: By which the uncandid Dealing of this Man must be very obvious; since, besides his Silence, and that he seems to shut his Eyes to our Explanation and Vindication of what we hold, from what he charges, he doubles the Perversions, by Changing and Misgiving the End for which the Scriptures were cited by me: For he makes us to quote them, to prove what we expresly deny, as a false Charge upon us; and carries them, at least beyond, if not against the Intent and Reason of their Quotations, which he knows deserves a black Name, since they were never quoted to prove *whole God and Christ to be in every Man,* or to be so in any Man: But that God, Christ and the Spirit were in some near Manner in the People of God. For the very Perversion runs it no farther than the People called *Quakers*; that every one of us are suggested to have whole God, and whole Christ, and the Spirit in us: Which is to improve, as I said before, upon the very Perversion.

Hear him. Pag. 58. *Christ says not here, that any Man, except his Disciples, shall have him in them; that Christ is in none but those that are in him; that he is not in Reprobates, so not in every Man; that he was not in the* Galatians; *that they must be new Creatures that have him; so all against* W. P's *Purpose.* But what was my Purpose, I pray? Hear the *Key* again.

" Yet, *in a Sense,* the Scriptures say it, and that is their (the Quakers) Sense,
" in which they only say the same Thing. What fair or wise Adversary would have been guilty of so ill a Thing, and so easily to be detected? Is any Thing plainer than, First, That *every Quaker,* and not every Man is in the Perversion?

Se-

Secondly, That I deny, in the Name of that People, any such Blasphemous Principle, as that every *Quaker has whole God in him,* but much the contrary; explaining our Principle, of which he takes no Notice. Thirdly, That yet we own God, Christ and Holy Spirit to be in the People call'd Quakers; but that it is according to a *Sense :* In what Sense do I say it? Why, the Sense in which the Scriptures say it.

Now, *Reader*, judge thou, and not I, what to call this Man, that with so much Falshood obtrudes upon us, the untruest Things and unworthiest Abuses, for the Principles of the People call'd *Quakers.* And to shew him to himself yet more plainly, he has provided me with the means of doing of it, which I toucht upon before, viz. *That the Quakers use to say, None but Believers have Christ in Union, but all others have Christ in them.* Which at least gives away the Point: For if Christ be in some Sense or other in every Man, yet he is not said by me to be in the foregoing Scriptures, in any but Believers. And he makes too bold with us also, in saying, in our Name, That Christ is in all Men; for we chuse rather to express our selves otherwise, as, *That a Manifestation of Christ is in every Man, or that the Light of Christ is within every Man*; and in so saying, I have, by many plain Scriptures prov'd, That we speak but the Truth, and that which is every Man's Blessing: And it were well all would prize it, and live up to it. For that is the *Gift of God* to Men for their *Salvation,* and the Convictions of it, the Day of their *Visitation,* and tho' *Tradition, Form* and *Formality*, in many Countries, as well as Wickedness, having darkned the Understandings of People, so that they seem more Solicitous about their Forms, than zealously obedient to this Divine Principle; yet there is none without a Sense of the Reproofs and Convictions of it, more or less at one Time or other: Which cannot be without *Light,* since all that is reprov'd is made manifest by the Light, *Eph.* 5. 13. But before I close this Subject, I must touch upon his Interpretation of some of those Texts before cited. p. 58. 59.

He says this Passage of the Apostle's, *Christ in us, the Hope of Glory,* is against me, *because it was only to Believers that he wrote.* Grant it, yet why may not Christ be a Condemner in the Consciences of the Wicked, as well as the Hope of Glory in Believers? However, it is not against me, since I cited it only to shew the Enjoyment of Believers: And since he allows Christ to be in Believers, I hope his Light and Spirit are there with him, which is more than the Effects of the perceptive Powers of their Souls, or outward Ministerial Help in the Business of Religion; a Thing he has so often denyed to any but the Holy *Penmen,* and here and there an extraordinary Person, that has had the *Power* of Miracles, to confirm the Truth of their Inspiration: *For if he has given us his Son, how much more with him shall he give us all Things?* So that our Adversary has herein granted what he has so often denyed and opposed.

The like in that Passage of the Apostle to the *Corinthians,* 2 Cor: 13. 15. *Unless Christ be in you, you are Reprobates.* This, says he, *proves, no Reprobates have Christ in them*; *How then is Christ in every Man, if he be in none of these?* But then say I, he is in all but Reprobates by this Man's Concession: And we can say no more. For if by Reprobates we are to understand a *Judas's* State; a *seared* Conscience; one that has absolutely *crucified* to himself afresh the Lord of Life and Glory, and has sinned the Sin against the Holy Ghost: In short, an *Apostate* or an *obstinate Opposer,* and *Perverter* of the right Way of the Lord; then, I say, our Principle of Christ being in some Sense in every Man (*viz.* as a Light lightning every Man) receives no Disadvantage from his Objection: For, therefore, *Reprobates* have not Christ; because they have finally blown out the Candle, extinguish'd Conscience, and are become dead to all Sense of Religion; which is because they have outliv'd the Day of God's Love and Mercy to them: They would not be gathered; they would have none of him; they would not have this Man to reign over them. But then *all others*, by this Text, and this Man's arguing from it, have Christ in them; and so it makes greatly for us, since it plainly concludes, That if all that have not Christ in them are Reprobates, then those that are not Reprobates have Christ in them; but such is every Man that cometh into the World, *therefore every Man that cometh into the World hath Christ in him :* For, to be sure, Men come not *Reprobates* into the World. They have a Day of Grace; God calls; his Spirit strives; his Long-Suffering waiteth, as in the Days of *Noah,* for their Repentance. And this is that which will give the greatest Weight in the Scale against the Rebellious, at the great Judgment, that they had a *Talent* ; a *Seed* was sown, *Grace* did appear, and *all had Light*, but such lov'd Darkness rather than Light, because their Deeds were evil. The last Scripture he would turn upon us, is that in the *Galatians;*

ans; My *little Children, of whom I travel in Birth again until Christ be formed in you:* Upon which he says, *The Persons spoken to then, had not Christ in them.* Thus does this Man walk in a Circle, and contradict himself. One Time all but Reprobates have Christ; another while the *Galatians,* tho' not Reprobates, had him not. But when he considers that there is a great Difference between a *Seed,* and an *Ear,* a *Plant* and a *Tree,* he may better understand the Apostle, and what he now says. For the poor Man, after so often allowing Christ to be in the People of God, says. Pag. 59. *But neither in Believers is Christ a Light within.* I wonder then what he is there, since he is the *Light of the World,* Joh. 1. 4. 9. and that *true Light that lighteth every Man that cometh into the World;* and yet not to be a Light within Man, *tho' he be within Man,* is surprizing. I shall leave it with my *Reader,* to do our Principle Justice; and I hope he will find Reason to think I have asserted no *Errors,* nor *prevaricated* with my Friends, nor *lost* my Point, nor acted with *Leger-de-main,* or *Meditated Temperament* to deceive; and that all the *Wards* of my *Key,* after his many *Strainings, Wrestlings* and *Forcings,* keep their Places, and answer the End for which the *Key* was first made (viz.) *To open to every Common Understanding, the Difference between the Principles of the People called* Quakers, *and the Perversions and Misrepresentations of their Enemies:* Wishing this Adversary, for all his Scoffs, Scurrility and Abuse, upon us and our Religion, Repentance to Salvation.

His Exceptions to our Refusal of Oaths, *And his Arguments for them considered.*

PAge 62. *To their* (the Quakers) *Scruple about Oaths I shall only hint these few Thoughts, because True Speaking is not only a Part of Honesty, but Religion; therefore not only Honesty, but Religion is engaged, with it's full Force to support it self: But if a Man engage all his Religion for the Support of a true Speech, he takes an Oath.*

If this be true arguing, then we swear as often as we say *Yea* and *Nay* in Evidence; since we acknowledge we stake the Credit of our Religion and Conscience for the Verity of it; and then methinks there needs no Dispute in the Matter: For it is certain we do, and that Swearers can do no more: And since that is our Principle, it is as binding on us, as Swearing is upon those that give themselves the Liberty of Swearing. But pray let us hear what follows. *I shall not,* (says he) *insist upon the Nature of an Oath, but consider it's Place in the Political State of Christ's Kingdom.*

If he will not insist upon the Nature of an Oath, I have no Reason to insist upon the Use or Disuse of it at this Time; since here it is an arguing upon an *Individuum Vagum;* a Nothing. He should first have ascertained us, what an Oath is; and when that had been adjusted and setled, then he should have proved such an Oath Lawful, and us unreasonable for refusing it upon all Accounts. However, I will both observe and answer his Notions of it.

First, he says, *He cannot understand how Swearing can be wholly put down, where People may Swear by Law,* as in *England.* True, unless that Law be repealed, that requires it. But it is a great *Bull* to say, That they who make a Law can't repeal it. If the Legislative Power is pleased to make *Yea* and *Nay* have the Force and Acceptance of an Oath, they may have it in any Government, and that is what the People call'd *Quakers* desire in this, for all of their Communion; and to shew him how much he is mistaken, the highest Judicature in *England* sits upon Honour and not Oaths, viz. *The House of Lords:* So Commissioners of *Oyer and Terminer,* that judge Life, are rarely, if ever, upon Oath. So that I have herein answered his Question, p. 63. *If an Order against all Swearing were not,* Ipso Jure, *Void.* He carries it higher than any Body ever did, that I have met with. It is with him the great Hinge or Axletree upon which Religion turns; and explodes my Reason as False, that I gave for the Rise of Oaths, viz. Want of Faith, either in him that Swears, or in him to whom the Oath is Sworn.

For, says he, *God the Father Swears to the Son,* Heb. 7. *where there is infinite Faithfulness on both Sides.*

But to this I say, That, strictly speaking, God cannot be said to Swear, for he that Swears, Swears by the Greater, Heb. 6. 16. So that it is call'd *Swearing,* that it might strike Unbelieving Man with the greater Assurance of God's Love to him. And tho' there was Infinite Faithfulness between God and Christ, yet it referring to Man, it is termed an Oath, to heighten and augment Man's Credit and
Confidence

Confidence in God, as to the Means of his Salvation, and not that God did properly Swear, or can do so.

But he tells us, *That Christ answered upon Adjuration before a Judge*, which is the way of Swearing in our *English* Courts.

I cannot allow it, since he does not prove that Christ Swore in his Answer; for all he said was, *Thou hast said*, Mat. 26. 63. Now that is putting it back to the High Priest; as if he had said, What need I answer that upon Oath, which thou thy self say'st? Dost thou first accuse me, and then query to confirm it? Thou hast said. But next, if it be said, That it was an Answer usual, and the Propriety or Peculiarity of that Language, so to speak, he should have proved it: For as the Words are in the Scripture, there appears no Oath in them: But if it were as he says, which I cannot grant, yet it concludes nothing against us; for as he was in the State of a Servant, a Jew of the Jews, made and born under the Law, *Gal.* 4. 4. He was to fulfil the Righteousness of it, and so might act as a Jew; as he did in the Instance of Circumcision, the Passover, *&c.* Yet after his Resurrection we hear nothing of an Oath, any more in Example than in Doctrine, that, with all other Customs of the Jews, that in old Time were practis'd, was, as it were, left with the Grave Cloaths behind, and he ascended, in his Evangelical Righteousness and Glory, Triumphing over Principalities and Powers, and vanquishing Hell, Death and the Grave, and brought in a better Hope, Sanctuary and Tabernacle, where *Yea and Nay* succeeded and superseded all Oaths. So that the very Basis this Man builds upon is unsound, and his Premises precarious. How then can he build well, or conclude rightly against us? But he says, The Angels Swear, which I conceive is more than he knows; for no Body can think by his Writings he is very conversant with good Angels. However, I grant that the Angels have sworn, but that is no Reason to continue Oaths among Men, if Christ, the Blessed Author of the Christian Religion hath forbid them: For the Angels, as well as Men must worship him, *Heb.* 1. 6. and therefore Christ and not the Angels are to be follow'd by us; but whenever an Angel hath Sworn, it hath been in Condescension to the Incredulity and Diffidence of Man, and to heighten his Credit of the Mind and Will of God; and is therefore an Instance for us, because it refers to a low and imperfect State, proposed as an Expedient and Remedy against Untruth; which is out of the Question, Truth leaving no Room for Swearing, which in it's Nature is but a Terrifying of the Mind into true Speaking; as in some Countries, in Default of Evidence, they use Racks to extort Confessions from the suspected Parties: An Instance of which we have near us, in the *Scotch Boots and Thummikins*.

He alledges also, *That the Apostles Swore*; but he has not mention'd any one of them, nor any Place; However, that I may not leave my *Reader* as much in the Dark as he has done his, I refer him to my Book, entitul'd, *The Spirit of Truth Vindicated*, from page 86, to page 91. where he may see how much softer Translations may be given of the Apostle's Expressions, than that of our *Vulgar Version*. Nevertheless, those extraordinary Ways of Speaking were in extraordinary Cases, and cannot be a Rule to others, but under the same Circumstances and Authority: And till this Author has given us an Authentick Definition of an Oath, he cannot justly call the Apostle's Expressions, *Oaths, or Proofs of Oaths*; unless he will allow that binding any Affirmation, or Negation, *by the Name of the Lord*, is an Oath; but if that were the Case, it differs mightily, to use the *Name of the Lord* to inforce the Verity of Divine Things, and to make it a Witness and Voucher for us in our Low and Temporal Affairs: A Distinction as old as some of the most Eminent Fathers of the Primitive Ages of the Church.

But he adds, *That all Christians take Sacramental Oaths*: Which is not True in Fact; for among the *Protestants of the Low Countries*, there is a Great People, *Who in any Case will not Swear*, as well as we, and yet we know no other Name, Blood, Power and Spirit by which we can be Saved, than *That of the Lord Jesus Christ*. Again, many of the Followers of *John Wickliff*, would not *Swear in any Case*; and divers also of our *English Martyrs refused to Swear*, upon the same Principle. And if this Man will call to Mind, he may remember, that some of the Best of the *Ancient Fathers* were of the same Judgment; believing it Unlawful for a Christian Man to take an Oath; which in my *Treatise of Oaths* may be seen at large.

Now, for what he alledges, Why Christ's Prohibition, *Mat.* 5. doth not extend to all Oaths, I think it will not be hard to shew it is slight, and concludes nothing against us.

First, He says, the Expression whereby the particular Law is suppos'd to forbid all Oaths, does frequently, in the Law-Books, signifie no more than False Oaths, or Swearing otherwise amiss; as may be seen by comparing *Matth.* 5. 34. with *Levit.* 5. 1. *Eccles.* 9. 2. *Jer.* 23. 10. *Zach* 5. 3. *Hos.* 4. 2. But this is rather against him than for him; since if Christ only forbids what was not Lawful before, his Righteousness rises no higher than that of the Law of *Moses*. But it is plain from the Text, *Mat.* 5. that Christ forbids such Swearing as was Lawful before, and therefore more than the Texts before-mention'd express.

Secondly, Page 64. He limits Christ's Prohibition to those Oaths which had no Sacredness in them, but which the *Pharisees* thought they might make and Violate without Impiety. This also is a meer Conjecture, for which he offers us no Proof; the contrary being evident, as before; for Christ treated of Oaths that were to be perform'd to the Lord, Were they not then Sacred?

But, *Thirdly*, for his Third Particular, it is as unintelligible as his *Gypsie Gibberish* in Page 10. and he must explain it before it can be answerable.

His Fourth Particular is this, *When he divides this Prohibition into it's Parts*, Mat. 5. 35, 36. *He does not divide it as against Swearing in all Cases, but sets the Bounds of his Distribution directly to oppose this corrupt Gloss of the Pharisees; for he doth not say,* Ye have heard that it hath been said, *Ye shall Swear in Truth, in Righteousness and in Judgment*; But I say unto you, Swear not at all; *for so far as concern'd Swearing by God, the* Pharisees *Doctrine was Sound:* But what does Christ say? *Why I say unto you, Swear not all; neither by Heaven, nor by Earth, or Jerusalem, or the Head. Directly contrary to Swearing by the Temple, the Altar, the Heavens, which the* Pharisees *taught to be Lawful to do, and not be bound by such Kind of Oaths.* Which in my Opinion is very Weak and Gross; for if it be plain, as it is, that Christ forbad such Oaths as Men ought not to break, but to perform to the Lord, then it was not such Oaths as the *Pharisees* taught to be Lawful to take, and not be bound by them when they had done. So that he forbids such Oaths, as he says, *The Pharisees Doctrine was Sound in*; because it was what they ought not to break, but perform to the Lord: So that Christ was so far from limiting his Prohibition to the *Pharisees* Oaths, by *Heaven, Earth, Jerusalem*, or the *Head*; which this Man says they made not Obligatory, that he forbids them, by forbidding those Oaths, that according to the Ancient Doctrine of the *Jewish-Law*, Men ought not to break, but perform to the Lord; that as every Major includes it's Minor, so Christ by his Prohibition of the Use of Lawful Oaths, includes the Prohibition of the Practice of Unlawful Oaths.

Page 67. His Fifth Allegation is every Whit as much beside the Matter as what he said before, *viz. That Christ did not condemn Swearing by* Jerusalem, *the Throne, the Foot-Stool*, &c. *Holily, but as Vainly and Unholily used*: Which is to exceed the Bounds of all other Writers; so very heartily does this Man love Swearing. But now I must tell him, that he has much wrested the Text, and perverted the plain and obvious Sense of it, and mis-represented the Mind and Doctrine of the Lord *Jesus Christ*, for it is evident to every considerate Reader, that Christ in that Chapter was not reproving what was Reproveable under the Law; nor was he exhorting his Auditors and Disciples to live up to the Righteousness of it, which was the Way of the Prophets, that were under that Dispensation; but Christ plainly introduces a *New One*; even the Dispensation of the Gospel, the Righteousness of his Kingdom; and that is the Difference between them, as in the Case of *Killing, Adultery*, &c. As well as of Swearing, *Mat.* 5. 21, 22, 27, 28, 33, 34. *Ye have heard that it was said to them of Old Time, thou shalt not Kill; but I say unto you, that whosoever is Angry with his Brother without a Cause, shall be in Danger of the Judgment; Yea, whosoever shall say, Thou Fool, shall be in Danger of Hell-Fire. Ye have heard that it was said, by them of Old Time, Thou shalt not commit Adultery; but I say unto you, That whosoever looketh upon a Woman to Lust after her, hath committed Adultery with her already in his Heart. Again, Ye have heard that it hath been said of Old Time, Thou shalt not Forswear thy self, but shalt perform thy Oaths to the Lord; but I say unto you, Swear not all.* Now I would fain know if Christ's Prohibition goes no farther than *Moses*'s; and, if he does not intend by these Words, *That the Righteousness of the Gospel should exceed that of the Law*: The Parallel runs thus: *Thou shalt not Kill, thou shalt not commit Adultery*, says Moses: *Thou shalt not be Angry, thou shalt not Lust*, says Christ. Now this was no false Gloss of the *Pharisees* in that Time, which Christ reprehended or reformed, as this Adversary would suppose; but a plain Improvement

ment upon the Righteousness of the Law, viz. *Thou shalt not Forswear thy self, but shalt perform to the Lord thine Oaths,* says Moses. *But I say unto you, Swear not all,* says Christ; *neither by Heaven, for it is God's Throne; nor by the Earth, for it is His Footstool; neither by* Jerusalem, *nor thy Head, but let your Communication be Yea, Yea; Nay, Nay; for whatsoever is more than these, cometh of Evil.* Upon which even *Beza* says, That by Forswearing, *We are not to understand a False Oath, but that it is Best not to Swear at all.* And that what Speech is of an higher Nature than this, is too much, and cometh of Evil; and *Tremellius*, out of *Maimonides*, says, *He is the Best Man that will upon no Account Swear.* And the Annotation upon this Place, of a Translation, *Anno* 1599, says, *Whatever ye Vouch, Vouch it barely; and whatsoever ye Deny, Deny it barely, without any more Words;* that is, Let your Affirming and Denying be Simple, and upon the Authority of your own Word and Truth, without going about to bind it by the Authority of a *Greater and Holier Thing,* which is not a Bare and Simple, but a Compounded Speech, and so more than *Yea, Yea*; and *Nay, Nay*; and *therefore cometh of Evil.* To which that Passage of the Apostle *James* aptly refers, *Jam.* 5. 12. *But above all Things my Brethren Swear not, neither by Heaven, nor by Earth, nor by any other Oath*; which is to say, *As by nothing else, so not by God: But let your Yea, be Yea; and Nay, Nay; Lest ye fall into Condemnation.*

One would think this Man had hardly ever read the Bible, to make Oaths so Essential a Part of the *Religion and Kingdom of Christ*; when Christ Himself makes it a Part of the Righteousness of His Kingdom, *Not to Swear at all.* Or is it Candid in him, to limit Christ's Prohibition to the then False Glosses of the *Pharisees,* when Christ looks over their Heads, back to the very *Decalogue,* or *Ten Commandments,* for an Instance, to shew, *by Comparison,* how much the Righteousness of his Kingdom excels that of the Law, that came by *Moses.* I could wish there was no Thing but Weakness to be charged upon this Man, in this Particular; but his Abilities look too considerable elsewhere, for that; as well as his Disingenuity too frequent; not to conclude it of a *Meditated Temperament* to force the Text, rather than not have his Ends upon us: But with what Success he has managed it, We must leave to the *Judicious Reader.*

His APPENDIX about BAPTISM, and the LORDS-SUPPER, (so called) Considered; and the KEY, with the People called *QUAKERS,* Defended; against His Exceptions in those Two Particulars.

OF Baptism he writes thus: *Baptism is a Rite of Admission into the Family of God, making Persons Citizens of Heaven, and Free of the Kingdom of the Messias. It consists of an Outward and Visible Sign, and an Inward Spiritual Grace: These are the Two Parts of the same Baptism, but not Two Baptisms.*

One would think that this Man had never read the *Third of Matthew,* or the *First of the Acts.* For in the first *John* distinguishes his Baptism from Christ's, as plainly as he does his Person (viz.) *I indeed Baptize you with Water to Repentance: But He that cometh after me, is Mightier than I, whose Shoes I am not worthy to bear: He shall Baptize you with the Holy Ghost, and with Fire:* Which shews their Difference in Nature, Excellency and Efficacy. In the last Scripture Christ himself, just before His parting with His Disciples, does very expresly and emphatically distinguish betwixt His own Baptism, and the Baptism of *John:* For, says he, *John truly Baptized with Water, but ye shall be Baptized with the Holy Ghost not many Days hence.* I shall not insist upon the Force of this Place and Context so fully, as by and by, yet nothing can well be plainer, than that Christ's Words imply Two Baptisms, *That the Water was John's, and the Holy Ghost His:* And that his Intention was to leave that Distinction upon the Minds of His People; not only that *John's* and *His* were Two Baptisms, but, *That Water was John's, and not His.* And this too after all, is granted by our Opposer himself, Page 89, where he says, *Can any Man believe that Jesus used John's Baptism, and not His own, in making of Disciples?* But he adds Page 78, *For neither is the Visible Part alone, or the Invisible by it self; but both in Union by the Divine Appointment:* But where this Divine Appointment is, he does not tell us. Again, Page 87. *John did the Outward Part, and Jesus the Inward Part the same Moment.* But surely he is mistaken, when *John* tells us, *The Baptism of the Holy Ghost was to come after,* not *to go along with his:* And Christ told His Disciples, *That it was to come,* (so that His and *John's* went not together) *and bid them stay at* Jerusalem *till they received it,* viz. *The Promise of the Father, which was the Pouring forth of the Holy Ghost;* as the *First Chapter of the Acts* informs us: And that was nigh Three Years after they had been Baptized, and Baptized others with Water: So that both did not go together, as this Man Dreams.

But he proceeds, *Page* 80. *For* John *admitted Men into the Faith of the* Messias; *that is, into the State of Subjects, owing, and acknowledging Allegiance to Christ. And Christ owns this Grant and Admission Valid in His Kingdom, and that they were Legally Instated in the Rights of His Kingdom, whom* John *Baptized: This being done by a Publick Authorized Herald of His Kingdom.*

But it's strange that *John* had the Power to admit Men into the Faith of Him, when at first he sent his Disciples to Him, *To know if He were the* Messiah, *or they were to look for another.* This is to give *John* the *Keys of David,* and to make Regeneration an Absolute and Necessary Adjunct, or Concomitant of his Water-Baptism. But those Baptized by *John's* Baptism, were so far from being admitted into the State of Subjects, and enjoying the Rights of Christ's Kingdom, that in *Acts* 18. *Apollos* is said *to know only* John's *Baptism.* And Chap. 19. Certain Disciples to *John's Baptism,* declared to *Paul, they had not so much as heard if there were any such Thing as the Holy Ghost:* So that when *Paul* askt them, *To what then were you Baptized,* they answered, *To* John's *Baptism,* by Way of Distinction from Christ's. And the Apostle's Question led them to that Answer, being founded upon a Distinction between the Baptism of *John,* and that of *Christ.* And lastly, I must take Leave to wonder how he can think to word upon us so great an Untruth: *As that of Christ's owning an Admission into His Kingdom by* John's *Baptism, and that such are Legally Instated in the Rights thereof,* because they were Baptized of *John,* when Christ himself says, *That the Least in the Kingdom of God, is Greater than* John; which implies, that *John* himself was not of that Kingdom: And because that cannot be understood of the Person, or Soul of *John,* for so he was certainly a Glorious Subject of it, it must refer to his Administration, which, He himself tells us, *Also must Decrease, and Christ's Increase.* Besides, Christ told *Nicodemus, That unless a Man be Born again, he cannot see the Kingdom of God:* How then is he a Subject, and Invested in the Rights of that Kingdom? Again, *Did* John's *Baptism Regenerate?* If it did, *What Need of Fire and Holy Ghost,* that *John* said was to come after? What Need of any Thing after *John's,* if it was so effectual, Or was he always attended with such a Power as is affirmed? Where now is our Adversary's haughty Assertion, *That* John's *Disciples, as such, were the Subjects of Christ's Kingdom, and Legally Invested in the Rights thereof,* when it is plain, that the Least of that Kingdom is Greater than their very *Baptizer,* the *Great Herald of the Kingdom?* But that Expression it self gives away the Cause, being well considered; *For the Forerunner ends in Him He Foreruns; and the Herald in the Presence of the King.* He has forgot sure, who it was that said, or that it was ever said, *The Prophets lasted till* John, and he ended them, but he did not *begin* the Christian Dispensation; that was Christ's Work. *John's Baptism* left Men in that Old World of *Jewish Rites,* where it found them; but 'tis Christ's that makes all Things New; *New Heavens, New Earth,* and *New Creatures, to Inherit them.*

But says this Author, *Christ declares, That being Baptized with Water, was a Part of Righteousness;* Which it could not be, unless there was a Law of the Kingdom for it. As if it might not be Righteousness without such a Law: For with his Favour, *There is as much to be said for Christ's Circumcision, and Eating the Paschal Lamb,* &c. Since that was to *fulfil* all Righteousness too; and yet there was no Law of the Kingdom of Christ for them, unless this be one, *That Christ was to fulfil the Righteousness of the Law,* which He did in General, to introduce the Kingdom of God. For *Christ's fulfilling of the Law and the Prophets,* of which *John* was the *Last,* made Way for the Kingdom to come, *which was not of this World,* nor are it's Rights, by Consequence; but of it's own Nature. That Christ did fulfil all Righteousness, in condescending and conforming to divers Rites, is so far from Ratifying, or Confirming the Practice of them, as this Man suggests, that it Discharges and Abolishes them. This appears very plain, in that Christ's performing of the Rites of the Law, was in Order to end them, *being made under the Law for that very Purpose.* So that *His* being Baptized by *John,* does not Establish, or any more Confirm that Baptism, than His being Circumcised after *Moses* does perpetuate

petuate Circumcision. On the contrary, it rather ends *John's* Baptism. *Moses* and the *Prophets* were 'till *John*, and *John* was till Christ; both had their Times, and both their Periods in Him.

I am not He, says *John*; but *John's* Baptism *is It*, says this Opponent, which is to put *John's* Baptism in the *Room of Christ's*; and *John's* Ministry, tho' not his Person, in Lieu of Christ's. Now *Moses* and the *Prophets* were as the *Stars of the Night*; *John*, as the *Morning Star*, the Forerunner of the Day. He rose last, but Shined most: But tho' the Morning-Star be the most Burning and Shining of all the Cœlestial Lights, and next to the Rising of the Sun himself, yet his Time is shortest, his Light is soon swallowed up of the Sun.

Page 81. But this Man tells us, *That Christ gave Commission to His Disciples to Baptize with Water*, Mat. 28. 19. *And that they did understand it so by their Practice.* But is it practicable, or possible, that any Scripture can reasonably be said to declare an Institution, or be the Commission of any Thing which it does not express? Now in that Text there is not a Word of Water, How then is Water-Baptism Instituted by it? I cannot help wondring, and this Man must allow it me, that the only Text to prove the Commission of so Celebrated a Practice in our Times, should not declare a Word of it. But I shall next shew, notwithstanding he produces following Practice, to prove Christ meant, and his Disciples understood it so, that the Text means it no more than it expresses it; and that Christ, that gave that Commission, never intended it to refer to Water. This is the Text, *Go ye, Teach all Nations, Baptizing them in the Name of the Father, the Son, and Holy Ghost*, Mat. 28. 19. Now Christ by this Commission, must mean His own Baptism of the Spirit, and that from the Nature and Force of the Words, as well as Comparison of them, with other Places to which they relate, and that are also lately Explanatory of them. The Words are not *In* the Name, but *Into* the Name of the Father, &c. Which must refer to the Power and Spirit of Christ; Water being too feeble to *change and wash a Heart*, which is the Import of Baptizing into the Name or Nature of the Father, Son, and Holy Ghost: That is, by the Ministry which is from the Spirit. So *Mark* 16. where Christ saith, *They shall Cast out Devils in my Name*; that is, by my Power, or by the Virtue or Force of my Spirit, which shall attend you for that Work and Service, That many may be turned from the Evil of their Ways, and made Heirs of an endless Kingdom.

In fine, after you have received the Spirit, you shall Teach and Baptize, or Dip, Plunge, and Interest them that Believe, into the Name and Power of God, unto Holiness, Righteousness, Mercy, Truth, &c. Qualifying them to bear the Holy and Excellent Name of Father, Son, and Holy Ghost.

And that this is not strained, but Natural, and no *Allegory* upon the Text, I shall desire my *Reader* to look forward, to the First of the *Acts*, and the First Nine Verses; which plainly expounds this Commission, and consequently resolves us what Baptism it refers to; particularly the 4th, 5th, 8th, and 9th Verses, *viz. And being assembled together with them, commanded them that they should not depart from Jerusalem, but wait for the Promise of the Father, which, saith he, ye have heard of me. For John truly Baptized with Water; but ye shall be Baptized with the Holy Ghost, not many Days hence. But ye shall receive Power after that the Holy Ghost is come upon you: And ye shall be Witnesses unto me, both in Jerusalem, and in all Judea, and in Samaria, and unto the uttermost Parts of the Earth. And when He had spoken these Things, while they beheld, He was taken up, and a Cloud received Him out of their Sight.*

In which Three Things are observable: *First*, That Christ *Distinguishes* his Baptism from *John's*. *Secondly*, That He assigns *Water to John's*, and the *Holy Ghost* to His own Baptism. Not that *John* and He had *Two Water-Baptisms*, yet *Two Baptisms*, but that *John's* was the Water-Baptism, and His the Baptism of the Holy Ghost. Therefore His is not a Water-Baptism, but a Baptism contradistinguished from that of Water, as much as the Person of *John* was from the Person of Christ.

Thirdly, by comparing the 28th of *Matthew* with this Place in the *Acts*, we may see that the Commission in one, is to be construed by the Qualification in the other, which is not exprest at all in *Mat.* 28. There they are bid *To Go*; here they are bid *To Stay*; that is, *Stay before you go, and have your Qualifications before you Qualify*; viz. *The Promise of the Father*, to wit, *The Baptism of the Holy Ghost*; that is to say, *Power from on High*. Why, Had they been Preaching two or three Years, and been Baptized, and Baptizing with Water, that this Man says is followed, *That Moment*, with the Baptism of the Holy Ghost, and yet had not been themselves Baptized with it, nor as yet received Power from on High to *Disciple and Baptize* any into Christ's Kingdom, with Christ's Baptism? This must be strange to our Opponent, and who can help it? But so it is, Reader. For that as one *Evangelist*, and one Part of Scripture, supplies and explains another, this in the *Acts* shews, that the Commission in *Matthew*, supposes the Qualification, mentioned in the First of the *Acts*, to precede it; else they were to go, before they were Qualified to Perform. If then it is Rational to suppose, that what past at *Christ's Farewel*, as rehearst by the *Evangelists*, should be all laid together, for our more plain and compleat Understanding of the Import of it, we must needs conclude, That the Disciples were to stay at *Jerusalem*, till they had received the *Promise of the Father*; that is, till they were *Baptized with the Holy Ghost*; and then the Commission took Place, for them to *Go and Teach all Nations, Baptizing them in the Name of the Father, Son, and Holy Ghost*. Now then, if in Order of Time, and from the Nature of the Discourse, it must be so, How is the Baptism in *Matthew* a Water-Baptism? *John truly Baptized with Water, but ye shall be Baptized with the Holy Ghost not many Days hence: Then Go ye, Teach all Nations, Baptizing them in the Name of the Father, Son, and Holy Ghost*, &c. It is plain, this is the True Order of the Discourse, not only from what I have already said, as to Qualification *preceding* Commission (for they needed no such to Baptize with Water, having done that Two or Three Years before, without it) But for that Baptizing stands *alone* in *Mat.* 28. 19. which would have been Ambiguous, had not that Passage in *Acts* 1. 5. preceded, which made it needless to tell us what Sort of Baptism they were to Baptize with, and what they were not; *For* John *truly Baptized with Water, but ye shall be Baptized with the Holy Ghost not many Days hence:* Therefore not with *John's Baptism any more*, but with the *Baptism of the Spirit*, Do you *Go Teach all Nations, Baptizing them through the Holy Spirit, into the Name of the Father, of the Son, and Holy Ghost:* Make them *True Jews, True Israelites,* in whom there is no Guile. And 'tis certain it was a New Scene and Part they had to Act; as much Superior to what was before, as Form is to Power, *Letter to Spirit, Shadow to Substance. Greater Things than these shall ye do,* said our Blessed Lord, *because I go to my Father.* I think I have not strained the Text, or extorted a wrong Meaning. I write what I believe, and take to be the Genuine Sense of the Place, without Partiality, or Passion. But our Adversary will have it, that the Apostles used *Water-Baptism*, in pursuance of this Commission; and instances the Words of *Peter*, in the Case of *Cornelius*, for Proof thereof. The Words are these, *Can any Man forbid Water, that these should not be Baptized, which have received the Holy Ghost, as well as we?* Upon which says our Opponent, pag. 82. *If it had not been an Ordinance, any one might have forbid it; therefore the Apostles accounted themselves obliged by God to do so; and that it was not in their Power to refuse it, unless they would resist God.* To which I say, as before: *First*, That Water-Baptism was *John's*, and not Christ's. *Secondly*, That Practice is no Institution. *Thirdly*, That the Apostle *Peter* did but continue a Practice, introduced by *John*, not easily left among a Ceremonious People, it having obtained Reputation among them, and was the Discriminating Sign, or Mark, of a Change of Dispensation at Hand; and this *Peter* could not but know, after those Distinguishing and Emphatical Words of His Lord and Master, *Acts the First*. But the Disciples having before been actually engaged in the Practice of *John's Baptism*, in order to call People to the Expectation of a farther Thing, continued it afterwards; not of Authority, but in their Christian Liberty and Condescension, as what had a Reference to the Christian Dispensation; inasmuch as *John*, whose Ministry concluded the Prophets, became herein the Forerunner of Christ, *whose Kingdom* John said, *was at Hand*, and the more Excellent Dispensation thereof. *Lastly*, The Reason of *Peter's* Words, *Can any Man forbid Water*, &c. referred not to the *Institution, Authority*, or *Force of Water-Baptism*, but to *Peter's* Caution about *Cornelius*, that was a *Gentile*, for fear he should give any publick Distaste to the *Jews*, whose Prejudices against the *Gentiles*, like some *Predestinarians* of our Times, excluded them any Pretence to Religion; insomuch that we see *Peter* himself, without a Vision, was not yet large enough in his Spirit, to credit *Cornelius's* Convictions and Devotion; as much as if he had said, *Why may not this Man, though a* Gentile, *be Baptized with Water, since he has received the* Holy Ghost, *which is the requisite Qualification of a True Christian; and that the Promise of the Father is to them that are afar off, even to all that the Lord our God shall call, as well as to the Seed of* Abraham,

Abraham, after the Flesh. So that the Reason of *Peter's* using those Words, was not to give Authority to *Water-Baptism*, as an Ordinance of Christ's Kingdom, but to excuse himself against *Jewish Exceptions*, that he feared would be scandalized at his owning of a *Gentile*, which, to them, was *Unclean*, *Prophane* and *Reprobate*.

His other Scripture in Defence of what he asserts, is *Acts* 9. 18. which says, *That Paul received his Sight, and was Baptized by* Ananias. But not a Word of *Water*, is in the Text, or the foregoing, or following Verses. On the contrary, there is Reason to believe it was not meant. *And Ananias putting his Hands on him,* said, *Brother Saul, the Lord, (even JESUS that appeared unto thee in the Way as thou camest) hath sent me, that thou mayst receive thy Sight, and be filled with the Holy Ghost ; and immediately there fell from his Eyes, as it had been Scales, and he received his Sight forthwith, and arose and was Baptized.* Now here is, first, *Sight* and *Holy Ghost*, to be given to *Saul*, by the Ministry of *Ananias*: Next, he received *Sight*, and was *Baptized*. Now must not this be the Baptism of the *Holy Ghost*, since being fill'd with the Holy Ghost, and being Baptized, are, by the Text, *Made One and the same Thing* ? Especially since it is past all Controversy, That there was such a Thing as the Baptism of the Holy Ghost.

His other Scripture, to prove the Authority of Water-Baptism, among Christians, is, *Acts* 11. 15, 16, 17. *And as I began to speak, the Holy Ghost fell on them, as on us at the Beginning. Then remembred I the Word of the Lord, how that He said,* John *indeed Baptized with* Water, *but you shall be Baptized with the* Holy Ghost. *Forasmuch then as God gave them the like Gift, as He did unto us, who believed on the Lord Jesus Christ, What was I that I could resist God?*

Which is so far from weakening, that it confirms our Sense and Assertion: For the Bent of *Peter's* Words is to justify himself, in going to, and communing with the *Uncircumcision*, and not to vindicate Water-Baptism. And that which he offer'd in his own Vindication to his Brethren, was, 1. His Vision. 2. *Cornelius's* Righteousness and Devotion. And, 3. God's owning of him, *in that the Holy Ghost fell upon him, as it had upon them in the Beginning. Forasmuch then*, says Peter, *as God gave them the like Gift, What was I that I could withstand God?* As if he had said, How could I refuse to own them, and have Fellowship with them that God own'd, and had Fellowship with, and Gifted and Sanctified, as well as the *Believing Jews?* Speaking not one Word, in his Account to the Brethren, of *Water-Baptism*: But, on the contrary, he makes it *John's* Way of Distinction from Christ's Baptism, by remembring and repeating the Words of His Lord and Master, viz. John *indeed Baptized with* Water, *but ye shall be Baptized with the* Holy Ghost. I appeal to every indifferent Reader, if I have not done Justice to the Text.

I shall next consider his Exceptions to what I say in my *Key*, in Defence of our Disuse, or Cessation, of *Water-Baptism*, &c.

Page 83, 84. The first Reason he makes me give for it, is, *That all Protestants are against Figures and Shadows*. To which he answers, *But* Baptism *and the* Lord's Supper, *being no Figures nor Shadows, all Protestants are for them; unless the* Quakers *are to be accounted Protestants, that disown all Protestant Churches, and are own'd by none.* This is all he quotes of mine, and this is what he says, on what he has quoted: So that they may be of the Nature of *Shadows* and *Figures* for all him; and consequently *Protestants* practise against Judgment. For he only denies them to be *Figures and Shadows*, and leaves us there. But he had done well, if he had given us his Reasons, and had also taken Notice of what I say, page 22 in *My Key*, which immediately foregoes what he has cited out of it ; viz. *That Practice only is no Institution*; and that is all he can alledge in Favour of *John's* Baptism. That which seems my Part to perform, tho' he presses it not upon me, is to shew, That *Water Baptism*, and the *Lord's-Supper* (so called) are of the Nature of *Figures and Shadows*, of which Christ was the Substance.

Now, that they are so, we must consider, That if Christ was the End of *John*, as *John* renders him, *Mat.* 3. 11. *John* 3. 30. and Christ himself suggests to us, *Mat.* 11. 7. to 12. then *Water-Baptism* was but a *Forerunner*, and shewed forth what was to come, *that which the Least in the Kingdom of Heaven exceeded*, and therefore not of the Kingdom, and consequently of no longer Force in Point of Institution. Tho' by being the *Observation* peculiar to *John's* Ministry, it had obtained Credit, and therefore was continued, *Ex Gratiâ*. But it is plain from Christ's own Words, *The Kingdom of God came not with Observation*, Luke 17. 20. At least therefore *Protestants* ought to be Modest upon us, with Respect to the Reason we render for our *Cessation of Water-Baptism*. And tho' he says, *We ought*

5 N   *not*

not to be accounted Protestants, *that disown all* Protestant Churches, *and are owned by none of them:* I would have this Author to know, We are *True Protestants: Protestants* upon those Reasons, that were the first *Motives* to that *Character*; and can compare, in our *Negatives*, with any Species of *Protestants*. And do challenge this Author, without Vanity, upon that *Head*, begin when he Will.

At the same Time, we cannot but have Charity for the Persons of *Roman Catholicks*, and would by that teach them the Truth and greater Excellency of our Religion.

And next, for our *disowning* of all other Protestant Churches, and *not being owned* by them; first, it is not upon the same Grounds that the *Roman Catholicks* disown them: And, secondly, Experience tells us, It is what *all Sorts of Protestants do to one another*; and therefore not so singular in us, as is suggested by this ill-willing Author.

But, he is mightily displeased with me, *For being against all Figures in the Time of the Gospel*; adding, *That we Mortals cannot think, or speak, or work without Figures*; distinguishing between *prenunciative and commemorative Signs*: Ridiculing me for such an Assertion. But if my Reader will turn to Page 24. of my *Key*, cited by this Author, he will find, I *only* deny, under the Gospel, the *Necessity and Service* of *prenunciative* or *forerunning Signs*; Joyning to Signs, Figures and Shadows; and promiscuously using them to one and the same Purpose, and therefore not all Signs, but Signs of something to come, and to be accomplish'd by the Coming thereof; as the following Words, he makes another Quibble upon, plainly shew; viz. *That the Nature of the Gospel is Inward, Spiritual and Eternal*. But he leaves out, *That therefore the continuing to practise Figures, Signs and Shadows, as still in Force, which forerun Christ and his Dispensation, make his Coming of none Effect*. For then he had given too strong a Reason for our Disuse, and disappointed himself of the unfair Advantage he endeavours to gain upon me, by letting his Reader see that I did not deny the Continuance of all Signs, but *prenunciative* or *forerunning Ones*: Such as are of the Nature of *Figures* and *Shadows*, and therefore can have no Commission to perpetuate them; of which I take *Water-Baptism* and the *Supper* to be two. For *Christ* as well as *John*, declares *Water-Baptism* a *Forerunner* of a more excellent Baptism. And one Thing wherein that Excellency of *Christ's Baptism* consists, is the durableness of it: But if *John's* is to last as long as *Christ's*, *Christ's* does not excel *John's* in Duration; quite contrary to *John's* own Discrimination and Testimony, viz. *He* (Christ) *shall increase and I decrease:* But if it be considered, that this Adversary would make me deny all Signs, as *Exodus* 7. 8. 9. *Numb.* 11. *Psal.* 77. *Jer.* 32. Just as his Friend *J. Faldo*, and some of that Ingenuity, have made us to deny all Scripture Commands, because some of us have said, in *Temporary* and *Extraordinary Cases* (as that of *Jeremiah, Jonas, Amos*, &c.) *That which is a Command to another is no Command to us, unless the same Spirit require the same, or the like Thing of us*; therefore *the Moral Law or Decalogue is no Law or Command to us, nor are we obliged to yield Obedience to it, tho' it be general and perpetual.* I say, they that consider the Justice of my Parallel, and Injustice of his Insinuation, will perceive he is not a fair Enemy, nor ought to have Credit with his Reader, to our Prejudice.

I am then no more against *Figures* than against *Forms*. We cannot, I know, live, speak or act without them: *But these are not forerunning Signs or Forms, Temporary and Shadowy Observations:* But such necessary and essential ones, as are coupl'd to our very being, and requisite Converse among Men.

But from this he falls hard upon me, because I say the Gospel is *Inward, Spiritual and Eternal:* For, says he, *without many Figures, this is not Sense, and with them, is either not true, or not to the Purpose. The Gospel being the new Covenant, is neither Inward nor Outward. Will* W. P. *never leave talking of Inside and Outside of Things that have no Sides?* This Language. I doubt not, will sound harsh, as well as light, to other People's Ears, as well as ours: And truly he is a daring and an adventurous Person, for till now I thought Truth had an Inside; if he had read the 31*st* of *Jeremiah*, he would have found there, that the Gospel is an inward State, and has an Inside; where God, speaking by that Prophet, of the Gospel, or New Covenant Time, says, *Behold, the Days come that I will make a new Covenant with the House of Israel, and with the House of Judah: Not according to the Covenant that I made with their Fathers in the Day that I took them by the Hand, to bring them out of the Land of Egypt (which my Covenant they brake, although I was an Husband unto them, saith the Lord) But this shall be the Covenant that I will make*

make with the House of Israel, After those Days, saith the Lord, I will put my Law in their inward Parts, and write it in their Hearts, and will be their God, and they shall be my People. And they shall teach no more every Man his Neighbour, and every Man his Brother, saying, know the Lord: For they shall all know me, from the Least of them to the Greatest of them, saith the Lord: For I will forgive their Iniquity, and I will remember their Sin no more. Now here is Truth with *both* it's *Sides*: Truth in it's outward Appearance, according to the low and carnal State of Man: And this may be call'd comparatively, the *Out-Side* of *Truth*. Here also we may learn, that Truth has an *Inside*; a more Spiritual and Eternal Part; and that is what I call the *Gospel-Dispensation*: Or that this more Inward and Spiritual Appearance of the Truth, is the New-Covenant or Gospel. What else did our Lord Jesus intend by the *Gospel of the Kingdom*, than the Blessing of the *Power of God*, to deliver Man from the Power of Sin and Satan, the Original of it? So the Apostle phrases it, *The Gospel is the Power of God to Salvation.* That is, the Power of the Kingdom of God, and that is the Gospel of the Kingdom. Now if this be not of an *Inward*, *Spiritual* and *Eternal* Nature, nothing can be: Which I presume, the *Reader* will, with me, think an absurd as well as unchristian Conclusion.

But he says, It is *partly Inward and partly Outward*. I say, it is Inward, but it may be Outwardly exprest by a Godly Conversation; and so far, and no otherwise, it may be said to be outward. Nor does this weaken my Assertion, or the Consequence I have observed from it; *viz.* That the Gospel, and New Covenant, came not with *Outward Observations*; and that *Water-Baptism* was such; *Therefore no Ordinance of the Kingdom of the Messiah.*

But if it be an Ordinance, as this Author says, *p.* 87. and that the Inward Part *keeps Time* with the Outward (for there he allows of *Inside* and *Outside*) then it would do so to as many as have the outward Part administred to them: But we have no Evidence of such Concurrence of the Holy Ghost. We have never found it in our selves, nor do we see it in others, that are in the Practice of it, but much the contrary; in that *Envy, Pride, Luxury and Covetousness prevail*, and little of the true Cross of Christ, Self-Denial, Dying dayly, or the New Creature appears: How then does the inward Grace make up but one Baptism, if it accompany not Water? But of that I have already treated before; and, it is plain, 'tis but *Gratis Dictum* on our Adversary's Side. He begs the Question.

Lastly, *p.* 90. finding himself a-ground about the Passage of the Apostle *Paul*, 1 *Cor.* 1. 7. *For Christ sent me not to Baptize but to preach the Gospel.* He endeavours to gloss away it's Force, what he can, from the End for which I cited it, and the Apostle writ it. The first Thing he opposes is, *That since Water-Baptism, was* Peter's *and his Brethren's Commission, which Christ gave them before his Ascension, to the End of the World— It is not to be imagined that* Matthias *and* Paul *were without it.* But in this also he begs the Question.

I have already shew'd that Commission is mistaken by him, and that Water is no Ways concern'd in that Text; and that *Water-Baptism* was *John's* and not Christ's; and that they were not one *Baptism*, or inseparable in their Administration. Also, that *Practice* is no *Institution*, and that *Water-Baptism* is a *prenunciative* Sign, and has it's Accomplishment in that *Baptism* of the Holy Ghost, as *John* had in *Christ*; *the two Administrators of the two Baptisms.*

But next, he says, *Paul spoke an Ellipsis, elegantly; meaning, that he was not sent only to Baptize, but chiefly to Preach*; citing two or three Scriptures, that he imagines Parallel, and illustrating that Place, as *Hos.* 6. 6. *I will have Mercy and not sacrifice.* And, *let Women adorn themselves, not with putting on Apparel*, &c. 1 Pet. 3. 34. Now, says he, *These Places prove, that the* Israelites *were not to sacrifice to God, and Women must go naked*, &c. (as some Quakers did) *with the same Evidence that* Paul's *Words teach, That Christ sent him not to Baptize.* He might, if he had pleased, have cut it all short, and like what L *Muggleton* once said of *Moses*, have told us, *Paul* did not mean what he writ. But these Places are ill apply'd by this Man, for when God said, *He would have Mercy and not Sacrifice*, he meant not to have Sacrifice at that Time, and in those Cases, wherein he called for Mercy. He would not be so put off, nor have Duties exchanged: That Speech is limited to, and to be interpreted by the present State of the People he spoke to, who were unqualified for Sacrifice, because they were unmerciful and cruel, and the merciful God in that State would have none of their Sacrifices. What is this to the Apostle's Words about *Baptism*, that denies it any Part in his Commission? There is no Parallel in the Case, but if any, it is for us rather than against us; for that of not putting on of Apparel, it is evident, for so the Apostle intended by "Ἐνδύσεως Ἱματίων κόσμῳ, as the Words themselves plainly import, viz. Garments of *Finery and Ornament*, and not useful Clothing.

So that the Apostle meant what he said in the Use of the Word, for such Apparel is not to be ever used by true Christians.

For his saying, that some of our Women have gone naked, 'tis affirmed with Lightness, tho' some few of our Friends have gone naked, for a Sign to this Generation, in Token of God's *stripping* some Persecutors of their Power, and in particular that Generation of the Clergy, that preceded the Restoration, which having risen through Persecution, forgat their Pleas, when they had Power, towards those that dissented from them, and testified against the same Evils in them, that they had justly inveighed against in the former Bishops Days. And now he may see we are not against all SIGNS.

To conclude: It is plain, the Apostle had no Obligation upon him to this Expression, from a Comparison any had made between Water-Baptism and the Preaching of the Gospel. Nor does he use any, tho' this Man makes him to do so, to justify his imagined Elegancy. The Occasion of this Expression, the Text shews, was the Vanity of some Disciples, that were comparing and boasting of their *Baptizers*; not a Word of Baptism it self, to over or undervalue that Tradition. Why then does *Paul* take Occasion, not only to knock them, but *Baptism* too? What had *Baptism* done to be so coursely treated? So Sacred an Institution; the very Rite or Door of Admission (says this Man) into the Kingdom of the *Messiah*, p. 80. Why, without Doubt, it was to let them see, that they had so little Cause to boast of their respective Baptizers, *(for who is* Paul, *and who is* Apollos*)* that they ought not to value themselves upon that very *Baptism*, since it was not what he had in Commission, but what he had used as a Tradition, that had obtined some Credit among them: Else the Apostle must not have had the same Commission that the other Apostles had, who yet said, he was behind none of the rest of the Apostles.

Again, Baptizing, in *Matth.* 28. 19. was as much the Apostle's Commission as Teaching or Preaching: Nay, the preferable Part. For though Preaching opened their Understandings, it was *Baptism* that gave them *Admission into the Kingdom of the* Messiah; made them Subjects thereof; and instated them in the Rights of it: Yea, the Seal of the Covenant that God made by Christ with Mankind, without which no Remission of Sins, or entring of God's Kingdom. Can such a *Baptism* (and such an one this Adversary renders *Water-Baptism*) be no essential Part of *Paul's* Commission, or not upon equal Terms with Teaching, when by it People are to be interested in the Sacred Name of *Father, Son and Holy Ghost*; that is, to be made, qualified, admitted and sealed *True Christians, Subjects of Christ's Kingdom, Citizens of Heaven*, and endowed with *all the Privileges thereof*. How little is this Man willing to allow *Baptism* to be, that he may keep it any Thing in Force, and excuse it from the genuine Sense of the Apostle's Words? Were there as much Difference between Preaching and Baptism, as between Mercy and Sacrifice, it might have helpt him better. But in as much as the Apostle denies *Water-Baptism* to be in his Commission, and that it is certain he had the same Commission the rest had, whatever was his Practice, in Condescension (as in *circumcising* of *Timothy*) that *Baptism* that is indeed in Christ's Commission, *Matth.* 28. must be the *Baptism* of the *Holy Ghost*. And this is the less to be doubted, since the same Apostle that denies *Water-Baptism* any Place in his Commission (which he could never, *If an Ordinance of Christ, and the Right of Admission into the Kingdom of the Messiah*) makes *Baptism* an Article in his *Epitome* of *Christianity, viz.* That there is *(Eph.* 4. 5, 6.*) One Lord, One Faith, One Baptism: One God and Father of all, who is above all, and through all, and in you all*. This *Baptism* being therefore Essential, must be that of his Commission, and consequently the *Baptism* of the *Holy Ghost, Acts* 1. 15.

But, after all, I know not what Right this Man has to argue upon the Head of *Water-Baptism* against us; since, if I mistake him not, he is of those that make Children the Subjects of that Practice, who cannot believe, nor be taught in order to it; and therefore not within the Scope and Direction of the Text. If it should be said, That Children may be as well *Baptized* as *Circumcised*; I say, no: For Faith was not so personally required to Circumcision as it is to *Baptism*: Nor are the *Covenants* or *Kingdoms* the same, to which they refer, therefore an improper and unjust Allusion. Upon the whole Matter, we let fall the *Baptism* of *Water*, as *John*'s, and not *Christ*'s; therefore, not in Contempt of a *Christian Ordinance*, the Lord knows, but in Honour of the *Christian Dispensation*: And the rather, because of the great Abuse of it, both *Sprinklers* and *Dippers* laying, as we apprehend, a dangerous *Stress* upon it: As indeed they do upon the Use of the *Lord's-Supper*; far beyond Signs, and as if they were the inward Graces themselves: too often referring thither, rather than to the *Obedience* of *Faith* in *Christ*; and falsely quieting their uneasy *Minds* under *Disobedience* and *Neglect of the Cross of Jesus*, with the *Performance of these Outward Signs* of *Inward Graces*, the Generality of them being but too barren of any true Sign of the Power of Grace upon them. But to that Little he has said about the *Lord's-Supper*, so called, I must say something before I close this *Treatise*. He tells us,

Page 92. *The same, in Substance, may be said of the Lord's Supper as of Baptism.*

Reply. Then the same, in Substance, may serve in Defence of the other He adds,

Christ celebrates it with his Disciples, signifying, That his Meaning was, they should perform this Service at other Times, after his Death, by constraining them to do it in Remembrance of him, which is a full Institution of this Service.

Reply. That which Christ celebrated was the *Paschal Lamb*, or *Passover*, which he told his Disciples he so much longed to eat with them. And this was the Jews great *Anniversary Supper*, in Commemoration of their Fore-Fathers mighty Deliverance from *Pharoah*, and passing at Night out of *Egypt*, towards the Land that God had promised their Father *Abraham*, he would give to his Off-spring. And it was also the Conclusion or winding up of the Course of our Saviour's Life; the fulfilling of the Shadowy Ordinances and Ministration he was born under (he being the Antitype); at the Close of which he was graciously pleased to intimate to them, that unwelcome and uneasy News of his Departure and Death, by bidding them eat that Bread, and drink that Cup, and so do the like, as a *Memorial, or in Remembrance of him*, viz. his *Death, 'till he came to them again*.

He did thereby,

I. Inform them of his Departure and Death, by giving them a Memorial of him, which was so hard for them to think of.

II. He tells them, That he will not leave them Comfortless, he will come to them again, and he will drink New Wine with them in the Kingdom of his Father, which, in it's due Season, should be made manifest to them.

III. That they were to look to that Coming, as an Accomplishment of that Memorial.

IV. That this must refer to his Spiritual Coming, as the Bread of Life; and that it was only to hold them up in their Minority, whose Weakness, Incredulity, and Doubting, were well known to him, and which, *Luke* 24. 11, 25. are enough observed; even after all they had heard and seen of the Power of Christ.

That this Practice lasted longer, I grant, but that it lasted of Authority, I find not, but rather of Weakness: Signs generally have a Resemblance of the Things they signifie or represent: There seems none in any other Respect to me, so proper and suitable, as of Christ being the *Bread that came down from Heaven*, John 6. and as such he came to his Disciples some Time after his Ascension, for as yet they were, as before observed, in several Respects, Weak, yea, Carnal, and to be stirred up and instructed in Sacred Mysteries by Outward and Sensible Things.

Page 93. As to what this Author says, *That the Apostle* Paul *had a Commission to administer this Sacrament*, 1 Cor. 11. to 26. It is his Mistake; for it was not a Commission but a Tradition. He tells us what he received of the Lord's Doings; but neither commands nor recommends it, only reproves Indecency, and requires more Respect in performing, *as often as they do it*. But if that Chapter be well read, the poor and mean Condition of the People he writ to, will be seen, to whom Signs, well understood, might be of Benefit. But that neither proves their Continuance under the New Covenant, nor their Service to those that were come to discern well the Lord's Body; what it is, and what it is made of, as Chapter 10. 15, 16, 17.

Page 94, 95. But our Adversary will have it, *That Christ's Coming is to Judgment*, at the End of all Things, and 'till then, this Sacrament, as he calls it, is to continue: Telling me, That when Christ said, he would not drink any more of the Fruit of the Vine, 'till he should drink it new, with them, in the Kingdom of his Father, Christ indeed means it of a Spiritual Wine, *but that the Kingdom of his Father*

Father was Heaven, and therefore the Sign was not to ceafe 'till that Kingdom began, which was not to be, *till Chrift had delivered up the Kingdom unto God, even his Father, at the End of the World.*

Reply. But he has forgot, furely, that in the fame *Page* he allows the Kingdom of God was then, among the Jews, tho' not in them, and fo come before the End of the World. And if he would have called to Mind the firft Sentence of *John the Baptift*'s Sermon, and the Drift of the Difciples Miniftry, that Chrift fent forth, he muft have found that at was, *Repent, for the Kingdom of God, or of Heaven, is at Hand*, as *Matth.* 3. 2. ch. 10. 7, Then not fo far off as the End of the World. Again, the Apoftle declared, *Heb.* 12. 22, 23, 24, the true Believers of his Day were *come to Mount Zion, God, the Judge of all, and to the Spirits of the Juft made perfect*; and alfo that they *fat in heavenly Places in Chrift Jefus*, which muft be an Attainment above Signs of invifible Grace; being the Life and Subftance of Religion, and fo the Period and Confummation of Types, Shadows, and fuch Sort of Signs or Significations as are in queftion. They that perfonally enjoy their deareft Friends will not repair to their *Pictures*, tho' drawn never fo much to the Life, to quicken their Remembrance of them. Chrift did promife his, That he would *come again, he would not leave them Comfortlefs*, and that he would drink of the Cup or Fruit of the Vine *after a new, or other Mannner* with them, even *in the Kingdom of his Father*. And in the *Revelations*, Chap. 3. he makes an Holy Proclamation, as it were with an *O Yes! Behold*, fays he, *I ftand at the Door and knock; if any Man hear my Voice and open the Door, I will come in to him, and SUP with him, and he with me*. This, we are not afhamed to fay, is our Supper, or the Supper of the Rifen and Glorified *Jefus*, which the People called *Quakers* do acknowledge, profefs and practice as the *Lord's Supper*; the *True Gofpel, New Covenant* Supper: The Supper *of and in the Kingdom of God*; which is come up in Thoufands, bleffed be his Name, and is coming more and more among, and in the Hearts of the Children of Men. And tho' the Seed of this Kingdom be fown in all, yet the good Ground alone knows it to grow to Advantage. Thofe that *obey* the Manifeftation of the Light of the Lord Jefus in their Souls, the *Seed of the Kingdom*, are the true and fenfible Witneffes of it: The Government of their Hearts and Affections being upon his Shoulders, according to that bleffed Promife, *Ifaiah* 9. 5, 6, 7. And fuch as can fay, *Thy Kingdom is come, and thy will is done, in Earth as it is in Heaven*. Even fo come, Lord Jefus, more and more fet up thy Kingdom in the Souls of the Children of Men; that the Holy Will of thy Father may be done in Earth, that Mercy, and Truth, and Righteoufnefs, and Peace, may embrace and kifs each other, fo fhall the Kingdoms of this World become the Kingdoms of the Lord, and of his Chrift, who is God over all bleffed for ever.

An ESSAY towards the *Prefent* and *Future* Peace of *Europe*, by the Eftablifhment of an *European* DYET, PARLIAMENT, or ESTATES.

Beati Pacifici.   *Cedant Arma Togæ.*

To the READER.

Reader,

I HAVE *undertaken a Subject that I am very fenfible requires one of more fufficiency than I am Mafter of to treat it, as, in Truth, it deferves, and the groaning State of* Europe *calls for; but fince Bunglers may ftumble upon the Game, as well as Mafters, though it belongs to the Skilful to hunt and catch it, I hope this Effay will not be charged upon me for a Fault, if it appear to be neither Chimerical*

nor

nor *Injurious*, and *may provoke abler Pens to improve and perform the Design with better Judgment and Success*. I will say no more in Excuse of my self, for this Undertaking, but that it is the Fruit of my solicitous Thoughts, for the Peace of Europe, and they must want Charity as much as the World needs Quiet, to be offended with me for so Pacifick a Proposal. Let them censure my Management so they prosecute the Advantage of the Design; for 'till the Millenary Doctrine be accomplished, there is nothing appears to me so beneficial an Expedient to the Peace and Happiness of this Quarter of the World.

An ESSAY towards the Present and Future PEACE of EUROPE, &c.

Sect. I. *Of PEACE, and it's Advantages.*

HE must not be a Man, but a Statue of Brass or Stone, whose Bowels do not melt when he beholds the bloody *Tragedies* of this War, in *Hungary, Germany, Flanders, Ireland*, and at Sea. The Mortality of sickly and languishing Camps and Navies, and the mighty Prey the Devouring Winds and Waves have made upon Ships and Men since 88. And as this with Reason ought to affect human Nature, and deeply Kindred, so there is something very moving that becomes prudent Men to consider, and that is the vast Charge that has accompanied that Blood, and which makes no mean Part of these *Tragedies*; Especially if they deliberate upon the uncertainty of the War, that they know not how or when it will end, and that the Expence cannot be less, and the Hazard is as great as before. So that in the Contraries of Peace we see the Beauties and Benefits of it; which under it, such is the Unhappiness of Mankind, we are too apt to nauseate, as the full Stomach loaths the Honey-Comb; and like that unfortunate Gentleman, that having a fine and a good Woman to his Wife, and searching his Pleasure in forbidden and less agreeable Company, said, when reproach'd with his Neglect of better Enjoyments, *That he could love his Wife of all Women, if she were not his Wife*, tho' that increased his Obligation to prefer her. It is a great Mark of the Corruption of our Natures, and what ought to humble us extremely, and excite the Exercise of our Reason to a nobler and juster Sense, that we cannot see the Use and Pleasure of our Comforts but by the Want of them. As if we could not taste the Benefit of Health, but by the Help of Sickness; nor understand the Satisfaction of Fulness without the Instruction of Want; nor, finally, know the Comfort of Peace but by the Smart and Penance of the Vices of War: And without Dispute that is not the least Reason that God is pleased to Chastise us so frequently with it. What can we desire better than *Peace*, but the *Grace* to use it? *Peace* preserves our Possessions; We are in no Danger of Invasions: Our Trade is free and safe, and we rise and lye down without Anxiety. The Rich bring out their Hoards, and employ the poor Manufacturers: Buildings and divers Projections, for Profit and Pleasure, go on: It excites Industry, which brings Wealth, as that gives the Means of Charity and Hospitality, not the lowest Ornaments of a Kingdom or Commonwealth. But War, like the Frost of 83, seizes all these Comforts at once, and stops the civil Channel of Society. The Rich draw in their Stock, the Poor turn Soldiers, or Thieves, or Starve: No Industry, no Building, no Manufactury, little Hospitality or Charity; but what the Peace gave, the War devours. I need say no more upon this Head, when the Advantages of Peace, and Mischiefs of War are so many and sensible to every Capacity under all Governments, as either of them prevails. I shall proceed to the next Point. *What is the best Means of Peace*, which will conduce much to open my Way to what I have to propose.

Sect. II. *Of the Means of Peace, which is* Justice *rather than War.*

AS *Justice* is a Preserver, so it is a better Procurer of *Peace* than War. Tho' *Pax quæritur bello*, be an usual Saying, *Peace is the End of War*, and as such it was taken up by O. C. for his Motto: Yet the Use generally made of that expression shews us, that properly and truly speaking, Men seek their Wills by *War* rather

rather than Peace, and that as they will violate it to obtain them, so they will hardly be brought to think of Peace, unless their Appetites be some Way gratified. If we look over the Stories of all Times, we shall find the Aggressors generally moved by Ambition; the Pride of Conquest and Greatness of Dominion more than Right. But as those *Leviathans* appear rarely in the World, so I shall anon endeavour to make it evident they had never been able to devour the Peace of the World, and ingross whole Countries as they have done, if the *Proposal* I have to make for the Benefit of our present Age had been then in Practice. The Advantage that Justice has upon War is seen by the Success of *Embassies*, that, so often prevent War by hearing the *Pleas* and *Memorials* of *Justice* in the Hands and Mouths of the *Wronged Party*. Perhaps it may be in a good Degree owing to *Reputation* or *Poverty*, or some particular *Interest* or *Conveniency* of *Princes* and *States*, as much as *Justice*; but it is certain, that as War cannot in any Sense be justified, but upon Wrongs received, and Right, upon Complaint, refused; so the Generality of Wars have their Rise from some such Pretension. This is better seen and understood at Home; for that which prevents a Civil War in a Nation, is that which may prevent it Abroad, *viz. Justice*; and we see where that is notably obstructed, War is Kindled between the *Magistrates* and *People* in particular Kingdoms and States; which, however it may be unlawful on the Side of the *People*, we see never fails to follow, and ought to give the same Caution to *Princes* as if it were the Right of the People to do it: Tho' I must needs say, *the Remedy is almost ever worse than the Disease*: The Aggressors seldom getting what they seek, or performing, if they prevail, what they promised. And the *Blood and Poverty* that usually attend the Enterprize, weigh more on Earth, as well as in Heaven, than what they lost or suffered, or what they get by endeavouring to mend their *Condition*, comes to: Which *Disappointment* seems to be the Voice of Heaven, and Judgment of God against those violent Attempts. But to return, I say, *Justice is the Means of Peace*, betwixt the *Government* and the *People*, and one *Man* and *Company* and another. It prevents *Strife*, and at last ends it: For besides *Shame* or *Fear*, to contend longer, he or they being under *Government*, are constrained to bound their *Desires* and *Resentment* with the *Satisfaction* the Law gives. Thus *Peace* is maintain'd by *Justice*, which is a Fruit of *Government*, as *Government*, is from *Society*, and *Society* from *Consent*.

Sect. III. GOVERNMENT, it's Rise and End under all Models.

Government is an Expedient against *Confusion*; a Restraint upon all *Disorder*; Just Weights and an even Ballance: That one may not injure another, nor himself, by *Intemperance*.

This was at first without *Controversie*, *Patrimonial*, and upon the Death of the Father or Head of the Family, the eldest Son, or Male of Kin succeeded. But Time breaking in upon this Way of Governing, as the World multiply'd, it fell under other *Claims* and *Forms*; and is as hard to trace to it's Original, as are the Copies we have of the first Writings of *Sacred* or *Civil* Matters. It is certain the most Natural and Human is that of *Consent*, for that binds freely (as I may say) when Men hold their *Liberty* by true *Obedience* to Rules of their own making. No Man is Judge in his own Cause, which ends the *Confusion* and *Blood* of so many *Judges* and *Executioners*. For out of *Society* every Man is his own *King*, does what he lifts, at his own Peril: But when he comes to incorporate himself, he submits that *Royalty* to the *Conveniency* of the *Whole*, from whom he receives the Returns of *Protection*. So that he is not now his own Judge nor Avenger, neither is his *Antagonist*, but the *Law*, in indifferent Hands between both. And if he be Servant to others that before was free, he is also served of others that formerly owed him no *Obligation*. Thus while we are not our own, every Body is ours, and we get more than we lose, the Safety of the *Society* being the Safety of the *Particulars* that constitute it. So that while we seem to submit to, and hold all we have from *Society*, it is by *Society* that we keep what we have.

Government then is the *Prevention* or *Cure* of *Disorder*, and the Means of *Justice*, as that is of *Peace*: For this Cause they have *Sessions*, *Terms*, *Assizes* and *Parliaments*, to over-rule Men's *Passions* and *Resentments*, that they may not be *Judges* in their own *Cause*, nor *Punishers* of their own *Wrongs*, which as it is very incident to Men in their *Corrupt State*, so, for that Reason, they would observe no Measure; nor on the other Hand would any be easily reduced to their Duty. Not that Men know not what is right, their Excesses, and wherein they are to blame,

blame: by no Means; nothing is plainer to them: But so depraved is Human Nature, that without Compulsion, some Way or other, too many would not readily be brought to do what they know is right and fit, or avoid what they are satisfy'd they should not do: Which brings me near to the Point I have undertaken; and for the better Understanding of which, I have thus briefly treated of *Peace, Justice* and *Government*, as a necessary *Introduction*, because the Ways and Methods by which *Peace* is preserved in particular *Governments*, will help those *Readers*, most concerned in my Proposal, to conceive with what Ease as well as Advantage the Peace of *Europe* might be procured and kept; which is the End designed by me, with all Submission to those Interested in this little *Treatise*.

Sect. IV. *Of a General Peace, or the Peace of* Europe, *and the Means of it.*

IN my first Section, I shewed the *Desirableness of Peace*; in my next, the Truest Means of it; to wit, *Justice, Not War*. And in my last, that this Justice was the Fruit of *Government*, as Government it self was the Result of *Society*; which first came from a Reasonable Design in Men of Peace. Now if the *Soveraign Princes of Europe*, who represent that Society, or Independent State of Men that was previous to the Obligations of Society, would, for the same Reason that engaged Men first into Society, *viz. Love of Peace and Order*, agree to meet by their Stated Deputies in a *General Dyet, Estates, or Parliament*, and there Establish Rules of Justice for Soveraign Princes to observe one to another; and thus to meet Yearly, or once in Two or Three Years at farthest, or as they shall see Cause, and to be Stiled, *The Soveraign or Imperial Dyet, Parliament, or State of Europe*; before which Soveraign Assembly, should be brought all Differences depending between one Soveraign and another, that cannot be made up by private Embassies, before the Sessions begins; and that if any of the Soveraignties that Constitute these Imperial States, shall refuse to submit their Claim or Pretensions to them, or to abide and perform the Judgment thereof, and seek their Remedy by Arms, or delay their Compliance beyond the Time prefixt in their Resolutions, all the other Soveraignties, United as One Strength, shall compel the Submission and Performance of the Sentence, with Damages to the Suffering Party, and Charges to the Soveraignties that obliged their Submission: To be sure *Europe* would quietly obtain the so much desired and needed Peace, to *Her harrassed Inhabitants*; no Soveraignty in *Europe*, having the Power, and therefore cannot show the Will to dispute the Conclusion; and, consequently, *Peace* would be procured, and continued in *Europe*.

Sect. V. *Of the Causes of Difference, and Motives to Violate Peace.*

THere appears to me but Three Things upon which Peace is broken, viz. To *Keep*, to *Recover*, or to *Add*. *First*, To Keep what is One's Right, from the Invasion of an Enemy; in which I am purely *Defensive*. *Secondly*, To Recover, when I think my self Strong enough, that which by Violence, I, or my Ancestors have lost, by the Arms of a Stronger Power; in which I am Offensive: Or, *Lastly*, To increase my Dominion by the Acquisition of my Neighbour's Countries, as I find them Weak, and my self Strong. To gratify which Passion, there will never want some Accident or other for a Pretence: And knowing my own Strength, I will be my own *Judge and Carver*. This *Last* will find no Room in the *Imperial States*: They are an unpassable Limit to that Ambition. But the other *Two* may come as soon as they please, and find the Justice of that Soveraign Court. And considering how few there are of those *Sons of Prey*, and how early they show themselves, it may be not once in an Age or Two, this Expedition being Established, the Ballance cannot well be broken.

Sect. VI. *Of Titles, upon which those Differences may arise.*

BUT I easily foresee a Question that may be answered in our Way, and that is this; *What is Right? Or else we can never know what is Wrong: It is very fit that this should be Established*. But that is fitter for the Soveraign States to resolve than me. And yet that I may lead a Way to the Matter, I say that Title is either by a long and *undoubted Succession*, as the Crowns of *Spain, France* and *England*; or by *Election*, as the Crown of *Poland*, and the *Empire*; or by *Marriage*, as the Family of the *Stewarts* came by *England*; the *Elector of Brandenburgh*, to the Dutchy of *Cleve*; and we, in Ancient Time, to divers Places abroad; or by *Purchase*, as hath been frequently done in *Italy* and *Germany*; or by Conquest, as the *Turk* in *Christendom*, the *Spaniards* in *Flanders*, formerly mostly in the *French Hands*;

Hands; and the *French* in *Burgundy, Normandy, Lorrain, French-County*, &c. This last, Title is, Morally Speaking, only Questionable. It has indeed obtained a Place among the Rolls of Titles, but it was engross'd and recorded by the Point of the Sword, and in Bloody Characters. What cannot be controuled or resisted, must be submitted to; but all the World knows the Date of the length of such Empires, and that they expire with the Power of the Possessor to defend them. And yet there is a little allowed to Conquest to, when it has the Sanction of Articles of Peace to confirm it: Tho' that hath not always extinguished the Fire, but it lies, like Embers under Ashes, ready to kindle so soon as there is a fit Matter prepared for it. Nevertheless, when Conquest has been confirmed by a Treaty, and Conclusion of Peace, I must confess it is an Adopted Title; and if not so Genuine and Natural, yet being engrafted, it is fed by that which is the Security of *Better Titles, Consent*. There is but one Thing more to be mentioned in this Section, and that is from what Time Titles shall take their Beginning, or how far back we may look to confirm or dispute them. It would be very bold and inexcusable in me, to determine so tender a Point, but be it more or less Time, as to the last General Peace at *Nimeguen*, or to the commencing of this War, or to the Time of the Beginning of the Treaty of Peace, I must submit it to the Great Pretenders and Masters in that Affair. But something every Body must be willing to give or quit, that he may keep the rest, and by this Establishment, be for ever freed of the Necessity of losing more.

Sect. VII. *Of the Composition of these Imperial States.*

THE Composition and Proportion of this *Soveraign Part*, or *Imperial State*, does, at the first Look, seem to carry with it no small Difficulty what Votes to allow for the Inequality of the Princes and States. But with Submission to better Judgments, I cannot think it invincible: For if it be possible to have an Estimate of the Yearly Value of the several Soveraign Countries, whose Delegates are to make up this August Assembly, the Determination of the Number of Persons or Votes in the States for every Soveraignty, will not be impracticable. Now that *England, France, Spain*, the *Empire*, &c. may be pretty exactly estimated, is so plain a Case, by considering the Revenue of Lands, the Exports and Entries at the Custom-Houses, the Books of Rates, and Surveys that are in all Governments, to proportion Taxes for the Support of them, that the least Inclination to the *Peace of Europe*, will not stand or halt at this Objection. I will, with Pardon on all Sides, give an Instance far from Exact; nor do I pretend to it, or offer it for an Estimate; for I do it at Random: Only this, as wide as it is from the Just Proportion, will give some Aim to my *Judicious Reader*, what I would be at: Remembring, I design not by any Computation, an Estimate from the Revenue of the Prince, but the Value of the Territory, the Whole being concerned as well as the Prince. And a Juster Measure it is to go by, since one Prince may have more Revenue than another, who has much a Richer Country: Tho' in the Instance I am now about to make, the Caution is not so Necessary, because, as I said before, I pretend to no Manner of Exactness, but go wholly by Guess, being but for Example's Sake. I suppose the *Empire of Germany* to send Twelve; *France*, Ten; *Spain*, Ten; *Italy*, which comes to *France*, Eight; *England*, Six; *Portugal*, Three; *Sweedland*, Four; *Denmark*, Three; *Poland*, Four; *Venice*, Three; the *Seven Provinces*, Four; *The Thirteen Cantons*, and little *Neighbouring Soveraignties*, Two; Dukedoms of *Holstein* and *Courland*, One: And if the *Turks* and *Muscovites* are taken in, as seems but fit and just, they will make *Ten a Piece more*. The *Whole makes Ninety*. A great Presence when they represent the *Fourth*; *and now the Best and Wealthiest Part of the Known World*; *where Religion and Learning, Civility and Arts have their Seat and Empire*. But it is not absolutely necessary there should be always so many Persons, to represent the larger Soveraignties; for the Votes may be given by one Man of any Soveraignty, as well as by Ten or Twelve: Tho' the fuller the Assembly of States is, the more Solemn, Effectual, and Free the Debates will be, and the Resolutions must needs come with greater Authority. The Place of their First Session should be Central, as much as is possible, aftewards as they agree.

Sect. VIII. *Of the Regulation of the Imperial States in Session.*

TO avoid Quarrel for Precedency, the Room may be Round, and have divers Doors to come in and go out at, to prevent Exceptions. If the whole Number be cast into Tens, each chusing One, they may preside by Turns, to whom all

all Speeches should be addressed, and who should collect the Sense of the Debates, and state the Question for a Vote, which, in my Opinion, should be by the *Ballot*, after the Prudent and Commendable Method of the *Venetians*: Which in a great Degree, prevents the ill Effects of Corruption; because if any of the Delegates of that High and Mighty Estates could be so Vile, False, and Dishonourable, as to be influenced by Money, they have the Advantage of taking their Money that will give it them, and of Voting undiscovered to the Interest of their Principals, and their own Inclinations; as they that do understand the *Balloting Box* do very well know. A Shrewd Stratagem, and an Experimental Remedy against *Corruption*, at least Corrupting: For who will give their Money where they may so easily be Cozened, and where it is Two to One they will be so; for they that will take Money in such Cases, will not stick to Lye heartily to them that give it, rather than wrong their Country, when they know their Lye cannot be detected.

It seems to me, that nothing in this *Imperial Parliament* should pass, but by Three Quarters of the Whole, at least Seven above the Ballance. I am sure it helps to prevent Treachery, because if Money could ever be a Temptation in such a Court, it would cost a great Deal of Money to weigh down the wrong Scale. All Complaints should be delivered in Writing, in the Nature of *Memorials*; and *Journals* kept by a proper Person, in a *Trunk or Chest*, which should have as many differing Locks, *as there are Tens in the States*. And if there were a *Clerk for each Ten*, and a *Pew or Table for those Clerks in the Assembly*; and at the End of every Session, *One out of each Ten*, were appointed to Examine and Compare the *Journal of those Clerks*, and then lock them up as I have before expressed, it would be clear and Satisfactory. And each Soveraignty if they please, as is but very fit, may have an *Exemplification*, or *Copy of the said Memorials*, and the *Journals of Proceedings upon them*. The *Liberty and Rules of Speech*, to be sure, they cannot fail in, who will be the *Wisest* and *Noblest* of each Soveraignty, for it's own Honour and Safety. If any Difference can arise between those that come from the same Soveraignty, that then One of the Major Number do give the Balls of that Soveraignty. I should think it extreamly necessary, that every Soveraignty should be present under great Penalties, and that none leave the Session without Leave, till *All* be finished; and that Neutralities in Debates should by no Means be endured: For any such Latitude will quickly open a Way to unfair Proceedings, and be followed by a Train, both of seen, and unseen Inconveniencies. I will say little of the *Language* in which the *Session of the Soveraign Estates should be held*, but to be sure it must be in *Latin* or *French*; The first would be very well for *Civilians*, but the last most easie for Men of Quality.

Sect. IX. *Of the Objections that may be advanced against the Design.*

I will first give an Answer to the Objections that may be offered against my *Proposal*: And in my next and last Section, I shall endeavour to shew some of the manifold Conveniences that would follow this *European League*, or *Confederacy*.

The first of them is this, *That the strongest and Richest Soveraignty will never agree to it, and if it should, there would be Danger of Corruption more than of Force one Time or other*. I answer to the first Part, he is not stronger than all the rest, and for that Reason you should promote this, and compel him into it; especially before he be so, for then, it will be too late to deal with such an one. To the last Part of the Objection, I say the Way is as open now as then; and it may be the Number fewer, and as easily come at. However, if Men of Sense and Honour, and Substance, are chosen, they will either scorn the Baseness, or have wherewith to pay for the Knavery: At least they may be watch't so, that one may be a check upon the other, and all prudently limited by the Soveraignty they Represent. In all great Points, especially before a final Resolve, they may be obliged to transmit to their Principals, the Merits of such important Cases depending, and receive their last Instructions: which may be done in four and Twenty Days at the most, as the Place of their Session may be appointed.

The Second is, *That it will endanger an Effeminacy by such a Disuse of the Trade of Soldiery: That if there should be any Need for it, upon any Occasion, we should be at a Loss as they were in* Holland *in* 72.

There can be no Danger of Effeminacy, because each Soveraignty may introduce as temperate or Severe a Discipline in the Education of Youth, as they please, by low Living, and due Labour. Instruct them in Mechanical Knowledge, and in natural Philosophy, by Operation, which is the Honour of the *German* Nobility.

This would make them Men: Niether *Women* nor *Lyons*: For *Soldiers* are t'other Extream to Effeminacy. But the Knowledge of Nature, and the useful as well as agreeable Operations of Art, give Men an Understanding of themselves, of the World they are born into, how to be useful and serviceable, both to themselves and others; and how to save and help, not injure or destroy. The Knowledge of Government in General; the particular Constitutions of *Europe*; and above all, of his own Country, are very recommending Accomplishments. This fits him for the *Parliament*, and *Council at Home*, and the *Courts of Princes and Services* in the *Imperial States abroad*. At least, he is a good Common-Wealths-Man, and can be useful to the Publick, or retire, as there may be Occasion.

To the other Part of the Objection, *Of being at a loss for Soldiery as they were in* Holland *in* 72. The Proposal answers for it self. One has War no more than the other; and will be as much to seek upon Occasion. Nor is it to be thought that any one will keep up such an Army after such an *Empire* is on Foot, which may hazard the Safety of the rest. However, if it be seen requisit, the Question may be askt, by Order of the Soveraign States, why such an one either raises or keeps up a formidable Body of Troops, and he obliged forthwith to reform or Reduce them; lest any one, by keeping up a great Body of Troops, should surprize a Neighbour. But a small Force in every other Soveraignty, as it is capable or accustomed to maintain, will certainly prevent that Danger and Vanquish any such Fear.

The Third Objection is, *That there will be great Want of Employment for younger Brothers of Families; and that the Poor must either turn Soldiers or Thieves.* I have answer'd that in my Return to the Second Objection. We shall have the more *Merchants and Husbandmen*, or *Ingenious Naturalists*, if the Government be but any Thing Solicitous of the *Education of their Youth*: Which, next to the present and immediate Happiness of any Country, ought of all Things, to be the *Care* and *Skill* of the Government. For such as the Youth of any Country is bred, such is the next Generation, and the Government in good or bad Hands.

I am come now to the last Objection, *That Soveraign Princes and States will hereby become not Soveraign; a Thing they will never endure.* But this also, under Correction, is a Mistake, for they remain as Soveraign at Home as ever they were. Neither their Power over their People, nor the usual Revenue they pay them, is diminished: It may be the War Establishment may be reduced, which will indeed of Course follow, or be better employed to the Advantage of the Publick. So that the *Soveraignties* are as they were, for none of them have now any Soveragnty over one another: And if this be called a lessening of their Power, it must be only because the great Fish can no longer eat up the little ones, and that each Soveraignty is *equally defended* from Injuries, and disabled from committing them: *Cedant Arma Togæ* is a Glorious Sentence; the *Voice of the Dove*; the *Olive Branch of Peace*. A Blessing so great, that when it pleases God to chastise us severely for our Sins, it is with the *Rod of War*, that, for the most Part, he whips us: And Experience tells us none leaves deeper Marks behind it.

Sect. X. *Of the real Benefits that flow from this Proposal about Peace.*

I am come to my last Section, in which I shall enumerate some of those many real *Benefits* that flow from this Proposal, for the Present and Future *Peace* of *Europe*.

Let it not, I pray, be the least, that it prevents the Spilling of so much *Humane and Christian Blood*: For a Thing so offensive to God, and terrible and afflicting to Men, as that has ever been, must recommend our Expedient beyond all Objections. For what can a Man give in Exchange for his Life, as well as Soul? And tho' the chiefest in Government are seldom personally exposed, yet it is a Duty incumbent upon them to be tender of the Lives of their People; since without all Doubt, they are accountable to God for the Blood that is spilt in their Service. So that besides the Loss of so many Lives, of importance to any Government, both for Labour and Propagation, the Cries of so many Widows, Parents and Fatherless are prevented, that cannot be very pleasant in the Ears of any Government, and is the *Natural Consequence* of *War in all Government*.

There is another *manifest Benefit* which redounds to *Christendom*, by this *Peaceable Expedient*, *The Reputation of Christianity will in some Degree be recovered in the Sight of Infidels*; which, by the many Bloody and unjust *Wars* of *Christians*, not only with them, but *one* with *another*, hath been greatly impaired. For, to the

Scandal of that Holy Profession, *Christians*, that glory in their *Saviour's Name*, have long devoted the Credit and Dignity of it, to their worldly Passions, as often as they have been excited by the Impulses of Ambition or Revenge. They have not always been in the Right: Nor has Right been the Reason of *War*: And not only *Christians* against *Christians*, but the same Sort of *Christians* have embrewed *their Hands in one another's Blood*: Invoking and Interesting, all they could, the *Good and Merciful God to prosper their Arms to their Brethren's Destruction*: Yet their *Saviour* has told them, *that he came to save, and not to destroy the Lives of Men*: To give and plant *Peace* among Men: And if in any Sense he may be said to send *War*, it is the *Holy War* indeed; for it is against the *Devil*, and not the *Persons of Men*. Of all his Titles this seems the most Glorious as well as comfortable for us, that he is the *Prince of Peace*. It is his *Nature*, his *Office*, his *Work* and the *End* and excellent Blessing of his Coming, who is both the Maker and Preserver of our *Peace* with God. And it is very remarkable, that in all the *New Testament* he is but once called *Lyon*, but frequently the *Lamb of God*; to denote to us his *Gentle, Meek and Harmless Nature*; and that those, who desire to be the *Disciples* of his *Cross and Kingdom*, for they are *inseparable*, must be like him, as St. *Paul*, St. *Peter* and St. *John* tell us. Nor is it said the *Lamb* shall lye down with the *Lyon*, but the *Lyon* shall lye down with the *Lamb* That is, *War* shall yield to *Peace*, and the Soldier turn Hermite. To be sure, *Christians* should not be apt to strive, nor *swift* to Anger against any Body, and less with one another, and least of all for the uncertain and fading Enjoyments of this lower World: And no Quality is exempted from this Doctrine. Here is a wide Field for the Reverend Clergy of *Europe* to act their Part in, who have so much the Possession of Princes and People too. May they recommend and labour this pacifick Means I offer, which will end Blood, if not Strife; and then *Reason*, upon free Debate, will be *Judge*, and not the *Sword*. So that both *Right* and *Peace*, which are the Desire and Fruit of wise Governments, and the choice Blessings of any Country, seem to succeed the Establishment of this Proposal.

The third Benefit is, that it saves *Money*, both to the Prince and People; and thereby prevents those Grudgings and Misunderstandings between them that are wont to follow the devouring Expences of *War*; and enables both to perform Publick Acts for *Learning, Charity, Manufacturies*, &c. The Virtues of Government and Ornaments of Countries. Nor is this all the *Advantage* that follows to *Soveraignties*, upon this *Head* of Money and good *Husbandry*, to whose Service and Happiness this short Discourse is dedicated; for it saves the great Expence that frequent and splendid Embassies require, and all their Appendages of *Spies and Intelligence*, which in the most prudent Governments, have devoured mighty Sums of Money; and that not without some *immoral Practices also*: Such as *Corrupting* of *Servants* to betray their *Masters*, by revealing their Secrets; not to be defended by *Christian* or *Old Roman Virtue*. But here, where there is nothing to fear, there is little to know, and therefore the *Purchase* is either *cheap*, or may be wholly *spared*. I might mention *Pensions* to the *Widows* and *Orphans* of such as dye in *Wars*, and of those that have been *disabled* in them; which rise high in the Revenue of some Countries.

Our fourth Advantage is, that the *Towns, Cities and Countries, that might be laid waste by the Rage of War, are thereby preserved*: A Blessing that would be very well understood in *Flanders* and *Hungary*, and indeed upon all the *Borders* of *Soveraignties*, which are almost ever the *Stages* of Spoil and Misery; of which the Stories of *England and Scotland* do sufficiently inform us without looking over the *Water*.

The fifth Benefit of this Peace, is the *Ease and Security of Travel and Traffick*: An Happiness never understood since the *Roman Empire* has been broken into so many *Soveraignties*. But we may easily conceive the Comfort and *Advantage* of travelling through the Governments of *Europe*, by a *Pass* from any of the *Soveraignties* of it, which this League and State of *Peace* will *naturally make Authentick*: They that have travel'd *Germany*, where is so great a Number of *Soveraignties*, know the Want and Value of this Priviledge, by the many *Stops and Examinations* they meet with by the Way: But especially such as have made the *great Tour of Europe*. This leads to the Benefit of an *Universal Monarchy*, without the Inconveniencies that attend it: For when the whole was one *Empire*, tho' these Advantages were enjoyed, yet the several Provinces, that now make the *Kingdoms and States* of *Europe*, were under some Hardship from the great Sums of *Money* remitted to the Imperial Seat, and the Ambition and Avarice of their several Proconsuls

consuls and *Governours*, and the great *Taxes* they paid to the *Numerous Legions of Soldiers*, that they maintained for their own Subjection, who were not wont to entertain that Concern for them (being uncertainly there, and having their Fortunes to make) which their respective and proper *Soveraigns* have always shown for them. So that to be *Ruled by Native Princes or States*, with the Advantage of that Peace and Security that can only render an *Universal Monarchy desirable*, is peculiar to our Proposal, and for that Reason it is to be preferred.

Another Advantage is, *The Great Security it will be to* Christians *against the Inroads of the* Turk, *in their most Prosperous Fortune*. For it had been impossible for the *Port*, to have prevailed so often, and so far upon *Christendom*, but by the Carelesness, or Wilful Connivence, if not Aid, of some *Christian Princes*. And for the same Reason, why no *Christian Monarch* will adventure to oppose, or break such an Union, the *Grand Seignior* will find himself obliged to concur, for the Security of what he holds in *Europe*: Where, with all his Strength, he would feel it an Over-Match for him. *The Prayers, Tears, Treason, Blood and Devastation, that War has cost in* Christendom, *for these Two last Ages especially, must add to the Credit of our Proposal, and the Blessing of the* Peace *thereby humbly recommended*.

The Seventh Advantage, of an *European, Imperial Dyet, Parliament, or Estates*, is, *That it will beget and increase Personal Friendship between Princes and States*, which tends to the Rooting up of Wars, and Planting Peace in a Deep and Fruitful Soil. For Princes have the Curiosity of seeing the Courts and Cities of other Countries, as well as Private Men, if they could as securely and familiarly gratify their Inclinations. It were a great Motive to the Tranquility of the World, *That they could freely Converse Face to Face, and Personally and Reciprocally Give and Receive Marks of Civility and Kindness*. An *Hospitality* that leaves these Impressions behind it, will hardly let Ordinary Matters prevail, to Mistake or Quarrel one another. Their *Emulation would be in the Instances of Goodness, Laws, Customs, Learning, Arts, Buildings*; and in particular those that relate to *Charity*, the True Glory of some Governments, where Beggars are as much a Rarity, as in other Places it would be to see none.

Nor is this all the Benefit that would come by this *Freedom* and *Interview of Princes*: For *Natural Affection* would hereby be preserved, which we see little better than lost, *from the Time their Children, or Sisters, are Married into other Courts*. For the present State and Insincerity of Princes forbid them the Enjoyment of that Natural Comfort which is possest by Private Families: Insomuch, that from the Time a Daughter, or Sister, is Married to another Crown, Nature is submitted to Interest, and that, for the most Part, grounded not upon Solid or Commendable Foundations, but *Ambition*, or *Unjust Avarice*. I say, this Freedom, that is the Effect of our Pacifick Proposal, restores *Nature* to Her Just Right and Dignity in the Families of Princes, and them to the Comfort She brings, wherever She is preserved in Her proper Station. Here *Daughters* may Personally intreat their *Parents*, and *Sisters* their *Brothers*, for a Good Understanding between them and their *Husbands*, where Nature, not crush'd by Absence, and Sinister Interests, but acting by the Sight and Lively Entreaties of such near Relations, is almost sure to prevail. They cannot easily resist the most affectionate Addresses of such powerful Solicitors, *as their Children, and Grand-Children*, and their *Sisters, Nephews*, and *Neices*: And so backward from *Children to Parents*, and *Sisters to Brothers*, to keep up and preserve their own Families, by a good Understanding between their Husbands and them.

To conclude this Section, there is yet another Manifest Privilege that follows this *Intercourse* and Good Understanding, which methinks should be very moving with Princes, *viz. That hereby they may chuse Wives for themselves*, such as they Love, and not by *Proxy*, meerly to gratify Interest; an ignoble Motive; and that rarely begets, or continues that *Kindness* which ought to be between Men and their Wives. A Satisfaction very few Princes ever knew, and to which all other Pleasures ought to resign. Which has often obliged me to think, *That the Advantage of Private Men upon Princes, by Family Comforts, is a sufficient Ballance against their Greater Power and Glory: The One being more in* Imagination, *than* Real; *and often* Unlawful; *but the other*, Natural, Solid, *and* Commendable. Besides, it is certain, Parents Loving Well before they are Married, which very rarely happens to Princes, *has Kind and Generous Influences upon their Offspring: Which, with their Example, makes them better Husbands, and Wives, in their Turn*. This, in great Measure, prevents Unlawful Love, and the Mischiefs of those Intriegues that

are

are wont to follow them: What *Hatred, Feuds, Wars,* and *Desolations* have, in divers Ages, flown from *Unkindness* between *Princes* and their *Wives?* What *Unnatural Divisions* among their *Children,* and *Ruin* to their *Families,* if not *Loss* of their *Countries* by it? Behold an Expedient to prevent it, a Natural and Efficacious One: Happy to Princes, and Happy to their People also. For Nature being renewed and strengthned by these Mutual Pledges and Endearments, I have mentioned, will leave those soft and kind Impressions behind in the Minds of Princes, that *Court and Country* will very easily discern and feel the Good Effects of: Especially if they have the Wisdom to show that they Interest themselves in the Prosperity of the Children and Relations of their Princes. For it does not only incline them to be Good, but engage those Relations to become Powerful Suitors to their Princes for them, if any Misunderstanding should unhappily arise between them and their *Soveraigns:* Thus ends this *Section.* It now rests to conclude the Discourse, in which, if I have not pleased my *Reader,* or answered his Expectation, it is some Comfort to me I meant well, and have cost him but little Money and Time; and Brevity is an Excuse, if not a Virtue, where the Subject is not agreeable, or is but ill prosecuted.

The Conclusion.

I Will conclude this *My Proposal of an European, Soveraign,* or *Imperial Dyet, Parliament,* or *Estates,* with that which I have touch'd upon before, and which falls under the Notice of every One concerned, by coming Home to their Particular and Respective Experience within their own *Soveraignties.* That by the same *Rules of Justice and Prudence,* by which Parents and Masters Govern their Families, and Magistrates their Cities, and Estates their Republicks, and Princes and Kings their Principalities and Kingdoms, *Europe* may Obtain and Preserve *Peace among Her Soveraignties.* For Wars are the *Duels of Princes;* and as Government in Kingdoms and States, *Prevents Men being Judges and Executioners for themselves,* over-rules Private Passions as to Injuries or Revenge, and subjects the Great as well as the Small to the *Rule of Justice,* that Power might not vanquish or oppress Right, nor one Neighbour act an *Independency and Soveraignty upon another,* while they have resigned that Original Claim to the Benefit and Comfort of Society; so this being soberly weighed in the Whole, and Parts of it, it will not be hard to conceive or frame, nor yet to execute the Design I have here proposed.

And for the better understanding and perfecting of the *Idea,* I here present to the *Soveraign Princes and Estates of Europe,* for the Safety and Tranquility of it, I must recommend to their Perusals, Sir *William Temple's Account of the United Provinces;* which is an Instance and Answer, upon *Practice,* to all the Objections that can be advanced against the Practicability of my Proposal: Nay, it is an Experiment that not only comes to our Case, but exceeds the Difficulties that can render it's Accomplishment disputable. For there we shall find *Three Degrees of Soveraignties to make up every Soveraignty in the General States.* I will reckon them backwards: First, *The States General themselves;* Then the *Immediate Soveraignties* that Constitute them, which are those of the *Provinces,* answerable to the *Soveraignties of Europe,* that by their *Deputies* are to compose the *European Dyet, Parliament,* or *Estates,* in our Proposal: And then there are the several Cities of each *Province,* that are so many *Independent* or *Distinct Soveraignties,* which compose those of the *Provinces,* as those of the *Provinces* do compose the *States General* at the *Hague.*

But I confess I have the Passion to wish heartily, that the Honour of Proposing and Effecting so Great and Good a Design, might be owing to *England,* of all the Countries in *Europe,* as something of the Nature of our Expedient was, in Design and Preparation, to the Wisdom, Justice, and Valour, *Of Henry the Fourth of France,* whose Superior Qualities raising His Character above those of His Ancestors, or Contemporaries, deservedly gave Him the Stile of *Henry the Great.* For *He was upon obliging the Princes and Estates of Europe to a Politick Ballance,* when the *Spanish Faction,* for that Reason, contrived, and accomplished *His Murder,* by the Hands of *Ravilliac.* I will not then fear to be censured, for proposing an *Expedient* for the Present and Future *Peace of Europe,* when it was not only the *Design, but Glory of One of the Greatest Princes that ever Reigned in it;* and is found Practicable in the Constitution of One of the Wisest and Powerfullest States

1695.

of it. So that to conclude, I have very Little to anſwer for in all this Affair; becauſe, if it ſucceed, I have ſo Little to deſerve: For this *Great King's Example tells us it is fit to be done*; and Sir *William Temple*'s *Hiſtory* ſhews us, by a Surpaſſing Inſtance, *That it may be done*; and *Europe*, by Her incomparable Miſeries, makes it now *Neceſſary to be done*: That my Share is only thinking of it at this Juncture, and putting it into the Common Light for the Peace and Proſperity of *Europe*.

A VISITATION *to the Jews: To the Seed of* Abraham, *and Houſe of* Iſrael, *after the Fleſh, where-ever ſcattered over the Face of the whole Earth, to whoſe Hands this cometh, Faith, Hope and Charity: Grace, Mercy, and Peace, be revealed and multiplied in the midſt of you.*

MANY Times have you been freſh in my Remembrance with tender Compaſſion and ſtrong Cries to the God of your Fathers, *Abraham, Iſaac* and *Jacob*, that the Time of your Captivity may come to an End, and that of your Deliverance, yea the ſet Time to favour you, may make Haſte, who were the natural Branches broken off through Unbelief, and which by Faith may come again to be engrafted, *through the Circumciſion made without Hands*, that the Hope of the Promiſe made to your Fathers may be manifeſted among you. Know ye, that ſo ſoon as I had looked over the * foregoing Treatiſe in *Manuſcript*, and obſerv'd it related to you as well as to *Chriſtians*, it came in my Mind to take this Opportunity to begin the Expreſſion of that Concern which hath for ſome Time reſted with me in your Regard. And eaſily foreſeeing the Objection you might be apt to make upon the Pains and Good-will of the *Author* of the ſaid *Diſcourſe*, I felt great Clearneſs to add this to his *Work*, to obviate the ſame, that ſo the Intent and Scope thereof may come with more Weight and Succeſs upon your Minds.

* *Note*, this was written by Way of *Appendix*, to a Book, call'd, *The Harmony of the Old and New Teſtaments.*

You will perhaps object, that the *Author* begs the *Queſtion* in what he concludes his *Harmony* from, in as much as you own not the *Authority* of the *New Teſtament* Scripture, and from Premiſes that are denied, nothing can be inferred that is concluſive upon you.

But if you have no Reaſon to deny the *Authority* of the *New Teſtament-Writings* any more than we have to deny the *Authority* of the *Old*, in which you ſo firmly believe, it is as reaſonable in us to expect you ſhould receive the *Authority* of the *New*, as that we ſhould embrace the *Authority* of the *Old*. For what have you to juſtify the Truth of thoſe Writings but the Impoſſibility of ſo many People's conſenting to delude themſelves, and being able and ſo wicked to impoſe upon their Poſterity a Fiction about the great and important Matters of Immortality.

For the Miracles recorded in the *Old Teſtament-Scriptures*, are as much above Reaſon, and conſequently as Incredible to worldly Men, as the Miracles Recorded in the *New Teſtament-Scriptures*, ſo that the *Authority* you have for the *Old Teſtament-Writings* is the Truth and Credibility of their Tradition. This, we ſay, we alſo have for ours. How could ſo many Men that you have not taxed with ill Lives, or Atheiſtical Principles, agree together to put ſo great an Impoſture upon the World, as the *Pen-men* of the *New Teſtament-Writings* muſt needs have done, if what they write were Fictions? You cannot deny, but that there was ſuch a Man as *Jeſus*, and that he was put to Death by your Fathers, though pretended as a Malefactor, and that he had Followers, and that thoſe Followers of his aſſerted and maintained the Doctrine of their Maſter; where is there any Confutation of what is affirmed of the Deeds and Doctrines of *Jeſus* by his Writers in the whole *Body* of your Antiquity, that he wrought none of the Miracles ſaid to be wrought by him.

Matthew, Mark, Luke and *John*, were Men, and ſome of them lived not the Periods of Mortality, the two firſt being reported to have been put to Death for their Maſter's Doctrines, and ſo died before their Time, by which Means many of

that

that Generation out-lived them: How comes it, that while they were alive, their Writings were not confuted, when it stood those Jews so much upon to do it? Historians make Jesus to have wrought his Miracles, not in Secret, but among (a) the Multitudes, as his *feeding Five Thousand at one Time,* (b) *and Five Thousand at another Time, with that which would have satisfied but a few Persons:* So that you have more than their Authority for what they say; for that is an Appeal to other Witness, by which Means his Enemies had it in their Power to have confuted them in their Days, if not true. But especially in the noted Places, as of the *Man born* (c) *Blind.* The (d) *Lepers cleansed;* the (e) *possessed with Devils.* And *the Man with a* (f) *withered Hand.* The *Daughter of* Jairus (g) *by Name, one of your Rulers, whom he raised to Life.* Also *the raising of* (h) *Lazarus from the Dead after he had lain four Days in the Grave, and so many Jews said to be by, seeing the Miracle: His turning* (i) *Water into Wine at a Marriage.* The *Conference with the* (k) *Woman of* Samaria *at Jacob's Well;* the (l) *healing the Centurion's Servant.* And *the High Priest's Servant's* (m) *Ear after it was cut off,* &c. We may add *the Story of* (n) *Zacharias, the Father of* John the Baptist, *the Fore-runner of Jesus Christ, and of the Soldiers Parting* (o) *his Garments among them.* And *that a Bone of him was not* (p) *broken.* And *of his Resurrection to the* (q) *Terror of the Keepers of his Sepulchre:* And our Historian convicts the Chief Priests and Elders of Bribery and Forgery, who, to belye his Resurrection to blind the People, bid the Soldiers say, (r) *his Disciples came by Night and stole him away, while they slept,* and which they would not have mentioned if Truth had not been on their Side, for Fear of being disproved, and punished, Power as well as Wrath being on their Enemies Side; also I may add, the *Passage of the* (s) *Shepherds, to whom the Angels appeared by Night, to bring them the good Tidings of the Birth of Christ, and with the Angel an Heavenly Host praising God.* And *the wise Men* (t) *that came out of the East to worship him, and of the* (u) *Star that then appeared,* from which a Religious and Learned Man at Cambridge, by the common and regular Rules of * Art, proves by the Disposition, Harmony, and Voice of the Celestial Bodies, that the Messiah was at that Time to come, and that Jesus was the Messiah. Also *his sending some of his Disciples in so extraordinary a Manner to fetch the* † *Asses Colt.* And *to take a* (x) *Room for him to eat the Passover, and the Owner's immediate Submission as to their Great Lord and Proprietor,* with Abundance more, as his Conferences with the Pharisees, Sadducees, &c. in which his Writers make him so visibly and convincingly to have the Better of them. And that he *cured a Man who had been lame* (y) *Thirty Eight Years.* And *another Man also cured by two of his Disciples,* (z) Peter and John, *who had been lame from his Mother's Womb, and sate Begging at the Gate of the Temple called* Beautiful. I say, that these Things, if they had been false, your Ancestors, to have justified themselves, would certainly not have been so Wanting to their own Credit, as not to have made it a Reason against the Credibility of Christianity, to the Followers of Christ or his Apostles, since so many were taken with them. But nothing in any of your Antiquities undertakes to shew, that those Historians have imposed upon the World, in the Account they give of the *Life, Doctrines,* and *Miracles* of their Master. Had they done it, we had heard of it among our Evangelists, that before, I observe, reported the Objections and Endeavours of your Ancestors to smother the Credit of his Resurrection. But all they said to his mighty Deeds, that they report, was, that by Beelzebub he cast out Devils.

It is true, above 200 Years after, *Tryphon* the *Jew,* and *Celsus* the *Gentile* caviled at the Christian Religion, and at the Meanness of the Appearance and Manner of Christ's Coming, rather opposing his Miracles with Miracles, to abate his Authority, than disproving of them. But they were answered at large by *Justin* and *Origen.* But not one Word of the aforesaid Adversaries giving this Account:

That whereas the Followers of Jesus affirm, He cured the Blind and Lame, and particularly the Daughter of Jairus, *and dispossessed Evil Spirits, and suffered them to enter into an Herd of Swine, and that the Swine ran down a steep Hill into the Sea, and that thereupon the* Gadarenes *desired him to quit their Coasts.* Also *about turning Water into Wine at the Marriage. Feeding the Multitudes. Curing the High Priest's Servant's Ear.* &c. *And that we have enquired about these and other Matters, and find them Impious, confidently imposed upon silly People by the Followers and Partners of the said Jesus.*

But where can you shew us such a Certificate or Contradiction to what is asserted by his Historians, writ in that Age, and Authentically proved, against the Au-

1695.

(a) Mat. 15. 30, 38, 39.
(b) Mat. 14. 14---21.

(c) John 9. 1.
(d) Luke 17. 12, 13, 14.
(e) Mat. 9. 32.
(f) Mat. 12. 10. 13.
(g) Luke 8. 41. 49. 51.
(h) John 11. 17, 36. 43.
(i) John 2. 7, 8, 10.
(k) Joh. 4. c.
(l) Mat. 8. 5, 13.
(m) Luke 22. 50, 51.
(n) Luke 1. cap.
(o) Jo. 19. 23
(p) John 19. 36. Psalm 34. 20.
(q) Mat. 28. 4.
(r) Mat. 28. 13.
(s) Luke 2. 8.
(t) Mat. 2. c.
(u) Mat. 2. 9. 10.
* See J. Gregory's Works p. 150---157.
† Mark 11. 1---6.
(x) Mark 14. 12--16.
(y) John 5. 2, 5. 9.
(z) Acts 3. 1---8.

1695.

Ignat. Epift.

thority of fo Ancient and Sacred a Tradition, as the Writings we call the *New Teftament*, that are cited by the moft eminent Writers fince the Time of *Jefus*, even as early as *Ignatius*, the Difciple of *Polycarpus*, if not of *John*, one of the Twelve Difciples? Add to this the Prophecy, in the New Teftament, is reported to have been uttered of the Future State of your *Anceftors*, their Temple and City of *Jerufalem*, mentioned by the Three Firft Hiftorians, that that Generation fhould not pafs away before great Diftreffes fhould overtake them, fuch as had never been before, particularly *Luke* 21. 21, 22, 23, 24, 25, and *Cap.* 23. 28, 29, 30, where Jefus bids the Women *weep for themfelves and their Children*, becaufe of the Diftreffes that fhould fall upon *Jerufalem* and that People; that tho' to be *Barren* was a Sort of Curfe under the Law, yet *they fhould blefs the Womb that never bare, and the Paps that never gave Suck*, becaufe of the Woes and Diftreffes that fhould come upon the Childing Daughters of *Jerufalem*. And indeed the Way your Fathers took to fave themfelves (not being guided by God's Counfel) proved the very Means of their Deftruction; for as they unreafonably feared the *Romans*, crying, the *Romans* will come and take away our Country, and made that a Reafon to put Jefus to Death, that *he was an Enemy to Cæfar*, to foften *Cæfar* to them, fo the Innocent Blood of *Jefus*, by the Judgment of God, haftned the Coming of the *Romans*, and the Obftinacy with which they refifted the *Romans*, who would have preferved the City, and Temple, and People, and offered them fo to do, would they *fubmit*, proved the Deftruction of the Nation, as * *Jofephus*, a Jewifh Hiftorian confeffeth; fo that if our Tradition, which makes your Anceftors to curfe themfelves and their Pofterity, faying to *Pilate*, *His Blood be on us and our Children*, were not true in Fact: The dreadful Things that followed, to wit, the unparallel'd Miferies that People fell by, in that Hiftorian expreffed, and the *long* Captivity they have lain under ever fince, has been as great and terrible as if they had put the *Son of God* to Death. And indeed if you did but confider how very like to Chrift's Parable of the Vineyard, *Luke* 20. 9. your Anceftors Cafe was, it fhould incline you to believe in that Holy Preacher of it, *viz.* that after the *Tenants had beaten and Stoned* their Lord's *Servants*, he fent his *Son*, and they *confpired* and *killed* him, and what Miferies thofe Servants drew upon themfelves thereby, which the Scripture fays *they underftood Chrift to have fpoken of them*. And comparing the miferable Exit and difmal Period your Nation made foon after, how can you but think he was fent of God, and that by fuch Doctrine he warned them of what was haftening upon them, and that hitting their Cafe fo exactly, as to their Anceftors, and their Sins, and the foretelling by that very Parable, not only his own Death, but their End and Judgment, as he did afterwards more directly in the two before-cited Prophefies; and fince that your Fathers at that Time expected the *Meffiah*, and yet then were *deftroyed*, inftead of being *reftored*, by the *Meffiah*, fhould you not confider if it were not fo, becaufe of their not knowing, but deftroying him, when he came? I know you think (and that mifled your Fathers) that the *Meffiah* fhould be known of all Men, and come with an outward *Irrefiftible Power*, and by Force overcome all the Enemies, and redeem you, and fubject them, and that the whole Earth fhould flow in unto him as a mighty Monarch of this World. But what then will you do with the 53d of *Ifaiah*, and divers other Places of the Prophets, that fo particularly and pathetically relate to the Paffion of the *Meffiah*, how he fhould fuffer, &c. What *Holy One* (a) was that (which came fo near, and yet) *was not to fee Corruption*? What (b) *Shepherd* was that, which being fmitten, *the Sheep were fcattered*, though he be called God's Fellow. Who was he that was to be for a (c) *Snare* and *Stone of Stumbling*, and a *Rock* of *Offence* to the Inhabitants of *Jerufalem*? But this was their *Stumbling* (d) *Stone* and *Rock* of *Offence*; they miftook the Manner of his Appearance; they were *Carnal, Worldly,* and *Degenerate*, and they had *Ideas* and *Notions* of a *Meffiah* accordingly; they looked for an *outward* before an *inward* Deliverance; and to be faved from the *Romans*, before they were faved from their Sins. They waited for a *Meffiah* indeed, but one after their own hard Hearts and worldly Wifdom, not after God's, and fo knew him not when he came. He came to fave what was loft; *firft within* and then *without*; they looked *without firft*, and fo fell fhort. Thofe that were deftroyed by *Titus Vefpafian*, you will eafily conceive were not qualify'd to embrace the true *Meffiah*: Had they feared God, and walked in his *Statutes* and his *Judgments*, had they had Hearts of *Flefh* and not of *Stone*, they had not been fo caft off; they had not been deftroyed as they were, but would have known him, that they rejected, to have been the *Meffiah*. O that

* See Jofeph. Antiquity of the Jews, new Impreffion. Fol. 755. C. D. D.

(a) Pfal. 16. 10.
(b) Zach. 13. 7. 10.
(c) Ifa. 8. 14.

(d) Rom. 9. 32, 33.

you

you would deeply weigh that terrible Period, and *lamentable* and *diſtinguiſhing* Judgment upon you as a Nation, by the Hands of the *Romans*, and what it is that could provoke God to such an aſtoniſhing Stroke upon his *once Beloved People*, if it could be any Thing ſhort of reſiſting his greateſt *Meſſenger*, his *Meſſiah*, the *Chriſt* and *Son* of God, for he hath not dealt ſo in all Reſpects with any People. And while you thus reſiſt, you will reſiſt your *own Mercies*, for at this Door you muſt come in, before the glorious Propheſies and Promiſes, that relate to you, are accompliſhed to you.; and I hope the Day is at Hand. Conſider with your ſelves what Sort of *Meſſiah* was to come according to the Scriptures, and how far the Life, Doctrine, &c. of our Saviour, accords to him; concerning which, I ſhall now hint but that one Place of *Iſaiah*, Cap. 61. 1. 2. 3. on which our New Teſtament-*Scripture*, ſays *Jeſus*, opening the Book, expounded it to the People, touching the *Work* and *Office* of the *Meſſiah*, viz. *The Spirit of the Lord God is upon me, becauſe the Lord hath Anointed me to preach Good Tidings to the Meek; he hath ſent me to bind up the Broken-hearted, to proclaim Liberty to the Captives, and the Opening of the Priſon to them that are bound; to proclaim the acceptable Year of the Lord, and the Day of Vengeance of our God. To Comfort all that Mourn; to appoint unto them that Mourn in* Zion; *to give unto them Beauty for Aſhes, the Oil of Joy for Mourning; the Garment of Praiſe for the Spirit of Heavineſs, that they might be called the Trees of Righteouſneſs; the Planting of the Lord, that he might be glorified.*

By which it appears, that the *inward* Work was to go *firſt*, and the End cannot be known where the Beginning is rejected: Conſider with your ſelves, I beſeech you, how this Character agrees with that Carnal Notion your Fathers had, and you have, of the *Meſſiah*.

This *Meſſiah* was a *Preacher*, not a *Soldier*, or a worldly Conqueror, and his Work *Inward* and *Spiritual*; and had your Anceſtors been true *Mourners*, truly *Meek*, of *broken* Hearts, ſenſible of their Servitude to the Enemy of their own Houſes, (Sin within) and had waited for ſuch a Conſolation and Deliverer, they could not have miſſed to have ſeen and received him. For his Sermon on the (e) Mount had an exact Harmony with that Prophecy, as alſo with the Eleventh Chapter of *Iſaiah*, becauſe the Doctrine he preached relates to the vanquiſhing of Sin and Evil Appetites, and becoming Pure and Peaceable, Meek and Harmleſs, and Holy, in the Sight of God and Men, to which thoſe Propheſies relate; if you will give your ſelves the Time to read his Sermons, you will ſee therein an exact Draught of Piety, and Man met with in all his Infirmities, being plainly and briefly laid open, and their proper Remedies; not like an Impoſtor, *which ſeeks himſelf*, for he ſought not his own Glory, but denied it, and taught his Followers ſo to do, which cuts up by the *Roots* the very Motives and Ends of all Impoſtors. For, conſider, his Doctrine leads to *Repentance, Humility, Meekneſs, Purity, Love* and *Charity, to the utmoſt* that Mankind is capable of; but if you will look back upon thoſe that have pretended among you to be the *Meſſiah*, you ſhall not find them carried forth with ſuch Sort of Doctrine, as well as that they had not that Power and Spirit. For, as *Iſaiah* (f) Propheſied, *He was of Jeſſe: He was an Enſign to the People, the Gentiles ſought to him, and his Reſt was glorious to them.* For you cannot but ſee the Succeſs that followed the Diſciples of Jeſus; how greatly they multiplied, and what Power they got over Countries and Kingdoms, and the Courts and Armies of Princes; not by Arms and Policy, but *Piety* and *Sufferings*, whilſt you were driven away from your own Land, and wandred up and down in the Earth. It is true indeed you may ſay, that *Mahomet* became great in his Followers, yet we will not allow that Greatneſs to his Goodneſs. The Caſe vaſtly differs; one's Kingdom was of this World, the others not; one gained his Intereſt over the Hearts of Men, by the *Purity, Patience, Humility, Mercy*, and *Charity* of his Doctrine, the other by Factions, and Force. It is true, the Chriſtians in general are much degenerated, to the Scandal of Religion; but this no more debaſes the Value of the Holy Author of it, than your Fore-fathers and your Degenerating can queſtion the Reputation and Truth of *Moſes* your Lawgiver.

And it is to be feared ſome *Terrible Criſis* is at Hand, with Reference to ſuch Parts of the Chriſtian World, as have out-lived their Religion; I mean a True Zeal and Love for Religion. For they have *Crucified Chriſt afreſh to themſelves*, by their Shameleſs Lives, and put Him and His Holy Religion to *Open Shame*, viz. *to Jews and Infidels*. Sad for them would it be, though well for you, if their Fall

(e) Mat. 5.

(f) Iſa. 11. cap. 10.

should be your Rise, as your sad Fall was their Rise: Wherefore it is earnestly desired that Christians would Repent and amend their Lives, and return to God with unfeigned Hearts. I shall conclude to you, that as your *Fathers* could never have fallen by so severe an Hand as they have done, since the Coming of Him, whom we believe to be the *Messiah*, had they been a *Godly People, of Clean Hearts and Right Spirits*, waiting in God's Way for Deliverance; so I do earnestly desire of God in your Behalf, that you may not lose the Blessing and Comfort of your Return, by an unprepared Frame of Spirit to receive the Divine Goodness in the Way of his Visitations to you. If you will but turn in your Minds, and consider that *His Divine Light Shines in you*, and shews you the Error and Vanity of your Minds and Affections, and if you would but give up your selves Conscientiously to obey the same, through the Course of your Lives, you would become a *Tender People*, and *discern the Law of God to be written in your Hearts*, which is nearer than that upon the Stone which *Moses* gave your Fathers; and as by this *Inward Work of the Divine Spirit*, you come to have your Understandings opened, and Minds Seasoned, you will quickly see where your Fathers mist the Mark, and what the *True Messiah* should be, and the Work that belongs to Him to do, in Reference to your Deliverance and Salvation. And *Hear, and Bear, this Word*, I beseech you, from me; you can never see, know, or have the Happiness of the Coming of the *Messiah*, till you come to a Prepared Frame of Mind. You must repent of your Sins, turn from them, and watch against all Temptations, not to commit them again; and in this State and Condition of Mind and Spirit, you will know a Fitting, to receive and own the *Messiah*, and enjoy the Blessed Benefits that accrue by Him, to all those that embrace Him. He did come Sufferingly, and will come Triumphantly; but those only can receive Him, and have the Comfort and Advantage of *His First and Second Coming*, that come to know and receive Him in *His Light and Spirit in their Hearts*.

And I testify to you, and I know my Testimony is True, *That you have a Measure of that Light in you*, that comes from Him, and by it's Works you may know it, *For it shews you your Sins, Convicts and Rebukes you for them, and will comfort you in your Obedience and Conformity to God's Precepts*: And if you would but give your Hearts to the Holy Conduct of it, that it may lead you and guide you to God's Holy Hill (as King *David* prayed, *Psal.* 43. 3.) you would not blame those called Christians, for acknowledging this Christ, to be *God's Messiah*; *but for the manifest disowning of Him by their Evil Lives, and contrary Practices to his excellent Precepts, that walk disorderly among them*. Prepare therefore to meet thy God, O *Israel!* Wash you, O House of *Jacob!* And make you *Clean*; put away the Evil of your Doings, and turn to the Lord your God, *with all your Heart, and with all your Soul*, that the Lord may turn away your Captivity, as the Rivers of the *South*. That your dry Bones may live, and the Hope that may be begotten again in you, God may answer, and he whom you look *for will suddenly come*, and will not tarry, and in such a Way as shall abundantly satisfy you: And the Fulness of the *Gentiles* shall flow in, and the Glory of the God of your Fathers shall be great over all the Earth:

Accept this small Visitation as a Token of Love to you, the *House of Jacob, and Seed of Abraham*, after the Flesh; for tho' the foregoing Book was not writ on Purpose to you (else it had been in a more direct and exact Manner) but to shew the Harmony of Scriptures, chiefly in Reference to Christ, for them that believe the Writings of both Testaments for their Edification and Comfort; yet as the Accomplishment of some of the Ancient Prophesies concerns you, you must needs be interested therein; and the second Preface and this *Appendix* are sent you, to intreat your Perusal and Serious Consideration of them. And the Great God give you Understanding, to discern the Things that are therein mentioned, which concern your Everlasting Peace.

And now to you called *Christians*, I direct the *Conclusion of this Appendix*; you have been long priviledged with the Mercies of God, as much above the *Jews* since the Death of Christ, as the *Jews* were priviledged above you under the Dispensation of *Moses*: Be you warned by the *Dismal Punishment of that People*, that you fall not under the same Sentence and Judgment. I have often, of late Time, sorrowfully reflected upon your great Abuse of the manifold Blessings of God; how little the Generality of you have of the Life and Power of Religion; how Formal, Covetous, Proud, Vain and Uncharitable you are, being Christians in Name, but *Crucifying to your selves afresh the Lord of Life and Glory, and putting Him, and*

His Holy Religion to open Shame, by your disagreeable Lives to His Heavenly Precepts and Examples; whereby you do *Despite to the Spirit of God*, that would teach you to *deny Ungodliness and Worldly Lusts, and to Live Soberly, Righteously, and Godly in this present Evil World:* And so Great and Scandalous has the *Apostacy* of many of you been, that *Jews, Turks and Infidels*, have been stumbled by your Evil Examples, against the Holy Name and Religion you profess, which is acting the *Second Part of the Jewish Tragedy* (you seem so much to abhor) upon the *Saviour of the World.* O *Hear, Fear, and Repent*, lest you come to suffer the like Judgment the *Jews* did. God has visited you in this Age, by the Testimony of a Poor People (especially in these Nations) in the Name and Power of the *Second Adam*, bearing Witness to *His Second and Spiritual Appearance in Man*, to wit, *As a Light Shining in the Inward Parts*, who was, and is the Light of the World, *and in which Light the Nations of them that are saved must walk.* To this you should have turned your Minds, and brought your Deeds, and conformed your Lives, which was the *Path, Rule and Armour, of the Ancient Christians*; but you have despised their Testimony, and persecuted them for it, and slighted the Light it self, calling it by many Reproachful Names, as did the *Jews*, when manifested in Flesh among them: So that it has often been in my Mind of late, and I have freely, on some publick Occasions, declared my Fears, that as it is now about the same Distance of Time since the Testimony of the Coming of the Son of God in Spirit in our Day, as it was between the coming forth of Christ in His Ministry in the Flesh, and the Destruction of *Jerusalem*, (which was the most terrible that ever was known amongst Men) so I fear Great Desolation (without great Repentance) is at Hand, because of the same Sin, *viz.* A resisting of the Son of God in His Light and Spirit in His Servants and your own Consciences; opposing as the *Jews* did, *Form* to Power, *Letter* to *Spirit, Ceremonies* to *Substance*, and *Scripture* to *Christ*: Doing Despite to Him in His Members, with an high Hand, though He would often have gathered you, *as a Hen gathereth her Chickens under her Wings:* O that you may be Wise, and meet the Lord in the Way of His Judgments, before his fierce Wrath be kindled, and an irrevocable Sentence be sealed against you, and you are utterly cast off, and God remove the Visitation of His Light and Truth to another People, that will receive it, in the Love of it, more than you have done.

W. PENN.

Primitive CHRISTIANITY Revived, in the *Faith* and *Practice* of the People called QUAKERS. Written in Testimony to the present Dispensation of God *through them*, to the World; *that* Prejudices *may be Removed, the* Simple *Informed, the* Well-Inclined *Encouraged, and the* TRUTH, *and it's* Innocent FRIENDS *Rightly Represented. By* W. P.

The EPISTLE to the READER.

Reader,

BY *this short ensuing Treatise, thou wilt perceive the Subject of it, viz. The Light of Christ in Man, as the Manifestation of God's Love for Man's Happiness. Now, for as much as this is the Peculiar* Testimony *and Characteristick of the People called* Quakers; *their Great Fundamental in Religion; That by which they have been distinguished from other Professors of Christianity in their Time, and to which they refer all People about Faith, Worship, and Practice, both in their Ministry and Writings; that as the Fingers shoot out of the Hand, and the Branches from the Body of the Tree; so True Religion, in all the Parts and Articles of it, Springs from this Divine Principle in Man. And because the Prejudices of some are*

very

very great against this People and their Way; and that others, who love their Seriousness, and commend their Good Life, are yet, through Mistakes, or want of Enquiry, under Jealousie of their Unsoundness in some Points of Faith; and that there are not a few in all Perswasions, which desire earnestly to know and enjoy God in that Sensible Manner this People speak of, and who seem to long after a State of Holiness and Acceptance with God; but are under Doubts and Despondings of their attaining it, from the Want they find in themselves of Inward Power to enable them, and are unacquainted with this Efficacious Agent, which God hath given and appointed for their Supply.

For these Reasons and Motives, know, Reader, I have taken in Hand to write this Small Tract, Of the Nature and Virtue of the Light of Christ Within Man; what, and where it is, and for what End, and therein of the Religion of the People called Quakers; that, at the same Time, all People may be informed of their True Character, and what True Religion is, and the Way to it, in this Age of High Pretences, and as deep Irreligion. That so the Merciful Visitation of the God of Light and Love, (more especially to these Nations) both immediately and instrumentally, for the Promotion of Piety, (which is Religion indeed) may no longer be neglected by the Inhabitants thereof, but that they may come to see and say, with Heart and Mouth, This is a Dispensation of Love and Life from God to the World; and this Poor People, that we have so much despised, and so often trod upon, and treated as the Off-scouring of the Earth, are the People of God, and Children of the Most High. Bear with me, Reader, I know what I say, and am not High-Minded, but fear: For I write with Humility towards God, tho' with Confidence towards thee. Not that thou shouldst believe upon my Authority, nothing less; for that's not to act upon Knowledge, but Trust; but that thou should'st try and approve what I write: For that is all I ask, as well as all I need for thy Conviction, and my own Justification. The Whole, indeed, being but a Spiritual Experiment upon the Soul, and therefore seeks for no implicit Credit, because it is Self-evident to them that will uprightly try it.

And when thou, Reader, shalt come to be acquainted with this Principle, and the Plain and Happy Teachings of it, thou wilt, with us, admire thou should'st live so long a Stranger to that which was so near thee, and as much wonder that other Folks should be so blind as not to see it, as formerly thou thoughtest us Singular for obeying it. The Day, I believe, is at Hand that will declare this with an uncontroulable Authority, because it will be with an unquestionable Evidence.

I have done, Reader, with this Preface, when I have told thee, First, That I have stated the Principle, and opened, as God has enabled me, the Nature and Virtue of it in Religion; wherein the common Doctrines and Articles of the Christian Religion, are delivered and improved; and about which, I have endeavoured to express my self in Plain and Proper Terms, and not in Figurative, Allegorical, or Doubtful Phrases; That so I may leave no Room for an Equivocal or Double Sense; but that the Truth of the Subject I treat upon, may appear easily and evidently to every common Understanding. Next, I have confirmed what I have writ, by Scripture, Reason, and the Effects of it upon so Great a People; whose Uniform Concurrence in the Experience and Practice thereof, through all Times and Sufferings, since a People, challenge the Notice and Regard of every Serious Reader. Thirdly, I have written briefly, that so it might be every One's Money and Reading: And, Much in a Little is Best, when we see daily that the Richer People grow, the Less Money or Time they have for God or Religion: And perhaps those that would not buy a large Book, may find in their Hearts to give away some of these for their Neighbour's Good, being Little and Cheap. Be Serious, Reader, be Impartial, and then be as Inquisitive as thou canst; and that for thine own Soul, as well as the Credit of this most misunderstood and abused People: And the God and Father of Lights and Spirits, so Bless thine, in the Perusal of this Short Treatise, that thou may'st receive Real Benefit by it, to His Glory, and thine own Comfort, Which is the Desire and End of him that wrote it; who is, in the Bonds of Christian Charity, very much, and very ardently,

Thy Real Friend,

WILLIAM PENN.

Primitive *CHRISTIANITY* Revived, &c.

CHAP. I. §. 1. *Their Fundamental Principle.* §. 2. *The Nature of it.* §. 3. *Called by several Names.* §. 4. *They refer all to this, as to Faith and Practice, Ministry and Worship.*

§. 1. THAT which the People call'd *Quakers* lay down, as a Main Fundamental in Religion, is this, *That God, through Christ, hath placed a Principle in every Man, to inform him of his Duty, and to enable him to do it*; and that those that Live up to this Principle, are the People of God, and those that Live in Disobedience to it, are not God's People, whatever Name they may bear, or Profession they may make of Religion. This is their Ancient, First, and Standing Testimony: With this they began, and this they bore, and do bear to the World.

§. 2. By this *Principle* they understand something that is *Divine*; and though in Man, *yet not of Man*, but of God; and that it came from Him, and leads to Him all those that will be led by it.

§. 3. There are divers Ways of Speaking they have been led to use, by which they declare and express what this *Principle* is, about which I think fit to Precaution the Reader, *viz.* They call it, *The Light of Christ within Man*, or, *Light Within*, which is their Ancient, and most General and Familiar Phrase, also the (a) *Manifestation* (b) or *Appearance of Christ* (c), the (d) *Witness of God*, the (e) *Seed of God*, the (f) *Seed of the Kingdom*, (g) *Wisdom*, the (h) *Word in the Heart*, the *Grace* (i) *that appears to all Men*, the (k) *Spirit given to every Man to profit with*, the (l) *Truth in the Inward Parts*, the (m) *Spiritual Leaven, that Leavens the whole Lump of Man*: Which are many of them Figurative Expressions, but all of them such as the *Holy Ghost* hath used, and which will be used in this Treatise, as they are most frequently in the Writings and Ministry of this People. But that this *Variety* and Manner of Expression may not occasion any Misapprehension or Confusion in the Understanding of the *Reader*, I would have him know, that they always mean by these Terms, or Denominations, not *another*, but the *same Principle*, before mentioned: Which, as I said, though it be in Man, is not of Man, but of God, and therefore *Divine*: And One in it self, tho' diversly expressed by the Holy Men, according to the Various Manifestations and Operations thereof.

§. 4. It is to this Principle of *Light, Life and Grace*, that this People refer all: For they say it is the Great Agent in Religion; *That*, without which, there is no *Conviction*, so no *Conversion*, or *Regeneration*; and consequently no entring into the Kingdom of God. That is to say, there can be no *True Sight of Sin*, nor *Sorrow for it*, and therefore no forsaking or overcoming of it, or Remission or Justification from it. A Necessary and Powerful Principle indeed, when neither Sanctification, nor Justification can be had without it. In short, there is no becoming Virtuous, Holy and Good, without this Principle; no Acceptance with God, nor Peace of Soul, but through it. But on the contrary, that the Reason of so much *Irreligion* among Christians, so much *Superstition*, instead of Devotion, and so much Profession without Enjoyment, and so little *Heart-Reformation*, is, because People in Religion, *Overlook* this Principle, and leave it behind them.

They will be Religious *without* it, and Christians without it, though this be the only Means of making them so indeed. So Natural is it to Man, in his Degenerate State, to *prefer* Sacrifice before Obedience, and to make Prayers go for Practice, and so flatter himself to hope, by Ceremonial and Bodily Service, to excuse himself with God from the stricter Discipline of this Principle in the Soul, which leads Man to take up the Cross, deny Self, and do that which God requires of him: And that is every Man's True Religion, and every such Man is Truly Religious: That is, *He is Holy, Humble, Patient, Meek, Merciful, Just, Kind, and Charitable*; which they say, no Man can make himself; but that this Principle will make them all so, that will embrace the *Convictions and Teachings of it*, being the *Root of all True Religion in Man, and the Good Seed from whence all Good Fruits proceed*. To sum up what they say upon the Nature and Virtue of it, as Contents of that

which

(a) John 1. 9.
(b) Rom. 1. 19. Tit. 3. 4.
(c) Acts 17. 28. 2. Pet. 4.
(d) Rom. 8. 6. 1 John 5. 10, 12.
(e) 1 Pet. 1. 23. 1 Joh. 3. 9.
(f) Mat. 13. 19, 23.
(g) Prov. 1. 20, 21, 22, 23. and 8. 1, 2, 3, 4.
(h) Deut. 30. 12. Rom. 10. 6, 7, 8. Ps. 119. 10.
(i) Tit. 2. 11. 12.
(k) 1 Cor. 12. 7.
(l) Ps. 51. 6. Isa. 26. 2. Joh. 14. 6.
(m) Mat. 13. 33.

which follows, they declare that this Principle is, First, *Divine*. Secondly, *Universal*. Thirdly, *Efficacious*: In that it gives Man,

First, *The Knowledge of God, and of himself*, and therein a Sight of his *Duty* and *Disobedience* to it.

Secondly, *It begets a true Sense and Sorrow for Sin* in those that seriously regard the Convictions of it.

Thirdly, *It enables them to forsake Sin, and Sanctifies from it:*

Fourthly, *It applies God's Mercies in Christ for the Forgiveness of Sins that are past, unto Justification, upon such sincere Repentance and Obedience.*

Fifthly, *It gives, to the Faithful, Perseverance unto a perfect Man, and the Assurance of Blessedness, World without End.*

To the Truth of all which, they call in a Threefold Evidence: *First*, The Scriptures, which give an ample Witness, especially those of the New and better Testament. *Secondly*, The Reasonableness of it in it self. And *Lastly*, A General Experience, in great Measure: But particularly, *Their Own*, made credible by the good Fruits they have brought forth, and the Answer God has given to their Ministry: Which, to impartial Observers, have commended the Principle, and gives me Occasion to abstract their *History*, in divers Particulars, for a Conclusion to this little *Treatise*.

CHAP. II. §. 1. *The Evidence of Scripture for this Principle*, John 1. 4. 9. §. 2. *Its Divinity*. §. 3. *All Things created by it.* §. 4. *What it is to Man, as to Salvation.*

§. 1. I Shall begin with the Evidence of the blessed Scriptures of Truth, for this *Divine Principle*, and that under the Name of *Light*, the first and most common Word used by them, to express and denominate this Principle by, as well as most apt and proper in this dark State of the World.

John 1. 1. *In the Beginning was the Word, and the Word was with God, and the Word was God.*

Vers. 3. *All Things were made by Him.*

Vers. 4. *In Him was Life, and that Life was the Light of Men.*

Vers. 9. *That was the True Light, which lighteth every Man that cometh into the World.*

§. 2. I have begun with him, that begun his *History* with him that was the *Beginning of the Creation of God*; the most beloved Disciple, and longest Liver of all the Apostles, and he, that for excellent Knowledge and Wisdom in Heavenly Things, is justly entituled *John the Divine*. He tells us first, what he was in the Beginning, viz. *The Word. In the Beginning was the Word.*

And though that shews what the *Word* must be, yet he adds and explains, that the *Word was with God, and the Word was God*; left any should doubt of the Divinity of the Word, or have lower Thoughts of Him than He deserved. The *Word* then, is *Divine*, and an apt Term it is, that the *Evangelist* stiles Him by, since it is so great an Expression of the Wisdom and Power of God to Men.

§. 3. *All Things were made by Him.* If so, he wants no Power. And if we were made by Him, we must be new made by Him too, or we can never enjoy God. His Power shews his Dignity, and that nothing can be too hard for such a Sufficiency *as made all Things, and without which nothing was made, that was made.* As Man's *Maker* must be his *Husband*, so his *Creator* must be his *Redeemer* also.

§. 4. *In him was Life, and the Life was the Light of Men.* This is our Point. The *Evangelist* first begins with the *Nature and Being* of the *Word*: From thence he descends to the *Works* of the *Word*: And lastly, then he tells us, what the *Word* is, with Respect to Man above the rest of the Creation, viz. *The Word was Life, and the Life was the Light of Men.* The Relation must be very near and intimate, when the very *Life* of the *Word* (*that was with God, and was God*) is the *Light of Men*: As if Men were next to the Word, and above all the rest of his Works; for it is not said so of any other Creature.

Man cannot want Light then; no not a *Divine Light*: For if this be not *Divine*, that is the *Life* of the *Divine Word*, there can be no such Thing at all as *Divine* or *Supernatural Light* and *Life*. And the Text does not only prove the *Divinity* of the Light, but the *Universality* of it also, because *Man* mentioned in it, is *Mankind*: Which is yet more distinctly express'd in his 9th Verse, *That was the True Light, which lighteth every Man that cometh into the World.* Implying, that he that lighteth not Mankind is not that *True Light*; and therefore *John* was not that

that *Light*, but bore witness of him that was, who *lighteth every Man*; to wit, the *Word* that took Flesh: So that both the *Divine Nature*, and *Universality* of the Light of Christ within, are confirmed together.

CHAP. III. §. 1. *How this Scripture is* wrested. §. 2. *That 'tis a* Natural Light. §. 3. *That it lighteth not all.* §. 4. *That 'tis only the* Doctrine *and* Life *of Christ when in the Flesh. All answered, and it's* Divinity *and* Universality *proved.*

§. 1. BUT though there be no Passage or Proposition to be found in Holy Scripture, in which Mankind is more interested, or that is more clearly laid down by the Holy Ghost, than this I have produced, yet hardly hath any Place been more industriously wrested from it's true and plain Sense: Especially since this People have laid any Stress upon it, in Defence of their Testimony of the *Light within*. Some will have it to be but a *Natural Light*, or a *Part of Man's Nature*, though it be the very *Life* of the *Word*, by which the World was made; and mention'd within those Verses, which only concern his *Eternal Power and Godhead*. But because I would be understood, and treat of Things with all Plainness, I will open the Terms of the Objection as well as I can, and then give my Answer to it.

§. 2. If by *Natural* be meant a created Thing, as Man is, or any Thing that is requisite to the Composition of Man, I deny it: The Text is expresly against it; and says, the Light with which Man is lighted, is the Life *of the Word, which was with God, and was God*. But if by Natural is only intended, that the Light comes along with us into the World; or that we have it as sure as we are born, or have Nature; and is the *Light* of our Nature, of our Minds and Understandings, and is not the Result of any Revelation from without, as by Angels or Men; then we mean and intend the same Thing. For it is *Natural* to Man to have a *Supernatural Light*, and for the Creature to be lighted by an *uncreated* Light, as is the Life of the *Creating Word*. And did People but consider the Constitution of Man, it would conduce much to preserve or deliver them from any Dilemma upon this Account. For Man can be no more a Light to his Mind, than he is to his Body: He has the Capacity of seeing Objects when he has the Help of Light, but cannot be a Light to himself, by which to see them. Wherefore as the *Sun* in the Firmament is the Light of the Body, and gives us discerning in our temporal Affairs; so the *Life* of the *Word* is the glorious *Light* and *Sun* of the *Soul*: Our *Intellectual Luminary*, that informs our Mind, and gives us true Judgment and Distinction about those Things that more immediately concern our Better, Inward and Eternal Man.

§. 3. But others will have this Text read thus, not that the Word enlightens all Mankind, *but that all who are enlightned, are enlightned by him*, thereby not only narrowing and abusing the Text, but rendring God partial, and so Severe to his Creatures, as to leave the greatest part of the World in Darkness, witout the Means or Opportunity of Salvation; though we are assured from the Scriptures That (a) *all have Light*, that *Christ is the* (b) *Light of the World*, and that he (c) *died for all*; yea, the (d) *Ungodly*, and that God desires not the (e) *Death of any, but rather that all should Repent and come to the Knowledge of the Truth and be saved*; and (f) *that the Grace of God has appeared to all Men*, &c.

§. 4. There is a Third Sort that will needs have it understood, not of any Illumination by a Divine Light or Spirit in Man, but by the Doctrine Christ preached, and the *Life* and *Example* he lived, and led in the World; and which yet neither reach'd the thousandth Part of Mankind, nor can consist with what the Apostle *John* intends in the Beginning of his History, which wholly relates to what Christ was before he took Flesh, or at least, what he is to the Soul, by his *immediate Inshinings* and *Influences*. 'Tis most true, Christ was, in a Sense, the *Light of the World*, in that very Appearance, and Shined forth by his *Heavenly Doctrine*, many admirable *Miracles*, and his *Self-Denying Life and Death*: But still that hinders not, but that he was and is *That Spiritual Light*, which shineth more or less, in the Hearts of the Sons and Daughters of Men. For as he was a *Light* in his Life and Conversation, he was only a *Light* in a more excellent Sense than he spoke of to his Disciples, when he said, *Ye are the Lights of the World*. But Christ the Word enlightned them, and enlightens us, and enlightens all Men that come into the World; which he could not be said to do, if we only Regard his Personal and Outward Appearance: For in that Sense it is long since he was that Light, but in this he is continually so. In that Respect he is *Remote*, but in this Sense he is *Present* and *immediate*, else we should render the Text, *That was the True Light which did lighten*, instead of *which Lighteth every Man that cometh into the World*. And that the

(a) John 1. 4. 9.
(b) Ch. 8. 12.
(c) Rom. 5, 6.
(d) 2 Cor. 5. 15.
(e) 1 Tim. 2, 4,
(f) Tit. 2, 11, 12.

1696.

Chap. III.

Evangelist might be so understood, as we speak, he refers to this as an Evidence of *His* being the *Messiah*, and not *John*; for whom many People had much Reverence. for *Verf.* 8. he saith of *John*, *He was not that Light, but was sent to bear Witness of that Light*: Now comes his Proof and our Testimony, *That was the true Light which lighteth every Man that cometh into the World*; which was not *John*, or any else, but *the Word that was with God, and was God.* The Evangelist did not describe him by his fasting forty Days, preaching so many Sermons, working so many Miracles, and Living so Holy a Life; and, after all, so patiently Suffering Death, (which yet Christ did) thereby to prove him the Light of the World; but, says the Evangelist, *That was the True Light, the Word in Flesh, the Messiah*, and not *John*, or any else, *which lighteth Every Man that cometh into the World.* So that Christ is manifested and distinguished by giving Light: And indeed so are all his Followers from other People, by *receiving* and *obeying* it. There are many other Scriptures, of both Testaments, that refer to the Light within; either expresly, or implicitly; which, for Brevity's Sake, I shall wave reciting; but the Reader will find some Directions in the Margin, which will guide him to them.

Job 18. 5, 6, & 21. 17. & 25. 3. & 38, 5. Pfalm 18. 28. & 27. 1. & 34. 5. & 36. 9. & 118.27.&119 105.Prov.13. 9. & 20. 20, 27. & 24. 20. Ifa. 2. 5. & 8. 20. & 42. 6.& 49. 6. 1 Pet. 2. 9. 1 John 2. 8.

Chap. IV.

CHAP. IV. §. 1. *The Virtue of the Light within*; *It gives* discerning. §. 2. *It manifests God.* §. 3. *It gives Life to the Soul.* §. 4. *It is the* Apostolical *Message.* §. 5. *Objection answered about two Lights.* §. 6. *About Natural and Spiritual Light*: *Not two Darknesses within, therefore not two Lights within.* §. 7. *The Apostle* John *answers the Objection fully*: *The Light the same,* 1 John 2. 8, 9.

§. 1. THE Third Thing, is the *Virtue* and *Efficacy* of this Light for the End for which God hath given it, *viz. To lead and guide the Soul of Man to Blessedness.* In order to which, the first Thing it does in and for Man, is to give him a true Sight or Discerning of himself: What he is, and what he does; that he may see and know his own Condition, and what Judgment to make of himself, with Respect to Religion and a future State: Of which, let us hear what the *Word* himself saith, that cannot Err, as *John* relates it, Chap. 3. 20, 21. *For every one that doth Evil, hateth the Light, neither cometh to the Light, lest his Deeds should be Reproved. But he that doth Truth cometh to the Light, that his Deeds may be made manifest, that they are wrought in God.* A most pregnant Instance of the *Virtue* and *Authority* of the Light. *First*, It is that which Men ought to Examine themselves by. *Secondly*, It gives a *true Discerning* betwixt Good and Bad, *what is of God, from what is not of God.* And, *Lastly*, It is a *Judge*, and condemneth or acquitteth, *reproveth* or *comforteth*, the Soul of Man, as he rejects or obeys it. That must needs be *Divine* and *Efficacious*, which is able to discover to Man, what is of God, from what is not of God; and which gives him a *Distinct* Knowledge, in himself, of what is wrought in God, from what is not wrought in God. By which it appears, that this Place does not only regard the Discovery of Man and his Works, but, in some Measure, *it manifesteth God, and his Works also*, which is yet something higher; for as much as it gives the *obedient* Man a Discovery of what is wrought or performed by *God's Power, and after his Will*, from what is the mere Workings of the Creature of himself. If it could not manifest God, it could not tell Man what was God's Mind, nor give him such a grounded Sense and Discerning of the Rise, Nature, and Tendency of the Workings of his Mind or Inward Man, as is both expressed and abundantly implied in this Passage of our Saviour. And if it reveals *God*, to be sure it manifests *Christ*, that flows and comes from *God.* Who then would oppose or slight this blessed Light?

§. 2. But that this *Light* doth *manifest* God, is yet Evident from Rom. 1. 19. *Because that which may be known of (God) is manifest in Men, for God hath shewed it unto them.* An *universal Proposition*; and we have the Apostle's Word for it, who was *One of a Thousand*, and inspired *on purpose* to tell us the Truth: Let it then have it's due Weight with us. If that which may be known of God is manifest in Men, the People called *Quakers* cannot, certainly, be out of the Way in Preaching up the *Light within*, without which, nothing can be manifested to the Mind of Man; as saith the same Apostle to the *Ephesians*, Eph. 5. 13. *Whatsoever doth make manifest is Light.* Well then may they call this Light within a *Manifestation* or *Appearance of God*, that sheweth *in* and to Man, *all that may be known of God.* A Passage much like unto this, is that of the Prophet *Micah*, Chap. 6. 8. *God hath shewed thee, O Man, what is good; and what doth the Lord require*

require of thee, but to do Juftly, and to love Mercy, and to walk humbly with thy God? God hath *fhewed, thee. O Man!* It is very Emphatical. But how hath He fhewed him? Why by his *Light in the Confcience,* which the *Wicked Rebel againft,* Job 24. 13. *Who, for that Caufe, know not the Ways, nor abide in the Paths thereof: For it's Way are Ways of Pleafantnefs, and all it's Paths are Peace,* to them that obey it.

§. 3. But the *Light* giveth the *Light of Life,* which is *Eternal Life* to them that receive and obey it. Thus, fays the bleffed Saviour of the World, John 8. 12. *I am the Light of the World, he that followeth me fhall not abide in Darknefs, but fhall have the Light of Life.* Now he is the Light of the World, becaufe he lighteth every Man that cometh into the World, and they that obey that Light obey him, and therefore have the Light of Life. That is, the Light becomes *Eternal Life* to the Soul: That as it is the *Life* of the *Word,* which is the *Light* in Man, fo it becomes the Life in Man, through his Obedience to it, as his *Heavenly Light.*

§. 4. Farthermore, this Light was the very Ground of the *Apoftolical Meffage,* as the Beloved Difciple affures us. 1 John 1. 5, 6, 7. *This then is the Meffage, which we have heard of him, and declare unto you, That God is Light, and in him is no Darknefs at all: If we fay we have Fellowfhip with him, and walk in Darknefs, we Lye, and do not the Truth: But if we walk in the Light, as he is in the Light, we have Fellowfhip one with another, and the Blood of Jefus Chrift cleanfeth us from all Sin.* Which is fo comprehenfive of the Virtue and Excellency of the Light, in Reference to Man, that there is little Need that more fhould be faid upon it; for as much as, *Firft,* It reveals God, and that God himfelf is Light. *Secondly,* It difcovers Darknefs from Light, and that there is no Fellowfhip between them. *Thirdly,* That Man ought to walk in the Light. *Fourthly,* That it is the Way to obtain Forgivenefs of Sin, and Sanctification from it. *Fifthly,* That it is the Means to have Peace and Fellowfhip with God and his People; his true Church, redeemed from the Pollutions of the World.

§. 5. Some, perhaps, may Object, as indeed it hath been more than once objected upon us, *That this is another Light, not that Light wherewith every Man is enlightned.* But the fame Apoftle, in his Evangelical Hiftory, tells us, that *in the Word was Life, and the Life was the Light of Men, and that that very Light,* that was the *Life* of the Word, was the *True Light* which lighteth *every Man* that cometh into the World, *John* 1. 4, 9. Where is there fo plain a Text to be found againft the Sufficiency, as well as Univerfality of the Light within; or a Plainer for any Article of Faith in the whole Book of God? Had the *Beloved Difciple* intended *Two* Lights, in his Evangelical Hiftory, and his Epiftles, to be fure he would have noted to us his Diftinction: But we read of none, and by the Properties afcribed in each Writing, we have Reafon to conclude he meant the fame.

§. 6. But if any fhall yet Object. *That this is to be underftood a Spiritual Light, and that ours is to be a Natural One,* I fhall defire them to do two Things: *Firft,* To prove that a *Natural* Light, as they phrafe it, doth manifeft God, other than as I have before explained and allowed: Since whatever is Part of Man, in his Conftitution, but efpecially in his Degeneracy from God, is fo far from yielding him the Knowledge of God, that it cannot *rightly* Reprove or Difcover that which offends him, without the Light we fpeak of: And it is granted, that what we call *Divine,* and fome, Miftakenly, call *Natural* Light, can do both. *Secondly,* If this Light be *Natural,* Notwithftanding it doth manifeft our Duty, and reprove our Difobedience to God, they would do well to affign us fome certain *Medium,* or *Way,* whereby we may truly difcern and diftinguifh between the Manifeftations and Reproofs of the *Natural* Light within, from thofe of the *Divine* Light within, fince they Allow the Manifeftation of God, and Reproof of Evil, as well to the one, as to the other. Let them give us but one Scripture that diftinguifhes between a *Natural* and a *Spiritual Light within.* They may, with as much Reafon, talk of a *Natural and Spiritual Darknefs within.* 'Tis true, there is a natural proper Darknefs, to wit, the Night of the Outward World; and there is a Spiritual Darknefs, *viz.* The *clouded* and *benighted* Underftandings of Men, through Difobedience to the Light and Spirit of God: But let them affign us a Third, if they can. People Ufe, indeed, to fay, improperly, of Blind Men, they are *Dark,* we may call a *Natural* or *Idiot* fo, if we will: But where is there another Darknefs of the Underftanding, in the Things of God? If they can, I fay, find that, in and about the Things of God, they do fomething.

Chrift diftinguifhed not between Darknefs and Darknefs, or Light and Light, in any fuch Senfe; nor did any of his Difciples: Yet both have frequently fpoken of Darknefs and Light. What Difference, pray, doth the Scripture put between Spiritual Darknefs, and Darknefs, mentioned in thefe Places, *Luke* 1. 7, 9. *Mat.* 4. 16. *John* 1. 5 & 3. 19. & 8. 12, 31, 46. 1 *Thef.* 5. 4. 1 *John* 1. 6. *Acts* 26. 18. *Rom.* 13. 12. 2 *Cor.* 6. 14, 22. *Eph.* 5. 8. *Col.* 1. 13. Upon the ftricteft Comparifon of them I find none. It is all one Spiritual Darknefs. Neither is there fo much as one Scripture that affords us a Diftinction between *Light within and Light within*; or that there are really *Two Lights* from God, in Man, that regard Religion. Perufe *Mat.* 4. 16. *Luke* 2. 32. & 15. 8. *John* 1. 4, 5, 7, 8, 9. & 3. 19, 20, 21. & 8. 12. *Acts* 26. 18. *Rom.* 13. 12. 2 *Cor.* 4. 6 & 6. 14. *Eph.* 5. 8, 13. *Col.* 1. 12. 1 *Theff.* 5. 5. 1 *Tim.* 6. 16. 1 *Pet.* 2. 9. 1 *John* 1. 5, 7. & 2. 8. *Rev.* 21. 23, 24. & 22. 5. And we believe the greateft Oppofer, to our Affertion, will not be able to fever Light from Light, or find out *two Lights within*, in the Paffages here mentioned, or any other, to direct Man in his Duty to God and his Neighbour: And if he cannot, pray let him forbear his *mean Thoughts and Words* of the *Light of Chrift within Man*, as Man's *Guide* in Duty to God and Man. For as he muft yield to us, that the Light Manifefteth Evil, and Reproveth for it, fo doth Chrift himfelf teach us of the Light, *John* 3. 20. *For every one that doth Evil hateth the Light, neither cometh unto the Light, left his Deeds fhould be reproved.* And the Apoftle *Paul* plainly faith, *Eph.* 5. 13. *But all Things that are reproved are made manifeft by the Light*; therefore there are not two diftinct Lights within, but one and the fame *Manifefting, Reproving*, and *Teaching Light within*. And this the Apoftle *John*, in his Firft Epiftle, makes plain, beyond all Exception, to all confiderate People: *Firft*, In that he calls God, *Light*, Chap. 1. 5. *Secondly*, In that he puts no *Medium*, or *Third* Thing between that *Light*, and *Darknefs*, Verfe 6. *If we fay we have Fellowfhip with him, and walk in Darknefs, we Lye*, &c. Intimating, that Men muft walk either in *Light* or *Darknefs*, and not in a *Third*, or other State or Region. I am fure, that which manifefts and reproves Darknefs, *cannot be Darknefs*. This all Men muft confefs.

§. 7. And, as if the Apoftle *John* would have anticipated their Objection, *viz.* 'Tis true, *your Light within reproves for Evil, but it is not therefore the Divine Light which leads into higher Things, and which comes by the Gofpel*; he thus expreffeth himfelf, 1 *John* 2. 8, 9. *The Darknefs is paft, and the true Light now fhineth. He that faith he is in the Light, and hateth his Brother, is in Darknefs even until now*; which is not another Light than that mentioned before, Chap. 1. For as Light is put there, in Oppofition to Darknefs, fo Light here, is put in *Oppofition* to Darknefs. And as the *Darknefs* is the *fame*, fo muft the *Light* be the *fame*. Wherefore we may plainly fee, that it is *not another Light*, than that which reproves a Man for *hating his Brother*, which brings a Man *into Fellowfhip with God, and to the Blood of Cleanfing*, as the next Verfe fpeaks: Therefore that Light which reproveth a Man for hating his Brother, *is of a Divine and Efficacious Nature*. In fhort, that Light which is oppofite to, and reproves Spiritual Darknefs, in a Man and Woman, is a *Spiritual Light*; but fuch a Light is that which we Confefs, Teftify to, and Maintain: Therefore it is a *Spiritual Light*. It is alfo worth our Notice, that the Apoftle ufeth the fame Manner of Expreffion here, Chap. 2. 8. The *True Light* fhineth, that he doth in his Evangelical Hiftory, Chap. 1. 9. That was the *True Light*; intimating the fame Divine Word, or *True* Light *now* fhineth; and that it is the fame *True Light* in his Account, that *reproveth* fuch as *hate their Brethren*: Confequently, that Light that fo reproveth them, is the *True Light*. And ftrange it is, that Chrift and his Difciples, but efpecially his beloved One, fhould fo often make that very Light, which *ftoops* to the *loweft* Step of Immorality, and to the Reproof of the *groffeft* Evil, to be no other than the *fame Divine Light*, in a farther Degree of Manifeftation, which brings fuch as follow it to the *Light of Life*, to the *Blood of Cleanfing*, and to have *Fellowfhip with God, and one with another*: Nay, not only fo, but the Apoftle makes a Man's being a *Child of God*, to depend upon his *Anfwering* of this Light in a *palpable* and common Cafe, *viz. Not hating of his Brother*: And that yet any fhould fhut their Eyes fo faft againft beholding the Virtue of it, as to conclude it a *Natural and Infufficient Light*, is both *Unfcriptural* and *Unreafonable*. Shall we flight it, becaufe we come fo eafily by it, and it is fo Familiar and Domeftick to us? Or make it's being fo common an Argument to undervalue fo Ineftimable a Mercy? What is more common than *Light* and *Air*, and *Water*? And fhould we therefore contemn
them,

them, or prize them? *Prize* them, certainly, as what we cannot live, nor live *comfortably* without. The more general the Mercy is, the greater, and therefore the greater Obligation upon Man to live humbly and thankfully for it. And to those alone that do so, are it's Divine Secrets revealed.

CHAP. V. §. 1. *The Light the same with the* Spirit. *It is of God; proved by it's Properties.* §. 2. *The Properties of the Spirit compared with those of the Light.* §. 3. *The Light and Grace flow from the same Principle, proved by their agreeing Properties.* §. 4. *An Objection Answered.* §. 5. *Difference in* Manifestation, *or Operation, especially in* Gospel-Times, *but not in Principle, Illustrated.*

Obj. BUT some may say, *We could willingly allow to the Spirit and Grace of God, which seemed to be the peculiar Blessing of the New and Second Covenant, and the Fruit of the Coming of Christ, all that which you ascribe to the Light within; but except it appeared to us that this Light were the same in Nature with the Spirit and Grace of God, we cannot easily bring our selves to believe what you say in Favour of the Light within.*

Answ. This *Objection*, at first Look, seems to carry Weight with it: But upon a just and serious Review, it will appear to have more Words than Matter, Shew than Substance: Yet because it gives Occasion to solve Scruples, that may be flung in the Way of the Simple, I shall attend it throughout. I say, then, if it appear that the *Properties*, ascribed to the *Light within*, are the same with those that are given to the *Holy Spirit* and *Grace* of God; and that those several Terms or Epithets, are only to express the divers Manifestations or Operations of one and the same Principle, then it will not, it cannot, be denied, but this Light within, is *Divine* and *Efficacious*, as we have Asserted it. Now, that it is of the same Nature with the Spirit and Grace of God, and tends to the same End, which is to bring People to God, let the *Properties* of the *Light* be compared with those of the *Spirit* and *Grace of God*. I say, they are the same, in that, *First*, The Light proceeds from the *One Word*, and *One Life* of that *One Word*, which was *with* God and was God, *John* 1. 4. & 1. 9. Secondly, It is *Universal*, it lighteth *every* Man. Thirdly, *It giveth the Knowledge of God, and Fellowship with* him. *Rom.* 1. 19. *John* 3. 21. 1 *John* 1. 5, 6. Fourthly, *It manifesteth and reproveth Evil*, John 3. 20. Eph. 5. 13. Fifthly, *It is made the Rule and Guide of Christian Walking*, Psalm 43. 3. John 8. 12. Eph. 5. 13, 15. Sixthly, *It is the Path for God's People to go in, Psalm* 119. 105. *Prov.* 4. 18. *Isaiah* 2. 5. 1 *John* 1. 7. *Rev.* 24. 23. *And the Nations of them that are saved, shall walk in the Light of the (Lamb.)* Lastly, It is the *Armour* of the Children of God against Satan, Psalm 27. 1. *The Lord is my Light, whom shall I fear?* Rom. 13. 12. *Let us put on the Armour of Light.*

§. 2. Now let all this be compared with the *Properties* of the *Holy Spirit*, and their Agreement will be very manifest. First, *It proceedeth from God*, because it is the Spirit of God, *Rom.* 6. 11. Secondly, It is *Universal*. It *strove* with the Old World, *Gen.* 6. 3. Then to be sure with the New One: *Every one hath a Measure of it given to profit withal*, 1 Cor. 12. 7. Thirdly, *It revealeth God*, Job 32. 8. 1 Cor. 2. 10, 11. Fourthly, *It reproveth Sin*, John 16. 8. Fifthly, *It is a Rule and Guide for the Children of God to walk by*, Rom. 8. 14. Sixthly, It is also the *Path* they are to walk in, *Rom.* 8. 1. *Gal.* 5. 15. *Walk in the Spirit.* Lastly, This is not all; It is likewise the *Spiritual Weapon* of a true Christian, *Eph.* 6. 17. *Take the Sword of the Spirit, which is the Word of God.* After this, I hope none will deny that *this* Light and *this* Spirit must be of *one and the same* Nature, that work *one and the same Effect*, and tend evidently to *one and the same Holy End*.

§. 3. And what is said of the *Light* and *Spirit*, may also, very well be said of the *Light* and *Grace* of God; in that, *First*, The *Grace* floweth from Christ, the Word, that took Flesh, as well as the *Light*; for as in him was Life, and that Life the *Light* of Men, so he was *full of Grace and Truth, and of his Fulness have all we received, and Grace for Grace,* John 1. 4, 9, 14, 16. Secondly, It is *Universal*; both from this Text, and what the Apostle to *Titus* teacheth; *For the Grace of God that bringeth Salvation, hath appeared to all Men,* Tit. 2: 11, 12. Thirdly, It *manifesteth Evil*, for if it teaches to *deny* Ungodliness and worldly Lusts, it must needs detect them, and so says the Text. Fourthly, *It revealeth Godliness, and*

and consequently it must manifest God. Fifthly, It is an *Instructor and Guide*; for, says the *Apostle, It teaches to deny Ungodliness and worldly Lusts, and to live Soberly, Righteously, and Godly in this present World, and herein a Rule of Life,* Tit. 2. 11, 12. Sixthly, *It is, to all that receive it, all that they can need or desire.* 2 Cor. 12. 9. *My Grace is sufficient for thee.* An High Testimony from *Heaven*, to the Power of this *Teaching* and *Saving Grace*, under the strongest Temptations.

§. 4. *Obj. But there is little Mention made of the Spirit, and none of the Grace, before Christ's Coming, and therefore the Spirit, as spoken of in the Writings of the New Testament, and especially the Grace, must be another, and a Nobler Thing than the Light Within.*

Answ. By no Means another Thing, but another Name, from *another Manifestation or Operation*, of the same Principle. It is call'd Light from the Distinction and Discerning it gives. *Let there be Light, and there was Light,* said God in the Beginning of the Old World; so there is first Light in the Beginning of the New Creation of God in Man. It is called *Spirit*, because it *giveth Life, Sense, Motion, and Vigour*: And it is as often mentioned in the Writings of the Old as New Testament; which every *Reader* may see, if he will but please to look into his *Scripture-Concordance*. Thus *God's Spirit strove with the Old World*, Gen. 6. 3. and with *Israel* in the Wilderness, Neh. 9. 30. And *David* asked, in the Agony of his Soul, *Whither shall I go from thy Spirit?* Psf. 139. 7. and the Prophets often felt it. It is stiled Grace, not from it's being another Principle, but because it was a fuller Dispensation of the Virtue and Power of the same Divine Principle: And that being purely God's Favour and Mercy, and not Man's Merit, is aptly, and deservedly called the *Grace, Favour,* or *Good-Will of God, to undeserving Man.* The Wind does not always blow fresh, nor Heaven send down it's Rain freely, nor the Sun shine forth clearly; shall we therefore say, it is not of the same Kind of Wind, Rain or Light, when it Blows, Rains, or Shines but a little, as when it Blows, Rains, or Shines much? It is certainly the same in Nature and Kind; and so is this *Blessed Principle*, under all its several Dispensations, Manifestations and Operations, for the Benefit of Man's Soul, ever since the World began.

§. 5. But this is most freely, humbly and thankfully acknowledged by us, That the Dispensation of the Gospel, was the clearest, fullest, and Noblest of all other; both with Regard to the Coming of Christ in the Flesh, and being our One Holy Offering to God for Sin, through the Eternal Spirit; and the Breaking forth of His Light, the Effusion of His Spirit, and Appearance of His Grace, in, and to Man, in a more Excellent Manner, after His Ascension. For tho' it was not another Light, or Spirit, than that which he had given to Man in former Ages, yet it was another and *Greater Measure*; and that is the Priviledge of the Gospel above former Dispensations. What before Shined but dimly, Shines since with Great Glory. Then *it appeared but darkly, but now with Open Face.* Types, Figures and Shadows *Vailed* its Appearances and made them look low and faint; but in *the Gospel Time, the Vail is Rent, and the Hidden Glory manifest.* It was under the Law but as a Dew, or small Rain, but under the Gospel, it may be said to be poured out upon Men: According to that Gracious and Notable Promise of God, by the Prophet *Joel, In the latter Days I will pour out of my Spirit upon all Flesh.* Thus we say when itRains plentifully, look how it pours. So God augments His Light, Grace and Spirit to these latter Days. They shall not have it sparingly, and by small Drops, *but fully and freely, and overflowing too.* And thus *Peter*, that deep and excellent Apostle, applies that Promise in *Joel*, on the *Day of Pentecost*, as the Beginning of the Accomplishment of it. This is Grace, and Favour, and Goodness indeed. And therefore well may this Brighter Illumination, and Greater Effusion of the Spirit, be called *Grace*; for as the Coming of the Son excelled that of the Servant, so did the Manifestation of the Light and Spirit of God, since the Coming of Christ, excel that of the foregoing Dispensations; yet ever sufficient to Salvation, to all those that walked in it. This is our *Sense of the Light, Spirit, and Grace of God*: And by what is said, it is evident they are *One and the same Principle*, and that He that has Light, need not want the Spirit or Grace of God, if he will but receive it, in the Love of it: For the very Principle, that is Light to show him, is also Spirit to quicken him, and Grace to Teach, Help, and Comfort him. It is sufficient in all Circumstances of Life, to them that diligently mind and obey it.

CHAP. VI. §. 1. *An Objection answered: All are not Good, tho' All are Lighted.* **§. 2.** *Another Objection answered, That Gospel-Truths were known before Christ's Coming.* **§. 3.** *Another: The Gentiles had the Same Light, tho' not with those Advantages: Prov'd from Scripture.*

§. 1. Obj. BUT some may yet say, *If it be as you declare, How comes it, that all who are Enlightned, are not so Good as they should be; Or, as you say, this would make them?*

Answ. Because People don't receive and obey it: All Men have *Reason*, but all Men are not *Reasonable*. Is it the Fault of the *Grain*, in the *Granary*, that it yields no Increase, or of the *Talent* in the Napkin, that it is not improved? It is plain a *Talent* was given; and as plain that it was improveable; both because the like Talents were actually improved by others, and, *That the Just Judge expected His Talent with Advantage*; which else, to be sure, he would never have done. Now when our Objectors will tell us, whose Fault it was the *Talent* was not improved, we shall be ready to tell them, *Why the Unprofitable Servant was not so Good as he should have been.* The Blind must not blame the Sun, nor Sinners tax the *Grace of Insufficiency*. 'Tis Sin that darkens the Eye, and hardens the Heart, and that hinders Good Things from the Sons of Men. *If we do His Will, we shall know of His Divine Doctrine*, so Christ tells us. Men not living to what they know, cannot blame God, that they know no more. The Unfruitfulness is in *Us*, not in the *Talent*. 'Twere well indeed, that this were laid to Heart. But, alas! Men are too apt to follow their Sensual Appetites, rather than their Reasonable Mind, which renders them Brutal instead of Rational. For the *Reasonable Part in Man*, is his *Spiritual Part*, and that guided by the Divine λόγος, or *Word*, which *Tertullian* interprets *Reason in the most Excellent Sense*, makes *Man truly Reasonable*; and then it is that Man comes to offer up himself to God a *Reasonable Sacrifice*. Then a *Man indeed*; a *Compleat Man*; Such a Man as *G O D made*, when he made Man in *His Own Image*, and gave him Paradise for his Habitation.

§. 2. Obj. But some yet object, *If Mankind had always this Principle, how comes it that Gospel-Truths were not so fully known before the Coming of Christ, to those that were Obedient to it.*

Answ. Because a Child is not a Grown Man, nor the Beginning the End; and yet He that is the Beginning, is also the End: The Principle is the same, tho' not the Manifestation. As the World has many Steps and Periods of Time towards it's End, so hath Man to his Perfection. They that are Faithful to what they know of the Dispensation of their own Day, shall hear the Happy Welcome, of *Well done, Good and Faithful Servant.* And yet many of God's People in those Days, had a Prospect of the Glory of the Latter Times, the Improvement of Religion, the Happiness of the Church of God.

This we see in the *Prophesie of Jacob and Moses*, concerning the *Restoration of Israel by Christ*. So *David*, in many of his Excellent *Psalms*, expressing most Sensible and Extraordinary Enjoyments, as well as *Prophesies*; particularly his 2, 15, 18, 22, 23, 25, 27, 32, 36, 37, 42, 43, 45, 51, 84, &c. The Prophets are full of it, and for that Reason have their Name; particularly *Isaiah*, Chap. 2. 9, 11. 25, 28, 32, 35, 42, 49, 50, 51, 52, 53, 54, 59, 60, 61, 63, 65, 66. *Jeremiah* also, Chap. 23, 30, 31, 33. *Ezekiel*, Chap. 20, 34, 36, 37. *Daniel*, Chap. 8, 9, 10, 11, 12. *Hosea.* Chap. 1, 3. *Joel*, Chap. 2, 3. Amos, Chap. 9. *Micah*, Chap. 4, 5. *Zachariah*, Chap. 6, 8, 9, 11, 13, 14. *Malachy*, Chap. 3. 4. This was not another Principle, though another Manifestation of the same Principle, nor was it common, but particular and extraordinary in the Reason of it.

Gen. 49. 10. Deut. 18. 15, 18.

It was the same Spirit that came upon *Moses*, which came upon *John the Baptist*, and it was also the same Spirit that came upon *Gideon* and *Sampson*, that fell upon *Peter* and *Paul*; but it was not the same Dispensation of that Spirit. It hath been the Way of God, to visit and appear to Men, according to their States and Conditions, and as they have been prepared to receive him, be it more outwardly or inwardly, sensibly or spiritually. There is no Capacity too low, or too high, for this Divine Principle: For as it made and knows all, so it reaches unto all People. It extends to the Meanest, and the Highest cannot subsist without it. Which made *David* break forth in his Expostulations with God, *Whither shall I go from thy Spirit, or whither shall I flee from thy Presence?* Psal. 139, 7, 8, 9, 10. Implying it was every where, though not every where, nor at every Time alike. *If I go to Heaven, to Hell, or beyond the Seas, even there shall thy Hand lead me, and thy Right*

Right Hand shall hold me. That is, there will this Divine Word, this Light of Men, this Spirit of God, find me, lead me, help me, and comfort me. For it is with me where ever I am, and where ever I go, in one Respect or other; *Prov.* 6. 22. *When thou goest, it shall lead thee; when thou sleepest, it shall keep thee; and when thou awakest, it shall talk with thee*: And I can no more get rid of it, if I would, than of my self, or my own Nature; so present is it with me, and so close it sticks unto me. *Isa.* 43. 2. *When thou passest through the Waters, I will be with thee; and through the Rivers, they shall not overflow thee; when thou walkest through the Fire, thou shalt not be burnt, neither shall the Flame kindle upon thee.* David knew it, and therefore had a Great Value for it. *In thy Light shall we see Light*, or we shall be Enlightned by thy Light. *Thou wilt Light my Candle; the Lord my God will Lighten my Darkness.* Again, *The Lord is my Light, whom shall I fear.* It was his Armour against all Danger. It took Fear away from him, and he was undaunted, because he was Safe in the Way of it. Of the same Blessed Word he says elsewhere, *It is a Lamp unto my Feet, and a Lanthorn to my Paths.* In short, a Light to him in his Way to Blessedness.

§. 3. Obj. *But if the* Jews *had this Light, it does not follow that the* Gentiles *had it also; but by your Doctrine all have it.*

Answ. Yes, and it is the Glory of this Doctrine which we profess, that God's Love is therein held forth to *All*. And besides the Texts cited in General, and that are as Full and Positive as can be express'd, the Apostle is very Particular in the Second Chapter of his Epistle to the *Romans, That the Gentiles having not the Law, did by Nature the Things contained in the Law, and were a Law unto themselves.* That is, they had not an Outward Law, Circumstanced as the *Jews* had; but *they had the Work of the Law written in their Hearts*, and therefore might well be a Law to themselves, that had the Law *in themselves.* And so had the *Jews* too, but then they had greater Outward Helps to quicken their Obedience to it; such as God afforded not unto any other Nation: And therefore the Obedience of the *Gentiles*, or Uncircumcision, is said to be by Nature, or Naturally, because it was without those Additional, External, and Extraordinary Ministries and Helps, which the *Jews* had to provoke them to Duty. Which is so far from lessening the *Obedient Gentiles*, that it exalts them in the Apostle's Judgment; because though they had less Advantages than the *Jews*, yet the *Work of the Law written in their Hearts*, was made so much the more evident by the Good Life they lived in the World. He adds, *their Consciences bearing Witness* (or as it may be render'd, witnessing with them) *and their Thoughts, mean While, accusing, or else excusing one another, in the Day when God shall judge the Secrets of all Hearts by Jesus Christ, according to my Gospel.* Which presents us with Four Things to our Point, and worth our Serious Reflection. *First*, That the *Gentiles* had the Law written in their Hearts. *Secondly*, That their Conscience was an allowed Witness or Evidence about Duty. *Thirdly*, That the Judgment made thereby shall be Confirmed by the Apostle's Gospel at the Great Day, and therefore Valid and Irreversible. *Fourthly*, That this could not be, if the Light of this Conscience were not a Divine and Sufficient Light: For Conscience truly speaking, *is no other than the Sense a Man hath, or Judgment he maketh of his Duty to God, according to the Understanding God gives him of His Will.* And that no Ill, but a True and Scriptural Use may be made of this Word *Conscience*, I limit it to Duty, and that to a Virtuous and Holy Life, as the Apostle evidently doth, about which we cannot miss, or dispute; Read *Verses* 7, 8, and 9. It was to that therefore the Apostles of our Lord Jesus Christ desired to be made manifest, for they dared to stand the Judgment of *Conscience*, in Reference to the Doctrine they Preach'd and Press'd upon Men. The Beloved Disciple also makes it a Judge of Man's present and future State, under the Term Heart, *For if our Heart Condemn us, God is greater than our Heart, and knoweth all Things. Beloved, if our Heart Condemn us not, then have we Confidence towards God.* Plain and strong Words: And what were they about, but whether we love God, in Deed and in Truth: And how must that appear? Why, in *Keeping His Commandments*, which is living up to what we know. And if any desire to satisfy themselves farther of the Divinity of the *Gentiles*, let them read *Plato, Seneca, Plutarch, Epictetus, Marcus Aurelius Antoninus*, and the *Gentile Writers.* They will also find many of their Sayings, collected in the First Part of a Book, called, *The Christian Quaker*, and compared with the Testimonies of Scripture, not for their Authority, but Agreeableness. In them they may discern many Excellent Truths, and taste Great Love and Devotion to Virtue: A Fruit that grows upon no Tree, but that of Life, in no Age or Nation. Some of the Most Eminent Writers of the First Ages, such as *Justin Martyr, Origen, Clemens Alexandrinus,* &c. bore them great Respect, and thought it no lessening to the Reputation of Christianity, that it was defended in many *Gentile* Authors, as well as that they used and urged them, to engage their Followers to the Faith, as *Paul* did the *Athenians* with their own Poets.

CHAP. VII. §. 1. *An Objection answer'd about the various Dispensations of God: The Principle the same.* §. 2. *God's Work of a Piece, and* Truth *the same under* divers Shapes. §. 3. *The Reason of the Prevalency of* Idolatry. §. 4. *The Quaker's Testimony the Best Antidote against it,* viz. Walking by a Divine Principle in Man. §. 5. *It was God's End in all His Manifestations, that Man might be* God's Image and Delight.

§. 1. BUT it may be said, *If it were One Principle, Why so many Modes and Shapes of Religion, since the World began? For the* Patriarchal, Mosaical, *and* Christian, *have their great Differences; to say nothing of what has befallen the* Christian, *since the Publication of it to the World.*

Answ. I know not how properly they may be called divers Religions, that assert the *True God* for the Object of Worship; the Lord *Jesus Christ,* for the *Only Saviour*; and the *Light,* or *Spirit of Christ,* for the *Great Agent and Means of Man's Conversion, and Eternal Felicity,* any more than Infancy, Youth, and Manhood, make *Three Men,* instead of *Three Growths or Periods of Time,* of one and the same Man. But passing that, the many Modes, or Ways of God's appearing to Men, arise, as hath been said, from the divers States of Men, in all which, it seems to have been his main Design to prevent Idolatry and Vice, by directing their Minds to the True Object of Worship, and pressing Virtue and Holiness. So that tho' mediately he spoke to the Patriarchs, mostly by Angels, in the Fashion of Men, and by them to their Families, over and above the Illumination in themselves; so to the Prophets, for the most Part, by the Revelation of the Holy Ghost in them, and by them to the *Jews*; And since the Gospel Dispensation, by his Son, both Externally, *by His coming in the Flesh,* and Internally, *by His Spiritual Appearance in the Soul, as He is the Great Light of the World:* Yet all it's Flowings mediately through others, have still been from the same Principle, Co-operating with the Manifestation of it immediately in Man's own Particular.

§. 2. This is of great Weight, for our Information and Encouragement, that God's Work, in Reference to Man, is *All of a Peice,* and, in it self, lies in a narrow Compass, and that His Eye has ever been upon the same Thing in all his Dispensations, viz. *To make Men truly Good,* by planting His Holy Awe and Fear in their Hearts: Tho' He has condescended, for the Hardness and Darkness of Men's Hearts, to approach, and spell out His Holy Mind, to them, by low and carnal Ways, as they may appear to our more Enlightned Understandings: Suffering *Truth* to put on divers Sorts of Garments, the better to reach to the low State of Men, to engage them from false Gods, and ill Lives; seeing them sunk so much below their Nobler Part, and what He made them, that, like Brute Beasts, they knew not their own Strength and Excellency.

§. 3. And if we do but well consider the Reason of the Prevalency of *Idolatry,* upon the earlier and darker Times of the World, of which the Scripture is very particular, we shall find that it ariseth from this; that it is more Sensual, and therefore calculated to please the *Senses of Men*; being more *Outward or Visible,* or more in their own Power to perform, than one more Spiritual in it's Object. For as their Gods were the Workmanship of Men's Hands, they could not prefer them, that being the Argument which did most of all gaul their Worshippers, and what of all Things, for that Reason, they were most willing to forget. But their Incidency to *Idolatry,* and the Advantages it had upon the True Religion with them, plainly came from this, *That it was more Outward and Sensual:* They could see the Object of their Devotion, and had it in in their Power to address it when they would. It was more *Fashionable* too, as well as better accommodated to their Dark, and too Brutal, State. And therefore it was that God, by many Afflictions, and greater Deliverances, brought forth a People, to endear himself to them, that they might *Remember the Hand that Saved them,* and Worship Him, and Him only; in order to root up *Idolatry,* and *Plant the Knowledge, and Fear of Him, in their Minds,* for an Example to other Nations. Whoever reads *Deuteronomy,* which is a Summary of the other Four Books of *Moses,* will find the frequent and earnest

Gen. 31. c. 35.
Exod. 20. ---
Levit. 21. ---
Deut. 29. 30. 31, 32. chap.
Josh. 22, 23, 24 chap.

Care and Concern of that Good Man for *Israel*, about this very Point; and how often that People flipt and laps'd, notwithstanding God's Love, Care and Patience over them, into the *Idolatrous* Customs of the Nations about them. Divers other Scriptures inform us also, especially those of the Prophets, *Isaiah* 44. and 45. *Psalms* 37. and 115. and *Jer.* 10. where the Holy Ghost Confutes and Rebukes the People, and mocks their *Idols* with a fort of Holy Disdain.

§. 4. Now that which is farthest from Idolatry, and the best *Antidote* against it, is the *Principle* we have laid down, and the more People's Minds are turned and brought to it, and that they resolve their Faith, Worship, and Obedience into the Holy Illuminations and Power of it, the *nearer* they grow to the End of their Creation, and consequently to their *Creator*. They are more spiritually qualify'd, and become better fitted to Worship God as he is: Who, as we are told, by our Lord Jesus Christ, *Is a Spirit, and will be Worshipped in Spirit and in Truth, and that they are such Sort of Worshippers which God seeketh to worship him, in this Gospel-Day. The Hour cometh*, faith he, *and now is*. That is, some now do so, but more shall. A plain Assertion in present, and a *Promise* and *Prophesy* of the Increase of *such* Worshippers in future. Which shews a Change intended from a Ceremonial Worship, and State of the Church of God, to a *Spiritual* One. Thus the Text; *But the Time cometh, and now is, when True Worshippers shall worship the Father in Spirit and in Truth*. Which is as much as to say, when the Worship of God shall be more Inward than Outward, and so more *suitable* to the Nature of God, and the Nobler Part of Man, his *Inside*, or his *inward and better Man*: For so those blessed Words import, *in Spirit and in Truth*. *In Spirit*, that is, thro' *the Power* of the Spirit. *In Truth*, that is, in *Realities*, not in Shadows, Ceremonies, or Formalities, but in Sincerity, with and in Life, being divinely prepared and animated; which brings Man not only to offer up *Right* Worship, but also into *Intimate Communion and Fellowship with God, who is a Spirit*.

§. 5. And if it be duly weighed, it will appear, that God, in all his Manifestations of himself, hath still come *nearer* and *nearer* to the *Insides* of Men, that he might reach to their Understandings, and open their Hearts, and give them a plainer and nearer Acquaintance with himself in Spirit: And then it is that Man must seek and find the Knowledge of God for his Eternal Happiness. Indeed, all Things, that are made, shew forth the Power and Wisdom of God, and his Goodness too, to Mankind; and therefore many Men urge the *Creation* to silence *Atheistical* Objections: But though all those Things shew a God, yet Man does it, above all the rest. He is the *precious Stone* of the *Ring*, and the most *glorious Jewel* of the *Globe*; to whose reasonable Use, Service, and Satisfaction, the whole seems to be made and dedicated. *But God's Delight* (by whom Man was made, we are told by the Holy Ghost) *is in the habitable Parts of the Earth, with the Sons of Men*, Prov. 8. 31. And with those that are contrite in Spirit, *Isaiah* 66. 1. And why is Man his Delight, but because Man only, of all his Works, was of his Likeness. This is the *intimate* Relation of Man to God: Somewhat *nearer* than ordinary; for of all other Beings, Man *only* had the Honour of being his *Image*; and, by his *Resemblance* to God, as I may say, came his Kindred with God and Knowledge of him. So that the nearest and best Way for Man to know God, and be acquainted with him, is to seek him in himself, in his *Image*; and, as he finds that, he comes to find and know God. Now Man may be said to be God's Image in a double Respect. *First*, As he is of an Immortal Nature; and, next, as that Nature is *Endued* with those Excellencies in *small*, and proportionable to a Creature's Capacity, that are by Nature *Infinitely* and *Incomparably* in his Creator. For Instance, *Wisdom, Justice, Mercy, Holiness, Patience*, and the like. As Man becomes Holy, Just, Merciful, Patient, *&c.* By the *Copy* He will know the *Original*, and by the *Workmanship* in himself, he will be acquainted with the Holy *Workman*. This, Reader, is the *Regeneration* and *New Creature* we press, (Gal. 6. 15, 16.) *and according to this Rule, we say, Men ought to be Religious, and walk in this World*. Man, as I said just now, is a Composition of both Worlds; his Body is of this, his Soul of the other World. The Body is as the Temple of the Soul, the Soul the *Temple* of the *Word*, and the *Word* the *Great Temple* and *Manifestation* of God. By the *Body* the Soul looks into and beholds this World, and by the *Word* it beholds God, and the World that is without End. Much might be said of this Order of Things, and their respective Excellencies, but I must be Brief.

CHAP. VIII. §. 1. *The Doctrines of* Satisfaction *and* Justification *Owned and Worded according to* Scripture. §. 2. *What Constructions we can't believe of them, and which is an Abuse of them.* §. 3. *Christ Owned a Sacrifice and a Mediator.* §. 4. Justification Twofold, *from the Guilt of Sin, and from the Power and Pollution of it.* §. 5. *Exhortation to the Reader upon the whole.*

Obj. 1. THough there be many good Things said, how Christ appears and works in a Soul, to Awaken, Convince and Convert it; yet you seem not particular enough about the Death and Sufferings of Christ: And it is generally Rumour'd and Charged upon you by your Adversaries, that you have little Reverence to the Doctrine of Christ's Satisfaction to God for our Sins, and that you do not Believe, That the Active and Passive Obedience of Christ, when he was in the World, is the alone Ground of a Sinner's Justification before God.

Answ. The Doctrines of *Satisfaction* and *Justification,* truly understood, are placed in so strict an Union, that the one is a necessary Consequence of the other, and what we say of them, is what agrees with the Suffrage of Scripture, and for the most Part in the Terms of it; always believing, that in Points where there arises any Difficulty, be it from the Obscurity of Expression, Mis-translation, or the Dust raised by the Heats of *Partial* Writers, or *Nice Criticks,* it is ever best to keep close to the Text, and maintain Charity in the rest. I shall first speak *Negatively,* what we do not own, which perhaps hath given Occasion to those who have been more Hasty than Wise, to judge us defective, in our Belief of the Efficacy of the Death and Sufferings of Christ to Justification: As,

§. 2. *First,* We cannot believe that Christ is the *Cause,* but the *Effect* of God's Love, according to the Testimony of the Beloved Disciple, *John,* Chap. 3. *God so loved the World, that he gave his only Begotten Son into the World, that whosoever believeth in him should not perish, but have Everlasting Life.*

Secondly, We cannot say, God could not have taken another Way to have saved Sinners, than by the Death and Sufferings of his Son, to satisfy his Justice, or that Christ's Death and Sufferings were a *strict* and *rigid* Satisfaction for that Eternal Death and Misery due to Man for Sin and Transgression: for such a Notion were to make God's Mercy little concerned in Man's Salvation; and indeed we are at too great a Distance from his Infinite Wisdom and Power, to judge of the *Liberty* or *Necessity* of his Actings.

Thirdly, We cannot say Jesus Christ was the *greatest Sinner* in the World, (because he bore our Sins on his Cross, or because he was made Sin for us, who knew no Sin) an Expression of great *Levity* and *Unsoundness,* yet often said by great Preachers and Professors of Religion.

Fourthly, We cannot Believe that Christ's Death and Sufferings *so* satisfies God, or justifies Men, as that they are thereby Accepted of God: They are indeed thereby put into a State capable of being accepted of God, and through the Obedience of Faith and Sanctification of the Spirit, are in a State of Acceptance: For we can never think a Man justified before God, while *Self-condemned*; or that any Man can be in Christ who is not a *New* Creature; or that God looks upon Men *otherwise* than they are. We think it a State of *Presumption* and not of *Salvation,* to call *Jesus Lord,* and not by the Work of the *Holy Ghost. . Master,* and he not yet *Master of their Affections: Saviour,* and they not saved by him from their *Sins: Redeemer,* and yet they not redeemed by him from their *Passion, Pride, Covetousness, Wantonness, Vanity, Vain Honours, Friendships,* and *Glory* of this World: Which were to deceive themselves; for God will not be mocked, such as Men sow, such they must reap. And tho' Christ did *Die* for us, yet we must, by the Assistance of his Grace, *work out our Salvation with Fear and Trembling*: As he died for Sin, so we must Die *to* Sin, or we cannot be said to be saved by the Death and Sufferings of Christ, or throughly justified and accepted with God. Thus far Negatively. Now, Positively, what we own as to Justification.

§. 3. We do Believe that Jesus Christ was our Holy *Sacrifice, Atonement,* and *Propitiation*; that he bore our Iniquities, and that by his Stripes we were healed of the Wounds *Adam* gave us in his Fall; and that God is just in forgiving true Penitents upon the Credit of that Holy Offering Christ made of himself to God for us; and that what he did and suffered, satisfied and pleased God, and was for the Sake of Fallen Man, that had displeased God: And that through the Offering up of himself once for all, through the Eternal Spirit, he hath for ever per-

fected

fected those (in all Times) that were sanctified, *who walked not after the Flesh, but after the Spirit*, Rom. 8. 1. Mark that.

§. 4. In short, *Justification* consists of *two* Parts, or hath a *twofold* Consideration, *viz.* Justification from the *Guilt of Sin*, and Justification from the *Power and Pollution of Sin*, and in this Sense Justification gives a Man a full and clear Acceptance before God. For want of this latter Part it is, that so many Souls, Religiously inclined, are often under Doubts, Scruples, and Despondencies, notwithstanding all that their Teachers tell them of the Extent and Efficacy of the first Part of Justification. And it is too general an Unhappiness among the Professors of Christianity, that they are apt to *cloak* their own Active and Passive *Disobedience* with the *Active and Passive Obedience of Christ*. The first Part of Justification, we do reverently and humbly acknowledge, is only for the Sake of the Death and Sufferings of Christ: Nothing we can do, *though by the Operation of the Holy Spirit*, being able to cancel Old Debts, or wipe out Old Scores: It is the Power and Efficacy of that Propitiatory Offering, upon *Faith* and *Repentance*, that justifies us from the Sins that are past; and it is the Power of Christ's Spirit in our Hearts, that purifies and makes us acceptable before God. For 'till the Heart of Man is purged from Sin, God will never accept of it. He Reproves, Rebukes and Condemns those that entertain Sin there, and therefore such cannot be said to be in a *Justified* State; Condemnation and Justification being Contraries: So that they that hold themselves in a Justified State by the Active and Passive Obedience of Christ, while they are not Actively and Passively Obedient to the Spirit of Christ Jesus, are under a *strong* and *dangerous Delusion*; and for crying out against this Sin-pleasing Imagination, not to say *Doctrine*, we are Staged and Reproached as Denyers and Despisers of the Death and Sufferings of our Lord Jesus Christ. But be it known to such, they add to Christ's Sufferings, and Crucifie to themselves afresh the Son of God, and trample the Blood of the Covenant under their Feet, that walk unholily under a Profession of Justification; for God will not acquit the Guilty, nor justify the Disobedient and Unfaithful. Such deceive themselves, and at the Great and Final Judgment their Sentence will not be, *Come ye Blessed*, because it cannot be said to them, *Well done Good and Faithful*, for they cannot be so esteemed that live and die in a Reproveable and Condemnable State; but, *Go ye Cursed*, &c.

§. 5. Wherefore, O my Reader! Rest not thy self wholly satisfied with what Christ has done for thee in his Blessed Person without Thee, but press to know his Power and Kingdom *within thee*, that the *strong Man*, that has too long kept thy House, may be *bound*, and his Goods *spoiled*, his Works *destroy'd*, and Sin *ended*, according to 1 *John* 3. 7. For which End, says that Beloved Disciple, *Christ was manifested*, that all Things may become New: *New Heavens and New Earth, in which Righteousness dwells*. Thus thou wilt come to glorify God in thy Body and in thy Spirit, which are his; and live to him and not to thy self. Thy Love, Joy, Worship and Obedience; thy Life, Conversation, and Practice; thy Study, Meditation, and *Devotion*, will be *Spiritual*: For the Father and the Son will make their *Abode* with thee, and Christ will manifest himself to thee; for the *Secrets* of the Lord are with them that *fear him*: And an Holy *Unction* or *Anointing* have all those, which leads them *into all Truth*, and they need not the Teachings of Men. They are better Taught, being Instructed by the *Divine Oracle*: No bare *Hear-say*, or *Traditional* Christians, but fresh and living Witnesses: Those that have seen with their *own Eyes*, and heard with their *own Ears*, and have handled with their *own Hands*, the Word of Life, in the divers Operations of it, to their Souls Salvation. In this they Meet, in this they Preach, and in this they Pray and Praise: Behold the New Covenant fulfilled, the Church and Worship of Christ, the Great *Anointed* of God, and the Great *Anointing* of God, in his Holy High Priesthood, and Offices in his Church!

CHAP. IX. §. 1. *A Confession to Christ and his Work, both in Doing and Suffering.* §. 2. *That ought not to make void our Belief and Testimony of his Inward and Spiritual Appearance in the Soul.* §. 3. *What our Testimony is in the latter Respect: That 'tis impossible to be Saved by Christ Without us, while we reject his Work and Power Within us.* §. 4. *The Dispensation of Grace, in it's Nature and Extent.* §. 5. *A farther Acknowledgment to the Death and Sufferings of Christ.* §. 6. *The Conclusion, shewing our Adversary's Unreasonableness.*

AND

§. 1. AND lest any should say we are *Equivocal* in our Expressions, and *Allegorize away* Christ's Appearance in the Flesh; meaning only thereby, our own Flesh; and that as often as we mention him, we mean only a *Mystery*, or a *Mystical Sense* of him, be it as to his *Coming, Birth, Miracles, Sufferings, Death, Resurrection, Ascension, Mediation* and *Judgment*; I would yet add, to preserve the well-disposed from being staggered by such Suggestions, and to inform and reclaim such as are under the Power and Prejudice of them, That, we do, we Bless God, Religiously Believe and Confess, to the Glory of God the Father, and the Honour of his Dear and Beloved Son, that, *Jesus Christ, took our Nature upon him, and was like unto us in all Things,* Sin excepted: *That he was born of the Virgin* Mary, *Suffered under* Pontius Pilate, *the Roman Governor, was Crucified, Dead, and Buried in the Sepulchre of* Joseph *of* Arimathea; *Rose again the Third Day, and Ascended into Heaven, and sits on the Right Hand of God, in the* Power and Majesty of his Father; *who will one Day judge the World by him, even that* Blessed Man, Christ Jesus, *according to their Works.*

§. 2. But because we so Believe, must we not believe what Christ said, *He that is with you shall be* in you, John 14. *I in them, and they in me,* &c. Chap. 17. *When it pleased God to reveal his Son* in me, &c. Gal. *The Mystery hid from Ages, is Christ* in *the* Gentiles *the Hope of Glory,* Col. 1. *Unless Christ be* in you, *ye are Reprobates?* 2 Cor. 13. Or must we be industriously represented Denyers of Christ's Coming in the Flesh, and the Holy *Ends* of it, in all the Parts and Branches of his *Doing* and *Suffering*, only because we believe and press the Necessity of Believing, Receiving and *Obeying* his *Inward* and *Spiritual* Appearance and Manifestation of himself, through his Light, Grace and Spirit in the Hearts and Consciences of Men and Women, to Reprove, Convict, Convert and Change them? This we esteem hard and unrighteous Measure; nor would our warm and sharp Adversaries be so dealt with by others: But to do as they would be done to, is too often no Part of their Practice, whatever it be of their Profession.

§. 3. Yet we are very ready to declare to the whole World, that we cannot think Men and Women *can be saved* by their Belief of the one, *without the Sense and Experience of the other*; and that is what we oppose, and not his Blessed Manifestation in the Flesh. We say that he then overcame our Common Enemy, foil'd him in the open Field, and in our Nature triumphed over him that had overcome and triumphed over it in our Fore-father *Adam* and his Posterity: And that as truly as Christ overcame him in our Nature, in his own Person, so, *by his Divine Grace*, being received and obeyed by us, he overcomes him in us: That is, he detects the Enemy by his Light in the Conscience, and *enables* the Creature to resist him, and all his Fiery Darts; and finally, so to Fight the Good Fight of Faith, as to *overcome* him, and lay hold on Eternal Life.

§. 4. And this is the Dispensation of *Grace*, which we declare has appeared to *All*, more or less; teaching those that will receive it, *to deny Ungodliness and worldly Lusts, and to live soberly, righteously, and godly in this present World; looking for* (which none else can justly do) *the blessed Hope, and glorious Appearing of the Great God, and our Saviour Jesus Christ,* &c. Tit. 2. 11, 12, 13. And as from the Teachings, Experience and Motion, of this Grace we minister to others, so the very Drift of our Ministry is to turn People's Minds to this Grace in themselves, that all of them may up and be doing, *even the good and acceptable Will of God, and work out their Salvation with Fear and Trembling,* and make their High and Heavenly Calling and Election sure; which none else can do, whatever be their *Profession, Church* and *Character*: *For such as Men sow they must reap*; and his Servants we are whom we obey. *Regeneration* we must know, or we cannot be Children of God, and Heirs of Eternal Glory: And to be Born again, *another* Spirit and Principle must *prevail, leaven, season,* and *govern* us, than either the Spirit of the World, or our own depraved Spirits; and this can be no other Spirit than that which dwelt in Christ; for unless that dwell in us, we can be none of his, Rom. 8. 9. And this Spirit begins in *Conviction*, and ends in *Conversion* and *Perseverance*; and the one follows the other. Conversion being the Consequence of *Convictions obeyed*, and Perseverance a natural *Fruit* of Conversion, and being Born of God; *for such Sin not, because the Seed of God abides in them:* John 3. 7, 8. But such, through Faithfulness, continue to the End, and obtain the Promise, even Everlasting Life.

§. 5. But

§. 5. But let my *Reader* take this along with him, that we do acknowledge that *Christ*, through his Holy *Doing* and *Suffering*, (for being a *Son* he learned *Obedience*) has obtained Mercy of God his Father for Mankind, and that his Obedience has an Influence to our Salvation, in all the Parts and Branches of it, since thereby he became a Conqueror, and *led Captivity Captive, and obtained Gifts for Men, with divers great and precious Promises, that thereby we might be Partakers of the Divine Nature, having* (first) *escaped the* Corruption *that is in the World, through Lust*. I say, we do believe and confess, that the *Active* and *Passive Obedience* of Christ Jesus affects our Salvation throughout, as well from the Power and Pollution of Sin, as from the Guilt, He being a Conqueror as well as a Sacrifice, and both through Suffering; Yet they that reject his Divine Gift, so obtained, (and which he has given to them, by which to see their Sin and the Sinfulness of it, and to repent and turn away from it, and do so no more; and to wait upon God for daily Strength to resist the Fiery Darts of the Enemy, and to be Comforted through the Obedience of Faith in and to this Divine Grace of the Son of God) such do not please God, believe truly in God, nor are they in a State of true Christianity and Salvation. *Woman*, said Christ, to the *Samaritan*, at the Well, *hadst thou known the Gift of God, and who it is that speaketh to thee*, &c. People know not Christ, and God, whom to know is Life Eternal, *John* 17. because they are Ignorant of the Gift of God, *viz.* a Measure of the Spirit of God that is given to every one to profit with, 1 *Cor.* 12. 7. which reveals Christ and God to the Soul, Chap. 2. *Flesh* and *Blood* cannot do it, *Oxford* and *Cambridge* cannot do it, *Tongues* and *Philosophy* cannot do it: For they that *by Wisdom* knew not God, had these Things for their *Wisdom*. They were strong, deep and accurate in them; but, alas! they were clouded, puffed up, and set farther off from the Inward and Saving Knowledge of God, because they sought for it in them, and thought to find God there. But the *Key* of *David* is another Thing, which shuts and no Man opens, and opens and no Man shuts; and this Key have all they that receive the *Gift of God* into their Hearts, and it opens to them the Knowledge of God and themselves, and gives them a quite *other Sight, Taste* and *Judgment* of Things than their *Educational* or *Traditional* Knowledge afforded them. This is the Beginning of the *New Creation* of God, and thus it is we come to be *New Creatures*.

And we are bold to declare, there is no other Way like this, by which People can come into Christ, or be true Christians, or receive the Advantage that comes by the Death and Sufferings of the Lord Jesus Christ. Wherefore we say, and upon good Authority, even that of our *own Experience*, as well as that of the Scriptures of Truth, *Christ will prove no Saving Sacrifice for them, that refuse to obey him for their Example*. They that *reject* the Gift, *deny* the *Giver* instead of themselves for the *Giver's* Sake, O that People were wise, that they would consider their latter End, and the Things that make for the Peace thereof! Why should they perish in a vain Hope of Life, *while Death Reigns?* Of living with God, who live not to him, nor walk with him? *Awake* thou that sleepest in thy Sin, or at best, in thy Self-righteousness! Awake, I say, and Christ shall give thee Life! For he is the *Lord from Heaven, the Quickning Spirit*, that quickens us, by his Spirit, if we do not *resist* it and *quench* it by our Disobedience, but receive, love and obey it, in all the Holy Leadings and Teachings of it. *Rom.* 8. 14, 15. To which Holy Spirit I commend my *Reader*, that he may the better see where he is, and also come to the true Belief and Advantage of the *Doings* and *Sufferings* of our Dear and Blessed Lord and Saviour Jesus Christ, who saves from the *Power and Pollution*, as well as *Guilt* of Sin, all those that *hear his Knocks, and open the Door of their Hearts* to him, that he may come in and work a real and *thorough Reformation* in and for them; And so the *Benefit, Virtue* and *Efficacy* of his *Doings* and *Sufferings* without us, will come to be livingly & effectually applied and felt, and Fellowship with Christ in his Death and Sufferings known, according to the Doctrine of the Apostle; which, those that live in that which made him Suffer, know not, though they profess to be saved by his Death and Sufferings. Much more might be said as to this Matter, but I must be brief.

§. 6. To conclude this Chapter, we wonder not that we should be mistaken, mis-construed and mis-represented, in what we believe and do to Salvation, since our *Betters* have been so treated in the Primitive Times. Nor indeed is it only about *Doctrines* of Religion; for our *Practice* in *Worship* and *Discipline* have had the same Success. But this is what I earnestly desire, that however bold People are

are pleased to make with us, they would not *deceive* themselves in the Great Things of their own Salvation: That while they would seem to own all to Christ, they are not found *Disowned* of Christ in the last Day. Read the 7th of *Matthew*: It is he that hears Christ, the great *Word of God*, and does what he enjoins, what he commands, and by his Blessed Example recommends, that is a *Wise Builder*, that has founded his House well, and built with good Materials, and whose House will stand the last Shock and Judgment. For which Cause we are often plain, close and earnest with People to consider, that Christ came not to save them in, but *From their Sins*; and that they that think to discharge and release themselves of his *Yoke* and *Burden*, his *Cross* and *Example*, and secure themselves, and Complement Christ with his having done all for them (while he has wrought *little or nothing in them*, nor they parted with any Thing for the Love of him) will finally awake in a dreadful Surprize, at the Sound of the *last Trumpet*, and at this sad and irrevocable Sentence, *Depart from me ye Workers of Iniquity, I know you not:* Which terrible End may all timely avoid, by *hearkening* to Wisdom's Voice, and *turning* at her Reproof, that she may lead them in the Ways of Righteousness, and in the midst of the Paths of Judgment, that their Souls may come to inherit *Substance*; even *durable Riches and Righteousness* in the Kingdom of the Father, *World without End.*

CHAP. X. *Of the true* Worship *of God in what it stands.* §. 2. *Of the true* Ministry, *that it is by Inspiration.* §. 3. *The Scripture plain in that Case.* §. 4. *Christ's Ministers,* True Witnesses, *they speak what they* know, *not by Report.* §. 5. *Christ's Ministers Preach* freely, *'tis one of their* Marks.

§. 1. AS the Lord wrought effectually, by his Divine Grace, in the Hearts of this People, so he thereby brought them to a *Divine Worship and Ministry*; Christ's Words they came to Experience, *viz. That God was a Spirit, and that he would therefore be worshipped in the Spirit, and in the Truth, and that such Worshippers the Father would seek to worship him.* For, bowing to the Convictions of the Spirit in themselves, in their daily Course of Living, by which they were taught to eschew that which was made manifest to them to be Evil, and to do that which was Good, they, in their assembling together, sate down, and waited for the Preparation of this Holy Spirit, both to let them see their States and Conditions before the Lord, and to worship him acceptably; and as they were sensible of Wants, or Shortness, or Infirmities, so in the Secret of their own Hearts, Prayer would Spring to God, through Jesus Christ, to help, assist and supply: But they did not dare to *awake their Beloved before his Time*; or *approach the Throne of the King of Glory, till he held out his Scepter*; or *take Thought what they should say*, or after their own or other Men's studied *Words and Forms*, for this were to Offer *strange Fire*; to pray, but not by the Spirit; to ask, but not in the Name, that is, in the Power of our Lord Jesus Christ, who prayed, as well as spoke, like one having Authority, that is, *Power*, a *Divine Energy* and *Force* to reach and Pierce the Heavens, which he gives to all that obey his *Light, Grace* and *Spirit,* in their solemn Waitings upon him. So that 'tis this People's Principle, that *Fire must come from Heaven*; Life and Power from God to enable the Soul to pour out it self acceptably before him. And when a *Coal from his Holy Altar touches our Lips*, then can we Pray and Praise him as we ought to do. And as this is our Principle, and that according to Scripture, so it is, Blessed be God, our Experience and Practice: And therefore it is we are separated from the Worships of Men, under their several Forms, because they do not found it in the Operation, Motion and Assistance of the Spirit of Christ, but the Appointment, Invention and Framing of Man, both as to Matter, Words and Time. We do not dissent in our own Wills, and we dare not comply against his that has called us, and brought us to his own Spiritual Worship; in Obedience to whom we are what we are, in our Separation from the divers Ways of Worship in the World.

§. 2. And as our *Worship* stands in the Operation of the *Spirit* and *Truth* in our inward Parts, as before expressed, so does our Ministry. For as the Holy Testimonies of the Servants of God of Old, were from the Operation of his Blessed Spirit, so must those of his Servants be in every Age, and that which has not the Spirit of Christ for it's Spring and Source, is of *Man*, and not of *Christ*. Christian Ministers are to minister *what they receive:* This is *Scripture*; now that which we receive is not our own, less another Man's, but the *Lord's*: So that we are not only

only not to *Steal* from our Neighbours, but we are not to *Study* nor speak our own *Words*. If we are not to study what we are to say before Magistrates for our selves, less are we to study what we are to say *for and from* God to the People. We are to minister, *as the Oracles of God*; if so, then must we receive *from Christ,* God's Great Oracle, what we are to minister. And if we are to minister what we receive, then not what we Study, Collect, and beat out of our own Brains, for that is not the Mind of Christ, but our Imaginations, and this will not profit the People.

§. 3. This was recommended to the *Corinthians* by the Apostle *Paul*, 1 *Cor.* 14. that they should speak *as they were moved*, or *as any thing was revealed to them, by the Spirit*, for the Edification of the Church; for, says he, *Ye may all Prophecy*; that is, ye may all Preach to Edification, *as any thing is revealed to you*, for the Good of others, *and as the Spirit giveth Utterance*. And if the Spirit must give Christ's Ministers their Utterance, then those that are his are careful not to utter any Thing in his Name to the People, without his Spirit; and by good Consequence, they that go before the true Guide, and utter Words without the Knowledge of the Mind of the Spirit, are none of Christ's Ministers: Such, certainly, run, and God has not sent them, and they cannot profit the People. And indeed, how should they, when it is impossible that mere Man, with all his Parts, Arts and Acquirements, *can turn People from Darkness to Light, and from the Power of Satan to God*, which is the very End and Work of the Gospel-Ministry. It must be inspired Men, Men gifted by God, taught and influenced by his Heavenly Spirit, that can be qualified for so great, so inward, and so spiritual a Work.

§. 4. *Ministers* of Christ are his *Witnesses*, and the Credit of a Witness is, that he has *heard, seen* or *handled*: And thus the Beloved Disciple states the *Truth* and *Authority* of their *Mission* and *Ministry*; 1 *John* 1. 1, 3. *That which we have heard, which we have seen with our Eyes, which we have looked upon and our Hands have handled, that declare we unto you, that your Fellowship may be with us, and truly our Fellowship is with the Father, and with his Son Jesus Christ.* I say, if Christ's Ministers are his *Witnesses*, they must know what they speak; that is, they must have experienced, and passed through those *States* and *Conditions*, they Preach of, and practically know those Truths they declare of to the People, or they come not in by the Door, but over the Wall, and are *Thieves* and *Robbers*. He that has the Key of *David* comes in at the Door, Christ Jesus, and has his *Admission* and *Approbation* from him, *anointed* by him, the alone *High Priest* of the Gospel-Dispensation. He it is that Breathes, and *lays his Hands* upon his own Ministers; he anoints them, and recruits their Cruise, and renews their *Horn* with *Oil*, that they may have it fresh and fresh, for every Occasion and Service he calls them to, and engages them in.

§. 5. Nor is this all, *but as they Receive freely, freely they Give*: They do not Teach for *Hire*, Divine for *Money*, nor Preach for *Gifts* or *Rewards*. It was Christ's Holy Command to his Ministers to give *freely*, and it is our Practice. And truly we cannot but admire that this should be made a Fault, and that Preaching for Hire should not be seen to be one; yea, a *Mark* of False Prophets, when it has been so frequently and severely cried out upon, by the True Prophets of God in former Times. I would not be Uncharitable, but the Guilty are desired to call to Mind, who it was that offered Money to be made a Minister, and what it was for; if not to get Money and make a Trade or Livelihood by it; and what Answer he met with from the Apostle *Peter*, *Acts* 8. 18, 19, 20. The Lord *Touch* the Hearts of those that are giving Money to be made Ministers, in order to live by their Preaching, that they may see what Ground it is they build upon, and repent, and turn to the Lord, that they may find Mercy, and become living Witnesses of his Power and Goodness in their own Souls; so may they be enabled to tell others *What God has done for them*, which is the *Root* and *Ground* of the true *Ministry*; and this Ministry it is that God does Bless. I could say much on this Subject, but let what has been said suffice at this Time, only I cannot but observe, that where any Religion has a strong Temptation of Gain to induce Men to be Ministers, there is great Danger of their running faster to that Calling, than becomes a true Gospel-Minister.

§. 1. Obj. *But does not this Sort of Ministry, and Worship, tend to make People careless, and to raise Spiritual Pride in others, may it not give an Occasion to great Mischief and Irreligion?*

Answ.

Answ. By no Means, for when People are of *Age*, they, of Right, expect their Inheritances; and the End of all Words is to bring People to the great *Word*, and then the Promise of God is accomplished, *They shall be all taught of me, from the least to the greatest, and in Righteousness* (pray mark that) *they shall be established, and great shall be their Peace.* To this of the Evangelical Prophet, the Beloved Disciple agrees, and gives a full Answer to the Objection: *These Things have I written unto you, concerning them that Seduce you: But the* Anointing, *which ye have received of him, abideth* in you, *and ye need not that any Man teach you, but as the same* Anointing *teacheth you, of all Things, and is Truth, and is no Lie: And even as it hath taught you,* ye shall abide in him. In which, Three Things are observable. 1*st*. That he writ his Epistle upon an extraordinary Occasion, *viz*. to prevent their *Delusion*. 2*dly*. That he asserts a nearer and superior Minister than himself, *viz.* The *Anointing or Grace* they had received; and that not only in that particular Exigency, but in *all Cases* that might attend them. 3*dly*. That if they did but take Heed to the Teachings of it, they would have no Need of Man's Directions, or Fear of his Seducings. At least of no *Ministry that comes not from the Power of the Anointing:* Though I rather take the Apostle in the highest Sense of the Words: Thus also the Apostle *Paul* to the *Thessalonians*. *But as touching Brotherly Love, ye need not that I write unto you: For ye your selves are* taught of God *to love one another.* 1 *Thess.* 4. 9. But Helps are useful, and a great Blessing, if from God, such was *John* the *Baptist's*; but remember he pointed all to Christ, 1 *John* 1. 26. *Lo the Lamb of God! I baptize you with Water, but he shall baptize you with the Holy Ghost and with Fire,* Matt. 3. 11. And so the true Ministry does. And while People are *Sensual,* and under such an Eclipse, by the Interposition of *Sin* and *Satan,* God is pleased to send forth his *Enlightning* Servants to awaken and turn them *from the Darkness to the Light in themselves,* that, through Obedience to it, they may come to be *Children of the Light,* John. 12. 36. And have their Fellowship one with another in it, and an Inheritance at last, with the Saints in Light for ever.

And as it is the Way God has taken to call and gather People, so a *Living* and *Holy Ministry* is of great Advantage to watch over, and build up the Young, and *comfort* and *establish* the feeble and simple Ones. But still I say, the *more Inward,* the *less Outward*: The more People come to be taught immediately of God, by the Light of his Word and Spirit in their Hearts, the less need of outward Means, read *Isa.* 16. 19, 20. Which is held by all to be a Gospel Promise, and the Sun and Moon there are generally understood to mean the external Means in the Church. Compare them with *John* 1. 13. *Rom.* 1: 19. 1 *Cor.* 2. 11. 15. 1 *Thess.* 4. 9: 1 *John* 2. 20, 27. *Rev.* 21. 22, 23, 24. All which Places prove what we assert of the Sufficiency and glorious Priviledge of Inward and Spiritual Teachings. And most certainly, as Men grow in *Grace,* and know the *Anointing* of the Word in themselves, the Dispensation will be less in Words (though in Words) and more in Life; and Preaching will in great Measure be turned into *Praising*, and the Worship of God, more into *walking with,* than talking of God: For that is *Worship indeed,* that *bows* to his Will at all Times, and in all Places: The *Truest,* the *Highest* Worship, Man is capable of in this World. And it is that Conformity that gives Communion, and there is no Fellowship with God, no Light of his Countenance to be enjoyed, no Peace and Assurance to be had, farther than their *Obedience* to his Will, and a *Faithfulness* to his Word, according to the Manifestation of the Light thereof in the Heart.

I say, this is the *Truest* and *Highest* State of Worship; for *Set Days and Places,* with all the Solemnity of them, were most in Request *in the* weakest Dispensation. *Altars, Ark and Temples, Sabbaths and Festivals,* &c. Are not to be found in the Writings of the New-Testament. There, every Day is alike, and every Place is alike; but if there were a Dedication, *let it be to the Lord.* Thus the Apostle, but he plainly shews a State beyond it, *for to live* (with him) *was Christ, and to die was Gain*; for the Life he lived, *was by the Faith of the Son of God, and therefore it was not he that lived, but* Christ that lived in him; that is, that *Ruled, Conducted,* and *bore Sway* in him, which is the true *Christian Life,* the *Supersensual Life*; the *Life of Conversion and Regeneration*; to which all the *Dispensations* of God, and *Ministry* of his Servants have ever tended, as the *Consummation* of God's Work for Man's Happiness. Here every Man's a *Temple,* and every Family a *Church,* and every Place, a *Meeting-Place,* and every Visit a *Meeting.* And yet a little while and

Rom. 14. 5. 6, 7, 8. 17. 1 Cor. 8. 6. Col. 2. 16. 17 Phil. 1. 21. Gal. 2. 20.

1696.

it shall be so yet more and more; and a People the Lord is now preparing to enter into this Sabbath or Degree of Rest.

Chap. X. Not that we would be thought to undervalue Publick and Solemn Meetings: we have them all over the Nation where the Lord has called us. Yea, though but Two or Three of us be in a Corner of a Country, we meet, as the Apostle exhorted the Saints of his Time, and reproved such as neglected to assemble themselves. But yet shew we unto thee, *O Reader, a more excellent Way* of Worship: For many may come to those Meetings, and go away *Carnal, Dead and Dry*; but the Worshippers *in Spirit and in Truth*, whose *Hearts* bow, whose *Minds* adore the Eternal God, *that is a Spirit*, in and by his Spirit, such as conform to his Will, and walk with him in a Spiritual Life, they are the *True, Constant, Living* and *Acceptable Worshippers*; whether it be in Meetings or out of Meetings; and as with such, all outward Assemblies are greatly comfortable, so also do we meet for a Publick Testimony of Religion and Worship, and for the *Edification* and *Encouragement* of those that are yet young in the Truth, and to *Call and Gather* others to the Knowledge of it, who are yet going astray; and Blessed be God, it is not in Vain, since many are thereby added to the Church, that we hope and believe shall be saved.

Chap. XI. Chap. XI. §. 1. *Against* Tithes. §. 2. *Against all* Swearing. §. 3. *Against* War *among Christians*. §. 4. *Against the* Salutations *of the Times*. §. 5. *And for Plainness of Speech*. §. 6. *Against Mixt-Marriages*. §. 7. *And for plainness in Apparel*, &c. *No Sports and Pastimes after the Manner of this World.* §. 8. *Of observing Days.* §. 9. *Of Care of Poor, Peace and Conversation.*

§. 1. And as God has been pleased to call us from an *Humane Ministry*, so we cannot for Conscience Sake support and maintain it, and upon that Score, and not out of *Humour* or *Covetousness*, we refuse to pay *Tithes*, or such-like pretended Dues, concerning which, many Books have been writ in our Defence: We cannot support what we cannot approve, but have a Testimony against; for thereby we should be found *Inconsistent* with our selves.

§. 2. We dare not *Swear*, because Christ forbids it. *Mat.* 5. 34, 37. *and James*, his true Follower. It is needless as well as Evil, for the Reason of *Swearing* being *Untruth*, that Men's *Yea was not Yea*, Swearing was used to awe Men to Truth Speaking, and to give others Satisfaction, that what was Sworn, was True. But the true Christians *Yea being Yea*, the End of an *Oath* is answered, and therefore the Use of it is *Needless, Superfluous and cometh of Evil*. The Apostle *James* taught the same Doctrine, and the Primitive *Christians* practised it, as may be seen in the Book of *Martyrs*; as also the earliest and best of the Reformers.

§. 3. We also believe, *that War ought to cease*, among the Followers of the *Lamb* Christ Jesus, who taught his Disciples to *forgive and love their Enemies*, and not to war against them, and kill them; and that therefore the Weapons of his true Followers are not *Carnal* but *Spiritual*; yea mighty, through God, to cut down Sin and *Wickedness*, and *dethrone* him that is the Author thereof. And as this is the most *Christian*, so the most rational Way; Love and Perswasion having more Force than Weapons of War. Nor would the worst of Men easily be brought to hurt those that they really think love them. 'Tis that Love and Patience must in the End have the Victory.

§. 4. We dare not give worldly Honour, or use the frequent and *Modish Salutations* of the Times, seeing plainly, that *Vanity, Pride, and Ostentation*, belong to them. Christ also forbad them in his Day, and made the Love of them a Mark of Declension from the Simplicity of purer Times; and his Disciples, and their Followers, were observed to have obeyed their Master's Precept. It is not to distinguish our selves a Party, or out of *Pride, Ill-Breeding* or *Humour*, but in Obedience to the Sight and Sense we have received from the Spirit of Christ, of the *Evil Rise* and Tendency thereof.

§. 5. For the same Reason we have returned to the first *Plainness* of Speech, viz. *Thou* and *Thee*, to a single Person, which though Men give no other to God, they will hardly endure it from us. It has been a great Test upon Pride, and shewn the *Blind and weak Insides* of many. This also is out of pure Conscience, whatever People may think or say of us for it. We may be despised, and have been so often, yea, very evilly entreated, but we are now better known, and People better informed. In short, 'tis also both *Scripture* and *Grammar*, and we have Propriety of Speech for it, as well as Peace in it.

§. 6. We

§. 6. We cannot allow of *Mix'd Marriages*, that is, to join with such as are not of our Society; but Oppose and Disown them, if at any Time any of our Profession so grosly Err from the Rule of their Communion; yet Restore them upon sincere Repentance, but not disjoin them. The Book I writ of the Rise and Progress of the People called *Quakers*, is more full and express herein.

§. 7. *Plainness in Apparel and Furniture*, is another Testimony peculiar to us, in the Degree we have bore it to the World: As also *few Words*, and being *at a Word*. Likewise *Temperance* in *Food*, and *Abstinence* from the *Recreations* and *Pastimes* of the World: All which we have been taught, by the Spirit of our Lord Jesus Christ, to be according to Godliness; and therefore we have long exhorted all, that their *Moderation may be known unto all Men, for that the Lord was at Hand*, to enter into Judgment with us for every Intemperance or Excess; and herein we hope we have been no ill Examples, or Scandal unto any that have a due Consideration of Things.

§. 8. We cannot, in Conscience to God, observe *Holy Days*, (so called) the Publick *Fasts* and *Feasts*, because of their *Human* Institution and Ordination, and that, they have not a Divine Warrant, but are appointed in the Will of Man.

§. 9. *Lastly*, We have been led by this Good Spirit of our Lord *Jesus Christ* of which I have treated in this Discourse, according to *Primitive* Practice, to have a *due Care* over one another, for the Preservation of the whole Society, in a Conversation more *suitable* to their Holy Profession.

First, In Respect to a *strict* Walking both towards those that are Without, and those that are Within; that their Conversation in the World, and walking in and towards the Church, may be blameless. That as they may be *Strict* in the one, so they may be *Faithful* in the other.

Secondly, That Collections be made to supply the Wants of the *Poor*, and that Care be taken of *Widows* and *Orphans*, and such as are helpless, as well in *Counsel* as about *Substance*.

Thirdly, That all such as are intended to Marry, if they have *Parents*, or are under the Direction of *Guardians* or *Trustees*, are obliged, *first*, to declare to them their Intention, and have their Consent *before* they propose it to one another, and the Meeting they relate to, who are *also careful* to examine their Clearness, and being satisfied with it, They are by them allowed to solemnize their Marriage in a Publick Select Meeting, for that Purpose Appointed, and not otherwise: Whereby all *Clandestine* and *Indirect* Marriages are prevented among us.

Fourthly, And to the End that this *Good Order* may be observed, for the Comfort and Edification of the *Society*, in the Ways of *Truth* and *Soberness*; Select Meetings (of *Care* and *Business*) are fixed in all Parts, where we Inhabit, which are held *Monthly*, and which Resolve into *Quarterly* Meetings, and those into one *Yearly* Meeting, for our better Communication one with another, in those Things that maintain *Piety* and *Charity*; that God, who by his Grace, has called us to be a People, to his Praise, may have it from us, through his Beloved Son, and our Ever-blessed and Only Redeemer, Jesus Christ, for He is *Worthy, Worthy*, Now, and Ever. *Amen*.

Thus, *Reader*, thou hast the *Character* of the People called *Quakers*, in their *Doctrine, Worship, Ministry, Practice* and *Discipline*: Compare it with Scripture, and Primitive Example, and we hope thou wilt find, that this short Discourse hath, in good Measure, Answered the Title of it, *viz*.

Primitive Christianity Revived, in the Principles and Practice of the People called Quakers.

A TESTIMONY to the TRUTH of GOD,

As held by the People, called *QUAKERS*: Being a short Vindication of them, from the *Abuses* and *Misrepresentations* often put upon them by *Envious Apostates*, and *Mercenary Adversaries*.

To the READER.

Reader,

OCcasion having been given us, which we never sought, we continue to improve it to the farther Explanation and Defence of our so much abused Profession; that, if possible, People may see, at least the more Sober and Candid, that we are not at that Distance from Truth, nor so Heterodox in our Principles, as we have been, by too many, either rashly or interestedly Represented: But that we hold the Great Truths of Christianity, *according to the Holy Scriptures, and that the Realities of Religion are the Mark we press after, and to disabuse and awaken People from their false Hopes and Carnal Securities, under which they are too apt to Indulge themselves, to their Irreparable Loss; That by our setting* Christian Doctrine *in a true Light, and reviving and pressing the Necessity of a better Practice, They may see the Obligation they are under to redeem their precious Time they have lost, by a more careful Employment of that which remains, to a better Purpose. In this short Vindication of our mistaken Principles, the Ingenuous Reader may easily discern how Ill we have been treated, and what Hardships we have laboured under, through the Prejudice of some, and the Unreasonable Credulity of others, and that we are a People in Earnest for Heaven, and in that Way our Blessed Lord hath trod for Us to Glory.*

A Testimony to the Truth of GOD, &c.

BY the Observation we are led to make from *Francis Bugg's* late Book, upon the Bishop of *Norwich's* giving him his Recommendatory Letter to the Clergy, &c. in his Diocess, to Relieve, by a Collection, the Necessities of that *Beggarly Apostate*; a Copy of which Letter the said *F. B.* hath published in his said Book.

And also by the Observation we have made on the Malicious Attempts of the *Snake in the Grass*, in his First, Second, and Third Editions, which is a disingenuous and unjust Collection from *F. Bugg*, and some other Deserters, of Things, for the most Part, long since answered; as also lately, by the Book Entituled, *An Antidote*, &c. (Though because his Second and Third Edition have some Additions to his First, and that being new vamped, for a better Market, he may expect a *Melius inquirendum* after a While: Yet should we follow the Example of this *Rattle-Snake*, against the Church, of which he pretends to be a Member, (but at present a suspended one) we might, in Retaliation, not only exceed the Cobler of *Glocester*, but the *Scotch* Eloquence, and that Master-Piece, the Ground of the *Contempt* of the Clergy.

And, lastly, By the Observation we have made on the Relation subscrib'd by some of the *Norfolk* Clergy, dated *October* the 12th, 1698. We cannot forbear thinking, that as their Confederacy is deep, so it aims at nothing less than the Ruin of us, and our Posterity, by rendering us Blasphemers, and Enemies to the Government, and to be treated as such.

The *Norfolk* Relation from the Clergy aforesaid, charges the said People with *Blasphemy*: First, *Against God.* Secondly, *Against Jesus Christ.* Thirdly, *Against the Holy Scriptures, with Contempt of Civil Magistracy, and the Ordinances which Jesus Christ Instituted, viz. Baptism by Water, and the Lord's Supper by Bread and Wine. And, Lastly, That the Light within, as taught by us, leaves us without any certain Rule, and exposes us to the Blasphemies aforesaid, with many others.*

Now, because this Charge refers to Doctrine, rather than Fact, or particular Persons, we think our selves concerned to say something in *Vindication* of our Profession, and to wipe off the Dirt thereby intended to be cast upon us, in giving our *Reader* a plain Account of our Principles, free from the Perversions of our Enemies.

But to manifest how uncharitably and unjustly the said *Clergymen* have reflected upon the People called *Quakers*, with Respect to the said Charge, we are contented the *Reader* goes no farther than their own Printed Relation, dated *Nov.* 12, 1698, not doubting but by that very Relation, and the Letters therewith Printed, he will meet with intire Satisfaction, with Respect to the Reasonableness and Justice of the *Quakers* Proceedings in that Affair, and how ready they were to come to the Test, and to bring the pretended Charge upon the Stage, and to purge themselves from the Guilt of the same: Provided they might be accommodated with what the *Common Law* allows Malefactors, *viz.* a Copy of their Indictment, but this could not be obtained. And tho' the said *Clergy* have thought fit to print the Charge in General, without any Proof, we think our selves obliged to vindicate our Profession, by freely declaring (as now we do, without any *Mental Reservation*) our sincere Belief of the very Things they most unjustly charge us with denying.

I. *Concerning God.*] Because we declare, that God is a *God nigh at Hand*, and that he is according to his Promise, *become the Teacher of his People by his Spirit in these latter Days*; *and that True Believers are the Temples for him to walk and dwell in*, as the Apostle teacheth; and experiencing something of the Accomplishment of this great and glorious Truth among us, and having therefore pressed People earnestly to the Knowledge and Enjoyment thereof, as the Blessing and Glory of the latter Days; We have been ignorantly, or Maliciously, represented and treated as *Hereticks and Blasphemers*, as if we owned no God in Heaven above the Stars, and *confined the Holy One of Israel to our Beings*: Whereas we believe him to be the Eternal, Incomprehensible, Almighty, All-wise and Omnipresent God, Creator and Upholder of all Things, and that he fills Heaven and Earth, and that the *Heaven of Heavens* cannot contain him; yet he saith by the Prophet *Isaiah*, *To that Man will I have Regard, that is poor, and of a contrite Spirit, and which trembles at my Word.* So that for professing that which is the very Marrow of the *Christian Religion*, *viz.* Emanuel, God with us, we are represented Blasphemers against that God; with whom we leave our innocent and suffering Cause. *Isaiah* 7. 14. 40. 28. 48. 17. 66. 1, 2. 2 *Cor.* 6. 16. *Rev.* 21. 3.

II. *Concerning Jesus Christ.*] Because we believe, that the *Word* which was made Flesh, and dwelt amongst Men, and was and is the only begotten of the Father, full of Grace and Truth; his beloved Son, in whom he is well pleased, and whom we ought to hear in all Things; who tasted Death for every Man, and died for Sin, that we might die to Sin; is the great Light of the World, and full of *Grace and Truth*, and that he lighteth every Man that cometh into the World, and giveth them *Grace* for *Grace*, and *Light* for *Light*, and that no Man can know God and Christ (whom to know is Life Eternal) and themselves in Order to true *Conviction and Conversion*, without *Receiving and Obeying* this Holy Light, and being taught by the Divine Grace; and that without it, no Remission, no Justification, no Salvation (as the Scripture plentifully testifies) can be obtained. And because we therefore press the Necessity of People's receiving the Inward and Spiritual Appearance of this Divine Word, in Order to a *Right* and *beneficial Application* of whatsoever he did for Man, with Respect to his Life, Miracles, Death, Sufferings, Resurrection, Ascension and Mediation; our Adversaries would have us deny *any Christ without us*. *First*, As to his Divinity, because they make us to confine him too within us. *Secondly*, As to his Humanity, or Manhood, because as he was the Son of *Abraham*, *David*, *and Mary*, according to the Flesh, he can't be in us, and therefore we are Hereticks and Blasphemers: Whereas we believe him, according to Scripture, to be the Son of *Abraham*, *David*, *and Mary*, after the Flesh, and also God over all, blessed for ever. So that he that is within us, is also without us, even the same that laid down his precious Life for us, rose again from the Dead, and ever liveth to make Intercession for us, being the Blessed and alone Mediator betwixt God and Man, and him by whom God will finally judge the World, both Quick and Dead: All which we as sincerely and stedfastly believe, as any o-

ther

ther Society of People, whatever may be ignorantly, or maliciously insinuated to the contrary, either by our declared Enemies, or mistaken Neighbours. *Deut.* 15. 18. *Mic.* 5. 2. *John* 1. 1, 2, 3. *Rev.* 22. 16:

III. *Concerning the Holy Scriptures.* Because we assert the Holy Spirit to be the first great and general Rule and Guide of True Christians, as that by which *God* is worshipped, *Sin* detected, *Conscience* convicted, *Duty* manifested, *Scripture* unfolded and explained, and consequently the Rule for understanding the Scriptures themselves (since by it they were at first given forth) from hence our Adversaries are pleased to make *us Blasphemers* of the Holy Scriptures, undervaluing their Authority, preferring our own Books before them, with more to that Purpose: Whereas, we, in Truth and Sincerity, believe them to be of Divine Authority, given by the Inspiration of God, thro' Holy Men; they speaking or writing them as they were *moved* by the Holy Ghost: That they are a Declaration of those Things most surely believed by the *Primitive Christians*, and that as they contain the Mind and Will of God, and are his Commands to us; so they, in that Respect, are his *Declaratory Word*; and therefore are obligatory on us, and are *Profitable for Doctrine, Reproof, Correction and Instruction in Righteousness, that the Man of God may be perfect, and throughly furnished to every good Work.*

Nay, after all, so *Unjust* is the Charge, and so remote from our Belief concerning the Holy Scriptures, that we both Love, Honour and prefer them, before all Books in the World; ever chusing to express our Belief of the Christian Faith and Doctrine in the Terms thereof, and rejecting all Principles or Doctrines whatsoever, that are repugnant thereunto.

Nevertheless we are well perswaded, that notwithstanding there is such an Excellency in the Holy Scriptures, as we have above declared, yet the *unstable and unlearned in Christ's School* too often wrest them to their own Destruction. And upon our Reflection on *their carnal* Constructions of them, we are made Undervaluers of *Scripture* it self. But certain it is, that as the Lord hath been pleased to give us the Experience of the fulfilling of them in Measure, so it is altogether contrary to our Faith and Practice, to put any Manner of Slight or Contempt upon them, much more of being guilty, of what maliciously is suggested against us; since no Society of profest Christians in the World, can have a more Reverend and Honourable Esteem for them than we have, *John* 4. 24. and 16. 8. *Rom.* 1. 19. *Luke* 1. 1, 2. *Tim.* 3. 16, 17. 2 *Pet.* 3. 16.

IV. *Concerning Magistracy.*] Because we have not *actively* complied with divers Statutes, which have been made to force an *Uniformity*, to what we had no Faith in, but the Testimony of our Conscience against? and because, for Conscience Sake, we could not give those *Marks* of Honour and Respect, which were and are the usual Practice of those that seek Honour one of another, and not that Honour which comes from God only (but measure and weigh *Honour and Respect* in a *false Ballance, and deceitful Measure*, on which, neither *Magistrate, Ruler or People* can depend) We say, because we could not, for Conscience Sake, give flattering Titles, *&c.* We have been rendered as Despisers and Contemners of Magistracy: Whereas our Principles, often repeated upon the many Revolutions that have happened, do evidently manifest the contrary, as well as our peaceable Behaviour from the Beginning, under all the various Forms of Government, hath been an undeniable Plea in our Favour, when those that also have professed the same Principles of *Non-Resistance*, and *Passive Obedience*, have quitted their Principles, and yet quarrel with us upon a Supposition that we will, in Time, write after their Copy; which, as nothing is more contrary to our Principles, Faith and Doctrine, so nothing can be more contrary to our constant Practice.

For we not only really believe *Magistracy* to be an Ordinance of God, but esteem it an extraordinary Blessing, where it is *a Praise to them that do well*, and *a Terror to Evil-Doers*: Which that it may be so in this our native Land, is the fervent Desire of our Souls, that the Blessing and Peace of God may be continued thereupon, *Job* 32. 21. *John* 5. 44. *Acts* 5. 29. 1 *Pet.* 2. 13. 14.

V. *Concerning Baptism.*] Because we do not find in any Place in the four *Evangelists*, that Jesus Christ instituted *Baptism by Water*, to come in the Room of *Circumcision*, or to be the *Baptism* proper to his Kingdom, which stands in *Righteousness, Peace and Joy in the Holy Ghost*; we are therefore rendred as Contemners of *Christ's Baptism*: Whereas the *Baptism* of Jesus Christ, of which he was Lord and Administrator, according to the Nature of his Office and Kingdom, is even by *John* the *Baptist* declared to be that of *Fire* (not *Water*) and of the *Holy Ghost*

Ghost, of which *Water-Baptism* was but the Forerunner, and is, by them that now practice it, called but the *Outward and visible Sign of the Inward and Spiritual Grace*; and therefore not the Grace it self; *which Grace*, as the Apostle saith, is sufficient for us, and which we believe, profess and experience to be come by Jesus Christ, who is the *Substance* of all Signs and Shadows to true Believers; he being no more a *Jew* or *Christian* that is one outwardly, by the cutting or washing of the Flesh; But he is a *Jew* or *Christian* who is one *Inwardly*, and Circumcision and Baptism is of the *Heart*, in the Spirit, and not in the Letter, whose Praise is therefore not of Men, but of God: And this *Baptism* Christ preferred and recommended at his *Farewel* to his Disciples: In Reverence and Duty to whom, to say nothing of the Abuse of *Water-Baptism*, we decline the Use thereof, Mark 1. 8. Luke 3. 16. John 1. 17. Acts 1. 5. Rom. 14. 17. Rom. 2. 28, 29. 1 Cor. 1. 17. 2 Cor. 12. 9.

VI. *Concerning Breaking Bread*, &c.] Because we also disuse the *Outward Ceremony* of *Breaking Bread* and *Drinking Wine*, which is commonly call'd the *Lord's Supper*, we are therefore rendred Deniers and Contemners of the *Lord's Supper*; whereas the *Inward and Spiritual Grace* thereby signified. viz. That Bread which came down from Heaven, which Christ preferrs to the Bread the Fathers eat in the Wilderness (which did not keep them from Death) and that Cup which he promised to drink *a-new* with his Disciples in his Father's Kingdom, we not only believe, but reverently partake of, to our unspeakable Comfort, which is rightly and truly the Communion of the Body and Blood of our Lord Jesus Christ, who said, *Except you eat the Flesh of the Son of Man, and drink his Blood, you have no Life in you*, John 6. 53. 63. For 'tis *the Spirit that quickens, the Flesh profits nothing*: It was also his Promise to all those that would open at his Knocks, viz. That he would *come in, and sup with them*; which Inward and Spiritual Coming, we have both known and testified to; feeling the blessed Effects thereof in our Souls, and knowing the *Outward Breaking of Bread and Drinking of Wine*, in the Way commonly practised, is no more than it is declared to be, viz. *An Outward and Visible Sign*: Why then, should any contend about it, and render us Unchristian, for disusing what themselves allow to be but *an Outward and Visible Sign?* And that none can reasonably believe to be an Essential Part of Religion, as is the *Bread* from *Heaven*; of which the *Outward* is, at best, but a Signification: But the Wine that Christ promised to drink with his Disciples *A-new*, it such an *Essential*, that without it none have, nor can have *Eternal Life*, Mat. 26. 29. Mark 14. 25. John. 6. 41 50, 51, 58, 63. Rev. 3. 20.

VII. *Concerning the Light of Christ.*] Because we assert the Sufficiency of the *Light Within*, it being the Light of Christ, viz. That if Men live up to the Teaching thereof, in all Manner of Faithfulness and Obedience, they shall not abide in Darkness, but have the *Light of Life and Salvation, and the Blood of Christ shall cleanse them from all Sin:* Our Adversaries from thence conceive, that we undervalue the Rule of Holy Scriptures, and *All* Outward Means, as having no Need thereof, since we have such a Means and Rule within us, and, *that this leaves us without any certain Rule, and exposeth us to many Blasphemies*, &c. Whereas the Light Within (or Christ by His Light inwardly Teaching) was never taught by us in *Opposition* to, or Contempt of any Outward Means, that God, in His Wisdom and Providence, affords us for our Edification and Comfort, no more than did that Blessed Apostle, who said, *You need not that any Man teach you, but as the same Anointing teacheth you all Things, and is Truth, and is no Lye*, John 12. 46. 1 John 1. 6, 7. 1 John 1. 2, 27.

VIII. *Concerning the Father, the Word, and the Spirit.*] Because we have been very cautious in expressing our Faith concerning that Great Mystery, especially in such School Terms, and Philosophical Distinctions as are Unscriptural, if not Unfound, (the Tendency whereof hath been to raise Frivolous Controversies and Animosities amongst Men) we have, by those that desire to lessen our Christian Reputation, been represented as Deniers of the Trinity at large: Whereas we ever believed, and as constantly maintained the Truth of that Blessed (Holy Scripture) *Three, that bear Record in Heaven, the Father, the Word, and the Spirit, and that these Three are One*; the which, we both sincerely and reverently believe, according to 1 John 5. 7. And this is sufficient for us to believe and know, and hath a Tendency to Edification and Holiness, when the contrary centers only in Imaginations and Strife, and Persecution. where it runs high, and to Parties, as may be Read in Bloody Characters in the Ecclesiastical Histories.

IX. *Concerning Works.*] Because we make Evangelical Obedience a Condition to Salvation, and Works by the Spirit wrought in us, to be an Evidence of Faith, and Holiness of Life, to be both Necessary and Rewardable, it hath been insinuated against us, as if we hoped to be Saved by our own Works, and so make them the Meritorious Cause of our Salvation, and consequently Popish.

Whereas we know, that it is not by Works of Righteousness that we can do, but by His own Free Grace is He pleased to accept of us through Faith in, and Obedience to, His Blessed Son the Lord Jesus Christ, *Heb.* 5. 9. and 12. 14.

X. *Of Christ's being our Example.*] Because in some Cases we have said, the Lord Jesus was our Great Example, and that his Obedience to his Father doth not excuse ours; but as by keeping his Commandments, he abode in his Father's Love, so must we follow his Example of Obedience, so abide in his Love: Some have been so ignorant (or that which is worse) as to venture to say for us, or in our Name, that we believe our Lord Jesus Christ was, in all Things, but an Example.

Whereas we confess him to be so much more than an Example, that we believe him to be our most acceptable Sacrifice to God his Father, who for his Sake, will look upon Fallen Man that hath justly merited the Wrath of God, upon his Return by Repentance, Faith and Obedience, as if he had never sinned at all, 1 *John* 2. 12. *Rom.* 3. 26. and 10. 9, 10. *Heb.* 5. 9.

XI. *Concerning Freedom from Sin.*] Because we have urged the Necessity of a perfect Freedom from Sin, and a thorough Satisfaction in Body, Soul and Spirit, whilst on this Side the Grave, by the Operation of the Holy and Perfect Spirit of our Lord Jesus Christ, according to the Testimony of Holy Scripture, we are made so Presumptuous, as to assert the Fulness of all Perfection and Happiness to be attainable in this Life: Whereas we are not only sensible of those Humane Infirmities that attend us, whilst clothed with Flesh and Blood; but know that here we can only know in Part, and see in Part: The Perfection of Wisdom, Glory and Happiness, being reserved for another, and better World. *John* 8. 24, 25. *Heb.* 13. 20, 21. *Heb.* 6.

XII. *Concerning Worship to God.*] Because we say with the Apostle, that Men ought to Pray, Preach, Sing, &c. with the Spirit, and that without the Preparation and Assistance of it, no Man can rightly worship God, (all Worship without it being Formal, and Carnal) From hence Ignorance or Envy suggests against us, that if God will not compel us by his Spirit, he must go without his Worship: Whereas nothing can be more absurd, since without it no Man can truly call *Jesus Lord*: Besides, it is our Duty to wait upon him, who hath promised, not to compel, but fill them with Renewings of Strength, that so wait upon him, by which they are made capable to Worship him acceptably, be it in Praying, Preaching, or Praising of God: And how warrantable our Practice herein is from Holy Scripture, see *Psal.* 25. 5. 37. 7. 27. 14. 130. 5, 6. *Hosea* 12. 6.

XIII. *Of God and Christ's being in Man.*] Because we say, as do the Holy Scriptures, that God is Light, and that Christ is Light, and that God is in Christ, and that Christ by his Light, lighteth every Man that cometh into the World, and dwelleth in them, and with them that obey him, in his Inward and Spiritual Manifestations: People have been told by our Adversaries, That we believe every Man has Whole God, and Whole Christ in him, and consequently so many Gods, and Christs, as Men: Whereas we assert nothing herein, but in the Language of the Holy Ghost in the Scriptures of Truth; and mean no more by it, than that as God is in Christ, so Christ by his Spirit and Light, dwelleth in the Hearts of his People, to comfort and consolate them, as he doth in Wicked Men, to Reprove and Condemn them, as well as to call, Enlighten and Instruct them; that out of that State of Condemnation they may come, and by believing in him, may experience their Hearts cured of the Maladies Sin hath brought upon them, in order to compleat Salvation from Sin here, and from Wrath to come hereafter. 2 *Cor.* 5. 9. 1 *John* 1. 5.

XIV. *Of Christ's Coming both in Flesh and Spirit.*] Because the Tendency (generally speaking) of our Ministry, is to press People to the Inward and Spiritual Appearance of Christ, by his Spirit and Grace in their Hearts, to give them a True Sight and Sense of, and Sorrow for Sin, to Amendment of Life, and Practice of Holiness: And because we have often opposed that Doctrine of being actually justified by the Merits of Christ, whilst actual Sinners against God, by living in the Pollutions of this wicked World: We are, by our Adversaries render'd such, as either deny, or undervalue the Coming of Christ without us, and the Force and Efficacy of his Death and Sufferings, as a Propitiation for the Sins of the whole World. Whereas

Whereas we do, and hope we ever shall (as we always did) confess to the Glory of God the Father, and the Honour of his Dear and Beloved Son, *That He*, to wit *Jesus Christ*, took our Nature upon him, was like us in all Things, Sin excepted: That he was Born of the Virgin Mary, went about amongst Men doing Good, and working many Miracles: That he was betrayed by Judas into the Hands of the Chief Priests, &c. That he suffered Death under Pontius Pilate, the Roman Governour, being Crucified between Two Thieves, and was Buried in the Sepulchre of Joseph of Arimathea: Rose again the Third Day from the Dead, and Ascended into Heaven, and Sits at God's Right Hand, in the Power and Majesty of his Father; and that by him, God the Father, will one Day judge the whole World, both of *Quick* and *Dead*, according to their Works.

XV. *Concerning the Resurrection.*] Because from the Authority of Holy Scripture, as well as right Reason, we deny the Resurrection of the same gross and corruptible Body, and are neither over Inquisitive, nor Critical about what Bodies we shall have at the Resurrection, leaving it to the Lord, to give us such Bodies as he pleases (and with that we are well pleased and satisfied, and wish all others were so too.) From hence we are made not only Denyers of the Resurrection of any Body at all, however Spiritual, or Glorified, but Eternal Rewards too.

Whereas, if it were true, as it is notoriously false, we were, indeed, of all Men, most Miserable: But, blessed be God, it is so far from being true, that we most stedfastly believe, that as our Lord Jesus Christ was raised from the Dead, by the Power of the Father, and was the first Fruits of the Resurrection, so every *Man*, in his *own Order*, shall arise; They that have done well, to the Resurrection of Eternal Life; but they that have done Evil, to Everlasting Condemnation.

And because we are a People, whose Education hath not afforded us an *Accuracy* of Language, some Passages may perhaps have been *mis-expressed*, or improperly worded: As for Instance, One of us hath denied in his Book, the Soul to be *Finite*, by which he plainly meant *Mortal*, or *Final*; to die, or have an End, which *Finis* signifies, from whence *Finite* comes, from hence our uncharitable Opposers have concluded, we hold the Soul to be *Infinite*, and consequently God: Whereas the Words before and after, as well as the Nature of the Things, shews plainly, he *only* meant that it is *Eternal*, and so not *Finite*; that is, not *Terminable*, or that which shall come to an End.

And also, because we have not declared our selves about Matters of Faith, in the many and *Critical* Words that Man's Wisdom teacheth, but in the Words which the *Holy Ghost Teacheth*, we have been esteemed either *Ignorant* or *Equivocal* and *Unsound*: Whereas it is really Matter of Conscience to us, to deliver our Belief in such Words as the Holy Spirit, in Scripture, teacheth; and if we add more for Illustration, it is from an Experience of the Work of the same Spirit in our selves, which seems to us the truest Way of Expounding Scripture, in what concerns Saving Knowledge.

XVI. *Concerning Separation.*] Because we are separated from the Publick *Communion* and *Worship*, it is too generally concluded, that we deny the *Doctrines* received by the Church, and consequently introduce a New Religion: Whereas we *differ* least, where we are thought to *differ* most: For, setting aside some School Terms, we hold the Substance of those Doctrines believed by the *Church of England*, as to God, Christ, Spirit, Scripture, Repentance, Sanctification, Remission of Sin, Holy Living, and the Resurrection of the Just and Unjust to Eternal Rewards and Punishments. But that wherein we *differ* most, is about *Worship* and *Conversation*, and the *Inward Qualification* of the Soul by the Work of God's Spirit thereon, in Pursuance of these good and generally received Doctrines. For 'tis the Spirit of God only Convinces and Converts the Soul, and makes those that were *Dead in Trespasses and Sins*, and in the *Lusts*, *Pleasures*, and *Fashions* of this World, *alive to God*; that is, *Sensible* of his Mind and Will, and of their Duty to do them; and brings to know God, and his Attributes, by the *Power of them upon their own Souls*; and leads to Worship God rightly, which is *in his Spirit, and in Truth*, with Hearts Sanctified by the Truth, which is a living and acceptable Worship, and stands in *Power*, not Formality, nor *in the Traditions, and Prescriptions of Men*, in *Synods* and *Convocations*, but in the Holy Spirit. First, in shewing us our real Wants, and then in helping *our Infirmities* with *Sighs* and *Groans*, and sometimes *Words*, to pray for a suitable Supply, for which we in our Meetings *wait* upon God, to *quicken* and *prepare* us, that we may worship him *Acceptably* and *Profitably*, for they go together. Now, because we are satisfy'd that

that all Worship to God, and Exhortations to Men, as *Praying, Praising,* and *Preaching,* and every other Religious Duty, ought to be Spiritually Performed; and finding so little of it among Professors of Christianity; the Spirit of God having not that *Rule* and *Guidance* of them, in their Lives and Worship, as It ought to have; and seeing them too generally satisfied with a Ministry and Worship of *Man's making,* being not qualified, nor led by God's Spirit thereunto; we cannot find that Comfort and Edification our Souls crave and want under so cold a Ministry and Worship. And for this Cause, and no Presumptuous Contempt, or selfish Separation, or worldly Interests, are we, and stand we at this Day, a separate People from the Publick Communion; and in this we can comfortably Appeal and Recommend our selves to God, the *great and last Judge* of the Acts and Deeds of the Sons of Men.

Lastly, Because at the Time of our Friends first appearing in this Age, there were a Sect of People, newly sprang up, and *truly* called *Ranters,* that were the *Reverse* to the *Quakers,* (for they feared and quaked at *nothing,* but made a Mock at Fearing of God, and at Sin, and at Hell) who pretended that *Love* made *Fear* needless, and that nothing was Sin, but to them that *thought* it so; and that *none* should be Damned at last, whose extravagant Practices exactly corresponded with their Evil Principles: From hence, some, ignorantly, and too many maliciously involved us and ours with *them*; and many of their Exorbitances were thereby placed to our Account, tho' without the least Reason, Truth, or Justice.

And because some that were convinced of God's Truth, afterwards dishonoured their Profession, thro' their *Unfaithfulness* to it; and that some, out of *Weakness,* perhaps, may have improperly worded what they intended to say, the whole Body of our Friends have been made *Criminal,* and the Religion or Principles we profess, have been condemned, and represented to the World as *Heresy* and *Blasphemy;* an Usage so Unjust, that doubtless, according to *Lex Talionis,* our Adversaries would think it intolerable to be so treated by us.

But as we desire not to render *Evil* for *Evil,* our *Great Bishop* having taught us *another* Lesson, and *better* Practices, so we desire God Almighty to forgive our *Causeless* Enemies, for his Son's Sake, as we most freely and heartily forgive them: Believing some may be zealously affected for their *Educational* Form of Religion, and as zealous against us for our Separation, and we are the more inclined to judge so, because many of us were once in the *same* Way, and had such Thoughts of those that were gone before us. But it hath pleased the Father of Mercies, to do by many of us, as he did by *Saul,* that *Zealous,* though *Mistaken* Persecutor of the sincere Followers of Jesus Christ, *Acts* 9. 3, 4, 5, 6. For as we heard an unusual *Inward,* but *Powerful* Voice, so we also had a more inward, clear, and distinguishing Sight, by the Illumination of that Light, which was more than Natural, and shined into our dark and sinful Hearts, 2 *Cor.* 4. 6, 7. Letting us see them, as they *really* were in God's Sight, which naturally *affected* us with *deep Sorrow,* and *true Humiliation*; making us willing to be any Thing he would have us be, provided we might have *some* Sense of his Love and Favour towards us. And blessed be his Holy and Excellent Name, we can, without Vanity, say, (generally speaking) We were not disobedient to that Heavenly Vision (*Acts* 26. 19.) we had of Him, our Selves, the World, and that Profession of Religion, where we had our Education. And since by that Sight God gave us, we saw he was Pure and Holy, and that without *Holiness* none ever could, or can see him, to their Joy, and that we were unfit to approach his Holy Altar; yea, the whole World lay in Wickedness; and that Profession of Religion, where we had our Education, was so far from having the *Power* of Godliness, that for the most Part it wanted the Right *Form*; from such, therefore, we had a *Divine Authority to turn away,* 2 *Tim.* 3: 5. Which we did, not in a *vaunting* Mind, but with great Sorrow; wanting to know where the *Great Shepherd* of the Sheep fed his Flock, *Can.* 1. 7. For we desired to be *not* of those that turned aside from the Foot-steps of the Flocks of the Companions. Nor was it Affectation to Popularity, Singularity, or Novelty, that induced us to a Separation; but a fervent Desire to know the Lord, and the Work of his Translating *Power* upon our Souls, being in Earnest for Heaven, tho' for it we lost all our Earthly Enjoyments, *Heb.* 11. 14, 15, 16.

In this *Solitary* and *Seeking* State, it pleased the Lord to meet with us, and gather us into *Families* or *Religious Societies,* according to *Psalm* 58. 6. And though it hath been a dear Separation to us, considering it cost us the Loss, at least, of all Things, and the great Sufferings and Afflictions that have attended us in this despised

spised Way, which Men have called Heresy, yet the Lord hath blessed us in it, with the Enjoyment of his Blessed Presence, to our unspeakable Joy and Comfort.

To conclude, As it hath pleased the Lord to bless us, in the Way we have hitherto been helpt to walk in, with that great Blessing which ushered in the Birth of our Blessed Lord into the World, *viz. Glory to God, Peace on Earth, and Goodwill to Men*: So we earnestly desire the *same* upon all our Neighbours: For tho' we may not be all of *one Mind* in some *Doctrinal* Parts of Religion, we must of *Necessity* be all of *one Sentiment* in the Great and General Duty of *Holiness*, or else we can never see God. And if that is our *Principal Aim* and Endeavour, we shall less fall out by the Way, about Words, Forms, and the Outside of Things: But *Universal Charity*, which is the most excellent Way, and without which the best of Creeds is but as a *sounding Brass*, &c.) will silence Controversy, and blot out all *Ignominious Characters*; remembring that the *Great* Judge, at the *Last Day*, will determine us, not according to our *Names*, but *Natures*; not our *Profession*, but our *Lives*; not our *bare Belief*, (though of unquestionable Truths) but *Works*; for *God will bring every Work to Judgment, with every secret Thing, whether it be Good or Evil*, Eccles. 12. 14.

Some Considerations *upon the* BILL *for the more Effectual Suppressing* Blasphemy *and* Prophaneness: Humbly Offered.

I. IF an Act be made, containing a Creed, and that Creed be not in the Terms of Holy Scripture; Whether this may not cause Ambiguous Disputes, and increase Divisions and Disunion in Affection, contrary to the Intent of the Act for exempting their Majesty's Protestant Subjects, dissenting from the Church of *England*, from the Penalties of certain *Laws* made *Anno*. 1. *William and Mary*.

II. If an Act be made to prevent *Blasphemy and Impious Opinions*, &c. — Whether such Creed Act, ought not to be in Express Terms of Holy Scripture, as being of Divine and best Authority?

III. Whereas the Bill enacts, *That if any Person or Persons, &c.. shall deny any of the Persons in the* Holy Trinity *to be God*; and makes it punishable by the same Bill: Were it not more safe and plain to put it in Scripture Terms, as instead of [*Deny any one of the Persons in the* Holy Trinity *to be God*] To insert, *If any one shall deny any of the Three that bear Record in Heaven, the Father, the Word, or the Holy Ghost to be God*. 1 John Chap. 5. Ver. 7.—— For many may believe and own the *Father, Son and Holy Ghost* to be God, according to Holy Scripture, and yet scruple the Term *Persons, as Unscriptural*; and thereby may be, by invidious Informers, brought under Severe Suffering for a Circumstance of Words and Terms, when they sincerely own the Substance in the Terms of Holy Scripture.

IV. Seeing the Holy Scriptures of the *Old and New Testament* are confessed to be of Divine Authority, as being given by Inspiration from God: How can it be consistent, with such Confession, to impose a Creed in Unscriptural Terms by a Penal Act?

V. Inasmuch as the Act made 22. *Car.* II. against Seditious Conventicles, hath been construed to Affect Religious Meetings, held for the Worship of God in a *Peaceable Manner*.

May not this Act also be liable to Affect those, whose Principles in this Matter are expresly agreeable to Holy Scripture; though they don't agree with the Terms of the Act.

VI. The Bill seems to be made only against any Person or Persons educated in, or at any Time professing the Christian Religion, within this Realm: That if any such shall, by Writing, Printing, or advised Speaking, deny the Points specified in the said Bill, such shall incur the Penalties therein mentioned.

First, Then, consequently, any Person not Educated in, or not at any Time professing the Christian Religion, within this Realm, may, by Writing, Printing, Teaching, or advised Speaking, deny any One of the Divine Persons in the Holy Trinity, to be God, or deny the Christian Religion to be True: Or the Holy Scriptures of the Old and New Testament to be of Divine Authority.

Secondly, Such Persons as are not Educated in, and professing the Christian Religion within this Realm, may, by this Act, take Liberty to make as many Proselytes

lytes as they can, against the Christian Religion and Profession, and be exempt from the Penalties thereof.

Thirdly, Any Person or Persons from beyond Sea, whether they have been Educated in the Christian Religion or not, may come into this Realm, and by Writing, Printing, Teaching, or advisedly Speaking, may deny any One of the Persons in the Holy Trinity to be God: Or deny the Christian Religion to be True: Or may deny the Holy Scriptures of the Old and New Testament to be of Divine Authority, and yet incur no Penalty by this Act.

A DEFENCE of a Paper, *Entituled* GOSPEL-TRUTHS, *against* the Exceptions of the Bishop of *Cork*'s Testimony. By *W. Penn*.

The PREFACE

Reader,

IT *was the Wise Counsel of an Ancient and Grave Prelate, of the Kingdom of Ireland, at a late Visit I made him there, to discourage Controversie, and endeavour to abate Strife among Christians:* For, said he, Heaven is a Quiet Place; there are no Quarrels there, and Religion is an Holy and Peaceable thing, and Excites to Piety and Charity, and not to Genealogies, Strife and Debates. *But the Bishop of* Cork *seems to be of another Mind, that could not pass by so inoffensive a Paper, as that stiled* Gospel-Truths, *(given him by me in a Private Way, at a Friendly Visit upon his own Desire) without his Publick Animadversions; and those express not with so much Justice and Charity, as might have been expected from him to his Dissenting Neighbours.*

I am, I confess, very sorry my Christian Visits to the Bishop have met with no better Returns than Controversie: But because that's his, and not my Fault, it shall be my Satisfaction.

I did indeed, perceiving him conversant in our Writings, and his Character to be Moderation, *casually present him with one of those Papers; but as the Nature of it is far from Provocation, so my Design in it was purely to improve his Temper, and not to excite his Contradiction. Nor was it writ for an* Exact *and* Compleat *Account of our Belief, but Occasionally, to prevent the Prejudices that the Attempts of a Course and Scurrilous Pen at* Dublin, *just before, might provoke in some against us, as to the Points touched upon in the* Gospel-Truths. *And though we have been so unhappy as to be therein mistaken by the Bishop, yet it's some Comfort to us, that our Christian Declaration hath had quite another Reception with the Generality of those to whose Hands it has come: And I heartily wish, That hath not been the most prevailing Motive to his Undertaking. However, since he has been pleased to fault it both with* Shortness *and* Error, *the first of which we thought Healing, at least Inoffensive, I esteem my self answerable for it, and shall, with God's Assistance, Defend it against the Force of His Exceptions, and, I hope, with Clearness and Temper: For though I may be plain, as he must expect, I desire to be neither Rude nor Bitter.*

I ask, Reader, but the Common Justice due to all Authors, especially in Controverted Points of Religion, to wit, Attention *and* Impartiality; *and then judge whether our Pacifick Paper deserved so sharp a Censure, and the Manner of it's being given him, so Publick a Return: Though I hope the Consequence will be Good. To Almighty God I leave the Success, and am in all Christian Obligation,*

Thy Real Friend,

Bristol, the 23d of the
7th Month, 1698.

WILLIAM PENN.

The TESTIMONY of the Bishop of *Cork*, as to a PAPER, Entituled, *Gospel-Truths Held*, &c. *by the People called* QUAKERS, And delivered to Him by an Eminent MEMBER of them.

[*The* PAPER *was as follows.*]

Sober Reader,

IF thou had'st rather we should be in the Right than in the Wrong; and if thou thinkest it but a Reasonable Thing that we should be Heard before we are Condemned, and that our Belief ought to be taken from our Own Mouths, and not at theirs that have prejudged our Cause; then we intreat thee, to Read and Weigh the following Brief Account, of those Things that are chiefly Received and Professed among us the People called Quakers, according to the Testimony of the Scriptures of Truth, and the Illumination of the Holy Ghost, which are the Double and Agreeing Record of True Religion. Published to inform the Moderate Enquirer, and Reclaim the Prejudiced to a better Temper; which GOD grant, to His Glory, and their Peace.

I. It is our Belief, That GOD is, and that He is a Rewarder of all them that fear Him, with Eternal Rewards of Happiness; and that those that fear Him not, shall be turned into Hell, Heb. 11. 16. Rev. 22. 12. Rom. 2. 5, 6, 7, 8. Psl. 9. 17.

II. That there are *Three* that Bear Record in Heaven; the Father, the Word, and the Spirit; and these *Three* are really *One*, 1 *John* 5. 7.

III. That the Word was made Flesh, and dwelt among Men, and was, and is, the *Only Begotten of the Father, full of Grace and Truth, His Beloved Son, in whom he is well-pleased, and whom we are to hear in all Things; who tasted Death for every Man, and died for Sin, that we might die to Sin, and by his Power and Spirit be raised up to Newness of Life here, and to Glory hereafter,* John 1. 14. Mat. 3. 17. Heb. 2. 9.

IV. That as we are only Justified from the Guilt of Sin, by Christ the Propitiation, and not by Works of Righteousness that we have done; so there is an absolute Necessity that we receive and obey, *to unfeigned Repentance, and Amendment of Life*, the Holy Light and Spirit of Jesus Christ, in order to obtain that Remission and Justification from Sin: *Since no Man can be Justified by Christ, who walks not after the Spirit, but after the Flesh; for whom he Sanctifies, them he also Justifies: And if we walk in the Light, as he is Light, his Precious Blood cleanseth us from all Sin; as well from the Pollution as Guilt of Sin*, Rom. 3. 22. to 26. Chap. 8. 1, 2, 3, 4. 1 John 5. 7.

V. That *Christ is the Great Light of the World*, that lighteth every Man that cometh into the World, *and is full of Grace and Truth*, and giveth to all, Light for Light, and Grace for Grace; and by his Light and Grace he inwardly appears to Man, and teaches such as will be taught by him, *That denying Ungodliness and Worldly Lusts, they should Live Soberly, Righteously, and Godly in this present World*, John 8. 12. Chap. 1. 9, 14. Tit. 2. 11, 12.

VI. That this Principle of Light and Grace, which is God's Gift, through Christ to Man, is that which shews us our Sins, reproves us for them, and would lead all out of them that obey it, to serve GOD, in Fear and Love, all their Days. And they that turn not at the Reproofs thereof, and will not Repent, and Live, and Walk according to it, *shall die in their Sins; and where Christ is gone, they shall never come, who is undefiled, and separated from Sinners*, Eph. 5. 13. John 16. 7. Prov. 1. 20, to 24. John 8. 24.

VII. This is that Principle by which GOD prepares the Heart to Worship him aright; and all the Duties of Religion, as *Praying, Praising, and Preaching*, ought to be performed through the Sanctifying Power and Assistance of it; other Worship being but *Formal and Will-Worship*, with which we cannot, in Conscience, Join, nor can we *Maintain or Uphold it*, Rom. 8. 26. 1 Pet. 4. 10, 11.

VIII. *Worship in this Gospel-Day is Inward and Spiritual*: For, *God is a Spirit*, as Christ teacheth, and he will *Now be Worshipped in Spirit and in Truth*, being most suitable to his Divine Nature. Wherefore we wait in our Assemblies to feel GOD's Spirit to Open and Move upon our Hearts, before we dare offer Sacrifice to the LORD, or Preach to others, the Way of his Kingdom. That we may Preach in Power as well as Words, and as God Promised, and Christ Ordained, *Without Money, and Without Price*, John 4. 23, 24. 1 Thes. 1. 5. Isa. 55. 1. Rev. 22. 17. Mat. 10. 8.

IX. This also leads us to deny all the Vain Customs and Fashions of the World, to avoid Excess in all Things, that our Moderation may be seen of all Men, *because the Lord is at Hand to See and Judge us, according to our Deeds*, Tit. 2. 12. Rom. 12. 2. Phil. 4. 5. Eccl. 12. 14. Mat. 16. 27. Rom. 2. 6. Rev. 20. 12.

X. We believe the Necessity of the *One Baptism of Christ*, as well as of *His One Supper*, which he promiseth to Eat with those that open the Door of their Hearts to him, being the Baptism and Supper signified by the Outward Signs; which, tho' we disuse, we Judge not those that Conscientiously practise them, Mat. 3. 11. Eph. 4. 1. 1 Pet. 3. 21, 22. John 6. Rev. 3. 20.

XI. *We Honour Government*; for we believe it is an Ordinance of God; and that we ought in all Things to submit, by Doing or Suffering; but esteem it a Great Blessing, where the Administration is *a Terror to Evil Doers, and a Praise to them that do well*. Rom. 13. 1, 2, 3, 4, 5.

This hath all along been the General Stream and Tendency both of our Ministry and Writings, as our Books will make appear, notwithstanding what Ill-minded and Prejudic'd Persons may have strained to mis-represent us, and our Christian Profession.

Dublin, the 4th of the 3d Month, 1698.

William Penn, Anthony Sharp, Thomas Story, George Rook.

Friends,

I AM *such a Reader as in your Paper you desire. I have Read, and Soberly Weighed the Account you give of those Things, which you say*, Are Chiefly Received and Professed amongst you. *And I will exercise so much Moderation and Charity, as to lay a great Weight on that Word* [Chiefly] *hoping these are not the Only Things, or All that you Believe. I should have been heartily glad to have found that you had been in the* Truth, *as I am well assured I my self am*; But, as I Professed, *when the Paper was given me*, That if I took it, you must expect I should Bear my Testimony Touching It, Or, Against It : *So I must now tell you, I think my self bound in Conscience to perform what I then* Professed; *and that upon more Reasons than I will now trouble the World with. You must not be offended, if I say, You have such a Way of Writing and Speaking, that it is very hard in many Matters of Religion, to know what you mean. But, as far as I understand you, I will candidly acknowledge what Truths you have sufficiently or tolerably exprest*: *I will shew you with Meekness*, How far your Faith, *if this be your Faith*, comes short of being Sufficient, or Christian; *and I will sincerely tell you, what I apprehend to be the* Cause of your Delusion, *and how* Dangerous a Condition *I really fear, nay, believe, you to be in.*

And First. *The only Articles in which you have express'd a Sufficient Christian Belief, are your* Sixth, *which is*, Touching Justification, and your last touching Government, and your Submission thereto. *I wish you may always stick to this Belief and Practice; and I heartily rejoyce to find you acknowledging*, The Necessity of Christ, as a Propitiation, in order to Remission of Sins, and Justifying you, *as* Sinners, from Guilt. *'Tis the first Time I have heard of it amongst you.*

As to all the rest of your Articles, I mean those which I understand, I must tell you, the Declaration of your Faith comes so short of what is required from People to denominate them Christians, *that except, under each Article, you believe more than you have declar'd, you cannot be accounted* Christians. *For first, in those Articles of Faith, which you have thought fit to mention, you have set down only some Little Ends, I had almost called them Snaps of the Article.* And, Secondly, *Many more whole Articles, of the* True Christian Faith, *and which are of no less Import, you have entirely omitted, waved, or suppressed.*

You acknowledge in your First Article, There is a God, *and you own His Providence as to the other Life. But that* He made Heaven and Earth, that He is the Almighty, and at present, by His Sovereign Power, most Wisely, and Holily, Governs, Orders, and Sustains All (by His Mercies, as well as Judgments, even in this World,

World, *not leaving himself without Witness*) you say not a Word. Creation *in the Beginning*, and Providence *as to this World at present, are not here acknowledged by you. We hope you believe both.*

Your Second Article *is wholly True; for it is express Scripture,* 1 John 5. 7. *But it is only what the Apostle there had Occasion to say, and what was to his Purpose, touching the* Father, Son, *and* Holy Spirit ; *far from being the Sum of what the Holy Scripture teaches of them ; and therefore is not a Sufficient Confession of Faith on that Head.*

In your Third Article, *You acknowledge indeed,* The Son of God to have been made Flesh, *but neither* Conceived by the Holy Ghost, *nor* Born of the Virgin *Mary*; *so that it does not appear, by this your Confession, but that He was at first an Ordinary, Corrupt, Sinful Person ; Nay, you own Him not so much as* Jesus, *or the* Christ ; *(the* Great Saviour, *who delivereth from the Wrath which is to come ; or the* Great Prophet, Priest, Lord *and* King, *of His Church :) You acknowledge him indeed,* To have Dyed for Sin, *but (not to mention the Articles inferrible from, and relating to, the Circumstances of his Death.) You have not one Word of His Resurrection from the Dead, or of His Ascension into Heaven ; which it may be proved, some of you have expresly denied, saying,* He is not Ascended into Heaven ; He is in us. *Nor again, Of His Sitting now at the Right Hand of the Majesty on High. And so you seem not to own any Thing of His Mediation, Intercession, or Appearing now in Heaven for us. Nor farther have you said a Word,* Of His Coming again to Judgment, at the End of the World. *Thus indeed, You have here neither owned the* Creation, *or* Dissolution of the World ; *so that it does not appear, by this Account of your Faith, whether you do not Judge it Eternal, and so otherwise Infinite. Yet again,* Not a Word of One Church, *which it may be feared you strike out of your Belief, because you are resolved never more to return into the* Unity of the Church, *but to make and maintain a Schism, or Party for ever. Nor farther,* Have you a Word of the Resurrection of the Dead, *which divers of you have been known to deny, and others of you only say,* It may be so. *And Lastly, Tho' you acknowledge* Everlasting Rewards for them that Fear God, *yet,* Nothing of the Everlasting Punishment of Wicked Men. *You mention* Hell *indeed (in a very Unnatural Place,* viz. *in your* First Article of the Being of God) *but whether you mean thereby the* Grave, *as most commonly in Scripture is meant ;* or, A Place of Temporal Punishment after this Life, *as some have done ;* Or, A State of Total Destruction and Annihilation, *as many now a-days do, no One knows.*

Upon the Whole : *As to the Sum of the* Christian Faith, *which you have been pleased to set down, there is not One Article of our Common Twelve, that you have owned intirely ; and Eight at least, if not more of them, that you have here totally suppressed, or waved. And how Influential to an Holy Life, those which you have waved are, and therefore how Necessary to Salvation, I must require and conjure you, on your own Eternal Account, to consider. I will only mind you of Two Passages out of the Scriptures of Truth,* 1 Cor. 15. 16, 17. If the Dead Rise not, *(that is, if there be no Resurrection of the Flesh)* then is not Christ Raised. And if Christ is not Raised, your Faith is Vain, you are yet in your Sins. *Hence it appears All other Points of Faith are in Vain, if this be not True. The other is,* Rom. 10. 9. If thou shalt confess with thy Mouth the Lord Jesus, and shalt believe in thy Heart that God hath raised him from the Dead, thou shalt be Saved. *This Article alone is of such Force and Influence on Men's Hearts, that if believed as it should be, such Belief will Save Men. But both Christ's Resurrection, and our own, are by you, in this Paper, left out of your Faith. I judge you not, but judge your selves, lest you be Condemned of the Lord.*

Your Fifth, Sixth, *and* Eighth Articles, *treat of what you call,* The Light of Christ Within Man : *This you have never been able yet, that I could find, to make out what you mean by. For you will not allow it to be either the Natural, Rational Faculty, or Common Innate Notions, or Natural Conscience, or Conscience Illuminated, by the Preaching of the Gospel, and the Operation of the Holy Ghost thereby : 'Till you can make us understand your Meaning, or indeed till you understand it your selves, (that is, till you are less Confused in this, the very Fundamental Principle, or Rule, of what you profess) you must not think of* Declaring, (*or* Publishing) *an Account of your Faith : See you understand it first. There are some Men who have a Faculty to speak Things seemingly profound, but in the End neither themselves, nor others, can make any Distinct Sense of what they have said : This we usually call* Banter. *And I must acknowledge, as far as I can see, your Discourse of this* Light Within.

Within, *is perfectly such. Take Notice, We in our Preaching, require People to Look Within, as much as you do: We strictly charge* All to walk according to the Convictions, and Light they have received. *We daily appeal unto Conscience: But then we Teach, that Conscience (opened by the* Holy Spirit, *under the Ministry of the Word,* Acts 16. 14.) *does, and must take in it's Light from Holy Scripture*; The Commandment of the Lord is Pure, Enlightning the Eyes, *Psalm* 19. 8. (viz. of the Mind, Eph. 1. 18.) Thy Word is as a Lamp to my Feet, and a Light to my Path, *Psalm* 119, 105. To the Law and to the Testimony; If they (even *Men in their Consciences*) speak not according to this Word, it is because there is NO LIGHT in them, *Isa.* 8. 20. *Now these Things are Intelligible. This Rule is fixt and certain, nothing of which can be said of* Your Light within.

In your Eighth Article you tell us, Worship under the Gospel is Inward and Spiritual. *If you mean hereby, that all Outward and Bodily Worship ought to be accompanied with an Inward and Spiritual Worship, it is what we daily Preach and Practice, and even in private Press. But if, as it would seem, you mean all the Worship* GOD *now requires, is from the Inward Man, or from the Spirit, this is abominably false: For Our Bodies are* GOD's *Handy-work, and Christ's Purchase, as well as our Souls: On which Reason,* GOD, *by his Apostle, commands,* Glorify God in your Body and in your Spirit, [ἅτινα] which (*in the Plural Number that is*, both which) are GOD's. *Not to tell you, that you your selves, now adays, perform somewhat of Bodily Worship. And indeed, if there be not a Worship of the Body, as well as of the Spirit, there can be no Publick Worship. This Article, therefore, must also be mended, to make it Christian.*

In your Ninth Article, You tell us of your Denying all the vain Customs and Fashions of the World, as also Excess in all Things. *I know no Sort of Christians who teach otherwise; I wish I could say, I knew none (even of* your selves) *that practise otherwise. It is one Part of the Catechism we teach our* Children, *to* renounce all these. *But there are many* Innocent and laudable Customs *which you call* Vain. *Would it not almost make a Man's Stomach turn to hear one forbear, in Point of Conscience, saying* You *to a single Person, because it is improper; and at the same Time, while he is speaking to his Superior, because* Thou dost, *sounds a little Rudely, to soften the* Thou, *and say* Thee doest, *which is commonly your People's Practice, and much more improper. Will you ever be able to prove, the Primitive Christians used a Dialect or Dress different from others of their Nation and Qualities, and placed Religion in it? Does not Christ require* Saluting even those who Salute not us? *And no doubt His and his Apostles Salutations, were in the common Form. In a Word, There is more Vanity in Singularity and Affectation, than in a moderate following a common innocent Phrase, Garb, or Custom.*

In your Tenth Article you believe (you say) a Spiritual Baptism, and a Spiritual Supper and Communion; *but acknowledge you disuse the Outward Signs, by us commonly called Sacraments: Now did not Christ command Water-Baptism:* Go ye and Baptize all Nations, *Matth.* 28. 19, 20. *The Baptism here commanded, was Water-Baptism: For Baptizing with the Spirit was* GOD's *Work, not the Apostles; and tho' the Baptism of the Spirit commonly accompanied Baptism with Water, yet not always, as in the Case of* Simon Magus, *and many others. Yet, Did not Christ promise to be with them (Preaching to all Nations, and Baptizing) to the End of the World? Farther, Did not the Apostles, in Obedience to Christ's Command, both constantly practise, and also require, Water-Baptism to all Initiated Christians? Can any Man forbid Water, that these should not be baptized which have received the Holy Ghost as well as we? And he* [*Peter*] commanded they should be baptized: *Acts* 10. 47, 48. *Then as to the Outward Use of Bread and Wine for the Lord's Supper, can any Command be more express than,* This do in Remembrance of Me? *Four Times repeated in the New (which you call the better) Testament. To which St.* Paul *adds,* It is a shewing forth the Lord's Death untill he come, 1 *Cor.* 11. 26. *Now if Christ and his Apostles have commanded this, who hath Authorized you to disuse it? Remember what St.* Paul *tells the* Corinthians, *he received from the Lord that which on this Subject he delivered to them,* 1 *Cor.* 11. 23. *And 'tis a severe Passage in another Epistle of his,* Gal. 1. 8. If we, or an Angel from Heaven, preach any other Gospel unto you, than that which we have preached unto you, let him be accursed. *That which lays aside so much of the Gospel, and sets up a New and Variable Rule of Faith, (we know not what Light within) is Another and New Gospel.*

To draw towards a Conclusion: I have written this short Paper in much and true

Compaſſion to you: It had been far eaſier to me to have ſaid more, than thus to have confined my ſelf: I look upon many of you as an harmleſs, well-meaning People, but under ſtrong Deluſions.

This your Deluded State proceeds from your making what you call The Light within you *(which is in many Caſes nothing but your own Preſumptive Perſuaſion or Fancy)* a Rule of Faith and Practice, Co-ordinate, *if not* Superior and Antecedent to the Holy Scriptures: *Theſe Words in your Paper* [Which are the Double and Agreeing Record of True Religion] *intimate at leaſt thus much, That you will not believe what Scripture ſaith, except the Light within you dictate the ſame, and ſo make a Double Record.* Now, my Friends, do not flatter your ſelves, GOD is not mocked; *you muſt anſwer at the Dreadful Day of Judgment, amongſt other Points, to ſuch as theſe*; and therefore examine your Conſciences before-hand.

1. Is it not your main End and Study, *by pretended Mortifications, and Renouncing the World,* (while there are no Sort of Men alive that more eagerly purſue it, nor have more effectual, wily, and ſecret Ways of getting Wealth than your ſelves?) Is it not, I ſay, your main Aim and End to make your ſelves a Party conſiderable, and ſuch, to which, for Reaſons of State, peculiar Privileges muſt be indulged?

2. Are not, *to this Purpoſe,* many of your Diſtinctive Characters, *ſuch as your* Different Garb, *(for it is plain, not a few of your People's Cloaths, as to Materials, are more coſtly than many of ours)* your Way of Speaking, *yea, even* your Looks and Geſtures, *aſſumed rather to make your ſelves remarkable, and at firſt Sight known from other People, than out of any Perſwaſion, Senſe of Duty, or Conſcience of Obligation?*

3. What reaſonable or tolerable Warrant *can you plead for waving,* ſuppreſſing, *at leaſt,* not confeſſing *much the* greater Part of the Chriſtian Faith, *and* Rejecting all Outward Poſitive Parts of Worſhip *(eſpecially Baptiſm and the Lord's Supper) which have ſuch plain and repeated Evidences in Holy Scripture. Your Light within, (or Senſe and Perſwaſion which you ſay you have, and are ſure is from Chriſt) foraſmuch as, in the preſent Caſes, it dictateth againſt Holy Scripture, can never be proved even to your ſelves, much leſs to others, to be from Chriſt:* But muſt rather, in all Reaſon, be reſolved to be one of the Heights or Depths of Satan transforming himſelf into an Angel of Light. And for any Perſons to yield to ſuch Conduct, (beſides or againſt Holy Scripture) *is plainly to* abandon themſelves to the Deluſions of the Devil.

In a Word, therefore, I again require you, *as you will anſwer all your Secret Arts and High Pretenſions at Chriſt's Tribunal, that you either* Embrace and Profeſs intire Chriſtian Faith, *in the Points wherein I have ſhewn you to be defective*; and that you receive the Chriſtian Seals or Badges, Baptiſm, and the Lord's-Supper; or elſe that you deſiſt to lay Claim to the Name of Chriſtians.

It is not for me to Judge you, but again I ſay unto you, *(truly from GOD, as His Miniſter)* Judge your ſelves. *This is the Caſe. If Men who* take away *even from the* Faith once delivered to the Saints, at *leaſt* Two Thirds, *beſides many main Points of the other Third;* who Equal their own Preſumptuous Conceits to the Divine Oracles, *and Revelations*; *who* uſe and diſuſe at Pleaſure, what Parts of GOD's Inſtituted Worſhip *they think fit, Even the very Badges of Chriſtianity,* (I will not here Interpoſe your Making Gain your Godlineſs) *but if the aforeſaid Men are in a* Way of Perdition, *what can you conclude of your ſelves? In the Name of* GOD Repent and Return: *And from my Soul I pray, That GOD will pleaſe to give you Repentance.*

Cork, July the 2d. 1698.   **Edw. Cork** *and* **Ross.**

A Defence *of a* Paper, *entituled,* Gospel-Truths.

I Have given the *Biſhop's Exceptions* together at large, as he did our Paper, and ſhall now Conſider their Validity.

He is pleaſed to ſay at the Beginning of his firſt Paragraph, *he is ſuch a Reader as in our Paper we deſire:* Words that gave me great Hopes, of not only fair, but friendly Dealing; and I heartily wish it had been so: But since it seems to me the *Reverse* of his Promise, he must not take it ill from me, if I stop a while, and shew him a little to himself, and how much he is mistaken in his own Temper, as well as in our Principles. For tho' he begins with the Names of *Moderation, Charity,* and *Meekness,* that's all: He quickly loses Sight of them, and forgets them, with himself, almost all the Way. And unless my Taste be Extremely Depraved, there is little Relish of those Virtues in his Management, or a tolerable Temper shewn towards us, respecting either our Belief or Practice. We desired *such a Reader* indeed as had *rather* we were in the Right, than in the Wrong; One that did not Prejudge our Case, and would give us (and not our Enemies) the *wording* of our own Belief: While the Bishop but too plainly shews, he would not have us in the Right, Even where he dares not say, (however freely he suggests it) that we are in the Wrong. Which appears,

First, by his *Unnecessary* Exceptions to such Truths, as we have declared in our Paper (and he cannot deny) as *imperfectly* Exprest, because we have not said all that might be said, to Branch them out, or Illustrate them; tho' enough to be understood by such as are not Captious.

Secondly, by *Suppositions Incongruous,* and that can have no other Service than to *Expose* us, and that in a very ill Manner.

Thirdly, by rendring us to *Deny,* what we don't Express in our Paper: Though indeed we Believe it.

Fourthly, in not taking due Notice of what is *Implied,* as well as Exprest: Which had been but Just.

Fifthly, in making the *worst* of what is not concurrent with his Belief, and not the best, where we believe the same Thing.

Sixthly, by Grosly Misrendring our Pretences to *Strict Living.*

Lastly, by Condemning us upon *Rumour.* All which is *more than Leaning to that Side,* that had *rather* we were in the Wrong, than in the Right; and Consequently not *such a Reader* as we desired. That this is so, let it but be observed, how he *Unchristians* us in his Third Paragraph; tho' Immediately in a *Contradiction* to what he just before Acknowledges in his Second. Nor will he allow us to be so much as *Deists* in his Fourth, or at most but very Imperfect Ones, because we have not said all of God, that may be ascribed to him. In his Sixth, he supposes us capable of believing that Christ Came of *Corrupt* and *Sinful Flesh,* because we say no more in that Place, of the *Manner* of his *Incarnation,* than the *Evangelist* doth, *John* 1. 14. Also, that we are *Defective,* at best, *Ambiguous,* about Eternal Rewards and Punishments. He makes us, in his Seventh Paragraph, to *Deny* the Resurrection of the Dead, at large, and *without Distinction,* though we there acknowledge a *Future State,* which implies it; and have not said one Word against it; but upon all Occasions, in Print, or otherwise, have Exprest our Belief of that Branch of Christian Doctrine, *according to Scripture.* In his Tenth, he derides our Plain (though Proper) Language, of *Thou to a single Person,* though it is what he himself gives to God in his Prayers. In his Fourteenth and Fifteenth, he is pleased to slight and render our *Stricter* Living, a *Trick to promote a Party,* and that our *Garb, Looks,* and *Gestures, are more to make our selves Remarkable, than out of any Perswasion of Duty, or Conscience:* As bad a Construction as he could make. In his Sixteenth, he tells us, *The Light within us, that we say, we have from Christ,* is rather *one of the Heighths or Depths of Satan Transformed, and that we are Abandoned to his Delusions.* So that We, and most of our Principles too, are stark Naught with the Bishop. In his Eighteenth, and last Paragraph, he suggests, *We take away Two Thirds of the Christian Faith, besides many Points of the other Third; and equal our Presumptuous Conceits, to the Divine Oracles, and Revelations, and use, and disuse, at Pleasure, what Part of God's Instituted Worship we think fit; Even the very Badges of Christianity. I will not,* says the Bishop, *interpose* (yet suggests it) *your making Gain your Godliness; but if the Aforesaid Men, are in a Way to Perdition, what can you Conclude of your selves? In the Name of God Repent and Return.* Thus the Bishop, upon a whole People, without any other Provocation, than has been Exprest.

I hope, after this, He will not Expect (I am sure he ought not) that any Body should think him *such a Reader,* as we desired, for our Gospel-Truths, and which he promised us to be; or that he has treated us with the *Moderation, Charity,* and *Meekness,* he made us hope for; since none of our Adversaries have used us much worse, in so little a Compass. I heartily wish him a better Sight of himself, as well as of us, that he may be less mistaken in both another Time; for I have a Respect for him, and desire not to be upon these Terms with him, any Longer, than he thinks fit to make it necessary.

The rest of his first Paragraph is only a Strain of Fair and *Pastoral* Promises, *forgotten* by him, and not to be remembred any more, at this Time, by me; and therefore I shall proceed to his Second. Only observe this one Thing to my Reader, and the Bishop too, that he is pleased to place *Moderation* and *Charity* to our Account, because he does not take us by our Word *Chiefly* to mean *Only*, or *All*, in Reference to the Things, by us believed: Which, under Favour, he could not do in Justice; and therefore he needs not bring us in Debtor for that, which is our Due, since no Body ever took *Chiefly*, for *Only*, any more than an *Eldest*, for an *Only* Son, or an *Arch*, for an *Only* Bishop. Nor does *Chiefly* imply *All*, any more than *Only*; for whether It regards Things Human, or Divine, It imports the *Best Part* of any thing, but not *All*: The *most valuable*, that which deserves and commands our Regard and Esteem in the first Place. And I leave it with my Reader, whether Believing in God, and Christ, and the Holy Spirit; and Believing the Scriptures, and the Necessity of Holiness, and Divine Worship, and finally of *Eternal Rewards and Punishments*, are not Points of Faith, *Chiefly* to be Received and Professed by Christians? And if they are such, the Bishop must have been Superfinely Critical, upon our Word *Chiefly*, as well as that he might have been a better Husband of his *Moderation* and *Charity*, and have kept them for an Occasion where they might have been *more* needed, and Consequently better bestowed.

His Second Paragraph allows us to have sufficiently Exprest our Christian Belief in two Articles, but with this Censure, that of Eleven, we are *only Clear in these Two*, viz. *Justification by Christ*, And *Submission to the Civil Government, wishing we may always stick to this Belief, and Practice*; and adds, *I heartily Rejoyce to find you acknowledge the Necessity of Christ, as a Propitiation, in order to the Remission of Sins, and Justifying you, as Sinners, from Guilt. 'Tis the first Time I have heard of it among you.*

If so: It is the Bishop's Fault, and seems to me, next to Impossible; since before that Paper was given him, he was pleased to Acknowledge he had read several of our Books; particularly, my *Rise and Progress of the People called* Quakers, taking it out of his Pocket at that Time; also *Robert Barclay's Apology*, which States, and Vindicates our Principles at large, in which the Two Doctrines afore-mentioned, are very clearly Declared, and Maintained, notwithstanding he seems to make this look like a *New Discovery*. But however, I am pleased, that the Bishop is so, at two of the *Gospel-Truths*: I am of Opinion, if he had well considered the Force and Comprehensiveness of our Belief concerning Christ, that pleases him so well, he might have saved himself the Trouble of what he has published to the World upon the rest of them: For, whoever believes in Christ, as a *Propitiation*, in order to *Remission of Sins*, and *Justification of Sinners from the Guilt of Sin*, can hardly disbelieve any *Fundamental* Article of the Christian Religion; since, every such Person, must Necessarily believe in God, because it is with Him alone Man is to be Justified. To be sure he must believe *in Christ*, for that is the very Proposition. He must also believe in the *Holy Ghost*, because, he is the *Author* of his *Conviction, Repentance*, and *Belief*. He must believe *Heaven*, and *Hell, Rewards*, and *Punishment*, and Consequently the *Resurrection of the Just and Unjust*: For, why should he be Concerned about being freed from the Guilt of his Sin, if if he were unaccountable in another World? So that Acknowledging the Necessity of Christ, as a *Propitiation*, in order to the Remission of Sin, comprehends the main Doctrine of Christian Religion; and as so many Lines drawn from the Circumference to the Center, *they all meet and center in Christ*: And indeed it is as the *Navel* of Christianity, and Characteristick of that Religion. I would intreat him again, to reflect well upon his own Acknowledgment, and *Commendation* of our Belief, concerning the *End*, and *Benefit* of Christ, to Mankind; and he cannot think us so Deficient, much less, under such *strong and dangerous Delusions*, as he has been pleased to represent us.

His Third *Paragraph* will not suffer us to be Christians, notwithstanding what we have said of our Belief in Christ, in our Paper called *Gospel-Truths*. In one Sense I shall easily agree with him, for I think nothing makes any Man a *True Christian*, but *Regeneration*, the Power of the Son of God *Revealed in the Soul, Converting it to God: For the Devil's Believe, and Tremble* too, and yet are Devils still; they Believe what is *True*, but they do not *Truly Believe* in him that is *True*:

1698.

They know and assent to the Propositions of Truth, or Articles of Faith, and knew *Him* to be Christ too, when He came of old, and called him by His *Name*, but this did not make True Christians *Then* of them: Nor yet does an *Assent Now* to all the Truths of the Gospel, *Truly Qualifie* Men Christians, *unless they feel the Power of them, upon their Hearts*. And I would have my Reader reflect well upon this Great and Essential Truth, tho' he were as Big as a *Bishop*: For a *New Creature* is the Business; an *Orthodox Life*, the *Cross* of Christ, which is the *Narrow Way of Self-denyal*. Yet I must say, That whoever declares, he believes in Christ as his *Sacrifice* and *Sanctifier*, which is to save both from the Guilt and Pollution of Sin, is a *Professor of Christianity*, and may reasonably be allowed to be a *Christian at large*. And that what we have declared, in our *Third, Fourth, Fifth*, and *Sixth Gospel-Truth*, comprehends the Belief before-mentioned, my Just and Sober Reader may satisfy himself in the Perusal thereof.

His *Fourth Paragraph* faults our first Article, as he is pleased to call it, *with great Shortness and Imperfection concerning our Belief of God*; for tho' he says we own his *Providence as to the other Life*, yet *we say nothing, as to the Creation of this present World, and Providence over it*: But, with the Bishop's Leave, He that believes in God, believes in all that's necessary to a Supreme Being. 'Tis what he, and all Christians, take for granted, and allow, as often as they hear any one say, *He believes in God*. For not to believe Him *Omnipotent, Omniscient*, and *Omnipresent*, is not to believe him to be God, being inseparable from the Divine Nature. I must appeal to the Bishop, whether a small Grain of Charity would not have excused us from his Reflection upon this Head. We have said more than *Moses* said to *Pharaoh*: For besides that, *I am*, is no more than, *He is*: We have added that *He is*, the Rewarder of all Men, according to their Works. We gave the Text, as it is, and the very Text seems express for a *Declaration of Faith in God*, viz. *He, that will come to God, must believe that He is, and that He is a Rewarder, of them that seek him*. The Text does not Enumerate and Require the Belief of all the Divine Attributes, and Properties that are in God, but the bare Belief of his Being, and what He is to Mankind that fear him. And whatever the Bishop says, this is enough for a Man to come to God, though not enough, it seems, to come to the Bishop in the Quality of a Believer: He must help the Holy Ghost to speak Properly, or we, that speak after him, must be *deficient* in our Expressions, if not in our Belief. But when any one affirms, that Man was created by God, is he Short, Fallacious, or Equivocal, because he does not say *how* God made Man, or *what* he made him? Is not his *Body, Soul*, and *Spirit*, his *Will, Understanding, Memory* and *Affections* comprized, and meant, under that Word *Man*? Besides, could the Bishop think, that while we own God's greater Providence, his lesser could be disbelieved by us? He that has the alone Power of *Rewarding* Men, in the other World, according to their Works in this, must certainly be the *Sovereign of Both*; and his Providence, in Justice, is to be so understood. And as it is most certain that we believe of God, all that the Holy Scriptures declare of him, and whatsoever is proper to that Great and Glorious Being; so, had we not thought it unnecessary to be more particular, from the Common Notion all Men have of the Deity, the Bishop could have had no Room left for the Exercise of his Charity.

In his *Fifth Paragraph*, he Blames us for being Defective in our Confession of the *Holy Trinity*: Though we give it in the very Terms of the Holy Ghost, 1 *John* 5. 7. If this is not a sufficient Text to prove the *Trinity*, that *Antiquity* Urges, and also *Modern* Writers of the *Church of England*, to prove it, I know not where to find one, in the Scripture.

It is Generally Believed the Apostle *John* gave this Declaration to the *first Christians*, to *prevent* their being deluded by *Cerinthus*. How came the Bishop then to render it but a *By-Passage*, and otherwise intended by the Apostle, than for an *Article of Faith* about the *Trinity*? Is there a Plainer, or a Fuller any where in the Writings of the New Testament? Three and yet *One*, is the Doctrine of the *Trinity*: And no other Apostle has gone so far, or been so Express: Insomuch that the Text has been doubted, and render'd *Apocryphal* by such as do not believe the Common Doctrine of the *Trinity*; and *Foisted* in to serve the Turn of *Trinitarians*: So plain it has been thought to their Purpose, even by the *Anti-Trinitarians*. How then is the Text defective with the Bishop? But he says the Apostle writ it *upon Occasion*: Doubtless he did so. But what other Occasion, I pray, than that of the *Holy Trinity*? He adds, *And it was to the Apostle's Purpose*, touching the
Father,

Father, Son, and Holy Ghost: But what Purpose could the Apostle have, but that of declaring the *Trinity*, and yet *Unity*? What other Use does he make of it? The *Bishop* must be very hard put to it, certainly, to shift of, and lessen our Confession in this Point, and rather than fail, render the Text it self short; which, with Submission, I think is a bold Attempt in one of his Station, if he believes the Thirty Nine Articles.

The next and Sixth Paragraph, relating to our Third *Gospel-Truth*, is large, and consists of divers Branches, and therefore I shall consider them distinctly and apart. In *the Third Article, You acknowledge indeed the Son of God to have been made Flesh, but neither Conceived by the Holy Ghost, nor Born of the Virgin* Mary: *So that it does not appear, by this your Confession, but that He was at first an Ordinary, Corrupt, and Sinful Person.* I think it is hardly to be supposed that we could intend so gross a Thing, or that it is inferrible from the Manner of our expressing of our selves, in *Reference to Christ's Manifestation in the Flesh*. Where Enough is said, to Comprehend the Rest, All is Meant, tho' All be not Express'd: We call him the *Beloved Son of God*, the *Only Begotten of the Father*: Pray what is that short of being *Conceived by the Holy Ghost*? To be sure, it is very far from a *Corrupt and Sinful Person*, a Supposition as remote from what we said, as from what the Bishop promised, *viz. Charity*. He that confesses the *Word was made Flesh*, confesses him made *Flesh by God*, and therefore made *Holy Flesh*: For God never made any corrupt or sinful Flesh. If the Place is read, as some do, *viz.* the Word *took Flesh*, the Flesh must be Holy, for he would not take, or dwell in sinful Flesh.

And had the Bishop well remembred what he *Acknowledged*, upon our Believing Christ to be a Propitiation for Sin, not many Lines before, he could never have suggested so Unreasonable, as well as Uncharitable a Conceit; since *Sinful Flesh*, or *a corrupt Person, could never be any Part of a Sacrifice for Sin*: So that in commending that Part of our Belief, he has sufficiently secured us against this Part of his Insinuation. But the Bishop proceeds to aggravate our Shortness in Expression, to a severe Imputation, *viz. That we own Him not so much as Jesus, or the Christ*.

This must be a great Oversight of the Bishop, not to say worse, when the very Fourth Head, *about Justification by Christ*, of which he declares himself so well satisfied, *Thrice* confesses him to be *Christ*, *viz.* in the *First, Third and Fourth Lines*. Again, we call him *Christ*, in the *First Line* of the *Fifth Gospel-Truth*; likewise in the *First and Fourth Lines*, of the *Sixth*, we call him *Christ*: We do the same, in the *First and Fifth Lines of the Eighth*, and in the *First Line of our Tenth Gospel-Truth*. How the Bishop came to miss in so palpable a Point of Fact, in the Compass of One Half Side of a Sheet of Paper, I cannot imagine, and am unwilling to censure. Nor would I willingly think the Bishop so trifling, as well as disingenuous, as to excuse himself herein, because we do not call the *Word*, that took *Flesh* by the Name of *Christ*, in *that Place*, since the Bishop repeats it from us, out of our aforesaid Fourth Head, about *Justification by Christ*, where we call him by the Name of *Christ*, as may be seen in the second and foregoing Paragraph of his Reflections. Besides, we have not confessed his Name less than *Nine Times* in that Paper. But if the Bishop could yet insist upon the Word *Christ* not being in our Third Head, I say the Thing is there, though the *Word* be not. For what is Christ but the *Word made Flesh*, and who is the Word made Flesh but *Jesus Christ*? Again, who is the *Beloved Son of God but Christ, and who else but Christ is the Beloved Son of God, and Only Begotten of the Father, full of Grace, and full of Truth*: For these High and Distinguishing Characters are to be found in *That* very Head of Doctrine, where the Bishop will not have us to acknowledge him to be Christ. So that unless a corrupt and sinful Person can be full of *Grace and Truth*, I wonder how the Bishop came to suppose a Thing, in our Name, so very gross. But he proceeds in the same Paragraph, *You acknowledge indeed he died for Sin, but you have not one Word of his Resurrection from the Dead, or of his Ascension into Heaven, which it may be proved some of you have expresly denied,* saying, *He is not Ascended into Heaven, He is in us*; with more to this Effect. I should be sorry to Tax the Bishop here of *Absurdity and Uncharitableness*; but who can help it? For if Christ be not Risen, He is still in his *Grave*; He is no more. How then do we assert him to be a *Propitiation*, and the *Light and Life of his People*? See *Gospel-Truth*, 3, 4, 5, and 6. Can that which is Dead, *Sanctify and Justify Believers*? Can the Dead give us *Grace and the Holy Spirit*? Or have we not said so of *Christ*, that he is the Giver thereof? And if we have said so, must not the Bishop be extreamly beside the Business? His Uncharitableness is as obvious, I will not say his Untruth; but I must

pray

pray him to reflect a little better upon what he has writ; for unless he would make us to mean the *Grave*, when we say, *That Wicked Men shall never come where Christ is gone*, Gospel-Truth 6. he must allow that we acknowledge Christ to be in *Heaven*, and consequently *Ascended*. What shall I say to his Story of some of our *Friends*, whom he makes to affirm, *That Christ is not Ascended into Heaven; He is in us*? Can it touch us, or should he have said it, and not have proved it? Is that fair and candid? Is it Charitable, supposing it were True, which does not appear? Or is it Just to insinuate it upon the People as *Dubious*? But let it be never so True, it cannot conclude the People, if not *Act of the People*. The *Church of England* has Doctors of very different Sentiments; would the Bishop think it fair the Common Belief of the Church should thereby be concluded? It is True, and a great and comfortable Truth, *That Christ is in us*, according to 2 *Cor.* 13. 5. *Gal.* 2. 16. *Col.* 1. 26, 27. but not *Confined* to Man: He is not so there, as that *he is no where else*, and least of all that he is not in Heaven. For the Apostle tells us, *Eph.* 4. 14. that *He Ascended far above all Heavens, that he might fill all Things*; then *he is in Man certainly*. So that our asserting that Doctrine of the *Indwelling of Christ in Man*, does not make void his being elsewhere, because he is every where: Tho' in Heaven most Gloriously, without Doubt, *being there Glorified with the Glory that he had with the Father before the World began*. And they that thus believe in Christ, cannot deny *his being at God's Right Hand*, which signifies according to Scripture, *Phil.* 2. 9, 10, 11. *the highest Exaltation:* Nor yet to be their *Mediator*, for that is inseparable from his being their *Propitiation*. So that tho' we did not dwell upon Points, but were Concise in our Expressions, *yet whatever is implied, or is implicable from any Assertion, Justice, as well as Charity, always grants*; and so would the Bishop have done, had they been uppermost in his Mind, when his Pen ran so fast against us. I must own it was not writ for *Criticks*, but for such *Readers* as the Bishop says he was, or should have been, to wit, *who exercise Moderation and Charity*; more of which, I hope he thinks as well as I, will do him no Harm.

But it disturbs the Bishop that we have said nothing of *Christ's Coming to Judgment*, nor *of the End of the World, whether it be Dissolvable or Eternal.* For the First, *It is implied in our making all Men Accountable to God, for their Deeds done in the Body*. For the other, it was not under our Consideration, being not objected to us. But they that say as much of Christian Doctrine as we have done, in those *Eleven Heads of our Paper*, did never yet, that I have heard, believe the Eternity of this World, *Heb.* 1. 10, 11, 12.

Yet again says the Bishop, *Not a Word of One Church, which it may be feared you strike out of your Belief, because you are resolved never more to return into the Unity of the Church, but to make and maintain a Schism, or Party for ever.*

These are very harsh Constructions, besides that they beg the Question, and in my Opinion would have past better from a Person, whose Office was less concerned in *Charity*, than that of a Bishop: But why, pray, *Must Interest and Obstinacy Rule our Dissent?* What's to be got by it, *Profit and Preferment* go the Bishop's Way, I will not say he goes theirs. But why not *Conscience*, tho it were mistaken, since we have been all along of the *Losing Side?* Which is not usually espoused by the *Men of Interest*, nor are *Men ordinarily Obstinate against their Interest*. Let us at least be Honest Men, and allowed to mean Well, though we were mistaken. But what Church, of the many Churches in *Europe*, is the *Bishop's One Church*, to which he would have us return? He has not told us. Methinks he that censures our Shortness so much, should not have been deficient himself in so Material a Point. So that if we are out of the Way, we must be so still for all the *Bishop*; since we are yet to seek what Church we Err from, or should Repair to. But I will suppose he means his Own, by which he excludes the *Lutheran* and *Calvinist*; the *Presbyterian*, *Independent* and *Baptist*, as well as the *People called Quakers*, from being of his *One Church*; to say nothing of the *Roman Catholick* or *Greek Churches*. But unless the *One Church*, as he phrases it, by which I understand him to intend the *True One*, may be of Two Minds, it will be difficult for him to recommend his own above the rest, because that is not only broken in *Sentiments, but Practice too, and which the Bishop knows is no longer a Secret*. I might mention the Differences warmly managed between the Doctors of it, about *Grace and Free-Will*; one taking the *Calvinist*, the other the *Arminian* Way; as they also do about the *Doctrine of Satisfaction and Justification*. Likewise the late Controversy between Two Famous Men of the Church, about the *Trinity*, who are followed in their differing Sentiments, by great Numbers of the Learned of the *Bishop's One Church:*

And

And for that Reason (if no other) I cannot be so well satisfied of his exact Correspondence with all the Articles of that Church himself. And I hope I am not beside the Business, when I say, *It would very well have become the Bishop to have told us what it is he would have us believe, when he found so much Fault with what that Paper says we do believe.* It would be too long, and perhaps he might think it besides the Business, at least the Brevity the Case requires, to give him the Reasons of our *Separation and Dissent,* or *Disagreement with the Church.* I put these Words together, because some were never Members of it, and so they could not properly be said to separate from it; but True it is, we may all be said to *Dissent, or Disagree*; and I would think the *Bishop* should not be much to seek for the Reasons of it. And yet where we are vulgarly apprehended to differ most, we Dissent least, I mean in Doctrine, which is the Reason so many have upon Occasion said, as indeed did the Bishop at the Visit I made him; viz. *Why we believe the same, 'tis what we Preach as well as you.* For except it be the Wording of some of the Articles of Faith in *School-Terms*, there are very few of them profess'd by the *Church of England,* to which we do not heartily Assent. And this I have exprest for my self, and in Behalf of my *Friends,* in my *Key,* and *Primitive Christianity Revived.* But of this, and the more Material Reasons of our Distance from the Church, I may have Occasion to express my self at the Closure of this *Vindication.*

But the Bishop proceeds in his Sixth Paragraph: *Nor have you a Word of the Resurrection of the Body, which divers of you have been known to deny, and others of you only say, It may be so.* I shall consider this immediately upon the next Paragraph, where he treats upon the same Subject, and apply my self to his Conclusion of this: Lastly, *Tho' you acknowledge Everlasting Rewards for them that fear God, yet nothing of the Everlasting Punishment of Wicked Men.* I think we do, and that the Bishop aggravates his Disingenuity to us upon this Head: For the Words of the Paper are these, *It is our Belief that God is, and that he is a Rewarder of all them that fear him, with Eternal Rewards of Happiness; and that those that fear him not, shall be turned into Hell.* The Scriptures are, Heb. 11. 6. Rev. 22. 12. Rom. 2, 5, 6, 7, 8. Psalm 9. 17. Now though *Eternal* is not joyned to *Hell*, yet Justice as well as Candor would have understood it so, and to mean the *Hell of the Damned,* the *Punishment of Evil Doers after this Life,* according to the Ancient, Common Belief. But the Bishop that seldom fails to make the *Worst* of every Thing for us, thus comments upon our Words: *You mention Hell indeed, but whether you mean thereby the Grave, as commonly in Scripture is meant, or a Place of Temporal Punishment after this Life, as some have done, or a State of Total Destruction and Annihilation, as many now a-days do, no One knows.* But with the Bishop's Leave, what if we mean None of these, may we not be in the Right for all that? For what if none of these are the Ancient, Common, and Scripture Belief, what will the Bishop do then? Since One would think that One of them is the Bishop's Hell, because he gives us and his *Reader* no more Room for our Meaning, or any other Belief of a Hell. And either one of these is an Article of his Belief, or else he keeps the True Hell to himself, and was not so Just as to include that in the Question with the rest, lest he should be thereby Guilty of supposing us capable of meaning the *True One* in our *Gospel-Truths*, viz. *The Worm that never dies, the Fire that never goes out, where is Weeping and Gnashing of Teeth for ever.* See 2 Thessalonians 1. 9. Jude 6. 7. And which, I think, is none of the Three the Bishop mentions. However, he abundantly shews his Inclination to represent us rather Wrong than Right, in our Belief: For if the Scriptures by us cited are consulted, they plainly shew we never meant the *Grave*, and that they equally refer to the Future State of the Souls of Men; viz. *That all shall receive the Recompence of their Works, and the Rewards of their Deeds, according to the Nature and Quality of them.* And if the Rewards of the Righteous are Eternal, then so must those of the Wicked be, or both must be Temporary: For the Holy Ghost makes no Difference as to the Duration of the one more than of the other. One Grain of a *Truly Christian Temper,* had saved the Bishop, and he me, the Trouble of this, as well as other Reflections.

I am come now to his *Seventh Paragraph,* the First Part of which, is a heavy Complaint of our *Shortness and Deficiency in expressing our selves.* We, it seems, are *too General* in some Points, and Wave in others; he is pleased to say, *Eight of Twelve,* but Instances only in that of the *Resurrection*; tho' he conjures us at the same Time, upon our Eternal Account, to consider what he says. Now if being General, and keeping to the Terms of Scripture be a Fault, we are like to be more

Vile with the Bishop: For Thanks be to God, *That Only*, *is our Creed*, *and with Good Reason too*; since it is fit *That* should only conclude, and be the *Creed of Christians*, which the Holy Ghost could only propose, and require us to believe. For if the *Comment* is made the Creed instead of the *Text*, from that Time we believe not in God, but in Man. I heartily wish none had been Wise above what is written, and that Generals had concluded Christians: Then Charity had been *better* Maintained, and Piety promoted: Wheras *Strains*, or *Refines* upon the Text, have thrown us into those Labyrinths of Controversie, that the Zeal which should have been imployed to suppress *Sin* in all it's Branches, has too generally been used to fire one Party upon another, till Practice, which is *Religion indeed*, was blown up by the Generality. So much for our *Shortness or Wavering*, as the Bishop calls it.

I shall now attend his only Necessary Point of *Eight*, that he thought fit to mention, which, he says, we either suppress, or wave, viz. *The Resurrection of the Dead:* I confess I did not think that any Body would have been so Uncharitable to us, after our *Acknowledging the Future State of the Just and Unjust*, since that implies it, and every *Medium* to it. However I will attend what the Bishop urges for Proof of what we don't deny, but always must the Slander of doing so. *I will* (says he) *only mind you of Two Passages out of the Scripture of Truth*, 1 Cor. 15. 16, 17. *If the Dead Rise not, your Faith is Vain, you are yet in your Sins.* Hence it appears (says the Bishop) *all other Points of Faith are in Vain, if this be not True.* And so say I, as well as the Bishop, and shall always say as he says, while he says no more than the Text says: For who can think, that allows himself to think, that we should not believe an *Immortality*, who have exposed our selves, and suffered so much, that we may obtain *an Happy One*. But the Question is not whether the Dead Rise, *But with what Bodies?* For if the Dead Rise not, then may we say with the Apostle, Verse 19. in the same Chapter, *We are of all Men most Miserable.* So that the Resurrection of the Dead is out of all Dispute with us: But with *What Body*, will, I believe, be One, *till the Dead Rise*.

Here it is we are *Cautious*, and tread *Softly*; remembring what the Apostle says to the Curious and Inquisitive upon this Head, Ver. 35, 36, 37, 38. *But some Man will say, How are the Dead Raised up, And with what Bodies do they come? Thou Fool, thou Sowest not that Body which shall be, but bare Grain.*—— *But God giveth it a Body as it hath pleased him, and to every Seed his own Body.* Here is the Ground of our Caution, which the Bishop is pleased to call *Suppressing*, *and others denying of the Resurrection*. We have indeed been *Negative* to the Gross Conceit of People concerning the Rising of this Carnal Body we carry about us, which better agrees with the *Alcoran of Mahomet*, than the Gospel of Christ. But *that there is a Resurrection of the Just and Unjust to Rewards and Punishments, we have ever believed.* And indeed we cannot but wonder that any should be displeased with us, for being *Pleased with that which God is pleased to give us*. Bodies we shall have, *but not the same*, says the Apostle, and so believes the Quaker; *but God giveth every one a Body as pleaseth him*, and that pleaseth us, whoever it displeaseth: For we had rather be called *Fools Ten Times by the Bishop, than Once by the Apostle*, which we think we should deserve, if we should dare to stretch the Text, or presume to define the Secret.

The other Scripture urged by the Bishop, in Defence of what we never opposed, is *Rom.* 10. 9. *If thou shalt confess with thy Mouth the Lord Jesus, and believe in thine Heart, that God hath raised him from the Dead, thou shalt be saved.* He adds, *Those who believe this as they should do, shall be Saved.* But, *that we have left out both Christ's Resurrection, and our own in our Faith.* In the First Part of his Note, I agree with him, that all who *Rightly* believe the Text, will be Saved: For that must be by the *Illumination and Working* of the Saving Power of Christ in the Heart, that he can so believe. But that we have left out *Christ's Resurrection and our own*, is a Mistake already observed, because they are both plainly implied; one in our Belief of Christ's being a Propitiation for Sin, and the Light, Life and Strength of his People, and in giving us his Grace and Holy Spirit, which that which is Dead cannot do: And our own Resurrection is sufficiently secured, in our declared Belief of Rewards and Punishments; tho' the Mode of it be not expreft: Nor was there any Reason for saying more upon that Head, with Respect to the Occasion of our Papers being published.

I am now come to the Bishop's *Eighth Paragraph*, which comprehends his Exceptions to Three of our *Gospel-Truths*, viz. the 5th, 6th, and 7th, which wholly relate

late to the *Doctrine of the Light of Christ Within Man*. And I am truly sorry to find the Bishop at so great a Loss, as that Paragraph shews him, about so *Excellent and Evident a Principle*; and which so very much concerns him, and indeed All Men, to know. And that my *Reader* may inform himself throughly in this Matter, I must desire him to look back, and read those *Three Gospel-Truths*, and compare them with the *Bishop's Eighth Paragraph*, and he will make himself much a better Judge of the Validity of the Bishop's Answer, and my Reply, and which of us Two keeps closest to the Doctrine and Language of the Holy Scriptures, that he in the same Paragraph seems so much to Respect.

His First Exception in this Paragraph, is at our Incapacity: For he says, *We have never been able yet, that he could find, to make out what we mean by the Light of Christ Within*. Perhaps the Bishop has never sought, or has sought amiss; which, as Great and Learned Men as himself, have done before now, and so mist what they have sought for: And then it cannot be a Wonder, that he has not found out what we mean by the *Light of Christ in Man*. But that a Bishop should represent this an unintelligible Doctrine, after reading so distinct and plain an Account of it in *Robert Barclay's Apology*, not to mention divers other Books; and which is of greater Authority, the *Scriptures of Truth*, is no ordinary Surprise to me. Has the Bishop forgot the *First of John*, and the 4th, 9th, and 16th Verses, where speaking of the Word-God, he says, *In Him was Life, and the Life was the Light of Men*.

This is that *Light of Christ* the *Quakers* assert, and desire to turn the Minds of all People to: For all must have it, if it be the *Light of All*, as the Text plainly tells us it is. The Ninth Verse is yet more express, viz. *That was the True Light which lighteth every Man that cometh into the World*; than which, nothing can be more expresst to our Purpose. And that the Bishop should feel no Share in this *Glorious Light of Men*, renders him very unfit, methinks, for an Overseer of them.

I know some read this Text otherwise, as indeed he did to me in *Cork*, viz. *That was the True Light, That Coming into the World lighteth all Men*; referring the Word *Coming* to Christ, and not to Man. But all the Versions I ever met with, and I have seen more than Twenty, render the Verse as it is in our *English* Translations: And all Criticks and Commentators, except the Followers of *Socinus*, Read and Render it *as we do*. And while we have so much Company, and so great Authority, I think we need not be Solicitous about the Success of this Point. But besides that the foregoing Verse tells us, that the Divine Life of the *Word-God*, is *the Light of Men*, which shews all Mankind have it in them (for it is the Light of their Minds, and not of their Bodies) it is impossible that Interpretation should be True in a strict Sense: For the Coming of Christ in that Blessed Manifestation, was to the *Jews* only: He says it himself, *He was not sent but to the Lost Sheep of the House of Israel*, Mat. 13. 24. Again, *He came unto his own, and his own received him not*, John 1. 11. And within that narrow Compass he could not be said to be the Light of all Mankind that *had*, *did*, and *should* come into the World, for so both the 4th and 9th Verse plainly import, viz. The Light of Mankind, without Restriction to This or That Manifestation of God to Men.

But the *Bishop* is still at a Loss what to make of this Light, and what we would be at; For, says he, *You will not allow it to be either the Natural Rational Faculty, or Common Innate Notions, or Natural Conscience, or Conscience Illuminated, by the Preaching of the Gospel, and the Operation of the Holy Ghost thereby*. We say, we would have it to be what the Scriptures say it to be, viz. *the Light of Christ*, the Son of God, who called himself, *John* 8. 12 *the Light of the World*; and if so, then *Every Man's Light*; *the Light of every Mind and Understanding*, and consequently the *Light of Christ Within*; too hard it seems for the Bishop to comprehend, and yet so very easie, to the meanest Capacity, that observes the Discoveries and Convictions of it in their own Hearts.

But since it is, as he rightly terms it, *a Fundamental* with us, we will follow the *Bishop*, in his Enquiries a little farther. We say first then, It is not the *Natural Rational Faculty* of *Man*; for then it would be *Man*, or a Part of his *Composition*, meerly as Man: But that It is not, but a *Manifestation* in the Soul of Man, of *Christ*, the Word God, the *Light of the World*, the *Second Adam*, the *Lord from Heaven*, the *Quickning Spirit*, who was full of Grace and Truth, and of whom Man hath received Grace for Grace: To wit, a Talent, a Proportion suitable to his Want and Capacity, to Convince and Convert him, to Renew and Restore him from his great Lapse unto God, his Blessed Maker, again. In short, our *Natural Rational Faculty*

Faculty is our Sight, but not our *Light:* That, by which we discern and judge what the Divine Light shews us, *viz. Good from Evil*, and *Error from Truth*. But as the *Eye* of the Body is the Sensible Faculty of seeing external Objects, through the Discovery that an External Light (as the *Sun* in the Firmament) makes to the Eye, but is not *That Light* it self; so does the Rational Faculty of the Soul see Spiritual or Immaterial Objects, *through the Illumination of the Light of Christ Within*, but is by no Means, *That Light it self*, any more than the *Eye* is the *Sun*, or *John* the *Baptist*, was our *Blessed Lord and Saviour Jesus Christ*, that was but Servant and Fore-runner of his Blessed Manifestation in the Flesh.

As for the Bishop's *Innate Notions and Natural Conscience*, if by them he means Impressions or Principles, which are born and come with us into the World, *viz. the Law of God in the Heart of Man*, I must tell him, first, that this is not the Language of the Law and Testimony he refers us to in the same Paragraph: And next, that as the *Work is not the Workman*, so they are not properly the *Light of Christ*, but the *Blessed Fruit and Effect of the Light of Christ, the Word-God in Man, which Shines in the Heart, and gives him the Knowledge of God, and of his Duty to Him*. So that the Innate Notions, or Inward Knowledge we have of God, is from *This True Light that lighteth every Man coming into the World*, but is not *that Light it self*. Just so the Bishop's Natural Conscience, must only mean a Capacity that Man has by Nature; that is, in his Creation, of making a Judgment of himself, his Duty, and Actions, according to the Judgment of God manifested to him by the *Light of Christ Within*. Not that such a Capacity is that *Light*, but that it sees or understands, by the Inshining of the Divine Light, the Things that belong to Man's Duty and Peace.

Nor is it Conscience illuminated, *By the Preaching of the Gospel, and the Operation of the Holy Ghost thereon*, which is the last of the *Bishop's* Constructions; but *That very Principle of Life and Light*, which illuminates the Conscience, and was the very Spring and Force of the *Apostolical Ministry*, and of the Conviction and Conversion of their Hearers; and which opened their Hearts to receive the Gospel when Preach'd unto them. In short, this Excellent Principle is in Man, but not of Man, *but of God*. The Nature of it is to discover Sin, reprove for it, and lead out of it, all such as Love and Obey the Convictions thereof. It is a Principle of Divine Life, that Quickens the Obedient Heart to Newness of Life: It Raises the Mind above the World to God, *and Searches out and Reveals the Deep Things of God to the Humble and Waiting Soul*. And be it known to the Bishop, and all that with him profess Ignorance about what we mean by the *Light of Christ Within Man*, This is *It* I have been treating of; and I have writ, I bless Almighty G O D, my own Experience, the Taste and Relish I have had of it's Excellency and Sufficiency, in the Course of far the greater and best Part of my Life.

But the *Bishop* must excuse me, if I say, I cannot but take it very ill at his Hands, to forbid us in his following Words, *to pretend to give an Account of what we Believe, unless we can make him understand our Meaning:* And because he does not penetrate our Sense, to call our Way of Wording that Blessed Principle of the Light of Christ in Man, a *Perfect Banter*. This to me is one of the severest Persecutions, because *Spiritual Things*, are only to be *Spiritually* discerned and understood. I would fain know how a Regenerate Man can possibly make a Carnal Man understand the *New Birth*? It is certainly the Gift of God to understand Divine Truths, as well as Rightly to Believe. So that supposing our Assertion of the Nature, Power, and Excellency of the *Light of Christ in Man to be True*, not to have Leave to say so, unless we could make every Man rightly take our Sense and Meaning, *Whether he be Spiritually Discerning or not*, looks Antichristian as well as Unreasonable. *We speak Wisdom*, says the Apostle, *among them that are Perfect*, 1 Cor. 7. 6. It seems others understood him not, must he therefore not have wrote of the Things of God? The very Preaching of the Gospel was Foolishness to the *Wiselings of the Jews*, and *Greeks*; they could make neither Head nor Tail of it, by their Way of judging of *Truth*: Must not the Gospel therefore be Preach'd? When the Apostle *Paul* Preach'd to the *Athenians*, some of the Men of the Gown, the Philosophers of that Time, opposed and despised him, saying, *What will this Babbler say?* But had they known what he meant, we cannot think they would have said so to Him. Was the Apostle then, or the *Athenians* in Fault, that they did not understand Him? Or, was it *Bantering* as well as *Babbling*, because he did not make them understand his Meaning; which is only the Work of the Holy Ghost to do? Who was it, I pray, that said, *The World by Wisdom knew*

not

not God? And can we suppose any Thing else blinded the *Scribes* and *Pharisees*, and the High-Priest of the *Jews*, from discerning the *Messiah* when He came? For they wanted not *Academical* Learning, if that could have enlightned them; nor yet the *Scriptures*, but they *Resisted* the Holy Ghost, their *only True Interpreter*, and so stumbled and fell. Let the Bishop also have a Care.

In the Second Chapter of the first Epistle to the *Corinthians*, he will find that the Apostle spake the Wisdom of God in a *Mystery, which the Princes of the World knew not*, with all their Wisdom: *For the Things of God*, says the Apostle, *knoweth no Man, but the Spirit of God*; by which those Christians knew those Things that were *freely given to them of God. Which Things also we speak*, says He, *not in the Words which Man's Wisdom teacheth, but which the Holy Ghost teacheth, comparing Spiritual Things with Spiritual. But the Natural Man receiveth not the Things of the Spirit of God, for they are foolishness unto him: Neither can he know them, because they are Spiritually discerned.* Now, according to the Bishop's Treatment of us, the Apostle ought not to have writ of Faith and Salvation, unless he could have made all that read his Writings *understand* his Meaning. And it must be a *perfect Banter*, to talk of speaking Wisdom in a *Mystery*, and not in the Terms that Man's Wisdom teacheth.

But the Lord Jesus Christ was of another Mind, when he said, *I thank thee, O Father, Lord of Heaven and Earth, because thou hast hid these Things* (the Truths of the Kingdom) *from the Wise and Prudent, and Revealed them unto Babes: Even so, Father, for so it seemed Good in thy Sight.* It is hence, beyond all Dispute, that God *hideth* the Mysteries of his Kingdom from the Wisdom of Man, while *Simplicity and Sincerity* fail not to *Reach* and *Understand* them. Here it was that poor *Nicodemus* was absolutely at a *Loss* for Christ's Meaning, when Christ said, *Unless a Man be Born again, he can in no wise enter the Kingdom of God*, John 3. Insomuch as he asked Christ, upon his Discourse of the *New Birth, How can these Things be?* At which Christ seems to admire, in a Sort of Reproof upon *Nicodemus, Art thou a Master of* Israel, *and knowest not these Things?* As much as to say, Art thou, a Man of thy Station in the Church of God, Ignorant in the Way to Heaven? Whoever reads that notable Interview between Christ and *Nicodemus*, will find that Christ resolves the Matter into *Two Births*, That which is born of the *Flesh*, and that which is Born of the *Spirit*, and these are Contrary: And therefore no Wonder if they *differ* in their Understanding of the Holy Scriptures, being a Declaration of the *Faith* and *Experience*, as well as *Doctrine* and *Practice* of the Servants of God that were Enlightned and Born of the Holy Ghost. Nor is this all; for *they that are Born of the Flesh, Persecute them that are Born after the Spirit:* So that when they can no longer commit Violence upon their Persons and Estates, they will Persecute them with their *Tongues* and *Pens:* They are *Hereticks, Blasphemers, Illiterate* and *Ignorant*, yet *Presumptuous; Enemies* to *Cæsar*, and *Disobedient* to Government, if they will not give God's Due unto Man, *viz. Conscience.* And if they chuse to deliver themselves in *Scripture* Stile, and speak earnestly of the Necessity of the Work of the *Spirit* of God, in order to an *Experimental* and *Saving* Knowledge of the Truth, declared in Holy Scripture; and that *Christ's Ministers* are made by the *Holy Ghost*, and not by *Human* Learning; and that the Worship, which is acceptable to God, must be *in the Spirit* and *in the Truth*; that is, with *Clean Hearts* and *Right Spirits, Kindled* and *Inflamed* with the *Holy Spirit of God:* They must be called *Enthusiasts, Unintelligible, Men of Cant and Banter.* And here I leave the Bishop, upon this Paragraph, desiring him to Consider, whether his Knowledge of God the Father, and Jesus Christ, *whom rightly to know, is Life Eternal*, John 17. be by the *Revelation* of the Son of God in his own Soul, since Christ himself Teacheth and Affirmeth, that *no Man knows the Father but the Son, and He to whom the Son Reveals Him:* I should be glad to see the Bishop's Evidence for this Knowledge. For in the Conclusion of this *Paragraph*, he turns us to the Scriptures, who, in the Beginning of it, makes us *Unintelligible* and *Banterers* in Religion, for Expressing Ours in the *Terms of It*; which may well merit the Bishop's Serious Reflection.

His *Ninth Paragraph* refers to our *Eighth* Article, as he calls it, of which he cites these Eight Words only, *Worship, under the Gospel, is Inward and Spiritual*; upon which, he says, *If you mean, that Outward Worship ought to be performed with Inward and Spiritual Worship, 'tis what we Preach, Press, and Practice; but if* (as it would seem) *you mean that all the Worship, God now requires, is from the Inward Man, or from the Spirit; this is abominably false;* for our Bodies are God's

Handy-work, and God, by the Apostle, Commands, Glorify God in your Body, and in your Spirit, which are God's. *Not to tell you, that you your selves, now a-days, perform somewhat of Bodily Worship.* Indeed we do, and Ever did, and Ever shall, I hope, while we have Bodies to Worship God in. We are so far from denying the Body what Share is due to it, that with the Apostle, 1 *Cor.* 6. 19. we say, *What, know ye not that your Bodies are the Temples of the Holy Ghost, which is in you, which ye have of God, and you are not your own?* Of which I would have the Bishop well Consider: For, if our very Bodies are under the *Influence* of the Holy Ghost, how much more reasonable is it to believe, that It dwells in our Souls, and that our Hearts must be prepared, and animated by the Holy Spirit, in all our Devotion towards God. But two Things I must Remark to the Bishop, First, That we did not give him the least Occasion to suspect we deny'd Bodily Worship, as appears by the *Gospel-Truth* now in Question: For 'tis plain there, by these Words, *Worship in this Day is Inward and Spiritual,* That we only distinguish'd between *Gospel* Worship, and the *Ceremonial,* and *Pompous* Worship of the *Law*; and that by *Spiritual* Worship, we understand *Praying, Praising,* and *Preaching* by the *Preparation* and *Sanctification* of the *Spirit* of God; which the Bishop does not, and, I hope, dares not, Deny: Yet Unkindly, and I think *Unjustly,* brings in His *as it would seem,* to make us by an Uncharitable *Innuendo* look to his Reader, as if we denied *Bodily Worship.* And yet, to avoid so hard a Chapter, as Maintaining this Aspersion would prove to the Bishop, he is forced to confess that *now a-days we perform somewhat of Bodily* Worship; as if we did not perform any formerly, and but a little now: Which shews not that Candour, that his Character owes us, and but too plainly tells every Impartial Reader, how much more Mind he has that we should be in the *Wrong* than in the *Right.* I must Confess we have *less* Pomp and Gaudiness in our *Worship,* as well as in our Cloaths, than is the Custom of some other Churches, and think it our Happiness, that we are freed from such an *Unprofitable* as well as Unsuitable Incumbrance. Whatever It be, 'tis such as we believe God by his Holy Spirit hath led us into: And tho' it be not so Entertaining to those who are governed more by their *outward Senses* than their Souls, yet, I hope it will be allowed us to be *Grave, Solemn,* and *Fervent.*

The other Remark I make upon the Bishop's Exceptions is this, That the Spiritual Worship he there allows of, seems to be but the Worship of *Man's Spirit,* and not of the Spirit of God, working upon the Spirit of Man. I would not Imitate him, lest I should be Uncharitable too: For if my Reader can make more of it, he has my Consent; but that seems to me to be the Bishop's Interpretation upon Christ's Words, cited by us, on this Occasion, *viz. God will be Worshipped in Spirit and in Truth:* Though there is a Truth in that also, yet this not being so *peculiar* to the Gospel-Dispensation, could not be the *Extent* of Christ's Words, whose Drift certainly was, to draw Men's Minds to a more *Inward* and *Spiritual Worship:* Not only to have *less* Ceremony than was Practis'd among the *Jews,* but to *feel more of the Power and Spirit of God in our Adoration and Praises,* than belonged to the Former Dispensation; and, with which, I heartily wish the Bishop a better *Acquaintance.* Upon the whole Matter, I am apt to think my Reader believes with me, he might as well have spared his Pains upon us, about the first Part of this *Gospel-Truth,* as he is Silent of the latter, *viz. That we may Preach in Power as well as Words, and as God Promised, and Christ Ordained,* without Money and without Price.

The Bishop, in his Tenth Paragraph, is pleased to Endeavour to lessen the Authority and Credit of our *Ninth Gospel-Truth,* relating to the *vain Fashions and Customs of the World.* His Words are these: *You tell us of denying all the vain Customs and Fashions of the World, as also Excess in all Things; I know of no Sort of Christians who teach otherwise: I wish I knew none (even of your Selves) that practis'd otherwise; it is one Part of our Catechism we teach our Children.* He first Concurs with our Doctrine, for he says, *he knows none that Preaches otherwise;* and that they do the like in their Catechism. So far, then, he allows us to be found. But he wishes he *knew none (even of Us) that Practice otherwise.* This is a Sort of Charge, and being not prov'd, looks like a Calumny. Some, perhaps, do not walk quite so strictly as becomes them, to their Profession; but are they own'd by us therein? Or Indulged it self? If not, what are we to Conclude but that the Bishop's Insinuation is to *Ballance* Accounts with us for the Failures of his own People? But, pray are our Excesses *equal,* or the *Numbers,* that in Proportion

proportion do transgress? I would not have him Comfort himself with his Uncharitableness to his honest and friendly Neighbours: As it will not excuse his less exact Friends, that any of ours live larger than they profess, so it cannot justly affect our Body, where so few are faulty, when 'tis so well known that such are sure to meet with due Reproof.

But he adds, that *There are many Innocent and Laudable Customs, We call Vain:* This is all in a Heap, and a Reflection by Wholesale. I can truly tell him, I know of none; and if he had been more particular, so would I too: Perhaps he thought Generals best to make his Reflection *Safe:* But if it were my Place to be Plaintiff, I could treat the Bishop with a large Catalogue of very Offensive Customs, that would concern him to think upon. However, he is pleased to be particular upon us in one of them, which almost turns his Stomach, he says, to think of, *viz. Would it not make a Man's Stomach turn, to hear one forbear, in Point of Conscience, saying,* [you] *to a single Person, because it is improper; and at the same Time, while he is talking to his Superior, because* Thou doest *sounds a little Rudely, to soften the Thou, and say* Thee doest, *which is commonly your People's Practice.* It is pity the Bishop could find nothing else to observe from us, that might have better edified us and his Readers: Yet if this be that, among the Laudable Customs which we call Vain, which is most Offensive to his Stomach, it shews him to have a very *weak* one. However, a weak Stomach is better than a weak Head, and such an one I should take mine to be, if my Instances were no more to the Purpose and my Reader's Instruction.

But I have somewhat to say to the Bishop, before I leave him, upon the *Old* Topick of *Sincerity* and *Charity*, in this Reflection, as I have had in most of the other, *viz.* That he makes the *Ground* of our Conscientiousness, about the saying of *You* to a single Person, to be only *Propriety* of Speech; which he (I was going to say) in his Conscience must know is not so: But that the true Reason of it is, first, That it is the Language of the *Scriptures of Truth;* and next, That the Original of *You*, to a single Person, was *Pride* and *Flattery*, being a *Plural* Honour to a *Single Person*; given first to *Potentates*, and then gradually to all Subordinate Ranks of People. In Ancient and Unmixt Tongues, *Thou* to a Single Person is kept still, as also among the Common People of the present Languages, and particularly in *that Kingdom* where he is a Bishop. I refer him to a Book, entituled, *No Cross no Crown*, where he will find other Reasons for our Tenderness in that Matter than he alledges, or we have Room for here; though the Bishop confines us to *Propriety*, as the *only* Reason of our Practice, that he might the better Lash us with the Impropriety of *Thee* for *Thou;* which yet he might have spared, since nothing is more common with all People, than to take the like Freedom in Speech, in Cases as well as Tenses; not excepting the *Learned* themselves. But be it so, we keep *Numbers*, and intend not clipping of Cases, and that's Our Point, though not the Bishop's it seems; which it should have been, would he have been just to us upon the Question. As for the *Levity* and *Scorn*, with which he is pleased to treat us upon this Head, I shall only say, it unbecame him, and Confirms us more than it Exposes us, whatever it does Him.

But I confess, I am surpriz'd, to find a Man of his Character, and Pretensions, propose so loose a Question as that with which he closes this Paragraph, viz. *Will you ever be able to prove, the Primitive Christians used a Dialect or Dress, different from others of their Nation or Quality, and placed Religion in it? Does not Christ require Saluting those that Salute not us? And no Doubt, He, and his Apostles Salutations were in the Common Form.* Doubtless, *we are able*, most easily and fully: And 'tis admirable to conceive how he could be ignorant of these Proofs, who ought to be so well read in *Scripture* and *Antiquity. I beseech you therefore, Brethren*, says the Apostle, *by the Mercies of God, that you present your Bodies a Living Sacrifice, Holy, Acceptable unto God, which is your Reasonable Service:* And *be not Conformed to this World, but be ye Transformed by the Renewing of your Minds,* Rom. 12. 1, 2. Again, the Apostle *Peter*, Chap. 1. 13, 14. *Exhorts the Believers, to Gird up the Loins of their Minds, and be Sober, as Obedient Children, not Fashioning themselves, according to the former Lusts in their Ignorance;* which was the *Custom* of their Country. And Chap. 3. 3, 4. *Whose Adorning let it not be that of* Plaiting the Hair, *and of* Wearing of Gold, *or of* Putting on of Apparel: But *let it be the* Hidden Man of the Heart, *in that which is not Corruptible, even the Ornament of a* Meek and Quiet Spirit, *which is, in the Sight of God, of great Price.* Thus the Apostolical Counsel to the Churches. But for all this, the Bishop

shop of *Cork* cannot tell how to think *We are able to prove, that the Primitive Christians differed in their Dress, from other People in their Country and Quality.* Nor was this only the Strictness of that Time; for the same Apostle adds, *Verse* 4. as an Argument to Enforce his Advice; for, *After this Manner*, says he, *in the Old Time, the Holy Women also, who trusted in God*, Adorned themselves. But can a Man of his Letters, really be at a Loss for a Proof of the *Singularity* of Primitive Christians, in *Dress, Speech* and *Behaviour*? Or is it to try whether we have any to resolve his Question? Or taking our Illiterature for Granted, that he puts upon us? I beseech him to Converse with *Ouzelius* upon *Minutius Felix*, and he will tell him that the first Christians were taxed, and despised for *Ill-bred* in *Manners*, *Unpolish'd* in *Speech*, *Unfashionable* in *Behaviour*; in fine, *Rusticks* and *Clowns*. As the Christians *Ironically* return'd their *Scorners* the Stile of *Well-bred* and *Eloquent*. This, and much more, he cites out of *Arnobius, Lactantius, Theodoret*, &c. and *Jerome* writing to *Celantia* and *Demetias*, Noble Women of that Time, sets them a *Singular* Form of Life from that of the People of their Quality: And *Paulinus* Bishop of *Nola*, was so far from pleading for Christians *Temporizing* with the People of their own Nation, or Quality, according to the Bishop of *Cork*, that he sharply reproves *Sulpitius Severus* for It, in a Letter to him; as the Learned *Casoubon*, in his Discourse of *Use* and *Customs*, observes. If the Bishop would look into the *Constitutions*, that go under the Name of *Clemens Romanus*, with *Tertullian, Gregory Naz. Clemens Alexandrinus, Austin, Gregory the Great*, and other Ancients, he would perceive the Care and Zeal of those Eminent Men to suppress the *Educations* and *Customs* of the Gentiles, and to encourage and recommend the *Simplicity* and *Moderation* of the Manners and Behaviour of the first Christians, which *Machiavel*, in his 2d Book of *Disputations*, takes Notice of, and is none of the least Proofs to our Point.

And to finish my Authorities, passing by *Petrus Belonius, Gratian, Cardan, Luther*, &c. I must recommend to the Bishop the History of the *Waldenses*, (an Early People, if not *Successive* from the Primitive Times) written by one *Perrin*, more especially concerning their *Faith, Worship*, and *Discipline*; and there he may, if he please, observe the *Simplicity, Plainness* and *Distinction* of that People from the Customs of the Countries they lived in, and those that have the Name of *Reformed* Ones now.

But he tells us, *Christ and his Apostles had Salutations*; and I tell him, so have We. But he will have it that Christ and his Apostles *Saluted after the Fashion of the Country they were in*; which is sooner said than prov'd. For Christ ask'd the Jews, *How can you believe that receive Honour one of another, and seek not the Honour that cometh from God Only?* Now this certainly must be Unlawful to Give or Receive, which hinders true Faith. And what was this Honour, but *Salutations* after the Fashions of the Times? As the Text shews, *Matth.* 23. and for *Calling, and being Called of Men Rabbi*, Christ was so far from Commanding, or Imitating them in such Things, that He expresly *forbids It*. But the Meaning of Christ's Saying, *Matth.* 5. *And if ye Salute Your Brethren only, what do ye more than Others? Do not even the Publicans so?* Is this; That in all Acts of *Love, Mercy* and *Goodness*, they were to *Exceed* the Practice of that Time: They were to take more Notice of, and to look more kindly and friendly upon All Men. But in another Sense, He that bid them *Salute Enemies as well as Friends*, also forbids his Disciples to *Salute any Man*, or *call any Man Rabbi or Master*; *for that One was their Lord and Master, and they were all Brethren*, Matth. 23. 6, 7, 8. and *Luke* 10. 4. And between such Relations Worldly Honours were of no Use, as well as of no Value. And did a *Primitive Spirit Prevail* in those that so much pretend to be the *Successors* of the Apostles, we should see them more *Exemplary* in *Self-denyal* and *Holiness*; Encouraging, and not Undervaluing and Brow-beating the Serious and Conscientious. But *Trees are known by their Fruit; for Grapes are not gathered of Thorns, nor Figs of Thistles*.

In the mean Time, if my Reader please to peruse the Ninth and Tenth Chapters of that Book, entituled, *No Cross, No Crown*, he will, I hope, be satisfied, that we are for *Honour, Respect* and *Civility*, according to *Scripture*; tho' *Non-conformists* to the *Empty* and *Troublesome* Ceremonies of the *Times*, left by Us, not of Rudeness, but *Conviction*; and forborn of Duty, and no otherwise of Choice. For, Humanly Speaking, that Contradiction to Custom cannot be pleasant to us. I have detained my Reader longer upon this Head than I expected, or perhaps he desired: I shall therefore proceed to the Bishop's next Paragraph, which contains his

Exceptions to our Tenth Gospel-Truth about *Baptism* and the *Supper*, and the last he has to take Notice of, the Eleventh about *Government*, being by him already granted in the Beginning of his Paper.

He begins thus: *In your Tenth Article you believe a Spiritual Baptism, and a Spiritual Supper and Communion, but acknowledge, you disuse the outward Signs, by us commonly called Sacraments: Now did not Christ command Water-Baptism?* Go ye and Baptize all Nations, Matth. 28. 19, 20.

He goes on, *The Baptism here commanded was Water-Baptism*: His Reasons are, first, *That Baptizing with the Spirit was God's Work, not the Apostles.* 2dly, *Primitive Practice*, Acts 10. 47, 48. in *Cornelius*'s Case; *Who can forbid Water?* But this is also *gratis dictum*: For the first Reason is no Reason, since it is *not true*: And the second seems to me *Defective* and *Short*. I am very sensible of the *Disadvantage* I am under, and that I touch a *tender* Place, and what I say upon this Head, as also anon upon the *Supper*, will be against Wind and Tide with the Generality. But, as I hope I shall express my self *Reverently* as well as *Plainly*, upon this Occasion, so I beseech my *Reader*, for His Own Sake as well as Ours, not to *Prejudge* us; as I am sure he will not, if he be a *Searcher* after Truth, and that I charitably suppose of him.

I say then, the Bishop's first Reason is not true; for God, by the Apostles, did Baptize Believers with the *Holy Ghost*. It fell upon them, through the Powerful Preaching of the Word: Thus, *Acts* 10. 44. *While* Peter *yet spake these Words, the Holy Ghost fell on all them which heard the Word.* By which, it is evident that *Peter*, in that Sermon, was the Minister of the *Spiritual Baptism* to *Cornelius* and his Company.

And *Peter* gives this Account to those of the *Circumcision* at *Jerusalem*, Acts 11. 15. *And as I began to speak, the Holy Spirit fell on* them *as on us, at the Beginning: Then remembred I the Word of the Lord, how that he said,* John *indeed Baptized with Water, but ye shall be Baptized with the Holy Spirit.* So that *Peter* evidently declares the Gift of the Spirit by the Ministry of the Gospel, to be the Baptism of Christ, or the Baptism of the Holy Spirit and Fire, which Christ promised at his *Ascension* into Heaven.

But the Apostle *Paul* puts this Matter beyond all Doubt, in his Excellent Account he gives of his *Conversion* and *Commission* to King *Agrippa*, *Acts* 26. where my *Reader* will find these Words dropping from the Mouth of the Lord *Jesus* to Saul; *Delivering thee from the People, and from the Gentiles, to whom now I send thee, to* open their Eyes, *and to turn them from* Darkness *to* Light, *and from the* Power *of* Satan *unto* God, *that they may receive Forgiveness of Sins, and an Inheritance among them which are Sanctified through Faith that is in* Me, Verse 17, 18. Now if this could be done *without* the Holy Ghost, let my *Reader* Judge. 'Twas with the *Holy Ghost* that *Peter*'s Hearers were *Prick'd to the Heart*, and fitted to receive more of it: And it was by the *same* Holy Ghost that *Paul*'s Hearers had the *Eyes of their Minds opened*, to see the *Mysteries* of God's Kingdom, and by which they were *Converted from Darkness to Light*, that they might receive the Forgiveness of their Sins, and Inheritance among them which are Sanctified. So that the very End and Benefit of the Apostolical Ministry was *Converting*, that is, *Baptizing them into Christianity*; in the Nature, Power and Life of It, by the Holy Ghost.

Now, for the Bishop's Second Reason, viz. *Practice*: I say it is granted that Water-Baptism having got Place among them by *John*'s Ministry, the Fore-runner, it held after Christ's Coming; but that was *Ex Gratiâ*, and of *Condescension*, not of Commission; for that properly ceases when his Ministration begins, of which *John*'s was but the *Fore-runner*. For *Moses* and the *Prophets were 'till* John, *and* John *'till Christ*. And this, *John*, the Water-Baptist, tells us, Matth. 3. 11. *I indeed Baptize you with Water unto Repentance, but he that cometh after me is mightier than I, He shall Baptize you with the Holy Ghost and with Fire*, see Mark 1. 8. Luke 3. 16. Here's a different Baptism and Baptizer, the *Servant* and the *Master*, the *Water* and the *Holy Ghost*. One *Transient*, the Other *Permanent*: One the End of the *Jewish*, and the Other the *Beginning* of the Gospel Dispensation. Wherefore, says our Lord Jesus Christ, *The least in the Kingdom of Heaven is Greater than* John, Matth. 11. 11. Why, is not *John* in Heaven? No Doubt of it at all, and a Glorious Saint too: But the *Least* in Christ's Dispensation, *viz. The Kingdom of God in the Soul*, the *Work* of Christ, the Baptizer with the *Holy Ghost and Fire*, is *Greater than* John, as to the *Nature* of his Administration. See John 3.

3. 30, 31. *He must Increase, but I must Decrease.* What! *John* Decrease, or his Ministry? His Ministration certainly, which he calls *Earthly* in Comparison of *Christ's.* So that the *Baptist,* in his Watery Dispensation, did but *Fore-run* Christ, in Reference to the Kingdom that he was to set up in Men. He pointed to Christ, and shewed what Christ was to do, *viz.* to *Wash, Fan,* and *Throughly Purge his Floor;* that is, His *People,* and Sanctifie them throughout, *by his Spiritual Baptism,* according to the Apostle, *in Body, Soul and Spirit,* 1 Thess. 5. 23. So that in short, *Practice,* Properly, can be no *Institution,* where the Thing Practised has *no Commission,* which I suppose the Bishop will not think fit to deny: But, says he, *It has a Commission,* Matth. 28. 19. which is, under Favour, but his *Say-so;* and that I think it is no more, I do with all Humility and Submission, say, First, I cannot tell how to reconcile it to Good Sense, or Common Usage, in Sacred or Civil Matters, that any thing should be in Force by a Commission that is not so much as *once named* in the Commission. I say, to me, it does not appear *Congruous* any more than *Cogent,* or obliging. And this is the Cause in Hand: For there is not a Word of *Water* in the Text alledged for Water; nor yet in the Context. And unless there were *no other* Baptism than that of *Water,* as there are several, it must at least be allowed to be a *Question,* what Baptism Christ meant in that Commission, when he said, *Go ye therefore and Teach all Nations, Baptizing them in the Name of the Father, Son and Holy Ghost.*

But it may be returned upon me; nor does the Text say it is the Baptism of the *Holy Ghost,* and so the Bishop is upon equal Terms with me. Grant it, that the Word *Holy Ghost* is not literally joyned to *Baptizing,* any more than the Word *Water* in that Part: But if I am able to shew that the Thing is there, and that the Baptism of the Holy Ghost was the *Subject* of Christ's Discourse, when he gave that Commission at his Farewel, I presume it will be granted me, that Christ intended a *Spiritual,* and not a *Water* Baptism; and that is what I shall do, I hope, with much Clearness. First the Fact, and then my Arguments. *Matthew,* the Evangelist, large in his History upon other Points, seems short and abrupt in the Context of this Commission, as the Reader may observe. And as it is usual for one Evangelist to explain another, which was the great Wisdom, as well as Goodness of God, that those Christian Memorials might come with less Suspicion to the World of any Human Contrivance; So *Luke* supplies the Shortness of the other Evangelist in his Context to this Commission. *Luke* 24. 45 to 50, particularly the 47, 48, 49, Verses. And *that Repentance and Remission of Sins should be Preached in his Name, among all Nations, beginning at* Jerusalem. *And ye are Witnesses of these Things. And behold I send the* Promise *of my Father upon you: But tarry ye in the City of* Jerusalem *until ye be endued with Power from on High.* Where, as it is plain that this Evangelist in his Account of Christ's Commission, to wit, *the Work Christ gave his Disciples to do,* Names no *Baptizing* at all, though that which it *Implies,* in my Sense of the Word, is there, *viz. The Promise of the Father,* which is the Power from on High They *were to tarry at* Jerusalem *for.* So is there not *one Word* of Water here mentioned, to induce us to think that Christ intended to give it *any Place* in his Commission. In short, it appears that the Disciples were to be *Qualified* before they were to go forth as His *Witnesses,* and that this Qualification is the *Promise of the Father,* that he would quickly send them. Now I must desire my Reader to turn to the *Acts* of this Evangelist, Chap. 1. 4, 5. where he farther opens the Manner and Matter of Christ's Discourse, and *Farewel* to his Disciples: And (Christ) *being Assembled with them, commanded them that they should not depart from* Jerusalem, *but* Wait *for the* Promise *of the Father, which,* saith He, *ye have learnt of me: For,* John *truly Baptized with Water, but ye shall be Baptized with the Holy Ghost not many Days hence.* It can be, methinks, no longer a Doubt what Baptism it is that Christ's Words, *Matth.* 28. 19. refers to, since we see not only that Christ distinguishes between *John's* Baptism and His Own, and between *Water* and *Holy Ghost*; but also he assigns Water-Baptism to *John,* as *his Baptism,* and not Christ's, and thereby declares the *Holy Ghost* to be his own Baptism, and none of *John's,* and which yet is no more than what *John* had said before.

So that comparing both Texts together, *Matth.* 28. 19. and *Acts* 1. 4, 5, we may see, if we please, that the *Commission* in the one, is to be explained by the *Qualifications* in the other, which was omitted by the first Evangelist. There They are bid to *Go,* here They are bid to *Stay:* That is to say, Stay, before you Go, and receive your *Qualifications* before you go to *Qualify, viz. the Promise of the Father;*

that is, the *Baptism of the Holy Ghost*, which is followed *by the Power from on High*, Verse 8. And indeed, had we not this express Force on our Side from the Text it self, the Word *Therefore*, in the Commission, (referring plainly to the foregoing Verse, as the Reason of what follows) justifies our Sense. For whereas the Bishop has objected against our Assertion, *that it must not be a Spiritual Baptism, because that was the Work of God, and not of the Apostles*: It is plain that our Lord takes off the Force of his Exception, since the Reason why he bid them *Go*, &c. is, *because*, says he, *all Power in Heaven and in Earth is given unto me*. Verse 18, as much as if he had said, *Go, do all that I have said unto you, and be not* Doubting *or* Fearful, *about the Performance of It, for* All Power *in Heaven and Earth is given unto me* that bid you Go, *and Lo I am with you always, even unto the End of the World*, Which need not have been said, as an Encouragement to them, in Reference to Water-*Baptism*, since that was practised by them, as well as by *John's* Disciples, long before.

Nor is this all; for the very Text, duly considered, will not have It to be Water, since that could Baptize none *Into* the Name of the *Father*, *Son* and *Holy Ghost*, and so the Bishop knows the *Greek* Text runs, εἰς τὸ ὄνομα. For they that are Baptized *Into* the Name of the *Father*, and of the *Son*, and of the *Holy Ghost*, must be Baptized with the Baptism of the *Holy Ghost*. Since it is to become their *Likeness*, and bear their *Image*, which is *Holiness*. And had not the Apostles understood their Commission as I render it, when they had Baptized with Water they would certainly have used the Terms that bore the Force of their Commission, viz. *In the Name of the Father, and of the Son, and of the Holy Ghost*; of which there is not one Instance in all the Scripture.

But that which farther shews that *Water* cannot be understood to be meant in the Apostolical Commission, is, that one of the Greatest of the Apostles, he that came behind (and was added to, by) none of them, denies It, 1 *Cor.* 1. 27. to be *any Part of his Commission*; for, says he, *Christ sent me not to Baptize but to Preach the Gospel*: And thanks God for that Reason, in the foregoing Verses, that he had Baptized so few: Which to be sure he ought not to have done; but on the Contrary, to have been sorry he had Baptized no more, had *Water-Baptism* been Part of the Apostolical Commission, *Matth.* 28. 19. Again, this Eminent Apostle, the *Great Grand-father* [not to say *God-Father*] of Gentile-Christians, delivered to them *for Doctrine*, *Eph.* 4. 5. that there was but *One Lord, One Faith*, and *One Baptism*. And if so, That must be the Baptism *of Fire and of the Holy Ghost*, which is Christ's Baptism, and *Proper* to the Gospel-Dispensation. Now, could any other make a Man a *True Christian*, or a *Child of God* then? Nor can any be so now without It. That Baptism therefore, without which a Man cannot be a *True Jew*, or *Christian*, or of the *Circumcision made without Hands, that Worship God in the Spirit, and hath no Confidence in the Flesh*, must needs be the *One Baptism*; but such is the Baptism of the *Holy Ghost*: Therefore the *Spiritual Baptism* is the Apostle's *One Baptism*, Rom. 2. 28, 29. Phil. 3. 3. Again; the One Baptism must be Christ's Baptism, but Christ's is the Baptism of the *Spirit*, therefore *That*, and not *Water-Baptism*, must be the One Baptism that's in Force, according to the Apostle. As *John* was the *Fore-runner* of Christ, so was *Water*, of the *Holy Ghost*: But that which Foreruns, in Nature *Ceases*, and that which succeeds, of Course *Remains*: Therefore the Baptism of the Spirit, is the *One Needful*, and *Permanent Baptism*.

Yet farther; If it be Gospel, *That he is not a Jew that is one Outward, nor that Circumcision that is Outward in the Flesh*; *but that he is a Jew that is one* Inward, *and that is Circumcision that is of the Heart, in the* Spirit, *and not in the* Letter; *whose Praise is not of Men, but of God*, as Rom. 2. 28, 29. Then unanswerably, *He is not a Christian that is one Outward, nor is that Baptism that is of the Flesh*: But he is a Christian *that is one Inwardly, and that is Baptism that is of the Heart, in the Spirit; whose Praise is not of Men but of God*. For indeed in all Ages Men cry him down, as a *Slighter* of God's Ordinances; but his Praise, however, is of God, let Men say what they will; and this is the Inward Christian's Comfort, in all Undervaluings and Reflections he meets with from Outside Christians. For it's not to be thought that the Apostle meant or designed to undervalue one Observation, as that of Circumcision, because it is Outward, and set up another Outward Observation *instead* of it, viz. *Water-Baptism*.

Again, *If in Christ Jesus, neither Circumcision availeth any Thing, nor Uncircumcision, but a* New Creature; as saith the same Apostle, *Gal.* 6. 15. Then by the same Reason, *neither being baptized with Water availeth any Thing, nor being not baptized*

baptized with *Water*, but a *New Creature*. I will repeat the Apostle's Discourse at large upon this Subject, in the same Chapter, because it is very Instructing, and seems Decisive in this Case; *As many*, says he, *as desire to make a fair Shew in the Flesh, they constrain you to be Circumcised; only lest they should suffer Persecution for the Cross of Christ.* It seems they were Outside People, that laid Stress upon Outside Things; or something else instead of the Cross of Christ; for they Temporized in this Matter, to shun the Shame and Persecution that then attended the Christians Cross: Which stood partly in laying down of outward Observations; and which they that *desire to make a fair Shew in the* Flesh stand most for. But the Apostle goes on; *For* (says he) *neither they themselves who are Circumcised keep the Law, but desire to have you Circumcised, that they may Glory in your Flesh.* They were not exact in the other Parts of the Law, it seems, as strict as they seemed to be for this Sacramental Practice, which is the Case of too many now: Yet they prest it, that they might glory and value themselves upon gaining others to be conformable to them, whether to excuse their Compliance with Custom, that they might avoid Persecution, or out of Love to Ceremonial Religion.

But, says that clear-sighted and plain-dealing Apostle, *God forbid that I should Glory, save in the Cross of our Lord Jesus Christ, whereby the World is Crucified unto me, and I unto the World.* If he rejoyced in nothing but in the *Cross* of Christ, then in no *other* Elementary Rite, Service or Ordinance, any more than in Circumcision.

But he proceeds: *For in Christ Jesus, neither Circumcision availeth any Thing, nor Uncircumcision,* but a *New Creature.* That is to say, for according to Christ Jesus, or in the Religion of Christ Jesus, neither Circumcision nor Uncircumcision availeth, *but a New Creature, a Regenerate Soul; One born again by the Spirit of God*: For the Apostle, in these Excellent Words, not only strikes at Circumcision, but all Outward and Elementary Observations: Neither This, nor That *Outward Thing availeth in the Christian Religion*, or according to *Christ Jesus,* but a *New Creature*: He does not say, *but Water-Baptism*, as some would have it, who tell us that It *succeeds* Circumcision by *Divine* Institution, by no Means: But that which availeth with Christ, and in the Religion of Christ Jesus, is *a New Creature, a New Man,* one *Changed, Regenerated,* or *Born again by the Word and Baptism of the Holy Ghost.* And, says the Apostle, (to confirm them in this Doctrine of *Inward* Circumcision, that is of the *Heart*, in the *Spirit*; which is the *same* Thing with the Baptism of the Spirit) *As many as walk according to this Rule, Peace shall be upon them.* So that We, the poor despised *Quakers*, take Comfort in this Apostolical Benediction, and can say, to God's Glory, his *Peace has been upon us* in our Belief and Confession of his Blessed Doctrine of the *New Creature*. It is what we have Aimed at, and has been the Great Drift of our Testimony since we were a People; and in order to it, we have directed all to the Gift of God's *Grace in themselves*, that by believing in it, and resigning up their Wills and Affections, and whole Man to the Teaching and Conduct of it, they may be leavened and sanctified by it, *throughout*; by which the State of the *New Creature*, which is Christianity indeed, will be *Experienced*, though it was and is a Mystery to the World.

As for the Apostle *Peter*'s Question, *Acts* 10. 48. *Can any Man forbid Water, that these should not be Baptized, which have received the Holy Ghost as well as we?* It imports, with Submission, no more than this; That *Peter* well knowing the Narrowness of his Country-Men's Spirits, was Cautious lest his Latitude should distaste them: For the *Gentiles* being *Unholiness to the Jews*, and even *Peter* himself without a Vision from God, too narrow Spirited for the Convictions and Devotion of that Excellent Centurion, *Cornelius*, it behoved him to ask if any Body had any Thing to say, Why they might not be Baptized as well as the *Jews*, being Proselytes to the Christian Profession? In all which he seems more concerned to save his *Own Credit*, than to recommend, or establish that of *Water-Baptism*. As if he had said, Why should this Custom be forbidden to the *Gentiles* more than the *Jews?* But this will not warrant the Practice in General, because Practice is *No Institution*, and that there appears no Command to make it one. So that asking who can forbid what was not commanded, strengthens his Question, instead of weakening it, since what was done of *Condescension*, could not have been forbid upon Authority. There needed not so much Care or Strictness in the Matter. And indeed, the Apostles themselves seem not to have been so clear about the abolishing of the *Jewish Observations*, as appears by the Want *Peter* had of a Vision, his own Apprehension of the Straitness of his Brethren, and their calling him to Account for what he had done, as may be seen in the same Chapter. But

But I confess I cannot see why the *Bishop* should assume the Power of Unchristianing us, for not practising of that which he himself practices so *unscripturally*, and that according to the Sentiments of a considerable Part of *Christendom*; having not one Text of Scripture, to prove that *Sprinkling of Water in the Face, was the Water-Baptism*, or, *that Children were the Subjects of Water-Baptism in the First Times*. And yet this is all the *Baptism* the *Bishop* practices, who seems so severe upon us. I think our forbearing of *Water-Baptism*, from a Belief and Sense of the coming of the Invisible Grace, signified by that Visible Sign, cannot be reputed such a Slight to *Water-Baptism*, as presuming to *alter* the Manner and Substance of it's First Institution: For then it was in the River *Jordan*, now in a *Bason*; it was then unto *Repentance*, now, *to Children uncapable of Repentance*. But that which perhaps misled the Doctors of the *Declining Church* first into this Practice, being at the Distance of some Hundreds of Years from the Apostolical Times, might be the Supposition that *Water-Baptism* came in the Place of *Circumcision*, and that being to Children, so might *Water-Baptism* too. But they forgot (among other Things, which even before that Time were crept into the Church, without Precept, or Evangelical Example) that Repentance was not made a Condition to Circumcision, as it was to *Water-Baptism*. I would beseech the *Bishop* to tread softly in this Matter; for if *Water-Baptism* should indeed prove a *Badge of Christianity*, he would be at a Loss for one that would pass currant in Scripture. Thus much for this Point.

What I have said upon this Head of *Water-Baptism*, may serve also for what is commonly called *The Lord's Supper*, which the *Bishop* reproves us for omitting to practise; urging *Luke* 22. 19. *This do in Remembrance of me*. And the Apostles Words, 1 *Cor.* 11. 24, 25. It is True indeed, Christ said, when He Eat it with His Disciples, *That they should do it in Remembrance of Him till He came*. And this seems much more of the Nature of a Commission, than that cited by the *Bishop* for *Water-Baptism*: But the *Limitation* Christ gives to the Practice of it, and a Right and Proper Consideration of the *Import of His Words*, and the *Nature of the Thing*, will best lead us to understand his Mind therein.

First, This was also a *Jewish Practice*, as well as *Water-Baptism*, and so in Nature of no Gospel-Institution, but Temporary in it's Use.

Secondly, Christ seems by this, to break, or open to them, what was so hard for them to bear, to wit, *His Departure and Death*, by a Token of Memorial till he should come to them again.

Thirdly, Christ takes Occasion from thence, to shew forth to His Disciples the *Mystical Supper* they should Eat, and the Fellowship they should have with him, when he came again.

Now we believe this Coming was *Spiritual*, suitable to that Saying of his, *I will drink no more of this Fruit of the Vine, till I drink it New with you in the Kingdom of my Father: And some here shall not taste of Death, till they see the Son of Man coming in his Kingdom*, Matt. 16. 28. Again, *He that dwelleth with you, shall be in you*, John 14. *I in them, and they in me*, Chap. 17. All which plainly imports a Spiritual Coming. Also Rev. 3. 20. *Behold I stand at the Door and knock, if any Man hear my Voice, and open the Door, I will come in to him, and will sup with him, and he with me*, which was said near Forty Years after his Ascension. Now since this is acknowledged to be an *Outward Sign of an Inward and Invisible Grace*, what can Outward Bread and Wine more properly Signifie and Resemble, than an Inward Supper? And if so, the Words may Reasonably be read thus, *Eat this Supper of Outward Bread and Wine, till I come into, and Sup with you, and be your Supper, that am the Bread and Wine from Heaven which Nourishes the Soul unto Eternal Life*.

Fourthly, The Kingdom of God being Spiritual, and in the Soul, *such* should be the *Ordinances* of that Kingdom. Now Christ tells the Pharisees, *Luke* 17. 20. *The Kingdom of God is Within*. And the Apostle *Paul*, Rom. 14. 17. saith, *The Kingdom of God is not Meat and Drink, but Righteousness, and Peace, and Joy in the Holy Ghost*: But the Outward Supper is *Meat and Drink*, and therefore not of the Kingdom of God, which is not *Meat and Drink*, but *Righteousness, Peace and Joy in the Holy Ghost*. And this was made Use of by Christ, in the State of *Humiliation*, before his Death, and the pouring forth of the Holy Ghost, to fasten upon his Disciples that were *Weak, and of Little Faith*, the Remembrance of him, till they should know him with them, and in them, by His Spiritual Appearance (as He was the *Lord from Heaven, the Quickning Spirit*) according to his Promise. For if the Scripture be consulted, we shall not only find that Christ *Reproves* the Apostles for their Infidelity in him, but after all the *Example, Precepts and Miracles* they saw by him, and that he had so very lately left them with such Assurances of

1698.

his coming to them again; yet when *Mary*, &c. brought them the Tidings of *His Resurrection*, it is said *Luke* 24. 10, 11. *Their Words seemed to the Disciples as Idle Tales*, and *they believed them not*. Which sufficiently shews the low State they were in, or that at least they needed a *Sign* or Token, as that of the *Supper* to Commemorate Him. But this Reason, which is yet True, does not Credit it's Continuation; for when the Spirit was come, or Christ in his Spiritual Appearance, their Eyes were opened, and they saw then it was the *Spirit that Quickens, the Flesh profiteth nothing*, John 6. 63.

Fifthly, Most certainly Christ meant no less, when he preach'd himself *the Bread that came down from Heaven*, John 6. 31. to 52. and that they that would have Life Eternal, *must Eat his Flesh, and drink his Blood*; That is, they must feed upon *Spiritual Food*; Not the Outward, but *Inward Supper*; the Thing signified, and Substance it self. For Christ opposes himself, *who is the Bread of God*, to the *Bread* their Fathers Eat in the Wilderness, who were Dead, which was of an *Elementary Nature*; therefore it can never be that such *Bread* as perisheth, should be the *Bread of the Evangelical Supper*, when Christ by Comparison, undervalues it to the *Bread* he had to give them.

Sixthly, Our Blessed Lord, *Mark* 7. 18. taught, *That it was not that which went into the Man, that defileth the Man, because it went but into his Body, and not into his Heart*; and if so, the Argument is undeniable, that it is not that which goeth into the Man, that is, into his Body, and not into his Heart, that *Sanctifieth the Man*: But *Material Bread and Wine* goeth only into the Body, and not into the Heart; therefore they cannot Sanctifie. The Import of Christ's Words is plainly this, *Meats and Drinks* neither Defile nor Sanctifie; *they neither Benefit nor Harm any one upon a Spiritual Account*: Consequently *Elementary Bread and Wine* cannot be the *Evangelical Supper*, but a Figure of it, which is ended in *Christ the Bread of God, that cometh down from Heaven*, John 6. 31, 32, 48, 49, 50. That a Man may Eat of, and not Dye: The Substance of all Shadows; for saith the Apostle, *the Body is of Christ*; and where that is, our Lord tells us, *Luke* 13. 37. the *Eagles are gathered together*: Where the Apostles Wise Men, 1 *Cor.* 10. 15. seek for the True Supper, which Nourishes the Souls unto Eternal Life.

Seventhly, But the *Bishop* will have this *Supper* four Times repeated in the Scripture of the New Testament, besides that of the Apostle *Paul*, which must be his Mistake ———— since there is no Command to practice it beyond that very Time, but in *Luke* 22. 19. if there it self. For tho' his Eating of the Passover is there related, as also in *Mark* and *Luke*, it was but *Once done*; and the Command, *This do in Remembrance of me*, is only *Once Related* among the Evangelists, as well as it is *Once Commanded*. And would we be strict with the *Bishop*, we need not allow him that Command to reach farther than the present Time in which it was given; for *This Do*, or, *Take Eat*, are equally in the Present Tense, *for thereby you shew forth my Death*. And the following Words, viz. *I will Drink no more of* This *Fruit of the Vine, until that Day when I Drink it* New *with you in my Father's Kingdom*, Mat. 26. 29. farther explains it. Thus *Mark* has it, 14. 25. *Verily I say unto you, I will Drink no more of the Fruit of the Vine, until that Day that I Drink it* New *in the Kingdom of God*. Luke 22. 18. gives it thus, *I say unto you, I will not Drink of the Fruit of the Vine till the Kingdom of God shall come*. Now it is plain that Christ refers them to the Spiritual Supper, which we Prefer and Practice, and which is the Supper *Signified by that of Outward Bread and Wine*, that was to serve *till the Kingdom of God came*, and then he would Communicate with them in a Way *Suitable* to his Kingdom: Which Kingdom as before said, is not *Meat* and *Drink*, but *Righteousness, Peace*, and *Joy* in the Holy Ghost. And as the same *Apostle* has it, 1 *Cor.* 4. 20. *The Kingdom of God is not in Word but in Power*; of which Power, and it's coming from on High upon the Apostles, Read *Acts* 1, 6, 7, 8.

For when they asked Christ, *Lord wilt thou at this Time Restore the Kingdom again to Israel*, and that He told them, *'Twas not for them to know the Times or the Seasons which the Father had put into his own Power*. He also adds, *But ye shall receive Power after the Holy Ghost is come upon you*, and ye shall be *Witnesses unto me, both in* Jerusalem *and* Judea, *and in* Samaria, *and in the uttermost Parts of the Earth*. This Power was the Kingdom of God, *For it stands in Power*, says the Apostle; but it seems he thought fit to wave their Question, as to a direct Answer, and left it a Secret to be revealed unto them, when the Holy Ghost should come, and the Power from on High should fall upon them: And thus he takes his Leave of them, and is immediately received by a Cloud out of their Sight.

Before I conclude this Paragraph, I would observe, *First*, That it was the

Paſſover and *Cuſtom of the Jews*, which, properly ſpeaking, we conceive hath no Juſt Plea to continue as a *Goſpel-Ordinance*, or Inſtitution, ſince it was a Type of Him to come, and therefore ended, as to Inſtitution, by His Coming.

Secondly, That the Evangeliſt *John*, the Beloved Diſciple, that lay in the Boſom of Chriſt, does not ſo much as mention it, or *Water-Baptiſm*, as left by Chriſt, to be continued by His Followers. Concerning the Spirit's Baptiſm, tho' he uſes not the Word *Baptiſm*, he is very full, *John* 14th, 16th, and 17th Chapters, where he tells them, *That he would ſend them the Comforter, the Spirit of Truth, to lead them into all Truth, and that he would dwell with them for ever.* I ſay it ſeems very improbable, if not incredible, that what the Biſhop ſtiles the *Badges of Chriſtianity*, in his 17th Paragraph, ſhould be wholly forgotten by ſo Great an Apoſtle of Chriſtianity.

Thirdly, And as the Beloved Diſciple ſays nothing of theſe *Viſible Signs*, which the Biſhop calls the *Badges of Chriſtianity*, ſo neither are they made an *Article* of any of the *Ancient Creeds Extant*, which certainly does not make for their Credit or Authority: Since had they been of that Importance they are now by ſome eſteemed, we cannot think they would have been forgot by the Compilers of thoſe Creeds.

Fourthly, The Apoſtle *Paul*, though he repeats the *Tradition* he received of the Lord's Supper, that Night he was betrayed, does not injoyn it; but as often as the *Corinthians* did it, he tells them, they ſhould *Do it in Remembrance of Chriſt:* Which is as far from commanding it, as it would be, if the *Biſhop* ſhould ſay to his Friend, *As often as he comes to* Cork, *he ſhould come and Eat with him*, an Obligation upon that Perſon to come often to *Cork*. So that tho' the Apoſtle bids them, that as often as they did it, they ſhould *Do it in Remembrance of Chriſt*, yet he does not thereby bid them do it *often*, if at all.

Fifthly, And whereas the *Biſhop* would make it a freſh Revelation to the Apoſtle, when he ſays, for *I have received of the Lord, that which alſo I delivered unto you,* I muſt diſſent from Him. I cannot apprehend that means any more than this, *That what Account he had received of Chriſt's Eating the Supper with His Diſciples, the Night before He was Betrayed, the ſame alſo he had Delivered unto them:* For what Need could there be of an *Immediate Revelation*, for ſo late a Fact, ſo well Witneſſed by the Diſciples? But if my *Reader* will peruſe that Part of the Chapter which relates to the Supper, he will find the Streſs lies upon *Remembring of the Lord*, which is indeed our Daily, Indiſpenſible Duty; and he that lives without it, may be ſaid to Live without God in the World; of which thoſe *Corinthians* at that Time ſeemed ſo Inſenſible, and as ſuch are ſeverely reproved by the Apoſtle, being *Irreverent*, *Greedy*, and *Drunken*, hardly fit for the *Sign*, and leſs able to diſcern the *Thing Signified*.

Sixthly, Nor does the Apoſtle ſeem to recommend this Practice, but rather reprehend the Abuſe of it; and if my *Reader* will look back to the foregoing Chapter, from the Beginning to the 18th Verſe, he may find a more *Spiritual Supper*, and *Myſtical Bread and Cup* hinted at by the Apoſtle, as well as *Mat.* 26. 29. *Rev:* 3. 20. by our Lord Jeſus Chriſt Himſelf: Which is indeed very Copiouſly expreſs'd by *Luke*, in the *Parable of the Supper*, Chap. 14. from the 16th to the 24th Verſe, where One that was at Meat with Chriſt, ſpeaking of the *Bleſſedneſs of Eating of Bread in the Kingdom of God*, Chriſt takes Occaſion to ſhew forth the *Goſpel-Supper* by a Parable, viz. *A certain Man made a Great Supper, and bid many, but they refuſed, upon divers Pretences, and came not; He ſent out a Second and Third Time to invite an Inferiour Sort of Gueſts, and they came to the Supper,* that is, they Received the Goſpel, which *is the Power of God to Salvation*; and the Evidence, as well as Means of it: Which Chriſt in the 27th Verſe farther expreſſes thus, viz. *And whoſoever doth not bear my Croſs, and follow me, cannot be my Diſciple.* Now the Croſs of Chriſt, the ſame Apoſtle alſo ſays, *Is the Power of God*, 1 *Cor.* 1. 18. All which refers to an *Inward and Spiritual Work*, and *Supper*, and that they who Receive Chriſt in Spirit, *Sup with Him in Spirit*, being the Partakers of *His Spiritual Supper*, which Chriſt promiſes, and prepares for all thoſe that *Open at His Knocks*, the Door of their Hearts unto Him, *Rev.* 3.

Seventhly, But beſides what I have ſaid, both from Scripture, and the Nature of the Thing, in Proof of *Chriſt's Spiritual Supper*, and Defence of our Diſuſe of the *Viſible Sign*, the Biſhop himſelf does the ſame Thing, in relation to another Ordinance: For our Lord Jeſus Chriſt did as Solemnly Command His Diſciples to *Waſh one another's Feet, as to Eat the Supper.* The Paſſage is large and edifying, and I muſt recommend it to my *Reader*, to peruſe in his Bible, *John* 13. but that Part of it which more strictly concerns this Point, between the *Bishop* and me, I shall repeat here, Verses 12, 13, 14, 15. *So after He had washed their Feet, and taken His Garments, and was set down again, He said unto them, Know ye what I have done to you? Ye call me* Master and Lord, *and ye say well; for so I am; if I then, your Lord and Master, have washed your Feet, ye also ought to wash one another's Feet! For I have given you an Example, that ye should do as I have done to you.* Thus Christ Commanded His Disciples, not only by His Authority but Example. Now does the *Bishop* and his Friends follow Christ's Example, and obey this Precept? He and they know they do not. What must I infer from thence, that the *Bishop is No Christian?* I suppose he would take it very ill from me, tho' he has treated me and my Friends after that Sort. But I will shew him a better Example, and suppose he thinks, that if Christian Ministers and People walk *Humbly* towards God, and one with another, they fulfil this Commandment, tho they disuse the Sign, by which the Lord Jesus express'd and recommended *Humility* to His Followers: Now that which excuses the *Bishop*, in Reference to this Ordinance of *Washing of Feet*, will also excuse our Disuse of the *Supper*, viz. *Our Eating of the Spiritual Bread and Wine of the Kingdom; the Thing Signified by the Outward Supper*. But it is an Error incident to Frail Man, to prefer the Practice of those Things that have a Shew of Religion, and have *least* of Uneasiness, and of the *Nature of the Cross of Christ* in their Performance. Just thus it is easier to Receive the Supper, than to be *Humble*, if not easier than to *Wash Feet*: For one is but a Memorial of Christ, but the other perhaps is a Reproach of present Practice, and to be sure a *Command to Mortification and Self-Denial*, the hardest Lesson in Religion. And who knows but for that Reason it has been *drop'd* so long; since it must be very uneasie for People to continue a Custom, to which their Daily Practice is so Visible a Contradiction: Though I hear the *Roman Bishop* mocks the Text Once a Year.

Eighthly, But in Relation to the Supper, we farther say, the Practice is varied; Then they *Sat*; now One Sort *Stands*; Another *Walks*; a Third *Kneels*, a Fourth *Lies down upon the Ground*, as in the *East-Countries*. The *Romans* have One Opinion, the *Greeks* another; and the *Lutherans* and *Calvinists* divide, to Great Bitterness, in their Sentiments *about It*.

Ninthly, Again, In those Days they were *Disciples*, such as followed CHRIST, now *All* are admitted that profess *Christianity*, tho' they do not follow Him, or forsake any Thing for His Name-Sake, or keep any of His Holy Precepts, *Matthew* the 5th, 6th, and 7th Chapters.

Tenthly, Nor is this *All* we have to say, to justifie our Disuse of this Practice: *It is too much Look'd at, and Relied upon by the People:* And indeed is become a *Kind of Protestant Extream Unction*; for if the Generality of them can but have it Administred just before they Die, they are apt to presume upon it for an Acceptance in the other World. And indeed it is very frequent, if not Natural, for many Men to excuse their Disobedience by *Sacrifice*; and where Ceremonies, or Shadowy Services are continued, People rest upon the Observance of them, and *Indulge* themselves in the Neglect of the *Doctrine of the Cross of our Lord Jesus Christ*. I need not look far, nor yet the *Bishop*, for a Proof of what I say; we can hardly miss, which Way so ever we throw our Eyes, the more is the Pity: And as this is no small Abuse of Primitive Practice, so no small Argument for our Disuse of it. For when the *Brazen-Serpent* was *Over-valued by the Jews*, God, that had commanded it, for their Benefit, stirred up *Hezekiah* to destroy it.

Eleventhly, Besides, these Things are become Matter of *Gain*, and made a *Sacerdotal Revenue*, not to say *Merchandize*; which has also help'd to Scandalize People of Tender Consciences, who think it a Prophanation of Religion, to suffer any Part of it to be Excised to the People, that ought to be Free.

Twelfthly, But passing that by at present, and supposing *Water-Baptism* and the *Supper* were not Antiquated, but still in Force, Who is there Qualified to Administer them? Who has Received a Commission, or the Mind of the Holy Ghost, and Power from on High to perform these Things? For if those that hold they are in Force, have no Divine Force or Authority, to Qualifie them to Administer them, there will be but a *Lifeless Imitation*, instead of an *Edifying Reality*. Which leads me to what I promised long since, That I would at the Close of this Discourse, say something of the *True Ground of our Difference and Dissent*.

I say then, that where we are supposed to differ most, we differ *least*; and where we are believed to differ least, we *most of all* differ: Which I explain thus. It's generally thought, that we do not hold the Common Doctrines of Christianity, but

but have introduced New and Erroneous Ones in Lieu thereof: Whereas we plainly and entirely Believe, the *Truths contained in the Creed*, that is commonly called *The Apostles*; which is very Comprehensive as well as Ancient. But that which hath affected our Minds most, and engaged us in this Separation, was the Great Carnality and Emptiness both of Ministers and People, under their Profession of Religion: They *having hardly the Form of Godliness*, but generally speaking, *denying the Power thereof*; *from whom*, the Scripture warns Believers *to turn away*.

Next, Ministers being made such, and Preaching, and the People Worshipping *without the Spirit*, confining the Operations of it to the *First or Apostolical Times*, as if these did not want them as much, or that Christ would be less Propitious, where His Gifts were not less needful. I say, an *Humane and Lifeless Ministry*, and *Worship*, together with the Great Worldliness of Professors, have occasioned our Separation; and the Persecution that has commonly followed it, hath abundantly confirmed our Judgment in that Matter. Hence it was we Retired our selves to wait upon God together, according to the Gift of His Holy Spirit, and as the Apostle *Paul* exhorted the *Athenians*, Acts 17. *We felt after Him* (with our Souls) *if by any Means we might find Him, and hear what God the Lord would say unto us, who speaks Peace unto His People, and His Saints; but let them never turn to Folly any more.* We could not, I say, tell how to think that such as God had never sent, but *Ran of themselves*, and were made *Ministers by Humane Learning and Authority*, not knowing the Work of the Spirit to their *Own Regeneration*, could possibly Profit, or Edifie the People *unto their Regeneration*: And yet that is the very *Work and End of the True Gospel-Ministry*; for no Man can guide another in the Way he never trod.

Besides, we apprehended the *Ministry* was very much a *Temporal Preferment*, and therefore few were to be found among them, that did not court the *Better Places*, I mean those that gave the *Greatest Pay*, and by those Methods mounted to *Worldly Wealth and Honour*, as the Rest of the World did: *Turning Alms into Dues*, and by Law, *Making Gifts Rents*; and vexing those extreamly, that for Conscience-Sake could not uphold them: Which we thought very Foreign to a Primitive and Apostolical Spirit; and *Short of a True and Through Reformation*. This is not said with any Disrespect to their Persons, or yet Calling, simply considered; *For he that desires the Office of a Bishop, certainly desires a Good Thing*; but the Holy Ghost in those Days, had the *Making of them*; and the Good Thing then was their Service, and not *Revenue*, or *Worldly Dignity*. They were then not only *No Lords*, (One being their Lord) *but they Lorded it not over God's Clergy or Heritage*, which was the People in those Days, for so the Word κλήρων signifies, tho' it is now ascribed to the *Ministry*. Then the Ground of Prophesie, or Ministry, was the *Revelation of the Spirit*, in those Ancient Assemblies, as may be read 1 *Cor.* 14. 29, 30, 31, 32. *For All might Prophesy*, that is, Preach, as the Spirit of God moved upon their Spirit, and gave them Utterance, both for Reproof, Instruction, and Consolation: Now *Study, Collection*, and *Memory*.

In those Days they Preach'd their *Own Experience* of the Work of God upon their Hearts, but most now Preach of the Experiences of Others, recorded in Scriptures, but according to their own and others *Human Apprehensions*. To be brief, we Ground our *Conviction, Conversion, Ministry, Prayer* and *Praise*, upon the Light and Spirit of our Lord Jesus Christ, as the Powerful and Effectual Spring of our Religious Performances, and that alone which prepares the Soul, and Enables it to Perform those respective Services and Duties in a Manner *Acceptable* to God. And that Ministry and Worship which stands *not* in the Spirit, and is not performed in the Preparation and Inspiration thereof, but according to the *Compilings, Traditions* and *Precepts* of Men, we cannot allow to be *Primitive* and *Evangelical*, and consequently cannot joyn in them. And we are satisfied that it is the good Pleasure of God, that all who profess the Name of his Dear, and only Begotten, and Well-beloved Son, should *Acquaint* themselves with the Spirit of His Son in their own Hearts, in it's *Reproof, Instruction, Conviction* and *Consolation*, that they may become *Spiritually Minded*, such as mind Spiritual Things more than Earthly Ones; and that Daily *sow to the Spirit*; that is, bring forth the Fruits of the Spirit, and become the Children of God, who are led by the Spirit of God. *Now the Fruit of the Spirit is Love, Joy, Peace, Long-Suffering, Gentleness, Goodness, Faith, Meekness, Temperance: Against such there is no Law. And they that are Christ's, have Crucified the Flesh, with the Affections and Lusts thereof. But the Works of the Flesh are manifest, which are these, Adultery, Fornication, Uncleanness, Lasciviousness, Idolatry, Witchcraft, Hatred, Variance, Emulations, Wrath, Strife,*

Seditions, Heresies, Envyings, Murder, Drunkenness, Revilings, and such like: Of which I told you before, as also in Time past, that they which do such Things, shall not Inherit the Kingdom of God, Rom. 8. 6. 14. Gal. 5. 16, to 24. Chap. 6. 7, 8. And under these Marks and Directions all People may examine themselves, and know their *Birth, Family, and Inheritance,* whether they are the Off-spring of God, and True Christians, or Children of the Evil One: Those that are *Born of the Spirit,* for whom is reserved an Inheritance with the *Saints in Light,* or the Seed of Evil Doers; for whom is reserved the *Blackness of Darkness for ever.* And truly it seems just with God, that those who love Darkness better than Light in this World, should have their *Fill* of it in the next; from which, God Almighty Redeem *Thee, Reader,* that thou mayst walk in His Blessed Light, *as He is in the Light, then thou wilt have Fellowship with the Children of Light, and the Blood of Jesus Christ* (the Great Atonement) *shall Cleanse thee from all Sin,* 1 John 1. 5, 6, 7. *yea, from the Filthiness both of Flesh and Spirit*; and being *Sanctified throughout in Body and Spirit, thou mayst live to serve God in the Newness of His Holy Spirit,* Rom. 7. 6. and come to be made a New Man; that is another Man: From a Proud, an Humble Man; from a Passionate, a Patient Man; from a Rough, a Meek Man; and of a Cruel, Covetous, Unjust, Lascivious, Intemperate, Vain and Ungodly Man, thou may'st become a Merciful, Liberal, Just, Chaste, Sober, and Godly Man. And where this Change, this New Birth, or New Creature is not known, Sacrifices avail nothing, Religion is but Formality, and the Peace of God will never be their Recompence of Reward. But they that walk after this Blessed Unerring Rule of the New Covenant, *Peace be on them, and Mercy, and upon the Israel of God,* Gal. 6. 15, 16. *who are the Circumcision made without Hands, in putting off the Body of the Sins of the Flesh, by the Circumcision of Christ,* Col. 3. 11. even that of the Heart, in the Spirit, *whose Praise is not of Men, but of God,* Rom. 2. 29. And who therefore Worship God in the Spirit, and have no Confidence in the Flesh, *Phil.* 3. 3. that is, in Fleshly Ordinances, or the Observation of Figures and Signs compounded of Outward Elements, which represent Heavenly Things: Wherefore the Apostle exhorted and commanded, *Col.* 2. 16, 17. *Let no Man judge you in Meat or in Drink, or in respect of an Holy Day,* &c. *which are Shadows of Things to come, but the Body is of Christ*; that is, Christ is the Substance of all outward Representations, and they that have Christ, have the End of all those Things: Who, *Reader,* we Labour and Pray, may be better known, received and obeyed, by the Professors of His Holy Name and Religion. That as He is Given of God to be our Priest, Prophet, and King, we may all Know, Feel and Enjoy Him such in our selves, and then the Kingdom of God will be come in us, and His Will done in our Earth, as it is in Heaven: Which God Grant, I most humbly beseech Him.

For the Conclusion of the *Bishop's Paper,* it is either *Repetition* or *Reflection*; the one needs no Answer, and the other wants a Defence. However, I will not have it said that I either wave or suppress it, and therefore without any Reflection I will consider his: Which should have no Weight with my *Reader,* but against him.

He says in his 12th Paragraph, *He pities us, thinking many of us Harmless and Well-Meaning, but under the Power of Strong Delusions.* And in his 13th Paragraph he gives us his Sense of the Cause thereof, viz. *That we make the Light Within, a Rule of Faith and Practice, Co-Ordinate, if not Superiour and Antecedent to the Holy Scripture.* To prove which to be our Sentiment, he cites these Words out of our *Gospel-Truths,* where speaking of the Holy Spirit, and the Scriptures, we say, *They are the Double and Agreeing Record of True Religion.* Now if the Light and Spirit agree with the Scripture, there is no fear of contradicting the Scripture, and so we can have nothing to answer for on our Account of that Expression, for what agrees with the Scripture, *Establishes it,* instead of slighting or superseding the Authority of it.

And tho' we used no such Words as *Co-Ordinate,* much less *Superior* and *Antecedent,* which is the Bishop's Gloss, to render our most True and In-offensive Expression suspected, and make Way to fasten his supposed *Strong Delusions* upon us, I will be very frank with him in this Matter, That we Believe the Scripture to be the Declaration of the Mind of the Holy Ghost, and therefore not Superiour to the Holy Ghost, but *Credited, Confirmed, and Expounded by the Holy Ghost*; so that without the Illumination of it, the Scripture cannot be understood by them that read it. The Grammatical and Critical Sense of the Words, and Allusions therein may be understood, but the *Inside* and Spiritual Signification of them, is a Riddle to those that are not Spiritually instructed therein, tho' they were never such Grammarians or Linguists.

Again,

Again, Christ says, *He that loves the Light, brings his Deeds to the Light, to see if they are wrought in God*, John 3. 21. which was before the New-Testament Scripture was in being; and this makes it both *Rule and Judge* of the Life and Deeds of Men. What says the Bishop to this? Also *John* 14, 15, and 16th Chapters, Christ promises, *The Spirit to lead them*, his People, *into all Truth*, and this was not the Scripture, but something at least *Co-Ordinate, if not Superiour and Antecedent to the Scripture*, which is more than we said before. Also the Apostle *Paul* tells the *Romans*, Chap. 8. *That as many as are led by the Spirit of God, they are the Sons of God*: Then the Spirit is to Lead Believers, or they cannot be the Children of God. And that which Leads, Rules; and that which Rules, is a *Rule* to them that follow it. And the same Apostle referr'd the *Galatians*, Chap. 6. 15, 16. to the Rule of the *New Creature* to walk by, and that must be the Spirit, which begets the *New Creature*, viz. *Christ formed in them*, of whom he tells them, Chap. 4. 19. *He travelled in Birth again.* And the Beloved Disciple expresly says to the Christians, in his First Epistle, Chap 2. 20. *That they had an Unction from the Holy One, and they knew all Things*; that is, all Things they had to Believe, Know and Practice. And Verse 27. he adds, *But the Anointing which ye have received abideth in you, and ye need not that any Man teach you, but as the same Anointing teacheth you of All Things, and is Truth.* If the Bishop will break through all these Scriptures to undervalue the Light and Spirit of Christ (for no other Light or Spirit do we Assert, Recommend People to, or Contend for) that he might render us Guilty of *Strong Delusions*, I cannot help it, but must be truly sorry for him. But I beseech him to have a Care that he does not, like the *Jews* of Old, undervalue, and indeed Blaspheme against the Holy Light and Spirit of God, by miscalling the Fruits and Effects of it's Power, *Strong Delusions, and Transformations of Satan*: For God will not hold such Guiltless, in His Great and Terrible Day of Judgment.

And after all, the Best and First Reformers and Martyrs, as well as Fathers, concur in our Assertion and Testimony: As *Zuinglius, Luther, Melancthon, Calvin, Beza, Bucer, Peter Martyr*, and *Erasmus* too. Also our own Excellent Martyrs, viz. *Lambert, Rogers, Philpot, Bradford, Hooper, Woodman*, &c. That the Double and Agreeing Testimony of the Spirit of God Within, and the Scriptures of Truth Without, is the Rule and Judge of Faith, Doctrine and Practice; yea, that the Spirit is given to Believers, to be the *Rule and Judge*, by which they are to understand the True Sense and Meaning of the Scriptures. Now let the *Reader* judge who gives the Truest Honour to the Scripture, the *Bishop*, or the People called *Quakers*? They say the Scriptures have a Double Record, that is, the Evidence of the Spirit of Truth in the Hearts of Believers, as well as their Own: Or the *Bishop*, who by his Way of Treating us, and our Principle, will allow us no other Evidence of their Truth, but themselves. For to say the Evidence of the Spirit of God, with that of the Scripture, make a *Double and Agreeing Testimony*, is with him to undervalue the Scripture, and the Ground, in his Apprehension, of our *Strong Delusions*. It must be my Turn to pity the *Bishop*, and truly I do it with all my Heart, to see him strain so Sound, as well as inoffensive an Expression, as that which he makes the Reason of our Delusion, that he might have an Occasion to lessen our Credit with the Professors of Christianity, and especially Protestants. Can it Dishonour the Scripture, to assert the Evidence of the Principal and Author of the Scrripture, to back the Authority of the Scripture? Or doth not he rather lessen the Authority of Scripture, that will not allow us another Evidence of the Truth of Scripture than it's own, for fear of Co-ordinacy, which was not so much as once intended to be insinuated by us, nor do the Words import any such Thing; yet it had been no strong, nor any *Delusion at all*, to give the Holy Ghost the Preference. But I shall keep to the Terms of the Paper, whatever the Bishop is pleased to do; knowing that whoever concludes an Argument in Terms, not in the Question, nor plainly deduceable from the Premises, is not *A Fair Dealer in Controversie*: In which the *Bishop*, if he pleases, may reasonably enough think himself more than once concern'd.

Blessed be God we have known the Power and Efficacy of this Holy Light and Spirit of Christ in our selves, and being in good Measure Witnesses thereof, we do not only speak by Report, but by Experience. We had the Scriptures in the Days of our Ignorance, and Worldly-Mindedness, but disregarding the Reproofs and Instruction of the *Light of Jesus in our Hearts*, we never could come to know the Power of those *Truths the Scripture declares of*. But when it pleased God, in the Riches of his Love, to cause His Blessed Light, that had Shined in Darkness, and the Darkness comprehended it not, *to Shine out of Darkness*, and *give us the Know-*

ledge of Himself in the Face (or through the Manifestation) of His Son Jesus Christ, we saw and bewailed our selves, and by an unfeigned Sorrow and Repentance, returned as *Penitent Prodigals*, towards our Father's House; and in this Turn, we were brought to Die daily to that Love and Satisfaction we once had in the Glory, Pleasures, Honours, Friendships and Diversions of the World, which now became *Burdensome*, more than ever they were pleasing to us.

Hence it was, and from no Sinister Ends or Self-righteous Conceits, that we became an altered and a distinguished People, in our Behaviour, Garb and Conversation: More *Retired, Watchful, Silent* and *Plain*, than formerly; equally avoiding *Luxury* and *Avarice*. I say, it was the Work of God's Spirit upon our Hearts, who by his Light gave us to see the just Difference of Things, and to distinguish between that which pleased Him, and that which pleased Him not. And this Holy Pattern he gave us in the Light of his beloved Son, which we design to follow, as did the Holy Ancients; and is a full Answer to the Bishop's Unfriendly Queries upon our distinguishing Behaviour, in his 14th and 15th Paragraphs, as if it were not out of Fear towards God, or upon a Conscientious Bottom, but to serve a worldly Turn? For he asks us, *Is it not your* main Aim, End and Study, by pretended *Mortifications, to make your selves a Party Considerable?* Again, *Are not to this Purpose your Different Garb, Speech, Looks and Gestures, and to make your selves Remarkable, rather than out of a Sense of Duty, or Conscience of Obligation?* Which, as it is the worst Construction that the most Irreligious and Prophane could make upon our Behaviour, so I beseech God to forgive the Bishop, and make him sensible how little such Treatment of strict and sober Living advances the Common Cause of Religion, and how much it indulges those that know no Reins or Check to their Excesses in his own Church. But to go no farther than the Bishop and his *Clergy*, pray who distinguish themselves more by their Garb from other People than they? Tho' I cannot say as much of their Behaviour. So indeed did the *Chemarims*, or black Coats of Old, and those that wore long Robes in our Saviour's Time, but, as I take it, they went not without his Censure, while I think the Bishop will find none in Scripture against our Plainness. But the Bishop's Pontifical Robes, do, in my Opinion, look much more like *Singularity* and a *Sight* than ours; for our Garb is like other Men's, only freed of their Superfluity. In short, I wish him a better Understanding of the true Grounds of our stricter Conduct, and Where and Who they are that make a *Trade* of Religion; that if he has any Shot left against *Mercenary* Religionists, he may not miss the Mark next Time, but may make it his *main Aim, End* and *Study*, to Expose Hirelings and Hypocrites in their Proper Colours: And some are of Opinion he need not go far to find too many of them.

It is strange the Bishop should be so unsensible of the Advantage he gives me by his *Queries*, and what a wide Door he opens to a Severe Retaliation; but I desire to be Modest, and to be Silent upon such Advantages, is, I think, to be abundantly so.

Howbeit, I must take Notice of one Expression, for it may too seriously affect us not to be observed to him. When he asks, *If it be not our main End and Study, by pretended Mortifications, to make our selves a Party Considerable?* He adds, *and such to which*, for Reasons of State, *Peculiar Privileges must be indulged*. If this were not more than Mockery, I should wave my Notice; but calling the Meaning of the Government in Question about the *Liberty of Conscience* we enjoy, He must forgive me if I bestow a few Remarks upon that Expression. It seems then our Liberty flows not from the Inclination of the Government to Liberty, less from Compassion, and least of all from Justice and a Christian Principle. Which Motives carry with them a Prospect of the Continuance of Liberty, if not for Liberty's Sake. But the Bishop believes no such Thing, and if he would not have us of his Mind, he did weakly to tell us so. Well, then, we are all of us to take his Advertisement, that our Liberty holds but by slender Threads, and a *Reason of State*, and not of Nature, Right or Christianity; which certainly is not to bespeak this *Considerable Party* to the Advantage of the Government: And for which I think the Bishop a very moderate Statesman, and the Government as little beholding to his *Politicks* as we are to his *Charity*. However, we will have a better Opinion of our Superiors Regard to Liberty, and conclude that their Inclination equals their Discretion, and that their Judgment, as well as Prudence, is on that Side. Let the Bishop say what he pleases. And tho' he deserves it not at my Hands, I could almost persuade my self to think that he does not begrudge us, and means not so loosly as he writes. But be it as it will, *That God that has upheld*

held us by his free Spirit to this Day, through many and great Afflictions, we firmly believe will suffer nothing to attend us, that shall not in the Conclusion work for his Glory and our Good, if we continue stedfast to the End, in the blessed Way of Righteousness, wherein he has so often and signally Owned and Preserved us; notwithstanding the Violence of Open Enemies, and the Treacherous and Restless Endeavours of False Friends.

His Sixteenth Paragraph multiplies Reflection, as before Observed, and Repeats what I have already largely answered; particularly that we own the Christian Faith, which he makes us to *Wave, Suppress*, or at least not to Confess; and have expressed it even in the Paper, he has faulted so much of Shortness, and that more fully, in all Points, than in the Creed commonly called the *Athanasian*; except that about the *Trinity*, which seems to me less plain by that Copious Way taken to explain it.

He also says, *We Reject all Outward, Positive Parts of Worship*, which we deny: For we own and use *Prayer, Preaching*, and *Praising in the Spirit*, without which they cannot be Owned or Joyned with; for they cannot be so performed to Edification by a true Christian Worshipper; since God, *who is a Spirit, will be worshipped in Spirit, and in Truth*, which Christ's Spirit must enable us to perform: And such Worshippers Only, God the Father seeks to Worship him: Implying he regards not other Worshippers.

But *Especially*, the Bishop says, *we reject Baptism and the Supper*. We say, we do not *Reject* but *Disuse* the Signs, because we felt the *Invisible Graces in our Souls* they were *Signs* and *Shadows* of; and therefore not in *Disrespect* to the Signs, but in *Reverence* to the Divine Substance they shew forth, we discontinue their Use among us. They obtained Place in the *Infancy* and *Twy-Light* of the Church; in her more weak and Ceremonious Time, directing, as I may say, that *Interregnum* between the Law and the Gospel, before the Dispensation of the Holy Ghost had *Fully* obtained Place and Pre-heminence in the Church. But of this I have been already very particular.

He grows *warm* in his 17th Paragraph and *Episcopal*; for he says, *In a Word, I again Require you, as you will answer all your Secret Arts and Pretensions at Christ's Tribunal, that you either Embrace and Profess the Entire Christian Truth, in the Points wherein I have shewn you to be Defective; and that you receive the Christian Seals or Badges, Baptism and the Lord's Supper; or else that you Desist to lay Claim to the Name of Christians.*

But first I must return the Bishop *his Secret Arts* and *Pretensions*, In all which he is grievously mistaken. For either I do not understand his Meaning, or I abhor it. Next, be it known to him, we *Wave not*, we *Suppress not*, but heartily Embrace and Profess, before the whole World, all Points of Christian Doctrine, according to the Mind of the Holy Ghost, as I have amply signify'd before upon this Subject: And where the Bishop takes Leave of the Text, he must excuse me if I leave him to keep Company with it. We did not Entitle our Paper *All Gospel-Truths*; but *Gospel-Truths*, which extended so far as we were Tax'd with Error about those Truths: And yet he must have but a little Charity that will not allow a Believer and Follower of those Truths to be a Christian. Nor indeed has the Bishop given us the Articles of Faith he says we *Wave* or *Suppress*, or told us his own, or that *One Church*'s Faith he would have us receive, as I have complained already. But that the Bishop *should forbid us so much as to lay Claim to the Name of* Christians, *unless we will Practice what he calls* the Seals or Badges *of Christianity* (which divers Churches in *Christendom* think he misuses) is very Uncharitable and Dogmatical. But, besides what I have said at large in our Excuse and Defence in that Matter, he produces not one Scripture that calls them either *Seals* or *Badges*. But yet there are other Things that are so represented by our blessed Saviour and his Apostles, which he takes no Notice of. As *Matth.* 16. 24. where, *they that will be reputed Christ's Disciples must take up his Cross and follow him*. Christ's *Cross* is a Christian's *Badge* and *Seal* of Discipleship. Again, *John* 13. 35. He said to his Disciples, *By this shall all Men know that ye are my Disciples, if ye love one another*. Likewise *Matth.* 25. 34, 35, 36. The distinguishing Character of the Last Day is not Water-Baptism and the Outward Supper, but *Love, Mercy* and *Compassion; Bowels* and *Charity*; not being *Ashamed* or *Afraid* of Owning and Helping the Lord's Servants in their Afflictions, viz. *I was an Hungry and ye gave Me Meat: I was Thirsty and ye gave Me Drink: I was a Stranger and ye took Me in: Naked and ye Cloathed Me: I was Sick and ye Visited Me: I was in Prison and ye came unto Me.* This is the Christian *Badge* that will be Recognized by our L d Jesus

Jesus Christ at the Last Day: We have his own Word for it. In all which he is so far from mentioning either of the other Badges, that, *Luke* 13. he brings in the *Unhappy*, that are on his Left-hand, using this Argument to engage him to receive them into Blessedness, *viz We have eaten and drank in thy Presence, and thou hast taught in our Streets.* A plain Instance they had the Use of such Ordinances as the Bishop reputes *Badges* of Christianity; but it is as plain that such Pleas would not do: For behold the Lord Jesus says unto them in the Parable, *I know you not, depart from me, ye workers of Iniquity!* I recommend the Perusal of the following Verses to my Reader, which confirm my Sense of the Text: For He spoke to an outside People, that counted themselves the People of God, and were Observers of *Meats* and *Drinks*, and *Divers Washings:* And that which was Doctrine and Caution then, is Doctrine and Caution now; for Truths holds the same to the End.

I might add Holiness for a *Characteristick, without which no Man shall ever see the Lord:* and that *neither Circumcision availeth any Thing nor Uncircumcision, but a New Creature*, Gal. 5. 6. Also the Fruits of the Spirit, *Chap.* 5. among which there is not one Word about *Water-Baptism* or the *Outward Supper*, with many more Passages that are Close and Cogent.

His Eighteenth and last Paragraph tells us, *He will not judge us*, and yet his whole Paper is but one Continued Judgment of us. But, *from God*, as he says, *and, as his Minister, he bids us judge our selves*. First, We thank God we are before-hand with the Bishop, having Judged our selves, and that by the Judgment of God upon us, and so have Right to Judge others according to that Judgment. Secondly, We have no Proof that the Bishop speaks from God to us: Nor can I tell how he should, that does not acknowledge the Inspeaking Word of God in the Soul. Thirdly, For his being God's Minister, he has not shewn us his Commission yet, and I fear it will not be from Heaven whenever he does. But if my Reader will take the Pains of perusing this very Paragraph, he will not only see a Judging Spirit, but that the Bishop holds out abusing us to the last, rendring us as bad as bad can be, *viz.* That *we Subvert the Faith once delivered to the Saints, and equal our Conceits to the Divine Oracles, Using and Disusing what Parts of God's Instituted Worship we please*; adding, *I will not Interpose your making* Gain *your* Godliness. But, as I have already taken ample Notice of this Charge, so I shall say no more of his Irreligious *Slant* at our Sincerity than this, That I cannot pretend to tell the Bishop what Tribe of Men, in *Christendom*, it is that have long made Gain their Godliness, and the Pretence of it their Worldly Inheritance; since he has been so much more Sensibly Instructed in this Affair than my self: But one Thing I am sure of, that if *Gain* and not *Godliness* was our Motive to be the People we are, we mightily Mistook our Way *when we left the Bishops:* For *Afflictions, Spoils, Prisons, Banishments*, yea, and *Death* it self, have attended us, since God was pleased to manifest his Truth to us: And if under all those Calamities that have followed us since we were a People, for the Sake of our Unfashionable Profession, the Bishop or any else is so Unnatural, as to envy us the Blessing of God upon our honest Industry, and to render that which is an Effect of God's Goodness, the Reason and End of our Religion, God forgive them. I could enlarge upon this Topick, but Time would fail, and the Discourse swell beyond Bounds, as indeed it hath already, beyond my Expectation; for which I should Excuse my self to my Reader, but that it was not Simply from the Regard I had to the Bishop's Sheet, since that could not have deserved this Notice from me, but might have been answered as Concisely as that was written, had I only considered his Undertaking and Treatment, and not my Reader's Satisfaction, in the better Knowledge of our so much Misrepresented Perswasion: Especially in a Nation where of late I had Occasion so Generally to Travel, and the Bishop's Paper hath been, I suppose, as Generally Dispers'd. I owe it therefore to My Profession, to My Self, and to the Country, to Vindicate the One, and to Express my Christian Regard and Acknowledgement to the Other; having received a more than common Civility from the Inhabitants in General: To whom I wish, as to my own Soul, the Saving Knowledge of the Truth, as it is in Jesus: That *Christians Indeed*, and at *Heart* They may be, to the Glory of God their Creator, and the Eternal Salvation of their Souls, through Jesus Christ, the alone Redeemer, to whom with the Father, by the Holy Ghost, be all Honour and Glory, Thanksgiving and Praise, World without End.

F I N I S.

AN INDEX TO WILLIAM PENN'S Works.

A Premonition to the Reader,

Candid Reader.

I know that the more thinking and inquisitive Part of Mankind, are sollicitous to know the Source and Origin of Actions, as well as the Reasons of Things; and therefore sincerely assure thee, that 'twas neither Vanity nor Affectation, that moved me to this Undertaking, but hearty Desires to further the Worthy Author's own Design in his Works, viz. *The Promotion of true Religion*: methought I could but lament to see WILLIAM PENN's Works come into the World without an Index, a Friend that deserves so largely at our Hands! *And who through the Multiplicity of his Business, wrote not sometimes with so much Method as might have been hoped for.* How is the Reader perplext to find all, or most of the Places where he treats of the same Subject, here casually, there ex professo? He is, I doubt not, often tired with the Search, before he has the Satisfaction of finding. A general, methodical and expressive Index, would I'm perswaded, have rendered them generally more useful and acceptable, and especially to the Busie, Idle and Indifferent; however, to supply the Defect what may be, I offer mine to the candid Acceptance of my Friends: It has indeed cost me some Time and Pains, but to their Service I dedicate it, and think it a Debt but partly paid, which I owed to the Memory of the worthy Author. As to the Method of it, the Reader will soon observe, that I have mostly made Use of the Author's own Expressions (than which in general, none could be found to express his own Sense better) and where I have delivered his Sense in my Words, I have endeavoured to do it in such as were both clear and brief. Where the Reader thinks it dark or defective, I ask his Charity, or Correction, assuring him at the same Time, that the uncertain and hasty Calls of Business, has frequently prest so hard upon my leisure Hours, as to oblidge me to run it over more superficially, than my self at first intended. Now, Friendly Reader, I only wish (but that earnestly) that this Help afforded thee, may, if not excite, yet encourage thee to read these valuable Works, with Gravity and Attention; that they may prove as instructive and beneficial to thee, as they have to me, may make as deep and lasting Impressions on thy Mind, as they have on the Mind of thy faithful and ready Friend in so good a Work

PHILALETHES.

N. B. The Numbers or References in each Article, are the Pages of the first Volume, till noted Vol. 2. and then the Numbers which follow that, are the Pages of the second Volume, till noted Vol. 1. for I have sometimes made a Transition from the second Volume back to the first, for the Sake of Connextion, and to express the subject Matter with more Clearness and brevity than otherwise could have been done; and I freely confess, that I have sometimes done it upon the Re-occurence of some Things which I had perhaps too transiently slipt over.

Vale.

A Catalogue of Authors quoted in *William Penn*'s Works.

A*RRIUS*	254, 746
Anthanasius	254, 553, 631, Vol. 2. 584, 795
Artaxerxes	375
Agathocles	375
Alexander	376
Antigonus	376
Aristides	377
———*Christianus*	Vol. 2. 747
Agasicles	378
Agesilaus	378
Agis	379
Alcamenes	379
Alexandridas	379
Anaxilas	379
Ariston	379
Archidamus	380
Augustus	383
Adrian	383
Alexander Sever.	386
Aurelianus	385
Ardentius	Vol. 2. 626
Anacharsis	392
Anaxagoras	392, 543, 556, 911
Antisthenes	395, 545, 558
Aristotle	398
Arria	404
Ambrose	411, 478, 636. Vol. 2. 130, 795
Augustin	471, 478, 481, 553, 592, 645 Vol. 2. 436, 476, 902
Acatius	418
Aquinas	476, 483, 690
Alphonsus a Castro	481
Antipater	546, Vol. 2. 583
Amiraldus	592
Andrews Bp.	Vol. 2. 631, 632, 666
Ames Dr.	600. Vol. 2. 347
Alexides	624
Ausonius	625
Antiochus	651
Ambrosius Ansb.	652
Albertus Mag.	653
Alexander de Ales	653
Anselinus	655
Alphonsus de Avendano	659
Abbot A-Bp.	745
Arminius	745
Alexander Alexandrinus	746
Acontius Jacobus	782
Arnobius	Vol. 2. 320
Atticus	Vol. 2. 583
Bias	390, 548
Bambycatii, who	391
Bion	397
Bellonius	412 Vol. 2. 485
Bacon Ld.	424
Bellarmine	470, 474, 481
Binius	470
Biel	474
Becanus	483
Bacon Nich.	679
Barnes Dr.	Vol. 2. 358, 394, 413
Bullinger	600. Vol. 2. 353, 413, 436, 592, 599
Bradford	Vol. 2. 391, 592, 665, 814, 913
Beza	663, Vol. 2. 107, 346, 427, 438, 476, 592, 665, 814, 913
Blandina	627
Basilides	627
Basilius Mag.	633, Vol. 2. 795
Blastaris	634
Beda	634, 651, 675, 677
Bernard	652
Brute Walter	656
Beveridge Bp.	Vol. 2. 760
Burnet Dr.	Vol. 2. 761
Bucer	Vol. 2. 913
Cleobulus	391
Causabon	325
Charron	345, 663
Cowley	346, 428
Cyrus	375
Clitomachus	377
Cleomenes	380
Cato	382, 559
Chilon	390, 419, 554, Vol. 2. 583
Chaucer	460, 655
Crates	398
Cornelia	404
Clemens Romanus	410, 633, Vol. 2. 485, 902
Chrysostom	410, 420, 462, 478, 553, 636, Vol. 2. 130, 630, 632, 748, 795
Cardan	412, Vol. 2. 485
Charles 5th Empr.	420
1st King *Eng.*	Vol. 2. 748, 762
2d Ditto	462
Caracciolus Galeac	439
Cassander	474, 481
Cyprian	481, 630
Clemens Alexandrin.	472, 552, 592, 593, 629, Vol. 2. 320, 373, 413, 425, 583, 584, 599, 795, 902
Calvin	461, 600, Vol. 2. 345, 346, 480, 592, 627, 665, 814, 915
Carpocratians	471
Clement the 3d	483
Cajetan	483, 650
Canus Bp.	484
Chrysippus	546
Cleanthes	546, 549, Vol. 2. 626
Cudworth Dr.	592, 911

Cameron	598, Vol. 2. 435, 582
Capellus	598, Vol. 2. 630
Clarius	600, Vol. 2. 325, 328, 373, 435, 439, 582, 626
Cradock G.	600, 605, Vol. 2. 328
Clinias	603, 623
Curtius Quint.	622
Cherillus	624
Cæsarius	636, Vol. 2. 795
Chromatius	650
Cyril	650
Cassiodorus	651
Camerarius	663
Crocius	745
Cæsar Julius	675, 677
Cambden	676
Cook (Coke) Ld. C. Justice	682, 687
Crellius	Vol. 2. 108, 109, 110
Curcellæus	Vol. 2. 110
Cave Dr.	Vol. 2. 320, 485
Castalio	Vol. 2. 325, 373, 582
Cicero	Vol. 2. 345
Collier T.	Vol. 2. 352, 355, 366, 383, 394, 420, 429, 592, 595, 596, 660
Canne J.	Vol. 2. 366
Codurcus	Vol. 2. 373, 435, 582, 626
Caryl J.	Vol. 2. 373
Constantine } Constantius }	Vol. 2. 748
Council of Carthage	412
Laodicea	Vol. 2. 800
Constance	476
Lateran	474
Demosthenes	378
Dersyllidas	380
Dioclesian	387
Democritus	394
Demonax	397
Diogenes	397, 558
Donn Dr.	426
Dominicus a Soto	461, Vol. 2. 485
Duplessy	592
Drussius	598, 600, Vol. 2. 373, 434, 435, 582, 626, 630
Diodorus Siculus	522
Damascenus	550
Druthmarus	553
D'ossat Cardinal	Vol. 2. 733
Dion	675, 677
Dell W.	Vol. 2. 328, 355, 366, 394
Downham Bp.	Vol. 2. 413
Dort Synod of	745
Erasmus	329, 598, 599, 657, Vol. 2. 325, 328, 347, 424, 426, 435, 583, 588, 599, 814, 913
Epaminondas	377
Epictetus	402, 624, 911, Vol. 2. 345, 626
Elizabeth, Princess	430
Eusebius	460, 593, Vol. 2. 320, 748
Euripides	560
Epiphanius	599, 636, Vol. 2. 352, 660, 795, 800
Æshilus	623
Esseni	625
Euthymius Zigal.	653
Episcopius	745
Everard Dr.	Vol. 2. 382, 395
Franciscus de Mendoca	660
Feber Jacobus	661
Featly Dr.	Vol. 2. 354
Fagius	Vol. 2. 424, 435, 521
Finch Martin	Vol. 2. 429
Gregory Magn.	Vol. 2. 902
Gell Dr.	Vol. 2. 629, 631
Gomarus	745
Gregory Thaumat.	630
Gauden Bp.	623, 667
Gnosticks	471
Goad Ch.	600, Vol. 2. 357, 382, 391, 394, 420, 429
Grotius	426, 461, 592, 598, 623, 665, Vol. 2. 130, 325, 376, 388, 626, 630, 632, 730.
Gymnosophistæ, who,	391
Gynæcosmi and Gynæcomoni } their Office	392
Gregory Naz.	410, 474, 481, 634, 902, Vol. 2. 795, 800
Gregory Nyss.	634, Vol. 2. 795
Gratian	412, Vol. 2. 485
Gondamer	425
Hall Bp.	Vol. 2. 632
Howel	330
Hippodamus	380
Hudson Dr.	Vol. 2. 763
Hippias	391
Heraclitus	392, 543, 560, Vol. 2. 582
Hilary	411, 462, 632, Vol. 2. 497, 747, 795
Hatton Sr. Chris.	423
Henry, Prince	424
Howard	430
Hammond Dr.	461, Vol. 2. 107, 476, 758
Hesiod	542, 622
Hieron	548, 911, Vol. 2. 583
Herbert Ld.	592
Hierocles	623
Haimo	652
Hooft	658
Hales J.	745, 757, 782
Horn Andrew	676
Hooper Bp.	Vol. 2. 665, 814, 913
Hobart Judge	Vol. 2. 345
Heylin Dr.	Vol. 2. 480
Irenæus	254, 472, Vol. 2. 413, 595, 599, 626
Justin Martyr	254, 420, 459, 474, 481, 551, 592, 593, 599, 626, 676, Vol. 2. 429, 435, 584, 599, 626, 747, 795

Jerom

Jerom	325, 411, 462, 599, 644, Vol. 2. 129, 630, 632, 748, 800, 902	Origin	254, 439, 478, 552, 623, 629. Vol. 2. 626, 627
Julianus	387	Oxcistern	425
Ignatius	420; Vol. 2. 429, 633, 676	Orpheus	542
Junius	426, 470	Owen Dr.	600, 605, Vol. 2. 373, 592
James 1st of England	462, Vol 2. 497, 748	Olympiodorus	651
Jewel Bp.	599, 600, Vol. 2. 352, 420, 592, 625, 660, 665	Otho Brunfel	653
Josephus	603	Oecumenius	653
Isocrates	623	Orange Prince of	669
Isidorus pelus.	649	Ouzelius	Vol. 2. 485, 902
Hispal.	651	Philip King of Macedn.	376
Jansenius	653	Ptolemy	376
Ironside Bp.	Vol. 2. 480	Pericles	376
		Phocion	377
Lactantius	461, 553, Vol. 2. 345, 497, 584, 747	Pausanias	380
Livy	459, 690	Pertinax	386
Lowther Anth.	443	Pescennius	386
Lipsius	329	Pythagoras	387, 543, 547, 555, 559, 603, 623, 911, Vol. 2. 582
Luther	270, 329, 461, 599, Vol. 2. 347, 355, 1591, 665, 913	Periander	390
Leonidas	380	Pittacus	391, 554
Lysander	380, 623	Plato	395, 545, 549, 559, 562, 623, 742, 911, Vol. 2. 580
Lycurgus	382	Penelope	402
Lucretia	403	Pandora	403
Langius	Vol. 2. 626	Protoginia	403
Latimer Bp.	330, 604, 606	Pontia	404
Lainbard	23	Pompeja plaut.	404
Lyricus menalip.	545	Plotina	404
Laertius	623	Pompeja paul.	404
Libanius	625	Paulinus	418
Lollards	657	Philip 2d Spain	425
Lodovicus Soto	663	Penn, a Sister of the Family	442
Pius Empr.	664	Sr. William,	442
Lotharius Empr.	665	Philo Judæus	436, 449, 603, 625, 911, Vol. 2. 373, 626
Laud A-Bp.	745	Polydore Virgil	481
Lambert	Vol. 2. 913	Panormitan	484
		Parmenides mag.	545
Marlborrough Earl of	427	Plutarch	550, 622, 623, 624, 911, Vol. 2. 345, 626,
Medina	481		
Marolat	325, 663	Philpot J.	606, Vol. 2. 329, 330, 665, 913
Marcus Au. Anton.	384, 625	Polycarpus	626
Mandanis	398	Ponticus	627
Malvetzy	459, Vol. 2. 741	Paschatus Ratb.	652
Machiavel	410, 690, Vol. 2. 485, 902	Plotinus	911, Vol. 2. 373, 583, 626
Montaigne	420	Polano	Vol. 2. 326, 328
Mason Sr. John	422	Perkins W.	Vol. 2. 595, 666
Momerancy Duke of	424	Paræus	Vol. 2. 626, 627
Mazarene	425	Pagnine	Vol. 2. 629
Mosconius	484	Proclus	Vol. 2. 747
Menander	549, 624	Pointz Sr. Robt.	Vol. 2. 761
Martyr	599, 605, 665, Vol. 2. 347, 354, 394, 435, 592, 814, 913		
Maimonides	625, Vol. 2. 730	Quintilian	624
Maldonatus	Vol. 2. 107	Quadratus	Vol. 2. 747
Munster	Vol. 2. 373, 435, 582		
Moor Dr.	Vol. 2. 435	Rawleigh Sr. Walt.	422, 461, 690
Minutius Felix	Vol. 2. 626	Richlieu	425
Melancthon	Vol. 2. 665, 913	Rivetus	427
Melito	Vol. 2. 747	Rochester	430
			Renty

(5)

Renty	443	Tayler Bp.	461, Vol. 2. 666, 759
Rainnondus	625	Triumphus	470
Remigius	653, Vol. 2. 627	Theodoret	471, 650
Ruffinus	653	Tolet Cardin.	483, Vol. 2. 107
Rogers	Vol. 2. 814, 913	Timæus	545, 547, 911
		Theognis	623
Sextus Senenf.	481	Thorp William	626, Vol. 2. 676
Scotus	474	Themiftius	746
Salmeron	470	Taulerus	777
Stephen K. Poland	462, Vol. 2. 733, 748	Thomas a Kempis	777
Socrates Schol.	460, Vol. 2. 747	Theophilus Antials.	Vol. 2. 320
Socinus	268, Vol. 2. 108	Tillotfon Dr.	126, Vol. 2. 761
Stillingfleet Bp.	268, Vol. 2. 344, 760		
Scipio African.	383	Vefpafian	383
Solon	388, 623	Vane	428
Socrates	394, 544, 548, 556, 560, 620, 831, 911, Vol. 2. 513, 583, 626	Vafquez	483
		Virgil	561, 562, 563
Seneca	394, 550, 690, 911, Vol. 2. 345	Vatablus	598, 600, Vol. 2. 328, 373, 434, 435, 476, 582, 626
Sidney Sr. Philip	421		
Selden	426, 680, Vol. 2. 482	Valinax	623
Salmafius	426	Varro	559
Sibylla	542	Valla	Vol. 2. 329
Sanders	Vol. 2. 814	Urfin	Vol. 2. 626, 627
Smith Robert	Vol. 2. 814	Villerius P. Lof.	663
Sprigg Joſhua	Vol. 2. 357, 380	Vifogoths	665
Slichtingius	Vol. 2. 108, 109	Uſher A-Bp.	666, Vol. 2. 758
Sophocles	548, Vol. 2. 582	Verfion the Syriack	Vol. 2. 113
Scultetus	593, Vol. 2. 599	Æthioptick	Vol. 2. 128
Sanderfon Bp.	599, Vol. 2. 345, 488, 595, 631, 632, 758, 793, 795	Arabick	Vol. 2. 113, 128
		Greek	Vol. 2. 113
Stobæus	623	Anglo-Saxonick	Vol. 2. 114
Simocatus	624	Chaldean	Vol. 2. 118
Swinderby W.	655	Septuagint	Vol. 2. 118
Sadler Ld.	657	Latin of Beza, Luther, Erafmus, Montanus	Vol. 2. 113
Sagareld Ger.	657		
Suarez	661		
Sibrandus	745		
Spelman	678		
		Waldenfes	412, 655, 902
Tertullian	254, 410, 451, 474, 552, 599, 627, Vol. 2. 435, 599, 627, 747, 795, 902	Woolfey	421
		Walfingham	421
		Wooten	423
Tindal William	345, 600, 665, 778, Vol. 2. 352, 355, 391, 394, 592, 660	Whitlock	431
		Wickliff	460, 655, Vol. 2. 827
Themiftocles	376	Weftminfter Matth.	675, 677
Theopompus	380	Woodman	Vol. 2. 429, 913
Tiberius	385	Wilkins Bp.	Vol. 2. 666
Trajan	385		
Turrecrementa	470	Xenophanes	376
Theodofius jun.	387	Xenocrates	397, 558, 624, Vol. 2. 513
Thales	387, Vol. 2. 582		
Theoxena	403	Zeno	399, 546, 558, 911, Vol. 2. 583
Theophylact	410, 652, Vol. 2. 130	Zegerus	598, 665, Vol. 2. 130, 325, 435, 476, 630
Tertian Barthol.	416		
Tacitus	459, 675, 677, Vol. 2. 675, 677	Zuinglius	Vol. 2. 329, 665, 913

THE INDEX.

Able-Man, it is by some thought the Character of an *able Man* to be dark, and not understood 845, if he is so by Disguises, 'tis insincere and hateful, if by Silence better, the honest Man that is rather free, than open, is ever to be preferred, and especially when Sense is at the Helm; Men thus dark and disguised, are the Reverse to human Nature, and to allow them the Character of able Men, is to disinherit Wisdom 846

Ambition, the worst of Distempers, always craving and thirsty, restless and hated, a perfect Dilirium in the Mind, insufferable in Success, and in Disappointments most revengeful 849, its present Danger and evil End *ibid*.

Anger, never correct in Anger, because the Way to strike thy self at last 833, the Allowances which our Reason makes by Reflection when our Passion is over, would afford us a Rule on like Occasions, 'tis a sort of Fever in the Mind, the Mob of the Man that commits a Riot upon his Reason *ibid*. return no Answer to Anger but with much Meekness 897

Apostacy, how it enter'd the Christian World, and its Progress therein *Vol.* 2. 52-3

Apparel, the Use and End thereof 349, 725 its gross Abuse *ibid*. the Trimming of the vain World would cloath the naked one 824, Meekness and Modesty, the rich and charming Attire of the Soul, and the plainer the Dress, the more distinctly and with greater Lustre Beauty shines *ibid*

Applause, see *Praise*

Art and *Project*, Art good where beneficial, *Socrates* wisely bounded his Knowledge and Instruction by Practice, beware of Projects, and yet despise nothing rashly or by the Lump, Ingenuity as well as Religion sometimes suffers from Pretenders and Despisers, many Hands make light Work, and several Purses cheap Experiments 831

Avarice, its Definition and Distinction 339, is a mark of false Prophets 341, a Reproach to Religion 341-2, an Enemy to Government 342, treacherous and oppressive *ibid*. the Testimonies of *Tindal*, *Charron* and *Cowley* against it 345-6-7, is the greatest of Monsters, as well as the Root of all Evil 824, much gotten by evil Methods, generally runs away as fast, and by as bad Means as it was heap'd up together 832

Baptism with Water, not of perpetual Institution *Vol.* 2. 59, 60, 475-6-7, Christ never was an Administrator of Water-Baptism, but that of the Holy Ghost 275 Water-Baptism properly of *John*, *ibid*. 786, *Matth*. 28. prov'd to signify, not Water-Baptism, but that of the Spirit, a making true Disciples of them, by being baptiz'd into the Power and Spirit of the Gospel 276, 'tis confest to be an outward and visible Sign of inward and spiritual Grace, this being come, the Sign necessarily vanishes 277, Water-baptism not evangelical, but only an introductory Ceremony to Christianity 403, the Practice of the Apostles as such, no Institution, for if it were, then Circumsition, Purification, Vows, anointing the Sick with Oyl, washing the Disciples Feet *&c.* might be perpetuated as well as Water-Baptism, and by the same Arguments 277, 474, why the *Quakers* disuse and think it ceased in Point of Obligation 535-6-7, 786-7. 829 to 36, 878, 903-4-5-6

Bearing, a Man in Business must bear many Affronts, and wink at what he sometimes sees, if he loves his own Ease and Quiet 829, a Man's Strength is shewn by it, *bonum agere & male pati Regis est* 833

Books, see *Study*

Bribery, ought to be punished with as severe Penalties as defrauding the State 837

Burial, how the *Quakers* bury their Dead 870-1

Business, to be very subtle and scrupulous in Business, is as hurtful as being over confident and secure 830, in difficult Cases such a Temper is timerous, and in Dispatch irresolute, Experience is a safe Guide, and a practical Head a great Happiness in Business *ibid*.

Censoriousness, we are apt to be very pert at censuring others where we will not endure Advice our selves, much of this comes from ill Nature, and inordinate self-love, they have a Right to censure that have an Heart to Help 823-33 they must first judge themselves who presume to censure others 843

Charity, has various Senses but is excellent in all of them, 1*st* it imports a Commisseration of the Poor and Needy, and extending an helping Hand to them 857, this Duty illustrated *ibid*. 2*dly* the best Construction of Persons and Things 858, 3*dly* Love to God and the Brethren *ibid*. Charity should have Bounds and what

what ones 823, all People charitable and forgiving when humbled by the Approaches of Death, which shews that 'tis not Reason, but Passion that maintains feuds and Animosities amongst Men in Health and Fulness 843, the diffusively benificent Effects of Charity 857-8, 904-5

Children, see *Education*

Christ Jesus, his Eternal Divinity asserted 267 *Vol.* 2. 418-19-20, 783, his Sermon on the Mount paraphrased 758-9-60-1-2, the End of his Coming was to set us free from actual Sin, and enstate us in Newness of Life 770-1-2-3, he is the perpetual and immediate Teacher of his People *Vol.* 2. 42, his Body was crucified without the Gates of *Jerusalem* for the Salvation of Men 65, 74, 506, his Humanity also confest 94, 231-2, 783, firm and obedient Faith in Christ gives Remission of Sins 281, there is no other Name given under Heaven whereby Salvation can be attained 670, the *Quakers* truly own the great Benefit of his Death and Sufferings 784-5, 869-70-77-80

Christians ought to be distinguished by their Likeness to Christ, and not by their Notions of him 767, None say the *Waldenses*, are true Disciples of Christ, but those who imitate his Life *Vol.* 2. 495, Margin.

Christianity, see *Religion*

Christendom, its Degeneracy from primitive Integrity 279-83, its Cause and Cure 280-1-2-3, an Essay towards a future and general Peace of *Christendom* 839 to 48

Church, what 781, *Vol.* 2. 480-1, as good, so ill Men are all of a Church *Vol.* 1. 842, the humble, meek, merciful, just pious and devout Souls are every where of one Religion: better be of no Church than bitter for any 843, what its Power, and how far extendible *Vol.* 2. 192, 697, 698, whether the Church has an infallible Spirit *Vol.* 1. 606

Clergy, the Etymology of the Word 336, their Pride and Lordliness, and the evil Consequences thereof 337-8, the Power and Sway they bear, and the Peoples Reliance upon them for the Knowledge of Religion, with the lamentable Effects thereof 774-5, to take every thing implicitely and upon Trust from them, an Effect of the Apostacy, every Man is a Priest to save Souls 790, the Opinion of *Hales* and *Acontius* concerning an implicit Subjection to, and Confidence in the Clergy 782 to 88

Colledges, see *University*

Commands, in Scripture all general ones of Faith and Holy Living of general and perpetual Obligation, but particular ones upon particular and emergent Occasions, not so, but upon particular and special Commissions *Vol* 2. 253-73-4 656 to 9 the Possibility of keeping the Commands of God, asserted by *Grotius*, *Sanderson*, &c. as well as the *Quakers*, 630-1-2-3

Complacency, never assent meerly to please others, nor contradict to vex others, the first shews a Mind servile and base, the last an ill Temper 828

Comprehension, see *Uniformity*

Conduct, see *Conversation*

Conformity reasonable, where Conscience does not forbid it, for 'tis at least a civil Virtue 855, the just Measures of Conformity 855-6

Conscience what *Vol.* 2. 661-6, 729, Liberty of, what 729, defended *Vol.* 1. 447-8, as consistent with the Nature, Practice, Promotion and Reward of the Christian Religion 448-9, as agreeable to the Laws of Nature, Reason and civil Government 451-2-3-4-5 to the Sense and Judgment of many great States and Personages of antient and modern Times 459 to 64, *Vol.* 2. 730 to 36-47-8 and to the Example as well as Doctrine of Christ himself 610, Liberty of Conscience pressed by Argument and Example 729 to 47 49 to 73, the Church of *England* not persecuting in Principle, as testified by several of her most illustrious Members 758 to 63

Consciousness what, and how produc'd in us *Vol.* 2. 666

Controversy, the different Designs of it with both good and ill Men *Vol.* 2. 668

Conversation, if thou think'st twice before thou speak'st once, thou'lt speak twice the better for't, speak pertinently, and to do so, consider both what is fit and when to speak, return the Civilities thou receivest, and be ever grateful for Favours; sundry remarkable Reflections on Conversation 827-33-4 beware of Affectation in Speech, yet speak properly and briefly 850 Sense never fails to give them that have it (the Dumb excepted) Words enough to speak it intelligibly, the Odiousness of Affectation and super Curiosity, with divers Remarks on Conversation 897

Correction (of Children) should be reasonable 740 Men of Fury rather ease their Passion than mend their Youth, Correction should not exceed the Fault, *Plato's* Opinion of Correction *ibid.*

Cross of Christ (metaphorically) what 284 how it must be born 285 what its Work respecting Man 286 this Doctrine of infinite Moment to the Souls of Men, because the Way to eternal Blessedness 274

Curiosity in Living, see *Life*

Customs of *Lacedæmonia* 281

Days holy, why the *Quakers* refuse to observe *holy* Days (so term'd) *Vol.* 2. 875

Dealing

Dealing, an honest Man is a fast Pledge in dealing 853, there are few Dealers but what are faulty, which makes Trade difficult, and a Temptation to Men of Virtue *ibid*.

Death, tho it be a dark Passage it leads to Imortality 841 yet Faith lights us even thro' the Grave, it is the Amends of a short and troublesome Life that doing well and suffering Ill entitles us to one longer and better, this is the Comfort of the Good, that the Grave cannot hold them, they live as soon as they die *ibid*.

Detraction, to be avoided and why 832 Virtue is not secure against Envy, for Men will lessen what they wont imitate *ibid* Detraction is destructive of Religious Society 896

Diligence a laudable Virtue, its Use and Extent 908-9

Disappointments, such as come not by our own Folly, are the Trials or Corrections of Heaven, and it is our own Fault if they prove not our Advantage, to repine at them is to grumble at our Creator, who entrusts us with the Use of all 822 God often touches our best Comforts, not always to take them utterly away, but to prove our Integrity, caution us from Excesses, and excite us to remember the Author of them 289

Discipline, if thou wouldst be happy and easy in thy Family, above all things observe Discipline 823 the Discipline which the People called *Quakers* use in their Church Affairs 876-7-8 *Vol*. 2. 774, 775, 875

Dispensations, of God to the World have been divers, and what the End of them 859-60-1-2-3-4 *Vol*. 2. 21, the Excellence of the Gospel Dispensation above that of the Law, and how 40-1, 631

Dispute, the Author's with *T. Vincent* 6, with *Richard Baxter* 49, with Dr. *Galenus Abrahams* 107, another 108

Drunkenness, the present and consequent Evil and Odium thereof displayed 722-3, is a reigning Vice, the Poor of *England* might be maintained by the Excess of the Rich *ibid*. a Drunkard no Man, because whilst such void of Reason which distinguishes a Man from a Beast 824

Education, that of our Youth much out of Order 738 the Industry of the *Jesuits* in Education recommended 739, a Method of Education propos'd, 1*st* that our Youth be carefully brought up in Morality 739, 2*dly* that they be put upon the more obvious Parts of the Mathematicks and natural History, 3*dly* the History of our own Kingdoms, and the Interest of the *Protestant Religion* and civil Policy, 4*ly*, that their Genius be not crost, 5*ly*, that they be rather allured than forced to Learning *ibid*. we ought to inculcate the Knowledge of Things into our Youth with that of Words 821 Men generally more careful of the breed of their Horses and Dogs than of their Children, those must have all good Qualities, but with these Money answers all Things 825-31, we ought to ward against that Passion in Children, which is more especially our own Weakness and Affliction 830, the just measures of Education in general 901

Election and *Reprobation*, absolute, the Doctrine hereof rampant in the Time of *Abbot* (i e King *James* 1st) but deprest in the Time of *Laud* (i e K. *Charles* 1st) the clashing and Bitterness of the contending Parties hereupon in the Synod of *Dort* 745

Eloquence, there is a Truth and Beauty in *Rhetorick*, but it oftener serves ill Turns than good ones, it is a good mein and Address given to Matter, be it in proper or figurative Speech 828, 'tis a reproveable Delicacy to despise Truth in plain Cloaths *ibid*.

Envy, a Mark of ill Nature, it lessens good Actions and aggravates ill ones 848, some Men do as much begrudge others a good Name, as they want one themselves 849, many of the evil Qualities and Consequences of Envy enumerated *ibid*. just and noble Minds rejoice in other Men's Success, and help to augment their Praise; such deserve to share in the Character of Virtue that do abhor to lessen it *ibid*.

Europe, see *Christendom*

Faith, what 591, Prayer ineffectual without it 304-5, Opinions often pass for Articles of Faith, and its mischievous Consequences, the Division of *Arrius* and that of the Synod of *Dort* in particular, 745-6

Fasts and *Feasts*, the publick, why the *Quakers* refuse their Observance *V*. 2. 875

Flattering Titles, see *Honour*

Formality, the Vanity thereof 299-300 Form good but not Formality 852 It is the Frame of the Mind that gives our Performances Acceptance, we should therefore lay more Stress on inward Preparation than on outward Action *ibid*.

Fornication &c. *England's* Declension in this Respect 723, Plays and Romances not a little conducive to this Evil 724, its abominable and destructive Consequences; the Unrighteous shall not inherit the Kingdom of God, neither Fornicators *ibid*.

Fox George, his Birth and Education, his many excellent Qualifications shewing

a divine

a divine not human Power to have been their Original, his Troubles and Sufferings both from within and without, his Christian Disdain of Death 878-9-80-1-2-3-4

Freeholders of *England*, momentous Advice to them about their Choice of Representatives to sit in Parliament, *Vol.* 2. 678-9-80-1

Friendship, there can be none where there is no Freedom 826, Friends true Twins in Soul, they speak and act freely and take nothing ill if not meant so, a true Friend unbosoms freely, advises justly, assists readily, adventures boldly, takes all patiently, defends couragiously and continues a Friend unchangeably 827 the Covetous, Angry, Proud, Jealous, Talkative and False, make ill Friends, Virtue the Bound of Friendship, they that love beyond the World cannot be separated by it 850

Frugality, good if join'd with Liberality, both makes an excellent Composition 823, cast up your Income, and live on half, one third if you can, reserving the rest for Casualties, Charities, Portions 898, the general Benefit and Bounds of Frugality 909

Gaming inconsistent with civil Government and Christianity, demonstrated by its many evil Attendants and Consequences 729

Gentiles, many of them believed in one God 541-2-3-4-5-6, that he hath imprinted the Knowledge of himself on the Minds of Men 547-8-9-50-1, that Virtue was the Way to eternal Happiness 554-5-6-7-8-9, the Doctrine of Immortality plainly deliver'd by them 560-1-2, they had a Foresight of the Coming of Christ *ibid.*

God, many of the *Gentiles* believed in one God 541 to 7, our Notion of Him mean by the Ways we take to please him 853, what Benefit is it to say our Prayers regularly, go to Church, receive the Sacrament, go to Confessions, feast the Priest, and give Alms to the Poor, and yet lye, swear, curse, be drunk, covetous, unclean, proud &c. at the same Time—can one excuse or ballance the other—or will God think himself well serv'd (by performing the external Parts of Devotion) where his Law is violated *ibid.* the Fear of God necessary to our well being 897

Gospel what *Vol.* 2. 675-6, is more excellent than the Law, and how 631, see *Dispensations*

Government Civil, the great Foundation and End of it prov'd to be civil Interest *Vol.* 2. 682 to 90, which can't subsist without an equal Ballance to all dissenting religious Persuasions *ibid.* the *Quakers* neither inconsistent with, nor troublesome to Government 788-9, 878, the general Design and End of Civil Government 840 *Vol.* 1. 834-5

Gratitude, what 907, there is something baser and more reproachful in Ingratitude than in Injustice, and why *ibid.* is an Evangelical Virtue and an indispensible Duty 908

Great Men (or *rich Men*) what their Obligations to Almighty God for his distinguish'd Goodness to them 856, 'tis a dangerous Perversion of the Ends of Providence to consume the Time, Power and Wealth which God hath given them above meaner Men, to gratify their sordid Passions instead of being good Stewards to the Honour of their great Benefactor, and the Good of their fellow Creatures *ibid.*

Hands, the laying on of Hands a *Jewish* Ceremony, those that plead for it must at least implicitely assert a successive Apostolical Church from the Apostles Times, with a Power of conferring Gifts *Vol.* 2. 484

Happiness temporal, if thou would'st be happy, bring thy Mind to thy Condition, and have an Indifferency for what is more than sufficient 831, many useful Hints concerning it 832

Hatred, dislike what deserves it, but never hate, Hatred being one of the blackest Qualities which Sin begets in the Soul 832

Hazard, in all Business 'tis best to avoid it, but where 'tis unavoidable, be not rash but firm and resigned.—'tis in vain to be troubled at what we cannot help 832, other useful Reflections on hazardous Enterprises *ibid.*

Heresy is an Act of the Will, not of Reason; a Lye, not a Mistake; else how could *Austin's* well known Speech [*errare possum, Hæreticus esse nolo*] be true 758.

Hierarchy, that of the *Romanists* inconsistent with the Example they plead, viz. *the Primitive Times* 484, the great Design of the *Romish* Hierarchy *ibid.*

Holy Days so called, see *Days*

Honour, what 316-17-18, what it is not 318-19-20-21, the Testimonies of *Marolat, Jerom* and *Causabon* concerning it 325-6, why the *Quakers* reject those Titles that express not some real Office or Relation, and the modish Salutations of the Times *Vol.* 2. 62-3, 130-1-2, 874, the *Quakers* truly honour all Men, treating their Inferiours and Equals with Love and Gentleness, and their Superiours with a modest and awful Distance and Regard 787

C

Humility

Humility, a great Virtue and how, is the Beauty of Religion, Chrift himfelf a moft eminent Example thereof 902-3

Idolatry, whence it proceeds V. 2. 715

Jealoufy, be not fancifully jealous, for that is foolifh, as to be reafonably fo is wife 830, the Jealous are a Trouble to others but a Torment to themfelves 853, the Rife and Confequences of Jealoufy *ibid.*

Jews, an earneft, expoftulary and reafonable Exhortation to them to embrace the true Chriftian Faith *Vol. 2.* from 848 to 853

Ignorance, many People come into and go out of the World ignorant of themfelves and it 820, the ill Confequences of wilful and fupine Ignorance in things refpecting another World 872, Ignorance the Mother of Devotion with the *Romanifts* 477

Images, how the *Romanifts* adore them, and by whom introduced 471, the Opinion of *Clemens Alexandrinus*, and the Council of *Eliberis* about them 472

Immortality, fee *Vice*

Impartiality, its Ufe and Excellence 838, the illConfequences of Partiality *ibid*

Inconfideration, is the Caufe of all the Unhappinefs which Man brings upon himfelf 822

Indices expurgatory, the Craft of the *Romanifts* in framing them 470

Indifferency, good in Judgment, bad in Relation, and ftark nought in Religion 838

Induftry (or *Labour*) good, for if we want it not for Food, we may for Phyfick, to keep a free Circulation of the Blood, a good Stomach, and our whole Body from Corpulence and Diforder 824, Induftry is commendable fupplying the Want of Parts 831, Patience and Diligence like Faith remove Mountains *ibid.*

Infallibility, how held by the *Quakers*, they don't fay that Man is infallible as fuch, but only and fo far as he is guided by the infallible Spirit of God *Vol. 2.* 69 let him doubt of his Faith that lifteth, fays *Philpot*, God give me always to believe that I am fure of true Faith and Favour in Chrift. *Latimer* to the fame Purpofe *Vol. 1.* 606, if no Certainty in Religion, then Preaching vain *Vol. 2.* 241, 328-9-30

Inquiry, is human, blind Obedience brutal 828, have a Care of vulgar Errors, diflike as well as allow reafonably. A mean recommended *ibid.*

Infpiration what, *Vol. 2.* 521, fee *Light* and *Revelation*

Integrity, a great and commendable Virtue, a Man of Integrity a true Man, few Difficulties infuperable to him 907

Intereft, has the Security tho' not the Virtue of a Principle 828, its Effects and Obfervations thereon *ibid.*

Jury, that of the Author and *W. Mead*, inhumanly debarr'd from Meat and Drink &c. fin'd 40 Marks a Man and imprifoned, for bringing in their Verdict contrary to the partial Opinion of the Court 15, 16, 17, 18, the Power and Office of Juries according to our Englifh Conftitution fairly ftated and refolved 499, 500-1-2, and from 513 to 520

Juftice, a great Support of Society becaufe an Affurance to all Men of their Property 852, of the Benefit of Juftice, its Ufe, Extent and Reward 906-7

Juftification, defined *Vol. 2.* 411, that by imputative Righteoufnefs refuted from Scripture and Reafon *Vol. 1.* 259, 260-1-2, its irreligious Confequences 263 Works as well as Faith neceffary to Juftification *Vol. 2.* 66, 522-3. Juftification fignifies being made juft and righteous 281, God's Goodnefs and Mercy and not any Works of our own is the formal Caufe of Juftification *ibid.* Juftification by imputed Righteoufnefs refuted by *Stillingfleet, Tillotfon, Sherlock* &c. 408, to 414

Knowledge, is the Treafure, but Judgment the Treafurer of a wife Man 829, He that hath more Knowledge than Judgment is made for another Man's Ufe more than his own *ibid.*

Language, that of Thee or Thou to a fingle Perfon proper, proved from the ftrict Rules of Grammer 326, *Vol. 2.* 64. the Cuftom of the Oriental and Modern Languages *Vol. 1.* 327, the Original of You to a fingle Perfon *ibid.* the Opinions of *Luther, Erafmus, Lipfius* and *Howel*, touching it 329-30, why the *Quakers* refufe You to a fingle Perfon in Point of Confcience 326-7 8-9, *Vol. 2.* 871, 901.

Law, the moral, notoriously broken by the *Papifts* in ufing of Images, difpenfing with Difobedience in Children to their Parents, in granting Bulls for Maffacre's, Licences for publick Stews &c. 482-3

Laws of *England*, their Excellency 674 by their Sanction we enjoy an undifturbed Poffeffion of our own 675 *Vol. 2.* 679, a voting of every new Law that is made 677, an Influence upon, and a Share in the Judicatory Power 679, the Laws of *England* ought to be inviolably and univerfally obferved, without Regard to Difference in Opinion, prov'd by nine fubftantial Reafons 688-9-90-1, the obfervable Curfe of the *Romifh Bifhops* againft the Breakers of *Magna Charta* 685

Liberty

Liberty, spiritual, defined and distinguished *Vol.* 2. 692, its Extent and Limitations 643-4-5-6

Liberty of Conscience (or Civil Liberty) see *Conscience* and *Laws of England*.

Liberality join'd with Frugality, makes an excellent Composition 823, Liberality and its Objects considered 905-6

Life, a Country one to be preferr'd, and Why 831, the Country is both the Philosophers Garden and Library, Food and Study, and gives him Life as well as Learning, is a sweet and natural Retreat from Noise and Talk, allowing Opportunity for Reflection, and yielding the best Subjects for it *ibid.* a private Life preferrable, and why 836, of being easy in Living 851, 'tis a Happiness to be delivered from a curious Mind, as well as from a dainty Palate; several useful Reflections on human Conduct, 897-8-9, 900

Light, divine and saving, (viz. *a Participation of the divine Spirit*) it leads Man to Blessedness 524, the *Antediluvians, Patriarchs* and *Jews*, even down to the Time of Christ had the Benefit of it 523, 533-4-5, the *Gentiles* also were illuminated 535 to 42, the Testimonies of many of them in Confirmation hereof 547-8-9-50-1, and of many of the Christian Fathers 551-2-3, the Universality, Divinity and Sufficiency of this Light proved 584-5-6, and from *Vol.* 2. 855 to 66, 899, what this Light does for Men when obeyed *Vol.* 1 894-5-6, how and with what Limitations the *Quakers* own it *Vol.* 2. 18, 19, 95, 96, 232, *John* 1. 9. Critically examined 113-14-15, 2 *Pet.* 1 19. *we also have a more sure Word of Prophecy*, &c. critically explained 291-2-3-4, 425-6-7. Rom. 10. 3. *the Word is nigh thee*, likewise critically cleared, 423-4-5. the Light proved to be saving, by several famous Authors 123-4, Bp. *Sanderson* calls it the Eternal Law of Righteousness, and a Rule sufficient to good Life 496, how tis variously denominated by divers *Gentiles, Jews* and *Christians* 626-7, whether it be improper or indefensible to call it a spiritual Substance, as *R. Barclay* 794-5, the *Quakers* don't say that this is given ordinarily to reveal past or future Contingencies, but the Nature of Things as to Truth or Falshood, Obligation and Duty, Good and Evil 815, this Light is not the Effect of the perceptive Faculties of our own Minds, but distinguish'd from it, 821-2, 897-8-9

Love, Religion nothing else but Love to God and Man 843, Love is above all, and when it prevails in us all, we shall all be lovely, and in Love with God and one with another *ibid.*

Luxury, what, and its Mischief to Mankind 347, it depraves the Bodies as well as the Minds of Men 349, Luxury consider'd in divers Respects 348-9-50, soberly and seasonably reprehended 725 6-7-8, 822.

Magistrate, whether he hath Power over the Consciences of Men, see *Conscience*, the Magistrate ought to carry himself upon a Ballance towards dissenting Parties, prov'd by eight substantial Reasons 692-3-4-5-6-7, 83-4-5, a sincere Promotion of general and practical Religion, the Way to take in all Perswasions 701-2.

Man, (see *Vain Man*) what he was created for 272, was made an holy, wise, sober, grave and reasonable Creature, fit to govern himself and the World 367, is like a Watch to be valued for his Goings 832, never esteem another or thy self the more for Money, nor the less for Want of it, Virtue being the just Reason of respecting and the Want of it of slighting of any one.—the just Measures of respecting Men *ibid.* Man is enlightned with a Divine Light, says several famous Men *Vol.* 2. 435.

Marriage, is honourable 725, but despised and neglected by many for evil Ends 724, never marry but for Love, but see that thy Object be lovely 825, prefer the Person before Money, Virtue before Beauty, the Mind before the Body, then thou hast a Wife, a Friend, a second self, one that bears an equal Share with thee, in all thy Toils and Troubles 825 6, 906, sundry observable Cautions about Marriage *ibid.* how the *Quakers* marry, and their Care as a Society therein 869, *Vol.* 2. 775, why the *Quakers* testify against Mixt-Marriages 875.

Master, ought to rule more by Discretion than Rigour 830, his Duty towards his Servant *ibid.*

Mediator, the *Papists* frankly own many Mediators 471

Meekness, what, Christ presses it in his own Example, *Moses* noted for it 903

Mercy, what, its most beneficent Effects 904.

Merit, how understood by the *Romanists* 472, in obeying the Commands of God, we obtain but not merit Salvation *ibid.* no Works of Man are meritorious 282, the *Quakers* say with the Apostle, *that Faith without Works is dead*, yet assert that Works are not, cannot be meritorious, and why *V.* 2. 785-6, 879 80

Minister, of the Gospel ought to be of Christ's making 839, his Life ought to confirm his Doctrine, he gives as well as receives freely, accounts Content with Godliness great Gain, and therefore makes

makes not a Gain of Godliness, he is exhorted to feel Life in his Ministry to let that be his Commission, Treasury, and well-spring upon all Occasions, and not to depend upon either Parts or Memory 885-6-7-8, the Meaness and Illiterature of much of the *Quakers* Ministry vindicated by the Example of the primitive Christians and *Waldenses Vol. 2.* 17, true Gospel Ministers must first be taught of God before they pretend to teach Men, they must first know the Work of Mortification in themselves, and then an immediate Call by the Spirit of God before they can be true and living Gospel Ministers 265, 782, the primitive *Protestants* were of the same Opinion 352-3-87-8.

Ministers of State, should undertake their Posts at their Peril 836, how they ought to be qualified 835-6-7, ought to be punishable when they do amiss, for the People as well as Prince will not endure *Imperium in Imperio*, those that serve their Country faithfully, deserve publick Marks of Honour and Profit 837.

Miracles, why used, and to what Purposes *Vol. 2.* 38.

Moderation, it were happy if Men could bound and qualifie their Passion and Resentment with Charity to the Offender 832.

Moralist see *Morality*

Morality, what, is very unfashionable among, as well as a common Enemy to Men of immoral Principles 766, a right Moralist is a great and a good Man, and therefore rarely to be found 845, the compleat Moralist begins with God, gives him his Due, next himself, lastly his Neighbour, is in short, one that loves God above all, and his Neighbour as himself 845.

Neutrality, distinguished from Indifferency 838, a wise Neuter joins no Parties, he only has Room to make Peace and mediate Reconciliation, yet when Right or Religion calls, a Neuter must be a Coward or a Hypocrite, we should never stand neuter when and where we can do Good 839.

Oaths (or swearing) absolutely unlawful under the Christian Dispensation, 10 Reasons why 614 to 20, a Cloud of Witnesses, both *Gentiles*, *Jews* and *Christians* of the same Sentiments 622 to 70, the prophane Use of Oaths a Sin against the Majesty and Dignity of God 731, whether the Greek *Μα* and *νη* are only and strictly Adverbs of Swearing *Vol. 2.* 128-9-30-1, the Foundation of Swearing says Bp. *Gauden*, is the Wickedness of Men 488 Margin, when the primitive Christians were required to swear, their Answer was *Christianus sum*, [*Christiani sumus*] I am a Christian, [we are Christians] 488, it was a primitive Maxim, *non oportet ut vir qui Evangelicè vivit, juret omnino*, it behoves a Man, who lives according to the Gospel, not to swear at all *ibid*. other Reasons why the *Quakers* refuse to swear at all 793-4-5-6, 826-7-8-9, those emphatical Expressions of the Apostles, term'd Oaths by some, are not Oaths, as say many famous Critical Authors 128-9-30, 794-5-6, 827-8

Ordinances, see *Baptism* and *Sacrament*, what is truly a Gospel Ordinance, the *Quakers* desire to, and do own and practise *Vol. 2.* 786.

Ostentation, do what Good thou can'st unknown, and be not vain of what ought rather to be felt than seen, he that does Good for the sake of Good, seeks neither Praise nor Reward, tho' sure of both at last 839:

Parents, see *Education*, next to God we ought to obey them, next them, the Magistrate 829, the Duty of Obedience to Parents illustrated *ibid.*

Partiality, of Men's Inconsiderateness and Partiality in general, with the Effects thereof 851-38.

Patience, its Use and Excellency, thro' our Civil as well as Religious Course, we cannot act wisely nor safely without it 903-4.

Peace of *Europe*, see *Christendom*

Penn William, his Birth and Education 1, enters Student at C. C. College in *Oxford* at 15 Years of Age, his early Inquiry after Religion, and Difficulties thereupon *ibid*. returns Home from the University 2, his Tour to *France*, his spiritual Conflict and Exercises, goes into *Ireland* and is convinced there, is imprisoned at *Cork*, writes to the Earl of *Orrery* ibid. his Discharge thereupon 3, his Constancy confirm'd by suffering, publickly joins the *Quakers* Society, returns to *England*, his and his Father's mutual Exercises thereupon *ibid*. a remarkable Instance of his Sincerity 4, is turn'd out of his Father's House, his Father's Anger abated, is call'd forth into the Ministry *ibid*. writes to an Acquaintance dissuading from a vain Conversation 5, appears first in Print Anno 1668, publishes his *Sandy Foundation shaken* ibid and is therefore imprisoned in the *Tower* 6, shews both Magnanimity and Resignation under his menacing Treatment there, and writes his *No Cross, no Crown* and a Letter to the Lord *Arlington* ibid. goes a second Time into *Ireland*, his Services there 7, returns to *England*, is committed to *Newgate* and tried at the *Old Bailey*

Old Bailey, where he makes a bold and memorable Defence of his Religious Principles, and the fundamental Laws of *England* ibid. disputes with *Jeremy Ives* 36, writes to the Vice Chancelor of *Oxford*, is apprehended at *Wheeler Street Meeting* ibid. and examined before the Lieutenant of the *Tower* 37, is committed to *Newgate* 40, and writes several Books there, as also a Letter to the Parliament 41, is abused by the Keepers of *Newgate*, and writes an Account thereof to the Sheriffs of *London*, writes to a *Roman Catholick* 42, is discharged 43, marry's and settles at *Rickmersworth*, travels into *Kent* and *Sussex*, writes to Dr. *Hasbert* of *Embden* 44, to *Lodowick Muggleton*, and against *John Morse*, *Henry Hedworth* and *John Faldo*, and answers *Faldo's* Challenge 45, writes against *Henry Halywel*, *Thomas Hicks*, 21 Learned Divines, *Samuel Grevil* and *Anonymus*, and writes sundry remarkable Letters 46, to — *Bowles* Esq; to the *King* 47, to the Senate of *Embden*, and publishes several Treatises 48, writes to a *Roman Catholick*, disputes with *Richard Baxter* 49, becomes a Proprietor of *West Jersey*, writes against *John Cheney* 50, goes by *London*, *Colchester* and *Harwich* for *Holland*, lands at the *Briel*, goes thence to *Rotterdam* 52, *Leyden*, *Haerlem*, *Amsterdam* 53, (writes to the King of *Poland* 56) goes thence by *Naerden* and *Osnabrug* to *Herwerden*, and makes a Religious Visit to the Princess *Elizabeth Palatine* 59, thence to *Paderborn*, *Cassel* and *Franckfort* [on the main] 64, writes there to the Churches of Jesus 65, thence by Way of *Worms* to *Crisheim* where he writes to the Princess *Palatine* 72, thence to *Frankendal*, *Manheim*, (where he writes a remarkable Letter to the *Elector Palatine*) goes thence to *Crisheim*, *Worms* 76 *Mentz*, *Frankfort*, *Hampack*, *Bacherach*, *Coblentz*, *Tresy*, *Cullen* alias *Cologn* 77, *Duysburgh* 78, *Mulheim* 79, writes to the Countess of *Falckensteyn* and *Bruch* 80, thence to *Holton*, *Wesel*, *Rees*, *Emrick*, *Cleve* 85, *Nimmeguen*, *Utrecht*, *Amsterdam* 86, *Horn*, *Enckhuysen*, *Workum*, *Harlingen* 87, (where he writes to a Noble Young Woman at *Franckfort*) thence to *Leeuwarden*, *Wiewart* 90, (where he visits the *Somerdikes*, *de Labadie's* Followers) *Lippenhusen*, *Groningen*, *Delfzyl* (where he writes to Friends every where) *Embden* 96, and visits the President of the Council of State 97, thence to *Lier*, *Bremen* and *Herwerden* (visiting again the Princess palatine) *Wesel*, *Lipstad*, *Ham* (writes to the Countess of *Hornes*) *Collen*, *Dusseldorp* 104, *Duysburgh* 105, *Wesel*, *Cleve*, *Nimmeguen*, *Utrecht*, *Amsterdam* 106, (where he disputes with Dr. *Galenus Abrahams*) *Leyden*, *Hague* 108, *Delft*, *Rotterdam*, (where he publishes several Epistles &c) *Wonderwick* 110, *Hague*, *Delft*, *Rotterdam*, *Briel*, (where writing to the Princess Palatine) he took Boat for *Harwich*, where after a turbulent Passage he arrives, writing thence to Friends in *Holland* and *Germany* 114, from whence he passes by *Colchester* and *London* to *Worminghurst* 116, writes to *John Pennyman* 117, the Commons of *England* ibid. makes a Speech before a Committee of Parliament 118, makes another Speech 119, publishes several Pieces 120, *Pensylvania* granted by Letters Patent to him and his Heirs 121, he writes an instructive and pacific Letter to the *Indians* ibid. draws up fundamental Constitutions of *Pensylvania* 122, goes thither, makes a Speech to an Assembly at *Newcastle*, and another at *Chester*, goes to *Maryland*, and his Reception there by the Lord *Baltimore* 123, defends his sincere Intentions in Government, describes *Pensylvania*, writes an Epistle to his Friends there, and returns to *England* 124, is undeservedly censured as a *Papist*, publishes a Vindication of himself 125 writes 3 Letters to Dr. *Tillotson* 126-7-8, writes a Defence of the Duke of *Buckingham*, and a Perswafive to Moderation 129, makes a Speech to King *James* the 2d. writes an Answer to *W. Popples* Letter, in Defence of his both Religious and Civil Sincerity 134, is examined before the Lords of the Council 139, a second time, & appeals to King *William*, is falsly swore against and retires 140, writes several Books and Epistles in his Retirement, is admitted to plead his Cause again before the King and Council, and is acquitted, his Wife dies, he travels in the Work of the Ministry 141, is interrupted at *Wells* 142, presents the Parliament with a Paper about Swearing 143, marry's again, his eldest Son dies, presents the Parliament with a Caution about the Bill against Blasphemy, writes an Answer to *Plymton*, sets out for *Ireland*, his Services there, visits the Bishop of *Cork* 144, arrives at *Bristol*, goes to *Pensylvania*, his paternal Administration there 145, makes a Speech to an Assembly at *Philadelphia* 146, returns to *England*, writes an Epistle to his Friends 147, visits the West of *England*, settles at *Brentford*, is unhappily involved in a Law-Suit, his last Travels in the Work of the Ministry, he removes to *Rushcomb* 148, is seized with an Apoplexy, which impairing his Faculties, he gradually declines, and at length yields himself a quiet Victim to the irresistable Messenger of Death, and was interr'd at *Jordans in Buckinghamshire*

(14)

the 5th Day of the 6th Month *Anno Domini* 1718, *Ætatis suæ* 74: His Soul (no doubt) being enter'd the glorious Habitations of the Just.

Penn Sr. *William* (Father to the preceeding) his high Maritine Offices, King *Charles* the 2d confers upon him the Honour of Knighthood 1, his great Concern at his Sons embracing the despised *Quakers* 4, dies perfectly reconciled to him 35, his remarkably Dying Sayings 432-3, Interment, Monument and Inscription thereon 35, 36.

Pensylvania described, with the natural History thereof, and an Account of the Natives or Aborigines, from *Vol.* 2. 699 to 708.

Perfection, from Sin or Regeneration, necessary to be known, because the Way and Condition to eternal Happiness, for no unclean Thing shall enter into the Kingdom of God 867, how the *Quakers* maintain it *Vol.* 2. 19, 492-3, 671-2, 781, 880, *Grotius's* Opinion of Regeneration 630.

Persecution, how inconsistent with the Laws of God, Men and Nature, see *Conscience*, the Christian Religion made illustrious by suffering Persecution 673, the Causes and Cure of Persecution 811, 12-13-14-15-16-17, *Hale's* Opinion of Persecution 813, those of *James* and *Charles* the first, Kings of *England* 817-18 the Church doth not persecute but is persecuted, says *Hilary Vol.* 2. 497.

Philosophy, no essential Qualification of a Gospel Minister *Vol.* 2. 56.

Plainness, in Apparel and Furniture, why the *Quakers* use and press it *Vol.* 2. 875.

Popularity, to be avoided and why 834 they that appear to be what they are not, raise an Expectation which they can't answer, and so loose their Credit when found out *ibid*.

Praise, we are more apt to love than deserve it 849, but if we would deserve it, we must love Virtue more than that, *ibid.* the just Measures of giving and receiving Praise 849-50.

Prayer, that of the *Romanists* in Latin, which is an effectual Method to keep the People in Ignorance (with them the Mother of Devotion) 477, Faith and Resignation essential to Prayer 305, as also divine Assistance *Vol.* 2. 50, 271-2, why the *Quakers* oppose formal and pre-appointed Prayers 474, the irreverent Practice of keeping on the Hat in Time of Prayer censured and why 192-3-4. why the Head ought to be uncovered in Prayer to God 207-8, the earnest Breathings of the Spirit of God, and not the Will of Man, ought to preside in Prayer 397, so several famous Protestants 398.

Preaching, publick, the Necessity and Use thereof *Vol.* 2. 35-6, the Example of Christ preaching from a particular Passage of *Isaiah*, no Institution to preach from or upon a particular Text. The Practice of the Apostles so far as recorded confirm it 49

Pride, what 306, the Causes thereof *ibid.* its evil Consequences 307, 311, is ever follow'd by Superstition and Obstinacy 309, is an universal Enemy to civil Society 312, the great Stir about Blood, Antiquity, Beauty *&c.* Effects of it 331-2-3-4-5, the Character of a proud Man in his several Capacities 335-6, Pride bad above all in Ministers, because the very Terms incompatible 337, the proud Man is curious to wash, dress and perfume his Body, but is careless of his Soul 822, other useful Reflections on Pride 854-5.

Prophaness, the Declension of our Age in this Respect 731, instead of being punished, it bodly lays Claim to Parts and Wit, the Prophane earnestly call'd to Repentance 732-3, an Address to the Civil Magistrate for Redress hereof, with three great Reasons why it ought to be given 733-44.

Promising, rarely promise, but if lawful constantly perform, the Consequences of hasty Resolutions 829 30.

Property (see Laws of *England*) no Conformity to the Church, no Property in the State, a Maxim with some 797, twelve Reasons why this Maxim is Antichristian and destructive of Government 797-8-9, 800

Proverbs, the Wisdom of Nations lies in their Proverbs, collect and learn them they are notable Measures and Directions for human Life, they save Time and speaking, and upon Occasion may be the fullest and safest Answers 899.

Psalms, of *David*, the singing of them as usual, opposed, and why *Vol.* 2. 60

Publick (or Common Wealth) has an Interest in our Estates 854, hardly any Thing is given us for our selves, but the Publick may claim a Share with us *ibid.* if the Taxes we pay are not to maintain Pride, to be sure there would be less [Pride] if Pride were made a Tax *ibid.*

Purgatory, maintained by the *Papists*, tho' evidently against Scripture, Reason and the Opinions of several of their own Authors 480-1, *Vol.* 2. 68, 69.

Quakers, why so called *Vol.* 2. 67, their Rise, and the Afflictions and Contradictions they met with *Vol.* 1. 864-5, their great Increase 866, their Characteristick or Fundamental Principle, with its Subdivisions *ibid.* they were at first noted for their Communion and

and loving one another 867, loving their Enemies 868, Truth speaking without Swearing, not fighting but suffering, refusing to pay Tithes, not respecting Persons 869, using the plain Language of thee and thou to a single Person, recommending Silence by their Example, refusing to drink Healths, their Way of Marriage and of Burial 870-1, the Qualifications of their Ministry, eleven Marks that it is Christian 873 4-5, their Discipline and Practice as a religious Society, with their Manner of Proceedings against erring and disorderly Persons 876 7-8, this People reminded of their primitive Integrity and Simplicity, particularly their Ministry 884-5-6-7-8, the young Convinced exhorted to Diligence 888-9, and the Children of Friends earnestly perswaded to walk stedfastly in the Way of Truth, having their Fore-Fathers for Examples 889-90, the meaness and Illiterature of much of their Ministry vindicated by the Examples of the *Waldenses* and Primitive Christians *Vol*. 2. 19, they are in Principle widely distant from the *Papists*, as shew'd in many Instances 68, 69, they own Civil Government and Society (with the Laws and Obligations of each) to be according to the Laws of God, Reason and Nature 72-3, their known Quietness and Submission to all Governments, demonstrate them to be not inconsistent with Government, as charg'd by some 878, why they became an altered and distinguished People from others 913-14.

Ranters (Followers of *Reeve* and *Muggleton*) their Ignorance, Errour, Impudence and Blasphemy V. 2. from 152 to 178, they had over ran the Nation had not the *Quakers* come says Dr. *Gell*, and a Person of Quality 208.

Reason, in all Things should prevail 851, 'tis quite another Thing to be stif than steady in an Opinion, this is reasonable, that ever wilful, the clearer the Argument the greater the Obstinacy where the Design is not to be convinced, Truth never lost Ground by Enquiry, because she is most of all reasonable *ibid*.

Recreations, those of the Times Enemies to Virtue 349-50, their Rise from Degeneracy *ibid*. the Recreations of the Saints of old was to serve God and their fellow Creatures 350-1, many of the *Heathens* of old esteem'd destructive of Sobriety and good Manners 351, what Christian Recreations are 354, the pernicious Consequences of Play-houses, Stages, Revels, Gaming &c. 357-8, had they been solid and necessary *Adam* and *Eve* had never been happy without them 362-3, those who pretend to Seriousness should be examplary in their Declension from such Latitudes 370-1.

Refining, the Uncertainty, Folly and dangerous Consequences of refining upon other Men's Actions or Interests 857

Regeneration see *Perfection*

Religion, (see Church) its Fall from Experience to Tradition, from Power to Form, and from Simplicity to Pomp and Ceremony 283, it is the unum necessarium to Felicity here and hereafter 701 2-3-4, is not to be propagated by Force 773, is the Fear of God, and its Demonstration good Works 829, to be furious in Religion is to be irreligiously religious 843, Grace perfects but never spoils Nature *ibid*. the Source of false Religion, and the Definition of true *Vol*. 2. 5, 6. 230-1.

Reparation, if thou hast done an Injury to another, rather own than defend it, one Way thou gainest Forgiveness, the other thou doublest the Wrong. True Honour will pay treble Damages rather than justifie one Wrong by another, true Honour and Submission not at all inconsistent 827.

Reprobation see *Election*

Respect, see *Man*

Resurrection, of the Dead, the *Quakers* believe it according to the Scriptures *Vol*. 2. 298-9, 438-9, 543-4, 670, 804, altho' they cannot believe with some, that the same Carnal, Numerical Body which is buried, shall rise again, for Flesh and Blood shall not inherit the Kingdom of God, *Origin*, *Jerom*, Dr. *More* and Dr. *Hammond* believe the same 438-9-40 1-2-3, 543-4-5, 881, they also firmly believe eternal Rewards, else think they are miserable 787, 881, 896.

Retirement, the Benefit thereof demonstrated by *Cowley* 428-9, recommended by Count *Oxistern* 425, earnestly prest by the Author 438, how conducive to help human Frailty 438, 897, little or private Men have the Advantage of great ones in having Leisure for Family Comforts 834.

Revelation, immediate, Miracles no certain Evidence of it *Vol*. 2. 38. what the *Quakers* mean by the Word [Revelation] and how they use it *ibid*. the Revelations of the Prophets of old were not always evidenced by Miracles *ibid*. Natural Revelation [or Reason] and Divine Revelation distinguished 48, immediate Revelations frequent in the second Century of Christianity 71, the Question resolv'd whether or no. Immediate Revelation is to be expected in our Time, and to the End of Time 331.

Rhetorick, see *Eloquence*

Rule, general of Faith and Practice, necessary to be known 591, it is not the

Scriptures, because they neither are nor have been general 592, because many Generations had them not 593, because as to Number they are still imperfect 594 because I may doubt of their Verity, and what shall resolve me? if the Scriptures that infers an Absurdity 595 (*Vol. 2. 590 591*) the many voluminous Cases of Conscience extant also prove it 596, the Scriptures are a Rule, but not the Rule 599, (*Vol. 2. 590*) the Eternal, perfect and universal Spirit of God, being the Rule of Faith and Life, as witness many famous Authors 592 (*Vol. 2. 96-7, 110, 338, 595*) Church Authority not the Rule for several Reasons 774, Right Reason says *Stillingfleet* and *Tillotson*, is the Judge of Controversy 344, the Writing in the Heart is the Rule, says *Irenæus* 595.

Sabbath (or first) Day, whether there be any moral Sanctity in it *Vol. 2. 51*, the Negative maintain'd 479-80

Sacrament, (so called) of Bread and Wine, the Discord of the *Romanists* about receiving it in both Kinds 475-6, the Word [Sacrament] not to be found in the Scriptures *Vol. 2. 20*, 'tis confest to be a Figure and of what 60, the *Quakers* confess Bread and Wine to have been given by Christ's Command to his Disciples, but believe it not to be of perpetual Obligation, and why 278-9, 476-7-8 why they disuse and think it ceased in Point of Obligation 406, 535-6-7, 837-8 879, 907-8-9-10.

Salvation, is not only a being saved from Wrath to come (the common Notion) but also from the Cause thereof, *viz.* Sin here 523, how we are to obtain it 526.

Salutations, the *Quakers* use civil ones *Vol. 2. 62*.

Satisfaction, the vulgar Doctrine of, refuted from Scripture and Reason 255-6-7, its absurd Consequences 257-8, Bp. *Stillingfleet* also against it 268, the *Quakers* believe that Jesus Christ is not the Cause of God's Love to Mankind, but the Effect, and why *Vol. 2. 867-8.*

Schism, what, 'tis not the Identity of Conceit which the Holy Ghost requires at the Hands of Christians, but the Unity of the Spirit and the Bond of Peace, says *Hales* 758.

Scriptures, holy, the Opinion of the *Papists* about them 468-9-70, they are a Rule, but not the Rule of Faith 599, how and to what Ends they are useful *Vol. 2. 37, 334, 670*, what Things are set forth by the Holy Ghost, requires one inspired with the same Spirit to interpret them *Vol. 1. 599, 600, Erasmus, Luther, Beza, Martyr, Calvin, Tindal, Jewel, Owen* &c. speak to the same Purpose. The *Quakers* do not oppose the Holy Spirit to the Scriptures *Vol. 2. 260*, whether the Holy Spirit or Tradition be the the Evidence of their Credibility 325-6, the *Waldenses* and many antient *Protestants* held the former 591, the Uncertainty of the latter 326, how some of the antient Councils rejected as Apocryphal, several of the Epistles &c. which are now received as Canonical 340, Dr. *Stillingfleet* and Dr. *Tillotson* against the *Papists*, assert, not the Scriptures but right Reason to be the Judge of Controversy 344, the *Quakers* own the Scriptures as they own themselves, *viz.* a Declaration of those Things most surely believed 781-2, and own the great Service they are of to true Christians 797-8-9, 800-1-2, 878-9

Secresy, 'tis Wisdom not to seek Secrets, and Honesty not to reveal them, the ill Effects of Openness 828.

Self-Denial what, and its great Importance respecting Salvation 286-7-8, *Abraham, Job, Moses, Isaiah* and *Daniel*, remarkable Instances of it 288-9-90, the *Romanists* Abuse of this Word 778, a Recluse Life no Gospel Abnegation 295

Servant, his Glory is Fidelity, which can't be without Diligence as well as Truth 830, his Duty in general, and in particular towards his Master, Master's Children and fellow servants, a true Servant is diligent, secret and respectful 853-4, how to be chosen and treated 901

Shifts, accuse not another to excuse thyself, 'tis neither generous nor just 828

Silence, the Benefit thereof 899

Sin, Christ came to take away not the Guilt only, but the very Act of Sin 770 1-2-3.

Society, see *Government*, a Fruit of it.

Speech, see *Conversation* and *Language*

Spirit see *Light*.

State, Service useful but not State 853 the least Thing out of Joint or omitted make the Stately uneasy, he that makes not himself cheap by indiscreet Conversation, puts Value enough upon himself every where *ibid*.

Study, have but few Books, but let them be well chosen, and well read 898 much Reading hinders Meditation, oppresses the Mind, and extinguishes the natural Candle, which is the Reason of so many senseless Scholars in the World 899.

Superfluity, an Address offer'd to the civil Magistrate, that the Money which is expended in Maintenance thereof, be collected into a publick Stock for Charitable and worthy Uses 373

Superstition, whence *Vol. 2. 5, 715*.

Swearing, see *Oaths*.

Temper

Temper, its excellent Effects 827-8, Truth often suffers more by the Heat of its Defenders, than the Arguments of its Opposers *ibid*.

Temperance, what 909, its benevolent Effects 372, is a political as well as religious Good *ibid*. we ought to eat to live, and not live to eat 824, strong Liquors good at sometimes, and in small Proportions, being better for Physick than Food, Cordials, than common Use 824, Temperance in general earnestly recommended, its salutary Effects with the destructive ones of Intemperance 909.10.11.

Thoughts, Man being made a reasonable, and so a thinking Creature, there is nothing more worthy of his being, than the right Direction and Employment of his Thoughts 848, employ thy Thoughts as thy Business requires, and let that have Place according to Merit and Urgency 200-1.

Time, we ought to be solicitous how we use it, because when once trifled away, 'tis irrecoverable 819, do nothing out of its proper Time, the ill Effects of mistiming our Affairs *ibid*.

Titles, of Honour, see *Honour*

Transubstantiation, the Absurdity thereof 473-4.

Trinity, of distinct and separate Persons in the Unity of Essence refuted 252, as inconsistent with the Scriptures and right Reason 253, the Doctrine hereof broacht by the Bishop of *Alexandria*, opposed by *Arrius*, was unknown to the three first Centurys of Christianity 254, the Decree of the Council of *Sirmium* Anno 355, respecting this Doctrine *ibid*. the *Quakers* believe it as delivered in the Scriptures, but reject the School Term [Person] *Vol.* 2. 18, 783, 804-79-85

Tythes, why, how, and to what Purposes given under the Law of *Moses*, *Vol.* 2. 56, were abolished by Christ *ibid*. revived again by the *Romish Church*, when and how 57, the primitive Protestants testified against them 58, when and how they came to be established by Law in *England* 482-3, why the *Quakers* refuse to pay Tithes 874.

Vain Man, is a nauseous Creature, he is so full of himself, that he has no Room for any Thing else be it ever so good or deserving 855, the vain Man's silly Disposition amply delineated *ibid*.

Virtue, the Support of Men and Kingdoms 734-5-6, content not thy self with being virtuous in general, for one Link being wanting the Chain is defective 839, perhaps thou art rather innocent than virtuous, and owest more to thy Constitution than thy Religion, innocent is not to be guilty, but to be virtuous is to overcome thy evil Inclinations, if thou wouldst not sin, don't desire nor embrace the Temptation, no, not look at it, nor think of it [divert thy Mind by meditating upon more noble and sublime Things] *ibid*.

Vice, the Destruction, as of private Men, so of common Wealths and Kingdoms, the *Jews*, *Assyrians*, *Persians*, *Greeks*, *Spartans*, *Athenians*, *Romans*, *Vandals*, *Goths* and *Brittains*, Examples hereof 734-5, the many Miseries that follow Vice and Immorality 737.

Uniformity, Coercion retards rather than promotes it 673, five Reasons against a Comprehension 699, 700-1, improbable to be effected, proved by the Instance of such an Attempt between the *Homoousians* and *Arrians* of old, *Luther* and *Zuinglius*, *Luther* and *Cajetan*, *Melancthon* and *Cassander*, *Bucer* and *Pflugg*, of modern Times 700, those who dissent for Trifles less excusable than they who do so more fundamentally *Vol.* 2. 187

Universities, those of our Times do not answer to the Schools of the Prophets of old, but are rather Nurseries of Vice *Vol.* 2. 55, 56.

Voluptiousness, the Sin of the old World, and without Doubt of the new 726-7, Voluptiousness and Delicacy reprehended, and its hurtful Consequences manifested *ibid*.

Waldenses, who, and why so called, *Vol.* 2. 53.

War and Fighting, the *Quakers* think it ought to cease, and why *Vol.* 2. 874

Wisdom, the wise Man governs himself by the Reason of his Case, and because what he does is best, best in a moral and prudent Sense 847, he proposes just Ends, and employs the fairest and probablest Means and Methods to attain them, he is cautious but not cunning, judicious but not crafty, equal and ready, but not officious, has always an Eye to sure footing, he offends no Body; nor is easily offended, and is always ready to compound for Wrongs, if not forgive them, he is neither captious nor critical, hates Banter and Jests, he may be pleasant but not light, is always for some solid Good, civil or moral, his Actions are all of a Piece, they'l bear the Touch of Wisdom and Honour, as often as they are tried, he makes Virtue the Measure of using his excellent Understanding, in fearing God, hating Covetousness, eschewing Evil, and loving his Neighbour as himself 848.

Wit, is a happy and striking Way of expressing a Thought [and perhaps a quick and apt one of conceiving it] 'tis not

not often that it carries a great Body with it, is fitter for Diversion than Business, where Judgment has Wit to express it, there's the best Orator 829.

Women, good and holy Women may preach the Gospel, since *Paul* had fellow Labourers in the Gospel that were Women, 'tis reasonable to think, that Women as Women are not prohibited by him to teach and instruct in the Way of Godliness *Vol.* 2. 133-4-5, *Grotius* pretty much of the same Opinion *ibid.* the Use and End of Women's Meetings amongst the *Quakers* 775.

Works, see *Merit*

World, our immoderate Pursuit thereof shews a depraved State of Mind 854, where Charity keeps Pace with Gain, Industry is blessed, old Men generally excel in their inordinate Desires of wealth, as if they would augment their Love in proportion to the little Time they have to enjoy it *ibid.*

Worship, spiritual, instituted by Christ 293, God's Condescension to the *Jews*, in allowing them a pompous and sensual Worship 293, Men's Inventions in Worship 292, true Worship proceeds only from a Heart prepared by the Lord 295 842, publick Worship commendable if well perform'd 840, serving God is not confined to the Acts of publick and private Worship (as People generally think) but concerns the Frame of our Spirits thro' the whole Course of our Lives, for God is better served in resisting a Temptation to Evil, than in many formal Prayers, if thou would'st serve God, then do not that alone which thou would'st not that another should see thee do, what true Worship is, and how performed 87 1-2-3-80.

Zeal, dropt in Charity good, without it good for nothing 843, they must first judge themselves that presume to censure others *ibid.*

FINIS.
